ISBN 978-0-259-53168-5
PIBN 10822067

1 MONTH OF
FREE
READING

at
www.ForgottenBooks.com

By purchasing this book you are eligible for one month membership to ForgottenBooks.com, giving you unlimited access to our entire collection of over 700,000 titles via our web site and mobile apps.

To claim your free month visit:
www.forgottenbooks.com/free822067

English
Français
Deutsche
Italiano
Español
Português

www.forgottenbooks.com

Mythology Photography **Fiction**
Fishing Christianity **Art** Cooking
Essays Buddhism Freemasonry
Medicine **Biology** Music **Ancient
Egypt** Evolution Carpentry Physics
Dance Geology **Mathematics** Fitness
Shakespeare **Folklore** Yoga Marketing
Confidence Immortality Biographies
Poetry **Psychology** Witchcraft
Electronics Chemistry History **Law**
Accounting **Philosophy** Anthropology
Alchemy Drama Quantum Mechanics
Atheism Sexual Health **Ancient History**
Entrepreneurship Languages Sport
Paleontology Needlework Islam
Metaphysics Investment Archaeology
Parenting Statistics Criminology
Motivational

RATIONAL

RELIGION AND MORALS:

PRESENTING

ANALYSIS OF THE FUNCTIONS OF MIND,

UNDER THE

OPERATIONS AND DIRECTIONS OF REASON;

THE FIRST, ELICITING THE NECESSARY, RATIONAL, AND ONLY RELIGION,

MONOTHEISM, OR THE RELIGION OF PRINCIPLES;

THE SECOND,

THE OBVIOUS DUTIES AND PRECAUTIONS OF SOCIETY.

BY THOMAS J. VAIDEN, M. D.,

OF ST. LOUIS, MO.

NEW YORK:
PUBLISHED BY THE AUTHOR.
1852.

TO

THE CITIZENS OF THE WORLD,

THOSE OF THE BILLION,

CONSERVATORS OF MIND, INSPIRED BY REASON AND TRUTH,

WHOSE REVERENCE FOR DEITY IS MOST EXALTED,

WHOSE DUTY TO MAN IS MOST BENEFICIAL, WHOSE ADHERENCE TO CONSERVATIVE

PRINCIPLES IS MOST EXACT,

WHOSE DESIRE FOR INVESTIGATION OF TRUTH IS MOST ARDENT,

AND WHOSE INTELLECTUAL, MORAL AND RELIGIOUS FIRMNESS, WILL INSURE

THEIR SOUL TO BE GOD'S, AND NOT MAN'S,

This Work is Inscribed.

TABLE OF CONTENTS.

THE SECOND PART,

OR,

THE PRACTICAL SCIENCE FOR MIND.

RATIONAL RELIGION AND MORALS.

INTRODUCTION.

RATIONAL MIND, pure and innocent to its available capacity, gift of Deity, is the subject of analysis for the world's exaltation ; not the perversion of man ; not the ignorant tyrant and corrupt engine of government, oppressor of the people ; nor the rabid evil genius of society, that riots in exploded customs and obsolete dogmas, the poor dependent on the bigoted opinions of the hour and brief authority.

But the independent assertor of immortal principles, and soundest practical philosophy of every-day life, acting with progressive improvement in the best lights before it, taught by the highest dictates of enlightened reason and liberal justice, and ever subject in its minutest errors, to the correction of truth's faithful representative, time, in its wisest tuition : that seeks to be wise in this world and to-day, that it may be wiser in the Universe and the future to come.

The Universe, the magnificent result of cause and effect, with its conservative principles declares the supreme character and name of its Author, in the great first cause, whose almighty attributes are centred in unity and perfection. The Creation presents past, present, and future theatre, for best fruition of intellectual and rational created beings.

The soul of the Universe and centre of universal sympathies is God, the preserver as creator, the ruler as organizer.

The analyst is Mind, moral free agent under the wise limits of universal conservative principles. The correct and immutable decisions of a sound rational mind of proper calibre and quality in a sound and healthful body, rest on common and proper sense, truth, honesty, justice, and science ; principles, the essence and standard of which are reason, and their test is experience introductory to the highest earthly tribunal, an enlightened public opinion of a world-community, wise in conscientious reason, and just in truth and virtue.

ANALYSIS OF MIND—ITS FUNCTIONS.

AMONG the invaluable gifts of the Universe, subject to the best appreciation and enjoyment of God's noblest creation, man, brilliant as the light of the suns reflecting their elementary greatness and superiority in their solar systems, inviting as the planets with all their richest treasures and gorgeous splendors, honored with satellites and encircled by atmospheres, embracing all their wonderful elements and philosophical agencies united in mighty concentric revolutions, in connection with all the systems of spheres around the holy centre, still above all is Mind inestimable in value, that takes cognizance of universal relations and results, itself emanation and inspiration of the Supreme.

Mind analyzes the facts of creation, and introduces itself into the appreciation of the first great cause, Creator of all, of the Universe through the sublime tuition of cause and effect. Mind is the only key to the analysis of man's nature and destiny,

1

and above all others that of its functions and of itself in the attainment of self, the greatest knowledge, an element of its unlimited powers only defined in the circle of the Universe.

Mind is the telegraph of Deity, to the Universe and eternity.

Mind is the best agent to secure immortality.

Without Mind man approaches the animal.

With Mind man approaches his God.

With Mind man reaches reason, an independent monitor, and entertains in its sublimest state an enlightened conscience, Mind's trusty guardian, God's best inspiration.

Without Mind man loses reason, degrades and brutalizes himself and becomes nothing, forgetful of his Creator and his highest, best, social duties and relations to mankind in general.

With Mind man governs himself and enjoys creation.

Without Mind man becomes the sport instead of the master of the elements, and the greatest wreck of the creation.

With Mind man does his duty, and reaches his dignity and reward, his highest self-respect and the best earnest for immortal fruition.

Without Mind man prostrates himself to the dust of the earth, and creates his own penalty from violation of universal conservative principles that vindicate themselves, and exact evil, the negative of good.

With Mind man masters time and soars to immortality and eternity.

The powers of Mind, the unsullied emanations of Deity are equal, if attaining its inherent virtues for its own rational conservation.

Mind increases in mental and moral endowments according to the appropriate cultivation and its richness of innate qualities, to the best exaltation and purity of conscience.

Man's moral free agency, or proper action of Mind accountable and responsible to attain its best purity, cannot be mistaken by Reason.

The qualities of mind made available if directed aright by the best cultivation, that declares the best lights of the world liberalized above all grovelling notions that cannot respect Reason, best exhibit the dignity of man's character and worth.

A pure mind must be filled with good, to avoid its necessary negative, evil.

Mind innocent and pure, is the unadulterated greatest gift of Deity ; its negative state is that of evil, to be avoided on the principles of highest safety.

Mind constitutes the chief of the living scriptures of an Immortal Deity, alone guarding in its purity its sacred temple from injury.

Mind has to work out its good, as self and free agent, without which position there could be no merit.

Who can do justice to this noble jewel gift and diamond attribute, above all price ?

To rational Mind, correct rational education and cultivation's pure light, are everything for its good, the only means for best appreciation of itself.

The operations of Mind are forever constant for good or evil, and should be furnished with the select treasure of proper materials.

The analysis of Mind discovers our errors, and secures the avoidance of their penalties in general, best on conservative principles.

Mind's best and satisfactory gifts mature on the attainment of general principles.

The brighter the light of Mind obedient to conscience, the more rational its enjoyment, and the brighter its reward.

The God of Creation has wisely given to Mind conservative principles, that are universally to be respected, for safety in physics, ethics, and all science.

Any other doctrines rest on no foundations and are demoralizing.

Mind can never yield reason to tradition, unless infatuated or unprincipled, misled or misleading by the wiles of sophistry and bigotry.

Any doctrine that requires or admits the least sophistry, that is a counterfeit of honesty to defend it, is dangerous to the rights of Mind in even an enlightened community ; is demoralizing and an imposition, a false pretence, unworthy of the respect of Mind and Reason, of rational religion.

The whole truth cannot be recognised except through Reason, Mind's constant and sure guide.

Take Reason, the patron, away, and Mind is lost in a fathomless abyss, without compass or chart.

Will the people whose free mind should elicit pure light, being entitled to a proper position in rational religion, submit to the trespasses of ignoble sophistry on their senses, and the outrages of bigotry on their rights, because the theme is Theology ? Every rational mind is held in abeyance, to the true wisdom of pure religion.

RELIGION.

Among the most sublime and magnificent subjects of the Universe is Religion, that properly refers rational Mind in all its duties to God and in all its social relations to man, productive of universal religion of principles and brotherhood.

Who can analyze this mighty subject?

Who has ever analyzed it rightly?

All rational and honest beings are vitally interested in Rational, the only True Religion, that causes the creature to appreciate with the highest adoration, the Creator of the Universe.

The highest-toned attributes of Mind, embracing in their amplest comprehension, morals, philanthropy and universal humanity, invoke the indispensable highest tribute, intellectual and religious of this world, to the proper investigation of this its most important theme.

This vital subject is addressed to all rational, particularly the most cultivated minds, the more religious as their civilization is more refined before the highest earthly tribunal of Reason and Truth.

Faith under such auspices, secures the right code of True Religion, that rests in the Bible of Rational Mind, that necessarily excludes all Bibles of Tradition of all pretensions.

Correct analysis of the rightful functions of the supreme gift of the Supreme Power, Mind rightly cultivated, shows wisdom the most rational fund for Religion in rational existence, to bless the highest rationality, the immortal soul.

Are intellectual freemen, the highest state of mortal existence in refined civilization, afraid to investigate this loftiest subject, because bigots, the slaves of slaves, proclaim their dynasty?

Will freemen never avow rightful professional universal views of True Religion, because of the dynasty of the false, but another edition of superstition?

Will they elude the very means of true wisdom through rightful investigation?

The God of Nature and the Universe has endowed his rational creation with religious as well as physical conservation, vindicating his glorious principles.

Can the Mind of Truth in good faith avoid any longer its investigation, because corrupt dynasties have sought to alienate Mind's rights, and bury truth under the false pretences of conceited and presumptuous faith?

Faith rises the more exalted as Truth justifies, and Reason confirms it.

All minds good and true looking to their duty, to human nature so fallible under the wiles of sophistry and the curses of fanaticism and bigotry, to the best interests of a world-wide subject that interests the affections of all minds for their best safety, for the security of all salutary institutions, should raise at least modest protests to stay some of the errors of the day, too prevalent for silence and acquiescence.

It is to be deplored, that so many of the supposed authority-minds engaged in politics, the press, peculiar faith, and the professions, are afraid to say their soul is God's alone, but as mere caterers to pre-existent customs, no matter of what calibre and quality, continue pretences the seed of future evil, when the light of the age, Reason and Mind, require so many fundamental changes.

The right doctrine is no creed fund, no manufactured discipline, no inquisitorial dogmas, but that which meets the demand of Mind upon the proper Faith of Reason, founded in the very character and essence of creation.

None other can be more essential or ancient, as it refers to the first origin and originator of all: hence, all other creeds are antagonistic and subordinate to extinction, as none of them reaches the correct position of the supreme, nor purely consecrates with faithful and intellectual reverence, his most characteristic attributes.

Man's nature demands religion that only comes truly and rightly through the wisdom and purity of mind, and mind must look to itself for truth.

All wise men confide from the satisfactory evidences of their senses, that were given them to lead to all correct conclusions and the proper reflections thereon by mind, that has the unbounded theatre of the Universe to read and analyze in a Creator and his conservative attributes, and firm in this knowledge, they dare not contravene them as due in full to the first great cause originating all such.

Rational religion acts then in all sincerity of conviction with all conscience, and is too pure for mortals to assail.

So enlightened is public mind in this free and intelligent Union, that if we were now to submit to its test, it is rational to believe that the majority would decide that all religious faiths short of rational religion are wrong.

An enlightened conscience affirms them wrong, in principle and profession.

But many systems may be built up on various materials, the main question especially in religion is, which is the right one, for there can be only one right? Rational mind positively, without the least risk of mistake, declares that, rational religion. Now, Mind has that to investigate.

Can it be credited that priestcraft has imposed so much superstition on the human mind not liberalized by education, that people are actually afraid in their stupid ignorance, to institute any comprehensive investigation?

All such minds are slaves of priests and superstition, especially, if they oppose to this very investigation the names of infidelity, skepticism, and free thinking.

Religion is a conscientious serving and duty to the Almighty in appropriate manner, for the certain safety of mind on earth, and the soul's security thereafter.

Without rational religion the mind overlooks its obligations, and the particulars of those obligations, and the noblest of all the object of all duty.

Without rational religion the mind loosely conceives of duties, but fulfils no direct obligations.

Rational religion then is, the rational binding of rational minds to the Almighty Being, for all rational duties during its consciousness.

The reward is the amount of life's benefits and soul's happiness.

The induction to the true belief of principles of paramount value, regards the Immortal Being, Author, Creator and Preserver, Almighty. The unity of these principles produces necessarily, unity indivisible and incommunicable to others, as division implies an equivalent imbecility. One Being who does everything by his own inherent attributes supreme and independent, cannot by reason of those attributes divest himself of them.

All good citizens are bound to uphold the proper institutions of the world, in their relations to their and others interest.

Then they must think wisely and essay to counteract those rabid self-interest seekers, who act all the time as if nature required a midwife, and that all the departments could be supplied by their important pretensions.

They just reverse Nature's acts and God's decrees, interrupting the beauty and strength in impeding the most substantial blessings and most legitimate capital, the inherent capacities of liberalized mind.

They must be reminded to make no trade or speculation of religious professions.

This is a sacred gift, so intended to all men that have rational mind as an innate quality distinguishing it from that of the brutes, to be used rightfully according to its endowing faculties, distinguishing grade of talents, that must never be perverted for any sinister purpose.

THE BIBLE OF RATIONAL MIND.

I stand committed in pledge, to a proper amount, for the correctness of the principles of the Bible of rational mind, through the blessings of rational religion. Our proper position will be thus defined:—Finding that there is no peculiar rational inspiration, it becomes mind most nurtured in culture to rear the best fabric of a moral and religious code. As to the people not being able to appreciate things aright, that is a great mistake. In popular constitutional government, we see that, as constituents, they are competent to teach their representatives, and rebuke them for their delinquency. They cannot know the world-facts too soon. It is because they have been taught by peculiar education, the perversions of mind to aid the cause of their false teachers, that the world has suffered so much and long. With the Peace Convention, the pacificators of the world cannot establish peace without principles; with them, they can procure peace without the convention.

This bible calls for science, knowledge, and wisdom, the best appreciation and use of principles. The present time uses as agents, or servants, the gods of the ancients, as lightning, and surely should define their peculiar bible to be effete.

This bible aids to break up the odious monopoly of evil customs and habits that do not seek what is right, but what is popular.

What is really sacred history, is that which pertains to the pure rights of God, who has written and endorsed all his own writings in the universe, by his supreme self-evidence.

The bible of mind only elicits the knowledge of the true God and his supreme characteristics, displayed by his unmistakeable and undeniable word, cause, and effect,—that introduce rational mind through the principles of causation,—that reflects the whole universe.

THE BIBLE OF RATIONAL MIND.

Now, nothing in the universe besides gives these facts, that are fixed and immutable. No peculiar book of man, of Jews or any other, can do it. It may be pretended that the world, mankind, would only get the idea of God out of their Jew bible, which is the most absurd of all fallacies. Various nations, as a part of the Egyptians, Persians, had just as good an idea. The knowledge of deity among all the ancients, Jews and all, was most clearly imperfect, and reflected their limited knowledge.

The statement of Josephus, of Aristeus, to Ptolemy Philadelphus, that the Egyptians worshipped the same God as the Jews, who "paid a peculiarly excellent worship to him," cuts down all pretences of the priestocracy. The bible proves who was their peculiar God, and all that assert the claims of the Jews to a pure view of the God of the universe, compromise truth, honesty, and intelligence.

The bible of rational mind proclaims that you can be nothing without monotheism.

I am gratified that I have adequately and most satisfactorily investigated for myself the subject of religion, and that monotheism presents the only position that will secure rational religion. It is essential for all mankind to know, that religion must hold all peculiar faith in perfect abeyance, which proves at once the whole position of monotheism, or rational religion. Let these be on one side, and the brightest of peculiar faith on the other.

Would you go to Mark's last chapter to wind up all the Christian believers at one moment, or would you soar to God's Word to reach the facts of sublimest action? It is even so; you go to Mark or to God's works. What a difference.

By God's Word you rule out Mark and all the tribe of impostors of spiritual knock-ings. God's facts are omnipotent. If you went to Mark you would be none the wiser, but be the subject of imposition, ignorance, prejudice, bigotry, and superstition, a world's age; whereas, if you went to cause and effect, you would defeat the whole humbug, without getting out of your seat. Now, what else but a participation in such crimes can you plead, who adopt such a felon as Mark? As good citizens you are bound to renounce all such at once, now and for ever.

You bible advocates may feel ashamed after your Wesleys and your Foxes are exposed; but you still persist in the participation of the foundation that is ever creating such vile impositions.

Agitation of the world by such a base, is horrible indeed. You have asked us to read your bible, and I candidly tell you the result.

The powers of ratiocination elicit the world-wide faculties to perceive that the standard of perfect, correct, legitimate, exact, sublime taste is religion, that points to the highest enjoyments of the universe, and the best appreciation of its God. As to peculiar faith, she is a murderess, tainted with high treason to mind and God, debauched in all the prostitution of priestocracy.

The bible of mind proves conclusively that all bibles are mere books, till proved bibles, otherwise they are base, ignominious counterfeits.

The bible of rational mind gives us the highest reverence for Deity, far surpassing all that Polytheists, including Trinitarians, can possibly have with their peculiar muti-lated gods.

The world is a mutual insurance company, that bespeaks the holiest purposes to be carried out on religious and social principles. Exalt yourselves, people of the world, to the right appreciation and action.

Monotheism contemplates rational religion, the comprehensive universe problem, that requires the immortality of the soul for its completion, and comes the nearest of all in proving it in the sublime data given. Peculiar faith deals in the metaphysics, mysteries, and detestable sophistry of faith, while religion looks to honest truth and facts.

She bids the world, rational mind, mankind, to seek the right position, and maintain it rationally, and to act with a zeal worthy of the best of causes, that of the First Great One Almighty. It is only religion that can put the whole frame-work of world society right. She must bring in her conservative revolution, enable the master analyst to correctly criticise all departments of life. To rid the world of all the malign antagon-ism that is alien to its whole interests, let all have all the fullest and speediest benefits of rational religion. All peculiar-faith, Christian, or any, is in the way of the legitimate currency.

How the world is imposed on all the time by the whole mock-faith. You must not discuss religion, say the priestocracy, and the people blindly obey those whose very name will be a by-word hereafter. The peculiar bible logic is the craziest of all things. It would wind up the creation at any time if it ever had a hold, from the imbe-cility of its peculiar gods.

Heretofore it was only sectarianism exchanged for another kind, all bad and without redress. Then all sectarianism and peculiar faith went for rational religion ; but this will not now do, as none is religion that is peculiar.

Now, because many do not believe peculiar bibles, they are not to be excluded from the higher obligations of principles of religion that the world, mind, mankind, must have. The bible if rational will bid us never take up a position without principle that will uphold us for ever.

Rational religion legislates for the whole world, and yields to mind its rationality, and to rationality all that are in the elements of eternal happiness. Why do men differ so much about religion ? Because they have never analyzed this subject aright. They advance doctrines, pretending them principles.

THE BIBLE OF RATIONAL MIND AND RELIGION, AND THE PREMIUM OF $5000 THEREON.

What can be advanced against the bible of rational mind ? An unprincipled opposition may affect that it is like the works of Deism, not right. Then if wrong, why not seek the reward ?

As all critics cannot be confided in because all do not rationally and religiously investigate, all rational minds should take nothing for granted from the priestocracy.

I would not only be happy, but am anxious to pay over five thousand dollars in negotiable paper, to any peculiar faith advocate, Christian, Jew, Mormon, Mahommedan, or any other, to prove the authenticity of any such bible, and if not competent to do so, to upset monotheism, all by rational principles.

That I may do full justice to this whole subject, I make the preceding offer.

I will be thoroughly a monotheist, and that I may be so, I comprehend all peculiar faiths known to the world, or that can be possibly conceived of by mind.

The reason is most obvious, as how can any advocate act with truth and fidelity if he cannot establish the authenticity of his bible ?

How can he religiously blame any mind for infidelity, if he cannot prove or demonstrate the faith authentic ? In other words, can any triumph over infidelity if they cannot prove or demonstrate the faith authentic ? The only triumph over infidelity, is through the authenticity of the peculiar bible. But if unsuccessful, then what becomes of conscience, that peculiar faith-advocates talk so egotistically about ?

If all peculiar faith bible-positions be utterly false, must not their advocacy be perjury ? The question is with all such advocates to disabuse the enlightened mind, or abide the explosion of the only infidels, for assuredly, if incompetent to demonstrate the truth of the peculiar faith-bible, they stand forth in bold relief as impostors, and are estopped from any abuse against those whom they assail with false pretences as infidels.

What intelligent world-citizen is there, that cannot see that no dependence can be put in peculiar faith-criticism ?

There are various reasons that cause me to commit myself to monotheism.

I will pay for the damages to the world and its society, in order to be set right if wrong.

Peculiar faith people will estimate this book with the prejudices, that they have to all other books not espousing their doctrines.

But are they not tired of their own profitless position that disturbs the world, and does not benefit any ?

Do you, citizen, wish to adhere to superstition, or change to the cultivation of religion ?

Do you seek the only rational means thereto ?

The universe read rightly, gives us the only correct edition of God's works.

Those not appreciating, may require the reason of my publication. My answer is, to have religion put on the proper basis of mind.

The more bigots oppose, the better, as they will use themselves up in the sublime facts of monotheism.

Were I to omit this publication, I might be more popular in Church and secret society, but a great and paramount duty awaits me.

My individuality is not to be looked at, especially when I claim no exemption from human nature's frailties. I pay this premium, if fundamentally wrong.

My good feelings can be perceived in the principles, as I deal with what militates against them.

If the whole set of peculiar doctrines are wrong, then no part of any peculiar faith can stand. Thus much of the proposed reward might be offered to the successful proof of a Devil, which would be a miserable failure according to the correct law of evidence. This premium is offered to any person of the five grand divisions of the whole world, that will prove without any sophistry, that the author is not right in the main, on the subject of rational religion, or the bible of rational mind. This certainly is the paramount question with the world, that ought to correct the errors or adopt the principles of the author. That question resolves itself into the enlightened inquiry of how far he is right, and what is essential to perfect the glorious system. Mind that is rational, sees no rational authenticity of any peculiar scriptures of the myriads of ancient bibles, and consequently the full failure of all their advocates to disprove the bible of rational mind. There can be no satisfactory proof of the authenticity of any bible of tradition in the world, no matter from which of the five grand divisions. The bible of the religion of principles, God's document, cannot be gain-sayed, much less disproved. The only proof that is required of the authenticity of the scriptures, is satisfactory evidence on the principles of sound truth.

But the author may be mistaken? Then this premium is for the mistake. I wish to be rid of all mistakes.

But why the reward? As many have prejudged. I am desirous of calling the citizens of the world back to right perception and judgment, and therefore offer this premium for orthodoxy.

What proof do I require? The authenticity must be unquestionable and satisfactory to gentlemen.

If I were offered this premium to prove my position, and could not do it, I would renounce that profession, certainly, as disreputable.

I consider that monotheism or religion of principles, is self-evident.

What good does peculiar faith do, but deceive the world, trading on the capital of the first? All is arrogant imposture.

All the writers on monotheism, must ever have its principles as paramount, while on the same subject seeking originality, they may still have analogous views, in some respects, differently, or even similarly expressed.

The platform that I maintain, upholds conservative principles. I have and can have, no antagonism to any that upholds them.

Have the priestocracy any to God Almighty?

Why do I offer this premium for what is so clearly plain? To meet bigots, most effectually.

If this book have truths unimpeachable, the world can see the premium safe; if otherwise, the prize is truth gloriously won.

The bigot would lay aside his views about peculiar faiths and Messiahships, before the sun-light was off his horizon, were he not a prejudiced bigot. Thus with facts so plain, the bigot will remain bigot, till monotheism diffuses its rays and dispenses its blessings. No one with successful solutions, can draw on me in vain. Good men will excuse me if wrong. I know I shall be excused at the right time by such. All objections to receiving this premium, can be met at once, for the amount can be dispensed, if fairly won, to all the best of purposes, and the triumph can be that of the noblest, most laudable, ambition.

The purport of this publication, is to secure the right faith by discussion freely and fairly executed.

This work was written in pure defence of religion, and to illustrate not christianity, but the brilliant and substantial effects of mind reflecting Deity's power, regaining her long usurped rights.

What true soul can I possibly offend?

If any have adopted bad faith or pernicious errors, no matter the name, of course they ought to be obliged to me to set them right.

Prove me wrong, and I will adjust all claims of right and order.

If I have become antagonistic to you or your rights clearly, convict me on principles.

But some people are afraid to read such books. No one that is wise and sincere is afraid to trust the selection of the true from counterfeit coin, to have a true report as the result.

But the perverted are afraid, those that hold the bad coin, tremble for fear and reproach. Forethought in all such discussion, will disclose the true point.

If the position of rational religion be not correct, what is easier than to win the premium?

If I have done an injury to the Church or the priestocracy, I will atone for it by that means, and act with the amende honorable. Without investigation, no one could rightly estimate how valid this position is.

RATIONAL RELIGION AND MORALS.

I let the subject carry me to its legitimate results, and congratulate myself on the amount of satisfaction. I am pleased to find my writings confirmed on reading the world before publication. Genius has consecrated her contributions, at the shrine of monotheism in more ways than one, for mankind, mind have devoted, however imperfectly their resources, in some way or other, in all ages and in every clime.

But as the premium being forthcoming, the peculiar faith advocate affects that I would not believe his doctrine if an angel from his heaven were to come with the proof. To all this the most valid answer can be at once returned, that my soul, my mind with its functions, has the deepest interest in all such.

I have as deep a sincerity in all this matter as could be elicited in all the treasure of the Universe. Who can have any deeper or more vital interest?

I am fully satisfied in my own confidence that there is but one God, a perfect Being, but to prove that I have no part of prepossession, I offer the premium not to defend myself behind prejudices, but to annihilate them, no matter where they exist.

After a number of years' investigating and thinking on spiritualization of peculiar faith, my mind all at once fastened on rational religion, as the only effectual means without prejudice or peculiar education. From these two words has grown all that is valuable to my mind.

I offer the premium on the basis of principles, sound honest sense and truth I offer it for authentic proof, demonstration, satisfactory and soundest principle that the whole world will recognise

If a bank note affirmed to be 'valuable, but unknown to us, were offered, the world of course in its wisdom would ask for satisfactory proof of its genuineness. If books are presented which their advocates pretended guaranteed deeds of gifts of the most important kind, and had besides what were considered genuine interpolations that affected them essentially, and no name signed, being perfectly anonymous, a sane man would not, could not receive them. Interpolations prove foul play, when especially, all are palmed on the world as genuine.

Who endorses their divine origin? Self-evidence cannot, as in God's works. The text is admitted by the warmest advocates, to be corrupted. How far? Of course, enough to invalidate them by their vitiations.

Is this religion that goes for honesty and truth? The world has nothing to do with such peculiar faith or its bibles, but truth is needed as the strictest justice to the world to anticipate all such evils.

I wish the smartest scholars to meet this question fairly and honorably. I would not mislead the world, hence this premium to be applied as the church sees fit when fairly won.

This offer is for the people, including the parsons. I wish to give the Bible advocates all the advantages they claim and prove, wishing to advance the highest morals of the world, and declaring for pure religion. All that belongs to rights and justice, I wish to accord.

If the world priestocracy cannot attack the main points with truth, they should not protract this world wrong any longer, nor vitiate the principles of refined civilization to effect retaliation. In the name of God let them adopt the principles of rational religion, and unite the world on the glorious basis of universal brotherhood. Liberality and justice will enable me to allow all the legitimate latitude of proof on the principles of reason in the world.

This work is an introduction to the magnificent subject of Monotheism that all minds should rightfully analyze, and not listen to the seductive and criminal sophistry of priestocracy. If there be any real error on any adopted faith, ought not its advocates who profess truth, be most signally obliged to any intelligent minds for exposures of its fraud or its imposition? To satisfy the most skeptical, I desire to be responsible and hold the world responsible for facts. I write not to incense any order, being no opponent but on principle.

RELIGIOUS MORALS.

Has the world any religious morals? It has peculiar faith morals in abundance, which pervert the world. Mind has to look to the illimitable liberality of rationality in religion to reach them. The desecration of religion is by peculiar faiths.

The idea of approaching God is by our best actions, words and thoughts.

Rational religion can establish the only basis of pacification throughout the world, and the best platform for universal civilization.

Do I have faith or belief in a God? Certainly. Why do I have that confidence?

RELIGIOUS MORALS.

Because this is a world most conclusively of cause and effect, and the proper analysis refers most positively to the great first cause. No rational mind can escape this just conclusion.

In the next place, I must define to the extent of my powers exactly what are the qualities, attributes and principles of God. These we can appreciate more exactly by philosophical science the more exactly we can define it, that is we can only define them exactly by exact philosophical science—none other, as all the false pretences of tradition bibles conclusively show. God is the exclusive Creator, uncreated and unbegotten. How can any claim of a begotten created son, be equal? The idea is preposterous to all that will drop the priest and become the man, the thinking rational being.

Religion, rational religion, is certainly not accountable for any slaughter of the human race in any age or country, in France, or elsewhere; if that were the case, God is amenable to man's censure, the most absurd position. All such evils are referable to peculiar faiths, all of which are of man.

Rational religion requires the full culture that implies the constant exalted exercise of conscience, the conservative of rational mind.

The only universally safe position in this Universe is on principles. You are after religion, and must therefore maintain in the best faith, intellectual, social, moral, religious, filial, conjugal and parental relations. You can obtain all by and through God alone and exclusively; by none other most positively. Is it religious morals to continue the propagation of inventions, made in the days of a world's ignorance? Let reason look into facts, and it must see that God has no room for a specific hell or purgatory. What is it to the people if the pockets of the priestocracy require them?

Mind has to regard the world, national and individual sins, according to the Universe ethics established by God. All this requires the supreme duty of all mankind.

The peculiar faiths of the world have finessed too much, and, destitute of principles as all are universally, they have lost the confidence of the truly religious.

As religion is the supreme of all supreme constitutional rights, it is indispensable that she be confirmed by all constitutional principles.

Religion goes for the greatest of all good, the whole public of the world and nothing less at all. What can imply more universal benefit accredited in all good faith? Carry religion into the world. It has it now. Let it be improved on, to make it as rational as the highest rationality can carry it.

In matters of religion the rational mind must elicit principles, not mere policy, to command the organic powers of the whole, or Nature. The whole classes of the world society form one harmonious whole. All reforms and revolutions should be invariably and universally conservative, and all then must be on rational principles to be permanent. The rulers of the world should bow to the majesty of religious not peculiar faith requisitions, however much of peculiar power and vanity they sacrifice.

When we speak of reform on conservative revolution, it is the right action of the world to recovery of her right position. None should be without legitimate principles.

Truth and honesty uphold all religion that sustains mind, but all peculiar faith starts with the reverse and necessarily ends in perjury. How horrible!

The world must stop the mere temporal policy of peculiar faith, and let rational religion have its noblest sway. The character of religion is desecrated, to dub peculiar faith by that name when all is so clearly disproved. The world cannot discuss too rationally all that is religion.

Carry conservative reform to the right point—far enough. This is a world-wide question.

What, freemen, reject rational religion? What were your free constitutional institutions for, but this in part? If any country do not positively assert her rightful claims to rational religion, assuredly she will be cursed with peculiar faiths. There is no failure. As the Jewish councils made Mosaic bibles or found them at convenience, so did the Romans make testaments, all patch-work. These characters not only endorsed those demoralizing lies, but ask the world to do so.

As great as was the creation of our noblest of all governments, because God-given by our illustrious ancestors, the most illustrious of all in the pages of heraldry, our nation now is equally concerned in the preservation of the most difficult of all—all solvable by religion that recognises the highest of morals, virtue and intellect.

Rational religion carries rational mind, while peculiar faith assumes faith. Religion decides on justice universal, before she affects any position, and rules out all atheists and polytheists as most superficial in most positive demonstration of their reckless ignorance or want of principle. Religion sustains the wisest statesmen, the deepest, soundest original thinkers, the firmest friends of rational mind, all the true and faithful conservators of the world.

...in omniscience and be comprehended by a wise comprehension, are criticism has claim on intellectual confidence. This world cannot furnish what is a universe problem, therefore monotheism introduces mind into the sublimest hope of immortal existence, to rightly appreciate its sublimest purposes.

RELIGION.

WHAT is the religion of rational mind? That which discloses the true duty of man to God, and puts down all base trading speculation of the world—the counterfeit. Though the world speaks about religion, its age, and have not principles, all is worthless. Though the world prides itself on faith, and have not truth and reason, faith's masters, it has nothing. To have the right faith, mind must be faithful to truth and reason, and to have the best security for all such, it must have rational education. Religion is for just views. All must be just to the God of the universe, to mind, the whole world and universe. She establishes on the best demonstration, that the only safety is through principles. The bible of rational mind introduces the religion of mind. That begets the deepest humility, and the supreme unbounded confidence in the Creator, as the supremacy of science is from Deity. He who speaks against that, is base and blasphemous. Stubborn bible bigots will suppose that you are to take their bibles to get religion. Nothing short of the Creator will do, and we have only to improve what he has already given. Religion is a pure, perfect principle; when matured, the soul matures and rests there in the bosom of purity. Religion rests on the eternal sublimity of her sincerity and simple purity, abstracted from all the violations of reason. What is more precious than woman's chastity, man's integrity, the world's humanity, mind's religion?

Religion strictly teaches mind to beware of all violations of principles, lust, drunkenness, avarice, and envy, as they produce murder, crimes, adultery, poison, all the misery of mind. How do we get righteousness? By grace and mercy of God. How the profoundest humility? By the deepest confidence in God, who is known by the best analysis that philosophical science discloses, to be so exalted, as to exclude all pretensions of polytheism. The deepest analysis gives the best confidence and humility. What can be said of Messiah righteousness? That it is as heinous as self-righteousness; both are self or priestocracy delusions. The religionist is to seek proper compliance with the requisitions of wise laws to promote sound morals, true duty, and the highest civilization,—to leave the world better than he found it. The mighty question of true religion is kept in abeyance to a union of church and state, the policy of empires, of power despotic in government. Peculiar faiths, their mouth-pieces, misrepresent all the qualities of Deity. Talk of them, when God is surely proved by his creation. Who would presume to libel God by bibles of tradition? We hardly know ourselves, till indisposition or sickness teaches us. Do we know of order, harmony, till we feel disorder, derangement? We are then for law, order, religion, and the Creator of all these. We do not know of organization till we know of disorganization, and we must then appreciate the Almighty Organizer of the universe. The world needs the broadest position of morality and religion, but not out of any peculiar bible, for its writers did not know them at all. The very idea of peculiarity kills all.

All owe a gentlemanly deportment to civilized society, and are under the highest obligation to offend it least by thought, word, or deed. The world must seek to maintain the soundest public opinion, to be universally conservative. Religion is the only thing that suits that, to create the world morals.

Those who have power have no mercy, if they have no principle.

What is religion? We only know some say, as others tell us. What are freemen with cultivated minds, and not know this subject? Have you ever investigated it? No! Why? Because my preacher tells me not! Is your preacher your master? Force of arms or device of sophistry is not the way to settle questions of the world to be civilized. Religion is the supreme wisest intellectual and moral power of the world. By religion alone can mind progress to one uniform standard, as to present virtue as uniform as mind can present it. The world will be better sustained as self-balanced.

Let us see where religion is, that is the good faith of truth and principle. Are you after religion?

All the wise, true, and good are after nothing else, and that in her purity and excellence. Religion affords supreme protection to all. Religion sees that you are accused, does she teach the doctrine of non-resistance? You are innocent? Then act to the promptings of an honest mind. Face the world and at once invoke, challenge the worst, defy on your position. Innocence can triumph over the world certainly. But do one bad or suspicious act, then you may be suspected for the worst,—as for instance, an adulterer. You will not then be too good to be charged as a poisoner and murderer, especially if the accusers have any hold of you for any such crime. In being an adulterer you become a perjurer. Religion leaves nothing to contingency.

All peculiar faiths are the work of man, but religion is the work of God. Religion exists, yet man affects other faith. He thinks that the bible of tradition has it! The greatest mistake in the world. Well may we say what a mistake; and then base men have taken horrible advantage of it. The fact of correct observation has been needed. Mind must exclusively rely on the justice, greatness, magnanimity, goodness, and all the essential attributes of God.

Man is a creature of social, moral, and religious feelings, of course the gift of his Creator.

To have the right cultivation, we must have proper education,—a true, practicable, rational knowledge of science, &c. Religion sustains the reality, not the romance of virtue, and calls for the tribute of praise and thanksgiving by appropriate benevolence to the destitute, proper deeds to the world. What an enviable fame would the good citizen get, to die aiding the helpless and destitute. Such will strive to succor the distressed, relieve the afflicted, protect the defenceless. Adequate reward will bless the mind that has principles; the curse of those destitute of them will be certain, as principles vindicate themselves.

All have more religion the more civilized,—this is an indisputable axiom; the less civilized the less religion, as the crusaders prove, &c. What more glorious measure can there be for the soul than doing justice to religion on the proper principles of mind? As having a free and intelligent mind in the glorious free agency of God, you have done justice to the investigation of this subject on both sides, as wise persons will not possibly put any bibles otherwise into the hands of their offspring, whose immortal souls have to be cared for in the most rational way. But the minister tells the world that the books that show up Christianity are dangerous. What do parents say? They do not investigate the books, for they are afraid. Afraid of the truth!

But have you avoided the subject? If you have, then are you and they traitors to the right use of mind.

But the world is afraid to oppose the bibles. Mind is crushed by the baseness of superstition. What clashes with preconceived constructions of the bibles, is what clashes with the priestocracy, deeply interested in their corruption; thus we do not recognise that God's construction is elsewhere than in his works.

You declare for such bibles, then you are at issue with God. Religion of mind progresses as mind is civilized. Peculiar faith, of peculiar education, usurps the province of mind, in assuming to dictate about religion. True devotion to God is inculcated by religion of principle. Benevolence inculcates the noblest acts under her auspices.

Religion is the most sacred duty, higher than bibles, creeds, and peculiar faiths, above all art. The God of Nature requires all adoration, worthy of the laws and principles of nature, of the purity of creation.

Mind is obliged to have religion, as nature has laws. The purport of religion is to lessen mind's and the world's misery, and teach the soul of man to look to a better future. The permanent action of religion must certainly revolutionize the ethics of the world.

Religion goes against polytheism, as atheism.

What is the best friend of man? Religion. What is that? A rational recognition of duty to the Creator. Who is the best friend to mankind? The Creator.

Man never can appreciate God all his life-time on this earth. The more he appreciates his works, the more he loves the architect of his own soul for its blessings. None can make idol of the work who appreciate the workman. Religion is the only thing that ever can impart pure devotion of feelings, of which the unworthy are deficient. Religion is the highest rational process. All the means of securing true faith are rational.

The great object of religion is to civilize man, render him fit for the human family, and adapt him for his mighty change. Religion looks to reason, judgment, sense, law and justice. There can be no religion of the heart, but of mind, that recognises all things of thought, word and deed. We can reach or embrace no part of creation, but by and through mind. As mind appreciates, priestocracy and peculiar or heart faith, depreciates.

Religion does not refer to the heart, but the affections, emotions and passions, the functions of mind. Such makes a person too religious to be in any peculiar church! The world should know its own powers through its own rights.

The religion of principles, is the object of all. Without principles nobody improves religion.

Mind culture alone, will not suffice for religion. It must secure the highest appreciation of all, and the practical illustrations. It must do its best practicable duty.

Religion commands all to avoid taking advantage of passions, emotions or circumstances, and characterises the best class of the world, as doing the most good.

The mere men of straw, military and superstitious, will not answer for the light of civilization. The world needs religion, the true effect of which is civilization. We have not to inquire about any man's faith, when we inquire has he cultivated his religion? What religion, it may be asked? He has and can have but one, and that from God. That cannot be mistaken, as faith and truth are analogous. As a rational being, we address you in all this matter. Religion, and bibles of tradition with peculiar faith, are two different things. Religion proves itself, but bibles of tradition disprove themselves. Principles only, can legalize religion. We should progress in the right views of religion. What is the true position of religion among rational men? Is it not rational religion? What is the most valuable element of religion? Justice to man and duty to God. Without it, one hardly knows how to begin action in the world, till he is nearly ready to leave it. What good does the world do him, then, temporarily, if not religiously? Why do not the people do right? Because they do not know, frequently, beforehand, and are victims of relative habits. They have little power of analysis of thought. True religion teaches that none should surpass in reverence to deity, who has the exclusive right to adoration of mind.

Is man an accountable and responsible being?

Then he is so only on rational basis, and on no other.

All morals are based on truth and reason, on no other. All religion is on principles, the most exalted.

When we begin to think, talk, and act on principles that are uniform, then we begin to enjoy the noblest, highest refinement and civilization.

True religion and morals must be upheld by the world's conservative patriots. The proper character demands trial, proper efforts and perseverance. It becomes the good citizens of the world to see what is the best protection for religion and their profession. It becomes honest patriots to inquire rightfully what is their duty and obligation. This inculcates chastity, eternal truth, avoidance of murder and crimes involving sympathies. To uphold religion, then, give God all due him. This is intellectual, religious honesty. The church-monarchical power and monetary influence, have prevented the just view of religion. Superstition and all its malign influences commenced before science, which is to eradicate them. The social world is singularly constituted, on account of money and power, ignorance and superstition. We know very well what malign influence of peculiar education is, and how it perverts mind. That is often a misfortune, rather than a crime or fault. But be it what it may, it should be corrected. The world is diversified, and needs the various best talents of honesty and truth, elevated science. As to faith, when rational, that is God's concern. Religious fortitude upholds the best resolves of mind and soul. Whilst she teaches us to exert ourselves for the best, we must strive to receive all as the best, and be best satisfied if mind do not demand correction. Who can appreciate civil and religious liberty, that gives the pure currency of thought the noblest reflection of actions? The world must have fixed just views of religion, as the only proper elevated standard of actions. What are the religious rights of freemen? The way to have them universally performed best, is to have universal knowledge on the subject. This business materially concerns all mankind, all minds, as they are the beneficiaries. How long will they suffer their rights of mind to be put in abeyance to exploded bibles of tradition and their peculiar faith? The most substantial, shortest road to happiness, is through the virtue, purity and innocence imparted by religion. The religion of the good when matured, will fill the world with its best position, rendering mortals most happy. Let it not be debauched by the bibles of tradition, and kept behind the age of freedom. We need the absolute conservation of social duties and relations. Be independent of the world, if you desire truth and virtue, true independence. How callous must be the world when it affects that some say; this is my belief, and that it may be perpetuated, however erroneous. Proselyte in good if practicable; correct and teach on principles; enlighten on science.

What is to protect man, but the great conservative social principles? If man infringe or encroach on social rights and duties, thus far is he injured, as others may do the same. If sophistry be admired, sycophancy must be practiced. Both are in antagonism to truth, as faith without religion. We desire religion that we can be pleased with, having affection therefor. If it cannot be a pure guide or light for safety, it is mere faith, worse to its friends than enemies. Religion demands candor and decision on honorable judgment, or silence where there is not certainty. Religion is the settled policy of the system of principles. Perverted is the wretch that would impugn religion or its sacred precepts. For universal brotherhood, the world should go as its greatest good, next to religion, the sacred indispensable duty to God. Religion is the moral sublime that requires well posting up in good deeds, thoughts and words. It is an immortal subject, to be taken hold of by all rational minds. True religion protects and commends itself to mind, for the world's purification, truth's verification, universal confidence. Public oaths can only be on the best affirmation, and that should be as sacredly held as the most serious declarations. Religion enjoins sanctity to words, as matters of fact not to be violated. What especial merit can any arrogate to themselves on the profession of religion, a necessary constituent of their minds? Rational education makes religion acceptable, and causes it to differ from superstition. What enable us to get the right advantage of the world?—Principles. The highest obligations are due society and religion. What has religion to do with party spirit or peculiar faith? Religion recognises the obligations of justice, as ever paramount. The world must go for the law of God, nature, mind, religion, reason and truth, and if all the bibles of tradition are antagonistic to them, they should be at once excluded the world. Why prate about religion, when it is essential to all. ˙It cannot be too cultivated, as evinced by civilization and character, the wisest and most intelligent legislation, freedom of enlightened speech and press. The common interests of the world are not alienated, unless the sacred rights of the people were basely violated. Religion is not for suppression of legitimate passions, as monks teach, but for their legitimate enjoyment. You need the only religion that rational mind can ask for, rational religion, and that you cannot mature without rational measures.

We seek that basis which is competent to build up what is right, not merely exclude all errors; to look up to country, parents, and the world, to do all that justice requires.

But the ostensible reason for peculiar faith, is on account of man's sins. Now that is an utter defiance of mind's analysis.

Religion has an identity with mind inseparable therefrom, and comprehends the whole duty of mind.

It is a constant inspiration of God's principles, directed by a true analysis of mind.

Sin is an accompaniment of man's nature, either untaught or uncorrected, and negatives as evil the proper result of principles of conservation.

Do the people actually know what they want or need?

Have they rightly analyzed all that is necessary?

Do they know what analysis of the subject is?

In their excitement about religion, they may look to a Messiah, but no true masterly analysis can affirm this, the pretence of a profession that thus seeks profit.

What is religion? The best duty of man, to God and man.

How does man show it? By enlightened mind and the most comprehensive reason that takes in the compass of all practicable principles, instituted for the physical, moral, and religious state of the universe.

What mind lacks of civilization, it lacks of essential religion. Then rational religion is a science the most exalted and cultivated.

The most energetic powers are most potent of good, if rightly directed, as those of steam, while the innate powers of mind are analogous for good or evil, by analogous direction.

Religion is then a self-regulating system, to prevent the necessity of paying forfeiture for any delinquency, if it did not soar to the most ennobling emotions and object, an eternal homage to the worthiest being in creation.

Assuredly religion is the true foundation for avoidance of penalty, that must requite for duties unperformed, and errors committed, the noblest guarantee of reward for duty done. He who violates any principle, must necessarily pay forfeiture, and has to make restitution.

Religion teaches the general avoidance of all suspicious persons and matters, that may corrupt if evil.

The best command of the elements of nature, an ever present subject, presupposes a proper knowledge of her, then religion to master her duly, must be the science of sciences.

This world's beauties and virtues are too often read amiss, by an unthinking and ungrateful people.

Their construction is libel, their appreciation is too often subversive of reasonable benefits.

Mankind seeks to improve religion that belongs to all minds, not to peculiar faiths.

We appreciate what religion is, not by feeling alone, but by enlightened conscience when it can refer to reason, for it requires a rational, not fanatical conscience, that towers above the animal feelings.

What is religion, then, but a binding again the mind that had become perverted from the innocence of infancy, and had to be rebound in the purity of enlightened conscience?

Religion is then the action of mind consistent with the philosophy in life, or to act best the philosophy of life.

Religion is the characteristic of mind in its noblest condition of life, and exerts her full sway on the human character as the right impress of God.

All religion improves the mind and soul, through inherent principles that guide reason, proportionately to the cultivation ; and none can perfect the conscience that does not full and equitable justice to both.

Faith that represents religion, but draws back from mind and reason, is unworthy the respect of either, and incapable of perfecting conscience, but on the contrary, must pervert it.

Neither peculiar faith, bibles of tradition, nor their professions, have anything to do with rational religion that stands on the merits of the Almighty.

This is a paramount question, not of bigotry and preconceived notions, the off-casts of ignorance and prejudice, but of religion, pure, vital, and rational.

Bibles of tradition cannot reveal faith of religion.

How has all peculiar faith been revealed ? By priestocracy. Is that worth anything ? Not the reading. All rational beings desire religion revealed by God, that is the only rational one of principles, and can be no other.

But in regard to religion, we should go to the party best acquainted therewith. Agreed—who are they ? The professors. Are they the possessors of true religion, or peculiar faith ? Are they interested for the maintenance of doctrines that are right, or professions that are profitable, influential and powerful ?

Shall we not go to mind that is universally endowed when sound, with the innate faculties and principles of religion ?

When we are told to seek religion, then we must rightly seek to improve it as possessed by all rational minds.

All nations have codes graduated to their state of civilization, that characterizes their real state of religion, not the fictitious one of peculiar faith.

It is utterly impossible to destroy the true position of religion, as God has endowed every mind possessed by rational beings with its elements, and that has to be improved while mind survives in its present shape.

What then remains for the world of mind to do ? To make religion a pure thing, peculiar faith must be abrogated, as the last has no reason or mind but sophistry, animal feeling and bigotry, the cause of fanaticism.

God designed religion to be universal, a covenant with mind from first to last in his own church.

The rite universal, is mind's appropriate cultivation in all the philosophical science attainable in the universe.

The Supreme requires no right impracticable, therefore he gives religion that is rational, to rational beings.

The circumstances of mind, and the context of reason, define religion.

The positive safe duty of man, is rational religion, and honesty and truth are the great corner stones.

All mankind has by the gift of creation, innate principles of religion that preeminently distinguishes man from the brutes, to be carried out by a correct, not peculiar cultivation of mind, else it is to be perverted by treachery to mind that may degrade nations, continents, worlds, a universe of nations.

Thus many lose sight of purity of conscience, from want of cultivated mind, that is liable to further degradation by continued perversion.

The Creator alone is the fountain and object of all religion. His perfect unity constitutes its purity. None other can be, else the creature is equal to the Creator. All religion must be pure and genuine, else the faith is wrong and useless, and the practice is inconsistent and hurtful.

You either seek true religion or the reverse.

If the first, it was instituted by God for universal good ; it will bear and court investigation through reason by rational mind.

If untrue, it is impious blasphemy, and ought to excite the voice of all good citizens of the world, in denouncing it by a general condemnation.

All mankind must have faith of some kind, for good or evil.

If we do not have the good, the evil must and will predominate as paramount.

Mankind has the innate principles of religion, from the Creator.

Ours must be the right culture of this invaluable trust fund, as ours is the harvest.

A consistent faith will insure good and consistent practice.

All rational minds seek the purest religion.

What is it ? Is it peculiar, or universal ? Investigation of truth only decides that it must be universal to belong to God, as all that is peculiar belongs to man.

Many think that faith will do, whether truth sanctions faith or not.

Does religion consist of faith and practice?

Let us analyze the first, that the second may be just and righteous.

Is the faith free? All is under truth and reason.

What is the only test for mind that is to be operated on? Reason. Can there be any other at all? None other with wise or honest people.

What has reason then to do?

She has to operate on facts presented.

But a part may be unseen?

Then her aids, analysis and analogy, alone can act for universal safety, otherwise a blind and dangerous hypocrisy results, and such errors as the history of mankind truly shows are more dangerous than a state of ignorance, for the state of the first must be crime, that of the last comparative innocence.

The book of knowledge is the Bible of Mind addressed to the understanding of mankind, and the innate monitor, Conscience, that is universal to rational man, will disclose on due and adequate investigation, the rejection of the bibles of tradition.

We must then adopt the light of mind and reason now, at once, and forever, as the only safe and sound-minded system. All others are those of the monomaniac.

Mind has the faculty of religion to be cultivated to elicit conscience, that can rightly face the Universe.

God initiated all minds into religion by innate endowments.

Religion that is true, upholds the Divine dignity of God in universal, not peculiar powers.

Religion knows what is law, and makes friends through the foundation of the law.

Wise legislation, one of her best aids, must cover all the grounds of deficiency in man's codes.

Have we a system of religion instituted that answers the demands of the whole world, that suits mankind in its most exalted character, and causes it to be united in one universal brotherhood?

None short of the true belief in one Almighty Creator of the Universe, clothed in all power, can answer and fulfil all such.

It is conceded that all nations have, as all rational beings or minds need, religion in elemental endowment. The great object is to give it the right direction.

True religion must be that of civilization to suit the whole world, and must be that of science and philosophy that support civilization the highest, all of which were written by God in his works, and stamped on mind. The bibles of tradition were written afterwards, thus proving themselves counterfeit.

Any other than true religion, is mythology.

We know God by his works; we do not know his word than by his works of the Universe.

Shall we be unpopular, to seek analysis of our religion?

We seek to establish religion, morals, and government, to meet the world-wide benefit of mankind.

To understand religion, is to look to the genuine resources of religious knowledge, and that promotes practical piety and vital religion in the minds of all.

A true conservative revolution will cut down atheism, polytheism, and all sectarianism.

Then we shall have no pilgrimage to pay devotion to the relics of the pretended dead saints, or to the absurd notions of ecclesiastical dictators, by penance or folly, finding the God of the Universe omnipresent.

And then we shall cut down the false pretences of the priests, who were the real beneficiaries of those pious frauds.

No less shall we attain, when we abolish auricular confession that creates the greater sin of the priests.

When one fraud is substituted for another, which is the gain?

Neither phylactery nor the priests' pretended praying off sins, nor their intercession for pardon, can avail one iota.

Man's must be the exertion, and by right actions.

Let us not mistake true religion.

Is it absolutely necessary to have a priest to obtain pardon, to confess the sinner and cause him perform the penances which are imposed?

Which is the greatest sinner of the two? The priest, of course, for he blasphemes God's rights, and swindles man's.

Does he do this at his own expense, or yours? This is no child's play, however fraudulently he acts; for, although he gains money here, he atones for it afterwards.

Shall even self-constituted councils decide that people should request "intercession of saints reigning with Christ in heaven;" when the omnipresence of God excludes all such as useless and absurd?

The faculty of religion is universal to mind that is rational, as sense of Deity is impressed on mind. It is a perception of cause and effect, and is a universal conviction that is perverted as mind is perverted.

Religious principles were instituted by God himself, elicited by deductions of reason.

Education must be rational to command circumstances, otherwise, peculiar as the result of circumstances, it perverts the principles of religion and misdirects them to self-interest.

It is enlightened, liberal, and just reason that is to free us from the rank errors of superstition and idolatry.

Life presents a perpetual struggle as to orthodoxy, never to be decided but upon this principle.

Religion has to steer clear of atheism, and polytheism of man and bibles, therefore must bow to the majesty of God by the fidelity of mind.

The beauty of it is, that all trinities of church, state, and the military, are the absolutism of polytheism and atheism, and all such are elegantly excluded by rational religion.

The brotherhood of the world is hastening by all legitimate means of truth, honesty, and humanity that bless mankind, to advance the principles of religion. Let a benevolent commerce carry all these throughout the globe.

Our religious persuasions bind us to show proper actions and morals, manners that decide for all rational beings who revere God and respect man.

If morals be not exercised, that individual has no practical religion. Theology is a free and rational subject, and ought to be discussed fairly and rationally.

There is as much reason now for the world to investigate as ever, the purest principles of religion.

How are all to be saved? As rational beings, by the influence of God's gifts that fell on all at creation, and gave to each the innate faculty of religion, that is a conscience that should be enlightened by the ways of wisdom, virtue, truth, honesty, and sincerity, with all the elements of thought and science to best meet the varied grapple of the world, and look in all its deeds to God and his pure attributes and none other, as worthy and competent to do all for mind.

All the office of a vicegerent is assumed, usurped, and affected.

God manages the managers, and sincerely rebukes such to death, for abominable blasphemy.

Thus, what is called the skeptic's acts, are the most worthy of the world's notice in the justice, efficiency, and sufficiency of God who created all, and is equal to its government as proved in that of the whole Universe.

The faith of religion is accompanied by truth and reason.

While religionists rely on thoughts, words, actions, and works to be recognised by God as the best practicable evidence to those interested, the advocates of peculiar faith refer all the time to their faith, and speak of works as intended for man's not God's appreciation!

Religion by profession is a silent manifestation of God's principles, while peculiar faith is noisy and a tell-tale for worldly speculations, a blustering bully to crush the world.

Religion glories in rational faith, that is approved of by God and man.

If we do not possess the best rational faith, we are liable to the impositions of fanatical faith at all times, for which we have to thank man worship. The sooner we get right in religion, the better for liberty and freedom of mind.

Whoso is opposed to religion, is opposed to God.

Whoso is opposed to superstition, and peculiar faith of all kinds, is for God.

Where dwells practical, vital, rational religion, but with those who adore the living God!

What else is opposed to God cannot be religion, but must be superstition and man-worship.

What is rational is just, and what is comprehensively just, is religion—the highest duty to God paid by rational mind.

The highest position attainable in religion, and that proves it, is that which brings rational belief and action all the time, as this best refers to the best standard—an enlightened mind. In whose keeping is religion?

In the minds of men who adore their God—Creator, and not in the hands of those after the order of Melchizedek the priest, who received the tenth of the spoils of war of

2

Abraham, who gave this power to take tythes, and to realize the salary of millions therefrom, by the imposition and blasphemy of peculiar faith—priestocracy, who enslaved the world by their false pretences.

Let religion have none of the habiliments of sordid inducements. The dynasty of the priestocracy has nothing to do with religion, that is too *sacred* for this *vulgar* clan.

The greatest humbuggery is carried out under the pretence of faith, that cannot exist unless rational; and that excludes all base pretences.

There can be no uniform system of religious principles on the doctrine of peculiar faith.

WHAT IS RELIGION?

A DISCHARGE of duty most faithfully to enlightened conscience.

Ought we to have organized associations to carry out its principles? That may be very well, but God has taken care of the elements, and man carries out its practical benefits throughout the world.

Truly religion is all over the world, where mind is, as there God can be truly represented. Civilization supreme can best impart its blessings, and expel the vileness of the dark ages from the world.

Do you seek pure vital religion?

Avoid all the errors and vices of superstition.

Then mind has to decide between them, by truth and honesty, humanity and facts of benefit.

All nations of the whole world are elevated in ratio to this mental elevation, that gives moral elevation; that is clear, certain, and proved.

All should seek correction of religious opinions at once; as all the errors, vices and violence of society have the elements of its destruction for the vindication of principles.

They are to be corrected ere ruin strikes down the whole.

Let us rid ourselves of all such, to exclude the pirates of society in general and particular, individuals and nations that must be rightly checked.

Our ideas of religion do essentially refer directly to the Supreme Ruler of the universe, on recognition of its organization, whose first cause is immutable as he is perfect; but man is changeable, as he is imperfect.

The fault is in the individual mind, referable either to disgraceful ignorance or bigotry, that pretends that the Great First Cause cannot be read by the eye of science in his creation.

The more correct the science, the more correct God's attributes can be thereby, and only thereby, portrayed. All others are false pretences, unworthy the rational mind of the world.

We are all accountable beings to the one living God, to whom the highest, purest principles of religion present the true emanations of mind in its loftiest aspirations.

Can there be any more genuine conversion of mind than its purest rational connection with the best reverence to Almightly God, in whom it justly confides with the most genuine Humility.

The bible of rational minds asks of you, a reasonable being, to reason on this the most reasonable of all subjects, otherwise to be silent, that strife be not recklessly engendered, where peace can be maintained.

The sacraments of religion, as prayers, are good actions.

True religion seeks to correct all wholesale errors.

In the great school of the world, the whole full duty of rational man is to mankind, and must declare the true issue of the whole religion to God.

• What else on earth can it do to correct these low characters, assuming to themselves the benefit of man-worship, excluding Deity from his rights.

Religion makes everything responsible to right principles. No priestocracy of peculiar faith can stand this test.

One peculiar system supplants the preceding as deficient, or the subsequent goes to aid the prior.

All good citizens need proper systems of government and religion; no peculiar code suits, as the code of God is supreme, all-wise, and universal.

We need a high morale for the bible of rational mind, that ancient records cannot give as adequate to the civilization of man and justice to Deity.

All the ancient systems of peculiar faith must be universally rejected, as inadequate to the morale needed at the present day.

Then nations will not seek to prevent others doing what they should do at home, that is, secure a government that give the blessings of constitutional and religious liberty.

The justice of the bible of rational mind does not stop at what is forced by rational law, or popular correct opinion. It institutes all that is right all the time, and commences at the commencement, rejecting delusions of the world, and what are too often miscalled time-honored customs, deeming all unworthy of freemen; adopting none but reason-honored, the wisest suggestions.

This code places it as the height of absurdity to take a half civilized people and make them and their institutions examples for all time to come, as models for morals and ethics of science and faith, when rational mind knows them to be preposterous.

Religion leads rational mind to view all things correctly. It teaches us that a supreme intelligent God rules nature and mind, and that materialism is utterly incompetent in the universe, and that all are in abeyance to Almighty God.

The principle of causation is ever present to rational mind, to correct the endless theories and speculations of the world, that otherwise can be perverted by atheists and polytheists.

This destroys the advocacy of all bibles of tradition.

Religion is due to the constitution of our nature.

He that resorts to peculiar faith divests himself of religion to that extent as he that resorts to small acts and cunning has no great parts nor wisdom. The sword or sophistry is the only means of propagating peculiar faith ; both are by absolutism.

What honest and truthful republican can adopt any such base means ? The light of religion is by rational instruction, and must be science, philosophy, reason, and truth, to reach the mind successfully.

Neither skepticism, infidelity nor peculiar faith can stand before the tribunal of rational religion.

Mystery is excluded by reason, that appreciates the right and virtuous power in society.

Genuine religion speaks to universal humanity, and cannot exist in the atmosphere of peculiar faith.

She establishes social relations on the right basis, exempt from antagonism; and refers to the virtues of self-government, and reliance on Deity alone.

She discards all mysticisms of peculiar faith, and all such systems.

She adopts mind as the universal agent for the universe, in regard to its relations, and thus establishes its only legitimate responsibility.

She enables us to enjoy the present, and be prepared to receive our change for other spheres at any moment.

She considers the principles of safety are to be duly estimated in the capacity of mind, and that sin is the negative of good, the antagonism of conservative principles.

She enables mind to dismiss its superstitious views and fears, and estimate the idea of hell-fire and brimstone as old as the volcanoes, and no doubt originating therefrom ; and that volcanoes, so far from being the evidence of a world's conflagration, that they are actually safety valves.

Satan, who is considered the god of evil, and enemy of mankind, extinct anyhow, has no locality if hell has no rational existence.

Would the atmosphere of the earth actually suffice to destroy it by conflagration ? How can that be accomplished ? Let the wiseacres' generations decide, as they have tinkered at all such things the lifetime of superstition and false philosophy.

But new stars have appeared, and old ones disappeared. What astronomer can pretend to more than that they are performing their revolutions in their mighty orbits.

What astronomer can pretend to assume the perfect knowledge of the splendid science of astronomy ?

Religion teaches us to inquire what would God want with angels to deliver messages on this earth, when principles perform the functions of the universe, representing a perfect omnipresence, as quick as thought, over the whole universe ?

With such powers as electricity, Deity can move the universe, and with principles he can command the whole, as they can vindicate themselves if not obeyed.

It is mind that acts, all the time obedient to those universal constituents, as principles can only be addressed to that faculty, otherwise there could be no responsibility.

God at first did all most munificently, that is falsely claimed for Messiahship all after pretences of man.

Religion is a necessary indispensable constituent of mind, and should be pure.

She considers good actions as prayers, and necessarily constant protection without hypocrisy or partisanship.

Conventions of mind may seek to perfect the standard of religion—rational religion— but at present that is impossible, unless rational mind could burst forth in its sovereign maturity of intellect and excellence.

Mind, in its inquiry for what is best to be done for society, wishes the best good faith sincerely carried out, else social qualities are mere pretences, and show the fragments of principles.

The best organized code must present liberal, enlarged, and just views, social, moral, and religious, as much as needed by enlightened freemen, that exacts enlightened public opinion and sentiment.

We need pure and fearless actions, as pure and enlightened views, else we only realize a very small proportion of our rights and interests.

It is not by faith, but by deeds and actions all the time, that mind's excellence, the only thing affording us cognizance, can be fully tested.

It is almost impossible with the finite mind, to define exactly for all future time, any exact code of morals and religion, as the progress of mind is upward, and its excellence and worth advance in its general science and philosophy.

It is for that reason that we must discard all that accords not full and fair principles.

Religion embraces professions of rational faith, and due performance of correct actions, as exact as science, and lovely as philosophy.

Upright, truthful, and honest conduct before the world is the best morals and religion.

The rational view of religion is the only best one in life, otherwise a reckless abuse of reason in sectarian faith may beget an analogous one in regard to God. You cannot serve God and Messiah at the same time, as Mahomet, Christ, or any others.

You cannot have religion and peculiar faith at one and the same time ; the thing is impossible for genuine purity.

The least that the bible of mind can propose, is mind's best reverence for God of the universe, who is worthy of all praise as the correct standard for mind to exalt its purity, and promote by his omnipotence its most correct appreciation.

The cause of religion is sacred and holy, and belongs to universal mind, with an enlightened conscience. Who dare pollute this sacred function of Divine right?

We shall never establish the safety and peace of the whole world on the equitable basis of civilization until we recognise the true principles of religion, that God has instituted.

True religion secures a universal brotherhood, the greatest universal prosperity that secures itself most successfully to individuals.

Religion has existed from and along with first created human nature. God does not exact of it sacrifices of victims—human or brute—as burnt, or blood, or mind offerings. but he does require the pure excellences of mind.

All that tolerate and practice all or any of these sacrifices are not his genuine adorers.

Rational religion does not tolerate or practice ceremonies that do not constitute religion.

A want of true civilization prevents the perfection of the bible of mind—the universal code for the world. Its completion must be sought in the mighty future.

In the analysis of the universal condition of the earth and man, we find that man's first simple hunter state shows a rude one of society ; where the wife is vassal, and man may be cannibal, with the grossest idolatry and superstition, as well observed by the Honorable John Quincy Adams.

The second state—the shepherd or pastoral, exhibits polygamy and idol worship.

The third evinces the state of agriculture, and the title of the soil begins to show the rudiments of better society : and the fourth, the citizen seeks to complete civilization. where science and philosophy can flourish, and religion triumph.

The difficulty has been from vassalage of mind, that by force of education bound to customs, has engendered castes in all countries:

Peculiar education is one of the most dangerous things to mind—the commander of the world's elements, and the aspirant to universal immortality.

Books of Tradition, Bibles, or any other as they are called, can then never do to rely on as authority, for they reflect the state of barbarism of their age and people.

The grade of anterior civilization in any of the four states of man,—the hunter, shepherd or pastoral, agricultural, or civilized,—is not high enough for mind that seeks the best lights.

The mighty soul of the world of time and sense, is enlightened intellect.

Mind, in the best state of civilization has to guard against the vitiation of a morbid taste, to which too many books cater.

Civilization, the highest state of man's existence, has to look forward and upwards for the noblest organization, and can never look backwards with justice. Paramount rights should be held to, as worth all the balance.

Wise laws, and those well executed, do away with much ferocious retaliation.

If we do not have wise, legal, rational institutions, we shall suffer by those assuming to take law into their own hands.

Not to properly resist injuries is to invite them.

We demand wise and just laws—national and international, and thus we render evils, in redress, the least.

How is it, that though all possess the innate principles of religion, that few can believe in miracles, prophecies, and mysteries ?

Because religion is divested of all such trash.

The minds that are rational and duly educated are so constituted, that reason only can prove to them all that is required. They must be hypocrites to own knowingly any other power.

All can be rational religionists, while the few affect to be spiritual, yet these two cannot be separated.

All the faith that can be given as evidence of things not seen or spiritual, is no less rational than of things seen, else it is irrational and fanatical.

Philosophy, not priestocracy, should introduce religion.

Genuine preachers are not politicians, but must adopt analysis of Nature, which is obligatory on all rational minds.

The organization of industrial labor, legislation, and improvement of religion, are to promote universal happiness that no peculiar people can appropriate.

The confined limits of pastoral and rude society in which the bibles of priestocracy originated, cannot begin to meet the wants of the world for labor, legislation, and civilization.

The mighty circumference of the globe must be embraced, and all conservative principles adopted.

We must address ourselves to the Universe when we seek the immortality of the soul, and all the means of self-preservation.

The religion of civilization cannot go back, when cultivated mind goes forward and upward.

There is but one true way of obtaining proper knowledge of God, and that by the purest reason.

Revelation is only tradition, both false, if not conformable to the law of reason.

Rational mind must subserve the purposes of the whole, not a part of the world.

The religion of all countries of the whole world, is that due one eternal God, to properly support alone the foundations of civil society.

A mediator implies a division of Deity's rights, a gross absurdity, not to say impiety. How can that be religion, in any sense of the word ?

Religion and civilization accompany each other, and give no sway to inordinate passions, but direct them in the legitimate track, requiring as the best guarantee for man's deportment, the most effectual responsibility.

No code of religious belief that puts off responsibility to another world, can be effectual.

The day of judgment, if deferred beyond the grave for indefinite time thereafter, is too long delayed.

The speediest is the most effectual of the two, as it meets all the functions of mind and soul.

The more successfully the world approaches uniformity in science, the more it succeeds in civilization and religion.

Mind well endowed and imbued in principles and manners, will do the promptings of humanity, philanthropy, and patriotism, of course, religion.

The most effectual help in this world, is that emanating from self, aided by God.

He that asks the respect of the world, must first respect himself.

Of all this before God, man must show himself worthy.

Pure religion ever addresses mind, the beneficiary, to secure the soundest views.

We need the only true great and sublime truths of religion, and never get them short of the only pure exhaustless fountain of creation's God, the sublime Creator of the Universe.

If you deny this position, you expose your vulgar ignorance and stupidity in belief of impossible things as miracles, that reverse the order of Nature.

The true gospel is what mind directs under reason's sanction, but the people are excluded from that by reason of peculiar faith, are libelled in their divine rights and are not justified as their own vindicators, but treated as children and slaves.

The word of the God of the Universe addresses the enlightened and accurate reason of mind.

Revealed religion, is by the revelation of rational mind.

Much is yet to be revealed in the progress of science and improvement of mind, that must finish its readings in the Universe.

The works of God and his best creation-gift, enlightened mind, teach mankind better than all other means.

What other than mind has claim to sacredness of character in this analysis?

No nation can have true faith but in the government and religion, that emanate from reason.

Good and evil are manufactured, as mind is enlightened or perverse.

· If rationalists are right, absolutists must be wrong.

Is not religion engrafted on mind, pre-eminently superior to all professions?

Pure and upright religion belongs to mind, properly nurtured in no faith but that of God.

Who can create any system of religion?

There can be only one orthodox, corrected by time, subject to reason's sway, not man's notions or notion's folly. That is the only one that can be catholic.

Such demands free, independent, and honest opinion, to convince the world of the justness of the faith advocated.

God addresses all rational minds to preserve the deep truths of duty, and none are left destitute of principles, or entirely to themselves.

All the Universe is operated on by God's inspiration constantly, by or through conscience, the vigilant monitor

God addresses minds all the time.

The bible of God is the bible of enlightened mind, whose aid is necessarily invoked for a world's age. Who, and what the authority is, what the whole documents and circumstances are, the Universe proves. Study it as to be mastered, on eternal principles.

Church membership is a fictitious advantage, and religion has nothing to do with peculiar faith contamination.

Religion elevates the standard of public morals to the most exalted capacity.

Religion is mistaken by the advocates of peculiar faith, for the inspiration of sanctification as an impulse; feeling, instead of reason, acted on through mind or soul.

Religion invokes all the aid of principles to meet best and most successfully, the trials, difficulties, misfortunes, and evils of life.

She teaches that mere revenge may degrade and injure her followers, whereas principles vindicate themselves and give the highest, the only moral victory. Any systems or creeds of peculiar opinions and faith that are antagonistic to the progress of just principles, are hyenas in society.

To meet the wants of the world and the majority of minds, we need a proper comprehensive code of religion, not peculiar faith, that will satisfy the whole globe, as mind is so organized from its constituent faculties, that reason must hold the sway, else truth and sincerity cannot abide. Such code will exclude the licensed tyranny and corruption of society.

But religion is not philosophy, the peculiar faith people would think.

It is the highest state of philosophy that recognises the accountability of all rational beings to God, and rendering due responsibility of itself, thereby proving its innate faculty available by the mind's inherent powers.

All enlightened minds will seek to be saved by the true salvation.

What is to save not only the world but the Universe? is the earnest inquiry.

Who can do so? None, but the Creator, who appreciates their wants, and provides for their preservation on universal principles.

Providence eternal, ever living, never dying God meets the points, and decides the whole question. Why are there so many stupid errors about religion, in every age of the world?

It was the base self-interest of the priests, and the degradation of explosion to the faith-notions of the profession, that caused its death-like support.

But let rational mind reflect.

Nothing can be done on earth without mind, then it is palpably absurd to say that reason has no hand in religion.

None but faith-jugglers can pretend to any contrary idea.

So far then as God and his attributes are proveable by his works, so far is religion proveable, the highest of all kinds of rational faiths.

The laws should take cognizance of all cases necessary in a free country; none being above the laws as above morals and religion, the supremacy of principles.

Man should not be so regarded as to permit false positions to create his own wrong and injury.

Those who reject reason in religion, are unwise and unreasonable. Are they honest men?

If mind and reason be left out, folly must be surely adopted. Pious frauds cannot supersede God's religion.

Philosophy is the height of all wisdom; it is the binding of common and proper sense with the best learning, the best and exact knowledge of science.

It constitutes then the most perfect code for religion, that venerates with the loftiest adoration, God, as perfect and pure, who could not be less concerned for man's preservation than for his creation.

As God created, he has to preserve man in the circumstances of free agency.

As to any other solution, it is man's work and pretences.

Mind and reason eminently meet all points and all cases practicable in religion.

The God of mind and reason cannot record these paramount claims to be superseded or discarded, by any minor ones, by books of tradition that have false science and system of faith.

Children, infants, show depraved and perverted minds, from perverted minds and depraved examples for generations. Now the only thing that can timely and properly counteract all that, is by proper cultivation of that very mind. That is, essential. But were it not for the bible of Moses, mind could know nothing of God ! This is the modesty of false pretences, with a vengeance ! The whole universe rebukes the infamous pretension.

The school-boy by causation or the commonest principles of cause and effect, can decide this question fully and satisfactorily, that there must be a great first cause, and all the rest created beings.

But the priestly machinery has been sprung upon mind in all ages, and instead of one great first cause, mind has been forced by brute force and ignoble government, butcheries, poisons, inquisitions, proscriptions, excommunications and all manner of ecclesiastical tyranny, to look to the number of Gods, whether of millions or Trinity, that best suited the reigning dynasty of the priestocracy, whose immediate interest was directly involved, including their cliques and foul crowds who have licked the dust off the feet of degraded priests, like men putting themselves in harness of brutes and asses, to haul harlequins and actresses about.

The world can see, if it choose, the amplest reason for the exclusion of the God of the universe by the world's priestocracy, as those of Egypt, and burying moral force, brutalizing mind in all respects, causing it to worship idols and animals.

All such creeds and bibles, just as bad from remotest antiquity, had been debased, deformed by horrid depravity, animal sacrifices, excommunications in this life, and eternal damnation in that to come. The potential power of priests, arms, and curses rarely forgave, so that the most reasonable of all reasonable propositions, the plainest and most direct truths to mind, have been degraded to its deepest perdition, enslavement and mastery.

Religion is necessarily a science, the exactness of which will be the work of civilization.

Rational religion meets the case of all rational beings, and institutes for them the order of universal brotherhood and union, that embrace the security and dignity of all mankind, causing it to look through creation to the Creator.

Religion causes all rational beings to rely on consistent conduct through life, and innocence as the only safe position. It is the comprehensive tuition.

An honest belief or faith can only embrace the result of God's attributes, the proper bible faith of rational mind.

No other bible itself can exist as true, therefore its peculiar faith falls off certainly.

The majority, fortunately, of the world at no time, has received one such faith, and it is reasonable to believe, never will.

All minds that are sane, believe in God with genuine faith. They thus prove themselves rational beings. But the most outrageous action is to arrest the advance of mind by condemning all the rational codes of religion to bibles of tradition, like arresting all constitutions of correct government that are never to be remodeled, because the first has been written. Can God or his religion be booked at once ? Are they both substantially appreciated in the dark days of superstition, ignorance and pastoral ages ? Can the world be civilized in one day ?

Does that accord with all the facts of the case ?

Science the best and perfect, and philosophy the most exact alone, enable us to see that our construction of God's attributes, mercy and justice especially, do not clash. When the Jews were the peculiar chosen people of God, having their lights and all the world else blank, then justice and mercy clash.

Then we can plainly see that mind's imperfect views, such as these, clash ; and that prove to a certainty, man being wrong. God is all wise and just, and gives a consistent religion. Then mind has to seek it of God, by the lights and requirements of mind's concentrated attribute, philosophical science, and cannot ever possess its first elements from a degraded priestocracy.

All rational beings are created with innate faculties of such religion that is elicited to mind by reason, that proves mind above all brute matter, and reflects a possession otherwise never appreciated.

The will and faith must ever follow reason in religion where freedom of mind abides. Reason can never be dictated to by the will and faith, which would be absolutism.

The great religious question carries in its bosom the solution for future blessings of the wide world.

The only fair, honest and honorable test of true religion, is the best performance of duty to the unity of the only eternal Supreme being. A belief in more, shows Polytheism, a detraction from the universal attributes of God.

What available prayers can wise and good men have, but their best communings with God, to correct themselves, not expecting to change God, but reform themselves with virtuous thoughts, words and deeds, doing as well as wishing the best for their country, and securing by good conduct the glory of such deeds.

When the empire of unity triumphs, then freedom does so. Religion does not, cannot, rest on sectarian peculiar faith, but on conservative principles. Such are adopted by rational religion. How eminently characteristic are God's liberal principles! They have no brute force, no compulsion, no blue laws and codes, and black ages to protect, no mysteries to conceal, no inquisitorial anathemas to enforce. All is gentle, kind and persuasive, through their legitimate basis the most lovely.

True religion is worthy of the most unbounded confidence and esteem of the world, whilst peculiar faith is unworthy the respect of slaves, and the sooner rejected the better.

Religious elements invariably and universally refer to innate principles and faculties at creation of each mind, while all the pretences of peculiar faith refer to the teaching of particular and partial dogmas, or especial tenets at subsequent time on the capital of religion.

After all the peculiar educations, God has erected one universal standard, the Universe, to disclose to mind, its brightest jewel, all that is rational.

Worthy citizens, begin at the point of peculiar faith, to feel serious about religion which all rational minds possessed.

But what have preserved them already from the ills and snares of the perverted world, but vital principles and God, their author, who are ever present to mind?

In the case of rational religion, principles govern the whole platform for mind, through reason up to God.

Religion asks the best recognition of intelligent minds.

Man's faith is laid in mystery for sinister purposes, but mind's, that is, God's religion, is anything but a mystery, as it is connected with the performance of duty, as plain as reason, and as honest as truth.

Resolve religion into its primary elements, and we must recognise truth, honesty, virtue, as all other constituents of a good conscience.

What have mystery and faith to do with these, that the better understood the better for the world?

Religion is to be cultivated with all upright intentions, but all the seeking to eternity will not improve it, unless on the right basis. The Almighty, who, as the Creator of mind, the beneficiary, must be the dispenser of grace that he alone created.

All kinds of faith, but rational, are incompatable with true government of God, mind, or liberal principles.

The world's fund is for mind, which, having the fund of due cultivation, presents the solution to the Universe in the harvest of time of true religion.

Among the worst tyrannies of the world, is the proscription of rational discussion and equitable decision about religion.

If mind's position be right in religion especially, what cares it an iota for free and fair investigation with rational discussion? The best rights are there rightly promoted, instead of abridged.

Religion therefore seeks all such, to best establish its paramount claims.

Innocence and purity never sneak from the contest in the conflicts of faith, certainly never get rid of the arguments by any but fair and honorable means, and leave abuse to the unprincipled opposition that needs it.

Public opinion enlightened must be paramount, as the people's rights are paramount.

Intellectual people seek to improve their religion inherent in mind by creation right, from the right source, by the right way, and at the right time, functions that cannot be filled except by the Giver.

Of course they cannot find any in any Messiah, as that is absurd and idle.

No Messiah short of Deity, could save himself at the last trying moment from the sin of blasphemy, how then save others by that heinous sin?

The world needs in religion an intellectual audience, tribunal or jury, to give a righteous verdict to God.

Most of the people, individually, lack several gifts of mind, by lack of its proper cultivation, in being able to analyze what is religion. The most are not competent in phrenological developments or mind, time, ability, to remove themselves from habits of thought, prejudices of education, customs, by want of maturity of science.

Then we must protest for anything but a fair and impartial analysis of this mighty question, as no man can be depended on from weakness of human nature, the ignorance and corruption of the age. Then, who can be satisfied without his own best exertions in this whole matter?

But the whole world seeks the mighty gift, religion, and where does it find it? Is it the gift of priestocracies and their peculiar faith? Or is it not the endowment of God at creation's birth, already possessed, but to be improved on for life?

Innate faculties of religion distinguish rational beings, the dignified character of the human species, from that of animals, and render them superior to all animated nature.

Religion regulates the affairs of mind, that is in abeyance to God for man's happiness.

The only divine government is that of God, and all of men must be identified with principles constitutional, have the right means to remain enlightened as by the fountain source, rational education, and all pure educational influences, as the press, &c.

If government must be pure, what else can religion be? In her teaching and illustration, most conformity to science has to be established, as acknowledging the want and actions of mind.

If religion have any officers, their lives must be pure, else she degenerates into peculiar faith-trickery; but the whole people are the only officials. The claims of religion and ethics are verified as true, as relating to man by God, a paramount and universal, not peculiar divinity.

This characteristic, written by its Master's hand, on the Universe, does away entirely with peculiar bibles, people, or salvation, or messiahships, which doctrines have been forced on the minds of the people by various insidious pretences of priests, have been dove-tailed and are hard to be eradicated.

Sophistry that deceives the world in every age by her countless wiles, urges the false doctrine for the true, of which most minds, from peculiar education, cannot distinguish the difference, or are afraid to attempt the analysis, however sound their private individual skepticism. The absolutism of church and state, with all their powers, alarms them.

God, the guardian of mind, can tell how much of the world has rightly improved its religion, whether called pagans or christians, or any other name of sectarianism. He only takes the will for the deed.

It is time that no fraud should be tolerated about religion that can only be of God.

It is the bounden duty of the principals of the world to institute a code of ethics, to see how far mind cultivated and civilized can universally reach to protect the rights of all. It is high time that it be done, as it is due the world.

The right code teaches honor to parents and country, principles and God, above all.

The bible of mind teaches to regard the rights of the people paramount, those of priestocracies and hierarchies subordinate, and not to forbear in the presence of the world for absolutism.

Toleration of opinion with freedom, has perfected the great principles of true religion, that is incontestibly best secured by free and rational discussions in freest governments. The rational definition of man, then, makes him possessed of the innate faculty reflective of ideas of religion, that binds indispensably and innately to this Supreme Being, who has shown his supreme intelligence by thus engrafting into mind this inextinguishable faculty.

The certain consequence is, that the higher the cultivation of mind, the purer may be its religion.

Truly, then, is a brute animal defined to be a being without innate capacity of ideas of religion, or that has no faculty to develope or exercise them.

To this exact definition, mind, when perverted, is more or less degraded in part.

Then there is no cognizance in sincerity of any mediator, for there can be nothing intermediate to mind but its adorable Creator, consequently, all offered as such, as Christ, Mahomet, Paganic, or Juggernaut, Confuciusic, Bhuddic, Mormonic, or any analogous, are imposters, and blasphemous pretenders by their imposition. The Almighty shows his characteristic supremacy by preoccupancy of the whole ground through omnipresence, and his work is heralded by the Universe.

Thus the mighty question of mind is at once decided, and analysis declares the difference between the false position of peculiar faith, that is to be superseded by rational religion. In the first, we see polytheism deformed by man ; in the last, the God of the universe portrayed in his master virtues. None but mind could see the God of the universe. Cultivated rational mind can see no mortal intercessor, as that is an imposition. Reason teaches this, and reason is truth.

The religion of God is for freemen ; free agency—free action—and ennobles mind.

Every person must attend to all final duty, ere life passes.

All things and works give a faith, in God alone.

All work into that universal belief ; whereas all work out of peculiar faith, is unworthy of rational mind. You cannot drag a rational mind out of the belief in a God ; you cannot drag the same into the belief of a Messiah, as you cannot drag it into an irrational faith.

All this is utterly impossible.

If the one be a principle, the other is antagonistical.

Now who has principles ? their universal author, or the peculiar pretender adopting what is ready made to his hands ? Conservative principles are concentrated in the right use and exercise of mind, that upholds religion as indispensable, but emanating from God.

Religion does not know anything of peculiar faith, but is sustained on rational faith, that is necessary, and must be supported by facts, truth, and reason.

What benefits accrue from affecting to feel religion, when peculiar faith predominates ?

Religion is the science of God-morals, and is the obligation the most enlightened due to God and mind, from mind, the noblest jewel of the universe.

What, then, is religion ? Let liberal patriotism, enlarged to the world's circumference, one of its duties, tell the wisest statesmen.

All the world's books—a world's age—will only begin the momentous subject.

This subject can never be booked ; and after all the oriental dogmas, fables, and legions of myths are buried beneath the ruins of their crumbling temples, then will pure religion rise in her glory, as permanent as eternity.

We go for religion that must supersede peculiar faith. Where do we go for such religion ? To rational mind, that belongs to rational beings, the emanations of Deity.

We must start right at once with truth and honesty, then manners of courtesy and politeness, kindness and love, bounded by no peculiar faiths nor globe localities.

Minds, properly constituted, will throw aside envy and sectarianism, for the noblest theme of religion.

All rational beings improve religion, as all such have it as a faculty—the more reason the more religion—the more improved and cultivated the better.

All must seek rational cultivation, that is truth.

There is no rational being that has reasonable mind, and having rational actions, relying on the best lights of cultivated mind, that can miss religion.

Mind has it in thought, word, and deed ; the better the more civilized and virtuous.

There is no fiction in religion ; that is a creation birth-right, and a life-tenure.

Religion proves itself from God, and is mind felt, and universally beneficial.

How does feeling of religion truly decide, when the feeling of peculiar faith is deceptive and fallacious ? Every mind must weigh well the character of equivocal morals, and of the means giving diffusion to them ; the mind feels assured on its rational foundation of the only supreme standard that the mind of the universe can reach.

The moral sublime endows mind with conclusive feelings.

Any religionist, so far from finding fault with rational discussion about religion, ought to seek it by all manner of means, to get rid of the errors of judgment, deliberately, unintentional or intentional, but otherwise unavoidable.

One outrage on mind is, that churchmen, members of any character of supposed power, should exclude such improvement. Mind that is rational seeks rational decision.

The truest enjoyment of mind results in possession of religion, that can only be appreciated as rational, as joy results from even enthusiasm, but much more from rational grounds of truth.

Mind needs a universal religion, to give God alone his power and rights, and mind its duty.

Some persons, bigots of course, are alarmed at the bare mention of authors who have destroyed the foundation of their creed. There is something in the thing, not in the name. There was as much religion in Rome the ancient as in Rome the modern, flourishing in its horrid inquisition, illiberal and cruel excommunication of persons for opinion, and dishonest confiscation of property. Which massacre is the least sinful, that by gladiators or that by inquisitions?

The walls of a Saint Peter, who flourished a saint in name, rise towering to God's mighty solar system, in the richest and most gorgeous architecture; but can all such reach the mercy-seat of the Almighty, as soon as if its costly prices were wisely dispensed to the suffering poor? This then is part of religion—duty to mankind and mind, that must be cultivated rightly, and humanized to civilization.

But few minds, where it is eminently the duty of all, investigate rightly the important points of religion.

The most important acts of one's life are, to pay due respect to religion, and be sure of the power to whom it is paid. How idle to spend one's life in superstitious worship, or anything short of pure adoration of God alone.

Religion appeals to mind's noblest and highest duties, in the use of principles that have done so much for the universe, but have been wofully overlooked for man-worship.

Religion is rational, and appeals to rational beings, through rational principles, and excludes dupes and hypocrites in faith most positively that has no particle of foundation, and bigots who affect to rule society by pretences.

Rational religion is the only one possible to exist, as all the rest is mere peculiar faith—the child of superstition and man-worship—the counterfeit of hypocrites who resort to smuggling.

Does not the world demand of mind not only a just but a generous—not only a wise but a liberal exposition of its capacity for religion? Religion is the true duty to God, that depends on nothing else than philosophical principles to its proper development, in reaching the right start—the Great First Cause.

Without analysis, some would suppose christianity was religion; others, that Mahometanism, and several that Mormonism was religion. Very clear of it all.

They have not the dignity of the name even; as they are all superstition and man-worship; all humbugs, having no underpinning of religion. Was the predecessor of all these, religion? Was Judaism aught but priestocracy, with all its machinery? Judaism, a miserable sectarianism, was preceded by countless myriads of sectarianisms.

The history of the world shows that one species of superstition has succeeded another —the polytheism of the moderns that of the ancients.

For centuries the christian peculiar faith was struggling for existence and power, till the power of the state, (then a monarchical autocracy,) of Rome breathed into it vitality. Mothers in seeking religion for their children, can only desire the best upright views for their tuition.

The liberal wise do not want superstition, or that which is connected to absolutism, to enslave and debase the human mind. Feelings short of rationality will never decide religion, that is certain, nor mere peculiar education; nothing short of the light of philosophical principles will answer. Principles, then, for ever!

All rational beings wish to be right about religion, not to be enslaved by superstition and the absolutism of its Church power, State power, and all its other malign powers.

Religion is the most endearing of all, the most sublime of civilization. It preserves the noblest elements of friendship, and extracts the most beneficial results from the mirror of eternity, giving the solace of the first, and the wisest teachings of the last, to which it is not in abeyance under its own triumphant principles.

It teaches mind to discard pride, but adopt an elevation and dignity of character.

It realizes the treasures of experience of life, and forbids their burial. It respects the real objects of generosity. It considers it absolute perfidy to impose knowingly on the world the interested and partizan acts of peculiar faith.

Peculiar faith is concealed, monotheism, is open and unpretending, and the purest monotheist comes the nearest of having the least cause of repentance.

Religion can never justify vassal slavery to faith.

Analysis of philosophical science proves religion due the God of nature, and disproves any peculiar faith.

Peculiar faith is sectarianism that has nothing to do with religion. The province of religion is to render mind correct and better, and to free it from contingency.

There is but one true religion having living witnesses to attest it. There are two paramount points: the first is what shall the affectionate parents especially do for their offspring, if they do not have religion?

But all rational beings have it by creation's birth-right.

The main point is its right improvement.

God has given it and mind to man. Mind must improve its free agency under the circumstances, the conservative principles of its creation.

None but true religion and its best improvement, will answer for the best civilization.

But as to investigation of religion, this is the last and least thing done. But little of absolute facts about religion, is investigated. The words of an interested and ignorant priestocracy, who neither know the nature of the God of nature, nor of mind, are taken for granted.

The main point, the object, the God of nature alone, is absolutely sneaked out of, and the parties are intentionally deceived. Religion is the comprehension of sacred duties, moral and intellectual, paid to the sacred Supreme, who has fashioned the universe in perfect wisdom.

Mind only needs a suitable audience to approve.

You inquire what are you to do for religion ? You have it, and have only to exercise the principles essential to its proper cultivation, to approach the nearest to God.

But the word of God is essential to carry us through life. Where is that word ? In the purest recesses of an illumined mind, that has been enlightened by the most exact philosophical sciences.

We consider it the deepest impiety and blasphemy, to consider peculiar faith-scriptures as the word of God.

All need the living and essential principles of religion. Whether bible, law or constitution, morals or mind are respected, good faith is the essential of religion, their essential.

Some affect that the obligations of society are not attached to the highest duty of God. How can we duly respect God without duty to society of the best kind ? The most honorable duty is implied, if not pledged by all its members, for the greatest good to all the greatest number, the foundation and essence of society.

What does God need of man ? Implied duties of his position.

The world should be now thankful for the present age by which the light of truth is extracted from so much darkness. Conceive it, citizen, to be your noblest prerogative, to perform deeds equal to those of God in similar circumstances. Reason is then the mighty fortress of mind, against which the adverse currents of life may beat in vain. True religion inculcates not the conformity of principles to thy peculiar faith, but thy peculiar faith to principles ; then thou wilt be obliged to adopt monotheism or rational religion.

Religion dwells not in the heart, but in the mind, the soul of mankind. What is religion but the payment of duty we owe to God, to whom all such is due ?

How could we pay all, if we divided it with usurpers and priestocracies ? Religion in the practical universal sense, is truthful faith and consistent action, not as a small part of one division, sect or denomination, but as the laws of God dictate. We wish to be right in religion. We depend on a moral and intellectual force.

Moral force to be available, must be rational and intellectual, to reach the foresight of results, and exclude ignorant fanaticism. Right religion is for intelligent freemen, but peculiar faith suits vassalage of mind. If there be nothing true and right to advance, science above all things is expedient, to maintain the principles of justice and mind. It is the province of religion to rationalize and generalize for this world, all her purest benefits. What is religion but the most sacred duty that mind owes and pays, to the adorable Creator of the universe, who sublimely holds sway by mind influence ?

Anything that detracts from this, is a false and corrupt position. We have no bad feelings to any peculiar faith, but feel bound to do justice to rational faith, in good faith to our own souls. The highest obligations of society insuring proper actions, involve good faith, and that is religion. Religion cannot compromise her dignity with the peculiar faith of all bibles of tradition.

Any individual that has not truth, honesty and reason, has no showing of religious dignity.

There are various systems of faith, but can only be one of religion, as truth and principles do not clash, therefore it is the diamond among trash.

But these faiths had their martyrs, and so has atheism had ; that proves nothing. Juggernautism, martial ambition and the evil passions have had millions of theirs. Martyrdom, then, must yield to reason in all analysis. But you have the true faith because you have the bibles of priestocracy ! Because you have the bible of tradition, it no more follows that that entitles you to religion, than your being in a nominal republic secures you honorable liberty.

We wish all to go as far as the farthest legitimately advanced in religion. As to conscience, that is wofully perverted the world over, by peculiar education. Who is to set it right in religion ? Priests, who have not improved the elements already possessed ?

We might as well ask sharp lawyers who are partizans besides being proxy and agents. Priests are peculiar faith-lawyers. Can the world be set right by such? The conscience is at the mercy of the world whether fanatic, superstitious, or dishonest, as the adverse circumstances may decide, and can be only freed by liberal mind fund of philosophical science that imparts the right rational education. The exalted state of civilized mind, will make bibles of tradition an obsolete idea, and will establish the true progress of civilized religion.

No bibles of tradition can take precedence of the great inalienable rights of mind. Order and justice of the whole world are only obtained by properly cultivated mind, not by erroneous bibles from unprincipled and wicked men. Honorable men must go for the dignity of principles.

What power, gifts and magnificent elements of greatness has the world to rear, her noblest elevation, and yet she does not appreciate them.

What a sophisticated state of the world exists, when subject to perverted mind.

In these enlightened times, we can have reforms of organic laws and constitutions, but minds made vassal to the most degraded absolutism, miserable bibles of tradition.

Is the moral and intellectual force of mind to be broken down by bibles of tradition, the nuisances of the world?

No such bibles can over-ride moral and intellectual force that upholds social and political order.

Religion must embrace a moral and intellectual force, that to be valid, must embrace all the inherent principles, else it is not intellectual and legitimate.

It is high time to decide between peculiar faith and religion, the pretences of bibles of tradition and the principles of bibles of rational mind. These are world-wide questions for intellectual solution, and no bible of tradition can take us out of this life's difficulties, when the base is wrong, and all such are miserable failures because they are false pretences plunging us deeper into quagmire.

Mind that radiates the best of civilization, will do the work the best and only best.

But you, bound to custom and its vassalage, can never lay aside man's pretences, and refer the great vital functions of principles to God.

Are not restraints and obstructions put upon religion?

What does that worse than peculiar faith, engendered by the bibles of tradition? As hope must be attended with possibility, religion looks to the practicability through God's attributes. She never places the God of the Universe in all manner of equivocal positions, as a peculiar god of man's creation!

Pure society is what the world needs, and that only pure religion gives. The world needs all religion that it can get, but no peculiar faith.

All that you want is religion, not false bibles, as the bibles of traditions. All the world needs in all religion is good faith, and nothing less, avoiding as it must, fanatic absolutism. No man knows what God said, except through cause and effect, that are appreciated by only what reason, truth, rational mind and honesty say.

Whatever system is God's, that mind can understand; hence, all lie that say, we cannot get the idea of the God of Creation from the Universe. We cannot get it from any other source. All such people must lie knowingly.

The greatest good to all the greatest number, involves all that belongs to society and religion, mind, and God, and courtesy to freemen.

Religion teaches implied honor in society; no half way action. Would she hesitate to accord to woman all the rights of soul that belong to the other sex?

To relieve the world of persecution, bigotry, false faith and doctrine, religion speaks through rational mind. Jew, will you for the sake of superstitution, still circumcise children? What can you promise yourself by this odious and degrading mutilation? The God of the Universe never did this! Your little peculiar God that was so fierce against the heathen in the conclave of priestocracy, did only as the Jew priestocracy dictated. Are you still enslaved to such vassalage? Grace, conscience, and mind, all go together in religion. These, not circumcision, give the hope of a religious man. Spare your children in this free country, this degradation. Do not enslave, debase their minds, mutilate their persons, or desecrate their rights.

God alone makes religion what it is. Society is to be instituted on the great principles of God, not the dogmas of man. Religion starts no subordinate question, but prepares man to meet all his duties as he ought, while peculiar faith disqualifies him all the time from commencement to the end, as he violates the first elements of religion towards God at once. The very moment peculiar faith advances, the systems of sectarianism begins and their elements of warfare are let loose. Religion begets the highest sense of duty, and recognises all's well that ends well.

She gives peace and equanimity, serenity of mind, to all that wish to secure the best moral certainty, and feel resigned to their situation and position. What can we do better than rely on the Author of mind, grace, mercy, and happiness, and its permanent abode? Let us seek that point where pure religion is, as she legitimatizes the whole elements of mind and its nature, to God and man.

What avail religion, if morals be deficient?

Mind only wishes such system that it can thoroughly, rationally, and most consistently believe in; that can bring no tinge or blush for its advocacy, but the world's satisfaction for its most substantial adoption. Religion demands a most rational investigation, to have the most rational decision.

Then, look at the best bible of mind.

As to the heathen and Jewish priestocracy, all missed the true appreciation of religion and morals, as they were more or less removed from civilization.

Religion gives us the clearest view of life and its duties, and its platform is the only constitutional one of the world and mind, that renders the possessor and improver as good as practicable, knowing that he is right, and that the foundation, as the only one, cannot be shaken.

The world's organization on universal brotherhood, must and will prevail to a practicable extent. Have you looked into this thing, of religion that depends on pure and honest truth, above suspicion?

If we do not succeed in religion with mind, we cannot in anything else. Religion is a theme that no menial critic can say aught against, as he cannot do so by principles. As we have a system of constitutional government that legitimately carried out will answer the demands of civilized mind, so let us have a system that defines religion to which we may entrust our lives, fortunes, and sacred honor. Let us have no cause for distrust.

The pure religion of God is commanded to man, by the luminous disposition of rational mind. The supreme love to the God of the Universe is proved and demonstrated most clearly, by the love of mankind in one universal brotherhood. This is the religion of rational mind and civilization. What can uphold better the dignity of rational mind?

Religion is not contaminated by priestocracy.

Integrity and conscientiousness are ornaments in the religious platform of God Almighty. Good habits, laws, and principles, are its most worthy assistants.

Religion gives an exalted state of belief in God, not in mortals. We discard the bible of tradition to establish religion of the highest and purest order. Religion must be consistent to be rational, and asks for correction by rational discussion, unlike peculiar faith that precludes it by inquisition or proscription! Such sneaks from all proper responsibility, at the same time libels religion. All laws and acts to do the greatest good to the greatest number, that is to all, must be predicated on those principles that are immutable.

But can any refuse this sublime subject? What can be more important to harmonize the world's interests and feelings? It can furnish world-staples, as love, honesty, and truth, that constitute its essence. What better is there? Is there any bible but that of mind? Prove any other to be the word of God. This proof, will secure its suitable reward, for it embraces the munificent works of creation as the legitimate comprehension, and secures the due reverence to God, the Creator.

You become excited for the first time about religion, when invoked by the priestocracy, and seek to get what you only have to improve. But you adopt for granted, by impulse, not rationality, and you become committed. Nine-tenths do not investigate, or change to the right point.

Now all the world should first investigate by the bible of mind. There are some things above the world's criticism, as that of religion, that will revolutionize the world, no matter sects, creeds, and opinions.

The only union of religion is that to freedom, as the greatest theme for each individual mind.

In all governments of the present age, the sacred rights of all citizens will secure the only purity in religion. Religion should give universal harmony, but peculiar faith disorganizes the world.

The necessities of the world require true religion.

What is really practicable for man in this life, to obtain the most happiness? To attain the best position through the virtue, intelligence, &c., of rational mind.

Religion is thoroughly rational, and induces principles as the rule of action the purest, not fear, as peculiar faith has it. The principle of religion is involved in the elements of science and philosophy, all concomitants of mind, the beneficiary.

Let the world start right, about religion. Let the first step be correct. She teaches mind to avoid everything that will make it principal or accessory to crime. While religion must be inherent in the human mind, peculiar faith must be expelled the world.

All the religion that the world has is right : but all its bible peculiar faith is wrong. By mastering principles, you may master all the contingencies, and rule the unprincipled demagogues, agitators, and dictators of society, assuming to know what they do not.

Let truth and honesty advance, no matter about the words of religion. What but religion presents the right sound opinion and sentiment, most beneficial to the world ? What a poor thing if God had not bestowed the gift of religion, in all existence and age, to rational mind, that improved improves its state of religion, but had left it for fraction of existence and age to the contingency of Messiahship, that might have been unknown to the majority.

But how is it possible that mind should have possessed religion without revelation of God ? That is the only reason that it does possess it in its purity. If God had not revealed it to mind, who could ? But mind is so helpless ! It is in an absolute state of ignorance ; but we must not merely reason from the past, but from the present and future, as regards the full knowledge of science.

At one time the world, by the dogmatism and despotism of peculiar faith, could only get to peculiar gods, as the Jews and Christians, who were and are all more or less polytheists, having two, three, and four gods of peculiar characters all of them.

The true God, in perfect unity, has been unknown to most of mankind, to the present times, by perversion of mind.

How beautiful and sufficient is the system of religion, that is God-gift—a creation's birth-right—a fore full and satisfactory thought ; whereas all others are contingent as after-thoughts—utterly ridiculous, absurd, and imbecile. It is the duty of all rational beings to analyze religion and mind ; to know what mind requires. The analysis of mind gives us the analysis of religion. Do we go for religion ? That is the reason that we go for a correct bible of mind, to attain perfect religion.

Impressions are everything that cause peculiar faith, and supersede facts. Now if the facts are not verified, of what avail or rational use is faith ? Of course religion must take precedence of all bibles of tradition.

We ask for the sacred deposit of religion, to be kept inviolable. None but she gives right impressions in time in this world. A good intention of the world's mind is to aid in all good undertakings, not exclude them.

Religion, as truth, must take precedence of faith, and cannot conflict at all with truth before rational minds. What is faith worth without faithful rational evidence ? Rational mind reveals religion, that teaches us that we have certain duties to perform, any how, in the greatest comprehension ; that we must not speak undeservedly of the world, nor do it ill, much less think ill of the same. We must correct it—better it— do not make it worse ; that is, we must act thus to ourselves. Religion is the high conservation awarded by Divine power, that protects all, and interferes with no speculation. She gives the efficient responsible power to endorse our actions—to have the proper and safe position.

The majesty of intellect is in religion. We only ask for all the legitimate fortitude of religion at the last final change. How shall we meet death ?

By religion, that teaches that principles vindicate themselves in retributive justice. Religion makes all principled, then they must act consistently, and conform to immutable laws. This prepares the way for universal brotherhood.

The paramount question with the world is, what system or code will give the greatest number the greatest amount of morality and true vital religion, the best essence and element of happiness ? Nothing but rational religion will, to be the true one. Then how can we best appreciate and secure it ? Free rational discussion is the only way to attain all, in its purity.

Reverence the highest cause, as to discard the bibles of tradition, as most irreverent and usurping.

True religion never has been rightly advocated.

She involves justice, while peculiar faith flees it under the special plea of faith.

By the authorization of religion, principles were made for all—the great conservatives to mind in all ages of the world. Religion puts us on the safe, the right side.

If honesty be one of the pillars of religion, peculiar faith then cannot exist at all, as it is untrue, a part of superstition. Religion makes all things right, hence the good must aid in the majesty of all proper laws and social rights. There is no black-letter God-written code of religion. but there is the counterfeit in man's bibles of peculiar faith.

Do I object to religion ? never, whilst my mind recognises duty to God and man. If the people do not have religion, they must have superstition, its substitute. They, in their ignorance, were never known to be without the last, therefore all should have rational religion, the more civilized the more rational. But none of this admits bibles of tradition, Christianity, Mormonism, Mahomedanism, or any other peculiar faith. If you start such system, that begets more, and keeps the world always wrong. But religion established rationally, not peculiarly, begets more rational religion, the more the people are civilized.

With the true faith of religion you can have no sects, no polytheism, idolatry of man-worship, or images, atheism, no speculation or trade, for all will be between one's conscience and conscience's God, proved by action to man, proved by social good.

It is not only not wrong, but absolutely right.

Religion teaches to think first and last of your Creator, exclusively so as Creator and Preserver.

You can get the only pure religion from the purest fountain, which nature's God gave thy mind. He is represented by mind and conservative principles, as the powerful agents in the universe.

Religion gives a social faith and confidence. It enables all minds to wish all the world to prosper, then it may prosper with all.

This position enables mind to see that the Creator of the universe is properly represented, not in a peculiar, but universal perfect power and character.

This is his character, support it godly, religiously.

No master's words, but God's principles, declare his own religion. The organization of the world's circle is to counteract wo, to comprehend happiness. Religion is national and universal, never sectional, but as lofty as patriotism prompts, to secure the order, peace, harmony and happiness of the world. It eschews pride, but ever adopts highmindedness. The mighty functions of time and supreme action over all, as the optimist, are hers.

Right and wrong, virtue and vice, sectarianism and religion, are not arbitrary distinctions, but have their lines of demarcation.

Among the beauty and munificence of mind, is one of the crowning virtues, forbearance ; that includes a host of virtues that ripen the soul for eternity.

If rational faith be wrong, what faith, then, can be right? Matters of government have been submitted to the people on constitutional properties, why not religion, that would institute the proper energies of moral and social duties? Religion yields the inalienable imprescriptible rights of duty by reason of creation. She alone, in the solution of the mighty problem of the world, gives the excellency of enlightened civilization.

This enlightened age should insure, on the best security, the most enlightened system of rational polity, for the most enlightened civilization. This is to render all satisfied, correct, and happy. How are the true ends of life attained? By the best of self-government. What is government for? For the best interests of society, by a proper inherent protection of its organic bodies.

The highest attainment is rational freedom, that confers its principles to nations, illustrated by enlightened and refined civilization. The blessings of all are the highest practicable steps. The teachings of pure religion will cause God to estimate mind, as the noble character acting according to the best of its nature, not in reference to the traditional legends of obsolete bibles.

Who are infidel? They who know not religion, but should know that it is the highest duty to the God of the universe, and nothing less. She knows no God less than the Creator of the universe. The bible of tradition and religion! choose ye between them, as the one is distinct from the other.

It is the least of evils, the best philosophy, to resign ourselves to satisfaction under matters of equitable government, though they particularly bear on us whilst they correct greater evils elsewhere. Religion enjoins this much on us. Would you individually keep yourself forever in a passion for what you cannot alter, and which benefits others as the least of evils? To analyze religion, we must analyze the universe, as its relations can be comprehended by it.

Religion is not worship, but adoration, if rational, it has no peculiarity. Man is necessarily a moral, religious as intellectual being. True religion must and will meet the whole demands of conscience. Peculiar faith subverts them.

Religion directs all the affections legitimately, maintains the best equilibrium of mind in support of duty.

She has no burdensome and expensive ritual, no gorgeous priestocracy, no ceremonies and rites, no miracles, no prophecies, no mysteries, no pretensions, but all glorious realities of mind.

None but rational religion has ever been in all kinds of times, and all ages of the world, in all states and conditions of mind, for its creation's birth-right. It is the perpetual religion, that had a contemporaneous existence with mind. Man cannot invent religion. Mere faith carries with it self-delusion, whereas rational religion carries with it satisfactory truths.

Why should there be penalties for society? If no more, the Supreme law of society, that of self-preservation, requires it. As the Creator is the one great Supreme standard for the universe, so religion must be the supreme standard for public opinion. What can be worse than a vague, miserable public opinion, based on no supreme conservative principles? The world, then, suffers. This helps to bring on irretrievable ruin.

Is the bible supreme over religion and mind? Rather, are not these supreme over the bible of tradition?

You seek to be pure with the best? Yes. The bible of mind comes to aid in the perfection of that purity. Why should there not be freedom in religion? Does it belong to anything but mind, the beneficiary? Some seek to act on mere temporal policy, to do the thing of intrigue and concealment, so as not to be found out! That is not the safe position. Do the thing of principle, on principle, to defy crimination of the world. It is not the being found out, but the competency to triumph over vice.

The noblest view, the highest value that is practicable by duty, is inculcated by religion. There can be no sanctification in peculiar faith, as religion only admits justification through grace, and mercy for hope.

We see merely one-sided views in the pulpit.

Rational discussion is the only fair position about religion, nothing short of it. Here is no negative, but a positive position. The rational takes precedence of the irrational; it is not cold nor deficient, when it is the only thing expedient. It is the creation of God, the substantial reality for the embodied soul, in all its duties and affections. Ours is to build up and expose the subtleties and sophistries of the presumptive substitutes. The great defect and error in mind of all, are the partial action as to our duty, religion— it lacks legitimate comprehension. There is an awful vacuum in morals and happiness, only to be met by mind in its wisest actions of legislation, rational education, &c.

What a singular idea that classes of people are sanctified, have gone as high as faith can carry them.

Now let us correct the priestocracy. If mind had attained perfection in science and wisdom, it were all right, but as we know that it is otherwise, it is all presumption and assurance.

The world has to adopt principles sooner or later, if it adopt justice. The world will not be right till mind be right, well educated and cultivated.

Reverence God's principles by reverence to mind.

In seeking after religion, we go for truth, to which faith and fable are in abeyance. One of the great secrets of life, of religion that imparts mental satisfaction, is to have no antagonism with the world.

How can the world avoid that? By the adoption of principles. It is rational education that teaches and enables individuals and nations to look to themselves independently. But for this, an insidious world will use them to the end of their lives.

Religion scorns the idea of idols or images in any respect whatever; it seeks not rites or ceremonies of faith, but goes in for the realities of mind.

Religion is rational, not cold, speculative philosophy, being part and parcel of all rational minds.

There is but one thing worthy of the name of religion, the pure adoration of Almighty God. Who had this? None connected with priestocracy.

Religion seeks the exclusive pure empire of God, who is universally supreme. The great essentials should be correctly appreciated in the world.

The social organization requires the perfection of religion in practice.

Religion is the best kind of law and justice, for the whole human family. The reverence due to God, and the paramount obligation to religion, have caused this work to be written. It is practical religion that is worth anything to the social relations of the world, that yields no individual hypocrisy, no rational aggression, no unnatural crimes, no world's distress.

It is of the utmost consequence that man have religion, and disavow all peculiar faiths for the best of reasons, universal brotherhood, that cannot be established without it. See the state of all peculiar sects that have deranged. dissociated and demoralized the whole world in all ages, and that cannot possibly be reconciled because they are peculiar.

Religion is all trust in the God of the universe, and the highest, most virtuous duty to society.

The elements of religion are in all rational minds.

The world has the best of reasons for rational religion to secure a universal brotherhood, to stop all the degradations of pretended prophecy, that may be any and every-

thing that human piracy can make it. Pure religion is confined to no locality nor age,
neither to sectarianism of Polytheism, Christianity, Judaism or Mormonism. Before
Christ was even thought of, for thousands of years since mind's creation, religion necessarily existed as a part of mind.

The Creator managed all this by forethought, whereas the priestocracy has interpolated their puny peculiar faiths, most spurious coin of after-thoughts.

The great question with the world, lies between rational religion and peculiar faith,
which may be Christianity, Judaism, Mahommedanism, Mormonism, but not religion.

To reach this, revelation of the universe must be appropriately studied, and the
proper adoption made. All the revelations of peculiar faith or tradition bibles, can
never reach religion, the essential principles of which are the birth-right constituents
of every mind.

The great question then is, rational religion or none.

Peculiar faith makes many revelations all peculiar, and many peculiar assumptions.
Rational mind has rational faculties or means to attain its happiness. If God has designed a future state of existence for mind, most clearly it is improbable that the perfect Creator should have given.several revelations to the world, and all so imperfect as
not accomplish his object by a majority !

All persons ought thoroughly to know religion, none peculiar faith. The main great
question you and the whole world are concerned in, is religion. But all the bibles of
tradition do not present the meagre pretence of justice to mankind. We may well say,
what a libel on justice ! Let it not be forgotten that morals, laws and government, of
the right cast, are a part and parcel of religion, that no peculiar bibles ever yet
presented.

As reformed faith advances benefits to the world, so will rational religion complete
the position. Religion teaches the adoration of God alone, in his purity.

What is sin ? Any thing antagonistic to God's immutable principles.

One of the most abominable is that of the priestocracy, to render God's government
divisible. This is contemptible. There is no legitimate ability to trade on the capital
of any peculiar faith offered in the world.

Religion is to carry out the highest obligations of civilized society. The whole
question of religion has never been truly solved, and the balance has been ignobly surrendered to peculiar faith, an unscrupulous usurper, which has to be discarded as a preliminary solution by mind, ere the world be rightly brought to its relative and absolute
position. The first English settlers of New England assume to have emigrated for
religion, not for bible idols.

What promotes the first ? Assuredly, not the last. Then the world is in error,
enslaved by peculiar customs and habits. Religion bespeaks the purity of intention,
and the intellectuality of design.

As to sectarianism, religion is not divided. When there is the spirit of division, religion is not there. Religion has no sectarianism. Wherever we see the last, the first
does not exist at all. In the place of the bible of peculiar faiths, she uses what is
available all the time in her utilitarian processes, in law, order and morals, establishes
the noblest institutions practicable for the world, and has them most faithfully carried
out.

The Jew, Christian, Brahmin, Bhuddist, Mahommedan, and Mormon, are personally
friends by direct commercial and world-interests.

Are these to be annihilated in useless and dangerous faiths, that never were worth an
iota to the sovereign people, being mere devices to uphold dynastics oppressive to the
people ?

They seek to know what to be at. They must adopt, what rational men only can
do. The whole world of peculiar faiths must lay them aside, and unite on the only
platform practicable, given them by God, who is the eternal standard. The question
of religion rises above all peculiar faiths. I go for the soul of religion, not the form
of peculiar faith. The mere intellectuality of man will not do in all this matter, much
less his opinion founded on the authority of other people's pretences. It requires the
soul, the mind, and its best functions, to make him what he ought to be. Mind has not
accomplished its mission, till it has solved the mighty question of religion through its
highest rationality. With that, peculiar faith or its advocates, have nothing to do.
But the term of religion some affect to be a re-binding again, as if man was ever cut
loose from his existence, or the Author of his existence. He may adopt any absurd
notion about faith, and affect to be under its superstitious protection, but that has not
absolved him yet from abeyance to the Author of his creation, whom he thus constantly
libels.

The world needs a sound, healthy, public mind. It can be only on the conservative principles of pure religion, not of peculiar faith, the highest, most refined civilization. Religion commands mind to investigate with reverential duty, its position, and not let the world plead in vain for necessary assistance.

She institutes all the proper offices of life. She requires all to treat the world courteously, but all must protect themselves against its machinations. Religion is that which unites the moral Universe, but any peculiar faith, Christianity, Judaism, or any, separates them wide apart, and renders them hostile! Citizen of the world, think of these things. Let the world master the subject of Monotheism, and then it will see the full benefit of rational religion.

Religion teaches all the social, civil and individual duties, the filial and parental, and all the kindred relations. The obligation to poor relations, sisters and brothers, are paramount to empty monuments that last but for a time.

Religion is essential to the cause of the right faith, or view of God's facts. All the peculiar-faith bible people are squatters on the legitimate premises of religion. This great question of religion ought to be satisfactorily settled before the world, that bible bullies may no longer blackguard those who choose to think rightly. The world should see a speedy end to all the pretences of all peculiar faiths.

So great is the intrinsic capital of virtue and integrity, that the whole world affects them when not inherent; therefore the standard of religion establishes the position.

Religion has ever shed its divine light more or less on mind, according to its cultivation.

No sect appropriates religion or its principles.

When we see human nature in its proper theatre, the trial of soul in matters of interest-absorbing transactions, then we can appreciate the character of the man who suffers none to excel him in good deeds, courtesy or politeness, the result of enlightened and liberalized mind, that looks at truth all the time.

God immutable, immaculate and infinite, ever must regard such characters with due consideration. Religion counteracts the most evil, and renders the suppression the main object of greatest good, to the greatest number, the whole. The world then has to combat most effectually the capital sins of pride, envy, anger, voluptuousness, avarice, idleness, gluttony, ambition, if it seek that happiness of mind that best insures the happiness of soul.

Religion promotes excellence, and enlarges the intrinsic capacity to meet the facts and circumstances for a successful mastery, and turning to the best account of mind here, of the soul hereafter.

Religion teaches the world to abhor the degrading sophistry of peculiar faiths that sneak from all manly views that look to principles. She teaches mankind to faithfully claim that their soul exclusively belongs to God, the sole creator, that they will not betray, traitor-like, but do their duty to all, country, friends and family, and be above all meanness, even to its shadow.

Let the world be rid of the horrid iniquity, the false position, the degraded prostitution of sincerity before peculiar faiths, and resume the God-given religion.

Suppose all the time, means, and pains devoted to peculiar matters were properly, at once and forever, given to all that is religion and universal brotherhood, the world at once would be in a fair way to progress rightly, by rational education. Religion permits only the proper independent resentment for self-preservation, and all that must be in the absence of principles of one side or the other.

If a person acts untruthfully or dishonestly, surely religion will not passively permit him to prosper thus. Reformation to be potential in its comprehension, must soar to the influence of conservative revolution, as much above the attempt of a Luther, as that of rational religion is above the pretences of peculiar faith, as much above passive toleration as universal temperance is above partial drinking.

Religion teaches the world never to be identified with other peoples' weaknesses, errors, much less their crimes. Religion is God-gift to mind, and is inseparable therefrom. How is man to be a gentleman ?

Will peculiar faith, that alienates mankind, perfect that character ? Religion teaches all to remember, never forget at any time the refined courtesies of life. You cannot make religion out of peculiar faith, no matter how you fix it. Religion is the highest, fullest, most complete performance of duty to God and man, in its primitive purity. Let the conservative principle and soul of religion prevail all over the world, let it have full scope, to increase the beauty and loveliness of expansive Mind. Religion allows of no equivocation in regard to the equity of Justice ; her advocates respect wise laws, order, honesty and truth. Here is the abiding spirit of supreme Good.

The question arises, why not have mind to come up to the defence of property, without lock or law, as religion is for world-usefulness and correction ? It is because

peculiar education perverts the mental organization, and holds the world in abeyance to
it. Peculiar faith has usurped her rightful possession, and cuts up the world into fragments, whereas religion blends them all into harmonious universal brotherhood.
The highest of all rational codes is that of religion, that has no contracted sectional
but broadest platforms. People should see their way clear under the highest code of
religion, and be fearful of doing any thing wrong. The sovereign people should be now
held responsible for the correct position of this whole matter. Get religion, say the
peculiar faith priestocracy. But what was mind about previously? That is the great
and vital question. The true secret of religion is the legitimate government of the passions. Religion tends to make perfect gentlemen, and the world most peaceable and
friendly. The world cannot contend at all about religion.
Come, reader, let us have the mighty question of religion settled ; it can be done
certainly by the best of truthful and good faith, the best of faith decision.
Religion requires mankind to pay what they owe at the time and way, patriotism to
their country, brotherhood to the world, religion, instead of peculiar faith, to their God,
their highest parental, filial, conjugal and social duties. Religion is to make us most
contented, happy and most extensively useful. Religion, the great law of nature and
morality, is incompatible with peculiar faith doctrines of Jew or Gentile. The priestocracy talk of spiritualizing religion ; that is the highest duty on this earth for individual, social, national and world morality. How will you like people of the world to be
deceived, deluded out of the only practical part of true religion, for all the false pretences of peculiar faith and all its priestocracy ? What are either of the last worth to
you ?
Religion is attractive and lovely, but peculiar faith is odious and contemptible. The
mass of the people have mistaken peculiar faith for religion.
Gratitude is a great action due from man to God, and should be paid to mankind for
the indebtedness to God. Citizen of the world, let us understand each other. If you
are disinterested, and not the bigot of superstition and peculiar bible faith, then you
must be a rational being, and if we both possess rational minds, we must agree on the
rational principles of religion, the highest duty known to rational mind.
The whole world should seek the best and highest individual, social, national and world
morals with religion to man and God. You ask for the purity of society, the chastity of your
wife, the elevated justice of the world, the universal benefit of society ? Then you
should have acted all your part to promote such excellence, such exaltation. All this
is pre-eminently embraced in the holy precincts of religion. Say what you will of this
kind of government, and that kind of peculiar faith, still is there that highest Supreme
Tribunal established in this earth, where a world's justice can be dispensed but with
religion ? None but pure religion can establish it. That spirit never yet has been instituted by all peculiar faiths, whose whole elements are not competent as they are not
inherent.
Because one disbelieves in the peculiar faith bible, that so far from exempting any
rational beings from duties, social and rational, obligates them more.
When the acts of nations become to be scanned as individuals by the world's tribunal,
whose enlightened opinion will become appropriately potent, then morals and religion
will take precedence as omnipotent agents for mind. To keep the world happy, at ease,
contented, and in the progress of mind's light, is the part of religion, but peculiar
faith seeks all it can for self, conspires and combines with despotic union for collusion
to deceive, enslave and render mind benighted.
I give credit to all mankind for all the religion they do possess, and that is Monotheism, or Rational Religion. The right soul throughout the world can only be rightly
maintained by rational religion. The world needs religion ; it demands the action of
the legitimate direction of all the holiest matters, also the exclusion of even the means of
useless popular excitement in peculiar faith, the agitation of impracticable and hurtful
world measures. Why do I come out so strongly ? To adjust the whole rights of mind, religion as due the Creator, to whom the only exclusive reverence is due, all else is blasphemy, impiety, sacrilege. The world needs the great vital principle of religion. I
know none but one religion, monotheism, one society, the universal brotherhood of civilized, refined mankind : all others are of the devices of man and will be finite. Religion rises equal to all the demands made upon it, whilst all peculiar faiths fall invariably below their dignity. Religion bestows universal and uniform protection to save the
world from antagonisms the most. The great world questions to-day are not whether
we can reach all at once the solution of the weighty matters to be accomplished, but
whether we can progress in laying all proper foundations upon rational principles and
no other.
Religion obliges men to do that which is right, to take the loftiest character and ac-

sion, without compulsion. She causes man to honor himself by advocating God's unity, all that is exclusively due it. Rationality connects us, with due appreciation of Deity. It is she that teaches us to duly estimate that adversity has made the world more virtuous. The religion of rational mind bids us put ourselves beyond the reach of vice. Can there be any improvements on truth and reason? .

Religion comprehends all legitimate pleasures. But what has the laity to do with religion? Every thing, as universal property of mind. .

But is it not the peculiar property of the priestocracy? That at once decides their claim not to be religion but peculiar faith, for religion is universal to rational minds.

The priestocracy may arrogate all their peculiar faiths as monopolies to themselves, but let them not diffuse one iota of such poison in popular minds.

Religion has permanent principles, that cannot be appropriated by any cliques or professions. All that pertains to religion must be immutable as principles.

The doctrine of peculiar faith, ever variable and changing, is a libel on religion. Confidence most rational binds us to the Great First Cause in genuine humility, and this constitutes rational religion to God, the supreme and universal standard, who is the author of principles for a universal guide. The God of nature is identified with nature, the rules of which are his immutable principles. The fixedness of principles is a guarantee, a bond of religion, between the Creator and the universe. Without such consecration of immutability, the whole would be subject to reckless contingencies and wrecks. What nonsense to forsake principles, that by religion bind all mankind to their Creator.

Atheism and polytheism are deficient in all this, for want of justice to the pure author of our existence. Religion as most philosophical, depends on the best science of rational principles, to become most rational.

She influences all rational minds, in ratio to their rationality and the appropriate rational education. If it were not so, why are those religious and good not possessing peculiar faith?

Nothing can obliterate religion from the universe. Let the mind be engulphed in all the horrors of barbarism, it will be impossible to keep it there, for the God of Religion indited it on man's soul for the noblest, most universal purposes. How often does much of the world affect that it does not concern them, to act their part in religion. Religion and its rightful state do concern the whole of mankind, and if carried properly and rationally out, would exclude all the equivocal state of morals, &c., growing out of its neglect by new doctrines and practices of spurious faith. If a man be of the right stamp, education, &c., all may be well. What an illustrious, noble theatre, had Washington, whose example will be honored the world's age. What an ignoble one had Moses and his priestocracy, to impose the deepest tricks upon the Jews for religion! The world needs religion, not Judaism nor any sectarianism, to exempt itself from crimes, faults and follies, that peculiar faith increases.

Let not superficial critics pretend that superstition and false faith were the only means to govern the ancients, when the God of mind gave the reverse as conservatives. The same might as well affirm that California gold mines had caused the world to sin, when it was the perversion of mind. Where was religion anterior to the institution of all peculiar faiths, Jew and others? Where it is now and has ever been, true representative of its author, God, supreme over all such pretences.

The Romanists pay more respect to saints, so miscalled, than they do to God, the effect of the vices of their peculiar faith. I seek to disabuse the public mind, and have all about religion right.

No peculiar faith or bibles, ministers, churches, or missionaries, one or all the aids employed, can begin to reach the main and vital question of religion, but they will mislead souls farther from the real and essential object. Dismiss all these as trash, and let the soul confide in all its deepest humility in its creator. Do you wish to be right? Then you wish not to be a bigot.

Religion is pre-eminent justice in the best of good faith, towards the God of the universe and man. It is most essential to know and premise what is religion, for the converse carries in its face fraud, untruth and dishonesty. The world has only very partially thought correctly on religion, as it has recklessly and heedlessly submitted to the mercenary speculations of an avaricious priestocracy. However it may have been duped for thousands of years by the advocates of the false position, it should not be ashamed to amend. Gratitude in all things is due from mind to its Creator, who is pre-eminently characterized by love, wisdom and perfection. The world has been too long injured and deceived, by peculiar bible sophists. The sooner mothers arrive at the most correct conclusion, the better for their offspring. They might linger for them in doubt and uncertainty, but for the universal care of the Universe Creator.

Religion is the consummation of correct knowledge and duty, to man and God. Principles are universal laws of nature, immutable and eternal, inviolable as equitable and just. Never violate principles.

Religion is one of the loveliest of matters, and the individual may feel all that he may expect to realize from rational actions and feelings. Religion governs minds, thoughts, words and deeds—is the only legitimate government adapted to mind's organization. She cannot vary, but has unity as principles that are universal. Religion calls for all the legitimate advancements of rational mind, the properly conducted unrestricted range of discussion on all appropriate subjects that will advance mind to the right point. Churches should be public arenas for this purpose and nothing less, to hear all sides to secure the right one. Religious fortitude can be defined, a firm maintenance of the best appreciation of the religion of principles. The question of religion is one of mind, that holds faith in abeyance to truth, and forever decides the world-wide agitation on rational principles, that of free agency. This consigns all peculiar faith people to non-existence.

Mind is in its legitimate element, when it is under principles. What system then, gives principles? Religion. We then have to investigate this superb, supreme, sublime subject, to reach the most legitimate conclusions.

Atheism allows mind to grope in the dark after a creator, and of course gives us none of his principles. Polytheism gives us false doctrines and positions, and both mere hopelessness. What is the difference between these two? That is of little consequence, for they are worthless. Of course all mind's circumstances the most elevated require the exercise of principles, and if mind be corrupted by peculiar education, it is most corrupted.

What a sacrilege are the peculiar faiths of polytheism entailing on minds. Being failures they permit it to run riot in vice and crimes, rather than concede the right instruction to monotheism. She teaches the true secret of life, to seek to be always satisfied, with the best the safest done. A virtuous life is the best insurance of happiness, especially in society that is so mixed as to excite distrust.

The progress of religion is arrested by the prejudiced bigotry of old exploded bibles —that of course must be put down.

ANALYSIS OF MIND AND ITS FUNCTIONS RESUMED.

Mind, well constituted and organized, well balanced by appropriate cultivation, can never surrender paramount principles essential to its vital enjoyment, or immortal action in more exalted spheres.

The due cultivation of mind is requisite to resist the fascinations of temptations, the deceits of sophistry, the various forms of superstition, and adhere knowingly to the protective benefits of rational rectitude.

Above all earthly considerations is the absolute necessity of mind eliciting the wisest national and self-governments, most ably sustained by the wisest legislation, to best effectually repel all malign dynasties.

Faith, reason, and truth, how recognised by mind? Faith is an act of the mind, to satisfy which we adopt the solution and test of reason to secure truth, by analysis and analogy.

It is impossible for it to be otherwise, from the very faculties with which we are endowed by the God of reason.

We cannot adopt faith on unreasonable testimony, as our minds are not so constituted to elicit truth.

All truthful faith must be sincerely embraced to be faithful to our highest rights, else the result is most hostile to our highest interest, misleading us into difficulties and dangers.

The proper functions of truth and reason require faith to rest on rational and proper testimony.

Mind is for ever the analyst, self and free agent to proper attainment of its security by reason, of facts under its cognizance, or solution through analogy.

Faith is not for assumptions, fables, and legends, as our tyrants to enslave or terrify, but the true friend of humanity on rational testimony to satisfy.

Faith never can go beyond reason—if so, then the richest functions of the mind are at an end.

Reason holds faith accountable and responsible to the functions of mind, else God never gave reason nor conservative principles to the universe, as they are useless if not appreciated by mind for its good.

It is impossible for faith to triumph over reason ; the minor or less would then be superior to the major or greater, an absurdity and a blot on the assertor's mind, a libel on Deity and his best gifts, the foul blot of fanaticism and superstition.

As all faith comes through the mind, all bibles as trustworthy must be the bibles of mind, amenable to reason and philosophical principles.

All others are the bibles of miracles, prophecies, and mysteries, all of which are inconsistent with reason and truth, and cannot possibly arouse proper faith, suitable for free and intelligent minds.

All such bibles are the works of insidious masters, and not of soul-ennobling principles.

No traditions of faith, ancient or modern, that are obsolete, obscure, or contradictory ; partial in time and space, and peculiar in all ; that appropriate phenomena of nature supernatural, unreasonable and unrecorded by God's works ; peculiar endowments of mankind with prophecy limited to the exposure of science that explodes superstition ; language misunderstood and liable to a multitude of misinterpretations, mistranslations and misconstructions : above all, mysterious of themselves, giving man's mysteries for God's elaborate and perfect wisdom : subject to contingency in hearing and excluding the constant monitor, an enlightened conscience, that teaches the perfection of the Almighty, whose noblest attribute is unity, from its highest duties of ever watching at the shrine of the soul, and substituting irresponsible proxies for hire and gain ; holding up their best lights and examples as universal corruptors of the people, by broken faith, repudiation of honest debts, termination in idolatry, murder, theft, adultery, and hypocrisy ; imposition of mortals, born and dead as mortals ; speculating in impiety and blasphemy offered for immortals ;—can have a proper claim to confidence, or the sincere faith of mind endowed with reason, to supersede God—immortal and supreme over all, by the mere pretences of men !

The functions of mind are to secure reason, guide of rational religionists or monotheists, believers in the one living God, and his principles conservative to his creation. This position is absolutely necessary to exclude the demoralizing doctrines of atheism, that pretends to a universe without conservative principles, physically, morally, and religiously ; also to exclude those of polytheism, or belief in any plurality of gods ; which last doctrine must have various antagonistic or inefficient dogmas, with analogous appreciation of mind, all of which must finally be referred to the supremacy of the only Great First Cause of all, whose conservative principles are paramount to all ; and certainly to exclude any system if indifferent to the conservation of legitimate, social and religious duties, relations, and virtues.

The doctrine or belief in any number of gods, infinite, trinity, or more than one God, is alike embraced in polytheism, all equally demoralizing and hostile to the unity, supreme rights and character of the Great First Cause, the sole creator of the universe, and by right of genius, the exclusive proprietor.

Any such faith necessarily introduces chaos and confusion into Deity's government, a vile usurpation on God's rights.

Such faith gives imposition to mind, and blasphemy unto Deity.

The conception of such impeaches mind and its best qualities.

The results of all such faith are proved by the history of the world to have been demoralizing, and productive of an immense train of corruption and evil.

Those who adopt such doctrine knowingly, present a corrupt doctrine of faith, not sustainable in any moral attributes of exalted social relations.

This confusion is plain in the world, from dreadful conflicts of false faith in all ages, acting on perverted mind, embittered by deadly feuds, animosities, strife, hatred, malice, injustice, reckless shedding of the blood of millions, sparing neither ages nor sex, outraging by exile and banishment ; and exterminating with the most ferocious fanaticism, the most vindictive butchery, murders, tortures at the stake by fires, and the most savage warfare on rights, reputation, and mind.

The only remedy is through reason, representative of truth, that refers to the unity of the Great First Cause, and erects on this, the only foundation—the unity of one brotherhood of the world, for whose universal benefit and stock, universal principles have been given by the Creator.

Through man's life, from youth to matured age, what else protected him all the time but these very conservative principles, adequate to representatives of Deity ? They were in existence from the foundation of the universe, that was chaos but for them, that silently and sublimely operate, physically and morally, and none but the Creator is the wiser, but through mind, his inspiration that recognises and performs what is necessary.

The atheist denies the existence of a God, then he denies the principles of the universe, whose wisest organization utterly condemns him, and of his own vital existence that he cannot violate without penalty.

The atheist must deny these incontestible proofs if he deny the First Great Cause. Is the mind of such a being sane?

Let a derangement exist between the relations of the sun and any of the planets belonging to his solar system, and the physical principles are clearly proved to be existent; but the wise and sound mind has already, with sublime contemplation, recognised those principles, in the prevailing order of such spheres, and especially in the sublime harmony of the universe.

Much more do the moral principles apply, when we see the derangement of man's nature from his vices. Then physical, moral, and religious moral principles prevail, and must be recognised by all wise and sound minds.

MIND—FAITH—THEOLOGY.

Mind then has to assert its dignity, independence of Feudalism or feudal vassalage, light, right, beauty, strength, greatness, goodness, patriotism and wisdom, to resist a blind and fanatic faith.

Faith, religious particularly, must be addressed to reason, to claim mind's belief and truth's assent, otherwise it universally merits its supreme contempt, for enlightened conscience is ever excluded by blind relief.

Freemen know no other avenue for honest men, ever since the days of American Independence, when freedom of government gave freedom to reason, and independence to truth, on all legitimate subjects, of which religious freedom is pre-eminent.

Theology is then ever free for discussion, as any matter of mind in all its bearings, from thought to action.

Mind demands proper reading of reason's language.

But the people are certainly lost, many affect, if they do not have faith of peculiar character.

Can any people be saved, without honest, that is, rational faith? Such faith is not peculiar, but universal. Those who do not believe in some peculiar faith, are damned! And yet they are to be saved by faith, honest or dishonest? Faith they must have!

Was there ever such imposition on mind?

Is the world to believe in religion, but what is rational and honest, to have consistent actions?

The sublimest system of religion calls for faith on its merits, without which none can exist.

For want of faith, the soul is to be damned, yet she is not to call upon the only Sentinel on the watch-tower of her liberty and salvation, but is to cast her off most absurdly with ignominious surrender to seducers and speculators!

Can the conscience and reason of enlightened freedom exist and flourish in any such faith?

The greatest variety of peculiar faiths may rise up, all intended to deceive and beguile the people, unless all such faiths are made subject to the majesty of reason, truth, and principles, that are the only safe protection for mind.

The more diversified faith in her various peculiar systems, the more is that faith to be scanned by reason, for if mind do not consult reason in this labyrinth of mere opinions, what else can it consult rightly and justly, to reach the only one of truth?

There is no safety in any peculiar faith, without reason.

What mockery of wisdom and religion, to exclude reason, the noblest attribute of mind!

What treachery to the noblest treasure of the Universe, free agency of mind! Free agency of mind cannot exist, without reason, a position that excludes the responsibility of mind, of soul.

Where can there be a juster and wiser faith, than in reason that characterizes truth and justice?

Such faith is the friend and beneficiary of mind.

FAITH FROM UNIVERSAL FACTS.

Things seen do declare universally the character of the Creator; the hand-writing is there surely, not to be counterfeited.

The systems of the Universe do declare their soul and first cause, which is name potent enough in character for mind, just and true to his exclusive attributes.

Analogy of philosophical analysis gives us the balance in the process of freeman's highest state, refined civilization. This is omnipotent faith, to mind progressing in the knowledge of science and thought.

Let none with the picture of iniquity resulting from peculiar faith and its attendant evils, arising as a necessary consequence for refusal to God his universal attributes, impiously and blasphemously mislead himself for the best years of his life, after a vain and particular faith that is to injure creation, marring its brightest lustre, and libelling its Creator.

Let none die, as millions of good citizens, thinking of adopting a faith, that their enlightened conscience refuses to their dying breath.

But let them, as worthy citizens, know that their Creator as great in preservation as creation, is fully competent to do all for his purpose, despite of all the legends of systems of man's opinions and libels.

Then all rational minds have the essential and inherent elements of true faith of rational religion, that honors, if rightly directed to none but the living God, and blesses the soul that it honors.

All rational beings are bound to one faith, honestly woven in their nature, by the God of Nature.

The only saving faith, comes from the Supreme Power.

Is faith competent to go beyond reason, then mind is competent to embrace a position beyond the great first cause ?

This pretence, would expose a universal imposition. Any tradition of this character, carries on its face the clearest evidence of its own destruction, and the means of its own refutation.

The constituent elements of religious faith refer exclusively to the Creator of mind.

THE GREAT FIRST CAUSE.

DEITY AND HIS RIGHTFUL ATTRIBUTES, FUNCTIONS, AND PRINCIPLES.

THE great first cause, is Supreme and Immortal God of Nature, to be recognised by enlightened mind, and best appreciated by soundest reason.

His names may be as diversified, as mind can portray God's supreme excellence.

God is Creator of the Universe and its eternal conservative principles, that vindicate themselves for his supreme power, that is Almighty, Omnipotent, and Supreme Ruler of Creation. There can be no other God, as all else are his created beings.

God's function is creation, to which all others are subordinate. His functions, attributes, and principles, render him omniscient, knowing all things in time, space, and eternity.

Omnipotent, existing throughout and occupying time, space, and eternity, the perfect Creator of the Universe.

God is not peculiar, but universal in his attributes.

God's excellence is unmistakable to enlightened reason, through which his only language is addressed to all created minds, that approach nearest with their essential qualities, to his best appreciation.

God's excellence is eternally proclaimed and vindicated in all his works, through which he alone communicates his qualities, and unveils his attributes.

God's presence is veiled to mortals, and can only be approached in a better, future, and more elevated state of excellence, through immortality, the exponent of the soul's worth and character, and of its blissful fruition.

God's word is the Universe document recognised in the tablets of mind, to be enlightened by reason as worthy analyst of the Universe.

The court of conscience which declares mind enlightened by reason, can only take cognizance of any affirmation or tradition of faith, on the just principles and proper analysis of truth. All others are preposterous and unjust in the sight of Omniscience.

Among God's Principles, written by the Immortal Hand of Infinite Wisdom, that the finite finger of mortals cannot counterfeit, are Purity, Justice, Mercy, Goodness, Benevolence, Immutability, Perfection, some of his attributes.

God's power is indivisible and adequate, therefore excludes any participation of his attributes in every respect. God is too powerful to need, as his attribute, Omnipotence, or Almighty, implies, and too great to admit any Vicegerent assistant or Messiah, mere creatures, but his conservative principles, that embrace universal good, and exclude its negative partial evil, ministers alone of his excellence, and exponents of all others as impostors of blasphemy.

Under those principles, the means of universal inspiration, mind acts on mind.

Man's crude opinions and insidious dogmas have superceded principles, and Messiahs with their minions, priests, preachers and devotees, have invaded the province of the Almighty ! Superstition enslaves minds and renders them vassal.

God's goodness and purity created good in its amplest extent, which is only limited in enjoyment by the operations of mind, that creates by perversion its negative, evil. The goodness and purity of God, exclude the original or subsequent creation of spirits of evil, as non-essential to his magnanimity or greatness, and antagonistic to the goodness of his soul, and the supremacy of his Omnipotence. Much more do these attributes exclude any seduction by sin from his pure presence, into which impurity cannot enter, of any beings, especially blessed souls, and happy in that blessing.

God's purity and immutability in that purity, are the best guarantees of immutability of happiness to beatific beings, that otherwise would be liable to temptation, transgression and expulsion, consequent thereon at any duration and period of eternity. There can be no greater libel of Deity and imposition on mind, than the code of machinery of devils, and the necessity of messengers or angels and messiahs in the universe of the Almighty, supreme in his perfection. Mind, inspired by the wisest philosophical science, can only appreciate the first elements of Deity's genius, in the sublime magnificence of the works of his universe. The very equilibrium of its sphere silences in the profoundest admiration, mind. Mind yields all its aspirations and intellectual claims of the loftiest ambition, in due voluntary submission of humility at the shrine of his Creator, beyond whom it cannot pass, and has to invoke for the solution of the mightiest problem, the self-existence of God, the gift of higher intellectual organs, and a nobler, an immortal position.

On this earthly theatre it is our duty to seek the right appreciation of Deity, for superstition that has such deceptive impersonations of religion, enables corrupt priests and preachers to libel Deity's attributes.

God's noblest work is the honesty of mind, and its immortal capacity for truth and happiness.

God alone, is the confessor of his creation. It is he that permits the mind to commune in the silence and solitude of its musings, with immortal hopes. Who, sinful mortal, shall usurp this sacred place of the Most High : who shall presume most blasphemously to his holy office ?

Who shall, destitute of principle, excommunicate God's people : who can foolishly arrogate this Supreme function ? Such presumption is accursed.

God's essence is universal good ; its negative is the position of penalty to mind, delinquent in duty and reverence. God's holiness of purpose must be recognised by mind, in the various deductions of reason, the means of truth. Devotion to this recognition, resting on God's immutable principles, the essential laws of the universe, bespeak respect to nature's rest, both of mind and body, that sustain injury by their violation. This is the supreme principle of humanity and philosophy.

One day is as another with God, who created all, and their light that reflects his supremacy, but the effect of various labor, mental and physical, from business of appropriate character, even of vital existence, must cause respect to the principle of rest.

The functions of sleep and advantages of general repose, establish a universal necessity for conservative laws for the mental and animal economy.

The present seventh day Sabbath, by habit, seems to fulfil the object generally, for humane and philosophical purposes.

The observance of many, not less than seven, distinct Sabbaths, all claiming origin from peculiar authority, best establishes their direct emanation from man, and incontrovertibly proves the peculiarity of his Bibles, characterized by tradition, that reason does not sanction, since truth is not antagonistic to itself.

God could only have had one universally over the world, and that would have been unmistakable to mankind in general. The sanction of refined civilization furnishes the best universal code for humanity.

We will find in the end that it is wisest and most humane, to reserve not less than the seventh day for rest.

It should be justly kept inviolable for man and beast, and no business that can be rightly avoided should be started on a travel just before that day. Do not hunt for stock or game on that day, for pastime. Let all have its best benefits.

God's purity and goodness, his attributes, require a superior goodness and exaltation of all, that have knowledge of superior cast, illustrating the universal purpose most consistently identified with the mass of mind on earth, advancing in one mighty phalanx, sustaining itself in eternal progression, and approaching in its improvement by proper results, the Divine character of its Creator.

The code of social and moral relations require as a paramount duty, that mind and conscience be enlightened at the right time and in the right mode, to establish its best attainable condition and position.

Mind's professions of rational religion, are from innate faculties, universal to mankind as rational beings, proved by conscience, that elicits in proportion to its successful cultivation at the right time, mode and natural capacity, the most successful possession.

Mind's professions of religion should be with God in direct reference to its best light, pure and unsullied by trade, speculation or power, and its actions towards the world, should be consistent and uniform, kind and just, in all things.

The certain and immutable principles are conservative for the religious moral as physical universe, hence the indispensable necessity of a correct faith for correct morals, all for correct rational action.

Knowledge is then power and virtue of mind, and the eternal result must be to universal good of creation.

The conclusion is irresistible, that mind's mission to the universe, has to develope these fixed principles in time, and apply them in their best solution to space and eternity, to secure in full man's highest blessing, the best purpose of the Almighty, who created nothing in vain.

Rational religion, that acknowledges the unity of a Supreme immortal first cause, rests with the mind, that should be embellished in all the loveliness of wisdom.

God's attributes, functions and principles, by which he brought creation into organization and being, keep it in eternal preservation, securing the universe in its perpetual action, and regulating all in order and harmony, represent him, and are his sole and sufficient ministers.

In all ages of creation, they are the pioneers of mind, to pilot all who are incompetent to decide best for their own good. Under the circumstances of moral free agency of mind, God is not heard by those who act vaingloriously for themselves or traitors for others and their own minds, while affecting to benefit the gullible sovereign the people, that can be easily coaxed into an immolation of itself, the tool of tyrants and the sport of menials, perverting most abominably conservative principles, all God's capital, by their deeds the veriest libel of God and mind. But God must be heard, and the people have to return to the right point, to listen to reason, the brightest inspiration of mind, to secure God's holiest blessings.

Then it will be perceived, that is the messiah, all-sufficient in its mission to do God's designs, and perfect his purposes. Elevate it to its loftiest powers and inherent capacities, that the soul may use its best capital, the life-gift.

God's works cannot be mistaken, all the time and space. The workman is characterized by his munificent works. Who, in sane mind, does deny them ? Rational faith reaches a point, in looking at the attributes of the First Great Cause, where the mind submits, impressed with the magnificent truths of God's creation of his universe, beyond which we cannot go by reason of our finite, earthly, mortal faculties, and want of data to reveal to our view.

Where the data stop reason is arrested, as truth stops, and imagination can do no good, then the virtue of humility, that teaches mind all confidence, all trustworthy faith in the Creator, places the soul in the bosom of the Eternal, who is sublimely triumphant as the God of nature, its ruler and organizer. In the Creator exclusively, then, created mind is estopped, and analogous principles are only to be embraced for life, and those only referable to God's attributes that are undeniable.

Mind rejects and impeaches all else, not compromising with imposture at any moment.

God stands alone, sublime in his majesty, that none others dare approach, much less fill in his universe.

In regard to any rival power in seduction of souls, if we refer to the origin, we must estimate it as fable too.

The mighty elaboration of God's purposes needs no angels, much less fallen ones, whose misfortune in the presence and place of purity, by transgression, a violation of eternal conservative principles, producing the most remarkable of all phenomena, revolation of conservative principles themselves, implies the most absurd imbecility of God's highest attributes, not only in permission of this horrible outrage, but incapacity of reducing this dangerous and opprobrious rival, too often successful in getting away souls from God, to even decent subjection.

Our respect for truth, ever consistent with herself, and reverence for Deity, cause us to discard such absurd credulity, not entitled to the name of faith, and all its nefarious propagators.

These are the vile heresies to mind that condemn them as most contemptible, to reach the object of priestocracy, who violated all that is sacred in their heaven, and polluted it by their treason.

We must believe the God of the universe is a perfect being, and we must not permit one single idea to invalidate it, as that invalidates our most perfect confidence in every respect in him.

So perfect is he, that his central residence is holy and pure. All souls that reach it, must be sanctified or they cannot enter, the best gaining soonest the appropriate prize.

·The transcendent magnanimity of God puts him above the seeking to estrange fallen souls or render them desperate, much less befoul his own high character by a penalty machinery that destroys the highest objects of creation. His magnificence is in his munificence, and that can never be better displayed than in the elevation of the soul.

Mind in its feebleness should be modestly silent, and bow in wisest humility to the majestic supremacy of God whose ways, presuming to define, it may libel. Their god of peculiar faith thus portrayed and caricatured, never was the Almighty God that reduced chaos into order when he was incapable of checking the worst of all disorder in their heaven, even where harmony had previously been established. All such, are priestocracy abortions. Such God-portraitures are unworthy the esteem of mind, and justly condemn the authors as degraded blasphemers. Now the attributes of Deity, creator of the universe, will admit of no such construction, unless language be changed. The creation of the Almighty proves conclusively his full supremacy, beyond which even mind cannot go, and less than which it should not presume to stop.

The idea is the essence of sublimity, of supreme majesty. Nothing can be more conclusive, for this idea concludes all; the universe and creation stop there in sublime silence.

His immutable power and essence are forever.

But, then, who knew there was a God or his name?

Who needs being reminded of the sun of this solar system, when his light and heat prove his presence? All the suns and their solar systems are effect of a great First Cause, the name, sublimely stamped on the whole universe.

Mind on the principles of its own action, that of ratiocination, or in tracing effect to cause, knew there was a great First Cause possessed of characteristic attributes. That is all that honest minds can know, or believe can be known.

We can more highly appreciate his character, whose universal attributes convict all the advocates of peculiar faith by principles that irresistibly lead to one universal rational faith that will shame them for their plurality of gods, or for the exclusion of the Creator from his creation, the greatest of absurdities, as corruptors of mind.

The difference between polytheists and atheists seems to be this, that the first only give the Creator partial and the atheists give no power to the God of nature, but all to nature. The first admits only part of a Creator, and the last admits none, both taking a wrong basis.

God is universally great and sublimely supreme; his universe and principles are his eternal agents and prophets, expressive of the living God, whom mind, God-endowed with free-agency, immortality-seeking to all ages, disposed to do right, cannot mistake.

God will amply guarantee for future bliss on the conservative principles of his loftiest attributes, otherwise none can be valid or safe in his august purity.

As it is, there can be no unity nor elevated morals in any faith short of unity, for society never can reach higher in the very highest of all others than the fragments of a disunited brotherhood.

Such will be its state in time, never prepared for eternity by the very constituency of its elements, that run them into quicksands and quagmires inextricable and irremediable.

Take all the systems of faith and its concurrent codes, and all, each and every one, past, present and future, or to come for all time, will fall short of conservation here, and eternal salvation, till they secure the proper conservative principles of an Almighty's attributes.

All wise men must observe and acknowledge all this.

It must be so, from the nature of creation.

All that we are, and can do, is by God; all that we can expect is from God, who supplies all.

God that made us, the First Great Cause, that mind and reason enlightened with just and true lights, declaring true religion, must exclusively adopt, is the true Ruler. He can never be superseded by doctrines of atheism, messiahships or any species of polytheism disguised in modern Trinity, or indefinite ancient numbers. The no-godism implies no principles, a radical and ultra want of system, order and harmony, policy, law and penalty, which is absurdly false to rational mind.

The polytheism or plurality of gods, a system that flourished in ancient times through the vitiated state of the priesthood, till the millions of gods have dwindled to three or four, is swept away forever, as the last but insidious absurdity, by the brilliant eclipsing splendor of immortal monotheism.

Let all their follies and crimes be buried with all their systems.

Potent reason reduces all necessarily, morally, justly, wisely, and rightly, to only the great first cause, that reigneth omnipotent and supreme in eternity.

What wise mind will defer the choice any more ?

If any has renounced the Great First Cause, their case is a bad one, for he is the only God, being the author of safety.

If others derogate from his powers, they do so most unwisely, and their penalties will be in accordance with their irreverence.   Every man's conscience must decide.

What one in his right rational mind, can reverence other than God ?

Is the mind of all perverted, prepared to appreciate all the evil consequences of rejection of reason's God ?

They do not, if they look at the results of the world for past time and the present age.

To whom but God alone, can mind, the only means of recognising the subject, resort ?

Abscond from its maker, when everything before it declares his authorship, and by the only and best titles, the ownership ?

Is that author, God, to be alienated by absurd division of his fee simple estate ?

In what enlightened court of conscience, will this be ever done ?   Who is willing to endorse the consequent perjury ?   Clearly, no good and wise man in this universe.

The thing is impossible to be done, in the calmness of reflection of any intelligent mind.

Animal passions, ambition, avarice and fear with their horrid and blasphemous fictions, theatrical representations and legends arousing the best sympathies of human nature by false pretences of degrading sophistry devoted to the most iniquitous purposes, may do it for the moment, but never designedly and knowingly, unless humanity is degraded to her lowest depths and stupidity.

The very foundation of such absurdities, is well calculated to create insensibility to the general interest of the world, insincerity and all the train of bad consequences to society, that daily observation points out.

Pure and strong must be the popular mind, to successfully resist them.

The mind must be rightly trained, disciplined, and educated in all proper lights that look to the universe and its conservative principles all the time, eschewing all the absurd subtleties of a credulous and most ignorant age, as angels; world of spirits, good or evil, and peopling the air.

All rational minds have inherent faculties of ideas of a first great cause, but tuition has to instil any other secondary cause that must be forgotten and eclipsed in the resplendent glories of the first, by the regular process of nature, the exponent of God's creation.

Nay, more ; this secondary thing, a rubbish of blotches, is perpetually clashing with the good of the first.

There can be no wonder when it ends, having the elements of its own destruction. The whole world, moral and intellectual, is conscientious in the belief of a great first cause, who must have proper attributes.   But a part do not carry out this principle in full.

Millions cannot be sincere in their professions of belief short of God, for they leave all other faith, and their conduct proves their absolute sincerity, and the agreement of that whole faith.

Unity of faith in the eternal first cause, would unite every mind in the bonds of proper affection.

There would be no repugnance of sects, as they could not form themselves into being ; their depravity would be apparent, and their antagonism to God most clear.

The scimitar of the Musselman would not have to meet the sword of the Christian, for the crusaders of the last could not point to any tomb but that of mutual enmity, nor would hierarchy in all her varied tyranny of absolutism disguised by siren sophistry, ever seduce the world freed from its sophisticated pretences, its sordid trade, its desecration of sacred things by speculation.   There could then be no ruler but God, whose watch-word is unity for all, and no ministry, no mission, but the pure light of mind.

Mind would have credit for construing his attributes, reason for appreciating him, wisdom in the confirmation.

If the peculiar faith-heaven be pure, Deity has full possession of his attributes.   Of course the creation of the devil befouls heaven in the quagmire of impiety, and dwarfs the original purity of the Creator who has to be perfect to organize the universe.

If by man's libel, intellect and reason, the proper sentinels would then face Deity with the rankest impiety, contradicting especially the attributes of purity, all his power and knowledge, all goodness and mercy.

That which is worth all the rest, fixed principles, would be of no avail, as a perfect failure is thereby implied in place of a governor affording adequate protection. The polytheist's god, is necessarily imperfect, as we have a creature fallen and degraded, then exalted, to be the eternal rival of his Creator in the seduction of souls! To what will not the corruption of priestocracy lead ? To the most consummate contradictions, ineffable, stupid, suicidal destruction of all the principles of reason and logic. No wonder that the peculiar-bible powers that be, expel her on all necessary occasions.

In this bible doctrine, we have two creatures endowed with peculiar powers. Everything is peculiar in this peculiar machinery. Where is the true piety towards God the Creator ? Monotheism originates in truth from God, the most elevated views of Deity, when we refer directly to him alone.

That shows a manly spirit and a freeman's duty, and religionist's character.

Where does any other view tend, but to make man a poor menial ? Not a freeman nor like an honest man, to face an honest and truthful being, but like an abject petitioner, he demeans himself to mortal, an impostor and a blasphemer. No, never does enlightened mind endowed with reason, take its religion second-handed ; never goes to inferior vicegerents convicted of direct imposition by all the laws of nature ever true to her God, mere earthly beings at best, in abject submission to the basest practitioners of false pretences, exclusive of the people from their God, when we can appreciate according to the lights of the age and our intellectual ability, God's attributes.

Sublime is the Creator's greatness by mind, that must reach reason to obtain its greatness in rational religion.

No sound mind can or will dispute this plain proposition.

Sincerity in God's creation must reign, as the test of his attributes. A messiahship, is a substitute most absurd.

The universe and mind are made as God willed, not as botches wish, or as dreamers speculate.

We have hardly begun to rightly estimate the object of creation as wisely directed by God.

Who are the witnesses of the living God ? The whole universe appreciated by mind and reason, as clear as the sun beams.

Any other, is false and contemptible, if peculiar.

All the first recognise the universe as proclaiming a great first cause, worthy of all the reverence of creation.

None but a very ignorant, deluded or perverted mind can begin to assert that any bible of tradition can meet the dignity of his attributes.

Cultivated mind has to be employed all its existence, to meet these demands.

It is mind that has to seek that which is worthy of universal esteem, and embrace it with the worthiest affection.

It must be in the acts of all minds that aspire to true rational religion.

The attributes of mind declaring innate elements and capacity of religion for its originator, honor the attributes of that power, and cultivated intellect requires the superseding all arbitrary means that tend to exclude that mighty quality of divine power.

While the sincerely religious minded, with feelings of superior reverence from constitutional organization, are to be duly estimated, at the same time they are to be appropriately enlightened as to the object of that reverence.

Reverence, to be honest, must be orthodox.

If God needs a messiah, then he is only part of a God, and must be inferior to him who aids, that is clear.

No prior occupant, with full fee simple rights, divides titles.

God's creation cannot refer to any higher than himself; if he were not independent of all messiahs and creatures, his creation would be independent of him.

What are the pretensions offered in competition with God ?

Those of atheism and polytheism, that is, no God, and several gods or substitutes in man—hero and idol worship.

Who has to take cognizance of these paramount subjects ?

Mind, the beneficiary, has to recognise these pretensions. If mind has the function as it has to adopt, it has the undoubted right to discard and reject the same.

How does mind reach the true issue, truth and fact ?

At the tribunal of reason, over which God presides.

There can be no other.

If there were no God, the universe could have no conservative principles, and all would be confusion. Therefore, the universe confirms most conclusively the existence of both.

Reason is the only power to prove conclusively that such principles apply universally in order and harmony, refer to the Great First Cause, and command mind to refer to principles and their first great cause.

If there was plurality of gods, the Great First Cause commands them absolutely on his conservative principles, as he is a perfect being, and must have perfect rule.

Messiahships make most foolishly imperfect rule, and are at most analogous to the exploded notions of plurality of gods.

Can any past remnant of peculiar faith, perverted views of superstition, be rightly modified, and made eclectic to religion? That would be most absurd. The attribute of immutability of God forbids it altogether. God's laws are immutable as he is, then they do not and cannot change ; but mind changes, and the error is in it. Man should take heed that all such be not libel, knowing the same to be error.

God, as universal, not peculiar, in all his attributes, comprehensive in his universal government, matures his munificent schemes in time, and will carry out for individuals also this last great attribute of mercy.

God alone must be perfectly worthy of adoration and esteem by the whole universe, that he made and sublimely governs ; and merits mind's true subjection, in its most profound humility, to his sublime glory.

All the universe could not eradicate the genuine devotion of a rational mind from its Creator.

All the universe could not create a genuine elevation of a rational mind, knowing the true position of things, for any Messiahship.

All the bibles of tradition and peculiar faith manufacture and create so small gods, that rational minds are not satisfied to adore them.

PRAYER.

Come, pure religionist, and indite yourself prayers, that are to be offered up by you, seeking purity at the shrine of purity.

You approach an unchangeable God, who has unchangeable principles and attributes. If you really seek to effect a change, that assuredly must be in yourself, for there is no need of God's character changing, that is impossible in the present order and harmony of the universe. He is pure and holy. He giveth all practicable blessings desirable to goodness, on universal principles. You surely do not seek to change these.

God reigneth over the universe, and must consider all.

But you are a sectarian warrior, and in battle array with the very banner of a faith, that of itself, if true, must inculcate principles that insure peace and universal friendship, that rebuke you to all eternity.

But, alas ! that banner is sectarian, and with all your crosses of Christ, as you are about to engage with your sister that came from the same parent stock of Judaism, which sister of the crescent is about to wield the scimitar, one or the other must be wrong.

God cannot be the author of war, however mythology had war-gods, especially to indicate his own religion, that is indicated by the ennobling triumphs of mind, that respects itself as it honors God's conservative principles.

But your gods invoked are peculiar ; then as they are the fictions of your priestocracy, to them belongs all.

You cannot pray to the God of the universe to defend you and the cross or crescent. What does the God of the universe know of either ?

What right have either of you to believe that ?

If you of the cross seek a mere sepulchre, that sign to him unfortunately is one of bloody warfare, piracy, and bloodshed.

But if you seek the conquest, as you did of Asia and the world, to prostrate it at the feet of peculiar faith, that victimized its foolish partizans without compunctions of conscience, then assuredly he, as the very author of justice, cannot grant your disgraceful and ignominious petitions.

God knows it not, no more than any other standards.

And here comes the other standard of the crescent, no more holier than its sister, but now carried in the defence of country and fire-side, that if not rightly won from possessors now passed off the stage of life, at least are possessed as rightly as by the ancestors of the very people expelled.

Many a bloody conquest, by Jew and Gentile, had been made alternately of this land before. It was one of the dark and bloody grounds.

The issue, you see, is decided by your address in the hands of justice against you, by a tribunal that respects no mortal, save as they respect conservative laws, that give the firmest action the best prayers.

You may have displayed all heroic valor and dauntless bravery, still the more just the decision then. You were the victim of fanaticism, or of the world's pirates.

But it is reserved for posterity to conquer that country by the light of true faith. Monotheism fights no bloody battles of the sword, as she wields the universal empire of peace.

In what an awkward state is God by the prayers of opposing armies placed, by mind's perversions.

Mind has to retrace all these errors for their correction.

It is the commotion of the world, but serene, no doubt, is the Creator in deciding justice, and all this is done by the agency of principles.

All this comprehension of justice is to reflect for the good of all, and retributive justice will be conspicuous.

National tyranny has remote effects, that come home for many generations. The world's history is full of it, and presents the sublimest philosophy, their correction by rational religion.

You can then commune with God, whose mercy is responsive to merit ; and in that you must be particularly correct. You must address principles, pure functions, and attributes, by pure thoughts, words, and deeds, as prayers.

Do we not believe in more than one God ?

We cannot possibly, and retain a rational mind.

Why is that belief necessary for polytheism, when God, the God of nature, Creator of the universe, is all powerful, knowing, and existent, with all the full attributes to the universal demands of creation ?

His attributes, characterized in bold relief by his works, prove that he alone is the only true God.

All others are counterfeits, and mislead mind.

We now ask you, does thy intellect tell thee that thou shouldst expect justice ?

Then do it yourself by just appreciation and its rightful action to the author of justice.

Let not God's eternal principles be monopolized by usurpers, as their thoughts and gifts, when reason decides, and principles are vindicated before God alone.

Do we ask to have truth revealed to us, and neglect the God of truth ?

If the world wish to obtain the full benefits of truth and principles, it must speak the first at all times, as disguise and ignominy follow falsehood, and the severest penalty comes for the violation of that and the last. The whole truth and principles are embraced in rational religion.

Man's just actions will protect him from unjust and unwise laws, fanaticism, bigotry, disunion of our country, craftship in its criminal guiles, nominal professions in peculiar faiths that abound for speculation by millions who follow vicegerents that are dead, instead of the ever-living God.

All that believe in God alone, truly possess a correct religious foundation. that if rightly cultivated, may lead to the speediest true happiness. Such actions without pretensions that are perfectly useless, must be worthy of God's regard.

This character is written of God himself in his own writings, as taught by enlightened reason. Will God lead us into temptation ? That idea involves a libel of God. God is a perfect being. and will do nothing derogatory to his exalted God-head.

And as to the devil, he has been proved a fiction, an imaginary being, however preachers and priests assume him as part of their indispensable machinery to be an existence. dealing in brimstone, the product of volcanoes, to terrify the timid, to secure successful extortions.

This character involves in the same category his residence, both of which must be ideal.

Eternal and pure adoration is God's the Lord omnipotent who sways the Universe with principles, and regulates all beyond mind's present conception.

He is the essence of true greatness, and his works are his prophets in the wide Universe.

God is the source and fountain of power, which is identified with the Universe, man included.

Mind is obliged to look to him or none.

What can the weak or incapable mortals do ? All are nothing before God, who knows our wants, and could only supply them all. His providence was prescient, in conservative principles.

The creation of the Universe presupposes nothing less than God's exclusive mastery.

It is idle to suppose any other plainly mortal, as plainly an after thought of vulgar minds.

God's actions are good and perpetual ; the evil of man is finite.

The creator is alone and unapproachable, except through the introduction of correct principles that lead man to his God. All created beings are then alike in this respect, and eternally condemned is all bible tradition. Their innate faculties necessarily refer to their Creator, for if mind had no inherent ideas of a God as taught by his universal works of laudation, elicited by action of mind on mind amid which are bibles of tradition, most imperfect specimens of exploded views, then we might as well say that mind had no existence, no functions, as that we could not get the idea of God from his works, his only sublime scriptures.

Most believe as it is their interest, without due investigation, and assent to a doctrine that there are no means of appreciating God without the bible of tradition in the face of God-proof, which position of itself necessarily cuts down the bibles of tradition, and all the advocates who have worldly speculation and profits therefrom.

But have we creatures any claim on God, to save and preserve us ? His prescient and universal providence at creation, answered that question.

We have the highest paramount claims, for the Creator placed us in his creation for his highest purposes, and recognised us at the creation, placing his recognition through religion in all rational mortals as his creatures, we may rightly expect what may be due essential to creation, by knowing what is duty.

We know no one else in this matter, as we can only know God by the creation, and if all give God his due, not make him a demi-god as possessed of part of his attributes, the balance being usurped for another, who proved by his death his mortality and consequent incapacity for them, they cannot possibly divide God's attributes as there is no plurality of gods.

Then we must perpetually look to God alone, the only one that had a hand in our creation, and with whom we can be acquainted.

God is immutable in attributes and functions, with principles capable of sustaining them, his powers, creation, and the Universe.

This faith is vital and rational, or else the God of the whole is below his creation, an absurdity that is criminal.

Rational mind may be beset with numerous temptations, but in its sanity and soundness never can it forget its Creator.

Its protection is mind's all in religious, moral, and intellectual culture, a finished education of that kind.

If God be not the supreme, there will be peculiar results and peculiar faith, which will disorganize the Universe, and demoralize the world results.

There is a supreme retributive power somewhere in the centre, operating to the circumference of space, else the self-decisions of the world would work its end.

WHAT IS GOD'S BIBLE ?

His works displayed in the Universe, that impeach and discard the Bible of tradition as paltry and contemptible, that advances all the time peculiar faith, and no true system of religion trustworthy of mind. Can you not easily appreciate why you cannot defend the bible of tradition ?

Because it is anti-God, and therefore of perdition, proved by its workers of iniquity.

God's bible proves that religion must embrace the whole range of science and philosophy, as far as all such refers to God and man.

The burning presence of mind's inspiration. towers over the dreamy notions of a mere substitute, or even worse, a counterfeit.

No mortal can put down God's works.

Who would wish to discard any that were right ?

Those that are mortal and wrong will put themselves down.

We only seek as good citizens to expose the errors of such, and as all rational minds have more or less the seed of religion, being endowed with its innate elements and principles from their creation, they should have the right direction and instruction to reach the balance. Principles are only needed to do that.

It is for mankind to sustain the severest tests of sense in the Universe, of adversity and prosperity, and remain true to their Creator and themselves, to investigate all this, and to undergo all not only without the least murmur, but with the most appropriate appreciation of Deity's motives, justice, and mercy.

The God of principles, Creator of the Universe, and Preserver of mankind, God of

4

mercy, glory, honor, and happiness to eternity, needs nothing to increase his power, and can permit in justice to his attributes, none to divide it.

It is impiety to suppose God incapable of preserving all of his creatures, or that he needs delegating his power to any who are almost clearly incapable of using it. This attempted reflection on God's character, only impeaches the libeller.

The Creator's honor cannot be put absurdly into the safer keeping of the creature.

Our reverence for Deity is so great, that we cannot permit ourselves to expect a division, much less a delegation of his power.

With no bias of schools, education, uninfluenced by profits of faith, mind must necessarily come to this position, that the great and sublime Creator of the Universe directs all by the sublimest science, and that there is no need of any other than his own Almighty preservation.

Who can affect to dictate against the adoration of God—Deity—whose character is only appreciable by attributes, functions, and principles, that are eminently displayed by his works?

If any bible of tradition be against this moral code, the only rational one of universe-ethics that cannot be overlooked, it well deserves to be discarded.

Why does not the world come at once to the point, about God? Why refuse him his full and proper adoration? Has it strayed too long from his fold for priestocracy? As God he has and can have no deputies, than his conservative principles.

All wise minds of every age of light must know that there is but one God.

What can it avail for more gods to be numbered? Who but the priestocracy is benefited?

One of the worst ideas of mind is, about God's attribute, immutability. It is man that changes, God is not mutable. It is man that pretends to translate God's actions, superseding them by his own feeble dreams and speculations.

Who can confide entirely in any being but in the God of rational religion? All else is made by fiction. What is any other worth? It is not worth the thought used. Is there any other but a partial demi-god divested of God's mighty attributes, impotent in his power and unworthy of reverence of enlightened mind?

Where would be the universe if the Creator were not ruler? The chaos that would ensue is in the mind of those supporting messiahships that are vain enough to claim a part of God's creation, and avaricious enough to speculate on it with the grossest injustice to God.

He that does not reverence God more than mortals, or their idols, mind or hand factured, is necessarily a deceiver, a degraded hypocrite.

God's attributes utterly preclude any copartnership, and necessarily include all religious duty exclusively.

All else is superstition the most stupid, and blasphemy the vilest.

Peculiarity is not the work of God, who delights consistently with his attributes in universality.

The first is man's device that must be referred to the vicious priestocracy, when analysis takes hold of man's actions.

What equity is there in ridding ourselves one moment from the sight of God's unity, whose eternity and uncreated self-existence, are unappreciable to all else that are necessarily creatures in the sight of this immortal, indivisible, the only eternal Being.

Our reverence leads us to the Great Creator of sufficient power.

Man must not in his ignorance undertake to limit God to man's circle and notions, to any absurdity, much less nonsensical sophistry, and still less of blasphemy, merely to get peculiar privileges by priest-works and craft.

Pagans will no longer sacrifice to the sun, seek to keep the holy fire, much less respect rain-doctors, when mind sees the false pretences that exclude the Living Almighty.

God's greatness and self-existence are not derivable, and in him after due investigation of organic truths, our faith is fixed.

God is not aided by others, as messiahships, that are in his way as useless, and must derange his system and position.

People do not begin to conceive of God's majesty. No wonder at their libel and slander in society. When we adopt reason we approach God, who is represented by reason, and is dignified by science and philosophy.

He who acts best on this light and knowledge, has religious cultivation becoming rational mind.

The Creator can do all necessary for his creation of himself, as he is self-existent. This self-existence proves his self-independence and sufficiency.

But what shall we do for the regeneration of man's nature?

None but God can renovate man's nature, and he is bringing it about in the process of civilization, science and philosophy.

So much for the world's charlatans, who assume the province of the God of Nature.

In this messiahs are nowhere, are out of place, as they do not deal in science and philosophy which were essential to our God's creation. Of course neither mind nor God want them at all.

The renovation consists in man's rightful actions, his life time. Thus messiahs cannot avail, in correction of man's nature.

As God is immutable and invariable, he is almighty. Who is to ride in the mighty tempest storm-cloud, and direct it properly, but he that rules all elements?

If vital principles be violated, we are burned, drowned, die or suffer physically.

We suffer the penalties of violating moral laws. Who can escape them, or rather, the Omnipresence of God?

We can be nowhere, that God is not; we can do nothing unknown to God.

Time is the gift of mind, that it prepares for eternity, by the wisest recognition of all God's institutions of the universe.

Let not God be robbed of any of his attributes, to be dwarfed a part of a God in his own universe, the result of his own genius and wisdom.

To know God, which we can only do by his works read by the science of philosophy, is to reverence him supremely.

Light and knowledge beget rectitude, that begets bliss. Whoever abrogates one part of God's unity, power or dominion, does as much for the creature's love, respect and reverence for God.

God would be imperfect, if he did not preserve mankind, after creating them by his Omnipotence in truth, not sophistry.

The wisest and perfect provision goes with wise Providence, that the Messiah-mongers belittle for God through their inefficient policy, as if God was to be troubled all his time with eternal labor about one world, when his universe, that is exhaustless, embraces all needful conservative principles. They act sublimely God's to the exclusion of Messiah's fortune, fate and destiny, by their order, direction and efficiency.

The inherent laws of matter, bespeak the Great God and an Omnipotent Providence.

The Supreme Being has all the time of vital existence, an overweaning influence in the universe, in regulating the conservative principles that characterize him an Almighty.

God's immutability is proved by his fixed, immutable conservative laws of the universe, that the wise see, and that position proves that miracles are impositions. Science of mind makes sad inroads into the bibles of tradition.

God's time disproves all prophecies, and these two facts proved beyond cavil, destroy all bible mysteries as impositions.

Man's libels of God must so recoil on himself, as to cause the modest to blush, and the presumptuous to be silent in works beyond their comprehension.

The bible of Moses libels the character of God, in making a space beyond reason for the postponement of man's creation, losing an amount of time of vast importance to creation.

The unity of God is one of his greatest attributes, and declares to the world that all polytheisms are a combination against the world's benefit, talents and truth, to secure advantage ground for superstition and man worship.

God has his own way of reaching the mind of rational beings, by light of science and morals.

To prove miracles, &c., militates entirely against God's attributes.

God is not the author of the evil on earth, that man's libel declares, when man's action accuses man.

All tuition must refer to God, the author of principles, that radiate and influence all the circles of the universe.

His sovereign power supersedes all.

What but most imperfect appreciation of Deity's attributes could have devised angels and messiahs as messengers and agents, instead of obvious conservative principles?

Any order of spirits of beatific beings is identified with another state of existence, and clearly incompatible with ours.

A rational reliance on the noble attributes, functions and principles of the Creator will best perfect rational mind.

His works are his ever-living witnesses, with all harmony in the microscopic and telescopic universe.

God is a perfect Creator, but tradition bible writers, as bungling botches, have caricatured him. God never created original sin, the negative of good actions. The future
penalty may be, negative enjoyment compared with the good.

None are perfect but God, a holy being, with functions, attributes and principles indivisible and identified, and mind has no innate inherent elements of ideas of any other,
especially a mere creature.

Too many minds cling to obsolete ideas, made so by exact science, of no existence
and actually feigned, but they actually contend not for these brainless phantoms, as
much as the self-interests of designing priests. Sinister policies, under all names, may
mislead and pervert mind unless it ever decides all questions on the only safe, which is
the only rational basis. As the patriot freeman looks to his government, so much more
all are to respect and adore their Creator. The idea of God alone meets all the immensity of creation, shows proper purity to do away with the terrors of hell, the machinations of the devil, as all fabulous and inconsistent, promotive of the delusion of mind
by the machinery of the ignoble priesthood, who are not needed, if God alone do his
own work : and here is proved most conclusively the vast difference between God
and man. Ignorant and perverted man has to invoke the aid of messiahships, whilst
God's works of the universe prove him, and only him, the Creator. So much for man's
libels and stupidity. The perfection of God is beyond earthly appreciation.

His universe without limits, with all its beauties and principles of admirable character, elaborated in all the finish and skill of exact philosophical science, no doubt is everlasting. Much more, then, is the soul immortal, the greatest of all creation, cherished
in the bosom of its Divine Creator.

God, as the Creator and President of the universe, must preserve all as his family.

He cannot admit any pretended adjutant that had no hand in this creation the important part, without derogating from his own respectability before the universe.

After all mind's best attainments in science, it knows but little if it knows not God
and God's rights. If it knows not God's rights, it cannot know God's attributes.
Mind, that knows enough to do full duty to God, is in the safest position of all. We
must give to God alone the sole glory and merit of his principles, without which the
universe could not move, and by which man exists and has his being. From God, the
policy and principle, attribute and function of kindness, goodness and mercy emanate,
and by him sympathy that unites mind to him is universal. God is infinitely wise and
immutable. What advances the peculiar faith power, but utter and reckless ignorance
of God's attributes and character ?

All creation is led most certainly to Deity the Creator, beyond whom, as worthy of
the sublimest adoration, none can go. This is conspicuous, and should have silenced
blasphemers of messiahships, unless most stupid, as to what their sublime duty was.

The more difficult to create, the more worthy of adoration is the creative Intelligent
Power, and the more is God self-proved. Philosophical science is to conduct us
through creation in its analysis ; all that reject her must be degraded. How insignificant, how degraded is faith without reason by her side, and the light of knowlege in her
path. Our senses alone can recognise the facts of nature, and they are best disciplined
by science. The senses giving intelligence rise above nature, and have his attributes
innate and refulgent with beams of irradiation to the universe.

The attributes of God are purity, that prevents the devil-creation, omnipotence that
prevents any vicegerent, almighty that supersedes priestocracies, and all their fancy corrupt stock of angel messengers, by conservative principles. People cannot analyze,
else they would not commit themselves so seriously in impiety and blasphemy. Reverence to Deity will not permit all such. Duty to man, sinful and helpless in his ignorance, will not permit us to leave an omission of his proper protection. This is the highest as the purest ground of conservatism moral and intellectual, that does not leave its
votary at sea without chart or compass, but still higher in the purest religion practicable, the most exalted duty and action.

On the true and essential merits of this vital soul-question, we must look into matters
and the nature of things, where all the difficulties and their remedies lie.

Deity should be ever honored in thought, word and deed.

All should tell most concisely to the point.

Principles as liberal as the age requires must be advanced, to do full justice to Deity..

Sin cannot begin to reach heaven if that be the great centre of purity. By what
standard of perfection can you try mind, but by the God of nature ?

You are indebted for constant grace to God as to his bounties in existence, and your
action in all such is as much a part of your religious as moral and physical existence.

If God be not your friend, who is or can be ? Do not libel him. A reliance upon
God's attributes prevents us from believing that the elements will melt with fervent

beat. It is true God can create and destroy, but he is supremely consistent with himself. He is immutable and perfect, and cannot be aided by messiahs nor priestocracies that libel him by such false pretences. The great improvement of the world shows the exhaustless grace of the Creator.

We adore the God of the universe, and ask only his purest blessings compatibly with our merits.

Who gives grace, but the Creator of all mind and grace ?

God is best served when best appreciated. Mind is bettered by the gift of God. The Almighty saves. The only peace is a right appreciation. The grace of God alone can reconcile all men to their lot, and to each other.

When that abounds enemies cannot be made, and where principles are obeyed, persecutions for peculiar faith must die out.

God's grace upholds us. In this sphere of existence, there is much speculation in peculiar faith, by which the world would be overrun, but for God's grace or principles. How shall we estimate God's blessed abode ? Not by the name of heaven, a most imperfect conception, but the great centre of the universe, where purity and perfection are permanent. What consummate libels are met with in the bible ! How much is pretended about God's wrath. Now, his mind is so balanced, his intellect so omniscient and his power so almighty, that it is any thing else but his wrath. This is the old tale of pagan superstition, and the bible is pagan. There is no sectarian dispensations or covenant that fulfils the design of mind, the demands of the world, or the obligations of the universe, as God alone in sublime science rules all in his majesty. With God dwell infinite knowledge, power, goodness, justice, mercy, love and perfection. You must not mar nor judge the world by your standard, as your education as one of the billion may be peculiar. There is only one standard in the universe, the Almighty, who conclusively, by the organization of the universe, presides in all its solar systems. What is the universal standard of truth, faith, reason, in a word, of mind ? God the Creator, whom all rational minds must appreciate from the works of the universe as the centre of perfection, whose influence extends to the circumference, whose attributes, functions and principles are perfect.

But then all rational minds emanating from him, ought to be perfect. Their purpose is final perfection without doubt. Is not this full proof of the immortality of the soul?

But all things emanating from God should be perfect. Why are they not so as far as practicable, and in the nature of circumstances ?

They are as God created them. To pretend that mind fell, is a libel on both. Who can give grace or mercy universal, in other words, conservative principles, but the universal author of these attributes and mind ? The God of nature, and the god and devil of Judaism and christianity, are two separate existences ; the first is the universal Creator, the last two are peculiar creations.

As God of the universe was most certainly never known to either of the aforesaid, the peculiar God's creation belongs exclusively to these discoverers. No enlightened mind disputes their rights, as they are exclusive.

There can be but one Creator, who as omnipresent, fills all space and time, and excludes all others necessarily. God would hardly occupy space with a hell, when his attributes could be better universally glorified. God's attribute of goodness, irradiates his creation. As there can be but one Creator, the peculiar God of Judaism is a fiction, and all its machinery necessarily falls, whether built up at that or subsequent time. This is the most certain and definite logic, unmistakably certain.

Principles are the avengers of God, throughout the universe. Define who God is. It takes the whole universe that exhibits his functions, attributes and principles, to comprehend that definition. We are obliged to take the decision of rational mind on rational data about God, not mere public opinion nor prejudices.

How has Deity emanated ? He is in relation to this universe, its great first cause, and that relative emanation utterly precludes by want of data, any investigation of mind, his creation. Humility and confidence unite in his adoration.

God has not only perfect omniscience, wisdom and goodness, but he has purity, perfection and immutability. If we cannot reach the God of nature in systems, we must go as near him as practicable.

God is so perfect that he does not create evil, but good, the negative of which is evil. Is this attributable to God or man ? The nearer right the world is, the least evil it has.

God does not require of us impossibilities ; he does not make us responsible for our minds not reaching a perfect state here, while severe penalties, the evils for natural laws violated, prove the necessity of our proper action.

There must be not only the wisest world-legislation, and the wisest execution of those laws, but the wisest and purest self-government, to escape sin as an evil, the negative of good. God's character is the very reverse of peculiarity, for it is universality. It is very reasonable that you should construe Deity's attributes aright, when you, unjust complainer, become his libeller.

Some croakers are ever murmuring, not able to be grateful to God, to improve on mind's defects.

In seeking the legitimate treasures of the earth and immortality, we will see that only one God supreme can be admitted, and that all others are unequal and unnecessary.

In taking proper thought for all such things necessary, we perceive most clearly that all the conceptions of the ancients fell far short of just appreciation of Deity's attributes and conservative principles.

Universal creation gives mind the highest appreciation of Deity's attributes, and this supreme respect engenders the most profound love for that creation-author, and the most comprehensive brotherhood of man, surpassing all the vain imaginations of pretended bibles. You can have unbounded confidence in God. The spirit and principle of soul-existence, are love to God and man, that creates religion and universal brotherhood.

How can you ungratefully overlook, stupidly not perceive the redeeming qualities of preservation in your immortal Creator? This power that was so perfectly performed for thousands of years before priestocracy and messiahship, now to be crushed by their ignoble pretences? We adore the God that created our forefathers, not such a peculiar being as they in their imperfect science conceived of. As to love to God, the soul could not keep from it, as it has in its deepest humility, unbounded confidence in the Creator. What best teaches humility? The idea of a supreme God so almighty, as to exclude messiahship. So transcendent in his existence, as to estop the most brilliant mind at that point. But is not the difference too great, between God and mind, without intermediates? Is not God the Creator of mind? Why then ask such a question, as conservation is implied in creation. That question implies false delicacy and position. Besides, what difference is there in a mediator made by the fiction of man, and man himself? What virtue in such? We do not understand the art to elicit, the art of this world to trace effect to the cause that depends on us, as there is the latent cause in this universe of cause and effect, up to the great First Cause.

Man should be modest, wait for gradual development of mind to irradiate mind. One idea will illustrate the whole circle. Conscience, principle, soul and religion, all refer to the only Supreme standard, the great first cause. Christ could be no fixed standard ; his mortality forbade that. How comes it that the God of creation is libeled as peculiar, when his every characteristic is universal? The mind of man can hardly appreciate his universality, as diffusive enough. The greatness of the Almighty decides his own character, and vindicates his unity by philosophical science and the facts of truth. None can usurp his prerogatives which are exclusive, unless the dupes are victimized and stultified by pious frauds. We must do justice to the supreme God of nature, in yielding him all the homage of an Almighty, competent for preservation of his creation ; all else is evanescent.

Rational appreciation of God's works. creates rational love to him.

We look through nature to nature's God, through love to the God of love, who has transcendent grace.

To know what God himself has promised, consult his only scriptures, his works, his book forever fresh and flourishing the universe. The world is one of the cabinets of Deity. God is at once perfect. The universe is a demonstration that tradition-bibles are a libel on God. Rational mind has to be irradiated in the mighty circle of the universe.

If God were deficient in the least conservation, he would thereby be at once characterized as imperfect, and perfection would not be his attribute. Thus preachers and priests do not know what they are talking of, when they advocate messiahship, for that very word personifies God's imperfection.

So far from reason ever being rejected, that her highest efforts through discipline of experience, is indispensable to investigate most sincerely God's attributes.

The unity of God alone is for universal brotherhood : God is displayed in his sublime universe, and reflected by the mirror of science in the face of truth.

After all the false pretences of substitutes, who can appreciate the preventions of injury in the conservation of Almighty Providence? That respects the moral as physical, the whole?

What mighty powers of periodical regeneration of nature.

God organized creation with the sublimest conception and wisest design that exalts all the time, not degrades the world. True faith must prevent the adoption of peculiar faith, looking to God, we cannot look below him to any pretender, impostor, messiah, nor can mind look above him.

The highest appreciation begets the highest adoration, purest of God's character, who performed the greatest elaboration in the creation, organization and conservation of the universe. When God spoke creation into existence, this was the intellectual, moral, and religious sublime, worthy of the God of nature. His whole work that we see, seems to have been finished. His principles are at work. Prophecy, his agent, time reveals, whose secrets philosophical science discloses.

Pray for others, says the priestocracy. Divide no affection, give the whole love and adoration that spontaneously arise from the sublimest conception of God's holy character and attributes. The self-righteous, say the priestocracy. Who but you are in this category? Who authorized you to act for us? Attend to your case by the best acts of your mind; you have no more grace than you can spare for yourself. Are your thoughts purer by divine excellence than those of others? Prove it. Actions concentrate words and thoughts. Have you a superior claim before us, provable? The foresight in creation of the rightful creation of this world in being saved without the loss of blood and life of a Savior, argues a perfect Deity, surely. Had such a Savior been necessary, the Creator had been imperfect. The matters of God are not abstractions.

Did the Creator possess the full and entire sovereignty over the Universe? Of course. Did he part with it by necessity? That decides the imperfection of God. Of what benefit was it to any less than God, if God himself was imbecile? But if not imbecile, of course he must have held to all his creative power. If the successor could do more, he could create and thus he becomes the creator himself, and that position conclusively proves his supremacy. But brought into the world by the function of procreation, his function could not be creation as his acts prove and confirm, hence we can only recognise one great Supreme, to whom all creation is subordinate. Of course there is but one limit and that at God, beyond whom this Universe cannot go, and this decides his supreme sublimity and grandeur.

God does not manifest himself in person, but is recognised through his works that are read by mind recognising science. What better proof can be given to each human being, than this position? Is there any honorable proof, that any person ever saw him the world's age? Must he be reviled as skeptic, because he asks for demonstration and proof conclusive on this essential point? Mind as honorable can asks for nothing less, and can yield nothing less if aught beyond it is demanded. As to all God's law and principles that are for mind, they are there still, not taken away or added to at all by any sectarian, for God gave them preservation. It is impossible that there can be in the nature of things, any other revelation of God than what he has given in the Universe. It is impious blasphemy to ask for more than the illustrious works of the Creator. The preservation of universal order, attests universal Providence.

The God of the Universe gave the world a greater munificence in its totality, and so of all its parts. Countries and people, the world and mankind, are cursed in any peculiar faith.

How do you reach the idea of the Almighty? Through mind out of his own magnificent Universe, and nothing less can represent him.

To not finally know God, the Creator, is not to know much of the Universe! That is not Monotheism.

Between God and man are principles. Did Christ originate any others? No; then he cannot supersede them. The most amiable idea we can have of the Almighty is, that his grace is universally, not specially diffused and effectual on merits of mind, without the taint of blood and murder.

The most appropriate name is the Great First Cause. We see the humbugs of the world nurtured by pretended revelation or atheism, that would be exploded by cause and effect arguments.

What truth has Moses for his narration, in the position of the earth? The polytheist and atheist who are the only ones besides the Monotheist, maintain a position of sophistry. Both stand on false data and premises. How can that of either be morals or religion, where there is no truth? The unity of design in the Universe, convicts both. This Universe is referable to cause and effect.

The atheist should comprehend all final or elementary causes, ere he disputes the First Great Cause. Their assumptions about the beginning of creation, will profit them nothing in the principles of causation. As candid, honest, and truthful people, they had better acknowledge their defect and inconsistency in all such premises, and as good and true citizens of the world, aid the Monotheist in the only tenable and upright position. The unity and preservation in creation, sufficiently answer both most conclusively. How absurd the idea with some sophists or their vassals, that if we admit the

existence of God, we must also admit that of Christ. The last is in direct antagonism
with, and detracts from God. God is perfect and needs no Christ's aid. The priestocracy needs the aid of such machinery, and they instituted all such for their especial
peculiar benefit. But the sovereign people, not the priestocracy, God not Christ, are
the source of delegated or original power, therefore truth, not faith, religion, not peculiar
bibles, are to prevail.

The whole category of Christ, priestocracy, &c., keeps God out of view. What
must be the magnificence of God's perfection? The Universe is an ever-present constant proof of its God, and that excludes all contingents as Messiahs alien to this principle.
Infidels! who are they? not those who believe in the God of the Universe, in the oldest,
the purest correct—the only faith. I advocate the supremacy of the unity of the God
of the Universe, of religion that defers to that paramount obligation, constitutional
liberty and rights of the world. God has given us a bible that Moses did not read, that
excludes him, Christ, Mahomet, Smith, and all the functionaries of peculiar faiths,
that yet admits them on the principles of mind. The difference between atheists,
maniacs, and polytheists, is this, that the second cannot use their mind rationally, the
first renounce the right use, and the last fall short of the rational use. The fault is, as
to the mind of all.

What enables mind to do best on earth? Monotheism, directed by the wisest Creator. Man can never appreciate God through peculiar bibles, much less pretend to correct one iota of what he has done. Man's dispensations dispense man's extreme
follies.

By what mighty intelligence and power has God arranged the universal cabinet of
Nature—placed in the bosom of the earth the seeds of vegetable matter, plants and
trees, preserve them for countless ages free from decay and exempt from vegetation, by
non-exposure to the atmosphere, and the process of heat and light of the sun? The
God that I believe in, cannot be libelled—by man. He is not in favor of priestocracy,
when the last are a set of hypocrites. He never ordered miracles, prophecies, mysteries, nor repudiation of honest debts, when an honest, truthful perfection of his works,
only honor him. He has no counterfeits.

The principles of causation, of cause and effect, unmistakably and absolutely lead
mind to the Great First Cause, that necessarily excludes atheists and polytheists.
Which of these two has the most perverted and ignorant mind? We must have most
imperfect views of Deity to suppose him a perfect being, and for him to leave others to
perform his functions! His principles do that. Both he and they are unchangeable.
How can man think of addressing him, for the purpose of change? Man does it from
the imperfect views of peculiar bibles. It is really opprobrious that God who created
the Universe, exclusively as the Great First Cause, also mind and religion, is not paid
by man, exclusive adoration. The wisest legislation emphatically follows the wisest
appreciation of Deity, as all produce the best religion. The laws of nature if made
right, are the ones to govern man rightly, most easily and successfully. How many
things are there in the world, if we look at cause and effect rightly, to remind us of our
duty. What a mighty contemplation of God Almighty, who towers above all ideas in
the creation of principles and the Universe. How sublime the thought. The mighty
unity of design, that none could ever carry out but the supreme majesty and unity of
God.

The world has to go wholly for the unity of God.

Who can dare say, that God ever created an evil?

Who will libel him, and stultify his own brain?

The conversion of mind, is not without the spirit of God. That is exclusively alone
effectual, and proves the unity of God. What would the world—the Universe—be,
without the spirit. the soul of the Creator, all the time? All the religion that Christianity and all peculiar faith has, is from this source. All else is not religion. As to
peculiar faith bibles, they all can be dispensed with all the time, but mind and rationality
that gives the only legitimate purification to mind, must be upheld as God-gifts to the
Universe. They embrace nothing short of refined rational education. How can the
whole world be converted, but by pure rationality on rational education?

Such must bestow genteel, refined, gentlemanly, individual, rational world-feelings.
For rationality to do justice, rational mind must be purely exempt from the malign
influences of peculiar education. I cannot think that God ever created an absolute evil,
as he is too perfectly pure and holy. The beginning of man is proved by the book of
geology, that proves man the last of creation, the highest order. The more mind's
intelligence increases, the more the Universe expands into greatness. Shall the conservative principles of the Universe be in abeyance to man's notions, ignorance, and
prejudice? God instituted conservative principles for the Universe, mind, and body,

and now whether polytheist, monotheist, or atheist, all the orders of faith that can exist, unless we blend the atheist and polytheist, and have only two in reality, have to adopt these principles. The polytheist has actually traded on this capital, and most ungratefully denied the true faith.

If the world assume that the sun or Nature causes all things that we see, it puts the effect for the cause, and stops very far short of all that is comprehensive. In regard to original sin bringing death into the world, it is perfectly ridiculous if we wisely and justly regard the objects of creation, the mighty functions of reproduction that would unquestionably cause mankind to overrun the whole platform of the earth's surface, if there was not a rational limit, that is, death. Creation would not stop reproduction, under its present position. All that about sin and death, is perfect legend. Preachers ought to stop all such.

Whence originate all mind, and all holiness of mind or soul, but from God, whose exclusive unity consecrates it and renders it most effectual by his divine grace? As to being prepared otherwise, is to get more and more unprepared. All this investigation leads us unmistakably to a supreme divine power, pre-eminently dignified in wisdom and consecrated in holiness, the appropriate standard for mind.

PROOF OF A GOD OF NATURE.

LET Aristotle, Xenophanes, Epicurus, &c., assert all matter to be eternal, still, as system and order are paramount, and principles are conservative in the universe, that universe is ruled by a Great First Cause, into whose Almighty authority all rational beings, duly impressed with his worthiness of supreme adoration, must, with humility and confidence, resign themselves.

By order, system, and organization the universe exists; without them, there is no universe.

He who is the limit of mind, causes mind to pay its most deferential respect to himself, the only standard.

Friendship, originated by such lofty intelligence, becomes the most exalted love, the more cemented on principles, that exclude all atheism and polytheism, however disguised by priestocracies, hosts, and trinities peculiar.

Philosophical science enables mind to prove our solar system, the order and regulation of that system; and enables us to embrace all systems of the universe, and its God, or Great First Cause, that originated, organized, and rules that system of systems, the universe.

The original of motion must have been eternal, and could only have rested in the Supreme alone, and thereby proves him the Almighty to a moral and religious certainty. What must have been the Almighty, to have created the universe!

The world reads, through philosophical science, the language of nature, that is universal and discloses her God; whereas books of tradition are those of men varying in sense and diversified in language, liable to misrepresentations, misrecords, mistranslations, and woful corrupt misconstructions, unsuited to mind as less exact in science.

Principles alone can elevate mind, the want of them alone degrade it. The bible of mind alone can impart those that hold mind on a balance and reputation of character at par.

The mind never can stop short of the Great First Cause, however defeated by priestocracies, with their sophistries and their superstitions, and above all by their polytheisms. Why not declare at once a Supreme First Cause in nature? That is relative only and only his exponent. Beyond the Supreme all is speculation, there mind is compelled to stop, where religion decides supreme duty due to the Supreme Creator.

Forethought will decide for us, that there is a God of nature, as nature only presents at best the elements. God is the prime mover, is the soul of motion, power, and intelligence.

Enlightened public opinion outruns book-knowledge in time, how absurd then was it to book by tradition God's word, that it takes the whole universe to contain.

The God that made our fathers is a different Being from any ever dreamed of in polytheism, however peculiar. The God of nature is a unit, sublime beyond the conception of priestocracies, who are ever distanced in all their ignoble attempts at their caricature of Deity. God stands alone intact, by all the vulgar priestocracies, the most corrupt of all dynasties.

The best of the ancients were ignorant of any responsible system of science, that explained the position of our solar system, much less that of the universe.

What miserable systems of the solar system were advanced! Tycho Brahe reversed the most correct view of our solar system, to suit the ignorance of the priestocracy's bible.

What did Moses, and all such priests, know of true science?

This is enough to humble the pride of sophists and dogmatists, and teach mind humility and an entire dependence on the God of nature, whose works alone can teach his attributes. All the bibles of tradition remove the mind farther from correct views of God. Modesty, humility and justice will make for mind its proper sphere.

The ancients were dogmatists, atheist, and polytheists, and of course had but little philosophical science, and could not appreciate Deity.

The facilities of the present age present a noble advance and progress of mind; enable mankind to become rationalists; remove atheism, polytheism, or any of its disguises as trinity; peculiar gods for peculiar people, with all the peculiar accompaniments of peculiar priestocracies; infidelity to God, reason, mind, principles, or any of their attributes.

God is distinguished by attributes, functions, and principles, among which is truth.

God cannot lie and be God. He cannot create and not preserve. Both powers are one and indivisible, embraced in unity, rejecting trinity. Preservation and conservation are identified with creation.

Creation must have had a beginning by the Creator eternal. This mightiest question is only partially solved. The very admission of the word universe, that none can deny with rational mind, discloses order, that premises organization of a sublime intelligence, characterized by the best attributes of supreme power and wisdom.

We infer most conclusively, by rational induction, these noble attributes. When we speak of nature we speak of the order resulting on matter by conservative principles. Matter organized is what we see of nature.

Who is the Supreme Organizer? Religion and morals refer again to supreme intelligence.

Matter alone could not form mind, that evidently needs morals and religion for self-preservation.

To say, that as the ancients could not appreciate God, that mind could not, is foolish in the extreme. The ancients could not begin to appreciate the system of systems—the universe; the moderns have only begun to do so.

Mind is on the progress of improvement.

Reason is the highest exercise of our mental faculties, and the more enlightened reason by exact science, the nearer we approach the God of reason.

All creation looks to the principles of causation. It is the right direction of motion, that rules the spheres of the universe, and that must rule the ratiocination of causation, and the attributes of matter, as mind takes precedence of matter.

God is an infinitely wise being, and self-existent.

The universe is infinite and uncomprehended by man, but God the mover, directing motion, is the comprehender, so much more above man, Almighty and Omnipotent God only asks the audition of reason, and if all the priests and teachers of polytheism were put down, then he would be truly adored.

The manifest proof of God is by his works universal, physical, moral, and religious.

Partial reason, under the pretence of faith, seeks the Creator in insignificance, and itself in blasphemy.

The Great First Cause is only known to us; we can grasp no secondary or satellite, that is totally inadmissible by the word and signification of Almighty.

There reason commences, in the universe.

The other volume for eternity has not been read, and therefore we must be silent in truth.

The universe involves processes, that involve principles wherever order and system are involved.

Neither atheism can detract from the Author, nor can polytheism add to him. These are the dangerous errors of the day.

The universal organization and order of the universe compel us creatures to eternal silence.

This is a sublime contemplation to the religionist, the rationalist.

The universe is a mighty constituency of solar systems, whose constitution was due to the originating power, to whom all creation looks as a perfect being, the fountain of all intelligence and power, the Great First Cause, the God of the universe, who is as much above the God of Judaism as the universe exceeds the little peculiar spot, Palestine.

Animated nature was created by its God, and could not have existed or been sustained and preserved independent of creative intelligence, almighty power.

As to the God of nature, we can only trace to him ; and having no more data, are compelled to stop as all, with the direction of motion and creation.

It might be vain speculation to attempt more ; we could not with propriety do less.

Nothing less than an Almighty could have ruled nature by systems, regulated by conservative systems that vindicate themselves and protect the spheres of solar systems, and those systems in one exhaustless universe.

Violate the principles of gravitation, and your fall proves the irresistible conclusion.

Human vitality can be injured and finally destroyed by fire, water, hanging, cutting chief arteries, poisons, mental disturbances, strangling ; over these preside principles that represent Deity, who requires the full dignity of rational religion. The God of nature can be only represented by the inherent principles of nature.

They are the circumstances of created rational beings, who have to conform to them by free agency of mind.

The God of the universe has been libeled by atheists and polytheists—equally bad, by priests and messiahs-mongers awfully and blasphemously. Can you define God, the Almighty, who spoke nature into the creation of a universe ?

What mortal can define the universe, a necessary preliminary ? Let its matter be infinite as much as you choose, have prior motion and time its consequent, still the universe that embraces that matter is all regulated by system and order, which were necessarily directed by supreme intelligence. There can be no atheist nor polytheist if their mind be sound, honest, and truthful. The universe may have had a universe of difficulties, then the more a God that triumphs over all.

God can claim exclusive paternity as self-existent to his works, and full almighty capacity for their preservation. All the bible-of-tradition-mongers never understood God's works or attributes, else they could not have committed themselves to so awful a falsehood about God's universe preservation. If the Almighty Creator was not the Savior, who then was the Creator ?

Be silent, then, ye degraded monsters of iniquity.

We approach the God of nature, and are duly humbled into supreme adoration of such adorable majesty.

We mortals have to ask of God another set of mental organs and data to reach him, much less proceed beyond him, whom we must style the Regulator of the universe, be the disordered elements in ever so great confusion and chaos. The name of Universe Regulator, then, surpasses Jehovah, or its prototype, Jupiter.

But do you back out from rational discussion, that involves legitimately the comprehension of the whole subject as found in the universe ? So far from religious men avoiding rational discussion, they will seek it, and be indebted therefor for light and freedom of mind.

Providence is truly divine. Let no human being presume to be divine, nor desecrate the idea. How can he aspire to be saint, prophet, miracle or mystery performer, or expounder. This is not a question of bluster or boast ; it is one of constant truth. It is the old regime of the priestocracy, often changed and varied in a new dress, but the substance is the same.

Need you ask about God's government, when you see how retributive justice follows in the wake of self-vindicating principles. Do you see in the western wilds and solitudes of America the reckless character calling himself a man, wantonly destroy a poor old Indian woman, a sex that his strong arm should have protected ? He prides himself in the power of his right arm, and the supposed strength of his party, his friends, his father, who helped to corrupt his morals and deprave his religion. from being rational. But see him arrested by the Indians, who seek the most summary vengeance, and compel this party to stand and see it. Principles had availed, but justice now is executed. This wanton wretch has aroused and maddened the sons of the forest, and they flay him alive.

See the reckless bully in Texas, that murders as an assassin and resorts to a judge, to compel him to a mock trial, that he may stand ostensibly and nominally clear before his country.

That wretch there meets with summary vengeance, and atones with his life for all his misdeeds. Enough of similar instances could have been recited.

What is the proof of God, the great first cause ?

The whole universe, that is all effect and cause.

To know what the universe is, mind must seek its proper analysis. All have a comprehensive adaptation, with design. What a diversity in nature, yet all promotive of one universal order.

The Creator's display is throughout creation by a diversity as rich, as design is demonstrable. This diversity is universal. The Almighty paints with light, writes with electricity, orbs his handiwork, the universe his system, with principles for conservation, and attributes for character. Law pre-supposes intelligence. We have direct proof of a God-presiding Providence, by the present operations of the universe.

All creation may look common after familiarity has been established, but all are on sublime conceptions of intellectual grandeur and system of principles. But the caviller objects that the distribution of this world's goods and possessions is most unequal, that many are wealthy and possessed of great if not unlimited power, whilst the reverse obtains with others. How many are worthy by dint of mind's merits, if not, matters soon return to their level. Your cavil reaches mind's vitiated perversions. The wealth of the father is soon squandered by the prodigal son, for others that may be meritorious to accumulate in the process of legitimate business, not of avaricious cupidity. All this proves defect in mind's operations. To scan all rightly, mind must understand all rightly. What blessings are oceans and seas, yet what robberies, piracies, murders and wars, may have been perpetrated on all, yet how many have been prevented by even the Mediterranean sea. To say that God authorizes such, is to libel him as the cause of evil. This is a world, not the universe scanned ; contracted views will not do. Where are the potency, the innocence of mind, its sublime satisfaction and happiness ? That must master all the elements of its circumstances, to carry out the principles of moral free agency, to their legitimate comprehension, to expel despotism in all its mind invasions. All the balance is but as the proof test of its character, triumph and glory.

God's omnipresence, omniscience and omnipotence, are as manifest as mind's functions are recognised in the body of man. Mind's functions have to subdue all the vicious elements of its perversion How do we know there is God Almighty ? If we could not know any other way, we could not mistake him in ruling out all false gods, Messiahs, Christs. Bhudds, Mahomets, Moses, Smiths, Tinkers and Botches, Priestocracies and all polytheists and atheists, witches, ghosts, spirits, knockers, Millers, affiliated oracles, all the world-tribe legion, though they be Belial in character and what not in blasphemy, by the potency of his word—his work, cause and effect, that define him unmistakably to be the Great First Cause, and all others caused or created. Obey the voice of science, mind—real light of God alone.

All the bigots and their nefarious inquisitions have not prevented mind from reading God's word and works. How vain are the impotent, silly despots, coxcombs ! Let the world be no more on contingencies. Have supposed great minds of the world overlooked God's scriptures, and acted the sycophants to man's ? Then that proves them the greater traitors to mind. They are the real Judas Iscariots in the world's toryism and toadyism, caterers to absolutists and priestocracies, when they vitiated their excellent gift, mind. Play not false to your country, constitutional government, freedom, law, order, for the whole world. No matter what position the christian, mahommedan, mormon, or any other peculiar faith takes, they all kill themselves the very moment they lay a foundation in their bibles. Rational education enables mankind to avail themselves of the principles conservative of the universe given to rational mind, but not used by the ancient fathers. There are some persons, I trust, that hold bibles in abeyance, that they may honor themselves in the right supremacy. How much of the world at their own arbitration acquiesces in what is before it, without seeking to correct or make better, palpable errors.

The ministry of the universe address mind, as long as thought can be exercised. The proper study of all life's comprehension, presents a few world-problems for mankind to solve. There is but one proper way to solve them. Are you the adorer of the Almighty Creator, or the worshipper of a created, peculiar idol god? Choose ye this day whom ye will. If you be of the first, you are to all honorable persons a monotheist conclusively ; if of the second, you are decidedly a polytheist, an idolator, irredeemably—irrevocably, by your own special providence, the acts of your own predestination, revoking most ungratefully your own God-given free moral agency. All should render the earth as attractive as practicable. Cease, polytheists and atheists, you vipers bite a file when you meddle with monotheism. In your existence you cannot touch one iota of it. Why do persons commit themselves to these two, atheism and polytheism ? They must be seduced by the partizans without investigation. Their object embraces so much, that mystifies weak or credulous minds. Proscription and ostracism in all the forms of despotism, have been in array for polytheism, perverting mind, bullying the world, robbing, pirating upon it. By the free moral agency of mind, God makes himself the modest President of the universe. There is now no reason for vain man to be more on earth, at the very height of his power and greatness. The very idea of peculiarity in God libels justice. God is not a just God, if peculiar. He is not omnipresent by the bible, as the Devil was his successful rival in his absence. As to monotheism, with all their effrontery the unprincipled opposition cannot say the first word or thing in truth against it. Cause and effect rule out atheism and polytheism. A spiritual being, however etherealized, must be appreciated by its substance.

Atheism presents a headless being for creation. All our ideas are derived from the senses, therefore cause and effect carry us to the great first cause. Farther than this mind has no data.

Both atheism and polytheism beg their questions. Their bibles address the vilest passions, an ignoble faith, and not reason of mind. Such books are the best evidence against themselves.

Omnipotence and perfection of Deity are necessarily united. He is God in perfection, otherwise he could not be God enough to meet all the metaphysics of atheists.

All this pre-supposes perfect attributes. Such a Being atheism does not upset, such polytheism cannot know or adopt.

It is easier to believe in a perfect God, than in an imperfect nature-creator. One or the other stands in this relation to mind. Why, atheist, use mind for legislation if nature be perfect? God has unlimited, infinite perfection.

It takes monotheism to overthrow all the imbecile sophistries of atheism and polytheism. The perfect omnipotence of God absolutely prevents his change of nature, hence he is absolutely immutable, and possesses infinite faculties.

All peculiar bibles, as peculiar faiths of polytheism and atheism, are caricatures of a perfect great first cause. Where do you get conservation of the universe from? How can you prevent one system of worlds or suns from invading another? If nature furnished the means, what prevents the aggression of major or minor bodies? Is nature thus intelligent? You affect matter from nature, but whence do you get the principles of matter? In using terms, do not pervert language. The modesty of the inquiring mind is in abeyance to the future development of facts. Monotheism is the only belief competent to live in a universe of principles. Atheism is no belief, and polytheism like it, is absorbed by monotheism.

Monotheism will absorb atheism and polytheism, the only antagonists, because the last two have no principles. It is impossible for any God of miracles to exist in this universe. Where would atheism get a standard of morals, but from the sublime creator of principles? Where will the polytheist get a standard for the construction of his peculiar bible, and the formation of conscience? Are not all rational views commensurate with principles? Without a God, how will you fix proper responsibility? What is God but the President of nature? He is perfect in his immutability—why then prayers? If there be space, what created it? Nature? How and when? What potentiality could nature have? By all the best definitions could she be adequate to overleap herself to reach a high-wrought performance? The whole nature of things in the universe, not in one world, much less one black letter book or bigoted mind, should be wisely embraced to comprehend the whole category.

The harmony of the universe demonstrates a Creator.

There can only be three views at first, Monotheism, Atheism and Polytheism, and only one at last—Monotheism, as Polytheism resolves itself into Atheism, that resolves itself into nothing.

This is a universe of cause and effect, and as such, addresses itself to the highest, best intellectuality of mind, that cannot be violated in an iota, however spiritual may be the views.

The God of nature is certainly not a peculiar God of any people, as that presents the worst of all false pretences; he certainly never entered into co-partnership, compact or covenant, with any priestocracy. No abstract propositions will answer, unless the whole comprehension has the conservative elements of the universe, therefore all peculiar faiths practicable can never fill the first function of religion, no more than abstract nature, hence both Polytheism and Atheism are nothing.

All with the Almighty is self-evident. The Trinity is not self-evident. God created the universe in conservative principles physically, morally and religiously, but no Jew or Christian Jew bible.

God Almighty stands unapproachable and unapproached, sublimely apart from all others, most self-evident forever.

As to the change of this universe, God is immutable, and Peter was too ignorant to know, and too perfidious to be trusted. Would you go to the best appreciation of God and his universe by all the supreme lights of science, or would you trust to the fiction of irresponsible ignoramuses, the priestocracy?

But you affect to be close followers of the bible. Why, if the bible revelation is before reason, do you refer to commentaries made by reason? You plainly go to mind in preaching! If you act not thus in your mind rationally, already you act the part of insanity. Why is a man recognised as compos mentis by the law, that does not recog-

nise him otherwise ? Is not this a proof, that reason, rationality, governs ? You trade
on this capital until your peculiar faith is cut up by it, and then you dishonestly and ungratefully discard them and your God. A man that is honest, is so by reason of principles, not because of church or peculiar faith, that are all corruptions. You can make
speculations of any doctrines, not of principles, hence you affect to sneak from reason
and truth after you are exposed as malefactors and felons by them.

God has no superior or equal. But why should he, a perfect being, create the world
with its apparently imperfect conditions ? It is a perfect world. Had it been an absolutely perfect creation, it had not been a world. The speculation of Atheism, as Polytheism, is impotent and impudent.

What do you call nature ? Prove it. Principles are immutable, is nature their immutable Creator ? She is ruled by principles.

The Creator manifests himself to all mankind, lettered and unlettered, by his word and
work of cause and effect. Polytheism furnishes the paternity to Atheism, for their disgusting pictures, caricatures of Deity.

The regularity of the seasons proves cause and effect to the Great First Cause, who
is the universal providence that rules principles as their immutable president.

The Atheist overlooks the want of data for all of his absurd metaphysics, whilst the
Polytheist does very little less, and more heinously in supplying his speculative trading,
mercenary notions on the world, for the reality. Man has a plenty of facts now, to do
right. He has to eschew the evils of both, and act as he can on the balance.

The Atheist affects by his assumption, that there can be no beginning of time. He
certainly does not understand the definition, which is only the measure of planetary
motions, and God could exist before all such time or space, of course. Time and
eternity are relative terms, with the Almighty, emphatically.

The universe itself gives the fullest proofs of cause and effect, up to the great first
cause, all that is needed by a sane analyst. But the Atheist goes into metaphysical
speculations, as idle as absurd. The most amplified volume of the great first cause,
meets all the demands legitimate of mind.

But the Atheistical metaphysician speculates in his crude vagaries about God's attributes, as his omnipresence. That can be most perfectly represented by his conservative principles, to fill the whole measure, and proves most conclusively God an Almighty,
on fixed and certain position. His omnipotence, as omnipresence and omniscience,
proclaim him Almighty.

When the Atheist asks mind to step beyond the great first cause, he requires it to
pass beyond the supreme obligations of religion and reason, into metaphysics, the data
of which are not given in this theatre. It is more than a universe problem.

The perfect justice of God demonstrates itself under the circumstances of his creation. His universe is not revocable, for he is immutable. He is the constitutional
president of principles. The ancient devotees to despotism in all its forms, could
never appreciate Deity in the purity of his attributes. They mixed up with their degraded and perverted notions, his divine nature. It is utterly impossible that the
moderns can follow all such, with the lights of mind before them.

Deity is like himself, and mind has to appreciate it with the holiest rationality. He is
unlike all the most incomprehensible of all creeds, the claiming nature and not Deity
for the supremacy.

Man is not to create Deity, but must read what his magnificent volume declares.

None but a monomaniac can deny the great First Cause. Mind can comprehend its
rational relations to Deity, enough to prevent the metaphysical speculations of the
Atheist. Those presuppose the necessity of the immortality of the soul, as a universe
problem for mind's solution. Instead of going beyond Deity, mind must not go beyond
man, for instead of metaphysical speculations, it has practical duty in their stead. That
is the province of mind and of monotheism to teach. God's conservative principles
represent him an Almighty indeed, and vindicate him as the wisest philosophy and science
demonstrate. All peculiar-faith systems are swindling speculations ; all priestocracies
are fanatics, a useless clique, entirely superfluous ; all Atheists are monomaniacs : of
all, the priestocracies are most dangerous, for they have ever enslaved mind in the worst
of all its fetters, for their monopolies and usurpations; mind under the best constitutional
liberty, has to extricate itself entirely from their grasp. The dynasty of superstition
is theirs that commences in fraud, ends in bayonets, inquisitions, bastiles and massacres.
Mind should never let these things be, while God is perceptible by his immutable principles that exclude all the blind assumptions about nature, over which his supreme intelligence presides, represented by conservative principles that vindicate it by or through
themselves. Nobody in his or her senses can decry the presiding influence of the
great First Cause.

Universal principles preside over nature, and they must refer to their cause, Creator, originator, ruler, president. The Atheist takes the effect, nature, for the cause ; she is passive. Can nature create, vegetate, without the seed ? The universe is a component of systems, that move with exact mathematical precision, and the systems of the universe are in abeyance to universal astronomical laws. What is nature ? The Atheist enters into suppositions about nature, a crude passive agent.

The facts of the universe extend to the utmost perfection of nature, a perfect actor, an existence with the highest perfect intelligence, a principle ruler and creator. Nature is in abeyance to principles that represent Deity, the Supreme who gives self-evident proofs. The Atheist speaks not only of nature, but in his misconception and imperfect analysis of nature ruled, and that by conservative principles. That is certain, now, perfect conservation bespeaks, proves, demonstrates the highest, perfect wisdom. It is not simple nature, but nature under sublime intelligence and laws paramount to nature, hence a decisive proof that a supreme first cause rules or presides. An Atheist is presumptuously blind, or fanatically bigoted, and aids his father bigot, the polytheist. The severest agitation and conflict of society, is by sectarians such as these.

The paramount question is, is nature ruled ? Of course she is, and supremely, else she could not be in the sublime form of the universe. Now is nature the ruler ? What an absurdity. Then nature is subordinate. Supremes, not subordinates, institute principles. Nature is passive under active rules, as self-evident through the diversified seasons. If rules from a ruler that had not supreme power were offered, they would be subordinate to destruction, and all nature would fly into fragments. They must be active, to insure the appropriate security and inherent action. Whenever nature then is named, it implies a universe ruled, and nothing less, otherwise it is a blind nothing. Look at this physically, morally and religiously. Mind needs a harvest, and as the active agent representing the Creator, plants them, nature, the passive, operates to maturity. Nature is then the passive means, and cannot originate ; otherwise new species, order and genera would arise infinitely. Now mind, if passive, might wish to all eternity, before its wishes were complied with.

Mind then is the especial providence that directs Nature originated by universal Providence.

The atheist contravenes all principles, when he makes Nature passive and active both at one and the same time, a contradiction in terms.

What are the fruits of atheism ? not those of principles. To an atheist, time, that has a simple solution, is incomprehensible. Rationalism will kill all atheism and polytheism. Where, atheist, do you get the universe conservative power ?

Is nature the passive agent adequate for all the Universe ? Prove atheism, demonstrate it, or upset Monotheism. On what data can the last be done ? The supreme intelligence is identified with the Universe, by all conservative principles.

What is the Universe, but the union of vast systems ? How could these preserve their admirable equilibrium, but for a presiding Great First Cause. The denial involves derangement of the brain of the recusant. It is only a change of terms, when we know by the lights of science that principles conserve.

Peculiar faith-advocates assume that liberal education will make infidels and atheists. Do they understand their subject, I ask with due respect to honest and truthful motives ? If they do, then I have yet to learn more of these savans. As to history, I must believe them mistaken—for the alumni of the most enlightened institutions that irradiate the world with science, as far as I know, are on the side of law and order, to say the least.

In their assumption against infidels and atheists, they define their own creed, that is, on pure analysis is nothing less than polytheism, not one particle beyond atheism.

As a Monotheist, I must ask on the noblest of all principles, that of religion, what creeds can there be but monotheism, atheism, and polytheism ?

Then the polytheist, as atheist, has no tenable grounds, and both are swept away completely in their own vortex. What, then, becomes of the term, infidel ? Of course, an infidel to polytheism or atheism, is one pledged in fidelity to Deity. Then necessarily, all present and future accountability is in abeyance to the supremacy of the Creator, including social, moral, and religious obligations.

Polytheists, as if to enhance their cause, tell us of the horrid abominations of atheism in France, but they must see all such in alliance with polytheism, the abominations of which are identified with a world's history.

As an offset to atheism in France, let the acts of despotism of church and state be truly represented. Who has not heard of the dreadful Bastile ? the horrid massacres of polytheism ? The French had been brutalized into atheism, by its fixed parent, polytheism. What better could be expected of either, when both deal in bloody revolutions, and not in the conservative one of Monotheism, exempt from dark and bloody deeds? The atheism of France was sown by polytheism, and the harvest matured in the blood shed by the first.

What was the condition of France, has been too much enacted over the world as their bitter fruits. What is the condition of Mexico? That of the finest country in ruins. Both countries were apparent republics, the one adopting atheism the relief from polytheism, the other the continued victim of the last.

Who were the conquerors, but one class of polytheists superseding another? But then, this is the work of Romanism, you may say. What is the condition of India, or Hindostan? Ah! but that was the ruins of the Brahmins and Bhuddists. Who completed it, but the Protestant English?

Polytheists, no more than atheists, have any claim to principles that are all conservative and of God, whereas atheism and polytheism are of bewildered and ignorant vulgar doctrines of men. The last especially, of the priestocracy, and to be exploded before the piercing rays of intellectual science. To appreciate principles is the work of rational mind, that must have rational education, the very jewel to be obtained in such institutions.

On clear analysis, what the polytheist terms an infidel, resolves itself into this, that such ferociously declares against those that conscientiously cannot believe his book religiously, and that the polytheist is an impostor. No, the polytheist has no right to the term of infidel, when his bible is untrue, as the polytheist is clearly and positively in the light of an impostor, before the light of the whole rational world.

Polytheists, are the peculiar faith world. Are rational minds afraid of all such schools? What, atheist, can you aspire to above the polytheist? If you get rid of polytheism, you are still amenable to monotheism. But the worst inconsistency is with the polytheists, who declaim against all others. How can they get rid of the whole offensive brood? By adopting the truths of Monotheism, and renouncing their whole errors. What nuisances are polytheism and atheism. All their positions are dogmas and assumptions. The world will get rid of the abominations of both, by first getting rid an important step of their whole priestocracy. They adopt the dog in the manger policy of keeping the world out of Monotheism, because it cannot swallow their peculiar dogmas. The world has to adopt one of these three. Polytheism blames the world for atheism, that she herself makes when she outrages monotheism. Is there such a thing as cause and effect? How far are they admissible? only just so far as peculiar faith chooses? Do they stop short of the whole comprehension? Do the peculiar bible advocates know what truth and honesty are? Do they not see positively and conclusively, absolutely, that peculiar bibles are incompatible with all such as with republican constitutions, human liberty, the noblest liberty of mind? What gives perpetual motion to the different spheres or spheroids of the Universe? Who bade time start, and eternity last, but the Universe Author?

All this was on the principle for that governed, of action and reaction. You polytheists complain of atheism, and yet with all your pretences and powers you cannot silence it or put it down. The world should examine, test properly all about monotheism, polytheism, and atheism, on their own intrinsic qualities, not on the pretences of priestocracies, whose voice should not be listened to an iota in this paramount investigation. The worst committalism and using up, is by one's own self, therefore, this premises the supreme caution of doing this excellently well and right.

Atheism is criminal in fostering the murder of mind—it does not do it justice, neither can polytheism. Both are murderous of mind. Who, then, wishes the follies of the priestocracy? The earliest rationalism on refined civilization the better, without monotheism, no mind is right, therefore it cannot be divested of its holy protection by the intrigues of polytheism.

Polytheism is as accountable as atheism, and both are opposed to monotheism.

Atheism may bring forward much quibbling metaphysics about an ideal something estimated Deity by it, but God is omnipotent in his perfection, and perfect because he can do all that is perfect, and remain perfect.

What a bigot monster of depravity is polytheism.

But, says the atheist, I go for nature. Does he go for licentiousness? · Nature is only an exponent of principles, that bespeak a supreme Organizer and Creator. Let the majesty of principle, the glory of virtue be appealed to. You cannot mistake your duty, atheist, if you wish. There are checks and balances in the philosophy of the Universe, but in the meagre, contracted, conceited bigotry of priestocracy there is no virtue. The ipse dixit of dramatic writers is to be put down, that mind may not be imposed on always. There must be a self-motive power, the originator of perpetual motion.

What of Providence universal and especial? The first belongs to the function of creation, the last is identified with the action of mind and principles, his special representatives. The bigotry of polytheism and atheism is clearly demonstrated, with regard to monotheism and the highest injunctions of rationality, by the complete overthrow of such people as had not advanced in the science of the times, &c. They go backwards. Infidelity is anti-God, the poor metaphysics of polytheism and atheism, that fall forever before the divine majesty of Monotheism.

THE GOVERNMENT OF DEITY; ITS EXALTED CHARACTER.

DEITY must elaborate and enjoy all that is excellent, possessed of his inherent elements of greatness, power and sources of happiness.

Must not then especial perpetual punishment yield to the superior government by rewards?

The first debases, the last elevates and ennobles character. The hope of reward, is identified with free agency, to raise mind to its best promotion.

But other considerations exclude the soul, and the divine purpose of its creation.

Human nature becomes depraved, corrupt and vitiated, from the corruption of the times, and the perversion of mind.

Much of it is seriously degraded and brutalized by the circumstances affecting it—some is debased despite of much effort to elevate it aright, hardly fit for vital existence, and yet as accountable and responsible, unprepared to die.

The conservative revolution of such character reflects the amendment expedient for mind.

Not only the counteraction of universal depravity, but the advancement to the highest state of elevation of mind, is the problem of existence. The benevolence of refinement induces the faith that perpetual punishment in a future state could not be instituted by the possessor of universal attributes.

The motive of adoption of the least of all evils, is the attribute of benevolence, as we must take nothing for granted, but on the most rational basis.

The value of the best minds best elevated is far superior to the rest, and must be duly estimated and shown. Their reward must be insured.

But mind is of too much value to be placed as a polishable diamond and then cast idly by, among dust and rubbish hopelessly lost, when possessed of available elements. The author must estimate and cherish his best work by the best care and solicitude. He cannot do justice to it, short of immortal functions bestowed.

Association and mixture of all varieties of character through all gradations of best to worst, is incompatible with ideas of propriety, and cannot be permitted by Deity, who has arranged the infinite number of spheres, boundless to man, after his own best taste and skill.

A distinction is drawn by the worst, and they must abide their own action in correspondent degree.

The enjoyment of existence must be consistent to its every gradation—through the various links of creation. There is much misery that follows as penalty on bad actions on this earth, but too often the guilty seem to escape condign punishment.

Sinners, as all are, most feel when others feel; misery begets misery; when others suffer we sympathize. It is our nature, and the great God of nature gave to us this feeling. Such sympathy induces the question, would it not enhance universal enjoyment to institute universal salvation? Then all enjoyment of happiness is promoted by the knowledge that all souls possess the position relative to merit.

But guilt of mind perverted exists.

What shall become of the dreadful and depraved tyrants of society, who have ruthlessly and recklessly crushed the noblest feelings and sensibilities of mind, and consigned it prematurely to another state of existence?

Who can be worse than all those who have committed trespasses of the most flagrant character directly with the worst blasphemy, against God and his rightful attributes? Among which are all the institutions of false, spurious and counterfeit faith, that pervert God's unity and impugn his prerogatives.

No less are social wrongs, of those highest in authority for a time over man.

All these may be punished in part on earth, but not adequately, for their crimes and brutal oppressions, for their slaughter of the human race most wantonly by millions, outraging all humanity on age and sex, assailing human life with all the direst calamities.

No less are the minor tyrants, who go to the extent of their power, to be corrected.

The peculators of the public, the oppressors of innocence and helpless people, defrauding them of their rights and depriving them of their privileges.

All the flagrant violators of principles must make atonements suitable and commensurate, nations as individuals, the whole world. Nations that do not heed principles will go down to the common tomb, and their names shall be erased from the virtuous.

Every degree of vice must remove the soul by degrees from the fountain of purity. Then intrinsic differences must be graduated between souls meritorious and culpable. The soul that feels appropriate punishment, makes atonement for misdeeds. The mode and measure are among the unrevealed realities of a future state. The Mighty One of creation enjoys that which befits consummate wisdom, spotless purity, and unappreciable magnanimity—whose space is the universe—whose duration is eternity—whose power is imprescriptible—and whose reward, as creation, is self-elemental.

His exile is sorrow and punishment, but his presence is happiness and joy, as whose glorious mantle is justice, without which the elements of creation had not been so elevated, so self-preserved and regulated in their eternal foundations.

This world, then, furnishes but one of myriads of apartments in the universe, and may be one of the spheres and theatres of mind progressing in its career towards perfection, tried by time and rewarded by eternity.

Who that is wise will not make the best use of time, most valuable function of mortal existence?

Mind in time becomes the soul in eternity.

The sublime creation of the universe saw also its true fundamental principles of government for its preservation, else it had not been creation, but chaos, without head, a consummation that characterized the loftiest unapproachable skill of the Immortal Architect.

The Creator then left all in a glorious state of blessedness and adaptation for future progress.

If God cannot save us, what are we to expect from feudal vassal office-holders?

Their platform is of self-interest, as directed by their leaders good or bad, adapted and qualified by the times, not of principles that originated creation. All the most beautiful creation of mind's fancy will not, cannot increase the matter-of-fact loveliness of God's creation, that should not be diminished by any of the deformities of mind in the priests' empire.

God vindicates his attributes, ennobles his works, and punishes blasphemy.

Not to give God all his attributes and qualities, is to attempt to impeach them, but the pretences thereon for desecrated objects victimize the impostor in all particulars inevitably and deservedly, in all the elements of ignominy and disgrace, of infamy and ruin complete.

Better would it be, if done designedly, for such never to have heard reason, for she will condemn him when her voice can be heard at the tribunal of the God of reason, if it cannot be audited in the forum of conscience, but stifled so as to originate the cause of curses of billions on his head.

Sooner or later a correct decision, and right action on that decision, must come, when reason holds her rule in the presidency of mind and conscience, at the tribunal of honesty and universal cognizance.

The God of the universe asserts his claims in their comprehension, and vindicates them in a masterly sublimity, that reduces all pretension of man to the lowest humility.

By reason he excludes all impostors, and often punishes, through avenging principles, the blasphemous pretenders by speedy death.

Let their deluded followers beware of his invincible might, and his omniscient faculty.

Let not not the gods of false faiths, or the priests, their oracles, affect his functions over mind, for they cannot survive the infamy that will finally overtake and overwhelm them.

The world will approve doctrines that depend on vital principles, as it is bound imperatively to all such for vital existence, whether we will or no, because of God's supreme wisdom; but it is needless to tell a sound mind that all things are possible with God, through a fool's exposition that tangles common sense and reason, and libels their author.

All the acts of wisdom are possible with God, but not a fool's faith. God does not contradict himself, as he is unchangeable and perfect from the start of creation; but the priests' bibles and peculiar faiths change this proper character of God, through their stupid imbecility.

Man's delusion and oppression led through the blood of all kinds of victims—man's included—offered up in groves, or on the altars erected by his deplorable and stupid ignorance and his horrid crimes, under the misguidance of priestcraft and man's omission of duty to his own mind, to the erection of mighty temples to the gods of polytheism ·

but the hand of Deity—time—has erased much of all such rubbish, and will scatter the rest entirely to the dust.'

The God of Immortality has created a living temple, that he continues as a constant memento of his own greatness, that lives and feels and has its being from the fountain of all life, and that is perfectly incapable of receiving a substitute. Disguised as peculiar faith may be, the trophy is only a senseless temporal speculation, a hypocritical pretence that cannot breathe in the pure ethereal atmosphere of the Supreme.

This living temple is immortal, under the successive renewal of endless life, from procreation, in the interminable link of human generation.

Where is God's temple better located than in the mind, having its mental appreciation from the time of cultivated consciousness of its author, the Almighty, who has vouchsafed and thus constituted an immortal guardian, as far as legitimate and necessary.

It is here that religion most rational can be enkindled around the family altar of friendship, love, and esteem, filial, parental, and social, comprehensive as earth, boundless as the universe, and respondent to all that can inspire adoration for the universal protection of him who sympathizes for all and with all, as meriting it.

What is there in the cold soulless pages of a priest-book of superstition, or the bible, so called, not of mind but of man, that can breathe the breath of love so pure, of appreciation so vivid of the Creator, as mind that eclipses all in the universe of creation, purified by a right conception of its duty and its proper execution?

God never left to contingency his mighty attributes.

The affairs of such condition and position indicate action too preposterous, thanks to Deity.

All such proves, if needed, that the government of this world would be tangled in worse than Gordian knots in a few seconds if left to the guardianship and guidance of all the priests, ancient and modern.

There can be no worship of God but true adoration on principles, that reflect the excellence of actions.

Special providence is not peculiar, but a universal providence; not of peculiar, but a rational faith.

The God of the universe is not the God of wrath and fury, as he necessarily hath an equilibrium pre-eminently his. Any other was a peculiar god, such as the petty Jew god described in the Jew bible. Persons that are good in or out of church are so on principles, rational religion, monotheism, the only thing that can keep mankind right. Now, is it possible that an omnipotent God would have ever permitted his chosen people, the Jews, to have been made slaves of by the people he had no liking to, and that he would have permitted his book to have been lost, had all been fixed upright at the start? The God of the universe knows no such peculiar god as the Jews claimed, no more than religion knows their peculiar faith from any other false pretence. All that adopt peculiar faith adopt idolatry, and cannot reach the proper adoration of the perfect Creator.

The world complains of the shortness of life, but who can complain of the shortness of principles?

The priestocracy and minions complain of infidels, those that do not believe their degraded book-lies, falsehoods and pretences, that libel the perfection of God, but they are tories to God and mind to take that position. The dispensations of the Almighty are compatible with the best preservation of the universe in its widest comprehension, therefore mind has to correct its errors, and be sure and not commit itself to the false positions of presumptuous priestocracies in no respect. Let the disposition tell. The analytic mind has to detect, to expose errors with moral firmness, to secure a conservative revolution, to reach all expedient as created to best govern itself. Why do they not let God govern by his conservative principles, instead of their botches and tinkerings? How few of the world do this? The only proper patience and resignation to the will of Divine Providence is inculcated by monotheism, that rejects all the tricks of degraded priestocracy. This position rejects suicide as an infatuation, a crime, a folly, a cowardice, a want of proper balance of mind, that has needed the highest protection of rational education. What shall we do in our death end? Why not ask for our life-time? Rational religion is the only thing that can satisfy a rational mind, at that and all times the most trying. All peculiar faith starts falsely, and ends so. Now, of what benefit is all that to a dying person, when not fit for a living one.

The most perfect and harmonious understanding throughout the world can exist by rational religion, that must finally exclude peculiar faiths of all kinds, and advance conservatism, that is, the preservation of all God's conservative principles, the true spirit that ought to prevail throughout the world. The abuse of the little brief authority in every department, particularly to the prejudice of ignorance and neglect of conservative principles, is counteracted by rational mind, that represents rational religion. The highest justice can be awarded to those people who are best disposed, while all should have equitable principles of justice, renouncing to be the unprincipled gamblers in the world's stock.

Religion of the God of the universe is just the reverse of the peculiar faiths of the peculiar god of the bible, who let his devil get man and woman from him after the creation. The close of this writing would just be the beginning, as the subject of God's religion is exhaustless to mind.

It seems sacrilege, in such an enlightened age as this, to miss the sacred object of God, whose holy deed has written his ineffaceable and unmistakable word, cause and effect, that is self-impressed as rational mind's universal standard.

All violations of conservative principles are unsafe, dangerous, and to be avoided. God has immutable laws and principles for his universe, co-extensive with creation. Man cannot deprecate them ; messiahships cannot modify or alter them by prayers : hence, how absurd was it for the ancients to imagine, and more absurd in the moderns to adopt any pretences whatever in this respect. The wisest conformity to all the sublime regulations of Deity during rational life, bespeaks the greatest wisdom of mind.

Is universal Providence especial? This position premises Providence and foresight in mind, to reach and attain its appropriate sphere.

When were they premised by a perfect being, who does his work at first forever without any necessity for a second touch, but at the creation, in the institution of principles conservative to the universe?

Analyze the state of that mighty design, and mind, under the perfection of reason and elevated by philosophical science, is introduced into renewed adoration of Deity.

Without these attributes of mind, man is as apt to run into danger as from it. He can only keep cool, by the best direction of mind as the best plan forever.

His, then, is the part for your especial providence, prudence and foresight. Principles must and will vindicate themselves, re-acting as God's general and especial Providence.

But is there an especial Providence? God shows his supremacy in the sublimest light, to cause His universal principles to act for him in all necessary capacities. Some of the incidents of life seem to support the idea of especial Providence on extraordinary vicissitudes, but the best efforts of mind duly cultivated, secure the best and that through conservative principles. The history of life seems curious, and offers much for philosophical, moral and religious contemplation.

When two men contend on a bluff and fall into the water, by which one is drowned, but the other, though then saved, is killed in a well a few years afterwards, the enthusiast may contend for especial providence, while the rationalist sees the effects of principles that were violated. The Providence of God is Almighty. Those who travel on steamers that are badly attended to by construction and engineering, risk their lives by drowning or being blown up. Mind then is to be looked to as responsible. Mind is mighty but finite, therefore it must resort to all the uniform expedients of science, and all the protection of principles. Many an apparently weak side is favored by its circumstances, and none better than by all the powers of mind in its innumerable expedients.

Revolutions conservative are always for justice and the good of mankind, but if mixed up with selfish ambition, and not directly carried out on intrinsic merits, may fail. The failure was incident to the means, not Providence. In the category of revolutions destructive, are to be placed all revolutions for peculiar faith doctrines. and all for messiahships. Wisdom can always predict their final downfall, for they have not conservative principles wherewith to sustain them. Sectarianism in peculiar faith always involves final ruin. When the Jews spoke of the rest of the world as heathen, they indited their own barbarism, and proved the worst practice and species of sectarianism an example for their own treatment by those nations that have repaid it many fold.

Their downfall is, then, the result of principles, for peculiar faith will never let mind advance to the requisitions of nature or herself.

A man towering in his vain egotism, possessed of power, is reckless of rights that pertain to others and himself.

Short sighted indeed must he be if he do not understand the results. Many incidents of history and biography will clearly illustrate.

Preceding a drove of cattle was a carriage, containing a lady and family, and following came a man in a sulky, dashing recklessly along as if he wished to scare the herd, perfectly independent himself, as he was behind, and supposed himself free from danger. But principles vindicate themselves in the whole circle.

When the cattle were about to drive furiously along, to the extreme danger of the lives of those in the carriage, the humane drover sprung before them, shaking his coat, that he had stripped off. They were driven thus on the man behind, whom they crushed down, breaking his bones, and ruining his sulky, to the very great danger of his life. What teaches brutal perverse minds, reckless of restraints and duties to society, better than certain penalties? Impunity licences to crime.

All society most look to this for self-preservation.

To secure the potent realization of Almighty Providence, mind must be enlightened by reason, referring to the lights of education, the reflection of rational minds illumined by the best lights of a liberal world that refers to enlightened public opinion, in an enlightened community of mind.

Religion arises spontaneously by virtue of innate faculties in all rational minds, and is subject to the influence and tuition of education, that ennobles mind if right by a just appreciation of Deity to rational religion, or debases it if misleading by perversion and corruption to superstition, idolatry, and man-worship, ostensibly and really polytheism, or plurality of gods, if more than one.

Rational religion that can be characterized by all the noblest attributes best, from the pure fountain of goodness, creating the most rational faith, and brightest, most substantial hope, that can be carried to the legitimate extent of justice to Deity's attributes and man's duty, teaches rational mind to survey Providence through the medium of sublime principles.

Rational religion credits all the legitimate claims that mind is entitled to, that God exacts, and that man can require or expect from the nature of creation perfected by God.

God's attribute of mercy is characterized by universal principles, and must produce universal fruits of salvation, proportionate and graduated to characteristic traits of mind.

The Almighty stands alone in his own perfection in the sublime dignity and supremacy of his unity in his own self-sustaining worth, grandeur and magnificence. He needs but virtuous intellect, to appreciate his glory, a fact that bespeaks the highest hope for immortality of the soul.

Rational beings must see and know unmistakably that God is the true object of their adoration, and as his creatures, that they must look for protection through their Creator, as in all the principles of justice and of his being, the Creator is bound to the best protection of the creation on conservative principles.

The Creator is under obligation to protect his creation, that is equally bound to him for that conservation.

The best obligation on both parties is implied.

Mind has been impressed with the right elements of religion, that must be sought of the right standard, the Creator, the protecting Providence.

Conscience introduces rational mind to the Creator, and is a sacred deposite from innate faculties in the holy keeping of mind, exalted at all times by the best lights and exercise of reason, herself the great emanation and inspiration from Deity, and establishing true rational religion.

Anything that interrupts man's conscience with God, or invalidates God Almighty's attributes in their full force and virtue, impeaches that peculiar whole faith as untrue, and its actions unfaithful to the Universe, that conclusively gainsays the same forever beyond mistake, as unworthy of reason and mind, the only beneficiaries.

Rational religion, true religion, rests with the right actions of mind, that is faithfully directed to all duty, by the conscience of the individual who must be a free to be a responsible agent.

Man must live and die with a pure conscience resulting from no wanton injury to creation, but fortified by acts of justice, love of kindness and humanity before God.

The conscience free from offence, guilt, and guile, and enlightened by reason, presents the best intercessor for the rational religionist throughout the world.

Without reason there is no conscience, and without its free agency there can be no responsibility.

On a different basis, the jurisprudence of this world, and the exalted justice of Deity must forgive crime.

Conscience is the crowning glory of mind, as a guardian genius enlightened by the best inspirations of reason, that gives man his triumph over malign circumstances.

Conscience asks, when rightly directed, if not smothered and murdered, always for correct principles.

Give, oh give, then, free and virtuous scope to mind, whose vacuum has to be filled.

How can conscience ever reach correct principles, without reason and the light of mind, that luxuriates in all the degrading crimes of a vicious education of the age, if not elevated above them by correct principles.

What is to restrain the unprincipled mind?

The spirit of the wild and savage state has its partial education and its principles, its partial rational religion.

A matured and properly organized conscience, is the full growth of mental reaction, and the entire comprehension of all innate principles, not a mere part to suit the present and reject the future, to suit time, but abjure eternity.

God has endowed all rational mental capacities with this blessing, that cannot be too purely and brightly cultivated in all the refinements of honesty, and all the fruits of rational religion.

Its blessings tell hundreds of fold in social, moral, and religious life in the world's welfare, and the people of the earth feel its kindliest aid and genial protection.

What man is entitled to in life's rights, pleasures and hopes, will be accorded by the right tribunal of conscience, as his just right under creation's claims, mind's merits, and God's purpose.

Every man's conscience asks for durable peace on eternal principles, and nothing less, if wise unto his own preservation. In the tribunal of conscience, then, neither he that wears the mitre, nor that is in power, can escape the remorse of the deepest guilt.

The God of principles judges those that defeated the elementary principles of true government, that giveth the rights for the full exercise of social duties and rational religion. Then they will not pass unpunished, after having sworn one faith, and meaning differently with mental reservations and moral obliquity.

The result of a guilty conscience presents the deepest penalties of remorse, that "without consuming burns."

How glorious is it that reason should shed her benign influence over free rational discussion and freedom of conscience, that enables intelligent minds to pay exact justice to all. How are all prepared in life for death, but by universal adherence to all the requisitions of enlightened conscience?

The consolations of enlightened conscience are one of the chief sources of exalted happiness.

On whom, then, but God alone does true religion rest?

But cannot others participate also with God in power? Not at all, if God's attributes are God's.

Why is not God exclusive ruler of all? enlightened conscience positively demands.

He is the first, the great and everlasting cause, that by pre-occupancy of omnipresence excludes the least rightful invasion.

Else, he is no God, much less a perfect being; but he is full proprietor by genius, rights the best, and can only be excluded in the vain, perverted, self-conceited, bigoted mind of false teachers.

The system of christian messiahship presents four gods, one expressly the God of evil, seducing souls from their Creator, and other vulgar absurdities.

Such a system is criminal before conscience, and absurd, contemptible, abominable before the light of mind.

What, then, holds the divine right, the only divine right of God's inspiration?

Mind, that leads to enlightened conscience, and its most enlightened, noblest system of rational religion.

What is the attribute of mind, in recognition of these principles of the universe?

Her highest wisdom attainable, which is reason, declares most plainly a full and proper action, that leads to constant performance of duty to the universe and its First Great Cause, Creator, Ruler, and God Supreme.

Can faith have any prior claim or superior respect in man's mind, in any of his duties, religious or social?

It would be the height of criminal absurdity if that position was the order of conscience.

There is but one tribunal of mind, over which reason presides, and she is the only representative of God in reaching faith. Any other is dishonesty, if not superstition.

The best decision arises in truth, that is indebted to reason's God.

Where there is deviation, it rests on mind's perversions, delusions, and deceptions.

The tortures of conscience are the worst of all penalties. Some delinquents are impeachable for weakness of mind voluntarily, that affect not to be able to recognise their full duty by stupid ignorance, whilst the real state evidently must be corruption.

Those who can know or find out, and choose not to investigate, but affect belief in errors of faith, yet are passive in good, must be amenable at the bar of conscience, whilst they pretend that the devil keeps them back.

The devil is one of the most demoralizing fictions ever perpetrated on mind.

The right speculation hands all this over to the right principle, without desiring, much less needing, intercessorships of priests or preachers to finish it to their notions.   God is the only actor, whose mind plainly tells these gentry to be distant.

What kind of conscience ought the world to have, but in its original purity ?

Analysis, the fort of the mind, tells us that the world is nothing without the right kind of people.

They must have wise firmness for life, and life's best interest confirmed on immaculate principles, duly recognised by enlightened mind.

Deity demands this of all rational creation, physically and morally, requiring adoration exclusively of enlightened minds, whilst he communicates the blessings to all.

This world is a scene of just relations, and is to be the theatre of conscience, that regulates and governs the actions of mankind.   Who, then, is the preacher but conscience?

Spare the holy spirit of conscience, do not violate its benign influence, and you will be spared remorse at the trying hour of purification.

To make right impressions, the conscience must be innocent, and the cause good.

When enlightened conscience acts, a pure religion is supported by rational mind, instructed by rational education.

God can only be addressed through the pure principles of reason, originating appropriate actions.

All as enlightened are religious in degree, if they have any conscience enlightened, and as full proof that faith becomes fanaticism when mind is debased by ignorance, history abundantly teaches.

Purity of mind best results from the light and benefit of light of science and philosophy, on mind naturally benevolent.

Conscience untrammeled and enlightened by reason, is the best criterion of moral rectitude.

Modesty and worth of character, are of no weight of estimation to the intriguer who looks to his own selfish ends in power and money ; but estimate, you that have conscience, the pains, penalties, forfeitures, confiscations of mind for vice.   The short comings and omissions are bad enough.

When collusion and combination impose penalties and sufferings, where but to a future tribunal of a just God can all look ?

Conscience if rightly cultivated, leads to virtue and its reward, but if perverted, leads to vice and its penalties.   Paramount duties must be premised and practiced, before all others, else the folly of the world is bad, and its corruption is worse, as a natural consequence, because certain knowledge and exact science are not its benefactors to rescue from degradation.   All rational beings have to obey the upright decision of enlightened conscience.

Repentance is on remorse of conscience, that must be enlightened through mind itself, influenced by the science of morals, ethics, religion.

Conscience makes calculation good and bad, fairly for both sides.   There are a great many things that a conscientious man will refuse, though permitted by law.

An honest man never considers debts out of date, that are not so in conscience.   He will never compromise debts when he can pay what he owes justly.

Absence of interested parties, no more than their presence, causes him to neglect his duty to them.   With him conscience is never stretched, much less violated.

He seeks progression in good, by safe rational education, legislation, rewards and indispensable penalties.

He will act well at home, in all the circles of duty.   He has no unreasonable conflicts about his affairs abroad, much less in the neighborhood.   He means right, acts and shows this disposition to be right.   Acting rightly, he neither embraces, conceals, appropriates or smuggles up all he has.

Such does not recur to personal abuse, for the defence of his position.

Conscience wishes to analyze religion, but peculiar faith disclaims the ability, and repels the attempt.   What does faith avail in true morals, if the base be perverted as peculiar faith is always, hence we should like to know how enlightened conscience comes, but from reason ?

Conversion is change of or on mind, and premises a pure base.   No commission of the principal can possibly supersede or dispense with his almighty influence.   His is the creation, and his must be the grace.   All else is inefficient from the very nature of mind's existence.

Conscience enables the world to criticise all on merits, not to crush them by libels, which is felonious.

How many restless spirits are there without peace ?   Have they been pirates on the world, with remorse of conscience still pursuing them ?   Listen to all the wise admonitions of conscience, to secure immortal happiness.

Lay aside conscience, and mind is tyrant. Is the right to liberty of conscience, full and fair in regard to bibles?

If not, it is an awful tyranny.

Blessed are they who seek to do right all their lives, by an enlightened conscience, a pure and cultivated mind, whose thoughts first and last on each day arise to God, and have the least of evil. The highest of legislation is that of an enlightened conscience. The history of the world proves mind's free agency under the circumstances of creation. But that kind of free agency is objected to. You then ask for something absolute, that does not pertain to God, who is consistent on his own principles of creation. All this position of mind revolves on the great centre, enlightened conscience. Mind is the existent principle, but the light of conscience is ever referring to the only infallible standard, to the Creator of the universe. The only safe motto is, do nothing of which you can possibly have any remorse of conscience. You are dissatisfied. Why? What can satisfy you? You have done acts that cannot be re-called. What are you going to do about it? Make all the practicable atonement by retributive justice. The world should take care how it trespass upon the expansive grace of the Creator. The bible of tradition subscribes to polytheism, whereas reason and mind's conscience uphold only one Supreme God of Nature. Conscience, to be most elevated, must be enlightened by philosophical science and truth.

All that is done in wisdom, is the supreme action of mind. If the pure conscience have God on its side, all messiahs may go. To-day sectarians would have an imperial ukase or edict, to proscribe conscience.

Cultivate conscience through mind-culture.

The conscience that is nurtured by rationalism is too pure to admit any of the forms of polytheism, as trinity, that causes atheism.

Conscience can only be elevated by the elevated lights of mind, reflected on by the education of philosophical, liberal science. Proper conscience can only thus be established. Retributive justice must bring remorse of conscience, on the seduction of innocence, the outrage of rights and wrongs done.

Conscientiousness can only be right, as rational education is right. That of peculiar education is more or less fanaticism. Man, perverted by peculiar education, faith, and interest, aggravated by all the world policies of ambition, avarice, covetousness and envy, and infuriated by all the evil passions of unrestrained and licentious will without equilibrium of principles, is devil enough.

Sinful thoughts may arise, but not dwell, certainly not mature, in the mind of those refusing action.

Conscience decides for immortality. What is freedom of conscience worth, if freedom of mind is embezzled by peculiar faith?

The conscience is solicitor for the mind, which is alone responsible officially to its Creator. The question at the proper tribunal will not be as to peculiar faith, which is alien to the subject of religion, but how much of the last has been duly practiced to the honor of both conscience and mind, man and God. The consciousness of guilt or remorse must be met at first by the right actions. The world must go for the liberty of conscience, that was hardly known to the best intelligence of the world a century ago. To live without fear and reproach is one of the best of all positions, but to live self-approving is happiness indeed. How are you going to counteract the thousand evils and ills of this life, caused by mind's perversions and short-comings? By mind's rational education, correct action and genius; above all, an enlightened conscience, comes from the most rational mind, most rationally treated. The highest, chastest, purest taste, is virtue, and that is the exercise of the highest legitimate functions on conservative principles. Consult then conscience, not peculiar bibles, the engine of earthly Belials, who convert the earth into their hell, pervert and dwarf all to their ignominious notions. Conscience is as to education, hence that must be rational, or the worst injustice is done it. As all peculiar faith is as to peculiar education, hence conscience must be only guarded by rational education. There are some unprincipled people that will take advantages, and care nothing for conscience or its paramount rights. Keep such at a distance, as unworthy of notice, contemptible and base, till they learn that they have to correct their beginnings, and hold themselves amendable to a right public opinion, based on rational principles.

The whole world should know if it investigate what is truth and honesty, that graces the start of rational religion. So some of the world get out of their difficulties, they care nothing at all for the balance. There are many things not defined on principles, that are sought to be by world-bullyism—mind-toryism.

THE IMMORTALITY OF THE SOUL.

Is there immortality of the soul, or does mind perish ?

As like produces like, affinities produce affinities, and only such, man shows a mental organization above the animal, towering above it on to perfection.

All animal's instinct is in accordance with animal organization, as finished at the start of their creation, as in the remotest ages.

But man's is not so. His body, the animal part, is so ; but not his mind and functions, the soul that progresses through the whole time of mind's existence.

The soul, the mind with its functions, has to recur to the purposes of creation to perfect them. These are not for mere man a flower to bloom and wither, but the whole purpose is for the soul, as mind that is capable to realize the everlasting truths of the universe, is taken hence. If for higher and nobler purposes, to whom is the accountability ? To nature ? What an absurdity ! It must be to nature's God, who is under best obligation to do it justice that absolutely requires, therefore, immortality. The proper variety of the universe is, without doubt, to be enjoyed by the soul. The justice of God demands, bespeaks the best future accountability of rational beings, hence the immortality of the soul. It is the individuality of mind that must be respected. Though the laws of gravitation compel the influence of earthly things—matter—is not the soul a universe traveller, coming by birth and going by death, yielding to the paramount laws of its being ? But why not of brutes also ?

They are not rational, and therefore cannot be embraced in the category. But some of them are learned animals. True, but they cannot impart their learning. All that they have is mechanical, and after all, their learning dies with them. The species to eternity is not thereby benefited. All such animals are only subservient to the highest scale of existence, that of man. But you deny the further advance, the immortality of the soul ? To do so successfully, you must prove that the existence of mind on this sphere was gratuitous, and strictly, rigidly confined to this earth. I speak of rational minds as contra-distinguished from brutes, that cannot appreciate religion, a thing that exclusively belongs to rational minds, and that binds them to the universe and its God reciprocally. If you, polytheist, make peculiar faith supersede reason, then you destroy the best hopes for proofs of the immortality of the soul, that you incontestibly place in abeyance to peculiar bibles, that are nothing. Is this mental machinery to perish, almost as soon as vitalized ?

Whence came it, and whither does it tend ?

What are the whole purposes of creation ? Mechanical and animal influences ? In justice to creation of mind, it should have a proper theatre for its deeds and merits, nothing less than immortality.

The soul is the quintessence of the being of nature.

Religion is inseparable from mind's nature, and rationally bespeaks immortality for the soul. This earth is a sphere of rationality, not spirituality. Death is only a change for souls to pass from one sphere of action to another—to carry out the universe-problem. The state of soul-spirits is forwards, not backwards. Whence come, and whither do they tend ? To carry out the paramount universal purposes of the creation.

A brute's mind is for specific animal, earthly purposes, and the whole only can be animals.

A brute is as much a brute in the first as the last part of the world's history. Not so man, progressive in every age, more or less, with an expansive intellectuality, refinement, civilization, and religion above all, he evidently needs other spheres of the universe to complete his most rational eternal happiness.

The exact language of God is by death, that bespeaks the onward, not retrograde progress of soul.

Mothers might linger for their offspring as departed souls, but for the universal care of the universe-Creator, that absolutely supersedes all such. This world, then, cannot be the theatre for spirits as they have been called, as it presents one for vitality, material, breathing beings. Who is the Author of the five senses, but the Author of the soul ? Could nature, itself creation, create a soul ? Prove there is one. There is the thinking, reasoning faculty, the source of thought and reasoning. The five senses are the recipients, and exponent organs. Does not this faculty exist as an individual element, that individualizes all to ratiocination and rationality ? God, infinitely perfect, should, in justice to mind, create it perfect. That it has to attain, on its working and merits. Has he not created it to be perfect by a universe-problem solution ? Religion proves that knowledge is by comparison. How could life's pleasures be enjoyed, appreciated, if the world were not as it is ? The innate principle in soul or nature of mind's character is identified with principles that are for eternal universal benefit. The universe is one mighty architectural design, that eminently displays intrinsic unity both for God and his highest purposes, the best exaltation of mind and soul. Nothing less than monotheism elevates the soul to the complete appreciation and enjoyment of this universal comprehension.

Death is nothing but a universal change, a part of this unity of purpose, not an eternal sleep, as mere materialism teaches in its grovelling and abortive conception of blind vagaries and bewildered phantasies.

God is prescient on principles, and has met the whole question of universal conservation as an universal savior. A mere world-messiah is then most preposterous. Appropriate retribution implies, from the attributes of God's justice, other theatres of existence besides this. Death is so far from being a defect in the system of nature, that as a great change it is the great blessing of supreme purposes.

As to spiritual knockings, the suggestion is gratuitous, and comes from mortals. What an idea, that spirits are declared, when touch and vision, or the main detective senses, are unapproached. Mind is only the embryo of soul. See the chrysalis, that becomes a beautiful insect. Give all animal creation all that belongs to this state, still it is subordinate to mind that rules it and the world, the universe.

The soul has its functions. If this universe cannot perish, with its immutable principles, why then should its diamond—the soul or mind, with its functions?

This world is identified with the universe, and the soul is indissolubly united by religion to its God. What an illustrious obligation has mind to rear on this conservative fabric, the best earnest of its immortal fruition and happiness.

The soul proves another state of existence necessary and essential to its supreme excellence.

All rational beings partaking relatively of God's nature as rational intellectuality, must inherit other relative analogous qualities essential to God, as immortality and wisdom, for their due conservation and honor.

All beings that do not partake of the attributes of immortality, cannot possibly partake of any direct inherent relation and connection with God.

They do not then owe any fealty of religion to him, which is impossible with mind's organization.

The great First Cause, beyond whom thought of mind cannot go, has not revealed to human vision the brilliant fountain of his own almighty character.

Here is the limit to human mind, that must feel and acknowledge in suitable humility the Supreme, but its aspirations premise something more in reserve. With no data, reason cannot arouse analysis nor analogy, that is ever true to these her noblest advocates.

Reason has looked through cause and effect to the great First Cause, who must command all with due and voluntary acquiescence.

Mind invested with mortal habiliments cannot look upon immortality; the highest and brightest intelligences, endowed with the best mental organization, thus situated, are incapable of the least such gift.

The scenes and powers of mortal embodiments are on a mortal theatre. The Creator of universal attributes endows such with no peculiar gifts, a fallacy confined to dark ages. Here embodied souls learn the elements of their own non-appreciation.

In another state of existence more advanced than earth, no doubt other brighter and nobler investing organizations await the mind, reared in the magnificence of the soul, more developed to reach a higher appreciation of Deity and his works, and secure a fuller enjoyment of Deity's benevolence and glory.

In this earthly state, mind's organization cannot obtain any certain or satisfactory solution of the future; hence it must ever trust to the pledge that is reciprocal of God and itself for the best insurance of the balance. To mind, as now constituted, it is and ever will be an unsolved problem, great and grand, never to meet revelation on earth—a sealed book, the seals of which can never be loosed in mind's present physical nature, so earthly, animal, sensual, sinful, and prone to evil, by peculiar perversions. This confirms the supreme, pure character of the Creator. This is the best position for mortally-invested mind, to have only inherent gifts, appropriate to its existence, to have no absolute knowledge of the future, as the evil would outweigh the good in man's life, if he knew his particular history, a matter unknown to all.

The picture of immortal fruition, if known, might render an earthly residence uncomfortable and unsatisfactory, unworthy of present enjoyment, and the present would be nullified in the future.

The gift of death is a blessing, a passport to a nobler existence, but if anticipated by prescience, must mar the pleasures of present existence, or increase the miseries of guilt.

Mind when ignorant, must modestly learn at the true source of wisdom, and test all by reason fortified by time's experience. The circumstances of each mind's test will best verify its merit.

Silence discloses all wisdom, where solutions may condemn themselves as libels.

Human nature participant of two elements, must be incompetent to elicit beyond her earthly province, and therefore produces results in mind's deductions only confined to its proper theatre ; the deductions of mind, unless regulated by the highest reason, must be one often fraught with error, especially when misled by design, self-power, and temptation of its circumstances.

Fallibility causes corruption that runs to degraded extremes in the code of a mere earthly existence, as accountability is partial, not efficient, and there stops with mere mortal materialists.

But the doctrine of a full accountability elevates us to a faith in the immortality of the soul, the best present and future position, safe and ennobling.

It becomes mortal's creation, subject to vital danger and abundant poignant anguish for misspent functions to comprehend at all times their earthly actions and immortal hopes. Instead of becoming self-inquisitors of the world's citizens, increasing their own penalties and punishment, and establishing the locality themselves, the agents, let them modestly perform their becoming duty, and duly estimate all that pertains to it.

The body was suited to the earthly existence ; the soul seeks future eminence, never satisfied with the present for permanent fruition.

Who can estimate in reason, the worth of an immortal soul ?

Who but human fiend, will thwart its best resolves, intentions, capabilities and its own best analysis of the state of facts through a proper discipline of rational education, liberal and untrammeled, to elicit its final, greatest, purest, best faculties ?

Who but bigot will bring the iron chains of peculiar faith, to imprison its noblest aspirations to the Almighty ?

Who can dare reject or thwart the pure teachings, admirable precepts, and wisest admonitions of enlightened reason, that upholds man's true greatness, the sure, proper and certain counsellor of mind, that does all for the soul and true religion ?

As well can the Atheist pretend to deny the existence of Deity, whose organization of creation proves an intelligent God of nature, as the caviler pretends to the non-existence of the soul, from the partial material existence of man.

What mind can take cognizance of that which has no materiality, and still an active independent agent.

To deny or dispute this principle of materiality, of the most subtle organization, etherealize it as you choose, is to deny most absurdly the existence of the five senses, the very gift of the creator, for all such appreciation of his creation known to mind.

Mind only acts in organization as known to our senses. The future veils the mighty changes, to clothe the powers of mind that must rise proportionately to the theatre of its operations and enjoyments.

Between this and the central and purest sphere, various gradations of rational existence must live.

The God of the soul, of mind, has created its full spheres of improvement to eternity, else his creation is in vain. As an all-wise Creator, he makes nothing in vain. The nearest approach to immortality of soul perceptible to our senses is in the mass of living matter, in the form of human nature, that propagates itself, and mind from age to age; creating on its own elements a hold in perpetuity, allied to its first character to this sphere, but with its animating principle advancing to loftier grades of dignity, approaching immortality.

The immortality of soul rests on the Author of immortality and creation, firmly guaranteed by religion.

The universe resting on eternal principles, yields in importance to man's mind, that is supreme in creation.

Most confident in the proof of eternal conservation of the first, the proof is conclusive as to that of the last.

The Author of the existence, commends himself through the principles and elaboration of the universe, for the guidance and guardianship of the soul in all things, that we can appreciate for our good, nor should we suffer them to be arrested by any intermediation or intermeddling priests and collusion of all others, however advantageous the result may be peculiarly to all of them.

Unlimited and untiring should be the effort by statesmen, philosophers, and good honest citizens, over the world, to give mind its best protection for the happiness of soul.

God is ever righteous and is proved uniformly great, in his whole system of creation, without express days for judgment only as identified with the vindication of principles and the disposition of their violators.

Let not trifles, conflicts, rubbish, or conceit stand in the way of an immortal soul, that wishes, with the best aspirations and feelings, to go the right way properly.

It is to avoid anarchy, chaos, and confusion, the nature and character of the animal, to see the clear light, that man, humble and unambitious of aught save his world's good, seeks to secure his soul's happiness on the only proper true principles, to bring about the best state of existence, and of the world's best feeling, of harmony, order, universal peace, that he seeks the best foundation on principles, in the adoration of their only author.

Where else can he find this pure and exalted treasure ? Common sense and honesty, that make up reason, certainly tell.

Save mind or soul, all else of man is nothing but dust.

Mind cannot reach perfection on this sphere, and is ever increasing in knowledge if suitably situated.

The scene of mind's action is not in a perfect theatre, therefore mind cannot be perfect here.

As well ask for a globe free from the vicissitudes of the seasons, the piercing cold and wet, the melting heat and fever, the action of electricity, the gravitation of the spheres, as to ask for mind free from all the vicissitudes of the passions, and the storms that their licentious gratification arouses.

The passions produce the only reproachful slavery, and mind has free agency there against all absolutism, by their legitimate direction, under the wisest rationalism.

The mind perfects itself here to the extent of its capacity and the capacity of its circumstances, for the future benefit of the soul.

The mind sows, the soul reaps.

Man, composed of body and mind, must be analyzed and estimated according to that combination, just as God made and intended him. The balance depends on man's own intentions, for introduction through his merit, to a nobler theatre.

We ask for all rightful faculty practicable, correct at the fount of wisdom in its purity fit to introduce to immortal bliss, using no other than virtuous attributes fresh from the mint of God, that shows a living soul and breathes with immortal youth, having an elasticity superior to earth all the time, that mortality cannot reach and death cannot limit.

With no possible access to deity but by mind's highest inspiration through reason, at least not till another state of existence which has its own appropriations, more intellectual introduction awaits our leaving this world for that state.

The beatific happiness of another state fit for the soul, would be incompatible with the mind ; the parts would not be in suitable positions.

We are bound to attend strictly to this, ere we permit an indulgence of one iota of complaint as to our location in this terrestrial sphere, which is adapted to our nature. He that would complain, is impeached.

God deals in the magnificence of the purest treasures, of brightest rewards, that belong to the universal power that we reverence, not in the magazines of torture and of penalties peculiar to man's perverted mind.

A sublime view is to be taken, a nobler theme to be estimated, that mind should exalt itself to God's standard, not abase itself in lowering that only divine character.

Mind in such contemplation is raised from its most moderate elements, to the highest capacity. The true position is that eminently consistent with itself, mind to soul-ennobling.

Its good deeds are elevated to rewards, the food of the poorest mental enjoyments rising by their elements to greatness. Analogy proves that.

Its arrested progress in all the allurements around it, even bespeaks a penalty, compared with its equals that have outstripped it in all the pure enjoyments of a legitimate fruition.

Time is their mind's best function, that must not be trifled with, but profitably employed in life's great cause.

All the rich gifts of mind, should be devoted to legitimate purposes, for soul's advancement.

Whether individuals will or no, omnipotent principles, as those moving the spheres, will decide and sweep all living minds in their current with a mathematical certainty, that mind cannot escape the conviction or the adoption.

The security is not put on penalty as the negative of good, that follows necessarily like confusion succeeding derangement of the solar systems, as the lofty and fair reaching of reward, the best incentive to a properly balanced mind, a durable memento for eternity.

What can subserve the purpose of a perfect being better, than the exactness of order, and the fulfilment of duty in its comprehension in all the Universe?

Wise unto its own salvation, the mind will not risk its titles to fee simple in happiness eternal.

Placed on an earthly theatre-without its own assent or consciousness by an all-wise Almighty, who, therefore, alone is the responsible and competent preserver, whom none that are wise can mistake, in the comprehension of conservative principles, its will and agency however free, must act consistently thereto, or abide the necessary penalties and place itself back in its career for a just felicity.

The bauble of peculiar faiths or the delusions of superstitions of the moment, cannot satisfy such immortal beings. There is nothing earthly that can meet its rational demands. It leaves this earth for another life without its own assent, as the laws of creation are immutable.

All that mind has to do, then, is to meet immutable laws by immutable principles, the nearest practicable to its nature, and analyze their whole nature in time as far as necessary and practicable, ere conviction of duty come too late, when hope is expiring, and all may be deferred or protractedly lost ere life's benefit be secured.

All need the proper policy of insurance, in the quicksands of life, for the veiled future.

What has best availed for rational man in this life, must be the best qualified means for eternity. Created as the Universe is, its parts form one grand harmonious whole in action, and mind must soar to its highest points by these means.

It must not desert them at all, else they will fail it when none others are available.

MIND AND SOUL: THE DIFFERENCE BETWEEN MAN AND BRUTES.

MIND is connected to all organized animal matter, supremely applied to man. Instinct, its partial form, is applied to brutes, that attain a certain degree of it at birth, peculiar to their species. Rational mind is universal; instinct is peculiar. Brutes are not endowed with innate faculties of religion, that is, then, the universal gift of all minds capable of being rational, the universal characteristic of rational man, that elevates him to his God, and bespeaks immortality.

If God has exhibited any peculiar favor to any chosen people, then that people had been distinguished by pre-eminence. But faithful history chronicles no such event, and truthful reason audits no such pretension. The remote nations of antiquity affected to claim for their gods a peculiar power, but this was all trick of the priestocracy, or of the people deceived by them, and seeking to deceive all others. It was only one of the many disguises of superstition mixed with patriotism.

The mind is the intellectual will, or that which takes cognizance of action. How important that all should be right.

The soul applies to man here and hereafter, and is indentified with mind, that characterizes it.

The soul is that part left of man after his earthly existence.

What is the state of existence immaterial?

That cannot be conceived of by rational and truthful minds.

It is needless for the world to hide behind mysteries, or that some theological questions cannot be answered.

There are points that reason can only approach by analysis or analogy, to a certain extent, and then stops as to creation, the universe, eternity, the soul, future spheres, &c.

The soul was not created in vain, and it would certainly only partially have solved its own immortal question to be limited to only this sphere.

It needs improved organization for intellectual capacity to reach the mighty problems, and other theatres.

Its greatest question is as to the security of future certificates. Its main great problem it can solve on this sphere. That problem its best sphere of action, social and religious.

What has been recognised, was so by the action of mind on mind, and all errors are subject to correction for ever by the same process, which peculiar faith absurdly refuses.

If rational religion did not only sanction but require this, she would not be the true religion, but an ignoble peculiar faith. Religion emphatically, supremely requires the immortality of the soul.

Who, then, can comprehend in their own minds anything existent separated from materiality?

We cannot separate the God of nature from nature. All such pretence of immateriality looks absurd in an extreme degree.

All things are comparative, but not less material in some degree, by mathematical and philosophical, the most exact laws.

The sooner we get rid of all such absurdities the better.

Grant the soul the subtlest organization, it must be material to be a soul, or vitalized existence. It has a noble organization, conceiving it to be the greatest gift of the universe, the brilliant diamond set in it, the soul, must be guarded with supreme care and fondest affection by its Creator. It masters progressively the attainable government of much of the elements of the universe, and is the master-work of creation. Immortality is essential for this performance.

The universe seems to be exhaustless to mind in its present organization, and is, no doubt, eternal, therefore the master-spirit of created being must have the greatest claim to immortality.

The reason of the soul's immortality is, it is co-existent with the universe.

Why should this magnificent creation of God's genius be extinguished, after all the perfecting elaboration of its potent munificence?

This must be the error of perverted minds, fond of their own vain conceits.

Its birth was the bright creation of its functions, its vital existence on this sphere was the free agency to display its character; and its passage through death was a purification, and an admittance to a loftier existence and higher theatre, a purer change from mortal organization.

The mighty genius of the Creator, that anticipated and satisfied all the loftiest purposes, immortal as mortal, of creation; whose mighty purposes elevate souls instead of sacrificing by bloody crucifixions his own attributes, a solecism as absurd as impious, will reveal the whole drama in consummation.

Mind is limited to time and its functions, and must be thereby limited in action for the present. The future belongs to eternity.

Though all material substance continues the same as far as our bodies are concerned in the world, yet that which animated them departs to a nobler sphere on its intrinsic merits.

None have history in matters beyond the grave.

Death parts the body from the soul, that departs to the appropriate sphere of appropriately organized beings, that can no longer dwell among those composed of body and mind, no longer associate with earthly beings.

How absurd, then, to suppose that ghosts and spirits can be appreciable on earth!

Sound intellects that are honest must deem that impossible; as mind refers to the present, soul, or immortal organization, refers to the future state of existence.

As to the position of the souls departed, that question must be wisely submitted for solution to God, who created them, not to peculiar faith notions that caricature all sacred things. But what shall be the scale of punishments?

They are more or less certain on this earth; but as some do not get their full penalty, justice requires other spheres of existence for the appropriate theatre.

The very means adopted to complete selfish designs are those of penalty and severest punishment to nations or individuals.

God is a perfect being, and perfects his exalted works in appropriate time. Among them the immortal soul is most conspicuous.

The concern of all conceding this should be to save it best and properly. To seek messiahs makes it worse.

Man needs God's power, mercy and purity to assist him in the best employment of his judgment and conduct.

None but a properly educated people yeomanry can stand up properly for their rights, and for the purity of the human soul, uncontaminated by vices, as perjury, murder, felony, and treason. The lazaroni cannot.

As to the soul, is there not a material existence involved? What else can we conceive of?

What conducts it in its genial position?

The same power that originated it, who can re-endow it or renovate it, in improved condition of appropriate organization.

If the universe be eternal, proved by its essential character perfectly strengthened by its constitutional union, how much more shall the soul be immortal, that is of more value than the universe? If the dissolution of the first bespeaks imbecility of design, what must that of the last?

If the condition of all in the future is equal, intense must be the purification as a trial ordeal ere that point be attained.

What is the soul if not identified with the mind, that must commune with God, for it is only by that his inspiration operates successfully?

This is the sensible inspiration of God's spirit, his principles in the best of enterprises, that mark their influence on the age and the whole world.

To suppose any other is to be deficient in faith and reverence towards God, the giver of all good gifts.

The constitution of our mind is such, that it is rewarded by the soul's happiness, if right, and punished by its sufferings, if wrong. The very nature of conscience's analysis proves the whole position, as that remorse inflicts the deepest penalties.

What is the soul? It is the immortal element and principle that refer to mind, that act with free agency, and is accountable for that action. Its existence on this sphere is exhibited by mind, that at death is more or less purified, and traverses other spheres as an organization congenial to its own kindred elements.

This earth is only a part, but peculiar faith sectarians make it most by peculiar appropriations.

An excellent proof the soul's immortality is, that is nothing is annihilated, therefore we have the best data that rational mind cannot be. Is not that the base, the flower, the soul, the matured fruit?

Is not the mind-element immortal, the body going to its original elements?

Nothing is made in vain by the Creator, and nothing can be annihilated.

That is all that we know of the resurrection, as we have no demonstrative proof otherwise, and have not reached a sufficiency of science to decide according to hopes of immortality with a perfect demonstration on facts verified. It seems a matter of omission of duty of culpable character, merely to look at the state of this earth, and use no exertion by deeds farther, for future happiness of the race of mankind, when the mind just begins to expand as a flower, the fruit not maturing for its earthly existence.

It seems, then, bad taste in all who must appreciate that only the human mind or souls can reach the holy centre, that man should not soar above the soulless state of mere brute creation.

As honesty demands the payment of daily debts in every respect, both in money and duty, we cannot escape those of gratitude and religion to the Creator, the universal creditor.

The earthy parts of man return to dust, but all that remains of soul and mind, the immortal part that scans the highest matters of the universe, must embrace the noblest destiny and purpose.

Immortality of the soul has come to be admitted nearly by universal consent of mind, or by the best conclusive evidence from the worth and essential character of mind that precedes in excellence, the universe.

The excellent perfection of God is proved in the perfection of the soul by immortality.

What is the human mind but the greatest gift in the universe? Is it not such as God created it? Let not the first be tinkered with, nor the last libeled by botches that cannot explain the first attributes.

The first is in a state of progressive improvement, from the mass of intelligence.

We must analyze and know the mind, the soul, its capacity, character and quality.

We all admit mind to be liable necessarily to corruption, as what could be baser when perverted? Then we must advance all the principles to prevent that corruption. Do not all those conservative principles refer to an immortal tribunal?

Any others, as peculiar professions, will advance its corruption.

Take mind from the universe, and the brightest light is extinguished. What then is the universe without it?

ETERNAL PUNISHMENT!

That seems cruelty unrefined, gross, vulgar and destructive, whereas God's principles are conservative!

Who knows of future punishment, of spirits, &c.?

Much has been advanced of a kindred spirit, to other imperfect views.

Does man, humble and ignorant, know God's attributes but by his works, to define them properly, and lecture on them skilfully?

Moses and his coajutors undertook this, and gave a miserable portraiture of the universe and its creator, a complete botch of presumptuous ignorance.

You must seek to be better off than priestocracies, in your bigotry in after ages.

Will you then punish a man forever for a few faults, and carry him back to eternal punishment? Will you undertake to affirm that all will finally be saved, after punishment?

If you have doomed them to your hell, such inmates will hardly be fit for any heaven.

Fortunately we are all under God's protection, and must act up to the best lights before us.

The best actions will insure the best and safest position. But where will the worst characters, as the wilful murderer, adulterer, tyrant, seducer, and other vicious characters go? The Creator of the Universe will manage all that, to the best benefit of all creation.

The soul must account for the misdeeds of the mind. God's eternal justice requires it. The Creator can master the point by mind.

Though cannibals have very inferior souls, in what are they worse than nations that destroy, by wholesale, thousands of the inoffensive people invaded, by arms and weapons of offensive warfare? Those nations miscalled civilized, too!

If cannibals have very inferior souls, what sort have the priests, who assume to be the necessary factors of God, who never asked such impostors once?

Who is best off, piratical nations of war, savage cannibals, or fraudulent priests?

However are proud nations and nefarious cliques, cabals, and clans, above man's punishment, God will decide that question appropriately. Bad and vicious men cannot enjoy divine favor, and God cannot contaminate himself therewith. They must be properly purified, ere they can reach his pure and holy presence, that is certain.

Peculiar faith among its many peculiar creeds may demand the doctrine of eternal punishment, that is hardly credible to rational religion in her liberal and just appreciation of God, who requires all rational, not slavish actions.

What rational minister could preach any of the doctrines of predestination?

Is man accountable here and hereafter? Yes, both, without doubt. I must therefore conclude, that the soul is then immortal, as many do not receive the punishment due them in this life.

The Universe cannot be annihilated, and that in its bosom must be eternal.

Man's body becomes dust. Where is the mind, the soul?

That must be superior to the Universe, whose elements it has to command.

Mind annihilates space and time, the difficulties of ocean by navigation, neutralizes the deadly effects of electricity, and masters it for the telegraph.

The atmosphere is rendered subservient to mind's power in steam and philosophy, and all this is surpassed by its competent command of the best principles of constitutional government.

Mind corrects its own errors, and acts its paramount duty in religion to God supreme. These are masterly deeds that reflect a gift analogous to creative power. And shall the sophistry of man control its superior power? For whom was the universe created? Mind or intellect. And shall that sublime creation burst into a life-death, a nullity? What is the soul, but the mighty controlling free agent placed on earth for a time?

What gave impulse to animal matter? Deity, the Creator.

Accountability does check all that transcend principles.

Accountability and scrutiny should run in all public matters, otherwise frauds can be perpetrated by impunity. Where is then the tribunal for all such?

Rational mind must do its part, its highest duty, in all its departments.

There should be no suppression of public inquiries.

He who wishes to come to the point at once in rewards, must abide by the appropriate penalties that must purify the offenders.

The idea of purgatory accompanied as it is by money, is corrupt, a base and degraded church speculation.

Religion is not a plan to make money out of the friends of departed souls. Speculation libels religion.

What is the operation of the spirit?

The influence that accompanies the suitable operations of mind. After all, it is no more or less than that of God. Our bodies go to the dust, but our souls that exalt man above the beasts, should merit of God their happiness in his Almighty's hands.

In the tuition of the bible of rational mind, exclusion from the presence of the Almighty in all future existence will be punishment enough.

Mind, the soul identified with body, seeks satisfactory knowledge for the rest of the soul when separate from the body.

We must read all creation, to learn our best destiny.

God could not have formed compatibly with his attributes, rational mind for evil— that is a libel.

It must have been for good, and the security of the greatest amount is in immortality. Rational mind seeks friendship for all the best purposes, but who alienates the good of society, violates the best principles of kind, and affectionate friendship of mind? Those opposed to universal rights of mind.

Mind, as ignorant of the future, must rest for immortality of soul on a just and rational hope, securing safety by virtue with the most active avoidance of vices.

The soul is a part that belongs to its author, and of course will follow the proper current of eternal principles.

The rewards and penalties of the future accord with past acts.

The dignity of the soul's salvation is established, not by especial but universal grace, and its right, through creation.

We should seek the best cultivation of true religion for our immortal souls, that emerge from earth as a transition from one state to that of another, that to become the immortal part must perform certain functions of mortality, as a matter of probation, for which mind must prepare mind and secure by the best deeds of merit.

These functions are the action of principles, and cannot be of mere abstract faith.

Principles are as eternal as the universe; shall mind, soul, their living superiors, be less eternal?

As to the soul, this being God's noblest gift to the universe, he will do the best for its happiness.

We must adopt the noblest view for this greatest gift, as appropriate for its exaltation.

Mind must return from this world all that can be embraced as the holiest offering to its Creator, worthy of its immortal endowments.

He who gave the soul must expect its most worthy tribute. Its immortal tribute is most worthy of Deity, its Immortal Creator.

All rational minds have more or less universal impressions in their souls, of God's spirit, and are to account for cherishing it in the best possible manner.

After all said and done, mind then does its duty.

The jewel of the universe is soul, that polishes mind, in whose preservation is conscience. What a blessed re-action!

Mind's future hopes prove all its best future responsibility and accountability. What can best secure social and moral duties, but religion that absolutely requires immortality for retributive justice?

But when is reform needed?

The people must seek all that is practicable at once, by all suitable frame-work.

It is not only for the past we must sorrow, but must wisely act for the future, during rational existence.

Illegitimate pleasures cause us to miss more than half of life's enjoyments and comforts.

How miserable is it to find that we cannot extricate ourselves after the deed is done. Innocence is a pure flower, a true blessing.

Life is a continual trial, therefore none are exempt, however situated, from an intellectual, moral and religious watchfulness, the eternal price of a man's soul.

Who can dream of defeat on principles, and with the mighty power of will?

A future state of the soul must disclose to more perfect beings, what it has only an anticipation in this life.

If we did not believe on rational principles in the immortality of the soul, then we might see the disastrous effects of self and mutual destruction, and a brutal degradation without conscientiousness of proper approbation, nothing to hope for.

But there are many circumstances to be regarded in this subject.

However partial, peculiar and unjust a God the doctrines of election make as miserable libels; however incompetent the faith, if universal salvation is to meet the case of pirates, felons and cannibals, blasphemers, traitors, human tyrants and demons, without the most exact self-atoning purification, still rational beings, cultivating their conscience, must feel accountable most justly for the future, and must hail the immortality of the soul, mind, a position that invokes, commands the practice of principles to commune with God.

There are many questions to be adjourned to the tribunal of the Supreme Ruler of all. Man has no ability to decide them satisfactorily. Time, the only prophet of God, will teach the wise.

The candid mind seeks the proper position in regard to the soul, faith, God, or any thing else.

It decides to believe the only living witnesses, God's sacred scriptures, which are God's works of the universe. This is God's book, teaching his sacred principles.

It cannot believe man's fictions, but God's facts.

6

All others are dead, absent, ignorant, perverted, impostures deep and full.

Man is demoralized to adopt, degraded to propagate, simple to rely on, and vicious to follow them.

Mind that is to be immortal should not be the stupid dupe of others, nor the rabid and bigoted partisan, for which it may repent.

Let mind look to a right cultivation of mind, and its right exertions—as the only agent of communication with creation and its perfect Author.

For the very reason of our faith in the immortality of the soul, and its accountability here and hereafter, we seek the true way, and can never yield the true for the spurious proprietor.

We can adopt no other, whilst our mind is sound and independent, and reason prevails.

The code of rational faith in regard to the soul is one to be realized in the chastest and profoundest view of its Author and attributes.

All the codes of peculiar faith fall miserably far short of justice to truth in the initiative! What must be their position at the conclusion?

All their references are the stupid caricatures of immatured ignorance, gaping at wonders, miracles, that science and philosophy abhor or contemn!

From the best rational observation of the operations of this world, mind must be drawn irresistibly to the conclusion, and acknowledge as certain retributive justice, adequate but rational, and reject volcanoes and Vulcans, hell and the devil.

Souls as immortal may traverse the universe to appreciate Deity, and while the purest may enjoy beatific spheres with inestimable happiness, the impure may have to be purified at first in more appropriate ones.

A correct appreciation and improvement of religion will prevent the correlative sacrifice of myriads, who have to expiate their sins by future atonement. Cannot God save all mankind and bless them with happiness? He has made all creation for the good of the greatest number, and that is the whole. To do it in the most perfect way, requires immortal fruition, especially as it was gratuitously created. God renders his universe available for good, and dispenses, not so much endless suffering, as a temporary purification by suitable penalties.

Where is the limit to retributive justice?

God alone knows; its universal result is for universal good. The greatest good of the greatest number in God's universe may embrace all rational beings in degree, consistently with God's capacity, and in all respects with his attributes.

All past speculations that invade the premises of God's attributes in the least, ought to be scouted from the face of mind and truth.

Beware how you teach and innovate on God's attributes, as you may become the libeller of a Being perfect in truth, honesty, goodness, justice, mercy, will, power and wisdom, immutable and infinite.

You can plead no bibles of tradition, no priestocracy for authority to libel God or his attributes.

What did God create mind for?

Not for eternal punishment and misery.

Future retributive justice will most certainly cause a separation of the good from the bad, else the good could not be in a pure enjoyment, and might suffer in contamination from the bad.

But the bad may be only relatively punished; God alone knows. The penalty of conscience by remorse, is worst of all.

The ideas of mind, that is, the gift above the gift of the animal, give mind the most powerful reason to believe in the immortality of the soul. The Bible of Mind is the safeguard to life and immortality, and carries in itself the genuine proofs of its own intrinsic character.

But the Bibles of tradition, the work of absolutism, in collusion against the people, were intended to deceive and delude the human mind and nothing less, to cut it out of its own proper Bible.

Under this despotism the sovereign people have been punished as heretics, who were purer and better than their judges.

The body, the organ of mind, enters the tomb of earth on death, but the soul or mind passes to judgment and due appreciation. Then comes the value of its capacity or philosophy in resisting all the various phases of temptation, all the improper influence of wealth, the delusions of vice, the fascinations of sin, in having looked properly to itself.

Well may it have been if the party concerned, the soul, may have never appreciated any scripture but God's book of the Universe, caring to hear, learn or read no other than what is rational. The soul then has considered all others as matters of contingency, unworthy its regard, not permissible in a vital and essential matter that requires certain proof of all points affecting such important rights.

The soul requires all things to be put on the broad platform of principles, and no contingency.

The right action of mind alone constitutes accountability and responsibility of mind.

Mind, that is the agent of the soul and body on this earth, cannot embrace correct principles, without an education appropriate, which is a matter of necessity.

What do the advocates of peculiar faith know or care for the correct analysis of mind, as long as they can secure the profits of self-interest in its circumscribed views?

A gradual amelioration may bring out safely all the souls of existence, as a proper retributive justice may leave the immortal soul to its capabilities and the ultimate attainment of the intention of its creation, the elaboration of the mighty theatre of its usefulness and sublime existence.

The end and means of this life, is to liberalize man's soul. Many are so contracted, that they seem hardly to have a soul.

This world is not the permanent abode of mind, that else had been matured on brighter auspices.

Why should there be a re-union of soul and body, at any final judgment day? All this seems the height of absurdity.

The soul here is mind embodied, elsewhere its organization appropriately suits appropriate existence. The final judgment day is still more absurd, as that is commanded by retributive justice more promptly and wisely.

A previous suffering and purification are instituted, under retributive justice.

Why should the soul, after leaving the body, not meet immediately appropriate final judgment?

Why should there be any intermediate state, except by peculiar faith doctrine, that seeks to be benefited? Why two judgments, when one can meet all the exactions of justice much better? Any other assignment of the soul implies that God is imbecile and unfit for his measures, and reflects on the puerility of those that dream in this way. How long shall peculiar faith libel God, in all his departments?

It will be, until the mind of science disperses all the fogs of her ignorance.

No doubt all souls needing it, are purified progressively by penalties.

God, according to his attribute of mercy, that shines most brilliantly, irradiated by his supreme intelligence, cannot seek the mere punishment of this world's people, so much as to purify them for reception of future and permanent happiness.

All must be purified, to reach the pure God, whose central residence is fortified by perfect purity.

But how deplorable is peculiar faith, fanatical and bigoted, that creates the worst features of its creation, to exclude God's creation from the fairest portions? It deals in currency so belittled, that mind revolts at its disgusting pictures.

Mental and physical retribution, must be paid by all created rational beings.

All good and true citizens are interested most deeply, to rectify religious faith properly, and divest it particularly of superstition and man-worship.

Its benefits will be estimated, when we see it is the most difficult matter for rightly educated minds duly cultivated and confirmed, to get their own consent to improper actions.

The evil-fund must be met by the mind-fund, that joy may be more substantial and misery less permanent.

The capacity of the faculties of the soul for ultimate perfection by the progress through the Universe, demands as a prerequisite its immortality.

Its character for perfection is indispensably fixed, at its advancement to the centre of perfection, the abode of Deity himself.

Who is recompensed on this earth for his duty and toil, slaving labor to man, but for reciprocal good and benefit in this world, as absolutely essential as keeping each sphere of the Universe in its respective orbit?

The hope of future reward in another state, is an invaluable recompense. Nothing short of God can satisfy an immortal mind, certainly not this earth nor all its treasures. The day of judgment should be every moment in mind, reflecting on itself.

Absence from God's abode that is in sight, or banishment and exclusion from seen extatic enjoyments of the blessed, would be the severest punishment inflicted, but all this might comport with the low views of a vindictive priestocracy, while the enlightened mind aspires to see the greatest good to the whole, and all practicable opportunities afforded erring and polluted souls to ultimately attain their best position through all necessary purifications.

The soul has to seek sincerely the highest attainable position, when it believes that all such abide in its appropriate sphere permanently and substantially.

The immortality of the soul is a thing of paramount interest to mind, that only begins its lessons on this earth. How can it expect less? It is mind that recognised creation, and appreciates all practicable, in the age of its existence.

Enlarged in its capacity, receiving purer and superior accessions of organizations, as it progresses in eternity, it approaches still nearer its adorable Creator.

The soul may be purified to the subtlest point, still it is defined by specification.

It honors nature, and thereby honors the Creator, the God of Nature, who honors it most by most honorable immortality, a justice that honors both.

What constitutes the mighty adoration of intelligence, the difference between the animal and man, between matter and mind?

Souls in the advance and progress of their improvement have congenial spheres, and a proper comprehension of their duty and the penalty.

What can be the proper position of the soul, short of immortality? It is our sincere belief and wish, that the soul be considered immortal. It is too short a time on earth to perform its functions; nothing less than eternity will answer or permit their maturity. An earthly sphere alone, cannot do justice to the soul-problem.

But the soul exists, and can the soul be annihilated? Is it less than the thinking principle? The soul is identified with eternal principles. Is the soul immortal? Who is not anxious, to receive demonstrative proof thereof?

It was made to little purpose, if mortal, to breathe a miserable existence short of immortal happiness. Could the Creator create an anomaly to himself?

One of its clearest defined positions, is all self-improvement on earth to its noblest elevation, and then all will be on the safest position for the future.

If all mortals should avoid giving unnecessary pain to brute, much less to human beings, extend sympathy to all suffering, and humanity to the really needy, how much more will the God of nature do justice to mind-creation? Religion is due between mind and its God, immortality and happiness are due between God and the soul.

Irreligion and immorality may prevail on this very point, that may make life wofully and decidedly unsafe and miserable, if there were no belief of the soul's immortality, and no future state for its accountability and responsibility.

The present question demands facts, not mere vague speculations, as in bibles of traditions. All things are made subservient to mind, that must be to its Creator who has regulated the universe right. Let mind do its duty.

This sphere is too contracted for its display. The soul leaves this theatre, ere it has accomplished its important mission. The body is only subservient to the mind on this sphere, and all creation is subservient to them, in a measure.

Mind is created for best and most efficient purposes, as the noblest work of Deity. It would fall short of all that, if mortal. What is the theatre for the soul's functions? Must it be confined forever, to the earth? Can it then reach the universe?

Does the soul have any reference to any appreciation of the universe? Did it not, it could not appreciate the noblest qualities of the Divine Creator.

Mind is the divine gift of the God of nature, and order, system, law and principle, are its theatre.

This world is to be made a blessing by mind, that is, to embrace by philosophical science all that civilization can expect. We adopt the immortal existence of the soul, as most just to creation of mind. Why is there virtue, if the soul be not immortal? For social good only? That is but a partial comprehension of the God-gift. To comprehend less than the immortality of the soul, brutalizes mind, and blasphemes God. Creation was no soulless enterprise in the matured elaboration. Be the classification of souls what it may of future existence, the divine arrangement cannot be less comprehensive of all the universe, to which mind is an immortal ornament and blessing.

Has the mind the soul to appreciate the character and attributes of Deity? Then it has to traverse the universe to do so, and must be immortal to meet this exhaustless subject that spreads to infinity as regards mind, the embodied soul, but not as to God.

See the aspiration of the soul or mind, never ceasing after happiness.

This world is not an adequate theatre. But it is claimed that the immortality of the soul can be proved by the bibles of tradition. Of course if it can, it will be a rational proof, and no other, and this is the category of all such bibles' proofs, as far as they have any to be relied on.

Fortunately those books are not proveable, and therefore they are necessarily discarded.

Prove any bible to be the word of God, and all the rest follows. If such be not proved, it is the most felonious imposition, because it involves blasphemy, hypocrisy and perjury. Of course all that pretends to be bible-proof of the immortality of the soul, is only an assertion, not proof, valid in the court of conscience. Queer book, that, that robs mind to prove the soul immortal.

You see your soul towers above animals, in having a higher and exclusive order and gift of organs.

Now are you the brute, that you are going to place it in jeopardy? Is your soul brutal, that it is to be annihilated? Can the thinking principle be annihilated? Have you forfeited by your extreme brutal crimes, all rightful claims to any immortal felicity?

Is your soul of so little account that it should perish? The best reward of the soul is a future dispensation that sanctifies its mighty character, and vindicates for all merits and demerits.

What is the world seen through the mere position of sordid interests, the grovelling of corporeal actions, unconnected with the noble connection, the mind, the soul?

All that is presented, is not above the mere animal nature. But let the true character of man, as mind imbued with the highest principles that rational education presents him, and the whole is embraced in truth and reason.

We must respect and analyze the noble defences of patriotism, the pure acts of benevolence, the personal risks of soldiers, sailors, mariners, firemen, and all such, the universal sympathy of nature, the worthy responses of the soul through the best tributes of the human family, and acknowledge that it quits its animal connections, to be allied to purer essences. The noblest deeds of man, reflect the sublimest impulses of the soul. If it was created for the perfection of the Creator's glory, surely its terrestrial initiative cannot give it by any means. Who so low as to believe that mind was created merely for animal purposes?

The idea is grovelling, low and vulgar indeed. Can low actions suit the soul in its individual or social relations? Individualize the soul all you can, socialize it all that is practicable, still of all feelings in their various vicissitudes, those of principle are they that delight the soul permanently. The fountain source is the Almighty. Rational beings must consider maturely how much is perishing matter, in this sphere of existence. What is the soul, material or immaterial? How can it be the last? Souls may be put back, but the worst is that souls put themselves back, in the immortal race. Now your mind was put in the right way by God, will you go to the perverted ways of man? Will you permit priestocracies tamper with your immortal souls? Will you act unworthy of mind? But what is mind? Is it the effect of electricity on mental organization? Electricity is the atmosphere of mind, whereby it reaches the universe. Electricity is one of the grand agents of the universe. Soul is more, far beyond all such. The soul passes through a series of purifications. Man, who is nothing less than soul embodied, was created by God for the most comprehensive purpose commensurate with his unit attributes. That most comprehensive character, is immortal felicity. The more imbecile soul is longer at arriving at perfection. But how is it with those souls that, like fruit, may rot ere matured perfection?

Has God created a soul in vain? Shall a mortal grant general amnesties, and not the Creator, who must love his creation? God the creator, must delight in his own works to the intensest affection that declares immortality of the best. God would have created man lower than the brutes, to have given him mind capable of immortal deeds, and yet incapable of immortal fruition.

Vast must be the difference correspondent to individual quality, in the relative position of each soul. While that of a Washington may be countless degrees above the Neroes and Caligulas, his soul may have to traverse a vast number of spheres, to reach the centre of purity. The materialist may speculate upon the excitement on the mental organs, by electricity, yet the power to create and originate thought, bespeaks a supremacy to gross materialism. There is no time in the soul's existence that it ceases to go on forever, if it do not impede its own progress. It must pass by reason of the change of death, to its immediate functions. Death is a mighty change in this world, and a veil that separates souls from embodied beings living on earth, is more or less a purification and preparation expedient for nobler operations. While on earth, we must talk of rational operations. Mind accompanies soul. The old idea is exploded, of soul returning to its last dust; no, it passes on to other spheres of existence. What can cause the idea of happiness? The soul-world residence in the centre of purity, must furnish a supreme state of happiness of course, where must be perpetual and perfect peace. What an idea of spirits remaining in the air, because some of the foolish ancients considered the heaven, the heaved-up, their place of abode.

Shall God exalt the stars of the universe, and not exalt thy soul? Shall he deck them in all their perpetual glory, and not invest thy soul, his greatest work, with all the noblest of his treasures? The great problem of the soul never was properly vindicated nor verified, till mind was untrammeled from all the dynasties of malign influences, was made a proper free agent, by having the only comprehensive means, rational education of both sexes. But why so concerned about your soul peculiarly? All else except the necessary cultivation of intellect and practice by the best actions in religion, are mere priestocracy suggestions. These stupid bigots must advance with mental science, to correct themselves. Who could promise himself much in correcting bigots? Who originated the soul but he who provides for its immortality, as well as all the time with superabundant grace, that scouts messiahs as impracticable, merely local? All this shows the God of nature, of creation. What botches are the priestocracies, to assume any of mind's, much less God's prerogatives! There can be no unmerciful punishment, much less excessive or eternal.

The followers of all peculiar faith will find themselves most awfully mistaken at a certain time ; as delinquents, they cannot go into the pure residence of Almighty God without their titles are exclusively prepared by him. God can put the mind to a better use than to unmerciful punishment. Can you analyze the nature of relations in this world, and the universe? You must rely in due humility and confidence on Almighty God, who provides therefor. Mind is the gem brilliant of creation, and proves by its supremacy its immortality. It has just begun to develope its energies and assert its triumphs.

But what is certainly known of the soul? Nothing on this earth, by any peculiar system. The only best earnest is provided by its almighty Creator, providence.

The soul, in state of purer organization, goes on through purification. Time is the great function of mind and life ; eternity is the great function of soul and immortality. Whence came mind, or soul?

Surely it is as easy for the God of nature to create its organizations of investment anew, appropriate for its sphere. The God of the universe has provided for the soul's future position. The mature development of Divine Wisdom is best attained by the immortality of the soul, that is part of its function. its best function.

Death is the mighty change of mortal man, to free his immortal part, is the purification for other scenes of existence more or less happy than this.

Because the rational mind is endowed with faculty of rational religion that binds the soul to God, it is endowed with immortality that refers to the immortal and total duties due to God. Religion only commences on this sphere of action, and is incomplete as its performance is incomplete of immortal action. The functions of the soul are to carry out this essential whole duty to God, and that is always, forever. If the soul be deprived of its immortal existence, God is necessarily deprived of his appropriate whole soul-adoration. Mind has a conscious existence. The very idea of free agency implies ability of diverse actions, and for the most comprehensive purpose, no less then than the universe and to all eternity. The mind has inherent motion, and a living power. What is the mind and functions, the soul?

The soul, however subtle its organization, must be respected as organized, sublimated existence. The elements are of organization, however subtle. We must follow truth and nature, not blind custom, nor faith that is absurd credulity.

This position does not involve any of the points of gross materialism. The Creator can even renew that soul in a far more glorious and exalted organization, of the loftiest intelligence.

The soul is the immortal part most sincerely believed in, the most refined organization.

Should we take a partial, that would be an unsafe view for the full comprehension of the right estimation of this whole subject? In future existence, the soul may appreciate Deity's magnificence—here it cannot. Brutes have an electrical, men have an immortal soul. Man's body goes to its original earthly elements, the soul or mind goes to its immortal elements.

What is the soul of itself nearest to? A God-like existence.

God having created us of his pleasure and supreme wisdom, doubtless will see and cause our souls to be cared for most effectually, by his own universal attributes ; less than that, cannot touch the subject or question. The soul-machinery of the world is moved by God.

As all rational beings are created for some highest purpose, and that could not be limited to this earth, but must be carried to the fullest capacity of a universal theatre, of course the Creator endowed mind with the freest rational exercise of its functions. The best souls reach the centre of creation's purity soonest.

The least good are doubtless longer reaching such purity, and pay proportionate penalties. God can purify by the functions that are expedient. Death, the mighty changer, is one, the law of our nature.

This is the sphere of our probation; other spheres are those of retribution and recompense, or where the triumph of immortality abides. The mighty attributes of mind, came from the President of nature, of mind.

Which can take care of a man's soul, his own cultivated mind taught to comprehend by exact knowledge its duties, itself the God-given guardian, or the self-given priest-ocracy, who may be by contingency also ignorant, depraved, corrupt, self-interested, and of no account as they have no such functions.

The world may constitute a guardian of mind as it is, but it can only be by principles, and so must be estimated all its citizens, else they are positively impostors.

Mind has to ever regard the final great exaltation, the access to the great central sphere of purity and perfection. The highest means of most happiness as of right and merit to man would be, the certain endowment of immortal existence, an immortal soul.

To secure this happiness aright, he must secure by the very best means of virtuous and religious character compatible.

God, the creator of the immortal soul, had the sublime conception and power to carry it out.

In what does man excel all the beasts? By an organization of mind that becomes soul appreciating God, endowed with religious faculties.

These are life-problems, the solution of which, is in the best life-actions, thus to resolve what is the living principle, the immortal principle, &c. We have to defer to God, and there our humility is perfect. This is something that is an adjourned question. Are you prepared to solve the whole problem? Are you ready, is your mind embellished enough for the future conference? The present life only serves for intro-duction to the next. Individuals can define their own introduction. Shall the acts of mind live, and not the substance? Mind conceives immortal principles, which animals do not know. Shall mind become extinct, when principles live? Shall the inferior survive the superior? The soul is in ever constant advancement from one desire grati-fied to another, the end the means, having unlimited enjoyment, and capacity progress-ive for that enjoyment.

How ignorant must peculiar bible-writers be, to prate nonsensically about idle mat-ters, being estopped about the God of the universe, they have only their own peculiar province to enjoy and that not possibly to be proved. The God of the universe rules out all peculiar gods. We do not believe in any such confined place as purgatory, much less hell, the chimeras, idle dreams of visionary monks and priests. The holy centre is for independent soul-existence, to progress in all compatable enjoyments. Mind em-bodied, is inquiring and analytic, but is not capable as soul-organization of enlarging in its intellectual capacity. Here we are confined to five senses, but how constituted and exalted, soul has to realize to solve by future data. Unless you give mind its inherent worth, you cannot give soul its consummate felicity. It is the priestocracy that assail its dignity, and detract from its worth.

This is only a mediate theatre for a nobler existence, for the embellishment of mind and improvement of soul.

The soul's work is self-purification on the merits, continued grace of its Creator, who left it his impressions, creation's birth-right; and who supports it in all its future progress. Let no counterfeits or pretenders step between them.

The soul seeks the greatest degree of happiness attainable, of which nothing is made in vain.

God's goodness, intelligence and power vest the plan of salvation with himself and self free practicable agency of mind. It is utterly impossible to vest it elsewhere. We feel satisfied and gratified that we came to know the right analysis of this subject.

God cannot in justice eternally punish a human being for effects of his weakness. Eternal punishment cannot be for temporal crimes. The soul only begins to blossom, to be something on this sphere, hardly getting the elements of its start, much less of its height of progress, and has to mature in other spheres. If this were a perfect sphere, where no vice or misery existed, then all had been right; but free agency, under the circumstances of creation, and a suitable physical state, evidently not suited to perpetual happiness, declare that a future blessing is in the last great change of man through death, which is to transport the disembodied soul hence.

There cannot be any enjoyment of equal felicity by the good and the bad encircled in the same sphere of soul-existence. The mind progresses in soul and self-purification, and its future state is best adapted for that progression. The universe is open for that purpose, and the result can only be verified by the individual organization.

There is no need then of encircling this mixture, when the universe is exhaustless. A future existence looks most rational, through the facts presented of the Great First

Cause. Can less be expected by rational minds? But the noise about the soul is the effect for the profit which is considered by too many as temporal. You need not find fault, when there is so much to amend. The Creator must have guaranteed the soul's highest interest, and that is nothing less than the universe. This earth cannot satisfy the mind, the soul; it cannot give, it was not arranged for immortal felicity. The greatest comprehension is that by the immortality of the soul, to reach which the paramount questions of the world must be considered.

That the soul is capable of existence in future, and not formed in vain, as resulting from its creation, it must be formed to sustain that existence in all its richest and glorious beauties and enjoyment. The more we appreciate God the Creator the more we love him, and the immortality of the soul, and its eternal happiness, must promote that in perfection.

The best earthly position of the soul only presents a dissatisfied gratification, a resulting inquietude. It has to solve a universe problem, and nothing short of it will answer. But do we mean absorption of the soul to God when it reaches his holy presence? By no means, when each has distinct individuality, having separate and distinct functions to go on to eternity to solve the eternal problem, with expansive intellectual progress, morally and religiously, to enjoy happiness, to gratify the expansive goodness of the Creator, who has created an infinite variety of spheres or orbs for intellectual residents. How shall the soul possess such locomotion? How came it to be created on this spheroid? The Almighty intellect that placed it here can remove it to its appropriate place.

There are universe agents, as electricity, light, gravitation of systems, and principles that move the universe. That is a minor question.

Neither can we enjoy perpetual happiness on this spheroid, nor appreciate, with our present intellectual organs. God is an immortal being, and has endowed man as the best of this universe, with an immortal soul, for the noblest object of creation. This is sustained by conscience, that proves the soul. Animal life attains the extreme of its capacity in this life and world, while the mind only begins its rudiments on this earth, its sphere is in the future, as nothing is made in vain. It is rational to believe that mind needs much of data that it cannot ever get in this life. The future must be for it. The immortality of the soul does not depend on the supposed proof of the authenticity of the scriptures. That is an independent question, that refers directly to God. It is desirable to have all proved that has a bearing on the immortality of the soul, to have admission as the fixed purpose of ethics. What is the human body worth without the soul, the thinking part?

Legitimate death is the great solvent to life's miseries, and procurer of future blessings. It is a glorious change, most wisely instituted by the Creator, to consummate supreme happiness of man. It should be brought about in the right way. No mortal can escape it. What will not retributive justice bestow on the murderer? What forbids his sustaining all the penalties of the murdered, that is deprived of future best changes? The systems of rewards and retributive justice, compatible with the circumstances of creation, are, doubtless, the soul's state. Death, with mortality, would be a bitter scene for the gifted and virtuous mind.

Each soul must discuss both sides of the question. But who will not look upon any dogmatist as a monster worse than Satan or Belial—character as pretended, to oppose such a principle? Who can explain the connection of mind to man? Is it material? Is it a part of God? Pantheism may speculate, but we conceive of an efficient existence, the subtlest organization created.

The soul has conscience, its sacred function, and reason to lead it to truth, proving it an element, a distinct though complex individuality. At death, the immortal part reverts to the decrees of God. But how about the proper distribution of the soul? That is God's business, not man's. God could at once renovate after death, as at first he creates its investing organization. Mind is ever inquiring, never satisfied short of immortality, as identified with the universe.

The mind's mission cannot be short of the universe problem. Mind in the world is like a diamond set in a large casket. Antoninus says, that "the faculty of the generative vitality is the eternizing principle." But this will not meet mind, an individual element. To elevate, not crush, is the attribute of Deity, who formed nothing in vain.

God created the soul without its concurrence, having done so for its best good. Surely to confine it in endless punishment does not accomplish the wisest, most humane, or just purpose. The soul's creation was for the best available capacity. One sphere will not answer—the best, because necessarily essential, is the universe.

What can be worse than the state of that soul that feels and knows it is doomed to some adequate, not perpetual punishment? What are all the world's treasures compared to a mind's innocence?

What is heavier than a soul's guilt?

Why do we live on this earth? To give our souls the proper culture; otherwise, this theatre would be a blank. The mighty problem of this life is more than world-wide, as great as that is to give the greatest good to the greatest number. This is in abeyance to mind, soul, virtue, religion, happiness. What is thought, but proof of mind and soul? It is the thinking part, that looks to immortality, and proves the superlative magnanimity and munificence of the Almighty Creator.

A belief of future rewards and punishments is essential to the best earthly position, the best security for mind's best appreciative action.

The soul or mind is created in vain if the soul be not immortal. All of the earth would be animal, and that adds no glory to God.

We shall have the real optimism only in another state of existence. Brutes think. They have memory, and that is part of mind, though animal. Brutes cannot be free agents, and cannot be held responsible therefor. If man be of any account, he has a soul that looks to more than animal, and more than animal's sphere.

How do you appreciate the soul is immortal? I believe that the proof is incontrovertible that it is immortal, because I believe most positively in the perfect justice of God the Creator, who certainly exists with pure attributes. He created the soul of his will, and will do it justice, which can only be done in the solution of the universe, not one world-problem. A rational being does a bad act here, is only partially punished, therefore retributive justice meets him in another sphere.

Many have comparative misery here, and can only look for reward elsewhere. To merely stop here would be most imperfect organization indeed.

In the punishment of the bad, some get not their rewards, nor are men capable of judging them correctly.

Many are misjudged, and suffer as victims to perjury.

The greater the mind, the greater the soul. Beasts surely cannot possess immortal souls, as they cannot be free agents.

They have decisively an animal sphere, a mould, as it were, that is exact, no more or less. All their tuition is imitation. Their mind is animal self-preservation, an earthly consideration. They are subservient to man's use, and best fill that as their destined function. Beyond that they cannot go. The greater the claim have they for man's humanity.

A God is mirrored in the magnificent munificence and construction of mind, that is so sublimely elaborated for genius, science, philosophy, and religion.

What are the mighty functions of the soul?

Death is a change from mortality to immortality.

There is no limit to the progressive magnificence of action by mind in the world, but the soul has to depart to sublime spheres, to solve its universe-problem. The soul is rational, and requires all rational means, not the credulity of faith, to reach its rational destination.

As fire has a quality of heat, so has mind a quality for religion, that best prepares for another state of existence. We believe in the immortality of the soul, because we believe in the exclusive unity of the Almighty, who makes nothing in vain.

Has man as a mere animal to sustain animal life, to have the refined sensibilities of his nature to perceive the relations of things, and be amenable to all the powers of thought, all the vast conceptions, to have all this in abeyance to the worst state of existence in all the vicissitudes of life, and to become extinct at the moment earthly existence ceases? Is not mere animal nature, that of the brutes, superior in that case? The soul must be an immortal entity. What can you make of a being, man, without an immortal soul? An animal? The conglomeration of the animal? What was that creation for? To dwarf God's glory? What a libel! To have the perfect creator, perfect in all his attributes of wisdom and intelligence, to have his most exalted earth-creations mere automata? To rise up and decay. What is the use, the good?

Man may teach the animal various mechanical things, more or less, according to its sagacity, but that animal cannot improve on it, nor teach its fellow animals. The animal is moulded to a certain routine, that the whole race thereof is distinguished by, forever.

But how can any prove that animals are not entitled to souls, and a soul's position? They are subordinate and in a specific sphere, for souls' use. Can they contribute to the exaltation of mind? Their sphere is limited definitely, and the first animal is as perfect as the last, except as to certain facilities of animal fibre, improved by animal advantages. If they were entitled to a soul's dignity, they should have the principles of ratiocination, but they are for certain animal, mechanical purposes. Are they for any thing more? If so, the advocates should prove it. The soul is for the universe-problem, the highest subject worthy of mind as of itself, and its mind is so constituted that it can only reason on phenomena with ultimate correctness. What are the functions of animals, but satiety of appetite and propagation of its species? Will these satisfy the immortal soul? The question spontaneously arises, at death, if not before, who and what are we? The animal extends next to the lowest organization of man's nature, and man extends, by mind's elasticity of ultimate capacity, to the highest order of organization. Where is that?

It is not visible as existent in this sphere.

What, then, are we to conclude? That it is in another state of existence. Death then must be a change, a passport, to that state of existence, of the immortal part, the soul.

The succession of generations keeps up the continuity of mind that thus always exists, but the reality of soul organization is elevated to its own spheres. God's creation is his pleasure, and that he will dispose of as almighty Omniscience knows best. What is the ultimate object of creation of the universe, of the earth? Can it be less than the highest attainable good? Can that be attained, by the shortest or longest duration? But how is it possible to render the soul immortal? This earth is not prepared for its immortal happiness. Then another scene is the one fitted. It is a singular phenomenon that any thing short of rational religion will not begin to do for mind. What, then, is the position? Ultimate relations, in the last great change.

One of the great principles of matter is, that it cannot be added to nor diminished. How then can the soul be translated to other spheres? By the best of course of the various universal means, most obviously. Our best affections originate a hope about immortality. Affection lingers around this subject, and rationality confirms the best appreciation of the rationalist. -

How came we here on earth? For some ulterior object? What can be fully accomplished here? Is not this a scene for future preparation, the state of chrysalis? Change of life is change of state. The universe is exhaustless, and could not God adapt mind, soul, as here? In this, God has illimitable power, beyond mind's conception. Will he not act to answer universal requisitions? Relative orders of intellectual rational beings may fill the scale of existence in the universe, from the lowest intelligence to that which stands next to God. How are these in regard to another state? Has there been no advance? Man's mind does not stand still, as about that time it declines. The organs'decline, through which mind's functions are displayed. The soul needs a better organization and sphere. It seems that the constant progression of mind from generation to generation will not answer for the soul's immortality or requisitions.

Religion is an institution of God for the human mind. Can brute animal mind recognise such? Is there, then, any thing in common for their final disposition? If any religious cognizance could be taken by the last, then we might discuss the final question as much as lies in our power.

The animal enjoys the good things of the earth, but the mind of man contributes to their origination, culture and multiplication, enjoying the subservient benefit of the animal. The whole makes unity of design. How can we prove that there is nothing made in vain by God? From his perfect character and attributes. But is man made perfect? He is made in perfect accordance of fitness to creation; were he a god on this earth, he could not be contented with his situation; as it is, he is desirous of a higher sphere. Mind is made then as it is, excluding all the false pretences of libelous bibles. Who can justly criticise one iota, the whole creation? The very attempt impeaches its propriety, as the whole question cannot be solved on earth. Nearly all nations, it has been remarked by others, seem more or less to have an idea of a future state impressed on their belief. The nearest we can come to the proof of a future state that I know is through religion, that only presents a partial completion of God's whole design, requiring the universe-solution to complete the problem. How can religion, God's own problem, be solved but by immortality of soul? How is it possible that mind should stop short, and neutralize God's whole comprehension? When the Creator gave life to rational mind, he instituted it as the noblest creation, and compatibly with his own sublime attributes gave the greatest good to the soul, and to comprehend the whole, that was for eternity.

Retributive justice must be equal, and equitable here or hereafter. If not practicable here, immortality is certain, and the soul is the illustrious being. This is well proved, because God is perfectly just. We know that proper justice is not dispensed here.

The soul is taken hence in all ages, and under all circumstances, to meet another state of existence. We know the God of the Universe by what he has done. This state of existence only advances the soul to prepare for action. Monotheism, practical, not professed, is a provision of the soul, to adjust itself most sublimely for all eternity without doubt. Conscience bespeaks the existence of man's soul. It may be callous by peculiar education, that teaches superstition and peculiar faith. Rational education can only fairly elicit, to the noblest aspirations of its creation and Creator. What conscience is in man, instinct meets the wants of animals. They are the conservative gifts of the Creator. Instinct premises self-preservation here, the soul both here and hereafter. What essential learning do we get of Moses of the immortality of the soul? This is an illustrious proof of the soul, through religion, the pure creation of God-inspiring mind. To elevate man to the highest, God doubtlessly gave him a rational soul. Man and brute differ in this, whereas both are created for wise purposes. Man may become irrational by peculiar education ; the brute is rational all the time of health by instinct. The law of nature is correct reason, to govern rational beings.

By the unity of design the mind is the recipient of the religious law, that is orthodox right reason or judgment, with nothing insidious.

We recognise in all rational minds, souls, the materials for morals and religion. I go for all the soul, that is possible to be proved and saved, and as I go for all the perfection of Deity and all the holiness and purity of religion, I cannot possibly conceive of a Messiah or a peculiar faith, other than the interested invention of the world priestocracy. Of these I have friends whom I respect only as men through God's kindness and grace, not through their supposed actions.

They speak of righteousness in peculiar faith, that damns itself and all its advocates by their blasphemy. If man can prove the immortality of the soul more clearly than what the facts of cause and effect warrant, then let him do so. But he can avail himself of no other truthful means, in the Universe.

Mind, soul, is a Universe problem to be thus elaborated. Mind's free moral agency, gives us the idea of the immortality of the soul. It is in the circumstance, of conservative principles. The immortality of the soul is necessarily the result of God's perfection, as he creates nothing in vain. How absurd, that He, the Creator of the Universe, as the Great First Cause, should endow mind, as the chief of earth, and of course of creation, with all the habiliments of destruction, misery and suffering, when as Almighty he could accomplish its infinite perfection and happiness. The thought is a libel on Deity.

Mind, the embodiment of soul, has to accomplish its glorious mission, by appropriate use of all its faculties, and seeking thereby the best earnest and security of all desirable in the future.

The immortal soul must desire the choice parts of the universe, and all that can render them desirable. Its main question is the appropriate preparation.

He who undertakes to deny the immortality of the soul, to first do so effectually, must deny religion, an utter impossibility that puts to the deepest scorn, the atheist and polytheist. Their feeble and meagre pretence must certify that mind's mission is only to the world alone, and not to the universe, that the supremacy of mind and the sublimity of the Creator most clearly confound.

The pure organizations of Deity, place a halo around the immortal soul.

Mortality implies injustice to soul from God, who requires of soul as the best earnest of immortality, its best religion. This, the universe police requires.

Rationality impels mind to its duty, where sophistry cannot, as exemplified in the history of the Jews, that ran after other peculiar gods besides theirs that the priestocracy invented themselves, composing the most efficient eating and drinking portion.

All peculiar faith is what is made by such, the world over. All their books and contents, all their teaching, are no more than other oracle false pretences. Churches or temples cannot consecrate, but partake of all their desecrated fooleries.

What a mockery of mind, humanity, creation, would mortality of the soul be ? No mind most rational aspires to less than the purification of the soul, its pure organization in immortal bliss.

We must look at the capacity and property of mind, the most elevated organization— an immortal element possessed of functions, principles, and attributes, elevated most by its most refined purity to reach most refined immortality.

Do the priestocracy treat the mind as becoming immortal, to continue it subservient to this odious, fanatical, degrading compulsion of faith ? And yet they take away reason from mind, the noblest position for religious attainment and elevation. Mind to reach its best state, has to be fully guarded against all such, the various schools of its perversions. It is utterly impossible for the mind to be inferior to principles, that are pure as God's functions and attributes that are immortal. Priestocracy trash, bibles and creeds, are unworthy the dignity and immortal purity of the soul,—for when we talk of reason and mind, we must embrace all their most legitimate and enlightened capacity by rational education on this earth, that must yield in due time its soul-treasure for ecstatic enjoyments. Mind, then, cannot be too guarded in such an invaluable jewel as the soul, committed to its most rational care.

FAITH.

The position of Faith without reason, would establish a miserable state of morals.

It would be inconsistent with the lights of mind, not enslaved by feudal vassalage and man-worship.

Who makes any proper impression, religious or other, without mind and reason?

What gives the brightest jewel in religion, an enlightened and pure conscience, but mind?

Can you successfully address any mind in religion in any other than rational principles? But faith is a mystery! Religion, then, is a mystery!

That position impeaches the character of the mind of those asserting it, the sincerity of mind affecting it.

Man's systems of peculiar faith affect to be mysteries, prophecies and miracles, while Deity's religion results in the purest and plainest best action of reason, proper sense and truth, that exclude all such clearly. None but the most arrant humbuggery can deny this—none but hypocrisy can knowingly do so.

God's works decide this test question.

Religion is rational duty—is that a mystery?

If peculiar faith, that is blind credulity, is to prevail, how can we know the difference and the merit between sectarianism and true religion?

Why was any reformation original or subsequent, unless founded on the vices of the parent stock, and the relative merits of correction?

Why prevail so many orders and sects of peculiar faith, in all ages and countries?

The inference to the contrary, is a suicidal position.

When peculiarity, selection, election, or partiality, is advanced in any system of faith, that moment all such is self-impeached, as libeling the universal attributes of Deity.

Intelligent freemen cannot overlook their own best advantages, the pure gifts of mind, that give the best faith by reason. All other faiths arise from improper sources, as fear, superstition, base passions, but what good can all that do? It must do harm.

Reason brings with rational religion, the adoration of God. All others bring in their train idolatry or man-worship.

All such being a host of evils, shown in the sorrowful history of the world, misdirecting the mind's devotion, character and communion.

And what is that character, among the best systems, short of the true faith?

Where is the intrinsic protection, but in the fundamental principles, that respect the only supreme authority all the time?

The essentials of faith are reasonable and just. Pure and sincere men aim to be right, but are too often deceived, misled, and sorely disappointed, under any existing regime, that leaves out principles essential and conservative.

Freemen need what mind can receive, adopt, and faithfully defend for ever, on true conservative principles, that have their full inherent and intrinsic elements, that always vindicate themselves and triumphantly protect all espousing them.

Our faith must be properly founded on the nature of creation and Creator of mind, the Universe of things, time, matter and eternity.

When time, that discloses the motion of each revolving sphere, and eternity, that sublimely speaks for that of the Universe, declare unmistakable facts, mind in due humility founds its unmistakable faith in the God of Nature.

Man's professions must be appreciated, as referring to silence, while his actions declare their character in all necessary respects.

But some who have not fully analyzed this whole subject, might think that it made but little difference what faith mind adopted.

A military despot who sought the conquest of the world, might affect this selfishly, degradingly, and hypocritically, in being Mahomedan, or Christian, or any others, as circumstances governed him; but a freeman decides otherwise on principle, as he respects dignity of character and the good and universal peace of mankind.

There can be from the very nature of things, but one true faith for religion in this whole world, as universe, and none but that can ever keep the people united in one brotherhood, peace and general good-will throughout the globe. As well assert that there can be two or numerous principles of gravitation for the preservation of the universe, as for man's pretences in numerous faiths to conflict with God's certain laws of principles, the very quintessence of rational religion.

What chaos and confusion at once there would be in the spheres, as what endless bloody results on earth do prevail from such false views of faith.

There may be innumerable faiths of superstition, but the unity of faith identified with religion, is as indissoluble as the unity of God mirrored in the universe, whose very name declares its character.

Superficial, nay, awfully deficient must that mind be, that asserts the contrary, an opinion not worthy the name of principle.

Yes, it does matter with mind what faith is adopted, for rational beings only, need and must have the right one.

If false ones be adopted, never can the proper elements of union be disposed of, as the volcano is always subject to eruption, for there are the materials in the magazine of conflict and war, strife and bloodshed, ever disregarded by charlatan bigotry and a soulless superstition.

Many are nurtured in creeds and faith of peculiar education, compelled from force of custom, habit, authority of the family, social circles, public perverted opinion, priests and state by absolutism, to do that which their reason revolts at above all things. Tyranny, essential despotism, has kept peculiar-faith alive.

Many are forever enslaved by ignorant custom and barbarous fashion, and most stupidly as most insincerely, adhere to any taught faith not inwardly respected nor duly respectful to the Great First Cause.

Unfortunately authority is brought as stupid, that one faith is as good as another, only let the believer be sincere. This is the language of irrational minds, in abeyance to peculiar-faith, tyrant of reason.

Hence we see many changing from one sect to another, and actually dissatisfied with all of that class, not independent enough to declare for the pure rights of mind and its rightful deductions.

No emoluments unworthy an immortal soul, whether in church or state, no public enginery of superstition and inquisition, should cause acquiescence in bible untruths, to restrict mind in full respect to God alone.

No future worldly rewards in any place or emolument, should bribe, no brute force should bully, no insidious sophistry should seduce mind to permit impositions by any bible of priestocracy, on the people.

How much in this world that should premise one universal brotherhood, demands mind's truly conservative exertions for correct faith and action !

There will be many opinions about peculiar faith, how can mind combat then successfully and rationally, to attain to the right one, as there can only be one right ?

Faith with no analysis or analogy of reason, is absurd. The Mormons, if cotemporary with the bibles of tradition, by aid of that credulous age that unfortunately is not peculiar, might have just as good authority by record, for if we believe their disciples, they have saints, patrons and prophets too.

They are only the younger, not less authentic tribe. It is only a peculiarly increased credulous age, of ignorance that is needed, to beget all the miracles of superstition. The light of science expels all this, as the sun dispels the fogs of night. If the world was deeply skilled in philosophical science, superstition could not exist. Let the lights of such science be then diffused. How then can we mortals distinguish all such peculiar faiths from the right ?

By one universal rule, by right reason, and that alone ; and when any person or sect advances, for a moment, faith over reason, that moment decides that character dishonest and untruthful, for it is irrational.

The greatest absurdity and difficulty of any age is to deny what conflicts with preconceived opinions, backed especially by self-interest, whether they lead to the worst of superstition or criminality. All such faith must be criminal.

What demoralization, to say the least of faithocracy that comes of priestocracy.

What can you do with any mass bigoted to peculiar faith, that enervates the mind and destroys its noble manliness and independence, inherent ? Truth is not sought, and religion is not improved ; hence the good of all is to be superseded by that of the first dictating opinion.

But, say some of the older faithites, the Mormons are superstitious. Are not all peculiar faiths truly so too ? being based on the rankest superstition ?

There is no difference, unless action decides the conduct.

But, then, the tenets of the Mormons lead to vice ? But do not the tenets of all peculiar faiths lead to the same, only as the light of mind prevents ?

Mind, the beneficiary, is in everything in the universe ; if perverted in faith, that faith is peculiar ; if good, that faith is rational, for its Creator is most rational.

We see the consequence of conflict of faith in Mormonism, that produced war and disturbance in several States already ; not that all the other peculiar faiths were less obnoxious to rational faith. Rationality is the only means to effectually get rid of all such.

If we allow due credit to the bible-faith of others, they must be bound to furnish proper reasons, or have that faith utterly rejected on that principle, the only path of safety for mind.

If others allow us due credit for our reasons, of course they can, then, say nothing about the certain conclusions. All minds must be in abeyance to reason and philosophy, and be silent to their teachings and requirements, consequently the faith that grows up is the legitimate consequence, and not manufactured to order of priestocracy.

But "faith is the evidence of things not seen, and the substance of things hoped for."

Now, all rational minds can only hope for reasonable, just things, and confide reasonably in unseen things. Any other faith is not worth the thoughts of mind, for its fruit will be of no account, but most noxious. Substantial results can only accrue on substantial basis.

Respect appropriate to all rightful authority is the first principle of rational religion necessarily to be right; then faith is identified aways with reason and reason's God, a fit companion in the universal whole, and can know but one God. Has peculiar faith ever acknowledged this principle? True religion investigates and reveres true authority.

Mind decides, on reason, that faith must be just and right to be faith, else faith becomes nonsense or untruth. Faith rests on eternal principles of right and justice, that rest on reason and reason's God, whose attributes are right and justice in their purest sense.

Hence, no messiah can be smuggled in at any time under the pretence of sophisticated faith.

God is immutable, necessarily consistent, never inconsistent. Wherever his authority prevails, and that is as far as the universe, man's error about faith must be corrected.

Faith and reason cannot possibly be inconsistent in any respect; if there be any error it is book or man's opinion. The book opinion, as man's peculiar written opinion, is abominably false.

The cognizant facts of faith and reason unveiled, rest for mind's cognizance on testimony that must be consistent, else the testimony is inconsistent, and necessarily to be rejected in the highest earthly court, that of conscience.

If any testimony offers plurality of gods, it is inconsistent with the conservative principles of the universe, the highest known to mind.

That testimony impeaches itself, as self-destructive.

There must be an end of such testimony, and it is ruled out in respect to reason's God.

That testimony is also convicted of impure morals.

That testimony involves impiety and blasphemy towards the Most High God, and imposition on man.

That testimony commits high treason towards mind, in destroying its independence of sophistry, in production of man-worship, that excludes the pure duty towards God, of mind from itself, to receive the tradition of others on their mere assertions and perjuries, without analysis of the facts on rightful reason, and reason's aid, analogy.

In faith, the sum total of belief founded on facts, else the faith is identified with the fraud, the right mind requires a sound decision, and God commands it eternally, or God has never given mind, nor its best protector, reason.

Faith received on any kind of tradition, that skulks from reason and reason's God, is demoralizing and criminal.

Proper faith can be most clearly defined, without mistake.

Could any organized resistance exist in the breasts of any refined people, who enjoy a correct and beneficial true constitutional representative government, to that government?

Never if that be wise, for all others fail to benefit the most with the greatest good.

If that position apply to civil institutions, how much more forcibly does the argument apply to divine rights of mind?

Who resists true religion, the highest duty to the Supreme? Can any sane person, if a good citizen?

Can any such resist the true adoration of Deity, and his highest, holiest attributes? None.

Well, who are they that do resist God in his exclusive attributes? Sectarians', and all those of peculiar faith.

What is to stop the whole error?

The conservative revolution of free intelligent mind, acting on mind rightly, productive of proper faith.

The highest victory of truth rests on moral and intellectual grounds, and on none other.

How, then can the advocates of pure religion call for blind, peculiar, impure belief or blind faith, but from fraud, superstition, sophistry, falsehood?

If the foundation be wrong and perverted, the result will easily be foretold as corrupt. The tendency and facility in all such communities will be most easy, and too common to perjury.

Such will be the inevitable result.

Banish from society all such banes as fundamental and organic errors and sophistries, then we institute the soundest judgment, and make the most important move to reach the noblest principles of truth and honor.

Then will good and wise men estimate all in the balance of morals and intellect, or mind, and the result will be right by proof of all.

Nothing less than this can satisfy the immortal principles of creation, that is ruled by its Conservative Creator.

No faith that is pure then stands the test but one that gives a wise and sincere adoration of Deity.

All others fail, as earthly.

Religion is made of principles, not maxims of mortals, not messiahships that cannot apply to the universe, but are most alien thereto.

Principles are the only safeguard in man's faith and actions.

It is very clear that no Messiah ever instituted principles, that constitute religion.

God instituted all at creation, and mind has to elicit from these God-given treasures.

Then all messiahs must be arrant impostors on mind, which they cannot save, and on God, whom they rob and blaspheme.

Most systems of faith have been the cause of deeper iniquities, and created higher necessity for penalties when they deviated from God-adoration.

Can history begin to paint to us all the blood of millions shed for such in past ages?

The people no doubt would have been much better, but for the false leaders who sought to pervert their minds under the fell influence of ambition and avarice, that have misled the world to its deepest punishment.

What was the character of inquisitors acting against those men who were too honest to prostitute their faith? They were rogues and impostors, killing others, their equals in faith, whose sacred principles cannot be violated on the basis of reason and truth.

Shall philanthropic world-patriots yield to the narrow-minded, weak, corrupt, and self-interested, when they ought to exert a proper, wise, and redeeming judgment?

There is no system of redeeming faith, but a proper creed in the one eternal Creator and his proper attributes, that can encircle all persuasions into a proper basis, confounding bigotry and sectarianism. Away then with all false creeds and heresies at war with reason and rational principles.

Give us all rational religion and science, or give us none, no superstition nor craftship of priestocracy.

Where once the pageants of absolutism through peculiar-faith and dictatorial power, mere factions of assumption flourished, rational discussion on the broadest principles of mind will rectify for the world's good.

Where power assumes her various disguises and wiles, sinister influences and corrupt practices, none but virtuous minds and manly breasts can be rescued by potential conservative revolutions, that can only flourish on principles. Faith of things unseen can only be analogous to reason, if it be not, then religion cannot embrace men of rational minds. When we take things on trust, it must not be blindly, but in a rational and trustworthy appreciation on rational investigation.

This thing of faith is a delicate question for fear of its being a false one on false data, that it must be, inevitably, if peculiar.

All rational beings must have a rational faith, that must be the invaluable diamond of religion. As religionists, they must positively assert their superior and infallible claim to true religion.

We have an infallible and tangent standard of orthodoxy, that will assure us all that we have, that which will prove faithful to the end. Now what is that? The only test is mind and reason, that can carry us all to the true issues and nothing else, whether our faith be that of superstition, man-worship, the Musselman, Juggernaut or Mormon.

Where religion begins, mystery, miracles, prophecy and oracles end; this is the proof universal to mind, that is not vassal to bigotry.

Now faith can be so perverted, that the powers of government and the pretensions to religion can be accounted by the interested people, natural, no matter how absolute!

The principals and the interested deluded people, are to be the judges! With them, there must be no rational discussion and decision.

Mind duly cultivated by suitable civilization, must come in, to repel all such delusions and perversions.

Those that say we should not reason on these points because faith is advanced, abjure all principles as unprincipled swindlers of the people's rights.

People are very conceited in their selfishness about faith, as if theirs was to be the best. However powerful for a time, no such position will be more than mortal.

Analysis discloses enough to actually astonish many, to find most of the world so vassal in most matters of opinion, not having the boldness to do otherwise than follow others who must speak first.

What but clanship will disturb society, till relieved of sectarianism?

Then watch yourself preferably to watching others, and adhere to universal principles, your conservation.

It is bad enough when man has no interest to deceive, as he has to watch himself to protect the truth in omission and commission.

What must be the necessity for watching, when his interest and that of others' corruption and errors mislead him?

It is difficult to divest ourselves of the trammels and modes of customs, but the wisdom is to get rid of errors. All faith emanates from reason, or ends in absurdity and crime.

The mere profession of peculiar faith makes nations at this day, hostile and inimical to others, though all claiming to be republican. How else could the French treat the Romans as they did?

The principles of such governments do not clash, but the faith does, therefore it has erroneous basis of religion.

Faith that comes to rational minds by reason, rests on eternal truthful principles.

Genuine faith must be an act of the understanding, that receives the right perception of all objects.

Divine faith is supreme assent, founded on the only revelation by God's works.

That faith declares that there can be but one religion true and rational, all due to Almighty God alone.

But this faith produces only one universal brotherhood, where then will be the loaves and fishes of the priestocracy? Appropriated to more trustworthy objects.

All faiths only approach true religion as they approach the requisitions of enlightened mind, that acts for God.

The Islam faith causes sincere protection of persecuted national refugees. What can the christian faith do more? This is religion despite of peculiar-faith.

Any other than rational faith being illegitimate, all foundations reared thereon are illegitimate and untrue.

Any faith that leads to belief of peculiar miraculous dispensations, divine inspirations, prophetic declarations and subsequent fulfilments, must be inconsistent with mind's true position on earth, and God's exaltation in his holy centre. All such is too peculiar for mind.

Are beings indisposed to change their tenets and sectarian views, it is because of relentless faith that modifies conscience as self-interest directs, and thus are they steeled against all kinds of conviction, all light and unreasonable impressions remaining inflexible to their opinionativeness and peculiar-faith, whether emperors or clergy. Bigotry is the coin of despots and dupes. They wish for no new light, the old faith must not be superseded by any evidence, no matter how rational, as the whole machinery of church and state power is the best for autocracy and peculiar faith, that cannot on the best analysis, be considered other than superstition, is with them religion. They never consider that true faith can only abide in reason and truth, the best ministry of God.

Who has the true faith? He who has the true reason. But what does absolutism care for that, provided that the faith perpetuates her powers?

Why does faith diminish, or become extinct? Such never can be more than peculiar, and because reason diminishes or has never existed.

Whether peculiar faith assumes to be imperial, as it is arbitrary, none can be orthodox, as it is not true.

No faith can depend on custom, authority of powers or numbers, but only on intrinsic worth and merit. No human dictation can control true faith, its essence is in God alone, the author of all good, otherwise there can be no end to the systems of superstition, miscalled religion.

The spirit of the age is only right as the reason of it is right. Unfortunately the world depends on the judgment of others, that too often requires almost absolute correction.

The ways of speculation in faith, the mere politician, are those of the hack and charlatan, perverted and crooked, not trustworthy.

Make honest capital, out of honest purposes.

Such persons employ their capital and labor in bad ways, with no profit, that if well employed might redound to fortune and fame of all.

Shall this thing of peculiar faith, the exploded humbug of priestocracy and the dangerous toy of absolutists, still prevent the rightful action of the world ?

Faith is a curious mental problem, becoming opinion, and deluding most of mankind that cannot investigate on all rational principles too accurately.

Innumerable faiths arise from varied caprice, whim, device, ignorance, error, malignity, vassalage ; speculations of interest working the whole, whilst there can be but one right judgment, and that predicated on enlightened mind's decision, reason.

With most, faith is ever paramount, as self-interest is paramount, as sophistry is paramount, with a bigoted speculation.

Humanity, truth, honesty, and science, will teach the only safe doctrine.

When faith unites all sects, that would otherwise be in violent hostility to each other, then there are unity of God and his principles exclusively operating.

In some countries the Jews as Jews cannot sit as legislators, as in parliament in England, while Jews and Christians can sit in a divan or municipal council of Mahometans.

Now a Universal brotherhood, through rational faith and its religion, would at once decide this paramount duty for the whole world.

The main question is not what opinion is your faith, but is it the pure faith in the one Creator ?

All confidence of mind, in faith, must be by truth and reason.

" The evidence of things not seen, and the substance of things hoped for," rest on testimony of unimpeachable character, no less than that of God, and determine in God alone.

God is a perfect Being, perfectly wise, as the First Great Cause must be self-existent, beyond which analysis and analogy, daughters of reason, cannot go.

The wisest humility, then, causes the rational mind to be at once and perfectly self-resigned into the glorious supremacy of the Almighty.

Men's assertion of their faith offers not the least reason for acquiescence in its supremacy, unless its principles practically prove it conclusively. Few have calibre of mind and character to warrant acquiescence, as their works and general character are to be estimated, appreciated, and deemed accountable, for themselves.

Mind has to depend on Supreme Principles, that exclude all usurpation and imposture.

The people must open their eyes in regard to faith, and judge properly for themselves.

Too many are followers, not original thinkers. We can take no cognizance of the truth or falsehood, but by mind and reason acting on the process ; all other pretences are demoralizing, hence faith must be degraded not to submit to this principle. The conscience is the guide all the time, and must not that be directed aright by rational education. God gave its innate faculty full and adequate to such reception, to mind's demands and reason's requirements.

Now as education is the discipline, and as that discipline may incline to perversion of self-interest and ignominious custom, then reason is to act and re-act forever, on the great funds, the treasures of mind.

The education in peculiar faith varies as men's faces, if not governed to the one great essential Cause, on which reason turns.

Even savages recognise laws, reparation for murder, all from mind, that in all its varied states, from innocence and purity to crime ; from ignorance to error ; from brutality to civilization, is in abeyance more or less to rational restrictions.

Even the Emperor of China, miscalled celestial, brother to the sun and moon, has faith, and that especially, to exclude what belongs to mind and reason.

To compel the faith-adoption of the reigning world-dynasties, absolutism of church and state ordains its various inquisitions.

To cover up its felonious brute force, it marshals all its miserable fanatic sophistry. Citizens, explore all.

What is the standard of truth ? Reason.

Through what means ? Mind, cultivated to the most exalted capacity of its intellectual qualities.

Why do you discuss, speak, or read, but on these universal principles, to convince and act out mind's part ?

Can you without mind convince, and can you best convince without the best exercise of reason ?

7

Mind and reason exalt from one state of society to the other óf the four, to the height that of civilization.

Mind and reason extricate the savage, for a more civilized state, from the errors of faith and its education, by their safe funds, to enlightened principles and their education; upsetting the tyranny and vulgar pretensions of peculiar faith in all ages.

But for mind and reason, with all their faith and its bibles, the past nations of antiquity would never have been rescued from the dark ages.

The faith of absolutism binds the world to its despotism, its mandates and its iniquities.

That of Russia binds the people to government of an autocrat and the church of the Greeks.

That of Rome upsets the will of the only sovereigns, the people, and crushes their only divine rights, under the rule of its brutality.

That of France has made her forget her own position, and caused her to play the hypocrite and tyrant of the world's privileges.

There is no end to its corruption, as there is no dignity in its aspirations.

Nought but the light of mind, of right cultivation and purified reason, can raise them to the dignity of Creation rights.

The only way to escape the subtle wiles of insidious sophistry, the degrading power of priestocracy and all its hierarchy, all the world's absolutism, that perverts, corrupts, or misrules, is by mind and reason, God's gifts.

The day that exhibits mind's reception of any faith, without its reason, proves that mind is reckless and wickedly blind, stupid in its folly and crime, and even more.

No genuine faith can arise without genuine and rational proof of the truth; the reverse is foolish, absurd, and false.

When faith is sought to be forced on mind without reason, that person is impeached for blind faith that he has already adopted; his sincerity is doubted, and his faith looks dishonest.

But faith in tradition affects peculiarity; that spoils all, and that mind cannot recognise.

All such articles of creed and dogmas rest on arbitrary views, whilst all that rational religion asserts, are triumphantly and liberally referred to the code of reason.

What reason stamps is a perfect passport—all else is rejected.

Faith is any and everything, as interest and sectarian education peculiarly dictate.

But some may affect that one faith may be as good as another, as the best may have the best Messiah, as Christians having Christ for the Messiah. That position is most conclusively condemned, as all such steps are acts of most disreputable disloyalty to God, divesting him of his attributes, and contracting his divinity to a sphere more limited than his creation.

The very idea of trinity, that is common to the Vedas and other bibles, not being a plurality of polytheism, is an absurdity, sophistry, subterfuge, an evasion of most outrageous pretensions.

Force your family, children, wife, or relations, the social circle, or your country, into dishonest faith, and you damn your world.

Monarchs, force your subjects to union of church and state, and you damn your state to intolerance, persecution and inquisition, inconsistent with free and just principles, and only tolerable as mind prevents the odious despotism.

God's theology is not to create man's theology.

All systems must elicit principles to arrest the illegitimate results of popular passions, and remedy the evils of society.

To wish the people converts to idle faith, is base faith.

Pretences to religion on faith not rational, are made to eradicate morals that are social.

Faith is to be kept between conscience and God, not between mind and mind, as all peculiar faith is. Faith has nothing to do with mind and mind.

If wrong faith exists, what else than sophistry can exist to support it? Sophistry will prevail, unless rational mind counteracts it effectually.

But the mystery of faith!

The God of mind gave reason, not mystery of faith. That is as clear as that reason governs life, if mind is to be respected.

When man tells the world, that it is not to reason in any respect about faith, that man is lost to reason, self-respect, truth, honesty, virtue, above all, to rational religion.

Impressions of faith should come by intrinsic merits, not by any foreign support, aided by sex, passion, nor improper influences.

Let us have no dogma, but all only as reason requires. To admit all that we can obtain on this source of God is enough as essential, for to go beyond or less does not redound to God's glory, nor our dignity of candor.

The ancient vassalage of faith was by misfortune and ignorance arising from the brutal and barbarous state of the times, but now it is more degrading from the people's own fault.

If shame attached to the ancients for their foolish superstitions, how much more so especially to the present priestocracy for their criminal continuance, and to the people for their stupid adoption, with all the lights of science before them.

The walled town of faith, cannot exclude reason.

The inside barbarians will have to yield the question. They can say nothing more than is justifiable by the state of creation facts, and consequently must keep their tongues still, as they are not and cannot be justified by honesty and truth.

If the intelligent world were called upon to estimate any one quality necessary for its good, it would have to say that it is truth all the time, the very foundation of all rational faith, for a lie originates false faith all over the world.

How, then, can that part of the world be better, till all concerned learn to speak and teach the truth ? Her primary benefits are universal, while the low habits of falsehood and sophistry, will lower the world generally to the end of infamy, that perjurers must sustain.

All belief or faith to be valid, is through reformation of mind, an act of inspiration on mind by influences productive thereof.

Those who refuse reason to faith, must refuse truth beyond doubt. There can be no faith established by God inconsistent with both, for that is impossible. Then faith, without truth and reason, is worth nothing at all. Who is the author of faith ? God. Will he institute any peculiar faith that rules him out of his power, and mind out of reason and truth ?

It is ineffably stupid to suppose it for an instant. Yet all messiahships do this ! Of course they cannot stand, while all rational things are possible with God. Then all irrational faith is credulity.

But then, faith may be historical, saving, or any other. If God spoke any such, all such must be most rational, all depending on the testimony of truth, his mouth-piece, and must be estimated accordingly. But all bible of tradition faiths are irrational, and therefore, never spoken by God. They are untrue. God's position rules them out as counterfeit.

But the abundant superstition of the world may oppose all proper duty of faith founded on reason, as that superstition would arouse much of the world. All this is in antagonism with reliance and confidence in omnipotent truth.

What rational mind is afraid to investigate, as that is the only way to reach the truth, by equal balances ? What is mind worth, not to act as mind should do ? The world asks us to declare for some faith—and if we do not declare for its purity, and discard all superstition, we are not just to ourselves or our minds, our duty, our God.

In faith, as in lands and worldly possessions, we have to look at the right titles, else the whole is not worth the time and thought devoted thereto, as all such are necessarily defective and imperfect.

Faith in God cannot possibly arise from prophecies, visions, oracles, types, nor figures, as mind alone can recognise the appreciation through his works.

Faith without rational proof, is absurd.

Faith embraces all the errors of bibles of tradition, while reason disciplined by philosophical science, expels them. Which, then, is the true friend of mind ?

Faith must be necessarily rational to be truthful, otherwise it is the basest and veriest humbug.

There can be no merit in faith, unless that faith can stand all the severest test and scrutiny of truth.

What depth of injury to the world in all ages of mind, has imperfect faith perpetrated ! One kind of faith has persecuted another. They must conclusively prove themselves all bad. The very moment faith uses any such, she ceases to be infallible, as she must be irrational and peculiar by such acts.

There can be no proscription in rational religion ; no inquisition by machinery for the body, nor of opinion for the mind.

Do not act inconsistently, hypocritically, and corruptly, about faith. All rational beings can obtain honest faith from honest minds, by truth and reason, not otherwise, else the faith is dishonest and alien by falsehood.

There can be no exception. Freedom, that is intelligent, disclaims the serfs of faith.

Faith of the state ! What false pretence, felony, and tyranny of absolutism ! If any such had been the true worship and right of conscience, there never would have been a disturbance.

Place your faith on no man or set of men, much less on the minions of peculiar faith; sectarianism is not for intelligent freemen, when it is not fit for serfs and slaves. The people are told that they must have faith. Can they have faith without reason? If they think so, either their advisers are deceived, or the deceivers. But how can we get the truth, when the parties are interested? If you do not investigate the truth yourself, you may get the trash. There is in truth no such thing as absolute faith, but confidence in truth or its representative. Faith does not remove mountains, only a knowledge of science, correctly put in action, removes them. Mathematical science is exact, and begets confidence, in the execution and operation under its proper cognizance, yet the materials or the investigator may be erroneous. Which is least, a dishonest belief or an honest belief? The first is hypocrisy, the last is honesty.

Faith cannot be a boast at all, unless it be in perfect accordance with the facts of science. It is all proveable at once, on the right principles of science philosophical. If we go at once to the highest source, we will reach only rational faith—rational religion.

We need that faith to live and die by. The true one is that—that only is rational.

Faith is subordinate to reason and truth. But the bigot exclaims, you must not inveigh against my faith!

What has the world to do with his faith, if untrue?

The quicker it is abolished, the better for him in his delusion. If all be not done right, do not attempt it at all. This thing of faith is not a speculation, but a deduction of facts, it is not a thing of popularity as due to various causes of interest to the people. It is essentially a matter of principle. This thing of faith may be referable to a false standard proved by psychology, as when minds are negatively placed they can receive impressions that are of false conception, so faith can be any and everything at the will of the operator!

But as to our having to exercise faith in all departments of mind, we must invariably exercise at the same time, the trustiest vindication of truth and reason, for its best and sacred establishment.

We know enough for all practical purposes to accept for mental satisfaction all practical applications, so as to condemn when faith is not good or trustworthy, but betrays its trust. But to what does all this amount? Follow no sectaries for self-preservation. Religion binds mind to God and gives it the faith of truth, and its inviolable rational preservation.

No peculiar bible faith stands the law of evidence. It is not mere faith, but good faith that is truthful and rational; that the world needs. Faith without reason, is an abomination to mind, the beneficiary. Faith without reason, is an ignis fatuus of the world. That thing faith covereth a multitude of sins; it is the scape-goat to many iniquities.

You cannot sunder reason from faith.

What right have any to dictate by social force to any, in irrational faith? Any that is not rational, is not religion. The great astonishment is that the world, the people, should be so stupid as to believe in faith that is not proved and is nothing of itself. It is a vice, when credulity or belief without proof. Self-preservation begets a proper belief on facts. Why, then, should the world be perverted by peculiar false education?

What are writings not endorsed by any truth for credit to be paid them, worth? It is wonderful that any analytic mind can credit them at all. No ancient oracle ever had less pretension. Both have no truth.

It would really be some alleviation if the present professors of faith could enact like the ancient oracle-mongers, but all this is gone. There is no proof of the least faith contended for, on either set of scriptures, and all the pitiful vestiges of oracles are gone. And because people are destitute of investigation, they now must continue destitute of consistency of truth.

Some have little or no opinions of their own in theology or faith, afraid to express them for fear of their not being right but unpopular, only ready to go with the current, sold to the customs, fashions and errors of the day, never able to get out of the mud of such pollution.

Why cannot the intelligent community of thinking men speak out, instead of being vassal to the stupid unpopularity? The world has its masters in all peculiar faiths and professions, and their dictation is law, by reason of their temporal supposed character. But the true faith only looks to the true standard of God, not the peculiar dictation of man. No faith can be good that has not good reason.

Who lives by faith alone? That is absurd.

Has faith or reason the power to reduce all things into their original elements? A person is to be damned for his faith, if he don't have it peculiar—or if he have it different! That destroys free agency and correlative responsibility, while the true owner of mind is silent, and lets mind carry out its free agency under the circumstances of creation. What is the difference, after all? Rationalists have principle, good faith, whilst all others have faith ordered to terms of credulity that is only analogous to peculiar opinion, no faith in reality. The lights of the world must give credit for its sincerity.

This constitutes a pure, brilliant and patriotic blessing.

This does not belong to the usurping impostor tribe.

The peculiar god of faith, is worshipped by the last.

This image-faith outrages reason and mind's rights.

Faith is worth something to kings; will they lay down faith? You may ask them to lay down their crowns as well. What, then, could be expected of their vassals?

There are two classes of professors of faith, one that honestly seeks the true one, knowing no better than that peculiar faith is the proper one; the other misleading, knowing better, but preferring to be wrong and misleading others. When the people find out this, they will repay with vengeance many fold.

A blind and implicit faith is necessary to establish a peculiar faith. There is no virtue in all this, as it produces extreme of sin.

The faith-men go to sleep on what has been carried out for them by rulers of thousands of years past.

How few read and understand the bible, or read it through? Of course they do not analyze it, and go by impulse to those affiliated, who advise as interest and feelings prompt! Are these proper safe-guards of mind?

How few ever think of the proper analysis of the subject, till their feelings bid them seek in the cant phrase of the day, that which they already had given them?

And instead of seeking in the whole comprehension of the universe for religion, they go to man's books, which are as fallible as their stupid writers and impostors.

A man gets excited at a meeting all at once, and he then is told about religion for the first time; he undertakes it without analysis, and joins the church! Yes, but he may express his sorrow that he ever read so much about the anti-elect, or the elect. What, afraid of truth!

The fault is, he has not comprehended the proper analysis of the whole subject. Peculiar faith only produces a minority, rational faith civilizes the whole.

We desire the world-wide question ended in peace of civilization, that shall carry the best of fruits to every mind, and the best of happiness to every soul. This mighty question of faith has been agitated in all countries, to the malign enmity of all, when the elements of good faith can bring a millenium, a conservative restoration to the whole world.

We need peace and satisfaction. We need the closing on the noblest basis, and that is rational religion. Citizens of the world, aid in its final comprehension.

But we must have faith, at the expense of mind; that is not rational; cannot be religion.

The greatest and purest of all faiths is that of truth.

Faith is a virtue, but it must have virtuous, noble, intellectual and truthful principles, otherwise it is an ignoble outrage. Prejudice is blind, as a blind man, having a brilliant light. No man should change from the faith of his father! Run out the analysis, and you will have it very high in superstition, as the very first start was in the commotion of elements and fear of a wrathful Destroyer. Faith goes with truth, else it is credulity.

The world is false to itself. What makes it so? Peculiar faith. What is a greater humbug than faith, which is faithless credulity if blindly adopted without due investigation and analysis. Faith is an idol.

Ere we adopt faith, we must analyze what is religion. All faith must be rational to rest on proper evidence. Orthodox faith is right thinking faith, that comes by enlightened mind, depending on no governmental machinery.

We are told to have faith. Who endorses their authority, that they should endorse for faith? It is foolish to adopt faith, not investigated and analyzed.

Truth is the exponent of principles and facts most sacred, to be first and last and all the time, truth before faith, as the unity of the God of nature before trinity of men's notions, that violate the truth of science and reason. Mind is so constituted as to believe rightly on proper proof. Then are sincerity, confidence and humility established. The great error of the world is faith, without value received. God takes the will for the deed of those who cannot know any better, but then it is their bounden duty to give the best and enlightened deed with the will, and that they never do with the faith of bible traditions. What does such faith amount to, after all ? Faith cannot over-ride truth, knowledge, science, common sense, the evidence of our senses and wisdom.

Every facility ought to be furnished the world, to learn the truth, not the faith, only as it accords with the truth of religion. Let reason triumph if faith sin forever, as it is trash unless upheld by truth.

Justice before liberality, mind and truth forever before faith, else the world is ruined instead of saved.

The world has been made fool of by faith.

There is but one universal faith, as one universal religion. Bible-of-tradition-faith swallows any monstrosity, because it finds it bible written. What credulity can be more foolish, what falsehood greater?

Patriotism, truth, reason, law, science, honor, rational religion, invoke a change. We recognise no right of faith over reason. We seek by direct, not indirect means to reach truth. Shall botchers in faith decide for freemen ? Shall the doctrine of election prevent the investigation of truth and reason ? If so, faith is fraud and false pretence. We have seen persons in conversation seek to force others to their belief, opinion or creed. What honor is in this, of a discarded system ?

This produces results injurious to truth and peace. Let the world of mind be duly informed and thoroughly instructed, before any action is had. The unity of God presents the true majesty to promote a universal brotherhood, and that is too important to be sacrificed to a clique, or what sects can do. The Romans have tried that under the pretences of catholicism, but the soul of unity was wanting. The world is cut up into clans of private societies, all availing nothing, serving to distract and delude the world. What has the world to do with the popularity of sectarian clans ? What humbugs! This is a matter of personal merit. When faith takes precedence of reason, fanaticism is the result. Not only peculiar faith then prevails, but all its errors and vices. We have all sorts of miracles, as the doctrine of the transubstantiation, and liquefaction of the blood of St. Januarius. The divisions of faith, if true, are never adverse to reason but corroborated by it. Matters are put not on their merits, but on profession of faith, not on the pure testimony of that faith. What dogmas of superstition have been too monstrous to be adopted ? What will not the mind, perverted by seductions and hope of power, do ? Stupid corruption only prevents the right decree. When faith is not established on reason, it is sheer credulity. True faith confirms, peculiar faith detracts from God's attributes. As to faith, your sense will decide, if your honesty will permit.

The nature of evidence, if truthfully carried out, would supersede all blind faith.

You can tell us much about faith ! The best is, to let alone faith entirely, and stick to religion.

What, is not faith, religion ? Not at all.

They are two different questions : peculiar faith is the reverse of religion.

Some affect that one faith is as good as another, but there can be but one religion the world over.

Faith is asserted to be proved by feeling, devotion or affection ! How deceptive, as paganism, as well as its branch, Christianity, is assumed to be proved by feelings. In all such, you must mind your own self-delusions. What sort of world morals are those that reflect antagonism and social proscription for an honest, sincere disbelief of peculiar faith ? How great the delusion is, to deceive the people, that one faith is as good as another. How false the assertion ! Then there is actually only one good faith.

How does the world clash so ? Either the world is wrong or the faith is, one or both. What faith is fully sustained by principles, free from sectarianism ? There can be only one, and that sustaining the unity, providence, attributes and perfection of the Almighty. All the universe centres in him. When faith becomes to be looked upon as a world wide question, then we shall hear no more of its peculiarity, but it will be absorbed into religion, a universal solved problem. We cannot believe in any system entire of ancient philosophy, nor faith, when there was so much defect in all and the means of improvement.

The moderns have a hundred brilliants to one of the ancients, and of course the moderns are proportionably accountable for their position.

The world is vitally interested in truth, honesty and religion, but none of faith only as it accords therewith. Faith can only be the substance of things hoped for, by the evidence of things seen. Faith or no faith, mankind should be properly convinced of the fact, the great leading fact. How otherwise can they be honest, truthful and fully satisfied, honorably so, that all is right and just ? How can you carry out the original idea of genius and mind with bigots ? You have to leave them in their stupidity, else they may ruin you. You may not change them, and they would murder you if they had power to produce that change. The change of the age of the world does not change the nature of the bigot, who is bigot still. The animal, is animal still. The nature of the beast does not change. Proper discussions on the facts will answer when the mind of the world becomes sound enough to reason, after breaking off from its past errors. A simple unsophisticated citizen of the world, of city or country, supposes when he hears the priestocracy affect all they are doing is for souls, that it is all religion they are specially pleading for. But it is not a word actually true, by the very nature of things seen.

It is all peculiar faith! Now what has all peculiar faith of the whole world got to do with the pure faith of pure truth? What a miserable state of world morals.

There are hundreds of millions of sectarians to-day in the world, and you could not get the truth out of any about their peculiar faith, clearly as it is that all such is antagonistic to monotheism, the only religion in God's universe.

No peculiar faith suits the country, much less the world, or the whole universe. Mind requires the pure faith of truth, and that is universal. There can be no such thing as peculiar faith, and none but stupid priestocracies of the world ever dreamed of such a thing. The very idea of faith implicit was absolutely required by all ancient teachers and philosophers, from pupils who were required to hear for years their masters without even questioning them.

Are moderns, children like the ancients, that they cannot question or analyze?

The world should have no faith but what is good, right and true, and comprehend too where all tends. It should have none of the vices of political capital. What are party and mere faith questions worth to the whole world, that needs conservative principles? The only faith is good faith, for the whole truth of religion. Faith is only good and true, as it accords with truth of universal facts. The time has now arrived when all intelligent minds should demand of the pulpit people, as the highest duty to purity of rational faith and religion, a proof of the authenticity preached, competent to satisfy an honorable court of justice, otherwise for all the preachers to be silent and leave the pulpit, and resign their churches for monotheism. The intelligent world is simple to let itself be trifled with, as has been the case heretofore. I do not know of any kind of faith, but what is good and consistent with truth and reason.

They talk of spiritual faith. There is no such thing abstracted from rational faith. It is all a pretence. Give us facts, truth first, then faith will follow. But it is foolish fraud to ask for faith anterior to these. No honest and truthful analyst can do it; none but debauched priestocracies, whose minds are bribed, and act collusively, can do it. The priestocracy affect faith and not works, a most demoralizing doctrine, if it can mean anything. They talk of helping their unbelief. That will help itself if the rational mind be left open to rational conviction.

Mind is so constituted that it is made the recipient of facts, on truthful conviction.

Faith without facts is credulity, and if that credulity has had motives, it is a world's curse.

Can you priestocracy act like honest people and stop, close your business, as you, your bibles, and profession, are conclusively convicted of false pretences? Do not mislead the world for a little pittance. Act like Americans. There were old pretended prophets of various kinds at Rome, pagans you call them. Who believes they told the truth? God had immutable principles at first, then he had no dispensations of paganism, Judaism, or Christianity, which are utterly antagonistic, though the latter, as Mahommedanism, Mormonism, depends on Judaism. There is nothing in names, it is in the thing itself. Christian, the Pagan is as truthful as you. You both borrowed, plagiarized on mind; you did the most and gave no credit for it, and are the greater robber of the two.

Faith is the representative of facts, otherwise it is not faith. There is no ridicule so effectual as that intrinsically identified with the solecisms of arguments on the facts of the case. You may have all faith, all else, and if you have not truth and honesty, you have nothing. Though the world talks about faith to the end of time, yet unless it is consistent with the facts of creation it is all a blind man's folly and imposition. The world may boast of any faith, but all such will be its bitterest curse and deadliest enemy unless it be good faith, consistent with rational religion. The peculiar bible faith is the soul-swindler's theme.

The good faith of monotheism is the only faithful friend of mind, directing it to its God Creator alone. Cherish it with all the holiest devotion, and the most sacred efficiency.

Reject reason! reject mind as well. As to faith, if not truthful, it is unworthy of mind, as below the dignity of truth, no matter what brute and sophist force commend it.

Holy peculiar faith is that of trained bands of smugglers, who, whether hailing from their pretended holy lands, books, men saints, all their holy days, can never be introduced to the recognition of one honest and enlightened mind.

No peculiar faith can go to the universe, religion, or their God. What are all bibles of peculiar faith but man's written peculiar faith disguised in all his felony on religion? There are two dangerous positions of mind; one that advances peculiar faith, that has no religion; the other, that has no acknowledgment of religion, exempt apparently from all its obligations. We can see both effects in overgrown vicious cities, as on the frontiers and wilds of new settlements, both theatres of robbers and pirates.

A CODE OF RATIONAL FAITH NECESSARY.

LET all citizens of intelligence or mind, and worth of character, act consistently with these gifts, and respond most gratefully for the best good of their immortal souls.

All should act as if they knew they had immortal souls, as the only safe position to elevate the sentiments of mind to its comprehensive duty and true allegiance. Hitherto few had any distinct faith of immortality, resting on a rational code, and certainly no correspondent action worthy of mind's immortal dignity, beyond the suggestions of their own views, prepared to receive that which is safe.

The most that had to be established was, that the individual believes in his own universal present and future accountability as a rational being, comprehending as well the past deeds; and that he is responsible at all times in that accountability directly to principles, or finally to the Supreme, therefore he acts consistently in the deeds of a good citizen; he believes in future rewards and punishments, and he knows that he has to refer to his Creator to enjoy the immortality of his soul-organization.

This, then, is the essence of the world's code of rational faith, if it ever consults the freedom and light of mind.

What more is wanting to put the soul on the safest footing than an exact duty to society and the best reverence to the Supreme?

The innate principles arising spontaneously from due cultivation of intellect give the proper direction to mind, that is directly indebted to God for all that is needed.

Had there been anything left out, where, from man's first existence to the most matured and expiring age, was his protection?

Could it possibly be in an extraneous faculty?

The God of mind has never thus constituted its circumstances. There can be no accountability in such position; it is absurd and puerile.

Some safe and comprehensive code is needed, built on a foundation never to be shaken, no less than on God's immortal principles, to meet all the necessary demands of mind.

As it is now, the majority of the world has no active distinct faith, neither affirms nor denies increase of faith; for however intellect has been addressed hitherto by persuasion and plausible tradition of bibles, still that majority remains unconvinced in mind and reason.

Its wishes must sincerely lead it to the best, the safest faith, but that faith stops at no declaratory act during the age of man, and must die with only that protection that shielded them and all rational beings alike, from the commencement of vital existence up to the period of their latest breath.

Such are the conservative principles of their existence. Assuredly, then, the world needs a code of its religious rights, arising from mind's duty and responsibility in man's most comprehensive and perfect accountability, that must declare the full duty, nothing less or more, and leave all wiser by knowing, and better by action. Then the feeling of the timid and the sex will not interfere with mind's just, equitable and everlasting rights.

Mind, in the assertion of a right code, will teach mind that never thought aright, or by right reflection, its true position and dignity, to adopt all protection from the great pale of its safety, reason and reason's God, who is the only object of rational faith, as Creator, from all rational beings alike suppliant to his mercy.

He that affects more than his position is an impostor to his fellow creatures, and a blasphemer to his Creator.

God's attributes eternally vindicate his exclusive right to mind's honest faith, and impeach all others as violative of every principle of justice and equity.

Let neither man worship nor anything separate mind from the purest adoration of its Creator.

Let no intolerant bigotry prevent, no priestcraft monopolize, no union of any power arrest, no sophistry corrupt it.

Bible traditions and man worship will be swept away most certainly sooner or later, when reason employs the right of mind.

God will assert his claims exclusively through reason's presidency. A rational system of religion must be maintained for right action and proper good deportment, for social and the world's good, extended to the greatest numbers, the whole.

The whole ethics of the world must be rational to be best accommodated to the wants of mind.

Let rational sense, truth and honesty forever preside at the world's theatre.

Man, as born a helpless infant, ignorant of the wiles of mind perverted and corrupt, subject to evil communications, the poisons of miserable and degraded education, abiding errors of ignorance and customs, misguided teachings of dotards and pretenders, invaluable time lost, eternal truths never attained, concealed or mistaught, all the dangers of temptation to ills and evils only known by physical ruin and despotic tyrannical habits, must have a proper code for the family altar, to the boldest consummation of true faith, the exertions of genius, and the happiest attainments of philosophy. His mind should be duly balanced, and his happiness best promoted by all the fundamental principles that can glorify his perfect Creator.

Then an enlightened conscience, the possession of all civilized beings, taught the ethics inherent to human nature and its best condition, reflecting the best lights of the age, will continue to bless mind's fruition. Rational education of all the nations of the world should be universal, and have the proper scope to all this for its full comprehension, that all may be justly dealt with and advanced to the legitimate elevation of mind.

But one true system of religion can stand all proper tests and satisfy mind, that is supreme in vital religion, as all proper principles direct a certain and unmistakable education for mind's present good and future happiness.

This question will bring the people of all faiths to a right solution, as there can be but one true faith resulting on inherent elements.

No system of faith can restrain the spirit of the wilderness unless sane by mind's civilization.

The mighty cities of the earth have even their dark and criminal corners and circles as well as the country, all amenable to mind's correction.

The only saving faith is that resting on the right foundation, and directing in the right way.

Mind of civilization must do that.

The rights of reason are to be heard when faith speaks.

"Faith is the substance of things hoped for, and the evidence of things not seen," says one of the bibles of miracles, prophecies, and mysteries.

But seen or not seen, reason guides the mind to the adoption of all faith on a right basis, else insanity and untruth would be the basis, and all tuition would be the quintessence of sophistry.

This position defines itself on truthful testimony properly endorsed.

Enlightened mind in its utmost sincerity must assert for its best good, that its purest allegiance is all due exclusively to the exclusive Author and Creator of all. His creation can never be misunderstood by mortals observing and reflecting on his works.

Who, under the influence of such undeniable proof, can reverence any dogma of man for a day, or even an hour.

The constitutional organization of a rightly balanced mind causes it to reject all dogmas, to recognise and analyze eternal truths and principles, and as a faithful sentinel to the citizens of the globe, it is bound not to stifle conscience for its own sake, or for the little lucre of the moment, custom blind, deceitful, erratic, blundering, and hurtful, or the more attractive emoluments through the rubbish of life.

The Immortal and Supreme Being needs no service but pure and unadulterated ways, honorable and just, that honor mind and must honor God.

With this basis, actions, words, and thoughts, with the right direction, are of rightful benefit, be they as humble as the modest flower "that blooms unseen, and wastes its sweetness on the desert air."

No species of idolatry, no man or mortal-worship, deludes the just man's devotions.

To God Almighty alone, as due, they are purely paid, the holy and only confessor, to reform on the past, to improve for the future.

The just man opens his mind to wisdom, his acts to virtue, his duty with his fellow man, his religion with his God. He knows no priest nor bible of tradition preaching. He commences with God, who is unchangeable, and commenced with his mind. He holds himself responsible to the progress of amendment, and renders social virtues to man; building his actions on the best foundations.

He looks upon truth as ever essential to his actions, that they may be rightly endowed with honesty.

His acts are fundamentally right, as his intentions are the elements of his happiness and fruition.

His deeds rebuke mortals who come short of duty, curtailing their manliness and capacity, their best titles and hopes, acting unwisely in seeking shadows, wofully missing the substance in their immediate circle.

MONOTHEISM.

WITH such a code, rational religion, or monotheism, unavoidably arises—it is utterly impossible for the people to think on this subject, without becoming rational religionists —that is most plain.   There can be only polytheism, atheism, and monotheism, all defining accurately the points of faith.   The first is absurd, the second incredible, and the last indispensable and unavoidable, the right concession to the majesty of God.   Many have decided against the gods of Christianity, Judaism, and all other peculiar faiths, most conscientiously, as unsuitable for the universe or this world, but lose themselves in the vacuum of a faith having no fixed principles; whereas they all must look to themselves all the time of consciousness, as most responsible for due observance of all conservative principles, if they in good faith invoke the God of those principles, as their God and Supreme Ruler.

If they grapple to his principles, before religion can be thrown, the universe dependent on them will also fall, and this at once destroys all Messiahships; for conservation of the universe embraces this as only a part of the mighty creation.   Such botches have been all messiahship tinkers, that they could not analyze the first principles of the universe, much less mind.   Eternal infamy is their portion, with all their pious frauds.

Most of those enlightened minds that are up to the light of reason, philosophical, not sophist, whether invoked to the investigation of Judaism, Christianity, Mahometanism, mormonism, or refined paganism, must be considered indifferent to all these existent partial and peculiar systems of faith, yet have no system perfected in general to concentrate their energies in proper union and strength.

The system of monotheism must be the only rational code, and deep be the sins of any peculiar faith-doctrine vassals that seek to set it aside, seeing that all else is a blank, that wise men will not deny and good men will deprecate.

Let not the want of union and knowledge exclude conservative principles, and the injunction of duty.

The insurance to the whole world, of the only beneficial code, depends on individual exertions, most important and essential for a right start and permanent action in life. Man owes it to himself and world, to select the right code.

Of course reason and mind are to be warred upon, tortured and silenced down by brute force or sophistry, the arms of absolutism in all her disguises.

They are not to be heard, for that is a loss forever to false rule and usurped power.

Does the world need a moral or intellectual light?

How can it obtain it, but by mind and reason?

Let mortals know their right, and do their whole duty, as the unchangeable requirement of God, of mind, that is only responsible.

Reason is God's favorite; analysis and analogy her assistants.   When such are absent there can be no truthful faith, for there can be no reasonable basis.

There can be none totally exempt from sin, none sanctified; but the best state is the least sin while life lasts.   God's forgiveness of sins may ensue by appropriate action of the delinquents, but all can only live improving the proper insurance on enlightened principles.   In this there can be no mistake.

God alone can only appreciate man in all his vicissitudes, and aid him best by his Providence Universal.

To inspire the right faith in belief, reason must inspire the world with wisdom, else the effect is only transitory and evanescent.

All previous modes of peculiar worship being destitute of all such elements, will finally yield to the noble impulses of mind.

Even fashion and custom must be upheld by reason, or time will efface them.

If we give up the faith of reason and rational mind, we have to submit to all the abominable doctrines of the peculiar faith of superstition.

All the codes for a bible but those founded on reason ought to be immediately abolished by all reasonable and cultivated intellects, in their mental appreciation, which decides them all nonsense, if not nuisances.   Mind that is rational must not only abjure, reject, and discard all the bibles of tradition as the most insidious fabrications, made as a conspiracy against the best rights of mind, but impeach all, as most demoralizing and treacherous to the majesty and dignity of God Almighty.

We all need the highest order of intellectual and moral religion, that disseminates itself in civilization.

Our faith must be liberal, however incomprehensible the principles of the universe, and modestly in accordance with reason that recognises inherent actions.

We have to be modest, and advance on the modest steps of reason.

We can know of no revelation, but through rational mind.

What an insult to cultivated intellect, to be asked its faith in such legends as bibles of tradition give us? Intellect recoils indignantly, at the proposition.

The necessary result will be forever, under the circumstances, of freemen not exercising their own judgment of mind in matters of faith, but go back to customs of ages, where pretenders and their minions acted most insidiously, that idol-worship will be at one point, man-worship at the other, of the whole globe. At the best, it will be hard for all such Jesuitical belief to die, most difficult to be killed off. Who can separate faith from reason and mind for his idol, is prepared for treason to human nature.

The noblest faith is obtained by the noblest reason.

Name principles to a monotheist, and he will feel himself bound to them, as others by law, for religion.

Rationality is the motto, that takes precedence of all low, vulgar proceedings. You are a member of society, and must pay a reciprocal obligation. The highest is through religion. I do not believe in man's bible, but the world must adhere to what protects mankind universally. Before any talk of having rational improved religion, they must show the essential constituents, truth and honesty, or there is no rational religion there. All have the elements of religion, but all do not make it rational. Peculiar faith just reverses and lies to get in, and all the time injuring all the elements of religion. Rational religion will answer for the death bed. It is the only religion, and can sustain the departing soul; who, as rational, must know all that is essential and beneficial.

The uniform protection to society is rational religion. The world and society are bound, in all the highest obligations, to act up to all its requisitions. As you seek all the benefits of society, you are bound to all for the best return. The nearer the world becomes one general commonwealth or common weal, the nearer perfection will be monotheism, the highest dignitary of all on earth, next to rational mind.

Mere atheists cannot speculate on the existence of a God, without feeling the necessity of having the full benefits of his providence in this world, the providence of conservation.

It does matter for every principle of humanity, that correct doctrines should be brilliantly illuminated by righteous actions, else man is a brute without innate organs of a soul approaching the Almighty, this is his earthly history in all ages and with all professions.

It is horrible to contemplate the bane of society, predicated on no comprehensive universal accountability. Atheism does that, and polytheism is a bigot to as miserable doctrines.

All reason and philosophy must plead for chance as effectually as the best doctrine of design, as mere names are nothing.

Man is clearly to all observant and reflective minds, held amenable and accountable in the circle of the universe, that could not be a universe, if not governed by the fixed principles that God ordained for universal conservation, physically, morally and religiously.

Man has ample free-agency of mind, that renders him justly accountable for the violation of these principles, beyond which he cannot go.

God's splendid works prove themselves by their government.

How false to society are all that pretend to believe in no accountability of mind, as they affect that man's life is mere animal existence; but rational mankind has innate faculties of religion that a mere brute has not, then that proves the supreme obligation of a supreme adoration and accountability to God, if not, the brute equals the man who acknowledges no innate responsive principles. Such people are grossly, blindly ignorant, or monomaniacs.

Many die without fear or reproach, believing in the God of the universe, and yet the preachers, divines we hear they are called, libel them at death.

Is this the way the noble question of religion is to be met? Sure the way that it is met, proves conclusively that "all the divines" are utterly vanquished.

Why do they not meet this question as men? They ignorantly and unprincipledly give them no credit for rational religion.

The preachers and priests affect all the time to persuade men about their souls, and yet are afraid for the people to discuss this on free, rational and enlightened inquiry. This bigotry cuts short religion. They denounce beforehand, all works that inquire thereof!

Priests and preachers that assume to dictate about men's souls, will be deeply accountable for their errors. If they had a rational claim, they would submit it at once to rational mind. But what do they care for all that?

Are any of them mentally responsible? Who believes that? The world must have no divine rights of absolutism, kings or priests, but all divine rights of the people, and those alone next to God's alone.

Wise systems of education and laws of social benefits, are those of man, whose interest is thus best subservient where it approaches nearest these principles.

The world must look at all such as making one mighty system of unity for mind, its true conservative position, and not let mere feelings and emotions in errors of education and prejudices mislead, but consider what safely address existence in all ages.

But here is a waste, where no code exists. Surely it is right that aid of the right kind should be administered for universal safety, to put mind on a higher system that honors its nature and character. The wise institution of universal principles must exclude sectarianism, in all its inconsistencies.

But sectarians object to rational religion as leading to deism, that is, it leads the people away from their flagrant errors. No matter where it leads, if deism or all advocated be truth. But that destroys the bibles of tradition. That is right, if they be the gods of idolatry that prevent sight of truth, facts and rational faith, or the banks of false pretences. No matter what is destroyed, if such bibles, if connected, as all are, with untruth and crime so universal, promoting the distrust and disunion of a peaceful world that learns to hate with a peculiar hate on the peculiar basis of sectarianism. The nearest approach to Deity is through deism, Monotheism; all others are gross and, vulgar departures therefrom. What an outrageous abuse of Deists!

Why is this? Instead of the priestocracy concocting this abomination, they would learn wisdom and truth from their position, and instead of reading out of a book written by priestocracies for their unholy purposes, they had better read out of the universe created for God's holiness and soul's happiness. All trinitarians view God as an imperfect being. When we get to the Great First Cause, we get to humility that teaches mind its moral obligations! Our moral obligations are derived from the laws that rule nature. Man was created for rational purposes. Monotheism willingly audits the pretensions of atheism as polytheism, that the wide world may be best enlightened on all relative claims. She is after truth, and fears no triumph of all such under this luminous banner.

My objection to polytheism and atheism applies to their pretence of principles; they have no principles.

What is the weak point in polytheism? They are all weak and rotten, having no foundation. The people of each audience ought in self-defence, in their rights of mind, to say to the preachers, declare the substantial proof or stop, be silent. What shall we do with the literature, as Milton and Shakespeare, all the poetry? Let the modern go as the ancient. Homer was the prince of such in his days, now it is as all are, romance and fiction. Truth must take precedence of fiction and poetry. Monotheism is not appreciated, as the ancients had no advocates. No ancient Monotheists? Where was Socrates? He had an accompanying demon, ordered the sacrifice of a cock to Æsculapius, and composed poetry in praise of Diana and Apollo. Where was Plato? Part of his metaphysics, and that of the Brahmin's and Bhuddhist's, make up that of the western Bhuddhist's, the christians. Where is Confucius? His went to the state faith of China, with spirits, the emperor for high priest. Where is the Indian's great spirit? Debauched by his imposing priestocracy. Monotheism has none of man's devices from imperial pontiffs down to any intriguing priestocracy. Emperors of Russia and China, Papa of the Greek faith, Pope of Rome, Lama of Thibet, the world priestocracy, do not help keep up the world cheat about faith not for your Creator, religion, the best good of mankind, but put away your false pretences, base, bad faith, absolutism, priestocracy, sworn enemies of mind's dignity, worth, independence, the value of the immortal soul that has to work out its own eternal problem. The only way to do it rightly, is the comprehensive solution of the whole problem. Rational mind demands exclusion of all peculiar views in religion, to establish universal principles for the whole world. The general welfare of all mankind is on living principles, not on exploded notions of dead bibles, or of the brief authority of man assuming faith to sustain his empire over the superstitious minds thus defrauded.

As to bullying proscriptions of church bible views against Monotheists, that is all wind—gas. Numbers only make many things tolerable, that of themselves are most contemptible and iniquitous.

Polytheists as atheists, are all equal to monomaniacs, they lack reason but have faith, the very thing the monomaniacs have. All bigots deal in faith, the counterfeit in religion, which is the highest duty to God and man, the quintessence of sublimest justice obligatory on all rational minds.

The polytheists and atheists might preach their lifetime, and not teach Monotheism, not the first point in God's word, cause and effect. Monotheism reflected through cause and effect, is for the world mankind to read. Everything that the priestocracy have done in their province, has detracted as far as in them lay from the providence of the Almighty. Instead of God's creation being remodeled, all was the miserable fixture of the priestocracy, whose after-knowledge kills them so dead with honest, truthful analysts, that they cannot breathe one breath more of libel on God the Creator.

ATHEISM AND POLYTHEISM: MONOTHEISM.

THE Almighty of Monotheism originated all of universal motion that is identified with time, beyond which the human mind cannot take cognizance. The atheist may rely on the position that matter cannot be added to nor diminished, created or annihilated, therefore it was in existence all the time from eternity.

Several points of profound inquiry necessarily arise, in this interesting subject. It is easy to contemplate matter as now presented, different from that anterior to its elaboration. Now it is nature bedecked in beauty and usefulness, then it was disjunct from that state. Time is a relative state of orb-motion compared with the self-existence of the Almighty, with whom neither time nor periods of eternity apply. If both are durations of motion, as the terms imply, time being intrinsic to our planet or other orbs of the universe, eternity that of the Creator, then God is almighty compared to each. He was independent absolutely of all universe motion or time, and is characterized by eternity that precludes mind's investigation.

God's creation of something in the form of matter wherewith the universe was created, transcends the wishes of atheists. Now where are the properties, attributes, functions and principles of matter of this universe, that premises subsequent motion to eternity?

These are, if anything, still superior questions, to the creation of mere plastic matter. The philosopher now speaks of nature with all her essential properties, and considers, most properly, that her matter cannot be diminished or added to, for the universe is perfect and independent of addition or diminution, neither can it be annihilated, as God's conservative principles are eternal protectors for its conservation. The matter that was in existence from all eternity necessarily refers anterior to creation, the time when universe motion began; then matter is originated by Deity for creation that informs mind through time, its integral measurer, of the Almighty elaboration, the magnificent effect the result of supreme and anterior causes. The lines and outlines of demarcation for the universe intrinsically, are too distinctly drawn to deny its creation, for pro-creation necessarily results itself the effect of creation that as all, must be universal, not peculiar. Time, the definer of universe-motion, is a demonstration.

Geology defines the bold outlines of creation, and characterizes them by universal epochs. This whole category of matter the first, applies most definitely to the Almighty, whose perfect functions, attributes and principles, are supremely displayed in the universe, and proclaim his eternity pre-eminently his.

If the atheist presumes to go beyond creation, he presumptuously essays more than universe, and assumes to affect cognizance of questions most abstract, not pertaining to mind's province, but Deity's organization, the data of which cannot be entrusted to that of mortal organization. They cannot both breathe the same intellectual atmosphere. To affirm that eternity should be identified with the universe, is to manufacture dictionaries as bibles, not subservient, but dictators to rational mind.

It becomes all rational minds to investigate properly all questions expedient, and take nothing for granted not in unison with truth and rationality. It has always to abide principles, and abjure all doctrines, no matter how, deemed orthodox, that do not accord therewith.

To let the atheist's metaphysics that refer to matter beyond Deity, a veiled speculation, be self-confuted, if we grant that matter was in existence, how can you get without the Great First Cause, soul or supreme intelligence, the beautiful and systematic organization of matter that moves with such mathematical precision, sublime adjustment, ultimate exactness and certainty? No such mass of matter could organize itself in harmony and symmetrical arrangements, from the magnitude of the mighty spheres of space to the minuteness of the atom, beyond either of which, mind created cannot think, much less act.   Nature is not, till the God of nature designs with attributes, functions and principles.

That is utterly impossible for chance, which is, however, but another name for an unknown Great First Cause.

Thus we prove, beyond doubt and cavil, of all inquiring, candid, and intelligent minds, that the Great First Cause acts supremely as the organizing infinite mind.

Not only has the God of nature organized as well as created matter, but endowed it with conservative principles and immutable laws, functions, and attributes.

He has endowed man with supreme qualities of mind, that can originate its own conservatism.

Atheism is a dangerous creed, gratuitous in its assumptions.

In France, it is supposed that three millions of people perished in ten years, during the first revolution, from atheism.   Yet how many billions have perished from polytheism, is not known or cared.

This same argument that cuts down atheism, excludes polytheism whether of many, or four, or three gods.

The mind that pretends that mind could not reach the recognition of the Great First Cause, is below its own dignity, and ought of course to prove its position.   We demand it, as a supreme justice to monotheism.

All other systems of faith than monotheism are polytheisms, even atheism that deifies created matter, and substitutes chance, which are all substitutes for an unappreciated Great First Cause.

FATE.

HE who can readily content himself on any basis of fate, in face of all the magnificent organization of the universe, is a humbug indeed, not trustworthy of his mind.

He succumbs to chance that has no existence but in his perverted brain, in a universe where Providence universal and almighty presides.

Fate and duty to social and religious obligations, are incompatible.   The first is contingency, the last is uniform.

The field, mental and physical, is utterly neglected by fate, that neither exercises nor justifies duty.

If fate decides anything, it is but a name and substitute for a nobler conception, that science, philosophy, and religion, exalt to the Creator.

If the criminal under the gallows was born for crime and penalty, what is the use of any preaching, for predestination presides where fate decides ?

Then there is no free agency of mind, which is as plainly contradicted by the works of the universe.

Thus in the extensive subject of religion, that accumulates in honors, we see all a beautiful consistency uniform in action and harmonious in all that uniformity.

There is no such thing as chance in the universe, that excludes the want of design, for all its parts the mighty solar system, prove that fortune and fate can only refer to the First Cause.

Atheism is irrational, the proceeds of mind so long crushed under the peculiar faith, despotism.   This was seriously proved in France, by the massacre of millions, all having been the stupid contrivance of the priestocracy, who set aside the only magnificent, brilliant, and indispensable revelation, and thereby brutalized mind, beforehand aided by the despotism of monarchy.   But it is considered by some intelligent persons, that an adoption of deism will produce or proceed to licentiousness !   How and why ?   Deism claims principles.

We must estimate atheists as monomaniacs beyond the domains of reason, and lost to its genial influences.

Why is a majority of the world skeptics ?

They are only so, on man's exposition through books of tradition, that become obsolete by the errors of their writers, not enlightened by the progress of enlightened mind.

God has provided for all this universally.

He has given mind innate faculties of religion, without which religion could not be appreciated, and whose mind is cultivated, his religion is rational, the very highest known to mind.

All minds are entitled to rational religion, that embraces all that is pure and soul-ennobling.

Rational religion is exhaustless and comprehensive as the principles of the universe, that suits all minds not constituted for understanding peculiar belief.

It addresses itself to the intelligence of all rational beings, for it is innate in mind and is evolved by God's works, and soul thoughts, words, and deeds.

It depends upon no man's creed, for it exists in nature of the best dignity, character, and benevolence, embracing the adoration of the Author of all the universe.

Atheism flies at her approach, abashed and self-rebuked as self-convicted.

The omnipotent hand of God has written the facts of the universe, and the sacrilegious finger of man shall not pervert it.

Mind perverted by atheism cannot look creation in the face, without expelling its degradation, and however imbued by superstition and polytheism, shall be circumvented about their pretended miracles, prophecies and mysteries, the libel of God.

The infidels should look at God's exclusive power, because of his exclusive genius and attributes, that determine his exclusive unity.

When they can digest his character, and refute his competency, then we will yield the thousand other points, all supreme as they are, to the polytheists and atheists.

What is the difference between atheists and polytheists? The atheist goes further than the other in atheism, and denies the existence of God, whilst polytheists deny the appropriate attributes to the Supreme.

Atheism is a denial of all religion, polytheism gives nothing that is true of religion.

The world needs a moral, social, and civil system, that can comprehend religion on just principles, and place it beyond the hazards of contingency, excluding partisan faith as blind and of no value. The destiny, fate, fortune, and chance, of the world, will be regarded as all embraced in the principles of causation.

If any men can be made atheist, it is the example of peculiar faith, false pretences to religion, which is practical atheism, for which its advocates are duly responsible. For instance, if the trinity is to dismember God's power, this is practical atheism in degree, for it detracts from the attributes of the Almighty in that proportion.

There are few monomaniacs that make an open avowal of atheism, assuming chance as their actor.

But chance is no agent at all, and the idea is at once stultified and annihilated by the exact operations of the universe.

The work of the universe requires the profoundest elaboration of infinite wisdom and power.

Conscience is the result of enlightened mind and reason, not of chance, but of the mighty principles of causation, excludes all pretensions of atheism, and is amenable to them, not to tradition, books of priestocracy, bibles, or any scriptures of polytheism, but those in accordance with mind, reason, and their constituent elements and essential principles. Conscience, an emanation of mind and reason, is directly responsible to them, not to man, and books only as they enlighten on just basis.

A correct appreciation of conservative principles must build up the best practicable code of morals and religion, and most effectually destroy licentiousness, and in the strictest accordance with a moral and religious conscience to promote every just principle in mind, to expel vice and immorality, to build true constitutional government, and secure all the blessings by such universal elements of good to all, to resort to mind and reason in the rightful exercise of their loftiest qualities, and above all to God.

The knowledge of the God of creation has not only filled the whole earth, one little planet, but exhaustless creation, that proves God's power, and all bible tradition writers are most insignificant, when they, as ignorant of the first principles of science, have committed themselves in regard to the Almighty.

Let mind assert its dignity, and the triumph of truth will be complete.

The very argument that the best of peculiar faith uses to condemn atheism, is most condemnatory of its doctrines for a partial polytheism.

But all bibles of tradition necessarily lead to skepticism, atheism, or polytheism, and nothing else.

All their degraded advocates thunder into the ears of the people, that they must believe in one of them, or be damned.

But the people when enlightened cannot in good faith adopt peculiar faith, yet they may be afraid to declare their soul God's.

If they touch rational, the only revealed and inspired religion, they leave the priestocracy, priests, preachers, and insidious hierarchies, that, alarmed for their very existence, damn all the world to save themselves. Vassal minds may disgrace themselves under this absolutism a little longer, but so help us God, we can and will adore only thee, Creator and Preserver of the universe.

Atheists are bound to the rule of mind as all rational beings, and have to yield to the order and harmony of creation, as having a head that organized matter thus.

Savages of the forest acknowledge the power of their Great Spirit, paramount to all other spirits.

Here is proof of their mind having innate capacity for the idea of Deity, either original or traditional, either view being equally valid as to the faculties of mind.

Action of mind on mind in process of time brought about science and the best views of God, most clearly estimated by the character of peculiar bibles that have more superstition the more ignorant their writers and authors are. Atheism and polytheism are mere subjects, in abeyance to rational religion—the more vanquished, as light of mind vanquishes ignorance.

But you affect to stop at destiny, fate, chance, nature, fortune?

We stop at the Great First Cause, where honesty of mind, truth, reason and rational faith place us, and where death or dissolution of life finds us.

You may affect to believe in a universal power only, as that of nature. But there is no supreme power without supreme intelligence. The division is absurd and impossible, atheist! How was matter created without both qualities? How organized as created, as universally admitted by sound minds?

All creation requires a Creator, the essential Preserver. Mind was created, and endowed with the noblest intelligence of creation. All organization requires an organizer. All causes require a causer; who caused the first organization? You assume the name of nature ; do not assume the elaborated materials of the sublime Architect.

Chemical as universal materials will form unions of order and character. Who arranged these materials, to secure all these wondrous positions?

What harmonizes that order, and beautifies that symmetry? Each solar system is organized in beautiful consistency with relation to the other systems of the universe, else chaos and confusion must necessarily arise. We observe comets that have regular circuits, and pass in mathematical orbits. Do they connect solar systems together, and perform functions of ethereal messengers? All this great work had a Great First Cause, who not only had the power that governed the inherent forces of nature, but intellectually directed and organized the whole universe.

His intelligence as power is perfect, and perfect is his character, but for all such the present state of things would be absolutely dangerous, had it even had an existence, and had not God provided comprehensively, that danger had told on the world, the universe.

Rational beings can only believe in rational faith and religion, consequently they must reject all the bibles of peculiar faith, and their demoralizing doctrines, and because they honestly do that, the advocates of these bibles declare, that if they do not believe in them, they are damned! This shows the height of dishonest dogmatism. The consequence necessarily arises that those who do not reason clearly, aided by all the rightful benefits of well regulated minds, will declare for some gross materialism, polytheism, atheism and non-entity of the soul after death.

Believing that annihilation of the soul takes place after this life, they seek to make the most of it here, and act cunningly in crimes and vices, and repel all religious cultivation.

Much of this abuse in life is due to the absolutism of peculiar faith, that thwarts reason and trammels mind. Peculiar faith connected thus with absolutism is the worst of all states, the dog in the manger policy, neither cultivating true religion, nor permitting the world to enjoy it.

Religion is a constituent of mind and man's nature, giving the mind the most exalted adoration of Deity resulting from appreciating his glorious attributes, that form a perfect character in power, intelligence and qualities.

Religion teaches the sublimest contemplation of all God's character, and the noblest obligations dutifully paid by mind to God, and as one of the loftiest parts of its sublime mission teaches the immortality of the soul, that is necessarily connected to an immortal Creator. If the world do not acknowledge religion, it does not pay due respect to mind or matter, or the Ruler, and the whole tells finally on the injury if not ruin of society, an incident too frequent in the world's history. Society is destroyed for want of social principles. A man's actions would contradict his assertions as an atheist, sometimes proving the existence and government of a supreme. All the speculations of polytheism, having trinity or more than unity, necessarily contradict themselves by actions, whatever they affect in words, as the Great First Cause is paramount, while monotheism sustains itself throughout, most consistently.

The geological epochs answer all such, and must improve the views of all earnest inquirers to a better faith in one God. Who can contend, in these serious matters, for the triumph of sophistry over facts? All good citizens must go for that doctrine, that secures all the necessary actions, duties and sympathies of life. But bible of tradition advocates will affirm, that if you do not believe their way, you are damned. This position of mere assertion for credulity, thus produces deep demoralization with some who do not analyze the whole subject. Not having minds constituted for credulity, they cannot assist in any such dogmas, but yet overlook necessary duties to be duly investigated by truth.

One part of the world must believe the other part. One part has to support the other.

One part of the world has to obey as a vassal, the other part or balance.

The world's society is cut up, by sinister influence, intrigue, more or less. The same is cut up by clannish, secret actions, that mar the justice to mind and morals. The mighty masses of the world, less ignorant in other matters, can be moulded to all the miserable humbugs and baseness of superstition, subservient to fear or custom.

Atheists are less injurious to society, bad as their doctrines are, than bible of tradition advocates.

Whilst all such are in the pale of God's religion, the last seek to usurp it by their peculiar-faith dynasty, for priestocracy speculation and trade. The first are passive, without the pretences of monopoly, and its odious machinery, to rule the world. What can be worse than the last, hypocrites before God, tyrants to mind. Wherever faith declares itself in opposition to scientific principles, that faith is worth nothing, for it is guilty of base doctrines.

Time and science have painted out the various defects in all peculiar-faith doctrines, that are necessarily condemned. It has been most important that the most miraculous tales should be invented, to cause peculiar faith to flourish, and this deception has to be kept up all the time. However palpable the falsehood, the knowing ones keep it concealed, and war on its exposition and exposure. How flimsy the base of that which seeks such miserable expedients.

The very moment that polytheism is admitted, as it is by peculiar faith, monotheism cuts that down, as no partial gods can work for the God of Nature, who stands sublimely a unit, neither needing nor permitting any co-workers, consequently monotheism, the only rational religion, cuts down all polytheism and atheism. We have a just idea of God indubitably by his attributes, if the God of unity. All others of no account to mind, need men's books for artificial support. But God only fills the test and measure of rational criticism and investigation.

The dogmatists hold that there is no God, or a partial God.

The rationalists hold that there is a God of nature, recognised by the most sublime science, and the exactest system of that science, as the prime mover of the universe. The universe, as far as mind can perceive, is already comprehended in system most beautiful and orderly.

This is rationalism to admit it, but the converse is dogmatism and atheism, that are in the same category as polytheism, that manufactures partial gods.

Mind must travel up to nature, recognise her constitutional laws, and appreciate her law-giver, not seek to lead all to its pre-conceived notions and imperfect desires.

Mind must dispute all wrong, and have proof of all that is right, to be rightly ruled by science. All that is right is provable. Mind thus reaches, by the principles of causation, a Great First Cause, to whom it resigns itself at rational discretion, not being able to transcend his bounds. Polytheists have made atheists, and from the sublime God they both fall to the ridiculous.

But much stress is laid to the opposers of the bible, as Robespierre and some other degraded despots, who were also the opposers of order, law and proper government! Let all these degraded characters be considered the tyrants of the human race, which these terrorists butchered without reason, and despoiled without limits. But who are opposed to the noblest of all governments, that of God the Creator, more than polytheists? The despotism of absolutism was, by the deep corruption of these people prior to the reign of terror. The people, truly, had been crushed, by the enemies of civil and religious liberty. What was all but a mighty reaction of wrongs long perpetrated? Monotheism deplores all such, whether commenced by polytheism or finished by atheism. There should be no deep-rooted attachments to exploded customs. If we give faith as the motto for our action, we may believe the atheists, who deny God, for there is Aristotle, who believed in no God.

We must try the whole atheists and polytheists by reason, as faith leads us to be what destroys us at once.

Reason must expel the irrational part.

All the bibles of tradition have irrational, defective points, abominable caricatures, resulting from the ignorance of the ages of the writers. No wonder these make atheists, as their advocates, the polytheists, falsely and ignominiously pretend that the world

8

cannot get any other idea of a God but from these book-libels! Should such ever see the light of the Almighty? To get on with the doctrines of atheism, a universe of mere assumptions and speculations is raised. We hear of the opinion that the earth, when exhausted of her impressibility to electricity, will undergo absorption into the sun, but then the solar system would be unbalanced. In all this there would be an effect, then necessarily resulting from a cause, which premises a design, and of course a designer. But atheists pretend that there is no omnipresence of God. They are, then, met more effectually, as God presides over omnipresence, which is commanded by his conservative principles, that act for him.

But, says the caviling atheist, who wishes to maintain his brainless position, God is not cognizant to our senses. His works, those of creation, the universe, the system of systems are, and the God of nature is, recognised through his attributes. It takes a refined mind to appreciate, a vulgar mind to deny, the existence of a God, that all nature most conclusively proclaims through the pure voice of philosophical science.

Leave out all but mind, and we see that that must be governed by principle, by the science of principle, without which the world is a blank; without both of which the universe would be chaos and confusion.

What is society? It is the bond and union of mind, that refers to the great principle essential to its good. All this should embrace the greatest good to the greatest number, that is all. This cannot be obtained without the highest appreciation and action for these principles, the highest of universal self-preservation.

And this question of society refers to virtue, and both to the comprehension of the universe. Virtue must be the proper, correct organization of society.

Why legalize marriage, why not pair off like a part of animated creation, if there be no God? The highest good of society must look to social order, law and constitutional rights, that are all included in religion, which comprehends the wisest economy of the universe. The best object is attained in best taste, by this process. The best good of society depends on the greatest mutual forbearance. The propagation of the species is a great law of nature, but with man it should be under all proper circumstances.

But for this, but for mind that belongs to the universe, prostitution had been tolerated. The love of the offspring is identified with their best protection most comprehensively, and as nature declares the position of legitimate action by the sexes being nearly balanced, virtuous marriage of the pair is proclaimed the immutable law of nature.

Grant the premises to the atheist or the polytheist, and the extremes of stultification are proved at once, and mind, the only beneficiary, is stripped of all that is desirable. Then there is no God, or as many fictions of gods as the imagination and speculation of man decide. Grant their premises that are begged, and anything can be proved, that principles utterly explode! The atheist recurs to spontaneous creation. to reach the noble creation of man. But as man is not now created, but procreated, if modest, he has to be silent, or give satisfactory proofs why the creation does not progress! Why not continue the same process as that of man, and in fact, all the rest? Here at once is an insuperable difficulty, for new creations should still be progressive, that would ultimately defeat the very object of creation! Polytheism and atheism thus wind themselves up, to be scouted by virtuous intelligence.

There is too much design in all creation, especially in man—mind and body, for mere nature to be the exalted only actor. She is the elaborated agent, representing a universe exponent of God. All other animated natures below man, declare a subserviency, a subordinate state. Mind is the head of all creation, and that mind was instituted by an institutor. Nature is only agent in acts of mind. She is not the actor. The body is moved as the mind directs. Rationality decides the question for all rational beings. The two great constituencies of man, mind and matter, decidedly demonstrate it. Mind elicits the truth from all the elements of nature of matter.

But objection is made by the rabid atheist, of God's attributes of his omnipresence. But how easily and better is that met, when we see that his principles, functions and attributes, preside over all space. He is the President over omnipresence, then. The bible of the polytheist, which is a caricature, makes atheists. The first has a peculiar god, of man's devices. The consequence is, that the atheist takes this peculiar abortion without analysis, and he is not believed in. When nature is assumed for all, then it is the ridiculous to mount to the sublime, for nature elaborated is only part of the whole comprehension, since we must go to the Supreme First Cause. But your mind O, atheist, is so constituted that you cannot see all the exact mathematical order and harmony in the solar system, then we will take you to one simple object. Whence the rays of the sun? They are effects. What produces them? You admit a cause, that necessarily leads in the principles of causation, if you understand logic, the rational use and meaning of language, to the Great First Cause. Whence he? That, now, introduces irrational mind to speculation, hypothesis and metaphysics, that belong to atheism and polytheism. but introduces rational mind to humility the most sincere, to stop there as the centre of all confidence, all love and adoration. The fool assumes there is no God, but the greatest fool assumes a partial God.

But atheism is clamorous for spontaneous generation, that produced man. Then why not continue the same?

Its position is gratuitous, and begs the question.

It is procreation that prevails, not spontaneous generation. But atheism says, the links of the whole first made an increasing order. Why do not those phenomena still exist? They do not, that is clear and final. A Supreme gives defined consummate order, symmetry, and organization of systems of systems, without whom the whole would be chaos and confusion—all disorder.

Whereas, how beautiful, how wise, and beneficent, the science of conservative principles.

We must speak of mind as it is, with its facts ; not as a God at present, but of created mind, that is to work out its own best problem of civilization and greatest happiness, on the elements and circumstances of its creation. Mind is necessarily limited, compared to God, and must have limited functions on this earth, the scene of its present action.

It has not mere specific limited scope, of exact but of liberal action—it is a free agent, under the circumstances of its existence. It is necessarily a creation, and must respond to all the organic laws of creation.

God, in giving mind its greatest range of free agency, has not created it a slave, but has enabled it to work out its own problem, and noblest elevation of character. Its created position and capacity of improvement must be respected, as the last leads to its nearest progressive approach to the perfection of its God.

Death is a mighty change of identity, and thus it has to progress through purification. The earthly action of mind refers to its merits or demerits, and involves the sublimest act of creation, its future existence.

Atheists advance all kinds of speculations—the extinction of globes of the Universe has been often spoken of. This is incredible to my mind, since neither their orbits are certain, nor the means to ascertain them. See the facts of the case in this history of the times.

A COMET ENDANGERING THE EARTH.—Southey, in his " Common Place Book,'" relates, that in A. D. 1712, Whiston predicted that the comet would appear on Wednesday, 14th October, at five minutes after five in the morning, and that the world would be destroyed by fire on the Friday following. His reputation was high, and the comet appeared. A number of persons got into boats and barges on the Thames, thinking the water the safest place. South Sea and India stock fell. A captain of a Dutch ship threw all his powder into the river, that the ship might not be endangered. At noon, after the comet had appeared, it is said that more than one hundred clergymen were ferried over to Lambeth, to request that proper prayers might be prepared, there being none in the church service. People believed that the day of judgment was at hand, and some acted on the belief, more as if some temporary evil was to be expected. On Thursday, more than 7,000 kept-mistresses were publicly married. There was a prodigious run on the bank ; Sir Gilbert Heathcote, at that time head director, issued orders to all the fire-offices in London, requiring them to keep a good look-out, and have a particular eye on the Bank of England.

Modesty becomes ignorance. We are bound in truth and honor, to the rights of mind, above all others. When some conjecture that mind is the result of electricity on the organs of the brain, an inefficient, unsatisfactory materialism is elicited. If the senses are organs to thought, thought is elicited—from an element, a God-endowed, individualized organization. The atheist assumes nature, and goes against rationality. Why should there be only a certain order in nature, when we see no creation that is arrested, and procreation progressive. Here are chaos and confusion at once.

Creation is assumed, for procreation. The God of Nature is its president—its organizer—its designer—and officiates in the highest attainable capacity.

When we look at mind as it is, on the facts of the case, the beautiful creation of the Universe is God's problem. Atheists may give an isolated, partial view, but they must embrace the comprehension of the whole. Have they done so?

To assert that there is nothing beyond nature, is to assume a dogmatism that betrays the character of mind.

The cotton plant helps the world to civilization ; that calls most for the whole people

to aid and assist each other. The mind, the most magnificent endowment of intelligence and adequate power—a creature of itself, of its intelligence—to promote its object,
takes hold of this one means, and carries out the mighty design. What is plain in one,
is so in all.

All the solar systems are in abeyance to one grand centre, the locality of supreme
purity, there abiding the Supreme First Cause. It is absolutely essential and necessary
to have a supervising head or ruler over the Universe, else chaos and confusion at once
ensue.

The Universe could not arrange itself into such admirable design.. By what principle
can the Sovereign of principles be excluded from the Universe, that reflects the conservation of those principles? Who heads those principles? Nature? She is commanded by them! This, at once, proves the position.

Can society organize itself, without principles? No. Refined civilization adopts the
best, for society. This proves mind. This is religion, in part, that binds us to our
duty to God and mind. All the multitudes of difficulties in the world are for mind to
overcome.

That was the object, the intention of Creation. But is that all? What less than the
Universe can be the wisest comprehension?

Polytheists and atheists have to assume positions, resort to imagination or fictions;
the rationalist is the only one that can stand the pure test of reason, standing on the
platform of facts.

The atheist and polytheist leave the world destitute of the highest principles.
What! no religion to God, that implies duty to man and society? Where would be the
standard, of so much importance to exclude polytheism and atheism? Mind must have
a standard, and that is in Deity. Polytheists have their miserable standards in idol fictions—atheists have theirs in idol imagination; both in false pretences, assumptions, and
positions. Whereas humility, acquiescence, is the order of rational mind generally, in
the Supreme standard, who is not a reckless dictator, but a law-giver of supreme immutable principles. How few understand logic, the use or true meaning of language.
Polytheist, trinitarian, or unitarian, how can you successfully combat or defeat the
atheist, but on the grounds of rationalism? Without ratiocination, you can do nothing
with him.

Are you going to use him otherwise? But you are classed necessarily together, on
the pure principles of ratiocination.

The systems of the universe are relative to each other, as those spheres of one solar
system.

All things are made impossible with God, the converse of his attributes and principles, both with himself and his creation. The function of nature is procreation; of
God, is creation. Here, atheist, is enough to silence you, and all polytheists. As we
can only appreciate the God of nature by his attributes, we all have to look to him as
the standard of the universe, for greatness and dignity. Mind, is to get right; to do
all things rightly, under the direction of science; all of which is needing in the world.
But who directs that mind? Who has originated that science? Come by nature!
Has nature such intelligence? The beauty of it is, that rational religion, our position,
cuts down at the same blow the atheist, polytheist, dogmatist, trinitarian, or unitarian.
In what, polytheist, do you differ from the atheist? The last robs God entirely of existence and attributes, the universe of principles, while you only rob them in the best
part, and insult God about his imbecility.

You have murdered all, by your peculiar faith.

Change speedily, all of you, the errors of your ways, that will bear witness
against you.

But electricity acts on mind, and elicits thought, but what causes mind to originate
thought; that shows something beyond materialism, good atheist?

But how do I estimate the monotheist? As all mankind, by his actions. If a fellow
calls himself even deist, and becomes a tool of tools, untruthful and unprincipled, breaks
his pledges made to temperance societies, I consider him the lowest of the low, unworthy to a great extent of the countenance of monotheism, that still protects him.

Why so many ancient atheists? Because the light of civilization, of astronomy, had
not taught the organization of the universe; and of course all polytheisms, as trinities,
are partial atheisms, and produce equally bad morals and social results. Whether
atheist or polytheist, names are nothing. All that are right will seek to be tried by the
proper court of conscience, and respect the righteous verdict of rational religion.

Mind is compelled to observe the works of creation, and estimate the Creator from
their organization and regulation, to the amount of its acquisition of science and philosophy; as in the days of Moses' bible, or that of the priestocracy, the people had ideas of

a little peculiar god that was so unsatisfactory to them that they sought after other peculiar gods. The priestocracy would not let them be rightly directed to the perfect God of the universe.

In the days of rational mind they have excellent ideas of this God of the universe, the Supreme First Cause who regulates its organization, and rules by conservative principles, being the soul-guardian.

All other views than a creation of nature, leave the mind in woful ignorance. That it was created, the book of geology, one of the leaves of God's volume, the world, furnishes distinct epochs as distinct proofs. The first was creation for vegetation, then animalization.

Now, where creation ceases, generation or pro-creation commences. Here the Almighty is self-evident to draw the ineffaceable line of demarkation, that rules out atheists and polytheists, by the last of whom was the conspicuous positive error of afterthought priestocracies, who conceived of covenants and messiahs, that were necessarily too late.

Original creation had ceased, and the only pro-creation was a mortal function, and all the results were necessarily mortal.

When God created and organized matter, he instituted conservative principles, for physical, mental, moral, and religious providence, universally and especially. These principles supersede the use of angels on earth, vicegerents or devils, and this destroys all the pretended functions of the priestocracy, who have foisted and palmed themselves on mind, the people, the world.

God, a perfect being, and having his residence in the centre and soul of purity, a perfectly pure place, where abide pure organizations of just rational beings, sin, an impurity, could not enter nor tempt, much less corrupt angels, much less archangels to devils. All these are fictions, unknown to rational mind. God was too good, my reverence tells me, to originate devils. The nearest to it is mind perverted in its free agency, limited to the circumstances of providence and perverted in various degrees of corruption and degradation. Mind is, as God created it, still rational, and capable in that position of enacting religion. Mind helps mind, that can help itself, and abjures bigotry.

What is the difficulty about the facts of monotheism? Partial appreciation may be a simple denial of messiahship and all such corrupt appurtenances, without any active participation in the duties of rational religion; such is mere passiveness. Monotheism is founded on the noblest reverence of the Creator, who must, by its pure tenets, have full adoration in his own right. She has objection to individuals only, because they are unprincipled, while she gives all minds her best and loveliest, holiest influence. This they may be, whether atheist or polytheist. The unprincipled of the world avoid being religiously improved.

It is the interest of the world, as it is the intention of Deity, to successfully adopt all that will promote principles and merit.

Nature is nothing but a consistent elaborate organization, proving the God of nature.

Its sublime harmony and order excite our adoration for him ; but the brightest organization of all, the soul, demands it as a duty supreme on the supremacy of principles, and the sublimest feeling of gratitude.

How much of the world is unprincipled, dishonest, without veracity ? When once the mind gets to this, there is little or no hope for adequate reformation. Unprincipled people are those that throw off all restraint of principle, and in all this the world is most vitally concerned. Actions and motives draw the proper line of distinction. There is such a vast dereliction in all these, that the unsophisticated mind believes that there is but little of the essence of rational religion governing them. This appeals not to the liberality, but the high-toned justice of all dogmatists. An atheist must see that we are obliged to be certain, in all the positions and deductions of the right premises. The universe is a system of systems, of cause and effect, referable to the supreme First Cause, in which there is one universal adaptation, that bespeaks the highest order of design of a universal President.

The atheist might continue a monomaniac as he is, while the polytheist that knows what he is talking of, may be a hypocrite or affected dupe, but the highest sense of religion bespeaks the highest interest in the numerous victims to the world's custom and fashion.

What principles then, are in atheism and polytheism, in the sight of their miserable world-pollutions and demoralizations ?

Analysis under the glorious and benign influence of monotheism, resolves all things into their first elements and principles that are essentially good, not to the original chaos, but where civilized man is or can be, and plants in the highest religion.

Yet the people are afraid to advance in conservative revolution. There is no latitude for monotheism, as it is indissolubly bound to principles, those of Almighty God. None can violate them and claim to be monotheists, whatever else they be. All the vices of creeds, are those of anti-god. If you speak truly as wise analysts of the world's injuries, you will admit all this.

He who recognises no God in the organization of one solar system, has no rational mind. He who does not recognise that mind to be the most endeared of all to the Creator, has no improved morals or religion, has no gratitude for the Almighty in his perfection, caring for all, and sufficient for the preservation of all.

Mind originates the idea of a God, proved by the Indians ; however, like all nations, it is mixed up with interloping pretenders, priestocracies. None can surpass their unadulterated integrity, before it is corrupted by the contact of pretended superiority of other people, like the unique beauty of monotheism, that gives the purity of religion. Mind could not originate less than the idea of a Deity, if it respects the truths of creation.

The order, harmony, unity of design, exact mathematical adjustment of the system of systems, the universe, proves a Creator.

Man's organization proves that in full.

We can only get access to mind through reason, as rational beings, by a rational religion, to the most rational God.

If we analyze chance, destiny, fortune, nature, however hard to define apparently, they must come under the definitions of order or arrangement, that will not benefit the atheist, as all have due respect to rational rights, all in abeyance to mind and reason, truth and God.

What, atheist, can you be thinking of about all these, that must be ruled, or ruin, if chaos rules ? The powers universal of creation, as electricity and gravitation, must be under creative intellect, else they might shiver the universe into fragments. All such must be controlled by an Almighty Ruler, Organizer, on the best conservative principles.

What are the properties of matter worth, if not most wisely directed ? Who but the Creator of the universe, can most wisely comprehend all ?

But you affect to criticize God's designs, yet libel them in your ignorance. They are all placed under the cognizance of universal principles, that must rule. Many are apparently unfortunate by the force of circumstances, that, if not carried out, might have rendered the results more deplorable. The philosophical monotheist will perceive that mind is too short-sighted to arraign God.

The polytheist should not be a bigot on irrational grounds, about his preconceived or peculiarly taught faith, that cannot possibly require actions self-sacrificed. Will bigots sacrifice themselves to a foolish faith ? The world can get no fair proposition from bigots. They do not adopt a rational, but sectarian position.

With them, everything bends to their peculiar faith, everything is peculiar ; all is distorted through that distorted and unfortunate medium.

The atheist seeks to be a moralist, and criticises the perfection of Deity. If the Principal of the universe is not correctly characterized, he is bound by all just and honorable principles to do them justice, or be silent in his utter incapacity of amendment.

Among the caricatures of character the polytheist is wofully amenable, when he adopts a bible that impeaches itself for such gross misconceptions, as God producing evil. God does not create evil. Mind is not evil, no more than the universe—all were intended for good and the benefit of souls. The very universe or creation implies that all have conservative principles, but if they be perverted or changed, the reverse is destructive principles, or the self-vindication of conservative principles of God, for their abuse by mind.

Only think of the sublime conceptions that balanced one solar system with another, and suspend all the universe in space. All the little peculiar petty sectarianism of polytheism or atheism, precludes the right conception of God, of sublime things even, by bringing mind to their little petty area of their peculiar earth. God is the only infallible standard, and he can only be known through his creation.

Nature alone gives us no standard as she is only creative agent, a mere creature, and this proves conclusively the supremacy of the head.

Silence, atheists, most becomes your petty misconceptions. But forced from nature and the universe, you object to the present position of things, as an effort to find fault if not to correct them. You object to him who has caused this. But you are silenced then in the wisest of all beings, and of course in all. But you persist, not appreciating your defeat. You object to excess of water over land.

Are you at all right, there ? The whole creation is not amenable to your criticism.

The mighty water brings you pleasurable temperature, delightful breezes, most expansive commerce, the amplest treasures of the deep, the most fertilizing productions of land, to feed or employ the most numerous multitudes. Nothing is made in vain: it is all right.

The idea of the God of nature irresistibly arises, from the positive organizations of matter. Legitimate free agency, perversions of mind and responsibility, surely accompany mind on this earth.

Do you not recognise relative free agency in punishment? Certainly. Then you are completely wound up.

The soundest reason not only produces the highest conception of God, but endows him as the most sublime, the supreme.

But licentiousness is greater in deism. That is, deism destitute of principles. But what is any profession, destitute of principles? The world cannot recognise any such in monotheism.

Let honesty and truth prevail in all that is worthy.

You cannot convict monotheism of destitution of principles. She is actually certain of God Almighty.

You must either take nature, or the president, organizer and creator. What else, atheist, is there that you can take? Nothing. Then if you take nature you adopt a partial cause, vague and most unsatisfactory, because it is an effect referable to cause, an organic agent. Your partial decision condemns you, as you affirm the principle of causation by your position.

The highest good sense enjoins your adoption of the Great First Cause, whereby we comprehend power as with nature, and all the intelligence of omniscience identified, that nature alone cannot have. This comprehends the only wise position, cause and effect, the actor and agent.

But here come in questions of universe character, as what is space? Where is the limit? This is an organic question, that carries mind to the organizer, the centre of all. When the universe alone solves the whole question, it is not to be expected that all the main points can ever be met in this state of mind. The soul will have to meet the highest, after its elaborate and protracted analysis. Every thing, every class, bespeaks the necessity of principle, a rule, system above all, a head.

When a man, atheist or not, comes to have thoughts, words or deeds, disrespectful of Deity, he sinks below the brute. As in our constitutional government, mind that violently plots treason thereto, is unworthy the respect of mind.

Roll on, countless orbs, countless to man, in the immensity of space, immense to him, and humble him by thy numbers, and convince him by the light of those so distant, that are just hailed for the first time since creation.

Ye can demonstrate beyond cavil, his sublimity, the genius property of Deity!

But minds of congenial reason, need not leave this planet.

What beautiful, philosophical, mighty powers of atmosphere! What could have caused them in nature, without the supreme soul of intelligence? Elaborated nature is the universe, that was created by the exercise of the highest functions of creative intellectuality, and has to be thus appreciated by mortals? The main question is not the how and where of Deity's creation, but the utter incompetency of the atheist to reason on them. This department is in that of religion, not in atheism.

The great standard of Deity in his perfect unity, and his universal elaborated nature, puts down atheism as a dream, as well as polytheism, more libels than inquiries. The universal character of God is written in action—works. We cannot see nature alone, without Deity.

Could the ancients ever have conceived of the universe, and of the sublime laws of its system of gravitation? Of its sublime author, and of his sublime system of rational religion, that as much exceeds all other systems of faith, as light of days does that of night, as Deity does that of mortals, to whom monotheism, the safest, in most trust-worthy confidence imparts its sublimity by practical operations in the soul, mind, by morals and religion without profession, itself the sublime provision to the soul, the execution of a God, not needing but excluding peculiar proclamations of the priestocracy.

And how beneficent the provision, when all christs as messiahs are self-condemned as begotten and positively mortal, as the function of all procreation is mortal. God's is creation, not procreation. Physiology decides the question, and expels this abominable libel of human lewdness from all pure minds. What is the atonement worth? It is a pious fraud; the least that can be said of it is, that it is disgustingly mercenary.

Regeneration or the new birth, the new heart, is as worthless, as the doctrine of miracles, prophecies or mysteries. But in monotheism there is a certain platform for all the faith of religion, that recognises the conservative laws of universal principles.

Comprehend Deity, atheist. First comprehend his universe. Know that each sun in his own solar system cannot be eclipsed by the universe of suns, nor its gravitation unbalanced. Think, then, of the eclipsing character of their Author.

Say what you will, you have to acknowledge the organization of the universe, and that demonstrates, gives full proof of its organizer, the creator, the Great First Cause. But a mighty war has been waged upon the religion of principles ; all the supposed highest authorities have been adduced to militate against it. "As to Deism," says Patrick Henry, quoted in Wirt's Sketches, "The view which the rising greatness of our country presents to my eyes, is greatly tarnished by the general prevalence of deism, which, with me, is but another name for vice and depravity." And this was the illustrious patriot and orator, the honored Henry, who at the time this sentiment was uttered was giving the noblest expression of rational religion, under the cover of another faith ! otherwise, that very view was antagonistic to principles that triumph for ever. If deism reflect principles, she is libelled with any such view.

For want of comprehensive analysis, vindication of principles is not satisfactory. The question is grossly misunderstood. It is difficult to decide which would be worse, the demoralization of bibles of tradition, or the vices of pretended deism, for the conservative principles of deism, or monotheism, permit no such thing as licentiousness. That is impossible. The fault is in man. One of the great principles of monotheism is to combat the licentiousness of all peculiar faiths, busied in upsetting the very principles of religion in libels of Deity himself. Revolutions that are conservative never go back. Now monotheism will meet the purest views of the purest mind, and confront it as prepared soul-organization to enjoy its reward of the highest order, with its God. She is without blemish, and is the production of God himself.

Where can we go amiss, to trace the First Great Cause? Where there is no effect, that is, nowhere. Look at any point, and the best appreciation will demonstrate its appropriate organization and functions, be it the minutest microscopic atom, or the most enlarged orb. See the mighty revolutions of the atmosphere, that so admirably fills all its departments. All creation does that, how much more does its Creator? Pettifoggers of mind, ye know not what God is, in your trifling cavils that disgrace you. The paramount proof of God, is the almighty organization of creation, whose unity is demonstrated by its conservation in the unity of design, which excludes and annihilates atheism and polytheism or trinities.

From my sincere conviction and deepest reverence of Deity, and respect to rational, his ordained religion, I cannot believe in any bibles of tradition, however plausible, given by any priestocracy, in the face of this universal sublime proof. Of course all their prophecies and miracles to prop up such pretences for man's least works, are the worst of humbugs. Who and what are antagonistic to facts of nature? Who but the priestocracy and their special peculiar bibles, that have various translations and interpretations modified by the mirror of time.

But all of priestocracy are most suspicious, and not trustworthy. All their designs were most corrupt, for temporal despotism, all they could get. Monotheism, that enlighteneth the world while she purifies it, civilizes nations, and proves herself a superior power that offers best rules for creation. She recognises the planets and suns, all the systems of systems to move in harmonious order, to organic laws that premise nature for nature's God. She reflects the moral organism, dependent on eternal principles that cannot be shaken, confirmed as it is by being total and exclusive property of her President.

But how wicked are some deists? They that are unprincipled, no matter of what profession, are base. But are the principles of deism in its purity, that of excellent monotheism, untenable? That's the question, for if they are demonstrable, from that moment I renounce all such. But that is utterly impossible, for she is the religion of principles, and the fault lies in the minds of cavilers, not critics, sophists, not philosophers. Were there any numbers of deists or monotheists who were to think previously and maturely on this subject of religion, they would all come on comparison of notes to the same primary essential conclusions of the unity of the existence and design of one Supreme. What less than principle could cause them thus to be supremely right? Deism then reflects principles that guide the world. What is wrong, then, in it? No mortal can reach higher than principles. But peculiar faiths differ essentially the world over, so much so, that the world's peace has been disturbed nearly all the time. All such have no principles, but what are essential to the very thing that they all traduce. What is wrong in them? They are all wrong. Religion must take in all minds, whether they assent to the name or not. Now peculiar faith never can take in rational mind that ought to be universal.

The world needs the want of moral and religious codes to carry the whole for unity.

Dogmatists, did you never violate all this ; prevent mind by this bigoted vice, while you sophiscated all practicable ? Faithites, you deprive yourselves of your own moral power, otherwise of religious influence.

You produce wholesale evils of peculiar faith and doctrines, earth's despotisms.

As to atheists and polytheists of all classes of peculiar faith, they have to become rationalists to reach the proper appreciation of God, the Creator. Mind needs a code to rule out and govern all such bigoted dogmatists.

Polytheism debauches mind, from the purest character of philosophy and science.

The animal materialism of the atheist that consigns the soul to animal mortality, comes into woful conflict with the justice of his God. How could he diminish the intrinsic worth of soul-materialism ? It is his sophistry, that affects undisciplined mind. What is his position ? It does not matter whether his faith or belief is acknowledged as any thing at all ; he has an existence that depends necessarily on principles, to which he is amenable for all that existence involves, now responsible for a certain amount, and that tells the whole tale, proclaiming unmistakable universal facts.

Now, his verbal faith is not to be the base means for his abominations and bloody deeds. His mind is to be used for weal or wo ; if not adverse to himself, it may be to billions of his race. He is a member of the universe society, and owes supreme allegiance to its best conservative principles.

If he cannot get his own wayward assent to his dreams, he is bound to advance only facts and their benefits. He affects to speak of nature, which is but an illustration of laws and elaborations emanating from the Supreme, and stop miserably short of the comprehension of the whole subject. So does the Polytheist who dwarfs the God of the universe boundless to him by his petty bible, and pretends that he has analyzed the subject, when he has not touched it at all. I criticise no effort of mind, for such praiseworthy attempt at analysis, is the very thing I seek, but for the pitiful pretences offered for that analysis. Their sophistry makes all such, God-libellers. The polytheist does not even talk of that God, but has booked a miserable apology, an abortion most rickety of a peculiar character, heathen and barbarian, for the sublime, supreme, with true effrontery of graceless priestocracy. The truth, the whole truth and nothing but the truth, in giving all that is liberal, from first of Genesis to Apocrypha, prove it all Apocrypha, and that there is no confidence in such pretended prophecy. Instead of proper analysis, the sophisticated priestocracy give all the go by. It was bad to see such from the ancients ; it is horrible to have it from the moderns.

One of the great objections to Deism is, that some Deists have been afraid by legal causes and social proscriptions, from telling the whole truth. I have not to cite the errors of deists against deism, a self-evident principle, but to investigate the facts of the case, difficult as it may be, pure Monotheism, which is not responsible for the errors, omissions and commissions of her advocates. The reign of terror, as that of atheism in France, is alien to Monotheism in every sense, as she contemns despotism of numbers and names assumed as sacred. Many points will be urged trivial in objections to the deist, but of no moment to overthrow deism, much less Monotheism that is thoroughgoing in principles, by the side of which dogmatic polytheism and atheism cannot stand. It is a virtue and religion to deny what is not in existence, but both are inequent in refusing a just appreciation to what is. That is their look-out, and con-signs them to their scale.

But the attention of the world is arrested at the charge of licentiousness of deism. If this be inherent, deism as all other illegitimate isms, ought to be silenced. But where can an iota of this accusation be laid ? By what fair means can it be properly sustained ?

Where can licentiousness grow up in Monotheism, that recognises all wisdom of all is predicated on their just principles, and seeks to correct the first by the last, by conservative, not reckless, bloody revolution. She breathes in the atmosphere of principles that never clash. It is she that defines the legitimate scope to all the vindictive passions of human nature. As rational religion, she is the concomitant of all minds, speaking attendance on thought, words and action, while peculiar faith, the noisy usurper allied to despots, has no such function. It is she that bestows the wisdom conservative of mind's own reflection. In her boon of universal brotherhood, all nations in safety universal, the largest honored in the bestowal, the smallest in the reception, while all are more or less equalized by her international continental unions. She considers all this time and all eternity, the amplest adequate protection for vitality of humanity, physically, mentally, morally, and best of all, religiously. With such a benign radiance that proves nothing less than God, can the atheist or polytheist exist any longer on their own pure ratiocinations of rationality, however deluded they had been by futile minds and their more imbecile books, when they rightly observe the influence of supreme light in general adaptation of means to the universal benefit of curtailing life to the present limit, thereby preventing excess of errors and power, the overwhelming accumulation of wealth, and its potent influence growing up in a few centuries, redundance of population dangerous to morals and vital enjoyment?

Turn where they will, this universal supremacy of intelligence and wisdom, superlative magnificence is conspicuous. All this is right, and of course the dogmatists are wrong.

Nature a God, atheist? You a part, represent her; are you a God? The defect is in your mind, by your abuse of reason. You have mistaken the work for the workman, the functions for the functionary.

Atheists affect that they have no God, yet they give all the functions to nature. They idolize the work, rather the conceits of their own opinions. But conceits nor opinions will answer in this most momentous subject. If the universal navigator is not invariably rightly governed by the universal chart, he will encounter breakers that may dash him and billions of compeers to atoms and ruin.

But polytheists have a peculiar god, whom they appropriate to their petty bible notions, and make consequently peculiarly imperfect. This has been the case with Jew and Gentile, who have entertained their peculiar notions. There is no essential difference between these two classes, as both are followers of their whims and notions, mere dogmatists. But the monotheists cannot permit themselves thus to act, for they have to read through cause and effect, to the final effect, the universe, and the Great First Cause, who is perfect and unadulterated, unmixed and perfectly pure.

Bible advocates have pretended to tell the world of the recantation of some dying free-thinkers, deists, who of course were of doubtful veracity, no matter on which side they were. But have they told us of the other side, that is in the majority against them, of course? Do they know, independent of notions, that principles are right, and that they are worth all the balance, and above all, are against them? But they pretend to claim mighty things about creation, because a book they call the bible, speaks about a creation which is evidently the fiction of man, and very ignorant and unprincipled at that, who of course violated all the principles of religion, truth, honesty and faith, in palming it on the world for anything.

The leaf of geology, one of God's books, proves facts of creation, difference in time of creation through the various strata, that make all such the modern pretences of the day. All the volumes of his book demonstrate all such black-letter affairs, as the most stupid and felon-blasphemies of the world, with which all rationalists are disgusted to nauseousness. The principles of Monotheism rule out entirely, all the doctrines of atheists and polytheists, but do not exile them from the whole people with whom she incorporates them all in all the noblest. She overlooks their follies, when she credits them as part of creation. She enables them to make as wise people, proper capital, and to give her all just and meritorious credit for their best duties.

The polytheist, from the crude notions of dark ages, made gods of the elements, whereas the atheist took, as he supposed, nature, earth, or what was apparent. Both are bigots, and took the effect for the cause, being undisciplined in rational science, and their bigotry confines them with false pride. Nature bespeaks an elaborate organization, and is self-evident by the finale to all creation, for the cause that generated in nature cannot be limited if once thus set agoing.

If man had spontaneous production, why is it not continued? All this idea was most vaguely conceived of nature as an independent existence at first, and has been preserved by correlative ignorance and want of analysis. When the term nature was used, language was indefinite, and analysis was paralyzed. Now nature cannot be less than the universe elaborated, which is clearly organized, and that defines the atheist to be completely ruled out. The worst of all is, that religious education is exiled from youth, that are nurtured in loose morals, from which emanates depraved and bad deportment at last. But the polytheist, by reason of the court favors of despotism, of royalty, and vitiated public opinion, mind-factured, affects to know and dictate all about this. He is the self-appointed guardian of the world, morals, and faith, and rules with the dictation of Sir Oracle, as he is, but a peculiar one, like his ancient brethren the soothsayers and augurs, his equals in untruth, effrontery, and popular imposition. Has the polytheist a conscientious adoption of rational religion? Mind most rational can appreciate by virtue of an efficient police over a mighty city, of a constitutional government over a vast people, that of religious police over the world and the universe. Then religion, the most efficient of all constitutional government by reason of its principles, functions, and attributes, cannot be divested from the universe by dogmatists, whether atheists or polytheists.

How could the ancients, as Moses, Christ, &c., be able to give a proper religious code, when they violated the principles of the universe, which they all, that is, their dramatic priestocracy, did not know, as proved clearly, most conclusively?

But the worst appropriation of religious and mental capital is by peculiar faith. Their advocates talk about the religious improvement of the world, as if it all emanated from Christianity. Now they should not libel mind and its rational, which is nothing less than religious improvement. That is only religion that takes hold of it in the right way by the right means. It gives me pleasure to accord to Christians as Jews, Mahommedans as Mormons, all that they are entitled to in religion, and that is pre-eminently monotheism.

In taking leave of this subject, it would be well to premise distinctions of mind and soul—materialism, and what is animal exclusively. Among the plausible sophistries about matter not being added to or diminished, the line of analysis must be drawn as to the universe mass, all matter, and its parts and components. The earth receives rays of universal light, dispensed by the suns of other systems, or universe suns. Is that any limit to universal means? And is not the soul above all such? The atheist, as polytheist, will have to be more schooled in the depths of philosophy ere they can make a decent showing against monotheism; but ere that, they can avail themselves best of its reflective light to irradiate their own deluded and benighted souls.

This is an inquiring, and it is to be hoped, a just age, and all that is now needed is for mind, in its best lights, to do full and ample justice to itself, in order to settle this question forever.

MIND.

What a fine thing it is to have a mind well cultivated, and possessed of all its native richness, having therefrom an inexhaustible fund for self-possession, enjoyment and satisfaction, for the possessor to have an independent and inexhaustible resource in all trying vicissitudes of woes, sorrows, and oppressions, to rise superior to all temptations, ever giving due glory to the Creator, ever competent to solve all the world problems, essential to prospective welfare.

The majesty of cultivated sound intellect, that best represents Deity, also represents man's duties and ethics, and embraces legislative, judicial, and executive responsibility. Such creates the downfall of all peculiar feudal systems, ever prevalent in all ages where mind and philosophical science are not justly represented.

An independent mind is all important to the world. The noble resolves of an independent mind bespeak the manly action, its inherent right and duty, in obedience to reason at all times, conservative of what is just, no matter how recent or novel, antagonistic and resistant to all however imposing by authority, that is evil, if enlightened and conservative to itself of rectitude.

The mighty object of all such minds, so constituted, should be to counteract the intolerant and bigoted fanaticism that interferes with the restoration of order and general brotherhood throughout the world.

This state of mind bespeaks high knowledge of what mind itself is capable by analogous review of past weakness, and criminal outrages in numerous modes disgusting to it, enlightened and raised to its elevated scale of reason.

In all ages, and in much of social intercourse, the weakness, follies and vices of mind have prevailed, under an odious feudalism, in all departments too where mind should be free and act independently.

From martial despotism to assuming criticism, this tyranny over mind is sought to be perpetrated.

When mind is brought properly to examine correctly for itself in the funds of cultivation, uninfluenced by any prejudice or improper motive, into the matured code of systems and principles all sooner or later practicable, then its universal assent will expedite what is so highly necessary to general welfare; and then, as wisdom increases, purity and independence of mind will necessarily increase and elevate themselves to a just position.

The intelligence and reason of mind are forever its best sentinels for its freedom, religion, and happiness.

By such position mind is valid to expose and rule out all hostile to its best interests and well-being.

Sound future improvement is thus premised as a necessary result on the proper operations of mind.

The excellence of mind is indispensable and invaluable for the best fruition of the present and future.

Man's best duty and highest intellectual action are a just appreciation of Deity's attributes.

This presents a fundamental starting point, that corrects much of fatal future deeds. This position is indispensable to give a correct and sincere faith, that none can ever renounce, but all must entertain with the highest exultation and hope.

It is the essence of wisdom, the triumph of mind, the purity of philosophy, the glory of religion.

None can recant unless mind subsequently becomes deluded, and reason is lost.

Man's duty is identified with commission and omission, that involve mind and reason in all transactions in the performance of good and avoidance of evil actions, words, and thoughts.

The beauty and strength of this doctrine are, its capacity complete to present to the world, in the full recognition of mind, true definition and apprehension of the subject, its moral good and bearing, its resulting blessing, the honesty of human nature, as far as the best can rest on the supreme effect of an absolutely identified and exclusive Creator.

This doctrine does away with all the elements of antagonism; ever willing to be right, it refuses no tuition for correction, and no correction for exaltation.

The reform of the world is progressive improvement, varied but increasing in the hands of Deity, that embraces all his potent agencies and energies.

All these, man should ever seek, with due humility, to analyze, not libel any of God's acts, by miserable views and assumptions of God's character; by his own botch-work and tinkering, seeking to correct a world of God's elaboration, and thus ignobly becoming amenable to self-impeachment in his own weak and erroneous impressions and perceptions. The first part of exalted religion was mind's humility and appropriate confidence in God.

Man's part is to begin rightly, with humble and modest but just inquiry, and refer the end and accomplishment to the Supreme, with the most liberal conception of God's universal power and virtues.

Nothing sectarian or bigoted, nor ever contracted; nothing short of fair and liberal investigation of both and all sides of all questions, to arrive at truth, rational and just, should cross his path, to build up a creed or faith correspondent, that will necessarily decay sooner or later, be the delusion popular or fanciful.

This is to be the platform of principles, whose comprehension is as extensive as the universe, as desirable as time to eternity, as conservative and universal as God's attributes, that are to be the only standard; for none other is genuine, or can exist!

Unless man adopts such, all will be vain in his short-sightedness, with improper, deficient, antagonistic. peculiar faith, that leads to idolatrous devotion or man-worship; that poisons mind and all its true sources of legitimate enjoyment; all which can never enter into true faith, recognised by mind, in its enlightened reason.

Amidst the toil of circumstances arises triumphant mind, secured a worthy government of true principles, for the toleration and direction of one's own opinions and rightful actions, with a freedom of discussion, a righteous decision, a fearless assertion of manly dignity for true religion, a proper devotion to the Almighty; that all wise and true-minded freemen will acknowledge and duly reverence, as a proper construction of duty.

Intellectual freedom of mind enables it to analyze, with the justest obligation, any doctrine, to discard any or all points that enlightened reason revolts at, without being libelled and classed with any others, than those who seek to maintain the noblest character and principles of true religion.

These are American rights and freedom's blessings, hostile to none but the enemies of God, and the deceivers of mind.

The enlightened mind of the world will shake off the vassal shackles of ignorance and superstition, and adhere to no custom not sanctioned by reason and justice.

The mind, of a liberal education, attains the height of its capacity.

No matter where mind exists, it is distinguished, guided, moulded, modified, characterized, and protected by liberal education, that is one of the holiest principles of monotheism.

Then the question very rightly settles upon no locality, creed, or platform of crude opinions; no inquisition, bigotry, fanaticism, dogma, nor assumption of temporal power, no exclusive divine rights, nothing peculiar, no expounder for the principles or thing expounded, but on a proper education fund at the right time, to give forethoughts ever, not look foolishly at impotent afterthoughts; to promote mind's right cultivation, to render it well balanced and self-sustaining, pure as to the past, innocent in all, fully stored for present and future demands, for all life's drafts in its immortal treasury!

The great and vital question is, is mind invaluable, competent and able to wrestle with the gigantic conflicts in life with all the varied powers successfully and triumph-

... .;.—M.nd. that has been so grossly imposed upon for thousands of years, and cheated by all antagonistic dynasties ?

Its panoply is in principles, that it must know how and when to use. It must give its own works, not peculiar faith, which is mere credulity that belongs not to the secret recesses of the immortal soul.

This is the paramount question for mind to consider all the time, and to reach. There can be none more important.

Then if mind has not made a right start, having right views, when conviction flashes with its vivid light, it must and will repent of time misspent, of faith misunderstood and misapplied, and of actions misdirected.

If untrammeled, as all mind should be forever, only aided by sound suggestions, it will seek its own best correction in referring as the most holy offering of its vows, its petitions and purity, its best actions to God, the only object of its adoration as witness.

The seal is by its best deeds and its most comprehensive duties, as its chastest designs, and the permanent resolution of its hopes and its just faith in him that only saves.

The light of one mind thus endowed and inspired reflects honor on mind, enabling the mass to become enlightened and rejoice, and gives an impulse irresistible to every age .. bound, on correct principles, to advance with firm and tenacious hold on the en- .... ned steps of its predecessor.

Great as every age of mind thus illumined, the future must be more so, if it be wise. Liberal education takes away mind's trammels, remnants of dark ages, the vassal .... that enslaves and darkens, and the glory of mind proclaims itself to the world.

The world has been most debased by tyranny of mind perverted in all the quagmires of superstition.

But brilliant lights of mind are bursting forth by the powers of liberal education, that frees mind enslaved by despotism of bigotry and superstition.

IN MIND'S PURPOSE;

Mind has to tower over all its obstacles to be itself.

In the world's school mind has to grapple, and on the world's theatre it has to declare its independence, and never be contracted to an odious localized existence.

A correct history of mind's analysis will show it, next the mighty potentate of the universe, rising forever to a higher sphere of greatness and happiness, with its progress through almost insuperable difficulties, that conquered, build up its tower, advancing to interminable elevation, to its future refinement, worthy of greater and advancing promise,—the end the means—the means self-generating.

In feudal times, only more obsequious than the present, when castellated towers gave earnest of the best protection to the mass circle, mind became menial, and individual liberty was merged into strong necessity and force.

Then was it that martial prowess was apparently omnipotent, and the iron weapons subdued the mental.

But all such games of life, too serious to be played with, showed the temporary defeat of mind.

The present age cannot plead such ignominy, unless by its own consent. Then it is a degrading step, when light shows the iniquity thereof.

Now victories of mind are the only ones of value, fortified by moral and religious fortitude.

Those of brute force are allied to neither worth or character before the author of evil.

The first are sublimated by purity : the last are degraded and sunk by evil results.

The duel and rencontre were decreed once, by the vices of past ages, the mighty tributes of correct decision, but now are never needed in a just and righteous cause.

How often have they been designed, and malicious assassinations, made so by all pre-meditated intentions and false pretences, from skilful use of arms and superior adroitness ? The tables might be turned when weapons are proposed that equalize the parties, or if the bully is not skilled in the use of; or when it is fixed that as one is to be vic-timized that both should die the same death, or run equal risks at once ; best of all by righteous legislation, where principles declare the best avenging penalties.

When man, individually or in mass, sees that he is participant of danger as well as of others, that he can do nothing important wrong without conviction and exposure, and being deeply injurious with impunity, then he is not only made to pause in even his mad career, but is arrested in his execution of serious crimes, by the interposition of the wise statesman's best veto, next to enlightened public opinion.

This new regime of self-government, of order from the powers of order, weaves a chaplet to mind's power and character, and the purity of the age.

What supposed evil is there but has a counterbalancing good in the mighty potency of mind?

Then let mind be duly and rightly instructed in wisdom's lessons at the right time, and protected by all its best guardians, the right ægis of wise laws, intelligent customs, and well ordered society, then mind is nearest right of necessity.

Mind is right by knowledge, and so by necessity of habit, that is the nature of things, if not so by the highest influences.—Let all such be pure.

In the development of mental light, like man's age, many lights are nurtured to create an effulgent blaze for the vista of time previously dim to man, as mind must have enlightened mind to create the master genius.

Bright lights preceded to help to form such a master mind, that looked intellectually so high as to assert the Great First Cause, and acted so candidly to avow it in the face of tyrannical superstition forever disgraced by the rejection.

No light burst into magnificence so pure and great at once. Time, no less than mind, is to be examined and analyzed to secure the right recognition of the adequate advantages of both.

The history of nations who have advanced as the world has proceeded, step by step, teaches us to be rational and just, and to profit by the useful treasures of mind and time.

Centuries of time have advanced the development of principles to their proportionate mastery, until the mighty accumulations of light mutually irradiated each other.

Time and light have brought mind to a point actually outstripping recognised written land-marks.

The lesser luminaries are lost amid greater lights.

Under the best and safest views, then, mind has to act for itself rightly, circumspectly, and independently.

The mighty mastery of mind is conspicuously needed to avoid, in this sophisticated, humbugging world, all the varieties of forms and peculiar kinds of faith, and select that which accords with principles, which are to direct it, the beneficiary, to the true and safe issue.

A pure independence of cultivated mind is absolutely needed to protect the world from all its tricks, and all its degrading and grinding tyranny.

A want of it has engendered a peculiar faith, blinded to reason; and peculiar faith engenders a world of iniquity. Such faith is horrible, and ruinous to universal bliss of mind.

Many good citizens, seeing all professed peculiar faith so defective, believe in not even that of God, that is peremptorily necessary for the law of good morals, and the religion of principles, in the happiest management of mind.

Illustrious mind, aided by philosophical science, marks out to all the household, friends, relations, and citizens of the whole world, to reject unsafe pilotage over the many breakers of life, having character and nature not of the right stamp for universal brotherhood and power. Whatever mortal affects any other, is an impostor, and impiously discloses his character at once.

Any other than those of mind are counterfeits, that cannot pass current however much good is affected, and however sophistry, prating about faith, no more nor less than miserable credulity and superstition, delude their votaries.

It is time that mind, exalted to the lights of the present time, should assert its dignity, and claim its rights.

Down with the sophistry and pretences that thwart mind in possessing its own.

Of all the races of mankind reflecting God's innate principles, all individually must have paramount claim through mind, in degree at least.

All their claims to God's notice can only be by or through mind, man's guardian and vital pilot.

Mind can only be reflected on by science, which is knowledge and inspiration of God's conservative principles, an inspiration superior to miracles, prophecies and mysteries of all tradition bibles, whose writers are limited to the state of the times. All persons can only be reached by created mind, and mind can only be reached by and through reason, that of itself is built upon mind sound unto wisdom.

All successful tuition and missions are predicated on these principles and faculty.

Mind is the conservative for science, and can never be superseded by peculiar faith.

Its claims were established when existence commenced, and its value has increased as man's best consciousness and recognition have been awakened to its holy dignity.

It truly represents Deity, its creator, and exhorts to reason, its friend and patron.

The light of mind raised itself up over the dull glare of imperfect peculiar false faith, and triumphs over fanaticism and superstition, bigotry and sophistry.

Let mind go on untrammeled under its only proper inspiration from God, and it will do the balance.

Mind perverted is to be counteracted and prevented by mind enlightened and correct.

The fund of mind is inexhaustible, from the inexhaustible treasures of the universe, proving mind a free moral and religious agent.

Every honest mind has a direct diploma from God, to whom alone that mind is responsible, whilst every dishonest and untruthful mind has comparatively renounced it, and has lost the best part of its privilege of using this most invaluable capital.

Those who see that the support arises with the God of truth and mind, resort to no false paintings.

It is the true interest of mind not to be misled by the devices of hierarchy, fanaticism or false enthusiasm—any blind misleadings or delusions of others or of self, however fascinating or seducing.

Let all conservative principles have fair play, obscured by no pretences, assailed by no influences, then, even with silent revolution, immortal good results to mind aspiring to immortality.

Every proper incentive should be furnished for proper action, and no evil obstacle interposed.

Principles, and all that they command the world through, must come sooner or later into pla . Bad minds may and do pervert their order, but such men will be silenced finally. y

The paramount principles of Deity will decide for the whole, and acquiescence will be wisdom for universal protection and illustrious benefits too elevated to be lost, too commanding to be neglected.

Wise men appreciate penalties as well as rewards, consequently with the liberalized advance and improvement rightly begun, with correct habits fixed and matured, a properly self-sustaining mind, their progress must be upwards and onwards.

The supposed weakness of the popular mass results too much from excessive confidence in the circle of mind, perverted and too apt to deceive them.

Profession of peculiar faith, and not that of principles, makes no difference. when latitude of power permits. All mankind must be tested, on fullest experience. Profession is a siren spirit, that has preyed on every age.

The people have the inherent means of correction amply in their own hands, if they will analyze truly that condition, and exclude the base factions hostile to them, when self-aggrandizement is the object.

The severest rebuke, the most effectual restraint on all the petty tyrants of society and of the world exists with the enlightened people, who should always make their country too hot to hold any species of absolutism.

Who can fear where facts omnipotent prevail, for the result must be happy, as all the good-minded, if unimpeded, will proceed to the right point.

The true shepherds are needed, as tyrants of all grades consider the mass like sheep or bees, obliged to follow leaders, who are too often misled by others!

The popular mass needs confidence in themselves, and much more in principles, their best protectors.

Their leaders are principles, not men above principles.

Cunning and designing men practice all kinds of deceit to get the people's confidence.

Such men are unworthy of it, thereby proving clearly their calibre.

Of course men, mere hacks when they assume to be what they are not, as proved by their course, cannot be repulsed and discarded too soon by the people. While the towering minds of the world feel above such intrigues, and rest on their talents and the principles that they respect!

Their virtues must descend, to be commemorated in their country's annals.

Mind of proper organization and natural endowments, having brains or organs expansive in depth and breadth, well balanced by judgment, conscience and will, able to impart much competent analysis of momentous subjects in the right way, should be duly estimated when possessed of virtuous patriotism.

The majority of the people generally may get out of the pale of safety, if they do not appreciate the public duties.

Can they be too well prepared to solve the difficulties that pertain to all public duties ?

Their mind, if cultivated in principles, prompts them to the adoption of the select, unless debarred by absolutism that may tyrannize in social circles of even free countries. All profound minds must concede that the world needs protection. Now what is that protection?

Is it in flatterers and sycophants, deceivers and absolutists? In storms, wise men do not trust to rotten planks. The mass needs guardians—a right construction of the guardianship of the principles universally the gift of the Creator, alienated from them by various means of treachery, when they can sustain all wisely and properly. Too many minds are now crushed and withering, by the pretended wisdom of conceited leaders.

When the touchstone of principle that cultivated mind honors, is preferred by all wise people to any man or set of men, then man-worship must be abolished, as the people will wish to be safe.

All public virtues should be duly rewarded, beyond that the people injure themselves. A wise people, duly enlightened, must ever inquire for correct principles.

Will they blindly submit to any set of mortals, all being fallible, to conduct them independent of mind, reason and principles?

They are then the vassal slaves of the worst absolutism. The absolutism over mind uncultivated of professions that are insidious disguises by names, is the most dangerous to the world's freedom and noblest interests.

Man's own action on the best light of mind should save him from the curse of omission and neglect that deluged for centuries continents in blood, for mad ambition, conquest and rapine and most wicked church power, from the curse of even seeing mind wrecked in the tortures of inquisitorial tyranny and bigotry of absolutism, therefore he cannot exert too much, on his own best resources, all the powers of his cultivated intellect.

Plausible bigotry upheld by brutal force, has been too prevalent in every age, disgraced by the effusions of the blood of millions shed for centuries over the world, for mad, reckless, and lawless passions, conquest and dominion. These are upheld by sophistry, that fostered the mad conflicts of contending ignorance and prejudice. And what a hold has sophistry on the world?

She paints with all colors, and subdues captive, the mighty mind that is to rule and reign over her superiors. What is this that deceives men? They deceive themselves. The mind of God is only recognised by man's mind; all instruction of the first, is addressed to the latter.

Mind can therefore rightly have no prejudice, as benevolence of man must extend to man, but could not, if its principles were not universal. It is the error and fault of education. True knowledge and science must be conservative.

Emanating from all compatible freedom, the mind seeks its own pure rights, an equal and general participation here, and an everlasting fruition on a base sure and certain to obtain it, a base whose purity possessed guarantees not only immortality, but that most desirable.

Without the ever watchful action of mind, no one is safe. All mind's prospects are uncertain for time and eternity, when all stop short necessarily of the true object of creation. The mind endowed with freedom with man, a free agent from its Creator, will rise higher upwards and onwards, to its ultimate titles in fee simple given by the exclusive proprietor, and will dash to the dust all that impede its progress. It is expected to act to the full, in accordance with a sound faith and professions, that are for man's safety, not for the world's direst oppression and cruel ruin.

Then let mind adopt by all means, the wisest and best, the only ones that can insure salvation.

Mind in every age and country, is analogously situated. Take away the light of reason, which means comparative refined mental knowledge with its inherent power, and mind is destitute indeed, and society most deeply injured. The progress of the social blessings is stopped, and to advance, the same circle has to be gone over eternally.

Thanks to the improvement and invention of printing, one of the inspirations of mind, the records of science are now fixed, and the records of vice distinctly mirrored. Mind must be totally blind, to overlook the reflections from such obvious truths. Its freedom and virtue rest on immutable principles vouchsafed by the Creator, and fortunately rest in the keeping of no sect or creed, but in its own illumined treasury. The great question how best cultivate these principles after they are ascertained, is unmistakably addressed to the world. The world depends on better means and capacity for improvement, than the botches of profession appreciate, whose vitiated and abominable doctrines mar its beauties, and condemn these workers of iniquity, of foul deeds, and ignoble ingratitude.

What is more becoming than for man to acquiesce in the fixed laws of nature, and devote them to their legitimate purposes? To all this cultivated mind must bring all its best powers, that vulgar errors should be duly corrected, however sanctioned by absurd customs. The masses of every age are unfortunately check-mated by the cunning devices of those who are bound to do mind justice, but who avail themselves of its weak points, render them vicious or perverted, to secure more important parts of their complete mastery.

Never will this be fully corrected till every mind is its own best committee of the world's affairs, to the extent of its innate capacity, untrammeled by insidious advice.

Self-exposed errors are the worst of all, and hardest to be eradicated.

The Creator gave organs of mind, and fixed them by laws that cannot be easily reversed after habit has decided. All the world's legislators should premise correct positions at once, and do everything right at first, always. All officials of constitutional government must address mind through Monotheism. Mind acting on mind, has passed on by the silent but effectual agency of thought inspired by its mighty author.

Mind must not disgrace its best gifts, its own talents and its own analysis, its self-knowledge and its self-government, its capacity for avoidance of merited penalties, and its meritorious security of rewards, by embrace of superstition in any of its delusive characters compromising escape of injuries terrestrial, and its immortal anticipations of things to come.

God made mind as it is, for mind to correct itself, that it might have merit when called to account for its jewel attributes.

Mind has to take its position in the midst of the universe, and perform with promptness and alacrity the right functions in the right soul, all that is required of it to reach the best future position attainable. That is the only safety. What are those functions? It has to learn in the school of the world, its only comprehensive theatre.

While mind is modest in its ignorance, discards errors, not libels itself, much less its author, God, the will may be taken by the God of mercy for the deed.

Deity never intended for mind to be deformed by superstition, or polluted by man's base speculations and traffic in professions, designs, intrigues, ambitions, corruptions that must as improper fundamental evils, run out to the final injury of all that come in the sphere of their malign influence.

God gave mind capable of being God-like, by reaching the perfection of its capacity and attributes. God is then to be appreciated by the best action of mind, not libeled by ungrateful demoralization of its nature. The question of its proper sense is not, why did God not give man a better sphere of existence? but, what sphere of future enjoyment shall he obtain by his merit on this present sphere?

Mind must not speculate in discontent here, while it has every reason, obligation and nobler impulses, to improve that condition.

Physical existence of itself, is not independent of morals and religion. Their union bespeaks the highest theme for mind to act on, to improve all as a faithful guardian, responsible to the proprietor universal, not peculiar, for that would be man.

Are the lights of mind in the van, battling against superstition? No, they are often full fed on its gorgeous pamperings. Such often act or say, that one faith may be as good as another!

In the dark ages, when mind was incapable of assertion of rights and protection of self, permitting wars of no principle. but ignoble purposes, plunder and conquest, throughout the world; we could expect no elevation of sentiment, but now the reverse of circumstances should cause us to put the reverse of the dark ages.

Then it was that mind's power and light were negatived, for reason held no tribunal. To the shrine of the mass thus corrupted, sectarian and bigoted views of selfish ambition sacrificed.

Ask one who has generalized his views, why there are barbarians, cannibals, &c.

The advocate for bible traditions may affect that it is for want of the gospel.

The philosopher who advocates rational views in the whole problem of life, will prove it is for want of light of mind and civilization. That light and reason will lead to the expression of religion and social duty of man to man.

The analyst will see but little or no difference between the cannibalism of savages and the butchery of those who affect the highest civilization, if it do not preclude the degrading crimes of slaughter and bloodshed, unless in the noble position of self-preservation, any other will put all into the same category of life-destruction. And is this the position of the boasted faiths of the present day, after all their peculiar pretensions instituted so many centuries for this and all other purposes of civilization. After all, the best of them are only an advance in peculiar faith, not in universal civilization, which it cannot reach, as it has been debarred from most of the world at all times! After

9

eighteen centuries of the earth's annual revolutions, the highest boasts of all such faiths cannot begin to enter where God's creation birth-right, the religion of mind, has been in existence all the time! The dupes of peculiar faith may not see all this, but any other knowingly affecting the supremacy of this faith before the real supremacy of mind, outlaws himself from the best benefits of mind. How many nations of the world have had no gospel of bible tradition, yet they were more or less civilized, as mind was permitted expansion in all·its glories, the true freedom of acting on mind by truth and rational discussion.

Many of the ancient nations, and conspicuously among them the Greeks and the Romans, improved in their laws and civilization, in the progress of time.

All countries will improve in time by the lights of the world, through commerce, navigation, science, industrial labor, manufactures, or fall back to dark ages, by abominable wars, that produce barbarism.

But the great question before the world is not, What shall be done with the scriptures, that are not only not essential to its happiness, but have been one of its worst detriments and nuisances, but, What has mind to do?

In the first place, mind has to assert and vindicate its own exalted supreme worth, as the greatest gift of the universe, and knowing the object of its exclusive adoration and all the appropriate functions.

In the next place, mind has to aid in ridding the world of all exploded and obsolete doctrines of messiahships.

Is it possible for any rational mind to believe that the Supreme would introduce any such system, that was not only a usurpation on his rights, but a stultifying himself by the proof too of his own imbecility?

This is the insignificant degradation of mind that peculiar faith elaborates.

How and when could this absurd nonsense arise, that reflects the knavery of the originators on the stupidity of all the propagators?

Give in rational religion forever all the full, decisive proof, that reason tells her high minded and intelligent faith to adopt, otherwise be wisely silent in refusal, as the faith that skulks from investigation is dishonest. This should be from the essential nature of things; for if such be not faithfully produced, then the mind is surrendered, as that of the juggernaut devotee, to self-delusion.

We then believe things on mere assertion, because it is called religion, and its characters of authorship gods, while at the same time, if our minds were free to investigate, we should speedily denounce the whole imposition, sustained by temporal force of absolutism, and the sophisticated one of superstition.

Mind when perverted sticks at nothing, sacred or profane, to attain its base purposes, especially if fanaticism and superstition excite it; there is no bound to its credulity, no more than that under the influence of psychology; then sound and correct minds must counteract all such, by all the conservative principles of their nature. Let no name or authority of mortals impose on minds, unauthorized on the unmistakable principles of mind. Mind owes it to itself to take cognizance of all belief, and scan all the circumstances.

Belief leads to action—impulse, weal or wo—proscription, tyranny—unless reason arrest at the right point.

It is obligatory on toleration to give due and liberal credit, for all minds seeking eternal salvation, for purity of motives, in all their peculiar creeds, however erroneous, until their light of knowledge enables them to do better. Propriety of feeling and freedom of mind urge all this in rational opinions.

The next question then, is, how put them in the right way? Appeal to that which governs the universe, reason forever.

None but deceivers, knowing it to be false, can pretend that the people cannot recognise what is their interest, if all the facts be duly discussed.

Equal liberality in faith is to be mutually accorded by liberal and enlightened minds, till reason convinces to the right one, as all are equally good till her decision is made.

In the past dark ages, not yet elapsed, anything but reason, when interest spoke, shaped the course of faith of all kinds; and that will ever be, until God's conservative principles master every demagogue, that affects to be master of peculiar systems, the most outrageous of all mind despotisms.

There are always two parties for mind's operations, and both have to stand to no peculiarity that can never exist, but to the right decision of reason.

The right stands to reason. All others are self-delusion martyrs of the true stamp, as Socrates, suffered for rights of mind.

Others, as the Juggernaut devotees and martyrs, so called, though acting under delusion, have suffered for a correct principle, unfortunately misdirected.

Their sincerity of belief, though wrong, proves their honest conviction of mind, but not the correctness of that faith, nor the light of that mind.

They suffered for the right of mind, the independence of thought, that was ultimately to see the clear light of rational religion, by rational discussion.

This martyrdom the true braves of the world suffer in many respects, political or any other; all subserving the noblest purposes at the sacrifice of life, when ruthlessly taken. Rodgers suffered for principles of thinking right, though he was under delusion. He was a martyr, as millions, to the freedom of thought, however misdirected.

The right point can only be attained by proper discussion, in time by philosophical science, proper freedom of principles, that vindicate themselves.

Is not mind disgusted with all the antagonisms of peculiar faith? She can end all this, once and forever, when enlightened. What right has any man to deny the rights of mind in any part of its domain?

Mind must be ever grateful to all that labor purely for rational views, for it owes no other obligations.

The clergy that operate by the benevolence of the age, that would rebuke anything less, are with mind and its rational labors.

The people are ever disposed to be on the right side, if they look at their best permanent interests; they cannot be anywhere else; but deep, designing, and base leaders, have misled them too often to their ruin and deepest regret. The spirit of God is always in advance, and beckons so plainly that all minds can take the best heed.

But here is the difficulty.

How can we expect mind perverted with priestocracy, those deriving personal advantages from the existing order of things, disposed to change voluntarily, when the government of all is in their hands?

As bad as absolutism is, productive of evil to the most, who expects it voluntarily to change for constitutional government, that gives good to the most, to all? Will any absolutism of perverted mind willingly yield?

The class of absolutism, a multitudinous number in conflict, and antagonistic with the best condition of man, brings forth collusions most insidious, to defeat the best efforts of mind.

Mind must be properly disciplined in science education, ever watchful, and aroused in its proper efforts, and must counteract all at the start, else it may be circumvented in toils of sophistry.

All resorts to sophistry the most cunning, the negative to true philosophy, will be used under all disguises, even in the name of rational religion.

We can see this system for victory constantly used in contests political as well as faith.

This plausible personage assumes the costume of philosophy, as well as her titles, until ignominiously expelled from her base pretensions, universally at the tribunal of reason and worth.

She dealeth in self-delusion and logical folly, but her footsteps are backward to monomania.

She is a destructive genius all the time, especially to those she particularly promises to defend.

Her slippery tongue promises successful results to basest characters, but she breaketh her promises as soon as made, for if she be bravely followed she is an exposed cheat and a miserably false-pretender, directing wrong and perverting good all the time.

Her wisdom is cunning, her cunning folly and deception, and the end ruinous and disgraceful.

All will be well repaid to look faithfully at the profound analysis of the human mind, the wondrous gift of the Almighty—from the infant's step, from innocence to reason and wisdom, bound to its physical encasement, inseparable and indivisible on earth, progressive in appreciation and enjoyment.

How beautifully consistent is the analogy of mind's structure, for future purposes under the proper direction.

There is no delusion worse than that of self-delusion, no injury worse than that which produces self-reproach.

Who so destitute in reason, that he has no proper base for self-protection, must receive it from public guardianship.

What gives law protection but the agency of mind?

What has any form of peculiar faith to do with this?

The principles of law and religion are indissoluble, but no form is requisite at all.

There might as well be a church for law as for forms of faith.

Both are executed in each other's temple, the mind.

Let the theatre of operations for mind be first mind itself. The innocent mind is not to be sacrificed as a victim to misguided education, so miscalled, to become the cannibal of society, the fanatic, idolator, or whatever the custom of circumstances imposes upon the benighted intellect. Such mind, modified by such circumstances, is ready to do the bidding of demoralizing superstition, to call an impostor master, and the possessor refuse the only allegiance to its own noblest gift, a sound mind, and to its most Omnipotent Author.

The possessor may blunder in the rubbish of prejudice, where he might reign triumphantly as a man, and claim mind's sacred prerogatives, if such being could appreciate his position.

Then it becomes all good citizens to plan for the best views that reason authorizes, to protect mind as self-preservation.

When mortals commune with God the Author of mind, to whom all their reverence is exclusively due, that mind owes and can pay at all, a debt of gratitude that is glorious to the debtor ; they commune with themselves, thereby exerting the most salutary influence in improvement of themselves in mind and its best improvable qualities.

In seeking that improvement we get the best standard, and secure the improvement of the whole, soul, body and attributes, to the limited extent of our nature and capacity of our resources.

Humanity, enlightened and instructed in the lights of mind's treasures, enables us to pay the appropriate tribute to all to whom tribute is due, in any area of the five grand divisions of the world where we toil for man's good.

Such humanity, good feeling and action, enable us to reach our whole duty to man, and constitute the excellence of the human character.

People, sovereigns of the world, must act up to the high commands of mind, that sublime gift of man, that is the possessor to its appropriate sphere, not a fanatical brute that demands faith-restrictions, and compels it by tortures for self-power or ignoble revenge.

Mind of this age is not to monopolize for a moment, as it will afterward be accursed in men's memories.

This is not the time for bigotry, that bends all mental materials with impious sophistry to superstition, rising from absurd and stupid idolatry to sacrifices of people's rights and feelings, and that has sacrificed human victims, in past times, without pity.

She has broken recusants to her absurd faith on the wheel of torture and death, butchered millions in civil and crusade, miscalled holy wars, has tyrannized in every age with brute force, subservient to blind acquiescence to the absurd notions and peculiar faiths of the day, that never thinks of one of the noblest attributes of progressive improvement and independent mind.

Due credit must be given to mind and facts, and the legitimate deductions that reason draws from them.

Mind must never be trammeled by any peculiar faith alien to its good.

All faith other than rational, that of true religion, is alien to mind's welfare and the world's happiness.

All sectarian faiths will subside on proper improvement of mind to a rational perception of duty, that enjoins then the belief in the one living God to be universal, as proved by all principles and all sense that is right in the universe.

Man must not act the vassal, like animals that follow a certain fellow leader.

He is constituted with mind, his leader to God his Creator.

Man, then, is not the leader ; man's work, bible tradition, is not the leader, but mind acting on mind and evolving reason.

All people have some errors, the wisest seek the least, except the adherents of tradition-faith to which they are blindly devoted by the worship of idolatry.

Most are not master minds to originate the true state of things, therefore the world has to review at every principal period of time, like individuals, its position.

Happy is the people that can secure the genuine free benefits of revolution, without its scourges. That ought to be the present state of mind, and would be, but for the curses of monopoly and usurpation.

In all the intricacies of superstition, mind cultivated to its liberal capacity, is expedient for the best correction. All depend on science, to be elicited by wise investigation and comprehensive elucidation.

By this process many of the strongholds have fallen. Most of the assigned virtues of the moon and stars, another edition of priestocracy, are either exploded or surely assailable.

The moon only presents mathematical appearances of changes in her form from the earth's shadows, not from any intrinsic characteristic changes.

Most all such of past phenomena, looked upon as influential, are analogous.

Eclipses have actually alarmed the minds of many nations, just emerging from barbarism.

Few of mankind can correctly analyze: they act by impulse and passive induction, and vassal obedience.

Potency of mind, sovereign creature of the universe, thou art to be cultivated with the most strenuous care and regard, to be the protectress of worth, guardian of rights, and the lever of character.

The potency of this mightiest element is for weal or wo, like other elements, and its errors must be mastered, else it may cast all to utter fragments, as misdirected steam.

The right cultivation is essential to the essential appreciation and enjoyment of life.

That individual nation or world only partially exists, that does not enjoy the pre-requisites of mind, whose powers most rationally cultivated are next to omnipotence.

The mind crushed by absolutism requires ages before men can refrain from being womanish, women childish by superstition, that may render all brutish.

No doubt absolutists, and all the adherents of power, the interested participants, and the host of menials that bow to those that honor them as office holders, all these minions had peculiar faith superstitious aids to bind the frail human mind under its weak and assailable points, to the governmental influences.

Mind with its full fund of elemental knowledge cannot be trammeled, in its rightful operations.

It cannot be excluded from the verdict of reason, that is universal protection among free and enlightened minds.

Mind was at first endowed with inherent and innate capacity, faculty, and function of religion by God, that can never be eradicated surely in a sound state, and their evolution is best facilitated by proper cultivation of mind that refers to all conservative principles.

Mind, then, has not science at first creation, that is rational, but its science is evolved by mind acting on mind; thus man has been elevated instead of fallen, as bible tradition would have us believe.

The Creator inspires mind to the best, and consequently, the idea of some that the Ruler of all things, making man as he is, entitled mankind to exemption from penalty of transgression, is not tenable to common observation.

Mind, in its kind and character, is influenced by education, that limits mankind to its character more or less; how important then that the fund of mind should be of the noblest calibre and quality.

Of all the blasphemies that could be possibly devised, of all the detestable machinery for punishment, what could be more execrable to mankind that aspire to the proper standard of mind, than the trammels of superstition that uses the brute force of the inquisition, and the insidious knavery of sophistry?

The good citizens of the world must have patience for time to correct all, that principles may be vindicated.

The conservative state of mind is an innate faculty fund of principle from the Creator, identified with mind, and all identified with education most rational.

Fundamental principles never can be divided.

Enlighten mind in the midst of the world's circumstances with the best funds of science, to attain its best possible triumph.

Mind is located in the centre of various routes and only one right; all the rest are those of sophistry and superstition. In the wilderness of uncertainty, mind alone, when rightly cultivated, can master the right one.

It will then discard the bigotry of traditional faith and the errors of chance direction, soliciting the rational only as the true faith, because it is the only safe one, considering all else false and finally unsafe.

Let the world act becoming the better progress of mind. Man's mind has been downtrodden for too many ages, and crushed by the severest circumstances of absolutism, governmental and church, and therefore must pass through its transition states.

Mind must learn the lessons of freedom and help itself by conservative revolution, to burst asunder the immense chains around the necks of the people who cannot otherwise be divested thereof, till the blood of millions flows.

Families of nations will arise to the feast of freedom that will lower absolutism.

The successor of those who exacted homage of royal heads, has been a petitioner for the aid of royal hands, but has obtained the favor of republicans so called, against his revolutionized people.

Principles are everything, professions nothing, in France, Italy, or the world.

Mind has not yet reached its elevation, where it has been so long crushed. One of the proofs of absolutism has yet been left in the ascendency, and this the hierarchy has given its insidious blow to freedom and the dearest interests of mind.

But thrones shall be as dust, before freedom and true religion, and peculiar faith in all its hierarchies will yet do obeisance to rational religion, that honors true government of the sovereign people.

God will favor strong minds and right actions.

The present age should dispense all practicable tuition to the world, and place the mind independent of feudal traditions, and secure the rightful benefits delayed by prostituted and imbecile criticism.

Where was criticism, that should honor mind and science much of past time ? Silenced and martyrized, one of the only true martyrs, a sufferer for the truth.

Rise, light and vindicator of the world, of God, of religion, of justice, and science. Teach man his true duty, and that his pretences, if unjust, are all vain and perishable.

All that obey thy pure precepts recollect that unprincipled man has been paid by the spoils of conquest, and the object is of little moment provided he attains them ; that the talisman of superstition, disguised under peculiar faith, has rioted again and again, without being yet satiated with human gore and human suffering : that it is the pay of speculation that makes these trades, about which the conscience of ambition, stimulated by avarice, has acted in past scenes. And what limit has such conscience, no matter how called or painted, no matter under what banner or sign ?

We might as well ask, what would be the limit of pirates, perjurers, and felons, but for the action of wise laws ?

Thine is the mighty function of conscience, free and rational mind, a province supreme over all the pretences of the messiahships of the world, that cannot begin to effect any such divine inspiration. Thus is the Lord of the universe able to characterize his supreme greatness, over all man's pretensions.

Mind, then, can adapt itself to its select choice, subject to the supreme supervising conservative principles ever existent and active.

Intolerance, then, is not to be put down by undue influence, but to be corrected by light of rational mind in rational discussion.

Mind should be protected against the weak and blind deception of perversion, perjury, &c.

It is science, and the God of science and philosophy, who act on mind.

Mind is the beneficiary, the self and free agent.

But are not the lights of science and philosophy the true friends of wise men, not as plain in all the other deformities of superstition ?

When will be their due present time, to be honored and crowned in triumph ? Will it be always the future ?

The solution of this paramount question belongs to enlightened freemen.

Are you free, and not enlightened ? Or are you enlightened, but timid to act ?

All nature cries aloud for man to assert his dignity with progressive intelligence, truth her sphere, then Deity will have his entire supremacy on the free agency of mind.

It is for the world to appreciate its treasure blessings, to evolve them, the trust-fund, the treasury exhaustless, by mind, potent representative of Omniscience.

Mind has to be ever modest to construe God rightly through his works, to which time will introduce it by science, otherwise it libels him and his deeds most vilely.

A sacred silence must preside over its ratiocination, when any other than due peace is likely to be the result.

Mind, not God, creates an original devil or a fallen angel. What a compliment, unworthy of its own powers of analysis that exalts Deity, not disgraces itself by impiety to the bible's heaven.

The world in good faith to its intelligence and its author, must unlearn all its myths that universally libel God. Who of sound mind and action, wants any of all the creeds of the faith world, but the proper one ? Of whom shall we inquire, but of God alone, by and through mind the beneficiary ?

How miserable may be some duped of their wealth by gilded baits through degraded men, or by some just means of retribution, but how much more miserable to be defrauded of their soul's immortal rights, by any bible games of humbug or electioneering, that are played in this world over mind !

When mighty baits are held out, the temptation is irresistible unless mind wisely counteracts them all. But the best thing to sustain mankind in life, is fair and honest dealing in truth, at all times for adversity or life's close, and all that is comprehended by rational religion.

Mankind must ever consider not what the world thinks, but what God knows is right.

It has to correct on past errors, and act rightly and consistently, with just duty.

The various ages of the world teach man much to benefit, for none are barren of the blessings of nature's wisdom.

This duty is to progress not retrograde, and enlarge the stock of previous intellectual and moral worth, obedient to reason's friends, virtue, &c.

The error of brutalizing human nature can be fundamentally corrected, in prior correction of mind's persuasions.

The strictest attention of mind discovers duty, and performs it.

The Infinite God originates all, but the finite creatures can only appropriate the result, and if with no thanks or justice, are usurpers.

What is the holy alliance but that of the people, to uphold the crushed mind of oppression?

Mind then has ever to regard its titles.

What proof does the history of sects afford, that furnishes the best evidences of mind's imbecility and corruption, but a piece of cunning machinery for priests' and preachers' benefit, however prejudicial to the whole people besides?

Here then is the highest proof of mind on one side, that of priestocracy, for ever antagonistical to that of the people.

Who can overlook the best displays of mind in the comforts of the lonely stranger Park, in Africa, among his colored guests, or the comparatively pure displays of conscience of the ancient philosopher Socrates, all showing the impress of one great Being Creator of the means to originate this mighty union of the world? Mind is the means of improvement, in all relations of God and man There can be no other at all, under God's inspiration.

It is the means of reward, and the cause of punishment, all of it at least in this world.

It is that which takes cognizance in conscience, and in a state of remorse suffers one of the deepest and severest punishments.

On the death-bed, much agony may be embraced in minutes even.

What is the bible of inspiration, but the bible of mind?

Is it not the act of the light of mind rising to its loftiest powers, self-government, that characterizes mind, as the endowment of the Creator on animated nature of man in various gradations?

Mind can detect the whole game of life.

When mind comes forward to assert its own, it is wantonly intrigued against even by its own household, and the various impositions to be the plausible substitutes, and made to assume by all the wiles of deluding and seducing sophistry, every appearance of the true claimants.

Reason having been called on, quickly decides the whole question of right, and gives the potency of truth her beautiful strength.

When persons ask what is to be done, if the substitutes for mind be taken away in the show of bible pretences and vicegerentships, seeing that they have the mighty power of mind their only true friend, they are like boys who wish to cleave very erroneously to bladders all the time, and are at a loss to know how they can possibly do without them for overcoming the mighty element, the ocean, though they have those main functions that mainly constitute them, adepts for self-preservation, their own strong limbs and powers inherent in the body combined with the nature of the element, so well adapted to the best processes of mind properly directed. They forget that their own ships are the appropriate means of navigation. Arouse mind all the time, assert thy rights that are the richest, and thy claims and merits that are invaluable. Thy destiny is command of souls; thy province is to reach immortality, through maturity of virtues: a blossom on this earth to fructify and expand in all the riches of thy glory, thy sphere cannot be confined to earth, when thou diffusest thyself among the universe, and thy duty is self-introduction to the pure presence of Deity, Almighty mind's creator, thy necessary monitor, only guardian and faithful preserver.

Mind then is to protect the world, not to fall under par to Deity.

Is the world to lose its right hold on science, philosophy and civilization of mind for peculiar faith, worth nothing after all?

The wisest institutions of mind all the time, must be made to head otherwise insuperable difficulties; hence, we see the necessity of honoring mind's action all the time, as the master agent of God, the only Messiah, to apply most wisely his doctrines. But for the self-preservation of mind, where would be the world, but perpetually at the feet of absolutism in all its wiles, and most inextricably so?

Nations of non-resistance would have to yield to base nations, who would tyrannize over the world in proportion to peculiar power.

Weak-minded individuals would be at the mercy of unreasonable people, who would become more unprincipled the more they obtained impunity.

All the peculiar advantages of peculiar action of mind would be dangerously carried out to the worst abuses of the world, if principles of mind did not withstand them.

But now, mind every day, is asserting God's principles that vindicate their position; hence, if right and justice be done, the reputation of the party is most powerfully sustained against encroachments.

Mind can overcome all the difficulties of the world, if mind be addressed through reason.

This, then, is the regeneration of the world, where mind's cultivation elicits the enlightened conscience, that comes on God's teaching and inspiration in the various conditions of man's being and feelings, as from national and individual positions. The death of relations and of friends causes man to feel, think, and experience reflections, that may often change the course of the worst habits.

It is time and principle, that work on mind.

Who is not wiser to-day than yesterday, has never been a beneficiary of mind, and presents a monstrosity in nature abhorrent to the universe.

Philosophy is common and proper sense, embracing mind, reason and principles. The progressive improvement of religion continues to arise from the simplest impressions, suited to the capacity of all minds, and is a stultified object of peculiar faith only a matter of degradation, if Messiahship be embraced.

Religion and philosophy, are the telegraphs of God's mind. They teach that mind must be honorable, and honest to God alone, for if it pay obeisance to anything more, it dishonors God and itself by abominations.

None go to infants, savages, or cannibals about religion, until mind can operate fully and effectually in all such subjects, through mental, moral, and science cultivation, for it is perfectly unreasonable to do otherwise.

Mind is, then, the noblest gift of God.

It is only mind that commences from or with God. Mind can only be rightly conscious of God, of no other power can it take equal or right cognizance.

Who, without full, fair, satisfactory, and intellectual energies, could conceive the iniquity of perverted and ignorant mind?

It is for mind to arouse up its energy and retain its truth, as most do not honor the last, and the least of the many possess the first as a rational friend.

The great end and aim of moral and religious science is to govern intellectually the whole mind, to embrace the circle of its cultivation, to comprehend its duties and its appreciations of God, whose magnanimity cannot be dwarfed by mind's incapacity, however mind exposes its own infatuation, foibles, and libels, from perversion of education.

Mind must seek its present good by wise restrictions self-imposed, making virtues of self-denial, forbearance and self-government, and secure its future happiness by adequate and worthy exertions, relying on right sources.

Who can appreciate all the inherent virtues of cultivated intellect?

What man resolves particularly to his immediate interest and narrow views, any day bad absolutely, when such cannot be in due consideration to an all-wise Deity, or to all persons of the world? God creates no evil. The God of nature gives the greatest good to the most, not to any peculiar people; and if the day be wet and rainy, the water promoted navigation, commerce, agriculture, and various healthy and necessary modifications of the atmosphere.

We must take the most comprehensive view in religion, morals, physics, and mind, otherwise mind is an eternal libeller of God.

No philosophical mind can believe that all men and women have their price. It is a libel on the race by corrupt men themselves of corrupt times, age, and circle, breathing a vitiated atmosphere.

The conservative virtue is in mind, that must be regenerated by the highest moral, intellectual and religious civilization.

Under the best state of such position, who believes that there can be purchase by money of friendship, that can be duly estimated by the world? Could all the world's gold have purchased the chastity of a Lucretia, or the friendship of Damon and Pythias? Partial analysis of mind and society causes their libels.

Who that hears of low life in large cities but must be struck with the bold fact, that society requires new organizations to correct errors and vices, from the unnatural division by fictitious, not genuine, distinction; not merits of mind, but demerits of dollars. The frame work of society is in an unnatural state, and demands correction. Crime, then, is in excess by reason of mind not asserting its proper empire. The proper tuition of mind demands precedence of wealth. By ignorance and resulting error it is easy to fall into vice; all can do that; very few can raise themselves at once into virtue. The world needs an independent start in life, and mind requires innocent culture. What have we not to gain in timely cultivation of the unsophisticated, candid mind, to prepare it to meet and triumph over the wily intrigues of perverted minds?

What a jewel is mind if rightly cultivated and polished!

Legions mislead in history, judgment, and tradition, therefore mind must have its own funds to create a sound judgment, a correct independence, exempt from all flagrant impressions.

Most minds would follow the physiological and phrenological organic developments, but for mental government, the best of all governments received from schools. Let, then, the best tuition regulate all minds.

With firmness, justice, and talents, rightly directed, mind towers in the world, therefore, a great triumph of mind is over the passions. Rational mind does that supremely best.

We consider that mind and its operations take precedence of faith of any particular, peculiar character, distinct from the true principles connected to mind.

Let faith be what it may, still, without mind where would faith be? and this decides at once and forever, without controversy or difficulty, that mind must invariably, for two reasons, take precedence of faith, as the object to be attained is paramount safety of mind, and through its own powers and qualities.

What would the universe be but for mind? A blank.

The universe was created for mind by God, that is more than its soul, as he is Supreme Intelligence itself.

Mind is God's chiefest good, and greatest care.

It is not miracles but life occurrences mind has to analyze, meet, and fulfil. Miracles are alien to its subject at this day of science. Messiahships cannot supersede mind in any respect, nor command the confidence and respect of the rightful beneficiary, an honorable mind; much less, then, can they supersede God's impression on mind, when finally corrected by the verifications of science.

Nothing of the kind uniformly protects, but is left to the action of time, a most uncertain contingency.

Such stand as parishing memorials, whereas God's is eternal, and endures as long as man and mind.

The progress and advance of mind are so extensive as to cause us to congratulate ourselves on the glorious results.

Mind enables us to reach the standard of respect, when we are right and rational; we cannot be far wrong when we seek to approach the same.

How can we protect ourselves best from the world? By being right, appreciated by mind's knowledge, that necessarily embraces the most philosophical science.

Good and true citizens will act to their and country's honor, independent of laws from principles, and superior to all absurd and bad legislation by the highest actions of mind.

The proper analysis of most things may be unknown to the people in general, but none can mistake the intention that to be right should always be pure.

The standard of public morals is not generally high enough in all circles of the world, certainly not in a corrupt society of what is called civilization.

The low bred are generally great nuisances in all countries where mind cannot become the rational leader, and take precedence of peculiar faith.

Is there aught but what cultivated mind is not the guardian?

Some tribes of Indians are as wise as the wisest in looking to the Great Spirit, if unrestricted in that position, without the aid of a more refined priestocracy; but they should be enlightened in philosophical science, if practicable, to render their minds the great beneficiaries of the world, benefactors in turn to mankind.

Mind's highest attributes and qualities are not the work of accident, but of uniform enlightenment. Its various organs are to be duly and constantly cultivated in the legitimate sphere, and pre-eminently as that of conscientiousness, that so conspicuously rules much of free agency.

Believing that the fundamental principles of phrenology, as defined by physiology, are magnificently great and elevated God-like endowments, whereby mind is thus constituted to act, the results, thought, understanding, and wisdom, cannot be too highly exalted.

The difficulties, dangers and trials of life are to be met by mastery of. mind, not by the battlings of brute force, that demoralizes the world.

We all need self and well balanced minds.

All matured minds that are rational, will admit the need of correct education and views of society that unfortunately too many never get till too late, if ever mind must be balanced, and ever independent of extraneous causes, to exclude bigotry, sectarian, and partisan tyrant.

Universal toleration of opinion goes really to freedom of mind and reason, that certainly are given to scan peculiar faith, that may involve antagonism to fundamental principles, according as men are influenced by peculiar motives.

Bigotry must be effectually vanquished by the light, independence and blessings of rational minds.

It becomes persons of mind to cultivate that mind in the best lights of liberal and rational conscience, that its cultivation may properly reach general and substantial science, in all that comes within their scope to enlighten and adorn.

They must recollect that honesty and truth are principles of religion, and not at all by excellence of church or sect.

Honest and truthful minds dislike the fellowship of the many stumbling blocks already there, men who might cast reproach upon them, and whose antagonism might be effectual, in a church trial, of not only traducing worth of character far above them, but even to convict improperly.

This may be a bane of society.

The world would be a penitentiary more than man's theatre, were it not for mind that avails itself of capital and labor for economists.

The duty of mind is to the Creator of the universe, its exclusive object of adoration.

Any other is untrue, and the error so dangerous to the public, as the sooner excluded the better.

Many several kinds are supported but with invidious sophistry, that usurps truth and beguiles mankind.

The only revelation of the God of the universe is mind's universal inspiration, lighted up at the temple of science and proper sense, through the creation, as recognised universally by mind and reason.

All else is false pretences more or less contradictory, and clashing with God's eternal principles.

God's book and scriptures are in the universe alike imperishable, that shows an Almighty Architect, Preserver and Self-sustained.

All others are an imposition and counterfeit in the whole system of truth.

The advocates of pretended revelation must let alone all systems of faith that do not do universal good to man, and accord the only glory to God, appreciating God's exclusive attributes.

All else is superstition, that utters constant blasphemy in giving part of creation to others by subtle sophistry, and raising up fictions about beings not in existence by God's creation.

All systems then of superstition are dangerous to mankind, and a mockery to God.

How can we reach the proper decision, than by mind and reason?

Why do we hear any sermons and how do we decide, but by rational mind? All preachers contradict themselves, when they advance other views.

It is not only absurd but dishonest to talk of any other mode of safety or salvation to man.

Most men are mind-vassals to some one individual. Most follow example without analysis, and the balance have some object of ambition in view.

ew are intelligent to separate themselves from the world's deceivers, or as good as intelligent.

Take no individualities and men's traditions before principles, or puritanism before science, to produce any perversion.

Condemned be the mind that perverts truth any way, but especially fundamental truth and principles in science. This all arises from man's peculiar faith, that cannot produce universal approbation.

When the organs of conscientiousness and reason are well balanced, the mind is so • constituted that it cannot be satisfied with less than respectable and trustworthy proof.

Such mind does not seek to know whether the position is popular, but right.

What shall we say of any set of men in this age seeking to destroy the majesty of mind?

The progress of mind is in the great power of invention and discovery, that no virtuous honorable man will see trammeled by the imposition of usurpation and monopoly, nor by the ignorance and reckless folly of criminality.

All such light will be exercised through the principles of ratiocination to overcome the prejudices of the times, to reform society into original elements of honesty and truth, to get right from all imposition.

If mind be just to itself, the world will honor it.

The paramount rights of the people are the decrees of nature's God.

" The greatest good to the greatest number," can only be accomplished by the rightful action of cultivated minds of the people who have always had, if they had known, this divine right.   The simpler this truth, the more fixed the fact.

It is not that you have talents inferior to the mighty question of religion, your highest duty, but of not doing justice to them, but permitting yourself to be hoodwinked by the priestocracy that have constituted one of the strongest links in absolutism ever since mind was its vassal.

Thus you should never forsake old friends, however humble, if avoidable by your minds.

All rational intellects then, properly imbued, must feel most reverential to Deity, so much so as not to divide his exclusive creatorship, and render his a demi-godship.

Thanks to Deity for the liberty and light of rational mind, as of the means to aid us, that of education, the press, that if untrammeled, will act for general good with the best results.

Mind must claim reason, if it can claim itself.

We go for conservation, not destructiveness.

Man has to work out his own duty by proper respect to his own mind.

There are many harassing scenes in life, many difficulties and trials to meet, and this can only be wisely done by mind liberal and cultivated over all the bigoted notions of the day, so fatal to the welfare of the many.   It is an outrage on mind's divine rights, that man should undertake to define the limits and scope of the mind, by the morose, contracted and narrow bigotry of any age, and pass that off for the only true faith, degraded as it may be by superstition and want of reason, guarded in its defects by all the effrontery of sophistry and errors, that have a most perverted influence on mind and its best interests.

Time must and will come, when all this will be swept away before the light of mind and reason.

Mind, when enlisted under the banner of civil and religious liberty, will advance national and individual benefits together.

Then we shall witness the success of useful inventions and discoveries as brilliant, as peaceful revolutions for a world's benefit and reformation, progress and prosperity.

The virtues and sciences mutually aid each other.   Organic principles are now advancing in this age of utilitarianism and substantial enjoyment, surpassing that of poetry and speculation.

Take mind from the universe, and the last is a perfect blank.

If mind be not perfectly cultivated, mind is a perversion, and the universe is more or less a blank to it.

Mind, cultivated to its capability, governs the elements of creation, and creates the elements of its own greatness.

Mind's discoveries and inventions of every age, among the most brilliant of which are the press, steam, electricity and true constitutional government, aid in evolving the blessings of civilization, that is advancing with advancing navigation, commerce, manufactures, mining and agriculture.

All the mighty trials and difficulties of life are given to mind as its circumstances to be overcome, whereby the mastery of mind may vindicate itself, and create its own greatness, and decide its own happiness and enjoyment.

Mind must be filled with suitable action to its light and knowledge, to tower over all the world's temptations and corruptions, that ensnare, enslave, and destroy.

Self-examination is necessary to self-preservation.

How can anything but mind realize religion at any time?

Who expects the exercise of idiotic, infantile, maniacal faith?

Why not expect such?

Because there is no soundness of mind for reason to act on.

And who can expect reason of intellect, perverted by blind and implicit faith and reckless infatuation?

Science, philosophy, and truth, are what God deals in, to perfect rational religion.

Mind has already entered into immortal functions, by the exercise of reason, in the analysis of parts of the universe, and in the performance of its duty.

A suitable, well-balanced mind attains the best judgment, that particularly distinguishes great men.

The corruption and cunning of the world are deep and hard to estimate, from the malign influence of feudal vassalage that prevails in society ; therefore mind must be fully enlightened, to meet this world-wide question.

It must recognise menials of power, money, fraud, avarice, and ambition, to escape the infatuation.

Who cannot observe the degradation of mind by lust, drunkenness, and all the low characteristics of meanness?

Our age is better when it improves progressively, as with the best light of mind come the best light of knowledge, and best results for universal good of mankind.

All hail, benevolent societies of the world, for universal good. Such can clash with no principles.

Thanks to the lights of an age of progressive civilization of mind, that makes deeds of dark ages felony and piracy.

Who can set limits to his own improvement, if he keep his mind always open to receive truth?

Both for himself and the world should man act, to secure the full blessings of mind.

Mind has gradation in organs, and is proved by gradation of improvement, as talents are proved by actions of those emerging from mental darkness.

But how futile the idea, that if the bibles of tradition were taken out of the world, that minds would have nothing else to rely on. This is the ridiculous, of the mighty sophists.

Where is God Almighty's bible? that of mind?

The first has defective translations, pretended revelations of mysteries, all for the priestocracy to decipher; and not for the people even to read!

Do not all these bibles deceive? All then are defective, weak, impotent, demoralizing, coming from a bigoted clique.

God's is all-sufficient, and calls for mind's best improvement, by science and reason. It is the only one.

We are all assured of the frailties of human nature, therefore we must protect those frailties at the right time, and point, by enlightened parents and wise legislation, and all the only means of rational mind.

Give us wise legislation, arising from the principles of matured mind enlightened, and give all the preachers of peculiar faith, to the greatest number practicable, all their peculiar bibles, and we shall secure an incomparably better world, despite of the preached hell and all its sulphur machinery.

But they preach, "Repent and be baptized."

The last is not essential, while the other is embraced in domestic discipline of morals and religion, all life-time.

Behold what can be done in the goodly land of mind, when missionaries are sent thither to convert the people to peculiar faith dogmas! To change from the practical efficiency of mind, to the nullity of peculiar faith.

The light of the Principal and not of the assistant must enlighten the people; instituting his glorious elements from the very creation.

Let the light of science enlighten the world.

These are necessary and universal truths, that cant or hypocrisy cannot deprive the mind of.

By the influence of perversion, sophistry may deprave, defraud, but the faculty of mind will assert its noble functions for freedom and purity of thought.

Mind, enlightened, must discover that faith without reason is a monster, most tyrannical and hideous.

The old advocates of peculiar faith, as the representatives and authors of Moses' Dispensation and Bible, usurped the province of mind, and the present canters of the day continue it.

The operations of mind insure the discovery of all pertinent to its own faculties, and must not be divested of its own legitimate functions.

The man that does it, is a felon.

The brain is the galvanic battery, and the will is to operate on the brain, that arouses the electricity that sets the nerves to action, and they move the muscles into play.

The organs correspond physiologically, and are modified by temperaments.

All this supports the doctrine of rational religion, that improves on the improvement of mind, and the advancement of science.

How then can bibles of tradition, that come to a dead halt in mind and science, have worthy elements to teach us moral truth; built, as they all necessarily are, on falsehoods?

All are grossly ignorant of natural science.

Either natural science is wrong, or the bibles of tradition.

We must go by exact science, if we go by God's works, to read correctly his book, that is in the universe, which is clearly libeled by the bibles of tradition.

God's works teach that God has all moral and religious attributes, else the universe could not stand.

God created all things, with reason, intelligence, science, philosophy and wisdom.

All wise provisions were elaborated by a perfect, sublime power, at the beginning.

All this is discovered by mind, not in one age, but in many ages of the world, by the progressive improvement in science, that comprehends finally the most practicable to mortals. Hence, it is not fair, wise, nor just, to say that mind did not tell all this at once, seeing that it did not attain the relative advancement.

GENIUS AND DISCOVERY.

He that originated thoughts of brilliant genius, that lifted the veil that concealed the mighty cabinet of God on this earth, has contributed more than all the bible of tradition pretenders.

He that taught the blind to read with their fingers, excelled all messiahs in miracles.

He that taught God's messenger, electricity, to telegraph the world's events to man, created a fund that out-did all mystery-mongers.

The improvements of the moderns have outstripped the prophecies of the ancients, and have subverted their obsolete views.

The inspiration of God is with mind, that respects the mighty science of nature.

The cunning of the ancient priests was not up to God's wisdom, nor the science of the moderns.

What new continent is that, new to all the rest?

It is one that modern genius has disentombed from the bowels of the mighty ocean, and science crowns with triumph.

Whence comes its light, that bursts upon the dazzled view of the Old World?

It is that of liberty, that spreads her refulgent blaze of rational mind, itself irradiated by constitutional principles, that render religious adoration to God.

What would have been the tyranny of the old world, but for the genial influence of the liberty of the new. All this is the inspiration of minds operated on by science, the mighty work of an Almighty.

Let the mind, conscious to itself of rectitude, look at the safe and uniform protection of principles, science and virtue.

Let all proper new lights burst upon the world, by all public instruction.

Science and philosophy can rear their best tributes as life-saving benevolent associations, life boats, mortars to throw rockets with lines attached, from the shore to the wreck, in cases of utter necessity.

Thanks to mind, after God, for the comparative blessings of the world in the comforts of life, as good clothing, nourishing and healthy diet and food, transportation safe, easy and expeditious, by ocean and land, over the world in definite certainty, in most instances of steamers and railroads; means commercial and national, interchange of productions of the world most effectual, preventive of famine; of news, facilities for mind's improvement, excellent government, protection personally and materially, leading to the highest enjoyment and spread of rational religion.

Who can criticise the wise economy of the world, must be able to scan the universe; mortals then have to maintain a wise silence, or the most circumspect reverence to the Creator.

Mind's supposed evils, are in the remedies of mind, by right actions. The province of reason is to investigate the principles of the universe.

Man has nothing else than mind to use to determine in the constant sophistries of the world's pretences, and is perfectly responsible for the right use of it. Then mind is absolutely compelled to abjure all peculiar faiths. Man is an animal in any other position.

Mind enlightened by reason, asserts its empire exempt from all pretences of miracles, to rescue mankind from the clutches of bigots.

Do not disgrace mind by superstition, but as long as peculiar faith continues, so long must prejudice and superstition prevail.

Have no inglorious surrender of mind to any peculiar faith, however popular at Rome or elsewhere.

Act in good faith to mind and society, and you who deplore the errors of fallible faith, should now select, with us, fundamental religion!

Whence arises the flourishing condition of free countries, but the benefit from free mind?

It is a libel, an insult to injury on mind, to say that mind could not originally conceive of the Great First Cause, a school boy's solution. It is one of the ignoble, false pretences of the stupid knavish priestocracy.

Mind by inspiration from God, does good, if mind's works are the result of good faith. But mind's works are the result of faith good or bad, as influenced by irrational or rational education. How faithful then ought rational education to be to the whole world, that is subject to such malign influences.

No creeds of predestination that carried man to the scaffold, could fix rational mind and faith there, because it was unreasonable, unjust, cruel and viciously criminal.

These men of peculiar creed and its faith, were the basest tyrants of mind, enslaving and vitiating mind's best qualities, brutalizing and victimizing it.

They manufacture a hell out of the earth's volcanoes that are its mere safety-valves, earth's cannons.

They degrade fictitious angels from their paltry heaven, and scandalize God's munificence with ignorant ribaldry, to cover up their own hideous deformities.

All exact and proper investigations, will expose them to their deserved contempt of mind.

The mind expels the absurd idea of book mysteries, when man desired to do what was necessary, and therefore must have had a plainer scope for correct action, therefore a mystery mocks mind's sense, God's attributes, and religion's dignity.

Principles are for all time and systems that are right. The originals stand in abeyance to the reflective progressive state of mind, in the advance of reform and revolution.

We need a system for religion that gives no countenance to, but counteracts any of the thousand forms of licentiousness, as mind in this liberal age of reason is still servile and vassal, being spell-bound to the car of sophistry, bigotry and fanatical superstition

At the first dawn of consciousness, mind may not be impressed with principles, but may be in the toils of sectarianism or of designing men, without any system of self-protection, therefore the necessity of rational codes.

The sophistry that we meet with in some form or other every day, and in most parts of the day, is to be counteracted by the richest funds of a sound and healthful mind, that are needed to fulfil mind's duty properly and correctly. Its destiny or better purpose rests then, on the omnipotent principles of causation.

The mind is the mouth-piece of God the Creator, the supreme gift that originates and selects the scriptures, is strictly eclectic, the only avenue for the scriptures of thought, the only link of connection between man and God, evinced in its purest concentration, the conscience.

Messiahship must necessarily displace mind or God, one or both, and is not only useless, but detrimental, an abominable nuisance of priestocracy.

As the picture of the object seen is painted on the retina, the expansion of the optic nerve of the eye in vision, so in mind's eye is the inherent appreciation of God painted by the innate faculty of religion. There is no learning of correct faith but with truth through mind, and the deep-felt conviction rests on the affection, the refined faculties of soul.

The passions avow sympathy that should be rightly directed on a rational basis, else it degenerates into fanaticism.

Physiology rejects any other than these; to her is the proper appeal, as philosophy referring to history of facts. The Creator having endowed mind as the master creation, never can truth say that any written document is supreme over mind, for it is the right and commanding function of mind, to receive or reject all written documents until satisfactorily proved.

Any usurper of mind's rights may pretend that scriptures are above mind, the minor above the major, but that is certainly a false pretence not worthy of mind. The mind is the best treasure of the world. The work of mind is superior to all books of tradition. There must be no forcing tuition prior to seven years, to make any prodigy or genius, over-burdening mind or memory, but let the book be last, the world-school most to insure ripe judgment.

Mind ever gets its innate reaction and reflection, and all the legitimate ideas of God the Creator, by his works.

All should bide their time as the least of evils, and consider mind when cultivated rightly, the means of conquest of all that is worthy of mind's attention. Mind and judgment must meet any crisis.

One of the greatest curses of the world, is by corruption of the mind. It will take a revolution deep and strong, of popular opinion the most enlightened, refined, and civilized, social and religious, before matters essential to the world's happiness are rightly settled.

Whatever custom the parents have transmitted to the children, mind should be consulted as the responsible enlightened free agent, improving in each successive age on fair advantages, ere that custom be valid by right, or enslave by the potency of its tyranny. Parents are bound on the highest obligations, as far as practicable, to render the mind of their children innocent and rational. In this way, mind asserts its noblest principles, and freedom her most high-minded legitimacy, all exploding the worst humbugs.

What mind is there with proper calibre and cultivation, that cannot conquer all practicable difficulties of the world, if that world will be just to itself?

By its best improvements and reforms, the world is regenerated first in the arrest of mankind's oppressions to continents and nations.

The wisest legislation pertains to the right action of enlightened mind, to counteract the bad and perverse actions of stupid and perverted minds.

The only revelation is that by mind enlightened, just and truthful, honest and virtuous in universal principles.

How can we overlook the characteristics of the human races, in their form of phrenological developments?

Can abstract or rational principles affect mind most? Nothing, is principle bereft of rationality, hence, peculiar faith is a nullity. Perversion of mind represents it.

What is mind capable of doing? What is its duty?

All the prizes ever attainable, were mind's inalienably by creation's grace.

God has given mind to fathom and attain all.

When and how? Reason and rational mind declare the constant mode, the only practicable one of truth.

They read the scriptures of an immortal God, undead and undying, written on the universe.

No doctrine contrary to reason, can be the word of God.

Mind requires a full exercise of God's principles, a part of creation with the universal elements, and we shall have all ever exacted by God.

We can have no more by any system, nor any less.

No system but that of rational religion, can give us all.

Mind, not peculiar faith, gives the defences of civil protection.

Where would American freedom have been, but for our civil revolution that is indebted to mind?

Where would have been the revolutionists, but for their admirable constitution, that sound minds elaborated?

Exalted science of mind reflects the most exalted of the world's benefits, an exact justice, in regard to the nature of mind and of the universe.

What have miracles to do with mind, but to prove its reckless ignorance of natural phenomena?

They form no part of mind's existence or blessings, but evidently are its curse.

The moderns are, no doubt, as a mass, better and wiser than their predecessors, and are so not by miracles or prophecies, much less by bible mysteries, but by mind, that entitles all to their full benefit when possible to be realized.

No wonder that the last discoursed so weakly and ignorantly about the heart, instead of the mind thereby superseded by ignorance.

If God governed by miracles the universe, then mind could not be rational: but analysis proves reason and not miracle to be the attribute of mind that rejects faith, if the last reject truth and facts.

Civilized enlightened mind, teaches man all that can be rightly taught on this earth. The Creator has so ordered it. His omnipotence includes mind's potency.

While human reason may commit mistakes that time may rectify, superstitious fanaticism and degraded bigotry commit crime, vices, and high treason, against the whole world. Will its present priestocracy continue all such?

While the faculties and functions of mind bid us hope, when no man is certain by tradition about the realities of another world, as all its assumptions cannot satisfy because there is no title but imposition, no one in his senses can deny to God the creation of the universe, that has its moral and physical preservation so conspicuous in conservative laws, that include all practicable redemption, from which man's libel on mind excludes Deity's rights!

Mind must be ever rightly employed all the time.

The tyranny of man has resulted by perversion of the great principles of mind.

Mind has yielded up its paramount rights, and tyrants have encroached by all the avenues of absolutism, till the unprincipled, degraded, and base intriguer, has but too successfully tyrannized over the world.

It is mind's fault, folly, and crime, not to profit by wisdom, when good and evil are so much in the possession of mind, according to its will and capacity.

Mind has to combat the vagaries of modern socialism and communism, to radicalism, and all the antagonisms of sectarianism, in all its dangers and fanaticism, to all the present advancements, as mormonism.

Mind has ever to be on its guard, or submit to the slavery and vassalage of brutal degradation, that with no principles has no mercy with absolutism.

Perverted learning, that makes mind dishonest or cunning, is to be shunned in all the departments of its theatre.

Benefit and usefulness to mankind are the great objects of patriotic minds, that cannot obey fashion, faith nor custom, independent of truth and religion.

Rational mind that comprehends all, seeks the best security to govern the worst passions.

Its domestic economy includes all that bears on safety.

It has the least trouble to govern domestics, where the reverse gives the worst or severest difficulty.

Under its legitimate influence, children know best how to obey their proper guardians. as taught all such.

Its light and action cause the world to flourish in freedom and riches, with the most satisfactory comparisons in life.

But the inquisitor of peculiar faith has exerted the powers of absolutism, by all the slavery and vassalage of mind, and by all its tortures to the stake and faggot, to stifle this noblest of man's rights.

When printing did not exist, what but a chaos of uncertain tradition prevailed in regard to science, and bibles of tradition? Then they could be mind-factured with all the licentiousness of reckless and bold myths and fable. Then man had power, that excluded the world's rights. Men were burnt at the stake, as Bruno, in 1600, for fair appreciation of science. Peculiar faith is the quintessence of peculiar cruelty and tyranny.

"The heretic had to expiate the crime of open defiance to the dogmas proclaimed by the church."

All indignities were practiced on heretics so called.

What country can flourish by peculiar faith?

Well is it, that mind masters it finally.

At best it is a mere incident, and certainly an impossibility, when peculiar faith of christianity has burnt books and destroyed authors, to arrest science, whose light excludes all such as its and the world's tyrant.

The varied benefits of reform, individual and universal, are needed, and the necessity of society shows mind's immediate responsibility and accountability.

Hence, from the deficiency of mind's action, we must consider its perversion.

Mind requires all to think for themselves, but how few of the world have done it! How many have been victimized for assertion of correct independent thought!

What little stock of reflective or original ideas is there among people, that submit to the wiles of perverted mind, whose embrace is more poisonous than the adder!

The highest power on earth, mind endowed with reason, impeaches this pernicious state of things.

Bigotry and superstition, backed by ambition and self-interest of the priests, have bound the ignorant mind, and debased, perverted, and enslaved it.

Give mind its weight and power in science, to civilize the world, and arrest the fanatic phrenzy, bigotry, and superstition of peculiar faith, while there flourish religious toleration and freedom.

All expedients to direct mind in faith are of absolutism, that seeks to deceive and enslave mind.

These must be counteracted by the mother and father, the rightful guardians; schools. societies, and associations, free and enlightened rational discussions, wise legislation, valuable books and codes.

All books that mislead by errors, are worthless trash.

God extracts good out of much apparent evil, and makes the mind agent for mind and good.

Why so much perversion of mind, but from self-agency of mind?

The analysis of mind must give with the analysis of the universe, the only just appreciation of Deity. His appreciation leads to the depreciation of all messiahships and originators.

By mind's illustrious free institutions the vassalage of most nations is ceasing to exist. as slavery ceases by mind's acknowledgment, when free labor becomes cheapest.

Let mind's whole position be equitably established, and the world will, as it must, become right.

Mind decides against amalgamation as the worst demoralization, and returns to the shores of the once barbarous, but now civilizing Africa, mind of African races ennobled. Mind will comprehend its own problem. The first part of mind is innocence, that requires the greatest cultivation for protection of its innate greatness ; but the intermediate presents by ignorance and error, bigotry, and all the evils and dangers of barbarism.

Mind is only to be treated in the legitimate way.

As no country can flourish without adequate improvement on religion, so none, we will prove, can secure it without mind and civilization, that exalt the world's blessings the more they are advanced.

God endowed man with the noblest gift, mind, and that has to endow itself with the noblest ornament, reason.

How sublime the liberty ; how chaste and refined the position. The people of the world do not appreciate their gifts, the very best of which is mind, that they permit their passions to enslave. The greatest slavery is voluntary.

The evils of corrupt education, as piracy, and all evil deeds, are to be corrected and reclaimed from, by reason.

This teaches us that restitution is by acts of mind, and its offerings are wisely to anticipate the penalty of blood, which is peculiar to those affected by sins that produce it. The loss of blood adds to sin, not detracts from it.

We do not address the idiot, maniac, infant, or savage, to proselyte, because we cannot reach their minds.

Next to these, are the wilfully blind, fanatics, bigots, those prejudiced by self-interest, corrupt and ignorant. They murder the light of mind, and should be deprived of their capacity for evil, as they are not equal to the demands of good.

All cultivated minds must see and acknowledge as honest, that the highest philosophy is the highest religion, that looks into the mightiest realms of the universe, where beams science in every point, the work of an Almighty, perfect in all attributes.

The divinest religious feelings, the most refined and the loftiest, are those ever given to man by mind, that scans by the best-light of rational education, the whole theatre of its action.

Mind alone approaches the matter of an exhaustless universe, and reason improves its religion as rational, as God's nature requires.

Mind is placed above the brutes, and has therefore the highest rational duties to perform.

Brutes have innate faculties, whence originate ideas and impulses, for food and drink, and can reason in that circle, and all the available capacities of self-preservation, as habits of range, or course, distance, locality and time ; but mind alone recognises religion, that elevates man above all creation.

Mind has nothing to do with any rite or ceremony, baptism, sprinkling or christening. This is all theatrical, in man's customs of peculiar faith. The moral and religious sublime, are from God's own innate gifts, ideas and faculties ; no other can put a genuine mark there, as mind is pre-occupied.

All the substitutes for God and religion are counterfeit, that cannot take proper hold, even when the best impressions of God and religion are worn down, and nearly obliterated.

Youth, should improve by the age and light of science, correct their parents' views, not adopt their absurdities, that show the small process of mind, and little or no brains.

It is not that parents know so little, or that children know so much, it is that science speaks, mind learns, God commands and teaches.

So far from sectarians exposing their ignorance and their exploded doctrines, they ought to thank the age for the mighty spirit of light, otherwise the progress of mind will be obstructed by prejudices.

The use of the mind must be exercised on general principles, else the most disastrous effects may ensue.

God has implanted the right faculties, and mind must produce the right action by these faculties on these principles. A perfect God has established the faculties of mind, capable of reaching perfection by a purification incidental, in the progress of its action through the universe.

Sound minds duly cultivated, will pursue principles.

This position establishes the proper appreciation of Deity. If weak minds submit to the perversion of their capacity and rights, if they seek the desert, the ocean or dangers unprepared by safe means, or reckless of food, and are caught in that folly, and suffer

10

from fatal hunger, then God is not responsible for the transgressions of these plain and obvious principles of life.

Trace out the legitimate results that bring famine, disease, and war, and mind must be abundantly responsible.

Mind is the beneficiary from God's benefits, and is its own defaulter in their negative.

Each man is as to the gifts and right cultivation of mind, constituted on physiological and phrenological facts.

Mankind is ever addressed through mind, in seeking its best judgment, or blind submission.

Mind has to look out for the breakers of life, the desert, ocean, famine, and adopt all life's mighty beacons, watch self, and avoid self-treachery.

It becomes the worthy great minds to counteract the arts of superstition; to do that, they must be rightly cultivated universally, to the legitimate demands of mind's-fund of science and philosophy. They must renounce all the pigmy, petty and paltry game of demagogism. This is the very best basis of equality to get rid of vulgar superstition and vassal sectarianism, and insure more universal happiness.

Fortified, as the world will thus be, it is a libel on the wise and good part of it, that they will scoff at the right thing in any respect.

It is said that the world is a humbug, but base and unprincipled minds have made it so, and stupid minds have thus adopted it.

The people are fond of being humbugged, only by perversion of mind, if that were not the case, the most would die out at once.

All such reflects on the state of mind that adopts miracles. The people are deceived by the antagonists of the genuine in all science, government and religion, that yield so much power, as power of all other powers. These are mighty stakes, and are played for by mind, by all the means, that perverted mind adopts in the most important games.

It is gambling on the most extensive scale, and is the most dangerous business. The people should seek to recognise their mental faculties, as the mighty gifts of Deity. Who can claim the title of Divine Right, but the universal people, who have it through mind by the universal title of God himself, author of the universe, recognised always by rational religion?

If minds were capable of peculiar national appropriation, then they might be peculiar people of God, which is disproved by all the facts of history, reason and truth.

. Some minds are perfect pirates in society, victimizers of all that is consecrated by mind.

Penalties should be adequate for proper correction and prevention. Is capital punishment demanded?

Mind is organized phrenologically, and one must be different from another, more or less by that organization, consequently all differently organized and constituted, could not have similar crimes, vices, or virtues, but all in the degree modified with its education. In this the world of mind is displayed, the richest magnificence of the organizer, the universe architect.

The aim of rational philosophy, that is religion, is the best effort of mind to obtain all knowledge, as well of God as man, as well of immortal as mortal things, to rely on analogy for the balance.

All things to be acted on must pass the action of mind.

Reason accounts satisfactorily for its own history in the analysis of mind, and rejects all miracles as neither God's nor mind's, but rank impostures.

Honest intellectual truth rejects unqualifiedly all such.

All truths are proveable before rational minds, while the reverse rejects reason, light, and truth.

God gave mind pure and innocent as this earthly theatre can permit, in the morning of its existence, to the guardianship of parents, who, then, must exert the potency of free agency with their children.

They should not pet them one moment and treat them as slaves the next.

Nurses are to be aids, not substitutes; mothers should look to this.

The greatest slavery is the delusion of mind in supposed religion, and in pursuit of evanescent wealth, in all which soul and body are worsted most unprofitably for life, without recompense or satisfaction, in hopeless mental servitude, the butt and scorn of a better appreciation.

Only think of being a vassal to a blasphemer, usurper, and counterfeit, instead of moral truthfulness in adopting the right titles of the only Supreme Sovereign.

In carrying out all the legitimate demands of mind at once, no one, however popular, can be entrusted with power above the laws, or any ways irresponsible to rational views of life.

Mind must take cognizance to put down all tyrants of all superstitions, as a bounden duty to patriotism, and the highest rights of humanity.

As to excluding the rights of mind and reason, it is no wonder when the rights of the Mighty God of the universe, all adorable as he is for attributes, are excluded by the false lights of Messiahs, assumed blasphemously.

We ask for the legitimate position for civilization, to give mind and reason fair play, not a Jesuitical stifling, assuming the darkness of past ages.

There has been no fairer test of either, in regard to the religion that emanates from the loftiest appreciation of Deity.

But attempts have been made to reach the right position as to religion the last century, but all were miserable failures when other means were used than the bibles of tradition.

The tyranny of the despots of Paris last century were for enslavement of their country; they did not care for God or country, or the highest obligations of religion.

Mind is as God created it, on a fit theatre, the present earth. If the earth was no better than it is, mind better than it is would be unsuited in its abiding place, and would be much more dissatisfied. The earth then could be no fit abiding place for superior intelligences.

The mind may be stultified and deluded on all subjects; what but mind can expose the whole?

We ask and commend, require and prescribe an indispensable duty to the whole world to educate mind of all rational beings by faithful parents, guardians, and scholars, in the best of schools, academies, colleges, and universities, above all in the world's school, aided by Lycea, societies, mutual associations, lectures, libraries and the press, only on rational principles; and when mankind travel over the face of the globe, they will find that peculiar faith assumes, in its mighty divisions, to have for itself the orthodox infallible peculiar faith, on which their minds, through reason, have to act, to escape the wiles and defects of corrupt education.

God takes the will for the deed, and will duly estimate sophists who assume philosophy, and hypocrites who make faith worse—enslavers of their country, as Robespierre, Marat, and Danton, who cared neither for God, country, or religion.

It is the deep thraldom of past ages, perpetrated by imperfect and imbecile minds, claiming to be leaders, but false lights, that have produced this almost inextricable vassalage of the present age.

Mind degraded, brutalized, loses almost the very instinct that protects animals. Mind is for true analysis. It is power. How can you use this power rightly without rational education? The spirit of protection to mind is mind competent to analyze, adequate to comprehend, qualified to declare all light and right before all the world.

On account of the imbecility of mind and reason, the safeguards of freedom, arising from the circumstances of the age, blasphemous impostors have been rewarded as those of Christ, Mahomet, Smith.

All peculiar faith must be excluded when we have no vassalage of mind.

When freemen get rid of all the corruptions of past ages, they will universally adopt God's religion of principles, not of mere particulars.

If some differ for a time, they will maintain the essentials of right.

The diversity of the human race, exhibiting the proper elements of mind and its highest obligations, evinces the unlimited powers of the creative faculty, that bible-mongers wish to dwarf to their paltry notion, to falsify nature's laws to uphold their falsehood. We need not refer to history, when mind is at its best illustration. I ask nothing of impracticable testimony in the face of the independent universe-demonstration, that annihilates atheists and all that clan.

Let the majesty of mind of independent people put down all the vassals of social cliques and clans, teach and rebuke them effectually as serfs. O mind, be watchful as well of those who call themselves holy and divine, as the worst of the world. Sacrifice not thy only divine rights, thy independent attributes, to those selfish curses of the world. Respect principles all the time for the conservation.

The ancients knew not the science of mind's rights, or its mighty inherent powers. It is the character of low, petty monopoly and usurpation to decry all the efforts of mind with which they conflict, if its genius-discovery aid the people over their ignoble pretences and vulgar contentions. Mind, enjoy thy rights, thy blessings, not create evils for all mankind, thy universal brotherhood.

The supremacy of rational mind, religion, then order, and law, will follow no names. Let mind settle at once, now and forever, this paramount question of religion. God has settled it.

The Americans, adhering to the quagmire of peculiar faith, have stopped awfully short of the imperative requisitions of mind. All the ancients were the most abominable plagiarists of mind in advancing all the false pretences of oracular faith as supreme, and the Jews affect to have done this peculiarly. All peculiar faith, as that of the Romans, despoils God's attributes even by language. All the world would be as bad off as the people of China and Russia, Rome and Thibet, with their head autocrats, pontiffs, high priests, if rational mind had allowed it. That is the only supreme providence for all such impostors. Americans ought to be most grateful to their Creator that religion is not in the corrupt keeping of such men, who know nothing of conservative principles, that expose them as degraded impostors, and vindicate the Creator, whom they effectually represent.

Mind then needs the solution of the Great First Cause of the whole creation, and can only best approach it by all the best elements of cultivation.

If any authority declare for capital punishment, of course it is bound by all highest obligations to cause the mind of the world to avoid violation of essential principles.

What is the paramount duty of citizens as parent, wife or husband, child? The first has not only the province of being the author of vital existence, but its guardian, teacher, friend and instructor. All such must respect the highest intellectual, moral and religious principles.

Thus fornication and adultery cannot exist in the code of exact morals. The best instruction is the best self-government of passions.

Parents are responsible for tyranny that may engender the deepest ruin of their offspring, and the deepest injury to society. The exactness of truth must be properly secured, not by forcing lies, but inculcating rational principles. The whipping arguments are silencing means, but may accumulate results much the worst for all parties.

Childhood must be rightly cultivated, never tyrannized over. The virtues resulting from the faculty of mind, are not to be expected by the cogency of force.

Beware, parents, that you do not pervert the minds committed to your charge, as to injure all, deceive all, and destroy all.

If you rear your children rightly they will honor you and their own minds, their soul being in unison with the best sympathies with mankind, but if you do not direct rightly the best energies of their souls in the legitimate channel, you may arouse the worst of dormant faculties among them, as revenge, the most odious, embittering your sympathies with the human race. Above all, beware how you force marriages, as little less than prostitution for money may ever be the curse. Parents should not crush the spirit of their children, nor the government do that for its citizens. Parents must not expect too much of their children to support them unnecessarily, and therefore should act intelligently and with mind in their own independence for life, at the same time helping their children in the real time of need, when they first start out in life, and when it is so difficult to get that first right start. Their offspring should not be pushed upon the world uninstructed in the use and value of money, time, talents, and mind's best functions, as green pigeons, to be plucked by every sharper, gambler, and prostitute, the most dangerous of mankind.

Parents should never deprive their children of the necessaries of life, among them the best mind-fund education, to leave them luxuries that they cannot rightly use. In having mercy on themselves at the right time, they may be spared the sight of much wanton injury to themselves and society through their children. The question of mind is not whether their children are disbelievers in any bible of tradition, but whether they are infidels in the only Supreme Being, who is duly appreciated by the right code of mind.

Reason, then, will exert the most potent influences of all influences in the right employment of that mind; that is the world's best and noblest protector. Let us have no overworked, overtasked or ignorant mind, to make existence a curse instead of a blessing.

It is too late after the deed is done in the whole annals of mind's injuries, after the crush of the feelings has been committed, and the victims of a thousand follies and crimes been made.

How much is due from mind to mind in rational education, that may correct the one predominant idea that may be the master and exclusive passion of all others for the time being, causing suicide, murder, crime, or indiscretion.

None should dictate in this world, as that is tyranny of opinion, but submit to paramount principles of truth and honesty, not as individuals interpret them, but as they interpret themselves.

Who can be the standard while all are amenable to sin, error, ignorance, caprice and perverse will, but the master standard of the universe, its Almighty Creator? Who but absolutists would confine, thwart or defeat genius or principles? Not only appreciate the best gifts of mind, but cultivate them to best advantage of right and wisdom. What but this governs the elephant and cages the lion of the world?

What mind is so doltish, that sees not that the universe revolves in science, and is lighted by philosophy, but the odious reptile, the mere bible bigot?

This work is intended as original as far as practicable. The author is indebted to advance of public sentiment and mind for the balance. The object is to render this a useful code for youth, especially those needing useful advice at first.

In analysis of this paramount subject of religion, we may have been anticipated in some things, but the legitimate may be elicited by most minds.

Freemen, are you actually afraid to read a code styled the Bible of Mind?

What are you afraid of?

That if the bible of tradition be superseded, that we shall have no other! All these were only bibles of mind perverted and debased.

This age enables mind to offer its bible to meet that difficulty, to remove away the rotten building ere the destruction of its inhabitants.

The bible of mind is the only one of God for religion; any other is by man for peculiar faith that is dust indeed.

There can be no one living who believes stronger than the author in the existence of an eternal Great First Cause, and of the absolute necessity of accountability in the deepest reverence to his holy attributes, and respect to his conservative principles; but then he distrusts, impeaches and necessarily discards the bibles of tradition, that were written at a time when neither science, nor mathematics, much less astronomy, were understood; but would not mislead others for his life, nor be misled himself; therefore he asks for all the essential proof of their divine authenticity. An honorable defence, based on the merits of the question, is requested. We advocate the cause of rational and honest minds.

The peculiar faith people ignorantly tell the world to get religion, to do what they know nothing about. All minds, if rational, have religion, and have only to improve it. The people, though, never look into the noblest operations of their own minds, but are misled by vassals as herds, flocks, swarms of insects. There are the fewest original thinkers. Can there be, after due investigation, any doubt in a rational mind of its supremacy in the world's civilization? Historical records and all the lights of mind conclusively decide that position.

When we contemplate the four stages of mind in its progress, every step admonishes most truly of that. What, are not the teachings of savage life in bibles of tradition, oral traditions, &c.?

Formerly, as the author is informed, he states that the Creek Indians burnt their deformed offspring, or infants, as decreed by solemn meetings.

Indians have their superstition, their rain-witches, &c. A statement was made to the author, that not many years past a Choctaw rain-witch, not succeeding to her ambition in procuring rain in a great drought, disclosed to her chiefs and warriors the important item that another rain-witch, living at a distance, had counteracted her efforts to procure rain, and that it was essential that she should be killed forthwith, whereupon these sage savages proceeded to the residence of the rival rain-queen and murdered her accordingly. Mind that is slave to peculiar faith and superstition, is vassal indeed all over the world. One of its horrors is the fear of volcanic punishment from its brimstone and sulphur; to be swallowed up is one of its fears.

Science will disclose its blessings, to relieve the natural elements of a greater disruption, ever present to vulgar ignorance.

Enlightened public opinion will be a mighty engine of mind and of God, in process of time. It will put down despotisms of governments and peculiar faiths, in one breath.

What was it but the exaltation of mind that put down absolutism within the last century, when its brute force and bribery were the means of tyrants, before persuasion?

What but mind, exalted, is to teach America her mighty destiny, the light to all nations, the benefactress to the world? How sounds benefactress of the world, before its conqueress? The one diffuses diamonds, the other sheds blood! What will America be, when her countless resources are developed? But what will be the whole world, impelled by the same universal principles?

Universal legislation, that may be bad in all governments, if not enlightened by wisdom, has to be exempt from all perversions. The vitals of liberty are overwhelmed by perversions of mind. Universal rationalism must correct and rule mind universally.

The antagonisms of universal society, the rich and the poor, can only be obviated on principles.

The day will come when it will have been better for absolutists to have been humble citizens.

A revolution conservative must arise, in the world's society. Families, as nations, should have the tuition of philosophers of science, not the sophists of peculiar faith. Philosophers of science are necessary to better the world, by light of mind.

What others can enlighten the world?

There may be wise and good people among ministers and priests, not from their profession but in despite of it, however incorrect the way they take to prove it. As part of the human race, they should devote the best principles in the right way to secure mind its appropriate blessings.

The process of induction, by thought, is the way mind learns; but that process must be unbiased and uninfluenced.

We have our senses, to teach us by objects, without which, as by protracted solitude in prison, the mind may become demented.

The intentions of the mind present best prayer in actions. Recollect that in all your millions of errors, you must not censure, blame, or libel God once. It is your errors, not God's, you have to correct; turn your mind to the correction, not harrass God, by greater imbecilities.

How then can you address God, but by actions?

The best appreciation of mind proves that it was created for the great purpose of religion, the sublimest subject of the universe. Shall mind be ever deceived, cheated, by false pretences, and bound vassal to the car of peculiar faith, when it can most ably repel the whole attempt, and expose the felony?

The mighty result of rational education, if free, liberal, and right, is to teach mind to think, and be mind.

Mind has its rights, powers and attributes. One of its greatest is knowledge, of which the consummation is religion in its purity. The faculty of mind is to receive ideas through the senses, not by insidious, peculiar teaching, nor brute force. As there can be no innate ideas, mind should be purely handled. No tinkers should botch its ideas.

Men of thought are emphatically men of reason, and would be the world's lights, if not trammeled by peculiar education, the worst vassalage of mind.

Mind, enlightened and pure, can best procure every reasonable blessing, and best shun every supposed evil.

One thing alone, principle, will give mind advantage of the whole world on right basis. Religion binds the mind-universe.

Without principle, the world has the advantage of mind. A better world can be obtained by the world of mind, and that cultivated and elevated by exalted worth. The constant use of mind is the preservation of mankind.

Mind enables us to prove and demand proof of every thing, in religion.

Mind is indebted to mind for science, itself inspiring mind; all inspired from God of Intelligence.

The tribute is due to science of mind.

God presides over our science and mind.

What mighty benefits await the world, through the best lights and freedom of mind.

What cannot the lights of philosophy, in government of man and mind, in agriculture, commerce, navigation, mining, manufactures, the schools of science, effect? The present position of mind is that of a subordinate, that must be self-ennobled to supremacy. The right one should honor itself by rational religion, carried to its highest legitimate practice, and all its societies ever referred to the mighty central standard.

What has mind done for rational religion, that has done for mind everything necessary and expedient?

Mind will be cowed by humbug, and crushed by peculiar faith; though possessed of right and power, yet it is to be silenced before its and the people's pulpit, by the pretences of base assumptions.

Intelligent freemen, do you stand to all this?

The light of mind excludes all ultraism, all extremes, and sectional interpositions, reflecting the noblest deeds and influence of its powers.

It is the full perfection of mind, that gives the full benefits of the social circles.

No system, however glorified by names, can tolerate a crusade against reason and rational mind.

Is it fair, honorable, and just, to exclude the rights of mind, and bind it to exploded, obsolete ideas?

The paramount duty of mind is due to God alone, in the true way that purity of mind can be displayed. The past history of the world proves the errors of mind, in obtaining the best means of happiness. To answer all the cavils of disputants and sophists, will be to countenance the libels of imbecile minds. Time and science will decide, all that may be the balance. Let mind be right, and act uprightly, and there is nothing more to do. Reason is the self-preservation of mind. No man is honest, that discards reason in any department that mind can recognise. Honorable minds should discard such as a nuisance.

There can be nothing inconsistent with the right action of mind, that rejects faith and all its associations, if devoid of truth.

What mind can recognise all this, without reason?

Shall mind ever be in abeyance to the dynasty of peculiar faith? Shall there not be freedom of rational discussion, to investigate satisfactorily for all minds, this most important subject of rational religion?

Can we get the honest people of the world to discuss it, in the right way, not by an ignoble blinking of main and essential truths? Are they not afraid to do it, from the suggestion of pious frauds?

Crush mind, tyrant, ere you deprive it of correct religion, or the proper means to ascertain the correct position.

Mind must not be paralyzed by either sophistry or martial prowess, that usurped the rights of ignorant people. What shall be the arbiter of opinion, that varies so much? Science. Opinions, unless based upon philosophical science, eternally vary.

But how is it that men of science differ so much in opinion? From this very reason, both parties have not been equally enlightened by philosophical science; that, as the vicegerent, or minister of Deity, probes all opinions. That is only freedom of mind, that recognises full improvement of intellect and its legitimate rational principles; for you cannot declare the position of intellect without reason.

When the bibles of tradition were adopted, but the fewest in thousands could read and write.

Now it is a misfortune, if not a disgrace, to be unable to do either. Then others were necessarily proxies; and mind, dependent on circumstances of the age, necessarily became vassal. But her lever of independence, rational education, has been raised, and the cover of imposition, fraud and imbecility, has been lifted; hence, discovery teaches the true state of things. The sooner the world gets out of its antiquated notions, and learns of philosophical science, the better. When mind is rightly improved, it is justly independent. But yet it is not elevated in the best countries, to its noblest degree of refinement.

The power of original thought is too much for the masses, and the fewest are the pioneers by high-mindedness, independence of thought and firmness, that being necessarily of the phalanx of conservative revolution to obsolete notions, are opposed.

There are minds centuries in advance of their age, but they are the objects of envy, and of course obloquy with those behind them adhering to the last, to their base usurpations and monopolies. The pseudo-moralists are alarmed at the state of their bibles of tradition, that must necessarily perish because of their errors and demoralization, without being able to see the imperative need, adequate sufficiency and potency of bibles of rational mind, for purest morals. What influence the statistics of crime, but the deplorable state of mind's ignorance, errors and need of rational cultivation, that all bibles of tradition never can relieve?

How do evils cure themselves, but by the free exercise of mind illuminated? Let all this prevail, and all irrational repudiation, sectional agitation and fanaticism, will die the death of ignoble mortals. Mind that profits by the intelligence of agricultural science, to provide for the world's wants against famine, that dispenses to the world a most benignant commerce, that invokes all the aids of philosophical science to counteract pestilence, and that avows all the principles of universal brotherhood to guard against the evils of war, bids man recur to the true fund of creation.

The mind still needs organization, and all proper protection. Does any know half of the corruption of the world? Let him commence in the right of his own inventions and discovery, and then he will see the dishonor, perfidy and felony of it. Let all be progress possessing a legitimate order, and seeking if not enjoying the government of constitutional law.

Mind is to render the world like a plant bed, a flower garden; beautify, embellish and fertilize it.

Mind is helpless at first, and the beauty is, that it must rise on its own exertions and greatness, and overcome all conquerable difficulties.

Mind is to be prepared for future good.

Vassals of the various professional characters, cause the mind to be like humbugs, most clearly. Mind is to analyze itself, as it may be the dupe of the world. But mind likes humbuggery—unless put right, it may become perverted. Who believes that the world-mind likes humbugs? Its perversions, bad, morbid taste, cause that.

God appoints every mind to address, adore and revere him, as he ought to be. Intellectual existence is a bright dawn of mind. Beware of envy, avarice, inordinate and unprincipled ambition and malice, by which mind is perverted and falls overwhelmed and crushed.

Do not forfeit your rights in mind. How few use the principles of mind, the only sure basis of safety.

In the trackless ocean, what is your only safety? It is in the means of safety, of approved and conservative character. It is in chart and compass; your standards are the universe spheres, by which you correct your reckoning and amend your errors. By rules of exact science, you steer. God is the Creator; whom else can mind have; by whom else can it be sustained? Mind owes nothing to peculiar faith, but has experienced many of its curses. Do you know how to appreciate aught of life's functions, but by mind properly cultivated, in civilization? Suffer a partial loss of one of your senses, as that of hearing, then you may thank your God for his mercies and grace.

Are you going to forfeit your claims to these? Then you do when you permit usurpers to use you as a vassal, and when you pretend to adopt an intercessor, messiah or priestocracy, who have no such functions over mind the beneficiary. It is only over mind the impostor or the dupe.

Do not unite with hypocrites, traitors and unprincipled oppositions. Priestocracy is a rabid tory-pulpit to mind, and a traitor to its rights.

Mind must have all the elements of its greatness, the dignity and freedom, light of intellect, liberality, rationality—truthfulness.

The human mind will become vulgar and low, if not watchful of itself. Analyze your mind, and do not be victimized by ambition, avarice, lust, envy. Keep your mind your diamond, intact from corruption.

Mind has to act compatibly with the circumstances of the universe and God, whether free agency be the question or not. There is no tyranny in this: the evil is in the reverse. The property of mind is the paramount question for mind; it has to look to God for protection, and exert itself as a free agent all lifetime, by universal means.

What is man but as mind makes him? What accompany that mind, but all its elementary endowments that the Creator gave? Hence there is no need of, as there can be no substitute. All such is folly, man's most stupid presumptions. How can mind be substituted? Without mind all your messiahships are nought. With mind they are worse than useless, and of course they are worthless.

Mind that appreciates its own pure analysis, scouts and scorns such miserable nonsense.

The mind is God's lever, and his principles are its fulcra or points of support. Show the superiority of mind over muscle.

No bibles of tradition can furnish correct models for mind, while it is indebted for all its principles to the God of its creation. A great class of the world, it is that of mind that arises on the potency of its own greatness. In the future generations of the world, the last part will be best, by the best polish of the mental diamond. God is in all this.

The inalienable rights of creation entitle every mind to expect an appropriate position of its Creator.

Rational mind is the preacher, reason is the corrector, conscience is the auditor. Do you hesitate one moment at the real benefit of mind in civilization? The steamboat invention has put commerce under obligations, that in turn has caused the world to be inappreciably indebted to mind. We are in the infancy of science. All the operations of the universe refer to mind, else the last had been created in vain, and still more to the immortal soul, the noblest of all.

Who can estimate the mighty potency of mind-fund, that teaches the true taste, that teaches mind; while all should seek to soar above to proper fame, a laudable object, all should seek to avoid mere notoriety.

But how is man a being of free agency? He is created without his own volition, and acts without his own consent. Hardly, as he knows the difference between right and wrong, and is capable of dignifying his own actions.

The history of individuals and nations proves this conclusively. The Creator is bound to adjust matters compatibly with his obligations, but then man has something to do; he has to improve that mind in science, to read the God of nature's works. Under the circumstances of his creation, he is to avail himself of all the lights, all the aids before him to progress in his own best conceived happiness, that he independently sketches out. He has the aid of God's grace, and God estimates the will of the world's mind for the deed ; but for that, what would the world be ?

Do you know the value of an intelligent, sensitive soul? Do you crush the true spirit of mind, of the world, of worth, of both? The whole crime of deeds is in mind's conviction. Mind of the mass cannot analyze under malign peculiar education, it is minion to others' interests, and antagonistical thereby to mind.

The chances that occur for greatness to be displayed by mind cultivated to its execution, place it as the agent among the greatest deeds of the Creator.

How much of the world is sacrificed to mental imbecility? A free and intellectual press, is mind's lever in the world. The improvement going on in the Sandwich Islands is considered by the advocates of peculiar faith, as due to their missionaries, but it is the merit of mind to which it is indebted.

There can be no standing, invariable pattern for mind, only as the munificence of mind, allows it for mechanical arts by the best cultivation of legitimate taste. The world, as the universe, comes under principles, immutable laws. The mind is the only effectual means of elevation in life. Do not neglect its mighty and sovereign functions, its noblest rights. Mind now makes government lighter, revolutionizing it from despotisms. What was the state when the Hebrews were subject to priestocracies?

It is difficult to tell how far vassalage of mind extends. It produces the worst defects and disruptions of society. Be not surprised at vassal mind, that is like a whipt spaniel ; it stoops after being crushed by perversions.

Mind is made straw, overrun, yet mind recovers from the peculiar faith contentions that blast it most deeply.

Which is best off as to peculiar faith, the heathen and the savages, all that have their superstition, or the most refined of those assuming to be civilized? The refinements of mind make the difference, and secure all rights. Mind must not be trammeled by any of the obligations of life's courtesies, as hospitality, nor by anything less than absolute rights. Modesty is becoming, and rational custom is obligatory for reserved rights. Let mind produce a generous and exalted rivalry of nations ; all on the most liberal competition. Commerce is for the world's benefit, and furnishes competition and improvement, a noble position. What was mind for but to expand on such brilliant means?

Brain, or material organism alone, does not constitute mind without the soul or supreme element,—the functionary mind does not recognise animal, but soul-materialism. Industry and surety of living means to maintain existence, begin now to characterize mind of the present age ; one of mind's triumphs.

Man in the world must be treated as a being of mind, not of mere muscle ; not brutalized, but exalted here on this earth. What bespeaks mind's dignity and freedom more than the votes of the people? That liberty of the people carried out, presents a brilliant solution of freedom.

How many neglect their health, body, mind, their souls. To neglect the mind is to neglect the soul. To soil the mind is to soil the soul. What vassalage of mind is in the world, in villages and circles, in cities that analyzed, present villages Vassalage of mind is the abuse on conservative unity. The best settlement of world-agitation questions is by the cultivated honest intellect.

Mind is created as God created it, as we find by rational experience and science, placed under the circumstances of creation, with free agency, to work out perfection, undergoing appropriate purification.

If mind was perfect on this sphere of action, we should be doubtful of its perfect bliss. Its sphere is that of preparation, not of consummation of felicity. All systems, even of monotheism, are amenable to the proper decisions of rational mind, that has to look to it, a perfect standard, as religion of principles.

You advance a peculiar system of some peculiar bible of some peculiar nation, claiming to have a peculiar God, all which pretend to denounce the balance of the world with eternal damnation if it do not believe! We claim the protection of a free agent, as American, before we can believe. We must be assured by proof conclusive that all is right, to proceed with a clear and satisfied mind, and eyes open. Mind is essentially important, there is more in man than land, world, or mere universe. The mind is in trust, and to be improved, for time and eternity. It is not excellent, then bad ; that is absurd. The bible writers were actually ignorant of the analysis of mind. In writing this work we draw on the great treasury of mind—the store-house of rational mind. It might as well be said that the human body was to be destitute of clothing, as that the mind was not to complete its own improvement by the unchangeable laws that rule nature. What a dangerous state of things would rule the world if mind did not now preponderate. Look at the despotism of peculiar faith, that would lay this world in ruins if not governed by the ruling forces of mind. Look at the Mormons, driven from

State to State, expelled by force of arms. What if they had numerical force connected with their peculiar social position? Would not the world soon learn by the motion and power of that force? Peculiar faith rests not on truth, but on numbers and sophistry. Where would be the Christian if the Mormon had his millions to back him? None such rest on principles, all must be propagated by fraud. This is now the time of rational, not vassal mind.

Preconceived notions injure the world when they do not accord with principles. It is only rational to suppose that mind is created as God created it, rather than it was good, and that it fell because of God's rival, the devil. In the first is proveable to a demonstration that the devil is not the successful rival of the Creator of the universe, and that, of course, he never caused the fall of mind. · The party who conceived of the devil had not the capacity of complex ideas, as the free agency of mind destroys all devils.

It is the imperious duty of all minds to investigate all important science before the world, and above all, the great enigma that they have made of mind.

What is public opinion but mind set in thought progressive ; a tyrant in its ignorance, but a blessing in its wisdom and rationality ? Do not overtask the mind by the monstrosities of its perversions. Mind must be modest in declaring, as it is slow in progress. Much experience is necessary to verify facts. Investigate nature, not adopt the errors of preconceived opinions, no matter when, how and where recorded, whether in the so called bibles or otherwise. The only proper record is in the universe. Who will act traitor, vassal to mind ? How much treachery is there to mind, to arrest all justice of light to mind !

The mind is originator of legitimate motion and power, if mental derangement, that also refers to physical, moral and religious derangement, is not insidiously introduced.

Congratulate yourselves that this is an age of mind's presidency, and its progressive lights.

Mind has to rescue mind out of its state of ignorance.

There is no messiah known beside that can act if honesty be consulted. The Creator Almighty is the head of mind, to be enlightened in physics, morals, and religion. Let mind obtain a mind-fund or capital, then it evolves the whole cabinet of its own treasure. Away with the villifiers, libelers of mind and God.

Mind is beautifully adapted to the progress of God's light, revealed in endless and exhaustless succession, that otherwise would require an endless succession of inspiration. None but mind can fulfil it for the time, and the whole.

See, now, how deficient always has been every attempt otherwise ; eminently proving man's incapacity, but God's perfection. Mind gets truth by successive inspirations of genius and mind, whereas the old messiahships become obsolete in the light of science, and state false pretences. Any other revelations are so extraordinary that it is not safe to mind and truth to rely on any assertion short of extraordinary proof.

The only evidence of divine inspiration is mind's appreciation of God's works by science, and by its own progress in excellency of civilization. The potency of mind is constantly progressing, with each end the means, the last irradiating the preceding, and enlarging the circumference, enriched at an exhaustless mine.

Electricity, that was one of the gods of ignorance, becomes obedient to the action of philosophy, and subject to the laws and wisdom of science.

Mind, rightly cultivated and directed, permits no hopes of any to be taken away, but gives the benefits of a right investigation. Mind ought not to omit any of the legitimate demands of civilization or religionization.

What does it remain to this age, that humbugs are actually necessary to be used by mind for faith ?

Would you not prefer the pure deductions of mind to the false bible that gives poison to, along with its other matter ? The mind of civilization rejects the bibles of tradition of dark ages ; and all are dark with superstition.

The reason of civilization can be satisfied with what is rationally satisfactory. Mind has a birth-right claim on Deity, provided its merits are adequate for safety. The sophisticated, morbid state of feeling and of mind is miserable. Only see the effects of Moses' legends about witches and ghosts ; such false impressions, made by peculiar education, are hardly ever eradicated properly. Well, whence did they emanate but from the source of superstition. That same fund for a world's morals, the bible, gives it its worst funds of superstition. We should speak all the time of conservation of mind, not of heart. As to public opinion, we want none short of a comprehensive and philosophical view, as less than that is what is made of bibles of tradition, as the witch murders were those of public opinion, founded on the false position of such bibles.

It is mind for ever that gets out of the difficulty, by free and rational discussion. Do always what is right, practice all the virtues that enlightened mind approves and requires. Let the people know what is right. Let all principles govern the fallacy of bigotry and sophistry. Lay a right foundation. The mind should have something good to do. Mind is for science, science for morals, and morals for religion, which cannot be for less than the soul's immortality and happiness. Mind must regard all social improvements, as those of public virtue and independence. The blessed virtue of patriotism, calls for all the legitimate demands on the world, whilst religion invokes those for eternity and the universe. We recognise improvement by the advance of mind in everything, but old obsolete bigotry and its explositions.

The great obligations of society include mind all the time. But for the light and inspiration of mind, where now would be the law for witches, the priestocracy, and all such? Mind must become wiser and better every moment, or not exist finally in the result of eternity, that commands the conservation of principles.

Justice and virtue require the advocacy of high-mindedness. As the treasures of the earth are developed by mind, so are mind's richest purest treasures to be developed.

Mind is the true and only inspiration through science and truth, which is inspiration. As mind will believe the errors of a false education, the truths of rational education must predominate. The only proper dispensation effected in bibles, is the covenant of mind, and that did not require the false pretences of any priestocracy.

If these ancient and modern blunderers, stumblers on plain even ground, had appreciated a complex idea, they would not have involved themselves in these absurdities. In improving mind, we lay proper foundations for all other improvements, as in country, race, law, all things expedient, and learn to appreciate with just knowledge, the utter worthlessness of kings, and the reckless pretences of bibles of peculiar faith.

Mind is conservative in the world's imbecility.

What is the fatalism of Mohammed, when compared with the free agency of mind, that monotheism inculcates? What is any peculiar faith before the omnipotent free agency of mind? What, at once, may we say, is error, compared with truth? It takes mind cultivated to its supremacy of rationality, to decide rational questions.

Mind is the mighty lever to remove popular ignorance.

How much injury of the world springs from the sheerest ignorance? The mind, next to God, shapes, the policy of the world, that should be based universally in principles, to meet vital difficulties, and secure its general prosperity and happiness.

What are all local superiorities and peculiar notions without the mind of science? Stay not back the value of potent mind, by any stay-laws of exploded bibles of tradition, the veriest trash, not fit to cover the shelf of an honest-minded conscience. Many men assume to know much more than cultivated mind recognises: mind must counteract their false opinions. Act only when ready by mind, and be very prompt to be right.

All the actions of the world are based on mind, that is ever addressed. Hail, rational messenger of truth.

Mind cannot define all facts, but it has improved progressively in its ideas of God, as science advances; hence, its rational religion has improved, and must become perfect.

Mind must seek correction of many terms obsolete, from the ignorant idea that introduced them.

The mind when disciplined and practiced, responds to the pure demands of civilization. At the stern with principles, it steers through the rocks and breakers of life.

The power of mind is to move the whole world masses, for mind's protection, not oppression.

For what object is religion, but to make mind act to the highest intrinsic capacity and calibre; no system hitherto has done that, for all declared have traduced and degraded it. The character of mind is to sustain its good faith to the world without any oath.

Perverted minds seek to make an apology of their sins, by a non-entity, the devil. Why continue the exploded humbug for the world's strife? Is not robbery of God's attributes enough, much less the episode of such fictions?

Mind should become the constitutional government of the world. Shall the agitators of the world disturb it, by the inculcation of such flagrant evil as its usurpation? The true analysis of mind is, what is needed for the world? The brain must not be excited too much by paltry faith; it must be balanced by right and faithful education. Never let your God-gifted mind be polluted by superstition and bigotry, the advocates of which have traduced, lowered and belittled it, and have made it dependent on the veriest trash on earth.

But mind establishes the world's great constitutional rights, that world-intelligence that is spreading over all.

Had they previously prevailed in centuries past, there had been much less of the world's bitter wrongs that have convulsed it. Rational education must guard against the fanaticism of the human mind.

Beware of the slavery of mind. When we speak of the difficulties of the ancients, we speak of the difficulties of mind unenlightened and uncultivated, whether pagan or christian. Without mind the world is blank, with it cultivated, it is all that God ever intended.

We abjure paganisms, all bibles of tradition, all that is in antagonism to rational mind, all that can be claimed of the false positions of Robespierre and all his confederates, all that is not mind rational.

Be tender with the human mind, as it may be crushed.

If the world's history was exactly written by the spirit of truth, mind as rational as it should be, how different would much of it appear! Mind cannot ever be too modestly and rationally cultivated, or aim too high, when by peculiar education it may fall too low.

The greatest creation God ever gave is mind, that over-ruleth all peculiar faith, that is necessarily false ; and yet there are no miracles, as they exist only in the ignorance of mind. If there could be miracles, they would be what the works of the universe are. As to individual perverse mind, where is the mass of the world-mind ? It is progressing better and better. Who but God elaborated mind ? The vassalage of mind prevents conservative revolutions. Next to God of mind, is mind itself. This world is indebted to its beauties and wisdom.

It was mind that took Columbus across the ocean to this new continent, compared to ancient civilization ; and that caused the Americans to rise from the oppression of tyranny to liberty.

By the improvidence of mind may come all its bankruptcy, as of property, character, &c. The peculiar heaven and earth have been moved to christianize the world, and convert it to its peculiar faith ; but all will not do ; they cannot usurp the functions of mind, that in its excellency of civilization will vindicate itself and God its author.

Call the world from its lowest degradations by science of mind. The most that can be accorded to all sects is, that they helped to aid by general mind, when not perverted, but then how could that be ?

The functions of mind or sectarianism are two different things. What ruins nations and individuals ? Want of cultivated intellect, mind, and the right use of it.

All minds should be taken out of the current of peculiar education, as antagonistic to their best interests when founded on principles, or what is the same thing, of all the errors the correction of which ought to be sought. People of mind must regard it the means to rebuke the world's iniquities, through God's principles. Is life to be a vulgar existence, in abeyance to all the vulgar impostors, charlatans of mind ? What less than mind can recall vassal cattle ? What less than talents can make this world the proper embellishment designed by God ?

And what is it that precludes us from seeing and realizing the hidden treasures of the universe, that would give greater perfection to mind's knowledge and wisdom ? It is the want of science and mind.

We have to resort to mind to make exceptions in the bible, and it is best for mind that is invoked to rule in its own right. We must go for the freedom, as purity of mind.

Mind has been betrayed, humbugged ; the worst is self-delusion. The prince of characters is he who rules circumstances on principles, without being governed by those without them. The great principle of mind's right cultivation gives the right principles of logic, proper sense, and rational science, with honest intentions, not obtained by mere church membership. The mind under peculiar faith, is at enmity with God, unless regenerated by rational religion. The history of the world, and all science, eminently proves, and that most conclusively, that mind is the agent through the grace and spirit of God. Mind is at antagonism, but science of mind teaches the error. What was it that elicited our noble constitutional government ?

Was it christianity ? She who had been, and is now, prostituted to the union of church and state, from the days of Constantine, the emperor ? When she, as all sacerdotal despotism, has been allied to all absolutism of church and state, bigots must see and acknowledge at once, that it was mind. But churchmen of America, aided in that revolution. Not as churchmen, but as lights of mind, and this can be affirmed of all their noble deeds throughout the world.

We wish only to be right, not in error against an iota of errorists. The mind that seeks the conservative revolution of the world, has much of· its unprincipled baseness to contend with. Mind elevates man's situation in civilization, puts down affected masters, and rouses up the crushed feelings of the peon, and bids him be a man. Only mind cultivated, unravels the mighty convolutions of its own life problem, and gives them their purest solutions to bless existence temporal and eternal. The ancient mind, as even that of the Jews, knew not God. They had not gone far enough ; had not science enough. The most comprehensive revelation of God, is to mind, by his creation. Cultivated mind could not have discovered the bible of tradition, for it is clearly the peculiar work of the priestocracy, who have pretended to many assumptions inadmissible on earth. Mind is to elaborate its own good, that is the difference with the old regime. It is clear, that it has none perfected at first.

It perfects it through life, as far as mind can.

It relies on God, who made and endowed mind, what it is. All the object of instruction and culture, is to teach mind to think rightly, to fill its blanks and complete its mission.

Do all things right by mind, that is to do all things right by reason and religion. Do not complain or murmur about God, much less libel him, and if things be not right blame your own agency, and redress through mind.

What causes the elevation of civilization; what makes the world flourish? The right direction of mind.

To overcome the various difficult antagonisms of obsolete opinions and vain customs, effete notions and idle pretences of faith, a conservative revolution must be accomplished. A moral revolution deferred must necessarily produce a physical one surely, or the reverse, both or worse. Do not let your mind run into sophisms, that have produced the sacrifice of human victims. What is the slaveocracy of mind? The mass is slave to demagogues, that flourish in every age on the ignorance, the servility of the people, who decide matters still by custom and usage, not by mind and exact justice to original thought. We are all identified to mind in all the departments of life, action by mind, pleasure or pain, hope and joy, all through mind. Mind that is brutalized, degrades itself below animals. Mind has to act for the world ; the ancients had mind, but they were behind in science. The moderns who adopt peculiar faith, make that take precedence of science in the full legitimate comprehension. Our governmental institutions have decided much, that mind must take precedence of peculiar faith. The faculties of the mind are perverted by peculiar education, that disturbs the just relation of society and deprives the world of its best rights. Yet what are we not to think of mind, when it fixes a telegraph, whose electricity, as the emanation of Deity, out-travels time as measuring the earth's motions? But alas, there are two conditions and classes of minds, the one exalted, advancing ; the other perverted, retrograding, going down to the sinks of misery. While its electric telegraph advances before time the earth's motion, and the time may be when it will be diffused as means of intelligence over the civilized world, and hold all intelligence in close and rapid union, aiding all rational means to promote one universal brotherhood, that mind must be rational to tower over, and command itself. What an achievement mind-culture bestows, when self-control is attainable. A mind well matured by culture, bestows the only practicable equilibrium. Mind is for universal purposes. Let man pay due respect to his own mind. The moral and religious, as intellectual world will get right, if there be no counterbalancing perturbations. We have too little of mind's protection, in all the operations of life. Mind has to exert itself. Mind must seek the best thought and ingenuity with wisdom, but candor and firmness to avowal. How does man rise superior to animals? By mind that decides his superiority, and still more does it decide for him among races, endowing with power and potency. Mind alone will reduce unprincipled ambition, that is not satisfied with the whole world, to its proper legitimate position of noble daring.

It is difficult to appreciate the value of enlightened mind. Mind is to enable man to secure the safest position in life, in all its legitimate matters ; among them is religion. Mind has to trade on the capital of the world, and rescue the world from all difficulties, and avail itself of all practical advantages that are legitimate. We must not permit ourselves to be cheated out of our rights, therefore we must presume on nothing, or take nothing for granted, in any of man's mind's professions. The more you rationally cultivate mind, the more it goes against mean influences, ghosts and witches, dreams and visions, moonshine bibles. So far from waiting on the moon and such stuff, agriculturalists will act when ready ; mind that is rational will act when right.

Mind-culture teaches to best regulate ambition on any excess of passion, as any violation of the laws of nature will bring signal penalty. What detraction can be greater than want of merit? The appropriate conversation is one of the great funds for mind's improvement on rational discussion.

There are many mind's so constituted, that they have to plumb the track of leaders. Mind must so regulate the world, that it may cause it to rejoice in its own general prosperity. Mind must be able to scan the malign advice of persons, meanly advising far-sighted

but selfish measures, to benefit themselves but not the undertakers. The world's history presents this! Mind gives us the luxury of thinking, and genius avoids the trammels of the schools and bibles of tradition, that belittle and degrade Deity—libel him.
The social parties of mind cannot be those of peculiar faith. Mind has to relieve the world's necessities, counteract its oppression, prevent its baseness. We must watch all the time the functions of mind and time. Mind must overcome the malign influence of passions. Command your own resources; your own, if a right way, through the excellence of mind. Without the best use of mind, the world may use you up.
Break all the fetters and bonds of mind that is vassal. Independence alone brings nations and individuals to their senses, for the triumph of mind, whose rights must not be usurped, whose duty must not be violated. The proper use of mind under favorable circumstances, ought to render most possessors rich enough, if they live long enough, at least independent.
The great error of mankind, is in not using mind to the requisite degree of analysis, not looking deep enough into matters. Mind is the master of all the social and religious relations, under paramount principles. Command circumstances by mind, as far as practicable, otherwise you are their slave.
Indulge not in luxury and effeminate ease, if you seek to hold intellectual vigor. Mind must counteract the intrigues of life. The little brief authority is always rising up, in every little circle, even of republicans. Selfish ambition too often takes precedence of principle.
It is time that mind be freed from its trammels and proscriptions. People have now learned to think for themselves; they cannot be humbugged much longer. All tuition is for mind's reflection and benefit; any proposition to the mind, the more serious the more it involves reason and the reasoning powers, of course; above all is that of religion. This, of course, includes good faith, as this is belief in proper testimony, and nothing less. The rational religion of mind, having enlightened conscience, is the only thing to abolish sectarianism—a blot on the human mind, martyrizing public opinion, and botching up mind. Mind must be a conservative revolutionist. We must arouse the independent, self-relying mind. Why is mind alone, not self and free agent? How long shall the world be in abeyance to her charlatans and botchers of mind? The world is to be made a garden, to be embellished with roses, instead of mere thorns and thistles; to supersede the slavish passions of ambition, avarice, lust, and intemperance, by virtues; war, by peace; ignorance, by philosophical science; superstition, by rational religion. Under fraud, mind loses its self-respect. The world is only to be known and acted on, through mind that is its own agent.
Mind is to give us independence, genius, to tower over, not be curbed by, ignoble brutes. Nothing is valuable, if mind, forethought, and forecast do not preside.
Mind, inspired with truth and reason, vindicates God. Then rational education will instil all, that can enable it to do it satisfactorily. The vassal mind can be made to do anything. Mind, when serious, cool, and calculating, will do justice to itself, and can well be mixed with mind ardent, impulsive, and candid. We go for the immense moral power of intellectual greatness. We must go for a strict adherence to the constitution of mind: the bible of tradition presents no such thing. Why do people govern themselves even, without forms of government? Because the good of society absolutely required this, as necessary to be done.
What can be worse than the tyranny of public opinion, oppressive to free and enlightened inquiry?
The bible of mind is intended for the bible of truth, reason, and rightful action. To remove most of the supposed evils of the world by progress of light, and effect of the mighty cause, we must have the religious crisis, that of mind. Remove the ignis fatuus of bibles of tradition, then mind can hew out, by inherent genius, its mighty resolves. But for mind, peculiar faith would have ruined the world long ago. It has perverted it for thousands of years. Once upon a time, martial prowess and all its adjuvants, necromancy, divination, prevailed; but now rational mind, the oracle of God, inspired by true philosophical science, speaks out truly. The billions rush to hear, to read, to heed, at the fountains of instruction; the world becomes wiser and more virtuous. For what, as responsible moral agents, are we indebted, but to mind, that has to operate on principles? Why preach at all, if mind be not addressed?
The resources of the mind are to be elicited by mind; that must be sustained on the functions of its means. Do rightly, consult mind, act intellectually, not be crushed to suicide, when principles will render all remedial and triumphant. Giant minds now mould and direct public sentiment, on liberal and enlightened principles. The difference of races shows the value of mind. Why do nations perish, if not from want of energy, provision, and forecast of mind? We can only approach the holy of God

through mind, not the priestocracy, who cannot analyze the distinction. The mind ought to be prepared now, by right culture.

Myriads ignobly conceal their right opinions. Mind must seek the triumph of mind, in all things. We should never neglect the blazing and brilliant light, in diamond mind, that has been desecrated for thousands of years to the most unhallowed purposes. To become the gentleman, the civilized man, all are interested in best restrictions, to govern his own wayward nature best. Mind can only begin the elements of its knowledge, and its existence. Mind is now indebted to mind. Let the plain proposition be stated of all things, submitted to mind, to investigate untrammeled for itself. The pure and sacred holy functions of mind have been invaded and usurped, blasphemously so. Let mind always decide, right and honestly.

When we analyze the human mind, what an amount of influences, actions, impulses, and interests, the position in society brings! The more peculiar, the more difficult for its rights to be maintained. Mind must expect one conservative revolution after another, as a necessary consequence of existence, till the mighty problem of life is solved. The mass of the people is very curious when it mistakes doctrines for principles. When one bolts, most bolt.

The wide world is made of sectional parties, that are deeply engaged in crushing the rights of the others, not in maintaining the justice of their own, the whole.

The right universal position of mind is to receive, at all times, right impressions, but repel all false pretences, rites, ceremonies, fasts, or feasts.

Mind, not messiahs, had the mission, whereby universal justice and action are done. Our minds are created as they are, to improve on the elements of right impressions already there, proportionately, as rationality is developed. Mind is not equal to its capacity, from peculiar education, as the sophists have taken possession of the world to a great extent. Justice must take possession of them.

The greatest power of mind is the true inspiration of genius, that cannot be too highly cultivated in all the primary blessings of rational education.

What is man but for his mind, rationally cultivated? What is mind but for the soul? What is that but for immortality; and what are all but for God the Creator?

A satisfied state of mind is essential to happiness; therefore, one should make up his or her mind to be practically satisfied with the world. The religious contributions of society establish that position.

Mind proves rational religion—no other can be proved. Mind, and that cultivated to its proper elevation, is the only protection to man. It is his holy guardian in religion. It was by mind usurped, that all the councils of the priestocracy voted in their bibles, having first thereby manufactured them. Now it must be by mind, that rational education of the world must correct all that. The present bigoted sociality changes and deranges the mind's noblest sociality. The present is venial, and derogatory to mind's noblest position of independence.

We must not forget what belongs to race, as gift of organization, and the endowments of science, that aid in concurrent reformation.

The mass of the people, if senseless, must be without principles, and therefore dangerous.

The world has grown older and better, as mind is cultivated which civilizes the world. All the means of mind-instruction is essential to this result; consequently, the fourth or last age has just been commenced to this elaboration.

The enlightened mind is clearest of idolatry.

Look at the physical, moral, and religious condition of the world. Mind has to operate on it for future good; hence, its liberal, moral, and intellectual agency is requisite and undeniable. As free agent, the mind was not enlightened by science at first.

When a man leaves the sublimity of mind's innocence, he has the degradation of brutes, and may be assimilated to their general natures, more or less combined. Mind must recognise the merits of all cases, as well of religion as of science.

When mind commences, it is to receive impressions, of course of the right kind. The object of all rational education is to procure the highest balance of mind. How ignominiously have mind's rights, qualities, and powers, been overlooked and crushed! How was Europe recovered from the degradation of the dark ages, but by mind? What has put America before the whole world, in the true principles of government, but mind?

What can we think of those bigots who have not the materials or elements of friendship, and will sacrifice to the false views of society at the anxious bidding of popularity, all that is dear and sacred to mind? The facilities of postage will enable the transmission of much improvable means by mail, to reach the universal wants of mind. We have gained much knowledge considering the difficulties of perverted mind; how much more would it not be, if all superstitious faith was laid aside, and the mind left free to act rationally ?   The mind is not left free, and never will be, till rational education liberates it.   Mind has disregarded religious science taught by God's works and word, as in his edition, not man's, and must rely on rational education.   The supremacy of mind comes into play everywhere, for the best good of the world.   Let this be menaced with many potent elements of trouble, yet let the gifted sons of earth arise superior to all.   What is it that mind must not take hold of in this world ? All that genius can invent, mind has to do.   Her very inventions and discoveries excite still new theatres. The mighty inventions pertinent to navigation, to steam, all demand further protection of mind.   The fatal collision of ships and steamers at sea, in night fogs, are among the first.

Mind should ever make triumph out of supposed defeats.   All proper relative allowances must be made for mind, under all its circumstances.   Should a steamer have appeared to the ignorant ancients without any intimation. it is likely that they would have worshipped it for a god ; yet the ancients made some great discoveries.

PHRENOLOGY ACCORDING TO PHYSIOLOGY.

But what is mind ?   It is not the mere functional action of the brain—the mental organ as known to mind somewhat analogous to the appreciation of Deity's attributes through the universe, but it is some element with functional attributes.   The mind analyst, then, can read somewhat of mind's characteristics through the phenomena.   It may perceive the individual calibre, and some of its qualities.

One of the best results is the appropriate cultivation of the various organs to benefit individually, socially and universally.   Beware of mind's abuse.   No overworked mind should destroy the brain, by severe intense action thereon.

The overworked mind, of authors especially, breaks down.   Southey, Scott and others prove this most sadly.   When mankind resort to stimulus, as opium, they may become its slaves, to the ruin of health, principles and character.

Night watching and study may be deeply injurious.   The best position in life is to have a well balanced mind properly directed in well balanced physical and mental labor, to secure the best safety for mind and body, to counteract the various passions and emotions, as grief and fear, that affect the nervous system.

Fortunately, a necessary abstraction of mind by natural causes prevents much injury that the possessors are not aware of.

Before genius lays aside her wand, let her inquire if the felon monopolists of the world are still holding the people's mind's-rights in abeyance, and let her properly direct the best organs to counteract them.

The organ of conscientiousness is one of the noblest in the whole.   That of firmness is next to that of conscientiousness ; cultivate both organs, as well as the intellectual, with the intensest care, as the best conservatives of mind's purity, innocence, greatness and magnanimity.   These important organs have a protective influence over man's noblest character, and promote the ultimate designs of Deity ; but what organ of the mind can be legitimately neglected ?

The world must be put on the basis of conservative revolution by mind, as it needs a high-minded independence to make the purse-proud and money-power loving and usurping know their places.   The world needs to be satisfied in mind, and should be.   Respect what cultivated mind enjoins, not to stifle its rights, but let it possess the benefit of rational education.

The most extraordinary thing in the world is, that the world should prostrate itself for the benefit of cliques and despotisms ; but it is even so.   Where is rational mind ? Will it never learn, and assert its rights ?   Mind should not remain imbecile and helpless, but must rise on its own exertions.   All matters in the world have direct reference by the wisest design to the whole world, which mind masters.   Mind cheats itself worse than the world cheats it.   Some minds, no matter the calibre, without education, rational of course, cannot reach their elevation.   With peculiar education the best minds are warped like crooked guns ; no matter the calibre, they dare not shoot straight, cannot get over the defects of sophistry.   With rational education, all rational minds can trade properly on the world's rational capital.   Now all peculiar faiths trade on the capital of rational religion, and most ungratefully deny it.   They act by aid of mind, and corrupt it.   The legitimate, pure, chaste taste of refined mind begets rational religion, and nothing else.   If God never created evil, as he did not, what then must be mind's perversions.   Mind must look rightly at the great world-capital.   The only aristocracy is that of mind, embellished in its noblest intrinsic virtues and magnanimity. The wisest actions of cultivated and refined mind are needed to meet the mighty fluctuations of contingences in the world. Who can come up to the noble requisitions of mind ?

Mind is the holy conservation of the Creator; therefore let not the priestocracy profane, pollute or corrupt it.

A proper cultivation of mind will decide nothing in favor of pride, but all for highmindedness. The world should beware of vulgar extravagance, enervating luxury, and the foibles of pride and vanity to keep up appearances, that may keep out independence. To appear gorgeous, one may make himself miserable. The only real aristocracy of the world is that of mind, and itself measured by the world-benefit and patriotism it produces.

The real sovereignty of mind bespeaks the noblest intellectuality. In regard to the rejection of all untruths, the bible among them, a plain honest duty is before the worldmind. The rational world-fund is for talents, genius, mind successfully employed.

But mind alone will not do, when we come to consider the real intention. Rational mind is the very thing, having the soul and emotions.

They who seek to bind mind to the bible of tradition, do the rankest injustice to the mind of mankind. The motto, never give up any thing rational, will bring the world to its sublime rationality. What is not rational on earth to mind is to be avoided. Peculiar faith is not rational.

The world will necessarily bow to the majesty of intellect, the aristocracy of mind, that must rule out all the vassal impositions. The debt of parentage and country is to promote the noblest good to the greatest number by rational education. When this is done to the world, religion, that is put far behind the progress of constitutional government, even in America, that now ought to be its equal and certainly must precede, is made to be in abeyance to the odious political capital of peculiar faith. Patriots and statesmen, sages and philosophers, do not permit it any longer. Even God does not make mind vassal, when he nobly endowed it with moral, intellectual free-agency, under the wise limits of creation; how then can even an autocrat do it ?

THE MIND OF INFANTS.

CHILDREN have the most pure and unadulterated minds, the reflection of Deity, and ask for the duty and purity of mind's action and right education.

The best impression of mind is already there in the purity and innocence of its capacity, identified with their creation and birth-right for the wisest and best purposes.

The world is fully interested in its preservation, and must exert all to spare the spoliation of such a noble gift, that has the most exalted innate faculties.

Wisdom and purity are enlisted to prevent its being despoiled for false gods, pretences, powers, and miserable emoluments, that lay waste the fairest portion of God's creation.

The world is deepest interested in seeing that such mind is not polluted by ideas revolting to reason and God, nor fall short of the fund that protects, defines, and renders happy.

The consolation on one's death-couch will be sustaining as one of the best in life's annals, to uphold the helpless and innocent mind, incapable of defence, against the difficulties and conflicts of a wrong faith or position.

If sectarian that faith, no matter how fanciful and richly painted, it will be hopeless, and the inherent expectations, however high wrought, will and must have an end ere long, in the universal power of the one living God, who looks alone to mind and reason. Of what moment will it be, to convert to an evanescent doctrine, that must perish before the bright light of truth ?

Children become the citizens of the world, to labor for the great ends of their Creator and his true glory, not as apostates for men's vain glory and dying pretensions.

Theirs, rightly nurtured, will be a true fame, and is a mighty power, to shield souls in safety by rectitude of mind.

Look to its principles, and invoke their best truthful tuition, and leave the balance to mind, that is accountable for its own choice.

The infant mind must be taught self-independence to look alone to itself, for its own accountability on the best performance of its whole duty.

Let mind be most liberally cultivated by rational education, that it may elicit its own glorious salvation from its own richest funds, with a freedom that is lovely, and a wisdom that is full and comprehensive of God's magnificent purposes of creation.

Such mind, if put right, will honor the true God, seek the true way, and be a true follower of true religion.

11

How difficult is it to eradicate false conceptions of peculiar faith, when once established : the noble mind should not be misled for priestocracy, sordid lucre, and false systems of faith, that truly analyzed, are abominable and demoralizing superstition and false, senseless worship.

Let mind be truly and nobly enlightened, that it may not miss the way that the purest inspiration leads. There is a right and wrong way as different. Both cannot be right.

A right cultivation rightly directs, as a plain sign-board, and has an unmistakable stamp, that no mortal can put thereon.

The other is necessarily counterfeit.

Whoever have been taught wrong, should not persist in the error of their ways, but rectify their errors by the light of their reason and philosophy, the shortest expression of proper sense, and then they shall stand amid the wisest and trustiest of the land. How accursed are those that mislead the mind of the innocent to wrong faith, no matter the object, but especially the bigot, the sectarian, and all that deny to God his just sphere and attributes.

The proper education and cultivation of mind from infancy to manhood, or mind's full maturity in the world's school, are to give the right direction and the genuine bullion, that each possessor can fashion by his or her own taste and genius, to the highest elevation in refined civilization.

It is to teach all to act aright under all untried circumstances, knowingly and satisfactorily, to escape the wiles and duplicity of sophistry, that ever takes her advantages, the counterfeit of truth.

THE MIND OF YOUTH

Is to be trained to eschew flattery and sophistry, and to speak boldly and candidly the truth in all its comprehensive bearings, when necessary for public good. It must have sound principles, the best guide for life and correct faith, whatever that faith may be.

Nothing, then, can be withheld in the compass of its whole duty, through craftship, or anything under the power of the Creator, to invalidate or control its first and constant perception of its duty.

Youth's mind is to be moulded according to its mental quality and inherent calibre, and come weal or wo to sects and denominations, truth must be adopted. Truth begets truth, whilst sophistry begets sophistry. The progeny must be like the parents.

Paramount truths should never be withheld from the world from paramount reasons, as the best and purest should be given as the portion.

Accursed be that tuition that leads to untruths, for perjury and corruption of the people have had their foundation at the same time.

All youths should have an independent mind fostered, to overcome sectarian views, that have been propagated by tradition recorded, as if book sophistry was any the less sophistry, and bibles were less fables, when fables and legends were their foundations, and faith any less than blind credulity resting on them.

What cannot stand the tests of mind, the analysis of truth, be it covered with the silver locks of old age, or the cobwebs of past ages, is unworthy of mind's respect.

Truth only is to be reverenced by youth in faith.

THE MATURED MIND AND SOUND JUDGMENT.

Does educated, cultivated, and enlightened mind, hesitate at its best good ?

Does such mind fear man rather than God ?

Such mind easily sees, when abstracted from all the malign influences too potent in blind credulity, that the present state of peculiar faith of the world is most accommodating and credulous, that adopts much of absurd and contradictory traditions, no matter from what source.

Such mind must see that all, when reduced to reason, and tried faithfully by her tribunal, are dissipated like mist before the meridian sun.

Such mind, triumphant in its intrinsic sagacity will aver most satisfactorily, that there is no supreme reverence due to any but to the Creator. That whenever mortals violate correct principles, their claim to mind's respect is cut off, on the rightful policy of truth and self-preservation. All wise minds will ever try all things, without exception, by analysis and analogy, reason.

If any exception be made, no matter in what, religion or any invaluable subject, then the position is blind faith, dishonest and stupid in full.

No enlightened mind can be spell-bound by any irrational faith, as it will always demand that all faith and all testimony be submitted to reason and truth. Hence, faith, no matter what, is worthless, unless substantiated on this basis of rationality.

The practice of the world is to test all others by such standard, if forced to assume honesty.

Neither Deity nor duty can be appreciated, except through the agency of cultivated mind.

The appropriate mental fund, matured in the richness of its own innate greatness, ripens a plentiful harvest of native independence, that divests mind of feudal vassalage, confines best to the strict limits that virtue creates, and avoids all the torturing penalties of vital errors, the most dangerous under the licentious sway of ignorance and vice.

The conclusive bearing of all these views, leads all, with ample and just confidence, to certain definite and ennobling results, that give the best independence and consolation. The paramount duty of enlightened reason arises therefrom, to refine humanity with all the graces of civilization, adorn her with all the courtesies of life that can bless mind; to liberalize the soul in its stateliest capacity, not only avoid all the results of equivocal character, in daily intercourse with the world, but to do most positive good to the greatest extent and number, and refer to the most certain and authentic genuine Author of all good.

He that views his duty and his secret professions aright, must not waver, doubt, or defer the right action, at the right time.

Man must, then, do his part dutifully and most faithfully, to secure the co-operation of Him who thus announces and secures the correct position.

THE DIVINE RIGHTS OF MIND THAT IS OF THE PEOPLE, THE ONLY ONES ON EARTH.

ALL children should learn to think, and speak the truth. But how can they, under this ignoble regime of absolutism, conceived most cunningly, for the good of the vulgar pretences of those mastering the divine rights of the people? Rational popular mind lays the foundation of the people's future usefulness and character. They can then reflect the greatest of all legacies, the principles of mind, on the past and the future, on parents and posterity.

All good states, the whole world, will be the mighty gainers.

This is what rational religion inculcates, all the time. All proper physical and mental development must be promoted; how can that be, if peculiar faith bigotry dwarfs and warps the mind by its peculiar sophistry. All sound, rational minds should have a proper, rational, scholastic education, and all should choose or be apprenticed to professions, trade, or business, as far as expedient or necessary, to maintain that healthy existence that nature requires, or that independence that social virtues adorn.

No children can be sectarian, without pretending earthly leaders mislead, or they pervert themselves from sinister motives, at this present age.

The numerous oppositions of sectarians affecting divine faith, to the genuine faith, can speedily die out, if peculiar faith be not inculcated prematurely in mind of youth, and made a part of the curses of sectarian education.

Let no tender mind be reared in fanaticism, social, moral, or religious, that separates the world with unsuitable antagonism.

What are all bibles and their teachers worth, that commend the slavish doctrine of divine rights of absolutism, for the only divine rights, those of the people? To whom should freemen, enlightened in their government, resort for tuition in religion? Surely not to any that show a vestige of absolutism.

Mind, that has obtained its dignity by the principles of freedom in its own fundamental institutions, should never place itself in abeyance to the enslaved mind of any country, degenerated by her luxury and overwhelmed by her imbecile faith.

The people of the ancient, or monarchical world, were and are miserably enslaved, by its priestocracy, in horrible superstition, and cannot give its peculiar faith to the free of America, when all is condemned by truth.

Religion is in proportion to national elevation, intellectual and moral civilization. America should exact the true. She should seek to diffuse the true light, that the stains of superstition on mind in every past age may be obliterated.

It is due to freedom of government, to secure full, pure freedom of faith, seen in rational religion.

The mighty power of the people should participate, in all rightful attributes.
Prospects may have been most gloomy, as those of freedom's past revolutions, but the result was most brilliant, for continents and the world.
The most liberal, rational, and just deportment, procures the best results to all the world in general.   Freemen, have you esteemed, valued, and availed yourself of your noblest liberty, privileges, and rights, in all the attainable points of life?
Have you helped to put down ignorance and error, repulsed bigotry, dispelled superstition, and overcome sophistry?
Have you sustained the defence of nature's rights, on her free and lofty principles?
The world has ever been overrun by vile and degraded demagogues, thirsting for power and self-interest, reckless of consequences; ready with their trainband vassals and retainers, to swear to any and everything base and perjured, in order to succeed.
In injuring mankind, we seek to injure their Creator.   To do justice to principles, we must comprehend the whole relations to their Author.

SOCIAL AND RELIGIOUS DUTY OF MAN, TAUGHT BY MIND AND TIME.   THE FAITHFUL OPERATIONS OF MIND.

MAN must look faithfully and wisely all the time into the operations and functions of mind, as their character alone safely guides to correct and profitable conclusions, essential to vital benefit and immortal happiness.
Man seeks the reward of his merit, in the various grades of its worth.   He clearly has to abide the penalties of demerit.
As certainly as virtue that is the practice of correct principles is rewarded on principles, in her various attributes abundantly on this earth, too plainly for the eye of philosophy to mistake, if principles be faithfully taken into the whole account, in action and estimation, so surely has vice, which is a violation of the certain laws of creation relatively to strict religion to God, and social duty to man, to sustain undeniable penalties for violation of such inherent principles-that vindicate themselves to assert the supremacy of their author, who is pure, perfect and almighty.
Those principles then become universal laws for all.   In the progress of time, a more correct knowledge of principles that are inherent, the growth of centuries matured, as philosophical science was developed, and man's highest duty, as his own best self-preservation socially and individually requires their most faithful observance, and is the promotion of their future eminence and elevation.
It is individually or in mass, that organic principles apply, and they decide authoritatively for mind's best good, if it act the part of true and enlightened wisdom.
The mind's powers were devcloping from age to age, each reflecting circles more or less enlarged, till they burst forth in development, in more universal good and liberal progress.
Minor lights had glimmered in the vastness of space and remote obscure durations of time, till master fires were enkindled in various mighty revolutions; then it was that the greater luminaries were conspicuous, and their beams beneficially effulgent, until now the whole series begin to be irradiated, and blind is the mind that will not see, stupid its constitution, that will not discard irrational superstition.
The mighty functions of mind and time co-operating, have taught men to think systematically, and respect principles that they cannot now overlook, as tending to the great ends of the Creator.
System that bespeaks science, finally brings man to know and record his proper codes of ethics, most essentially important and absolutely necessary, and seeing their comprehension in the world's wide theatre to an endless eternity, mankind is better enlisted to the proper performance of all duties to God and man.   The world, whose large majority, unless perverted by habit, is disposed to act up to its rights, seeks to know them rightly, to perform them appropriately.
None but bigots, cowards and blockheads are afraid of science in theology and in all matters.
In the morning of his days, man enters the beautiful edifice of his existence; innocence supplies the place of severer science, and throws the mantle of its noble protection over his halcyon moments.   His mind realizing the benefits of reason, leads him finally to the conception and exercise of its best functions; good habit secures the certain results of his duty, and patient perseverance joined to true confidence, rational faith, arising from true knowledge of the laws of his nature, give him a triumphant vital career.
Perfecting sound science by seeking true wisdom, it becomes all men to test by ex-

perience, which is testing light of mind by time, his whole position, and declares the manly intention of being wiser in future. Mind's first and last duty ever points to its Creator and attributes.

CONVERSION.

THIS is claimed to be a change or a new birth, in a second human nature. Now can there be any change but by light of mind, that comes by rational education? When is the victory for individual mind, in the whole world? It must embrace conservative principles, otherwise it has an uncertain tenure of elements dangerous and suicidal.

Religion then, is, when deciphered, mind yielded up by reason into the embraces of soul and emotions, but all must be under the commands of mind's highest and soundest duty. Religion is the true expansion of the human rational mind.

Without this, the world is strange, because perversion of mind perverts it or makes it strange.

Religion then, sets the proper seal on mind.

Where is the limit to any doctrine adopted, but reason? Can you as a good and true citizen, exclude mind's best friend, reason? You may affect spiritualization, enthusiasm, ecstacies endorsed by feelings, zeal, devotion to martyrdom, but all must be tested by reason and Monotheism.

The perverted world can get up any creed of any peculiar faith, but for reason, all the time mind's protector. But reason may mislead.

Reason as all others, must be ruled by the universal standard, to be right. But reason has been rejected by faith.

Now we see where priests have misled us, where we and the world are.

Faith and reason are two great principles of the God of nature, and cannot possibly clash. The clashing is all from mind's perversion.

Faith has superseded reason, and of course faith of all kinds we have with a vengeance.

The world pays the expiation of all this treachery to God and reason, by billions of humanity sacrificed on faith's bloody altars.

How can we thus erect enlightened public opinion, that is the supreme ruler, as high as man can go? It is hid under faith's sneaking pretensions.

There are some inhumane, almost lost to all conventional rules of society. What of that?

The bigot in peculiar faith is apt to be a brute in friendship, ungrateful and stupid. Have you ever analyzed human nature, the world?

Were you always in affluence, so as to look at the sunshine only, and not at the shade?

Why is there education of mind, if entirely and absolutely a free agent? It is to give it command of circumstances of creation, the universe. To do so, the soul has to perform its universe-solution problem.

To train and evolve rightly the affections along with the intellect, the mind, with all its appropriate functions, is the work of the most comprehensive education. But let the question be fairly stated. Reason that operates, if perverted by malign effect, with valid perversion on society, is to possess its equilibrium on all just educational principles, to do justice to mind and Creator. When the question of the judiciary is asked, is the culprit insane, or of responsible mind, the full amount of free agency under the circumstances of its education is admitted. Free agency of mind implies a liberty of will and choice with a becoming knowledge, to insure a proper responsibility.

When the soul governs adverse circumstances, that is what a right rational education is for, to be the true director of reason. An enlightened free agency, results from the religion of principles; thus the mind is ever under the influence of peculiar or rational education, in the first of which it is misdirected by faith, and in the last, guided by religion. Adam and Eve, the Jew bible pretended first parents, were perfect, and put into an Eden, a paradise so called, and yet fell in their perfection. That is a libel on mind and its Creator.

THE PRESIDENCY OF MIND.

MIND was ruler when time began.

Do not let the world injure you. How will you prevent it? By the proper use of mind, that calls for a wise legislation, administration, and due execution of proper laws, that are equitable, just, and constitutional.

The world must yield to rational mind all that it is entitled to.   To whom else can the tribute be rightfully paid? Mind is to solve the problem of life and soul.   Do not be tory to them—to the noblest principles of the richest legacy and heraldry of the universe.

Absolutism is a world-tory conspirator against the rights of mind, the people. Is the world tory to mind? Rationality is to govern rational minds, that know no faith but through that channel ; all else is false and bad, perverse, wicked, and evil.

Embellish mind, the earth, society, duty, government.

It is for sovereign mind to explode that old dotard, the old regime, the tyrant.   Meet all the world-questions with mind, not as charlatans.

Have discussions every seventh day, to perpetuate the blessings of mind's progress through science, philosophy, and religion, in their sublimest principles known, not as now, in hearing what does not improve mind, but renders it bigot.   The universe is always in motion, and time, the exponent, declares that, and requires of mind proper action.   If rational universal education be not universally fostered, then the deficiency reflects on the world in all the departments, and in none less than in religion.   Each mind must be rationally cultivated, else it may degenerate into horrid superstition, that is only graduated by the light of the times, even to human sacrifices.   The sovereign people must not relax their comprehensive vigilance, through the proper operations of the human mind.

The last best rise on earth is that of rational mind to its highest rationality.   This teaches the world that the height of logic is not to use rhetoric, but argument ; not to resort to sophistry, but expel it in its most insidious world-coils, under its most extravagant disguises and assumptions.

When mind declares its world-independence of peculiar faith, it will be the most glorious day of refined civilization.   Mind is to overcome all life and world difficulties.   The mind has God-elements of religion, and knows its Creator by its five senses, operated upon by the universe.   Any other view is peculiar, and is the result of peculiar education.   However sacred be feelings, still soundness of judgment ought not to be alienated for minor objects.

The recognition of God is by and through mind. How shall this question be otherwise properly decided? It must be decided by supreme rationality, referable to the supreme standard of the universe. It does not depend on man's books, that cannot touch the question in their present absurdity. All that exclude the civilizers of the world are guilty of high treason to mind—rational education.   Do not turn traitor or tory to the noblest intellectual rights of mind.   Cultivation of mind by science and philosophy is expedient all the time.

Give the proper liberal expansion to rationality of the world. I have a duty to perform to my mind, the world, that must not be omitted. Let rational mind have no trammels of the bigot partisan, but obey the high behest of principles.

In eliciting the proper resources of mind, we elicit the proper resources of the world.

All rational minds should have nothing short of a rational education.   Mind that has no laudable curiosity has necessarily great ignorance ; the more bigotry it has, the less rationality.

FREE AGENCY OF MIND.

On the best principles of free agency, the intelligence of mind, in perfect equilibrium, would correctly decide that question ; but these bible worthies write as if this was the only world, and that mind could be here perfect ; a perfect nonsense.   This is only a perfect world, and mind can only attain through life a perfect state at best comparatively. That is the great question, how far that worldly perfection can be attained by mind.   Now as to God's not giving mind the proper issue, the proper direction, that is a libel, as proved by the religion of principles.

All minds are bound to act from the circumstances of the universe, and act with the best taste, that moral spirit is the only true test of greatness.

Mind has free agency for good or evil, as it is properly educated to maintain its just equilibrium on rational principles, that master all up to the circumstances of creation.   What creates a sound public opinion? That which builds up the noblest light of mind.   What are mind's attributes? Those of Deity must be considered to solve the question. All in the universe subserve the noblest inspirations of mind and soul.

It has been said that Deity has not given mind light to reach the solution of its purpose.

This is a libel, for these are the universe marks, too visible to be mistaken, that is, the consecration of mind and soul's physical, moral, and religious being, that leads to the sublimity of universal happiness, and the avoidance of individual misery. The Great First Cause adopts all as instrumentalities for future good.

In the present corrupt frame-work of society, mind, the superior, is held in miserable thraldom to creeds and notions, all being false of course.

The supremacy of mind is proved by making the best available legitimate capital out of one's errors, follies, and crimes. Mind must not depend on others to do its own best correction, to redress its own wrongs and injuries, when its capital is the best in the universe, that of principle. In all institutions rational mind can most satisfactorily protect itself, its best reputation, by a proper check and balance. ,

The necessity that compels mind is that for the universal comprehension of principles. It is the area of fruitful religion, that consummates its eternal happiness. Mind is a free agent under the wisest dispensations, else God the Creator had been responsible for moral delinquencies. God is responsible for the complete comprehension, and mind is bound to embrace it in the purview of its immortal fruition. To have mind fully right, it must have full and complete rational education, in full and complete maturity of time and ways. Educate the mind rationally in time, to eradicate superstition.

Supersede churches by all the noblest means of rational education. Spread all the best lights of principles, and the world must and will be duly enlightened.

What can compensate for the loss of functions? Money ; trash, shadows!

Provided that mind acts consistently to its enlightened functions, the whole world could in a short time be fully vindicated from the thraldom of ignorance, and the curses of perversion. The mind's perfection cannot be attained on this stage of being ; other portions of the universe are requisite.

God, infinitely perfect, should in justice render mind adequate and equal to the reformation of its own abuses. He has clearly done so. Free agency of mind is to secure the noblest results. The highest tuition of the universe is religion, that teaches in the beautiful and consistent principles of cause and effect, all forming the noblest circumstances for mind's illustrious triumphs.

An innate principle, cognizant of right and wrong, presupposes an enlightened conscience that is best matured by self-denial and education. It is not that education will mislead, but that rational education should comprehend all the available principles of intellect, morals and religion. Take cause and effect out of the universe, and all the theatre of reason is annihilated. Will bible bigots underrate all these because their monomania renders them crazy? It will not do to say that mind is the creature of necessity, and acts by impulse. That is only a part of the mighty subject, that looks through the universe to its Creator. If the immediate assigned influence of sensual gratification should cause the deplorable viciousness of mind, why there is the master countervailing influence of penalty, if mind did not look to a nobler influence of religion.

Say that in Europe the pauper could not command enough to eat, the master influence of eternal hope would counteract bad impulses, when his presence in America decides the special providence of mind. Now, call it nature, what you choose, a blind materialism you cannot make it, when all the Great First Cause is Providence, whose exponent is principles, the consummation of which is religion.

The intricate question of free agency should teach mind the noblest position of Providence, universal as to God, and the most rational, if special, as to mind or soul.

By the magnificent power of mind man has to solve the problem of religion, the soul and the balance, and to do this a universe problem, a rationality, is expedient universally. Is mind a free agent, or does it not act from necessity? Whatever is, is right with God, who created the universe on certain conservative principles that constitute the especial circumstances for will and action, that should be according to an enlightened conscience, an innate consciousness of right from wrong. As to all sin, that implies a departure from universal principles, and is to be corrected by their best appreciation. All this implies the right exercise of the whole powers, or means in power, and to be attained. The broad platform of monotheism implies all this, and predicates the proper position of rational education.

If free agency of mind was only according to peculiar imparted education, then the position of self-improvement would be fallacious. What is the rational world doing? Improving the mind by all rational means of education, as discussion. The paramount object is to reach the most elevated, that has paramount influence. Why are all the organs of penalty for infraction of principles? Because all moral and religious, as physical, must be obeyed implicitly when appreciated. The State must see that all its constituents must have the best abiding practical interest in rational education. There is the richest treasure, the capital of which realizes compound interest. Rational education commands all commandable circumstances.

Religion, the most exalted of all teaching, puts every thing on principle, which solves the whole question. Principles command all Christs, Mahomets, Smiths, Tinkers, and all their mongers.

To make mind fully responsible, educate it all the time rationally, that its functions may be rightfully employed. Mind has its functions, and is responsible for their appropriate exercise.

The responsibility rests somewhere, positively. Freedom of choice, will, volition, implies responsibility. When people sin all their lives, and at the last dying moment, when retributive justice was impracticable in this world by wanton wicked life, then by fiction of the priestocracy they are forgiven. This is not, in the nature of the universe or things, real.

Mind has free agency under the circumstances of creation. Then it has to inquire, what are those circumstances, that freedom, and that responsibility? There are no mysteries in well defined duties, and what can be better defined than by uniform principles? The bible people did not understand their subject, and committed themselves wofully and ludicrously.

The Jews fell, as all the ancients did, and all even the universe would, because they needed the religion of principles. The moderns thrive, the more deference they pay to mind and its holiest purposes. Has mind used all the means available in its power to rescue itself? If it do, assuredly it will put down witches and world-spirits, superstition, priestocracy, and all their odious, contemptible, infamous bibles, all the abusers of trusts of the most valuable character, being burlesques on religion, and its violation. Mind has weighed them in the balance, and found them wanting.

As to mind's free agency under the circumstance of creation, we must give the proper analysis. The proper functions of mind present an independent individuality, the soul placed on this theatre to master all the elements subservient to its purpose through rational education. In this sense, it has a perfect free agency. Does mind act from necessity, a mere creature of circumstances? A partial view would consider it in abeyance, but a masterly comprehension renders it a triumph—the position of mind and analysis of its functions, of thoughts, words, will, deed or action. It enters into the audience of three beliefs, that act for general weal or wo. Now all should be presented fairly, for correct appreciation or adoption, as it can only select one as the best: it discards the others.

Mind is brought forth to battle with the elements of creation and master them. This brings us into cause and effect, without which nothing in the universe can be done or thought of. That at once decides rational belief, for monotheism alone takes proper cognizance of this whole subject, and comprehends rational mind in its guardian care. The functions of mind decide its commissions and rights. Mind presents in its agency all the best considerations, educational, legislative and judicial, and invokes the noblest talents of most expansive minds to this particular.

The great emblem of mind and its functions is the self-adjusting capacity of maintaining its proper equilibrium over all evils that beset its dignity. What can be more disgraceful than the attempt to make mind responsible to bibles of peculiar faith, that is totally irresponsible to truth? Mind should adopt the most enlightened associations to discuss the truths of religion, to which it is ever in abeyance.

Man's free agency of mind would be nullified, and his sins would be superseded, if they originated from an evil genius, and a monster without responsibility; and God, the essence of purity, would be a party to the guilt of imbecile mortals, and of corrupting immortals; to such absurdity and crime, do evil systems, of worldly-minded speculation, lead unthinking minds.

If Satan was a fallen angel, then an impurity, sin, a mere negative quality, not a positive existence, can enter a pure place, and the presence of a pure being, a palpable absurdity, and contradiction; and Deity then could not help himself in his imbecility, against the misrule of his evil cabinet, stupidly adopted and countenanced, nor his choice spirits, or even his future charge, though billions! Where even, is his own protection? For all this false pretence decides the Creator's impotency, which, if true, the universe would demonstrate.

O, mind perverted! that could impeach thyself so low, by such demoralizing fictions. Where was thy blush?

This delusion and wilful stupid blindness, apparently impeaches God, but certainly emanated from impiety, and a host of errors, by self-elected teachers, or blindly permitted by reckless constituents, whose actions and misdeeds directly impeach the minds of all its asserters.

This assertion is most absurd, for the bible's heaven is made to yield its best treasures, and most glorious rights, and strips God of his best attributes, to gloss the less pretensions of mind, whose free agency is necessarily subject to the best of character, under the circumstances of its earthly creation, necessary for the formation.

Where there was no temptation in heaven, there could be no sin and no demerit, as no characteristic action is implied, and no appreciation can be formed.

The time for temptation had passed ; the eternity of reward had arrived. The state of embodied mind had ceased, that of soul had been commenced. The mortal had merged in the immortal, the part of human nature had been put off—an immortal spirit had been realized. There could be no temptation, where nothing could be gained, and all were to be lost.

In the full fruition of happiness, all was sagacity and wisdom, and as sin was folly, an impossibility, is fully assured of a fall. God created no temptation, and the whole pretence impeaches and demonstrates itself false.

The character of soul had been formed and matured, elicited from previous trials of its nature in the incipient existence of mind and body, its various soul-organizations, and the success of its resistance to supposed evil in all its minority.

Any other position involves the responsibility of the tempter, not only the successful but triumphant rival of his Creator, and imposes upon the Creator, the necessity of the tempter's punishment, and that for triumphant rivalry ! What jesuitry ; what object could God have in placing imbecile mortals in the bible's garden of Eden, to play a farce that his fore-knowledge, a part of his Omniscience could have prevented ? Of course then, there is no responsibility in such position.

It is then the powers of mind that are potent for good, and magnificent in its greatness, but full of evil if perverted. We must take the facts, as they are clearly presented us in this world, and scorn all bible of tradition legends.

Mind must then have a suitable theatre for self-agency : it must be untrammeled to be responsible.

The nature of universal existence implies a positive good ; the reverse, physical or moral, is a negative evil. The author of all, is a conservative Creator.

A correct knowledge of human nature, sees it as a matter-of-fact existence, endowed with passions and emotions, that are lawful, if rightly directed and gratified. Their gratifications on legitimate principles, are those of conservation and protection, but on improper basis, lead to disastrous results, and ruinous destructive consequences. This is the nature, and must be the law of creation. The best appreciation of these laws, establishes the best code, on the most refined taste and civilization, the highest state of man's earthly action.

But what triumph awaits mind in its wisdom and purity, to rise above error, master difficulties, conquer ignorance, surmount prejudice and bigotry, and attain the final general perfection practicable.

Free agency of mind declares the wisest philosophy of rational religion, an epitome of sound, common, and proper sense, that directs according to the best lights of mind, in all moral and physical bearings of this whole subject, and renders unto God all that are his truly and dutifully, and unto man all that blesses and guides him aright to his Author and Creator, safely and satisfactorily. Free agency of mind, implies reason as accountability.

Whatever system of peculiar faith prevents all this, that does withhold any of God's least possessions, is spurious and counterfeit to all eternity, and should be contemned by mind, as its seal of condemnation from God is plain to all reasonable minds in the world's history, shown in wo and misery.

The poison of nature is to be counteracted, and turned to nature's benefit, and mind's triumph instead of their injury, but mind's poisons made in numerous ways most insidiously, are its greatest evils.

As bad as the tyrants and oppressors of the world are, mind that acquiesces and created them is more heinous still.

The tyrants of the world can be held now, in abeyance to mind that asserts its glorious independence.

The exposure of the world's tyranny is the prerogative of mind under freedom's banner.

The least of all its evils is, to conquer all as far as practicable, by its competent forces of available cultivation, of correct instruction, fortified by correct habits, and enlightened principles.

To sin the least, is the best that mind can do, in its present state of existence.

What system can teach more correct doctrine ?

It is demoralizing to pretend that mind does not err, and hence does not sin.

Our enlightened faculties teach us, if not perverted, that mind is fallible, and much of human nature is corrupt, and has to be guarded with all the solicitude of affection, the care of wisdom, and the best protection of reason.

Where then was the necessity of adding positive evils, to increase the difficulty of mind?

The fallen angel is a fable indeed.

Such a being is unnecessary on earth, as an angel or messenger, and a stigma on mind and soul, as incapable of blissful enjoyment if degraded from heaven.

Conservative principles are angels for earth and the universe; happy spirits are fixed in God's holy centre. Any other view is most irrational and contradictory.

This earth presents a scope for mind free agent, in self-avenging principles, that promote mind's felicity, if pure, but counteract it if corrupt, sooner or later, individually or nationally. This is surely not evil but universal good. Rational mind scans rightly. Past ages, dark, ignorant, and ferocious, portray to us another more formidable avenger, and another more horrid abode, resorting to mind's contradictions.

God must have blessed creation, as his own lovely work, coming from the fountain of love and mercy. A local curse must have created universal sympathy. All matters are only relative.

The most favored of all, was the pure, the holy centre, a perfectly pure place for a perfectly pure being.

Into this abode, what impiety it would be to conceive any entrance, without perfect and spotless purity.

Who then was Lucifer? Fable or history, that is consistent with reason, must represent him as one of the brightest of beatific intelligences.

To be characterized as a select being in the holy centre, he must have been essentially pure, to enter an essentially pure sphere.

All that entered therein must be pure and holy.

Then, for impurity to reach a perfectly pure being, in a perfectly pure sphere!

If that were the case, what now would prevent the awful catastrophe, from reaching any or all, at any period of eternity? God's imbecility demonstrated once, is an eternal imbecility, as it is inherent.

Are not each as liable as the highest and most intelligent, who must have appreciated much the best of all the blessed, pure beings, the horrors of perdition, the loss of all blessings, the gain of extreme misery and unceasing remorse?

What a reflection to the character, not of him, who, as in the holy centre, still better must have appreciated the result, but of those who write themselves the stupid authors of fables, with no sense and morality, terrifiers of mind, and libelers of the Creator! With them is the inherent imbecility, not with God.

Can he who had honor, glory, and happiness sure, realized by an exalted light of soul, tried in all the gradations of spheres up to the highest, be taken out of the purest of all, himself most purified when received there?

Was not this exalted character best, after reaching the holiest, the highest abode?

How came he there, if not pure and meritorious?

Any other character was unworthy of entrance. For the holy centre never could, as pure a place as defined, be a recipient for a moment even, of impurity—no never; that would, must be, an aspersion on Deity's purity. Then it is Deity, not Lucifer, that is to blame.

What kind of a compliment does it pay Deity's omnipotence, omnipresence, and omniscience?

That the libelers of God were recklessly ignorant and miserably blasphemous.

It may be said temptation caused his fall; if that be so, was he worthy of such a trial? But the Creator is not mind's tempter; that is a stupid libel.

But the day of temptation had passed—that belonged to spheres of inferior character or less purity.

But temptation in the holy centre! That is the abode of enjoyment, rest, repose, and glory!

Temptation, then, of what, how, and why, must be asked; seeing that happiness and joy were his, were before him?

What more could he, if pure, promise himself? And if not pure, say, could he or any other being reach the presence of the immaculate Deity, in his immaculate realm?

Mortal! Thy mind has slandered the holy residence, and blasphemed thy God; erecting a monster, a fiction, with the peculiarity and contradiction thine; thus libeling the nature of creation and its Creator. What sphere, then, so unfit for Satan's reception?

Was there any location prepared, any before accursed, in the wide expanse of space of creation, instituted by a Creator of blessed attributes, not previously filled already?

Would God resign his own means of bettering the spheres of creation, by resigning any space to the majesty of an evil genius, his successful rival, to hopelessly degrade mind and himself beyond the redemption of the Almighty?

Shall the creation of unspeakable sublimity, where the order of genius most supreme reigns pre-eminently, be blighted with a monster of no responsibility, taking away all from the victims of his seduction, by reason of his conquering influence, when he ruins God's fairest creation, mind, but enjoys all such as the spoils of victory and reward?

Shall this fictitious being, who never was of any greater value, at his best, than the least human soul, riot in the ruin of souls innumerable, subject to his fiendish seduction and agency? There is no reason at all in the supposition.

It is much more rational to suppose that Deity would have raised beatific souls above the holy centre, if the souls merited that distinction, than that he would let them fall below.

But the noblest views arise in the liberal expansion of free and moral agency of mind, that bigots are afraid to trust, in the unbounded ocean of its greatness. Among them is

GRATITUDE.

To commence with the Supreme, is not only the highest privilege of mortality, but a pleasure and happiness that define the eminent character of mind.

It is that serene state of beatific composure of mind, that renders sacred the time, and gives the best sanctity of life.

All rational beings are endowed with this glorious privilege, that invests the contemplation with sublime aspirations at any moment of life.

It is that which renders human capacity available on its own resources, by relying on self-advancement to the utmost capability, and leaving the balance in the hands of an unchangeable being, who asks for the purest adoration, and the best grateful emotions.

Such a state of mind disproves the doctrines of election and predestination, as stupid and unworthy of God, who is made responsible, instead of man.

Man had then been a mere machine, and the mighty mind, that is ever present, acting, working, practical, pilot and guardian—if rightfully cultivated, ever grateful—is a mere machine; has no free moral agency; thus contradicting what every moment disproves! Lost and hopeless must be that man, that does not feel abundant sources of gratitude to Almighty God, for his favors and kindness; and this every mind feels from free agency.

This earth might present a happier state, if this feeling of gratitude were duly cultivated, and could present the nearest approach to universal salvation, in the shortest duration, by universal mind being better.

Gratitude ought to preclude any, that are refined, from allowing others to excel them in courtesy of just feeling, or kindness of manner, in life.

What does more good, than this desire for good?

It renders humanity lovely, wise, and of noblest value. It repays a thousand fold its numerous blessings, in the family of man, through its wide diffusion among the nations of the earth.

Here is portrayed an index of soul, that delights the analyst of character, and assures us that mind is ennobled by the liberal principles of a right education, civilizes nations, and renders lovely the earth. And if mind be thus just to man, much more will it be to God, whose every attribute and character must present the clearest evidence of such a debt, due by mind to mind's Creator.

As great as the munificent artist has shown his skill in the construction, no less is his greatness in the richness of mind's endowments, and destined purposes of action.

Its most exalted is devotion, without alloy, to the mighty Author of its existence; its next is to itself, in all the varieties of its characteristic circumstances, and especially in its duty to that of others.

A true, sincere, and exclusive allegiance to its worthy Creator, endows it with the loftiest and justest conscience, of its consistent duties elsewhere.

Thus is the soul refined, and started on the only true basis of its own inappreciable salvation.

The future furnishes an earnest, full of the most attractive inspirations, to the most determined perseverance.

Its commencement was in permanent principles of conviction; its resolves arose on the purity of its devotion to the best of causes, and the most exalted of Authors.

FREE AGENCY OF MIND AND PREDESTINATION.

Is it predestination that puzzles you ?   Do you pretend that no matter how you act, God commands you ?   But you have a free agency of mind under the circumstances of creation that contradicts that.   What more can you have ?   God himself is only God under the consistent circumstances of his attributes.   He has made himself a free agent under them, and less nor more cannot exist.

But what is this thing, predestination ?   Is it, on true analysis, the compulsive force of a supervising Power in all the vital actions of man, or is it not surely the most enlarged, liberal, comprehensive providence of the universe ?   As sure as there is a Creator, his almighty, just and perfect providence has devised a uniform rule of government, the most appropriate government, that presents the noblest conservation.   If there be any excess or diminution, impinging on this conservation, the inherent results necessarily follow.   Man has his prescribed functions in life to perform, and if he do not enact them as duty, his failure is attended with appropriate forfeiture.   .

His being is identified with social and religious relations, and his mighty life-problem is most elevated when it reaches the dignity of rationality.   He is bound as a rational being to come up to rational and religious principles, for the best present and future self-preservation.

This thing of predestination is, then, not the petty arbitrary rule of the Creator, but the comprehensive problem of the universe, and man must adapt himself accordingly. Every thing in life proves the necessity and utility of mind's best action.   Mind is the artificer of its own position under the circumstances of its creation.   You believe in improvement of mind, to enable it to improve the world.

That implies more than a simple, blind acquiescence in predestination, that leaves a creature merely where he began—a mere animal that has no free agency.   An animal has certain defined limits of instinct to perform, and in all ages he is an analogous animal.   All the tuition of mind has not changed the nature of the beast, the maturity of his instinctive intellect.   Predestination leaves man a mere animal, but free agency under the circumstances of creation takes man where predestination leaves him, and carries him to the dignity of mind's functions, duties and merits, and gives the best earnest of immortal functions of creative thought.   Your vessel, under common circumstances of navigation, goes to your chosen port, under appropriate circumstances of management, varied and diversified by incidents.   It goes as you direct.   But you assume that God pre-ordains, and that you are only a passive agent.   How is this, when he gives the functions ?   It is yours to employ them rightly.   You speak of predestination any how, as a creation-obligation, for which God alone is responsible and mind only in abeyance.   Why, then, do you punish ?   You are self-condemned as a tyrant, if this bigoted view is to be the order of the times.   Why, then, is there mind ? Why was not man a mere animal, to reach in all stages of the world his certain defined sphere ?   Of what use is reason, the thinking part ?   Predestination, then, is your bigoted, contracted definition of peculiar faith.

We see that the world presents four stages of mind's condition, and the last the ennobling one of civilization, that proves most conclusively mind's mastery, by the most general advantages of its circumstances.

If there be only predestination, why do you differ so essentially with mankind, and censure them for their position, their opinions and actions ?   On your position, you must exercise forbearance and toleration.   Persons of ignorance cannot do as you.   Why is this ?   The difference is in mind, in the state of that mind.   Instruct and enlighten the whole, and then you may expect better things.

What has been vainly and ingloriously considered predestination, which is equivalent to appreciating the creator of mind as unjust, is mind's inglorious own.   Mind has to act to the best of its ability.   The world observes that talents differ and make up an agreeable diversity ; some talents are not as great as others, but greater than many. What does that signify ?   That mind can excel the creator of mind ?   God is perfect and perfectly just.   You cannot construe his deeds until you can analyze them, otherwise you would libel him.

You must plant, improve and embellish, to do justice to your position and duty.   You must not stop short of rational principles.   God does the balance.   Now you see what you aim to explain.   The most sacrilegious impiety is perpetrated in making God responsible for man's sins, follies, crimes, murders and wars.

When two armies, about to enter into conflict, engage in prayer to the same eternal God of the universe to favor their side of the question, how can the supplication, of one at least, be otherwise than hypocrisy ?   After all the logic of sophistry, the whole affair is naught but that of principles which cannot clash. Either one or both are wrong; how then can the offending party, with show of sincerity, affect prayer? Prayer is in the place of self-examination, and does no good under such circumstances. The world must do away with all punishment, all censure, ere it can dispense one iota of libel on God. It must seek to analyze the whole position, and be silent, if not right, about God.

Predestination misleads to the narrowest bigotry, and the most absurd conclusions. Have you a will? If not, why leave any thing by testament, preceding death? You are self-condemned already, if you do not do it as becomes a righteous rational mind, and the dignity of reason. Can you exercise your intelligence? Is not that free agency? Your mind may be perverted by drunkenness, that involves your reason, or by ignorance, that cannot analyze it, by error, that distorts it, or physical inability, that invalidates it. It is your bounden duty to master all this.

If you are unfortunately any of the degraded characters by predestination, you are surely punished by predestination. If you understood principles, and their vindication, you would drop that word predestination, the property of bigotry, foolish fanaticism and despotism.

But you ask, is man created equal? No. He may have a rickety constitution, and die speedily. Whose fault was this? Not the victim's, surely, yet do not libel God, who created no positive evil. With him, "whatever is, is right."

Does predestination teach to sit passively in the quagmire of despondency, and exert not the plainest dictates of reason, the best action of correction? For what purpose was mind, of what use is reason? Their functions are to vanquish all these illusions. Look at the horrid iniquities of all peculiar faiths. How shall we ever extricate the votaries, devotees, victims of their errors of faith, vices? Mind and reason have to show them what religion is. Of what use is that tuition without the action? The bible libels God about predestination.

Do you refuse the influence of mind, science and genius, by the proscribing predestination? You deprecated the inequality of man, and it is their union that enables man to reach the dignity of his creation. Fire arms and gunpowder have more equalized man, as one of the best results of mind in its creative genius. Other weapons of war will insure that equality to that degree that peace instead of war will be the universal object, as now more beneficial. But are such evils the means, in the face of conservative principles, even by the very best of them violated.

What makes man? Mind. How then can predestination subsist? When the good of all is legitimately secured, then predestination is dissolved in free agency of mind under the creative circumstances of Providence. If predestination be true, why preach?

Why do you teach people to think? To do right? Does that not involve the principle of free agency of mind, that renders the world what it is, so far as man is concerned? The whole world is bound to acknowledge it. Predestination indicates senility or puerility, if not imbecility, the doctrine of superstition that proves mind in its leading strings, its dotage of errors.

The people have to act up to the demands of mind, ere the world is revolutionized. Though we are yet in the infancy of knowledge, we know enough to correct the world and extricate it from the toils of superstition and its prolific family of errors, if we do justice to mind. When predestination is mentioned, profound analysis will eject it as unworthy of mind, that has to secure to itself purity of taste and correctness of judgment. Individuals and local differences, bespeak a greater strength of the whole. The southern clime has what the north cannot produce, but all is a harmonious whole rightly estimated.

The predestinarians tie themselves up every way, and make a long circuit about evanescent trifles. They disregard the noblest attribute of mind, free agency, under the circumstances of creation that are the most certain and proper position, like liberty, that is the most dignified and freest under appropriate laws and order, otherwise it is licentiousness that ruins by excess. But great objections are made, that equality does not prevail in the world. How in the present constitution of the universe, could there be uniform equality among the people? Who would serve? The organization of the whole must be changed, to conform to man's opinions. God has consulted his own wisdom, and acted accordingly. Tell us no more of predestination which bespeaks the fetters of mind by immutable proscription, when the world gives such substantial proofs of mind's capacity for action and its progressive execution.

The world has progressed, by the efforts of mind; that demonstrates the whole absurdity of predestination. The faculties of mind prove most conclusively, that predestination, confined to the limits of the bible, is as absurd as that book. Conscience proves man's free agency. The very position of the world, in regard to accountability, decides against predestination.

All are created so as to prove, on maturity, the efforts of free agency of mind. What can you make out of predestination? That is a base absurdity, and exposes the authors as the most ignorant libelers of Deity. All things of creation are right, however divergent man is made by peculiar education. Mind must not read God under peculiar opinions, prejudices of peculiar worship, reflecting the damnable bigotry of the priestocracy, under any of its peculiar ways, but the right way, as God acted. The rational mind, under rational education, comprehending universal relations, only can perceive the right way. More injury has been done the world, on this basis, than enough. Let us give the greatest latitude to mind's actions and improvement, under the farthest legitimate comprehension, the circumstances of its creation.

The very position of mind proves free agency, in the accountability, the means used. Admit that the people are not equal in intellect, &c.; but does that argue that we can justly appreciate all the balance of their case, that may give a correspondent equilibrium of advantages? What mortal can gainsay this? The very circumstances of man's existence on earth pre-supposes him to be a moral free agent, under the circumstances of his creation. Some say, as to predestination, God certainly did know who would be saved or lost, according to the bible. Then the bible doctrine consigns the balance to a localized eternal punishment.

What sort of morals does this bible inculcate? Has it any morals, when the writers knew they violated principles and mind, and affected familiarity with Deity, who can only be approached that way by immortals? Creation implies preservation, correspondent on merits personal. What superior claims then have one to exclusive privileges and prerogatives, when all have rights that cannot be abrogated? No bible can set them aside. All future positions may be modified, but cannot be annihilated. The doctrine of election is miserable. What is predestination, and all such stuff?

Is the world to maintain the authors of such monsters? God created man on this earth for beneficent purposes. Under those circumstances, he could not particularize an isolated little obscure nation, who evidently disproved such guardianship, evinced in the bible, time after time, by their bondage, and especially by the loss of the ten tribes!

If any thing were wanting to the proof, their miserable civil wars, and horrible piracies, to the bloodiest extinction of the tenderest age and sex, of the rightful possessors of the soil, give it to overflowing. To give a colorable picture for the last, the priestocracy manufacture the false pretences of Noah, and the incest of Lot.

The bible, and its want of morals, will break down all its pretenders. There is great objection by the predestinarians of the great differences of individuals in life, as to fortune, gifts of mind, &c.

This is getting into the first causes of things that are out of the reach of finite mind. Man elevates himself by the means, that elicit his best exertions.

Mind, under the circumstances of creation on this earth, must resign itself to all the results of nature, only doing its highest appreciable duty. Be it then supposed misery or real happiness, under such action it will all come out right in the end, that is referable to the immutable laws of God, that regulates mutable animal nature. Perfect happiness is not created for this earth. What avail contentions about the First Cause of all things, as God's foreknowledge? The first causes of things cannot be resolved by mortals, without involving man's finite mind. We may trace all more or less to them, and there leave them, in due confidence, with God. The chemist analyzes water into oxygen and hydrogen. What are the first elements of these? God knows. God is not an autocrat, but a constitutional president of his universe—a perfect standard to the world for its example. The free moral agency proves that. Predestination carried out is a libel on God, founded on the bible, the disgraceful father of God's libels. The murderer can say that God, not he, did the crime, and therefore he is not accountable. If God predestinates for one, he does for all, murders, as all acts. Can there be worse morals? Is God the author of evil? God is a universal providence, and as such, no select, especial people, Jew or gentile, could have been entertained by God. There are a great many things we must leave to God, without committing ourselves. What do you want with such bible, Mr. Predestinarian? We cannot speculate about God's supreme government. We need not fear that the bible writers would dip into the grand hidden mysteries of nature by revelation or inspiration. They are very clear of that, as they have tied themselves altogether in a dilemma. What mortal ever looked into the first causes of things? The bible writers are not able to analyze such; that science has done since and exposed them. Metaphysical, biblical pretences will not do in a system of facts. Providence universal enables moral free agency of mind under the circumstances of creation, to carry out his almighty decrees. This excludes guardian angels, genii, demons, and meets the requisitions in the circle of certain and almighty providences. As God is immutable, the general laws of nature have been, are, and will be immutable. Particular providences are desirable to bible of tradition men, which will yield the proper view of moral free agency of mind under the circumstances of creation. God's conservative principles vindicate him in vindicating themselves.

Bible metaphysics must be dispensed with.

Does not the world look to mind and reason in all improvements? What is moral free agency for? Will predestination justify the priestocracy for all their blunders, the bible, as to all one's deeds? A great progress will have been accomplished in civilization when the powers of mind, rightly directed, shall have their legitimate scope and influence. Then the thousand and one perversions of mind, bound to the car of superstition, will be legitimately directed to the right channel, and we shall have no more of the absurd pretensions of obsolete despotisms. The principles that vindicate themselves represent the especial providence of God; how much more I do not know. They humanize, civilize, and refine the world.

Has God created evil? This seems perfectly incompatible with a perfect Creator. Is not all such that appears so attended with matters that evoke man's genius for protection, to attain a greater and a more exalted good, a stimulus that leads on invention from necessity, and a new triumph from its success.

Mind is to master the elements of creation; and what seem the most appalling difficulties eventuate in the most illustrious benefits. Man's perversion of mind renders abuse an evil to himself; but then that is an abuse of the mental faculties, under the guidance of free moral agency. If all creation move on in one harmonious whole, where is the evil? If man relax his duty, and suffer by imbecilities of his own creation, conservative principles are only vindicated. Mind negatives its own good, and that negative is evil. Did God ever establish a positive evil? What mind can impiously and recklessly pretend to such assertion?

What one thing can be denounced out of this world? There is fire. Can that form one iota? In cold we are warmed, in cooking we are supported, and by appropriate uses the world participates in the benefits of this element. If a man choose to insert his finger into the blaze, conservative principles only vindicate themselves.

What is done by means of supreme providence through mind, legitimately though? With the bible gentry mind is nothing, a cypher; but miracles, prophecy and revelation, all impossibilities, non-entities, demonstrated, are everything,—the very reverse of truth, and disgrace of mind.

The idea of God giving laws to predestinated persons, who affect the faith in the scriptures, is most preposterous for them! Why should God punish them, whom he had already predetermined to be lost? Can mind, after thousands of years of the deepest reading of God's scriptures, his works by philosophical science, now assume to be critic, when yet it is not a competent analyst?

Any slight view of Deity's character might betray an attempt at impeachment, which of course, so far from being just, that God cannot in any wise whatever be assailed by his creation, but causes the converse, that forever impeaches the assertor, and disgraces him as a libeler. Our analysis of creation is very finite, and consequently very defective, but the correction ever rests with us to better amendment, and that corrective is progressive improvement. The pretensions and assumptions of man too often betray the attempt to libel Deity, which attempt forever recoils on himself.

All the pretensions of predestination are odious, as they subvert the noblest principles of mind, and libel God.

What a miserable vassal doctrine that keeps up false notions in the world, through peculiar bibles, about the essential difference in mankind, the basest libel of the God of the universe. No one can conceive of the miserable sophistries of monopoly and usurpation. The world has been full of such.

Rational truth is not to be heard in the category of peculiar faith and predestination. They were made for another circle. All sophists are Jesuits, and all peculiar bible advocates are necessarily so. You talk of predestination, when the world is for the best exertions of mind and body.

You speak of God's creations of evil, as if you were familiar with all the comprehensive facts of creation. Now the self-vindication of conservative principles takes precedence forever; and though in their rectification paramount laws take precedence, how is that an evil that holds minor obligations in abeyance to all supreme?

Know the order. Necessity, is this the great law of self-preservation, that reigns paramount in nature. Do not, then, idolize your own errors worse than the pagan idolists, whom you have complained of. There is no positive, absolute evil. The effects of peculiar education prove mind's moral free agency, that must necessarily be in relation to its circumstances of creation to be invariably understood. But from this position smatterers and quibblers wish to escape, to be free from all restraints; a thing impossible in the inherent laws of matter, intrinsic or relative to its circle. Man must do all for himself by the best light of rational mind, and then all else will follow. Religion teaches self-reliance to the highest point of independence. Who is to blame for tyrants' acts and crimes? The people are responsible in a great measure. Mind is subservient, and the world must place all things beyond that contingency. If we knew positively that the soul was immortal, moral free agency and reason had not been disinterested, hence bible sophistry and priestocracy effrontery.

Evils prove the perversion of mind endowed with free agency, relative to the circumstances of creation.

God never created evils, or an evil genius as an agent. The free agency of mind is most clear, and it has to elaborate its own chief good on its merits, to correct the evils of its peculiar perversions.

What is the substitute of mind, as all the peculiar bibles are incompetent, as untrue, to meet the mind question? Your liturgy reminds God of his duty, and invokes miracles he does not do! God's grace is universal as mind and creation, and identified with, and to be elicited, by the highest and most worthy rationality. You libel God to invoke the aid of peculiar faith ministry; an indirect action, that cannot be done directly.

The noblest blessing of mind is its free agency. That indicates no sudden change of heart, but a rational change of mind for man, individually and mass. Talk no more of evils and predestination, but conquer all practicable difficulties by mind, most rational.

The state of the world is for two things at least; to create rational mind, and means for independence of God's noblest work, mind—the embodiment of soul—that it may create its own future elastic exaltation.

Use providence of mind in the wilderness, ocean; avoidance of perverted mind's evils, as war.

Avoid antagonism, conflict with the world. How? By avoiding all contingencies, uniformly recurring to principles, counteracting by the best intellectual ability all that mind, under the circumstances, should and can do. Rational education is the best pilot to free agency of mind.

RATIONAL EDUCATION, THE PROPER CULTURE OF RATIONAL MIND.

EDUCATION from tradition, that is not amenable to rational deductions, becomes peculiar, teaches mind innumerable errors, biased opinions, perverted conclusions, ruinous habits, sectarian interests, and bigoted prejudices, without number and redress, and none but enlightened reason can recall mankind to correction, and that on clear knowledge of their particular errors.

There is a rational government in education, reaction of mind's light resting on the pure gifts of mind, conservative of good, otherwise of latent evil, as separate and distinct as the national blessings of American independence, and piracy on the high seas.

Women as well as men, should have colleges and highest seminaries, to enlarge the comprehensive capacity of mind, but all must ever be only on rational principles.

What mean those lofty piles of architecture, those churches, monuments of superstition? Are these the means of peculiar education? Are they to hand down to mind the mementos of false faith and doctrines, too contemptible for it to think of, much less embrace?

Why not turn into the legitimate channels of right use, their costs, for mental improvement? Make them colleges for science and mind's fortification in true thought, the greatest adoration that ever was paid to Deity.

Let all the world be truly benefited by the excessive outlays, and let excesses go to their legitimate use in science, her rewards and best attainments. Let there be no absurd and wicked teachings of wicked cunning men, to distract, divide, and embitter the world in false and superstitious notions, and all absurd copyings of degraded fables, received with implicit faith by infatuated multitudes, sharing the folly and crime of mind perverted in all parts of the world, usurping and monopolizing by the self-interest of impostors and blasphemers, what is really the duty and sincere actions of mind.

Let not missionaries carry back to Asia, absurd and corrupt copyings of their own base and degraded superstitions, but let America, that gave the brightest light of liberty to the world, in the mighty principles of free government, give to those lost sons of superstition and tyranny, the bible of rational mind for rational and true religion. She is not only the lovely bride of annexation on her own continent for governmental institations, but she should be ready to respond to all other main divisions in the mighty bonds of religious brotherhood, the only proper union of the rational world.

This position will meet the requirements of mankind, of the world, that is a miserable abject slave and menial servant to ignorance and its consequences, but when master tyrannical, purse-proud and overbearing, yet a correct agent only when taught its duty by mind, that enlightened, can counteract it errors and frailties. Of what value is the education of bigotry and peculiar faith? Educate men of mind in all the power of science by the money appropriated for such gorgeous buildings, and as living temples, let them go into the dark points of the earth, and teach the principles of science pure and unadulterated to unsophisticated minds, to create the right germs of thought and give right scope to action.

All nations becoming civilized in the right way, will be glad to receive all such, to scatter the mists of minds and their errors, superstition and ignominy.

If the facts were now told by the missionaries from Asia, they might say that the priests there are laughing at the idea of their people being taught only copies of their own superstitions, allied to absolutism, to render church and state omnipotent over the people, the true sovereigns, mere abject subjects. Discoveries aid discoveries, as points for future advances. Science begets science, philosophy evolves philosophy. Due respect to the lights of mind will put down superstition, negative the quagmires of the dark ages, proscribe all absurd bigotry, and declare religion as proper duty of man to man and God. To secure all this, education is indispensable, and that must not be peculiar.

SOCIETY AND ITS RIGHTS.

Society depends on natural laws and principles, that premise the most legitimate taste, and comprehensive results.

She teaches the counteracting influence of benignant education, and directs talents to their legitimate theatre, the whole earth.

She regards the misdirection of talents as a public evil, and sustains the best practical effects of rationality.

She reminds of the loss of invaluable time for years, by putting apprentices under poor and incompetent workmen and poor trades, at which hardly bread can be made.

She directs and rewards the industrial pursuits of the nations of the world.

The man of energy, repentant of misdirected ambition, that seeks a triumph over the world's rights, under her fostering care may aspire to the noblest vindications of science and philosophy.

The assassinations brought about by revenge, resulting from the vices of the powerful, who injure with seeming impunity, the other by the weakness of the sufferer, may be directed into channels where no such disastrous cause should be given, as legal justice will avenge the injuries of the humblest citizens.

The best cultivated mind of education in science and philosophy, understanding the proper rights of society best promoted by religion, can understand all the varied forms of superstition, the works of priestocracies, whose collusion has been imposed on this world, the age of mind.

The world will never be right, till a conservative revolution in society, establishes the equity of principles.

ANALYSIS OF PRINCIPLES.

A correct education gives the best introduction to this position. Without it, prejudice forms one of the worst barriers to cheat the mind of its rights, and God of his attributes. The sooner we reach the analysis of principles, the better will be the performance of our duty, the more certain our safety in all the present and future prosperity.

Principles must be understood, not mystified at all, to secure the best legitimate good to society and all, who, truly religious, have nothing to fear, and less to object, but all to hope when undeniable principles are advanced. All wise men should know before they start, that all is safe, to insure their safety.

Religion exists in its elements, not in the advances of opinions, but in the Author of, its principles, who is recognised in the organization of creation.

Religion only exists with its principles, that must emanate from the Supreme, innate for all objects of preservation, ever since mind was formed—then no after action is

12

wise at all, hence messiahship, that is subsequent to creation of the universe and mind, cannot begin to meet the question, admitting the necessity for it, which there is not in the universal presidency of the Almighty, therefore cannot be recognised by wise or sane minds.

All such are a horrible and impious blasphemy and imposition, can be nothing less than a gross libel in the region of reason.

The organization of Creation is an eternal witness, that the Almighty rules supreme in his unity, and annihilates every bible of tradition as basely false.

Natural and simple, then, are the provisions, secure and lasting are the foundations, that look only to God.

Men of principles and true science must see that no individual, no community, can exist, without fundamental good as premised.

For what were the universe and its conservative principles instituted, but for mind, the mighty free agent of the Creator? Shall libelers of God enslave it for their degraded purposes? Past history of Jews and Gentiles, show this too plainly.

Rational religion is certain to rational minds for its principles, as mathematical science, that no botches can affect.

This subject is unmistakable to all of every civilized nation, and dwells despite of all other peculiar faiths, ready to be called up by reason for ever.

Who will pervert these principles for a worldly gain?

All must see the effect of personal responsibility in the presumption of tampering with the rights and destinies of mind, that may constitute the brightest emanation for immortality, or the severest curse in result.

Who will forfeit the first, or incur the penalty of the last? Who is not already condemned in the attempt?

The intellectual and moral state of the present age, demands a proper exposition and vindication of every principle affecting the liberty of the individual, the prosperity of the state, and the future happiness of all.

Monotheism can never be passive in such matters, inculcating on all, as she does, a just adoration, by eternal principles of their Almighty Author, the one great and Living God; she requires their essential and indispensable adoption.

The obvious means for conservative light of reason, are those furnished at the mint, that wise, good, and true citizens, recognise mind-cultivation, rational and universal education, right education of mind, as pure, and innocent as God made it in attainable capacity, education in His other gifts, the principles of science and philosophy, to render unto mind her purest, brightest attributes, the worthiest faculties.

Such education is for wisdom, and not mere learning.

Wisdom to learn, to know, to act, to apply the richest treasures of mind to the right place, at the right time, and all appropriate means of observation and science.

Then, the days of tradition, uncertain, vague, and fanatical, subject to a thousand aspects moulded in the hands of demagogues, flatterers for favors, treacherous to the dear people, whose souls they affect to love, and blasphemous to the eternal, with her varied impositions, oral or written, from the authors to the publishers, will be rightly numbered.

Then, the tyrants of society, cannot seek to bind and coerce its members by all the unhallowed acts of fiendish ambition, when bigotry will be silenced, and may not wantonly add again her now expiring siren delusions.

Without a right education, we see in every age, the incapacity of man for uniform, and adequate protection, for society in general.

Assuredly the elements of this evil are not in creation, where libelous ignorance in her impudent assurance, places so much of self-exoneration, as that implies mind's faulty analysis, and impeaches the attributes of Deity, but in the faulty action of mind and its dereliction, to meet the legitimate demands made upon it, to correct the evils of the world.

Most of the case, is in this position—now instead of complaints, murmurs, repinings, and libels, arouse to correct action, mind of mankind.

Thy earthly province is a high and plastic destiny.

To whom shall we refer? Assuredly to expanded and expansive minds, those, all of them, whose interest it is to enlarge the capacity of a liberal and expanded freedom.

Can sound mind ever refer to any species of absolutism, that betrays its character in increasing the difficulties, instead of the blessings of society? On what basis of ethics is the logic founded? We can never refer to those wedded to preconceived opinions, and invested in their professions to abjure all progress of mind.

Little should we avail, if we estimate by intimate knowledge of human nature and character, if we sought this idle and worthless futility.

This analysis enables us then to receive with caution, any of the extraordinary gifts of absolutism.

From the first idea of innocence to the extremest depths of iniquity and crime, man's education involves analogous results.

This mighty principle was instilled for the wisest purposes. Its good tendency, as conservative, is by God's benefit; its bad impulse is by man's perversion, and is his penalty.

See the difficulty of change from its fixed character of first impressions; how immense is that of revolution for reformation in most worthy objects, even through this avenue rightly directed, and how deplorable the difficulty of what is wrong from bias perversion! Many has been the effort to overcome this difficulty, but light of each mind itself, the rightful guardian, presents the only solution. Start right to end safely.

Man is a being created for the most beneficent purposes, as God made him subject to the modification of circumstances and education.

The world's light cannot be too bright to benefit man.

The primary benefit is to ensue on true refined education and its elements.

Such a state of things will teach that man's professions are to be with his God, his actions with man, and only to be estimated by his proper conduct through life; hence, man becomes a rational religionist.

With the most expansive freedom, freemen ought to have the best education of science, else they may, if licentious, abuse it the worse, and degeneration be thus effected.

The substantial true education of mind at the right time, is to overcome the amount of sophistry, the order of the day with lawyers, preachers, doctors, and a great part of the world.

That education goes to the depths of philosophy as high as mind can reach.

It commends the giving all minds proper training to the legitimate extent, a life-fund to grapple with all life's difficulties.

Such means will expel feudal times, and false social views, and secure the best attainable refined social and moral intellectual state, requisite for man's good.

It is the leadership of mind that must be in the mastery of principles.

Coercive leaders, military and civil, are only to be respected in their places, to attain pure and unadulterated views of duty and proper security, for their just performance.

All intelligent inquiring minds will admit that the world needs education, varied as its subjects, to extricate mankind from the horrible vassalage of peculiar faith error, that infects with moral contagion, all within the sphere of the terrible malign influence.

Of the billions of past rational existences, how many would have received the truth of mind, if they had had the means of appreciating it?

Then all this matter is one of suitable education.

How desirable and absolutely necessary is it for parents, friends and guardians, to guarantee a proper education for the child, as wise citizens render the state prosperous, and themselves worthy of it.

Education alone enables us to handle principles properly, to attain to that sublime equality, fraternity and liberty, that bless the world.

What is education? Simply the evolution of mind, on science, and philosophy; all else is its counterfeit.

Education that comprehends the master funds of mind, correctly carried out, protects us against, and defends us from the world's wiles, all peculiar faiths that positively emanate from peculiar education.

The education of the world does not impart at first to children's youthful minds the right appreciation, consequently right habits are not fixed from depraved tastes and vitiated results.

Nations, as the world, suffer, as both are concerned.

Education must expose all the machinery that embraced ghosts, witches, and hobgoblins, as the exploded pious or impious frauds of superstitious notions of barbarian ages, existing only in the brains of dreamers or designers.

It is important to use rational education, that introduces science and philosophy, with practical good sense, else the possession misleads, as a thing hurtful among a host of blessings.

She tells us the folly and idleness of animal excitement prevailing in churches, the hardened folly of bigotry, the wanton stupidity of faith sophistry, all of which have some peculiar custom and government.

Wise legislators will find the palaces of education cheaper than cabins for jails.

Education of right principles is not a forced power, but is ever characterized with the loveliest qualities.

She promotes no ambition misdirected, but causes pride to be rightly directed, as a high-minded sentiment divested of variety.

She rightly cultivates the moral tone and mind of society, and produces the best fund for life-enjoyment.

She will teach peculiar faith to be so heinous as to inspire true men with the resolve, that it shall be the least if not last of mind's trammels, if practicable.

She directs to the improvement of the natural acquisition of religion, that her constituents can best appreciate.

With her, religion will not be forced as in a hot-house.

The analysis of mind cultivated by liberal education will rightly tell us, that the doctrine of non-resistance cannot apply to any part of mankind by education.   Non-resistance can only invite aggression, insult, or injury ; then the quickest way is to give the delinquent aggressors their penalty ; as the hotter the war, the sooner peace with principles.

But by resistance is meant defence, not the wrong of aggression, that does not involve the lofty character of self-preservation, ever founded on principles.

There are many things deeply injurious to feelings, and they may crush the best characters, unless proper resentment be made; therefore appropriate penalty may be best for both parties.

It may make the evil the least, and correct most evils at the right point.   A wise precaution is the best in all things of life.

It is not non-resistance, but justice for evil and oppression.   Mind seeks and obtains its best protection by principles, that are the only thing that show the mathematical precision of science, the correct action of morals.

Doubtlessly, the time is approaching when cognizance of principles will be so exact that the highest state of correction of the world will at once arise, from their inherent potency and reflection of light; hence an enlightened public opinion is now the highest sovereign arbiter of all earthly standards and tribunals.   But it can never be so elevated as long as obsolete bibles of tradition are the tyrannizers of society, and force faith, whether destitute of principle and reason or not.

Now if there were any cause of difference of feeling, &c., between persons, two or more, they should face each other calmly and state their grievances ; and if insult be the motive, then a more consistent and proper resentment can be shown, and only that justified by the highest soul-principles ; or a better correction can be most promptly and properly had on the same basis, to lay aside erroneous impressions and unsound prejudices, and promote a better state of society.

Act, then, in this paramount matter, manly and candidly, openly and above board at once, and decide permanently, and in the best honor and peace.

The best action of society is that of knowledge, that results from science, which the key of rational education, the proper discipline of mind, reveals and inspires.

Then all rational minds must be satisfied that the world can only be in her happiness, greatness and prosperity by the flourishing state of rational education, through philosophical science.

The people, the rational minds of the world, must institute a new era for their best position.

By the blessings of science-education subsequent ages will put into the shade much of past improvements and discoveries.

Optics have advanced astronomy.   When we reach something that will advance optics, and that displayed by subsequent improvements, then we may begin to appreciate who God is, his mighty funds, and the agency of mind that he created.

Science and philosophy, the more accurately known, cause us to approach more accurately to God, in the advance and progress of mind.

Without the characteristic traits of universe-education, the only safe one, the vortex of speculation is one that destroys myriads that do not depend on their own manly action, best, matured, and honest judgment, but unfortunately depend on the verdant, unnatural, and often interested advice of incompetent men, who will most stupidly shrink from all gentlemanly responsibility, and sadly leave the advised to deplore the brazen ignorance and baseness of the advisers.

Judgment is the quintessence, the concentration of the senses after all said and done, and that can be only wisely matured on the basis of conservative principles.

How much of advice is tendered, and how little of it is disinterested or good !   Then think and act judiciously for all and thyself.

There is hardly one original genius—one genius thinker or analyzer in millions; then mankind should distrust all equivocal pretensions.

Without education we are subject to the contingency of chance, not the uniform protection of science and philosophy, in our daily transactions, and liable to be swindled by every unprincipled man that comes about us.

How, otherwise, is the ignorance of the world to be overcome? `

You have an organized brain, a rational means to learn, and it must be so applied in all subjects, religion especially.

By this fund we obtain a definite system, a meaning and point in every thing we aim at, to counteract all perverted advice.

Carry on your schools to propagate good sense, and all that it commands, as the moment they go down liberty dies.

All minds are confirmed by habits of education, and rarely change; then have that most rational.

Liberty itself is to be directed by the lights of rational education, that it run not into communism nor licentiousness, that all belong to absolutism or sophistry.

All ought to protect the altar of their country, and elicit the worth of science, for the blessing of the human race, that should not feel the despotism of monarchy, nor of the majority.

A rational education enables us best to invoke justice, wisdom, honor, and virtue, to counteract the disgusting and low intrigues of cunning and vice, that may supplant the good by wretched policy and criminal design.

The world, in its honest ignorance and exemption from suspicion of all the horrors of tyranny, will suffer self-delusion and public imposition.

Parents are accountable to their children for the correct instruction imparted, as the conduct of the child reflects on the parents.

Children should, then, be firmly accountable to such parents.

Society and states should hold all parents reasonably accountable for correct instruction, and themselves responsible for all the facilities necessary, as they do for all the penalties inflicted.

It is better to build up systems and means of liberal, rational education, than those of punishment.

What a pity it is that parents do not resist, candidly and firmly, the downward tendency and progress, that may ruin their children.

They indulge their children unwisely, and see them first perish from abuse of morals.

They undertake to govern their children, and fall below their esteem.

Children have all the faculties of copying the example of their parents.

Those parents are bound to give them a correct copy of principles, but, alas, that copy is a miserable failure.

Do not cow or pet children; they, as all, must beware of the first step, and should be invariably governed rationally.

Education, that teaches cultivation of independent thought, presents what religion requires. What do predestination, baptism, Romanism, protestantism, Greekism, or any other church division or peculiar faith, present to mind, but the errors of peculiar education?

Youth, sincerely installed in the light of science of mind's principles, learns that liberty of conscience that shows respect to mind, and proves true sincerity in religion. Such minds must best honor truth and honesty. All people have it, where mind exists, Jew or gentile, Christian or pagan, if they would cultivate its right precepts.

Ignorance of mind, and its false government of passions, particularly the most common, as avarice and ambition, make bigots and fanatics.

Education of the world, with the whole of the reasoning faculties, elicits the mind-fund for thought, enjoyment, independence, action, and progress, and goes for sound, pure, and loftiest religion.

No impressions can be made, then, by all the designs of superstition, however politic and visionary.

Proscription by names, under the mask of pure religion, will not avail, to commit outrages on mind thus fortified. Education must teach so as to satisfy the inquiring mind, explaining and solving all essential things.

Mind is truly to be consulted in the solution of all the questions of this life, for all time; not in one but in all centuries. States hold all their citizens accountable to them, then they are responsible for correct morals and their rational education, that mind throughout the world may be adequately supplied by all the means and facilities of its happiness. Rational education teaches mind to think for itself, and that correctly, whereas peculiar education causes it to obey the peculiar opinions of others. The first is of God, the last of man.

Let the millions annually expended, for the last, be devoted to the first, then mind would be enlightened, and the world happier, because better. Peculiar education is promotive of peculiar prejudices. Educational purposes may embrace monumental, to celebrate the victories of the illustrious dead, in this utilitarian age.

But what will compare with one brilliant mind, superbly and rationally educated? Monuments, erected to worth and merit, may promote that very education. We must make due allowances for those schooled in their peculiar education, and wedded to all its institutions, that look at the customs of their fathers.

Education should be so rational as to quarry out a proper amount of action for life. The world is so cut up by sectarianism, secret societies, &c., and the difficulties of mere public opinion are so intricate, that rational education must preside, to obviate all such.

All must have no education of peculiar, but rational views. Rational instruction and education are the conservatives of the globe, while ignorance is the father of errors. Poor persons are too much excluded from mind improvement, by the dictation of the priestocracy—they are in its leading strings, as its minions.

What are the curses of false education and faith? The cultivation of mind by rational education has brought the age far beyond what any bibles of Moses or his priest-fathers could do. Only think of the inhibition, virtually, by all interdiction, of any change of such scriptures, on a proper appreciation of astronomical science so recklessly declared in those works.

The science of education is entitled a regular commission, embracing all practical subjects, as agriculture, customs, examples, laws, and opinions, that must be referred to the Almighty standard, by rational education.

The moderns have the best educational means, general protection of laws, all the means of mind concentrated to one great object. Educate, to eschew peculiar faith and narrow views. He who depends on mere professional school-knowledge will be humbugged, deceived badly—miserably. Such is not for advancing, but for failure. But the odious distinction of poor and rich can be well obviated, as far as practical, in the order of universal brotherhood; we can see the good effect of a liberal rational education. The superfluities of the rich, the ornaments of houses of extravagant order, had better be devoted for the benefit of the poor's education.

All that is essentially necessary for mind is universal, and commenced when mind was created. Rational education must do its duty by it. The support of public schools cannot be too extensively entertained.

The race of mankind is compelled, in self-defence, to seek the best legitimate rational education. If bibles of tradition stand in the way, expel them. Rational education corrects the dogmas of the schools, causing them to be permanently right, and never to be reversed! Who, in his innocence, does not believe that the world is nearer right and truth-telling, justice doing without peculiar education? Rational education is to enable us to see, and correct all fallacies, practicable.

It will put away all the trammels of the schools, and will finally produce the desirable and necessary social regeneration. The obligation conferred, renders mind capable of leaving society no worse than found. The great rational means of improvement are all educational; but letters are not the absolute means, however we deplore their absence in any one case, while common sense is to be elicited by things and subjects. Ignorance is preferable to error. It is hard to find out at this time any part so unenlightened, that proper sense may not be elicited. Peculiar education differs over the world, while rational is universally uniform in principles.

The first imparts faith in devils, angels, witches, ghosts, miracles, prophecies, and mysteries peculiarly revealed. What is more absurd, or untruthful?

Once the clergy had nearly the sole means of education; moulding public sentiment: forcing it by inquisition; perverting it by sophistry; silencing it by poisons and dungeons, by the blackest imposition, the most detestable superstition. Who can wonder at the world-wide perversions? There was but one edition of clerical imposition, in Rome, Greece, Egypt, India and Asia, the whole world. When and where will all this stop? When rational education of the world gets the mastery, and mind asserts its full rights!

Rational education can correct all the malign effects of peculiar education, if the world will do right.

Phrenology physical presents relative exception to responsibility, unless the organs be rightly cultivated; hence, a liberal and just education is expedient. The state owes this. Some people do not appreciate the good effects, the necessary obligations of a liberal education, that enables us to depend on our own judgment, and the best facts of the case. Those do not understand the subject they affect to decide on.

The world cannot possess too much of independence; and as to success in various professions and employments, the novice has to ask some preliminary questions, as if the village or social circle is free or is rented out, belongs to a few dictators? Every essential that promotes rational education, must be sacredly protected. What is done with all the school funds? Are they properly used, well employed by the head men, for the benefit of the poor? Are they added to, instead of diminished? The world needs a proper system of rational education. All cultivated circles ought to have libraries of most select and valuable books, debating societies, if practicable ; all the approved substantial means.

A respect to the best feeling on this subject bespeaks the effort for justice. This subject should be fully comprehended, by the inherent right of self-protection. The object should be to obtain a true republican education, that will prepare youth to do justice to mind in all the various relations of country, science, and religion.

REASON IS THE PROPER STANDARD OF TRUTH AND RELIGION.

Deity underwrites his own character by creation, organization and conservation of the universe : if man contradicts this position, he perverts his own mind, libels God, and impeaches himself, as degraded, wilfully ignorant and blind.

Such views, involving treachery and high treason of the Divine Being, and his imbecility for the past and future protection of all creation, recoils in fearful retribution on the authors of such obliquity of mind, more disgraceful than heathen mythology, all of which has been swept away from enlightened minds.

In the name of God's attributes, purity that admits nothing impure in his character, of omniscience that recognises sin, the negative of good, and expels it as evil, and of omnipotence that faithfully interdicts all such, mind, enlightened, pure, and free from vassalage of malign influences, looking properly at the essential attributes, must protest forever, with suitable reverence of Deity, the eternal Creator.

There can be no peculiar nor original creation of an evil genius, when the sinful genius of mind perverted already, resulting necessarily on its free agency in circumstances of a world of earthly character, exists enough.

Such original, peculiar, particular creation, would be a contradiction and absurd analysis of Deity's essential attributes.

Deity has created the greatest good, whose negative is evil, as destruction is the negative of conservation, and his perfect character extracts the greatest good out of the supposed greatest evils, the most worthy example of mind to imitate.

The more perfect the mind, the more valid is its good.. Such mind enlightens the world, and blesses it by the best fruits.

Any particular malign creation of an evil genius would imply the same perversion of mind of the Creator, and necessarily impeaches his character.

Ignorant and self-willed, avaricious and ambitious mind, wilfully and knowingly blind, self-important, degraded in affectation to render mind vassal, libeling the Creator at every step, a botch in conception, has to retract its horrible conception, and must retreat to its demoralized and corrupt insignificancy.

Mind's errors do not arise from pure thoughts, and liberal world-wide views of creation's nature and obligations.

God's inspirations rest on noble thoughts, and his best blessings fructify such candid exposition of truth and reason.

No: the errors that assail the world in bitterness, degradation and wo, arise by corruption of mind, self-delusion, wilful blindness and imbecility.

The day that proclaims faith peculiar of any character especially to advance the pretended divine rights of kings and churchmen, is to be admitted without reason, witnesses in its broad light an admission of reckless tyranny and guilty sophistry, the like of which cannot be conceived.

Enlightened reason informs and teaches us the value of conservative principles, for which past legends substituted the pretences of angels, a mere fiction in the brain of dreamers.

Angels were as necessary to uphold the solar systems of the universe, as to convey messages for Deity to its rational beings in the enjoyment and exercise of mind, the only medium of communication.

The universe was created on a system of conservative principles, and must be governed by them in the physical, moral and religious elements. Who but reason prostrated the fell purposes of idolatry and superstition, with their attendant sophistry, forever misleading the people and seducing their noblest exertions?

She can rear the best fabric that mind can institute.

Who but she befriends man in his best capacity, when he is duly aroused to give best
heed to her counsel, and improve by cultivation to the best talents ?

Can impudent peculiar faith stand in the presence of reason when she rebels against
her tribunal ?

Every trustworthy, truthful man is aided by his reason, whose justice and protection
he feels conscientiously bound to invoke forever to sustain himself, posterity and world.
Who asks for or can obtain better security ?

This foundation is sure to eternity, resting on eternal principles as old as time, durable as creation, conservative as God's attributes.

Reason can never adopt traditions of any character or profession as truthful and
worthy of honest faith, no matter of what part of the world, marred by feudalism and
vassalage, imposed on ignorant credulity, scarred and disfigured by legends, fables,
bigotry and fanaticism, wars for centuries to master the world by its absolutism, blurred
by iniquitous inquisitions of fiendish character, proscriptions of the sovereign rights of
the people revolting to man's dignity and purity, all to deceive and procure the absolute
sway of government of man on earth, to procure wealth, aggrandisement, vainglory
and power at man's expense, blood, deepest suffering and mind's ignominy. Already
has mental reformation rescued mind from much of the thraldom of superstition. Then
came correct constitutional government, that blazed high with a brilliant and increasing
light, irradiating religious freedom by severance of church and state, and lastly comes
benignant reason to crown the triumph of mind.

We all seek universal protection from imposition and its treachery ; what standard
can be universal for protection but that of reason ?

The highest practicable authority of man, past or present, is only tradition, oral or
written, and can be only rightly estimated by the only tribunal possible in the nature of
creation to mind, and that tribunal is, or ought to be, must be, reason.

What else is it ? All of mortals, all that they say and do, no matter how wise supposed, must be tested at this tribunal. It is not what men say or can say, but what
mind, enlightened mind, whose best result is reason, says.

Man records all his tradition, his bibles or scriptures, but mind recognises them all,
otherwise man would be worse off than brutes that have instinct, which he has not,
but in whose place an Almighty has vouchsafed the glorious attributes of reason.

As it is, mind has the noblest faculty and function of appreciating its God, and that it
performs through reason, not faith, unless in abeyance to reason.

Undoubted proof establishes facts to our satisfaction.

Pre-eminent caution and care are expedient, when the humbugging world has
abounded so much in fabulous, imperfect and deceptive story, especially that miscalled
sacred. that might be named desecrated.

Much of such pretended history, if not to be discarded, is doubtful, of no value, only
as satisfactorily established.

Ordinary facts, in the regular course of nature, require this course. The world humbugs itself about faith—worse than others humbug it. It adopts bibles of tradition,
when they are certainly proved the veriest fables. No wonder priestocracy clearly war
on reason, that satisfies a wondering people, that the extraordinary phenomena exist
only in their brain, like the phantasmagoria of psychology, as when analyzed are only
ordinary phenomena, seen in the distorted rays of credulity, misnamed faith.

This is the decision of incontrovertible principle.

When we come up to the capacity of enlightened minds we reach the sublime dignity of reason, that peculiar faith-sophists the world over, during all its ages, have hated
with a deadly hate, as adverse to all their nefarious humbugs.

So far from knowing the facts of reason, they have not begun to appreciate the essential elements of mind.

The majority of all rational men believe in no tradition independent of reason, as
they most conscientiously consider all such as most corrupt decisions and impositions,
especially all that fear the light, considering hierarchy in its numerous forms of power,
yet they feel a necessity of a better state of things, to obtain which they are disposed
to act with all reasonable men.

What is to be done ?   How can they be reconciled ?

Tortures and ostracism, inquisitions and proscriptions, are not competent for enforcement.

You may preach all the doctrines that tradition can give, all the dogmas that men
can invent, you cannot reach their case by all sophistry that proclaims " every knee
shall bow." All peculiar faith doctrines cannot reach them.

These people, the majority of this union and the world, must not be left out, when
justified by reason, rational mind.

God fortunately has not left them out, though peculiar faith doctrine people have separated themselves from them, and proclaimed with an unholy proscription, their damnation for unbelief, not of the truth, but of their peculiar faith.

The first are devoted to the God of the universe, and cannot take the peculiar gods of the latter.

Libel of a system that meets their case, the case of all, every case, is not the emanation of mind seeking light.

The immortality-aspiring mind universally feels its own innate character, if unadulterated to be rational, and has a bullion that it cannot knowingly surrender for dross—but seeks the pure mint-coin and rejects the counterfeit, too plain for any by reason to mistake.

This faith tested true by reason, that dignifies because it humanizes the world, needs no means as some peculiar faiths had for thousands of years, of which very children should be ashamed for the debasement of mind, and the enslavement of the world.

Freemen are now looking aright manfully and fearlessly to the one sublime and mighty temple inherent in mind, that points all true adorers to the Almighty through the true way of reason.

Nations of the earth, hasten to enjoy this holy and worthy offering, one that your posterity will thank you for most gratefully.

Reason may be smothered by all the crimes of the anti-God, that fanaticism can invent, and all the errors that idolatry can adopt, still, all these, time her mighty hand-maid, will supersede.

Down then, with all the absurdities of bible tradition devoid of reason and truth, as unsafe and ruinous to the world. Let reason assume her tribunal in rational mind, wisely governing the sons of men in duty to man and God. God holds all accountable to reason and her attributes, not peculiar faith and her dogmas.

Argue as others may against this, plead all they choose about peculiar faith, they are self-condemned by their impeachable sophistry, themselves wound up in abundant contradictions, and their best hopes in fragments scattered to naught and dust. All the strongholds of peculiar faith are yielded by time as false and untenable, exposed under the conviction of reason.

In science of government, national or self, individuals can exercise thought, mind, reason, as they ought in all science of life, all vital matters, but in religion that requires the most of thought, as the true science of life and life's thoughts of mind, the pretence is set up that its function is too sacred for any but sacred persons, so corruptly called, by sycophants, traducers of their own sacred rights; God above all, can only take cognisance !

Wise, patriotic, and philanthropic statesmen, should see to it, that reason have her sway for the good of mankind, and not have an enlightened public opinion to be elaborated by corrupt division of the spoils, all to be extracted from the dear people.

All such men are compelled to cast away, of course, all that does not accord with enlightened, rational, and true principles.

Why do you send your gospel to the Pagans, who have been nurtured in similar and analogous condition of faith ? But theirs is not a rational faith ! Now are you caught. Your faith in any messiahship, is as unreasonable and blasphemous.

How, then, are you infallible, if they are in error ? When you opened the door to your peculiar faith, you gave a wholesale passport to all peculiar faiths.

You have not the first principles essential to proselyte, worthy of mind.

Do not stupidly persevere after being caught in full, on your conceited and adopted position against reason.

Self-sufficient mortal, learn true wisdom from wisdom's only source, reason, that alone gives you safety in true principles that constitute the bible of mind, the only safety.

Do not adopt reason in full, in all but one point, faith, and leave out that the most important.

Be a freeman, and have all the benefits of a freeman's mind.

When reason is a guide, let her be a moral, intellectual, and religious one—to be the safest. She cannot be rightfully divested of any essentials of these.

At the present age of the world, the best position from the advanced state of knowledge must be rational. If ever the ignorance of the age permitted the dictatorship of masters, that assuredly is not the case now, when mind can think by science that expands on reason.

Mind cannot be getting worse with the better lights progressing, as it must, if open to light, get more enlightened. This is a true axiom, and what is true of individual, must be so of aggregate, as the age means that.

Then do not trammel rational mind in free discussions about religion, the most rational of all subjects.

Men of matured age tell me, that they have been actually afraid of the free discussion of this subject of religion, so plausible are the arguments against the bible of tradition, as if that was the only tenure of morals and religion!

Do they think that the world will come to an end as to morals and religion, when such bibles end, as they will? The vices of the peculiar bibles will destroy all of them. But is not all this social tyranny, the vassalage of mind, while some fear from previous influence of others' opinions, that their minds may be set wrong, and have an improper bias, when their minds may be at fault, and not the bible! How do they get all those ideas? From any sound rational disinterested mind?

But who is the author of religion, God or the bible?

If God be the author of religion, as Creator, then any bible that denies him exclusive omnipotent unity therein, is adverse to the purity of both.

The bible of Judaism gives mind up to priestocracy, and is not the representative of God, because no principle of God clashes with another principle, but this bible clashes with many principles that mind recognises. All bibles, built thereon, are equally at fault.

The God of this universe is the author of religion, a universal constituent of rational mind, as he is the author of innate faculties of the mind, the rightful beneficiary, through conservative principles, without which religion could not exist, as it could have no Being at all.

Therefore, these men ought to read and study a bible of mind, to free their souls from blasphemous error.

Are men afraid to look at the bible of mind? They, then, are afraid to look at truth, for one is essentially the same as the other.

When their declaration is analyzed, they have been told that the risk of such investigation is irremediable, and their souls are lost, because the parley is temptation irresistible.

Was there ever infatuation so absurd, sophistry so evil? Rational minds must hail the time for free rational discussion of religion, as more important than of government; as superstition, the certain substitute, controls not only man's government, but mind, by absolutism, in this world, and renders it unhappy, by the most awful forebodings, in the next. It makes mind vassal on earth, and soul a slave in the future; awes both, and fixes them in a channel, assuming to be universal dictator, now and forever.

This very day millions are afraid to reason on religion, the very thing that their minds need most of all.

They have not shown themselves competent, with sufficient virtue and principles enough, to carry out the behests of God Almighty, as displayed in mind and conscience.

They stupidly embrace an obsolete bible, that stings them with its foul embrace, and causes their murder throughout the world, which it had outraged as long as it could hold it in absolute abeyance.

This might answer for slaves of the dark ages of the world, but not for freemen of this century.

Our excellent institutions require better things of religion, that promises to be our blessings, not our curse.

Either reject the decision as wrong, or admit the tribunal.

Less cannot be expected of freemen. Slaves are forced out of reason to carry out, by want of principle, endless incongruities that arise in all systems of peculiar faith.

In all their sermons and writings what do preachers invoke all the time, by every word spoken, but reason or sophistry? If they receive peculiar faith they are obliged to use sophistry in her train.

Rational religion only gives full audience to reason.

Sophistry is most disgraceful; then reason must be appealed to.

Faith is only to be trusted through reason, else the mind of the individual adopting may be fanatically savage, or to be pitied for its dependence, or want of the powers of discernment.

When mind rejects faith of reason, the God of reason rejects mind's wayward thoughts. We need proof that reason must be satisfied with.

In relation to any tradition without analysis into the supposed facts of the case, or the character of the testimony, or of the analogy to which we are compelled necessarily to resort by the very nature of the case, what is such belief or faith worth?

It is not entitled to the name of faith, as it is mere credulity; and is that worth anything?

If our faith be adopted independent of reason we have a foundation that has no reason.

We are the beneficiaries, and if irrational, are the losers; therefore we have to inquire into the motives and influences of others, probably subservient to measures that they cannot scan, and pretences that they cannot truthfully uphold.

All the time that the advocates of any peculiar doctrine preach, though reason is invoked in the exercise of mind, their position absurdly excludes both from their faith.

They can never expect to have the proper respect of either.

Where is the end to all their trifling absurdity?

Mankind universally admit reason's proper guidance in all things submitted to mind, except in the part that suits some few! Then the exception excludes the rational part.

Enlightened justice, tempered with benevolence, allows all due respect to others' faith, with the highest respect for their immortal souls; at the same time they must submit the question to enlightened reason, or they may fail, miserably fail, in the reality for which they have ardently and sincerely striven.

Religious sentiments are inherent, but are diversified by circumstances of education, schemes of hierarchy, mythology, that unbiased reason alone can rectify.

All assumptions must be expelled when based on no reason, yet affecting the mysteries of nature.

All wise laws should be paramount and obeyed, therefore those of creation are the documents of a Supreme Immortal God, who must be adored exclusively as supreme.

The laws of God are written in an enlightened conscience, that none but uncultivated minds can reject, thereby declaring themselves of brutal character, and a miserable mass for corruption and perversion.

The pure and great minds of the world must counteract all these bad results, that lead to the worst of crimes, of perjury, &c.

It is not faith but reason that looks at the nature of things.

No hope or faith can stand a moment but on reasonable premises.

Reason and conscience enlightened are the best codes for life-rights, and if priests and preachers reject them for peculiar faith credulity, they are the enemies of mankind.

Moral ethics are intellectual and rational, and demand reason.

Much of the world has been so situated that it is vassal to the other part, depending on their leading, too often their misleading.

Then our interpretation of truth must rest on the facts of the case, never on sophistry or its appearance, that must be an abomination in the sight of the God of the universe.

If you throw away reason in faith you are condemned, because you throw away principles.

If you adopt peculiar faith you are condemned already by reason.

Thus reason decides, that if faith be not true, that she is a curse procured from the toils of superstition of some kind, nurtured in the bosom of absolutism, base and deceptive, to circumvent the people for sinister purposes of power, ambition, and crime.

What power on earth can decide but reason as to genuine faith, leaving to God to test all men's minds therein.

What is the great standard of morals for the whole world? Religion, that rests on truth and honesty.

One part of the world excludes the faith-ethics of all the others; what, then, is the great regulator but reason for ever, and that in all parts?

Exclude her, and we are at the mercy of tyrants and imbeciles, unprincipled demagogues of all kinds.

We need the great balance-wheel of mind, regulated by reason in all things, but especially in vital and rational religion.

As all time-pieces are referred to the revolution of the earth in its imaginary axis for a standard, all analogy decides that rational mind should have reason as the umpire universally for faith in morals.

This is the only means to do justice to religion on this earth. All just policy demands it.

Who has the true faith? They who have rational mind and philosophical reason on their side, of the highest order and most magnificent character of its exercise.

But this produces skepticism, atheism!

The very reverse is proved and demonstrated, as it disproves all such.

The order and harmony of the universe are the most irrefutable evidence of its organization and regulation, directed by one great architect, who orders and maintains in beautiful and perfect system exhaustless millions of worlds and systems of worlds, without the least confusion or disorder.

Two witnesses are enough to testify for justice if they be trustworthy, but here are innumerable witnesses of one God, whereas all other pretensions have mere forms of inorganic, decaying matter.

Well may the question be asked, who were the testimony, but those all interested in all things, companions of deceivers, traitors, and perjurers.

Every sermon that is preached, if rightly analyzed, should make the sound mind assured of its own faith in one living God.

A faithist never reasons ; what sort of animal is he ?

He affects to reason till you get him to faith, then he stumbles or bolts.

What is the world but a mixture of herds, flocks, swarms of the mass vulgar multitude, led by the bold, reckless, and intriguing ?

So far is the bible of tradition from being the word and revelation of the God of the universe, that the comprehension of the reason cannot be there obtained.

That would prove man's perfection in mind, the very reverse of which is fact, as all wise men know.

Theology can only be considered a system of principles by reason, not of faith only, as reason sanctions.

We must look always at reason before faith.

When you speak of your faith, that you do not approach by reason, and assail the doctrines of other peculiar faiths, reason is the only weapon, and that you have just deprived yourself the use of ; your position fixes you side by side with Mormons, Mahometans and Pagans, all of whom, have only faith-doctrines.

You have but one way to rid yourself of your own quagmire, and that is by reason.

Reason improves our nature, and best elicits the happiness of mankind, as she relies on the certain principles that must be exercised most certainly.

Reason bespeaks the only weapon of toleration and freedom.

All systems of peculiar faith, tried under the standard of reason, that all minds obey, must come to an end

Any system repugnant to reason must be repugnant to truth ; and all such become pretences, false and corrupt, begetting lusts of dominion, ambition, &c., and clash with each other, contrary to God's principles.

Once the ancients instituted oracles and auguries, in which the ignorant confided, as their feelings were ingrafted into superstition and its rites. This was one of the peculiar faiths.

From that time flourished the inquisition, the proscription of depraved public opinion. The people did not perceive that all the systems of erring man, must be under the domain of reason, that establishes the true religion.

Is spiritualization a power to destroy reason ?

Who have this pretence on this earth but impostors ?

Death, inherent to all animal creation, shuts out the dead from the living, and kills all bibles of tradition.   Surely our reason is better than the improbable testimony of interested persons, distant centuries past in the dark ages of the world, under the various fascinations and temptations of promises and self-delusions.

All intelligent freemen must place reason above faith to make truth.   Reason analyzes nature by the enlightened senses, to reach the proper actions of life, to secure propriety by experience and knowledge.   But this is a world-wide and world-age subject, and mind must traverse the universe, ere it can appreciate the God of Nature.

All rational beings are concerned in the good actions of rational mind, to preserve universal order in society.

Theological subjects are judged of by the world, through feelings, not reason.   How deficient are the first !

We are told of faith by the ignorant world, and on analysis, find that feelings dictate it !   What have feelings to do with reason ?

Reason, not faith, then can alone appreciate justice, and reaches in process of time, by operation of mind on mind, the true position.   Who wants a system of faith that he cannot prove to be generally approved, or right intrinsically ?   Thou shouldst not do, what thou cannot justify.   What is your faith worth, if built on a vague, instead of an accurate investigation ?

Of what use is science to faith, that depends on things unseen ?   Of the same use as the mariner's compass.   The mariner is in the wide trackless ocean, and without that, is destitute of the true means of safety.   If expert, he may regard some of the bodies of the universe to know how to steer.   He seeks any way, a regulator standard.

Reason has universal empire over faith, peculiar or general : this is an axiom.   What comes to our notice or cognizance, is through reason.   Whatever looks to reason, ever approaches the nearest to the safest position for mind and man.

ANALYSIS OF RATIONAL RELIGION.—MONOTHEISM, OR THE RELIGION OF PRINCIPLES.

Derry's best light of mind, the elements of rational religion or Monotheism, that is, rational faith and confidence in the First Great Cause, soul and ruler supreme of the universe, and consistent actions and works in conformity thereto, are universal to rational minds in all ages and countries.

This principle cannot be effaced with all practicable evil designs and mind's perversions, by all the machinery of inquisition and proscription, as it is the inculcation of an innate and indestructible faculty, one identified with our being, the living monitor of living rational minds.

Its right directions have been perverted to man's worst purposes and passions, and most iniquitous uses.

Superstition, with her thousand false pretences and sophisticated darkness of mind, may retard, idolatry may mar, false faith torture and pretend to counterfeit it, still the work of the Almighty progresses to the triumph of his agents, mind, time and matter, a beautiful union of the powers of a true trinity, such that faith and reason recognise as self-evident. Rational religion wins the best and only affections of enlightened man's best aspirations, bows to the tribunal of the God of reason, in the sublimity of silence and conviction, encircles in the most exalted manner, mind's best interests and highest, purest honors, enhances its true character, its best confidence, and consequently must embrace its candid faith.

Rational religion ennobles man's nature at the right time, by a correct cultivation, comprehends most certainly all mankind in one mighty universal brotherhood, united on proper principles, in conflict and antagonism with no creed that mind and reason recognise; at war with no sect, for none of hers can exist, protective of all races, however diversified, bound in general interest of love proportionate to the wants of mind, universal in its application and salvation of all worthy rational beings, requiring them as free rational agents, to elicit their own safety ; marked with no peculiarity as an imposture of man and a libel on Deity, and competent to secure under its benign and sufficient influence, universal good feeling, the loftiest benevolence and permanent peace.

Monotheism comprehends works consistent with such noble and exalted faith, and all consistent with reason, exalts itself most liberally and justly the more the test of reason applies to it, and is only in existence by reason's legitimate authority. She delights universally sincere minds, that wish to find the rational true way without doubt. She pilots mind through the mazes, labyrinths and mysteries of peculiar faith, through the trying scenes of life with the' eye of true faith on the refulgent light of the universe author, directing the best deeds of conscience, an independent, not a vassal monitor, to do the bidding of a freeman, not of a tyrant and the part of a coward, and waits with the exaltation of true hope on the dying mortal, and assures such of the most honorable close of life. She does the amplest justice to this world, and gives thereby the best earnest for the universe. But rational religion affords no pleasure to any that seek to profit by perverted worldly speculation, under her banner assuming the province of mind, as they are utterly condemned for acts inconsistent with her pure teachings, when they bring the trade of conscience before God's tribunal.

The diffusion of rational religion omnipresent in all rational minds, whose elements are possessed by all as deed of creation-gift, has been operating in the world all the time, through the inspiration of God on mind in general ; but impostors of peculiar faiths have assumed all the praise from the one eternal Supreme and only sovereign, whose omniscience and purity do not license any to speculate as better than the world. God himself is judge of all minds, and has only yielded any capital of his divine attributes to any creature, as part of the universal share.

The diffusion of rational religion over the wide world, suits the pure and essential wants of mind, and no means under any pretences, should arrest them to secular power and aggrandizement in God's republic.

Ignorant fanatics have run wild, blinded by peculiar faith, reckless of universal good, for their selfish purposes. All this must be counteracted by universal philanthropy and patriotism, as all rational beings are deeply interested on the score of social duties, benefits and morals that embrace them.

Rational religion is embraced in man's whole duty to God, its best adoption and practice towards man, and including all imperative bounden obligations to both ; nor can these matters be mistook by those adopting " honesty as the best policy."

All this duty elicits the best and full code of ethics written, embracing the elements from the foundation, essential in all societies, not after, but forethought and action.

All these are to be recognised by enlightened reason and truth, and all should be embraced in faithful action, the correct decision on which rests with a tribunal universally, no respector of persons, only as they are respectors of Deity's conservative principles.

Every mind, then, having its rationality and innate faculties, a part of its constituency, must have its religion, which should be rational religion only, to be acceptable before the rational God of rational beings, to honor him alone, ruler omnipotent.

All rational religion includes all spiritual religion practicable and genuine, that is legitimate. But spiritual peculiar faith cannot embrace rational religion, which condemns all such at once as wrong in conception, irreverent and impious in the sight of purity.

In all peculiar, that is, spurious faith, sophistry and bigotry must necessarily all the time supersede truth and liberal justice, with all possessed of fundamental principles.

It is impossible for peculiar faith to render this universe moral, pure, or happy.

There is wanting the great central sun, reason, that balances all creation, that is to expel all the elements of superstition, and correct the conscience so much misdirected and misled.

Rational religion has to give due credit to all the great cardinal virtues of man's nature endowed by the author of all that is estimable, which is preferable to mere peculiar faith that vaunts beyond correct action, that implies correct principles. All these when rightly directed to enact necessarily religious action, must be caused by the necessary possession of mind's innate faculties.

If rational religion do not have her true government of mind, then come superstition, idolatry and man-worship, from which emanates a multitude of spurious systems, the more degenerate as mind is enslaved by ignorance, and debased by superstition.

All such systems are eventually overturned by reason illustrated by philosophical science, God's best vicegerents, else they overturn the mind debased and degraded, below reason.

The conflicts of opinions among the various sects of peculiar faith, ever antagonistical, prevent a consistent invocation at the same time, by direct antagonism to the throne of grace, and evince a reflection on the mind that wars on reason, that reflects on the age of reform, and presents countless obstacles to man's true happiness.

Be our faith what reason adjudges, our actions are the rule to be judged by.

Monotheism, or pure rational religion, will carry mind into the full and diversified theatre of its action, words, and thoughts, its social and intellectual existence—to enlarge its virtues and direct its moral and religious culture—to improve its reason, on its present relations—and its loftiest duties to its Creator.

The sublime character of Monotheism, or rational religion, cannot permit it to be of any peculiar phalanx, sect, denomination, or creed, or claim community of interest less than what is general and universal; a world-wide position, high as the holy centre of the universe, and as deep as mind's needs, to recognise standard wisdom and illustrious reason.

In the blessing of humanity to the minutest fibre of sensibility, she is ever alive, and must feel most deeply as she is duly interested, with a mother's care and a daughter's obligation, invoking the purest sympathy of soul. Sensibly alive to the wants of the whole human sphere, surely she is identified with all that pertains to the Creator's benediction.

She seeks ever to be enlightened by the effulgent rays of intellect, itself enlightened and liberalized at the fountains of philosophical science, securing satisfaction at the shrine of genius and of all mental light, whose mighty universal blessings of inspiration and revelation she solemnly and in good faith invokes.

Her faith is that of reason, arrayed in all the glories of mind and in the beauties of truth, fit offering for Deity, and worthy of freedom of mind : a pure resident of earth, best prepared for immortality, man's holy guardian, God's universally acknowledged minister.

However the flights of fancy may please, and the visions of imagination may delight the superficial, yet it is only the sublime truths of reason that enlighten, instruct, and amend her most substantial institutions.

Her interest-share in the fund of eternity is equal and deep to her constituency, and she never sacrifices with wanton sacrilege at the shrine of vanity, ambition, power, vain-glory of the world, the jewel-gifts of mind, the freedom of conscience. She is ever aroused to extricate mind from the bigotry of all ages, the mazes of feudal vassalage, and the intricacies of insidious sophistry, bedecking superstition in her thousand varieties of false colors.

On this sublime and majestic greatness of mind's happiness, she knows no worldly interest of sordid lucre, obeys no ambition but that of pure faith, though thousands of train-band clans may dictate, and thousands of bibles of tradition of miracles, prophecies, and mysteries, may affect to teach her, to forego the nuptials of her holy wedlock.

She hails with exultation of innocence the rational decrees of divine inspiration, appropriately recognised through God's works, and the mighty behests of wisdom, legitimately deduced in divine legislation by mind and reason.

She feels at all times the profound impressions of the character of the Creative Architect, reflected in the radiant magnificence of the universe, the sublimity of the exact machinery displayed in the splendid elements of the solar systems, and the crowning magnificence of the whole.

She is fain to credit on such testimony, too clear to be mistaken, too mighty to be eclipsed, too majestic not to be appreciated, the universality of God's power and munificence, his exalted wisdom, illustrious, matchless genius, and surpassing beneficence.

The great First Cause is self-proclaimed by the magnificent revelations of his sublime creation, organization, and conservation, the holy trinity, that mind must fathom in its glorious inspirations.

The worth and intrinsic character of rational religion asks for no contracted solutions, only liberal elucidation. With a reverence of Deity, most profound in conception and duty, she looks upon the Supreme Spirit as no localized and peculiar exclusive, that delights in the bloody strife; producing no incongruity of two belligerents addressing the holy throne of grace, mercy, love, justice, peace, and omniscience, at one and the same time, reciprocally hostile.

But she refers to correct actions, as the available prayers of the whole world, at one and the same time, that premise conservative principles never antagonistic, that accompanied the creation of the universe, as the best, because the only inherent means of preservation.

What those are, let wise philosophy and intelligent goodness point out.

Rational religion does not leave us to mere contingency, but to uniform and certain protection of God, the author over all existence, who best saw and gave what was needed; and she peacefully and in sublime silence does this, after all the systems of peculiar faith have been promulgated, that still leave mankind suffering from cardinal causes of injury.

She stands pre-eminently modest in her majesty, over all systems of faith, triumphantly looking to the pure sources of mind, adorable by reason, on which she waits to insure safety with God.

Well might she exclaim, O man, thou art an incongruity, conforming thy views too often to thy devoted interests!

Tragical, ever, must be thy systems, where principles consistent with such virtues as mentioned, do not abound.

Beset thou the fetters of ignorance, superstition ever assuming the mantle of religion, and passions, vile passions that enslave; instead of promoting the destructive fascinations, exalt all the legitimate powers that bless and uphold thee.

Rational religion will cause thee to exert thy potency, annihilate the dire tendency of passions that destroy thee, and the best interest of the world, by due and legitimate restraint.

She will teach thee to learn to govern them and thyself with all practical wisdom, that declares beforehand her laudable position.

Rational religion introduces mind to a consistent and immutable God, not an incongruous deity, a partial inquisitor, or a peculiar avenger to any particular nation on their enemies, who are the rest of the world, the whole human race, begetting the faith of a butchering fanaticism, but a suitable director of mind's energies in the best sphere of understanding, reason, and peace, justice, knowledge, and wisdom, to the grand organic principles of our existence and happiness.

Religion, to be becoming to the loftiest civilization, pure and satisfactory, a competent and universal teacher to all, must permanently bless them, as far as the capacity of our nature and mind will allow, with exceeding wisdom, deep and lucid knowledge, practical and available, with justice in her acts, mercy in her love, and humility in her deportment before the God of existence.

Religion is universal in her attributes, teaching the principles of the universe and the creation of God.

She does not minister to measures of men, and substitute any being's opinions, absurdly expressed in bibles of tradition, exploded, when written most absurdly for God's principles, as all spurious and counterfeit faiths invariably do, but she renders unto God his exclusive rights, and obeys implicitly him as the only sovereign.

Rational religion is strictly monotheism, its right term, and rests on the right truths of mind, presenting the religion of principles in regard to God and man, and can present no other, in her wisest guardianship of her charge, man—composed of mind and body—through all the vicissitudes of life ; the best evidence that principles command and direct her difficulties.

The tribunal is ever constant, as principle is ever needed to the faculty of a religious conscience.

The highest emanation of mind is rational religion, seen in man's varied best actions, and is restricted to no forms, but diffuses itself over all the brighter points of character, correcting and amending it, with faithful and wise watchfulness.

Religion has no system but what is rational, as all things of appreciation can only be recognised on this earth, but through rational mind that must be faithful in duty.

The more rational the practice of religion is, the more correct it certainly must be, else faith would run wild into superstition.

Banished for ever must be that senseless and stupid doctrine, that reference for authority must be made to any book of tradition, and no where else, as the primary originator of thoughts, independent of mind the only beneficiary.

The mind that asserts such rubbish, is senseless, stupid, and corrupt in analysis, its mighty shield, and is unworthy of its own glorious attributes, is guilty of treachery to its inherent rights, just reversing all reason and justice, twin sisters in religion.

The rational religionist can triumphantly refer the professors of deluded faith all over the globe, to the general conflict of all such doctrines, and in answer, all such, without exception, will have to resort to devices and sophistries, ever to be discarded, and absolutely refused, as incompetent to explain this inextricable solution.

All such professors have ignominously to assail the first principles of the great first cause, to uphold the pretences of faith, short of reason, forgetful of fundamental principles, that absolutely preserve the universe in equilibrium, mind in balance, truth in justice, and all. just relations in harmony and order, exposing necessarily the reverse degrading and demoralizing.   .

But rational religion invokes the best and wisest reason of enlightened minds, with implied honesty, truth and judgment, to reach the pure solution, the simple facts for man's best good, ever discarding all sophistry, and excluding its likeness even.

All mankind cannot fail to see then on the appeal of calm reason, that the best and only consistent faith, rests on a Universal Creator, who harmonizes all in order and union—that the Creator depends on no mortal representative, or created being, a desecration of the noblest virtue of Deity, that must must arouse an impiety and ruinous evils in its train, and bring shame to modesty.

The sublime qualities of true religion, require us to be certain then, and reject all trifles, and mind must refer for ever with earnest affection to monotheism, as the saving faith.

Rational religion existed from the creation throughout time, declares God's fore knowledge in omniscience, and his perfection in his omnipotence and omnipresence, and expresses through monotheism, the exposition of whose rational principles have been already moderately under consideration, as establishing the only sound faith, the only one possible, practicable, practical, working as the purest, most elevated, and suited to immortal souls.

If no more, its practical and valuable benefits, excluding the darkest evils of society, and the foulest blots on its foibles and crimes, establish its universal claim to reverent respect, the highest obligation for its recognition and the essential security for its adoption.   She can look upon all others as usurpers, and monopolists, counterfeit and spurious.

Under her auspices, reverence for Deity finds a proper resting place, as she can never tolerate the grossest impiety that assails his attributes, and characterizes God too gross and sensual for refined humanity, much less for an immaculate, almighty, all-wise, and all-in-all.

Under her holy influence, mind exalts its majesty, reason its dignity, soul its worth, and mankind vindicate their character and obtain their position.

Under her guidance, woman attains her loveliness, preserves her chastity, and honors her station.

Rational religion can know no individual being greater than mind, unless it be its author ; knows no koran, vedas, books of Menu, nor bibles of miracles, prophecies or mysteries ; of course is under superior obligations to God, to reject all messinhs, Christs, and all the machinery of superstition, as anti-God.

Proper, rational, and free religion, causes mankind to yield reverence, just and due, to God alone.

It is the homage of mind, the adoration of soul, the tribute of the universe to its Supreme Ruler.

All other than such religion is idolatry, impiety, superstition, imposition, untrue faith and pretence, man-worship.

Try all this proposition by mind, in its best condition from reason, and the response is affirmative all the time.

What is rational religion but all practical correct deportment to God and man, the proper objects ?

If that religion gives not the true essentials in name and attributes, most respectful, the full question is at once decided against its purity and supremacy.

The Supreme alone, commands supreme control of mind in time, and soul in eternity, for his supreme excellence in creation, organization and conservation.

Whoso detracts from God's exclusive attributes, the same detracts from himself, and is self-impeached before the highest of all tribunals.

Reason, enlightened reason, for ever employed by mind, most rational, to secure the proper decisions for mind, declares the code of rational religion, that is for ever the true one, and can be spiritualized to the greatest practicable extent by all the genuine and legitimate bursts of enthusiasm, that the fullest confidence in true titles, from the only liege lord, can inspire towards the eternal centre of this moral universe, upheld by truth and philosophy, encircling the altar of the soul in the immediate and constant presence of its immortal author.

An ennobling justice yields most candidly, that this light enters the soul of all in degree, to their final benefit proportionately, if properly fostered.

The principles of religion interest all, as true and undoubted.

The first do interest every mind to 'their full possession, as·its innate constituency can never be satisfied with less, and must exclude the balance.

It cannot be otherwise, from the true history of mind's organization.

All the acts then of a mind, enlightened on these principles of its duty, must be consistent with this position, for none without due investigation, can settle this or any other important question otherwise.

Practical monotheism is essential to rational vitality.

All rational beings are practical monotheists, if they ever think rightly, while, but few that advocate other doctrines, are truly and consistently sincere, beyond the purviews of circumscribed limits, that are always too restrictive to " do the greatest good to the greatest number."

It is impossible for this doctrine to clash with God's, as it is one and the same.

God cannot be against himself, and no sound mind that reviews the organization of the universe in its admirable relations, can advocate atheism, that implies no great first cause, a matter that is evidently self-contradictory and suicidal ; much less, can any one consistently take up polytheism, or plurality of gods, the advocacy of a partial first cause. A first great cause, of whom still exists, and renders all the other god-heads subordinate and secondary to even his conservative principles, and the doctrine odious, contemptible and futile, no matter what may be the combination, what the pretensions, whether there be trinities, hundreds, thousands, or millions in one, the absurdity is all the greater, the mythology nothing less unsatisfactory and childish. Ages that could invent the superstition of polytheism, were also as culpable in the stupidity of atheism ; both are the descendants of barbarous ignorance, maintained by vulgar bigotry.

Deism cannot be cold-minded merely to speculate and criticise, and not correct, and supersede by a better faith and practice, as such bald doctrine advances but little in leaving the minds of the world uncared for and unprotected. The human mind, without due exertion, makes but little advance on its destined course.

All minds are interested in the highest cultivation of their rational and just faith, and a secure and satisfactory protection, that will accompany all from birth to death, giving all the best instruction for life, all the best consolation at death, all the most elevated hope for the future.

The system of religion that the world wants must be all that mind and reason are justly entitled to ; is that on which all classes and conditions of life can lean in all its parts, with no peculiarity and partiality in time or place as to faith, that only wakes up thousands of years after creation has been blessed by its all-wise and almighty Creator, who has been, and will be by necessity and right, the protector of all the universe, in all time and eternity. All peculiar faiths, then, are idle and absurd dreams, the most visionary.

All such stupid doctrines of God's want of fore-knowledge ever show man's miserable pretensions, impositions and defects. They will be duly silenced.

Let man's libel of God shame man into silence.

No matter what the names of religious systems are, unless their innate principles are universally in mind at creation, commencing with and centring in the Creator, the

13

protection is mockery, the means illusory, and declare the vain aspirations of mortality. Monotheism, rational religion, that satisfies all minds of the existence and universal worth of God Almighty, of the existence of his potency by principles, and of the necessity of their right inculcation in mind, to raise man to his God, and equalize him with himself, his legitimate position no more nor less, to cause him to do and know the extent of his rightful duty, all having a foundation not to be shaken, is the only mighty power that can unite mind in the whole world to one great unity of purpose and amity of feeling—the universal sympathy of soul—in the universal dispensation of mind's Creator.

Ever faithful is this doctrine to her high commands, to the position of being always right, and amenable to the only rightful tribunal known face to face with mind, in the audience of reason.

All other doctrines than that of monotheism that teaches the existence and attributes of God Almighty, a God possessed of all his exclusive attributes, eternally clash with each other, and the whole present in their fall to earth the fragments of a broken brotherhood.

One system of this kind is arrayed against that of others, all having unreal pretensions, except in the minds of those thinking themselves interested, and all having mortals for heads, or in lieu of principles.

Much of the time of its existence the world has been trifled with by self-delusion or corruption, ignorance and crime, sordid and selfish lucre, or unmanly fear, while polytheism, the monster of fiction in man's mystified forms, arises, and spreads her unhallowed hands over the fairest possessions of the globe—exhausting every device of fraud, every fiction of sophistry, tyrannizing over mind, and claiming for the benefits of her clergy and priesthood a large portion of man's property, rights and dominion, implicit and blind faith, a permanent fund for mind's oppression, interweaving herself in all the fastnesses of power of government, all the rabidly excited passions, especially of ambition and avarice, and all the mighty influences of mind perverted from its own mastery to inglorious and ignoble servitude, the degrading servitude of pretenders corrupted and debased, the wilful contriver of its own chains, and seducer of the happiness of others, recklessly ignorant of the mighty advantages that it betrays.

Defeated and prostrated in her vain attempts at full imposition over mind, into which floods of light are constantly pouring by the progressive improvement of the world, the forms of theocracy are changed, and a moderate but unique plurality of gods is left, giving mind of the world still in the peculiar power of the priesthood, rendering mind more or less vassal to an odious servitude, and separating it from its own just claims, its direct claims on God, the exclusive owner.

Corruption floods the world with her horrid train under all the disguises, but the eyes of mind are not opened, till deeds the worst are perpetrated, as wars for centuries have followed their conflicting faiths, with all the furious passions of maddened ambition and insatiate avarice, exciting the sword of the Crusader and scimetar of him of the Crescent, to master continents and thereby secure the conquering faith, ending in deadly hatred after the lapse of many hundreds of years. So far from conquering, some have divided and subdivided into ominous fragments; the Greek church separates from the Roman, affecting catholic power of the world, still yielding those remains of power to the protestant, a successful rival. The dissenter separates from the state-church man, all against each other. The loss of millions of lives tells a fearful tale for the doctrine of peculiar faith. Peculiar faith begets clans over the face of the earth, makes the church members side with their clique in profession, and opens the widest door to corrupt fanaticism, alienating the best feelings of the human bosom, a part of the human family from the balance.

Churchocracy constitutes a corrupt combination, that, if universal as to its sects, would erect a standard of peculiar faith, and proscribe much of the world not of them.

What a fine thing that churchocracy is not universal as to the various sects, as a serious retaliation might ensue on the part of some of the world.

Each sect now erects its own inquisition, assumes to be infallible and orthodox, condemns the balance to perdition—proscribes where it cannot prescribe. All are infallible, no matter how pagan and superstitious any system, with a sacred mystery for the talisman, and with no tribunal of reason and no correction of justice to make any right, whilst the proper faith could have saved mind from such fiendish deeds.

You cannot touch these bigots, for that moment they throw before their professions an enormous shield, on which is inscribed peculiar faith, their castle.

Gracious God! are these to be the lights of the world, who have struck out the most brilliant of all lights from mind, that of reason?

The world needs not opinion unenlightened to create a reign of universal terror and despotism, but that foundation-principle that creates and organizes conservation to society, and all honor to God, the supreme.

But then the priesthoods of the various systems could never be interested in yielding to the people, to mind, their rights, nor become of the people.

It is the nature of assumed power to increase the assumption, never to acquiesce in the rights of others, till the sword cuts the gordian knot.

When rational religion is displaced, superstition and tyranny act. Religion, the elements of which, are implanted by God in rational mind, must be made most rational. Monotheism then, from wise observation and satisfaction in a universe of God's power and rights, beautifully commands us to give unto God, all that are his! This is the wisest command imperative to mind, and is most just.

Strict obedience is the best source of happiness on earth and in life, and gives the best earnest for the future.

Here then the mother can well compose her feelings, inward fears and horrors at the dread of a wild waste, when she asks for herself, her husband, and her beloved children, all their fullest protection, she finds that protection of her whole household from the source of all mercy and perfection in the true course of nature taught.

But where had been all, had not that very protection been accorded the universe by its perfect Creator, before the conception of their bodies?

O, man, think of thy weakness! do not increase it by thy presumption. Aid a just cause in expelling all the base libels of thy all-wise Almighty God.

The mother, the tenderest of all rational beings, has her best and purest power aided by God alone, to whom she can address her devotions, and direct those of her household, all united in adoration to him, with the most comprehensive duty to mind. But she will not expect, if wise, to change an immaculate God.

She must change herself to pure feelings and thoughts, and purer actions, her most impressive prayers that change and elevate human nature to God that rules it. Her reason and feelings are then addressed to the only Supreme, and more than that, are satisfied. All rational beings are thus satisfied, as more could not be done.

Monotheism, then, never aspires to the vaunting inconsistency that ends in atheism, that leaves the world to itself, and mind to its delusion, destitute alike of those ennobling principles that govern all creation, if left to the right perception of things; much less does she descend to polytheism or plurality of gods, whether of millions or of three in number, under any name, pretence or disguise of numbers above unity, with priestcraft-up confused, conflictive and antagonistical, seeking the life's blood of the deluded people who are treated as the veriest dupes unworthy the gifts of God, or any system that contradicts itself before it can explain with consistency and truth, one attribute of the Almighty, thereby depriving God of his divinity, to clothe impostors with it, that they may triumph over the multitude as in all past time!

The triumph of doctrine in unison to Monotheism, will not be for a mortal or earthly consideration, but for God Almighty and the worth of immortal souls, worth all worlds and their gorgeous treasures, secured by no power of martial armor, no insidious theologian pretences to popularize absurdities, and uphold crime and iniquity, but the unappreciable noblest panoply of eternal principles.

Rational religion cannot clash with the people's rights, nor mind's purity, reason or right; and so far from conflict with sound government of the people for whom all good and wise governments are primarily instituted to secure the invaluable good of the largest number, that it upholds all that is just and true.

Then religion will not, cannot, be for the temporal good of the few, but the eternal benefit of all that have mind, and avail themselves of reason.

Religion, holy and pure, modest and retiring in her dignity, asks innumerable times to be heard by her messenger, reason, that is, to be appreciated merely.

She was fulfilling in the dark ages of mind, her duty for the soul-ennobling science of promoting the good of all, by universal freedom in God's devotion, by the best light of truth before mind and reason.

Intellectual freemen are then bound to dash down as mental poison, the idolatry of man-worship in any of the sophisticated forms of polytheism, that embraces mind of all by her thousand wiles and evils, and binds so cunningly, that the coils are unseen and unfelt, till the delusion is effectual, and the injury unavoidable, inevitable and fatal.

Monotheism as the interpretation of enlightened reason, teaches the world must pay due and appropriate respect to the sincere motives of all those believing their peculiar faith to be the true religion.

Rational religion regards the sincerity of piety of all who seek to find their soul's salvation, but cannot ask to supersede any faith without full and convincing reason, requiring as she does all the time for mortals, the right faith, and its best, because its only safe pilotage. She concedes all the wisest systems of laws, that fill up man's duty to man, and his exact duty to his God, all codes that mind requires in equity and justice to himself and God, and all that wise statesmen and worthy humanists will positively institute, all that mankind require in the universal relations of the whole world, faithfully executed.

What all such are, let time, the best prophet, teach ; and man's conscience enlightened most ably in the treasures of mature and ripe experience, decide.

A man of true principles, no matter his faith, will not act without due respect to them, possessed as he may be with any brief authority, because in his mind has been instilled the power of true light.   Principles presuppose rational faith.

His deportment in a few brief minute particulars, defines his character, that "honesty is the best policy," carrying out his belief in action and duty, to an elevated state of refinement that characterizes the true gentleman and best religionist.

His language is a representative of his thoughts, his action of both, and all accord with the best performance of duty to man and God.

True faith looks not at forms and professions, but at the soul's actions in substance and spirit, not for one, but all time, to no final, but ever present day of judgment, making no respect to persons, only as self-respect and principles eternally win.

Confidence is given not for past conduct exclusively, which is simple and demoralizing, but embraces the whole subject and scope of man's life, written at his death and without concealment, favor or reward.

God's innate principles of religion are implanted in all rational minds at initiative existence, and are capable of being elicited at consciousness, and more or less practiced as directed by light of mind, influenced by tuition, and various circumstances constituting a code for action.

Of this fund, all systems of peculiar faith extract a part and parcel, as more or less graduated in its excellence, not originating any of it, but explaining their peculiar views more or less successfully as approaching or assimilating rational religion, trading on its, God's capital.   Then all systems of faith, no matter how superstitious, how foul and depraved, are cloaked under the disguises of the true belief that incontestibly belongs to the one being, who as God of the universe, must have unity.   The safety of all creation, is indebted to the conservative innate principles of God alone.

This position of innate conservative principles remains with the world of mind, and can only be masked by man's artifices, by deceived or corrupt minds.

Let no sophistry answer for them, as this is a holy subject, and requires the holy answers of a world's actions and deeds untrammeled and unbiased.   Professions cannot supersede the actions of life.

As no faith can solve this whole question but that of reason, truth requires her support in due humility and candor.

All systems of faith otherwise built up are partial, defective, vitiated, and most hurtful to mind, that it sophisticates.

All such cannot stand the test of reason's solution, and will be effaced by the great luminary of mind.

The wise should aim, in the great vital drama, at the immortal luminary.

The most conscientious faith, and sincerest appeal to reason and reason's God, are made through mind, his means of avenue, and only inspiration, that proves the true rational faith.   Monotheism requires no official organ but God's noblest gift, purity of mind, to see, feel, and adopt the legitimate universal treasure.

Profession of all is with God ; the reward is in immortality ; the speculation and trade on both are not of this world.

This earth presents nothing to give in lucre for mind's worth, but presents a field ample for all labor, not for self alone but for all a glorious theatre of manly action.

It is a sacred republic, endorsed by conscience, where no church dignitaries are needed to perpetuate what the Eternal has written on mind, that succeeds wave after wave in the ocean of life.

Monotheism is gentleness itself, having no blood and guilt-stained conscience, no blurred by misdeeds, distorted by vague pretences, nor cloaking anything under other names, and availing itself of other people.   She is what she seems, and has no reason to be anything else.

She fawns on no absolutism that she excludes, deceives no man, and avoids all that looks like deceit, untruth, and dishonesty.

She claims what is right, perpetrates no continued wrong.

She matures her judgment by facts, and adheres to moral firmness with modest confidence

She institutes protection by enlightened public opinion, that no man can escape
Hers is the bible of rational mind.

Absolutism on the throne, with the mitre, by brute force, insidious cunning, with sophistry and degraded licentiousness, may affect to disregard it, but the retribution will follow.

As high as absolutism may pretend to be above it, wrong assuredly as it is, it can be effectually checked by mind.

Mind is the master of absolutism, when it is the subject of principles, a fealty to the Almighty.

The summary punishment by conservative revolution from the people, who are forced to take this part of the common law into their own hands, often proves a retribution.

The bands of counterfeiters, forgers, pirates, and robbers who may escape prison or judiciary punishment, by collusions of confederates prepared for rescue, even to perjury, or by the weakness and corruption of officials, do arouse up this summary punishment of the people, especially in new countries and states. But the majesty of principles should command the efficient majesty of law.

Individuals, as adulterers, violators of social principles in various ways, often feel this in a speedy manner.

Nor does the curious law of retribution stop short of vindicating the principles of their Immortal Creator worthy of him, enough to cause every libeler of Deity to sink into immediate insignificance. Conservative principles require a uniform recognition by the wisest laws, and their execution in the world.

There can be no religion save rational, and no faith but what is its universal agent.

The God of monotheism is the God of the universe, whose endowments to mind of reason and principle universally give wisdom.

Citizens of both sexes, is it not your highest advantage to have full monotheism of mind over the polytheism of dreamers, visionary devotees of absolutism?

Has not polytheism ruled the world to its ruin, with her superstition and her fanaticism, bloody and tyrannical, long enough?

The world must analyze the proper elements of language, and must be held responsible to this point, as capable of complete decision, as in innumerable others.

No other construction can be admitted by reason or right.

It is utterly absurd to deny this. Then all such peculiar faiths are wound up, as entirely unworthy of resurrection.

Ask ingenuous youth, too pure to have their motives assailed, what do they think of religion?

They may not be aware that the question is paramount, and involves a paramount essential of their vitality, and of a Deity that implies allegiance to the right source.

If wise, they will forever seek that which is pure.

It is an allegiance to God, Supreme Creator, who endowed them with the elements essential at creation.

It cannot be to gods of creation, for all others have to acknowledge one Creator, thanks to monotheism, that rules out all other faiths, no matter how loud or boisterous, for they all are counterfeit as their base superstition.

How, then, is God to be found? As he is omnipresent, all are inquirers, through their own minds the analysts.

Where is this pure religion that gives certain faith and action to insure certain protection? How will they find the right way? Mind answers all these, all necessary questions.

Mind knows that it has to improve its own elements to the best calibre, capacity, and comprehension, to finish the whole solution, the problem of life.

What need has mind of priests? What is a priest? An impostor, if not an imbecile; both ought to be silenced of course. Will man take such men's word for it? That is unwise.

It is not the wisdom pertaining to mind, but the world, as the world has many faiths, diversified by contingency. But the inquirer is after truth, not contingency, consequently he cannot trust to any priest, who relies on human contingencies all the world's age, who is bound, as priest, to lie all the time for his faith, that lies all the time for him.

Men's words may lead to a plurality of gods, more or less to several millions. Is that safe or wise?

The wise man will forever, in all things, especially sacred things, take only reason; if he do not, he will forever desecrate sacred functions of mind, and then he is liable to become an advocate for atheism, polytheism, or plurality of gods, including man-worship and a host of idolatry, with attendant evils, diffused through the world.

Reason only admits monotheism, the God of which is worthy his universe; try him by all the rules, laws, and principles of mind, the only means and power with us, by us, and for us.

Give the world God Supreme, who teaches the best happiness, and the best means t
secure it, with the avoidance of most supposed evils.

Then we must point it to the code of mind, to God in his purity and exclusive majest
who cannot be represented by messiahs, priests, prophets, nor their clan, who are to
low to represent mind, much less the God Creator of the universe.

Man has to perform the complete fulness of his duty to his fellow man, in though
word, and deed, that it may be best with him in his dying hour, that he may sustain n
conscience-pangs, no consuming remorse for wrongs and injuries done in private, o
with recklessness, next to irreparable then.

He has no code to depend upon, that licences any to spend a life of beastly larcen
vice, and criminal licentiousness, and at the last moment to embrace a full treasure dr
pite of his reckless crimes, by the compliant pretences of money and power-sycophant

To embrace all the dispensations of virtue, he must carry out the supreme regard t
the majesty of virtue.

If he have luxuriated in all the beastliness of degraded nature, deceived by the fals
doctrines of false bibles, to commute at death, he must abide his own decisions, and su
fer for the penalty to principles, that certainly vindicate themselves in their whol
legitimate circle. Let no false faith incite to such life. While there is time to do goo
let none be in despair. What is worth the travail at the last moment? The constitu
tion of man may not consign him to hopeless misery, while his best actions will b
suitably rewarded, his worst must be suitably punished.

A true religion is only supported by true constitutional rule, that gives restoratio
and security to principles, reason, and their proper attributes, that bravely place abso
lutism, personal and social, in abeyance.

What other than true rational faith can avail ?   Good and faithful citizens of the worl
cannot now recede, for they can never get any other; all else is fiction. But while all creed
of peculiar faith are decaying under the crush and crash of their own destructive element
rational religion invokes the full practice of duty and humanity, and while she abjures a
wicked superstition, however refined by all the tricks of sophistry, adherence to worship of
dead mortals, she requires a rightful action for conservative principles, their immediate
and only representative, mind and their Creator, that all living men have to respect.
Our belief must be perfectly sincere, resting on sincere incontrovertible foundations, o
else there will be an eternal conflict discoverable to the world, as is plainly discovera
ble to be the case in every creed, sect, and denomination of peculiar faith, when refer
red to deeds.

The belief will never be one moment's value, if our deeds to the whole circle of our
duties do not consistently conform thereto, practicable for human nature under proper
honorable constructions. What value is our faith to us, if not available on a rational
basis, the only right one ?

Of what value is any, short of the unity of God ?

It destroys the more it is announced as peculiar.

Its existence then piles up the elements of the believer's destruction.

But pretences are set up, that the people cannot carry out the very things their duty
enjoins. What absurdity !

God gave mind its superior endowments to carry out this very purpose, all life's.
purposes.

Man thus libels the people for his low purposes, and above all, the Creator. This is
the case with the world's curse, of monopoly and usurpation.

It is always the case, when power of the few is interfered with. The difficulty in
worldly polity is not so much the elevation of the people to proper representation, as to
counteract the evil designs of men, whose talents are great, but whose minds have been
perverted, and their collusion thousands of years in various editions of the same miserable code. Mind has to keep the world from taking advantage of it.

In mock dignity it may be asked, what are to be the flame and torch, to sustain the
light of the religious world in a rational manner ? The dignity of rational mind enables
rational religion to sustain herself on her dignity, independent of the speculation and
trade in God's world.

She sustains herself in all the pure minds of good and true citizens, at home and
abroad, in and out of the pulpit, or any altar.

The inherent virtues of the Eternal Ruler of the universe, have furnished the right
means.

The universe has ever had those means from its foundation, independent of vain man
. and all his adverse schemes, else chaos and confusion, instead of order, had been its
portion, despite of all peculiar faiths. Conservation is as sublime as Creation, when
the last premises supreme unity, and the first, that it has no division.

Peculiar, as false faith, absolutely differs with rational religion, that cannot differ with herself, as the true representative of unity itself.

Nothing less than the Supreme could have indited this, his own sublime character, so indelibly.

It is impossible for the glory of his eternal consistency to be eclipsed with rational minds.

Let not freemen shrink back from the workers of iniquity, who unite all their efforts for error guided by self-interest; let them know their rights and vindicate them by reason.

The object attained is a glorious victory indeed, never seen yet on earth, for a reconcilement of men's differences on the best, the only ground not visionary, because it is one of principle, and one universal faith and that alone in Deity, Creator of all, and whom the civilized world should justly appreciate in all his glorious attributes.

The object is union of mankind universally, in one grand brotherhood, on the altar of true faith to a God owning all, that religion, which is true allegiance to him alone, calls for, pure and undefiled as his property, thus proving that the perfection of the soul is accomplished by its own perfect solution.

All virtual indebtedness must be intrinsically on merit, and must be due in all respects that reason and justice invoke, and will be paid on their certificates by grateful and honest debtors, with the prompt feelings that reverence can inspire.

Some suppose that the speedy change of character, is vital in religion.

Surely, this can take place better in true than in absurd faith, as then the reason is convinced in faith rational and confirmed, beyond cavil to satisfaction; when both are satisfied they are immovable.

With this foundation, sure and certain, hope and joy rising to all that is legitimate of enthusiasm and spiritualization, as near sanctification as God permits human nature on the earth, with a pure faith, pure in God, may inspire the professor to his mind's greatest content.

But with what satisfaction and honest zeal can we subscribe to faith, not justified by sincerity or reality, or to sectarian or peculiar faith, that is not liberal enough for the spirit of the age, or of our own excellent institutions—a species of superstition that is circumscribed in time and place, occupying in reality, little or nothing in the great drama of life?

In utmost sincerity, we cannot do otherwise than reject all peculiar faith, as long as five senses are retained, and language is limited to their verdict.

Then let all good men aid in enlightening the world, but let none assume anything beyond this, as there the ministry of rational mind ceases, and imposition begins, and then, too, it is impious imposition of the worst character, with which all co-workers are identified.

Those observing the difference between superstition and rational religion, and the serious effects of the first, must not stand by now careless of results.

Rational religion commands only obvious and necessary duties, while the first demands unnatural ones.

Religion is, in nature, the highest supreme duty—is the soul of mind's duty.

The Creator must be reverenced through the fixed conservative principles for his whole creation, and their constant action and influence pervading all intellectual animated existence.

There can be no religion without mind, as there can be no accountability, and no responsibility without its reason, that has to elicit the only true object, the Creator. When will man adopt right views in respect to them, since he is involved in their adoption as a right appreciation for his own proper action, words, and thoughts? Without this position clearly evinced and proved before the universe, all the constituents of life's agency would be utterly contingent for ever.

Now is the hour for the world to rescue itself from its culpability, for citizens to rouse up and proclaim their rights and their best of blessings.

If wisdom give a right direction, the balance will be right.

All that monotheism, rational religion, can ask, is to have this momentous subject put before the world, free from any of the malign influences of absolutism of kings or priests, and nothing more nor less.

If rational religion had its true position on earth, the superfluities would meet the necessary demands, and the beggars of the world might be duly supported in comfort, and their minds too, cultivated, vice more effectually excluded by the true light of knowledge and science, if social and religious matters were put right.

Discussions about peculiar faiths would cease on their certain extinction, the pure beams of a pure faith would irradiate a noon-tide day, and disunions of countries making nations otherwise brothers, cut-throats, would cease, and the blessings of universal union would disseminate universal strength.

But the bigot and fanatic, giving the same kind of execrable inquisition that the worst vassal times of dark ages ever saw, equal to the stake-burnings, command all simpletons fearful to call their minds reason's, their souls God's, bid them not discuss rationally the subject of religion, or read what enlightens them. Then the world belongs to these wiseacres, and it might as well be theirs in the next, unless their responsibility will give them enough to do in accountability.

Then mind is of no account and contrary to reason but for the folly and crimes it is made to commit, a position that libels God as making! O mass of absurdities and contradictions.

All things in the universe are for free rational discussion, that mind might rightfully embrace them.

The sooner truth is embraced the better. The sooner falsehood is exposed and rejected, the better for all mankind.

None but absolutism denies this by her base actions, for her argument is in fragments, and is nowhere whole.

Absolutism of any species, for they all are in collusion, kingly or priestly, may cant about faith, which is only credulity, if taken out of the reason of mind, but absolutism is a hypocrite, and when she rejects any work for free rational discussion by her fears or will, she shows her utter disgrace.

Away then with absolutism in all its forms, from the despot, with all his sycophants who trammel mind, down to all priestocracy with its myrmidons who sophisticate it, and cannot do it justice in investigation.

The weak systems of exploded ignorance and prejudice must yield to the superior lights of the day, by which the world was to be enlightened and will improve.

Take away all false lights and their teachers, and let the best inculcations of true lights illuminate the dawn of life, then its meridian will be fruitful, and its evening a blessing in the land of adoption.

Let a liberal and diffused patriotism prevail, to cover the whole lands and oceans of the globe.

Let a worthy spirit of humanity be permanent.

Sacrifice all minor things forever, before fundamental freedom and its securities are sacrificed to degrade mind and rational religion.

If there be any failure, assuredly it is not in God's principles that cannot clash, but in the wiles of absolutism that pretend to the divine rights of church and governmental despotism.

Rational religion does not permit, with impunity, the ends of justice to be ignominiously defeated by sophistry or perjury. She has the potency to correct miserable and abominable states of society, where false pretences and hypocrisy exist and social tyranny predominates.

She permits no loose views, but holds up all the world at once to the supreme obligation of rule on principles. She draws no imaginary line defined by men, but holds universally mind subject to universal principles, that all rational being must know and be responsible for.

In her presidency she overlooks no persons high in power or rule, but in all the grades of society, and in all its circles, private or public, whether in the supreme temple of God, the universal brotherhood of principles, or in the little churches of man, all that cannot begin to be trusted, unworthy of trust or going wrong all the time, not doing justice to truth, chastity or moral virtues, whether emperors or kings, popes, bishops or laymen, governors or governed, are to be reminded that they are unworthy members of society, and cannot be worthy of future felicity. She inculcates the only mastery of mind, the supremacy of God, the mighty Unity, all obligations, social and religious.

Hers is the intellectual tuition that those miserably raised in the world in the school of its vices, its follies or its crimes, whose history is evil, the penalty for violation of the good, must mend in her presence and under guidance the error of their ways as the best practical faith.

Religion is ever rational and consistent, and always appeals through mind to mind by reason up to reason's God, without worldly speculation in church, state or any regime. She delights in the blessings that reason ever gives.

She knows no divisions of men, and does not know herself, unless mind can be satisfied by the recognition.

She makes no division in The Holy Centre, for she ever looks to unity in God and men, and can recognise no other state.

Her earth is superior in universal brotherhood to the heaven of peculiar faith, whose sectarianism has, by fiction, caused its God to exclude rebellious angels. Peculiar faith loses caste on earth, and forgets the truth in her heaven.

Religion teaches truly that when the unity of the God of the universe is transcended, principle is violated.

Hence it is that peculiar faith in heaven or on earth begets peculiar trouble to its peculiar people.

Did monotheism admit of any peculiarities, then her extinction would be certain, as her intention would be mortal, and she would be unworthy of herself as the representative of an Immutable Omniscient Being, pledging conservative and eternal principles.

The religion that God of the universe established is the only appropriate one to be used; all others are peculiar faiths, hurtful, and in the way of the true. Mortals must recognise all such.

The perfect Creator, wise at creation, gave her a creation-birthright, inherent faculties, without which no rational being could exist.

The universe will meet God's requisitions. Can all this be properly accomplished, without the immortality of the soul?

Vain and ambitious mortals should not seek to prevent it their brief moment and their expiring hour, for retribution will expose their corruption and unveil their disgrace.

All should be wise to honesty, and honest unto just reverence of the Supreme.

This code is written in mind, and mind's understanding can honestly comprehend duty, needing no pretender to help it do for itself what mind can alone do.

No real due value of rationality can be mistaken for mere enthusiasm and its visionary spiritualization, affecting the fruition of better spheres, that must be superseded for time-serving worship of the moment.

Exalted thoughts and aspirations for the immortal creation and eternity's benefits, can only be manifested by proper adoration; nothing else is genuine.

Any faith short of monotheism is necessarily sectarian, and is fundamentally wrong. If it be divided into minute divisions of hundreds, so much the worse.

The more division the more proof of errors and erroneous elements, and evincing the finite being of man's work of most moderate efforts, if he forsake principles for peculiarities, mind and reason for priestocracy and their particular faith. Religion does not need priest but rational mind for practical illustration.

The only way of correction is in one God, supreme, immortal, omnipotent, and unmistakable in his attributes, that characterize him as ministers in the universe and its universal relations. The sublimity of his character is portrayed in the sublimity of the character of rational religion, in the utter impossibility of reducing the unity of either, for when the vain attempt is made by impotent mind, the position is untenable, suicidal and fatal.

How much, then, is rational mind indebted to monotheism, and the means to obtain it, sustaining its dignity and securing its happiness.

Without this friend of mind accorded by God, there is a purgatory of conscience built up on earth by false systems, calculated to immolate victims worse than in their blood, when ceaselessly tormented by imaginary evils, the chimeras of impostors.

What a real blessing to get rid of all these curses.

The constant accountability and responsibility that wise and good men invariably acknowledge to God, imply a proper service, and the protective defence against the torturing state of such conscience.

When we get rid of superstition, and sophistry its inseparable companion, then we may obtain monotheism, the sublime religion of God.

It is she that will urge the wisest comprehension of each individual penalty consequent on the violation of God's laws, not to destroy but save universally, and institute the most elevating system of rewards that will necessarily produce an illustrious code of ethics to protect mind in general.

She invokes all laws consistent to the permanency of good legislation, to rise to the dignified and beneficial character of the world's benefactress.

What better views can enlightened mind have?

Whither else can it go but to the wise practical functions of reason?

With all the wildest enthusiasm of our nature, the feelings and emotions of soul, still religion is a certain, definite, paramount duty towards God.

Man may feel aroused to the highest expression of emotions, under consideration of his having religion, a possession in common with rational minds, but all improvement thereon must be submitted to the calm and serious tribunal of philosophy and practical life, the test of mind-embodiment for soul-organization.

when peculiar faith cannot qualify one want of one world. Mere words of the pulpit are things of no consequence.

The essence has been diffused in every rational mind, as sunbeams, being the true communication of Deity, and the active self-agency of mind.

That a subject and requiring only truth, simple and unadorned, banishing forever as unnecessary and degrading, that sophistry that is used necessarily in all other creeds of faith, because that faith, whatever else it is, rests on sophistry all the time, and that can end in nothing else but superstition.

And else can a sectarian faith beget, but a stupid or dishonest result!

Where reason cannot dwell, as peculiarity occupies her place, where peace is always variable with herself, where all are infallible, but none orthodox, by their own position and assumptions mental!

Better and more minds never heard the preaching of peculiar faith, better have your ears disagreeably shut, than to receive the doctrine that you shall not use the reason that God gave you.

If you are not heed to reason, better will it be in the day that decides on the merits of this vital subject, that you never had it, for then reason's God, by your own un-answering action cannot then own you as a reasonable subject. Your soul will have to be justified by all the necessary preparations of reason.

Are you to be satisfied with less than a reasonable God to decide on your own defects and demerits?

If you have merits, with whom can they be better appreciated than by the most rational God?

Monotheism calls for rational faith, in the only true living God. This religion has all things that reason and truth elicit for mind, neither in omission nor commission.

She assures to represent God universally, offering the world the best that can be found, as God made, recognizing no other.

All others are peculiar, finite in time and space.

And but deceive yourself, much less others; you will not, can never conquer life's diffi-culties under any other banner than that of God.

Monotheism resorts to no Asia with her numerous systems of peculiar faith, and her millions of divinities. She abjures the depravities of perverted minds.

The best sources of all good minds on each continent, have religion in degree, but their highest duty is not paid directly to God as it should be alone, but unfortunately to God's usurpers, not representatives, who can claim only to be his ministers and crea-tures.

But the egotistical enthusiast, ranting and raving in impulse, filled with animal passions for grace, rational, devout, and spiritual, sanctification etherealized too pure for earth, aroused to zeal too impatient to admit the common avenue to glory by death, needs all these institutions, denied him, he may pretend to think, by the pure light of Monotheism.

But pure rational religion meets all this false position, and grants the petitioner all that his mind of personal titles calls for, honors all genuine drafts in full measures, to the greatest joy and satisfaction of recipients at the trying hour when all such are needed.

All claimants get all that they are fully entitled to. They get all besides, that they never thought of.

They reach the sublime triumph of reason and philosophy, to guide their honest and judicious zeal.

They are ever commanded to mind to counsel them in all thoughts, to counteract all else but the best and purest inspirations, and to reject all else as the teachings of the weakest, the visionary or the monomaniac.

Rational religion furnishes the strength of a wise cabinet and bosom friends, council-lers, reason and truth.

As to the flaming love of the fiery zealots, all will burn the brighter, the stronger the inspirations, the more lasting the fountains, the more permanent the source.

None can transcend the true understanding of the pure analysis of God's attributes. They are mysteries only to those that make them so.

We see in the plain truth of the honest understanding, that comes through mind all the time. It is mind's practical operation.

That must not then pervert the perfection of those attributes, knowing as thou observest that omniscience, which is knowledge of all things, belongs only to an Almighty. Thou must know that Almighty asserts all practical operations or capacity for omnipotence.

Thou must know that omnipresence embraces these two attributes with a perfect union, and excludes by its unity all other combinations, which would destroy the character and principle. All trinities, antagonistic as they must be to these, are false and futile.

And further, thou shouldst know that Providence crowns the perfection of the whole at first, over all the future special acts of mind, and is self-demonstrated Almighty, that bespeaks all perfection.

If thou appreciate all these simple things, impart truly the blessings of thy belief to thy fellow-man.

Thou then wilt not impeach thyself nor dishonor God under false pretences, to reach the worldly treasures of the five grand divisions of the globe, with their appurtenant islands. Thou mayst overrun the world with insidious faith, but then thou hast thyself to save, a work that needs thy constant attention for time, that thou may not be lost in the world's gain for much of eternity.

The Creator is most highly pleased in the truth and sincerity of his creatures, their honesty as one of the great platforms of true principles, and he adopts all such most readily for ever, but frustrated and brought to naught are all those destitute of principles that vindicate themselves above all other primary foundations.

The general providence of God, the vindication of these principles, aids the good will and faith of man, aids him in all good tendencies, so far as not to defeat God's own good purposes of mind's free agency, which bespeaks a freeman's responsibility.

Man has to take hold of things in the right way, at the right time, and with the right spirit.

Unlike all peculiar faith, rational faith has no exception whatever, on true analysis of the whole subject, as its antagonism is the pretence of false faith forever. If there be exception, there is nothing real, as God has created, and all his are certain.

Whether others affect spiritualization and grace to enthusiasm and sanctification, or any other dogma of faith resting on the personal feelings and bigoted education of the individual, doing our whole duty to God, the great soul of the universe, embraces full faith, creed and man's necessary practice.

God exacts no worship, but the pure adoration of mind, having an enlightened conscience.

When man does his duty, his whole duty, and nothing but his duty, then he embraces the mighty subject of his earthly mission, the truth, the whole truth, and nothing but the truth. Created by God, all his duty is absorbed by duty to the Creator, whose unity takes supreme precedence of all trinity.

Monotheism has prevailed universally from creation of mind. All other faiths are peculiar to a season and place, to a peculiar incarnation or idolatry, man, animal or image, then die out in a series of time, all being antagonistic to monotheism, as they are antagonistic to supreme principles.

Monotheism must last for eternity, as it rests on eternal principles, all co-existent and co-equal.

Monotheism rests on truth, and is ever consistent, otherwise the solution has not been rightly appreciated by mind, and its correction is ever readily received with gratefulness.

Faiths not dependent on eternal principles are peculiar, and had their origin in man's peculiar notions and superstitions, are antagonistic to exposure, and uselessly vindictive for the attempt which they repel.

Monotheism invites enlightened rational discussion on her principles or her faith, as she is the true friend to mind in securing all the benefits universal.

· Faiths not dependent on right and justice are suspicious of any intellectual questions, involving the fundamental principles, and pretend most falsely that it is dangerous to investigate too deeply the primary points essential.

Monotheism asks for calm and philosophical investigation to satisfy the conscience of rectitude previously to adoption, to maintain firmly and most consistently the right position under the most intense feelings of our nature.

Improper faiths ask for impulse, and retire behind assumed mysteries, non-existent miracles, false pretences to prophecies, all untenable doctrines.

Religion is not only spiritual, but rational ; she cannot exist otherwise.

How comes religion at all ? By the creation of innate faculties, by which her principles act on mind.

If reason predominate, the result is rational religion, but its substitutes, sophistry and peculiar faith, mislead to superstition, and from the unity of God.

The spiritual and rational are all emanations and inspirations.

The brute, as soon as man, could become religious on other conditions. This principle of religion properly accords with the physical and mental organization.

Take religion that is rational from the world, and the world is not only divested of her loveliness, but is brutalized.   Her banishment presents only the ragged and jagged fragments of worthless peculiar faiths, that misrepresent God.

Superstition repels civilization ; science accompanies to the best of philosophy, that causes mind to steer best to its highest duties.

Free citizens will now take nothing for granted that is not rational, and that pure analysis cannot solve, yielding nothing to blind, selfish infatuation.

Rational religion does not martyrize on the faith of blind devotion and superstitious Juggernautism, but adheres to the light of reason and the impulse of sincerity, its essential creation, bending neither to fancy nor custom irrational.

Had this noble spirit prevailed in times past, had but her voice been heard by the Crusaders, a savage and relentless war of two hundred years, and much blood of millions slaughtered as victims on the altars of peculiar faith, had been spared.

But now too, as much as ever, is the time that her voice should be heard, and the qualities of the eminent artist available, that all should be beloved of God and man.

The institution of the right principles will effect this, what no messiah could reach before, for all such scattered the fiery elements of distrust the world over.

The true faith can be selected by the enlightened Judge, who needs not appearances, but wisely referring to the inherent and exquisite qualities that endow the rightful possessor to be loved of God and man, to the future decision of time, as the proper test for the best religion.

Peculiar faith has appealed to papal dispensations and the sword of military chieftains, from which it had no higher tribunal.

The Mahomedan won Jerusalem and yet retains it, his country still.   The war of conquest was sought by peculiar faith.

Once custom decided the' justice of the world by the sword.   What could monotheists say to this, but in rebuke ?

God was then, as now, the ruler of the universe, this earth included.

The sword has been used by nearly all of peculiar faith, yet that faith has not been decided by the martial tribunal.   All the messiahs that make the peculiar faith, and all its false positions, are perfectly worthless, as they are obnoxious to the world's peace and welfare.

Such faith has appealed to swords, and not to reason.

God of the universe deals not with the sword,. as base priestocracy have misrepresented him, but with reason.   With reason he electrifies, and manages the universe.

Mortals are truly taught by rational religion not to put themselves between Deity and his creation, with any arrogance or imposition.

Was not the ordeal of savage crusades enough to teach the world that all that were of earth are earthly, that all that were born, lived, and died were mortals, and none but self-deluded people can affect more ?

But when had bigotry any ears ? when had peculiar faith any reason ?   What have they ever learned ? what have they ever forgot ?

Those of any age that go beyond the doctrine of rational religion are no better than savage crusaders on man's sacred rights.

The unholiest fanaticism and the worst piracy for the world's conquest were hid under the specious garb of false pretences of peculiar faith.

The hand of the Almighty cannot be mistaken by reason.   Simplicity and beauty are its seal, and eternity its attribute.

In his palm, conscience presides with a moral triumph.

Without illustrious actions before him, prayers are but a mockery.

The martial prowess of the church !   That defines her position, with corruption and iniquity her birth-rights.

When the voice of rational religion is heard in the world, ·martial prowess, that oppresses with cruelty, whose vindictiveness cannot be used with impunity, and calls for avenging, will be excluded, as then peace will define her position; therefore the world will come to a definite view of things.

Rational religion seeks fundamental principles already in existence from creation, for the elements of general good, eductive of harmony in the wildest moral chaos.

Our only true system of rational government has laid the foundation for future expansive good of mankind; and religion that is rational has sealed it.

Why, then, is the world shamefully made to rest on individual and peculiar authority of men and books, when the dignity and universality of principles in religion and government tower above all these ?

All faiths except rational religion must be self-convicted in many respects, before the tribunal of philosophy, that all false and peculiar faiths most terribly hate and fear, for reason of exposure.

If rational religion be not correct, those who introduce her exposition must learn themselves.

She is ever right, because God is right.

If a sincere aspirant seek her best institutions, he goes far to cause a speedy termination of all that is spurious and hostile to human good.

Philosophy must decide what is rational religion, by her comprehensive investigations and universal acts.

Then rational religion has it forever.

Her deeds expand as her faith, both universal, and universally securing the affections of the world, exempt from conflicts and sectarian views, that when presented are discarded as not of her faith.

The very moment rational religion approaches, all the godly virtues attend her, possessed in perfection, otherwise she is not predominant.

It is a counterfeit, sectarian or bigot, that assumes it.

She considers the demoralization of the world, and gives light of mind, at home and abroad, to correct it.

She seeks to be judged by the true issue, and if general peace be not of her banner, then she is libeled.

She introduces true analysis into all subjects, seen as far as the minds of her friends can go, and she seeks true analogy of things, unseen by the light of reason, that is the best light of mind.

She is not peevish, much less vindictive in the rational discussion of all rational subjects for mind to investigate.

With her there prevails no such idea that sin can reach the holy centre, for the creation of the devil involves contradictions to all her creeds, that are used up if mind and reason, the only means to reach them, be properly exercised.

Rational religion rests on the highest morals and intellect, that takes cognizance of all the best appreciation of duty, and the most suitable action.

The duty must be inquired into as it is fixed by God's attributes, and the circumstances of the universe decide its character.

Due inquiry and investigation, must be made at all times, as otherwise mankind cannot decide between superstition and religion. That is provable daily, even in the deaths of all creeds and peculiar faiths.

We see clearly that there can be no conflict of opinion, while faith is fortified by reason, and cultivated intellectual liberty in the belief of God's supreme elevation above all these contingences of imbecility.

We see clearly that the people need a uniform system of social and religious faith, resting on nothing supernatural as against truth.

Religion is most rational, and seizes on the rational part of mind and frees it for Deity.

The policy of nature and of human character, rests on a guarantee for correct codes, to be best filled up by wise and discreet philosophy.

That guarantee, the best of all, liberty for free man, is to have a free and intelligent mind.

All that observe must realize, that religious essence imparts a faith to every human being, as relatively enlightened and elevated in the scale of philosophical principles.

All have to realize this subject in a proper spirit.

All must respect enlightened views about religion. while they deplore erroneous lights, and must acknowledge that the present views may answer for past ages, but will not, do not, and cannot, for the people of liberty, possessed of minds free for liberty.

The people's every feeling will be duly aroused the very moment rational religion is sustained, and will expel monopolists and pretenders.

Reason claims rational religion, founded as disclosed on analysis of mind on its innate capacity, without which God is unknown by mind; but by peculiar tradition, peculiar faiths are promulgated as of Christ, the messiahships, &c.

The first is natural, certain, uniform and truthful; the second is mechanical, fortuitous and factitious, and depends on sophistry always.

The pure attributes of God, creator of all, insure his power exclusively, and the obedience of all, however perverted the mind in recognising it, must be in abeyance to that power or none.

Peculiar faith claims that obedience and its prophecy pretends to proclaim it, but reason shows that a large majority of the world has ever disproved it.

So much for prophecy of any bible.

Rational religion is needed in every mind, and God's omniscience, omnipotence and omnipresence, had provided for all this at mind's creation, a matter not perceived by the stupid pretenders of priestocracy, whilst no other can occupy the same mind at the same time, without trespassing on religion, which act is an abominable injury in the sight of God and man.

How little intrinsic worth in the world can we hold to as substantial, among all its evanescent things, when we are deprived of rational religion.

She is ever true to mind, when it is true to itself.

All enlightened at the fountains of wisdom, cannot be put back in their duty by the affected or pretended mysteries of priestocracy, as they will discard plausible but erroneous theories.

Did rational religion rely on anything else but the purest wisdom, she would fly from the proper discussion of truth, and her own existence.

It is she that asks, is truth ever injured by intelligent and rational discussion?

Mind, as a creature of education, has to refer to this tribunal as a necessary constituent of that education for freemen.

Rational religion implies mind, in its best sense, reason all the time of life's consciousness, and thereby, effectually shuts out all priestocracy's peculiar faith.

Our mental position implies but certain duty, merely the purest intention of doing and acting right.

Monotheism looks to God, to whom the universe looks. She has but one great God, all powerful, almighty.

Rational religion sits calm for rational discussion, that she always invites, wishing to profit herself by rejection of errors, and give important substantial facts to the world. This is the action of her enlightened advocates.

It is her spirit that inquires, where does the tyranny of absolutism ever stop?

It is she that considers the deplorable state of the world as tributary for too much time, to some form or other of superstition, and invokes the notice of that world to this sad state.

She gives the only consolation in God alone.

She ever requires honesty and truth in her essence, else it all goes for nothing, however the professors of any peculiar faith may mouth a ,messiah.

It is she that recognises multitudes of other peculiar faiths, elevated to a high-toned character, despite of all those faiths, living according to an eclectic action, showing mind in its beauty and strength, however their bibles of tradition may invalidate those very principles. By her light, they may be the lights of the world.

She recognises the prosperity of free institutions, resulting from mind and its purity.

She deplores the miserable state of all peculiar faith, as that of the worst errors of the world. When we speak of the Mormon faith, that is due to peculiar faith, that begot Mahometanism, and had for its ancestors, the dogmas that gave rise to the vedas of Asia, we only embrace the beginning of what encircles much of the world.

So much for peculiar faith, the child of superstition.

Rational religion teaches man all this, and the correction.

She informs us that miracles, prophecies, mysteries and enigmas, prove that man, not God, had anything to do with their bibles. All those snares are too small for the God of the universe : they are only the means for the gods of peculiar faith.

One of her main objects of inquiry is, whether the mind is not the only priest and preacher of religion, by the divine rights of the people ?

If so, as really is the case, priests and preachers are impostors and charlatans.

Rational religion requires for herself the same tribunal of justice, that she allows others, and demands correction, not skulks from it, on principles established on their enlightened and liberal position.

She recognises a pure conscience, and upright conduct, emanating from proper principles.

It is necessary that they have a proper foundation for light, in a liberal and just education.

Rational religion looks to no mortal, has no creed that mind does not recognise, and reason approve, and adheres to nothing but rightful duty and substantial principles, that bless mind and honor God alone.

She takes precautions against the evils that affect morals, intellect, and government.

She is modestly silent, when peculiar faith gives her antagonistical constructions to most of Deity's dispensations, oftener libeling them, explaining or solving his mighty deeds of good.

She holds herself in abeyance to correction of all errors of faith, and can never take umbrage thereat, as her good, not her speculation is to be attained, therefore, she rejoices. What is apparent adversity, she wishes to consider universal benefit.

Under her auspices all minds should so act, as to cause all adversity to redound to relative prosperity if practicable. With her the admonition is not to be disregarded that time gives, and she truly conceives that more is oftener saved by prompt rendition of justice, than by any equivocal action that finally involves all in ruin.

The best of civilization is the best of rational religion, that constitutes the best adoption and execution of the noblest code of duties of mind to God, and this is best done on best analysis and by consistent action of mind. Religion is of paramount importance but then it must never degenerate into peculiar faith, that spots, taints, and corrupts it before the whole universe.

Mind is for science, science for morals, morals for religion,—the highest act and thought of mind that is thereby effectually introduced to its God.

Religion we see must rest on universal principles that constantly apply to their originator, who sees all the universe.

Man is already bound from creation to God alone, by that supreme birthright, religion, and when he moves out of that sphere of his only safety, he takes a false position by false faith, in a counterfeit that comes of peculiar faith.

All God's principles vindicate him, in vindicating themselves and religion, sooner or later.

All men must know this, to be sure of the only means, ever given the universe, much less one of its spheres. Now the conclusion is inevitable, that what is done by conservation for this world, must be done for the universe. As God's principles are universal for conservation, this world cannot be excepted ; consequently the doctrine of Messiahship, as most worthless and noxious, falls to the ground.

Religion must be rational, and displayed by mind that should exhibit its best activity, not in sounding pretensions, but in ennobling actions.

The world may add all enthusiasm, and all the exciting feelings of spiritualism, that are inherent and to the purpose. But what can all avail if any of the passions transcend reason ? Use all that is legitimate, to the highest intensity of feeling if necessary.

Religion must be rational however spiritualized to the deepest enthusiasm, and purified in all attainable sanctity ; and such cannot mislead us by bigotry or any improper weakness, as the governing power of mind will prevent in the audition of philosophical reason.

The influence of monotheism or rational religion, pervades more of human character than those of peculiar faith will admit. But is peculiar faith ever just? What has made men honest, virtuous, patriotic? Innate principles have done these, especially when aided by domestic education, that elicits the best conservative principles the better the higher they are carried.

Peculiar faith is any thing else than right, if it acts knowingly. Idle opinions may be entertained about one's conscientious views, as if a loose and idle speculation without base or capital ; but none of these are available, as all must depend on certain principles.

A comprehensive knowledge of the world, will show us the proof. The whole life is pre-eminently in this momentous question, for we only know life after its passage at the dying hour.

Rational religion gives the firmest faith to live and die by. There are no blind footsteps that mislead us. She is independent of the least improper motives.

All that we can rely on is on God and his attributes, to whom mind's whole duty throughout life must be directed by its own best functions.

She calls for no excitement of animal passions, no sway of terror or fear, no vindictiveness.

The principles of salvation are universal and uniform from creation down, and incite the paramount duty to man and God. To have them variant in time or space, demonstrates false positions of imperfect perverted minds only.

But the faith of monotheism avows itself responsible, at the same tribunal of reason that condemns all others.

She teaches to like all in one brotherhood and God, and acts most consistently with circumstances and her ability.

She contemns all impostors, and countenances no blasphemers.

She bids the world ask all, if they be rational beings, what kind of religion must a rational God have instituted, for man did not institute it ?

Man is rational, or expected so to be in all other things, must inevitably be so in religion.

All wise rational men should educate mind against peculiar faith, especially all that conflicts with reason, or in direct antagonism with rational religion.

Who could oppose monotheism ? as well expect opposition to God, who instituted its pure principles.

She institutes no absurd views to kill with the fear of superstition in her fictions of hell, or to defer duty with superficial expectations of a promiscuous assembly of universal mixtures.

She commands actions as merit, and requires merit before rewards, soliciting social duties for man, who must pay the adoration of religion to God, but abjures all man, hero, and idol-worship.

She considers infidelity the state of opposition to the Almighty in favor of atheism or polytheism, both of which she negatives, in whatever form of numbers the last insidiously appears. With her supreme excellency of character, all other faiths are undeniably pagan.

She considers the plurality of gods as abhorrent to fidelity to the Supreme, and a violation of good faith to reason.

She considers atheism a desecration no less absurd, and only another apology for the idolatry of nature-worship.

In her reports about peculiar faith no matter where located, she accords all delicacy respecting feelings of unintentional wrong, and would take the will of intentional good for the omission of the deed : but she considers the paramount nature of the case demands official statements to approach the facts of truth.

The true representative of God, monotheism, is not appreciated because God is not.

When peculiar faith boasts of missions, rational religion can well ask what do missions avail, before science and mind understand each other ?

Why not address now the world in its tongues as claimed before, and promised in the last chapter of Mark, when the same or greater necessity exists among its many hundreds of millions ? Why delay now in China, with its three hundred millions, to make efficient progress before many millions die ere its very language can be mastered to address the balance ? Why not perform the necessary miracles to make the paramount impression among its many people courting the most auspicious faith all over the world ! Shall we not conclude that the master and his followers have assumed the falsest pretences, about unknown tongues and mind-affected miracles. Then this position condemns before rational religion, all the fabrications of christianity as the veriest mockery of honesty and truth. What an abomination when we hear men speak, do we not consider what they say ?

Does the subject make any difference as to this requisition ? Do preachers speak to savages and those of different language, without acting on the science of language ? If the speaker be not understood, he induces no faith. We all appreciate understanding, through the mind. How then can any kind of faith induce any exception. The advocate of the contrary, is unfaithful and dishonest.

What was faith of the dark and bloody ages of antiquity, but consistent with their science that had but little elevation ?

When science expands to rational philosophy, civilization adorns rational religion.

The true missions are those of cultured mind in all legitimate functions, commerce, trade, and as much science as philosophy can inculcate. Religion will follow as a legitimate consequence.

God has planted the principles, and man must cultivate mind to recognise them by reason.

All rational minds need freedom and light of conscience to exclude the tyranny of peculiar faith.

All minds should have pure, holy, vital religion, and should be duly protected in such religious freedom ; but let all be between them and their God without speculation.

Wise statesmen should take away all cause and pretence for temptation by private or public advantage. Of course, then, there can be no state-faith—which is state-despotism.

Pure religion is to protect mankind against encroachment of bad passions, acting in themselves or from others. In the existence of rational religion, when the varied storms of life assail the mind, its principles adapted for their propulsion, insure the triumphant victory. She can well say to the obsolete systems, let go old errors, and to their followers, do not let them ruin you. She makes due allowance for blindness of mind of the ancients, who were only partially impressed with the sacred obligations and the duties enjoined respecting religion, involved in essential errors from want of science as they were, and were misled by governmental demagogues. She now declares the light of the present day, blessed by the effulgence of philosophical science.

We all need her pure principles to save the world in its various errors, to circulate for the world's currency potent and self-evident indexes of enlightened philosophy, to eradicate peculiar faiths and all their substitutes of vicegerentships that arouse worse vices than they can extinguish.

This is proved even to nearly this present moment by the hostile imperial armies affecting conservatism of mind, to put down the liberties of initiative republics of the world, and to reinstate its corrupt priestocracies and political despotisms.

Why do not rational religionists say, religion of the heart, and not of the mind ?

Because faith of the heart is one of mechanical impulse, if any thing, peculiar enthusiasm, peculiar faith and doctrines; but that of mind, the only religion, carries reason and reason's God along with it.

The government and religion that give the greatest amount of good to the greatest number, are most rational.

The character of rational religion has an aristocracy over all other aristocracies of faith, when viewed by enlightened intellect.

She invokes the firmness expedient in all good things, in order to attain and maintain the fixed application of the greatest good.

Her position constitutes the only universal brotherhood now that all nations can recognise always in time and with affection of mind, that universally saves in time and space.

Her principles begin at the source, and endure with an endless creation.

Sectarians of all creeds and systems can lose their errors and names when they rally under her best light, where dwell peace and liberty. She knows no sectarianism in her spotless purity.

Nothing short of this position will satisfy an immortal mind, aspiring to God, participating in freedom here, and expecting fruition for manly and honest action hereafter.

Man has to avail himself of all wisdom to appreciate what is due the God of purity, before whose presence, which is The Holy Centre, all sin must fly the farthest.

When impulse, not mind, is foremost, especially with mothers, whose causality is small and mentality not deep, but whose maternal feelings are strong in the presence of children whom they have already committed by peculiar catechisms and sunday schools, this noblest gift to mind, arousing no ardent and noisy enthusiasm when she is entitled to silent courtesy, commends feelings that are deceptive, to be held in abeyance to reason, that is ever nearest right.

Though she estimates God's light as worthy of equal respect, but as the present sabbath suits our functions, the laws of nature and creation to promote mental and bodily elasticity, to protect from sensuality, to promote contemplation, observation, and commune with proper spirit, devoting one day in seven particularly to the consecration of divine thoughts on the Creator, to advance the cause of humanity and country, of civilization, popular associations, it is essential that wise laws should consecrate it to all such blessings without violation, except to indispensable business.

We are willing that this may be one of the great tests of social freedom and religious refinement.

Our night is a proper sabbath for the twenty-four hours for rest, one-fourth of that time consecrated by nature to the most delightful refreshment of sleep. The sabbath, as a day of rest for bond and free, man and beast, consecrated to the holiest purposes of humanity and the greatest blessings of mind, to secure the happiest results of civilization, and the greatest exemptions from barbarism that curses mind with its deadliest blast, should be rendered holy by wise legislation on the wisest principles.

Some people in the civilized part of the world, that ought to know and do better, work every day in the week, and do not regard the sabbath for any principles. There are no reasons that the superstitious require, but the soundest philosophy, that upholds the most stringent legislation under the wisest dictation of humanity.

God created all days alike, provable by works of creation, that moves on to all eternity.

The seven or more different sabbaths, and referring to the same thing essentially, declare that had God decreed an especial sabbath, the proof would be irrefutable by nature's works, that cannot be wisely suspended. All this nonsense about God's day is the fraud of the priestocracy.

There is no arrest of the revolution of this globe for that time, but all time is alike to God.

Philosophy, reason, and humanity bespeak rest of mind and body in regular business. All such may be properly suspended for recreation.

That may be a day for the whole world to observe at the same time, as far as practicable, but the main functions of time must go on without any sabbath.

It is remarkable that from the revolution of the globe in twenty four hours, that the same sabbath would differ much of that time in the sphere.

But monotheism bespeaks no sabbath, and great particular days for good deeds, as she exacts the best actions all the time.

Civilization and religion will not permit less than monotheism.

There are seven Sunday sabbaths in seven days by as many peculiar faiths, five of which at least, if not six, cannot be right or necessary on the principles of philosophy. Which did God make or mark? Only on philosophical and political or civic principles can such be established, for the rest of muscular created, not creative, power. With God such is absurd, as neither does the Creator nor his conservative principles rest. Of course all bibles of such tradition bear prima facie evidence, the highest proof of their own falsity.

Now of all the errors of the world, the statement of the head of the family, generally held sacred, (if sacred by science, but not otherwise, through truth,) is longest maintained in the family archives. Superstition and ignorance uphold them. Men seek to be led, but in the name of God let them be led right, as the evil deeds of ignorance and vice prevent good actions.

We need the eternal, permanent, and immutable institution of principles, that will prevent any injury to the world, from the turbulent pretences of those incapable of abiding their imperative duty without penalties.

The voluntary choice and adoption of principles confer dignity, while compulsion presents ignominy.

The sabbath can be instituted for rest by mind, for the best blessings of mind and its physical circumstances, that must elicit its own best condition on this earth, as the highest tribute to, and the best evidence of free agency, the gift and endowment of the Creator, who should receive the adoration of the soul, tried in the theatre of adversity. We should, at least, devote every sabbath, one seventh of our time, to the proper contemplation of the God of nature, and the refined duties of social and religious discussions. Let us try to have the world avoid its, as all days', desecration, to the unholy purposes of peculiar faith in any respect whatever.

Some do a very small business when they complain of sabbath breaking, but not conscience breaking, in the usurpation of a messiah over God.

A day of rest is natural, desirable, a part of civilization. But it must be confessed, that one of the most powerful and singular exhibitions of superstition is the observance of sabbaths for the reasons assigned. Was this too one of the filchings of priestocracy from religious philosophy. Give all operatives rather two sabbaths than none, as that position will enhance and prolong their religious, physical, and moral worth and character, and sustain humanity. We are to duly estimate the best effects of mind's wisdom on human nature, and act to the best under all circumstances. We must give legitimate issues to all that is expedient.

What sabbath can God have compatibly with the analogy of man? Time does not qualify Deity, who ruleth eternity by his presiding supremacy.

"And God blessed the seventh day, and sanctified it."

Christians, do you sanctify that day? Do you believe the Jew bible? Is Christ's day preferable to God's? Do any of you adhere to the original, except the seventh day Baptists? Do you not, by rejecting the santified day, reject the bible, on which you assume your testament is founded? Did not the bible writers find the sabbath day established before them, by the natural divisions of the moon's quarters? The division of time into weeks of seven days dates as far back as Hesiod. If the Jew sabbath was established as holy and sacred, how could christians violate it at all? The violation of the Jew sabbath was punished with death by their laws. The christians have changed Judaism with as much reason as they changed the sabbath. It is clearly all pretension and sectarianism.

Monotheism speaks for herself, doubtlessly when she rightly would go legislating to maintain the great principles of humanity, if it were not interference with citizens' or the world's rights. If practicable with the world's rights, adequate protection ought to be extended to all needing it, beasts as man. But no greater wrong should be perpetrated by legislation under the guise of aiding peculiar faith notions. The great principles of religion, God-instituted, when once rightly appreciated, will be so conducive to the world's benefit as it will be to its entire civilization, that spontaneous adoption will follow necessarily. There will be no need of the Levites' sword, nor papal inquisitions, nor despotic excommunications. None but rational religion will ever institute society aright. All else is false pretences.

It devolves on the whole world to carry out these doctrines as speedily as practicable, as soon as justice will permit. Proper attention to the subject of the sabbath should be paid, to do justice to man's nature, under the most elevated view of religion. Enough action can be legitimately taken to make any people happy and flourishing. The people of the world can rejoice on that day.

The social ability of man is to be promoted by all legitimate, to make him a useful, honorable, and cheerful member of legitimate benefits.

To put social happiness beyond a contingency, humanity, a noble humanity to all creation, requires the best enjoyment, every sabbath, to man and beast, if practicable. The safest error will be to give more holidays than proper civil institutions call for. All animal fibre must be duly relaxed, and at no time over-exercised in common labor.

The master is responsible for all undue invasion of natural laws. The over-use of iron by friction is as bad, if not worse, than rust or oxydation by inaction, and teaches mind a lesson.

Will the peculiar faith man spend every sabbath day of his life to teach the false pretences of his faith, aye, even to his own children, fellow citizens? How degrading! Is it possible that parents will teach through the bible, the witch story of Saul? What low speculation! Is it possible that a cultivated mind can be found in the Union to believe all such miserable stuff? It is disgraceful. But the world will not use its right mind, but entrusts all to the priestocracy, who are interested in the most ignoble false pretences. Have you wisely employed time and talents, your mind justly to proper adoration of the proper object? otherwise you have blasphemed by idol worship. Your own peculiar bibles, corrupt as they are, condemn you. Desecrate no time to peculiar faith institutions.

As long as the God of monotheists exists, which will be forever, the universe will subsist on the conservative principles wherewith it was created, but the peculiar Jewish God could not create his heavens to last, if we believe the lying priestocracy, who affected to be very familiar with him. They knew as much of that as the colors of the sun and moon, affected by the atmosphere, falsely attributing them to those bodies.

Mind then could never entrust itself to their ignorant guidance in time, nor principles of eternity.

But how can we get at the conviction, that is worth nothing without practice?

Monotheism will fill a point unattainable to christianity, or any other earthly schism, sect, or dogma, and attain a dignity and worthiness lofty enough.

This will be conceded by intellectual refinement, that the purest minds can only exhibit.

It seeks man's universal adoration to his Creator Supreme, and needs no vicegerent but that of mind.

When the world is thus united it is impossible to better it. Philanthropy must acquiesce in its pure character.

The influence of religion honors the sceptre of executives, the wisdom of legislators, the purity of judges, and the justice of the people. Its true restraints are felt in every land.

But for this, the rights of a world-wide commerce would be preyed upon, and contracted to the piracy of the social circle.

Smuggling, that debases national morals, is checked by its conservative virtue; and the merchant or citizen assuming to fail, assigning property to fictitious or preferred creditors, having means to live on plentifully, and even in luxury, is accountable to this mighty power.

If there be no clue on the debtor, who is all fairness in getting credit, advancing false pretences, then he has no shame and no sense of guilt; and where there are no such principles recognised, you have no course of redress on his feelings or sense of conscience, and but little elsewhere if public sentiment be not sound.

When we see smuggling avowed by any legislators, then that country is corruptly governed indeed.

This endowment of mind, then, is the mighty conservative of man's noblest qualities. But the state of mind is not up to her glorious requisitions. The legitimate expedients of mind must be realized in full capacity for general good.

When we see bigamy with the laws, what would it be without them. Give us wise laws, and their wisest enforcement, but above all, give us that which holds all in abeyance. If peculiar faith allows polygamy, what but religion can correct Judaism, Mahomedanism, or Mormonism.

Mind has become degraded by tyranny of government and peculiar faith, despotic customs both of obsolete ideas, till its nature is brutalized, and best condition is unknown to most of the world.

The greatest injustice next to these potent injuries, has been done it by scandal and libel.

The present condition of general society has been thereby disorganized and vitiated, in much of the world.

We need a sublime and conservative code of morals and religion, as a solace for all rational minds; the friend and adviser of the humble, a corrector of the haughty, and guide to all the world, to promote universal wisdom and liberty. Where is such? Is this because mind shrinks from its own?

Tell us, nations oppressed by debts, the interest of which you cannot fairly, yearly meet, and the capital of which you cannot extinguish. Did ye spend all that honor required and policy dictated, pouring forth every generous tribute of mind that is yet held subordinate ?

Tell us, history, for what so many millions have been slaughtered, so many billions expended, for vain man, ignoble and ignorant after all his assumptions and vainglorious ambition ? Was it for those baubles that cannot be held, peculiar church and state faith despotisms ? It was because philosophy, the height of proper sense, was not heard in the revelry of false faith and government, that have oppressed and crushed mind's holiest rights.

What cared the ancients, but for conquests or peculiar benefits ? Was it not the triumph of their peculiar faith ?

All sects and divisions will eternally contend with each grand system, as well as with each other, clash and conflict ; but all that believe in Deity alone, and his attributes, will be ever unable to contend at all about rational tenets, but must live in general peace and good will to all rational men.

Rational religionists have no popes to give away the inheritance of the nations of the globe, because these nations are not sectarians.

Their creed is not to war for religion, but to reason for its improvement.

They bow to no degrading man and idol worship, but adore God with the profoundest reverence.

They have the illustrious authority of philosophy, in her retinue.

Good ideas only be suggested by true religion only. What can prayers do ?

Do they move God, that is unchangeable and above all shadow of change ? A God of principle, that is to govern the universe ?

God cannot change his principles, without change of the universe ! What then is to be changed, but man ? Before we say aught we must seek to make ourselves worthy of the audience of extraordinary purity and justice.

We must look to our own best deeds and actions, as the very best prayers to be addressed as respectors of principles before the tribunal of the great author of them.

Mercy may be yielded by the soul of nature, to the right petitioners, who cannot have vicegerents or substitutes.

But we must recollect that we have to appear in the audience-chamber of principles, that rightfully introduce us to the divine majesty of the Supreme.

We have to cherish and cultivate most faithfully their acquaintance, to reach all desirable and rational expectations.

Mere enthusiasm, spiritualization, messiahship nor saintship, will profit us nothing ; it is principles alone that will safely conduct us.

All that rational religion teaches, is the improvement of individual self ; it requires each to get better on times reading by seeking the attainable good.

It suits and is adapted to the true physiology and phrenology of the mental organization, and scouts the corruption that is introduced by priestcraft, in lieu of the original position and nature.

All the world should philosophize upon its necessary position, as equal in knowledge to the best, who are the veriest impostors to do more.

The principles that direct the belief in God, direct to proper sincerity that unites all minds, and must convert them if independent of malign influences.

What shall we do to make man right ?

Peculiar faiths that involve false positions and hypocrisy, if not ignorance, will never rectify him surely. Then man must be altogether, on correct whole principles that vindicate themselves. Such will carry him through to the holy Deity, centre of residence, or the attainable point of future happiness.

Then down with all others that ruin the whole world. They are tolerated, till mind can rescue itself.

Man was created on physiological and phrenological principles, by which he is governed universally. This caused the world's worthies to die like men. No one can do more ; if he assume it, he is an impostor.

There is but one God, and he rules by inherent attributes, his creation is supreme unity.

Unity reigns triumphantly in the excellence of its supremacy, while trinity or polytheism is a botch of mind that jars in discord, and reigns in imbecility. All its creeds are devices of art, and all are purely matters of perverted sophistry.

Its numbers may be indefinite, all assuming to be infallible, yet the mind corrected by proper principles, and left free, to exercise the best just judgment, discards them all as trash.

They all begin wrong, and confound the noblest tuition.

Children under their guidance must be badly raised, as they are suffered and shown the way to become vicious in deceit, untruth and dishonesty.

Who can wonder at the defects of society?

Habit in them as in all, is hard to eradicate. They are sophists from their cradle, and bigots in old age.

Happy is the youth that can escape such toils.

See, then, statesmen of the world, that there is then a correct exercise of mind and body.

But science and philosophy will not answer to decide for religion! What else have we to correct "the average of mere public opinion, a mere collection of prejudices, foibles and errors?" This pretence is advanced by the thoughtless vassals of priestocracy, who place the last ignorant and interested instead!

These are they who absurdly advance the opininion that nothing is impossible with God.

With the God of the universe, all things are not possible, as vicious imbecility of permitting his creation to be governed by man's messiah.

God can do nothing under the present declared position, without science and philosophy, his attributes in or out of religion.

Hence they are absolutely necessary and essential to expel false faith, and that causes impostors to commit themselves most absurdly. Then it is utterly impossible for all such libels to be acceptable to God. It is utterly impossible that God can like them.

What government and religion are best, but those that ever give to the sovereign people the greatest good, not only to the greatest, but the whole number?

We must all live a pure and upright life, that is blessed by correct principles that govern the social circles.

True religion enables man to tower over despondency, as she only gives the triumph of correct principles.

Unity in religion will embrace unity in government, two of mind's greatest blessings.

When science reaches the greater unity of language, as far as possible, then several of the most brilliant annunciations will begin to be realized on the unity of God's principles.

Religion itself depends on science and philosophy, the highest and deepest, to evolve it rightly, showing the best diligence of rational minds.

Religion, then, must be of itself the surest philosophical science.

Conscience, that directs it, is enlightened at this fountain. Religion has grown best, with right education, that elicited correct principles, which were all the gift of God.

Religion is a latent quality, best shown by rational mind, not by irrational minds. It must be most elevated by cultivated science.

It is not the gift of industrial organization, conferred by churches, as it is universal in its foundation where rational mind can be developed.

When most rational, it displays the security of just reward, for the mental labor.

It is a constitutional, or conservative revolutionist, not the passive reformer.

Show us the bible of mind, that of God's inspiration, and you will inspire us with the holiest reverence for it as God's.

The bible of mind can be the only bible, and can counteract the usurpation of bibles of tradition, that have created a host of petty despotism, by the little cliques in their bible way, blue laws and all.

Thus we see that this slavery of mind horribly vitiates it.

Religion will protect all, but it must be rational and vital religion, such as God alone justifies.

It sounds like purity to have its principles from an immaculate Being, creator and protector of his universe, having the affection and the power.

If we make the application of the right test, that circumstances allow, religion is admitted to be love to God and man, with comprehensive active benevolence.

Resistance to resistance may be necessary, from the depraved state of man's nature, but when expedient, what forbids the comprehension of the only policy to civilize and embrace the whole world in the ample folds of its protection. If we adopt the right and righteous principles to govern the world, we adopt God's righteous government, instituted therefor.

Let all, then, know neither Jew nor gentile, Christian, pagan, Juggernaut, mormon, nor any but the true belief in one eternal God, who needs no vicegerents, and excludes all in his present government.

God does not let his works be mistaken by man's right mind, that comes in with prior claims to establish the right polity, his duty to God and society.

In religious duties we can supersede with no blank and omission, but must act up to the full commission and duty. The whole is to be filled up aright.

We require and give proof for all things, the most valuable above all.

Where error prevails, let all go, as worthless.

If mighty mortals fall, let truth stand ; then philosophy and science will prove the facts of the world to the entire satisfaction of the beneficiaries.

Let all principles stand, and no more than their truthful code ; then no matter about time and custom, as error is so much the worse, the older.

Truth is all, no matter how young.

All men are to be estimated by their deeds and constant actions, as the best letters of commendation are the proof of one's own deportment all the time.

But we must refine, on our present improvement of age. All the systems of the world, past, present, and to come, can only go for what they are worth, before the tribunal of God, whose unity decides the whole question of religion.

Let us seek, by the powers and principles of mind, for the noblest and best appreciation that can be elicited. Let principles be espoused and all vain error rejected, no matter how identified with power and influence.

None but eternal principles can answer.

Sectarian views, in anything, will not answer at all, as they do not touch, much less comprehend the subject. Our views of civilization are always in respect to proper testimony of the mind. The freer the mind, the purer its civilization.

The right basis and test must be ever present, as rational religion cannot pass the impassable gulf of sectarianism, but endowed in the rich exclusive gifts of God, exclusive only to wilful impostors, she can soar to the circumference of the world on expanded wings of comprehensive benevolence, and embrace the whole universe by her beneficence. All codes of true faith are behind her times and the necessity of human nature, in too many particulars. The subject of religion is truly behind the age. It is her voice that inculcates her principles, those of the God of the universe, not of any messiah, who never originated one iota of principles, that were correct, if misleading from the adoration of the Supreme alone. She teaches man to eschew all undue passion and improper emotions, that affect the serenity of temper, or that disturb the equilibrium of mind, and thus removes him best from fear and anger, as best from superstition, to the trust in supremacy.

In listening to the tuition of science and philosophy, he best respects her voice that nobly sustains his strongest confidence and hope in the one efficient Power.

Who but that divine Power created him ?

To whom does the creature belong but the Creator ?

It is not the name of the thing, but the thing itself, that the eternal wise intelligence of the Almighty respects.

What is religion, but the duty of the creature to his Creator?

From whom do the gifts of the creature emanate, but from the Creator ?

Whence beauty of person, talents, gifts of mind ?

Are they not God's ? You have never analyzed this subject rightly, else you could not miss the right conclusion.

Self-denial comes in for a large portion of due attention from the truly religious, the worthy patriots and humanists of the world, who practice it, under the benign influence of rational philosophy, to be exalted by rational religion, that gives it the best and complete direction.

All good and wise philosophers will affirm, that an enlightened way of regulating mind on universal principles must be adopted, for successful regulation of all ; but before that time arrives, minds see differently, and require all the wisdom of wise legislation and education to help settle the difficulties of the world.

Rational religion is the only one, simple and complete of itself, from God and for God, ever existent in every rational mind, whose capital has been stupidly usurped by priestocracy, as if its own.

This, as a proper science, needs no enlightened code of ethics, for all mankind to act justly, on the just relation of things.

All have religion that have rational minds, that are under the Supreme obligation of making it rational, and improving it according to their gift of reason.

A cultivated science of rational religion gives the world the very best attainable, relative to the state of mind cultivated.

Religion is the science of sciences, and must be proportionate to civilization, mental culture, and talents.

Truth and honesty are the corner-stones of religion. Those who violate these can hardly possess the balance, as these are the platforms.

If these principles are admirable, how adorable must be their Author?
What a difference in things prevails in all peculiar faiths, that present the reverse of adoration! True religion is exalted by its noble Author.

Peculiar faith degrades its adopters, who imitate only the counterfeiter and usurper! What mind can hesitate, in the choice of the two?

Much censure then can be avoided for candor and friendly feelings. The true appreciation of things can be nearer approached, and will be much better practiced.

Money, by her criterion, will be only valuable for the proper independence, not excess and plethora of wealth that enslaves the possessor, engrosses his best time and qualities, and prostrates his best virtues, unless he have proper guards, enervates his prosperity, and may deprive him of seeking a sound education, and means of suitable promotion of mind's noblest gifts.

There are few exceptions.

Above all, money or wealth should never be any where, much less in a republic, a means of absolutism, defying enlightened public opinion, outraging and escaping conviction.

Money is valuable for the proper independence, secured in commanding circumstances, and equalizing all in glorious virtuous republicanism.

Such a state should be realized in chastening opinions by practice, in the vicissitudes of life.

True wisdom is that which can direct to the best advantage the proper usages of society, and the best progress of improvement, best promoted by freedom of mind, that has thus its best scope.

All good intellectual circles ought to advance and estimate all this.

What produces a right sincerity in religion?

A right exemption from temptation to do wrong by speculation; none, but the unostentatious practice of the sterner virtues and principles, because they produce the only best and true ethics, founded on the great laws of nature, and nature's God and soul.

Should not rational mind attend to all this?

But religion is a science, abstract and difficult.

It merely requires proper sense and honesty to work it out rightly.

Some have not been taught principles except through penalties, while all should get them by precept and example, and imbibe them rightly, otherwise their imperfect and contingent indoctrination may involve the delinquents in all the difficulties, and penalties of vices and crimes,

How much of God's funds are passing in this world, unobserved and unappreciated by mankind, if heard of?

The vast funds of mind have to lie dormant under the regime of bibles of tradition! What an outrage on the principles of mind!

The trust-fund, a creation-birth right, can never be fully appreciated, nor used in mind's present vassal state and mode of acting, when deprived of its innate energy, to exercise its innate principles for the best function of its gifts.

Mind must be taught to feel that the God of the universe is exclusively the God of conservative principles, and that it must depend on uniform and consistent principles of rectitude for its best guard, protection, and defence in life.

Cultivated and rational mind has yet to learn that mere coalition of church members, is not the quintessence of these principles.

Creeds will not begin to answer, unless they subserve the whole purpose of constitutional principles of religion.

Manners that bespeak the outward demeanor, as flowing from polished courtesy, good proper sense and feelings, are essential to man and society, but a loftier purpose arises in duty to God.

Reason, with her best aids, analysis and analogy, leads us to the extreme limit of God's existence, where data fail, and honesty stops, then mind cannot act further, after all the false pretences of peculiar faith and her legends.

But if some affect that morality and mind are not to be respected, as the essentials of religion, they can tell us the reason to separate this family.

Will any honest, truthful mind, pretend to see such a distinction, without the reason for the difference?

In God's philosophy, both belong to the same family.

But then, if rational religion prevail, where is spirituality? What is that but God's inspiration in all truthful and honest minds?

What more spirituality can exist, than that rational means should prepare the immortal spirit, by the best purposes for immortal fruition?

Rational religion must speak of things as rational.

Rational minds must learn to drop all images of fanaticism of past ages, that had so many obsolete ideas.

A very small portion of most church members, may be as good as human nature can be under their circumstances, but the balance certainly not as good, but worse than religion asks for.

What will spiritualization do for either of them, half as well as rational religion, that is the exact science of their being, and only adapted to their sincere and rational improvement that necessarily embraces all that is spiritual at the same time?

Rational religion only asks for mind's rational improvement.

Mannerism differs entirely as much from manners in being an adherence to customs and fashions of customs, as distinguished from innate courtesy and benevolence of mind, the liberal soul of man, as peculiar faith does from true faith, which is rational religion.

Peculiar faith can only be an imitator at best, and a disguise at the worst, of religon.

The action of true rational religion has been on earth with mind's existence, however silent and unobserved by the superficial and the fanatical, still she has done help in all circles to promote the teaching of virtue, morality, and good state of morals, that are claimed to prevail by excellence of peculiar faith! Who can overlook the virtue of mind?

The light of mind is the pure gospel after God.

Religion calls for the protection of conscience above all things of interest, as the good effects of a sound mind, not misled by vice and its temptations.

Conscience is then best fortified against the haunts, as the hands of others seeking advantages.

The most energetic proof before the world, is that we should so act privately as publicly, as to make all relatives, friends and citizens, satisfied with our actions.

Rational religion requires the highest humanity from rational beings. None lose by civility and courtesy to all, much less by kindness to servants. The very beasts are more profitable by great humanity.

No committee, or authority official, can legalize doctrines not established in the Divine Code of God, much less annul any principles. All the councils of earth could not make a peculiar bible of any force and virtue.

Many may and do deceive themselves in regard to all the acts of their peculiar codes and faiths, but all such have no peculiar principles appropriated, as God's system has all the principles known.

Judgment concentrates several virtues of the individual, and repels the effects of fear and other depressing emotions, that operate injuriously on most of mankind in sickness, of various difficulties innumerable, counteracting the destruction of virtue.

It enables its possessor to keep an equilibrium well balanced, and on guard all the time, above fear and reproach, least excited by passions, that ought to be controlled.

All possible superiority of virtue renders the possesor equal to the world, capable of facing bravely all its opposition.

With the man of judgment, the functions of times can be most present, as he can always promptly consider those things that require proper timely action, that once lost, cannot be recalled.

This faculty bestows the best recognition of life-time affairs, and none less of rational religion.

We need religion without superstition, never enjoyed hitherto generally, on account of peculiar faith, as well as government without tyranny.

A conscientious individual desires nothing equivocal or contingent, when he has to draw on a fund of uniform principles. He seeks wisdom and all practical common sense, and ever shuns cunning as contemptible. He seeks a liberal rational discussion to improve the qualities of mind, not merely to come off victorious in sophistry.

He cultivates good qualities, to avoid the bad. With such position countries become less corrupt the older they become, as possessed of rightful means they necessarily improve.

He seeks to analyze the difference, between religion and peculiar faith.

The first he finds to ennoble, the last to degrade the nature of mankind : the first to demand truth, the last to require power. Gratify the first and she blesses ; yield to the last and she abuses her trust by persecution and bloodshed. Monotheism invokes the soundest reasons to close all errors, if mind leaves improper constructions of her immutable truths.

Sulphur and brimstone sophistry, will not do it. Monotheism takes the only tenable right course in things and holds it to the end, never to desert the God of nature, or be deserted by his noble principles.

She asks for no military renown or glory of chieftains, no gorgeous outlays of power, and instead of worldly pomp and display, requires that the money legitimately raised be appropriated for school-houses and teachers of science, to invest mind with its best calibre, quality and capacity.

Her light excludes the propagation of peculiar faith doctrines, that her's eclipses.

With her, the sooner equality of rights is given the world by conquest of mind, the better.

With her, toleration is the friend of man.

She promotes proper self-government nationally and individually, as the highest dignity of all governments. There can be no opinion for there is no analogy, to affect this position.

Monotheism requires no political or faith propagandism by particular missions, except through the science of mind whose benefits are universal.

Wise statesmen cannot oppose this, as they are the best agents, not the corruptors of the people.

It is right that monotheism should disabuse the mind of the world on the subject of religion, that the mind of the world should disabuse itself.

She must be independent of speculation and powers of government, as it ought ever to be and must be the noblest as purest of actions, separate from all the adverse machinery of priestocracy.

Monotheism is the great leading question; all others are sectarian and led.

She considers it right to believe that God can do all the works of preservation after all the principles established prove it, without being taxed above the measure of the ability of the operating power, that the creation imposes.

God will certainly not dishonor the right draft.

We can well appreciate what kind of religion presents the very highest order of morals and ethics.

If we cannot find truth and reason in the bible, where can we expect to find it in its peculiar faiths?

Which is orthodox but rational religion, that increases only from the purest culture of mind, looks to all such immutable principles that vindicate themselves in penalty of vices, presents the highest views of all science, and illustrates by physiology its benefits?

She refers man's thoughts, words, and actions, to the highest earthly tribunal, when pure and enlightened, that of his own conscience; that reflects all the pure operations of his own mind and reason, corrected by enlightened public opinion, their highest exponent.

Her's is the security for the best condition of life in this world, and in the future.

The best promotion of all such, is the best science—education. All should be pleased to respond to the just demands of nature, illustrated by the highest civilization of mind, and fulfil the requirements of all the affections; filial, parental and conjugal, to soothe the paths of aged parents, to enlighten children, and fulfil the highest obligations to families, in the course of life with becoming dignity and action.

Our obligations to our country, the world, universe and their Creator, should require a higher elevation of our daily thoughts, by meditating on the vital blessings of that happy land where freedom of mind dwells and rational religion abides, where we can aspire every way for the best earthly happiness, undisturbed the least to meet death, one of nature's noblest and greatest functions, the soul-purifier, with a conscience least void of offence to God and man, as the action of a wise and self-studying Being.

Such theatre, gives best scope for effort.

Thus all rational minds have much duty to perform, as all things of earth require of an immortal mind, the bright light of a bright age that looks to God.

We need mind-ethics, and must look to the great laws and principles of an immutable infinite Being.

Belief in one true God unites all faiths into one religion, destroys all sects and creeds of sects, makes men candid, moral, virtuous, independent of all kinds of faith-craft, cant and hypocrisy, as aliens to religion, as it takes away all the temptations, shows truth, and excludes sophistry with bravery, diminishes perjury, places man at once in the presence of his God, whose providence superintended his actions all the time, and rendered his life as a moral agent more or less accountable under his peculiar or personal circumstances.

The reverse is verified by the doctrines of peculiar faith, that publishes to the world as its own, what is the property of God.

Why should not rational religion be silent in God's presence? What have availed all the babblings of peculiar faith? The silence of rational religion effects all good, while peculiar faith has been blustering, brutalizing mind, outraging its rights, misleading, by her infatuation, bullying it with her brute force, deluding it with her abominable sophistry.

With all this load of iniquity, man not God, has to change. Religion asks for no dangerous peculiar school, but that which is safe, pure and just, most rational.

The citizens of the world have to rid themselves like intelligent freemen, of all feudal habits, and seek liberal, rational, conservative principles.

Under these circumstances, rational religion asks for no weak, meagre and doubtful or doubting faith, but inherently just and adequate.

Rational religion is the only representative of principles of God, and they constitute an impenetrable phalanx. To do justice to this whole subject, nothing can be more important than a well balanced and cultivated mind, in all the social and religious obligations.

This individual state refers back to the general principles of phrenology that is founded on the eternal and fundamental basis of physiology.

Scientific people can appreciate all this, and cast off the shackles and false pretences of the fraud of monopoly, no matter from what source.

Thus the destiny of the world will not be referred to fatalism and occult astrology, demonology, or lunacy, but will be left to rest on the eternal principles of philosophy, as given it at its creation by the Creator.

Analysis in a court of justice shows human nature's characteristic, the action of perverted mental organs.

Rational religion gives mind its full rights, corrects it, raises it to its best capacity. She is the only cure for trickery, and charlatanry of thought, and vanity of earth, under the best view of proper sense, and enables the world to estimate man's action more than his words, but herself estimates both rightly.

While she fosters eclecticism on the principle of will for the deed, until toleration can be superseded by conservative revolution, that constitutes her order of mind, distinguished for refined intellect, she teaches principals the knowledge of the government of their families.

She directs the world not to sacrifice to mere fancy, and informs us that religious duty will enable all rational mortals to meet in a rational way the dragon of superstitious terror, and breathe with conscientious satisfaction in the universal mirror of truth.

What do mankind need, as soon as reason dawns and mind acts? A mantle to cover their physical and mental nakedness. They need a moral code to be at the same time intellectual, to protect and defend their weakness. Who does not wish to be guarded from the blasphemy of feeling, thought, word, or deed, as from misanthropy?

It is wonderful that we do not commit greater errors than we do, influenced and misled by the superficial and crude opinions and errors of others, who assume to dictate their views and interests on society.

WHAT IS CONVERSION, BUT A RATIONAL IMPRESSION?

Conversion consists not in mere outward changes or speculations, but internal conviction resulting from the lights of conscience on the necessity of reformation, and using the conservative principles, by a proper respect and compliance with their requisitions to the best of personal ability.

It is not fashion or mere opinion, but satisfactory facts and their proper fruits; a proper deportment in thoughts, words and deeds.

To whom does it show fealty, by man?

To God alone. There can be no real benefit from mere excitements, and impulses of intense passions.

Religion is and must be a principle of due and adequate action or practice, paid truly to the great and living God, as reason construes, united with all the feeling that conscientious right actions can impart to one satisfied with doing the best, hoping the most, fearing the least, but confiding, as safest, under the loftiest and highest protection of the Almighty Architect of the universe. It is built up on the noblest principles conservative for rewards, self-vindicative for penalties.

The best confidence is the most rational, built on a wise comprehension of duty and its noblest execution.

But the doctrine of falling from grace, an opponent says, produces "fatal delusions in regard to conversion, and the mind bewildered and distracted amid the storm, is rendered utterly incapable of deciding, with judgment and accuracy, anything as to its operations or experience"! And reason at last is admitted.

"Many enter the church unconverted," admitted by churchmen.

Conversion will do, so far as mind is capable of right action, without "forced faith," and no farther for us. But the opponent of falling from grace admits, that this fatal delusion of "the many that enter the church unconverted," may extend to the fourth time, or even oftener, and yet this prevails in the operations of minds seeking after immortal happiness.

The correction of this potent evil is called for, by the advocate against falling from grace. The potent evil, is the base most radically wrong.

Radical errors can be corrected only in looking to God alone, and his attributes, by rational beings.

Gratitude that ennobles the manly independence of mind, is due to God alone, as Creator.

The highest reverence is only shown by admission of God's functions, faculties, attributes, and principles. To divide them out, is to lessen that sense and feeling.

All his qualities unimpaired, beget affection and love ; and constant obedience arises as a matter of unerring certainty.

God can arouse the noblest emotions and actions on principles, due him from the mind thus instructed in the highest and best.

All others bring blasphemy, and their contradiction impairs confidence, and bespeaks low degrees of feelings.

We leave out fear and blind faith that govern the slave of superstition, but appeal to reason and mind, that dignify the freeman.

The mind of man is taught to estimate purity, by that attribute of God.

It is his power alone that saves man all the time, when blasphemous vicegerents were naught, and have become less.

Mind's fidelity is due to God alone, expressed by rational religion.

Duty to God and man begets rational religion, gratitude, and love, takes away terror, and substitutes confidence, supersedes contingency for uniformity, gives a universal brotherhood for fragments and sects ; science and education for ignorance and feudalism, an Almighty God for an imbecile vicegerent mortal, the freeman for the slave and vassal, mind for blind submission, and reason for guide and helm ; sincerity for self-delusion, elements and principles not to clash, for clashing dogmas and schisms—and above all, that the eye of an Eternal Ruler is ever present, and a ready providence ever potent.

This will teach man to act as best comports with his nature, doing what its capacity enables and its character justifies, advancing in light of mind and liberality of feeling, improving in the fruits of knowledge that enlargeth the understanding.

Our religious creed places us, unalterably, at monotheism. Should we advance any farther ? How can we do so, as that position reaches to God, the supreme ?

The bibles of all traditions will be most demoralizing and fatally immoral, whereas rational religion is and can only present the safe faith in the bible of mind, that must seek to be critically exact in moral, religious, and physical science and philosophy.

The bible of mind pays no respect to authority, but as that authority accords with reason—any other cannot suit even slaves.

No freeman can give in his adhesion to any, but rational religion.

She teaches whatever be thy impulses, let them not carry thee ever beyond reason and principles.

Farther than that, is not the path of safety.

She teaches us, then, to look in the might and majesty of mind, to the might and majesty of God, to the power of reason, and the purity of principle.

To adore none, no authority written, oral or personal, but what supreme reason commands mind, when it looks devoutly to God Almighty alone.

The only rational religion, as the only true path of safety, consists in being reasoned into faith and belief.

The bible of rational mind alone, gives us the safe and correct moral, intellectual, rational, and religious faith.

No other bible excludes the thousand and one bibles, that innovate on principles of the God of nature, the right and virtues of rational mind.

No other bible excludes iniquity and sin, in the true and full legitimate comprehension of perpetual safety.

Hers is the tuition to turn all passions into their legitimate channel, and use no enjoyment thereof, other than what accords with true principles.

No genuine confidence in any other than rational faith can be at all conclusive to any proper religion.

Pure religion increases in the growth of wisdom, the benevolence of deeds, and in the truth of science.

Let religion flourish by the disinterested system, that spiritualizes the world through God's universal inspiration.

How many ignorant people in the world affect to know all about religion, the science of all sciences, the sympathy of all sympathies, and yet have hardly one idea in their minds about any of its dignity?

Knowing ourselves sinners, let us seek ever to sin the least, as the safest position practicable for all souls. Most can avoid extremes of sickness if they will timely correct their case, so in law and sin.

Our sickness, adversity and prosperity should be wisely estimated as blessings in disguise, and should elevate the thoughts of the creature to the Creator.

Our life may be spared out a few more years, and let that be a benefit to our fellow citizens and creatures, not an oppression.

The great institution of religion, God's best principle, ought to create the most enlarged views and actions of the virtues.

The best exercise of religion results in rightful actions of mind, through reason to God alone.

Can those advocating rational religion differ? They can never differ materially, for they all believe in the essential doctrine of God alone. Where they seem to differ, they will find the error theirs, one way or the other, not very material, and that such have not investigated the whole subject. Who has?

Good men and true can be nothing less than monotheists. What is there to mortals, but the immortal God's gift, religion? What nobler benefit can there be to mind?

The secret societies that apparently divide the globe into so many clans, antagonistical to the enlarged and liberal benevolence of the world, must give up their cohesion of clannishness, and attend to the invocation of universal brotherhood, that looks to the sublime majesty of principles. The whole world must do this.

Who can give greater safety to all than the helm of God, who is the First Great Cause?

The people must not overlook their own responsibility in this life, at all times.

Give us reason, mind enlightened, liberal and just laws, right and freedom of the people.

Can the people be more justly dealt with under God's guidance?

WHAT IS SPIRITUAL RELIGION?

It cannot be of peculiar faith at all, most assuredly.

Can there be any but the only rational religion, and is not that co-existent with the very first creation of mind?

Mind is identified with it forever, most clearly.

To best elicit all that is legitimate, rely on reason, not tradition, as the highest of all earthly authorities. Persevere in correct principles, whereby you may reach good ripe fruit; otherwise the fruit may be bitter, green or decayed by rot.

Theology, then, cannot be too pre-eminently a free subject for rational discussion, but the human mind has been not only trammeled in all its best powers, but superstition and bigotry to suit the times, and the gods of idolatry, with the interest of the minority, have forced to increase their absolutism, by even military brutes forced mind to the enslavement by peculiar faith, that acts as a fashion of the season for a few centuries, and is no more.

More misery has been entailed on the billions of the world from all this degraded machinery, than all others. This is one of the great bases of all evil. It has been like cutting off the head to direct mind, which it has outraged by usurpation of its rights. It has depraved and demoralized mind all the time, with some few exceptions.

Let him who affects to claim aught for peculiar faith show any of its intrinsic fruits, above what good minds and true, rightly civilized, can effect.

Billions of minds have never heard preaching in their lives; has God not provided them with mind's tuition nevertheless?

The fault is in the people, who must not deceive themselves about the means of their own action, civil and religious, then others cannot deceive them.

Her faith combines all that is reasonable with what is just, arousing the proper qualities of mind, the intellect, in its best views of wisdom.

Not otherwise can we prevent absolutism, combined as state, church and military despotism, the most powerful and odious tyranny.

Religion is the right action of minds to God and man. This subject is universal, to mind and the world.

Rational religion imparts all that is great in goodness.

It corrects those who might be incorrigibly dissolute and vicious, but only on rational principles.

The prime and the whole of life are well spent in their exercise, for she asks for no impracticable faith.

She requires the best of good works in an unpretending manner.

But the supremacy of rational religion is gloriously paramount, and vindicative of God's attributes, when she triumphantly rules out and silences, by her august presence, all the false pretences of all ignoble peculiar faiths.

She alone is the only true exponent of the God of nature, Creator of the universe.

She tries all by her own just tribunal, of her own standard of merit and trustworthiness.

It is she only that rightly responds to the question, what proof is there of any divine writers or writings? Her just analysis declares, none, for all is imposition. Monotheism alone can save; her institutions, without speculation, should be reared for the world's benefit. Let her press and teachers do their duty.

Let her permanent benefits be felt throughout the world; causing mind to rejoice in the purest joys of existence, as the landscape of nature's rearing reflects the joy of the birds that sing and carol on trees in the rich green of spring, and the variegated gorgeous display of autumn. Let her acts be strict justice of mind to be cultivated, and reflect on the happiness of mankind, feeding the hungry, clothing the naked, and comforting the blind, aged and helpless, as an indispensable, legitimate duty. Let wise organic laws fix the equilibrium that will dispense what is to be done. Let her rebuke the false expenditures of pride, rearing palaces and churches for fifty and one hundred millions of money, while the mind of the people is uncultivated, and their organic constitutional rights unredressed.

Rational religion suffers no sophistry of faith to pollute the inmost recesses of the minds of her followers, nor prevent the right perception of their judgment, nor degrade their right action by any malign influence or interest.

She will produce rational and individual righteousness, that consists in the purity and honesty of purpose and actions, and calls for positive laws, to be executed for life; all the blessings of civilization, that excludes wanton injuries, violence, murders, that go unpunished among cliques and clans on account of the temporizing mockery of corruption and of sophistry, in all their wiles.

We need to be exempt from the contingency of deception.

What can do that but rational religion?

The code of rational religion destroys any idea of skepticism, as that code is definite, and rests on definite principles. The only remedy for schism, is reason and rational mind. The standard for unity, is the God of unity.

The Romanists number some thirty-four schisms in their church.

The great schism of the west, lasted forty or fifty years. Who are the christians, but a great schism of Judaism, arising as a sect on other sects, as Samaritans.

What greater hatred was there than between the Jews on one side, and the Christians, Samaritans, &c., on the other? And are these characters pretending to teach mankind to follow them? Do they want more vassals?

All main advocates of peculiar faith, are hostile, as Mahometans and Christians. Where then is their love?

God's conservative principles do assist man to good, and are a restraint upon evil actions, as they constitute the constant circumstances.

Where then is man's pretence about other vicarious means that are perfectly nugatory and idle before God?

Rational religion advances in the best lights of rational mind's solution, a fixed fact as old as creation, but dependent on mind, the beneficiary for evolution. She asks for improvement of the bible of rational mind, with the best of sincerity. We all need this, as the bibles of tradition prove no valuable characteristics of worship, much less of high-minded adoration.

How can such bibles prove the immortality of the soul, when they are not endorsed by proof of themselves?

The thousand pretences of miracles and prophecies, are no proof. They are all false pretences.

We may be told as if in triumph of some being fulfilled, as we hear of the winnings, not the losses of gamblers. No mortal can claim to be prophet. The intrinsic character of such claim proves him impostor.

How many thousands of Hebrew, nay, of the world's augurs, are unknown, as ignobly false and degraded.

That province so foolishly looked for by the world, was never given to mortal or earthly inhabitant,—never. The human character becomes debased too low for appreciation by the corruption of sectarianism, which is rebuked most severely by the moral triumph of rational religion.   She teaches the world to bow to universal rights, justice, courtesy and liberality.

She teaches woman's elevation equal to man in all countries and in all governments, and that her education be not perverted by imperfect and imbecile systems, superstition, ignorance or prejudice.

Analysis of all things is essential to truth, hence the absurdity of any faith that receives all for granted.

Rational religion requires restitution of all overpaid, as the duty of the debtor, without limit of time, what conscience enlightened requires.

To injure no character sooner than property, and hold all such sacred by the laws of God and man.

All systems of faith short of rational religion, are imperfect, defective and vicious, when tried on this position.

A universal benevolence by the universal brotherhood, is the order of rational religion, that unfolds new beauties and worth the older creation grows, a universal beneficence of rational mind.   The whole comprehension of this subject is in good faith, nor can any part be basely withheld by peculiar faith, whose doctrines prove that the whole code should be constantly embraced.

The only faith that religion that is rational can know, is good faith to be carried out in due faithfulness.

Mankind are too credulous and disposed to take for granted as truth and science, what requires the fullest investigation and elucidation.

Impostures at every age, especially in the dark and ignorant, have been most wantonly propagated by men whose conscience for truth was measured by self-interest and sordid inducements; above all, by the sophistry and power of governmental despotisms.

Monotheism comes to cut down the atheist and polytheist, and establish the only principles of rational religion.

She modestly submits all to the light of mind and reason of rational beings, and claims nothing but what is self-evident.   No messiahship can be her companion, as she proves all counterfeit, and utterly unworthy of her and mind.

She goes for no fancy, fashion, custom or institution of that kind.

She invokes solely God's principles, to govern mind in morals as the universe in physical potency.

Rational religion asserts no pre-eminence, for all have it, and good minds can improve it more or less in all parts of the world, thanks to the Creator of religion as well as mind, its recipient.

By works, all are proved in truth and reason to reach faith.   All that are sincere cannot be hypocrites, as rational religion offers no speculation, but demands exclusion of all that can corrupt mind, and especially all that can delude it.

Rational religion is the universal greatest good for all, and must take precedence of all, just as much as the Creator, its only object of adoration, takes precedence of all others who must be his creatures.

Wisdom, science and learning, take precedence in defining religion that is proved by the superiority of its character, that must be necessarily rightly formed.   Above all, is Monotheism, that must exclude all peculiar faith the day that science and philosophy triumph.

It is the part of science-advocates to record facts, and modestly hold themselves in abeyance till further discoveries verify the solution.

The creed of rational religion is as old as mind, and the best that legitimacy and genuine purity can make it.

We absolutely need rational religion to govern fanatical atheists and monomaniacal blasphemers; neither can survive in her pure atmosphere.

She commands the sword to be sheathed that has been uplifted for the world's age, and invites the pen of reason that has been banished all, except the civilized world.

But for the remedy of rational religion, the age of superstition triumphs, and that of atheism must follow.

The sacrifice of reason by sectarianism, invokes humanity, philanthropists and statesmen to analyze all this for their good and the benefit of all.

The wise men of legislation must counteract by superior states of mind, and meet the axiom that God extracts good out of supposed evil.

What but reason should elicit the best views of faith, when the philosophy of exact science alone decides the highest religion.

Is monotheism, that is rational religion, the friend of mind without mistake?   Is this what the world has to cling to?

It is that which teaches of God all the time, in his purest attributes and loveliest purity.

While peculiar faith, even christianity degrades its heaven to a hell, and angels to devils, this the friend of creation espouses its Creator and exalts mind to its God.

Light will give religious rights to the people, therefore the suppression of investigation is base indeed.

Whenever rational discussion is evaded, or its books proscribed, then a black felony pervades the priestocracy that cloak the peculiar faith.

All the world is concerned to know the truth, the whole truth, and nothing but the truth.

Why make any fuss about getting religion at any time, that all rational beings have by creation birth-right, that cannot be alienated, only injured by their perversions of mind! Like the genius of discovery, let all such be free as air.

Rational religion cannot be a creature of state policy, for its origin is the most exalted, and its object the noblest for rational mind. She is built on God-given elements, through the best mental elaboration. She is advocated by no vassal or feudal schoolmen.

Let us live at once aright, not to deplore and repent, but prevent the necessity of repentance.

Rational religionists wish to be right, and desire no victory but what is exalted, moral, dignified and intellectual, and will accept of no other.

Monotheism was the first, and will be the last religion, and all practicable faculty will be her's.

She commends that the gifts of mind be not accepted at the expense of independence, or being crushed. She enables the world to observe whether priestocracy, or mind cultivated to its rational capacity, should rule the world?

Which is competent in time and constancy, a responsible agent, ever present, as mind, all over the world, at all ages, from its creation, ever imbued with the principles of religion, ready to be evolved at the right time and by the right mode, long before priests and their bibles were ever thought of; both being filled with mind's perversions?

Rational religion can ask no advance of her principles, unless they are clearly those of mind, God's works and book, incorrectly read at first, better and properly appreciated at last.

Rational religion requires rational faith and consistent practice. A religion of principles pays all duty to God and man. She requires children to be dutiful to their parents, respectful to their teachers; and parents to be faithful to their offspring, and not desert it under any circumstances—of course avoiding its illegitimacy. Above all, citizens to be faithful to their country. Under her auspices, husbands and wives will be faithful to each other; guardians and teachers will meet their responsibilities with faithfulness. Friendship will meet with gratitude; the country will be served with patriotism; mankind will be justly dealt with, and the whole world will be harmonized, under one universal brotherhood. Those that take all advantages will be counteracted by wise precautions of mind, and the weak will not have to succumb to the strong, as adequate world-legislation is progressive by the wisdom of mind.

Rational religion enables mind to say its soul is God's, not man's, whereas all peculiar faith compels mind to the stupid acknowledgment of a master, an imposition on the world, instead of revering God at once, as the source of purity and wisdom.

Thus man, with all his bibles of tradition and peculiar faith, is the author of folly and wickedness, as often as of his sickness and its intensity, because his mind does not adhere to reason and its attributes, but to exploded nonsense.

What genuine assurance is there of any spiritual religion, independent of rational religion?

How can the first exist without the last?

We might as well expect to see the pretence; that mind need not recognise it; for if it do, it must be rational or absurd.

We ask for certain evidence and proof, that cannot be furnished.

There is full ground, not only to doubt of, but exclude all, except rational religion, that is adapted to mind, soul, spirit, and hence is the only spiritual faith.

Rational religion, then, causes rational and universal liberty of mind.

In rational religion, no rational being can now mistake, as all can appreciate principles, the guide and pilot all the time.

She has amity for the whole brotherhood of the world, that is united in eternal principles. The world should understand, to appreciate and enjoy.

If mind be unable to get the idea of a God from the universe, the first and only accu-

15

rate idea that necessarily and absolutely, on the principles of causation, presents itself to a rightly cultivated intellect, it would be utterly incapable to appreciate his attributes and the obligations imposed thereby, on mind. There could be, otherwise, no universal standard.

· Rational religion, then, resorts to science and philosophy, God's genuine emanations, to ascertain her right duty, and declares reverence to whom it is rightly and exclusively due, in her faith, and invokes no wild conjecture in reason, her guide.

Polytheism, with all its messiahships and all its pretences. starting with its various comprehensions, has split into fragments, and is now withering before eternal principles, to be recognised by monotheism.

None can stand in opposition to conservative principles, that keep the universe in order, harmony, much less this globe, a position that all messiahs can never reach.

Rational religion inculcates and instils all the principles and actions of a gentleman, as its characteristic is the most gentlemanly conduct.

The best advocates of religion, if they do not possess what is rational, can adopt no other but peculiar faith, and must fraternize with the most inveterate enemies of all religion.

All the world, when civilized, will embrace the universal comprehension of rational religion alone, as the only practicable and safe ground, since it is utterly impossible for there to be any other.

We need its moral aphorisms, to do away with all sectarian dogmas, to exclude the idea of satanic temptations, no matter how metaphorical, figurative, or substantial; melancholic, ominous forebodings; visions and dreams; faiths and creeds in many absurdities, as in astrology, alchemy, &c. Speculations and rational religion are unconnected.

Can any deny that there is any such thing as rational religion? Give us a proper audience, tribunal, or jury, of honest, intelligent monotheists, who must have rational religion, as rational beings, created by a rational Creator.

God's book, the universe, is the living witness, that proves exact harmony of system. an abeyance to its conservative principles. The jewel of the universe, the mind, proves it most conclusively, too.

You cannot supersede the mind that is inextinguishable, by dead books, the bibles of tradition—dead as soon as conceived, much less finished—no more than supersede the living faith of religion by the peculiar faith of dying priestocracies.

Rational religion is correct as rational beings are accountable, if for no other reason. It will be the happiest moment of our lives, to die monotheists, rational religionists.

What respectable monotheist, having enlarged patriotism and philanthropy, but wishes all the blackguardism of peculiar faith abolished, on the enlightened principles of mind, whether Jew or Christian, Mahometan or pagan, are concerned.

It is incompatible with the light and spirit of the age to continue any incompatibility, to have any party or right crushed, lowered, or dispirited.

OATHS FOR JUSTICE,

Can only be administered in the faith of God, who is omnipresent, in this wise. I, the witness, affirm to the truth, the whole truth, and nothing but the truth, of what I shall now state in this matter.

Who could safely make oath, but on solemn affirmation? As there is no divine authenticity of any scriptures, there is no truthful authenticity. Hence the oaths administered on them are not only absurd and criminal, but blasphemous. There should be no cursing or vulgar invocation of Deity; and who that is rational would hail the plurality of peculiar gods in all their scriptures? Who can object to God's system of rational religion, but those devoted to the vagaries of peculiar faith, committed to take for granted all about the ancient fables and legends respecting hell, assimilated to volcanoes, &c.?

Peculiar faith resolves all other faiths out, including, most unjustly and untruthfully, certainly most unreligiously, rational religion, while that the only pure one, the world's republic, resolves the world in, and cannot be destitute of its principles.

Contingency, then, sticks to the first as accident of peculiar education, and discloses her pretences or presents them, while nothing prevents the primary main part of the last possession. Right improvement and cultivation are only needed. Rational religion enables us if we err, to do so on the safe side, and being the only religion of rational beings, she only uses universal means of reason, truth, and honesty, for ever.

Rational religion institutes the essentials of social relations, and recognises that God is always with us.

We require rational religion associations, on the principles of universal brotherhood. There is no need of fanaticism with rational beings.

As the world will declare for rational religion, the sooner we establish her principles the better.

The highest species of civilisation, is that of rational religion.

Monotheism adopts only one right bible, and that of mind, that declares the perfect unity of God.

Rational religion calls for reformation all the rational life-time, on the highest principles of rational education. She is the mutual obligation of God and his creation—in perfect consistency—all peculiar faiths are in antagonism to that, and must be in blasphemous rebellion to principles. All mysteries, prophecies, miracles, come under this category, with their peculiar bibles of tradition and all their designing priestocracies. Be done, miscreants!

Rational religion reconciles all doctrines of pure religion, upon the principles of reason submitted to the sublime standard of the Supreme perfect being.

There can be no difference of opinion but on the scale of ignorance, as speculation cannot breathe in her pure atmosphere. No doctrine can be permanently adopted by rational men, unless it be rational, and therefore must be principle. Rational beings need a system that has principles and elements conservative, that will place the whole above any of the authorities of priestocracy, absolutism, or sophisticated superstition.

Rational religion will exclude all the peculiar faiths of the world. Universalism is a small incident in monotheism. Rational religion will permit nothing in the dark, not at all.

The world must, necessarily, become monotheist, when the right principles can be appreciated, and when the right spirit of the people commanded. Monotheism is obliged to prevail and triumph.

Rational religion requires of all, when anything is personal and they are not certain of the purport, to inquire modestly, not assert boldly and then become recklessly responsible. The right performance of duty to ourselves, as all, takes precedence of passion.

Now, if rational religion clashes in its principles, stop : it is the error of its adopter's not of its author, whose principles do not clash. The days of peculiar faith are numbered by rational religion, that can expel any number of its advocates. True analysis, the profoundest of all profound subjects, not attainable by common minds without proper pains and exertions, declares, as sure as the empire of ignorance yields to the empire of mind and reason, so surely does the empire of peculiar faith yield to rational religion.

The day has been when more attention was paid to the moon and stars in astrology, than to reason in the various duties of life, in the heart rather than the mind. In such times, peculiar faith usurped all the rights of reason.

The bible of rational mind must be that of universal brotherhood. In doing justice to the analysis of the position, psychology proves rational religion, that needs only a right statement of facts for self-demonstration.

The Creator of the universe has duly impressed mind, and no messiah can remove that impression.

The head of the universal brotherhood, not church, is He who ought to be, no less than God himself. The only spiritual religion is rational, and nothing less. We profess to be monotheists, believing in one eternal, immutable Almighty, that rational mind traces to the first Great Cause. We believe in the bible of rational mind, that is the greatest gift in the universe, whose adoration of Deity is rational religion.

The bible of rational mind must adhere to principles of truth, reason, and the God of the universe, or such bible is non-existent. People may not be afraid to take hold, as monotheism will support them.

The province of rational religion presents the noblest of principles, which is a pleasant duty.

Peculiar faith is always in restraint, to support its inconsistences and its sophisms, the devices of the priestocracy.

Monotheism, illustrious conservative revolutionist of the world, should never be outdone by advance of progress of mind. We defy sectarianism to be born of monotheism, that would have excluded all the piracies of peculiar faith wars, all the inquisitions and proscriptions of church tyranny, all the bayonets of despotisms. Rational religion places woman on her only elevated and dignified sphere ; gives her mind and soul—the first of which man has not got by even christianity, or any other peculiar sectarian pretension or dynasty. Monotheism asks you to assist mind by your most rational discussion, the best for rational minds on rational subjects; she knows nothing but what is right—to have all right; knows not herself except by rational position. She is out of existence when not right, for otherwise she cannot exist.

Where one says there is falling from grace, another that it never was possessed, she composes the conflict, a war for centuries with peculiar faith, by affirming on the true averment, that the elements of religion were original, cotemporary with not only birth, but a creation-right—and improved as mind is enlightened and civilization refined. Morals can only be secured by rational religion. This argument cannot be evaded.

Rational religion begets the deepest conviction that there is a God, whom humility in the sublimity of her silence, acknowledges the Supreme, and to whom confidence in her deepest reverence, confesses the loveliest adoration.

As phrenology or psychology is to physiology of mind, so is rational faith to its obligation in morals and religion, all else is mystic metaphysics that beget the subtlest sophistry, and create infidelity and disbelief. We leave the chaos of conjecture a partially discovered system of judaism, blurred in superstition and clerical despotism, in christianity, man and image worship, where priestocracy stalk in all their horrors.

And what philosophical science does monotheism present? She kindly leads mind to the contemplation of the mighty vista of nature, she takes away the veil, and introduces to a nearer and juster appreciation, the God of nature. Superstition, however refined her every faith, is unworthy to have the audience before rational mind. She never can be else than false faith, when she is superstition. At first ages, man hardly had abstract ideas, and the proper analysis had not been then made. Now, rational religion stands alone in her sublimity, unapproachable by all peculiar faiths.

The difference between monotheism, rational religion, and peculiar faith, is this : the first is after truth, the last is after faith! Rational religion needs nothing extraneous ; thus she rests on her dignity and grace.

Rally for her in this approaching age of civilization, and we shall soon see a triumph indeed. This rally is not for her, but yourself, world, grand and glorious. She is the independent minister of God. How can you live a religious life? Only by rational religion. None have dignity till civilized by rational religion. Monotheism is the only rational faith, the only religion—that enables us to get rid of church bigotry, sophistry, tyranny, expulsion and excommunication, and all the idle dreams and visions of the supralapsarians, who cannot fall from grace! what peculiar faith never had, but on her borrowed yet unacknowledged capital.

Rational religion rids the world of faith tyrants, and all such petty evil doers, and while peculiar faith cannot reconcile only two persons differing on her premises, she holds a brotherhood of billions, responsive to the bursts of manly feeling and love. This bespeaks the sublime magnificence of the God of the universe, itself united in indissoluble union. But for the supreme wisdom and power of the Creator, this mighty bond of man, religion, had been burst asunder, by the odious and vile machinations of myriads of peculiar faith that assumed her province.

Rational religion needs no martyrs; she depends on truth, that will render the world generous to create the noblest links of peace and happiness. Monotheism calls for God's grace. She causes her advocates to meet the views of her tuition by proper elucidation and discussion, hoping that mutual benefit will accrue.

Rational religion directs the legitimate use of all the passions among their towering ambition. The world has grown,wiser and better under her noble auspices in rational morals, that define her peerless excellence over peculiar faith.

Who but she is the protectress of true science, as she ever aims to be right, and lead all aright? No peculiar bible, or its minister, can teach monotheism. If the people were enlightened, and willed right, perfectly untrammeled, all would have rational religion. She teaches the rescue by inherent benevolence, the risk of life, when necessary for exertion of the noblest feelings.

There can be no other but rational religion, all else is idle and absurd, a nullity.

Monotheism has sublime principles, above all bibles of tradition ; and whilst she challenges proof for the last, that never has been given, she yields the best analysis of herself.

With all the courtesy of toleration, we must have uncompromising resistance to all human plans destitute of purity of mind, that does not recognise the unity, and the almighty omnipotence of God.

Why monotheism? Because there can be only one correct view of God ; all others are more or less species of superstition, reckless polytheism ; but monotheism presents the bulwark of principles to all, rich or poor. There can be no hypocrites in rational religion, as she recognises no profit in profession, and no speculating professors.

She has no speculation in worship, nor worship, but adoration of God. God is not to be worshipped by any rite or ceremony, but adored in the purity of mind.

It is she that separates government from faith, and proscribes faith or church proscription. The mind can only conceive of rational as true religion; any other is superstition.

This question of rational religion is paramount, and above bibles of tradition, that cannot teach, as their writers did not appreciate it.

Rational religion never quarrels. Anything short of rational religion is superstition. Rational belief is true, irrational is untrue. You have for rational religion elements already, if you be rational, to satisfy the most rational mind. Why, then, change the real genuine for the counterfeit? Appreciate at once and forever the right functions—those of time, of sense, rational action.

Who could not glory in being a monotheist, free from bigotry, ready to reason, and bow to the decrees of rational religion? Who wants irrational faith, when none but rational religion is true? We can only ask for this as the purest to hope, live, and die by. Rational is the legitimate, real, and substantial. You desire the best triumphs of rational religion, then seek the most rational to be the most successful means of their attainment. Rational religion unites all the fragments of society, all sects into one universal brotherhood. It is the noblest duty of every rational mind to investigate the subject of rational religion.

Define monotheism; it is that which defines the correct adoration of one Supreme Being, in his strictest unity of character and design.

The subject is so deep that it cannot be exhausted, and rises in confirmed sublimity on the advance of mental light, that will illuminate the world, the universe.

The bible of rational mind and religion is the only one that can be given the world; there can be no other. The world's happiness requires principles.

Rational religion is demonstrable, whilst all the rest is mere peculiar faith, nothing but dogmatism, vicious superstition, idolatry, bigotry.

The only thing consistent with herself is rational religion. In the essential points of their faith, all monotheists are obliged to agree.

Rational religion cannot be secured by any bible of tradition, but secures the people their rights. It is the only, the safe side. Monotheists adore God, the highest act of the highest religion. They are honest to acknowledge that they are indebted to mind's action upon mind for progressive light on mind, next to God. Liberal, generous, cultivated, refined, civilized mind is concerned for the perfection of monotheism, not to be caviling or quibbling about its minor errors, that will correct themselves. Monotheism is perfect, and requires mind's perfect appreciation. Can this be done on this earth?

Rational mind can only believe in one Supreme, identified with unity of existence and design.

Monotheism inculcates, that if there were no law written, that with the present organization of the universe, rational mind is bound to act rightly on its noble principles. Peculiar faith could not exist on this noble rationality.

Who meets fairly and honorably the arguments of monotheism? The advocates of sophistry?

Rational religion demonstrates herself, whereas all peculiar faiths resort to all the low intrigues of sophistry to reach the position of imposition.

Rational religion thinks or originates as rational mind directs, by the right standard, whereas peculiar faith of superstition, the highest that can possibly be attained, binds to her car the worshippers of self-interest and fear. The difference between rational religion and peculiar faith is so vast that mere children can analyze after their attention is rightly fixed. The first starts with the premises of God, the glorious universe; the last starts with man's premises, the inventions of the priestocracy. The one shows her revelation in creation, the other a meagre black-letter pretence; christianity and all analogous being false, because sectarian. God's revelation is written in the annals of creation's records, forever brilliant, as forever true.

It is written by God's grace, that towers above justification by blood, that is conceived in ignorance, and perpetuated in bloody iniquity, following in the footsteps of its ignoble predecessor. Peculiar faith trades on the capital of rational religion for good, as it must embrace principles to reach the comprehension. A part of every bible of peculiar faith has a part of religion mixed with it. The situation of the world requires the full and comprehensive exercise of religion, not base mixtures, as was and is done at Rome, in China, America, the world. All the morality, religion, and good ostensibly derived from peculiar faith, as Christianity, Judaism, Mahomedanism, Mormonism, Brahminism, Bhuddism, Confucianism, Lamaism, are derived from God's fund, religion. All this is by the immutable laws of nature, that display God Supreme, sublime in intelligence, power, and goodness. Christianity has its pretended revelation, as Judaism; but religion must look to the universe, its annual and eternal record for the truth. Short of that, mind cannot find it.

Mind has the world-machinery, now let it put it into motion most certainly, as otherwise useless to the people, who should act at once, constantly and rightly. What is rational faith? You need not be alarmed that any of the degraded examples of compulsion or seduction of peculiar faith will be imitated by rational faith. She abhors all such. When there is anything wrong in her circle, it is improper construction, that must be amended. Her voice, not that of her advocates, her principles, not their policy, are to be canvassed. Natural religion and revealed faith do not harmonize. As they clash, one is surely wrong. The first cannot possibly have any sectarianism; the last is made up with it, blasphemous to God, unjust to man, not dealing in fact, but in sophistry and cant. Revelation takes away free agency of mind, and makes no merit in reason. Revelation is not begun by books.

The highest moral or religious reformation is rational, with God for the standard.

The ancients are quoted to us as if they had fathomed all science, whereas they knew but little of it accurately; hence their miserable blunders about faith, morals, and above all, rational religion.

Peculiar faith alone was known to them. None knew of monotheism in its purity, for the priestocracy was in every thing the alloy with pure metal. Rational religion is before the age, if the priestocracy will let alone what is right.

It deals in facts of reason. It is obligatory on the world, the people as patriots and citizens, good and true, to carry out the rational and religious principles. How have they been met? Have the people made themselves acquainted with them, as essential as the noblest principles of freedom? Will the priestocracy begin to do justice to such a sublime cause, when they are in the quagmire of their own peculiar self-interest and correspondent faiths? Do they pretend to meet any real issues when they take hold of the little unessential points of controversial errors, not the pure and immutable principles?

Rational religion teaches to realize the beauties, strength and virtue of the world, to read it as it is, and elicit therefrom all that is practicably good. Have you put yourself on investigation of what its system is capable? Do you know the relative capacities of the different systems? The chaste aspirations of rational religion tend to produce a generous rivalry throughout the world, while she is competent to arrest and silence all the collisions of sects, no matter where and how widely diffused, relying, as she does, on obvious plain facts, and a convincing demonstration.

Her great triumph is, that souls cannot, otherwise than by her inherent elements of uniform protection, be best prepared for close of life, either by contingency or in the natural course of events, and that by fiction of peculiar faith that usurps her capital.

That thing of contingent repentance by preaching of the gospel or not, believing or not, is unsound and irrational, and nothing after it is supposed to be established. The soundest state of the world's mind requires proper proof, and ere that be given of the gospel, that never has been properly proved, the soul passes into another state of existence. Where would the soul have been but for its inherent elements of religion?

Mind had not been able to meet all this contingency, if God had not instituted an almighty providence. The pretence of the gospel men that theirs is the only way to be saved, is an insult to a freeman's mind. The horrid picture they draw of monotheism, as certain to destroy a man's soul for present and future happiness, is unparalleled imposition.

Rational religion teaches us to act so that all ages may be satisfied that justice is done, that philosophy approves, science portrays and conscience confides in. After all the sectarian denunciations of monotheism, you will find the most awful ignorance of principles, not only among the people, but their ministers. Now, cannot they be at least modest in all this matter! They affirm to the monotheism of the Jews' peculiar faith, as it was, and deny that of the perfect unity of God, pure and immutable as mind can now make it! While the whole of Christianity have to advocate the peculiar faith doctrines of the Old Testament to reach their own position, they most inconsistently betray themselves in regard to the only pure religion, which they libel. Monotheism commenced with mind and time, for the good of both, whereas peculiar faith commenced long after both, with the priestocracy to corrupt both. Who would give the title-bond indisputable of the first for the counterfeits of the last? The theological sophists have tried to supersede rational religion by their own peculiar faith. Unless we institute rational religion as a consummation, we stop short of the ultimate final earthly dignity, as we would mar the soul's dignity by merely closing with mind. There can be no true humility but through the recognition of God. This produces the only true conversion, as it begets the most entire confidence, and the most conclusive resignation to his divine will, that is supreme in justice and intelligence. All this position looks relatively at all mankind, in regard to merits and retributive justice. The doctrine that a child or person is prepared for future happiness under a certain age, or of a certain way of belief or faith, and beyond or out of that, no matter how close, condemned, is odious, detestable, and abominable, revolting to all principles of justice and intelligence. The world has to adopt the system of rational religion sooner or later, as " the truth, the whole truth, and nothing but the truth," for the people, the whole people, and nothing but the people—for mind, rational and religious. Then things will be called by their right names. Under this position, the church, the hierarchy, the priestocracy get all that honest and truthful modest people ought to ask for. The people are the proper guardians of the world, and should act for each other in all legitimate constitutional ways. What is a worse animal than man, when irrational? He is a mixture of nearly all the animals, when debased. Surely, the whole comprehension of rationality can best protect him. What state in this world is that wherein the people can get along with the least evil, sin, difficulty and antagonism? Is it Christianity, or any best of peculiar faith? All such, as sectarianism, presents antagonism. As a necessary consequence, it is monotheism. Wise, honest, truthful and faithful people ought to give up the useless contest. The wise man will not commit himself to a bad cause, nor leave a good one; therefore he will adapt himself always best to the circumstances of his creation, with proper reference to present and future improvement. What is harmful in rational religion? Is the parson's objurgation any argument? If monotheism be right, as rational mind must conscientiously believe, is it not the most infamous blasphemy to oppose it? By this position only can justice be done all nations. The advocates of peculiar faith assume their usurpation. Religion should cause the world to avoid all sophistry, let alone all false pretences in faith. Monotheism is the only correct view of the Almighty Creator of the universe. What can give a more exalted idea? All peculiar faiths are ungrateful prodigals, that have to bow to the majesty of monotheism, their mistress. Theirs is a false position, of subordinates.

What can all the peculiar faith people do with monotheism? Their best efforts are futile against this, the only religious doctrine of God. Well, say they, their bible doctrine must be true, and the only word of God, and that those who dissent must be against their God. The only proper answer to any question depends on the nature of it, discovered on correct analysis. Now, all their position is not only the most dangerous sophistry, but it is really right down blasphemy.

The bible-god only has one flat four-cornered world, that rested on pillars, and a hemisphere of heavens for his creation, and peculiar characteristics besides. He is the God that for four thousand years restricted himself to one small people, the Jews, and left the balance of the world and creation to shift for themselves. Then he left even on this globe alone, some one hundred and thirty-three generations of the people, allowing two hundred millions for each of thirty years, some twenty-six billions of mankind, most recklessly for that time. To such absurd results do all the peculiar bible-mongers come. This is too great a God-libel for the most vulgar unsophicated mind to accept. People have not thought of these things. But they pretend that all the combined wisdom of the ancient philosophers and systemizers never could originate the idea that the Jew bible did. And what does that prove, after all? Religion? Not at all: only that Judaism was a peculiar faith doctrine, and even that not original, as Moses, the writers affirm, was skilled in all the learning of the Egyptians. Surely, it would pester any rational mind to follow, much less invent, such absurd doctrines. No wonder the Hebrews were always wrong in this superstition, when they were misled all the time from the right influence of mind.

They were not permitted to use the noble and independent prerogatives of mind, but were ignominiously tied down to all vassal restrictions of mind. How could they extricate themselves? They could not escape from military, political, nor priestocracy-barbarism, and are suffering to this day, the bitterest dregs of that odious and abominable superstition, the remnant of a denationalized people, an exotic on the globe. What a curse to their nation.

Where, in the mean time, was that pure rational religion, that exalts the world, and ennobles mind? The Jews never possessed it.

What, after all the boastings of the priestocracy, all their falsifications of history of the world, this was not possessed by the world?

All their pretensions about the philosophers not finding it, are absurd and silly, for all their systems fall short of it. What is christianity? Aye, one of the worst of sectarianisms, and pagan at that, all of which have the elements of death in themselves. The whole brood of Judaism down to Mormonism, is in that category.

What, the Son of God, sectarian and pagan? Yes, as much as Foe, Fohi or Bhudd, his prototype, many years before him. All are ignominious sectarianisms, distinct from monotheism or rational religion, the only one legitimate or in existence.

How, but by usurpation, effrontery and monopoly, have they triumphed? They have crushed and silenced the lawful heirs, because the mind of the world was not competent to defend its rights.

Have not mind and science done all that we see done, by the conservative principles of God? The Jews had no just conceptions of the God of the Universe, certainly not of his attributes, nor of rational religion, that is the best action of duty on the highest appreciation to God and man.

There is no just idea of a God, but in monotheism, and that of course, the Jews did not have. Their whole doctrine was of a peculiar god, that had a peculiar people, that claimed him as their peculiar protector against the world, and thus setting the whole world at variance with itself and religion! Were there ever such ignorance and presumption? Such blasphemy, unless with the modern priestocracy, who do not know what they say, when they affect the Jews had pretensions to religion, much less the God of the Universe! when they did not know either? How stupid is even the worst Jesuit, to commit himself on these false pretences! The lights of monotheism will disclose at once the whole idea of church sophistry, which no man can duly estimate, till he sees and hears the whole. What is their faith? Peculiar. They act against monotheism with perfect assassination, having broken into the chambers of religion, and carried off a caricature, a pretended original, peculiar faith, to oppress the world. With all seeming fairness, they befouled the whole world.

The bible-people cannot touch the subject of monotheism that towers in the sublimity of its own greatness, established by its immortal author.

All that they say against it impeaches them, because all their side is of men, not of God, for they continually libel God. Monotheism was the first and only religion necessarily instituted, all others are pretenders; then peculiar faith, as Judaism, and all her brood Christianity, Mahommedanism and Mormonism, are all pagan, parricides and assassins. The opponents of monotheism, often do not understand, and the bible-partisans misrepresent the object, as if it were a pity that sectarianism, peculiar faiths, and their bibles, should be put down. But, as the last cannot stand, but must fall, monotheism must be elevated to her dignified rank in the world. Her purity was never conceived by the adherents of Judaism nor her offspring. Her dignity is above all peculiar faiths. Yet their ministers pretend that a change from the peculiar bible-faith, would necessarily result in atheism.

That is not the fact at all, but the reverse for the better, if the truth be followed rightly. Polytheism and atheism are convertible—monotheism is above both. Such pretend that all the so-called wise men of the ancient world, could not devise a proper system of religion, and that God devoted all of four thousand years to their trial. All this is perfect nonsense. All these pretenders, with their philosophers, stuck in quagmire. Action of mind on mind, only evolves in time the appropriate results in all matters that concern the world. Will these ministers fix time and mind-limits, by their absurd standard? All the peculiar faith philosophers, with all their bibles, have done nothing for the God of the universe. Under the misrepresentation of polytheists and atheists, who have not their eyes open to their own blindness, monotheism cuts short immortal hopes in a future state! The simple question might be asked, are the unprincipled opponents mind-deranged bible-bullies? Some of polytheists deplore under the state of ruins, necessarily arising from the destructive elements of their faith christianity, that atheism will be the result. Atheism is as good as polytheism, both are absurd. But monotheism results, if man have the whole truth, and trust the balance to the God of truth. The bible stands or falls on this proposition, that it must be the truth, the whole truth, and nothing but the truth, which is not supported by true time for the author of even a part of those scriptures. It is utterly impossible for Moses to have been the sole author of the first five books as claimed, since no man can write his own obituary, and other matters subsequent to his history.

But the polytheists will not let monotheists die peaceably, but advance their pious frauds, as if that altered the correct position of religion.

When polytheism resorts to such shifts, she is nearly run out.

Too many people, on their supposed death-beds, have proved a triumph, satisfied to resign their spirit to the Creator alone. Indeed, what other is the safe position? All the clan of priestocracy, along with their laity, may pretend otherwise, but is it not an insidious malign pretence to deceive the world? Neither polytheists nor atheists, with all their advocacy, can touch monotheism that was God-written from the first, that has been most awkwardly imitated, and most ungratefully libeled by the two first. But how are heresies, the heterodox faiths, to be managed? By the orthodox. Facts only declare for monotheism.

The world will be savage, barbarous and hostile in parts, till that is universal; of so much consequence is rational religion to decide mind's refined rationality.

People may talk of polytheism and atheism, but monotheism is what all are bound to come to, if right be the world. Mere toleration will not do : the world has to act right, the sooner the better. This declares that the True God can only be read of through the universe by mind.

Then this matter of monotheism is God's, not man's, that renders it truly holy, just, good and true. Are not the principles of monotheism conservative, and of God? Let any opponent deny this, truthfully, if he can. His own utter ignorance will alone save him from being considered unprincipled. As nothing but principles will carry a rational being properly through life, then monotheism, that authorizes and enjoins them, is absolutely essential. The principles of monotheism permit no popes nor priestocracies, peculiar gods, people, nor messiahships.

Monotheism sanctions no position at all, of unprincipled characters, who renounce bibles to get rid of moral and religious, civil, social and relative duties, but requires all rational beings to improve in all principles, to the most refined civilization.

What immorality in those who object pretendedly to monotheism, that they cannot touch, to support trash that cannot support itself without hire, bribery and corruption to perjury. Let the whole truth be told.

The errors of mind are not to be put to the account of monotheism. The last is perfect as of God ; the other is more or less objectionable, as of men, as it departs from the noble principles of the last.

Monotheism is unapproachable by atheism and polytheism, in their devices and ramifications. Then let no good citizen define monotheism by mind's errors, but by God's principles.

Those who think a pious fraud by the scriptures no sin, had better take up the truth, the whole truth, and nothing but the truth, of monotheism, the only way that God reveals himself to mind.

I invoke the sublimest protection of all that mind can rear, for refined civilization of the world, all that true religion, monotheism, can do for mankind. It is she alone that is hallowed by God himself; let all blasphemous idolators and libelers beware how they encroach on God's sacred functions. It is the cause they must look at, not the advocates. How few can see the remote, proper, comprehensive bearing of subjects, especially in monotheism? The minister of peculiar bible faith, berates that position, sophisticating the whole subject, seeking to prejudice the people, and winds up after all, self-exposed and condemned in the infamous attack of a subject, that he, all his aid, the whole world's peculiar faith cannot touch.

The priestocracy are wound up by the sublime subject of monotheism. Man must not forsake his judgment for any man, when it is founded on right justice and reason, otherwise he cannot form it.

Mind must avoid bigotry, injustice and intentional error, as it most conclusively does in monotheism.

The world should possess an honorable analysis and action, despite of all social, civil or ecclesiastical despotism. Can we expect the world to do itself justice, when it does not know what is justice ? The whole world should be able to think justly for itself, in all matters of mind and religion, which is the height of refined civilization.

Monotheism originates all the virtues of all the peculiar faiths, without their vices, errors and crimes. Religion ought to reflect as a mirror the attributes of God, and noblest elevation of mind. None but monotheism can do that.

If there be one only truth on earth, it is monotheism or rational religion. It is the loveliest of all principles, as it comprehends all—all truth practicable for mortals. The priestocracy that oppose it, expose themselves every step, not only their nakedness, but their deformity and obliquity. They think themselves the privileged class to attack it, but in that is their greatest weakness, as all theirs is the veriest patchwork on previous botch-work. Monotheism can gloriously triumph over all prejudices, all sectarianisms; all uncivilized fragments of peculiar education. It is the interest, the highest duty of all intelligent minds, to lay hold of it, to put down all sectional, sectarian demagogism of the whole world, especially of the priestocracy, which ought to be discarded as its cause, the way they oppose monotheism. The whole world ought to know analytically what monotheism is, and most gratefully thank their God that they can do so. Monotheism is sacred, is God-created. Its sublime supremacy is over all peculiar faiths, it rises the only representative of the God of the universe, pure, innocent and unsullied, though unsung, yet most honored and glorious. Stop, priestocracy, your vulgar blasphemous babblings.

Monotheism is the only means for the world to adjust itself to all the developments of time. She is God-given, adapted to the best faculty of man's soul, his conscience, and is the highest duty to God and the universe, to mankind and the world.

The bible bullies cannot touch monotheism, though their language is vulgar, and their intentions blasphemous. That is monotheism that ever perfects the best system of most refined civilization of mankind, throughout the world. The world owes it to itself, to analyze its position. Release not your creation-birth-right rational religion, for all the peculiar faiths of all the world priestocracy, who should not succeed if they were to pay the world to accept their pretences. Monotheism is something worth looking at, whereas there is no truth uttered by the priestocracy about peculiar faith, that has no existence. The monotheists must be organized. The books of monotheism have no peculiarity or any mysteries. They teach that the people of the world are bound one to another. That man is a social being, and would go right in affections without antagonism, unless others excite a contrary interest. The world has been harassed time out of mind, by supposed contrary interests for church and priestocracy speculation, whereas monotheism unites the whole in one paramount necessary duty, that of rational religion. Therefore the world has never analyzed this subject faithfully. Give the world the subject of monotheism, and all will have to come to the same main conclusions. Religion is to civilize the world, now how can you by peculiar faith, bring all the others to civilization? They will reverse it.

Having completely satisfied myself of the validity of monotheism, considering it one of the most high-minded of my life, it now remains for me to introduce it before the whole world, as most worthy of its notice and adoption. This subject of monotheism is endless. The monotheists have their minds in constant abeyance to true humility. confidence and gratitude to the author of perfection, and go for thanksgivings, humiliation and abstemiousness, not fasting, all the time.

Some minds may affect or act as if God had no particular care : if polytheists find fault with any appreciation by monotheists, they will please help amend all that is imperfect. They should know that monotheism expands, while peculiar faith contracts the characteristics of God and mind. But mind has not taught men right. There is the point of difficulty, which has but rational mind under rational religion ? What has all the pretence of revelation done ? What were more contemptible than the Jewish notions of an adulterated priestocracy speculation that was as far from religion as their peculiar god was removed from the God of the universe ? As wrong as that, christianity, that is founded on it, is worse. The Jews made one peculiarity, and the christians make several, whereas monotheism declares for no peculiarity. She teaches that God established all his immutable laws, of course, at the creation of the universe, of which this world is only part, when all matters were created.

But how shall all this matter be fairly decided ? Bigots and priestocracies will put down all books not of their faith, as they are after their peculiar faith, not truth. Will they not run from the advocates of monotheism, or evade the justice of the position by proscribing all their books before as much of the world as they can influence to a false position and opinion ? •

I have seen the advocates of peculiar faith avoid monotheists, to avoid meeting their propositions on premium to prove the authenticity of their scriptures. Monotheists have no peculiarity about their principles ; for if they possess anything of this, there is something wrong. The principles should be modestly but firmly advocated, by dissemination of facts. All peculiar faiths unite speculation, while pure monotheism excludes all such. It is one of the most difficult things for some people to take a correct and firm stand, and hold out to the consummation, but on this platform mind can hold most conscientiously and knowingly. There is no doubt about all this.

I know that the vulgar, who adopt the loose ideas of deism, as trammeled by previous restrictions, or those that libel the correct position, think that it is to cut loose from all moral and orderly restraints, but the highest of all monotheism puts no such constructions, as it feels bound to the noblest principles of rational religion. It is no more accountable for loose constructions or malign libels, than one peculiar faith is accountable for the peculiarities of the other faiths. She holds no peculiar dogma, nor can hold any, and if it be put in her sacred precincts, mind, refined in its noblest civilization will exclude it. We are not spiritual but rational beings on this earth, hence religion is rational that includes all that may be spiritual. Rational religion teaches mankind to attain the highest of all that is lofty, magnificent, and sublime.

What is the good of monotheism ? All good, to cut down all the false pretences of polytheism or trinitarianism, and nonsense of atheism, all paganism.

If there were no other means for mind to do better in belief or faith, then I would be silent; but here is the glorious rational religion deserted for a false faith, and all that is degrading in the frame-work for perjury, if carried out, and does cause millions to damn themselves by perjury, and risks their souls any way. Is this manly, American, or republican? Can any honest mind require of the world a sacrifice of all that is sacred before God, for the minor, base considerations of no value—devices of mankind?

Rational religion gives justice, and deals in beneficence. Monotheism has conservative principles of the universe, adores the Creator in his supreme and eternal unity.

All defects apparent are in the mind of the receiver or the imparter, and not in the position.

I do not declare my individual opinions, only as the exponent of rational religion, and abide all correction that is legitimate. All the unprincipled opponents of religion, advocates of peculiar faith, ought to remedy all the defects of monotheism's exposition, which is not monotheism, if wrong. She depends on her principles, God-given, not fails on man's exposition. She has no priestocracy. All, as people, whether they will or no, are under the holy banners of religion. Will they, as rational minds, improve it, to the loftiest rationality?

I know that rational religion is the right and safe side, God's, nature's, truth's, reason's, that of the universe. Rational religion forever, and nothing less.

All questions of rational religion can only be answered properly by the whole comprehension of the universe, the world, mind, all God-relations. Nothing short of that will do for the immortal soul. This world and universe-wide problem has to be solved. Then how can a petty, paltry book called bible, meet the correct position, condemned, positively convicted, by line and precept, of being anything else?

Religion covers the whole ground of rational mind victoriously, as the God-gift from mind-creation, while peculiar faith only pretends to help the peculiar possessor, an intruder into the legitimate premises of the first, that is as ancient as mind, while peculiar faith sprouts up like a mushroom, a mere fungus, a parasite of the moment, and always subsequent to mind's functions, that clearly rule all its nefarious innovations, as futile and impotent.

This thing will not do at all. When we say rational religion irradiates rational mind, we mean mind cultivated to its proper state, regulated by conservative principles, that guard it strictly against lust, drunkenness, absolutism, especially peculiar faith, and the obnoxious peculiar education.

The world needs religion of principles, to cause mankind to solve the noblest problem of mind, that has not been accomplished by any one nation. The United States commenced the problem, now the way is clear, let their actions in clear light prove.

No extraordinary tradition can be truthful as of religion, as all such are incompatible with the immutability and perfection of Deity. As all honorable religious positions are necessarily truthful, they cannot be less than rational. All religion is in order, none can be extraordinary.

All bibles affecting tradition, that are not rational, are not truthful, therefore not religious.

All rationality is compatible with truth, and all faith that is not compatible with the first must be excluded by the last. There can be no religion but what is rational, and all faith that is good must be consistent thereto. Who has religion? All rational beings; they that do most justice to their fellow man extend it in the scale of rationality.

Is not Christianity religion? Not a particle of it. How come Christians to excel the world? They do not. Those that are good, are so by mind that is relatively rational. What is Christianity? Western buddhism, and all, paganism. All are equal, and differ only in the relative state of mind that is either more or less rational.

The monotheist knows certainly, that God's word, cause and effect, declare to the whole universe what religion is. Now peculiar faith has none of it, but is in conflict thereto, and as it is antagonistic to principles, as a culprit and felon the blasphemy of all, excludes all. Their stupidity prevents their seeing. Instead of being hostile to the author, they ought to be grateful for the exposure, and amend their ways by the illustrious light of rational religion.

Let an intelligent, honest press do me, itself, God, mind, justice. If people were to perpetrate crimes on government as they do against religion, by peculiar faith, they could be rightly adjudged monsters of iniquity, fraud, deception, tories and traitors. They do not act man-like nor God-like, but priestocracy-like. It is not partisan feelings, but justice to be evoked, in this momentous subject. Let all the feelings legitimate be aroused, but let them be established on just views.

Whether principals or protestants, you go for religion? All of it, in its purity, but none of peculiar faith, bibles, or people. But does monotheism conflict with peculiar faith? No, sir. The last has counterfeited it all the time, and libeled truth. Peculiar faith perpetrates fraud, and sustains it with bloodshed—religion elevates the mind and the world, all the time.

Why has the world deserted rational religion? Is it on account of fool-bibles, bible-bigotry, bigot priestocracies, priest-kings? Put down all such stuff. The world has to put them all down by conservative revolution, the sooner the better. The rational world must not let all such take advantage of it any longer. Do you call this their profession, religion? Are you a monomaniac, or is your mind so imbecile, so degraded priestocracy, as to impose the base fund of polytheism and atheism for monotheism, on the world? Are you so tory, as to sell all that is noble in mind and principle, for their abomination? Cannot the American people carry out the great life, mind, soul, universe-religion, the God-problem?

Religion, that is rational, is the sublimest of all creations; next the immortal soul, it towers to the height of mind, the depth of creation.

Instead of making skepticism, atheism and self-sufficiency, monotheism institutes at the start rational religion. It has none of the speculative mysteries of atheism. Religion is no mystery: it is the highest rational duty. As man is rational let him have proper discussions, liberal, &c., for best improvement.

The question is not as to the popularity, but its correctness. If popes were to consult the propriety of religion, they would not be prisoners to their own creed. A fair trial and nothing less, that proper justice may be done mind of the public, is demanded by monotheism. The principles of protection, are for the paramount good of the world's society. All religious, is as expedient as political discussion, to reach the right appreciation. The truths of monotheism are sacred.

In justice to creation of mind, it should have a proper religion of principles as suited to the whole human family, but peculiar faith is unsuited to all. Responsibility of mind's agency is comprehended by monotheism presenting a proper potency over the will, the most characteristic of good qualities. The rights of rational education embrace religion, that gives the most exalted conscience.

What is the difference between deism and monotheism? Deism, the opponents say, has been incompetent to defend religion or meet its question, and monotheism by Brande has been wofully misconstrued as peculiar faith illustrated as such. I adopt monotheism as defining most exactly, all that pertains to rational religion.

She only makes the refined gentleman, in all senses of the word when she invests rational mind with all the purity of rational religion. One can only live religious on principles, all others are trifles. Monotheists above all others have to be extremely thoughtful and cautious in all their duties, else they may sadly err.

The practically religious, are the rational religionists. Social, moral, and religious duties, with knowledge, are implied in rational religion.

Nothing less than monotheism can take proper care of conscience, therefore individual responsibility must demand at once the absolute expulsion of all peculiar faiths. Prevention is godlike, far beyond counteraction, good as it is, and this monotheism does as there is no honesty or sense in faith, as mere faith is all nonsense. The professors of such faith have no bible—poor blockheads, only the humbugs of the priestocracy who have published their false pretences. They have no bible of their own, but seek to make hypocrites and sophists. Mind can see the world debased by drink, peculiar education and faith, and all the peculiar results. Now what religion can all these shadows of peculiar endowments present? They end in trash, instead of leaving mind to secure the high purposes of creation. The religion of principles causes all rational minds to come the nearest, to be a law unto themselves.

In respect to God, taking him for all in all unity, the least of all mistakes and the least of all atonements expedient therefor would be committed. No one but the priestocracy would start their metaphysics, and none but their dupes affiliated could receive it. Again, what of all systems, including all theirs, if this be wrong can be right, or do less error? This is the paramount question, if speculation was necessary, but we have omnipotent facts that preclude all such. What is practicable, in all that can be started? To the God of the universe is due adoration, gratitude for the divine faculty of religion that has no abuses, no defects, that are referable to peculiar faiths of fallible arrogant minds, as of popes and priests.

The ennobling sentiments of patriotism and philanthropy emanate from religion.

Reason may then be the God of monotheists? Not at all, as it is the agent to appreciate rightly the God of all. What would the world be but for monotheism, rational religion? That is nothingariness. How can that be, when all the religion, not only in the world but in the whole universe, is that? All that peculiar faiths have is taken altogether from this fount, and trade on this capital. When detected in the stealth, they, like convicted sophists or bigots, fly from reason into passion, instead of from the last to the first, and disavow honestly, abjure truthfully all the blasphemous plagiary which does not avail them, but impoverishes mind indeed.

Monotheism commands entire disbelief in all peculiar faith's bibles and priestocracies, as especially their peculiar god, and sincere trust in religion and the God of the universe.

But some do not wish a change from their vicious errors of faith, deeming that blindly adopted as taught, enough. Such minds do not wish to become wise in wisdom of God, but stupidly persist in the detected, exposed, and exploded false pretences of dishonest men.

Establish a proper view of the religion of principles, and then all whining and cant about faiths would be at an end, and all would have fixed principles. The atheist is defective in the comprehension of the whole subject. What principles have atheism and polytheism? This earth, as universe, abides on conservative principles. Atheism and polytheism abide in their fixed dogmatic bigotries, man's conceitedness. The monotheist adopts universe facts, and uses them for the greatest good to rational mind. The absurd positions of the others can only abide for the time of bigotry.

What year shall the monotheist adopt? In the absence of better, it will be well to adopt the year of American Independence, till that of universal mind is proclaimed by monotheism, the presidency of which will establish a perfect independence for the world.

Monotheism furnishes the only standard of God. It is the principle advancer of conservative peaceable revolution, whilst polytheism and atheism cause bloody revolution. Rational education only calls for conservative revolutions, the best of arguments for universal light of mind.

Are you after intellectual, honest, rational truth, or are you a vassal of priestocracy and their invention, peculiar bibles? If for the last, then are you tory to your God and mind, for the bribery of a peculiar god.

Monotheism stands on a platform commensurate with the universe, and is the only advocate of the religion of principles; and this is the potent silencer of all peculiar faiths and bibles, people and dogmas or doctrines that split the social world into fragments, instead of imparting the universal brotherhood of monotheism, that blends all in one harmonious unity, consecrated by universal peace and dignity. Socialism is only when legitimate, a constituent.

Is it not absolutely essential, then, for refined civilization, for this last best age of man, that rational mind should be educated rationally, to attain rational religion?

How long before rational analysis will demonstrate beyond contradiction that peculiar faiths, however numberless, are all false, and that there is but one religion—the creation's birth-right of rational mind, the diamond of the universe, and that on principles established as an element by the conservative Creator of the universe, a perfect being, whose prescience and omniscience precluded subsequent covenants, the after-thoughts of priestocracy, or tithe-monarchs.

Where was all religion prior to such characters, for thousands of years? Then as now, independent of them.

In the whole comprehension of this magnificent subject, hasty and partial views may have caused mind the commission of errors that are incident to all fallible mortals; but as a monotheist, I ask to have the correction on the highest principles of rationality.

Whatever is wrong in this work is so from the human mind, and not in monotheism. That is unlike polytheism which uses all kinds of inquisitions to manufacture opinions at variance with principles, and the universal benefit of mankind. The first never desires any decisive measures to be taken to check the progress of principles. Principles belong to the God of the universe, and are universal. What fallible mortals can gainsay that?

Monotheism discards all men's bibles, and urges the adoption of religion's.

What are the purposes of creation? Of the highest, noblest, most universal, monotheism begins and ends with the Creator; socialism begins with mind, that has to solve the mighty problem. I do not know about the present popularity of this subject, but I know I am right, as far as I can know anything by the universe-proofs. Monotheism enables us to make all legitimate capital out of misfortunes. She is the only means to effectually put down all peculiar faiths. With her, now, the people truly have the mastery in their own hands, over the most insidious priestocracy. The only question for the people is to know, is it right? The result will tell, and silence all the ignorant cluns of all sects and denominations. It will take away their foul game of humbuggery and imposition.

God is the vitalizing supremacy. Mind needs a correct standard of moral and social laws, with religion. It can never attain them short of monotheism. All peculiar bible systems caricature them, do injustice to God and man. The feelings of enthusiasm and fanaticism will be cut down by monotheism, that furnishes all harmonizing principles of philanthropy. Mr. Brande undertakes to define monotheism, and misrepresents it under the dogmas of peculiar faith most unjustly. Mind is to disabuse the world, discover and remedy the evils of peculiar education.

This is a universe of rational principles, that are active.

How did nature, that is passive, do that? Here we see the confounded notions of the atheist, whom also mind must silence.

To make rational mind rightly responsible, it must be so at the bar of rational principles: it can never be so at the bar of peculiar doctrines, as peculiar bible advocates would have us believe. Free agency is in abeyance to reason and rational circumstances, not to credulity and peculiar views, more or less monomaniac and crazy, absurd, despotic, smuggled, or exploded. There can be no infallible guide to conscience but through enlightened principles, that emanate from an infallible standard of unity. A rational conscience is indissolubly united to rational principles. Principles alone can carry the world with safely and happiness, and principles are concentrated in religion. What can avail over the worst of crimes, the most licentious passions, as lust, revenge, and ambition.

The main question with all minds is not, are you in a church, but, is your mind in abeyance to any principles?

All minds are as the universe, now that allegiance, that religion, is sacred. You then have not to cultivate faith or churches, but religion. What will carry mind through life? Money, power, friends? only that which is identified with conservation of the universe, principles, that which will do it in this and all future existence. Mind only can be sure on this position.

Do you wish never to doubt your religious position? Then see and feel the ennobling beauties and universal blessings of God-given religion, monotheism.

I could conscientiously choose my friends from those who are conscientiously wedded to rational principles, the religion of principles. These exert the only conservative influence on society. Monotheism is that I wish to live and die by; this is it, for the world, for it unites the universe to its God Creator. In what do monotheism and faith differ? If the faith be good there is no difference.

The position will prove the difference, if the faith be bad. Deists yield too much to Christ. Monotheists do not admit him at all.

The moral sublimity is in monotheism, that gives the only happiness in its principles. All others, as peculiar faiths, have no principles except what they select from monotheism, and most ungratefully without acknowledgment.

I desire to have the whole world act in conformity with monotheism, that can only absolutely restrain individual and rational passions, or put them into the legitimate direction.

It furnishes the only system of religious morals to master all world piracies. Atheism cannot do this at all, for it has no standard, no principles. Polytheism comes short of the sublime supremacy of a perfect God-standard.

Monotheism furnishes the only purity of morals—to govern man necessarily, to break up his unhappiness in this peculiar doctrine, his doubts, his death-bed of misery and recantation. The life of peculiar faith is a bad and vicious criminal one, derogatory to mind and its God, Creator, Almighty of the universe.

Monotheism should make men true gentlemen.

When you see the advance of monotheism, then you will see the full blessings of liberty, civil and religious. Is mind prepared for its mighty change?

If monotheism do not prepare it, that which cared for it from creation-birth, what can?

Monotheism does not ask for charity of the world, but requires justice. She does not deal in the coin of fanaticism, but in the bullion of religion.

What enables mind to attain right but the elements of religion? What objection can be found against monotheism? None valid. It is maligned because it confutes all the faiths of polytheism, as Christianity, Judaism, &c., as utterly false. They made their own false position, and monotheism only exposed it. The world has to adopt it as the only good faith—the faith—true and genuine. She that invokes the noblest cultivation of rational mind by the most scientific rational education, can civilize the world to its most refined gentlemanly rationality, or rational refinement. Ladies, above all, should declare for it, as the best protection of their holiest rights.

Monotheism knows no such absurdity and despotism, as priestocracy. Forethought for ever, premises the effectual conservation of all as taught.

Monotheism has the highest respect for man, woman, and child, mind, mankind, that it disabuses the world about the crimes of peculiar faith.

She forbids any to rebel against one of God's laws, with that position, the only legitimate one. All peculiar faiths conflict at once, that can only maintain themselves ostensibly, so far as they can be upheld on that basis, by uniting with the pure elements of monotheism. There is now a world-crisis that must be respected by mind for its own advancement.

Peculiar faith-people, the priestocracy, with their special pleadings, act as if their faith was the light that directed the world to civilization, supplanting mind and monotheism in all that is good. A man is only elevated to the highest scale by monotheism. All minds are bound to do justice to religion, monotheism; and if that be done, all is safe. It is matter of moonshine whether religion is professed or not, the acts of life are. if rational, predicated on that element. It becomes the most rational minds to inquire for their most comprehensive duty.

How often is the term principle abused, misconceived, or misinterpreted, equally as much as that of religion, that comprehends all principles.

There are many things to be fixed hereafter by a world's convention of monotheists, but only the representation of the sovereign people, for the year, names of days and the best appreciation of all other important duties needing. There is much to do for national, individual and world etiquette, subject to progressive revision of rational mind. If the world cannot agree on a universal common year, let it consecrate the day of universal brotherhood as the commencement of that year, and let it drop all the barbarian relics of past ages,—a disgrace to mind. The base of all rational education, is to instil the religion of principles into all rational minds who should be competent to comprehend them. The truly sincere, those desiring religious benefits, have entirely mistaken the means, when they appeal to any doctrines or means of peculiar faith, the last thing to be sought or the first avoided. The world or mind can never grow old into decay, under the protection of conservative principles. Monotheism not only aids mind to obtain a just equilibrium, but to manage crime, and thus obtain a free agency on the influence of principles, that promote all mind's legitimate purposes.

All the acts of monotheism, possess a proper unity. Constitutional government is only part of its principles, that rule mind. The universe must be enlightened by sacred principles, but in becoming of peculiar faith the devotees become sworn sophists, and hardened bigots. Who can become with the lights of conscience a conspirator for peculiar faith, when principles are involved for the universe. The peculiar faith of churches takes hold of policy, while monotheism is based on sacred principles—that perfect mind the noblest work of God,—while the first degrades it, having a vacuum never to oe filled, confined to time and space, while the last has no limit of either, but is universal. Monotheism is blessed with the sacredness of purpose from the eternal creator, while the other is stained with blood or effete explosions, abominable doctrines. Religion belongs to mind, not to the priestocracy, who cannot take charge of it. They cannot do justice to it: it is not in their element when they practice an impiety.

Monotheism is not understood, and is effectually libeled by peculiar faith demagogues. What will not the religion of principles meet? She does not deal in metaphysics, mysteries, but facts. She acts for all times, the future especially, if not appreciated by the present. She may be called free thinking, but her liberality carries her to what is correct comprehension, and she proves the only infidels to be anti-God. She analyzes, to reach correct thinking, no matter how free, so it is accurate; now if that be orthodox, it is rational.

What can promote the greatest good? If that be monotheism as it is, it is established on immutable principles,—stained with no reproach, she has no fear, and is worthy of all admiration.

All associations must be select in faith as in companionship, to insure perfect safety and eternal happiness.

Monotheism elevates, atheism belittles, polytheism perverts nature, the exponent of its creator.

When you appreciate what defence a police is to the city, the country's army is to it when invaded, you can know what the moral force of religion is, over all the despotisms of peculiar faith-world. She meets the wants of the world-mind, the universe, the creator's purpose.

If you go for the right base of religion, this will secure it; you cannot go for anything better. Not only go for religion, but a religious platform: then all will end well, and happily.

This will invoke the right actions, that will cause the world to approve, give right, just, due credit to all your sincere, pure motives. Monotheism specifies accurately, its position.

Religion is the only means that can pilot the soul, that is thereby like the magnet, safely to God. She will give the filling up that can be made by thoughts, words and deeds. She asks in her jurisprudence, does any injure by invasion of social rights, let him abide the penalty of principles. She regards the endless progression on earth of mind, that of immortality of soul-organization. If mind do not do justice to its soul, it commits the worst of pollutions. The denial of immortality to soul, reflects back the miserable bad government of mankind, who have to be ruled, and must be, and if they depend at all on that, such code of religion must be filled up. There is not only hideous deformity, but vacuum there.

In regard to mind that operates to self-destruction or murder, when the proper government of all preservation is interrupted, the function of all is invaded, and if the view of immortality be thus invaded, the correction must follow.

Monotheism predicates the sternest fortitude of religion, its most illustrious results.

In the abstract and pure solitary inspirations of mind, that expose in all its ablest resources of itself, all the degraded contradictions and the absurd stories of the bible, mind decides correctly, but then enslaved to custom, society and opinions of others, it forfeits all pretensions to freedom of mind, and betrays itself most treacherously to its very best teachings.

If religion be universal, how can it be peculiar in time or space ? If God and religion occupy the whole of both, who or what can supersede them ?

Monotheism is the superb work of constitutional liberty, both the brightest emanations of rational mind, the most illustrious of all embodiments. Monotheism teaches to be a man, the height and depth of religion, all honest means, if liberalized, such as the bible of rational mind and constitutional liberty, republicanism, not of toryism, mind-treachery and smuggling, not a question of man's bibles, but of religion, not of man, but of God, Creator, not man's creation. Improper advantage has been taken of man's feelings, to take possession of his senses and rights, superseding mind by faith.

If the ignorance of the priestocracy be arraigned, what must be their duplicity, complicity, conspiracy against the world, to condemn it with all their maledictions of superstition and knavish bigotry, for daring to think aright about bibles to analyze and rescind their false pretences to religion ? They have stopped at nothing to fabricate the whole beastly proscription.

Monotheism has the most elevated of all standards, rational mind and God the universe Creator ; peculiar faith of all shades and tints, its antagonistic, has fanatic man's creation, his bible and gods. The first is of the soul, the last is mercenary. The first carries out all the policy of religion, the last the policy of despotism. Mind has to look up to the first ; man degrades himself in looking down on the last.

The rational world has to rally to the proper rescue for social, moral and religious economy.

Monotheism imparts sympathy of soul, she teaches that there is no enjoyment without independence, no peace without innocence.

Speak not of fictitious plaints of Christs, but see most wisely the demands of the world for religion. Enough is in the world, nay, in the universe, if rightly directed, to secure the benefit of all. Tell us not of charity ; pay, due justice to the imperative demands of the soul. Monotheism gives mind incorruptibility, and soul immortality. Can anything be wrong about her ? Is she not sublimely right ? She permits no sectional factions against government. If anything be deemed wrong, seek redress by overt patriotic acts, as a noble Judge Curtis, not preach treason to government, and perjury to mind in the pulpit, as Parker, of Boston. She bids counteract all the ills of life, by mind. The poor to exhibit no ill-will towards the rich by envy or libel, but properly direct mind-to all that can be legitimately accomplished, to subvert obsolete regimes and empires by rational republicanism. After all, mind will not be found if properly investigated by the lights of monotheism so bad, as we must allow for the bad impressions and false views from the false frame-work of society. Philanthropists will amend the last, with all the sagacity, the wisdom and protection of mind.

The proper tribunal and standard of the religion of principles, is the standard of principles.

She is consistently competent to meet the enlightened test trial, and prove mind and reason as well as herself, that have been all vilely libeled by polytheism, competent for all demonstration, as principles do not clash, all that are these are sublimely thus demonstrated conclusively so.

What is the mighty reaction of religion on the soul, estimate the beautiful reaction of modesty and emotion, that is the mighty response of nature exalted through the sexes. If peculiar faith does as well as its advocates pretend, what will not the religion of principles, the substance, effect ?

Rational religion can meet and defeat, all the sophistry of atheism and polytheism. All that they say of themselves is sophistry, any other is from rational religion, her capital, and to be honestly credited to her unity and identity of mind, no matter about the body.

What can be more fascinating than to live and die a monotheist gentleman, distinguished for religious excellence of character in all that adorns man and mind? It is she that determines non-intervention, holding sacred international treaties, municipal laws and government, by principles of universal justice.

Monotheism will cause rational mind necessarily to respect character, and it institutes ever consistent with itself, a correct view of things, far different from peculiar faiths that differ with each peculiarity. She carries peace ever. She that teaches the highest confidence, that of humility in the Almighty, imparts the principles for the firmest confidence to mind and men, a great desideratum to mankind, while peculiar faith exhibits confidence betrayed.

Can you cavilers or critics object legitimately, to rational religion? Then you are unprincipled, positively, for she is only the consummation, the religion of principles. You are anti-principles as anti-Creator.

Monotheism is pre-eminently conservative and progressive, and has conservative revolutions for her eminent excellent civilization.

Of all nations, this has the greatest materials for national exaltation, and to do it effectually, it has to secure the everlasting benefits of monotheism. It has to cherish it with the deepest affection. Mind in its individual capacity is ever to guard this, for its chief good. How can man ever bear up best and most independently against all the storms of life, without this holy protection? How shall the stranger in all the vicissitudes of life, meet all arising difficulties, without proper references founded on appropriate deportment?

The American mind should seek that which ennobles and makes wise, imparts popular confidence.

Monotheism honors every honorable draft, meets all the requisitions of mind, refers universally to universal relations, and meets universal obligations.

Religion gives the commandments of the God of the universe that have universal, not peculiar relations, which, if mind refuse, that mind is liable to a suicidal negation of universal benefits.

Now the universal commandments satisfy and qualify all the universal wants of mind up to the soul organization, and not only silence all opposition, all criticism, but win the highest tribute of gratitude and adoration.

Not so is it with any of the patch-works of peculiar or pagan faiths. The highest claims of any faith besides that of monotheism, can only be pagan all the time, pagan in nature, and results, self-evident.

Monotheism makes this avowal by the best appreciation of the author of this book, that there is this about Providence, that his own special representatives, conservative principles fully and ably vindicate.

Let the most comprehensive views be taken of this whole subject, and much of it will be apparent.

Try it any way. Is it fornication, promiscuous or special. What are the results, but most specially nugatory of future good?

The parties that are led astray are victims of that or future acts of worse habits. They are not protected against further aggression on principles, as they may commit or suffer murder, infanticide, foeticide, disease, death, infamy, and a host of ruinous consequences, the character ruined and blasted, as that of their family, more or less, the mind affected, deranged, the feelings gone, the sensibility undermined. Is it rationally that we look, then we see a vast vista of good lost and advantages destroyed.

While the crowning triumph of republicanism is monotheism, exalting Americans free and happy to be men, as monotheists, seeing the loveliness of their constitutional government, that is most closely allied to their greatest temporal advantages, yet should they forego the highest obligations of a proper international code, they may alienate too extensively their future permanency.

The best of nations have to guard most strictly their sacred non-intervention from aggression, into the municipal regulations of others, in the great sisterhood of nations. The sword of retributive justice, is one that cuts every way, and prostrates the proudest.

The means of degradation, conclusively the worst and last, that turned the scale against despotism, was peculiar faith, the dupe of mind, the despoiler of its purity, and will sink all to practicable perdition.

Monotheism commands the dignity of nations, the worth of individual character.

She permits nothing privately or publicly that will cause nature or men to blush to own. If this be your motto, then you place your dignity in the highest order of conservation.

What renders ages, nations, pre-eminent?

All the lustre and intrinsic worth of mind best put into practice. She permits no armed interventions, no crusades on friendly nations, for any false pretences of liberty that is piracy—no peculiar faith, factious, or demagogical spirit, under any pretence, to disturb the government of its country.

All such must be considered as palmed on the world, the greatest subverter of its peace.

It is not the apparent impunity, but the real immunity, that religion regards. She comprehends all relations as the wisest foresight of Deity at creation, and she bestows the wisest foresight on mind.

Mankind must not mistake with after opinions.

She does not permit any ascetic condemnation of earth to reject the best, when it is then best profound legitimate direction.

The proper uses of the world by mind is the beneficent and wise purpose of creation. She permits not the abuse when she institutes the whole comprehensive use.

But the gross corporeal materialists affect that all such is for present use, as all obligations cease with what they call death, the last earthly change.

The mighty weakness is in their appreciation.

They, like all special peculiar pagan faithites, reflect on their own abuse or misuse of their mental faculties, involving their whole category with other conjunctions. They only take the animal views of the question.

Monotheism considers death, instead of being the close, is another brighter and more auspicious beginning of immortal existence.

She considers the mind-organization cannot possibly be inferior to the earth, and superior at one and the same time. To say that its elements can master the facts of the universe, yet all of its best powers, functions, and faculties to be subject, in abeyance to earth, is self-contradictory. Mind can master all the elements of earth, conducive to vital existence, under appropriate circumstances. Man roams the earth, traverses the oceans, navigates the air, dives into the bowels of the earth, and extracts therefrom her richest treasures, commands electricity, and overcomes space and time thereby; controls the winds and waves, and renders all tributary and subservient, through the science of mind, that scans the universe, and measures its sublime relations, that proves a capacity to meet questions of other spheres above the universe, when it boldly presents to itself the mighty question of its own self-existent Creator. Here, it finds an adjourned question, that overlooms time and soars to eternity. These prove a God perfect, and a mind, a soul that aspires thus to be.

It tortures the mighty problem, and demands data that cannot be given in mortal existence.

These too clearly demonstrate that corporeal functions of its brightest embodiment, however evanescent, however the only proof, self-evident of its termination, that it only presents an isolated and partial view, and leaves out the balance of the relations of the universe previously discussed.

Its illustrious conservative principles cannot be destroyed, however their functions are suspended ; it was only a gross material that became defunct.

That all such was mechanical, as the perpetuity of its principles are renewed according to the proficiency of the soul. The architect is sublimely supreme, and has rendered himself responsible for the perpetuity and supremacy of mind-element, renewable in soul-organization. One of the best earnests is his gratuitous creation.

Life's best appreciable function, the soul, that possesses reason, conscience and will, is an independent individuality, the actor using time, itself and matter. Its future immortal improvement is clearly fore-shadowed in the immediate improvement of mind itself. Whilst mentality of the soul is ever progressive in cumulative improvement, it is essential that it possess all the necessary area appropriate. There can be no limit to mental advancement, only in the essential facts furnished.

Animality never can exceed a definite limit, and needs no transfer. Its organic action is not mentality, and therefore such a theatre is inexpedient and superfluous.

The organic action of mind renders organic areas essential to its position. It is clear that mentality was not created exclusively for animality, when such does not begin to satisfy its taste.

Nothing short of a soul-organization, and its appropriate spheres, can give the satisfactory solution to the whole sublime problem of creation.

The change of pagan worship, from age to age, as the light of mind progresses, eminently proves the progressive appreciation and adoption of monotheism—that will displace all such in time's and reason's progress. Time will be, when all peculiar advocates, will drop all the messiahship machinery, and advocate that entirely of rational religion, that must absorb all faiths as religion. What is the opposition to her principles from the priestocracy, but brutal, vulgar, and unprincipled, from selfish despotism? She decides by mind's civilization, that Solomon in all his sensuality, was much of the animal, and that all his temple professions were idolatrous. Those that are destitute of proper cultivation of conscience, are the animals in all ages of society. What can you do with all such? What is man, having mere animal materialism? All the brutes have all real defined natures, limited by instincts, certain animalities known, the mould of their nature. All creation is thus limited, as all mere animal nature has a defined routine instinct of action. The universe has definite physical principles, that if violated, destroy it at once, but mind clearly having free agency, the richest gift, as a gratuitous creation, is necessarily amenable to the deepest penalties. Otherwise mind might affirm that it could not help itself, but its free agency exonerates the responsibility of the Creator, and creates its own. As to animals, the more valuable they are, the more subservient are they to man's purposes in the whole scheme. Now there is nothing but definite instinctive existence in all, except mind, whose free agency enables it to follow its best qualities, and select its own future good. Why is man made responsible, but for all his mind's functions?

Every point of time, past, present, and to come, benefits mind. And what must not mind anticipate from the paternity of the Creator, to his universal creation? Conceive of the natural affections, then, of the Author of all existence. All animated nature is subservient to the best of purposes, that must have the most expansive area. The animality is left on earth, the mind and soul organization change to a fitter sphere.

Rational religion holds all peculiar faiths and their propagators in perfect abeyance, as man is a being ever in abeyance to physical, moral, mental, and religious principles. As excellent chemists decide animals to excel vegetables in the multiform organisation, so man excels all other creations by excess of religious organization, that proves the immortality of his soul-organization. Man cannot be less than a religious being, which demonstrates immortal existence. Rational religion is any way, worthy of God, the Creator. It is this that renders consolation to the intellectual rational mind deprived of a portion of the five senses. The blind has the function of the past, as he possesses in his mind an individual element, that regulates its storehouse of mentality. Rational religion is the only catholic faith: all others are peculiar by the full confession of advocates.

This establishes a proper code for penalty of the culprit, and at the same time does exalted justice. Insanity is often plead in justification of high crimes, and defeats justice.

A plea of faith could be one of insanity. Mind may be corrupted by the peculiar scriptures, the worst of all involving hypocrisy, deceit, double-dealing with God and man, self-delusion. What is the state of mind, that has such base? Mind may of itself commit endless errors, therefore all its responsibility must be referred to the highest and perfect tribunal. It can only entrust its best safety to the consummation of the best tuition, that is of monotheism, rational religion.

What interest can it have in peculiar faith, that to the religious eye of science, has not one attraction? It is certain that no peculiar bible of this world can give religion, therefore the immortal treasure must be furnished by monotheism.

MONOTHEISM HOLDS UNIVERSALISM, AN INCIDENTAL QUESTION.

But can the doctrines of universal salvation prevail? The correct answer of reason must refer to the present world, in part, and the perfection of the Creator.

A vast diversity and variety exist among the human mind, graduated in intellect, character, and cultivation. The first best reward for merit accompanies, throughout life, mind refined for virtue and its practical action.

In seeking to render others happy, the action necessarily reflects on the appropriate centre.

Where, even before reaching their dying couch, is the position of the worst of all characters, the tyrants and oppressors of society, the pirates on the rights and feelings, those who delight to crush the human mind in its tenderest sensibilities, the low, debased brutes of vilest crimes, whose company disgraces on this and other spheres the first great character, an honor to man and the delight of Deity? The universal correction is somewhere.   What shall be considered of those, who cheat their God by hypocrisy?

The mighty defect is in mind's perversion, individually.   The correction is in mind's true intrinsic virtues, and capacity for correction.

After all the professions and pretensions of peculiar faith, mind rises triumphantly to the inherent powers elicited by rational religion.   After all bad deeds, mind triumphs, taught by true wisdom the true points essential.   To reflect on the errors of the past, and remedy the aggressive causes, teach the wisdom of the future.   Mind must vanquish all supposed evils.   God knew what man's nature and capacity were at man's creation.   Mind will only know them after the universe-solution.

Who can criticise God's creation of man?   Bibles of tradition blasphemously attempted it, but their authors were exposed, by their own folly and wickedness recoiling upon them.   Who is possessed of the facts of creation, that enlighten us on that sublime action?   The priestocracy have blasphemously pretended to it.

Be the relation what it may, all created rational beings, however endowed, are only actors from certain fixed principles circumscribed in creation, and perfect consummation perfects the organization.

God is the supreme—his providence is universal.   The very facts of creation bespoke the end and purpose.   Mind acts best according to the lights of reason and science.   The world suffers according to that perversion—this necessity must arouse its best action.   Comprehensive intelligence teaches us that retributive justice, in varied relations, is self-vindicated in the world, and that only commences the solution of the problem.   Happiness on earth is graduated, then, in proportion to the best attainment by mind.

Nothing but equal individual merit can equalize all, in the varied states of existence.   Enlightened minds, with freedom of religious faith, must redeem themselves from the miserable libel of dark ages on Deity, assert the progressive advantages and character of their own age, and triumph by their own best lights.

They can well rejoice then, all the time, in their Creator, who has made nothing in vain, and cause the future not to be ashamed of them, but rejoice.

All minds will be illumined as far as mind can be, to the verge of its capacity, not trammeled by the defects of idiocy or monomania, nor by the degrading beastliness of savage lowliness, much less by a cowardly acquiescence of the people in the horrid depravity of ignoble tyranny and piracy on the rights and feelings of mind.   Then it is not so much the deeds of individual baseness that statesmen have to regard, as the spirit of tame, passive, and humble submission, that vassal mind of the many causes.

Society must be regenerated, on the conservative principles of the universe.

The world will be peopled by civilized beings, and its citizens will be cosmopolites, dispossessed of selfish views less than its circumference, when benevolence is presented aright.

Man's nature, as mind, will embrace its largest scope, and be exalted to its vastest limits.

Then his righteousness can best speak, in the circumference of his ability and peaceful acts.

The triumph will be over selfish considerations, that mislead to ignoble deeds of injustice and bloodshed.

Then nations or individuals will not tyrannize, and debase the human mind.

Constitutional rights of the world will teach mind its rights, and all their duty, the honor of principles.   This best performed, will entitle to the fruition of happiness, emanating from purity.

All rational minds must then look forward with the brightest hopes, of realizing in the future all that belongs to mind's fruition.

The pledge of rational mind to merit, and of its rational God, for reward, bespeaks reciprocal obligation, that invokes the highest rationality for consummation, which of itself bespeaks the noblest of all happiness, that of itself radiates to the circumference of the universe, and the munificent duration of eternity.

To take less than this view incontestibly dwarfs mind to instinct, the soul to dust, and circumscribes the universe Creator to imbecility—when that universe demonstrates him possessed of exhaustless elements of creation.

Rational mind seeks the religious improvement, not defined by old regimes of priestocracy, a re-binding to their notions, but the consummation of God-given, written, executed, mind received, reason improved.   Thus, catholic will be the glorious rational religion—not as the Romanist, that has pirated every way.   Would God put mind-created on earth, to prepare it for punishment?   The idea is absurd—much less for extinction, for that is barbarism.   Man cannot solve the soul-problem short of a soul's

theatre. Is this theatre adequate? Not at all : far from it. The soul must be then
immortal, and have an adequate universe-theatre.

The moderns have one vast and mighty duty to perform to sacrifice superstition and
their bibles, and all their machinery to the sacred holiness of rational religion. Ask the
priestocracy to resign, to depart the pulpit and all its hoary sophistry for ever. The
world is of the universe, and that refers to God—the soul refers to God. Thus teaches
monotheism. But cannot she be refuted? That is impossible, as rational religion is
God-given and protected.

Free rational discussion, is on rationality.

The way to return God grateful thanks is by doing the best justice to that mind that
he has given us, making it rational, its bright embodiment as pure as possible as the
charge that he has given us, to rid the world of superstition, idolatry, priestocracy, absolutism, despotism.

Religion inculcates the idea, the obligation, not to leave the world or society worse
than found.

Is religion a reality? As much as mind—the universe—individuality, all of which
are held together by inherent conservative principles. Take religion away, and the
key stone of creation-arch is destroyed. Now peculiar faith, has not, and cannot have,
one particle of religion, no matter the imposing name, Christianity, Judaism, Mormonism, or Mahommedanism.

What does Brahminism produce but the degraded popular castes, the ruin of Asiatic
society ; what Bhuddism and other peculiar faiths leave of it? What Christianity lacks
of this disgusting barbarism, is all due to mind that is getting the ascendancy of all these
myrmidons. How is all this conclusively demonstrated? Because of the world's taint
from analogous peculiar faith, one of its accursed evil genius to mind, principles and
religion. Peculiar faith has divested the world of all these, as far as practicable. The
world needs refined civilization, and that is only got by the consummation of rational
mind in religion, the consummation of man's duty here, the highest aspirations of the
future.

Nothing is out of date with monotheism, that is not out of the protection of principles.
The more sacred the subject, the more rational investigation it demands of all rational
minds. Religion demands most of all, by freemen. The peculiar faith-man, refers to
his bible as the standard. The rational religionist refers to the Creator, as exemplified
through the universe as the standard. Command your own best self-respect, on principle. Promise and act, on principle, the highest order of morals and religion.

Never let money stand between you and morals, much less religion. Let your word
be your bond, and that on principle, not on impulse, to get you into any difficulty. Pursue the path of principle in defiance of the world's seduction or its influence. Always
understand matters properly, before commission. This thing of power of any little brief
authority, is most clearly to be considered, before any proceeding or acquiescence. Let
nothing be conceded without principles. All grants of power must be constitutional, to
be rightly used as trust, otherwise there is abuse of principles. We do not know so
much of theology, as of religion that is implanted in all rational minds. What is the
limit of an honest truthful mind as to temptation, but what is eternally based on principles? Who can tell, better than time, that convicts pretended prophets? Can aught
save the world but religion, in the most essential points of society? The whole of the
opposition to monotheism or rational religion, is unprincipled.

Monotheism after all the analysis of bible and church-matters of peculiar faith, decides that none such have religion. It remains for the Americans to prove to the world,
that they have solved the problem of religion. The Holy Book of God, is his universe.
Any black letter book, a peculiar bible, is a false picture. No master can be safely followed. Adopt principles.

Religion must be rational, and demands rational education, nothing short of it. But
what shall we do for the Christian religion? There is no Christian religion. It is all a
misnomer. There is only rational religion, but christian peculiar faith, and what does
that all amount to but paganism most genuine? If the advocates contend for their faith
being religion, then their own game is eternally blocked on them by the world gamblers
in the balance of such stocks. Calling things by names, does not establish its first principles. How much is the world deceived, by all such fooleries. The world must expunge all its false position, to do right on its theatre fully and satisfactorily, to be entitled to the best earnest hereafter. Nothing else can answer, as nothing else is a test.
Every base of ill feelings and will, and all malign influences, must be removed from the
world, at the instance of rational religion that commands the moral intellect of mankind.
When any world-citizen talks of religion, he can only speak, write, think of and act on
rational religion, and if he be not strictly truthful and honest, he cannot start on more

than the God-given elements of religion that all rational minds have as creation-gifts, but which he has most basely perverted.

He must ever stick until he speaks the truth, and acts honestly for ever. Now what is the state of all peculiar faiths? Not a particle of truth is in their first or last points. What others they have, they have smuggled and embezzled. They will have to disgorge all their infamous plagiaries and larcenies.

Rational religion improves on her virtues, while peculiar faith holds to her odious and exploded vices and crimes, sinking lower to her lowest depths. The progress of rational religion in America, will prove the gratefulness to the winners of pure government. The vipers of atheism and polytheism bite a file when they assail monotheism, rational, the only religion. Can monotheism make the perfect gentleman, the accurately religious, the best aspirant to immortal fruition? Can it cause the enactment of perfect justice, to the absent? Who are the dignitaries of the land? Those who have the dignity of rational mind. Those who honor self-respect of mind, their word, obligation, honor and life, above all, religion rational. With them, the whole world adopting conservative principles, the details settle themselves. With them, truth and honesty are matters of habit as they are settled principles.

Rational religion requires the world, mankind to act so as to make every day as a holiday, every thought, word, and deed, winged messengers of future joy. The highest exercise of mind on earth, is the consummation of rational religion.

If a man die in his sins, he will be damned, say the peculiar faith bibles. What sins? Because he does not believe the rickety sophists, the priestocracy? Now rational religion inculcates the highest legitimate actions, words and thoughts with the best appreciation of nature's laws, God's laws, as the right position when carried out on the chastest taste legitimately furnished.

All others are false.

But for religion there would be no consummation of virtue, of conservative principles, to keep all in abeyance, &c. By the wisdom of rational religion, the world has due respect to innocence of mind that is as bold as truth, that is the boldest yet the most modest. She teaches the world not to contravene the customs of nature and nature's laws, but those of erroneous man not in abeyance to rationality. There can be nothing more of a dignitary on earth, than a perfect monotheist.

ANALYSIS OF FAITH, HOPE, REASON, TRADITION, RESURRECTION.

PECULIARITY in faith, hope, &c. necessarily condemns all such. God's attributes being universal in their power, indite universal character, authority, faith, and all essential principles, and stamp their universal acceptance to all rational minds.

Peculiarity of faith, then, is originated by mortals in bad faith, is inconsistent with God's universal attributes, is basely unjust, and must meet with universal reprobation and rejection by all rational and enlightened minds.

Mind of rational beings is universal, and takes cognizance of universality as legitimate when Deity is considered, and worth of mind is assessed.

Reason, not tradition, takes proper cognizance of God's works, that universally speak to mind.

Faith and hope can only refer to God through mind, most reasonably, truthfully and honestly.

Tradition, then, does not embrace nor cover time and space, clearly proving its untenable position, that reason amply supplies in eternity universally over time.

What can reason say for man's resurrection?

All that can be said in truth on this earth.

What can tradition do for that, anterior to its cognizance? Tradition must fall on imposition to affect any knowledge beyond this world.

The way to meet this question truly is to be prepared to meet the Author of creation by the best course of life to God and man.

Reason can say, and sincere and faithful minds must abide her supreme decision, that the resurrection of man is certainly in the right hands, those of his Immortal Creator only, who is sublimely omnipotent in man's creation in the endowing the attributes of mind.

Where is proof direct of any resurrection on this earth? Is any recorded, that will pass the ordeal of an enlightened mind, capable of justice?

Will any honorable court of conscience authorize the faith of reason in any resurrection days after death, which must prove conclusively, all it can prove, its immediate execution?

It is the highest proof to see the defenders of any such doctrines avoid the condemnation, by shirking the main questions, the proof of authenticity of all the bibles.
The balance are of no consequence now.

Was Christ's resurrection proved, when no positive proof is exhibited of his body
being positively in the sepulchre, when the door was sealed? How can we take that
for granted?

No court of justice will affirm that much, when dissolution proves the immediate departure of the spirit from the body.

Who does not wish to stop the father and mother of base superstition, sophistry?
Kill that, and the world-monster is dead.

To do so, give mind its legitimate triumph.

In the name of God of the universe, let not minds, aspiring to be enlightened in a
free world, suffer themselves misled by such base superstition.

It will be an everlasting disgrace to freemen of the world, if intelligent, who are prepared to accept such humbuggery. the offcast of a degraded part of the globe.

Natural phenomena being most obscurely appreciated in the dark ages of the world,
the mere imposition and pretence to miracles, divination, divine inspiration and prophecy were assumed in all the circles of priestocracy through mythology.

All their bibles are those of mythology, while the bible of rational mind espouses the
only true principles of rational religion.

After all the pretended objections to science and philosophy in faith, how can they
be dispensed with by the wisest, who seek a full knowledge of natural phenomena as
essential to combat successfully all the difficulties of ignorance, error and prejudice,
backed by bigotry.

The fault is in the people, who are humbugged about peculiar faith and all its peculiar frauds, when they can master the powers to control the degradation of their own
nature.

INSPIRATION, REVELATION, PROPHECIES, MIRACLES.

The veils of the future are a bliss bestowed on mind for the best of purposes, for
man's own internal peace, constituted as he is by emotions in regard to death, hope and
fear for punishments, and the penalties for improper transgressions. If mind take cognizance of this subject rightly, the world that is so much disturbed by the Romanist
view will be at rest.

That view is a very slavish doctrine of mind. The universal Creator has cognizance
and exclusive power over natural phenomena, and these he has subjected to conservative principles that represent him, both unchangeable. To reverse them, or execute
miracles would be a change of himself, an impossibility in his immutability, and be the
God of the universe; also unsafe, inexpedient, unwise and unnecessary, for all wise
minds, in the dignity of philosophical science, recognise his supremacy best by their
consummation in the universe. No one but impostors on the best rights and interests
of the community of the world could seek to perpetrate such degraded frauds, under
the assumption of peculiar faith, as none but the Creator can have any power at all on
the phenomena of creation, and no worthy member of society can put forth any pretension to appropriate more than what mortals universally have. Every man in his own
mind well knows how incapable and incompetent mortals are to perform one single
function of a miracle.

The whole constitutes false pretences, and the most wicked humbugs of the world.
If peculiar faith had not been stilted on such, it could not have breathed at any time.

While the world may have to deplore past transgressions of the degraded impostors,
it has to exert its most intellectual exertions from being the dupe and transgressor in
turn, lest it make itself the curse and laughing-stock of posterity.

The reverse of principles implies miracles, or destructive negative qualities, the exercise of which, not understood by man presuming to chronicle God's government, impeaches at once wisdom and creative attributes.

The fair creation is often read with error, if not with impiety, the necessary and inevitable result of all systems of peculiar faith, that mislead from the only True One,
recognising the unity of an Immortal Supreme, as those systems produce a constant sophistry, that mislead from truth and beget bigotry in their followers, antagonism if not
contempt of the rest of the world for all such, and a culpable indifference to the requisitions of what is genuine and most worthy.

Baffled forever and entirely exploded are the tenures of those supposed strongholds
if the zealot will persist in asserting them. He has to learn that miracles cannot pos-

sibly exist before the light of mind, as they are now forever superseded by a knowledge of natural phenomena. They are all as baseless as the peculiar faith that originated them. All such are false and foul pretences.

Miracles have never existed. Their record has ceased, because popular ignorance has abated.

A recent sect, the Mormons, as preceding ones, tried miracles, but they could not flourish in this or any enlightened age.

Then the age or authority the more affecting religion, mind, highest duty, the more disgraceful, and is impeached forever, that does assert, much less propagate, the doctrine of miracles, that always derogate from God's divinity and perfection.

Baffled to the last points in the category and links of corruption, the zealot refers to prophecies.

But here he is estopped by the undeniable fact, that time is God's only true prophet, and most benevolent at that, in only disclosing fast enough for man's good and feelings; hence prophecies are a libel on God's attribute of benevolence, to say nothing of the blasphemy of the false pretence.

The priests' God is not the God of the universe, painted as he is in false colors, and indebted to the priests'·miracles, prophecies, enigmas and mysteries; of course the doctrine has to be dismissed as that of superstition. The talisman of science, the sceptre of the true God of the universe, silences not only the priests, but their god, all very corrupt and bloody, wrathful, and worst of all, a very changeable being.

Baffled to the last, with consummate impudence, arising in ignorance and bigotry, he refers to peculiar faith, mysteries, and enigmas; and fearful of not escaping if located on earth, he puts them in other regions.

But God made the universe, and wrote down all the characteristics with his own hand of electricity, all readable in simple appreciation as far as needed; of course, then, no mysteries but to ignorance.

The faith that reaches God is only the faith of reason, that can go no farther. Any other than rational faith is credulity, dependent on false positions and interpretations.

When God speaks to man he uses plain facts.

Priestocracies use mysteries, and veil them in enigmas, which the experience of best histories incontrovertibly proves impostures.

The mystery turns out a simple duty, that honest minds appreciate. The enigma or mysterious revelation of priests is needed to have that guessed at which proper sense tells straight forward, unless arrested by the trick and cruelty of the interlopers, who want pay or power for interpretation.

The cobwebs of the dark ages, and their darker workers, all the sphinxes, must be swept away forever and at once, as dangerous to the rights and morals of mind.

But reason is not the coin used by absolutism. That did not aspire to all the best means on earth. It affected to be divine, so miscalled, to maintain itself. 'All that are on the right side can well show it. All are meant, that their own position proves. The history is too plain to mistake absolutism for aught but an enemy to the rights of mind.

All are acquitted that reason acquits.

Absolutism, then, does not refer to reason, but to faith. How comes faith of any peculiar character?

It is the faith only of absolutism, that carries its point by the bayonet, or by malign sophistry.

But it is asserted to be the faith of the bible. So much the worse! It is corruption the blackest, that fawns on absolutism, unprincipled, and acting in the worst of bad faith. Faith, then, means any and every thing that credulity chooses to believe, and absolutism dictates.

But the degraded sycophancy of the world, that clings to the casts-off of sophistry, assumes that miracles have ceased, as if ever performed in good faith, or otherwise than by jugglery, legerdemain, or ventriloquism.

The miserable imposition is on the present mind, as if such things ever did take place, and never emanated from a lying priestocracy, always intent on popular deception for their own immediate emolument. Kings and priests have combined, and succeeded in deceiving the world.

Whoso propagates such sophistry is responsible for the frauds thereby committed; but what do an unprincipled priestocracy care for all if they can escape detection?

Every agent and preacher who help to propagate these doctrines are morally guilty of crime, high treason, and perjury.

Well can it be affirmed that miracles have ceased, because they never existed but in the brains of wiseacres, and the tongues and hands of pious knaves.

They only appear to cease, because stupid and blind ignorance, credulous of nonsense, has abated, and the phenomena of nature better understood by science.

Various hoaxes are often played now upon the people, and have been in every age, for all the seducing emoluments and gain to be derived therefrom.

The fact is, the people act their part too well in this senseless imposition upon them. They are the dupes, so intended, to obtain from them their invaluable treasures of mind, to reach those of their pockets.

Will they be sold without redemption to such impostors; will they play their part in this iniquitous game, make senseless ignorance as culpable as unprincipled knavery, and worse than the deluded vulgar of more than eighteen centuries past; will they continue the currency of the base counterfeits, after being taught that this is spurious coin?

The people, if the subject be addressed successfully to their animal passions, fears, and ignorance, and most cunningly too, in the state of the conscience too often guilty, are ever credulous.

The other phenomena of bible of tradition-ethics, like that of the star locomotion in Christ's times, are more than remarkable, beyond any credence of rational faith. The canopy of heaven is naught but thin atmosphere; beyond, are the hosts of bodies of the universe.

Nothing but meteors pass on or near the earth, and they are projectiles of volcanoes, more or less, if solid.

The success of these abuses, indoctrinating the credulous part of the world into pretended miracles, brings forward unlimited faith-perversions.

The peculiar doctrines of Judaism, originating from eastern peculiarities, without doubt, most probably from Chaldea, where astronomy was cultivated, and priestocracy predominated, was the peculiar mother of a prolific offspring, the end of which is not yet.

On that arose Christianity, with her hundreds of divisions. On these two arose Mahomedanism, with its sects. Again, in these latter days, has been thereunto added the Mormon peculiarity.

The others, older sisters of superstition, desire to disown her, but the sisterhood is indelibly established, and what is a good ear-mark, they are all pagan, a foul crowd.

The priority of age is nothing at all in all such faiths; the characteristic superiority is in successful sophistry.

The world has to be deceived into its deception. "The greatest art is to conceal the art."

If the Mormons spoke with new tongues, what else could Christians expect, whose master asserted that "these signs shall follow them that believe."

Although hundreds of Mormons might have sworn and perjured themselves, that their prophet did not die without resurrection to them, still all their miracles and pious frauds fell still-born on the intelligent, for want of an ignorant age.

If intelligence heeded the Mormons, it was only perverted, as in all systems of miracle faith, by hope of rewards.

In what respect, then, are the Mormons less than their other peculiar faith brethren of the world?

But the greatest miracle is, it is surprisingly strange that the people, sovereigns as they are of mind and its cultivation, of the mastery of thought, should permit themselves to be led about by a few characters, as if a mighty elephant governed by his keepers, with this difference, that the elephant only succumbs to his friend the keeper, whereas the people succumb to masters alienated to their true interests, else the priests have no concert of action, and do not know what they are about.

Where is mind all this time, asleep or infatuated?

The miracles are mockeries and trifles, not fit for children; when the author is most wanted now, in time and space, he is not present, nor are his memorials, through his works, before us to represent him to the satisfaction of mind, honesty, and reason. Miracles cannot elucidate for mind, that looks for reason. Miracles are not rational.

But God's works are always before us, day and night, material and spiritual, that shame into confusion the impostors.

Miracles cannot be when the word of God comes through science, his messenger, that can only expose usurpations and monopolies, that are always jealous of talents and virtue in opposition, as all such rest on a false base, and never can be safe while reason and mind can combat them.

When phenomena are offered to our respectable credence, then they must be analogous to what reason requires, as philosophy teaches. All phenomena are for the five senses to recognise, that all refer to reason, and faith through reason.

The natural causes must be rightly traced, and none assigned that are not supported by nature's facts.

Phenomena, co-incident to any event, are not identified with it, as an eclipse of any sphere is not connected to the various births and deaths, marriages, and all vital business cotemporary to such phenomena.

Analogy, that takes the place of analysis in her absence, will set all right if true science be truthfully carried out.

Mankind must be enlightened by mind's light, reason, not to mistake the phenomena of the elements of nature, and give due credit to the creative power.

Faith of all kinds must have the truthful testimony of science in all cases of doubt, to satisfy man's mind.

Grant that all the sects of peculiar faith could not rise to a better state, and that only those have survived that conformed most to mind's advance, we have outlived those times, the days of miracles, when all that ever depended on miracles ought to die too.

Let the believer in miracles look to science for a solution of natural phenomena. The Jew bible says that "the windows of heaven were opened!" What was its heaven? "The firmament" that held the waters!

In those times of the tradition, the arch of the blue ether heaved above, was considered heaven, until wise astronomers lifted the veil. and by teaching man to look beyond at the millions of systems of worlds, that truly speak the only words of God, who created the universe, plainly prove the ignorance of those asserting this fiction, as heaven is as much antipodal as above us. So much for priestocracy inspiration, that is unquestionably priestocracy ignorance.

Now the telescope as improved by mind, recalls daily more and more magnificence, and shows space unlimited only by mortal vision, the universe exhaustless filled with the expansive riches of creation. While at the same time, the microscope, the work of mind too, displays to the minutest points, another part of creation of minutest greatness.

Did the botches of bible tradition ever dream of this philosophy? No wonder that they were afraid of the mirror of God, that reflected so strongly their deformities of mind. What can miracle-mongers expect of the Supreme?

What shall we think of those propagating such stuff at the present day?

All wisdom proves conclusively and incontestibly that we take nothing for granted that mind can test, prove, or easily investigate.

When any character pretends to deny this position, then his faith and philosophy, which simply mean the purest wisdom, rest on no foundation, and are negatived on all good principles. He may pretend to mysteries, and that the eye of faith can only see things after experience of peculiar character. But he actually forgets he stands on the platform of universal nature, and cannot escape by any pretences, spiritual or temporal, whether he assumes anything divine or of the heart. It is not as he wishes, but as God of nature has done.

Our part of analysis discloses the whole matter, that there can be no mysteries that contravene reason and her assistants, analysis and analogy, then how can the experience of the heart be philosophically correct, when the mind and the standard of reason utterly contradict and condemn all such?

This age is too enlightened, and owes it to itself to disenthral all, as far as practicable, by a better and wiser code of morals, when facility of faith, that is credulity, goes to corrupt the world in weakness of intellect, as many cannot distinguish but as they are directed!

Many tell us about passages of the bible read, as if that was proper evidence; they have been over the books, but was mind there, and was that mind fit to be trusted? Immortal minds seek the analysis of immortal truth, not the contemptible trash of ignoble ignorance.

Has mind's reverence been correct, its intelligence sufficient to see what an impotent God this bible made the Creator, divested of his intrinsic attributes and virtues, at the very time that it did its best to make miracles, a perfect libel, but self-impeachment of man? This is detestable for this or any age, however the world likes humbugs, which all wise and honorable men will arrest.

There is the resurrection that many good people believe actually took place! Would that all was right, and if it were right that the fact was unmistakable. But the Almighty never permitted blasphemous false pretences to have but one position, to define their own exposure and felony.

Joseph is said to have laid the body of Christ enveloped in the cloth, in the sepulchre, but who watched all the time, till Jesus was missed?

If the facts were tried to-day before an intelligent judge, the verdict would have to be, that there was no decisive proof at all that the body of Jesus was identified in the sepulchre, and that the resurrection ever took place from the sepulchre!

The testimony of the adherents about seeing Christ's spirit cannot be correct, for no spirit can be seen by mortal eyes, much less angels, whom God needs not as messengers, when he has mind and his principles to minister to it. That is an utter fabrication, about ghosts. When will the world shake off all this chaos of fraud?

Christ with the mission of a God, could have invited the whole world to witness his master miracles, could have called the planets, even the sun from his system, and could have caused the most public exhibition of his body laid out before the world, and then shown his triumphant resurrection, a mighty miracle indeed. But here eighteen centuries afterwards, much of the world is actually at a stand from doubt about any one of his merits, if they have not actually seen his demerits.

And this the being for mind to embrace, not doubtingly, but affectionately and devoutly? The world needs no better evidence of folly, than such credulity.

Why cannot we have miracles and prophet-inspirations now, as all such are as much needed in every age and country?

All such were laid low, because ignorance has departed, except among ignorant savages who have their rain-kings and war-prophets.

Happiness needs no mystery, to flourish on universal morals. What is inspiration? Some think it a supernatural gift of God to that man, who is this chosen one.

It is supposed to be a peculiar endowment, a miraculous influence by the operation of the spirit. But the God of nature is universal, not peculiar, else he was not the God of the universe.

What nation is there that had had specific peculiar faith, but thought theirs the chosen one of God, as the Jews, Druids, Christians, Mahometans, Mormons?

Science and philosophy discard all these, as preposterous dogmas. Inspiration, then, cannot be peculiar, but universal, graduated to the talents, their successful improvement and employment.

· Mind that is cultivated by science and philosophy, conductors to the fountain of God, is the better instructed and rightly employed, the nearer it approaches to the fount of wisdom. But mind best endowed, yet perverted, is wicked, profligate and degraded, and though a master genius, may be one of evil to the world and the race of mankind. The Mormon faith is as much as any peculiar faith, and in using strange tongues as gifts, they could not in this age of science and philosophy, inspire the faith of others too rational for that, but believers in past pretences no better, because it is reason that governs modern acts in all other matters among present believers, but superstition that rules their faith in such ancient institutions, no better, in truth. Thus we see where the doctrine of inspiration leads us. Hence all are responsible for any peculiar faith that misleads the world about inspirations.

The bible of tradition, a mass of contradictions and false pretences, fills the world with errors arising necessarily from the ignorance of the supposed inspired writers, who could not embrace full knowledge of science and philosophy, which the bible-followers had to outrage through hand-maids of God, to seem right before the vulgar circles of the world.

Mind then has to advance a bible of rational mind, as mind progresses in science and philosophy.

There have been many messiahs, but all must be false that cannot perform any inspired functions necessarily, because messiahships encroach on God's dominion.

The more you inculcate the messiahship, that much you detract from God and his attributes.

Monotheists oppose all inspiration of peculiar faith, and monotheism is the only system of religion that admits the providence of God universal on principles, and accountability of mind for the immortality of the soul through its spirit, by its moral free agency. •

The mercy of Providence bespeaks pardon for transgression on repentance, and future rewards for practice of good deeds. This is all in the course of secure results, through conservative principles.   ·

What especial revelations have been made to mind, but by or through reason that renders it rational? What rational mind of respectable weight can seize on any other, but through reason?

Where, then, is peculiar inspiration? Is it at last the sole creature of peculiar faith, ready to do its bidding, abased by all its peculiar corruptions?

The world cannot be governed by all such peculiar institutions, that are necessarily the works of man and corrupt at that, when the universe has a claim on it as a sphere subject to its universal, not peculiar laws. Sectarianism cuts down the possibility of its being right

Inspiration of bible writers! The first commenced in fraud and deception; and the last ended in imposition and blasphemy. Who endorses the endorsers, but impostors?

We cannot commit more heinous sins of iniquity, than to blaspheme God with such infamous superstitions.

PROPHECY.

THE veil that obscures the future can only be lifted by an Almighty, who has placed it over the same for the best good of all, to prevent all the incidents identified with such a position, otherwise, suicide, murder, and misery, might be a part of the result. Let any man know his destiny that it might terminate here, and that he was the more miserable, the longer he lived.

He might seek to end the existence of himself, and all that caused his misery.

Hence, all are impostors, that pretend to prophecy by authority of the Creator.

None but the wise can appreciate the future by the past, from analogy by analysis with the aid of reason. There is no inspiration but of mind and reason that must be enlightened, to appreciate the ways of general Providence.

The idea of peculiar providence has begotten the most peculiar outrages on the whole world.

All peculiar faith advocates have sought to monopolize, pervert, and coerce mind, and have degraded all things by their peculiar pretences.

Inspiration and revelation came, it is said, by the ministry of angels. Now that we hold impossible, to supersede conservative principles.

All peculiar faith is defunct, for there can be no especial revelation or inspiration.

But the authors of miracle, prophecy, and mystery doctrine, affected them, some think to carry the day. Corruptly and basely, rational minds must say.

Moses affected to meet God at Mount Sinai; Mahomet sought Gabriel, and so did Numa Pompilius seek Egeria, the goddess so called, as if the people were to be told the truth about religion, by having the utmost false pretences of miracles and prophecies advanced for their belief.

Who but the base and vulgar ignorant, can believe them essential to religion?

Who but the same can believe peculiar faith anything else, than the deepest curse of the world.

Who cannot see the difference, while reason and truth regulate religion, sophistry and falsehood intrigue for peculiar faith?

The bible of tradition speaks of particular prophecies; do we actually know the lineage of the nations of the world, by any such authority? Who will endorse it as worth the reading?

A few cities are spoken of, but where are the cities of the world? Real prophecy would have embraced cities, buried for thousands of years under their rubbish. Are there not several ancient cities, that have been traceless as to their ruins? Did not general causes operate on them?

What is there of Egypt, that is uncommon to most of the countries of antiquity? It is no worse than might be expected of uncivilized countries, however the Jews might have inveighed against it and eastern cities, by feelings of intense enmity for past captivities.

Is it still tributary and subject to strangers? Is that true?

It has its own sovereign, and that proves a high position for that country. What was such prophecy worth? To gratify the malignant feelings of the Jews? What have the moderns to do therewith?

But how much of the prophecy is left to conjecture and speculation of an ignorant posterity? What is all such worth? The affiliated have to help out the pretences.

There is prophecy, as supposed, against the Roman church. What is there against the Greek church, that is equally guilty? Against Grand Lamaism, their prototypes?

All such tends to beget a curious and restless spirit of superstition, to carry out by Millerism, and other absurd notions, the fulfilment of pretences all false. Is mind so weak, as to be imposed upon forever by written superstitious legends, when the original pagan oracles have passed off the stage of action?

All bibles of tradition, the work of false pretences forever by the necessity of their nature, are run into the pretended mystery and power of a peculiar God, to escape the conviction that natural phenomena do not admit of miracles. The sophistry is to make the vulgar wonder, responsible for miracles. The veracity of the God is affected to be disputed, if the lies of the tradition are exposed! What degradation. The veracity of the God of the universe is proclaimed by its organization, never to be contradicted by sound minds. Assuredly He has no need of such paltriness as miracles. Their calibre is too small for him.

Science lifts the veil of wonder from phenomena, that miserable ignorance once proclaimed miracles, as a mere boy knows more now, than wise adults did anciently. Science in one department, enlightens the whole circle.

Mind has to appreciate all this rightly, or it fails in duty. Once it was a system by the pretence of divine rights of absolutism of kings, priests, and soldiers, to keep all in ignorance; now the divine right of the people proclaims its majesty, and makes science common stock.

None can learn too speedily and practically, for universal benefit.

In more ancient times, the people had but few books, and they were as silly as the bigoted minds of the authors were perverted. The vices of the times upheld abominable errors.

Much was submitted to tradition of self-conceited bigots, hence, errors, frauds, and ignorance prevailed, for centuries upon centuries, and without help, especially too, where conscience, the noblest faculty to nurture the principles of religion, was deficient, in her triumph of a just and enlightened mind.

Kings could not read, and the people had but little of the benefits of rational minds. The priests had the learning, such as it was, dwarfed to the narrow precincts of bigoted minds, and of course they had the feeling to misuse it.

The gullibility of ignorant people is always counted on by bad men of all classes.

Of course, the priestocracy held to all the mysteries, miracles, and prophecies, all the jugglery of mind, all the secrets of psychology, to enslave the multitude.

The platform that superstition and despotism reared, was that of iniquity, and will finally sink itself, or finally sink all that reared it.

What shall we say of pestilences, that decimate the world?

What else than our iniquities either to the great principles and laws of nature directly, or to the Creator of the universe, could have occasioned such by means of natural causes?

Minds perverted have excluded Almighty God from his own universe, to which the creations of his own genius entitled him. Strange god-idols, man-worship, have been introduced, as an abomination, before his august and supreme power—dovetailing them into his essence and being, most absurdly and blasphemously. This was the most vulgar trick of polytheism. What worse was atheism?

How could he refrain from destroying the world, for its unholy actions, sins of blasphemy—the chief of sins—but for his mercy, that has prevailed, with his voluntary creation of mind, entrusted to its own free-agency, under the circumstances, the conservative principles of the universe? His immutability saved all, from the very counterfeits of priestocracy, miracles, &c.

Repent, men of superstition, idolators, and man-worshippers; turn to the living God, the only Creator and God. The light of rational mind scatters miracles and prophecies, as ignorance ceases.

Thus the world is wiser, therefore there is less imposition; and the world is better. The whole world, by the light of reason, is becoming utilitarian, and makes mind more rational.

What numbers are deluded to seek prophecy and miracles, and to interpret the unfulfilled prophecies and judgments? the problem never to be solved. The pursuit is as vain as that after the perpetual motion. And what fanaticism of Millerism, &c. follows! The devotees are willing to consign the minds of the people to a pervading superstition, and the world to destruction, that their foolish solutions may come to pass, as they told us so.

All peculiar faiths may have their fire and brimstone, that they get from volcanoes—all their devil-angel ministers of evil, that they get from Vulcan, who originated volcanoes, they pretend; but the exploded doctrines of the mythologists cannot stand before the modern analysis of natural phenomena.

The narrow prejudices of superstition and vulgar errors, the contracted faith of witchcraft, that murdered millions of citizens upon citizens with fanatical fury, and all the wretched machinery, arousing the fears of the world, must yield to science and philosophy, the true friends of mind, the lovely daughters of religion.

Prophecy adds to mind's misery and evil, hence it is not God's work, for time is his prophet.

Who, of the present day, ever saw the miracles? And none but peculiar faith ever claimed such false pretences, denied to all ages.

What sound mind is there, that is not satisfied, that they are all humbugs.

Pious frauds, however the capital, are not to give Moses—the priestocracy—weight with cultivated mind, about the oddest mixture of all animal creations blended in one house for months—the smallest peculiar insects crossing the deepest and widest oceans to escape the very thing they thus encountered, in getting to the ark.

The plainest sense and best philosophy contradict the idea, that all the waters should rise, by a general deluge, to flood the whole globe at once, however they acted on the four-cornered plane, their creation.

What will it profit that mind to pretend to belief of such absurdities, to gratify the morbid taste and false philosophy of a priestocracy, at the same time knowing all such to be false, and damning its own purity, to an unnecessary purification, for such abominable perdition? Let the world look to its duty, above all things, and not become contemptible by credulity.

God deals in reason, through rational minds. Man affects miracles, most stupidly, victim of superstition, ignorance, and error.

Where is the consistency, in right and justice?

God alone is our instructor, but modest alone must be principles that elicit his aid. On what do you rest your faith?

On revelation, miracles, prophecies, and mysteries. But revelation can only be by tradition, that is absurd; the others, of course, must be false, as all other deductions therefrom claimed. And, as false, all good and true citizens would wish them exposed, and if true, to see them confirmed.

Miracles, prophecies, and mysteries, bespeak collusion on the part of operators and writers, and gross, vulgar ignorance on that of the believers.

God created all the universe, as natural phenomena in their current proper action; such has been and will be the order of things universal. If miracles were to exist, conservative principles would terminate.

Miracles reverse order, and produce disorder, which is unsafe and inconsistent with safety. Who believes that an all-wise Almighty reverses this order of nature, when his universe proceeds best when right; which fact not only convinces of supreme power, but creates the most exalted conception of the Creator? The very pretence that miracles have ceased, proves mutability, that is inconsistent with God's immutability. What necessity was there of miracles, to prove a God, who is universally and supremely proved? What pretence has a miracle in face of the whole universe, that is God's document? All the miracles in creation could not prove a mortal a God.

What proof of miracles, past or present, is there, in all creation? Such in this universe would disprove God. We have none that is worthy of enlightened mind. And yet the proof-marks would have been unmistakable, as God's works; hence, all is folly, untruth, and libelous, that God reverses the order of creation, to accomplish what he can better do otherwise, and what is not practicable, in fact, while he is God. All this is man's libel of Deity.

Volcanoes are mere safety-valves, and a correct appreciation of them and all the fearful phenomena of nature, renders a blessing of mind.

The leviathan is a fiction arising from the gross ignorance of vulgar minds, prepared to receive miracles, and not prepared to appreciate science, electricity, &c. With the Almighty, nothing in this universe is a miracle, where order and harmony universally reign. If they did not, chaos and confusion would arise, showing God imperfect and imbecile, the reversal of nature's laws, not miracles, that cannot exist with conservative principles. All this is the worst libel on the immutable perfection of God, and nature's laws. God can no more make a miracle, that destroys the consistent preservation of the universe, than he can act inconsistently, and maintain his character.

God is not the God of miracles, prophecies, and mysteries of priestocracies, nor the peculiar God of any chosen peculiar people, a mere machine of fable. A miracle is an inconsistency physical, and involves a moral inconsistency of God.

Nothing is impossible to the God of nature, within the sphere of his universe; but he is not the God of man's notions. We could no more expect of God a miracle, than wanton sin of a wise and good citizen, in his right senses and corporeal functions, who sought the greatest good of his world.

It is, then, all nonsense about miracles : worse, if anything, about prophecies and mysteries.

These are the designs of knavish, and the belief of credulous, people. The world must by this time see that there can be no miracles; the thing is in us, or the deception in those assuming rank imposition.

Astronomers agree on the order of the universe, and we might, on that order and system, affirm no God, as miracles. If there be a God, as the noblest systems of systems prove, then there can be no miracles; for his conservative principles totally prevent all such.

Miracles certainly impeach the Creator of the universe of imbecility. The polytheists, miracle-mongers, detailers of false pretences and small scandal, make themselves atheists the very moment they cut God out of his high estate, as his rule is then imperfect and imbecile. If miracles had been the means, they might have been too clear for mind to have mistaken them.

Proper sense impeaches all miracles, and all bibles of tradition for miracles, proving that systems of faith without reason, as miracles, are those without honesty.

Miracles are against the order of nature; then it is in us, not in miracles, that cannot exist thus. The God of the universe, would be actually unjust to himself, to entrust the power of divination and prophecy, fore-knowledge, to individuals, when he gives universal powers. He does not violate his own glorious attributes, functions or principles.

This inconsistency unmakes the God of the universe, and dwarfs him for the peculiar god of priestocracies, whom mind enlightened, cannot respect, revere or adore.

Such characters could usurp power as the priests sought, and be invested with extraordinary qualities and endowments of life. What rational mind analyzing its own defined position, can believe all this a moment?

All honest sense impeaches any work of man as divine revelation. It is all rant and cant, about the third heaven, improperly so-called. What is prophecy but the old plan of divination, by dreams, visions, oracles? such as pagan augurs and soothsayers' used. The adopters are as bad as these.

All the bible-miracles being impossibilities, need absolute confirmation for constant and current time.

They are all denied as positive falsehoods, and the proof is demanded or the assertors will be pronounced felons and perjurers. Miracles are not natural, but effects have been misinterpreted as supernatural, when they all had only adequate causes of nature, acting under the conservative principles of the universe. There can be no miracles, as all effects must have adequate causes. Miracles are unnatural. Now we see nothing, hear or read nothing that is unnatural. All else, is false history assuredly. If the perfect God of the universe had inspired about creation, he could not have been so unjust as to libel himself and creation. God cannot be inconsistent with himself. All purported miracle histories are libels of God.

The great objection to prophecy was, that so much was false. · All was false clearly. How was it possible for prophecy, God's function, to exist?

We have been told of some prophecies—how can any usurp the functions of time? How many millions have proved false, but they were left untold. No doubt, many volumes of such stuff were written and destroyed. Take the chief of prophets. as an example of truth not told. Isaiah, ch. ix. v. 7, says, " of the increase of his government and peace, there shall be no end upon the Throne of David," &c. He was a false prophet, no matter of whom he wrote.

Who endorses lying prophets? Where is the prophecy that has the remotest bearing on the legitimate latitude of proper, not forced construction and comprehension, in the old testament on the new?

All the inspirations coming from God, a perfect being, must be perfect, have no possible antagonism with himself, truth. reason, and philosophical science, else they are the false pretences of false prophets and priests, of a peculiar god. What confessional of inspiration can be carried out? That is an impossibility. Every prophecy is a direct antagonism with God.

How many pretended prophets, as Isaiah, have the priests tortured, to elicit the prophetic signs about Christ; but all in vain, say honest, common sense, and the Jews, who, above all people, ought to understand their own peculiar doctrines.

They would feel bound to yield to supposed facts of their bible, as they are peculiarly interested. Now, instead of prophecy, it is all priestocracy, imposition and pretence, of the present day.

The vassal sides with the priestocracy, and is enraged against their vileness when his eyes are opened.

There is no prophecy to the point, and all the times are ambiguous. What guesswork. The christians build up their sect, and swear to it, as authorized by the old bible. The Mahometans build up their sect, and avow it from both, and from Mahomet. The Mormons erect their latter-day-faith, and prove that all are equal. They all fight, not like men, civilized, but barbarians, like degraded sectarians. Get out of the world, if ye cannot unite on one eternal principle of brotherhood, and one eternal standard, that of Almighty God, of the universe. You do not act like men. Religion makes men.

All inspirations and revelations, and all peculiarity, disclosed under that category, are necessarily most exact communications, and most accurate science tested on all the principles of philosophy, or they are the most outragous fraud and false pretences, whether poetry or history, there can be no license, as all must be true inspiration, or for ever to be discarded.

Church-men have said before us that they conceived all the bible inspiration to direct erring man. If the bible be taken as inspiration, none of its contents can be excluded.

It is very evident that such pretended inspiration, presents the worst antagonism with truth, justice, mind, and the God of mind.

The best revelation of God to mind, is by his works of the universe. No book revelation can compare with this.

Peculiar revelation makes known to us a peculiar god or gods. All book revelation does this, and destroys itself for ever. But you may affect to believe implicitly, the fathers of the church, as they are called. We have seen how one of the chief. Eusebius, was caught about Josephus, the historian, and now we may form good estimate of Irenæus, who says, "Miracles even from raising of the dead, down to the casting out of demons, were, in his time, frequently performed by Christians."

The word demons, must cast him out of the credence of any respectable mind. What can be worse than the legends of the fathers, except the bibles on which they are built? But the time for miracles is stopped. How do you know that? Because it never began!

Mind only knows, as mind enlightened by science and philosophy, reveals to it: all else is guess-work.

Physical causes prevent any reliance on man's position about miracles, granting that the bible was less suspicious than it is. Psychology explains much.

God's inspiration can only be to mind through his works, not by bibles, that present peculiar faith necessarily, which clashes with rational faith, a thing that betrays the error, as no two principles of God clash.

His works prove universal, not peculiar principles to any select few or nation, and therefore nullify the bibles of tradition. All that we can say of the phenomena of nature is, that however wonderful relatively to the state of science and mind, they are not miracles. But the world is not yet reformed by all the priestocracies' pretences about revelation.

It has to advance many more steps in mental elevation. Mind is God's, only of course best agent in general, for his revelation and inspiration.

God has no other, and does not make distinctions.

These were made by the oriental priestocracies.

The very action of mind proves that. Where, is even full and satisfactory proof of any, but mind-revelations? If God committed this peculiar power of miracles to individuals, then no peculiar proof will answer. It must be truth-proof. If miracles were ever performed, then the miracle testimony should be left not dependent on man's record, but God's record. God has left a fair and unmistakable record, which is his works of nature, but man's, is books.

God needs none but his works, as the main demonstration proves him to the confusion of all atheists or polytheists, that pretend to advance miracles, prophecies, mysteries and peculiarities, and decides by its paramount importance, the whole question for ever.

What are all miracles and prophecies but positive falsehoods from the very nature of things?

All miracles and peculiarities reveal superstition, not religion. No miracles are expedient, for God's works eminently prove his authorship, attributes, and conservative principles. All natural phenomena are universal, and cannot be appropriated by any peculiar sects, therefore, there can be no especial miracles.

All pretences to miracles, no matter what the occasion or the propagator, have in their very nature, the full proof of their falsity. Miracles are essential to all false systems, and take away the miracles which are necessarily false, and all the systems will topple.

Shame to the senseless propagators of all or any miracles, thereby teaching to mind no truth, reason, or God of the universe. As pretenders have not changed the nature of things, they must abide the analysis then, and the true miracles, that is, God's power, condemns them. No priestocracies' dramas can prove a miracle.

It is not rational that God would yield miracles to defeat his own exclusive empire, as these bibles of tradition involve themselves. Instead of one messiahship in the old, there were the priestocracy a whole. In the second or new, not only Christ, but all his priestocracy.

What are the miracles of the Romish church? Ridiculous falsehoods and pretences. Rational mind gives us the only, the best revelations of God. There can be no other. Peculiar faith gives us peculiar trifles. How accommodating it was. The prophecies would be nothing, if peculiar faith, urged on by peculiar interest, did not meet them. 1 Kings, c. xiii. v. 11, The "old prophet in Bethel" had to inquire, 12, "what way went he? (the man of God,) 14, and went after the man of God, and found him. 18, He said unto him, I am a prophet also as thou art; and an angel spake unto me by the word of the Lord—but he lied unto him. 19 v. So he (the man of God) went back with him," contrary to his orders, and did not know it! What prophets! These be they, O world, which are the truthful. The one a liar, the other ignorant! and the liar had prophecy after that! v. 20, " The word of the Lord came unto the prophet that brought him back." The first had healed the dried-up hand of Jeroboam. 33, " After this thing Jeroboam returned not from his evil way, but made again of the lowest of the people priests of the high places ; whosoever would, he consecrated him." The highest were only of that class at best, could be no others. As bad as Israel, Judah was worse ; c. xiv, v. 22, " Judah did evil in the sight of the Lord, above all that their fathers had done 23, For they also built them high places and images and groves on every high hill, and under every green tree ; 24, and there were also sodomites in the land. 25, The king of Egypt, Shishak, invaded Jerusalem successfully. 26, He took away the treasures of the house of the Lord, and all the treasures. 30, And there was war between Rehoboam and Jeroboam all their days." Of course the priestocracy referred the corruption to the surrounding nations. And the speech of the prophet Ahijah to Jeroboam caused war between the people of Israel and Judah, and their several kings, for a long time. He excited him to revolt against his own king, Solomon, because the last subdivided the kingdom of the priestocracy ; and another prophet, Shemaiah, promoted the success, in stopping Rehoboam from seeking his own. Thus these men of god made and unmade kings.

What a detestable degradation was the pretence of prophecy. See the bitter fruits of this barbarian sacrilege. And Baasha, the son of Ahijah, conspired against Nadab, the son of Jeroboam, and destroyed all the house of Jeroboam. And by bible acknowledgment, Baasha was as evil as Jeroboam.

Jehu the prophet proclaimed against Baasha and his house Elah, against whom conspired Zimri, who was successful. Were not the prophets fomenters of discord in the country ?

Zimri destroyed the whole house, as the prophet spake. Then there was war between these two people of one family. Then Israel was divided into parts. One of the subsequent kings, Ahab, served Baal, and worshipped him.

False prophets, they were all false prophets.

Elijah was a humane prophet to tell Ahab that it should not rain for these years, but according to his word, as the Lord God of Israel liveth. Where were the people all this time, the innocent women and children, as well as men ? Were they all to be sacrificed to the vanity of prophecy? Religion is an accompaniment and constituent of mind, as creation's birthright, uniformly and invariably from God, but peculiar faith is the mere contingency of peculiar education, varying with places, circumstances and people. The triumph of religion over superstition is the first law of God.

1 Kings, ch. xvii. v. 1, Elijah said unto Ahab, "There shall not be dew nor rain these years, but according to my word."

He was fed by ravens! He brought a dead child to life. These juggleries might be explained away, if the bible was not false. He slew hundreds of Baal's prophets, and those of the groves, I presume nearly a thousand in all ; and here we see the crusades of the prophets, bad enough without involving the world. These prophets are strange beings—the priestocracy-jesuits. Strange to say, that he could not satisfy, but enraged Jezebel by so doing, and fled her wrath. What bitter animosities, persecutions and massacres prevailed among the prophets.

Ch. xix. v. 9, Elijah had to tell the Lord, who inquired of him " What doest thou here, Elijah ?"—that is, the priestocracy involve themselves in their labyrinth—10 v. " and he said * * for the children of Israel have slain thy prophets with the sword, and I, even I only, am left"—and the poison worked both ways with the priestocracy, who were " very jealous for the Lord God of hosts." 16, Again the prophet is true to his functions, setting up other kings and another prophet.

He, Elijah, anointed Hazael to be king over Syria, Jehu king over Israel, and Elisha the prophet in his room. What a sprig of despotism. The unction of priestocracy was expedient for despotism ; both are one and the same, republicans.

Though Ahab was evil, yet he whipped the Syrians twice dreadfully, but, ever true to their vocation, the prophets had a hand in it ; and yet their bible only speaks of " the

17

servants of the king of Syria," who were their pagan priests, advising about success untruthfully. Their casuistry is ever ready to make themselves the conspicuous actors.
They were complete masters of the kings, as they write it. The whole key to this bible
is, that it was written for the despotism of the priestocracy. Elijah humbled Ahab. C.
xxii. v. 20, "And the Lord said, who shall persuade Ahab—21, and there came forth a
spirit ; 22, and the Lord said—and he said—and I will be a lying spirit in the mouth of
all his prophets. And he (the Lord) said, thou shalt persuade him, and prevail also:
go forth. and do so. 23, Now, the Lord hath put a lying spirit in the mouth of all these
thy prophets." This was what Micaiah the prophet said in part. The hand of the prophet was in the third battle, when Ahab was slain. When a person was saved, and no
damage done after the false prophecy, it was because of repentance. What do priests
differ in ? They all lie outrageously. We may ask triumphantly in detail, as in all,
what proof is given that " Elijah went up by a whirlwind into heaven" ? Who saw all
this ? The bible speaks of witnesses : but who endorses these ? No one. It is false.
   2 Kings, c. iii. v. 14, Elisha said, " were it not that I regard the presence of Jehoshaphat the king of Judah, I would not look toward thee, (the king of Israel,) nor
see thee." No wonder the popes put themselves over kings. What a mighty influence they wielded, the victory enured to their acts as coming from the Lord. What kept
the priestocracy down, even as much as it was ?
   Because they were mortals, and committed themselves as mortals. Elisha had to
inquire of the Shunamite what was the matter, as " the Lord hath hid it from me, and
hath not told me." C. v. v. 15, And he (Naaman) said, now I know that there is no
God in all the earth, but in Israel! and positively no such god elsewhere ; hence mind
cannot know him. Elisha made Gehazi a leper, as white as snow, from Naaman's leprosy. The prophets ought to have repelled the invasion of enemies, have civilized the
world, possessed of such potent power. But this petty capital of theirs was of a different calibre altogether, existent in the atmosphere of bibles. How this false pretence
defeats itself.
   The juggle of the peculiar god who only lived in Israel, is a far different thing from
the unappreciable dignity of the God of the universe. The priestocracy of course is
correspondent. They only let this peculiar god, this Juggernaut, speak as they spoke.
Thousands and thousands of men were engaged in this legend. Will the world ever
thoroughly analyze this curious dynasty ? Gehazi saw his master lie, and what else
could he do but lie ? That was his trade. But this is an episode, to give the boldest
relief to the position of Elisha. How curiously this net-work is woven ! Are you
preparing for the ministry ? You must be a sophist, positively. C. vi, 6, And the man
of God said, where fell it ? And he showed him the place ; and he cut a stick, and cast
it in thither ; and the iron did swim.
   This is only a small slip. Where is the necessity for the man of God to inquire ?
The writer only outdid himself ; he was asleep when he wrote that small circumstance.
C. ix, True to his vocation, Elisha had another prophet to have Jehu anointed king of
Israel, to avenge on Ahab's house the blood of the prophets at the hands of Jezebel.
It was dangerous for kings to resist prophets, who were not sophists for nothing. 14 v.
So Jehu, the son of Jehoshaphat, the son of Nimshi, conspired against Joram, for the
whoredoms and witchcrafts of Jezebel ; c. x, v. 16, and he (Jehu) said, see my zeal
for the Lord. 17, He slew all that remained unto Ahab in Samaria, till he had destroyed him, according to the saying of the Lord, which he spake to Elijah. He
caused seventy of Ahab's children to be beheaded, and excused the assassination by the
·prophecy of Elijah, " for the Lord hath done that which he spake by his servant Elijah." What a dangerous and ferocious union of church and state ! Wo to the man that
lifted up his countenance against the priestocracy. Is the world asleep ? Is it so detestably corrupt as to be the perpetual tool of such ignoble myrmidons ? Is the history
of the Jews aught but one revolting and disgusting scene of conspiracy, through the
priestocracy, against the rights of the people ?
   This same sneaking and cowardly Elijah, who could not face the living Jezebel,
caused his tool Elisha to promote his tail to perpetrate the most vindictive revenge
upon her descendants ; and the excuse, ever sovereign, was, thus saith Israel's God!
Jehu carried out the creature. He destroyed all the priests of Baal, between whom
and the other priests there was war, and to prove it conclusively, he followed after the
golden calves of Jeroboam in Bethel and Dan, preferring them to any other. Of course
miserably corrupt were the whole, without exception. Now, if these were true prophets,
they had no function to select pure kings. C. x, v. 32, The old excuse is assigned, as
"Hazael smote them (the people) in all the coasts of Israel," that " The Lord began to
cut Israel short." Ch. xi, v. 9, Jehoida the priest commanded, v. 12, and they made
p.him (the king's son) king, and anointed him, and they clapped their hands, and said,

"God save the king." Jehoida, the priest, had the Jew usurper killed, and destroyed all Baal's house, &c., by the Lord's people—that is, the priestocracy's people, full proof that the Jews belonged to the priests. Jehoash was the priest-advised king. Let the pretended prophets hide themselves behind mysteries; let them tell their own curious tale, mix the probable with the improbable and the miracle, and the system is complete for verdant people, to enjoy the peculiar God of the Jews and all such machinery, all the Elijahs to sustain him, but then they horribly neglect the God of the universe, who needs no more than that which is enough to prove himself. This pure Being does not change. He is immutable. He does to-day, what he did alway at first. He is perfectly immutable. If he be not, if he ever offered miracles, he is obliged to give them now, to be consistent. But this perfect Being acts the very reverse to miracles, to prove his exalted character.

Did not the kings retain prophets in their cabinet of councillors? They appear to have acted as the dictators, the secretaries of state. There should be perpetual momentoes of miracles to be for every generation surely, as all generations were the beneficiaries, and had the absolute right to demand these miracles. After all the tinkering and botching of the world's priestocracy, they had not the sagacity to see, or the honesty of truth to acknowledge, that it was mind through which God of mind has maintained his conservative action through the universe.

But how came the priestocracy not to make more miracles, and better, at least less liable to detection and exposure, as they had the universe to draw on? They never could have originated them at all at first had science been exact, and mind honest. It proves conclusively that mind and science were in a miserable fix at the first stages of existence, by perversions that took all advantages of that ignorance, and that none on God's earth have ever been baser than the priestocracy. None can be worse.

That sophisticated state now prevails over much of the world; and instead of honest patriots seeking to put it down, most are actually nurturing it!

Let any gypsey be brought forward, and now crowds flock in some places to see her prodigies. False pretences are advanced, and the wonder-loving, sight-seeing, superstitious people feed and fatten their own fictions.

Only to think of a pig drawing crowds of people to hear their fortunes told in 1850. The pig separated its master's tales, separated even married people, and was sacrificed to their fury. What should have been done with the master, the most guilty wretch? But is nobody else amenable to censure? Who are the aiders and abettors, that give comfort and aid to all this stupid senselessness, this bullion of imposition?

What senseless fury of the people, and what nonsensical faith or credulity! There are no limits to foolish faith. The people should at least analyze all that pertains to this point, and know that if they did not furnish the vitality that all such humbugs would necessarily die of themselves. What malignancy attends prophecy. What a spirit it engenders among the wise-acres.—I told you so.

What was that of Ishmael, with "his hand against every man, and every man's hand against him." That is a caricature of human nature, and the basest libel of its author, God. To this day the Arab is libeled under this prophecy and peculiar-hating faith.

There is nothing in the prophecies, that we can see, beyond what may be expected from those savage times. What horrid sin of the prophets? One superstition is put for another superstition, one pagan idolatry is substituted for another. As to the prophecies, if there had been any, it was too easy to establish by them most conclusively.

The truth was not spoken by the priestocracy, who lie always.

All the bible dramas among the people are jesuitical throughout. What do you want with prophecy? Can anything make mankind more miserable and corrupt? The government of universal providence repels the idea.

Does God create misery or evil? The priestocracy does that too much already, with its calibre for ruin.

But you wish by all means to cultivate the wonderful. It is you that make miracles, that is, wonder at what are merely common phenomena on the solution of science on adequate analysis.

The most that can be said in favor of prophecy is, that it is the clairvoyance of somnambulism, a diseased state of mind. How far can that go? Is that in reality, after all said, anything?

It is asserted of some, that they could tell important events then transpiring at distant places. But could they foretell the future, the deeds of other spheres? That looks impossible. We have no authentic accounts, and believe that much imposition of this character has been practised.

When we are told of heaven, it is the detail of men's dreamy thoughts, amounting to nothing after all.

The prophets assume because they speak by their writings.

The world has been ambitious of the marvellous, the miraculous, of prophecy. All wisdom can point out analogy, wise foresight, but not insight, as all pretence thereto is imposture. Be the advantage of ventriloquism, voice and hand jugglery, what they may, but mind-jugglery covers the whole ground of false pretences.

There is no effect without a cause, and though we cannot account for it, yet this principle is universal to God. Every ancient nation has had its gods. The system that describes some of them is a bible. To make them most impressive, legends of miracles, prophecies, and mysteries are common. Now, does it follow that such are right? How do you know that they are wrong? Try them by the only potential jury, mind and reason, and they can give this only righteous verdict against such. You deem them right, because your education has been peculiar, you have been taught to believe implicitly in them by a blind faith. Now, all the education and faith were false, the pretended miracles were false. You did not question the first position, that your duty to mind absolutely required. You sacrificed your mind's rights at the altar of the priestocracy of superstition. You have been wofully deceived, and that by mind and self-delusion.

The question of mind is paramount to all others, and should hold them in abeyance. How, then, can you resign yourself to such subtle and designing impostors as those who fabricated such unprincipled plans?

The question of mind and reason is not advanced as a rational one, but by sophistry, in defence of superstition. It has ever been so with the priestocracy. Are they more truthful now than previously, except so far as science compels them? Be not their blind victim, to be fleeced and derided by them and posterity.

You appreciate augurs and soothsayers; they are the priestocracy, all analogous. Magicians and astrologers of the world in the days of ignorance prevailed, as humbug is the creature of ignorance. When we cannot account for miracles, or any wondrous events in the universe, the difficulty of solution is in us, and it is not in existence as to the miracles which cannot possibly have a being in this creation. Miracle, prophecy, and mystery are the creatures of ignorance, that has a prolific brood of humbugs, let off in every age of the world to the present day. Of course, then, none such are of God. Who endorses the miracles. When people speak of a miracle, it is their direct admission of ignorance of nature's laws and phenomena. The science of all natural laws destroys all miracles, prophecies, and mysteries.

Miracle is a thing to be wondered at, that cannot be defined as to its nature and character, though a natural phenomenon that exceeds the knowledge of science in the philosophy of the miracle-maker. It is the ignorance of the audience that makes the miracle, not the man pretending to operate.

Revealed religion! who revealed it but mind?

What is more, is false pretences. Where, now, are your prophecies? This is a test question. A great attempt has been made about God's mysteries. All that are priests' mysteries do not enlighten the world. The world is none the wiser whether they be God's or not, by all the bibles of tradition, nay, farther removed from them. As to prophecy, all that is practicable is by the inspirations of mind through sound sense and philosophical science, can be thus only consummated. What does somnambulism add to the proof? Where mystery prevails, there the bible false pretences prevail. The world is after making something by abuse of man.

There are even now the omens of birds, from which auguries are drawn! Of what avail is the mind without rational education? The mind that has instilled into it superstition, can rarely eradicate the evil of peculiar faith or credulity in such things. The idea of ghosts, not the ghost, haunts the mind of the credulous vulgar. The world, in the folds of peculiar faith, speaks of miracles, and there never was one; even the great creation of the universe, and the mighty creation of mind, if you are sincere in miracles, must be only a paramount problem; and this has proved the authenticity of the Creator's bible, whose volumes are its mighty solar systems, that your soul has to read to appreciate the divine author, and realize the divine presence, the Holy Centre.

It is clear that mind is supreme of creation, and therefore must be the particular centre of due honor that can never be paid short of immortality.

Rational mind needs no prophecy of man's black letter peculiar bible, when the most illustrious document is in bold relief most patent.

The only seeming prophecy is entrusted to the function of time, the measure of motion of each orb.

When the immortal soul has read through in eternity, then the universe-problem will be solved.

It is impious to ask of man miracles and prophecies, when the problem is elsewhere in proper course of solution. Were the pretenders crazy, or those that believe them prophets?

Prophecies and miracles should not close at all, but should continue, as they are as necessary now as ever, for the influence is to be on mind that cannot take cognizance thereof unless submitted to all the proper tests of the senses. That is the nature of honorable testimony, of truth and honesty. The priestocracy pretend to the assertion, and they first originated the whole legends. Was it because they had no legitimate offspring of religion, that they were reckless of the effects of their falsehoods on posterity? It was their profession, that was enough.

Of what use are the pretended prophecies, their bible and patriarchs as they were called; all that, when none can be or are proved? Why this best of proofs omitted? Who endorses all such? The affiliated. What the interested sophists? Can a sworn sophist tell the truth? That would be a miracle indeed. This bible will not stand the test of morals much less of religion. What was Noah's prophecy against Canaan for? Surely he never made such but by subsequent operators. Much stress is laid upon the position of Canaan, and enough to have fragments of hostility thereby in the human family.

Now if I understand his story rightly, as far as presented, the children of Shem were in the worst bondage to Ham's descendants in Egypt, for four hundred years, if we allow that statement of the bible, which clearly proves prophecy futile; and when it states, too, the same people were in subjection to the Canaanites for years.

Could morals be worse, than credulity in such a book-curse to the world? The writers were the most pitiful pettifoggers in the drama of human events, and confined their bigoted contraction to their little circle, not even of facts, but of their miserable fiction. In the so miscalled universal empires, those of Shem and Japheth, the pretended bible first stock, after its deluge, alternately were the subjects, and are yet, so far as that implies. Now what has been worse than the vassalage of the Jews, for centuries since then? That was a theme for a statesman. I do not believe that any such tradition is correct, any more the prophecy, all one, and the same. The bible ancient lineage is as false as the balance pretended. It bears the ear-marks of the priestocracy, and in no part of the world, and in no age, did they ever rise to the dignity of men, but sank far below the rights of mind, ever. What, then, is all biblical prophecy worth? Before we can be assured of the first prophecy of Noah, that reflects on the justice of God for punishing Canaan for his father, Ham, who had other sons, we should have it proved that the whole earth was known to the writers at that day, which is clearly disproved by their making it a plane, instead of a globe. It is even improbable, since a great portion of it has been long since their time discovered to the moderns, the discovery of which enabled them to pronounce its rotundity. Was there ever such a man as Noah? What mortals can endorse it?

Now what sort of justice was there in condemning a race of people to perpetual servitude, on account of a drunkard's nakedness being seen by his son?

Did the God of the universe have any hand in that? Is this inspiration? Was vision itself so unpardonable? Was it any personal action done to Noah? Had it been a parricide, the curse could not have been greater.

Is this bible-morals; certainly not religion?

It seems that one of its patriarchs, Noah, got so drunk that he stripped off his clothes and exposed his nakedness to his sons, and not content with all that, he cursed about, and worse than all, like a stupid beast, he cursed his innocent grandson!

How could Noah be a just man and perfect in his generation, walking with God, if he cursed the Canaanites in his drunkenness? But he did it from divine impulse! That adds impiety to blasphemy. It brings down the character of God to degraded man, and causes him to perpetrate an irrational deed.

The nearest version is, that because fanatics sought Canaan's land, the last were pronounced accursed to justify land piracy, murder by the wholesale, and all the accursed abominations of barbarism.

Is this the loveliest attitude of prophecy, that brutalizes man, and libels his maker? When one superstition was only to be superseded by another, a prolific crop of paganism to the remotest times. What was in such? There is no excuse, much less justification, because the priestocracy fabricated this impious felony.

True is such prophecy? Man of mind, republican, can you be so far lost to your rights to believe such?

Having disposed of one of the patriarchs, let us try another. What can be more untrue than the prophecy of Abraham, a prophet as called by the bible, respecting the Israelites, Gen. xiii., 14, and the Lord said unto Abraham, ch. xiii., v. 15., "For all the land which thou seest, to thee will I give it, and to thy seed forever."

But, say the affiliated, this Abramic prophecy was subsequently modified. Agreed, says liberal monotheism, to all the legitimate extent, and then all modifications are st'll stronger against it, the afterthoughts of the priestocracy. What shall be said of Moses, the dictator of the priestocracy? His prophecy is not proved though : Deu. xxxiv. 10, "There arose not a prophet since in Israel, like unto Moses, whom the Lord knew face to face." We will try him by Joshua, his prime minister, who assuredly will do him justice : Josh. ch. xiv., v. 9, "And Moses aware on that day, saying, surely the land whereon thy feet have trodden, shall be thine inheritance, and thy children's forever, because thou hast wholly followed the Lord my God." Was Moses the world-maker, or the Creator ?

What can be not only falser than all the preceding affected prophecies, but more abominable blasphemies ?

Where the Turk rules, is that the undisputed possession of the land of Canaan forever, by the Jews ?

These prophecies were the purest and most unadulterated of any ; why not fulfilled ? Because it was utterly impossible for God to have ever made any such. No—never. The God of the universe is not like man's creation's gods. What can be more untrue than all this ? The pretended prophecies of Noah are equally futile. Who can endorse a universal deluge of this globe, in the face of impossibilities ? None of these pretences can be modified without blasphemy, as the God of the universe is the God of foresight. Any other category makes him a god of afterthought, peculiar and imbecile, clearly a priestocracy's work.

Those who prophecy of the final restoration of the Jews are Moses, Isaiah, Jeremiah, Ezekiel, &c. How comes the prophecy already quoted of the grand patriarch Abraham not fulfilled ? That cuts all these subsequent prophets down at one blow, from which all Jewry and its bibles cannot recover. That is all of a piece in the whole humbug.

What could have been of greater value than the lost tribes ? Why were they not recovered and united to the nation ? Does pretended prophecy represent any elevated character, of policy or statesmanship or world government ? It seems that the last is supreme over it. It did not begin to render them or mankind susceptible of mental improvement, but debased it. When we duly estimate the false pretences, the balance is immeasurably against all such.

They all necessarily present falsehoods. The books of Moses from Genesis to Deuteronomy, contain several remarkable interpolations, the last of which proves particularly them written very many centuries after Moses is said to have died. Deuter. chap. xxxiv., v. 10.—" And there arose not a prophet since in Israel like unto Moses, whom the Lord knew face to face."

This would not have been written in justice to truth till after all the prophets so called lived with whom the comparison is made. If written after all, they are forgeries, if before, they are false. What profit then, can they be to the world to whom even prophecy is a wholesale forgery and falsehood !

No matter by whom written, the books are anonymous, and unworthy of credit as vitiated by interpolations if not by legends originally.

That is too plain to miss, after what we have seen of Moses.

As to prophecies we see the oracles of the heathens claim them, the Philistines, Pharaoh, Nebuchadnezzar, Balaam, and even his ass.

The pretension to divination was a profession among the ancients. Now as to the prophecies of Moses about the Jews, all that had transpired up to the time of writing the last word in Deuteronomy must be embraced. Of course the story presented is like all priestocracy's work, after-thoughts. Can enlightened minds of the present day be entrapped by such scurvy tricks? They would laugh at the Roman, Greek or Egyptian mummeries of augury and soothsaying, yet can take in all that of the Jews, that of course is worse, by being knavishly fixed up.

Do not the moderns need the policy of prophecy which would be immutable, if the God of the universe had instituted it ?

That such should become extinct proves a change only in character, with the Jew peculiar God.

It is worse than children's play, to talk about prophecies. In what a miserable dilemma and transgression does the admission place the moderns, who not only stultify their own exalted minds in taking and endorsing these false pretences of the priestocracy, but blaspheme their God ?

What are the credentials of divine mission ? Miracles. What honorable proof has the world of them ? None, but false pretences.

Do they establish anything then, trustworthy ?

All the miracles in the world as assumed, cannot repel for a moment any sectarianism ancient or modern, Christ's or Smith's ; that invalidates and vitiates all titles claimed. All sectarianism thus declared is antagonistic to God's unity, that must not be violated, else creation is violated in its preservation. So of course prophecies are perfectly worthless, a dead letter, analogous to all its bibles.

I need not particularize how defective all this is about Christ, till I reach that particular: or of the false positions of a Paul, who reminds us of the astrologer who knew a.! about the distant stars, yet proved his utter ignorance by falling into a near pit.

What can be falser than John's revelation ?

John that proclaimed to the seven churches of Asia, proclaimed the absurdities about the bible's heaven, which destroy the false pretences about Christ's greatest miracles. Thus they perpetrate murder on others, and suicide on themselves.

John only told too much, and in making a peculiar heaven for the peculiar gods, he put the last blow of destruction, and toppled it all over.

Are the prophecies of Daniel understood by the best minds ? If they are, why do they differ so essentially ? Those prophecies cannot be interpreted alike, by the moderns. Of what use are they to the world, that looks at truth and not oracles, that are all analogous from those of the pythoness to those of this monomaniac ?

The genius of best minds is rendered impracticable in his quagmire about the accounting for the kingdoms, at the miserable guess-work, at the blasphemy of this trash, for Asia as well as Europe. Thus it is the most ludicrous, the most ridiculous position of the amateurs, that they now require a prophet, to unravel the prophecies of the past ! These be thy gods, ye idol-worshippers. How could this prophecy be true, when " The fourth beast shall be fourth kingdom upon earth, which shall be diverse from all kingdoms, and shall devour the whole earth, and shall tread it down, and break it in pieces." Where was there a universal empire ?

What can be falser than this, if the fourth empire, that is assumed to be universal, is assumed to be that of Rome the ancient ? Her power, as imperial as it was, did not extend east beyond Babylon. How could it be a universal empire, to leave out a majority of the world's population, and one of two continents ? The limits of that empire were fixed by Hadrian on the western side of the Euphrates, or on the very borders of Chaldea. How can this last part be true ? Where was China, with her one-third of the world's population ; India, with her eighth ; Australia—when America was not even known ? When was Arabia wholly subdued, that the bible defenders evince was subject to no empire ?

Is this prophecy against prophecy, and that in the same bible, the modern Daniel against the ancient patriarch Abraham ? But worse than that, there is a fatal collision between the last and Christ ; for if Ishmael " will be a wild man, his hand will be against every man, and every man's hand against him," how will Christ have " the uttermost parts of the earth for his possession ?" " To whom every knee should bow," and becoming united, they should " love the brethren." This kingdom of Rome was equalled, if not excelled by that of the Saracens, after it.

Consistency is a jewel, that such bibles cannot attain. The Millerites, who have had awful and fatal panics, in several of their corps, given to some of the timid, to causing their deaths, can now well appreciate the impracticable prophecies, and find the difficulty on the other side of the proposition ; for assuredly, if they never reach their ultimate place of rest till the decyphering takes place, they will have to look on the other side of eternity.

The bible speaks of false prophets, as if all were not so that pretended to prophecy. If they are not so, the fault does not lie with them, but those that affect to think otherwise.

What else but the lying sort can prophets be ; so far from knowing prophecy, they do not come up to the facts of creation, or of truth.

There are no prophecies but are all matters of a piece with the vitiated books of Moses.

There is nothing certain in the peculiar faith bibles, not even their heaven, whose very God changed and repented. All the conception of the priestocracy reflected, as a mirror, the utter insignificance of their peculiar faiths and bibles. Had not the Creator impressed on mind all the elements of its duties, all that man could do would be totally inefficient.

Peculiar faith and prophecies present a sad view of the earth's history. To estimate the earth's desolation, we have only to notice their ancient conflicts. Martial piracy was much identified with their persecution. Vandalism prevails throughout these scenes of violence. The priestocracy were universally after power, and all that can I procure it. It is ever in this light that we must study them. When it is said that Genseric, the king of the Vandals, the most bigoted, persecuted the orthodox Christians, it was of a character in his overrunning and plundering Rome. The world presents an analogous condition of peculiar faiths suffering in turn from each other, unrestrained by the enlightened benefits of mental toleration.

Rational religionists desire to exclude the vandalism of all such faith, now too abundantly despotic.

Let not bible interpreters pretend to solve prophecies by any bible legends. They should attend to a better theme. Who does not recollect the savage Portius Cato's famous "Carthage must be destroyed."

When ready to become subjects, the citizens were excluded from the city, that it might be destroyed. The savage Romans burnt this city of seven hundred thousand people, razing it to its foundations. Even the Roman general wept over its ruins.

It is faithful history that embraces science and philosophy; that presents the right causes and effects—not oracle prophecies, a thing of no existence—that rational mind needs.

What do the Jew oracles say of the destruction of this, one of the most splendid cities of the world? This was a remarkable event in the world's history and time's annals, in which the pure priestocracy could have dilated for a world's benefit. But Jew, as well as Canaanite hands, were reeking with human sacrifices.

Did we see Jews coming forward to civilize the balance of mankind, in the arrest of such things, when other nations established it as a compact, and proved themselves longways ahead of Jewry in civilization?

What! the Jews not helping to humanize the world, when they boasted of having a peculiar God, that did all peculiarly for Jewry?

No; they sunk into the lowest barbarism themselves, by the effects of this very prophecy, and devoted their own proud city, Jerusalem, to be sacked by Titus, and sacrificed on the bloody altar of this same prophecy more than a million of their own fellow-citizens, immolated by the delusion of an oracle of their degraded priestocracy. What was prophecy and all the accompaniment for, but the best civilization of the world?

Has such mission ever been thus proved?

Not an iota, for the reverse has been established, in the fearful annals of humanity.

A mighty inspiration was that which left out of sight of the world, some of its best portions, one of its two continents! That ignored the form even of the globe, the philosophy of its position, the reasons, &c. Ah, but these things did not concern the Jews. Come Jew, christian, prophets should tell us, then, where were the lost ten tribes! This was a question of importance, for the proof of prophecy. Has it been answered? Better was it not expedient to have that loss prevented? If the Jews were selected for the world's benefit, assuredly all world questions are essential.

The only best way for the world prophets and all, to do best and right, is to act on principles of truth and independence. Has it been done? Very far from it.

God has not superseded mind by prophecies that require prophecies to interpret them, nor inspiration that requires science to correct and rectify it. God deals in the facts of creation, man deals in the fictions of fictions. God certainly would have protected his chosen peculiar people more particularly than he did, as they were overrun and captured by so many different nations. They were, of course, vindictive towards their captors, and painted them in their worst colors. If his power was peculiarly manifested about such things, protection was best.

Why was pretended prophecy so much behind the wants of the world, as not to have America preached to? All this, kills the doctrine of peculiar faith completely. Where were the cities of Central America so long depopulated, that their desolation could not have been prophecied about? Surely the Gospel should have preceded science in the discovery, if faith be superior to mind and reason, and the magnificent enjoyment awarded the Jews as something worth while. Prophecy should have been for the world.

Why did she not enlighten all Asia, as China? Why not prophecy to all? What desolation has come to the country of her protection? Such should not be desolation, but the noblest triumph of intellectual and moral greatness of all nations that we would expect to see realized. And has it come to this, that the potency of peculiar faith has ruined, instead of elevated the Jewish character? Yes, this is the proof, that the Jewish mind has been debased by its peculiar faith, Judaism. What a reflection of self-congratulation, for comprehensive rational religion! The world has to come to this decision, the sooner the better, that any peculiar faith is a despotism instead of mind's blessing.

If the pentateuch had been written after the Jewish captivity, then it was easy to describe the Chaldeans and Babylonians, that had birds' wings on their beasts. As to the straits and reductions of famine, they were not uncommon in those days of barbarity that was exercised to the conquered.

The height of agricultural cultivation was not so elevated as to preclude it, nor was commerce so extensive as to prevent it. They were to be carried into Egypt and sold for slaves. What, a second time? What then becomes of Canaan's curse? Here is prophecy against prophecy again and again. Where is, then, Abram's perpetual possession of land? Sandys says, as to "The Holy Land, here be also some Jews; yet inherit they no part of the land, but in their own country do live as aliens."

But the Jews are a peculiar people—so are the gypsies, neither is a nation, but its remnant. What could we expect of the ancient cities that have decayed? We must analyze the facts of nature. They were dependent on commerce, that has changed abundantly in our days, and left nations most known for others, that have just entered into notice. America, then unknown, has the greatest commercial marine on the globe. What can be worse to the world of mind, than the errors, the vices, the crimes, of any pretended revelation? Its gain will furnish no profit. Says the thinking priest, I cannot reconcile the justice of predestination of the accursed part, destiny, with that of the saved. That proves itself all of man's folly, through the pretence of revelation. The bible advocates skulk the question; so far from prophecies, they have not even science.

It is shameful that the world should be so meanly imposed upon by the base. The greatest was no miracle, nor is it right to call it so, and that must supersede all others, that is, the universe that was established and can be read in universal language, by men who might speak millions of different languages, and is forever to prove its illustrious Author, the test of its creator.

As to any miracles, they are spurious, all false pretences. Moses' miracles cannot exist, because they would violate and displace God's immutable laws of nature. God has recorded in the self same act all that mind could think of calling miracles.

I have selected the greatest principal prophets, and all have seen them prostrated by their own pretences.

Let us analyze all their positions, that if proved would be testimony. God, of course, is the essential witness. Does he affirm any such as the interpretations of Nebuchadnezzar's dream? Not a word of it. All this looks very clever if Daniel produced the proof. But what impious false pretence! We have that proof.

It is not prophecy, but rationality of mind that God deals in. The word of God was ratified in the sublime universal language of the creation, that people of all tongues, however diverse, can and do construe alike. Down, impious blasphemers, after this. Miracles by God will be miracles, if intended, no matter how long past. Had a miracle been ever performed by an apostle it had been enough to convert the whole.—This is all overlooked, as disproving all such pretences. When things ought to succeed, of course "God hardens their hearts," to defeat the very purpose.

Does the world believe in popish miracles? No. Yet, have not many books for such false pretences been multiplied and attested in past ages? Why are not they entitled to faith, as any bibles of faith? If Jesus had done a tenth of the miracles ascribed to him, he ought to have convinced the whole world. It would have flocked to him most certainly, particularly the Jew portion, as having such before its eyes.

What good did Christ's or others' miracles if they were not conclusive for final and complete success. The tale of his miracles kills itself. He performed miracles plentifully, yet they did not convince the Jews, who were to receive all the whole benefits. Of course such miracles were most abominably false.

What was this Messiah for? To do this very thing? Then if he did not do it his mission was an imposition, fraud, base false pretence. Out of their own statements the whole are condemned.

Miracles and prophecies interfere with God's arrangement of free agency of mind. Speak of prophecies, do they not need another series to explain the past? Commentators the most learned fail, as they differ much about revelations, not being able to agree among themselves about Paul, much less Daniel. Is not the whole world, Jew and Gentile, contending about such stuff? There are various interpretations given by several, varying with nearly every writer! Has not the world been tortured enough without keeping up this bible delusion to all time. It is not the prophecy, bible, or faith, that are all false, it is religion we need. Were not the Jews the chosen, pet people of God, the peculiar God? Of what benefit were the prophecies if the peculiar chosen people of God could not obtain, through them, the real benefit of the second dispensation? If mind be at fault about the prophecies, the prophecies are at fault. Of course the Jews have proved again and again their readiness to adopt all the blessings of such a dispensation, having adopted several messiahs to the death by tens of thousands of their people. The question well arises, was the first messiah ever announced, but by fiction? It seems too clear for refutation, even contradiction, after the manifestation of the spirit by the Jews, who were ever ready to do justice to their peculiar faith.

Of course, prophecies have proved a curse to God's own chosen people! What a senseless absurdity! The bible is so insidiously written as to split both sides of human events, by oracles that evince this double dealing. At first, with Abraham, the prophecy is, that the land of Canaan should be his and posterity's forever; in other instances, as time rolled on, time proved the necessity for reservations, and reservations were made. Covenants on covenants, new systems of faith are originated. The interpretation is left with the designing priestocracy. It is time that the world acted, as it has to act, in self-defence; it should put a correct end to all such false pretences.

God's magnificent attributes can be better manifested through the works of the universe than by pretended prophecies, that seem to stand therefor with the ignorant ancients, who had not mind-science enough to originate such an idea. The moderns ought not to seek to be sillier.

The expounders of the prophecies affect that we should wait on the fulfilment of the prophecies, that is, on the functions of time. That is, that an exposition of their failure must be overlooked.

All this belongs to time's functions, and was only abstracted therefrom by man's silly pretences.

Take up all the prophecy expositors, and what do they prove? Only that this subject is still mystified, and they cannot unravel it.

Time is not only usurped and monopolized, but lost by all this chicanery, in all such bibles.

What are considered prophecies are no prophecies at all. All expositors differ, and all agree only in this, that they know nothing about it. Even the greatest minds have been lost in the labyrinth of priestocracy, and its quagmire of sophistry.

What is very remarkable, the expositors, the affiliated, had to prophecy themselves, to help the book-prophets out; that has been overlooked prodigiously. To the overthrow of mind, they inquire exultingly, can the Ishmaelites ever be reclaimed from their wildness? I ask, has fraternizing ever been adopted? Have these people been properly educated at the best institutions of science of mind, in its noblest faculties of proper training? Some have proved themselves scholars.

Let not religion be sacrificed on the altar of prophecy. The ancients issued oracles; the moderns swear to them!

The ignorance of the ancients made miracles.

Miracles are the fictions of ignorance and superstition. The prophecies are obscure oracles.

Superstition was an accompaniment inseparable from the government of the ancients. Which of the moderns is exempt? It is true that a legal separation of church and state has been established in this Republic, but is there a genuine freedom from the undercurrents of superstition? See how easy the Mormon proselytes have been gulled?

Are prophecy and miracle for mind, as is pretended? Then they should be universal as mind. They cannot be, and there is an end to all such false pretences. If these facts are worthy of a free and sovereign people, let them circulate, and be honorably, honestly, and truthfully avowed and discussed.

Prophecies and priestocracies are ineffectual when science, teachers of mind, legislation founded on wisdom, and all the rational world-wide funds, are to instruct and enlighten. Prophets and priests, preachers and ministers might talk till doomsday if the minds of the people were enlightened; of what benefit can all such be to the world, but to mislead it on false pretences?

Facts triumph over interpretations of prophecies.

What was the object of miracles, but to correctly influence all mankind. We must so infer if they emanated from God. The Joshua miracle was enough to have Judaized the whole world at once. If you are interested in truth, analysis of the whole bible proves that so far from the Jews influencing the world, that they have been dispersed throughout it by the curse of their peculiar faith, in the very face of their pretended prophecies, that they should possess the land spoken of forever? Of what use were miracles? Can all such preserve the world's morals by falsehoods! Are the priestocracy so stupid as not to see that? The same efforts of miracles done for the whole world, as related in the bible of Judaism, would have been effectual if they were proper ones. God comprehends all by the fewest means at the same time.

The prophecies that established land piracies were libelously called the word of God, invented by the priestocracy to gull and deceive the people.

When was the prophecy of Noah made? At the time specified? Who can believe that? Why cannot we believe it? Because Noah was only a man, and debauched at that, exposing his physical and mental weakness.

Most all the ancients made emigrations, and did not stickle at conquests. To get hold of the land of Canaan, the priestocracy give just such a pretext as the priestocracy alone could invent. God, they assume, gave the revelation, but did he give it with such blood, murder, and iniquity, and partial corrupt language, that died out before the Jew nation; only think of that! When he had already given it to the whole universe of mind, located in billions of orbs, in a language universal, eternal, chaste, and unmistakable, in the most magnificent tablets, without blot or blemish, let alone blood or conception of injustice, partiality to one set of people, much less one globe, which was one of the whole, without the necessity or use of a second edition, which his omnipotence, omnipresence, and omniscience precluded.

Are the priestocracy worthy to appear before the books, much less the author.

John proves in what absurd relations the prophets involve themselves:—"And the stars of heaven fell unto the earth, even as a fig-tree casteth her untimely figs when she is shaken by a mighty wind." Again, "and the heavens departed as a scroll when it is rolled together." Chap. vii: "And after these things, I saw four angels standing on the four corners of the earth, holding the four winds of the earth." Chap. xx. 11: "And a new heaven and a new earth succeeded in the place of the first heaven and the first earth, which passed away at the general judgment." Haggai ii. 6, 21: I will shake the heavens and the earth." An earthquake to shake the heavens!

Before you settle subsequents, premise preliminaries; before you leave particulars, settle principles.

The interpretation of Daniel's prophecy and John's pretended revelation give the protestants a fine chance to worry the Romanists. If Romanism has grown of christianity, the whore of Babylon, what must christianity be?

What confidence did the Jews put in their prophets?

How did they treat Jeremiah? Like a tory!

How many thousands of the prophecies were missed, now unknown? If America were to buy a whole lottery, as she often does, she gets all the prizes,—the large ones are heard of, like good fruit; the blanks, like withered fruit, are lost to knowledge.

These prophecies, as published, keep up a peculiar malevolence of feeling at this day, analogous to despicable proscription. Would it not gratify protestants, if not in malignancy of feelings, at least to the height of vanity, at this day, to see the speedy downfall of the Latin if not of the Greek churches? They have good authority, modern prophets assume, for the decision against Rome. If this be true, then the Romans should yield. What becomes of the protestants who are their offspring? The Christians in a body would prefer the downfall of Mahomedans, who, with the Mormons and Jews, would pay the Christians back in full measure.

Is this a proper correct feeling? Is it religion? And yet these sects have it, as a habit naturally so. Prophecy is at fault no where worse than in the most essential particulars of mind's loveliness, innocence and purity, and yet you adopt the bible, because of the fulfilment of the prophecies. Will you prefer man's bible to God's word, prophecy to religion? You are not able to analyze them, else you would see their fruitlessness and clashing. What demoralization prophecies inculcate and generate!— Would not the prognostication pretended affect much of the world's happiness for man's vanity, much less of his envy and malice? Would not the Christian to day sacrifice much of the world, to attain Christianity for the world? How many fanatics would not still plunge the whole world into another miscalled holy war, to attain such an object? Would not many a Christian gloat, to see Mahometans perish? Why should a miracle be enacted to derange the proper universe, when the proper order seems all expedient and designed? Must this world be deranged, for a deranged set of metaphysicians and priestocracy? It is not by miracles but mind, that governs. All such are the false pretences of the priestocracy. The very thing of a miracle proves superstition, not religion at all. This is a universe of cause and effect, that puts down atheists and polytheists, as it bespeaks the unity and supremacy of one God exclusively, and has no miracles or prophecies, else the God of the universe did not exist. Miracles, prophecies and messiahs are in antagonism to God. The proper analysis of the question comprehends this position, otherwise we are incompetent to its appreciation. Even now there are pretended miracles wrought in the Roman church, but who believes them? Miracles are all the coin of the priestocracy, the basest counterfeits of the whole world. As I believe in God's perfection, I cannot believe in miracles that affect all that position. Many believe the scriptures because they consider as they have been told by interpretations made by the priestocracy, that the prophecies are fulfilled. All that is the trick, of the trade, of the speculation. As regards miracles and prophecies, we cannot take the opinions and statements of interested priestocracies, their inventors, when God's document proves the contrary, exhibited in the principles of causation, which if we disbelieve or overlook, we divest ourselves of the only tangible proof of the God of the universe. The priestocracy mislead us from the true point at issue, to their trifling trash.

A miracle never could have so important an end, and worthy of its author, as the principles of creation in the universe. If an author speaks of a miracle, as he calls it, being seen by millions of people, does his statement prove anything? Have we those millions of people present to substantiate his statement? Are we possessed by their or his statement, of the truth or the false pretence about them? Of course the last. Is the ignorant world competent to decide on miracles? The ancients were as ignorant as superstitious, and under such circumstances are not competent witnesses of truth. The whole of the bible writers were as much affiliated as any of the oracle-mongers of polytheism in the gross.

When any bible says that "God said, let there be light, and there was light," four days in advance of the organs of light, the whole foundation of the principles of causation are broken up, and the whole document of bibles is self-impeached. The whole world has not credit enough to establish one miracle, and need not make itself a blockhead on that score any longer. I say this in the presence of God and mankind, that the whole universe is God's witness. All that the pretended revealed faith knows, it is indebted to mind and the evidences of the universe. It then acts ungratefully, like a parricide. The whole world would have rushed to Judaism, had its essence been the pure characteristic, but connected to its priestocracy, miracles and prophecies pretended, its peculiar God, its creation was a fabulous monster. The performance of miracles, carries a lie on its face. We ask not for solution in magic, but in the false pretences of the priestocracy. People are busy about accounting for the magic. The mystery, the art of the mystery, rather than the fiction, the painting of the legend. People, sensible people, overlook this, until they commit themselves, and then sorrowful to relate, feel too mortified to correct their false position. The world-masters declare for faith that is united to the government, and the mass obey. A false color is given to the whole, in the pomp and gorgeous splendor of the various orders, and the world is captivated by specious appearances, and most of all, by supposed self-interest.

I have written as if things of this kind were presented. The people may spare themselves much endless and useless trouble, thought and time, about all this matter. But how govern the people? Not by false pretences, for that is not morals, much less religion. Govern them by the consistency of truth. But miracles prove no consistency, as their publicity was equivalent to imposition. But God gave the proof, the whole proof, and nothing but the proof, in his universe. No better, no more proof, was wanting. Will the people read? This last age will be the best as evincing progressing refined civilization, through the contined triumphs of mind. It is not rational to suppose on the principles of causation, that God would impeach his own attributes by having the pretensions of prophecies, miracles and messiahships to rule out his supremacy, when he had already created all on conservative principles, and of course ought to have had the appropriate reputation. We might as well suppose that God had need of millions of angels, to hold up his orbs, as to convey messages of prophecies or aid in miracles. We must make all due allowances for the ignorant state of mankind, the wants of the ancient times, the moral atmosphere tainted by despotism and superstition, that prevented the egress of sovereign mind. A visit to the East to-day, would teach us the usurpation of peculiar faith in all its disguises, modified by oriental despotism.

An ignorance of natural causes betrays itself clearly in the whole bible, from the conception to the close, the priestocracy stick out all the time, in the worst kind of blasphemy and imposition. It is all pious frauds, a stereotyped edition of falsehoods as old as superstition, only advanced as far as mind was competent to burst the darkness. We must speak of things as they are.

It is impossible, with the principles of causation, that God should select a peculiar people to do what they plainly could not and did not do for themselves, much less for the world. Judaism and Jew christianity, as all paganism, are failures. All the machinery of prophecies, miracles, dispensations and covenants, rites and ceremonies, make the monster "whose light has been taken away," still more a monster. If their priestocracy deceived them, let them, cursed as they are, no longer deceive themselves nor the world, that if intelligent cannot be deceived. If we find out all these falsehoods in the bible, about the prophets in their own book, what could we not do with the whole priestocracy, if we had them, with all the historical facts that were suppressed, in the most honorable court of conscience.

In that court, only, can the world obtain enlightened justice. They would sink, with
all their brassy impudence, into eternal insignificance! Many useless tubs are thrown
to the whale, the people, to engage their attention, from the main, primary matter, as
by the priestocracy, with a thousand pretences and pretexts, from their bibles of tradition. How absurd, though, to commit themselves, on what cannot be defended. How
came Ahab to consult the four hundred prophets, as they were called? Their prophecy
was false, for Ahab king of Judah, and the king of Israel, were discomfited by the Sy-
rian king. Did not the party antagonistic to these prophets write the tale? Where are
now your prophets? All are killed dead by the light of popular intelligence. It is because rational mind writes that history now. Where is all the attendant advantage
that prophecy should bring? Why was not the world elevated to mind's rank? Because prophecy was not rational popular education, but was built on supposed popular
ignorance. What an awful tale true history would tell of the ancients, could she speak
to-day. She has been suppressed. Before the pretended prophecies are trusted, as
worth anything, we are to consult the natural character of things. What had the Jews
to teach other nations of prophecies, when they were not beneficial to their own people,
now so humiliated before the whole world? Is not this enough to teach even the most
Jesuitical priestocracy to withhold, ere they seek to injure the world, by such false
pretences? Tyre and other old cities are done for. Well, what can make cities, if the
countries be kept worthless, by a miserable set of sectarian, superstitious nations?
Have not all these countries been ruined again and again, by all the hordes of barbarian
bigots and fanatics? Wars, pestilence, and famine? Have not the Christians and
Mahommedans helped to do it?
What part of God's earth can stand all the protracted perversions of mind? Has not
the commerce of the world changed, and are not the mighty oceans now the highway
of nations, instead of mere inland seas? All the causes that are now operating locally
and generally, the cause and effect, are not disclosed by the prophecy-mongers. Why
could they not tell the truth, the whole truth, and nothing but the truth, from Genesis
to Revelation? That would kill their book, their profession, and them. The interpretation of prophecy by the Jews and gentiles prove at once, in regard to Christ, that the
prophecies were perfectly worthless.
The Jews had a notion of Christ being a mighty temporal prince, that they were to
possess the empire of the world, and that Jerusalem was to be the seat. The Christians assume that he was spiritual. Now of what value was the prophecy? Who had
the best right to know? The peculiar people, or those excluded?
The very name of prophet or messiah implies false pretences, an imposition. It is
self-impeached, the moment of annunciation. The very idea of inspiration bespeaks
false pretences. Mahommed is said to have prophecied that his people would take Constantinople, which was done. Then the result of this prophecy ought to prove his doctrine as correct as any other dependent on prophecy. Is it so very difficult to introduce
prophecy of some kind, about future events! Prophecy of the world's affairs might
now produce some truthful events. Prophecy begets a ferocious spirit of speculation,
that has not true benevolence from vanity. The prophets knew no more the true character of the Jews then they did of prophecy. The bible advocates affect prophecies, as
if they had an existence, when the very foundation declares a horrid evil that God does
not create. The most benevolent institutions of God's withhold prophecy from the
world, as one of the best states for it, without which free moral agency would be wanting in its best proportions—to combat with unseen dangers and vicissitudes of life.
The spirit of bible prophecy is a horrid fiendish spirit.
Has the whole history of all these subjects pretended to be prophecies been eluci-
dated? Have deserted maritime cities, whose harbors may have been filled up or
ruined by the action of the sea, had their whole history laid open? Has not a world's
commerce sought other channels, and does not a world-wide commerce now adorn the
mightiest oceans that the ancients dared not encounter? Of all the niggardly commentators of true history, the miserable priestocracy are the worst. They dwarf every
thing from the bible of the universe and world, to their petty conceits. Fie upon it,
be men: let alone the gold that you sell the world, your souls, your only religion for!
Have these men gone into the solution of cause and effect, that they always absurdly
overlook for an accursed pretence of non-entity, prophecy they call it, and told us that
the whole land of the east assumed to be in the category of their prophecies, has been
cursed by a series of peculiar faiths, the followers of which have been ferociously vindictive to each other, and lost true sight of that invaluable jewel-mind, that would make
all lovely as a garden?
Where now are the miracles? covered up by the peculiar bible sophistry. " The
sceptre shall not depart from Judah, till Shiloh come." Was this ever intelligible to

mind? Talk of miracles. All such is folly, legends, false pretences, as the universe is one of cause and effect. All are the legitimate province of science, not of the assuming ignorant priestocracy, who assumed all such for monopoly and usurpation, that would be ridiculous if it were not a serious fraud on the world, a felonious imposition on the people; a degraded swindling of the soul's rights, a miserable superseding religion by the petty larceny of peculiar faith. The whole universe is in constant motion : time, the act of universal motion, and their conservative principles, are the prophets. The world has been governed, and sought to be governed by superstition, but another name for all the peculiar bible-machinery. Those who are of it, do not like to talk of it. Alexander sought too late among the Greeks, who were too civilized to think him a god, but he commanded the aid of the sycophantic priestocracy, who, in Africa, hailed him as the son of Jupiter, and this was immense capital for future conquests. Napoleon tried the priestocracy, it is said, in Egypt, by becoming a Mussulman. But what did it avail? Cromwell cherished superstition in his camp, and aroused the enthusiasm of his men, who signally aided him in his victories; while these military chieftains were men of policy, Washington was a man of principles ; the one lives in the affections of his country, the world, mankind ; the others will shrink into insignificance by the just awards of monotheism.

When church-faith resorts to tricks of miracles to uphold it, it is tottering. Is not the whole from first to last such a resort? Principles all the time for an honest policy, the world. Inspiration of what? To make men deceivers. How dangerous is pretended prophecy, as the result agreeing with I told you so, conspires with the wish and effort to have it so!

What are the prophets of the Jews worth to strangers, when their own people and kings disregarded them, according to the best pretended prophet's showing. How came Moses to portray the rebellion of so many, but for that very cause? Was not Christ put to death by disbelievers? Was Isaiah treated with decent respect by his own king, to whom he affected to deliver a sign? Jeremiah's scroll was thrown into the fire by Jehoiakim, his king, who had imprisoned the same. Can Americans be fooled, when those present scouted the pretenders? All the old oracle-mongers built their faith on prophecy, without which they could not have arisen; and all the present priestocracy built up their power on this basis. What were the augurs, soothsayers? Will the moderns know that they are all complete masters of the ancients in all their superstitions, if they will just use their honest truthful senses? But the tory priestocracy tell them not to read the very book that God has written, and that his own word, cause and effect, positively declares. All that the most virtuous and honorable monotheism can do, is to appreciate it to the very best of its intellectual abilities.

The God of the universe declares himself as all rational minds can read, but all the priestocracy, to have their peculiar profits, pretend another view, with most crazy sophistry. This is the result about miracles : Judges ii. 10, "And there arose another generation after them, which knew not the Lord, nor yet the works which he had done for Israel." That required peculiar education—were the bibles lost, or not yet written? 11 v. "And the children of Israel did evil in the sight of the Lord, and served Baalim." Did they not do this eternally? 17, "And yet they would not hearken unto their judges." The people had none to depend on, priests, prophets or judges, who they knew had deceived them. Ch. iv. v. 2, And the Lord sold them (the children of Israel) into the hand of Jabin, king of Canaan. Where was the slavery of Canaan? 3, "And twenty years he mightily oppressed the children of Israel. 4. Deborah, a prophetess, she judged Israel at that time." Another pythoness. God does not avail himself of angels, prophets, miracles nor mysteries. What a great age of the ancients! Their polytheism disproves that they had any notions of rational religion. The Israelites were fanatics against the citizens of Judea. Were not all of Palestine so? Ch. i. v. 19, "And the Lord was with Judah ; and he drave out the inhabitants of the mountains ; but could not drive out the inhabitants of the valley, because they had chariots of iron." Rather a poor war-god—not equal to Mars. 21, "And the children of Benjamin did not drive out the Jebusites that inhabited Jerusalem ; but the Jebusites dwell with the children of Benjamin in Jerusalem unto this day." Exodus, ch. xxxii. v. 2, "And I will send an angel before thee, and I will drive out the Canaanite • • and the Jebusite." x. v. 11, ' And the Lord said unto the children of Israel," v. 13 v. " yet ye have forsaken me, and served other gods ; wherefore I will deliver you no more." Ch. xi. v. 29, " Then the spirit of the Lord came upon Jephthah, 30, and Jephthah vowed a vow unto the Lord." 32, "So Jephthah passed over unto the children of Ammon to fight against them ; and the Lord delivered them into his hands." And that vow was the sacrifice of his own daughter as a burnt offering to this peculiar God, who delivered the Israelites after all the priestocracies' false pretences !!!! Yes, this bloody and impious book of the Jews, desecrated with the name of bible, presents the horrid blasphemy of their peculiar god's bribery and perjury, with a human sacrifice! Then it was that the Jew Christians could tamper farther with him, in causing him to be a murderer and an adulterer—all such iniquities recoiling upon themselves, whom I this day impeach as the most nefarious of all nefarious priestocracies. Jephthah was one of the judges.

Of course, an intelligent God, immutable, could not perjure himself, much less permit a human sacrifice, knowing too what it would be. What savages!

The world will be cursed as bad as these human-sacrificing and God-blaspheming Jews, if they continue to adopt their nefarious books. It will be cursed till it becomes rational, and has rational religion and its sound principles. Ch. xxi. v. 25, " In those days there was no king in Israel : every man did that which was right in his own eyes." Was any nation more idolatrous, more degraded in morals, than this book presents of the Benjaminites ? Were there ever worse barbarians in any land on earth ? What do prayers avail when mind is lost to its own dignity and duty ? It is not priestocracy, nor their pretended revelations ; all such cheats will do no good, before the conservative principles of the universe.

Samuel, ch. viii. v. 3, " And his sons walked not in his ways, but turned aside after lucre, and took bribes, and perverted judgment." Now the people preferred a king to judges. A king, bad as he was portrayed by Samuel, was the least of evils compared with the priests. The priests monopolized the Lord's flesh. They desecrated the sacrifice, and the chastity of the women. The people could not stand them. Let not Americans stand all this bible profanation of the God of the universe. It is a Belial work. Every rational mind needs rational religion, that comprehends all that mind in the universe, to give the only passport, as all rational minds have the principles and elements, and only need their evolution. There are too many sacrifices to judicial and other bigotry. Give mind power, no matter priest or prophet, king or judge, and they will pervert, and make all the pretences that will hold the world in abeyance to sophistry. After all the efforts of the priestocracy, whether good, bad or indifferent, we see how deplorable was the state of morals of the Jews, practising their most unnatural, not to say ungodly sins that polite refined minds of the present day would blush to name in public. All this is worse, and in part arose from the priestocracy fixing on the world the most ungodly faith.

If the world had not been put back by such ungodly faith of Moses and Aaron, the world-priestocracy, the world, might have been far in advance of its present state. The priestocracy were the belials, with their ungodly wars. What is the best proof of the scriptures ? Prophecy. Whose ? Isaiah's. He was a libeler of God. Any person on earth, on the authority of God's word, cause and effect, and rational mind's supreme authority, stands self-declared and convicted as a dupe, or worse, to assert that there are, ever were or can be, miracles, prophecies, messiahs, mysteries, angels good or bad, hell, purgatory, any need of priestocracy or any such machinery.

Messiahs, so far from originating new principles, did not, could not, inculcate any of themselves, for their very position destroys all principle.

The universe-knowledge was lost to the priestocracy, on account of messiahship ; they disregarded all creation-teaching then in existence. as long before, hence afterthoughts were in their minds, and they substituted them for those of God, who is basely misrepresented by libelous bibles.

It takes rational mind to give, as analyze, all facts of creation. hence no apostles of peculiar faith are honorable, worthy, creditable witnesses of universe-facts, when making them appear miracles, prophecies, mysteries. The whole truth turns not at all on mysteries, prophecies, miracles, bibles, but on the perverted versions of the degraded writers who act degradedly below mind's character, in aspiring to be of the priestocracy. Let religion flourish, but the world's nuisance and curse, peculiar faith, with all their froths, be ruled out of rational minds.

It will not do to speculate of the future. until we do the amplest justice to the present life, this world and its people. Let mind tower in the sublime greatness of its own inherent worth and use. Had the ancients had the knowledge of mind now of the moderns, they would have fixed up a different messiahship, if the honest, truthful ones had not adopted rational religion. If any doubt after all written, and only on prophecies, as they are pretended, let him see the touch-stone in the most pointed peculiarity, that of the messiah, who was the diamond before mind, and not to be mistaken, if pure. Yet truth discloses the false stone of no value. It was as usual about trifles. The spirit of pretended prophecy is an odious evil kept up in families, to reflect the supposed wisdom of those presuming on brief authority, but really the folly of their own badly trained minds.

If rational minds reject human sacrifices with horror and shuddering, the miserable delusion of perverted minds of degraded priestocracy, they must loathe with ineffable disgust, all the pretended immolations of Christs and messiahs, and contemn, despise the priestocracy concerned from first to last, as ineffably barbarous and iniquitously degraded, corrupt, vile, stupid, their own hell deserving as belials, all the time. How dare they invade the sacred rights of mind?

All bibles of peculiar faith are made up of dove-tailed, disjointed stuff, called prophecies, the greatest of all frauds, impositions and blasphemies.

The immutability of nature and nature's God, convicts all the priestocracy of the present times, in felonious falsehoods that miracles, prophecies and mysteries affected in the bible have ceased. Before the world they are this day fully and satisfactorily convicted, as they never were performed. If they ever existed, they would certainly now exist.

Miracles are the reversals of the order of nature, and of course could not exist in a universe that recognises all the time, cause and effect. Peculiar faith people forget that miracles reverse the order of the laws of nature, and convict themselves. The popular idea is, that there are spirits, ghosts, witches, &c. Why? Would a perfect God create all such stuff? An idle brain, or that of superstition, creates all such.

Prophecy is a part of the peculiar creed of peculiar faith, that with or without it, is nothing. Now prophecy is only essential to help make out the false pretences of peculiar faith, that is all. The performance is feigned, not perfected. This is where the world is deluded by such blasphemy. All such bibles have story and some history to sustain their story, this is by cunning and sophistry, that enlist all the affiliated priestocracy. The history is hard to find in the story. All the book, kills itself. The world has been afraid to handle it right—on account of the sophisticated bullying priestocracy, who were posted behind the world's bullying despots. Even in modern times this ferocious faith is portrayed. What was the course of republican France under Louis Napoleon's presidency, towards Rome? Was it any less by the vile dictation of polytheism, than under the vile rule of atheistical France? The names of things are nothing, it is the thing itself. What government can assume dominion by the grace of God, defender of the faith? The very position is self-impeached, as base fraud.

Could the world ever have found near as much ill, but for miserable false pretences of bibles, priestocracies, and prophets? What upholds peculiar doctrines and prophecies? Bibles. What upholds them? Faith, frost, fog, mist—to be dissolved by the light of truth. The peculiar machinery of bibles is miracles, prophecy, and mystery; all these are indispensable to such.

But all these have to be submitted to rational mind. To talk of receiving any message at all without recognising by mind, rationality, is foolish in the extreme, as much in faith as in all other things.

All the bible aspirants about miracles and things of their heaven affect much, when they could not tell rightly of earth. Let them now give honorable, high-minded proof, that such things are true. They cannot, for the immutable principles of God pronounce their miracles, mysteries, and all their peculiar bibles and people, all the priestocracy detestably, ignominiously, and degradingly false. They are not to give the priestocracy fixing up, on mere bible statements but documentary demonstration that all such is positively true, or be forever silent. A free and intelligent people should silence all pretenders and pretences forever. The least iota of detraction from God's perfection or immutability, renders him imperfect and that much no God. That is the inevitable result in moral, physical, intellectual, and religious position. Now, if there were miracles or prophecies at any time of creation, they are now in their full force and vigor. Are the stupid priestocracy and affiliated minions so far gone in iniquity and corruption, that they cannot see this? They had best stop, and seek, by repentance, to become honest and truthful people for the balance of their days. II. Chronicles ch. xxi. v. 7. "Howbeit the Lord would not destroy the house of David, because of the covenant that he had made with David, and as he promised to give a light to him and to his sons forever." Is this promise fulfilled an iota? This call prophecy? This was the priestocracy, speaking always to be understood for their peculiar Jew-god, made by priestocracy jugglery. Now the God of the universe before whom all such are impeached, made his covenant with the whole creation of mind in the universe at creation too, so far does the last incomparably exceed the first as God exceeds perverted mind. Why so much difficulty among the priests and prophets, as they were called? Because the people abundantly saw through their hypocrisy and false pretences.

Now the world does not investigate for itself in one of the most important of all matters, religion, that elevates it to its sublimest sphere. Well does it regard prophecies as the prop, but little does it investigate them. The pretended prophecies deceive many moderns, palmed on all, and after all the fixings up by the Jews were and are no more than the oracles of other nations as of the Romans. They are done with all the sophistry of the priestocracy, backed by false governments and their belial times. They have distorted the God of creation, by all the degraded investments of peculiar forgery and fraud. They are characterized by all that can pervert the truth, and degrade mind. Ch. 32 and 33 of Exodus clearly prove at once the whole imposture, besides many others. They affect to make belief of things that they did not ever know, and never could know, nor could possibly have seen. The world ought to be told the truth, the whole truth and nothing but the truth about the bible's pretended prophecies, which are all false pretences that would have died long ago, had the priestocracy not been false pretenders. The superstitious people idolize the bible and its idols, as if the world would come to an end if they were destroyed. The key of the death of the new testament is in 17 and 18 verses of 16th ch. of Mark, and what can all the pretended prophecies of all faiths avail their own suicide? and the same fact conclusively applies as the key of suicide to the old testament, in ch. 32 and 33 of Exodus, where the peculiar God kills off through the priestocracy, all the foolish prophecy foundation of all such bibles, that are thus blown sky high. A factitious importance is attached about some Jew oracles, respecting a few old cities, Babylon, Nineveh, and a few countries, as if the whole world's destiny was anything to be regulated thereby, when the Jews had lost at the seige of Jerusalem by their own pretended prophecies their million of people, and ruined their nation.

If ever there was a stupid and infatuated people, the Jews are they. Many still adhere to that degraded superstition, the most abominable because the most murderous to them. Are the priestocracy completely crazy, that they wish to ruin the world in the same way? All this iniquitous folly should be estopped by intelligent freemen. The world should not be sacrificed to such degradation. Jew oracles lied as all other oracles, and they that deny this, lie as endorsers. Oracles are nothing at all, but to gull and defraud the world.

Analyze the ancient world, and a pretty set of piratical barbarians they were indeed. One old city pirated upon another, one nation on another. Babylon grew out of Nineveh, that the Medes and Babylonians destroyed. Then Seleucia eat up Babylon, that its enemies ruined. The mighty problem that gives the solution, holds all the priestocracy and absolutists in abeyance. The mighty question that they could not solve overwhelms them in their pitiful ignorance. Tell us, world-philosophers of this age, how many cities have perished in that old country of Assyria? Who were the first aborigines of that country? How many countless generations existed before the priestocracy's Adam was ever heard of, nay, how many passed off the world's theatre. Yes, tell us how many Babylons and Ninevehs, and then the priestocracy will be scouted as impostors truly.

What was the case of the old country of Italy, where races had pre-existed unknown to all the ancients? Is not that the case in America? Tell us, priestocracy, of America's ancient cities without one inhabitant, and then you can claim to be more than you are now. Absolutists and priestocracies have played into each other's hands. They have stifled the truth, bullied the world in miserable falsehoods.

All bible prophecies and oracles are like the priestocracy, that have conspired to delude the world. What are Babylon and Nineveh to prove? Have we the facts of truth told us, as rational mind requires. How many thousand untruths have been told to fix up all such trash? Are they not reactions of cause and effect? Cyrus ruined Babylon by changing the river, flooding the country. What a mighty dead-list of ruined cities would the world's history present us, enacted by savage warfare. Have there not been thousands upon thousands destroyed? If the bible has been true the whole world could not be kept from believing it, for it would have presented mind the first principles of things, and the true history of pre-existing races, which it cannot do, as its writers, the priestocracy, did not know.—Ask for bible proof, and man speaks; ask for God's bible, and his universe responds with true sublimity. Where, bible prophets, are the ancient cities of Egypt? They are now in ruins. Are they prophecied of in the bible? The bible, if of God, had necessarily told us of the world, and nothing less, to comprehend a just revelation; but we have none of this. It does not do justice to the smallest part, much less mind, that it assails! But you bible advocates are bible worshippers, faith polytheists, believers in devils, angels, ghosts, wars in your heaven; but you dwarf the God of the universe; no, that cannot be, but you dwarf your own mind in blasphemous conception and description of him who needs no aid of his creation, priestocracy, or pretended prophets, who is blasphemed in the pretence down to the little peculiar overseer god of Jewry. Shame upon you, that you sacrifice the lights of the present age to all the false pretences of Jew idolatry and oracles.

Do you really sacrifice your religion to all the false pretences of slave Jew bibles and faiths? Shame, freemen of the world.

18

Where are the mighty ancient cities, races of the earth, anterior to all bibles? What shall the world do for that history, that bible pretences cannot reach? To disprove the absurdity of these bible pretences what veritably endorsed authority have we that Jeremiah prophecied against Babylon. It is expedient to give truth endorsements before prophecies. Bishop Newton says, "Jeremiah sent his prophecies concerning Babylon to Babylon by the hands of Seraiah," &c.—(Jer. li. 59.)—"There is, therefore, no room for skepticism."

What stuff!' Thus are the people gulled by the modern priestocracy. See the vile imposition:—

63. "And it shall be, when thou hast made an end of reading this book, that thou shalt bind a stone to it, and cast it into the midst of Euphrates.

64. "And thou shalt say, Thus shall Babylon sink, and shall not rise from the evil that I will bring upon her: and they shall be weary: thus far are the words of Jeremiah."

Which was the biggest blockhead or mind-juggler, Jeremiah or Bishop Newton? Did not the last know that such false pretence to evidence would be laughed out of an honorable court of justice. Jeremiah also said, v. 43, "neither doth any son of man pass thereby." Capt. Keppel, in 1824, visited the ruins of Babylon. So much for Jeremiah. If all the facts of all peculiar faiths, bibles, and priestocracies were laid before the world, the most ridiculous of all impositions would appear with the most flagrant murderous outrages on mankind, of all the Belial-world outrages. The world with one united voice, the priestocracy and minions always excepted, would accurse this lowest blasphemy.

Instead of prophecies, read impositions. The moderns must not regard the few old obsolete cities, Babylon and Nineveh, &c., as if they were the world. They are dead; let them be buried; and let not their ashes be desecrated by the priestocracy, who are lower than they are. We should never have heard of them in any such light, but for the vindictive fury of the Jews in resentment of their national subjugation. That is not a laudable spirit, when these Jews butchered the world when they wanted its land.

They talk of prophecies, and all their category of deluge and fallen cities bespeak their stupid fall in science, ignorant of obvious natural causes; yet the moderns stupidly keep up the ignominious game, disgraceful to novices in truth, honesty, and science.

Now the subject of peculiar bibles, and all their peculiar machinery, is impracticable to their advocates. What did the bible give of the pyramids of Egypt? Of Thebes, famous for its hundred gates? It has ferociously exhumed the world's vices, and buried its virtues.

How many thousands of years before the bible Adam did the human race extend? How many races of mankind were extinct, and their very name lost in the distant vistas of past pre-existent ages? A bible of God's inspiration should have told of first principles, and of things before tradition, not of tradition, which is man's.

As to prophecies or oracles, what ancient nation did not have them? Rome and Greece luxuriated in them. Among the Greeks they were used in all important public matters. The name of the thing does not change the thing itself.

These Jew prophets were all impostors, who were ignorant of the most essential causes, that wrote their history on the deeds of the ancients. They sacrificed their nation.

Transfer, republicans, no such paganism to your blessed country.

The world should be able to tell by this time what is the worth of rational mind and religion; not of peculiar faith and all its accursed train, that has to be scouted from the face of this earth.

What do mankind need of any bible prophecy to give the highest glory to God, that requires the purest duty of mind to the world and God. Surely all the polluted Jew bible examples cannot begin to teach them. What is religion? The highest function of mind illustrated by action, the committal of the soul, mind, spirit, to God Almighty.

What does christianity embrace? What, western Bhuddism? Is that any better than the eastern?

All are fictions of the priestocracy, that sought to rule the people, No peculiar faith is any, unless mind has bestowed its portion of capital for civilization, then it is monotheism unacknowledged. True prophecy is it, when no ancient nation ever furnished us with a true history of itself.

It yet, at least, remains to be proved.

The Jew prophets, &c., poured out this hatred against Egypt and Babylon particularly, that conquered them. Not only Babylon is fallen, but Judea and Jerusalem.

Gen. ch. xvii. v. 1: "The Lord said unto Abraham 'I am the Almighty God;' 8. and I will give unto thee, and to thy seed after thee, the land wherein thou art a stranger, all the land of Canaan, for an everlasting possession; and I will be their God." As the Jews have not an everlasting possession therein, it was only the priestocracy God that spoke, that was all.

Alexander burnt Persepolis. Ancient countries were ravaged with fire and sword, the adverse parties doing themselves and their peculiar gods service in doing so. Think of that, ye blind devotees of Jew idolatry, peculiar bibles. What city of the ancients was not destroyed, at one time or another?

Athens was burnt by the Persians. Has true and authentic history detailed all the facts, about the utter destruction of all these cities? What were the natural causes? That the pitiful bible sophists could not tell, no more than the other oracle sophists of the day. Their trade was to detail available pretences, and have themselves screened from the exposure. The special providence of perverted minds has left a burden to that of rational mind to clear the world of.

Is the whole history of the world-facts laid open to us? if not, then all such peculiar bibles are peculiar nuisances. Now what did all the Jew prophecies amount to, admitting that they had any such character, which cannot be honorably proved in an honorable court of justice? After all said and pretended, all evaporates and discloses that the world is going on as God created it. They availed naught, and were worthless, and therefore to be disregarded, as flagitious and base. Some of the pretended prophets, that the bible presents, affect to treat others as lying prophets ; now if we were to hear both and the true sides, all would be convicted as base, lying prophets.

The evil of prescience, in prophecy, outweighs the good—does not suit the functions of mind. What blockheads all oracle-mongers were, to leave their posterity at the mercy of such abominable vices and crimes. But God's immutability prevents miracles and prophecies, that if he required yesterday, as part of his conservative principles, he does to-day. But these are mysteries. No, that is the absurd answer of the bible bigot, who disgraces his own mind and God, as far as in him lies, by false pretences of false bibles, priestocracy, and their affiliated, duped, or dependent vassals. Now if God fore-knew he fore-ordained, but all that is abeyance to mind's free moral agency, under the circumstances of creation, that bespeak immortality of the soul as a part of eternal justice, and God's immutability on conservative principles. This question of religion is the highest inquiry of philosophical science, and bespeaks a sublimity too triumphant over all the pretensions of miracles and prophecies. Bible bigots have opposed the idea, because they were thereby ruled out. Who countenance and support the absurd miracles of the present day, of the world, but those who sustain the foolish bibles and churches built on their premises? Now if you do that by belief and presence, you are culpable and amenable. The ancients, in their comparative ignorance, resorted to miracles, to explain what they could not appreciate. The power of the press would have passed with them for such. Now the people perform what would be considered innumerable miracles, compared to which Moses was only a juggler.

All miracles are phenomena ; however consistent with nature, were unknown to the ignorant barbarians, who did not know even whence the rain came, by their own bible, that, instead of being a perfect code of science and religion, is a stupid memento, recording the national degradation and vassalage.

Take the article of manna, of Moses, and let it compare with the billions of pounds of sugar evoked by the hand of the moderns, elicited by science, and the comparison places the last far above this necromancer's dream.

If he were to-day in this city of New York, he would affirm that he was a mere school-boy to modern savans, and that his advocates were blind fanatics.

What is pretended to be miracles and prophecies are in abeyance to the laws of evidence.

The very attributes of the great First Cause destroy all miracles and prophecies.

All religion is that of principles, cannot be that of miracles and prophecies, and must be submitted, on the nature of evidence, demanding the full recognition of what is rational.

In this plan of peculiar bibles, the pretended prophets played the knave ; all followers, faithites, are desired to play the dupe.

The idea of prophecy, would embrace the whole category of full time. Where is proof of any such, but in the pretences of subsequent impostors?

All such is the vilest imposition. The people should not be throwing away a lifetime on trash, much less actually committing a sacrilege on the Creator, for which nothing can atone. Many affect presentiments, under improper appreciations of prophecy, and act disreputably to correct good sense.

The priestocracy bible, the word of God! What a libel. But stay, it is only the word of the priestocracy's God, that is, of the priestocracy.

These simpletons forgot that miracles were enough, expedient to force the faith of the people, when they resorted to church bullyings. The God of the Jew bible is the Jew idol god—of the priestocracy—not of the universe, universal, but of peculiar faith, peculiar. The peculiar one deals in miracles. The Author of the universe deals in principles, not miracles.

Do you believe in miracles? Then, you do not believe in the Creator of the universe, that cannot be made up of miracles, but cause and effect, the result of principles to which miracles are antagonistic. Of course you believe in the humbugs of Jew idolatry, that has their peculiar god. A peculiar god does not belong to our universe. Credulity or credulousness is heinous; it is mockery on the intellect of the world. Miracles belong to supernaturalism, an absurdity and sacrilege on mind.

All creeds of faith that admit messiahs, prophets, and miracle-mongers, necessarily exclude the God of the universe, for all such are the false pretences of the priestocracy.

When cornered, bible advocates refer to mysteries, faith, metaphor, miracles, and prophecies' fulfilment.

But none of these, as their trinity, are self-evident.

None, but the unity of God, who is consistent in the unity of design. '

What destroyed Babylon? We might well ask, what destroyed all the ancient isolated countries? Was it not for want of principles in government and religion? Instead of the sacred protection of universal brotherhood, they all fell victims to the fragments of peculiar errors and faiths—Palestine as well as all—even the mighty conquerors in turn, were overthrown by universal vindication of principles.

The universe could not last unless it were based on conservative principles. God gave them equally to the world, but mind's perversions have stood in the way. To have full principles in the world's government, let it have all of religion of principles. Does any part of it, though blessed with the freest of governments, have? That is utterly impossible in the vagaries and crimes of polytheism. The mind must be perfectly rationalized, and the press—public opinion too much wedded to customs, must be free from malign influences of monopoly and usurpation. Publications, schools, discussions, associations, libraries, &c., should be liberally subservient to all the legitimate demands of the mind of the world.

Prophets and inspirations are impositions and frauds. But the christian, par excellence, demands faith, because of miracles and prophecies. Then he furnishes the best argument against himself, for Judaism claims priority and originality over him, the borrowings from sectarianism of predecessors—certainly of nobler views by corrupt, venial and mercenary priestocracy.

The Mahommedan claims a subsequent covenant, and that arouses up the Mormon, who vows, as the latter-day saints, that they have precedence, and thus the subsequent blasphemer is to win.

But the christian affecting a mock dignity from his familiarity with despotic power, that upholds him in strengthening itself, a custom time out of mind in the annals of nations, assumes to talk of learning and science, and thus he is completely triumphed over by reason, to whom the braggart appeals, for he, as all his compeers, have usurped in this all the rights of monotheism.

But as a last dying effort, he conceitedly tells the public that the world will go into the jaws of atheism, if it be not under his protection. This is always the case with consociates of illegal and collusive action.

How can the world be worse off than under all such despotic regime? Well, now for the atheist.

How prove a God? he asks. That is easily proved by reference to cause and effect, that lead us to the great first cause, in whom mortals, all that are rational, must confide in due humility.

What then? says the inquirer. That proves an Almighty, for we cannot go beyond the Almighty Creator of the Universe till out of it. What does all this knowledge avail? All intended. The religion of principles that produce all, that is the wisest purpose.

This protects the purest conscience, for its immortal happiness. As to the when and how of the universe and of its Author, these are all alien to our data and powers. Nature is in abeyance to principles, that are so to the God of nature; this suffices for mind's noblest aspirations and brightest, best and most beneficial actions.

Rational mind can comprehend enough of the attributes of God, the Creator, to carry out rational religion. The when and the how of the atheist in creation are absurd, as his denial of the Creator.

Prophecy and miracle are the machinery of man, maniacs, crazy fanatics, and more crazy menials, vassal followers, the counterfeit currency of unprincipled priestocracies. Which is the worse, the denial of a God of the universe, or the peculiar dwarfing him below his own attributes? From Deity the monotheist learns, appreciates that still higher is his purpose. Religion and priestocracy are incompatible. Cause and effect lead mind to the Great First Cause; and religion, the inevitable result of humility and rational confidence in him, confirms it.

It is not the when and the how, but the what is to be investigated in due adoration of the Author of perfection and happiness.

The Author of principles must be the immutable standard for a religious conscience. Mere matter and the universe are two very different things. If all were mere matter, then senseless as atheism, but it reflects its glorious Author. The atheist is bewildered about matter, the monotheist is enlightened and exalted about the universe.

The very idea of miracles and prophecies destroys all religion, as far as in them lies, being suicidal of principles. If the Jew priestocracy were capable of prophecy, why not proclaim the real substantial benefits of time to the whole world, as the discovery of continents then unknown, sciences then undeveloped, all the present and future means of civilization and its best blessings? These are the very things that prophecy could have done, a theme fit for the noblest statesmanship, patriotism and philanthropy, instead of the degraded tricks, not competent to dupe school-boys.

The Jew pretence to prophecy is the veriest humbug, and burlesque of humbug, the coin of knaves or fools. When you speak of prophecy, you speak of the suicidal curse to soul's happiness, mind's ease, quiet and earthly equanimity. If mind ever required direct revelation, it does it evermore,.universally.

That difficulty annihilates the whole manufacture of miracles, prophecy, &c.

But the prophecies about cities are heralded by the affiliated moderns as if that was any thing, destitute too even of its proof! As to their decay, that is only the history of the world—often by notorious causes, abundant among the ancient barbarians, whose pride and glory it was to destroy them.

What part of the world is exempt?

Of course, if prophecy were any thing above the paltry tricks of the priestocracy, we should have heard of major not minor local points—all that would have civilized the world, not have stabbed and assassinated with peculiar faiths, that are as old as sin itself.

Monotheism will justly accord all the biblical modifications of varied and subsequent prophecies, from Genesis to Revelations; that, however, will not avail all the advocacy of peculiar faith, for that incontestably proves the revelations of the peculiar god, not of foreknowledge, but of after opinions, and thus of man and that of mind perverted conclusively and surely.

Thus she meets all the legitimate demands of her duty in silencing, with the most exact justice. all the fictious of faith, and giving the full benefits to rational mind of the purest religion.

THE PROPHETS, PRIESTS, &c.

Let the prophets declare the character of their brethren. Micah ch. iii. v. 6, "And the sun shall go down over the prophets, and the day shall be dark over them." Of course, they were found a useless machinery. V. 7, "For there is no answer of God." V. 11, "The priests teach for hire, and the prophets divine for money: yet they will lean upon the Lord." The prophets and priests, mere seers and diviners, did not set out to write anything but fictions and falsehoods all the time, with whom the tribe was in collusion. That was the very character of the undertaking. How much they borrowed, and changed with the advance of mind, whose rights they always usurped under their blasphemous false pretences of claiming their peculiar God for authority. The apotheosis of the Pagan Emperors as they called them, eventuated in the canonization of the Saints, all paganism.

Zephaniah ch. iii. v. 4, "Her prophets (Jerusalem) are light and treacherous persons; her priests have polluted the sanctuary, they have done violence to the law."

Zechariah ch. xiv. v. 17, "And it shall be, that whoso will not come up of all the families of the earth unto Jerusalem to worship the King, the Lord of hosts, even upon them shall be no rain." 18, But as Egypt have no rain, "If it went not up it was to have the plague—also the heathen." O prophet, did you not dream in all your visions, that mind is the mighty means before the Lord of the universe? The universe! Let that name startle you more than when you were awakened out of your sleep. You Israelites, appropriated the God of the four-cornered earth, and the scroll heaven, and could prophecy as much as you chose. But your prophecy was after the event, or as little account as this which is false, and the best of you would have been the worst exposed, if all your dark pretences and falsifications had been written with the pen of truth. But your train-band in collusion, kept up the profession. Who of all was more zealous than you, for the priestocracy of Jerusalem? But out with the truth, and the same you say of others is applicable to all of all ages. But no, you are faithful to your household.

Malachi ch. i. v. 14, "For I am a great king, saith the Lord of hosts, and my name is dreadful among the heathen." And this peculiar God who was a great king, and whose name was dreadful among the heathen, is indebted to Malachi for the publication. Who endorses Malachi? But hear him, ch. iii. v. 8, "Will a man rob God? Yet ye have robbed me. But ye say, wherein have we robbed thee? In tithes and offerings." Malachi, thou wast a true priest, but a false man. This was priest robbing man, through his peculiar God. The very essence of the profession.

JONAH.

THE whole of this, as all the balance of this Pagan bible, might have been anticipated by the fact, that no such mission was necessary, as God of creation does not change, for his attributes are immutable, and the principles of the universe are fixed. Of course, wily priestcraft tries to play the whole drama. No matter the absurdity, it makes a fish story for Jonah. It was easier for Jonah to have lived three days, after swallowing'a fish himself. That is more truthful and rational, any physiologist would say. The bible violates all principles of physiology and religion. Jonah must have swallowed a fish and lived better than three days, than in the other condition, for then a fish and not Jonah would have lived. The people swallowed the fish story.

Ch. iii., "And God repented of the evil that he had said that he would do unto them; and he did it not." What blasphemy—men said—God did not say. What a miserable character Jonah was, for a prophet, disobedient, refractory, and envious! He a pure being, through whom God spake? Very clear indeed. He was very angry. Now prophets should not get angry; much less God. But the peculiar bibles can draw any peculiar caricature. Jonah was nearly guilty of the crime of suicide, as he wished in himself to die! But his crime of all crimes, was his libel of God's veracity.

Daniel ch. iii. v. 25. If this miracle had occurred, the world could not have kept Nebuchadnezzar from adoption and adoration of God, him and his nation, and as a proof, the Jews would have obtained then and there, their freedom.

Ch. ii. If this dream had been such, then they also had been convinced of God. But all the peculiar God people forget that God should not have done generally, if he had acted by miracles, as they could have been universal. How much easier was it for the God of all, to have acted at once for all. This is the way the God of nature does act, but these butchers of honest truth affect otherwise, and damn themselves forever as the worst of men.

Ch. vii. v. 8, "But I kept the matter in my heart," says Daniel, a wise inspired man surely.

Ch. viii. v. 10, "And (the little horn) it cast down some of the host, and of the stars to the ground, and stamped upon them." What good did all these mysteries of this ignorant simpleton? Like the oracles, intended to deceive. By all these stupid characters, one general idea is conveyed, that of cunning.

Let us have all this nonsense stopped. Mind, had these fanatics ever listened to it, would have taught and enabled the Jews to have excluded all the pretended prophets, and an ignorant set of astrologers and jugglers. Let this fellow be tried by the laws of nature to entire conviction and condemnation, from respectable society.

Hosea ch. iv. v. 1, "Because there is no truth, nor mercy, nor knowledge of God in the land." V. 6, "My people are destroyed for lack of knowledge." V. 9, "And there shall be, like people, like priest; ch. v. v. 1, (God spake) O priests, ye have been a snare on Mizpah, and a net spread upon Tabor." Ch. vi. v. 9, "The company of priests murder in the way by consent: for they commit lewdness." The greatest piece of false pretence was, that the Jews were a peculiar people, thereby making their God a peculiar God, and causing their peculiar professions assuming to be prophets to eternally lie, a peculiar curse.

Ch. x. v. 13, "Ye have ploughed wickedness, ye have reaped iniquity; ye have eaten the fruit of lies; because thou (the people) didst trust in thy way, in the multitude of thy mighty men." Give up all abominable peculiar faith, O people, to be safe.

Ch. xiii. v. 4, "Yet I am the Lord thy God from the land of Egypt, and thou shalt know no God but me; for there is no Saviour besides me." Had the God of nature spoken, he would have said he was of the universe. But the peculiar God only spoke, as the oracle-mongers spake. What a God!

Ch. xiii. v. 16, " Samaria shall become desolate : for she hath rebelled against her
God ; they shall fall by the sword ; their infants shall be dashed in pieces, and their
women with child shall be ripped up." Had not the Jews set the example to the original possessors of the soil ?
This creed of prophecy, the indispensable result of Judaism, a peculiar faith, falls in
with that faith. How abominable is any such, made by hypocrites and dissemblers !
This pretender was as rabid a fanatic, as blackguard could well rant. What nonsense, impiety, and blasphemy, for a mortal to pretend to inspiration for himself and
others about divinity. The man that assumes that any such should be believed, is either
deranged or unworthy of an honest fame. We can well see what was the character of
all such, by reference to Josephus' translation about Archælaus, who sent for the divines
in Judea, whose study was employed about dreams. And while some were of one
opinion, and some of another, (for all their interpretations did not agree).
How many are made miserable yet in life, about dreams !

AMOS VII. 10.

AMAZIAH the priest, and Amos the prophet fell out.
Amos wrote his own book, and told his own tale.
Amaziah's is not here. This contention proves corruption, among these professed
people of God. No, they had not a universal brotherhood, certainly not. Why ?
Because they knew not the pure God of the universe. They overlooked his mighty
attributes, and disregarded most ignorantly an investigation into his principles, and substituted false pretences about prophecies, an impossibility. How easy was it in all the
military dynasties, to foretell much of the fate of the world, of races, much less one
nation. But how came they not to prophecy better? Because they were not only
men, but wretchedly, stupidly ignorant of science. Ignorance was the state of the
times. They were sadly deficient in all science. What good did all such prophecies ?
Did the people believe in them ? Their authors abundantly prove, that they were discarded.
All prophecies are incompatible with the conservative principles of the God of the
universe, and as the Jews only knew their peculiar God, they had to feign prophecies.
to juggle the people's minds, that of course were most wofully corrupted by this source
of evil. The prophecies only benefited the priestocracy, apparently, but they finally
involved them in one general ruin.
No such short-sighted policy can benefit any in this world, much less in that to come.

EZEKIEL.

EZEKIEL, as Ezekiel says, ch. xiii., " And the word of the Lord came unto me saying :
2. Son of man, prophecy against the prophets of Israel that prophecy, and say unto
them that prophecy out of their own hearts : 3. Thus saith the Lord God, wo unto the
foolish prophets that follow their own spirit, and have seen nothing !" And this very
pretence of Ezekiel, is now turned against him. Out of his own mouth, he is positively, justly condemned. All the prophets enacted their pretences through their heart,
how else could they ? Rational mind revolts at the bare idea of such action. Before
the highest tribunal of rational mind, rationality tries, rebukes and condemns them,
properly consigning them and their followers to obloquy, as they have " followed their
own spirit, and have seen nothing."
The worst of all, is that corrupt and designing moderns wish to make all the available capital out of all this obsolete paganism, for their nefarious and foolish purposes.
Not being able to perpetrate their own, they appropriate the thunder of predecessors.
If they have no blush of modesty, will they not spare their country, their posterity,
their iniquity ? They are not only wrong, but heinously so in all their pagan business,
that is totally irrelevant to religion.
And the whole land is bigoted, ch. xliv. 9, thus saith the Lord God, " No stranger,
uncircumcised in heart, nor uncircumcised in flesh, shall enter into my sanctuary," and
the castes of priestocracy were horribly defined, as in all Asia. 24. " The priests in
controversy shall stand in judgment. 29. The priests shall eat the meat offering, and
the sin offering, and the trespass offering : and every dedicated thing in Israel shall be
theirs. 30. And the first of all, the first fruits of all things," &c. Discuss this matter
at all times for light, truth and satisfaction. Bigots are afraid to discuss, but hide themselves behind faith, as they call it, but as truth estimates it, credulity. These priestocra-

cies paved the way at the earliest day, to mind's perversion and the world's corruption. What, layman, do you join in with the priestocracy, to help cheat yourself by peculiar faiths? Have you like an intellectual freeman, demanded of the priestocracy, proper proof of the authenticity of any bible of tradition? As they cannot give it, will you continue to endorse bible or gospel falsehoods? Will you give currency to counterfeits? Will you stand by and see the world cheated, and not lend a helping hand? What must be the infamy of intrigues, to put down worthy citizens who use worthy means?

The writers have brought the pretended prophecies, but have left out the full proofs of their authenticity. Who endorses them? The Jews must have scorned the pretended prophecies, but what could they do? Freemen, now you can and should act.

Was ever there such a dynasty as that of priestocracy, on the face of the earth? Ezekiel, xiii. 4, " O Israel, thy prophets are like the foxes in the desert. 6. They have seen vanity and lying divination, saying, the Lord saith : and the Lord hath not sent them." All this is fixed up, collusion of priestocracy, an abomination to the world, mind, freedom. These are after-thoughts and after-prophecies : ch. xvi. 43, Jerusalem is said to be addressed by God, " Hast fretted me?" Ch. xviii. 31, " Make you a new heart and a new spirit." The Jews can appropriate this over the Christians. Ch. xxii. 25, Jerusalem, the bloody city is addressed, " There is a conspiracy of her prophets in the midst thereof, like a roaring lion ravening the prey ; they have devoured souls ; they have taken the treasure and precious things ; they have made her many widows in the midst thereof." 26. " Her priests have violated my law, and have profaned mine holy things," &c. None but a corrupt government could have ever polluted the world by this abomination. 28. Her prophets, divining lies unto them, saying, Thus saith the Lord God, when the Lord hath not spoken." This is the true portraiture of the whole tribes of priests and prophets of superstition, ever, from that to this day, as long as such faith exists. 29. The people of the land have used oppression, and exercised robbery, and vexed the poor and needy ; yea, they have oppressed the stranger wrongfully. Ch. xxiii. 39, " For when they had slain their children to their idols, then they came the same day into my sanctuary to profane it." The Jews were savages. Ch. xxv. 14, " And I will lay my vengeance upon Edom, by the hand of my people, Israel : and they shall do in Edom according to mine anger, and according to my fury ; and they shall know my vengeance, saith the Lord." This is all the fury of false prophet Ezekiel.

The Philistines, Moab and Edom, are threatened for their insolence against the Jews. Why are not the present world-nations, as there is as great a necessity? Ch. xxxiii. 26. Ye defile every one his neighbor's wife." A world of such priestocracy, would adulterate the world. Ch. xxxiv. 8, " But the shepherds fed themselves, and fed not my flock." Ch. xxxvii. 21, " Thus saith the Lord God, behold, I will take the children of Israel from among the heathen, and will bring them into their own land." 25. " And they shall dwell in the land forever." False prophecy, Ezekiel. Ch. xxxix. 21. " And I will set my glory among the heathen, and all the heathen shall see my judgment." The Jews spoke this, not God. The balance of the world did not appreciate the peculiar God of the Jews. The whole world appreciates the God of the universe, and cannot possibly desire such information as the Jewish priestocracy vouchsafed to it. It did no good, but all harm to the Jews, and would ruin the world, if participant therein. The priestocracy were aroused to the perception of their certain destruction, and desired to avert the odium, shame and ignominious reproach of their misdeeds and crimes, by criminating their people. but well has it been said, like priest, like people. The Jewish faith, all peculiar faith, is an abomination to refined mind, cultivated in the richness of rational education. Ch. i. 1, "The heavens were opened." Is that the abode of God, the ether, the heaved up?

Criticism that is just, must call all to a strict account, when the glorious light of mind is to be invaded by arch intriguers. If they did not understand the earth as clearly proved, how did they learn of God's residence? Ah! but that was only a prophet's license. Then let it have a prophet's infamy. Ch. ii. 3, " To the children of Israel, saith the Lord, to a rebellious nation that hath rebelled against me." The rebellion was against the spirit of the Jewish peculiar code, that no nation could abide and continue rational.

As they did transgress, they proved that they had the soul of monotheism, and the constituency of men's souls. If there was any other rebellion, it was that of Ezekiel against truth, for this national rebellion condemns him and all his ignoble tribes of false teachers and legislators, conspiring against popular rights, committing high treason against them and religion, against God himself. They are all conclusively condemned on their own arraignment, and must be consigned to condign obloquy the most absolute.

JEREMIAH.

JEREMIAH the prophet, the son of a priest. He has already been disposed of in regard to his prophecy of Babylon, but he shall have still more ample justice. What good did the prophets? They of course were in collusion with the priests who were in collusion for themselves, against the people in that respect. Did the people appreciate any real benefit? Never. Ch. i. v. 4, "Then the word of the Lord came unto me, saying"—Who endorses all this? The folly of superstition. Ch. ii. v. 7. "He tells the people they defiled their land, and made God's heritage an abomination." He does not include the main reason, that the people were not governed as rational beings but as brutes, that had no free agency of mind. 8. "The priests said not, where is the Lord? And they that handle the law knew me not; the pastors also transgressed against me, and the prophets prophecied by Baal, and walked after things that do not profit." That is, the whole priestocracy. 26. "As the thief is ashamed when he is found, so is the house of Israel ashamed; they, their kings, their princes, and their priests, and their prophets." Let the truth come, Jeremiah, though you convict yourself too certainly. 27. "Saying to a stock, thou art my very father, and to stone, thou hast brought me forth:" and to the priestocracy's book-idols, the very same—" For they have turned their back unto me." (God.)— 28. "But where are thy gods that thou hast made thee?" God-making was the especial trade of ancient priestocracies; their endorsement that of moderns. " For according to the number of thy cities are thy gods, O Judah." Hear that, ye weak imitators of Jewish idolatry of this day. 30. "Your own sword hath devoured your prophets." A terrible retribution, that their peculiar faith and sects with bigotry, fanaticism, and want of toleration, excited. Ch. iii. v. 8. "Yet her treacherous sister Judah feared not, but went and played the harlot also." Civilized moderns, do you need these ungodly teachings?

Ch. iv. v. 22. Saith the Lord—" for my people is foolish, they have not known me; they are sottish children, and they have none understanding: they are wise to do evil, but to do good they have no knowledge." They were bad pupils or had miserable teachers, and a corrupt lesson. The last two abounded, I most conscientiously believe for the honor of God, of the universe, and the legitimate capacity of mind. Ch. v. "Run ye to and fro through the streets of Jerusalem, and see now, and know, and seek in the broad places thereof, if ye can find a man, if there be any that executeth judgment, that seeketh the truth:" v. 2, " surely they swear falsely." And is this the people that presents a bible, the base of the testament? If the first be a corrupter to the people, what must be the second? 9. "Shall I not visit for these things? (adultery), saith the Lord: and shall not my soul be avenged on such a nation as this? 13. And the prophets shall become wind, and the word is not in them." All this was, because mind did not have the proper sway. Monotheism does not require prophets, for mind has to perform its constant functions.

No! God did not place the inhabitants on the earth for thousands of years, all the time in fact, without mind's protection. From all the statements of the so called prophets, they never could get it from them. 31. "The prophets prophecy falsely, and the priests bear rule by their means; and my people love to have it so." This is the whole solution of superstition. All the world of priestocracy of the present day plays into the category of the ancients with all the best lights before them, having too much of mind vassalage.

Ch. vi. v. 13. "For from the least of them even unto the greatest of them every one is given to covetousness; and from the prophet unto the priest every one dealeth falsely." Well done, Jeremiah, that is consistent without any exception. As the son of a priest you speak officially, as you had seen all the drama behind the scenes. The world will get at all the truth expedient, without much difficulty.

Ch. vii. v. 18. "The children gather wood, and the fathers kindle the fire, and the women knead their dough, to make cakes to the queen of heaven, and to pour out dumb-offerings unto other gods, that they may provoke me to anger." Now this was only a change from one pagan worship to another. When the priestocracy presented their creation an imbecile peculiar god, who could not govern his chosen people by direct inspiration then, as mind governs the world now, who can wonder that these pagans should worship the moon, Diana, as the Greeks, Romans and Egyptians, who were as enlightened as they and more so, clearly proved by science, arts, and philosophy.

V. 35. "Since the day that your fathers came forth out of the land of Egypt, unto this day, I have even sent unto you all my servants the prophets, daily rising up early and sending them: 26, yet they hearkened not unto me, &c."

Now we have the official declaration from the peculiar god himself, that both he and his prophets were of no account, that is, they are both analogous.

What the prophets were, so was their God; it was like priests, like people, like god.

This is the climax of ridiculousness. If a priest ever saw that, he should then stop. After all the early rising of the Jews' peculiar god, he could not rule them.

Why did not this god come in person, as he labored so hard to rule them, and they hearkened not?

As the proxy did not avail, why did not the principal act?

It was the safest, easiest, and most effectual way. To him of any potency there could be no denial.

And here is the official document that there was something wrong, either in the peculiar god or in the prophets. If it were in either, the facts are proved that they were of man, as the facts declare them so to be. The mind of the people was then where it was purposed, and still all the special acts could not do. It is clear, that the universal action was not in it. The vitality of the living Creator never sanctioned all such stuff. Where is the world's sense—its liberty—its mind?

The bible is full of iniquity and blasphemy against the God of the universe.

This was not the Jews, but the god of the priestocracy. The last never invoked after this fashion the God Creator of the Jews, but dealt treacherously and deceitfully with him always. "28. Truth is perished, and is cut off from their mouth (the nation's.) 31. (The children of Judah) to burn their sons and their daughters in the fire." Will that do for you, mothers? Is that the kind of faith that your refined sensibility adopts? You must choose this day one of two things, the proper rational use of your minds, or the implicit espousal of that bible that portrays its tuition in what the Jews did. You cannot escape the dilemma of the last.

Ch. ix. v. 2: "for they, my people, be all adulterers, an assembly of treacherous men." And this the people that had all the especial care of their bible, priestocracy, and above all, their peculiar god, who got up early in the morning, in fact, "daily rising up early." That did not permit himself to sleep after a certain time, for the mighty correction was needed as,—"5. and they will deceive every one his neighbor, and will not speak the truth." Then one of the greatest things in society was wanting. The people had plenty of priests and prophets, who were so abundant that they killed off each other by hundreds out of the way, and plainly could not establish social confidence. Then, in them the soul of society was wanting.

And this was the chosen people of God! Of a peculiar god most certainly. Who has ever yet appreciated rational religion? Who has yet ever duly estimated monotheism? The true belief of the unity and purity of the God of nature, that which man calls nature, the elaborated cabinet of God's universe.

The world has to come to it; in all its beauty and loveliness, its exactness and fullness. It should not delay, for the excellency of its character is supreme. All peculiar faith is false, and makes its followers false to their God.

Ch. x. v. 10: "At his (God's) wrath the earth shall tremble, and the nations shall not be able to abide his indignation." Jeremiah, you libel the Creator, for his perfect Godship is ever in equilibrium. With all the lights of their prophets and priests, the Jews, ch. xi. v. 10, "refused to hear (Moses' God's) my words; and they went after other gods, to serve them." It is very clear that all the platforms of all the priestocracies that ever were and to be in existence, cannot begin to fulfil the requisitions of a rational mind. Inquisitions and despotism have tried it in all ways that torture could invent, backed by all the proscriptions of society, then, as now, without availing.

V. 19. "And let us not cut him off from the land of the living," said the opponents of Jeremiah. Now, they would have reversed all this had the people been duly impressed with the truth; and how easy was it for all true prophets to have convinced them at once. Miracles could have been successfully invoked as part of the appurtenances. All the artists of this peculiar drama forget that they are estopped in the incapacity of its execution. To say that there are prophets, a miracle, and not have the effects, is to stultify the narrator's mind, and falsify his words. As to the hardening of hearts, that is all solecism.

Thus the scriptures commit clearly their own suicide.

To affirm that prophets were sent to perform miracles, and that God defeated the impression by such process, is too scandalous for mind, much less the Creator.

But the time-serving bigots pretend they do not understand them. Of course they do not wish to do but their way, and slavishly follow the devices of the reigning dynasty, be they what they may.

But here is their miserable error. They are accountable for all such decision at a higher tribunal than any they have chosen, one that cannot know them only through their adoption of the religion of principles.

It seems that the children of Israel had several gods, but never reached the true one, of course, as all were peculiar. Did they lose the true bible as well as the true God, and give mankind the spurious ones?

Ch. xiii. v. 13 : "Then shalt thou say unto them, thus saith the Lord, Behold, I will fill all the inhabitants of this land, even the kings that sit upon David's throne, and the priests, and the prophets, and all the inhabitants of Jerusalem, with drunkenness."

What a peculiar god, that is, what peculiar prophets. Was Jeremiah drunk when he wrote this?

It will have to take a drunken man to receive and endorse it. Why did he and Isaiah —ch. ix. v. 7—come into collision? There is here prophecy against prophecy.

What is the testimony of Jeremiah respecting the priestocracy of Palestine.

Ch. xiv. v. 14 : "Then the Lord said unto me, the prophets prophecy lies in my name, I sent them not, neither have I commanded them, neither spake unto them : they prophecy unto you a false vision and divination, and a thing of naught, and the deceit of their heart." Now, the monotheist asks, who of all the bible-prophets prophecied truth? Prove that, and the whole discussion ceases, for I yield the question then.

Ch. xviii. v. 18 : "Then said they, come, and let us devise devices against Jeremiah ; for the law shall not perish from the priest, nor counsel from the wise, nor the word from the prophet ; let us not give heed to any of his words."

Ch. xx : "Pashur, the son of the priest, smote Jeremiah the prophet, and put him in the stocks." V. 6. Jeremiah accuses Pashur of having prophecied lies.—Jeremiah would be put to it to prove himself the pure one. V. 7. Jeremiah said, "O Lord, thou hast deceived me, and I am deceived ; I am in derision daily, every one mocketh me." Here is impiety for the world. This man affects to have told the world of events beforehand, an impossibility, becoming outrageously blasphemous, in asserting and palming off his pretences for prophecy, and then out-blasphemes blasphemy in palming off his false pretences for those of his god! Was there ever such an outrage on God?

And this comes of tampering with false pretences, that were blasphemy. Now, what could have been the conscience of all such, short of vulgar perjury, to address his own God thus? He was evidently in the category of a false prophet as all, only badly caught, detected, and exposed, so that the people could not believe him, else why did they mock and blame him in the very face of such peculiar endowments? Had he been successful, he had been honored by the applause of a convinced people, who could not shut their eyes and ears to omnipotent facts, expressly delegated to them.

No, it is all an imposition, deducible on its very face.

I will by no means conclude that had not the Babylonians been victorious we should have heard no more of Jeremiah, but I am fain to believe, on the best facts of this and all such cases, that had the correct history been written, that all such would have shared the fate of the balance, their brethren, the augurs and soothsayers of the world.

Cannot the people be suffered to die in peace on their death-bed, without disturbance of priest-faith?

Ch. xxiii. v. 13 : "And I have seen folly in the prophets of Samaria ; they prophecied in Baal, and caused my people Israel to err." One prophet against another. They recognised deceivers in each other, and wrote the true history, nothing less.

14. "I have seen also in the prophets of Jerusalem an horrible thing ; they commit adultery, and walk in lies : they strengthen also the hands of evil-doers, that none doth return from his wickedness :"

This was stronger than I bargained for, really.

Here is enough indeed. The anti-prophets truly could not have known, as none knew till the events transpired. All these writings clearly prove that the whole of the prophecies were the most degraded of impostures.

I have already adverted to his Babylonian philippics. The spirit of revenge spoke there. I animadvert only because I do see such evil peculiarly obnoxious to religion. All such is history antedated.

When a prophet pretended to prophecy against the people, and the Lord did not destroy them, it was a part of the prophet's machinery to say that they repented. Ch. xxvii. v. 8: "And it shall come to pass, that the nation and kingdom that will not serve the same Nebuchadnezzar the king of Babylon, and that will not put their neck under the yoke of the king of Babylon, that nation will I punish, saith the Lord, with the sword, and with famine, and with the pestilence, until I have consumed them by his hand." What danger was there in prophecy? Was this treachery? Did not his subsequent treatment from the Jews result from this opinion of him.

9 v. "Therefore, hearken not ye to your prophets, nor to your diviners, nor to your

dreamers, nor to your enchanters, nor to your sorcerers, which speak unto you, saying, Ye shall not serve the king of Babylon :" Was Jeremiah less than these, and a traitor at that? He was of course not a prophet. He was as a prophet means, a falsifier of history. Who endorses such?

Ch. xxviii. Hannaniah prophecies differently from Jeremiah. There are but two sides to every question, and he that is talent-endowed, and studies with the closest observation of nature and science, will be oftenest right, that is all ; but all those devoted to such an ignoble profession, were necessarily of small calibre. All that has been protective from universal exposure, has been by, and through the collusion and conspiracy of the priestocracy, who wrote, and kept the books.

Ch. xxix., v. 23. Jeremiah defines the false prophets, villains, and adulterers. And what else can be the condition of the world, when hypocrites affect to believe them? A revised false statute edition, is all that the world has of bibles of prophecies.

Ch. xxxiii., v. 5. "Whom I have slain in mine anger, and in my fury." Less than the fury of the critics, that raged high, when the storm of the inquisition came, and the mighty mind was crushed under the power and weight of the church and kingly despotism. V. 21. Jeremiah threatens the Levites, the priests, the ministers. The people paid no attention to Jeremiah's prophecy. What a burlesque.

Ch. xliv., v. 16. "As for the word that thou hast spoken unto us in the name of the Lord, we will not hearken unto thee." Prophecy is the veriest abomination to mind, uniting humbug with blasphemy.

Ch. l., v. 34. "Their Redeemer is strong ; the Lord of hosts is his name." Vindictiveness is proclaimed upon all nations that had conquered the Jews. This is very politic indeed, as if other nations did not know as much of that matter. But their peculiar god was a priest-mind image, mind-idol. This was a theme for all the clique to expend all their small thunder. Let an example be given for all bibles of tradition to yield all the mockeries of superstition. Religion will triumph on her modest merits. Mind would have profited the ancient Jews more than priestocracies. Hear him. Ch. li., v. 37. "And Babylon shall become heaps, a dwelling-place for dragons." Will you be bigot still? Will you cry faith, when it is only credulity? Will you call a dragon prophecy when it is a nonentity?

Lamentations, ch. ii., v. 11. "My liver is poured upon the earth." Jeremiah was as conversant with physiology as he was with natural history, and knew as much of both as the world knew of religion.

Did the Jews then have any religion when they knew not the true God? Hear him. Ch. iv., v. 11. Fury and fierce anger of God are spoken of ; that will decide, v. 13, for the sins of her prophets, and the iniquities of her priests. To ask for all the subsequent modifications of prophecy in its advocacy, is to commit suicide on its self-contradictions, not to mention all the defenceless category. Integrity acts on principles. Choosing peculiar faith, and its prophecy the adjunct, you cannot take principles that uphold not only you, but the universe. You are only between them, and cannot take both. One of the best evidences of the superiority of the Greeks and Romans to the Jews, besides the facts of civilization, mentioned in this work is, that all their peculiar faiths only pass for what they all honestly were, all auguries and soothsayings. The Jews can form no exception.

But the worst of all is, that most of the moderns that affect to be so learned and pious, that they have the pure faith, none of your pagan, are most stultified.

What would all the Jew prophecies be but one mass of contradictions, most suicidal and futile, but for the elaborate interpreting prophecies of the affiliated, who are determined to keep up the miserable fallacy as long as popular mind will permit them?

The moderns may affect this position, but they cannot do it with integrity and good faith, however they may pretend to it in their faith.

To uphold the spirit of prophecy, by the spirit of sophistry, is very questionable morals, to say the very least of it. To establish the frame-works of society on such basis, carries out the corruption of mind in its worst features, and saps the vitals, when advanced for spurious speculation. The Jews were overrun by the most powerful and successful conquerors, but to apologise and avail themselves of apparent pretences, the priestocracy seized hold of the sins of the people as the cause. What charlatans! The prophets assumed all their peculiar God's sense. With all the supposed aids of the Jews, they were a miserable nation of hypocrites, and all that done by their priestocracy, that overrode the whole people. It takes them, however, to tell their own tale. Let Isaiah denounce the result of what his clique enacted.

Isaiah, ch. x. v. 6. "An hypocritical nation" is the Jews. With all their aids, this people did not prosper, because they violated the first principles of rational mind. xi. 7. "And the lion shall eat straw like the ox." Is this inspiration? It is that of stupidity. Strange, that the people should have had the mighty prophecies, but yet had not the true teachings of mind. Now natural history will never permit such a metamorphosis of nature. What ignorant pretenders, what an ignorant, stupid set of listeners; what a degraded set of followers! xiii. 10. "For the stars of heaven and the constellations thereof shall not give their light. v. 21. And satyrs shall dance there. 22. And dragons in their pleasant palaces. xiv. 29. A fiery flying serpent." What did the prophecies amount to, with such stupid effrontery on all truth of natural history and natural laws?

The mind has a particular mission in life, honorably pledged to social and religious existence. But these prophets were not competent to comprehend that mission, as they sought by their own false pretences to solve the universe-problem. The modern priestocracy are just as stupid, and more shameless.

The world should rule them out affecting to be masters, where they should not be slaves. These are they that assume the peculiar province to interpret. What peculiar vices have peculiar faiths, all of them without an iota of an exception.

It is their dictators that assume peculiar prerogatives, to indite and interpret all such peculiar nonsense.

Isaiah, ch. xxx. v. 9. "That this is a rebellious people, lying children, children that will not hear the law of the Lord. xxxiii. 20. Look upon Zion—thine eyes shall see Jerusalem—a tabernacle that shall not be taken down. xxxiv. 2. For the indignation of the Lord is upon all nations, and his fury upon all their armies." What ranting! What truth about Jerusalem! What faith! 4. "And all the host of heaven shall be dissolved, and the heavens shall be rolled together as a scroll : and all their host shall fall down!" Where shall they fall? Of course on the earth! Wonderful astronomers, if not wise naturalists. How contingent is prophecy! xxxviii. 8. "So the sun returned ten degrees!" No, the sun of God did not certainly—the prophet varied so many degrees from truth—as a sign that Hezekiah should live fifteen years longer, after Isaiah's God had said he should die. Did God or Isaiah say so? Isaiah said it. xl. 22. "(God) that stretcheth out the heavens as a curtain, and spreadeth them out as a tent to dwell in." How wisely described. 28. "The Creator of the ends of the earth"—created as a peculiar God, many peculiar creations, among them were prophets, peculiar animals. Isaiah, ch. xliii. v. 10. "Before me there was no God formed, neither shall there be after me." The God of the universe rules out all peculiar gods, Christs, and Christmakers. 11. "I, even I, am the Lord; and besides me there is no saviour. 12. I am God. 14. Thus saith the Lord, your redeemer, the holy one of Israel: 15. I am the Lord, your holy one." Had God spoken, he would have said, I am God of the universe, and of course he would not have said, 21. "This people have I formed for myself." It is all false. God spoke only through the universe and mind, not through the miserable priestocracy, nor their abominable books. The universe declareth its Creator's speech and work.

Isaiah, ch. xliii.—Much less did God say—v. 23. "Thou (Israel) hast not brought me the small cattle of the burnt offering. neither hast thou honored me with thy sacrifices." All this was too small a capital for the God of the universe. I tell you plainly and candidly, nations of the earth, assuredly this was the peculiar God of the priestocracy, that spake the oracles through his priestocracy. xliv. 6. "Thus saith the Lord, the king of Israel, and his redeemer the Lord of hosts; I am the first, and I am the last; and besides me there is no God." God is no king of Israel, however kings and priestcrafts dictated this. This does not authorize any Christ, I presume. Then the old and new testaments are positively in conflict. The priestocracies must have thought the whole world fools, or have made much of it so, to think that it would believe them. 8. "Is there a God besides me? Yea, there is no God; I know not any." The God that priests invoke, that is God! But how far below the God of the universe! They give lies to the people! 24. "Thus saith the Lord, thy redeemer, and he that formed thee from the womb, I am the Lord, that maketh all things; that stretcheth forth the heavens alone ; that spreadeth abroad the earth by myself; 25. That frustrateth the tokens of the liars, and maketh diviners mad ; that turneth wise men backward, and maketh their knowledge foolish." Hear that, ye priestocracy—God will confute you. xlv. 1. "Thus saith the Lord to his anointed, to Cyrus." Cyrus is too small. What folly on earth ; to falsify history for prophecy, maketh prophecy positively falsified history. 4. "Israel mine elect." That makes a peculiar God, certainly and conclusively. 5. "I am the Lord, and there is none else, there is no God besides me. 18. I am the Lord, and there is none else." How often is this repeated in Isaiah. We mention this for the benefit of conscience, priest-stricken people. Why should there ever have been any enmity between the Jew and Christian? Are the felonious priestocracy and bibles between them? What simpletons! 21. "And

there is no God else besides me ; a just God and a saviour ; there is none beside me.
23. I have sworn by myself, the word is gone out of my mouth in righteousness, and
shall not return, that unto me every knee shall bow, every tongue shall swear." England, as other countries that have union of church and state, advances her prelates
of that church to the peerage, over and above all other denominations. She creates civil
disabilities, even over those for whose forefathers these words were said to have been
written. The civil disabilities of the Jews should be removed ere there is freedom.
What would become of the world were it not for laws and legislation ? It might be
overrun by despotic bibles and minions, but for mind. xlix. 26. " I, the Lord, am thy
saviour, and thy redeemer, the mighty one of Jacob." Take one, take all. What other
than universal dispensations can be made ? lx. 3. "And the gentiles shall come to thy
light, and kings to the brightness of thy rising." What condescension in the church,
and how much the world owes Isaiah for the declaration. lxv. 17. "For, behold, I
create new heavens and a new earth ; and the former shall not be remembered, nor
come into mind. 25. The lion shall eat straw like the bullock—saith the Lord. lxvi.
19. And they shall declare my glory among the gentiles. 20. And they shall bring all
your brethren for an offering unto the Lord, out of all nations—to my holy mountain,
Jerusalem." Which is most to be looked at, the presumption of this priest-prophet or
his vulgar ignorance ? The last always begets the first. But will the people of this
day let such a low character make fools of them? 21 and 23, what priest-jockeying !
Was all this the bribery, to such gross, licentious babbling ?

If there be an honorable man among the priestocracy, can he honorably maintain his
profession before the light of the present day ? The longer he holds on to his berth, the
longer he justly exposes himself to the world's tribunal of rational mind, and the penalties of future retribution.

If m nd receive this pretence as prophecy, then it yields its proper function of rationality.

If the sophists pretend to explain that such is only typical, figurative, metaphorical,
they then are the first to desert their own assumed platform. Both positions are not
tenable. When they advocate all such, they have a mountain of straw, that increases
and leaves no room for the grain. The moderns are not to let the Jew fables be palmed
on them, nor their own fabulists get the advantage over them, as augury and soothsaying endorsers. What are all the miracles of a peculiar God of the Jews worth, in the
universe of a God, who is not peculiar, whose immutable principles preclude miracles?
God does not change them for miracles.

FAITH-DOGMAS, PECULIAR AND SPECIOUS.

THESE are all insufficient if they furnish an absurdity of belief or creed, for all will
and must be a faithless salvation, if sincerity and truth, that ever sustain themselves in
all things by conservative reason, are not the foundation as well, even better, in religion
than in all things else.

How and where can these be secured, that ever accompany religion, short of the full
attributes of Deity, in his omnipotence, purity and perfection, that require a strict interpretation by language, the correct sign of our ideas, that owe their origin to mind ?

Neither church membership, nor the mind inadequately balanced by defective education in essential duties and habits, are enough to arouse man to his proper sphere.

Mind must be civilized in all the best comprehension of reason, and must have its intrinsic fund to reach its noblest destiny.

If any faith could have answered, then the dark ages for centuries were the best
theatre to prove the fact, but mind had to work out in the lapse of time its own bright
merit and true glory, triumph in science, and above all, over superstition and idolatry,
the very constituents of all peculiar faith.

Such elements of the injury of mind prostrated, overcome by correct mental cultivation, that incontestibly vindicates itself as part of religion that saves, prove mind to be
paramount.

The history of faith, as expressed in various creeds, evinces correct mirrors of the
time, and the degree of refinement, and proves that such creeds, not being on the broad
platform of God's principles, are stumbling blocks and hindrances if they be not of the
right kind, to the just attainment of mind's rightful position.

In the faith professed, the great and independent question arises, does the faith advocated advance religion of the Supreme Being in all essential characteristics ?

If it fall short of any essential particular, then assuredly that faith is wrong in principles, and must inevitably be in the result.

Nothing can supply the radical defect and deformity. No pleasing pliancy, no subordinate compliance can rectify material and fundamental errors, and the only way of correction is to renounce all such at once. The Creator requires his own exclusively, and any peculiar faith that withholds irreverently the least iota, and does not pay the Creator, is unworthy of his smiles, favors or blessings, and must incur his displeasure.

The payment must be made to the genuine creditor. The payment and homage to a created being, instead of the Supreme Creator, are a mockery.

What honest and intelligent judge can say the debt is paid?

The mind when enlightened revolts at such pretences. What could the holy and just God vouchsafe to those that fought in the wars pretended to be holy for ages on both sides, but death to most in slaughter, that they madly provoked for peculiar faith or conquest, lust, ambition and rapine? What was the pretended sepulchre of some impostor at Jerusalem, Mecca or in Hindostan, to avail the good of mankind?

Was that the disguise to unholy ambition, to general conquest of the world?

What was the system of peculiar faith to be built up, affecting to be the blessing, but the curse of the world?

Was it plunging that world into deeper darkness by such wars for centuries, or deeper misery by all the machinery of proscription by the fiendish inquisition, to torture the body, to coerce and enslave, debauch and darken the mind? Was that the best of all faiths that elicited the greatest ingenuity in such sports of degrading tyranny, to be best entitled to the holiest position of happy and immortal fruition?

And as the deadly wars of races and of creeds for centuries were not enough to glut the horrid morbid appetites of the priesthood, civil wars of more ruthless vindictiveness were aroused to perpetrate general carnage and slaughter, to excommunicate the people from earth and the Holy Centre, and confiscate their property to their own uses amid the general wreck.

Can faithful history, that portrays the thousand horrors and crimes of the degraded times, be placed in the hands of ingenuous youth, without enkindling the deepest curses upon that degraded body of human depravity?

What has not the priesthood done in every government that its insidious wiles could influence? See it in the oracles and soothsayings of Rome, ever faithful to its own selfish interest.

Are there not thousands of acts of cruelty and tyranny that disgrace all the lights and blessings of mind?

But for the mastery of mind, enlightened mind, the human race would be at the humblest and most degraded point of vassalage, to the curses of superstition that has assumed religious livery. Where can any such lumber and rubbish be placed but out of sight of mind, as weak traditions commended by no proper virtue of mind, but misdirected by perverted minds deceived by vain authority, or misled by the bribes of lucre and profit of the same profession, that present many delusions to the people, who, in such matters of momentous importance, are unable to rise in their majesty and assert freemen's rights?

The followers of a more presumptuous sect affect to scorn the pagan on the standard of reason, and yet all such flinch from their own tribunal!

For the lights before them, are the modern as good as the ancient pagan faiths? What, the christian-pagan? Does the advocate put that faith below paganism? Is it more than equal?

Vain mortals, clergy or laymen—nothing but principles can be consistent; therefore peculiar faiths are all pagan.

All the counterfeits have the elements of their own destruction, and the christian as all others.

This very tribunal is self-impeached, self-condemned, and its sceptre has been passed by its own decree. Stupidity only prevents the correct vision, and the record of the right judgment and verdict.

Mind may collect all the systems of peculiar faith that have been in existence for thousands of years, hallowed by customs of revered ancestors, sealed with the blood of the miscalled martyrs, except as far as they go for the imprescriptible rights of conscience, and testified to by all the false saints of earth, yet they all promulgate the elements of contradiction, that cannot be reconciled by all the benevolence and justice of mind.

To what point can mind turn of the five grand divisions of God's globe for its inherent rights?

The ardent devotees of Asia, the prolific mother of peculiar faiths, may refer mind to her rites and customs of worship, hallowed by time from the remotest antiquity, and received by their most eminent priests, of whom the learned Brahmin points to his vedas, the mufti to his koran, many of the Chinese to the books of Confucius, and other Asiatics to pagan worship, and to the other faiths of tradition.

Alas! mind revolts at all such faiths, that engage the attention of half the human race, five hundred millions, as soon as mentioned.

The rest of the four parts of the world are mostly beset by the conflicts of speculative peculiar faith, superstition and pagan idolatry! Alas for the condition of mind, that the best of all such has a miserable tenure by miracles, prophecies, mysteries and enigmas, all non-existent!

•

SUPERSTITION AND IDOLATRY.

PECULIAR faith is identified with these monstrosities of mind, influenced by the worst of passions. Superstition battling for assumed claims, resorts to arts of stratagem, and invokes her hand-maiden, sophistry, for a thousand expedients.

Baffled in the bland arts of flattery, she uses all the forces of tyranny, into which so many of her outrages run. Superstition is ever inseparable from tyranny of mind, and the worst is that self-imposed.

Peculiar faith is upset by reason in all the assumed mysteries, all of which, when translated by a cultivated mind, mean, that belief in religion, a plain constant duty, is beyond the people's comprehension, and that therefore the priests, though it is a plain duty, are the only ones competent to decide and solve these questions!

But all intellectual minds do see that self-interest, power and influence, do always decide in the priests' favor, not the peoples'.

When we come to the last strong hold, and ask why the after-thought of messiahship so many thousands of years subsequent to creation, since God's fore-thoughts decide his character as a perfect God, his immutability and omniscience necessarily presenting unity and his perfection, preventing any after-thought thousands of years after creation of mankind, millions and millions of whom have sunk down in death without any but the only true aid from their Creator, always sufficient, to doubt which, is sacrilege, save when official priesthoods assumed by diverse peculiar faith, his prerogatives; we are told that Christ was the Lamb whose blood was shed from the foundation of the world, that is, from creation!

We ask for the proof conclusive, not assertion of that pretence. Words alone are given us, but words alone will not do here. The only proof that is necessarily furnished us in the conservation of creation, is by God's unity that such is untrue. The organization of the universe clearly disproves it, and that is the highest authority. No expost facto creation belongs to a perfect God.

If there were ever such a being as a fallen angel, then that evil genius invented peculiar faith, engendered in superstition. But mind perverted, is the only corrupt evil genius.

Superstition reaches her lowest state by sophistry, then such is an evil genius in the business of after-thoughts to after-thoughts. The whole system of peculiar faith, thus ever falls. Had it been let alone for free discussion of mind and rational toleration, all peculiar systems would now have been in abeyance to reason and mind, enlightened.

All systems of peculiar faith are compelled to perish, as false. All such have gone, or are going to the dust to be remembered no more, but for their iniquities, above all, for their hateful and vile blasphemies to God.

Great as was Diana of the Ephesians, yet all her greatness is buried, and few so poor, that is if men to-day, as to do her reverence. All such will be with Diana. Other gods and goddesses, and other such machinery of crude mind's conception, had passed on mind's stage time after time, before, in the long lapse of ages, and had passed off the stage with those nations, evincing sufficient proof of deplorable imbecility and perversion of mind.

Superstition, idolatry and man-worship have done their utmost, and in their expiring moments, before the progressive light of mind, have enacted many a fearful tragedy for human nature, that recoils now aghast, at the miserable picture of such horrid deformities.

This will ever be the case with all such works of mortal stamp. But man's tyranny with bigoted self-interest, enacted all these over the globe.

The blood of human victims is shed without compunction, by the fiendish priests of barbarians, and that rite is only superseded by the blood and flesh of animals, while this folly only yields to the light of mind itself, ever finally triumphant, but ere that, most awfully sacrificed, victimized, at the feet of superstition, by the oppression of unholy power of theocracy, diversified in form and polity all over the world.

Why delay, men of mind, the hour for the complete triumph of truth by one universal accord and concert of action? Has not superstition in her various forms insatiate with sacrifice, been not enough filled with human blood for thousands of years, not only shed at the altar of the priests, but at the altars of the country's despots?

Shall a deeper and bloodier sacrifice, a deeper and deeper atonement of the world, for outrageous blasphemies to the pure God of the universe, be necessary for the crimes and stupidity of past and present generations?

If God proclaim his recognition, it must be to condemn. That condemnation must be proclaimed by punishment. The duty then is yours, patriots of the world.

Spare, mind, not your energies, in this mighty and most laudable effort, to rescue mind from the deeper error of its ways of self-delusion, and aid in giving mind its worthy tributes, and let reason assume her legitimate character.

Fanaticism has swept over the earth time after time, and has overwhelmed mind's best sources of instruction, and despoiled the world of its fairest fruits. In their ruth-less vindictiveness, fanaticism and superstition sacrificed the brightest stars of philoso-phy, and the noblest religious advocates for the times, in the persons of many true martyrs to mind's rights and freedom. What such fanaticism and superstition can be, the worst oppressors of man and man's mind, under all the lurid wiles and disguises practicable, too many centuries of time bitterly felt.

What they have been with the sword, inquisition, with mind's torture and proscrip-tion, they have been again by the bayonet, brute force and insidious wiles of sophistry and credulity for true faith, and will forever be, if we give tyrants of mind the power, and suffer its rights and lights to be perverted and corrupted.

No blind creed should be ever adopted, that separates man, the equal in character, from his fellow citizens, and advances that view untenable, because impracticable. The question with the world is to be settled for the peace of all, their ease of mind and vital enjoyment.

Who wishes to see mind ever harassed by mysteries, mere idle, if not cruel pre-tences, involving no good, but ever a fund for uneasiness?

The philosophy of life decides certainly, for what is only available for the Creator's paramount claims.

All intelligent good citizens will finally know this, without any faith of a peculiar character, but what the pure reason of liberalized mind gives.

This causes the globe to smile in loveliness, and repel the foul waves of superstition. Take away the self-interests of absolutism, and the degrading corruption will cease.

The absurdities of peculiar faith are very palpable. Why did God, being no re-spector of persons, seek to destroy thousands of his subjects for one monarch, as David, an adulterer and murderer?

The solution shows incapacity of sophistry, to pretend to reason on the peculiar faith that includes any man-worship, as an inconsistency that commits suicide. When pecu-liar faith is adopted, reason exposes it. Nations are necessarily punished on this earth as individuals, as we see too often by their rise and downfall, from their own misdeeds or by the misdeeds of rulers that represent or ought to represent them. But then each individual is still amenable for proper retribution.

The military code of ethics adopted by the world, is too reckless of principle, and brings weaker nations at first under the dominion and injury of the stronger, and the last, finally, under its own traitorous factions.

Arms, the resort of barbarous nations, can never decide principles, that seek the forum of conscience, but other ingredients of the mixed cup of national vices, may elaborate the results of penalty.

The misfortune of subjection to absolutism, is the adoption of its follies, and the pay-ment for its crimes. Here the one-man-power involves the mass in difficulties, and the nations of the world must risk the suffering sustained in the extrication, as a certain law of nature.

Is the condition of superstition, only chargeable upon past ages?

The main bulwark is faith so called, behind which, most professors throw themselves. That will not do.

All faith that is not rational, can be most easily demolished, as it is credulity. Su-perstition originated what priestcraft has continued.

When the minds of children are filled with superstition, we observe the effect of shameful deterioration of better morals. The highest patriotism prompts to the correc-tion of superstition, that is, sectarianism of rationality.

One's own vices produce fears, that play into the hands of superstition. Fear and superstition have played into the hands of peculiar faith, which reason and science came after to correct for the dignity of religion.

19

Superstition has paid court to ancient heroes as worthy of worship, very far inferior to our own Washington.

It is ignorance of the people and much of it corruption, that make demi-gods of mortals. What degradation of the apotheosis of emperors, canonization of saints, the sooth-sayings of augurs.

The herd, the vulgar prejudices of the rabble, enrage and stultify the people. What superstition about days, especially Friday!

Sailors, above all, have a horror about this day, and the transportation of corpse. What superficial views!

But for fear and superstition, the sword and bibles of tradition never would have progressed.

Advantage has been taken of the world, through its superstition. The sword and power of Constantine as of a Mahomet, have forced peculiar faith on the world, and vassal minds ignorantly retain it.

Why do the adherents of peculiar faith and superstition lay themselves open to assaults, on their motives or their mind? All church membership is not done for effect, mere capital for influence.

Would that it could be said to be from pure reason, sense, justice and religion.

But mind under the noble influence of philosophical science, will not continue vassal. Neither military conquests, empires, nor peculiar faith, have been or can be effectual. Mind that is mind revolts at the blood of victims, or the senseless messiahships. Philosophical science cuts down all miracles, prophecies, mysteries and enigmas ; does not leave plausible belief of one.

By the blessing of mind, enriched by previous benefits of science, children know more science now, than the ancient philosophers or Pauls, who trusted to dogmas,—not science. This is all through mind cultivated in the truths of science, and then not a particle of bigoted sectarianism can prevail, as that detracts from mind's worth.

But as philosophy and science cut down all prophecies and miracles without any exception, therefore those bible advocates seek to cut them down, but most outrageously for truth and the God of truth.

But all this will not do, as none properly raised can permit false gods imposed on the world or mind.

The first impressions are important in the noblest gift of mind, that no false steps be taken, no false impressions be made, no false pretences be propagated. It is one of the most arduous enterprises of patriotism, to extricate from the clutches of superstition.

The combination and collusion of despotic government with superstition, have prevailed from the remotest times of power to the present, and fastened the most usurpations. Every rational being can plainly see that religion asks no union with government, much less with absolutism that ever presides with superstition and peculiar faith. Every age, and nearly all countries, have seen and felt the awful consequences of the last. It is a horrid state of affairs when the people of the country are not able to perceive the position of their rights, the actual existence of their wrongs, indifferent to the policy of political machines that move governments and the world.

Is mind to be kept in terror and thraldom, about abstract superstition ; the idea of hell feloniously got up to rule it by fear? Some may deem it expedient to have such ideas still supported.

All partisans go for their profession in clanship, as long as profitable. Omens, apparitions, visions and dreams. are a part of her fixtures.

One of the superstitions of the world is presentiment of death by forebodings, &c. All delusion.

I have seen a patient who affirmed that he must die of his fever at a certain hour—so also a friend, both from forebodings, the last having a remarkable dream, but both survived clear of all such most certainly. We eternally hear of the winning, but most rarely of the losing side.

Another thing is spirits or ghosts, a part of the machinery of pious frauds. Who sees spirits in the day time? We are familiarized to many peculiar faith absurdities, and find it most difficult to be extricated from the darkness of superstition.

Monotheism alone, can free us from superstition. But then renunciation is said to take place on the death-bed. Of what? True religion! Was there ever such a deed in mind that was sound?

Pious frauds may affect some pretension or assertion entirely worthless, for how can renunciation ensue on a sound basis? Where is any proper proof?

False pretences however affecting piety, prove nothing. The greatest astonishment may arise, to see intelligent freemen worshipping with superstition and bound to those that follow in her footsteps.

There should be no fast days, or partial fast days—that is absurd unless decreed by nature. Physiology decides against them. No terror of superstition in any way devised is to induce mind to decide most vital questions, by policies that go beyond reason. When people get scared, then they rush to messiahships and all such false pretences. The creation of such a being as the devil arose in the darkest ages, when particular messengers were put into the place of God's principles, giving too much importance to such a being, and detracting from the attributes of God. Among the miseries of superstition, may be ranked the many witch murders. One butchery of this kind was perpetrated in the colony of Massachusetts, as related in "a concise account of North America, by Major Robert Rogers," who says "about this time a most shocking tragedy was acted in this province, several persons being accused, tried, condemned, and executed for witchcraft, and others imprisoned; but the next year they celebrated a public fast to beg forgiveness of the Almighty for having murdered the innocent the year before." Where did they get this idea from, but the bible of peculiar faith?

The ignorant ancients could be easily gulled and directed by vicious superstition, but does it become the American people to be humbugged by such pretence? The world has been governed by superstition long enough. Where superstition in peculiar faith prevails, the most absurd credulity abides in many things, as the mind has not its power of analysis. Thus cholera may be considered the cause of witchcraft, as said to have been in Russia. Now what better could be expected of a people, whose mind is held in the lowest abeyance to peculiar faith superstition? Away with all false faith of churches and the priestocracy, and all the arch-heads with them. The spell of witchcraft in Africa causes extensive murders, in the form of trial, by poisonous wood. All such proves that mind has not begun to reach the first main principles of rationality. Asia has her various degrees of peculiar influence; and embraces among them the Hindoo Thug assassination, a most extensive code execution of wholesale robbery and murder. But the captain of an hundred freebooters was a robber, while Alexander who commanded one hundred thousand, was a mighty conqueror. The Thugs are assassins, but England, who has subjected her 140 millions of Hindoos, is the moral ruler, defender of the faith, by the grace of God.

Some of the world are so superstitious, that their ideas refer to the age and state of the moon and stars, particularly sirius, whose days are very ominous indeed. All had their star-astrology, the trick of priestocracies and absolutists. The age is hardly past that heard this idle false pretence, from one of the world's aspirants. They believe in enchantments. The collusion of the world has been great in upholding all degrees of this pretension.

Among the means, the royal touch of kings has been maintained by men of letters, who ought to have known better. Superstition and ignorance in the first ages of the world, misguided the most, who were alarmed at the natural elements! Now, many are the conspirators against philosophy, that sets the world right in this whole subject. Bigots get caught in their false position. No such habit of lying so offensive and so perverted, that when telling the truth the functionaries cannot obtain rational credit, passes with impunity.

What nation is there in its rude state but has superstition? Government, instead of suppressing all the incentives of superstition, actually support much of its nonsense, and especially the pretences of the prophets. Such act knavishly, to take advantage to tyrannize.

The ignorant, superstitious man, hath said, that there are more gods than one; there is the trinity. This thing of trinity, keeps up the old exploded notions of polytheism, under a disgraceful and ignominious sophistry.

It is the basest blasphemy on God, and has been the vilest imposition on man. The bible is one of the frame-works of this superstition. Most, the greatest sophistries in the world are propagated through superstition. Why? Because power is connected therewith, and premium is appropriated therefor by the world. If the superstitious were to think, they would not adopt, could not tolerate their absurd conclusions. With them, how many things become mysterious, as the recent knockings, the most arrant humbuggery. Visions of ghosts were commonly believed in by the ancients. The mass of the people is a peculiar monster, some liking show, popularity.

The most are bound to the car of superstition, and though convinced of errors of peculiar education, yet cannot see the honest dictates of rational religon.

PECULIAR FAITH—PAGANISM.

ABSOLUTISM has bound the world to its iron chains in temporal and sacred things, and has thereby invaded its most precious rights. None but senseless fanaticism can fail to see or be ignorant of its ruthless injury.

All good citizens must seek by all earnestness to be independent of all the wiles of hierarchy, as hostile to all the best interests of social and religious duties.

The world is obliged to consider by its sufferings its collusion in its diversified forms of power, wealth, and influence.

In their absolutism, the priestocracy have given no reason in the absence of all documents, proofs and vouchers, for all the miracles, and prophecies claimed, but imperiously advance credulity, that they most absurdly claim to be faith upon the consciences of mankind.

Though God's works, that speak for him to all eternity, deny all this as flagrantly obnoxious to sense, virtue, and decency of mind, still " cloaked in their little brief authority" of mind's despotism, they fruitlessly usurp time in persisting.

What wise man can adopt that which cannot reach the court of conscience with any protection ?

What authority of mind has the result, emanating from the fabrication of the cunning and the credulity of a mass; extremely and grossly ignorant, being web adapted for such materials, by which shrewd and unprincipled ambition operated ?

Have not nations felt enough of this cruel drama, in blood freely drawn in every age by varied tyranny ?

If we analyze these facts, we must be forced to reason on them by the present state of worldly faiths.

What interminable disputations, controversies, quarrels, and equal intolerance of sects, and vices of clergy, peculiar faith-persecutions, and bloodshed, about the non-essentials of religion, but the road of ambition to power.

The lights in all professions have to be corrected as originated at the true fount of wisdom, the mind.

The right nature of mind must be studied to be cherished, then we find that all, except the true faith, that is in the keeping of mind, not of priests, (wolves cannot protect the sheep,) is deformed by iniquity of insidious members, of all sects, all over the world, acting with subterfuges, prevaricating and equivocating, addicted to private, if not public vices, in face of their absurd pretences and protestations.

It is their immediate interest in the circle of peculiar membership, to secure some petty and puny object over the mighty benefits of universal brotherhood.

All this faith, without exception, is degraded by vassal character before this light of day, requiring ignoble vicegerents to do what mind, the functionary of all mankind, was purposed to execute by its Almighty Creator, not unlike to having mental midwives from the chief to the subaltern, proving corruption and imbecility, one or both in man. God did not create mind to be thus miserably prostituted and abused.

Rouse up, soul, and honor thyself, by honoring thy God. All this discussion is not for derision, but amendment, that is profitable for the universe.

Not to deprive of peculiar faith, delusive as it is, and leave a blank, and desert inextricable, but to ask proper investigation of all sound minds into the character of their immortal life-funds, and those, the only ones, to be considered by intelligent freemen.

But what is it that absolutism, aided by self-interest, that fosters ambition, that prompts or promotes, fanaticism that enrages, and passions that encourage it, will not do in the controllable crowd ?

But mind that is played upon, is made to feel all these elements, till the spell masters it, as in all ages, mind seeks the best way, but is too often misled most ignorantly or designedly, as the multitude go with their immediate interest in union of sacred matters with civil government no matter how absolute, all such union made the stronger, cunningly designed for its increase and sustenance of power, over those adopting holier purposes, but doing as taught, to lisp from infancy, and revere by infantile custom various names and characters, in place of God's one authority.

What chance has there been for the world under her worst circumstances ?

Yet all could not do under the inspiration of mind, receiving its holy light from Deity, for mind revolted, and burst the bars of superstition and idolatry.

In her pure analysis she does wonders to her ignorant self, not miracles, a thing that cannot exist, but in the false notions and position of priests' stupid language.

Thinking is a function of mind that ever secures truth, when it secures reason, the highest proof of that function and attribute, the ability to separate truth from falsehood.

Thinking mind could not believe in monstrosity, that defied mortals and degraded God, that outraged modesty and revolutionized reason and facts.

Thinking, enlightened rational mind, sincerely rejected all such imposition.

The testimony of truth which is rational faith, the exact position of true, the only faith, that mind and religion, its highest function, can recognise in its existence, what mind has to believe, was adequately established from the foundation of creation, by the Creator's works.

The Creator is not entitled to his supreme functions, if this were not so in the universal fitness of all things.

If false peculiar faith was adopted, it was not the fault of the works, but of perverted mind, that misconstrued those works. Mind, as free, moral, rational agent, must correct its own perversion by the universal functions and faculties. It must begin anew or again, that is practical availability.

Peculiar faith leads to all absurdities and crimes of false doctrines and systems, that produce as the result of false faith, all the iniquities of superstition, that misrepresents and counterfeits religion.

False or peculiar faith, under her various colors, produces many crimes, that history takes cognizance of. False doctrines come in for their share. The result of false doctrines in part, is natural conflict and direct hostility in creeds and their practice, instead of the unanimity of purpose of rational religion.

Fortunately for itself, mind has counteracted this injury of superstition by toleration of opinion, that does away with much of barbarous outrages on its rights. But a deep under current, most prejudicial, still prevails.

The torch of superstition is still lighted. Short-sighted adherents still affect that the best system of peculiar faith is theirs, which they modestly ask of the world to adopt, at the expense of mind's vassalage, and the world's ruin.

This is all self-delusion, a monomania, a one idea, for the basis being all wrong, the foundation unsound, the building however diversified and embellished, must fall. The world, full of messiahships, does not alter the truth.

'Tis needless to speculate in face of facts.

God, as Creator, is alone to be adored.

All other doctrines will clash, and break each other to pieces and fragments.

There is no peculiar faith to truly represent religion for any chosen people, the idea is absurd and monomaniacal of some despot priest, as the God of the universe has a universal religion, since he has a universal people, under the conservation of universal principles, by reason of his Almighty unity and perfection.

Man has made the world contracted, illiberal and clannish, while God's world has the circumference of the globe, with liberal and just proportions, and life to the people.

The god of peculiar and select chosen people, can be absurdly moulded, as has been the god of Judaism to the ignorant, false pretences of priests, who managed their men of straw, Moses and Aaron, as necessary.

The christian's god is the example of whoredom and seduction, that gave the wife's imposition on the husband, the blasphemy of her son, that caused him his life, and death error, and many crimes to the people of the world, miserably affected by such horrid superstition, the end of which cannot be told by wise men, much less by prophets.

But the God of the universe sublimely towers in his own Holy Centre, too pure for peculiar faith, the adherents of which, as Moses and Aaron, never dreamed of in all their pretences, much less approached the confines with their odious and noisome sacrifices of the blood and flesh of victims.

The God of nature rules out all the dwarfed little gods of peculiar faith, not jealous of them, no matter where worshipped, in groves or altars, because he is the approved God of mind, the God of conscience, purity and all the attributes of supremacy, eternal and unapproachable.

Where he exists, there can be existence for none other, as his seal is on mind, rational and religious, excluding all else, as mind is the concentration and reflection of divine inspirations by the attributes of God.

Vast and unlimited have been and are peculiar faith doctrines of the world, but they are distracted by divisions from the nature of their elements.

One faith only is right and that is not peculiar, for it is built on the solid foundation of eternal conservative principles. Had any other been right, there could have been no division at all. Any division assumed of the true one, is that of a counterfeit surely and certainly.

God cannot be divided, for he has a perfect unity.

Man, the botch, has made his gods, and fights the world to compel its worship.

Man's god is one of blood always, deformed by passions. The God of the universe is distinguished by the intrinsic characteristics of equanimity, impressed on mind the beneficiary, that realizes all due it by the sublimity of peace and justice.

Where all peculiar faiths' are essentially and radically wrong, is it worth while to question which division of the mighty host is right?

What are the test and standard, seeing that reason is abjured and rejected by all the founders who assume credulity for faith?

Conscience is invoked, but she can only appeal to truth, honesty and principle. These constitute the only aristocracy of religion, and place faith in abeyance, subject to her betters, reason and truth.

All professors of religion must seek to meet this only honorable basis, which none can avoid at all.

If any avoid these, then indeed is sinful man bereft of his only true friends that are authorized to introduce him to his God.

In this ocean chaos, the compass of reason alone guides in safety. First came all the rough drafts of superstition, with her horrid human sacrifices and disgusting multiplicity of idol, animal, man and hero worships; finally mind with obscure views of the directing agencies of the universe.

Myths and fables, legends and fictions, danced attendance in the mighty drama of priests, who supervised the whole. In all these, mind and reason in their weakest state, were stilted, and with truth played a subordinate part to peculiar faith, no matter how monstrous, iniquitous and degraded, provided that the priests manufactured correspondent oracles of their pretended deities. Any thing with them was especial and peculiar providence, without conservative principles. They were the judges and kings of kings, for their oracles manufactured for the occasion decided the fate of man and empire. They were and have been dangerous parts of government. In some countries the deepest feuds and wars were the result of their antagonism, till victory of the one annihilated the others, and cowed if not crushed the empire and people. Mind of course in competition at home, and among other nations, all espousing a reigning priestcraft in some form or other, improved under all these malign circumstances. Successive ages obliterated the worst of the preceding. The main features, the desire for power were never lost, never relaxed, but grew stronger, while the defects of the previous administration of priests were lessons of experience to increase that department. Among myriads such, comes first in priest character and strength, Judaism, with her god of miracles, prophecies, mysteries and enigmas—all imperfect of course. Nothing could be done without the priests, the judges of the people, intermediates between them and the god of Judaism. This peculiar faith paved the way for others. In process of time, there came many messiahs, with after-thoughts to better man's deceptions, delusions and imperfections.

The Christs, Mahomets, Smiths and Tinkers, all seeking to supersede the prevailing faith, on the basis of speculation that condemns the whole unequivocally, in the face of monotheism, that is upheld by principles.

As mind rules the world, so rule they, bible or no bible. In successive ages, not many hundreds of years hence, the mormons may supersede the christian by their peculiar faith.

Where is all this vile imposition to end? How long shall insatiate superstition bathe the world in iniquity and blood, and outrage the high Holy Centre of the gracious Creator of the universe? Her empire will be as long as ignorance rules with her iron hand and corruption of bigotry, as long as mind, forgetful of its rights, duty and mission, will permit them overstep the modesty of innocence, negligent of the worth of high-mindedness and exalted sensibility.

All this is seen well enough, but absolutism subsidizes corruption of the public faith! Perverted mind acts tory to rational mind and religion.

Much of mind is bought off in promotion to church livings, and all the emoluments of importance. The benefited portion will hardly directly impeach itself.

All other than rational faith is from man, and therefore cannot stand on the immortal principles of consistency.

The world is deeply interested in being done with all peculiar faith forever, as dangerous and demoralizing, never safe or trustworthy, speedily and in time ere it be too late. Down must go all but God-adoration, if raised be man's dignity to repair, by a just reverence of God, all that can be done by rational mortals for a wise advocacy of his attributes. A false faith will ever create false views of religion, nothing better than superstition.

It has been claimed that some at least of these systems of peculiar faith, as Christianity and Judaism, go along with science, and remove the system, and the last or science perishes.

If this pretence were so, the fact that established it would fix and prove its innate principle.

This position, if true, would undeniably prove its imperative claims to conservative principles, and would link it forever in the league of creation's best and perfect gifts to man. It would have been ever identified at mind's creation, whereas as subsequents, it is all impeached as illegitimate.

Surely, all matters established since the creation are undeniably excluded from the genuine character of innate principles, and are imperfect excrescences offered for such.

Thus, among innumerable reasons, decides God's perfect exclusive prerogatives. Being excluded by reason, it is irrational and excluded from science. It is alien to science. This is no fancy sketch, but the most serious facts.

The peculiar faith dreams and visions of the ancients must be superseded on the analysis of science, by the facts of modern rational religion.

The light of science was best held by the Greeks and Romans, pagans though called, even over the Hebrews in their palmiest days, and that light was handed from them to the Christians, who established the Roman and Greek churches.

The priests were the keepers of the records called sacred, and were also the authors, by authority of the nation.

They ought to have been the most learned, if not the wisest of the world, having peculiar power. But alas for any peculiar faith, science was obscured with a decreasing flame, and though the orthodox of that peculiar faith burned out in popular enthusiasm for crusades, science had to hang her head, for her friend and patron were disgraced at the court of truth. Strange to say, in the war of conquest, the sword yielded to the cimeter, and the Christians were behind the Saracens or Mahommedans who mostly had the best of science in the dark ages of the world, when the light of Christianity and Judaism shone dimly, and the whole world was more or less obscured in science and perverted in miracles.

Where, now, is the superior light of the Saracens and Mahommedans, of any peculiar faith, apart from the advancement of mind and reason ?

If christianity were pre-eminent for her gifts of learning, and her refinement and courtesy had been equal to expectation, then she would have a high claim to mind's regard, if even her legitimacy had failed.

But silence for this arrogant claim, is preferable to history of many misdeeds and foul acts.

Who would not wish the veil of silence drawn over church or peculiar faith history of the world ?

Fanaticism, that discloses the action of bigotry on unprincipled ignorance and vindictiveness, foul passions influencing a darkened, lowering, and beclouded state of mind, preaded over much of that ignoble part of the world.

At the time of its ascendancy to its defeat, it ruled, the tyrant of the human race, and made its influence tell most potently ; also, most malign were the effects that darkened the ages much more.

But now the jesuitical casuist tells us, in his sophistry, that all that was false faith.

If so, the question is yielded by them, for we know no other responsibility of the doctrines involved than through those assuming to be their professors, to the practicable limit of those doctrines.

If that involves not the question, that peculiar faith had no existence, as none such can have, it trades on capital of mind never acknowledged.

Incidental to the war of conquests, rapine and pillage, comes the deepest corruption of the people by sale of indulgences to maintain those bloody love-feasts.

Never after this can we expect the learned scholar of truth to pretend to speak of the light of the world being due to the darkness of peculiar faith.

When science arouses her head, and speaks through the mind of a Galileo, peculiar faith tyrannizes by his imprisonment, to arrest the mental and popular light, and the truth of science is held in abeyance to the errors of bible despotism.

A few hundred years after the bloody crusades, that involved the best part of the world in deadly strife for fanaticism, miscalled religion, the lovely and amiable christianity is employed in the tortures of the inquisition, and all the blights of real worth are caused by this unholy faith, affecting claims to science.

Mind at last partly rescued itself by revolutions, partial, but tending to a mighty crisis in the world's benefit.

This very faith was bettered by this light of mind, the only lever of the world, that she wishes to obscure and deceive by her varied sophistry.

Despite of peculiar faith, under the most arrogant pretensions of christianity, or any sect, mind is working its way to a purer triumph ; the watch-fires are blazing over the wide expanse of space. Where can we find ignorance? Where mind has not been duly and liberally cultivated?

Countries now, with their millions to-day sounding one mighty peculiar faith, as that of the state, that ostracises all others by intoleration, an intolerable evil to all, though claiming to have the light of liberty, however freed from that of the pure conscience, show populations whose majority is uneducated.

And what country that nurtures as a social blessing any peculiar faith, but is cursed by the proscription of bigotry and affected piety?

Where intoleration by the laws dares not show its odious head, a proscriptive unpopularity stalks by favor of church dogmas in regard to peculiar faith, that holds the supreme rights of mind and mind's God in abeyance! Such a state needs correction, not argument, that yields to omnipotent facts.

Are not peculiar faith and its church aristocracy an ostracism of the world, that cannot subscribe to its doctrines?

No individual, if honest, can deny principles, that govern peculiar faiths.

A conservative revolution for the better must come; deferred it may be, but cannot be prevented in the progress of mind.

Patriots and statesmen, good and true, of both sexes, are invoked for this holy enterprise, in which the good of the world, of society in general, is at stake.

For general peace, never otherwise affected; for reason, that is legitimate, the virtues of mind, that needs it; true religion of God the Creator, that commands it; arouse, citizens of the world, and lay aside your lethargy.

Paganism, idolatry, superstition, and man-worship, more or less over every land, have to be supplanted by rational religion, introduced by the purest precepts of mind cultivated.

The true faith that asks for the freest discussion of her own sacred rights, to appreciate her correct principles, should be established for success and conscience.

None other can succeed, if we take analogy, the test of experience, for the balance.

The time is now, for there are millions asserting to no dogma of tradition of peculiar faith, not submitted to reason, in every country where the best prevails.

With the minds of freemen they are candid to hold aloof, satisfied in their conscientiousness that they have a better state than the adoption of any notion that they cannot faithfully support, or reasonably and justly recognise.

If reason do not supersede peculiar tradition, the light is in darkness forever with too many already, ignorant to appreciate, or corrupt to amend.

What legend tradition, then, under the sanctity of age, may not be adopted, if the test of reason be excluded?

Ask the uninitiated if they believe in these traditions? Some will affirm to a partial, others to a peculiar faith in such.

Do they faithfully practice their precepts as believers?

The position of the last contradicts their faith at once. What is such faith worth! Ask them for the reasons of their peculiar faith? Can such peculiar faith give mind's honest reasons?

The first disclose the true character of the work, as a mixture of legends, fables, connected, of course, to a part that is probable.

If all fiction had been used, the whole object of the designers had been defeated, as none could have believed it.

But there can be no peculiar faith short of superstition, consequently there can be none short of false faith.

All that come not under the banner of rational religion are necessarily the adherents of superstition and peculiar faith.

They can know now whether others do know their whole position. Many have been sincerely deceived.

The present state of the world is one of vast consideration, vast responsibility resting it seems with none more than with each individual, self-independent of all advisers except enlightened conscience, but the effects of that responsibility fearfully telling on man and his habitation, the world.

Then, a system of rational faith is needed, that candid man can in the clearest conscience acquiesce in, and do full and strict justice to. He needs only read the documents of creation, by the light of reason, which is aided by truth.

Fundamental errors have been overlooked too long, creating the whole family of evils, warring upon the best interests of mankind, where a correct faith would engender perpetual sunshine and peace.

It is not to be expected that the doctors should lay aside their doctrines; not at all, however erroneous.

Their vital interest, profession, living, pride of consistency, all are at stake.

Some are consistent and sincere, if their minds be partially informed and capable; while others are more or less constantly identified in these errors.

Where is the limit ?

The bigoted generation must pass off the stage of action.

Gross as those errors, still that generation will embrace them by inextricable custom and habit.

Many a battle for conservative religious revolution has been already fought, but the duty and light have not been embraced.

Mind must see its way clear by reason and principles, after its affections had been previously enlisted another way, for successful revolution, and above all, with many, the persuasion most be for vital self-interest.

All analysts will see, that choose, that it does not make an honest difference about faith in absurd notions and religion, for the sake of the world's benefit, and man's dignity and peace. Sophists in religion or science assume faith, but philosophers require truth, reason, and facts.

Faiths, as governments, that have warred or do war on man, in body or mind, for lands, money, or church power, are false, and the propagators are fiend-minds.

The pure God of Monotheism permits no such obligations. It is bad enough to have the false opinions of peculiar faith, but horrible to have its tyranny in the world.

What better can we ever expect, constituted as human nature is, and perverted as it can be, than such tyranny, when the opinions of faith or credulity mature into actions ? The only correction is in mind's precaution : the fault is in mind's vassal and abject submission, from blind faith, after the chains are rusted and the spell broken.

At the bidding of peculiar faith, how convenient is it to reject reason, when it emphatically condemns the whole, and yet all are bound to use it in all things of mind and principle, for universal safety.

Shortsightedness adopts reason, when profitable, in part. Wisdom forever clings to it, as universally necessary. When is it ever to be rejected in this life, in anything ? What creed is not self-impeached forever, unless its reason rest on the platform of immortal principles ?

All creeds condemn each other, where principle is needed ; then we need travel no farther than to upset the whole foundation, of which all such constitute a part.

The military chieftains, who assert faith of any kind on their brute force, are unworthy of the countenance of good and true men.

All civilians that assert peculiar faith of any kind by sophistry, are degraded and debased to the dust. These misdeeds are a lasting injury to the world, most difficult to be rectified, and the sooner abandoned the better. The world has to be guarded against all such ministers of peculiar faith, as those of peculiar power, military chieftains and all. The world or they to perdition must go, by the great law of self-preservation.

All professions of civil chieftains who affect to be religionists, spiritual or any other, but adopting any but the true God of the universe, are condemned already by their own basis.

But who pursues doctrines that terminate in false positions, absurdities, and crimes, with satisfaction, much less safety. Rational beings have immortal souls, that must not be debauched by false faith or doctrines.

Grapple to man and his notions, destitute of principles, and all such will come to the dust, principal and followers. Co-equal are all peculiar faiths, and they contend with each other on the veriest trifles.

What is all such faith worth, but to deceive and humbug the people, and promote impostors over their rights? The practice cannot be superior to the faith.

All peculiar faiths are counterfeit, full of deceit and mockery, with the elements of their own destruction.

Away with the gods of such faiths, and all their priest-machinery, but give us forever the God of the universe, with his universal attributes.

Thanks, at the same time, to all honest and truthful men, no matter who they are, that aid and direct properly mind to its correct duty.

Alienated from all improper influences, such are to be respected, whoever and wherever they may be.

False faith cannot corrupt them, nor despoil them of God's innate gifts, their only property at birth, and of which no absolutism, no priest pretences ever dispossessed them, in life or death.

They have been found in the battle-field of American liberty, advocates eloquent, and brave defenders of freedom.

Adorned by her light of mind, they have sought to diffuse her amplest blessings among the races of man.

Many absurdities of peculiar faith have been noticed already, but this is proof conclusive enough to stop, were it not necessary to elucidate the subject in various lights, to suit the minds of the world.

This peculiar faith, but another name for false faith, puts itself down effectually, by its own irremediable antagonism. More than six hundred kinds of dissensions have already prevailed under one branch of messiahship, with no prospects of its limits or universal reconciliation, as it is diffused instead of contracted.

Coercion by proscription and bloody massacres, has been attempted in vain.

False faith engenders false doctrines, and false positions lead to false modes of reconciliation of particulars, that never can be effected except on the platform of principles, that peculiar faith, no matter how imposing, has not got.

What a commentary for religion, that the God of religion cannot approve !

The fundamental error rests not personally with many professors, who, for aught that the world knows, are as good individually as the best, and as liberal minded, but the whole issue turns, without exception, in contravening God's proper and exclusive attributes, functions and principles.

Rectify all this preliminary man's blunder, gross and bloody, and then the system is bound to be right in all essentials, and then if there be difficulty, it will be by misrepresentation.

Worst of all we have society cut up into clans, with bad feelings and pent-up ill will, the banding of cliques of peculiar faith, contracting the world's interests and benefits to their narrow circles.

Mind has been too confined to narrow, small circles, to the limits of puerile creeds, instead of taking the whole globe for its theatre, the whole universe for its circumference, to do its whole duty and mission.

Upwards and onwards its progress in time must be, to properly reach eternity and mature happiness.

Yes, all the subdivisions of peculiar faith, and all its grand divisions, can and must yield to a universal faith.

But the priests, preachers, prophets, and messiahs, all its peculiar machinery for peculiar advantages, must be merged in the universal interest of that universal faith. The crescent and the cross, the Brahmin and the pagan, the Jew and mormon, the bhudhists and those of Confucius, can be in one moment converted into the only true faith, that must prevail forever, when all others and their founders are trampled in the dust, as vile, to be forgotten, and remembered no more.

They all can be reconciled to each other, if the intelligent people will decide, for what the whole world is bound indispensably to do, and let mind act that considers no creed venerable by time without truth, as Christianity is in the same category with mormonism, while the whole world, at the very name of the Eternal, forms a band of universal brotherhood, in the pure standard of indissoluble union, love, and the best fraternal feelings.

This sublime position, universal brotherhood. practicable above Utopian schemes, looks to God to seal it with his almighty principles of conservation.

The ignorant man is a presumptuous libeler, while the liberal mind of science only realizes the only practicable humility before an appreciated God of nature.

Universal brotherhood! What a millenium, the only one that can come! brought about by no local messiahs, who can never rise above locality or time, but by an Omnipresence, that commands time and space, and stamps its indelible character on mind worthy of it.

Let all the good and the wise adopt the necessary measures to speed and welcome its glorious triumph, and guidance to all nations of the five great portions of the globe, with all their appurtenant islands, adding also the blessings of constitutional government.

All are now contending about trifles of no moment or value, catching eternally at the shadows of peculiar faith, that disorganizes and demoralizes the world, but leaving the substance and universal blessings of rational faith. Let them not unite the cynic of the manger, too, to exclude a better state of things, and unable to do justice to a world-wide subject, let them, so far from impeding, aid the mightiest epoch of time, and the advent of the rightful and supreme only Lord of all.

The gorgeous splendors of man's towering temples of various peculiar faiths over continents, built with the wealth of many millions, have to decay and moulder in the dust.

Time will ere long point the world to the wrecks and fragments, and the lowliness of those suppliant for restoration by force, instead of what true principles inculcate by peace and the happiest aspirations.

Little can we expect a ready submission of men to rational principles in practice, when they affect to assert the correctness of their adopted professions in peculiar faith, dependent on a reckless credence in what is virtually non-entity.

No doubtful heresies nor spurious orthodoxies can avail, in any peculiar faith that is necessarily false.

There are various kinds of peculiar faith professions all over the world, but all are destitute of the one foundation, and cannot be true to God nor man, hence none such are rightly established yet among nations, who owe it to themselves and each individual, not only to seek the true, but secure it as soon as possible, and exclude all the false thereby.

Are we told not to investigate this subject? As well might we be told by the robber, not to investigate the rights to our property which he affects to claim. No freeman can be satisfied with such false pretences. Slaves of mind and simpletons, cannot even be passive any longer, after a manly feeling is excited.

The whole families of all peculiar faith, forever contend with one another in the most odious rivalry and degrading opposition, to rise on each others' ruins, thereby disproving forever their disinterestedness.

Even the mother of one tribe and a numerous family, has been quarrelling and fighting with her daughters for centuries, previously fighting for centuries unsuccessfully with those of a different master and faith, representative, as she assumed to be, of the principles of peace! Had she an element in her composition, of any such character? All this has been disgusting and nauseating, to the true advocates of proper principles. But what could they do? The human mind has been fettered in science and faith, by usurpers who assumed to monopolize the whole to themselves.

Have not false faiths caused more blood to flow than all other causes in the world?

And the conflicts of the daughters with each other, a very large and noisy family, by-the-by, are no less endless and unpleasant to the feelings of a brotherhood, much less of an amicable sisterhood.

And will all these lessons of awful experience be lost upon a free and intelligent people, whose glory and honor are in their own hands as far as their interest directs? Will such a people take up the miserable fragments, instead of seeking their own glorious and sumptuous repast, the most salutary viands by the true host?

Shall the mighty teachers of the world in true government, not finish the munificent crown of glory by dispensing also a true system of rational religion? Better never had we any pretensions to this momentous subject, as then the evil results would cease from cessation of false faiths. The practice of the necessary demands of civil society, would be essentially a vast constituent of religion. But creation of a supreme innate faculty, requires a fuller policy in the advance of civilization, as a necessary and indispensable constituent of the whole existence.

Eternal wisdom has decreed a full and exclusive adoration, and eternal power must be reverenced by mind, whose humility advances with appreciation of the Almighty.

Every mind has religion from the smallest element of light, to the brightest rays of effulgence.

No dogma of peculiar faith can satisfy such mind. Priests and monks, preachers and mountebanks may pretend to such, but the intelligent world will expose them as degraded false lights, unworthy of mind. But peculiar faith has grown with infancy, that was taught to consider it anything in life or death, and mind is too often precluded from its free investigation by the bigotry of social dynasty.

This most oppressive case must be met as the greatest difficulty. It is the slavery of infant mind, and exclusion of the habituated mind of man from due appreciation of the foundation of the faith.

Revolution, to stop half-way, is treason, and not cause the true estimation of names and position.

It must be bold and spirited to the full maintenance of mind's rights, to be hailed its worthy champion and avenger.

Constituted as all false faith is, all sectarian creeds are the sport and opposition of each other, of the philosophical facts of creation which they violate, and all the insidious injury accrues to the world for its conceited superstition.

The conceit of man, as bad as it is in common business social matters, is many fold worse than tolerable in his peculiar faith, that has so many peculiar notions and whims to uphold it, which above all, he is responsible to reason for.

The more untenable that peculiar position, the more sophistry and absolutism are needed to enforce it. This should not be on a sphere that must recognise man's mind supreme, to recognise through its cultivation and amendment, the immortal mind, the soul of creation between the creature and his Creator, the first rightly using, the last, generously bestowing the deed of gift.

All peculiar faith betrays the ignorance and darkness of past ages, the puny works of men.

In all such, an immortal soul will never be satisfied, as leading to contradictions ever absurd, teachings most gross, results ever dangerous, and consequences ultimately ruinous.

All creeds that pay higher reverence for masters than principles, run into man-worship, and are a species of idolatry, thus forming what has affected mind in all past ages, corrupting all sources, and poisoning all religious enjoyments.

Peculiar faith, however it clashes in its thousand vagaries over the wide world that it burns with its destructive torch of disunion, has unity in its evils, and among them is classed as one of the chief, fanaticism.

When mind runs riot in its wildest recklessness, it degenerates into fanaticism, truly a bloody tyrant, whose reign leaves a bloody progress, and its deeds of foul evil recorded in the agonies of society.

Millions of many nations have been corrupted at this poisoned fountain, to deal vindictive tortures on others, or its curses on themselves and posterity.

This fury has libeled reason at every step, and has debased mind in every age.

She has blasphemed God in hypocrisy, and has usurped man's prerogatives by her unhallowed devices.

She has misled youth by her deceitful sophistry, to their ruin, and revelled in all the seductions that overwhelmed youthful modesty and merit.

Cunning and fraud are her attributes, for when wisdom is present, she sneaketh with her siren breath.

Her ends have been selfish, the means deadly and fiendish.

She hateth innocence, and exchangeth the poison of vice for its destruction.

She is a companion of ignorance, and associates with her friend and relation, error, and doeth the bidding of superstition.

She buildeth bonfires for evil, the incendiary of mind's peace.

She deceitfully promiseth, but kills by the performance.

Her history is known by her injury ; her reward by anguish and crime. She knoweth not the circumference of brotherhood, but is well known to prevent it.

In the honesty and simplicity of their innocent nature, good citizens have not dreamed of the evils of deceit, that have been perpetrated more or less in every age.

Man can hardly realize what he is subject to in this life.

The game played on his credulity, called faith, is that of absolutism, either in the small or large circle.

All that he has possibly to counteract, then, is the best cultivated mind and the right use of it, that scan motives and traditions, and severs the chaff from the essence-grain of mind. For his life and honor, his present and future happiness, he must not part with it the least ; if he do, he is so much weakened.

Let not those of peculiar faith flatter themselves that they will do much more ; their days are numbered in enlightened mind's tribunal.

Much of the world may resort to their churches from fashion, convenience, motive, and a host of other peculiar reasons, the prime cause of all, but the true faith in one God.

All the rational part of mankind sees too plainly that the other various believers throughout the world conflict with each other's creeds, faiths, bibles, and persuasions, most reasonably, and only from reason, that can be the only chief and decisive cause for this difference. A rational position can only unite all. God has mocked all such in the face of reason and mind.

If the rational religionist could see no possible relief, better should he leave each such persuasion to think its crystal a diamond ; but as he sees but one genuine diamond, and all else he knows certainly are crystals ; it is impossible to mistake the false jewels compared with the genuine, and wrong to be silent under the momentous circumstances of the whole world.

The question is not that each is silently progressing in humble faith, and performing its vows of devotion in peace and general benefit to all mankind ; very far from it, indeed.

Observe the power of the state that is dangerously and insidiously united with most of such persuasions, to crush or deceive the best and purest freedom of mind.

The mind of history recoils at the sight of the iniquity.

See the past power of the clergy, one of whose professed corner stones was humility ; yet, when their absolutism was to obtain mastery, kings were their servants, people their abject menials, who secretly and fearfully submitted to their sway, glad of the honor of permission to crawl or kiss themselves into the august presence of mortals as degraded as themselves, the one in wishing their feet to be kissed, the other doing it. Did any but the most contemptible idolatry and superstition ever have a foothold in this? Such men gave away, under false pretences, temporal as spiritual continents, and submitted the fate of their population to unmitigated cruelties for their false faith, ruling the so called civilized world with relentless tyranny, doing their peculiar gods service in their dispensations.

The petty despotism of confession of faith, arousing the marvel of the vulgar multitude by petty miracles of tunics, liquefying blood, blood flowing from pictures of messiahs, of building sacred fires, of whipping the people about by priests, may serve the petty tools of superstition for their season.

But let the present age atone for all such past blindness, that would be wilful if now adopted with its present lights.

The candid belief in the one Almighty unmistakable, can only reconcile the innumerable conflicts of peculiar faith-parties, and that at once. What a step in refined enlightened civilization! Such would heal all fundamental world-errors, and give the only elements of perpetual union of one universal brotherhood.

It is thus necessary and obligatory, apart from the paramount duty to the Creator, as false faith engenders false views and practices of superstition, that diffuses the worst morals and results to the whole world.

Citizens of the world, be not of any multitude that does not avow God's innate principles, that can defend society.

The proper social principles, will ever carry the world through in safety, and their right avowal, if rightly adopted and practiced, will redound to the greatest good of all. But proselytes to peculiar faith will affirm that the greatest question with the world is, what shall we do for faith evangelical?

Evangelical refers to angels, and there are none such on earth, if the God of nature, a perfect Creator, uses as he has instituted, conservative principles.

Any faith that is true, must preserve its supreme unity, and we must refer to truthful testimony therefor, to render it respectable and worthy of mind. We must ask to be introduced to reason, the favorite of God, who looks upon it equal to truth passing through mind. Mortals can never decide faith any other way. But never was there a nation yet, but that had some system of religion? Never did any have such system, when analyzed. They all have had a system of superstition, a peculiar faith, that is antagonistic to God and his attributes, his conservative principles, all producing sectarianism, and cutting out one of the noblest results, universal brotherhood, for which defect secret societies are instituted.

The present state of sectarian faith is, that it is cut up into many little sects and factions, many of them continuing to divide and subdivide with rancorous hate and trifling controversies, perpetuating elements of disunion among the social circles, with no confidence in each other, and impressing the whole community with less or least, for themselves.

How long shall mind, the God-endowed, be subject to the injurious fallacies of peculiar faith?

For two centuries, the sword of the Christian was turned so unsuccessfully against the professors of the Mahomedan faith, that believed in the cimeter, that the faith and action of the last triumphed. And the ordeal of battles decided justice to the successful faith against the Christian. And yet after all, neither was orthodox. Cimeters or swords could never solve this universe problem. The beauty of it was that the power of mind arrested or diminished at last the fanaticism of both, running into piracy, butchery and conquest, and stopped the ungodly and irreligious wars. Still both are infallible, if you hear them tell it, and yet both tried on principle, are utterly condemned.

When will stupid peculiar faith ever learn wisdom? She has no reason, no propriety of thought.

She affects in her mad ambition and lust, the empire of the world, and deserts the only true empire, that of mind, that should rightly represent the Creator.

She has tried the sword in vain, to decide world-wide questions that belong to mind. She never will know her incapacity for good.

She has used all the petty tyranny of puny perverted minds, but their base inquisition has not been able to drive man to the confession. Bribery, corruption, all tyranny failed.

This question rests with the world's committee, that will pronounce the facts slowly, but surely.

Already she disavows past crimes, but clings to iniquitous errors of the present day. What have we left to-day, of all peculiar faiths, with all their priestocracy machinery and messiahships, but sects and factions, and fragments that are to be scattered before the luminary of God, mind asserting its rights.

At the present day, the sectaries of the world can make no excuse of not having a better faith.

Those that make such pretence, are anti-God.

Humanity, the true friend of man, scouts at them.

In subjects on religion, we hear too much that is superficial, that does not comprehend the subject.

Feeling or sympathy, custom of forefathers, mere opinions or force of absolutism, except the true principles of mind, cannot decide the question of religion.

It is not a question of faith, but of truth, and to be heard on such testimony as truth forever decides on.

Faith, however peculiar, and peculiarly represented inconsistent with reason, is so with truth, and is surely a falsehood.

What is grace of peculiar faith, but a fallacy?

Grace of peculiar views is defined, favor for sins pardoned. What mortal knows that? What test is there if reason be excluded?

This tale is often told by the thousand and one, who go back to the world in their sins. The whole solution, that which can only be true is, that all minds sin more or less when reaching a state of rational accountability, and that being the only best state that presents the least sins.

This is all the grace that can abound, in the conscience most void of culpable offences, and most abounding in its richest fruits of self-approbation arising from the best consciousness of innocence and good actions.

If sinners entertain notions of grace, it can be only graduated, otherwise from the character of human nature it is self-delusion, if not worse, going into public deception.

What other than this view arises on the analysis of the subject, and what more correct version of it can be adduced?

A mind that is conscious of rectifying itself by the inspirations of mind through God, must feel most satisfied.

That mind may consider in its enthusiasm this the favor, the best state of mind, when conscious of rectitude as old as the pagan Romans so called.

Falling from grace, is founded essentially on the character of mind, that has to fortify itself against all invasions, as it is liable to sinful conflict every moment, in thought, word, and deed, and has to be defended from falling below the level of its own inherent and essential dignity.

Here again is another interminable conflict between churches, some affirming that it is demoralizing to preach the doctrine, while others truly affirm that such doctrine is founded on our nature.

The whole difficulty can be resolved into this position, that mind possessed of the intrinsic elements of religion, is ever dependent on its proper inherent capacity for light and the proper exercise of that light.

Does it not argue weakness in the God of peculiar faith, to have a select few, the elect, and of those in the church, none of the best are presented?

Here is a war, fortunately for the age, only of words, but the feelings are bitter, and reason is in conflict.

We see clearly, now, that the world has been regulated by fanatical pretences among all nations.

All are false to themselves, to withhold their only standard of protection under innumerable errors.

What standard but that of the one Holy Being can regulate mind, and whose lights can shine in every soul, till true teachings expel the darkness.

All things that oppose and affect rational religion, have the elements of disunion and antagonism. Peculiar faithites not only renounce reason, but the God of reason in his purity.

Do not perjury and deceitful action, as hypocrisy, short comings of truth, as well as its abundant violation, and constant sophistry, presented in a state of society cherishing peculiar faith-worship, made the standard of actions and words utterly at variance with reason, necessarily arise?

Now, those in the world not seeking the true and sincere salvation, are liable to all this evil, in or out of the churches.

The good part of mankind are morally exempt, until they persevere knowingly in all such dangerous errors.

With the best of good will and patriotism, as comprehensive as the world, and a philanthrophy as expansive as its duties, they should see the bearing and correction of this important topic.

Can any sectarian faith furnish universal benevolence?

The language that decides the position of the first, decides against that of the last as an impossibility.

Where are the acts, the only proper proof?

The world's history decides conclusively against all sectarian faith, as impracticable and pernicious for the good of all.

Peculiar faith is then not the good faith of the world.

In this matter no assertions on its part, no sophistry can repel these serious facts, as all such are unavailable.

No flippant criticism can supersede the high-toned greatness of soul-speaking wisdom.

Some may feel the highest impulse of enthusiasm, and seek spiritualization, sanctity, and holiness, but how can any sectarian faith rightly impart any such?

Deeds of gifts from spurious proprietors may cause momentary excitements, but they all are worth nothing at all. They must refer directly to the purest object, God, who is in the purest position.

What then remains to be done in the world-waste for man's good and mind's ease, as the thousand-and-one dogmas and creeds about all kinds of peculiar faith, all fall short of satisfying the very wants of the mind, that it begs, implores, and entreats to meet?

Know the God of the Universe and his functions, principles and attributes, through mind, that will rectify itself through his inspirations of wisdom.

Terror is presented the mind, as it is threatened with eternal damnation if it adopt any rational faith no matter how superior, but that faith, that mind, if rational, does not inherently in good faith adopt.

The sectarian, that is the professed follower of peculiar faith without disguise, readily inquires, on whom do you rely? There can be but one correct answer to all such error forever.

On the one wise and all-powerful Author of the universe and all its conservative principles, that from the creation embraced all subjects of preservation, especially man in all his different positions of being from time to eternity, from life to death, all the time of mind's existence.

But all other reliances are impositions on their face, with counterfeit the rankest and titles most defective, for in place of being universal from the creation in time and place, both are limited very long after creation, embracing in reality but a small portion of each, and that on the capital of religion counterfeited.

Out of these evils of antagonism of false faiths, creating civil and general wars that blot so many pages of the world's history, has arisen much universal good by the countervailing influence of all these governing principles.

What supposed evil is there, that God of supreme intelligence and might, does not cause to redound to universal good.

A general superintending Providence is essential and important to the universe, but the especial acts of mind are most essential and important to decide the world's good. What nation or individual ever yet perpetrated crime with impunity? It is the same as the violation of principles, that from their very nature vindicate their Creator.

Impunity stimulates the criminal, that rouses up avengers even on principles.

Felons consider themselves most intelligent by enacting crimes with temporary impunity, when too late they too often find that the path of wisdom was better than the path of cunning, as honesty is the path of safety.

Throughout, all sectarian systems are defective, antagonistic to each other, and all opposed to the universal harmony of creative elements, at war forever with the just relation of things.

No wonder the principles of philosophy and reason were opposed, when science showed all spurious faith revealed by bibles of tradition.

Whoever heard a sermon, but was necessarily made up of sophistry in part, in any faith that did not look to God exclusively and his pure, unsullied attributes?

How much daily sophistry is employed in the world, to uphold corrupt systems?

All such vital questions must be left to reason's mind.

In peculiar faith is centred all the species of idolatry of man and hero-worship, what every such faith this day pays with disgusting misconception of mind's dignity and independence.

The miserable result is, that if cannibalism does devour, or brutal superstition does slay the victim directly on the altar at once, that man-worship of all these grades in antagonism only prolongs the slaughter more indirectly, and slays when let loose in mad fury and ambition with bloody fanaticism, her millions in wars, miscalled holy, inquisitions, crush of minds and tyranny over freedom of conscience.

Usurpation of peculiar faith is seen in the world's injury for orthodoxy of power, whereas God alone decides at his tribunal, who is worthy.

False faith, when in power, that it always usurps over reason, which she will not yield to, assumes the spoils of the earth for its possession, directly or indirectly, and returns the poisoned cup to the lips of those whose hands transacted for its temporal promotion. Where is an exception?

What a concentration of iniquity, corruption, and disgusting cruelty, in the papacy, to give away unknown countries of the world, though peopled, if those inhabitants did not possess the Christian faith?

Where did this complication of felonious crime end?

What an amount of perfidy to the nations of the world, to give dispensation for the most licentious tyranny, as far as physical and mental weakness permitted?

Where did the sale of indulgences, perquisites of state powers, licenses for crimes, and iniquity, end?

What must be the pitiful condition of those hacks' minds, with degraded spirit, that have to uphold with party sophistry all this, as religion?

If this be religion, God help the world out of the quagmire.

► What generous spirit does not pity the poor, ignorant wretches, that have to do their part, for their bread?

But is there a menial so pauperized, that would not scorn such, if possessed of the right views?

Where is the spirit of patriotism in the mind of man, that will not scorn to see his country so prostituted?

What can prevent all the secret vices, degraded crimes, assassinations, corruptions of female chastity, perjury, and all such consequences of prostituted moral power, that should forever take precedence over all other, in the right performance of indispensable duty?

The moral power of the world must be kept sacred. Perish at once, and forever, all peculiar faiths before it.

The insincerity of belief must characterize the public mind. How can it escape such iniquitous contamination?

All false faiths being insufficient to arouse the world's unity, or to command its proper respect, it is the duty of patriotism and philanthropy, an enlarged duty, that man owes his fellow-citizens of the globe, to stop or arrest the malign influence, if nothing else was elicited thereby, of the spirit of insincerity, that mars, blots and blurs the purity and excellence of mind, ever kept thereby in the most degrading feudal vandalism and vassalage, indecorous for reason.

We should get rid of a reckless faith, inconsistent with reason, and productive of the worst consequences, from the fell spirit of insincerity of belief.

Freemen owe to themselves this justice, to see that an amendment is effected in proper time, way, and spirit. Benevolence, enlarged and liberal, that honors home and all its virtues, in all the pleasures of duty, and the fruition of affectionate regard for household benefits, and then radiates from home the happy sum of its wise operations to the circumference of this world, compels the full allowance for mortal's frailties and weakness, and therefore premises their best correction.

Bigotry is a horrible incident in the character of man, and impeaches, as it is not an attribute of a mind enlightened by true faith, that is rational religion, the character of the faith, and decides its blighting curse on the mind darkened by it, and all the circle affected thereby, to the latest malign influence.

What justice or truth is there, in the circle of bigotry? But the bible faith, that is the supreme idea!

What faith can there be in the whole universe, the Supreme particularly, no matter how peculiar, that is not subject to the proper investigation of reason and truth, with their best aids, analysis and analogy? If any faith could be supreme over these, then that faith is supreme over God, assuredly.

But we must take the Trinity. What is peculiar in that?

Three Beings, but all in one! What language is that?

Three beings distinct in location at times, and all one!

Is language understood right? Is the foulest sophistry to dethrone rational mind?

All questions are addressed to mind and its understanding, and must be answered by the understanding, which is reason. Then no understanding that is honest can affirm to this absurdity or monster, neither on mathematical principles, a part of the conservatism that governs the universe, nor by the language of mind.

Whose mind is so peculiarly constituted as to receive this rightly ?

We are in the thorny and stormy paths of life, a direct way is to surmount its various difficulties, and to do this, mind with its completest understanding and wisdom is the agent, and reason the pilot that directs.

If we forsake these, our position is below the slave's—our mind vassal.

The followers of peculiar faiths are mistrusted in foreign lands, while if they were true, they had been universal. The followers of Judaism are mistrusted in most countries where prevail the Christian or Mahomedan faiths, though all these have referred to Judaism originating theirs. As there is a conflict of feeling and interest not only among all those, but among their seceders, and the world full of peculiar faiths, that assail and restrict each other in their privileges, all are necessarily hostile more or less. This is not religion, but the curse of peculiar faith. Man is in this, not God.

The sooner they all get out of these conflicting faiths, they will become united in one brotherhood and not before. Such advocates have to learn what religion is. They will have to abjure and unlearn all that they profess peculiarly, and the sooner done the better for the parties and the whole world.

There is no need to have had the Nestors sadly butchered, nor should there be any enmity however laid up for future miserable ambition in Saladin's country. All will forget the deplorable evils of the past of peculiar faiths, in the blessings of monotheism.

Times have their peculiar vices, and in ancient feudal times, men did look up to civil and military chieftains almost universally, and dearly did they. Noble mind was betrayed. It was the iron law of custom from apparent not inherent weakness, not of the helpless orphan who is now protected by the law of mind, but of the stalwart giant man that knew not his own mighty concealed strength, because he knew not the gift of his mind.

The partially civilized state of the world had him bound, when might oppressed right.

Self-government had advanced, mind has improved its powers, but has been misled in the quicksands of peculiar faith, that is deplorably and obstinately behind the advance of science, arts, civilization and commercial advantages of the world. Let intellectual truth mirror all that is visible for mind's correction.

While mind is advancing, the mystic notions and follies of peculiar faith are counting her beads and preserving her relics, contending for rites, forms and ceremonies, excrescences of a decayed mass, that belonged to times when millions of warring Christians contended against millions of Mahomedans for centuries, for seeming trifles, a spot of earth not worth a pauper's notice till his death ; all to gratify the church's ambition, avance, papal hierarchy, craftship ostensibly, as well for personal fame and the world's conquest.

No wonder the hostility and the enduring hate between the Mahomedan and the Christian, the best evidence of the fallacy and ignominy of both faiths.

How can they compare, with that which belonged to mind ? They cannot be maintained in reason.

No wonder the Hindoos hate Mahomedans and Christians. No wonder the hate of the whole world of peculiar faiths. Which of any such would not tyrannize over the world, if not prevented?

What a barrier is mind, the enlightened mind of science and philosophy ! These aid the supreme religious principle, the mighty moral force that truly represents the wishes and purposes of the Almighty.

Do not all count the profits of their professed faith ?

In opening the door to peculiar faith resting on miracles, prophecies, mysteries and enigmas, the world is subject in process of time to an everlasting flood of similar faiths and traditions, that are only limited by the state of mind, whose ignorance and corruption alone originated them.

Various have been the attempts in all systems modified by the circumstances of mind's light for ever.

Mind alone guards its own holy citadel from superstition, but it has to be most rational to do that most successfully.

Mind is constituted for religion that can be counterfeited on the ignobly ignorant, only in part, however, as deeds tell.

It has been its history to suffer thus from its incapacity to distinguish the genuine from the spurious.

The adherents of true faith are modest and tolerant for truth, but those advocating the spurious are brazen and impudent tyrants of the world.

Under this banner, befouled with blood, all pretences are advanced, all clamorous for professions, that should be in perpetual abeyance to actions the best prayers.

The five grand divisions of the world are beset with them.

Among the latest, the Mormons recently arose, assuming to do so, on the miracles of the panacea faith, of visions, of miraculous gifts, and prophecies.

But what man can possibly believe them, unless incited by delusion of worldly feelings?

Certainly, neither the wise nor the honest, can be placed in this category.

Thousands. would not all of them, without hesitation, establish wonderful or miraculous belief about the death and resurrection of their prophets, by direct testimony, equal to any others' about miracles? Would they not forswear and perjure themselves for their peculiar faith? But the materials of mind are needed.

In process of time in future ages, who can affirm that this peculiar faith will not supersede others, especially if the sword be successfully wielded by the faithful followers of some fanatical warrior? Is not this the world's history of all such faith! Peculiar faith has no reason or truth.

Has peculiar faith any peculiar limits to her ambition, short of the complete vassalage of mind throughout the world?

How truly dangerous as demoralizing. to help keep up the bibles of peculiar faith. Are not you, citizen, somewhat culpable, for a part of the sum of all the false faiths of the world, and their horrid deleterious consequences. The veto of proper, sound, honest sense is invoked.

The infatuated will not listen to the voice of mind, but may fall by conflict with other peculiar faiths.

The faith of the creed may be carried out to the broadest extent of absolute faith, and tyrannize socially and religiously over the world.

Peculiar faith has no limit to its ambition.

Its days are limited by the force of science and cultivated mind. Where do you hear of faith, the loudest?

In the haunts of ignorance, and the wilds of error. where people have no schoolhouses, and cannot direct you the plain way of the country, much less even the analysis of mind.

The days of miracles are past, because the days of deplorable ignorance are past, one of the many proofs of the improvement of the age, that is the only reason to meet the views of contracted minds, while liberal minds feel as confident as in their existence, that no miracles ever existed, as miracles prove imbecility of ignorant minds, that wonder or admire in every sense whatever but the right one, at the ordinary natural phenomena of the God of nature.

Liberal minds truly see that the truly great deeds, the nearest to miracles, are the right creation, sublimely organized, and its regulated subsequent actions to endure for ever.

The only true sublime standards for admiration, belong to the Great Supreme, and their functions invoke and challenge, as they should, the highest adoration of the whole world in his unity.

Solve all the secrets of nature, then mysteries and miracles cease in the true acceptation of reason.

Where can we find any tyranny more awful than the tortures of body to operate on mind and conscience, in behalf of faith? What is that faith worth, but the worst engine of cruelty and fanaticism?

How careful then should all good citizens be in arousing up the fierce spirit of sectarian creeds, never to be sincerely and patriotically realized in a free country.

No true rational religion, but dark fanatical superstition, ever could arouse so many wars between sects of different leaders.

No one adopting the correct tenets of God-religion can fall out; it is impossible, as unity is union and agreement. God is never inconsistent. Man libels God, but is self-impeached if he dare the libel of such assertion.

What has peculiar faith ever yet done among the Indians of the world? The millions of Asia? The whole world bewails its sight, by blood and treasure untold and countless, sacrificed to the gods of its idolatry.

Such faith in our own America must have been shamed by the faith of the red men of the forest, who believe in the Great Spirit. Before the pretences of peculiar faith are urged, let the rights of rational mind be audited.

Not able to sustain themselves on the only foundation that the Creator ever gave to honest minds—reason—the advocates of the first turn to weak mind's folly and the slave's creed, and tell us in this century about a stupid and senseless non-entity of faith, that does not admit of analysis! Whenever the test and ordeal of reason are skulked by any minds, it is proof most positive that the position is not honest, or the intellect is miserably stupid.

Just like the charlatan doctor, who stupidly claims all medical practice for his ignorant and impostor tribe, and leaves unfilled a circle of most urgent and necessitous
claims, and that too by the only rightful claimants, the sufferers in the first access of
disease—the beneficiaries by their own scientific-directed exertion in points, that this
pitiful herd never can see or correct.

Now, the majority of mankind is not in the pale of any made faith, while all minds
bow down from innate principles, instilled for the wisest and noblest of purposes of creation, and necessarily to be filled.

All peculiar faiths are generally in the minority of the world.

One of the differences between peculiar and rational true faith is, that the first requires the world to look after her interest, whilst the other refers to the interest of God
all the time.

Does peculiar faith depend on intrinsic virtues, or has she not for her life-time ever
sought all the protection of brute force?

Never say, if you admit a polytheism, more than one God, that your age is better
than the Greeks, for you have four gods, a trinity and an evil genius—they only had
more. Who of you are better off? As to the improvements of the age, they belong
to mind, which your faith discards.

It is wise that the whole world should understand its position, and mature its views
—define by language what it affects to say.

But why not conform to the world's ways, and not encounter the antagonism of these
peculiar faiths, but let them all ferment and work their own purification?

It is the supreme duty of good citizens to act well their part, as the highest specimen of rational religion, and counteract all false faith as base superstition and man-
worship.

Can intelligent freemen cower to man-worship, and thus participate in the degraded
blasphemy?

A due reverence of Deity cannot permit us, without sinister motives or influence,
to suppose that his perfect attributes needed a vicegerent in this or any part of his universe; his omniscience must have foreseen and his omnipotence anticipated. All such
is the vagary of peculiar faith.

There has been shed the blood of millions from false faith, that aroused the most
damnable passions of human nature, and caused ambition and avarice to tyrannize over
the human mind the worst of feudal despotism, exciting the worst penalties of the feelings here, and inflicting most poignant anticipations of a horrid future, at least in falling
short of blissful rewards.

What picture is more horrid than this, philosopher?

No wonder the dealer in peculiar faith should avoid philosophy to decide on its merits; truth courts the light. What can wipe away these stains of peculiar faith, existent
for so many ages? Nothing but its entire extinction. Of what sect or creed is your
faith? The orthodox. Now we hear you. What is the orthodox? The right
thinking.

If language mean any thing, orthodox must be the rational. What does the rational
invoke to suppress all these difficulties but mind and reason, most comprehensively and
philosophically? Orthodox can only be rational, and that impeaches peculiar faith forever.

If our belief be as good as God can make it, who can make it any better? What
does that teach but a right use of a rightly educated mind? That is infallible orthodoxy.

The position of peculiar antagonism is from peculiar faith. Rational orthodoxy is
legitimate, and treats antagonism with contempt.

Peculiar faith looks to messiahships, to which perverted tradition pretends. Can this
be right?

She has four gods or more, and many demi-gods. As to polytheism, her creed is an
abomination before the Great First Cause. Instead of her hideous peculiar favors,
superior wisdom is shown by God in giving light, more or less, to all, in the beauty of
simplicity and the strength of safety, if mind act as mind should before God.

Now where, mortal, would have been thy blessings had God been a peculiar god,
giving peculiar favors? All greatness and goodness would have been in abeyance to
contingency. The god of polytheism never could have been a creator; that is certain.

Trammel neither mind with peculiar notions nor God with peculiar libels. Peculiarity bespeaks the rankest absurdity, the most impotent imbecility.

Do ye of peculiar faith believe that all others of their peculiar faith will be saved,
after worshipping God Almighty to the best of their lights of that faith?

Your answer, affirmative or negative, condemns you all.

If you say that they cannot be saved on account of that faith, then you are involved
in that category, for no peculiar faith can be orthodox, infallible, honest, or true.

What saves you? Because you are Christian, Mahomedan, Brahmin, Mormon, Bhuddist, or Pagan?
Which of these, or any analogous peculiar faith, is orthodox? Apply the right and only truthful test, not peculiar faith opinion. Honest rational truth condemns all for ever.
Do you, or any of these, represent rational religion? If not, then none are orthodox, none correct.
Time was when God took the will for the deed, but this cannot now apply to those knowing better.
Peculiar faith winds itself up every way in innumerable times by its constant sophistry, untruth, absurdities, contradictions without end, its predestinations without justice, &c., in its bible of tradition.
Are not its professors of well raised character ashamed of all such?
With what impudent assurance and reckless effrontery can they knowingly face their God, who provided for all generations of mind prior to all messiahships.
If God did it as he has always surely done, and will forever, by what untruth will they persist in undoing his work, that condemns forever all arbitrary dynasties of messiahs, invented in books?
Is the untruth any more sacred in a book than in the mouth of men? Is it any more consequential because these legend-books add the crime of curses on mind for refusing them as false, and seeking the solemn truth elsewhere?
All this needs reformation; but no important reformation will do short of conservative revolution.
The god of peculiar faith is not the God of reason; that is clear.
Reason does not know any other than rational religion. She cannot know peculiar faith before God and man, as there can be no such religious faith.
All such is the faith of superstition.
The light of the age requires rational religion, as the only right and just religion of the universe.
If there be any other faith, it is unsound, and has unsound basis.
Whatever is deficient is erroneous. All peculiar faith is deficient, and must therefore be ruled out.
All sectarian creeds rest on the genius of some mortal, are carried out by the vassalage of his followers, who submit to his pretensions, that however connected to custom, must be finally all absorbed by general principles.
What myriads of immortal souls have not sought a faith worthy of them and their Immortal Creator for the best of a life-time, without attaining anything at all of all peculiar faiths known to them, or only the veriest trash, unworthy of a serious thought?
They have been wofully deceived as far as the preacher's statements went, as they could never attain anything worthy of God.
Such in the sincerest consciousness of the soul's dignity have had to conclude that God alone is the giver of every good, the author of all that is good, that elicits good out of apparent evil, by his principles that vindicate themselves, or right evil consequences.
But some may affect to think, that the system of peculiar creed had best be carried out in this wicked world, to keep the people rightly to the point, else there would be no living for most, therefore the idea of a hell, with all its potent machinery, must be held up in especial reserve. This is the worst of bad doctrine.
Man is a rational being and must believe in rational principles, therefore must have rational religion and nothing less, consequently must be truthful, honest, liberal, just, and ever seek to exercise the best construction of sound, honest, proper sense.
The rational being must certainly reflect on his obligation, though the preachers or expounders of gospel doctrines acknowledge this, yet when their peculiar faith is touched, they fly off this only position that justifies all professions of faith.
Now this clearly proves, that most men do not know their own minds about religion.
On this principle all the advocates, priests, and preachers, are entirely wound up and silenced.
All people of all peculiar faith do not know what they do believe in, and if they run out their doctrines they will find them and their bibles clash in their peculiarities from which particular sects arise, thus no peculiar faith can stand before God and his works, the highest evidence of things not seen, and the only material substance of things hoped for.
Despite of all peculiar systems of faith, false positions and gods, the world advances in improvement, thanks to the superintendence of a Providence universal, not peculiar.
All this is recognised by rational religion, that feels bound for the greatest amount of

good on principles that must be advanced and taught, to save the majority of the world from gross errors and their penalties.

Where would be the conservative state of mind of mankind in general, if it had universally to depend on the belief, the faith of any one tradition? Ruined at once and forever. Be grateful that you have a God of the universe to adore, not several peculiar gods to contemn.

Peculiar faith is nowhere, religion is everywhere, and represents truly an Omnipresent God.

How vain is the effort to fix on creeds, that do not comprehend the subject of religion vast as the universe.

There can be no safe platform, on other than rational basis.

Creeds short of full comprehension, result in vain pretences.

The whole matter returns to duty and that, mind teaches as the most useful learning, the best to live and die by.

The small circle of eminent and conscientious preachers can estimate this, as an undeniable principle.

What delusions, terrible indeed, has fancy painted by her creation and fiction of hell, that premises predestination, and excludes responsibility!

Everything has to be reduced to the standard of reason in the universe, else Universalism would give us all kinds of mixed spirits in the holy abode of Deity, in the same company, as if God was not just to the best aspirations of the purest who could not associate rightly with all kinds of characters.

Universalism, when rational, is a part of rational religion, and will graduate penalties as rewards proportionately to individual merits. Purification will prepare all for final abodes of purity.

Wherever peculiar faith stands, sophistry upholds her, and wherever sophistry is studied, she misleads, and prevents all that fly from truth reaching substantial attainments.

Where fancy and ingenuity are studied for cunning, good sense is needed. Individuals, personally, may be respected, how much soever they may be deluded by peculiar faith; but intelligent freemen must condemn palpable errors, of all doctrines.

What wise mind will not perceive the false security under faith, when omnipotent reason is not left free to combat it?

All intelligent minds see that reason is proscribed by the whole clan of priestocracy, who have not the very thing they affect to respect—a liberal soul. Where is the end to all the stupid ignorance of peculiar faith? Among its monomaniacal notions, is the destruction of this world.

If its peculiar God, that made this the principal sphere, and the rest for its lights, was the God of our creation, then it would speedily perish; but the God of the universe made it.

How, then, can this world be destroyed? Libels will not affect its perpetuity. The question will be as wisely put, as to the destruction of the universe, therefore why not ask if the universe will not be destroyed? Can a wise mind believe such nonsense? This position of destruction is allied and identified with other fictions of world-governors, alias world-botchers. It may be put in the same category with hell, purgatory, devils, spirits, ghosts, witches, and other characters, communing with mortals as messenger angels. The sooner we get rid of all this abominable nonsense of mythology, the better.

It is worse than vulgar, it is demoralizing, to maintain all this machinery of superstition. All the worlds of such fictions will of course perish, with all their peculiar faith. Mind is slave enough, by self-delusion of ignorance, to be degraded by all the errors of false faiths, and have parts of the world tortured by fear, exciting by even present-day false prophecies of its destruction.

This is an age of science, and her legitimate functions, as God's noble inspiration of mind should be credited.

This, and many other follies are impiously kept up, to uphold past errors of ignorant writers.

Philosophy would get the better of superstition, if mind would do its duty, and lay aside the pretence of sophistry for the substance of truth. An enlightened philosophy and astronomy would tell us, that the earth could not be wholly covered by water at the same time.

There is a certain level of water at present; where, then, could there be water to deluge the world from the water-level to the extreme height of mountains?

All must see the absurdity of a universal deluge, if they see at all, or can reason at all, on the rotundity of the earth. To suppose it possible, we must take the ignorance of the ancients, who supposed it one vast plane. Of course this proves it a false position, for the rotundity of the globe, with a little variation, is well established. Bigot sophists will pretend that now the destruction of the earth is to be made by water or fire. We have considered the impossibility of the first, as the inherent earthly character cannot permit water to affect a universal deluge.

Water would have to come from some other sphere, but God's beautiful harmony of · order does not permit that sphere to be so accommodating, as that would leave it in a state of injury most essential.

It is a wonder if those old writers ever appreciated God as the author, much less the providence of the universe. They could never have had a right conception of such God. Their god was a little god, of one world, and that the earth; and that earth belittled, as a plane, with the winds at the four corners. This god had heavens above, but no where else, when the bible of tradition was written; of course this peculiar god is the god of a hemisphere of heavens, for the sun moved round the earth to light it!

The God of the universe was thus dwarfed to the god of a hemisphere of heavens, and yet those who do know better, avow this infamous book to be right.

A worse libel never was conceived of God, except to rival him with the god of evil. The mere school-boy of reason, would never have consecrated such a god, while his first thought could not miss the God of the universe under the lights of mind matured in philosophical astronomy.

The water may encroach on land, and land on water, but there can be no universal deluge under the present form of this spherical or spheroidal globe.

But as the ancients thought it flat, the bible-bigots would swear their thoughts were right, because the book says the deluge was universal, by waters on the whole earth. Water might easily, then it was thought, deluge a plane. But the spheroidal figure of the earth disproves then the bible, in the essential nature of Providence, who demonstrates himself the creative and preservative faculty. But after thousands of years of mind-torture about deluges, the fire is now to consume the earth, the botches think. Is this stable earth never to rest from the reckless nonsense of superstition? Must all its pleasures, it hopes and treasures, be all sacrificed to its insatiate appetite? Is that to devour by its jugglery, all that is fair of mind? All that is noble, of God the Creator?

Yet matter cannot be annihilated, nor fly out of the attraction of gravitation, one of mighty conservative principles. Did all the ignorant, stupid priestocracy, ever think of all this, once?

Why then should it be vitiated by the God that created it. Fire has constant sweep in volcanoes, that throw out melted lava, &c., and yet we have no consumption.

Who can say after seeing the action of fire in the earth solidifying and rendering it more compact, after driving off the water or moisture, that the earth can be consumed by fire in connection with its own oxygen? On what principle can the eternal fire of earth find existence without oxygen, the supporter of combustion, or why if existent at earth's creation, has it not already shown its action thus supported?

Shall man in his utter ignorance, add disgraceful error, and continue to libel God for his noblest principles of conservation, the very internal means so dreaded?

Let the ignorant hide their peculiar faith before man, nor dare vulgar libels before God.

Independent of all this, where is the balance equipoise of the earth, in regard to the rest of our solar system, and where are the conservative principles of the universe to be affected, when its equipoise is affected by derangement of solar systems?

But did these petty priests ever know, that a single world was in existence, but this earth?

And if this derangement take place in the physical, what must be the chaos in the moral universe, if its ruler only relax for the idle dreams of whimsical botches?

Who is worthy to uphold the sceptre of his Almighty hand, that commands the organs of light, before whom, darkness cannot dwell?

Monotheism could not exhaust this endless theme.

How unwise is the sectarian feeling of peculiar faith towards all sects not its own, in claiming to be orthodox or infallible, a position perfectly unattainable by it! Sectarianism on this special plea alone, excludes the idea of religion, and destroys all principle. But peculiar systems of faith engender hypocrisy, deceit and perjury, most assuredly, among too many of its votaries.

All its hierarchy and prelacy tend to corruption, by speculation, one of the worst of temptations, and individuals are only exempt therefrom by just inspirations of inherent elements of rational religion, that will display signally its noble spirit, unless too deeply silenced by complete treachery to conscience.

Where there is no chieftainship in peculiar faith speculation, there can be no serfdom for collusion and oppression in any form with state.

Let then mind in its purity extricate itself from vassalage to such things, that may otherwise govern it.

If peculiar faiths cannot respect each other, how can rational religion, which they have usurped respect them?

The Christian, Bhuddist, Mahomedan, Brahmin, Mormon and Pagan faith, is all peculiar, and all in this category.

Their own sects, of the same peculiar faith, hate, and have warred with each other, time after time, to the horror and ruin of the world, and their utter disgrace.

How long will all this superstition involve mankind in its difficulties and troubles, its permanent contests and conflicts?

Fatal wars, for hundreds of years, have prevailed for these faiths.

How many continental wars of the world have been surely aroused on the score of fanaticism and bigotry?

How much of the noblest, general good feeling, has been sacrificed the world over?

We have recently seen hierarchal absolutism affecting conservatism by the sword and bayonet, when popular conservation, governmental and religious, rest on principles, that peacefully vindicate themselves.

Shall force and tyranny overwhelm man's reason for ever on this account, that ought to bring eternal blessings instead of curses?

Better let all the forms of peculiar faith die the death of the felon, than have mankind cursed and crushed in this form.

What a pity it is, that superstition, under so many promising forms, should still affect man, by reason of those interested in upholding it for profits; that all chief actors in the faith-drama have alienated, usurped, and monopolized the proper rights due to the pure Deity alone.

Hierarchy or priestcraftship has existed more or less in all its craftiness and absolutism, in all ages of man known to us, in all the vile forms of superstition, terrible by its effusion of the blood of human victims, or disgusting by the sacrifice of animals, rapacious for spoils, and ferocious for murder.

Her tyranny, that malign passions could arouse, has enslaved and degraded the human mind under the falsest pretences, and the most assuming disguises.

Her impiety all over the world, whether Roman, Greek or Protestant, Christian or Bhuddist, Mahomedan or Brahmin, Judaism, Mormonism or Paganism, that dares assail the immaculate purity and attributes of Deity, and ignorantly or insidiously assumes doctrines to libel his government of the universe, should be indignantly rebuked and silenced before rational religion, that has been so vilely imposed upon.

Vile impostors all, of any peculiar faith, that pretend to this degraded impiety of libeling God.

Those who cannot analyze thoughts, as few of the world know what original thought is, or where it leads, much less what it comprehends, are not to be condemned as the conscience-hardened offenders, in this offensive position of peculiar faith.

But all are to be condemned if they will not trouble themselves to discover and retract the error of their ways. Enough is now before the world for rational mind to appreciate rational religion.

Where peculiar faith dwells, there is little reason, and where there is little rational religion, there is little honesty in the world. The social frame-work of the world needs the best regeneration of rationality.

What surety has the world on this basis from disturbance?

If disturbed by force, neither principle nor anything else, can reinstate its equilibrium. It must be revolutionized for the world to get right.

Peculiar faith leads to inextricable difficulties, duly estimated in the empire of reason.

In the empire of peculiar faith, the idea is that power domineers in its day, and reciprocity of the favor is right.

Infallibility belongs to her every claimant, but to none in fact, as religion cannot be seen for peculiar faith of the Hindoo, Pagan, the Mussulman, the Juggernaut, and all others who dispute the palm on their basis.

We are infallible but you are wrong, is said by nations. So say the Protestants and Romanists to each other.

The only millenium will be the union of all in one faith, through the God of mind. Mind will conduct that affair better than armies, for it is God's decree.

Men will be thus, and never otherwise, united.

Universal faith depends on universal reason, and must be in a Being not mistakable, in whom all feel concerned, and this exalted faith will be for all a precedent.

We should have all nearest right in most matters at once, on that equitable and indispensable basis.

There is always the utmost necessity of strict integrity of honest and truthful religion, that can promote proper compliance with all the relations of life.

This is the base of a sound public opinion that should correct the world, as the best of all tribunals.

But piety is shocked if anything is advanced against peculiar faith! That is all the affectation of hypocrisy. Bigots of peculiar faith obstinately refuse the tuition of reason.

We advance nothing but the true piety and morality of God's rational institutions, for the good not only of our fellow citizens but of mankind. We demand that justice be done the subject, and that you prove all your positions, if you dissent. All must see eventually what deplorable injury all the systems of peculiar faith produce, but for God's light of mind that enlighteneth all the rational part of mankind.

As habit of thought is by education, surely that cannot be right by sectarian faith.

The different sects of faith-superstition contend all of them most passionately about creeds, that they if wise would care less about than for the power to be secured.

What profit can false faiths and messiahs do the world? All the sectarian views of all the creeds can never establish the proper principles of religion—never.

Their disagreement at once shows this the general error.

Any one that is trammeled in absolute rights by customs obsolete by false position, serving and watching the signs of the times, is no man, certainly no American.

Too many are misled by the false pretences of others, their crude opinions, designs and vicious leadings.

Such are some of the serious humbugs of the world. It takes proper independence of mind, to be obtained by a suitable education of science, free and unbiased by errors and unfettered by profits and emoluments to resist them.

How can you reconcile sectarians on their basis, that has no foundation of science and philosophy, the hands of the eternal God?

What wise and good citizen will feel an iota for peculiar faith, when the paramount question of mind's freedom is awaiting solution?

What is peculiar or church faith worth before the august tribunal of mind?

Peculiar faith relies on sophistry, and always comes short of God.

Mind may analyze this position in all its common treasury, and must, if sound, elicit this fact, but the human mind is so sophisticated now by peculiar faith that the truth cannot be got at it readily! and where does such faith throw the responsibility? Before the rightful tribunal of God.

Have its followers ever reached the dignity of faith in a God supreme, that rules the universe?

Have they ever mastered the greatest of wisdom, in the powers of analysis, or senselessly followed others? Peculiar faith cannot possibly be religion, but must be a great humbug where it is not a known treachery. Religion rests on eternal principles of an eternal God, confiding in no mortal or messiah individuality.

Sectarianism is the exponent of peculiar faith; that proves the hate of sects and denies the love that has been advanced as proof of religious feeling.

Be done with this murderous faith, that has such pretences as to the expulsion of the demoniacal possession, and give priestocracy the command over mind in its most delicate relations: that regards their altar as the place or part of the machinery for the mind, as important for conversion.

We object against the propagation and colonization of any doctrines of peculiar faith, of any church apologist of absolutism that spares neither age nor sex and renders partisans pensioners.

When peculiar faith rails at science and philosophy, it is a certainty that it has superseded them by sophistry.

Falsehood or sophistry is the gangrene of all society. What is worse? It is the agent of absolutism in its worst state.

Under cover of sophistry and casuistry, myriads are lost or rendered miserable about trifles of faith, that supersedes all the noblest traits and essence of rational religion.

Peculiar faith, as all church faith is, the counterfeit of rational religion, as messiahs, are the counterfeits of the God of the universe.

How difficult is it to remove the prejudices of bigotry. Descartes removed the canopy of the upper firmament, and disclosed to the vulgar gaze, the universe.

Thus it is that science and philosophy alone can remove bigotry, that keeps company with dotardism.

We have to learn their teaching in the various good schools of the world, and profit by all that is valuable.

All this time there is open or latent marked hostility of sects of peculiar faith, the under current of feeling being most malignant, only kept back by mind.

Can such rest on fundamental principles of right and justice in religion, that has no such mind-mark of sect at all, that knows no sect, no peculiarity in this world? If any faith has sect it proves to be the counterfeit, the spurious mark of religion.

However races differ in color, mind and body, they are all from God, who has no distinction of persons, but as distinguished on principles of honest and truthful deeds of life.

It is the mark that false faith for ever creates, that sect shall be against sect.

All over the world, race, kith and kindred differ about this thing of faith, that cannot be peculiar but universal from God.

They differ in non-essentials, in institutions of worship, of doctrine, whether of the week or the sabbath, because that may cause sectarianism which is the negative of rational religion, therefore a curse and an evil.

If language have its legitimate meaning that all candid minds must give it, then we have an odious system of polytheism in the world, and if the plurality of gods was confined to the invisible world, then all would be less objectionable, but an unholy alliance of man in all the shapes of power that self-interest could create, and self-delusion of the multitude would permit, has fastened its fangs upon the worthiest traits of society, and is perpetrating its odious and insidious poison in every breath.

An odious abstraction of just rights has perpetrated the inception, that misleads mind from giving due credit for its religion to God the governor of the universe.

It is the thing itself, not its name, that offends.

Man for his false systems of peculiar faith, must do rank injustice.

With sectarians God does all—that is of principle. What is wrong is theirs. Yet they acknowledge predestinarians as the most rigid are, that mind must work, and that the messiah works!

What absurd contradictions, to disorganize the foundation pillar, accountability, that God has instituted for the good of all, else he never made free agency. But peculiar faith then is an usurper and pirate, if it dare to usurp truth and honesty. But peculiar faith only asks to make her impression on mind's credulity. It is her function of prostitution; and she uses her capital.

Bigotry is united with peculiar faith; both are degrading.

What is bigotry but the obstinate adherence to peculiar faith and superstition. Rational minds will correct their own errors.

We are compelled, as rational beings, to have the reason of truth, instead of the sophistry of superstitious faith, that stretches conscience beyond all probabilities and reason. What can faith do? What has it ever done worthy of mind, independent of reason and truth, with the human mind?

We ask for manly and suitable proof, that rationality accepts.

Is it not the perquisite of office and profit that stretches faith? Peculiar faith doctrine is the world-iniquity and curse.

What peculiar faith having union of church and state from the time of the old soothsayers, who had to be consulted necessarily if they were to be believed, to the present date, ever benefited the world?

But who can appreciate the curses therefrom arising?

What do we need of peculiar faith for " The high bishop to have a procession, the people falling upon their faces and bowing down to a man?" Blasphemy most intolerable; mind-vassalage most disgraceful.

Can any mind of worth, dignity, and freedom possibly perceive any necessity for all this?

What shall compensate for all this manly sacrifice? Gorgeous shows, paintings, and churches towering in the air; but mind, noble representative of Deity, grovelling in the dust of iniquity and ignorance!

Do all the bribes of such prostitution compensate for the vices and degradation.

The first act of all peculiar faiths, that produce necessarily false systems, is to defraud the Almighty Creator of his attributes, reducing him to a demi-god, or partial, peculiar god, divested of his intrinsic powers for the degraded vicegerentships of man-power, usurped most blasphemously.

The second act, of course, can be nothing less than to cheat mind of its attributes, divest it of its innate and intrinsic powers, deny their legitimate potency, and basely substitute man's pretences, and mock necessary aids, that are detrimental to the whole family of interests, and the whole human family.

What a prostitution of mind's virtues and talents, on trash! What an outrage upon the rights of the Creator and his universe.

He that is hypocrite to God must be hostile to man's good.

The deplorable consequence tells on mind, kept back thousands of years from its true greatness, subject to all the lacerations of miserable misrule, and most wicked policies of tyranny; and made almost to crouch even in the days of its regeneration, and of its improving appreciation.

Never can peculiar faith, that grew out of superstition, arise in minds not constituted therefor: then must not this position and constitution yield to an honest faith? Sectarianism cannot stand; it must fall.

What is the cause if you dissent one iota, that you do not address children, next to infants and savages, about religion?

Because their reason is not matured ripe enough for suitable fruit; the fruit and the attempt would be green indeed. The soil, the mind, must be prepared for the seed. But you treat the matured mind like that of infants, and deny it its freest legitimate exercise.

Say what pretenders, dolts and charlatans can, still the world is governed by reason, graduated to the state of mind's capacity for its reception.

All their present systems of faith are those of peculiar notions, and are like those of usurpers in medicine, insufficient. They claim to think and act for rational mind and religion. What audacious infamy and felony.

They cannot begin to meet the wants of mind of mankind; but their advocates wish to monopolize and raise up antagonistic powers to any principle that seeks to present rational impressions.

What a spirit, that seeks to crush the best value of mind itself, the very matter in question about its light and happiness.

If any previous system had been discovered, commanding all the principles of religion, and their head, short of God, was the embodiment, then the disciples might appropriate the world; but up to the present time all claims to supreme power are an imposition. The question is therefore open alone to God the Creator, and his creatures.

What claims to the discovery of a new religion, are valid? None. What claims to that of a new creation, are worthy of notice? None. What claims are there any way? None but those of an impostor. All such are false.

It must be admitted that some errors may occasionally be made by the fewest, but that is the veriest trifle to the thousand ills irremediable otherwise.

Investigation of Romanism discloses inquisitions of horrid deeds, dark and bloody murders of many of the human family, male and female. For what? Can any at the tribunal of mind, answer for what? Religion that is rational and spiritual, asks for what?

The worship of several countries under that peculiar faith, show most superstitious modes of worship of the saints, and invocation to images, prayers for the dead, celibacies, vows, sacraments, public prayer, the scriptures, written by and for the priestocracy, to command their dupes, the people, the only rule of action by faith, elaborated by the peculiar views of absolutism, myriads of fanatical miracles and such creeds. These are not fit for animals, much less rational mind.

Art, intrigue and accident, supply peculiar faith, that of course, does not depend on truth.

It had been a wonder that peculiar faith had not corrupted the world much worse, but for the existence of a God who rules creation.

Then the existence of the God of nature, prevents the existence of any miracles.

Peculiar faith is governed in its ideas of right and wrong, by the course of the messiah founders, not by the principles of God. Priestocracy edicts, false pretences are to govern the world. Wonderful legislation and government, that! It does not regard the development of mind in all the richness of its faculties, as it arose in the darkness of the past, when topics and ideas were meagre, the people illiterate and ignorant. and mind was vassal. What pretence can such faith claim to mind's light, when it depends to propagate its doctrines on mind's darkness?

Why is there antagonism in peculiar faith; is there in mind?

Antagonism to truth, cannot exist in mind uncorrupted by peculiar faith, as the purpose of deity gives mind that is rational, adhesion, love and fondness for facts and truth. When mind has antagonism to correct views, it is because it has not self-government, nor proper government of principles.

This is easily proved, as principles do not clash, hence sectarianism, Roman, Greek, or Protestant, is radically wrong.

Mere reformation does little, where conservative revolution is needed to exchange the radical basis.

All peculiar faiths are putting themselves down better than others can, that is, God does it.

A man puts himself down, nobody else can, if he be right. Principles universal, cannot be put down, but peculiar doctrines and pretences can.

The very chief temples of peculiar faith easily change hands by conquest, the spirit of which has been aroused thereby, and the conquered are subject to the mortification of their faith-mutations, while those of true faith are already the same everywhere, not only insuring a brotherhood universal in rational religion, but the safest general position to prevent all the ill consequences of wars provoked. Rational religon does not institute any wars.

Party spirit of peculiar faith, only sees one side of the question, and that its own.

Rational religion is the silent messenger of God, unlike peculiar faith, that characterizes mind's perversion. Have religion, then, not peculiar faith, and there can be no necessity for repudiation, and this age will hear no more of peculiar faith doctrines, but will rise from a subordinate to a God-like position, that of the noblest triumph of mind. Thence arises the means of an exalted censorship of society, that will command all the just powers of the mind by the press, &c., what no bible of tradition can impart, an enlightened conscience.

The ignorance and stupidity of peculiar faith, cause hate in the world, that would be united, but for its quagmires that prevent the transition state to rational religion.

The worst argument for the adoption of peculiar faith rests on the example of particular men, instead of universal principles, that recognise reason as paramount and omnipotent. Principles are of God; peculiar faith is of men, and refers to their pretended opinions, as authority for the world! If reason be not always most safely appealed to, in the name of God what else can be honestly?

Romanists and protestants can decide rightly for each other's peculiar position, but they cannot be reconciled on the great principles of religious freedom, as they have not the permanent principles of rational religion.

The God of the universe can meet any draft on his funds, for that reason our reverence for him obliges us to discard the vagaries of peculiar faith.

Mind, that looks to its improvement and duty, can respect no custom, no more than cobwebs that are to be expelled; the moment they become nuisances, they are to be abated.

God's principles cannot possibly clash at all, but the creeds of sectarians forever clash, and their doctrines forever involve difficulties of logic and reason; hence, they seek to avoid reason, and recur to sophistry, affecting faith for credulity.

One sect says that falling from grace is the preservation of its church, while another sect says that this doctrine is demoralizing to churches.

The doctrine of falling from grace can only be purely met by rational religion, to put every man on his merits for his life-time, liable to sin in degree more or less, by temptation; and exempt as his nature is purified by a correct education and action in the correct appreciation of conservative principles, that promote the best possible condition of conscience. This is the only safe and pure doctrine, about falling from grace or having grace. All living beings are liable to sin, in degree.

Shall absolutism still decide the question of peculiar faith despotism over most of the world? Shall the organ of thought, the mind, be held in abeyance to man's notions? Shall religion be dependent on peculiar faith? Shall that be the absolutism of custom, or state power? Shall the existence of Christians, Mahomedans, Jews, pagans, mormons, or Juggernauts, be due to the contingency of citizenship, and the peculiar influences bearing thereon?

Reason is the only proper avenue, through the empire of mind, else men might be pirates and murderers, from the customs of barbarian faith.

Open the door for superstition and its varied peculiar faith, and all their curses can pour on us. There is no limit, as men's notions and licentiousness dictate.

You cannot stop the mormons nor pagans, who only have peculiar faith as you have, by brute force, but by rational measures, that exclude your as well as all theirs. What a sublime power is that of moral force, that bespeaks rational religion and its God. Then be done with peculiar faith, if you are good and rational citizens, and pay no court to any but the legitimate doctrines of monotheism, that demonstrates the sublimest power of the universe. Be wise!

Disrespect for God is engendered by any system of peculiar faith, that affects to impart any of his attributes to any other being. Rational religion claims potency adequate, of omnipotence, the Almighty.

God being self-existent, all others are created, and necessarily inadequate to the government of creation.

Peculiar faith superseding religion, is the most disastrous thing to public morals, as it deranges society.

It is the basest fraud to deprive the world of its inherent rights in religion, by all the false pretences of peculiar faith, that will die the death of the felon of superstition.

Base is any character, to think of the usurpation, much less to execute it.

To whom can the distressed friend apply, in his difficulties of mind about religion?

To the base intriguer, who cannot analyze this momentous subject?

No assassins are to strip off physical rights and inherent equality.

We cannot, as rational beings, permit such serious humbugs as peculiar faiths be imposed on the people, in disgraceful obloquy of mind.

The curses of peculiar faith go into all social and national circles, as we now see that with all the blessed light of civilization that emanates from rational religion, the master spirit over party spirits, how one nation mistreats other nations, seeking to force on them a government analogous to the one it had itself got rid of, such has been the conduct of France to Rome. Peculiar faith is one of the most dangerous enemies to mankind, as it is one of the most reckless bigots of tyranny.

Mind enlightened, not empirically, but by the means that nature demands and reason sanctions, will seek to carry out the noble and upward tendency of free institutions, a mighty conservative power of the world.

There are innumerable systems of superstition and peculiar faith, but only one rational religion.

The way to that is by mind and reason, truth, honesty, fidelity and integrity, not through priestocracy.

The Lord deliver us from sectarians and bigots, who only look to superstition for their motto, and a miserable doctrine for faith, for which they commit themselves in all their iniquities.

All such must end, as man's deeds, as thousands of their predecessors. Man, be wise in time.

How many innumerable and inextricable contradictions do the sects of peculiar faith produce?

It is absolutely important that we should have a system of rational religion, that gave full and ample confidence in its universal powers and virtues.

Where is any such after all the boasts and pretences of peculiar faith, that begets peculiar difficulties?

Have we, the people, any proper system of rational and vital religion that imparts on spontaneous innate faculties, inherent principles, that inspire in the breast of all mankind, having rational minds, true confidence? None at all, for we have only systems of superstition.

The principles of religion, not the doctrines of peculiar faith, are for ever important to live and die by.

But then it is claimed that the christian or some peculiar faith, has the pure and genuine possession of grace. What proper proof can be given the world, that has the best right to ask it? None. It is only mere assertion, without any honorable proof. Why the humbug?

Positively all peculiar faith has sectarianism, and that certainly excludes the main idea of grace, universal love for God, and his people.

Do the advocates love God alone, who is the sole Deity?

Do they love that people, with whom they cannot commune by their articles of faith?

The only position then of grace is rational, not peculiar.

Do not libel mind and reason, and then you will not libel God.

All, but the true faith, have many superstitions and contradictions in faith and creeds.

It is the duty of all enlightened free minds to seek that which is entirely free from clashing, as God's principles cannot possibly clash, if they do, assuredly the work is man's.

To correct the wrong, we must know the right.

Action on principles all the time will effect all right. Action on peculiar doctrines will affect right but effect wrong.

The world absolutely requires what God decreed it, religion, as peculiar faith deranges and ruins all its relations.

The code of mind's ethics will best protect the world. How base the world can be about its peculiar faith.

How puerile, imbecile, yet furious, fanatic superstions, yet call peculiar faith religion!

The virtue of the world is too often forced; its hypocrisy disgusts human nature, its corruption degrades it.

The world is too clearly governed by all the present codes of interest rather than of principles.

Peculiar faith is a non-entity in religion.

All faiths in spirits and ghosts, demons and exorcisms, peculiar endowments of grace, are unreasonable and unworthy rational minds.

There can be no peculiar exclusive form of religion in this world, nor any doctrine peculiar or mystified, beyond God's eternal and universal principles. Any others are absurd, the belief blasphemes God, and condemns itself as the work of priests.

There can be no peculiar god-head, no spirit or holy ghost, that unites any vicegerent to God, and man to the vicegerent.

All such faith is absurd, and betrays the assertors as impugning the rights of mind for degraded purposes.

Any denial of reasonable views without a proper refutation is dishonesty, and can only be the act of a perverted, weak, and ignoble mind.

Any faith that circumscribes God's actions to any one nation and its pretences, making all a peculiar nation, is utterly absurd, and negatives God's attributes of universal omnipresence to a peculiar little god of the world, made by priests' brains if not by their hands.

Any mind professing peculiar faith, must war with other advocates of different faiths and war for the false sovereignty of the world, and therefore shows improper spirit destitute of love to God, who is universal in his attributes throughout the universe.

What can the antagonism of the world full of peculiar faiths avail one soul, knowing their false position ?

It takes all the elements of religion, a God-gift to the soul, to save it from the effects of peculiar faith that deceiveth the world, and renders nugatory much that is good.

But what is the condition of the minds that are much perverted, to have the serious difficulties of peculiar faith to contend with ? How few can escape ? Why, then, should the best of the world use the counterfeit, when they are already in the enjoyment of the genuine at once at the mint ?

Any one mortal that dies meriting condign punishment, or penalty for misdeeds, presents a state or condition deplorable, hence a change should be made at once and of progressive improvement.

This can only be done by consent of mind, to be enlightened by truth, and matured by wisdom.

Accursed, then, must be he who misleads, trammels, and perverts the mind of man, whose immortal soul is invaluable and inestimable.

The absurdity of faith made of blind belief, that is only taught as custom taught the teacher, is most culpable, sinful, and degrading.

Any hope that rests in it is imbecile and impotent.

All such must be demoralizing, and in the best proof, an appeal can be made most faithfully as to past and present fruits.

What can the future promise ?

History shows us murders and butcheries innumerable to correct heresy, as it was called, by burning, forced conversions by inquisition-generals.

Who shall decide this greatest question ?

None but the Almighty Creator.

Who represents him ? Mind enlightened.

Peculiar faith is made the means of hiding a multitude of pretences, designs, and sins.

The world is wicked enough without all these !

Peculiar faith gives us the mixed plurality of gods.

Nations seek true government, but must have their rights trespassed upon by the usurpations of peculiar faith, worth nothing to the world.

Who wonders now at the thousand deformities of society, when primary wholesale injuries abide in goverment that unites church and state ?

Butcheries of the people must be perpetrated to establish the temporal power of the popes, by the worst of political hypocrites.

The crisis of the world's history makes men, who as good and true will unite to secure it from the fangs of superstition and its effects !

They know that high-mindedness, honor above all vulgar prejudices, will elevate the world to its pinnacle.

Peculiar faith generates in all ages, immense vices and crimes, consequently it is the rankest absurdity, when estimated as religion in any age.

Has any form of peculiar faith, that sets out with false pretences to God affecting to be religion, done otherwise than as a virtuous institution, then it was an ignoble superstition, claiming to be what it was not, and being what it should not have been !

In countries even claiming to be free, faith, unless conformable to the existent national peculiar faith, denationalizes the recusant parties, who are ever excluded from national councils, after their election, by being unable to take the oaths required.

In England, the Jews, though elected, could not become legislators for this reason. There is no end to peculiar faith heresies while its several bibles of tradition as of Judaism, Christianity, Bhuddism, Latter Day Saintism or Mormonism, Mahometanism, Brahminism and Paganism give them utterance. Is it necessary to ask which is right, when all rational minds can see them all wrong?

And yet what rights have the citizens, but under the recognised national peculiar faith of those countries so silly and corrupt as to adopt them? If the evil be intolerable, even in England, what must it not be elsewhere?

What country rights have they but by adoption of their abominable creed?

Put down, for God's sake and mind's rights, these the rankest heresies that war on God's creation, and creation's rights. Even proscription of opinion in this Union, the mere reflection of the dying monster, precludes delicate liberty.

Let not this stupid invasion of mind's freedom any longer exist. Enjoy all the genuine exaltation of purest rationality; that is the purest incorruptible liberty.

The one peculiar faith of the slavish government is arrayed against all the rest, while religion holds up all, modern and ancient, polytheism or trinity, as unworthy the countenance of honest minds.

Do you wish to get rid of the errors of Romanism, you must revolutionize Protestantism.

Relieve the world, in God's name, and by his principles! Let us go with those that go the farthest in religion, no matter whether we rouse absolutism, or the women and children, so we be right. Rational women and children wish to be right; let them now learn it.

The world would have been much further advanced in science, philanthropy and the real greatness of humanity, if there had never been any pretensions to superstition and miscalled religion.

For whom was the institution of peculiar faith from the first ages of the world to the present time? For the priestocracy, priests and preachers, kings and their minions. The good of the many was not consulted, who were made subordinates to the peculiar faith order. Despotism, not religion, was the purpose of the most ungodly ambition.

See their iniquitous enslavements of mind, by all the vices of absolutism. See their iniquitous wars for conquests of soul and body, lands and money, powers and principalities, throughout the world.

The world of peculiar faith is ambitious of rising, right or wrong, on the ruin of others.

This is not a religious but an ambitious spirit. We must be guarded by principles, the only conservative basis. against the impudent pretensions that affect the world.

Peculiar faith can never exalt to the Supreme Creator, as all such has emanated from the savage, vassal, ignorant and barbarian state.

Savages revere the sun, but as far as the Creator exceeds the sun in majesty and brilliancy, so does religion excel peculiar faith, that can be nowhere before the God of the universe.

It is not altogether the fault of new doctrinists of peculiar faith, new sects, as the Mormons, as the ignorance and corruption, the bigotry and superstition of the masses of the people, who ought to have investigated this comprehensive subject, and to have seen that peculiar faith doctrine is not religion, but is the very reverse, and the peculiar curse of mankind. Past ages have been disgraced enough by the wicked heresies of all peculiar faiths.

The pretenders have been enough illiterate, profligate and licentious epicures, loose and vicious, to curse the present also.

Let a Numa institute his god's temples, altars, sacrifices, and rites of worship, declaring idolatry under the care of their priests; let the East Indian build his pagod temples for his worship, with his vedas for his bible, and the tyrannical Brahmins for priests, but let world-freemen, that are intelligent, revere truly and mindfully the only being, the God of nature, who could create, organize and ·regulate matter by sublime principles, that render his attributes above all, as the great sole First Cause of the existence of things.

And the beauty and strength of this position that triumphs above all others, are, that all God's creation tends to good if appropriately appreciated by mind, whose actions must be correspondent.

But in what horrid position is the world now? Who will rescue it from the snares of peculiar faith?

Various and opposite faiths are mixed up in the same government, and thus the whole world is wofully cut up thereby. It is so in China, Hindostan, Asia, Europe. Where is it not? Its waves after waves, with fiery martial prowess, enslave the fairest portions of the world.

The Brahmins ruled India, then the Bhuddists, producing civil and horrid wars, then the Mahometans govern, and all in turn, submit to the Christians, while in Arabia, &c., the Mahometans rule over Christians and Jews, all producing their peculiar hostility and injuries.

The Pagans of Babylon conquered the Jews, and transplanted them in the east. Did not the Jews learn from the Egyptians and their conquerors, the Babylonians, their peculiar faith?

Other conquerors with diverse faiths, people with them, several cities of Asia and Egypt, and caused them to be diffused widely over the world, where they are not cut off by persecutions of enemies of peculiar faith. In this, the Jews were treated better by the outside barbarians, as they murdered their enemies, and spared neither sex, nor age, nor property!

Who had the most orthodox civilization? All the ancients, Jew and Gentile, possessed only peculiar faith.

Martyrdom, severe as it was itself, was much of a speculation, for proposed benefits.

Now toleration, the lovely daughter of civilization of mind, that rebukes all the boasts of Christianity, and all peculiar faith affecting to be the only light of the world, as withholding the noblest blessings of mind, is its universal protection.

Instead of toleration, christianity has given in turn, persecution, inquisition and proscription, peculiar faith for religion.

Toleration is a defence against a world's persecution, that arises against all peculiar faith, its necessary concomitant.

What protection better to conscience, Jew, can be offered you, than the adoption of rational religion?

You have tried thousands of years, your own peculiar faith, and have been the cause of many new ones, no better diffused over the face of the globe.

Your predecessors laid iniquitous foundations, and you have sacrificed deeply on the altar of superstition, and most deeply have you atoned therefor.

Arouse, ye descendants of Joseph, and assert the dignity of character that belongs to mankind, united in one universal brotherhood.

You can never attain peace and happiness on this earth by your faith, that can never reach the dignity of religion.

You can never assert a union with mankind, from whom you have been estranged by the follies and crimes of past ages, but by the eternal principles of the God of the universe, who ruled your peculiar gods.

Consider, remnants, fragments of a nation, so much persecuted for so little profit, after all, your duty and happiness.

No vows of such a faith that is peculiar, will be estimated by the Almighty, for religion.

You may see the errors of other peculiar faiths, but by your education so peculiar, you fail to see your own.

However you esteem yours, its peculiarity will never render you safe with your peculiar god.

The integrity of your mind before all blood offerings of victims, can only be acceptable to the God of the universe.

While all sacrifices are superstition and nonsense, from the blood of animals to that of pretended messiahs and Christs, mind alone atones as mind ought.

It is in your power to interdict your civil and religious death and oppressions.

You have sacrificed long enough to the false peculiar faith of your fathers, who were ignorant and fanatic. Forsake their barbarism in the lights and blessings of rational religion.

You are now diffused among most nations, and nearly in all lands.

This you have chosen, that lies between the two mightiest oceans, commanding all continents and their wealthiest commerce. Aid in rendering an example of the most brilliant light to all the nations of the world.

No one of peculiar faith can expect to triumph in this mighty country.

What military chieftain will be fool-hardy enough to try his ambition, when a nobler field of glory awaits mind in its richest rewards?

By the side of this land the ancient republics stand half civilized, as they had not representative constitutional governments, the first principles of freedom.

Appreciate, then, to enjoy your best boons of national happiness, and lay aside the exploded pretences of peculiar faith, that ruined your forefathers.

Where peculiar faith ends rational religion begins, and where the persecutions of the first stop, the blessings of the last commence, covering the whole earth with happiness.

When all other persuasions are done, rational religion flourishes, and mind reflects the attributes of its Creator.

The persecutions instituted by those advocating peculiar faith and doctrines, have immolated hundreds of millions of victims over the world.

This was the degradation of base self-interest, and proves conclusively that there is but one true faith, that is rational.

If one peculiar faith perished, another triumphed.

This spirit among all corrupt classes of man has immolated for all kinds of power upon the base altars.

There have been horrible persecutions of christians by those of the same name; that proves conclusively that christianity is not religion.

How many did the reformation of Luther cause to be anathematized and excommunicated, to be butchered!

Much of Europe suffered in the attempt to overthrow the reformed church, by civil and international wars.

To this we owe the infamous massacre of St. Bartholomew. For this, popes decreed that a jubilee should be published throughout the whole christian world, " to return thanks to God for extirpation of the enemies of truth and church in France." " The whole city of Rome was illuminated with bonfires."

Under fanaticism, all the atrocious and revolting indignities can be perpetrated upon human nature, as the rape of the modest virgins and matrons, the murder of all ages and both sexes, even of infants and sucking children. Even an unborn child burnt for heresy, the exhuming and burning of the bones of reformers buried for nearly half a century, as of Wickliffe, not to mention the confiscation of property to millions in amount.

Who can meddle with peculiar faith with impunity? Her history is horrible to contemplate.

She has to invoke the power of absolutism to aid in the world's tragedy; the power of kings and queens to do the base office of fanaticism, to become the dirty tools of destruction, by burning people denounced as heretics by assassins.

The rights of conscience are lost sight of, and both persecutors and persecuted, the regulators and moderators, the executives of peculiar faith, become mutual victimizers, and butcher the world between them.

Both sides persecuted, and will persecute forever, if you give them power and impunity.

What were not butchered were exiled, banished, or forced from unceasing persecution to expatriate themselves to various parts of the world, and America in particular.

Again we repeat the question, how many hundreds of millions have been massacred and butchered, to the fanaticism of peculiar faith. The most atrocious tyrant, the bloodiest butcher is peculiar faith.

One sect has been accused, long ago, of destroying sixty-five millions of people! Yet they are called Christians!

Well can we say, that without truth, honesty, and humanity, none have religion by profession.

The religion of civilization, to be what God requires, excludes all these actions, as no part of her creed.

Have not most of the world's wars been perpetrated for peculiar faith?

Her errors and tyranny put to shame and confusion.' Who can uphold them? The world detests this felon, its deadliest enemy.

To renounce her vices is to renounce her bloody flag.

None are safe under it: pirate of the world!

We believe that false philosophy, with false faith, should be guarded against, by the revelations of rational mind and reason. All else is dangerous sectarianism.

Allowance must be made for education, that perverts all the advocates of peculiar faith, retards the world's improvement, enslaving mind and imposing on its credulity.

All the jealousies, ambitions, and warfare, between the different sects, prove all sectarianism to be destitute of religion.

Fanaticism overlooks morals, religion, all patriotism, in the horrid curses of her own peculiar faith.

No violence is too severe, no sophistry too base for her purposes. Hers is the bloody flag, that crimsons the world.

Blindness of faith is the one dogma, with all kinds.

All the prominent leaders of peculiar faith have suffered a miserable or felon's death, for their impiety and blasphemy, expiating by their own blood their own iniquity, of basest character.

Nor is this all : would that it were.

One of the conclusive arguments against all errors, are the disunion and warfare among the sectarians. Their views and interpretations being after the manner of men, from the imperfect organic base of their principal, directly war on each other, with a perfect hatred and hostile ferocity.

Some of them must have a blind faith; whilst many adopt a very convenient faith; whilst none have the true faith, pure and uncorrupted.

Then it becomes all honorable patriots to resist with manly energy all the errors, crimes, and injuries of superstition, and repel all her malign influence. It emphatically belongs, as a paramount duty to the people, who are to resist all such absurd evils and immoral misdemeanors, to save us from any secret, or all associations, whose clanships defile the rational society of the world.

The hundreds of divisions of peculiar faith can never unite on messiahs, much less on doctrines, when they have such peculiar views, that subdivide all the time into peculiarity.

Will the moderns be never done with the exploded notions of the ancients, about the science and philosophy of peculiar faith, while they reject their science and philosophy, when abstracted ?

All such institutions are erroneous, having a false position and platform.

They have not the elements nor principles of union, hostile and aggressive as sectarianism, gory in blood, is.

How much less can it unite its antagonistics, Mahometanism to Christianity, Mormonism to Judaism ?

All are peculiar, and all must necessarily be antagonistic.

This peculiarity has destroyed all, and must destroy all, forever.

It is too selfish, and cannot comprehend the interests of the whole world, embracing those of the mortal masters for the God Creator.

Any faith short of the last cannot stand, for it is false and must be defective.

The people are the beneficiaries. Who shall thwart them ? Priest and preachers ? Who are they, but those acting for themselves ? The whole world-people absolutely require a rational solution, to their world-problem.

If probably one of the hundreds of sectarian divisions of all the systems of peculiar faith be nearly right in form of doctrine but most wofully short in sight of practice, where is the balance who are directly antagonistic to this one ? Where is the peace of the world involved, when religion has no antagonism, no war ? Which one is that, of all sectarian creeds and doctrines ?

Must minds act by direct interest, according to the present teaching of sectarianism. They may be crushed by want of success.

Many act by blind impulse, hope, interest, misleading, want of correct opinion of themselves or others, false ambition.

There can be billions of peculiar faith, and every one necessarily must have bad faith, antagonistical to all others, and all to reason, the act of rational mind. Shall the peace of the whole world be at issue, when religion secures it at once ?

Then reason or mind enlightened can be for the wisest system, the only standard, the Creator God with no priestocracy, no worship but a true rational adoration.

That faith that was sophistry in sermons or dictation in power, ought to be silenced by reason.

Then one form of peculiar faith only differs from another, if it be not the true one as monotheism, as grades of superstition.

At this age of the world any one affecting faith independent of reason and the best guides of rational mind, should be scouted as an enemy to God the giver of all such.

It is deplorably lamentable that so much superstition and sophistry to uphold it, still prevail among the supposed best circles of the world.

Centuries hence if reason do not assert her empire, thousands of forms of such faith may prevail for their season, superseding each other by base intrigues or bloody wars. They must all diverge from religion. The handle to the peculiar faith, shows the impostor.

For thousands of years, this game has been played upon the unsuspecting honest people, under various forms of expiation adopted, as by the blood of animals or by blood and water baptism, then came the blood of the so called messiahs, and preceded by the blood of millions of victims of the dear people who listened to the fatal words of peculiar faith.

20

So abominable is peculiar faith before the light of truth, so odious is its perversion of God's rights, that its followers all expiate more or less for the folly, delusion and blasphemy.

Its god is an improvable being who is wiser in time as man, more so since the creation!

Is this possible when the God of the universe is unchangeable, and has omniscience? What a libel on Deity!

Who was the weakest of mankind, the priestocracy that invented and propagated all such stuff, or the receivers? The knowing receivers, are as bad. Will the world overlook this position, is it blood of beasts and men, or mind that adores God, the God of the universe? Is it blood or mind, that is to be appreciated.

The code of peculiar faith presents antagonism of sects, all professing Christ, even in the same church: of governments, as absolutism against Republicanism. Who can wonder at this, when such governments embrace church power and union!

BRAHMINISM, &c.

WAS there ever a greater curse on the land of Hindostan than the Brahmin faith, degrading man into four castes, and unmanning by its deepest curses on him. To what but this faith that arrested the march of mind to its sublimest conceptions and aspirations, do they owe the present subjugation of their mighty country, that shames from its mighty national fortresses, the imbecility of its one hundred and forty odd millions, one-eighth of the whole world, to the intelligence and bravery of a few thousands of Europeans? As long as they nurture this faith, so long will they be imbecile and at the submission of men of mind.

THE HINDOOS.

No wonder their corrupt empires fall, as they only have the fragments of society cut up and ruined by peculiar faith.

They have been overrun by Mahometans and Christians, and have had civil wars for the peculiar faith of the Brahmins and Bhuddists. What nation could stand all these peculiar curses, backed by martial piracy?

In the administration of justice in India, "the value of the bribe determines the cause," excepting when the case is so manifestly proved, as to brand the failure of redress with glaring infamy. The first is peculiar faith-justice, and rational mind makes it.

"Of the host of Hindoo Divinities, Brahma, Vishnu and Siva, are the most exalted.

The Hindoos have distributed the creation and government of the universe among these three, styling Brahma the Creator, Vishnu the Preserver, and Siva the destroyer." This position bespeaks the want of analysis of the profound subject in their minds.

What claim has the old and new testament to originality? Is it not indebted to heathen mythology?

Is it not all mythology itself of a peculiar kind?

We clearly have here, God, Christ, and the devil.

The system of the Hindoos gives a universal deluge.

The mythology of the world has absurdly undertaken too much, mixing opinion with fiction for reason and facts, causing absurd, peculiar faiths and ceremonies, to usurp the place of religious principles.

The whole world has to be now revolutionized on the loftiest conservative principles of rational mind.

The pure morals of society must be preserved by suitable institutions from the bible of rational mind. All other bibles are not only unsafe, but most dangerous.

Have we any creed or action in pure faith, that has accomplished the legitimate demands of religion?

The Brahmin assumes to rule all other orders of society, their rights, justice and laws, and becomes a despot of the worst character, for sacred purposes, and degrades society in the most licentious manner.

This Hindoo peculiar faith and tyranny, present a prototype of universal priestocracy, if mind of the world would have submitted to its vassalage. It only needs the power to act.

Woman, you thoughtlessly adopt the bibles of peculiar faith, and they are they that degrade you. Unite with rational mind, to secure to your best rights, the best endorsement of their protection.

In Hindostan, the women are degraded as servile, and the most outrageous position is established by unnatural orders in society, enough to force the conviction that all such superstition and tyranny are incomparably worse than no professed faith, the world over.

Proper laws would be the glory of glories to it.

What can be worse than the government of priests?

The progress of mind has been impeded by them for thousands of years, and has been deprived of its potent rights, and just character, crushed and overwhelmed.

Such a state of things has rendered India, with her one hundred and forty millions, the abject vassal of as many thousands, and she has none to thank for her suicide and parricidal curse and ruin, but the abominable jesuitical priests at the expense of their country.

This curse of all curses, has been upon her.

What can any people be when church is monarch?

It blights any country, the fairest of the globe.

It is even bad at any time, at the very best, when church and state are united, as oppression will prevail, till all corrupted, most certainly fall a prey to the worst passions and despots of the world, enslaved by them.

The advance of the Hindoos, in social improvements, was just enough to enslave them with the most abject submission to the car of superstition and absolutism, possible to be conceived of.

Any priestocracy that rules, is well calculated to ruin any country.

Let us analyze the books of Menu and the vedas.

We now can see that all but the bible of rational mind are false, as the codes of superstition.

All other bibles are mere copyings of each other, of false gods, plurality of gods and demi-gods, man's libel of Deity, who cannot be a peculiar god, to suit peculiar notions of priestocracy.

"The vedas are called the sacred book of the Hindoos, and are believed to be revealed by God, and estimated immortal."

What numbers of systems can arise that mind has to analyze ere the right decision can be duly made.

If we had never heard of any till all were placed before us, we must resort to the best appreciation.

The Hindoos are believed to have had the faith customs of the Egyptians.

They were conquered by the Egyptians, Mahometans, and Christians, in succession, and what but idolatry was the result? Asia, let alone Hindostan, has been overrun by peculiar faiths.

With the Hindoos, Brehm was the great god of all ineffable.

The peculiar faith was that of polytheism.

China may have been originally civilized from Hindostan. Bhuddism, the great heresy of India, prevails very commonly among the Chinese.

The military castes ruled over India.

The priestly or sacred caste governed where intellectual functions were not effectual, as in Egypt.

The eastern Hindoos did not know Jupiter's son, Alexander, or knew him too well as a humbug to recognise him, especially as conqueror.

His army took a panic, although his court flatterers would have the world believe that he was its ancient conqueror.

The Egyptians, who carried their worship to Greece, northern Africa, and perhaps Italy, transferred it also into Hindostan, according to authors.

The Hindoos had the worship of human gods and heroes, and rivers with them were sacred.

History enables us to extract, that "The Egyptian theogony enfolds a very perfect psychology, and the purest science of their day, in a system which began with the identity of God with his work, and ended in personifying every least species of existence."

Zendevesta, the bible of the ancient magicians and modern Perses, teaches that there is a Supreme Being, eternal, self-existent.

The Persians entertained the purest form of heathenism, and abhorred the worship of idols.

With the Hindoos, a whole and extensive class, the Brahmins, is sacred, and an object of worship.

When does a priest ever relax his absolutism over the people? The light of independent mind only stays it.

Civilization does not need priests, but philosophy, science, mind civilized and refined, rational religion.

India, the finest country on the globe, has been a prey to priests, and has thereby been sacrificed to soldiers and priests. It is priests all the time. Citizens of the world, do not help to pollute mind.

There is every kind of peculiar faith in Asia, and what good has it done her? Rather say, what harm has not been perpetrated? The end is not yet.

Man is the same from mind everywhere.

Already has Asia, the most of the world, been victimized by peculiar faith. Let, then, mind seek to arrest its curses.

All its bibles have their prophecies, miracles, and mysteries, mysticism, mythology, romance, fables, and legends.

There has been a constant antagonism of all such faiths, but all their virtue has a very low scale of morals.

The Bhudda faith displaced the old Brahmin faith of India for a season, then the Brahmins, by a new dynasty, persecuted and drove out of Hindostan their Bhuddist antagonists. Would that the people had driven out all, that the world would silence all priestocracy.

The Hindoos afterwards had a dynasty of magician kings, that terminated. It was the state power sought, all the time church and state union.

And this is the history of the whole world, time out of mind. The only rational remedy is rational religion, that ends all antagonism and sectarianism forever.

The Bhudda faith "denies the truth of everything invisible." It is materialism exemplified in idolatry.

The Brahmins have their prophecies.

"Brahma seems to be the supreme reason, and originator, corresponding with the Egyptian Phtha."

"Indra, the brahminical faith, resolves all things unto God."

The Hindoos have fables of gods being married to mortal females. Even their literature is enfeebled by mysticism. Hermits reside also among this people. The history part is taken from Whelpley.

According to the vedas, every sacrifice has a particular and proper value attached to it, and within its proper limits is infallible.

According to the authority of Menu, Brahma is the principal person of the three that emanated from Brehm, the vast ineffable one.

Creation was the work of Brahma, who, the first of created gods, gave origin to the world by conceiving it in his thought.

Has not the cosmogony of Menu been followed by Moses? Menu, the legislator of the Hindoos, is claimed to be among the most ancient of men.

The book of Hermes was predecessor.

In the book of Menu, there are four castes or classes. "The Brahmins are sacred with him, and their very birth is an incarnation of Dherma, the spirit of justice; for that the priest is born to promote justice; and by the right of primogeniture, (being first created,) is the virtual sovereign and possessor of the world." Menu takes especial care to impress the sacredness of custom;—declaring that it is transcendent law, and commanding all twice-born persons (as they revere the divine spirit that is within them) to observe it with the utmost reverence." Menu was of the priestocracy.

The Brahmins at first were beggars. They turned out to be the worst of tyrants, enslaving their own fellow citizens.

The code of Menu blended superstition, and was to uphold the good of the priestly order.

"Among the laws for reading the vedas, each time the preceptor must pronounce silently the mysterious O'M., the initials of the unknown name."

When was it that the priestocracy overlooked mystery?

Repetition of prayers is inculcated on all occasions where any pretext will serve to introduce them.

The repetition of the prayer of prayers is alone sufficient to expiate all sin, and secure immortal bliss. Tho Supreme must be adored silently.

The morals inculcated are fine indeed.

Courtesy to the Brahmins insures celestial beatitude.

The marriage code is excellent, especially for the priests. Marriages must not be contracted within the sixth degree of consanguinity.

Penances are apportioned, and torments are threatened in the world to come.

Every unexpiated offence has its punishment appointed in the future state; and the degree of purgatorial pain is fitted to the enormity of the sin.

The idea of the Hindoo purgatory may be traced to the Egyptian doctrine of transmigration.

All conditions of life are regarded by the vedas as probationary.

The redemption of souls out of purgatory is supposed to be effected by the prayers of their children.

Hence, in the ancient poetry of India, woman is named the giver of heaven; for, by her, the son is born, whose prayers and offerings shall redeem the soul.

Offerings to the manes are inculcated.

Demons and evil spirits are believed in.

We cannot avoid asking here, what effect must all such books have had upon the minds of ignorant, deluded and superstitious people?

Devout Brahmins must keep a sacred fire perpetually burning in their house. The manes are to be revered as gods. It would take a man all the best time of his life to observe all these particulars—and strict attention to such subjects must exclude important knowledge. How ignorant must these people be generally! A Brahmin must not shed the blood of a Brahmin.

Evil, once committed, fails not of its fruit, if not in the father, yet in his children, to the second generation.

The fifth chapter is of diet, purification and women. Many kinds of animals are enumerated as unclean. Every thing is pure which a Brahmin has either praised or sprinkled with water.

Married women, for the hope of paradise, are commanded to honor their husbands.

Devotion, the life of a hermit, the modes of self-torment, are detailed to severe ascetism.

Religious suicide by penance, is commanded, and to die under torment, is a surety for paradise.

Kings must be held sacred, and treated with respect, even in childhood.

The code of Menu, like all others that have emanated from an ascetical or fanatical legislation, aims rather to control and punish the individual, than to protect him in his civil and moral freedom.

To Brahmins, the sovereign must make many and splendid gifts, to secure his happiness in this and in a future world. His council is that of priests. He must be always guided by their advice.

The advancement of the priests is inculcated.

He is commanded to enlarge his empire, and to subdue neighboring nations.

Advocates and attorneys are very numerous in the Hindoo courts, for all ranks of the people are exceedingly litigious.

False swearing is a very common and trivial offence among them, and for a trifling sum, any number of witnesses may be suborned; nor do they esteem forgery a crime, but count it among venial offences.

The usages of law, not equity, are considered.

Immemorial and barbarous custom, is the force of law, with these people the most of all nations.

This trait, the same as with the Egyptians, causes the wonderful duration of their governments. Caste and sect preserve this feature.

False oaths are commanded, to save the life of light offenders.

Menu cautions the king against offending Brahmins, "who, without perishing, could provoke those holy men, by whose ancestors the all-devouring fire was created?" Confession is equivalent to expiation.

The priest's own power which depends on himself, is mightier than that of the king. This power consists in curses and incantations against enemies; the holiest of the vedas contains a great number of these weapons, in the form of prayer.

The penances may be by walking on a tedious pilgrimage, or repeating the whole vedas, &c.

The least insult to a Brahmin, is met with a severe penance.

But no penance is comparable, for power, with the repetition of the vedas.

"A priest who should retain in his memory the whole kig-veda, would be absolved from guilt, though he had slain the inhabitants of the three worlds."

"As a clod of earth cast into a great lake, sinks into it, so is every sinful act submerged in the triple veda."

"The primary tri-lateral syllable o'm, (or a. u. m.,) in which the sense of the three vedas" (i. e. the unity of the Divine Being) is comprised, must be kept secret, like another triple veda.

He knows the veda, who distinctly knows the sense of the word.

A knowledge carefully concealed from the people, for whom it was esteemed fit that they remain idolators, unconscious of the divine essence.

So in Egypt, the knowledge of the one God was hidden from the people, and they remained idolators.

The priest only saw in the sacred idol or animal, a symbol, and not a presence of divinity.

The final absorption of the soul, is believed.

Millenia of torture by fire, are taught.

The opinion of one priest learned in the scripture, is declared to be more powerful than the voice of all the people.

The esoterical doctrine of the Brahmins, may be communicated to those only who are twice born.

The Brahmin must consider the supreme omnipresent intelligence, as the sovereign Lord of all; by whose energy alone all exist."

"All nature must be considered as existing in the divine spirit."

The supreme soul, the most high, eternal spirit, is present; the highest essence, the vast One, shall have the souls of mankind absorbed into himself.

This law recognises one God, but reserved that knowledge for a class, elected from the beginning, to be saints and sages; conniving at idolatry.

The government was absolute, from sovereign to all the local lords. In the administration of justice " the wealth, the consequence, the interest, or the address of the party, become now the only considerations—and, excepting when the case is so manifestly proved as to brand the failure of redress with glaring infamy, the value of the bribe determines the cause."

The trials by ordeal, which distinguished Europe during the dark ages, holds a high rank among the Hindoos."

There are three great powers among the Hindoos. Brahma is the main one.

The pagan priestocracy is equal to the Roman.

Can anything be more Jesuitical? Priestocracy is the same all over the world.

We are forced to exclaim, that better had there been no government with such absolutism and such unholy superstitions.

The Hindoos have the greatest tyranny over their women, or wives. What better could be expected from the slaves of slaves?

The filth of their towns is great.

Are the Hindoos equal to American Indians, who believe in a Great Spirit?

Their lower orders are degraded by their laws and their people.

In Hunt's Merchants' Magazine, May No., 1849, it is said that " No where among men have the laws and ordinances of society been more exclusively referred to divine authority, than by those who instituted the theocracy of Hindostan."

The first legislator of the Hindoos, whose name it is impossible to trace, appears to have represented himself as the re-publisher of the will of God.

He informed his countrymen, that at the beginning of the world the Creator revealed his duties to man in four sacred books, called Vedas; that during the first age, of immense duration, mankind obeyed them, and were happy: " that during the second and third they only partially obeyed, and their happiness was proportionately diminished; that since the commencement of the fourth age, disobedience and misery have totally prevailed, until the Vedas were forgotten and lost; that now, however, he was commissioned to reveal them anew to his countrymen, and to claim their obedience."

Their Vedas speak of the longest lives, compared with which Methuselah's is nothing.

The division into castes, made by the author of the Hindoo laws, may fairly be considered the first and simplest form of the division of labor and employments.

The priest is a character found among the rudest tribes, by whom he is always regarded as of the highest importance. He is the supposed means of propitiation, between the supreme power and the victims of superstition.

The Brahmins or priesthood are generally found to usurp the greatest authority in the lowest state of society.

It is only in rude and ignorant times that men are so overwhelmed with the power of superstition, as to pay unbounded veneration and obedience to those who artfully clothe themselves with the terrors of religion.

The Brahmins, among the Hindoos, have acquired and maintained an authority more exalted, more commanding, and extensive, than the priests have been able to engross among any other portion of mankind.

And this despotism of superstition has told awfully on the people.

As great a distance as there is between the Brahmin and the Divinity, as great a distance is there between the Brahmin and the rest of his species.

The sacred books are exclusively his.

The slightest disrespect to one of this sacred order is the most atrocious of crimes.

"For contumelious language to a Brahmin," says the law of Menu, "a sudra must have an iron style ten fingers long thrust into his mouth; and for offering to give instruction to priests, hot oil must be poured into his mouth and ears."

If a sudra, the fourth and last class, or caste, sits upon the carpet of a Brahmin, in that case the magistrate having thrust a hot iron into, and branded him, shall banish him the kingdom; or else he shall cut off his buttock.

The following precept refers even to the most exalted classes :—

" For striking a Brahmin, even with a blade of grass, or overpowering him in argument, subjected the offender to the obligation of soothing him, by falling prostrate."

Not only is extraordinary respect and pre-eminence paid to the Brahmins, but they are allowed the most striking advantage over all other members of the social body, in almost everything which regards the social state.

Although punishment is remarkably cruel and sanguinary, for the other classes of the Hindoos, neither the life nor even the property of a Brahmin can be brought into danger by the most atrocious offences.

As much the largest portion of existence, among the Hindoos, is engrossed by the performance of an infinite and burdensome ritual, which extends to almost every hour of the day, and every function of nature and society, the Brahmins, who are the sole judges in these complicated and endless duties, are rendered the uncontrollable masters of human life.

Thus elevated in power and privileges, the ceremonial of society is no less remarkably in their favor. They are so much superior to the king, that the meanest Brahmin would consider himself polluted by eating with him."

The Brahmins are a sacred class.

What a blighting influence peculiar faith has had on the oriental authority; her ridiculous fables have been for time's duration, and are only modifications of the same object, the elevating the priestocracy, but degrading the people, country, and world.

They have had in the largest circles their destined result, a malign influence, inducing the most feudal vassalage of their votaries.

For thousands of years the devotees have endured the worst of all servitudes, that of mind-vassalage, the most degrading of all.

Mind, then, has to examine the trinity of the Vedas, the prototype of subsequent bibles, and finding different trinities, will have necessarily to exclude all, as inconsistent with each other, that their advocates desire to displace, and above all inconsistent with God's universal attributes.

The Hindoo trinity, emanating from the ineffable Brahm, was Brahma, the Creator, Vishnu, the preserver, and Siva, the destroyer.

Brahm, the original, was self-existent, a mystery not to be spoken of. This position was no doubt taken, because the impostors could not analyze the subject, and stupidly concealed themselves, like all the priests, under mysteries, when pure philosophy is to be resorted to, with all the candor of truth. Siva was the evil genius.

Vishnu was to have ten avatars or incarnations. He has had nine, and when he comes the last time will be the armed avenger.

In one of these incarnations he appeared as Bhudda, the god of the universe ; and again, in one as Juggernaut, at whose festivals the hostilities about their faiths, between the Brahmins and priests of Bhudda, are suspended, and all castes are amalgamated, or not separated.

Incarnations are quite common, and can be manufactured in priests' legends.

It is a shame that the world should be imposed upon, when the light of God should and can prevent it !

The peculiar faith of the Brahmins is placed, by the admission of Christians, next to theirs, however it has degenerated from its exalted originality.

That faith flourished three thousand years, according to the conjecture of Sir William Jones.

Now, the traditional unwritten part may have commenced thousands of years preceding, and run back into the dark vistas of antiquity.

Abraham is considered by Brande to have been of this faith. Indeed, there was a circle of the earth, including Western Asia, Eastern Europe, and Northern Africa, involved in the communism of priest professions, craft and policy, each peculiar to his own country, but all potent for the priests, who claimed the chief benefits, as an exclusive caste of people, lording it over the people.

Peculiar faith has all the picayune squabbles of the world—very low and degraded. It is not a peculiar, but the universal order of the whole rational world that is concerned in religion, that binds all mankind to each other, and the whole to God.

If faith were peculiar, as the advocates pretend, then God is peculiar—but religion is universal as God; hence peculiar faith is a false dogma, enslaving and deceiving the world on false pretences.

All those thousand and one tales about spiritual actions, are as a tub to the whale, the great people, all idle gossip. Sophistry carried out is perjury. In physics and morals, do you uphold faithfully the exclusive adoration of God? As you do not, rational mind should neither adopt or uphold your doctrines or you. Mind could never have been sunk so low but for priestocracy's movements. No one should foster mere preconceived notions, or a false position to maintain, as he and all such will be prostrated before principles.

There is no slavery like the vassalage of mind to peculiar faith. The acts of peculiar faith are in collusion, that if submitted to rational mind must be totally condemned.

What of all that ancient mass of worship of peculiar faiths remain but the forms and machinery of superstition? And all such are detestable to rational mind. Some peculiar faiths are the most vulgar and obscene. The bible shows it plentifully.

The very members of peculiar faith now proclaimed in the world subversive of each other, present the amplest refutation of the reality of all, and exclude themselves from belief of pure conscience.

They are like pirates of usurpation around the people. Most unquestionably the hopes of reward have excited cliques of usurpers, who would have had to support their false pretences by final perjury.

Who are the witnesses proposed for the peculiar faiths? Dead. What! a god to have dead witnesses? Are they mortal? How could they testify of God's adoption?

The perjury would be complete, if carried through courts of justice. If not, they would be miscalled. If the bible were not upheld by the dynasties of usurpation, it would be kicked out of decent society. When bibles of peculiar faith reign, conservative principles are not abrogated, as they are God's, but are overlooked by an iniquitous clique of pretenders. The suspicion of one bad deed or creed leads to general involvement.

Peculiar faith domination is one of the world's worst slaveries. What is social proscription in America for proper views in monotheism, would be acts of the hottest inquisition, if mind were to succumb and permit it. All peculiar faiths have left the world barbarian and antagonistic, which rational religion must correct, humanize, fraternize and civilize to all practicable refinements of mind, enlightened by the holiest of God's documents. No wonder the world, as China, &c., has declared its parts outside barbarians, when a barbarous inside peculiar faith dictated all such, to the estrangement of mind's noblest blessings, a universal brotherhood. For that reason, all secret societies are hostile to the world's greatest refinement and civilization.

Peculiar faiths endow churches, enrich a bloated priestocracy, and increase peculiar privileges; while religion, endowed with rationality, diffuses the world's blessings, and honors God in the happiness of mankind. What is bible faith is of no more value than the balance, a false pretence from first to last.

All peculiar faiths are antagonistic to each other, as they are to principles; hence they could not uphold toleration, as they are all intolerant bigots, the best even saying or pretending that he who does not believe shall be damned, and it acts accordingly.

Citizens of America should congratulate themselves that they are in a land enlightened by rational mind, to the free and liberal discussions of which from the first the world is indebted.

You need the noblest guarantee of your rights in religion, but you can only get a base surrender of them by peculiar faith. I now consider the mighty question solved amply enough to satisfy the world, that all peculiar faith is a miserable humbug. It is the most execrable pirate of society, the world. Of course, when individual man renounces his conservative principles of God, he is beyond as he is below mind's censure. Was there ever such a prostitute and harlot, such a murderess as peculiar faith, that is any and all things to the world, in its insidious sophistry? She has prostituted all practicable of the mind, and murdered its purest conscience, which she has seduced. She has tortured the world's peace, and has degraded its honor. She has bribed sectarianism with its own gold, and pierced universal brotherhood with her own deadliest weapons. She has mocked all that is of religion but its purity and innocence, and has upset all with the deadliest deception. If peculiar faith were not allied to the deepest sophistry and governments, it would be kicked out of all decent, intelligent society at once. But it is an ally of all practicable in despotism.

Peculiar faith has no patriotism, no sympathy. The inside barbarians are worse than the outsiders. Peculiar faith excites the worst passions, when she should master them. What Robespierre did for France, peculiar faith would have done and would do for the whole world. World patriots, stop her infuriate, mad career. Peculiar faith has no inherent principles, only peculiar doctrines to suit many degrading peculiarities. Analyze all peculiar faiths, and it will be clearly seen that they were for despotic sophistry and misrule. Are the world-people so blind as not to see all this? Will freemen, blessed with the loveliest land and the happiest government, that reflects the freedom and rationality, the pure religion of God, forget all this? Peculiar faith makes emperors high-priests, as those of China and Russia, Thibet and Rome, and their people low laity, the gambling policy is the first being high, low, Jack, and the game. 'Tis false to rational mind to say that the people must be governed by priestocracy, superstition, or monarchy. The world has to fight two brutal monsters, despotic force power and the jesuitical sophistry of the priestocracy. It might well commence with the highest, and put down emperors of China and Russia, and all others of that stripe, high-priests of their nation; also the Pope of Rome, and Grand Lama of Thibet. What was Russia but for the conflict of mind, habitually free? The whole machinery of the world's peculiar faith would be a miserable farce if it had not been its bitterest tragedy! Peculiar faith cannot solve the universe problem of union indissoluble.

She stands in the way of the only means of soul-safety, rational religion. As to that thing of contingent smiles, dependent on the whim of power, let good intelligent mind deliver us; from all priestocracy, church wiles, and chicanery, mind, good and true, deliver us.

The special acts of mind are the conservative special providence. Peculiar faith shocks the whole moral, intellectual world. Who is the God of peculiar faith? Not the God of the universe; therefore the advocates of the first have no God to offer us. The god of their selection can do us no good, and they are estopped from the God of the universe. Christianity, and all that emanates from peculiar bibles, are of peculiar faith. Let all be defined, as it defines itself. How miserably tied up, caught in their own peculiar nets, are all such? Polytheism, atheism, all peculiar faith, are amenable to correction, as they are utterly destitute of conservative principles. If a pastoral people were unfit, are a barbarian people competent to civilize and refine the world? "The Bhuddists believe that there will be rewards and punishments hereafter, and, therefore rack their brains to devise fitting torments for the damned in the infernal regions." In all countries of less than constitutional government there is a state faith, as of China, Russia, Thibet, and Rome. Faith with them is everything pretendedly, being human law compulsory to man's conscience. With high tyranny, state governments resolve the whole, which can only exist in truth, fact. and reason. Novel faiths, in some, would overturn the existing government. Where there is a state faith, all the rest, even rational faith, that is religion, is discarded. Now, just government and faithful rational religion can only abide. Lamaism prevails in Japan, &c. This is something like Asiatic popery; or is not Roman popery like it? Its name obtains in Thibet. Fohi in China, or Bhudda in Hindostan, is the other name. This creed has the mysterious trinity.—Opposed to him is an evil principle. The Son of God of the Thibetians was born of a virgin in Cachemir, and was one thousand years before Christ. He is the principal object of divine worship; also incarnate god; wonder working prophet. It is doubtful, as of Christ, whether Bhudda ever existed. Several have assumed the name. Thibet presents the prototype of the Greek and Roman churches. It is said that the Jesuits were very much astonished at the ceremonies of the priests of Fohi in China, when they first came there. They only had the same editions. The people of China pay disrespect to the priests of Bhuddism, while they adopt their state faith.

The whole subject of peculiar faith is the same all over the world. It has no principles, but is petty grand larceny on the world, religion of man, mind, the world, the universe. God's own religion makes a man of principle, the most perfect and faultless gentleman. But peculiar faith gives demoralization.

Never give up the armaments to guard against perversions of mind. If principles do not avail, what will? Peculiar faith men will oppose rational religion, but the world will not consult tories, nor surrender to traitors their diamond rights. Let not the sovereign people of America speak of the peculiar faith of our fathers, but the religion of our God! That is the sublime position of mind.

Peculiar faith begets the most extensive hypocrisy in the world. All the latent effects of bad morals, carried out by peculiar faith, is mind's cannibalism throughout the world. Religion ennobles, while peculiar faith degrades mind.

The nature of peculiar or false faith is such, that the world cannot get rid of its false peculiar prophecies, until all are swept away by rationality of cultivated civilized mind. Peculiar faith affects to be Catholic, but with pretences as false as the foundation, whether Roman, Greek, or Protestant, all are retiring from a field in which "every knee should bow" to its institutor. The time will come when all such will be known no more, but as the dangerous toys of absolutists and priestocracy to delude and cheat the people their sovereigns, if they only had exercised their mighty jewel, their brilliant, their diamond mind, whose triumphs would give unfading lustre. It is your duty, highest, wisest world-minds, statesmen and all, to put me down if wrong, but to uphold my writings if right. Let the whole world look to it.

The pope, papa of the Greek church, lama, &c., are at the head of, and premise monarchical doctrines. Will freemen act tory to their republican liberty of mind, for these aliens to mind?

All the moderns may commit themselves about any peculiar faith of the ancients, but all Jew and Gentile were only ignoble, peculiar, unworthy of rational mind in all their peculiar faiths. All the ancients had only a smattering of religion, the Jew and Christian as little as any, as far they renounced rational religion. All peculiar faiths renounce religion as far as in them lies, and only retain what God first imparted of the elements, though sadly deteriorated. The ancients, even Aristotle, could not separate complex ideas of the God of the universe, the preserver, as well as the creator, the organizer. They could only comprehend the evil, not the effect of derangements of conservative elements by perverse mind, or as defective appreciations and misapprehensions, but as emanating from powers antagonistic to the good. Thus, all such stuff run through all peculiar faiths, most sadly deficient, degenerating into absurd metaphysics, whether upheld by eastern or western sages, even a Plato. The atheists were, and are, as good as the polytheists, for the first make no God, and the last make equivalents. There can be no Supreme, where there are detractions therefrom. The Jewish priestocracy first make a very inferior creation, correspondent to their ignorant position of philosophical science, and have the creator miserably deficient. As all such systems are amenable to philosophical science for correction, all the affiliated absolutists preach up for faith, to sustain the whole monster deprived of light. All their charlatan priestocracy preach against philosophy and science, as they can most successfully assail such false pretences.

It is needless to talk about the Jews of all the ancients having the idea of one God, when they necessarily had only peculiar faith, and did not have the idea of the God of the universe. Their god was peculiar to their nation, of course was the peculiar workmanship of their priestocracy brains, the stone-stupid tablets, to make an idolatrous people subservient to their government, and their unholy, and ungodly, selfish interests.

Cannot the whole modern world see through their iniquities? If it cannot, it is hopelessly lost to all rationality, the unappreciable God-gift.

The world has been martyrized, victimized enough by peculiar faiths, its bloodiest enemies, the blood-hounds of mankind. If mind was not peculiarly blind, by peculiar interests of absolutism in its peculiar forms, it would soon see it.

All peculiar faith has no peculiar claim at all to religion, all such being man's device, superstition for peculiar purposes, the merest counterfeits gotten up by the priestocracy of the world for worldly purposes. All the advocates having surrendered reason for peculiar faith, they have no tribunal but that of the ruling dynasty of bigots, and the last never had any justice or its right, rational perception. They are all gone, indeed, on their own self-willed position. Let us have no peculiar faith, the best that mind can devise, as all Confucian or any, are ungodly.

If individual peculiar faith be a curse, what must not national peculiar faith be? Just in proportion to its means. What outrage upon the world, mind, people, God.

The mildest monarchical governments have state faith, that tells its own tale, as rational mind of the people permits; if there be autocracy, the emperor fools, cheats, the people, as head priest. Priest is synonymous with cheat, as by him, the world is cheated. As to subjects of monarchies, however great their intellects supporting peculiar faiths, are they not doing their duty as loyal subjects, carrying out their double duty to peculiar education that has formed a second nature? When, then, any bright intellect is named, allied to such faith, we must analyze the whole peculiar influences that tyrannized over his deepest nature. The wisest nation will institute nothing less than the best rational education, as the highest duty to its citizens, who will repay the world, mind, religion, God, many fold. To give then peculiar education, is next to an unpardonable sin. The world can give no credence to the priestocracy, that are the pulpit sophists. Absolutism sustains worse, and is answerable for all its misdemeanors and crimes. Did I ever say all these acted felony to man? I say it was worse, all was blasphemy to God, the God of the universe. They shall not mistake me, and have any mental reservation that it is their peculiar god that they seek to palm on the world. The world should act like freemen, worthy of a Jefferson, Franklin and Paine. Ah! but you affect some conscience, as these men were not perfect. Are you looking at the perfection of man, or the conservative principles of mind? If you discard for personal considerations, you are most ingloriously condemned, as all your bible heroes are mock characters, the disgrace to mind and its beneficent principles.

When you decide your god for a mock system of faith, you do the same by your conscience. You dwarf both. But you affect to draw out of the category of polytheism, as you are a believer in trinity. That defines your position positively in that category, and you are either hypocrite to deny, or dolt not to perceive the absurdity. Why do you not act like a rational man, since your Creator has endowed your mind with all the mighty elements of rationality? You not only have one-third of a God, worse than atheism, that makes all nature God, a mere substitution of terms at last, that is unequal to the devil, your own distempered creation, as prince of the power of the air, a most foolish idea, but you have other partial gods, angels, spirits, ghosts, witches, wizards. You not only make your bible an idol, but you idolize nothing but the priestocracy creation, as the contents of that infamous book. You go further in your maniacal absurdity, that is as foolish as perverted mind of priestocracy can get to be; you say the world could get no other idea of God, but from your exploded bible. I say this is the most absurd of all idiocies. The world of mind never could get your bible ideas of God's perversions, without the obliquity and perversions of your priestocracy and bible; but it could not miss the God of the universe, to read his creation by his science and philosophy, vouchsafed to rational mind. Peculiar faith people cannot define rational religion, and of course they cannot practice it. much less possess it. The deadly hostile feuds among the grand divisions of peculiar faith, not to mention those of the same families, bespeak anything else than love to neighbors, much less to God, who is cut up, divided and sub-divided, conspired against, blasphemed and outraged by the priestocracies. Its messiahships are the fooleries of the world.

That peculiar faith that gets the ascendancy and suits the reigning dynasty, is the pretended true one. The Confucius of China rules out the Eastern and Western Bhuddhism, and is administered by the emperor who assumes the high priest office, under whom are the priestocracy the mandarins. But some approve of the civil officers holding also the peculiar faith, yet all such is odious corruption of government as well as religion. The world needs no priestocracy, much less civil officers of government which is necessarily corrupted. It becomes American freemen to teach the humbugged world as much in religion as constitutional government. To do so, they must have the highest rationality and purity in both. If the world of peculiar faith were not to swear to the truth of their faith, for which they sacrifice themselves as far as in them lies, they would be hypocrites. And if they do swear, they would be perjurers. Priestocracy peculiar faith is one great piece of patchwork, on the ancient oracles a great excrescence deformity, that botches, tinkers and cobblers have manufactured to meet the market, the peculiar market of the world.

As to the cause, all the world, talents, cannot uphold it, but if committed thereto must sink with it. Peculiar faith is a deformity on the world, has no principles, truth or rational faith—all borrowed capital, and ungratefully obtained on false pretences of religion that is basely slandered and its author robbed, his universe miserably imposed upon. It is the ignoble priestocracy that keeps the world in difficulty about peculiar faith, when rational conscience propels to religion. We have an illustration by the Mormons, Mahometans, &c., how peculiar faith can grow like a mushroom on false pretences, on which all is built. Intelligent virtuous freemen ought to be the last people to adopt, and first to reject peculiar faith tory and unprincipled, smuggled in by the pirates of mind, the brute force of absolutists, and the malign sophistry of priestocracies. There are millions to-day devoted to this world-curse, that would victimize the whole world by peculiar faith, that would see it murdered under that plea, and would perjure themselves the worst to have it fastened on all minds. No age can render the past vassal as it was, the master of the future. No slave of past peculiar faiths can be any example for freemen. Mind and rationality are inseparable in the universe, that is exclusively and rationally addressed to rational mind. All peculiar faith is to the world, like the fatal gift of the poisoned shirt to Hercules, as the fable moral has it. How absurd to have to go to the intermediates, messiahs and priestocracies, who have to go of course not to the creator of the universe, but to their created peculiar God! What benefit is that to you, or any rational being? The work of sectarianism is manifest, all over the world. The Bhuddhist thinks in his miserable bigotry, that he is too pure for the rest of the world! He not only will not permit the touch of others if avoidable, but has most difficult regulations and tedious rites and purifications to redeem his supposed pollution about the touch. Is his food touched, his utensil used by others, they are polluted! Is this ungodly and inhuman pollution of peculiar faith never to be expunged off the face of the globe, by rational man? No wonder that this, the first country of the continent, Hindostan especially, has been ruined by this bitter curse of the priestocracy. Yes, the priestocracy can curse with a bitter, a horrible, and impious curse, and its blight falls on country and all alike, made abject vassals. People of the world, renounce all such curses, the world over.

How, church member Republican, can you convict the autocrat, the head pontiff, high-priest that rules his people with military despotism and bible superstition, when the last appeals to faith, a part of his government? How can you dissent from your own position? You are then self-impeached by a clash of principles, that convict and utterly condemn you. Retire from your senseless and ignoble position, and never pretend that you are pure in government, when your impurity in bad faith entirely silences you for ever.

The bloody piratical tory flag of peculiar faith has to be surrendered. How dare these peculiar faith demagogues of the earth to deform it, by such outrages on God and man! We are indebted to the Jew as well as others, for all this intolerable abomination, peculiar faith. Down with this world-curse, nations of the earth. A citizen of one country cannot go to another country, without this abominable curse staring him in the face. He cannot participate with the people, nor associate without the most abject vassalage. No mind degradation is the adoration of the Creator. Down with this relic of barbarous ages, the most contemptible of the world usage.

Religion by peculiar faith, is the tool and instrument of tyrants. Peculiar faith is a smuggler all the time. The world needs religion most rational to hold all the whims. crimes, and sins of peculiar faith in abeyance, to tell all the priestocracy, the Imperial Pontiffs, Popes and Papas, Grand Lamas, and all the tribe, that they are the vilest of the vile world. Impostors and swindlers of souls, not only denounce them and all their fool false pretenders, but silence them at once by the majesty of truth and good faith, to the only faith, the representative of nature's facts. The Bhuddist peculiar faith unsettles the world, disorganizes and deranges in its harrowing agitations.

What peculiar faith has not this peculiar vice? Rejoice, O rational mind, that you can secure the proper analysis and solution of this world-wide, this universe problem. Peculiar faith has various dyed garments of patch-work, bedecked in all the tinsels of a world's gewgaw. In what a quagmire is peculiar faith, about each other's creeds. If the world believes them, they are the worst of creation. By their own position, self-declared, Christians are Jew parricides.

I fear the gifts and givers in peculiar faith. Rational mind would have to play the hypocrite, to pretend to adopt it; so much then for the supposed authority of supposed great men's example. What is all such worth? Suppose the whole world were to pretend to such. What corruption. What ill-will and crabbedness, prevail between those of peculiar faith. In the same village, those of different churches generate a miserable state of things. Church bigotry is the absurd worship of peculiar faith and bibles, the priestocracy, instead of the adoration of the Almighty God. What is the world? Much of it is peculiar faith. Peculiar faith people do not know what religion is!

Peculiar faith commits highway robbery and spoliations on the world. The comprehensive liberal justice of rational religion excludes all contracted caucus, and frees the mind from all improper earthly sophisticated allegiance. Peculiar faith is one of the alloys of the world, having not the least intrinsic element of religion. The Jews, the Hindoos, have been ruined by their peculiar faiths. Let the balance of the world beware for itself. Rational mind under its glorious munificent mission of free agency, is to rescue the world from mind's perversions and abuses. What are they? Absolutism, with all its diversities and variations of sophistry, bigotry, usurpation and monopoly. We do not need peculiar faith and its bibles, but religion and its code, the bible of rational mind—no speculation but facts. Peculiar faith has retarded the noblest benefits of mind in all ages, pushing forward its own ills and evils. Is that religion, that raises the whole machinery of bullying institutions, proscriptions, and ostracisms, excommunication, wholesale butcheries and massacres. to perpetrate its ignoble peculiar faith? How do Christians, Mahommedans, and Mormons feel exotics on an eclectic, that if right, kills them, but as wrong, all are killed by rational faith? They are dead any how.

Religion commenced with God, peculiar faith commenced with the priestocracy, obliquity, and iniquity of mind, that worshipped the servants of rational mind, that commands the universe problem, that does justice to itself, to its God of the universe. We do not want a faith to exist to trample as a despotic master, where it is not fit to be owned as a slave. All the peculiar faiths arouse all the means to sophistry as clairvoyance, superstition, with their thousand false statements, as knocking to be heard. All peculiar faith must be knocked in the head, then all sophistry, all village and world-bickerings, will die a wholesale death as true peculiar faith. Where did you get peculiar faith from? Its age makes no difference, and it matters not, as all of it together is of no account, being counterfeit.

The priestocracy are the same everywhere. Both come from false pretences. But the Confucian is more philosophical than others. O, no, the Emperor of China has it for a state faith, assuredly for all the arts of government. He has excluded all the others as state faith. The prejudices of the people are enlisted by superstition of course. As concerns all peculiar faiths, so far as they are concerned, their poison is analogous, and would be relatively pernicious unless counteracted by mind. Christianity is what we have in Bhudhism. India has given it to the world.

Jew, what do you say? The Brahmin or Chaldean has given you your bible ideas—probably through Egypt. What can you make out of peculiar faith? The works, collusions, and combinations of king and priestcraft, to gull the people to pay taxes and tithes, and bow their neck to vassalage. But could man do that? Have priests any conscience? No more than all their faiths in all their forms have any foundation. Did God ever sanction one of them? Not the God of Creation, and if their peculiar god did, it was all the creation of the priestocracy who created the peculiar petty idol, and all he spoke, they manufactured by mind-jugglery.

But why did God not sanction? Because he had previously given the universe a sublime and soul-exalted dowry religion. All that peculiar faith presents, is false pretences. The bible-man affects that all things are possible with God. This is false—sophistry. Pulpit sophists of the priestocracy pretend it. The solution given by man, is false. God has his way to have all things possible, not man's folly, that involves crime, evil, negatives of God's good. Peculiar faith, with all its iniquitous disguises, and false pretences about religion, is nothing but an insidious form of despotic government. Most of the peculiar faiths have been handed down without analysis. The ancients could not analyze the complex ideas about good and evil, that the last is the negative of the other.

It is mind's perversions and deficiencies that cannot comprehend these things. God might as well have a million of angels to prop up this earth, as only to carry messages. An angel means a messenger. Now, if he needed one angel for any such business, he needed then the whole crowd, and the whole fabric of the priestocracy creation, would have gone to the speediest chaos. What blockheads, the dramatists, not to carry out the whole consistently. The whole creed is utterly defective, and falls to the ground. If any defender seeks to uphold it, he will make it and himself utterly ridiculous. The very thing that the world should discuss properly, the facts are there withheld by the false pretences men. What is the position between the main sects of peculiar faith? Will a christian love a Jew? Why not? O, he is of different faith. That kills the objector dead.

Why does not the monotheist approve: why are there any conflicts? The monotheist has no temporal interest in the priestocracy speculation, and if there be conflicts, they come from the peculiar faith-priestocracy, who seek loaves and fishes.

Will all the world peculiar faith people never learn that they are stupidly, constantly exposing themselves and outraging God, by perpetrating fooleries, pretending to miracles and prophecies, to impeach pure religion and render her odious, discarding the unity of God in his sublime supremacy? Was there ever such suicidal policy with any but maniacs? Who but jesuitical priestocracies could have ever devised such absurd abominations? All peculiar faith corrupts the world-mind. What can we learn from peculiar faith pulpits? Mind is misled all the time from God of the universe to the peculiar god of the priestocracy, who must be represented by them and their bibles, else they would drop into insignificance and annihilation at once. That is the difference between the God of the universe and the peculiar god of the priestocracy, and their cliques and minions, that the first embraces religion, whereas peculiar faith people and bibles have to sustain the other. What a god, people, a monstrosity, that draws the sword, and puts the father against the son, makes the sectarian christ quarrel with his father Jew, the Protestant quarrel eternally with his father the Romanist, puts the people of the world together by their ears and hearts, by their low, degraded feuds, pits a large part of the world against another part, that seduces the world from the true faith to which it is antagonized by the bribery of the priestocracy, and bribes conscience to commit blasphemies, perjury, surrendering the best only fund, God-given, the best future happiness for an earthly non-entity. Where is mind? Crushed by its own heel. made by despotism and sophistry. As peculiar bibles beget peculiar faith, what is that worth to rational mind or its God? Who can define peculiar faith? Is it definable? It cannot possess the rational mind, of course. What a monster, then, with which the light and peace of God cannot dwell.

It has taken mind thousands of years to master peculiar faith, the intruder by toleration, how long will it take it to reach rational religion? The ancients sacrificed ostensibly millions to peculiar faith. What do the moderns sacrifice? The idea of making mind and people peculiar, could only have originated with the degraded jesuitical bigotry of priests' selfishness. How correct it? By church? That has no principle. Principles must correct it. God proves his own record; how then can he prove man's? Man's only proves itself by conforming to God's principles, from which, if divergent, its perversion is self-marked. A conservative revolution in all this matter must arise.

A peculiar education may be peculiar seduction of mind. Various are the opinions about the disposition of the soul. The Hindoos would have a different location for souls than the metempsychosis had they been acquainted with the universe.

Give us religion, but no peculiar faith, no such bibles, or priestocracy, or churches. All peculiar faith advocates have diversified pretensions to what is right on the globe, and falling short of universal justice, which is religion. Religion is the consummation of unity, of correct universal appreciation of right.

Let religion advance. Peculiar faith people have had a miserable non-appreciation of it, however desired. The mass of the world mean right about religion, but they have been defrauded, swindled out of their rights. The absolutists and agitators of the world are foolish, thereby cutting short the very cord that binds man to his noblest elevation. They go to bloodshed and its attendant trains, war, pestilence and famine—barbarism. The degraded dwarf-circle of bigotry is in the same dotage for all lifetime. Do not sneak. Adopt principle, and you can face the world. You can triumph over the whole world by one principle. Where does peculiar faith rule? In the pockets of the priestocracy. Where does religion prevail? In rational minds.

Are not the abuses of peculiar faith, most oppressive to mind and the rights of the world?

What but the worst abuse caused the putting down the free state of the Romans, by miscalled brother republicans, for doing the same thing as the last?

The more tyrannical a government, the more influence does church have with state.

All but principles beget creeds, that have the elements of confusion and their own destruction.

Look at the clash of all creeds in the world, and of the world, not of God, whose principles clash not.

What is the difference between any professions of peculiar faith? It is all in degree and variety of alloy.

While one interdicts the bible from the people, all interdict rational mind in faith, and rational discussion, preferring their own blasphemy in interdicting the universal and appropriate rights of God. They exclude the possibility by their traditions, so fast by fetters on the human mind, of obtaining all the legitimate benefits of progressive improvement, from the bible of rational mind, the mental, the only true one.

Their dogmas exclude the humanity of genius, and weigh down mankind by all the iron sceptre of clannishness.

But why the scowl on free rational discussion of religious doctrines, and proscription placed on the correct conclusion?

What do the mere laymen followers of the church know, but to adopt what is called faith?

Can any peculiar system be placed on the merits of reason, before the people? They can only seek faith that betrays the rights of the people.

No rational being can withhold reason about faith, if he do, then all are withheld from him as absurdly.

What difference is there, whether there be thousands, three or four Gods, all is polytheism?

But what curious character the prince of the power of the air, has had by authority of the bible.

"Satan is said to have fallen from heaven with all his company." The bible's heaven is not equal to the modern earth. He is the evil genius of the world; of course, if the bible's God permits this, he participates in the act: what a libel.

Peculiar faith in all ages of the world, mythical or fanatical, seems to be the deepest conspiracy of mind perverted to override mind, crushed by brute force and sophistry.

It had to improve, as the mind of the people improved, by regular gradations, and its burdens from the building of pyramids to that of temples, was in accordance thereto. The peculiar faith of foreigners, is called that of heathenism, as if they were the only barbarians.

Peculiar faith that admits Polygamy as the Hebrew patriarchal dispensation, demoralizes most ignominiously, the world.

Rational law that emanates from rational religion, excludes all such peculiar faith, and its felonious customs.

Constitutional representative republicanism, requires rational laws that legalizes marriage according to the arbitrament of nature, that approximates equality of number in the sexes.

When peculiar faith prevails, the people are liable to any amount of false steps and position, as any amount of such faith may be added.

Reformation will never heal the corruption, as it is too partial, therefore conservative revolution is necessary to exclude the errors of faith, that are too powerful for reformation.

All peculiar faith is priest faith, from which we might ask the good Lord to deliver us, were it not useless to ask delivery from the worst of all corrupt governments, when the world's people make themselves participant in their corrupt ignorance and degrading superstition.

All that adopt peculiar faith, have never appreciated the universe author, and may expect to be cashiered by the holy chancery, if they knowingly continue the error, along with all those that join peculiar faith churches from any but pure motives.

There are low characters of all persuasions, that are reckless of the laws of God and man, conscience and mind.

All priest-faith dies hard, with its many heads this dragon has to be cut down.

CONFESSION.

Confession is boasted of as a triumph in peculiar faith, when securing by remorse of conscience a few dollars overdrawn.

Rational religion prevents all that at first, by one of its chief attributes, honesty.

Do we hear of the numerous murders concealed and confession withheld; the thousands of corruptions unknown and unredressed? The priestocracy's confessional the most desirable of all, to be made for the highest of all crimes, blasphemy to the God of the universe.

Of the fornication and adultery, that may lead to murder and many miseries.

Are the principals themselves guiltless?

What confessional of faith can sin make to sin?

Arrest not by reckless impiety God's attributes, sinful, weak mind.

Thou canst reach the very elements of proper sense, to assume this character.

Undertake not to define the limits and character of God, the fountain of all wisdom.

Recall thy libel, and repent of thy iniquity and blasphemy.

Let us hear only of religion that reason can hail as affording all the elements of greatness of mind, dignity of character, performance of duty, and rendition of highest allegiance to the Almighty.

It is idle, useless, and absurd, to expect any other means than through the responsible mind of each rational being, to overcome all obstacles in life, and reach all that belongs to it in its whole duty.

How important, then, is confession to a mortal!

We can neither speak to the world, nor indite a book, without recurring to the requirements and responsibility of rational mind that denounces all such stuff.

All we say and do, are by, through, and for mind, not ignorant stultified priests. But all this is of a piece, with the other ridiculous machinery of priestocracy and peculiar faith.

When the world becomes enlightened, then peculiar faith cannot exist.

It will die an ignoble death, the tool of absolutism.

Citizens, patriots, and philanthropists, decide this mighty question, the sooner the better.

Then the narrow and contracted policy of nations and societies can be liberalized, and the whole world march onward to true greatness and its inherent glory, by its most extensive comprehension of unity.

Then the remotest parts of the earth will come to know each other; and even China will open her ports voluntarily to the good of all; and the inside, as the outside barbarians, will unite in its completion.

There will be no violation of the trust of the mighty boon, mind; and all nations will impeach and discard all other bibles but that of rational mind.

They will adopt what is now instituted, The Order of the Universal Brotherhood, that embraces all the essentials and principles becoming to all societies, for it embraces all.

The Order of Odd Fellows and Temperance, Masons, and all can now unite on this mighty basis for universal good, and be necessarily absorbed thereby.

Peculiar faith has been a curse upon mind wherever it has been introduced. There can be no exception.

The history is that of sophistry and absolutism, forever antagonistical to mind's rights.

The Egyptian faith supplanted the Hindoo, and much of Europe and Africa.

The faith of Bhudda supplanted the Egyptian or Brahmin for a time, but was finally expelled from the supremacy.

The doctrine of Bhudda has invaded China, but the state faith of Confucius holds it in abeyance.

Christianity was introduced there centuries ago, and yet makes no progress. Mahometanism supplanted much of the faith of Asia, and kept military rule over Hindostan, till christianity comes over the same country, by the sword, pure military power, to rule out Mahometanism and Brahminism.

With all, there is a mighty jar, and but little proselytism. All exclude rational religion, and its lofty social adoration of God the Creator.

Mind to-day, has to seek the true faith, that rules out all by most potent reason.

Judaism has been divested of much value by Christianity, Mahometanism and Mormonism, superseding it.

Judaism has but little to complain, as she innovated in rational faith.

The christian faith soon splits as all peculiar faith. The potency of councils is invoked in vain to preserve its unity.

Arianism splits the church into fragments—that are with difficulty collected—after mutual triumphs and losses, massacres and bloodshed.

Not only many bishops are exiled and banished, but the Crusades were gotten up by false faith-people.

The bible is upheld by the vile sophistry of false-faith people. The idea of hero-worship, demigods, a mere matter of sophistry and flattery, arose in the days of popular ignorance, when deep cunning prevailed over true wisdom. Religion, most rational, must rule the mass, human nature, and all its speculation. Put yourself on principle, and you are fortified in defence against the fiercest assaults of the world, and competent to meet your God-creator. This is what is called virtue, and is certainly rational religion. The world must get rid at once of all the fool systems of peculiar faith.

Every world-patriot should scout that miserable position that causes talents and creative genius to pay obeisance to it, instead of exalting themselves and the world to its designed elevation.

The Roman absolutism, armed with the potency of infallibility, loses nevertheless its eastern churches, that became Greek, and finally many of its western, by protestantism.

Its pure orthodoxy is rank heterodoxy at the tribunal of mind, after all the sanguinary contests to secure it.

She warred by crusades, ineffectually, for centuries, to obtain conquests, but her gospel was put back by Mahometanism, and now the pope has been a curse upon his own country, seeking to murder republicanism, to maintain an usurpation.

What first principles of humanity or religion has this power, that has prostituted all at the shrine of mind's basest corruption?

More injury has been done the whole world, under the pretence of faith, than by all other means whatever.

The world would have been far happier and better, without any peculiar faith at all.

All such faith has only presented the world the shattered fragments of a broken brotherhood, that rational religion justly revolts at.

What is the world benefited by the persecution of dissenters, the bloody tragedy of the Vaudois, the rebellious clergy?

Whether "the interior of Asia, for many hundred miles square, had never been visited by any christian missionary" until 1849, or not, rational minds have the assurance that God is omnipresent, and that mind is the rightful guardian.

What matters it whether the Brahmins profess to teach science by divine authority, if the ignorance and superstition of the world did not enslave mind to believe their pretences?

All such imposition would die of itself if mind rightly counteracted it.

The light of mind-science never irradiated the crusade ages, and consequently superstition and bigotry, not religion, prevailed.

If mind could have had the mastery all had been right.

But peculiar faith cannot be enforced by the sword, nor propagated sincerely by all the delusion of sophistry.

How can the God of religion, favor any species of superstition?

Efforts have been made in all continents, but arms and conquests will not do.

Rational religion decides against peculiar faith, and she will, ere long, be scouted from the face of the earth.

The Indian of America believes in a Great Spirit, the Great First Cause, that puts to blush the asserter of the plurality of gods.

How impiously and blasphemously has God been treated, by the peculiar faith barbarians!

How cruelly have God's creatures been treated by them!

What, for centuries, was done for the millions of Indians? They have felt the force of the peculiar faith dispensation of the whole—the fire-water and the arms of the whites—something more potent than the gospel, to give them a receptacle to the spirit land. Yet they cling, with a laudable tenacity, to the Great Spirit.

Is not conquest made of all pagans, and would it not be of all other sects, by the sword, had the sword been available on the day of trial?

But the cimeter of the Mahometan was too strong for the sword of the Christian at that time.

Now, when civilization has spread, the Christian only wars on the pagan, and the partially civilized in creed, as the natives of the various continents, if they are behind in the use of weapons of war of the present day. But it is all still pagan against pagan.

Who can deny the crimes of bibles of tradition, that gave each sect inheritance of all that it could get, as the propagation of their peculiar faith accompanied the conquest!

To possess the lands of the heathen, the elect did God service in the action of possession!

The majority of the world is not aware of the remote consequences of these real heresies on principles.

What but the sword will define the rights of orthodoxy of peculiar faith? What shall stop the progress of such crime? Principles alone define the true extent of that position, that must be placed on the highest grounds of justice.

We can see the miserable delusion of sectarianism, when one sect seeks wars, unlimited in country and time, on others, to stay the proselytism that was going forward, and the conversion of the people, by an eternal enmity.

Races of men are not natural enemies, neither are professors of religion—the farthest from it, but all are natural friends, and would continue sincere friendship, but for faith charlatans, the real enemies of both and mankind.

Which ought to be put down?

Give us the value of enlarged and liberal views, without any bigoted policy of the age.

It is our highest duty and right not only to abolish all others, but institute all that is necessary, legitimate and correct.

We should have, at all times and occasions, a foreshadowing forecast, a judicious analogy and analysis.

All classes are invoked and identified by inseparable interests and indispensable duties and business, from the physical laws of nature, that are paramount to man's pretences.

The balance, or equilibrium of the universe, as paramount, can demand the right revolution and orbit of any system of worlds, that all harmony be maintained, and all right be executed.

No less, in the moral world, has mind the right to restrict and require the same rule, to exclude the many avenues to base, degraded usurpations, and monopoly of tyrant powers.

The best of those, avowing peculiar faith, cannot justify themselves before God.

Even christians admit that they have many and stormy doubts about their having religion. This is honest, and would be consistent, when they find that it is utterly impossible for them to have any on any such impracticable basis.

Who could doubt the rational position advanced in monotheism, that reverently and righteously only asks the aid of the God of nature.

On our last day, and at the last moment, this position will present the only justification before God.

Let not remorse, bitter and little availing, be yours on that important occasion.

22

You must act up to the possession of your belief of the soul's immortality and responsibility.

You must perceive that sectarianism propagates and disseminates doctrines at enmity to God.

The benevolence attributed to peculiar faith is through the innate principles of religion.

It is idle to say that one system of peculiar faith exceeded another as better, when all are deficient in primary and paramount virtues and attributes.

Wherein is any better? In departing from religion and God, and overwhelming by its greater influence the divine rights of mind?

The peculiar faith that is best appreciated has been most destructive to the lives and interests of the sovereign people?

The human mind is in a progressive state of improvement, independent of all such incidents of faith, and should have the intrinsic characteristics of religion.

Did any author of any such system discover any principle, other than the constituent of the universe, all of which belong to God? No.

Then all such are no creators, but usurpers and blasphemers of the Creator, impostors on men, only fit for vulgar belief, amenable to heaviest penalty.

But what harm would ensue from belief of revelation, though false?

It stands, as all false faiths, in the way of truth and rational religion.

The extreme proof has been at Rome as elsewhere, all over the world.

All on earth are punished for errors, more or less, and this thing of peculiar faith affects the whole world.

Our errors beget penalties, more or less, and remorse is no little part at times.

Reform belongs to the light of enlightened mind, and is constituted by repentance necessarily.

Now, repentance for what, as expressed by peculiar faith? It is duty to God and man that constitutes religious and moral sentiments.

What is the revelation of peculiar faith worth?

Is it anything like religion?

As to all the science of peculiar faith, we must make allowances for what mind has done, and cannot, possibly, omit to mention its illustrious deeds.

What shall atone for the omissions of peculiar faith, that pretends to usurp the claims of mind, through science?

Which are most abominable, her pretences to religion or to science? Peculiar faith is the vilest impostor on earth.

When we hear of the uncivilized embracing peculiar faith, that is evidence that they have not realized the proper benefit of civilization.

The history of paganism proves this.

Palestine has been ruled by the Jews, Romans, and Mahometanism, and has not yet seen the light of civilization.

All Judaism, with all its pretensions, could not civilize the Hebrews?

All the peculiar faiths of the world could not civilize the world!

Civilization is an act of enlightened mind, not of peculiar faith; the first comprehends God's principles, the last the faith and acts of individual leaders.

The result of peculiar faith tends to cause bishops to grow rich in a country of starving poor, that die poor by the million.

No matter the injunction of peace, when self-interest dictates, we can observe popes. the professed representatives of peace, urge nations, monarchical or republican, to war, and even receive their own papal power in bloodshed of their own fellow citizens.

The true analysis of mind will prove the doctrines of peculiar faith fully carried out, as leading to bloodshed, and this proof is in the appeal to history.

What were the murders of New England and Europe for witchcraft of all ages and both sexes, but from fanaticism of faith?

The Quakers of that province were awfully persecuted, no less the dissenters, who were exiled to Rhode Island. It is mind, not doctrine, that has been falsely claimed, that imparts the noble principles of morality and religion, nothing else will on this earth. It is folly and stupid nonsense, to expect any other source.

Faith must be subordinate to civilization, when it is peculiar.

The best as it is by excellence claimed, makes its God one-third or one-fourth of an imbecile being.

Men are better, as they are wiser, at this day, when a school-boy that has not had any peculiar education, contemns any murderous peculiar faith that burnt scholars at the stake for opinions in science!

Peculiar faith is an impostor, dictating in science and government.

What would she not do to-day, if mind permitted her?

Any peculiar faith is as deep in the mud, as the others are in the mire.

The novelty of a faith is no proof of its truth, which no custom nor fashion, but analysis, decides.

All kinds of peculiar faith, the best that can be devised, perform the bloody oblations of superstition in human sacrifices, through all ages of its existence.

Tory is peculiar faith by her fruits and deeds, not by her professions and faith: is one any better than the rest?

Is there any proof of superiority, but as the emanation of a better age and more improved mental cultivation?

If mind under any culture of peculiar faith, was peculiarly better a saint on earth, then we admit the superiority absolute, but we have to deny all the premises when the results are inadequate.

What essential difference of goodness is there between any such faith?

Opinions or faith of men doubtful and uncertain, not trustworthy, do not alter God's position of things.

What can be peculiar to any system, that is common in God's principles?

If mind carry out the principles, it elicits the best already, for its good and best happiness.

Much good may be effected when mind has the ascendancy, but take mind away from the peculiar faith, and faith becomes fanatic and tyrannical. As to government of passions. the sins that are evils, resulting as the negative of conservative principles, science and philosophy teach their correction.

What can peculiar faith avail with them, when mind has no control of the self-government?

What is the difference between good citizens well educated and well behaved, and those the best of any peculiar faith?

The excellence and light of rational mind, equalize them.

What then becomes of peculiar faith on its best behavior, and that under the restriction of civilization? But in its worst behavior, it is the fanatical scourge of the world.

Unlike fire, it is the worst of masters, yet it is not fit to be owned as a slave. You cannot trust it with any power.

It is useless, and has failed to meet the puffs of its advocates, but increases the sum of human misery.

What can we do with it, when the attributes of God preclude its admission, its own demerits preclude its retention? Misery and evil, its concomitants, will result to human life, rational religion makes them the least, and the most of human happiness.

The last invokes the aid of science and philosophy as the more wisdom, the less folly and wickedness.

The earth has its mixtures and alloys, and rational religion can best temper them.

Universal happiness cannot inure to man's soul while on earth, but a right education and morals can remedy the greatest defects and errors of mind.

God has given the functions, mind must exert the actions and exercise.

Peculiar faith ever degenerates into superstition, man-worship and imposition, when the whole comprehension of the subject is not in abeyance to the faculties of intelligent mind, the only beneficiary.

Conscience all the time is to preside over this vast subject, and necessarily excludes all such faith that is too peculiar to be true

Ignorance presided at the first start of peculiar faith; now the best philosophy is most substantially the best supporter of the best religion.

We can easily challenge refutation when miracles, the product of the grossest ignorance, are referable to imposition.

Magic powers of psychology can be the cause of mental illusion and delusion; when analyzed are the beautiful exhibitions of natural phenomenon.

The modern adoption of all pretences of this kind, as recognised by ancient fictions, has but little apology for the advocates.

Rational religion, as directed by science, ought to preclude all such now.

Mankind needs religion, not peculiar faith, as the first blesses, the last curses the world.

All religion does promote honesty and truth, and will exclude peculiar faith that nurtures sophistry and false pretences.

Men interested particularly in peculiar faith, that necessarily and universally depends on false pretences, will go to the extent necessary for that interest.

Are the advocates of any peculiar faith any better than the rest of the world? In what?

Do they excel in mind, deeds and morals, well behaved citizens ?

There never was a system of peculiar faith, messiahship and all, but what there was the greatest zeal to have it estimated as infallible and orthodox, to surmount all reason, and reason's God, if necessary. The object is to make it live, if all others die. No object can be stopped short of, that will obtain it. Will perjury, force, ambition be despised in its consummation ? Never.

What partizan priests ever abjured their peculiar faith ?

The great object was, through the influence of moral doctrines that accorded passports to heaven the most captivating, besides all earthly anticipations, if the faith was successful.

Christianity, that was persecuted for centuries by other peculiar faiths of polytheism, persecuted with vindictive fury the world, as far as practicable, when she came into power.

It is too late for any attempt to render any peculiar faith dignified with orthodoxy, against the inalienable rights of conscience and reason.

Many forms of peculiar faith avail in barbarism, as savages have not attained the right use of reason. Races are to be estimated, as some cannot rise far into any scale of civilization, by reason of their natural talents.

Phrenology proves this on principles of physiology. While Greece, Rome and a few others had grown into much comparative civilization for their ages, eighteen centuries or more ago, many nations fell below it. The world has to abide and suffer from all the miserable systems of faith teachings and doctrines, and cannot help itself from the dogmas and false pretences of its teachers, who recoil at the loss of self-interest, not at the sacrifice of the world.

What but fraud and imposition gave license and authority at first for peculiar faith, that has existed under all the forms of superstition to the present times.

Superstition, the inseparable companion that invariably attends peculiar faith, ever abides with all states short of civilization ; and, of course, civilization can never be governed by the faith of uncivilized mind.

The world acts blindly from interest, fear, and custom, without reason, that governs in civilization.

All the peculiar faith of Judaism and its posterity, Christianity, Mahometanism, and Mormonism, with its progenitors the Egyptian, the Brahmin, &c., emanated from the three imperfect states of mind, the hunter, pastoral, and tiller of the soil ; and have dwarfed the God of the universe to the provincial peculiar god of each, that had the sacrifice of victims in their own blood.

Peculiar faith aspires unwisely to unsolvable problems, wild as the perpetual motion is at present.

After all, there is only a minority now on any one side of peculiar faith, or gospel side, and shall that, erroneous as it is, rule the large majority of thinkers for themselves, and aiming to be right ?

Good and true citizens of the globe must see that mind be not perverted by false teachings.

They must investigate the whole purpose of their being, and not be divested of their birth-right.

Peculiar faith can easily render multitudes of mind vassal, and that decides the necessary facility for fraud, perjury, and complete deception.

One of the perversions of mind by the sophistry of peculiar faith is, if we doubt we are damned.

This is one of the most iniquitous pretences to logic, reason, and religion.

The only faith that is worth thought is through the principal only true and living God, and that reason teaches through present science.

Another vile piece of arrant humbuggery and sophistry is, with God everything is possible.

This is in the mouth of every pretender to interpretation of God's universe, no matter the defective system of science or reason. Is folly possible with God ? What libel, O vain and ignoble man.

Make the whole question of theology refer to God, mind, science, and the universe, and then the world will all see the dignity of religion, that gives all capable of receiving all the advantages of progressive improvements of the spirit of the age.

Rational mind is independent of the elements of peculiar faith, and repels priests and preachers, only receives, as they are identified with the whole people, who are the beneficiaries before God and religion.

Modern statesmen treat the people as sovereigns, while the ancients mistreated them as vassals, to stand at a distance from things called holy.

What need we of a gospel scheme, that adopts man instead of principles, peculiar faith for rational religion, blind faith for enlightened mind and science.

Peculiar faith refers to a messiah, an irresponsible deputy; religion refers to the principal, who is responsible for his creation, and bound to preserve mind to the best of his attributes for appropriate happiness.

Let us hear no more of the contingency of such imbecile substitutes.

No peculiar faith is exact or certain, because it is booked; an adherence to its mere partisan conduct can hardly be justice.

Nations that have governmental peculiar faith do not follow the principle of returning good for evil, but if their conquests are criterion, return evil for good in many instances.

Who can trust his life, happiness and rights of mind, at all, in the power of peculiar faith?

Peculiarity of nations, persons or churches, shows the peculiar designs of man, but universality shows God.

All peculiar faith persuasions have had so many failures, that man's peculiarity is conspicuous.

Mind must set about something else.

It is high time that mind's rights should be heard, in defence of the truth of its position, that all the defects of peculiar faith, that outrages so many and abundant facts in the world's history, be exposed.

The butcheries of peculiar faith, without number, and inquisitors creative of all the violations of the very attributes and essence of religion, rational and true, revolting to all reasonable minds, should be repressed.   Dissentient in her thousand divisions of secession, assuming to be divine in all, she pursues with a unity of tyranny her speculations in the world's richest treasures.   Her bibles accumulated in all kinds of mythology, under all the deepest devices of cunning and Jesuitry, have been handed down, with constant care of her pretensions and assumptions, that could not be counteracted nor resisted by individuals, or isolated exertions, that were feeble and impotent, against her collusions.

Citizen, are you battling for peculiar faith, spell-bound to the delusion, whose malign influence you cannot appreciate?

Have nothing to do with a cause, that debases and corrupts mind, the world.

But you believe in revelation, you may say.

All kinds of peculiar faith are peculiar, and have peculiar revelations—all are fictions, necessarily.

What is the evidence of your position being right?

You will have to seek a circuitous route to that point, that will be worth nothing, after it is advanced.

All such can never be proved, for it is disproved by even God's attributes, at once.

How dangerous to the world's liberty and happiness, are the shackles of peculiar faith, that pretends to be religious faith, yet the most oppressive of all the world's tyrannies, and subversive of religion.

In this respect, most of the world do not assert their proper rights, if they know them.

When reformation took place in peculiar faith, the light of mind called for it, not peculiar faith.   Now conservative revolution is demanded, by all the lights of the world, over all peculiar faiths.

Institutions of mind must be properly sought, to change spongers, idlers, and drones, into industrious and responsible citizens, well raised and well behaved, by equalizing popular rights, and lessening the difficulties of making a living, and giving more legitimate facilities to the people at large.

Why the reformation of Luther, if mind and reason had not triumphed over corrupt peculiar faith?

Why or how does one peculiar faith displace another, but on this principle?

If the Hebrew peculiar faith was that, by excellence, to save the world, what was it doing for thousands of years, if that was the chosen one of God, the light and salvation of the world?

The silence of this savage chosen people decides the inutility for all nations.

Whose hosts of people suffered so awfully by their superstition, from first to last, as the Jews?

Of course, they rejected, by the despotism of their priestocracy, mind and reason, and have naught—the bibles of tradition being impostures.

In the differences of peculiar faith, that distract the affection of families, society, and country, the whole world is not only unpleasantly but disastrously situated.

But party is the life of the world—what would it do, if all were of one peculiar faith?

The party of principles, not the faction of peculiar opinions, is essential in all rational discussions, where light is needed.

When the universal action of rational mind is predominant, then rational religion is in the right position. While the only victories in religion must be gained on facts, not in casuistry, the feelings of the world are still situated as partisans for peculiar faith, not yielding readily from bigotry, prejudice and ignorance to the facts of the case.

Hence it is not the authority of men, but the principles of the faith that meet the world's wants. But the mind cannot comprehend all about the mysteries of peculiar faith, and it never will, never should, if priests permit its foul impositions.

Pure religion has no mysteries, prophecy, nor miracles, but plain matter of fact views. The advocates for peculiar faith seek the reason in referring to the tree, the grass, the flower, the growth of vegetation, for mortals to tell the process. What sense is there in the appeal, presenting neither analysis, analogy nor parallel point in the statement?

The word of God is addressed through God's avenue, reason, to mind, for mind to understand by plain facts of science. The advocates of peculiar faith expose themselves, in refusing all this to enlightened mind.

But what rational mind can yet explain all about God's universal documents, the solar systems? that prove conclusively a perfect God.

We see and believe vegetation to grow, from inherent enlargements and the products, and the fruit decides the value. All this is a part of the universe proof of its God.— Such is proof positive, but the book men affecting miracles destroy all pretence to truth, for God rules creation by conservative, not reversed or destructive principles.

There can be then no miracles in creation, otherwise the Creator is imbecile.

The advocates of peculiar faith object to phrenology, but as the system of physiological phrenology does not conflict but agree with rational religion, we are bound to admit its exact appreciation, however peculiar faith is in antagonism with both and all the facts of creation.

Peculiar faith does not look to the zenith of intellect, but to nadir of self-interest.

Some never attain, while others pass it and become puerile.

As all men's systems of peculiar faith have failed and will for ever fail, let reason and the God of reason have theirs, and as God and reason are above man and folly, so will be the first exalted to the most sublime of virtue and her noblest blessings.

The intrigue, malice and hypocrisy are antagonistic in peculiar faith, and defeat themselves.

Minds, blinded by peculiar faith, cannot appreciate rational religion.

Any other than rational faith, places mind more or less in a psychological state.

People think of the profit of self-interest, not of the good part. Are the revenues, the profit, the inducements and power of the church, nothing to influence? But what are all such to the people's rights, thereby violated?

The reward immortal is conditional and only contingent in peculiar faith, and perverted minds hasten to secure their's on this earth.

We desire no peculiar faith that drowns reason and enslaves mind.

What is the value of peculiar faith to those who backslide or err? Yet all that look to principle cannot err intentionally, otherwise true religion is necessarily unknown.

Under the auspices of principle and science, the best position is obtained for truth, honesty, sound judgment and modesty.

Mystery about the seed vegetating and the word of God is all dissatisfactory, as all present no analogy nor parallel. All systems of peculiar faith are for the benefit of the priests and their dynasty. They bespeak that man's qualities and attributes are too selfish for general good, if they be perverted. He cannot displace but must control them, by the will of enlightened cultivation.

The idea of sect is not innate to true religion, but to peculiar faith, and never can be anything else. Any other opinion is utterly preposterous. The Roman affects the name of Catholic and rejects the proper position in substance, at the same time being utterly incompetent to attain universal principles in peculiarity in faith. His position never can be catholic.

God's attributes are universal, and any faith not to be antagonistic, must be of universal constituency and nothing less.

Analysis will prove conclusively that reason, unity, and universality catholicism, characterize God.

Peculiar faith and bibles of tradition are of the same character, all are worthless and treacherous.

But thanks to God of mind, all false systems carry within themselves, the elements of their own destruction. The sectarianism of peculiar faith is fast developing that

result, in most of its secessions of the present day. The true spirit of prophecy which
is analogy from reason on the world's analysis, declares their progressive ruin and
extirpation, for all these are perverted minds' deepest collusions that shall mould, whilst
the ever living authority of Deity becomes more vital and immortal.

The peculiarity of sect adheres not to the liberal universal spirit of rational religion.
The very necessity for separation of church and state, impeaches the parties as
involved in corruption. All peculiar faiths are thus amenable.

The best code of peculiar faith selected from the world of their systems, can only
lead us through partisan faith to the chief propagator, and what does all such avail the
world's age?

Rational beings must see which of the two, peculiar or rational faith, can best govern
the world's whole interests. The pious frauds committed in behalf of peculiar faith or
of their authors, are beyond conception. The very first acts of such proselytes is that
of cheating their God by faith, to swindle mind of its rights, in most detestable ways.

They must know as clearly as they see God's works, that God is present everywhere,
and may be called upon by appropriate duty ever necessary and expedient in thoughts,
words, and deeds, actions rather than by words of prayer.

The prayer of duty can only be made through the prayer of thoughts, words, and
deeds, the prayer of action towards mankind, yet mind perverted leaves the author of
its existence and benefits, and recurs to the pretences of the priestocracy, and thus
cheats itself, at the same time opens the door of future injury for its conscience that
may be or not violated, only to be answered by motives to be judged of at the supreme
tribunal.

If, then, all churchmen's first steps are those of self-delusion, deception, or intentional
imposition, what proper guarantees can the conscientious persons have in adherence to
such faith?

Many sectarian peculiar faiths are split into hundreds of fragments, surely so, as
blind faith not on analogy and analysis of reason, precedes works that alone are to be
looked at by mind.

What is the enemy of constitutional liberty?

Absolutism in peculiar faith, government, and aristocracy of money. All these are
in abeyance to aristocracy of mind. The world is cut up into fragments of clans, that
if they do not aid beyond their own little circle, fail in best actions of the greatest good
to the greatest number.

What wise man will give anything for peculiar faith, that is all things to all men all
over the globe?

Is there any faith that separates you from the unity of God? Depend on it, it is an
evil that you cannot rightly embrace. What guarantee does all such give mind on earth
equal to principles?

Who would give, if wise, one iota for any character that overlooks principles; and
who do that more than messiahs?

What guarantee for good character has any in all peculiar faith professions?

If peculiar faith was an abstraction, we might be satisfied to let time remedy without
interpretation; but it is a troublesome superstition, that becomes bigotry, fanaticism and
tyranny.

When peculiar faith becomes speculative, and unites with absolutism, all-governing
authorities in excess, and when does it not do all these and more if permitted, then mankind ought to put it down as the worst species of tyranny?

Its false tastes are not quite so bad, but eventually malign, when it may run into
ridiculous states of invoking from the universe intercessors, other than God, may affect
belief of visions, and exhibit the various influences of trifling with the souls of the world
by pretended miracles, mere sleight of hand or mind-jugglery; but all denote a contemptible, obnoxious influence on the human mind.

How long shall it be ere such vulgar prejudices and superstitions are superseded by
the reflective part of mankind, who are truthful and honest? Not until original thinkers
exert themselves as freemen, free from electioneering and corruption, and act as intelligent and correct-minded citizens.

Such will observe that the creation shows order and symmetry, the work and design
of a Supreme artist, who moves it with electricity, and balances it by gravitation.

The best regulation of the world will be by principles; and all society is best regulated
when it resorts to full principles, as all its members are best benefited thereby. You
ask for the greatest good of society, and yet you practice its greatest evil, peculiar
faith!

However abundantly peculiar faith prevails, what does that profit religion?

Mexico, ay, even England, that is so conspicuous in the world, are surfeited with a state peculiar faith, and present a large class of their population ignorant, and of course superstitious.

With all your peculiar faith, show us an ignorant people, and we must see a superstitious and degraded set of people.

Some countries with state faith do not even tolerate other faiths to any participation of citizenship. Where is the freedom of mind? If, then, peculiar faith produces all these evils, away with all such abuses, that help to crush the world.

· If any wish us to adopt his views and faiths, we must first have the full proof of their worthiness ; God did not give us more than five senses, hence they require proof, else he would have given us a sixth sense, which inspiration of revelation, with its false pretences, affects to supply.

God's works prove him the Creator and Preserver, so that none in their senses can deny them.

The world has been blasted by speculative peculiar faith. It has been seared by its horrid crimes.

When advocates ask the world credence in their faith, without satisfactory reasons for that faith, then they act dishonestly at once, and do an injury all the time to morals, truth, honesty, and purity of mind, the greatest desideratum in the world for both sexes.

If we preserve truth and honesty, we preserve chastity and dignity of human nature.

Are we to take peculiar faith of the Asiatics or Africans, who could not give freemen laws?

The peculiar faith of miracles, prophecies, mysteries and enigmas is an abomination in the sight of God and his religion, a degradation to mind and the human character. But there has been no superstition so absurd, no rites so cruel or barbarous and criminal, no peculiar policy so tyrannical, but that they have, at one time or another, had followers, who carried out successfully for a period the misdirected perversions of mind.

What part of the world has not been beset by superstition? Let us rid the world of it, and man-worship. How? By reason and religion.

By this time intelligent, unprejudiced people must see that it is superstition that still stalks her hour on the stage of life, and ought to be expelled.

All good and true people ought to unite in arresting the downward tendency of morals.

We address those of independence of character, not faces of wax, or people of straw.

The mind of the ignorant mass in all ages is assimilated ; hence it is difficult to eradicate old or new impressions.

We must desire minds enlarged and cultivated, that can protect themselves through God's light and spirit.

What power has peculiar faith with the last, when all such know positively that it has need only of universal religion, which is dignified, as it comes from God?

If the light of any peculiar faith blazed, the blaze was that of fanaticism, not of science, for centuries. Its absolutism flourished on the soil of serfdom, and nations have to undergo a transition state to be rescued. To extirpate heresy to peculiar faith, Francis the First of France issued an order that any person that refused to sign the confessions of faith, should be deprived of all offices, and burnt alive without further trial.

This produced the massacre of the Huguenots of France. The sanguinary persecution of the protestants overran much of Europe.

The design was to exterminate heresy by fire and sword, and to extinguish civil and religious liberty. The dynasty that assumed this prerogative was composed of state and church absolutism, and contained in one felonious mass judges, accusers, prosecutors, witnesses and executioners.

The persecutions of the protestants in Holland were most dreadful. The spirit that prevailed was the malign demon of peculiar faith, for protestants that were persecuted to exile from Europe, in America persecuted a more peaceful sect.

And what saves the world now from the ferocious piracy of this fell and dangerous tyrant? Any church association? That is the very thing, if possessed of power, to play the tyrant. It cannot be trusted one moment, for it is the most dangerous tool of barbarian cruelty and vindictiveness.

There is no virtue in any of it, vile and degraded in corruption and vulgar ignorance as it is.

It is the great evil genius of the world and mind. It mistakes superstition for religion, credulity for faith, and the oracles of priestocracy for the enlightened principles of the Almighty.

Its peculiar notions cause its peculiar god to speak as it chooses. In the sight of its fanaticism, patriotism had no virtue.

What, then, is heresy? It is an error of opinion about religion, not to be corrected short of the science and philosophy of civilization.

Of course, then, those that issued orders for confessions of faith proved themselves exempt from the holiest inspirations of religion in its purity.

Had the dynasty of peculiar faith thus propagated its doctrines, the world had been depopulated.

Where would mankind have been, but for the blaze of science? In the toils of hypocrisy, or the ruin of the world. But peculiar faith has the peculiar assurance and impudence to lay peculiar claims to science! The christian particularly, assumes this peculiar greatness. The state of science depends on the state of mind, and its facilities for civilization. This is the whole solution.

Science, if to be appropriated, is indebted very much to the Pagans, who outshone all, in some things.

The moderns are indebted much to the Roman law. "The equitable doctrine of Salvage, came from the Roman law," says chancellor Kent.

While peculiar faith appropriates all to its peculiar monopoly and usurpation, religion diffuses to the whole world, by its agent, mind, never proscribed, but advanced in all its legitimate civilization.

Where is the evidence of high principles of sound religion, but in the general benefit of the world?

No form of man-worship yields the point, giving the tears and ruin of the world, instead of its blessings.

The functions of the world can create its rightful possession of happiness, that peculiar faith frustrates, mars and degrades.

Religion is to insure the best results of rational education or cultivation of mind, that is to make man useful and happy, and should embrace all expedients necessary.

Who could stop the heresies of Millerism? None that had faith in the bible of tradition. Thus the heresies of faith are proved by rational mind, to be demoralizing. What heresies can arise but from the false positions of peculiar faith, that has disturbed the world for centuries, on this peculiar point? Its numerous votaries are ready to swear on their creed, and yet all would be antagonistical to each other, and to the only basis of God and truth. Numerous Mormons would no doubt swear that Joe Smith has been seen since his death, that he did not die till his time came, though pierced by many bullets. Their position is analogous to that of the Christian. Both are superstitious.

His oracles when consulted, told as Joe Smith spoke or wished. What more could be desired, but an ignorant people in mass to propagate more successfully this peculiar faith?

These are rich scenes for the world, did they not enslave and corrupt it.

How long shall the best interests of the world be sacrificed to peculiar faith?

Is it right or honorable, to put down right by sophistry, the perversion of truth? Is peculiar faith occupation the return for constitutional religion?

Shall the priests' substitutes of peculiar, prevail over universal good?

There is no reason or principle, for peculiar faith.

Over part of the world the voice of usurping absolutism, not of the sovereign people, is heard, and causes all its curses.

The world from paramount interest, is bound to do away with all that can indoctrinate mind in the least corruption, sway or intimidation.

All secret societies and peculiar faith doctrines, fail in promoting the greatest good to the greatest number, which is universal.

The great struggles between peculiar faiths that have enslaved the world, must die out.

On true analysis of mind passing through its gradations of relative ages of cultivation, we are necessarily convinced of the pernicious effects of superstition, engendered in the diversified theatre of natural phenomena. The tumult of natural elements, as the tornado, hurricane, earthquake, volcano and electricity, have excited ignorant ages to regard them, though the agents, for the cause. As science advances, peculiar faith and superstition recede.

How many of the present systems of peculiar faith have been received by the simple, unthinking world, as the very best that could be proposed, all which the world of absolutism, at one time or another, has conspired to impose on the balance, with all devices and pretences! Peculiar faith is an act of sophistry, that misleads mind. But the advocates of peculiar faith affect that they have the only right one, orthodox or true.

The followers of Christ, Mahomet, Moses, Smith, Bhud, &c. affect all this!

Have they any idea of the only true God, who is to be truly adored by the best actions of mind alone?

That is the first thing enlightened mind has to learn, as the Great First Cause, else the school-boy, or the Indians who believe in the Great Spirit, will outstrip it. The names, whether Hebrew or Greek, of Deity, are not material, when all convey the proper idea of the supreme Creator. All minds are naturally compelled to have ideas of religion, crude or enlightened; they should perfect them in the pure mint of mind, unadulterated with any of the sophistries or absolutism of hierarchists.

All the wise and good should separate themselves from this ignoble crowd, and secure pure ideas of God all the time.

What can we expect of any peculiar faith, but the legitimate fruits of deception, fraud and imposition?

Analyze all peculiar faiths, and this is their correct history. The Christian is as deep, in this obnoxious quagmire.

What other is the Roman, but a system of deep and peculiar faith swindling? " Roman catholic divines had argued, in their writings, in favor of equivocation, mental reservations, perjury, and even assassination." Also, says Macauley, "The clergy were the king's worshippers, and the judges his tools." What cannot absolutism do! Charlemagne assigned to the benedictine Alwin the high office of preparing, from the various sources within his reach, a perfect codex of the holy scriptures."

Peculiar faith has been a system of tything, a taxation for false pretences, and the priestocracy have been peculiar brotherhoods in all ages of mind's perversions. We can well say what corruption prevails by union of church and state, in the case of " Charles II., who refused the Eucharist from the hands of the English church, and died a Roman catholic."

The advocates of peculiar faith must not expect us to believe their doctrine, unless they prove the same to universal propriety, an impossibility forever.

The world may well differ about peculiar faith excitements, but if all do not improve religion on right principles, better had they never existed; for assuredly they do injure society in its most vital parts.

Let none stifle inquiry respecting these principles, whether protestant, Roman, or any other.

When they come to see the matter in its true light, they will adopt the position as the deepest interest to mind, and will discard their own. The world will see the right, if not trammeled.

The Jesuit Journal, The Universe, says, " So long as religious unity exists, civil intolerance is the duty of government." Where would have been his peculiar faith, had it not superseded the preceding one of the country?

Plenary indulgences disgrace the Roman hierarchy. What are phylacteries, but part of the superstition and its imposition? All these are the veriest' trifles of mind. The power of the pope can be only upheld by liberal views, tolerated for a time, then go down, as mind marches to its elevation. In principles, mind has something to contend for.

What superstition can be greater, than praying to angels and saints, all priest manufacture?

What corruption can be greater, including the imposition on the people, who are to be preyed upon.

The dominican and franciscan friars before the reformation, were, what the jesuits have been since. They were the most contemptible of all the different orders of the priesthood. The barbarous superstition and ignorance of the multitude, raised them to the supreme state of peculiar faith-influence. " They discovered the most barbarous aversion to the arts and sciences."

The idea that converts to the creed of peculiar faith being competent to decide on its validity for the world's recognition, because they profess such faith, and are members of some church, is too absurd to be entertained.

Do they actually know the definition of religion?

Most do not know the difference between peculiar faith and religion! You affect much merit by songs of praise and thanks. But you pay them in words to a mixed Deity.

Your prayers, as fervent as peculiar faith-devotion can make them, are not paid to the right source.

All are best evinced in actions, and those are due to the God of nature, the Almighty alone.

Your grace before meat, and for the reception of all blessings, can also be expressed louder and more effectually than words, by your actions rightly addressed.

But of what use are prayers for the dead?

Appropriate burial service should be performed by a civil commission, that the living may be benefited, and act rightly, and that relations may do proper justice to their feelings, the rights of humanity, and the proper obligations of civilization.

What avails peculiar faith-phrenzy, but to aggravate her world-wrongs? What can devotees do for the world-blessings that they altogether contravene?

What authority has any king or potentate to assume the title of defender of the faith, catholic majesty, any more than the popes, who assumed to depose kings from their crowns? All these are the tricks of church and state absolutism, to cement a lasting influence.

What piety have any of these superior over the world?

All the laws of psychology and physiology, allow of no infallibility to any mortal. There is no fatalism that has given it, as that does not exist.

Libations were superstitious rites.

It will not do for the moderns to claim any prerogatives for their peculiar faith over any kind of ancient superstition, all of which must succumb to universal principles and their Supreme Creator.

Mind proves before any proper tribunal its own agency and superiority.

After all, peculiar faith has nothing to boast of.

So great was the light shed by the minds of Socrates and Plato, that the first fathers of the christian church, praised them both in some measure as christians.

In what did they, and Origen, the greatest of the christian fathers differ, when he believed in the transmigration of souls?

What has degraded the best institutions of mind but its perversions, and which of these can be worse than those of peculiar faith?

"The most fatal wound of all to the Swiss League" was contention about peculiar faith.

For this, for a long time, they had civil wars.

The disturbances in India have been the worst, from the different orders of Brahmins and Bhuddists.

Nothing can protect nationality and humanity, when lawless, reckless, and faithless pretences of national peculiar faith prevail.

Instead of the ruins of empires, and the destruction of mighty cities, brought about by peculiar faith, and recklessness of principles, religion causes mind to rear its mighty empire over the globe, on permanent conservative principles.

There can be no pure religion in peculiar faith by the nature of things. But smart people, professors of peculiar faith, affect that they certainly know.

Yet how can they, as they have not investigated, nor can they know the whole circle of history and science?

They cannot know intuitively, as that is impossible, therefore they must prove their position, especially messiahship, satisfactory, otherwise they are cut off from any foundation, and their mouths are effectually closed. But what tenable proof can they adduce, after deserting reason for faith?

But converts rely on hearsay, which comes from interested and ignorant partisans whose oath could not be valid as interested.

The errors of peculiar faith are hard to be divested of.

Even Napoleon had his astrological superstition, and spoke of the star of his peculiar destiny.

Numa, the great law-giver of Rome, affected to have sybilline books, to impose on the people whom the cunning world has always treated with contemptible imposition when impunity was practicable.

This has been the door, for all kinds of peculiar tyranny. How much were the poor ignorant barbarians of ancient times imposed on by the necromancers, who pretended to learn of the dead?

Peculiar faith presents no genuine diamond or crystal, nor similar ring. Good citizens, should have no counterfeit or any such means, for agitation of the world.

All this doctrine is supported by special pleadings, sophistry, mental reservations, and the deepest pious frauds. What infamy!

Peculiar faith only advances the pretences of superstition, whose doctrines must be utterly exploded by rational religion that tolerates no messiah. She has no history.

The supposed history of peculiar faith, is a peculiar story—it is one of persecutions.

The one that is persecuted by other species of superstition, uses persecution in return.

It has the nature of the beast, never to be regenerated. A perfect hyena, it persecutes mind, its very power, and robs God whom it has always blasphemed. Peculiar faith has fought in various ways for thousands of years, with peculiar weapons of faith!

What intelligent freeman is not ashamed to have peculiar faith, that should be left to the serfs of absolutism and superstition?

Reason is rejected only by the ignorant, or by fools and knaves. Some may estimate that if peculiar faith do no good, that it can do no harm. But do we truly estimate the invaluable loss of time, the perversion of habits and vices for virtues, the future enslavement of our passions and superstitious fears? Philosophy has ever been attacked by the false pretences of sophistry and peculiar faith, the enemy of mankind and its highest right. The story of miracles is a pretended appeal to facts, and must be analyzed by philosophy that alone analyzes truth, to analyze the nature of things.

Philosophy ever discards the phantoms of peculiar faith. Every system of peculiar faith is a libel on God, and an imposition on mind. Do we undertake philosophy that only deals in facts of reason with mere faith, or does it not result in experience and observation through the senses by ratiocination?

Advantages will be taken in faith if yielded, forever.

All peculiar faith people are bigots and egotists, of most unjust character. Sectarians! whom can you blame for opposing peculiar faith, that is sectarianism in general, yours included, when you attack all others, to protect your own? We attack all on principles, you act for self-interest. You have to be silent, or self-condemned. There can be no greater humbug than that of peculiar faith, that is dangerous and oppressive to the world, which knows so little of it in all its insidiousness.

Peculiar faith disorganizes society and the world.

She gives curses where she dispenses supposed blessings. Parasites, flatterers, and retainers, may descant on this topic, but all the merit is unequivocally due the real and intrinsic character of God's boons.

It is on his capital that all the effect is produced.

His are the magnificent institutions and prerogatives, the duty is mind's.

What peculiar grace has peculiar faith of any kind imparted to the world, that she should find peculiar favor in its sight?

The rites and ceremonies of peculiar faith are bad, oppressive and tyrannizing to the citizens of the world.

What liberality has sectarianism, that thinks all others have not as good a faith, as they have not its faith? Sectarianism cannot decide, as it does not stand at the right point, but must transcend or fall below it.

None but the right standard can give mind the qualification of right judgment.

Peculiar faith is the result of dark and benighted ages of absolutism and priest imposition, whereas rational religion is that of rationally cultivated minds, elevated to and ennobled by the best blessings of civilization in all its glorious and pure excellency.

We permit no short sighted polic of peculiar faith, that follows a master of absolutism, receives the dictation of sects, adheres to creeds of opinions, but violates the principles of rational religion.

Any persons may change from peculiar faith, from the Roman to the protestant, or from either to the Mahometan, but no rational mind can leave rational religion, the God-gift.

Who desires to know all the vices of peculiar faith? This reflects from its corruption, all the superstition and bigotry of ages thus darkened over the world. It is she that presents all messiahships, and those in antagonism with the great laws of nature. Principles cannot be excluded by peculiar faith, no more than the Creator by messiahships.

But how can peculiar faiths be the policy of any, presuming on their potency? Do they blindly mislead themselves, without knowing where their own dogmas actually lead them? Peculiar and easy faith arose in an age of darkness and superstition, and has never been eradicated.

"Mahomet, who lived in the sixth century, considers Christians in the light of infidels and idolators throughout the koran; and, indeed, had not Christians worshipped Christ, he could have had no shadow of a pretence to reform their religion, and to bring them back to the worship of one God."

Can the world begin to appreciate the amount and extent of persecutions for peculiar faith in the world? Barocaba, who pretended to be messiah, murdered heathens and Christians. In Christian countries there have been persecutions to murders without mercy. In France, multitudes of Jews were burnt.

In Germany multitudes of them were murdered by the myrmidons of the eight crusades.

In Persia, the Tartars murdered multitudes of the Jews. Neither paganism nor polytheism is extinct in the world of peculiar faith, that invades the sacred precincts of civil liberty, conscience and philanthropy. Will you stand by, citizen, patriot, and not aid the exigencies of the world in this essential matter? Some people have no sincerity, as their minds have become perverted; they are thankless as they have no gratitude.

Can all these cultivate the right spirit in the empire of peculiar faith? How will they compass such impracticabilities?

But you cleave to your faith? Of course you found it upon the bible? Now, certainly, you must unmistakably prove the last, to be honest and truthful in your consistency. What are the proofs of your bible, as to its authenticity? You do not know, nor do all your ignorant misleaders! It is astonishing to find how few do know this, as priests cannot know or prove it!

Are you betrayed to the loss of the genuine for the counterfeit, throwing away your soul-gifts for the shadow, what you can never reach?

Are you thus caught so stupidly, when so shrewd in business and life transactions otherwise? Do you cheat yourself, or do you permit others to do it, which amounts to the same thing?

The false position of peculiar faith is always apparent on proper analysis.

On the fragments of peculiar faith arise the splendor and magnificence of rational religion.

At her dawn presided science and philosophy.

Patients are often harassed, are deranged at times, about peculiar faith. For God's sake, let the world and souls be in peace. There is no peace in peculiar faith, that has no brains, intelligence, or magnanimity.

The miserable patients who are disturbed at death, wishing for a faith, should be gratified, but enlightened too. Not only ought ministers, who come to advise, have purity of morals above reproach, but intellectual correctness too; above all other things they ought to tell the truth about the authenticity of their gospels, which, if candid, they are obliged to say cannot be done, as they are not authentic. Are freemen slaves to peculiar faith? Is that so? There has been war upon Jewry for eighteen centuries nearly, by the children that came from its womb.—How parricidal is peculiar faith, when anything opposes her selfish interest. She is created in the froth of sectarianism, and is equally meretricious as her prototype in fiction.

Where is the end of all these things? One superstitious wave succeeds another. The Mormons have created theirs. Every new system does the same. The motives are all similar, never can be vastly different.

Is there no money nor speculation in all this matter? There is hardly anything else when all seek power.

Allow all the motives that prompt, and take away those that are not in the secret, who suppose good faith all the time, and the balance is nothing but blasphemous corruption forever.

Peculiar faith will do for scary children, hysterical females, imbecile men, cunning priestocracies, and despotic autocrats, that rule the world by a devil, a very pious and religious duty! Peculiar faith is inseparable from sectarianism; both are identified.

But the world must have faith. Is that a particle of virtue? Is there one particle of virtue in peculiar faith? Is not faith a necessary result of investigation, and only in proportion to the facts of the case?

The sectarianism of peculiar faith keeps the world apart, and thereby clearly proves its peculiar vices. All peculiar systems of faith are imperfect from the essential nature of the materials: now mind needs a perfect system, that mind may invoke as religion —the model system of religion. The same peculiar faith that gives a devil also gives a messiah, proxies of priestocracies, all anti-god. Peculiar faith corrupts all communities. What a blood-thirsty tyrant is peculiar faith. Such mere faith stultifies its followers, blinds their senses, and brutalizes their nature.

Sophistry of peculiar faith, thou hast no limit; as envy, thou hast no dignity. The system of electioneering against all principles for reasons of their temporal popularity, when it was to their disgraceful advantage, show the extreme length that peculiar faith goes. Who can doubt of the false pretences of peculiar faith? The very position implies the most blasphemous falsehoods. How can you expect less than millions of lies and liars to sustain it all over the world. Peculiar faith sides in argument just as it suits self-interest. Do we respect truth or justice when we speak of peculiar faith as a faith? Who has the orthodox, the infallible, of all such? Can its corrupt elements beget any such?

Judaism and Christianity are the parents of Mormonism, as well as of Mahometanism. Which, then, is most sinful? They are all peculiar faith, which is only modified more or less in each. If Mormonism be a corrupt daughter, Christianity is a corrupt mother, as Judaism is a corrupt grandmother.

As peculiar faith advances, so does a hypocritical age, then rational religion recedes. It is a false position to refuse to get out of your heresies of untruth and bigotry.

If you wish the world further humbugged, let the mass still be vassal to any demagogue. In all kinds of government they have but to continue this thing of peculiar faith. When the leaders are influenced by sinister motives, blindly selfish, the balance can be easily found. Which is peculiar faith worse in, impudence or ignorance?' What gives tendency to scandal and libel more than this position?

Is peculiar faith never to end her impious evils, and rational religion never to begin her illustrious, godly blessings?

Shall mind be subject in any respect to the odious vassalage of any peculiar faith, the peculiar tyrant of the world? Shall property be confiscated, and persons be excommunicated. Shall both be subject to violence? None of peculiar faith-men ever conceived properly of God : it is utterly impossible. All this pulpit peculiar faith is exparte, one-sided, giving suppressed statements or one-sided sophisticated, and filled with a thousand delusions. Reason and rational mind can rear the proper standard.

Where can we get a rational discussion of religion by peculiar faith-people? All peculiar faith derives all its honor and respectability, from mind, that makes it what it is. Peculiar faith was to rule the ignorance of the world, to secure all power-influence, pretending that society only could exist but by fears of future punishment, and yet the world is overrun by these very nations, claiming to be elite or select, in piracies, martial and naval murders, and robberies. It is impossible to civilize the world by peculiar faith, that has not its first elements—a universal brotherhood!

We may cherish the best feelings to all the citizens of the world, as part of God's creation, but not for any of their peculiar errors, among which is one of the greatest, peculiar faith.

The christian innovation was once to the Jews, what now the Mormon faith is to the christians. What is wanting to the last power? What is wanting to all peculiar faith? Truth. An affiliated is not debarred from giving testimony, but then he, and all the world, cannot establish one pretended miracle.

Peculiar faith has devils ; rational religion has none.

The bible of peculiar faith unites prejudices, passion, credulity, sophistry and superstition, to overwhelm the human mind, and involve all mankind in its ruin. With all your toleration of peculiar faith, your Mormon would or could not live in peace among christians. Wars have arisen between them.

This proves most conclusively how delusive and dangerous is any peculiar faith : behold the snake is not killed, it is only scotched. If the Mormons be a dangerous people that seek a vindictive retributive justice, for the deep wrong due them, how much more so is the peculiar faith that originates all the tribes?

The great danger is, that too much of the world will have too low views of duty and action through peculiar faith. Their acts are grovelling—undermining against their neighbors, seeking advantages. But this you may affect is not so. But how did you treat the Mormons? Oh! that alters the case. Did not the Pagans treat your ancestors thus intolerantly ; besides, you set the Mormons an example to plagiarize a peculiar faith.

Why so many sects in faith, and so many systems of faith in direct collision and antagonism?

There is but one religion most certainly. There cannot be any two principles clashing—nor any two faiths—for assuredly, all are false that have the elements of antagonism. All peculiar faiths, christian particularly, as well as the Mahometan, are in antagonism to religion.

It is the paramount duty of the enlightened religionist to denounce all false faiths as false positions.

But the cause of sympathy, is that of some of these peculiar systems. All do not weigh one straw before the rights and dignity of mind, the true beneficiary which has been crushed by them for thousands of years!

Peculiar faith advocates pretend, that they have investigated the whole subject of religion. Have they touched the first position, the supreme obligation to the Supreme? Are they disinterested enough to do justice to this subject?

But then the feelings of wives and families are to be consulted in faith. The right position is paramount with wives, children and family, and that is only rational faith. Any other is a curse to the whole country. We congratulate ourselves in the due investigation of this subject, and that reason is on the Lord's side, and can only see this as the safe side.

We seek to live and die in this the true faith, as confirmed converts, exempt from skepticism. Those who advocate peculiar faith can only be the veriest skeptics.

If we sided with priestocracies that conspired against God, as atheists or polytheists, trinitarians, unitarians, or luke-warm optimists, we should feel that he was against us in the end as well as all the time.

Do you expect virtue, &c., in a people wedded to peculiar faith and its tenets? In the best and fairest portions of the globe, peculiar faith, its education and dogmas, poison up the blessings of life. Most of the world will go it blind for peculiar faith. They will swear white is black, if expedient. Exemption from all peculiar faith will add dignity and grandeur of dignity to the world. Mind has been falsely, treacherously brought up to yield the question of peculiar faith hitherto, bound to the car of superstition. Has a fanatic, bigot, any reason about him in peculiar faith? Conscious of extreme weakness, he becomes a decided despot of humbug, and throws himself on the dignity of toleration—if he cannot repel all such by vindictiveness. What wanton felony. What train-band mind and society-spoilen victimizers!

So sectarian are some village schools, that even ladies of the same town hardly give to each other the street. This is civilization, with a vengeance!

Joe Smith found, it is asserted, his golden plates in New York; Moses found his stone tables at Mt. Sinai. Which has the best claim for truth? Neither. One has the oldest lies. That old bible, for which sophists and autocrats battle, is a fine example for freemen to seek. Of course it is right, is it, for freemen to copy after all such? Is the world to adopt the word of bigots, the most odious reptiles? Are they not the thousands of harpies preying on society, having but little unison of interest?

What a position of the world, that much of it is priestocracy, a fraud or deception on the world by peculiar faith!

The main question arises, is it done knowingly?

The true analysis of the world's position is not yet fully written. The peculiar faiths are cut-throat to each other; while rational religion is happy to be defeated of her errors by rationality. Even now the world is so soft and verdant as to believe as told. This is the effect of peculiar faith, called Faith. Ignorant of the earth, they are ignorant of spirits and angels who they assume are its visitors.

Do you believe in haunts, they inquire? We do, in those of guilty conscience. But in spirits, ghosts? They have something else to do than abide in that capacity. Their functions commence in other departments as soon as changed by death.

Rule superstition to proper obedience, and science makes her the noblest mind-agent.

Know and think of the differences between religion and peculiar faith. Can the last be honorably adhered to, while so far from backing out as in pure love, all must get stronger inclined in the true faith, with which all the advocates will identify themselves, it being the nation's interest, the world's glory, and all that is needed is the proper opportunity of securing the world through mind's civilization.

What rational man will refuse to display his mind's greatness and purity? Let us not have the dynasty of peculiar faith—it is the scourge of the world, the mind, spirit, the soul. What an impotent, imbecile state of non-resistance does the thoughtless world oppose to the unreasonable pretences and tyranny of peculiar faith. Can any rational beings be opposed to the true exposition of the baseness of this faith, when they ought to be most thankful for doing so?

Peculiar faith is ashamed to let go at once, as she would be exposed in her deformity.

It seems that the whole system of peculiar faith has been wrought out very cunningly, but not usefully, as all its elements are perishable.

False faiths are little hells of little minds that propagate or adopt them.

Is there any faith that is peculiar too absurd for the deluded mind of fanatics? There are even the devil-worshippers in the East. The whole idea of demonology is monstrous, as displayed in the bible, one of the greatest libels on Deity, as to their possession of human souls over God! How monstrous, absurd, ridiculous, miserable, mean and degrading to rational mind!

Evil beings, living in human bodies! As good as the origin of the conception of messiahs! All utterly at variance with the first principles of physiology and pure morals. Let not your prejudices intervene between the twilight of science and bigotry.

But the idea of the devil is figurative. But as to that of legion, that was a spirit, of course not figurative. There can be no halting between two opinions, for here is the most marked decision.

Christianity is only peculiar faith, with less alloy than some other counterfeits. Peculiar faith is a stupid, sottish superstition. How demoralizing are peculiar faith and its bibles! They propagate the falsehoods about demonology, ghosts, spirits, with craft and all the heinous tribe of superstition. But, if you explain by figuration, the expounders assume the exclusive right, and then you are told to take hold of the real substance, and if you seize that, they refer you to figuration. Why not drop such a rotten system of sophistry and superstition, that cannot protect its friends, and cannot longer deceive the candid world? Better for the whole world that it had never seen peculiar faith in any form, as billions have been injured most deeply by it.

The real existence of angels, good and bad, is one part of the bible machinery. If it be the bible and not mind that directs, how is it that you affect figuration?

Some construe, as the universalists, as figures; you deny them. Large parts of Asia, as south Asia, are devil worshippers, the slaves of priestocracy.

Under this dynasty of faith, what little of the world is worthy of the real light of rational mind?

How many millions commit themselves, even to perjury, to oppose mind's innovations, as adverse to their peculiar interests and faith! How many believe in evil spirits! A trial for bewitching was held in Alabama not many years ago, in a Christian council, I am informed by a pastor of a church! What but the bible originated, and the priestocracy uphold it? Mind arrested the burning, of course.

One nation has conquered another, and what love is there yet established on any peculiar faith? But all peculiar faith is suspicious, as it is, and cannot be true: it is false security by a false position. Of how many is the lifetime spent, without any peculiar faith! Where was the pure faith all the time, but with them, more or less?

But what can we do against the world's peculiar faiths? If you aid, you break the charm of improper teaching. The noisy are to be rebuked, by rights of the world.

Does bigotry ever forgive opposition?

But few sectarians contend for truth, they are after their own wordy victory. What needs the world of any peculiar faith, that, on analysis, it must be fully satisfied, is not only of no benefit, but a positive evil and injury?

I have been particular about Hindoo faith, as incompetent as any, that though the world be full, still it is of no avail. But they all do evil, and dangerous powers should be counteracted. Why attack all peculiar faith?

Because they have assailed the rights of mind, depriving it of all its best principles. Analysis will tell that the propagation of doctrines has not depended so much on rational as interested views, that may reflect the profits. The pecuniary emoluments are to be considered, in the peculiar faith expenditures. What else can be expected? If you have money to expend, it is well.

In opposing peculiar faith, I am only doing what every patriot would do if he could. The taxes of the people should be appropriated for their benefit, not forced, for the curses of peculiar faith. Suppose that all peculiar faith people were to carry out all their peculiarities, what sort of a peculiar world should we have?

The Bhuddists avoid contact with the Christians, and cook exclusively to themselves. Names are nothing in peculiar faith, whether quaker or Bhuddist, all are bigots, in which character they all unite!

All is contingent by peculiar bibles, that the world may never know; but God's documents cannot be hid, as his works prove. These are facts outweighing all bible rhetoric, addressed to the five senses of every rational mind. But the peculiar god speaks and hears, as the peculiar caste says! Sectarians, if not hostile, are antagonistical to each other. There is no orthodox opinion about reforms from absolutisms.

If religion was not the mistress of peculiar faith, the last, would master the world. Peculiar faith is a libel on religion, as is christianity. Peculiar faith brutalizes all that it touches and sticks to; it contracts the bigot to the fanatic, and him to the brute, and changes all so that its best friends cannot finally know them, if subject to its comprehensive influence. What can be worse than the priestocracy, that uses this means against the world?

What is the state of rational discussion now? Is it not proscription by the priestocracy? Is not the exclusion of the bible circle brought to bear? Is there not evasion of friendship, and direct hostility? Is this a proper position in society, free and intelligent? The peculiar bible opposer is an infidel! What is an infidel? It is an unfaithful being. To whom? He cannot be to God, whom he reverences. But he is to the messiah! That he should be, otherwise he would be an infidel to God. All that sustain robbery of God are infidels. This is the true position when true advocates impeach infidelity, for the whole must be comprehended to reach the right basis.

Peculiar faith doctrinists can be bitter, but it is not the bitterness of proof, but of blackguardism on mere assertion.

Infidelity is robbery all the time to the unity of God.

What are all the pretensions of cliques but resting on this unprincipled position, that authorizes the sincere belief that millions of perjuries could be perpetrated for peculiar faith in the world; for what member or advocate would not swear to it? And yet all would perjure themselves. Does not the professor appropriate much of his lectures to all the sophistry of his faith?

Cowards, hypocrites, and robbers of society oppose rational religion, and are loth to say aught against peculiar faith, as it is in the ascendant! We could forgive them if they could not analyze the truth. Peculiar faith could not last the attack of mind one Sunday if the world would do its duty. Peculiar faith peculiarizes its each individual interest. Now the world is after its own self-interest.

How can you give us liberty in every sense of the word, whilst you are under the iron fetters of peculiar faith?

The paramount good of society of the world absolutely requires that no dynasty impose its peculiar faith on the same. Peculiar faith causes even individuals, let alone nations, to estimate themselves peculiarly endowed. Peculiar faith has corrupted the world of mind about ten to one hundred fold worse than it would have been without it! The perverted world will not fight you honorably; it has no principles, only peculiar ways, faith, and action. What if the chief or archangels were in the seventh or best heaven if sin get in, and angels there become devils? We cannot help your having adopted peculiar faith; that may be your misfortune when not your fault; but the time may have arrived when it may be your fault and not your misfortune.

The dogmas of peculiar faith prove no orthodox faith, much less religion. How much time is fruitlessly spent by peculiar faith in plotting against the balance of the world, in every disgusting way! What is peculiar faith as regards God, the universal Creator? An unprincipled opposition, the veriest humbug! Think of that, ye conscience-men.

Among fanatic enthusiasts we have the Swedenborgians, who believe in revelation to Swedenborg. Are they not as true as all others, as Mormons, &c.?

While we reject peculiar faith altogether, we seek to cultivate what is rational. The peculiar faith dogmas and dynasties, with all their machinery, are contradictory of each other and themselves. They have the basest intention of fraud.

But why not let peculiar faith prevail? No convict or culprit should in this world, that requires religion.

Such faith is counterfeit and has all its curses. Let this humbug, as dead, be buried. It is for the people to have it interred. The bias of sophistry of peculiar faith warps the mind sadly. As to martyrdom, what is not due to antagonism of other peculiar faiths, that without exception, are despotic with powers. One peculiar faith is as good as another, till exploded. What can one individual do in a corrupt society, that will libel and sophisticate? How is the world to be rightly benefited?

By discarding not only all errors, but all oceans of errors, no matter how estimated from the cobwebs of antiquity. Did we come out to satisfy peculiar faith-people or truth? Mind has no innate ideas, but impressions through the senses; ought they not to be correct?

What can be worse than the materialism, the depravity of mind. The infidelity, the skepticism of peculiar faith? What can be more savage than peculiar faith, that fights all other sectarians, and the true and only faith?

Her parricidal character is degradingly odious and vicious.

All peculiar faiths clash, thus proving their position wrong. No peculiar faith can establish its position, with all its peculiar characteristics.

The very idea of peculiar faith expresses the elements of peculiar views, that are false to universal principles of God. How could they be established but on false pretences, violations of truth and reason, alias miracles, prophecies and mysteries, but sophisticated visions of the same thing. 'Tis needless to say, that we cannot take cognizance of the acts of our own mind; suffice it to say, that we know enough of the partial operations, to fully carry them out in good faith. The ancients interdicted examination into first principles, and required, as now do the advocates of peculiar faith, to have them taken for granted.

By this course, we only have less degrees of superstition, arising from the elevation of mind, not being untrammeled. Well may it be said, reformers correct yourselves, as well Hebrews, as christians, all are in the same category. Peculiar faith has peculiar sophistry.

There can be millions of systems about peculiar faith and its miracles, all analogous in falsity, but there can be but one right system of religion, that duly estimates the God of truth and honesty, whom no nation has ever yet recognised. The system of Judaism revealed innumerable untruths about their peculiar god, with their priests, prophets, and pretended miracles.

Let us give proper credit for all conscientious members of any peculiar faith-association. God takes the will for the deed. A world-wide evil is peculiar faith.

People set out in life, determined to be sophists, not to be convinced. How often does society invoke all its perversion to defraud itself of its own rights.

· 23

Society is now made up of sects, clans, and secret clubs, all having influence, good or malign, the worse, as it is more peculiar.

All good citizens must eschew all the sub-electioneering of society against universal brotherhood.

All peculiar faith-labor is lost; it ever begins, never ends, forces, but does not satisfy. Of all corruptions, in this corruptible world, corrupt peculiar faith ousts all.

What are all the Robespierres, all the wild, reckless, fanatic bedlamites of tyranny, in all ways, the enemies of their race, stupid in crime, their minds perverted by peculiar faith and education, and crushed into all the degradations of brutes to the advocates of peculiar faith. Do they not recognise their brethren? Are they so stupid as to deny their analogy?

How many thousands of years has mind been extricating itself from the wiry-serpent-folds of priestocracy and polytheism? The polytheists made their devil of course, that they had of the devil-worshippers, a suspicious pedigree. Next to an idiot, a maniac, an atheist, a polytheist, save us from faith-bigots.

All are sectarians that are not rational religionists, and the fact that Christ was necessarily sectarian, conclusively proves him mortal. The proof of sectarianism is self-evident. What can we expect of the world about peculiar faith, when its bigotry has no justice, and it would cut each others' throats, but for the civilization of mind. What war has peculiar faith stayed? What, rather, has it not excited? The government of the universe, this world included, is in fact, and right, in the Creator of mind. Some see interminable difficulties among various sects, but see no end. Where is the remedy?

In rational religion, universal brotherhood, that look to one God. The knowing any depravity and adopting it, is a bad state of sin. How comes it that the people do not know better. It is the most difficult thing, to reach the right analysis of a world-wide subject. Isolated points of material importance are known by thousands, but the fewest know the whole connection. Peculiar faith leads to so much worldly deception practiced, till habit is confirmed to a dangerous position. While some faiths are better than others, what are all peculiar faiths worth? They primarily transgress the chiefest points in usurpation of divine rights. The priestocracy mislead the people, who willingly submit to their degraded dictation.

Skepticism and infidelity should only apply to atheism and polytheism; peculiar faith is irrational.

Strange how much reckless fatuity prevails about peculiar faith, and the treacherous desertion of mind that cannot be superseded. Bring back all, to this point. The only difference is, that some peculiar faiths cannot conceal their baseness as long as others, nor any from God. All are robberies of God. One foolish goes after another, as mind advances. If mind did not advance, these would increase.

But what avail missions of peculiar faith? Look at the contingencies of missions, how much time is lost in learning language, laws, superseding and quarreling with other peculiar faiths.

It is thought by some that the author of Swedenborgianism scarcely had sound mind, as he professed to enjoy open intercourse with the world of departed spirits. He is said to hold that there is a trinity, and yet denies its personality. All peculiar faith presents dreamy delusions: all are visionary, gratuitous. The laws of Sweden are said to be that " Every individual leaving the national church to enter another communion, was liable to lose his property, and even to be banished from the kingdom." This is a Protestant country. Peculiar faith was always the great aid to absolute ancient or modern governments. No faith was worth anything, that did not aid government. The ancients sought peculiar faith as capital, and is this vulgar gewgaw any the less avoided by the moderns? What can furnish worse morals? But you mention the glorious triumphs of faith at the last sad close of life. Why should this change be sad? It is the harbinger of another brighter birth, into a more glorious immortality, the more illustrious as the soul recognises the exclusive unity of a perfectly pure Creator. This attends the most rational consideration of this paramount subject. But as to any other idea, can there be any greater bursts of enthusiasm than those of the Juggernaut, who voluntarily victimizes himself under the wheels of the car of his peculiar god? All such as the last is fanaticism, but the first, the only true effusion of religion, exalts its position. With what peculiar facility can peculiar doctrines of made bibles be propagated, mormonism is proof. It is sectarianize now, not originate, except among the ignorant class that stupidly never inquire into the proof of the position. They overlook this, for want of proper cultivation of mind.

The code of peculiar faith is that of the equivocator. Peculiar faith says to its equals, parents or closest relations, ye all are infidels, that is outlaws.

With the proper use of their mental faculties, they cannot be more vassal, to audit such libels.

All peculiar faiths are peculiar powers, a part of usurpation of absolutism, nothing less; is this expedient to make people better?

Peculiar faith always has mysteries as a part of its humbugs. Peculiar faith is a tyranny over mind, and is handed down as the perpetual constant tyranny of superstition and sophistry. It is forgery and a counterfeit; it is no hand jugglery, but the jugglery of mind, that pays by a dash of the pen, millions. It is wholesale and retail, a perpetuity. But it is cruel to dispossess one of even a crystal, unless you can give him a diamond. Yes, we invoke the diamond of pure religion. Destructive must be superseded by conservative principles, that revolve in religion.

Let not the people sacrifice their independence of mind and morals, when they hold the treasures of both.

Religion knows no difference between Jew and Gentile, she eschews sectarianism, and points to the unity of God. All peculiar faith is declared by man, but this is not what reason and mind need and tolerate.

Why is there infidelity? Your peculir faith is in part responsible therefor. What an outrage on the world, to make peculiar faith an inquisitorial power.

Peculiar faith may talk all it chooses about love to members of each, but the part is not practicable nor beneficial. "The Hindoo and Musselman population in the city Majeeruab, had risen against each other, under the influence of religious fanaticism, and the city was destroyed by fire." The Christian had at last subdued both, and was master. Peculiar faith offers all felonious false pretences.

What is peculiar faith knight-errantry worth?

Great is the Diana of all peculiar faiths.

What greater evils are perpetrated on the world, than those originated by peculiar faith? Sectarianism sees no merit. But each has its own elect! Who are they? The egotists. Has not peculiar faith had something to do with every ancient war? Has it not compelled man to look on his brother as an alien, an enemy? With the world any one especial faith is orthodox, infallible, christian or civilized, whilst all the others are those of minds at enmity against God, that is their peculiar God, as they are heathen, naturally pagan outside barbarians. All peculiar faith doctrines are a desecration to God. Peculiar faith people value themselves on feelings, excited by enthusiasm. What else is it. What value is it, if this be no foundation for messiahship. The works of peculiar faith must introduce evils, because it mistakes principles. The very position means an impossibility: when faith is to supersede reason, then the fabric of virtue goes to death. Peculiar faith never can find the true God. True principles are libeled by the professors.

Seeing that you cannot attain purity of faith your way, will you deny the only practicable one because different with yours? You ought to help remedy the defects of that advanced on proper principles, not advance the defective system however adroit its sophistry.

Reason must-obviate the poison of peculiar faith.

Much has been said of infidelity, but what can be said fair for peculiar faith? Rational religion asserts the only claim to good faith, no other can.

Peculiar faith of the world is no where; it is an imposition, humbug. Where the most power is invoked, there the most vitiation of it arises.

Peculiar faith antagonizes the feelings and interests, rends them asunder from that God that joined them together in the holy wedlock of one universal brotherhood.

Let's be done with all this folly and crime.

All sectarianism, all peculiar faiths, stand in the way of constitutional liberty, one of the great elements to its injury. The diversity of opinion may be honestly entertained on both sides, but both cannot be right. What sort of morality do moralists use adverse to reason, proper sense, justice, honor and truth? One form of peculiar faith is only preferable to another, as the least of two evils. Christianity, Mormonism, are all superstitious evils and crimes.

No custom, plan, or design should restrict the world, to any set of peculiar faith dogmas.

The popular sovereignty of this world must decide this paramount question, and to do so let it be presented in all proper light. Peculiar faith tyranny has convulsed the world. There can be no national or church peculiar faith. But what shall we do for some peculiar system? True rational religion will do all that is needed—all that can be permitted by the Almighty.

Who wishes to see society cut up into clans, cliques, vassals, as it will necessarily be by peculiar faith that degrades and embroils it? Let us give a world-wide protection against peculiar faith, peculiar power, peculiar dynasty, peculiar humbuggery, to deny which a man's face must have a shield not only thicker than a rhinoceros' hide, but even than Homer's Achilles' shield.

What is the revelation of John, but a gross priestocracy compound of deepest ignorance assuming mystery, making beasts of the heavenly host, rather a beast of himself?

If he had said that he saw an animal there that should have had long ears, then he would have spoken the truth for once as an ass. He is true to his vocation. Ch. v. 8, And when he had taken the book, the four beasts and four and twenty elders fell down before the lamb, having every one of them harps, and golden vials full of odors, which are the prayers of saints !!! The priestocracy sticks out in everything.

The saints! Who are they? Can mortals declare them?

This was the heaven of the peculiar god, and this peculiar man saw it! Ch. vi. 10. And they cried with a loud voice, saying, How long, O Lord, holy and true, dost thou not judge and avenge our blood on them that dwell on earth? Well, and who are these they, that cried? 9. The souls of them that were slain for the word of God, and for the testimony which he held! What vindictiveness in heaven—another worse state, than when the devil fell. This was the second sin there. And what did all John's sights amount to at last, but a monomaniacal rhapsody? 13. And the stars of heaven fell unto the earth! Inspiration teaches exact representation ; now, John, a school-boy can correct you, though you saw all this in heaven. 14. And the heaven departed as a scroll when it is rolled together. Worse, John, your visit, revelations and inspirations, betray you as the greatest ignoramus of all monkish pedants. O John, you lied too bad! John, you mistook the scroll for a host of starry orbs in boundless ether. Your vision was visionary.

Ch. xii. 7. And there was war in heaven : Michael and his angels fought against the dragon. 9. And the great dragon was cast out. Worse and worse. The object is to fix the host in heaven, of those claimed to be saints on earth. 4. And his tail drew the third part of the stars of heaven, and did cast them to the earth! Now, if any one will affirm that the scriptures are true, we will give him up as a hopeless bigot.

But some may pretend that this is all metaphor. Then, why employ the world about such silly metaphor as the bible?

All peculiar faiths have peculiar country or people, god of course, privileges, laws that are tyranny, surely. The gods were part of the strength of the country ; their name was to strike terror into the opposition, to create panic. There was great hatred among the ancient nations, Egyptians—Jews, about their gods.

The Egyptians had implacable wars, about their gods and peculiar faith.

All this matter wants a start, to put down peculiar faith. Its advocates use no argument that is rational to support it. The Jews were shepherds and had to leave Egypt, the hot-bed of priestocracy, under the guidance of priests, governing them by a code of their regime. There is a delusive charm in all peculiar faiths, among the ignorant. The object should be to get rid of all, as mind advances, and then the universal rational faith religion triumphs.

What enmity of sectarianism is there, whether Christian, Mahometan, Jew, or Mormon.

All peculiar faiths are impositions. Who can be saved by peculiar faith that speaks : are not all lost so far as that is concerned? Peculiar faith claims to be heart-faith, all that we can know is mind-faith, that results from honest conviction of mind. All peculiar faith has been devised by priestocracies. It is unnatural to man, and can only be propagated by devices and force. Though the world is full of peculiar faith and superstition, there is but one religion ; there can be no other. What if the world has been wrong in its faith. It should drop it, if proved satisfactorily to be spurious, not adhere to it like a bigot if wrong, to make inconsistency apparently consistent.

Be not self-deceived. All peculiar is superstitious faith, and so far as it has its self-right, it is only that much of mind.

It is impossible for any peculiar faith, Christian, or any, to be universal. It has not the essential elements.

All have been too ready to embrace all expedients to promote their elevation, from the use of the sword to the dollar, from the king to the debauchee.

It sacrifices, even at this age, glorious republican institutions of government to its hierarchy, and makes sister republics, so miscalled, her tool! O, what a falling off was there, our world-citizens? It makes kings and autocrats unite, and issue ukases, to enslave the world, by its superstition. its peculiar influence, and its degradation. All peculiar faiths have useless rites and ceremonies. The affiliated knowing ones do not like to see it exposed. Sin is error, or wrong, all sincere knowing ones should seek to correct. All peculiar faiths are invented for some sinister object. Peculiar faith eagenders coarse, vulgar bigotry. How much insanity is there in the subject of peculiar faith? Let not the world cultivate any sneaking self-system, that will lower its intrinsic merits, and all that should elevate it. Carry out this matter about peculiar faith far enough, and you will necessarily be convinced of its error.

Peculiar faith makes God peculiar, endows opinions with superstitious notions, and imparts such code of its object. What sort of peculiar faith doctrine does not imply sophistry, falsification, and imposition?

What an absurdity, the offering of jealousy and envy, in the different orders of peculiar faith!

It is difficult to decide, in some matters, which proves most civilization? We have to look at the matters of fact. Which is more civilized, Christian England or pagan China, in the opium matter?

Sophistry is everything in life with some, but we can detect it always, if we bring principles to bear.

Peculiar faith degrades its followers below principles. Some meet by fraud, sophistry, and collusion of the world in peculiar faith. Do these satisfy the intelligent and honest mind of freemen? We come not to attack your good but your credulity: we defend all your religion, but impeach all your peculiar faith.

But the professor's feelings are peculiarly claimed, as proving the faith, especially in Christianity. All peculiar faiths can claim feelings; where then is the superiority? Rational beings are perfectly satisfied to retain the only maintainable position that is rational, to live and die by. What more can be said, or done? The only object of proper standard is God, and to be recognised, not by feelings but by mind's operations.

Fanaticism is the cut-throat incendiary of the world.

God fixed man, who fixed himself in a false peculiar position, from which he has to recover himself.

The whole world's history amply proves that superstition and peculiar faith will never answer for the world's welfare. Some people think how well, how beautifully they can perform: they had better consider how well they can omit the malign misdeeds of the bible. Who continues this abominable system? The profession of the priestocracy, who have taken such pains for centuries to mislead the world.

What is peculiar faith worth? It is faith misdirected. Self-delusion may cause you to seek peculiar faith, whilst at the same time none has principles.

Professors of peculiar faith assume all the morality, despite of the supreme rights of mind! What base sophistry! Puseyism, Romanism, Greekism, Protestantism, Polytheism, and Atheism, are all combating religion. The greatest engine and machinery of corruption to the whole world is peculiar faith, its cause. What malignant feelings, "acts of faith," torture by fire, and mutual persecutions, of Christian, Jew, Mahometan, have prevailed, when power permitted.

Who could trust himself to the tender mercies of peculiar faith? The sooner we get rid of peculiar faith the better. What good faith has peculiar faith?

We overlook the character and functions of human nature, created by God for noble and elevated purposes.

Heresies will arise in peculiar faith the world over, which can never see right in this matter.

The world must observe the enmity of peculiar sects, all the time of their existence, for thousands of years.

What is their redeeming quality? None. All that is valuable is mind, whose rights they have crushed.

We see it between Christianity, Judaism, Mahometanism, Mormonism, Bhuddism, Brahminism, or any other form of paganism,—all. The power of each church hierarchy, once greater than the civil government, has aided in all this. Whole massacres of Jews or other sects have been witnessed more than once by light.

No one can reason, enslaved to love peculiar faith or fanaticism, on the especial subject that overrules them.

Peculiar faith doctrinists seize upon the human mind as their peculiar property, and tyrannize over it as a heretical vassal. Without principles man is an animal: and with peculiar faith man deserts principles of science. The highest proof of want of science is the position of peculiar faith.

These peculiar faiths and sects alienate the various portions of the world from each other.

How many try, pretend to get peculiar faith, and fall back. No rational being can retrograde from rational religion, while mind thus enlightened is so constituted that it cannot receive peculiar faith. Now rational religion is for all, consequently this is the only faith of religion. Society is so constituted by peculiar faith that individuals take base advantages of it. The base act badly when permitted with impunity; but when society is deprived of its best constituent principles its safety is in abeyance to improper influences. Then feelings are shocked, and principles are outraged, without proper redress. As man can only live to sin the least, so his position to be most successful must be relative to such.

Of all the humbugs of the world, that about peculiar faith is the greatest and most culpable. What prejudices are addressed, what vices are aroused, what ignominy is accomplished. The pride of opinion may cause antagonism of error with truth, but no humbuggery is available permanently on a false capital. Hypocrites cannot appreciate true devotion. Their too much devotion in idol-worship blinds and causes the world to trade on the capital of the position that is made false.

This is the age of bigotry with all of peculiar faith, not of refined noblest feelings. This is one of the things not worthy of acquisition, as we have necessarily on the best principles of existence to look on all the heads as deceivers. Well can it be remarked that adults are grown up children, The whole tendency of mind under peculiar faith is to sophistry. The lifetime on this basis presents a continued evasion of right. This tribunal has proved itself totally incompetent to settle the great question of religion.

Peculiar faith is the faith of superstition, the parent of a prolific world brood, whereas the faith of rational religion is that of reason, truth, and facts.

How comes it that so many world-people believe the statements of peculiar faith about the future, but yet refuse absolutely to become of that faith?

There is something singularly wrong in all this.

Peculiar faith sophisticates the world, and causes most to see mostly one side of doubtful questions; and what is worst, to uphold all such by bigotry after their explosion when interest is involved.

Peculiar faith is one of the great questions of agitation to the world. The best social relations are interrupted by peculiar faith and sects.

What a fine thing it is that the peculiar faith people do not go as far as pretended in most instances, else the world evil would have been greater. Its hypocrisy, as bad as it is, may be a fortunate ingredient.

What does peculiar faith constitute but a series of clanships, as destitute of real merit, to vanquish by base intrigues? While each peculiar sect has honorable people by the blessings of God-given minds, the elements of all are most dishonorable and unworthy. Our rights are not to be compromised at all by any such organized felony of after for forethought.

The state of the Mormons is one of the emanations, and consequent on bad faith doctrines. The world is inundated by base doctrines. Can there be any systems of peculiar faith without the vitiation of superstition mixed up with it? All would be well if they were passive, but crusades are made of conscience misinstructed.

The responsibility of peculiar faith is inappreciable for its evil. It has not been in the power of fanatics, &c., to get the world ruined by their peculiar faith doctrines. Time secures a better and better conservatism, and the God of nature reveals his supreme character.

Peculiar faith affects all parts of the world, while affecting much good that the tuition of mind, however under disguised pretences of the first, is the legitimate claimant. This should not rob mind of its character, nor God of his rights. Where peculiar faith predominates, there is so little independence of the balance that sophistry obscures, or mind is vassal to obedience and acquiescence. Patriots, philanthropists, freemen, to the rescue of mind, your noblest jewel. What an evil to see with other people's eyes, thoughts, analysis of mind, forced by the current to adopt a creed of peculiar faith, or be proscribed all the benefits of social and civil rights! True patriotism, intellectual and noble, revolts at the idea. If now we feel the force and tyranny in this country, separated as church and state are of clerical influence, what must it have been for ages and centuries when invested with sway of undefined powers. The clergy were the teachers, moulding mind, influencing will, assuming to be the guardians of education, necessarily made most peculiar. What could escape the potency of such sacrilegious usurpation?

The peculiar faith doctrinists project their creed as universally applicable, and peremptorily admissible. They have usurped by dictation, proscribed, dictated by inquisition. There are many good people, though they have adopted peculiar faith. How much better could they be if they were to adopt the only true faith. It makes no odds whether christians or pagans, they are on equal footing. It is only the state of mind's elevation in their country, that is indebted to science, that makes the real difference. One idol-worship is as heinous as another.

In what a category peculiar faith leaves her votaries. Would not one hundred and forty millions of Mahometans swear that Mahomet is the true prophet? Two hundred millions of Christians would swear that Christ is the only true messiah. From five to seven millions of Jews would swear that there is no messiah. Five hundred millions of pagans would swear for other messiahs! Now all contradict each other. Who is right? None. All this brings about a bad state of morals. Is it any less than a world perjury? When heads of families show no particular care how members of families progress in life, whether they have good morals or not, so they have peculiar faith that is advanced, it is very bad. The world has been imposed upon by peculiar faith-mongers, who set the world to quarreling and fighting therefor. Get religion, says the sectarian. All minds have the elements of religion, the more refined in civilization the more possessed of it. When they improve it, it is rational, and nothing else, not peculiar. What enormities from false pretences about religion, about the forms of superstition, that begets a world of lies and falsehoods. Peculiar faith is the concern of the priestocracy. Instead of aiding peculiar faith, men should thwart every effort but that of perfecting a bible of mind, the only one between God and mind. Peculiar faith people ruin a good cause, given them by the Creator, for the cause of the priestocracy, who are most conceited, and ignorant of the analysis of mind.

Every peculiar faith man is obliged to start on false pretences, which he, as not in the secret, may not have known. The world is full of systems of peculiar faith, but there is only one rational faith, religion, that Deity wrote on the human mind.

Let a world unite on it, and the result is the same. How dangerous and demoralizing is peculiar faith, by peculiar education trammeling reason, as any error may be propagated, the individual becoming a pirate, murderer, as faith, without inquiry, curses.

No science should bend to peculiar faith.

Peculiar faith bewilders the mind, while rational faith enlarges it; the first is antagonistic to the last, which is conservative of the world, the universe, the immortal soul.

Man is forced to suppress his honest sentiments and conviction about peculiar faith, that is no faith at all, if it be not believed in. If a man previously satisfied, when in his final sickness is made to be excited with his family and friends, about his faith, unless he has a very balanced mind, has thought of all these things, and is well prepared for them, he, and all such, may spend the balance of his days miserably. The peculiar faith-people have had it too much on their side, and use all pious frauds to perpetuate their doctrine. How comes it that the world do not fully believe that the peculiar faith-people all lie, when they speak of their doctrines? They can do nothing else.

Now, people do die most abundantly without a qualm of conscience in monotheism, trusting alone to the powers of their God, from whom, as they detract in attributes, they render themselves proportionately atheists or polytheists, who are about equal. People in all ages, have decided to be humbugged, time after time, and tyrants have destroyed myriads, seeking to prevent them.

Let us have no peculiar faith at the expense of freedom, conscience, reason, science. Peculiar faith is the fruit of bibles of tradition, that are ever false friends to mind, and destructive, not conservative, antagonistic elements of social and religious life. It is a mighty work, to eradicate all such errors, with all her machinery, wiles and corruption. Peculiar faith must be defined mouthy; knows but little, and betrays itself, miserable in acquisitions, and worse in enjoyment.

Opposition in argument to peculiar faith, influences the bigots, and arouses its basest tyranny. The majority of the world will outlive any one peculiar faith, no matter of what pretensions. As all Pagans have various peculiar faiths, none have had a majority.

Peculiar faith is the essence of bigotry, and the food of fanaticism. The world needs no peculiar faith or tradition bibles, to sanction or sanctify usurpation and tyranny.

The cunning, short-sighted, peculiar faith-people, think that they can escape detection, when they vainly sacrifice mind, time, to unavailable doctrines. They are the worst sufferers.

Their platform discloses at once the doctrines of that faith.

Under its auspices, have originated some of the monstrous iniquities of the world; among them was the French revolution, which was a full comprehension of proscription of social relations and virtues. And what has peculiar faith done for the soul? She has scattered the vile weeds of sectarianism over the world, causing universal antagonism.

For thousands of years, her sword has been drawn, and she waged war for two centuries, for one object, the war of conquest, ambition, power.

There were Christians and Mahometans, not religious, surely not. contending. each affecting to draw from the one fountain of Judaism, itself sectarianism. What better could be expected from the children? Sectarians would rather principles should perish and religion cease, than that their peculir faith-bigotry should not prevail! It is dangerous for any such faith to prevail, as thereby bad men come to wield a dangerous power, who are able thus to set bad examples for monarchy. The peculiar faiths of all mankind are directly in conflict and antagonistic to the best position of mind.

Who is safe on the side of the destructive, that negative what is good, permanent, and rational?

Of all outrages, sectarianism of all kinds can excel the world. When a person seeks to convert us to his faith, that has no rational testimony, we have no faith in him only as a rank impostor. If you bring peculiar faith forward, as the test of one single thing, you make bigots for all things. Peculiar faith is a murdress, foul and degraded. Keep the elements of mind right, else everything·is made to bend and conform to the iron despotic rule of peculiar faith of bibles of tradition.

Well may the world look out for all the despotisms of Judaism, Popery, Mahometanism, their awful conflicts not yet terminated after many centuries of antagonism, if any had the ascendancy. Have we forgotten the conflicts of the Mormons? See the case of Bhuddism and Brahminism. The history of such faith is analogous, and presents danger to the world, wherever peculiar faith exists.

What does peculiar faith do for the sovereign people? It is like imitating the cries of the young, inveigling through superstition that imitates rational religion. But for the benign spirit of toleration, which is one of the brightest reflections of mind, the horrors of the dark ages of peculiar faith would still triumph. Who doubts it, let him refer to the last views of Italy and Spain. In all the fury of fanaticism, the triumph of mind holds its sway through toleration, whose beauties and strength are hardly appreciated.

The fanaticism of peculiar faith diffuses a malign spirit over all the social relations of life, and the world. It is the exercise of bad faith to man, and blasphemy to God, repudiation to man, dishonesty to God.

By accustoming themselves to the sophistry of peculiar faith, the mind of the public is vitiated for abundant sophistry. On this basis the world decides, and merely from conceit. which is disgusting and contemptible.

At the most, faith, however peculiar, must be the subject of reason, and yields most certainly to universal faith. To whom are we indebted for the inquisition? To the doctrines of peculiar faith. Can you institute any law but that of reason? Is not the inquisition the law of peculiar faith, that of peculiar tyranny, sheer nonsense, if it had not been sheerest oppression? You cannot bring the masses, the clans, the cliques to rule, unless you rule them on principles. Christ's spirit is claimed in all the hundreds of christian sects, yet they war on each other! Our indignation might be aroused at the apparent inconsistency, if his nature had been truly depicted by his fabulists.

What humbuggery and vassalage have the people suffered by their masters, foisted on them by the same acts.

Who can attend all his life to the precepts of peculiar faith, with benefit? He hears but little else, as all else has been proscribed and anathematized by it. There are millions of martyrs to peculiar faith, bibles of tradition, fanatics. priests, preachers and ministers, bigots, popes and their minions. You cannot arrest the right action by peculiar faith. It is God's, and is rational religion.

The wise must go for reason and religion.

Peculiar faith draws drafts on mind in the treasury of God, without due acknowledgment. We must refer to such bare-faced pretences. The world secretly laughs at peculiar faith, as an imposition. Can rational beings sincerely believe in it? Do they not make a profession, policy of it available their way? The sooner blotted out of the world are all peculiar faiths, the better for soul and body, religion and God.

Those who adopt crazy doctrines are as bad as those who originated them.

Peculiar faith begets peculiar notion and opinion, that vary with or nurture peculiar interests! What sort of a vitiated society does it beget? What are people to do! They do not, cannot believe in all such matter that enslaves mind. They proscribe principles in defence of the worst tyranny ever invoked ostensibly for God, as the authority, but pretendedly, as is in the bible, when the very reverse is the reality.

It is singular, that the real intelligence of mankind should be superseded by their superstitious fears. The opinions of affiliation corrupt the perverted and ignorant. It is the   st arrant credulity to believe peculiar gifts of the past, that should exist now, if ever. Those of the. moderns, that advocate such idle and absurd pretences, are worse than th ancients. The malign influence for peculiar faith is in government, that arises;

in usurpations needs all the arts and devices of humbuggery to uphold it. All the odious enormities of such vile imposition are overlooked, by the bribes of hush-money. This very thing, peculiar faith, is nauseous and noisome in the eyes of proper sense and honesty. Who that sees the right analysis of the subject, but must believe that all peculiar faith is most abominable and degraded.

We attack no pure being, who is never identified with the odious crime of peculiar faith. Because you have joined its bonds that is no fault of mine. It is your misfortune, and you should, if wrong, retreat from its insidious folds.

And you, intelligent freeman, knowing better, as you see better, by the vision of true science, adopt all these degradations! When the wolf is to be expelled, we must not take him for the sheep. We cannot be caught by names—a meagre substitute for Deity. What a stumbling-block is peculiar faith, that proves only removes of mind, in superstitious rites and ceremonies.

Peculiar faiths cannot meet the contingencies of the world. While monarchies are local tyrannies, peculiar faith tyrannizes over the world. The howl of despotism is for faith, but a faith treacherous to the rights of mind and truth, a bad faith to the world and mankind.

What iniquity has been committed by peculiar faith. If mind had full justice done it, all peculiar faith would in one moment terminate! And that not a miracle. You cannot usurp the world, by monopoly of peculiar faith. No person, able or in power, should assume vulgar privileges.

How much the peculiar faith world differs in the expediency of correction, as it differs in the points of correction. What a pity it is that the world has not a full code of knowledge of all important points, to properly and timely guard against.

The worldly cannot see religion for peculiar faith, not only doing wrong, but seeking to put others wrong. Peculiar faith brutalizes and debases mind. Can there be anything meaner or worse than peculiar faith, that daily utters some hundreds of millions of falsehoods? People are misled in the mass, and yet they are willing to submit to the humbugs of the priestocracy. That miserable state of bad feeling, enmity or animosity of the world, about peculiar faith, is to be deprecated. See what peculiar faith has done already, in Judaism, and her prolific brood Christianity, Mahometanism, and Mormonism, and these only a beginning.

When these die out, as they will, because not built on science, then religion will prove her brightest light. It is the fault of peculiar faith that we condemn, as it has no principles, without which no universal system of good can be accomplished. That catch-word, faith, deludes the world. Faith is rational conviction. Our object in life should be the pursuit of truth, but when peculiar faith is adopted, it is on a false position, and there is no standard to prevent a falling to a lower depth.

The abstract maxims of peculiar faith will not do. Do not be wheedled, swindled out of your creation-birthright, religion, by the false pretences and position of peculiar faith. To maintain any peculiar view, rationalists have to leave their noble position, and give up the substance for the shadow.

The world has been overwhelmed by false faith and misrule. Commerce and religion unite the whole world. Why separate it by any false pretences of peculiar faith? The intelligent patriots of this Union sympathize with the unfortunate patriots of Europe on the eternal principles of universal brotherhood; and is this inefficient, hurtful thing, peculiar faith, that separates the world with hundred fold animosity and causes its bitterest ruin, to stalk to the end of time over mind? Let us, in the peace of man and love of God, be done with this heathenish barbarism of the ancient and modern world, that lies crippled or crushed beneath it bitterest poisons. The whole world needs correction.

It is not only China, but other extensive countries of Asia, subject to despotisms, and what is as bad, the first tottering under the piratical smuggling of opium, and that by the most enlightened of European nations who boast of Christianity! that should be the theatre of conservative revolutions, not of missionary petitions of peculiar faith, but of the real means of civilization among the Asiatic nations, especially the Arabs of the wretched country Palestine, and all the country to Babylon and Ninevah, peculiar faith is an article too abundant. All Asia needs rational religion.

Let us not wonder at the jealous policy of Japan, that fears the awful vicissitudes of peculiar faith in Western Asia, that has had such awful lessons taught them. And shall all this be lost on the wise of this generation of this nation, that is so blessed with a large share of the world's commerce and its happiness? Well may mind observe the question, Does it wish to appreciate the effects of what peculiar faith has been and is now? Let its attention be turned to Asia, Eastern Europe and Northern Africa, and after you have trodden the classic ground of its best contributions to the world, now desolate in much of its area, then you will still be better satisfied that much of Africa, however ignorant, has been spared some of the world's ferocious improvements. Africa has exported her barbarians for a better future, while conquerors, as Tamerlane, have reduced the country of the Euphrates and Tigris, and erected on the ruins of Bagdad a pyramid of ninety thousand heads! The Tartars and Saracens, as the Romans, have despoiled indeed. Sectarianism is vicious, criminal. The world ought to be rid of insidious impostures of peculiar faith. We now cannot trust any peculiar faith people with the faithful records of history. How much has been altered! The source is poisoned to garble cursed bibles of priestocracies on the world! The vile persecutions of the world are not done with. They are arrested more by the power of toleration than by any merits of peculiar faith. It is enough to make misanthropes to see the effects of peculiar faith.

The world will never be rightly governed till universal brotherhood is established. The world-poison is in the thing sectarianism.

The people are individually to be bettered. How can they be fairly and justly dealt with by any such, as the human mind has been crushed by the world's despotism for thousands of years? In getting rid of all peculiar faith and its education, we shall be exempt from all that fund of the world's evil. The functions of peculiar faith that assumes all, cause the question, who and what is the heathen world? All that does not belong to other particular peculiar dynasties. All peculiar faith, as Christianity, Mahomedanism, &c., is pagan idolatry, nothing more or less. All peculiar faith, where practical, has usurped temporal powers, and we see the evils of all when each is specified, as that of Judaism, in the bad fruit of a bad tree, the base of sectarianisms. The world has made itself a perfect blockhead about peculiar faith, that has been its worst point, whereby it has been overwhelmed, oppressed and ruined. Every little village is now divided by sectarianism in Christianity, between that and Judaism, &c. Apocrypha is an elegant illustration of peculiar faith, a test of faith between the Romanists and protestants. With rationalists, all is sure enough as apochrypha. If any peculiar faith be the true one, how came it to let the others get the start of it? If true, how came it not possess the whole world? None but fanaticism of peculiar faith could consider it essential that Christ should die by the million at Jerusalem, and leave the world most oppressed by other faiths, pretendedly for prophecies.

What world morals! Let the world throw away all the curses of peculiar faith, and its infamous sophistry.

As the chicanery of faith as all peculiar faith is false, how then can we promote religion by any other than rational means, as all bibles of tradition that represent peculiar faith are necessarily false?

Do not most set out determined to believe the faith of the country, however preposterous or absurd?

What was and is the character of the Egyptians and Hindoos for truth? What has been that of the Jews? Has it been most high-minded and honorable.

All countries had their tutelar deities, and necessarily their peculiar faith. Which was right? None. Which was wrong? All. Which was apocryphal? All. They were all not only worthless, but deeply injurious. Truth cannot be told where peculiar faith abides. Peculiar faith is the most childish trifling in place of religion. All the dispensations of peculiar faith, as Christianity, Mahommedanism, Mormonism, come from man most positively. If one peculiar faith be admitted, all must be, and thus the most irrational category is created, misleading mind. duping the world, and falsifying God's word. Man mars what ought to be left entirely to the Creator altogether.

What a scene for othodox peculiar faith people to contemplate, when their opponents, the Mahommedans, drove the Christians not only from their holy sepulchre, but from their eastern capital, which they have retained for several centuries.

The Romans built a temple to Jupiter Capitolinus where the temple of the Jew god, in Jerusalem, had stood.

The peculiar faiths had to contemplate a war, that ensued, wherein more than fifty Jewish cities were demolished; nearly a thousand of their best towns were destroyed; more than half a million of soldiers were slain by the sword; and in the end of the war the Jews were banished Judea, by Adrian, upon pain of death if they returned. What had not peculiar faith of the Jews to do with the destruction of Jerusalem? What could have been more wretched than their situation after Jerusalem was taken by Titus.

All peculiar faith is contingent and subject to corruption, as Judaism by Antiochus Epiphanes, and the Romans after him; but rational religion is above all when mind, reason, and rational education guide mankind. The whole wise world is interested in maintaining good faith and destroying the bad, which is peculiar.

The majority of the world does not think for itself, but is blindly misled by demagogues in the pulpit, politics, martial piracy, &c.

Many were the tricks and expedients for peculiar faith.

What a potency peculiar faith exerts over the world yet; what must have been its mighty influence once? What greater corruption can be exhibited of mass of muscle in abeyance to it. All undue advantages have been taken by it, in all forms and conditions of life. Tenants at will are hardly free, and despotism of government has made mind a tenant at will!

By reason that mind is prone to perversion by peculiar education, let us have no system that will promote that end; let us have the only proper means of rational education, that is from rational principles.

What are peculiar faith and its bibles but what past ages consumed thousands of years in mystifying, and in which thousands to come may be fruitlessly consumed in unraveling. After the use of all the talents, bibles of tradition, and time, the world is not as well off at the end thereof. And what have been the aim and scope of peculiar faith in general? To originate the power of superstition, to rule the devotees in this and other worlds. What good people do this? Who are good in this world? The peculiar faith people? How do they prove that?

The earth was for man, but the way the peculiar faith people act, they make miserable and degraded distinctions. The select few appropriate what does not belong to them more than others. All distinctions on earth should be on merit, among the same tribes at least. Peculiar faith seems to advance cities as well as men, in regard to holiness. A local charm was attributed to such city. One of the great reasons that actuated the Christians, as suggested by an intelligent citizen of Gainesville, Francis Walthall, was seeking a holy city for worship as the Mahommedans and other nations had. Fanaticism and lust of dominion or conquest I think, were the great reasons too. A man may be all his lifetime at peculiar faith, and he will be worse off therefor than when he commenced.

Reason alone can tell us the difference between true and false faith. The very basis of argument faith helps each peculiar faith, to its own silence or its own defeat. Any one peculiar faith is therefore undeniably incompetent to proselyte other faiths, and has to yield all to rational faith. Do you decide, that we must go by faith? Then we may go for all peculiar faiths, as there is as much obligation on us for adoption of such.

All peculiar faiths are corrupt in conception and tend to corruption; the best Christian as others, was deeply corrupted by imperial unions. What improved it but mind, that directed reformations and revolutions in faith and government. To reach the highest proper position, it has to reach the highest state of rationality. The wretched state of ignorance conspired to aid in the promulgation of peculiar faith. All earth and its demoralization, have been moved about this thing of peculiar faith.

"Mahomet never asserted a falsehood" say the orthodox, when he asserted nothing else in the koran. Mahomet lied about his night journey from Mecca to Jerusalem and thence to Heaven, and would have ruined his whole design, had not his friend Abu Becr vouched for its veracity. This fiction made his fortune. Now but for the accommodating credulity of the world called faith, we should get rid of all peculiar faith. When peculiar faith is dependent it is mild and asks for toleration, but when in the ascendant, then it is dictator.

It creeps, by words, and progresses by the sword; after that it is upheld by sophistry, sustained by superstition and secured by bribes and sinister government. Thus with Judaism, Christianity, Mahommedanism. Moses held his power by superstition and an armed priestocracy. If his superstition did not avail, terrible as was the imposition, the swords of the Levites did the balance. If persuasion and art did not establish Christianity, the union with the mighty Roman power did. Rational religion is independent of all these designs and machinery of priestocracy. She is independent of prophecy and miracles, and can be demonstrated clearly and conclusively by the highest universe. There never was a peculiar faith, but what lied into existence, and was indebted to the same for its maintenance. Among other things the most conspicuous have angels, a most senseless invention. "This whole doctrine concerning angels Mahommed and his disciples have borrowed from the Jews, who learned the names and offices of these beings from the Persians, as themselves confess." Talmud Hieros. in Rosh hashana. Sale's Koran.

What a light the world would have if we had the books of the people preceding the Egyptians and Assyrians, or if literature be not accorded their predecessors, what if we had theirs?

All peculiar faith, is humbug, certain. Part of the world is humbug any how, and that is necessarily from that source much the larger part.

What awful schisms in the world have grown up by peculiar faith, none of which can possibly exist permanently with sectarianism, whereas if any of the last arise with supposed monotheism, it is proof positive, that it is not monotheism, but peculiar faith always. Judaism was sectarianism rank from its ignominious predecessors, and we see how little the Jews agreed with the ancient world. Who warred on them? Was not peculiar faith the cause of many ancient wars? Christianity and Mahommedanism have had bloody work with each other; both of them have had parricidal assaults on Judaism, and all with their own offspring. How many bloody battles had Mahommedanism to sustain itself against what were called false prophets? What furious and relentless animosities still prevail? Is not this the case with all kinds of peculiar character that has reared its impudent face? No matter what be the garb of peculiar faith, it is a world's curse as its delusion, the sooner dropped the better. A few instances of Mahommedanism will suffice, as they are not so familiar to this part of the world. The sectary Bâbec cruelly put to death a fourth of a million of people, "it being his custom never to spare man, woman or child, either of the Mahommedans or their allies," says Sale. What dreadful deeds were perpetrated by the people called the Ishmelians, or the assassins. When Moseilama was killed, ten thousand of the apostates who followed this false prophet, were left dead on the spot. What wars can be more relentless?

As Abraham's prophecy declares the land should be the Jews' forever, what if under that prophecy the Jews should be always fighting the Mahommedans therefor? One may be perfectly disgusted with society, human nature, as society may be, and acts on a false basis. Society is mapped off by clique and kith circles. Has the majority of the world under the present defective organization of society, proper morals when it clearly has not pure religion? Peculiar faith necessarily alienates one portion of the world, from all others. What superstitious rites can be a rule of faith to mind? What nation has ever risen by peculiar faith, to the full demands of religion? Let the world answer. No peculiar faith is disinterested; all have their speculation and priestocracy. These little petty sectional views, must yield to the large ample continental world comprehension of religion. It must have no selfish subdivisions, when the world requires enlarged liberal views. The highest temporal objects have been sought by peculiar faith, that despoils mind of its noblest characteristics and best rights. Society is deeply corrupted by petty peculiar faith organizations, from which it has to be freed, ere truth and justice are done the world.

All revealed systems of peculiar faith, are made by the ignorance and superstition of the people.

In peculiar faith, the sovereign people are forgotten. The education of their minds is overlooked, as the main pillar of science and virtue.

Who can comprehend the objects and intentions, the net-work and dove-tail of various unions of peculiar faiths? Well, what distinguishes all peculiar faiths? Sectarianism, that kills them all dead, christianity or the very best. But to overcome the difficulty, they all lie outrageously, to make the world fool enough to believe that they are the real pure divine inspirations. No matter what absurdities, they must all be swallowed. Of course the concentrated energies of centuries are in their bibles. Fishermen did them? Who is verdant enough to believe that? The most expert of the priestocracies, clearly worked in them. What can the doctrine of such revealed faith teach the heart that is ignorantly put for the mind? For many centuries, the world has been deceived by peculiar faith. It should learn now, what is religion.

Peculiar faith does not suit the rudest state of uncivilized society, and is at variance with the fundamental principles of the best society. Peculiar faith or bible revelation, does not approach rational religion, that secures the highest protection to society, and, therefore, such faith proves itself of mortal pretensions, consequently it could not have emanated from God. Peculiar faith begets many world evils as legislation, for forms of faith or belief, and to exclude unbelievers.

Religion is to save all rational minds.

There should never be the first advance of any such proceeding as peculiar faith, in any part of the world.

If this world were to act about anything else, as it does about peculiar faith, it would be considered deranged assuredly, and justly so.

The process of peculiar faith distorts the human mind, and renders it a miserable machine.

And the functionaries of peculiar faith assume to it, all that belongs to mind, that is crushed under its poisonous influences. The capital of peculiar faith is used as the pillars of despotism for the world. Yes, emperors proclaim peculiar faith to the people as long as they are verdant enough to be thus deluded, but how can freemen be blind enough to receive such? It is by a continuation of imposition, of sophists, whose sectarian spirit has crushed the noblest aspirations of rationalism. Pure religion does not breathe in the atmosphere of peculiar faith. All the people, of one peculiar faith, cannot agree, how then, can you reconcile the Mahommedans and the Christians, when their forefathers fought for two hundred years, nearly. For what did they fight? Conquest?

That was incompatible with rational principles.

For the sepulchre of Christ? That was fanaticism. And have not the Christian and Jew oppressed each other for nearly two thousand years? And will they not, for two millions, if they could exist?

The only end to them, and the blessing to the world, is by the majesty of mind, the most illustrious action, rational religion, this the world has yet to learn.

Is it that christianity boasts over philosophy, that the last was incompetent to govern the world? In what has she then proved herself superior or adequate? The sectarianism of sophists, has misruled the most of the world. It is that spirit that murdered a Socrates, expelled the philosophers, as they were called under the Roman Emperors, and has basely maligned, and excluded the hallowed spirit of rational religion, the only conservative of the world. The advocates vociferously speak of the pretended civilization of peculiar faith, especially christianity. Mind claims, as just to the whole world, the refinement of civilization, and that rational religion alone can give.

It is not in the nature of any sectarianism, of which christianity is an impudent part, to give pacification to the world. How are the peculiar faith-people sophists? Because they advance the idea that deism would ruin the world, that cannot otherwise reach a higher position in morals and religion.

They are in perfect antagonism with deism, that they must destroy to survive themselves.

The humility of monotheism is the greatest, as its sincerity is complete, and its confidence in God universal, comprehending all the soul especially.

Does any peculiar faith rear any temple of virtue, and practice odious iniquity behind it?

What is the difference between Pagan and Christian? The first had open idolatry, the second has book-idolatry. How can the world break down the errors of peculiar faith that horribly assails it?

The glory of mind's light must do it.

The strong arms of powerful monarchies of the world support them; money and its pernicious influence sustain them; the people love them—women worship, men fear, children look up to them. The humbugs of the ancient priestocracy are nothing to the modern, who affirm them to be the essence of morals and religion. Bibles of this faith, are the coins of priestocracy. Patriots of this world correct all this. All the worst false pretences have been sought to establish peculiar faiths. Citizens of America, complete your freedom from these, the glorious refinement of civilization through mind.

Why do we speak against all the peculiar faiths of the world? Because none of them have any pure religion. In this, then, mind should not let the world get the advantage of it. Why is there antagonism in the world, about peculiar faith? Is there not enough, about other things? There can be none about rational faith, pure religion, that unites the whole world into one grand brotherhood, and harmonizes its dignified union. Had the ignorant ancients, the presuming priestocracy, left many things alone, they had not imposed so many errors on the world. The moderns must modestly analyze, and refuse credence to peculiar faith. But what a bore on the world, that is outraged indeed. Families have to conform to the vitiated peculiar faith of the day, else be ostracized. Men, in our circle, so far from asserting the dignity of intelligent minds, in speaking out what their independence entitles them to, sneak out of all responsibilities, and are actually afraid to read, much less discuss, the important truth of the world!

Peculiar faith must corrupt all countries, without exception. All its churches have no principles inherent, as all must be united on a false position. What virtue is there in all that? Proscription attends opposition thereto, and where it has union with state, so much tyranny it has displayed, by persecution and punishment, or peculiar influence and power. A new conservative organization must prevail, to have public opinion most enlightened, and rational religion most elevated. Let the world not only aim to be right, but lay the sure foundation to appropriate it. All the foundations of peculiar faith have to be broken up, ere public opinion is right, for the world to uniformly assert its own rights and correct its own wrongs. It will not do, to let others decide in all this matter exclusively for mind.

Who is qualified in integrity, talents, and disinterestedness? By the people's taking for granted that irresponsible priestocracy would act up to their pretended good talk, usurpation commenced, and having its hold sustained in state power, will not relax it. What, then, is the difference between atheism and polytheism? Has either of them any correct principles? The difference between the atheists and polytheists, who go for more gods than one, is this. The first deny God and the duty to him, that is religion, and of course duty to man. The last deny a correct, faithful duty to God or man. They impart a false worship in peculiar faith, a blasphemy to God, and a most ungodly despotism on man.

All polytheists go for revelation, that is necessarily based on false pretences, as it is obvious to all the rational part of mankind, that mind is the agent of God on earth. Nearly all the ancient philosophers, and peculiar faith people of all ages, are so superficial, that it is absolutely dangerous to follow them, in their metaphysical pretences.

All peculiar faiths are contingent, which clearly cannot suit mind, in all its various permanent conditions of life. Atheism or polytheism is the necessary result from all peculiar faiths, it seems to us. Peculiar faith has not scrupled to manage God's affairs, and interpret for him most absurdly; it cannot meet the necessary demands of the world, and of course is exploded. It cannot begin to satisfy the world ; its end is worse when all see it—no form, no kind, no pretension will answer. But none must oppose it. It is an unpopular step, especially with the women. All its advocates profess to have its peculiar revelation. If that be so, let it be provab e, and reliable, as genuine. After all the pretences of revealed faith, it is all founded on the teachings of perversion of mind respecting the universe, and all for the sinister purpose of absolute rule and tyranny.

Mind comes short of the proper comprehensive analysis. As to feeling being the test for peculiar faith, that must be all a pretence of the party advocates, the partisan priestocracy, as all claim that much.

How much history is made to bend to peculiar faith? All the bibles of peculiar faith are old legends and myths, and every one of them analogous, all relying on unity of false pretences. What will not peculiar faith do ? Will it not excite in the world a peculiar state of immoral feeling, most difficult to be eradicated ?

What did not the military spirit of the ancient world, with its ferocious exhibitions of embittered feelings? What did the gladiatorial shows at Rome do less, than finally expose her as one of the bloodiest butchers of the world? Did not peculiar faith demoralize the whole world, Palestine included, when she sacrificed her children to the fire of Moloch ? What had she to boast of but her degradation, if she had ever been presented with the true worship of the God of the universe ? All such faith corrupts the mind. But how is it possible that in all countries where any peculiar faith prevails. that people get along in that faith ? They succeed in the universal principles of mind, the elements inherent to life, granted by the immutable God of nature. The followers of these peculiar faiths do many fantastic tricks before God, they pray to him, sacrifice and seek to appease him as if he was a mutable priestocracy idol. All mankind have to watch over their own actions, and commune as rational beings before God for their own correction as they are the mutable beings. What have they to say to the immutable Deity ? Instruct their mind.

They can be thankful and grateful, and should cultivate all such refined feelings. I thank my God that I have such a splendid governmental liberty, to write what I consider just for him and all mortals. You wish to travel over the globe peacefully and religiously. Can you declare your peculiar faith without offence to the law of God and man ? No. But civilize the world, and then you and the rest of the world lose your and their hold on all peculiar faiths, and all will adopt what is just to God and man, rational religion. No other will safely convey you all in this world.

But you boast of the numbers flocking to you. What does that signify ? Raising up sects is nothing. Mahomet raised his, and the number comprises now nearly one-seventh of all mankind, it is said. The Mormons are very recent, and number several thousands. Their sect has flourished on the same platform as Christianity and others, that of peculiar bibles, and if they had the sword they would find the followers by the power. The whole world would be actually Mormonized, if they could dictate terms to-day. And so would it be under the sway of any peculiar faith, capable of mastering it by brute force. What conscience has any ? Is it in Christianity, that fought for its very existence. and afterwards for this very purpose, some two hundred years continuously ? What virtue is there in peculiar faith ? Is it not a barren fig tree ? The fault is in the people who do not reason, but look forward for sinister purposes, &c. They put themselves into the power of the artful and unprincipled intriguers of the world.

As long as peculiar faith exists, principles cannot accompany. Though the world does not fight now generally, fortunately being governed by the light of mind, still, peculiar faiths keep it in antagonism. Peculiar faiths will alienate the various portions of the world from each other, that can be united by religion. As with bad and unprincipled lawyers and doctors, so with parsons who could not give me any of their peculiar faiths with all their delusive premiums of bribery and corruption, in exchange for rational religion, which they clearly have not got.

How much valuable time is spent in the world by peculiar faith people in hearing, reading, and using controversial writings about peculiar faith, that of itself is worthless. What does it all amount to? Science ought to be discussed and lectured on instead, as that will not divide but harmonize the world. Then a universal brotherhood will prevail. Where will peculiar faith longest linger? Among ignorant people and despotisms, union of church and state. There is the charm. The adherents of peculiar faith argue in this way, we might as well gather the fruit as others ; but they should not gather it illegitimately and blasphemously.

A man that is under peculiar faith doctrine becomes a bigot. The mind, and not the heart, is concerned in the investigation of truth the world over, and if it be not rationally concerned it is irrationally. Peculiar.faith does not look above the priestocracy. No peculiar gospel of any bible of tradition can be upheld in truth, honesty, or reason.

How ridiculous is the contest of peculiar faith people, that some of them are better than others.

That argues against the first, who had the best means, and therefore are not as good, relatively.

How comes it that the best are in such a perversion of light, in which there can be none good? The first and only true question arises, is monotheism right? If so, then the whole world must come into it ; the sooner the better; lay aside all peculiar faiths. This is the religion of the whole universe, none other can suit at all.

Christ or Bhudd, Mahommed, Lama, or Smith, if potent here, never would get through the exhaustless universe ; of course, then, monotheism is the position forever.

Who is chargeable for the atheism of France? Peculiar faith despotism, that had crushed rational mind, and had invoked the stupid flock of faith.

All peculiar faiths, as the Christian, Jewish, &c., are of human invention, but monotheism is of God.

All the advocates of all the peculiar faiths combined can never fill up the awful chasm in mind, that is left in mind ere their particular faith takes hold of it, thus proving the whole an imbecility, a blasphemy in the sight of the pure God who created, endowed, and preserves all minds. O vile, wicked, degraded priestocracy.

The adoption of peculiar faith is the blasphemy of the Almighty, slander of his religion, and catering to the worst demoralizations of the world.

You cannot reform religion, but you can reform youselves and your faith. No peculiar faith can stand. How often are intense efforts made to cover weak and corrupt priests.

There are many systems of peculiar faiths, all emanating from superstition and her speculation, all more or less absurd, none religious.

No peculiar faith can prove the authenticity of its own scriptures, nor say aught against monotheists.

The extensive establishment of any peculiar faith as Christianity, Mahommedanism, Mormonism, Bhuddism or Brahminism, is no proof of its authenticity, since the world has been div. led mostly among such faiths. All may flourish. None of it has a living principle.

Peculiar faith has an awful quantity of infamous vices that affect the world. This country now has the Mormons, Christians, Jews, Bhuddists, Atheists ; all must embrace rational religion, toleration will be very partial.

What virtue peculiar, has peculiar faith?

This world is now filled with poisonous, bitter, deadly feuds, of sects and peculiar faiths arrayed against each other, the representatives of which they had rather see perish, than one jot or tittle of their pretended prophecies, or their exploded demoralizing books, called bibles. What an idle legend is peculiar faith : what stuff about infidelity.

That religion had nothing to do with peculiar faiths, the whole of their history for the world's age will prove, if nothing more. Has not all the calendar of crimes been committed? Has there been ranker ambition, deeper avarice, more relentless pride and revenge, more malign by inquisitions? Under the name of religion, all the world iniquities have been practiced.

Peculiar faith begets a false confidence—hypocrisy. To say that the ancient philosophers could not find out peculiar faith, is contradictory to history, as they had nothing else but peculiar faiths that are polytheisms diversified only.

Peculiar faiths have no peculiar virtues ; all have their vices.

The law protects all peculiar faiths claiming the name of religion, and all that is not too monstrous to be permitted, is protected by law. The pulpit is the arena, and the people can adopt or reject, without any benefit of testing the correctness. Very rarely is that side heard, as the discussion of the truth is interdicted. There is religion in the world, and has been, necessarily, from the first rational mind, from the nature of things, but no thanks to peculiar faith. There is plenty of religion in churches, but no thanks to churches. Rational religion was before churches. People are too disunited in the universal matters. The appropriate legitimate means should be fairly, rightly and universally used, to rescue mind from its agrarian peculiarities. Can there be anything meaner than bigotry ? A female bigot hates, with all the fury and meanness. You might do her all the favors practicable, but such a bigot is a bigot still. Though the talents and merits might be of the first order, they would be the best reason for bigotry to assail. Peculiar faith tells you to look to the master, religion reasons you into conservative principles. The spirit of ill-feeling is kept up in the world by peculiar faith that has its own peculiar interest. How can any be exempt from suspicion of motives, when they persist in that non-entity, peculiar faith ? What will not peculiar faith do, when united to all practicable despotisms ?

Can freemen overlook the eastern barbarism of degrading man to the Eunuch, and possessing the liberty of murdering slaves ? What degradation of the east, yet ! The exposure to sale of women, for wives, or worse, concubines, by their own relations. The world must act for principle, not for fanaticism, plunder nor blood, as the peculiar sects and faith people do. The phalanx of peculiar faith people, is a great one, and their conscience is hardened, because they are steeled by monopoly and usurpation. All that is irrational in peculiar faith, has no existence in religion. Now all we are, and have in this world, is based on rationality. The world cannot always be fanatic. All peculiar faith is purposeless.

Let us have all the good faith that the world is entitled to. What if two conflicting armies about to engage, having peculiar faith, were to offer up their petitions, as they are called ? Thus peculiar faith is such a monster, that both armies would be sacrificed to its unholy requests ! Prayer is to reform the petitioner, not the petitioned. There is where the world has been mistaken so long. As to prayer, two hostile fanatic armies meet to fight, but first pray as the Christian and Mahomedan, and if God hears the prayers of both, he will have to destroy both, annihilate them ; thus peculiar faith is such. It brutalizes mind, to the lowest beastiality. As an evidence of the effects of peculiar faith, the priestocracy cannot or will not give a fair analysis of religion, but assume that they have it, and make war with contemptible antagonism on monotheism, as if that God-given inheritance was to be excluded by their ignominious monopoly.

Their priviliges have only been tolerated by the stupid ignorance of the people, for monotheism was the only God-creation in this respect, and all that are after truth can see it by the fairest comprehensive analysis. But how many have sold their birth-right for a part of the millions of dollars that the world is plundered out of yearly ? Society is cut up and many cut out of its universal rights, by peculiar faith documents and bibles. This exclusiveness ought not to be at all.

Can the fanatic bigot become a good citizen, after he is informed of better positions than his peculiar faith, that has no existence ? Who that has rational education is not perfectly astonished at this state of things in an intelligent country ?

On what can Christians and Mahommedans, Jews and Mormons, peculiar faiths of all kinds unite?

On principles ? They have no conservative principles. Where did they get them ? Monotheism had all them from God ! On faith ? That separates them. On revelation ? Which ? The latest ? Will the Mormon do it. after expulsion from three states, and confidence in none ? The Christian says the Mormons have no pretensions. On what basis ? Reason. That excludes the Christian ! If a few able and patriotic men come forward and do their duty, Monotheism, the law of the universe, will be carried out in this age, and not be deferred. Let bigotry cower before the altar of religion. A man that is exclusively devoted to peculiar faith, becomes nearly infatuated on that subject. One party finding another party peculiarly recusant, is still worse excited. What a world spirit ! Where are the great and legitimate bonds of brotherhood of this world ? Has accursed peculiar faith produced them ? How can even this country be united in brotherhood, without the principles ? How few of the world know that all peculiar faiths, as the most valued Christian, or any, are all humbugs, and yet the people expect something of the kind, and will have the humbugs. The priestocracy and the peculiar powers of united state or government, profit by the popular delusion.

If the world were to investigate peculiar faith, Christian or Jewish, Mahommedan or Mormon, it will find all such nothing—a counterfeit, spurious coin not worth the paper written on! I know one thing, that all such is humbug of the worst kind, manufactured by the priestocracy for their peculiar benefit, and they have to fight it out with all that controvert their position by all the falsest pretences.

All peculiar faith is not worth noticing or receiving, even on premium. All are deceiving. The only true way is that which does justice to the unity of God, that does not derogate from his dignity, worth and perfection. All peculiar faith men make the God of the universe imperfect. But this is their peculiar God, in their bad faith.

All such christianity, or any reduced to truth, renders itself ridiculous and absurd, and the advocates foolish; they know little or nothing but for mind, which they libel and outrage. Most of these peculiar faith people read but little, and analyze less. What will they not do? The vilest bigots, and yet they do not know that they are the veriest infidels to rational religion and God! What, christians infidels? The very worst sort, and nothing less.

Let all peculiar faith people discard the follies and crimes of their peculiar faiths and bible, and all unite in religion. The first has been the strong arm of despotism, nay, despotism itself; when the last has modestly borne her meek honors thick upon her.

Not only does the world sustain, by reason of peculiar faith, undignified contentions, but hypocrisy.

The spirit of love for the world and mankind is entirely eradicated by the world nuisance, peculiar faith.

Sophistry is a part of this world's magic invariably.

But for peculiar despotism and faith the world now would be deeply united. Science unites much of the world now. Truth, reason, mind, will exclude peculiar faith and all its bibles out of society. Experience proves that all such bibles are the explosions of an age long since past; unsuited to the moral, social, national, and world mind. Let there be no alienation of good feelings in the world; we should diminish all such.

There must be no pandering to partisan, sectional or peculiar views. The world can take new starts on conservative revolutions. They will come; do not arrest them, for it will be like damming up mighty rivers, and the radical injury, the radical revolution, will be the consequence. The most hypocritical electioneering is brought about by peculiar faith. This is not really American. Give us, besides the noblest American constitutional government, holy religion. No! give us not one iota of Jew religion faith, no more than of the Jew government, or his barbarisms. All these things have been stolen from mind, whose noblest rights have been oppressed.

Christian peculiar faith talks of civilization, and it is quarreling with each other's professors in every country among themselves, and with the whole world of peculiar faiths.

What can you do with peculiar faith or medical bigots? You may do them any and all favors, and their black ingratitude can see nothing but their own peculiar prejudices and interests.

The world has been thousands of years, and has not yet got to pure religion, impeded as it has been by the adulterated self-interest of peculiar faith. Peculiar education begets prejudices all peculiar.

The world needs unity of love, and how can it get it?

Peculiar faith has not the elements, as material necessaries. God intended for no speculations in religion. As much was the ancient world short of the full comprehension of true geographical position before the discovery of America by Columbus, as peculiar faith bibles are of religion without the bible of the universe. The world possesses the right elements of religion, pure and natural; it must drop the speculations of peculiar faith to do right. The intelligent and thinking religious world should be cut out of all means of mind perversion as far as practicable, hence exclude peculiar faith matters at once. All peculiar faiths will go down necessarily as the principles of religion advance, and rational education gains the ascendancy of mind. Peculiar faith, as christianity, is sectional, sectarian, partisan, whereas religion is comprehensive as the globe, the universe, adequate for mind, suitable for all mankind and nurtures the world's union and peace on principles most conservative to rational minds.

The world, the universe, cannot be benefited by peculiar faith policy. Let the intelligent and just world teach the whole professors of all peculiar faiths the noblest lesson of religion, that has naught to do with such stuff, but recognise all mankind, as far as practicable, as one universal brotherhood. No one can be a true friend to the brotherhood of the world, that goes for peculiar faith. All this peculiar faith is the real despotism of mind. There should be at this age among citizens no enslavement of mind. What is the condition, under absolute governments, but this establishment, a sacrifice to one-man power ? The colossal power of Russia centres in her czar for emperor and pope-god of his church. With absolute military and clerical imperial sway, he assumes faith when he is showing the most horrid bad faith to religion, and of course to the world. If he did it ignorantly or wickedly, ho should stop it.

What is the emperor of China perpetrating, but the same despotism ?

The world needs the noblest characteristics of human nature, the noblest specimens, the worthiest conception of rational mind, that render human nature the most lovely. In what light do these emperors appear before the world ? Peculiar faith distorts what is rational, and proscribes what is right, the dupe, the bully of superstition. The opinion of the supposed great who uphold the bibles, their power, is preferred to the truth of reason. You emperors have it in your power to teach your numerous people, your population of many millions, to be men, to forego all the hypocrisy of peculiar faith, and take hold of all the requirements of religion. All the heads of government are bound to advance their people as mind, in all the legitimate precincts of rational educa-tion, government and religion. But the glorious legitimate amity of the world is broken up by all the curses of peculiar faith, that does the rankest injustice to mankind. It is one of the vestiges of ancient barbarism, and has escaped the shrewdest perceptions of the people by its sagacious and unprincipled sophistries.

Religion has to be put in abeyance to peculiar faith, that does the greatest injustice to the world's peace and dignity, its loveliness and welfare. How comes it, Christian, that you war on one hundred and forty millions of mankind because they are Mahom-medans ? Suppose, now, the world was equally divided, half Mormons and the other Christian. Would there not be the bloodiest war that the world ever saw—ending in the most outrageous barbarism ? If the Romans had power to-day, the inquisitions past are nothing to what the world would suffer.

If the pope had his own people slaughtered by French bayonets; what would he not do with strangers ?

Well has it been that the Roman pope is bereft of the power of the Greek church pope. And mankind has assuredly mistaken all this for religion ! The world cannot stand at what it is. It must go forward. It has stultified itself enough, and dearly paid for its experience by too much of its blood, treasures and sacrifices of mind. What an idea of separating the world by such lines of demarcation. There is nothing rational about bigotry. A bigot in a republic or monarchy is a bigot still, and is as proscriptive in either as power permits. To counteract all this, the permanent organized plans of mind's progress through rational education must be arrayed. Ex-clusive control of religion is claimed by the advocates of peculiar faith, one of the falsest pretences imaginable. Why such claims ? Does feeling that is a delusion not verified by facts, give it when the principals are false ? What a collusion between sophistry and bigotry ! What a compound has the Asiatic become, a vassal to despot-ism of peculiar faith. The Brahmin expelled the Bhuddist, by whom he was expelled, both giving India the blessings of civil war instead of religion; and thus it would be in England, if mind was not too enlightened for the bigotry of peculiar faith that fills the world even now with civil commotion, when it cannot embroil it in odious civil wars. Has not all Western Asia been ruined this way ? Has Egypt ever recovered from the *baseness of the priestocracy dynasty*, a blasting kingdom wherever its inquisitorial and proscriptive despotism is exerted ? Mind has been worth nothing under its most odious and execrable dictation.

The preservation of the public is more important than peculiar faith. Of course, the people do not know, but have self-delusion about peculiar faith, all of which is in the same category of error throughout the world. Lay aside all the bibles thereof, and learn of the moral sublimity of rational religion.

Peculiar faith embroils mankind, in families, countries, world, and universe, unfit for all. She is the pest of society, and the curse of mind. She is not trustworthy in the humblest cottage, nor the royal palace, where her sovereign rules her out, and turns his back on her for another pet, no more correct, but more subservient tool, to his whims and his despotic policy. All such creations are unknown to the Creator. Her little brief authority is most dangerous in the extremity to the tyrant, who exercises it thus improperly. In the name of religion, the universe, mind, God, repudiate all such.

Matrons, who make sacred family, and consecrate mind, by religion, to your God, take not this conglomeration of serpents to your bosom, to render man a conglomeration of all the worst of animality.

The religion of principles will restrain all bad acts, and elevate minds, always to be relied on, as sufficient. Cultivate this in your household, and you will render it the happiest, by the Creator's blessing. Then the world's despots will have no base to pretend to a faith false to all humanity, and abominable to all the purity of honest and truthful minds. Such despots will all be scouted from the face of ,the earth, and will be remembered for this their deadliest mental poison.

Nicholas, imitate the example of Peter of Russia, and give a constitutional government to your people. Cast aside that church sanctuary, and come into the rational church of God. Do not be associated in peculiar faith, with the inside barbarians of Asia. I am one of the sovereigns of America, your equal ; conservative principles are paramount to, and take precedence of all peculiar faiths and bibles, and necessarily exclude all such as in antagonism therewith.

There were peculiar faith tests, to hold office, until very recently even, in New Hampshire, that has abolished them by the present constitution. That is, only a protestant could hold office ! How green the people about religion ! Have they ever considered the impositions of the whole world, and that the priestocracy are the heads of the most damning faiths ? The fixing up of this world after man's fashion, not God's ways.

You, Jew and Christian. complain of Mahommedans and Mormons. You have taught them the degraded way to deceive man and brutalize woman, to outrage mankind and degrade humanity.

The peculiar faith people have no foundation whatever for their bibles, not a particle but false pretences. Peculiar faith has been setting the whole world at variance, in odious, murderous, criminal hostility, and yet the whole adopting it cannot prove its first point. Let it get out of the pulpit, and depart degraded. The world antagonisms, through peculiar faith, are as abundant as the collision of solar systems, if deranged. What section of the globe has not peculiar faith, its bibles, and priestocracy set at variance, pitting father against son. the household against itself ? What part of the world is not full of vulgar deadly conflicts of peculiar faith ? The whole world has labored but to little purpose, to get only peculiar faith. A wise and just man looks to his proper duty, not his peculiar faith, to mankind and God. Now peculiar faith certainly does not give any peculiar guarantee to the whole world, that has no particular safety but principles that are conservative for the universe.

How can you put the world at peace ? By the noble principles of rational religion. But peculiar faith obstructs all that, and causes improper conflicts. Take away such, as all means of antagonism. History of the world now tells the tale, paints the facts. When the people, under christian influence, drove the Mormons out of Missouri, Illinois, &c., if the last had had the full power of the sword, what a bloody war would have deluged America.

Would the world have seen an end to it for an age ? Has it yet seen the end ? The feud is silenced at present.

Why then, not stop all such stuff ; we will begin at the fountain-head. Can you call any such religion, that sheds blood ? That of God ? It was evolved by the worst passions, the most flagrant outrage on religion. Peculiar faith, christianity. Judaism, or any other has no truth, no honesty, no foundation, all built up to fool and defraud the world. Give us the dignity of religion and liberty, that comprehend the proper courtesy due the whole world, the official acts of the world-brotherhood. As often as any other peculiar faith is built up, so often is a base for peculiar squabbles, conflicts and antagonism, with the pure principles of rational religion, and the unity of God. Nothing short of rational intelligence, virtue and religion, can elevate the world, and keep it at its rightful point. All peculiar faiths are exclusive to their disgrace of having religion.

How many millions ruin themselves by partisan views?

It is all to no purpose that peculiar faith prevails.

The wise and virtuous world must look through all such designs of man, lustful and ambitious, to God. Religion is the highest link carried out in all its practical duties, that binds mind to Deity, the moral world with the universe. The peculiar faith-people, and their bibles, have no pretensions to principles, consequently their frame-work for society is destitute of truth, honor or honesty. Which is most destitute of these, the priestocracy, pettifoggers, who seek to cloak all the pretences of law, or the doctors of the old regime, who impose on the people their fraud, that the people cannot cure diseases ?

What can correct all this ? Conservative revolution.

The unprincipled, so far from thanking, actually war on conservative reformers.

Those who adopt peculiar faith-bibles, are prepared to advocate fanaticism, and all its absurd dogmas.

How much longer can the world be gulled with peculiar faith-bibles. What rational mind would ever think of making them the rule of his faith or practice ? My reverence to God and truth, forbids. A total conservative revolution alone can effect what is needed, as everything is wrong with monopolists, who usurp the support of the world.

Why are all peculiar faiths in such deadly animosity, antagonism to each other? Is it for holy zeal to the God of the universe, or is it to the god of profits? Are the people blinded, that they will not see all this? The God of universal conservative principles, desires the best of universal brotherhood, but the elements of all peculiar faiths are alien to all this. As some of the monopolies that have overrun, they have corrupted most feloniously the whole earth.

The advocates of peculiar faith act like aliens to each other—deadly hostile, and this they call religion, that unites the whole world into one universal rational, honorable, most friendly brotherhood.

Kings, and the priestocracy, have broken up the world's brotherhood by usurpation, and monopoly, among themselves, and no doubt, have secretly gloated at the peculiar faith mock-auction farces.

As one little Jew peculiar nation is to the whole earth, so is their peculiar faith in ratio to religion.

Peculiar faith and its bibles all absurd, incredible and blasphemous, that desecrate God's functions and creation, are due to the degraded regime of stupid, abominable ignorance, and despotism, that profits thereby. As go despotisms most certainly, so go all their machinery, as state faiths, and their livings, bibles, and all that fatten on the spoils of the people, the world, who are defrauded, contemned and laughed at, as fooled. Who could expect less than opposition from all the tribe, that is so unprincipled?

All the advocates of peculiar faith kill each others' faith.

Do not adopt any peculiar faiths that arise from the school of ignorance and fraud, that cause the priestocracy to support it by sophistry and falsehood, the people to maintain it by sectarian hatred and conflicts, to teach children the same, to the disgrace of parents.

There is no peace, nor can there be, between the different peculiar faith people. Under the influence of peculiar faith, bigotry, an unmitigated vassal of usurpation, runs through all the social rights, a curse to man's character and the world.

Peculiar faith will create millions of peculiar lies. What but the silence of their churches must follow? Stop the desecration of morals and religion, that are too holy for preachers and churches. They are the holy property of mind. I will do church-men justice, as possessors of mind, what they do not do themselves, their souls, minds nor God, justice in the first best capacity. If all will carry out uniformly the unity of God, then they will act consistently with truth and facts.

Peculiar faith takes away mind's merits and worth, and presents in the eclipse of mind, the darkest storms of fanaticism. Religion cannot possibly arouse up the storms of the world's conflicts, for she calms and soothes men's passions by the most legitimate rationality.

She holds all peculiar faith in abeyance, as a vile caricature, a detestable, contemptible demagogism. And all its bigots will carry out their infamous conspiracies upon the rights of mind, the conservative principles of the universe.

Peculiar faith talks of idols of heathens, the outside barbarians, under the dictation of its priestocracy. What odds does it make whether the idols be of stone or flesh, whether manufactured by hands employed in statuary, or fiction of imagination? Whether books called bibles, or images of any kind? Whether the polytheism has many gods, four or three? Whether in America or Europe, Asia or Africa, India, China or Japan, whether called Christian or Pagan, heathen inside or out, backwoods or forewoods, barbarians?

Who to-day, is defender of the faith? What faith? Peculiar faith. That is a piracy on religion, a petty larceny.

The spirit of perjury is extensively diffused throughout the world. Why is this? Because the foundation of truth is not permitted to take her legitimate sway in rational mind. This is the evil that peculiar faith diffuses over the world.

The proper and efficient system must be established, to abate the abominable world-nuisance of peculiar faith. That is the world-wide legislation on principles, and that is religion. What a conviction is forced on the world, that has been harassed its age by peculiar faith difficulties, that rational religion alone will vanquish the whole proposition.

As to the intelligent people of the United States, they have not investigated the subject of peculiar faith, being scared off by the ministers, the priestocracy. Let this matter be wisely discussed. All good men, whether deceived priestocracy or not, ought to seek consultation of mind's light by the best investigation, and drop their errors, if discovered, or adhere to truths.

What are the crimes, the taints, spots foul and reeking with gore of peculiar faith! She commenced with human sacrifices as her spoils, the weak, those in the way of others, and thus her infuriated morbid appetite reeking with gore, cried for more. She slaughtered millions of adults. Did she ever sacrifice in America? Yes, among the outside and inside barbarians, in every land. She erected the demon's altar, and Christians presided, and horridly did they perform the oblation, for two hundred victims were the offer! That was not all—that is not all—that will not be all. They have sacrificed all over the earth. The only protection to man is through rational mind, rational religion. Send missionaries to Pagans. Let missionaries be sent to Christians. As long as the demon peculiar faith stalks over the earth, in Christian, Mormon, Jewish, Mahommedan, Brahminical, Bhuddist or any other cloak, man's life, property, reputation, conscience, religion, is not safe. All are at the mercy of the demon. Take rational education away, and man must see, for man will feel. Toleration goes, and intoleration with her base proscriptions ensue. Let the last strong hold of gigantic world-sophistry, be dissolved, before the light of the Creator. How curious is it, that the world with all its mental improvement, adheres to the juggler's superstition of all peculiar faiths, and think that they are something. Why does not every wise patriot in the world, rise in the majesty of rational intellect, and put it down? Because hitherto, it was only a change of peculiar faith, for some other as iniquitous. They are all flagitious, and will be superseded by rational religion, the only thing to sustain the perfection of laws and the proper position of mankind.

The rational soul could not receive any of the pretended gifts of peculiar faith, with all their bribes, no matter what the slander of human nature by sycophants, that every man has his price. But the priestocracy affect spiritual faith.

Peculiar faith has no kind of religion, therefore it has none spiritual. She is a potent engine of deception and injury to the world; is a dangerous thing to handle, both for professor and the world on which it is used.

All peculiar faith, as Christianity, Mormonism, &c., is sordid sectarianism. All that is valuable is under the banner of rational religion. Analyze peculiar faith.—All that it is worth is the borrowed, yet ever unacknowledged capital of rational religion, the balance is its own peculiar vices. Its virtues are those of rational religion, its vices and their results are its own. Who would own such for a slave? Peculiar faith has filled the world with iniquity, dissension, and ungodly antagonism, perfectly irreconcilable for ever.

No peculiar faith people can convict another clearly. They are all equal, but have to bow to the majesty of monotheism, that convicts them all of petty larceny on her domains. Why are the Jews silenced? They are not allowed to speak in their own rights. What verdant people; when all might act as men, honestly and truthfully, in rational religion. The peculiar faith tuition can never teach the world its duty, for it has not the elements.

To whom can mind apply? To peculiar faith, that has wronged it so much, and crushed its rights? All peculiar faith people miserably neglect impiously the word of God. There is no evidence but what is rational. God is the only standard in all this matter.

Conversion is necessarily rational. Profession of faith, is it? The operation of the spirit is so powerful, as some pretend, as to cause the hysterical to faint, jerk, &c.

Who is at fault, the preachers that preach, or the smart people who desire it? Will you, good citizens, pay a preacher to help cheat you with the most wily sophistry, and both cheat your God; no, that cannot be done; cheat yourselves, truly. You have to admit that it was bad faith that set the Christians and Mahommedans together in arms for two centuries.

Now, what is that which keeps you Christians from a feeling well disposed towards the Jew, Mormon, and Mahommedan, on the one side, and the Gentile on the other? Because of the sectarian spirit wherewith you were inducted into your church, the vile spirit of antagonism to rational religion and the unity of God. In all peculiar faith there is no intrinsic religion.

These peculiar faiths commenced in the deepest corruptions with false pretences in oracles, auguries at first, and have become worse steeped in guilt as they have grown older. They have some plausible sophisty, if they had not God's only universal word contradicting themselves the world over. Peculiar faith makes polytheists, who make atheists. Rational religion makes monotheists. Every peculiar faith has degraded the God of the universe. Not at all; they have blasphemed him and degraded themselves, substituting their peculiar imbecile god therefor. How long will the people hire them to do so much wrong?

As to peculiar faith, which is to believe any things the priests told, that is too un-

civilized, too peculiar. for my mind, constituted as it is, for the reception of universe
facts, to believe or know. The present age needs civilization and religion, not peculiar
faith nor its ignoble priestocracy.
    What is the difference between Jewish idolatry and peculiar faith, human sacrifices,
butchery of mind, and those of other nations? There is no history in peculiar faith as
Christianity, it is all story. All peculiar faith is totally unprincipled. Peculiar faith,
like a base usurper, is not grateful to mind, that she has conspired against in all ages and
governments. The world does not need any more church or world idolatry, to ruin
mind by the sophistry of peculiar faith.
    Superstition is dovetailed with ignorance, both of which must be removed by rational
education, the great world lever. All bibles are built up by superstition and ignorance,
and retained by bigotry and absolutism. Peculiar faith of the world is dead through rational mind, and it is for the American people to act first in the burial, the sooner the
better, that the world may reach an equitable distribution of its own rightful perquisites.
Peculiar faith is destructive, cannot be conservative, it is a doll, a vulgar and dangerous
plaything. It is a humbug, as irresponsible power of all kinds is a humbug; so also is
military prowess piracies of all kinds. What can the world-freemen care for peculiar
faith, the world's deceiver, enemy and curse? The world has been fooled and injured
by it long enough, to banish all such to non-entity, by rational education.
    These peculiar faith people, Romanists and Mahommedans, bullied the world, Asia,
Europe and Africa, for nearly 200 years, producing the worst of fanatical wars, bloodshed and massacres. What they did, their posterity can do, would do, but for mind that rebukes them. We need not go out of our own country. The puritans drove the quakers and
baptists away. The Christians drove the Mormons out of Missouri, Illinois, to the
western wilderness. Did the Egyptians drive the Jews out of Egypt, to the Arabian
wilderness? That is the question? Now if the Mormons had had equal numbers, the
world might have seen bloodshed for centuries. As it is, who can answer for the result? When did peculiar faith absolve itself from power, without compulsion?
    Leave off all the pretences. Poor bigoted villages—yet cities are made up of villages
—that is the world. Let the potency of rational mind rise in its might. Persons must
be weak minded, to adopt any peculiar faith. It shows a vitiated depraved taste, to
seek error, as all such faith unquestionably is. The world has to avoid most clearly,
soul-smugglers. I consider all peculiar faith nonplused. The priestocracy have introduced a harlot before the world for religion, and the two first have destroyed millions
of the people and deranged with mad superstition. Give us religion, and remove all
these the farthest from us. Do not give us absurd copies, or copyists.
    Who could trust their rights willingly with one who would deliberately affect that
faith as an equivalent for credulity, was a governing principle. The present peculiar
faiths are permitted by sufferance, not received. I would not commit myself to a cause
that could not defend itself, and that required sophistry to deceive its adherents. The
ancients could not distinguish between individuality and peculiarity, in their polytheism.
The Jews were as bad as any, and the adopting moderns are still worse.
    As to getting religion, the notions of all the pulpit sophists, the priestocracy, through
their peculiar faiths, are positively absurd. How can one get what is not elementary,
not there—a non-entity? Polytheists and atheists cannot defend one single point of
their peculiar faith, for both stand peculiarly affected to the God of the universe. All
that they do is to uphold all by sophistry, false pretences, the curse instead of mind's
blessings. What perfect absurdity is there respecting these would-be world-guardians,
when they are destroying their own best prospects by their own perversions? But
what if the advocates of peculiar faith go wrong, how can the matter be remedied, without a right and competent standard? How came all to differ so exceedingly, if there
were a right standard? Suppose one is not baptized right, ye rigid sticklers, what if
false preachers, as some baptists, have been excluded the pulpit after baptism of others.
Was that valid? This question should be submitted to the only competent, because
only proper tribunal, rational mind's supreme functions. The whole family of peculiar
faiths is a desperate set of fraud-mongers, manufacturers, and inventors. You emperors, brothers of the moon, in your lunacy of peculiar faith, pontiffs, you are held in
abeyance to the religion of God, who estimates man not for brief authority, but for
personal merits. None of you can govern yourselves right, much less your people.
Resign, and act like men, not as world-impostors. Down, all ye priestocracy absolu
tists and all, in your vilest, basest ignorance. How many forms of peculiar faith-super
stition, as Millerism, have deranged people?
    Peculiar faith will not do for any government of mankind, as all the world absolutely
needs Monotheism. The social circle is cut up by sectarians, overrun by secret societies. Peculiar faith is dangerous to the world.

The world is fanatic enough, but it was as much as a man's life was worth to oppose the ancient faith. Now he is looked upon as accursed—recently he was burnt at the inquisitorial stake, and in the times of Moses, as Korah and the nobles, their lives paid awful forfeits for defence of popular rights by proper discussion. Is this the truth on which the gospel has been admitted, when blood was the forfeit for its resistance. At first and last, blood and sophistry were its defences. The dynasty of the priestocracy is felonious and despotic in the extreme, that offers up human sacrifices in the ignorant ages of the world, and keeps it, when mind knows better, bound as a vassal to the accursed car of superstition, bigotry, and sophistry.

Do not disturb this faith, as it has a hold. That is the doctrine of monopoly and usurpation. What is worse, Jew-bibles, faiths, priestocracy, or the council-smuggling of bibles, or the priestocracy-smuggling of sophistry ever since? As to society of Americans, people think such, protection; truly none is, unless principles are uniformly adopted.

The spirit of peculiar faiths is demon, arising from perversion of mind peculiarly acted on. All such must be corrected by the spirit, soul, religion, that evolves high-toned sentiments, and the manly actions becoming the light of mind. What would the world be at any time, now or for the future, but for enlightened public opinion, that keeps down the power of peculiar faith and malign influence? Mind in its best ration-ality must be ever invoked by the liberal spirit of mankind, the world, to protect against bible-clans and absolutism-bullies, above all the covert, concealed, insidious, ensnaring priestocracy-treachery.

The vulgar idea of keeping the people out of the only means, philosophy and science, which are keys to detect all false faiths, is a doctrine of the jugglers of mind, the priest-ocracy. What good will false positions of faith and morals do the world? Abolish all such, as bad faith and injurious morals, to the whole world. Let them be blown sky-high. Of all the absurd talk that ever was uttered, this thing of faith, the food of the designing priestocracy, beats all. There is no sense, truth, or honesty, in it. It is the craziest, most rickety sophistry of all the world sophistry.

Mind needs the highest improvement of mind, acting on mind, instead of that false pretence of self-sufficiency claimed by the priestocracy, who affect the perfection of their old rickety bible; that is all the reason, despite of all these miscreants, in the progress of mind's expansion, why the modern peculiar faith excels the ancient, being a nearer approach to monotheism, as to all improvement most rational. Now there is no reason to delay the full improvement at once, in discarding all peculiar faiths, as a world cancer or incubus, an ignis fatuus. There can be no distrust of religion, but there is of all peculiar faiths. There is no hope but on facts, as faith. Any rational mind knows that no peculiar faith-bible can be sustained, and if any member chose to have joined the church without knowing anything about it, that is another question; that is his difficulty. Peculiar faith enabled the absolutists to carry out their base de-signs better. The Druids, who were priests, commanded the people in all things. They sacrificed human beings to any amount. Of course they were savages. All the excesses of temple expenses, are robberies of the proper world treasure. The world requires justice to the people, not a vain and idle idolatry. All peculiar faith is analo-gous and untrue. How many wars have not been excited in all countries, for peculiar faith, miscalled sacred?

The world has groaned under them, for centuries. Greece can tell the hor-rid tale, that her liberty was desecrated to that unholy spirit, and was swept away by Philip, king of Macedon. What cares peculiar faith for victimizing mankind, barbarizing him, so she gets her ungodly aims? Sacred wars. Accursed were they, indeed.

Will you sacrifice yourself, soul, highest interests, religion, God, to peculiar faith and myrmidons of any kind, no matter the name, that are entirely worthless? There is but one religion, and that is rational, and that you can only have by one universal Creator, too powerful for a messiah, too pure for a priestocracy. Nicholas and Chinese empe-ror. lama, pope, and papa, bishops, and all the tribe, you make yourselves lower than men, to be one of the priestocracy, and prate about faith that is the foulest blot on man's mind, the craziest of all thoughts. Do not desert religion for peculiar faith. It is not opinion nor any peculiarity that is to prevail, in regard to the bible

All are matters of facts, not opinions or manufactured faith. The change cannot be contemplated, when the certainty is fixed. Peculiar faith bibles have nothing to do with religion, no more than counterfeits have with the currency.

Let the world, mankind, decide on what is religion, and their deed, by a firm resolve, is done. Religion is a practicable universe problem, while peculiar faith is nothing, trading on false pretences, false capital, and in a constant false position.

The will indomitable, arising from free agency of mind, is that to meet the religious solution. You speak of enemies to the Christian or peculiar faith? How came you an advocate of any such faith, but by the devices of man, tory, traitor, deserter, base, execrable deserter, to monotheism, pure rational religion? You talk of its defects, who have no religion. Why, sir, monotheism has no defects that you, deserter, ought not be ashamed to help to remedy, when arising from imperfect state of mind, that much short of rationality. Is Japan partly cut out by priestocracy sectarianism from most of the world? While rational religion exalts the world in all its highest expansions of greatness and magnanimity, peculiar faith debauches and ruins. The world has no need of the last, while it has to pay bounden duty to the first.

The contingency of peculiar faith depends on peculiar education, both monsters of iniquity, that can be anything and everything as dark ages permit, and cannot possibly form any part of the uniform possession of religious elements in every mind. Peculiar faith debauches mind, but religion enlarges and liberalizes it to its sublimest expansion of rationality.

The first does not enable mind to reach the true resources of man's intended position in the universe, and must be dropped as utterly faithless and worthless. If any peculiar faith was true revelation the whole world could not be kept from it, as part of the functions of mind. On that view, then, rational religion should secure rational minds. So it does, in proportion to the rationality of mind. That is certain. This subject is exhaustless, and impregnable by peculiar faith in every mind, that has been effectually exhausted, and only proves the assaulters impious traitors to God and mind.

Dispensations is it that the peculiar faith advocates claim, and that always the last. The Christians took precedence of the Jews, who doubtlessly had theirs of their older neighbors. Next, the Mahometans take precedence of their predecessors, with the doctrine " to fight for the faith was an act of obedience to God." Since then, the Mormons are the orthodox, but all hold on to their faith or their interest.

How many hundreds of years has England been harassed between factions of contending faiths, neither party having aught but peculiar interests and motives in view? In what country have not the bitterest feuds prevailed respecting peculiar faith? All the large grand divisions of the world have sustained the deepest, bitterest feuds. France has had her portion; India, England, China, even free America. And how often have countries had to change their peculiar faiths! Of all the most atrocious butcheries of the world, that of Paris was the most barbarous, not less than of 70,000 people. Now, can any one inform the world that such was one iota for religion, but that it was just the reverse? Peculiar faith brutalizes and debauches mind, while rational religion commands, civilizes, enlarges, and ennobles its faculties. Not but pure rational religion and mind prevent the false claimants, the peculiar faith people from constantly agitating and deranging the world; thus the whole of mankind must see that they constitute not only the duty but the highest only protection in mind's especial providence.

What are the court faith and Romanists now doing in England, that has had, such dissensions for centuries? Now most of peculiar faith people are perfectly psychologized in all the self-delusions of bible follies.

What a miserable framework of society, the people of free governments are slaves thereby to superstition, all in abeyance to perjury to swear to it.—Traitors, if not supporters; hypocrites, if not sincere; and perjurers, if upholders and endorsers.

The world cannot be too guarded against all the evils of peculiar education, that kills off billions of the human family. Peculiar faith bibles were to fool and cheat the world, mankind with.

Good, honest, truthful citizens, do you want such? Will you endorse your character worse than your worst enemies can do that? What can you be thinking of, to despoil your own soul of its God-creation birth-right, the elements of religion, for robbers and pirates, the priestocracy?

You church vassal, what are you, though in name a freeman? Would you refuse to-day the exposure of peculiar faith, tory-like, to have your selfish folly concealed? You help to fool yourself in helping cheat the world out of right government and religion. Think of that, emperors of vast empires. You present mockeries not worth trash. Peculiar faith approaches the most masterly of all supreme sublime subjects, and has been mistaken in all past ages, even the present, for religion. This subject has not been analyzed, and now only proves a more exalted state of rational mind, progressing to an indefinite series of happier solutions, the mighty creation-gifts of a perfect Almighty. What can polytheists, who are crazy about peculiar faith, know of religion?

Atheists are deranged about nature. All their tribes will be dissolved, when religion will be self-portrayed as indissoluble to all eternity. The bibles of all peculiar faith are necessarily the most arrant forgeries and false pretences. Now, will not the world have to sustain, as long as it permits such, all their combinations and collusions to maintain the whole swindling operations? There are some members of the peculiar faith persuasion, even members of the church, that are not corrupted by the association. Some people at first know not how to decide respecting their faith, and only had as all the world had it. by peculiar education ; hence their motives cannot be impugned. Let not your vulgar peculiar faith pollute the soul of man in any respect, nor let its bibles taint his lips, nor its demoralization influence his actions.

What a monster is peculiar faith, reeking in bloody, murderous sacrifices of those sacrificing, in place of religion, that consecrates the pure soul to God—that, with the universe-problem, consecrates the soul's immortality. I impeach all peculiar faiths as the most murderous and blasphemous trifling with souls or minds.

All peculiar faith doctrines cause the world to be still in barbarism, to build barbarian walls around nations, families, and though Christ did not draw the sword, his followers have too awfully done so, and that not for two hundred, but nearer two thousand years, and will for two millions, if mind will permit. Now, the world-problem must be solved by mind in sincerity of soul and zeal of spirit. Take away Christianity and Mormonism, Mahommedanism and Judaism, Brahminism and Bhuddish peculiar faith from man, the world, mankind, and how can any quarrel? How many peculiar faith people act outrageously wrong at times? What better can be expected when churches present no principles by peculiar doctrines. Do not blame the churches, but the priestocracy, who, if they do not know better, ought for that reason to quit the pulpit as a case of hopeless ignorance, and if they do, they should quit for want of honesty ; they should quit any how.

It is utterly absurd to expect aught of peculiar faith but the base elements that injure the world. It is impossible for peculiar faith, that is conceived in fraud, to do good. Give no excuse for felony. The world has no excuse nor apology for peculiar faith or its bibles, as rational religion is the only proper basis.

As to peace conventions, you may have them to eternity, but if you do not take away this earth-curse, peculiar faith, you cannot get a brotherhood. Take all such away, and the mighty question is solved, for the world will rush to it. The proper choice of life calling should be made, that no reproach be sustained.

Sectarians reproach each other with charges of spurious and corrupt faith. God help all such, when the whole faith is counterfeit. Stop this deliberate fraud, this sacrifice of principle, this means of hypocrisy or duping, for intelligent preachers cannot believe what is preached.

I protest against all flimsy reforms of peculiar faiths, as nothing short of entire utter expulsion will do. Rational education is the only very thing to accomplish it fully. Let the youthful mind be fully instructed in science, then it can choose for itself. What kind of morals has this kind of faith, when all the preachers are smuggled impostors on the world, without any license at all.

All the peculiar faiths in the world, cannot demonstrate the first part of God Almighty.

It is your fault and crime that your audience cannot subscribe to your doctrine. Give up all such ignoble policy, and let monotheism teach you and them. Your polytheism furnishes the paternity to atheism. You are doubly accountable for both sins. Your denial of the last does not absolve you, when you are guilty of the iniquities of the first. It is your caricature of God, that forces the revolting and disgusting picture on mankind. The people are to blame when they can rightly investigate for their imbecile credulity in all such characters.

The very primary possession of God's perfection, precludes all peculiar bibles, all covenants thereof. What is light? Is it not a universal attribute? Is discovery of all science at an end, consummated? Hence I ask correction for faith fallacies.

When was any fanaticism ever routed, but that it aspersed the means that did it? When truth is violated for fanatical origin, it will be murdered for its propagation. A code of monotheism declares that no ultraisms should be advanced.

Peculiar faith engenders fanaticism of itself odious. Do fanatics hate the taking the life of opponents? That is disproved by their bloody world butcheries. Do they ever forgive? They hate and war in proportion to their bigotry, &c.

How, Christian or Mormon, Jew or Mahommedan, can you exclude all other peculiar faiths, unless by rational principles that exclude your own? How can you exclude the atheist?

Give peculiar faith power, and whether Romanist or Protestant, it will vindictively, ferociously and piratically use it, desecrating religion of principles, whether in Massachusetts, Sweden, or the world, killing hundreds to millions of innocent children, women and men, their own fellow citizens for witches, expelling others for their faith, or destroying them, whether in Connecticut, voting the poor Indians out of their peaceable possessions of lands and themselves in, as the saints of their peculiar god, preventing mothers from kissing their babes on Sunday, and other outrageous deeds, or whether in South and Central America, destroying millions of Indians because they were heretics.

When the black catalogue of the peculiar bible pirates shall be unfolded, then we see the most abominable of all worldly abominations.

Faith revealed by barbarian Jews: will that do for us? Polytheist, how can you talk of conscience and morals, when you have neither truth nor honesty in your platform?

You call yourselves reformers and Protestants of Catholics, why not reform yourselves out of all the vicious dogmas? Why protest against a part? If Catholic, why do you cut up the social world into fragments? Why cannot you establish universal Catholicism? Because you cannot change universal principles to peculiar dogmas.

The ways of peculiar faith that does not answer to the mind or world's demand, are delinquent. If its bibles were true, truth conquers; but if untrue, as proved, the advocates should do justice to truth in rejecting them. The figurative language of all peculiar bibles, fills the vacuum of imposition. Too much of it is made to mean, as the guesser intimates.

Peculiar faith gives us the trash of men, not the pure intrinsic blessings of religion. It trades on the capital of monotheism, and then acts the assassin. All peculiar faiths are instrumentalities, as far as they comport with monotheism, with the exalted religion of principles. They may seek to appropriate it, but they will be scouted and defeated in the ignoble attempt. They may clothe their intentions in all kinds of false colors, bedeck them with all kinds of garments, still they will be disclosed, and will. in the tide of time, be exposed as usurpers, and monopolists. Religion has stamped in her acts the full character of universality, while peculiar faith has only a temporary and fading locality, and that in spots, that blur and disgrace the originator and followers. as the vassals of untruth. Peculiar faith has nothing to commend her hideous deformity.

If any good be ascribed to her deeds, it is because they are misunderstood. If any value be attached to the crusades, they can be met as too expensive, for the drama is bloodshed of millions of victims, and virtue and religion were mocked and defied.

However all peculiar faiths fill the pockets of the priestocracy, still they can never rise to the dignity of religion, nor possess its richest purest gifts to mind or soul.

Their divinities are all daubs by the vulgar hands of the priestocracy. They are neither human nor divine, for they are fanatically inhuman. Their highest appreciations of their impostor-masters, fall short of the noble principles of deity. Peculiar faiths are incompetent to draw the proper distinctions between the elements of virtue and vice, and pander to all the worst fanaticisms of reckless enthusiasm. They are ignorant of the noblest purposes of creation of mind and soul, and pander to the ignoble fables of peculiar bibles.

What peculiar claims has any peculiar faith? Has Romanism? Look at the pretensions of the Asiatics as the Faqueers. Peculiar faith has no principles. As regards Protestants finding fault with those of the Roman church for idols, have not both, and all such followers of peculiar faith, the rankest idols, as bibles, faith, and church? Who were the ancient people but serfs, and vassals, that dared not think for themselves, having but little means of investigation, few books, and little learning?

The religion of principles impeaches all peculiar faith, and its bibles, all emanating from paganism.

Peculiar faith is the vile offspring of superstition and toryism—treachery. Do you wish to be right? Religion addresses itself to the whole man, through mind the most rational. The absurdities of peculiar faith are endless. They only have doctrines, no principles.

The church, peculiar faith and bibles, have bullied the world, and driven much of it to the rankest infidelity to God the Creator.

Where is an enlightened philanthropy, when peculiar faith always makes fragments of society first, and of itself afterwards, while religion establishes a universal brotherhood, and confirms for eternity?

What are morals and faith built on false bibles worth? They never can reach the dignity of religion, a holy element of mind's purity and excellence.

Peculiar faith has to yield up its tory doctrines to the religion of principles. It is treacherous to the greatest good of the greatest number, that is all.

The teachings of all peculiar bibles and faith, clash with principles, that rule them out, as demoralizing and libelous on nature and nature's God.

Peculiar faith shivers society into fragments, while religion builds up a harmonious brotherhood of this world, prepared to greet those of all other planets of the universe. The peculiar faithites should surrender their commissions that are false, and their churches should be made schools for religious discussion and rational education.

Peculiar faith advances only peculiar doctrines, while religion, the sublime consummation of all duty, is the evolution of universal principles.

While the first never can attain the last, the last never descends, condescends to the first.

The world must start right or not at all.

Whom does peculiar faith suit best, hysterical old women and imbecile men, afraid to investigate the indelible truths of Monotheism?

All peculiar bibles have their peculiar faith, peculiar causes, antagonistic to religion. What can you get by exchange of all the first for the last? The highest purposes of creation.

The Mormons, &c., are religious not because they are Mormons, but because they have the elements of rational religion. None but Monotheism will answer as God intended, since all others, as peculiar faiths, the peculiar policies of vain and ambitious man, have been fully tried, and are self-convicted as peculiar curses. There were thousands of bibles more than nations, for the Romans had many, so did the Greeks, the Egyptians. What do we need of them, their documents, when their people, as the Jews, were below the scale of civilization? All were idolatrous, and their bibles represent that idolatry. They of course do not teach religion, that has been advancing all the time by God's universal means of mind. It is all wicked nonsense to adopt such. Is not peculiar faith the result of peculiar education, then a man is Christian, Pagan, Jew, or Mormon, as peculiarly taught? What, then, is to correct him, but rational religion, that gets the only proper standard from the unity of God? Coldness of faith, amounts to coldness, poverty, want of truth and facts.

How convenient are mystery, faith, &c., yet how disgusting and contemptible is the sophistry that employs them. Is the cunning bigot, bigot because he revokes the rationality of his mind, aware how much he cheats his own immortal soul, when he is conceitedly seeking to evade and equivocate on the valid and unanswerable objections of monotheism? When the sophist is cornered, then he does not understand the scriptures. Does he go for rational understanding; does he speak rationally and understandingly, or does he equivocate to commit himself·to the falsehoods of the priestocracy? The man who equivocates about religion is ineffably stupid.

Will you force the conscience of children in not only doubtful but false positions? What crime.

No country, no matter how much thought to be a republic, can be entirely civilized or free where liberal discussion cannot be duly had to investigate and exercise the first principles of religion, &c.

All peculiar faiths are necessarily behind the science of the times.

As all peculiar faiths are utterly false, their advocacy is dishonest and dishonorable. What effrontery in their priestocracy. that chide and berate their gods.

Prayers to God are dictation of mind.

Peculiar faith brutalizes mind and libels the God of the universe. The degraded murderer, Moses, upbraids and rebukes his own god! His idol.

Take away all the whimsical vicious shackles of the social framework of faith that is peculiar, and let faith, the rational monotheism, the reality, supplant as she will polytheism and atheism, the shadows. Pursue all that is legitimate.

Can anything but peculiar faiths beget fanaticism? Can á hysterical woman reason comprehensively? She causes the doubt by her perverseness, when mind compromises itself and dearest, noblest interests of soul for bibles of peculiar trash.

The funniest part of peculiar faith is, that each adherent quarrels with the others about the untruths, and they are all hostile, and act like people that lived in glass houses. The truth could not make them do this. Their faith cannot cause them to see principles, for which they have mistaken untruths.

Man's passions are natural, and are liable to perversions and perverted enjoyments. Now, what is to restrain them as lust, murder, and above all, revenge, that is so sweet? Atheism follows blind nature, the apparent plane, and a mere custom of faith rules polytheism. What is to correct all this? Comprehend all the dark and defective points of both, and see where they tend. All these are, with their codes or bibles, most peculiar, most contemptible, below criticism, were it not for the social evils executed by them. Their subsequents falsify their position, and commit suicide of all, murder all. Nothing but rational religion, ever referable to its standard, is immutable and conservative on principles. All peculiar faiths are nuisances to society, the intellectual religion of monotheism. How can the world get rid of any peculiar that is allied to the state or clique influence.

See what a host, a countless family of nuisances from peculiar faith, as Judaism, &c. It is a vast crime, not less than sacrilege, to misunderstand peculiar faith for religion. God has given full evidence of himself in the universe, the fault is in mind's peculiar perverseness, &c. So far from man falling, it was the fall of the priestocracy, who fabricated the fable of man's fall.

What interest have the sovereign people of the world in peculiar faith, that makes hypocrites and knaves? She is a horrid deformity and base speculation in all the pretensions of the priestocracy. All peculiar bibles have no platform, while that of religion stands on the platform of the universe. Where was the world thousands of years before the institution of all such malign influences? Where was Christian conservation the eighth century, under the supremacy of Saracen Mahommedan learning? How dare any tory peculiar faithite assume one iota of merit, when his faith's demerits are those of the impostor?

Peculiar faith is separable from mind's organization, and alien to it, while religion of principles, a totally different gift, is the only sure guide, as the reflector of the universe creator, to mind to form and insure the perfect soul. Peculiar faith fills the world with sycophants and hypocrites, vassals to untruth and dishonesty—governed as time-servers for timely policies. Is this religion that acts independently of all such trash, ennobled as she is by divine institutions—love to God—justice to man, to whom she presents the hope of best future bliss? Can bigots change? No persons wise and prudent should compromit their dignity in expecting reason from fanatical bigots, who subvert reason by miserable peculiar trash, and are, tory-like, pledged to uphold it at the world's expense. If peculiar faithites were to act in good faith to religion, they would resign all the false pretences of such faiths, and act under the auspices of religion. She should make a gentleman complete, in all the refined courtesies and intellectual duties in life.

Why are so many liars in the world—so false and dishonest? Because the framework of society identified with peculiar faith, is thus predicated.

These are the forfeits that vice pays to virtue, faith to religion, after all the disguises of brief authority and despotism now exposed. The advocates of all peculiar faiths are not at all entitled to the term of infidels for their opponents who conscientiously disbelieve their bibles, as they themselves are in the light of impostors till they demonstrate their own position.

Religion is the supremacy of principle to the majesty of which, peculiar faith should bow as long as reason is in the ascendant. Infidel to what? Falsehood, or Truth?

Of course if your peculiar bible is destitute of truth and proof, there is no infidelity, but the bible is an imposture, and the makers, aiders and abettors are impostors. All the illegitimate tribes of peculiar faiths are absolutely dangerous to the peace and dignity of the world. The miserable frame-work of society predicated on false pretences of bibles, cause deception and hypocrisy, and that enables the intelligent to see that there are no real foundations to all such, and the profligate of these seeing that, act as if exempt from all social, moral and religious restraints.

Can there be a worse code than that of the ecclesiastics who are unworthy of such office before the people if they knew no better, and most certainly unworthy of all such if they do, being ignoramuses in the first, and deceivers in the second. The sooner all such are got rid of the better, as the cause of religion is injured by them all the time.

All peculiar faiths are inanities, non-entities, direct impositions, of course all their agents act impostors. Analyze them as you will, still they have no intrinsic religion or inherent merit—not a particle.

Why cannot the world learn to tell the truth in religion, and not turn traitor to itself in its own best interests—is it possible that it submits to be swindled so easily, by all such false pretences? Put all that go to build up false faiths, to rear the most splendid fabric to philanthropy and humanity.

Only think of the family bible of peculiar faith! It had best be called the family folly of peculiar credulity, a nothingariness for religion surely. Its inspirations are all false. Peculiar faith confessional, hurries the priestocracy to the worst of impiety. Is the world determined to be imposed on? Then let it keep up the peculiar faith no matter the name, and its impostors.

The best of all things, the purity of your conscience, is surrendered to those that violate its holiest functions. Never violate conscience for all the priestocracies in the world. The peculiar faithites are disposed to abuse their best friends for peculiar exploded bibles, a libel on God, mind and religion.

Calvin is adored by his followers, murderer as he was. Reformed peculiar faith! The only way to reform all such is to exclude it altogether from mind.

Why do all peculiar faith advocates bring forth trivial matters, when they fly the only essential, an indubitable proof of the authenticity of their scriptures? Why will they not, as gentlemen, quit their sophist theme, never to be proved to the satisfaction of any gentleman? Whence did all peculiar faiths get their bibles? Out of the lying priestocracy. The difference between any peculiar faiths, Roman or protestant, Christianity or Judaism, is nothing, when all are positively pagan, utterly false before religion. That they call religion has no truth; monotheism presents the only infallible authority to rational mind, acting on the unity of the Creator.

The best argument of fallacy, or that destroys the whole position, is furnished by one peculiar faith against all the rest. Come, priestocracies, all to the proofs of your peculiar bibles, that if given decide the question, but if not proved, as they cannot be, estop you and your commission, so much so that you are disgraced to appear at all more in the pulpit.

As peculiar faith people have resorted to thousands of tricks in the invention and fabrication of their bibles, or oracle-codes, as the ancient priestocracy universally did, they have had to adopt all the ingenuity imaginable to carry them thoroughly out or through. The doctrine of mental reserve is that permitted, adopted, advised by churches. What can be a greater perjury, except the perjury of making their bibles, for the other is only the consistent performance of it.

Mind, that has been espoused into the adoption of the scriptures of peculiar faith, has been libeled, bribed, seduced or bewildered. The world-scars show the marks of peculiar faith persecutions all over it. All peculiar faiths commit sacrilege on monotheism. A convention of all the sectarians would destroy all polytheism, and establish atheism on its ruins, unless they could hear the voice of reason, as monotheism arrests all this fanaticism. Peculiar faith is murderous and corrupt. All sectarians, and they are all so universally, that feign, adopt or advocate peculiar faith, go for trash, trifles.

However churchmen affect to be infallible or orthodox, their position is entirely that of peculiar faith that has no infallibility, purity or religion. I concede to all church sincere people, seeking their supposed soul's salvation, all proper deference to good motives and sincerity of good faith, but candidly declare to them that they have adopted a false bad faith to preserve it, which the sooner laid aside the better. They are in the foulest crowd, that has taken the worst advantage of them.

Morals, religion and world's good are all unsafe in the keeping of all such bibles and people.

How could it be otherwise, when there is no proper capital for principles that are vitally conservative for, or bind the universe together? The only thing that commends monotheism is, that she is the true exponent of religion, the only conservative of a world's morals.

Let then all church people, that are sincere in good faith, come forward to this only right platform, and secure all the greatest good to the greatest number, that is all.

Peculiar faithites are incomparably worse than infidels and atheists. Are not their peculiar bibles the base of many evils? They have no honorable, rational proof at all established of such pretences, and all this can be most easily demonstrated to rational mind, on the clearest principles, rules and nature of evidence.

There can be no rational honorable difficulty, on this point. And yet these people persist in imposing their counterfeits on a credulous people. They must know them counterfeit.

Would you cheat or swindle mind for a false faith, to benefit false teachers, world sophists, the priestocracy? God forbid—rational mind forbid. Act for mind, mankind, the Creator.

The world should not go it blind, as to peculiar faith. When the advocates of peculiar faith speak of principles, they should know that such faith and principles are perfectly incompatible.

The question is not to find out anything of recent revelations, as the one contemporary with creation was the only one, and that was by and through the universe. As to revelations, that is most absurd, for they can be pretended and renewed all the time. There is no end to all such cursed foolishness.

God's plans are being perfected on conservative principles, and time on their execution reveals the facts.

How are you to comprehend all rational minds, within the pale of safety? Are you to wait for their peculiar conversion to peculiar faiths, that is doctrines or pretences, with some impostor their head, and some church their demagogue, or adopt the religion of principles, which alone guide and govern the universe forever? All peculiar faiths are but editions of each other, all from oracle-mongers, the pretended soothsayers and augurs; the Jew or Christian no better than the Egyptian or Persian. They are all pagan to religion—all idol-worship, scenting of priests and priestesses—vile impostors.

It is not only the good faith that rules, but action on that faith. There can be but two kinds of faith, good and bad; the first universal, the last, peculiar faith, that is made by peculiar education. Universal faith is by God, for mind. Peculiar faith usurps that of God, gives a false construction to things, propagates false doctrines and tenets, and produces bad actions, evils of opinions and feuds; of course, never can be right. A man, with such faith, to talk of getting religion! Such a fellow has not foot-hold, much less a platform, for religion. Religion is of the soul, while peculiar faith may be of the heart! as the advocates pretend.

All peculiar faith people make imperfect gods equal to no gods, for they are the priestocracy's gods, and none else; hence they play into the hands of the atheists, and affect passion for their own imbecility. But sophists never know what is right, and bigots cannot change, if bigots. What a hopeful pair! The bigot refers you to the book, the bible. Why so? Because of prophecies and miracles. But there are neither miracles nor prophecies, for they are all lies. All the old soothsayers and augurs of all nations pretended to all these; but they, of course, were frauds, to tickle the credulity of simpletons, willing to be fooled.

Is there anything lovely or novel in pecular faith, that had its drama in every ancient nation, the world's age? Is it because it divided the Jews into sects, old Jews and Christians, and has set much of the world together by the ears for eighteen centuries, as pretended in era, and likely to keep all in commotion for its period of existence, until it wears itself out?

Long after the existence of man, priestocracy and tyrants rose, and devised this corrupt and despotic thing, this blasphemy on religion, this begetter of sectarianisms, peculiar faith, and sacrificed mind to its heathenish and bloody dogmas, its horrid statutes. How are we to get out of the maze, labyrinth of errors and false doctrines? By the brightest standard of reason, the supreme standard of Deity, and the proper exercise of mind.

The world is pointed out the advocate of bibles of peculiar faith in monarchies, as if that proved anything, but that such were tories to mind, if they knew their subject, and so much the worse are their imitators in republics, that were traitors as tories to mind, when they were instituted to free mind. Such are vassals indeed. All the ancient nations had their peculiar faith, and of course their bibles or codes of that faith, oral, or written, all analogous, all at war with nature's God.

The moderns, more silly, through their more stupid priestocracy, have adopted them, instead of analyzing for themselves, and eliciting God-written monotheism, the holiest conservative of mind.

With all polytheists who can do nothing without the priestocracy, the last formed a part and parcel, inseparable from polytheism, for their dictates are part of the decrees. It was so in Judaism, it is emphatically in papacy, the more imperial the more despotic. Now all peculiar faiths, all lies and pretences, have been policies or kind of tory government of mankind.

There is only one constituent in faith, that makes it good, namely, that of truth, for if it be false, it is bad faith, and unworthy of mind.

Now the advocates of all peculiar faith are bound to demonstrate this essence of its vital existence, or be denounced as impostors. No wonder they assail the disbelievers as infidels, when they seek to hide their impostor character by this vile cheat and charlatanry. Lies are dangerous for faith-makers and smugglers, in all the departments of mind, that can expose them as felons.

Let all peculiar Bibles, Jew, Christian, Mahommedan, Mormon, Brahmin, Bhuddist, or Atheist, as exploded, lie in the tomb of all nonsense, error and imposition. Do not let the foolhardiness of any modern disentomb them. The world must trust to principles, not fallible human nature. This is the proper and only protection entrusted and vouchsafed by the Creator, who finished his work effectually and perfectly, at that period.

The standard of gentility never can be too high; but may be too low. While despotisms, monarchies, and priestocracies, fall short by oppression of mind, republics, through . monotheism, can bestow it.

The days of priestocracy, peculiar faith, and mind-despotism, monarchy, are numbered.

To have the false position of peculiar faith of any name carried through, the whole world must be swindled, seduced! So far from adopting, it had better never know of any such.

Uniform principles for ever estop peculiar faith-bible people from speaking of infidels.

As all peculiar faith-dogmas and bibles, are ignoble failures, endangering the peace and happiness of the whole world, it becomes the paramount duty to organize on the highest God-given document, that of monotheism self-demonstrative.

This is due the constitutional organization of mind, that must have all the benefits of sublime rationality to reach its culmination.

If the world is endangered in becoming idol-worshipper, as it is most positively under the ignoble guidance of the delusive doctrine of polytheism, it becomes such advocates as seek the truth to renounce it, and all its errors, and adopt monotheism, and all its truth. She has no metaphysics, no subtleties, no labyrinths, as atheism, and polytheism. Bible and faith-peculiarities, are alien to mind—non-existent as facts. Are you an American republican? On what principle can you advocate peculiar faith? If you can possibly invent any argument that is applicable to all tory doctrines of universal despotism, and resolvable into sophism. The last faith-discoverer is the true latter-day saints, and that may be the very last speaker, alias impostor. If the metal is a base alloy, of course all the currency must partake of that character.

Why do you, so careful in business, permit illicit traffic in peculiar faith, that was originally smuggled, and never has paid the tariff to truth, when the perpetrators are swindling priestocracy? Peculiar faith, its bibles and priestocracy go into the sordid speculations of earth, while monotheism soars to the loftiest arch of religion. Well, says the enthusiast, I will die in the faith. Good, if he will let it be pure and good, not idiotic, bad faith, not a faithless doctrine to blind and stupify dupes.

What are the statistics of peculiar faith? Her various wars of bloody deeds and costly expenditures will disclose the mere commencement of the world-tragedy. They are too great for the passive toleration of the world. The present light of the world's mind demands the discarding of all peculiar faith bibles. Social civilization demands religion. What but she can oppose the mighty avalanche of delusions of Mormonism and all peculiar faiths? Christianity and Mahommedanism, two vile sectarianisms, emanating from as vile a source, caused the world peculiar faith accursed wars for two centuries. All the good done the world has been through mind's and monotheism's capital. Idolatry, is it, that any of these sectarians complain of? They never dream that they too, the best of them, are in mud and mire.

And sectarians refuse, too, to be educated in each other's schools, though entire ignorance be the result. What a base of fragments!

Peculiar faith is a debauching political enginery and machinery for the corrupt bargain and sale of souls. This real treachery to monotheism is worse than the pictured one of Judas.

As conscience is to be the guidance of mind, and to fulfil this faithful function must be fully enlightened, how can peculiar faith be trusted, that can impart no such light?

All analysts can well appreciate that it arose in the dark ages of most stupid ignorance and bigotry, when there were few or no books, and those the works of sophists; when there were few readers and still fewer writers. Most books were perverted from truth to suit the miserable reign of terror, or misrule of despotism, the vagaries of blind faith. Now, when most can argue, reason on facts of science, on the mind-platform of liberty, peculiar faith, that affects to be all light herself, imposes her bibles as the perpetual barrier to religion's rational progress.

Down with all the peculiar faiths and their books; they are all felons, tories.

The commissions in peculiar faiths are most detestable, and beyond all mental endurance short of conservative correction. There are many people, and they are myriads, revoking all faith, allegiance to peculiar institutions, that need the firm conviction of rational conservation. It is these that are inhibited from proper deeds by the odious, brutal expulsion of religious principles by such faiths.

There are many people revoking all faith, allegiance to religion as it is called improperly, yet evincing most clearly by their actions that they are actuated by God-given elements. All this must be looked at and analyzed. Separate priestocracies from religion in profession, as they are utterly incompatible. Define peculiar faith as monotheism positively defines it, no religion at all. Monotheism is divinely authorized, as that is a God-written document, self-evident in the universe.

There can be but two classes of believers, those, deceivers or deceived. Which is which, reason declares. What is the world to you if you have no confidence in its faith, and what can impart confidence, short of conservative principles? The world people are made to ostracize each other through peculiar faith, when the whole universe cannot be disunited in religion, the universal civilizer, refiner.

The advocates of peculiar faith wish to put down all others but their own. Now let them first put down their own peculiar faith follies, and then they can act rightfully for all, in putting down all. 'Tis idle to cry Mormonism or Judaism, when the professor adopts christianity. Let all the world peculiar faith yield to monotheism, the God-written, not man-written document.

All the councils ecclesiastical, are smuggling circles. Peculiar faith smuggles her dynasty of the priestocracy. There is no sense in peculiar faith preaching, as there is no virtue in the faith. Let us have none of such, to have no world-butcheries or massacres prematurely. Let us have no such horrible feud.

Peculiar faith will fall more and more into disrepute, as science advances in the world. Let all proper purposes be carried out, while all improper ones should be carried off.

All peculiar faiths have been basely smuggled, palmed upon the world by despots and their minions. Is there one plan or base of such operations, but have been fashioned by despotism or fanaticism?

All peculiar faiths are a failure to promote social, moral and religious law and order, but give general hypocrisy or dupery to the world. Why is all this? Because they all are faithless, have no good faith or intention to act up to religion, the quintessence of good faith.

The people, mind, already possesses the right elements, that peculiar faith cannot evoke, but monotheism can. Now the world should be prepared in cultivating what it possesses, qualified to do full and ample justice to all the universal demands made on it, and anticipate in fact all such. The victory is assured to monotheism over all the vices, and can never be to peculiar faith that is unworthy the confidence or countenance of a single mind the world over. For God's and mind's sake, spare the world the silly and felonious invasion of peculiar faith, that fills mankind with countless absurd impositions and mock pretences.

No wonder the smugglers of peculiar faith should seek to excommunicate all other faiths not congenial to their own, but when they do all this in the establishment of their own, to the exclusion of monotheism, they have committed the most heinous blasphemy, and have ruined the world and mind, as far as in them lies, of the holy essence of religion, for they meddle with a God-written document. The advocates of peculiar faith have sacrificed religion to their faith.

The best rites of peculiar faith, are a mockery of religion, as masses for the repose of souls, and money to rescue them from purgatory. What a mercenary prostitution of the agent souls who thus commit sacrilege and blasphemy.

The mysteries of the ancients consecrated peculiar faiths, and subtle metaphysics inveigled, befogged the community into their enthusiastic support. As all the virtues of peculiar faith are from monotheism God-written, the advocates must not sacrifice ungratefully, religion to their peculiar faith. The very existence of peculiar faith is a nuisance to the world, as it is the ostracism of rational religion. But which of all faiths peculiar, has the firm undoubted position? None—they are all weak on an untenable basis. Christians are no more than all other peculiar faiths people. They all doubt, because they have no basis of their own; it is all in that of rational religion, what they have of it. But how is it possible that so many can be mistaken, and especially those devoted to sincerity and truth, cannot speak the truth on this subject? Because they are certainly mistaken, and seek to be consistent, declare for what they do not know. They use faith-sophistry, a sin indeed, and to prevent the proper recognition, the priestocracy-faith-perjurers, conspire against all means to disabuse the world on this subject. What is certain, all peculiar faiths corrupt the minds of the people, as all other depotisms.

Peculiar faith reflects the vices of perverted mind, and positively libels Deity, the Creator.

She is delible, whereas religion is indelible. See the myriads of peculiar faiths of the ancients, that have passed into oblivion with all their originators. Nothing of all this miserable family will be left, when rational religion triumphs forever.

Most dangerous is peculiar faith every way, when the conscience cannot beware too much of the first encroachments, the first aberrations from rectitude, as the end may be the deepest curse, and such faiths are making their encroachments perpetually.

They do not fear to sin. Then mind must eschew peculiar faith as the greatest sin, and the propagators are the greatest sinners.

It is important to begin in time with rational education for correct actions, to conform the cranium to mind's organs and functions, to what is right, to fix right habits. Such faith pretends to give us a bible for religion: all such pretences are utterly false, for the bibles are of peculiar Jew or Christian faith and pretences.

Let not mind pretend that I am hostile to it, when I oppose peculiar faiths that enslave it—no such thing—as the bibles bent astronomy to peculiar faith for many centuries, they eclipsed the universe by their four cornered earth. When wares are offered for sale, their qualities are to be wisely inspected and recognised by the interested purchaser; now peculiar faith is essentially of this character, and is for sale to the highest bidder. It is a world church-priestocracy, state-despotism affair at auction. Its bibles are so much waste paper.

The best functions of the soul are lost on peculiar faith. What schisms, false doctrines, heresies, and conspiracies, mislead from religion?

Your preachers are eternally complaining of the insuperable difficulty of making the people believe the bible tales—yes, it was making by despotism and sophistry. Get religion, say the faithocracy. That is all trifling nonsense, self-delusion.

All kinds of despotism are perishing before the lights of rational mind, and this, its vassal, goes with it. You need not fear any opprobrium, by a wise change. That change is only horrid that proves want of principles. The faith you affect is sacred, any how you may pretend. It is not at all, but the reverse. You desecrate faith, by adopting false pretences that convict it of blasphemy and felony. What claim has polytheism on the world?

The base desecration to mind, now, is peculiar faith, the detestable incarnation representative of religion. Peculiar faith is constantly presenting strife of its own offspring, spreading disruptions of society, of itself, its fragments are always in view, fragments first, its own explosion last.

Freemen, can you touch this odious tory?

Religious education with peculiar faithites implies, sectarian. Religious agitation is ever in all sectarian church and state countries.

Peculiar faith, when passive, means sectarian bigotry; when in influence, peculiar despotism.

Who can be held responsible for peculiar faith? You, and to your own mind, the most illustrious embodiment. Can you separate your physical from moral and religious existence? Then mind is bound to first examine the principles of unity.

There are some excellent people in peculiar faith churches, and the only way that they can be accounted for is, that they have been the least corrupted by their doctrines. Monotheism, that predominated with its saving influence, has saved them, assuredly. What a fine, excellent thing it is, that they kept their honest, healthful senses, and had God, their creator, to protect them and the universe, instead of man's botches and creation.

Indeed, well may they, all patriots be pleased with their noble country and its illustrious institutions, that they can reach monotheism in its best purity, whereas in peculiar faith they had forgot, overlooked religion.

While rational mind leaves nothing to contingency, bigotry, the stubborn hybrid of superstition and peculiar faith adopts both, and maintains them with fanaticism, when infuriated.

Religionist, do you know what you are talking of, when you affect the company of peculiar faith? That she is a bloody tigress, a reckless prostitute of souls, and that all priestocracies are her tools and menials, herself that of despotism?

When mind is told to seek religion under the auspices of any peculiar faith, the advocates of which tell it that its efforts, then and there, have been crowned with success, by their influence, at that very moment falsehood and imposition are asserted by them, for false pretences, as all that mind possesses is by its own inherent faculties, God-given, and must be mind-improved, and so allowed. The imposition and world-demagogism is still carried farther, when the neophyte is enlisted ostensibly under that peculiar church-banner, instead of ascribing, with most grateful emotion, the mind-existence of their invaluable gift, then and there desecrated and polluted by a series of frauds.

Are not these tender mercies of fanaticism as bad as the domains of lust, unholy ambition, unbounded avarice, beastly drunkenness? The worst and most execrable deception is in taking advantage of emotions, passions, deep recesses of the soul's innate, intrinsic feelings, by unholy, ungodly counterfeits. Of all this the world has to be aware, in all the reckless disguises of sophistry and all its degrading alliances. All bigotry, in its best appreciation, is erroneous education, as it is a species of monomania in faith. All peculiar faith is that assuredly, nothing less, in the wisest analysis. In all this, the world is more sinned against than sinful.

Deny peculiar faith to be monomania? What is fanaticism, her child, but of that character? Like begets like, affinities beget affinities, and only such. Monotheism begets or is rational religion, that begets immortality of the soul, the loveliest family of mind.

Go to the widest oceans, the loftiest mountains, the sublimest cataracts, to secure the liberal expanse and impulse of humanity, the soul's emotions, and to religion, for the munificence of the Creator.

25

No peculiar faith dispenses herself in this wise, when she dwarfs her mind in the attempt against the God of the universe.

What she calls mysteries are metaphysics. What can she promise the plaintive and soul grievings, the remorse, the deep feeling and anguish that lacerate, the penalty-appreciation, the mental dissatisfaction, when she violates Almighty Providence by messiahship, a perfect incompatibility. If it had been decreed from the first, as is pretended, then the complete mission deferred predicating omission of time and space, precludes its perfect character, and demonstrates it the worst of all impositions. The great holy centre cannot know peculiar faith, that religious people will be ashamed to mention there. What is miscalled sacred history is mostly mind-factured, as all the oracle-peculiar faiths. Mind has nothing to do with cross or crescent, but soul and its religion.

Peculiar faith goes where it is not wanting, and can do no good anywhere, but harm. God's universe rebukes all such. She daubs everything with her peculiar sophistry; appeals to purses, and tythes, and peculiar missionaries. Peculiar faith is ever in the rear, with hypocrisy most brazen before and ignorance behind. Let her gather her cliques and clans, sections and factions of sections, she gathers only fragments of fanaticism. Her garments are died in blood. She carries dissension, distrust, impotency, imbecility, and mortality. Peculiar faith of all sects and denominations can be rightfully branded as the ungrateful guest of monotheism, the tool of despots, tory to constitutional liberty and light of mind. Where is her glorious example of patriotism for this union?

In her disunion and fragments of churches?

Why cut up the world into fragments of petty societies, cliques, cabals? The world cannot unite too strongly on religion, its highest duty, a universal brotherhood, its greatest interest.

Hard and imperfect is the tuition of peculiar faith, that has to travel too much over the same path.

All precept should enjoin proper investigation of all subjects submitted to mind. Those submitted for despotism are different. Is that not the bible of peculiar sophistry?

All the fair criticisms most legitimate against peculiar faith are to profit the mind in rationality. Peculiar faith cannot establish her doctrines endorsed by all world-despots, as she cannot appropriate principles, the universe-fund that God created.

The only way for peculiar faith of the greatest genius to be eternally founded is for that genius to invent, nay, to create principles. As all on this earth are creatures, proved by birth, life, and death, a vital existence identified with atmosphere, the whole fabric of such faith is the veriest fraud on earth, too plain for a school-boy to mistake. Now, rational mind can see most plainly the reason and demonstration of the religion of principles, created by the Almighty Architect of this universe. That settles the whole question at once and forever.

Now, mind ought to be mature enough to appreciate that it is instituted under providence at creation, as adequate for all questions occurring in the universe, and that no peculiar faith can furnish any materials for such solution.

Those who pay homage to their peculiar god cannot expect rational minds to apostatize from the God of the universe, whose supremacy is his unity.

A pagan always claims exemption of his faith from reason, because honest, truthful reason condemns all pagan faith as untruthful in position.

We expect nothing from peculiar faith, that only presents the poorest, the fragments of faith, as she is imbecile, impostor, usurper of good faith to the world, mind, universe, and their God.

She is not trustworthy; mind cannot know, the Creator cannot own, the universe cannot trust her. She is an outlaw, heinous and demented.

Her bibles are all pagan, with bloody statutes; her gods, numberless, are all fictions and caricatures. She knows no true way, sinning and causing all her followers to sin, causing retributive punishment for her folly and crimes. She is a political hack, for her kingdom is that of despotism, unprincipled in all things; she is of the earth earthly, born of mind debased, spurious and illegitimate. She has no functions for she has no titles thereto in any respect foisted by false pretenders; her every breath is mortal, her every acts of that character. Of superstition, she is brazen as bigotry, seeking for ambitious power, which she of course always abuses.

Her perversion of mind is too dangerous for any one to be intrusted with her available intrigues, as she urges to perjury as traitors who called for perjury, false positions and influence against their own government, to which they acknowledged no intrinsic indebtedness. Peculiar faith is a part and parcel of government machinery, and is always dressed in the garb to suit the complexion of the times, being an arch-enemy of mind, ever despotic, ambitious, thirsting for power. She is a dangerous thing to meddle with. The world should never know her, and only knows in its self-delusion, superstition, ignorance, ruin or ignominy.

Republicans above all should have nothing to do with her, as in despotisms she forces herself on mankind and forces them to support her in the most sumptuous cathedrals, palaces and the extreme of tithes.

And her books, man-mind, self-deluded, call those of religion ! What desecration of thought, what a prostitution of mind ! Religion only asks of mind justice, that is to do itself justice, that it may do justice to her and through her beneficence to God. This is all her own, but peculiar faith seeks all that is not hers, and grasps all with her iron will that only asks for power to be enforced at all times. She is the after sight of perverted mind's creation, vaunts herself in the demagogism of affected republicanism, the greatest friend of the dear people, caring for their souls.

You affect not to be amenable to any of the obligations of public opinion. But you are to all social obligations. It has been decided that man rational, is not mere animal the brute, unless peculiarities make you so, therefore you are not to act whilst in rational society as it does, for your sphere is urged by its appropriate principles to remain there. So you are bound to all obligations that comprehension of principles embraces, not stopping short of the universe. Do not pretend to escape the past follies of mankind, as expedient. You thus adopt folly, with crime. The universe can no more rest on the isolated principles of one solar system, than your position can be sustained by ex-parte social doctrines. You must take all, or none. You expect most rational protection from all principles, thus you are bound to exhibit the best of good faith contribution, as your part necessary for the whole consummation of universal safety.

After all, what is peculiar faith ? Analysis will demonstrate that peculiar church and state-faith-despotisms, are inseparate and indivisible. Both are peculiar nuisances to the world, and must, will be abolished by mind when liberalized by rationality and religion, vindicating, asserting its own immortal dignity. Peculiar faith people follow the teachers, not the principles, but the policy, doctrines and measures : their mind is psychologized by peculiar faith bibles and worships its idols.

If the advocates of this doctrine had ever considered the measurable difference of mind over its pretensions, they could not hesitate a moment.

See what mind has accomplished for constitutional government in this union ; what it is accomplishing in all of life-problems.

The mind has interminable difficulties with peculiar faith in predestination ; its doctrines are tortuous. and cannot be straightened. They must die, and let those already advanced under mind's glorious free agency be properly estimated. I grant that the adherents know their faith but not their religion, they cannot assert any thing more. But all their coin is counterfeit, for all their metal is dross, not pure. The intention is every thing ; if the motive be wrong all is wrong in mind. Monotheism alone carries out the legitimate blessing of free agency of mind, while an inconsistent predestination is peculiar faith's.

What finer exhibition of mind can be given than its adequate appreciation and responsibility by conscience, firmness, general and particular. Whilst, personally, I feel a gentlemanly courtesy towards all people, I must desire to see the serpents of peculiar faiths to be securely handled at once, or not attempted.

The proper function of mind is rationality, not faith, unless admitted thereby. If it gain admittance at all, it is on these premises ; and if not true rationally, it must be spurious. Custom is one thing, and principle another, in regard to all sham-faiths.

We have to make principle sacred, for the more faith is talked of nominally, the less religion : all such is counterfeit. It is man-worship, mind, and soul-sacrifice, these faith-mongers are dealing in all the time.

But you profess to be in horror of atheism ? Then you should unite yourself to the only tenable position of science. Instead of bibles, you might tell the atheist to scan first the universe, solve that problem ere he could understand godology. He should fathom the depth of creation, ere he could penetrate the character of the Creator.

That science is too deep for him, when he had not fathomed the elements of mental rudiments, that of mind. He who denies conservation in all respects, physically, morally and religiously, denies to God his creation.

What good mind, with a world's patriotism, wishes to see that vindictive spirit unbridled and let loose all over the world ? Does that harmonize with religion ?

The world is indebted to old Asia for despotism, monarchical, ecclesiastical, military, vast ruins of edifices, and above all is mind's prostration to the vandalism of all these. Such scenes of iniquity, that this trio trinity, the triune of peculiar god-head, has enacted is enough to arouse any republican man, woman, or child, to never let the accursed books of that detestable compound of sophistry, superstition, and faith, darken their doors. All of it, is belial indeed.

Let freemen, America, teach the world religion, and its purest principles. What redress has the world if it violate principles, that will preserve it to eternity otherwise? Is it not complete suicide? Is it not the duty of the soul to make their sincere acquaintance?

Adopt no faith that will cause you to think reproachfully of your maker, whilst your mind is rational, but elevate it rationally to the very best supreme of purposes.

Now, what less than monotheism can make a man God-like? He can well say, I am a man, and what monotheism made me, and all this, through republican constitutional principles. I only asked to be estimated in that light, no more nor less. What despots can be more?

I am opposed to peculiar faith, as it is opposed to civilization. Mind has to look above peculiar faith, and all life's errors, especially all associations, if suspicious.

The moderns must know that all peculiar faiths are unquestionably pagan and superstitious. The pulpit sophists have been taught a faithless faith and depend on it. They have chosen a miserable false position, the fault is in them, their perverted minds, whose proper functions all the time is best wisdom.

Now, they should not sleep one night, much less die in that fix. When was peculiar faith ever modest? She usurps mind's rights, and then scouts at reason.

The world is initiated into peculiar faith by peculiar education, and thus indoctrinated, is utterly incapacitated to rationalize the subject; you cannot do justice by reason of sectarianism; cannot investigate it for your bigotry, self-interest, and superstition. You have put your bible between you and religion—between mind and religion.

The worst of all is, that peculiar faith debauches the whole world! What can be expected of individuals, when the platform of the whole world is thus prostituted?

It is a wholesale evil, and that too when there is not only not a particle of necessity, but on the contrary, is an obsolete necessity for its expulsion and exclusion. Peculiar faith, is it? Rather peculiar curse. Regeneration is too small a calibre, when conservative revolution of rational, not peculiar faith, is due mind. Peculiar faith is actually dangerous to the world, as if mind did not counteract its unholy objects, unceasing blood would flow. To establish any peculiar faith, no matter what, the worst of human nature has to be invoked: the worst of passions, superstition, false pretences, blasphemy, sacrilege, the worst imposition of mind, instead of the praiseworthy straightforward course of honorable, high-minded religion. Now, good citizens, you are not identified with all the most malevolent position to your God and country. You only need the proper view. Investigate independently of all influences, and decide religiously in good faith, to your own mind.

Gentlemanly deportment is the height of monotheism aspiration, justice to mind, world, God, religion. Has peculiar faith done all that? Has she started in truth and honesty aright? One of the most singular exhibitions of the world is to affect mind is not right, not in the right pursuit, is deranged, when genius attempts conservative revolutions of old exploded customs, ways, faiths, and of all the pitiful hacks of life, and in this, the monopolists and usurpers act the worst for their miserable and corrupt self-interest. If they did it with reason, truth or justice, the thing would be right.

Peculiar faith that has always libeled mind, is indebted to it for putting an end to most of her evils. Mind will close the balance by closing all peculiar faith, when reason can get audition. In being the peculiar god of the Jews, the peculiar superiority must be shown, or the avowal stamps the assertors claimant as unmitigated stupid impostors. From this dilemma they cannot escape. Peculiarity of god or gods, stultifies the claimants invariably and absolutely. How does this thing stand by the side of monotheism, that directs mind with the noblest, purest. chastest thoughts, exacts justice, beneficence, no superstition instead of religion? She exacts justice in place of charity, that is a trifle to the poor, who are to be cared for by the best acts of state and mind. She inspires all with true confidence, and tells them not be dispirited.

Atheists, you have to come by the side of your own abused compeer polytheist; you are a nature-worshipper, the other is a partial creation-god-worshipper, both pagans. All the intrigues of creation, the most unprincipled ingrates who seek to libel God's character, cannot invalidate his claims.

Rational religion presents a smooth road, while peculiar faith's is beset with quicksands. It is hard to avoid vice, unless the other side of the picture presents rational education to counteract always. All governments and states should furnish an adequate one, not empirical or peculiar, the curse instead of the world's blessing. When you educate peculiarly, to teach to hate peculiarly, you give an impulse, a wrong bias and influence to mind, the potent lever of the world. How little of the world can be depended on? Why is this, but from the malign influence of peculiar faith? How can we resist evils? By peculiar faith? What, the prolific authoress?

Upon what principle can peculiar faithites arraign rational religion, one iota, when they are amenable in both honesty and religion? When the monarchical head turns his back on all but court faith, and persecutes, expels, dishonors, maltreats or insults the balance, as is now done in all the five grand divisions of the globe, then the curse of this world abomination, comes home to the deceived. There are no people in the world more interested than peculiar faithites, in putting down peculiar faith that trades on their capital, as that of mind and religion. What in the name of the Creator can they want with the very means of their own degradation? What is to stay all this abominable ungodliness of self-interest, but principle, and what better than its consummation, the religion of principles? The majority, the world, as far as it properly uses rational mind, uses monotheism, while religion exists without peculiar faith, that has to borrow her main plumage from the former. How was it when Luther arose against Roman-ism? Was that peculiar faith against herself, or was it not most clearly mind against her iniquities?

Cause and effect will rule out all of peculiar faith, that cannot get a foothold in rational mind of this whole universe! Polytheists as atheists, her defenders, can be nowhere.

When their minds err, religion still sustains them, as the gift by God's mind; the fund is still there.

As the position of all peculiar faith is diametrically opposite God's principles, to carry it out is perjury certainly. But peculiar faithites affect a devil is necessary. It is in their devil-machinery, not in God's, nor in that of monotheism; their position is too much of their devil. Let it all go, especially to get rid of all such.

The priestocracy, above all, have repentance to seek. If you do not wish any corrupt evil faith to arise, do not corrupt the world by your peculiar faith. You have to act thus, most certainly.

Your very existence depends on principles, social, physical, moral, religious, to be conservative. Now, you have to find out these, to render you conservative. You, sir, are not to clash therewith in any of your opinions or acts. If you adopt peculiar faith, that decides you have a false position.

When partisans tell us that past scenes and acts of peculiar faithites were not sanctioned on their platform, that all such are not pagan, they do not speak the truth, only as they admit that the whole category is wound up by plenipotent rational religion, monotheism. The real position of religion is in every rational mind.

All that check peculiar faith is mind, the better as more rational. She has the worst evils in peculiar education. Education to be really good must be most and only rational, not peculiar at all.

The world mistakes in supposing people are so rational, just, good and true; it must take nothing for granted, and grant no powers but the most necessarily rational; else they will be awfully abused where peculiar will rules. All the peculiar machinery most corrupt will be put in requisition to sustain it, as prophecy, that is, for which must be read always sophistry. Mind can be God-like on principle, supreme completely to the extent of its capacity.

Now, it is not for the benefit of churches, whether cathedrals or not, priestocracies, nor their peculiar faiths, their paganisms, all their temporary advantages, made for that express purpose by the original intriguing designers, but what will be the elevation of your immortal souls, and the promotion of the religion of principles identified therewith and its Creator, that binds both in one indissoluble amity and unity.

You have nothing to do with peculiar faiths, priestocracies or their churches, much less their follies, crimes, strifes, bickerings, tithes, despotisms or foul designs, but you have with religion, rational discussions, universal brotherhoods, and all the highest promotion of the world's benefits.

You are bound as a member of society to exercise your best religion, and carry out the legitimate purpose. Reason, that holds all peculiar faith in abeyance, is the creative power, with the certain elements of solid happiness, emanating from rational religion. The last will give mankind the nearest approximation of perfection. Her innate qualities are adequate for the whole universe. Her word to the wise is sufficient, and her capital creates wisdom, not peculiarly but universally.

She will enable the valiant to rout ignorance, superstition and oppression, and aid the zealous by her principles. It is perfectly useless to pretend about faith of any kind being an absolute matter. That was the tory assertion of the smuggling tyrants that introduced it, a miserable imposture on the world, a false pretence to uphold a false pretence, taking advantage of the God-gift by their treacherous enforcement. If you receive any such by surrender of your mental citadel, how are you going to get rid of all the insurmountable difficulties your own produced? Religion cannot possibly regard peculiar faith, no matter how blazoned by meretricious ornaments, as a rival, when she has plenipotent supremacy.

We must estimate the false glare of the world's treasures, powers and possessions, that influenced and perverted mind, that oppressed the world for the purpose, losing its equilibrium.

Rational religion must now restore it.

CHURCH MEMBERSHIP OF PECULIAR FAITH: PAGANISM.

A LOOSE state of morals, arising from insincerity of more than a majority of members, it is said by good observers, evinces the relative state of peculiar faith doctrines throughout the world, from a want of truth at the foundation, and hence arise a general use of sophistry, and its attendant bigotry, among most of its professions of life.

What can all mortal messiahships avail the world, or those not absolutely rejecting, yet not adopting; not in the pale of safety, though belonging to the various churches?

Millions thus neutralize their own good, taught certain family and church worship from youth, they do not dissent, yet in years of reflection and maturity they do not assert or avow the doctrines that they cannot conscientiously believe. They die, martyrs to custom of inherent nothing, abstracted from the true and essential belief, the eternal ever living Almighty, the universal Savior, because the universal Creator, having a power equal to his goodness.

Such persons neither adopt nor reject the doctrines of messiahship, but live and die good citizens, certainly no avowed believers, yet indebted to their Creator for every breath of life, and every elevation of mind, whom they overlook most ungratefully and irreverently.

Past teaching, and habit in such tuition, all over the world, thus present an immense number of the human family of doubtful change, yet preserved despite of all these circumstances by their Creator.

Pride, habit, the wish for consistency, the institutions and laws of the world, fix the opinions but not the conscience in all false positions of education that asks for peculiar faith independent of reason.

The sincere faith, certainly the pure acquiescence of the mind, triumphs by reason, the only acceptable and worthy offering before its Organizer.

Church membership confers power; but—

Each clique and sect cuts up society into clans, and curses it with its foul breath.

God Almighty never made such a world.

Let sects and clans unmake and undo their deeds.

Trifles of mere puerile contention will be erased, because the corrupt base will be discarded.

Some sects look on others with perfect contempt, and hardly recognise them as anything at all; in fact, exclude them, as not orthodox, from communion.

But the eternal principles of universal brotherhood, which are those of God unmistakably, admit all rational minds within the pale of safety. What a glorious position!

Here there can be no conflict, whether water by sprinkling or by immersion be the way, when the purity of the soul will be the acknowledged universal means of eternal safety.

There can be no contention whether the elect or any peculiar sect in place of all shall be saved, for no particular merits of the believers, as the leaders of all such doctrines, the originator of such faiths, are all sinful mortals, mere created beings, alike infatuated and corrupt, who pretend that universal safety is approachable to such that have rational minds on rational principles, through a rational God.

In peculiar faith there may be no end to trifles, as there is no end to mind's corruption when it is perverted. Mind is always subject to perversion, under influences arising from all power; and that of church power is too great to be missed.

Before God, what matters it whether some are excluded from communion with others in peculiar faith? God cannot recognise in the foundation any other than corruption?

SEVERANCE OF STATE FROM CHURCH.

BRIGHT was that day that American freedom saw a severance of state from church. That act constituted an element of popular power of mind, the richest in the annals of rational religion, the noblest friend of man, that gives to freedom of mind all that is hers, the kindest for mind, the most triumphant for reason and God.

Rational religion yields this as a sacred right of the people, of mind, and reason, and God, and asks only for a rightful participation throughout the world. None better could have been done by wise statesmen for religion, as rational religion only asks for the good of souls for all past and present generations and posterity.

She asks for due and prompt atonement to be made for past errors accursed by the blood of millions, by aiding man to find the most direct path to his God, and to take away all means of mind's perversion.

If monotheism asked more or less, she would be unworthy of God's countenance and man's confidence. Of course, she asks to be independent of any corrupt priesthood. She does not wish any such to be her ministers.

The annals of this glorious day ought to be had in rememberance by the nations of the world, where civil and religious liberty has her votaries, and enlightened mind her friends.

It is a day that God blessed, and that freemen will consecrate with love and appreciation.

Her light was holy, and her atmosphere pure and vital. It will be known as one of the great days of freedom and rational religion.

The benefits shall go abroad on the earth, and the globe shall be blessed with their presence.

The mind of man and of the human race shall praise it, and honor its sacred name!

The present age has witnessed that the papal Roman states had asserted their freedom, and had exchanged the errors of the past for the improvement of the present, having excluded their pontiff from temporal government, whose see was once so powerful by mind's delusion and infatuation, man's corruption and degradation, that its mandate governed much of the world, to the astonishment of subsequent ages.

But what availed the acts of these noble descendants of worthy patriotic sires, in their assertion of fundamental principles essential to the only kind of correct government, constitutional republican representation, clearly showing as a necessary consequence, that religious faith is truly placed in the minds of the people, not in the power or possession of assuming rulers, who are hostile to the best interests of the people, if those rulers be connected to speculation in rights and principles?

But popish faith has not responded to true civil and religious liberty, and its malign influence has caused even a sister republic to aid in crushing with horrible inconsistency and iniquity, the birthright of freemen. This is one of the execrable abominations of peculiar faith.

This is the most conclusive proof among hosts of all kinds not to be invalidated, that the peculiar faith of any sect, and under any form, is incompetent to the rights of man, and has nothing of religion.

Sectarianism so far from benefiting mind's rights, has crushed them with the iron heel of absolutism for the most part of her existence, after possession of power.

All proper blessings will redound to mind in a true republican constitutional government, excluding all shackles of any character on mind, that must be true to itself, to be true to God who made it.

All blessings will follow in order eventually, as the mind of man is more generally enlightened.

What a step Europe had already taken, under the example of her younger and energetic sister, America! Had the hundred millions of free-thinking people only been united, and used the appropriate moral and intellectual power, they had thereby effectually overcome all the malign influences of absolutism!

What a step the balance of the world has to take, to assert first principles, already enacted from the foundation of all things!

If all the world to-day, in its present state, could be in the church of partial and defective doctrines and peculiar faith, none could be assured of any nearer approach to a full and sacred fruition, from the character of the elements, that have no especial claim to him who created the purest, as all deny his purest Almighty attributes.

How can such believers face this supreme God, with just hopes, or conscientious minds?

Their God is not the pure, perfect God of happiness! In fact, most are, from the essential character of their peculiar faith and worship, farther removed from God's approval, did he not take the will of the ignorant for the deed of the best enlightened.

The Creator, then, is the only being that can recognise the proper analysis of mind, and all its character. The best compliance with his requisitions, is the strictest conformity to the requisitions of his great principles. Thereby all other masters are necessarily ruled out.

Church membership opens, in its present organization, the door of temptation to corruption and hypocrisy, by giving decided preference and clanship to the members, without reference to merit.

Many are proved, by the best documents, to merely pretend to membership. Why so? They are doubters.

The conduct of several expels them, not only from church, but from society. Many stumbling-blocks remain.

But all such are arrayed in false character, many joining the church for sinister and worldly motives, become workers of iniquity under such a banner desecrated.

What can prevent it? Enlightened conscience will tell.

Priests and preachers' churches of peculiar faith are those of superstition and paganism, and their ways have been those of violence. Let not their acts cause any more curses on the world.

Their churches are mutually condemned by members of the same representative, who proves no diploma from God, fit for credence in any intelligent court of conscience, enlightened by reason and principle, either by his presence, in time or space, before the present world, where reason proves the Creator to be unmistakably prior to both, or the existence of creation.

The contentions of co-churches, under this representative, are endless, and bitterly antagonistic.

What but for worldly power do they feel hostile?

Can they act thus for religion? That is impossible. Such is of the world, worldly. What is the world to all such, proving themselves thereby most amenable to correction, but for worldly considerations?

Who wonders, on the analysis of peculiar faith, that not only its sects are arrayed against each other, but that all the primary peculiarities of the world are deadly hostile to the death of all the other faiths?

Though some have begun to admit that others can teach the ignorant barbarians of the world some good, they will not admit that principles and truth are common, and are the appropriate sphere of mind, that sheds the light of the Universal Creator.

They will not admit the truth, that is adverse to their position, but direct the common property to secular and peculiar benefit.

The protestant leaves the mother church, as he asserts, on account of its articles of faith, and corruption, that is depraved action, growing out of that faith ; and thus contends with co-equal protestant churches for demoralization of self-agency, and the possession of power over dissenters!

One church affects age for distinction, as if truth depended on years, and character rested on mere time.

It is to be regretted that the beauties of creation, the glories of immortal mind, are thus marred, in silencing mind, whose right to tell the whole truth is best and indisputable.

Let us not sacrifice, with blind infatuation, the noblest qualities of mind to the erroneous customs of the day, neither upheld by reason or light of philosophy.

What, has it come to this, that in the most enlightened age of the world, that the professors of peculiar faith cannot trust each other, all claiming a common vicegerent and representative of God, or affecting to claim? How can they expect the world to trust them?

The members of one church are afraid to trust their children at academies, perhaps rightfully too in most instances, to the tuition of teachers who are members of other churches.

As this distrust in several matters is very serious, it argues the absolute necessity of the world righting itself, the sooner the better, in all such matters, on universal principles, and then if there be difficulty in intrusting youth for education, depend upon it the objection is necessarily, conclusively and rightfully personal, which reason can be entirely valid with the world.

How can ministers give up their calling, their church power and possession, custom and supposed consistency, however forbid by paramount truth and wisdom, when power, reckless of justice, rarely yields at the last, not gracefully, but with vulgar resistance, especially after so much bloodshed by false faith, with all her horrid tortures and ignominy, her savage butchery in many ways?

When the wars that were engendered by and about church faith are referred to, as most barbarous and outrageous for even superstition, dark and ignorant, the greatest curses of the world, church members become indignant, if such be not ascribed to false faith.

This admission uses up the whole category, having its exposure at last, that false faith, the very point we condemn, engendered the abuses.

When we convict of interminable abuses the whole spurious systems of faith, in the name of God, how can any such system be exempt from censure, as it has inherent elements of abuse? The elements of abuses are referable to the nature, the incurable nature of the systems, that must be eradicated.

The abuses of any system being unlimited as these, can only end in the system, no matter how modified.

A system that begins its foundations of libels on God's uprightness and attributes, engendering blasphemy, is full of evils only curable by its termination.

Are the conflicts of churches done with? Are all rightly settled? Are there no bristling bayonets to uphold any of its representatives over citizens seeking right government?

Are there no gorgeous salaries to enslave human rights?

Are there no poor people, with but little property, heavily taxed and burdened for its support?

Has peculiar church faith no peculiar interest with the state power?

Is there no exclusion of sister churches from equal rights and privileges? No desperate and ungodly bloody intrigues?

By what honorable standard can this measure of state-policy be instituted? Are not all social and religious principles violated?

Is not this certain proof of the acts of absolutism most complete? Is not all, the institution of ecclesiastical and monarchical despotism?

Do all church professors act for the pure love, unadulterated love, of the dear people? Do they then live without hire? Is it for the souls of the people, or the interests of the churchmen, and the despots, tyrants, kings and monarchs, that union of state and church is established?

If for the first, all is useless, as all such are vain.

By what authority is all this done, and still maintained?

Has not time corrected all such views as outrageous and hostile to the sovereign people, destitute entirely of religion?

If disinterested love were the case, why do not they prove the facts by absolute refusal of all pecuniary, church and state power? Let no intervening object cause the loss of sight of the one pure Being. How could the loudest professions be otherwise than very suspicious?

Has the question ever been submitted fairly to rational mind, by free investigation and inquiry, or rather has it not been scouted upon, and the investigators been libeled by priests and clergy, and all their vassals?

Have proper measures ever been taken to have the free people institute all researches and proper best means for mind to reach, by rational means, the true issue of this paramount subject, before a competent committee of disinterested citizens in convention?

Is this momentous question, the most important of the world in all its bearings, to be blindly passed by, and left to the incompetent and interested stock-jobbers of the world's morals to botch and tinker with for indefinite ages to come, without redress?

Is an intelligent and free people prepared to suffer all this in satisfaction, without saying their souls are God's?

Forbid it justice, peace, mind, reason, that are to be consulted.

True believers in God Almighty, of duty to man, with no church emoluments for their proper and satisfactory belief, could never begin to war therefor.

The thing is impossible, because fundamental principles prevent it.

The whole world, so far as rational religion is applicable, would then be in peace. Who would not go for such a glorious result?

Will your omission of duty, your neglect and silence longer prevail, to rebuke you for your priceless advantages?

You are one of a billion of voters at the ballot box of conscience, enlightened and liberal, to decide to-day for the settlement of this principle forever.

It is absurd to say that the people will not act on it.

That is the siren song of those that misled the people to their injury and wrong, to the interest of the leaders, who assume to think and act for, and dictate to the people.

Let not that exploded doctrine be repeated before a self-governing people.

We seek to rid ourselves of all exploded doctrines of absolutism of church and state, and adopt the only safe principle of mind for the sovereign people.

No one can libel this position, to which none save tyrants are antagonistic, for the pursuit of right and title beyond doubt, otherwise that very position supposed of right is error.

Freemen seeking such invaluable rights are antagonistic to none who are advocates of justice, honesty, and patriotism.

Counterfeits are not to be passed as pure jewels on them, or to their detriment.
Freemen are of the billion to legislate on the pure currency of the world. All good
citizens are thus interested, and intelligent freemen acknowledge none true but such as
is of the right mint and genuine coinage.
The right stamp easily proves the genuine.
Again and again is the attention of all good citizens in life, of elevated and refined
qualities, worthy of the world's respect, and of their race and kind, invoked to aid in
sealing and closing the world-wide difficulties, conflicts of peculiar faith opinions, and
the consequent interruptions of peace, in rescuing the state of society in its noblest base
and object, in the exaltation of man's dignity, greatness, and happiness.
The end of religion is not church membership, clannish or sectarian, doubtful or
visionary, but sound and substantial views, with definite and wisest prospect.
The Creator of all has vouchsafed the best co-operation in the institution of inherent
principles, that distinguish man from animals, and elevate mind to soul from time to
immortality, and that bespeak the union of all minds of conservative character.
As wide as the most conflicting differ, still the divine author is pre-eminently characterized by a universal virtue that can harmonize and tend to universal good and union
on principle, and that alone.
On principle, man is linked to man, and all to their Creator, who thus endowed creation with self-preservation.
All the sects and denominations of the world can never unite but on one single platform,
that of principles as universal as creation, to which all nations must look, and by which
all wise ones will abide.
Come to this all must; the sooner the better; there is or can be no other. .
God has instituted it, man must not usurp it.
Man is the worst of his race to deprive that race of it.
It is clear that the improved state of general mind needs an exalted system of civil
and religious code, that may rally mankind to their true feeling and duty, to realize
what all need universally.
Millions this day cold and indifferent in action, put on hostile feelings as to the points
of faith that they are conscious are not of the true character for mind, are sensible
that they owe allegiance only to their Creator, but they are silent when the still small
voice of conscience speaks for that God.
It ought not so to be in any country, much less a free one, where at least free and
open discussion should be elicited on all subjects, to rescue true thoughts and their
originators.
But individual attempts are frowned down, their works are banished or libeled by
impudent and outrageous arrogance, accompanied with as much assurance as if all were
divine oracles, and that all decisions of exploded custom and men's opinions, were all
right, and that lay freemen had not a sovereign right yet to be investigated, acted on,
and matured by the only way of reaching the subject, the proper analysis of mind and
its functions.
If religion be in the keeping of church membership, characterized by this spirit and
faith, what is to become of the large majority who can never be professors to such
creeds?
Why should there be masters of peculiar and partial creeds? Because mind is universal, not peculiar or partial, then faith, an action of the mind, must partake of mind's
character.
No, it is not possible that man should be excluded from the pale of safety or society,
because he cannot enter the pale of faith and church, believing most sincerely and truly
in the only living God, ruler omnipotent.
He who believes in more, believes in a plurality of gods, and is compelled to admit
a solecism, a contradiction, the existence of their Supreme, an Almighty, the Great
First Cause. That great first cause has attributes beyond man's vain notions, and must
command his highest deference.
Men's professions, independent of shining actions, that tell with unerring certainty, in
the course of a long life, are never to be taken for granted until proved.
Mind cannot decide the whole question by professions, that wise men ought never to
entertain exclusively.
Life is made up of professions and their practice, all to be estimated church or no
church, duty in life is plain, not to induce evil, the negative and antagonist of good.
of the we cannot safely take anything for granted in common matters of little moment,
This admit professors of the sects, how then can we expect safety in regard to the
faith, the very hierarchy, that does not practice in unison, that is proved to be distrust-
from youth to end of life, under the evils reflective on its character?

What advantages does all church peculiar faith offer, that can equal her world-wide evils, either in the great primary benefits of life by government or religion? Under all her auspices, the results reflect on each other.

Hierarchy gives us promises of supreme advantages under dictation on earth, of its creeds, but unfortunately does not recognise with certainty, the character and person of the payer.

The hierarchy presented the people dealing in prescriptions on this earth, and in promises that must be inefficient in another state of existence, seems not to have drawn on the only payer that mind can recognise through reason.

The hierarchy known to us, bows ever to a plurality of gods, or worse, makes a man born and died as a mortal, a god, and inevitably libels God, imbecile as man. In the face of all such hierarchy, the belief expressing the pure teaching of monotheism that gives mind its best inspiration, adopts God Almighty, not god imbecile.

All principles are common, the exclusive property of God their author, that only require a right tuition and direction in their employment by mind.

Has hierarchy any exclusive pretension to their appropriate tuition and direction, when she does not meet the wise tuition of proper honest sense?

How does she prove her position right? She proves the reverse.

Hierarchy has been sundered into fragments by her corruption, and the fragments are running out in minuter divisions, in objection to inherent elements of corruption.

The whole foundation is baseless, and must run out.

What more than name, have many church members?

Is it in the unimpeachable veracity and honesty, and the secret actions of such? While they only act to the promptings of their own uncultivated and perverted minds, miserably balanced and fixed in that miserable state of bad habits, that grown and strengthened to their matured and ripe age without due correction, prove the necessity of continued light of mind, to guard properly all its avenues. Whilst the best church members are no worse than the the best members of society in general, they are no better in respect to true chracter. Both are preserved by the same principles.

Membership in peculiar church society confers no new principles, but detracts from the purity of God's perfection.

The most extensive theatre for mind's correction is that which embraces the whole legitimate comprehension of God's perfection.

Nothing but a right action on universal principles that recognise no peculiar faith as an exponent, can bring back all actors to the right thoughts and actions.

The right position in any society is to be sought by a recognised and practical society and certain base.

Belief and action are mutual, and reflect on the actors.

What else can possibly result than that too many of mankind are deceivers, on the present code of justice and virtue?

Look not to what tradition says, but in unison with mind and reason, all to be proved by the result.

Patriots, philanthropists and philosophers, men and women of common and proper sense and honesty, are reminded to assert the dignity of mind and the pre-eminence of rational duties.

In self-defence, a proper analysis of this whole subject is necessary. The ignorant ancients had too little of wise knowledge, to be examples to the moderns.

Man is not in general prepared to see his case, he must investigate it, and by the true lights alone.

Look not to mankind's opinions, only as recognised by tested truth and facts.

Man needs the superior developments of enlightened mind for ever, as he is subject to the loss by perversion and collusion of others in his own ignorance, the prey to all that seek to obscure the gain of mind's light.

Man then enlightened must ever hail the hand of Deity too plainly needed to be mistaken, in all man's pretences that he can discover, to be miserably, stupidly defective.

Then by observation he can correctly see that many in the churches are stumbling blocks to others, by affecting sanctified conduct and looks, unnecessary and impracticably beneficial.

Social rights are violated in regard to different persuasions, as conflicts arise not so much from personal as professional pretensions; principle alone can heal or have prevented them.

Such church proceedings engender among the people a state of insincerity that is ruinous, and requires the highest elevation of character to counteract all the malign and evil tendencies of all such radically erroneous systems.

The people have the command of this mighty subject, in looking to its true anaylsis and themselves the proper means for correction, and have only to permanently institute principles. Millions in such circles have no idea of belief in the church dogmas of the day, yet it is most obligatory that all the world should be civilized and know who is God, and what he requires for man's highest duty in regard to all, for social and personal safety.

Mind owes it to itself to decide rightly and act on that decision in all such matters, as the signs of the wolf besides his howls, are too clear from the blood-marks and wounds.

How in society, where means are ready and furnished for wide-spread and incurable evils delusive yet most insidious, can mind ever rest satisfied in leaving such momentous matters at the mercy of relentless elements, to be lightened at the shrine of fanaticism so often used in the world under high sounding names and pretension?

To the everlasting regret of the good, men are possessed of such fanatical intentions enacting them too often in the present age of the world after all its boasted light, and are sustained by military force to perpetrate them, in defiance of the true sovereigns of the land, the people, by union of church with absolutism, or civil and military despotism under the hypocritical name of a republic.

The state acting this degrading drama, that ought to protect all alike! The best codes of all duties ought to counteract all this, that the people cannot do and know too soon.

Do all the church members, even many of the very preachers, believe in the bible of peculiar faith? How can any enlightened mind do that?

Can any affect it but those whose mind is peculiarly warped by peculiar prejudices and peculiar education, unknown to the recognition of purity?

Can any pretend to such, but those whose trade and vocation cause them to speculate in such faith, in the face of reason and paramount truth?

But do they act honorably to the author of their mind, that he has created for reason, truth and honesty?

Do they act honorably to their fellow-citizens of the world, whom they viciously seduce and contaminate?

The Romanist considers the Protestant a heretic, unworthy to be thought entitled to the rights vouchsafed to the christian.

The Protestant thinks the Romanist is too corrupt and ignorant, ever to see his heaven.

While the numerous subdivisions of this whole persuasion, including the Greek church, and all other christians of any pretensions, exclude each other necessarily, by their peculiar notions, from all the pretensions of orthodox peculiarity.

Now, what must be the inevitable righteous decision of rational religion, and its author, God, who knows no other, but that none of these, according to their own showing, possesses it, especially if we go to their various sects?

Where then is the rest of all peculiar faiths, and all absurd theologies, pagan, or any claiming more than pagan, but no higher than man-worship?

No wonder that the corrupt peculiar faith-world, the most iniquitous of all, should call to its aid the worst of tyrannies, and the most insidious of sophistries.

But all such have not availed, however they sought concealment.

The day of reckoning has come, and the decision can be had.

The concealment is like that of the ostrich, that hides its head, it is said, but its body is disclosed.

It is absolutely right, and at this time, that the millions now held in, should be freed from thraldom of peculiar doctrines, as they, but for shame and tyranny of misdirected public opinion, would be among the lights of mind.

One church is opposed to another, as heretic, esteeming itself only orthodox, because of the youthful age of the other, as if truth required age to become respectable.

Such is bigot opposition, having various pretensions to its own orthodoxy, and no base to true faith, affecting that its peculiar faith is the only true way, and that the world must be indebted to that for its safety.

The Creator has made no such world or faith, nor has he thus constituted mind.

From want of feeling and experiencing such faith that cannot be fortified by mere words or sophistry, in the time of need, when the only God, and his facts, are wanting, an immense number of church members of these persuasions, thinking in the excitement of conversion that they have the true faith, as the priests tell them they have, doubt at last, whether they have any or no.

It is not their deeds that are to be scanned, as they, when good, are as good as the best of the world, but the foundation on which they lean unknowingly.

When they know that position, they have found that they have left God for man-worship, a pretended messiah or prophet, and what an exchange!

A mortal blasphemer for the only Immortal Supreme God!

What grace is there in that membership?

What is the grace of God?

The prayer of good actions, correction of one's self, by the aid and inspirations of mind, lessening the evils, and increasing the universal benefit of the world, causing love of a universal brotherhood, best representing God's mind.

Persecution and bloodshed necessarily result from all the licentious spirit engendered by church governments, as compulsion and sophistry, not reason, have to be used in propagating such doctrines.

Much of church membership that has no pretensions to the dignity of faith, is brought about by various causes. Temporal preferments of diversified character, come in for a very large share.

The custom and fashion, the fault and vices of the times, of being "all things to all men," as the popular current directs, not as mind but as the social dynasty says, bring about many world-conversions to church membership.

Church-belief and association often result from feelings, and them by sympathy, aroused animal passions, the fear of superstition, with all the thunders of fiction and ambition too, no less than sinister designs, and credulity aroused and captivated by theatrical representations and recital.

What extreme youth is taught as household words, are fastened, if possible, in the circle that is interested in carrying out the peculiar faith, and the power of the priestocracy.

We see that many sects arise and fall under such influence, and though they rose like the morning star in their faith, they fall by force of true faith that must supersede all others.

Religion must be rational to exist at all, as it depends on the attributes of mind for sustenance, and is not, never can be, of church or state, but is identified with the soul's incentives, and the deeds of the conscientious individual who does right.

It breathes too holy an atmosphere to be trifled with by the vulgar intermeddlings of priestocracy, for if its essentials be lost in its own positions, it is lost in the quagmires of such odious vices.

All differences in church can and will subside, when honesty has her sway and religion her brotherhood.

Even in this union, distinguished for elementary fundamental principles of government, that the enlightened world recognises right by progressive adoption, where mind is untrammeled by absolutism, the most of church faith is no test of sincerity or protection, as but few members are absolutely sincere professors of pure faith by action.

All churches are subject to the infatuation of priestocracy, as fundamental power for their incorporation.

There are many individual exceptions in all such, that are more or less removed from improper motives, but they all are liable to improper positions and resulting injury; of course, they must be weak-minded.

Well educated persons of proper standing, add nothing to their standing in the church, except on the principles that have reared the blessings of their minds.

But the analysis of their position is not clear to their minds.

Many carry all their blessings into church-membership, and are a means of raising the most of the balance to their standing, but then they could elevate that whole position on the basis of rational religion.

But there are also stumbling-blocks in such churches, from the popes and bishops to the humblest layman, and unfortunately, they have their influence by church-membership to a certain extent.

It is not in the power of church elements to do justice to the world.

Their vices are ever extreme and revolting to social principles, that can never overlook, as the soul of the whole question.

The ignorant are often prejudiced, not by what results from a proper system, but are superficially misled by the inherent defects of previous bad ones.

All the intelligent minds of the world untrammeled by errors of peculiar education, and the influences of intriguing power, acknowledge the correct principles that a constitutional representative government gives to the people.

Why, then, is any church power expelled, and depending on gunpowder influence for restoration, if her faith is in accordance with the benefit of the greatest number?

Shall all possessed of absolutism, finally be utterly destroyed by the very influence it has invoked. to secure universal freedom?

Shall the noblest attempt of the brave citizens be its perpetual disgrace, through its excommunication of those people?

Freedom of religious conscience is incompatible with one-sided decisions of compulsion!

We observe here, that church government stands against conscience and freedom.

God creating religious and governmental freedom, never made them inconsistent. One or the other is wrong, and should be corrected, by proper submission to and decision of mind, most rational and free.

Enlightened freemen sovereigns, who act, or ought to act for themselves, can alone decide a sovereign question. There is no other rightful decision of mind and reason. The principles of religion and government being for society, morality and God, are compatible, or else a good and evil are mixed, which is an absurdity.

The correct analysis of rational mind, in her universal operations, insures the right decision.

The great good that has been accomplished in the world, is very clear of being due to forms, sects, or denominations of peculiar church-faith, but oftenest in defiance of them, when they have interfered.

Church peculiar faith-sophistry is not to usurp anything of reason, under any pretence whatever.

Much good, that has been accomplished in the world, has been the result of natural causes, that always have a conservative result, else the destructive would predominate. It has been the great result of social intercourse, where mind has acted on mind, stirring up the mighty latent powers. Commerce, also, has brought about an intercourse of sentiment, a knowledge of science, facts, and truths unknown, reflecting vast and mighty improvements in the condition of men, and in despite of errors and their narrow prejudices, encumbered with the deepest impediments of all alien designs.

Too much has been ascribed to others, that are legitimately and solely due to the principles conservative of the Creator, who has been unappreciated by vain men, and their vain and evil intentions have been paraded, as something for the gratitude of a world, injured by them!

The absolutism of the church is the worst of all, as hypocrisy is there. Her pretensions have been palmed on the world too long.

What have the adherents to respect, but force or sophistry?

The whole hierarchy, built up, as it is, by hands, is rubbish, and that on the fee simple grounds of others.

Why cumbereth it the ground? Honorable minds, answer. All previous church governments, with their gorgeous hierarchy and priestocracy, in all the fascinations of wealth and power, to bewilder mind and beguile reason; in the pomp of courts, the beauty and grandeur of architecture, the lustre of paintings, with the magnificence of statuary, backed by all the state powers of absolutism, securing potentates, armies and navies, their protectors, combined with exalted talents, aspiring orators and eloquent defenders, and untiring zeal subsidized, have failed to procure its greatest jewel, unity.

Without unity there can be no sound basis of religion. The unity of God Almig' requires unity of religion.

Principle cannot present antagonism with itself, that is impossible. The first chu' of Judaism had dissensions, and the second church, Christian, had dissension, an successive periods it has been divided; and the whole Judaic, Christian, Greek. M metan, Mormon, Protestant and Roman, are the church, divided against itself, that i fall in time. All peculiar faith churches, throughout the world, are divided.

The reformations and their wars have proved the falsity of the faiths.

The subdivisions have been continued, among each kith and kin. Faith-anta₂₂ has become the duty and the game of each other, and all are a spectacle to th' Unable to secure unity, much less to strengthen the church, they fail to comm₂a! necessary moral and intellectual power of the world, that, however needed, it impossible for them to possess.

They have traded on the principles, the capital of God, without referenc legitimate authority, thereby acting unwisely and dishonestly, without ackn' to the God of themselves.

The times that saw kings travelling barefoot to the holy city, so miscalled. ...ᴧᴧᴧg days for audience of the pope, to get absolved from his curse, are thought to be past, ',ɪt the dark clouds are yet lowering on the horizon. Of course the more humble subjec₁ were subject to more awful tyrannies, and not the least was the pope's excommunicat:ᴏns, that even at this day are fulminated with all the vindictiveness of bigotry. Only t₀ think of the holiness of the pope, so miscalled, united with such a curse! The ,ᵦurning to death, to create religion! And these claim to be the source of science and ₁ɪlosophy for the world, in whose keeping mind is murdered, and its most worthy attri-'cs crush.ᴧ!

'₀ᵣ many years, the predominant absolutism was that of the pope, whose very feet were worthy the lips of other potentates, who thus degraded their lips below their feet, and their minds below them! And all this, because mind did not assert its rights, mind that was sovereign to rule the world, was ignobly ruled by its lowest minions.

And these the keepers, self-assumed guardians of mind's richest treasures!

Talents then were buried for fear, as they were dangerous to their owner.

There was mind all the time, but its tyrants exacted the deepest curses of men of talents.

No science or philosophy could rear its head that did not agree with the dogmas of superstition, and her sophisticated ignorance advanced in the bible!

Can mind begin to feel the infamous tyranny of the priestocracy that excluded all science and philosophy, if they presented the conduct of these worthies as antagonistic? The dungeon or the faggot was the tribunal!

Disgusting relics illimitable in amount, outrageous legend, ignoble miracles assumed, were the science of those days. May they never be repeated. May they now end.

We must cling with the more sincere tenacity to rightful principles, and invoke their best protection, whether spiritual enthusiasm or peculiar faith regeneration be diffused or not.

It matters not whether all such unholy notions be the prevalent dogmas of any day, if men be broken on the wheel for conscience, or libeled now for its correct maintenance.

Absolutism will insinuate itself into every department of human rights, and above all, the human mind, then becoming perverted, leaves its rights subverted.

The combinations of peculiar faith to exercise collusions and insidious designs, are numberless, and hardly credible. Never will this matter be appreciated, till the purity of truth be duly elicited by sagacious analysis, which cannot be too highly estimated.

Mind must lay aside its abeyance to the master, and resume that to principle, and give up its devotion to the assertion of the dogmatist, no matter of what standing, and adopt the faithful portraiture of its own facts.

How long shall vain and puerile, but hurtful trifles, occupy as toys, the minds of grown-up children, who lose sight of the substance that men need?

What need is there of church prerogatives to the world, except so far as duty to God prevails, and that, these impostors have essentially failed to impart?

The people do not need them for temporal, and they are useless, perfectly so, for spiritual governments.

What benefit are they to foster all the ambitious views and intrigues of numbers, many of whom make religion subservient to their selfish aims, faithless, reckless, and of no account, reflecting on their connections with the church or state, contending for non-essentials in forms, rites and ceremonies, made by man and for man?

What does the pure mind of man care, whether a part of the body or the whole, should be bathed in water; whether the opinion, that the elect should only be saved in place of all seeking safety, by self-agency of mind, in its best aspirations, unless it deplores the miserable position superseding correct duty?

What does this all arise from, but degraded designs on the one part, and on the other, fundamental ignorance and error, never to be corrected, that go from bad to worse, till all shall be swept away before the Almighty, the only object of pure religion, that only satisfies the wise and virtuous?

What character so base, that will defeat the right direction and tendency of what so controls man's happiness?

The department of all sectarianism shows an irreconcilable antagonism to each other, horrible and depraved, for the worst purposes.

But some sectarians hate sin, that is, vice and iniquities.

Do not all good and wise citizens hate the same, if well raised and bred, their brain balanced, their education right, their social circles of elevated thoughts, which bespeak the reason of such position?

Learning, is it in the church faith, causing all countries, receiving its peculiar faith, to flourish as countries never flourished?

The very best evidence of the reverse is the fact, that a counterfeit faith, a superstition is adopted, showing the ignorance of people, not knowing it instead of religion, showing the unsoundest state of science, where the very first principle is violated, and ferocious and insidious absolutism has been, and is invoked in all its forms to carry it out.

Is that an honorable position of learning and science, where faith is made use of over mind, faith superseding religion and truth, causing the most odious church vassalage?

Absolutism that advocates any such divine rights of potentates, civil or ecclesiastical, must be discarded.

Protestantism, as advocating such, though the least of evils, as to Romanism, and other peculiar faiths, only as it emerges from superstition more, and gives more latitude to mind, as it commands the reading of the bible, when Romanism had excluded it once, is more tolerated, but the conscientious freeman is yet frightened by its libels, as old women, and children, against free rational discussion of the essential principles of rational religion, and the visionary position of its faith.

Is that freedom of mind, when reading of intellectual works. about free agency of mind, are prohibited by all fanatical expedients, creating church member vassals, and degraded ciphers of thought, of demoralized pupilage?

If that faith be sound and just, honest and truthful, membership will be high-minded to meet all opposition as the best thing for all the world.

But opposition, that is principled, defies all church faith that is or has been the avowed enemy of mind, as long as free thought and independent action can be estimated, as the noblest position of man, and execrating all forms of peculiar faith that have crushed man's spirit, by all basest expedients.

What is rational free discussion for, but to clear the whole world of its rankest errors, and its most obvious prejudices?

There is no limit in this world to its varied superstition, in any age or country, except by the light of mind, that rules out the bigotry of action.

What wise head of any church faith would wish it established by intrigue, malign influence of military stratagem, bribery?

Are such appropriate to create the solid foundations of any faith?

What is thus established by such force is the work of fraud, and is amenable to the tribunal of the highest justice. What is established by force may be speedily prostrated thereby.

But all such never can suit civilized man, or any state of man who needs the best gifts of civilization, not the curses of superstition and barbarism.

Man has a social and religious duty rightly to perform, from his organization the innate foundation therefor.

No church faith personal or absolute power can alter or endow this, the pure gift of an untrammeled conscience.

No wise observer will wonder to see that all church power has its days numbered, by the spirit and action of science. The wiles of hierarchy and the papal potency suffered badly, when the light of philosophy truly dawned.

Its meridian light will scatter all such by a total eclipse. When its blessings are diffused, all the ambitious aspirations of superstition yield their temporal pretences to those of heroic virtues as patriotism and self-denial, exhibited by the greatest men devoted to enlightened mind's institutions.

Enlightened codes and precepts properly prepared are the safe-guards of the social world, enabling all to appreciate their duty, and to feel the necessary penalty on social and moral violations.

Time will be known as the great vindicator of eternal truth, when man knows himself practically.

How many numerous oppositions do sectarians show to each other, and still they affect religion, doing duty to God and man, fostering the very elements of strife; any thing else but good feelings of mind you may call all such.

Where is that courteous toleration, nay, rationality, that adopts what is rational, that suits the rational spirit of this age of freedom?

We are bound to give all due respect to the feelings of all true members of all churches, though myriads do not believe, but join from various impure motives, hence all such faith originates the curse of hypocrisy on man in all departments.

What good citizen will affirm this to be right?

All have innate faculties, functions and principles of religion, and if rational religion exist, these professions must be sound and pure for ever.

Religion and worldly affairs as church professions, must never be mixed, but invariably be separate. The priestocracy have nothing to do with religion. Not only separate church from state, but from money and all peculiar power that intervene between mind and God. We must nurture such morals that science can originate, reason approve, and philosophy seal.

All these are proper resources, and will do to fall back upon.

We must have just action on belief and adoration of Deity, to cut down selfish sectarianism, bigotry, hypocrisy, impiety, blasphemy, man-worship, polytheism in all its disguises of members as trinity and idolatry, under their various and disguised forms.

All the church establishments are money-power engines.

What benefit can they impart to the world? The preachers have "calls."

Who can dispute their thinking so, if they choose and if the call be profitable?

When the true adoration of the true living God will supersede the various worships of superstition, and destroy hypocrisy by his immutable principles that keep the universe in the proper sphere, and direct moral agents to their proper duty, we shall be puzzled to see what preachers and priests can do for mankind.

All had best retire forthwith, as unneeded at all.

Analysis of mind leads men to appreciate its principles and ideas, that lead conclusively to God a fixed fact of all facts, but many church people have partial conversions to messiahs and fall back soon afterwards. What do all such avail them?

But what rational mind can fall back from its recognised God? As well ask for the destruction of the universe.

What protection is the church against evil, sin, or vice, independent of the vital principles of God?

As far as churches embrace conservative principles they do good, but those principles are universal to mind, not peculiar to any individual body. Churches corrupt the right impression about those principles.

The foundation of all those very principles must begin rightly with mind, not church membership.

Principles, then, have acted the world's age, where messiahs could not possibly be heard of, and where they could not possibly go, and that all over the globe, consequently messiahship is inefficient, defective, deceptive, and degrading to all minds, churches, or any body corporate.

When the mighty hand of time shall sweep all traditions into the dust, as the folly and crime of mind perverted, then shall arise the beauties and strength of mind enlightened, and God's temple shall be in such mind, and all will acquiesce in one universal brotherhood, that will be appreciated on the principles of universal union.

Then churches, faiths, creeds, or sectarian clanships shall be no longer a shield for bad members.

Then society will be on the right basis, and God's blessings will be aroused in a more sacred cause.

Then the necessity for all secret societies will be dispensed with, and the great objection to all such having a malign influence of some popular members oppressing others, and interfering in some of the social relations.

Then crimes will be punished as they deserve, and universal society cloaks will be stripped off as unworthy mantles before the majesty and honesty of mind, that leads man to his God.

Then the sophistry that a school-boy can detect, of God's character not being recognised by his works alone, will be silenced effectually, whether coming from open atheists or those in the disguise of any kind of polytheism or priestocracy.

Then the base impositions and abuses of God's works, dwarfed into a bible of tradition, under the false pretence of sacred character, will be exposed as ignominious acts of degraded men.

Then the thousands of disreputable people of all nations, that have never sworn the truth on the bible in a Court of Justice when it was not their interest to do so, will learn another code, to speak the truth from their infancy, and affirm it, not swear to it, in their manhood. He who speaks the truth will do so without a bible. He who is perjured in conscience will not speak the truth if to be compelled by bibles.

Then we shall see the difference of a wise education, that teaches mind its first lesson, that of truth, and that gives it its last blessing on this earth from the truth.

Then the ignoble distinction that engenders sectarian differences of reaching the truth, whether on a cross or on a bible, will be swept away, as swearing of any kind is worthless and degrading, but that affirmation is truthful, endurable, and consistent, because it rests on the only principle, a sure foundation, a right tuition from the mother's breast!

Intelligent citizens whose age and observation entitle them to due consideration, speak the sentiments of many, that more than a majority of the christian church members join for sinister motives; while other citizens, high in the estimation of their circle, speak the opinions of many when they say, such very people are these that they have to be watched most above all others.

Due credit must be given to all worthy people in or out of churches or peculiar faiths, according to their motives, as proved by their deeds, not professions; the only true estimate, actions.

Let none complain if there be hypocrites in their church, the sooner they are exposed the better, as stumbling blocks. But the sooner the fundamental position is corrected that makes hypocrites, the better.

We do not complain that there are hypocrites and evil doers in all churches, as they

26

are more or less abundant; they would be greater, did not the light and lustre and worth of mind guard them so well ; but that the only position is not secured that makes the least.

But all churchmen will find it impossible, under a peculiar faith, to have any other than those of peculiar motives.

As long as the system of peculiar faith is sustained by trade and speculation, the highest bidding for hypocrisy will be made, unfortunately for the race of mankind.

What will not absolutism do, under all her disguises ?   Now the issue should not be left open at the mercy of the elements, when all liable to injury have immortal minds, that should not be thus perverted and necessarily corrupted.

Romanism has sought to prostitute principles to its peculiar purposes, but corruption drove to secession and Protestantism, that has itself been subsidized into state-church-ship and all the various secessions.

All these have been distinguished in the annals of persecution, hatred or ill-will.

There can be but one catholic church, that must recognise God as its head, and all members as equal, no more.

There can be no aristocracy of power therein, for corruption will follow necessarily otherwise.

The errors of churches otherwise ordained have been so open, that all that open their eyes cannot mistake the signs.

But the fundamental error creates all the difficulties, as the door is wide open for future errors, from the doctrines, precepts, maxims and practices of peculiar faith.

In our time, new sects have arisen with all their novelty and fiction, but the Mormon faith is only a branch of the old superstition.

A previous branch was Mahommedan faith.

Upon what tribunal but that of mind will you put down all peculiar faiths ?

Then you must, as good citizens, adopt rational religion.

The Mormons are as good as any peculiar faith, no Christian faith or sect at all excepted, if they use the same light of mind and all its proper teachings.

But this reformation is not adequate to the demands of mind and civilization.   Nothing short of conservative revolution can rescue out of all such quagmires.

To get rid of all other peculiar faiths you must first get rid of all yours.   You need not hesitate, for you only lay aside the trammels of superstition.

And, patriots, are you not most vitally interested ?

The Mormons may vanquish the regular churchmen, standing for centuries before, on doctrinal and biblical arguments, to their greatest triumph.

The older churches cannot object to the Mormon platform, as all stand equal on fiction !

How is this, men of truth and mind ?

All look upon the Mormons as impostors, who pretend to have found a new bible and golden plates !

A plagiary from the novel of some preacher !

A preacher a novel writer !   Are not all preachers in this category ?   Is not every sermon a novel, if connected with any bible of tradition ?

In Mormonism it is only a little plainer that thousands are deceived or deceive themselves, if not others.

Had it existed thousands of years past, and had commenced by improvements in mind and morals, testified to by assumed authority of pretended saints, affecting miracles and revelations, it had been reverenced much of the world over.

Now, people in these latter days may begin to see the curses and fruits of superstition.

Wars and conflicts have arisen therefor, and the advocates of this peculiar faith have been driven from several states, one after another, and finally to Utah, where they seek to emerge from a new and distinct territory, with all the functions of government and their faith.

Now, church people, you see only Mormonism, one of the errors—and you have it in power to arrest your part of it.

Touch not the impurity of peculiar faith ; for you cannot tell whither it will lead. You can only head it by monotheism.

Pity it is that we had not had conservative revolution for reformation, for then all such impositions drive us back irresistibly to mind, as having the best data, and that recognises all rights, human and divine, through reason.   Reason is then, the divine attribute of rational religion.   Without reason, no such thing as religion can exist, the miserable opinion about faith, by botches, to the contrary notwithstanding.   The interested tinkers are not able to analyze the truth.

We would have the beauty of their curse, in this our age, if the Mormons were equal to half of the people of America. This country would have to take war, or adopt their superstition more extensively.

What if the various hierarchies of peculiar faith had the mastery of the world now, what but the dark and dismal days of superstition would be the result? Let any one get the supreme ascendancy of the world, and farewell liberty of mind, as well as its light; even the proper and necessary benefits of toleration would be abolished, and the most horrible of all tyrannies would be repeated the world over. World-patriots arouse, for your present and future safety.

Let not the church sectarian lay any flattering unction to his soul, as he ever stands on slippery ground. It is his highest and best interest to correct the miserable state of things, in peculiar alias false faith.

The great object of religion is not to alienate, but be enlightened, or enlighten beforehand friends to be made, not foemen worthy of the steel, to be slaughtered and butchered.

All rational beings must accord to all the worthy people of the world, who have adopted their faith about religion, the sincere intentions to save their souls, knowing as we do many church and pulpit members to be most worthy members of society, as now directed by mind.

How could they otherwise be by this universal standard, at this age, with their organization and education?

Their peculiar faith proves nothing at all—no addition to the benefits of such society. They may expect that their church professions prove it? But not at all.

They love the brethren, but hate the other sects?

If not, why attack sects then, and say all the things said?

We cannot refuse the sectarians, however mistaken, their claim for their faith, but we must say that peculiar faith has no peculiar claim; that all rational minds must see.

How often is the same church at loggerheads, and split into several factious divisions? All had better quit then. What is a church? Is it anything of mind, then it is at once what is rational religion, so far as that mind is rationally free, otherwise it is vassal; hence the interminable difficulties and squabbles, and consequent demoralizations. All these are not the fourth of mind, only as it is perverted by peculiar notions.

But the feeling is taken for the evidence of religion. That will not answer. What church factions and squabbles, showing that one party have no principles. Cases of accusation about unchastity may occur, and the most partisan views are advanced, to promote vice as well as doctrines.

When the fact is affirmed that a church member of standing is converted to the Mormon faith, and stated that she never had before any religion, this thing of feeling is no test, but self-delusion and fallacy.

When many converts of all churches fall back, and have to be converted over again, then the world can put its own estimates on all such.

When long standing church members fall, and fall disgracefully, the whole question is yielded that all such systems only fail, as others analogous fail before them. All must fail.

But church organization embraces trade and speculation, that are hardly expedient in God-given religion.

The tithes of the people are better appropriated to the best light of mind, and would go far to the civilization of the world.

What expenses of religion could there be if the experience rest, as it should, with the possessor, who is the professor before his God?

Honesty and truth, the foundation of purpose, would never show any half way designs.

Youth would not be committed about creeds, but would prove her sincerity in acts from generous impulses of religion.

Many church members deceive under the broad mantle of profession. Never should there be credence for aught but good works and upright behavior, based on pure religion, that is rational.

Correct views are to be estimated forever, in language that gives due weight and appreciation of man's actions.

We must arrest the facility to vice and perjury, that is too common.

The members of churches are members of the human family, no better, no worse than most of that family in similar circumstances; but it is a miserable policy to have abuses in the world that can be corrected, and to have them aliens from unity universal.

The church emoluments are an incumbrance upon the face of the earth, and an evil of corruption to freedom and equity of the people.

Mind should duly estimate those affairs that bring so much reproach upon the churches, as adultery, seduction, fornication, &c., whether by ministers or lay members.

If, then, all church members are as amenable as human nature like the world, what can protect better than conservative principles rationally avowed and adopted?

As no one but God can know of another's religion by profession, whether the individual seeks membership by design or purely, and in the first case acting the hypocrite, the worst of characters, we have to take him or her by their conduct for life, not their profession, consequently the system of reception on experience of feelings must be utterly fallacious.

All must be truthful and honest, otherwise they cannot be religious, for truth and honesty are the foundation attributes of religion that requires humanity and other virtues.

How, then, can we know of religious feeling but by conduct?

Some churches initiate members on personal experience, and declare them religious; but if the members do not act uprightly they are excluded as defaulting.

As their church advocates the doctrine that converts cannot fall from grace, these members are considered never to have had religion! Peculiar faith has, then, no test at all.

The advocates admit persons as fit members on their assertion and profession of faith, and then exclude them as never having possessed the very essentials of admission! Here is a total failure of peculiar faith and its pretences.

It reduces itself to probation in or out of church, which probation excludes very many.

Some leave in process of time, believing that they never possessed religion; others are expelled for various unmemberlike conduct.

Many of the balance, more fortunate, are not turned out till found out.

Of course, then, they are not indebted to church membership, but the principles of God evinced by rational religion.

This all proves that religion should be between man and God.

Now, if church members of the various sects and systems, to an extraordinary extent and number, have no sincerity in their profession, but by profession from policy have joined from various impure motives and designs, as increase of influence, of power, money, self-interest, matrimony, combination, clanship, collusion, the sooner such a state of things is exposed the better. All societies that interfere with social principles are nuisances.

The pure who have joined for pure motives will certainly see the necessity for looking to a purer source than man's foul designs, that all perish.

They will feel the harm it does to have a Christ instead of a God; an usurper instead of the Proprietor. The present-day papers show a spirit of proselytism to or from papists and protestants, yet all will not avail against the final decay of peculiar faith, protestant or Romanist.

Look at the tithes of state churches, their gorgeous incomes and the pretences of their priests.

Some of the churches have arrested this in part.

What deadly hate and rancorous animosity prevail among different sectarian churches, even of the same country.

The mutual scandal will hasten their death-blow.

The exile of the pope of Rome showed the feelings of the people, who ought to know best, though excommunicated by their pope!

Which is the true, the infallible, the orthodox church? None. Rational religion can tell the balance. What would it avail the world, if we were to seek only to reform the faults of the protestants, or the vices of the Romanists, and not to revolutionize for the true adoration of the everliving God?

As to the length of time the Romanists have been in existence, for eighteen centuries, we see pagans have existed thousands of years before their commencement, and are not overthrown by Romanism.

Judaism, the parent, and Mahommedanism, another offspring, still pursue their course.

How can one superstition triumph over another?

Here rises the youngest born, Mormonism, as good as the best, if she conform as well to outward appearances.

Polytheism, in some form or other of idolatry, is still before the world in its disgusting characters.

The penitent is in a troubled state of mind. His anxious state of inquiry is met by those who have been over the ground. As preachers, of course they must speak the truth, for who does suppose that "divines" stretch their conscience? The mediators are at hand, whereby the penitent can only be saved. He is not able to investigate, in his new-born zeal, and must act as told by custom, interest, influence of the peculiar predominant faith. What despot ever made greater vassalage of mind? The church-gospel is unquestionable, and the authority of its expounders is dictatorial for the poor neophyte. He is duped at first, and of course must be consistent in his inconsistent and untenable position of faith. Where would be the world but for Deity, where else but in chaos and confusion?

All feelings about church-faith may be perfect illusions, as we may see at times of revival, when, out of fifty thinking themselves converted, hardly one-fifth persevere in that conscientious belief?

And of these, how many are really the religious? Have they started with the first correct point? Is their position not the farthest distant from religion? For, if God be considered the Creator, as no sound mind can dare deny, he has provided universal means of the best happiness, and that thousands of years before a pretended messiah was ever thought of.

The priests and preachers affect to know all about it, as it is their profession; but this is all false pretence, necessarily of the worst character, to mislead mind and gull the people. They are the most ignorant analysts of the whole world—a disgrace to mind.

Because some have been members of churches, they think they ought to know all about their peculiar faith, of no account to the world.

But they have been under self-delusion. There can be no such thing as church-faith, from the nature of things. There is church-faith enough that is peculiar, and to spare, and all that is man's, certainly, opinions.

What and who are church-members, if they be not as the best circles of civilization guided by social benefits? How often is it, that church-members show no compunction of conscience, hardened in guilt, and steeped in iniquity?

What hold can the world have on such portion of men in payment of their debts, if destitute apparently of property, if, above laws made for debtors, they are below honor?

Sectarians say they know they have a saving faith, because they love the brethren. What brethren? Those of the same church? The stumbling-blocks and all? But what do they mean, when they hate those of other sects? "When they would not stay in a church. only a few years over a century old"?

If time be the criterion, then they must go to the oldest, though the most corrupt in peculiar faith.

If protestant, they hate the Romanist with a bitter hate, for that has perpetrated horrible wars in protestantism.

If they truly seek the most ancient and trust-worthy, they must seek rational religion. The world, then, is only on the safe side surely, when it seeks the great ever-living God, Creator of the universe, whose soul expands and sympathizes throughout creation. If we adopt God, as necessarily sound minds must, we must adopt his universal works that require universal, not peculiar laws.

Again, we recognise in all other matters, the highest kind of best evidence of sense and science, but in faith, that is the highest attainment, a blind superstitious belief is to be foisted on the intelligent minds of freemen, who are not to be deceived out of one living God of justice and mercy, by any of the frauds or frailties of poor human nature.

Should they be defrauded, or scared out of their life-rights? All virtuous, high-minded, and honorable citizens will ever seek to protect the society of the world, to keep people from being hypocrites.

They must have them all judged properly on principles of sense, honor, and honesty, not by professions, but by deeds that speak.

None of God's principles can permit hypocrisy, therefore the means that lead to that result by temptation, are to be excluded.

No pure men can tolerate any speculative priestcraft, or preacher-craft, that results in that.

Hierarchy is a petty monarchy, the most tyrannical government without soul, as it is without sympathy, basely hypocritical and criminal, especially with inquisition,—intolerance. a most hideous tyrant.

With all the boasts of church-laudation and priests' pretences, for their centuries, we see yet how deplorable and sad the condition of the world, only to be improved by mind directed in her best efforts.

Feeling has been pretended as a means, the spirit of God witnessing with the spirit of man, but all this, if peculiar faith. has been a failure in churches, and proves nothing.

All that is addressed to man, is through rational mind, by a perfect not peculiar God.

Are not the rich and influential persons pre-eminently sought for, by the ministry? Is this religion?

How shall we estimate the customs of churches as essential, when some shout, others do not?

Some shout at church, join as members, and then leave the membership.

How far is this all from self-delusion, mere excitement, or enthusiasm aroused by sympathy?

How far does this theatrical representation, by shouting, avail in rational religion? What has it to do with God's religion?

Why should it prevail, when at revivals the preachers tell the shouters to stop, the noise generally soon ceases.

Youth is generally taught to look at much of this as the only safety, and it becomes a part of their education, and at last they assume it as an indispensable matter.

Others, through sympathy of relationship or feeling, join them, and even men of minds, that ought to know better, shout.

Who will admire the locomotive worship of the Shakers and Jerkers, as essential to any but their peculiar doctrines?

Predestination is pitted against the free agency of mind, and then we see the antagonism of sectarianism in the last or in both, as the advocates narrow it down to their peculiar notions, and in the way the first is used, it does away with the responsibility of mind.

God's spirit bears witness with man's spirit, that is God's inspiration, is the only one on mind all the time, and all others are excluded.

When did God's cease? To say that God's spirit or inspiration is not with man's spirit, is a horrible libel on Deity.

O, but as you have never been in our particular church, you have not our particular spirit! As if there could be more than one in God's universe, and of course not his. This is part of the quintessence of church sophistry.

Every nation of old had its particular gods, that, in their opinion, were better than the gods of other nations.

Now, the churches have—well, we submit this case to respectable people, who had been members of a church, claiming free agency of mind, but who become Mormons, and declared that they had never known what religion was before that feeling!

Did they have religion then? Who believes it? Feeling cannot prove it, except with the principles of God, that prove it completely, and satisfactorily.

The sense of the soul is not by feeling, but by mind, that has the universe to analyze, but has been most cowardly deserted for the most miserable false pretences.

Church membership cannot create anything essential, that is not in the universal principles of God.

Messiahs and their ministers, may pretend to monopolize for a time, but their pretences are false, and will fail.

Religion, the advocates of peculiar church faith, assume must be spiritualized, or taken in a spiritual sense.

Do we know what we believe? If we do not, but intrust ourselves in the power of suspicious and badly-raised characters, we are in the chains of absolutism.

As to churches, it matters not, as to age or creeds, since sectarians need not contend about either, as all is peculiar faith. Triflers will contend about trifles.

The divisions are abundant, and the contentions will continue to demoralize on their basis.

Rationality, the best essence of mind's functions, does not seek churches to hear of Christ, but hear all proper principles of God, who governs men's best actions.

But "that change of heart" is to be effected.

What is that, but the proper effect of the light, previously existent of Deity in the mind and soul?

It must be the mind and soul, and not the mere heart, a mere blood-organ, that is represented.

But the natural man cannot see; it is the spiritual!

The mind of every man that is rational, recognises things, rational or spiritual, on this sphere.

No obstruction that is valid, can be raised by bible sophistry, that is derogatory to reason.

It does not become an authority, not yet established on rational proof, after all its pretences, to dictate instruction to mind, its superior.

If man were all spirit, it might do to talk of the spiritual man, but his is a mixed state, spiritual and physical, corporeal and mental.

The Spirit of God that pervades all space, operates on mind. Whence conscience otherwise?

The purer the conscience, the brighter the light and deeper the inspiration.

In great excitements about religious revivals, the animal feelings may be deeply aroused by fear and other kindred passions, that move speedily to superstition.

When cooled down, the individual experiences a change in his feelings, but of what kind?

This may be a speedy education, and that depends on the circumstances among what peculiar faith people he happens to be.

He joins himself with what he is taught is the house of God, and acts to his appreciation of duty that may lead to the future reward.

All that are intelligent and honest in or out of churches, know that there are many brave people of the world, in or out of churches, with no honesty that adorns all good institutions, above all things, names at least. Then church-faith is a non-entity, and cannot have any existence at all.

What men are despite of church-faith, they can be much better without it, putting all the best at the best appreciation.

Peculiar faith revivals show sometimes forty or forty-five out of fifty, return back to their original position.

All such are mere excitements, and yet all the forty-five had religion purer before the revival. Did they know this?

The five left are retained on more peculiar considerations, evidently so, but the balance are preserved on the best principles of rational religion, whose inherent elements they can never eradicate.

Sectarianism cannot be religion, for it hates and wars, as its name proves, on the brethren.

Do the brawls and fights of church factions, of whole churches affecting to be leaders of light and peace especially, their splits, divisions and subdivisions, prove less than the inability of all such polity reaching the essential point, a proper brotherhood? All such have not the very first principles of right. The people see all this, do they properly heed and correct all such? Rational religion can eradicate all this, certainly. But cannot church membership and meetings do some good?

The meeting of the sexes and of all classes of genteel society, on the Sabbath, produces a state of civilization of itself, high-mindedness and sentiments.

The messiahship thus promotes the improvement of social virtues, when rightly put to account. All this is enjoined by monotheism, the only promoter of civilization.

How often have been deceived by members of churches, in payments and settlements of money? Does church membership make any preachers or members any better? Freer from violation of promises? We should estimate the numerous schools of the world that influence mind, that is independently good, despite of church influences?

What creed of responsibility and restitution, like the certain punishment for crimes and sins, will deter some? Do we get that from churches, or their founders?

None but that founded on the best appreciation of principles, can be obtained.

Do principles belong to God, or messiahs? All sound minds will admit, to God alone.

What then can messiahs do? Where is their employment? In churches? Mind if cultivated in principles, can find no manner of use whatever, with them, their antagonists—away, then, with the imposition.

A proper knowledge of the world and man, gives us the best insight into duty and science; such will show us that most affect more than is real.

Many amusements of innocent character have been precluded by creed abiding persons, as they think that they are required to act with an eye single to God's glory, but in peculiar ways.

But such must recollect that in promoting the true physiological principles, all do that in a universal way, the only proper one.

Now where monotony and dullness can be well relieved, where actions are seen teaching wisdom, arousing exhilarating spirits and feelings, an important part is obtained even to drive hypochondria away.

God does not know sectarianism, as that is anti-god, hence a reformation of reformation, a constitutional conservative revolution is needed.

Why should members of different churches fall out about apparently mere business transactions, that ought to be settled by a court of conciliation?

Even members of the same church, of several denominations, including the most peaceful, fall out and fight each other, in respect, too, to their own church matters! Correct principles of mind can do better.

Ask one of peculiar faith how he knows he is a christian, and he replies, because he loves the brethren.

But they are brethren who believe in the same messiah, and yet sectarianism cuts down this test at once! For do they love other church members? All the world, with all its various peculiar faith doctrines, are brethren, disjunct because they believe not in the same God of the universe. How can sectarianism abjure all its prophets and messiahs and peculiar machinery to reach the universal brotherhood?

They have to sacrifice all their pretences of superstition to reach the sacred precincts of rational religion, that can only induct them to the right position. They must doff all the machinery of peculiar faith to reach rational faith.

Whoever is of rational faith, and all the world must be to be right, must be of a universal brotherhood.

In what respect can any faith exist that conflicts with our views of rational religion, that inculcates the divine grace of the God of the universe by inspiration of mind, and the very best lights to cultivate, cherish, and adorn it in full?

How many Jews and Gentiles convert themselves for the temporal rewards! Take away all the world-machinery of corruption.

How many ignorant and deluded people fall into the Mormon miracles, that would have filled volumes had not the present age been too intelligent from science and philosophy for them?

How many intelligent minds perverted by lucre, power, influence, passions of ambition, and various inducements, cater to the morbid taste of the customary fanaticism?

As it was with all the lights of the age hundreds of times better than the dark and bloody ages of antiquity, when at best the fewest could read, and less could write, how many poor minds prostituted themselves for want, to this superstitious order of people?

But this is a day when the people's mind, befriended by science and philosophy, can counteract the base efforts of priestocracy.

The more the intellect diminishes, or is less enlightened, the more feelings are displayed as a part of the exercises.

This proves that the less rational the less religious.

Shouting, of course, must be indulged in as the blessings are felt, for with some this is the only best evidence of God's grace shed abroad in the soul.

But mind, the only beneficiary, conclusively proves that the feelings are utterly deceptive, and that reason alone can decide on facts, to which alone imposition can demur.

But the advocates of peculiar faith doctrines affect to object.at the impotency of reason reaching a God's appreciation, and the proper means of man's salvation, without the gospel dispensation.

They have absurdly regarded the impotent conclusions of sophists of ignorant ages, when their own ignorant dispensation was assumed for mind, and its purest blessings, reason.

They have not analyzed the paramount question, not understanding its splendid principles, nor its glorious results, all the time dwarfing mind to all the vain circles of their narrow bigotry.

They must begin rightly to do justice to God and mind.

We need take but one simple proposition thereon, in which all mankind are most concerned.

What are the guarantees of best societies? Are church ethics? The ethics of any church that has not the very first elements of true faith, truth, and honesty, the proper award to the God of the universe, who fills all space, all the inherent attributes of omnipresence, that by all the principles of mind excludes all messiahs? What other guarantee can meet the world's demands but rational religion?

The science of all sciences, the philosophy of all philosophies. rational religion, that necessarily makes the best of good citizens, who look at the sincere good of the many.

In rational religion there can be no hypocrisy, no deception, for speculation is not a part of her trade.

Her purest motives are above suspicion, and beyond envy.

Her advocates are the pure adorers of God, a perfect and pure being, who needs no advocacy but pure reason.

She looketh to the universe for her residence, and to immortality for her home.

They now see that it little avails to have a church faith, that produces stumbling-blocks in and out of the same.

They see that a wise institution of general principles, is what God intended.

The censorship of the inquisition will pauperize its faith, ere it ever enrich the world with any religion.

Madeira may drive out her poor exiles, and torture her worthy citizens by persecution for reading the bible, till the day of retribution, not to be very long deferred.

What, peculiar faithites afraid to trust the word of their peculiar god to the light of truth?

What a stigma on her name and character!

Who that visits the scenes and dungeons of the inquisitions, can otherwise than execrate these horrors of iniquity and superstition!

When will civilization, religion, and truth, assume the mastery of this world?

The answer can be given, when intelligent freemen act up to the analysis of the case. No other position answers.

Who rule out that bible? Reason and mind, the gifts of the universal God. Here is an awful clash : the peculiar is done.

Some of both sexes join the church and seem above suspicion, after a life of prostitution, fornication, adultery, murder, &c. It is well, if this be not during the continued perpetration of such crimes.

Reformation of errors, vices, and crimes, is essential, but exemption the most of all in moral deportment is worthy of God's attention and reward.

All that enjoy the right benefits of a good liberal education, received at the proper and right time, and way from parents and society, cannot do less than exhibit a sound, natural, ripe, and honest judgment, that is one of the superior faculties of the mind along with conscientiousness, that characterize the man so eminently.

A zealous member of a church admits that persons of ignorance and small minds, knew but little of moral and christian obligations, as most of such members proved their incompetency for religious appreciation from intellectual weakness.

This concedes the question that peculiar faith has impracticable difficulties, whereas rational faith addresses all rational beings, the uncivilized as the philosopher, and is received with facility by the universal mind of rational beings.

After the triumphant testimony advanced, of the capacity of mind for rational religion, from the improvement of which it has been perverted by all varieties of peculiar faith, of priestocracy, deeply interested in its monopoly and usurpation over the rights and minds of the people, we now refer to one more sect, "the Druids, who were the priests or ministers of religion, (so called) among the ancient Gauls, Britons, and Germans. The honors of their birth, &c., procured them the highest veneration of the people, as the interpreters of religion, and the judges of all affairs indifferently.

Whoever refused obedience to them, was declared impious and accursed. They were the priests, poets, augurs, civil judges, and instructors of youth.

Their high priest had absolute authority over the rest, and commanded, decreed, and punished, at pleasure.

The Druids believed the immortality of the soul, and worshipped the Supreme Being, who made his abode in the sacred groves of the oak, governed the universe," &c., according to the acknowledgment of "their religion."—*Buck.*

These people were as much the chosen people of God as the Jews. Who can pretend to dispute this opinion?

They worshipped the God of the universe, that none of peculiar faith now can surpass. That is certain.

Religion has been constituted a matter of rites and ceremonies by all of peculiar faith. The Druids consecrated the misletoe as "the peculiar gift of heaven."

Rational religion sublimely consecrates the mind, as the sacred gift of the omniscient Almighty, and only thus enables it to reach its immortal fruition.

That mind is not to be misled by enthusiasm of feeling, but must be enlightened by the potency of reason.

In the chief priest of the Druids, we ask, what more fearful power could exist, than the union in the same person of priestocracy and civil government? Who could withstand that powerful influence, of temporal tyranny and spiritual superstition? But these were pagans! Who are the best of others? Christians. What is the difference, before the God of the universe?

The one consecrated the misletoe, the others consecrate a mortal for a God! The last exclude the first by aid of the martial power of Rome, that had the imperial sway. It was the power of the sword then that gave the mastery; now it is the insidious power of sophistry, superstition, and social despotism.

Imperial power of absolutism adopted Christianity over the Roman rites of augurs and soothsayers; the various sects of the world then as now contending for supremacy of mind's vassalage.

The four great sects of the world, the Christians, Mahometans, Jews and Pagans, with the hosts of minor sects, are hostile, with deadly hatred and animosity against each other; yet all are analogous, and in the same category.

Their world has lost sight of mind, that is the eye of the universe, and that must take cognizance of all things therein, either now or hereafter, in time and eternity, with a full and proper employment of all its resources.

These sects, the world, must reverence deity alone, do duty to man in all parts of the earth, and mind in its true analysis.

These sects, all, cannot ever absolve themselves from the least of these universal duties, as mind is the bright particular creation of the God of the universe, must have his best particular care, and may be thereby entitled to his particular preservation, for future improvement, leaving but little more than the elements of its ignorance behind it, in this world.

Never, then, can there be any peculiar people or mind, when the creation and purposes of mind are universal.

This cuts down dead, forever, the pretence that the God of Nature ever had any peculiar chosen people.

The god of Judaism was necessarily a peculiar god, whom it is essential that intellectual freemen should never know, as he is degradedly abominable.

The peculiar gods of the world, ancient or modern, are the creatures of creatures of the God of the universe!

How unspeakably magnificent, then, must be the majesty of the universe's Almighty!

His immutable laws demand the duty of man to man, and God, involving universal love, fidelity, and purity.

Where, then, is sectarianism, in its duties?

The polar star for all on this earth is " the greatest good to the greatest number."

Corrupt society, under its present organization, has reversed this memento.

Peculiar motives originated all peculiar faith, whilst universal principles caused religious faith.

The more ignorant the ancients, the more peculiar their gods and their character, the more peculiar their faith. All polytheisms have peculiar faith.

All honest minded wise men can never be convinced that it is indispensable to be in a church to have their souls saved. Not at all. They can never see the utility, much less the necessity of putting society into clans, and promoting individual views and interests, at the expense of demoralization, whilst the whole nation, the whole world, demands mind's universal assistance and rights.

The peculiar faith that calls for social organizations distinct from the world, has not rational religion.

Those of philosophical science wish to see religion's benefits as universal as the world, and know that universal principles alone secure its execution.

The primary principles of religion were implanted in every rational mind at first and cannot be superseded, therefore all others coming after are pretensions as they are after the time and necessity of the case.

Many persons are taken in on probation and trial, in church-government. The church endorses members, but who endorses the church?

The necessity is proved to be direct and absolute, when we come to observe the fearful state about oaths, that result with facility in perjury.

In or out of church, this state of things prevails.

We can easily find members of one church, speak of the perjury of their own church members!

What horrible iniquity is otherwise practiced by admission of peculiar faith-worship by sects, that arise every age or so, a false branch on false stock.

Sectarianism cannot come up to its promises, the wants and expectation of the world, but religion can as designed by the Almighty.

Take fanatics or moderately educated persons, and shouting can be secured in churches. Is enthusiasm rational religion?

The Jerkers will show muscular contortions, the Shakers dancing, and the Mormons may exhibit a delphic prophecy or oracle, unknown tongues!

What has all this to do with religion?

Will any honest man in church or out of it in the world, ask for faith in any thing without sound logic.

What are all claims of sanctification, regeneration, and justification, but sinless perfection, and therefore arrogant? Rational religion upholds reasonable views identified with earth, and forbids any set seals of demarcation except for conduct.

No peculiar faith can be other than presumptuous, to affect any lives growing out of faith. God alone can decide, in mind's purity and merits.

What mind is there not sinful, or what mortal can live without sin? Consequently all that arrogate the title of saint or holy one, increase their sin.

Where would you look for the greatest and best characters? In any church? No more than elsewhere. We must try all men on earth covered with breast-plates of honors, only by their actions in the case. The full science in all the schools of human nature in the world, warrants nothing on trust or granted, but all on trial in all professions church or not. As life is a continued trial ordained by God, let not vain man presume to define it different.

His is the part of humility at the fount of philosophical science to learn, not dictate, much less affect the world with false delusions.

There can be no saint, as there is no perfection.

There can be no sanctification, from the real nature of mind. Hypocrisy would take precedence, if pretended. What produces so much corruption in the churches directly professing these things of virtue, yet most obedient to the deepest degradation of vices as lust, avarice, violations of truth?

It is the sin of hypocrisy that degrades all churches of peculiar faith, and proves most conclusively, that no system of peculiar faith can come up to the requirements of mere fancy or peculiarity.

With all its prepossessions of prejudices, what rational mind could now desire any established church or clergy, as all such are dangerous to individual and national liberty?

Wherever it is established, absolutism is rendered more severe.

Who had greater power than the patriarchs of ancient times, in civil government, domestic policy, and peculiar faith? They had the offices of priest, king and prophet, that gave unlimited sway over the lives and liberties, the persons and property of their subjects. What could rational mind do, with such an avalanche of despotism?

All the nations of antiquity were under analogous dynasties. The most civilized, as Greece and Rome, had their state and faith policies. What now, is the case in the world?

The koran is the imperial code, that governs nearly one-seventh of mankind in law and faith.

The druids were the autocrat sovereigns of a great part of Western Europe, being their priests and judges, and these were prototypes of the papal supremacy.

Who have borne greater sway over one hundred and forty millions of Hindoos than their priests? And what enslaves and reconciles the mind to all despotisms worse?

In China, the emperor is sovereign pontiff. Under such regimes of mind-vassalage, most of the world is unfit for liberty.

The Incas of Peru, it is said, claim that the ancient faith is still preserved, and its rites are still celebrated in secret, even amid the apparent devotion of the Indians to the worship of their foreign masters.

They have their ancient prophecy and mysterious lore, to the confusion of the assertors that the Christian faith has excluded all others where it has taken hold. Power is the same all over the world, and assumes all the pretences to advance its usurpation. In no department can an exception be made, for the greater the sphere, the greater the exertions and the corruption to uphold it.

Who could be a partisan, on the principles of justice? Inaction in all instances would be preferable.

A higher order of rational mind forbids the union of church and state, in order to put down the potency of both tyrannies, that effectually filch from the people millions of money and treasure, lives, and all that life is worth.

Let the anathemas of such corrupt dynasties of superstition thunder, what rational mind cares?

With money, and its concomitant power, enough, people enough can be found by the thousand, whose minds are perverted, to perjure themselves for all crime and corruptions in church and state, to oppress or deceive man.

Why did the Romanists take away the bible from the laity or people? Why exclude their flocks from the use of protestant bibles? Because mind could see the entire falsity of such a work.

Why do all sectarians exclude the people from the bible of mind, the free and rational discussion of the subject? Even people of mature age, not in the church, are so ignorant of all this principle, that if you talk of excluding all this corruption, they will expect to drop into perdition right off! Was there ever worse superstition? The old women and children will crouch before her dogmas and despotism.

The mere singing and shouting are acts of the mind, that avail nothing unless accompanied by the solid and substantial sincerity and honesty of mind.

In peculiar faith pretences the adherents assume a standard, and seek to tyrannize over all others, to whom they dictate by the standard of their assumption.

It is not only absurd but criminal to be merely taught any faith or belief.

As to the "love of the brethren," if that love be not as comprehensive as mankind and the globe, it is partial, sectional, peculiar and sectarian, and subverts God's attributes of universality and general love.

But the church may offer some protection better than the world? What fallacy!

Those in the church may commit many errors that lead it to crimes. Why add church and faith-crimes to life's sins?

Innocence of those out of the church is preferable to error in the church.

One church sect affects to act, as if it thought all the rest of the world would go to perdition without any redemption at all, surely.

What miserable envy prevails among sects.

What kind of a world would they make it, if they had their way? It would be thus unmade in a short time.

If the Calvinists, those who say that a certain number was predestinated from eternity, was to be exclusively saved, were to preach this doctrine, the articles of their faith and creed, they would have but very few to hear them, as where would be the reason, seeing that all the balance were to be damned?

This savors of doctrines that make priests indispensable to the performance of various rites, as funerals, &c.

Now we see the schools of different sects, possessed of jealousy and opposition to each other.

Parents will not send to each other's schools, if possible to prevent it, and this rivalry runs through all their business transactions.

Sectarianism is bad enough, but hypocrisy is the worst of all characteristics, as the actor is prepared to do anything needed.

Now let the faith-pretensions be exempt from all this temptation, and we will even cut down hypocrisy.

Let there be no speculation in professions of faith, as the practice is with the conscience of the individual, and his God, and no more.

What has the world to do with a man's religion, except that he conforms to rational conservation of society? Before the world, profession is mockery.

Before the God of Nature, religion is the highest and most sacred obligation.

As to orthodoxy, who can claim that in peculiar faith?

There it is a farce, when it is not a tragedy.

The Greek and Latin churches deny it to each other, and their Protestants, and the last repel the first as corrupt. The whole world of peculiar faith denies it to all not of their creed.

If all be in this fix surely neither can be right.

Rational religion affirms this. All such faith is positively in direct antagonism with her and God.

A republic, so called, caused her soldiers to butcher a sister republic for dismissing absolutism, and adopting a free faith feeling, independent of temporal power. This is the worst species of hypocrisy.

Rational religion asks for all that is legitimate, good and just. It certainly never can butcher individual, much less national liberty.

Toleration is not a boon, but freedom, bold, and independent.

Already, many a church has been split to pieces by internal elements of discord.

We see that some of the great churches of this union, of the very same persuasion, are now separated, and with bitter feelings of hostility. This has helped to foster disunion, a parricidal blow at our noble constitution.

But can we maintain our position, free from division of sentiment, when we advance the religion of civilization? Religion has no peculiar faith or divisions.

She organizes mind-institutions on a different basis.

How many corrupt people are received into the church? What good will they effect?

All this is worthy of the deepest investigation.

If the God of Nature be for us, we have enough.

It will profit us naught if the world be with us, but God be not for us.

No church-institutions can be available, but through God alone. Who is infallible? God.

It is enough to make rationality excited, to see the degraded tyranny of hierarchies, whose heads assume God's privilege, infallibility.

What stay deity's electricity, but his universal principles that vindicate him?

None can be free till they discard all such sectarianism and peculiar faith.

Who is a bigot, but a base charlatan and slave, that seeks to crush every noble principle of mind?

Who shall be punished by fallible mortals for rejection of peculiar creeds, that have involved the world in moral, intellectual and social darkness and misery ?

The infallible God of nature has given plain facts and laws to the point. Who can mistake them ?

It is the height of folly for any to talk of sanctification on this earth, as there cannot possibly be any one not sinning in thought, word or deed. To sin the least, is the best security for mind in this life. This is religion that constitutes the most exalted actions, according to light and knowledge.

Why should there be any intervention, national or individual, to assault the independence of mind of a republic or the world, in any faith that is between conscience and its Creator ?

Can any but blasphemy prompt all governments or faith advocates to any such ?

The triumph over such people and hierarchies employed in such base acts and intriguing designs, is their shame and disgrace before the best benefits that they seek to destroy.

Truth will scatter all such, to their confusion and ignominy.

What shall insure confidence in the world's community, as we see all professions fail ?

Hold all perfectly accountable for their conduct, and answerable for their actions at all times.

It is strange that those of unsound mind are exempt from responsibility for lack or defect of mind, yet rational men are free from penalty for superstition at the tribunal of man, who affects to advocate rational principles.

Bad governments with assumed powers and union of tyranny, depress the people to their downfall, but the blights of superstition are unnoted, till the people are degraded or rescued by the popular mind.

The great object of religion, is to stop sectarianism of all peculiar faiths. . Freemen should know their highest duty. Has the christian or any other peculiar faith done it ? Not at all. Then all such are not trustworthy.

The hatred of the Greek and Roman churches, is proverbial, no less than between them and their Protestant brethren, and no less so between all these, and the followers of Judaism. They despise the Jew, but take his bible. Yet prophecy is the sacrificial altar for all these iniquities, and that, God's word denies most positively. All such must be false prophecy for a messiah, for whom the Jews and the world have suffered awfully for centuries, by the loss of millions of people.

What distinguishes sectarianism above all others of the world ? Love, they claim.

But hear the beloved sects preach, though all professing Christ.

They impeach all others, reviling or slurring them, thereby condemning themselves on the inherent elements of their own category.

This is a sore point, and no wonder that all the machinery of inquisitions and despotism have been employed to silence all but themselves.

The New Englanders were the scions of European persecution, yet they cruelly persecuted the Quakers, and through idolatry of the bible, they disgraced mind about witchcraft.

We have to judge all mankind by their deeds, not by professions of church, or any other than orthodox faith of rational mind, that looks to the unity of God, and his divine attributes.

None of the human family have exemption from frailties, in or out of churches. Church membership adds to them when it involves hypocrisy.

It is all sophistry and hypocrisy to pretend otherwise.

If any claim it they are all degraded impostors.

The improved age proves the necessity of looking to the right point of mind, and the true deed of God.

Does not the very existence of denominational strife decide a warfare base, degrading and unholy ? Do you call this religion ? So far from it, that it is its desecration.

All superstitions are an abomination before the Almighty ; and all church impositions on men are base, no matter the pretence.

What is more obstinate than the prejudice of church bigotry ?

It is self-willed, vaunteth itself, is proud, arrogant, and full of errors.

Modesty, then, pre-eminently becomes the sectarian, when the Greek is against the Roman church, and both are against their Protestants ; the church-statesman is against the dissenter, and the last against the reformer, and all against religion.

All the religion that you can possibly have in purity, in or out of churches, you had at first by God's principles, that impeach all preachers who affect that it is obtained at their churches.

And if, then, they corrupt the fountain source, how can they ever carry out the noblest gift of things to mind, whose brightest ornament is thereby obtained? Church or no church faith, rational mind can only show the best actions as the best prayers.

Much is said about charity, but dignity of mind and soul, as man is constituted, will preserve the best charity in justice and benevolence, right actions.

Associations on rational religion may do good, but when we see the church squabbles and divisions among members, criminating and recriminating with all manner of accusations, some proving their unworthiness as to be discarded by their church-creeds, that make them hypocrites who never had improved rational religion, whilst others are discarded as falling from grace, a demoralization as the first change, then we are highly gratified at the decided triumph of mind vindicating itself before God.

Have not the christians by gross infatuation and crime, involved themselves in war for centuries with other grand divisions of peculiar faith, and with still greater butchery to their own sects, horribly perverting correct and good governments, and the blessings of social existence?

The church has been a part of the state, the machinery of absolutism; abolish one and the other falls.

The perversion of education, that makes most bigots of superstition, results from peculiar faith.

The very idea of members being in churches does not render them any better, but worse if they join with sinister views, and affect to be better than the world that is civilized. How can any be better?

People become bigots and narrow minded the moment they affect that any sectarian union is going to save them.

Will the whole church-world continue to conceal all the iniquities of peculiar faith, that helps not the excellence of the world?

Thus sectarian creeds cause inquisition over their fellow citizens.

Do any people thus governed need anything more than power to show their character? The bloody statute of Henry VIII. that denounced death to any that should deny the doctrine of transubstantiation, or that auricular confession to a priest was not necessary to salvation, proves to us the absolutism and meanness of bigotry.

It is not church membership that does good to rational mind, but a whole soul-justice is needed for all the world in its comprehension, lofty and noble character. Every honest common-sense person can see at once how much imposition and fraud have been practised.

Let all good citizens draw the line of distinction between ignorance and imposition on one side, and science, with sincerity, on the other.

Every thinking mind has its own ideas about churches and their derelict members, their half-concealed crimes and meanness, unworthy of members, if not of churches, at least of society.

Then church membership comes far short of the universal good of society.

Investigation will show many stumbling-blocks in most churches, many dark clouds too, that would blush to see the light of God.

How many conspiracies are there in churches?

Do not drunkenness, lust and brawls invade the soul of too many preachers and laymen?

To usurp and feign the divine right of church-faith, superstition enacts all that is wonderful.

The statue of Jupiter was changed by false pretences, by some mysterious power, into that of Peter, at Rome, by one of the popes.

Its great toe is kissed by the Romanists. Is this religion?

Where does the ecclesiastical oppression, characterized by so many forms, stop? Mind must act universally upon its own dignity.

In the inquisition at Rome, the book called the Solecetarione shows the government lately expelled made use of this tribunal, strictly ecclesiastical in its institution, also for temporal and political objects, and that the most culpable abuse was made of sacramental confession, especially that of women, rendering it subservient both to political purposes and the most abominable licentiousness. "By means of confession, the most odious licentiousness was insinuated in the confessionals."

Will the protestants stand on half-way ground of reformation, when the exposition proves the necessity of conservative revolution?

But is all this denied?

Then there is something wrong in the accusation, unworthy of rational religion.

In church and private life how much hostile enmity prevails between Romanists and protestants?

Ay, even among protestant churches?

"The presbytery and episcopacy are declared to be two opposites, as the presbyterian system involves error in fundamental doctrines." If it had been declared that all peculiar faiths were in this category, the truth had been told.

All peculiar faith does. Are the people asleep?

Who is infallible but God?

Is it any other than man-power that institutes a pagan superstition-worship, and calls it religion! That pretends to have as many mediators as there are angels in heaven, and saints in their calendar, with altars to the saints, and adoration of their images and relics! Purgatory, with masses, a speculation, is an abomination before God.

The order of universal brotherhood can organize suitable universal societies of general and public character, that may cause the universal good contemplated, with which all the peculiar societies are nothing in comparison.

Such are the world's societies, and no peculiar people or order, not even the peculiar people of God, could have assimilated the world, as all peculiarity in faith acts unworthy of the mighty comprehensions.

God's designs must be duly appreciated by mind to lead it to its true glory and power, through benevolence, humanity and liberal justice to the world. God's principles serve to unite all into one general mass, more or less, certainly not render them hostile and belligerant.

Assuredly mind's corruption through its perversion has spread many awful blights that the good and true citizens of the world must arrest.

There are general and world's sins—as the present universal idolatry, man-worship, money-worship, and guilt-worship.

The world, assuredly, has its scourges and penalties.

Who expects to see order and beauty of order, if the system of the worlds of the universe be disturbed?

Who, then, in the moral world of mind, can do less than preserve that equilibrium, that advances the full dignity and best perfection of mind?

The high tribunal of reason has cognizance of all mental things. She, in the best reference to herself, best holds the balance, for the world and mind.

But the word Catholic takes with some, who have not investigated this whole subject carefully and sincerely to their good, and the best, noblest interest of their country, but have adopted peculiar faith by force of a peculiar education.

But words are shadows, actions are substances.

Religion and constitutional government must accord, not clash. Catholicism and democracy are the property of the world-people, of none peculiar.

Then why did not the government of Rome accord with the rational faith, the popular catholic faith?

The citizens, as sovereign, with their rights as divine, had the only decision of that government, and established it on the principle of the greatest good to the greatest number. Then this peculiar faith was hostile to mind's highest interest, dignity, and right.

Moreover, another so-called republic forced the people, by brute power, to nullify their government, which was protective of the rights of the people, for the power of the pope, the inglorious minority.

The world cannot have its eyes too open, its mind too erect.

Discuss this as a world-wide subject, and all peculiar reverence must bend to universal reverence, to God alone, as the only Catholic rational religion.

All others are usurpations and sophistries, bloody and despotic, a world's age.

What shall we say of him who adulterates ardent spirits, but that he was a base poisoner, and how much more shall we estimate those who poison common sense of mind?

But then Romanism is so extensive, the pope must be maintained.

The Roman is only the twin-sister of the Greek Church. Which is right? The Romanists are the most numerous, and the Roman pontiff was a greater sovereign.

That only proves the evil to be greater. But the Chinese peculiar faith exceeds that. The Chinese emperor is the high priest of his nation, that has nearly one-third of the world's population. Yet he worships his heaven, and sacrifices to it, with incense and victims.

The emperor-priest is worshipped with divine honors, and an homage, like unto Deity.

His edicts are law, his power irresponsible; the government is an absolutism, and a system of centralization.

The Chinese state-faith has ethics and politics derived from the system of Confucius, that inculcates the worship of their heaven and the earth.

The priests of the state-faith, subordinate to the emperor-priest, are the court-priests.

What are all such morals, when rational religion is held universally in abeyance to priest-craft and king-craft?

From their bigotry, the people have not advanced to the science of the times. Force has caused them to tolerate other faiths; a contingency dependent on imperial whims!

But many Christians suppose that it was absolutely essential that their dispensation was revealed especially by God, otherwise we could not have had the partial apprecia-tion of him thus obtained!

What professors of peculiar faith can believe in their own peculiar dispensation, as an especial favor of God, when it is all from the world's priestocracy?

All this has been done through mind's perversion, most plainly, assuredly, certainly, and conclusively.

The only dispensation of God is through mind that is rational, and that reveals a uni-versal rational faith, as the indispensable function of rational mind.

What delusion in sanctification, what senseless ambition to become a saint! Yet how idle the effort to all mortals, and how much false pretences about them and their relics! What could the leader, the head of ignorant multitutes, the monarch of the little circle, to be enlarged to their most ardent hopes, have of any divine power when it was not rational religion?

It assumed to be spiritual, but could not be of the right stamp, when it was a tem-poral absolutism of revelations or miracles!

This is no new thing at all. But sectarians affect to be better than all others. They can affect, that is all. Are they more patriotic, humane, intelligent, honest, truthful or sincere? Do they know that the world appreciates them now in their doctrines of pecu-liar faith? That their mantle is stripped off them?

The advocates persecuted each other to death, and even at this day, republics, so called to their eternal shame, persecute sister republics to their utter ruin. What con-fidence can freemen put in peculiar faith?

Do you call any such, religion?

The Greek faith in Russia, teaches that the Czar represents God on earth. It is here that priests are often drunk, and passports are made out by the priests for the dead to go to their heaven! And what sort can it be?

Here czars have been buried in churches, the image of the virgin has wept tears of oil, and a second coat of Christ has been found! Which of the sister churches are the greater evils?

Here foundling hospitals are reared, where children are matured that know not their relations, and lose sight of the propriety of the laws of consanguinity. Incest may be one of the incidents.

With rational mind, no morals can be worse than what results from superstition and the dictation of hierarchies, and it acknowledges no code that permits absolution of sins from any priestocracy, that is thereby still more corrupt and sinful by their false pretences.

The prayers of liberalists and peculiar faith doctrinists, when they are in mutual conflicts, cannot be both right, as they are antagonistic! And this is the perpetual state of the world.

By the same rule, preaching must be vain on its present basis, and its advocates are ignorant, corrupt or debased, worse or more ignorant than their congregation. Their doctrines are constantly clashing, as predestination against universal salvation.

"The Jesuits sought in Russia to increase their power. The impostor to the king-dom had the assurance of the pope of the support of all Catholic Europe in exchange for his promise, to unite Russia to the Latin Church."

What a character the pope is, who pretends to excommunicate the people from their inheritance, at the same time when all the world is equally entitled to all the blessings of mind, by a universal Creator, and much more after his imposture and blasphemy, or his degraded usurpation.

Love characterizes especially the christan above all, it is assumed. But does it, like the charity of too many, only remain at home? What especial claim to love has chris-tianity over any other such faith? What is the circle of the love of religion, but the comprehension of the whole globe? Nothing less is God-like.

Where was the love to man by christians, when one-half of the world was embattled against the other, in the crusades?

The world is the church of God, the mind of man his temple.

All institutions of rational religion must be established on the principles of mind. All their functions are in reference to mind, and all the time, reason presides. Religion then presides where there is rational understanding, and nothing less, if real, genuine, true, rational, not spurious nor mere stumbling-block, but good faith rules.

The spirit of God Almighty, the architect and preserver of the universe, communes with mind; neither God nor mind requires any intercessor, as that would be an imposition.

The moral as intellectual light of God proves itself, and that principles from the nature of creation can be the only messiahs, to execute the commands of the Creator for all.

Let none deny by prayers any of God's all-sufficiency, man thereby intimating that God ought to do more than he does do for mind. Prayers addressed to God in mere words, are rank impiety and blasphemy.

Mind has to do a greater part in the world, than has been ever executed.

No church can be pure where impure doctrines are advocated, as of the messiah, a useless, inefficient and blasphemous non-entity, that cannot exist at all before the attributes of Almighty God.

Some of the Roman clergy take the bible from the people, and preach up a creed of saints, &c., to act as mediators, but there are no half gods before the Supreme. Let these ignorant pretenders be silenced by the wise voice of the world's rational mind.

Miracles are always a part of their dependence, as that of the holy fire at Jerusalem, all unworthy of notice by rational mind, that knows them to be falsified by God's word, cause, and effect, in his whole universe.

In Spain, oaths are taken by some military orders, "to defend the conception of the Holy Virgin."

Virginity of a woman is thus entrusted to perjured oaths, and not on the principles of chastity!! The military followers are involved in perjury, as the chastity is negatived.

What protection have the people in church-membership? They have complete falsehood and sophistry in the pulpit, exceeding all the balance of the world, and that sophistry is self-desecrated by perjury.

Peculiar faith, though of church, is divided into many and endless secessions, construing its ideas of faith differently from all others.

All make sectarianism, none of which is religion, that pays due respect to the Creator exclusively.

Sectarianism separates the natural affections of relations, friends, and citizens.

The papal kingdoms, Roman and Greek, are deeply iniquitous for enslavement of mind; would that this were near all. Such religion is it by peculiar faith?

Who has not sought unsuccessfully, religion, for years, under all the guises and pretences of peculiar faith, that has ever led the mind away from the true object of its devotion! Will an ignis fatuus do for the world's light? Let mind-analysts declare.

In what part of the earth can religion be found, but as a rational and just view of Deity, his creation-gift, that has only to be cherished and rightly cultivated, to become the most rational of all rationality?

The death-bed scene fixes the true fidelity, by her creed. The world, sooner or later, will cherish her holy spirit. Even now, legions are increasing, with the light and freedom of mind.

Her substitute will be discovered to be a deformed and ghastly being, miscalled in her name, but really, superstition, whose attire is steeped in blood.

Her speech is fair, but foul—her thoughts are wicked—her ends selfish—her devotions are earthly, and her faith idolatry, man-worship, and even beastiality: all her ends are seduction, and her termination misery. In anguish and sorrow, mind enlightened turns away from her thousand fields of carnage and savage butchery.

Who will not discard superstition for God's religion, that is made up of forethoughts and principles, the loftiest aspirations and the noblest aims?

Man's faith is made up of after-thoughts and ruin, instead of pure principles, having a world tinkered on and botched up with peculiar faith, by which it is bankrupt.

Religion has operated from creation, all the time silently and modestly, even by moral influences and conscience.

Peculiar faith is only for a time guided by force, sinister devices, self-interest and delusion.

Religion yields all the very best system of accountability for the wants of mankind, sets forth all the legitimate influence in the world, from which result the best governments.

"About 606 the most profound ignorance, debauchery, and superstition reigned. From this time the popes exerted all their power in promoting the idolatrous worship of images, saints, reliques, and angels.

27

The church was truly deplorable ; all the clergy up to the most flagrant and abominable acts of licentiousness.

Places of worship resembled the temples of heathen, more than the churches of christians." Of course the improvement is due to mind in civilization : what else?

To propagate their doctrines, the anabaptists sought by holy fraud, which being ineffectual, they had recourse to arms, declared war against all laws, governments, and magistrates of every kind, under the chimerical pretext, that Christ himself was now to take the reins of all government into his hands.

Sermonizing is not argument for religion, and does not touch the point or question. It is all one-sided, the most warped at that.

What is the world about to suffer it ? Its duty is to fully investigate the other side.

Does any church of peculiar faith stand on the truth ? Does priestly domination prove it satisfactorily ? All proof must be rational ; there can be no other in the universe.

Can we forget the stumbling blocks of churches, the ministry silenced or degraded by lusts and all human nature's inquities, with their vows broken !

Of all the sophistries in this sophisticated world, is the presumption to supersede mind, the only pilot of the world, and the sole means of communion with the universe and its Creator, by the bibles of miracles, prophecies and mysteries.

The only bible is that of mind, commenced with all rational beings, more or less with creation's birth, and vital existence.

Why do church people affect to be better than the rest of the world ? They are stupidly or wilfully ignorant of their false position.

God is the judge of all, not church people, whom he cannot know in that or any peculiar light.

When all nations are judged, the people will show some dark spots left of dark and sinful ages.

The proper result decides the question in the most available characteristic under the whole circumstances, as wise men prefer those for their general best character, not adopt church membership for the selection. Which of the many churches contending for orthodoxy, is orthodox ? By what test shall the solution be made ? Faith will not decide of course, without mind and reason, that bring out all the mental and soul capital, and resources.

In orthodoxy, mind and reason, not faith, decide.

Faith will be false as interest inclines, therefore mind and reason must counteract it. The exclusive test of utility is reason.

The mental seed must be good, or the harvest will be spoiled : now orthodoxy is right thought, and that implies rational mind, whose banner is reason, not faith.

The last is foolish, not correct thought.

But the bible exacts a peculiar faith, else the damnation threatened by the makers, aiders, and abettors follows.

The idea of our God negatives any peculiar faith, as his attributes are universal.

Any one who believes the bible not written by man's collusion and designs, cannot have an honest but peculiar faith.

God is too pure to require any but an honest faith. Wise and good men wish no other.

Our immortal interest guarantees the best, and that is in God.

There must be reason that follows the will in such a decision of mind, for all must be truly convinced to believe truly.

If miracles are performed now by the members of the Roman church, how came the pope not to prevent, as a supreme minister of peace, by miracle, his own expulsion from his government, to prevent the slaughter and butchery of thousands of his countrymen by foreign bayonets, of a sister republic, clashing with a sister republic before his restoration, and save the clash of principles, one of the mighty difficulties that would have benefited all his people? Then was the auspicious time to have stayed the effusion of blood, and have performed a miracle worthy of mind and the world, for its universal conversion ! But all peculiar faith is ever in conflict with God's principles. How long can smuggled faith supersede religion and reason.

Do not expect much from the peculiar faith of any preachers who play cards, or commit any licentious and lustful vices, though they may show many beautiful bibles, or noisy church membership.

With christians, their good are saints, but they estimate the good of the world besides, as sinners. Who made them competent judges ? Have they analyzed the world-wide subjects, that mind in its most exalted civilization can do ?

Mind must be thus false on preconceived notions, however exploded the absurdity, therefore mind must counteract all such.

A devil is superfluous, an abstract non-entity, and unnecessary, as mind, when perverted, is its own worst punisher, individually or nationally, by retribution of conservative principles, that vindicate themselves.

The division of several churches on sectional and national sectarianism in this union, the adherents of a part over-riding the constitution, display the malignancy of peculiar faith, and render her subversive, by example, of the liberties of the country, and the best hopes of the world.

We never will get the world right till we rid it of its corrupting influences. Do you wish purity? Then be pure yourself, in thought, word, and deed; proved by example abstracted from worldly speculation. Waver not, when principles require it, and be above self-reproach, much more above the reproach of the world, that should look at the principles of religion instead of the delusions and chimeras of peculiar faith.

Follow no church authority, that is individual, but act in accordance with principles, that are universal.

Neither sex is exempt from degrading and demoralizing nature in the church, and some are actually worse for church membership. Some are better by their honest natures realizing the virtues connected with proper mental discipline under rational religion, whilst most reflect the vices of peculiar faith and its partisan zeal.

Church vices and despotism are enormous.

They have crimes worse than inquisitions.

The basis of their creation excludes God's sovereign rights and attributes.

What church, then, has not necessarily bigots?

The discipline of the church is paramount to many paramount universal principles.

What can be worse than the present tyranny of the Roman hierarchy, embracing its inquisition.

There is something worse the cause of such institutions, peculiar faith. All bigots are inquisitors; then they are abundant even in this country, this republic.

Protestants are imprisoned for refusing to uncover their head while a Roman procession was passing.

What is the position of woman under the tyranny of peculiar faith but that of a degraded being?

She owes her exaltation in this country to the liberal light of mind.

The adulterer is a part of the peculiar faith, and can dispense with its obligations. The interpretation rests with him at confessional, who rules the wife and virtue, or principle. So much for Roman peculiar faith.

But independent of absolutism, principle causes such adulterer to put himself in the power, not over the power of the offended party, and forfeit his life if he choose its risk.

All main crimes, as adultery and drunkenness, are under the abeyance of principles, not of faith, where mind has its influence.

In vain may mind seek their correction by getting good stock and causing it to be well improved, independent of property, the last and least consideration; but the means of peculiar faith may destroy and annihilate all such exertions, and reflect on the miseries of the balance of the world. Then mind, that sees the world as it is, must desire the world's, not priests' prosperity. What errors are committed by churchmen! Millions join the church and have to leave it, or disgrace the church worse by continuance.

Their faith is not improved religion.

Church memberships by myriads, show that the word preached, is only received as that of man's. It is impossible for sincerity to act otherwise; hearing the word is a contingency the world over, but its right adoption is the thing for mind to recognise. That word is the result of rational religion.

The acts of mind portrayed in conscience, are constantly and uniformly proved to be by the only true word of God, cause and effect, for correct analysis of mind and its truthful sincere adoption.

Conscientious minds devoted exclusively to God, to whom all adoration is due, actually would refuse church-membership to any peculiar faith.

Men of principles can be made no better by joining any church.

Are none made worse by joining a perfectly useless thing? The great divisions of the church recently enacted in England, and more particularly in this country, appear a disgrace to those of the great church, so called of the world, always holding the genuine majority.

This position in this union declared in not less than two great divisions, declares a miserable example for its citizens, and familiarizes them to the accursed spirit of disunion. Such agitation is a hideous, but dangerous burlesque in religion.

The people at large are growing more and more sectional, from that degraded cause, and that, too, when the elements and light of mind are now best prepared to elicit more universal brotherhood. Where is union in church, but for union of interest? The light of faith in churches, is behind its proper position in the circle of liberty and mind. The position is not tenable, and has to be eradicated, expunged by truth and reason.

This mighty nation, to have the most powerful light of all nations, whose brilliancy from its glorious confederation, must reflect on the world at all points, at once, with gigantic strides to civilization, must take the noblest stand on all great conservative principles.

Already is she pouring in her noble offering, the best of mind, that atones for the original sin committed at first by a half civilized mother, whom she entreated to spare her this horrible crime. But relentless self-interest saw naught but profit over man's rights.

Through the influence of both nations, and the avenues of mighty commerce, Africa begins in earnest to reach civilization, by the only practical effects of mind. Already has she in part become regenerated from barbarism, at the best practicable point, and many of the descendants, Americo-Africans, who from thousands have become four millions of human beings, advancing on the blessings of mind, have established a free government, and already man-piracy is arrested for a large extent of coast.

What shall we say of the balance of the world? All peculiar faith dogmas and doctrines, will avail it naught, till mind rears its majestic influence, and its potency will rear a fabric for the glory of rational religion. All its churches are naught, and built on materials robbed of mind and religion, that direct man's chief good by intellectual and moral light, most refulgent.

What shall we say of that faith that produces change or conversion in a moment?

We must analyze the state of all minds, in this passion.

There is deep excitement, then a composure ensues, as the feelings will run their course and limit.

Some church professions exhibit no such show; as far as we can appreciate, the Romans and Episcopalians do not.

Wo unto all churches and members of churches, especially their heads, that hide the light of science under the pretences of faith.

You can never open your mouth against the atheists, as you reject the light of reason, that cuts them all down, and all your bibles of tradition, and all its doctrines of polytheism, or faith in more than one God.

It may seem singular, but it certainly is true, and vouches for the masterly handwriting of the Supreme God, who never lets mind, that has executed its trust, mistake the proof.

Nor need you fear the results of Mahometanism, Mormonism, or any analogous fanaticism or superstition.

They or you can never succeed, before the religion of God. Did you and all your fraternity not give an impetus to those very fanaticisms?

Have you not forwarded man-worship and superstition? Did you not believe in superstition, and what is that but a base for all such peculiar faith vagaries? See how the Christians love one another?

Which of the sects—for see how some sects detest and hate the others? All divisions of sectarianism think themselves orthodox, all infallible; of course, all others fallible, and to be put down.

How bad is it for churches of the same persuasion to be litigant. Is there any love there? Who believes it?

What can be worse than all the petty church priest tyranny? What, under such regime, does it matter about exclusion from confession, excommunication, &c.? Where is the mind-benefit?

Priests are tyrants, popes are murderers, and antagonistic to republican principles, avowed by their citizens.

What does mind need of these, to aid its progress in virtue. Church services stop on time, but mind always acts for itself, if left sound to do so.

What shall we say of the secret vices of the churches, of many members?

Have the head or leading men of some churches ever supported the means productive thereof?

We may counteract much of the world's nuisances and crimes, but not break up or eradicate at present, when there is so much corrupt collusion in the old overgrown cities. What is all church protection worth, to poor, ignorant females, who neglect the supremacy of mind?

No youth, females especially, should go to cities to live, that can be properly supported in the country. Not that they should not go thither, but when they go to cities,

.t advice of discreet friends, they lay themselves liable to suspi-
·l considerations and laudable·objects.
n is always suspicious, it is especially so in town residence, thus
ys keep sacred their right position above suspicion. What good
.ic perfection attained by, but a trifling against God and his natu-
.l osteology, the holy tear of Vendome, and all such ignominious
.t the proscriptions and butchery of past ages were perpetrated,
.nd the world confounded and oppressed?
.elieve in all such, though sanctioned by any church? Who can
.hinery of Christ, if his mind duly investigate this comprehensive
·eatly?
.emoluments be thus won, we do not wish them at the expense of
.gion. Mind must counteract what the time may not exactly suit
.rsede, by innovation, reformation, or conservative revolution.
.ghtened public opinion in republican constitutional freedom, in her
progress, to perform? Mind has to do the world the proper justice.
do in this respect? The most they can effect is their own peculiar
.erpetuate their own unredeemed abuses. But what avail the world
.nizations, that are made for the peculiar institutions, not the whole
.ertain.
.he elements of dissension, not only against each other, ·but actually
in Europe, America, all over the globe. Peculiar faith wars are the
.e is necessarily the enthusiasm of bigotry, the most fanatical of all

.hemselves to church clans, that are identified to their exclusive inte-
.hers, not having any love of principles, but principals before their eyes?
.e feelings of some independent thinkers to find themselves liable, as all
investigation, at the pleasure of members?
.d private societies helpers to bind their members to the same power,
.te bible traditions? Are they doing the universal brotherhood of the
.at justice that religion enjoins?
.ardened sinner, full of years and iniquity, is converted in the deep infir-
.l and mind, probably at his death-bed scene, who can believe that his
developments are properly changed? Are not such changes the gradual
.e? This justification is at the bar of conscience and reason, and must be
.u the utmost difficulty, as some are of the lowest organization. Intelligent
.s are bound to see all this, and correct all necessary as they live.
.ot a question of feeling, but of religion, the highest reason. Most church
.e so bigoted that they talk of the world as no one but themselves having any
.ere are God, mind, and its God-gift, religion? Some professors are worthy,
.most are unworthy members of society.
.n all the tenets of church doctrines avail when the organization of churches
.ondation?
.vail baptismal regeneration, when there is no valid baptism? " Dr. Musgrave,
.p of York, in his primary visitation, distinctly disavowed the doctrines of bap-
.'generation."
.aa we expect of baptism, when there is no baptism? There is no mission but
.nind, no commission but for its rational religion. All else is irrational, vain and
.y. What church of peculiar faith is there but is troubled, and if old enough, divided?
.r deplorable has been the state of the Roman church? To what abominations
.nd degradations has she not resorted as long as mind permitted her?
.some priest-ridden countries, oppressed by intolerance of Romanism, one has to
.a his knees before the procession of the host which passes, and conform outwardly
.oervances which are exacted of him. This is honor and respect to mind, the
.est part of man, with a vengeance.
.time will be when this slavish felony will be duly estimated, and the priestocracy
.sled on earth.
.Are the worship of the figures of the virgin, &c., the institution of the holy sacrament
.d miracles, the procession of the miraculous wafers, the assumption of catholic majesty,
.efender of the faith, all these tricks and impostures the less to be deplored and objected
.a! What peculiar faith is to be, can be defended?

Are whole nations to be committed to an ignominious credulity, and the peace of the world disregarded therefor? The history of the miraculous wafers discloses an awful tragedy. The object was attained by killing the wealthy Jews in Brussels for their money, which the clergy obtained. Is not this felony still enjoyed?

All persuasions persecuted each other most abominably once under the peculiar faith garb. The priestocracies incited this, and enjoyed it over the ruins of the world, as much as Nero in the fire of Rome.

What a felony, then, is the base of all sects!

The working of miracles would rise to-day, if popular ignorance licensed it. Who needs the actors?

The actors are prepared, if the audience could be found. Poor imbeciles, who cannot estimate the value of their own mind. What greater blasphemy can arise than from hypocritical peculiar faith?

What good comes of any institution that erects an inquisition at this day at Rome? If this prevail while the press speaks, what were its horrors when there was none to befriend man?

Of what value to society are nunneries and such societies, but to entice the holders of property to bestow it as a legacy on cunning priestocracies?

How much better to the world would it be, that all this should be the world's fund for mind and virtue.

All church property should be appropriated for educational purposes, and then we would begin to be right. Then church-faith would go with speculation to uphold it, and no state-church-supremacy would blight and blast the honest effusions of mind, and its religion.

The fund for bickering and opposition, even to rebellion, wars and crusades, would become extinct.

Citizens of the world, it is yours to decide this momentous question, to still the world-wide agitation.

Have no state and church endowments and preferments.

What would Juggernaut be without his car and his brute parasites, priests, and their minions?

What better are those that adopt the mummeries of church pretences?

What division of the world's bigots has the least vindictiveness when clothed with the brief authority of power? In protestant countries, the laws against popery were brutal in olden times.

In the year 1700, the Assembly passed a law to hang every popish priest who should come voluntarily into New York. Think of that, in these times of mind!

All sectarians swear they are right; of course, all others are wrong. What then is religion, and to whom is it due? It is the sacred obligation of mind to God most directly, not through messiahs or priestocracies. All that is a false position of peculiar faith.

Bigots and fanatics, the world over, will assume to decide this mighty question of religion, that they do not begin to appreciate or recognise, by their feelings of enthusiasm and narrow prejudices, exclusively by the doctrines of peculiar faith, that do and cannot touch the question at all. They persist that they are better by their faith, impudently arrogating pretensions not supported by their actions.

Religionists only claim to believe in the immortal God alone. Polytheists, called Christians, believe in four gods, many angels and spirits on earth, while one of their main ones is a mortal, on the laws of physiology, and illegitimate at that!

On the laws of the highest religion, he is a blasphemer. Ignorant of the earth's figure and its conservative principles, they, Jews and Christians, stupidly substituted ministers, angels and spirits in their place.

But no matter how absurd all this, it is peculiar faith, and that is sought to be made unquestionable, not however by any law of civilized mind.

The true faith must ever be in duty to God and mind. Peculiar faith believes in duty to gods, and that causes wars among men, who have their notions about these things, that if in power must be carried out, however repugnant their false views to society. Duty to God alone has naught to do with trade and speculation, whereas peculiar faith lives by them all the time.

The sooner all this is taken away, the better for pure religion and the universal good of all mankind.

What avails the prayer of the priestocracy, said over dead bodies for the redemption of their souls? It only avails the pockets of these pretended functionaries?

The question was decided by the decision of principles at the end of life, for the immortal soul.

So far as it concerns the balance, the pockets of the priestocracy are better filled, but those of the soul's representatives are emptied by gulling speculations of an ignoble and debauched set of blasphemers.

This vicegerentship is an absurdity, and heinously is the doctrine corrupting. All emanates from the priestocracy. God's attributes cannot be invaded for a moment, much less to be thus explained away. Individual accountability must be met by retributive justice for that particular mind, the soul embodiment, to produce the best happiness of the spirit embodiment, that may be a spiritual etherealization. An intolerant church is a butcher, all sectarian churches are nuisances. But evils have their end, that is a means to produce good by the manifest providence of conservative principles.

Persecution arouses up all the latent energies and zeal of mind, that is certain. Crush a man's spirit, dispirit him by misfortunes, and you arouse his ambition and talents, if he be of the right standard.

If obscure preachers are convicted as nuisances, vilifying other sects, what can we expect of their whole position.

Falling from grace is affirmed by some, and utterly denied by other churches. When members of churches fall or sin, they are considered by the last brethren, as never possessing the faith, and of course never attaining the point of correction.

This position implies that the position of faith is according to opinion, and that opinion, unless the result of science, reason and cultivated mind a serious mistake, or a degraded hypocrisy.

Give power even to persecuted protestants, and they will persecute most horribly, as the people that settled Rhode Island, an outcast from her sisters of New England can tell!

What superstition can induce the belief that it is in the nature of mind, to have sudden complete conversions?

Is there no ground for suspicion in some; is there no prompting from passions, as avarice or ambition? Are there no preferments to be expected in, by or through the church? But how about revivals? The world may have all that are legitimate.

The world is better, and improves on its improvement.

More crime is apparent than ever, by its superior general intelligence, and its varied excellence of means over that of past ages. How many of the superficial of the world, set themselves up for analyzers?

Past and ignorant ages gave in to the predominance of military ambition, but ere long a new era will burst in upon the world. Between Fulton and Napoleon, a few years hence, a decision will be made for science of mind over the butchery of mankind, the exalter over the corruptor of nations. What a distance is there already, between Washington and Napoleon?

If all societies, secret or others, fostered the greatest good of the world, which is the most, as it would be, of all, then they could not be clannish, or sectarian, or segregated. The justice of life is to be universally diffused. The christians can appropriate the claim of exclusive protectors of science for several reasons, as they were its bitterest unprincipled opponents, especially whenever their faith came in antagonism to science. The Saracens protected learning, in the 9th century. All this was nothing beyond the force of circumstances of ambition, lust of power, and the inherent capacity of principles.

How was the christian church recovered at various times from its deepest heresies, corruptions and schisms, but by the potency of mind, that will eradicate all, in time? When churches, creeds, faiths and the perverted cliques of the world, seek to extirpate natural improvements, they must first seek to extirpate mind, the world's active guardian, after God

But the church-converted, are the only people to be saved! Who are they? Of course, those in the peculiar church are meant. But the main question remains for solution. Are they of the church of God Almighty? Did they not eschew him when they adopted others?

As feeling presumes to define and decide this pretence, analysis decides it is not correct, as feeling is erroneous as peculiar education that originates it, when reason has not been heard. What avail church organizations, when the policy is worthless? The policy of mind is, to be honest and truthful.

Some people are bad enough, any how, without being disciplined to insincerity. Church people should look to that.

The clerical statistics will show an immense decrease of clerical persons, in ratio to the population, more than four-fifths, it is affirmed, in France, in less than an hundred years; three-fifths at Rome, and an immense decrease in less than a century. Principles will put the world right, in time.

What squabbles and quarrels were there among bishops, with the corrupt factions at the council of Nice.

Can smuggling make gentlemen? What church quarrels most disgraceful to gentlemen, let alone ladies, the world over.

Do the people know what they are about, when they go to join churches, and confide in a messiah? They are tories to their God and mind.

Have they had means to investigate the whole subject, by deep and sound inquiry, from authentic sources? Then so much the more culpable are they.

Have they not confided in those who are involved in interest and feeling, having committed themselves, and having too much false pride to reverse their own published deeds? What can churches impart, when none of peculiar faith has the right elements of religion?

Why a ceaseless agitation, to render the world dissatisfied on all that is of no account? What class of mind, men, or profession, can be trusted as granted? The priests? They who never could be depended on from the first ages of the world, from their most exorbitant deceit, fraud, deception on mind?

Thousands are sincere in joining the church, but if we were in a church and saw the gross errors as we do, and the imposture of all messiah church salvation, we would renounce them as blasphemy. Churches and secret societies form peculiar brotherhoods, but the brotherhood of the world is founded on the principles that govern the world and are universal. This is exempt from all man's misrules and petty tyranny.

The Romanist excommunicates the Protestant as no minister at all, as not having the apostolic succession.

Rational religionists can consider no such professions as these, of religion. The worship of golden images, of Jesus, &c., does not differ from that of heathen idolatry : all, of course, is paganism.

Wake out of the dream, that the good church members are any better than other good people. But people join churches to get better. How can that be, as the very step to messiahship excludes the whole position?

Rites and ceremonies are not religion! The house of God is not the house of the priest of peculiar faith.

But how could any fall from grace, by reason of their church position? They could not, as they did not have it, by church peculiar faith that cannot impart it. They mistake the source, that is all!

But their feelings tell. Tell what? All sects claim all such. Millions on millions are deceived, thinking they had both as God-gifts to their minds, better before they started! Nevertheless, as they are in the church, they may think in sincerity, that others ought to be there too. Never was there a greater mistake.

Hear them! But my child may become an infidel, and I would rather follow him to the grave!

What nonsense—blasphemy—degradation!

Does your church clear you of infidelity to your God, whom you oppose by espousing a mere fiction for a messiah who cannot exist in God's universe?

If your child be a rational being, you are bound to desire him, bigot as you are, to adopt all rational conclusions comprehending this whole subject. This position defines a balanced mind and morals, on principles that promote fidelity to God, and discard the blasphemy by peculiar faith.

We except all church members that keep pure, despite of all church corruption and pollution.

Some members in the church are much worse than others out of it, surely. How can the church render any better? Many join innocently, and purely to be better ; that they could better attain by being out.

What good does church peculiar faith do the world?

The authors of all peculiar faith cannot begin to better any church members, since inherent principles of God operate on their minds. As to any maxims of doing to others what we would have them, under similar circumstances, do unto us, these are all social principles, discovered long before the birth of any writers of any man-christ, with whom they are not original, as all social principles are all God's assuredly, which mind has been enjoying according to its excellency in civilization. Confucius used this maxim, that was in use by Chinese legislators as long, it is said, as five hundred years before such a being as Christ was thought of. There can be no usurpers of social principles, as they are degraded by that pretence worse than men. Affecting to be messiahs, they become the most arrant impostors.

Joining of church of peculiar faith is a fashionable custom, warranted by no rational consideration, but forbidden by purest patriotism and the loftiest humanity. What good do all church peculiar faith rites and ceremonies do? Among them is fasting all day, to which are opposed the best physiological principles, that are undeniable.

Let us seek to promote the paramount principles of health, the work of God, not destroy it by any errors or devices of perverted mind, and miss the means of its future restoration. But the sudden and speedy change of the soul from the hardened sinner to the refined convert, upholds the faith of the testament of Christ. Then your faith, that looks of course to a foundation, is self-sustained, independent of any such foundation. All this is fiction throughout, as analysis discloses.

The mind, influenced by habits and perversity, has lent reflective image to the face which is too often influenced by the hardihood of crime. Phrenology of physiology decides, to a certain extent elegantly, that the moral and intellectual character is confirmed, and when fixed is hard to change. Now the bible of mind insures this physiological rational fact, and does not deny any fact as fact that seemingly clashes with preconceived notions. Some church members talk and act, that you cannot possibly have any confidence in all they say or do. But your pious frauds declare that no one can view death with complacency, except their peculiar faith is analogous to yours! Now, the falsity of this is most clear, as nine-tenths of mankind die in direct antagonism to your faith! Will you never see, bigot as you are, the iniquitous falsifications of mind that you ignobly practice on your deceived church members? We hear of persons in your peculiar faith, ay in the church, and become skeptic, as you call them, of course acting in sincerity, and dying as calmly as possible. There are too many of these facts for you to commit yourself any longer to this deficient defence.

We are all as much interested as any of you can be to have the right position. We defend the pure cause of rational religion.

Persons of liberal expansion of intellect ought to abstain from church; thus the matter of church speculation and superstition would die of themselves.

Some studiously avoid rational discussions, or even allusions to their church faith, or allude to such in a defective and objectionable way. Why is not all this question rightly met? The way it is treated is downright murder of mind's rights.

You wish to be satisfied and happy on your death bed. We are assured of this fact, through God's grace.

But none can take proper cognizance of all this but God. Therefore it is not speculation but religion to maintain an enlightened virtuous public opinion in the world. Enlightened mind should never be gulled by any church member, as member. Only act toward him as a man. Our mind has no misgivings about the propriety of our situation to die with in rational religion. That is the only safe one, despite of all the pious frauds of the world to the contrary.

Some church people cheat, lie, act the dissemblers, hypocrites, have learnt their trade for speculation surely. If God had not helped the world by principles before churches, the universe had been bad off indeed.

But it is claimed now by peculiar faith that these are the people of God, as if he had drawn a line of demarcation around them. All are the people of God, through the bible of mind, to the exclusion of peculiar faith, that has nothing to do in the matter.

Mind, infuriated to-day by all church misrule, is not to be trusted by mind that is rational.

Your church-membership is no presumptive evidence of your virtue. It is against you, in religion most clearly.

If death was not certain, how few mortals, churches or not, would be at the point of their conceived safety?

In seasons of affliction and adversity, church-memberships become abundant; but in the plenitude of prosperity, how great is the falling off! Religion is as constant as principles, that never can be absent.

We have always to examine if there be no cheat or imposition on the world. It is a burning shame that superstition so rank, stupid, gross, and vulgar, should not be seen through. There are many we cannot credit in or out of churches, hypocrites as they are. Take hold of one of those old lying, hypocritical, church stumbling-blocks.

What a tough old case, indeed, of sin and corruption!

But repentance is the great idea of church doctrine. How preposterous, that a man by mere repentance could expect as high a reward as by the life innocent? What demoralization-doctrines! The base should be abolished. Let the law of retribution be applied.

God's grace sustains the universe, but mind's merits must do all practicable for the rescue, by nature, of its organization and functions. But it cannot be expected that christians can be entirely exempt from sin—certainly not. All people sin; the least sin is the best attainable position. But christian church-people have stupidly separated themselves above the world as God's people, as if the whole world were not his creation. This is the absurd conduct of the Bhuddists, Jews—all that pretend to peculiar faith. They have made themselves a mark to be shot at. What bigots! what ignoble, contemptible impudence!

If the best can only sin the least in this life, how then can any one be holy or sanctified on this earth? How preposterous! But all christians are not demoralized—only no better. The church furnishes no criterion. Man is what his mind makes him, under his circumstances. But some preachers of some persuasions have little pay. Any pay is too much in a faith that has no real foundation. But how good are the benevolent associations resulting from church establishments! What Samaritans are the nuns! It is all well if ending well, and they have no expectance, no sinister or peculiar influence to establish their orders, their powers, or causing them to retire from a world that their blasted hopes cannot permit them to enjoy. All this proves the noblest features of civilized mind, that can accomplish much more for the world.

There is not any test of character, except a man's actions. How often is it that we hear of church-members and preachers prowling, at night, in the sinks of perdition! How often have they been caught in disreputable scenes? How much is left hid, but to God alone? No, let us have no such pretension, when mind is already possessed of the genuine religion, only needing cultivation. What is the main question in life? How much trouble and tears, blood and sorrow are caused the world for want of a proper code of faith of religion! Church faith is not religion. But of all the great curses of life, is the support of unions of church and state. Is it right that dissenters should pay to the state church, when they disbelieve in it, and not have their prelates advanced to peerages? Is it right for mind, that man should be imprisoned for writing his views on the fraud of priests? Is this freedom of mind, the present day? How long shall the world be burthened by tithes, the tenth of the produce of the soil? How long shall church-rates be one of the nuisances of priest-ridden countries! Church property should be confiscated, only on a right basis—not by repudiation, but when appropriated by law as obtained by false pretences. Members of churches have told the world the most barefaced falsehoods, to get the least private advantage. If they have this habit, will they not swear to them? How unseemly are church differences! How often do the members hate each other? There is no necessity for any churches that do no good, but much harm. Let patriots decide that the church-world shall not take any unprincipled advantage any longer, if they can prevent it.

How long shall the world, much of which has been forced by proscriptions of one kind or other, brute force, by all the libel of language, be kept in abeyance to the farce of church pretences? What an ignominious contention of those in the church, who slander each other?

What shall the world think of the numbers who affect to be dead to the world, yet desert the highest platform, that is, have no principles? Church is not principle. Who would give up conservative principles for any church membership? But what of conversion? Is there no deception? What internal witness? None certain, for all professors of peculiar faith have the same. What external witness? None more than any other of the same profession of peculiar faith.

But all have one pure standard alone, that decides by actions, and those alone. Professions will not do without them. One God Creator is worth all the universe of messiahs.

We must live up to the best lights before us, that is all we can do.

All are excluded from censure in this work except those who knowingly advocate the corruptions of church doctrines. But how much more imposition is there than delusion?

Pious men must assume to be honorable men, yet how often are they not only disposed to acts unworthy of mind, but actually compromise their church relations!

"We learn from Vienna that the church question will be one of life and death, so exasperated are the minds of men upon the subject." Members of churches have to be reconciled after the severest quarrels. What worse specimen of humanity can be given? Take away all this ignoble base, and the world will be exempt from its results.

All kinds of characters are certainly in the various churches. What proves them right? Of course church members will say, church membership! But no! that is a cloak, a mantle for the baseness of the bad.

It is bad association. Then, of course, principles are the only proof, and these are only found in rational faith.

What is the character of the common mind, illiterate members in churches? Are not too many corrupt of all classes?

To whom would you apply for correct deportment? Any sooner to churchmen? Not at all. Would you go to churches to look for an honest and truthful man by excellence? Very clear of it; for there we have often been bit the deepest by assumed characters. We can only take those positions where character and personal worth, not professions without substantial possession is held up. Whom would you select in preference, the man for guardian and administrator, without security? We ask for the test questions of life. Then peculiar faith only offers, at the best, only low professions and empty possessions, the credit claimed that exclusively belongs to another department. Some churchmen affect to look upon deists avowing their doctrines as lost. Where are churchmen found? Under protection of principles. What are we to think of ministers seeking seduction wholesale of the world's souls on a faithless faith? Have proper trials been had, any expulsion of the defaulting preachers for many flagrant offences upon the world's society? How few have been known. How many various cases of odious character stain the ignoble churches.

How many seductions, adulteries, and fornications by the heads of the church, with notorious impunity?

What a shameful thing it is that men of talents, who ought to know much better these days, should play the vile hypocrite, to state and church-power in some form or other, all over the world.

What but the worst public morals, corrupt bidding at the auction of popularity, can be expected?

What higher conservative revolution can be desired than in all this? Do you wish to put down the Mormons, who, with their socialism, may help put down the Christians? Put down all the chimeras of superstition, put up religion, that will put down all such by its innate virtues.

Give us no churches, but cultivate rational religion.

Good as you affect church organizations, is not deference oftenest paid them to the influence of power of peculiar faith, than to truth? While absolutism lasts, be it what it may as names are nothing at all, the mind perverted defers to it in some way.

How noisy church members are, affecting to be so good, when it is an utter impossibility from the nature of the whole position. Some of the worst deceptions have been practised on the community, by members of churches. How many in churches are incompetent, to do justice to common principles? How antagonistic and clashing are they, between pedestrianism and free agency?

But the church and all such only have peculiar faith, with the elements of their own destruction.

Sectarians or peculiar faith church-men never seem to dream, that their church or their faith is amenable to the elements of condemnation that they pass on all others. We now know that members are abundantly in the church as bad as the worst in the world or large church. They have two crimes, hypocrisy and blasphemy, in addition to their others. What can render a mind worse?

The various grades of martyrdom are analogous to those of enthusiasts and fanatics—as juggernauts.

Is it not within the experience of nearly all professing christians, to have doubts about possessing conversion? By rational religion we know that we have to depend on facts not doubts, on God, not his inefficient substitutes. Even the same churches, can not maintain unity. Now, the brotherhood of pure principles could not absolve themselves if they would, from paramount obligations to duty. They could have nothing to do with dissolution. How can they? Who wishes a mere church-right, when all have a universal one? Who asks for the counterfeit messiah, when he is compelled by honest truth to acknowledge the full rights of the Creator? Some church-members seek license for licentiousness, estranged from God by peculiar faith.

It is the most difficult thing to acknowledge our errors.

. The worst deception, is by church people. You may have enthusiasm, and may arouse sympathy for your imaginary cause, but you should avoid all your difficulties by uniting to the principles of God's unity.

Why are Protestants less bigots than Romanists? Because the light of mind is better diffused among the masses. But if they are bigots, that relative stain of soul sticks to them.

Why is there so much hatred of protestant, by Irish Romanists? There is an implacable hatred, that has emanated from various peculiar causes. The very church and peculiar faith organization, produces the elements of hatred, not love.

Why did the protestants succeed in Germany? Because the light of mind had preceded. They only commenced the light of reformation. The light is in rational religion, monotheism.

Do all the Romanist priests permit the reading of the scriptures, the bibles? They do not. What does this prove, but the fact of their falsehood? That the priestocracy are afraid to trust the people therewith.

It is asserted on the authority of a protestant paper, that in Portugal and Madeira "more than a thousand converts have fled before a merciless persecution for the bible's sake from Madeira, and five hundred of them are now in this country!" What a theme of reflection for religionists. France, a republic, has destroyed the Roman republic, for peculiar faith! Whereas in France Romanism and Protestantism prevail, there is the battlefield for strife, contention and absolutism. How many thousands and tens of thousands of protestants have been destroyed about the edict of Nantz? Millions have been destroyed in France, Ireland, and in Poland, about the christian peculiar faith. What prevents in this free country, but the potency of mind?

Animal feelings and excitement prevail in most of all converts, in forty-nine fiftieths, said the elder of a church before us. He ought to know.

Why revival shouts; do all christians do that, as the episcopalians, romanists? All have peculiar ways. This elder said that only one in fifty had a true religious influence in revivals. All else were deceived or hypocrites. His friends and relations had withdrawn from church. Now, as he thought best of his own church, of course all other churches were no better. A dishonest man will act in all the character that will best carry out his low schemes.

Church missionaries are ever too few, they are not enlightened enough. This is one of the efforts of mind, but a corrupt one at that. Why not adopt the thing itself, mind, that relies on science?

All seek to render their own sect good and great; that is a false position. Let them erase and expunge all this, and let them rear on the universal standard of creation. There are two grand divisions in all churches, the good and the bad, as in the world, and both as mind directs, by exaltation or perversion.

Now-a-days, much of church business is the adoption of the popular, not the invention of a new faith.

We have proof of an experimental professor of peculiar faith changing from one church to another, and from one sect to another—first Christian, then Mormon—had tried two prophets or Messiahs, and then declared that all such was a humbug!

The world now presents a real difficulty, as so many designing fellows have brought forward their schemes, to inveigle their race; it does not know what to do. It is in the quagmire of doubt.

The most are unable to analyze, yet the weaker part is inclined to superstition, and most are alarmed for life about the state of their souls, that would have done better, or well, if they had been let alone by these alarmists and agitators. The church has been an usurper all the time, as representative of superstition, superseding mind's rights, and counterfeiting religion.

Some you can hardly tell are in the church; some escape the penitentiary all their lives, as they are not arraigned for violation of social law and order. They are not tried fairly before the world, and possess an equivocal reputation. Some of these are the luminaries of the church : dark, indeed, must be that church.

The whole doctrine of election is only gotten over by rational view of rational religion. What are we not indebted for to this, that takes us out of such ungodly quagmires? Matthew, ch. x. verse 5th. These twelve Jesus sent forth, and commanded them, saying, Go not into the way of the gentiles, and into any city of the Samaritans enter ye not. 6. But go rather to the lost sheep of the house of Israel. 8. Heal the sick, cleanse the lepers, raise the dead, cast out devils. Could the master cast out devils? Did he not leave sectarianism, a greater devil? 14. And whosoever shall not receive you, &c. 15. Verily I say unto you, it shall be more tolerable for the land of Sodom and Gomorrah in the day of judgment, than for that city. It was priestocracy all the time; and the whole world was to be cursed if it did not receive them, and was most awfully cursed for having done so. 35. For I am come to set a man at variance against his father, and the daughter against her mother, and the daughter-in-law against her mother-in-law. Then these sectarians, for it was the priestocracy that were speaking, were committing their worst suicide, for here is the most awful clashing with principles, that excludes them from God. 34. Think not that I am come to send peace on earth; I came not to send peace, but a sword. 36. And a man's foes shall be of his own household. Not only sectarianism, but the lowest and bloodiest, as wars for Christianity, by the sword, testify. The very worst violation of God's principles, that negative religion. These were the truest words that the fanatic dramatists of this tragedy ever wrote, to portray their own bloody deeds. 41. He that receiveth a prophet, in the name of a prophet, shall receive a prophet's reward. That is, make priestocracy master of the world, and ye shall be its minions; give it the larger, and ye shall have the less loaves and fishes.

Christianity is indebted to the sword, and was placed under its patronage, for its final propagation and power, a union of church to the state, of Constantine. That is certain : that sword has never yet been sheathed. The blood of millions has flown, by this tyrannical sectarianism. What substantial foundation has church-membership? The members of churches are repeatedly falling from grace, and have no principles.

How can man, sustained only by man in church, be any better than man out of church, sustained by God? All are God-sustained, after all church sophistries and antagonisms. But the efficacy of prayers. Let a man's life, actions, proclaim all the performance of practicable duty. There are millions of honest church people from the principles of mind, who only need the proper teaching of truth, to go the very best practicable for mind. They are deceived into' the belief or faith, that church union imparts all essential to their soul's salvation. But what self-delusion. All they are through the grace of God, who alone gives it, is by mind and its faculties. How many persons join the church not possessing any practical experimental faith, but desirous of it' How preposterous! Authors and writers have flattered the prejudices of the peculiar faith, church and state-faith. But peculiar unions are not for nothing, they not only procure bread and salary to the chosen for themselves, but they dispense favors for all adherents, &c., making a system of machinery. From emperors of China, Russia, Rome and Thibet, high priests assuming thereby most divine rights to all the gradations of priestocracy, one indissoluble peculiar sworn band of tories to religion exists.

How do you know that you are one of the peculiar faithful? Our feelings teach the members. Feeling proves any faith that is peculiar, one kind as another, all self-delusion. The christian faith has been introduced into the eastern part of Asia, as China, twice at least, heretofore, by the Nestorians, who also carried it into Tartary, and by the Romanists, and originated as claimed in Western Asia, and yet all has been extirpated by the more successful court-faiths. What better evidence do we want than the world's history, to prove that all peculiar faith is evanescent as its base is false, and that none but rational religion can sustain itself, as it always has done correlatively to mind. Where once the Christian faith is claimed to have started in Palestine, the Mahomedan faith triumphs, and hardly tolerates Jew or Christian. What a commentary on peculiar faith! It is time that the world-patriots and mind-statesmen had acted aright. Let mind be duly and honorably represented. Are partisan questions to settle justice? They are often started to defeat it.

Well, if we omit church-discipline, faith and the peculiar redeemer, what shall we do? will we not drop into non-existence? Can the world stand? Will it last a day longer? Will not Satan reign? Calm yourself, bigot, fanatic. Adopt as honest and truthful people, mind-discipline, brotherhood, membership on principles, and the Creator, and lecture on science every seventh day, set apart by wise legislation for physical rest, but mental culture. Peculiar faith will produce endless difficulties; we might as well call things by their right names; peculiar faith is superstition, and churches cannot prevent the least of that. Churches are torn all to pieces by divisions. Sectarianism will beget sectarianism. Members become mutually hostile, and amenable to a miserable jury of peers, for a too artificial state of things. Expectations are raised that cannot be realized. Look how the animal passions are excited in large camp meetings. Much is theatrical. How can we break with the church people? We cannot see people unless we go to church. I admit that man is a social being, he should have amusements and enjoyments, though we may at first thus cut ourselves off from society as at present organized. But is there no pleasure in conservative revolution, and the company of a few kindred spirits? Is error always to be popular? Is rational religion to be kept back? What errors are promulgated on the absurd dictation of peculiar faith? The christian is told to live a life of penance, and disregard the main points of this life. Cities as the country, furnish intelligent, but some depraved citizens, men of mind perverted. How is this? Men look at the outward standing as if above reproach. People join the church and act in defiance. What is to remedy all this? any possession of faith? Not at all; but action of principle that looks to a full comprehension of rational religion, morals and civilization. Has the Christian faith any of these? Ah! but its missions have done good in the Pacific. Mind has done it. and thus faith claims, usurps all the credit. Mind ought to be ashamed of permitting this.

A man's character was above suspicion, reproach; but then action before character alone proves this.

How did man get character but by action? His standing, like faith, is worth nothing, if unsupported by proper action. The gentleman is only written by life-action. What has church to do with all this?

We cannot well renounce at present meetings, as they present social life. What can we do? Society must be revolutionized. Missionaries to continents are boasted of, when the dark and dismal points of all countries are fit positions for mind to act. Among the corrupt of the land are preachers and priests, leaders of their circle, who commit adultery, seduction. The best can only claim to be new, and actuated by the best principles. No code of tradition presents them. Will church discipline, rules, or management regulate the affairs of the world-morals? Not at all. We see that there is a miserable defect. What is to be done with those members that use enticing means for injury? Expulsion. What retribution does that produce, seeing that it leaves the injury unredressed? The church aristocracy is hard to oppose.

What an influence it yields! The church party may be the governing party in too many social circles in the whole society. It often governs talent, subsidizes and and support. It has a factitious and fictitious importance. If the government particularly combines with it, many of its offices that are lucrative are under its dispensation, and all the dignity of society is turned that way.

Through this, the world is playing at games at which it cannot hope to win. What is momentary gratification? Instead of subscriptions to foreign missions, let us have all this satisfactory before we do anything for them. We should be well assured that we are teaching the correct doctrine. If we do not teach correctly, we ought to stop.

What do we need more when we have as now the christian faith that progresses in the world? It did not progress of its own intrinsic merits, as it is indebted to the union of church and state under the banner of Constantine, in an empire that embraced supreme sway over the then best-known parts of the western world. We impute no bad motives, as we wish to have every thing exactly right in seeking the best system of faith for the true way to life eternal. But what a curse is there in the province of Judaism, when the disciples refer their greatest persecution actually to the scions of sectarianism growing out of it! Animal bravery is hardly ever lacking, but where is moral bravery?

When people sing out, "Come and get religion," you may be sure they are after humbugging you, for they cannot give you what God has already endowed you with. You have to cultivate the immortal gift.

But that change of heart? What has the heart, the blood vessel, to do with acts of mind? This is another of the gross errors of the ancients. But the efficacy of prayer is thought to be great. All is effectual through thought, word, and deed of mind intent on good results. See the case of General Washington, who was found on his knees by a quaker, as reported. As to Washington, who is a noble example of exalted patriotism, he was made by mind-culture and by rational education. He was unquestionably a believer in the Almighty, and ruled his own mind in equilibrium. But as to the success of America over England during the revolution, that was a matter of principles that vindicate themselves, if properly sustained by mind. America did this, aided by many circumstances advantageous to her. What can prove the position of the right view of church faith? The triumph of the dying saint, the blissful feelings of the living christian. All professors of peculiar faith are on an equality. The Juggernaut votaries even victimize themselves, exulting in future blissful hopes. Of course these are true martyrs as any, and have the best passports, sealing their own faith with their own blood for saintship. Why had I not joined the church? I thank God that I was not influenced by any sinister motives, and therefore am not hypocrite enough to join I have not calculated the chances to float on the tide of popularity or power. I seek not to calculate the advantages of church-membership. Principle and duty are paramount in truth, and all kinds of pure actions. There is but one pure faith, one religion; whilst there can be no admission to peculiar faith in any one matter.

It would be a monstrosity in creation, if there was. An analytic mind in or out of church must know, that peculiar faith will not do. Who can sacrifice his soul to any species of peculiar power, without remorse? There are some in the church that may practice all manner of deception and fraud, blasphemy and felony, and yet have no fair investigation of their conduct, much less turned out. How can individual exceptions be made for blasphemy, when the whole church-world is founded on it. How many members will falsify their word most basely. The Protestants say the Romans are not Christians. From whom but them, did the former get their bible? The fanatics at Athens, caused Socrates the philosopher, to die, for his opinions on Deity: was it the influence of the sophists that helped the Christians expel the philosophers from Rome? It was the first at Athens, that caused Socrates to drink hemlock; it could be no less than they, the antagonists in all countries, that drove out the philosophers at Rome when Christians got the ascendancy, and it is they, in every age, that dispute the princi-

ple of reason and philosophy. Who are now the sophists of the world? Do they not put truth in abeyance to faith?
There could be no better proof in the whole world.
How are they the friends of science? It is impossible.
It is policy that causes church-membership: let a man in affluent circumstances be reduced to poverty, and how readily he joins the church. While many have the sincerest objects in view, subsistence, promotion, ambition, avarice, are the objects of the hypocritical.
The world is forced by social relations to act in the popular faith, no matter how peculiar, if that part of the world do not act independently as mind ought.
Many members of the church will speak untruths too quickly, if it be their interest to do so. The whole foundation is in falsehood, fraud, and imposition, beyond cavil or doubt. Do not expose human nature, unnecessarily to it.
Enlightened patriotism ought help explode it.
But we have seen men of mature age, not depending on the world for their bread, afraid as they acknowledged, to read books calculated to enlighten. Would they not forbear, in being convinced? Afraid of truth and reason! What is life profession, at best? Sons of the same family go, as policy and choice direct. One chooses a profession in the army, the others, in law, medicine, theology! All are mere livings. As long as millions are given to peculiar faith men, so long will such faith survive. It is the sugar that supports the flies, not the flies the sugar. As long as humbugs are paid for out of the pockets of a verdant people, humbugs will flourish. As old as the world is, is it yet too young not to know all this? The most intelligent of the priestocracy know better; they are obliged to know that all such is false pretence, but yet their senses are bribed and seduced to seduce the world for despotism.
The language of Almighty God is in his universe, unmistakable to mankind, universally understood without mysteries, that are men's machinery. The clannishness of church membership is like peculiar socialism.
But all my positions may be good for life, but may not be for death! That is impossible, for both are consistently supported by rational religion. Pious frauds and lies about the death-bed of those believing only in one God, can only be work of the belials of peculiar faith. Why will the world persist, not only in its folly but its crimes? The world has to come to the right point, and why not at once and forever? Is it because the vile sophists of the world have conspired in collusion against it? How comes it that no peculiar faith has not flourished better? That under bibles has been upheld by sword, state, intrigue, and money, all the despotisms of perverted mind. Any cause that permits such, is unsound. Bequests under such influence have been abundantly made, large amounts of money, and what but bribes for more proselytes who overlook their rights of mind. It is hard to dissolve such associations, however made in corruption. You have drunkards in the church, that is a respecter of persons, not principles. If they are turned out they are only drunkards, and are less sinful as not hypocrites. Those of the church who act knowingly, are base men. Reason is the means of arriving at truth, beyond which we cannot go.
Many join the church because of fashion, interest, policy. Will any trust another merely from the fact of his church membership, and thus obtained? Not at all. The history and custom of the world, prove the contrary.
Does church membership enable the dying man to make his peace with God? How can any of peculiar faith that removes mind farther from God? Church members are multiplied, and sectarianism is engendered, but where is religion? All depends on faith, which depends on truth, which cannot be known without reason or reasonable testimony, correct investigation and conclusion thereon. The church-people are disposed to horrify the human mind against the position of monotheism. Why do they go to mind, if they refuse reason to faith? They act as monarchists against republicans.
Church-membership confers power proportionately to the church hierarchy. A person on the excitement of the moment gets into the altar, and as pretended, gets religion! Well, that he has had before, but he has never cultivated it properly : now he horribly mistakes, on the affirmation of ignorant pretenders, that it is not God, but his vicegerents, of whom they are part and parcel, that are to bring his soul into the fold of safety. Is this mind, that of progress, the effulgent beam of a bright free institution of the nineteenth century? It would do once for the wilds of Siberia, the serfs of Russia, the dupes of the priestocracy, but not for intelligent freemen.
Rational minds can never exchange their certainty for such pretensions. Inspiration through science, knowledge and wisdom, love, gratitude, light of mind, all are agents of the author of mind.
Responsibility of mind accompanies unmistakably moral agency. The path of

innocence is the only path of safety. Mind is bound to do good not only the best for the present, but the future generations, only by principles that reflect on the priestocracy and honor the Creator. If there be any society that refers in foundation to God, participates in universal principles, seeks to diffuse universal good, then that constitutes the only one that will last for eternity, and that is the one that all should unite on for one universal brotherhood.

It will not do to pretend that the heart is independent of the mind in religion, any more than the feelings are independent of sense and faith independent of reason. The bad men in the church are worse than the bad out of the church : for this reason, they add the crime of hypocrisy, the most wicked and blasphemous, and sophistry of faith the weakest. Now, all are obliged to have rational religion, a part of one's existence. If actions do not prove that, use mind-culture. Rear your church-domes as gorgeous as wealth can make them, still your case is not improved. Not only have the ecclesiastical bodies split into sects, but those sects have become sectional local segments and fragments of an ill-assorted brotherhood, none being able to maintain their unity, as they have not the appropriate elements of unity at all.

Let them all go as they will go, to nothing in time. The great first cause has unity of being, and design in all his creation, and his representative, monotheism, has all for a universal brotherhood.

We have had botches down to the present time clothed in the sanctity of faith, whose province could not bear scanning. Whenever you hear at a distance there is something wrong, there is something rotten in the state of the church.

You speak of missions and missionary societies, for what? · That you may be accursed by posterity? How can lying church-members act straight, who have no principles to go by? Judges have perjured themselve for this, as quoted by Jefferson.

We are not in antagonism to the good and virtuous of the world; just the reverse. But how can we get along without the faith of the heart? That is a nullity, as the whole is faith of mind, that has action on belief or faith ; all else is nonsense. But men of mind, of talents, are wicked. Yes, they are perverted by peculiar education, as emanating from peculiar bibles. But many that believe in the bible are excellent persons. Grant that they are good, they were so constitutionally and phrenologically by rational education, the chief part. But the voice of the people is the voice of God. That is only correct when all is truth and right ; not when a bible and its faith are preferred to truth and its best analysis. It is the aiding and abiding in false pretences by the world, that has to be reprobated. Why are not both sides of man's supposed duty advanced fairly and dispassionately, instead of concealment, libels, bullyings, and inquisitions, social, moral, and political. When churchmen have not aliens to contend with they worry each other.

The church has talents and worth misdirected, and profession misemployed. Better are church members than the world, are they? Who now presents most cases of crim. con. accusation? Whilst now writing, there are two awful cases of crim. con. of parties wholly in respectable churches, so called.

What intrigues there are in the world, through peculiar faith. Who claims to be orthodox? The Christians, by excellence. How did their actions quadrate? When Jerusalem was taken by the Christian crusaders, all that were not Christians were put to the sword. They massacred seventy thousand Musselmen, and burnt all the Jews.

When Saladin took it, he let the Christians redeem themselves with money. He tolerated even the oriental Christians, restoring to them the church of the holy sepulchre. Saladin showed that much of religion. Where is the Christian's? Have Mahommedans gotten the start of Christians in religion?

The Mahommedans in Palestine and Spain gave the Christian world the brilliant example of toleration. Can we duly estimate the ferocious barbarism of peculiar faith without the most accurate history of the facts? Only think that for nearly two hundred years that the wars of the crusades agitated the most important parts of the then known world. All christendom was excited by the most horrible passions of revenge, malice, all the basest passions of ambition.   ·

Individuals, nations, the world, should so act that no just exceptions can be taken to their deportment by the world of any age and profession. There are universal principles intended for all mankind, that can sustain themselves fairly, honorably, and justly before the whole world, at all times, and countries, and people. Buck says, that " when the Moors conquered Spain, in the eighth century, they allowed the Christians the free exercise of their religion ; but in the fifteenth century, when the Moors were overcome, and Ferdinand subdued the Moriscoes, the descendants of the above Moors, many thousands were forced to be baptized, or burnt, massacred, or banished, and the children sold for slaves ; besides innumerable Jews, who shared the same cruelties, chiefly by means of the infernal courts of inquisition. A worse slaughter, if possible, was made among the natives of Spanish America, where fifteen millions are said to have been sacrificed to the genius of popery in about forty years. It has been computed that fifty millions of Protestants have at different times been the victims of the persecutions of the papists, and put to death for their religious opinions." Toleration was not enjoyed in England " untill William III. came to the throne, who showed himself a warm friend to the rights of conscience."

Toleration properly restrains persecution. "Twenty-two thousand persons were banished from England, by persecution, to America." Such record declares the extreme barbarism of those causing the banishment.

All the petty societies have to seek their dignity in universal comprehension. Missionaries are sent to the heathen, the outside barbarians. What correct impression was ever made on the savages of America, as they are called, who yet rebuked their civilized teachers in their creed of the Great Spirit? What good have the missionaries done in the depopulating Sandwich Islands? Call things by their right names. The covetous desire of popularity renders many anxious bidders unprincipled.

Sectarian combatants! where are your actions when you preach of prayer? When you address God, do it by principles that are conservative to the universe. Before you say one word, reconsider your position. You speak of love as a universal influence in Christianity, how can you Christianize Mahommedans, or Judaize both? There is but one adequate solution to this otherwise impracticable problem. The whole world can be rendered rationalists in one day, one hour, one minute, on the highest authority, the Creator of all. If the scriptural moral law be love, how came the Christians to war on the Mahommetans and persecute the Jews? Debate on faith, is it? What good does that do? The church advocates return, persuaded his or her own is particularly right, and probably influenced against the others for denial! How many in the church are deists? Are there not very many that are proscribed for opinion's sake in this most important matter? During church existence, we see its contentious lay members against the dictatorial clergy, dissensions, divisions, wars and bloodshed.

A great deal is said about the martyrs and missionaries of the church. but what of them? They have been all mistaken in their pursuit, and when the world's history is correctly written or read, mind will see it. Those of the church often err for want of principles. How then is this? Safety is not of the church, but in mind that uses principles. Is the church, then, an infallible personification to save mankind? No. All have to recur to mind, any way that it can be fixed.

We must give credit to many for their action in or out of churches, but have they ever sought to know that the laws of nature are those of God? If the world trades on no one's capital but its own, then what can church membership fairly avail its people? People may assume much for the church, but the most intellectual analysis decides against its morality, rational intellectuality and faith divided. that I cannot begin to call religion. This course may be unpopular now, but that is nothing at all. The world enlightened will discard all unprincipled objection, as most ignominious. If a church member is not right by union, he positively adds hypocrisy to his other sins! Interest and policy cause union to church. Can that create a healthy state of morals, from the highest prelate in the realm to the lowest menial of such dynasty? Is it not one entire system of corruption and speculation? One sect secretly hates another. Can this be denied? Interest and policy force to union of church, and if the first are invalidated by opposing sectarian interests, where are conservative principles? Nowhere. Has this sect, the Christians, all the order, decency, because it assumes that faith?

Are Christian people ahead of the world in morals and practical brotherhood? A Christian nation, with her queen defender of the faith, attacked China, that, for two thousand years, had maintained the policy of peace. What were the motives? Were they the honorable ones of commerce, or for their violation? If both had had proper principles, there could have been no war.

What does the church-member learn! Sectarianism all the time. The church admits to its bosom members guilty of crimes, of which the party culpable affects to have repented. Admit their repentance, but no implicit confidence or reliance can be put in men prone to badness. A rational education can enlighten on a peculiar education, but however we credit the repentance of past errors, the only confidence we can give for office is to those worthy of it by general good deportment. They, at least, are most removed from suspicion. The people, under unions of church and state. raise funds to bribe, for keeping themselves deceived about the real truths of religion! Volumes could be written on this point. Despotisms of church and state have played most shrewdly into each other's hands.

What an amount of pious frauds have been perpetrated through the world—and such

28

frauds are the most flagrant crimes, as the deification of men, and canonizing mortals as saints—the most heinous sycophancy. Had not all peculiar faiths been vulnerable, most positively, we never should have heard of inquisition murders.

Was not Christian church association at first a socialism, a community that benefited the poor, trodden down by oriental, occidental, and world-wide despotism, social, civil, and individual? Hence the accession of numbers, that were artfully used by intriguers. Where did not ancient tyranny of man and vice prevail, after all the boasts of civilization? Every century now is more and more disclosing its partial blessings, through mind. Why does not Christianity influence the Indians of America? Here is a theatre to prepare the foreign missionaries in. How comes it that they are not christianized?

The demands of the church, in past ages, were exorbitant, in getting all power and money practicable out of the people.

What has Christianity to do with comprehensive science, when she is in antagonism to it? Her peculiar faith has excluded religion. as far as in her lies, with perverted minds. Christians do not favor true science, as long as they prostitute mind to faith— mere credulity. The fathers at Laodicea adopted the gospels, and their decree is blindly assumed as mandatory to future generations, to the end of time. Can there be a more shameful imposition, a more revolting despotism on the world? Shall ecclesiastical false pretences, then, overrule mind's conservation?

To what effrontery have church conventions reached. Their assemblies at various times, have sought to denounce the proper laws of the land.

Christianity the organizer of science, was she? Was Copernicus a Christian, when he forebore for thirty years to publish his system of astronomy, that he might escape her oppressions?

Was Galileo, when he was imprisoned for supporting Copernicus's system, and made to abjure it? Was that the light of the bible, that kept this system, before declared by Pythagoras, who got it at the East, beyond the Jews, in abeyance for thirteen centuries to the ignorant bible idea? We have but one authenticated proof of God, the God of the universe, and that by his magnificent system; and is this to be kept in abeyance to a dwarf black letter bible of tradition? Is this the boasted science of mind, that excludes all proper science of the universe? By God's system we can only get intellectual and moral sincerity, and religious sublimity. How much of valuable life of the world is lost, in trifling with miserable peculiar faith, that is of no value, but an abiding injury to the world. The peculiar scriptures nurture fanaticism, superstition, miserable bad feelings, disruptare of brotherhood, even in the same families, nation, country. But what odious vassalage of mind, that the world must believe the way of the scriptures, if not, it must be damned.

But how ignorant are the priestocracy of human nature, thus left to an impious impossibility. There are thoughtless people, who conscientiously cannot believe that way; and as all others are recklessly excluded, most ignominiously so, by the ecclesiastical despotism over mind, for faith, the consequence is a loss of morals is established, most disastrous. In regard to the Roman church proceeding, it has basely fabricated, interpolated, and forged documents in its possession. What has it not done, to sustain this ignominious imposition over all mankind? What can be a worse state of morals? Before the public, the presiding preacher of a district stated that he sincerely believed that forty-nine fiftieths of converts had backslid. Afterwards, it was said by an opponent, yet member of his church, that three-fourths of the ministers of that creed ought to be expelled from the church.

What shall be said of raffling at fairs, for churches? Is there no vice engendered? Is this not gambling? If the world will permit it, churches will be political machines. What else were they? Have they not now made moves that tell disastrously? What are the church-fanatics now not doing, in opposition to constitutional laws, exciting the country by deep injurious agitation? They have split from union of churches, and is this union of country sanctified with the glorious recollections of the past, the most animating inspirations of the present, and the most glorious world-results of the future, to be injured by them? Many in church quibble, prevaricate and equivocate. They are not perfect by the church, nor less good out of it. What should hinder all those expecting to reach their heaven, from being most honest, so much so that a lock and key, legislation for law and order would be a reproach to them? The peculiar faith people talk of atheists, of others, only different a few shades. They talk of the bloody days in France. What was more bloody than the days of Salem, and other witchcraft, while it lasted? I have been told that some two hundred fell victims, of all ages and conditions, and both sexes. The accusers of innocent persons who were amenable for ill-will, and hostility or unfriendly feelings, had them tried, convicted and executed in a few short hours. It was equal to the bloody days of the French directory. And one of the best impediments was the vital danger of the felon accusers, some of whom paid forfeit for their crimes, by their lives. The result began to work on them too strongly, as their common danger brought them to their senses and humanity. But there have been millions massacred for this bible-faith in the world? The Christian churches oppose each other, much less the other different peculiar faiths, though their motto is "love thy neighbor as thyself." How came the Salem witchcraft butchery to stop? By effects of the bible? That gave the foundation, and was the very code of laws that originated the murderous fanaticism. Did that bloody transaction stop by faith? That was what started and excited it, next to the bible.

Was it not triumphant mind? What gave rise to the horrid inquisitions? Superstition, bigotry, bible-faiths, are the fathers of inquisitions, that would have overrun the world, but for mind!

Those who have been members of churches, will acknowledge that all such was a delusion. The crime is that all peculiar faiths are as great delusions.

Church union begets an improper alliance alien to universal principles. In Asiatic Turkey, the Turks are prompted to fanatical excesses against the Christians. In European Turkey, the Christians and Mahomedans are contending for political supremacy, and the last have massacred the first. In Switzerland, the Romans unite with the radicals and socialists. Have they not excited bloody deeds in that country, within the last few years? In England, the peculiar faith agitation still continues unabated, about the English and Roman churches. Is it any better in America, when Baptist synods seek to dictate about constitutional laws? Let the world and rational mind, deliver themselves. How many great difficulties are there not, about the Roman church? But such a man is a republican, a churchman. He is only a man. Act with the world on principle. You can depend on principle, but not without. All plans of churches, secret societies, are failures; none but principles are the thing, and they not without rational religion. There are some persons of the world that cannot be corrupted by church machinery, but some are deeply in for all that they can get. Do not tell me about the excellency of the church, when it is a part of the machinery to govern the world.

With what propriety, reason, or justice, can we go to churchmen for truth or honesty, when their whole foundation is otherwise? But the churches do not make the converts right, as they do not stick generally. But God has made religion natural: churches make it artificial.

The best illustration of priestocracy is the union of church and state in the same head, as the emperors of China, Russia, the grand lama of Thibet, &c.

All things were common in the primitive days of christianity. Who was ever a greater bully than the church, as shown by proscriptions and inquisitions? It had no mercy, when it has no principle.

It is important to decide right, to escape the clutches of church tyranny, oppression, and exaction.

When people lie to us every day, whether in or out of church, for a little interest or money, what will they not do when impelled to swear? Would they not perjure themselves? What a class are some of the lawyers in that predicament! Is there any reason that any one should prostitute his soul to falsehood for mere petty, trifling, or great considerations? Every act, thought, and word of mind should be rational, look to reason, else they may look to the reverse or ruin. Society must be respected as a harmonious whole, and must therefore take precedence of church and secret associations. It must then have the proper basis to realize it. There must be no real cause for discontent, but there is now necessarily, as the world needs an honorable position. What made the christian and other faiths, as the Mormon, so popular, was the common stock arrangements, from which the rich backed out among the first.

The constitutional laws of principles furnish the proper protection from rational religion, that gives justice instead of contingent charity, that requires a proper homestead for all destitute families, that requires rational education for all citizens, and puts all in an honorable harmony, not local or sectarian antagonisms.

What are church organizations worth? To propagate bible heresies and advance the interest of demagogues. Church national disunions are tubs to the whale.

How can church-membership give religion, what God has already given to every rational mind? Destitute of principles that direct to him exclusively, it must make many bad or worse, while those that are good would be better out of it. But as to church-membership, no pledge should be given but what is honorable, and that must be honorably sustained. Can any honorable pledge be given or sustained, when there is no honorable foundation? The word of God most luminously, conclusively declares for the supremacy of religion the only conservative, and rules out peculiar faith as inimical to and destructive to mind.

Every church-member, by his or her position, scowls on all others,—else why a difference? There are some in the church I could not trust with anything I possess. Who are they? They are myriads. Why? They have not the rational principles of rational education. So far from feeling compunction of conscience, they do not know what conscience-religion is. I could not trust my soul with one of the whole tribe. No peculiar faith, polytheism, or atheism ministry, can teach principles that belong to rational religion or monotheism correctly. That is certain.

Because their existence seems prior, is that an evidence of the exactness of their truth? They had affected the capital of rational religion, and were indebted for all available good-faith capital.

The feeling engendered in villages, in the same circle, for the peculiar half-a-dozen sects contending for life, reflects the great world agitated by the ungodly peculiar faiths. Whoever subscribes to any church of peculiar faith, has violated all proper principles of truth and honesty that such faith has certainly violated.

I know that this is the boldest step to arrest all such, and requires the highest moral firmness. Put down the felony. The protestant is as deep in the quagmire, as the Roman or Greek churchman, Mormon, Brahmin, more so for the lights of rational mind.

What harm do churches? The houses do none, only take up ground by worship of polytheism, better employed in adoration of God of the universe by making mind rational, inspiring it with the best of rational religion. Union of churches and secret societies, were for factitious purposes and advantages. Do they benefit the world at large or its component society? What factitious importance is there in societies and churches? Look at the millions of converts of all characters that backslide or fall from grace, commit sin, &c. Now, all this elegantly proves that rationality is all in all in religion. All that we can know is by mind, that must be relatively rational for all rational enjoyments.

The baptists do not participate in their sacraments with other denominations of christians, thus increasing the subdivisions of sectarians.

As to heart-holiness from Christ, all that stuff is common with the Asiatic Brahmins. Have not the juggernauts all that pertains to experience? Are not their martyrs as much entitled to credence as those of any other in the world? Now, mind, rationality, change, comes of God, the universe ruler, who becomes the dignity of his station by assigning constitutional rights to mind by moral free agency, and acts like the constitutional president of the universe, not an autocrat of an empire. But if the world breaks up the priestocracy, all this would break up too many fine choirs, churches, organs, book concerns, charities, missions, collections, and livings. What are churches? Do they make people any better, when the priestocracy do not? Some are worse. Ah! but how shall we worship God? The rational mind does not need idol-worship nor lip-service, nor priestocracy performance.

Many church-members are all church malign influences, that cannot be injured thereby.

If the church present such men as Paul describes, what character had they for veracity, &c.?

In the land of bigotry, where church-ridden people are, there are only the forms of freedom.

What can rickety church-establishments avail in religion? Let a free, fair and liberal discussion be enacted, not avoided. Religion demands this, as the friend of truth and reason, not of faith and policy, mere pretences of oracles. Religion does not know faith, but through the right avenues of truth. What avail all the benefits of a crank-sided rickety church faith? Are there any principles intrinsic in any association? I know members of churches that stand as high as the world can make them, for honesty and honor, their membership not hurting them, being safe before they joined.

But the house of God is expedient? Where is that particularly in this world, this universe? See the various difficulties in churches. All that is best decided by enlightened public opinion.

What divisions of families who go to different churches. All this is miserable man's devices. What a noble thing it is that church-members are not corrupted by their membership.

Now, as to the church, does that make religion? Who made the church? Man. Has the church any specific pr nc ples? What has the church to do? It is only man's devices, as priestocracy and bibles, faith and all its machinery. What good do all churches do after all said and done? They are split into factions, divisions, and subdivisions.

As to being in the church, that does not avail, for that is founded on false pretences, σa bibles that are a binding of lies, and its peculiar faith is a part and parcel thereof. All membership has to be strictly watched, else ecclesiastical or church power will aspire to supremacy ; therefore all such is objectionable as partaking of man's polity. The world has some hard old sinners to deal with, and the worst are those in the church, especially the licensed heads, as bishops and others that feel themselves licensed to take licentious liberties.

The priestocracy have the worst morals in the world, except they be checked by the best lights of mind and rational civilization. Each peculiar church assumes peculiar prerogatives that destroy with its own elements. You protestants declaim against the auricular confession of the Roman church ; what less sin is your assumed sanctification ? You, Christian, complain of the Mormon ; did you not show him the way, when you adopted peculiar faith, a thing that has no being but in the false pretences of superstition ? Who are many of the church officials, but those seeking loaves and fishes by church-people-communion ? Associations in churches should discuss the subject of religion, the only way to reach the most correct views. The only church is the temple of the world, as part of the universe, and mankind the audience.

Churches that offer only one-sided peculiar views of sleepy sophist lecturers or preachers, instead of popular associations for truth discussions, diffuse the worst of mental, social, moral and religious suppressions, the worst of all peculiar poisons to the human family. Can you confide justly in any persons because they are in the church ? You cannot in truth, as the worst hypocrites may be church-going.

But there must be some criterion for public confidence. What is that ? Personal merit, of course ; then it is not church-merit. To be confided in justly, the individuals must be thoroughly known for consistent honorable bearing.

In separation of church and state, religion allows of no church at all, for that is a political engine, a hobby, machinery, of no pretensions to religion. Such churches have millions of property, as the St. Louis Roman church, the Trinity church, New York, and too many elsewhere. Apply all these incomes to the right use of religion, not of churches. Apply all annually to the right correction of the world, that can be rectified in a few years, for billions will be withdrawn and devoted to God's, not man's purposes. Put down all despotisms of church and priestocracy monopoly, by conservative revolution.

Every churchman ought to resign his church-faith as derogatory to religion—if it be of religion, he can prove, as it will prove itself beyond a doubt the authenticity.

But freethinkers are the anti-church party ; and what does that sophism all avail, churchmen ? The anti-church party is not the anti-religious party ; if it were, it would not be rational.

It is religion, not superstition, that rational mind, sane and sound, needs. It is utterly impossible to eradicate religion by all the efforts of the peculiar faith church-party.

Love the brethren, says the church advocate, proves the position. Do Romanists love protestants ? Does the massacre on St. Bartholomew's day prove it ? Peculiar faith always has a false position.

All that is corrupt is in churches, that should be best appropriated to the benefits of the world, and discussions held by associations of monotheists.

Politics and ecclesiastical policies are mixed up in church regime to the disturbance and agitation, strife, animosity, difficulties, and sectarianism of the people of each government and the world—as in Canada, Great Britain, Italy, &c.

The maintenance of peculiar faith is abominable. It was bad enough to have to receive the counterfeit. Religion does not need money, but mind-maintenance, no established churches nor hireling officials. The rational world asks to be free of all this. To do so, let each rational mind free itself at once and forever of all peculiar faiths, bibles, all priestocracies, all the vilest humbugs. Let there be no ecclesiastical regimes—no ecclesiastical nucleus for frauds, imposition, and despotism. The appropriation of property of the people, or what ought to be theirs if any, to churches, is sacrilege to mind, God, and religion.

All the establishments of world-peculiar faiths are frauds, sacrilegious frauds, that corrupt the people unqualifiedly. Where church benefices are, principles and the religion of principles are abandoned.

Let there be no kind of feudal tenures, nothing to check world and mind's improvements.

If it is not a pity to desecrate all churches of the present day to paganism, it is certainly wrong to devote mind to such trash, and that is adequate argument.

Are you a churchman ? Then you sustain despotic, ill-gotten, and worse retained power. The world must estimate things as they are.

But you are at a stand, halting about the best to be done. What is all of peculiar

faith that is adjudged a felon worth, having committed blasphemy against God ? N
reformation of protestantism will answer ; nothing short of conservative revolutio
What a pity it is that the diamond owners, should desire to swap it for false stone
That had been a gospel if rational, but it has murdered all its pretensions by her
peculiar. As having a peculiar god and gods, it rules itself from rational mind, and
only fit to keep company with barbarians that originated it, or half civilized tyrants the
smuggled it into the world.

Monotheism is legitimate, and carries out all legitimate purposes. She is faultless.
Peculiar faith as illegitimate, has been palmed for God's, on the world. That is wh
it has been so reverenced. Religious protection is what the world needs.

Peculiar faith is still the old prostitute with all her meretricious ornaments, to inveigl
and deceive. She is with absolutism.

The love of mankind, Christian, takes precedence of the petty love of a sect : tha
is as clear as monotheism, religion takes precedence of all the earthly mortal peculia
faiths : besides, she gives justice before charity, as the first travels over the world, th
universe, the last to home and its kindred interests—that is the charity of all sects, an
the Christian has no more feelings than man can have under his circumstances.

How can that be protection of church-membership, when the recipient is deceived
deluded, and misdirected, from his own excellent possession ?

The noblest suggestion of religion would be, take no advantage of the situation of
mind—but has not peculiar faith done this enough to the world, to declare her ignobl
character to condemn her ?   The wise Author of the universe has put it out of the
power of man, to trammel mind forever in its religion.   He has taken care of all that

All peculiar faiths cannot prove religion, but all are certain evidence of peculiar, perverted, weak state of mind—that of corruption of the whole, every way by absolutism,
a false weight that shrewd minds ought to divest themselves of, only what the world is
capable of.

The world does not require, and cannot abide ascetism.   Let all that is legitimate,
be consistently carried out, no more or less.

Man has no business with any capital, that can be turned against him, as peculiar faith, all others of which war on his, that is in direct antagonism with religion.

Come, citizen, can rationalists be hostile, with her banner ?   Teach them right, and
they, doubtlessly, before God, will abjure the wrong, the day proclaimed ; then they will
confirm it as respects anything about peculiar faith being the right way, superior to rational religion.

All vice is an ignis fatuus, and at the head is peculiar faith. If you will not act
straight about rational faith, stop your crazy, rickety monomania, for posterity will
curse you with the bitterest curse. As an evidence of the uncertain basis of peculiar
faith, Christianity the modern, most remarkably eschews previous acts of Christianity
the ancient ; proving incontestibly that it is all in abeyance to mind, that has become
more rational, civilized, and essentially religionized, not faithized. All peculiar faiths
faithize, not religionize—that is certain. How can any carry mind beyond what it cannot carry itself ?

By the admission of the professors, then, Christians, instead of wisely espousing rational religion, that is identified with rational mind, and gives all true expositions, have
to resort to the deepest and most humiliating mortification of expunging the foulest blots
of Christianity, that was barbarous as barbarian sectarianism could make her ; and, worst
of all, in debasing mind, now, at the very moment of its acknowledgment, in the expunging. Will the feeble egotists of peculiar faith never see the stupid and endless
degradation ?

Not only God, but rational mind can evolve, out of apparent evils, its consummate
good.   Let wise souls of the world at once attain all the legitimate blessings of religion, constitutional government, universal brotherhood.

Billions die out, that peculiar faith does not practically reach, that, but for rational
religion, would be brutes.

Christianity the advancer of true science, whose very first step, is the exclusion of
the science of all sciences, rational religion ?

Whose eighteen centuries of exertions have been fruitlessly employed, to put down
the true science of the Great First, the only Cause, sublime in his unity ?   What can be
more brazen, in the wide world of ignorance and impudence ?   The very initiative of
her own position excludes and estops her from all such special pleas and claims. Peculiar faith of churches cannot monopolize or usurp the world, endorsed as she has
been by all abominable despotisms ; and the sooner she gives up the place she cannot
fill to rational religion the better, that looks over this earth and all the future. The
wise existence of life requires a comprehension of what are requisite to be done.

HIERARCHIES.

The head men of hierarchies have the advantage of the world, and will rule it, one way or another, until the lay people know what and who they are. Will the people investigate and decide, in all the potent empire of mind, that they are the only sove-. reigns, and have the majesty and sovereignty of rights? How verdant the world-people are to be imposed upon, at this meridian-time of light, by priests and preachers, the priestocracies, who assume to have divine missions! There is no imposition or blaspheming greater, in or out of the world. How the world is befooled and defrauded about religion, by what is only a degenerate thing, peculiar faith, that is lauded above reason and religion. If you doubt their orthodoxy you are damned; if you refuse it, you are proscribed by all their brute force. When self-willed, what limit has been placed to their tyranny, that is bad enough at the best? ∗

They are impostors, and become tyrants of the human mind. Their bibles are libelers of Deity, mind and man.

What a destruction of books in the world, both by Christians and pagans! And yet science and philosophy are pre-eminently indebted to Christians! What a libel on mind, on truth, on reason, on sense!

Hierarchies subsidize talents in their support, and invoke all the potency of perverted mind to their aid, but neither the inquisition of the ancients by banishment, death by hemlock, tortures, availed to exclude mind from its right course.

These hierarchies claim to rule, not by the aristocracy of mind, but affect to be infal-lible, a most degraded and gross absurdity, when they take faith for reason.

For the supremacy of sects, protestant or Romanist, the nation, the world must be convulsed time after time. The worst of intoleration has prevailed, when church and political power has been united.

The tenets of church-power are subversive of a constitutional government. The non-conformists have been subjected to intoleration, persecution and prosecution by judicial and military murders. Fear and hate of the churches have involved nations and their rulers into the worst of miseries. Why did the Romanists withhold their bibles from the laymen? Is hierarchy supreme over the world's mind?

" The English Romanists have now the whole bible in their mother tongue ; though it is to be observed, they are forbidden to read it without a license from their superior." —Buck. " In 1532, Tindal and his associates finished the whole bible, except the apocrypha, and printed it abroad ; but, while he was afterwards preparing a second edition, he was taken up and burnt for heresy in Flanders."

" Notwithstanding, however, the excellency of this translation, (king James' bible,) it must be acknowledged that our increasing acquaintance with oriental customs and manners, and the changes our language has undergone since king James' time, are very powerful arguments for a new translation, or at least a correction of the old one." Let it go entirely down, and build up that of mind. God's bible never changes.

" After very violent opposition from the (Roman) clergy, the court of Spain ordered Spanish bibles to be printed by royal authority in 1796, and put into the hands of people of all ranks, as well as to be used in public worship."

" By the statute of England, he that denies one of the persons in the trinity, or denies Christianity to be true, &c., for the first offence is rendered incapable of any office," &c. " These laws, however, in the present age, are not enforced"? The burning to death for heresy! Huss was burnt alive in 1415. Then there was war be-tween the two parties. What terrible wars there were about the images! Image-worship debauched the priests, only a little more so.

Rites and ceremonies take up too much time uselessly, analogous to all the balance of hierarchal pretences. The Roman hierarchy affects to keep no faith with heretics. Which is greatest, the ignorance or cruelty of priestocracies? They burnt heretics in England by legal warrants. In France, they murdered recusants without the pre-tence of law. During the reign of Charles IX., on the 24th of August, 1572, was the massacre of St. Bartholomew. They massacred all ages and both sexes. They took no prisoners in civil wars, and pope Pius IV. commended the author of such murders. What prevents the repetition of all the malign felony of priestocracy now? Only the want of power.

Take away the pretence for absolutism, that gives all false pretences and no good from the nature of things.

In the massacre of the Huguenots, " seven long days was Paris one scene of pillage, outrage, and cruelty, which would have disgraced a horde of the wildest savages. Men might be seen stabbing little infants, while the innocents smiled in their faces, and played with their beards. According to different historians, from 70,000 to 100,000 protestants were butchered or perished at this time; and Pope Gregory XIII. ordered thanksgivings for the victory of the faithful; and a medal was struck to commemorate the event, with the head of the pope on one side, and a representation of the massacre on the reverse."!!

Citizens of the world, will you embrace this crime of crimes, peculiar faith, in any shape, form, or design? Will you stupidly hug the rattlesnake to your bosom? Will you nurture the strong holds of despotism, the most ruthless, to tear out your very vitals should the days of despotism ever again obscure your horizon? Will you permit its existence among you? Is this the hideous and dangerous thing that ministers of the gospel tell you you should get, to reach its peculiar god? Will you give up the pure God of the universe, your Creator and Preserver, for all this worthless, bloody trash? Do they, ignorant and stupid, overlook the proper analysis, and seek to draw the whole world by such ignominy?

Henry VIII. of England, who at first was a bigoted papist, burnt the famous Tyndal, who made one of the first and best translations of the New Testament.

" The higher orders of French clergy enjoyed immense revenues." " The clergy, as a body, independent of their titles, possessed a revenue arising from their property in land, amounting to five millions sterling annually; at the same time, they were exempt from taxation."

" The religious orders, viz : the communities of monks and nuns, possessed immense landed estates."

The preachers and priests know whether there is reality in peculiar faith or no. The reality of their livings determine that question. But it is a pity to impute to so good a set of people such motives. None but vassals can say that. As all kinds of sects are debased and debauched for such rewards and speculations. What do names prevent? In the name of religion, the greater the felony.

The clergy in every country have sought and held great privileges. Who would not be without analysis of that order, to reach honors and titles, and such emoluments. Analyze the whole, and you will soon perceive, even in one point, the dire iniquity. Only think of the blasphemy, the absurdity of remission of sins, by confessing priests!

Are these the advancers of arts and sciences, that now reduced to systems, contend faithfully against, and expose truthfully those abominable superstitions? The author of "Italy in 1846" states, that the public debts of the church of Rome have been accumulating a long while. The public instruction is in the hands of the priests; not less than 30,000 of her men of letters have been violently destroyed or driven out of Italy. That is her science.

The Roman church assumes to be catholic; that is a perfectly absurd presumption, as she cannot be till she is rational, and that absorbs her into universal religion. Hierarchies are nurtured in the blood and treasure of the world; they are dangerous pets.

In what do hierarchies differ essentially in purity, when all are anti-god, all apocryphal? They cannot be self-elected, which they are now, assuredly.

In what do paganism and popish worship differ? In names. What stupid assumption of cities and hierarchies over the substantial knowledge of the country.

I read recently of a painting, styled the Apotheosis of George Washington! The preservation of the memory of his illustrious deeds on this world, is worth all such stuff. Recently, it has been stated that the pope has just canonized two new saints—a jesuit missionary, who died 200 years ago, and a secular virgin, a shepherdess. The pope to assume this blasphemy! The pagans persecuted the christians, as one peculiar sect persecutes another. That is the history of the world. The force advanced by the sword of Constantine in behalf of christian faith, proves that it was corrupt enough to go upon that basis; and this was when it had not been established as the Latin or Roman church. So that it was corrupt, any way. All peculiar faith has the necessary elements of corruption, for it cannot depend on the elements of intrinsic merits.

I am of the opinion that Justinian's code, on the authority of Gibbon, has a law that had been previously decreed, that the christians should destroy all publications against their doctrine. Never let them hereafter say that they are the exclusive protectors of science, when they are its worst tyrants. Truthful argument is the only weapon that rationalists could ask against such publications. How often have peculiar faith-people brought opposition to new science—as geology—that clashed with their doctrines; but finding that ineffectual to arrest mind and science, its adoption is sought, as if upholding the scriptures. What a morale in the social world!

Church-advocates stretch their theories and science to extremes, in regard to all peculiar tenets of their bible.

Tycho Brahe was mistaken about the sun's revolution around the earth, to help support the bible of Joshua, and he may have been also mistaken about the extinction of a star in Cassiopeia, to sustain Isaiah, ch. xxxiv. v. 4.

The mighty hierarchies of Babylon, Egypt, Rome, the Druids, have fallen. Others are deeply shaken, as of Judaism, Christianity, Brahminism, Bhuddism, &c. They will all go by the board as the supremacy of mind is established.

The only durable hierarchy is that of mind.

No one should be slave of vows, habits, or priestocracies.

The tyranny of the Romish church is very apparent when she proclaims that marriage should be her institution, as ceremonies, masses for the rest of the soul!

What mighty nonsense has been perpetuated by the claims to transubstantiation, or change of substance!

Is it possible that imprisonment is legal in England for deciding, by rational discussion and writing, that Christ is an impostor—the worst of characters, who, or his priestocracy romancers, excited the most outrageous blasphemy and sectarianism, to disturb the world? Romanism gives purgatory a worthless residence, created by priestocracy for its profits, not for soul's benefit. What capacity in that pent-up condition can be shown for due improvement, one of the great objects of mind's creation?

There can be no infallibility, no catholicism, but of rational religion. What evils will not hierarchies create! We learn by newspaper, that at Rome " the houses of the English residents and others are being closely searched for bibles, not even excepting the British consul's."

The Romanists sell indulgences for a time, and swindle the poor ignorant people.

There should be no licenses for popularity and insidious designs. What has not been the tyranny of hierarchy?

The rights of mind have been proscribed in all variety of ways, even to the excommunication of books.

Hierarchies embrace circles of mind subservient to their machinations. Asia went for absolutism—anything but mind in her Oriental vassalage. She has reaped the bitterest fruits therefor.

Who, without true analysis, can have true ideas that the world is ignorant, mean, and pretending, when it can rise to a state of dignity in science, worth, and reality?

Hierarchies interchange and reciprocate all they can.

The protestants overran Ireland over the Romanists.

In the union of church and state, no greater affiliation can be secured than by induction of the highest officers of the last into those of the first. Constantine was baptized, and was in every respect identified.

The hierarchies confiscate property, excommunicate the owners. Shall hierarchies longer disgrace nations that tyrannize over sister republics, and cause exclusion of the only kind of free government?

An elected member of Parliament, because a Jew, cannot obtain his seat! Who is superior, the Christian or Jew?

Who can pretend that Baron Rothschild is not excluded from the full rights of a free Englishman?

What, like the purchase of absolution of sins, has contributed to a greater dissolution of popular morals?

All the expedients of art and vice have been gotten up, to perpetuate hierarchal power. But what is all such worth?

The world's attention is whiled away on these ingenious trifles. What are all the rich paintings of scriptures worth? Are they not, in one sense, talents devoted to humbugs? O, had all this been mind truly devoted to the triumphs of sacred philosophical science, how much better, had God's benefits been diffused over the world! Hierarchies had large property, of the people of course. When national, they show not only intolerance and ill-will, but cruelty.

In some hierarchies of the Roman order, no other preacher dare say a word in the pulpit, or have any voice in the government. What provincial tyrannies are endured, under some regimes! How degrading the passport!

The beauty of the earth is equitable institution of government and its equitable administration, otherwise the loveliest country is deformed and degraded, and God's blessings, mind's rights, are prostituted.

Some of the Romanists do not like to see protestants, as immigrants, bring their bibles with them. Is it possible, that those who become citizens have to be Romanists? What folly, what tyranny is more execrable? Is this in Cuba?

What a monstrosity, then, is the bible. What a weak lever for justice—what a potent one for demoralization and the worst of crimes.

We have to increase its power, for benefits, that mind alone performs, whose place it has usurped.

·Will you become the hypocrite defender of a peculiar faith bible? How can you be anything else, if you be republican? The triumphs of such a faith are those of bigotry, of tyranny.

What do her paintings avail the world? What has any hierarchy to do with the name of catholic, much less holy? If hierarchies be the depositories of science, they dwarf it as sadly as they dwarf Deity, by messiahship. How comes it that the pope did not vaunt triumph of the church over Napoleon, as he humbled the pope?

Was not the fall of Napoleon the effect of his blasphemy, against the power and vice-gerent of the Trinity?

We presume that it was more the result of unprincipled ambition. Constitutional governments cut out all feudal tenure, all laws to promote confiscation of property, and is always referable to a standard of sense, honesty, and nature, forever. For what can the world wish to sustain any such institution? Is it to uphold the errors of public opinion and vice—the errors and prejudices of peculiar education, that presents the errors of faith?

What parties of the world are to blame, more than these?

Church-power is one of the most dangerous to the world and mind, that it awfully perverts and circumvents.

The very elements of church hierarchy are rotten to the centre. This has been accomplished by delusion, sophistry, and much of it by brute force. What are the anathemas of popes, but the maledictions 'and curses of Christ-authority? Was that pure, holy. or just, that gave it? Are we to depend on the fallacy of Christ, for such evils? The evils are greater than any promise? As evils, they are to be universally discarded.

Church-dynasty is connected with all popular influences. Little did the pope think that, when his myrmidons were preaching crusades for conquests, that his successors would see the crusades of liberty against them.

Conquests have enslaved the world; the lust of dominion perverts it. What felonious dispensations have been granted, from the head of churches, for the most nefarious purposes—for piracy and conquest.

Conquests and piracy are indebted to this thing, peculiar faith. Some people think the pope is a direct vicegerent with God; and that their souls will have to pass through the priest's hands. What an influence to preside at birth, marriage, and death, all the best intermediate time. What less than infatuation can take place? Where is glorious mind, all this time? The acts of the pope have been against the light of civil liberty of his own citizens. There are associations of people, in the world of hierarchies, as others, the honor of human nature; among the first are the sisters of charity. Protestants refer to the church of Rome, their own mother, as the whore of Babylon! What must the progeny be, but illegitimate, of course?

The gorgeous splendor of temples, as that at Ephesus, of Diana, "whom all Asia worshipped," proves the influence of peculiar faith, and its pernicious consequences. Christianity has not spoken peace to earth, nor taught a law practically of universal love. "A funeral service will be celebrated in Chantilly, on Monday, for the repose of the late king Louis Philippe." The records will condemn enough.

What shall we say of the tyranny and farce of the church in trials of members? The world, in its freest part, America, is yet a slave to all such power, a thing most easily proved to a proper conclusion. The errors of judgment result by the fault of peculiar education, as in England and all countries subject to a peculiar state of national affairs, not the crime of intention.

What does the mass of any people know without the light of cultivated mind? They are perfect animals the way they conduct themselves—mere animal machinery, under the worst and most corrupt influences of dynastic psychology. Inquisitions, social proscriptions are to prevent liberal discussions, truthful expressions of religion!

What a potent hierarchy was that at Rome, when magistrates were priests, that adopted six hundred different kinds of peculiar faith.

No wonder that hierarchies and their ministers tell the world to hush up in silence about the inconsistency of bibles and peculiar faiths.

The exorcism practised by the Roman church proves how the scriptures is interpreted about Christ's expelling devils. It made a considerable part of its superstition. The greatest split of the christian church was into the Greek and Latin, with insuperable hatred. Then came the Roman and Protestant grand divisions. All sectarianism, and having its essential elements. The original split of Arianism and the orthodox was characterized with the bitterest animosity, and all this history conclusively proves that the ingredients of love to neighbors is not entertained, much less of that to enemies.

And is religion never to rise in hierarchies above the base grovelling superstition that seeks to avail itself by traffic on the rights of insulted and perverted mind? Praying to this woman, Mary! They might as well pray to Venus. O, says the Protestant, the Roman faith is a perversion! Yes, and he contributes to the very fountain sources, that condemn him as badly. What sort of a bible and faith are those that can be personated so long, and with impunity not only, but great temporal honors? The imposition is not only tolerated by honest minds, but honored and rewarded. Is it not time for the world to open its eyes, and give intellectual justice its due?

What but the spirit of sycophancy of the world upholds the pope, who excommunicated whom he anathematized, and executed both by his degraded inquisitions? ruled kings as subjects, and subjects as vassals, the vilest. How was the pope made, but by that usurpation that upholds despots? Was he not created by the kings of France, one of whom, Charles, was made in return, emperor? Charles decreed "That his holiness, being God's vicar, could not be subject to the judgment of man." This, above all, caused Charles to be made emperor. A mutual smuggling of despotism on the world, that has cost France and Italy millions of lives! Where is the end?

Can high-minded republicans tolerate all this? Can they be fooled yet centuries more, by the senseless and stupid assertion that they ought to avoid all books but the bible, the very thing that has degraded the world? As bad as the papacy is, still it claims its whole authority from this very book. Christ is the authority. They have the worship of saints and angels. In what do the papists differ from the Pagans? In more adroitness of policy! Peculiar faith has been made available as practicable, by ambition and avarice. It has made itself all things to all men, in all countries. When Rome could not rule the world by tyranny, she has fooled a large part of it by sophistry. But for this, France would have been less bloody in her first assertion of freedom, and less hostile to free institutions of others in her last. Has not the ambition of the hierarchy prompted it to expect nearly all power to pass through its folds? Anything that partakes of sectarianism, partakes of the elements of destruction, and well is it that many things are disconnected therewith.

The church even in this union, disjunct as it is, reflected back by social relations and moneyed influence, has a powerful hold on the world, by all the aid of superstition and sophistry. What are its influences from its peculiar union with state in Europe? The people have been bullied by the union of church and state in regard to expression of views, and dared not write, speak or discuss church matters that were thus rendered more sacred than truth or first principles, those in power assuming for the shadow what belonged to the substance.

We shall never be done with the tyranny and despotism of hierarchies, till we get rid of the hierarchies. What are the sovereign people of the world waiting for? Are they not yet satisfied of the absurdity of the whole category? This country is now receiving the Portuguese exiles, emigrants, on account of alleged religious persecutions. Religion never persecuted. There was but little to be gained by the humble followers of Christ? What dynasty has been more powerful than that of the priestocracy? Can any one appreciate the benefit of clergy? How many centuries ago has it been in England that any man that was "clericus," who could read, but had the benefit of clergy, and thus escaped the penalty of death, that others who could not read, found guilty of similar offence, suffered? There was no greater forgery or usurpation, than the ecclesiastical power. The world can scarcely believe the false pretences of the priestocracy. There are forgeries everywhere, not only for the peculiar faith, the messiah, but of the authority for the pontifical throne by the pretended donation of Constantine to Sylvester. Perjury then is the whole of all peculiar faiths. What is the history of some of the popes, but the most revolting indignities on human nature? These are some of the chief sources of upholding this iniquity. As bad as the popes were in the crusades, they were worse in civil society. No doubt the ecclesiastical phalanx laughed at the chivalry of the world, as the Asiatics at the western missionaries of the present day, who came to teach them what their forefathers knew many centuries before, and with whom the doctrine emanated. Both have analogous faith, but misguided faith. The most horrible machinery, is the papal fixtures. The very resurrection of science broke the powers of the church-despotism, especially of Rome, than which none is more tyrannical, none more detestable. Some think more of their pope than God. Of the world in mass, many aid and abet the spiritual imposition. What impiety is there in transubstantiation? What speculation and trade in purgatory? Did the Christian church trade in indulgences of vices and crimes? Then can the world trust it in any honorable sense? She that dishonored the world, has forfeited the liberty of access to the company of the virtuous. She vitiated the world, and corrupted mankind! Where is mind? asleep? "The Church of England, through their bishops and clergy, seconded by journals, are calling for penal enactments to extinguish •new titles assumed by the Roman hierarchy."—*Washington Republic.*

To meet all the abuses of peculiar faiths, the world needs the thorough organization of Monotheism. What must be the state of doctrines in the hierarchy, when the ordination of the priestocracy is a forgery on religion, and the basest imposition on morals, the world? It does not touch the subject of religion. They have not touched it at all, and never will. All is a false mantle. Pope, where are you, in the position of mind? Insignificant! You are representative of peculiar faith, that precludes religion! Will you, who have' been educated, it is true, by peculiar education stand by and see your God libeled and religion supplanted by peculiar faith? Look at the excitement and commotion in England about the hierarchies, Roman and.English.

See the pope and the English peculiar faith attempt to dwarf God and man, the universe and the world, feelings and principles, to one idea peculiar! What effrontery is in clerical pretensions, that are antagonistical to the sacredness of obligations to country under the constitution. When was it that clerical and priestocracy's assumptions have not prevailed? Are they not as old as the oldest despotisms, of which they are part and parcel? The people's wrong is seen and felt under the odious fanaticism of Moses, whose slaughter of Korah and friends, the advocates of liberty, damn the whole as the basest degradation!

The history of hierarchies proves that they are after political capital and machinery What are the Roman and English hierarchies now doing in Great Britain? In the most ardent competition for religion? Very clear of it surely. What pollution. Let' the English and Roman churches contend, as these hierarchies are endowed with many privileges. What peculiar faith agitation is there between the Roman and English, the Swiss Protestant and Roman churches. See the massacre of Christians recently in Turkey, by the Mahommedans. Peculiar faith has one universal sin, universal agitation.

Whither can we turn but the disaffection of hierarchies and peculiar faith is world diffused? Suppose the Methodist church had been united to the government, what sort of split union, north and south, by this time should we have had? The world ought to look at all these hostile feelings engendered, and boding no good at all. The hierarchies cannot keep themselves in order, how, then, can they ask to regulate the world? Their incapacity is wofully plain.

The church of Rome saw its head expelled; of course it was indebted to perverted, degraded mind for reinstation. By this time the intelligent and honest ought to be ashamed of all this miserable complot against the noblest rights of the world.

The potency of rational mind is to rule the world, when the last becomes elevated to its proper dignity by rational education. All depends on the whole sovereign people.

Time has been when the hierarchies would have burnt authors at the stake for writing these sentiments. Is that the reason that the clergy have such an ascendancy over the people's minds? That is the deadly spirit hostile to true religion, and that destroyed all reformation as far as practicable. England is now in a ferment about peculiar faith, that is, about peculiar power. Is not the world always agitated by it? There are riots in England about the two hierarchies of a most serious character, as the mobs drove out the legal authorities.

The whole frame-work of society of the world has to be remodeled by rational religion, the only means practicable. We see the effect of two hierarchies clashing in England, on a subject the most sublimely lovely and attractive for the whole world, but, taking the wrong view, they are antagonistic and driving to riots, and the magistracy and the police before it. This is on a small scale. What would it be now before the whole world, if coequal with the world's theatre? What a horrid conflict of mankind it would be. Are we never to have an end of all this disgrace to mind, what was conceived in fraud, and continued in infamy?

The hierarchy is the mongrel of ambition, peculiar speculation. But they have sustained science, and aided in the arts. Christianity has laid the world under a debt of gratitude, to its best promotion of science? Did Christianity build the pyramids of Egypt? Those and the embalming of the dead were doubtlessly in the hands of the Egyptian curators of science, who represented the imperial and ecclesiastical faculty. The people were nothing then, as now, being vulgar before the pretenders. But better had the world never heard of them, than to be reared at the expense of mind's most valued qualities. Hierarchy has reared a St. Peter's church, and its prototype of polytheism in ancient Rome had reared many fine buildings to the objects of its idolatry and superstition, enacted by collusions.

It is questionable whether ancient polytheists did not exceed the modern, in the magnificence of their temples, but all the gewgaws of peculiar faith hierarchy are nothing before rational mind's duties.

The peculiar faith of the priestocracy and hierarchy robs the people of their Godgift, religion, and substitutes the vilest pretension in its stead. The various expedients of sophistry use with a horrid vengeance the proffered bribes. Thus the world is cheated, fooled, swindled out of its best life-rights. It will be the fairest for all to say, as I do with pleasure, my mind is indebted for preceding light of mind. I go for no peculiar faith or church, messiah, saint, or hierarchy, or any of its pretensions, robbed of rational mind, but for my country, mind, world, and God the creator, who must be exclusively adored in the sublimity of his unapproachable unity, that stands out in the boldest relief, rebuking all man's devices into utter insignificance. All hierarchies, as their peculiar faiths, are a curse.

Let there be any clique in power, church-hypocrites or hierarchies, and there will be despotism proportionately to the licentiousness yielded by the people. It is the people that are blockheads to permit any indulgence to any mortals. Church-people of any name are degraded impostors, if you permit them.

Rational mind is the only thing that keeps them at bay. See the fuss 'about Chargé Barton at Chili, made by the Romanist archbishop, who claimed peculiar privileges. Barton was not of that church. No, it is not the peculiar faith, if it were not for the peculiar power. A bigot never learns religion, nor ever forgets peculiar faith.

Rational mind must speedily get rid of all the world nuisances. Have not the hierarchies claimed and assumed every thing that sophistry and speculation could assert, the very days of the year? What are all worth to the birth-day of a Washington, or the natal day of a nation's liberty?

CHURCH POWER PERVERTED: OPPRESSION AND CORRUPTION,

THAT I have been writing about all the time, when I mention churches, that were instituted in fraud and corruption.

In the reign of Charles II. eight thousand non-conformists died in prison. Sixty thousand suffered to the revolution. What corruption is that, when non-residence enabled clergymen to receive emoluments, without ever visiting their parishioners.

"An Irish bishop, the late bishop of Limerick, Ireland, lived abroad for the last seven years,—received nearly three hundred and fifty thousand dollars for doing none of his duties as a bishop ; and died at last, leaving his cathedral windows unglazed."—*Southern Christian Advocate.*

Did ever the Spanish inquisition luxuriate in the barbarity of a figure of the Virgin Mary, that when criminals embraced it cut them into fragments ?

"The anabaptists of Germany followed the patriarchs in polygamy, sought to be mere radicals in society, excited wars in which perished one hundred thousand by the sword. They had visions, revelations, and predictions, divine impulses, and power of working miracles."

These miscreants had as just pretensions thereto as any mortals.

Do eleven bishops receive nine millions of dollars in Ireland ? When millions of their countrymen are in beggary ? Can rich men do as much wrong as poor men ?

The controversies about predestination, Roman assumption, and Protestant bigotry, have caused reckless bloodshed.

The most horrid and bloody statutes against heresy, as it was called, have been devised to put down rational discussion and religion. All these were of absolutism.

What is worse to individuals, as estimated by vassal minds, than to go forward with conservative revolution, with which clash all the old felonious dynasties of usurpation? The world has to obviate much in kith and clan intrigue. The kith may be bad enough without the clan.

The church is an enormous cloak for vices, crimes, and misdemeanors. Organization of society should be such that no order should have too much incident power. When society is predicated on general principles, that is protection enough. Peculiar organizations are invasive, more of less, on public rights, when the abuse of sectionalism prevails as it is seen all over the world, under its present organization.

Church societies speak for evil, even in opposition to important laws of the land. Start a new conservative revolution on principles, and how does the usurpation monopoly party meet it ? By the most vulgar meanness. They will lie, affirm anything but truth to impede its progress ; even affirmation of derangement of mind.

Infidels, say the usurper and monopolist. Deists, say the priestocracy. Consign them all to perdition, says the bigot. Kill them, says the fanatic. Don't talk of them, say the vassal. Don't read their books, say most. Are they not atheists or heathen, say the superstitious? They are not orthodox, says the churchman. Excommunicate them, says peculiar faith, that poisons the morals and peace of the world. Peculiar faith has invoked the strongest armies. How many millions to-day would perjure themselves for it? The whole moral feeling of the world is outraged by it. There is no limit to its perversion, only by the limit that mind legitimately gives.

The Romanists appropriated nearly all the days of the year to their pretended saints. What stuff! They appropriated all mind's rights. The world must know the extent of usurpation and monopoly. It must get rid of all its organic evils, resulting from the organic perversions of mind. All this proves that hierarchies catch at straws. Some affect to be squeamish about the least things, as the social accomplishments of dancing, that graces society with all the engagements of civilization. Church bigots will do this, and set the world on inquisition-fire? Religion and peculiar faith. What a difference, no matter the form of the last—Christianity, Mormonism, Mahommedanism, or Judaism. The first exalts mind to its noblest capacity, the last degrades it to the extent of peculiar views, involves all bad faith, and ruins as far as depends on itself. Bigotry is brainless, as it is mindless.

A vain, unprincipled, avaricious ambition will carry absolutism of autocrats and priestocracy to the greatest enslavement of mind, in the most sacred rights.

When a party, as the pope, is smuggled into power, he will forego no unprincipled means to sustain that smuggling. Who of peculiar faith is exempt from the false pretences and crimes of that smuggling.

The Romanists and Episcopalians are quarrelling in England yet for supremacy after hundreds of years of bloody difficulties, and think it nothing to agitate the world with their senseless nuisance. If they were small petty pirates they would be put down. Where is the moral and intellectual power of the world people? Is it still dreaming in this land of visions? Do you feel interested in keeping the world improving, then keep out of war. Had the hierarchy of Rome been possessed of religion, it had no war with the Mahommedans to advance any church matters. There is an idea for you. The world to fight for peculiar faith, and call it religion!

Only think of Trinity Church in New-York city, with her millions of property, a perfect nonentity of faith, causing exclusion of religion to that extent. What a monstrosity, in language, before the tribunal of rational mind! Well may many people be impoverished, pauperized by such solecisms.

What church quarrels and squabbles, and yet the church pledges are to renounce the world, the flesh and the devil. Now, if they were to renounce, as a primary matter, all sectarianism, that of itself would be a most valuable and efficient principle. That of itself would negative all churches, and cause the next revolution to renounce the bible.

As the church pledge stands, is it less than perjury? The bible stands between rational mind and its creator, assuredly. I am altogether for the God of the universe; but the bible—Christ says he that is not for me is against me. Then he puts himself out of God's category, particularly as the perfect God of the universe cannot possibly need or require a Christ, as his almighty functions will not begin to permit such a mighty sacrilege for a moment; therefore this of course is the peculiar christ, who belongs to the peculiar god of the peculiar people, and none other positively and conclusively. Now, the priestocracy enact this perjury, and cause the compliant world to enact it. What an iniquity! The world was not aware of what it was doing, much less how degraded the priestocracy to have it perpetrated. All this is the rickety, crazy priestocracy patchwork. But, say the church-people, I must belong to the church. That is only an association, a device of men. It has no new principles no more than secret societies ; all are sectarianisms, and therefore cannot be honorably endorsed as they are self-undermined. As the renouncing the bible is that bigot the devil, the rational world will have the purest protection. Any kind of bibles can be made correspondent to peculiar faiths ; hence renounce all of these, and cleave to the sacred religion of God. This leaves no remorse, or self-reproach at the dying hour, when rational mind can be only sustained by monotheism or rational religion.

But join the church, and we are under the full protection. What good does that do, when it cannot prove its own position or protect itself?

The church is then an arrant impostor. In what respect is the church then a protection for public morals? Were it not for the church or their profession, the priestocracy would be intolerable. That is the very reason they are so.

THE AUTHENTICITY OF ANY SCRIPTURES.

· THIS is the most essential of all positions of any bible, that if properly sustained by truth, may be the most elevated means of faith, or if rejected, may be the veriest degradation of contempt.

If God had written any book-bible, he would have told the world plainly and unmistakably all about it, as he has done in his volumes of the universe, his only book. But as that is amply sufficient, all else is unnecessary and objectionable.

Man's bibles of tradition have left most to conjecture and imposture, doubt and evasion of mystery, where all should have been clearly defined for mind that is rational, that above all others rejects them.   We must take nothing for granted, no matter how imposing by especial names, as the more extraordinary the assertion, the more expedient, the more extraordinary the proof.

Any one question touching the authority of the scriptures, rests on the whole proof of the authenticity, whether you understand them or not, whether you affect mysteries or not, you have to come to this point, and shall not evade the main question of their exposure.

The whole history of all bibles of tradition, is more or less analogous.   For a vast duration of years or time, the suns of creation had given light and heat to their solar systems, the mighty principles of the universe had been conservative for their permanent functions, when a little tumult arose in one of the lesser planets of one of these mighty solar systems, where man's blasphemy by mind's perversion, seeking fatal ambition, sought to assail God's attributes, producing interminable differences about creeds, and false bibles of peculiar faith that then were fabricated.

Blasphemy makes nothing better than ambition fatal.   The preachers and priests, the hierarchists, seek to explain the difficulties, but they mystify the whole subject more.   Before they preach any more, they should not only prove their commission is divine, not of self, but their authority, and not from sophistry, but such proof as will suit the most fastidious court of conscience, and the conscience of the most equitable court of justice.   But if this tumult comes from the priests, preachers and hierarchists, to disturb our earth with their base tricks and intrigues of priestocracy, what can be worse for them ?   They preach the patriarchal and mediatorial dispensations, the first characterized by mere offer of blood on the altars, practiced by the priests of Judaism, as a prototype.   What was that but the idolatrous victimizing of a pastoral people, just emerging from the second humble state of society, one remove from the hunter state ? All this was the work of priests, who claimed a corrupt machinery of prophets with their miracles and mysteries.   The result was another kind of peculiar faith added to the long list of worthless priest deceptions, with the falsest pretences of a peculiar bible, making a god who owned only one four-cornered and flat, this earth that had all the rest of creation to light it, and his heavens besides, so peculiar that he is used by the priestocracy on all necessary occasions.

The last dispensation, as peculiarly absurd as the first, indicates an offering, the lowest state of superstition, the remission of sins by the effusion of Christ's blood. Will the effusion of Christ's or man's blood shed for his blasphemy and imposition in the days that knew no toleration of faith opinions, be more effectual ?

But then there is his triumphant resurrection !

So far from its being proved, it is not satisfactorily established that his body was in the tomb on the second day, or that it was identified as Christ's or any other.   If his resurrection was like all mortals, no more or less, it was not equal by this fable. as the soul is freed from the body by death that purifies it for other existence.   It is then alien to all earthly things, but of this, these sapient priestocracies knew nothing.   So far from remaining three days, it could not remain three seconds, for its last breath signs its passport for other states of being not cognizable to mortal vision.

All the dispensations of peculiar faith, by incarnations of Bhudd or Christ ; all those of superstition, by sacrifice of blood, through the miserable subtleties of priestocracies, the world over, are obsolete ; as mind, acting on mind, has exploded all such, adopted the entire unity of the God of the universe, meets what will suit the present, discards the errors of the past, and improves for the future ; pre-eminently meeting all just points, by sweeping away the rubbish of the ancients, and vindicating the comprehension of enlightened mind.

The world will thus best see that all rational beings must have religion, but not superstition, certainly not blasphemy.

The teachers of the scriptures think that good souls stay till judgment in a place appropriate, and then depart to their heaven, while they place the bad souls in appropriate punishment, and then in hell.

Then can there be any final judgment, if the universe is inexhaustible and indestructible, as philosophy seems best to teach? What knew the ancient mythologists, only mythologists, the best of any faith, in their utter ignorance of a universe that preeminently displays God's unbounded creative and preservative power and attributes?

Can you burn the earth or dissolve it, to nonentity and annihilation? As you cannot, by all the principles of philosophy, beyond which your finite mind cannot pretend to travel, extinguish this globe, much less place it beyond its sphere of action and functions, that ever protect it, otherwise you then encroach on other spaces, spheres, and appropriate functions—of course, then, this universe, of which this earth is part essential, has its eternal conservative, not destructive principles; the elements of its destruction being counteracted by those of conservation.

To suppose universal destruction, supposes blasphemy, in libel of God's imbecility. God's universe goes elsewhere, to others, if possible, when his character is imperfect and lost. What absurdity, and how idle, to cause fear among the credulous weakminded, in regard to destruction of individual worlds. Look again, astronomers, and correct your reckonings, ere you assert the destruction of worlds. No doubt, the spheres are there, that impiety, to protect false bibles, removed, but you cannot see them till you know their orbits and their revolutions.

None but God knows or manages the preservation of all creation. It is his glory and feeling to manage it universally to the best, and that forever.

How insignificantly low are those who affected to know all about God, yet only know a little of the four corners of this spheroid, which was with these sapient characters the most of creation, after their heavens? Mind had to know the principle and the extent of creation in the universe, before assuming to be able to decide on covenants, dispensations, circumcisions, and messiahships. Silence, most foolish priestocracy, and assume no more before the world that you are wise.

But you think it ungodly to impeach the bibles of tradition. You do not understand the subject, as proof will disclose the reverse.

We know, not think it ungodly, to impeach God's bible. Which is that? The volumes of creation, of the universe. If that stand, as it must and will forever, it is ungodly to license those of peculiar faith; that libels God's most outrageously, and mind continually. The pulpit priestocracy affect that we cannot ever reach the idea of God without their peculiar bibles. Their peculiar bibles only give their peculiar gods, not the universal God of nature, and that nature alone points to. The hand of freedom has never touched this paramount subject.

All the solar systems have harmony for themselves, and adaptation for the universe, all in abeyance to the Almighty Ruler.

The question of peculiar bible pretension to authenticity, does not admit of proof that can be only more or less ingeniously, not more truthfully handled. If a bank-note is presented us, we would require proof of its authenticity, before its currency could be established. Have we any documents to prove, that there have been no material alterations and add t ons to the Scriptures? Let us have this paramount question of religion settled. i i

Give the bible advocates all that belongs to them. Are all the prophecies above suspicion for purity of authority prior to, and during all time to the present? Are any of the books of the bible cotemporary with their record of events? It is well known, that of the gospels do not begin to be. The solution is answered in Constantine.

What was the Council of Nice for? All to smuggle bible felony on a too confiding world.

No event, no incident of the bible, but mere matters of history that are history only, can be reasoned on as fact, till proved as fact, which has not been done, since the authenticity of the Scriptures is now asked for most sincerely.

Are there not bribed writers to a large number, under government of church and state? Is not that a corrupt influence that results from promises, or extorted by threats and proscriptive monopoly?

Europe and Asia, have enough of them.

The very first covenant was sectarianism, that kills all peculiar bibles at the bare mention. How could God be the author of self-antagonism?

The priestocracy made all sectarianism, that is incompatible with all the necessary dignity in action on principle. None but the exclusive unity of God, excludes incompatibles.

The accompanying proof of the whole book, disproves its biblical character for truth and honesty.

The discrepances of the bibles in peculiar faith, prove them men's works for man's pretences. The authenticity of such scriptures is asserted, not proved. It cannot be satisfactorily proved. The world must know this. It requires sophistry, special pleading, to establish the second covenant on the first, or both on truth. While the peculiar Jewish dispensation was being enacted for twenty-five centuries as claimed, what became of the excess of the world not in the pretended pale? Did the God of the universe and universal justice permit this injustice, that the vast majority of the world for twenty-five centuries should be excluded the light of his countenance and protection, for the sake of a most contemptible clique of fanatics and a contemptible peculiar faith, that ruined its followers and enslaved its advocates? The last in point of numbers sinks below insignificance with the first vast amount, as bad as peculiar faith sinks below rational religion.

Whence could we obtain pure records of the authenticity of any bible of tradition? From the sworn adherents of false pretences, perjury? Was it at the city of Jerusalem with the high priesthood, that was bought by the highest bidder, of Antiochus Epiphanes? As to the world's peculiar revelation, what else have we than that of peculiar faith, which possibly can be of any national or world interest, when the very elements or commencement of all, at once destroy all pretensions to the truth and correct religion of God, who has vouchsafed the only one by his creation-records.

The best preacher may preach all his lifetime on the authenticity of all peculiar traditional bibles or scriptures, and he will be no nearer the proof than when he commenced. His whole lifetime will be thrown away, on the basest soul-prostitution.

The Scripture oracles had more sophistry than the Pagan! Those of Daniel have puzzled all the learned sophists, and made them greater sophists.

You give me an introduction to the bible, as the word of God. As an honest man you cannot wish to palm this on me, therefore, prove it. You cannot do it, and as a just, good, and true citizen, you are bound to discard all such stuff forever.

Judaism was a polity of union of church and state, enough to induce all zealous cooperators to advance for its support. Its prophets lie, one after another, and thus endorse each other. Let us examine Charles Buck's testimony as to the purity of the scriptures, on the article "Septuagint Chronology, the chronology which is formed from the dates and periods of time mentioned in the Septuagint translation of the Old Testament. It reckons fifteen hundred years more from the creation to Abraham than the Hebrew bible. Dr. Kennicott, in the dissertation prefixed to his Hebrew bible, has shown it to be very probable that the chronology of the Hebrew scriptures, since the period just mentioned, was corrupted by the Jews between the years 175 and 200; and that the chronology of the Septuagint is more agreeable to truth. It is a fact, that during the second and third centuries, the Hebrew scriptures were almost entirely in the hands of the Jews, while the Septuagint was confined to the Christians. The following is the reason which is given by oriental writers; it being a very ancient tradition that messiah was to come in the sixth chiliad, because he was to come in the last days, (founded on a mystical application of the six days' creation,) the contrivance was to shorten the age of the world from about 5500 to 3760; and thence to prove that Jesus could not be the messiah. Dr. Kennicott adds, that some Hebrew copies, having the larger chronology, were extant till the time of Eusebius, and some till the year 700." Again, in the article II. Bible, history of—" Prideaux is of opinion that Ezra made additions in several parts of the bible, where any thing appeared necessary for illustrating, connecting or completing the work." But others must have done something besides, as " Malachi, for instance, could not be put in the bible by him, since that prophet is allowed to have lived after Ezra; nor could Nehemiah be there, since that book mentions (chap. xii. v. 22) Jaddua as high priest, and Darius Codomanus as king of Persia, who were at least a hundred years later than Ezra." " The Jews, at first, were very reserved in communicating their scriptures to strangers; despising and shunning the gentiles, they would not disclose to them any of the treasures concealed in the bible. We may add, that the people bordering on the Jews, as the Egyptians, Phœnicians, Arabs, &c., were not very curious to know the laws or history of the people, whom, in their turn, they hated and despised. Their first acquaintance with these books was not till after the several captivities of the Jews, when the singularity of the Hebrew laws and ceremonies induced several to desire a more particular knowledge of them. Josephus seems surprised to find such slight footsteps of the scripture history interspersed in the Egyptian, Chaldean, Phœnician and Grecian history, and accounts for it hence; that the sacred books were not as yet translated into Greek, or other languages, and consequently not known to the writers of those nations. The first version of the bible was that of the Septuagint into Greek, by order of that patron of literature, Ptolemy Philadelphus, though some maintain that the whole was not then

translated, but only the pentateuch; between which, and the other books in the Septuagint version, the critics find a great diversity in point of style and expression, as well as
accuracy." Here is a curious episode upon the bible : "IV. Bible. rejected books of.
—The apocryphal books of the Old Testament, according to the Romanists, are the
books," &c. " The apocryphal books of the New Testament are (among others)
several spurious gospels," &c. Under the article of Priest—" This divine appointment (priesthood) was observed with considerable accuracy till the Jews fell under the
dominion of the Romans, and had their faith corrupted by a false philosophy. Then,
indeed, the high-priesthood was sometimes set up to sale, and, instead of continuing for
life, as it ought to have done, it seems, from some passages in the New Testament, to
have been nothing more than an annual office."
    Buck says " the Hebrew copy of the bible, which we Christians, for good reasons,
consider as the most authentic, dates the creation of the world 3,944 years before the
Christian era. The Samaritan bible, again fixes the era of the creation 4,305 years
before the birth of Christ. And the Greek translation, known by the name of the septuagint version of the bible, gives 5,270, as the number of the years which intervened
between these two periods," &c. When we deny the authenticity of the scriptures,
we deny man's assertions and advocacy, whilst we desire to hear all of God's, that has
not been revealed.
    So peculiar was the God of Israel, that they preferred images to him! Why was
he called emphatically the God of Israel, if he was not their peculiar God?
    The bible at the bottom of the priestocracy machinery, has no sincerity, but was
made to swindle the people, most clearly so. Moses was the chief of swindlers, and
so are all the world peculiar faith priestocracy. They are the most base, claiming to
govern the people by pious frauds, as if frauds were not felonious, coming from the
priestocracy. The bible brings about the inquisitions, as part of government.
    None can support the bible of peculiar faith, on any just or conservative principle.
Such bible has no principle; it is unprincipled. What must be its advocates? God
repented that he had made man : he then had no fore-knowledge? What a libel. The
people of America and the world, ought to make the preachers prove that the bible is
the word of God, else stop and silence them as circulators of false, base and ignoble
coin, for which they should be held responsible to the highest laws, justice of mind, in
the deepest penalties. They are the alloy-mongers, the hoary sinners of mankind.
Bible, is it, the world needs? Anything else than peculiar faith bibles. But we truly
need a bible to protect us from the invasion of all peculiar faith bibles that outrage all
that is decent in mind, and influence its worst animal passions. Under the pretended
protection of any peculiar faith bible, you are under the peculiar organization of its
clergy, its priestocracy, and out of the pale as far as that can make it, of the conservative principles of God. You ask for protection. You can get none more uniform than
principles, that bespeak all that can be insured of God, the most potential. No peculiar
bibles, and they of tradition are all in this category by their author's defined position
and admission, can stand before rational mind. What a libel on God, when the bible
affirms that sin penetrated to his holy centre. That implies that God is not perfect,
but as the Jews and Jew Christians were only acquainted by their confession with their
very peculiar faith god, who of course is imperfect, they are estopped from any just
claims on him of the universe. As they have drawn the distinction, let them positively
abide their own lines of demarcation. Is a lie any less because it is in a book called
the bible, the assumed holy word of God? Is the infamous swindling of the priestocracy any less because their blasphemy has brought it about?
    The bible, as interpreted by peculiar faith advocates, caused expeditions of crusades
against the holders of the soil of citizens not initiated into bible mysteries, but shaming
the bible-butchers by the highest of all faiths, their best attainable belief of the great spirit.
The world could never have had toleration from bible bigots, if mind had not become
rational and intervened. Can any intelligent freeman, American, stop half-way in the
mighty problem of mind, that his illustrious forefathers of '76 solved to attainment of
the real free platform of independent freedom of action in the noblest solution? Shall
he act as tory for all this peculiar bible system, whether Druid or Pagan, Christian,
Jew or Mahometan, was to govern the sovereign people blindly with the vilest of all
machinery.
    Take all your peculiar bibles, that prove not only the worst of ignorance, but the
most reckless bigotry respecting mind, God, the principles of the universe. Are these
the petty trifles, most noxious, to teach mind what their authors did not know themselves? Are the moderns so stupid as to put such dangerous poisons into the hands of
ingenuous youth? Of all sophistries, that of the priestocracy is the worst, because their
ignorance of science and philosophy, God-given aids to rational mind, is the most stupid-

The bible makes its god successfully rivalled by the spirit of evil in seduction of mankind, and then makes the priestocracy not only the privy councillor, but the predominant spirit in that council.

If ever there could be more infatuation in fanatical stupidity and blasphemy, it is in the blind idolatry of the moderns in adopting and sustaining all, after mind-light is on the world-horizon. Well, I make war upon the bible. But do I go for religion? That is a different thing; the bible and its priestocracy are in collusion against that.

Constantine and the priestocracy, a potent imperial power, were in collusion to sustain the bible, a detestable world-crime. The priestocracy used sophistry,—impious, blasphemous sophistry. Constantine employed brute force, or all its malign influence. See the result of the council of Nice. Arius was banished. That was no display of armed potency? Thus absolutism of despots and priestocracies have despoiled mind, crushed and ruined it. Leave all the juggling Constantines, and ignoble toady clan of priestocracy. It is not bibles of tradition, but light of mind most rational, that you need, prove yourself worthy of it. The old plan, ancient toryism, of looking to names is most dangerous. What is there in the name of bible that is efficient? One conservative principle of God is worth all the word of peculiar bibles, that of Christ's, who, as well as followers, are disorganizers of the world stamp. All that the bible says and does represents the priestocracy saying. doing, and acting. The disciples, rather their puppet ministers the priestocracy, had no qualification to prove their bibles the word of God. I give credit for good intentions of millions; but when priestocracy's bibles are advanced or called the word of God, then a libel is declared. Positively if the whole world were to speak on the present position of bibles, all would would avail nothing. God has so fixed it that he is self-proved as created, and all that puny man can do is nothing to the contrary. . But you affect to think that I would not believe though one rose from the dead.

I believe the only credible witness, the whole universe, the result of causation, in the conservative principles of cause and effect, and that bespeaks a Supreme Majesty in unspeakable sublimity, for they rule out all messiahs and their pretended witnesses. This is the nature of God's evidence. Now, what is the nature of man's? He asks credence in his bibles. Who makes them? The printer, man. Who wrote them? Of course, man. What did he write them for? For truth? All the universe rebukes that, as a false pretence. Then he wrote them for bad purposes. Did God ask man to do this? No, in truth. God had no need of them, as his are eternal in the universe, that requires no translation. God requires no aid of bad men.

There is no fulcrum for all the adherents in peculiar bibles. All are heresies to God, palmed on the people. The poor old bibles of peculiar faith cannot define who God of the universe is, whom they defame and libel from first to last. The old bible gives no honorable code to the world, but debases mind and outrages its rights.

Who had the handling of the bibles? The priestocracy.

That is enough. The first devised, the subsequent endorse; all false. Moses' books were lost, and others were found, and of course fabricated. How many thousand editions of peculiar faith, all analogous, have been published to the world? That subject was handled for many ages by the priestocracy. Various dispensations were needed to the after-thoughts of mankind, and various book editions were expedient. The priestocracy, that could commence the holy fictions, could do the balance. But the bible is the subject. That is only a book—if superior, it should be proved, or the assertors are impostors. It impeaches itself, as a decided imposture, and all its advocates are necessarily in that category, whether ignorantly or wilfully, their persistence will prove. All peculiar bible advocates are impeached, when their bible cannot defeat its own impeachment. Their bible does not apply in morals, but violates, with the deepest crimes and misdemeanors, a murderous policy, the highest interests of the whole world. Its petty details cannot be received, as only the comprehensive bearing of all questions in the universe, world-wide, and truth sustained, can be entertained. As free and intelligent Americans, invite all that are stupid enough, in peculiar faith, to affect that is the way, to prove in the pulpit the authenticity, and to retire, as they will have to do, on incompetency to prove it, on its inherent incapacity. The game of absolutism is the deepest on earth, for perversion and peculiar privileges, usurpation and monopoly, that excite the deepest perjury—the most iniquitous felony, the basest blasphemy. Nothing is too sacred for its vulgar pretences. Bibles are its cards, and priestocracies are its gamblers.

Well could Milton, an adherent of such, write of paradise lost. A universe regained was beyond the vision of these mongers, as the noblest triumph of mind yet to be celebrated. How these priestocracies play into each other's hands. If the bibles of any peculiar faith be assumed to be God's, they are blasphemously false, as the universe presents his exhaustless volumes, that cannot be supplanted by man's words or books. If they affect to be those of mind, they are ignominiously and wickedly false, as they supersede mind's function, reason, for fictitious faith. Do you, peculiar faith infidel, unfaithfully deny the bible of your God Creator, for the peculiar bible of any peculiar set of liars, false teachers, world-impostors, known and proved, conclusively demonstrated to be such?

This bible-fanaticism spreads all over the social, political, civil, and rational world circles. Monopoly and usurpation, with their hideous monstrosities, overwhelm mind, and assault all improvements in religion and philosophical science.

Do not deform society by such outrageous bibles or codes, of ignorant barbarians. The world does not need or want the Jew codes or institutions, and the stupid priestocracy ought to have seen that long ago, at first, if their senses had not been stupidly and ignobly in their pockets.

All peculiar bibles have no principles, but have innovations thereon. And all this fuss about bibles, of Jew, Christian, and other peculiar faiths, has been made by the tory-world absolutists, kings, autocrats, emperors, priestocracies, and all their minions, when rational mind could have been credited for the eternal principles of illustrious God-given religion, the consummation.

Superiority of the ancients is it, when the servants of modern science were the gods of the ancients! Think of that, ye blasphemous priestocracy. Had the ancients in their barbarism any solution of complex ideas? What are all their abstruse metaphysics worth, when it confounds the blockheads in their folly, and confuses the confusion worse confounded?

They had but little correct data, and of course could not reason rationally, from want of rational data. Their compounds were often false, and their simples untrue. Ought this perverted bible to be in the hands of any person, children especially?

And after all, are all the bibles of peculiar faith, the felonious mock pretensions of this world's government, by kings and priests, by which mind has been bullied or defrauded, through world's sophistry, fit for free minds?

The very day that the world banishes bibles of peculiar faith, it advances one half in civilization and religion; mind then becomes faithful to itself, its best charge, and acts in the best good faith to God and man.

If the bible was put down, society would not be resolved into its original elements, but will be elevated on the noble sublime platform of religion.

Train up a child only in the way that is rational, therefore never give it the fanatical Jew bible, or the peculiar faiths of collusion therein.

All that is sought to be done by bibles, the world has to resort to mind for one way or another. Of the so-called bible : here is a book. Does the world know what it is, by any one exclusively of its five senses intrinsically?

If it did, that book is peculiar and has peculiar claims. If it did not, then that book is like other books, and submits to mind that concentrates the five senses, all in abeyance to its reason, not to faith, which is absurd. Here then the question is positive, and conclusively settled, decided. Here is conclusive demonstration, that ends the whole matter at once and forever. It is idle, it is most dishonest, for any advocates to affect a single idea further. They are mastered and exposed; they have to yield the question.

I mean all the peculiar faith people of the whole world. The world must not suffer any longer by the miserable contingencies of peculiar faith, that gives its contingent doctrines and no conservative principles; hence the world is cut up into its petty factions and sectional differences, without any standard of unity and proper execution of the proper actions for mankind.

If this book had been peculiarly a world-book, then it had originated a world-faith, but as a miserable failure of one exists, the other, the balance of the failure, must follow. The world has to yield all such bibles and their priestocracy, or never talk of religion more, as it is not peculiar.

The advocates have to abandon language or truth, honesty, honor. The present age of civilization cannot permit the bible of peculiar faith to trade on the capital of religion, a higher theme. The height of refined civilization is to know how to discard all exploded errors, and not retain them too long, no matter how valuable they may have been considered. But the world's notions differ essentially, as the component parts have been raised differently; but notions have nothing to do with the question that looks at the most solemn facts. All principles are the same to all rational minds. I grant you that your bible is peculiar, which you could not give any rational mind. It is not conventional matters of society, but the mighty organs of it that are under consideration. Of course the people of the peculiar bible are peculiar, and their God is peculiar.

Their whole creation is peculiar. But it lays claim, unjustly, to more. What, religion? No, sir, you were estopped at peculiar faith. There can be no peculiar religion; that is a solecism in this universe. Religion belongs to the God of the universe, and of course is universal, intended for all rational minds or beings in that universe, on universal not peculiar principles. Nothing, then, can be more universal than religion.

I will credit the motives of some, that they aimed at religion, if they aimed at rationality, truth and their language. But I must not say anything against this bible. There you do not defend religion, mind, nor the God of the universe, when you oppose my position. Do away with all fool bibles as nuisances. Let there be wise organic laws, to put down all nuisances by all-wise institutions, superseding them by rational toleration, but by superseding their use. We must abate such, by the wisest rational substitution. What shall the world do for a universal code? One that all will adopt, none rational can refuse, that will put to scorn the atheist or polytheist, who refuses to put away the gods and images of their idolatry, and cause all to acknowledge what is right. The world can refer to the same inspiration of religion, of rational mind, and adopt the unity of God for the standard.

Many ancients were atheists because they did not know by science the universe, or were polytheists because that little was perverted. The bible shows perverted astronomy, peculiar characteristics, the inspirations of 'ignorance. The ancient and modern sophists pervert language and ideas, make bible heresies all over. Monotheism allows God to create himself, and recognises his documents through his universe, cause, and effect. Polytheism creates gods of her own, and atheism supersedes God of nature by nature, putting most absurdly the effect for the cause. But you suppose that it was all right by the bible-makers, that they did not show the hand of their game in any of their councils composed of priestocracy and absolutism, the one to conceive, and the other to enforce?

In analyzing character, do you suppose that such pirates on mind can compare with yours, raised to rational standard of conscience? Do you think that the priestocracy who have a peculiar standard, can compare with the universal standard? The whole world may be psychologized in its ignorance in some matters, peculiar faith especially, under the treble engine of fraud. Do not sacrifice yourself, religion, to exploded bibles. All peculiar faith bibles leave their followers at sea, without rudder, chart, or compass, but rational religion gives mind all it needs in its sublimest standard, the Creator of the universe. Some who have only listened to pulpit-sophistry, may think that the bible is an impregnable fortress of religion, when it does not touch religion on its own basis, only as it invades the sacred precincts of mind. The bible furnishes a world-fund for bigotry, whereas the world-wide demands should be met by religion and her appropriate means, to satisfy each mind. Let mind do right for itself, the world.

What was the bible written for? The benefit of absolutism, including as a part and parcel thereof, the priestocracy, all in collusion. It is a very dangerous thing. The sovereign people ought to know it. What, convenient capital of "heart-hardening," Holy Ghost, spirit-prophecy, &c. made to order, to assume so many interpretations. How were the moderns indebted to the ancients for religion, when they had not science, morals, only some idle metaphysics? They could not have been atheists to do so much injury to the moderns, if they had had the proper science, much less could they have been polytheists. Let not the moderns adopt the criminal vices of the ancients, who would not have had such, if they had known better.

Be honest and truthful, or see the bible has no malign provisions for the world, as it is its nuisance—its disgrace. Its makers were its belials.

Moses was a very smart man. Yes, a little too smart for truth, as he wrote his own obituary. The whole secret is, the bible was fabricated to mislead and misgovern the people, by priests and kings, a vile caricature of God and truth, a base fraud on mind.

Do you believe the bible? Only in part. That condemns it as corrupt. It is history and story mixed, as bad as any other similar book. Would you now believe any man who would tell us, that he had commanded a river to divide, and it did so? No modern would be such a fool! Then how believe Moses or his bible? All such faith shows the bigger fool. To act on such foolish belief, is the practice of imposition, dishonesty, and knavery. The people get the priests to help cheat themselves. But what shall we do for religion, if we discard the bible? Do what the bible never yet did do, cultivate rational religion given of God exclusively, aided by rational mind. Moses was not as smart as Korah, who desired the people to be governed with conservative principles, and thereby disproving the false assertion, that the people then could not govern themselves. Korah was a republican philosopher, and had the wisdom to appreciate the immortal conservative principles of mind, over all the degraded disguises of Moses' priestocracy, which includes him dictator, priests, prophets, as pretenders, and all affiliated machinery.

Religion rebukes all the fanaticism of peculiar bibles. God's book speaks for itself and him, whereas man's bibles require the priestocracy to speak for them, but without avail. If you know the nature of evidence, you must know that all this Jew bible matter is a base, scandalous fraud, that would not pass a pure court of justice, much less that of enlightened conscience. Now, if the priestocracy wish to keep the people from discussion, and profoundly knowing this subject, they act a most dishonest and untruthful part. They should, as honorable people, ask for the truth, the whole truth, and nothing but the truth, and all this they plainly seek to conceal. That religion, that sneaks from truth, when truth can be had most honorably? Stop that Jew bible. You have been deceived, undeceive yourselves. Such bible profits you, the people, the real sovereigns of the world, nothing. It is folly, crime, to trust to it.

To establish any peculiar bible, the makers must destroy the characteristics and attributes of Deity, especially his immutability and perfection, hence prophecy is the lowest of all things, and like the whole bible; its authenticity remains to be proved, as the most sagacious prophecy is a positive falsehood. It is losing time to trace up all the obscure points. It devolves on the bible-makers to prove their foundation.

Choose you this day for good morals or bible demoralizations; the God of the universe, or its peculiar god; religion, or its peculiar faith.

As to the dispensations, one lie is told, as usual, about the creation and the fall of man, and another, worse, has to be told to support it. The dispensation lies are all in the category of the priestocracy creation or fiction. It is astonishing that the world should have any such in credence, respectable keeping. The fact is, the most outrageous advantages have been taken of mind in this respect; and what is worse, they are all kept up. Americans, abolish such. But what must we do, ask the mothers, for our children, if you take these bible dispensations away? Be sure that you will not murder your fellow citizens, in fanaticism, for witches. You cannot do any worse than that. You hardly need bibles to lie for you, who are to be held subject to the bible priestocracy. Be free people every way, especially that which presents the purest taste. Teach, mothers, your children the purest religion, and that, be assured, is rational, nothing else. That, no bible of Moses or Christ can present. Religion is too holy for the polluted hands and corrupt minds of the priestocracy. It is a thing of God, the Creator, for rational mind. Tell the impious blasphemers depart, like the vulgar mind assassins, from the holy and sacred presence of free minds, whose rights they have outraged. In regard to all claimed of God's actions in the bible, God is the only competent witness. As it is clearly proved by these scriptures that it was most positively and clearly none other than the peculiar god of the Jews who claimed: therefore, to be his chosen and peculiar people, the God of the universe is not the one, as he is positively not peculiar, but universal, as his own word, his deed, cause and effect, satisfactorily proves.

All peculiar gods speak by peculiar ways, as they differ from the God of the universe. and that is by the priestocracy. They cannot speak or act otherwise. Not to understand all such in this light implies that the modern priestocracy are more heinous than the ancient. But if bibles be put back, what shall become of the churches and ecclesiastical literature? The bible having story and history, rational mind can decide as to their usefulness. The Jewish bible has right to peculiar property in its selfish excommunication of the rest of the world, but no more. Of course, what folly was the pretended law, that thou shalt love thy neighbor as thyself, when it had not the elements of religion, self-excluded by its peculiar institutions; of course the stupid writers had not the right use of the element of language. What business have the moderns with the peculiar property of the Jews, who excluded the rest of the world? As it has a peculiar god, it had a peculiar fall for its peculiar people. Do not overlook the bible quibbles.

The person that would undertake to endorse the authenticity of the scriptures, would require endorsement himself for sanity of mind, morals or intelligence.

Any one who undertakes to defend the scriptures, undertakes sophistry of the vilest kind. His mind is corrupt. What then has the world to protect itself by, if we take away the scriptures? Will you require a bible? And that bible forged? Now what good does a forged bible do? Principles are not forged, for they exist by God's positive appointment, and their consummation rational religion, exists by the same, most assuredly. All these are the highest, holiest obligation, and no mistake. These are as potent as nature. As long as nature exists, these exist. You cannot abrogate them at all. Now a bible of rational mind and religion, meets all your question. Make all minds rational, as all have an abiding interest in the common weal of society. A man of no principles, is nobody. Without principles, no society exists; without reliion there is no virtue, and without truth and honesty, there is no religion. Truth and honesty must be inviolate. Peculiar faith violates them, always, therefore the first has no religion. What virtue is there then, in its bibles, that bear the full record of all such falsehoods? Society is best off without such, must get rid of them. There are no bibles, unless sustained by God's principles.

The universe gives us a sublime and magnificent view of Deity, who presides over all, whereas the peculiar bibles give us that of his caricature, the most ineffably stupid. The bible-advocates do away with everything satisfactory as the foundation of God, and institute all that is sophistry, perfectly worthless. They alienate self-respect, and reverence of things worthy of it. The rational bible holds all accountable, to all that is rational responsibility. What is mind's highest, best interest? The consummation of principles, religion. When you renounce all such, you renounce your best allegiance to your God-Creator, and the universe. Do you pretend to assail me about your lying scriptures, that the world has lied to invent and establish? Are these the morals to uphold, the moral part of mankind? These the pitiful means to advance the holiest views of rational mind? Win the just confidence of rational intelligence, and institute thereon the appropriate fabric for society. The bible's caricatures of its peculiar god, remove us further from the God of the universe, which is the mirror that reflects God the Creator. The peculiar bible cannot do so, for that reflects bad degraded men, the priestocracy's deformities. These men had the same selfish interest in writing and upholding this book, as the Pythoness had for her oracles. The pride of consistency now pervades the affiliated. Millions upon millions in the world are yearly subsidized to uphold all their peculiar faiths, peculiar governments and bibles.

Absolutism, the world-bully, has an awful hand in this, backed by bayonets. Rome and France prove this, conclusively. What has the whole world to expect of peculiar faith bigots and devotees? All book systems as the bibles, are to be adjudged on their merits, and condemned on their demerits.

What good did bibles do the Jews, whose minds were behind the most humane acts of civilization, the most polished heads, their kings performing human sacrifices? If the Jew bibles were the thing of divine inspiration, then the Jews are thereby impeached as the most savage barbarians, making war most blasphemously upon humanity, and of course directly impeach the bible that affects them the chosen people. What do the people need of the priests' bibles? As much as they need of crown jewels, the gewgaws of royalty. That is only a small part of the question. In fact it is not the question. You listen to the priestocracy that are lying all the time in their pulpit. They are obliged to lie, shame for truth and God's truth.

What is your proof of any peculiar bible? You have none. You cannot pretend in truth to one iota : then do not lie about bibles of tradition any more. Stop all such disgraceful positions.

What is the difference between the polytheists and atheists, when the last make nature God, and the first make no God. The tory bible of Moses represents the man, who was a tory to popular rights that he warred upon. Can the freemen of America respect such tories as these? Is there any reason in such absurdity? What extraordinary world-good has Moses done that he should be esteemed anybody? He murdered to enslave and enslaved to murder his own people, by the wiles of priestcraft and jugglery. He repudiated, by the priestocracy's own showing, honest debts; he substituted idolatry of their peculiar god, for the adoration of the God of the universe, to build up the priestocracy. As to any peculiar acts, they are the absurd trifles of fanatics. Moses made water come out of a rock. That is nothing to modern science, that masters it hundreds of feet below the rock. But the others were miracles. No, sir ; that is your mistake, only miracle lies. Now this clique affects inspiration, which mind-science exposes as the vilest fraud. So much for inspiration, that is all gas—like that exploded at Delphos. You whine about peculiar faith bibles. Of course, you cannot need religion, for they do not contain it. They do not contain the great popular rights, principles, as the assassination of Korah and his illustrious associates satisfactorily proves. This bible affects supernatural matters, and these are self-impeached invariably and immutably as story. Discard all obsolete bibles and their explosions, pretensions, in order to reach the principles and elements of rational religion. The Jew or Christian bible is the very reverse of religion. The people acquiesce more in the bible than approve of it. They are silent, when, if asked their honest and truthful opinion, they candidly declare that the bible contradicts itself, is absurd. Now, this does not present a healthful tone of public sentiment, that is silenced if not sacrificed to the good of the tory world.

What good pure mind wishes to see bible worship, much less mind sacrificed on the altar of faith, as it is necessarily done. Shall the belial-makers become the belial-actors to the world ?

The first and only step is to prove your bible. If you do that, the whole certainly follows. There can be no greater libels on God and mind than peculiar faith bibles. The world's citizens are basely libeled by the bible advocates as infidels ; now, the first are bound to prove their case honorably, before they ask belief, or can say aught against infidels, and even leave the pulpit as impostors, on failure. What an incongruity that their god could not stop their devil from corrupting the world. Their devil got away the peculiar god's creations. The ancients were poor creators, as their ignorance shows that their patchwork is rotten, and constantly needs remodeling. Peculiar bibles are non-entities, that cannot protect their existence, but absurdly invoke the aid of God's entities that have universal protection, that at once impeaches the bible as entirely worthless of itself, and only apparently beneficial, as it can trade on mind's capital.

As the peculiar attention of the world is invoked to the Jew peculiar bible, we will first inquire about the Jews.

The Jews were early diffused among the nations ; at the æra of Christ's supposed birth were in every part of the known world. What Jewish authors have written on faith, but the recording priests and prophets, the rabbis, and all their affiliated hosts ? Who but the Jews are best competent to decide on the faith and interpretation of their own peculiar bible, who have been denounced therefor by their wise and righteous persecutors, their parricidal offspring, Christians, Mahommedans, and Mormons ?

The restoration of the Jews to the country of Palestine, is an important item in peculiar faith. But over this country false government and faith have made their horrid marks, and their prime ministers have indited them. It is to be hoped that the Jews will carry the blessings of constitutional government and rational religion, upon their restoration.

Can you ever expect, Jews, to hold that country as your fathers held it ? Can you ever rightfully expect to go there, as possessors ? Your fathers outraged the rights of hospitality, the comity of nations, the courtesy of humanity. You cannot appeal to the God of the universe, for you outraged and alienated him by your peculiar god, that was imbecile. What is the benefit to go thither with your peculiar faith, that has been tried by your ancestors, and has proved a miserable failure, their and your curse, in which too much of the world has participated ? The land has been in abeyance to conquest after conquest. Rebel tribes now overrun the country, that needs the blessings of cultivated mind, government, and a universal brotherhood.

Your ancestors lost, after gaining that country from military conquests, that are not tenable before a world's religion. To reach the incipiency of restoration, on the proper permanent basis, you have now to give up your superstition, from rational motives, and cease to be antagonistic to a world's interest.

What would cause you to care for the site of Solomon's temple, on which has been since erected, by Omar, a Mahometan mosque ? If you chose to feel revengeful, you will discover that a chapel was dedicated to Venus, on the spot claimed to be the place of the death and resurrection of Christ. The condition of Palestine shows only natural results, otherwise an imbecile, peculiar god. As to any prophecies, this is the apology of a stupid people, who could give no other.

The eye of philosophy must see natural results, the effects of not less than twelve conquerors. One wave of conquest has followed another. Which was the best ? Can any be worse than that of Moses, who set so many miserable examples of piracy, and horrible peculiar faith, of which Mahomet particularly availed himself, in founding his ? His is but a second edition of Moses' peculiar faith, suited to a military chieftain. The curses of peculiar faith are heaped on Palestine, because the blessings of rational mind are outraged and silenced. The bigots will cry out prophecies, prophecies, while the rationalist must see the execrations, the abominations of peculiar faith, that despoils, desolates and defiles the world.

That is the way to tell it—let nothing be kept back. Do you, bigots, pretend to talk of the desolation of countries, mentioned in your peculiar bible ?

Why do you not turn your comprehensive attention to the whole world, and philosophize on the essential reasons ? Are you as much below this, too, as your bible is below God's ?

How long will it be, before you begin to learn wisdom ?

What is Jamestown, in Virginia—its first settlement—but a spot, to show the first settlement in that state. Tell us, what are those deserted cities of Central America ? Were these prophesied too of, by the Hebrews ? Was even the country ever thought of, till mind discovered it ? Yes, mind, that lays low all the pretences of prophecy, as false and absurd, impious and blasphemous, by the word of God, cause and effect.

Where is Italy. that has been overrun by successive races, that became extinct, or blended with the conquerors? Do we hear of the whole world explained by the bible, in its geological causes? Such bible is a miserable abortion of truth and philosophy.

No, it is not prophecy but philosophy, not faith but religion, that exalts nations, and causes mind, the world to triumph. No, the poor Jews are to be placarded all over the world, divested of the world's rights.

You speak of the desolations of countries of the East, because the bible can be stilted up to satisfy vain speculations that do not touch the subject.

Where are the mighty injuries of provincialism under haughty and rapacious con-querors, who drained countries of all their wealth to concentrate in imperial cities for luxurious emperors, rapacious and reckless of the world's dignity, peace or love of mankind? Tell us. ignorant bigots, ye pitiful priestocracy, had the Jews under their peculiar faith fanaticism been able to have been universal conquerors of the world, where would the world have been? Let the iron age of her oppression tell.

The world cannot be too grateful that rational mind is rearing aloft its munificent empire.

Were the civil wars and captivities of the Jews evidences of civilization? Who had the worst civil wars, ay, about kinds of priestocracies? Civil and general wars, mere piracies, were the ancient world's acts. What a blessing to the world that the Jews were scattered.

Thus reason declares, before all the pretences of prophecy.

The world now begins to appreciate what good goverument is in city or country. We plainly see that much of the world is subject to abundant riots and massacres, from its many subdivisions that should be subject to one body of municipal laws and rulers. It needs one proper government, not the pretension of several petty municipalities.

What better could have been expected from Babylon, that luxuriated in all the vicious errors of the times, and only excelled the ancients in the magnificence of her vices and crimes. Thus it will be with all tyrants. Principles protect the world, before the mightiest walls of Babylon or her superiors.

Babylon, with all her prowess, was taken not less than seven times, enough to have destroyed any one city with all her mighty resources. When Seleucia and other rivals were built out of her ruins, and the upper country, instead of aiding her commerce, oppressed and enslaved her, then her fall was certain as natural.

Bible prophecies are the veriest world-fooleries.

Does the bible tell of the ancient and mighty cities of Eastern Asia? Of the mighty revolutions of the earth, with which all mankind was interested? Has it given us all history, prior to the right culture of mind?

Alas, it has given us its worst perversions, the legends of the priestocracy who sought the worst dynasty. It speaks of the owl living in old deserted dilapidated towns, and wreaks its vengeance on Babylon, because of her power over them. This is below the schoolboy's theme.

The commerce of the world makes and unmakes cities, either in ancient or modern times. Mightiest oceans have become the course of trade, instead of overland, as navigation improved. Isolated and interior cities may be upheld by court and local influences, by manufactures and other adventitious causes, but the real magnificence of wealth results from the domains of commerce. Where was the necessity of prophecy when mind fulfilled the best and noblest, the only functions of Deity, and telegraphed for the world? Did it take any vaunting of pretended prophecy to make known the God of the Universe to the heathen? That was the peculiar god of the Jews that required that. The God of nature was already sublimely represented by his own im-mutable works, the dignity from all which was awfully detracted from when God was localized by the Jews.

What better, then, could we expect from any such people, who affected superiority in peculiar faith, that actually weakened them in their essential power, and rendered them unpopular with the world.

All the bible proofs intended for sophistry, essentially prove all this. Palestine was devastated by the Chaldeans, who carried away captive all its people. It was im-poverished by the kings of Syria and Egypt. It was utterly ruined by the Romans, who destroyed more than a million of its people when Jerusalem was destroyed, and carried off the balance, or made them subjects and tributaries. The dynasties of brute force and peculiar faith prevailed over the ancient world, and brutalized it. Is it to this state that the modern priestocracy would wish to see the world brought? What number of conquerors passed over this land! The Persians, and among the most ferocious are the Arabian tribes—the Crusaders, the Mamelukes of Egypt. It has been ravaged by Tamerlane and his Tartars, and is now subject to the Ottoman Turks.

The Jews characterized all their enemies as vindictively as possible. They were a hopeful set, including their historians. A vast extent of the populous world has been doomed to the lawless fury of man's basest passions. The greatest conquerors were no less oppressive than the smallest. Nearly a third of a million of people of Seleucia were massacred by the Romans, who sacked and burned the city.

Man has blasted the earth, and cursed its beauties.

No wonder that Eastern Asia, with her hundreds of millions, is so cautious of man, who has proved himself the greatest curse of the world, when invested with peculiar power and faith, necessarily destitute of rational education. The Romans, under Julian, devastated this noble country of Chaldea. Among the curses of this part of the world, at one time, were the Abassides, the assassins and enemies of mankind.

After all, can the greatest conquerors, the Romans, be considered in any other light than the greatest robbers in the world? The Jews did not reach civilization, by much. Would not the world be in a far superior condition but for Moses and his progeny, Christianity, Mahommedanism, and Mormonism? What were the wars of the ancients but for peculiar faith corruption? What those wars of the crusades but for peculiar faith and opinion, superstition, bigotry, conquest, and piracy. Who were worse teachers of sectarianism than Moses and Christ? What is sectarianism? learn of the sixty-five millions slaughtered by one branch of Christianity, the Romanists.

In the Jews, behold a picture of peculiar faith.

What a scene for the world, suffering the direct antagonism of its own peculiar faith. Let every nation have its own peculiar faith as deep rooted as that of Judaism, and what a world the whole would present! Every nation a fanatical bigot, having a peculiar god and priestocracy. What has not the world suffered already by its vulgar obstinacy and opinionativeness on this subject? The warfare of the ancients was cruel and vindictive, ferocious and exterminative. What had peculiar faith not to do in all! Did it not aggravate, if not originate most? It peculiarized all the world into clans, and embittered each against the other. This is what the tinkering of a botching priestocracy has done, from which it is so very hard to get rid.

Ancient peculiar faith had the least of the spirit of toleration. You, Jews, possess but an inferior rank in the scale of national elevation, degrading intellect to base superstition. Shame upon it; come forth for the universal brotherhood at this enlightened day.

Why do you idolize Moses? Did he act like a true member of the human family? Did Christ, Mahomet, Joe Smith, Brahmin or Bhudd, Juggernaut, Lama, or the emperors of China and Russia? No, none of it. Palestine has been scourged by at least a dozen masters, and mostly on account of peculiar faith and barbarism. And what less than ruins of the ancient cities should follow in the ignominious train? All such are from natural causes, that must have their effects, else why those in central America, that were never prophecied of by the ignorant prophets? Tell us this, as you pretend to those of Asia! See you not, superstitious bigot, natural causes? No pretended prophet can be God's prime minister as long as peculiar faith scourges the world, and transforms it into a hyena; devoid of universal brotherhood, so long shall this curse prevail, and desolation, not of one faith, but of all in time.

Did not the Jews procure the desolation of Canaan? Did they not first desolate their own national union by sectarian feuds, even to extermination of sects? What else could they expect but their present denationalized state?

Is this the real state of things, that the peculiar god of Judaism, after using the Jews for a peculiar specific purpose, has turned their descendants out to the world for its scoff and their misery? If the Jews answered that purpose, would their peculiar god have served them so? If they did not answer the purpose, what obligation is there on the world to obey their impracticable peculiarities?

If the ancients were punished for their treatment to the Jews by the mighty desolation of their lands, what must be the fate of the moderns who deal so hardly with them?

Rational religion supersedes the necessity of restoration of the Jews to Palestine, a perfect absurdity, as great as making all the pairs of different insects cross the ocean to get to the ark, thereby encountering the very dangers in reaching the means to preserve them. Now, the diffusion of the Jews will be their blessing, especially in this glorious Union, that gives the world such magnificent govermental institutions. The great absurdities and foolishness in bibles of tradition kill them. How absurd, before the enlightened tribunal of mind, appears the peculiarity of the Jews, gypsies or any such! Rational religion most honorably prevents any from being heathen, or outside barbarians. The whole human family is cut up into factions and fragments of sectarians, who cut each other's throats and ruin the world.

Many such are not raised. They may have property, but have not found manners or courtesy, and never will under the evil banners of sectarianism.

No prophecy or miracle could come short of national elevation of character and mental excellence.

Did the Jews excel in these? No. Then all is gratuitous about their bible. But agitation is kept up to this day about their restoration to Palestine.

Modern writers affect that the Persians and Russians may become "instruments of Providence in the restoration of the Jews"! How? By trampling on the rights of the Turks! Is there never to be an end to the curses of peculiar faith bigotry?

The Arabs, in their various tribes, are independent even of the Ottoman supremacy, and they are to be ruled out ere this can be accomplished. Do the world's peace and happiness depend on peculiar faith or rational religion. a mere locality or universality? If the Jews are wise, they will disregard the land that ruined their ancestors, and not envy the predatory tribes that rob one another, though of the Mahomedan faith, whenever it is their interest to do so, and enjoy the blessings of civilization in this and other countries of the noblest governmental institutions. Who were more degraded on account of that very Jerusalem, than the Jews by Titus? Were they not treated most ignominiously by the Romans of all conquerors, destroyed by wild beasts, enslaved, sold into slavery, destroyed by such treatment as questions the civilization of the Romans? Of all places on God's earth, the Jews have been treated as the greatest aliens in Jerusalem.

The Jews were enslaved and ignorant, and were best governed, as some think, only by superstition. That may do for Moses and his friends to tell, but how will it suit enlightened religious freemen? Was it not a universal empire the Jews were after? The Jews are so peculiar. The gypsies are scattered among nations—are there any prophecies of this peculiar family of people?

Have not the Africans been also diffused for two centuries among nations of America, and Africans still, except to nativity? Do not all nations render themselves peculiar by peculiar institutions? It proves that their world-intercourse was less than others possessed, who mixed with the world. Are the Jews an especially favored people now? Are they distinguished over and above the intellectual race of mankind? It reflects on their intellectuality, that they were so befogged by false pretences about inspiration. Who does not recollect the weak state of mind exposed on the reading of the book of law stated to be found in Nehemiah? Were the people cognizant of the laws? Who found the law? How came it lost? How came they not to know it? The very idea of assuming to be a peculiar people, cuts short truth and intellectuality. Fine revelation, that separated one nation as peculiar, from the rest, making God peculiar, and rendering the second dispensation a peculiar polytheism afterwards! What a fiend, to divide the world, and make each division a faction and sect.

What nation was it that was not heathen to the Jews?

How great is the absurdity of all bible-advocates, particularly of the Jew, who must have known, if he saw at all in his life, that his forefathers' country was ruined time after time, by this state of things! Is he going to die by what they could not live by? The Hebrews seem to be any. other than the select, the favored people of God, as they were peculiarly cursed instead of blessed, by their own acts. They cursed themselves, what better could be expected from their institutions, that governed them most imperiously, as most ignorantly? The iron sway of the priestocracy, the tax of the same to one-tenth, their polygamy that opened the door to a multitude of crimes, were enough to ruin them. Debase woman, and the country is worthless, as its public virtue is destitute of respect. Thus Asia has been ruined by the despotism of the men, the legal prostitution and debasement of the women. What a horrid picture of vice is the regime of women! To complete the misery of the whole, the priestocracy have added their curses of desolation to the land, by their own actions. Thus has the world been debased. deranged, tortured, crushed, by ignominious vassalage of peculiar faith, that is dovetailed in the very essence of malign evils. Is free and intelligent America going to submit to this? Will Asia, the world, be reformed by peculiar faith, always identified with inherent vices? The sword carries all those, but this is not the age of the sword, while mind can carry religion. If Deity had expressly inspired Abraham, Moses, and selected the Hebrews as his chosen people, it looks most reasonable that he would have given a more select country, exempt from invasions and the tyranny of the rest of the hostile world. It is remarkable that both bible dispensations are most deeply tainted with blood. God could have conducted them to the new continent, where they might have reared an overwhelming empire to astonish and convince the world. Here Moses might have reared his priestocracy in all its magnificence, apart from the collisions, murders and piracies of Palestine, to have been like a radiant star in commerce and faith. Had the Jews been the peculiar people of the God of the universe, the whole world had been convinced. That it was not, is the most conclusive proof against it. Which is worse, the false pretences of the ancients in regard to them, or the moderns in basely upholding them? What nation can be more flagitiously wicked than the Jewish in the time of Solomon, whose base misdeeds have formed a prototype for Mahomet, who does not begin to touch this vicious ruler? Jews, when we address you by that name, we consider you deplorably superstitious. We address you as men. Seek to be such, and enjoy all the benevolent blessings under that title. Act to the dignity of man, not to the degradation of perverse superstition, that has cursed you and your forefathers for many centuries.

You must see that you can never atone adequately to the world till you dissolve the bonds of superstitious iniquity that has done you such gross injustice, and the world such horrid injury.

How terribly corrupt were the Jews, the prophets tell! What can the superstitious Jews now expect of the world, that is progressing in science of mind and its universal relations? Can they expect the world to turn back to their exploded errors, or will they not feel bound to rational principles to advance along with them? They had better rush to mix themselves with an enlightened people, and give over all their nonsensical bible stuff.

We must make allowances for the vices of ancient times, and that ancient wars were recklessly made, without international treaties, for robberies and conquests. The code of the world's morals was very low, and emigration was recklessly practised. Was there any virtue in this piratical vice of the Jews? Ancient emigrations devastated the world, but now they constitute annexations under the laws and protection of the country sought. The world-morals have produced the most beneficial change for the better.

How has the world estimated the Jews? Their present position in society tells. Who would wish to adhere to a superstition that, instead of blessing the whole world, has awfully cursed Abraham's seed? The Jews might have been better by this time—as a nation, no doubt would have changed for the better—had they not been interrupted and broken up. But let not the world receive any such superstition that they could not live by.

Jew,—you who expect a Messiah,—give over all such. Be not hardened in superstition, nor connect yourself to false expectations. What can the Jews promise themselves by a peculiar faith that has cursed them all the time? They must be the most infatuated of all people. Really, it seems that the Jews have cursed themselves for their impious superstition in assuming to be the peculiar people of God. Though the Jews elected their judges, yet they could not stand them, being from the priestocracy, and preferred the despotism of kings. What a commentary on that order! Surely, if not competent for government, they were less so for religion. It must have been their corruption, not the people's inconsistency, that brought about this mode of government. The priestocracy tried their best to dissuade them from it, but the people preferred any government to them. If the ancient Jewry could not stand their government, how could the world stand their faith? Did the Jews have an equitable government? Anything less for the sovereign people.

Is not Judaism wearing away among the most intelligent of the Jews as they become enlightened? Their rights, the world's rights, are in monotheism—that is, rational religion, not in priestocracy-faith. Moses foretold, it is claimed, that the Jews should be removed into all the kingdoms of the earth—"scattered among all people, find no ease nor rest; be oppressed and crushed always."

Could any people be more greatly cursed than the Jews for their superstition by the Chaldeans and Romans, who slew them with much slaughter, and carried them off from their country? The world treats them as aliens now, because they act as aliens. Their peculiar superstition distinguishes the Jews. What is all their superstition worth to them in God's own residence or in theirs? And yet they absurdly cling to it, as if available. Scattered were they to teach other nations superstition? Reason induces me to belief to be taught by the world, to divest themselves of all such stupidity.

What is a Jew's life worth in Turkey or Persia, and indeed in many other places? They occupy an inferior grade at this time in the world for an obstinate adherence to blind superstition. Get rid of all such, and be useful members of the chosen community, and glad of the chance. Lay aside your absurd customs.

Did Judaism render the Jews a respectable or virtuous nation? Josephus speaks of their enormous iniquities.—De Bell. Jud. lib. v., c. 2, § 5, and c. 13, § 6. The Jews are the beneficiaries of both Testaments, as any, and could not have been choked off if it were all right—all their hatred, prejudice, and Christ's exposure of their vices, to the contrary notwithstanding.

It is the basest imposition from the pulpit to affirm that the Jews had a proper notion of the God of the universe. They had no idea of the universe, much less of its God, the last of whom never can be made known by any priestocracy. They were not ruled by reason but by superstition, the most difficult thing that made them so foolish, for their minds were left uncultivated. The priestocracy, who have not a true knowledge of God most clearly, are as stupid as the Jews, to affirm to their having a true knowledge of God. The priestocracy cannot endorse about any true knowledge of God. It is mind, under the inspiration of genius, science, knowledge and wisdom, that attains to this pre-eminent position. Why did the Jews persecute their own prophets if they held sacred functions?

Why did they resist Moses, if he performed miracles? The answer is inevitable, that these people were arrant impostors, and did not hold such functions as they claimed. If they had differed so remarkably from other people in this respect, they had differed mentally and physically, beyond doubt, and the whole world would have acknowledged their pre-eminence. All such is self-impeached.

Sectarianism had so contracted the Jews that they held other nations as accursed. They acted no friendly part with any. The brotherly tribes were divided into two large national, sectional factions, most of their time fighting more or less with each other, thus weakening themselves most stupidly on their peculiar faiths, killing the priests, and rendering themselves so much weaker against the attack of foreigners, who enslaved them all easily, even fighting against their neighbors, whom they professed to love as themselves.

Were the Jews any but a national banditti, libeling God by declaring his orders to murder the people of the country and take their land.

Had one man done this, he was a murderer and pirate, an assassin and felon—no matter his excuses; if his bible had claimed such, he was a hypocrite. Is God to be libeled this way by any bible? Therefore is the bible the most demoralizing of books, that excites nations or individuals by such felonious outlawry.

What could constitute worse national iniquities than the sins of murder, piracy and blasphemous libel of God? No wonder the people were expelled the land forever. They were unworthy of mind's blessings.

The Jews' bandits destroyed the poor inoffensive Canaanites, and ignominiously libeled their characters, adding insult to injury. Many moderns are ready to endorse such conduct. Why? Because the felons said that their peculiar god directed it! Will the moderns approve and adopt the libel of felons, guilty of blasphemy against the God of the universe?

The Jews were an obscure and inferior nation, and never have extricated themselves from that category. As to the special people of their god, not to advance any other better. proves a bad choice, a poor specimen of humanity. The Jews even lost the use of their language, the Hebrew, in which the law was given.

If the Jews were outrageously superstitious on account of their peculiar rites, what must be those who now adopt them?

What an enmity between the Jews and Samaritans, the last of whom are of the intermixture of. the ten tribes with the gentile nations.

What the Jews might have known of the true God, their priestocracy spoilt, and made it all then as now, superstition. The priestocracy were clearly in the way of their being religious. Much has been claimed for the Jews, who nevertheless were not a learned nation. They had the advantages of the Egyptians and Babylonians, by whom they were enslaved, according to their own accounts. Who ever went to the Jews for learning? Pythagoras, and other Grecians, went to the east and south for learning, not to Palestine especially, as far as I know. As to learning from the Jews, we had better attribute to their masters what little they did know. They were slaves over five hundred years, according to their own accounts. Are slaves to teach freemen? What can they teach? Superstition. Peculiar faithites cannot teach religion. We see emphatically that the government of the Jews was not salutary to prevent outbreakings and internal divisions, as when Moses is said to have presided, we see that Korah went for the rights of the people withheld.

Nor was it any better in Judges, nor in monarchy, when ten tribes were divided against the other two. But we are compelled, if we believe the priestocracy, that everything is due for the faith of the Jews. If no nation but the Jews had the idea of their peculiar god, then the assertor damns his own position, if he condemns the Jews or assumes any other. As they are good authority, as quoted by the preachers claiming that their idea of God was correct, then why did the Jews reject their position of Christ? Either one or the other is wrong. The Christian conclusively makes himself and Jew wrong forever. Was it not because Christ did not believe as the Jews did, in their priestocracy's god? Christ's view, of course, was sectarian, and was undoubtedly wrong, if the Jews' faith was right. No preacher can escape from this dilemma.

Who would go to the Jews for science? In what age did they excel the world? Was it when their wisest man, not the wisest man of the world, Solomon, had his harem of one thousand women; or the temple of the sun? Was it when he had to get Phenicians to instruct his people in architecture? Think of that.

Some of the nations of antiquity were passing out of the stage of existence, when the Jews were coming into it. Had they no faith about the Creator?

Was there ever a nation that had any science, that had no such idea? What must be the state of doctrines in the hierarchy, when it received what the Jews rejected? The Jews were ignorant, surrounded by nations learned compared to them. The very fact of circumcision proves the actual barbarism of the Jews. What they call faith in this matter, I consider anything but religion.

Did not the Jews show their vile vindictiveness of revenge on the Egyptians, and expose, also, their own dishonesty by their own history, when they repudiated their debts? Did they not make a contract specific with these people, and clearly violate and falsify it by cunning and dishonesty?

What does the world value the Jews for? For their refined morals? In what did they excel? In worship? Which kind, idolatry or superstitious priestocracy? In science? Where is the evidence, when they had to engage the Phenicians to build their boasted temple? And to what use did the builder, their wisest seraglio-man of one thousand women, devote it? Was it not to the worship of the sun? And did not Solomon, like the pagan Romans, adopt foreign gods?

What did these Jews know of physics, medicine, science? They could not advance to one point in the circle, unless correlatively to all that is clear in the circle of science. They should have enlightened the whole world had they been prominently enlightened.

The best thing the Jews could do, would be to incorporate themselves with the people of the United States, who came much nearer being the favored people of God than the Jews, who were so odious to the ancient world. Had the Jews been the favorite people of God, they ought to have been assuredly the world's nucleus, whereas they were the world's nuisance in some respects.

These Jews had little or no commerce, a little pent-up country, subordinate at that time, much less this. Are this people's fragments to teach the world now, when their best could not teach the world then? No: it is not they, but the priestocracy of the present, always of the present, ever looking at the profits, not the principles.

What sort of government had the Jews? Despotisms, monarchies, and judiciary, all under the control of the priestocracy, who bred all the national disturbances in sectarianisms. See what slaughter they aroused, about the superstitions of the day Is all this fit to enlighten and bless the world? The world should get rid of all such the quickest.

As a great and righteous God of the universe had he made his inspirations, would they not have been of the most exalted intellectual character, providing most divinely, wisely, and of course universally, for the noblest elevation of the human race? The very peculiarity of the Jews, most clearly and conclusively condemns them forever. None but bigots could exhume such, or priestocracies busy themselves about them. Instead of barbarian incursions with exterminating wars, ferocious butcheries, and land piracies, assigning as a reason for the odious idolatry of the nations whom worse idolators destroyed, the holiest brotherhood would have sprung up with love, instead of such odious feuds and hates of the world.

Now we see that the more the intelligence of the world is truly rationally diffused, that all things are for the better. Peculiar faiths of all kinds, teach one another's advocates the deadliest hate. Thus the world is kept apart, when commerce, trade, science, and religion, unite the whole in one indissoluble bond. As human institutions, all were failures more or less, with all the wrongs and sins of the nation thick upon the Jews; that the world should be so weak as to believe all such, when unworthy of notice.

While the Jews are no worse, considering their circumstances, they are no better than the balance of mankind of their day and times. They were the victims of superstition—the remnant of a people now no nation. What is their faith, but one of the superstitious remnants of the past? What great learning had the Jews? Was that original? Who, of the Jews, knew that the earth was a globe? Did Moses, when he absurdly wrote of the division of light from darkness, when light and darkness are constantly on the earth during a certain number of hours, days, or months, relatively to the sun, whose presence as the especial organ, makes light, and absence darkness through the effects of his rays? The East surpassed these Jews in astronomical science, most clearly, as the doctrines of Pythagoras, since adopted by Copernicus, clearly prove. Of all the systems, that of the Jews was most absurd. And if ignorant in the sublime science of astronomy, how much more in religion.

Did not the Jews lose their very laws, while at Babylon? To whom but the Babylonions and Egyptians were they indebted, for most they did know? What science had they? Their Moses, no doubt, was a considerable man, but not as dressed up as in their bible. That would spoil the whole character of the American Washington, the hero, patriot, and statesman, the illustrious defender of his country. Describe Moses, what reason admits, and all would be right.

The Jews loaned their money for what they could get—exercised usury as they called it towards strangers, yet not to their own people who could reciprocate favors of all kinds. Of course, they had no principle. It was only a policy, and a miserable one that has disgraced the annals of the world, in making all strangers outside barbarians, heathens, and even this sectarian policy was adopted by Christ, who "came rather to the lost sheep of the house of Israel." There is no palliation for such an absurd law, as all money is worth just what its uniform value calls for, no more nor less, and any opposition made could be made justly, only on that ground. All else is unjust, and cannot be legitimate nor honest.

The Jews, as a favored people, should have had prophesied all matters pertaining to the world, and won the confidence, and enlightened it; whereas they were the most despised, and had the confidence of the world the least. Will the Americans, who are giving the moral sublime in government, submit to be taught by the Jews, who had to learn of other nations, by their own confessions? But God taught them! What, the peculiar god of the priestocracy? That was of course, most positively, the priestocracy themselves. That was no teaching! Jews, stop your filthy circumcision. The world must get rid of its antiquated notions, and learn of philosophical, not traditional science. Where now are commerce, wealth, and greatness? Not in such a country, destitute of civilization. What it had, was transferred by various causes. What was the judicial light of the Jews? How debauched were many of their judges. Their kings were as debauched as any. Even David, whom flattery had elevated after the likeness of their god's character, was a contemptible debauchee.

The bible of the Jewish priestocracy could not uphold their nation, but helped to involve them in inestimable difficulties. Their history is, that they were actually cut up into sectarianisms, that caused the deepest antagonisms. They had had little commerce, which advances any nation, as the English and Americans, to the height of practicable intelligence and civil polity. From this reason, islands above all, ought to possess superior advantages. The Greeks did. Now as to the government of the Jews, we are led to believe that they were miserably governed, and that the light of mind was too far behind the peculiar light that they affected to claim.

How absurd was the belief of the Jews, that this earth was the only habitation of man or mind, and they the peculiar people—of all people the least so. All their pretences are utterly false, abominable, contemptible doctrines.

No ancient nation survived the various antagonisms of the old world, having no conservative principles of rational religion and government. The world has not yet seen the true equilibrium of principles, carried out rationally and universally. Had the Jews had the immortal principles of God the Creator, they could not have been peculiar, but would have had the universal principles of brotherhood, the want of which condemns their priestocracy as the vilest impostors, and those that adopt their false pretences of passing their (the Jew) counterfeit coin on the world—the impostors of impostors.

Now the world hates the Jews, and yet it seeks the very platform that made them detestable, their peculiar false pretences. What ignominious inconsistency. All such can be attended only by one sad result, to render the world as miserable as the Jews, who were first demoralized and then denationalized.

The Jews experienced the most sanguinary revolutions, and their catastrophe is enough to warn all sectarians off from all their peculiar institutions, as the just retribution of want of correct principles. No priestocracy alone can flourish: if mind be not there, the people will sink. No Jewish superstitious worship can answer at all.

The Jews and Christians are punished, or used rather as the world, by the just self-vindication of conservative principles. Who are the Jews, but a denationalized people, once fanatics and pirates—and their bible teaches the world to continue so? Tell the truth, the whole truth, and nothing but the truth. Piracy was the policy of the ancient world, and superstition its faith.

The Jewish nation was cut up, by sectarianisms, and that of Christianity is positively one of them. The first members were, by their own showing, Christian Jews, sectarian Jews. The Jews trifled with their little, peculiar god; let not the moderns absurdly imitate these priest pagans, forfeit their claims on the God of the universe. The Jews were from Asia, that gave all the forms of her peculiar faith most suspiciously savoring of oriental despotism, and popular degradation.

Are a people under despotic government, of ages rude, universally barbarous, without general commerce, science, arts, literature, philosophy, one of the world's civilizers? What has the world to do with such an abortion? If you would not believe in such a people, would you confide in their obscure bible? Universal perjurers in affairs of peculiar faith, cannot affect religion, the noblest dispensation. Would you barter the benefits of exalted genius, the deepest wisdom, the most refulgent philosophy, for all such paltry, worthless wares that would disgrace enlightened people as the circumcision?

Has not the character of the Asiatics particularly, been ruined as to the finest trait of mind, by their peculiar institutions? What do you want of Jewry? It was ruined by its own peculiar institutions, as all the ancient world, destitute as all were of permanent principles. You cannot get anything of it worth the notice of an enlightened mind.

The gypsies, fortune-tellers, were probably descendants of the priestocracy, and have as much peculiarity as the Jews in many things. How stupid are the Jews, denationalized as they are, scattered and diffused among the people of the earth, to be calling themselves the chosen and peculiar people of God, in face of God's denial most positively, from his word, cause and effect, and among nations to which the Jews were nothing. All that moderns are indebted to them for, is a stupid priestocracy, insolent impositions and fraud. The Jews never had rational religion. The old oracles taught conquests, piracy and plunder, that was the custom and fashion of the times. Surely that was not religion rational. As to rites and ceremonies, how foolish before God in the place of justice of man to man. Duty here on earth as required by rational mind, is a part of religion. All their vile tales about dispossessing the original people, the aborigines, was a swindling through the priestocracy and prophets, as great blasphemous felons. Did not the Jews let the Persians into Babylon, and then were they not rewarded by restoration to their country? The Jews propagated petty larceny on religion; that is what the world is indebted to them for. They have been treated contemptuously by the world therefor. and have caught it. Now as God's people having rational minds, let them help do away with all such base frauds of their fathers, to whom the stigma alone should stick. The height of all rational religion, which is the only evidence of God-given elements, is to do away with all peculiar faiths and their false pretences that have stifled truth as far as practicable. Are you Jews of those that are the chosen and peculiar nation? Where are your peculiar blessings? You are not a nation, and have no country! Even your very peculiar bible is peculiarly turned against you by parricidal hands, as yours turned against its predecessors, and you are expelled aliens from the superstitious scene of your forefathers, fugitives, wanderers and aliens on the face of the earth.

You discard religion, and of course its God, as you lay claim to your own creation, one that the world-wise in wisdom cannot dispute with you, who are not benefited by the whole machinery.

You and all Jewry are estopped as far as you are concerned, in claiming the Creator-God of the universe, who cannot possibly be dwarfed into a peculiar God, as then he would cut himself out of his almighty attributes, which the perfect Almighty would hardly do for the Jews, when he was committed most justly to his whole creation. As God, he could not be peculiar, therefore it is certain that another subordinate god of polytheism is claimed by the stupid Jewry.

If any nation were blessed, that is the United States of North America. But what she is the whole world can and will be, not by priestocracy, your awful solecism, but by mind, that will solve in time its universal problem. Now you have to get out of your most contemptible peculiar faith, that altogether degrades you and the world, and cuts you out of the legitimate benefits of religion, the noblest brotherhood. Think of that, Jew, and see your forefathers' miserable blunders, and all your foibles, not to name them harsher.

Do not render yourself ridiculous in your contempt. Avail yourself of all the light of the God of mind, and let alone your priestocracy falsehoods. Shame the stupid part of the world that takes now the shadow for the substance—that affects your old cast-off garments, too rotten to conceal the deformity of the iniquity. Yes, the word of God, cause and effect, most conclusively demonstrates that your pretended Moses and all that tribe were the veriest impostors of the priestocracy-clan, clique, or tribe, that includes all priests, prophets, and all the oracle-machinery.

The Jews do not begin to come up to the point of a fourth-rate nation among the least. Are these they to teach rational mind rational religion, neither of which they had when they most miserably debauched themselves by peculiar faith, the direct antipodal antagonist to religion?

The Jews may forever look by reason of this miserable peculiar education to peculiar faith, that will, like an ignis fatuus, mislead them from rational religion. The Brahmin faith is as good as the Jew faith, if not better. All peculiar faith is counterfeit, and only improves as rational mind improves, by ruling out its peculiarities and instituting correlative rational religion.

One of the worst things, the worst of all, if the Jew lies when he sells to aliens not of his peculiar faith, setting the most odious example, that is repaid in contempt a thousand-fold in evil. Now, of course, this is not the beginning or spirit of religion. This shows the odious vice of peculiar faith. Why an odious distinction of usury to the world ? All is not on the equitable principles of commerce that has uniform, open justice. The Jew has no one to thank for all this hideous deformity in the body politic but himself, and he is only excusable on the ground that he was ignorant of any faith but the peculiar Jew one. As to swearing by the bible, how can the truth be told when the advocates go for faith, not truth, as they are lying all their synagogue and church life-time about it ? What sin is there in numbering the people ? Was that the province of the priestocracy ? Is not a census one of the most valuable statistics of the world-government ? What ignorant and degraded barbarians those Jews were who over-looked the glorious free agency of mind, that has to elaborate its best circumstances nationally and individually !

And did the Jews devote their spoils, obtained by repudiation of the Egyptian laws, to the holy ornaments of their peculiar god ?

The Jews were a kingdom of priests, well expressed indeed, while the people were petty dupes.

The Jewish and American governments cannot be mentioned together the same day. All this results necessarily on the conservative principles of rational mind. If the Jews, as pretended, sacrificed whole nations to their faith, they were the greatest savages, worse than cannibal-monsters, of the world.

Affecting to be the world-lights, they were the world-butchers. The Jew notion of religion is very inferior, low, and degraded, especially when the Jews claim to have discovered it, as if mind had not been created. What a burlesque on religion ! The world descends from the sublime to the ridiculous, to pretend that Jew or any other peculiar faith is religion. If you prove that the Jews were the only beings that had mind, then they are then proved to be the chosen peculiar people of God. Prove that, and all is proved. If the Jews had been the peculiar chosen people of God, they could not have been kept back from conquering the whole earth. That is too plain for the world to miss seeing. They could not have been kept back from the triumph. Instead of Canaan, the whole world would have graced their triumph. Hence their prophecy-pretensions by their national flatterers to obtain the same by their savior.

As the Jews did not tower over the world, they were impostors and their bibles are impostures, and the priestocracy that are idolatrous enough to worship their bible, idolize this faith, and are the greatest blockheads on earth. Were not the Jews a mixed race of people ? Where were the intermixtures of the aborigines of the provincial conquerors ? Are they not a motley race of the ancients ? Where are the Egyptian, Chaldean, Assyrian, &c. Races but diffused through some of the present races of mankind. There are mixtures—ii. Kings, ch. xvii., v. 18. Therefore the Lord was very angry with Israel, and removed them out of his sight. There was none left but the tribe of Judah only.

They were absorbed among the Assyrians, &c. 23. Until the Lord removed Israel out of his sight, as he had said by all his servants the prophets. So was Israel carried away out of their own land to Assyria unto this day. 24. And the king of Assyria brought men from Babylon, and placed them in the cities of Samaria, instead of the children of Israel. The priestocracy could always assign a cause of sophistry why the people were removed for their sins, as if the Jews were ever any better under their hypocrisy to Moses. They forgot the prophecy of Abraham. Were not the old Druids as good in Groves as the ancient Jews ?

But the first were devoted to human sacrifices. What less did the Jews do when, 17, and they caused their sons and daughters to pass through the fire, and used divination and enchantments, and sold themselves to do evil in the sight of the Lord, to provoke him to anger. 2 Chronicles, ch. xxxiii, v. 6, and he (Manasseh) caused his children to pass through the fire in the valley of the son of Hinnom. 9. So Manasseh made Judah and the inhabitants of Jerusalem to err, and do worse than the heathen, whom the Lord had destroyed before the children of Israel.

Now, if the bible told that the Jews were actually worse than the heathen whom their peculiar god displaced for them, what if the world had the whole history, out of all the imperfect story of the priestocracy. The whole world ought to rise and put down all such pretences. Now, the best part is unwittingly told by the Jew-Jesuits, for Manasseh changed after he had been to Babylon, from idol and human sacrifices. Were not the Babylonians most civilized? In a few years the book of the law was found. To whom were the Jews indebted for all these changes? It actually seems that the priestocracy are actually afraid that the people will see for themselves how degraded the bible is.

If the priestocracy seek to hide all the book and faith iniquities from the world, then they are the endorsers of all, and are responsible to the whole world for all the blasphemous felony that they seek to palm on the same. Did any of the priestocracy appreciate the horrible position of their profession ere they adopted it, human nature must have revolted at the black and dismal picture.

It seems that the kings were respected by the bible as priest-partizans, and as the chief priests held the bible, of course the records were made to suit the complexion of their profession. How many kinds of bibles did the Jews have as a nation? That is the question. Was the human sacrifice diffused to more than one time? Of course. 2 Chronicles, ch. xxviii., v. 3, and (Ahaz) burnt his children in the fire, after the abominations of the heathen, whom the Lord had cast out before the children of Israel. Between the human sacrifices of absolutism and priestocracy, the world has felt enough indeed. The bible chronicles abundance indeed. The barbarian Jew-kings thought it nothing to slaughter, as Jehoram, "all his brethren with the sword." If the kings sacrificed human beings, of a surety the people did. We cannot reach how low the ancient polytheists were, only by seeing the modern adoption. No wonder atheists were made as the savage cannibalism of the polytheists made them. It is really surprising that the whole world did not turn atheists, to escape the savage cannibalism of polytheism.

Will this idolatrous generation of priestocracies never stop? Will it pollute the presence of free and intelligent mind, with their afterthoughts of their affiliated tribe, who sacrificed children in human' sacrifices, and ended as they begun, in blasphemous impositions on God and man?

Of course, Jew, you sincerely believe that the Christian is the very devil, and you hate him. Now, there is no love lost, for he hates you with a bitter, scornful hate. You both hate the Mahommedan, who hates you too. The Christian hates the Mormon, and wars upon him, for serving him as he served the Jew. They are all an amiable family all around, and yet they are all impostors, having no religion, but in positive antagonism with monotheism, which only represents rational religion.

The eleven patriarchs, sons of Jacob, were true to their stock; murderous in their thoughts, they sought first to slay Joseph, then they sold him. The people were greater calves to follow such men as Moses and Aaron. As the Jews were denationalized if their peculiar god deserted them, it was for their corruption, and surely their peculiar records must have been too corrupt to help other nations, as they did not avail the Jews. Do the Christians browbeat the Jews because the first live in a glass house? All are in similar houses when they build on peculiar faith.

Alexander's dream about the Jews was all of policy, like the visions of the Jew prophets; he wished to conciliate them. Moses made the people hypocritical and sinful, Solomon made them more corrupt, neither of whom showed wisdom in that. These men perverted their nation, and helped to ruin it.

No ancient nation had the essential principles of rational mind. The ancients had little mind, and were slaves and vassals of their false leaders.

Who were the Jews? Warriors. The American savages are that. Did kings wish to invade dominions; they had but to consult their gods, most peculiar, to inspire enthusiasm among their bandit followers, that is the priestocracy, whom bribery, corruption, and compulsion could bring over to their will and wickedness. Did even adulterers wish to succeed? Were they rich enough, or powerful enough, the chastity of matrons was then, as now, a small thing in the attempt? O priestocracy, base instigators of crime untold, the bully of the people and of kings till compelled to be their sycophants, the tool of tyrants, and vassals of despots, ye have corrupted and ruined the world as far as in you lay. The way the priestocracy talk, one would hardly know, unless by strict investigation, that human sacrifice was ever instituted in this idolatrous nation. Were not the Jews from Chaldea? Was not Abraham acknowledged from that source? The Chaldeans excelled the Jews, who did not know that the tower of Babel was for astronomical calculations. Abraham might have been a renegade. We have only the account of his affiliated tribe for it.

These old regime world-curses injure the moderns. Our fathers did so? What did rational mind do? The Jews had a peculiar education to consider their books and faith right, therefore they have the greatest difficulty to become rational. The ancients were more or less taught their peculiar faith, as the Greeks. All peculiar faiths were about on an equality only as they embraced rational doctrines from mind. The circumcision of the Jews is nothing, for most of the neighboring nations, as Egyptians and Ethiopians, did the same.

I presume that the Jews were driven from Egypt as the Mormons were expelled by the Christians.

Of all the oracle-mongers, the Jews and Jew Christians had their part. Now will the moderns be so soft, as to partake of all such folly and crime?

I think the moderns are greater blockheads than the Jews, who made a little overseer peculiar god, whom the first take instead of the God of the universe—and, as a proof, they have to help him, with messiahships and priestocracies. They have to endorse all, by the most abominable pretences. What a god, that his own peculiar people have to lie for him all the time! The present Jews are withheld, by their peculiar prejudices and follies, from participating with a nation truly blessed.

The Jew-bible is not good enough for the slaves that it was written for, however much they revived it, with some exceptions, as Korah and his illustrious compeers. Now, if the Jews revolted at it, what must the intelligent modern freemen do? But Josephus proves this book. Indeed—when he only translated the books that affect to endorse it, and them written by whom? The very Jew priestocracy? What did Apion say, if Josephus is thus introduced? Is not that enough to condemn the Jews? Had we the ancient books destroyed, what facts would appear.

The very fact of Solomon being a polytheist, proves him far from being the wisest of men, else that very authority disproves the authority of the scriptures.

It is most evident that the idolatrous Jews, who sacrificed human beings, became like the world in process of time; and by improvement of mind, more humane and civilized, and less barbarous. This is the whole history of the world. When were not the Jews slaves? Were they not under vassalage for five hundred years, by their own showing, and were they competent to teach mankind—the ancients, much less the moderns—the precepts of rational religion, when they were barbarians, idolators, repudiators, and sacrificers of their own offspring? Did not all the ancients hold slaves, on the martial tenure?

Were the Jews any better in peculiar faith than the Romans and Grecians, the two last of whom had no human sacrifices in their refined days, while the first had abundance? The Jews had polygamy, that the Romans abolished in their empire, including the Jews.

Are modern freemen willing to have the Jews for masters in peculiar faith, when the ancients did not wish them for slaves? The ancients were incompetent to the solution of religion, and all the Jews had no religion. They had superstition and its peculiar faith, and shall that be the bribe to the modern world for its religion soul-elements?

The further back all history goes the more fabulous, and even the more modern has been basely corrupted.

Were the Jews an exception to the frailties of mankind? Are they of the present day more honorable in trade, more truthful and faithful to the comprehensive demands of religion? Do they even know what religion is? Have they proved it by their abominable sectarianism, that was repaid them many fold by their parricides, vindicating the principles of retributive justice, especially for their infamous blasphemy? I can prove, by Plato, that other nations had an idea of God, at least equal to the Jews, who were polytheists, having god, devil, angels, and priestocracy—not to mention the balance of peculiar faith—that proves them, by their civil polity, their worship in their inhuman sacrifices, inferior to the most civilized. They were the vulgar slaves of superstition, as the history of their Christs proves, by the bloodiest massacres, and to their prophecies pretended. Never was there a time but that the Jews were idolatrous, and all that adopt the Jew bibles are the rankest idolators.

The Jews sacrificed human beings, their own offspring, as burnt offerings to ignominious superstition—so do the moderns as vilely sacrifice their religion, and mind's nobility, to the barbarian Jew's debauched bibles. What a stigma on the world's freemen.

Rational mind, to reach the excellency of its rationality in refined civilization, has to put down all peculiar faiths, and all the secret associations and institutions identified therewith, all over the globe, and evoke the noblest religion, and her institutions of universal brotherhood.

What were all the Jew governments but absolute despotisms? They were the most factious of barbarians, assimilated to the Chinese—excluding the outside, and butchering all the world practicable.

As the Jews were a peculiar people, favorites of their peculiar god—Gen. xv. v. 13. And they shall afflict them four hundred years—they were to be slaves to the Egyptians that time! But God doeth as man doth not, it may be pretended. Then man, not God, delivered the pretence that the Jews were his favorites; for that slavery condemns such bible.

In regard to Jephthah's bribing his peculiar god to commit perjury :—Jephthah makes a burnt offering of his own daughter, clearly making his god participant in his crime of murder also. Now here is clearly proved, that the peculiar god could not be the omnipotent God, as then he was criminal; and not being omniscient, he was peculiar; and the whole is an imposition, a fraud, of the priestocracy. Not only Jethro, but the devil was greater than this peculiar god. The Jews were so utterly ignorant as to weep, when they should have rejoiced, at the reading of the laws, as pretended. But it proves that they did not know the laws and ordinances, that were peculiarly prepared, no doubt.

Does not the soul of modern freemen feel the deepest disgust at the idea of having to go to the infamous pretended bibles of Jews, of Judaish sectarianism, with all its patchwork from barbarian idolatrous worshippers, to find that which neither they nor their priestocracy ever had, pure rational religion? Will it not feel indignant, to get less than by the purest sources of most rational mind, that is growing in the divine grace of rationality? Would you go to the barbarian Jews for the principles of government?

You would think that perfectly absurd and ridiculous, much more then would it be preposterous and outrageous to expect what is more sublime, and that identified with the noblest of all constitutional governments, self, national, and universal, for one universal brotherhood, when these same Jews were the most selfish and sectarian of all the world. What is their bible, but poisoned up with the same malign results? What are all the progeny of Judaism, as Christianity, Mahommedanism, and Mormonism, other than hundreds of monstrosities, from whom light has been taken, but hybrid! Religion consecrates mind in all its beauties, strength, and greatness, but not Jew pretensions.

The people that adopt the Jew government, pretending to praise it, are the most deceived or greatest deceivers on earth, tories to mankind, country, and the God of the universe; all of whom they would sacrifice for the benefit of the priestocracy, the most contemptible of every curse on earth, without any exception.

Do you worship Jew idols, their bibles, faiths, peculiar god and messiah? Who were the Jews, but ignorant barbarians, pirates and jugglers of their time? But the Jews are so peculiar, distinct from all other nations. Yes, the Jews are most peculiar, so much so, that their peculiarities of their god, bible and faith cannot be appreciated by other nations. They knew not rational, the only religion. Barbarians, ignorant and superstitious as they were, and never reaching more than a fourth or fifth rate nation, at their very best. They never presented, in their selfish peculiarity, any but pretensions to the claim of superiority in the world. Neither their country nor themselves occupy a prominent portion of the world's history. They were neither distinguished for commerce, arts or science, religion or government, and modern despots alone have given their faith consequence in seeking their own power. By the showing of the Jews, their peculiar faith suited the barbarian complexion of the times, as self-interest and despotism prevailed.

As to Jephthah, that commentators affect to explain away, all that proves the barbarian, heathenish superstition of the Jews, who have pretended to religion, worse than the false cry of the hunter, that imitates the voice of animals to inveigle and destroy. What the Jew assumes about his god is peculiar, and cannot be transferred. The world, mankind can only participate in universal attributes and principles; all else is fraud, deception, imposition and delusion about an ignoble faith, abominable superstition and vile, canting hypocrisy.

To the peculiar faith people, Jews and Christians, the world is indebted, as well as ancient nations, for the terms of heathen, infidels and barbarians. The Chinese, bringing this ancient custom from remote ages to the present time, call all others, outside barbarians, and with just as much justice. If any people is entitled to the name of sacred and religious, their immense antiquity gives them the most substantial claim, but that is all nullified in the presence of monotheism, that started with the universe.

The minds of intelligent monotheists are too often outraged by the impudent pretensions of those Jew barbarians, unless they estimate them with a cutting analysis. David, their adulterous, murderous king, is represented as "a man after God's own heart"! What god? The Jew god, of course. This man was an adulterer, murderer, bandit, who fostered an ignoble priestocracy; this vile character to be the fountain for false messiahs and prophets, this character to be approved of by the world? Forbid it, light of mind and liberty.

This fellow, that combined the tricks of the priestocracy and monarchy, the vilest union of despotism! Forbid any such example, freeborn Americans, who would laugh to scorn the Jew government, much more can the monotheist the Jew faith, alike destitute of principles.

Jew, you have no excuse for your pretences.

Do you need law? Would you prefer Moses, the barbarian, self-convicted, to the accomplished codes of the present times?

You should prefer religious and moral force to physical barbarism. You are made to study your bible, so called, and a few things pertaining thereto, and you become tainted more or less with odious, mean sectarianism, that forever divides you from all the pure lights, benefits and blessings of monotheism.

You thus divest yourself of the glorious rights of universal bootherhood, and can obtain nothing an equivalent therefor. Renounce, from this day, your fanatical bigotry, your abominable seclusion, your nothings for immortal benefits not otherwise attained. As Jews, you can promise yourself nothing good.

Put down the principles of monotheism, or maintain the doctrines of peculiar faith.

The priestocracy have degraded their creator to a peculiar anomaly, to subserve their base and dishonorable, selfish and lying purposes.

The light of these times informs you better.

The nation of the Jews was not even rational, much less religious. It was mostly running after the gods of other peculiar faiths, as it was swayed by circumstances, proving that the people were barbarians, and had no rational conception of religion or good rational government.

No matter if the god peculiar of the Jews was pretended to be the God of the universe, the very peculiarity destroys the character of their god, and renders him the peculiar idol of all the priestocracy, however self-concealed the last be. This nation boasted through this source, and let it enjoy all the peculiarity with all its peculiar ignominy. This is a peculiar creation, and has all the vices of such peculiarity. The priestocracy, if nothing else, vitiate the whole peculiar theocracy. Monotheism has no peculiarity about it, and therefore is of God.

The priestocracy of all the ancient and modern world were and are below science and patriotism, and never could appreciate, from their bigotry, principles God-honored and religious. They are unsafe guides at all times, and ought, should be scouted from the face of the earth by all honest men.

If the Jews had no more respect to their god than to liken their King David to him, let modern monotheists at least have the justice to place the God of creation above all creation.

Did the Jews ever have the remotest vision of the blessings of constitutional republican government, much less of monotheism? How came Samuel when importuned for a king by his fellow Jews, who absolutely refused the rule of the priestocracy Judges, he himself refusing monarchy, not proclaim with prophetic vision the sublime majesty of mind, so pre-eminently displayed in illustrious constitutional liberty, that would have elevated his nation so conspicuously above all of the whole globe, and given it a renown and himself a glory, eclipsing all the theocracy of Moses and his colleagues. And what little civilization the Jewish nation had, did it not get it from the Egyptians and Eastern nations? Joseph had an illustrious character somewhat, but that is recorded by the priestocracy, and is part of all. Well, where did he get that but from the Egyptians, who civilized him?

All peculiar faiths are of an analogous character: they are all deception to acquire power. They do no good, but detract from mind's excellency. The moderns are so far from being indebted to the ancients for faith, that they have been most awfully cursed thereby.

All of the Jews, as all other ancient nations, will be finally consigned to the tomb, as the folly and vice of a barbarian age.

Those advocates of peculiar faith that object to the unnatural and ungodly circumcision of Jews, still receive their bible that enjoins it—a reproach to civilization; to mutilate the body is base, but to immolate the mind by any peculiar faith is detestable.

And you, christian, have been persecuting the Jew for centuries, to effect a change of his faith, and what faith can you secure him? From that, rational religion deliver us all. If the curse is on the Jews herein must be the greatest, that they have abjured the God of the universe for their little peculiar jew-god of priestocracy, and rational religion for tory peculiar faith. But all such is the curse of the world.

REVIEW OF THE JEW OLD TESTAMENT.

THE predominant idea or passport of confidence to the world, respecting the scriptures as they are assumed, is inspiration and revelation by the god of covenants. Proper analysis and the highest respect to truth and religion, compel the most exact and just language. That they are inspired by the Creator of the universe, must be gratuitously admitted or taken for granted, but mind most rational and of right culture, is compelled to hold all this in abeyance until proved and demonstrated conclusively and satisfactorily. All such inspiration must be exact and perfect as God, who is perfect. If such scriptures be not perfect, then they are not in exact accordance with philosophical science, that convicts them of false pretences. Divine and direct inspiration, then, is a proper substitute for science, wisdom and philosophy.

Mind invariably owes it to itself, as most honorable thus to act, to decide properly and faithfully on all propositions, for in the multiplicity of the world's bibles that were more numerous than the ancient nations, and that flourished relatively to the state of auguries, soothsayings and oracles, to analyze this whole subject fairly, that it may not be imposed upon by false pretences that will mislead it to the most disreputable and dishonorable company, the association of which may be regarded most justly before rational mind, as most felonious, and before the perfect Creator, most blasphemous. None that are fair, honorable or just, can take exception to this correct course, but those whose dishonesty and untruth will be necessarily exposed to the whole world that is obliged to be identified in the glorious subject of religion and morals. As a universe-question, this whole matter must be resolved on its illustrious and eternal principles, and on no other. The very first chapter, nay, verse, of Genesis, proves the scriptures to be an uninspired book, and that too, in reference to the most important points, God and his universe, otherwise science has to be sacrificed before inspiration, which is an imposition, though it be from ignorance and any peculiar god of the writers, with whom the universe cannot possibly be acquainted on its principles, functions or attributes.

In the first place, I will premise that there is no unity between the old and subsequent testaments, new or more recent, first, intermediate or latter, as now presented by Christians, Mahommedans and Mormons. Such last testaments are bound to the old, by a mere rope of sand, and all rest on no foundations. The old speaks of one peculiar god, the new speaks of trinity and prophets peculiar, and all of their peculiar machinery of faith. The question of all sublime questions of honor, justly and rationally arises, are those scriptures endorsed for mind's conscience and soul's reception? When submitted to the only test of the whole universe, they are all refuted as false pretences. The creation's God has recorded his self-evident, neither refutable nor deniable by any rational mind.

We now advance to the most prominent matters of the first, the Jew Testament so called, and among them the analysis of the creation, by submitting it to rational mind, its master-spirit. Whose creation is this, to which we are now introduced by this so-called bible? It is positively that of the priestocracy, who ostensibly are represented by Moses. All that we have, proves that mind originated sham designs of intellectual but perverted creation, for the emolument and selfish purposes of the priestocracy, that had then a preponderating ascendancy in mind's affairs.

God alone prophecies always by time, acts constantly by the universe, the consummation of cause and effect, his work and word represented by its principles, functions and attributes, all matters of fixed and immutable facts cognizable to mind, an individual element whose exponents are five connecting organs, those of sense, and thus invites all by his eternal truths of universe facts.

Now, if this matter submitted had been true inspiration of the creator, the author would have enlightened correspondently to the munificence of this sublime subject, conformed more in accordance with exact science, and instead of such peculiar bible-defective communication, would have indited a universal language, as much above all that pretended, as God is above Moses.

God, in his perfection, has, exactly in conformity to his august and divine majesty, thus enacted, and left the eternal record unmistakable to the universe.

For bibles, partial representations of science, philosophy, astronomy, and wisdom, he has left their divine essences indelibly impressed on the universe itself. He has given it the real substance, and left rational mind to elaborate from those munificent universal treasures, exhaustless and evolved, proportionately to the innate capacity of mind's improved rationality.

In the beginning, the great first cause created that universe, his own seat of purity the holy centre, and all the abodes of rational mind, that can appropriate all that is legitimate in universal language and facts, all eternal.

This universe is a system of systems, reflecting effect to cause all to him, its supreme consummation, and the earth a planet that belongs to our solar system, and is directly indebted to the sun for its light, that reflects the supreme luminary of suns, and that ever shineth on this planet in its revolutions that make the day and night, the year and seasons of the year, and its own mighty results during that year.

The elaboration of this universe, exhaustless and immense to the brightest embodiment of mind, that characterizes it as nature, which analyzed, is creation elaborated with principles, functions, and attributes, is due to the creator's almighty potency, intelligence in perfection, for the glory of himself exacting the adoration of his supreme work—man's mind, in soul and spirit, that are to elaborate their perfection in this mighty theatre.

Any system that pretends that nature is adequate for the creator, is destitute of the first principles of its comprehension.

The creator adapted all the elements of creation to each other, each solar system balancing itself by its inherent properties, and all for an harmonious whole that necessarily and exclusively respects its almighty standard, whom all conservative principles represent and vindicate.

The chief purpose is religious comprehension of mind, that can unite universally on this consummation. Before all this, all partial and peculiar bibles sink into utter insignificance. Its authors absurdly sophisticate natural results, cause and effect, and give no credit to universal principles that represent the first cause.

A partial or peculiar creed or bible, when we are introduced into the audience-centre of the perfect creator of the universe, is worse than none at all—incomparably worse. That is miserable morals to palm all such on the world for the inspired one. From the sublime subject just presented, we have to descend to the grovelling, mercenary, and ridiculous one of the bible, mind-factured by the priestocracy who represent in every age of the world and division the soothsayers, augurs, and oracle dispensers, pagans all. All that they can possibly present are only diversified editions of the same mighty subject, to which their pretences are as irrelevant and inadequate.

THE BIBLE OF THE JEWS.

GENESIS, ch. i. 1, gives "God created the heaven and the earth." What was the heaven, but what was heaved up? Does this creation of man, define God's creation with philosophical science? If it were the best that mind then, or at any other time, from the nature of information as it was, could only give, then I would hail it as the best offering of religion; but when it is palmed on the world as the offering of inspiration, I feel bound to test it by the claims advanced, and not of its relative potency of mortality.

The very start premises a downfall. If the writers, assuming as they do inspiration, be ignorant on that, as in social science, what must they be in religion, when they cannot define the God of creation, nor the most obvious parts of creation?

The creation is not defined by the word heaven, which means heaved up, in the opinion of the bible writers, who were ignorant also that it was relatively heaved down, or that the revolution of the earth constantly presented the same kind of exalted concavity. When we ask where is heaven, who can pretend to locate ether for heaven, much less is it a firm frame-work built up by the ignorance of the priestocracy, who assumed to fix the frame-work of science, that has upset all their impudence.

Their idea of the earth, was as far from science. Some of the self-inspired men pretended that this earth was a plane, with four corners or ends, an idea that was conveyed to the sailors of Columbus, when they feared they might drop off, or from it, if they sailed too far west.

Circumnavigation only proved the rotundity of the globe. All the resulting ideas were parallel. The ancients not only conceived of heathen, or outside barbarians, that did not belong to their peculiar god, but they also viewed the land as heathen. The errors at the first great source made many more.

The perverse bigotry of peculiar faith is indebted to this source, as even the Christians by excellence enlightened, adopting the peculiar errors of the peculiar bible, that represents its peculiar god, seek to have the ineffably stupid pleasure of introducing him by their gospel to the outside barbarians, that is the heathen, who they overlook or are totally ignorant, have their minds from the God of the universe, whom no such pretenders represent by faith.

God Almighty is represented by religion, not by faith. To return : the heaven of this bible was only half a vault or concavity, as the earth was on pillars for its foundations. They never dreamed of the rotundity of this earth, much less of its various motions or revolutions, that reflected as in a mirror, a boundless scope of solar systems.

As they are self-exposed, assuming to be the peculiarly inspired pensmen, it is the duty of rational mind to notice it in its own self-preservation. 3. And God said, let there be light : and there was light. 4. And God divided the light from the darkness. 5. And the evening and the morning were the first day. 7. And God made the firmament. 8. And God called the firmament heaven. 16. And God made two great lights ; the greater light to rule the day, and the lesser light to rule the night : he made the stars also. 17. And God set them in the firmament of the heaven, to give light upon the earth. 19. And the evening and the morning were the fourth day.

God made the light the first day, yet he did not create the two great organs of light till the fourth day ! This is a universe of cause and effect, we must ever keep in mind, so that winds up the bible.

"And God set them (lights and stars) in the firmament of heaven to give light upon the earth."

All was a firmament or firm fixture, in which the stars were fixed as lights to the earth, as if lamps.

The larger lights, the sun and moon, moved, for the purpose of lighting more brilliantly the earth.

The sun or moon rises, because they were thought by these inspired, as they assumed, to move around the earth. This error, with others of greater magnitude, has stuck to the present times.

But these lights "divide the light from the darkness." This looks science ! Inspiration could have cleared up this, by revealing the reason for mind's light, that where darkness ceases, there light begins, or the reverse. But the oracle did not speak, as it was analogously situated.

The bible's only objects, main ones, of creation, were heaven, the earth, and its people, the chosen ones, peculiarly, to which all the rest was subsidiary.

The firmament is no firmament at all, when verified by exact science, that only discloses ether and innumerable stars that are suns of their solar systems, besides the planets of our solar system. Where the ignorant bible writers located heaven, we locate ether, a space without limit, for all is the universe undefined to mind, the end is the means, the last the means without end. What exhaustless munificence.

So the stellar light was for a more magnificent object, directly at least.

But the magnificent philosophy of the atmosphere was as unknown to Moses as to Peter, and this ignorance rather desecrated heaven, for 7. And God made the firmament, and divided the waters which were under the firmament from the waters which were above the firmament : and it was so. 8. And God called the firmament heaven. And to this we are indebted for rain !

Was the bible view adapted to the mighty universe, when it discloses, among imbecilities or puerilties, the stars to be lights as lamps to the earth ? The beauties of creation had not shone on the writers of those days, as philosophical science had not presented much of her treasures and discoveries in optics ; proof conclusive that the moderns are before the ancients, inspired or not.

Science decides most conclusively that inspiration has been brought forward by the false pretences of the priestocracy. The leaf of geology, one of the volumes of God's word, discloses that the earth in the fulness of time was lastly prepared for man, who has the ascendancy for all, by the supremacy of his mind. which, as its history discloses, works its own elevation to the standard of its divine Author, who is eternal. Geology then proves the creation of the universe.

All creation is as God elaborated it. Can it be better or more correct ? That devolves on Deity, not on the priestocracy to define.

I feel like descending from the sublime to the ridiculous, in coming from the contemplation of the Creator in the mirror of the universe, to that of the peculiar god in all his peculiar bibles, reeking with impudent ignorance and vulgarisms of man's images and idolatry.

What would be the surprise of Moses and his tribe, if they were to stand by the falls of Niagara, in the glorious light of the sun ? How rebuked would those barbarians be by the spray that sends forth its rainbows, and no doubt has taught the forest sons of America of the almighty power of the Great Spirit.

Ch. ii. v. 1. Thus the heavens and the earth were finished, and all the host of them. v. 2. And on the seventh day God ended his work which he had made, and he rested on the seventh day. Now, did it take God six days of this earth to create the universe? If so, by what principle was this peculiar time of this earth for six days, God's measure, in preference to any of the universe? Is the earth the superior planet? If so, does man's situation of imperfect state permit the idea? This idea is condemned at once. Is God so imperfect a being that he had to rest, as a created being? This betrays at once an imperfect appreciation of God that is the emanation of man's brain. We should have the sign unmistakable of the proper sabbath, as there are now no less than seven sabbaths. Which is the proper one, if any be more than man's ordination? What should we do, if peculiar systems made every day a sabbath? Do what we ought to do at once—use wise legislation.

The heaven was the abode of the peculiar god of his peculiar people, who certainly were indebted to the mind of predecessors and successors for this very imperfect knowledge of creation. As to the light which they ignorantly divided from darkness, as two separate existences, not conceiving the last the negative of the first, as sin or evil is of good, they misled themselves into the mists and fogs of their own twilight, which obfuscated all their moral as intellectual faculties. Now, the bible writers are estopped from the God of the universe, as they claim all the peculiar benefits of their peculiar bible, its god, &c.

In the creation of man, respect was had to his adaptation to the diversified conditions of the earth.

Several varieties of the same species best accomplish that purpose. It was as easy for the Creator to produce as many as the great grand divisions of the globe required, and at the same time identified through mind. It was not corporeal existence that God respected, as mind was his master creation, his chief workmanship. Both mind, soul, spirit, and their embodiment, were the objects of his divine providence and eternal regard. All are as God created them. His creation implies preservation, correspondent to their merits. Mind, the soul or spirit embodied, was endowed with its chief creation birth-right, religion, the chief end of its eternal existence, a problem that requires the universe and eternity for its solution.

Mind, then, only has the elements to elaborate for future good. It has to work its way through science, through nature, up to nature's God. The only inspiration is to itself, and that must, can only be through the mouth-pieces of the Great First Cause, who speaks by cause and effect.

Mind, then, does not at first repose on a bed of luxury, till it has won it by its merits, through the gracious boon of its Creator. ·It has to embellish itself by the best of culture to civilize the world, and render it embellished a true purpose in all its comprehensiveness.

Mind has to make its own creation for its own enjoyment. The idea of happiness being first is absurd, on the analysis of mind. As to the river and garden of Eden, all is clearly a fable as much as any. All such is an absurd fable, that belongs to the peculiar views of the brains of the priestocracy that wrote the books of Moses, and caused woman to be taken from man.

The leaf of physiology declares for the exhaustless genius of creation in woman as in man, as civilization declares for the equality of both. The diversity of human creation meets the whole case, obviates any necessity for incest, and glorifies God as a perfect being, who is libeled by bible-fables.

If God took one of man's ribs to form woman, then man ought to have one rib less, by physiology.

" 25. And they were both naked, the man and his wife, and were not ashamed." They, of course, were not civilized, by indirect admission. It seems that the man had to work after all, for—" 15. And the Lord took the man, and put him into the garden of Eden, to dress it, and to keep it." But in the 28th verse of the first chapter, man and woman were positively commanded to subdue the earth, that implies labor! besides, they were told to look for supplies to the whole earth. Eden is an afterthought in the diversified chapters of the priestocracy fixings.

" 16. And the Lord God commanded the man, saying, of every tree of the garden thou mayst freely eat: 17. But of the tree of the knowledge of good and evil, thou shalt not eat of it: for in the day that thou eatest thereof, thou shalt surely die." Ch. iii. The attributes of God declare against any monster creation of morals, and their antagonism, the Devil, or Satan serpent. This is a fiction also of the aforesaid visionaries. " 4. And the serpent said unto the woman, ye shall not surely die :" The serpent had more influence than God, for—" 6. She (the woman) took of the fruit thereof, and did eat." All the idea of man's fall is a libel on mind, as the seduction of the evil one is a libel on the Creator, who is necessarily deprived of his omnipresence, as of his Almighty power, by a superior antagonism. All this proves conclusively the priestocracy's peculiar god not almighty. God walks in the garden and inquires about the matter.

The diversity of the species of the human race, and the universal attributes of God Almighty, not here conceded, preclude all this pretension; even to all the bible characters that have been invented. Tradition could not recognise any such at all. None can tell of Adam or Eve, or such. It is folly and blasphemy. The idea of the Creator coming down subsequently, after all was ruined, and rebuking poor mortals for what he should have protected them from, particularly his powerful rival, the serpent, that "was more subtile than any beast of the field." of whom he is not mentioned as cautioning, declares an awful omission of duty on God's part, is a disingenuous legend of those who knew nothing of what they pretended to write.

Now, it most clearly is proved by analysis, that mind required rational education, and not receiving its full comprehension, that it erred. The impression of a Supreme was not satisfactorily made by this peculiar god, who has to be dismissed for the God of the universe, the God of mind. As to any antipathy at first between mind and serpent, that results from education. As to the woman's sorrows being multiplied in child-birth, that is by no means certain, not even probable, as her organization is as created originally. The less luxuriously the mother living, the less laborious the child birth, to a certain extent, as the more it is assimilated to animals.

The curse of the man is relative, and negatives the bible's falsity, for his labor that produces the sweat of the face, also sweetens the enjoyments of life, gives a relish for the taste, and health to the body. As to the fear of the Lord lest man should live for ever, all that is legend, and does not portray the imbecile character of the peculiar god, as it discloses the decided ignorance and assurance of the bible writers, who knew not the God of the universe, nor the great laws of nature, that comprehends unity of design, and required a universal change from what it now is, had that prospect been practicable to man. The bible of inspiration truly, if of ignorance general.

All created animal existence had to change by death, or the world had been unfit by reproduction.

"21. Unto Adam also, and to his wife, did the Lord God make coats of skins, and clothed them." The first state or stage of life.

"7. And they sewed fig leaves together, and made themselves aprons." Still a savage state, though in the Eden: The dramatists wind themselves up completely. And they were so simple, so verdant, as to trust the serpent. How could they appreciate God, who was with them so much?

This Adam and Eve were weak-minded and ignorant, a very poor specimen of humanity; that is, the writers of the bible were. The last clause of the third chapter of Genesis implies, that Eden was left guarded by cherubims, both non-existents, all fabulous. All are fables about Eden. Angels could not supersede conservative principles. Which was the best, peculiar god or devil?

After God Almighty created the elements pertaining to earth, from the least organization to the highest man conceived in his forethought, he committed all to the conservation of principles, that bespeak most that belongs to providence.

And as books called bibles, or by any other name, are man's, all that pertain to any tradition, are afterthoughts, that betray their own absurdity, the absurdity and infamy of the priestocracy, who are more apparent in the subsequent progress of this work. Ch. iv. v. 2.

The most conspicuous display is next made, in the history of Cain and Abel, all priestocracy inventions for the purpose, who are both represented as priests offering sacrifices to their peculiar god. The main object is to show that this god had his select chosen peculiar priests.

"And Abel was a keeper of sheep, but Cain was a tiller of the ground." These are the second and third states of society, as that of their parents was the first.

How came Moses, or those having this man of straw, to know aught of tradition for so many generations back? It is impossible among all such tribes as the Indians, who represent an analogous state. The peculiar god could not know, hence the priestocracy lied blasphemously. V. 3.—"Cain brought of the fruit of the ground an offering unto the Lord. 4. And Abel, he also brought of the firstlings of his flock, and of the fat thereof. And the Lord had respect unto Abel, and his offering." Well done, priestocracy, here you planted, confirmed your mighty origin. To identify it still better, Cain is made to slay Abel about their offerings! This work for the profession was instituted in blood said to have been shed.

This has been the centre of immense bloodshed. "17. And Cain knew his wife." Who was she? Who ever heard of her before? Were the writers incompetent or ashamed to tell?

Now, if God of the universe created, as reason tells us, five or more varieties of species of mankind, he obviated the crime of incest.

So much for the bible demoralization.   Ch. v.   The ages of mankind assumed by the bible, prove, by all the laws of physiology, ignorance of the times, and leave us uncertain whether years were months or not.

When the world was destitute of science, it proves itself inaccurate in most of its important points.

The ancients lived several centuries!   What fixed the years for that obscure period? Was there science to decide whether the years were not months?   Have we any authority but tradition; and is not tradition fable when it is not history?

Instead of degenerating, man is actually improving in the social circle of being. "24. And Enoch walked with God, and he was not, for God took him."   What an absurd falsehood about Enoch!   The direct translation of Enoch to God is against all the principles of life.   If they pretend to mean God Almighty, they lied outrageously, as his word proves.

All mortals die, by the principles of physiology.   The change of death is essential for spiritual existence.   Death is one of the works of God Almighty.

Every page of this bible teems with preposterous falsehood.   It is most difficult to decide which is most absurd, the familiarity of God with man, his inability of resistance to the serpent that spoke a reptile low in intellect and morals, or his translating Enoch. All this is priestcraft.

The bible is an idol worship.   Faith is an idol, because power and money are the idols.   Only get the mass to believe, that is all that is requisite.   This is the world. Who can dare affirm that man is exempt from death?

All things are possible with the peculiar god of the Jews, even to lies.   For the peculiar god always read their priestocracy.

V. 29.   Because of the ground which the Lord hath cursed.

If the God of the universe had not had omniscience and forethought, then he might have done this.   As a god cursed the ground, it proves afterthought of the priestocracy who wrote for their peculiar god.   But how imbecile and self-contradictory, when he "saw everything that he had made, and, behold, it was (not only good but) very good."

Curses and evils are not the God's of the universe, hence they belong to this clique.

Chapter sixth of Genesis gives us a fabulous view of the marriage of the sons of God with the daughters of men.   If all this does not prove a second race, a diversity of human species, then all such book is a mixture of fable and confused history. What better could we expect of shepherd writers, men of the second age of the world, preparing the mind of the faithful, the credulous, for miracles, prophecies and monstrous stories?   People lived to most extraordinary ages, had most extraordinary size, excessive wickedness, all by the mind-jugglery of the priestocracy.   Their god only saw by experience and after-thought, what was only the property of man, if we believe the bible stories.   His forethought would have told him what man would be, and clearly proves that all this is an absurdity of man's fictions.

To say as the bible says, " and it repented the Lord that he had made man on the earth, and it grieved him at his heart," is to propagate a libel on God's attributes, especially as   " God saw that the wickedness of man was great in the earth, and that every imagination of the thoughts of his heart was only evil continually," so contradictory to the statement previously made, " and God saw everything that he had made, and, behold, it was very good."   And the Lord decides by this bible statement, to destroy all animated nature, except that of the sea.   Why was that reserved :   Because the bible, alias libel authors, could not devise in their absurd schemes and pusillanimous minds, any plan to destroy that?   Their peculiar god had to compromise on that position.   Was that humanity, to destroy the land-brute creation, for men's sins.   How much better was it that the God of the universe presided over the world's conservation, despite of the peculiar pretences!   " But Noah found grace in the eyes of the Lord." And was it not as easy for the world to find grace in the eyes of the Lord in all its ages, as well before as after Noah, Christ, the priestocracy?   What had they, mortals, to do with any grace but their own?   Nothing could possibly prevent the reception, as long as the creator of mind could dispense grace.   But " Noah was a just man, and perfect in his generations, and Noah walked with God," however contradictory to all truth and its reason, in walking with the God of the universe.   Noah was of the pulpit-priestocracy, and had the telling of his own tale, however impossible it was for tradition to be accurate as regards the vast generations of men, unsupported as it is clearly by any god-inspiration that is worth mind's attention.   All was the inspiration peculiar of the priestocracy, not any inspiration at all.   V. 17. And, behold, I, even I, do bring a flood of waters upon the earth, to destroy all flesh, wherein is the breath of life from under heaven : and every thing that is in the earth shall die.   18. But with thee will I establish my covenant.   19. Two of every sort shalt thou bring into the ark.   20. Of every creeping thing of the earth after his kind." How preposterous was it to conduct through oceans of thousands of miles in width, two of every sort of animated nature of the earth, the very thing that was to be avoided by the ark. Had these wise men ever conceived of another continent and ocean? How are they caught. Some animals are covered with heavy woolly coats that, when wet, would sink them. All had to forego climate, and all the peculiarities of animated nature, to the silly conception of an addled-brain priestocracy. To what world-absurdities will not peculiar faithites reduce themselves? But how could there be a universal deluge? They had declared for the theatrical exhibition of their peculiar preacher, Noah, who was most righteous, and yet who could only be one least free of sin—not certainly exempt, according to human nature. Nothing is impossible with their god, in the eyes of these men! But all things consistent with his godship are certainly impossible with God the immutable, and cannot be consistent with himself, as he is a perfect being. The earth of the priestocracy was a plane, easily deluged, but circumnavigation has proved God's earth to be nearly a sphere or a globe, and that has spoilt all their pretences. Had the writers dreamt that the waters were oceans instead of seas, and that their four-cornered plane was a globe, they would have fixed up the universal deluge more cautiously. The same waters of the earth could only be used after all—they could only return to the bed of the ocean, absorbed therein compatibly with the nature of currents. Where are their brains? As the earth is, all the waters collectable in the clouds could not drown the whole earth, and the abstraction of more water from other globes would derange the universe.

So all the matter is quieted at once, as an impossibility.

And God's creation of earth, but the ark and contents, was destroyed, when a wiser action could have prevented that creation, as God is just and perfect. Honest sense on this, if on no other point, decides the right position.

Ch. vii., v. 20. "And the mountains were covered." This kills the deluge, as all this is conclusively contradicted by exact science, God's mouthpiece.

The ante-human world was when water and earth separated to their right position. "There are frequently found, in places leagues from the sea, and even on the tops of high mountains, whole trees and bones of animals; even fishes entire; sea-shells petrified and sunk deep under ground, which the best naturalists (geologists) are agreed could never have come there but by the deluge."—*Buck.*

Where are the bones of man? Are they found there?

If not, of what avail is the theory of the deluge?

All ancient nations had an idea of floods and deluges from these signs first mentioned. "In India, also, Sir William Jones has discovered that in the oldest mythological books of that country there is such an account of the deluge as corresponds sufficiently with that of Moses." Or is it not that of an anterior doctrine? Geology proves man the culminating point of creation.

THE DELUGE.

WHAT the barbarian writers of the peculiar-faith bibles mistook for universal deluges was only a mighty universal operation or elaboration of conservative principles. To these same worthies the world is indebted for the sun rising and setting for the earth exclusively. What humanity was it to destroy all the brute creation for man? Even in Egypt, in regard to the cattle. Surely the priestocracy are a curse to all animated creatures, which they sacrificed on all occasions, but the fish, and those defied and defeated the poor stupid dolts. No thanks to them that the fish were not drowned or burnt up, as with all their ingenuity it could not be brought about.

The fish defeated the priestocracy, as the peculiar devil defeated their peculiar god in the peculiar creation. What a peculiar set of numbsculls!

We can see what kind of earth the priestocracy had. 1 Sam. ch. ii., v. 8. "For the pillars of the earth are the Lord's, and he hath set the world upon them." 10. "The Lord shall judge the ends of the earth."

What an absurdity in talking about the universal deluge, which the Jew bible pretends to, when history well discloses, which is well evinced by the immense numbers of people soon after the time claimed, to be false. Of course all things are peculiar with the Jew-peculiar people. They had a peculiar deluge. It could not have been a universal one, as it is eternally estopped from all such by God's earth, which is different from the peculiar-bible creation, that presented a four-cornered prodigy or abortion, resting on pillars.

According to Rollin, who quotes Callisthenes for carrying the origin of the Babylonians to one hundred and fifteen years after this deluge of the bible.

That is about the time of Nimrod, the father of Ninus. He enlarged his conquests by his own troops and powerful succors from the Arabians, conquered a large extent of country from Egypt as far as India and Bactrians, " which he did not then venture to attack." Why build Nineveh so large and with such powerful walls, but for the populousness of the times. Nineveh, the city he built, was fortified and adorned with fifteen towers, two hundred feet high. After he had finished this prodigious work, building the city of Nineveh sixty miles in circumference, he resumed his expedition against the Bactrians.

Ctesias, who had access to the court of Persia, states that his army was over one million nine hundred thousand men. "Ninus made himself master of a great number of cities, and at last laid siege to Bactria, the capital of the country," which he took with the aid of his wife, Semiramis, finding therein a great treasure. Now the people of the opposing side were vastly numerous, and bear evident marks, by numbers and treasure, of a high antiquity. Not only that, but we must look at the real state of mind so cultivated as to bring about all these grand results, indisputably above the Jews in their best days, and of course showing a better peculiar faith. Now the Jew must have gotten of this very source. Eight people, according to the Jew bible of the peculiar flood, replenish the Jew earth in that time and to that extent, when it took four hundred and thirty years from the time of the peculiar promise to Abraham, who had then a large household, to increase to six hundred thousand persons! But the jesuitical caviller may affect to estimate the peculiar longevity as some aid; but that remains, as all other bible peculiarities, to be proved. The thing is as bad as the insects crossing the ocean, to avoid the very difficulty that they thus thereby encounter. Of all the impostor-dolts, and blockheads, the bible writers exceed all, not only for foolish legends, but for striving to make the world as ignorant and mean as themselves. They not only seek to render the world ignorant, but to keep it at that state to promote their nefarious views.

We have panoramas of the deluge that amount to only fancy sketches. The ancients could not analyze anything complex. They saw traces of local and partial deluges, but those were not universal. The very tides of the ocean would repudiate all such solecisms. The world has to get rid of all such miserable rubbish, fit for barbarians.

V. 1. For thee have I seen righteous before me in this generation.

How does this compare with Noah's drunkenness, and cursing an innocent grandson?

Ch. viii. 20. And Noah builded an altar unto the Lord; and took of every clean beast, and of every clean fowl, and offered burnt offerings on the altar.

Noah proved himself a good priest in building an altar unto the peculiar god, who was pleased by smelling a sweet savor, to say in his heart not to curse the ground any more for man's sake. So great a priest was Noah. So great a revolution was thus effected by Noah, that "while the earth remaineth, seed-time and harvest shall not cease," whatever Elijah said to the contrary. Thus will the bible priestocracy tie themselves forever, and contradict themselves most disreputably for inspired men. Honest truth would become them.

Ch. ix. 9. And I, behold, I establish my covenant with you, and with your seed after you. 12. And God said, 13. I do set my bow in the clouds, and it shall be for a token of a covenant between me and the earth. 14. And it shall come to pass, when I bring a cloud over the earth, that the bow shall be seen in the cloud.

But the token of the covenant is the rainbow, a natural phenomenon on the reflection of the sun's rays on a cloud, and which, fortunately for the bible, belongs to the effect of the rays of the sun on the particles of water thrown up even by an engine, a natural phenomenon illustrated by a prism. All this is below the dignity of mind. The writers were numbsculls.

The writers of the universal deluge affect to know, that the rainbow was a compact against any more such deluges by God. Now, mere prisms of glass prove the refraction of the sun's rays, and the school-boy excels their Moses in true science. It is a shame, not that Moses and his priestocracy knew so little, but that the moderns should know no more, and be gulled by impudent impostor priestocracy.

The deluge has been more of blood than of water, for peculiar faiths. The world would never have heard of the first persecution, blood, massacre, had any been true. The result reflects on the partisans, their vindictiveness, passions, and all that.

As to the division of the earth among the sons of Noah, it is not also in the power of tradition that is remote, to give us an accurate account. Who can affirm of tradition? Who can testify to its first settlers, when ancient history is so deficient?

21. And he (Noah) drank of the wine, and was drunken; and he was uncovered within his tent.

Alas, the drunken priest! That Noah was a righteous man, his drunkenness forbids when his nakedness was exposed, and his unjust curses of his son's son were blasphemously uttered. What will not a priest do? It was important to state the power of priest's curses, however unjust on an inoffensive unborn generation, however ferocious the fanaticism. Does a priest ever forgive aught against himself, though he foolishly condemns his own posterity of which his high-mindedness should have prevented right minds.

But it was essential to curse Canaan to get at his land, as if the priestocracy could be possibly justified in such iniquities. And he (the priest) said, cursed be Canaan; a servant of servants shall he be unto his brethren. Who can say aught to this as correct, or to any abomination growing out of it as prophecy? 26. And he said, blessed be the Lord God of Shem; and Canaan shall be his servant.

The children of Israel, descendants of Shem, were servants, by Moses' account, for four centuries in Egypt. 27. God shall enlarge Japheth, and he shall dwell in the tents of Shem; and Canaan shall be his servant.

The Canaanites were conquered, slaughtered and despoiled of their lands, by the Jews who libeled them with savage ferocity. Of all the abominable stupidity, that of the priestocracy is the meanest. The children of Shem, were Elam and Asshur, &c. And the Abrahamites were also in captivity for seventy years under the Assyrians—worse than that, they were also under those very Canaanites.

Ch. xi. 1. And the whole earth was of one language, and of one speech. The difference of language proves different races, and natural causes acting thereon.

To make out the unity of the human family, it was expedient to make out the unity of language, and if the preceding race destroyed were more wicked, surely those that were left, were the most foolish. What is the tower of Babel? A fable? 4. "And they said, go to, let us build a city and a tower, whose top may reach unto heaven; and let us make a name, lest we be scattered abroad upon the face of the whole earth." What ignorance in the people, having no science? Who? who but the priestocracy? Where and what is heaven? Surely not the concave ether. Lest we be scattered abroad: that is what was essential, necessary and unavoidable. But the worst was the peculiar "Lord came down to see the city and the tower, which the children of men builded," and it was concluded by him, as the people were one, and they all had one language, that nothing would be restrained from them which they have imagined to do, unless there was a confusion of tongues.

So their language was confounded, and the people were scattered from building the city Babel. And yet unity of language is one of the very best benefits that will promote civilization of the world most speedily. It is the game of priestocracy, to disunite the people.

The diversity of language helps to prove the diversity of race. What a libel on science, the bible is! Its seal of condemnation is on its face forever. This was the little god of Judaism, the little sense-god. The people were scattered from the best natural causes, and have built thereby the cities of the world. The authors assume to be very particular about the old names; now if they could not give true histories, how could they give true traditions?

As Abraham, the head of Judaism, is taken from Ur, of the Chaldees, it is very satisfactory to conclude that the tenets of this circle, originated from that circle, modified by the changes of time and the knowledge of a more diffused circle, that is as mind advanced. To build up a foundation, it was expedient to refer the priestocracy to the peculiar god's own acts.

Thus we have the calling of Abraham, and the origin of the Hebrew state. And now we see the curse of prophecy; Abraham was introduced into the land of Canaan, who had been cursed by the priest Noah, alias the priestocracy writers, and because his grandfather cursed him, an inoffensive being, in his drunkenness, Abraham was to be blessed by robbery of his possessions! This is priestocracy's logic. Abram, &c., went forth from Ur, of the Chaldees, to go into the land of Canaan: xii. 5. and into the land of Canaan they (Abram, &c.) came. 7. "And the Lord appeared unto Abram, and said, unto thy seed will I give this land." Who endorses this pretence? This land now belongs to the Turks. This, then, is a false prophecy fully condemnatory of the bible. 7. "And there builded he an altar unto the Lord, who appeared unto him." Well done, priest Abram. This was not the Lord of the universe, who is the God of rational beings.

And building altars in this land by Abraham, did not prove the rights of the priestocracy. But the priestocracy's right by their peculiar god's deeds of gift, is supreme, "And the Lord said unto Abram, for all the land which thou seest, to thee will I give it, and to thy seed forever;" a death blow to all prophecy and its peculiar gods. Now

Abraham proved himself a good priest, as he lied about his wife, when he came into Egypt. But the customs of the ancients might be plead in Abraham's justification, as there was perfidy among mankind. But then the peculiar lord of Abraham had blessed him; yet doubtless he had lied about the Lord, as he had about his wife. When a man, priest particularly, transcends the limits of truth intentionally, there is no end to the violation. None can be a priest, without personally by the very act lying. It is very clear by Abraham's lies and actions, that the world had been destroyed to little purpose, as perfidy of mankind was prominent. So the peculiar god who had a peculiar creation of heaven and earth, had peculiar labor, his peculiar deluge, in vain. If the worst part of mankind had not been left, it at least was equal to its predecessors. The peculiar organization of man's brain had to be altered, ere deluges did any good. As there is no proof that mind's organization was altered, it is conclusive proof that the priestocracy lied about the deluge. 17. "And the Lord plagued Pharaoh and his house, with great plagues, because of Sarai, Abram's wife."

Who endorses all this; who affirms this to be truth? It seems that Pharaoh rebuked Abraham, for his duplicity and dissimulation, the characteristics of priestocracy. All this was natural to Abraham. But we suspect that the author's lies about the whole affair, are the worst of the whole.

As a proof that God had left a very bad set of people, this bible tells us, "But the men of Sodom were wicked, and sinners before the Lord exceedingly; and moreover the iniquity of the Amorites was not yet full. Ch. xiv. v. 18. And Melchisedek, king of Salem, brought forth the bread and wine : and he was the priest of the most high God. v. 19. And he blessed him, and said, blessed be Abram of the most high God."—The highest peculiar god; the God Creator cannot have priests. One priest endorses the other priest; but who endorses this statement? Who can truthfully, and in good honest faith, endorse the whole? But the best is to follow—v. 20. And he gave him tithes of all. Here is Melchisedek, the tithing priest. Here is the foundation of priests confirmed. The proper appreciation of Melchisedek is that he was of the priestocracy, a chief actor in the incipient drama. For his peculiar blessing on Abram, Melchisedek got the tithes of all. Here was the institution of tithes. And shall the dissimulator, the incestuous, the adulterer Abraham, be in a better position than the rest of the world, merely because the bible says, "And he believed in the Lord; and he counted it to him for righteousness"? Who endorses this for truth? After Abram falsified his word, he could not be believed. All rational minds will believe unmistakably in the God of the universe, if they look properly at the works of that universe, and most purely too, without any taint or corruption of priestocracy.

Shall bible visions and dreams be preferred, as in this instance, to the highest demonstration of God's creation before the universe?

As a just and immutable perfect being, God gave all mankind, of all ages, their mind, with all their science of demonstrating his rule and religion. If the priestocracy had been honest, they would have acknowledged that it was mind, not they, that found out all such things. What an exhibition of the priestocracy, who have sought to prove their mission divine, by their own false pretences? To prove their own exaltation, they have sought to disgrace the God of the universe to a peculiar imbecile god—that is themselves, not God, as that is impossible. Ch. xv. v. 1. After these things, the word of the Lord came unto Abram in a vision. What of that? 6. And he believed in the Lord; and he counted it to him for righteousness. The whole rational world can easily be placed on the safe ground, not by visions, but by the highest proof of principles. That word of the Lord would be current to-day, if mind would permit the priestocracy.

Ch. xvi. The adultery of Abraham caused strife in his household. Polygamy is felony with us—yet not with this righteous patriarch, who is any and everything, as the dictatorial priestocracy decide, whether adulterer or not. They have lied for him, calling his concubine his wife. The priestocracy will do anything. 7. And the angel of the Lord, &c. God has conservative principles, not angels, to do the commands of the universe. He could have hardly sent after an adultress. The pretended inspired authors miss a figure here certainly. 11. Ishmael; because the Lord hath heard thy affliction. Now all this is legend. How could he give all such reasons? If Ishmael be the Arabs, the prophecy against him is against the Old and New Testaments; a death-blow to both. 12. And he will be a wild man, his hand will be against every man, and every man's hand against him. Whom had he to thank, but those that ought to have been his rightful protectors?

C. xxi. v. 20. And (he, Ishmael) dwelt in the wilderness, and became an archer. What was he but an outlaw? What less could he be, but a robber? Who made him thus but the author of his existence, Abraham?

Who can affirm to the severance of the race of Ishmael from their common progenitor?   All looks plausible, but is it provable?
The conduct of Sarah, to both mother and child, does not show that she was reconciled to the act of her adulterous husband.   But then this was only an orientalism.   If she had consented, she acted in virtue of the bad faith to the woman, and lied to God to his face.   Both she and Abraham are not exempt from the iniquity of this adultery, and the crime of expulsion of the unfortunate, whom they had corrupted.   They were worse than Hagar.
So much for the Patriarch Abraham, the world's pattern!   But, worst of all, the Lord of the bible is the patron of its demoralization.
Ch. xvii. v. 1. And the Lord appeared to Abram, and said unto him, 7. And I will establish my covenant between me and thee, and thy seed after thee in their generations, for an everlasting covenant, to be a God unto thee, and to thy seed after thee. 8. And I will give unto thee, and to thy seed after thee, the land wherein thou art a stranger, all the land of Canaan, for an everlasting possession, and I will be their God. Is this prophecy, as pretended, fulfilled? It is all false pretence.
Circumcision of every man-child was the token of the covenant.   If God had required this, he would have caused nature to put the mark on mankind in general.   How preposterous, that the female should be exempt!   All this is man's folly, all the false pretences of the priestocracy.
Ch. xviii. v. 20.   And the Lord said, because the cry of Sodom and Gomorrah is great, and because their sin is very grievous ; 21. I will go down now, and see whether they have done altogether according to the cry of it, which is come unto me ; and if not, I will know."   This was the peculiar god, who of course was not omnipresent; and that he was not omniscient, the sixteenth verse, last clause, proves, as " Abraham went with them, to bring them on the way"!—god, or his angel, was actually located with Abraham ; that proves it conclusively.   We should close the book, but for the necessity of doing justice to those who have not investigated and will not for themselves.
What an extraordinary influence the priestocracy had, even with god, this chapter is brought forward by them to illustrate.
23 v. And Abraham said, 24. Peradventure there be fifty righteous?   26. And the Lord said, If I find in Sodom fifty righteous, &c.! and thus they communed, until the Lord said, v. 32. " I will not destroy it for ten's sake."   What miserable imbecility, and how complete.   The Lord not to know how many righteous in Sodom!   Can the climax of the peculiar god be carried to any greater effrontery?   Ch. xix.   And after all, who will dare say to-day, that the destruction of Sodom and the cities of the plains was not accomplished by natural volcanic causes?   As to Lot's wife, that is all a legend of the priestocracy.   And shall the drunken, lying and incestuous Lot find grace in the sight of the Lord, and shall not the world too, when God has magnified his mercy to the same?   What are the means but grace and mercy to a repentant world from its Creator?   On just analysis, we see that the rescued are miserable, unworthy of notice. Fine people, were Lot and his daughters, after being spared the destruction of Sodom and Gomorrah, to commit crimes of drunkenness, lying and incest!
Who were more vindictive in libeling the Jew priestocracy in assigning them wicked and disgraceful origin, and most ignominious ends of existence? Their wrathful peculiar god was invoked against all the heathen who sacrificed to other or their gods.
All the natural events, as this story of Sodom, were stupidly seized upon to promote their blasphemous pretensions.
Ch. xx. v. 2. And Abraham said of Sarah his wife, she is my sister :   This is the second lie implied, and involved Abimelek, who is represented as saved by a dream from god.   Thus the stupid superstition is maintained from this bible to this day, and the world has been visionary on the dreams of the priestocracy.   All is written to produce the conviction of sacred persons. 7. Now therefore restore the man his wife ; for he is a prophet, and he shall pray for thee, and thou shalt live.   Though a prophet he did not know, and had to resort to a subterfuge, thus proving that he lied either way, for if a prophet, he knew how the event would result, or he lied that he was a prophet. It was not God of the universe, but the priestocracy of the bible we mean.   As a prophet assuming, he was true to his vocation. 11. " And Abraham said, and they will slay me for my wife's sake," whom he thus obtained by incestuous marriage.   God does not permit any false statement ; thus Abraham stands convicted.   Noah was a prophet, and is certainly convicted of falsehood, as no universal deluge could take place on this globe. He might have been drunk at the time that he assumed a deluge, whether it was when he stripped himself and cursed Canaan we do not pretend to know.   Whether

he dreamed that he was on a planisphere, or lied right out, the priestocracy can judge. Dreams and visions could place the whole on their four-cornered earth, where appeared a peculiar god, who spoke to the hearts, and not the minds, and this was the earth that the sun moved around. We propose to send the priestocracy on a voyage of exploration; they have already gone as far as the land of Nod! We have to take the words of the writers about tradition; who endorses? Who can endorse, if they wished? The priestocracy? Assuredly they would most awfully commit themselves to, and convict themselves of, perjury!

17. So Abraham prayed unto God : and God healed Abimilech, and his wife, and his maid servants, and they bare children." What circumstantial falsehoods.

Abraham was so much in the habit of lying that he could not get over it, in his lying about Sarah. He had previously made out, or his foster priests had done it for him, that he had feasted angels at his house, and that he had made such impressions on god by his entreaties, that god acquiesced in them all about Sodom, if he found so many righteous within the city. Now the chief object of the priestocracy is, to show on all occasions all the miracles, and this adventure of Abraham is introduced for such. It is to prove that Abraham was a prophet besides a priest. The poets take all manner of license with language, but they could not hold a hand with the game of such a profession.

And this Abraham is the founder of a code of morals and faith for the world! Ch. xxi. v. 33. "And Abraham planted a grove in Beersheba, and called there on the name of the Lord, the everlasting God." Is the everlasting God the peculiar god? Is the peculiar god the God of the universe?

All the gods that Abraham ever called on were peculiar, as his nation.

The God of the universe has no peculiar priest or grove.

What, then, is the difference between the grove of Abraham and the groves of the other priests? We can most easily perceive the difference of the gods in this, that the everlasting God of the universe had all omniscience, without temptation; but the peculiar " god did tempt Abraham." Ch. xxii. v. 1. It seems that he only knew by this how it was, as v. 12. "And he (the angel of the Lord) said, For now I know that thou fearest God." V. 17. "Thy seed shall possess the gate of his enemies." Why libel God? Do the Jews do that, with shame to the lying prophets? 18. "And in thy seed shall all nations of the earth be blessed, because thou hast obeyed my voice."

That he did not sacrifice his son in place of an animal, is due to the improved light of mind; but sacrificing an animal proves that the God of the universe had nothing to do with it.

The Creator asks not for the blood of animated nature, neither knee, nor lip, or body worship; but mind's adoration, its supreme duty in life. The shedding of any blood proves a position adverse to all this.

The burnt offering that Abraham made in the place that he called Jehovah-Jireh, eminently proves the sacrifice of polytheists and the name of Jupiter.

The angels of the peculiar god were the intermediates.

So neither in morals or religon have we anything to irradiate mind from the polygamist, adulterous patriarchs. What, in the name of God Almighty, do you want with such bibles? To murder with?

This same patriarch Abraham lived with concubines in adultery. Ch. xxv. v. 6 : " But unto the sons of the concubines, which Abraham had, Abraham gave gifts, and sent them away from Isaac his son, (while he yet lived,) eastward, unto the east country." Was this, also, a colony of outlaws and robbers, of miserable morals, and peculiar education? Were they, too, authorized to become wild men, their hands against every man, and every man's hand against them—a prophecy called, but a vocation under that authority, for lies, robbery, and plunder on the world? Is Arabia, then, indebted at this day for her licentious code of morals through this patriarch, cut off as she is from redemption through mind, by want of intercourse from the rest of the civilized world. by her peculiar-faith curses? But what an example of Oriental licentiousness the patriarch leaves for imitation by justification of this faithful morning star!

And Isaac, the son, lied, like his father, for which he was justly rebuked, as well nigh causing adultery.

It is a principle in morals that when a man betrays one of their best ingredients, truth, that he renders himself obnoxious to all its legitimate disadvantages, that of not being believed when he speaks it. On this principle, we surely cannot begin to believe any of this kith and kin, this profession, whenever it is their interest to lie, and that is much of the time. Ch. xxvi. v. 24. "And the Lord said unto him (Isaac), I will bless thee," &c., " for Abraham's sake." Why? What substantial proof of all these traditions? None. What a righteous character Jacob was, who took advantage of Esau and bought his birthright, circumventing him by selling what was necessary sustenance

31

their maids to him. All participants in the crime of adultery. The felon used adultery with polygamy, and he ignominiously excited jealousy between the two wives who were sisters. Is this to be followed by pure republicans? Is this the faith that the world imitates so closely? Are the people so verdant, so insane, or are they slaves? Can they as rationalists, act on principles, or must they follow such cattle as masters? And Jacob's god was the god of his father, and the angel of this god spake unto Jacob in a dream, about the cattle. The 12th verse of chapter xxxi., is equal to that of the New Testament, where the holy ghost appears unto Mary. 19. "And Rachel had stolen the images that were her father's." His chief wife a thief and liar; his children deceivers, nearly all conspiring for fratricide or the murder of their brother, being intentional murderers, and some were incestuous. The household were idolators, and this is the bible that was not only to delight delicate matrons, but lead refined daughters in the most exalted of mind's attributes, functions and principles. Save them, the sight even of such a nauseous compound. Why will virtuous and good citizens persist in forcing this odious compound of absurdies, contradictions, and abominations, after all its explosions of mind on mind? Why will they conspire with world-despotisms, to perpetrate such felony? Ch. xxxii. 24. "And there wrestled a man with him (Jacob), 26. And he said, let me go, for the day breaketh; and he (Jacob) said, I will not let thee go, except thou bless me. 28. For as a prince hast thou (once Jacob, now Israel,) power with God and with men, and hast prevailed. 29. And he (who? God) blessed him then. 30. For I (Jacob) have seen God face to face," &c. This beats Abraham all hollow. Abraham headed God in argument, but Jacob outwrestled him. Pin the priestocracy close, and they affect metaphor in that particular verse or chapter, thus they would dissolve the whole bible by figures. But this is a figure missed; the priestocracy have been too anxious to show off, and overdrawn on faith, that convenient morsel to a monk's pretences.

The bible, too indelicate for chastity, is too low for mind and religion. We can well exclaim, not only what absurdity, but outrage on the Creator of the universe. The certain and irresistible conclusion is, that if Jacob prevailed with his peculiar god, that he was superior any way, and of course saw this god, as he said; proving enough for us, that the God of the universe was not in that wrestling scrape. How is this proved? 32. Therefore the children of Israel eat not of the sinew which shrank, which is upon the bollow of the thigh, unto this day: because he touched the hollow of Jacob's thigh, in the sinew that shrank. There it is, proved! But this is monk's proof. Who endorses it? Of course, God should. Well, how does he do it? By his word, the bible. All this is in a circle. What is all such worth? In conclusion, how do we know all that? The bible says so, but who endorses the bible statement? If God does, he must be its witness. Is God a witness? His universe contradicts it entirely. The true analysis is this: that the priestocracy outlied themselves in this affair of Jacob, over that affair of Abraham. The sapient dupes have outlied the pettifoggers, and have befogged themselves and world in inextricable blunders.

Ch. xxxv. v. 2: Then Jacob said unto his household, and to all that were with him, put away the strange gods that are among you, and be clean and change your garments.

What cumulative proof about Joseph, who was to enact a conspicuous part of the drama. Ch. xli. 56. And the famine was over all the face of the earth. 57. And all countries came into Egypt to Joseph, for to buy corn; because that the famine was so sore in all lands. Who can believe all this statement? That very statement bespeaks a grade of civilization founded on science and mind culture, that did not exist. At that time navigation had not advanced to the mariner's compass, that enables man to steer across the trackless ocean. This statement is unquestionably disproved, as false. One of the great characteristics of biblical narration, is identifying its tales by plausible reasons. Its language betrays the ignorance of the writers, that laugh to scorn the idea of inspiration, as xliii. 30. For his bowels did yearn upon his brother. About as physiological as the understanding of his heart. The world might have written all such stuff, but it is another thing to believe it.

Who believes that God talked to the patriarchs? If he knows any idea, he knows that it is only the peculiar god. Ch. xlvi. 31. And Joseph said unto his brethren, I will say unto him (Pharaoh) 32, and the men (his brethren and father's house) are shepherds, for their trade hath been to feed cattle.

The second stage of life cannot teach the light of civilization to the fourth and last age, that is absurd in the extreme. Ch. xlvii. 20. And Joseph bought all the land of Egypt for Pharaoh. 22. Only the land of the priests bought he not; for the priests had a portion assigned them of Pharaoh, &c. 26. Except the land of the priests only, which became not Pharaohs. The priestocracy and the king had a community of interest. 27. And Israel dwelt in the land of Egypt, in the country of Goshen.

Ch. xlviii. 3. And Jacob said unto Joseph, God Almighty appeared unto me at Luz, in the land of Canaan, and blessed me. 4. And said unto me, and (I) will give this land to thy seed after thee, for an everlasting possession. And sure enough, this impostor is rewarded, for time proves him a false prophet about the Jews and their residence. He that could not tell where his son Joseph was, nor anything about him, as he said, " Joseph is without doubt rent in pieces." " For I will go down to the grave unto my son, mourning." After this, if any one can say that a bible prophet is a prophet, then he knows not God of the universe, nor his noblest attributes, truth and honesty.

Yes, but here is a mighty mistake, the bible minions may say—for Jacob said that God Almighty appeared unto him at Luz. And does that pretence mend the matter at all ? This peculiar god was all in all, the almighty, but his peculiarity is proved by Jacob himself, in the very speech quoted.

He has peculiarized him, and of course the bible has defined its own position, so the mistake is with the advocates altogether. But they may affect to be thunderstruck about the supposed blasphemy, and there again is their own mistake.

All the bible assertions are predicated with the supposed holiest sanctity : then all the lies of their fraternity, as of Jacob, are all perjuries; for they are all attempted to be fixed as irrevocable, by all the curses of the priestocracy, on those that attempt to revoke them at all. Now it is not so much the inextricable blasphemy of Jacob, bad as it is, as the verdancy of the moderns adopting what idiots ought to be ashamed of.

Who can believe that chapter forty-ninth was ever fixed up by Jacob, if ever there was such a creature in substance ? If it was, he portrayed the character of the priestocracy, who have portrayed their own likeness. The man that does not know his own grandsons affects to be a prophet ! But all these blunders are chargeable to the dramatists, whose patchwork could not hide their peculiar deformity : their mantle was too rickety for truth.

But Jacob speaks from the facts of the case, when he speaks of Simeon and Levi—instruments of cruelty are in their habitations.

" 6. O my soul, come not thou into their secret; (hear that, preachers,) unto their assembly, mine honor, be not thou united. 7. Cursed be their anger, for it was fierce; and their wrath, for it was cruel. 10. The sceptre shall not depart from Judah, nor a lawgiver from between his feet, until Shiloh come ; and unto him shall the gathering of the people be." The dearth universal, except in Egypt, of course is a fiction, ingeniously devised to invent the tale for the bondage in, and to the same source of invention is due the deliverance of the children of Israel out of Egypt. Besides the fanaticism of pretended prophecy, engendered in arousing up the enthusiasm of this people, was the additional motive of recovering the land where the bones of their ancestors were buried. But neither priest-altars, nor wells, nor groves, nor all the pretences of priestocracy's words, entitled the children of Israel to the possession of lands occupied by others, and to say the least, deserted by their ancestors. What sort of a covenant was made with Jacob ? Was he honest enough to keep one ? As patriarchs, so is the bible worthless.

EXODUS.

Who was Moses ? Born of incestuous wedlock, and when grown, a murderer; when ruler, a repudiator ; and when competent to dispense his peculiar faith, an idolator and pagan. Moses married a priest's daughter, and necessarily became imbued with all the character of a priest, having such previous education in Egypt. He makes an admirable start as a man of genius, intending to play out mind-jugglery. He clothes his superstition with the sublime wonders of nature, and resorts to the volcano to add to the influence on mind.

But the mighty solution is in the bible, that gives the priestocracy for god ; but the lord god of Israel is certainly not the God of the universe, as is proved by ch. iii. v. 7. And the Lord said, 8. And I am come down to deliver them (my people) out of the hands of the Egyptians, &c. All the people of the world are those of the God of the universe; any other language is untrue.

The God of the universe does not have to come down to earth, as he is omnipresent, and has his conservative principles to represent and vindicate him, excluding necessarily the angels. What proof is there that God sent Moses to deliver the children of Israel ? All lied. Moses sent himself; as God had as little need of him as of angels to act divinely for the Hebrew nation. The whole nation lied, claiming any divine mission, proved by the works of God in the universe.

Moses and Aaron were the greatest mind-jugglers, the most astute of their priestocracy ; and the whole of all peculiar bibles are mind-juggleries. If the world had con-

THE AUTHENTICITY OF ANY SCRIPTURES.

temporary history of all such bibles of tradition, they would be proved and confirmed by
science, as the worst of all iniquties. We are conscientiously convinced this bible is
an abominable fable, made up of degraded lies. The priestocracy are all self-commis-
sioned, and endorse each other.

The pretence is, that the object was to smite all Egypt with all God's wonders; and
if they had been performed as related, not only all Egypt, but the whole world would
have been Judaized. The lies are told, but the omission of rational effects convicts
them all. The most reckless opposition could not have possibly withstood all such, as
coming from God.

The last verse of this chapter violates all the principles of religion, for it libels God,
as advising and suggesting repudiation. As like priestocracy, so was their peculiar
god, who spoke and knew only as the first. What does chapter the fourth prove?
That God proved Moses for jugglery? What mind is so verdant? Would God have
disciplined Moses or the priestocracy, when he could better do it through the minds of
the world; a performance that was purposed at creation?

That is the way that God has been operating during his administration, but the dynasties
of the priestocracy have assumed a different thing, to their disgrace.

God has a direct way of doing things, the priestocracy has an indirect way, about
which they have to lie continually to keep it going; and when that is done, all is done.
The moderns have to aid the ancients. One of the worst features of this libelous bible
is, that God said unto Moses that he would harden Pharaoh's heart, that he should not
let the people go! The terms of ignorance in which this libel is conveyed, betray the
science of physiology, as of religion, enough to confute the whole forever. The very
signs and wonders that caused the Israelites to believe, would have been irresistible to
the superstitious Egyptians. The legend commits its own suicide.

There is, no doubt, something latent here, as the ornaments thus obtained, that went
to the Egyptian peculiar gods, were or could be devoted to their Jew god.

Ch. v. v. 3 : And they said, the God of the Hebrews hath met with us." This had
been anticipated by Pharaoh, who knew not such a god. Had the God of the universe
been proved, there had been no sectarianism between the Hebrews and Egyptians.

It was a thing impossible to convince one ancient nation that another cotemporary
had superior gods, when exclusive proprietorship was claimed, and their national priestocracy were ever on the alert. Had the universal God been proclaimed, then the difficulty
had been obviated; assuredly this was the case with the Hebrews and Egyptians.

The Egyptians were bound to believe their peculiar faith superior to that of the Hebrews, as their masters, from whom, at last, the Egyptians had to run away by the best
rational view of truth. If half was true of the slavery of the Israelites, then they had
a most woful time of it, and of course had not time or means for mental improvement.
Are these miserable people they who are to give the enlightened, of two ages before
them, the highest code of civilization? The very idea is an insult to the light of mind.

Ch. vi. The talking about his names, that are men's, proves that God had nothing to
do in all this matter. Had God's omnipotent arm been directly in this matter, he might
have at once met the question. Can any one, on the true analysis of this subject to-day,
say that the Egyptians were not as dear to God the Creator as the Hebrews, or any
other mortals? If the negative be adopted, then let a sufficient reason be given; miserable world-agitation does the bible morale impart. What, will any rational being to-day
say, that the land of Canaan, wherein the Israelites were strangers, should be their
heritage? The thirtieth verse evinces the language of the priestocracy too plainly to
be mistaken,—"I am of uncircumcised lips,"—emanated from the whole soul, probably
the heart, of these spiritual speculative people. Several of the succeeding chapters
are of that spirit, and are endorsed in their black letters as prominently as can be. . Ch.
vii. And the Lord said unto Moses, see, I have made thee a god to Pharaoh; and Aaron
thy brother shall be thy prophet." Can priestocracy do more than that? Thus, these
low-bred, incestuous characters lorded it over the Hebrews, and all others that their
little brief authority could reach. These were a hopeful pair of brothers! Go, priestocracy, to all the world, for all you have now to do, is to prepare the simple minded to
believe a book called the bible, because it is written therein, " thus saith the Lord of the
Israelites." Ye are an affiliated band of professors, whose sworn duty is to deceive the
whole world, and not enlighten yourselves out of your hybrid bigotry. What matters
it whether it be right; it is your profession? What matters it whether this chapter
contradicts all human nature? Your faith, with your vernacular heart, your perjured
sophistry, can set at defiance all the legitimate criticism of the world. Is not your
power the union of church and state, that ruleth mind, purse, and sword, that setteth at
defiance the ingenuous wisdom of all ages? You will convince Pharaoh's mind, but
his heart belongs to you! And miracles were the game that these men played with!

Ostensibly in the jugglery of serpents. V. 11. The sorcerers and magicians acted with their enchantments." But the Hebrew men outdid them, because they played another game, the jugglery of mind, not on the Egyptians, but on the multitude of the world, silly enough to believe, to play at the game of faith. The Hebrews had the last throw, and that game is played in their bible jugglery. What say the Egyptians? Have we their statement? Was ever this scene perpetrated before the light that shone on the land of Egypt? If so, it was written in the closet of some monk of that order.

13. And he hardened Pharaoh's heart, that he hearkened not unto them, as the Lord had said." Said what? Libels from beginning to end, both of nature and nature's God. This book disproves itself, that it was neither mind nor heart. What did these bunglers know, but trade on the low speculation of their degraded profession? That Moses and Aaron were mind-jugglers, the chapter proves, that they prove themselves. It is not in the power of human nature to oppose the manifestations of divine power. For that produces the true humility. This is the true result of religion.

20. And Moses and Aaron did so, as the Lord commanded; and he lifted up the rod and smote the waters, &c.—and all the waters that were in the river were turned into blood.

22. And the magicians of Egypt did so with their enchantments, &c. Where is the proof conclusive now that all this is true? Who believes it? If the magicians of Egypt could do this, what excelled it, proves better magic. But it is the magic of falsehoods, that knaves and fools play with. The magicians could turn water into blood! As Pharaoh did not believe it, it proves that some magic was used of which we have not the true history. We have heard of its raining blood, but then that blood came from a man's hands.

Ch. viii., v. 7. And the Magicians did so with their enchantments, and brought up frogs upon the land of Egypt."

But the magicians could not bring forth lice with their enchantments. We can all say this is the finger of the priestocracy, their trickery surely. It is not for the Egyptians, but the verdant people of the world. Who was worse, Moses for lying imposition, or infamous priestocracy for their inquisition to enforce these infamous lies?

Sacrifices and burnt offerings were so convenient for the priests. Ch. ix., v. 27. And Pharaoh said: The Lord is righteous, and I and my people are wicked; yet, 34: Pharaoh hardened his heart. What had the last to do with the convictions of mind! Ch. x. But here is the beauty, kings and people must be humbled before and by the priestocracy. The world must bow down to them! V. 17. Now therefore forgive, I pray thee, my sin only this once, and entreat the Lord your God, that he may take away from me this death only." Thus was Pharaoh suppliant to Moses and Aaron, if we take their words for it! 21. And the Lord said unto Moses, stretch out thine hand toward heaven, that there may be darkness over the land of Egypt, even darkness which may be felt"! That is pretty strong. The lying increases, several coats thick. Ch. xi., v.1. And the Lord said unto Moses, &c. V. 2. Speak now in the ears of the people, and let every man borrow of his neighbor, and every woman of her neighbor, jewels of silver, and jewels of gold:" What a libel on God! What felonious theft of Moses the repudiator! Ch. xii., v. 15. Seven days shall ye eat unleavened bread, even the first day ye shall put away leaven out of your houses; for whosoever eateth leavened bread from the first day until the seventh day, that soul shall be cut off from Israel." A human sacrifice for a rite of superstition! This a particle of religion! Would that millions had not been sacrificed by the people, who make the greater sacrifice to the impositions of the priestocracy.

V, 26. And it shall come to pass, when your children shall say unto you, what mean ye by this service? 27. That ye shall say, it is the sacrifice of the Lord's passover, who passed over the houses of the children of Israel in Egypt, when he smote the Egyptians, and delivered our houses." Did God of the universe ever do so? Were the Egyptians a part of his creation, or were they the real estranged heathen whom he did not create? Were the Hebrews so heathenish to mind's analysis, that they committed themselves to a peculiar bible, that adopted a peculiar god for them and no others? 29. And it came to pass, that at midnight the Lord smote all the first-born in the land of Egypt, and all the first-born of cattle." Priests, how can ye say so? Can ye come to the truth this time? Where did the first-born of cattle come from, as in the very grievous murrain, ch. ix. v. 6. And the Lord did that thing on the morrow, and all the cattle of Egypt died." Liars ought to have good memories. V. 35. And the children of Israel did according to the word of Moses: and they borrowed of the Egyptians jewels of silver, and jewels of gold, and raiment. 36. And the Lord gave the people favor in the sight of the Egyptians, so that they lent unto them such things as they required: and they spoiled the Egyptians." This is the source of repudiation.

What a fine thing it was that these Hebrews only knew no more such people! The God of the universe never knew such a people, as they claim acquaintance. 47. All the congregation of Israel shall keep it (the ordinance of the passover.) 50. Thus did all the children of Israel, as the Lord commanded Moses and Aaron, so did they. The children of Israel were merely stupid grown up children, to believe it. Here is the secret of priestocracy power.

This nation of the Jews was doubtlessly matured enough, to obtain through numbers and the employment of stratagem, their national sovereignty. They left Egypt successfully; how, we cannot possibly tell, by their miserably corrupted bible of tradition.

Ch. xiii. 1. "And the Lord spake unto Moses, saying." The decree of this priestocracy was as absolute, by their own showing, as the ukase of the Russian Emperor.

2. Sanctify unto me all the first-born, whatsoever openeth the womb among the children of Israel, both of man and of beast, it is mine." We observe once for all that when the priestocracy spoke with their greatest authority, they said the Lord spake. Then there was of course no reversal of that decree, unless they chose to entreat the Lord to speak differently, and that declared itself according to their notions of things, under peculiar secret influences. What a formidable power, the colossus of the world, by which the world has been overwhelmed and mind mastered. Their rites and ceremonies bound the devotees by the strongest ligaments of superstition.

The old priestocracies sought to gain the first, now the modern ones seek to maintain and manage all better, by the worth and wealth of the whole born, whose deepest feelings are peculiarly enlisted and linked. We may reasonably conclude that the course pursued as in second verse gained over the friendship and combination of the people, whilst the last added to their abundance and enjoyment.

The priestocracy's power is powerfully developed in this chapter. Power of government can always find expedients to assume prerogatives. V. 15. Therefore I sacrifice to the Lord all that openeth the matrix, being males; but all the first-born of my children I redeem. 17. God did not lead the people through the Philistines' land; for God said, lest peradventure the people repent when they see war, and they return to Egypt." Where, outrageously lying priests, are your miracles to stop them?

This is another proof that this God was not omniscient, as the God of the universe does not use the guess-words peradventure, since he knows. Whether the generals were timid, and put all on this category, this untruthful account does not enable us to discover satisfactorily, but it looks reasonable if they did not march straight forward. But their wilderness story is a miserable legend most doubtlessly. Who can substantiate as to a pillar of a cloud, or a pillar of fire? None. Moses or his book-makers have lied. Ch. xiv. v. 4. That the Egyptians may know that I am the Lord." It seems this peculiar god was very ambitious to be known to other nations, by taking penalties on them in behalf of his people the Jews. 5. And it was told the king of Egypt, that the people fled. 8. And the Lord hardened the heart of Pharaoh king of Egypt, and he pursued after the children of Israel, &c. It is no more reasonable that men taught by miracles, as related, could have done this, than the miracles could have been performed, or that the sea opened for one to pass, and the other to be drowned. All this is infamously false. The Egyptians and Pharaoh were not the creatures of God, as these pretences would have us believe. No, not at all. They were a part of the outside barbarians. The heathens that should have been butchered up for the good of the peculiar people. They were only reserved for the priestocracy to try their hands on, to prove their peculiar god. Mind had nothing to do with the priestocracy: they deal in faith and miracles. 17. and I, behold I, (the Lord) will harden the hearts of the Egyptians, and they shall follow them, and I will get me honor upon Pharaoh and upon all his host." What honor is comparable to the loftiest government of mind, what is holier than religion that knows the people of the world as one brotherhood? 18. And the Egyptians shall know that I am the Lord." The world best knows the Lord, through the best culture of mind.

Now for the priestocracy. 21. And Moses stretched out his hand over the sea, and the Lord caused the sea to go back, &c. 27. And Moses stretched forth his hand over the sea, and the sea returned to his strength." Who so powerful as the priestocracy? They were the master-spirits of the world, for lying!

How explain? How believe, sir? Who so verdant, eh? As to the prophecy of the Hebrews, did they not prophecy against their dispossessed enemies? The statements must be first proved, else it is irrational to ask belief. It is not religion nor honesty to require faith where there is not rational proof. I ask for indubitable proof that exact records were made, and all such kept above suspicion and reproach.

There is no such proof at all. Those who could lie about the past, could easily lie about the future. Chapter the fifteenth displays proof of direct antagonism to chapter thirteenth, respecting not going directly to Canaan, and indirectly against the statements of the fourteenth chapter as regards the miracles through the red sea. Ch. xv., v. 16. Fear and dread shall fall upon them, (expressed in preceding verses, especially 14 and 15,) by the greatness of thine arm they shall be as still as a stone, till thy people pass over, O Lord." And yet this man, Moses, was called an unsurpassed prophet. Some knowledge of chemistry kept as an occult science, might have been possessed by the priestocracy, but that is only an incident to the main drama that required more potency from them than that to sustain them. Moses changes the character of the waters; that may be. Who, of disinterested witnesses, can tell us? We should never have heard of this, but for more weighty matters. Who certainly proves that all these things were done?

The bible specifies all things as real! The particular conversations of God disprove all the bible, that Moses, or those who sustained the man of straw, could not sustain.

It carries the elements of its own destruction. It is hard to know the truth from the fiction of these deceiving priests, and fortunately it is of little interest, as the sure word of God, cause and effect, annihilates all priestocracies. Ch. xvii. Water was obtained out of the rock of Horeb by Moses, accompanied by the elders of the children of Israel. Water can be easily gotten out of a rock, if the party be prepared for it, but whether it was by a rod or by the pen is unknown to us. All the elders of Israel are affiliated, dead and buried, and so will be their bible. 11 v. And it came to pass, when Moses held up his hand, that Israel prevailed; and when he let down his hand, Amalek prevailed. 12. And his hands were steady until the going down of the sun." Why was not the miracle of Amalek's discomfiture done at once? The world must submit to this all-powerful dynasty, and let it construe all things their way. Was the hand of the priestocracy or of the general the most effectual? The writer's was potent. Can the people believe all?

But what sort of morals and religion would any such memorial as this be? 14. "And the Lord said unto Moses, write this for a memorial in a book, and rehearse it in the ears of Joshua: for I will utterly put out the remembrance of Amalek from under heaven." Was their conception of Jehovah much removed from the name of Jupiter? They had not clear views of God's character; very far from it indeed.

What morals were in this? 16. "For he said, because the Lord hath sworn that the Lord will have war with Amalek from generation to generation"! If the Israelites could not conquer the Amalekites otherwise, of course it was called prophecy, but written undoubtedly after full trial of the facts of time. Is man more than man; is mortal more than mortal? Moses was having many fold as historiographer, the best berth for the future.

The moderns will not take this into proper consideration.

He and his clique fixed up all the drama, being all in all with Israel—judge, dictator, master, and all that autocracy could ask for. What can equal the dictation of the oracles of the peculiar god of any country? They are uttered without restraint, and executed as expedient. Nothing on earth is equal to its power, and it carries all before it. The terrors of a French Directory are nothing to it. Has the world ever appreciated half its character? C. xviii. And Moses judged the people, making them to know the statutes of God, and his laws; but Jethro told him that the thing that he did was not good. 19. I will give thee counsel." The priest of Midian advised him to appoint his inferior judges, and himself the supreme judge of great matters. 24. "So Moses harkened to the voice of his father-in-law, and did all that he had said." Here then is an acknowledgment of the superiority of mind, though it is one priest advising another. The truth will speak for itself, and the defect of mind prevented a better condition of things.

Ch. xix. v. 5. Then ye shall be a peculiar treasure unto me above all people; for all the earth is mine; v. 6. And ye shall be unto me a kingdom of priests, and an holy nation." Would not the priestocracy delight to have the whole world in this position? But the God of the universe does not rule it that way. His conservative principles do not call for priests or angels, devils nor bibles of tradition. Moses went up to the mount unto God. All priest impostors had their secret places. The people were too vulgar to come near to gaze. They were not to know the mysteries. The dictators of the priestocracy were to be only in the secret. All the strikers were to keep at a proper distance, under the penalty of death. Who, then, but these dictators gave the moral and ceremonial law on Sinai? It matters not whether Mount Sinai was volcanic or not, as "Mount Sinai was altogether on a smoke—and the whole mount quaked greatly"; so that the people were smoked, and whether that voice was ventriloquism or not, as long as the dictators presided over the pen, and wielded the sword. That mind is to be pitied at this day that pretends not to see what potency irresistible influenced the whole records. Are the Jew records any better than any other mythologists'? In what respect? Ask honest and truthful sense if it would not have been best to convince this rebellious people Israel, by the real majesty of Almighty God, than to have had such ineffectual means through their dictators, who were viler than the rabble? Would it not have saved the life of thousands, ay, of millions? But the hands of bigots have received the traditions of bigots, and they run wild with their pretences. Ch. xx. v. 19. " And they (the people) said unto Moses, speak thou with us, and we will hear : but let not God speak with us lest we die"! Mind, thou art watching the Jews—guard thyself. Awake. Was this not the very soul language of the priestocracy? If the people will not maintain their rights of mind, will the priestocracy do it, combined as they are against it? 24. An altar of earth thou shalt make unto me, and shalt sacrifice thereon thy burnt offerings, thy peace offerings, thy sheep and thine oxen." This verse conclusively proves that this bible was written by men, and not inspired by the God of the universe, who only requires pure adoration of mind, whereas the priestocracy desire the flocks of the people, and commit perjury to get them. Ch. xxi. v. 6. And his master shall bore his ear through with an awl. Ch. xxii. v. 18. Thou shalt not suffer a witch to live. 28. Thou shalt not revile the gods. 29. Thou shalt not delay to offer the first of thy ripe fruits, and of thy liquors : the first born of thy sons shalt thou give unto me." How most demoralizing is the bible in regard to some primary matters! But how about the chief matters of laws? Many are necessarily good, otherwise the whole had been easily exposed. But why seek to maintain an exploded system, that cannot be sustained in justice to mind? We prefer at once all that is due the world. Chapter the twenty-third is quite to the purpose of the priestocracy. 10 v. And six years shalt thou sow thy land. 11. But the seventh year thou shalt let it rest and lie still." How peculiar! This certainly came from their peculiar god. 20. Behold, I send an angel before thee to keep thee in the way, and to bring thee into the place which I have prepared." This angel is to be truly obeyed, and then he will cut off the Jebusites and the other occupants of the soil. V. 24. Thou shalt not bow down to their gods : but thou shalt utterly overthrow them, and quite break down their images." Moses reserved to himself the right of coming to his god, who spake as Moses dictated, and he did as his book-makers ordered. They pulled the wires. It is quite curious to see how the nations were to be treated. 27. I will send my fear before thee, and will destroy all the people to whom thou shalt come. Ch. xxiv. v. 2. And Moses alone shall come near the Lord ; but they (the priestocracy, &c.) shall not come nigh, neither shall the people go up with him. V. 3. And Moses came and told the people all the words of the Lord." And Moses came as near the Lord as the people of Israel ! 10. And they saw the God of Israel : and there was under his feet as it were a paved work of a sapphire stone, and as it were the body of heaven in his clearness." Wonderful description ; mystified mysteries of the priestocracy. How much it enlightens the mind about God ! 17. And the sight of the glory of the Lord was like devouring fire on the top of the mount in the eyes of the children of Israel." Was it any thing less than a volcano?

But no matter ; our author, Moses, can make it any thing.

13. And Moses rose up, and his minister Joshua." Does Joshua help the truth, who could not tell it about the sun? 18. And Moses was in the mount forty days and forty nights. Ch. xxxiv. v. 28. And he was there with the Lord forty days and forty nights; he did neither eat bread nor drink water."

All this time? This was man's work. God acts by electricity, and in the time could have made several universes. What became of the one all that time? Of course, Moses and his coadjutors are convicted of libel of the God of the universe, wishing to substitute most ignominiously his peculiar god therefor. Has the world waked up yet out of its Mosaic sleep? Is it still in the vision of the priestocracy?

God ordered all the particulars about the altar, tabernacles, &c. Aaron and children, as priests, were to be clothed with very fine dresses, and Aaron to have a plate inscribed Holiness to the Lord. Moses was the master of the ceremonies, to " consecrate and sanctify the priests." Moses was in fact the autocrat of the people, and the master of all the little despots. With such a power, despotic and absolute, as Moses had in priestocracy, he could do any thing with the people, the mass, and ingraft superstition so deep into them that it could not be gotten rid of for thousands of years. What can be a greater curse !

Ch. xxxii. While all these means of elevating Aaron as priest to the peculiar god of Israel, were progressing, he was making a calf-god for his ignorant people, and building an altar to it, to which they sacrificed. It was quite easy to change from one idolatry to another. This is a curious chapter of incidents, for Moses rebukes and reminds his god of his oath to the patriarchs, to multiply their seed as the stars of heaven, and the gift of the promised land, that they should inherit it forever. Whether the writer affects that his god forgot this oath when his anger waxed hot against his people, he tells us that the lord repented of the evil designed; which, if done, would have placed that peculiar god in an awful and inextricable difficulty. If Moses had let the lord alone he would have consumed the people. In fact, Moses makes' the dereliction, the crime of his peculiar god, perjury. I am at a loss to know which is the greater, the priestocracy's god or the priestoracy, as represented by Moses. Abraham proved him destitute of omnipresence and omniscience; Moses proves him both. Their peculiar god was only as they represented him; the God of Creation is as the universe represents him: that is the inappreciable difference. To find out the peculiar god, we need only unveil the priestocracy; to know the Almighty, we have to solve the mighty problem of the universe. O, how disgusting is this priestocracy, reflected on their corrupt mirror, the bible. 16. And the tables were the work of God, and the writing was the writing of God, graven upon the tables." O no, Moses, this was all your work. God's works would prove themselves, as those of the universe. His pen is electricity, his books the spheres of the universe, that as much exceed your stone tables as religion exceeds your Judaism. 24. Then I (Aaron) cast it (the gold) into the fire, and there came out this calf." Which was the greatest liar, Aaron or Moses? Who stood up to help murder the people? "All the sons of Levi," of the priestocracy. 27. And he (Moses) said unto them, Thus saith the Lord God of Israel, Put every man his sword by his side—and slay every man his brother, and every man his companion, and every man his neighbor." Now the awful thing, peculiar faith tyranny, works, and Christ's words can be well understood.. If any autocrat of absolutism can devise more tyranny than that, then he ought to be master of a verdant world. And whom did this ancient Jesuit, this monster of inquisition, this leader of sectarianism, slay? The head of the sectarians? Very clear of all that. 28. And there fell of the people that day about three thousand men." Men of the world, talk no more of inquisitions, of papal despotism, or fanatical bigotry; ye support it all, who support such a base book. The priests' laws and swords enacted all this tragedy.

And who, on the side of the priestocracy's god, shed all this blood? Who but the priestocracy, of course? All the sons of Levi. And Moses called it consecrating themselves to that Lord, to slay every man his son, and his brother. Let it pass now, that Christ came to bring the sword, and to set the household in chaos and confusion. Fanaticism can never stop till religion rules, and sectarianism is no more. And who but the monster of persecution and intolerance could atone for the sin of the people, before the priestocracy's god, who did as the oracle-master directed? Yes, this murderer of three thousand people, whom he blinded with peculiar idolatry, and left in their woful ignorance, could talk of sin, when there were any sectarians to his sectarianism; and any opportunity to show off his pretensions. 35. And the Lord plagued the people, because they made the calf which Aaron made." The God of the universe is no respector of persons, and would have taken hold of Mr. Aaron the first man, as the greatest calf of the whole. Who was it that spoke in verse 34? Most clearly a man, and one that had lost his equilibrium. Ch. xxxiii. v. 1. And the Lord said unto Moses, Depart—unto the land which I sware unto Abraham, &c. 2. And I will send an angel before thee. 3. For I will not go up in the midst of thee; for thou art a stiff-necked people; lest I consume thee in the way." And the peculiar god is thus again proved destitute of omnipresence, by his own peculiar dictator, who used up both himself and god, worse than all others can besides! 5. For the Lord had said unto Moses, Say unto the children of Israel, Ye are a stiff-necked people: I will come up into the midst of thee in a moment, and consume thee." Beat that, autocrats of the world. But even this threat had not the proper influence in the place of suppressed rights of mind, for before we get through this bible, we shall find this imbecile complaining most awfully of impotent power. 11. And the Lord spake unto Moses face to face, as a man speaketh unto his friend." John said, no man has seen God. Was John right? Moses could not be. 17. And the Lord said unto Moses, Thou hast found grace in my sight." Why not the whole world find grace, before the God of Creation? It has found existence, itself a grace of the Creator, and mind his constant beneficiary. The priestocracy, not mind, spoke. 20. And he said, Thou canst not see my face: for there shall no man see me, and live.

Ch. xxxiv. "And the Lord said unto Moses, and I will write upon these tables." If God ever wrote on these tables, he wrote them eternal for the world, else the peculiar people were the sole world. Where are those tables? Are they not in dust, as their language? What was the language? Hebrew! Has God created in Hebrew? Is his universe in Hebrew, or in unchangeable universal language, that mind in all ages of eternity, and all variety of nations, reads and glorifies as the only book? Ye that have opposed Mormons, do so no more. They prefer golden plates. Of tastes, who can dispute? There is no other position that the world of superstition can dispute.

Although God was going to do marvels before all the people, no man was to come up with Moses, when God wrote. Now this was the greatest of all marvels, and the worst of all suspicions, had the whole been a fact, instead of fictions. 11. "I drive out before thee, the Canaanite—and the Jebusite." 13. "But ye shall destroy their altars, break their images, and cut down their groves." Go it, ye sectarians, most pagan of all pagans. "And it took God forty days and forty nights to write upon these tables?" Not an iota, as you shall see by 28th. "And he was there with the Lord forty days and forty nights; he did neither eat bread, nor drink water. And he wrote upon the tables the words of the covenant, the ten commandments." If any doubt remains about who is the last he, the 27 explains, "And the Lord said unto Moses, write thou these words." Merciful God of creation! What a faith! to sacrifice their universal God, to their peculiar bible-god, all for the world. Sin of sins, thou, sin of blasphemy, art the blackest. In the hands of the priestocracy, everything that is honorable and just, even the veracity of their peculiar god, is sacrificed to their unholy purposes, to show off their peculiar brief authority. That is the last sacrifice, and when the day comes, when come it must, that their tricks are fully seen, none will or can be, more contemptible. They humbugged the world to make it believe, and sacrificed all to retain it! In faith they sacrificed religion, in idolatry they blasphemed God, and in bigotry, fanaticism and superstition, they immolated mankind, and crushed mind. Were the blasphemous priestocracy after all, afraid to say that the last tables were written on by their God? What sort of a cork-screw mind had they? It was peculiar, unlike all others, perverted by their sophistications. They have helped divide mind into two classes, and have well defined thus the artificial one. They have taught mankind what taxings are. It would be a curious problem to know how much have been paid them by the world. Ch. xxxv. 2, "Whosoever doeth work therein (the seventh day), shall be put to death." What more bloody statute could despotism devise? This is equal to another one, "Whosoever toucheth the mount, shall be surely put to death. There shall not a hand touch it, but he shall surely be stoned or shot through; whether it be beast or man, it shall not live." 3. "Ye shall kindle no fire throughout your habitations upon the Sabbath day." The elements of temperance were made to bow to the inexorable demon of blasphemy. After this, if never before, when the bible is put into our hands, the primary question arises, what proof is it that it is a bible, since its own household is divided into three Sabbaths?

Pile up your burnt offerings, and give "the remnant" of the meat offering, "to Aaron and his sons," but no atonement was ever made, by offering sacrifices of blood of animals or mankind. It is absurd. One of the great sins is, against the full jurisdiction of the Creator.

Leviticus, continue on, Moses, in your absurd regulations of priestocracy, as emanating from God Almighty. Desecrate his attributes and principles, to promote your object. Ch. vi. 7. "And the priest shall make an atonement for him before the Lord; and it shall be forgiven him for anything of all that he hath done in trespassing therein." All the priests' bibles will tell us so, but who that reflects the true nobility of mind, will believe it? Ch. vii. 35, "This is the portion of the anointing of Aaron." Moses was the consecrator, consecrating and sanctifying the priests. What can be a greater curse of a people, tied up to such ceremonies and obligations? The effects are now before the world. Little dreamed Moses or his coadjutors, that the best protection against idolatry was mind cultivated in philosophical science. There is no fear of images, when man thinks, speaks out justly and independently, by the rules of refined civilized society that is thereby best fortified. Does the bible talk of idolatry? Who was a greater idol than Moses? Ch. xix. "And the Lord spake unto Moses saying, 27. "Ye shall not round the corners of your heads, neither shalt thou mar the corners of thy beard." It might as well have been said, ye shall not use soap nor water for cleanliness. Ch. xx. 27, "A wizard shall surely be put to death." What an existence was this, for a rational being? Who was so circumstantial in all the details of the ark, tabernacle, the vestments, the rites and ceremonies? What are they all worth? Not the notice of an enlightened mind, much less the details of God Almighty, the Creator. Wise legislation, such as improved mind originates, must be the best corrective of all irrational trespasses, united with the most rational education, rational religion.

We see most clearly that man is ridiculous in assuming perfection in any bible statutes, much less claiming it as of God.

Ch. xxv. 4. "But in the seventh year shall be a sabbath of rest unto the land, a sabbath for the Lord: thou shalt neither sow thy field, nor prune thy vineyard." Why

was there not a sabbath to the earth also, so that no fructification could be in existence
every seventh year? What did this man understand? The proper principles of geology? The mind that is now enlightened of the husbandman in agriculture, causes him
to divide his fields, and rest one while he works another, not so much that, as alterna-
tion of crops on all his fields.

Can any mind that can analyze ideas, read this book without the deepest execration
of the writers? It will not be very long before this will be said of the adopters who
know better.

V. 21. "Then I will command my blessing upon you in the sixth year, and it shall
bring forth fruit for three years." Never let any candid mind after this, pretend that
the Jews were obnoxious to the deepest reproach in forsaking their peculiar god, for the
gods of their neighbors, when they must have been wofully taught by want and famine,
of this obnoxious statute. No: the result does not appear in the priestocracy's bible;
do you find them disclosing secrets that would convict them?

Ch. xxvii. 30. "And all the tithe of the land, whether of the seed of the land, or of
the fruit of the tree, is the Lord's: it is holy unto the Lord. 32. And concerning the
tithe of the herd, or of the flock, even of whatsoever passed under the rod, the tenth shall
be holy unto the Lord." The priestocracy shall be taken care of, is the decree of Moses.

Numbers, ch. i. The males are numbered as God said to Moses, but is there any
evil or plague therefor? Was not the plague in David's time, an incident of history,
unconnected with the numbering? Who can suppress his indignation at the stupid
ignorance of the priestocracy?

Ch. iii. 10. "And the stranger that cometh nigh (the tabernacle) shall be put to
death"! What can be worse than to have the secrets betrayed? 38. "But those that
encamp before the tabernacle toward the east, even before the tabernacle of the congregation eastward, shall be Moses, and Aaron, and his sons, keeping the charge of the
sanctuary, for the charge of the children of Israel; and the stranger that cometh nigh
shall be put to death."! Is not the secret of the priestocracy worth more than the
blood of the people? Who are the last, at best. but vulgar, compared with the dictator?

Had Moses really been a great man, this nation could have become much greater and
better; but no mere priest-nation ever flourished well. The sin-offering was an equivalent for the atonement made by the priest, who had all the perquisites possible.

Ch. v. 9. "And every offering of all the holy things of the children of Israel, which
they bring unto the priest, shall be his."

Ch. vi. 22. "And the Lord spake unto Moses, saying, 23. Speak unto Aaron and
unto his sons, saying, on this wise ye shall bless the children of Israel." God help
the blessing of the priestocracy.

Ch. ix. If the passover was not kept by those in a proper situation, they were to be
cut off from their people. What a burden to life, what oppression and tyranny! 15.
"The cloud covered the tabernacle." This was to deceive posterity, you, even you, if you
are green enough. 23. "They (the children of Israel) kept the charge of the Lord, at
the commandment of the Lord by the hand of Moses." And Moses acted as Moses
thought. Ch. x. This was a military priestocracy.

V. 31. "And he (Moses) said, leave us not, I pray thee: for as much as thou know-
est how we are to encamp in the wilderness, and thou mayest be to us instead of eyes."
Why did Moses want Hobab for eyes, if the angel was sent by God who said besides,
"My presence shall go with thee, and I will give thee rest"? Also, 33. "And the ark
of the covenant of the Lord went before them—to seek out a resting-place for them."
Moses is convicted abundantly, of availing himself of mind all the time.

Ch. xi. The people complained. No wonder; they got enough in having this military priestocracy. Why should the people be blamed for doubts and dissatisfaction,
when their consecrator, Moses, chides his god right out in verse eleventh, and tells
him indirectly about his doubt of his god's veracity, in verse twenty-one and two, "and
thou hast said, I will give them flesh, that they may eat a whole month." 23. And the
Lord said unto Moses, is the Lord's hand waxed short? Thou shalt see now whether
my word shall come to pass unto thee or not." No, Moses, the burden is of another
kind, that will pronounce you a blasphemous desecrator of the God of creation. These
plagues are very convenient to the bible writers; they prove conclusively the sins of
the people, as if mind could be exempt entirely, and be kept perfect.

Ch. xii. What amiable people these priests and prophets are? Aaron and his
wife are envious of Moses. V. 3. Now the man Moses was very meek above all other
men which were upon the face of the earth." He was very meek when he caused three
thousand of his people to be slain for mere sectarianism. This chapter is one of the
greatest efforts of priestocracy. And now, though Moses himself wanted Hobab for
eyes in the wilderness, we find that the Lord came down and stood in the door of the

tabernacle, and proclaimed the chief Moses as above all vision-prophets, for Moses received all directly from God.   To fix this as certain that god did come down and do all, Miriam became leprous, white as snow.

And Moses caused her to be cured.   Many a pious disposed soul will think this all so!   Not a word of proof is brought.   The mere statement of a book that was gotten up, merely to uphold the dynasty of Judaism.   And the priestocracy of much of the world wishes it to uphold all the dynasties practicable to be raised on its capital.   That is the trick.   Of course whilst all this is available, the affiliated will affect to believe it, and no longer.   They must laugh at the people, the vulgar herd, in their sleeve, to be such simpletons.

Ch. xiii. Remarkable indeed.   The peculiar god directs Moses, as Moses says, to send men that they may search the land of Canaan.   Why so?   Moses needed the eyes of these twelve men to cause his peculiar god to speak.   Moses used this god as he chose, being a privileged question.

V. 19. Whether it (the land) be good or bad.   20. And what the land is, whether it be fat or lean.   What! Moses, doubt thy Lord, who said it was "a land flowing with milk and honey."?

V. 33. And there we saw the giants, the sons of Anak, which come of the giants ; and we were in our own sight as grasshoppers, and so we were in their sight.   Who blames these liars, when taught by the bible of their peculiar faith, about the giants and children of the sons of God and daughters of men?   But who believes others than the pensmen told the tale?

Ch. xiv. Proves that the people sought to return to Egypt.   What, Moses, after all your miracles and the display of your peculiar god!   We believe this proves conclusively, that you did not truly inspire them at all.   You could not.

V. 11. And the Lord said unto Moses, How long will this people provoke me?   And how long will it be ere they believe me, for all the signs which I have showed among them?

What, God not know this, but had to inquire of Moses?   The people believed these spies, rather than their God?   What a remarkable point this is in this bible?   It proves that this god had not made the impression that belongs to the God of the universe. Well might a second God, the mortal Christ, call him father, for both are human dramas.   Both are dramatized by the stupid, blundering, botching priestocracy.   12. I will smite them with the pestilence, and disinherit them.   13. And Moses said unto the Lord,   14. For they, the Egyptians, have heard that thou, Lord, art among this people ; that thou art seen face to face, and that thou goest before them, by day time, &c.   15. Now, if thou shalt kill all this people as one man, then the nations will speak, saying, 16. Because the Lord was not able to bring this people into the land which he sware unto them, therefore hath he slain them in the wilderness.   17. And now, I beseech thee, let the power of my Lord be great, according as thou hast spoken.   20. And the Lord said, I have pardoned according to thy word.   The intercession—no, the pretence of Moses, carried the day with Moses—that is, the priestocracy's action was different from the world that has the past, as theirs is future.   We should suppose that God would prefer his own oath, to all Moses' words, and the opinion of the Egyptians and all the nations.   22. Because all those men which have seen my glory and my miracles, which I did in Egypt and in the wilderness, and have tempted me now these ten times, and have not hearkened to my voice.   If any body else had stated it, it would be perfectly incredible, that God could not influence his peculiar people, after his most earnest endeavors.   This necessarily results that this was not the right kind of a God, or he mistook his people, in either case proving his imbecility. But Moses and his priestocracy authors were the ones mistaken, and mis-stated.

23. Surely they shall not see the land which I swear unto their fathers, neither shall any of them that provoked me see it.   Did god make any reservation of these people to Jacob, when he said, "And the land which I gave Abraham and Isaac, to thee will I give it, and to thy seed after thee will I give the land"?   Did god make any reservation to Isaac, when he said, "I will perform the oath which I sware unto Abraham thy father"?   "And I will make thy seed to multiply as the stars of heaven," saying to Isaac, "for unto thee, and unto thy seed, I will give all these countries."   What reservation did he make to Moses, when he came down to bring them unto a land flowing with milk and honey?   When he said to Moses that he had established his covenant with the patriarchs to give them the land of Canaan, swearing to give it to the patriarchs, to the Israelites, for an heritage?   'Tis needless to multiply words.   The position proves afterthought of man, not of God.   Men swore, and perjured themselves blasphemously before the God of the universe, who is immutable.   The prophets were caught as false, that is all.   45. Then the Amalekites came down, and the Canaanites,

494 RATIONAL RELIGION AND MORALS.

which dwelt in that hill, and smote them," &c. How convenient, yet how utterly worthless is prophecy. The Lord did not assist them ; nay more, Moses " departed not out of the camp." Ch. xv. But why, 18 v. " speak unto the children of Israel, and say unto them, when ye come into the land whither I bring you," after the preceding chapter? Caleb and Joshua alone were reserved, of the numbered males, to see the land.

Was Moses competent to take the people into Palestine? Was he not timid? But it makes very little odds in this drama, this story.

Ch. xvi. Now we see the supreme power of this priestocracy. The republican Korah and friends sought to establish a more equitable order of things, for the sovereignty of the people, but these two hundred and fifty princes of the assembly, famous in the congregation, men of renown, whose spirits might have been as patriotic as a Washington and a Hancock, a Tell and a Warren, and a host such, asserting that the dictators "took too much upon them, seeing all the congregation are holy, every one of them, and the Lord is among them : wherefore then lift ye up yourselves above the congregation of the Lord ;" made vain efforts. The people were not prepared, and the priests circumvented them. These were sons of Levi, Korah particularly, and they asserted enough proof, for they saw the humbug. These men of renown felt the deep oppression. Were these men maniacs, that they forgot all the wonders of the Lord? Who believes that these men, famous in the congregation, had ever been prepossessed by any such impression, else they would have committed any other suicide. This is too good a point to overlook ; this is enough to prove most conclusively that these men could not digest this odious fanaticism. Whether it was ventriloquism or no it matters not, a more potent pen-power was used. The priestocracy is uppermost. They have a charmed power.

Let us notice these points. 19 v. " And the glory of the Lord appeared unto all the congregation. 20. And the Lord spake unto Moses and unto Aaron, saying, 21. Separate yourselves from among this congregation, that I may consume them in a moment. 22. And they fell upon their faces, and said, O God, &c. 35. And there came out a fire from the Lord, and consumed the two hundred and fifty men that offered incense." And this last puts the noble resolves of these famous men on the ground that none but of the seed of Aaron were to come near to offer incense before the Lord. But after all these reported terrors, enough to make the earth quake, Behold, 41. " But on the morrow, all the congregation of the children of Israel murmured against Moses and against Aaron, saying, ye have killed the people of the Lord." Now are they going to kill these two murderers? Not at all.

It is only the platform of the priestocracy, a higher story. 42. "And it came to pass, when the congregation was gathered against Moses and against Aaron, that they looked toward the tabernacle of the congregation ; and behold the cloud covered it, and the glory of the Lord appeared." Well done, Moses—the stroke of the pen is better than the stroke of the sword. Moses turns from the wrath of the people, to appease the wrath of his peculiar god. That is something worth while ; that of the people was too vulgar. 44. " And the Lord spake unto Moses, saying, 45. Get you up from among this congregation, that I may consume them in a moment. And they fell upon their faces." What was to be done? Of course the atonement of the priestocracy was to be made. Moses and Aaron only killed fifteen thousand lacking fifty by their pen. Did they have a plague? It was sent by the angry god ; and if one cause was not good enough, another could be invented. As they had little artistic skill, it was best to have the deaths all caused by the Lord. Their peculiar god was their great peculiar refuge for causes. The greatest plague was the priestocracy surely. We have their account only ; but where is the people's account? We have only false pretences, all the time, of these murderers. What could the poor ignorant people do? We see here, how impotent their chiefs were. Moses was clothed with the most terrible of all power that superstition could give. What influence could be greater than what Moses wielded? When he said unto the congregation, depart, they got up on every side.

Had these priest bigots souls above their censor-pots, they would have given more credit to Korah, as a patriot. But did they ever dream of constitutional liberty? Of that the world had not true visions of, rightly, till 1776. Much of the world's history has been dark and lowering, proving the supremacy of usurpation over mind. If it were not for modern Moses and adopted bibles mind would be happier.

The whole majority of the world, nay the whole world might testify to the bible, but it would only perjure itself, not confirm what of itself was not tenable. If any one were to tell the world that the bible was true, he, as dupe, could know nothing of what he asserted.

He betrays his want of sagacity or honesty ; one, if not both. Let it be affirmed by

me that Moses wrote all ever claimed by the bible advocates, what does that prove ?
That the bible was true ? It proves that Moses was one of the most degraded of the
priestocracy, an infamous libeler of his God, a base calumniator of truth, and entirely
unworthy of trust.

Now, whether bible lies go under the name of prophecies, miracles, oracles, mysteries, they as lies ought to be impeached and discarded by the honest world.

Well, it is most difficult to get a portion of the world to believe that the priestocracy
lie.   They cannot see the object.   Was not one-third of the land of Egypt enough to
corrupt the old hive, and taint the new swarms, as Moses was taught in all the learning
of the Egyptians, at the head of all which, of course, was that of the priestocracy ?   Has
any curious investigator analyzed this whole subject, and seen the immense bribes to perverted mind, that maketh and unmaketh the gods of its idolatry ?   " The revenues of
the Mexican clergy exceed twenty millions of dollars a year.   The value of their real
estate is enormous.   In the district of Mexico the total real estate is worth fifty millions
of dollars ; half of it belongs to the clergy."   Now, this peculiar faith superseded that
of the Aztecs, who enjoyed great privileges.   The land has not changed the tyranny
and bribery of peculiar faiths, in changing owners.   The real discontent causes must
be remedied—but no radical ultra views can be a conservative revolution, that requires
conservative principles forever, to confirm its justice and necessity.   All faith is bad,
that does not full justice to conservative principles.   Do full justice to the Creator, and
then the world will know that the bible is a blasphemous libeler of God.

The world needs the true spirit of conservative reform.   Did Moses establish a republic ?   It was a military despotism, as potent as any autocracy on earth.   His ukase
was the most plenipotent, that carried fanaticism therewith, the end of which is not yet
come.   The remnants of his nation will have to learn of higher and purer themes, than
through the degraded code of barbarism that they now have.

Moderns with shame, if not with wisdom, will have to quit the field, to which priestocracies are utterly incompetent, else they will have to let the exploded vulgar barbarisms,
the Jew oracles, get the better of them.

NUMBERS.—XVI. 26.

What more formidable decree could any sovereign of earth make, whether righteous
or not, when it was the displeasure of the priestocracy, that was enough ?

Now, be not more verdant than these poor, deluded, priest-commanded wretches.   The
main machinery, ever to be borne in mind by the reader, is false pretences, and nothing
else.   43. "And Moses and Aaron came before the tabernacle of the congregation.   44.
And the Lord spake unto Moses, saying."   It is a matter of no moment whether these
two men went near the tabernacle to aid a ventriloquist or not, it was all the same to
the corrupt priestocracy, who fixed up this whole history to suit their profession, as they
were perfectly irresponsible to any power, let alone truth and reason, as they have
invoked a still higher power, the faith of a credulous world, and that is all necessary.

Give the priestocracy this power, the faith of a credulous people, and they can make
a fanatical world.

45. " Get you up from among this congregation, that I may consume them, as in a
moment.   And they fell upon their faces."   And to control the meeting, Aaron was to
make atonement by the advice of the chief, who said,—46. " For there is wrath gone out
from the Lord."   Where is the proof of the plague ?   The jugglery of hand was some,
but the jugglery of mind is most.

The priestocracy could never have succeeded unless they had lied, and lied exceedingly and greatly all the time.

Short of all that, was too common an affair for their credence.   As they were to be
paid for lying, they sought the most profitable lies ; and the lies of the priestocracy have
surpassed all in profit, surely.   Behold, they have done much, they have only killed in
these two matters, very nearly fifteen thousand people.   But, after all, the worst plague,
that of the priestocracy, was left.

They then resort to another miracle, the rods !   Had this plague, that might have
happened as a pestilence on the tide of time, been so murderous, it was enough to convince any rational, much less peculiar people.

Bible mysteries, miracles and prophecies are all right.

Twelve rods were selected and laid by in the tabernacle, and examined " on the
morrow," and buds, blossoms, and fruit of almonds were on one.   None of this was prepared by the time ?   But how came so many thousands destroyed ?   Were they truly
destroyed, or is all this part fiction, legend, history of jugglery, legerdemain, one of the

most curious pieces of mosaics ever propagated in the republic of letters? How much collusion was there among the Jewish masses affiliated, whether of the priests or people?

Can we be asleep to the state of the present dynasties of priestocracies? Do not the present people help aid? Can the drama, the disgrace to the world, be kept up without all the actors? Can the play go on without the audience? Superstition is the master genius, and credulity is the substitute for faith.

Why are these things not kept up now as of old, as human nature, and the God of human nature are the same, as God is immutable? Falsehood has to be framed to get around all this. God does not teach by miracles, they are the pretensions of the ignorant mass. He teaches by science and philosophy, that caused God's character to be truly appreciated indeed.

Behold the function of the priests, ch. xviii. 3, "only they shall not come nigh the vessels of the sanctuary and the altar, that neither they nor ye also die.   4. And a stranger shall not come nigh unto you" (Aaron).   7. "And the stranger that cometh nigh shall be put to death."   Could Brahmin furnish a baser division into castes?   Is there any greater species of downright murder than the injunction to the stranger?   8 and 9. The Levites' portion.   12. How rich "all the best of the oil, and all the best of the wine, and of the wheat, the first fruits of them which they shall offer unto the Lord, them have I given thee.   13. And whatsoever is first ripe in the land, which they shall bring unto the Lord, shall be thine."   What oblations of meat offerings, too. These were the deepest curses of taxation.   17. "But the firstling of a cow, &c., thou shalt sprinkle their blood upon the altar, and shalt burn their fat for an offering made by fire, for a sweet savour unto the Lord."   As if the God of the universe could be pleased with vile sacrifices of blood of animated nature.   None but the most stupid priestocracy and their degraded minions, could ever pretend to this base libel made through the mouths and pens of hypocrites of a peculiar imbecile.   18. "And the flesh of them shall be thine."   21. "And behold I have given the children of Levi all the tenth in Israel, for an inheritance."   Of this, a tenth part went to the chief priest. What greater enslavement to the world than is here embodied?   22. "Neither must the children of Israel henceforth come nigh the tabernacle of the congregation, lest they bear sin, and die."   That is, lest they find out the degraded tricks of the priestocracy, who say, thus saith the Lord, and never once wished the people to appreciate the majestic silence of the real Almighty, whose works alone speak to mind.   Ch. xix. The ashes of the red heifer, a purification for sin!   What ridiculous rites and ceremonies, even with savages.   Coming into a tent where the dead was, made unclean for seven days.   Was there a worse priestocracy-despotism?   If the person called unclean did not purify himself, that soul shall be cut off from Israel.   Who are they that seek to bring this foul despotism on freemen?   Are they madmen, or felons?   They are felons, to honesty of mind.   When these people murdered the possessors of the soil, they did mountains of prodigies through their priestocracy.   But what should induce the last to do so?   Ambition, avarice, that prompt the world forever.   The tithe of everything in ten years, counts one hundred per cent.   In Alabama, estimating the worth of the cotton crop at twenty millions of dollars, we should see that amount in the hands of the clergy in ten years.   But we must not forget that the chiefs also had the first choice, and a large amount besides.   What a revenue!   What a revenue now, is there in church countries.   And for what?   A non-entity.   Ah! who would not be eloquent for such an amount?   But let now this be a disinterested thing, a voluntary matter, without speculation and trade : let it be decided that when a cent is collected, that it detracts, and our word for it, this delusion, this imposition, this superstition, would die out in one generation.   Let pure patriots think of these things, like good citizens.

Deuteronomy, ch. iii. 23. "And I (Moses) besought the Lord at that time saying, 24. O Lord God, thou hast begun to show thy servant thy greatness, and thy mighty hand ; for what God is there in heaven or in earth, that can do according to thy works, and according to thy might."   This speech of Moses and his wise men, kills all their virtue about their proper appreciation of the universal God.   Ch. xiv. 2. "For thou art a holy people unto the Lord thy God, and the Lord hath chosen thee to be a peculiar people unto himself, above all nations that are upon the earth."   This decides that none but a peculiar god, could have a peculiar people.   The bible authors and advocates are most welcome to their own position, and cannot with any logical consistency, permit him to be appropriated by the rest of the world that had already the God of the universe.   It is a peculiar position that claims a peculiar god.   Hear the imperial decree of the priestocracy.   Ch. xvii. 12. "And the man that will do presumptuously, and will not hearken unto the priest, &c., even that man shall die," &c.   This was a glorious republic for the absolutism of priestocracy. Hear the fiat of the savage, and take the bible, take all.

Ch. xx., v. 16. But of the cities of these people, which the Lord thy God doth give thee for an inheritance, thou shalt save alive nothing that breatheth. Ch. x., v. 19. "Love ye therefore the stranger." Is this the world policy now? The Jews were polygamists, and maintained the right of primogeniture.

The priests were judges. Ch. xxv. If there be a controversy between men, and they come unto judgment, that the judges may judge them; then they shall justify the righteous, and condemn the wicked. 2. And it shall be, if the wicked man be worthy to be beaten, that the judge shall cause him to lie down, and to be beaten before his face, according to his fault, by a certain number." The judge-priests had power enough to create their own influence. 5. What a low bestial law, to force a brother to take his brother's widow?

What enlightened lady would entrust her rights in marrige to the tender mercies of this code, that gave power to the husband to divorce himself from his wife, when "she found no favor in his eyes, because he hath found some uncleanness in her?" This would occur enough often, without this despotic temptation.

Who wrote the Deuteronomy after Moses died? Ask who wrote the numberless bibles, and their diversified editions? Who endorses the statements as facts of the five books? None—not one. Ask not this question, for it cannot be answered. But all such seemed so good. Did a state felon, Murrell, never preach for sinister purposes? Did world-felons, the priestocracy, never perpetrate their codes for world-power?

Joshua, ch. vi. The priests blew with their trumpets, and Jericho was taken! The priests always had the blowing and the lying, 21. They (the people) utterly destroyed all that was in the city, both man and woman, young and old, and thus Joshua acted with several cities.

Ch. x., v. 13. And the sun stood still, and the moon stayed, until the people had avenged themselves upon their enemies. Is not this written in the book of Jasher? So the sun stood still in the midst of heaven, and hasted not to go down about a whole day. 14. For the Lord fought for Israel." The solution is partly in 12. Then spake Joshua—"sun, stand thou still upon Gibeon, and thou, moon, in the valley of Ajalon." Who endorses this? None less than God. Does he? No. Then it is false, as lies of priestocracy.

The writing in the book of Jasher is no more to the fact, than in the book of Munchausen.

Where is the fulfilment of the prophecies about the everlasting possessions of the Jews, and about the Jebusites these days? Nowhere. There was no prophecy to fulfil.

Judges, ch. ii, v. 12. "And (the children of Israel) they forsook the Lord God of their fathers—and followed other gods. Ch. iii. 7. They forgot the Lord their God, and served Baalim and the groves."

The children of Israel were enslaved for several years by the neighboring nations; from the Midianites they fled to dens, caves, and strong-holds. The chief men of Israel were polygamists. Gideon had many wives. That proves them unworthy lights of civilization. Ch. x. v. 6. The children of Israel served many gods—as the gods of Syria. 8. (The Philistines) vexed and oppressed the children of Israel eighteen years, &c. Afterwards for forty years. The tale of Sampson, his strength being in his hair, is a gross fable, not physiological; also, as is the destruction of the house, by taking away the two pillars. xvii. 6. In those days there was no king in Israel, but every man did that which was right in his own eyes. There was necessity for laws, not for kings. Sampson had been a great judge of Israel. Enlightened people, those judges. xviii. 7. And there was no magistrate in the land, that might put them to shame in anything; they put nature to blush in their actions; even their Levites were open fornicators, and could seek to go "to the house of the Lord." Had they ever seen that house, in Israel? Take away the shame, that such a code be presented in gentlemen's parlors, much less in the court of conscience. Good citizens do not wish to return to the days of barbarism.

I. Samuel, ch. ii. v. 2. There is none holy as the Lord: for there is none besides thee." These offset all prophecies, affecting to give credence to the New Testament. Astronomers know no such earth, and monotheists, of course, can know no such god as were peculiar to the Jews, and evinced in this chapter. 10. The Lord shall judge the ends of the earth." We know none such nor the pillars, that inspiration affected for the earth. 12. Now the sons of Eli (the priest) were sons of Belial." These were one of the great sects of priests in Judea. 14. All that the flesh-hook brought up the priest took for himself. One of the encroachments of the priestocracy.

Ch. iv. v. 11. And the ark of God was taken." And this was sacred, was it? But the Philistine gods were made to fall before it—if we are to believe this side of the tale. Where is the account by the Philistines? Samuel advised the people to put away strange gods.

Ch. viii. v. 3. And (Samuel) his sons turned aside after lucre, and took bribes, and perverted judgment. The corruption of the judges or priests induced the people to prefer a king to rule over them, as the least tyranny. 21. And Samuel heard all the words of the people, and he rehearsed them in the ears of the Lord! And this seer or prophet made the king. Samuel commanded Saul the king. xv. 33. Samuel hewed Agag in pieces—whom Saul had spared.

The power of the pope was once greater than that of foolish kings, that submitted to it.

Ch. xvi. v. 4. And Samuel did that which the Lord spake; and came to Bethlehem : and the elders of the town trembled at his coming, and said, comest thou peaceably !" No wonder, poor fellows, it was as much as their soul was worth to resist this supreme dictator of the priestocracy. Hear how wisely he speaks. 7. But the Lord looketh on the heart (in regard to David). 14. But the spirit of the Lord departed from Saul, and an evil spirit from the Lord troubled him.

What a libel on God—of course this is not his word.

Samuel was dictator—and held the selection of the kings, and anointed them. Ch. xxiv. v. 6. And he (David about Saul) said unto his men, The Lord forbid that I should stretch forth my hand against the Lord's anointed." God save the king—the king can do no wrong. The witch of Endor raised the dead Samuel. What is easier, for a psychologist to make the passive mind believe it sees such sights? That is practicable surely. But mind-jugglery, under false pretences, is the capital. How easily did the priestocracy appreciate everything beneficial to themselves. The capital of false pretences was the stock of the priestocracy.

PSALMS.

Ps. xi. David alludes to himself. Why address God, who needs not his vaunting! The god of the Jews was addressed by David, but also sounding his own praise and affectation of glory.

David affected to be on very familiar terms indeed.

He speaks as if his god would make him the chief of the whole earth. The peculiar god was impotent.

Ps. xxix. Give unto the Lord, O ye mighty, give unto the Lord glory and strength. David could sing, or cause others to sing for him, beautiful psalms, not do fine actions. Is not this the world?

Ps. xl. v. 9. I have preached righteousness in the great congregation.

The height of this peculiar god's ambition was against the heathen. As the Jews thought and spoke, so thought and spoke this peculiar god. Fine prophets, these. Nathan prophecies to David about his guilt, adultery, and murder. Then David prophecies to the Jews and all enemies!

He is agreeable, but deceitful, not trustworthy! A hypocrite in society! We must, surely, if we know the world, decide on the best analysis of all the varied relations that try the souls of men, all this for king David. And we look at both sides.

David seems to be absorbed about his enemies, and abundantly invokes his peculiar god on this subject. It is very clear that this Jewish god was as peculiar to that nation as the gods of other nations were peculiar to those nations, and what is conclusive proof, enlightened mind cannot appropriate any such peculiar god.

Was David the especial favorite of the God of the universe? No one in his sound mind will pretend to any such absurdity.

The words of David's psalms are for himself, yet the meaning is wrested therefrom by insidious priestocracy, as to other leaders of sects. David's psalms are pretty, but what were his deeds? lxxii. v. 1. For Solomon to God. 11. All nations shall serve him." Not so fast, David. Flatterers might say that. 7. In his days shall the righteous flourish." Was that near the truth? lxxvii. v. 18. The voice of thy thunder (God's) was in the heaven." The peculiar Jewish god. with all the priestocracy, never could keep the rebellious Jews right. Now, he must have had little intrinsic power, as mind and the God of the universe can keep the whole world right. The marvelous things boasted of could not be effectual, whence we must necessarily infer that all miracles, prophecies, and peculiarities were mere gewgaws for grown up children of that dark age and country, not for the present light of science, that teaches the division of the world into continents and oceans, and of the universe into a glorious union of solar systems.

The priestocracy could not make the people believe in this god, to whom, when associated with the trio of others of the trinity, the whole world cannot be dragooned, despite of all the barbarous brute force of its odious tyranny. lxxviii. v. 22. "Because they believed not in God. 32. For all this they sinned still, and believed not in his wondrous works. 36. Nevertheless they did flatter him with their mouth, and they lied unto him with their tongues."

The only sincere religion can be between mind and the God of the universe ; all else is nothing.

This peculiar god was often angry ; how could he be otherwise ; his mouth-pieces and wire-pullers, the priestocracy, could not make their machinery work as well as they wished ; it was not so available, and of course they got furiously angry. As to mind, that governs the world, they had thrown that overboard. 58. "For they provoked him to anger with their high places, and moved him (God) to jealousy with their graven images. 49. He cast upon them the fierceness of his anger, wrath, and indignation, and trouble, by sending evil angels among them." The peculiar god of the Jews had to have angels in his machinery of world-government, but not so the Governor of the universe, who lays the first on the shelf. 48. "He gave their flocks to hot thunderbolts." Wonderful science even of a king, who, though assuming to be inspired, appears the ignorant impostor. After all their bibles, they know not the God of the universe, the only pure God ; they talked with brassy impudence and blasphemy of things they knew not of. How often did they arrogate to know God's secrets, libeling him about his anger and various qualities. How often did they change the resolves of the Immutable God ! But their peculiar god was a changeable being. lxxxvi. v. 10. "Thou art God alone." But the priestocracy made him a part of themselves, a polytheism. lxxxix. v. 6. "For who in the heaven can be compared unto the Lord ? 11. "The heavens are thine, the earth also is thine." But the universe was God Almighty Creator's. 4. "Thy seed will I (God) establish forever, and build up thy throne to all generations." This god had no such gift ; as proof, there is no such result. Was the world to be deceived into the belief of perpetual royalty ? Was the bible a tory perjury-book, to fasten for all time to come, on mind kept in leading-strings, all despotic errors ? 3. "I have made a covenant with my chosen, I have sworn unto David my servant." Here we see the vices of orientalism, that flatters kings, and records the most blasphemous lies to uphold them. Here is union of church and state, the most insidious of the world's tyranny and man's vassalage. Mind requires us not to look after David, the adulterer and assassin, whatever vulgar faith teaches, corrupting his own brave general, Joab, to murder, but use its own religious resources. How comes it that David, an adulterer and murderous assassin, should preach for the world's benefit by inspiration ? What humbuggery, what morals of such bibles ! If repentant, he was a culprit, unworthy to appear as God's messenger before the world. He was the messenger as all the ministers of any peculiar gospel of a peculiar god. legitimately subject, as he was, to the world's criticism. But inspiration carries with it enough to kill all pretensions to any exalted aspirations before the God of the universe.

Ps. cxxxv. What sectarianism against the balance of the world.—This the people, uttered against Egypt.—Great nations and mighty kings, whose land was given for our heritage. All this was paid back by two daughters, the Christians and Mahometans, who despised the Jews and each other.

Ps. cxxxvi. "(The Lord,) that made great lights : 9. The moon and the stars to rule by night." All pretending to astronomy must know that the stars and moon, even, know no such false position. Inspiration premises certain and exact science, as the source whence it comes. If god knows, then inspiration is true. This inspiration is false, as the peculiar source whence it came. But the priests, prophets, and kings may affect more sanctity ; who has sanctified them especially ? They give no proof at all ! How are they peculiarly better, seeing that they affect something peculiar that is worthless. They are condemned by their false doctrines and pretences, that wind them up. They caricatured their peculiar god as angry with lightning. We believe this is a consummate libel. The equanimity of God is utterly above all that.

Ps. cxlvii. v. 11. "The Lord taketh pleasure in them that fear him ! 19. (God) he showeth his word unto Jacob, his statutes and his judgments unto Israel. 20. He hath not dealt so with any nation ; and as for his judgments, they have not known them." Vain and ignorant egotist ! How superficial art thou ? The wise of the world would earnestly pray that they had not known them. cxlviii. v. 3. "Praise (the Lord) him all ye stars of light."

Are the stars obedient to his peculiar god, or to the God of the universe, who does

not look to prophets, but principles? Hear him further by inspiration on astronomy :—
2 Samuel, ch. xxii. v. 10. David says of God, " He bowed the heavens also, and
came down, and darkness was under his feet." That is, the top of this plane, earth
resting on pillars, was only shone upon. As David was so refined to write poetry, let
us see how refined he was to the world. 1 Chronicles, ch. xx. 3. " And he brought out
the people that were in it, (Rabbah,) and cut them with saws, and with harrows of iron,
and with axes : even so dealt David with all the cities of the children of Ammon."
Only think, that seventy thousand men fell of Israel, because David numbered the
people, provoked by the devil, yet—2 Sam. ch. xxiv. " It was the anger of the Lord."
Ch. xxi : 17. And David had to reason with his peculiar god, ere the angel arrested his
slaughter. But mind, this is one of those episodes that display the leading characteristic of the whole book-priestocracy potency.
Absolutism is the same everywhere. But let us hear all about that numbering. In
1 Chronicles, ch. xxi. "And Satan stood up against Israel, and provoked David to
number Israel. 2 Sam. ch. xxiv. And again the anger of the Lord was kindled against
Israel, and he moved David against them, to say, Go, number Israel and Judah. 10.
And David said unto the Lord, I have sinned greatly in that I have done." And for
this numbering, which we cannot define as sinful, seeing that the census of countries
aids in their statistics : 15. " So the Lord sent a pestilence upon Israel. 16. And
when the angel stretched out his hand upon Jerusalem, to destroy it, the Lord repented
him of the evil." What a libel on mind, reason, God of the universe.
David did, indirectly, unto Shimei, by Solomon, what he swore against. 2 Samuel,
xix. 23. " Therefore the king (David) said unto Shimei, Thou shalt not die : And the
king sware unto him. 1 Kings, ch. ii. 9. Now, (David charged Solomon,) therefore,
hold him (Shimei) not guiltless ; but his hoar head bring thou down to the grave with
blood." What a perjurer. Solomon had him slain finally for disobedience ; but was he
not himself the perpetrator of perjury through murder, as also in the case of his brother.
David was an open polygamist and adulterer, corrupting the people, the world.
2 Sam. ch. vii. 10. " (And Nathan said to the king,) moreover, I will appoint a place
for my people Israel, and will plant them, that they may dwell in a place of their own,
and move no more ; neither shall the children of wickedness afflict them any more, as
beforetimes." Nathan was a false prophet, and committed perjury for his god. 13.
"And I will establish the throne of his kingdom forever, (Solomon's.) 16. And thine house
and thy kingdom shall be established forever before thee : thy throne shall be established
forever." Perfect oriental flattery. 24. " (David to the Lord,) For thou hast confirmed
to thyself thy people Israel, to be a people unto thee forever." Is all this a true prophecy?
David was a man after God's own heart, yet he committed adultery, and assassinated
the husband, Uriah. Then came incest and murder in the house of David, his household conspiring against each other, his son Absalom killing his brother Ammon, and
then conspiring against his father David.
As flattery made David after God's own heart, a very foolish and senseless expression,
it was the petty peculiar god that the priestocracy committed themselves about, in the
adultery with Mary. As David had no rational principles, he had no correspondent
religion. No more than church faith is not religion, not an iota.
. Solomon had no religion in his polytheism. There is no religion in any peculiar
faith-bible under the sun. The curse of the world is the old monopoly regimes. How
comes it that Moses could number the people—N. c. 1—on the express command of
his god, and no exception could be taken thereto? Was it with David because there
was pestilence thereafter so remarkable, that the stupid priestocracy had to assign this
ignoble special pleading casuistry for the cause, and thereby enabled themselves to make
capital, as usual, and show off to their advantage? What is the world to think of the
best biblical examples, the most corrupt of David and Solomon.
It will not do to make the world lie, through this bible, about peculiar gods any more.
It is ungodly, pagan, heathenish, worse than outside barbarianism.
What is there in all the bible worthy of a religious mind? Nothing before the Creator of the universe. There is nothing in the bible or people that is trustworthy.

ECCLESIASTES.

How came Solomon to be the wisest man estimated? Was that by universal consent
of mankind, or was it by court flattery of hypocritical courtiers? We have no authority
but the Jewish books that are not proved as anything but their own statements. Did
the Jews know one-fourth of the whole world at any time? Was not this work to sustain
the union of imperial and church dynasties? Let facts be submitted to a candid world,

just to itself. Ch. viii., v. 2. "I counsel thee to keep the king's commandment, and that in regard to the oath of God. V. 5. Whoso keepeth the commandment shall feel so evil thing."

2 Chronicles, ch. vi., v. 38. The people when captive are to be directed to pray toward their land, and toward the city, and toward the house which I (Solomon) have built for thy name. Some of the Israelites and Judahites were the worst sort of polygamists. Solomon, 1 Kings, ch. ii., v. 20, violated his promise to his mother, "for I will not say thee nay," in killing his brother Adonijah, who had nearly raised up extreme civil war previously. Solomon's idolatry was conspicuous. Jeroboam's idolatry was great also. 1 Kings, ch. xii., v. 28. The king made two calves of gold :—"Behold thy gods, O Israel, which brought thee up out of the land of Egypt." After all, were the Jews but a miserable idolatrous nation.

Solomon's seraglio. O that mine enemy could write a book. It was sufficient for the exposure of this demoralization of the idolator, a degraded sensualist adopting Asiatic despotism.

If this of itself be considered, it is enough to decide honorable intelligent preachers that they should leave such a bible, as wanting the pure light of science and morals. They should learn of school boys, if they are too hoary in error, and cannot see all such.

Job, ch. ix., v. 6, says of God, which shaketh the earth out of her place, and the pillars thereof tremble. Job knows about the peculiar god, but who endorses Job's knowledge about the God of the universe?

Ch. xxvi., v. 7. And hangeth the earth upon nothing. Ch. xxxvii., v. 3. He directeth his lightning unto the ends of the earth, says Elihu, v. 4. After it a voice roareth; he thundereth with the voice of his excellency. 5. God thundereth marvelously with his voice. Ch. xxxviii., v. 1. Then the Lord answered Job out of the whirlwind, and said, v. 4. Where wast thou when I laid the foundation of the earth? This was clearly the language of the peculiar god of the priests. The God of the universe had spoken, but Job had not told his tale. V. 6. Whereupon are the foundations thereof fastened? Or who laid the corner-stone thereof? 18. Hast thou perceived the breadth of the earth? 19. Where is the way where light dwelleth? And as for darkness, where is the place thereof. 36. Or who hath given understanding to the heart? This all spoken by a creator God? What inspiration! Never let the names be desecrated thus. Ch. xl. Here is the sublime of ignorance, wrapped up in pedantry. Ch. xli. This beats the preceding chapter surely. What shall we say of Leviathan? V. 20. Out of his nostrils goeth smoke, as out of a seething pot or caldron. Israel, Job, thy peculiar god? No, thy priestocracy did not quite understand natural history. They laid their minds, their honesty, their honor, all in the shade. How they lied most blunderingly! 21. His breath kindleth coals, and a flame goeth out of his mouth! Well, Job, if you lied so badly in your afflictions, what would you have done had you been in health?

Ezra, ch. vi., v. 10. The re-building of the temple : That they may offer sacrifices of sweet savors unto the God of heaven, and pray for the life of the king, and of his sons.

Ch. vii., v. 12. Artaxerxes, king of kings unto Ezra the priest, scribe of the law of the God of heaven. 26. "And whosoever will not do the law of thy God, and the law of the king, let judgment be executed speedily upon him, whether it be unto death or to banishment, or to confiscation of goods, or to imprisonment." What is more clearly displayed, than the union of Church and State. What mighty sounding titles are named.

It would be a repetition of contradictions of all the bible characters in their most essential points, to whatever extent this discussion might be carried. Had all the data of facts been before the world, there had been no necessity of my saying as much. I shall conclude this part by another small review of the illustrious Daniel.

Ch. ii., v. 39. "And another third kingdom of brass, which shall bear rule over all the earth."

There was no such kingdom, neither Macedonian nor any other, and this man had a brazen impudence in writing, as his supporters have in sustaining it.

44. "And in the days of these kings shall the God of heaven set up a kingdom, which shall never be destroyed." This monomaniac speaks untruly, for the God of the universe had fully anticipated all that, the little prophets of the world in all ages and their peculiar god.

BIBLES OF TRADITION.

THE ancient landmarks so conspicuous once, so defective now, as recognised by a superior age of mental calibre, have to be remodeled or superseded, and the bibles of miracles, mysteries, prophecies, and enigmas, must yield to those of mind.   The inventions of the clergy must yield to the principles of the God of nature.

No codes of religion, if not rational or of morals, unless identified therewith, are worthy of the name or the age of mind.

Mind in its progress of light has outstripped the records of all peculiar faith, and shames them as miserably defective into actual silence, where reason holds her sway; hence, the first miserably libels the last, the best friend of mind.

The time is rapidly hurrying when all such rubbish of bibles will be left unheeded as a curiosity.

Cultivated mind will adopt only that one that becomes consistent with proper principles that are always new, bright, and adorable, from time to eternity.

Ask men of liberal minds liberalized·by the best lights of philosophical science before them, and they will tell you, if they speak candidly, that they cannot subscribe to any peculiar faith or its pretences now before the world.

A majority of the world that should be ready to subscribe to all that is right in religion, and withhold from that which is wrong, will tell this, and thus decide as far as reason can decide, that no documents are valid that are exceptionable in parts, to an ultimate self-contradiction and condemnation.

Principles cannot contradict nor be antagonistical, but forever strengthen each other, and resist successfully all opposition that must be necessarily unprincipled and invalid.

It is time, when illustrious fundamental doctrines have so long preceded in creation, that the part applicable and practicable should most rightfully and unquestionably follow.

Mind must not be vassal but entirely free, to have this elevated dignity so justly due, conferred on the world.

No tradition hallowed by time, custom, and social ties, if unprincipled, can be legitimate. The world cannot approve of any such, and all present and future generations are justly bound to absolve themselves from their misrule.

The objections to bibles of miracles, prophecies, mysteries, and enigmas, are innumerable and valid to explode all such, as the worst humbugs of the world.

What is true of the best of such bibles, is much more applicable to the worst.

Among the glimmerings of past ages, is that of Judaism, that in the most liberal criticism can only be estimated as wretched superstition and despotism.   All the learning of past centuries of Egypt, Chaldea, and all the eastern countries of Asia, gave instruction in the dogmas and crude notions of the times and peculiar faith.

We are not able to appreciate all the preceding lights, but must know that the state of knowledge was very defective, traditional or written, among the people, who were deprived of the best facilities of printing books, and liberal discussion of toleration, to reach correct views.

The great defect was want of reaction of mind on mind, for the decision was too often conclusive and final, on the dictation of individuals whose interest decided them!

The rude state of the people proves that they were prone to receive passively, and without inquiry, what those above them commanded.

The world was vassal, for its free agent, mind of the mass, was ignorant, and ah ignorant mass is vassal.

The best of nations were destitute of high and noble principles, were piratical, warred upon the weak and enslaved their prisoners whom they did not murder and victimize, unprincipled in most wars for conquests and plunder.

The misery of it was that mind was crushed, and had to rescue itself from a long lapse of time, darkened and blurred by its most perverted depravity.

All the vices of ignorance, and all the crimes of error, carried into the extremes of superstition and prejudice among all the nations of the world, had to be corrected.

The greatest bondage was and is, that of mind.

What a mass of corruption and ignorance was that of the Hebrews, prepared as most of the ancients to blindly receive the dogmas of Judaism, a confused mass of superstitious peculiar faith !   A blind peculiar faith, under the most ignoble despotism of mind.

Then, lawgivers were not very liberal, if skilled in the rights and mighty potency of mind.   If not the first, they betrayed the noblest rights of sovereign man. and if not the last, they are destitute of any claim in both on the confidence of mind, in having any peculiar gifts from the Author of mind.

The question properly arises, not how far this character should be censured by criticism enlightened and just, but how suitably all the defects and flaws may be pointed out, to break the unfortunate spell on the dark minds of the superstitious, who are not conscious of the mighty hold on their minds: as to the balance, the case is desperate for human correction at present.

The polity of church and state governments has been one of the mighty means of enslaving and debasing mind, in all ages and countries practicable, under the most insidious forms.

It has always been a strong one addressed to the interests of mind by policy and corruption in this life, and of fears for the next.

Rational religion proves that no national polity can be permanently prosperous, but on eternal principles, in regard to state governments, religion, and social rights.

The more any national polity departs from them, the sooner it ends.

The authors show a reckless ignorance of the pure character of God and his works, unworthy the respect of the wise and honorable.

They libel all, and impeach themselves and their book.

They misrepresent God as a localized existence, and personally their companion.

They misrepresent his qualities, as similar to man's.

They misrepresent his universal polity, as peculiar and contracted to that peculiarity most unwisely so.

They betray their utter ignorance of his conservative principles, adequate for the universe, and mind in all its states to the most sublime bliss and immortal fruition, and put angels in their place to execute God's wishes and messages, good angels for conservative, evils ones for destruction, the negative of conservation.

They have created a system of their faith, and defined that for man; whereas, mind rejects it as spurious, and reason excludes it as counterfeit.

The religion of God Almighty is liberal and universal; their faith belongs to a chosen peculiar few, and can go no farther. It can be transferred to no rational nation of people.

They restrict God to one race of men, whereas the facts of physiology cannot stop with one, proving the illustrious genius of the Creator, in his unbounded resources, and the limited knowledge of the writers, whose imposition is clearly exposed to the wise.

They, charlatans of mind, affect that man was not made right, and render his situation truly deplorable, by their ignorant botches of pretended correction.

They have to learn the first principles of physiology, in appreciating that man was made expressly as God made him, and that man could not alter man by any contrivance foreign to his nature, character, and mind, without corrupting and degrading all such.

Therefore conceited priests and clergy have to drop all such false pretences.

So far from a right conception of the God of nature, they have actually libeled nature, misconceiving her plainest attributes.

Mind must first learn nature, to appreciate the God of nature, through his philosophical science to reach his most sublime of all sciences, religion.

Mind must learn all accurately, to be right, and know that all are right.

What a libel on God does the line " in sorrow thou (the woman) shalt bring forth children," declare! The woman's travail is in her nature according to circumstances, more or less modified by her time and mode of life, &c.

The sweat of the face or body, so far from being a curse, is most conclusively the greatest of blessings to balance the health, diffuse the secretions, stimulate the vital organs, prepare the sweetest of appetites, and procure the most refreshing slumbers, and above all, preserve that beloved innocence of mind. freed from the curses of idleness that begets lowness of spirits, dullness of ideas, and seduces idlers and loungers to the most perverted mental corruption, for want of better employment.

This position applies to both sexes, and all ages available, all conditions of life. from which none are exempt.

Failing in two of the most important and material points, God and man, the most essential concerned in this whole subject of such bibles, which had been already banished the world as unworthy of it, retarding its civilization, destroying its peace and affecting its benefits, had man not acted as vassal, and mind declared its independence, we turn to further expositions of their sheerest ignorance and perversion.

The cosmogony or description of the earth's creation, is most awfully deficient, if the principles of geology and astronomy be duly estimated.

Taking partial and contracted views in all the elements of substantial science, they betray invariably, their short coming and perversions.

In natural philosophy, they fail most signally, in the fable of the deluge of the whole earth at once, as an impossibility for want of materials to execute it. Inspiration and revelation with faith, are the talismans that the adepts of peculiar faith employ. With this knavery, the dupes of the world are to be made. Who endorse all these? Can we find one endorser where we find innumerable conclusive proofs, that it is all false as corrupt mind could conceive.

What circumnavigator of the globe at that time, could be adduced as furnishing one iota of proof? They have cut off all witnesses to their own legend.

We invoke the proof from God, and he plainly denies it in his unmistakable evidence.

All minds of science can see that the earth cannot be covered by water, without intrinsic revolutions unthought of by the writers, and surely none in their senses can deny what God's works prove, that all such imposition is a libel.

Their writings, then, betray the grossest ignorance of natural phenomena, which they misrepresent as miracles.

Partial deluges are common, more or less, to all ages or centuries, as one a few years ago on the great Yellow river, of China, that destroyed or affected millions of people in life and property.

The most absurd ignorance is invoked, to save the species of all creeping things that must necessarily cross and recross the ocean waters, to be saved in the ark, thus encountering a difficulty worse than these botches of mind obviated.

But it never entered the brain of these dreamers, that the species of animated life was at all different in different continents.

But was the mental state of man bettered by such a deluge that destroyed one portion of the animal creation, but necessarily left out the fishes, exercising a miserable distinction from miserable incapacity?

What wise man will say that the case is altered at all, as to man's nature, that is intrinsically the same all the time? Then we see the utter fallacy and abominable wanton cruelty in devising such pretences. Had human nature been altered, the unity of design required the alteration of all; then, it had been a conservative revolution instead of an absurd destructive universal deluge. That conservative revolution established by an all-wise Creator, has been constantly more or less progressing in mind that is preparing for elevation.

With an afterthought that betrays man's foot-marks all the time, as contradistinguished from God's forethought and omniscience, an all-wise and perfect wisdom before creation even, we have to deplore this pretence run out in a second attempt at bettering man, who is made inconceivably worse by the exploit of messiahship, conceived in impiety, and executed with blasphemy.

Vainglorious man, modesty had better kept thee in silence! for thou art exposed in all thy folly, and when thou aspirest to God's province, thou art deeply punished.

Again, another miracle is invoked, where a volcano may have destroyed Sodom and Gomorrah.

The very crime of incest committed by the drunken man Lot and his two daughters, who are saved, impeaches the character of just integrity of morals of the times, and casts a verdict of condemnation of its especial favor for purity of conscience.

In Melchisidec, we see the acts of the priesthood selfish and tyrannical, appropriating the tenth of warriors' spoils, no matter the source, so the priests were paid. Who can wonder that they excited the people to wars, and incited them to plunder and conquests. All the muddying of the waters, cannot excuse the first, nor save the undertakers to smother their iniquities from the contempt and condemnation of good citizens.

The patriarch of the Jewish nation most stupidly lays the foundation of circumcision under the guise and name of religion, actuated by the most iniquitous superstition and criminal selfishness, to ostracize his nation from universal nationalization and brotherhood. He has created a most horrible state of national sufferings for his descendants most inglorious, and defended by no human, natural or rational principles.

The act was unnatural, and the object has proved disastrous to the people for thousands of years. It has separated them from mankind, by a device that God abhors, and has made them the scorn of the world, merely the result of circumstances connected with their superstitious polity, cruelly forced on them by the cunning priesthood.

The sooner it is laid aside, the better, that they may diffuse themselves among the citizens of the world, and be comprehended by universal bonds of brotherhood, on the rational principles of nature and of mind.

Let no superstition widen the breach any longer. This same patriarch enlarged the capacity of the priesthood, and added to the potency of their machinations, like the ignorant superstitions of all lands, advancing from the offer of the blood of animals, instead of man, who was sacrificed because mind was barbarous enough to permit it.

The best principles of physiology have been violated by the senseless adherence to peculiar faith in their intermarriages, corrupting the blood, and enervating its intrinsic superiority.

The safe line of the select and chosen is maintained in the fraud of Jacob over Esau, and is one of the thousand condemnations as libeling the character and purity of God, through their imperfect peculiar god, necessarily their priestocracy.

The resident Hebrews, Jacob's descendants in Egypt, are entertained most hospitably by the people, and become inhabitants.

By their own showing, but for their superstitious circumcision and rites, they might have become a part of this nation, but they excluded themselves from national participation, as they have always done.

They show nothing but a distinct nation. As to their oppression, that is a natural consequence.

Now arises the principal historian, Moses, who may be a fiction or man of straw in the hands of the priests, who seek to make him figure in their history, the mighty vicegerent of God. And first, what is this history, but mixed with legends and fables, as all such are? We have to reason on a part of their peculiar faith, and exclude much that is too gross for mind, or that cannot be, as a code, fit for civilized man. Nations mixed their peculiar faith, the necessary result of an ignorant and barbarous age, done all the world over, time out of mind. And what morals, too!

With his hands stained with blood, the pure God is made to adopt him, without qualification and purification.

Nothing can be done without Moses. He is all but god; only that they unwittingly make Jethro a greater man than Moses, and a more successful adviser than god! O priests! you were nodding then.

Moses and Aaron commence jugglers before the Egyptians, and by the bible showing they are the princes of jugglers in this juggling country and age. It was the dynasty of the priestocracy. And it is most difficult to say, whether there is better sleight of hand or mind, did not the intelligent world know, that the priestocracy use the last when interest requires.

A deep ignorance of natural phenomena is betrayed, and the bible distorts and interprets them its way, proving them jugglers of both.

What reliance can be placed in such clear perversion, when the first pre-requisites of accurate history, those of truth, are clearly and unequivocally wanting?

Priests, clergy, is this the book you ask the confidence of mind in? Are you honest, are you truthful to do so? Can any honest man, looking at all the facts, say but that the highest imposition is assumed when it is asserted that all this man's sayings and doings are from God? What worthy companions, Moses and Aaron, associates in popular imposition.

What are the tenets of peculiar faith worth, if they are not believed? Rational religion can see that it was better that Moses should have told the truth, but that did not suit him, a wily Egyptian-raised juggler, for the truth violation was his aim. It was sought to govern the people by the nett proceeds of untruths.

Rational religion was not his faith; it was too sublime for such people. It was not profitable. What is any peculiar faith worth, if the requisite power is not instituted to reap the full harvest? Truly have heads of government and peculiar faith conspired to head the people in mass, who were to be taxed to the height of their credulity and endurance. What can we do with this fabulous tradition, that no man in his senses can believe? Mortals have nothing but this report, and that the mighty word of God, cause and effect, gainsay.

The priests never would have written these monstrous legends had they known that the great God, whose eye of reason is upon all, could contradict them most successfully and triumphantly, unless they were so hardened that they cared nothing for the exposure, after filching from the people the success of their crimes. What care hypocritical pirates for public opinion, if they be successful in their abuse of human rights? Is it not now the word of many that though a robber, he was a mighty one of the earth? It is the success, not the obloquy, that false opinion of the world is misdirected to.

Who that analyzes this subject properly and comprehensively cannot proclaim, most conscientiously, that the immortal word of God proclaims the jugglers, through Moses, all that untruth can make such degraded caterers.

God does not operate by miracles. The universe gainsays that. Miracles show a revolution in nature, proving God's imbecility. This is a universal truism. God's greatest deeds are his regular works. What was Judaism? Was it a sincere belief in a God of principles, the only one that can exist, or was it not a god after the manner and thoughts of uncivilized men, characterized by low passions, groveling propensities, and puerile imbecilities, all the reflection of the priestocracy libelers?

The best of analysts can correct this if wrong.

Then the polity taught caused the blind followers not to examine with true, honest and rational belief, but adopt with blind credulity and superstitious faith.

Man-worship of course was a necessary ingredient in such a chaos and substitute for truth in peculiar faith. If God gave no such commission, as it is clear he did not, then the priests instituted man-worship in all its horrid demoralization and depravity.

All this is too clear to be disproved by reason and truth. All the fruits of man-worship were messiahships. The priests make Moses messiah, and what a counsellor. By their own showing, his character was that of a degraded, very degraded being, below that of a man.

He had not the first requisite of rational religion, truth and honesty.

This being corrupted the Hebrew people, unfortunately for their character, at the start of Exodus, by causing them to obtain a loan of the most valuable ornaments of gold of the people of Egypt, which proves that people's kindness, whose forefathers had so well treated their forefathers, and caused the children of Israel to adopt a dishonest repudiation of their just debts. Here was neither truth nor honesty.

The peculiar faith of Moses and Aaron, a polity that all cunning tyrants and priests aim at, of church and state governments, the strongest for grinding and insidious power, so far from ever being effectual in restraint of the idolatry of the ignorant multitude, established marked corruption, at all times, more or less to be expected in every such unhallowed union, and caused its woful increase.

God has instituted, through reason, that is always right, the important principles of government, that should be always right for the happiness of the people, but this conservative basis, the curse of all such power prevents.

The rulers, no matter of divine or worldly name, have nearly always brought false pretences against people's rights, when they could govern them with impunity and absolutely.

The error lies with the people, who should correct their rulers.

At that time when mind was vassal, and popular rights were superseded by the cunning of craftship, when governors were masters, and lords and priests were gods, the fault was more with the rulers than with the people, though to become, through rational mind, the sovereigns of the world.

At this time such imposition implies error, corruption, and the faults of the people, who should correct all such at once, when guarded against them. As bad as the world-humbugs are, the worst of all is that created by self. The people humbug themselves.

Hitherto, where a proper analysis has always been wanting, the error is not so much with the great mass of the people. as in their representatives, the original thinkers of the world, who usurped or permitted power to be usurped.

Priest-usurpation, such as that of Moses, never yielded power rightly, till compelled.

All lawgivers that are enlightened on principles must prefer, if sincere, to entrust the people at once with proper representative government, as the most just to the many, and the best to the whole for self-preservation.

The government of principle is the choice of a providence directly superintending and of elevated character, but the selfish lawgiver never looks further than what secures the government through his own dynasty.

No adherents of absolutism need argue against the capacity of man for self-government, as liberalism arouses the best of minds for that best order of government.

No government could have been worse than the past. Not only did the wily and arch Moses overreach the Egyptians, but he ungraciously and ungratefully overreached his own people.

Such a peculiar polity as he is said to have instituted was not submitted to the people, as if they had minds, but merely bodies, and they were treated as they generally have been, where they do not interpose their protests to their high treason tyrants, as mere subjects, slaves, vassals, and cattle, not only in government temporal but spiritual. They were asked for their credulity, that did not amount to the dignity of faith. In all the modifications, priestocracy still maintained its ascendancy.

It was too much in advance of the times to expect popular government for Judaism, and no peculiar faith at that day could be devised as better than the one given. As all peculiar faiths are bad, no fundamental correction could follow. Conservative revolution had to be instituted, but that has been reserved for this time and country. The chivalry for mind could not arise, where all was vassal.

Many a dark and bloody ground had to be passed, ere the people, the best assertors, could reach and vindicate their rights, as sovereigns.

The people were not thought of as equals, or only thought of, to be made beasts of burden, by those that could rise into power, by trick and pretences of all kinds.

No; the people never could govern themselves, whilst others could attend to that matter, to govern them. The time was always ahead, never to arrive, when popular government could be instituted.

It is difficult to say, whether priestcraftship or kingcraftship has committed the highest treason against mind.

Through all such, the corrupt source of power has operated. This is a theme that none but the freest people can analyze, and which they can never analyze too closely, as they may ever be still subject to its misrule.

'Tis needless to trace all the Hebrew polity, in its various corruptions, any more than the details of miracles, alias impositions. Too much of the best, presents a woful picture of perversions. The perpetrators set out to act them, and they succeeded but too well, to hand down its bitterest curses to their present generations, whose alleviation is due to the very spirit of liberty, that this polity opposed—to that mind, that it crushed, deceived, cheated, defrauded, imposed on, and ruined!

Peculiarize the human mind, indeed!

Traitors to all its noblest rights, the miracles that your Exodus delineates, portray impossibilities, all that are directly contradicted by the light of philosophical science.

The very condition of the Hebrews, now and for centuries, give such history most irrefragable contradiction.

In any authors, such history of their pilgrimage in the wilderness would brand them as the degraded falsifiers of true history, the veriest, most stupid fabulists.

All such would have died out, by its intrinsic weakness, but for the craftship that had to live, and fan its vitality. The continuation of the fraternity under the peculiar mystic ties, has upheld the code.

The rock yields to the smiting of a rod, pure water. Such is not a miracle of God, but the mere jugglery of man. Artesian wells yield now water, hundreds of feet below the surface of rocks. Jugglery is science concealed under art. Water would flow, if a plug was struck out of a rock even. It is brought now from under rocks, and yet no miracles. When will humbugged mind stop, with its own fooleries and impositions? It is the key to all the false pretences of paganism, of which this is a great part. It is afraid to think, to read, investigate, even to talk before bigots. Do these bigots hold any claim on the people's souls? Is superstition so powerful to enslave, that the remotest generations cannot extricate themselves from its direst curses? Is there no tory despotism, no treachery to mind, at the bottom?

The man Moses goes up to the mount, to have God deliver his commandments, about which he was forty days and forty nights; rather long for sacred action. But this was always the case with oracles. Do any differ? The jugglery of the priests exceeds all other jugglery, for they have deceived the world for thousands of years. Their humbugs are the most durable of all humbugs. The fire of the mount, if fire, was volcanic—the locale, no doubt, was in the brains of the priests. There is no witness. The people saw it, but do these people tell us with any positive documents. Who endorse these, endorse fictions. All this is the work of impostors—not one, but enough in collusion. Their morals were easy, their falsehood reckless and facile.

An honest mind gives and demands proof, or gives up the point, as honesty requires.

The laws were only the work of mind.

At this very day, parts of the civil or pagan, so called, laws, are so superior to the common laws of lands adopting peculiar faith, that they are preferred in a state of this Union to all others. The last laws prove that mind is in the ascendant, and any exclusion of it, is in the basest treachery to God, the basest imposition to man.

We see the malign effects of want of principles.

Falsehoods were ever the coin of such peculiar faith. Moses lies about meeting God in the mount; Aaron and the people worship the golden calf, that Aaron lies about, in saying that he put the gold into the fire, and it came out a calf!

Moses lies about the brazen serpent, and though the greatest of all prophets, turned out a perjurer, as he aware falsely about the land to Caleb—and involves his god in perjury, about his oath to all the three patriarchs, that the Jews should "inherit it (the land) forever." As such is all false pretence, Moses or his peculiar god must settle it between them, and all will have to bury prophecy, that they killed on that occasion.

We need not mention the other prophets, particularly, except in some essential points, as Moses, the chief, was a perjurer: the others, his creatures, could not do less.

What could we expect, as the result of such a polity, but that the people would be characterized accordingly? When principles are violated nationally, the nation has no basis of national virtue.

The Hebrews, a peculiarly righteous nation, make a system of wars and pillage. They invade peaceful nations, expelling them from their lands piratically, no better than the world, though God's chosen people. That very position constituted the reason for piracy.

So the whole inspiration is clearly disproved at once, especially, too, when the holy ark, God's own, was taken and kept among their enemies.

Numerous were the horrid wars, conquests for plunder, acts of treachery and cunning, a fatal example of world-piracies. Did these people better the world?

They were secluded, more than the present Chinese or Eastern nations, keeping their virtues to themselves, if they had them, but their vices were most grievously oppressive to their neighbors, by their own accounts.

Their god was horribly stained, belittled, and dwarfed, by their painting, substituting him of superstition.

Cheerfully can it be said, that it was not the God of the universe.

Very incorrect notions of justice prevailed with them, as with other nations of that day and time. There was much to condemn, but little to approve, much less to adopt.

Had the priests let their deeds been buried with them, their frailties could not have been exposed, to so great a degree. As a peculiar superiority has been claimed for them, let the facts of their inferiority be displayed, enough to prevent all imposition. Beyond this it is needless to proceed.

In what did this peculiar people prove an illustrious peculiarity of mind? In its light, when they affected to a mighty miracle, of stopping time, but substituted the earth for the sun and moon—stultifying themselves by their blasphemous ignorance of astronomy and the fixed laws of nature, before God, who will vindicate himself, despite of all the pretensions of peculiar faith, the most contradictory and suicidal.

We can well estimate how matters were, when their best of rulers, as he was called, David, a man after God's own heart, was a murderer most ingrate, and an adulterer most vile, in religion a hypocrite, the worst of all characters, presenting the inconsistency of his not building the temple of God, and yet Moses, with his hands stained with murder, was the face to face companion of that god of Judaism. All this proves that the peculiar god was no more than the priestocracy.

This is the inconsistency of man, not God, who is deceitfully libeled in these pretences. Hypocrites can act most deceitfully.

The temple of Solomon was dedicated to the god of Judaism. What was that but dedication to priestcraft and superstition, the benefit of the priests?

How were the people benefited? By offer of the blood of animals to God? Does the God of Nature drink or inhale blood? Shame upon such superstition!

Are these the foundations, for mind of the present age?

Change, priests, your absurd inconsistencies, before a consistent immaculate God, whom you do not know.

Ages of improvement have passed on, mind has improved mind, and the present one in a civilized circle, does not permit such a polity, without protest or redress. by counteracting the misrule of absolutism in all its insidiousness, and moral infraction in all its turpitude.

There is no divine right of absolutism in any form of monarchy or peculiar faith as ancient Judaism and modern Papacy. All must recognise the divine right of mind, swayed by reason, carried on in wisdom, balanced in justice, and submitted to universal constitutional principles.

And, at last, who was the builder of the temple?

A vicious and licentious king. Solomon has been presented to us as the wisest most absurdly, disproved when his own acts proclaim him one of the weakest among mankind, enslaved by his passions and degraded by his vices, with a morality very low, and only limited by the loss of functions, hence all was vanity and vexation of spirit with him. The comprehension of his and all other characters at death, seals the true decision.

Despite of all the court flatterers that ever fawned on absolutism, forever linked in its foul embrace, and ready to do its bidding by all the insidious assassinations of sophistry that begets falsehoods on every step of peculiar faith, stupid and reeking in guilt, we see the horrid glare of iniquitous polity, in which priestocracies, absolutists, and their creatures make a Trinity.

As to this nation, the peculiarity of its especial favor of being the chosen people of God, is directly contradicted by God's universal attributes, the paramount influence of which compels the inevitable question of benevolence. What had the other nations, of all this especial faith, but the deadliest hatred and bigotry to combat?

God is a just, not partial or peculiar God, which last is impossible, therefore all nations do participate in universal favors, and those only through mind, reason, and merit. Mind has to act as free and moral agent, otherwise God is peculiar, and responsibility to him is peculiar. Man's polity destroys the unity of God and his universe. O, man, your credulity has superseded your reason, if all this be true.

Above all, too, such idea of peculiar favor of being the chosen people of God, proceeded from the pious frauds of their leaders, all the men of straw, Moses and his creatures and co-deceivers, and is flatly contradicted by this nation's career among victorious nations, till its final subjugation, captivity, and dispersion throughout the world. Anything else but a chosen people were the Jews.

Looking philosophically at the peculiar mark of circumcision and its faith, the conclusion is inevitable, that this nation thus renders itself peculiar and alien to all others.

What else can result in nature, but the very facts now connected with that nation?

All nations, without exception, have had their own superstitious worship, to which they have pertinaciously adhered, and for which the false position of martyrdom, one of its evils, has been most stupidly attached, fostered by the priests, who affected patents to their heaven for all such.

Never was there such a hold on earth, that the world-wide dogmas of superstitious faith have.

All kinds are antagonistic, and eternally in conflict. A monster itself, it produces all monstrosities.

Deprived as the Jew is of many national advantages amid the world by his peculiar mark and tenets, many of them yet persevere inflexibly to notions and opinions conceived in miserable error and enacting miserable scenes; but some of the wiser part, as of all peculiar creeds having no just principles, are abating in faith that was only credulity.

The philosophy of rational religion will teach man his true interest, and best prepare all for their happiness.

The picture then of the family of such bibles, the very best of them advocating such doctrines, is stained with absurdities and crimes, presents a most woful false position to man, imposition of incorrect philosophy at the creation, and is full of blasphemy, when at last God is degraded below the standard of man's morality, to create an assistant, a blasphemous usurper.

Sectarianism at last proves conclusively that the right worship was not in Judaism, that awkwardly affected to know and worship the God of Nature by priest-worship. But the change is in another set of priests.

All are such guardians of the dear people, that they will not give the God of mind a chance to take care of it.

Physiology or reason cannot permit the idea of the Almighty, a perfect being at creation, being superseded after great lapse of time, by any mortal vicegerent who affects the reformation by causing the first light of mind to succumb to man-worship, the loftiest intrinsic principles being lost sight of.

Any bible implies a horrid and squalid ignorance, too, when it affords food for faith in ghosts and witches, fostering a horrid and cruel superstition.

Is the bible of Judaism, or of Christianity, any bible of tradition, a third power peculiar, a specific characteristic of Deity, or does it merely represent Deity's characteristics?

All honest sound minds will affirm to no peculiar characteristic, unless the bible is a sixth sense, that ought to advance itself, then all bibles are subordinate to reason, not faith, and must be held in perfect abeyance to mind. Why then do you advance the gospel?

To produce proselytes. Religion premises the right basis.

How do you make converts, by the bible or gospel?

By addressing mind, through mind. Then you are indebted to mind and its best exponent, reason; and by your own showing you are condemned by reason, which you invoke in all conversions through impressions of every mind converted.

You are then involved in your own contradiction, which is the same when you say, "Faith comes by hearing," implying brains, mind, reason, for some of the five senses the ministers of reason are then addressed and men are taught to think; if the contrary is asserted, then full imposition governs all the time.

Thereby all other bibles but of mind and that most rational, are necessarily ruled out.

The last triumphs over the bible of Judaism and Christianity, or any other of similar character openly and boldly, and impeaches such for their deficiency and actual want of correct principles, the bad state of ethics, social, moral, national, and religious, inculcated.

The bible of Moses was deficient, and the bible of Christ was to amend it with vengeance! The world, full of all such bibles, would be necessarily incompetent to the task. God's portraiture is defective, because these and all other such bibles are defective; the bibles, not God, are defective. Bibles of patchwork should be all ruled out.

They are the bibles of absolutism, not of liberalism, of the priests, rulers and creatures, not of the sovereign people and mind, whose benefit should be invariably consulted and maintained forever.

The good and true citizen cannot believe in any such, knowingly, yet a right code of mind is needful to protect the innocent from the world's injury.

Correctly disposed minds, the majority, need correct codes for their families, to protect all best.

It actually becomes every good citizen, to aid society in reaching correct principles of religion, as of government.

No good citizen of cultivated, civilized mind, knowingly, can tolerate any such mass of absurdities, that lead necessarily to oppression and tyranny of the worst kind, that of mind, without an effort to rescue it.

The very object of such machinery, was made to enslave, not befriend mind in its purity, sovereignty, freedom and independence. It is the work of absolutism, whether crowned with state, or church, or creature-authority, and has to do its own execution. It unites delusion to oppression of mind, and sways a potent energy and malign influence.

This machinery, with all the elements of decay and destruction, requires all the art of its cunning supporters, to uphold it from the death. It changes its form. It causes a large part, the immediate beneficiaries, to separate with dictatorial power, and war on the balance. It falsifies where it cannot enslave directly. It stops at nothing too low, to foster its designs.

But pure honest minds may have never thought of this important and vital state question to command power and secure influence, and may have had a vague idea that the bible was the book of inspirations, and absolutely essential as the corner-stone of society, which, losing that foundation, would be dissolved into its original elements. This is the priests' pretences, to keep back mind. Very clear of all this, from the first best of reasons, that God the divine architect, upholds not only society, but all the mighty universe.

God is the supreme ruler and omniptent governor of the whole, much less of this small globe, a small portion. He governs all safely, wisely, and above all, religiously, the highest state of wise government.

The peculiar bible is not to be put for the doctrine, the principles of God's pure character, for it libels God's character, and impiously strips him of the only true essential object of his adoration, his inherent power and attributes, and yet the writers call it the official organ of God's court and authority, thereby adding insult to injury, before high justice. It trades on the capital of mind and God, and appropriates their benefits to itself!

God gave to all nations, mind individually, to furnish their best offering to him, in the best actions throughout the world, but perversion of mind offered a thing that men called bible of tradition, for usurpation of mind.

The God of the universe flourishes forever, independently of all court and official documents, except through his works alone, his only court and official organs, that the immortal mind must seek to understand, and thereby prove itself worthy.

The world also, would flourish its part, independently of all such foul pretensions, but is reckless of God's rule and the right agency of mind, his gift, cultivated mind most of the time under whose wise influence act wise legislators and statesmen, with their best view of fundamental principles of government, that give the highest purity for man's duty and its performance.

All student observers must clearly see the bad effects of the Hebrew polity in that nation, considering itself the chosen people of God! What absurd and heinous egotism! And is it possible that rational minds can be so stupid as to confide with rational faith in this absurdity, not to say criminality? It is bad enough for one people, let alone the world, believing in such stupid nonsense. This doctrine was not monotheism, that liberalizes man's mind to the circumference, the depth, height and breadth of the whole universe ; that exalteth the soul to all its duty, that comprehends the citizens of this world, whom, if man exclude by his polity, he impeaches his own justice and liberality to the balance of creation, and neutralizes and annihilates at once the principles even of religion.

Judaism built up the god of the Hebrews, a god that repented, was changeable, was irascible and imperfect, adapted to the narrow limits of a sect and their country, of time and the prejudices of man. Man's tradition-bible of God's creation, had to be amended from time to time, to correct the imperfect legends of the ignorant bigots propagating them, a position that was false, and laid the foundation for all sorts of creeds and innovations on the principles of reason and mind.

This bible was no doubt delivered in monographs. The first, was when man was placed as pretended, in the garden of paradise. But as man was sinful, the second had to account for it, correcting it as Mahomet's bible, each part reviewing the preceding. The chapters divide into books, more or less. But as the world was not made right by man, man had to make a deluge to get out 'of the difficulty, and was lost in the deep ocean of difficulties. In subsequent ages, the priests in whose hands the records were all the time, adapted these books still better, down to their conclave, at the council of Nice, and probably subsequently.

So imperfect is this priest-bible, that its god's imbecility permitted even mortals to interfere with the machinery of the priestocracy-creation, and his attributes were revealed as crude and unmatured. A school-boy, now, if adept in true science, can correct all such bibles as imbecile, not God, of course.

The peculiarity of God's people, that is, a few millions of Hebrews, being chosen and upheld, not for extraordinary personal virtues and intellectual genius, while hundreds of millions equally good on parity of creation for liberty, equality and fraternity, were not known as fellow-creatures, shows the most stupid absurdity on its face, while all God's works are universal at the same time.

If this bible was a painting, the caricature would be plain.

This bible is an abominable libel on Deity's attributes, unquestionably. This result comes of deception of a murderer and a repudiator, turned juggler, politician and dictator, aided by all the cunning of priestcraft in its subtlest wiles on mind of all ages. It is well that the Hebrews, despite of all these, have done so well. They have been separated from the world by this ruinous polity, that exposes them to its scoffs and contempt. The sooner they lay aside their superstition and its rites, the better, and diffuse themselves among the honorable of the world.

They must lay aside circumcision and all their conceit of peculiarity, the choice people of their imbecile god, and unite themselves to the people of the God of the universe.

They are invited not to revere the money-god, that has been worshipped in every age and by all nations, but the holy God of the universe, that mind recognises and adores. His decalogues are the mirrors of truth, elicited by analysis of social and religious principles and profitable thought, addressed in all their purity to man's sincerity and action. All peculiar faith violates the most of them.

The resulting acts decidedly and conclusively prove this, that neither Judaism nor Christianity, Mahometanism, Mormonism, Brahminism, Bhuddism nor their equivalent, Paganism, nor any peculiarity of faith can ever stand before rational religion, the language of God universal.

Without any teaching of bibles, but in despite of them, to the noblest triumph of mind, the Indians of America believe in one great spirit, and at God's tribunal, such orthodox faith would condemn that of the Christians, who assume to dictate to the whole world, most presumptuously, and appeal egotistically to the arrogance of ignorant credulity. Their faith rests not, as the poor Indian, on reason, but they have forsaken that which guides the savage in his wilderness, and gone to fictions of a bible that disgraces faith. But all the impostors have overlooked that God does not write as man, but by divine painting, totally unapproachable to man's counterfeits.

God's work is sublimity itself, for his pen is electricity, his canvas the universe, and his colors sunbeams.

But the imbecile pen of man, in his pitiful patent bibles of tradition, dwarfs creation and the Supreme Creator. It will not bear the audience of common science and common sense.

If we talk of more than one dispensation or covenant, that after-thought of man put for God's, impeaches God's perfection; and all such, if there were thousands, being of course man's, are utterly incompetent, as clearly proved by their own position to meet the case, since all dispensations of bibles leave out forever most of mankind who cannot be included by all the statistics of the world. All such authors of bibles are most stupid, criminal, blasphemous.

Their peculiarities are antagonistic and subversive of each other, and all are so to the only universal one of creation.

It is not bibles, that cannot be present, but the ever-constant and faithful mind, man's true friend first and last, all the time for man, that is his savior, redeemer, intercessor, proxy, free moral agent unmistakably.

It is this gift, worth all others from a pure God, that changes man to his unchangeable and perfect God

Proper sense and truth will estimate mind as endowed, but patent bibles have fallen short of them, and cannot possibly meet the great points at issue in life for the world.

The only thing that can possibly do so is mind, whose treasury is to be ever equal to life's drafts, the world's age.

Mind must be responsible for the policy of the world ; the bibles are not, only as they conform to mind's obligations. Those that impose the contrary, impose their own accusation and direful condemnation.

A truthful rational mind demands full investigation of any faith presented, that if adopted it wishes to rest on no slender base, doubtful or invalidated, as the bible of the priests present.

How dare vassals offer freemen any other but what can be universally approved ? Away with all vassal bibles, that have done the work of slaves and pirates.

Intelligent freemen need a better, and invoke the God of mind for mind's bible. The unity of God secures the unity that characterizes the bible of mind.

Neither Moses nor Peter, the representative of Christ, the authors of the dispensations as claimed by the managers of the peculiar drama, can be proper or safe authority for pure religion to rest on, very clear of it, as they previously perjured themselves at certain times.

All the advancers of peculiar faith unquestionably perjure themselves. Moses swore to many pretensions claimed in his bible ; Peter, especially, was convicted, when the purest are found present and right in need, and by the only fair test, the trial of purity.

No aspirant to peculiar-bible faith can be entitled to a just and righteous court of conscience verdict of acquittal before mind's highest tribunal, surely.

Then Mahomet, Christ, Smith, and all other notables are convicted as blasphemously perjured, or those who managed any men of straw.

It is wonderful how all these things were ever tolerated by any honest mind, since they cannot be denied nor overlooked as mere contingencies caused by self-delusion.

Mind ought to be ashamed of itself, if rightly cultivated, for the adoption of any such imposition of superstition, much less for the guilt of its propagation.

With the lights of the age, who can subscribe to the bigotry and superstition of bible-peculiar faith, much less to the thousand wiles of ambitious, intriguing, and deceitful hierarchy, no matter of what form, from the most delusive idolatry to the most brutal sacrifice of life, or mind—worse still—bad as preceding history presented is ?

Let us, an enlightened people, get rid of all the thousand and one errors that disgrace, mar, and murder mind in its loveliest attributes.

Let us extricate it from all the vile rubbish disgraceful for the age and damning to the people, subversive of their rights and of the gifts that should grace them.

Tradition, then, uncertain and absurd, peculiar in place of universal character, and that from the only reliable source, mind and reason, self-convicted in its impiety, cannot pass the review of the only real beneficiaries, mind and reason.

All such has to be smuggled through a thing some affect to call faith, as if faith in things seen or unseen, hoped for or realized, could exist but on any rational basis, and that of truth, mind, and reason.

For any tradition worthy of faith and the record of truth, a freeman is bound to give and necessarily demand reason, invoking truth in her best candor to uphold what is just, or exclude the reverse.

He asks for proof undoubted, full and satisfactory, in all things of this universe that includes all spiritual and temporal, in order to rightly appreciate them, according to the ways and acts of truth.

All the world is concerned, but above all the wise of proper feelings, those that deal in mind and extract the real benefits of mind.

He that affects, by his own word or through books called bibles, which are only equal to the state of mind and morals of their authors—mere men, the effects of which prove them very bad—to revolutionize and correct the created nature of man, impeaches himself and libels the Creator.

As all this has been done in all the bibles of tradition, both they and their authors are irreclaimably put in the lowest category of ignorance and stupid arrogance. They are their own accusers, and necessarily culprits.

A high-minded respect for the world's ethics and religion would, therefore, cause such entertaining it to render all rational minds worthy of that respect, by rendering the world candid and sincere, the faith to be established true, that will make the bibles the offspring of mind, not its usurpers and tyrants, being the inspiration of the living God.

But God makes individuals responsible for principles, not books, that peculiar faithites adopt as bibles.

What a reflection on intelligent freemen of this country and century!

And those books of the bible adopted are behind the age of this country in morals, laws, government, or rational religion.

Can freemen stand this baneful imposition? Have not the effects told on every position of society?

As false, those books were behind the progress of mind the very moment of publication—ay, of conception; consequently, they are thousands of years obsolete in truth, honesty, and right time.

The bible is ever obsolete, if quoted as authority for absolutism.

The world should not be misled by show and pretences. If pure and holy, reverence pure and holy will be universal. Is that the case in the world?

As impure and unholy, the bible of tradition has been discarded by men of mind and patriotism.

The gospel of God is unmistakable to all sane minds. All the universe preaches God's sublime principles. The beauty, symmetry, order, and grandeur of the universe universally prove his creatorship.

God unveils what such bibles stupidly call miracles and mysteries by natural phenomena the more exact the more sublime, proving the nobler science of the Architect who magnificently created all, or organized it into the mighty universe; and all these phenomena, in their position of order of time, are the only prophecies and revelations to creation.

They are all the legitimate functions of this creation.

Fundamental propositions affirm only this, in the strictest principles of reason, clearly and indisputably.

The gospel of God rests in the court of conscience, approved for all minds, as all others are disproved in that court.

Where, then, stand all the codes of tradition cleared up by no proof that reason recognises?

Messiahships have usurped God's rights; their miracles, prophecies, and mysteries counterfeit the functions of his conservative principles.

If you tell the world of any book superior to the code of mind reared in truth and reason for religious duties and instructions, you must introduce it rightly, as all other approved documents or acquaintances, and be responsible for that introduction.

You must guarantee that introduction rightly, or you become the base impostor and charlatan of the world.

If you introduce any such book, you must introduce it through the most correct avenues of mind, or you are the most degraded of impostors and blasphemers. If this be a code for instruction, it is only the code of mind, and can only be introduced as the code of reason, to claim what is asked for our highest respect and due appreciation as you value your own reputation for reason and candor.

You expect the world to give a merited reception and respect, to the best of its ability, to this bible.

If you be a just friend to both parties, you can expect or exact no more than your vouchers call for, as a demand on my most enlightened reason and judgment. There can be no other. Let this be honorably demonstrated.

If you deny us this only test of honesty, we must decide you a dishonest designer, as all are impostors to claim belief or faith before the position is proved worthy of faith. If such frail faith as is required be given, who wonders at the unsound or frail character of the whole institution? It cannot be worth the mind's thoughts of an honest man. We should lose our self-respect to expect any other view.

But what shall we do with the bible of tradition?

As God does not deal in tradition as a peculiar subject, but operates on living mind by mind and its characteristic operations, have nothing to do with it, as it cannot be right or prove its doctrines right.

Imposition is on the face of it, and its doctrines are of faith of equal character, that cannot present the gospel of God, who never gave any but what was written by foreknowledge, omniscience throughout the universe.

As it brings after-thought, its man's imposition kills it dead at once for blunder and fraud.

This book, called the bible, contravenes the highest principles of God in the universe and of his dignity on earth. What can be worse than all that?

It is clearly the bungling work of man, gotten up for corrupt and unholy purposes, and objects most sinister.

33

Can there be a correct introducer of this book, before man or God, that cannot be shamed at once and forever? He is utterly condemned in innumerable ways.

How can he appeal to God, whom he thus outrages by blasphemy?

How can he face man, whom he deceives by imposition? How can he ask remuneration of earth, which he defrauds, and how can he regard the universe that he so offends?

Freemen have to look to their rights, and not to this impotent offer that cannot stand the test of reason, nor abide the decision of principles, the only conservatives of mind.

Mind that is considered so weak, that has been so basely libeled to get it out of the way for a degraded priestocracy to rule the world in body and soul, is the sovereign of its own treasures, pure and abundant, on which it must rely.

They are sufficient; if not, man can get no more genuine. If he is offered more, they come from mortals who have no more nor better than he has.

Let man be no more deceived and betrayed by all the humbugs of bible pretences.

Before man suffers any to impose on him, or pretend to create more, they have to destroy mind most ignorantly, and usurp God's rights most impiously.

What a conspiracy on the world, and for thousands of years, against mind, merely to promote the degraded designs of people affecting to be peculiar people of God, and turn out to be no nation at last. What better could be expected?

Reverence for Deity and respect for mind will not permit the world to be humbugged any longer.

What did not ignorant writers of the bible affect under the disguises of infatuated superstition, under the assumption of inspiration, the revelations of the falsest of all false professions of the world. What but this could make them so stupid to pretend that Joshua, a mere mortal, could have arrested the course of the spheres of the universe, the chief of our solar system, even the sun himself, that would have required a power more than one million times greater than that of our earth to have commenced it, provided the location was given to do it from, and all this for one petty battle on earth, and more important still, arresting the mighty conservative principles of creation, the universe!

If ever this superlative nonsense and egregious stupidity were transcended, it is in the minds of those that adopt the faith of it! What ignorant bunglers to wind themselves up in such inconsistent nonsense.

Where was astronomy in those days, that forgot the mighty results to the universe by such arrest of systems? Equal to the assurance of faith is the impudence of sophistry, that all things are possible with god!

The God of nature presides on his own conservative principles, that protect all creation. Change this basis, and you change the order, system, harmony, unity and integrity, the conservation of that whole. After this, let no sophists affect that it is possible that God can be inconsistent with himself. It is their inconsistency. It is the peculiar god, not God the immutable.

The successive ages of the world, in reference to mind, must become more and more enlightened on the subject of creeds and system of the universe; let then no bibles of peculiar faith or priestocracy exclude the progress of improvement by their fables and fictions, and the immovable bigotry engendered thereby.

Homer, the poet of ancient mythology, is eclipsed at his own game by such bibles and advocates.

Religion requires mind to advance, but bibles of peculiar faith force mind to retrograde, and sacrifice it to their own brutish calibre of ignorance and bigotry.

Mere tradition of any thing will not do for mind, as it is no better than mere fable, if it do not abide the truth of fact; it can only be the falsehood of absolutism. Such absolutism is the enemy, not the friend of mind. Such things can never satisfy a cultivated intellect.

The bible of tradition has usurped the province of the bible of rational mind and of conscience. The whole ignoble family must be exploded.

None but sophistry of superstition could cause all this.

Those of the present age are most condemned, if they permit such iniquity on their race and family. They are bound to protect them as good citizens from all peculiar bibles.

The Hebrew faith and priestocracy system must ere this be constantly weakening in the essential confidence of the intelligent portion of that community even.

Moses the lawgiver, and Aaron, both arch-priests for their times, used no doubt all artful polity over the ignorant multitude to establish Judaism.

These men, or their wire-workers, adroitly united church and state government over their grossly ignorant people.

Moses was a wily politician and historian, and could easily operate on the masses, ready, from their blind confidence and dependence in their rulers of absolutism, to receive the most that was offered them.

If they had been in previous bondage, so much the more easily did they succumb. Moses could easily make his own record. Who is here now to call it to an account but the omnipotence of rational mind? Its jurisdiction is masterly over the recusant priest-ocracy. Did wily absolutists ever have conscience about results of power to peculiarly benefit them?

An analyst, who takes hold of assailable points not sustained by facts, can point with mathematical certainty to the defects, and well asks, are these the fit standards for intelligent and high-minded freemen of this state of civilized mind?

In a miserable light do stand these Hebrew men at last before the highest tribunal, light of mind.

But the wily politico-faith hack may affect that the people could not have been governed otherwise. This is ever the delusive pretence of absolutism.

These men, and all in the collusion, show by their oppressive hold on the people, that the people could have easily dispensed with all their pretences to divine rights.

This Moses stands in the category of absolutism.

How many stultify themselves, and by vitiating man's better nature to gratify their selfish ambition, are self-impeached? So stands this priestocracy before the highest of all earthly tribunals, responsible rational mind.

The philosophy of all things of life stands on the platform of reason, truth, science, and justice, and this then, embraces the whole question.

So far from being a god-like liberal government, embracing all the legitimate blessings, this priestocracy was conceived in the bigotry of the times, and partook of superstition, and priest-rule and craft.

Frauds, imposition, hypocrisy, and blasphemy, were on the very face, corrupting masses, orders, and individuals, to the nefarious traffic in the holiest of purposes.

It was so flagitious, that others arose of equally false pretences, and abominable false positions from that time to this, and would be endless if rational mind did not interpose.

The God of the universe breathes an atmosphere too sublime for their conceptions.

Superstition upon superstition has been put down, but that, evil men have appropriated for their ambition.

From many such malign causes, but moderate good has been accomplished from age to age, on its own legitimate capital.

It has been reserved for after ages and later times, to rally more potently, and point out more correct views.

How came the Jews so narrow-minded, but from the Mosaic polity? The Jews were taught to believe, that they were the peculiar people of a god as peculiar as themselves. This people, otherwise, was not peculiar by any virtue as a nation, if equal to the enlightened ones of Greece and Rome, the best ancient republics. Such peculiar views invariably elicited all their peculiar vices.

The answers have been already given.

The sanction of superstition of the Jewish peculiarity, sophisticated most awfully that nation's mind, and reflected the consequences in all their social relations.

The priests eternally perverted the minds of the people, and in every age are only more or less varied editions of the same book. The only variation is by and through mind, correlatively rational.

What a mass of crime was thereby propagated.

In the most liberal spirit, the mind of intelligence is obliged to find as the least of evils, much of the bibles metaphorical and figurative, but that will not meet their intrinsic evils and difficulties.

All of them have to be discarded as organic evils.

What else of evils of their magnitude introduced by peculiar motives to the notice of the world, could not be repelled as unworthy of its universal regard? No peculiar reception will meet the question. Have they not been elements of conflict to the world, and productive of many evils?

Ask candid men who undertake to interpret them, their solution?

Will one of them say that they believe or can understand the whole, much less practice the same understandingly?

This is an important paramount question to all.

A book of books, it is pretended, has been given mind, to which it is most dictatorial and despotic, and that inculcates a faith not to be reasoned with, language not understood, and of course, affecting duties involved therein. This at once condemns it as negativing the very functions of mind, and the quintessence of religion.

Ask all its ministers, and do they not make the difficulties greater, the quagmire more miry from the nature of the elements?
Many put you off without reasons or solutions.
You may be told that such are sacred things, that you must hold and go no further, that some events were to come, that they were not past!
The proper time for right investigation and inquiry may never come, and this state of things is to be fund for future imposition and false pretences!
Patriots must appreciate, that the mind that will not take heed of its rights that are universal in or out of bibles, that existed and flourished before all the trash of tradition of superstition was ever devised, is tory in withholding allegiance to its maker. But there are some things that may be true in that bible, while others stagger the faith of the most faithful. All that is true, is capital of mind, falsely appropriated by the priest-ocracy.
The position of the balance in which no candid honest mind can confide, invalidates the claim of the bible to man's adoption, for the whole must be taken or its character by partial rejection is impeached, as God is perfect, and would give a perfect original to mind.
Man gives imperfect copies, therefore the bible is man's imperfect tradition.
Cannot we believe that Adam and Eve were our first parents? Bibles of tradition cannot truthfully go as far back. Indians cannot, mind cannot.
Prove their color, compared with the diversity of the human race.
If white, whence came the black or intermediate colors?
Hundreds of years have not changed either, under most appropriate circumstances. Neither are the colors contingent or fortuitous, but follow after their kinds. It was as easy for the Creator to diversify the race in five varieties, as to make five large grand divisions of the globe. All that, proves him Almighty.
Philosophy will not permit a limited or isolated view of this mighty subject, very far from it indeed.
She, as the right science, is the strict constructionist of accurate language, necessarily, while at the same time she is a liberal constructionist of action and motives, as far as right and justice require, and will amend if misled by others. Her potent voice should not only be heard but obeyed.
She enters into the disquisition of this important subject, to secure the most suitable position of truth and reason. She would do injustice to her own rights and self-respect, if she did not thus act.
She respects the feelings and honest principles of all religionists, while she must accord to the nature of the subject the most candid exposition requisite.
She publishes views deliberately entertained, as the best for life and death, being the true friend of the people. Her reverence for Deity is of the highest quality, and cannot see his attributes affected, or his exclusive claim diminished by any worship of men, or any intervening object.
She leaves this momentous question and subject, with the conscience of the enlightened, who can decide whether tradition could impart correct views of the first parentage, in names or character.
Neither the memory of philosophy of the first rude ages of man, could meet truthfully this question.
Fiction has been resorted to to fill up the picture. Grant that there were Adams and Eves in ancient times, and that they were sinful people, digressing from established principles, still no peculiar faith has any guarantee or privilege to enslave the mind of the world to its peculiar homage. That is absurd in the extreme, for priestocracy to render the world vassal to its idolatrous legends, to secure unity of race for the maintenance of their pretended identification and power.
Every continent may have had its Adam and Eve.
We might give due credit to Moses or his priest-fathers, for some improvements in his code, if we knew the whole Chaldaic, or that its predecessor was less, but then the Mosaic, however curiously dovetailed, is sadly corrupted by the times. It is doubtlessly an abominable plagiary on ignominious priestocracy predecessors.
Did they not corrupt the Hebrews in causing them to borrow the valuables of the Egyptians, and then dictated repudiation of the payment? They teach this heinous code, whether it transpired or not. We have the code of their morals. Was this honest or truthful, the two first characteristics of true religion?
All that the Mosaic code can ever be, is that it is the result of corrupt peculiar faith.
Is not this enough, at once, to satisfy an honest and truthful mind, on the invalidation of this history of Moses, by this moral delinquency, an unsafe doctrinal teacher?
But then, is it right to believe a part, without taking the whole? It is impossible for

rational mind to receive what is irrational, as part of the bible, that might be gross legends inserted according to expediency of priestocracy at any or all times suitable.

All sectarian dogmas have their circle of malign influence, that should never by honest and truthful men be prolonged ; the life of this dishonest doctrine is now destroyed on this position.

People now have light enough to cast aside all the pretences of Judaism, or any peculiar faith, analyze their superstitious points, and not forget their duty to man, in blind devotion to self-professions and fanatical feelings !

Could not the Jews purchase and win to-day their beloved Jerusalem, for a few millions, and by citizenship ?

But think you they would wish to leave better countries, that give them much good civil, commercial, and faith-freedom ?

But they can do far better, as they can rid themselves of their false position, imposed on them by prejudices of a peculiar faith, and avow themselves the recipients of the noblest, and fraternize within an universal brotherhood. They can now adopt a pure and rational religion.

It becomes the wise of their people to show the beauty and strength of wisdom, and avow the God of the universe, and abjure the puny god of Judaism, imposed on them by a base and fanatical priestocracy.

Unfortunately, the weak-minded of the world can be rallied on false positions sooner than on the true, as many are ever ready to call by sophistry and names, to secure the ready profits of all worldly speculations.

The bible of tradition cannot be satisfactory to the world, as a transcript of its true position, imperfect and erroneous as it is, after contradicting the facts of nature, and outraging truth in many particulars.

Then the notions of its peculiar character, asserting the superiority of one people, condemn it as an outrage, and its ignorance as a libel on Deity, whose character is grossly misconceived, and authority usurped.

What can science say to its astronomy, when Joshua commands the sun and moon to stand still ?

What effect would this have had on the great conservative principles of the universe, thereby also intercepted?

What shall we say for its ethnology, geology, and phrenology, or the science of the races of man, of the earth, and man's nature and character ?

What moral maxims, at the best, did it institute, that were not the characteristics of mind, in its various degrees of improvement ?

Its moral maxims could not, by any means, be peculiar, and they were in abeyance to mind, laid up in its treasury, to be evolved by the best powers of its genius.

The famous one of Christianity, " Do unto others as we would have them, in similar circumstances, do unto us," was hundreds of years sketched by several prototypes in existence at the time of Confucius, and were necessarily suggested by the proper appreciation of the best social relations and duties.

Every age tells of heroes, that have done their missions—but why any hero-worship ?

Axioms of tried benefit and good, establish and vindicate themselves, whilst the rest pass away.

There is but one mighty system, instituted by God, and to be rightly read and appreciated by mind, that can stand all test in the world of intellect and motives, and that is rational religion, the inspiration of a living and undying God.

Most of the superstitions, mythologies, and kinds of polytheism, have gone down; the balance will, sooner or later, end, never to rise, as long as reason holds her sway.

Rational religion cannot perish, but will put down all errors, as the one true light, before all systems of earthly superstitions, that are unworthy, degraded, and to be excluded from the folds of true protection.

What peculiar claim has the bible of peculiar tradition to man's universal esteem ?

Does it give mind the character of the God of the universe, when it portrays him as the peculiar god of Judaism and Christianity ?

Does it not give us superstition for religion, priestocracy and hierarchy for freedom of religious opinion ?

Does it not make peculiar tradition to be placed before intellectual and moral conservative principles, that none but eclect ethics or the best morals will vindicate ?

Does it not increase the various superstitions of the globe, and yield the apologies for them ?

I desire no such book, that teaches the worship of the powers of nature, of mortals, to supersede the adoration of the Power Supreme.

Man is at the bottom, ministering to usurpation and monopoly, the pretensions of the priesthood.

Designing men seek, through this, for power and its attributes.

The sacrifice is too costly. The victims of intolerance are too many to the wiles of hierarchy and the duplicity of priestocracy.

In all this darkness, mind is crushed, befouled, and injured, if not silenced. Philosophy, mind, and science gainsay the bibles of tradition, most triumphantly.

Can mind learn correctly from any people, whose faith was the grossest superstition, whose knowledge was deep errors?

Can we copy, in honesty, from Moses, who corrupted his own people, by the most dishonest repudiation of debts contracted, for jewels borrowed, and of the brightest lights of rational religion?

Can we estimate the dire effects of these morals on the priest-ridden people, to countless ages of such superstitious faith?

Can we estimate his morals, with the blood of murder on his hands, and never wiped off by any penalty?

Was this the peculiar prerogative of his peculiar institutions, to make differences and distinctions of guilt, only as persons, not as the guilt, differed?

Can we copy from him, in mind, when he instituted a priestocracy to overwhelm mind?

Can we copy from the Jews, who believed in sacrifices of victims, effusion of blood, arrogated to themselves national superiority, without attaining it, and finally denationalized themselves by their vices, crimes, and errors?

What reflection of light did they cast, on the balance of their cotemporaries? Does priest-ridden Jerusalem show sound views of science, laws, and jurisprudence, the glory of the world?

Due credit is given to the Hebrews, who reject Christ; because if their faith, Judaism, were right, Christ was wrong; but rational religion exclusively proves Judaism a non-entity, and all entirely wrong.

They were intrinsically interested in securing the safest worship, according to their ability of defective education; but clearly they were not convinced by any rational proof of any other peculiar faith better than their own. Why then should they change the original for the graft?

If God had been previously disposed to any peculiar people, could he possibly suffer them to miss the right messiahship? That is the most conclusive proof, that the messiah was never before the people, more than the Almighty, who was there when creation was willed into existence. This position is enough to kill all such ideas forever.

Considering that the Hebrew had an immortal soul, as God's chosen people, how could God permit that part that lives after death, to miss so great and indispensable salvation?

God is incapable of less than immutable principles, that self-creation and immortality fortify, therefore this position of peculiarity evidently destroys the whole fabric of messiahship.

What need we any book of tradition to affect a caricature of God and his attributes, when the works of creation are the only mighty evidences of nature, and time performs the functions of prophecy throughout the universe, and plain matters of facts, the whole truth, the only oracles of wisdom, proclaiming the Creator, and enabling his creatures to proclaim and adore him, supersede mysteries, enigmas, miracles, and prophecies pretended?

Mind, that looks to cause and effect, will be the only means of discovering the supremacy of the Great First Cause, to the shame and confusion of hypocritical cant, that stupidly libels God and mind, when it asserts the contrary.

Bible tradition tells, that mankind sprung from one source, and all this is worth nothing, if we cannot advance our faith up to these absurd legends. No wonder that faith fills so much of the deeds of mind confiding in them!

Facts show characteristics that mark mankind with such variety, that the ethnologist must ask from which color, white or black, was that source? Absolutism alone affects to answer, by inspiration!

Mind has advanced to such a glorious state of intellectual independence, that it pronounces any inspiration not recognised by reason as the false pretences of folly.

Mind alone can recognise all inspirations. It is at its tribunal that all books of tradition, purporting to be such, are condemned.

The next base pretence, after inspiration, is peculiarity. This tradition tells us that the Jews were a peculiar people, eminently favored and cared for by God.

Reason on the facts of their history, not secretly kept by their priesthood, but known to the world, proves to us that they had no peculiar virtues or characteristics above other people of the world ; that they were as vain-glorious and selfish, as much of land-pirates as other barbarian nations of antiquity ; as vindictive and ferocious on their enemies, and no less idolatrous, or iniquitous in their idolatry.

They suffered losses by wars, that were frequent; and were carried into captivity, where they suffered as other nations. Their years of captivity prove the power of their enemies.

But the eternal jesuitical sophistry of priestocracy comes to the rescue. In their misfortunes they had sinned ; in their prosperity they had acted with no less sin. Will any but a stupid analyst affirm the contrary ? When was Jewry ever clear of sin? I will defy honorable minds to show.

Did they communicate the blessings of their peculiarity to other nations? They concealed them as long as practicable.

In fact, their cotemporaries did not estimate them very highly, if the Apion of Josephus permit us to judge. If we had Apion, he would speak for himself. The world has been robbed of truthful literature.

A nation peculiarly beloved by God must have excited high respect among neighboring nations ; but the reverse is their case.

What peculiarity had they but what man made, and priest at that? Are not the Mormons a peculiar people ; are not all that adopt any peculiar faith?

The world is not concerned except in its sufferings about peculiar faiths, but has the important problem of universal brotherhood given its magnificent solution of benefits to mind and the whole world?

Judaism, at its very best, is not the beginning of rational religion, that is never stained with blood, or corrupted by priestocracy, much less outraged by absolutism.

How much infatuation prevailed then about national peculiarity, when their country fell so often into the conquerors' hands, as the Assyrians, Greeks, Romans, Turks, &c.

Tradition claims peculiar faith with spiritualization, enthusiasm, grace, and sanctity, the doctrine of election, predestination, &c.

But the tradition becomes peculiar, and on the principles of the universe, that acknowledges but one God, as our solar system has but one central sun, it is absolutely invalidated, is entirely worthless. All that depends thereon is in the same category.

How, then, can peculiar faith, that only repeats the story, decide these positions at all ?

God's omniscience and omnipresence, much less his omnipotence, must not be libeled by such, as either attribute excludes peculiarity.

God is not local or peculiar, but universal.

Give us a God worthy of mind's reverence, fit for civilized society of the whole world, to be supremely benefited by his transcendant guidance, not one evidently characterized by barbarian pencils, an irascible being, having peculiarities too monstrous for mind !

Give us an immortal being, not the creation of Judaism, but independent of man's imbecile conceptions, the lovely perfection of philosophical science.

Rational minds are obliged to dismiss from serious consideration the absurdity that constantly hangs on the bibles of tradition.

That God cannot manage his own creation without the aid of his creatures, the priestocracy, from the flood, a most absurd history, and above all, that souls are indebted to their prayers and their exertions, as he cannot prevent the god of evil, his degraded rival, from interfering with his greatest work, mind !

In all traditions of bibles, unless the First Great Cause is the universal type, there is nothing but peculiar acts, and these incontestibly condemn them all, surely, as impositions.

Do not even the enlightened Jews now consider their bible as a mere history ? Has it any of the dignity of history ? Would that it was even a good history, correct and to be relied on ; but assuredly it, and all its emanations, are digests of most obnoxious and objectionable materials, compounds of most revolting absurdities.

If all these were abstract, isolated machines, kept in a museum for curiosity of the dark ages, one might tolerate the enormities.

What is the bible of tradition but a scheme to uphold the dynasty of priests, and all connected with priestocracy?

It fails to teach us the elevated, liberal, and just views of government and religion, that invariably recognise the greatest good to the greatest number. .

Pure religion did not commence with the Jews, nor at Jerusalem, nor in Egypt, but with mind's existence and creation in the universe, in the mighty dawn of its glorious initiative.

Of course, then, all such bibles are horribly iniquitous, for pretending that religion was a peculiar favor, when it was as old as mind, and inseparable from it. So much for these bible botchers and libelers.

All such systems of peculiar faith dwarf mind, and keep it in abeyance to ignorance, prejudice, and bigotry. These originate the heresies of mind, that disgrace the weak and dark states of the world.

The bible neither transmits science nor instructs rightly in the rules of life, but trammels the world.

Where is its legal or moral science, that is best of all?

If the writers of the old and new Testament had no correct knowledge of the sciences, as they clearly had not, it proves that their statements are traditionary myths, and that the balance is to be most truly scanned, as to Christ's assumed divinity, and the saving points of christian or its peculiar faith.

It is mind that scans divine laws, and exposes counterfeits.

Science stands by us, moderns, to eradicate what is most difficult, and the last, as the first, degraded superstition.

. Science enables the world to shake off the bigotry of education, and teaches mind that no peculiar faith is adapted to meet the wants and requirements of mind all the time.

Without philosophical rational science, how impossible would it be for mind to shake off the fraud of tradition that oppressed the ancients.

How thankful ought the moderns to be, in having science as a friend to rescue them from the foul grasp of superstition and absolutism, in their various disguises! Not in words, but in actions, that truly decide for the world.

It is science, philosophical and rational, that beats down all the sophisms of peculiar faith doctrines, and teaches that mind always is the recipient of God's inspiration and grace, and that there would not be any such difficulty about religion that silently acts, if it were not for the priests and preachers, who confound the world, and minister to the despotism of absolutists.

Many cherish by mere impulse, a faith on tradition, because that tradition promises everything to procure eternal life. But who justifies and warrants that tradition? None. Is there any living witness of the facts? There is, but the tradition-sophists resort to all evasions to silence the proper means to procure it. That one is God, whose works utterly condemn all such as false; his works, cause and effect, being his true word.

Where are other god-written documents? There are none but by designing priestocracy, and the affiliated know it is so.

Have we any true and undeniable records, written and verified at the time, beyond mistake or doubt? Not one!

Are we to yield to the treachery on mind, whose essential functions are thereby usurped by factions, that have governed the world too much in every age?

But no book-promise of this kind is poss b e, short of God's power alone, and his inspirations of mind promise this to mind's satisfaction.

But do the Jews need return to Judea? That is the question.

The civilized world's philosophy teaches liberal and cultivated minds, to regard religion as of universal principles, to be improved by individual address to God alone, regardless of time or place.

What, then, care the Jews about returning to Jerusalem, while they can do well in any land of true freedom?

Will not their wise men prefer to lay aside all the superstition of their peculiar belief, and seek the nationality of the whole world?

They are then more concerned if they be wise, in the rationality of religion.

Why delay they to help to secure their own happiness? . God is no respector of persons, and he cannot be of nations or worlds, only as they respect his universal principles.

There is a mathematical certainty in principles for the universe and mind, to the whole government of which God is equally competent. The Jews are no exception.

Nothing less than a great conservative revolution is arriving for God's rational vindication, and for the certain establishment of a proper code of morals and religion for mind. Bigots may thwart it, but bigots will pass away.

If the bible be the word of God, it must be a perfect book, and its treatise must be perfect, otherwise it is conclusively the work of man.

" But the bible is the inspiration of God," say its advocates.

The bible is imperfect in all its parts, and is therefore impeached as unworthy substantially of the divine rights of mind, and is conclusively the work of man, and the perversion of mind.

Then the bible of tradition is discarded entirely ?   Certainly.
But what shall we teach children, the world with, if we do not have such a bible ?
The same that will make them men and women in God's sense, the best bible of mind.
The best morals, science, and legislation contradict the bible of tradition, consequently it is certainly demoralizing and vitiating.

The pagan Romans looked to mind, and had such highminded morals, that the chastity of Lucretia, one of their ladies, was the admiration of the world.

Scipio, though pagan, secured the noblest triumph of victory, in the victory of his own passions, when he yielded the betrothed Spanish bride, unharmed, to her lover. Now what nation on earth can exhibit any truer individual test of monotheism ?   Moses was unqualified for religion.   Now both of these acts were the noblest deeds of rational religion.

And in what light does the Jewish people, governed by this bible of tradition, appear by their own history, as far as it is true, for they would put their own conduct as meritorious as practicable, to get it as a universal rule among all nations ?

Their invasion of other nations equally as good as they, and some even more civilized, and with whom they had no cause of war, at the instance of their priestocracy, plainly proves their code of morals far below the universal code of religion, especially when we duly estimate their ruthless barbarity, reckless of all restraint and humanity, to sanction which, they libel God.

The history of the world proves in countless instances, like those of the Romans mentioned, the triumph of mind from God's inspiration at a dark age of the world's history, when civilization had not reached her noblest refinement.   Religion has operated in all ages of the world, but the best efforts have been arrested by the priestocracy.

What will be the glorious result, when the mind reaches the loftiest aspirations of genius, reason and philosophy—when its rightful tuition shall expel the assumed inspiration of perverted intellect, as the false word of God, itself adorned in all its loveliness of monotheism that requireth truth and honesty, justice, liberality and humanity, a good faith, national and individual, with the addition of honor, chastity, and universal affection on relative merits ?

Mind now realizes its blessings in seeing a constitutional government put forth all its legitimate functions, to restrain any invasion of peaceful neighbors, and carry out in the best of good faith all national and world obligations.

If these authors be convicted, as they are especially in the fiction of the devil, that plays so conspicuous a part in both bibles, then both are silenced in the position of truth, morals and religion.

" But, nothing is impossible with God," repeat some of the initiated !

It is utterly impossible for this statement to be true !

Nothing under reason, truth and godship, characterized by his attributes, is impossible with God.

Of course, then, this book that contradicts God and his attributes, is not God's word.

But the priestocracy would not let him govern his own genius creation himself, in justice to mankind that needs his constant almighty universal providence.

They must needs keep constantly watching all, to reap the greatest harvest by taking dishonorable advantage of the people's ignorance, and now keep up all the humbuggery and fraud that sophistry, and the subsidizing and bribery of absolutism can administer.

The simple assertion of nothing being impossible with God, of course, is absurd, unwise and untrue.

It is impossible for God to change his nature and character as he would do, and be a God at the same time.

If God were not immutable, he would not be the God of the universe, and his conservative would be destructive faculties, and the functions of all would be imbecile, being the author of evil instead of universal good.

But is there not morality of the bible of tradition ?

As far as that conforms to the principles of God, and the bible of mind, and no more, does it contain one particle of morality or pure religion ; then all is borrowed, but unacknowledged capital, a mere but most dangerous plagiary.

What sort of morality is that, that authorizes the invasion of peaceful inhabitants of the world, and wars upon them to utter destruction by the basest libel of God, that destroys thousands of its own people, to uphold the despotism of its priestocracy, that opens the door to all the errors of peculiar faith, whose followers enact civil dissensions and wars for many centuries, with the bloodiest contests among the races of mankind, that could otherwise have been united in one universal brotherhood, thus putting asunder those whom God had indissolubly joined together ?

What sort of morality was that which made hypocrites of republicans, and made their savage despotism available in the present light of mind, before all Europe?

No people are freemen, that cannot adore God, after the dictates of conscience, reason, truth and honesty, much less be compelled to church-worship and its pecuniary support.

Thousands and millions for education of mind in rational science and philosophy, but not one cent to any church faith. Such is the worst of absolutisms.

All are hypocrites and vassals, deceivers, that pretend to the contrary, and put themselves under the throne of absolutism, slaves to its bidding, and suffer themselves to be kicked and cuffed by charlatans.

What insidious underminings in general, of liberty.

If the bible of tradition, or anything else, be the abuse in the name of God, let it be disused, to say the least.

What an idea of morality, to suppose that such a corrupt fountain to many sects, divisions and subdivisions, can send forth all pure flocks!

There are various institutions growing out of the abuses of the bible of tradition, not tolerable to sense and virtue.

The convents, nunneries, shakerdom, &c., are sought for by weak and vicious; all are miserable apologies for life. Some few individuals seek a refuge from the world. Let all such be individual recluses. Suicide may be committed individually, but let no community seduce or mislead people, to commit acts against the laws of nature or against the good faith of reason and justice.

The world has been overrun again and again, by military and superstitious despotism dragooning it into vassalage. What was the priestocracy of Moses but this? Whole nations with most of their leaders, can file into column, and live for centuries and thousands of years, without many rational investigations and conservative revolutions.

As to lights of mind, they may or may not, tell the difference from sophistry, and it is all the same in faith that assimilates religion.

Where does intolerance stop? Not where superstition prevails.

Where is all this senseless and wicked contradiction to end, among all the sectarians of the world? In rational religion by conservative revolution, that declares for one God, adored in purity and unity.

All bibles of tradition kill themselves by their absurd caricature and portraiture of God, whose character is inconsistent and changeable, irascible or liable to anger and wrath, in accordance with that of the minds engaged in this perversion, this blasphemy, this imposition and false pretence.

The bibles of tradition cause antagonism to God and his conservative principles, therefore they must be condemned.

Where were the millions of the world for many centuries, that Judaism was prevailing?

What bigot of this day can dare avow with reason and truth, that these millions, Pagan, as they are called, were peculiarly out of God's protection? All are Pagans that have not rational religion.

What did all the peculiar form of worship of the world amount to? Which is now ahead of others?

Let analysis tell the fact, that all such are undeniably superstition in degree, and pagan, all.

God's works universally prove all this.

If you dissent, satisfy the world what proves the bible the word of God? Does the bible itself?

That is impossible, by the law of testimony, as it is an interested witness.

Besides that, it stands condemned by the works of God, the only God-documents construed by science, equally addressed to mind as the only bible of inspiration.

Science and philosophy are opposed, and their progress over mind retarded by the bible-advocates, that suit bible of tradition-theories that are most absurd.

The very wisdom of mind condemns the bible-advocates, before the God of the universe.

Especially does the obsolete, vulgar and absurd ignorance of its writers, impeach it fully.

The advocates cleave to the bible of tradition, that represents peculiar faith as the last stronghold of superstition and absolutism, though defeated conclusively by all the essentials of reason and truth in the bible of mind that represents the Almighty.

Its conception of creation is clearly the defect of ancient mind, not the first refulgence of divine inspiration.

Worse still, these same propagators of most irrational errors, after all their idle boasts of the learning of the church that preserves the science of the world, even now advance the doctrine that this world will be destroyed by fire, and will be superseded by a new earth in its place.

But can they, then, supersede all the conservative principles of solar systems of the universe?

Such step destroys gravitation, which was unknown to the ancients, who conceived the world a plane resting on some prop, and that the most that God made! What planet of this solar system has yet been expunged, or could be, on any principles of the Creator?

The universe might be in chaos, and God might be nonplused by this miserable set of botches, because they think or assume that the bible says so.

What contradictions, in this bible of Moses, about the best rational and philosophical principles of Babel! Was it anything else but an astronomical tower? Was not the division of language a peculiar characteristic, consequent on the dispersion of man on the face of the earth, and the last a most certain consequence of necessity and the circumstances of his nature? In fact, was not the diversity of races one of the great constituents of the law of his nature in this very respect?

This dispersion is going on constantly all over the globe at the present day, as well as the alteration of language even of the same country.

What wiseacres these bible charlatans were, who affected inspiration of God about every thing, and yet were incapable of telling the most common facts of natural history! And are these the leaders for all time to come of mind in all the principles of religion, that they plainly know nothing about, but gave us a most contemptible counterfeit therefor?

And did Joshua stop the sun and the moon by the permission of God, that he might destroy his enemies—that is, the enemies, of course, of God, the peculiar god of the Israelites? Mankind are not the enemies of their Creator—that is certain.

Every ancient nation had its peculiar gods, that aided them in all national affairs, wars, worship, &c.; and these gods were superior to those of other nations.

It is strange that the Israelites should have sought so often, if they had a god so manifest, for the strange gods and groves of other nations.

Joshua would have stopped all the universe, but that was unknown to the fabricators of this story. And they were so ignorant as not to know that their infamous falsehoods would be disclosed by science, that avenges, as a principle, its Creator.

The modern affiliated seek to stave off the exposure as long as possible, but it will be to their final disgrace.

All the priests are interested in advancing the truth of God of the universe, not the falsehoods of bibles of tradition; for just as sure as they do advance them, the people now can brand them as infamous as the writers in the times of Joshua.

They furnish them arguments, plausible and sophisticated by false interpretations and various devices, to the deepest commission of crimes.

Their wholesale murders for papal regulations, restorations, and enactments, are accounted for the good of the church that its citizens have repudiated; and of course not for the good of the people.

Are they not, then, a wholesale license for bloody guilt?

The papal power is capable of excommunication of the person, and of imprisonment in dungeons, of confiscation of property, of the tortures of the inquisition, arbitrary over the virtue and person of the miserable sufferer. Whence does he get his authority? Is it less than out of the bible of tradition?

The cannibal, from oppression of hunger and dire ignorance, satiates his morbid taste on his victims; but what are individual victims to masses under ferocious vindictiveness of such peculiar-faith cannibalism—bible cannibalism?

The world must see that all this is not religion; it is only a pretence. And all are pretences that have peculiar faiths, as all tend to serious abuses.

Now, there is the utmost necessity for a final covenant, as the two first bible ones never will do, since many cannot understand the bible, they say. Deity would have made it simple and efficient, if his work.

It would, if his work had been written for all to comprehend.

He has written a better, before all bibles of tradition were ever thought of by priests: the bible of mind.

That is for the whole world to construe with reason; but most of the world is guided at present by impulse of peculiar faith, not by reason and truthful logic.

Few possess, under all trying circumstances, these greatest characteristics of true greatness of intellect.

If no nation ever flourished without the bible of tradition, how came the Jews to have such a remarkable fall by its very means? How did the nations, with Spain and Mexico, &c., fall with it?

It presents failures most disastrous, from Rome down; and results most humiliating. When man deserts mind for such bibles, God is not approached. God stands where he always stood, on his platform, ready to be approached by mind on its platform.

Now, the true question is not of the bible, but of the principles conservative and innate. If they fail, then all fail.

What has mind to do with the legends of this bible, its peculiar faith or its peculiar gods? As much as with those of the Philistines—just as much.

However sectarian Socrates was, he fell by the sectarian and peculiar faith inquisition of Athens, by its bible.

People have lost sight of conservative principles, when they take up bibles of tradition, which are the bibles of absolutism, to defraud the rights of the people, and bind them to the car of violence and superstitious men-worship.

There is corruption by perversion of mind all over the world enough, without the world raising a fund by such bibles, to exhibit it by membership, by reason of gorgeous temptation, to revolutionize still by such means for character exhibition.

The Hebrews made a partial peculiar god to themselves, as selfishly as other nations who also had their peculiar gods, at first made from earthly characters and heroes, with a stock of superstition from all the priest deifications.

The priests corrupted the Hebrews, who, as well as others, were punished, in not allowing the attributes of God to extend to their legitimate results.

All nations of antiquity, but little civilized, wished to appropriate the godhead to themselves as the particular favorites. This is the custom of barbarian nations, kept up by barbarian moderns.

The God of the universe never knew any chosen people, under his peculiar protection.

The Hebrews sought to conquer, as pirates, the lands and possessions of all the nations they could, though those nations had not injured them, contrary to their own commandments of not desiring or coveting the property of others, no less obligatory in national than in individual ethics. The Jews then were the violators of their own bible.

But universal domination and conquest were the spirit of the age and times, and however vicious and criminal, the Hebrews were not at all exempt, except by an incapacity for martial prowess to that extent. What a libel they perpetrate on God, by assuming that he thus directed such iniquities!

They remorselessly dispossessed the owners of their soil and murdered the people of all ages and both sexes, sometimes not sparing those unborn, and in battle they invoked their irascible god to destroy their and his enemies. And this is the felonious code that the modern barbarians wish to impose.

How were all these people, their fellow-creatures, subject to the same God, the enemies of God?

Were they his enemies because they were not Jews and worshippers of the Jew peculiar god?

And does the priestocracy of the present day desire this to be a code for civilized man? This a code of religion, and the Jew bible its exponent?

They obtain the aid of the sun and moon to delay, for a full punishment by slaughter of their enemies.

Now, the injury to the solar system would have been at the cost of conservative principles, worth more than a whole universe of victories. What nonsense of barbarian stupid paganism.

Can any be found so stupid as to believe all such, an extreme universal injury to be sustained, when attainable by more appropriate means?

They are not identified with any, because of their exclusive peculiar faith, that amounts to nothing more than other paganisms.

If they were not superstitious, as all pagan sectarians are, they could not be excluded out of the family of mankind, all of whom are most deeply interested in the principles of universal brotherhood.

They must give up their abstract notions of peculiar faith as all sectarians, and unite with all that profess rational religion.

They must acknowledge that their pagan forefathers had only peculiar faith that excluded them from rational religion, or the true God of principles and the universe.

The bible of tradition clashes with philosophical principles, above all with the bible of mind, the true friend of man, to be fully developed in future ages.

Does the peculiar faith of any bible of tradition agree with the republican constitutional principles, as now advocated? How, then, can men clash as they do, in the practice of them as recently at Rome? The fault was in the men, not in the principles.

None of the principles of the one Supreme Being clash; if they did, the fault lies in the interpretation or exposition, that is certain.

Superstitious worship of any kind clashes with mind's purest offerings in its most dignified adoration.

Are the worthy followers of what they deem the true faith seeking in earnest, to meet all points for the morals and good of the world? Will they learn of God? Then let them read his only earthly inspiration, cause and effect.

They will have to forsake the errors of the bibles of tradition ways, and adhere to rational bibles.

But the mighty talisman of this bible was, the divine rights of kings and priests!

The only divine rights, after God, are those of the whole people, consecrated by mind.

Citizen of the world, there is danger in taking any such authority as the bibles of tradition, as the sole rule of our faith, moral, social and religious practice. We must not regard any statement of men, when their object is to be attained at the disregard of facts and truth. Truth is omnipotent over all scriptures, that do not respect it.

Their examples are heinous, and their doctrines poisonous.

In the first place, God is horribly insulted by imposition, then society is deceived by a loose state of morals and untruth. Then came the clash, hate, wars, conflicts, and dangers of sects, orders of peculiar faith, as Judaism. Those of Christ, Mahomet, Smiths and tinkers.

Thereby the great truths and attributes of Almighty God's works of creation are neglected for minor points.

Also, the value of mind, that should be ever regarded as superior, that recognises all creeds, pretences, policies, opinions, and dogmas, is lost sight of at the most important time of man's life, and the world's history, when its faithful and manly aid is needed to oppose all these vices by the mighty standard that God has reared, reason, that can only estimate all these truly.

Mind, that has just appreciated the mighty dawn of the world's conservative revolution, is banished when it has to do justice to its potency, virtue, and character, excluding all fanatic, ignorant, selfish, and contracted views, rearing its just, wise, and enlightened cultivation for morals, religion, obedience to God's justice, instead of the bigotry of his self-perverted creatures.

Do we need proof in more than the ordinary occurrences and employment of life, of mind's universal value, power, will, and paramount functions?

Then take your own bible history, absurd as it is, of the two first human creatures in the garden of Eden, and undeniable evidence is furnished yourself of corruption, from temptation operating on these two ignorant beings, from want of mind to appreciate future evils in their full force and virtue, and want of firmness in those minds in resisting the inroads of invading forces, to become hostile to mind's best interests, peace, and aappiness.

But it is natural for opposition to the bible to prevail. So say its advocates, who pretend that infidelity to that book of tradition cannot cease till all, Jew and Gentile, are converted to it!

That will never be, as long as reverence to the God of the universe is paramount, and as long as he is Supreme.

When God yields supremacy, then the world will yield the question, and chaos, physical and intellectual, will predominate.

No opposition but that of principles is effectual, and that cannot be overcome. As to infidelity to the bible of tradition, that is fidelity to truth, mind, reason, and God. Infidelity, then, is the exclusive property of the bible advocates.

Has fanaticism any reason, any honor?

Some think that the Mosaic law is the general law of the land and nations.

Did the Romans adopt that law for the hundreds of years of their various governments, consular and others?

Did the laws of the Medes and Persians, of the Greeks, of the Chinese, derive their origin from that source?

Is our organic law, as set forth in the principles advocated of the rights of sovereign citizens, in 1776, a copy of the Mosaic law? Are the modern advocates the blindest of the blind, to pretend to all this?

We must allow for feudal ages, the prevalence of tyrannical times, when the human mind was truly enslaved, more or less, by force and custom, all great enslavers still.

But how far is this degrading vassalage to be carried?

A wise selection has to be made in the world's book, to bestow the proper tribute to mind, in its vast and prolific power.

Why did God permit his Israelites, who were his peculiar chosen people so many centuries, as bigots pretend, to be out of the pale of safety?

All this betrays imbecility of God, were it not the stupid imbecility of dramatic priestocracy.

It is the picture of a peculiar god painted by Judaism, surely and truly the work of craftship, that necessarily betrays itself.

But the bibles of tradition must confirm the tradition. If they be unreasonable, they violate truth, and cannot be God's works. All such do violate truth most abundantly.

Wise men agree in condemning such bibles, it is said. Do they not agree in other things also?

But wisdom, not men, must speak. It is not opinion, but the soundest and most truthful facts to be announced.

If any bibles stand in opposition to truth, let them go, as they cannot rightfully stand. Truth must and will annihilate all such, their originators and followers.

We all are interested in overthrowing all that opposes truth.

The greatest usurpation is that of the bible of tradition, and faith that it originates on God and mind.

But the bibles of tradition have stopped human sacrifices with savages! And introduced wholesale butcheries of nations instead.

What difference does it make to arrest individual human sacrifices, by sacrifice of the people by thousands to establish church rites and despotism, that outraged the continents of the world by dispensations of their people and their lands?

"Prideaux is of opinion, that Ezra made additions in several parts of the bible, where anything appeared necessary for illustrating, connecting, or completing the works; in which he appears to have been assisted by the same spirit in which they were at first written."

"To the same cause, our learned author thinks, are to be attributed many other interpolations in the bible, which created difficulties and objections to the authenticity of the sacred text, no ways to be solved without allowing them."—*Buck's Dictionary.*

Sacred text is it, that is fixed up as suited the priestocracy?

Is the constitution of our United States due to the priestocracy system, that deprives the people of their sovereign rights? of constitutional liberty?

Say, do not the lights of American intellect reflect the inspiration of the Almighty God of the universe, operating on mind?

Is the civil law of Louisiana, adopted as the Roman law, due to the narrow contracted code of Moses, or the fabricators of the Mosaic dispensation?

But if we take the bible of tradition away, we can have no system of religion.

Our answer is, that with that, or any bible of tradition, we have no system at all of religion!

In fact, mind is the only example of laws of inspiration, and the progress of mind proves the progress of inspiration.

We will thus have the only and best system of religion, all that is legitimate, that flows from the inspiration of mind, and is hallowed by reason, inspiration, and rational religion.

Ours will be the only moral law, resulting directly from conservative principles, and as to society flying to atoms and fragments, all the good citizens, from sense of mental safety, will feel bound to fly to wise and adhere to fundamental laws. Society will be thus properly cemented.

Our laws, defective as the basis now in existence, are for the good of society, and are upheld by the redeeming sense of citizens good and true.

None of our laws can be essentially sustained, unless upheld by mind and reason. Bibles cannot, when they controvert principles.

Essential good and wise legislation will be more important, and better executed, without so much curse of society, respect to persons, by combination and collusion.

The prompt equity of the admiralty courts takes its character from the civil law, and invalidates any pretended opposition as nugatory.

All such flourished, by the magnanimity of mind.

The copyists of bible traditions reverse this noble quality, and honor not God of Mind, but the little gods of men-dreamers.

Mind accepts, on the highest of all earthly authorities, fortified by religion, a God worthy of contemplation, reverence, and adoration, that rules out bibles of traditions, bringing forward myths of most disreputable degradation. Rational mind is sublimely the master of the whole theatre, and the master of impeachment.

It seeks to supersede, as impeached most justly, that bible, with better social, all religious principles, having no sectarian and bigoted quality, but to be put on their merits, and to be self-condemned, if on their demerits, for such is rational religion.

All will feel bound to do all things rightful, as self-agency of mind is constantly recognised, and the original is presented from a living God, for mind to imitate.

All have to be made sensible, on the highest basis of appreciation, that all that commit errors have to suffer equivalent penalties.

This doctrine truly inculcates on all strict accountability, and holds all amenable, and exempts none—predestinarians, universalists, atheists, deists, or polytheists—who are completely estopped thereby, and by no other.

This is the real and only compact that the God of the universe has vouchsafed to man. In the deepest wisdom let it be read, and subscribed to by humanity.

The greatest proof is brought, that principles hold mind all the time accountable, the more free-agency is permitted, and reason makes it responsible to the laws of justice on earth, and the God of Mercy in the universe.

Reason, that is rational thought and action of mind, tells man, that if he seek to diverge from the path of rectitude, in duty to God and men, propriety of conduct in society, honesty in morals, with less than truth on his lips, and sincerity in his mind, that he is gone to paths of perdition in sin and degradation, and is in a fair way to be lost and undone for time and a part at least of eternity, or lost, to a difficult point to recover from, on this sphere.

But how shall the world reach this supreme and independent tuition?

With supreme care, by the lights of mind, uniformly brought to all minds, and not left to contingency.

By whom? By the faithful parents, friends, and guardians of the individuals, by the wisest statesmen of the state, at reason's dawn.

Whose word shall it be? That of the Almighty Creator.

We must analyze the nature of mind, to know the whole capacity, the results and due progress.

Laying a right foundation, we can then proceed more speedily and safely.

But has not all this been a slow process?

It is the only safe and sure position, as it is the base. Purity in principle will best insure safety in the result.

The bible of tradition is not the book for the enlightened eye of science and philosophy, of government and of morals.

When it was written, those that could read and write were considered highly gifted, and endowed with peculiar privileges, if not with pretended inspirations. These mind-privileges were not diffused among the people.

It was an endowment for the learned, especially the priests, the so-called sacred depositories of the so-called sacred records. The very word hieroglyphics defines a meaning of sacred symbols.

Let intelligent freemen amend all such, to the best of their ability, and put an end to this imposition.

The bible betrays deepest ignorance of commonplace principles; a book that should have blessed mankind in the mighty benefits of God, had it not been endowed with the curses of man.

Is all this book-superstition to be kept up, from no cause of absolute good that it, the book, does?

The understanding can never be perfected to wisdom under such dominion, for sophistry predominates, and arbitrarily rules; consequently mind and reason are badly tyrannized over.

Tradition is a matter of false pretences, and speculation, if it do not rest on the facts of truth, that looks to purity of reason; therefore tradition must be rational, to be worthy of the credence of rational minds.

How does the bible-god stand before the august presence of the God of nature, creator of the universe?

No wonder the charlatan priestocracy were bewildered in the mazes of light that eclipsed their absurd darkness, when they placed the balance of creation to be mere lights to this little earth! What a miserable idea!

No wonder they betrayed themselves in disposition of mind, whose highest dignity they betrayed by dealing with the devil, the father of falsehoods all their own.

. They, in all their interlinkings of self-interest for thousands of years, have never raised the voice of reason to enlighten mind about the miserable legends, but have reached farther and farther into this wretched quagmire.

Their tradition affects a curse by prophecy on one of the sons of Noah forever!

What miserable degradation and corruption!

What standard curse has nature?

But you say that you cannot permit yourself to doubt of the authenticity of the bible of tradition. Is this the safe way, or the intention of mind, thus to act with passiveness in any life-question—to waive necessary inquiry, or to crush its falsity? That is not religion.

Will you disregard the necessary precautions in a matter most paramount, as it is, beyond all questions, to be investigated, whether official, genuine or spurious.

But what test have we as to this mighty question? The only test at the tribunal of the beneficiary mind, by a free, enlightened and rational discussion, that necessarily leads to the adoption of whatever is right, and excluding all of mind's perversions.

Whatever God ordained is right, and what that is, mind must inquire truthfully, not with sophistry to decide in bad faith, tory to God.

But you may pretend that the mysteries of that bible may not be for mind.

That is one of many reasons of its own impeachment and self-condemnation.

It is not possible that the wisest being, God, could have given mysteries to the world when he desired the strictest obedience to his word, that had necessarily to be divested of all mysteries to be plain enough to be understood by mind; therefore, also, as mankind perverts bibles of words, God put his word into his works, that cannot be mistaken nor successfully perverted by man.

It takes rational minds and the best reason to divest ignorance of her mysteries, the only ones known.

None but the wilful blind can avoid seeing; none but the wilful ignorant can deny this.

But then you demand a code of morals for your children and family, the world.

To whom can you permit the guidance of your children but to God, whose guardianship is supreme by principles?

But a code of rational mind will insure them this, and prove that the unprincipled always get into difficulties.

The bible of Judaism inconsistently makes God changeable, an utter impossibility, as God, from his character as God, consents to be immutable by principles, that are immutable as truth, virtue, &c.

All the bibles of tradition last, because they have propagated doctrines to the support of absolute governments, and its advocates help to promote union of church and state. Such is an interested and corrupt policy.

The design is to embrace the worldly interests, and influence the feelings of the advocates.

Their sophistry, though jesuitical and subtle, is too glaring to pass unnoticed by the mind of intelligence.

That they should attempt to portray the mighty character of God, and libel it in its essentials, at once condemns them all to utter contempt, as all vain, if mind itself were not adequate to its functions!

No form of priestcraft faith, however upheld by all such bibles, can be right, as no pure religion can flourish in the world, its theatre, destitute of constitutional religious freedom, no more than a union of free states can have a freedom of government in a central power of any one of them.

Strange to say, that God's peculiar people should suffer the universal evils of the world, as all other people, and should be peculiarly excluded from the so called Savior's blessing, for the whole time, from the first moment to the present. How is this?

No sophistry can avail with the magnificent author of munificence, the only imperial supreme in his genuine sublimity. Any people that was the peculiar favorite of the God of the universe, must have had a peculiar organization. Did the Jews have such? Then of course they were never the peculiar favorites, as their whole history proves most conclusively.

They merely had a peculiar god, as all their cotemporaries, and from that peculiar god, have been formed other peculiar gods, endowed with the name of trinity, the Mahometans, Mormons, &c.

There can be no direct inspiration of providence, except through the best agency of mind in principles that directly represent Deity.

Has Moses violated truth and honesty, the two first principles of religion? if so, he is unworthy the confidence of mankind.

It is proved that he has put himself in this category. Much more then, is the work growing out of it.

The first duty of the bible-advocates, is to prove its authenticity, as carrying all other proofs to mind's conviction, conversion and adoption.

In defence of such bibles, the present age must see silence or sophistry.
But what good will it do to discard and impeach the bibles of tradition?

As much good as any world-benefit, because we have thereby, religion for peculiar faith, the God of nature for impostors, and then our preachers will be of and for the people, not of and for themselves, and the people can institute lectures on the science and philosophy of man's duty and religion, inculcated by wise legislation, morality, truth, honesty and virtues.

All rational minds must seek to exclude such books, because they are in antagonism to the bible of rational mind, that inculcates monotheism, that seeks to take the shade and shadow of meanness out of human nature, and elevate it to its best attainable character.

Can conclaves of men at councils, vote out the authentic from the genuine books, centuries after the matter is said to have transpired? All that they can do on all such occasions, backed by all the world-emperors, is to smuggle false bibles of absolutism.

This bible has the most outrageous and vicious toryism to obsolete and exploded dogmas, on the divine rights of the people, and causes its worst errors to be a miserable and horrible fixture on mind's progress, constituting an incurable evil.

Mind that does not progress, must retrograde, therefore the sooner we get rid of such corruption, the better.

Take the texts, contexts, whole chapters, the whole book, all, to give the fairest, best exposition, and it excludes itself without redemption.

What a libel on the God of the universe, who permits any people to merit their own destiny, and govern it for the better. He could not be God, otherwise.

But what a god does Judaism create!

Mind, to be a free agent under its circumstances, looks back to the past, observes the present, and contemplates the future.

Let none wonder at the false pretences of the bibles of tradition, made so by the priestocracy and its minions of the present day.

What was the most of ancient history, but a compound of truth and fiction, before printing?

Even now, it is most difficult to separate the two, so much does self-interest degrade it by sophistry.

The Jews have been forced into their belief by all the peculiar powers that can influence man, and yet a part of the Jews feel under little obligations to it as religion, and as to returning to Jerusalem, some of them laugh at that idea.

The prophecy about Ishmael at once cuts down the prophecy of every knee bowing to Christ, for that involves love and peace of all mankind, not hatred and war, much less piracy and degradation. This all proves how ineffably stupid were the bible-mongers.

But who were the Ishmaelites?

The proof of ancient genealogy by Moses, is analogous to all prophecy of the eternal freehold inheritance of the Jews.

Now the king of Muscat, part of Arabia, recently, like a perfect gentleman, though Mahometan, cultivated the friendship of these states of America, having a different faith.

This does not show a deadly hostility to the rest of the world, but excludes the bible's prophecy.

We do not object to the bible's not teaching astronomy, geology, phrenology, ethnology, or psychology, but to its misteaching, or teaching them wrong, as the bible was written by men for priestocracy very ignorant of science.

The mind of analysis is needed for improvement of mankind by science, and will exclude the bible, as it must respect truth before the bible.

All the prodigies, as crossing the Red Sea, the food of manna, all must be taken in a priestocracy sense.

I would quote an article about manna now found, but it's of no use, as no sane intelligent mind can believe any bible of tradition worth more than the currency of priestocracy.

We cannot rely on the bible as a correct history, much less a safe system of religion, for various reasons.

"The precise number of the Hebrew manuscripts of the Old Testament is unknown; those written before the years seven hundred, or eight hundred, it is supposed were destroyed by some decree of the Jewish senate, on account of their numerous differences from the copies then declared genuine. Those which exist in the present, were all written out between the years one thousand and fourteen hundred and fifty-nine."

Chronology is very different in the bibles.

34

This is a fine thing for revelation and inspirations, and proclaims a corruption too potent for rational beings to receive as rational faith.

As to the authenticity of the scriptures, the preacher can make no successful point.

But what shall we gain to discard that book of books ?

Instead of the fourth part of a dwarfed peculiar god, we obtain the Almighty God of the universe ; and in place of puny mental nurses about man's footsteps where they are not wanting, we are put in the right views, and possess the power and majesty of Deity exclusively, that give the power and majesty of mind, that is thereby entitled to its full dignity on its worth and merit.

What, if you displace the bible, would you do with the people, the majority of whom are so vicious and ignorant ?

It is useless, then, to retain the bible of tradition in this condition of things, that adds to the amount of ignorance and superstition.

Every man ought to help support the proper demands of the community, hence, he should expel all nuisances. What greater can there be than these bibles ?

All rational minds will then be necessarily referred to the best representation, and seek out the best mental government, as was done so brilliantly for freemen's organic laws in 1776, by the United States of America.

The wisest legislation should be called for, and that too, to rule out all odious vices on the best conservative principles.

Ennoble your own free institutions. Teach the people to rely on their own elements of power, greatness and capital, principles and intellect, that combine best for best power.

The bible of rational mind is the only inspiration of God.

This can fulfil the faithful performance of all trusts, as guardians of all agencies.

Identified with its own best interests and feelings, it has no subterfuges, whereas one subterfuge of the bible of tradition has produced very many to support the first. There is no end to its false faiths, creeds, and notions. Their name is legion.

Mind's free agency under the bible of rational mind, then carries its own responsibility for mind's management, and mind approaches Deity by his only dispensation, its own proper elevation and dignity.

Under this basis, sectarianism cannot arise, as the principles that direct education cause rational religion, that is the same with Jew and Gentile, Christian and Mahometan, whose names are lost, and whose union is blended into one universal brotherhood.

Are you right or wrong, then recur to your self-examining rational mind, that tells, the bible cannot, for that of tradition is conceived in fraud and written in ignorance, by the writers who excluded most stupidly, God's conservative principles, superseding them, as all mythologists, by material beings as angels, messiahs, prophets, and priests.

The whole contour of all such bibles, decides most conclusively their own death-warrants, as they are clothed in the stupid habiliments of ignorance, error, and abominations of priestocracy.

Where would be the creation, but for those principles ?

How can mind be corrected, by as corrupt a basis as this bible ?

It gives us the most erroneous views of God and his works.

What tinkers of mind, and what libelers of God these writers !

It affects to give a correction of God's own works, and pretends to his dispensations.

It most absurdly undertakes to account for a universal deluge, to destroy the whole race of mankind, except a priest and his sons with their families. The worst of all.

How preposterous indeed : what absurdity this bible.

The first dispensation is murderous indeed.

Its second dispensation presents a miserable state of crime still. To support its vile pretensions, the worst murders were perpetrated.

And after eighteen centuries we have not reached their end, nationally or individually

Forty thousand bayonets, even in this civilized age, are aroused to butcher at its command the sons of freedom. Will the world never be free from the ignominious, degraded bible of tradition ? Can history begin to describe its horrid iniquities ?

And is this the religion of mind, that mind revolts at ?

No wonder that the priests and preachers eschew science and philosophy, in its discussions.

Their sophistry and proscription now, are equal to their bloody bigotry of past piratical ages.

A witness that lies so generally, is excluded from his testimony in an honorable court of conscience.

As to the opinion of part of the world, that the bible of tradition is the word of God, the whole world must look at the intrinsic merit of the whole question.

The bible, all rational beings will acknowledge, without much investigation, is partially self-evicted for falsehoods, and we have to exclude the whole, not a part, as when a witness knowingly perjures himself, he is to be ejected. It is not to select three points of four that are suspicious, but in all such pretences reject the whole as tainted. The bible is the child of perjury.

But then, we are not to be met with the foolish and absurd false pretence, that nothing is impossible with God. The peculiar dramatists of a peculiar people, can violate all rational principles, and yet the minions of absolutism are green enough to believe any falsehood.

The physiology that rational beings recognise on this earth, is the work of the God of nature who does not violate his own principles that are conservative thereof; if he did he would be a peculiar god, but that he cannot be, as he is the God of the universe, that the bible-writers did not know at all.

Man would have to have a peculiar organization, to meet the peculiar views of the bible.

Part of the peculiar priestocracy have lied their bible into existence, and others have had to lie its present maintenance. Besides all this, the powers of absolute governments, kings and monarchs, have disgracefully aided in all the abominable baseness of its continuance, abetting the degraded priestocracy in luxury and pomp, on the property of the people, and corrupting the minds of the world in all its circles.

Can such a violator of morals and truths of science be a safe pilot for conscience, that if not a free agent, must be deadened to all sense of shame and ignominy.

When conscience is drilled and trained by this bible code, God help the free agency.

Its legitimacy is odious vassalage.

No wonder at this day, that its advocates, butchers of the human family by wholesale. in the midst of the divine rights of the people, rouse up sister republican nations against each other, because of a different peculiar faith.

Where is the first principle displayed by them, of rational religion?

A high sense of duty is necessary for elevation of religious character, all that has to ever respect truth, the free principles of which ever survive and can never be extinguished, as long as the universe exists.

All such guarantee the people's best happiness, and all constitutional and essential rights, for the best inherent reputation, and will leave to no man or set of men under any devices of power, the dictation of any opinion except in accordance with principle.

Eloquence cannot justify the bibles of tradition, for truth is absent, and conscience is excluded.

How many bibles were made at various councils, as at that of Nice? Of course, was not man the maker? As the advocates of the 'bible assume it to be the organ of God, it, as well as all its knowing supporters, should be held strictly accountable for all the abuses resulting therefrom.

It presents disorganizations in morals, mind and social governments, all over the world. It pits one faith against another.

Its errors in peculiar faith produce serious evils in bad government, all of which must end.

The faith coming by its persuasion must be sophisticated to suit the perverted testimonies.

What particular fall of man can there be, when there can be no Satan or evil genius to tempt beyond perverted mind, that is not peculiar but universal, unless corrected by particular exertions?

Man overcomes the difficulties of his nature in the universe, especially those of ignorance, by the light of science that exalteth mind.

Alienation from God can be only mastered by the very best efforts of mind in resignation to his supremacy, that records God's divine will and purpose.

It is by the lights of rational mind that he overcomes all the vagaries of superstition, and its mercenary faith, that pretends to mysteries and miracles, that would upset the globe for natural causes, that enlightened philosophy recognises through good sense.

The whole bible category resolves itself most positively into the highest principles, of the proper position of which it is not a competent witness.

In morals, laws and religion, rationalists must know where is mind, God's immediate representative.

Our laws are taken from pagan codes in part, as from Rome, but all from mind.

Whence the Mosaic laws but from the first same-source, after all the false pretences, and probably coming through dozens of nations?

This bible forever inculcates sectarianism, because it portrays the distinct separation

·of the Jewish nation, that selfishly affected to be the chosen people of God, thus making him a peculiar god of this world.

Its separation causes the followers to separate from the people of the world. What can be worse?

What knowledge had the prophets of the God of the universe?

What kind of benevolence and good morals can such bibles foster, that offer no security to the sovereign people, but invade their rights through an ignoble priestocracy?

Where the bibles of tradition prevail, unless their abuse be counteracted by organic laws of mind, there we see superstition, bigotry and persecution.

When mind does not rescue itself by its own intrinsic powers, we may see persons of all ages and both sexes destroyed for witches, and sectarianism triumphant, and excluding professors of other peculiar faith by the rigors of state-faith despotism.

Unless the light of mind progresses by the school-house, the press and free rational discussion, peculiar faith, however exploded and obsolete, still prevails.

As to God's inspiration, science, philosophy and truth can best invoke all available for individuals, nations and the world.

After all the efforts of the multitude of absolutism that have had their hands on the bible of tradition, none can give us trustworthy proofs of God's supernatural inspiration. All are a complete failure.

Revelation, as it is called, is too meagre for God's word, as it stops short of history, most important to man, as it has not upheld the character of any of its heroes or messiah above that of mortals, presenting them as jugglers and impostors, unable to speak but the language of the priestocracy, and incompetent to comprehend the science of principles of the God of nature. That is too bad for teachers of the world.

It has been the means of abuse, that enabled bigoted princes to apply their power, subservient to the church, and subversive of the people's rights.

The horrid machinery of the papal hierarchy to put down opposition to the obsolete bible, is reproachful to intelligent minds.

She has sold the most revolting indulgences, and licensed the most atrocious crimes, for a sum of money.

She commands a blind and implicit faith about the messiah, and perpetrates the most grievous iniquities for the institution of her avarice and ambition.

Much of the past history emanated from dark ages of barbarism.

We ask the effort of the pure and intelligent to rescue the balance from superstitious feudalism and vassalage.

Truth, honesty, justice and integrity, universally and forever, by the refulgent light of mind, cultivated in the principles of liberty, philosophy and science, will advance, and all the legitimate efforts of genius and mind will be recognised on the globe, and thus reflect on all preceding barbarians who have adopted all the machinery of priestocracy.

The ample revelations of time alone, the only true teacher, present the highest proof of the utter incompetency of all bibles of tradition meeting the wants of the moral and religious world.

Their defect is proved relatively to their writers' defects.

All created minds are the beneficiaries of their Creator, who is omnipresent and almighty, and requires them to look at all faith through truth, not the idle opinions of interested men, ignorant and prejudiced.

What does the intelligent world want with effete works of tradition?

All such bibles were written by half civilized people, and are now utterly unfit for cultivated minds of this age, time, and country. They are obsolete.

It conclusively demonstrates that bible revelation is behind science, to which, as the pure revelation of God, it had been certainly equal. Such had been the science of sciences.

Now, had any revelation been by divine power, assuredly his omniscience would have appreciated all this, and had the whole completely right.

It would have taught the purest morals, and the sublimest principles universally admitted.

Religion is exact science, and nothing less; yet nothing kills any such book with more certainty than her revelations.

What fatal absurdities about the solar system, that use up the old exploded book most awfully, as well as all the abominable priestocracy, so impious to impose it, so blasphemous to publish it as God's work.

Of all the foolish and degraded thoughts, the idea of the sun going round all his planets at the same time, instead of their revolving at one and the same time around the great centre, and on themselves, is enough to blast this ignorant and abominable body of pretenders for a day after eternity, if possible.

And with all this load of folly and consequent guilt, will any rational being pretend to uphold it? Will any half-witted honest mind believe it?

The leaves of the great book, geology, put down all such bibles. Which was written first? Geology. Who wrote geology? The God of the universe.

Who wrote the bibles of tradition?

The most contemptible of priests.

For what purpose was geology written?

To promote the sublime conceptions and purposes of the mighty Creator of the universe.

For what purpose were the bibles of tradition written?

For corruption and perversion of mind.

All are to force peculiar faiths, that are all of the same family, founded by ignoble priests, only differing as they build successive stories, as that of Judaism on the Vedas and ancient systems of the east, that of Christianity on the first, that of Mahometanism on both the last, that of Mormonism on the same.

God's universe is doubtlessly inhabited, as nothing has been made in vain by him. Will it ever be destroyed? It is unreasonable to suppose such a thing.

Matter cannot be annihilated, but gravitation, a conservative principle of solar systems, will be deranged by the tinkering of man, who will destroy the people with the earth to promote bibles of tradition.

Geology proves creation, that gave regular gradations of the earth's investiture, in elevation, in the simplest to the most complex, up to man ; and his representative, mind, is in progressive improvement by all the developments of pure history.

But look at the light of the gospel!

It found Rome flourishing abundantly, and so far from advancing the light of the world, that even that already existing went down for many centuries, and has aggravated the burdens of the world.

That is the true analysis of this whole subject.

Books had their depositories among Christians as Saracens, but are we especially indebted for science and philosophy, the very things that faith expels?

The gospel has given the world the curses of peculiar faith, and abstracted its noblest blessings, rational mind, reason, and truth. Where are the discoveries of genius?

With mind universally, not with peculiar faith.

Darkness now prevails in church faith, that does not advance at all with mind, to establish the noblest rational religion of civilization, but holds back on that peculiar faith of superstition of the dark ages, partially civilized at the best.

The world has been divided and cut off from communications with its nations, on account of peculiar faith.

The Christian, Jew, and others, know, or ought to know, by the teaching of rational religion, that peculiar faith has been the butcher of the world, the persecutor of mankind in the sacred precincts of conscience and truth. Where is the exception in any gospel?

All its peculiar faith can be branded with the basest ignorance and falsehood, the most degraded treachery to mind, over whose rights it has tyrannized.

We must read not only the books of mind most liberal and rational, but the whole universe, as far as practicable, to decide by enlightened mind in religion.

But there is so much diversity of opinion respecting earthly things, and there are a fashion and custom on opinion that some think should be entertained. What folly and nonsense, when principles are outraged.

All this must be corrected by the only safe standards, the freest use of science and philosophy, that require and impart unity ; by that, we reach the correct precepts and position of rational religion.

What conception of Deity did the Jews have?

A very imperfect pagan notion indeed, when they unwittingly made God their peculiar god—an idol-pet of priestocracy.

After all pretensions to this one peculiar god, the Jewish princes incorporated different pagan vices and practices, ignorant notions and idolatry of their pretended worship, into the Jewish faith.

What especial claim has any peculiar faith to our reverence and approbation?

Does Judaism present it in the impurity of the patriarchs, who were polygamists and assuredly adulterers?

Did not the other pagan Greeks and Romans excel the Jews in this respect? Then it is the name of the thing, not the thing itself? Where is that?

Can this abominable imposition of peculiar faith, in any shape, be pushed any longer on the world?

If you really wish to bequeath the best legacy to your children, you cannot adopt the authority of the patriarchs, who were felons, tried upon the principles that govern our more civilized world.

If you also wish them honest, and act honestly, you cannot resign them to the creed of those who did not recollect what they borrowed, or who did not act as they ought, in borrowing and obtaining others' property under false pretences. They dishonestly withheld it.

What can you think of those who play off mind-jugglery for miracles? Is it not most dishonest, of all?

In Moses and Aaron, the Hebrews seem to have had no confidence, on various occasions. Can the world now have?

Shame on the faculty of mind, to be imposed upon so basely!

Would we learn of Moses, what were the pure laws of true government, of which he and his compeers had not the least idea? Can freemen learn wisdom of bigots, freedom of despots, religion of the priestocracy?

Could freemen learn truly what true government is, short of mind and reason?

But we impeach, and discard the bible on that impeachment, as we can only use the bible of rational mind, that you seek to impose against itself.

We seek to let it speak for itself, and thus prove our position, that the bibles of tradition are all impeachable, and not trustworthy.

We have the God of the universe, of which mind is pre-eminent, and takes cognizance of his creation and titles, repelling all speculation.

But for the bible, who could have thought of God? What God? All peculiar bibles are essentially estopped, on all claims of the God of the universe.

Developed, rational mind could not have thought of anything else, than the universal God of Nature.

The legitimate results of civilization will endow this God, according to its light and knowledge.

The bible was incompetent, of course, to rescue man in the dark ages, nor did it enlighten him to the light of knowledge that blesseth the world.

Even the peculiar people of god, as styled, have not been able to realise their most peculiar benefits, as they could not carry out this pretence by a peculiar bible.

Another bible supersedes the preceding, but does not satisfy those beneficiaries on the spot and scene of action.

Another covenant is advanced, after-thoughts are annexed, in this drama of priestocracy.

Can the moderns, the mere gentiles, decide for them, eighteen hundred years after the pretended events?

Is that reasonable or just, when the Jews were unbelievers, though the chosen people, the very elect?

Cannot the whole priestocracy patch up this Mosaic work, to suit the world? No! for that is God's province; God's work cannot be superseded.

But we could not get any idea of God, but through the bible! That is not only untrue, but absurd, to say that nothing else could advance that idea.

Then the mind of one set of men, is to doom the rest, forever, to vassalage.

Mind is the noble agent all the time; the beneficiary for and by which all such ideas have been elicited, without which nothing of the kind could have been elicited.

All that all priestocracies have, is their own peculiar creations, idol gods, subservient to them, as all pagans.

Was, then, it possible, for the universe and the supreme Almighty to be appreciated at all? But their bible is a matter of faith! Falsehood. Defeated by truth, science, philosophy, rational mind, and religion, the bigots resort to sophistry. What virtue is in that?

We can only reach definite views by principles inherent to creation. Instead of principles self-active, the bibles give us, absurdly, angels—nothings.

By their authority, one tribe had the priesthood, that added to its power, by subtracting from the rights of the people.

They bring us false systems, of peculiar faith.

They maintain them by false persuasions and dogmas.

Will such answer for a world that needs probity and dignity?

All systems of peculiar faith have to be built up on the pretence of prophecy, hence pagans, idolators, &c., have had their pretenders to it, to the disgrace of the age.

What were the prophecies for, but impositions? What value, but deception? Dreams, visions and angels were part of the machinery of prophecy, the whole being the mind juggler's substitutes of reason and mind, only requiring faith or credulity.

Prophecy caused idolatry, and degradation helped to ruin mind, the honor of the universe, if rational. No wonder that this nation fell a victim to its superstition, that left the mark of the beast.

We will defy rational mind to prove rational religion, by such blind faith.

How came these prophecies, not successfully used to convert neighboring nations who enslaved the Jews?

They little honored the Jews for their peculiar faith, whilst they could not have been kept back from due reverence of Deity through the Jews, the mighty object, if wisely designed. Had this faith been genuine, the world would have adopted it universally.

Their faith was to benefit the world by sacrificing the lives of nations to it, more hideous than Moloch, more relentless than savages.

The faith of inspiration, as a supernatural agency, violates universal principles.

Our fidelity to God supreme, prevents forever, faith in any prophecies.

The code of Judaism involves glaring errors and horrid iniquities. Talents and truth that belong to Deity in perfection, are here miserably prostituted to priestocracy. The god of Judaism is peculiarly coupled with Moses and all the priestocracy, hence he is of course the peculiar god, a mortal idol, like all others of peculiar faith.

The God of the universe has been therein most grossly libeled, and the world's people most basely imposed upon. But oh! the virtues of these bibles of themselves, some would affect.

Could mind do right with bible tactics, and no mental or legal tactics?

That is an impossibility, for mind then does not act. The globe would be overrun, has been overrun, and that without seeing it, if bibles were to be the dictation. All their peculiar followers and fabricators would have peculiar constructions, and tyrannize over mind. Then all such are funds of despotic licentiousness.

Where now is the limit in the place of absolutism, that prefers bible of tradition faith to rational faith, organic laws, order, mind, brains?

But where is indisputable proof of mind's appreciating the God of nature without the bibles of revelation?

The triumphant proof is in the correction by cultivated mind, of all the peculiar faith perversions of the appropriate character of the Deity of the universe, who has universal attributes.

Judaism had not one of the glorious attributes of rational religion, humanity, towards other nations through the principles of universal brotherhood.

But the Jews were the chosen people of God.

What God? The God of the universe has never had any chosen people. The whole universe is his.

The god of the Jews is not the God of the universe, then. The God of the universe did not claim them to be the light of the world at all.

They showed no superiority of good nationality over all nations. They practiced pagan idolatry with their god.

The world's facts condemn all peculiar faiths as the deepest curses of the world of mind.

The divine rights of the world's people are too sacred to be trifled with.

Now shall the advocates pretend that such frauds are invested with any attribute that should repel exposure? Is there any sacred felony?

If so, then is the God of the universe vilely libeled by these base characters, who cannot be silenced too soon.

What fatal errors have the Jews sustained, who have expected a messiah by false prophets?

Was there ever a prophet that was not false?

Have the Jews not lost millions of people by messiahs already?

At the assumed time of Christ, the Romans held Palestine, into which their faith of polytheism was carried, and there were greater materials for the revolution of peculiar faith. The time was propitious for such revolutions, amid the vast variety of so many faiths concentrated in the Roman empire.

The temporal kingdom of the Cæsars, the union of church and imperial absolutism, forbade any others of their empire, and only permitted a spiritual kingdom.

The loyalty of the people has been promoted by all the force of power, and all the sophistry of perverted mind; all things have been invoked to preclude all others. But rational mind scorns all these degraded impositions, on the face of the earth. No wonder the Jews could not believe to the present time, about any messiah of the many offering themselves, though the chosen people, the very ones to be saved. This proves them not only not the chosen people, but the falsity of the whole pretence.

Can they not yet see that false men assuming to be their leaders, have pretended to divine inspiration and prophecy, all proved to be utterly and ridiculously false in the essential particulars?

After all this abominable imposition, will they not get rid of all the prophecies as false, to do themselves and world, a mighty good?

The peculiar chosen people of God, are proved to have been the unchosen, for they sacrificed to superstition and a peculiar god, thereby libeling the only true God, and convicting themselves as peculiar faith upholders. This is the position the prophecies were false in, for there can be no chosen people by God the Creator universal. And well did they prepare the way for Christians, Mahometan and Mormon heresies of peculiar faith.

But the exclusive priestocracy, the true inside barbarians, never allowed once for the billions of the world besides themselves, before, then and to survive their most iniquitous and odious peculiar faith.

But few, outside of the Jewish nation, was thought of or cared for during fifteen centuries, as any thing but the heathen, who, as an abomination and objects of hatred, were dispossessed of their rights, property, and heritage, where these Jews could do so with impunity.

And well did the balance of the world return them the cup of their own preparation, drained to the very dregs of misery and retribution.

Their egotistical opinions of themselves and peculiar faith seem to be an heir-loom of priestocracy, that has corrupted the fairest portions of the old continent, particularly Asia.

By the same code of Judaism, with all its odious superstition and despotism, imitators justify themselves.

All the codes of peculiar faith, no matter how presented, are counterfeit, and present always clans and factions, parties and sects in churches, for the minority themselves, instead of the greatest good to the whole globe.

All sectarians have warfare, for all clash. Is this religion?

But how absurd that the peculiar covenant god should leave his peculiar people for want of faith in the messiah? Was there ever such suicidal sophistry?

Then he should have made them faithful for being his peculiar people.

Did God ever overlook the wants of a single mind to make it actually dependent on a bible of tradition, that may be read or not by the individual or friends? God has met all these things beforehand, some way in all minds.

The seed and elements of religion are therein; now for the right direction. And can the bibles of absolutism give that to the world? All such results from mind, that must be put in its highest state of excellence by the most approved rational means in the world.

Show us the children brought up in this wise by wise and intelligent parents, and we will expect, in a country invested with appropriate civil and religious institutions, all that human nature is capable of, no more nor less, under similar circumstances.

They will teach them that the unprincipled character of untruth and demerit never maintains the confidence of the people. Such impair their birthright.

An honorable people will invoke their direct attention to honesty in all their difficulties, as she will be a self-sustaining principle, pure and untarnished.

Human nature is the same always, and has not changed, except through mind's progress of improvement in science. That is the solution to the whole false pretences of faith.

Will rational mind receive what is valuable by reason, and reject all that is bad, however commended by the force of custom, authority and power of paganism?

Resolution and presence of rational mind are the very best protection to know and defend our rights.

Judgment is the highest prerogative, guarded by conscientiousness of rational mind, being the critical part, the quintessence of all others, and enables us to do full justice to creation.

Is it possible, then, that false pretences, booked as occurring thousands of ages past, are less degrading than those assumed for the present time, that is too refined to permit their existence?

Are booked false pretences any truer than verbal ones?

Rational mind must exert itself benignantly invariably to reach the only way to read from documents, to comprehend all that bears on the subject, and illustrates motives. Any catches are unworthy of a great and pure mind, and will, must be, forever discarded by all such.

Where are now the people of Israel, the pretended chosen and beloved people of god? Were they never possessed of the grace, or have they too fallen from it?

Have their gross infatuation and bigotry caused them to lose the beauties of a national existence ?

It is time that they lay aside the first, that they may attain the superior dignity of the last.

Have they not yet seen enough of the curses of peculiar faith in their case, from first to last, to teach any rational minds of the reckless folly of its impotency and worthlessness ? What is all such peculiar faith but the most abominable curse, folly, crime, the poison of priestocracy ?

All that are the bibles of tradition are impeached by the bible of rational mind, that best befriends mankind in all ages and circumstances.

Reason prevails in the bible of rational mind, as reverence for Deity the highest is inculcated most sincerely and truly.

Without the bible of rational mind, the noblest principles of human nature will be abused.

What can be a better standard for the whole world, that commends all to act worthy the liberty and the courtesy of true government, for justice, the decision of liberty? The world now acts on it.

It commends freemen to act for the best, independent of unjust blame, to seek properly the correction of the entire whole, as a wise legislator and statesman, and to rise to the height of wise principles, not fall below low opinions.

With it, the sin of omission is as great as that of commission.

It is its tuition that God alone is infallible, and that all else are fallible, and that absolutists, of which they are a part, are very hostile to mind's noblest dignity.

Did the assumed chosen people of God rise above the superstitions of the whole earth, or did they institute a faultless system of religion?

They instituted the peculiar god of priestocracy, and sacrificed the blood of animals on their altars of superstition. They, as all, were pagans.

Civilization relies on the lustrations of mind, as the purest offering before the Lord of the universe.

The scope of all the scriptures was to puff the Hebrews as the peculiar people, and secure the available profits by government of the people by priestocracy.

They have little true philosophy but the stupidity of the doctrine and of rejection of science, a demoralization without reason that God has placed in mind, as the cure for sin. Self-knowledge will teach all this.

Sin is a transgression of the immutable laws of nature, and results from violation of the principles of life and obligation.

The most unpardonable sin must be a denial of God's sovereignty, that is, his sole property indivisible, absolute, universal and eternal, and relative action thereon. These scriptures commit that enough. This idea results from the best proof, that all nations can reach.

God can only be appreciated in the purity of rational mind, uninfluenced by any except the proof.

Where the idea of God does not prevail, there no creed, mind nor universe can dwell. It is mind, not books merely, that upholds the idea of God. All priestocracy's bibles uphold only idol gods, not God.

The priests of the world, whose duty was to teach mind truth, if men have sought professionally to do anything else, may appropriate by false pretences their views of Deity, but after all their efforts colleagued with absolutism, can on analysis disclose only peculiar gods.

It is rational mind alone that can proclaim in the sublimity of its developed supremacy, the pure conception of the Immortal Organizer of universal matter. Who can endorse the writers of the scriptures, when their works condemn them ?

They plunged the Jews into deep idolatry and impotency of mind, instead of rescuing them. They gave most foolish notions about God.

The Hebrews are indebted to the world for not being still lower in superstition, not to their bible that libels God as imbecile, unjust, and deficient as a God.

The God of the universe never would have compromised with one small nation of the world, when the whole universal family was his, and which he was equally able and competent to save and appropriate, thereby proving himself the worthy God of the world, not a peculiar god of a small part.

But all had some defects. That resulted from the state of the world not enlightened, by rational mind not being imbued with the full lights of science.

The bible of tradition has been claimed to correct the darkness of the world, but unfortunately added to the darkness, and is now adding to the disgrace of the world, that cannot reject it too soon.

What has corrected the world but civilization, and what effected that but mind, through exact science? Let no peculiar bible thwart it.

The mind that pretends to peculiar faith being the cause of light, is insane beyond redemption.

What but the bible's advocacy ever countenanced "witchcraft, that was universally believed in Europe till the 16th century, and even maintained its ground with tolerable firmness till the middle of the 17th. The latest witchcraft phrenzy was in New England in 1692, when the execution of witches became a calamity more dreadful than the sword or pestilence."

The question with the world is for mind's rational dignity, not for priestocracy.

Rational minds cannot be seduced by any emoluments, to take the bible doctrines.

When they are offered, the whole truth, and nothing else, should be told. The bible or its priestocracy cannot tell it, as they are neither competent nor acquainted with it.

The world now observes the awful fruits of those abominable pretences.

All must be taught the proper improvement of mind's noblest faculties, not by peculiar but rational education, the elements of correct deportment, that will teach them best at once, how certain will be their want.

Mind, innocent and pure as practicable, has to be taught, and that by the very best code of mind, advanced to all the improvements of developed science and philosophy. These bibles never had these, and of course are left far behind them.

Let mothers, fathers, relations, guardians, and friends, above all, individual mind, correct at the start; all starting right will have the fairest prospect of ending right.

Let all children, much more youth, have their minds well grounded in all necessary noble principles, that they can only get of the Creator, and then they will return the source, honor and glory.

How else can you properly check youth at maturity? Can you teach them to lay aside old habits?

You may have suffered flaws to mature, and the rust of vice may have eaten into the soul, hardly to be reached in its corruption.

Much of correction in the latter days is too late, not only absurd, but wicked and criminal if recklessly delayed. The correction may never come in this world. These bibles offer no adequate means, and are absurdly in the way, as well as all priestocracies.

Let us ask for intelligent freemen's rights, the highest thought of, to do as best comports with nature, and the world's social system.

Young people will love to learn wisdom, and will produce the properly matured results.

Old people will, if perverted, hate all such, and will adhere to folly and hoary-headed error.

Theirs, then, will be a bigoted conceit.

Give us a liberal and rational mind, that looks to the highest and purest sources for its sanction and authority, not bringing fallible man to a single test of this or that creed, for public or popular favor.

Let its acts be as pure as its thoughts are elevated.

Who that rules children can uphold their vices for the present, without realizing the issue in crime, and the disgrace in penalty?

Whether from disease or vice, the parents may participate in the fault, their conduct in the first instance being the cause of disease, or of penalty in the last.

Neither fate, destiny, fortune, nor fatality are to be considered, when we duly appreciate the vindication of principles.

With all the bibles of tradition, what country in the world is safe without laws, after all the code of peculiar faith, that emphatically demands peculiar prerogatives?

No matter the character of the people, they may talk of their churches till doomsday, we must abide by the moral laws of society and rational religion for universal safety.

What teaches us that? Rational mind, assuredly. Intelligence, observation, and experience of the world.

Peculiar faith, with best morality, can be tolerated no longer than civilization can alter it.

It will not do to make any more present capital therefrom, political or otherwise, as all the world suffers from its tyranny.

This is the work of peculiar faith, not of religion.

Was it expedient to perpetrate libels on Deity, whilst if left in his universe-majesty, his perfection is above all criticism? Was God to be thus degraded, that the blasphemous priestocracy were to be exalted?

This makes him commit crime in his imbecility, and decides that all such is not the true God, but some of paganism, and a copy at that!

If you acted on the principles of religion, you could do no less than we do, but your bigotry prevents your religion.   Why do you not analyze your whole position?

The bibles of tradition are inadequate to describe creation, as to give the moral laws of mind.   They are worthless.

Their writers were deeply ignorant of natural laws, of the true analysis of mind, and that the first of mankind had a nature analogous to that of the whole race.   The adopters ignorantly or basely act.

We have in the bible examples of oriental vices, and are the American people willing to credit it, as their moral and religious code?

All such peculiar faith proves all its advocates still uncivilized, unworthy of rational mind.

But this bible declares the existence of a God, yet peculiar.

The Vedas assert the existence of a creative God, yet peculiar.   All the world gives peculiar gods, even Indians.

Roman priests were to read their bible, and only the Brahmins are permitted to read the vedas, while the universe can read the universe, the only proof of its God!   Down with the false books of false authors.

What shall we think of this work, the bible, that tolerates belief of absurd and impossible things?   That is not as strange as its peculiar polity-faith for a peculiar god.

All its testimony must be competent, full, perfect, and undoubted, not only unexceptionable, but satisfactory and convincing, for that is the purpose intended to convince mind in its highest analysis.

If any question will not bear analysis, it will not bear confidence.

All miracles are only vulgar wonders of natural phenomena not analyzed.   They cannot exist as substances at all.

A true history of the world, is the history of its science and philosophy, and must detail rational facts, or its injustice is unworthy the minds of freemen.

What shall rational minds think, of those assuming faith, to dictate to the world, of facts?

A faith imposition details miracles, that do not belong to earth or the universe; a chimera of fanaticism and paganism.

Happily God has left his works in the universe, and all the proofs unmistakable, that will recall mankind from bible vices and priestocracy.

This property, that so munificently declares the God of nature, is that of the God of the universe, by all universal, not peculiar rights.

All bibles of tradition detract from, instead of honor him.   All their faith is vulgar and suicidal, savors all the time of designing priestocracy, after their own emoluments, not God's or the people's good.

The truths of nature and religion do not clash, but statements from the bible do; therefore, they must be rejected as worthless.

No minds, enlarged and liberalized, can stop short of reading the world, the universe and all, for themselves, to attain proper decision.

Who can justify bible mysteries before the world of mind, God's gift, that can overwhelm all their imposition?   All creation, the universe attests as the witness of the living God, for religion.

It is absurd, to believe that mortals could tell us of inspiration, when they failed most ignobly in their history of creation.   There is no failure of mind sacred.

But we see the deplorable effects visible in the world, by fanaticism.

The terrors of all superstition are hard to overcome, as fear operates on weak and ignorant minds, in the exhibition of extraordinary faith and consequent actions.

The revelation of the bible of tradition cannot satisfy us.   That revelation is only endorsed by non-entities!

The Jews are no more peculiar than the Arabs, Chinese, or Hindoos, all devoted to ancient superstition, the most difficult to eradicate from the human mind.   Their situation among nations is analogous to that of the gypsies, who may have descended from some priestocracy.

But the main prophecy is falsified, about the Jews holding possession of their land forever, by their dispersion in other lands, their greatest benefit, where they can be rid of their superstition and peculiar notions.   This one answer closes the whole bible pretensions and faith.

If language can be changed, and forever does not mean always, then prophecy may begin to be noticed; but neither Judaism nor any other peculiar faith has any peculiar claim to the world's veneration one moment.

To sustain the overwhelming defeat, the priestocracy, ever true to their vocation, their only truth, are after altering language. They would ruin the world for their bible.

Shall mortals, that wish to have wisdom, virtue, and truth, ever cater to such morbid taste, that degrades mind, libels God, and outrages religion and decent society.

Such a bible can be given all the advantages of its priestocracy, and can be silenced at once by science and the attributes of God.

But after all said, the ancients and most moderns can only claim an imperfect view of a peculiar god.

All the ancient code of laws, as of faith, betray imperfect systems of their ages and time, absolutely needing amendment. This is the condition of mind undeveloped.

Is the boast of such faith to preclude the useful works of conservative revolution? Let justice forbid!

What wise friend can advise free and intelligent citizens to adopt codes that cannot contribute to the full protection of all classes of people, nor advance the highest qualities of mind?

Laws should not be demoralizing nor superstitious, and should embrace the world's benefit, promoting honesty in the payment of national and individual debts, counteracting all fraudulent transfers of property, and all purchases under false pretences.

Woman, as well as man, the citizens should be protected in their dearest rights and feelings, by all the exalted views of civilization.

Wise legislation must contemplate adequate retributive justice, but no vindictiveness merely.

Bigoted ignorance absurdly premises, and adheres to her dogmas.

In what respect can the ancients be our code teachers?

Their very pastoral and partially civilized state, precludes all confidence of those in a higher state of civilization.

Man's notions and pretences about peculiar faith must be in abeyance to rational religion, that none such do touch, but counterfeit.

If we analyze the ignorance and corruption of the world, of the people on one part, and the priestocracy on the other, we cannot begin to wonder at its superstition, false faith and pretences.

How can it ever get rid of all such, as long as it is profitable to delude the ignorant part of the world?

The true, vital and genuine is the rational part, and the only argument in the world is effectual only by reason, justice and truth.

If God had preferred all such bible machinery, they would be unmistakable, not in book monuments, but irrefutable as the sun's qualities and functions, the constitutional elements of the universe.

What greater tyranny was inflicted, than by the Moses of priestocracy? The modern priestocracy are equal.

Yet, with all his tyranny, priest-faith and craft, when he was absent—after all his proofs sufficient, if they happened, for obedience—the Jews rebelled, not for reason but greater idolatry, so much had they been hopelessly estranged from reason, that their minds were subverted by superstition and sophistry, inseparable companions. Moses perpetrated the greatest guilt of idolatry, perverting the minds of his people.

The minds of this stupid and ignorant nation had been so perverted by the monstrosities of fable, that they were ready to receive the greatest falsehoods of Aaron.

By this one statement of the bible's own showing, the Jews were dwarfed in the lowest idolatry.

They had not the faculties of analysis, as they had little science. But is that day not now passed, when the moderns presuming to be more enlightened, trade on all such foolish capital of paganism? We must make great allowances for the people of the ancient priests' regime.

How few means of enlightening their minds did they possess? The means were used, to increase popular ignorance.

How few laws, how few just ones, and what few copies in the hands of the people! How many copies of laws did the people have? None, but in the hands of their priestocracy, who could act arbitrarily as their peculiar god spoke!

The priestocracy are the proxy of absolutism, when not the principal. The exception shows mind, not faith; the man, not the priest.

What little popular knowledge was there in the whole world. Kings could hardly read, and thought to enslave mind instead of ennoble it.

No wonder the people so often transgressed, as they were so ignorant and superstitious, and rendered more so by their bigoted priestocracy.

In a contest of memory and books, who could dare deny but that books would prove triumphant, especially in the hands of the makers, framers and interested interpreters, who could change as their assumptions of power and interest dictated.

What was easier to the piratical masters?

Some things were held too sacred for the people, called vulgar, on that very account. The people could not see nor touch sacred things. Levites were judges, even in all civil causes, and it was death to resist their sentence.

In what hands during many ages were their bibles, but in those of the priests of Judaism and Christianity? After all, their first position cannot be proved. They might as well have destroyed all, and pretended that the proof was thereby lost.

The difference of opinion between the Jews and Christians, elegantly prove the inconsistencies and futility of their bibles, and this is much the case with all such bibles. Their bibles cut each other's throats, and their advocates did the same for each other, to prove their bible-loyalty. Their tales of superstition are available to subsequent sects as Mahometans and Mormons, ignorant and corrupt people, but to be deprecated by all, especially by men that a purely intelligent press reaches.

The bible of Moses had a social fanatical force and creative power of despotism, bible life guard, promoted by the peculiar speech of the peculiar godhead.

Almost all ancient nations have the accounts of their origin lost in fabulous tradition, and bibles that detail such are only man's books.

Man assumes great exploits, and if his legends are right, god is not immutable. In all fables, bible fables and all, man is god.

The talents of many minds have been perverted and prostituted to the propagation of those impositions of the priest world, in absolutism especially.

The Jewish nation has been wofully misguided by imposition, that has left us a bible, but a bible fable.

What nonsense in any rulers to build up a nation of impostors, to be punished for ages afterwards.

The advocates of the bible of tradition mar the beauties of the universe, and libel the character of its creator.

The deepest absurdity exists, when it is pretended that God assists one little nation, and leaves out the balance for thousands of years.

God's especial providence is blended and diffused, in his universal Providence, reflected through his universal conservative principles.

Have we, then, authentic records of necessary particulars, confirmed and accurately proved beyond all doubt? Far from it. Religion has reason, not tradition.

All bibles of tradition give attributes of deity repugnant to deity, as to justice, goodness, or his power and government. The treasury of reason has no such suicide. What has canonized some of the books of the bible? The opinions of man's councils! That is smuggling, not canonizing.

Rational beings that are fortified by reason and philosophy, necessarily reject all such. The god of Judaism is a very small god, whose mind is undeveloped, and who talks to the select very familiarly. The universe cannot recognise him.

This priestocracy worshipped a peculiar god of miracles, fear, terror, wrath, not of rational mind, and dwarfed him below the dignity of the God of nature.

Man consults his reason in everything else in this life; why, then, should he lay aside reason in the most essential part? Why can any one be so infatuated to act on tradition and revelation, that refer at last to the same position of reason? The corrupt dynasty of the priestocracy answers.

The bibles of tradition suit the character of their peculiar gods and priestocracy, but libel the true God in all his moral attributes. Bible pulpit-sophists pretend that we are indebted to bibles for ideas of Deity!

Such bibles speak only of a peculiar god, not of the universe.

We need not names, as that of the Great First Cause answers best. Rational mind, then, cannot know such bibles, that are tory to its God.

First causes are elicited best by common sense, philosophy, for all things; and of these peculiar bibles have no account.

If bibles could go beyond this, then such bibles, if true, would be the work of God.

But all the present bibles usurp mind, that looks through nature and her soul, to God or the first organizing cause, which is all that earthly faculties can do.

Now, this proves that mind is superior to bibles of tradition, that must be held to the abeyance of truth by this the only means. Bibles are amenable to mind, and both to God of rationality.

All the bibles of tradition have originated no new principles, but their violation, the ideas of the priestocracy.

To affect more is absurd and untrue.

Theology, like all other subjects, is before mind, and must be rightly analyzed, not by books, but by mind.

No sophistry of priestocracy, or their bibles, which represent it, is available before science and philosophy, as they constitute the greatest test.

Peculiar or priestocracy faith has been a fruitful theme for perversion and corruption, fraud and imposition, at all the three first ages of the world; but civilized freemen of this day and time owe it to themselves to overwhelm such superstition, and reject all unworthy of them.

Moses knew not as well as modern men of science, of the ancient progenitors.

He sought to amplify his own authority, and that of the priestocracy, at the expense of the divine rights of the people. He, or its foster fathers, were perfidious impostors, and tory traitors.

The great ends of principles will be ever perverted when men are followed as men.

What can all laws avail, if dishonest and incapable men have to administer and execute them, much less enact them?

The sources of power, no matter the name, are delusive, and ambition in all grades of professions, to become the dominant party, will incite mind to much that is suspicious, if not objectionable.

In religion, as in government, we must look to the final result. Let us have her full benefits, as of justice, not one side view.

Judaism, as all other peculiar systems of faith, is defective, vitiated, and demoralizing.

It is the foundation for any, the most monstrous doctrines, as the possibility of a progeny between God and mortals.

Let us have no such ideal monsters, hybrids, impossible procreations, no idol-creations.

Away with such libels, to prejudice mind against the highest esteem of its adorable Creator.

The right action of mind, that is to govern the world aright, must not be thus perverted.

Then let all minds, good and true, in mass, aid in the expulsion by their most rational wisdom.

There can be no God subsequent, or book idea of mutability in the universe, as God's universal attributes exclude all such.

There can be no new creation by mind, as it only acts on data of Deity, who thus excludes all others as pretenders. The conservative principles, attributes, and functions of the universe exclude all novelties forever.

Hence all systems of peculiar faith, and peculiar bibles, are cut down as analogous, effectually, at once and forever, by this position, and there can only be rational religion, that bespeaks the consummation of conservation.

The influence of God's spirit, word, and works are the operative power on mind all the time of existence, therefore meet all things by this enlightened mind.

No other view, but that man is as God created him, can answer to the present position of things, otherwise the earth, mind, and all else, would libel Deity.

Mind's depravity is only relative to circumstances of life throughout the globe. Perversion of mind peculiarly educated, creates evils; uncultivated, weak minds cannot counteract them.

All histories, whether called bibles or not, are analogous and parallel, as their detail of events is to be analyzed and estimated on that and only that analysis.

All books and bibles, as books, can only detail events that must be true or false.

None but a priestocracy need miracles, and their record bibles, for false pretences; none but their minions can be fooled by them.

Good faith must be observed in all good societies, on which they depend, for the proper benefit of the whole world, and is maintained by Deity's comprehension, to which mind must look. The good faith of mind must banish all bible peculiar faith.

What then, is any bible worth if untrue? If true, it cannot rely on the falsity of faith.

We impeach, then, all bibles of tradition, for the improbable and impossible codes for civilization. As civil history, what is it worth to us moderns?

What miserable sophistry it inculcates, quibbling and equivocation about false faith!

The delusions are perfected by falsehoods, pretences, and frauds. No confidence can be maintained in all such, destitute of the principles of truth.

Its veil is that of darkness, and necessarily requires ignorance.

Its power enslaves the world, bound to it by obligations of superstition, and to wily hypocrites.

Moses was so far from being a prophet, that he became a perjurer. Prophets are impostors. Prophecy can only be perjury. The advocacy is.

His false pretences are analogous to those of other priests of any oracles, Pagan, Jew, Gentile, outside or inside heathen.

What is easier than the forgeries of the priestocracy, the keeper of pretended sacred rolls, their authority so far from being questioned, that it has been ardently sought for by the uninitiated, who desired to be mind-enslaved?

Literary forgeries were once abundant, and successful to the last century, and are as old as authors.

As to inspiration, all minds act by God's best principles in the best universal deeds, truths, not fictions.

All bibles of tradition hold out false lights, to create belief in messiahs, men of straw for priests to swindle the people by, playing into the hands of absolutists.

We ever need enlightened mind to emancipate from all pious frauds.

Pretences, the capital of priests, the only foundation for all such bibles, having no reality, necessarily destroy the validity of the bibles that act in bad faith to the world, mind-enslavers and deceivers.

The abuses of this superstition, and peculiar faith, are made to cover practicable felonies on the world, to expel by false pretences to divine authority all minds from their lawful functions.

What is the material object? To deceive and beguile the whole world for the very means of benefit.

Is it possible to produce any result that would annihilate the world? In a word, can the earth be destroyed by anything except by the Creator? He is pledged to its conservation on principles that bible men did not know.

So says rational mind, the only power authorized to speak, from the wise revelation of reason, which rule out all the bible ignoramuses forever.

The pretences of the world's destruction (as universe, or any of its orbs) disprove all the pretended revelation of scriptures as nonsense.

An enlightened conscience will only support rational religion, and will exclude all bibles of tradition, and their authors, as not trustworthy.

The bible of mind requires that the organs of the brain be rationally cultivated, so as to overcome all that looks like predestination.

She requires nothing to be taken for granted but what accords with reason.

All bibles that invalidate the omniscience of God, predicate the elements of their own destruction. All bibles but that of mind do blindly contradict the omniscience of the God of nature, and consequently overthrow at once their only foundations to mind's confidence, by advancing the doctrine of messiahship.

The most wily of priestocracies continue to supply the defects of the books by all the sophistries of mind, to suit the complexion of the times.

This peculiar faith doctrine was sought to be built up as the Jewish hierarchy, for the full benefit of Moses- and friends.

In regard to assumption of divine powers of commissioner, Moses was a perjurer, and so are all his coadjutors.

On this authority rest the Old and New Testaments, and all their posterity, whose foundation having given away, saps the foundation of the New Testament, the Koran and the Mormon books, as all others.

The prototype, the vedas and book of Menu, of course have the like category. All such are equal.

All the spurious pagan faiths run out, having the elements of their own destruction, they cut themselves out or up.

They will answer as no good codes, for all fall short of human and God-nature, to unite or place mind where all are at first placed by God's endowments.

They are systems of priestocracy to displace mind, and usurp its best and sacred divine rights.

All these systems of faith are antagonistic to each other, and the progress of just principles of the universe.

What little piety has the daughter, Christianity, for the old bible, and the Jews, its adherents, and what love have they and Mahometans, who have another offspring? Their position has been a deadly hatred. These bibles and peculiar systems mistake religion for peculiar worship of their peculiar gods.

How preposterous then was it for Moses and all other authors of bibles of traditions, to define God's province and character, which requires the circuit of the universe, before the soul is adequately enlightened, or admitted to the presence of God's magnificent attributes.

Intelligent freemen, and ladies of chastity and virtue require the enlightened code of religion, that God has written as brilliant as sunbeams in his exhaustless universe. How can rational mind overlook it?

This pure and perfect Spirit has dictated for mind, that libels God to receive any code that authorizes miracles, prophecies and mysteries intrinsically pagan. No mortal Moses, nor any, should be trusted any further than analysis of truth authorizes. The authority of reverence of any less than God is base and degraded.

Intelligent mind recognises only the intelligence of mind for authority, and rejects as essentially wrong the espousal of others' opinions that may be a false position with partisan views.

The Jews have been punished, persecuted, basely robbed and plundered, for many centuries, for adhering to their peculiar faith-creed—no worse than all other pagan superstitions. What but curses is it worth to them?

Their forefathers were the greatest bigots of antiquity, and treated the nations dispossessed of Palestine in the same style, under the false pretences of their peculiar faith.

The bible furnishes full proof against such and the faith-machinery.

The disbelief of the so-called chosen people of God kills all as to the messiah, and the belief in the New Testament conclusively proves that there is no pretence of priestocracy but can be believed, to mind's degradation and confusion.

The failures of Miller and others respecting the bible solutions. prove conclusively the same confusion of the scriptures. When will all this infamous game cease to be played on the world? When all such paganism is silenced.

What do the ladies of America think of the polygamy of the bible? Any modification does not affect the rotten foundation.

We cannot tolerate the domestic vices of the patriarchs. Why then tolerate their absurd superstitions and paganisms?

America refuses to learn government of Asia, much more then can she refuse peculiar pagan faith, both of which arose from mind, not only undeveloped, but that most wofully perverted by oriental absolutism, pollutions, vices and degraded priestocracies.

If we refuse the originals, how can we tolerate the copies, or the subsequent stories? When the advance of mind and reason explodes the pretences of prophecy, we are met by Jesuitical typifications as to the exploded points.

Casuists, not reasoners, are brought forward, for authority, in decision.

Who are they, if not honest interpreters of all scriptures?

Who would give aught for all dishonest faith evasions?

When Moses pretends to testify to the peculiar gods, swearing to the inheritance of the land forever, we only ask for the interpretation for the version that embraces the present time. Such will prove perjury conclusively.

All depend on mind and reason in all things, of investigations in theology or interpretation of its scriptures. It is absurd to deny it, a dilemma inextricable.

All the bibles of tradition are necessarily imperfect, from the imperfect state of mind, unenlightened by reason, of their writers.

They are all a fraud on mind, and rely on fallacy of human nature, invoking the greater fraud of the moderns, to uphold this paganism.

But how can mind decide for the world, when so few have worthy minds for all purposes of life?

The minds of the priestocracy are incompetent to meet the requisitions of the world, that needs more than they can comprehend by sinister designs.

There are head minds among all nations, to govern them, aided by the government of the Ruler of all, who can be found, if sought in the right way.

The wants of the universe can only be met by God, principles and mind.

But where did we ever see a country flourish by civilization, without the bible? That must be, after all pretensions, the bible of mind.

In the first place, what country that has books, and mind able to read them, but has bibles of tradition? And what country, thus situated, but has priests?

Is any part of the world exempt from these wiles of priestocracy? How can bibles of tradition, that imply imposition, be the means of civilization?

Our own country flourishes in freedom, in despite of the bible, as blessed was that day that separated church and state.

The Roman empire had the bible, and flourished less than before. Her proudest days were when she had no such bible. All the world uses more or less the bible of mind. That it should make rational.

Mexico has the bible or priestocracy, but her ignorance is proverbial, and her degradation is consistent.

Why did not the bible prevent the world from the dark ages and centuries? The world grew worse, despite of all peculiar faiths, till it run down to brutal butcheries of the human race for near two hundred years, and this on account of two kinds of bibles. It took the world several centuries to recover, by rational mind. Peculiar bibles have outraged mind, in all its rights.

What restored the world to its present civilization, but mind, in its rational advancements? It was the bible of rational mind, correlative to its light.

The truth of history must be sustained. All that is in the world is referable to mind and its reason, or its perversions.

The bibles of tradition, chimeras of mind perverted, are evidences that mind must be truly and duly cultivated, to be equal to its position, the world's guardian. Mind cannot use the universe, except by rational education, that lays low all peculiar bible pretences.

What can an uneducated mind do in a world, that may triumph over its rights? What but a right education, can duly protect mind all the time? When mind is rightly educated, it will necessarily see all the world's iniquities practised on it.

Again, of the two states, the non and peculiarly educated mind, the state that God, through free-agency, intended most clearly to counteract, cannot be entrusted with its own or the world's rights; it is utterly defenceless.

Let the world be crushed by the absolutism of bibles, and can bibles restore it to its propriety?

The faith of superstition, the peculiar faith of bibles, keeps mind and reason out of their legitimate fruits, and behind their noblest performances.

What then can you do in any country before civilization, that premises the highest state of mind, reason, and just morals, a right code of ethics?

If mind be true, as it should be in all things, to be right and true, mind and reason are bound to support it; but if untrue, mind and reason are bound to dissolve it. I will submit these questions, in answer to the objection that the world has been at most times abundantly in error, in regard to mind and reason.

I. Is not the advancement of mind progressive and gradual, in all the relations of science and philosophy, as clearly proved by the comparatively recent and first establishment of the unbounded blessings of a constitutional representative government, which freemen enjoy, and that gives them the greatest good to the greatest number, as a test; and yet this was not established till 1776, by the United States, that had to receive the experience of practice till 1787, before they realized the natural blessings of mind?

Yet still, by the constitution of the latest state, California, that results on the Union's experience, have we only discovered the true principle of governing the financial administration of a country on honesty and freedom of good faith, by pledging the vote of the people prior to the expenditure.

The test of the world's experience now declares that there should be no important state debts, except the people, who are taxed, vote previously upon the measures.

The actual history of the world proves the slow development of mind's rational greatness, in things as they are by nature, and not as the world's dreamer's imagine. Now it is for patriotic minds to cherish mind, for its world-wide developments, and not see it frustrated by conspiring priestocracies.

II. If mankind was destitute of the bible of tradition, especially from the creation, as they were to the time of the New Testament, except those of Palestine, &c., what was its substitute but mind and reason, at all such periods of time, thousands upon thousands of years, according to the book of geology?

Again, what is the condition of the world's majority at this time, let alone all past ages, and what in the meantime, of hundreds of years, is to be done, before they all receive and appreciate the bible, whose circulation cannot be completed for many ages of the world, and not adopted after its circulation?

Sectarianism is trying its best, in antagonism, respecting the great peculiar faiths of the whole world, to cut down all but itself, as infallible and orthodox; all others being fallible and heresies.

Even in the Christian faith, there is a prohibition of even protestant works—ay, even bibles—calling them vicious editions, in some of the countries where the Roman faith is predominant.

The peculiar faith of the state precludes a fair and free liberal and rational discussion of other points of faith, and is a tyranny wherever established.

Omnipotent as God's truth is, still there is no exclusion of aught of faith, till rational mind declares the proper position, which implies the justice of the case.

35

III. Are any bibles of tradition, the bible especially now impeached and discarded, endorsed by approved contemporaneous history, a well-authenticated proof on its own analysis, to the satisfaction of mind; not by affiliated conspirators, but disinterested and competent witnesses, which would be nothing less than divine creatorship?

This question cannot be answered by the whole world, and has nonplused all the best debaters, to whom actually we are indebted, as means, in the defeat of the bible especial.

Were not the books of the bible especial, voted on as to their supposed genuineness or spuriousness, by a majority of the council of Nice, clearly proving the action and cognizance of mind, but mind of those interested?

Now the majority of the world's disinterested theologians, the men of mind, has voted it all the time in a minority; of course, then, the best of all decisions after that of rationality, is the republican one of majorities. The world cannot see its majority for any one peculiar faith or bible.

IV. Do not the exact order and system, the harmonious arrangement of the universe on conservative principles regulated in all its functions, prove incontestibly the rule of a Great First Supreme Cause, only discovered by the gradual progress of mind's improvement in causation? You cannot dare deny it, if so, you are a degraded atheist, a being that denies the very sublimest principles of rational mind.

But sophists and bigots will assume that their bible especial, can only point out the god. It is all pretence, which they know to be false, and is defeated by the third question, which is unanswerable.

But you will deplore the condition of the world, as if God did not govern it, and declare that the world cannot be safe and survive if we do not obey the doctrines of your especial bible. This is the fraud of priestocracies.

We must examine by proper analysis, the scriptures on your gratuitous introduction, and we must let them abide their own testimony, which their failure of proof, their contradictions imply.

If the only code of morals and religion existed in any especial bible of tradition, then we might be justly alarmed at the idea of its impeachment and expulsion, but we have clear proof that the best code of ethics and morals exists by the exact light of mind and reason, reflected by science and philosophy, that God has given all diligent investigators, aided by rationalism, consistent with the advancements of the age, and developments of mind.

Now what does any rational being want with the scriptures, that cannot stand the pure test of truth; how then can they be truthful, when defeated by intrinsic and extrinsic proof, and thereby necessarily impeached. And this is emphatically the position of all peculiar faiths.

There is no just cause of withholding the exposure of all, when no mind can justify past superstitions of all those that conspired against its divine rights.

What can justify the collusions and duplicity of priestocracies that are an abomination to the God of creation?

What shall justify their frauds on mind, to book God's divinity, thereby libeling it, with their vanity and deception, and restricting mind for all time to come, in the littleness of their own degradation?

Bibles of tradition are criminal codes when they not only do not come up to the appropriate demands of mind, but actually contravene its best and holiest requisitions.

The Hebrews, even the patriarchs, the head of the whole, as the orientals, practiced polygamy, while the Grecian and Roman republics excluded it to the shame of the Jews, the peculiar chosen people.

With all the precepts of that bible, how came the Hebrews to sacrifice their children to the devil, Moloch of the fire, but that they were below the proper standard of mind, truth and religion, the worst devotees of superstition?

What are all their peculiar bibles, if they were peculiar savages? Of course their bibles are savage codes.

Will any modern now, be so stupid as to endorse their superstition for religion? How then can he adopt more stupidly, the impositions and superstitions founded thereon? Does the world know what it is doing? Does not the state of the Jews show the want of civilization, only to be accomplished by mind in its loftiest triumphs of rational development?

Where then is the superiority of this people, who are assumed to be the chosen people of God? What God? Moloch?

Does not each bible show the best exhibition of the mind of the writer?

All the priests' bibles must expose mind's perversions, and the bible of mind must exhibit the rational views of religion, or it is self-condemned.

The priests' bibles are not God's, and their delineation of God's character is such, conceived in the imperfection of the minds of the writers, as to display him a peculiar god of them, not of the universe. That is certain. God was the creator of all such men, but not as they described him. He was above their pen. That decides the question that the peculiar faith of their inferior states of mind, is not to be imposed on a better state of civilization. Tradition was imperfect in the hunter, a rude state of society, how then even in the pastoral age, in the absence of written documents, not peculiar and pertinent to those ages, could any history be correct?

If we analyze the condition of the American Indians, we at once see the impossibility of their transmitting the code of ethics and correct chronology of the first ancestors. All that is impracticable, is an imposition. All the conceptions about Deity of each age of the four states of society, exhibit the relative state of mind most imperfect, at first, at which time its imbecility in duly appreciating the attributes of God especially is proved, incontestibly by gratuitous theories most fabulous, assumed for peculiar faith.

The oral pretences of the ignorant ages are advanced by the priests in books of tradition reflecting all such conceptions, whilst the most exalted character of Deity is daily proved above all booking, for whom adoration increases for time, until eternity unveils his mightiest qualities.

We can set no bounds to mind's elevation and appreciation of God, as has been absurdly and wantonly done by the priests and hierarchists, thus proving conclusively their base corruption.

The misfortune is that bibles of tradition having the faults and vices of each prior age, transmit them as setfasts to the last, that of civilization, that labors under inextricable difficulties to rid itself thereof.

All the prejudices of the people, and all the self-interests of the priestocracy, with the idle superstitions of both, conspire in this ignominious collusion. The people, mind, is thereby defrauded.

Future civilization will better reveal mind's present imperfections, and cause it to rely forever on liberal and just principles only, to which point we are approaching.

Such a state will lead all the world to liberty, intellectual and religious expansions of mind; all bible authors have gone to the works of creation, for display of their authenticity, those of tradition have laid hold of peculiar views as miracles, prophecies and mysteries, like ignorant pagans, but does their testimony accord with God's book?

Is God sole genius of his own creation, when they claim tradition of faith from inspiration, and commit wholesale frauds?

How difficult has it been for mind to extricate itself from the toils of priestcraft, their spoils system?

Such bibles cannot be owned by God, and cannot be current with honest minds.

We could forgive Moses and his associate priests for imperfect bibles of mind, as a necessary consequence, but not of tradition palmed on the people as that of God, who is thereby basely libeled.

All such bibles of tradition are ineffectual to restrain atheists, and produce polytheists, if we take in the comprehension of the whole subject that is legitimate.

All things should be properly represented, to inspire full and perfect confidence in Deity.

All scriptures of tradition are dangerous books, as they are sectarian, and must clash with each other and the universal catholic interest of the world.

The old bible of Moses, that advocates a peculiar faith says, " Look unto me, and be ye saved, all the ends of the earth, for I am God, and there is none else. I have sworn by myself, the word has gone out of my mouth in righteousness, and shall not return, that unto me every knee shall bow, and every tongue shall swear. Surely shall one say, in the Lord have I righteousness and strength." Isaiah, xlv. 22, 24. " Thou art God alone." Psalms, lxxxvi. 9, 10.

Now all such bible authors are false witnesses, they are perjured, for the God of the universe universally addressed rational mind, but never spoke to man any such words— much less to prophets. The God of all science and wisdom never spoke so that his own science could correct him about his solecism of the ends of the earth. And God never swore about the eternal inheritance of land to the Jews, as (Exodus, xxxii,) Moses stated, to be detected by his own function, time.

God's conservative principles exclude saviors, angels, messengers, and messiahs, and execute his plans and systems, thereby proving his exalted character as Almighty.

But open the door to any bible of tradition, and innumerable such are mind and handfactured, no matter how contradictory. See what contradiction is involved, by the next bible emanating therefrom. Do not the prophecies and the declarations of scripture clash?

"God sent not his son into the world to condemn the world, but that the world through him might be saved." John, iii. 17.

Why has it not been saved? Why all this libel on God, impeaching his imbecility every way, first and last, and all this contradiction proving corruption and perversion of mind?

Here are two positions, that prove the contradictions of two bibles and the condemnation of both.

Here one peculiar bible lies, and another peculiar bible does it also. Who is the son of God? God does not procreate but create, then this impostor is nothing but a creature, a mere mortal, and his biographers are perjurers.

If God's wisdom and power are infinite, then all messiahs and priestocracy are excluded, and his universal book, that none but a Divine Being, a God could write, teaches that. But, that the corrupt priestocracy could not appropriate.

What held the universe together for thousands of years in their absence, but conservative principles of God, that apply most magnificently in all the physical, social, moral, and religious departments?

Clearly, then, all these are useless and injuriously in the way, and must be rejected. To the preceding is opposed Isaiah xliv. 8, "Is there a God besides me? Yea, there is no God; I know not any: 6. I am the first, and I am the last: and besides me, there is no God."

These points destroy each other, as the Jews who interpreted the scriptures, as a peculiar people had a peculiar right, decide by their actions.

If the Jews are right, the Christians are wrong, but if the first are wrong originally, of course, the last are so incidentally, then the Christians are wrong any way it can be fixed. So much for building one story on another, and sectarianizing on sectarianism.

What does it all amount to, when it is not the God of the universe spoke, but Isa. xliv. 6, "Thus saith the Lord, the king of Israel." No, the God of the universe never knew one of the pretended prophets of Israel, from Abram through Moses to Christ; he could not belittle himself by such trifling peculiarity,—never. Thus the Christian has cut himself loose from the Jew bible, on which he pretended to hold, and loses all of the Creator. None can rely on prophecy, for if the peculiar god attempted it he perjured himself in Exode, and if he did not, which is the true position, then all the bibles and every man of them are liars, and are all excluded by their own perjury, that amounts to the worst of blasphemy, for attempting to palm it on their peculiar god who had nothing to do therewith. Thus are the priestocracy the most degraded of human nature, and the modern sect is the worst of the whole.

The world has to search but one scriptures that are authentic, that are God-written as created, and none other—they are they that testify, of all mind's perversions. Rationality declares all this with unerring certainty, that sacred scriptures are created, not written.

Was it ever intended to recover mind from idolatry? Before you can stop idol-worship, arrest your man-worship: but then your bible is idol-worship.

As to the bible's proof of a God, it sinks into utter insignificance before the sublime system and harmony of the universe, that no rational being of this age can pretend to deny.

All scriptures of tradition are naught but assertion, and no more but tradition, and conclusively prove that prophecy is a false light indeed, and only sustained by perjury. When all the chief prophets and their peculiar god are caught in oaths proved false by time, that shows the expulsion and dispersion of the Jews from their inheritance forever, that cannot be modified by any who thus perjure themselves to unperjure their bible. You have no perfect example to point to.

Instead of a David an assassin, point your citizens to a Washington, a purer and better character.

The bible has caused, by its tenets of predestination, the horrors and iniquities of the inquisition, and interminable agitations for future punishments.

Under the assurance and brassy impudence of the priests, such views have been carried out, to the disgrace and violation of human nature.

Their bible is most flagitiously false, treacherous, tory to God and mind, as the world has no other means but mind to approach God.

No such bible can begin to approach adequately the ignorant heathen, idiots, insane, and infants as rational beings. God therefore takes the will for the deed, as far as rationality is concerned.

The justice of God must be consistent with God's other attributes. Whether there be five varieties of one species of mankind or more than one, is not essential to the solution of this mighty problem of rational religion, that yields to Deity, that could as easily to create them as the several five grand divisions of the earth. The bible creation only makes one species or race of mankind, though there are several diversities of the race.

Man may have been created in various portions of the globe—in Australia, Africa, America as in parts of Asia—since the God of Power can thus easily display it greater, as competent in diversities of races, as continents, and as much assimilated. Several individual varieties of the human species must have been created by the great first cause. Do we know how many became extinct in the world's age?

The immensity of this subject affords a plenty for originality of discussion by cultivated minds, without encroachments.

But it may be objected, that the Greeks had not previous knowledge of the god of Moses. The objection might extend to the gods of the Philistines—of the world.

Paul found an inscription " to the unknown God" at Athens, and thereby clearly proves that this was not so, as he undertakes to tell them who he was, but most falsely.

But miracles must be now performed, no matter how much they violate natural laws, else the commission of Christ is falsified and the church is extinct.

But no miracles ever were performed, therefore the church of Christ had naught for its foundation that is trustworthy. His prophecy of miracles is conclusively false. It has been a pet system by its nurses, and can define no particular miracles worthy of the faith of one immortal soul.

In the best countries, how yet are the Jews still treated? and what causes the outrage still upon that people? In some of the freest monarchies of Europe they are not permitted to enjoy civil rights!

Thus, neither is there freedom in monarchy, nor virtue in any peculiar faith. All such is pagan.

The forefathers of the Jews sacrificed their children to the gods of their idolatry, while succeeding generations of mankind as moderns, sacrifice all ages and both sexes of immense numbers, to the tyranny of unprincipled opinions.

Self-interest of peculiar faith now rules too far, and gives no chance to the heretic, who has to receive perdition beyond purgatory as his place.

The mind of the world should not lead itself into difficulties, when it can keep out of them.

God's works prove the bible's fallacies and falsehoods. Principles do not clash.

Shall such bibles, and their absolutism, be fixed on the world by the barbarism of the ancients, at best but little removed from half civilized savages, piratical on the possessions and rights of both sexes and all ages, and incapable of enlightening in morals and wise legislation?

Truth, honesty, and above all, mind inspirited to do right and wisely, by inherent qualities, will stand before all bibles of tradition, and will secure the unity of the world, as necessary, as mind has unity, and above all, God has unity.

Now, all sectarian faith fails in unity, as their heads have none.

The idea of a bible of mind, the only fact of bibles worthy of mind, never crossed the mind of Moses, or the profession of priests. It did not belong to their sheepish age.

They would be as much astonished at mind's progress as its many modern improvements, as steamers, &c., that overwhelm the minds of the Indians.

What mind does, a dishonest priestocracy assumes.

Now, Moses, no more than these sons of the forest, could know by tradition from the first ages of the world what was exact history. He did not know their ages, names, nor the most important matters.

Our aborigines first found in America could not tell what races preceded them on this continent, whose graves and mounds arched the mighty land.

And Moses, or all the authors of bible tradition, knew not of preceding races to their bookings. The more we go into tradition, the more fable and less facts of mind are presented.

Tradition, then, if not true, as most of it is fabulous, is utterly an injury to man, in the true principles of rational religion. It is a conspiracy and collusion on mind's rights.

Resolve all such national records on the globe, and this important fact flashes on the enlightened mind with vivid light.

However immoral, untruth and legends of individual nations, affecting to be peculiar, are, still, if succeeding generations are not verdant enough to adopt them, it matters not so much.

It has been asserted that no country ever flourished without the bible! Where was Rome hundreds of years ago, going from conquest to conquest? Her bible kills the other bibles if that pretence applies. With her own bible she rose, with the Christians' she fell, if bibles are to be considered.

Where were many others, that also flourished for a period as ancient empires, without any such bible ? Where, now, is China, that has flourished for several thousand years without any such book? She has her own peculiar faiths, however corrupting they may be, like all others, more or less in truth.

Mexico was flourishing in her partial state of civilization, on her own resources, without any such book, prior to its conquest by Cortes, and well had it been had she not received its embrace. It is mind, not the bible of tradition, that keeps back mind, that advances the world.

Individuals and nations, the world have flourished from creation's dawn to the present time, only by comparative blessings of mind.

Their condition has corresponded to their improvement, through the essential principles implanted in human nature. Peculiar faiths flourish by reason of those very principles, that are the elements of pure religion. No advocates of peculiar faith, Jew or Gentile, Christian or Mahometan, Mormon or Brahmin, can have peculiar principles distinct and characteristic. There are peculiar doctines, but not peculiar principles. All principles are the property of God, and silently but effectually operate.

The priestocracy faith must fall into disrepute, as good as the best may seem to have been, inadequate to protect a free and intelligent people, from want of due respect to principles, that freemen prize, only answering for enslaved and vassal mind, especially of the orientals.

This is the highest authority practicable, after the undeniable position that all this was fiction.

Its peculiar gods spoke as the peculiar oracles, the priestocracy, directed. This is the only proper solution.

Patriarchal custom, dispensation or covenant, is absolutism of the priestocracy, under all its disguises and pretences. As the priestocracy are in conflict with rational religion, they and their peculiar bibles are ruled out.

Whoso seek protection under such auspices had better stay where they are ; and as to obtaining religion under absolutism, all had better absolve themselves from such delusion, stay where they start, unless the bridge of principles, sound and suitable for emigrants. be adopted. As the bibles of peculiar faith kill each other, monotheism, upheld by God's word, protects mind and the world.

Is astronomy to be prostituted, like everything else, to the false positions of bibles of tradition, that violate the first principles of conservation ?

The advocates of such bibles believe part in reason, and part in faith, that affects to rule reason !

That is not good morals nor logic, to deprive God of his rights by mortals ! The whole bible reflects the extent of what the priestocracy knew—their obliquity and ignorance.

God's principles can vindicate themselves in judgment of men, singly and generally, at the court and tribunal of conscience, and ever present a judgment, more or less, all the time.

Sectarians have the soul to lie torpid, instead of passing at once, in uninterrupted series of existence and characteristic position.

How could they have any exalted, right views of the future, when they could not analyze rightly first principles, but limited the universe to one sphere plane, demoralized their heaven into a hell, a scene for brawls of vulgar angels, and dwarfed their creation to a peculiar god? Any other faith about the adjournment of judgment day seems a contradiction, and could only apply to peculiar faith, that is made up of a mass of contradictions and miserable absurdities, handled by men-children. The sophists had no philosophy, the faithites no bible.

Why the necessity of a final judgment to the Almighty, who has omnipotence and omniscience ?

We do not believe at all in the machinery of priestocracy, that brings forward the destruction to annihilation of any one planet, much less in that of all the universe, an absurdity and imposaibilty in God's character, and the extra fears to increase extra profits for the priestocracy. As to any other god of priests' creation, that only produced abortion, I have nothing scarcely to add to my previous reviews on that.

God's book lives with him, and is the great part of his best proof. The priestocracies' book dies with them, a base and iniquitous conception.

God could not have written man's books of tradition to libel himself, conspire against his own empire, and degrade his own brightest jewel, mind.

He could never have committed himself in all science, nor left out important parts essential to man's faith and well-being, for if religion be blotted out of the universe, mind must go with it.

When Moses flourished, there were many populous countries, showing an older state of the world, that might have seen many previous races of mankind die out.

Of course tradition, or its bible, is comparatively worth but little any way.

The Jewish circumcision hardly suited those barbarian times to prevent amalgamation; as even with that peculiar custom, ten tribes were lost certainly. This peculiarity does not suit the present advance of civilization, but has prevented the diffusion of this superstitious people among the more civilized nations of the earth, and has injured this nation time after time, arousing the world's prejudices.

If the Jews had any thing worth being peculiar about, it might do, but all are the pretences of superstition. The truth of history must be asserted.

The bible of Moses authorizes the most absurd pretences of priestocracy, and enslavement of mind about criminal absurdities, that must involve the severest penalties. God is not served by such fanaticism.

The state of ignorance is innocence, compared with the crimes of such errors.

The bible of tradition teaches miserable superstition about ghosts and visions that take a first hold on the human mind that is with extreme difficulty disenthralled therefrom.

Its morals about witchcraft and wizards are miserable, causing destruction and butchery, without limit, of women, children and men, that are even helpless.

What cruelty and barbarism! The people that have received the tradition are hardest to be rid of such opinions. Let not peculiar education be fostered in any way, to supersede most rational education and rational religion.

If right opinions and morals be inculcated, the people will be right. But such bibles will never do that : we have advanced considerably, but mind is the mighty lever of the world's morals.

Why are politicians so selfish and corrupt as not to seek to correct all such?

Fostering such tales is superstition, that destroys the integrity and organic purity of mind.

Where are statesmen, patriots and philanthropists, that they surrender up the vital question, instead of enlightening the dark circles of the world?

But the world cannot appreciate wisdom previously to knowing the value, taught from the necessity of the case. Now you advocate that horrid book, and these are the bloody statutes, ready to be vitalized when despotism bids.

Have you ever thought of that? That, with this viper, you have all its poison? All is wanted is the chance!

Most may not thank authors for teaching what will benefit, but a paramount duty has to be done. Let not the good forget to decide and settle the mighty question of the world's morals, stay the decline of mind and nations, and establish the sound institutions of God's religion, and that it is the neglect of these that has so long delayed the highest civilization. Religion cannot flourish without rational education, a wise and enlightened legislation.

But some affect to look to the bible, as if religion had been booked by priests. That is an impossibility. The bible's detraction from mind's and religion's rights are by the earthly considerations of the priests.

The prophecies of the bibles are all killed off in several respects, especially by the proof of the bible perjuries in Exode.

All the prophecies are nullified or are ineffectual by the disbelief of the chosen people, who had cognizance of the scriptures and all the circumstances, being the best able to decide whether Christ died a God or mortal, if such a being ever did exist.

If they had been convinced that Christ was God, they could not have been kept from him, whether the poorest that poverty could make.

But the chosen people have decided against Christ, and of course that the whole is a felonious fabrication of him. Religion decides as much for all the world of paganism.

Had Christians a proper analysis of mind, instead of fanaticism of peculiar faith, they would at once have seen through all this base humbuggery, and given the Jews credit at least for sincerity in a matter that supremely arouses it in all pure minds.

The only question so often adverted to that could possibly be included or arise, is as to the availability of messiahship. and that is clearly refuted by the attributes of God. The centre of gravitation of all the universe, that includes all this mighty question, is God, who must be for himself, and not divided, to be held responsible for its satisfactory preservation.

The bible of Moses hardly begins to look at the world as at present constituted. It presents the character of the priest and his affiliation above that of other men, whereas it has degraded it far below. With what face of honesty can the presumptuous priests offer the world the pretences of any such bibles?

All sectarians that have been enlightened by the tuition of time, as the Jews, ought to see, that they are no chosen selection of any god, and that they are doing the God of the universe injustice to longer refuse diffusion among the world's people.

All must see that there cannot possibly exist any reality in any faith independent of that only that acquiesces in the exclusive majesty of the Author of all.

Will God hold any guiltless that propagate any other to derogate from his character, attributes and sovereignty? Why are they propagated?

Superstition and all the machinery of absolutism, perversions and stupidity of mind, amply explain or give the solution.

Ignorance and imposition at first were the means of their propagation. The sword was tried for hundreds of years, but the cimeter repelled its conquests for a time. The bibles turned the sword into the vitals of civil society, and civil wars arose in civil strife. Now, the most forcible illustration was carried out, especially by the very peculiar chosen people, who claim paternity to bibleocracy of tradition.

Science, philosophy and civilization, the mighty results of rational mind's action on principles of God, have come to rescue the world from the thraldom of bibles of peculiar faith. The church, then, must all be separated from absolutism, and religion from peculiar faith of hierarchy.

Even in this union, as free as the mind was in some things, the separation of church and state was not relished, and the names of those engaged therein were scowled on.

Sagacious and insidious casuistry and jesuitry of the whole ancient world joined civil and faith government, church to state power, and united all the circle by force and sophistry, with an influence that triumphed for the superstition of the world for future being.

The custom of the ancients was deference to the word of man, clothed in brief authority, in all the departments of his dynasty. It was not only unquestioned, but had the most respectful approval. Orientalism that luxuriated on people's rights, decided without appeal, and the terrors of the future crushed every latent opposition by the brute force of man over the mastery of mind. It was mind perverted by tricks and bribes.

This degraded position of a world's prejudices had to be broken down, either by reason or the people's bayonets. If mind had its legitimate sway, conservative revolution would ere this have triumphed.

The most that has been done to the present time, is that one superstitious pagan faith has superseded another, all to be superseded by rational religion. If the ancients had little philosophy, that proves the state of rational mind that defined little religion.

It is the principle that makes the rule all the time. We would have no right to the exceptions, but for principles that hold all creation in abeyance.

No matter what peculiarity is the choice, God alone, that marshals the universe, must rule the universal mind. All the moderns would be pagans, if rational religion did not give them the sublimity of civilization.

To meet the best question that can be entertained about what can be done for any peculiar faith, we say look to the God of nature alone, and appreciate the rightful way of his government of the universe as far as practicable for mind.

If the world tolerates one bible of tradition to mislead it, it has to suffer by paganism, as it opens the door to all similar abuses. The same pretensions that admitted the Jews or Christians, admit the Mormons, who are only like the balance, and have just as equitable a foundation.

Their future strength may decide the contest by force or strategy, the only weapons of peculiar faith, not principle, that rules out all such forever.

Peculiar faith may establish as its bantlings any community of women, even worse than polygamy, under all the hideous deformities of radical agrarianism and communism, the chiefs heading those below them, and all enjoying one great brothel of concubinage and prostitution, unless the conservative law of the majority rules out all this abomination to rational religion. What was the patriarchal age, but a degraded fanaticism tolerating polygamy?

The faith that any peculiar bible inculcates shuts out reason, that should shut out any, all bibles, but that of rational mind, that ever looks to the highest rationality, the universal standard, and that condemns all peculiar pagan bibles.

But smart men have said that they believed in the bible of tradition, and have been in the church of their country. Of course this very position has subjected the world in all its parts to the peculiar faith of that peculiar part, no matter how flagitious and vile.

Is this reason? The various people of each country are held in abeyance to the peculiar forms of faith predominant, as pagan custom and power have decided.

But are any of these abuses to decide in this important matter, when the God of the universe has demonstrated the hideous fallacy thereof?

Could Moses or any other priest, interested as all were in assumption of chief power, be trusted with rights that they have always abused, perjuring themselves for?

In enlightened ages they would have had to conform to the requirements of enlightened public opinion.

Shall that opinion, which they and all bible advocates basely violate, be forever asleep?

God deals in omniscience and forethoughts, but the bible of Moses has fallaciously libeled him as dealing in after-thoughts, as the priestocracy writers were wofully ignorant of their whole subject, and caricatured the whole botch, that is, themselves.

But priestocracies and their cliques who take all they utter for granted, like debased vassals, affect to know that there is nothing like the bible that is the main idol. Take that away, say they, and we have nothing left. That is a libel on the whole truth. Where is mind, that institutes mind's civilization?

But we cannot know how to proceed. Where is reason, that looks through nature up to nature's God, his word, cause, and effect, to the solution of the whole problem, the universe.

The actual history of the world and mankind, proves all this position most correct on correct analysis.

Of course all such bibles cannot be available as superior to honest mind, even superior to God.

Mind shows the only best inspiration from God. But bigots affect to claim that they know nothing of God but by these bibles.

They should speak only for themselves, blunderbusses and ignoramuses, as they know anything else but the God of the universe, the god of their creation only, not their creator.

If they were not wilfully and stupidly blind, they could only know God through his works, by and through mind, whose inspiration is the true point.

Bibles of tradition multiply mortals into teachers and dictators of their tuition, in place of mind's inspiration, that must supersede all such pretenders.

There can be only two kinds of bibles, those of tradition and of the dark ages, to be superseded by that of mind, enlightened to the height of civilization, as the savage sons of the forest are ruled out by the sons of cultivated intellect mind, that is the proper master after God of the world, creation.

How ignorant the bible writers were of all the great functions of principles! They have libeled most. They make out that death is the result of man's fall, all a mere fiction of theirs.

Life is a debt that mortals have to pay in passing through on this earth, and death is a debt of nature, not the curse of sin, which is absurd and false, but the decree of God.

The first requires the best philosophy and religion of self-denial, the best exorcism of supposed evil through reason and reason's wisdom, the best affiliation to parents worthy to protect and defend their charge—and at its close for the actor to be conscious of life well and gloriously spent in good.

Then man's life is that of living, not a lesson of despair, to be preyed upon by the impostors of souls.

Man has to look to the great author of life, not to poor mortals, the lowest of the low lying priestocracies.

We see that Moses needed reason to govern the children of Israel; much more stupid was the priestocracy to assume the government of the world.

He and others that fixed up their bibles, were ambitious speculators in the stock of mind, avaricious gamblers for the souls of men, blasphemous hucksters in the drama of evil.

What claim have all faithloquists, hand and mind jugglers, to the world's respect? What is such history, so unsubstantiated by the facts of nature, worth?

The bibles of tradition are incompetent to produce refined, pure religion at all, and are unworthy of mind's respect, even for slaves, to be regarded only as successful jugglers for the world's age of popular ignorance and sophistry.

God gives ideas and principles, and all the elements capital of mind. Bibles of tradition advance words of demoralization, the basest desecration of truth.

To be above criticism, do you believe in such bibles?

You say you do not understand them, the bible especially. There are some parts you do not and cannot believe; then that position destroys its validity, as " not one jot or tittle can be left out."

There are several views obvious to children's minds in this bible, that utterly condemn it. The ancients were the children of ignorance and the victims of imposture, and their dictators did not expect that the future would disclose so plainly and unequivocally those absurd pretences.

There are no rewards so universal and supreme, as those of mind.

The bibles of tradition cannot enable us to give any appreciation and adoration to Deity, as they give us mere man's creations and idols always, nor can they keep pace with mind's elevation, or the truth of facts that belong to the God of nature.

All bibles of tradition give us the caricature of God, the moment tradition is advanced by priestocracies.

The less cultivated the ancients, the more they substituted hypothesis of theory, and the last for facts, heaping masses of error on error, whereas verification of facts alone build up proper systems and truth.

Such mere personal authority will not suffice for facts. The code of Moses could never have answered at all, for those that could not help themselves, a people just emerging from half-barbaric state. Error is not fit for mind at any time. Thus the moral power of the world is identified with its intellectual position.

All that the world is—if any thing excellent, it is by mind, intellect, soul, that make the people of their proper account ; then let the world use right minds.

But what is the use of a general convocation of the universal dead, as fire is to destroy the earth ? What then is to become of the souls and bodies, that are to inhabit the new ? Where must they be, before the new is fit for their reception ? We must have the same principles of gravitation, or else away goes the universe into chaos, as it would any how, if the bible of tradition tinkers have their absurd notions carried out. Where will be the new earth, when the old is being destroyed ? The most proper principles of philosophy are most wofully violated, by these writers, who eternally commit themselves. These science pretenders bullied the world, and thus made a horde of atheists, who should have been monotheists.

Who that estimates these and all analogous doctrines of the bible, but must at once say that the bible might as well be cast away ? Instead of destroying the earth or the universe, destroy the bible, and all will be right.

Those minds that are constitutionally good, or improved by rational education, can be so, anyhow, by inherent rights of creation—while, those perverted, cannot be anyhow bettered, by all peculiar bibles, or any other false system. All that preserves the moral world, is its moral conservative principles.

Reject such bibles, as unworthy and incompetent to answer any good purpose for the world.

Man is bad enough without those bibles of tradition ; with them, his iniquity is monstrous to the height.

A bad spirit is embodied therein, and has to be counteracted by the wise purposes of mind ; as fostering malign influences, it must be noticed and corrected.

There are many fears, of all the timid, about the expulsion of the bible of tradition. Now we will have, in process of science, the bible of mind ; that is the only safe means to the world. We can have no other.

That has been due the world ; usurpation putting in the despots' bible.

Good men, without egotism, by all rational discussion, at any time, will be obliged to impeach the last, as demoralizing, and seek to institute in its place the right means, decreed by God, mind's right actions, as wise education and legislation.

As demoralizing as the bibles of tradition are, they are even pretended to be superior to the mind ; an outrage on God at once, an insult to the people, the deepest injury to all. The introducers took care to have their race in the pale of their protection. Taught sophistry, as mind is, by this system, it becomes the most unprincipled, and will contend to the last, unless hemmed in by reason.

Such minds will not only stretch reason but conscience. All such examples cannot be hid from the church ; and if the head men practice it, as they are obliged to do, unless they utterly discard it, the members must be deeply tempted and corrupted at times.

Any one who supports, knowingly, sophistries, improperly miscalled divine, will lie, when expedient, and for a cause always. He will lie like his devil, to support his peculiar gospel lies.

St. Paul, that could lie as other priests, could not be authority for mind. The world owes it to itself, to settle the accounts of peculiar faith. It will have to be done as mind alone can do it, as God alone is creator.

In the full ripeness of time, the world will be rectified by its conservative principles, that vindicate themselves. The great career of mankind is not to be defeated by bibles, that have radical errors and crimes running through them. What incidents there are, in some bibles. The bible Georgian is in the ancient language. That language having become almost obsolete, and the Georgians in general being very ignorant, few of them can either read or understand it. Did God leave this contingency, when he left mind?

" The bible Gothics. It is generally said that Ulphilas, a Gothic bishop, who lived in the fourth century, made a version of the whole bible, except the book of kings, for the use of his countrymen; that book he omitted, because of the frequent mention of the wars therein, as fearing to inspire too much of the military genius into that people. We have nothing remaining of this version but the four evangelists, printed in quarto, at Dort, 1665, from a very ancient manuscript." How many of the savage nations have any bible? O, sad indeed. How many of the individuals of the best nations are destitute, or loathe it?

The bible English. The bible of Tindal, who was burnt for heresy! The Jew Jephthah made a burnt offering of his daughter for the demon of war, and the English made a burnt offering of the scholar Tindal to the fell demon of fanaticism. Who was worse?

But the ancients and moderns used the bible for a cloak, then the abuses of this book evidently condemn it as base, demoralizing and degrading.

But mind, man's supreme adviser on earth, would detect all this, had not mind been superseded by a means to be used as a cloak. Take away all such cloaks forever, as the means of superstition and corruption.

It dwarfs the human mind, causing it to be hypocritical, deceitful, designing, clannish.

The bible caricature of the God of the universe, propagates other obvious errors: in giving one peculiar god, it engendered the whole family.

Of what advantage are all peculiar dispensations, when one universal dispensation of creation meets most becomingly, the proper demands of mind?

But that did not suit priest-machinery.

What did all its writers know of any dispensation, when they did not understand the analysis of the mental organization, and substituted the heart for the soul? But if all the bible doctrines be discarded as impeached and protested against, what are we to do then? Do right.

We had at first and have at last, nothing but mind to overcome all difficulties of life, to balance and settle all its accounts.

Wise men look to the powers of mind, to prevent starving in the desert. The compass in the trackless ocean and mighty deserts, enables mind to triumph over all its dangers and appalling difficulties. These are part of the bible of mind. And shall bibles of tradition claim exemption from universal obligations? So far from their being able to stand still in error, science excludes them forever, therefore sectarianism cannot exist.

Would you go to the Indians only having tradition, for exact history, or to exact documents unmistakable. The first demands foolish faith, the last furnish facts and truth. And are Moses and those of his priestocracy, any of his age and time, more competent to give the exact history of just such ages of hunting and shepherd men?

Can these men pretend to advance one iota in the presence of the holy and eternal God-written documents? But they were inspired. They were inspired with false pretences. What proof is there of any inspiration? None at all. Are they present? No! Who then endorses them? None. Then all is a dead letter. Is that dead letter, that false inspiration, to be the world's tyrant in the hands of despotic hierarchists and priestocracies, who are to mould mind as they can mould it? But how account for the rod-serpents of Moses and Aaron, swallowing the rod-serpents of the Egyptians? Moses had only to swallow his conscience, and the people could swallow his lies, as we would account for any lies; and the people of the world will be verdant, to swallow any serpent or fish story that the false priestocracy devise, and make their minds vassals to false pretences. We have only the legends of the first. Mind-jugglery was and is, and ever will be, as long as permitted, a part of the great game of priestcraft, and if any proof is thus advanced, it is that the Jews were greater jugglers than the Egyptians. The God of this universe does not deal in priestocracies or prophets, much less in their jugglery.

The very idea of the existence of a devil, pays too high a compliment to fabulous legends.

Volcanic action is a constituent element of the earth, and gave to the ignorant ancients their idea of hell and vulcan or the devil. But the hell of mind is a place for torment, and the devil is the mortal artificer. Mind then carries within itself the means of its own advancement, or of degradation. It is supplied with elements of happiness, or of much misery.

What science is there that vulgar prejudices do not still prevail to the libel of mind! In natural history, this has been for time out of mind. In ornithology it is so. Migration is one of the greatest characteristics of various birds, but as the small ones are not seen to take their flight, but do it noiselessly, the most extravagant vagaries are surmised to obtain the solution.

If we study nature, and then review our studies, we may become enlightened. Do you believe the bible and practice its precepts? Some affect they believe the bible, but do not practice its precepts. Then that amounts to nothing, worse than nothing, as that already condemns your inconsistency. If you did practice all such, you would be the deepest culprit. You are either for the whole or none at all. Belief without practice, is nothing at all.

Who is accountable in the first five books of Moses?

The one man, the author? Who endorses him? Can anything than mind do that, and as it is rational, not peculiar faith that results, the whole bible is necessarily ruled out, yet the ignorant and corrupt tribunals of the world exclude that, and libel all that attempt it?

Can any author be vouched for as correct, without documents?

As his own witness, the chief of prophets, he is degraded from giving testimony. He has blasphemed his own God buried in mausoleum of prophecy, ch. xxxii., of Exodus, by perjury.

Are the Jews paragons of excellence by their peculiar faith, for all the world to follow after? In what respect do they excel? Superstition or inhumanity?

How do we know anything of the bible miracles?

They say so; the bible says so. But who endorses they say so, or the dead-letter of the bible? If the bible authors are ruled out by perjury, the bible is the perjury.

What are the present faiths of all bibles of tradition, but modifications of pagan mythology? The ignoble proceedings of sophistry to skulk dishonorably paramount questions, produces the agitation of the most obnoxious measures.

We impeach and discard, as the present foundation to much of the world's iniquity, all the bibles of tradition, all the codes of peculiar faith, for reasons that are conservative, virtue's, law's, order's and religion's sake.

The Druids advocated as much as the Jews of their god, forming a peculiar priestocracy. But all the ancients made their god peculiar more or less, relatively to their stage of civilization that is the light of mind.

The Jewish bible and other bibles, as that of the Brahmins, have a considerable analogy.

Which is the copy? What is the world of such bibles worth to mind, that appreciates what is religion?

Bibles of tradition are all founded on one another, or are more or less analogous. The Jew originates the Christian bible, both have their prototypes in the vedas, and Fohi was the eastern Christ.

These two enable Mahometan and Mormon faiths to help agitate the world.

All have to resort to the expedients of the worst falsehoods, else they could not get an existence or be credited by their advocates. All are indebted to pagan false pretences.

What infatuation! That the mind cannot credit a bible of tradition, without it has the most outrageous false pretences of prophecies, miracles and mysteries. What can be a greater lie than gospels? Is not the audience culpable, that fosters and countenances such?

All these false faiths, ungodly perjuries, are indebted to the sword, the brute force of absolutism, or all the insidiousness of sophistry.

The sword of Moses is as conspicuous as his pen, in the propagation of his false pretences.

No wonder this chosen people were rebellious, and hearkened no longer to the peculiar god than compelled. Korah and his compeers saw through the imposition, and so can all not in collusion.

The Koran established a military priestocracy, that was corrupt and administered to the desires of sensualists.

The christian dispensation arose by military despotism over the rights of mind, the usurpation of false faith over the justice of reason. The sword and sceptre of Constantine were united to the sophistry of the priestocracy, to advance it.

Are such books as vedas, korans, and bibles of tradition of ignorant and enslaved ancients, to be the standard of taste for enlightened moderns, constitutional liberalists, of mind that is free? Are these legends to terrify the world from its exact propriety, . by their portraiture of terrible deaths, and misgovern rational beings?

The koran contradicts the christian bible abundantly it is said, and very probably paved the way for their terrible military conflicts for very nearly two centuries, most bloody and disastrous. No peculiar faith can bring peace and religion to the world : that is certain.

All these and all analogous are full of glaring contradictions, inconsistencies, absurdities, and errors. How could it be otherwise, when all started with ungodly perjuries, false pretences, and abominable blasphemies? Will not the enlightened world see all this, after all the efforts of absolutism to crush its exposure, all the devices of sophistry to conceal its felony? The world will expose it, and spare not. Of course, they are not of God, as they give depraved faiths, all necessarily antagonistic. They all are ungodly paganisms.

The Mahometans regard the koran with superstition and awe. They idolize the koran as all peculiar faith advocates do their bibles. They affect that it is supernatural. Why should not the Mormons affect the very same. The most modern has as much right to claims of superstition, as any, while all are in that category. So great was faith-intoleration with the Mahometans, that they sought to burn all books but the koran. But authors have been burnt by the world of faith. Has not the Christian intoleration amounted to odious criminality, when besides, it has sought to prevent the publication of the light of science, by all the practicable and basest proscriptions! Christian, as Mahometan bigots, are as corrupt as any, they are all degraded indeed.

The idol of a world's mind is a bible of tradition, as that has already, by iniquity, procured power, and the first is unquestionabie, because the last is sought to be held as indisputable ; hence the feuds of sects.

It is bible-power, not the simple bible—the priestocracy care nothing for that, means only vulgarized by the pagan minds of the deceived.

The world must cut adrift not only all unions of church and peculiar faith, but all kinds of consequent speculations.

Genius and philosophy are to be housed by this dwarfing monster. As an evidence, all true men of science see that there could be no general deluge at one and the same time, for obvious reasons of philosophy. As basely as Columbus was treated, mind is even worse situated, and all its honest rational suggestions silenced for this demon of credulity, by these ignorant barbarians.

As to the deluge, by the Mosaic account, " The mountains were covered" some five miles high. Whence did these wiseacres get the waters for a universal deluge? From their heaven. the storehouse of their blasphemous lies?

But, says the sophist-bigot, all things are possible with God ! Ask him the abstract question, if the Great First Cause operates by cause and effect in this universe, and he will be compelled, if of sane mind, to respond in the affirmative. Then, as an immutable being, this has been an organic history of the universe. Thus he actually makes his god bend to his bible, and himself to the depraved iniquity.

As the bible resource fails when heaven is put for the atmosphere, that cannot, on all rational principles, overdraw itself; hence this is point blank proof of four conclusive confutations that they knew nothing of creation, confirmed when they put heaven for the rain storehouse, and nothing of a universal deluge that could not come from the atmosphere, inherently limited, as the mighty lever of the Almighty for defined resources and measures of the earth's waters, and all declaring, demonstrating to a conclusive, positive certainty that they knew nothing of miracles, of which they could not of course prophecy, nothing divine of mysteries and enigmas, their pretences, because they would, as plainly caught, supersede natural phenomena, of which they were as now incontestably proved utterly ignorant and most consummately false witnesses.

Are the world's priestocracies now satisfied that they know nothing of peculiar faith, and that they are estopped about all such, and had better, as honest and faithful adorers of God Almighty, close all such bibles that libel him and convict them forever?

Who believes that mankind ever lived much longer than the present race ? Who can affirm that the year was defined correctly in the undeveloped, the barbarous and ignorant ages of antiquity, when science and philosophy were unknown to so great a degree that they stated the earth to have four corners, and of course conceived it to be a vast plane, not revolving, but resting on pillars for a foundation, a firmament, to use their biblical pretences. What did they know of years then on such views, that clearly prove that they had no correct notion of astronomy, when a flat earth cannot make years, that result by motion and revolution of itself around the sun that their ignorant and perjured Joshua made to run counter, thereby involving the statement of years as a perfect non-

entity, when they could not calculate them, having no proper rules or laws, no astronomy for exact computations.

People must have been at first ignorant of astronomical calculations, and reckoned then
by moons.

The science that bespeaks the true yearly period convicts all such tradition as the
veriest pedantry of ignorant second age of men, that is, shepherds, who knew not the
laws of the solar system, evinced by Joshua, &c. and much more by Isaiah and Joh:.
who testified to the falling of the stars.

In all this, the bible becomes thereby self-impeached.

Man has naught but mind and reason that his wisdom recognises in every breath
drawn, and all else about bibles is imposition and fraud upon the world. It could net
have been otherwise when priestocracies had their sway so triumphantly.

The condition of all faiths and philosophy is necessarily the only one deficient, as the
mind was undeveloped. The bible of mind cannot be completed till its rationality is
perfect.

No other bible is competent to lead us, or analyze our true state. Any other just
reverses mind's progress, and renders the last stage of civilization in abeyance to the
second of ignorance and barbarism. The condition of mind itself proves the world yet
destitute of refined civilization and its religion.

What is the difference in the gospel speculations but the worst gambling on false
pretences?

How can you safely rely on man's scriptures, that differ so materially in interpretations? Are any such scriptures worth translation, the thought of interpretation, after
their exposure on exposition?

But you still affirm that you believe the bible. Which, as there are several of tradition? That of Moses. But why not the others? The authority that rules out the
others, or any peculiar ones, is that of supreme principles, that rule out this and all
other such books. They cannot stand, as every page is full of perjuries and false pretences. All such are only the demoralizing expedients of priestocracies that harass
the world, whilst the world has to look to the mighty principles of God, that are silently
available as beings are rational.

But the bible of Moses relates such wonderful miracles about the passage of the
Israelites over the Red Sea, and about the pillar of fire and cloud.

It is you that make the miracles, the pagan wonder, as God has none at all of this
kind. He has no peculiar or other miracles, but universal truths for mind throughout
the universe to receive the benefit. All else is fabrication base.

Had a steamer, with its cloud and column of smoke and its furnace of fire, with its
certain and speedy progress against wind and tide, been discovered at that time, the
ancients would have boasted of a miracle indeed, that could have laughed to scorn all
the pretences of Moses and the whole world of priests that were in collusion to dispossess mankind of their noblest attributes. Yet all this is the triumph of mind and
science over all the boasts of ancient miracles.

Ere long the world will be ashamed to hear of such a thing as a bible of tradition.

What other certainly is language than of human origin or invention? We overlook mind when we come to at learning. Where now are all the sacred deposites,
as arks? Gone the way of all priestocracy's perjuries to annihilation. All their falsehoods could have never had one moment's hold but in ignorant minds, that were self-
deluded, and that most shamefully.

Assuredly these relics might have rescued the poor bibles, that will soon join them,
from the obloquy of perjury.

The bible's creation is nullified by the developments of cause and effect.

Instead of six days for creation, our reverence for the Deity of the universe would
give him, as a perfect being, power at thought not fixed to time.

He spoke most assuredly all such into being as a perfect God, willing the developments from the inherent characteristics. When the functions of an Almighty rest in
eternity, earth does not define his time : mind perverted has dwarfed itself by the
attempt to define creation by pretended inspiration.

In looking to the function of reproduction, all institutions must have virtue and
consistency in the human race.

God's function was creation, that of man is procreation. Their functions are as
separate as God is from man.

For priestocracy to contravene any principles is the deepest blasphemy, and to support it by sophistry is still worse. How libelous is it to affirm that nothing is imposs:-
ble with God, thereby making a licentious and absurd appreciation. All things consistent with God's character are possible.

This world, as one of the exhaustless universe of spheres, presents only a mixed state, fit for a mixed condition of mind embodied; therefore the mind, referring to the soul spiritualized and separated, asks for a nobler sphere.   Death is the universal passport, and the lot of earthly existences by their nature, disproving any bible of tradition assuming that any mortal ever escaped its certain signet.

None can put Moses ahead of the works of the Egyptians, whose pyramid architecture, more than two thousand years past, was the admiration of Grecian historians and philosophers that visited them in person.   They furnish the hieroglyphics before Moses, who was barred in Egyptian hierarchal policy, that, the world over its whole age, is necessarily more or less analogous; Moses then was not, could not be, possibly original.

Nor must we overlook the ancient Persians, among whom the Jews dwelt, thus having opportunities of selection.   If both sides of history be asserted, we shall find that in the ancient circle of best civilization from the Indus to the Mediterranean sea, from Egypt to Persia and India, Chaldea, &c., that the empire of peculiar faith, however diversified, had many analogies of commanding supremacy.   The Jewish could only be borrowed at best.

There were numerous secret associations all over Egypt that had reference to priestcraft.

The trade of India is beyond all historical records of nations that had literature, and Egypt and India knew each other before the time of historical record.   History says so.   They resemble each other in the division of their people into castes.   The ancient monuments of India show its mythology, equally ancient and similar to the Egyptians.   The Indian rocks, enormous works of sculpture, were symbols of an obscure mythology, for which the Hindoos have hereditary veneration.

The Egyptians had hieroglyphics.

Pythagoras introduced into Greece the Indian doctrine of the metempsychosis, one of the earliest of their belief.

In India, it was the first article of faith.

Egypt and India had strong coincidence in mythology.

The Hindoos are as peculiar as the Jews, both surviving the ruins of nations.   The possession of peculiar faith will assimilate the wreck of nations.

The two great divisions of the Hindoos were Brahmins and Sameans, according to the ancient Greeks.

The last is most recent, essentially hostile to distinction of castes, and the exclusive authority of the Brahmins.   They have been extensively, received into Thibet, China, and whole middle and northern districts of Asia.

Schamans denote the priests and sorcerers of middle and northern Asia.

The god of the Hindoos, Brahma, had Menu for his prophet, lawgiver, spirit, creative thought.   The code of Menu is the most ancient of the Hindoos.   Almost the whole of Indian mythology is to be seen hewn out of rocks, sculptured writing, whose antiquity is at least as great as that of any Indian poems now extant.   They have no hieroglyphics, according to Schlegel's History of Literature.   How many centuries did tradition prevail anterior to symbols and hieroglyphics?   Moses is no where among the ancients.   His Adam and Eve are lost in the vista of antiquity—are modernized.

The Phenician alphabet, as those of western Asia and Europe, were formed from hieroglyphics that preceded them, but the Indian alphabet was hardly so formed.   Decimal cyphers had their commencement in Hindostan, a very great discovery of genius.

The book of Menu has proofs of the highest antiquity and perfect integrity.   Jones' opinion gives its appearance of an age between Homer and the twelve tables of the Romans.   Alexander may have seen it.

The idea of a threefold godhead originated with the Hindoos, long before the christians arose.

They had the term, new-born, or regeneration.

What claims have the Jews to priority of idea of their god?   As their godhead is necessarily peculiar, it is a species of priestocracy, which makes the peculiar godhead act and speak at its will.

The Persians acknowledged one God, a good godhead, and an evil one like the Jews.   Was not that of the Jews, like that of the ancient Persians?

The Persians overran India prior to Alexander, and their faith and that of the Jews resembled.

The godhead of the Jews embraced a considerable machinery if we analyze their bible; but the Jews abolished human sacrifices.   They sacrificed, according to their own showing, a host of their own children to Moloch, for many centuries.   Even one of their own judges sacrificed his own daughter to the god of war! The Greeks also abolished human sacrifices, as the Greek Gelon in his treaty with the Carthagenians had an express stipulation, that they " should abstain in future from all sacrifices of men." And so did the Persians, for. their king Darius had also forbidden that.

This pre-eminently proves that mind finally triumphed over the superstition of priest-ocracy in this degradation of humanity. Its full triumph has to come yet. Let Americans will it, as they at once ought, and that triumph will be glorious.

But how much then have the prophecies of the Jews been lauded? In what did they excel the oracles and soothsayings of the balance of the pagan world? In mere asser-tions, and not in their excellence. Bibles do not justify, for all had codes or their bibles. If you have been caught thereby, that is your misfortune. How much have those been caught in the laudation, been victimized from the thousands to Miller and his followers? What avail pretended superior prophecies any more than oracles, if they cannot be deciphered, but befool all that attempt it? The magnificent empire of rational mind must overrule all such pretences, in the fragments of peculiar faith! The observation of national customs, gives some further tuition. The Egyptians embalm-ed their dead, and must have poured an immense revenue to the priests from that source. Living or dying, their dynasty ruled with fearful and ominous supremacy that was most flagitious.

What mighty revolutions are going on among nations, creeds, and localities of those creeds.

Countries that were once Jew, are now Mahometan. Those that were once Chris-tian have been long since Mahometan, as, Armenia, Syria, Egypt, Ethiopia, the Otto-man empire, including a portion of the Greek church still christian. The mighty city of Constantinople, founded by the arch-juggler Constantine, is that of the Mahometans. Egypt has had no less than three kinds of peculiar faith. Their literature is alto-gether perished.

How came it destroyed? Was not this the work of pernicious peculiar faith? The Persian is but little and imperfectly known, except through other ancient literature.

The Jew literature has been rarely subject to exact criticism, as the critics have been afraid to touch it rightly, so great is the influence of the day and time on the side of church and state.

How came ancient mythologies overthrown? All that is accomplished, has been by the light of mind. The balance that is left is by the perversion of succeeding systems of peculiar faith, all to be overthrown by rational religion, in the organic conservative revolutions of the world.

The establishment of most, if not all, has been by the sword; of one of the main ones is especially due the sword of Constantine, who established Christianity as the faith of the empire, and whose vices have been overlooked therefor.

Philosophers were banished from the empire by Justinian, to promote Christianity. All peculiar bibles are smuggled contraband counterfeits.

What are all bibles but the emanations of mind, in every way prepared, adopted, main-tained or rejected?

If those of tradition, they are those of its perversion.

It was mind, though perverted, that decided by the censorship of the Rabbis, what was the bible; and that decides all such bibles are governmental policies.

Bibles are voted on by mind, in caucus, written for the deception of mind by per-verted mind.

Mind interprets and plans, the peculiar machinery.

With what face can any honest man ask to impose the code of ethics of a half civil-ized people in their shepherd state, as the Jews, on whom " Moses, learned in all the learning of the Egyptians," imposed it along with others originally?

With all their learning, what but barbarism could afford the Egyptian idea of a god so peculiar, as having a son by a woman, a perfect incongruity? Why do not philan-thropists and patriots, philosophers and monotheists come out, and teach the people aright? Are the most culpable, sharers of the spoils of the people? or more supersti-tious than they? Wisdom calls for principles, as eternal all the time. Rational mind takes proper cognizance of councils of Nice, and their designs, and exposes them as vile collusions on the world.

Now the god that wrote bibles, or dictated them, positively perverted peculiar minds of the chosen peculiar people.

Mind peculiarly perverted, did all that. If this be denied, let the first be proved, as it ought to be always, for the satisfaction of mind universally. All God's functions are universal.

The world, the universe-marks would prove it—known to all nations, of course; not coincident, but caused.

But the whole was rightly and wisely done at once, at creation; and that disproves all men's bibles.

God's bible is the universe, for mind to study.

But the superstitious fear of hell fire, pious frauds, church power and earthly vassalage, and such influence, hold the dependent mind in bondage on all this subject.

But philosophy decides this subject, and has nothing to do but expose all their bibles! The bible!!

Which of the various bibles of tradition claim this exemption? That of Moses, and its affiliated new testament? Upon what grounds? That of inspiration!

What is the proof? If that proof be truth, your answer must be that; philosophical science has nothing less.

We have to listen to the voice, wisdom, and rationality of philosophical science to prove the God of nature; and we must not drop this absolutely necessary position of philosophy, because it excludes all bibles of tradition at the same time.

Then the bible is only pre-eminent by a greater amount of pious fraud, more successful competition and absolutism. Many affecting to lean to traditional. persuasion, have candidly to confess that they only believe a part of the old testament; and of course invalidating the whole, assuredly including the new testament that depends on the old testament, and has its underpinning knocked from under it.

All bibles of tradition are the base works of priests, and are a part of the machinery of absolute government.

What a tyranny of mind to yield to the bible of any peculiar faith, the power of governing mind about religion, exclusive of reason!

The time has passed nearly among civilized people who are free, that military priest-ocracies or miracle-mongers can trifle or traffic away the senses and liberties of the people. I seek to assail no true bibles.

But you, citizens of the world, claim that the writers of the bibles are inspired. Whom did God inspire?

Each claims a peculiar inspiration as right. Which is right?

The amount of your mutual condemnations, is a sum of moral, social and religious evils. The iniquity of all bibles of tradition is directly proved, their integrity impeached by their self-contradictions, and, above all, by the supreme testimony of nature, the noble representative and exponent of the Creator, who elaborated it with his creative genius, and presides over it most sublimely by his conservative principles, functions and attributes most perfect.

But you interpose that the Jews were a peculiar people, and still are so, though diffused among the nations of the earth. And are not many of the orientals, as the Chinese, Hindoos, Thibetans, also the Gypsies peculiar people too? The last were probably oriental, formerly of Egypt, and are now emphatically distinct from the nations of Europe, among whom they roam and sojourn.

Peculiarity begets peculiar vices, not virtues.

What was behind Moses' works, but the peculiar power of absolutism? There can be no inspiration peculiar, as the only inspiration is that of mind by genius and science, not found in bibles of tradition.

The Mormons have as much authority for their bible, which comes as near to inspiration, as any other tradition.

But tradition absolutely kills inspiration, as they are both antagonistical!

If books already printed were handed man by God, we then might call them God's word.

We require positive proof direct that such could be the word of God, as who but God could endorse it?

All else is perjury. To whom has God's word been revealed? Who can truly endorse that, and swear to it without perjury? Destitute as Moses and all others such were of true science, will you entrust them with the deepest science, that of mind and religion, when they only exhibit peculiar faith, not the shadow, nor its shade? There should be no faltering in this position. All bibles of tradition have kept back all suitable improvements in ethics, whilst we are actually in debt to mind for the sustaining them, when these bibles cause perversions, sophistry and violence to the rights of mind. There is no bible but that of rational mind, and that cultivated in supreme civilization only thus limited by philosophical science. You must take into consideration, who endorses all the bibles of tradition. Their endorsers are perjurers. The education about all such books may be as peculiar and false as they. Mind enlightened on its own trust fund only, can correct it. A liberal rational education always is needed, to meet this world-wide subject, to secure the conservative principles of virtue, to save us best from the malign influences of supposed evil, and prevent society from being disorganized. These bibles offer no advantage any ways equal to, much less independent of principles; and they do not, cannot define principles with an ever watchful integrity.

Enlightened and honest minds disapprove, dissent from, and censure most justly the bibles of tradition, without exception, that are to be accursed by enlightened ages.

But narrow contracted minds can assert with ignorant rashness and impudent reck-lessness, that their particular one is the one of God! They quote blindly that God's word is true. But it is man's word—priests' word.

We are after the facts of the case.

The priests and preachers have played on the sympathies of human nature, and takes advantage of it.

What is the testimony of God on this earth?

Only his works of creation—the universe.

God must prove to us that any bible is his word.

Man cannot prove it, however he asserts it.

Who endorses his assertion? Dupes or hypocrites.

Tradition of unlettered people is not certain—it is not of valid certainty, and can be no testimony of creation. It is any thing else, as its ignorance and error are clearly impeachable. All such tradition was for effect on weak minds. It is the faith and tradition of priestocracies intending to deceive and lie by bibles.

What can all these bibles of tradition inculcate, but the miserable errors of the whole world?

What bible of tradition can compare with the constitution of this Union? What have all these bibles to compare with the moral and intellectual power of the declaration of independence. Is there any bible of tradition, the word of truth? You cannot get at the truth by tradition—that is an impossibility. All historians know this. Consult all savage nations for a direct proof.

If bibles of tradition are true, prove it by the proper documents. That of inspiration proves the bible of Moses. Without proof as it is, bible inspiration is only assertion.

Now, what proves and endorses the inspiration? None!

If God were concerned in the inspiration he would speak, but he is silent, while his works prove all his.

No testimony that contradicts itself, as all these bibles, is valid. There are many errors and absurdities, the grossest falsehoods and intolerable ignorance scattered over the best bibles of tradition.

Can divine writings show any errors and contradictions?

Time, the very best authority representing God's inspiration, has contradicted all and denied their authenticity, and of course has put an end to them all before the tri-bunal of enlightened and honest minds.

All their miracles are fortunately mere mind-jugglery, its most vulgar fictions, else creation would have been ruined, as miracles are destructive not conservative.

All their prophecies are assumptions, and if right are only the analogy of proper sense, but self-disproved by their own clearest perjury. Are these writings those of the authors assumed. Who endorses all such? If not, how were they inspired? Have not these records been falsified? The writers are perjurers.

Do we hear of the thousands of men assuming to be prophets, that were unfortu-nately not authors, and therefore not known? Were not the oracles of the heathen equally in this category? Who are all the authors of bibles of tradition? All are mortals of perverted minds, practising the worst deceptions and falsehoods. Who will commit themselves to such a position? The slave, coward, ignorant dolt and corrupters.

After all the pretended divine command of circumcision exclusively to the Jews, Herodotus asserts, on the authority of Gibbon, that the Syrians of Palestine, who were the Jews, according to their own confession had received from Egypt the rite of circumcision. The best portraitures as drawn by peculiar faith, deform all the bibles of tradition.

The god of Judaism is very imperfect, because those people had but little in the advance of civilization and science of their times. In fact they retrograded, as all such impostors will ever do. The prophecies and miracles of Mahomet were founded on these and the new testament, another emanation, producing a faith that has now one hundred and forty millions of followers.

It is time that freemen should rid themselves of all the fables and legends of antiquity about bibles of tradition, such as all these three, and all the absurdities and impositions entailed thereby as by the Mormons.

The Mahometan faith is destitute of priesthood or sacrifice, but is made of ceremonies and rites, arising from a victorious fanatic, who substituted them for idolatry, and which were confirmed by subsequent wars. He was the sovereign pontiff.
But an available pilgrimage is instituted, as a part of this faith. What does it all avail the pilgrim?
Is there any evil latent in the human mind, any species of passion, any action of fanaticism, that peculiar faith does not arouse or engender?
We have the old, then the new testament, then the bible of Mahomet, the koran, then that of Joe Smith, with many efforts to build up intermediately hundreds of other faiths. Open the door for the first false position, and the whole world is liable to be overflooded without limit and mercy. Bad as the imposition was at the first in the darkest ages, it is degradingly worse now if propagated in the face of mind's progress.
To arrest any one, we must arrest all this felony. Neither age nor custom can legitimatize any of it. The paramount sovereignty of mind and morals, demand all conservative revolution. Moses, and all like him, were ignorant blundering priests, or the tools of priestocracies. The bibles of tradition are to enslave, and have enslaved, not render free and enlightened, but to pale the light, corrupt and demoralize the mind.
Circumcision is a vile custom of superstition and priestocracy, and an absurdity provable by physiology.
Can pseudo-moralists adhere to any exploded and obsolete ideas, because their ignorant forefathers called them the fixed ones of a bible, itself a false pretence from beginning to end?
What higher obligation than that of universal justice, principle and reason, can demand the exclusion of all such? If this be an age of principles and rational light of mind, it cannot be that of any bible of tradition. Any one that opposes this position is a bigot and sectarian.
The bibles of tradition are thought by some to supply food for the soul, but they have not the proper base.
Where, bible tinkers, would be the soul or mind in the mean time, unless it were under the especial providence of God's principles, that are adequate for eternity?
Every mind or thinking faculty, from conception to the time of reaching instruction of mind by its varied rational education, must have its vacuum filled, and that can only be by God. The objects of sense appreciation are all his created works, and can be only recognised from him.
Entirely worthless as peculiar faith when exposed is, yet some pretend that they have found out what philosophy never had and could. Then all their discoveries are certainly worth nothing, for if philosophy cannot recognise it, it is killed dead by its own worthlessness.
Moses, affecting to have God talk face to face to him, cannot be considered less than a perjurer. After all the wonderful fictions, letting the priestocracy lie all it could about the bible, self-condemnation is written on every page. The Jews, by their own adopted history, are portrayed as wicked. They became pirates on neighboring nations, between whom war was almost a trade. They fought among themselves for ages, with civil wars as sets of barbarians, and their peculiar faith figures most conspicuously in this matter. They practised idolatry, and were enslaved often by neighboring nations. They united church and state, to the odious feature of their despotisms.
Idolatry and impiety were constituents of their peculiar faith. The Jews were often in captivity, and suffered for treachery. They became scattered over the world from this cause; vast numbers remained at Babylon and never returned to Palestine. Vast numbers were settled at Alexandria by Alexander.
Many were carried into captivity into Egypt by the Greek king, and many were settled in many Asiatic cities, as subject as the world to universal causes and effects, thereby convicting their bible of perjury.
Why the persecutions of any, especially the Jews?
Peculiar faith answers to all others. Millions have been persecuted for their peculiar faith, for which they were victimized. They have been sadly misused, in nearly all lands, for centuries. It was not the fault of their peculiar faith intrinsically, as it was the misfortune of their position to prevent the impunity. There is the secret of intoleration.
The Jews are merchants generally, incapable of satisfying the world of peculiar faith, rarely seeking agriculture or civil offices. Apply the mildest views, yielding figurative and metaphorical language to scripture, instead of the proper exposition of facts, yet this will expose, by truth and honesty, the duplicity of this foul code of priestocracy. The bible versions give but meagre and diversified accounts of creation, after all the puffs of affiliation.

Their different periods of creation are too essential to be admitted. Can the great differences be the inspirations from God? They are of bibles. The one and the same God cannot differ from himself, however peculiar bibles may be. The adoption of his authority is the admission of his unity, and that decides the utter condemnation of all those different pretences for bibles. They are only apologies for bibles, no more, most conclusively. Their peculiar creations are a peculiar god, of a peculiar earth, and heavens still worse, that can be rolled up as a scroll, and whence angels were driven, where devils were made!

The whole ever proves an abortion, as all have to be renewed, and this idea renders man dissatisfied with his lot, and a miserable skeptic in God's unity, goodness, and perfection.

There are no such monsters, in the God of Nature's creation. None but priestocracies, as blasphemous as ignorant, and both as avaricious, could have originated all these ignoble fictions called bibles.

Shall the Orientals, who made eunuchs and mutilated the body by circumcision, committed unnatural crimes, odious vices, debased the mind, deprived woman of her rights and privileges, with an arrogancy most degrading, that finally embraced the horrible idea of denying her a soul, enslaved freemen to menials, characters so odious, be esteemed masters of morals?

You hear the constant theme of inspiration and revelation from the lips of those pulpit people, who can give you no satisfaction on that, the first and last, the only essential question in the whole subject!

The great question is, whether the account given is the true account? You can make nothing out of all the bibles of tradition, but they are fictions of priestocracies. Some of the names of the authors of some of the books, as the evangelists, are not really or substantially the authors, but fictions, doubtlessly used by the priestocracies.

Some people believe no more than what it is their interest for them to believe. This is too great a subject to have the world deceived in. Are you, citizen, going to entrust to the priestocracy to investigate for you your lifetime, when they originated the whole systems extant, and are bound to sustain the faith collusion at every hazard and by all means?

Is that wise or right? Why do you not all begin to do right at first, dismiss all your blasphemous priestocracy humbugs, peculiar faiths, superstitions, as messiahships? The bible of Judaism distorted God, and defined matters that betray the ignorant position of its writers, as heavens, heart and ends of the earth, the prince of the power of the air. No wonder other priests made themselves familiar with the peculiar god of Judaism, who was so compliant with author priests.

Judaism idolizes priestocracies, and their idolatrous creations. Had this bible been an humble effort to describe God, as mind thus understood him, all had been well, for it had been the only true bible, assuredly the bible of mind; but the God of Nature was caricatured, polluted by priestocracies, libeled throughout nature, in his characteristics. The bible of mind can convince any mind at once, if honest and truthful, and not disgraced and polluted by the craftship.

The bibles of tradition have libeled nature and mind; of course the God of nature and mind.

The gospels were written several years after the events are said to have transpired, by the foster-fathers of the so-called evangelists. Clement is supposed to be Matthew, Eusebius is Paul, &c. The world must get rid of dire false pretences, most detestable bible of tradition heresies, such bible despotisms, such absolutisms of priestocracies, conspiracies against good morals, religion, and the rights of mind, all the low quibbles of social obligations, all the Oriental vassalage of mind.

Jews, you can do the world some good at once, by stopping the false Old Testament, that stops the New Testament, that is false. as well as the koran. and the bible of the Mormons. Freemen, intelligent minds of the world, will you shrink from your religious duty of analyzing your proper position? Let truth and honesty be your motto, if the universe fall. People of the world, can you analyze your position, that of the world?

The bible of mind preaches its own doctrines—satisfactorily. Complex ideas cannot be nurtured much in the savage state ; hence we have the meagre and confused account of the creation, as given by the bible of Judaism.

But you ask for justice to be done poor Moses, who might not have existed, as far as we know, except through the priestocracies. Would Moses know himself, if he were ever on earth, and to reappear? How many different dresses, how many editions, altered editions of priestocracies, have there been about all this affair?

Is it less than hundreds? Are your eyes open yet, citizen? Do not shut them to the pretences of any such faith. If the authenticity of the scriptures is proved, all the world ought to join the church. If not proved, as they are not, most clearly and conclusively, then no falsehood will benefit God, and then all ought to adopt truth and honesty. If the scriptures were authentic, the world could not be chained from their adoption.

When one peculiar faith supersedes another, it is conclusive that the one superseded has radical defects—as the Christian is in antagonism to that of Judaism, the world can see how both are deficient at once.

The bibles admit of constructions, and are most Jesuitical the less carried out in good faith. The new depends on the old, yet supersedes it. Both are negatived by truth.

Bibles of tradition are explained away by each sect.

The bible of mind is progressive as mind, in order necessarily, as we have just commenced exact science.

Such will drive out all bibles of tradition, those of superstition clearly. Now the explanations of such bibles, as advanced by their advocates, are doing clandestinely and partially, what the bible of mind does by conservative revolution, in full, at once, and with the strictest justice to God.

The scriptures require explanation, that is as difficult to many minds. The bible is not consistent with universal good and proper morals.

We charge home upon you, Judaism, for high crimes and misdemeanors, for which we impeach you before a God you never knew, the God of the universe.

Can construction and explanation be scripture, when there are hundreds of ways or systems for them?

Has any people, assuming to be a peculiar people, or not, been greater sufferers than the Jews, as well in Egypt as in Syria and in Palestine, also from the Assyrians and Babylonians, Persians, Macedonians and Romans?

Has not this suffering been, much of it, through peculiar, their peculiar curse—half civilized as they were?

Were not their kings as foolish and corrupt as most of the Orientals at that day—their priests and prophets any less corrupt and degraded?

We are no skeptics, but feel assured, indeed, that we are right, in the great principles of mind, reason, and facts.

Bibles of tradition and their peculiar faith, with their advocates, aiders, abettors, and supporters, giving aid and comfort, have been wholesale murderers in the world, for hundreds of millions of lives.

That a bible of inspiration, that invalidates God's omnipresence and omniscience?

The Jew records were called holy or sacred: what ancient priestocracy's works were not so called, as they named them?

Is any such, is Moses or any such, superior to mind? But the zealot does not like any one to attack the bible. If the bible be true, it can defend itself. If false, it ought to go down, and you, zealot, ought to scorn the upholding such an ignoble perjury.

Sectaries will violate all the principles of logic to reach their faith, which is a mere delusion, as it cannot be a fact; consequently, it is not worth mind's notice, as it is not a fact, and cannot be religion; therefore is the bible a culprit.

But the Word of God is the bible. What bible?

The bible of tradition, bible of Moses? That is the bible of peculiar faith; that is of course not religion; hence not a true bible. The bible of mind is the only bible, and monotheism is the only religion. There can be no other. But that peculiar bible declares that the devil and all his angels shall not prevail against God. For that reason we declare for God alone. Let perverted people seek to be devils and their angels, we will reverence God alone.

The bible of tradition is framed in contradiction to God's attributes and principles that are in common to man's nature, that is common, not peculiar.

The bible of tradition makes all but the chosen people the heathen, the outside barbarians; yet all are the children of the God of nature. Mention anything of the bibles of tradition, and the advocates can see no error. Bigotry has closed their understanding. The pulpit people preachers and priests leave off where they ought to begin, for they have but this one sermon to preach, the full and satisfactory proof of the authenticity of the scriptures. The balance will preach themselves.

Moses was skilled for his side, of power. Was the Jewish nation of any respectable standing among the nations of the earth? Was it not reputed for extreme superstition?

Search the scriptures! How absurd to think that these scriptures could delineate the God of the universe, who fills all space! Analyze, by mind the most cultivated, this exhaustless subject, and if at any time hence you find an error, amend it before the proper tribunal of mind, that all creation should not stop from being corrected, unlike the bigoted priestocracy's bible that interdicts correction!

The chief thing of all bibles is the proof. If you expect us to believe the scriptures, we demand of you to prove them, honestly in good faith, beyond a doubt, or never to utter a word about them afterwards, as you are an impostor if you do. We can be no skeptics or doubters, when we speak knowingly that all such are conclusively false. As to any supposed deists, who have failed in their whole duty, being alarmed at death, that does not prove anything for you or your bibles, that if true, would have anticipated and counteracted all that. Why, sophists, can you not drop your small artillery, your petty calibre puerilities?

We rely on God alone, in life and death. On whom else can the world rely? Prove your position, or be silent. If you prove your position, with Christ and God on your side, you need not fear at all.

But if you take Christ, and do not prove, as you cannot, any connection with God, assuredly your position is miserable. You have no documents to uphold you! Where are you now? Do you know? If you do not, you ought earnestly to investigate. God could not be particularly identified to one spot of earth or one globe, much less one people, when he is universally identified with creation, as he is the God of nature.

The Jews suffered, after all their priestocracies, peculiar faith, and false systems, deeply and horribly as a nation. Their god is made peculiarly vindicative, furious and wrathful by the Jews, as other peculiar gods. Here seems more policy than principles, that characterizes their actions. They did not comprehend the dignity of the God of nature, as the only safety is universally in principles that vindicate themselves.

The time-serving bigots will pretend, if cornered, that they do not understand this bible of Moses. Do they understand principles, truth, or honesty? Where are the hundreds of thousands of people who are said to have seen the law delivered to Moses? Who endorses them? None! Then all are pretences, the worst sort of false pretences. It is not for a bible, but for religion, safety, greatness of satisfaction before the God of nature, that I write. And if this bible of tradition be a true one, let it stand on fair and honorable terms, for truly were it the word of God, man's word could and should not prevail against it. Bibles of tradition cannot be the guardians of the world, nor can be the functionaries of priestocracies.

God of the universe is omnipresent; that is, he fills all space or presides over it by principles that represent him. His residence radiates from the centre of purity, and comprehends the centre of power and intelligence.

Rational beings must come to the conclusion very clearly, that the old writers of the bible, so far from being inspired and knowing about the future and happiness, did not know truly the affairs of earth for their time, and least of all, of science. Inspiration implies a perfect knowledge of all that is to be communicated, in all its particulars. All this is above criticism, as it is above correction. It partakes of the divine nature, and is as perfect as God's perfection can make it.

The scriptures have no virtue if the essential foundation is false, as all is of any peculiar faith.

The bible people spend their life about an obsolete book of exploded doctrines, intended for imposition instead of science.

Judge of these so-called revelations according to their merits, and they are worth nothing at all. What do they reveal? any science? Nothing can contain more falsities than the gospels.

Figure or metaphor will not express their character, nor avail the advocates who affirm to explain away the whole, or much of it, as figurative or metaphorical. On that basis, the whole bible can be explained away jesuitically; therefore, let us consider and meet all as really intended, on the pure, proper principles of truthful logic the most satisfactory of all.

Had God revealed himself in any bible, as he has, he could have called himself no less than the God of the universe. But as ignorant men wrote it, they call him the God of a peculiar earth!

The world has pirated on the example of this book, by popes' dispensations.

Is the bible of tradition, or that of mind best capable of directing aright, the proper faculties of the soul?

What is the soul, without mind? Both are identified—not with the bible of tradition surely, that cuts down mind.

Bibles of tradition, as the arms of absolutism, are of design, upon mind and its rights in the world.

All the bibles of tradition are worthless, totally so. They tell us that the bible is the word of God. As such, we feel bound to require proof. Is it so? What is the word of God? The commencement of God's bible is truth, and that would tell that the God of nature is the God of the universe, not of one world and its hemisphere of heavens with all others lights, for the earth. All descriptions of God's language and appearance are all false. There is none able to give a full description of him on this earth; consequently there can be no truth in any bible of tradition, as it begins in ignorance and ends in perjury! What is a greater enemy of all righteousness? What produces worse temptation and example from doing that which is right? Action justifies pure foundations, and condemns this. Does it teach sinners to make white their robes in the grace of God? In God's righteousness? Any other is counterfeit, either a peculiar god or his peculiar messiahs. Mind that is enlightened does not wish to know what the bible tells, as the priests tell who wrote it. One jot or tittle of all such faith credulity cannot stand the test of reason.

But what a spell of superstition binds the world!

Some would not disbelieve in a devil for all the world, and yet all the world could not prove a devil to exist! The belief of a devil does not keep people out of penalties, nor the jails freer from culprits, but helps to render the world worse.

God did all things as seemed best to him, but the bible of tradition makers did not and never can do more than botch and tinker. Their bible may tell us of some things, but its extinction is preferable to all their dogmas. It had better be left out, than put in. It deceives the world, most seriously. The God of our fathers is claimed by all filial and affectionate children, but the advantage is taken of them as by hunters who imitate the cry of the young, to inveigle the mothers.

Let all analyze, and they will see that it is to know the God that created the race of our fathers. We are indebted to that woful state of public prejudice, for these bibles of tradition. The first ages recognised were corrupt, as any were. We can concede indulgence to their abstract pretensions, but not superiority as the adoption of priestocracy scriptures imply. Let us all aim to be right, and we are obliged to see the old testament fall, and of course, most assuredly the new does for the sins of both. The sins of the scriptures are the deepest of all, through their authors. You add to them if you make yourself subject to their pretences.

· Can we not add to the scriptures? We must discard them. The bible of mind as wise laws, may be then advanced. Any book that claims to be sacred and has no such proof, has to be closed by the command of truth and reason, God's vicegerents. The world would speak rightly to the Jews, but for its own superstition. What can the bible of the Jews tell us, of moment to the world? What of philosophical sciences, does it communicate? What of all the ancient race of the world? Did it know of but three small parts of all five, of the whole world? As far as it missed the world's geography, so far did it miss the true principles of religion. All the bible advocates are bound in the first place to give their hearers undoubted proof of its authenticity, especially in the old testament. In the second place they should prove satisfactorily, how the devil could have been made, compatibly with the purity of their heaven and the perfection of the God of their heaven.

In the third place they are bound to prove a sufficiency of prophecy in the old testament on the most undoubted purity, written at the time, and properly preserved without alteration to the proper time, that warrants in the fullest comprehension the whole matter beyond doubt or equivocation. The very object of bibliocracy of tradition was to deceive the world, both in conception and adoption. Potentates of the earth have so conspired. Mind only needs a proper audience of mind, to eradicate the false impressions. In the first ages of orientalism, when mind was abject, allegory was considered useful, but since age has become more refined, and mind is entrusted with its rights, in the name of God let it resume all properly.

The bibles of tradition cannot remove the sins of the world; it is mind that must act. What proof is there, of all bibles of tradition? It cannot be given, at all.

The assertion of Moses or his dramatists, is no more than of other irresponsible falsifiers. All is the work of priestocracy, for the worst of purposes. All cannot hold a respectable hold in decent society, when mind's rights are audited. If there had been any prophets especially of Christ, all would have been accurately and exactly told. If God had inspired, that inspiration would have been correctly defined. God would have had an appropriate bible representing intellect and power, and most perfect. But the stupid priestocracy did not understand that their bibles superseded mind, their messiahs and peculiar gods superseded God, their peculiar faith superseded religion, all their peculiar creation superseded the creator's. What was so plain before them, that time was God's prophet, and that wise minds could anticipate it only on principles that define prophecy a false pretence in conception, a perjury in conclusion. Will the moderns stupidly put on the cast-off mantles of the ancients? Do we know the true history, from these oracle-monger priests and kings, all in collusion before the people? What was the dynasty policy, was easily spoken by the mouth of the priestocracy who assumed to have the mouth of their lord, the most available mouth-piece the world ever used, who was a peculiar god, became very peculiarly pliant in the hands of the dramatists. This was the great idol of priestocracy—now of the world. The bible of tradition makers are falsehood propagators. The peculiar opinion of the Jews being the chosen people of God, made them sinful indeed. It was all political speculation, their eyes on other people's possessions, their priestocracy hands in the Jew pockets. the Jews seeking to fleece the world, their priests fleecing them all the time. Did the Jews show themselves particularly worthy in breaking their covenant, worshipping images, sacrificing their sons and daughters to them to be devoured? How like the most degraded savages, no less than cannibals! We perform a mercy to them, and all such, to relieve them of their numerous contradictions.

But we are constantly met by questions, What will the world do for bibles? That is really bible-mania. Murders flourish, when laws permit, bibles or no bibles, and so of other vices. An increase of power, results in remedial means. When peculiar faith prevails, repudiation flourishes. Where are the morals? What protection is any bible, if wise laws do not sustain society? Did bibles protect the Jews? The world from inquisitions? But then the French revolution showed the horrors of no bible! It reflected the brutality of bibles. That proved that mind had been crushed and brutalized by the three most powerful arms of absolutism, monarchy, church and soldiery. Look back comprehensively, not partially—that is not fair.

This was for want of mind-cultivation of the whole people—religion, order and law. Civilization and religion go together. It is not man's bibles, but God, who is above all, that we seek to appreciate.

In regard to the French Revolution, much of it was involved in the mighty conflicts of masses, brutalized by bible sophistry and despotism, that, pent up by absolutism for centuries, broke loose the other way into licentiousness.

The world has been treated as an overgrown animal, not as mind at all. Hush! do not speak against the bible. No, not of God. That is, of the universe.

But the Jews' peculiar god could not fill all space, for he was absent at man's peculiar fall, so absurdly related—the most to be pitied of all when he found it out—and present at a nonentity's creation, a peculiar heaven and earth. As a god of tradition, he is among the obsolete things of tradition. All this requires the foolish consent of mind, brought about by the artful duplicity of perverted mind.

Who can have implicit faith or confidence in any bible of tradition? Who can have as much in the writers? Who could endorse them? Ignorant men, yea, very ignorant priests, wrote these books; they were priestly inspired writers. The light and philosophical science of mind and bible of tradition, will not do to mention together the same day. It is pollution to connect them together. But what, for a code? If your rational mind, your country's institutions and righteous laws do not furnish, aided by all the benefits of rational education, go to the wild Indian chiefs that are the most refined in mind of forest growth, and ask them for the constituents of society. Why should the world have the peculiar faith of priestocracies, when its society is swindled thereby? Those who are wise, can see why the need of inquisitions, to uphold their iniquities.

They need all the tools of the world in their ignoble machinery of superstition, that damns the world and mind.

I impeach and discard the scriptures for various reasons: that they are most contradictory, rest on false pretences, and are most demoralizing, anti-religious. Among their many pretensions, a foul libel, I mention that there is no devil, and, of course, no local hell in God's universe, whatever there might have been in the Jewish peculiar superstition. This is proved: that no people can be chosen and peculiar on earth, without making their god and their scriptures surely peculiar, and all of no account, proving the whole a despotic polity to manage a defrauded people. Which is worse, for the world to denounce a thing without investigation and analysis, or adhere to their own explosions? But the scriptures are important, they fulfil an important point. That is, they sustain bigots. What use is there for me to go on with my bible opposition, you will say, as the world must believe in some faith? I go on to help promote rational faith. But what opposition to the bible is effectual? The intelligent patriots of the land know, but you cannot appreciate it, because your bigotry has no reason. Lay aside your bigotry, and then you will see what religion is. I reject all bibles of tradition on account of religion, to get rid of their peculiar faith—to reach the pure and essential demands of mind. But infidelity is a robbery. It is indeed to God, therefore all such bibles should be positively excluded. With the triumphs of innocence the purest, we extricate ourselves out of wholesale errors, or the perpetual cause of them, the bible of tradition.

But this is an extraordinary work. It is an extraordinary imposition, and should have extraordinary proof, or be discarded by the advocates, who should have extraordinary silence and retirement.

Some people's minds are so perverted that they cannot rid themselves of sophistry, so degraded that they cannot extricate themselves out of their bigotry.

If religionists, men must discard peculiar faith and all its heresies as bibles of tradition, and adopt that of the bible of mind. While the world is full of public improvements, it is a shame that this most important subject should be kept in abeyance. This is the age of reform and conservative revolution.

Analyze, for no bigots have ever yet investigated this whole subject. We ought to abolish all bibles of tradition, as absolutely abridging and restricting the proper means of mind to improve the creation funds of religion. The bibles of tradition can never be the standard of what mind ought to reverence, as they have no proper constituent elements for the world's peace and happiness!

But instead of extraordinary proof, we have extraordinary imposition by the peculiar scriptures. What is mind for, but to expel and not receive all such impositions? No wonder that the priestocracy arrogate that faith is not under the domains of mind, else they would have been blown long ago, sky high!

The only thing you have to decide is, as to any scriptures being peculiar; if so, as they clash necessarily with one another, and with that of mind that is universal, then they are hopelessly corrupt and to be discarded.

The mind has to respect universal, not peculiar principles, that do not exist. The ancients knew not the principles of astronomy, and betray themselves by the grossest ignorance of placing the stars in the firmament, which firmament was not ether, but a firm work for mere light to the earth, instead of their being the suns of solar systems, having their own planetary and cometary orbs revolving round them in beautiful harmony. It is worse for the world to be mastered by peculiar bibles, than to be ruled by the decrees of imperial Rome. It is taken for granted, because of the assertion about the holy scriptures, that all is true, unquestionably so, that it is the word of God. These two things are potent and talismanic; but when we affirm that God does not entrust his sacred word to priest's hieroglyphics, or to man's writings, any contingency, but in his own adorable keeping in the immortal, everlasting works of the universe, we are met by the supposition that God has not left anything less. But suppositions that have blasted the world so often, will not do. We must have facts, or the bible-pretenders must be forever silent on this world-wide subject.

The facts are demanded in vain. But the brass and stupidity of the imbecile mass have outlived their exploded bibles. They did not know that they have no bible in truth or fact. Their bible is a contingency, and bears unmistakable evidences of man's works, as it is liable to be lost, erased, misinterpreted, mistranslated, not preached from, after being made out of priests' lies from beginning to end. But how do we know the facts of any history, as history? All that is accredited and approved as national archives, exempt from doubt or suspicion, and free from the least improbability, presented us by those whose authority is unquestionable, and whose veracity is unimpeached, can be considered history. But none is history that convicts itself by the facts of science and philosophy as violation of both, that runs counter to nature's truths, reason's and principles' laws, and when its faith sneaks out of reason's court. This is the case with every bible of tradition. But the stupid objector foiled in supporting the bible of tradition, affects that in a court of justice one hundred years hence, when there is no living witness present, after a man was convicted, on the proper testimony of witnesses, of murder, and executed, that we may not have any better evidence than the bible.

If kept as a matter of record, most safely in the clerk's office, it would be correct history; but otherwise it would be only tradition, and estimated in worth accordingly.

Has the bible this position of record, faithful and true above suspicion? No! for if kept sacredly in a proper deposit from the time of the pretended Moses, it would kill itself, from the reason that it has impossibilities of miracles, prophecies, mysteries, and peculiarities proved to be perjuries.

But, says the simple advocate, hundreds of thousands of people saw Moses receive this gift of God! If all this was anything more than their peculiar god, who proves or endorses that now? None. Yet as God-gift, it requires God-proof, but gives none. Then it is untrue, false as fiction can make it. But the bible advocate begs for time to prepare for all the defence of the old bible, his ability not furnishing more argument, and his circumcised superstition still urging him on.

As much time as he may have as needed; but does he do anything further? How can

he, when the thing is impossible? But the bible is God's word! Then of course
God is the witness. But all this is utterly denied, for the God of nature does not
answer, and is clearly libeled by its caricatures!
. Freemen of America! to you especially is entrusted the sacred deposite of mind, as
much as to any free nation
    Give it its legitimate scope, and its holiest capacity.
    Other countries make it penal to declare the facts.
    Arise, freemen, and declare the true independence of mind, over all bible dynasties!
The authenticity of the bibles of tradition is the main question.
    The very moment that inspiration or tradition is announced, they are to be investiga-
ted. What miserable morals prevail in the world, to preclude the mind of children
from investigation of all bibles, and permitting a correct decision! All errors should be
corrected on rational information, not the correction prescribed by inquisition, nor
sneaked from by evasions.
    What could we expect from slaves, of Egyptians, Babylonians?
    The Jew books affecting prophecy were vindictive, very naturally, against these people.
Was it from Babylon that they got the idea of Babel, that was built for astronomical
observations? Were they so ignorant as to be quizzed as to its real use, and most absurdly gave the story of its causing the dispersion of nations and diffusion of language
on the earth, when those were from the most obvious processes of nature?. Was their
law formed after return from captivity? Did they not lose their laws, records, institutions, and even language, and adopt much of the eastern people? Are they not indebted
to them for their legends about the devil, whom they have exalted to a direct and successful antagonism with their peculiar god? What has the civilized world to do with
all their absurd superstitions, when it has to recur to rational religion that never was
theirs, by their own story?
    Are these people to be considered peculiarly interesting, over and above the balance
of the world, the hundreds of millions of people who flourished at their time?
    Was it a just Creator of all, to separate the Jews from all mankind? The Jews did
that, not God. God of nature would have destroyed all such at once, by their amena-
bility to destruction. In the east they had two geniuses, a good and evil one. What
was easier for them to manu-and-mind-facture from these prototypes? They must have
copied from some source, as they had not science to originate the true position. Their
bible is an extraordinary doctrine, that derives more notice from the character of mind
of its advocates, than from its intrinsic truth and virtue. But the proof of its authenticity is a stumbling block. Man should have a proper code of life, and he certainly
should be prepared to meet the summons of death, come when it may; and appropriate
the best of days to his proper improvement of mind. Ours should be a wise action in
life. Now we have not the first proof of the bible what is the safest to be done!
    But the people are good nevertheless, all the time.
    How is this? What shall we do for a bible, if this be discarded? and yet it has not
been raised to the dignity of proof, of truth! What an imposition!
    All its authorities for proof are mere assertion, and no proof!
    We willingly meet all offers for proof.
    What a contemptible position for mind to survey!
    Its bible no bible, but a collection of books of imposition. Its god a peculiar god,
known only to the Jews.
    Its heaven so impure as to cause its angels to rebel, and to become devils; and its
messiah affecting to cast them out on earth!
    The bible of mind presents the sublimest of all positions in the universe. It regards
the perfection of God the Creator to radiate perfect purity, as God is a perfectly pure
being, therefore a pure soul or beatific aspirant before such pure presence never could
become a devil.
    Revelations, ch. xii. v. 7, &c., to 13, prove themselves anything but the truth, ema-
nating from the God of the universe. They would be a base libel.
    Shall bibles of tradition be paramount to religion?
    Let us have no juggling for bibles.
    Give no gratuitous assertion, or stop; arrest all the false pretences continually grow-
ing up therefrom. Analyze, do not take for granted, merely because peculiar domestic
education and impulse cause it. But you say none must contradict the bible of tradition.
Can any but the vassal of the priestocracy say that? You must have faith that is
blindness of belief, a fruitless nothing, credulity.
    But the bible of tradition bigot pretends that mind cannot conceive of a God; that it
is left to conjecture about his attributes, and one's own soul.
    This sophistry is the most shameful, false pretence.

If there were no universe, this absurd pretence might be advanced.

In the first place, the best and only positive proof beyond doubt is the self-existence of the Great First Cause, and his attributes are only proved beyond doubt by his works; and the soul aspires to be equal in existence, and to have universal sphere of action correspondent to its relations with the Creator. Whereas, bibles of tradition are all priest robbery, pretences and imposition, and their contents are trash, and ruin the state of the people, unless beneficially corrected by God's greatest gift, man's guardian, mind. A majority of the Jews seem to have had no moral principles about them, according to their own books, their peculiar bible. They become degraded by superstition that is enough to ruin any people in the world, when the bible makes it imperative on all the nation. How glad the world should be to escape such a despotism!

What did these people know? Let the statement of Nehemiah disclose.

Here is one evidence of their intellectual stupidity.

Nehemiah, ch. viii., v. 9: "And Nehemiah and Ezra said unto all the people, This day is holy unto the Lord your God, mourn not, nor weep. For all the people wept when they heard the words of the law." In ch. ix., v. 27, he says, the Levites speaking to God of the Jews, "Thou gavest them saviors." The Jews were not so stupid to misinterpret this sentence, whatever such words may mean with others. They have learnt that there are some things that will not pay. All patriot minds should be resolved that no bible shall impair the rights of individuals to rational religion.

The bible of peculiar faith is not true, and the world ought to know it. But who has thought of all that? Why have not the clergy, the priestocracy taught all this? It was theirs to teach the belief in, not the untruth of superstition in this form.

What confidence, now, can be placed in a world full of all such, where constant deception is practiced?

Better have no bibles of tradition, that afford bad faith, hardly fragments of good faith.

The world is creeping on to its rights, through the energies of mind. "Lord John Russell has again introduced the bill to allow Baron Rothschild to take a seat for London, by removing Jewish disabilities." The peculiar god of the Jews talks familiarly with Satan, who talks in Job as defying this god. We must recollect that in this great eastern country there are yet devil worshippers. Mind was there undeveloped; and yet, if we believe the bible, everything was peculiarly great in this peculiar country. Solomon was the wisest, that is, if their prophets and priests had not been the greatest falsifiers on the face of the globe. Singular as it may seem, yet truthful analysis tells, that the bible did the devil's lying, that is, the priestocracies.

But how will we get over the difficulties for want of this peculiar bible, for oaths and marriage? Let a proper legislation establish a suitable law for both, affirmation in the first, and a solemnization of the last by a magistrate. Never hereafter, whilst in my senses and freedom, will I swear on any such book. I desire no marriage by any priestocracy. All such must be civil.

After all the boast of the Jews, where is the ark of the covenant, the particular select spot of their peculiar god? Where else is it, but gone after that peculiar god who only existed in the delusions of the people, and the shameful impositions of their head men priests, pretended prophets and ignorant kings? After all the advantages of the Jews with their peculiar god, their pretended prophets and self-appointed priests, with all their peculiarities of miracles, they were the worst off actually: much worse than the present nations of the world, that begin to use the better developments of mind, and with whom they could not begin to be compared.

It is the necessary result of undeveloped mind, that miracles or wonders prevail in all first ages, which premise mind's ignorance of the common principles of science. The more miracles and prophecies are tolerated, it may be conceded the more superstitious are the recipients.

When all such are excluded, then the world begins the best proper maturity of mind's development, civilization and religion. Then rational mind begins its existence to some purpose. The receivers of such superstitious relics are as bad as the original barbarian inventors. What can the moderns promise themselves from ancient Jew pagans, but to continue pagans themselves? How much can the slaves of Egyptian superstitious masters teach the moderns? Their subsequent history does not lend any charm to this obscure and low-rated nation, that pirated upon other nations, as all of antiquity did, when they had the power. After their improvement by seventy years captivity at Babylon, granting that they brought back the best code, their present bible, were they still half civilized, even half as civilized, or as great as their masters? Advance much beyond their very best, still it is an incongruity to establish stay-laws of mind-development by such preposterous explosions.

The world asks in vain from an impudent priestocracy, who are more brazen than their own Satan and Belial in the pulpit, for one single evidence of proof, that this bible, bad as it is, is an inspired book.

There is but that sermon to preach, and because it cannot be delivered, are all to be damned ?

Will the preachers seek by such books of tradition, to violate the conservative principles of the world ?

This question involves the peace, dignity, and safety of mankind. This is one of the world's great evils, brought about by perverted minds of the priestocracy, and as such, ought to be abolished, not continued, by enlightened mind.

But conservative revolutionists may commit any sin, but correct false bibles. The only proper correction is their exclusion ; nothing less.

Why not alter the balance of the universe, as well as this earth ? The last covenanters could have permitted God the Creator to alter that, better than being in a messiah, but then the speculation in their creations could not have been carried on : the priests were after the profits.

Common honesty would have accepted God's gift pure, better incomparably so, but this was not the policy of the sapient priestocracy, who were after the rule of the world, no matter how devised, how much the popular mind was agitated all the time therefor. Although the developments of mind have exploded the whole of all peculiar bibles, even if there were a million of them, although astronomy demonstrates the sun a million of times larger than the whole earth, still they would wish to stop him by their earth, to show out the powers of their order. The best powers of genius and mind, its noblest characteristics, reason, truth, and honesty, have been made to bend ignobly, to their infamous assumptions.

As man's work, they are amenable to supreme laws. As a nuisance, it must be treated as such.

In recognising the authenticity of religion, the diversities of peculiar faith, the counterfeit will be variously presented, but never under any of its disguises to be received by a rational age of the civilized world.

The whole, modern or ancient, is paganism, and can be no other. The names may be altered, but the thing itself cannot be changed.

Adrian erected a new temple at Jerusalem, which he dedicated to Jupiter. Which was less pagan or heathen, his or the one of Judaism ? But the Jews spoke of their god. The universe knows no such pretence, any more than the local Jupiter. The most rational analysis knows no difference in paganism. Now, if there be a superiority, all the advocates of such bible are bound on every principle of honor to prove it. The Jews claim that their god was familiar with their patriarchs, men of low character ; now the God of the universe cannot be thus known by the best of men, for his principles only introduce mind most rational, and that through the audience chambers of the universe, consequently the Jews have no claim to be respected as truthful, and their bible, their mouthpiece, is conclusively a false pretence, a book of perjuries. They or their modern endorsers cannot escape this dilemma. If the last wish to escape the ignominy, they have to renounce the Jew perjuries. This is clear analysis. I only expose or discover what was written.

In the creation of the devil, or adopting him from the east, Moses puts his own mind as Belial in that category, and exposes the peculiar god's inferiority, but characterizes the whole as a pigmy creation, the priestocracy included. Religion acknowledges no such. The progressive developments of rational mind, exclude all of satanic creations as those of superstition.

The peculiar bible writers did not understand language nor the sciences to which it applied, and libeled mind, woman, and the god of both.

What thanks have they to such abominable absurdity, palmed on mankind by their standard ?

Rational mind challenges the essential proof of any real fall of man.

Mind must have supreme cultivation, in all the rational education of excellent civilization, to be properly right. The mind of mankind becomes the agent of impressions from infancy, as education, rational, peculiar, or mixed, directs as psychology teaches.

As man's fall is all an absurd fable, an afterthought of base speculators, what atonement was necessary ?

All peculiar faith doctrinists are supporters of this false position, but as they are not disinterested witnesses they cannot be believed. They are reckless to establish it, as they are otherwise cut out of their vocation, but as honesty is the best policy, they had all better stop at the proper time, that is now, ere they excite the deepest execrations of an injured world.

Sin is an evil, the negative of good, and is a necessary incident to perverted free agency of mind, that has to build up its future state by its own exertions on the substantial materials furnished.   If mind act rationally, conservation results, but perversion engenders evil and premises elements of destruction.

The logic of priestocracy is sophistry.   A bible cannot be history; it is religion.   If not that, it is no bible at all.   Bible faith is not religion; that is positively true.

All the church and the kingly governments kept the secret, the mystery, dark as those affiliated, besides which, proscription's powers of brute force, and all the machinery of corrupt society and corrupt books, were brought to bear.   The dynasty of the bible has thus been kept in the ascendancy.   Genesis, ch. xxii., v. 11. "And the angel of the Lord called unto him out of heaven, and said Abraham, Abraham; 12. For now I know that thou fearest God."

Can this book-assertion be endorsed, when the trial had to be made ere God knew Abraham?   This after-knowledge kills the book and peculiar god.

It is the part of the public to suffer the greatest outrages by their unprincipled cliques. Have you, freeman, investigated all necessary?   No.   Why?   The pulpit people tell me, and that is enough!   Do you hear the other side?   These pulpit people tell us that we must not even read such books, if we do we are gone.   Do you belong to the pulpit people, who alter all their pulpit bulls, sophistry and edicts?   Are you and they afraid of the truth?

Is not all this the wicked trick of the priestocracy?

Are you freeman, and act thus?   But as a slave or minion of other slaves of opinion, you decide wrong against science, and of course humbug yourself and the world.

But the immortality of the soul could not be known without the bible!   What a pretender and usurper is that, which is indebted to mind all the time for existence.   An ungrateful parricide to its parent.

Did not Socrates know as much of the immortality of the soul as Peter?   But Socrates sacrificed a cock to Æsculapius, and Peter sacrificed his truth and honor before the cock crew thrice, if the gospels are taken.   How does the bible prove itself?

But they were killed by bible perjuries and must be buried.

What can bibles of tradition avail—peculiar faith avail?   They have been upheld in their various forms the priestocracy's ages, by not only the despotism but the venality and felony of criticism.

Moses did not know of any but a peculiar god of his peculiar people, but of what benefit would all such be to us?   As to revelations, John was visionary.   He was dreamer agent to the priestocracy, in all of whom there is no truth.

He only saw the peculiar heaven of such peculiar god; of course he never saw the universe residence of the God of the universe.   That was a little beyond his visions, and those of his brotherhood.   In the last there could not enter any sin, much less come out any devil, much less would God create a devil another God as the god would identify himself therewith.   This is no figure or metaphor.   We take the bible as it is in all its peculiarities, and the God of the universe in all his universalities.   All peculiar bibles require peculiar faith sophistry for the credulous, or all must die.

When we cut loose from bibles of tradition, and all their inherent evils, we seize necessarily on the basis of principles.   You cannot stand still in science, you must advance all the time; but the old bibles stand, fall back, exploded—all terminating as mortal emanating from mortal—yet all their aiders disgrace themselves about them.   You should hold yourself ready to be convinced on the facts of the case.   We perceive how the world has suffered by bible psychology, as one can have an influence or impressions on another's mind, when the last is in a particular state of passivity: all this is certain, and cannot be doubted, by any rational mind investigating.

The doctrine of Moses ruined the Jews, by severe, rigid superstition; giving more attention to little forms, rites, and ceremonies, than to substantial principles.

What miserable, degrading, stupid ignorance is presented, if this bible be now referred to our moral code.

Its visionary themes present endless controversy—not of mind in its sublimest conceptions.   The whole is puerile.   But cultivated rational mind cannot believe in the bible!   It is no hypocrite, and is it to be condemned therefor?   Is there any justice, in all such?   Many test a faith by the adoption of popularity at the time, of custom, public opinion.

Destroy only bad doctrines, confirm that which is correct.   Is the bible true?   Who has seen it proved?   But we have been taught all this from our infancy, the result of impressions and peculiar education.   No true principles clash; if they do, one is not a principle, or improperly stated.

No correct bible and rational religion clash; if so, that bible is wrong.   Ezra took it

upon himself, it is no doubt, to alter the bible.   All ancient nations had their romances
—each sought to excel by ancestral origin.
   All books are as fallible as their authors.   All that seek to advance on humbugs are
most fallible.   There was a faulty position, in revealing to a few minds, or peculiar people, when the greater benefit would redound to the whole by the direct revelation.   This
was the idea of undeveloped mind.   All God's revelations are to the whole of rational
minds, graduated to intellect and its relative improvement.   The height of free moral
agency is elegantly thus carried out.   Had the Jews received any peculiar inspiration
and revelation from the God of creation, their prosperity physical, moral and intellectual,
would have afforded comments to the receiving world, which could not have been kept
back from adoring this peculiar people's god.   But true analysis strips them of all this, and
exposes the vile imposition.   Their peculiar god, if omnipotent, would have caused them
to conquer the world, instead of Palestine.   What a pitiful and cumbrous machinery this
peculiar inspiration was, that proves its destruction, from its inherent elements.   The
scriptures are not only under the clearest suspicion, but they are impeachable for ignominious falsity.   They have no doubt been edited in direct reference to all subsequent
criticisms practicable.   .
   All this was for the protection of the interests of the priestocracy, no matter the
means, if plausible to the people.   Policy, not truth, was consulted.
   The support of the present day is an heir-loom of priestocracy, linked in with society,
around which the spell of superstition is most clearly woven, and it takes gigantic efforts
of the people to rescue mind therefrom.
   But the bible hath internal evidence of non-appreciation of God and his works, that
kills it dead, to all good purposes.
   We are unbelievers necessarily, from the nature of the case, when reason is contradicted, and not alone reason, but truth.
   Palestine had idolatry, from human sacrifices to the most beastly sensuality.   The
worst was too bad to be written.
   If anything exceeded the Jewish idolatry, it was their savage barbarity.   Moses
commenced with false pretences, superstition all the time, enacted the human tragedy
of his own countrymen, and planted the horrid harvest.
   2 Kings, ch. xv. v. 16. " Menahem, the usurper Israel king, smote Tiphsah, because they opened not to him, and all the women therein, that were with child, he ripped up."
   Ch. xvi. v. 3. "Ahaz made his son to pass through fire, according to the abominations of the heathen."   Were the Jews less heathen or barbarian than the rest of the
world, before the God of the universe?   They performed human sacrifices.   Are these
miscreants for mind's examples?
   In what were the Israelites better than other nations?   If they had the true God,
their minds were not satisfied therewith, else they could not have altered.   With the
true God thus acting, they prove themselves the worst of the world's creation.   It is
conclusive that the Jews did not know the true God.   They neither believed their peculiar god, nor his prophets, nor seers, with all the lights before their eyes.   How
could we now?
   They made them molten images, even two calves (like the Egyptians), and made a
grove, and worshipped all the host of heaven, and served Baal.   "And they caused
their sons and their daughters to pass through the fire, and used divination and enchantments, and sold themselves to do evil."   These were the people that had human sacrifices of their own children.   Here is want of mind, and after thousands of years the
Israelites are not advanced in the greatest progress of mind, that of religion rational—
the only true test of greatness of character.   So much for Judaism, paganism, and idolatry!   Are the degraded modern priestocracy, after selling themselves to this fiendish
machinery for pay, going to sacrifice the world to such sacrilege?
   The king of the Assyrians was much more refined than the Jews, for he did not kill,
but transplanted them; keeping his faith the best of the two.   After many and various
repetitions, the peculiar bible lord could not get his own peculiar people to know him
at all.   After all, his peculiar pains were in vain.
   Hezekiah, of Judah, (2 Kings, ch. xviii. 4.) " brake in pieces the brazen serpent that
Moses had made : for unto those days the children of Israel did burn incense to it : and
he called it Nehushtan."   "Unto those days," from what days?   Those of Moses?
Was he worse than Aaron?   Will the truth leak out after all efforts to hide it?   V. 3.
(Hezekiah) did that which was right in the sight of the Lord.   13. "Now in the fourteenth year of king Hezekiah, did Sennacherib, king of Assyria, come up against all
the fenced cities of Judah, and took them."   So the peculiar god overlooked Hezekiah's righteousness!

This king paid even sacred tribute to the Assyrian, after all his goodness. The Assyrian had the mind of his adversary. When the peculiar god of Israel spoke, it was after the manner of men.

Ch. xxi. v. 11. " Because Manasseh, king of Judah, hath done these abominations, and hath done wickedly above all that the Amorites did * * * made Judah also to sin with his idols."

The Amorites were heathen! The God of the universe is a God of mind, that comprehendeth the soul, and causes it to comprehend his attributes and principles. He has blessed us abundantly, not peculiarly. He has enlightened mind, that has separated church from state.

The sectarian priestocracies could not be kept down, though there was union of church and state. The most despotic tyranny and intoleration prevailed in Palestine on this subject. What is remarkable, though, the king Josiah put down the idolatrous priests, and the horses that the kings of Judah had given to the sun, and burned the chariots of the sun with fire, and the high places, &c., which Solomon, the king of Israel had builded for Ashtoreth, the abomination of the Sidonians, &c., and slew all the priests of the high places that were then upon the altars, with a deadly fanaticism; yet he was slain in battle. Was it because he believed he had a charmed life, that he could not be killed, because Huldah, the prophetess, said, " thou shalt be gathered to thy grave in peace"? See effects of prophecy. Why not? Did Josiah set up any better than he pulled down? It was all superstition, and the extreme of persecution and malignant intoleration. The Jews were intolerant and most vindictive where they had power. Neither the Egyptians nor Assyrians destroyed the Israelites after conquering them.

Chronicles, ch. x. v. 13. " So Saul died for his transgression, also for asking counsel of one that had a familiar spirit, 14. and inquired not of the Lord : therefore he slew him" ! In all this, the most abominable artifice of priestocracy is apparent. They sought, like the people of peculiar faith of the present day, to appropriate all the profits appertaining to all such inquiries. They sought to keep it in the line of safe precedents.

What is the faith worth, if its bibles are worthless? It is this very particular that causes us to dissolve the ignoble fetters, as they are not legitimate on principles that legalize an enlightened public opinion.

2 Chronicles, ch. xi. v. 15. " And he (Rehoboam) ordained him priests for the high places, and for the devils, and for the calves which he had made. Ch. xx. 7. Jehoshaphat, " art thou not our God, who didst drive out the inhabitants of this land before thy people Israel, and gavest it to the seed of Abraham thy friend forever" ?

How miserably has the world been thus humbugged by false prophecies and perjured bibles ?

If the Lord acted as the Israelites claimed, the people of the earth, the heathen, would have been afraid not only to encounter, but even invade them. This tale defeats itself. Jehoram caused sin to Judah, for which a great plague is dogmatically threatened by Elijah.

The Arabians and Philistines spoiled Judah. Thus was the sophisticated priesthood ever ready to assign its causes of all that transpired ! The law of retaliation was constantly being executed among the ancients, as they enjoyed the proper wished-for opportunity.

Moses said in the same bible, " Every man shall die for his own sin" ; the plague of Elijah to the contrary notwithstanding. Ch. xxv. v. 14. Amaziah brought the gods of the children of Seir, and set them up to be his gods, and bowed himself before them. Ch. xxvi. v. 5. Zechariah, who had understanding in the visions of God. 18 v. 20 v. The priests expelled Uzziah from their office of sacrificing. The priests and prophets were ever potent, even against kings. They have not lied to no purpose to govern the verdant world.

Many advocates seek to explain away the bible meaning, ashamed of its false positions and statements.

That shall not be done. Let us attack it as assured of all, and therefore exclude it. The bible is one of the despots of public opinion.

The bibles of tradition are impeached by clear violations of veracity—they were advanced as the ablest artifices. The fabricators do not stickle at any or all expedients to carry out their views. Now the principle in a court of justice is, that when a man perjures himself in one point, his testimony is discarded as invalidated. The very motive and object are to secure sinister despotism. The bible of Judaism has peculiarized the Jews to that extent that they are actually denationalized, and are now suffering, many centuries after, from their peculiar faith, furnishing more by which they and the world have been awfully outraged.

Their priestocracy was most potent, even above kings, and certainly above mind, the sovereign people.

Samuel made and unmade kings, as Saul and David. The first was his vassal as much as the worst vassals to the pope of Rome, who had probably this prototype for himself. The history of the Jews, as emanating from the priestocracy, was a peculiar history of course, and it made truth peculiar of course. That is undeniable, as long as the people were undeniably peculiar and chosen of a peculiar god. The peculiar administration was the priestocracy, and the appeal to truth is now made in due respect to mind's rights. The idea of evoking Samuel from the dead is an awful falsehood. But mind, that is and was in abeyance to superstition, is verdant enough to believe it. And what sort of popular mind had the Jews, a poor superstitious sect?

. Just let them have sway, and they become the rankest idolators, having been so used to idolizing the priestocracy. Were they hardly semi-barbarians, going in for wars of extermination of neighboring peaceable nations, justifying these acts perfidious to the comity of nations behind the commands of their peculiar god, who spoke as their arch and wily jesuitical priests sophisticated the tortured oracle? This priest Samuel figured a lie to anoint David, and involves god, his peculiar god, in the equivocation! To such a pitch did this priestocracy reach. It was the part of the children of Israel, like a grown-up child, to obey, without any questions to the priests. The ancient pupils obeyed the word of their masters without any questions. That now does not suit intelligent mind. The priests were more or less corrupt in revolutions. The priest was along with Adonijah in aspiring to the kingdom. The prophet Ahijah excited Jeroboam against Solomon the king. What was the bible, among this half-civilized people, but a bloody code? What else is it among any nation that adopts it as a bible of tradition, and carries out its commands? Even Solomon, the man of peace, was a man of blood, slaying his own brother Adonijah, by the hands of another. The bible of tradition is discarded by the bible of mind, that invokes pure rational religion and its Creator, to whom all adoration is due by rational beings. All bibles that advocate peculiar faith are unsupported by reason, mind and truth.

See the dying patient most miserable, as he knows not what to believe. The bigot will be only convinced by the powers of numbers.

I could not desire to say aught against this subject, unless it were actually wrong. I do not seek voluntarily but truth. The dynasty of bibles ensnares instead of preserving conscience, that licenses dynasties to tyrannize over man's rights under all insidious disguises. The bible of tradition is an awful means of deception. There are substantive rights to be analyzed and respected anterior to all such bibles, that are a nullity and the acts growing out of them, the usurpation of imposition and fraud. Before the light of truth no such bibles can be permanent. Civilization can acknowledge no allegiance to them. When people talk of receiving them on faith, they prejudge the whole question.

Faith of such is no faith, if fact be not in existence.

This bible is intended for the vassalage of the world, without question or doubt of authority.

All things of exact science prove the world to have been in rude, ignorant and barbarous stages. Reason vindicates herself in process of time.

We impeach the bible as a fraud, vile and base, and throw it on its proofs. Analyze. You admit portions of the bible that are incorrect, not credible. But let us take them that are.

But which are they? Precepts. Then go at once to mind, the true intellectual source. Touch not the bible of tradition, if we have to take all its pretences. Touch not poison, nor soil thy fingers with dirt. Look to the noblest inspirations of mind, in all constitutional matters.

Nothing subverts religion more than faith bibles of paganism. No argument can be more highly conscientious.

All such bibles are the greatest libels on the God of the universe. They are the shrewdest, most jesuitical works that could have been written to uphold priestocracy. with its living train band of superstition to uphold them.

The bible has the highest support from despotism, but all that does not absolve its organic defect. Mind must go to mind more improved than when bibles were written. Let the world's convention of intelligent mind aid for public morals. But in the mean time, as the motives of its writers are bad, its morals are hideous unless in abstraction, its mysteries unintelligible, the result of its faith sectarianism, we should act to the extent of our ability.

We have only to be convinced to the proper extent of reason and facts.

How often did the Jews show themselves idolators? Was not much the most of their national existence enough to prove that they had several peculiar faiths, and some of the most debasing and revolting kind? Is this degraded state of mind vassalage such, that the victory of sophistry is preferable to the conviction of truth ana reason? Yes it is so, and by gospel preachers! Do you call that religion, or good morals, or faith? It would be fastidious to follow out entirely Numbers, ch. xxxi. What miserable morals and logic of Moses: v. 15. "And Moses said unto them, have ye saved all the women alive? 16. Behold, these caused the children of Israel, through the counsel of Balaam, to commit trespass, &c.   18. But all the women-children keep alive for yourselves."

How, with justice, could the Jews appeal to their god, after robbing the nations of land, lives, property and virgins?

Do not uphold any rotten system of exploded paganism, of any bible of tradition. Do not bide from the aforesaid light.

What is any affiliated support of bibles of tradition worth? Is not all support more or less identified therewith? How few are really civilized, and is it by bibles of tradition, when the very commencement reverses the immutable laws of God's unity, "The Gentiles spake against the Jews as evil doers."

Were they less polytheists than any of the ancients?

The various perversions of mind, the worst of priestocracies, abounded with them. Is the bible practised to a gentleman's morals? That is utterly impossible.

How came so many nations to triumph, especially the Roman, over the Jewish? It was on the principle of mind and race, not of any peculiarity of God's institution. They were ruined by the superstition of their priestocracy. Could we know all the secret history withheld, we should see the whole vileness of that class. The bible can prove nothing about a flood that was general, as it does not prove a general knowledge of the earth. If the writers assume that God gave that description, we at once see them condemned on the vile ignorance of the earth, and as God of the universe could not have given that, the peculiar god people gave all. That is too plain to be mistaken by honest and truthful minds. It was like thousands of other floods, only partial. It was all a lie of the priestocracy, and it is shameful that false pretences should be held that it was otherwise.

All bibles of tradition of peculiar faith are absolutely dependent on the falsehood of the miracle mongers.

The whole is an abominable and degraded false pretence throughout—nothing less.

How much wiser do the old and new testaments make the world, especially in exact science?

Mind will crush all the bibles of tradition.   Candor and honor must invoke their expulsion, for the benefit of all their victims, the victims of bad morals, faith and laws. Speak of the supposed supremacy of bibles of tradition, but what an unmeasurable difference between a writ of habeas corpus, and the priestocracy assumption of Moses and Aaron rioting in their vindictive slaughters!   Moses was not a ruler so much of the people, as for the benefit of the priestocracy.

Did he not make faith a trade or speculation?

His bible is a dead-letter, before the right spirit of mind.   We would not give the self-religious and moral conservation of mind, the work of God, for all the bibles of tradition under the sun.

Will the continuance of these bibles produce any real advantage to the world?   In singing the requiem of all bibles of tradition, mind has to sing at the same time all of superstition, absolutism and sophistry.

This terrible trinity is hard to eradicate.

The responsible world should truly understand this.

Circumcision is foolish, absurd, cruel.   God would not have given any part of the flesh of the body to be cut off.

That condemns the whole, as God's word.

God is true, but priests and men of the pulpit, your books are untrue, and you are involved in that category.

Shall free and intelligent minds adopt any bible, the vestige of absolutism, that enacts court corruption after the manner of the Orientals or Eastern despots?

What a mighty talisman on earth that peculiar people, the diamond of nations, to whom all might rush, and embrace their priestocracies.   But did the world find them inspired by the God of the universe?   No.   It was only by a peculiar god, no—only by a peculiar priestocracy.

You find among them a mixed worship, of polytheism and idolatry, mixed paganism. What poorness of intellect, that their peculiar priestocracy had less of superstition than that of the rest of the world.   What things of superstition did this nation, its kings, priests, and prophets worship!   Ah, but these were false prophets and priests!   Yes; they all were so, most clearly proved by the nature of the case.

All is a hideous, peculiar faith, no religion.

The bible of tradition is God's libel. It is the most effectual system to libel God, and advance priestocracy. •

Only think of the legend, that mind, at the height of its elevation, fell. Then it was, the peculiar god had to inquire—showing undeveloped mind, not of him, but of the priestocracy—why the first two fled his presence? Worse than that; his omnipresence could not keep back Satan, who got the advantage. To meet the great question of life, is no proof at all of the scriptures, but one directly superseded by the rightful action of mind. What shall the world do, if it have not bibles of tradition? Constitutional liberty and freedom of government, that protect with good laws and order, will do the world best good.

Religion is to make mind wiser and better. It does not require any of the machinery of peculiar faith, but is the end to the means, and means to the end, the last, best platform to rise higher. It is improved and developed on rational education. It is the intellectual, moral, and happy position. How idle is the value of the bible!

We should dispose forever of the causes of the world's irritation, the mockery of piety, these bibles. Are they not the work of belial minds? No bibles of tradition will ever meet universal approbation.

The bible of rational mind will meet agitators of the bible of tradition, which must yield to paramount duties. Judaism has ground down its victims, by superstition.

Are you a patriot? Help to rescue the world.

The advocates of bibles speak of the Jews, the select people of God! What was the state of the Grecians; was it not far above the Jews? Were the last free, a century at a time?

It is priestocracy, logic, and history that always speak of tradition when proof is absent, but not of reason, that is ever present to mind. Their bibles add to the long list of the world's grievances.

How the Jews fall before the Romans, when we have history to detail it. What was the slaughter of the Jews, by the Roman, Titus? Were the Jews freer from diseases, as leprosy, than all other nations; were they peculiarly smarter, or happier? It is only a peculiar falsehood to say they were.

The works of God are the true; the false and counterfeit are the bibles of tradition. We cannot vouch for what is probable; of course we do reject all else as contemptible to mind that is cultivated. Reader, this is for your good.

Angels and devils are the bible machinery, with miracles, prophecy, and mystery. This may suit imbeciles, but not rational minds. Shame to it all.

Let us know what we are about, when such bibles are pressed on us.

If you say that such is not fiction, there is no fiction. We must get rid of all hypocrisy.

We do not believe in Moses, nor the so-called prophets, nor the dead, nor the living Christs. We discard them all, as the puppets of the priestocracy.

No bible of tradition can delineate the proper character of the true God; that is an impossibility. It gives only a peculiar god necessarily, and peculiar machinery of the priestocracy. The bible cuts out the pure spirituality of the godhead in its God and Christ, in the war of its heaven; the pure omnipresence in regard to the fall of the first parents, so called when Satan tempted Eve, and as to the incomprehensible and mysterious trinity, as there was no Christ or Messiah, whilst the God of the universe, the new revelation that science has made, reigns almighty, there, of course, could be none of that. It is a conceited nonentity. But you affect that the bible is an inspired book, and children are taught, by their unfortunate peculiar education, to take for granted all its contents. How hideous a sophistry! Enough to bias, pervert, and ruin the world! The obsolete bible to be the world's master, when it is not fit for its slave, surely not its use.

An inspired pen would have recorded, in the days that knew not astronomy, all that astronomy could ever teach. As it did not—but its advocates sought to enchain its errors on the world—it proves that there is no such kind of inspiration, and that the world is indebted to mind and mind's coin, exact science. The tribute that some claim for the bible, above all human productions, ought at least establish exact science that it has not got.

The talmud is said to be a mighty encyclopædia of commentaries on the old bible, most ingenious nothings of many writers seeking black letter, not the spirit of the authors. But the bible authors are nothing. They are clearly convicted, by their ignorance of exact science.

They are affiliations when not priestocracies. If any good can be extracted, it is only as from mind.

٭ god, made by the Jews!

٬re authority than Joe Smith!

٬.un, all of it. How many hundreds of sectarianisms were there of

٬٭rous warfare between the various kinds of priests and tribes! It

٬cution and massacre, bloody fanaticism, as each or any got the

٬٭ been the aspirations of their affiliated in Palestine! All the an-

٬ques, clans, adherents, train-bands ready to perjure themselves, and

٬es and crimes the worst, the world over. If we see these execrable

٬tocracy written, what must have been the balance, concealed or un-

٬tory of the world, written in truth, would be a very different affair.

told! what false pretences of peculiar faith so felonious, so treacherous

٬٭ The party, Mosaic writers, &c., are eternally estopped from invok-

٬tions of Deity, who rules the universe. Their fiction, curiously inter-

٬tains only the peculiarities of a peculiar people. Subsequent preachers

from the universe. Be theirs the honor and the use of employing

٬l Belial, as they are the responsible god-fathers to all this ignominy in

٬l. Such is their ineffable pleasure. Who that looks at the purity of

٬would pollute their lips with such desecrated books, in taking an oath!

٬ throw themselves on the dignity of affirmation.

answer for the mysteries; we do not understand them, but we believe

onest or safe? Shame upon it! Though such bibles as presented

٬made by legion, if you, the friend of truth, analyze, you must know that

٬egin to touch the subject. We must not forget that the claim of this

on, and that is perfection, exactness of science. On this we have joined

٬e that the bible of tradition is no bible at all; it is that of fraud and im-

tradition is, by the side of the so-called pagans and infidels, destitute of

٬e best that can be said of it is, that it is an ignoble institution, an awful

ligion.

٬ble must ever look at the great constituent, fundamental principles of

s is the code of rational mind of proper rectitude, but can never be com-

٬ect until it attain to all that religion, the supreme duty to the supreme

res. It is then a right code of appreciation of God.

r bible the Jews were as sinful, ten times more so, than the heathens

that are mind enlightened. By the by, they presented bad morals for slan-

٬he world. The bible pleadings are special pleadings.

٬ht mind, rightly instructed in the great principles of sound logic, that

imary proof, can abide any such book as peculiar bibles, whether the vedas,

٬ How easy is it to make a bible of tradition, but how impossible to conceal

ons and abominations.

٬e priestocracy who claim the manu-and-mind-facture, the use of the elements,

prophecies, and mysteries. Is that all? You must give them disseminators

must be paid, and honored with power equally interested in the propagation;

e all you must furnish a credulous people, who must yield at bidding or on fear,

٬h. You must have church vassals, and despotic bullyings.

to think of the absurd stories that the Mosaic tablet of legends weaves, that

dren of Israel were forty years in the wilderness, when the distance from Egypt

٬tine is only a few days' travel! The greater the time the more lies were told,

٬ how profitless, as the people disregarded all such machinery, and even preferred

culiar gods of the Groves, Baal, Belial, &c.; even their wisest man, Solomon

red other gods to their Mosaic imbecile! What a contradiction, that is com-

y successful. What do you think of the bible? Some pretend that they are

al. Why! They do not understand a part of the mysteries, and do not believe a

٬ What is such, but a corrupt vassalage to bibleocracy? What is such book

٬h is honest truth? Are you prepared for the correct position, analysis, and its

٬er results? No: the mind of such is neutral, and its position in the world is

erable, as truth cannot be advocated because it is unfashionable to do so! How

ny bibles have been written, and how often have they been altered? Because I

٬h to see the world better, I advance principles compatibly with what I deem right,

be tested as principles.

The world certainly wishes to be right, therefore all things should be removed, capa-

٬e of injuring it.

We need the best bible of mind to avoid all false positions, never to desert a correct one, but do all practicable therefor. What was the manna of Moses as a miracle to the teeming productions of earth, her mighty treasures in the hands of the Almighty enough to rebuke all of peculiar faith?

What was the twilight of Moses to that of the present times? The world has not really considered its happy fruition. Truly, this is truth, the inspiration of mind, to counteract all the false pretences and counterfeits of false leaders of mind, as those who worked the men of straw, Moses, Christ, and Apostles.

The Jews, all the ancients were terribly superstitious; it was the fault of the times inculcated by the vice of the priestocracy. They were idolatrous. What prevented them from man and hero worship? This was the great vice and error of antiquity. The visit of God to Moses to have his mission, could easily have been dispensed with. It added nothing to his power and influence, that were set aside so often by the disbelief of the Jews, that were abundantly complained of, on that very account. Now, the God of the universe who has never appeared to man on earth, as proved, rules rational minds. That is the difference between the two. The God of the universe dispenses with his personified presence to all, by the force and inherent power of conservative principles.

"And he came down to deliver them"! that is, Moses' peculiar god came down by a dash of the pen.

The children of Israel suffered evil of four hundred years. Why? It was so prophecied that the word might be fulfilled. It was so written that the lie might be told fully.

The bible of tradition is the many-headed monster.

What gave bibles their presented ideas of God?

Inspiration. If of mind, the fact is admitted—if of any other way, the fact is dishonestly advanced.

The egotistical Moses is forever blaspheming the attributes of God, belittling him. No greater absurdity could be advanced if millions of angels were necessary to prop up the world instead of conservative principles, than to make one a messenger for God.

The principles of gravitation, of electricity were not dreamed of, by these visionaries. Be done, sapient scholars, aping these wiseacres; the trammels of the schools the worst of tyrannies, when not in accordance with the real progress of mind. We want no royalty bibles, as the bible of mind must put all morals and religion, on the impregnable position of reason.

Let not the world seek to square science to the bible; let astronomers correct their reckoning. Has one star lost its glory? Let meteors pass, with the ignorant, for fallen stars. Bible writers affect much; what do they know? Enough, to expose themselves to the ignominy of exposure. When they mystify, their designs are sinister, and their treachery to mind is certain. They are serfs and vassals to superstition and absolutism.

The peculiarities in the world are increased by perverted minds. The bibles of tradition are their emphatic propagators and would be decided the veriest deceivers, if reason could have a showing, and most visionary at that. Let us have truth, if all bibles of peculiar faith perish, as all will undoubtedly.

The injury of souls, mean time, should never be in abeyance to obsolete bibles of tradition, certainly not those of royalty or cabinet bibles.

The devotees adhere to obsolete ideas, and force the infidels as they call them to no morality, not permitting that of reason. Which is best morality, to adhere to gospel that is false, or the laws of God, tried by reason and intelligent mind, that always come the nearest to truth? The bible is a dead letter before morality, that is shamefully violated in a wide extent of absolutism.

There is a morbid sensibility about bibles, which are a principal barrier to justice and rational religion. The world is entitled to a right constitutional position on this subject, the sooner obtained the better. It is because we are for sound morals and rational religion, the mighty union of one universal brotherhood throughout the world, that we go against all bibles of tradition as the elements of evil and feud.

What has Judaism done towards civilizing mankind?

The covenanters should be questioned aright.

What baseness of making things agree, with preconceived prejudices of bibles! What sophistry! All this is subject to a conservative rational religious faith.

The bible is below elevated criticism, and standard of mind. Prove to us the bible, the word of God. It is the master book used in courts to swear by! As well perjury as truth. But that is only custom. Satisfy us and we will not only be silent, but defend it. It is our highest interest to see it right; we wish to know our correct position. Great men have heretofore opposed it, and their temporal interest was identified. We cannot see the truth through this medium, only through the disinterested medium of truth.

As a rational free agent, I am bound to ask for satisfactory proof of this bible, otherwise mind is vassal. But all can not openly declare against an improved bible, however worthless it may be. Better had they live on bread and water, and do justice to God and man. We know of the tyranny of social dynasties, to proscribe recklessly in this matter.

There are bible despotism and priestocracy enough, God knows. Admit all the bible statements, who endorses them now as certain? Of course any affirmation, ought to be most valid. Would any man risk perjury, for such trash? Was there any thing in Judaism equal, much less superior, to the Amphyctionic Council of Greece, for great national objects?

Are the Jews worse than those of other peculiar faiths?

Some are honest. Now can a man in his honest senses affirm, at best, to but a partial belief in all the Mosaic fables?

A partial exclusion of them in belief, by bible advocates, destroys all necessarily, so the bible is ended thus.

Any other is the faith of priestocracy; that is, simpletons would rather credit the priests, who sought to move their hell and heaven to carry their day over mind.

And is the world to be displeased with any candid enough to tell it not to be taken in by all the false mysteries, &c., of the priestocracies, ancient and modern?

The bible of tradition prevents the practical action of mind, and trammels it down to obsolete ideas. You may complain of severity of criticism towards Moses, or his authors, who were as good as their cotemporaries; but they were all barbarians in these matters, and if you resuscitate them to be applied now for the advance of mind, be the sin at your door. We must look at matters as they are now situated, not as then. The question is not now whether Moses is tolerable, but whether the paramount interests of the world do not require his complete expulsion.

Moses, if now present, and a worthy intelligent citizen, would rule out Moses the priestocrat perfectly defenceless.

Take from creation through the deluge, to his swearings.

How could the effects of a deluge be universal, over a globe nearly round as this earth? How could the effects of a partial deluge be fatal universally?

Is the whole science of mind to bow to untruth? Is the whole world to be made subordinate to Palestine. a very small portion of it? Is the billion to be ruled by one autocrat of bigotry? Is that any more just, that religion should be in abeyance to peculiar faith?

The person that pretends to say that any bible or scripture tells things without the cognizance of mind, does not speak the truth at all. What is a nation of bigots, sectarians and fanatics worth? There can be only two kinds of faith in all bibles, partial or peculiar, and good. The last is contained in bibles of mind, and the first in bibles of tradition.

You are taught implicitly to believe a lie, by taking for granted the assertions of bible of tradition and their advocates. What miserable morals and sophistry!

Parents, do you teach such abomination to your children? You will be proportionately accursed for this sin.

What is the true great principle of life? There must be no sacrifice of truth or health. But our ministers tell us not to read any books opposed to their bibles! Are you the slaves of your ministers? You are the mind-slave, the worst of all slaves, if you obey them so foolishly. There is no arrogance, no despotism so vile, so great as this. You are an American, and tell us this command, order, ukase of your master ministers.

Do they intend to cheat you out of your mind's rights? Will such an outrage on mind's light and rights be thus perpetrated? Will you, patriot, good and true citizen, investigate. turn your attention to this the most important subject of the world? Have base pulpit men wished you to be wrong in this matter? How do you know you are right. unless you investigate?

We tell you that nearly all the pulpit men do not investigate thoroughly, nor do justice to this whole subject, and of course they cannot tell you honestly in the pulpit—cannot prove their position, to save eternity. Do you not rather prefer to list yourself, your children, your family. friend and countrymen, the whole world, to truth and honesty? No bible of tradition supporters or advocates ever outwent the science of their own times; they do not come up to them, as much as they are always behind them.

The Jews could not shake off the priests and prophets. They stuck to them, as all the ancients, like leeches. No doubt this made them prefer kings to corrupt priest-judges. Of the whole evils, they chose the least. Even the kings could not shake them off, and now the world cannot easily shake them off. Ahaz resisted Isaiah, who pushed himself on the king.

The bible of tradition is below criticism; God's works are above it. Such books unsettle the world, as Christians have looked for universal destruction; and subsequent writers, as Miller, have excited the credulous and timid to a superstitious dread. They have proved thus that they did not understand what the pretended prophets did not themselves understand, and never wished to be understood in times and half times, if resulting prejudicially to their pretensions.

The modern priestocracy are thus caught, affecting to interpret what they pretended to believe as prophecy.

The scriptures are inconsistent, contradictory, mere trifles, if they were not the dangerous games of despots.

Either the Septuagint or the old Hebrew testament is false, one or both. Buck and the Christians say the last!

What minute specifications of times, places, events and persons are made in the bible, as if they were true.

One of the objections to man's writings is, that language constantly changes; but God's word, that is, his works, do not change, that mind can mistake them.

I object to the doctrines and practices of scriptures.

Why a second revelation in the new testament, if the old one were perfect; and how could it be divine revelation if not perfect?

After-thoughts are not God's, but man's works.

But the peculiarity of the first kills it, as the balance of the world is heathenized thereby. God is just, and no respecter of persons, but the peculiar god of the bible is necessarily a respecter of a chosen people.

All bibles of tradition are totally imperfect, not reaching principles. The new testament is a succor of the old—illegitimate, a parasite, a mistletoe only. The first tells us of a false messiah; the last tells falsely of man's fall. Past times favored the imposition of bibles of tradition, when mind was stupidly verdant and ignorant, credulous, ready to receive all for granted, or be forced by regal power, and seduced by intrigue and sophistry of the priestocracy. Do we know how many books were rejected that were written for the old and new testaments?

Science is of divine origin, but the bible advocates require the rejection of the first for their pretences. Was there ever infatuation like this?

The bible does not begin to comprehend all that is legitimate and relative. There is too much of the avenger, as in most all peculiar faith that is analogous to superstition.

There are two kinds of gods, apparently; the one, Creator of the universe, known only to mind, through reason; the other, known only to priestocracy, by faith—a peculiar god of a peculiar people. The bible-mongers have been talking of their mysteries, when they botch creation. God never spoke in the bible of tradition, a work of blasphemy; he speaks most sublimely in the creation of the universe.

The rational religionist reads the last, the polytheist reads the first.

But if we discard the bible, how shall we have the date of the year of the world? Have that of the bible of mind, or of the Creator of the universe, fixed for future and past true history.

You cannot mistake the character of all such books, therefore do not act perfidiously to your mind, the great gift of God. Have you ever investigated this subject? if you have not, it is high time that you had set about it. But our preacher, our pulpit dictator, our priest objects! All such are traitors to their country, mind, and God, not to advise the investigation so essential to the welfare of the world. As no prudent man will throw away good money for bad, a certainty for an uncertainty, religion for peculiar faith, valuable time for trash, the Creator for the creature, so he should know that the bible of mind must not be superseded by any other pretence.

Yes, but you object to the whole bible; now are you to use its language against itself: Because it condemns itself, on that language. All denizens can enjoy this right. But the wisdom of the ancients did not elaborate who God was! Nor did the Jews, who made him peculiar, because their god was for them, a peculiar people.

If that god destroyed them, as their bible decides, or was inclined against the rest of the world, as heathens or outside barbarians, for the Jews, his godship exerted himself peculiarly to recover the lost Israel. But God's system is universal, not peculiar, therefore all peculiar systems of faith exclusively belong to the people adopting, and cannot be transferred, on the conservative principles of mind. All the peculiar gods belong to the peculiar systems, undeniably. As to the wisdom of the ancients, not knowing God except through the bible, the mind of the world had not reached science exact, and not knowing his works, could not know the workman. God is only known and truly known through his works. It is very clear that the bible-writers did not know God, for they did not know his works.

THE AUTHENTICITY OF ANY SCRIPTURES. 583

No truly inspired man would have ever mistaken the mighty orbs of the universe, of solar and primary character, for the miserable caricature of candle or lamp lights, for one little orb, the earth! And that the only place of creature man, whom God had to come down to visit. Let the world be diligent to know his works, to be correctly introduced to the Almighty Architect. Mind, then, has to work, to reach this glorious position. The unmistakable, unchangeable word of God is cause and effect, that speaks through the universe : all else is man's. You say God cannot lie. Why, then, do you assert that the bible's pretences are God's words, when they are the lying words of the priestocracy? The idea of selecting a chosen people promoted the idea of chosen rulers, kings of course, God's anointed. The bible of tradition is tory to the people, the world may be sure of that. As republicans, we want none of it. Moses makes out his father-in-law Jethro greater than God, in advising about the people, and suggesting counsel, not even thought of by God, in the wilderness. This clearly condemns all, as the pretences of the priestocracy, all man's writings. What need of Hobab in the place of eyes, when Moses had the ark of the covenant to go before them, and the cloud of the Lord upon them? Clearly here was something wrong, unexplained, only that they were doing as mind directed.

If Moses or his constituents had told all wonders or miracles, the legends would have been incredible ; but by mixing the probable also, more may assent to it.

Some simple-minded honest people say that they believe a part; that is the reason, on the nature of evidence, that no honest intelligent minds can believe this fabulous mixture. Testimony in a court of justice, that is in part incredible, vitiates itself.

This bible sets out to be not only correct, but most exact, by the inspiration of the perfect Supreme. It clearly vitiates itself, and betrays itself unworthy of the confidence of the world, of mind.

This priest Mosaic-work is one of the greatest pieces of tricks and knavery of the priestocracy.

But it may be advanced, that the bible is a code for the peculiar people of Moses ; if so, then are the advocates of peculiarity estopped from any universal benefits. The people should have been accustomed to the best popular right government of them-selves : they can do it better than anybody else. The usurpation of their rights has been done through perversions of facts.

But the Jews were not a very advanced nation, not very intellectual, over and above. That is the very reason that their codes should not be imposed on this age.

But this code furnishes the only means whereby all can be saved. That assertion should be proved, before it is ever repeated. It cannot be proved, and is certainly untrue, when it acts the impostor before mind, its master, this day declared. Yet we could get no idea of God but from the bible. We only get the idea of a peculiar god there. From whom did the bible get even that? From a line of priestocracy, through mind.

It has perverted what was real science to its own peculiar purposes.

The priest bible teaches the people to worship the priestocracy. The bible is the worst of all books, as it teaches robbery of God, blasphemy of man, hypocrisy of mind.

But the bibles tell. They only tell all that they got from mind, that represents the senses, the only avenues for inspiration, as earth has inspiration.

Now what is better and more honorable, to confess at once that the bible of rational mind is that of religion, and that the peculiar bible is false ; as any other than truth is the old dynasty creed?

Where is the Indian, who believes in a Great Spirit?

Who taught this son of the forest, but the great objects of nature? Science will cause the Great Spirit's independent attributes to follow most clearly, as mind causes science to be developed, in its own rich culture. The Great First Cause, the God of Nature, are supreme names. The bibles all borrow from mind, and have not the honesty nor the truth to say it.

All the bibles of tradition dwarf God, whilst reason gives expansion to his sublimest greatness.

Man's botches, the bibles of the priestocracy, make God imperfect, in amending the world, that he had not made right at the flood ; again at Babel, at the messiahship, and above all, at man's fall in Eden—all the veriest fables. It was my will to have been convinced by the bible. I sought it, but at last rational religion burst upon me. Any other idea is all the greatest fallacy and humbug. Prove the bible is from God. I cannot demonstrate, you pretend, or that I cannot know of Deity correctly, without the bible of tradition? That is a gratuitous and an unwarranted assertion. I affirm that bible causes us to know more imperfectly than reason, to which it is indebted for its best knowledge, however it and advocates have libeled reason and God through that.

They claim by assertion, without proof. Analysis will truly disclose how all this was. The priestocracy was too anxious for the little brief authority; they affected to have science by inspiration. All that was treacherous imposture. One age has not astronomy; it is a science of sciences of thousands of years growth. That teaches that the earth moves around the sun; but the bible assumes the reverse. The bible never claimed this, without reason. Its basis is to obtain credulity of the world, ostensibly for the knowledge of Deity, but really for its influence and power. Is any bible a talisman, that it should be above reason? If so, prove such character, and I yield the question. The divinity and holiness of the bible are gratuitous assertions. There is nothing divine but mind. Then prove the bible so, not assert it. Call for the only witness. How could the bible be less than a mixed fable, written at the time it was, when history of the present time hardly tells but a small part of the truth, unless closely reviewed. It is frequently now but a mixture of fiction—too often—and of misconception. I prefer truth to all the bibles in creation, and all the priestocrats, their authors. The mind, you assert, cannot attain to a true knowledge of God. The Indians have a better knowledge of God than the New Testament gives in its pagan trinity.

When they say the great spirit, they characterize him as a warrior. So did the Jews the god of Judaism.

The mind of civilization characterizes him as the perfect God of monotheism. Let not the onesided views of the bible of tradition adherents decide. No wonder that the bibles of tradition about God were so defective and yet so proscriptive, so consequential, so arrogant, for science was in that category.

The bible adherents are used up, and have none to blame but themselves, as they assumed to curse even those that disputed their foolish false pretences with the false blasphemous assumptions of their god.

All this may scare off foolish simple people, but cultivated mind can see through the blasphemy.

We must take nothing for granted that the bible tells us, nor take uncomprehensive imperfect views.

We have the world's view that has been at it for thousands of years. What does the conservation and organization of our solar system tell, but the almightiness of the great first cause? What can not the whole universe tell, to confirm this in the ratio of its numbers of solar systems? But some fearful prophecy has been advanced by the bible, about the disappearance and melting of the stars. It is claimed by some astronomers, that stars have disappeared as consumed. But is not this the fault of the astronomers, their ignorance or their error? Because we do not see the stars, are they gone?

Were not some enthusiasts and fanatics, that changed our solar system to suit the bible? As they did this, their pretensions are at least suspicious.

Irrational beings look to peculiar faith that makes peculiar gods, with peculiar minds. It strips them all of their rationality, surely.

The rationalists go to the light of that luminary that enlighteneth suns, the bible-men to that of their candles in a closet where they concocted it! The devil is the father of lies, as the bible to which he owes paternity says; but lies were expedient to create him.

The physical state of the world has nothing to do with bibles, much less its moral and religious condition. If we did believe such a bible, we could not believe in the perfection of God.

How many authors of remote antiquity are free from many falsehoods? Was Herodotus? The more remote generally, the less attested. Those affiliated to the pagan myths, have known them false. We need not much of analysis to convict them clearly or false pretences. It is foolish or dishonest to deny them. The history of records was with the priests, as the hieroglyphics prove.

Priests were abundant among the ancients, as all despots. The Jews had their high priests and prophets, to take care of their records; they had access to Babylon, surely, as the captives. Did not the priests have access much of the time to the court? Did the priestocracy change? Josephus says in his 1st book, sec. 7, against Apion, "they being only prophets that have written the original and earliest accounts of things, as they learned them of God himself by inspiration."

What an irresponsible power, with an unconscientious and unprincipled clique. Does rational mind want more light into the nature of ancient regimes? Surely this is enough, for it is a world's history.

The power of the so-styled prophets was beyond any autocracy on earth. It is easily accounted for.

An ignorant and superstitious age had yielded them all with the blindest submission.

Human nature, without responsibility, is with impunity. The minds of those men were finally blinded, as much as blind 'fanaticism could perpetrate. Assuming to be from their God, they concluded their dynasty never would be amenable to mortal power. Ignorant as presumptuous, they were blinded to the discoveries of science when they assumed legends or tradition.

As to the prophecies, what proof have we about their not being ante-dated, instead of being post-dated? They all, of every age, name and pretension, are the clearest perjuries, that the perpetrators cause to suit their case. They are the great stumbling-blocks, the decoy ducks, for the unthinking world, verdant and credulous, who say I must believe the bible because I believe the prophecies. Well, was there ever a greater suicide of reason? The bible is an arrant perjury, and the prophecies, most arrant perjuries, are its endorsers. A complete circle of the clearest perjury!

The result of all ancient captures and conquests in those barbarous and corrupt times, the whole world being of that character, would be analogous, dreadful and barbarous. All iniquitous morals, including all the theatrical and despotic acts of faith exemplified by oracles and priestcraft, were enacted according to impunity. Now, whether all the capital was directed to faith or government, so it was available as now, was the object. Who wonders, on proper analysis, at the iniquities of a Nero and Caligula? Think you that the iniquities of the faithites, the pagans, did not come in for their share?

If the Jews truthfully submitted their conduct at that time to a proper decision, we have to make allowances for the state of mind generally, otherwise they must be condemned as assuming superiority.

If the people did not do righteously, they were unfortunate, the prophecy was accordingly. What a safe policy, not prophecy!

Of course, when captive sufferers, they had not done right, as no superstitious nation could. If they had escaped, the prophets sophisticated the history, and all was right.

How much does one man in thousands investigate of the bibles and their commanding subjects, but leave them most stupidly to an interested party.

The acutest mind must see the bad faith of the priestocracy, that act unworthy of men.

Will their impeachment not open the eyes of the world? In impeaching bibles of tradition, are not the advocates of them impeached?

The bibles are not self-sustained, but impeached by the testimony of Deity's works, an unmistakable and unimpeachable verdict, always before the world for it to read for itself.

The first and indispensable inquiry we have to make is, as to the truth and authenticity honorably proved of the bible? Who endorses all the authors? False faith endorses—easily proved. Why should there have ever been any exclusion from reading the bible? Nothing but the untruth of the bible should have ever caused it.

The clergy should go with the bible. Give mind light, liberal as the air we breathe. What is the proof authentic, of the scriptures being the word of God? God's own testimony! Well, where is it? What proof is there of that? None at all. Is there not direct proof to the contrary? Most clearly.

The organization of the universe, including mind, the self-free, moral, intellectual agent, destroys the whole category of prophecies, miracles, and mysteries. God has no direct communications with mind, but through the inspiration of science and genius. This power of Moses' priestocracy was dangerous, by its own showing.

If bad in those times, they are execrable now, in the light of truth and science that condemn their impostures.

With what holy horror some people affect to treat the analysis of the bible, when that bible has violated every pretension to a gentlemanly claim on the affections or respect of the whole world?

But you pretend that I deny the bible, which proves itself by its work that progresses. So does the work of other bibles progress, as the Mahometan.

Shall we submit to any exploded bible system, that demoralizes man, is certainly untrue, and oppresses the world by speculation in that untruth?

Some have design, as they know better, like Napoleon, who is said to have adopted the star of destiny and the mysteries of fortune-telling. All have superstition, as peculiar education promotes it, or as interest of self predominates.

If the bible writers had had science in the several departments described, they never would have written the degraded book, that betrays ignorance and recklessness of purpose. But what shall be said of those having all the lights of mind and its science-culture at this age, that will absurdly persist in its exploded errors that the writers now would be ashamed of?

Then a wiser legislation due to mind-culture that prevents this uncivilized proceeding, takes precedence altogether. Why, then, talk of the half civilized Jews, when we are in a civilization that takes supreme precedence of them? The more part of the Jews appreciate the peculiar god, the less they liked him. He, that is his prophets, were eternally complaining of want of respect. No wonder, as he, rather his priestocracy, had been so often inadequate. The trial has been made to supply the deficiency, by more gods, rather their apologies. Thus it will ever be with polytheism, to have more peculiar gods. The bible bigot is the greatest idolist.

The bible is not correct in science, language, mind, the universe or God. We can only stand by that bible, that stands by religion.

But we must not construe God, as man's imperfect mind thinks. For that reason we construe not as one little bigoted book decides by imperfect mind, but we seek to comprehend the whole universe, the microscopic as telescopic combined. It is the absolute duty of wisdom to embrace all, the minute as the greatest; the practical and practicable, the rational not the unreasonable position; nor to expect of God any thing analogous to irrationality.

Prophets made their pretence, their profession. The prophets did not even wait as with Ahaz, Isaiah sought and even forced on him his sign, that the weakest minds are trying to force on the world despite of reason.

What pretensions have these patriarchs to lead the morale of the world? Jacob did enough to put him into the penitentiary by the laws of civilized society for polygamy, so Abraham and Lot would have certainly gone there. And are these men fit associates of angels? Of course they were, for the bible angels.

The angels were the inmates of their heaven where war and riot prevailed, in the time of John the Revelation writer, the abode of the peculiar god. What a low idea did the Bible writers have of religion and purity!

But Lot was made drunk, by his daughters. Yes, but the immutable laws of morals decide irrevocably that he who acts by another, acts himself. If drunkenness made Lot commit incest, then drunkenness is an intense crime.

The perpetrator of the act was capable of knowing better, and must be basely guilty as a culprit. The conduct that the world shows toward the Jews, results from the effects of the bible, the superstition engendered, and the prejudices of pretended prophecy and sectarianism and the Jewish seclusion. Could the Jews then be better off, by such regime?

This thing of superstition and its bibles, is the hardest to wipe out. Is it possible that this could be the God of the universe, wrestling with Jacob? He must have had something more important to do for the universe.

What a miserable conception of the God of the universe.

As a proof that the bible was not essential to the world's prosperity, more universal empires prospered and included Palestine in their government. As to morals we can resort to other nations, for equal light of mind.

The Chinese inculcated the most respectful piety towards parents, so did the Romans. Who were the gods of the last peculiar beings? Who was the god of the Jews? A peculiar being. It is impossible to have the bible heresies to succeed. We can never reach any other idea, but that of a priestocracy's god.

Yes, the Jews are a peculiar people, so far as they bear the impression of the priestocracy yet about their maimed persons, the emblem of superstition. You may talk about your bibles of tradition. Yet what would the world do, but for the supremacy of wise legislation, a part of the constitutional code of the bible and light of mind? While peculiar faith has been rearing her peculiar laws and codes, the wisdom of mind has been rearing, under the auspices of God, much for the progressive benefit of the world in true morals and religion.

The bible is obsolete, and to defer discarding it, is to defer the evil day. Its peculiar faith continued to distract the world, to put the household at variance with itself. All the world citizens owe a duty to a common world, to promote world morals and religion. Perseverance in such, will bring out the world.

What an imposition, whilst the capabilities of mind even yet in its infancy, to attempt to crush it by such ignoble means as bibles of tradition, to secure that narrow, contracted, bigoted feeling of the world arising by peculiar faith. We must establish the world facts, on the mighty broad platform and permanent basis of conservative principles.

The bibles of tradition are potent elements of strife over the world, producing all disunion, where brotherhood should be universal. Such a rule as Moses had, was the most outrageous despotism and autocracy.

This book, if we believe some of its prophets, says that the lion shall eat straw with the ox! Does physiology declare that the gastric juice of a beast of prey of animal flesh, will act on vegetables! Will it not act alone on animal fibre?

Mind has to make the world a flower garden, like clock work, embellished with all that nature can give. The scripture evidently violates the truth of history about the whole earth. We have now an artificial state of the world cheated into the faith of a faithless bible, that does not and cannot do God justice. Then, what less than immortal principles can fix mind?

For what can the true mind want such a bible, that renders God imbecile as to Satan and the first parents, and a murderer in a savior? If he was the first, he could not be efficient in the last. This antagonism is irreconcilable. If justice accepts as propitiation of capital crime, the life of an innocent person, it is actually making justice iniquity by a participation in crime. How many prayers are a libel on God!

What in the bible is called firmament, is no firmament at all; and sure enough the bible has no firmament to its knowledge and science. Stripped of its mantle, it is the work of impostors and hypocrites. Belief or faith will thus characterize the adopters. It pretends to give its peculiar god, for the Almighty who cannot be booked. The peculiar god can be booked by his peculiar priestocracy of course. God can be written of by mind, but not revealed by tradition.

The books of Moses, Joshua and Samuel are books of the bible that speak of events post dated for their assumed authors, and are false pretences that destroy the purity and the validity of its character.

Why does the world believe in the bible? Because it will not investigate what the bible is.

It has had its time-flatterers, as in criticism. What corruption in critics. What constitutes virtue? The gospel! What nonsense!

Armed with all its panoply of inquisitions, tortures, dynasties of government, of women, and all influence, it is a contemptible fraud, that helps pollute the state of society, being after-thought, not fore-thought.

Bibles of tradition are the most deceptive things ever devised by cunning impostors. Geology and astronomy, physiology and analysis correct such. Geology proves the creation of animals long ere man was created.

The bible has abstract propositions that will pass in the code of morals, but why resort to such a suspicious mixture, when we have the whole funds of mind that furnish the best originals in its purity?

Both gospels inculcate the worst of sectarianism, the propagation of doctrines by the sword; ay, and that too under the administration of the meek Moses, and the very words of the Savior, so-called. What can possibly establish the authenticity of the scriptures? Some of the main books of the bible were not written at the time, nor by the persons purported to be its authors.

Such are the books of Moses especially, that are a blasphemous libel on God, and a base imposition on man on their very face. It was written by one of two classes of men 'It was written by wicked men to perpetuate the power of priestocracy, and this assertion has a most beautiful consistency. It is claimed by friends espousing it, to be a perfect code of moral precepts.

Wickedness is there exposed, and the self-condemnation of the very characters aspiring to heap the heaviest denunciations, and expose the awful consequences of sin, is so forcibly illustrated, so fully and positively depicted, that rational men would not venture to seek any other assertion than that it is written by wicked men.

With whom can repudiation of jewels, borrowed of the Egyptians by the Jews, and subsequent devotion of them to their peculiar god by this peculiar people in worship, be sustained but by wicked men?

With whom could the slaughter of thousands of men, married women in all conditions of pregnancy, and infants, with the appropriation of all the virgin women-children, in number thirty-two thousand, by their male captors, be sustained but by wicked men? With whom could the dictator of the Jews and the murderous sons of Levi, who slew three thousand of their fellow citizens for sectarianism, be sustained but by wicked men? With whom could the reckless murder of the republican Korah and his associates, recklessly destroyed by the dictator, as the people accused him and brother, be enacted, but by wicked men?

And this last but opens the chapters of pious frauds and false pretences, a sacred felony.

That it was not written, most clearly evident, by inspired men, their writings that are inconsistent and inaccurate every way, inevitably decide. The ethics of civilization decide against all such.

What can be more highly exceptionable than the lives and conduct of the patriarchs, the fountain heads of this peculiar world-evil?

But that was the custom of the times. Then this refined age should not be forced by any code emanating from these characters, who are stained by several degrading vices of their times. Did not Abraham drive his son to the wilderness, where he became an archer ; that is, we presume by his history, a robber ? Who cared for his morals ? Abraham ? He was preparing and sending off another such colony to the east country. That they were not all robbers, no thanks to Abraham, the father.

Who endorses the statements of the bible ? Would you swear that they were facts ? Could you conscientiously swear such a thing ? If this were a book of inspiration from Almighty God, who is perfect, the facts would have been in accordance, most accurate and self-evident. Are they ?

The writer of creation is not ostensibly known, if it were not Moses; and it is impossible for it to have been Moses, who must then have written of his own death, burial and character, his own obituary, which vitiates the whole matter beyond redress. Of course the priestocracy mind-factured the whole. The first start kills all its creation, and the last winds up book and authors.

But the so-called prophecies are instanced especially about the Jews, who were claimed as predicted about 3000 years ago, that they should be a peculiar people, scattered over the face of the earth, that they should be oppressed and peeled. When a nation sets out as having marked peculiarities, whom had it to thank but itself?

How could the Jews escape being a peculiar people, who were made so by priestocracy ? They were circumcised ! Did God have this done ? How comes it that others also have done it ? If it were necessary for the human organization, would God have left it out ? If it be done by man, is it not man's acts ? Were the Jews any other than a peculiar people, before the assumed prophecy ? Have they got out of all their peculiar superstitions yet ?

So far from being scattered over the face of the earth, the peculiar god of Abraham tells, in the same Pentateuch, " For all the land which thou seest, to thee will I give it, and to thy seed forever."

No one, after this, can pretend to reconcile the pretended prophecies. If he do, he marries himself to falsehoods and perjuries.

But then the subsequents, the modifications should be added. Agreed. They prove various editions of time, and destroy the very character claimed.

Aaron, the chief priest, seems to have been every way worthy of the chief dictator. What shall we think of the purity of the idolatrous liar, wearing the inscription " Holiness to the Lord !" Many hypocrites do the same. Search the scriptures, for they are they that testify against themselves, and against their writers.

With what justice could God render himself peculiar to a very minute part of the world, and leave out more than nine hundred and ninety-nine parts, to gratify the peculiar part ? Are they the diamond of creation ? The way the world treats them causes us to estimate them differently.

In what a category are all that adopt and propagate all these bibles, without proof and rational faith !

I glory in exposing the bibles of tradition, as the most sinful books ever devised. What does the mass of the people know of analysis ? But fanatical fury is ready to burst upon any that disputes the bible.

You hallow the remains of pagan idolaters, but forget the noble duty to mind, the noblest representative of its Creator, God. The writers of all bibles of tradition prove themselves by their errors, notwithstanding all their impostures, to have been wicked men. The mysteries of bibles are all frauds to deceive the people, who have been imposed upon in all ages. Will you join the ignoble crowd of world plunderers ?

Who endorses the proof of inspiration of any writer ?

The object is not to investigate facts, but prejudice the world against them when adduced. How is this ? Is this the honorable way of truth ? Is burning incense to God anything but the highest folly ? Are then such blockheads to impose their pretences on us ? Actions are man's best morals. He must look to God for a standard, not at all to messiahship. The Jews have been insulted, their property confiscated, their synagogues burnt, and themselves compelled to be banished, or destroyed, or baptized by a hypocritical compliance.

" St. Cyril, the patriarch of Alexandria, endeavored to suppress Judaism by burning down the synagogues and expelling the Jews from the city, rewarding the ' soldiers of the cross' for their pious exploits with the spoils of the exiled race." " When the Crusaders passed through Germany, on their way to the East, they murdered the Jews, without distinction of age or sex." " The papal decrees against the Jews were very cruel and absurd."

How many varieties of the same species of man have been created in the absence of correct history ?

The analysis of the whole subject discloses several. The work of God is plainly seen in the sterility of hybrids, or that of hybridity, but the variation of the species only proves the genius of the Creator.

Bibles of tradition have been the worst causes of a world full, promoting the worst sins of blasphemy and hypocrisy.

God and man are libeled by bibles of tradition.

Conscience and sound faith compel all rational investigating minds to reject all such.

Geology does not disclose the era of man's approach on earth but as the last of all creation, and therefore the best. It discloses the fixed design of creation in development. God created all as they are, with no curses about it. We disbelieve the bible, discard and protest against it, as long as honesty is the truth of mind, as its creation of earth or heaven is incompetent for man. In adopting the peculiar faith of any bible, the vassalage of mind is completely established.

But if you find fault with God's word, you find fault with God. That is unquestionably true, and undoubtedly applies to you. God's word is alone in his works. People that seek to carry their theory as the bible botches, will too often sacrifice too much for its support. They have sacrificed religion for their bible. The bible that they uphold, is in antagonism to the universe. They are then at issue with the last, and that decides the question conclusively. They have to reconcile all that, or renounce the whole at once.

The Jews had a priestocracy deism; the oracular peculiar god of priestocracy. Rational religion only bestows the purity of deism, monotheism, distinct from sinister influences. What can be greater sophistry than all the bible articles about faith? You who have been blinded by peculiar worship and faith, cannot see without aid with correct vision.

What a ferocious sectarianism was that which induced the Jews to slaughter women in the most tender conditions of life, to violate the noblest virtues of chastity, and commit the most ferocious piracy on the owners of the soil, whom they sought to extirpate?

But the oracles of Judaism have claimed that such were the commands of God. What god, but their peculiar automaton, that spake as the bible-mongers dictated?

Does the God of humanity, purity and honesty command a nation to act the felon and perpetrate capital offences, for which that very bible caused individuals to be executed? Is the world never to get rid of this supreme felony of felonies? Is the code to be revered, though it militate against the loftiest conservative principles of the God of the universe, whom it audaciously, recklessly and blasphemously libels? Shall this hot-bed of poison, reeking with the evils of centuries and hoary in crimes, that caused one nation to aim eternal hatred against the world for fanatical sectarianism to their species, be still tolerated by mind? What intoleration could have been worse than Judaism? Shall its whole brood that murders the world be left in its bosom to tear out its very entrails? Humanity proves religion. Where is the humanity in the world's extirpation?

That the Jews did not extirpate the world on their own position is, that they had not the power. If one nation was to be extirpated because of their peculiar faith, how much more necessary was it to extirpate the whole?

As it was not humanity, it was not religion, nor was it of God. Religion begets a universal brotherhood.

Was this the divine essence of Judaism, or of any of its offspring? Their faith was that of a corrupt priestocracy. If it ever were a deism, it was so bald that it was destitute of principles. What a base for any offspring! If the bible had been inspiration, the just rights of the sovereign people would have been respected, as that gives the greatest good to the greatest number, but the priestocracy and their creations are the centre of worship. If you hold on to the bibles, you hold on to the false position created by them.

Is it possible that lovely, intelligent, virtuous females can tolerate a book that speaks so complacently of the appropriation of thirty-two thousand virgins by their male captors? Of Solomon the lewd as wise, who luxuriated like an animal on woman's gifts and charms, and then reviled the sex after his base abuse of power, like a world's despot? Was this a system that gave woman her rights, or mind its purity, in its oriental imitations?

Does the geological history accord at all with the bible? No. What true history does? The church and all hierarchies have stood in the way of all science and constitutional liberty, until mind forced them along despite of themselves, and now they have a series of beggarly elements. They withstood astronomical and geological science, until ashamed. The facts and principles of all science must be truly carried out, and they must expel all bibles of tradition. Then what shall we do for faith? The bibles have done all practicable for peculiar faith, but religion must act now for good, true, and inviolable faith. We must recur to facts, the science of truth and reason, like rational beings.

Antiquity necessarily blends truth and fiction, fables and legends, in correct tradition. History was not safe till science spoke. Bibles of tradition constitute the trash era, having nurtured the worst designs of ambition, avarice, and lust. Galileo was anathematized by the Romish church, and imprisoned for years in a dungeon, for denying the futile errors of the bible, and avowing the Copernican system of astronomy.

The adherents of the bible are refractory, opposing science as astronomy, and geology that corresponded with true religion.

Bible-advocates sustain science, when its pensmen violated the highest principles of physical science, in asserting miracles.

Such revelations are false pretences.

After all, what does the bible teach? Does it approach what mind has advanced? Mind cultivated now corrects these bibles, written by ignorant and unscientific but cunning men, a fact that shows mind's perversion and corruption.

Impenetrable mysteries there are of their god, but impenetrable for all the priestocracy's bibles, and all those of tradition. We are none the wiser in truth for all such.

As to the Jews, &c., having the divine words of God, and the rest of mankind in darkness, that is utterly inconsistent with God's universal attributes.

These bibles are the most foolish, absurd, the blackest impositions devised to perpetuate usurpation and power.

How many self-contradictions are there in the bible? How often is its sophistry received when truth is rejected? They talk of bible revelation! What is revealed but priest-sophistry? Of inspiration! What is inspired but fraud? What is revealed of mystery, but confusion worse confounded? Fables and legends, falsified doctrines and pretences.

Any and everything can be proved by the bible.

The bible is authority for nothing, except as borne out by characteristic morals of mind.

The age of refined civilization cannot be the age of bibles of tradition.

What can be worse misconceptions and butcheries, for the glory of God? The statement is impeached, for its testimony is worthless on its face.

Such bible morals are dangerous, as they have a counteracting malign influence on the light of the times.

There are thousands of evils in all such systems as that of Moses.

Principles alone are conservative, while peculiar bible of tradition-faith is dangerous and impracticable. All such are instruments of evil, only held in abeyance by enlightened public opinion. Let none dissent or adopt, but be convinced by truth from the omnipotent. who is not only supreme, but possesses all the attributes of unity and its comprehensive sovereignty.

To think merely of a messiah, detracts from his attributes. It is infatuation to assert messiahships.

Whilst toleration and forbearance are great virtues, the faith in blasphemy is intolerable to God.

We cannot read the universe without science, certainly not correctly.

None but reckless assertions are made, when it is asserted that Moses is right. Such is not fair, legitimate, or liberal.

The social, political, and national ameliorations have been carried far beyond Moses and his fellows, who ruined instead of blessed nations. Science institutes true benevolence, aids and blesses. But the gospel plan of salvation is the only plan, whereby mankind can be saved through priests and preachers! But mind is paramount to both, as God is to all messiahs.

What has the world to do with any such, when it emphatically needs universal talents, gifts, and endowments.

Why have the learned of the world been so silent, with but few noble exceptions, to the disgraceful ignominy of this bible? Have most been bribed?

God has only given one edition of his works at creation; all others are counterfeit. The bible is man's writings, that are worthless by tradition. The world needs a well-defined code of ethics, moral and religious culture. Creed and faith are the playthings of autocrats, the dreams of visionaries.

I would scorn to say anything against a good book or authors. But who, in his sound senses, after an honest and truthful investigation, will pretend to believe this of this book or its authors? As much above Moses as is the state of mind now, so is the present superior to the past of his country.

No peculiar bible is available for popular progress.

It is confirmation strong as proofs of the cause, that all writers on rational religion must mainly reach the same consummation. They can reach no other than God.

But such books are absolutely dangerous. To bibles, or truth? Of course, to bibles.

Of course, bible or peculiar faith-advocates are not going to give any one the means of overcoming them, truth or no truth. Why? Because it is life, or death. Will the christians do this?

None have proved it more strongly. How can they get over all this? As they have done before—declare it is not so. How can they do all this?

They are the world's sophists. What care the priestocracy for truth, as long as they can hold the reins of power in their own hands? While they laugh at the verdancy of the world on one side, they will extract their revenues on the other. What care the priestocracy for the world's opinion, as long as they can deceive not only the world, but make it contribute to that very deception?

What care they for the unity of God, while they can speculate on their trinity, and have not to disgorge their revenues and honors, however dishonorable?

What care they for retaining thousands and tens of thousands, if the majority are pauperized into many beggars?

What care they for conscience, when the government of usurpation and monopoly use them, or bribe their consciences? Will they ever see, if the world will close its eyes? Who of sound mind and uncommitted to its speculations in this world, through all the finesse and intrigues of the priestocracy, but must decide on the highest analysis, and come to a satisfactory conclusion that it is a base imposition? The world is sought to be bribed or forced to give faith and credence to it.

That defeated, on the thousand points, the bible sophist affects one more: that God must have a written word to point out the way! Having deserted the rights, he seeks to sap the very essence of mind. I say that he overlooks the beautiful free-agency of mind, that has the most rational invitation, not an imperative command to analyze the universe of God, who has delicately tendered mind its noblest conservation, without compulsion.

Could the God of omniscience create this world subject to the contingency of Adam and Eve's caprice, and all mankind in abeyance to these last two foolish people?

No! It is the libel of monk's brains; it is the most stupid folly of the priestocracy. All such bibles are no sort of account at all; and whether they flourish thousands of years or centuries, their end must and will come. The God that we adore is different, from the fiction of bibles. He does not write books as men indite, but wields orbs of the universe that is made up of suns, planets, and comets. Had the world been described by God, he would have told enough of its grand divisions and form, to have described it accurately. But he has consigned its best appreciation to mind's functions.

If the truth be violated by the bible, how does it support religion that is based on truth? We will then use, as always, wisest legislation, and its wisest administration all through rational mind. The bible of tradition is the worst prostitution of mind, to enslavement of the world.

But rational discussion, which is the very life of truth, is shunned. Is any freeman afraid of investigation?

God's language is universally uniform, and easily read by all nations, who now speak thousands of languages.

The orbs of the universe, in their relations of gravitation and revolution, are universal to all that know as much by science. The language of the bible of tradition is not worth understanding. Who, but blundering man, wrote it?

If anything be perfect in the bible, it is that the legends are perfect. Mind has been embarrassed and paralyzed by the policy of bibles of tradition. The policy of the bible of degrading sectarianism, and that has made murderers and robbers.

But the bible is looked upon by a mass, a circle, as holy and sacred. Is this proved? It is proved a humbug.

It has most woful abuses, and is the prolific parent of many others, without limit. They must be all corrected, on the noblest toleration of mind.

Away with its stupid perversions of mind, and stupid demoralization of intellect. Mind must not condescend, but must avoid sectarianism as barbarian.

For years past, say one-quarter of a century, it is believed that bible construction has become more and more liberal, till the whole will necessarily be construed away. If this be not the case, the world will be full of vassals of mind, afraid to say their soul is God's.

We must take the whole bible or none, yet the bible people, if honest, cannot believe, as they have to reject parts of the bible! That proves conclusively the action of its honest friends' faith, is conclusive proof against it, as a part vitiated vitiates the whole, as a witness that is partly perjured ; they are all patched up affairs.

The sons of God took the daughters of men for wives. This is the old mythology of polytheism revived. No bibles of tradition can arouse the mind truthfully—philosophically to God's lofty purpose.

Mind takes precedence of all such bibles. They are for different ages and pursuits, the mind vassalage of the country where manufactured, not refined civilization which they disgrace. They are received with mental reservation, proving their fallacy. Why does not mind do justice to itself, impeach and discard all such at once and forever ? This has to be done. The conservative spirit of the world, is the highest intellectual spirit. There can be no substitute, by the bible of mind. Bibles of tradition do not begin to be at all, for they are a source of corruption and depravity.

What has any black letter to do with the rights of mind, which it clearly violates whether in bibles of tradition or any other ? I can take no scriptures, and accept no errors, for they are too many to license them to perpetuate this fraud, assuming the power of the Divine Authority, to which the most substantial, shortest way is, by truth of mind. What a demoralizing set were the patriarchs, also Moses, Aaron, David, Christ.

They conspire to make a serpent beast, greater than God. To undo this blasphemy, it is right to impeach and discard the statement, the authors, aiders, and abettors, those who give comfort to the fiction and false pretences. How easy is it to write such bibles ! Many are over the world, all deluding by their false pretences.

Mahomet succeeded, and was as great as Moses ; he lied as bad as his prototype about his heaven, the moon, and quick travels. In fact, he outdid Moses, for he as mortal went to his heaven, a thing that Moses never did as he told. Joe Smith affected to be prophet and had many followers, but Smith had less materials for fraud. As long as the world will not choose to be philosophic but sophist, so long will bigots be unreasonable and generally ignorant.

Philosophy kills superstition. Whilst ever tolerant, she gives all information for the unwary as a true friend to mankind. But the peculiar faith doctrinists affirm to the belief of their bible, and war on all opponents. While the Christians have no better authority for their bible, than those Mormons, yet they drive them out, and would drive the rest out of the world, if they had the brief authority to do so. Of all vindictiveness, that of peculiar faith when enraged to fanaticism, is the worst. Take the bible altogether, and it is corrupt. Some believe only part ; that condems them.

Is it right for men to impose these frauds all the time in theology, and still all be right ? We have gained our liberty to but little purpose then, if our mind-rights are not respected.

The most refined of civilization are more inspired the present age, by true science, than all the bible worthies together. I impeach and discard all bibles but those of mind. Both kinds cannot stand certainly, as those of tradition or truth.

Where is honesty of truth, one of the main principles of life ? There is a lack of virtuous firmness, on this basis, that nothing can restore. Neither law, testimony, nor truth, are on the side of the bibles of tradition, which, consequently, are deeply injurious.

But a person reads his bible with first impressions inculcated, to which we see added the appliances of the priestocracy, to force conviction, and oppose by all means any other light of mind ! Before the mind has analyzed both sides of this most momentous question, it is forced captive to a peculiar faith, that cannot bear scrutiny, and recoils at investigation.

What can be a worse libel on the goodness or the omnipotence of God, than the legend of satan ?

All bibles of tradition are vile libels on the Almighty. Whose is less ? The Mormons ?

The Jews, under the dynasty of Moses, Joshua, and others, went for conquest and plunder. under the name of the Almighty, like fanatics—so did the crusaders—into the holy, the accursed land, having the example of each peculiar faith predecessors. Who were the Jews ? Were they more civilized, intelligent, wise, virtuous, just, noble, scientific, humane, rich, than all the rest of the world ? No just analysis will affirm this. No theology can be sacred that will support it.

They were a priestocracy-accursed nation.

There can be no good, pure faith in any bible of tradition. Infidels, is it, monotheists are called ? See how far the fanaticism of prejudice carries ! What is an infidel ?

One who cannot believe in any of the impositions and frauds of any of the various bibles of traditions in the world, but who believes in that of mind, the code of the purest, enlightened conscience, as he believes in the unity and supremacy of the Almighty.

But the blindly credulous of the world are enraged against the infidels to their bibles; then, of course, they are furious towards one another, and can never have the first principles of universal brotherhood.

The true definition is, that what is called infidel is opposed to the blasphemous, pretended messiahs, and is necessarily so, to have fidelity to God, who is perfect, and possessed of every attribute of preservation as well as of creation. But for toleration, there were no infidels, for the fagot and the various artillery of inquisitions would exclude them out of this world. The sects would rise infuriate with blood.

Who but Calvin destroyed Helvetius, and who but such would consign all opponents to perdition?

Which is best, an infidel or a libeler? The last the fanatic is, to man and God, when he arraigns man as an infidel, and God as needing a messiah for man.

Let the world full of bibles of tradition perish, rather than truth. Perish all such bibles, ere organic principles are assailed with obloquy. Is it not a shame that bibles of prescription should tyrannize over freedom of mind? Do you go to the bibles of tradition to learn science, or to mind? And is it not the science of rational religion, the most sublime, and requiring all the energies of mind? Were the Jews distinguished, peculiarly, by all the blessings of government? They were ruled by a despotic priestocracy, deceived by their guiles and false pretences. It but little profited, that bravest and best patriots fell for our freedom, if it be trammeled by bibles of tradition.

Liberty thus, was but half civilized. We have more than all the bibles of tradition of the world can give us. We have mind and the eternal principles of the Creator to elaborate the perfection of the soul; principles ever abiding, never dying or ending, enduring to eternity; whereas, bibles wear out and decay, like their authors. The great and paramount question of a bible is, to produce the greatest and highest cultivation of mind for religion. Can bibles of tradition do it? Not at all. The mighty problems of life, of the world, may be solved in the progress of light of mind by time. All bibles of tradition break into fragments the universal brotherhood of mankind. Principles vindicate themselves, and rule out all such bibles. We need those bibles that suit the rights of the world and mind; those we have not heretofore had.

With bibles of tradition mind is made to lose by their usurpation, as if anything could be done without mind.

Intellectual investigation will portray the priestocracy, the Jesuitical lawyers of peculiar faith.

It is the mind mission, not the bible mission. Priests take the last; philosophers, who really benefit the world, take the first. The world does not understand all the comprehensive bearings of some things called bibles of tradition, that are obsolete ideas with mind capable of analysis, if not with priestocracies and their vassals.

Why is there a superstitious veneration for all such bibles, when the world can attain incomparably nobler and better means?

What is the paramount question in religion? Not bibles, but principles.

Will you adhere to obsolete bibles and a lean meagre minority, a fragment of the world for believers, or on principles with us, take the whole world that can gloriously unite in one mighty brotherhood?

The ancient incapacity of mind's doing justice to itself caused the sale of the debtor for slavery; now modern civilization, elevated to the noblest principles of mind, gives a homestead to the family that cannot be taken or touched for debt. Rational mind will take care of all that are too imbecile to help themselves.

The old regime gave bibles of tradition, now modern civilization of monotheism expels them as obsolete, and triumphantly vindicates the rights of mind, and the glory of God, by the purest emanations of mind.

All countries are blessed by the civilization of mind, that looks to God's principles, the noblest standard of religion, the benefits of commerce, the lights of science, that asks to get rid of bibles of tradition, and have for them pure rational religion, sound honest sense of sane minds. The mind that affects such bibles is most unjust to itself.

The friend of law, order, right, religion that is rational, must ever decide against all such bibles. There can be no self-surrender to such dissolute codes of morals.

The God of justice would have inspired in every language of the world all the bibles. But what then would have become of free agency of mind, the excellency, the beauty of the universe, that has enabled the God of mind to meet the whole question of creation. For the bane of life, the antidote is in an enlightened mind. Yet bigots would say, do not read or investigate certain books, thereby proving themselves unworthy of rational mind. How can the subject be honorably investigated, if but one side is told! Does it hurt to hear the truth? If there are any books that óppose the bible, they are in the category of approbation or censure. In either way they, as the efforts of rational m:nd. should be known, on their merits or demerits.

The world seeks conservation only obtained through mind, as bibles bring destruct.on. What sophistry, now that such bibles teach us, and not mind teach as God directs it. What instituted the bibles, then? God. Who proves that? None. This is ;' the pretended inspiration of priestocracy, that the inspiration of philosophical scienc must counteract. The priests' interests revealed it.

Better had its record perished; but God permits mind to guard the world agains all such that would have been effectual if despotism had not governed. You sb i not only understand, but analyze all you read. Thus saith the Lord! It is an ins''..·· ous declaration that the God of the universe said it, when it was the god of Judais:. the god of the peculiar bible that said it. The bane should have the antidote, for t.. people's rights and their preservation. God's scriptures cannot admit of special pl .:.: ings and sophistry, that are of no avail in the primary position. Speak of peculiar p : ple of God, when justice requires no distinction in the same nation only as pers .: merit exalts, does it in the world, one of the great objects of regard to the Creator?

But as to the scriptures, if you reverence mind, you cannot estimate them. Levit '. ch. xxvi., v. 3, "If ye walk in my statutes, and keep my commandments, and do th.:.' (as a consequence,) v. 6, "and I will give peace in the land;" v. 7, "and ye shall :.- your enemies, and they shall fall before you by the sword;" v. 12, "and I will u .. among you, and will be your god, and ye shall be my people."

Though the peculiar people, yet they did not better themselves as well as those :· peculiar. Their peculiarity ruined them. They were more tenacious of circums: than of the improvement of mind. What a blur on mind! Is there any peculiar, n'·· terious power about man, greater than man's mind that is inspired by the principl..·' God? The proof of the Creator is the greatest good to the greatest number, u::· includes the whole. The bible is an imposition, proved by the reverse, of the pee. · care for a few million of Jews, whose intellectual mark was not equal to many cot.:: poraries, while the rest of the world was proscribed.

The god of Judaism is undeniably the fiction of superstition, idolatry and bi: ·· How does the bible of tradition compare one moment with the press, one of the :·· levers of the world's mind? The superseding bibles by principles will introduc .· highest order of action of mind, as no dependence will be put on other than our · exertions. Let writers, historians, reviewers, orators, lecturers, statesmen, pat:·· help the universal cause of truth, reason, morals and religion. At present, favor.'.· fashion, custom, and a base compliance therewith, a miserable sycophancy, rather "·- principles prevail.

Nothing short of discarding the bibles of tradition will answer. Why, says the :·: culiar faith bible man, do you attack our bible? Because that violates God's truth.· nothing less, by its impious antagonism. Now we invite all the world to attack :·· bible of mind on the same principle, if there be anything wrong, and not let it sta.. · minute. We therefore should also seek to get rid of its primary errors.

The use of angels by the peculiar god in the universe, betrays clumsy and ineffic: :: machinery. Light flies in eight minutes from our sun to this planet the earth, but i :· long would an angel be traveling as a messenger? What stupid processes of u·"· invention, sharpened by his wits for self-interest! The worst is to get a stupid mass,· believe in all this!

If the world really need a code, over and above what is now doing in our spl:·- government country, the best one is the pure, genuine bible of mind.

How can that of Moses civilize the world when it brutalized his own citizens, a·· sacrificed the potency of mind?

Sectarian, bigot and tyrant, it ruled out justice and religion to the lust of dominion a·· ambition, and fell a suicide thereto.

Monopolists cannot control the markets of the world, much less its mind.

How could the bible be God's inspiration when it has not even mind's science, ·· any principles?

God is perfect and immutable, hence his inspiration conveys a true exposition of :: character, which his universe most certainly does.

Truly may it be said that God has made himself almighty, by one revelation an! that the universe. There can be no revelation of God known to man, constituted with five senses as he is, but through God or his representatives, his works that characterize ··· his attributes and principles.

We can know nothing of God's writing but by electricity; none of his volumes ad:

the orbs of the universe constituted as mind is now. The universe that reveals full evidence fills all man's senses; but how many senses does the bible supply? It takes the revealer to prove revelation, that has no testimony after all. All the assertions about God's word in all the bibles of tradition, are worth nothing, without his proof.

God is a universe problem not to be solved in men's looks, and mere earthly matters. The peculiar god of the peculiar heavens, reflects the character of the peculiar people, all to be rejected by all rational minds. Who can be a reader of the whole bible? One that can analyze it in most of its parts. What then results? The utmost satisfaction that it is the most outrageous kind of book, ever published to the world. If the bible be corrupt, what must be those who knowingly support it? Who will argue, if in his senses, that one iota of advantage ought to be permitted to it or its advocates? And nothing but advantage has been taken by it, all the time of mind.

There are interpolation after interpolation in the scriptures, collusions, manufactures of sentences, all to no purpose, as all fell still born and obsolete.

The world is not intrinsically concerned about obsolete bibles but religion, to promote the best social condition of the world. The ubiquity of thought can only be through mind, not through books or even printing which are contingent.

If we had one book that all the world could read in the universe, in one unalterable language, that would be revelation, and that sure enough God has perfected for mind. As I am responsible, I seek to be correct. Who is responsible for the bibles of tradition? Would any foolishly commit themselves therefor, to perpetrate perjury? What an idea, that the bible advances that a part was predestinated from eternity to be saved, and a part to be damned, when some of the last, though not having the peculiar creed of the first, may far excel in virtue, truth, honesty and sincerity. The honest part of the world has been grossly imposed upon in many ages by these things, when its every object is truth, honest truth.

The poor world is so simple minded as to be caught by the lies of a book, because it states that God said so and so, when it betrays itself at once by those very statements, as God does not address those of this earth but through his word, cause and effect elaborated in principles evinced in science.

Korah was greater than Moses, as he advocated the rights of mind. He was far in advance of such a bigot.

But the bible of Moses is expedient for the organization of society. Where was the social organization of the Romans in their civil polity, that in the opinion of the learned in law, as T. Reavis of Gainesville, Ala., and Kent, who particularly refers to the excellency of the civil law, but in the supremacy of mind?

The Romanists do not wish the bible read by the people, as they know that it is not true.

All defenders of the bible are only skilful sophists, from the nature of the case, able if any could, to maintain the authenticity of the scriptures, but incompetent from the nature of the subject. What is the best policy in such a position? To let it all alone, as an impracticable subject. It cannot be defended by any honest mind conscientiously, that must necessarily compromise itself. Then mind must fall with an untruthful bible advocated.

Where is the first effectual defence of the authenticity of the scriptures? Does not all prove a flimsy attempt from the nature of the business. and all the defenders turn out mere sophists? Those that are strenuous take up a hundred unessential points, and advance them with a pertinacity worthy of a nobler cause, seeking bibles for religion, faith for truth, feigning pious frauds of people apparently dying, then recovering and telling tales of the spirit-land, of some in their delirium seeing sights and interpreting some at the last stage to suit their unholy purposes.

The very first verse of the first chapter of Genesis, has neither the truth, the whole truth and nothing but the truth, and this is the case to Apocrypha. The whole bible is apocrypha. Judgment is the thing in all matters of life, and that of others should be consulted, if ours be deficient correspondently with the facts of the world. If any one of rational mind will read the bible critically and exactly, he or she will be bound to reject the statements as corrupt and vitiated.

The Creator premises and presents exact science, on the principles of truth, the whole truth, and nothing but the truth—in the universal creation, his revelation—the whole universe his inspiration.

The bible advocates ought to be ashamed of the whole pretence. As advocates of sophistry, they maintain it at all hazards, without conscience or truth. We impeach them all—if ignorant, of error—if knowing, of crime.

All the defenders of the bible expose its deformity worse and worse, before the critical world, and render rationalism stronger every day.

I have asked again and again for proof of the authenticity of the scriptures, of those peculiarly educated; and though defeated in giving anything valid, yet by their peculiar faith, as about ghosts, they were unable to leave the poisonous spell, and stuck to their idols.

Jacob defrauds Esau of his birthright, to whom he afterwards basely cringes, as a sycophant. By this position it is sought to defraud mankind of their birthright, religion, superseding therefor superstitious peculiar faith.

The Jews were benefited, without doubt, by being carried to Babylon, as several refused to return to their native country; and that invalidates much of the supposed influence of their faith, seeing it all a farce about the Mosaic dispensation, worthless as that of the Mormons.

The moderns attach more importance to the bible than the cotemporary ancients. The moderns have made themselves blockheads about this, overlooking the progress and position of mind, that is the whole to be looked at. It is the fault of the people, that will not see what is so clear, thereby making themselves pagan, to uphold corrupt paganism.

All the efforts of all the sophists expose the weakness and corruptions of the bible, plainer every day.

After all their failures, it will then be their bounden duty to help civilize the world The bible is not worth sending to the heathens, much less retention among an elevated society!

It is a perfect impossibility, that God should ever have selected peculiar faith people or bibles, to be in antagonism with his peculiar functions and principles.

Did Moses or his manufacturers seek to take proper care of the human family? That is what they could not do.

You fear touching the defence of your bible. You fear you will lose your religion. No: you will lose, as you ought, peculiar faith, but you will get a nobler gain, which is, rational religion, that peculiar faith and bibles do not touch.

When ministers endorse this bible, they endorse all its heresies and frauds—devised most cunningly for collusion and deceit. Admit that it was the best of the priestocracy, that is not the best for the world to receive; therefore let it keep its place, out of mind. Let it keep the circle of bad company. God does not need such man's endorsement, as this libel of priestocracy.

Nothing less than the whole bible is to be taken by rational religionists, to defeat it entirely, and at once.

One single prophecy, of possession of the land of Canaan forever, to the Jews, will meet all the subsequent pretences of the bible most effectually in bold relief, and annihilate it. It is a fraud on the world that the corpse is not buried. The bible is far more modern than it appears. Its first five books are vitiated by interpolations, and corrupted by alterations, if not originally a base book! The bible, so far from being an aid of civilization, retards it.

Does Orientalism ask for mastery, to carry out peculiar views? What is the object of the bible of tradition?

Power and dynasty to the greatest practicable extent, embracing ambition and avarice, not neglecting revenge and envy. Have we any proof that the people of Israel, so far from seeing Moses receive any book of God, that they were in existence? How can you sustain this fabric? The question is not as to its destruction or annihilation, as theologians after the truth must see the entire contradiction.

What shall we think of the tears of the people, shed, as related by Nehemiah, at hearing the law read? Could any of them have ever known of such a thing before! As the first set of books, the fundamental and essential five of Moses, is vitiated, all the others are undoubtedly, also. The object is attained by the priestocracy, if they can fool their generation, and that by the most cunning sophistry! And yet, in how many departments is this carried out, as far as practicable! The advocates may parade their abstract rules and Mosaic pretensions, but one usurpation kills all such, stolen from mind, and ignorantly paraded as their property. All the bible is stolen from mind, whose rights have been basely and ignominiously usurped by mind's perversions.

The whole is a fraud on mind from mind, and the worst is, it is the lowest despotism, deep cunning, yet ignorance of mind. Its art has been studied, for the world's deepest .deception.

As to Abraham's faith, as reported, what merit is there in that, when he, as the bible says, had his god to create it, by prophecies and miracles? Give us no idolatrous polygamy of lustful patriarchs, for a bible. The god of Abraham conversed with him, who did mighty things, that would have stamped Abraham recreant to all the principles of human nature, had he not been faithful, as the book purports. But what merit is there in all that, then, provided the bible was truthful? The functions of Abraham's faith was aftersight of the miracles stated, not proved.

But moderns are not in similar or analogous circumstances to adopt such position, but must reject all until proved, as the part of wisdom. Now it is as little as the bible advocates can do, if there was ever one miracle, to prove it in their bible; and to do that they have first to prove the bible. If they do not, they are impostors.

The faith of Abraham is essential to his circumstances, as he is affirmed to have been an eye-witness; but it would be the height of folly, madness, or hypocrisy, in those not enjoying Abraham's sight and hearing, to have analogous faith, not even having sight and hearing of proof, much less of the demonstration. No: the world is not to be fooled that way, and that man is foolish or knavish to expect honorable credence of the world, without he gives honest, truthful, honorable proof. None such has been given, though mind can have no testimony without miracles, that, as extraordinary in nature, must be performed, to be believed. Any minister, then, that fails, is dishonorable, that seeks to palm the bible of tradition on the ignorant mass of the world. Miracles or their honorable proof is the first step in all sermons, that are perjuries otherwise.

Now the bible advocates will affect to say, that we say the word of God ought to be rejected. Certainly we say no such thing, not an iota of it. The word of God will not, cannot be rejected. Here is the difference, the honorable difference. The book, the bible, gives not an iota of proof of its being God's word. It is not an alphabet towards it, not at all.

What is sacred history, as written in the bible? That of superstition! Will you pollute your language? Are you not freer than the slaves of Orientalism? Why, then, not act up to your high rights and privileges? Sacred history is the true record of rational religion.

We seek the validity of proof, of this bible of tradition. It is God's word! What is that? Are you to suppose it the voice of a being? No! It is that which addresses mind, originates thought.

Believe the bible to be God's word! We can believe no ancient or modern story, that has improbable things. How do we know them improbable? By the best test, that of cultivated, scientific mind. I can know no book by name, only on truth. Faith without truth is foolish.

In reading any or all books, no matter the name, we must adopt this as one of the infallible standards of truth. All that defends the bible of tradition is sophistry, with its despotic and mercenary policies, not principles. That policy is reckless of rational principles, in the quagmire of superstition, bigotry and blasphemy.

A mighty solution was that, as most of the bible is, in giving the reasons for the destruction of Sodom and Gomorrah, the cities of the plains, that like all the world is subject to natural causes.

Angels. Sales in the preliminary treatise in the koran says, " that the talmud acknowledges the Jews to be indebted to the Persians, for the idea of angels."

Then of course, the whole bible is an explanation even on that position.

Esau sold his birthright, preferring to lay aside as the eldest born, the teaching of the doctrines of his fathers.

What a rebuke was here.

Jacob was an unprincipled, avaricious wretch, that went against the doctrines of his father's faith, to usurp that right that could not be transferred.

Did God countenance or connive at the transfer thus purloined? Not if made by fraud consummated as stated, by the intrigue of Rebecca, otherwise all the faith and morality are of a piece. The peculiar god only did that, that is the peculiar priestocracy did. What good did it do him, when he cringed to Esau, after all that Isaac had predicted? Jacob acted as the servant, cringing like an inferior, and paying tribute. Jacob's peculiar faith is positively stolen from rational religion.

Do the preachers sell their birthright of religion, for peculiar faith? Do they seek to deceive the world on that point? The gospel is the tidings of sophistry, the libel and caricature of the God of the universe.

The inspiration of the bible is that of men, not of God.

Yes, but God wrote for the people who were ignorant. He certainly did not write to make their ignorance error, as the ignorant writers who betray themselves, for the truth and science are the plainest of all to be understood. Man, not God, has mystified the whole. To criticise the bible properly, we have to take it as presented, substantially and as it reads. Is the bible of tradition, a true picture of Deity's mind, attributes or principles?

It is all assumption about direct revelation. The world has not made the right use, nor asserted its rights of mind. Revelation as pretended, has not perfected man's happiness nor wisdom. It has not done as well as mind's wisdom. How are we any wiser, by the Mosaic theogony?

Direct revelation takes away free agency, and leaves mind nothing to do, and destitute of merit.

The revelation of the universe is the thing.

All bible advocates assume that their bible is correct, and that their peculiar faith is right; very clear of all such. As to some of the ancient philosophers being assumed as wanting revelation, it must be proved that their philosophy was up to science; it was not—clearly so. False positions are taken in philosophy and faith. Philosophy is only advanced as the knowledge of science is, and the world knows that mind has only opened the position for investigation. The question has never been analyzed, much less answered. We can most clearly and conclusively rule out all revelation, by analysis of the very first verse of the first chapter of Genesis. The whole proof of inspiration of any book, is its truth, whole truth, and nothing but the truth. No person should decide any such question till properly investigated by him or her, to be convert of truth and religion.

In reply to bible advocates, we say a Divine revelation is needed to most, who claim that they have a revelation. The morals of individuals and churches prove it. All their present bible revelation does not lead them to the true God or religion.

Bible advocacy, priestocracy lied for kings, who burnt mankind for them. What thanks does mankind owe both these, their arch enemies?

How can the bible be a book of religion, when it violates the very first principles? Before people start on the authority of this book, the advocates must be properly assured of its authenticity, or they are in the category of holders of bank notes that are spurious, counterfeit, which they issue ignorantly or knowingly.

Esau was a better, honester man than Jacob, who defrauded Esau of his birthright, as the priestocracy seek to defraud the world of its birthright religion, superseding it by peculiar faith. Do you call that religion in Jacob, where fraud prevails?

The race of Esau was finally conquered and absorbed like myriads of nations. That of Jacob has been repeatedly conquered, enslaved, cruelly oppressed, partly exterminated, scattered over the world, persecuted on all hands, and now are not at peace with the whole world, contrary to the principles of God, who has no antagonism in all he does. The antagonism of the world and Judaism, disproves and condemns the last, and all founded thereon.

Now where would be the Jews, if the world had treated them as they treated the owners of the countries they pirated on? They would have been exterminated totally.

The ancients looked not at principles, but for masters, whose dictatorial words they dared not dispute.

A book then passed current for a time, because it was a book! The scriptures do not begin the record of religion, because they are the most positive record of peculiar faiths and after-thoughts of man, therefore they do not reach God's fore-thoughts. They are thus absolutely condemned, unquestionably and unequivocally. There is but one sacred history of God, and that is his works that are read through the correct translation of science, at the same time in ubiquity by all of billions of worlds.

His word is cause and effect: the result, the universe.

The Jew circumcision is a vulgar barbarism without the least pretence to civilization, the highest test on earth of religion. Circumcision then condemns Judaism, as the most contemptible of peculiar faiths.

The Jews now have enough to provoke war among those with whom they sojourn. It is even in this free country, but a miserable toleration.

As to the one race of mankind, the world must speak not by any book pretence, written by ignorant writers, who have impiously palmed it on the world for God's; but of the actual variety of the human species. Was Adam white, black or red? Was he not red, from his name?

The bible absurdly makes a mixed race with the Adamic, of gigantic size. We have the black or African, Indian red, the white, besides intermediates, not less than five in all.

How many more that are extinct we do not know; as we do not know the world's history, I dissent from the position that it is a true exposition of the race of mankind, any more than telling or writing of a miracle is conclusive at all.

The nature of bible faith requires prior performance of the miracle, as it is certain the writers knew nothing about it. The statement in the bible cannot elicit belief, as that is necessarily credulity. If miracles be essential to faith, of course to prevent collusion, such mind must have them performed. Man has falsified God's province in regard to prophecies, that his agent, time, alone decides. The scriptures of ink are too paltry to testify of God, creator of the universe that alone testifies with its billions of orbs and systems of suns. God's word, cause and effect, destroy all pretences of miracles; prophecies and their bibles. The repudiation of the Jews of the loans, as acknowledged in the bible, was a theft on the confiding Egyptians, who were friendly, as proved by this very act. Was it not the king that was absolute, who was to blame? How could the poor Egyptians help themselves? Why is it that this nation of Palestine, that had such illustrious peculiar advantages, did not enlighten the whole world, and make known by prophecy what was unknown to it, a whole continent of unredeemed souls, who had not the bread of life? If they did not know of it they were knaves, if they did, they were impostors, in both cases unworthy of the world's confidence.

Why was not the same essential good, equivalent to that claimed for the Jews, bestowed on the whole world cotemporary? Did not God create all? How were the balance more culpable or less worthy than the Jews?

Did they all have peculiar revelations, to try their souls and faith? This question decides the crime of such doctrines, and the miserable condition of the Jews to this day proves the effects of those errors.

Why will the modern priestocracy still debase itself before this ignoble idolatry, so vain and ineffectual for the good of the whole? Both sides of all this question should be heard and known, through lectures to the people. The American people ought not to let it alone any longer. All such bibles were made expressly for deception and collusion, to benefit monarchical and hierarchal participants over mind's rights.

Strange, indeed, that mind has to refer to the little country of Palestine, and its half-civilized people, for an example of civilization which they did never possess.

The bibles of tradition are out of the way statements, and require analogous proof. They cannot be demonstrated true, as they have not the dignity of truth. God has said, that is, it is assumed, to have given them to man. Now, where at present is God speaking to man? Where is demonstrative proof that God ever talked with man, past or present time?

God does not appear to us, therefore it is all false. Does half the world actually know what is essential to faith, when it mentions or discusses the authenticity of the scriptures? No wonder the priestocracy, that includes the host of pulpit men of all grades and peculiar faith, sneak from this question. Many of them, if intelligent, must be secretly deists or rank infidels, as they call deists.

It is too bad to quiz the world as the preachers are doing, and make it pay therefor. Now the quizzer ought to pay for the fraud-farce. What prior right or superior claims has any one, by books or pretences that are false, to claim any respect of the world?

Have they not cheated the world, the people, mankind long enough?

If all bibles of peculiar faith are overthrown, as they necessarily must be by the light of rational religion, then the peculiar faith, with its collusive priestocracy, goes too.

We are for this religion. But the priestocracy pretend that, if we deny the bible, we unequivocally deny any history. Not at all; as all true histories prove themselves, being sustained by cotemporaries on reasonable facts; but the bible is not history, nor a portraiture of rational facts.

It assumes more, and for that assumption cannot be proved by its best friends. It would kill the reputation for veracity of any of them, knowingly to justify its false pretences. No peculiar faith story can be justified.

The bible of tradition, doubtlessly, will become a museum curiosity, to be wondered at in future times.

Of the many advocates, how few would be left if they were to investigate the truths of creation.

That is the way the world of mind will believe, when the way is made rationally plain.

When we look at the world, we must have due respect to its analysis of the different races and their capacity. If it be pretended that ancient Africa offered no reason of her present debased state, we may see at once the force of the reason.

The northern portion was peopled in part, by a first race of people, as the Carthagenians, the interior by a wild and uncivilized set of barbarians, who murdered their prisoners or sold them as slaves. Slavery has been one of the means of humanity, and as the light of mind increases, will be alleviated.

Partial investigation into the authenticity of the scriptures, is worse than none. Bibles of tradition are after-thoughts for the peculiar faith of priestocracy. Is it not meritorious to expose the impositions of bibles of tradition?

The bible is God's inspiration, adapted to man as he was.

That is all false pretence. It was man's work, proving itself adapted to his state of ignorance. It is man's inspiration of man, and ignorant, botching man at that! As to the bible, the only thing rational about it cannot be had, that is proof of its authenticity.

Shall any dare say that we scoff at religion, because to get at it we exclude the bibles of tradition and peculiar faith that stand in the way?

In going for religion, we go for all that is rational and just. The bible of tradition is the chart of sophistry, humbuggery, imposition, fraud, and false pretence.

It is easy enough to decide all this question of reference to truth and facts, for all relates to peculiar faith that does not relate to rational religion. .

The inadequacy of pretended revelation is manifest, as is clear to every mind but to men base and degraded as Moses, Abraham, and hosts of such.

These men did have religion revealed directly by God to them. What God? The little peculiar god of the Jews! He did not have it to give. All such peculiar machinery was peculiarly impracticable.

All the potent means of revelation, as printing, the electric telegraph, and all proper appliances would have accompanied direct revelation, to give .the greatest good to the greatest number.

Direct revelation implies the most direct gifts to man ; but as he did not get them, of course he did not get such revelation. The art of printing is more of a revelation of genius of mind.

What does it prove, that the ancient philosophers admitted the necessity of a revelation ? Its authenticity ?

The observations of those called philosophers only proved that their philosophy was defective. If mind, the beneficiary, take proper cognizance of all the bible matters in all its essential comprehensiveness, it will find that God alone is an unexceptionable and indispensable witness of the authenticity of the scriptures.

Out of the very great number of particulars of time, place, persons, &c., mentioned in the Old Testament, is proof drawn against, not for it. How far has the bible been corrupted ? Of course not less than peculiar interests required. Three bold and glaring interpolations detected, serve to prove the vitiation of the whole, as several perjuries in a witness's statement serve to exclude him from all honorable courts of justice. That is all that is necessary in such a tribunal, that cannot be required to expose every idea. Genesis xxxvi. 31 is enough of itself; but when we add the last chapter of Deuteronomy, the matter is most conclusive. Is it not most dishonest to let this imposition continue? The books of Moses alone, are vitiated enough for all.

Yet the unblushing and brazen priestocracy, who are bribed and feed on the part of governments united to church for greater despotism, will contend that the books are genuine ! Are they also authentic ?

An authentic history is one thing, a bible is another.

The advocacy of the Mosaic bible cannot refute the corruption, to say the least of the Pentateuch.

How far that corruption extends, we do not know; but suffice it that it is corrupt. What a pitiful state, to have to feign answers to refute positive facts in the bible ? Is truth, the whole truth, and nothing but the truth, pure religion ? How, then, can the professors countenance all this infamy ? They have to yield bible or religion, for both cannot go together. All the words—divine, testament, covenant—are all forgeries.

What patriot does not desire his noble country exempt from such foul imposition ? God is so supremely greater than priestocracy's corruption, that his works and word all came together, and excluded miracles and revelations of after-thoughts. His mighty structure begets admiration in mind, that must truly adore the author.

The bible of tradition supporters have considered what is politic for dynasty and power, not what is true and beneficial for the people. This, like every other subject, should be open for popular discussion. No pretended feelings should beget false positions and views. The bible cannot elicit the respect and confidence of the world, and ought to be dismissed and discountenanced, as it is not a work in good faith to benefit the world. It is the injury and disgrace of mind.

The bible of tradition advocates are nonplused. Honest men must see their corruption, and must acknowledge and expose it, or be silent. The strategy of subtle sophistry has been used by the bible advocates, till it will not avail them. They have made hypocrites, and dupes or atheists, where the mind was not well balanced to espouse the sublime truths of monotheism.

Now, after the first five books are vitiated with interpolations fixed up with false dates, the whole dependent thereon must fall. Are not the advocates confuted ? Will they not, as honest men, retire from their own overwhelming defeat, but mingle with the corruption—identify themselves therewith?

What a botch the ignorant but designing priestocracy seek to make of God's universe—

only of themselves. The bible is Jew and Christian oracles—cunningly devised and kept up. Unwarrantable licenses have been taken in writing and corrupting the scriptures, to suit the complexion of the times.

Are not the interpolations of the pentateuch of this order? Bible superstitions are as hard to eradicate as ghosts' superstitions. Grant the fabricators the deepest learning, which is not admitted, it is sophistry or learning prostituted. There are no forgeries in the bible! It is all a blasphemous forgery and libel on God, made up by collusion of priestocracy, bribed and seduced by mental prostitution. through money and power. It is a fund for world sophistry. The origin and advocacy of the bible came from pretensions and assumptions of the priestocracy. To that, the world is indebted for the advancement of faith, not merely historical, but saving, otherwise the hearer is to be damned.

The bible was a dead-letter, necessarily, in its conception, much less its propagation. Part of it is proved, it is asserted. as regards the deluge, by the phenomena on the earth. Those phenomena are doubtlessly due to organic causes, not to incidental contingences.

Who represent the witnesses, the Jews, who saw Moses perform the miracles? Dead letters!

What, do we deny history? Not at all; we only deny its counterfeits. That the Jews did receive laws, as no nation can exist without them, is not denied, but who proves their identity with divine inspiration? I admit the laws and history as human, and very poor ones indeed, if we look at the witch part, &c. But more is an imposition and fraud.

When the arch priestocracy affect to talk to their God, how imposing it seems, yet this is not religion at all. The man is furthest from it. very clear of it. Socrates was as near, when he required the sacrifice of a cock to Æsculapius. When we strip off the mantle of pretensions, we can see the proper analysis. Why were the Jews so idolatrous? The view just embraced explains.

It was all the idolatry and false pretences of the priestocracy, who took the degraded view of low human nature for immediate profits. The Jews did not know enough of the God of the universe to do any good. They knew the peculiar god of priestocracy. Neither covenant was correct, as they clashed with principles through sectarianism. The God of the universe has no such machinery as covenant, prophecies, &c. The tyranny of the bible and the priestocracy over mind, is execrable. All the bibles of tradition are most dangerous, the source of which cause more bloodshed and ill will and rancor in the world, than all others known. This and analogous verbal oracles are and were leading causes all over the world, when resolved by the beauty and strength of analysis into first elements. Jews, as well as nations of the earth, owe it to themselves to see justice done them in government and religion. The polygamy of Abraham, &c., misled Mahomet and others fabricating bibles of tradition, as well as the licentious inclined in all circles.

Do I say that the bible of Moses is among the most demoralizing books in the world? What is the Mahometan faith, that emanated from this foul and disgraceful source, the foulest blot on human nature? What is its vice about women? How many are divorced by one husband? According to Dr. Paulding, who resided among them, the Mahomedans can marry and divorce wife after wife.

The Ishmaelites look up to Abraham for polygamy. and what is all that but legalized prostitution with oriental despotism? The Mahometan faith enslaves and prostitutes women. Is it not better to have wise laws framed to virtue, that is, the recognition of principles, than base bibles framed to vice? Dr. Paulding declares that the guilt of any falsehood, in the opinion of Mahomedans, is immediately expiated by the repetition of two words. The corruption of polygamy is awful. It elicits with the Mahomedans the most unnatural and degrading vice, not to be named in the civilized circle.

Congratulate yourselves, females of America and part of Europe, that you have the blessings of mind diffused over your happy land, and that you can rejoice in the name of wife, children, freedom, and virtue, and that you have a home indeed, all of which render sacred the family. All this is due to the illustrious stand of enlightened man.

To reform people of other faiths, you must faithfully reform yourselves. We demand of you in the first place, before you quote the odious bible for offence or defence, to prove its authenticity, to adduce its authority, otherwise we require your positive silence. No bibles of tradition can prove a Creator; then they cannot prove themselves, after the foolish assumptions of advocates. The first step is false, and therefore all is ineffectual. The bible is called the Word of God. God himself must testify to that assertion, else it devolves and recoils on man as a base and infamous fabrication. The bible of tradition cannot prove a Creator, while it libels him.

The bible can never get the confidence of rational mind, as it fosters the one idea of peculiarity of faith. Rationality is not peculiar.

Could the world ever be half civilized by all the capital that bibles usurp or abstract from mind ? They are a great and profound mystery. Rather, a profound sophistry. The burlesque of the Jews about God is evinced in the Talmud Berachoth, "Alas! that I have laid waste my house, and suffered my temple to be burnt, and sent my children into banishment among the heathen," &c.

We take nothing for granted in the bibles of tradition, or any thing that priestocracies and their affiliations can say.

If the old and new scriptures were a perfect harmony, there would be no difference between the Jews and Christians, and all would only be followers of peculiar faith.

Why is there any difference between your sabbaths ? Because men's opinions and interests differ.

"Thou shalt love thy neighbor as thyself." Christian, do you love the Jew, Mahomedan, Mormon ? Do ye not ardently study to get ignoble advantage of each other and the world ?

The bible is irreligious ; it does not make God any thing of the great God of the universe. The more peculiar it is, the more it diverges from God. Piratical opinionists and usurpers do not listen to reason.

There is no fallen condition of man. It is a libel on God and man. It is an uprising of mind all the time, more or less. The bible is potent for evil. When a man is cornered about his faith in the bible, he places his peculiar faith in mystery ! Men in the pulpit assume that God has written the bible ! What a profanation, a desecration! God has been pleased to declare his will by his works ; that is demonstrable.

Bible writers make mysteries, so that the advocates cannot solve them, about predestination, trinity, &c.

Moses had to drub his people into superstition, by slaughter of thousands. Ah, but he had witnesses of his deeds and miracles, to satisfy his people, it is pretended. Where are they ? Will all such statements go through as authenticated proof, in an honorable court of justice?

Any direct revelation from God would commend itself universally, as his character is universal, not peculiar. We have the very best evidence how the scriptures were fabricated from the miracles of the Romans, as the liquefaction of the blood of St. Januarius. How came the children of Israel to believe Moses ? On the same ground that the whole world came to believe in its whole systems of polytheism. All the artifices, the frauds, force, sophistries of priestocracies brought it about. It is idle to affect that bad men could not write such bibles, when that was the profession of all ancient priestocracies.

The bible is a complex thing, a mixture legend of history and peculiar faith, the first being in disgraceful company. How, then, can rationalists be honestly asked to believe it ? Some advocates affect that the fabrications of the bible or scripture impostors were too good to do such a thing. The facts prove them to have done the very thing. Has not the world been engaged in all such, time out of mind ?

Are not all these mere editions upon editions of pagan idolatry, and all the concomitant despotism ?

There have been analogous efforts in all ages known to us, correspondent to the conditions of mind.

But the advocates for revealed faith bind themselves to the car of its idolatry, and worship at the shrine of its superstition, never seeking to be wiser. Can any thing be more ridiculous than the ignoble pretensions of faith, that is a perfect nonentity, unless backed by reason and truth ? All the book false pretences about revelation and inspiration cannot compare at all with the sublime proof that God has left of himself in a universe of cause and effect, making himself the Great First Cause. If there be revelation or inspiration established by God, he would not let such fall through because of proof. Now, where are the indisputable proofs of both ? Do men of mind, patriots of purity, need any better proof or argument of self-delusion about books and all their pretences, than those furnished by the Mormons?

All writings are analogous, and must be put on analogous position. If not authentic history, but purporting to be revelation and inspiration, of course we must have the proper proof of such, ere any honest sound mind can begin justly to believe them. If any book is set up above history, it must have correlative proof. Who gives the interpretation and solution of bible mysteries, prophecies, &c. ? It is mind, which conclusively proves that that alone is the medium, through science, for reason.

How comes it that monotheism or deism, in which the world is primarily concerned, as regards religion, is postponed for pretended bible revelations ?

Has social proscription established her inquisition?

How comes it that the people cannot hear both sides of this mighty question fairly and honorably, ere partisan views are taken? It is to the world, the people, that this subject must be addressed, who must analyze for themselves the whole position. How shall we explain all the difficult passages of bibles of tradition?

Do you, intelligent American, complain of fanatics growing like weeds, in this lovely country?

Did you not proscribe rational, the only religion that would save all from fanaticism? The only fair way, both sides, is literal interpretation of the scriptures. We must avoid all metaphor, as far as practicable. Can the morals of the world be amended or governed by any revelation or inspiration that is pretended? Can any answer be adequately but that which approaches the soundest principles of reason, responsive to the best standard of Deity?

All such bibles are the emanations of priestocracies and despotisms, the union of collusion, most conclusively so. If the fountain head be notoriously untrue, how can truth be honored? The bible is too antiquated in its peculiar characteristics; mind does not require mere notions, crude and absurd, but universal principles, and the appropriate progress of those principles. All the bible shows man, the priest man, the priest's peculiar god. This has pretended to tell of conversations had, and many particular things that never were mentioned or transpired since the universe was made as it is.

The world has to guard against all these.

All its prophets are false, and cannot admit of anything but false pretensions and interpretations. Half the world has been slave vassal to demagogues; monarchs and a host of right-invaders influence writers, to prevent the people's good. Of what use is pretended revelation, when all bibles of traditions present only false pretences of inspiration? So far is revelation from revealing the future, it does not define the present. God would not use locally a second imperfect means of all languages to do what his sublime genius had consummated in one mighty universal language for time, ubiquity and eternity. What is pretended to be revealed faith is impotent and imbecile.

Rational religion teaches by bullion; the author is counterfeit throughout. What the bible has, it has usurped from mind. The world needs true capital, not base counterfeits. God is to be adored by mind, not worshipped by superstition or idolatry. The change of God, in which the scriptures abound, is a libel, as he is immutable. The change is to be in sinful beings. Man is mutable. The scriptures, so far from being a mirror reflective of God's word, is its worst caricature. They, on that basis, must be untrue, as God could not caricature himself.

The bibles of tradition do not touch the subject of religion, for they are treatises of peculiar faiths, with which the civilized world has nothing to do. Such concerns the priestocracy, not the people.

Moses' bible purports to give a creation of the world, fall of man, universal deluge, a brief history of the race of man till that event, also an account of the separation of a particular family, the germ of a nation. All this is fable, much of it is truly false science. The second dispensation affects abrogation of God's law. God does not abrogate any law; but man does, in his after knowledge. The bible presents, in its portion, desertion of solemn principles; it then has no principles, but sectarianism. The people should read, know, understand and discuss, for full knowledge all such subjects. None can believe all the bible, yet faith in all is enjoined as an absolute and positive injunction. Full faith in such bibles is hypocrisy, deficient faith is invalid. No freeman should ever think of making up his mind until he knows both sides of the question —all that the subject of religion admits of. All rational beings should analyze this whole matter.

What produced fanatical piratical crusades? Peculiar faith of bibles of tradition and martial ambition. The whole bible was then, as now, but totally inefficient with its own partisans, much less the world, to effect a universal pacification or love. Then, mind had not been enlightened. If this scripture do not tell the truth, the whole truth, and nothing but the truth, according to the most dignified taste of jurisprudence, it is vitiated, and unworthy to stand before man, much less God, whom it libels.

The world should strip off this false coloring, this infamous covering. The defenders are not only special pleaders, storiographers and sophists, but most deeply prejudiced. The bibles of tradition do not remove man from the brutes, for they do demoralize and brutalize man, by all the iniquities of peculiar faith. This kind of book familiarizes the mind to the pusillanimous perversions of reason and truth, substituting false pretences and faithlessness. All this would have been long ago exploded, but for the pecuniary bribes of salaries, of official influence, and worst of all by court proscriptions and inquisitions of governmental despotisms.

Religion is no book-jugglery. The decision against the bibles of tradition is made by this conservative question of mind, Is this action correct, when we wish to do all that is right? Talk of inspiration and revelation, when we have neither moral, physical, intellectual, or religious science, by any such! No bible of tradition throws or can throw any light on the subject of religion, for it is exclusively on peculiar faith. All the bibles of tradition carry on their face the facts of their own refutation. It is idle and absurd to say, that they were held authentic by any anterior to us, when the proof of their falsehood is borne on their pages. We cannot look at any such work as history, or analagous to history, that reaches the truth as near in being the word of God, as that any people ever conquered the world. Analysis corrects all such. Moses reflected the despotism of the times, having been bred at court, and a priest in his mind. What could not a courtier, a priest and pettifogger do? Six hundred thousand men saw Moses receive the law from God. Where are they now—are they here to testify —will any prudent mind endorse that statement as fact? If all the world's people, the world's age in the face of cause and effect were to endorse it, the perjury is sealed surely.

How did the Israelites become a nation? How came the Indians on this continent? All people had an analogous start, and must have lived somewhere. It is very unreasonable to suppose them forty years in a wilderness, destitute of the ordinary process of living, as well for their cattle as themselves. the priestocracy cattle. What, do we disbelieve the word of God? Not at all, we do not, cannot credit the legends of Moses, that is all. And if we believed some little of the probable, we could not take the balance.

The arch impostors affected the depths of antiquity, and on the face of their book the legend sticks out.

How did he rule the Jews? By priestocracy, sophistry, law, and sword. His own statement shows how many were sacrificed to that despotism. How came he to get such an ascendancy over the people? By the despotism of popular ignorance, that is most conclusively proved, when they wept so at the reading of the law that was said to be in a book found, that is, written by the priestocracy.

Among the worst features of this matter, are the most outrageous and unnecessary false pretences, as the Nile river turned into blood! How degraded must be that mind, that calls this veracity of Moses, who only carried out the oracle game. All peculiar faith bible of tradition oracle-writers were conspicuous in the ancient world, for legend and fiction. All such, of course, expected advantages, as Numa, Romulus, &c.

When the people consulted oracles, they thought the lie that the priestocracy spoke. What nation was without them? It is an exception to truth to exclude Moses, as Jew, Christian, Mahommedan, and Mormon, are all profiting by his pagan pretences and rules. The history of priestocracy to the present day is this, that they invented superstitious faith beyond the time of true history, and the followers endorse it as true. The priestocracy are the pagan perjurers, the people the endorsers.

And what odds does it make for one or more to play the oracle game of collusion? Is any so verdant as not to see it? Who are here to contradict them, of all that the pretence is recorded?

All this can be asserted with impunity then, but only with ignorant, corrupt people, who cheat themselves.

Yes, all the acts of these pretended men are blazoned forth. Who, of the moderns, can endorse their deeds? Is martyrdom offered as proof? Fanaticism begets that, even among the Juggernauts.

Is circumcision offered as proof? The Egyptians, Colchians, Ethiopians, Phœnicians, and other ancient nations, adopted that.

Are miracles proof? The creation of the universe, the word, the deed, cause and effect, stands sublimely above all such, and invite mind, the beneficiary, to the recognition of the First Great Cause.

Are rites and ceremonies proof? All ancient nations had them. They were church speculations, and liable to gross abuse and misconstructions.

They have been transplanted to countries of their adoption by the resident or emigrant advocates, as well as to posterity, by church membership, the easiest thing imaginable.

Are persecutions proof? Have not all important peculiar faith systems had their day, their mutual persecutions and heresies, and their temporary power departed forever! Such will be the case with Judaism, and all its progeny.

It takes no prophet to tell what the wise judgment of cultivated mind accurately knows. God created the universe, and his almighty providence is identified in the sublimity of its magnificence. How do we know anything of this? The universe is the result of cause and effect—is referable to the Great First Cause, the Almighty.

Were the divisions of time into weeks, proof of Moses' superior claim? Was not that extended to many of the ancient nations, time beyond authentic history? And was it not referable to the quarters of the moon? As well might the year, the time the earth performs its annual rotation around the sun, be the property of the degraded Jew. What could the world gain, after the exposure of the whole peculiar bible's impositions? It will gain the purest possession of religious dignity. A part may encounter the bitter secret hatred of impracticable bigots, who are unchangeable because they would involve themselves in the renunciation of erroneous opinions, that a false pride precludes.

The mass, misled by priestocracy demagogues, would swallow a whole world of bibles of tradition and peculiar faith, enlarging the dose with devils and hells, witches and damned spirits most congenial, before they will duly investigate and think for themselves in the pure regions of truth.

And what has the bible of Moses, or those that represent him, the priestocracy, done? It has imposed on his own people and the world peculiar faith for religion, false pretences of man for the word of God, the sword for rational mind. If we are called upon to make allowances for the state of those times, we cannot overlook the ample abuse of their errors, especially by the moderns, who must knowingly propagate the heresies of faith.

Bibles are the means to help cheat the world, that cheats itself the worst of all, by self-delusion, out of the noblest benefits of mind.

Where, world, is mind that you have so long disregarded, oppressed and crushed?

Solomon was considered after wisdom; he certainly proved that he was after idolatry more.

To have this bible God's inspired revelation, it should be certainly proved by him, and nobody else, if his word, as clearly as the God of the universe proves himself. Exact knowledge ought not only to be imparted in it, but such knowledge most positively proved as coming from no other source. As to the Jews having the idea of one God, many ancient nations had, more or less, the highest supreme, as Jupiter; and the others were less divinities. What did Judaism have but a peculiar god, and the priestocracy as intermediates, thus corrupting the fountain source most abominably? Now all the other schisms or sectarianisms of Judaism, as Christianity, Mahommedanism, Mormonism, have multiplied the difficulties of Judaism, and only varied the polytheism. The interpreters were the autocrats of the oracles. On their basis about one God, the offsprings are inferior to Judaism, have proved a prolific sectarianism, that has constant schisms.

There is no stopping in any, as their elements force that conclusion, whereas all monotheists absolutely agree in man's essentials. In his unity, God is the adorable standard, standing sacred in his sublimity.

A universal discussion of this whole subject and nothing short, always identified with the statements of both sides, will soon put the world aright.

How can the truth, the whole truth and nothing but the truth, reach universal mind, but on universal principles. What I advance is predicated in the bibles of tradition, which are to be investigated. I call for the whole investigation. I am bound to be completely sincere, and must take the whole books as absolutely meaning what they import. I hold myself to the comprehensive analysis. I wish to give the bible advocates any or all the advantages requisite, expedient or honorably expected, and then they are in inextricable difficulties. Like a razor without mettle, after its very best, finest edge is obtained, what is it? No belief or faith of ancient or modern supposed great men, no opinions of any man, no matter who, should change mind at all in rational matters, where truth is primary. We do not know their individual peculiar influences. That is enough. Peculiar faith unjustly involves peculiar influences.

What is mind for but a correct judgment? The world then should not forfeit its noblest claims to mind. We have to think and act for ourselves, and do so rightly, and for this we are accountable.

The position of the world declares that the authenticity of the scriptures cannot be proved, for the world would irresistibly come up to it. As it is, many that appear to be satisfied are clearly not, for if all were satisfied, nothing under the present order of things could keep them from it. Where is my soul's protection in the meantime, to proving the scriptures? Must it be balanced in doubt and uncertainty its earthly existence, and never, never attain it, for it is perfectly unattainable? The protection is somewhere, and certainly implied in its creation—its creator and preserver. God has not left it without protection, as he does not create the universe that way.

Inspired revelation not only teaches all essential and important things truly and exactly, but what no mind can reach as mind. All this must be only through God. All this is to be verified as surely from God; that it is his word, and not the priestocracy's.

When the world says I believe a part, the balance is a mystery that I do not believe, what is this but rejection analogous to a vitiated witness? The world takes for granted much of the bible, and reads it as it were so. How many read the whole book, without suspicion of any thing wrong? Resort to no tricks, but all the noble powers of discussion, and discard the very idea of improper cogitation. Let us have a fair analysis, under just conclusion. Bible advocates, are you aware that the bible of tradition is on one side, and truth on the other? What do you say to this proposition? We should exclude what is mere metaphysics in a bible of mind as far as practicable, and go to the facts of nature. The world suffers from the pedantry of the schools, as the ignorance of the mass is. What can be worse than that of the bible school? What ethics! To curse the world, until compelled by mind rising in its supreme majesty.

It was for want of philosophical science, that the ancient world stumbled so. The moderns are worse than the ancients, to pervert reason and mind by their peculiar faith errors. Mind is a mighty engine, for good or evil. Now is the time to be a greater man than Moses, Christ, Mahomet, Bhudda, or Numa, by proving the authenticity of any scriptures of their peculiar faith. And if this be not proved, as it cannot be, what will be the result when the bible is excluded? The death knell of superstition, and the universal birth of religion. How came the bible ever written? Was it mind perverted or intellect of inspiration that revealed it? Take it altogether, it presents the worst features of human demoralization and depravity, in caricaturing and libeling God, and imposing the most blasphemous frauds on man. If mind had not been perverted, how came man to write the bible and fill it with his ignorant false pretences? God never adopted, much less wrote or dictated peculiar faith, that excludes his universal attributes, libels himself, all such being positively absurd. All that the bible contains, is submitted to mind, that must honestly take cognizance of the whole and decide on its facts. How few lay members of churches study and analyze the bible? They take for granted what the affiliated peculiar faith preacher tells them. If there be not contradictions and clashing, how came so many hundreds of sects?

But there is opposition to monotheism, to which there is antagonism of all peculiar bibles impelled by peculiar self interests. Do you really make your bible your idol? If not, how can you be in opposition to principles? You have to give up one or the other. Which was in existence first?

Principles time out of mind as the permanent conservatives of the universe, moral and religious, as well as physical. We would adopt the bible of tradition if compatible with principles, but it is not; therefore we adopt that of rational mind and religion, as being compatible. Our adoption is on principles. Your opposition is without principles. Then the bible of tradition is in antagonism to them, and of course to God. Where can we expect to see the temple of virtue, religion, truth, reason and happiness? In the sacred precincts of monotheism. But you are opposed to it. Can you be on principles? Why? You can give no rational solution. The highest conscientiousness of all attainable on earth is obtained, must be imparted by monotheism, if mind understands and acts up to all its religious obligations and requisitions.

But peculiar faith adopts policy for principles, bibles for religion, takes the master's words for granted, as exact truth for science; and the clannish advantages of sectarianism and membership for personal merit and the substance of science. The comprehensive mind alone, looks at the whole ultimate bearing of what bibles ought to meet, not at what the priestocracy pretend them.

Moses' bible neither suits one nation nor the world; neither mind, man, nor God. His ignorance, if not his fanaticism, cut short the legitimate comprehension. It is an abortion, and of course is obsolete. As the priestocracy read their bibles for their peculiar interests, the people of the world as one universal brotherhood, should attend to their general interests, the proper demands of rational religion.

No bible of tradition or peculiar faith can ever adequately and wisely meet the paramount demands of mind, that requires full thought during its existence. What was done for mind, if such bibles be indispensable, prior to the time of Moses?

Was it not essential to mind, in error at all times, and would it not have been as indispensable and available then as now? Mind ever required its Creator's protection, which was identified with his creation, thereby giving the noblest proof of conservation. How can all this be got over by the priestocracy, who are the fathers-general to the world's guardianship, with impudence and assurance equal to their ignorance and avarice?

By what were the people of the world benefited, if God withdrew to the peculiar family? The world is made up of families of nations. Admit the balance were most wicked and abandoned, was not that a paramount reason that God should act for them too, as a part of his creation? Their goodness invoked his love, their evil actions bespoke his clemency, and all required his grace. The universal deluge implies an imbecility in the Almighty, unworthy of immaculate and immutable attributes of mercy and omniscience, much less of his omnipotence.

The harmony, peace, and dignity of the world, only to be maintained on the conservative principles of rational religion, is never to be trespassed upon by the vulgar bibles of peculiar faith. The world must look to the unison of principles. The sense of mankind may rest assured and resolved, that the universal peace of the world cannot be obtained on the basis of any bibles of tradition or peculiar faith, and that it is high time that mind, irradiated by the light of science and brilliancy of genius, look to the expediency and practicable availability of principles, so indispensable to the government and conservation of the world.

Who can complain, that a free discussion of principles injures the body politic? Are they of the people? We seek to protect them by principles. Is it the priestocracy? We seek to have them right. Your bible cannot compare with the noble efforts of mind, as the Declaration of American Independence, and the establishment of the American Constitution, that afford so many noble elements of conservation to freedom.

Do we wish to take away revelation from the world, you may ask? No. All that is revelation is our property too, but not the pretensions. We only wish to take away the pretensions. No bible of tradition can give revelation. The whole history is this, rational religion finds God in his universe as the great first cause, and pays all due respect and adoration to him. Thus, several ancient nations knew of God, as much at least as the Jews, and if they did not know more they were poorly off indeed.

In your kind nature, you think the bible makers were mighty men; that is, only as you take for granted. There was the mightiest rivalry, in the ancient world especially, to establish the most popular system of peculiar faith, the most sacred bible, to which all the sophists of priestocracy contributed all they could, by pious false pretences.

All such systems are founded on sophistry, by sophists. But the bible-mongers could not fix things right. They had to keep pace with mind's progress, as their after knowledge invariably betrays man usurping the foreknowledge of God.

For this universe capital they give counterfeits. They destroyed the world by the fall of man, which is utterly condemned by God's attributes, that anticipate all their covenants and dispensations.

They destroyed the world by a deluge, for man's sins, and yet make the chief, Noah, a drunkard, who exposes his nakedness of body and deformity of mind. Like all stupid debauchees, he curses away at the innocent Canaan, to justify the piracy and butcheries of the priestocracy, and belies his own prophecy.

In exposing their bible heroes, the priestocracy expose themselves; for if Ham was worthy of the curse, was he not unworthy of being saved, having an irredeemable wicked character, though not developed to man, still to God, who scans the quality of mind, in its deepest and inmost recesses; but this the cunning priestocracy were afraid to declare, as catching them in an inextricable dilemma.

Yes, all such books are the works of the priestocracy, who were prepared to do anything to propagate and maintain their doctrines. Perjury was a trifle; and, as proof, how stands that horrid state with hundreds of millions?

What was the whole world doing, while the Jews were kept the elect? Is it possible that no inspiration, no revelation was accorded all the others? Can any man in his senses believe this of God, whom the bible thus libels? Who would thus disgrace his mind? God is all wise and perfect, and he devised mind, all its existence, its own guardian, under his grace and guardianship.

The bibles of tradition are the greatest libels, blasphemous libels of God. Will the priestocracy of the present day degrade mind to all the bible iniquities, to keep the people in ignorance?

Will the people themselves continue so verdant, to keep mind in such abeyance to the bibles, the oracles of superstition? We might only expect this in monarchical countries, where mind was fettered by all such shackles, to keep down the people. But the dignity of mind is identified with the noblest solution of this whole question. The very creation of God implies preservation, for he gave conservative principles to the universe, and above all to mind. These mind has to use, as its legitimate capital. Mind has been assailed in the most wily and insidious ways, not only by bible-mongers, but even by the pedants of kings, as Aristotle and Plato, that have been unduly revered. Does calling or writing the bible of tradition the word of God, make it so? Here is the foundation of vice, when the whole world should know that it is the word of man. Principles of truth and honesty are to be invariably nurtured, and let all the bible falsehoods go to their merited end. We must make all proper allowances for the ancient world. In parts books were hardly in possession; as but few could read, much less write. We all know what power there is in the press, that still does not meet all the demands of mind. What then shall we think of its knowledge, when we know the whole ancient world did not take a single newspaper? Then, of course, they took all the fabrications of inspirations and revelations of church and state.

What ignorant mass ever resisted their combined conspiracy and collusion? What if the world now sees the imperfect pretences of all bibles of tradition? Will the intelligent, who ought to know better, hold it to the false pretences, and give up the lofty and solid protection of principles?

Let us get rid of all this miserable and evil condition of things, and adopt the full benefit of God's principles, in place of Moses' false pretences.

Could we wonder to see very bad results and people, under the regime of exploded bibles? No such state of things will satisfy the world. Revealed faith, with all its pomp of office, and all its retinue of sophists, is incompatible with rational religion. The bible is God's word! Prove it satisfactorily, and we will unite mind and hand with you.

Six hundred thousand witnesses saw God deliver it to Moses. God has left the protection of that proof, then. Is his testimony present? No. Where then is his representative in the truth, the whole truth, and nothing but the truth? It is not in science or in fact. Who of these people knew God, when they certainly did not know truth? How could we believe liars? Who wrote the first five books of that bible? Moses. What! could he write of his own death and burial—his own obituary? Would the bible blockheads make us believe this foolishness? Has the world lost its senses with its morals? Was there ever such absurdity on earth? Can the whole world show any greater madness, than this whole bible insanity? The bible was made by the priestocracy, who sought their peculiar advantages. Can you promise yourself morals thereby? The priestocracy have bullied the world, where they could not delude it.

The bible was written by very ignorant men indeed, ignorant of the mighty conservative principles that alone could guide the world right.

But, as weak as that bible is, we may be asked by weak pious minds, if we will take away all the hope of salvation from man? No. We wish to give the world the only one that was first, last and all the time, the only one of God, that the world has overlooked on account of the priestocracy. The very conception of bible-revealed faith is an abominable iniquity, absurdity, and ignominious fabrication, whereas rational religion elevates mind to its true dignity, its loftiest character.

Who wishes to know the partial and imperfect law of Moses or his peculiar god, the priestocracy, when he has that of the God of the universe?

We will take your own position:—what persons in their senses say, honestly and truly say, that they can believe all the bible? Who but say that they can only believe a part? That discredits the whole testimony as vitiated.

The bible of Moses speaks of God most familiarly to us, who need the proof. How are we to believe that it was God, who, by the description of Moses, does not come up to our ideas of the God of the universe? We cannot take his statements for truth, as they certainly are disproved by God's word, cause and effect. The Jews gave God angels; the heathens, as they are called, added many gods; the Christians, a few gods. What is the difference, when the principle is the same? Demonstration in the universe overcomes all the difficulties to mind. The present age ought, in self-respect, to dismiss all the explosive ideas of the ancients, of the whimsical mysteries of metaphysicians, all the astuteness of logicians, and all the insidiousness of the sophists.

Enlightened man must regard the proper organization of society. The priestocracy fixed up both Moses and Christ as men of straw. Their bibles are, if not without dates, as good as not certified to in truth. Are they not mostly without certain authors? We do not know when, how, and by whom they were advanced. They were canonized, that is, smuggled on the world, long after being written, and how many deemed apocryphal were left out of each sort, are not certainly known to us. That convention was totally irresponsible to all the world most concerned. Then, republican, how can you take a book that violates your rights? All this most naturally concerns mind, that has no rational cognizance of the same. Can irresponsible councils decide for the world's mind? Is this the first principle of reason, of constitutional right? Rational mind has to decide on the authenticity itself, and not trust absurdly to the vague and interested opinions of cliques and partisans, who smuggled their faith. Did the people, the whole people, and nothing but the people of any age, rightly delegate to these councils any such power? Can any such assumed power usurp for all time to come, the world's rights? Who would have entrusted the world's rights into such ignorant bigots' hands?

This is God's function that has been invaded by the priestocracy of every age, that would enslave mind to their ignominious idols. They preclude mind from ever liberating itself by their infamous course, about amending the bible! What felons—yes, what world-felons and culprits! A simple protest is too inadequate, it must be full impeachment, and discarding of all on that impeachment.

Of what use are our reasoning faculties, if the peculiar faith councils held centuries ago, without mind's approbation much less delegation, are to tyrannize over the world? All what is called revelation, is the imposition of priestocracy..

In what respect can the bible take precedence of mind? Who was Cain's wife? Are the priestocracy ashamed or too ignorant to tell? Was this libel of God the cause of incest? Or was there in a foreign land another race, of whom Cain's wife was one? Again, how the priestocracy have involved themselves, in the sixth chapter of Genesis! In this evidently another race appears.

Was this the character of the Delphic oracle, to split both sides? If the sons of God ever took for wives the daughters of men, what else were they than another race? How could the sons of God become as mortals? If they were as pretended, how came they lost? Shame to the priestocracy, who have sunk their reason and sense in their stupid faith! Christ, as the son of God, is made to hold to resurrected immortality. How came the sons of God so wicked as to be destroyed? Was that possible? But if we take away the bible, the people will be lost.

What and to whom can they look? To God the Supreme. Will not the people resolve themselves into first principles? No. They will go as laws and order permit them. The world will be more like one people united in government, language, and religion. For what can they contend?

They cannot clash on principles? But in France the awful tragedy of three millions slaughtered by atheism, is a terror to the world. They adopted atheism, which is akin to polytheism.

But theism, deism, or monotheism is the position of principles identified with Deity, who governs the universe on that position.

As to the canons on the bible, they are unconstitutional and inefficient. They lack the first principles of truth and right. The actors were not constituted by the constituent beneficiaries.

The mind of the world has the right to revoke that one-sided distorted thing, and amend for the better state of the world. The highest reverence for Deity will exclude this bible-dwarfed concern. Why did the Roman church stop the lay people from reading the scriptures?

To prevent their utter discredit.

God has been treated by these bible worthies, as only capable of improvement by experience. Whereas it is they that expose their nakedness and deformity, obliquity and stupidity. But there are some abstract passages that are good in the bible.

Yes, but mind pays too dearly for them, its own, at the expense of its virtue, purity, and independence.

The world is precluded from the truth by the bible, that it is considered sacrilege to handle for that very delinquency. What impiety! That the bible is such an idol before God, that its lies are protected by the power of despotism with perfect impunity! The bible pedantry seemed to have mixed up the astronomy of others, without understanding them as the Pleiads, &c. The Jews did not know the nature of their four-cornered world, much less the balance.

Their Moses might have given some of these institutions, that no doubt were abundantly added, changed, &c. All the bibles of tradition can be picked all to pieces, as they are the work of man of perverted mind. It is wonderful that they had not been exploded long ago in the circles, not corners, of the earth, by minds, not hearts. But what shall we think of a bible that is fixed up so, that a whole brood arise from it, perfect parricides, and the bitterest hatred ensue, and is kept up for all time of their existence? If the old bible is true, the Christians, Mahomedans, and Mormons, outnumber the original devotees, the Jews, more than ten for one. Will numbers this time prove it? The peculiar god cannot help himself, though the patron called. If the Christian bible be true, the world outnumbers them more than five to one.

Which is orthodox, in point of majority, in the world? Mind has it, and should keep it for ever.

In what is called a christian land, how many true believers are there? How many unite themselves to church, for policy? The world is filled with sectarians, but yet how many of them are indebted to principles of monotheism? Is not the whole world after all said and done, indebted to this vital principle? Where would the world be, if it were not for it? Give monotheism the correct position, and sectarianism would be no where. Who could see sectarians to monotheism? They would have to publish another universe in imitation, ere they could establish their first position successfully. Monotheists may differ on non-essentials from circumstances of mind, but they cannot materially err. When will sectarians that are wilfully perverse, hear reason, and act to the requisitions of mind? We wish to get rid of all the base views and terms of superstition. What can we think of the prince of the power of the air?

All bibles of tradition are the statements and fictions of their peculiar priestocracy assuredly, not God's, certainly. What blasphemy to believe them his?

As to only one race of mankind being in the world, how came the isles and the continents peopled? Would it not be as absurd to-day, that the balance of the world besides Asia, had to wait for the increase from Adam, as that mind should wait upon contingent dispensations of one little people some thousands of years afterwards! Was that a correct principle to have the whole world of mankind dependent on either of such remote contingency? Even five races now plainly obvious, may have had several cotemporaries, or have been preceded by others. If there be another race besides Adam, what becomes of his peculiar fall as pretended? Prove that his was the only race, ere we can adopt that Adam's fall reached the whole world. We think it was the fall of the priestocracy, and thereby Christ is innocent of the sin of Adam's fall, and has his own to answer for. If Adam's stock had not fallen, then priestocracy stock had not risen!

But the bible can give a faith to the world not otherwise obtained. The world cannot possibly thank the bibles for all their peculiar faiths. Too many of the ancients believed in the Supreme Being, for any bible bigots to deny the faith; no matter how corrupted, it is as good if not better than any of theirs. They have no pure faith that will stand the test of monotheism. Scholars can now know that. No bible revelation tells of pure monotheism, therefore the whole pretences of peculiar faiths are false. None need ever boast any more of bible revelations, as they are too impure to mention. The great question is, what is religion, and that no bible solves. That the moderns have to use the best. The Jews might have been helped by mind, had they continued a nation, to solve this question. We have to recur to mind cultivated in rational science, to reach this solution.

But how many thousand years has it taken mind to reach such solution? How long has it been since a Newton demonstrated the best science of astronomy known to the world?

But if the bible be not true, how came the Jews to receive the text as true? How came the Mormons to receive so implicitly their peculiar faith? The Mahommedans have received theirs. How comes the world to receive its various peculiar faiths? The greater the lie, the more sacred the legend. That is the analysis of such bibles that invoked too successfully the greatest despotism of sophistry and brute force.

The greatest reason for saying the bible is the word of God is, that it is the most unconscionable tissue of falsehoods. What good did it do the Jews, who are no longer a nation, but scattered over the face of the globe; thereby proving all bible prophecies, perjuries, however all subsequent affiliations perjure themselves to defeat their own bible.

Compare Jews with the Chinese, whose sovereign is pontiff or high priest, and which seems superior? Both present the pitiful crimes of blasphemy; was ever a nation free from its penalties?

The priestocracy and their people vassals shut their eyes to the plainest facts; are they committed blindly? These bibles of tradition prove the weak state of mind relative to the present state of the world. The ancients coveted to be considered as having great antiquity, particularly.

The books abound with the corruption of the ancient records, to suit for the pretended antiquity. Was the record of the Jews exempt? No, certainly not. An exact knowledge of geology might elucidate this whole matter ere the Mosaic account could be rightly credited. Deluges are from natural causes; of course the bible manufacturers have falsified science. Would you denounce him who seeks to correct the world errors. We all have whatever is a just inheritance in any authentic bible, and could not possibly be hostile to a document that would impart it. Who could be hostile to a testament that would define for an heir his proper quota? Could the whole world exclude him, on his authentic proof at the right time and mode? Have you not been convinced by this time, that the bible has falsified every department of science? The rain-bow is a very obvious falsification, being a phenomenon from the fixed laws of refraction and reflection of the sun's rays in drops of falling rain. It is high time that the world looked mainly to philosophy, and let alone such bible nonsense.

If geology, or any natural science support facts against bibles, of course, let the last go by the board as counter to God's word. What is affected to be inspiration, falls below science. The bible-mongers have invented, can invent no religion, a thing that emanates from the eternal Author of that and the immortal benefits. All the bible legends are most silly. Plain, honest, truthful citizens are at a loss to estimate why it was that such good books that they take for granted, have nothing in view but the elevation of God's kingdom, should be otherwise intended. They measure all other characters in faith, as they purely intend themselves. But that criterion will not begin to do. Fiction and evil ambition have luxuriated in all this field. It is hardly possible to judge the ancient by the modern world. Once, not long since, the upas tree was considered by the world, to have had a wonderful poisonous influence for a large area around, and now it is known only as other poisons of deleterious character. It is from the east we get such absurd stories. Almost all unsophisticated persons will affirm that they cannot believe all the bible, and if they could analyze all, they would not, could not believe any, for all is the perjury of blasphemy and despotism.

What was to be gained by bible falsehoods?

The most possible of any, it was the road to power, sought by unprincipled men who were reckless of any conscience. It looks too absurd that we should give up the only rational document—the universe—God's own gospel, for man's black-letter counterfeit, that cannot tell of the first. Considering the bible immoral, the world should not only resist but discard it. Since science has superseded mere statements when demonstration follows proof, this age is too enlightened to rest satisfied with anything less than proof, and demonstration on proof. Such an important matter as religion must be conveyed by unexceptionable means, but they are not furnished by any bible of tradition. The universe alone demonstrates religion. But comparisons are often made, as to ancient histories. We believe only the facts of all histories, beyond them it is dishonorable in any body or set of men, clergy, or any to advance their pretences. We believe the history of Julius Cæsar's assassination, but not the ghost story about Brutus. What is legends we do not believe, whether put in bibles or histories. The clergy should look at all this, and consider how much more the world should bear with their iniquities and false pretences, ay, their base frauds. I am now advocating the paramount rights of mind, the people. and all that is honorable therein is secured the aforesaid gentry, all the world. Will they assume more? Then they are vile, base, and degraded impostors, and must, will be ruled out surely.

The bibles of tradition are deceitful, taking away the proper characteristic action of mind, and sophisticating the moral sense of the world, thereby put below both unquestionably. What worse can they do? How artfully written is the bible? The false and the possible are mixed designedly. After all the noise about the bible, give us conservative laws and rational education, and burn all the peculiar bibles; then the world will do what it must have to do, act by rational religion.

What is testimony appropriate for the bible, to enable it to be self-sustained before the world? It is claimed as God's book, and as such, must be clearly and satisfactorily proved as all of God's documents. That's the fair question.

God himself would cause it to be proved as clearly as the universe proves himself. Now is that testimony that Moses wrote, that six hundred thousands saw God deliver the law to him? Is this testimony of these people, or merely the priestocracy's statement, and even that on supposition?

Does the bible hang on mere statements, suppositions? The world actually—the sovereign people—are blockheads to compromise their best interests, morals, and religion, for bibles of tradition, to say the least of no manner of account.

By discarding all the ignominious bibles of peculiar faiths, we shall approach the question of religion by the action of the bible of mind, and exempt the world from agitation and its evils.

The bible means brutalize mind, through faith.

To what is the world indebted, but mind and science? The vulgar cannot yet, or do not seem to be convinced, that the world revolves daily on its imaginary axis. The ignorance of the bible-men is just as vulgar. What a remarkable position, that the worst lies told are the most sacred, and the culprits, that ought to have been hung, rewarded.

Some of the faithful assume that a part of the bible cannot be comprehended, and that they dignify with the title of mysteries, as if that exonerated the bible falsehoods.

That is a fine way of extricating themselves.

They cannot possibly believe the whole bible, and the falsehoods are mysteries! What would expel a witness from credence in a court of justice, is held to be a bible mystery; that is, a bible perjury. We are told to be charitable, if the bible readers are pressed too hard in their false position for the weakness of human nature in the bible writers. Justice ever takes precedence of contingent charity, with monotheism. But we do not hear that they ought to do justice to the people, whose confidence is improperly invoked. No honest man can sympathize with a priestocracy bent on deceiving, and on false and perjured pretences. If they were to discard this infamous book, then the thing would be different, and they might invoke justice of monotheism. They claim that all is God's inspiration, which, falling through, we must excuse the writers for. But they do not rightly stop at that plea. They continue the bare-face imposition. We must exclude all such, as condemned on rightful impeachments.

If of God, the book must flourish; but if of man, it must fall. But does the world use the means of mind to decide the position, whether it be of God or man, and decide the question promptly and at once? Shall the world be cheated out of its rights by this stupid pretence, age and century after each other, as if fired premises were to be let alone to see whether the fire would abate of itself? Action on duty is requisite, as the very vitals of society are preyed upon. What sort of religion is that which binds men's consciences to the car of superstitious faith, and maligns their rights to protect obsolete bibles? The statements of the Jews in the bible do not excel the select opinions of the ancients in regard to the God of the universe. All that the bible contains are Jew oracles, that are analogous to the ancient oracles. The Jews, no more than any ancients, had no correct appreciation of Deity. I prove it most satisfactorily by their own books. The same power claimed for rights of preachers, for the councils, for construction of canons, establishes for the world undeniable construction for the truth or untruth of the bible.

Did the bible hacks know that?

Party-advocates for the bible must recollect that they have the affirmative, and must prove all authentic, either as a whole or its parts, as they go, to obtain an honorable credence of respectable minds. If they cannot prove most satisfactorily their position in the premises, they are certainly wound up. If they continue it, they are disgraced. The world will not take for granted any demand made on it by priestocracies, any more than from any other source.

The bible of tradition is the mother of superstitions, and renders ignorant minds amenable thereto. To the bible the world is indebted for everything that it knows of morals and religion. Which bible? That of mind, or tradition? The last, the bible of Judaism and christianity, does not teach either. The world must look at it comprehensively. What do we know of the bible? That it is demoralizing, and should be discarded as utterly incompetent to teach of the God of the universe. All such bibles only teach of the god and gods of the priestocracy and their morale, that goes against God's morals. That will not begin to suit the world.

But great men have believed the scriptures.

What has greatness to do with justice and right? Are they superior to the Author of Greatness? I prefer being with the God of the universe, to all the supposed great men of the bible. With them, God did not make the world right. Then. of course, the universe was wrong. If the universe was morally, it was physically wrong. Now. all this is disproved, by the harmonious action of the whole, beyond man's bible pretensions. This is the weakness of the priestocracy.

They preach a doctrine at variance with truth, honesty, science, knowledge, or wisdom.

Judaism and christianity are nothing, after all.

The immortal spirit is wanting to the scriptures, to breathe into them the breath of life. Unto dust they will return. Offering sacrifice is base superstitious idolatry. The patriarchal dispensation shows the relative condition of undeveloped mind. The king of Salem, Melchisedec, had a worship, analogous to the faith of Abraham. So other nations than the Jews, had such pagan faith; what can be greater fanaticism than to square the God of the universe with the bible that had a peculiar god, that of the priestocracy? What a blasphemy! Men cannot see the truth through blind faith. They may say God is Almighty by the bible, but then all that is killed by being made the peculiar god of the priestocracy.

The bible god, is not the God of the universe. Every thing is killed when the presumptuous, blasphemous priestocracy talk with God. The priestocracy should not make any of their profession, tell any more falsehoods, commit any more perjuries. The whole trick is exposed before the world, that has only now to act becomingly. The world has despotism enough any how, by neglect of mind over its own rights, without all the priestocracy's.

By the Mosaic laws with the advance of mind, the world would be in the deepest degradation. By their law, the domestic despotism of parents over their children was complete, to taking away their lives for certain offences. What brutal despotism!

Though they had, "Thou shalt love thy neighbor as thyself," Lev. xix. 18. The proper proof is before the world, what their treatment was to the Canaanites, the lords of the soil. What good did such a law for individuals, when the whole nation violated its principles? They traduced these people, and then extirpated them by a fanaticism as ferocious as the sectarianism engendered out of their bible, displayed in the Crusades! Instead of loving, the Jews actually hated mankind the more, by those very dispensations. And the sectarianism that grew out of their sectarianism, proved, and is now proving its hate to the death for centuries of fanaticism. Is this the principle of the creator of the whole people of the world? Worse than all, every sectarianism begets its peculiar elements of injury to the world. We are talking of the world morals, not the little pretensions of the priestocracy. What was God doing with the rest of the world, while he is libeled as tied down to his select people the Jews? What a disgraceful blasphemy, to have the God of the universe libeled as thus employed! Where was the balance of the universe? In the pockets of the priestocracy! O, bible advocates, blasphemers! The peculiar god of the Jews must have been very imbecile, not to have improved the Jews no better, when the Egyptians in Hadrian's time refused to buy them for slaves. The very segregation or sectarianism of the Jews by their peculiar bible doctrines, made them most obnoxious and fully amenable to the power of the conquerors.

The second and third dispensations are the patch work of priestocracy, on the botch of predecessors. In what contemptible light do all such appear before the God of creation, who designed that all rational beings should know him by rational means of mind? What mind can receive a covenant that is faulty, as God's? Then as God made none such, all go by the board surely and truly. What caused the division of Jews and Gentiles—out-side barbarians, but an abominable sectarianism? Thus God is most ignominiously libeled by the bible, when using such sectarianism by the two first covenants, and as much by closing it by the last. But lo and behold, all this machinery of covenants will not work.

God threw, by the bible account, a fire-brand among the people of the world by two covenants, and by the third, is to throw it off. He divided the people at first, and then he is to unite them. But there is the rule, and this proves enough to rule out the whole category of such pernicious bibles, the advocates of which, to hide all their effects and crimes, cover them up by the general thing of mysteries, when caught in perjuries. That convenient pretence is the means. But after making Jew and Gentile, God cannot unite them on any ground held to day, and that proves the Jewish peculiar god ludicrously imbecile, and their faith all sectarian, selfish and unworthy of mind. The principles of monotheism alone will unite, and never would have permitted their separation. This pre-eminently declares for the Almighty of the universe. The whole world has been tyrannized over for thousands of years by bibles of the priestocracy, when it had only to read God's scriptures in the universe. All the expedients of power in church and state have been used by the propagators of their peculiar faiths, as by Mahommed, Numa, Moses, who all blended church and state, and two at least used the sword when they deemed necessary. The first made a nation of robbers; the second made his still more superstitious, and the last prepared them for denationalization!

What sort of righteousness but that of pagan did Abraham have? The whole bible prates about things it cannot prove! What is such a pagan bible worth? A counterfeit bank note. By the priestocracy, I prove the bible false. God is a perfect being, and made all creation adapted with perfect fitness. But the dispensations of the bible prove an unfitness, and of course not God's, clearly so. After all the bible bubble, where is the proof?

The annunciation of the pretended bible inspiration by its own statements, proves most conclusively and clearly, that it is a false pretence.

How absurd are all bible dispensations? Man had ever to fulfil civil, social and individual duties. Mind then had to evoke the solution, which is admirably progressing. It is needless to talk about bible abstractions. How has the world been managed by the bibles? They awfully violate on nearly every page, the very principles of truth that necessarily exclude them as unsafe for protection of person, property and reputation. They abound in false pretences. For such evil of such bibles, monotheism offers her good. The bibles of tradition do away with mind, and its free moral agency—its mental agency, and brutalizes the soul. But the bible of rational mind—monotheism—is to give unto the people, what are the people's.

The peculiar god's past dispensations separated the Jew and Gentile, and his last was inadequate with all the help of Christ to get them back. The most reasonable conclusion is, that man, not God, was essentially wrong in all such matter, and that the priestocracy had been ignominiously meddling with a business for private lucre, their usual course all over the world, that they had nothing at all to do with, and could do nothing with. Are you, patriot and good citizen, perfectly satisfied with the bible? That it is the only way to advance the good of your country, socially civilly, and individually? First though, are you perfectly sure that it is honorably, truthfully, and faithfully proved? You cannot be, because you know you cannot believe in all its statements, and that is enough to destroy its credit at once, with all the honorable intelligent part of the whole world. But whether you consider them that you do not believe in as mysteries, legends or fables, if you cannot faithfully believe in every word, if your conscience sticks at some things, then you are bound to ask, Is there another bible besides all the proud or bibles, and is that the word of God? There is, and that is certainly proved. When you take the universe as a system of cause and effect, then you have God's sublime word in full. You are then to read and study it, with mind. What I am doing, is to give you the first elements; you are to do the balance.

At most, the bible is an odd mixture of peculiar faith and superstition. What does it teach mind of the real cause or elements? The fall of the creature impeaches the imbecility of the Creator.

Man is not to libel God. The highest glory to God, is acquiescence in his works, and a confidence in his glorious purposes of creation in his own edition, not in man's counterfeit editions.

If anything be amiss in this world, physically or morally, then the Creator is impeached, and the whole universe is involved, but the pretence is false, proved by the harmony of the universe.

One of the noble dispensations of Providence is, his withholding all revelations but through mind, that reads his universe-book.

When the bible is called God's word, it is man's word, priestocracy's word that says that.

Nobody proves it; and the priestocracy sink below the dignity of truth. If the authenticity of the scriptures is not demonstrated, we know no proper evidence before us for belief in them.

The scriptures may be confuted, for they have never been proved, but the priestocracy will shamefully declare that all is right.

A singular weakness prevails in the minds of most not cultivated, that they do not know the nature of evidence or testimony. They should know that all that is asserted by the bible has to be proved authentic, or it is no bible. If the general authenticity is not vouched for by competent testimony, all the statements are perfect perjury.

Is there no chasm of this peculiar bible after the death of Nehemiah, for more than two hundred years? Is this nothing? Where are the sacred Urim and Thummim, the ark itself, and all the gorgeous appurtenances of the Jewish worship that would testify to this dead bible? Are they all gone the way that all their peculiar superstition will go! How came the profanation of burning their books of the law by Antiochus and the Romans, the burning of the temple of Jerusalem not enough to have caused their peculiar god to show how terrible he was to such profaners? Then was the opportunity to prove his power, even better, by a timely anticipation. Nature's laws are God's laws, that are universal and immutable. What if a man, as Moses or Christ, Mahomet or Joe Smith, Bhudd or Lama, tells the people that they have, through him, especial peculiar select laws handed them by their god, would not every truthful and honest soul affirm that he was an impostor of the worst calibre?

If you want a quiet, easy, and facile life, go for the bible, what is popular, if not right.

Speak of the political condition of the Jews? What must have been the severe condition of their people, governed by the priestocracy, when they, with one voice, rushed to monarchy, pictured as it was a despotism?

The bible-people had no world morals, murdering the holders of the country on false pretences, thereby inculpating themselves in blasphemy, and alienating themselves from the balance of the world. The Jewish nation had their ideas moulded to peculiar faith, and out of all such they could not travel. The bible allowed no room for genius or truth, no matter how pure is monotheism.

God does not do works of supererogation for proof, when one fully demonstrates all as clear as sunbeams.

If the bible had been God-inspiration, it would have taught us the final causes and principles of things, but it has not—that is reserved for future lights of science, knowledge and wisdom, or the future existence of the soul.

The great scheme of redemption, as the priestocracy absurdly and nonsensically call it, is comprehended in that of creation, which necessarily includes cotemporaneous and eternal preservation, all the work of the God of the universe. Who put the dates to the bible? The compilers. By what authority? That of assumption, guess-work. That is the way the bible is made up. With all their boasted inspiration, they could not write the revelation right.

What man of wisdom, then, will attempt to prove the authenticity of the scriptures? How very ignorant are all peculiar faith people of the real attributes of God, as the Jews and Christians after all their boasts.

If man had had a revelation, it would have taught him the mighty truths of world governments, benignant with principles. All that we have thereof, is too puerile for God. It is too small, descends from the sublime to the ridiculous. Admit that the whole ancient world confessed the need of revelation, still where now is less need by any book revelation false capital offered?

The bible supplies no god revelation. It is all the false pretences of the priestocracy.

The starting self-certificate of every prophet bible-writer claiming to be of God, impeaches his own veracity, implicates his honor, and involves his integrity. The very idea is a demoralization, the most blasphemous imposition, and impeaches the whole book. The whole of the bible is made up, as a preceding dateless legend, about which no question should be asked. Things passed so recorded, were to be a history, if the people were verdant enough to take it for granted.

Who could disprove it, when inquisitions or imperial arms bristled?—when councils banished—empires exiled—the church proscribed? The fiat of that church was powerful, the league potent, and the collusion great. The bible is the mother of blasphemies, but as the mother of a faith dynasty, all else was overlooked.

The idea with many people of the world is, that the bible goes back to creation, and is the fountain head of all books. It is the fountain head of priestocracy errors—mere legends—false statements.

Is there any copy of the old testament before the year seven hundred? Not only were the writers of the bible, but the seventy translators of the septuagint, are claimed as inspired!

Having seen all these bibles tried to disgust, nothing remains but to discard them, having the true means. Would not the world laugh at the pythoness, or the oracle-mongers for claiming orthodoxy of inspiration? What better are any prophets or preachers professing than they? Are they not analogical? Has the world forgot the one, that it should trust so implicitly the other?

The bibles of tradition are not only the most demoralizing books in the world, but they are outrageously so, absolutely dangerous to man, woman and child. They constitute the bibles of the priestocracy, and their criticism repels many, causing them, though no believers, to account for the difficulty of bibles in mysterious, a most convenient way of escape. But bible-mysteries are ever bible-perjuries. The priestocracy have libeled and blustered much about infidelity, but that is not an essential issue with the world. The issue is not infidelity, but the authenticity of the scriptures on satisfactory proof, and the true position, monotheism. Before any bible-advocates arraign the world for infidelity, they are honorably bound to prove satisfactorily the authenticity of their peculiar faith and bible. Who, then, would call that religion, to libel opponents that were so on religious principles? Before any peculiar bible-advocates can say one word about infidels, they must prove conclusively that all is right about their authenticity, which has never been done yet, all peculiar faiths being indebted to rank fiction in the inception, creation and life-support.

Rather than believe contrary to the facts of nature, I must believe that all miracle-mongers lie, and that all moderns that pretend to support them, lie as outrageously.

What is the history of the apocryphal books? Those that were received as orthodox were only admitted at the fourth session of the last council of Trent, along with the old and new testament. The western church only admitted them. Protestants excluded them as uncanonical or fabulous. It seems the writers played the same game on their predecessors as the Mormons on theirs—outlied them. That is all. Unfortunately they contradicted the older books, and admitted too little of inspiration, and thus excluded themselves, till a severe probation of centuries rendered them of some authority by antiquity. Their history proves most conclusively to the world, and persons of reflection must see how all this bible writing is done. The successful liars are canonized or smuggled, the unsuccessful are excluded in part. How much longer is the world to be treated to all this odiously silly infamy? All bibles of tradition are apocryphal to monotheism, clearly so. When will the silly followers learn all this? Not till the people's treasury is exhausted. It is really astonishing that the people overlook such plain things, that Moses wrote his own obituary and the circumstances of his death and burial, and his comparison, with all the prophets, as they were called. This beats all the apocrypha all hollow. Much posterior authority is quoted in the scriptures, to help prove their authenticity; but that will not begin to do.

Cotemporary authority is the one to be considered of most respect. I believe that all the priestocracy that have written to help sustain their bibles have misrepresented. Some few have done it by too much confidence in others, who did it designedly. Advocates of the scriptures evade the necessity of proof of their authenticity, because part of the world affects to believe them, or takes them for granted that are true!

If the advocates do not prove the authenticity of the scriptures, but libel the opponents as infidels, they add two untruths to their sins and blasphemy.

I consider all the bibles wound up entirely.

The road to convict infidelity is through satisfactory proof of the authenticity of the scriptures. The pulpit priestocracy may try to stave off the proof by flaunts at monotheism, but they must be held to it by the people, or kicked out of the pulpit.

Man is inclined to leave the adequate elements that nature gave him, and fly to others of no value.

We believe all bibles of tradition the most palpable forgeries, and that forgeries and false pretences are kept up to this day, to uphold them.

Talk of inspiration, indeed, when one sees ignorant preachers! The bible produces blunders upon blunders, perjuries upon perjuries. The world has idolized blasphemous Moses, Christ, Mahomet, Bhudd, Joe Smith, Lama, &c. Why have these men tempted so unnecessarily the ignorant mass of mankind? Why have they plotted the dispensations of the world? By such you ask for a perfect world, and life enjoyment. How are you entitled to that superlative distinction? How have you merited such? How have the peculiar faiths and their bibles been sustained? The world's history shows. England, free as she has been, nearly all Europe, make it penal to publish a full statement against the bible! How many writers, as Bolingbroke, were restricted in their systems, when they wrote? What is more odious than book despotism, especially of old exploded notions not fit for freemen? Is the world to be thus enslaved by them? Who undertakes to settle matters of first and exalted principles of the world? Monopolists, who, above all, have no rightful pretensions, and should be silenced. Were the writers of peculiar bibles competent to personate the God of creation, when their ignorance of natural phenomena is so apparent? The igneous and aqueous revolutions by electrical, chemical and other moving forces that are constant and powerful, are clearly overlooked in the geological condition of the earth; and a specific deluge, with specific dispensations, is introduced to cover up that ignorance. Instead of a clear elucidation of the mighty secrets of astronomy, to enable the devout student to fix the proper era of time, all is more or less a miserable blank, making fools of false astronomers and themselves. Mind is left to conjecture, or discover, how solar systems of the universe are united, and even correct the false positions and delusions of meteoric appearances, mistaken for stars falling! The whole bible is wrong. Monotheism teaches the sublime of duty, to exclude all bibles of tradition, peculiar faiths, priestocracy and superstition. The time ought to be now, when proper discussion of truth ought to take place, where truth can be illustrated. No peculiar faith untruths, in or out of bibles, ought to go unwhipt of justice. The world ought to know at once what is the truth of religion, and nothing short of it. Clear up the bible as a preliminary, but as it is obscured by a fog, a mysticism, exclude it.

Let the world only think of the horrid iniquity of supporting bibles of peculiar faith by inquisitions, bullyings, crushing of man's life-rights out of the world. Can anything be more iniquitous in the world? What was all that for? Because these bibles could not support themselves! Is it possible that the world of people and mind is to be ruthlessly sacrificed for such pitiful things as bibles of tradition? Even so; it has been done long enough. Away with this shadow and delusion, the bible of priestocracy; it is one of the basest impositions on the world. It does not even give the world first principles. Society can work its own good, on proper principles. Mind has to adopt what God gave of the universe, not what man conceives in scrub-bibles of ignorant barbarian tradition.

What constitutional justice is there in imposing such stuff on mind, the world? What presumption is there about the bible, that is asserted to be the head of all books and authorities? On what right is this assertion? By the privilege of the priestocracy? It is the interest of the unprincipled holder of a bank note, though spurious, to pass it for genuine. The fault then is in the receiver, who is identified with the fraud and the crime of the man that passes him the bill. The bible is old enough to speak truth and prove it, if it has truth. But it has none, and ought to be nailed to conscience counter as a base fabrication. It is indispensable that the bible holders should prove their book, or be silent.

How dare they libel infidels, as they call them, when they cannot prove the book disbelieved? Faith is it, that is demanded? Is it not the faith in faithless demagogues and priestocracy, who act in most miserable bad faith to God and his holy sacred writings, the portraiture of cause and effect?

The peculiar bible is all man's plans of patchwork, but all the doings of priestocracy will be no where.

I have in vain sought for the vital, genial food of mind for the whole world, in the bibles of tradition. Let Moses tell the tale, and he was a greater, more consistent character than his bible god, who was going to destroy the Jews several times but for Moses, who is pretended to remind him of his promises, and particularly his oath; yet, after all, both, as all the bible worthies, perjured themselves, and the bible is the record. How changeable was this god, with Jonah and with Moses! No such thing; the world is to behold the influence, the potent influence of the Jew priestocracy, with their bible god. The God of the universe never changes. When cause and effect lead mind to the Great First Cause, they will bring about man's legislation.

After all God's getting up early in the morning, he could not get the prophets and his people to go right—that is, either the people were not as represented, or their god was imbecile. It is really astonishing how little the world knows of the peculiar bibles. How few read to analyze, but take all as the infamous priestocracy declare in their vilest of impositions; yet how ignorant the priestocracy are, who cannot analyze mind most clearly, attributing to the effects of their faith a non-entity, what is certainly due mind. They assume to know all, but monopolize and usurp by pretences.

We owe allegiance to mind before peculiar faith bibles of men, sanctioned by councils of men totally irresponsible to the present age or people, or to religion. The question is, whether peculiar faith and its peculiar bibles shall be put down in the world, or rational religion? Who decided on these books, at the councils? The priestocracy united to imperial despotisms. Mere men! What right then have any to declare them the word of God, when men alone sanctioned them? How dare any impostors to pretend these books the word of God?

If the world's verdict could be made up about all such bibles, it would be against them, and put down all the evils engendered in the bible and maintained to uphold it. The admission of that bible through various councils, or having it passed upon, is full proof that God did not introduce it.

The bible begins and ends in false pretences.

We may find the world very ignorant of the bible, so much so, that we may be utterly astonished to find how came so many such in their church, and are forced to believe that peculiar education and discipline, interest, ignorance, and prejudice, besides superstition, have caused much of it. The world is actually afraid to say any thing against the bible, for he who adds to or takes from it, shall lose his part in the kingdom of its heaven, &c. Many actually believe all this stuff! Some believe that the bible is every thing of a book. They read a few chapters, as coming directly from God—not with any analysis, but that all in the bible is really so without any doubt. Even to doubt, is beyond the pale of safety.

The scriptures need but this one sermon proof of their authenticity to preach themselves to all the world, that will rush to the faith. The bible of truth cannot be hurt by a searching analysis; only that of peculiar faith, bullies on proscription and inquisition to prohibit it. The bible has produced disquiet and endless evils. What a farce it is to expect the people to help carry out the principles of conservative revolution. Of the people that secretly do not believe in the bible, where are their morals? Many of them in their pockets. What a demoralization of the miserable degraded priestocracy, who assert, that there is no other way whereby man acts.

No wonder at the ruinous state of the world morals at this day! The poor deluded people of the priestocracy-governed world, never dream that all the bible is the greatest outrage on reason, mind and justice. Why do I disbelieve the bible? Because religion bids it. She bids us not violate nature, much less its God. The bible vilely libels both God and man.

Is the bible of any peculiar faith true? If it be, the world should rush at it, and universally adopt it as the only safe code. But if none be true, as it is not by the very nature of cause and effect, then it is the worst species of imposition, and its priestocracy knowing it to be false necessarily, are most degrading under such blasphemy. They are after some of the hundreds of millions of dollars appropriated unworthily by the world to such ignominious proceedings.

Can any one blame me for exposing the true state of the truth about all peculiar bibles? They ought to be grateful to escape from such evils, and all will, but the priestocracy and their minions, who look for the millions of dollars that the poor deluded world has annually to raise. It is a burning shame that the frame work of society is made up of such corrupt materials.

In what position of it can we expect truth and honesty, when religion is basely counterfeited, and all warred upon for the exposure? The people of the world ought to open both eyes.

The advocates of the bible, are not to estimate any assault upon it further than the facts warrant.

How absurd it is for the present generation to think of undergoing the impracticable responsibility of carrying out the old exploded bibles of peculiar faith?

To what is the world indebted for its discovery?

Mind, and nothing less than that perverted. Had it been otherwise, it would have been a rational code of truth and facts, not of faith of false pretences. Had it been mind rightly cultivated in science, the gift would have been religion.

Tens of thousands of citizens hold off about all the bibles of peculiar faiths. They do not wish antagonism of a bullying bigotry. The immutable supreme laws of nature, rule out all the petty bibles of despotic codes. In the name of religion, rational religion, monotheism, I impeach all such before the tribunal of conscience.

No monotheist seeks at all to do away with the bible of religion, but to decide on what that is. Every mind has a right to review what councils have pretended to make, and if finding all false, impeach and discredit it. Thus I do. The Jew bible, was for Jew land, and none else. The Jews were for no one but themselves. How foolish is it for the moderns to commit themselves, to uphold an exploded bible that cannot uphold itself. It is bribery, corruption.

What is the framework of such society worth? the spirit of conscience corrupted for bible faith!

But the bible says so, and they tell us that the bible must be right, as it was the first book, and reflects the true history of the world. Which bible, as people of their peculiar faith, make several?

As to any bible that is peculiar, is it not as peculiarly perverted as its priestocracy? What is the difference between a degraded priestocracy and all their bibles?

Do not all such books speak as falsely as their authors? If the authors lie, their books are to be judged accordingly. If true, the bible ought to be sustained, but if false, the whole world should put it down.

Churchmen, priestocracies and all, are bound to the supreme allegiance of their pure Creator, who rules in unity. All other pretences are polytheism or atheism.

The world must go for the religion of his spirit, not of priestocracy's books. There is no peculiar bible religion, but there is mind religion, and that the peculiar bible writers never dreamed of. For that ignorance all such must be impeached and discarded.

But the ancient bible has all matters, many think, on which the history of the world depends. None of it can bear the analysis of truth. In Lev. ch. xviii. v. 3., Moses refers to the ordinances of the Egyptians and Canaanites, to be avoided by the Jews; who, of course, only had another kind of paganism. Many of the nations of the world were doubtlessly dead and buried before the Jews began their national existence.

How many people, that do not believe in the bible, go with the crowd? Is it not a majority?

Popularity, not rectitude, is of faith; that religion reverses.

Did you ever, by reading your bible, perceive the contradictions? If you did not, you never read it understandingly. You must have seen that such could not have been the work of God, who does not contradict himself. How does the world read its bible? It receives it of the priestocracy, who tell it, it is the word of God; it reads the bible on that false position! What various shades and degrees of guilt and perjury in all that! What blasphemy, what false pretence, what demoralization! If the unity of the human race is untenable, then the bible goes; for the fall of Adam could not embrace the balance, out of unity; but the bible is ruled out of the world's confidence, not only by rational, but philosophical education, that teaches mind to look into cause and effect. If the world do not maintain a conservative, it will have to undergo a radical revolution. It must progress in rational, not peculiar faith education. No peculiar faith bible is an exponent of religion. The bible of Moses is the exponent of peculiar faith— a mere nothing. What idle absurdities are now-a-days told of the spirit land. How many believe in all such as ghost stories, when they are all superstition. All the idle tales about the knockings are no more than the idle dreams of visionaries. They tell no more than mind tells, and mind perverted at that. This is the creation of the bible, the father of such abominable nonsense and imposition—of millions of such superstition and faith, that have been imposed on the world's credulity. The world adopts the bible worship, modern idolatry, the worst of all vassalage.

This miserable bible, to which the loveliest features of intellectual and virtuous mind are so grossly sacrificed, is adopted by much of the world, to cheat itself.

What horrid iniquity? The bible is not a legitimate document, nor legitimately applied.

All the thousand and one humbugs of superstition will never be suppressed, till the peculiar bibles are excluded the world; then we shall have in the land of science, morals, religion, and good honest sense.

The bible is believed by millions, who have never investigated, to be almost cotemporary with the world, and to be the head of all histories, and the origin of all original ideas. That we are more indebted to a mere man book, for an idea of God, than his universe! All this is the basest sophistry of priestocracy.

These are the follies and vices of having bibles as gods. What is the difference between the verbal oracles of the old priestocracy from the bible oracles of the present?

They are both equal, vile, and base impositions on the world, and ought to be ruled out by rational mind.

This most absurd idea, of doing by mind now what mind is said to have done before, no matter how partially, and with what imbecility obtained, reflects on the world, that can investigate on the lights of science that this age presents. Will the sectarians have the magnanimity to see more clearly, as they have better means than their ancestors? By this time mind should recognise, on the true principles of causation, God, in the munificence, the magnificence of his sublimity. I now go against all infidels, and would be ten times stronger if I could. Revelation is it? Is it any less than that of the priestocracy? Conceive, citizens, of the priestess of the tripod. Which is worse? Of course the modern priestocracy, as better lights, should have prevented all these false pretences. All peculiar bibles are the covenants of the priestocracy. The bible advocates sillily try to uphold the peculiar bible, that ought to uphold itself.

You ask me to respect Moses and Christ.

It is you and your bibles that have desecrated their personal virtues, if they had them. You adopt the false pretences of the degraded priestocracy, that, to fasten their vile despotism on the world's mind, sought all the wiles of odious bigotry, all the meanness of lying and deceit, united with all the lowest intrigues of the world, to build up a false position, substituting the pulpit for the tripod, their peculiar faith for religion. All this is the stuff that sophists sport with, to master the noblest prerogatives and rights of mind. Many bible critics have condemned various parts, enough to decide all.

Rational mind can parry them all at one blow, as well as their prime originators, the peculiar bibles.

I was friendly to the best received notions of bibles, till I thought for myself. I advocate what I am now convinced, most conscientiously, is the truth.

As to the opinions of supposed great men, about the bible, that is a subject of mind's pure analysis. Do we know all the circumstances and perversions of peculiar faith, its briberies, corruptions? Its history is parallel with most of the world and its governments. Too much of it has been part of the govermental machinery. There would be no merit in bible believers, if all the authenticity of the bible was proved. How, otherwise, if not fully proved, should we then ever know the proper distinction between the bible of imposition and the one that is rational and true? That of imposition would be ever veiled in the false pretences of mysteries, that the God of the universe does not deal in. The only one is the bible of rational mind and religion. All others are self-condemned the moment of conception, as peculiar, whereas the God of the universe has naught peculiar in that respect! So far are these writers from doing justice to God, that they foolishly exclude a correct view of God's works, as regards their heavens, that they curtail of half the proportions. Is there no necessity for revelation? None at all, as all are as God created, and his cause and effect revelations are more glorious than priestocracy can appropriate. The bible has interpolations, that betray it as a bungling botch of priestocracy, a mere patchwork; so far from one covenant following another, as those of God, an after-thought, all, the bible additions; and all so far from being the work of inspired men, that all of them, principals and seconds, agents and actors, are impostors on the people, including the apostles and messiahs.

But we cannot question God's plan, as to Christ being not sent but unto the lost sheep of the house of Israel: Matt. x. 24.

Of course, if this was God's mission, I would support that. Give the people the proof of the authenticity of any bible, for them to know that the characters—priestocracy, ministers, and preachers therein employed—are not impostors. For there may and can be innumerable systems of faith from first to last, each having the justification. They are all systems of faith, and if the followers can even believe the most horrible of them, that one is the right one. Such is the odious and impeachable doctrine of faith. When bible-advocates are cornered about prophecies, then they admit they are vague and mysterious, the very cloak for imposition, perjury. All peculiar faith-bibles are bound to go down. Some of the bible critics are dangerous, unless they comprehend the whole subject, that betrays itself. What an absurd idea, that a book called the bible, issued by the priestocracy of peculiar faith, should establish the religion that God gave through principles.

The bible is the parent of usurpation and monopoly, and keeps up the worst collusion of the priestocracy, by superstitious bigotry and bribery of millions of dollars. To say that the merits of free, moral agency is lost by full proof of the authenticity of the scriptures, is not begging but sneaking from the question! What miserable abstraction of the peculiar bibles that mislead on trifles, impiety. What desecration of mind!   ·

As all such bibles can only be purified by fire, make a bonfire of all such. Instead of the world losing time about such bibles, it should have principles to regulate it.

The peculiar world is governed by policy, not principle. How absurd is it that our forefathers should bind their generation to exploded peculiar bibles! What criminality!

The legends of the Aztecs, which are equivalent to any bible of peculiar faith, tell of four successive revolutions that, at different epochs, destroyed mankind.

The bibles of peculiar faith are all pagan legends and follies.

The Jewish bible is the folly of a people that lost its nationality by it, after losing its rationality. It was a part of the machinery of government. Shall mind be held in abeyance to all the little bibles of peculiar faith?

All peculiar bibles were made to swindle the world, mind, in regal and priestocracy governments, which have bullied and proscribed free inquiry.

Do not desecrate God's holy name, by the unholy, ungodly bibles of peculiar faith! Never!

No man should commit himself about any bibles of peculiar faith, for if he assert any is holy or is the word of God, and cannot prove it, a thing impossible, he stands before the world, condemned as an impostor and a supporter of false, perjured pretences. He is condemned already, as supporting untruths most impious.

To call the bible the holy writ, is horrible impiety.

That is a profanation, a desecration of God's works.

All such are peculiar works of the priestocracy, and contain their oracles. As to mysteries, were any such bible the word of the living God, it would unravel them as the highest proof of his intellectual work.

If God's inspiration had appeared in any such, there could not possibly be any mysteries.

These bibles supplant the noble, pure·actions of enlightened mind, and retard its progress to refined civilization. No peculiar bible can be the unerring guide of rectitude, when it is conceived in false pretences all the time. It is neither truthful nor honest, nor purely devoted to the God of the universe. All bibles of peculiar faith are conceived in sin, fraud, false pretences, and grateful thanks to our illustrious civic, constitutional institutions, that enable me to affirm it to the world. Let not the world hug to itself delusively the phantom of any peculiar bible: all a desecration to God and mind·

The verification of the facts of nature, kills every bible of peculiar faith most conclusively. No book, call it what you please, bible or holy writ, forms an exception to general principles. All such must be proved, or go by the board of proper sense, truth and honor. Now, no such book should be a part of the machinery of any fraud-pious, kingly or priestly, to supplant the noble rights of mind. All such imposition must be put down, by mind that duly respects and honors itself.

The fundamental policy of all bibles should be religion, that shows the purity of mind's duty and supreme obligations, equity and justice to all the world, and supreme, exclusive reverence to God the Creator. But all the peculiar faith-bibles are conceived in fraud, and propagated under false pretences, promoting man's devices, not God's rights. Nothing can be worse.

As all present bibles of peculiar faith are below par in the just demands of civilized mind, it is right and necessary that proper investigation be made for the true one. Omnipotent facts prove it to be conclusively the bible of rational mind. Religion truly sinks all bibles of peculiar faith, for the only one, that of rational religion, rational mind. The bible of peculiar faith is a blasphemous caricature of the Creator, whom, if any painter had thus delineated, he would have been considered a contemptible daub.

In talking about the bible of peculiar faith, the weak-minded affect to be pleased that they are not infidels.

Now, infidels are they, who cannot believe in any such rubbish, who show intellect and virtuous independence in non-adoption of such tenets?

What do we drop, when we drop the bible of peculiar faith? Fraud: the device of fraud
What do we gain? Pure religion.

That none but the Jews, a petty, obscure ancient nation, ignorant and barbarous, should only have a correct view of God, when they maimed their bodies by an unnatural custom, and sunk their nation in miserable superstition, vassals to their priestocracy! What absurdity and nonsense. An infidel to all this is the wisest, the most virtuous and honorable of all. I thank the God of the universe that I am an infidel.

What is all such bibles for, but the vilest machinery to uphold monopoly and usurpation of power?

The king says none but the royal rulers have the right to direct and govern the world. Why?

Because of divine right. How so? You believe your bible? Of course. Well, that upholds kingly power.

Where did you get your bible? Speak truth, or leave the pulpit, and shut up the church. If you speak truth, you will have to leave the pulpit. If you speak lies, hoping to remain, you ought to be driven off.

Will the people pay ministers to lie for them, deceive them? Is this American? Stop, oh, people! all this accursed frame-work of deception! If the book had not been wrong, a fraud most damnable, the Romans would not have stopped the reading, but compelled the people, had compulsion been needed.

Shall the whole world be brutalized for such an imposition?

The proof of the authenticity of the bible ought ever to be kept in view, in regard to all that is preached. If that were the case, the whole pretensions of bibles of peculiar faith would necessarily die off. They have no base. These bibles do not enable the world to take the highest ground, at the best. How can you conscientiously adopt any bibles of peculiar faith, when you would certainly perjure yourself in swearing that they were true? The upholding the bible by various combinations, proves that it cannot uphold itself.

The world seems improving, and will decree the bible obsolete.

Abolish all the petty bibles of peculiar faith, as prejudicial and antagonistic to the highest interests of the world. Of all the blockheads, those who cherish the idea of a bible-devil, are most nonsensical. No public lie ought to be tolerated. All the preachers of peculiar bibles are necessarily compelled to preach lies, and if intelligent, must know them to be such, as pious frauds all are unmitigated falsehoods. All peculiar bibles inspire church lies and sophistry—the world-corruption of the worst sort.

It matters not how hoary-headed the error, the older the world-fraud the worse, for all such bibles. In what can the ancients be safe models for the moderns? In morals? In what did their pre-eminence consist? What, in science? When we have just opened the mighty treasury of nature? Had mind reached its limits in government? The idea is seen to be preposterous, when the constitutional representative government of America was established, and when such becomes continental in the five grand divisions of the earth, with their insular appurtenances, then mind can see how preposterous the claim of the ancients being models in one thing for the moderns. They had some discoveries most brilliant for genius, that is common to all ages. If the bible were true, there would be a rush of honest innocence to its support, but it cannot be upheld. It is a counterfeit. Cunning, base men have joined in with sophists to uphold monopoly and usurpation, that have corrupted the frame-work of society so badly, that perjury is one of the easiest things imaginable by and for the bible. Perjury, by the corruption of society, is most practicable in the world.

As the bible falls short of universal conservative principles confessedly, it cannot meet the demands of mind that requires nothing short of them, consequently, it is a deficiency that must go by the board. The bible advocates affect that it upholds religion, when they broke up its deep foundations to establish the bible. They speak of the God of battles, as if a peculiar God. What blasphemy.

But the bible has mysteries. It is not mysteries; it is a petty larceny, not only on man's but mind's rights. It was the Jews that fabricated all such false pretences, the curse of their nation, and all adopting it. Teach any ingenuous mind all the tenets of the bible from youth up, and when at full maturity, though a believer in its contents, yet it will doubt and deny its doctrines as it diverges from a peculiar to a rational education, though the bible be the same. Now all bible teachers have to resort to the corrupt influence of peculiar education to maintain the feeble hold. Then, of course, the teachers are amenable to the world, for its corruption. The ravages of time will scatter such bibles and teachers before the glorious triumph of mind most rational. It has no evidence worthy of consideration. As to the sanction of the Jews, it is worth

nothing. There can be no ratification, as there can be no son of God, and the testimony of the affiliated is worthless, as they are not competent on honor as men.
The idea of a skeptic being opposed to the bible, is all trash. There would be no
skeptics or infidels, if that was the word of God, who would have left it unmistakable.
even to atheists, who affect to substitute nature for God, whom they necessarily per-
sonify. In this they only equalize themselves with the polytheists or trinitarians, who
make a partial god, that, of course, is worth as little as the atheist's god.
There is but one revelation of God, who endorsed it, his work, the universe, by his
word, cause and effect. All others are false lights, that mislead mind wofully. This
bible black letter book is the story of the priestocracy. No subject is treated justly by
it. Its touch is pollution, its contact demoralization. Take away the bible. and some
affect that the very foundation of the world is destroyed, and that the world returns to
its original elements, and that even God is removed! What impiety and blasphemy. the
demogogical, radical, rabid priestocracy will arouse. They ought to know better. and
that none but the most ignorant and most credulous at that, can believe such nonsense
But the base priestocracy would stop the universe, rather than their bible should be
exploded. They are reckless, as their profits will be annihilated.
It is a very gross and vulgar book, and displays the idolatry of a foolish people.
affecting to be peculiar, and having a peculiar god. There is the God of the universe.
but their peculiar god of their heaven is too petty for rational mind to think of. The
Jews must have been the silliest and most superstitious people of the world, or the
moderns are, to attempt to palm all this silly bible trash upon rational mind. The bible
has no religion—not at all. Its peculiar faith cannot impart any. Rational religion is
not inculcated at all in the bible, and there can be no other.
Bibles of tradition are tory priestocracy sophistry. All their main prophecies present
falsification, and absolutely worse than that, they are destitute of all such character as
bibles, hence they are gross and vulgar libels on truth. God's word, cause, and effect.
kills the whole of them. They are dead, and it remains for the world of rational mind
to bury them. Who does not wish to put an end to all impostors? All bad people.
You do not wish to bear false witness against your neighbor, but you idolize the bible
that bears false witness against your God. Is that just to the Author of universal, not
peculiar justice? You surely have never analyzed this universal question. All your
peculiar bibles are false steps, that you and the world cannot honorably support.
Fishermen were the New Testament disciples who called Christ master: and shepherds were the Jews who obeyed Moses: no wonder they had such a stupid bible.
They may have been good fishermen and shepherds, but they were botchers in bible-
making.
The bible of peculiar faith is the organ of evil. It has non-entity as heart-faith.
and sun-rising, &c. It is rational mind that is to be represented, that rules out heart
and sun-rising—the last for light appearing on our horizon. The light of mind separates also the wall between darkness of faith, and light of religion. Rational mind has
to discard all the physical and moral nonsense of the priestocracy. How much ignorance, and how fatal! How many billions have such bibles caused to be ruined, by
Moses and the world priestocrats?
You talk about the bible: is that a right beginning to govern the world? If so, why
extra laws? Is not all this an effort most strenuous of mind? And if mind is requisite in such important sense, how then can it be wanting in any of the departments of
mind's functions?
The Jews made out the Moabites, from incest. Did they even speak well of any
people, that were their enemies? In regard to Babylon. Isaiah says, ch. xiv. 9. "Hell
from beneath is moved for thee, to meet thee at thy coming." Ch. xix. 5. (Of Egypt)
"And the waters shall fail from the sea, and the river shall be wasted and dried up. 14.
The Lord hath mingled a perverse spirit in the midst thereof." A vassal may err,
but can free Americans mistake? See what a libel of Deity, this fanatic utters. The
brazen serpent of Moses proves the brazen impudence of the priestocracy.
Hear Isaiah, ch. xlv. 7. "I form the light, and create darkness; I make peace. and
create evil: I, the Lord, do all these things." This is a base libel. None such of the
bible is true—God Almighty never created evil. Moses created darkness of his creation.
The book of Job is false, ch. i. 8. "And the Lord said unto Satan, Hast thou considered my servant Job, that there is none like him in the earth, a perfect and an upright
man, one that feareth God and escheweth evil."? In the first place there is no devil,
and secondly, no perfect man.
The Jew bible and testaments are bad copies, as the people were poor scholars. All
bibles of tradition are blunderbuss, as all kings, especially emperors and popes, that are
ministers of peculiar faith.

The god of wrath, fury, jealousy, is the toy of superstition ; the God of monotheism is above all that.

Peculiar bibles are peculiar expedients to fall with. Of course the ancient Jews, who had but their one little earth, besides the bowl of Heaven for creation, put their hell where volcanoes are, and their devil was Vulcan. Where else could they put them? See how full of libels the Jew bible is, of the God of the universe, whom moderns supersede for the petty overseer Jew god. I Samuel, ch. xvi., v. "But the spirit of the Lord departed from Saul, and an evil spirit from the Lord troubled him." Exodus, ch. xxxii. 12. "Turn from thy fierce wrath, and repent of this evil against thy people." This blasphemy of Moses, beats any thing in the annals of priestocracy. The fellow that accuses his god of forswearing, 13 v., "Remember Abraham, Isaac, and Israel, thy servants, to whom thou swearest by thine own self, and saidst unto them, I will multiply your seed as the stars of heaven, and all this land that I have spoken of will I give it unto your seed, and they shall inherit it forever." 14, "And the Lord repented of the evil which he thought to do unto his people." 35, "And the Lord plagued the people, because they made the calf which Aaron made." That is, 'the thus saith the Lord of Moses, set the fanatic sons of Levi to slay the Jews, who fell three thousand that day. Well, this calf was destroyed, being made from part of the gold stolen by borrowing of the Egyptians. What a bible, what a people, what a god, is portrayed! The man Moses, made the devil the best of the two with the woman, and he, the man, is the best of the two among the priests. As to the omniscience of the peculiar god, Moses beats him throughout, and as to keeping his word, Moses excels, if the world believes his way of telling it. The world could do no better than make one bonfire of all such stuff at once. Do not delay a moment, put down such idolatry, such priestocracy perversion.

Some -people take great pains to render themselves miserable, by peculiar faith. Would you, professing humanity and rationality, give such a bible to a child? Do not give such immoral poison, full of sophistry and evil libels. Beware, O mortal, what you do. If moral and physical science had been right, the world would never have heard of bibles of tradition, but one code, the bible of rational mind and religion. With the bible, the world became fanatic ; one half arrayed to cut the throat of the other half, and that not for a little while, but for its countless centuries, when ordinary passions had time to cool, but this was fanned by the most unholy fire of peculiar faith; the most deadly bitter hatred, malice, envy, revenge, ambition, lust and avarice, pillage, carnage, devastation, plunder. The end is not yet seen. The demon of destruction was roused and identified with its standing or marching armies, and wars were without limit, till the means were exhausted and the whole country impoverished. The world ever needs the best appreciation of principles, and no peculiar bible can give them. If we do not have rational education forever, away goes mind that is to rule the world, and the world may see an awful repetition of human sacrifices without limit. How is it now in the world, with mind-sacrifice? To the bible is due a horrid world tale, a complete cannibal faith. It has lit up the most horrid depravity. That feeling of pronouncing those at a distance savages, heathens, outside-barbarians, kindling up the spirit of wars, sycophancy, hypocrisy of faith, the poison of society, the sword of disunion, the perpetual quarrels of sects as of the Protestants and Romanists. I cannot see how it is possible that any rational mind can possibly believe, can be entrapped by any bible of tradition that can impart nothing of any benefit. The mother can teach her children, and will continue to do so, her affections are untiring if of proper character, she only needing the proper mind-fund—that no peculiar bible can possibly give. As the Jewish covenant was peculiar and pagan, all built thereon as Christian, Mahommedan and Mormon, are alike inefficacious. All peculiar bibles then rule themselves out. In asking the world to be rid of peculiar faith bibles, I ask it to rid itself of all the abominations of superstition, but it must cultivate all the principles of rational religion.

If God had fixed up the Jew bibles, for Christ was Jew, as well as Moses, as he has done that of the universe, man could not mistake or gainsay it.

The bible is destroyed by man, who cannot touch the universe nor its facts, that are there forever. What tricks have the priestocracy impiously raised to destroy its parts. Compliant astronomers have burnt up with fervid heat some of the stars. One has made a queen's hair, even a star, to suit the reigning dynasty.

If the priestocracy could manufacture stars out of women's hair, assuredly they could manufacture all their bibles needed. Peter and his fanatics seek to ruin this world, and then burn it up.

They would render their poor sun and moon useless, turn them into blood, ignorant of the atmosphere, by their sectarian lunacy.

What department of faith has not been invaded by absolutism and priestocracy? How silly are they! They can prove no truth of bibles, but affect all sophistry and false pretences, convict themselves, and get farther from God's truth every word they say. Give it up, and act religiously, like an intelligent freeman ought to do—like a person of refined civilization. All peculiar bibles are impracticable ideas. The bible is false, giving the world no consideration, but actually obstructing the best elements of mind. It is a matter of curiosity about the Jew bible, customs, story. The Jews were or are no more than other nations, and it is a false pretence to assume them to be more. Christianity, as Judaism, out of the same priestocracy school, is no more than another sectarianism. To prove how positively corrupt society is, there are many false positions prevailing, and yet, if exposed as they ought to be, as the bible and all its corrupt machinery, yet they are pertinaciously adhered to as if all were virtuous, good and true. What are all the invidious forms of douceurs and briberies in the world? Is this whole secret laid open to the just appreciation of the people? What verdant person can receive the whole of any peculiar bible as sacred?

As a citizen good and true, you would wish to have a bible truthful and honest, or not at all—that is the ardent wish of all rational beings. A false ambition and faith are opposed to high-mindedness, as displayed by the American Washington. The other side presents too many examples of perverted mind. If you attempt to force peculiar faith bibles as the only means, as the priestocracy pretend, on rational minds, the ornament of the world, you disgust them even with any idea of what is mind's inherent obligations in rational religion.

You, as a rational, honest, truthful and honorable high-minded world citizen, cannot justly expect me to subscribe to that tory doctrine of your peculiar bible, that is not entitled to house or mind room, much less the respect of mankind. What do I estimate the bible? It is only as the preacher or priest dyed in the depravity of peculiar false education, tells the people, who, instead of believing the ungodly Belials, ought to know the truth, the whole truth, and nothing but the truth. Now, would you take the word of the most interested forger and passer of counterfeit money?

Or would you wisely investigate, know before you took the spurious coin, the only thing the man had; and is not religion incomparably sublime above money?

But this the priestocracy have not to offer. All rational minds should improve their religious elements, to rational religion. The category of the counterfeit bibles runs all through them. How do you know of Christ? Only as the Evangelists tell. They cannot sustain themselves, much less Christ! Their position is that of story, not history even. What does the world absurdly want of the petty Jew-god, faith or bible! Such ruined the Jews as a nation, and would ruin now all absurd, insane, deluded followers.

Had God ever given aught to his chosen peculiars, he had assuredly fixed up all on the most permanent conservative principles, as he had already fixed up the universe, but the old dotards overlooked or underlooked all this, to get at their little brief authority. In the name of God, the people, the whole people, and nothing but the people, ought to discard all such as the wisest action of rational mind and religion. The Jew-dispensation had been immutable, if an immutable God had dispensed it; as it was not, the juggling priestocracy established it on their false pretences.

The old tory bible desecrates the sacred right of the sovereign people, whose minds were betrayed to superstition instead of religion.

As regards the diversity of language as recorded, the very reverse of science and universal benefit exists. Can the world stand all this bible nonsense and fraud much longer? Surely, if the scriptures be genuine, none can rightly deny them; but, if bad, none should accept them or let them pass current any more than a counterfeit. How can we tell without honorable, fair and proper investigation and discussion, and yet that is interdicted, but on one-sided scowls and criticism. Society cannot be much more corrupt, as far as depends on peculiar bibles, the abrogation of which does not resolve society, it only establishes it on its inherent proper basis, that of God-ordained principles. You complain that the world is insensible to your bible, infidel to its commands. There are several bibles; which is true? If any had intrinsic superiority, that one would declare itself and its author. Now, that is really so, for God's bible, the universe, magnificently proclaims its illustrious author.

You are talking of a bible. What bible? The Jewish bible? Is that proved? No, and never will be. If not proved, it is no bible. Do not flatter yourself that you can assume that any book is pre-eminent over any other. Your perjury statement cannot make any book a bible. If absolutism and sophistry arrogate all this, there is assuredly no foundation, and the world, the people, cheat themselves awfully. The people are filled with sophistry not to sustain truth and religion, instead of exploded bibles and priestocracy, with neither of which, as tories to mind and God, they have to do. To read the bible prayerfully, is to do so most rationally, and that conducts you to God. You say, minister, that you have a bible. Prove it. You cannot do it. Then it is no bible. It is a mere book, and you are an arrant impostor for a barefaced assertion, with falsehood on its face. Now, sir minister, never assert before your audience your lifetime that you have a bible, unless it is demonstrated, else you impeach yourself as impostor, and rational religion proclaims you a culprit and perjurer before the God of the universe. If false bibles are put on the public, it is dishonest, robbery, piracy.

The obsolete bible is tory, crazy. These poor ignorances could not see, had not the mental light to divide darkness from light. All this proves the priestocracy ignorant, but impudent, whereas the true inspiration that comes by philosophical science, had not come to them.

If the head or fountain is wrong, impure, muddy, then the whole is wrong. Without the bible, none could get the idea of God. We cannot get that idea at all, nor religion from the bible. All that such bibles give, is a peculiar god and faith, that the world cannot recognise. But are not such revelation? Of what? All priestocracy revelation. What have the world, mind, mankind to do with that? They should not begin to touch it, as it is tainted corruption of mind.

But all the world would be in idolatry, superstition, bigotry and blasphemy, without the bible. It is exactly in all that by the bible. But for the bible, we could not be the people we are. The bible was in Rome for centuries, yet all the world ran down to barbarism lower than Roman paganism, and then it was that the world butchery commenced under the bible, and the vicegerentship. Now all that is valuable is and retained so in the world, by rationality of mind in its free agency.

All perversions of mind, are by peculiar education. All we need is the universal standard, obtained by the creator of the universe, proved the great first cause on principles of causation, by cause and effect. But the bible clears the world of sin. What sin? It plunges it deeper into the quagmire of its priestocracy, the worst as the most blasphemous of all sinners.

But the bible brings redemption, preservation, and salvation of a ruined and lost world. All that remains to be proved, as it is utterly condemned as totally false by God's only word, cause and effect, that proves the world just as he created it, and with which such bibles are intruders.

Prove that any but God of creation had the godly commission. That last would prove God an incompetent witness, as it would actually degrade him most blasphemously. No, it degrades all the impostors concerned therein as blasphemers, who absurdly give up the only God capable of carrying out his own unappreciable Omnipotence. But the bible faith and dogmas, are in opposition to God.

What nonsense and stupidity about the bible god, so peculiar that he selects a barbarian nation, idolatrous and criminal with human sacrifices, ay, even to him as in the case of Jephthah, who is represented as sacrificing his own daughter, and this god had previously manifested himself as most familiar, does not interfere to arrest the horrid sacrilege, enough of itself to condemn all engaged in this bible as the degraded manufacturers of the bloodiest iniquity. What odds does it make with the modern adopters, who are more guilty as they have more light of rationality? But the last dispensation avoids that! When the last is predicated on the first, and more bloody reeking in the bloody sacrifice. This will not do to tell rational minds of freemen.

The selection was positively by the idolatrous nation, and the peculiar god and gods are all their creation; all their gods are mind-factured by mind-juggery to suit the case. Sacrifices of any kind are no part of God the creator, who permits no worship, when adoration that rules out priestocracy is supreme. The Jew bible makes the petty Jew overseer priestocracy god. Doubtlessly, the Jews got their notions of their god from the Chaldeans, who as astronomers, had the best knowledge of creation. Their second edition was a bible found, after their return from Chaldea. Melchisedeck was of the same persuasion, conclusively proving the idea of god not being peculiar, which is absurd in the extreme. The Jews must prove by their own bible notions, that they were as bigoted and conceited a nation as ever was on earth.

The scriptures cannot provide for mind ; but God, whom these scriptures misrepresent, has provided fully and adequately, by his elements. He made the universe right, and rules out all the priestocracy, whose bible creation is a caricature. The bible issues all patents for blasphemy, in its rickety sophistry. Any other idea than a pure God can be got out of the bible.

The bible advocates laud piracy, debt repudiation, usurpation of mind, monopoly of priestocracy, blasphemy against God. Each ancient nation had its peculiar gods, always better of course than others ; hence came the Jew peculiar overseer god, not even an original idea.

40

The pretensions of the priestocracy make their bible and dispensations imperfect, and in their outrageous, arrogant blasphemy, they packed it all on God, and speculated on a deluded, seduced people—the world.

That we could not get only the idea of God from that Jew bible, it must be proved that the Jew nation signally excelled all other nations, that it had religion, science, arts and happiness, the reverse of facts, as they were the most bigoted and conceited.

The difficulty about Moses fooling the Jews with his false pretences about his peculiar faith, is only apparent ; nothing was easier. over the ancient ignorant world, at one time. A Numa did that for the Romans ; a god Apollo had his oracles delivered in Greece. All had a beginning, and that was an epoch of the people's folly, as it was of their ignorance, and violence done that ignorance by the degraded priestocracy. The worst is, that the moderns are fooled, to receive such false pagan pretences, when the light of rational mind clearly directs to rational religion, and none other. The priestocracy are affiliated, and, as interested in the false pretences, ought to be silenced and scouted from the people, that ought to scout such fooleries. The present age of this date has no excuse whatever. Inspired men of the bible, that is assented to or asserted by the moderns : that is worse foolery than the imposition on the Jews, or of Numa on the Romans. All such are clear lies, and the priestocracy must know they lie, if they know anything they pretend to. The best evidence of God, who is the great first cause, that permits no effect without a cause, convicts Moses, the bible Christs, as liars, and above all, the priestocracy, for supporting all such low and degraded stuff.

Not only did the whole Jewish nation, but all the ancients received all the false pretences of peculiar faith, and the whole world murdered with the most vulgar intoleration and bigotry.

The worst feature is, that too much of the malign influence is left. How many do it now, when the means of rational, the only religion, bid, command them better. How was it in Switzerland in the last few years between the Romanists and protestant*; now in Italy, Rome—now in England—in America, between the same, and the Mormons and Christians? The ancients are more excusable. They could not analyze, could not tell the truths of nature ; they could not separate complex ideas, and receive principles for vulgar idealities.

The moderns cannot adopt the truth, bound down by the corrupt spell of old false-hoods.• Look what fools the Jews are represented, before Ezra, reading out of the priestocracy's new book

Do the bible maniacs libel the ancients, or seek to captivate the moderns? Will any modern, less than tory or maniac, attempt defence of such impositions ?

Never tell us more that the Jew, or any such ignorant nation, could not be fooled or forced by the priestocracy. when they were fooled and disgraced by human sacrifices— as that fellow, Jephthah, sacrificing his own daughter, as a burnt offering to the Jew peculiar god—who never would have permitted it, had he chosen the people, as pretended in the bible. Now all the blood of human sacrifices of the world are not before the God of the universe, in any other light than as murders ; and the felon priestocracy are thus accountable ; so that this bible presents a false, degradedly false position, in not declaring them to be such. A priest is a priest, with all his characteristics ; his bibles are priests' bibles, to suit the state of the world in every part and age. Is all this folly never to stop? God never libeled himself, much less mind ; of course, as the bible is a constant libel and caricature, then it is self-impeached and ruled out. It is bad enough to have all the bible errors.

What did the ancient bible storiographers know of natural sciences? Did they know that water could burn in part? Let us get rid of their ignorance and their tyranny, their nuisances. Let us sacrifice such nuisances to religion, the highest, purest duty to God. What absurdity are their abstractions, " Thou shalt love thy neighbor as thyself." How, Jew or Christian, is this, more than an abstraction, when you both have the destructive elements of sectarianism? What are all the elements of any peculiar faith but the suicidal perversions of mind, that injure all eventually? Only institute that bible and its precepts that can certainly render mind that is capable of soul, mind, and spirit religion, to mature for the benefit of all.

Moses could not write his own obituary ; of course, could not have written the first five books—if he did, they are necessarily false—if he did not, they are false, feloniously so, any way. All is story, not history ; not hand, but mind-jugglery, of priestocracy, and these books, of course, employed the pen of several of the priestocracy. They are the fathers of the invention, and priestocracy help sustain these falsehoods, in the form of bibles.

But you ask me to go for a bible. Yes, I go for the bible that is right, religion that is pure, faith that is rational, truth and honesty that are sacred and holy.

But you do not go for the right bible. You go to uphold the priestocracy ; then you go for less than your country, world, and God. As the ancients could not analyze complex ideas, they gave men's assertions and the master's dictation to be unquestioned, for principles ; and the moderns, in their bible, are absurdly and slavishly upholding that absurdity. What proves, Mr. preacher, the authenticity of the bible of Moses? The enemies of it, and Josephus. All that, minister, is no proof. They cannot do an impossible thing. Now you go for the priestocracy, not the true bible. Moses had no bible. All was the jugglery of mind ; all then was the jugglers' book. Now as no one man could write the first five books of the bible, most positively they were written by the priestocracy, who were debauched to most peculiar depravity, of crazy ambition, of fanatic sophists.

You must, then, know that the whole false pretence was the work of the Belial priestocracy.

Organize, monotheists, for the best good of the world. Carry your principles to the circumference of the globe, and the centre to that circumference will be right. Press on, your cause is that of most rational mind, devoted to the problem of the universe. The solution is for rational religion, the gift of the Almighty. Yes, give us a bible, but let it be that which seeks to delineate the features of God Almighty by his attributes, not their caricature, most ludicrously, as all the peculiar faith pretences do. You speak much of bibles ; which is best, the Jew, Roman, Greek, Chaldean, or Egyptian bibles? Which of these idolatrous faiths are worth notice? The moderns need religion, not idolatry. It is not a Jew bible, nor idolatry, nor sectarianism, the world needs.

But you tell me that I must not attack your bible ; I must not destroy it. Sir, it is self-destroyed if destitute of principles, but self-preserved if sustained by them. The last are God-sustained.

But I need not do that which you deprecate ; I only expose it as self-destroyed. You have to bury it, and it is to be hoped, all its deadliest curses to your race, world, mankind in general.

I believe that Washington lived and acted, as that is history. I will give the bible of the Jews credit for all its creditable history, but not for statements about God Almighty, of which it was utterly incompetent to speak at all, whereby it is self-impeached as story, and forfeits all just claim to the world's confidence, as a perjured witness, who had to use the connections of facts to reach the tissue of perjury.

Such bible and its authors deserve the pillory, without redemption. Now, what must those deserve, that adopt and endorse those perjurers?

You pretend that some went so far as to count the letters of the bible, to verify all right.

That only proves them triflers ; counterfeiters doubtlessly count over their money also ; that proves nothing. The only question is, does this bible do justice to religion, to God? No ; for it stands self-convicted on the most flagitious, blasphemous frauds. But it has been received by much of the world, for ages. That is only by sophistry the most crazy, peculiar education, that makes parents traitors to mind, and children dolts. Such a course defames, defrauds, deludes, cheats, and ruins mind.

Why do I attack the bible? I expose the self-impeachments of that man's devices, for defence of religion, merely to set the matter right, as such bible disgraces the age, mind, its light and rights, to do the duty due from my soul.

You join the church ; that is founded on the bible, and that entirely false.

How can any profit by virtue, when they start on vice, and continue in fraud?

The world, as honest and honorable, should make every preacher prove the authenticity of his bible as from God, or make him quit the pulpit, by the honorable refutation of mind, without force, compulsion, or intoleration, but merely by honorable, rational discussion. The ministry should prove their pretensions, or quit for an honest and truthful employment. They might as well be engaged in passing counterfeit money, as counterfeit bibles, and are as amenable to the pillory. They should know what they are about by this time, and the people more than they, as the sovereign guardians of the whole world.

The priestocracy have possession yet of controlling influence more or less malign, of most of the literary institutions, and much of literature, that they have awfully vitiated.

The Jew god was too petty and small a calibre for free, intelligent Americans to bother themselves about. Polytheism sprung up from the incapacity of the ancients to analyze complex ideas, and its adoption proves as much on the moderns, most conclusively. What is the defence of the bible? All that you, the priestocracy, can maintain, is self-impeachment.

If the Americans and the world's freemen do not stop all such tory frauds, by the proper vindication of enlightened public opinion, they are unworthy the blessings of their constitutional governments. The affiliated make themselves blockheads, to help sustain them by their vulgar sophistry, instead of acknowledging, like honest and truthful people, that they know nothing of the subject.

Who could once question, doubt, much less controvert, the bible of the ruling dynasty? It was a hieroglyphic, a sacred mystery.

What ingenious explanations could be elicited about Moses, the leader? He lied, or the priestocracy did for him, whenever expedient.

His system did not proselyte. The ancients duly appreciated it. Even the Jews, when left untrammeled, chose other systems themselves.

Their bible is full of their divergence.

Even their patriarchs are destitute of principles, and resort to subterfuge and untruth when they suit their purposes. But what morality results?

Abram's lies to the Egyptian king, caused the last, and not the first, to be punished! What contradictions are involved most repugnant to principles.

To talk of acknowledging the bible, and not doing so; that it contradicts itself, and then can stand, is an outrage on religion. It becomes a wise man to recognise facts, and act accordingly. The idea of taking hold of any sect or order, to advance temporal interests, is outrageous hypocrisy.

The bible bigots contract their views to a petty Jew bible, idol as it is, overlook the God of the universe and religion, that consummates man's honorable duty. The world should not rest satisfied with less than the best. To whom does this world belong? Not to the orders of sectional societies, who are not to cut up the universal brotherhood.

Had God revealed any such thing, not only all the world, at one and the same time, would have been the participants and beneficiaries, but the universe and all would have been antedated instead of post-dated to mind's wants; and, above all, it would have been conveyed in language always used by the Creator, needing no translation but universally read.

Priestocracies, be done; ye are nothing but degraded actors in impious deeds.

No peculiar bible can possibly contain religious morals, for all such subvert them by their very existence.

That created by God, has the function of enlightening the universe and mind, and supersedes all such. Let all demand the proof of authenticity of all bibles, as clear as the light of the universe, else scout them all as impositions the vilest.

When a preacher complains in his pulpit that his church is not attended, he can be met most triumphantly at once, that if he were to prove the authenticity of his bible, bars of red hot iron would not prevent any from attending, and as he could not do it, that he ought to be the first one to leave, as he was acting the vilest impostor, if he did not act candidly. A people perfectly free in mind, will clearly see this.

The religion of principles excludes all peculiar faith as imposition, whilst the creator God is self-evident in his creation.

Inefficient covenants furnish irrefutable arguments against all their peculiar bibles.

Disbelievers of the bibles are the very ones to be held in abeyance to conservative principles that govern the universe.

All of the Jews were of an ignoble faith, that presents their first bible a piracy on their own people's rights, and the second a robbery on that of their peculiar god's— while both are flagrant impositions and fraud on the world, and the basest libel on the God of the universe, the means of other degraded peculiar faiths, Mahommedan and Mormon.

Bibles of peculiar faith are the written lies of the priestocracy, who have always betrayed and swindled the people, tory as they are, for they and monarchy travel the same road.

What but falsehood to defend them?

Are peculiar faith exploded bibles not a mockery in religion? There have been thousands the world's age, but God Almighty only wrote at creation his one magnificent, that all mankind have been reading since. There is only one question to ask, is the bible presented done by man's means, and subsequently to creation of mind? Then it is spurious and counterfeit, for God never inspired pagan bibles; had nothing to do with the Jew, Christian, Mahommedan, Mormon or any such peculiar pagan bibles—mere shadows.

All peculiar bibles have neither virtue, truth, religion, nor the idea of a perfect God. What better could we expect, of ancient bandits and pirates? Did their system civilize mind or debase it?

In regard to man's fall, that is all folly. He was created as man—no more or less.

He was not in a fallen state, man was created just as he is, else he was not man. The creation otherwise, was that of the priestocracy. God gave conservative principles, and no evil created.

If machinery be good, there are conservative results ; but if otherwise, these are destructive, hence mind must enact as a responsible free agent the whole solution.

What is the proof of the bible of the Jews, or Christians ? It proves itself. No. It cannot be self-evident. But those not knowing the principles of logic suppose, that the denial must carry the proof of the negative. The affirmative must prove what is affirmed to be true. Who can endorse the bible as true? None that is competent, therefore it is false. God endorses all his works, and proves them by self-evidence. God cannot endorse any other.

Let the preachers be candid or silent, if not able to speak rightly. They should not undertake to answer unanswerable things. They who thus commit themselves, thus undertake what commits them to horrible disgrace, and awfully wind themselves up. They do not advance the cause of religion, but expose themselves to everlasting infamy. The collusion of their fellows may absolve them at present from a felon's penalty, but theirs is a felon's shame.

No bible of peculiar faith can be sustained a moment. It is self-impeached, and impeaches all its advocates to condign conviction. Every rational mind must hold all to the proof of the authenticity of the scriptures. But that is impossible ; then they should be held as incompetent to preach positively, as soul-deceivers and deluders—impostors.

All peculiar bibles make mind traitor, tory to its species. Next to the priestocracy the most contemptible of all things, are peculiar faith bibles, that destroy freedom of mind, thought. They are tory.

If fidelity is sacred, authenticity of commission should be equally so. To what absurdities do bibles carry themselves—that is, their writers? They speak of the bottomless pit. Did Divine mind ever inspire that idea? What an utter absurdity in the location of such a place, and so absurdly conceived. The most exquisite torture, is that of the mind or soul. Nothing transcends that as the deepest, most identified penalty.

To sustain peculiar bibles, is to sustain an eternal element of perpetual lies and dishonesty in the framework of society. All such of all creations of mind, perverted as it was, are twilight to the sunlight of monotheism.

The main paramount question with the world about faiths and bibles, is, are they honestly true of religion and of God ?

If God's word, they are self-evident and religious.

If God had written a peculiar bible, it would not have been a failure, and he would never have entrusted it to the priestocracy, who are such stupid and fallible men. The bible an inspiration! Where was there ever an inspiration in such thing, but that of evil?

The infallible truth and unity of principles, direct mind unerringly to the Creator. This is the only rational inspiration.

All other revelation and its inspiration are false teachers. All peculiar bibles are heresies to truth and honesty.

The word of God is infallibly true, but that must be searched for in cause and effect, not in priestocracy's black letter bibles. All such bibles give infallible demonstration that they are not the word of God, ruler of the universe, for their peculiarity at once commits them to suicide.

Is the peculiar bible purchased at the expense of religion of principles ? If so, away with all such forever, and their degraded priestocracies.

Are all the gorgeous churches, Sts. Peter and Paul, Mark and Luke, Notre Dame, Trinity, purchased at the sacrifice of popular corruption and violation of religion, that honors the unity of God ; then appropriate them only to the purity of religion by popular discussions.

The peculiar bible people have not only sacrificed principle, but the religion of principles for all such faith, the substance for the shadow—the poisoned shirt. What an indignity.

There is not the least particle of confidence to be placed in such faith, for it is not at all entitled in any respect to any. That is not religion that clashes with principles as peculiar faith does ; that is clear and certain.

Mind believes the dogmas of peculiar bibles, because it has not comprehended the proper relations of rational education and principles. Taught the holy principles of monotheism, it cannot resist the matchless powers of its teachings. Monotheism goes to the highest of all authorities, the Creator of the universe, whereas polytheism affects or invents a divided authority, and on its own basis must fall, while atheism can go to none but subordinates. Neither is authorized to speak for the universe. Religion will be self-evident, present intrinsic proof of which there can be no doubt, much less difficulty with rational mind. Bible-impostors cry infidel to hide their own infamy.

Bible bigots have a mind, but they close it to rational light. Search the scriptures, black letter books if bibles, and they are they that testify of their peculiar gods. Search the Creator's volumes, and they are they that testify and demonstrate the supreme ruler of the universe.

Bibles for what? To prove the stupid blunders of the writers, not to instruct mankind, mind in religion.

Are you after truth and religion, or falsehood and peculiar faith? Choose which you please, and be consistent. The last you cannot defend at all by truth and religion, that is clear.

That proves conclusively that man had alone this botch in his own brain.

"God in his word says," say the preachers, who assume this word of their priestocracy. They pretend that mind cannot refute this, their mere pretence. All that they advance on such pretence, is fallible conspiracy against mind. They must first prove that the God of the universe ever wrote in black letter, otherwise they are self-condemned, self-convicted conspirators, which they are to all intents and purposes. Whilst they address in their pulpits the people, they commit sacrilege and blasphemy. They should stop all this impiety and outrage on the purity and intelligence of mind, and let the truth, the whole truth, and nothing but the truth be advanced. What cares the world for perjured faith?

How can freemen tolerate all this sacrilege on truth?

Sacred bibles! They are desecrated lies, a sacred felony, only in the advocacy of such stupid dupes.

Swear by bibles! Can governments countenance such for a moment, to have witnesses testify on bibles that are false and utterly false in their positions? What country, then, can be free from perjury, and the horrors of organic vices?

The God of the universe does not write in black letter, but by worlds or systems of worlds—a universe.

What he writes is stamped with the self-evidence of his authorship, and cannot be counterfeited.

Some persons only desire an excuse to hide or cloak their nefarious designs. Shall the bible be the cloak of despotism and crimes? Will the sovereign people be fooled any longer by peculiar bibles, that are an insult and piracy on mind in all respects? For what trifles is the just friendly confidence of the world forfeited? How can you cause people to tell the truth? Not by swearing on a false bible, that causes them to lie all the time.

Virtuous world-minds, do not pollute your lips with such contemptible felonies.

Suffice it for you to know that all peculiar bibles are perjuries. Should the bible consecrate felony, because it wields the brazen face of monopoly and usurpation? Religion forbids all that.

What is the defence of peculiar bibles? Nothing less than their disavowment. The foolish sophistry invoked, injures all.

The Jew bible god is a creation, not a creator—that is certain—no more than all pagan creations.

There is then an end to all bibles of faith peculiar, for that is a pagan code—a pagan lie—that is too plain for a rational, cultivated mind to miss.

Washington freed his country, a shining example and light for the world; Moses made his people the slaves of the priestocracy to peculiar faith, that has enslaved and cursed the Jews to this day, and cast its base fetter on every land that has ever received the execrable codes, the Jew and Jew-christian bible. The proper sphere of such bible is banishment. Bibles, heh!—men's fooleries, booked! Will you sin, behind bibles? Can any code of piracy absolve the pirate?

Will you, republicans, as you call yourselves, presume to offer, before the light of God's sun, all your desecrated bibles, the fabrications of perfidious tories, smuggled in councils by emperors and priestocracies, with their hirelings, soldiery, and vassals forced on the world, to your enlightened citizens? Those bibles that have deceived, falsified, betrayed, outraged mind?

All peculiar bibles are books of false pretences, and ought to be presented by intelligent juries, in their rational verdict, as world nuisances, to be abated by rational mind.

The peculiar bible-writers were ignorant of first principles that are supreme and conservative, and thus betray themselves as false to science, truth, God, and mind. Theirs were base, selfish devices, most evidently combinations for supreme power and despotism.

Which black-letter bible did God institute? Would impostors' words be taken? How, then, can their writings, that increase that imposture, as all peculiar faith bibles, be less culpable and criminal? Cannot all the people see through all these bible falsehoods, because they were fabricated in vulgar and dark ages? But the miracles of Moses; are they not wonderful? In stupid minds, that have not analyzed their history, how produced and how untruthfully recorded. What are some of them to feats of modern—if truthful history could present them—but, notoriously as they are to exaggerate priestocracy, despotism fabricated by the fraternity, adopted and propagated by their vassals, what chance would fair analysis have with the affiliated sophists and bigots? What are all miracles as pretended, the deceits of mind, to the acts of mind aided by science? Let history give facts, and all bible mongrel pretences vanish as abortions of corrupt priestocracy. This bible dispenses with religion for faith, and the truthful annals of mind-science for its tricks, an odious crime, and demonstrates mind perverted. What avail all its perjuries of miracles, before the pure mind—religion. Bible sophists, preachers, priestocracy, what is all your iniquity of bibles and faith, before the code of Monotheism? Mind does not know bibles peculiar nor their priestocracies, Moses, Christs, Pauls or Peters, Joe Smiths or Mahomets, from other impostors, but it knows principles and the religion of principles, the universe self-evident demonstration of God its creator. The advocate of peculiar bibles, polytheist, affects dogmatically that if his false position be rejected, that atheism is necessarily to be adopted. Now is this the result of his deep and damnable corruption? Is he in collusion with atheism or sophistry? All this is hideous bad morals. He has no valid excuse, for an honest and truthful adoption of monotheism will meet all points effectually. What is the difference between a lying man, and a book of lies written by such?

NEW BIBLE VERSIONS.

DOCTRINES grow old, but principles are ever new. The first, as those of old bibles of peculiar faith, present erroneous translations of God's book of the universe, false grammar of his eternal language, and obsolete words of their own. Require a new version, do you, of what? Your own fables analogous to all of augurs and soothsayers, originally smuggled by brute force, ordered by kings to be read in churches that were all founded for kingly government. You consume immense sums of money in printing erroneous bibles. Self-defence and preservation render all bibles subordinate to religion.

Will any pledge to bibles obviate all these? Never. Do not give us a priestocracy abortion.

In new versions of the bibles, new doctrines are expedient. It is a new resurrection to them. That detestable incarnation of priestocracy's fraud, will not answer for the principles of mind, new versions of the bible : it is new bibles; that is the mistake. The priestocracy themselves then admit the necessity of new versions, but they are just waking up to their senses.

All old monopolies, like old obsolete imbecilities, wear out as old despotisms.

Do not expend any money in vamping up, patching up all such trumpery. Cast the offal to the dust, and humble yourselves in adoration to God, true justice to mind. Do not be bigots and fanatics the world's age, your old age.

Learn wisdom not from the corrupt fountains of man, but the immortal works of Deity.

The priestocracy have been quarrelling, massacring each other for old bibles—rather peculiar powers all the time, only qualified by the state of the times, much more by the state of the times, than despotism. So your obsolete bibles have given out. Take God's bible now.

The laws of despotism recognised witchcraft, even in illustrious England, that boasts of liberty and science.

What had witchcraft to do with religion? Don't, freemen, disgrace mind by such ignominy of adopting scriptures that recognise witchcraft?

All peculiar faiths are trades, not of that high order that attaches to all minds as pure religion.

The scheming and the powerful, have seized but too successfully on it as their cormorant prey, too plainly in all past history. The bible has not been written in good faith. And is a position above the very nature of things, that calls for the abeyance of bibles to have the pre-eminence? Do such bibles make self-evident such pre-eminence, when their own tawdry ignorance condemns all forever? Who is to be believed in all this matter? Of course, an honest and truthful mind sees at once, else that mind is brutalized. None but a vulgar ignoramus will deny all this. All such bibles put the world where none of its friends can help it, and they all have to wade through quagmire to reach such a state.

But so many minds are blinded by the sophistry of their supposed best advisers, respecting the supposed value of such bibles. But who are the presumptuous advisers? Are they possessed of supreme gifts, self-evident to the advised? None of all that. Because they live near them, or are in some office, are they any more trustworthy, when especially they may have surrendered all the noblest characteristics of reason, to effect that change? You can only expect the priestocracy to praise their bantlings, and all advisers are the affiliated.

The bible has on its impudent face incontestible evidence to rational minds imbued with truth, honesty and reason, of its base falsehoods. All its advocates signally fail to disprove them, or remove enlightened reason, that they ungratefully and ignominously for religionists, war upon.

If this be a peculiar bible of a peculiar people, what have the whole people to do with it? The world-problem, in which all rational beings have the most extensive interest to work for the better evermore, is not therein contained. It presents no title deeds that are for that loftiest object. It is counterfeit on its face, and should be nailed to the counter by all honest, intelligent minds.

It presents no honorable and rational hope to mind. It would not do to use-mind in all other matters, and make an exception to bibles of tradition, that would be an ignoble surrender of mind's rational functions.

All constitutional government is from representation—but here bible despotism is palmed on mind without assent or consent. Can liberty abide, where pure and enlightened mind does not? Surely where such bibles are, liberty and mind are incompatible. Give us all that mind requires, all religion, but no means of corruption as the priestocracy or any of their pagan augur or soothsayer bibles. Give us religion and its bible, that is what a free and intelligent people want, only want.

But some affect that they do not believe in rational religion. They cannot then believe in their own existence, for both are identified. There can be no other. If then they have any mind and its competency for use, reason, the object the soul, honor, patriotism, respect for themselves or others, any honesty or truth, they are obliged to believe as good citizens in social obligations that imply morals, law, order, government, and all these imply all supreme duty. Now it is needless for such to cavil here. That will do them no good, but expose not only their abuse of mind and its functions, but the worst want of decency. The party must be destitute of mind and mind's obligations, to stop short of mutual or reciprocal obligation, and if they carry out their heinous doctrines, they war on society and all the honorable relations of mind and mind's excellency, soul. Now, what makes the priestocracy heinous?

They worship their bible and its idols instead of the Creator: its faith instead of religion of God; its crimes and opinions, instead of mind's obligations and facts; their pretences and pretended ministry, instead of mind's. A man that refuses obligations to mind, society, religion, or morals, law, order of government, truth, honesty, is dangerous, culpable, black, and criminal.

If he refuse the light, he is heinous. Any one that proscribes others for not following his bigotry, sophistry, superstition, and bibles, is irreligious as far as rationality can decide, and that is final.

Any one that smuggles pagan bibles, and seeks to palm them on mind, or adopts them smuggled and palmed, knowing them to be such, commits trespass on mind, and a blasphemous nuisance before the whole universe. Any one that advocates all such is pagan to all intents and purposes, is the tool of despots, and hostile to mind's excellent light and liberty.

Now, there can be but two kinds of bibles before mind or the universe. That of mind, rational religion, religion of principles, and pagan. The first cannot differ at all, for unity is its standard, and that is as durable as the Creator. The last, pagan, is as diversified as peculiar faith, originates from perverted mind, and having no foundation at all, has no permanency, and must go down to dust "unwept, unhonored, and unsung" in time.

As well deny existence, as its obligations.

What is the covenant of subsequent bibles on those of the preceding, but the clearest proof and acknowledgment of the total inefficiency of the first? That all Judaism, Christianity, Mahommedanism, and Mormonism, all others are totally wrong founded, as they affect, on a predecessor which must have been radically wrong, and therefore no base, which makes all subsequent thus founded radically wrong. No, says the clergy, ministry and priestocracy, the people must not read any books that speak of these things; that is, freemen must not exercise their senses or mind in discovering the exposure of their rotten, corrupt, and exploded nothings. The sooner the world reaches monotheism, the better for all these short-sighted bigots.

Your pagan bible has sinned an unpardonable sin, libeled God the' creator, and teaches others to do so.

It makes the earth one great arena of contention, agitation, sophistry, and evils; separates man from his fellow, mind from its functions, and all from God the creator to gods the creatures, making the earth one vast slaughter-house in political peculiar faith. Such bible writers cannot be excused by all the sophistry of modern advocates; then that closes such books for ever and estops their progress. There never was any absolute necessity defined to the absolute wants of ancient thought. All that is gratuitous and vicious, for the injury to religion is the deepest, and the whole category any way is the finale and expulsion of all bibles of priestocracy of peculiar faith, as the most detrimental to the peace, intellect, morals and religious improvement of mankind.

Enlightened mind does not desire the pagan bible, the very best that peculiar faith can give, that makes the soul idolatrous, and that God's functions had to be indebted to angels that were indebted to mortals to show them.

There are all the codes of despotism taught as a system, to obtain all unprincipled advantages.

Mind, intelligent and principled, asks for the purest perfect codes of religion, but no pagan bible and codes—as all revelations are such that deify man and dwarf God. By such, hundreds of thousands of people in France, Germany, Switzerland, England, and balance of Europe, were said to have been burnt as witches, not more than two or three centuries ago! The Roman church started it, it is said. What more pagan institution.

Republican, what can you be thinking of to worship a bible so pretended, exploded, counterfeit, that despotism deals in. Will you surrender so ignominiously to your detractors? But you are after religion. Then you have taken the back track. But you are following your neighbors; then you are following the dupes of designers. Parents, do you not know the futility of lying when a person crosses the bounds of truth once, and will you give your offspring the bible-means of lying all their lives? The Jew-bible and Jew-Christian bibles, morals and faith, are the invasion of God's religion, as that is of principles, truth and reason. To meet the whole subject, its false pretences of miracles and prophecies have already produced violent disorder in the moral universe. What would they have done, had they had existence in the physical? Miracles cannot exist in the universe, therefore they exist in the priestocracy's creation, and prove nothing but mortal pretences.

You must look to the year of the priestocracy's creation. They have violated principles, by which, if you trespass, you are amenable. You cannot revere the Creator, and the priestocracy's bible creation. They are inconsistent.

Nature is an elaboration of principles, and miracles reverse the last, invading God's principles, as prophecies do his functions, mysteries his attributes.

Past stories and legends, as the peculiar bibles, disclose to us that mind was grossly ignorant and perverted.

Is the bible-faith anything like what it was when the witches were burnt—when the people were burnt for witches? No, would say the bigot. Why? The bible is the bible. He would have to affirm, or admit the difference which is only in mind.

Well, we are better off now in commerce, navigation, manufactures, schools, liberty, and in light of mind.

Did the bible do this? The bible caused people to be burnt for witches: that is certain, and may do it again by the bible statute. Where is the difference? In mind, the bible did not enact the burning. What then? Mind, under its influence.

Mind has victimized the bloody sacrifice. The difference is in mind, rational or perverted mind, superstitious, bigoted, despotic, fanatical. Give the bloody code of Draco, and the scenes will be repeated if mind is debauched by ignorance. Thus countries reflect back the state of mind. Better have no country a bible that has anything of the least license of evil, as injury to public morals and peace may result. Mind will act, and as endowed with good elements needs only the right direction to have all finally right. A peculiar bible is the most dangerous of all things, to the world.

He is a monster that would destroy religion. Would you do it as much as in you lies by peculiar faith bibles? You have done it. All literature is embittered with the errors of peculiar faith, that requires strong and firm minds to combat. The objection to reason by those advocating faith, is clear proof that their case is destitute of truth and reason, the platform of religion. Some cannot analyze. If you disbelieve a peculiar bible, the advocates are pretendedly shocked, as if you had declared war on religion.

They identify their bible with religion, an utter impossibility. They are two different things.

Which is truest, the Jew oracles or the Roman?

Which people had most virtue? Which had pre-eminence in any supreme peculiarity over the rest of the world. None. Which bible is the truest? None: as all are false. The Romans had sybilline books. What is the Jew bible? A book. Is it any truer? It is, if anything, less true. Who endorses it? The modern priestocracy? What are they by that endorsement? Counterfeiters. What is the difference in morals and religion between passing counterfeit books and money? The worst is in the books. Then all such priestocracy·are most heinous and culprits. They are unquestionably, and not only amenable to the world's condemnation, but to the bar of conscience, religion and God. They certainly did not understand the vile pollution of absolutism, that has vitiated all it ever handled.

Supreme tuition comes from a supreme teacher. No bible of tradition can give posterity principles—only falsehoods. The bibles are all horribly corrupt, and would be thus estimated but for a corrupt priestocracy, who adopt all the ancient sins, false to modern society, with the empirical light of peculiar false education. All the bible pretences are pretendedly adopted—which one can be verified?

Universal deluges are guessed at, because there have been so many partial ones, and the appearances on the globe warrant that belief. But they have not been analyzed.

Thou shalt not let a witch live. Let not such bibles live, for they have enough murder in them to be executed for world, universe felony. There is no satisfactory reference in them of virtue.

Heresy is it to the bible of Moses about witches, millions of people being put to death in the world therefor?

This bible feeds on too much crime to be sustained by religion. Superstition unbooked is bad enough, without the blood of human victims.

Absolutism has cursed man and mind enough, God knows, by all her other devices, but this thing of its bible tyrannizing over free countries where the masters cannot come is too bad.

To have the minions and vassals is too mean—the world neither needs absolutism in any shape of bibles, or any other way.

What is ethics? In commerce and morals, it means the correct conscientious action, &c. In peculiar bibles, the utmost sophistry to avoid detection. It is tortuous.

Do you believe the Jew and Jew-christian bibles, the Mormons and Mahommetans? Why not all? Do they differ in fact from the old Roman's, Greek, or Egyptian, or Hindoo? They do not. All had oracles, that is, divination, augury, soothsaying, that is priestocracy false pretences, the whole. All were pagans. The Jew ones have modern pagan endorsements—a double series of false pretences. He who passes such a counterfeit book, palms such false capital on the world, ought to be more amenable for violation of God's laws, than the money counterfeiter.

The innumerable witnesses of the Creator Almighty, every one of which is adequate, prove all the peculiar bibles legions, though they be and all their originators, writers, and authors. tory and treacherous as their aiders, abettors and smugglers, the monarchs, military chieftans, sword in hand, lording their mission with brute force over popular mind, all the advocates affiliated, all perjured witnesses with the clearest demonstration.

My greatest reason for being so strenuous against peculiar bibles and their advocates is, that all such are in the way of civil and religious liberty.

Prudence, which is but another name for mind's providence, should be strenuously exercised. No mind that is rational will put itself into any man's power, as is too often done for this bible.

Moses, as the Egyptians, were all jugglers: the whole priestocracy by their own admission practiced all manner of deception in their day, and the worst condemnation is in their own records, that they were destitute of the first essentials of religion, truth and honesty. All the pretenders of peculiar faith have had to resort to all species of jugglery to make it take with the world, and the most effectual is false pretences, mind-jugglery.

They are the serfs and minion agents of despotism. There has been the utmost latitude to originate, adopt, and propagate all peculiar faiths, all despotisms that mind will swallow. All such bursts out in latter days in Millerism, Mormonism, Knockings, as previously in necromancy.

It is in ignorant and superstitious circles: bible-ruled countries. In such, Paul's sophistry was philosophy, and tended to upset half-established science. We can hardly, bad as ignorance is, even in this Union in places, begin to realize the extremes of the ancients, when all kinds of mind's perversions prevailed. Now, for former philosophy and wisdom, read sophistry, as for religion, read peculiar pagan faith and superstition.

It is positively a fact, that faith is a necessary incident of facts in the universe, and cannot be excluded when they have any peculiar manufacture, for all peculiar faiths are necessarily peculiar falsehoods—all false pretences. Now a world of peculiar faith presents the strongest proof of a world peculiar perjury.

Such must be the exercise of faith, without conscience ; and what is all such worth when it must necessarily be without reason ? As conscience is necessarily the vigilant committee of rational safety, it must ever be the regulator of rationality.

There can be no faith valid, unless rational. Consequently, the world has no exclusive claim to faith. as foolish bigots or faithites pretend. All have to learn in life, all that the light of life bestows.

The only proper decision of all things in the universe, can only be by the comprehension of their character, and the only right decision of conscience is, when its correct judgment is exercised on its correct knowledge.

By the two Jew and Jew-christian bibles, you get all their peculiar faiths, but by the rational bible of mind, you get the munificent religion of God, the Creator. The one peculiar faith, the exhausting mind-fund, the other exhaustless of religion.

Will bible advocates adopt the bible boldly and recklessly on bible doctrines ? Which of all the hosts, legion as they have been, is by excellence *the* bible ? How will you establish it ? On faith ethics ? The Jews' morals impeach their bible, for if the chosen people of God, they had peculiarly chosen excellency of personal qualifications.

You anathematize the Mormons for polygamy ? Did not the excellent patriarchs do the same ? How can you get rid of the dilemma, if you hold to the Old Testament ? But you aver that you have a new dispensation. Take care, my soft one, you have bumped your cranium awfully. You are between two insuperable difficulties that will overwhelm you. That is the very victory the Mormon has over you : defeated by man whom you have affected to loathe as of yesterday, the very thing that preceding sects did with you, you are overwhelmed by the Creator, who does not dispense dispensations, but mind and its functions.

Are you idiot or crazy ? One or the other you are compelled to be. Taking your bible, do you admit the witch policy ? You must take it of course, and all the millions of murders thus perpetrated by and through your friend, the bible, that subsidized them. But you say, there are no witches these days. Then there are no bibles. If you take one, you are bound to adopt all, thou softer-softest. So you see, the very moment you speak of subsequent bible dispensations, you kill yourself by subsequent ones to yours, even that of the Mormons, as well as by prior ones, as all Judaism, all are innovations on a perfect being.

If you seek to vitalize your peculiar bible, you thus detract from your Creator ; that is, you only blaspheme for your bible, that is nothing after all. You do not know where you are in such a category, as you are never safe with all such peculiar faith, a nullity. You may affect all bibles, christs and gods, but is that religion that is imposition on mind, yours the worst all the time, that has the force of despotism, the pretence of sophistry, and the reign of terror of superstition. Can your bibles survive, because they have modern endorsement?

Were it bible, it might be better ; but it is the corrupt mind of the priestocracy and of despotism behind all such, that seizes the world-torches of its own incendiarism.

But things in the bible have died away ; that is the highest possible proof that the bible is dead, proving bible fraud not inspiration.

Millions of people have been sacrificed to obsolete bibles and peculiar faith, that could not uphold themselves. All such are the disguises of despotism. How the world-people are self-immolated on the altar of superstition, to please despotism that always mocks the glorious rights of mind.

For perjured Jew bibles, you have forsaken religion.

The regime of the priestocracy predicates that of popular ignorance, peculiar faith, and exclusion of religion. The hieroglyphics of Egypt tell not for the excellency of popular institutions, as the memento is a durable monument of popular grievances. Their government is partial, most despotic in ignorant ages, that yield to all the fascinations of power. We must see the relative state of mind in the world, and the relative state of despotism accompanying, where superstition abounds. If any bibles are intended to improve or lessen the difficulty, they increase it, as the future is dwarfed to the vilest regime of the past, and mind is moulded, not elevated, by genius to the expansive demands made on its energies.

The ascetics whine about bibles of the Jews, when that position abjures religion, but establishes only editions of auguries, soothsayings, and oracles, the paltry traffic of priest impostors, all rendering morals worse, and perverting, weakening, and corrupting mind.

Ah! but the courts have adopted the bibles.

What courts? Those of despotism; yes, and of America. The republic separated church and state—one of its wisest actions—but it has failed to separate religion from the bible of peculiar faith. That defect the world must correct.

I admit the peculiar Jew bibles and all they claim of their peculiar Jew gods, as that is their exclusive property, in which the balance of the universe has no part nor lot; but when they claim any thing peculiarly of the God of the universe, my Creator, a totally different being, a complete after-thought with them and moderns, then I admit what they can only incontestibly prove, otherwise I pronounce them, and all their endorsers, from autocrats to the beggars, the veriest felons on earth. Establish the honest, truthful, religious claims of any bible; do not sneak, equivocate about the proof; act like religion requires.

The peculiar bibles are really too bad. The more I see of them, the more detestable and contemptible they become, as peculiar faith becomes more odious when religion becomes more lovely, and proportionately as rational mind does justice to itself, man and God. Had any peculiar bible been the true one, it would have been adopted by the world; but as that is not the case, especially as the adoption has preceded the truth, after all the greatest efforts of mind, its veracity is disproved clearly. Even in England, several persons have been burnt, for reading the bible. The Lord Chancellor, Sir Thomas Moore, condemned to death, by fire, those who sold it.

This thing of bible proof is too serious for the world to be trifled with and put off by the temporizing priestocracy, who are felons for palming it on the world, knowing it to be false; they cannot know anything else, if they know proper sense. They can offer no valid proof, and are disgraced by their false pretences. They and their bibles are nuisances.

Modern interpreters claim all the benefits of modification in their biblical prophecies, and they are utterly confuted by monotheism at her first appreciation, that all such, the subsequents especially, are inconsistent with the perfection of the Creator, who acted once for all.

The sword and pen of the priestocracy, with the credulity of the world called faith, might crush mind forever. But there is the God of mind and religion to counteract all such. What can compare with the verdancy of the moderns? Their credulity is heinous, sinful. Their professions of faith are utterly culpable, criminal, when the light from the universe's luminary sheds its effulgent beams over all. Did the fallible priestocracy indite and keep the records? What more power could be desired? They have left nothing undone for the world's age to the present time, to secure all their dynasty. If God kept the records, then they are pure. He has kept his pure records, that no rational mind can mistake. This is what I desire to call the world's attention to.

Even Jew bibles had, in their times, to change, to conform to mind, and so different were they that the exploded left the people foolish when the next were read to them.

The bible true? The chief secretary—the unsurpassed prophet—and the peculiar god with the chief patriarchs, have all sworn to the everlasting possession of Palestine, the lands of the Jews; but as they all have falsified in their own bible, that bible is false if there be, as there certainly is, a true God of the universe. The endorsement of all such bible falsehoods by modern priestocracies does not make it right, but a greater wrong, disgraceful to them. All bibles are in the same category. If the Mormons had existed long enough to be better appreciated as more world-deserving, that is, more capable to attain a wider credulity among the people, that would be more iniquity.

The self-government of man is what Moses and all Jewry never dreamed of when he was harassed about government. It was a failure from beginning to end, as all the forms of despotism.

Constitutional and rational liberty, and religion, forever to the world, as the Creator intended.

The whole bible question now turns not on the past transactions, as they are all exploded, but on the honesty and truth, the gentlemanly action of the present advocates, who falsify all by their continuation. The moderns attempt to galvanize the corrupt, decaying mass of prophecy, that Moses and his peculiar god killed in exode.

The proper functions of the tradition bibles are not religion, but priestocracy plans. The good of mankind is supposed as with a proper conscience; but all such is best but a fishy story.

God does not deal in tradition, but in principles that he consecrates as inspiration.

The bible is a representative of biblical perjury. Let it not be inferred that I have taken any liberty with peculiar god or gods—it is the absurd creation of perverted ignorant bigots—the small coin of smaller counterfeiters, with miserable mental calibre. This absurd bible keeps the world from knowing better, if it looks at this false light. It does not take hold of things in the right practical wisdom. The bible of tradition can not be of history or religion, for it usurps the functions of both.

Now the most unerring proof of it is, prophecy, pretence. The moderns would invent gods enough, if rational mind would permit them. All bibles that have equivocal basis, or without principles, must be ruled out. Don't let them go too far; nor presume on any thing from them. The bible is a false witness of deity, and all its advocates are false in upholding it, to the proper appreciation of the creator, through his bible, cause and effect, word and work.

Religion is nobler than prophecy and faith, as the last are of a barbarous age, the first of the highest civilization of rational mind. The last have more than superstition, it is despotism behind them their subsidizing power. The Jews stole their peculiar god. The bible mirrors the errors of the days of its authorship, reflects the defects of mind, its own defects before the perfection of the Almighty.

Let us get rid of bible fooleries, crimes and all. Religion cannot be sold, bought nor booked. All of peculiar faith is at corrupt auction of despotism. The advocates of exploded bibles, all of which in the world are necessarily exploded by their peculiarity, are base citizens trading in smuggled wares all the time. Religion impeaches all such bibles and advocates—all prelates—all. But the bible has the evidence of its own divine origin. Then it has its full evidence of its peculiar god and gods, evinced by the priestocracy, who constitute gods, bible and faith, as they choose to construe all.

When the priestocracy go to the pulpit with any such, they sophisticate all the time; cannot do any thing else. They talk in a circle of sophistry their life time, and have to cite all their pretended evidences of the affiliated; as to any of assumed deists, it's all the same reduced to that point by bribes, dupery, or pretence. Now a monotheist is different entirely. He is obliged to listen to the admonitions of rational mind, that all peculiar faithites destroy, alienate or invalidate, actually making that false black letter book, mind and hand-factured by perverted man for sinister purposes, an idol beyond his mind, soul, &c. All peculiar bibles have to live in the vitiated atmosphere of their peculiar priestocracy, who spend their life time in lying for them, their faith. What barbarians!

Ever ask for the essential proof of their peculiar bible, and it is not, cannot be given. They equivocate in the false pretences, that one particle has ever been given. Such bible, faith, course, priestocracy, cannot teach religion at all, for it has no principles as truth and reason. They are the most dangerous professions of all on earth. But strike out the bible, and of course you strike out the mock sun of their firmament, their creation, not that of the universe, not at all. What will be the result? They will be put down necessarily, as all such that have no principles, but mind will see principles.

Superstition was the deified creation; mind rationalizes on the creator's. Silence, priestocracy, forever. You are unworthy to appear before God—use rational mind that you have basely betrayed. But all impeached scriptures, are estopped introduction to rational mind. They are impeached for perjury; they are tainted with inherent impeachment by religion, and are unworthy of audience, till a rational verdict acquits them, a thing impossible, as that has convicted them. What is to be done? Invoke the aid of monotheism, that cannot be impeached. If any peculiar bible can alter and destroy God's attributes, functions and principles, libel himself and his whole creation, setting all mankind at variance with each other, and destroying the universal brotherhood, supersede religion by faith or credulity of seduction, devices of despotism for morals of rational mind, all sophistry for truth, then I can be persuaded that the impeached bible has shaken off its disreputable abominations.

Why do Christians or any pagans bluster about their bibles, when they positively define their whole position? They declare themselves necessarily peculiar and positively pagans, for religion has no peculiarity. If they aspire to be religious they can neither have peculiar bibles, faith or priestocracy; but must defer to principles that are universal. Of these two points they can choose, but they cannot hold both at the same time. The whole bible question is here as elsewhere ended in its own defeat, and that through the impeachment of perjury by religion. The creator cannot possibly know such a hybrid. But there are some fine passages in the bible, and that forsooth is to exculpate the world culprit! Because the high treason criminal has fine language, that is to absolve him in the court of conscience! That is the best evidence against him, for misdirected and perverted talents, for it is certain that such bibles were fabricated and smuggled to order of absolutists, despots and their minions, monks and their vassals, world intriguers and their fanatics. All religion is for the benefit of mind to rationalize

the world, not for the bible to peculiarize and brutalize the priestocracy. If this were
a question of priestocracy and their bibles, and not religion, then they might have it all
to themselves, but as it is exclusively of the last, then the bible of mind excludes the
two first entirely, and reinstates rational mind to its brilliant and original ownership.

The Christians need not affect that the ancient philosophers were of small calibre
when their pagan faith cannot yet give them religion! Their faith is smaller calibre
than the ancient sophists' philosophy. They have yet to learn what religion is, most
positively.

The whole world's holiest and truest interest every way is identified with the munificent plenipotency of monotheism, that does justice here and hereafter.

When monotheism presents her loveliest humility, she gives the sublimest confidence
to mind. She directs the best taste of constitutional republicans. But the bible is full
of the evidence of divine inspiration. It is full of the inspiration of false pretences, as
gaseous as impudent, as assumptive as ignorant. It has not one whole truth of the
creator, but presents the priestocracy creations.

The whole bible teems with their falsehoods, as all sermons do with those of the
preachers seeking to uphold them. The new testament presents the functions of men.
No such bible can present the divine functions of religion, being the prostituted hireling
of faith. All such bibles are the stock jobs of the world's priestocracy. It is a wonder
that the American constitutional republicans have been inveigled with this tool of despots.
In getting rid of the curses of polytheism and atheism, they will reach the holiest blessings of monotheism ; the sooner the better.

God gave her to guarantee all the blessings of life, present and future. All others
are false pretences. The Americans should never know a preacher, or minister of the
ungodly gospel any more. They should not be corrupted by them.

The blasphemous gospels and preachers, as most ungodly, should be put down as
nuisances to God, mind and world.

The very first thing that the bible of the Creator would give, this bible of the priestocracy's creation does and cannot give mind hold, hence its false pretences of faith,
which is a most ungodly perversion of truth, honesty and religion. Bible-faith is
ungodly perversion of religion. Then all such gospels are the creations of creations
most perverted, ungodly idols and images—they are pagan false pretences, and the
advocates are pagans and false special pleaders.

The subject of religion should be discussed most religiously every seventh day
throughout the world forever, by those competent to do so. All the world capable of
attending should invariably seek to be present, and do justice to their God, country and
rational mind. They should discuss then as ever, as well as practice rational religion.
Proving, as has positively been done, that the bibles of peculiar faiths are all false
pretences, it is essential for self-preservation to claim the benefit of the whole victory,
for assuredly if they are as certainly proved fallacious guides in physical science, they
are so essentially as proved the unsafest guides for moral and religious science and
philosophy. Nothing can be clearer or more demonstrable than all that. ·

All the dangerous omissions of ignorance, all the insidious commissions of peculiar
faith and education, must be counteracted, by the conservative influence of rational
education, the only means to satisfy the world on the main essential parts. But,
advocate, you positively said that the bible was against itself in contradictions, and that
you could not believe a part as too improbable for credulity. Then, is not the bible a
false witness?

How can you believe such? The preacher who asserts the bible true, assumes an
unenviable responsibility.

He starts with a step condemnatory, for, if an honest mind, he cannot believe any
such thing. He cannot assert anything in direct contradiction to truth ; his calling, his
position, anything extraordinary only gives two falsehoods for one. His belief assumed
is hypocrisy, and his faith the same,—all false of course,—he will perjure himself to
sustain all his false steps, instead of retracing them like a wise, honest, truthful man ;
to sustain all them he perjures himself for perjuries and perjurers. There is no end.

Will he proscribe to endorse, to force and deceive ?

After all he has lost all, losing himself, pretending to be for others in the pulpit, and
he writes himself a blockhead. It is mind-adoration to God, on the most excellent proof
that only mind of all creation can pay, and cannot be represented, for religion cannot
be represented.

Did you know, sophist, who have gone on with your professions to the ruin of your
mind's perception, that you cannot make choice of any bible on mere faith ?

How do you reach the bible ? Is not all through rational mind or its perverted substitute of sophistry, the hypocritical counterfeit ? If you act right, as a man, a gentle-

man, you have no counterfeit; if you act otherwise by faith, then you are deceived necessarily into the counterfeit. If you set up any peculiar claims, then you rule yourself as well as all out, by rational views that exclude what you desire excluded counterfeits. Faith brings you in a counterfeit, unless you are crazy, and then you are a monomaniac.

The poor idolatrous, conceited Jew-priestocracy thought or affected they would escape the light of God and man by their false pretences to peculiarities, and many no doubt were fooled into that absurd belief; but the light of science, the vindication of principles, not only exposes their nakedness, but their deformity and vulgar obliquity; now, let the world beware, else it may get the jackall's share.

The day will come when a belief in the bible vulgarisms will be equivalent to mind's stultification, a by-word and reproach, ere they be swept away in the current of oblivion. I find it utterly impossible to settle on any bible of peculiar faith, as ere I can possibly reach that point, rational religion claims her rightful possession. I must obey the guide of my moral free agency.

But Joe Smith's bible is a forgery; then all of peculiar faith are certainly so, only one gets the better of the other.

The question never arises which is right, can be depended on, but which is most available. Moses' calf killed Aaron's, because he had most to help him; this is the world. You adopt faith, a faithless pretence. You are excluded by faith, that has power, court, and popular favor. It is singular how visionary the world is in this matter. How can you defend your position? Your books are as faithless. In vain may the vassals affect they will not investigate other's merits and be blind to their own demerits. By reading yours, I came to the certain inevitable conclusion, because I was thoroughly convinced of its fullest errors, self-evident, self-convicted, that none such could stand.

Away with them. The affected learning of peculiar faith may delude the world with its false glare, but the real wisdom of rational religion is the intrinsic concern of mind and soul. What good could millions of bibles do, identified with peculiar gods?

And the bible lies for and by the devil, acts by and for its peculiar god and gods, by and for the priestocracy, by and against the world and people. What a book! Its creations are its images and idols, the standard for and against mind. It mind-factures faith and speculates on its profits, and sacrifices religion and the God of creation. No bible owns faith, that is all pretence. No true bible invokes the falsity of any faith; bible knaves do that. The world has more important matter to attend to, that of monotheism.

As good citizens, you have no part or lot in false bibles, they are all pretence. You can only invoke the faith of credulity, not that of truth. There is no faith but that of truth, and it comes through reason and facts.

To own a bible, you must disown religion and mind; above all, language must be corrupted. and you, sir, are the corrupter, the defiler, the perjurer.

Bible-faith is estopped in the court of conscience as an illegal witness, as impeached and convicted of felony, blasphemy and perjury. All its advocates are impeached impostors. The games of bibles peculiar, faiths, miracles, prophecies and mysteries, are those of perjury. The players are perjurers. The bibles of all priestocracies, necessarily corrupt, look back to fabulous ages, the more untruthful the farther back, while the bible of rational mind seeks to evoke religion from documents of the Creator.

The world needs the chronology of monotheism, as the one of true science. All that it has is that of paganism most conclusively, which proves no exact science. The very name of gospel denotes perjury, as peculiar faith is pagan peculiarly and necessarily so. Where are the bible concomitants to uphold its authenticity and carry conviction to a subsequent world of mind, that as true to its souls must ingenuously demand them as prior to conviction? Their absence as vouchers in the silence of the principal, its peculiar god, proves the bible advocates as false as the bible.

Where now is that peculiar god thus boasted of? Dead as the priestocracy, his representatives, proxies and personalities. As all peculiar faiths are perjuries when carried out, all bibles, their representatives, are perjuries too. Now, when God has endowed all the universe with principles, will you take less when you are actually entitled to them, the only safety fund?

It is not faith, but the sagacity to comprehend the truth, elicits faith. This bible murders religion for bible faith; it has no principle. Its assertion for inspiration must be absurdly taken, when the name and not the substance is pretended. It comes in competition with God's word, and must give best proof or else be ruled out. It is religion, not history.

Prophecy and the bible are the most audacious blasphemies, and the quintessence of perjury. There can be no pure pacification of the world till all such are interred in the tomb of the world's errors. You cannot teach the world religion through the foulest codes of despotism, as such are incompatible. Have the bibles of peculiar faith psychologized the world-mind? All bibles of tradition refer to the past, and exclude mind's progress from development, thereby creating awful evils greater than any pretended to be remedied.

The world has to try faith and its bibles by religion. That is the only standard to get a righteous verdict. All that the advocates of the scriptures can say, is that upheld by sophistry endorsed by all available despotism. There can be no other for bible perjury. No intelligent freeman in his senses can receive a pagan bible for religion, for that book to be desecrated to the corrupt purposes designated by its clique. No such species of despotism can be tolerated.

I am not to consult your belief of the scriptures, but their facts; not bible faith, but God-facts.

You assert that religion should speak for the bible, as the bible advocates assume to her friendship. Now she goes directly against all such. God will not condescend to support such, then they are estopped, and ruled out of mind's confidence. Their advocates have to be silent. That bible is proceeding to its dotage, decay, and extinction. Bibles got the world into difficulties about wars, witches, and crusades: what got them out, but mind? But then, there is no grateful acknowledgment of all this.

All peculiar bibles, make castes. All such bear internal evidence of false pretences, the reflection of the. priestocracy. No bible of peculiar faith can do justice to the world, the wants of mind, or the requisitions of the soul, and as such is iniquity, it should never be palmed on the world, being the counterfeit means of religion. Surely after eighteen centuries' preparation, the bible affiliations ought to be able to prepare some plausible proof of their bantling. I am actually surprised to see the intelligent freemen of the land using such a book, tory to every principle of constitutional and religious liberty. No wonder that the adherents of monarchy, the one main power persist for it, when it is the best card in the pack of despotism. It carries the game, and sweeps all in its insidious folds. Its sophistry is more capacious than the anaconda, for it embraces in its serpentine power all the verdant and treacherous of the world. The possession of any peculiar faith and bible, is that much less than religion, and puts the supposed possessor that much behind.

The Jews acted as if monarchy was to be a perennial mode of government of the world, including its union the church, thereby proving that prophecy was a nullity, a degrading pretence to keep the world in darkness, political, and religious.

It is strange the advocate of one peculiar faith sees the glass-houses of all others but his own, probably the most brittle of the whole.

I could not wish to be one-billioneth the sinner in adopting any priest's bible, to be exposed to all the ignominious life of its defence. No bible has the merit of toleration, but bears the mark of a brute beast as it is.

All the bible advocates have to rely on now, is a miserable subterfuge of sophistry called faith, that when run out legitimately, is the rankest, craziest perjury. Mind is married to rationality, but meretricious and mercenary faith separates them by base adultery.

Now freemen can see, why inquisitions to burn and torture mankind.

Peculiar faith trammels, while rational religion expands the excellency of mind—the soul. God has organized the universe by conservative principles, functions, and attributes—of which we are an essential part, and therefore most wisely hold ourselves cognizant of and obedient thereto—the social and soul problem is an endless progression of consummate perfection and happiness, through adequate means. to their attainment—a never ceasing exertion.

Had not the world been butchered up, by so many bloody bible statutes, to force it on the world, the evil might have been less.

When such are written or adopted, that proves the undeveloped state of unenlightened, irrational minds—if the Jew corruption had been all—but that was the platform to an endless, ungodly brood.

Had constitutional liberty prevailed, when the first bible had been written, that necessarily had been that of rational religion, the only one.

The world has had the bible and faith of despotism, let us henceforward have the bible of religion of the people of the whole world. Peculiar faith so estranged and corrupted the ancient world, that the peculiar advocates estimated the balance as heathens, and unworthy of soul benefits. What but the immortality of the soul could enable the world to possess its intrinsic brotherhood? The best abstract proof of a God of rational religion, is the chaos and confusion of the whole world full of peculiar faiths, that divide and subdivide, instead of making the world right: when monotheism representing the unity of God, identifies therewith the unity of man. Where do you find the worst morals? Where the priestocracy have the most influence with the people.

The proper principle of the soul, that should deal in principles all the time, is, never to rely on that which has no principles or responsibility, as the priestocracy or their bibles. The only inspiration and revelation is an exact bible of mind, not of priestocracy, that is certain and exact by science and principle, the consummation of principles, the religion of principles. Had true physical and moral science prevailed in the days of peculiar bibles, we should have never heard of priestocracy's inspiration, that made all their creations worse off than at first found.

All such bibles prove moral and intellectual obliquity of the authors only. What a caricature of themselves and authors, who come not only far short of Deity's character, but of common sense science.

The authors were perfect blockheads, whether aiming or not to impose on the people. The bible falling short of the character of divine inspiration, as purported, proves itself, is self-evidence of its own perjury, involving the character of all its authors and advocates in that category. Religion requires the speediest expulsion of all peculiar faith bibles, as self-impeached, and discarded on that impeachment.

All such bibles are man's foolish work, and are ruled out by a higher inspiration of rational mind, that thus proves their usurpation and imposition. One of the very best proofs against all such bibles, was the fall of mind by them, only to be rescued by rational mind. Nothing could have been more insidious than such bibles, simulating false friendship to mind, that it crushed.

The bible is the most ungodly book in the world, and betrays the most vulgar ignorance, reflecting the absurd obliquity of the times and authors, the most miserable caricature of God the creator, mind the free agent, and the most bungling creation. Either their peculiar god or the writers have been left out; the adorers of the true God can tell.

The bible, as the worst sort of perjury, cannot begin to suit children. The proper portraiture of the Jews has been much adverted to, as mirrored in the bible of their priestocracy, that reflects their national imbecility, corruption, and idolatry, them dishonest repudiators, having no pretension to religion, as destitute of humanity and all godly virtues, insidious scourges to avenge themselves on mankind, as their enemies, thereby violating the world's brotherhood, adding the worst libel on their unfortunate victims, for idolatry that only was pagan as that of the Jews; barbarizing and prostrating, brutalizing human nature by utter reckless piracy, debauching their prisoners, if not nefariously butchering them, and holding out their false lights to the modern world, that should stoop to notice, by imitation, their national felonies.

The bible sophists assume that the philosophers of the ancients did not discover what religion was—nor did all the affiliated tribe of the priestocracy, in all their pretences, under their pagan regime.

Religion has been practiced in all ages and countries where mind acted as mind, independent of all systems and their pretenders.

There have been many Scipios of their passions, in not triumphing over prostrate virtue, and many unknown, practicing what humanity required. Better had the world know not such advisers, if they affect to teach religion.

What keeps up now that piratical spirit of martial prowess, but the degraded example of such bibles. Let the mighty continental governments be instituted, and the necessity for even annexation, much less conquest, will be annihilated. The Jew and Christian bibles are the most corrupt bibles of paganism.

Let the whole rational world decide at once that all peculiar bibles are, on the conclusive facts of the case, their own priestocracy prophecies, perjuries, and act becomingly on rational, the only religion, and the world would see, in the shortest practicable time, one of the greatest evils coming to an end, and the noblest liberty maturing to her most magnificent splendor.

I oppose the world of peculiar bibles from the highest intrinsic principles, their consummation that of religion, to exclude all such and their concomitants, their world evils.

I can take no higher basis, and can have no wanton views of injury to any being. I seek to vindicate my unassailable position.

Bible faith is it? Any can be manufactured out of that bible, that contribute to any species of despotism under such a curse. I cannot admit any such faith, that contravenes that of God the Creator, and overwhelms man's, the full and undeniable one of right.

After all the best analysis, the bible inculcates at the very start a violation of truth,

41

honesty, and religion, a priestocracy perjury. A pure soul wishes none of all that. The bible needs a dispensation, and that is its entire and speediest banishment, as the most unworthy of a world's notice for a moment.

Yes, a constitutional liberty mind must expel it, whilst the despot invokes its tory aid to his collusion. Would any mind less than a crazy monomaniac conspire with perjured fraud, to uphold such a rickety perjury as the bibles of peculiar faith? The bible sophists, manufacturers, and advocates falsify all science, religion, the universe, to uphold that sink of perdition. Faith, is it, about these bibles? Yes, let it be faith, of course, the world over; but let it be fully comprehended; let it not stop short of the whole analysis of the faith subject, and then you will see the faithlessness of such bibles.

You have not begun to see the whole question of faith.

Your priestocracy with insidious friendship to inveigle you, only showed you their black letter part, but the God of true and religious faith has a universal picture that your false guides, wolves in sheeps' clothing, have not shown you, but falsified the whole in failure. Their omission is a perjury indeed. Tell it to the world that I oppose and discard the bible, but the reason with it always, that it is for principle, religion. So far from the world's being backed out by bible mysteries, it had only to investigate them fully to discover the whole a mystified perjury. Give the world the faithful comprehension of bible faith, and it would have nothing to do with it. The bible covenants falsify the universe covenants of God, and of course falsify themselves. What a world false capital the bible is. It trades all the time on false capital of mind, is used by despots for government, and by world-hacks to manage social circles, by mercenary designs.

Bible barbarism and paganism. The adoption of any such bibles, stultifies the adopters.

As I have proved satisfactorily that all peculiar bible inspiration cannot be of the God of the universe, his inspired bible, then it results that ample reference be made to that of mind, the only means available for all other inspirations that must be necessarily either those of undeveloped and irrational or rational position, and reflective thereof.

I have proved that the last can only produce a bible of mind and religion, and therefore that all such peculiar bibles result from the revelation and inspiration of the other side of the proposition, that necessarily determines the answer and their extinction, for as all conventional rules of society are determined by their legitimacy of principles, all others are extinguished by that decision.

The very idea of the universe, requires universal standards, and to cut mind out of them, is the treachery of toryism. Thus, is the world victimized. The world has nothing at all to do with the relative antiquity of any peculiar faiths of Moses, Menu, trinities, incarnations, as they are all pagan and not religion. They are the special pleadings of special priestocracies, the meretricious and mercenary efforts of world traitors, to rule the abject mind.

They would blight the universe by their seductions. False bibles require all falsities for their support, most ignoble at best.

It is the deepest reflection on mind, that the world does not move harmoniously as mind most rational can make it, on principles the purpose of creation. That furnishes conclusive evidence to exclude all the world peculiar faiths and their bibles with all their appurtenances.

Suppose the whole world, like New England, had been in one universal witch massacre at that time, directed by what its advocates claim as the world's guide, the black spirit the bible; the terrors of French massacres are nothing to it.

Nothing has kept down that and other analogous evils, but the relative rational light of mind. We cannot be too cautious in regard to all such bibles, as they are the evil-errants of the world. God's own conservative principles, the great blessings of the universe, might as destructives be turned into its greatest curses, and thus with such bibles.

Nothing is safe but religious principles, and religiously carried out. God does not know any peculiar bible, nor any persons under such banner ; even his principles are unknown to them. All the advocates to be rightly received, must rally under monotheism.

I feel myself compelled to adhere accurately to the text, throughout the bible of rational mind. All conservative revolutionist authors must prepare to encounter the abominable prejudice and odious view of the world, that had instituted the monopolies. The purest motives cause me to make these inquiries. I feel most deeply interested to have all free of mistake, much less error. I wish to be critically exact.

One idea, rational religion, led to all this work. Man is a rational being, and must have the highest respect to rationality. The world's attention is called to this point.

If you do not respect your rights, investigate, know, and defend them, what part of the world will? As to the priestocracy, they are most interested in the converse.

All peculiar faith persons, Christians or Jews, Mahomedans or Mormons, Brahmins or Bhuddists, or any other, prove your position satisfactorily, on rational principles to rational mind, and the world will be fairly gained. Then you will overturn this system of monotheism, that is, the bible of rational mind and religion.

Peculiar faith has undue ascendency in the world, by undue ascendency of the world's ignorance. Justice cannot be done the system of religion, even by criticism, that is corrupt as the times will permit. As it is, I offer this to the honorable world, for a solution.

Bibles of mind have to be appreciated and adopted by the world.

Prejudiced and affiliated critics can be met by propositions of two distinct points: the first requiring positive proof of the authenticity of any bible being the word of God of the universe, submitted to the priestocracies and laymen of all peculiar faiths of the world, which, if not answered, impeaches all the peculiar faiths not defended. The second requires, on failure of all defence, to successfully overthrow the bible of rational mind, to be not the right bible.

I will give any church the noblest triumph, if it can gain it. I do not know that the world is yet prepared to advance with me to my point in faith confutation.

The bible of refined civilization is due rational mind. Matters of the world have to be estimated to the most refined civilization, the highest rationality of cultivated mind. If these problems are not met, rational religion impeaches the whole position. Rational religion invokes the most refined civilization, the glorious, triumphant advance of conservative revolution.

The proper triumph of the cause before the world is most desirable. I am interested in the truth of the whole matter. The just and equitable relations of life are advanced by the bible of mind; but the bible of priestocracy keeps up an unjust agitation and an outrageous infraction of mind's rights.

The world needs not only a proper analysis, but a liberal discussion respecting religion.

I challenge the whole world, every sect and denomination, creed and profession of peculiar faith, laymen and all. Come one, come all, and break your intellectual lances with an open and undisguised opponent. I do not attack any person's religion. I uphold that, but I assault the world's false pretences of peculiar faith. I do not attack the bible of God, for that I uphold, as that is self-upheld like its supreme original; but I assault the priestocracy pretended bible, that they have palmed on the world for their peculiar gods.

I will bind myself to act as a monotheist to any one that proves the authenticity. Now all of you who are in the church, should be obliged to any one to set you right, if practicable, as all mankind are perfectly incompetent to prove the authenticity of the scriptures without God's testimony, that is indispensable to the validity of securing what is rational and just. Impeach one single point in rational religion, and that is effectual. If you cannot say aught against monotheism, you cannot say aught for Jew bibles.

This enterprise will bring the world to the proper view in making a transfer, that it take proper care that it lose nothing, as in exchanging rational religion for any peculiar faith. Rational religion cannot own peculiar faith on any principle.

The demonstration of all faith has to be on rational principles, self-evident on the rules of evidence.

A total failure to sustain peculiar faith, requires the proper effort to maintain some other that is best.

That is clearly monotheism, the original, pure one.

The infatuated advocates of the first will seek the successful overthrow of the last.

All such is to be fairly and honorably decided, to insure the facts that are trustworthy by mankind.

To elicit the best that can be advanced for religion, the author invokes in this matter the ablest talents of the world's most expansive minds, to whom the most satisfactory exposition will be given.

The bible of rational mind elucidates the religion of principles. It is not to affect the piety of one individual, but to direct to the right investigation, that ought to be instituted by all, in order to reach the correct and confidential decision.

Our object is only to displace all peculiar faiths, and establish religion. There are frequent changes of faith made for sinister purposes, or mercenary designs, but nothing can change religion.

A proper code of morals and duties cannot be too correct. A proper codification, free, fair, liberal and just on discussion of principles, will unite mind, the world, on all subjects that have unity—religion is emphatically one of them. She renders man as near a perfect man as mortal can on earth attain. Her divine inspiration forbids all bibles of priestocracies. as creative of base idolatry of the book and its contents.

The sacrifices thereto, through its belial creations, are evinced in all the despotic devices of inquisitions and hypocrisy, exclusive of all the legitimates of mind and soul organization, whose priceless birth and creation's rights cannot be alienated, forfeited, or prostituted by all their belial machinery.

All minds can and will write on this sublime subject, in one harmonious brotherhood. Religious principles will rule all peculiar faithites, and expose their false position about orthodoxy. Why will the world, peculiar faithites, oppose treacherously nature and nature's God, forfeiting the noblest merit of souls, for the untenable deed of the ignoble priestocracy? It may be pretended that this question embodies the difficult one of faith, and as such is a matter of exquisite feeling ; but my mind is so constituted that it cannot be humbugged that way. The established rules of evidence can decide best this whole question in all its bearing of faith, which represents facts predicated in truth or falsehood. There is no recorded code of religion before the world up to this time. You affect the bible, that which is subversive of all the principles of religion. Do you go for such morals to give world felons, the chiefs of despotism, infallible excuses, and perjurers royal palliation ? Will you violate thus all the noble qualities of mind and religion, and uphold the felon, blasphemer most sacrilegious ?

If you adopt a barbarian bible, you barbarize your own mind, country, as much as depends on you.

But the bigot may say, that he or she may not read any other book whether bible or not. That position at once premises the worst bigotry of peculiar faith not of religion. What will not prejudice do ?

Peculiar bibles teach obstinate believers to be hypocrites or bigots. They obstinately adhere to exploded notions, and are afraid they will be upset by reading and investigation. Now these last are the very way to arrive at truth, which is the foundation of religion.

Whether there could be prophets or miracles cannot be pertinent to less than truth, that decides against all such as the idle tales of augurs and soothsayers.

But you refuse to read this bible. Why ? Because it exposes all pagan bibles. It arraigns them for bearing false witness against God Almighty, libeling his character every way profitable to its impudent anthors the priestocracy, who, with all their affiliated brethren, have taken unwarrantable liberty with their creator. And they have made their base capital the very means of entrapping mind, dealing the worst treachery thereto.

The affiliated may affect, of course, that they cannot see anything wrong in their bible or the priestocracy. But their self-interest and possession of powers as perverted minds, may affect blindness, and are really possessed of moral and religious blindness.

If despotism be wrong, of course its mental offspring is, and all their bible's acts are thus predicated.

Women of godlike mind and fortitude, invoke your sacred household and family to defend their principles, their religion of principles on the bible of mind ; to live with, to die by, and feed it, and your domestic glory will eclipse all that despotism can erect in all its gorgeous trappings and assumptions. The bible of mind illustrates these principles :

1. Thou shalt not have any gods besides the creator of the universe. Thou shalt not have any of the creation peculiar gods of the priestocracy. Thou shalt abjure them all.

2. Thou shalt not have any of their bibles to mislead thee in false faith, idolatry, or the evil sacrifices thereof.

3. Honor the creator and his functions, attributes and principles, then thou wilt honor all expedient, and his principles will honor thy attributes and functions.

4. Thou shalt do justice to thy mind, and above all creation to thy soul, the immortal part.

5. Thou shalt sustain the sacred brotherhood of the world, and nothing less.

6. Thou shalt go for the world's constitutional, civil and religious liberty, by the purest conservative revolution of monotheism.

7. Parents and children shall do reciprocal justice to each other, that the first may inspire the last with love and reverence, due respect for rational principles inculcated, evinced by the profoundest, permanent filial gratitude.

8. The family shall be sacred in all its social, moral, and religious principles, as endowed with the noblest functions and attributes of society.

9. As all principles are sacred, religion, their consummation, consecrates all of rational mind, to a more exalted fruition in the future.

10. Let the reckless affect to divest mind of all future organizations, still its social relations are paramount to harmonize the earth, and render it, on principle, all ever purposed, and that constitutes an identity of universal harmony and beatitude that bespeak a co-relative, expansive identity, and annihilate doubts and unprincipled pretences where a universality is essential. conceding at death as at birth, the supremacy to the creator, and his perfect conservation for eternity, consequently no messiahship or pagan materialism can encroach on the soul's sublimest rights and attributes.

MESSIAHSHIPS OR VICEGERENTSHIPS OF PAGANISM.

THE omniscience and immutability of a perfect creator, above all, his foreknowledge, utterly preclude most absolutely, and without the least doubt, any intercession or messiahship.

Creation's nature resting on immutable principles, utterly precludes any created beings, from the character of Messiahs, intercessors or vicegerents.

All created beings are endowed with the inalienable character of creation, and incontestibly prove the unity and supremacy of God the Creator.

The whole universe, as the elaboration of his genius, attests the complete titles to God's sole ownership and management, as it perfects the exhibition of his adequate and competent power.

Then, no physiological endowments of creatures, as all stand in that relation to God, can create the necessity or power of an intercessor, a reflection and libel on God, as all created beings of rational minds, start with the innate faculties of rational religion, and are directed by best cultivation of the qualities of mind to mature their fruits of happiness.

The intercessor, messiah, or vicegerent, is a character necessarily mortal, and is resolved by all the elements of creation necessarily to the ordinary character of every day life, most potent in the essential position of individual mind. The intercessor then becomes a preacher, teacher, or expounder of peculiar systems that he pretends to discover, that necessarily must be essayed on their intrinsic merits, and assuredly all such must be condemned, as they have not pure principles or that can be appropriated as his, that he can never originate, for such principles are universal, and were conservative to the universe before his creation, only requiring mind's analysis and appropriation to the right purpose of rational religion, that cannot possibly admit of any power less than God's and his unity ; all else is necessarily pagan, of which messiahships are a part.

The subsequent action of messiahs universally proves them the basest impostors, and declares that intercessors were perfectly useless, where philosophical science was established by Deity to disclose all these principles. Undeveloped mind of ancient priestocracies caused all the error for an ignorant people.

Having no claim whatever above creation with communication of Deity, the whole power of intercession, with all its worldly machinery of speculation, is flagitiously fraudulent, and necessarily surrenders to mind that asserts its own birth-claims, all its best rights, titles and emoluments, that had been usurped and monopolized.

The false position of intercession can never be available one iota, but produces evil, as it detracts every moment from the legitimate proprietor most blasphemously.

The world has been outrageously imposed upon for thousands of years, by various editions of peculiar faith, and worship, and messiahships, all to create pretended divine rights of monarchs' and priests' union of state and church, all of whom conspired against the liberties of the people as long as they could impose on mind, that can put an end to all this atrocious and abominable fraud.

The value of mind in its glorious rectitude, is conspicuous for its own pre-eminent and virtuous independence. Mind commits blasphemy in ascribing as tradition the corrupt policy of men any such earthly action of deity, who operates through principles, his attributes, that gainsay most effectually before all rational tribunals, all traditions, and messiahships of bibles.

Faith contradicts reason, all sound, honest, common and proper sense, when it invokes any aid, for a being eternal and almighty, who is above all conception of aid, and equal to all demands of creation. Any other position is most impious, and impeaches the supreme as destitute necessarily of his attributes, and reduces him below the standard of omnipotence, and the character of God unworthy of mind.

The same contradiction applies in full force and virtue, to any permission or inability to prevent any corruption in God's immediate presence, of any worthy or holy being under his charge at that or any future time.

Worst of all, such faith renders the creator imbecile, his supreme attributes and functions worthless, and his principles most refractory and disobedient to their Creator! There can be no religion but what is rational, for that embraces the operations of mind in good faith, that necessarily excludes all Messiahship.

God's omnipotence excludes any peculiarity of assistance, for his imbecility in one iota implies a universal deficiency, and the earthly residence of any being necessarily confines his operations peculiarly to earth, and excludes them universally, and establishes imbecility for both, and incapacity to preserve the universal organization.

If the residence of more than thirty years was necessary to constitute an incipient Messiahship in one sphere, the labors of such an intercessor must be employed for exhaustless time, granting the universe to be exhaustless, and consequently leave no time for enjoyment of the bible heaven. The center of the universe will be unapproached, by such imbecile. But the universe gives no proof, that its Almighty creator is inadequate to the functions, attributes and principles of its government. All the assertions of the priestocracy to the contrary, will be fruitless, as they cannot prove any in the face of a confronting universe.

No messiahship can be God's but what is universal to time, matter and mind, that must universally and clearly to its full satisfaction recognise it.

No mind would be left in doubt by God, when needing the true confidence of faith, if any messiahship had been intended for all minds capable of reason, that sees God's gifts universal, not peculiar in any respect or with any exception, but in degree.

The construction of mind causes it to recognise universal truths by reason, consequently as well any true knowledge of messiahship; that when peculiar faith tradition is merely proposed, the proposition involves the false pretences of man originating peculiarity of faith.

The peculiarity of all messiahships in portions of time, space and mind, universally will condemn them forever, as unworthy the attention and respect of mind, that if rational, must be certain, that their necessity is perpetual and should be ever present in ratio to God's imbecility.

All tradition by bibles presents all messiahships confined to time, space, and executed by mortals, that universally betray themselves, and are therefore inadequate for any universal mission.

On this primary and only rational view, where are the messiahships' benefits to the billions of created minds in the whole world, anterior to these messiahships for thousands and thousands of years, cotemporaneous with them in the largest part of the world, or space which they never even visited, much less converted, embraced or saved, and subsequent to them in all time and space, not filled from the necessary defect of their character, the contempt necessarily arising in enlightened mind, in respect to their intrinsic mission deemed worthless and unnecessary, that usurps God's prerogatives, and impiously blasphemes his holy attributes of omnipotence, omniscience, omnipresence, purity and perfection!

Messiahships were originated and appropriated, that such originators might get the ascendency and the peculiar benefit, as being the peculiar priests of this peculiar the only saving faith. Their oracle was the greatest. Who, or what can be the intercessor, messiah or vicegerent?

All such according to the proper meaning of language, however liberal the construction, can never overcome the primary and paramount difficulty of created beings.

All created beings are more or less equal, and can never attain to more than a certain dependent relation to their creator, whose omniscience and immutability prevent any messiahship; and none can be available from created beings—all persons born on earth are created—God's function is creation, not procreation. Surely there is an end to such idea at once. Any assumptions of messiahship, imply contradiction and imposition.

It is utterly impossible to procure a universal and primary character, short of the creator. All others must be impotent and useless, necessarily counterfeit and spurious.

No tradition or history can be correct that contradicts the light of mind, that is always addressed through reason. What good will partial mortal intercessors avail?

The very attempt utterly condemns and impeaches all engaged as principals, believers, or seconds, of vile blasphemy, and themselves most needing repentance by such highest crime.

Mind needs no messiah assertor of opinions, but God's principles themselves, no deputy but the principal, no creature mortal, but the immortal creator, and above all, it needs the full code that reason gives.

All mankind have universally and fully, a conservative influence of the magnificent principles of the Almighty, that will surely work out their future good, if their cultivation be directed aright to promote an enlightened and correct conscience.

Parents do their whole practicable duty, in teaching their children proper principles that will do the whole good, and the work of their creator, who uses universal means. Such position prepares best for accountability, and its day of judgment is not that deferred last great day with the wise minds, for such day is the present, now and forever, to create a wiser future.

All missions from God are to and through mind, the only avenue, all others are pretended, otherwise, all honorable and intelligent cultivated minds must become indifferent instead of active, in a fund of life, interesting to all if properly instituted.

All creation is the Almighty's by the best of all rights, the right of his own genius; and the creation implies constant obligation of preservation.

None then can pretend to appropriate it, in part or attributes. If so, then the universe is divided, and the creator is imbecile and imperfect.

The universe can only be taken by usurpation or monopoly, and the invader to think of it. the most that could be done, would be base and unworthy.

The universe would rebuke the blasphemous wretch from its presence. If deity yield it, he yields up his characteristic as God, and becomes imbecile, all which self-impeaches the mind so stupid to conceive any such absurdity. The universe in its eternal harmony, rebukes all this as impious.

All look upon the pretensions of a private soldier to command, as an usurpation, when asked for his authority, to sneak behind the pretences of faith, which means you must believe implicitly his assertion, or as an absurdity to assume mystery, which means you must not ask that question!

What other just question than to prove his authority official, can all wise minds ever ask then, as they all are equally interested and have the right, duty and highest functional obligation as the beneficiary, if benefit accrue, but the miserable dupe if imposition and fraud be practiced.

Shall censure arise if their minds, constituted by the creator, cannot be satisfied with any thing less than his unity and attributes, and are they to be silenced by the impostor bibles of tradition that deceive the people?

Surely it cannot be in a righteous and just God's character, to add penalty upon his pure and upright adherents that seek to be consistent with most conscientious scruples, who look upon him exclusively as their God, because he is the creator of them all, for the pretences of impostors and condemned therefor, not for the demerits of the persons.

All such exposures of the priesthood should be made rightly, and at the right time at once, to prevent mind from being unfortunately kept back from its rightful duty, and the right employment of its talents and man's vital time.

Let mind be spared the delusion and imposition of priestcraft the world over, under all its forms and machinations!

This whole subject is to be met with the proper spirit and candor of immortal minds, who should investigate all the facts of their rights and existence, not with subtle sophistry, and fanatical bigotry.

He who skulks this vital question in mock dignity, under pretences of mystery and of peculiar faith not to be reasoned on, but to be blindly admitted, or by abuse of monotheism, is unworthy the gift of mind, and the name of a reasonable being, boasting of the gift of an immortal or rational mind, is unworthy of the countenance of a man whose dignity he violates; is unworthy the respect of mind, as he violates all its best attributes.

Convince the world on the proper bulwarks of truth, and conquest is not only sure but universal, not only safe but triumphant, not alone of the weak for popularity of the cause advocated, not only of the credulous and timid worshippers of the day, but of the wise and sincere, the virtuous and trustworthy; men of mind that can rightly decide when facts are presented properly to them, not for a moment or day of gorgeous mortal power, but for mind and its glorious eternal happiness.

The comprehension of the creation involves absolutely all the universe, to which alone the Creator is responsible, and competent as a perfect Creator, an idea that at once excludes any other character of any world that is so small a part of that universe, and man as part of that universe can only resolve his safety through the Creator, who scans and preserves all as they merit. In this after thought of messiahships and bibles of tradition, antagonistical to God's attributes of Omniscience, how is salvation of the immense mass of human beings preceding that gospel and messiahship to be secured?

How is that of all absent from its teaching, past, present, and future, the greatest majority all the time to be attained? Do you answer as to the first question, that the Jews had the prophets before Christ? That does not apply even to them, as those prophets were false—unquestionably perjured. But what had the other nations of the world, who knew not the Jews, much less Judaism? Did the Jews dispense the proper blessings of mind, when they slaughtered the possessors of the soil without seeking to convince them of the errors of their peculiar faith?

Were these nations sensible of their wrong knowingly, when they were butchered by their savage invaders? Was that religion the highest duty to the Creator of the universe, when it was the worst of its reverses?

All these questions are answered at once, for all creation, in the gospel standard, libel of God!

That the word of God, that libels his own attributes, that divides his government, and divests him of two-thirds of his exclusive Omnipotence!

Let the tyrant botches of the world, look at their own picture.

Can any good citizen estimate the character of an intruder into his rightful and sacred possessions, no matter how artfully he pretends to proper copartnership, in any other light but a base enemy?

None but a person most stupid or most base, can otherwise estimate it.

Of all the opponents of God's universe, there cannot be found in the annals of time and the world, a creed more effectual to usurp God's rights.

Who can wonder at the pernicious results to mind?

Why was the dramatized Christ killed? Humanly speaking, from the state of the times that created intolerance of faith, that did not accord with the interest of the party in power, engendering, as always, cruelty and barbarity, these assuming superior piety and an orthodox faith, avenged the blasphemy, however false or just that piety, and however short of just views of Deity, as Judaism no more than christianity is rational religion.

Did Christ know the character of Judas? It is assumed that he did. If Christ as described knew the character of Judas, why did he associate and suffer his disciples to associate with such a degraded being, as such character corrupts morals? But even this important view, yields to one paramount. This was the very character he came to save—the chief of sinners, but he utterly failed to convert him!

This one point effectually destroys his pretensions to full messiahship, for as is asserted, if Christ were God, and all things are possible with God, he would have saved him surely and certainly. But then it is replied, that it was necessary that Christ should be betrayed and killed—that an effusion of blood should take place. This is worse and worse quagmire of sophistry. A bloody murder had to ensue, and that foreordained, proves imbecility and outrageous crime somewhere. As God is perfect, it proves it with man surely. As it denotes blasphemy, and is clear that it cannot be with God, it must be with anti-god. But the elect only could be saved, is the doctrine. That proves injustice, as God is just, it throws it back on man, ignorant man, to say the least, if not wicked. If the bloody murder were necessary, then Judas is necessarily absolved from responsibility, for he is not a free but a forced agent, as all bible-monk-creations. There it is again, the full sophistry of the priestocracy. All can be viewed in no other light, than a human transaction, that human as it is, admits predestination, no self agency, and excludes mind's responsibility, the greatest demoralization subversive of society.

Who does not abhor to see an attempt to impose on the minds of mankind and defraud them of their faith, in way most horrible, worse than their treachery of Judas?

Liberal toleration of mind acquits for the thousandth time the good meaning of all peculiar faith followers, who are good in despite of, not by them. But why do the good of all such refuse the true rational faith, and thereby abjure all the good, and increase beyond appreciation the evil?

How often, times without number, do the spiritualists doubt, demur and abjure most conscientiously the faith in messiahships, and reject all such as impracticable, because deceptive?

But who ever heard of a pure rational religionist, rejecting a deliberate conviction on this subject? Will such resign his God? That is impossible. The world will come to this fixed fact.

But where will be the present professors before God's tribunal, if Christ with the other messiahs and prophets of the world, are usurpers and impostors?

God requires no prime minister. He acts his own premier, as none but his conservative principles can do his bidding under his present regime and organization.

If messiah-mongers should decree a different one, there is no doubt but that their god will act if they establish it.

Pull down the gap for messiahs, and innumerable hosts will enter along with their prime ministers, the whole corrupt family of paganism.

Let no mortal born of a woman be worshipped as a god, being necessarily excluded by reason that excludes atheism, and all the sophisticated insidious pretences of polytheism.

The whole plot and contrivance about God's vicegerentships, are absurd, and wind themselves up directly by their imbecility, if not previously blown up for their horrid and vulgar blasphemy.

Those who are concerned, for who is exempt, should recollect the impossibility from the nature of God's creation, for any creature ever usurping or monopolizing God's mighty attributes, without the most disastrous consequences, as has been most plainly proved already by the inextricable difficulties attendant on past and present crimes, and their enormous world wide penalties?

The ancients attempted it in their myths, but wisely saw the fact under the fable of Phæton driving the chariot of the sun and setting the world on fire!

What better evidence do we want that nothing but true faith, and its happy prerogatives of universal peace and best results, can stand without failure, than the present order of things, that creates a wider breach among the nations of the earth? Can anything be worse than messiahships and their engendered peculiar faiths? What world-evil is greater?

But for the conservative light of God-science, mind and reason, this confusion would be worse confounded.

The world most of man's age has had the unavailing peculiar faiths, under those who assumed to wear the holy mantle of God, to represent him as vicegerents, claiming extraordinary powers as princes of peace, yet failing necessarily from inherent elements that analysis discloses as necessarily defective, no matter how high the vice functionaries of even absolutism commanding kings, thrones and principalities. There is a world fanaticism in all this, clearly not of religion, that is consecrated by principles above despotism.

The god of all such is made a murderer by bristling bayonets, but such is not the true God, who needs no implements of warfare, to corrupt and murder the world's citizens.

The faith in the God of the universe rests on incontrovertible grounds, the sublimest position of unity.

All faiths in messiahships beg the question, and rest on not only ever controvertible but untenable basis.

False pretences and sophistry are ever abundantly brought forth, that the people are incompetent for life rights and duty, the very purpose of their creation!

That is, if analysis speaks, that they are for a period incompetent to counteract the evil designs of most seeking to exhaust the people's rights and treasures, is meant.

A new science has arisen, thanks to the almighty organizer of the universe and mind, that bestows the science of the people's protection against all false governments.

We wish to start right, and hold to the substantial means, and surely we have the best earnest in the author of our existence. We have no other, and of course desire no pagan.

The conservation of the universe depends on principles; how then can this or any other sphere be benefited by any messiahship that excludes those very principles?

This position is contradictory and suicidal to its ruin.

Shall the very author of self-preservation of the universe be libeled by his creature, man, in his little sphere world, in his little bibles? What little business!

Mind, thou wast not present in thy majestic greatness; reason, thou didst not preside at the sanction of credulity, for mind and reason were never, when allied, rebels to their God, much less libelers.

The author of the self-preservation of the universe, need a messiah for one little sphere! Then, he needed a guardian for himself and could not be even a god.

The thought is so very small, my mind, constituted as it is, cannot grasp it. The very exclusion of perfection of God, annihilates the whole perjury.

God could not delegate any of his attributes, that would unavoidably be abused. What could messiahship do in a work elaborated by a perfect God? Let wiseacres answer; for wise men cannot imagine in the honesty of their minds. This petty dwarfage can only be understood by pusillanimous priestocracy.

The majority of the wise do not accept any messiahs, whom they must consider degraded impostors, without the least respect or claim of respect from mind.

Away, then, with all false and impious doctrines, that enslave and demoralize the mind.

No wise rational being relies on botches, when he can secure the divine architect, who has presented master-means and embellished master-work with principles well calculated to suit all natures, to rear in the place of these chaste and pure fabrics, dilapidating structures made by mortal hands.

The genuine, whilst they rebuild on the rubbish of desolation that pretending work-men have imposed on the world, repair the unnatural wastes of howling fanaticism, for the future security in all time to come.

The atonement due on perpetuation of this blasphemy of the assumption of God's attributes, that progresses in enormity proportionate to the lights presented the mind, has been signally executed in most of the cases.

Will a wiser posterity observe the errors, for timely correction of such stupid wickedness ?

If the people do justice to themselves, the whole will cease of itself. It seems they may reform in other matters, but in this that calls the loudest of all.

We must insist that time was unprofitably filled before Christ's mission, and that it required equally, if not more so, the same benefit of correction for thousands of years, provided that any benefit could be thus administered.

But no sophistry certainly can meet this question, after all the false pretences of Jesuits of mind.

In the first place, an omnipotent God is impeached for his imbecility in not making the nature of man better, if we can believe the world menders.

In the second place, his omniscience and fore-knowledge are impeached, as he was not perfect in world-making and mind-forming.

But unfortunately these botches, like weak pagans, have left the whole period of man, from the first creation, to Christ unredeemed and uncorrected, one of the most imperfect of systems.

But a mighty fiction is used by casuistry, that the whole is embraced from the foun-dation. If that be the case, that ought to have sufficed. In the hands of a perfect God, it does suffice, and none but blasphemous characters seek to arrest it out of his hands.

At best, an almighty Creator has to be superseded by an imbecile creature.

But how is this known? By peculiar prophecy.

Most of nations know nothing of these peculiar prophecies, that even the Jewish nation, the very assumed peculiar nation, cares nothing for even to this day, and there-fore kills it. If the peculiar nation cares nothing for the prophecy, what ought the other nations of the world to care, after others had so much peculiar pretences in both bibles.

" These twelve Jesus sent forth and commanded them, saying, go not into the way of the Gentiles, and into any city of the Samaritans, enter ye not :

" But go rather to the lost sheep of the house of Israel."

But then he enlarged the sphere, afterwards, to the whole world. Surely with an after-thought, that kills all.

Many has been the nation that has passed over the scenes of life, ignorant and bereft of all such messiahships.

So much for man's after knowledge, that he presumptuously and sillily affects to advance by the side of God !

What imperfect peculiar pretence, that neither commends itself by time nor space.

It is pretended that there were a spot in Palestine, and a time less than half a century, where and when flourished all the wonder.

Was much of the world, even at that time, any the wiser, or benefited thereby, that world then needing the mighty reformation, if ever ? Where is the messiah proof?

Was it like a god that he irradiated the whole of the benighted world, that absolutely needed the light of a God ?

Was God unfit for his universe ? What mortal will dare assert this in his impious blasphemy ?

Man is simple and stupid to pretend to defeat the best objects of creation the better-ing the mind, nay, he is brutally and vulgarly blasphemous.

Of all characters, then, a priest that is necessarily hypocritical and that adds to his blasphemy, the capital crime of victimizing souls to his ignominious mind botchery, is the most degraded.

We cannot escape the consciousness of the presence of God, at any point or at any moment. He fills all space, which excludes all messiahs. Where nature is, there its God presides. Where, then, can a messiah operate ?

The motion of our sphere is our time, and its space is the domain of nature.

Who is independent enough to declare that on the opinions of others that they could have wished to believe in the necessity of messiahs, but that their imposition and blas-phemy, on their own candid and manly investigation, were impassable barriers for honest faith ?

That they sought truly the substance, and not the shadow. This would be a proper position.

Such worthy common sense citizens would deplore that so many preachers wander in their sermons from the true subject, God, and such strange medleys of controversial arguments, distinguished by mystified meanings of words, dependent on sectarian interpretations, books, and dictionaries, with the endless divisions, all esteeming themselves the only orthodox, exacting hate in place of love and pure religion.

And how many lives are spent in vain in all this idle metaphysics!

All this arises from want of analysis in the use of principle. God acts most almighty with principle.

Without it, what man can address God? This relative position is only maintained by this sacred communion.

What principle, then, is there in the usurpation and imposition of any messiahs?

No messiah can affect mind's prerogatives but its Creator, who gave it innate faculties of religion, which are only true to him, recognising no other whatever.

Mind that performs its duty, is equal to any, before Him who is no respecter of persons, and who alone bringeth mind to himself—none else can.

He is a monomaniac to think that any other power, necessarily mortal, can, and none but impostors can presume to think so.

Thus good, inappreciable, has the Almighty, as a master, done his work, that in the court of analysis, all such imposition can be easily rejected, as the delusion of mortals.

God's works are universal, and universally applicable to mind, and utterly preclude and exclude all partial agents, such as messiahs, as mortal pretenders.

All messiahs must know what mind cannot conceive more, that is, originate new principles, a thing impracticable, and never yet done, or to be silenced forever, before mind, that represents God.

All systems of God's principles are only made by men, graduated according to circumstances, intellectual, moral, &c. Science vindicates God, and now declares all such messiahs known, as vile impostors.

Innumerable systems may arise, debased by idolatry of every species, as every peculiar faith will be, but they all will come to naught before God.

Man, his creature, is excited by the loftiest aspirations for what is true, as all truth is the true friend of mind, thereby showing what God's character is.

False systems, the work of corrupt minds, involve man in all the penalties of their iniquities, requiring force and power as checks to themselves.

All such systems beget an irritable, morbid state of feeling among the citizens of the world, that caters to their prejudices, and worst state of bigotry, incapable of social toleration, much less union. Surely every rational mind must wish to see religion put upon the true basis.

A dead God! What an idea! O folly, thy climax was uttered then.

All that pretend to mediate between God and mind, are impostors, from the very nature of the case.

Analyze it with all the intelligence of philosophy, all the scrutiny and vigilance of freedom, and all stand on other basis than God, its victims in the dust, and their souls in penalty, unless by the mercy of God.

All minds have to investigate, and see to all this.

The worst of all is, that in the midst of all the messiah doctrines offered the world, wherein certain damnation and destruction are preached to all that refuse their offered faith and grace, still belief has been refused, denied, or referred to a time that never comes.

Horrible pictures are detailed of torments of mind about to launch into eternity, under conviction of their sins, and destitution of repentance, but still belief could not come.

Wherever such gospel of messiahship has been preached, fears the most dreadful of superstition, must have been awakened, and every feeling aroused on this subject, that entered into the very essence of the soul and mind, to the worst agonies that could be elicited—still that belief has not come. Why is this?

Is God the giver of faith, so peculiar that it must be agonized for in such difficulties, and impracticable even at that, or is it a voluntary act of mind, in its own ideas?

Where the faculty is innate, faith easily follows, from the character of the mind.

Surely something is wrong, for God's handwriting is universal gifts to all the universe.

Clear as his is, if the truth be not obvious, and such be not presented, all then are spurious.

Never tell a rational mind, if you claim to be honest, of a faith that reason cannot adopt, and that philosophy, that is the plainest of reasons, and proper sense fortifying reason, cannot permit, under all the awful thunderings of exaggerated superstition.

662 RATIONAL RELIGION AND MORALS.

What one, in his senses, will not prefer, always, the rational account, as the only true one?

Who then, in his senses, that is conscientious, in this age will dare detract from God's qualities, and aid by thought, word, or deed, in the usurpation of any messiah?

Who, therefore, will affect to make or govern the world, better than God himself?

Yet all other systems but that of monotheism, that essays most modestly to read God as he is, assume God's functions!

Who but Almighty God has instituted principles that exclude all messiahs as degraded impostors, as those principles are the silent but effectual agents of measures and polity, equitable and just in themselves, evinced by universal order and harmony ultimately!

Tell us where religious principles do not exist in degree throughout the universe, and you will point us to a part yet to be created. What did messiah-mongers know of the conservative principles of the universe, when they did not know of the universe?

The advance of the proper views of those right principles has not been before mind, has been retarded by the various perversions, for temporal not spiritual interests.

It is not so much superstition as corruption and intrigue.

Mind fails, from its own powers not being brought by discipline to the right view, when it concludes that faith should be peculiar, and contracted to man's creeds or opinions, to the presumption and jurisdiction of mortals, to pretences and blasphemy, and not raised to the proper principles of God.

If liberalized, it will read the noble science exactly in all nature, from the songs of the feathered tribes, the gambols and maternal affections of animals, the cheerful action of insects, the gladsome and refreshing labor of the husbandman, to that of the brave, dying for his country's honor and good, and be ready to respond, with its own qualities. the best actions of mind, as durable and solid, as pulpit or pious ardor can evolve elsewhere.

But you are now breathing on a part of the universe; to whom are you indebted but to the rational Creator thereof? In what respect are you indebted for this, to a messiah? Did that messiah create you or mind? No! All the previous messiahs are dead—all but the God of the universe.

What does death imply? The immediate change or dissolution. The mortality of all that felt it, most certainly.

Does death decide the mortality of all messiahs?

It cannot decide anything else, in the language of the God of nature, cause and effect.

Which is to be believed, death or the bible of tradition, that makes miracles of natural phenomena, and attributes their cotemporaneous action to a peculiar action, contrary to God's universal purposes?

Before reason's tribunal, of course, all such bibles are impeached, as untrue and incompetent to give testimony worthy of credence and mind; and before death's tribunal, all such bibles of tradition are successfully impeached, for they libel the God of nature, as imbecile, the very moment they introduce a messiah.

As reason impeaches all messiah faith and all peculiar bibles, the peculiar advocates of priestocracy are for excluding reason, thereby impeaching themselves.

What new principles did messiahs ever originate, to prove their mission that of a God? None.

Of course, messiahs are compelled to advance original principles, if they come to aid an imbecile God, and as they can bring none, they are all self-impeached as blasphemous impostors. As they are only equal to the Supreme, if he be imbecile, messiahs are certainly. If he be not imbecile, as the God of the universe is not whom ignorant priestocracies do not know, messiahship is foolish.

But, of course, as messiahs are decided by death to be created beings, born of a created being, both of whom physiology decides as necessarily mortal, they can advance no new principles, and are impeached all as impostors.

But physiology also decides that the natures of a God and mortal are incompatible, and are separated by lines of demarkation that utterly preclude their mixture.

We have no authentic information as to the likeness of the God of nature, and that is one of his own secrets.

But as to the effusion of blood? What else could ensue? That resulted from their own mortal veins, when they died. The God of nature could not have died, blood or no blood.

The breath of the messiahs being stopped as with all mortals, decides them like all mortals.

Mind in its senses can make no other correct decision.

The blood of man has no more to do with man's salvation, than the blood of animals, all mere superstition. If there was any blood shed, it was a foolish murder. The priestocracies were fools any way.

Mind's salvation depends on mind's purity inspired by God, not on the bloody worship of the priestocracy, as they, impostor-like, had the world to believe.

Who, in his conscience enlightened by the proper lights of cultivated mind, looking at the facts of creation as made plain to reason, does not believe that the Creator has provided all the means intrinsic in the minds of his rational creatures adequate for conservative actions? But perverted, degraded man, has excluded his fellow man by the iniquitous measures of messiahship.

But you would appeal for proof, in the blood of martyrs.

You ask is there nothing due to the blessed blood of the martyrs? Who were they, of what country, for what object? They are those who claim especially as being sacrificed by the world, for the Christian faith! But how many true martyrs have that and all other peculiar faiths made, that have been upheld by the power of absolutism, by sacrificing the world to its proscriptions? It is a pity that paganism has made so many.

Martyrs are men, and women, and children, as well as those who bled on the plains of our Union, for freedom of government, civil and religious, as on all continents.

Then all good men will most gratefully honor them, in their most honored graves.

Their posterity has the freedom of civilized religious principles, that they cannot appreciate too highly.

But no one of mind can subscribe to the bigotry of sectarianism merely, that has little to commend itself.

The self-delusion of such as of the Juggernaut victims, sounds as the history of infatuation to the grossest idolatry and man-worship. Are fanatics martyrs?

They died the fool's death, and got their reward as to that.

What patriot and statesman can envy them?

All other martyrs to partial and sectarian faith may have been more elevated, but more or less bigots, as they were more or less removed from pure religion.

They all died as to religion under a faith as bigots, but then they died not martyrs for the true faith, but to that noble innate faculty of mind, for the principle of universal freedom of mind.

But among the highest of all known to us, is the true man, Socrates, that shows his character and mind.

He was martyrized for rational principles, considering the state of the times, and that by bigots and an accursed priestocracy, whose envy and murder were for their base trade, and speculation in false faith and gods. This is the only kind of martyrdom that lives.

Rational religionists adore nothing but God, who is able to protect all rightly, in peace universal and good will to all. He asks for no sacrifice of blood or of mind. There can be no martyrdom in all this, nor never can be. All martyrdom proves conclusively, the most opprobrious reproaches on predominating false faiths.

The mind disdains all martyrdoms but that for true principles, as for rational religion now, and repels with suitable defiance, all pretences to claim on its esteem; all martyrs, patriarchs and prophets, are disguised priestocracies; so are messiahs and peculiar god and gods.

The elevated position of the people of this union, that gives the blessings of civil and religious freedom, furnishes the best standard for estimating the innate qualities of messiahship faith.

Much the largest majority of all the population is unconnected to any church faith.

Now the impress of Deity was given every mind at its creation, rendering it capable of religious feelings and duty, on suitable evolutions of mind's elements, the fund of its capacious action. All such elements otherwise directed, prove God's capital misapplied.

The subject has been placed, with untiring zeal worthy of a better cause, before the American people, who had the option of securing their choice.

Constituted as the mind is to receive such as reason declares, there never can be an honest change on such people's mind but by the true faith, rational religion, which is monotheism.

If left to themselves, the inherent vice of faith-assimilation, prevails, subject more or less to error, as they have never fully analyzed this subject.

Many have a properly-balanced, well-educated and disciplined mind, and are the ornaments of the land, living and dying like honest people, but cannot adopt truth in the original, whilst custom and fashion are so powerful. But many have not even such advantages of mind, and need more resources of education than it was their portion to receive.

More lights of the genuine character are due the world. The common elements of education will not do; the vacuum has to be filled from the purest treasury.

Millions have been taught the faith in messiahs, but have been compelled, by conscience, to defer all their best, only affections, to the one God exclusively, from their mind's exclusive adoration of his holy attributes.

Whose business is it that more should be believed in?

The priests' and other orders of absolutism?

Then they should clear the world of conscience difficulties, and extricate themselves from the hosts of objections, that are an eternal barrier against the world's conviction. The assaults of all absolutism only bring this matter to the focus of the sun's light.

All the knowing advocates of messiahship are deep buried in the stupidity of their own quagmires.

God had fixed all this, at his first creation, on his principles, that will confute them to perfect silence.

Who of these myrmidons can stand before his own self-creation, that they have so often libeled?

The supreme, who does this, surely and certainly can never need the puny arm of messiahs.

The conception of self-existence, utterly condemns and forever precludes the idea of messiahships.

The various and diversified attributes of Deity have been mistaken and perverted into absurd and cruel polytheism, instead of the efficient simplicity of unity in the Great First Cause. But that was too great a surrender of usurpation, maintained in some form or other, thousands of years by the priestocracy, who fathered the profits.

The polytheism of the bible number is cruel, since it causes the spilling of man's blood, instead of the adoration of the true Messiah that cannot die, and is therefore a most dangerous faith, anything else than moral and safe for any sphere.

Its absurdity is vindicated in the punishment of the blasphemy of traitors to God's rights.

God's hand never wrote this doctrine, murderous and suicidal.

It, a counterfeit, shows the puny, false pretences, self-impeached, of ignorant, designing man.

The creation of vicegerents implies impiety to God, obscurity and absurdity in the origination of the idea that necessarily detracts from God's perfection.

If God needed a messiah in this part and time, he must have needed him in all, as incompetent to preserve his creation. But as the universe is considered exhaustless as to man, that messiah would be all his time to eternity acting the mediator, and thereby cut himself out of his mediatorial seat, for he could have no time to fill it; moreover the balance of the universe suffers necessarily. What an impracticable botch!

Thus this position cuts the doctrine out of existence.

But if God needed a messiah who acted, then God's imbecility is demonstrated, and his attributes are imperfect, consequently he is not a perfect God. All this proves a God, unknown to the universe, who is a perfect God.

The whole only proves the imbecility of the minds of the impostors who advanced this doctrine.

What sane mind could have irreverence enough to suppose, God's goodness permitted him to unmake his heavenly angels and create hellish devils?

This god is a monstrous fiction, any and everything with the blasphemous priestocracy. Man's own perverted acts have done all this, as much as practicable, in operating on mind.

The highest veneration of the supreme living God, is the original position, with the purest reverence without any intermediate object to usurp his exclusive rights.

God's rights can never be usurped, if mind do its duty. It is mind that is usurped by the priestocracy, who made their heaven a hell. Free agency of mind then absolutely devolved on man, and excludes all messiahships most clearly.

As all messiahs must be on their circuit to other spheres of the exhaustless universe, the most rational conclusion on foolish premises, mind must look out for itself, and look to that God, that can by his exclusive genius-right, look to us.

God alone is enough and to spare, if any way to see all the universe at all times, can estimate all actions past and present, and provide for the future.

Now the omnipresence of Christ was wanting most conclusively, to fill the functions of a God, proved beyond cavil, by his timely existence on this the only sphere of mortals as was supposed by the ignorant ancients.

Those on earth, who pretend to any character above mortals, are inferior to good souls.

All messiahs then, are inferior to good souls and can have no mission but that of fraud.

A messiah is not in the category of rational religion, that mind had more or less in degree before the consciousness of existence, as a creation birth-right; what then can mind need of that which is not only useless, but in the way?

But not being able to meet the conclusive argument of messiahship, involving after-knowledge and imperfection of God, the advocates resort to an absurd fiction, that one of the messiahs was designed from the foundation to be slain! This scents of the old blood sacrifices for intellectual mind to adopt, and its clash of religious principles renders it an abortion forever.   No blood sacrifice of one, can atone for guilt of another. That cannot by any analysis of mind, be reconciled to any principles of justice.   Then there is an end to it.

Now it was only little more than eighteen centuries ago, that one was said to have been crucified, (that was the Roman punishment,) and if that crucifixion was fore-ordained, crime had to be committed in doing what is assumed a sacred thing, and God is libeled by man as one of the guilty parties!   No wonder, when abstract views of justice in the times of these legends were very corrupt.   Now corrupt priestocracy had the fixing up of the whole affair.   The reproach of guilt adequately recoils on these stupid bunglers.   All persons ought to decide about their religious positions by correct analysis, and know whether they adore an almighty immortal, or worship an idol nobody : worse, a creature of fiction, whose creatures impose on him tyranny of superstition and tythes of tyranny, and manufacture for him future views.

It must necessarily create hypocrisy of the worst kind, to keep up the miserable appearance of fictitious personages.   All intelligent minds must appreciate from the time of proper consciousness, the constant protection extending from his creation, of God's inspiration, that is all sufficient for one sphere, and all the universe of spheres. What then must all intelligent men think of the system of intercessors, to go between the people and the messiah, who is between priest or preacher and God!   What document does God give us of messiahship?   None.   No truthful, honest mind can see the first sign in the universe, where God keeps all his records ; that there is a false record fabricated by corrupt men.   What proof and documents does man give?

Fortunately for mind, a position that proves the pre-eminence of a God of the universe over the little gods of peculiar faith, man only gives those that convict all concerned, in the deepest imposition on others, and it is to be hoped of the deepest delusion on themselves.

Man can not mistake or overlook if he will, in this day of science, and this land of freedom, his position, that must only be in principle.   He is obliged to learn of the universe, that knows no priestocracy.

God instituted principles of the most exalted character, in the most conservative manner, involving no crime, but creating perfect precepts, a divine system of the loftiest morality and the soundest religion, that commends itself to the world instead of adopting the fiction of redemption, of most objectionable features and frailties of man stained by bloodshed, the affected murder on the cross or crucifixion a theatrical plan for sympathy, an iniquitous, botch as a foul and dark spot of anxious bidding of absolutism. This is no new trick of priestocracy.

The augurs composed part of the government, connected to state superstition at Rome.   So did the ancient Druids of England, who had an ecclesiastical government over several other countries of Europe.

The powers of priestocracy were ample, and their pretences as false.   They and all their tribe of any pretensions, along with their foster children, whether messiahs, incarnations, or lamas affected miracles, that science at once ever condemns, scouting at the faith that pretends to them, for the foundation rests on mortal machinery, concocted by mortals to deceive the whole world.

Such characters are anti-people and anti-god, and value the good of man on earth only in proportion to their own advancement.

The main points of imposition are forever to be condemned for their peculiarity, which furnishes the best proof always of the difference between God and man.

God is universal in his endowments and agencies, and if an exception can be incontestibly furnished, then the whole question is yielded at once and forever.

Man is always peculiar, proved in his notions about bibles of tradition, the peculiarity of which is exclusive as his work.

But tell us, advocates of sophistry, for such are your gods, how can this odious peculiarity be ever remedied, of the loss of billions born before the birth of any such being? Of the loss of the billions during his age, born in other countries that should have gloried in the reception of such glories and indispensable conservation ; and of the billions since born, to whom even his very name is unknown, and that portion, the majority of the world, in every age of the world ? Shame upon the stupidity of this false system. But they all were saved from the foundation ! Then why the necessity of any mission, much less one of blood, a relation too to God, involving God ? Yet foundation or no foundation safety, no tradition of bible touches mind in the majority, while all are universally touched by God the rightful creator.

His master hand did this, in the silence of his majestic powers. God's principles are his efficient vindicators, that must arouse an irresistible reverence for deity, that cannot permit any such encroachments on his divine and holy rights.

What a libel on deity have the pretenders to his peculiar bounty propagated, in affecting to excommunicate their fellow men from the universal gifts of God ! They commenced knaves, and ended tyrants and despots. When rightly established there should be no change, but now we see constant changes in process in regard to faith, in the various sectarian denominations, clearly proving it peculiar, and that principles are not established.

Yet these changes, however minor, are pretended essential in place of revolution that must come, to uphold the fundamental principles of rational religion, that peculiar faith awkwardly imitates, counterfeits and assimilates to maintain her foothold with mind.

What rational mind can consent to the preacher or priest going between himself and another called a mediator, and that one to go between the priests and God for man !

All but God of the universe are mere men, and less, affecting all this.

And cannot the Creator have his own rights ?

Man may call the continent of America after an impostor, though the true discoverer was ignominiously chained, and robbed of the honor of even the name, but Almighty Providence can at the right time avow himself through principles over the absolutism, crime and folly of man.

As to the people's estimate of Deity, all their talk and actions to uphold the false pretences of messiahship, are mere specks in the balance, as to God's works that are eternal records of those pure in intentions.

Man had best absolve himself, as fast as practicable, from his impiety and blasphemy, in regard to God's attributes.

Rational philosophers can well appreciate all the facility of crimes that result on such wrong positions, a vitiated, demoralized, sophisticated, peculiar faith.

The facility of various transgressions follow as perjury and iniquity, when true principles are not the supporters of faith.

Let a person's faith be what it may, but do not let it be a source of speculation for one, and injury to the world's citizens.

Let it be put on higher, loftier, and holier grounds, and that none mistake the meaning.

It does matter what mind's faith is, when its sectarianism injures or corrupts the world, and agitates its peace to the deadliest convulsions.

How can this be prevented ? By legitimate conservation. By reason acting on mind, that must act rationally in all things, thereby securing rational religion.

Who can say that any Messiahs can be without sin and guile, when they commit by assumption and imposition of the character the greatest in both ?

Take all the Messiahs, from the most ancient learned to the most truly modern pagan and shrewd Yankee, who manufactures a little of most things under the sun, and all their doctrines must clash, and run into one wild chaos of absurdity and crime. Neither the Jew, Arab, Christian nor American, can agree on a disagreeble thing, messiahship.

Whether the priests officiate as a part of the drama, or subsequent doctrine of vicegerentships, shall be extended through a host of apostles, saints and martyrs so miscalled. aided by angels and spirits. till polytheism arises in all the deformities of priestcraft and policy all the time, in its wily, but low and trifling plagiarisms or current editions from ancient mythologies, legends and fables, woven and dove-tailed, suited to all ages and nations, engrafted in all the devices of cunning, all is the same vitiated pagan worship before a perfect God of all.

The pure worship then is not in blood, or burnt or money offerings, where mind is victimized all the time, but as the happiest result, is the pure adoration of mind elevated to God, and him alone.

The offering is by the purest light of mind that institutes the best code of morals, that indicate their tuition by the best preaching to mind, to arouse to man's religious duty adoration of God, united to social, moral and intellectual relations of man.

Other than this doctrine is not the religion that blesses the people, however the faith may benefit priests.

Who has greater need to investigate this sublime subject than the people who have suffered in every age and country by misgovernment and untrue faith?

The necessity for religion is absolute and self-evident, because God has ordained and impressed it in the mind; but then it should be the purest faith, not the worst—a peculiar faith or system of vicegerentship that enslaves the human mind. Rational education will save mind from peculiar faith. The last is leagued with hierarchy and priestocracy, an artful government from the chief down to its lowest servant, who are all in collusion, or subjects of it by others.

No matter what the chief knows, he does not conceive it his duty to hasten the appreciation of the people, who may know or not that all government should be on its intrinsic merits and influence.

He thwarts the best government if it thwarts his peculiar faith, that he and his clique, not God, substitute for the people.

No matter if the wisest and best citizens observe that such a state of usurpation gives no proper protection, radical or organic, against perjury, idolatry, fornication, and all the worst crimes and vices, if it be not a sound body politic, with wholesome statemen's laws, and them wisely and impartially administered, with proper penalties enforced for infractions, that is not his business, for he has to support the customs of ancient ideas, however obsolete they may be.   He goes behind a thing he calls bible, the monster of despotism.

The most high-minded exertions of the patriotic citizens are outlawed at his hands, and their property confiscated, if they oppose this complex despotism.

The grand defence and support of peculiar faiths are the mere professions of them, aided by governments of states, and all the emoluments that affiliation creates.

Such representatives of ancient vassals will not learn that none will do it properly, as it all rests on a false position which is indebted to absolutism and perpetual sophistry.

Let a wise circumspection, and an equity with consistent laws be enforced, as no respecter of persons.

The world can depend on no other.   The temporal must be separated from the spiritual, says rational religion, else the speculation is clearly naught but peculiar faith, a peculiar corruption of government.

What shall we think of a hierarchy, however high the authority assumed, as the professed recipients of the keys of their heaven from Saint Peter, when bristling bayonets are used to reinstate them, at the expense of blood of thousands of their brethren in the same Messiah Christ!

In letting open the door to messiahs, they make a whole list.   First, next to Christ is the worship of the Virgin Mary, a woman who had borne a child of which she was pregnant before marriage.

That is a virgin in the double sense, of exquisitely correct language.

The saints seem about superseding the messiah!

Has its messiahship got down to St. Paul with the Lord that may aid the people?

And are the Holy Virgin, that we cannot know by language at all, and all the saints who are worshipped to aid the messiah, to aid God?   Is the pagan god growing less?

Where does impiety stop?   In the unintelligible language of the trinity?

But why not receive a messiah?

We cannot possibly know him, if we know God rightly.

All the creeds of messiahs discard themselves in discarding each other as antagonistical heresies.

All messiahships are pecular, and all invalid.

There can be no such thing as a messiah before God, the perfect God of the universe.

There can be no God from the nature of things, if there be a messiah.

All pretences about it degrade instead of improve the world.

The world is misled by impulse about it.

When the world comes to pay a just adoration to the just and only proprietor, Deity, then there will be no cheating the Creator, and less fraud in man.

At present Deity is awfully cheated under horrid sophistry.   How can the priestocracy be honest or truthful?

Put all on a right foundation, and then man will wrong his fellow-citizens of the world less, if just to God.   The greater necessity is created by the bibles to correct its evils.

Half the world requires laws to keep it in subjection, under the present regime of social institutions.

The worst state is to permit pretences to lord it with such effect.

It is bad enough to permit wealth and power to insult with impunity, and continue the world's wrongs.

42

No doubt honesty is the best mediator and intercessor, as Deity must affirm to the vindication of his own established principles, by immutable truth.

All this conservative position excludes all messiahships, for honesty of faith is the honesty of truth.

The adherents of peculiar sects hate each other with a bitter hate, and contend severely with each other, all needing the proper characteristics of proper religion, credence in one ever living God, and the practice of his invaluable precepts, as taught by his attributes.

Sectarians worship mortals miscalled gods, or those of equivalent character when alive.

By the very brightest gifts of God, in all ages, most of the world dies without being disturbed by a messiah belief, whether of Christ, Mahomet, the Smiths, or Juggernaut.

All these messiahs will most speedily die out in the light of mind, as the exploded doctrines, once the light of a part of the world, about the numerous mythological deities.

The relics of the saints, the tunics, bones, blood and wafers, along with mothers, child, and saints, must always perish before that light.

The sooner mind discards all that trash, mummery, and adopt the adoration of Deity, more than soul of the universe, the author of principles, the better.

Let this age reject all errors of past ages, seek God, avoid base actions, assert the manly and noble independence of freedom, and rise superior to all the little local cliques of peculiar faith, church intrigues, and petty ambition.

How is it that the people are not fed by officiating priests?

We must analyze language, and never permit it to be sophisticated in all this matter.

Where are the signs falsely promised the apostles? Christ was a false prophet. All prophets are false; their advocates also.

We have no proof of any divinity, but God's.

Men may affect to testify; but what can ignorant men do, who are to be testified of themselves, wanting character, as proved by that very testimony that introduces them, against God-documents written in the universe?

Did these stupid boobies ever think of all this?

Who testify of these men, ruined in character by their testimony? Who will endorse, who will uphold their awful perjuries? The priestocracy made all these men of straw, and are self-condemned, though advocates falsify their word to protect them.

Take care you do not commit perjuries, that never can be cancelled in your heaven's chancery, and will bear witness against you, forgetting God and his attributes. That is the main and essential question.

Why permit nine-tenths of the billion of unbelievers to be sacrificed every age, when God is omnipotent?

Everything is possible, with an omnipotent Almighty, is it? If it were, he could not be an omnipotent long. All folly of man is inconsistent with God's character.

The omnipotent needs no aid in his universe, most evidently of his creatures; but they all need aid of him, to read correctly his works.

What could they do for him, with all their messiahs—what for themselves?

The Roman cross, Mahomedan poison, and American fire-arms have told for three, if not more.

Nature's works prove a God, from the universe down to the first germination of vegetation, through all the microscopic world, a principal supreme, not secondary, who never yet has instituted innate faculties, and, as a conclusive proof, had to adopt the principles of the Creator.

Messiahship is not only of minor, but of no importance. It is the false conception of addled brains. All its ministers are imbecile, from their ignorance of primary principles, and must be arrant impostors, proved by their blasphemy.

The saintship, that is part of its machinery, is degenerate too, degrading all peculiar faith people by its sophistry, that pervades the world.

Some minds are so constituted that they cannot analyze, but believe as their interest, or that of others direct, or as they are told.

All such are obliged to see that, if the messiah was a right principle, that there could only be one faith, that is certain. Sectarianism, or its hateful and hostile feelings and passions arising under messiahs, have nothing to do with religion.

All such is not religion; if it be, it is humbuggery, nevertheless.

Rational religion participates in love, universal as far as practicable, exempt from all sectarianism.

It would take more than a universe of peculiar godheads, trinities, and messiahs, with all their peculiar virgins and saints, miracles, prophecies and mysteries, to begin to approach, much less equal, the God of the universe, whom all peculiar faith-advocates never have known at all.   Their doctrines and worship so peculiar, prove all this conclusively.   They all constitute the lowest cabinet of creation.

But some may affect that it does no good to pay exclusive reverence to God!

What can we do, if we relax our highest reverence to God?   We diminish so much of God's rights, and that too in the face of God's works, for we can certainly discover God from his works, but no messiah at all; just the reverse.

Are we to believe them God's works, or man's books that cannot reflect them in portraiture?

No messiah can start any new principles; then he is impostor, and can only file into the ranks of mortals.

What mind, in millions, ever fully analyzed this subject?

The anxious inquirer is told by the "divine minister," who says the truth, of course, as divine, that he has religion.

He is told to believe in the messiah, and is baptized.

Did he ever investigate this subject, with learning and wisdom enough to do so?

After he is initiated, he is affiliated by pride of consistency that will rarely permit change, unless by errors of habits.

Any monopoly or usurpation raised by messiahship, cause confusion and strife, sophistry with tyranny, perjury with disgrace to all. a defeat in misery and infamy.

A messiah must be a creator, else he is necessarily an impostor.

Priestcraft and humbuggery pretend that the messiah aids the spirit of God to man's spirit, and man's spirit to God; but all such position is pre-occupied by an Almighty and his vicegerents, the consummation of principles.

The spirit of man is rightly directed by a right education, and the result is rational religion, that a messiah knows nothing of.

If the messiah is mightier, then he is the God supreme.

But the Creator, not the messiah, is Almighty, and that language doubly excludes the messiah.

A messiah cannot be almighty, nor creator; consequently he cannot be more than a creature.   This is the inevitable, right, and absolute conclusion.

Principles alone can best govern the world, in mass or in particulars.   An ignorant community speaks of messiahs!   What is a universe full of them, worth?

We need no messiahs, but faithfulness and truth, to carry out the honest convictions of mind.

We need no mysteries and enigmas in God's word, as his works from day to day most plainly tell.

All systems tell for themselves.

Had Christ, and all other messiahs so-called, been humble disciples of Almighty God, in the ways of purity and principles, they could not have needed body-guards, that betrayed themselves by falsehood, treachery, and desertion.

God's unity outweighs all the jarring, nonsensical trinities, that humble mortals laugh to scorn, while they revere God's unity, and solemnly reverence his exclusive attributes.   God's wise conservative principles declare his Godhead by no messenger but mind the beneficiary, by no interpreter but reason, while the Messiah's pretences jar by sectarianism, become as bad as Judaism.

What but truth, can we substitute for all such!

As the Messiah's all peculiar faith is antagonistical to rational religion, all such is the substitute, and we must exclude it certainly as hostile to mind's best interest and happiness.

What absurdity is it to pray to God, to give us ability to pray!   How can we implore Mary after God, to supplicate Christ, no matter the priest's authority?   How could any sound mind ask of any earthly authority plenary indulgence for all sins, whether royal families are the recipients and popes the givers?

All such pretences come under the errors and vices of man's opinions and blasphemous superstition.

There is but one God: all else are blasphemous impostors.

As the majority of minds from their constitutional organization in every age precludes entirely their adoption of any Messiahs, can any better proof be exhibited of their total imposition on and attempted usurpation of the rights of the Creator and ruler of mind?

An enlightened age must prostrate this base substitute of hypocritical pretences, and will offer up its purer adoration in sincere faith to God alone the legitimate claimant.

As to Messiahship, would not the mere offer for sacrifice made in good faith have been more worthy of all the parties, than the effusion of blood analogous to Isaac's case?

Should it have been the very cause of Christ's condemnation and penalty, if pure and free from high treason against the supremacy and majesty of the Almighty?

All such is absurd and suicidal, seeing that the will for the deed was efficient in Abraham. Here is an inconsistency that destroys the validity of both, as man's device. No effusion of blood can be necessary before the God of the universe; neither form or rite, but a pure mind and conscience unsullied by blood or any crime during life.

The sacrifice of sins and adoption of virtues, are what the Supreme requires of mind.

Mind has no blood to yield. What has mind to do with effusion of blood? Correct analysis yields no blood. What can Messiah-mongers find to do in God's universe, what God had not already done in the best style? What else can they do, but skulk out of their position in which they will but show their low character for deception and pretences?

Now, neither language that is the sign of our ideas, nor mathematics that truly defines precision of numbers, can be modified to express that trinity is unity. Both are immutable, and truthful minds are obliged to acknowledge these facts, or be accounted dishonest and held as propagators of gospel falsehoods, worse perjuries. Which is the greatest foolhardiness: to commit murder to reach purity of mind, or perjury to sustain the scriptures? Can the stupes get out of their lowest depths of iniquity? If we were to be benefited, especially by any direct mission or Messiahship, it would be universal if God had caused it, and it would be written by universal beams of light, otherwise it will be peculiar, partial, and confined to man's circle and invalidity.

That benefit could not be deferred to the last dying hour to convince the skeptic, but all would profit by clear and unmistakable light. The world needed the effulgence of rational mind, not the effusion of blood that degraded it still more in iniquity. The God of the universe has no vicegerents, as he needs none, and as God can have none, man's efforts vitiate the whole character, morally and ph s call . God's power is sufficient for the functions of his universe. The stupidity of the priestocracy, prevented vision. Man must claim the discovery of another universe ere he institutes another kind of government alien to the unity of God. All the universe can be reconciled in opinion and practice, in reverence and adoration to him.

All mankind can agree on his worthiness, and none can fall out of unity.

But the vicegerents cannot govern one church, much less one village, one country, least of all a world in unity, that does not belong to them at all.

All they offer the world, are doctrines and works of man.

If the Messiahs are wrong, all their followers can never get right. No Messiahship can cover the ground then.

The Almighty Creator is to be excluded by vicegerents, or he is to be made a trinity, demi-god, and this uncreates the universe that absolutely required the Creator, whose highest characteristic is unity.

Mind is to be degraded for feudal tradition and fable.

Reason is to be victimized for reckless peculiar faith.

Truth is to be annihilated for sophistry.

What was the atonement of blood worth?

All that ever was shed on earth on the altars by priests, was not only inefficacious, but entirely useless in purification of sins of all calibres.

The intention of an upright mind is seen in wise actions to benefit the world, not to be humbugged out of its rights.

How many countless defects are then in any vicegerentships. All such are superstitions, that show their counterfeit character by their peculiar inability to save universally. The most of all such is the burden of ancient history and mythology, abounding in errors, resting in fabulous traditions and senseless views of natural phenomena, considered miracles, before the mind was disciplined, much less schooled in science.

No wonder that the advocates of revelation of the bible retire in dismay at the very name of science and philosophy.

Any vicegerentship makes God imperfect. imbecile, and unworthy of his position as Creator, much less of preserver of his universe.

Now as preserver of the universe, much more trustworthy if possible is he of this globe.

So far is the bible a revelation, that is a felonious compound of errors.

Any mind that does not assent to this, is unsound certainly. Then if there were any necessity for Messiahship on this earth, as much was there for the whole universe, which is as great an absurdity. Any identity is universally functional. None then can perform the functions of a creator but the God of Nature, who rules out all impostors. All the sermons due to vicegerentships, must be blasphemous or sophisticated. Show us one, otherwise than a perjury. How much suicidal contradiction is involved in the creeds that emanate from vicegerentships!

It is time that a dreaming world should awake from this stupid reverie.

One tells us that mind's exertions are nothing, and that it must put its trust in a Messiah. Yet if all things are not prosperous, if large accessions of numbers are not made to churches, the poor sinner is then to be shaken over the burning lake for want of personal exertions, as if they were not made ineffectually when faith could not be anchored in any thing short of God alone. Mind must inquire and investigate in full, and seek invariably to be equal to the upward tendency of things, and not resort to obsolete ideas of effete peculiar faith, any faithless pretence.

What rational being would talk to freemen of proxy, when it is contemptible, vile, and detestable? God and his conservative principles are what mind has to learn, having nothing to do with vicegerentship. It shows unprincipled corruption to impose them on the world.

Mind must not ignorantly pervert, nor capriciously impair God's principles. Who so interrupts popular intelligence interdicts popular safety.

But all Messiahships have left the world in worse difficulties and confusion, distress and derangement, than where they found it.

What vast sources of abuses, horrid and abundant, flow in upon mortals through all such avenues. So far from the Creator sending agencies, his scheme of creation cannot admit of or tolerate any such. His conservative principles are effectual, in the physical and mental world. All the defect is in the preacher's mind; he has certainly mistaken his calling; manual labor suited him best.

Who can suppose enough angels and messiahs, all creatures, to prop up one world, as this, to keep this solar system in its philosophical equilibrium, motions and functions, and yet this absurdity prevails no less in the moral than in the physical world.

It is all the little work of little men, who undertook, in their cunning and devices, to characterize omnipotence, at the same time the greatest libel on his character, and the display of their own monomania. No bigot's mind is sound.

Rational mind must look to the future state of soul, to ever appreciate its Almighty's perfection, as great in the microscopic as the telescopic worlds; his systems so well balanced that they may revolve about Him, their mighty ruler, equilibrium, centre, in exhaustless concentric circles, displaying the unit standard of the universe.

But this God, whom man cannot begin to appreciate, saw man's weakness, and displayed his attributes through a messiah; which doctrine indirectly pays a higher compliment to the power of the Creator of a messiah, as God's absolute control is forever implied.

But what messiah—as several have been before the world, that has seen so many peculiar faiths?

The Mahometans tell of a different prophet from that of the other pagans.

Wily and cunning was the trick, to appropriate and monopolize God's spirit by any exclusive faith, that there was but one Holy Ghost and one Son, and that all the world must look to them, through the priest's bibles and only ways, not by God's ways, to mind's rights.

Of what value is true analysis! How difficult to attain in this mixed world, where ignorance of the majority abides, and the deceits of the minority is to regulate and rule it. The world is taken by appearances, as some once imagined the sun to rise and move round the earth, and fool sycophants of an exploded bible bullied the world to maintain it.

Look at the deeds and end of beings claiming messiahship, though mortals. They all lived and died, nothing but mortals.

All such agencies are useless, forever before God, whose omniscience establishes his immutable perfection.

The very impossibility of miracles prevailing now, when there is most need of them, than ever, to incredulous man, proves the imposition of messiahships.

All messiahships will perish, as the messiahs are impostors and blasphemers. What are their followers?

All intelligent minds now perceive, that simple assumed or delegated power, that usurps all conservative rights, is the part of felony, that involves all the actors. Instead, then, of a messiah, the world can declare such in that category.

All such is tyrannical, wherever it opposes the progress of liberal and rational principles.

Let all patriotic and philanthropic citizens do their duty, as subordinates to Deity.

After all messiahships, they are man's absurd and roundabout ways of blasphemous idea, of doing what God did at first and at once, at creation.

It is time to stop the millions of falsehoods about messiahships. God, the creator of the universe, excludes all creation from participation in his government, that would otherwise unbalance all that came under the pretension.

The light of mind, from natural causes, is the only inspiration; hence, God's light enables us to appreciate him pre-eminently, without bibles of tradition, and to dispel all such works of man, as not of God, however the bible-mongers may affect to treat mind, as incompetent to do its duty.

Mind can recognise all the priestocracy as conspiring against its rights and unworthy of its confidence.

If all the messiahs had been all possibly meritorious, still being mortals, they could only be accounted superfluous ministers. After all their bibles of tradition, there is no proof of messiahs. There is no proof of either.

No messiah has advanced original principles.

They or their priestocracy, to build up themselves, have advanced new systems, all having some pretensions, but all deserving, by their demerit, condemnation, where they assume God's province, as they blasphemously do in all. Intrigue and cunning generally recoil on the actors.

There have been very many messiahs, for whom millions of people have been deluded, slaughtered, and massacred—anything else but messiahs—and singular that the loveliest has cost most blood, of millions.

Who more than the Jews should look to all this, as their people have so deeply suffered by them?

But has the whole world been exempt from the deepest suffering, on account of all this superstition?

What faith that nurtures such iniquities is trustworthy?

The followers of messiahs have been known to perjure themselves to sustain them. Do not all of every peculiar faith do that? Now you understand why the Romanists forbid their laity reading their scriptures.

Messiahship necessarily results from polytheism, and is one of its absolute errors and crimes, that are the last to become obsolete.

The propagation of the gods is analogous to human generation, and thus betrays the jugglery of man's mind, in the vulgar conception.

Man or creature is not adequate for messiahship, that is implied in creatorship, but he is a botch for all, as a libeler of God and his citizens, at every step.

Begone, botches and libelers, to your degraded insignificance, and no more derange the world with your insidious designs.

Blaspheme no more the most high God.

Make no more trinities with the three powers of iniquity, unjust government, peculiar faith of church, and military despotism—corrupting all elsewhere, not able to cope manfully in open light.

Avaunt, base men. Your vicegerents must come through very much iniquity, and imposition on the people, blasphemy to God, folly, in reason, and blind misleadings of all.

Our Maker is the one to help all directly all the time; and no one else, assuredly, can.

This God is no less great in doing the last, the preservation, than in the creation of the universe, and is only a perfect God by such perfection.

· How small and low is messiahship, that tinkers at one world, and bunglingly excludes mind for an absolute book, the doctrines of which are exploded, while Providence has given his sublime impress on the universe.

Conservative principles are the vicegerents of God all the time; of course the ignorant ancients never estimated this position, when all fell short of the proper appreciation of the God of the universe, in their little peculiar gods, and the moderns must stupidly follow them, in their after-thoughts and bungling botches, that do not belong to God and rational minds, but show man's imbecility and corruption. How few minds are original thinkers!

All the faiths that are peculiar to messiahs, are false to the rights of the world.

They are in the way of God, as another sun would be in the way and derange this system of worlds, that might have three suns, to illustrate the pretended trinity.

You cannot, by any vicegerentship, secure rational religion; it is impossible and impracticable. That concludes the proof.

God's works are his oracles. His justice, goodness, and power are infinite and perfect; hence, a vicegerent is an impious pretender, especially when the proof is pretence of God's inspiring man by supernatural means; whereas

This universe is governed by natural means.

What is there, then, that a messiah, as mortal, can offer?　Conservative principles exclude all messiahs.

Analyze truth and all the constituents of religion, and you will have to invoke your best powers of mind, that necessarily recognises the whole, and represents God.

From first to last, the doctrine of messiahship is a fraud.　All must have seen its utter impossibility as to God's permission, as that would proportionately detract from his attributes and character that are perfect.

All the parts of the messiah's history are a fraud; as to the very last, relating to the resurrection, there is no proof whether the body was not secreted in the subterranean recesses of the sepulchre, or was not present when the seal was put on the door.　But that is needless, as there can be no proof of his existence, for no such power can exist. Who testifies to these facts of verification?　No one can.

The laws of God cannot be those of peculiar faith, and therefore our creation knows nothing of messiahships.　This doctrine advances discoveries or systems; are they due to faith or mind?

All such gives up the world to excitement of enthusiasts, and unsettles the philosophy of life.　That is fanaticism.

One sect seeks to counteract the progress of the others, all being for the same messiah!

If they cannot confide in each other, ought the world to confide in them or their messiah?

There are not only feuds among the different sects, but among those of the same faith and church, only as situated south or north.　What absolute danger lurks in such divisions to our union!　See this card of a bishop:

" We have waited the operation and effect of church-law contract, honor, conscience, and ' expediency,' in the north, for a term of five years, only to meet now, with a universal denial of claims and right, so promptly admitted, and fully provided for, by the general conference of 1844.

"H. B. Bascom, Ch'n. B. S. Com'rs.

" Lexington, Ky., June 25th, 1849."

Franklin exposes, in a celebrated letter, the character of the church of England, that refused to the American clergy episcopal prerogatives, after the emancipation of the North American states from the civil and ecclesiastical power of the British crown, unless they took the oaths of allegiance!　Where was mind's religion then?

Americans should see the concealed treachery to the world's rights.

Positively, to-day England would be split into fragments by the Roman and Episcopal quarrels, if mind did not give the equilibrium; the whole world would be in as bad a fix by peculiar faith.

Absolutism will be prominent.　The world cannot possibly be rid too soon of delusion and fanaticism, as any society of communism, any whimsical St. Vitus' Dance or jerking superstition may be originated upon its abuses.

Take the following :—

" As for miracles, it has happened to ourselves to be addressed by a near neighbor, who had seen the dead restored to life; on close questioning it turned out, indeed, that the patient had only suffered a suspension of his existence for about a quarter of an hour, so that his resurrection would have been thought no great marvel by the servants of the humane society.　Our informant, poor fellow! was a Mormon."—London Watchman.

That is a recent peculiar faith, but let us see what better is that which claims the best distinction for age :

" In a severe storm encountered we noticed one Irishman, who, taking from his chest a vial of holy water, and sprinkled over the ship.　In the honesty of his superstitious heart, he believed its power to save.　We endeavored afterwards to convince him of his errors, but in vain."

What was once the fanaticism of Romanists for relics of saints, for which they had formal worship, and so universal was the demand for them, that a profitable commerce grew up, and even theft was engendered for this lucrative traffic.

What must be the character of the scriptures that are confidently quoted, in the justification of such contemptible superstition?

But what ratio does that bear to asking forgiveness through confessors, who need much the most forgiveness of a common Creator for their blasphemy?　And all this from messiahships!

It seems that this church that claims to be infallible, can learn no principles, in common with the world's benefit.   She seeks to restore the tyranny of the inquisition, and the order of the Jesuits.

It was her inquisition that stayed the reformation in all lands, where she could make her influence felt.

So despotic and cruel is the spirit of peculiar faith, that is to be trusted in no sectarianism of this world!

What wars and conflicts were there in the reformation?   Before that reformation, the Pope claimed universal power, and assumed to be the sovereign of the world.   The pretension to Catholicism bespeaks the vanity of the Roman hierarchy, and arrogance of the Pope.

The power of mind has lessened his power, as it has limited the days of miracles and prophecies, and those of oracles.

All professing peculiar faith differing from him, were to be subjected to the arrogant presumption of this representative of the messaiah, a fraud on fraud.

And horrid wars were excited without provocation; on that account, the different continents were parcelled out to his friends.

What cared enthusiasts and fanatics for civil wars or oppression, so they gained their worldly ends?

Are other peculiar faiths any better?

They differ only in the relative amount of alloy in them.   The church acquired wealth, power and participation in absolutism by various strategems, and now all conspire by pious frauds and sophistry the vilest, to manufacture any horrible tragedies to those who have no confidence in their bibles and ways.

Admit all their benevolent institutions and association, for the needy in some places; let their benevolent societies rise still higher, as all have no balance with their paramount transgressions that oppress mind and world.

We this day impeach all that know better, and do it not, for low and sordid designs.

The messiahs were human.   Did they have the honesty of men?   So far from being equal with God, they were inferior to honest and truthful mind.

All of them were grossly ignorant of the conservative principles that could unite the whole world in one brotherhood, and hence blasphemously advanced their own selfish doctrines before the wants of mind and the world.

They have abused the world and vilified mind, whilst robbing them of their glory.

They have degraded mind whilst pretending to its mighty functions, by the corruptions of faith and selfish holiness.

The   chased away other systems, but have brought storms of vengeance on their followers.

They have taken away the blessings of God, that could make the sympathy of the world universal.

What can be a greater reign of terror than the curses of their peculiar faith that for centuries upon centuries deluged the world in blood and butchery, and now rules much of it under sophistry and absolutism, horrible and gory?   ·

Shall the mortal who deals in spirits and angels claimed to be God's messengers, affect messiahship?

This is all dispensed with, by the appreciation of rational mind schooled in science.

How can there be a vicarious sacrifice, justly and wisely instituted?   The greatest ignorance of analysis of mind could only pretend to it.

God has instituted principles, and defined the character and position of those transgressing them.

Is it his attributes that established the sublimity of his greatness, that are to be superseded or alienated by a mortal pretender to messiahship, or rather by the ungodly priestocracy?

The wisest messiah was clearly a very ignorant man, else if he had been a good one, he would have adopted principles not mastery, hence his disciples fled from him, betrayed or denied him, when he was first taken, proving that they estimated him a mere mortal.

What did he tell, that was not known by even the Eastern Asiatics, centuries before?

What systems of peculiar faith did he or his authors study in Africa and Asia?

The world owes it to itself to act consistently with rational mind, to ascertain what is clearly necessary; to get rid of the abuses of the messiahship, a fanatical priestocracy.

Such discovery is one of the paramount blessings of genius, to be enjoyed in a land blessed with constitutional government.

Do we believe that there ever was any messiah?

It is utterly impossible, if the god of nature is perfect.   History declares that great men as statesmen and warriors existed, but not that any were inspired or preserved by particular inspiration, other than by their own prudence or providence, that best invokes the conservative principles of Almighty providence.

It becomes analytic minds to sift all history for the truth, which is more obscure the more ancient the history.

Providence is more especial by mind. and universal through God.

What messiah can be earthly, and supreme above nature's laws? Nature could not act as constituted by a messiah, that would destroy instead of save.

Mortals assuredly all die where human nature abides. Neither Enoch nor Elijah escaped this common passion. The supernatural is courted by all minds prone to superstition. The marvellous is the heroic.

In battles, chiefs are noticed for particular wounds, while the soldiers are rarely heard of.

Truth should be preserved, though it kills off all messiahships, as it effectually does, at the tribunal of rational mind.

All messiahship is too much of an after-thought, both as regards the preceding ages of the world, and the position of every mind prior to its adoption. The world would be irredeemably lost, before messiahship can take hold of each mind.

How then can the egg be remedied, if addled?

A sound, mature and correct judgment is the best faculty of mind, and insures most genuine benefit to the possessor.

Such mind will always decide, that vicegerentship for God is the silliest thing on earth. the vilest and most blasphemous, the most hurtful instead of beneficial, the most destructive instead of conservative. God, as the enlightened honest mind's God, that does not need church power or pretences, governs all his own, without man's pitiful libel, intrigue and priest over-reaching.

Such priest faith has been the disorganizer of public peace and tranquillity, blinded by selfish profits, sacrificing country, friends and relations, the world to the demons.

The world's theatre will be wisely governed by its author, and well is it, that the supreme ruler of all is at its head.

What absurdities does messiahship ever present, having the peculiar god of a peculiar people, who were only a few out of many millions all equally dear to him, when the world does have the God of all! Worse still, that after all that this god and messiah were unable to save a goodly minority, after all the express missions for the purpose of universal salvation! Still worse, in the sight of billions perishing all around, and yet this peculiar god had put his abundant power of grace out of his own hands, and became utterly incompetent to unite and save all when expedient, because he had committed the trust to a hopeless means!

All this clearly proves a peculiar god, and him of faith's creation, the foolish curse of the world.

Of what value is a peculiar god to this one world, and peculiar messiahs to help him, when the God of the universe perfectly presides?

Is the present world satisfied to exchange its God, the creator of the universe, for a dynasty clearly of usurpation and imbecility? Enlightened mind must clearly reject all such as fable oppressive and ruinous.

Can you ever give up a certainty in God, for any lame substitute?

It is awful to think of the reverse, that is blasphemy.

All messiahships are due to mind's invention, and are attributable to an utter ignorance of God's character and attributes, the conservation of the universe. All such results from fool obsolete bibles.

The innocent cannot suffer justly for the guilty, that is no atonement but a palpable perversion of reason. Two wrongs cannot make a right.

There can be no messiah for moral or physical reasons, as God is perfect in his creative faculties. No two beings can exist in the same identical space and period of time. No absurdity of transmigration would authorize this monster of physiology.

You cannot exempt the slightest point of matter in the universe from the omnipresence of deity, who has not only presence but omnipresence.

Vicarious sufferings and atonement in sacrifice of fire, by blood, animal or human, are the result of superstition and brutal degraded barbarism.

The negative of good is evil, the penalty of error.

All can only obtain a certain aggregate of the goods of this earth.

They may be caused to decrease, which increases the evil. What is the remedy on earth for supposed evil?

A wise action of mind all the time, requiring a wise duty and the virtuous exercise of principles.

What benefit can any of the forms of superstition, a bloody tyrant confer on mind, when her influence is a horrible terror ?

The Jews were as much concerned as any people on God's earth about the messiah, and surely decided as honorably as any set of men could possibly do under their peculiar faith circumstances, and better than the moderns now do, who accept on mere tradition that is unproved and untenable by honest minds devoted to God and his righteous injunctions. All such false position gives bad customs, habits, ideas and influences.

All vicegerentships are founded on imposture, false pretences or monomania, and determine in perjury. All is blasphemy, of the most demoralizing character. All affect miracles, prophecies and mysteries as the works. What kind are they?

Are they worthy of honest belief, when the plainest proofs of their imposture exist?

All have to refer to such extraordinary machinery, to gull the world first out of its senses, to exclude its rights.

And yet with the effrontery of priest artifice, the advocates pretend to tell us that " to doubt is to be damned."

Can any honest mind that is rational, do less than doubt the whole of all such fables, that never were and never can be rationally proved ?

Can we have no truth, by philosophical discussion for it ? But no ; this is a question not settled by philosophy and science!

Then it is settled by falsehood and disgraceful fraud. Why messiahs confine themselves to inferior miracles ? Why did they not call on the whole people to witness and investigate openly and above board, all their extraordinary powers, and for the undoubted proof the facts to be clearly the record of witness competent of investigation, and worthy of confidence ?

But all could not bear such inspection, as the nature of the universe flatly contradicts the whole, and is the competent witness of their falsehoods.

Idolatry and man-worship that originated as the vestige of hero worship, has to be stopped universally, as they libel the true adoration of God.

The proselytes set out to establish their system of peculiar faith on miracles that could not possibly exist.

They manufactured all they deemed expedient, which all wise men reject, because science and philosophy reject them on all the proper tests of mind.

Time declares her province usurped by impostors, and honest proper sense will affirm the imposture of the felons.

All rational beings have religious feelings and promptings, that if not properly cultivated, will degenerate into peculiar faith, as superstition, man-worship and barbarism, like a field, however fertile, will cause weeds that choke the grain, unless cultivated and prevented from perversion.

All bible revelations and inspirations necessarily resolve into natural phenomena, that contradict completely all such pretences.

Mind-jugglery and imposition are the miracles, of course. These are not fit for rational beings, yet all revealed inspired faith has to appeal to these impostures. There is no possible exception.

The persuasion of messiahships rests on false position, as all the principles of the universe were established at the creation of the universe.

The last were and are adequate. There can be no new principles created nor devised since, as that destroys the perfect omniscience of the Almighty, dishonors and libels God, and that winds up messiahships.

As there can be no new principles, there can be no new power, no messiah or office in this universe for messiahs, the blackest libel on God and mind.

Messiahs should be sent to the whole world to complete the most magnificent mission, but the God of the universe cuts down all such as a pitiful idea.

Why did Christ confine his mission general to the whole world as it is pretended, to the little insignificant, obscure country of Palestine, compared with the whole globe, when all circles of the whole world were to be convinced ? Was he ever in America ? Was he treacherous to the world's mission ?

What did this party do, if ever in Egypt, but extract therefrom, as the prolific parent, all kinds of jugglery and this system of priest-faith government ?

No, all was concocted easily with the priestocracy. Palestine then furnished perverted means enough of peculiar faith.

Why did not the author leave written evidence of his system, at the time, to prevent inculcation of imperfect and false doctrines ? Was it then too trifling to be described, too contradictory to be risked with the age of its performance, that could have been most successfully contradicted as too visionary and sectarian, abstracting the rights of God by the false pretences of a mere mortal ?

He, as god-man, was the only proper conductor of this matter, and should have had all the necessary documents inscribed indelibly on the universe. Where are the world-signs but in the fragments of broken brotherhoods, and the torn banners of a peculiar faith enclosing the elements of its own certain decay ?

Was not such scheme or drama worked on by the despotism clan for ages, as Jew—all pagan bibles ?

This character had no new principles to operate with, and is thus disclosed as an impostor mortal.

Analysis, the only proper decision, decides for the potency of mind, to discard as impeach all such pretences.

Surely, the world is wofully ignorant of the true position, and of its invaluable treasure of mind, so miserably overlooked for its usurpers.

The very name of Providence, pre-supposes an actor, suited to the demands of creation and its conservation.

The universe Providence Almighty, though then in existence, was not appreciated by these most contemptible charlatans.

Are we deserving of the blessings of our illustrious civil institutions, to submit to the sacrilege of messiahship ?

Can any mind be more criminal, when it blasphemes God by messiahship ?

Who but visionaries and dreamers could assert on earth, themselves as head of religion, the exclusive property of God, impose themselves the heads and creators of God's conservative principles, and involve themselves in blasphemy ?

All messiahships are frost and fogs, vanishing before the sun of light and science, as all messiahs are assumed, and affecting to be more than mortals.

Infidelity to vicegerentships and messiahships, that are of no account but to harass the world, constitutes fidelity not to be shaken to God.

Taking nothing for granted, and investigating all tenets of peculiar faith, constitute this fidelity, their direct impeachment. What folly and wickedness to introduce messiahships in the face of the God of the universe.

The ancients referred everything of peculiar faith directly to some embodiment or personification, hence messiahs, as Christ.

God would not let the people mistake his purpose, if that messiahship had been his. No wise mind can mistake what God has done.

We cannot mistake that messiahship is man's, and is a libel on Deity, and an invasion of his best attributes and noblest prerogatives.

It becomes the people of the present age to change the error of their ways, their iniquities to God, ere it be too late.

One organic crime as this begets a multitude, and the messiahships have produced a mighty calender under the name of saints, a corrupt institution as bad as any.

Many miracles have been pretended, as the liquefaction of the blood of St. Januarius, &c., enough to condemn their prototypes.

But the error of supposing that if we let go this hold that we had been taught to consider for granted, all creation would be a blank and a curse to us, instead of looking at once to God, has deluded mind to its ruin and the world's shame.

We have best right of principals, God, mind, and science, and have gone after strange substitutes, messiahs, traditions, feudal vassalage, blind pagan belief of all ages, whether ignorant, false, or dark.

Do not let us take second-hand, and under poor testimony, when we have always before mind the best proof of all creation, that comes home to us.

Do not let us take erring man's, when we have God's all the time.

The best testimony of creation is above all of man, a corrupt vassal, imbecile in his ignorance, pretender, vain boaster, self-conceited, as he is.

It is mind that must overcome all this, and prove its exalted worth as a lovely and innocent bride, in the morning of the soul's resurrection.

It is not sacrifice, much less or least of all of blood, but the loveliest tribute of character that God requires.

Martyrdom proves nothing of truth, in peculiar faith, but the soul's determination to die for what it estimates rightly.

But all messiahships prove impossibilities as imbecile or juggernautism.

The world should not be the vassal of pretences, but the master of truth.

The state of the earth proves man's original mortality ; the triumph is in mind to conquer its own weakness, ignorance, and the difficulties of life.

The whole God-gift of mind is not complete in this world, and depends on its own free agency, to render it most acceptable in the next stage of existence.

All messiahships are obliged to be put down, by the very inherent principles of the universe, the principles of God. Enlightened and public opinion will appreciate enough, to say there can be no messiah, if there be one Supreme Ruler of his own creation.

All that advocate a messiah, advocate pretences against God's attributes and principles, their own mind's stultification, falsification, and disgrace.

All victims fall victims in consequence of enlightened public opinion, exposing all their impostures.

All messiahs must fall victims to their own impostures and humbuggery.

All honest people cannot deny that justice should punish all such impostors, for as purely religious to the true God, they must clearly see the blasphemy of such impostors.

Truth is sacred, and nothing that is antagonistic is sacred, but is accursed, therefore no infringement of the laws of nature and of principles can be permitted with impunity.

All messiahships are got up to deceive the world, that is liable to be deceived by vain delusions and gorgeous shows. All facts, justice, and equity, will exclude all such, as unavailable.

There can be no love where there cannot possibly be personal respect, and there can be no respect where there are imposture and blasphemy of messiahships.

Any messiah is an impostor, and must usurp and alienate the principles of the universe. No rational mind can reverence such.

God's omnipresence identifies man in the most superior degree for his salvation, better than any substitute, whom the circumstances of omnipotence necessarily exclude.

Who could be a substitute for the God of nature, who is identified with time, space, and eternity? A little located being of this world, appertaining to one sphere for thirty odd years, when the power claimed involves, necessarily, identity with the universe!

What absurdity, of the grossest ignorance and most bare-faced humbuggery, too glaring for mere school-boys of science to miss.

The conservative principles of the universe embrace man under the circumstances of creation, and prove God's all-sufficiency by their functions, that exclude all other substitutes as impostors.

What infatuation, to think of substituting vassals or individual mortals for principles that are God's, and proclaim his attributes all over the universe, at the same instant, with the sublimest munificence.

Did any individual, assuming to be messiah, proclaim any attribute beyond his own located precinct as mortal?

The idea of the contrary is preposterous, and rouses up the just indignation of enlightened mind.

The more we appreciate the God of nature, the less we can respect the peculiar messiahships of peculiar faith, peculiar bibles, much less of peculiar priestocracies.

All pretended messiahs are mortal and die; but God lives evermore.

It is absolutely absurd, and an imposition, to pretend to messiahships. Who will save us?

The only one who ought, is the Creator, whose goodness must show will—whose power proves the result necessary.

Who, of the numerous messiahs, can be the right one?

As none can be effectual, none is right. The whole universe proves the Great First Cause, and all right.

Mahomet found his system of faith in a dungeon. Joe Smith, the Mormon, discovered his in the ground; and Christ, not being found in the sepulchre, was the supposed means of establishing his system.

But all died on account of blasphemy.

Christ was the worst of all, blaspheming God, and died therefor.

On physiological philosophy, if begotten of God, he was immortal, and could not die. If created, he died as other mortals, and had no more power than any other mortal. Who, of mortals, is perfect?

The innate principles of religion require no messiah to develope them: but, like ripe fruit, the Creator rightly developes them.

"Take care of my children," says the dying mother; "prepare them for heaven, by saving grace."

What is to be done for the poor mother, who wishes to rely on the only safe basis, a saving grace, and leave the same faith to the offspring?

On whom can all creation of mind rely, but on the Creator alone forever, as he is the proprietor of saving works and faith, the author of all grace and mercy?

But must not mortals have a mediator?

It may be for the immediate benefit of the mediator and his priestocracy, not of the world party, needing aid no less than from the God of nature.

Did any messiah ever show any omnipotence, by creation of worlds or man?

Did he ever resist the elements of destruction in any world?

As he did not, he is necessarily proved mortal and an impostor. As a germ of the old stock, he could not be less than a demi-god, who—as the ancients who knew their mythology, the original type for this—tell us died, he could only be a peculiar, not universal power.

Now Christ, who is assumed to be the greatest, as he is said to have put out their lights, ought at least to have lived immortal, if he had the functions, attributes and works of a God to perform! But that is assumed.

Who have put out the lights of mythology, but the superior lights of mind, that overcome all such errors, one after the other, in the natural process of civilization? Rational mind is then another kind of superior savior, under God, to all others assumed as Christ.

The last, with the deepest sophistry to its support, still lurks in the best civilized lands, a glaring polytheism of four gods, assuming the province of mind that civilizes the world.

But Christ performed miracles!

Did that make him a God, or juggler? It makes the asserter, at this age of science, a fool or knave, as he ought to know better.

Why not call for all the works of a God at once, before the public? Because Almighty God's works had been already finished. Then, of course, the juggler's was to be performed. The world needs no messiahs or jugglers.

If he had performed, as a real messiah, the functions of a God, then he had done satisfactorily all.

But miracles, as juggleries, are to be estimated, no matter how satisfactorily performed, and the audience, the people of that or any other day and time, could only be estimated as wonderers at art's deeds, not the true reporters of nature's facts.

An ignorant people may have irresistibly believed in any one for what he was worth; but is God ever to be libeled by such imbecile pretences of jugglers?

Mind, the beneficiary, may be wofully deceived by political and peculiar faith doctrines, time out of mind; but, in the name of science, let there be an end of all these false pretences of the priestocracy, the patrons of mind-jugglery.

It is the modern jugglers that galvanize the dead corpse, and use it to decoy a credulous world. The world must notice rightly these last, the true offenders.

The correct impeachment of all bibles but the right one of mind, will be their successful overthrow, downfall, and entire demolition.

All will certainly follow, before the tribunal of cultivated mind.

Individual exertions will not be available at once, as in case of Socrates, who was overpowered by numbers, partisan to exploded customs and faith.

What are sins that Christ can relieve us of?

The greatest is blasphemy, the usurpation of God's rights of his own attributes and universe, and that he, himself, committed.

The next is hypocrisy, pretending to faith that is not genuine. If Christ had no such mission, how can he be free from this second category, and so of all the worst category of sins on earth?

Where, then, is his potency to relieve, from his own created quagmires; so far from bettering the world, he has plunged it into all the miseries of the worst sins, criminating all involved in his awful pretences.

The third great sin is governmental faith, that is the strength of absolutism, which involves the head of the peculiar faith: in the fourth, that is the usurpation of the people's rights, and mind's property.

Why the messiahship?

Is God deficient in his powers, that this should deny the whole attributes of God?

All the attributes of the God of nature are eternally exerted, through his conservative principles.

God shows pre-eminently his perfection, by action independent of all messiahs or messengers.

Instead of blessing all the kindreds and families of the earth, millions are daily and hourly cursed, and many have been butchered by slaughter. What a contradiction!

All churches established on these messiah abuses and nuisances, are abuses and nuisances.

Some are so ignorant as to put a messiah even before God, that is, the creature before the Creator. What iniquity!

They libel God as imbecile by all such positions.

They pretend that God had to amend the world at first by a deluge, then by the blood of a victim creature! What impiety! And their peculiar god paid forfeiture for his imbecility, the priestocracy's forgories.

The world must not let them smuggle their peculiar god for the God of the universe, whom they did not appreciate and did not know.

The world, the universe, all stand, and prove that they are as God created them, on conservative not destructive principles, morally as physically.

The mansions and appurtenances are the builder's, by every equitable principle of construction and fee-simple, and the whole proprietor and residence furnish, and have always furnished from the first, all inherent, possible, and worthy accommodations to the numerous guests; but in the long lapse of time here come jockeys and speculators, self-enacted pretenders, who blasphemously affirm with extreme imposition, that all the guests should speak to them and their servants first, as they assume to be the only ushers into the presence of the mighty host, affirming with reckless blasphemy, that they and a host have a co-partnership not expressed in any documentary evidence, that can go through an honorable court of conscience, not written in the unmistakable handwriting of the great and munificent artist, but in doubtful and botch-vulgar scrawl, betraying most clearly the counterfeit, all the time affirming that they are the best friends of the host, misleading some honest, simple-minded people, and uniting most that are already corrupt, who seek to use this means to deceive and corrupt others, till they wake up at a certain time, and find the worst deception is in themselves.

Could you call these pretenders, who were not only never needed at all, but who are in the way, all the time disfiguring the buildings, and belittling the sublime architect, friends?

Now this thing of vicegerentships is an after-thought, whether expressed as it was many centuries in the Avatar or incarnation of Vishnu, prior to the incarnation of Christ. All inherent principles are forethoughts of omniscience, and eminently designate the two characteristics in language as clear as sunbeams.

How conclusively then are all messiahs excluded by these potent representatives?

Then these pretended friends are anti-god, and are in the way as stumbling blocks.

They do harm every moment, and no good; as do their aiders or abettors.

Then it is most important that every mind should know what it was about to do, when it asserted the first article of its faith, for that is something of the greatest importance to itself, and the whole universal mass of the world's mind, of which it forms a valuable part of unity.

Have minds investigated the whole analysis of this immense subject of God and the universe, ere they have accorded their faith, or have merely followed in the wake of simple and credulous minds?

Was the mind of the ancients competent to comprehend this subject by their science and philosophy, when their bibles evince its ignorance, imbecility and perversion? In truth and conscience enlightened to supreme reason, mind can only assert its faith in one living and eternal being. When more or less is added, then comes the deepest injury to conscience, truth, justice, piety and religion, by nothing less than a hardened imposition and reckless blasphemy, and the evils and ills of vices thus inconsistently and inconsiderately licensed.

The God of the universe is thus excluded by man's libel, to whom it was easy to preserve all souls as create them, as creation implies that much under the circumstances of mind's free agency and God's redeeming grace.

The exercise of illegitimate pretensions, whether by sacrifice of animal or man's blood, makes no atonement for the world's sins that must be met by the individual delinquents to be valid, but actually causes their increase. We not only deny but impeach all pretences to the contrary.

It is all superstition before God.

What inducement could the Creator have to lose his power, and divide his universe with a mere creature in regard to this world, when he could do it more satisfactorily alone? Incomparably more?

But messiahship of this world renders the balance of the universe that is exhaustless in an incompatible state.

What rational being could expect Deity to lay down that power pertinent to himself and inherent to his creative action from the beginning, and peacefully divest it to satisfy the vanity of man, to create more sin and do more harm, and take up in the remoteness of time, long after the first necessity existed, if any did exist, the character of a mediator dyed in blood, and that character to be very partially assented to, by the mind of the people at all times a minority?

This was man's provincial puerility, and no mistake.

Such legends belonged to the dark ages of ignorance, and ignorant corrupt priests at that. All this reflects mind too little developed, to develope rational faith.

Was there such infatuation with earthly beings, much less than affecting revelation, divine things and miracles?

If God had chosen a redeemer for his aid, at man's reputed fall was the intellectual time, and certainly before the destruction of the world by the deluge. But all such inconsistencies will cut up the foul legends of the priestocracy.

A savior must prove satisfactorily his mission by his ability to meet the demands of the universe, not of a part of it as a mere world, for the Creator being deficient in one was necessarily deficient in all. The mission of a messiah declares the incapacity of the Creator.

The ancients put the world for the universe; now all such books prove there is nothing proved, except their own libels and ignorance, themselves miserably exploded.

Where is the proper proof of authenticity of the scriptures?

Man may figure out messiahships, but he admits one species more of his own evils and tyranny, and opens the gap for any number or an innumerable amount in time.

No messiahs have any claims on our respect, much less our love, because God is the universe ruler, being its author, magnificently endowing it with order and unity of design. Involve this order, diffuse this unity and reverse this design, and confusion with injury ensues. As there can be no two suns in this solar system, as there is one great centre the point of equilibrium that must be disturbed and disordered by a second, so there cannot be two creators of the self same universe, when one Almighty is the creative centre that originated it, himself the centre of all perfection. The centre for messiahs is derogatory to the centre of the Creator.

The pagan god of polytheists and priestocracy, as of Christians, could not save by their creed manhood from their sins, then how could his creatures? Can the less do more than the greater? Even if equal, one could do more than the other equal. What fallacy and fraud then, to bring a pretended equal to an impracticability?

The Jews were most deeply interested, and of course were on the look out for this messiah and savior, but after all could discover no trait nor test of his godhead, for had they done so all the world would not have kept them back from embracing him. That is clear, certain, and beyond doubt.

All creation bears it in mind that there is a God, and he almighty supreme.

None rational can be dispossessed of this idea.

All other beings claimed to be above mortals originally, are all fictions as to their nature, reality, and, above all, their necessity. It is impossible for them to exist, if God be as he is a perfect being.

The sons of the forest wilds of America generally refuse the ideas about Messiahs, while they universally have to acknowledge the existence of the Great Spirit! As the mind is thus proved the receptacle of God, it must be entitled to future elevation correspondent to its theatre. Messiahship is too vulgar a theme for unsophisticated rational mind. The more magnificent that theatre, the more magnificent its operations. Nothing less than the Creator will satisfy it. The whole universe can only bound its innate greatness. In the trackless ocean, rational Providence guided Columbus, the discoverer of America, and gave a new impulse to the era of intellect.

In the trackless ocean of life, the same guides us all. Where can Messiahs operate?

The Messiahships are an after-thought, man's of course.

If Christ were the Messiah, then his advocates are right, but as an after-thought none can be right, then Christ was an impostor, and his followers are blasphemous on this imposition, and are farthest from right, the farther they leave the unity of God.

How can any local Messiahs supply the demand of an exhaustless universe? How came any on this, earth, if universal? The false pretences of the priestocracy put them here for sinister policy. When the priests go, all will go. The supply in one department involves the functions for all necessity.

Yet they stupidly affect that God was inadequate to preserve his creation. How puerile is their pretence, how imbecile its pretensions!

The calibre of inherent capacity must disgrace all these pretenders and impostors.

The proper maintenance of paramount principles must silence them forever in the light of one solar system. What would the light of the whole disclose? Who but the most stupid dolts, the most reckless tyrants or pedantic dreamers will declaim against the most obvious principles?

Vain mortal, so far from being able to dictate about another God, thou couldst not even fill or know where was a vacancy in the chain that belongs to animals. Perverted mind, thou art ever exposed as impostor before rational mind.

But you say that sane men disclaiming Messiahships in life, at death renounce those principles.
That only proves the want of equilibrium of brain of individuals. Rational religion discusses principles. Then it was opinions, not principles, renounced.
This is the reverse of many, who professing peculiar faiths in such in life, at death renounced them as insufficient. Here was faith renounced for principles. As to some people having compunction of conscience on their death bed, they may have that on account of their personal sins. The majority of the world dies that way every day in the Union, out of the pale of any such peculiar faith. What can be said of the high heads of churches often convicted of crimes, and gross misdemeanors? But as to the death bed change, much of that is a pious fraud. That is too small a capital for mono-theists to engage in. Of what value is Messiahship of creatures to any dying soul that violates the highest principles of reverence to its Creator in one moment's atten-tion to it? If mind have as the God of mind must enact free agency in all of the universe, then it becomes more or less perfect, more or less perverted and corrupt, and as this Messiah would be travelling for ever as the universe is exhaustless to man, what is mind to do requiring such guardian that it may reach the great central essence of perfection, not being dishonest enough to believe the imperfect sketches of his imperfect deeds on earth? Faith such as this, without truth and science is ignoble, is not faith at all, but credulity, the merest folly, the alchemy of religion. Messiah-mongers are the craziest.
As to the Messiahship, what is remarkable, you can get but few Indians to believe it generally, but most all believe in the Great Spirit.
Such means is a cumbrous and complex machinery, hard to be understood, and harder to be believed. Do those whose minds are among the poorest of all, really understand it as it ought to be understood to be practiced?
Fortunately they do not, else the worst consequences might ensue, as they have done already to much of the world. They all understand God though, as school boys can easily embrace that proposition.
In God's mathematics, three are not one; in God's truth one is unity, and two are superfluous, and in God's principles there is no clashing; then Messiahs are no where, and this ungodly perjury is exploded. The question of Messiahship will never be understood by honest minds, that if adopting it must in the reflections of their dying or expiring hour, feel the deepest remorse for misspent and misused talents, for a life devoted to sophistry. It is religion, not priests' faith, that will sustain the departing. Then must be felt regret with the deepest anguish that so many expedients have been used to draw in all classes of persons as proselytes into the church folds, without duly honoring God by such membership that actually estranges from true adoration. Well may all question what church teaching, that is sectarian necessarily, can give universal good. The thing, they must see, is impossible as taught, by the experience of eighteen and half centuries.
Then if peculiar faith put on such cloaks, it is time that they be taken off, that the people be divested of them. Rational religion ever prays or acts to be rid of her errors, that her noble virtues may be more brilliant, whilst peculiar faith assumes pompous airs of importance, having all her abuses identified with her speculations that are inseparable. Principles declare alone God in his universe, that are interfered with by imbecile Messiahs, interlopers that produce conflicts, where confusion ensues and chaos reigns in and out of the body originating it.
All such are man's botches, and affect only his own sphere of action. Why had not God supplied at the time of the greatest necessity of a mediator, when man more wicked fell, instead of at a subsequent period when more improved? The first stage of mind's existence must have been through an ignorant and rude state: the last best state of civilization is that which the world is now approaching. It is expedient that all good citizens should rescue the world from the chaos of superstition resulting from the earlier imperfect states of mind. Innate or inherent and conservative principles were instituted by God, and all pretended messiahs have to use them, which they can-not conceal nor supersede, therefore they prove themselves beyond all doubt impostors in their use of God's principles. • It is mind that takes hold of the whole world, not the messiahs. Messiahship, to prove itself conclusively, has to prove the origination of principles, not the use of God-given. Then an original universe had to be created. As no messiahship has done that, all are frauds on mind, for which God instituted his principles. Messiahships ought to be dropped in decent honest society.
The actions of mind refer inherently to its own individuality, and must offer its own retributive justice as on every principle bound, therefore no blood of victims ever puri-fied sin or brushed it away.

Messiahships then are the weakest things ever talked of, all nonsense, imposition and fraud, as the bible records are all the same.   All about their visions and their third heavens, or any heavens, are to fill up the vacuum necessarily left respecting the immortality of the soul, and aid in priestocracy imposition.

Hypocrisy and deceit, sophistry and imposition follow, in regard to messiahships.

The name of the Lord is taken in vain to abstract his rights, and appropriate them to the abstraction of the people's rights.   This was a system of proxy gotten up by priestocracy, to manage the people, and the world through the people.   There can be no retribution by the blood of another that is innocent.   That is murder, in all participants permitting or enacting it.   Where is the cowardly judiciary that will not uphold God's light and mind's right?

The messiahship is void, and of no effect and virtue, by the nature of things in God's creation.   All such things are the speculations of priests and preachers, and had better be let alone as correct appreciation and morals, not errors, should be diffused among tho world.

Would you swear to the efficacy of any messiahship?   You should do so, if in earnest ; if you do so, you are perjured.   Then if you did, you would perjure or foreswear yourself.   But you and all the followers are in the worst category, by your present and past affirmation.   Is that less ?   Why do you hazard paramount rights, by means clearly iniquitous, and surely inefficacious ?

You seek to be very good through irresponsible messiahships ; now then, you commit greater sins or evils in robbing God of his attributes.

The position of the God of nature is supreme almighty, that cuts down all messiahs, or assistants, as impostors.

If you acknowledge an Almighty, you contradict yourself when you speak of a messiah.   All messiah power has to be discarded, as in the way.   As to piety, when we bring in a mediator, it kills all religion at once.

We have to give God all his essential attributes, therefore messiahships, whether through Christ, Mahomet, Smith, or Bhudd, cannot affect God, nor avail man, but injure all parties.   All such are nonsense and imposition.

There might be millions of messiahs, and the people spend their lifetime in devotion to them, but their every step would put them further from religion.   The Jew paganism is less idolatrous than the Christian.   It was bad enough with the priestocracy, but messiahships added, are intolerable.

The very moment you have to admit messiahship, the supremacy of God is dissolved, polytheism of all kinds runs into atheism.   Through the senses of mortals ideas come, and that proves conclusively the whole matter forever, as Christ's and all messiahs' ideas arose by their senses, the senses of their mind-facturers.

There are only innate ideas in the God of idea creation, who deals them to mortals, through their senses.

What ignorant botches of mind the priestocracies were.

Are you, citizen of the world, possessed of the glorious advantages of progressive mind, luxuriating in the lights of philosophical science, stooping so low as to vulgarize and stultify that mind in all such superstitions of pretended messiahships?   Are you going to let other people, clerical or governmental, ruin you, by bible faith?

Can we adopt any bible-people or heroes, who proved by their acts false pretences to inspiration and man-worship—who were all messiahs and prophets, whether called Moses or Christ, if to be estimated in that capacity?   They were the machinery of juggling impostor priestocracies.

If they were worthy of worship or homage, did they manage the affairs of the world worthy of mind ?

The dramatists have caused their hero Christ to be foiled, ere he had proceeded but a few years in preaching—causing him to leave, as the facts of the world's history prove, the pretended mission unaccomplished.   Incapable of his own business, is he capable of managing ours, the world's, much less God's?   For thousands and thousands of years such a thing as messiahship was never thought of on earth, and inadmissible forever by God, from the exalted perfection of Deity, the God of nature—then Christ, the man of straw, is necessarily an imposition of the worst kind, for exposure of which the world ought at once to be thankful.   If messiah be not God, then the worship is idolatry and the faith blasphemy.

In God we exist ; yet although almighty and omniscient, all wise and perfect, in all attributes and principles, for the universe, and all things therein contained, mind receiving its God-gift, grace and religion, yet a pitiful messiahship is advanced, that libels at once the attributes of the all-wise Almighty.

Before whom art thou, sinner?   Before God alone.

When you adopt aught else, you do not reject all libels on God's attributes as a solecism.

In the ignorant ages, the ancients might affect to talk of mere nature and messiahship, but the miserable non-appreciation, in themselves, made this a burlesque. Now science puts all this to scorn, as a fog, at the least. But how is the world to get along, with the unprincipled felons of society, reckless of laws, till forced? Surely not by making greater felons, by peculiar faith.

Science of mind must meet all this question properly.

No speculations of priestocracies will avail here, when mind has to use all the principles of God. and most rightly. Were there ever such tinkers as these messiahmongers? You affect to have no libels, but you idolize your messiahship, that is not only a fraud but a blasphemous libel on God, the very moment you utter it. You do not actually know what you are doing. When we speak of religion, we necessarily speak of a subject that comprehends the world, the universe, in abeyance to God the supreme, as God is committed, identified to his creation, far beyond all messiahships, that cannot and never will touch the question.

All such is ignoble trifling of dramatists and copyers of dramatists. Messiahships are in vain, a mere mockery, the currency of priestocracies, the counterfeits of knaves.

Before the universe, you messiah-mongers are arraigned. You ought to be rebuked into utter silence before that majesty, much less of its magnificent Author.

How can you be so weak as to suppose such a thing in your extreme ignorance? What could be the idea of putting a messiah in a subordinate planet, far removed from the great centre of universe systems, when he would exhaust himself in an exhaustless universe of suns, ere he reached the beginning, and never could do anything? The proposed messiah, scanning the question, might well say, save me from my self-interested friends, the priestocracy. As Christ, &c. did not scan their impracticable position, that furnishes conclusive proof of their pagan character. When God finished his work, it was all complete, as expedient.

To touch it, man, was thy abortion. Stop, cobblers of mind, and go no further—use no more imposition.

Know and recollect this, that God could not part with the functions of universe preservation, consistently with his paramount position of Creator.

There is one place for messiahs where God is not, that is nowhere. Many have believed in modern messiahs.

Why advance messiahships, that cannot supersede principles? Then, if you make messiahships, you make all sins deep enough. What are the functions of messiahship? Can it have one? What are its claims to immortality, when it has none that are mortal or earthly? They can form no part of a conservative companion.

All messiahships are peculiar, cannot possibly be universal. What has the world, the universe, to do with such peculiarities? God is the creator, and is the only natural guardian and patron, from creation life.

What efficacy can there be in any effete messiahship, when all the supporters have to acknowledge the power of God's grace, as sovereign. The dramatists of Jesus are thus caught, by his pretended prayer.

The mediator is not only needless and superfluous, but an outrage on the rights of mind, that subordinated even God's rights. Messiahship is a shadow, for the substance. How many Christs and messiahs, how many peculiar sects and bibles has the world seen?

And after all of them, dead and buried, their epitaph is, The Curse of the World— as of the balance, to be buried. Locality proves all messiahs mortals, whereas omnipresence proves God the supreme almighty.

It required demonstration of the messiahship to the world, the beneficiary of course, else it was not available—certainly not. This matter of messiahship, all the bibles should prove the truth essential, without controversy. No system of man, however gorgeously disguised by hierarchies and priestocracies, no peculiar system will avail, to make man any better than God Almighty created him, who had the elements of religion at his first creation. The best in all sectarian institutions are good, despite of all their policy, but no better than the best, independent of all sectarianism—that is clear—and for the good, they are certainly indebted to monotheism. Appearances and assumptions are most with some people—much, indeed, of the world—that cannot analyze much of the affairs of life.

It is with many such, that demagogues of all kinds, political and otherwise, have such influence.

When God created the universe, he then completed it perfectly. How then could a messiah, and he subsequent to creation, be available? The thing, as an impossibility and utter absurdity, is the lowest imposition.

God's creation birthright to all minds, forecloses, as principal, all substitutes or messiahs, as alien and inefficient. From the very nature of things, there can be no messiahships.

Messiahships affect much; yet do nothing.

No one that was born, lived, and died, as mortal, can be a messiah. That is impossible. It is man-worship—is criminal idolatry. We cannot mistake the God of nature nor his laws; we cannot, therefore, know any mediation, which is too small a business for the Almighty of the universe.

The words of any sectarian master are dangerous.

God needed none to perfect his attributes, as messiahship implies! The ungodly object was abstraction from God and man, by priestocracy. If ye love God ye cannot adore any other as a substitute, for he is the one perfect God.

Do you stupidly pretend to an intercessor and yet commit yourself, claiming that God is responsible for all that is necessarily incident to our creation? Think rightly in all this comprehension, not as a vassal, but as possessed of an immortal rational soul. Let us ask you, as a free and intelligent mind, how childish it was to pretend to think of declaring God's power on earth, when the universe most sublimely declared it. What had the earth done thousands of years before the messiah, but for mind? That is the only living witness and fact.

The messiah tinkers could not analyze the brain, and yet stupidly push their pretensions on the world. They are not only pagan but fanatical.

To have a messiah does carry not out the legitimate functions of mind, stops short thereof.

Messiahs are useless cattle like priests, in the way of mind's purity. Of course the peculiar people had peculiar judgment to know their messiah, who could not be defined by the pretended prophecies, else Jews would have known and appropriated him as peculiar. They have decided that he has not come. Of course all that prophecy pretended, as all others, to of him to them, is false. What is all such peculiar faith worth that the priestocracy had to dispense? Prophecy has to be prophecied of to be valid. Bible-bigot sophistry hangs on affiliation and collusion.

What sane mind can think of giving a positive good for imaginary pretensions, at best only temporal?

The jurisdiction should have been proved pre-existing and acting, not subsequent. There can be no preservation distinct from pre-existing creation. It is a perfect absurdity, to think otherwise. Having no power over creation, it is criminal to propose messiahship as essential to any of its forms. When you speak of a messiah a peculiar messenger to a peculiar people, spoken of in a peculiar record or bible, you are necessarily estopped forever from referring to any but the peculiar god. You may be sure of their object, that the tale is peculiar and invests faith with peculiar false pretences.

Investigation discloses supreme contempt for all messiahs; supreme love, admiration and adoration of God the creator—and due respect for mind, the embodied soul or spirit.

Messiahships never have approached the majority of the world; but the Creator acts on all minds of the universe.

Would you, impious blasphemer, exclude his holy influence? Yes, impotent, imbecile deceiver, you would if you could. If the messiah, a mere man of straw, did not speculate, the managers did and do, and their drama is protracted beyound credulity's age.

It has committed blasphemy to God, treason to mind, perpetrated the deepest frauds, and executed the most ignominious tyrannies. How de you know the true from the false messiah? We know of no distinction.

They are all suspicious as counterfeit. We can know no messiah, while we know the God of the universe.

The true from the peculiar god is known by the universe of the first when all effects are referable to causes, and all are honestly referred to the first great cause.

We must not permit, as it is not worth while to attempt the position partially. If God was ever so imbecile, he would have hardly told mortals—that is clear. The priests only heard the voice of peculiar gods, worked by their own peculiar mercenary machinery. Bigots of superstition do not know when they have no ground or platform to stand on; they speak of love to a messiah, when that messiah cannot exist before the supreme God of the universe, that recognises effect and cause, from the least to the great first cause, that rises in unity the more he is appreciated. The admission of devil or messiah is suicidal to God, that is to all mind's peculiar pretences and conceptions of God.

An elevated moral sense will not permit messiahship, which is but another name for old priestocracies time out of mind. The lowest standard of morals and undeveloped mind, is messiahship. God Almighty is the standard of morals—all else is low and imperfect, vulgar indeed.

As we believe in the supreme God of Nature, we cannot honorably believe in any messiah.

Is there any intelligent, well-meaning person, that would wish to see free persons vassals, to the degradation of messiahships? Then, why urge them?

More than the God of unity does not benefit but confuses nature, and renders her imbecile and impotent, and confounds all principles of justice. That confusion has been too seriously proved, in this world that has bled at every pore.

There can be no greater tinkering than messiahship—the merest retrograde step in the world's morals.

That folly and crime should be done with forever. Messiahship impiously removes us farthest from God.

A man's piety is condemned by truth, if in messiahships. As to injury, where none is hurt by leaving all to God's principles, billions are injured and relatively ruined by messiahships.

When we leave principles, we leave the path of safety. On them, all God-sufficient, we can rely. All messiahships detract that much from the character of deity.

The first false messiah, that is the second pretended messiah, was hailed as the true one by the Jews, millions of whom would have perjured themselves on that position.

One hundred and forty millions of Mahometans do perjure themselves this day, that Mahomet is the true prophet.

Millions of Christians, in the sacrament, perjure themselves about Christ. And so of all other pagans. Paganism is a perjury. Now we know what inquisitions of despotism, the foulest blot on the world, were established for, most hostile to rational mind.

If there be any divine mission to the world or mind, it ought to be clearly and satisfactorily proved—conclusively so, else it will be truly considered an imposition, and very low and vulgar at that. God could make all his missions clear and satisfactory. As he is immutable, he would certainly not give two covenants, when he had given mind the only recipient. God has forethought, not afterthought, which decides and proves man's position.

God's works represent him, but who authenticates any other credentials? Do the works which prove a Creator, prove any more? Certainly not. Man's writings are too small for God. What a superb idea to have the feelings by messiahship, and that messiahship disproved by the non-existence of the messiah? The doctrine of redemption is one of the most demoralizing, ungodly, and irreligious. When we declare messiahships, we lop off so much of the attribute of Almighty.

If we allow God to be almighty, we contradict ourselves at once in all our senses, the only avenue for reason by imaginary messiahs. Here then is the force of bible assertion, most worthless. The veriest ignorance of God's conservative principles substituted vicegerents, assistants, and messiahs for them. God would not let us mistake the right position if we would. The preserver is identified with the Creator, and it is a libel on God to pretend otherwise. No abstract doctrine of the Creator will answer, when the least of all messiahships is needed.

We are after the superior obligations of social relations, the supreme standard of religion. Detract from the Creator one iota, and you that much become atheistical. You must yield all the attributes of God, to know that he reigns supreme. He never could have been the Almighty, had messiahship been the least constituent in his existence. The messiahship cannot supersede principles. Principles must be totally inefficient in the universe, ere messiahships can take effect, and that only constitutes most absurdly a new creator on opinion. We have not an iota of proof, that the first principle has been defective. On the contrary, we believe most conscientiously, that the universe is as valid as ever, and that its Creator is perfectly so. Before such testimony the whole priestocracy ought to be silent, as by it they are disgraced. Everything points to the unity of God, throughout the universe. Who knows what he is talking of, about messiahship? You may have the universe full of gods and messiahs pretended, a diversity of pagan idolatry, yet there is their supreme of his own creation. Destroy the relations of supremacy between the Creator and creation, and there is an end to the universe. So messiahships, like all other priests' work, miracles, &c., are any other than godly and conservative, for all are evil and destructive. But this the bible-mongers could not see; for when they forged and smuggled bibles, science of course was in disrepute.

Mind will triumph through the press, one of mind's inspirations, that has been in operation over four hundred years, which is more potent than all messiahships.

Who can possibly advance any messiahship on the faith of the old testament, which says expressly that "the fathers shall not be put to death for the children, neither shall the children be put to death for the fathers. Every man shall be put to death for his own sin." The old testament kills the new, and godliness kills both.

There can be no vicarious atonement by any blood, as that vitiates the whole proceeding by a greater crime; the nearer it be pretended to God, the worst guilt, as the Almighty is perfect in all his attributes.

Nothing intermediate or mediatorial, should estrange or separate us from God. For the messiah Christ, some hundreds of millions of people have doubtless been destroyed. For some of the 24 other messiahs, one, the first, Caziba or Barchocheba, the Jews themselves allow, in their war against the Romans in his defence, they lost five or six hundred thousand souls.—*Buck*. We should think the Jews by this time, were tired of messiahs, especially a peculiar faith, the hot-bed of such vicious nurture. For David el David of Persia, who was beheaded, vast numbers of the Jews were butchered for taking part with this impostor. "Ten false christs arose in the twelfth century, and brought prodigious calamities and destruction upon the Jews in the various quarters of the world." The civilization of mind only saves the world from analagous scenes now.

The year 1666, was the cause of much deception, of course from the bible. Sevi set up for a messiah, and his history shows how easily he procured an Elias or forerunner, and deluded followers. "Four hundred men and women prophecied of his growing kingdom." When he could not perform a miracle, the people lied about seeing a pillar of fire, "and after some had affirmed to it, others were ready to swear to it, and did swear it also, and this was presently believed by the Jews of that city." Most of the Jews of Europe flocked to him.

The most absurd lies were told of him, when he was exposed as an impostor—to uphold the faith, though he turned Turk! But the first was so obscure, that the falsehood was sprung upon the world, before it knew of him. The doctrine of mediation was not at all original with christians, for it was old as Hesiod. Mediation was one of the doctrines of the times. Plato speaks of demons as interpreters between men and gods.

Demons were a favorite idea, who were looked upon as angels good or bad. They were messengers, of whom Mercury was chief, as a god. This is the doctrine among the Bhuddists, who have their ninth incarnation in Bhudd. Messiahship is a work of supererogation, and that God does not do. His works are done when created. Intermediates are the work of the priestocracy. All messiahships are effects, not causes, hence not effectual.

The messiahships involve all difficulties of truth: around this is the armor of the priestocracy, whose forte is the most jesuitical, sophistry has played.

All messiahships and their priestocracy imply an imperfection in deity, who is proved to be perfect by the harmony and unity of the universe, therefore the first are impositions on false pretences, and must be silenced by time and truth. If they survive now, it is all the monument of mind's imperfection and impurity, cupidity and folly. All messiahships are the fictions of sophistry. What is to save souls? Not the priestocracy. but the creator, who is necessarily preserver and savior. But how about the messiahship? As about any other imposition. except that it is an infamous blasphemy, a nullity, a creation, a fiction of perverted mind of the corrupt priestocracy.

But as to God's promises? They are recorded in the universe. As to any peculiar god, Jew or any other, that is too degraded for the world to think of. All such are not worth the paper printed on, as they are all spurious. Are you issuing counterfeits? You are then a felon, and as God and mind are to be cheated, you are an infamous blasphemer. All such pretended promises in any bible of peculiar faith, are those of the same gentry. As all they call his word, which is theirs, fall to the ground, all contained therein, so self-contradictory and imbecile, are annihilated.

What is asserted of messiahship, is an imposition, and therefore nothing. The bible is a libel of the God of the universe, to enable the detestable priestocracy to pretend that their peculiar god was something. The messiah is the blasphemous usurper of his rights, the machinery of knavish priestocracy, to dupe the world's blockheads. One star for the messiah, speaking astrologically. Now astrology is as baseless as messiahship—both have gone to the land of shadows. The amiable priestocracy tried to appropriate every thing to their unholy and ungodly purposes. No matter the blasphemy, provided they fooled the people and got the iniquitous results. Whereas the universe of stars belonged to God, not one to any one else. Not one star could be monopolized by these gentry, no more than messiahship could be ushered into this world by such boobies or grannies. Their devil is a successful rival to their peculiar god, and their messiah is his competitor, all chimeras in companionship of a corrupt and ignorant

imagination of a debased and ignominious clique. All messiahships detract that much
from God, who is perfect. The priestocracy have spoilt all they touched. By making
man fall, their peculiar god fell, and the devil outdid him. By botching their creation a
second time, they killed their demi-god mortal, then reason and truth kill them dead.
The messiah had nothing to give, beyond a mortal : of course it was a false position.
Which was worse, the conception of the idea of a messiah, or the sophistry necessarily
enlisted in its support ? Do I believe history ? Yes, that which is authentic. Why
not believe that about Christ, the messiah ? Because that is story, not history, and it
makes out the case of Christ the impostor.   •
   All such is not history of a world's light. Christ railed at the Jewish priestocracy,
only changing one kind of sectarianism for another, himself ordaining his own, as sectarian and corrupt, as any in the world. All sectarianism is corrupt, and all that peculiar
faith furnishes is sectarianism. Instead of rectifying all these petty exploded pretences,
this is not now the era for the conflicts and antagonisms of world's peculiar faiths, but
that of the triumph, the illustrious triumph, of rational mind and religion, the world's best
institutions. Why do these abominations keep back mind from its created functions ?
   Polytheism has flourished in all her diversified silliness, and her faith is still such
diversity. It might be astonishing to think, that wise people that investigate, can be
deceived by any of her diversities, were it not notorious that it is not investigation that
the world institutes, but blind credulity they call faith, put in the priestocracy, who he to
it all the time. The church audience do not investigate peculiar faith or church faith,
they sleep while the preacher lies. Now it is positively so, that all polytheism and
atheism can ever say, cannot contain one word of truth against monotheism. Yet all
their absurd blasphemy is perpetually bandied about by the gulled sovereigns. The
greatest of all earthly characters should be conservative revolutionists, who call the
people to principles God established, and who defend them with their best abilities.
   It is perfect nonsense, the party exposes itself to the worst species of fanaticism to
talk of loving an impostor, an object unworthy of adoration, love or respect. There is
no high-mindedness in all this.
   What miserable bad morals is it, let alone religion, to speak of Christ as a savior, and
not possibly be able to prove his mission authentic. How can you love, whom you
cannot respect ? How can you love an impostor Christ ? Prove him a messiah, and I
will obey, but all commit themselves to perjury otherwise. Vicegerentships are failures,
as despotisms are worthless. Society is so dove-tailed, that the world has to investigate
for itself or be often deceived.
   There are some things that no man can speak of as first principles, messiahships; if
he do, he commits himself to perjury most conclusively and absolutely.
   Analysis gives the theory of the middle men go-betweens, when all peculiar faith
was for state and personal peculiar interests and purposes. No wonder the Jew christians had to have a messiah, since their petty peculiar overseer god was so incompetent
to their creation. He could not manage as a God one flat four-cornered earth and his
half a globe of heavens. He could deluge the flat trencher, but he could not touch the
fishes, he could not drown or burn these. Why ? Because their creator protected all
them. O stupid dramatists !
   This proves positively if such were needed, that there was a God above all Jew
ethics ; and that the real savior was one, that all sectarians could not know of or vulgarize. Now the messiah that was efficient, could never have been located on earth,
for the God of creation whom he came to assist, is the first great cause of the universe.
He was needed at the holy centre.
   All the christs and messiahs could not adopt God's laws as mortals. Then they were
not messiahs or christs of any availability ; there can be none where God is. It is
utterly impossible. God actually prevents any messiahship. Religion holds all such
most contemptible, as the lowest of all radicalism, rowdyism ; none but the stupid brains
of the corrupt priestocracy could have thought of or devised such.
   Revive the messiah ! What messiah ? There can be none, from the nature of the
universe. After all the metaphysics, the sophistry, bigotry and superstition of the
ancients, the moderns have to discard all self-impeached, peculiar faith, views, and
learn of cause and effect the word and deed of the Creator, who and what man is ? If
you do not do this, you inevitably ask mind to be tory to its God, just all that much that
you ask for a messiah. The priestocracy might as well have asked a messiah to nature
in general, to all her universal operations, as to man.
   Open the door for this pretence and the whole flood of evils will arise, from which it
will take the noblest exertion of mind to rescue the world. Who has forgotten the sale
of indulgences, that caused the church of St. Peter at Rome to be built, and at the same
time the commission of the worst of crimes? This is the way that purgatory was in-

vented, to reap the harvest of money by getting souls out of it. What else than power to raise money was the object of all such?

The very definition of providence, who sees beforehand with universal foresight, omniscience, cuts short all the false pretences of messiahship. The balance is left to the especial providence of mind, that must use the universal conservative principles. All messiahships are false pretences that bring much retributive justice. The parties ought to be punished by the adequate penalty.

But the messiahship represents the new covenant, its advocates claim. That defeats its own pretension, for the newer the covenant the more estranged from God, who only made one at creation, and that with universal mind.

What was not only the world, but the universe, doing, from the creation of the same to the millions of years, when Christ is assumed to have come?

What all since have done relied on the Creator.

There can be no mediator, by the nature of things, in justice to the Almighty, who is omniscient. His principles do all for us entirely.

All who have to do with man's gods and mediators, are not self-sustained, but require peculiar teaching, that utterly destroys their credit at once.

God alone is self-evident; all else is trash, unworthy the notice of an honorable soul. All the spiritual knockings are a part and parcel of all this machinery, are as a tub to the whale, the people. What a rotten cause, to ask for such frauds to prop it up.

Do you believe in Christ, Mahomet, Joe Smith or Tinkers, as prophets? Then you do not believe in the God of the universe, that has no such aids of a degraded priestocracy. If Christ came myriads of years after creation of mind, then what need of any mission, as the intermediate time could not be possibly filled up by him, thus proving himself as unworthy as imperfect, in time and functions, for if the world needed him, so would the balance of the universe.

The most effectual criticism that destroys Christ and all his pretences is, that he did not represent God Almighty of the universe, for he truly misrepresented principles. In regard to his carrying the sword into the family, setting the family at variance, that incontestibly proves him alien to God, because alien to principles, as they cannot clash, and hence no persons, much less those of the same family, can be in antagonism. He represented that same little peculiar Jew god of one earth, and that a four-cornered plane, resting on pillars, somewhere in the dreams of the contemptible priestocracy.

Christ could not come up to the demand, much less the excellence or sublimity of principles. They prove a god of the universe, are self-evident, and disprove all others as the basest impostors.

It will not be twelve months before the whole world will come to this, if treated aright. It will be for the immortal felicity of all to do so.

Nations of the world have not heard of Christ and such, that being a proof of their utter inutility, for God can be self-evident to all nations, in some way of mind-appreciation. The more civilized the more they will appreciate him, as possessed of perfect wisdom and reason, judgment, consistency and goodness, not of peculiar faith at all, as he presides over mind or soul universal. A mere world-messiah is most perfectly preposterous, as that implies the supreme necessity for a universal one, that is the work of supererogation, if possible, with a perfect creator. Any advocate of a world-messiah positively disbelieves in the perfection of a universe creator, or falsifies his knowledge of the subject treated on.

The pretences of vicarious atonement are at variance with the immutable principles and laws of nature. All that can be asked of Christ is, was he anything to mind universal? As he was subsequent, he is clearly an impostor. Cause and effect prove the God of the universe, that depends on conservative principles, that characterize an Almight .

Christ was a false messiah, as a false prophet. Impeach Christ? Yes, most successfully, in the basest theft in the world, that of religion, and the worst of libels on the Creator for his perfection; for the most superstitious view of religion, in giving false pretences for miracles, a total impossibility. As a part of the priestocracy, was he honest or truthful? He, as they, is heinously, by his very position in the category of base conspiracy on man's rights and God's functions.

Down, impious and sacrilegious world and deity-infringer! When Mark, in his last chapter, speaks for a Christ, a man of straw, surely the people are deluded, for the whole position is base and iniquitously false. All such peculiar faith bigots are the most criminal, keeping the world in vicious ignorance, preventing investigation by their degraded libels on religion, mind and deity. Their peculiar faith is a libel on religion, while all of deity is self-evident and unapproachable to such impostors.

For eighteen centuries the christian faith has been dividing and subdividing the world, and agitating the worst human passions, not allaying, but exciting them. Thus all other peculiar faiths proportionately.

To nurture one peculiar faith is a nuisance to the world, and the people have to act necessarily in their own self-defence. Can there be any worse morals, when the fathers of the church are appealed to prop them up, and to do so with falsehoods and the statement from the chief of them, for its justification?

The world does not want lies, but truth and honesty. It does not need a church of one-sided sophistry, but proper associations for discussion of facts, not peculiar faith, but religion, and has no excuse at all, when it has from the foundation of the universe, monotheism.

To get at the supposed orthodoxy, the house is divided. This is christianity, and, by its own showing, must fall, for it is all sectarianism. We do not want such degradation to mind ; but, as freemen, let us choose the facts, not be forced by an irresponsible set of priestocracy to decide for us.

The sectarianism of Christ, or his makers rather, cannot face the religion of principles.

Conservative principles, ever since the creation of the universe, have been protecting that universe physically, morally, and religiously ; how, then, could anything be wanting in the plan or system of a perfect God to all this? How could more be done ? The thing is utterly preposterous. The secret is, the priestocracy had to live, and this lie had to be supported, or these gentry had to be annihilated. Let them be, says the righteous verdict of rationality. All the peculiar bibles were written to deceive. He is very stupid now, not to know all that. What else were they for, but to defraud mind ? How could they be believed, if they were rationally analyzed ? They were written by liars, and have to be propagated by liars all the time. There are no attested miracles, nor prophecies, but are the false pretences of most ignorant priestocracy, who did not, of course, even know natural phenomena. 'Tis the highest test of religion, to expose the peculiar faith of the priestocracy.

Christ could not possibly use aught but of God's created elements, social, moral and religious.

But Christ, having performed such miracles, is entitled to the position claimed. If he performed them, he is.

Who endorses them ? Those who lie for him. Their ipse dixit must be taken, ere the faith be maintained. But the writers are pirates on religion, to deceive the people. Can the endorsement of pirates be taken ? and that when inalienable rights are to be bartered away?

All the pretended messiahs and prophets cannot begin to be compared with George Washington, the universally acknowledged father of his country.

There is no such thing in the economy of the universe as messiahship or peculiar faith, as they reflect the fractions of eternity, a thing utterly impossible, and, of course, cannot belong to the world as a component of the universe. All rational minds should know what they are about. else they may commit themselves to blasphemy. If God is established, that was enough ; and if man, that was superfluous, and must be abrogated as peculiarisms.

All but exploded bigots can see this. Religion is to meet all the drafts of mind.

If there ever was such a being as Christ, say, does not his death bespeak the result of principles avenging God's holy perfection on his blasphemy ? What do we see but the hideous, blasphemous, monstrous caricature of God and man ?

As God's function is not procreation but creation, and as the man Joseph found his wife pregnant without his knowledge, according to these writers of their new testament, mind that is rational, not deranged, must pronounce the issue illegitimate to all intents and purposes, by all the principles of physiology, and principles that are the word of God, the highest of creation. No! God is ignominiously libeled, most grossly imposed upon by the heinous fraud of the priestocracy, heinous for the adoption and imposition on the world. 'Tis needless for any mind to speculate, demur, cavil or spunge, on life's existence, that is self-evident, having principles of existence as well moral as physical, as religious as rational, and not be held amenable to them. 'Tis too late in the day. The people will take it into their hands, that all minds must be rational as faithful, as faithful as religious ; that rationality as religion is part of existence, and can never be separated ; that both are mind's functions, and in good the only faith must be consecrated by exercise.

Christ or his authors said, a house divided cannot stand ; therefore, peculiar faith, the division usurping, will not, cannot. Do you doubt it ? Myriads of such, more than nations even, have gone, and all the balance are but diversified editions. As you cannot serve two masters, therefore God rules out Christ and all such pretenders. Rational mind cannot have but one God as one universe, otherwise it would have to travel beyond; but it is estopped ere it begins. So unity of God is eternally fixed, self-evidently defined. All others go with their devils and all their divines; they cannot 'go with the supreme unless repentant, and be introduced by monotheism that represents the God of the universe. All the worshippers of the other are pagans to all intents and purposes, no more or less; therefore all the powers of inquisitions to prevent their exposure.

Do you seek religion? Then you must seek the truth, the whole truth, and nothing but the truth.

Do you seek faith, the whole faith, and nothing but the faith, then truth, reason, faith and religion, are indissolubly united forever.

A mongrel breed is it? Whenever a person premises a savior different from the unity of the creator, he commits himself to the worst stultification of mind. Let not this packed commission of electioneering disturb the equanimity of your mind, now at ease. The last stronghold that you mistook for prophecies will clearly turn out false, and be undermined. That was your stumbling block. You sincerely thought, as you had learned from the affiliated, that prophecy proved a bible, when prophecy could not sustain itself.

As to the star of Christ, that really winds up the whole document at once.

In regard to estimating the keepers of the holy books as miscalled, let the christians who were thereby benefited, decide. Monotheism, as the religion of principles, represents mind; messiahship cannot represent anything but imposture. As the most abundant proofs and demonstrations exist in the universe of God's grace, love, powerful gifts, the universe is full of them to mind, and rules out the pretences of messiahships.

The soul is one of the highest proofs, as also the definite form in which all matter is in. Christ had nothing at all to do with all this fiction, no more than the reality : it is all that of the priestocracy. The bible or pulpit sophists affect in their reckless disregard of truth and honesty, that Christ is or was the representative of human nature, by which they stultify their own minds or that of their Creator who formed every thing perfectly at creation, therefore nothing subsequent to it could have such admission, that is an impossibility, much less could he represent principles physical, mental, moral, social or religious that were coequal necessarily, consequently he was mortal, and an impostor. There were no noble band of peculiar faith martyrs, as they were enthusiasts to a false cause, as their position involves.

The polytheist in relying upon messiahships beyond God, is as bad as the atheist.

You may rest satisfied that the whole of this matter is futile, as the function of God is creation, and that of mortals procreation, while mind is plenipotent to exclude all other means than its own to solve its own life problem under its own circumstances. Messiahship is it? Yes, there is one, and that is immortal by the creatorship, that is self-evident in the universe. No mortal as Christ can claim it. His advocates need atonement for past errors of their peculiar faith, without seeking to involve the world in them too.

Which of the four families of conservatism, physical, mental, moral, or religious, was so defective, that a Messiah mortal was needed by the universe? If you prove that, you disprove the perfection of the Creator which would then be a useless function, and you would have had chaos and confusion to confirm you, but as it is, you have conservation' to expose you as a blasphemous impostor. The horrid results, defects, omissions of mind are impracticably relieved as they are caused by peculiar faiths, and there again you are totally defeated.

The great proof against any messiah is, that he misleads from the adoration of the only Creator and conservator. But then the Messiah is the savior. Who endorses? Prove all. But the world needs mercy, and justice cannot furnish it. That is a monk's libel, for our very existence premises all that. Rational religion itself is the great grace of the Creator, the exhaustless fund of his beneficence to rational mind, that constitutes a universe of mercy. The universe is an exactly properly regulated sense affair, and premises two points of demonstration to rational mind, the only beneficiary of its rules that are in abeyance to a ruler the president of principles.

Give us then all religion, but no peculiar faith or any of her officials.

After all said by every diversity of thought, peculiar faith only presents a world's resources; of those in reserve we have to reverence the Creator for.

Christ was only dramatic, clearly so, one of the best of pagan characters, an improvement on paganism, sectarianism, all editions of which, however diversified, are analogous bibles, one pagoda on another, all not even crystals, much less diamonds. What do we need of false crystals, when mind has the constant rich flow of God's grace, religion, which it can appropriate according to its rationality? But the pretence is advanced, that so many for eighteen centuries have believed in him, that therefore there is something in that. That is nothing, as for thousands of years preceding up to this period, billions have believed in despotism and all its varieties of peculiar faith, all claiming protection ander its wing in some form, of which this is one.

It is not that the world cannot give peace compared with Christ, or any assumed messiah, all of whom were clearly mortal, and of the world, but principles of religion that vitalizes the soul and its holiest affections, the mind in her constant support.

There can be no comparison between all such, very certainly. It is religion to render the world lovely, that peculiar faith has lost and destroyed. The true government of the world has yet to be learned, by all the charlatans of peculiar faith regimes. The wholesale bullion funds have been thus originated, and all the minor agents are at work. "Spiritual rappers" as they are called, are part and parcel of this diversified and endless mortgage. The world begins to see the effect on mind as in Millenism. &c., from the deceit and hypocrisy. Here is a young girl in the Eastern States, that lies about this petty larceny-miracle, the effect grows on her mind that becomes thus so perverted. that she even murders her half-brother to sustain that fallacy, and especially prophecy of his death. You, the people, have never contributed to this game, when you gave your countenance to miracles that could not result in this universe!

But you still persist in the game of faith, the worst of all gambling operations. Your faith, says the seducer, and he ruins innocence; your faith, says the swindler, and he pockets the profits; your faith, says the despot, and he despoils the work; your faith, say his tools, the priestocracy, and they pervert the globe. The agencies of life, causes and effects, the elements of soul's actions on its scenes, are unnoted and unknown.

But why had Christ apostles, if more than man? His acts, miracles and prophecies, were best of all to herald him to a converted world. To the conscientious, intelligent part, I address myself: quit your ungodly pretences, and invoke the only powers of God, who created this universe, and all the powers that rule, of which mind should be your chief in enacting consistently with its religious agency. Do not, republicans, stand side by side with despots, in peculiar bible acts. It is not that mind is so universally selfish as that cannot satisfy mind, but because it does not begin to appreciate its highest order of purposes, and put them all into legitimate channels. For many centuries the world of peculiar messiahships, has been offering millions on their bloody altars.

What can be more costly than such hierarchies of despotism that pauperizes?

Taking the difference of the age, Joe Smith was as great an impostor as Moses or Christ-makers. Are the modern interpreters as good as Joe Smith? The last invented, the others adopted the false pretences of faith. As wise as the best pagans, as Christs, Moses, still they were only men. The world must revive the principles that they have failed in. It is not idolizing mind, but it is the consecration of principles that religion directs.

The world, the universe, needs religion for the good of the people, and that all needed they have undoubtedly by the grace of the Creator, that implies all savior for ever. The world cannot know or use a world messiah, while it cannot dispense at all with a universe savior. What Joe Smith has done for Mormonism, thousands in the pale of all churches, have done under the mantle of the peculiar faith. This was only a reckless, bold innovation, hypocrisy. So was Mahomet, Bhud, Christ, all others, chief or minion.

The world needs religion. What is christianity? That is paganism, as all other unprincipled peculiar faiths. Will not christianity answer for the world? Certainly not. Why? Because it has not principles. If one be irreligious, he is that much unprincipled.

Besides, the universe can only be reached by principles that unite the world and all therein to the universe, so religion is an exact thing, not to be silenced by brute force, nor seduced by sophistry. If you conform necessarily to the laws of society, much more so are you bound to those of the universe, that is religion. Thus you can see the full comprehension. The very introduction of a messiah kills the Creator, who is pledged to the conservation of the universe.

Priestocracy commit the most absurd solecism at once. Which was greatest, their ignorance or corruption? Can an intelligent people stand such a faction, God-conspirators? But the Christian, who has basked in the sunshine of court faith and living, feels indignant to be ranked pagan.

Does he believe in miracles? If he do not, then is he that much divested of paganism; otherwise he stamps himself with a brazen counterfeit of religion—all such being the exponent of himself.

No pagan faith, Christian or any, should monopolize God's funds any more. Mind must not be so recreant, in the constitutional freedom of the world.

Let the world be rationalized, and religious principles will render this earth far more lovely than any bible Eden or paradise, that evinced undeveloped mind, and the imbecility of its use. Christ turned his back on religion the very moment he commenced sectarianism. Had he been clothed with any mission, how fruitless has it been for eighteen centuries, when it is not difficult to affirm that the evils of Christianity, in the slaughter of millions of the human race, have outweighed all the pretended good. Had he possessed that deep foresight of a world's statesman, he might have invoked the inestimable blessings of monotheism. He would then have had some claims on the world's respect and gratitude, whereas now it will be, when the world rightly appreciates the belial character of pretended saviors, through the profits of the priestocracy, that of unmitigated scorn and contempt.

The end is not yet, but the day of reckoning will be, when the counterfeits will come home to such.

The wars of the different faiths kill all their religion.

Christ was only the chief of sectarianism, as apostles were only of that. All sectarianisms can only go to the certain limits of crime, at the very best.

There can be no Christian virtues, when all, civil, moral, and religious, are those of the Creator. He could not meet as much as was instituted, as the immortal soul's standard could only be in that of perfection, the Creator, nothing less.

The undeveloped state of the soul and its relative possession of the universe treasures, best prove its inherent capacity, illimitable and nascent.

The best proof of the scriptures being mortal is the relative ignorance of the writers, whose circle of science must have been of a grade correspondent to inspiration. The only state that can take precedence is the excellency of the soul's developments. The principles, functions, and attributes of its nature were clearly unknown to all the varied tribes of sectarianism.

The charity of any faith, any sectarianism, is not what the justice of rational religion requires. Christ did not rise to the dignity of religion. He, of course, could not practice all the religious virtues. The very doctrines were not principles—could not do social much less religious justice. No sectarian can, for that very platform estops him. Christian charity is not religious justice. The doctrine of passive toleration is social injustice, to self and the principles of justice. The equitable principles of monotheism exclude all such, and take universal precedence. When you speak of any virtues of Christianity, they are only pagan peculiarities, that cannot meet the wants and aspirations of the soul, that has no pagan faith road to religion. The Jew peculiar faith was peculiarly for the chosen people : how could the additions be other than spurious ?

The very first position that Christ-dramatists took was absolute ignorance of the fundamental principles of religion, which they violated with reckless impiety.

As to exposition of man-dogmas, religion cannot compromise with any such, short of principles, her legitimate position ; hence, Christ never advanced religion at all. When the Athenians advanced the principle of " the unknown god," they expressed most of all the pagan world, far beyond the Jews, as clearly implying that all heathen worship was incompetent to the subject. For want of analysis, the ancients and all the moderns, as pagans, could not know that there could be no tradition of creation, except through God's works, cause and effect, that address mind in all ages, that rule out all man's idols, hybrids between a peculiar god and mortals ; all such being invariably pagan, and monsters. And what is all this for ? To build up another and another false faith, that will divide and subdivide, destroy the world.

Is it to leave millions to soulless church corporations, already gloating in wealth, the dispenser a millionaire, who cannot see the protection of the poor needed, in beggary ? A full knowledge of what we are about, in everything, is to know all by correct analysis. We must give and require the principles. When we speak of a savior, that implies religiously, and as physically. Now, the universe could not exist a moment without the last ; that proves a power potent enough to exclude all such, pretended, moreover, all pretended messiahs, saviors, Christs and all, the very best compromised short of principles, and that fell short of the requisitions of this earth, much less the universe that includes it.

Rational religion takes care of all contingencies, to be cared for by mind.

As much as the light of the present age exceeds the twilight of any ancient days, so far does our rational religion exceed all faiths, a test and standard of excellency.

Your very Christ was the founder of a school for fanaticism, as all teachers of peculiar faith, sectarianism. This is what a proper analysis of the whole comprehension tells the world ; and bids it beware, and look to the propriety of monotheism, that excludes fanaticism and all her fragments. Patriotism, humanity, and religion, invoke the whole world, in God's name and blessing, to rally on monotheism. Where are the

world's statesmen, seeking to be mere political hacks, pandering to some of the corrupt
forms of peculiar faith, to reach the best auction of popularity? Catering to the morbid
taste of vulgar bigotry.

Christ was from a corrupt fountain, the priestocracy dramatists. It is utterly impossible for Christ to faithfully represent the Creator, for he misrepresented his principles,
a self-evident proposition.

The proper protection of all is to give and require principles, to and of the world, to
exact and pay justice a certainty, not the contingency of charity. Rational beings are
content with the universe creation, but others affect to introduce their creature, that
God's ministers his principles, cannot even know. How can you get him to God even,
when God cannot know him or you but the vilest, most blasphemous impostors?

The whole world may bring in their millions of best messiahs, introduced by billions
of incarnations, and they will fail in all essentials, in their impositions on a perfect God
Creator, who would be annihilated if it were otherwise, as all physical are reflected
in moral and religious principles.

You talk tory to mind, as if that was inadequate in the Creator appointed functions
of free moral self-agency. It is your priestocracy system that is deficient, entirely so,
as it is defunct, still-born. The full functions of mind, the diamond, are there, like
the world and man, both as God created and purposed them at the creation, and all
that is in it is the immortal religious use you, man, mind, the world of mind puts it to
ever. That is all the question, the whole question. Now you have desecrated it, by
foolish, impracticable messiahships, not worth the thought, much less the action of
mind, entirely above, as supremely, sublimely independent of all such. The priestocracy have entirely, utterly mistaken the whole category, and their bibles, their record
evince, mirror them, the biggest dolts of nature, the most degraded and vile.

Let the glorious record of God eclipse, erase for ever the ignoble ones of perverted
mind, idolatrous in such faiths. Let not the high-minded world overlook that it has
illimitable amounts of bullion evils for perjuries, that rational mind can and only meet,
as all irrational mind-bibles create that amount of such ignoble stock.

What is the difference between the Jew and Christian, them and the Mormon, them
and the Mahometan, them and the balance of the world's pagans? They are all
pagans, as all that diverge from monotheism, the only God-standard and that religion.
There can be no intermediate ground; all are compelled, from the nature of the
universe, to be monotheists in purity or pagans.

Who is Christ? The priestocracy, as the peculiar god, and the whole peculiar
machinery.

Moses was the same, and bibles only their peculiar records. They all have rioted in
the halls of peculiar faith, where the verdant people pay for the keeping. Are the kept,
the pampered, going to have the same, as long as the people honor them? They will
preach charity, when the justice of monotheism demands their expulsion.

Justice requires the world spoliations should be stopped. You pretend to ask the
credulity of the world to believe your disgraceful plagiaries on pagan idolatry. Let
fastidious honor be satisfied, ere you can honorably ask aught of the world. If you are
honest, prove your case, otherwise maintain an honest silence as you ought. Are you
in the universe, or out of it? Do principles command and preserve it, or does your
priestocracy? If the first, when did it begin?

How long shall the life-rights of freemen be ruled?

Much of the whole world has conspired in collusion, but it cannot reconcile Christ
with principles, much less with God, their perfect author.

Before you libel me, prove your book.

Christ or his dramatists hid their light in sectarianism. You may paint the noblest
earthly messiah, clothed with the mission of all world dispensations and all conceivable
incarnations, make him most excellent. Still you have only a mere mortal and pagan
at that, his excellency only exceeding that of mortals. You do injustice to your mind,
the direct messiah of God, under his wisest best dispensation to your soul. Christ left
the world worse than he found it, for over fifty millions of people have been sacrificed
by one branch of his followers to their doctrines and inquisitorial despotism. The
excellency of principles as much exceed his sectarianism under which he ingloriously
obscured his light, as the God standard does that of the Christ, the fanatical model of
monk dramatists.

All sermons now preached at best in sophist pulpits, are mixed part of monotheism,
the balance paganism of the worst sort. The effort of mind is to escape from all this,
as proof all the mixed paganism is one story on another, the last published is the
Mormon. Yet how vain. Why not reach at once the illustrious offspring of mind, the
best system of monotheism, and so predicating mind's exertions as to reach constantly

to the beau ideal of excellency in all its departments? The very disbelief of the Jews is a living memento against christianity, only proves it another sectarianism, which the very rays of light, the sunbeams, prove.

Principles prove conclusively the utter futility of messiahships, as all things in the universe, whose physical principles alone rebuke the imbecile clergy. As to the Jews killing Christ, that only proves the want of toleration, the vices of the times. Christ fell far below the whole characteristics intended by his plagiarist dramatists, whose fault was their weakness, resulting from imbecile undeveloped mind, self-condemned, as a wise science mind would have had the innate modesty of silence in appreciating the luminary of universal luminaries. They all mind-factured a monster hybrid without light.

What a botch, instead of having all right at creation, and be done with it. If the physical principles had not been simultaneous, the whole universe had not been simultaneous, had never gone into operation. Are not the clergy as learned, rebuked for their utter stupidity. Yet they affect in their pulpit as if perfectly unapproachable there, like the old dictator master, mind-facturing his data to be unquestioned by his pupils, that this is the only religion, and that only of Christ!

Will the priestocracy ever say less, whilst the breed lasts? Will not the whole world of them be wedded to all their idols and the appurtenant perjury?

Make it the best, and it is only on the very best analysis a mixed paganism, an idolatry from which the most rational mind of the world is trying to escape, proved by non-attendance of the people at churches, showing empty pews and benches. Why is all this? Because the whole pagan faith, modernized by all the patchworks, is only a botch.

Give up all ungodly pagan faiths and go at once to religion, that enlighteneth rational mind, and civilizes the civilized. All pagan bibles and revelations are the most stupid, ineffably stupid botches. All the pagan messiahships and messiahs are only pagan, fix language as you choose, are from the idea of only one earth. The ancients never could have fixed up such, as the error would have been exposed at once and never taken hold.

But various brute causes have conspired that revelation of a barbarian age of mind, on the world.

Developed mind revolts at the monsters of iniquity, in all the departments of undeveloped mind.

Some of the ancient despots assumed to be divine, assumed to make science even this, by power of paganism among them. It was a profession, whilst superstition flourished. It was the impunity. the irresponsibility to the tribunal of science of God its representative, made the odious hot-bed of such vulgar absurdities, of which modern brazen priestocracy ought to be ashamed, and would, but for the bribery and corruption of peculiarly educated mind.

The very idea of peculiarity kills all Christ's pretensions to a universal savior, and proves him self-dwarfed to the petty municipality of local sectarianism. Let him or his pen-holders make a tremendous agitation among the bible devils, the money-changers, the speculatists on patriarchs, prophets and martyrs, with all their accompaniments, but let this intelligent age of the world do itself justice.

What more presumptuous than the arrogant claims of peculiar faith on God and man? She is utterly incompetent to receive facts of the universe, except through reason; bible faith is deaf to reason.

A perfect God creator could not do justice to his creation, with all the ungodly creations of pagan or monk's all the same messiahs.

Claim no more that mind required such missions, as they blot and blur it, disfigure it under all its odious pagan shackles. Religion as government, all the acts of mind, require the most appropriate discussion and wisest decision thereon, independent of all the criminal, vicious, social, much less inquisitorial proscriptions of the world the beneficiary.

The very Christ is fixed up by his storiographers, however he may have been otherwise as a plain half-witted man, makes the whole a perfect Judas Iscariot business to the world. There is the treachery, and that by the priestocracy.

The poor dramatists bring Christ forward for their purpose, proclaiming his mission as the advent of peace and good will to all men, yet they violate their own position, and place him and themselves in constant trouble. They murder principles and religion to sustain their pagan idol, and the world has been tortured to help sustain their monster that they botch, mental-midwives imposed on the world, contrary to all the holy sacred divine organic functions of mind, whose highest glory is to attain the brightest rationality.

The very conception of a murderous evil greater than existent, annihilates all messiahships as impracticable solecisms of obsolete language.

All the modern pagans desire to shake off the name, as if monotheism did not brand them ineffaceably. They give us all that mind would permit them, modernized and mixed as far as practicable. I would not corrupt my mind with its ignominious sophistry, nor desecrate my soul with its impracticable blasphemy. In your progress in soul organization, you may affect such pagan mixtures, then you may get the tallest fall, as principles can never know any such. The mercenary and reckless priestocracy may affect much cant about the fiction of a fanatic, a sectarian Christ, but will they care after entrapping your soul for it?

How come you to educate the human mind with aught less than the facts of God and religion, by your pagan faiths that cannot last? I am but a man, but can be improved best of all by monotheism, the very thing not only for the world but the whole universe. It is the mind that you have to treat aright to reach the soul, not adduce bibles obsolete before they were written, much less nonentities, messiahs, and the whole criminal clique. Now after all said and done in this world, every rational being is more or less a monotheist, as far as rationality permits. I write to carry out this whole position, as the only tenable and prepared one of deity.

If the world be not governed by principles equal to the physical department, it is that much short of the divine purpose. If any persons offer messiahships to the world for truth, they act either dishonestly or ignorantly. Go for principles, not faith, that is vile without the first. As monotheism has the work of the world to accomplish, why then does not it resort at once fully and unconditionally to it? Because the devices and sordid interest of the perverted part prevent.

Gentlemen of rational mind and conscience will positively see, that it will not begin to answer, to sustain this iniquitous corruption, peculiar faith, a world's nuisance, perjury and ruin, as that every brood adds such relative ratio, until it dies out. None can live, but produce enormous evils anterior to death. Monotheism alone in perfection, will exalt the world to its legitimate supremacy. You care for your body with all the improved comforts of civilization, yet you mistreat your mind most shamefully. Give up all the ungodly bibles, their odious creeds, and turn to the adoration of the ever living God. Rational minds and souls only can decide this question, by the developed religion of God. No bibles of peculiar faith can, for all such are and will be the reflection of paganism, not religion, minds undeveloped. All peculiar views to supersede universal ones, are necessarily undeveloped ideas, no matter the age of the world. All messiahs are pagans, and have pagan mortality. I impeach all preachers and clergy, for claiming any messiah for the God of the universe, as they are undeniably perjurers, for their only record claimed, is for the peculiar messiah of the Jew peculiar god. They are basely and blasphemously perjured, to offer the present world any other.

They have no proof of any messiah, much less of the perfect creator of the universe. His one attribute, perfection, convicts the whole world priestocracy, as worthy of the pillory, for their degraded perjuries about him.

Mind has no business with any peculiarity in the universe about its creator, as it meddles with what has no religion, and can make none but false conceptions and abortions, monsters of iniquity that beget monsters, all fruitless but for evil to the world, world annoyances. Fanatics pretend to tell with false sympathy of the self-immolations or world punishments of messiah, when they overlook the horrible agony of a butchered world, bleeding at every point, for thousands of years, from all these false, bloody impositions upon its peace, and the life of its billions in the excruciated suffering of humanity. The greatest proof of want of religion, is the adoption of messiahships, that exclude most ungodlylike all principles most conservative of religion and the universe. There never was more infatuation, stultification, crimination, immolation of mind, than to receive all such frauds and perjuries.

CHRIST—THE MESSIAH—PROPHET—A PAGAN IDOL.

WHAT does the universe want with such a being? Its organization proves conclusively its Creator and his conservation.

There is nothing else to prove with mind as mind.

Has any one ever affected to be a messiah? Priestcraftship pretends to this vulgar absurdity. What became of him? He died, they say. No wonder that such character expiated ignominiously this atonement, for his own heinous blasphemy. Was the law of priests' Egypt necessary to help reveal this drama?

Prophets foretold his coming, but the prince of prophets swears himself into perjury, that time reveals.

And all the others, his creatures, fall, of course. .

The miracles connected, are ruled out on the same triumphant principle, that perjury cannot be heard in the highest earthly court, that of enlightened conscience, totally discountenanced and disproved by the best proof, that of God's universe. The advocates seek to avail themselves of the present benefits, the faith of the world; then they are bound to give purest, undeniable proofs, as the world-marks that are wanting.

What star, the ruler of a solar system, could fix a messiahship next in greatness to creation?

The stars are balanced by gravitation, as all the universal host, and that balance had been lost in the universe, if the miracle had been performed; the balance of the miracle has been left out, most wonderful of all, that only could escape the intellect of the ignorant devotees telling it.

Now, this would furnish the chronology of a God, but the mark, that should have been ineffaceable in time's history, is unknown to astronomers.

What, the Creator not put this eternal mark in the universe, after such a gift! This infallible sign!

But how could he cast out devils, when there can be no such character?

But faith is essential to this redemption. Mind's stultification is, only. Sane minds must have faith in the Creator, from the mighty organization of the universe, and his unity absolutely essential, for if there were not faith in such a God, there would be in priests and devils. The two propositions are entirely inconsistent, as a perfect Almighty excludes, necessarily, any messiah, good or bad, and employs conservative principles, his superior. The extreme ignorance of the priests, prevented them from knowing all this. The present age should not suffer itself to be gulled by such speculations of ignorant priests.

The eternal jugglery supplies much too much of priests' bibles, which are adopted with impiety and blasphemy, that would usurp the very universe of Deity.

Why did not Christ expressly declare himself the enactor of all deeds, competent of proving himself the very messiah, before the whole world? The world's faith is demanded, and the world's satisfaction should be previously established on all this point. Was he incapable of this proof?

Why did he confine himself to so small a country as Palestine, and but portions of even that little country, when his mission is assumed to be to the whole world, if not the prince of jugglers?

Why not submit to the most satisfactory tests of regular committees? The Jewish committee rejected him.

He ought to have satisfied the whole world, above all, the most intellectual, if any preference were to be given, that he was what he wished to be thought! It was not to one class, but all, that such doctrine, if true, came. It was his duty to have proved the matter conclusively, because he must have had the power if he had the mission.

If prophecies were to announce him, if miracles were to prove him, he should have settled that question forever before the world, master as he was, as is assumed, of ceremonies, and of the whole drama.

The game was for immortal souls, worthy of the highest proof, that has never been given.

But he never submitted to the world, to prove himself as an Almighty, for nothing less could have answered for such a universal deficiency as assumed by the priests.

Why did he confine himself to any age or country, as the greatest of all miracles, he could not and did not perform, of satisfying the world's faith and conversion, for which his mission was pretended? This kills the whole.

If his mission was peculiar to Palestine, then he might, as he is assumed to do, have confined himself peculiarly to it; but the world was essentially and universally interested, and should have been secured by a universal mission. Now Christ's mission, if it ever took place, was peculiar. That will not answer for all mankind. The best of faith, secured by the best of reason, the only genuine currency of an honest mind, declares this nothing more or less. The whole position defines, among God's exhaustless attributes, that nothing less than the Creator is identified in the conservation of the creation. Otherwise another master was, and is needed, whose place could not be supplied. Like his preachers, Christ answered when no one called.

One-sixth of his companions were depraved characters, the chief a perjurer, the other a traitor, both corrupt, all deserters, and the Master an impostor, thus proved. He was unable to spare his own effusion of blood, in an ignominious death for his blasphemy, a horrid forerunner of the immense shedding of blood through the world, by the human race, enraged and degraded for the false positions of peculiar faith and their engendered fanaticisms.

But his resurrection—what of that?

Did he wish that proved, to the satisfaction of the world, the beneficiary? Why, then, did he not do it openly and above-board, in the face of all? Why was not the most candid exposition universally made? It was to be a substantial enactment, in good faith, to insure the best conviction, and could have been most satisfactory for the world, had it been universally proved. But alas! it was such that no one in the high court of conscience, can truly say was properly substantiated. There is no proof of Christ's body being identified in the described tomb, by those who "made the sepulchre sure," after his historical death, in any of the four gospels. This miracle is not conscientiously proved. None affect to have seen his spirit but those in this peculiar faith; and the historians, not they, testify to all such stuff, and that God's word, cause and effect, disprove, as the spirit evidently leaves the body forthwith on death.

Do you ask me to believe in that creature, that had to expiate to God for his blasphemy, by his death?

Is the whole world to suffer for that blasphemy, after millions have been bled to death, for centuries, from wars resulting from such faith?

All Christs and messiahs can only be an usurpation of mind and God, misrepresenting both, inadequate for the ministry.

All such beings are assumed personifications of some mind capable of some reformation, but always misdirected, or not enabled to receive a right mental direction from their peculiar position.

No doubt, by the vices of the peculiar faith of the world, all such minds were perverted.

Owing to the obliquity of the peculiar faith of Judaism, any license for peculiar tradition could be taken, and we see several of the horrid results of such position.

The door had been left open for all this and subsequent creeds, portraying the sad history of a depraved superstition.

Would that we could say that some were before their time.

The people of those times were miserably ignorant, degradedly corrupt, and furiously vindictive, from fanatical policies.

Through all the vista of those ages, the age of mind is not permitted to palliate their asperity nor obliquity.

What if any, by bible statements, are represented abstractly pure and good, the blasphemy claims what no mortal, in his right, honest senses could affect, thereby forfeiting man's respect, or God's approbation, a horrid example to man, and a curse from the God of his existence.

His doctrines have been asserted as if he created man principles, and his the only code for man, thereby causing him to estimate the author of universal existence but a subordinate part in the salvation of the universe. All this is miserable morals for the world, that seeks to do right by the best rational light.

Those doctrines have been perverted by selfish collusions of aspirants for power and self-interest, men that stopped at nothing calculated to benefit themselves.

Men have actually forgotten the God of power, and his unity, overlooking conservative principles and their author, mistaking the creature for the Creator.

All this is below the dignity of reason, and the purity of mind.

The scorn of reviling and of ridicule is not the object, because omnipotent, enlightened mind, endowed with reason, and illustrious by the conscience, irradiating the highest civilization, the only true representative of God, commands the adoration of that God exclusively.

Many who have listened in vain for years to become believers in what was asserted the true faith, believing their souls immortal as other mortals, for weal or wo, were at stake, and dependent on the true issue of faith, but for their lives and souls had to act sincerely, yielding to the truth and sincerity of faith on maturest conviction of reason, that there is but one immortal being, and that all others are his creatures.

The whole world will forever, when reason is right in all sound and honest minds, assert this faith for Deity's attributes, not because it is faith, but because the highest truth is thereby declared, and all contradictions are thereby impeached.

The crime of blood-effusion is the object of his assumed mission by his God, to secure the fee-simple to his character! Instead of mending man it degrades God by man's libels, by the murder indispensable to this miserable drama.

No sane, enlightened mind, can acknowledge any necessity at all for such mission, without invalidating its claims to all decency and sound sense.

That position, of itself, decides the puniest finger of man in this matter, that does not show mind, but depravity.

The effusion of blood of animals, and of human victims, is analogous superstition, and condemns the whole faith that supports it, as most contemptible, before enlightened mind and conscience, as an abominable curse before the God of mind. All such is unworthy of the sacred name of religion.

His miracles were too peculiar for an object so universal as his mission to all men, and too circumscribed by time, past and future, that were effectually closed to his personal mission. This betrays the ignorance of the impostor.

A God should certainly have certain knowledge of natural phenomena.

The first intimation of his advent is by a star, that stood over the spot! A star is a sphere of the universe, performing its revolutions; if a planet, around its central sun; or if a sun, having planets revolving around it; or if a comet, performing its elliptical circuit. An action of this kind would have brought its host of stars. Of course there can be no single star. But then the whole universe would have been in commotion, and none less than the earth, and all would have suffered from gravitation, beyond all manner of previous phenomena.

We hear of none of all this, though the earth-marks would have been indelible, and the sign might have been fixed in the bible-heavens, for all the universe to see, approve and admire.

Above all, the potent Herod would not have dared to act the least of commission, but he would have met all omission; and for his life he would not have thought, much less said or done, aught to hurt the character, much less the person, whose mission of glory was thus heralded. The whole earth would have rushed over all impediments to the declared character.

Have any natural philosophers of those times left any history of such mighty deeds? Who knows of any, that is chastely authentic, and justly entitled to honorable credit? The story kills itself, and all those present or past have been the most affecting capital.

This speculation ruins the whole history at once.

It might do for a monk, dreaming of legends of the dark ages, to tell before very small children, but his conscience must be very Jesuitical to face science with it. O, preachers of the present day, before you tell the balance, please explain this.

Let astronomy speak her facts. If it were a meteor, the pretence is still more visionary.

Deal no more in fables, but speak the truth of the living God, with a mind that responds to the bible of conscience, which carry with you, instead of that of tradition.

All history and tradition require certain proof for the mind, to embrace them with satisfaction in religion, else it rejects all such as unworthy of credence, and mere passports of imposition.

The power of reason, as the power of truth, breaks through all these thin veils, as furnishing nothing effectual on previous principles, universal and almighty, to satisfy by their proper application the demands of man's nature.

This epoch of the world would have been too remarkable, for the birth-day to have escaped the certain knowledge of the world, of which it is entirely ignorant. The chronology, so sublime and durable a miracle indeed, should have been fixed by an immortal sign in their heavens, unmistakable to man. It was only a vision of some visionary, that none but world visionaries will pretend to repeat.

God creates and leaves his creation for proof, that no pretender-messiah or priestocracy can circumvent; but messiahs come and die, and leave no proof worthy of mind. Surely the step from the sublime to the degraded, was intended by God as a mark upon all such impostors. Ambition may be tolerated till it reaches blasphemy.

It was necessary that Christ should be betrayed! That his priest-dramatists might make fools of devotees to faith.

Where will all this category of crime and perdition stop?

First it was expedient that a virgin should be seduced; then a god to disgrace himself, of course the god of peculiar faith, by her seduction; then the husband was deceived; then the effusion of blood to victimize the demi-god; then the people were to commit unpardonable sins in that commission, in which was the betrayer of Christ! What a clumsy, stupid machinery of crime! Instead of raising the people out of their sins, it has actually plunged their god deeper in, and has actually produced the worst of crimes, an interminable effusion of blood since, and the most degrading absolutism, above all the most stupid sophistry. The god of peculiar faith is made a seducer, adulterer, or husband-deceiver, an imbecile, a murderer, and a participator in interminable crimes. from that to the end of peculiar faith. Does the world know the minor part of the crimes of such a stupid, peculiar faith?

The poor Jews, who stuck to their peculiar faith, are to be harassed for that whole time, and as they did not adopt the faith, they helped to execute the mighty behests of murder, of which the god of peculiar faith was president.

To carry out the so-called divine rights of kings and priests, martial laws are in every land possible, and an armed soldiery, overwhelming the land in blood and carnage, the rights of the sovereign people in the dust, crushing them and spirits with abominable and endless taxes, defiling the rational codes of morals and ethics, proclaiming the law of brute force, and banishing that of intrinsic virtues. Where priestocracy do not create the chains of despotism, they tightened those of mind, and where they have not been able to bully the world into submission, they have placed the many hydra-headed monster-snake coil of insidious sophistry.

Well, the betrayal in this priest drama was fixed upon, yet meritorious as was that act to the drama of crucifixion, still of course the actor was to be punished !

Punished, for what ? Can man explain this absurd contradiction, that has neither brains or virtue, when Christ could not fulfil otherwise his mission ?

What a tissue of absurdities and contradictions, man makes of attributes that were almighty, but which he has basely prostituted to corrupt ignorance.

Treachery is a crime, that the true traitor should rightfully expiate by deserved penalty.

The traitor to God's attributes should above all expiate for his crime of blasphemy. All generally do, sooner or later. What associates for a god! A traitor and a perjurer, one-sixth of the disciples, who were all perjurers. But then, he came to correct. Well then, he missed the very miracle expedient to correct such a man, this was the very one he should have bettered. Alas for his frailties, to become their victim instead of their master. Here was the right theatre; to obtain the mastery over such, would have proved something of his divine mission.

Last of all, did he know his own powers to be so feeble? No, it is not a god acts, who is born and dies, but poor, feeble man speaks for him. The priests stick out in all, showing nothing but human nature miserably covered over in dirty rags stolen from their brethren of mythology, Asia and Africa, as well as Europe.

But the supreme traitor to God's position of supremacy, expiated for abandonment of the only conservative principles God's unity.

This is a terrible thing to approach blasphemously, for many assumed God's messiahs and prophets have expiated by their death, and the people have suffered by millions in slaughter, and yet the end has not come. We can hardly go amiss. The world has wept in mud mired with blood, for this iniquity of degraded superstition.

Man's acts, as contradistinguished from God's, are seen by the slow progress of revolution, which if conservative, are so many epochs of right inspiration.

The present system of christianity has been before the world some eighteen hundred and odd years, as claimed, and still a small minority of the thousand millions of minds is only in the nominal circle.

And yet proselyting the whole was the very miracle he came to perform, clearly proved impracticable and unworthy of adoption all the time.

What impudence on God's earth, and before man's face!

There is more than a majority of the whole world that believes in no one peculiar faith, but more or less as pagans so called, but in whom in part God's light more or less beams as he is realized as the Great Spirit, whom they will not exchange for the Christian's gods, nor the gods of any other peculiar faith.

Then most of the balance are Mahomedans, Jews and others of peculiar doctrines.

But millions and millions are bound to no peculiar faith, which they reject as disgraceful to mind and the God of the universe, and abhorrent to rational religion.

As the last think, so will all mankind when most refined in civilization think, as this enlightened faith shows the impress of truth of Almighty reason.

But how did the wise men of the East know that the star in the East was the star of Christ ?

Who endorses their wisdom beyond that of mortals ?

Who endorses the endorsers ? What honest, sensible mind will to-day, believe this statement ?

This fable of the star betrays the utter ignorance of astronomical principles, and much more when the windows of the bible heaven are claimed to be opened.

The expression for the location is stupid in the extreme. Did half of the world see it ? Could this local incident interest the world ? The workers of this drama undertook more than they appreciated. They could lie successfully for thousands of years in earthly matters, but were nonplused in God's business.

The people of the world, from its commencement to the end of time, were all interested in this mighty phenomenon, that could not have excited less than a hemisphere to its mighty display ! Where is the mighty sign recorded !

It was a world wide interest, was intended for the world universally, and therefore must have the indelible God-prints analogous to all that the Creator does among universe phenomena. Its absence marks it the basest fraud attempted on the mind of man.

Where is it, astronomy, speak thou, one of the bright daughters of science to ignorant men?

Mortal was Christ, and mortal he died, if he ever lived.

If minister for good, he took false steps to show it, as evil, unlike that good that pure religious principles give, has come out of it.

Look at the wars, tortures and tyranny of its peculiar faith. It is reasonable to suppose that the deep designing men of this messiahship machinery corrupted the views of this man of straw, Christ, to their greatest extent for the temporal interest of priestocracy.

How does Christ stand by the side of Socrates, who died for the most rational faith in his times? Socrates sought most disinterestedly an honorable faith, claiming no more than a citizen's right. Christ assumed the God, and is convicted below an honest man!

Many have been called martyrs, who died for peculiar or false faith, but they can never reach that title or dignity, unless they claim martyrdom for the rights of conscience. But few who died fanatics, can claim the dignity of martyrs.

Now, if any man of any pretensions to candor, can claim more for Christ than a mortal, then the intellectual world can envy him neither his morals or intellect, as the rectitude of both is directly self-impeached. The obliquity of mind reaches the state of monomania, or he cannot rise to the right point of mind, that gives the inherent exalted views of social virtues, taking hold of noxious trifles when he could reach universal results, and could look through the phenomena of nature to her God, the God of all.

The name of Christ is used by many weak or deluded followers, as if that name had a charm above all principle, all works. Such people have lost sight of all principles, especially when they tyrannize over their fellow citizens of the world in such a name.

Away with all such characters that forget that principles must be respected, as they respect the Great Head of all.

Who are said to be Christ's particular ancestors?

Jacob, for whom this peculiar dispensation is procured at the expense of his truth, honesty, and honor, thereby excluding the very result contemplated, purity of character.

The boast of Christ's descent from David, is not effectual for unsullied virtue, that distinguishes exaltation of character.

Such descent has to answer for man, but if that mortal assumes prerogative of a God on this basis, he becomes a condemned impostor, a great deal worse than having claims to such polluted iniquity. Reason and truth clearly decide this. But after all, how is Christ proved to be the son of David, if Joseph his lineal descendent had not the paternity of Christ? Want of such lineage, the thing pretended, kills the prophecy and himself, and stamps him the false Christ.

If Christ assumed to be more than mortal, he blasphemed.

As mortal, he usurped the province of mind.

That conception of Christ originates a blasphemy of vulgar character and licentiousness, unpardonable in the authors of the assumed inspiration.

The mere fact of mortality, shows an imbecility unworthy of God, who cannot and never will die.

Such a fable falls short of heathen myths, which it poorly copied.

What contradiction and stupid nonsense! He was man and God! A solecism in language, and imbecility in power! God cannot die, man cannot escape death. No other proof is needed to the world, to appreciate this subject, truth tells, analysis decides fully, that such is a monster in physics, an impossibility in physiology, more to be avoided than sought.

Physiology decides the whole blasphemously false.

And what miracles for the messiah, in abeyance to facts. Among them all stand conspicuous those that caused expulsion of devils from man.

Some rational people take this bible figuratively and metaphorically, wishing to explain the whole as the most rational exposition of a good intention; but faith dogmatists, after all their mysteries, use the term of devil, angel, witch and sorcerer, &c., literally; then we must adopt no construction, suited temporarily to explain away anything of theirs, so tenaciously adhered to, but meet all, fairly and squarely, liberal in all, and fair in the whole.

No explanation of jugglery, of hand or tongue, will answer, because all this work is the jugglery of mind ; it is the mysterious psychology that is to lead mind and soul, as the masters direct, in this mysterious machinery.

Christ was not content to expel the legion, but he even caused the innocent swine, to the amount of two thousand, to rush into the sea, under its fury, and to be choked ! And, in all his just actions, we do not hear that he ever staid to requite the wronged owners, who to this day never cancelled this debt ; but were all glad to be rid of such men.

Now, with this position we overturn this whole priestocracy, in their highest enthusiasm.

We protest against the existence of devils, on their own boasted showing and advocacy, from the very character of a pure Deity. and Almighty Creator omnipotent.

The proof, by their own documents, in any worthy court of conscience, before all good intelligent citizens, binds the world to reject the imposition, come from what sources it may.   And the man or set of men that humbug in one instance, as in this clear case. will do so in a hundred thousand, or millions, if necessary, to carry out their nefarious designs on the minds of the people.

No matter what testimony of their own affiliated cattle is adduced, the position is proved more clearly, as false.   And what can be expected of the progeny of such corrupt parentage, the world knows to its deepest sorrow and most poignant anguish.

The whole of the disciples were at one time deserters.

Peter is quoted as the founder of the church, yet he, at the time worth more than any other, committed perjury, in the denial of its head.

His weakness, the weakness of human nature, can be excused, but his crime of perjury cannot be overlooked ; for the man culpable of its commission is not trustworthy in the word of so much conscience as religion.

The perjurer may be tolerated in his silence, not in religion, that he affects to establish for the whole world.

His peculiar faith people have excused him for the perjury, but monotheists must consider him doubly unworthy of credit, and that he cannot be believed.

Well had it been if the character of Christ had been a true reformer, purely for the good of all ; but he set up a kingdom for himself, anti-god to the pure God.

His personal ambition ekes out on all occasions, and instead of correcting, in his direct conflicts, the vices and the corruption of the times, he merely rouses up the hostility of the Jewish priesthood, who immolated him on the altar of their idolatry. involved as he was in the crime of his own deeper blasphemy and sectarianism.

Nothing less than this state could be expected of peculiar faith, that by its familiarity brings its gods into contempt.

The true spirit of reformation can only be rightly seconded by the best men, who must seek the most enlarged circle of action, speedily accomplished for the Author of good.

We might rest this great question on this single and solitary position, in the court of analysis, the court of conscience—that if the universal object of Christ's mission, for the salvation of souls, was peculiar to his time, a period of man's life, and one small section of country, at the same time he being asserted to be able to perform miracles— that is, perform the functions of God—not securing the whole world at that time, by personal action, analogous to that assumed, then he loses the best hold on mind ; as he neglected or was incompetent to the universal mission, or acted treacherously to the wants of the world.

His function was the salvation of all, and leaving that undone in most of the world, he left undone the only true miracle expedient for the world.   This position is truer than his gospel, that cannot be fulfilled by its own inherent elements, now shivering in fragments.

But miracles are not the functions of the God of the universe, who directs, not misdirects, his works, that prove his Godship to all rational minds, that would act most irrationally and stupidly to require any other.

The affected performance of miracles is unnatural, and can only belong to the drama of peculiar faith, an unnatural monster.   The God of nature works with her, and cannot be antagonistical, therefore does not perform miracles.

But miracles are created by the functions of ignorance and superstition, and are excluded from all codes of rational minds.

Miracles, then, can only have existence in ignorant minds, blinded to superstition and idolatry of bibles of tradition, which are better worshipped than the God of the universe is adored.   The performance of God is recorded by God-marks in the universe ; the performance of such mighty deeds, as claimed, are entitled to equal record as the works of a God, by God's marks.   Where are they ?   They could be the only proof.

But the bible of tradition is man's mark, that time, God's mark, sweeps away. Vain priestocracy, did you think of all this !

Now, if competent to control natural phenomena, as absurdly claimed, Christ's authority clashed with that of the God of the universe, that is regularly managed, or managed by rule, not by whim, or caprice, or the time, but by regular set, fixed, conservative principles—never by miracles. As one has to fall, rational mind can easily decide who.

We do not seek to know how the gods of peculiar faith manage their empire, in their peculiar way, as that is peculiarly claimed to be the peculiar province of peculiar minds, peculiarly affected ; whether with monomania or design, the God of the universe knows.

It is not to be disguised from inquiring minds, that Christ has only executed in a confused, bungling performance, a partial and moderate portion ever since of his universal mission, and that only to a very small portion of human beings, and all that on borrowed capital of God, when clearly a part of the majority of his cotemporaries was the very worst of savages and desperate cannibals, the very people to be speedily reformed.

But he had a special mission, is it pretended, to the peculiar people ? Were they worse off than the rest of the world ? What then becomes of God's especial peculiar providence over this peculiar people, that that peculiar providence made his charge worse ?

If he did not have a peculiar mission, then he is culpable of unpardonable guilt, in not saving all the world, while his life lasted, "before the time came when no man could work."

If he did have a peculiar mission, then what shall we say of the billions before he came on earth, most of whom neither knew him nor the bible of the Jewish nation ? Worse than all, his legacy has created rival sectarian creeds and faith among different denominations, that hated and killed each, without love or mercy, for the Christian ambition of having the ascendency in propagating their peculiar orthodoxy, that state and church might flourish aright, according to their notions.

And still worse, it has left one of the world's peculiar platforms of faith, to annoy and divide mankind, that God's principles can unite in universal brotherhood.

Christ's imbecile incapacity, under such striking circumstances, to help his friends, the sufferers—people needing, as he affirmed, the object of his mission—affords the best evidence that can be furnished of his mortal and vain pretensions, and decides conclusively the certain mortality of Christ's peculiar faith.

But admit that he encountered the most rebellious opposition from God's own peculiar people, who by their prophecies, as assumed, were bound to expect him, let that opposition be in innumerable folds, more powerful, to the extent of man, and the world, and the devil and his angels, all, still, if a God, how magnificent a triumph, which, lost, not only proves him a mortal, but a degraded, blasphemous impostor.

The issue is then joined most promptly and sincerely in comparison by monotheism, the adoration of the Immortal Being, and the sincere tuition with pure action necessarily inspired, from the only proper sources.

Monotheism compares triumphantly in regard to the union of all mankind, on her immortal principles, the only ones of God. Where is the union of any peculiar faith, Christ's, or any ?

The grand divisions of the church of Christ, began with its dissentient elements. The feuds about Arianism, show what it was in its earlier days. The writings of Paul prove disturbance at the earliest. The hierarchy split into Greek and Roman papacy, conclusively proving how peculiar power managed its affairs.

But it may be affirmed that Christ was for union and all its lovely virtues, then he missed too intellectually for a God, and thereby places himself irrevocably in the category of a mortal, and one ignorant of the true principles of human nature. It is needless to affect that his constructionists did not act for him, as both were rebellious to the nobler principles that insure universality. Christ defines his own sectarianism too clearly to be missed, thereby proving himself mortal conclusively.

But the code of Christianity has some excellent traits.

With pleasure I admit them all as coming from mind, and am sorry that they were not universal, and fulfilled the mighty mission of mind. But those traits are abstract. It puts itself in antagonism with rational religion, and its ministry have to defend or leave it.

So have all other important systems, but what of that, when all peculiar faiths violate the greatest fundamental principles, the rights of the Creator, usurping his and creating no new principles at all.

We must not stop short of a wise comprehension, that uses up all their abstract doctrines forever.

It is this partial view of abstract doctrines that has sophisticated, whilst the unavoid-able evils of the peculiar faith have ruined the world.

We had better resort at once, as we ought universally, to the rule of conservative principles, which embrace all the abstract truths of the least value in all peculiar faiths that are necessarily indebted to them, and exclude most masterly all their evils, and in so doing we can, by the only conduct alone approach the God of the universe, other-wise we delude ourselves, and deceive the whole world by the little god of peculiar faith, an insignificant and worthless deity.

Christ or his daubers have marred the moral sublimity of the picture of humanity. not liberalized, but degraded by mortal frailties. for he is the object of idolatry, instead of the one pure God exclusive. Some may affect that it was essential to institute this faith and elevate him to this supremacy, to get the faith of the people confirmed. But this is a flimsy expedient of absolutism, disguised in all the forms. It is the low trick of priestocracy to secure that absolutism.

The Thibet lama makers have done nothing worse, compared with the lights before them.

These divisions, sects and denominations, are due the faulty system that Christ is said to have originated, and proves that position without the redemption of contradic-tion.

The subject, man, originating from Deity, can never be satisfactorily and properly indoctrinated in any faith, less truth and reason, to fulfil the object of his destiny.

The standard of idolatry can never bring man right to unity. Nothing less than con-servative revolution will. The subject does not admit of any eclecticism, for the mass is totally corrupt.

The banner to suit man's nature needs the immortal fixed principles, that now im-peach it before the universe's high court of conscience, in its soundest piety and highest veracit .

That is of man-worship, and of the most vindictive character, as history of crusades, inquisitions, and treatment of reformations, to the amplest satisfaction of wise men prove.

But among the last dreamy evidences, some may think that the blood of the martyrs and saints, so called by priestocracy, ought to carry out their drama and prove the mes-siahship of Christ. Not at all.

Who were they? All such were mere men of various characters, of course, that died for freedom of opinion.

Thousands and thousands, no less so, died in our revolutionary war for this very rea-son, at the highest shrine of mind, its glorious freedom.

Millions have died for it, for many centuries over the world. It is to be deplored that their martyrdom was not in the noble cause of rational religion, instead of the bigotry of peculiar faith, that must die out.

To cite strongest pagan proof, the martyrdom of the Juggernaut car, can be safely introduced, to show that man can die most readily from self-delusion and fanaticism, for fallacy of opinion, as easily as for the most confirmed truth and principles.

The imitation voice of the offspring will rally the noblest impulses of the mother's affection, and the most timid animals risk and sacrifice their lives in their defence.

All such martyrs have died under self-delusion of peculiar faith, operated upon by true influences of nature in the defence of their supposed duties.

Analysis puts the whole matter right.

Though all the rest of the world, if civilized, sees the fallacy of the Juggernauts, yet who could persuade the priests to stop this horrid delusion, while the profits raise a bulwark to all attempts at reform ?

What care these fanatics for the loss of life, the degradation of humanity, the vassal-age of mind, to the most glaring and obnoxious murderous superstition, or for the peo-ple, if their priestocracy can flourish ?

An intelligence superior to all the base shackles of mind, a patriotism supreme over the selfish sordidness of all such speculation, a religion supreme in refined civilization, will teach mind that all such martyrdom betrays a fatal antagonism of sectarianism, hostile to the best sentiments of the soul and its Creator, and conclusively condemns the damning errors of their propagators, and triumphantly leads them to a position that gives universal union and love for such fatal puerilities.

What can faith in Christ avail, if Christ be unavailable ?

Faith is the confidence in reasonable and analogous, therefore mind principles, other-wise, it is only credulity.

All faith must rest on undoubted facts, to be worth respect of mind, to which all is necessarily submitted.

The greater the subject, the more satisfactorily is that faith to be established, on not only indisputable but irrefragable testimony.

All faith in peculiar system comes short of the unity of God, and can never be established in mind that he owns.

Faith of a proper and honorable character, cannot possibly enter into any absurd and unnatural views in any respect.

All things submitted to mind, must be received on the principles that govern mind.

All kinds of faith are especially submitted to mind, and nothing else.

Mind can know nothing of religion but as a truth, therefore, its faith in that must be undoubtedly true.

It is utterly absurd to talk of the heart-faith, when mind has the sole province, duty and responsibility, to decide rightly.   The heart is a blood-vessel, and is mainly concerned in the functions of circulation.

Religion, to be true, must be mind-felt, conclusively proved a rational faith.

Faith beyond reason, at all times, leaves analysis of folly that leads to crimes.

Faith must depend on the purest principles of philosophy, that represents the most liberal proper sense and science, the best of religion that causes mind to comprehend the most enlightened duty.

Hope rests on the same foundation, ever confident in science and true knowledge, always referring to God supreme.

Benevolence necessarily recognises the path of such faith, end owed with the noblest attributes of humanity.

Linked with the sublimest mercy, she cannot force out an improper and irrational faith, which would be criminal as unjust to ourselves and the just relation of things.

When all this doctrine is fully investigated and tried in the court of conscience, mind will acquiesce in that as wrong, not compatible with right principles.

No sound mind can reject reasonable decisions, as it must understand itself, that is necessary prior to appreciating God.

We must understand mind to understand the universe.   Language must be understood fully and properly, and be strictly correct.

Faith either relies on reason, that is, truth, or self-delusion ; she cannot rely on any other.

Faith with reason absolutely rejects all vicegerents, messiahs, Christs, prophets, miracle-mongers, mystery-pretenders, by one of the plainest attributes of God.

With self-delusion and insidious persuasion, what is called faith, receives the most inconsiderate and worthless doctrines, unworthy of the age and its virtues.

Christ's messiahship, or any of the best far beyond his, could not be mistaken if sent by God, for then they would have been universal in space and in time, past, present and future ; cotemporary with creation, not peculiar to any age or small circle.

Christ's mission had not the passport and genuine stamp of God on it, else its seal would have been universal, accompanied by its unerring proofs.

The stamp of peculiar character, unerringly condemns it as counterfeit.

When truth is intentionally and wantonly violated by any disciples or church-members, then who cannot see that there is a violation of the principal foundation of all religion that is rational ?

What, then, was the state of Peter's mind ?

Was it rightly imbued with rational religion ?

What honest mind can think so now ?

Were the disciples worthy of mind's confidence, when they all deserted their master of peculiar faith ?

This bespeaks a degradation however pardonable for the weakness of human nature, is inadmissible certainly, for leaders worthy of the world.

The possession of pure religion, and its author, God, cannot be truly denied by any rational mind.

No God walks the earth as mortal, that is unreasonable, as well as adverse to the principles of physiology, while the mortal may expect to aspire to nobler existence. God exalts.   And all such impositions of a messiah rank and absurd, bear further deeper stain, that of impiety and shameful blasphemy.

The gods of the ancients were miserable fictions, characterized by the mind of the writers, that the priests could mould as suited their interest, or that of the dictating conquerors, with which collusion they all acted in the falsest faith to the people, who were to be the vulgar dupes and exponents of absolutism.

If the most ample bribes were not effectual, the compulsion of victory and conquest was to secure the flattering answers of the oracles so common to the ancient world. The oracle-mongers were as compliant as bribes and power could create.

Among the peculiar faiths of even Asia, is that of a Confucius, who lived centuries before Christ, and offering sentiments that were doctrinal even with that, as the foundation of proper social principle, " Do ye unto others. as ye would have them do unto you."

The modern fanatic in his degrading notions of his own self-important powers, ignorance of those valuable and immortal powers in his own mind if secured from bigotry, filled with a disgusting man and idol worship, prevalent in every age that bows to power where its brief authority prevails, will wonder in stupid surprise at the origin of this sentence. Let him learn true wisdom displayed by mind's exhaustless powers if independently sought, the treasures that have been perverted in all false systems of peculiar faith, to correct which he must respect himself as the faithful representative of God.

Let him learn that all these came from the true mint that coins, that have been amalgamated in spurious, false, and counterfeit currency.

Let him seek the fountain, that mind becoming potent, reason drinks of, and keeps it forever pure.

From what can we learn of Christ, but that of imposition and blasphemy, too plain for mistake ?

What has his mode of faith done, but demoralize the world, exciting wars for centuries, civil and general, continent against continent, nation and family against each other, strife all the time of its existence, the most vindictive and evil passions of men stirred up thereby, the people impoverished, demoralized and enslaved, to a papacy absolute in proportion to the light of mind ?

The principal faith has been so corrupt, that reformation, the noble light of mind, obscured and crushed, had to be mixed to make it tolerable by the world !

If Christ be peculiarly sent to the peculiar people for their salvation, how comes it that these peculiar people did not receive him ?

But that holiness of the new creature being born again, the benefits of the new birth, regeneration, how can soul receive it, ay, the Holy Ghost, without it receives the peculiar faith of Christ ?

The priestocracy were wide awake, to have the peculiar benefits only expressed through their peculiar province, as all priestocracies that are cunning, to degrade their world, not wise to save it.

All that can come effectual, is from God, if truth be told, and the best of mind is God's own light from his omniscient inspiration, or none at all, in the best sense of the term, can come. The degraded priesthoods ought to know that, if they analyze mind and its relations to mind and God.

The Creator is certainly most interested in affection for creation. To attempt denial of this, libels God's and man's nature.

True analysis, however difficult to reach, decides all these questions in favor of God supreme and only sovereign.

Imperfect analysis alone can assent to those interested in the treacherous impediment of mind's noblest perfection, intellectual independence, that shows the only dependence on God.

But civilization and christianity go together ?

Where was civilization in the dark ages, centuries after christianity flourished ? In those dark times, when the church invoked the sword instead of mind's light, to attain the true conquest of the world. Did she save the ancient world for centuries, becoming more and more bereft of mind's light ?

Is not christianity one of the usurpations of God's attributes, and of mind's virtues ?

Did the church advance science, when it imprisoned Galileo, the astronomer, persecuting him and hosts of others, for advancing science as now required ? Does not this fully settle the whole question, at once and forever ?

If we admit the splendors of the Vatican, enriched with her seventy thousand statues, and a library fourteen hundred years old, eclipsing, by such perishing masses, the gifts of all gifts, the freedom of living mind, denied at this day by brute force, before that building, facts of history declare that civilization abides not with christianity, for mind's freedom thus oppressed is proof conclusive.

But, then, the Protestants deny the proper position to the Papists, and declare that they have the true civilization. The last are indebted to the lights of science through mind, for the very reformation they boast of.

It is mind all the time that acts, but peculiar faith affects to be its guardian. When will truth be spoken in the world-wide history ?

Did not science better abide at one time with the Mahommedans ?

But science never can flourish, where there is want of light and freedom of mind.

This is indisputable, that science only flourishes in degree. Her loftiest flights must be her freest.

However powerful the hierarchy and priestocracy, still their superstition should never stand for a moment, before the light of the present science of philosophy and rational religion.

Why do not the free nations extricate themselves at once? The intelligent good must act wisely for all.

They can analyze the true state of things, and decide most knowingly, that messiahship reverses civilization of mind, but the rest of the world should act understandingly, not do as bid by predecessors, who were prompted by peculiar views, interests, influence and even prejudices that must not arrest the progress of mind.

Here was Christ, that confined himself to a small spot of earth his whole life time, instead of devoting that life time to the whole world, the very object of his mission!

Why if he could work miracles, did he not as a master convince the chosen people of God? Was the assertion withheld, because the falsehood would have been too plain, for the world not to see it?

Why did he not work his miracles universally as a God, to universal conviction?

Were these miracles any more than bible machinery, jugglery of mind?

Did he ever remove mountains, or command the elements of the universe to attend him as a God? Where is certain proof?

If Christ was co-equal with God from the foundation, where was he when angels fell? If he could not rule in the peculiar heaven, how reign on earth?

But this angel fall, was worthy of correction in the supreme, and yet how imperfectly did this peculiar god manage his peculiar heaven. This is a peculiar tale, and requires peculiar minds to believe it.

Can his peculiar heaven be a fit place for souls, that seek no temptation there, and be entirely exempt from fall? The God of the universe is the God of all.

Now when man fell, then was the fit time for Christ surely to free him at once from the curse. Then he was familiar with God, and would have accepted at least the remission of sins, as these people, Adam and Eve, had been personally concerned.

The atonement was placed at the wrong end, and as God does things right, man's hand is in all this, and the corrupt priests' at that assuredly.

Again, why did not God use Christ, when the bible says he destroyed the world by a deluge, and thereby give all the world a fair chance to start with a messiah?

Man botches God's works eternally, instead of learning that God governed the universe by universal principles, as well physically as morally, mentally as religiously.

Had mind appreciated this position of God at the time tradition gave her bibles, then we had been spared this faulty conception of messiahship, and the debased character of the priests not overcome the science of the people. As it is, the priestocracy has spared nothing sacred in their peculiar heaven, and has desecrated all on earth, and tradition, merely priest fable, has made God incapable of ruling one world, much less the universe without an overseer. But in what is he delinquent? Can any of these base minded men, point out aught of the supreme's deficiencies? They have debased every thing their mind could pollute, from Egypt to the whole world.

God exists everywhere, and he cannot be excluded.

Mind is particularly the gift of God, and is inspired by him. On what then can the mission fall? On matter? God is there, for he is the God of nature.

In the dreams of these fanatical visionaries, they might have deluded themselves with the faith that another universe needed their missionary, and forgot after their sleep where it was their messiah was wanting?

God's splendid works prove by their government, that they did not come by chance, which if thus miscalled, is a complete system of creation, that eternally excludes the very idea of messiahship.

What was man's sphere? To exercise free agency of mind, but only in the limits of the conservative principles of the universe that could not exist even in name, if those principles did not govern it.

Where then could a messiah act? The universe is a perfect whole, that excludes him.

God himself is bound to his own principles, and has elegantly prefigured to man his correct and disciplined course. Though there are from the nature of creation precipices, yet man can see the landmarks.

Principles were violated in the family of Christ, that nothing could have caused, had these disciples been of God.

On what principles of judgment was Christ's death necessary to produce universal redemption?

If that be so, on what principle can the traitor be condemned?

The predestination kills all systems of messiahs. Who is to meet this predestination that kills free agency of mind?

The proof universal of God's works, referring directly to the great first cause, excludes messiahs conclusively.

What else was it than a mortal influence, that embraced twelve men, whom a god so called, selects?

If his followers could not esteem or adhere to him sincerely when he was with them, what could he do more in his absence?

The God of the universe convinces, having as creator certain fixed and immutable principles for his creation, adequate and efficient for its preservation, and to command the respect of all rational minds.

When there is failure, it was the fault of a mortal, who could not command the esteem of twelve men, much less convert them or the world.

In the dark ages, centuries after the institution of the christian peculiar faith, the deepest superstition and bigotry prevailed, whereas, had intellectual light and reason prevailed as God's endowments, men had been better as their minds had been enlightened, and the rulers instead of vassals of peculiar faith.

All exertions were made by Christ or Christ fathers, to generate a system, and popularize it before the world.

It was a dangerous enterprise, before God and man.

He gathered around him an imbecile ignorance, unworthy a God, characters none of the best, as Peter the perjurer, Judas the traitor, the rest deserters.

All perjurers are incapable of inspiring credence, as the virtue of truth is forever lost to them.

Hence Peter, on whom Christ's mantle fell, to whom the keys were delivered, is unworthy by perjury to face the world.

There is, then, truly, an end to that system.

All traitors are base and fit company for perjurers.

Now all the balance of the disciples were deserters, and are traitors to truth and the best feelings of sincerity to human nature, most grateful to its creator. Alas, what poor company to be found in, but then this was the very kind most needing amendment, but chosen as most easily moulded for this vile humbug.

What is any soul's interest in all such worth?

All such systems have essential elements, that degrade them as vile.

Judas had no business there if he had no faith in Christ, who could not unfortunately mould the very man most needing it, and could if a God had known him at once. If he did not know Judas he was no god; if he did, then his selection condemns him worst of all.

But if Judas discovered all this design of Christ to be a vile assault on mind's rights, who can condemn its exposure? Which was the worst treachery, to the world's best interests? The traitor to Christ, or the traitor to God?

All this was the peculiar work of peculiar faith, that can only do little at the time at one isolated point, and in few minds.

God that rules the universe, has his work better done, not operating on mere individuals, but all nations and on all minds at once, not merely small circles at Palestine, but the world at one and the same time, and not merely the world, but the universe! There is the test of sublimity, and sublime power.

The christian is no more than the Jew with God, yet there is prevailing a distinct separation. How can this be?

Even the bible of bibles has copied the heathen mythology in placing the rich man in hell and Lazarus in Abraham's bosom, as if there were two or more divisions in certain regions for all departed spirits, till the final day of judgment. What, then, did Christ know more than mythologists? He and all the bible writers have been very ignorant in the most important subjects, and were the exponents of priestocracy so wofully ignorant in natural philosophy.

Christ left others to do what he plainly could not do. And this is the fine messiah, for independent, intelligent mind!

The very effort to correct creation by a messiah, at that very moment stultifies the enterprise, and renders it a complete abortion and dissension, as the bloody history of the world shows.

Then God can commit crime and folly, both of which he would do, in having such a messiahship as pointed out.

The originators must try their hands at another botch, for all the past are miserably stupid and imperfect. The covenant makers are all botches.

It would be folly for a full-faith proprietor to have a co-partner when the proprietor was the only one to act, and could only govern the universe of himself.

It would be perfect folly for a master workman, after having a perfect machinery working admirably and adequately, to institute another part totally unnecessary and totally subversive of its harmony and order.

God could not commit the crime of seduction or whoredom, and against his own laws, morals and religion, on his own world race, the worst of all crimes, on a mere mortal woman.   Physiology decides against that, especially in the absence of all evidence of God's organization.

But God sent the Holy Ghost!

That makes the matter worse, for death comes in as a witness, having separated the ghost, spirit, or soul from the human body, leaves no access of the two distinct existences, much less a union between a spirit or ghost and living mortal.   It is clear that none such can be seen or felt.   Of course the function of God is creation, not pro-creation, and this decides the whole question.

Of course there is but one way left, and that is by birth, as all mortals.   Physiology proves the whole then, to be a miserable fabrication of priestocracy, who did any and everything for avarice and ambition that degrades man's nature.

Then God created Christ, if there ever was such a being, as all mortals, and no more.

God is incapable of crime, as a God, then he acted as a God in creating all alike.

God's providence superintends, but God's work was finished before messiahs, preceding Christ many centuries, were born.

The messiah-makers have God a daily laborer, even sabbath-breaker, to uphold his works.

His conservative principles and universal providence prove God more supreme than any other position, after the supreme organization of mind or soul.

If God's conservative principles apply, an intercessor cannot supersede them.

If they do not apply, they place God in an imbecile position, striving to do what he could not do.

His principles uphold his universal works, from creation.

To attempt an alteration by messiahship, involves not only contradictions, but the most absurd blasphemy.

If an intercessor apply, he must of necessity supersede God's principles, and must not only regulate the safety of man, but must protect the universe.

This deduction absolutely and necessarily follows, and displaces God or renders him futile ; to such miserable positions, not God, but stupid priestocracy is reduced, and has its aiders and abettors at this day and time before the light of science, that shames them as the most degraded of beings.

Providence, then, has provided at first not last, a good and adequate provision that all priestocracy cannot alter, much less improve on.

Who dares libel God on this point?

Who dares defraud man of this treasury of mind?

Will humanity, one of the first principles, permit any?

What was Christ's humanity able to affect, staying pent up in Palestine, a small country, giving him all else round about, when the whole world needed his immediate assistance?

This at once declares the nature of the deception, and that his system needed time and aid of others, as all mortal plans, when in a moment the God of such mission could have operated by inspiration to flash conviction, conversion, and regeneration in all rational minds, as he does when they are not perverted.

Coming to do extras, Christ could have brought an entire new and original stock of principles, thus best proving himself a god.   Did he do it?   He not only did not do it, but fell miserably far short of the universal application, of what God had given creation.

Instead of a universal brotherhood, he left the very worst elements of dissension and sectarianism.

Critics have been bribed by the seductions of powerful influences, or awed by the terrors of inquisitorial ferociousness, where they have not been destroyed by all the malign absolutism of church and state despotism.

Did he not increase instead of ending superstition?

Instead of one devil, he originated legion, and added to the horrors of mind already tinctured with this fiction.

How could he institute judicial reign, without full cognizance of every thought, word and deed, and how could he get this power but as Deity himself?

The works of creation fill every rational mind with adoration to humility for their divine author, God, but cause every sane one to revolt at the idea of any other being concerned therein.

The author of mind's existence never dies, as he is immortal.   His sphere is the universe, and he is always cognizant of all.

But whilst this assumed messiah was on earth, in Palestine or Egypt, he could not be in the balance of this world, much less in all the universe.

If in other parts, he must have operated as messiah, but this is not his history, as he is expressly located, and that location defines him too clearly as mortal, for rational mortals to mistake him at all.

Priestocracy corrupt at that, may affect to do so. He did not operate over the world as its messiah, that is clear.

How could this local Christ act on the balance of the world conformably to his mission then ?

If he came for that purpose, and did not do it, then it proves him a deserter of his own cause, or incapable—a woful position for a messiah.

His whole messiahship is thus annihilated as a false pretence and nonentity before a perfect God.

How could Christ recognise the transgressions of those born anterior to him ?

How fill the interval of the days, that were concerned from the time of conception to birth, to maturity of mind, and the days that it is assumed he lay in the sepulchre ?

This is an impassable barrier for peculiar faith. But peculiar faith leaps many a barrier, that reason revolts at.

Peculiar faith is a rebel to mind, that owes a primary good faith to reason and God.

The Christ-killers are dreadfully censured by some, yet how could the atonement by Christ's blood be otherwise effected ? The fault lay in the dramatists.

As to the co-workers in this bloody fiction drama, what senseless contradiction and stupid effrontery to arraign them ? Somebody had to do it !

They should be considered co-workers, and have their position accordingly.

But were they murderers or executioners of the mighty behest ?

If they were murderers, then is Christ's death naught but a murder of a mortal.

If they were the enactors of a necessary drama, who can arraign them ? Can predestination, herself most guilty ?

If Christ suffered for blasphemy, who can libel God, whose principles vindicate him and his universe ?

But why not have Christ, the Messiah ?

Because God is a perfect being, and has perfect attributes ; therefore it is a perfect blasphemy to do so. If God were not a perfect being, then messiahs might be tolerated: but that is the perjury.

Prove to the world the reverse position, or yield it in silence, and forever, that Christs are perfect humbugs.

Your peculiar claims for peculiar faith, come under this same category, by the soundest logic.

It is not Christ, nor christianity, nor peculiar faith and doctrines, that enlighten the world, but they darken it, indeed. That it is all a forgery, in pure language, to say that trinity can exist in unity, and be one or the other, as sophisticated dupes may pretend.

God never made such language, for it is not truth ; consequently he is not the author of such absurd doctrine. The pure in mind will believe in an ever-living God, in all his perfect purity, uncontaminated with such foul untruths or moral blemishes.

Analysis tells us, too plainly for mistake, of the meagre poverty and failure of all pretended redemptions, none of which ever reached a majority of the world, at any period of authentic history known to the wise.

All such peculiar systems are criminal, as they hinder the progress of rational religion.

But Christ died for all ! Why do not all say so ?

Where are the eight hundred millions of the billion, every age or two, that are not benefited ? and worse, this matter may end to the very ignorance of his name, in a few more ages in the world, except as a curious history of superstition.

It is utterly absurd to suppose a mediator-general, yet so peculiar that he cannot have an efficient mission.

He did this, confining himself to Jewry, a little country, and only a part of his own short age !

A brave and efficient messiah ought to have said : Follow me to the whole circumference of the globe-land.

Command me, world-citizens, as to your choice of miracles, that prove a God most satisfactorily.

Ye are the beneficiaries, and ye shall behold and direct all necessary to exhibit the Godship.

The mission is to convince and convert the whole world, and then it is done and finished.

And as you may have all doubts removed, death shall seem to invade this God; but the triumph shall be proved before the whole world.

Nature shall suffer, and the God-marks shall be left for a proof, all time of these conclusive miracles. History shall subscribe to the facts.

The character shall be fixed in nature, and she shall carry in her bosom all the arguments.

Mind shall not wait to be preached to, but shall reason on the mighty seal, fixed with God's works, and imbibe the trinity, not unity, of the Godhead.

But the very blood that, if he were mortal, he could not help shedding, and if God, could not have shed to death, is most absurdly to save the world, in one of its obscure points!

None, but the potent arm of Deity, can truly do this. And that proves the God, without the blood.

The presence of blood proves the mortal; the absence declares omnipotence. What an absurd drama!

All else belongs to the polytheism of an exploded mythology! The best proof of his mortality is, that he could not save himself; how, then, save the unvisited world, when he did not save the part particularly visited?

If the effusion of blood was expedient, there were the guilt and crime of murder in its execution, as the penalty of a Judas, the advocates of christianity affirm, prove.

Can any analyst admit that the purity of the God of the universe, the God of mind, could plan, in his infinite power and perfection, a murder, that is necessary to secure the character of this Messiah?

No one in his senses can submit to such contradiction of language, that portrays a murder and not a murderer, a trinity that is unity. When can sophistry beat all this? This is the deepest of sophistry, conclusively. Sophistry can go no farther.

Would that it were murder of language and sense alone.

Fanaticism and bigotry assume the province, and despotism of faith rears her obnoxious standard.

No matter for consistency. the virtue jewel of mind, the appropriate exercise and legitimate sphere is faith, however mere credulity, from which there is no appeal.

How can we trust to the false Peter, to testify about higher matters, in which his ignorance betrays him, or about matters of truth, when his testimony was invalidated by prior perjury? He cannot be at all, a worthy witness.

God asks not, nor permits, such witnesses and outrages on reason.

His signet is science, that impostors cannot lose, and his sceptre, philosophy, that blasphemy cannot mar. But how could the world dispense with the christian dispensation? How do without it? The universe cannot receive it, and that closes the barrier upon the whole world forever to its graceless pretences.

The majority of the world has ever done without it entirely all the time!

What part did the minority have? Not only that part, but all the balance of the whole world were upheld by God, thousands of years before any such pretended dispensation was ever cunningly devised, despite of all this, and all stumbling-blocks of all men's systems of plurality of gods, to have officiating priesthoods to expound their peculiar mysteries and faiths to the people.

But the Son of God must draw the soul!

What did those billions of souls, prior to the birth of Christ, eighteen centuries ago, do for that drawing?

As Christ had not died prior to his assumed crucifixion, which was considered absolutely essential for the satisfactory atonement, how could those anterior to his suffering, receive the benefit?

If the crucifixion had not been executed, as his advocates maintain, then none could be benefited.

The doctrine destroys itself plainly, and is sophistry, all.

Either, then, God is not God, or Christ is not the Messiah.

The works of the universe prove the first, and expel the last.

And is there any necessity, but in the monomania of fanatics, that sophisms and libels should be thus perpetrated on the Almighty, that he cannot be known by his works?

What base and blasphemous libelers!

We prefer the ever-living God, the true and only proprietor.

We do not need two powers, no more than two suns for our solar system, as they might confuse. What could a trinity of suns do? No doubt there would be a trinity of suns to solar systems, if there were a trinity of the Godhead. Where, botches, could ye put another? Answer that before ye advance a step farther.

God is enough, if God be the God of the universe.

What could existence be, but for God?

The controlling authority is the creative authority, of course.

The resurrection of the immortal part was not connected to the advent of any peculiar dispensation; a perfect absurdity, as the doctrine necessarily cuts off preceding souls, but only proves by the impotent pretence, God's universal power that acted thus omnipotently from the creation. There is doubt as to Christ being the lamb, slain from the foundation, for the remission of sins by his blood, that this blood that is not capable of saving a majority of the people after the advent, should save all before it.

There is then the greatest absurdity, since he has never been able, as far as good proof that is most essential goes, to convince a majority, at any time since, much less save the whole before his advent.

This proves an absurdity, and impossibility.

Parents can do more good by teaching their children correct principles, than any lessons about all messiahs and christs. Time will come when Christ will mean a deceiver. Why?

The Creator, man's only God, has endowed the universe, mind included, with all necessary principles, and all the christs, apostles, saints, martyrs, pretenders, past, present and future, on earth, can only teach the same, but not as well, for the same reason that medical doctors cannot act for patients when first attacked, because their absence forbids the same at the right time.

After all the pretences of the whole systems about faith, the best can do more than teach correct principles, that God gave for all rational minds to use. If mind cannot find itself having all the functions of capacity, then the province of reason is silenced indeed.

All the christs possible add nothing to principles, but invalidate their good effect, as has been proved, that two suns, much less three, would bewilder and confuse our solar system.

Mind needs the ministers of science—education, embracing all funds necessary to be known, not corrupt impostors. But Christ, who died for his own actions in his mortal functions, died for all!

How do you prove that Christ died for all, by any truthful and unexceptionable testimony?

You are estopped on all but feeling, which is mere animal excitement in polytheism, and all that cannot be by any means any test for religion.

If test for anything, it is for peculiar faith, that is worth nothing in rational religion.

"As in Adam all died, so in Christ all will be saved," is a doctrine that now falls also, and with it all its errors of universalism, that must be graduated to mind, merits, and all through the Creator of the universe.

The doctrine of accountability reigns triumphant, on triumphant principles of individuality and free moral agency.

Christ cannot be an infinite being at all, as his existence was local, not filling immensity of space; therefore he cannot possess infinite power, that is essentially necessary to save all, and positively cannot be a God.

Christ was identified with time and locality, and was their subject, whereas the God of the universe embraces time in eternity, and locality in boundless space, and is their master.

The infinite eternal must have created all others christs and christ-makers, and masters; that is, God gave existence to all created beings. He is the only self-created. All others have only mortal powers.

Did Christ partake of the nature of the Father, that is God?

Christ partook of the nature of his father, that is mortal, and proved it by his birth, life and death. Born of a woman and of earth, he was no more than other mortals.

Can any preacher partake of God's nature?

At most Christ, if ever such lived, only not as fiction, was only the author of a system of peculiar faith, he or his friends; it is impossible for it to be otherwise.

Did Christ originate anything characteristic of a God? Did he create a living being? Any body with perpetual motion, as God's creation shows? If he did not, then the mind, the beneficiary, is not to be hoaxed.

No peculiar hoax will answer now in this all important subject. As represented in the peculiar bible, who was Christ but a mind-juggler; well educated in Egyptian mysteries of that country's priestocracy? What better subjects did the whole world present at that time, for all kinds of imposition to be practiced upon them? The moderns cannot properly appreciate the extreme ignorance and credulity of the ancient people in mass. People in those days of extreme ignorance, were very credulous of phenomena that they could not explain, and looked upon as miracles. How could they do otherwise, when masters were bewildered in the mazes of metaphysics. Of course, miracles then were very common with such a kind of people. The cunning part, the priestocracy, made speculation of all this capital of superstition. How many such characters have arisen since, with success correspondent to the ignorance or improved state of the world?

Mahomet, six hundred years and more afterwards, triumphed in this very system, adding thereto his own works and miracles.

Prophecies need not be very interesting after the prophet Christ is annihilated. It would be well for the world to know when some were written? Were not all after the events? Of course, and long after the pretended life time! No special pleading will touch the question about that of the temple. Time, that prophecies, will best answer all such without error, and will destroy many other temples of peculiar faith, that is plain.

To whom but the author of time do honor and glory belong in the highest, as the Creator of the universe, and all intelligence, or mind, the greatest of all?

It is for intelligent mankind to discard all such impositions at once.

Mind has most ardently sought in its purest sincerity to estimate Christ as the greatest reformer, but it discovers that all messiahs are impostors and swindlers : and if peculiar faith was not represented by absolutism, identified with relations and friendships personal, besides the spirit of the corps, it would hardly be countenanced by men of science any less than the false pretences of impostors.

Did Christ propagate science or philosophy, to exalt the character of mind as Socrates, or scatter the seed of sectarianism and elements of dissension, by referring to himself as master, when the Creator alone was the chief of his own universe exclusively? The question arises, not to be resisted, how do you obtain conviction of sin, but through mind?

Mind must be enlightened to perceive, and independent to act. Did Christ advance society through God's principles in science and philosophy?

What is the character of him who appropriates from the public treasury of God, abundant funds without due acknowledgment, and misapplies them?

If miracles were expedient for proof, why not leave the world, the universe, duly Christ impressed?

But they are God, not Christ, impressed.

How many mountains or continents are Christ's?

Not one.   How many souls, minds, are Christ's?   Not one.   They are God's.

Instead of presenting us the facts of rational religion, Christ's system adopts polytheism, no less than four gods or powers, adds to it sex and numbers of assistants! Saints even at this day—all paganism of the worst species.

Christ was a man, and might have been a great reformer of his day, if he had acted as mortal, but attempting more, he was an impostor.

The acts of Christ, lead to blind and savage fanatical infatuation.

What were the crusades, but magnificent robberies and murders for conquests, under the impulse of abject superstition? The bible added to the delusion, and nurtured the opinion " that the thousand years mentioned in revelation, c. xx. were fulfilled ; that Christ was soon to make his appearance in Palestine to judge the world."

" The pilgrims meet with a rough reception in Palestine from the Turks, who derided the sacred mysteries of Christianity."   " Pope Gregory VII. had formed a design of uniting all the princes of Christendom against the Mahometans ; but his exorbitant encroachments upon the civil power of princes had created him so many enemies, &c."

" Pope Martin II., with Peter the hermit, excited four thousand ecclesiastics and thirty thousand seculars, besides the greatest prelates, nobles and princes, to rescue the holy city from the hands of the infidels by war."

" It is deemed the will of God," was deemed a divine impulse to influence Europe, now " sunk in the most profound ignorance and superstition."

The ecclesiastics had gained the greatest ascendant over the human mind ; and the people who committed the most horrid crimes and disorders, knew of no other expiation than the observances imposed on them by their spiritual pastors."

Next to this, feudal law prevailed.

" All the great lords possessed the right of peace and war, and valor was the only excellence."

The first army of three hundred thousand men, was a multitude " that found themselves obliged to attain by plunder what they vainly expected from miracles, and were slaughtered without resistance."

The crusaders of the confederated army, amounting to seven hundred thousand men, were successful in taking the holy city as it was so miscalled.

Other crusades had its defeats as well as victories.

"M. Voltaire, as quoted by Buck, computes the people who perished in the different expeditions at upwards of two millionŝ." Some good, of course, grew out of all these evils, and by the time, as "the rage continued for near two centuries."

"But the worst enemies the croisaders had, were their own internal feuds and dissensions." Their three states at Jerusalem, Antioch and Edessa, made war on each other, and other Greek emperors, and thus became an easy prey to the common enemy. "They committed horrid cruelties, as barbarians inflamed with the most bigoted enthusiasm."

"When Jerusalem was taken, the inhabitants were massacred; no age or sex was spared, not even sucking children."

The monks and schoolmasters superstitiously encouraged the croisades of children, who were betrayed by their base conductors.

And yet all this was not enough to satisfy the fanaticism of "several popes, who have attempted since that period to stir up the Christians to such an undertaking."

Once we might have been perfectly enchanted with the chivalry of the croisades, now we are disgusted at their fanaticism, superstition and bigotry, that caused abominable cruelty, without a redeeming trait.

What were the inquisitions, but the most brutal and savage tyranny, that the most superstitious fanatics ever got up?

After such displays, and utter incapacity of peculiar faith to hold up her head, messiahships can well be pronounced of no account as unavailable.

Had Christ or any other messiahship affector established the right principles, they, not men or disciples, would have vindicated themselves and him before the universe and its God, and would have established the incontrovertible faith of rational religion.

We go to the best and highest authority to prove that as the bible of tradition, so all peculiar faiths are impeached and utterly discarded. Then we see the utter absurdity of expecting anything from messiahship.

The commission of the Savior, as he is called, was to the apostles to preach to the whole world, whilst he who assumed to have the power of a world's conversion should have executed it in his lifetime, and perfected his mission. Who could have executed his promise to redeem the world better than Christ, if practicable.

But infants, deaf persons, &c., who for ages were not more than infants before science taught them, could not be preached to?

They cannot be taught faith—that is unavailable with them.

Their innocence is the pleader in the court of conscience before God, who was their creator, and they must be his beneficiaries. Any church rite is a mummery, where belief is not attainable at its institution.

Children cannot be damned because they do not believe the scriptures, supposing them at all efficacious. Shall the infant that is excluded from the church, be excluded from the bible heaven?

If there was an efficacious covenant by the Jewish polity, that, if a basis for universal salvation, should have been primarily so. But who does not know that it was absolutely confined to Palestine or its emigrants exclusively? and that it caused an absurd prostitution of rite on nature's laws, that is, circumcision.

Had the Jews established a universal empire by the sword, then that faith might have flourished as other peculiar faiths, that were peculiarly indebted immediately or otherwise to the sword or imperial influence, for propagation and institution, as imperial policy dictated.

As the first covenant of Judaism was too peculiar to be the world's benefit, the last predicated on that false position is entirely nugatory.

Whether these covenants be continued or annulled, they are both too peculiar as man's work, for God's blessings. Both have been the severest curses to the peculiar people adopting them. Any faith that refers to them, is as corrupt as the base.

Where was the Creator's covenant with mind, from its creation? A birthright stamped by the immutable laws of nature as this, could not be annulled.

All man's Christs might affect to offer their covenants of grace and salvation, but the seed could not fall on any but a barren soil. All that was of the universe was the exclusive property of Deity, and of course was pre-occupied.

Among the many proofs of gospel false pretences, are the great differences between the old and new testament dispensations.

The old dispensation is superseded by the new dispensation, on the annunciation of the messiah.

Now, God is perfect at creation, but man is imperfect in his conception of it, and advances in the progress of mind's science his various systems of peculiar faith.

Man's systems of two covenants were ever superseded by mind's covenant, the bible of rational mind.

The God of the universe set up his presidency at creation's birth, as universal as space, as durable as eternity, and proclaimed that covenant to be best recognised by the highest appreciation of civilization and religion.

The ministry of all men's systems of peculiar faith, however ordained, will not meet this holy question of God's institution.

The ministry of God is not of man, for it is principles all the time, and they are only God-ordained.

Repentence arises on conviction, that recurs on intellectual recognition of what are the best views of principles.

These principles supersede the necessity of but one master, and that of the universe. No local Christ, can be.

No commission looks honest, when the commander omitted to execute the mission. All was a failure, if a God, an imposition, if a man; both positions decidedly negative the virtue, in the sight of the God of nature. Of what benefit are peculiar gods, to mind?

Who, but an irrational bigot, cannot now see that the commission did not extend to this world?

John, the relation of Jesus, the son of Elizabeth, cousin of Mary, mother of Jesus, cried in the wilderness, to prepare the way for Jesus, and endorsed him.

Now, who endorsed John? Oh, but he was a prophet!

Does that endorse John? The bible endorsement is worthless, as it cannot be authenticated. God proves that.

Correct principles, when justly appreciated, can be the only prophecy that is universal to the truly wise.

Reason analyzes principles, that endorse themselves as God's works, and nothing else.

All things that occur, are fulfilled by the prophecy of time alone. What proofs are there of Christ?

He healed the sick. The doctor does that.

He made the blind to see. When blinded with cataract, the surgeon causes them to see.

But he raised the dead. Jugglery of mind and hand can do that, and the balance claimed. Who endorses Christ as the universal savior of the world? His success? That utterly condemns him. What does the God of the universe say, who is superior to any peculiar god peculiarly interpreted?

His words are universal and eternal, having respect to past, present, and future, and do not pass as tradition, that cannot be a faithful exponent of the God of nature. His words, like himself, are living, and cannot be written by any but himself, in his great spheres of the universe.

His words are engraved, by his eternal means, in his works.

All others are the words of bibles of tradition, the evanescent words of man.

Christ is ever claimed as omnipotent and omniscient.

How come the asserters of this imposition and blasphemy, to escape some marked punishment?

Angels, and a star, heralded him. Who heralded them?

They are all impossibilities, declared by God's word, cause, and effect.

The prophecies are falsified, the miracles are nullified, and mysteries annihilated as enigmas and oracles, by the first principles of mind, their master.

Truth and reason are triumphant over all such stuff; therefore it was that you cannot, and must not, reason on this bible.

That inquisition, the denial of reason, is the worst of all infamous inquisitions, and its absurdity, to govern by faith, is worse than the bible story of the fish swallowing Jonah, who lay in him three days, and then escaped alive. If any fable can beat that, then we yield the question.

What can intelligent moderns think of such dregs, worse than heathonish superstition?

People need religion, not nonsense and sophistry of a tricky priestocracy, who sought to rule, or ruin, the world.

THE TRINITY.

THE science of mathematics defines the truth of numbers. Now, who would pronounce three fingers of the one hand, one finger?

No wise or sound mind, much less, say that the hand had not four fingers, instead of three, as it is the polytheism of four gods of the bible.

Christ had no principles peculiar for a trinity.

Common sense and benefit are the cream of the world's sense, and they decide that the mode the Holy Ghost operates is unappreciable.

All negatives are proved by affirmatives, and, in this matter, ignorance and stupidity will prevail, though the institution is too peculiar for universal benefit. It commenced in sin, and was conceived in fraud.

Why do christians, whose creed is love, differ in hundreds of sects about creeds, but by reason of peculiar views, tastes, and inclinations, that prove human pretensions?

The Mormons now appear to the Christians, what the Christians once did to the ancient Jews, mere innovators.

Every time that Christ is preached as a vicegerent, so often is the deepest blasphemy preached against God, the Creator, and the vilest imposition practiced on men, the creatures.

Why so many differences of faith, if true principles, that belong to religion, were the foundation?

Who, but a peculiar God, could desert his son, when to be executed as a common malefactor between thieves?

The God of the universe has universal dignity and power. And yet effusion of blood was a part of the compact of this peculiar god-drama, and those that produced it were punished. That is peculiar-god ethics.

What greater absurdity and crime can be perpetrated?

To wash away the guilt of a world, the blood of a mortal was shed! Murder was to atone for it; crime was to wash away crime!

This was the messiah for man, made by God, who is bound to preserve to the demands of creation, which messiah could not save himself!

Man, who cannot save himself alone by good works, loses himself, by bad deeds, after Christ's help!

All ground of confidence, for the present or future, is false, but in God.

All minds are from God, and have the elements of religion as a creation-right, and all can improve them, more or less, by improvement of conscience.

Good and wise laws protect society, and no good, wise citizen will forsake them for reckless speculations in bad laws and worse systems of peculiar faith.

Man's nature belongs, in part, to earth, and it can only act as mortal, sinful to death only in degree.

It is remarkable that the greatest miracle that Christ came to perform, as said, to create belief or faith, is the one least accomplished, and that grows beautifully less, as science of the world advances.

So far from forcing the people up to the creed and belief of their salvation, they could not be forced from such, if convincing miracles for belief had been created.

Of course, then, all such are false pretences.

Rational, or reasonable people, wish to believe that way, that indicates a reasonable and just faith, which the God of nature never would permit the people of this world to mistake.

They cannot mistake him in his real books of the universe. That is utterly impossible.

The heir that has a fee simple, or a perpetual life-right title to an estate, could have no better claim from all other sources.

If anything, those titles might invalidate it.

The Christ offers, perpetual life, salvation?

On what reasonable grounds of proof, after his own mortality was so clearly proved on the cross?

Who sent him; where is the proof of his mission?

It is not in his life career, that was evidently that of a mere man, tricky and assuming.

It is not from God, whose almighty functions of creation are clearly sought to be usurped by any such monopoly.

Who can give us undeniable and full proof, that is incontestible, worthy of truth and rational minds?

The christian says: To the altar, to be prayed for.

What is to be prayed for? Religion? That you have had at creation. You need to make it most rational. Can Christ avail, when faith is invoked against rationality? In what light shall we address Christ, then?

As a reformer? Then was his mission as a man, and must be viewed through mind.

When he is sought to be placed in a higher light, as all rational beings have had the elements of religion already, without which no such subject could be entertained, then there is collusion among the people, that is tyrannical in the state, and the whole becomes an imposition and a blasphemy.

Weak minded bigots, ignorant and obstinate, and the self-interested, may be easily misled by similar perverted minds, but there is no excuse that you should act the bigot.

Two wrongs do not make a right, in the case of Christ.

His sins added to those of the people, will not avail, but press down the heavier.

But the christian bible is true, because all the prophecies have come to pass about the downfall of nations. The bible prophecies are all pretences; but little is revealed about them.

When that bible was published, man was barbarian and uncivilized. Nations warred to prey, and pirate on each other. There was no stability in national affairs, and one nation fell after another, like wave upon wave.

Wars for conquest, mastery and power, were the games that all played at. No nation can be stable without principles that are permanent. No ancient nation was permanent for this reason, therefore the Jewish fell.

The lust of the flesh was bad enough, but the lust of avarice and ambition, mastered all. The ancient world was composed of absolutism, priestocracy and military despotism, all having the elements of their own destruction.

This is human mind uncultivated, rude, undisciplined.

It will ever be so, under analogous circumstances, and the events can be well foretold. But bible prophecy is a perjury.

Then it is only the philosophy of history, where it is not its fiction, and not prophecy. Wise men can foretel thousands of things by analogy, and inspiration of science on mind.

Then let mind counteract all imposition, by its ample and proper means, that can avail effectually to the honor and triumph of mind irradiated by intellectual light.

Scourges of war, pestilence and famine, make a sad havoc of the erring nations of the world, for the self-vindication of principles, that should have kept them in their moral and intellectual orbits.

True observation of statesmen's minds will teach them their duties and actions, to banish deceit from their councils, and to accurse demagogism among the sons of men on the face of the earth, in order to drive feudalism of mind to nonentity.

But polygamy was excluded by Christ: a new thing. We believe not, when the world had the laws of other pagans, the Romans and Greeks, who had only one wife. The Romans had possession of Palestine, at that time, and ruled by their laws.

Were the superstitious Jews, who had polygamy even among their patriarchs, to teach their superiors?

The numeral equality of the sexes, teaches the exclusion of polygamy as an abuse of nature's laws.

Was there ever such a being as Christ?

We do not know the exact year nor the season of the year, month or day of the birth of this chief, or Christ's nativity.

He appeared many thousands of years, after the world stood in need of a savior by the pretended fall of the bible Adam, surely. Who announced him? The jugglery of mind, obedient to priestocracy. That was his precursor: the man that dares deny it, is reckless of honor, truth and religion.

It matters but little about ventriloquism, " the daughter of the voice," or the jugglers of hand, when the jugglery of mind is omnipotent on the ignorant and corrupt masses.

With the paternity of priestocracy, the jugglery of mind, and the movable mob masses, the world at one time was identified. Does any truthful mind deny this? Let the ancient oracles tell. The Jew oracles are no better-schemed with more art and duplicity.

How easy was it by ventriloquism and psychology, to work all the machinery of priestocracy.

Any pretended manifestation of the will of the peculiar god could be supernatural, when their machinery announced "This is my beloved son," &c.

It is the duty of every patriotic, intelligent mind, to expose all such imposition, as of all prophets, sorcerers and magicians who were false.

All oracles, the pretences of priests, should be exposed, no matter the authority.

The proper rational instruction and improvement of mind will discard magical operations, prophetic visions, ay, any oracles of Urim and Thummim. The only true prophet to be consulted is time, and that has exposed all the false pretences of all the world priestocracy.

But christianity claims the only decency about religion!

The Mahometan Moors taught the christians toleration in Spain, during the eighth century, yielding the rights of conscience when they conquered the people, but the Moors were treated in bad faith by the Spaniards, who reconquered their country in the fifteenth century, and refused them this principle at the expense of their lives.

Who could expect any thing of any profession, that resort to unprincipled faith for an existence?

We cannot be safe by the traditions of any books, that interfere with the principles of conscience and mind; in other words, with love, benevolence, philanthropy, justice and affection.

We must believe and know that God exists, and in the difference between vice and virtue, good and evil, justice and injustice, that we are bound to principles by conscience, else remorse must ensue.

We can espouse no system of man or books, but what reason sanctions, rational mind maintains, and nature demands, with becoming modesty.

God's conservative principles cut out Christ and all such pretended angel messengers and messiahs, and place dignity to his glory.

Had the ignorant priestocracy known all, and the revelations of science, that exposes the frauds of all mortals in time, then they would have been modestly silent. Their vicious book utterly condemns them.

If the godhead was perfect with Christ as is asserted, "I and the Father are one." in union with the godhead, it must needs be imperfect without him for the rest of the universe.

The time employed on earth is absurd to think of, as the rest of the universe must and would suffer in Christ's absence; this is a difficulty impracticable, to the priestocracy.

We hardly think the fabulists thought of all this, when they manufactured the story of messiahship.

Of course, they easily falsified any amount of matter, to carry out the drama, but their sophistry recoils at last, and transfixes them forever to exposure before the world.

The jugglery of mind, hand and voice, will explain the whole fabric of priestocracy, in all its most difficult points.

We need hardly ask, is it very difficult to cause persons to act most difficult dramas. if all matters were previously prepared, when the writers by a stroke of the style could manufacture all the dramas.

What cannot collusion do, by clanships?

The proof of Christ is pretended to rest on divine inspiration and prophecy, the falsity of which is well proved by the rejection by nearly the whole world, few of the Jews excepted, that is the peculiarly chosen people of course, of a peculiar god to be so asserted.

This of itself is authority, against such blasphemous imposition.

Thus it has been, with all other kinds of superstition.

Nations may take from their founders the kind of peculiar faith, and lose it in the ocean of dogmas.

The Romans adopted all kinds, and excluded by imperial power, what was suitable to Constantine, who enabled the christian peculiarity to progress, in that wide spread empire.

Should the Mormons last one hundred years by reason of the world's darkness, which God forbid, their prophets and faith may have equal claims on the credulity of the ignorant masses, and the vulgar bigotry.

Citizens of the world, noblemen of nature, aid in putting down all peculiarity of faith and bigotry. Talk of mind and reason, and the sycophants will tell us, that their prince cast out devils.

Did he cast out himself? If not, the assertion proves the falsity, as there can be no such beings, if God be pure. But he did many miracles. So can only the mind juggler. The Mormons claim all that kind of peculiar faith, and more too. All peculiar faiths claim mind jugglery, hence it is the juggler's faith.

If such pretence be used for a part, the whole is condemned. The fact is, no intrinsic part of peculiar faith can be approved. The balance is unworthy of notice, when a part is destitute of foundation. All of peculiar faith, is worthless.

As to sins, what are they?

The actions of deviations from settled principles, conservative if followed, but more or less destructive or injurious, if rejected. Mind is identified with the relations of creation, and must act consistently. Sins proceed from mind, ignorant or perverted, the last knowing better, but addicted to bad habits that enslave. Then rational education must teach and correct the world, to approach the best position, and that must accompany the dawn of reason, rational mind.

All the proper influences that rational mind recognises, should be brought to bear in the world to preserve its noblest position.

How absurd then the sacrifices of Judaism, or any peculiar faith, in the blood of animals?

What availed the cruel, murderous sacrifice of human victims, as burnt or blood offerings?

What crime did all such conceal, or what pardon for sin propitiate?

All the pretended sacrifices of messiahs or christs, are worse than idle; they are ignominious.

Are the bibles that speak of human sacrifices worthy of our veneration or respect, when all rational minds must consider them as the barbarous rites of mere cannibals' minds?

But if mortal rewards are desirable, how much more are those that are eternal?

Are not these the proper incentives to minds refined by cultivation?

We must be certain who has the right to bestow the whole. We certainly could not be expected, if sane, to look to those not having the power.

We seek not a frail, but sure position. But what shall we do for repentance?

Let all act to the dictates of the best enlightened conscience, for ever the best; look to the future, and correct the present. But what is the universal standard? The bible of rational mind, that improves on the best refinements of rational civilization, looks to the unity of the Creator all the time, and appreciates that standard by a universal comprehension. The faculty of conscience, enlightened at this tribunal, teaches most that the eternal principles of truth, honesty, humanity and justice, are some of the first duties for all rational minds all the time, and that they must act by a duly instructed mind.

The mind of man is operated on by the mind of man, in the court of reason and conscience.

Mind looks through natural phenomena to the author, having the innate faculties of adoration, but is liable to distort their appreciation by the perversion of ignorance and superstition, the last of which, under the guidance of the priestocracy, speculates in them as world stuck for miracles.

What kingdom could Christ set up, that God had not already anticipated in man's mind, by his presidential institutions?

As to the doctrines of regeneration, sprinkling, baptism, and the host of ceremonies and rites, they will all fall with the principals, who fall of themselves, without redemption or resurrection, before a rational world.

But is there not one peculiar faith of so many, that must be the true one? No more than a selection of many falsehoods can make a truth.

The best Christian, or any other, is no more than the Mahometan, Brahmin, or Mormon.

If Christ had been the messiah, Judas would have suffered himself to be cut into thirty pieces of flesh, and Peter would have died at first, before either would have acted as they are said to have done, the one by teaching, the other by perjury, and all by desertion.

The Jews could not have been held back by force, if the true messiah had been announced to them, being on the look out. The history of twenty-four other pretended messiahs prove this, as six hundred thousand Jews lost their lives for merely one of them.

How much collusion and delusion have there been for messiahs and their priestocracy, the greatest curse of peculiar faith, the worst iniquity of the world.

How many testified falsely to messiahship?

That was an easy matter, when the materials were so abundant. The people, especially the ignorant, were easily deceived by supposed miracles, particularly when they were previously prepared by false prophecies, that were one of the world's weaknesses.

With all such, witchcraft, omens, magic were the same thing, mysterious.

If miracles and prophecies ever were necessary, they are so now, most especially in the progress of opposition, to eradicate the effects of the vedas and the oracles of the other pagans, who swarm by hundreds of millions in Asia.

Now is the time to arrest this mighty influence. But alas for them, they are killed by the light of mind that rises up to-day, to reclaim its last possessions over all mankind.

Why were three days for the resurrection of a messiah, when this takes place as soon as the spirit of immortal life leaves the body?

If such resurrection was practicable, then was death impracticable to that being.

Fanatics advocated such doctrines, that rational religion cannot possibly recognise. The rational mind, therefore, rejects all such, and seeks the speedy purification that is rational.

Christ, his parents or his godfathers, the priestocracy, may have learned for him from Egypt and Asia, his systems of peculiar faith. Asia furnishes the prototype in bhuddism. The West had the full benefits of travels to the East. The Egyptians were capable of proselyting the world with priest-faith, and did, much in this way.

Their priestocracy was a part of the nobility, and enjoyed great and peculiar privileges.

Ignorance takes meteors for stars, and wise men, that is, priests, without any proof of names of such character, are merely asserted to travel therefor.

It may well be asked, who but priests were they, of the affiliated order, and astrologers, confessedly jugglers, at that?

Shall mind not close the theatre of deception, that invokes operations on the passions, fears, self-interest, faith, &c., of credulous people?

"The Platonic argument goes on the ground, that man existed in some celestial region before he was born of a woman." If Christianity be not Western Bhuddism, does any one need be told that this was the fact for the origin of Christ, who was the greatest of sectarians? But surely the priestocracy could make their fiction.

All should seek a uniform function of judgment, and have no pre-conceived opinion, much less peculiar education.

Had Christ done his mission like a master and a God, could he have lost Judas?

Would any but a monomaniac have resigned an eternal crown for thirty pieces of silver?

And who but monomaniacs will now resign an heirship of God, for that of mortals?

Christ could have easily proclaimed to the whole world, that he was master of miracles, and boldly challenged the opponents, and thus convert the whole nations of the earth, for subjects.

Did he do any God-like actions, that the people had chosen for him, to be convinced?

Was he master enough of human nature, to appease the anger of the pharisees, and soothe them into a proper change of mind, which he could have done, had he been its master?

But his foster-fathers wrote this drama, and filled it with an earthly corruption, and sowed the seeds of its own destruction.

There has been more boldness in the advocacy of some peculiar faith than in others, and in this particularly.

But what does all such pagan superstition amount to?

The wisdom is to discern the principles given by God, and practice them. The material business of all mankind is with the best duty of man to man, to reach the height of religion to God.

The best duty to God is the very essence of all religion, pointed out by reason.

Rational religion, that only comes of God, teaches the nearest approach to perfect morality.

The spirit of instruction and light went, with reason, to all rational beings, thousands of years before such a creature as Christ was ever thought of.

A divine mission, though superfluous, on this basis of the world's and creation's facts, could not have been mistaken at all, and would have called divine interposition in its favor; but none such is avowed or proved in the nature of things.

How beautifully and majestically the machinery of the whole universe is progressing, and all at the original institution of the Creator!

Many have been the priests' devices, to extract from the world, under the guise of miracles and oracles, most of the world's worth.

But Gods cannot be made of mortals.

The object of miracle-mongers has ever been to convince the people; an impossibility, as they have not the first elements of truth in their composition.

If from God, with whom all possible things are to be realised, the people would be convinced.

The world's history abounds in such, as impostures.

The majesty of mind exposes now, to the contempt of true science, all such as false philosophy and the worst demoralization.

There are myriads, millions of systems of worlds in the organization of the universe, doubtlessly most inhabited or preparing to be by intellectual beings, evincing the greatness of the Creator, self-living and all sufficient, as on this earth, for their complete and perfect conservation, as Creator-endowed.

He created all on conservative principles, physical and moral, to which. mind, endowed with the highest attributes of free agency, must conform, and they exclude all messiahships, that never would have been heard of but for priestocracy, a perverted peculiar order of world pirates, that feed on souls-speculations.

Intellect could not if it would be independent, any more than all the physical bodies, of these principles.

Mind, that is rational, should be properly silent, where it cannot see its way clearly, as it may libel, where presumption abides, against that all-wise being who is the supreme supervisor.

Man, as all animal beings, is created conformably to perishing nature, in part, participates in the relative state of his being and circumstances, and must be wisely directed to avail himself, through this free-agency, limited only by the constituent conservative principles of the universe, of all mental, moral and physical, and religious means, for the best realities of future existence that his Creator vouchsafes.

The history of the twenty-four messiahs, of all peculiar faith, ancient and modern, down to the mormons, proves that false faith can be easily imposed on masses of people.

The springs and impulses of human minds are alike, under all such circumstances, as interest, passion, ignorance, prejudice, credulity, terror, bigotry, sophistry, superstition and imposition.

This is the constant course of such peculiar faith, in man, as mortal, throughout the globe, all the time.

When it is otherwise, people reason with analysis and analogy.

What nation has not been misguided by imposition, in superstition?

The motion of the star, at the birth of Christ, could only have been from a meteor; that is a frequent occurrence all over the world, near volcanoes, when it does not arise from the pretensions of priestocracy.

The body of Christ was not identified in the sepulchre, an essential part; and the soldiers would be self-impeached, as outwitted by the Christians, were not a part of the world outwitted by the dramatists, who wrote long after the period when such events are said to have transpired.

When was stealing of the body? If it ever took place, it must have preceded the sealing the door of the sepulchre.

It was deception all the time preceding birth, and even of death.

All are base substitutes and counterfeits, other than the innate cultivated self preservation religion, due to the Almighty alone.

The greatest miracle of Christ was to convince and save the world, even after his pretended resurrection.

Nothing should have prevented Christ from saving the world, and this, the real miracle, was never performed.

Many were the occasions for him to have triumphed as a God, as when the priests essayed to slay him.

He was only an ignorant, misled fanatic—that is, his dramatists were.

Why should the early Christians, who were few, be preferred to be confirmed and converted by miracles, when the moderns, billions in all, are totally destitute of all such aids, that would be effectual, if performed?

This is surely the best reason of the miserable imposition for miracles, that are no where to be found, when most needed.

The whole foundation is in stupid ignorance and imposition.

Prophecy is exercised, for what and whom?

God does not need such false pretences.

What is there in all, but what the page of history and philosophy daily unfolds?

Are sinful prophets, impostors, to be preferred to mind?

By their own showing, Christ was unable to satisfy many, but a very small part of a whole nation among which he died, that he was a God and God sent, and for this the world must take their pretences.

His followers alone saw him, they say, after his supposed resurrection! Why show himself to the affiliated only?

Because the affiliated only fabricate the story.

How many pretended miracles are there analogous?

Was one of the twelve apostles, ever converted by a messiah?

Was there ever such a thing on earth?

Were not all deceived by or about miracles?

Priests affect in their insidious story, that all other worship was closed after the birth of the true messiah. Who was the true messiah? Let that be proved.

Do the moderns feloniously endorse the pious frauds of the ancients?

The present and past history of the world condemns that falsehood, as more than a majority is under other faiths. The degree of intoleration during the first stages of christianity, proves the power of heathen mythology. The intelligent portion of mankind is culpable, to suffer the priestocracy to propagate such falsehoods with credit.

We have not got rid of polytheism, the very thing instituted by the trinity, and never will, till rational religion excludes all pagan sectarianism that now overwhelms society and the world.

It is impossible to deny successfully the existence of Almighty Providence, that denies and impeaches the truth of all messiahships.

It is impossible to prove the sight of God as a demi-god, to any mortal—or that demi-gods can die.

This is a world-wide subject, concerning all.

The fault of the world is for the personal, instead of the truthful authority, the mortal master instead of the God principles. But the last are not so profitable to the priestocracy.

Is it reasonable that the whole people of Israel, should not have been the best judges of their own immortal benefits? They, cotemporary, deemed it so trifling, as to leave genuine no account of the pretended god, from whom the whole world could not have been kept.

They were as much the beneficiaries as all the rest of the world, and better judges, as eye-witnesses.

It is false conclusions to say that God would not protect his own peculiar people, by unmistakable evidences of the mission, the very object of his peculiar position, if it were ever taken. But as this adoption of the messiah would be their function, the whole category of fraud is most clearly proved for both dispensations, and all the peculiarity devolves on their ignoble priestocracy of both sides.

Who are the believers in the legitimacy of Christ, the assumed chief of messiahs?

Those who are as wise as Joseph, the husband of Mary. Who was Mary, the mother of Christ?

A common woman, rather too common, as she and the priestocracy have caused mind-prostitution thereby.

The pretences of priests make out Mary to have been immaculate, after all her impurities.

If the dignity of the Lord God of the universe was concerned, we would protest against this libel, but as it was the peculiar god of Judaism, we let it pass now with contempt, as we cannot know that god at all. The gods of polytheism were adulterous. Now, in free, intelligent countries, where the christian faith abides, has the majority any practical faith in christianity or Christ?

Is not the majority of the people in this Union, indifferent to the christian faith?

Have they any practical hope or faith therein?

"He that is not for me, is against me."

Does the majority practice, if it believes?

But it may be suggested that some at least have somewhat a theoretical faith.

If they believed in Christ, they would keep his commandments.

All theoretical faith is contingent an incident for a life time, whereas the masterly character of God is impressed more or less on all from their vital existence, and will continue to the end; whereas, too, the other is too often lost, mislaid for a convenient time, or never adopted. Let rational education teach all rational minds, who God is. None then will ever lose sight of him, adorable beyond appreciation. God's is a part of mind's constituency, and cannot be divested or eradicated, however perverted.

The world is only one of the universe, that is considered exhaustless. What has been done for the balance of the millions of worlds by Christ? Thirty-three years spent by a messiah on each, take up too much time for the rest to be reached. But man's cumbrous idea of preserving worlds by personal locality and suffering, will not meet the question in one world for all its ages and circumference, much less for all the universe. God met the whole demands of the universe at creation. The corrupt priestocracy are those that see not. To judge of all by analogy, that as God was incompetent for one, he must have been for all, why should not the balance of the universe be in analogous condition, if the Creator was so imperfect in this world?

God the Creator must feel most deeply on all physiological principles, for the safety of his people, the universal, rational inhabitants of all creation.

Their preservation is implied in their creation.

But if the assumed true messiah Christ got his trinity from the Hindoos, whose dogmas and precepts did he teach? He and his friends had access in Egypt to all theirs, and the doctrines of Asiatics, among whom was Confucius, who taught, "To do unto others as we would have them do unto us." Also to the Stoics, whose tenets were the prevailing ones of the most virtuous ancients, and who flourished three hundred years before him. They taught the conflagration, that christians preach.

It would be strange that the priestocracy did not know their position, with such power and influence in their hands, all over the world.

Even remote nations of Siberia, as the Shamans, believe in a Supreme Being, but their system permits inferior powers, good and evil, the last of whom are malignant deities, the priests affect to propitiate. But Christ's resurrection from the dead, is what astonishes the credulous, who are alarmed at death for themselves. It was any thing else than a resurrection, as it was deferred days after death!

Is it possible to prove by satisfactory analysis, that it was Christ's body that was laid in the sepulchre? That might have been a very material and essential point, but for positive certainty that messiahship is obsolete. Has it been proved at all, much less satisfactorily, that it ever was identified all the time in the sepulchre? Was there no substitute, no collusion about Christ, when it is certain that there are the most extensive collusions and frauds practiced for peculiar faith throughout the world, by the assumed gospels, and statements of its authors? It seems to have been a granted point to the priestocracy to let them lie all the superstition they could, as their mindfacture was to save the world. Had there been no previously prepared sepulchre with subteranean passages, in purview of the event of the death of this impostor?

Why did not the advocates expose the body before the whole world, who might watch and witness the mighty spectacle, that the incredulous Jews might see and believe, or that the opposition might be confronted and circumvented? But above all, was there no collusion in the rumor, the stories? Was the testimony proved on the spot, so substantiated that the world could not doubt, or was this tale appreciated as others preceding, written long after, giving all opportunities to mature the plot and add all impostures that were deemed necessary?

Mind scorns all such as contemptible, when it was written not at the time that truth can be proved, but years after, when fiction and falsehood could be successful.

Is the letter of Pontius Pilate, if ever written, any proof of the divinity of Christ, but only introductory of the rumor that was described? Is it authentic?

Is the request of Christ's likeness by the Roman Emperor, to be placed among the Roman gods, any other than a continuance of their customs, to adopt all the gods of their conquered nations, the whole one grand imperial polytheism to concentrate the feelings of the world, and excite its curiosity? Is that also, not a forgery?

Did ever Judas the traitor, so called, recognise Christ as God, when he took thirty pieces of money for his information? That very action proves Christ mortal, for Judas would have suffered himself to have been cut into 30,000 pieces of flesh, and gloried in the martyrdom, had Christ been a God.

Did not the rock and chief, the very founder of the church of Christ, perjure himself; and what better could we expect from his followers, who have degraded human nature, by licking the dust off the feet of the Pope?

What now are all other points worth, in the absence of truth and honesty, before God? Nothing.

Whilst Christ was on this earth for thirty-three years, what became of the balance of the universe for that time, but for conservative principles? As they preceded him, and were and are adequate, they undeniably take precedence of this impostor. This very one thing ought to convince every rational mind of the fallacy of peculiar faith.

It is claimed that ignorant fishermen instituted the apostleship; but that position is banefully carried out by wily priests of half-civilized shepherds, increased by subsequent affiliations. The sources and means, as those of ignorance and corruption, are most objectionable.

History, that is true, only furnishes us an account of mortals on earth. How, then, can mind have any just confidence in books, that violate the first principles of religion, truth, and honesty, in palming off on us fictions, when all are mortals that are born, live and die as mortals?

All mortals are creatures, and any one is a blasphemous impostor to affect anything beyond a creature's province.

How can he be honest or truthful, assuming to be messiah, an impossibility from God's attributes and the essential principles of the universe? Who can, true to his own soul, receive such felons?

Mind has wisely to consider the state of mortals, and the earth-theatre of their existence.

They are wisely adapted for each other, in a state of mortality.

Mind must make the best of it practicable, not libel Deity for its not being better.

Do you, mortal, idly complain of such? Seek the noblest immortality.

Mind can only seek that in a better, a future state of existence, and must seek to merit all such forever, by going to the Supreme, who has the title deeds.

The interfering about man's redemption, other than by the Creator, is a libel and impeachment of God's attributes, as mind declares, still more, man's presumption.

The doctrine of the trinity involves, in itself, a real and complete contradiction.

The few who do believe in Christ, must see that Christ could not be a messiah, if he would.

Of what efficacy is their faith, founded on fiction?

Will they not thank any proper authority for disclosing the whole fallacy, and exposure of the fraud?

Christ did not expiate his own sin of blasphemy. How, then, could he atone, in his condition, for others?

Beware how you adopt his blasphemy!

The christian priestocracy say that Christ died for one world! Where are the millions of worlds, all equally under the one Supreme, who, if imbecile in one, is so in all! But Christ died for all mankind.

As an after-thought of after-thought is utterly impossible with the Creator, the foundation is worthless. A man that dies the death, cannot possibly expiate for others, by all moral and physical laws of God and his universe.

So far from messiahship being right in the bible-heaven, it cannot be right for earth.

But how could God die in part, the one-third of the trinity? Again, the world was destitute for three days, while the action of minds, millions upon millions, needed their guardian.

Where would mind have been in that interval, but for the creation rule of omnipotence?

Is there any mind so stupid as not to see the full light of this heresy to reason?

Where was mind's protection, physical, moral, and religious, during the abidence of Christ in the world, and his minority? In the competent hands of God Almighty, and that ends the question most conclusively; for, if the Creator were competent all that time, of course, by his inherent rights, he was equally so for all time, as well before the conception of this after-thought, as since. This concludes the honorable argument. But can bigots see how many times they are wound up? Will they murder the universe over and over again, to institute their pagan idolatry?

Man affects that Christ died for all. That positively condemns the position; dying thousands of years after the creation of man, could not meet, but cuts off the previous question, which effectually cuts off, and out, the whole priestocracy, machinery, and sophistry.

God is universal in his kind attributes, and would not have permitted that peculiar and partial pretension, as part of mankind is cut out.

Messiahship is inadmissible in God's perfection, as it takes away God's omniscience and omnipotence, thereby rendering him imbecile and imperfect, consequently unworthy of universal adoration.

Then all creations called gods of peculiar faith, are defective, and use up the whole doctrines, as the God of the universe could not have created it, had he been as peculiar faith advocates characterize him. The death of any messiah for all, is an impracticability, by the character of time, whose functions of past, present, and future, entirely exclude all such as false pretences, and is in direct antagonism to God's functions of Creator, and to the only one rational and uniform ever-existing religion. We would ask for undoubted proof of that position, that Christ died for all.

It is not in the nature of any superior being to subordinate his own master-claims to an inferior being of his own creation. It is not in the nature of intellect to stultify itself, by allowing all the consequences of such supreme folly, for the Christians have four gods, among them, him of evil genius, equal, if not superior, to God-creator, in seducing souls, and undoing all most valuable. How absurd!

Christ was the promulgator of his system of peculiar faith, a completely deficient system for the good of the world, for, so far from showing a suitable God, it betrays the frailties of an ignorant bigot, and the fraud of a knave, to be exposed to the scorn of the world in its days of science. Analysis is the key that detects all such impositions, and proves the God of creation every way worthy of its adoration, the more he is known.

But the child of God has been vouchsafed to all creation.

Where is the proof, for that is injustice to God, and cruelty to his creation, deprived so much as that is worth of God? Not only Christ, but nearly all Christ's disciples, suffered violent deaths, according to christian story. For their blasphemous propagations, was it not?

Rational religion can cause none of this, unselfish and devoted to God alone as she is. It is she that arrests all this superstition and wrongs.

Why disturb the world with the wild vagaries and fanaticisms of superstition, to harrow up the mind to ideal and unreal views? For whose benefit is all this?

The priests!! The primary matter and commission cannot be approached at all by messiahships.

God would alienate his power to that extent, and lose that amount in the rule of his works.

Peter's frailty shows the directly imperfect conviction of the christian doctrine, and but little confidence in it. This doctrine fails to give support to an immortal soul, leaving it destitute of confidence, but leaves it in doubt, and often in despondency, most certainly in perjured corruption.

It betrays the state, most certainly, of undeveloped mind, of an age of ignorance, both of natural phenomena, and of the human character, above all, God's character.

It acts as if this was the only sphere for mortals, and priests were the beneficiaries; dwarfs man to a pusillanimous vassal to adopt them, who puts himself between mind and its maker.

Under malign influences, the vassal mind of the nineteenth century, has itself bound to do many odious things. Unless mind, that needs correction, get its wants supplied at the best source and origin of science, the inspiration from God, all the balance would be insufficient and ineffectual.

Its protection has not been secured throughout its creation, by any other than its Creator's Almighty conservation.

There are intervals of time not taken up by all peculiar faiths, that are not conservative. God is conservative all the time, through principles. The earth has inherent elements that prove the conservative power of God all the time.

Christ or his priestocracy, had to resort to the heathen mythology, in his fable of Lazarus and the rich man, consequently his system proves its own deficiency.

Mind seemingly needs to know of all this, more than mind can tell us as some suppose, but the God of good veils all in the future, and reveals only what is truly of world interest.

Christ does not tell us what rational mind can tell, by analysis. Though Christ assumes God's capital, he is not the capitalist for mind.

Mind from the time of its consciousness should be impressed with all that satisfies in after life, and none can do that all the time, but that from God, who permits no interval to be left out.

If humanity be true to itself, it will avail itself of this munificent capital of God alone.

Who knows of the world's or the universe's future termination? Is not all this evil speculation by ignorant and designing men, for base capital? We have seen Millerism die out. What is all prophecy, independent of its certain perjury, worth, that is so mystified, that none can reason on its results?

It proves, most conclusively, that man's fingers have indited it, one of the sacrifices of perverted mind to the vassalage of superstition.

The scriptures, advocating all the entangled sophisms of dreaming priestocracies, tell us, that we are to have a new earth, and that the sea is to yield up its dead. All this is absurd, as the third day resurrection.

The christian peculiar faith has four gods, instead of three. The fourth is an evil genius, and so powerful as to take away souls from their Maker! What other paganism is any worse?

The past and present actions of the Roman church, including all their pretensions, have no legitimate claim to the title of the true infallible orthodox faith. Their founder, Peter, on whom they count so much, who received the keys direct, and handed them down to the church, as pretended, was a perjurer, that would be deemed an unworthy witness in the especial court of conscience. Protestants may affirm, that their position is certainly better. How can it be, when Peter has the whole fraternity? Besides, that has sectarianism, clannishness, and the clans war on each other, even to this day, with angry and even with bloody conflicts at times. That is not religion. The sectarians are denied by the Romanists, who, in turn, are pronounced wrong by the protestants!

All have pagan man-worship, a species of superstition, all of which must be thrown away surely, ere pure religion is secured to honorable high-minded freemen.

There must be no trade, no speculation, no priestocracies, no mental midwives to go between the mind and its God. All that is worse than useless ; it is criminal, heinous, foolish, base, degrading to the mind, that should look forever up to God, the Supreme Being alone to be adored. You cannot detract from the perfect character of God, by any messiahships. Put away your false gods.

Does God create hybrids ? Are not these the work of mind perverted ?

Can a God be born of a mortal ? What incongruity !

Can an immortal originate from a mortal womb on this earth ? What false physiology !

The genealogy is most stupidly ridiculous, when it assumes God to be the father, and yet claims Joseph ! It proves itself ineffably nonsensical. A mystified perjury made by jesuitical minds.

No principle of physiology or of reason, will permit such a monster. It is too light and merciful, to call all this mere inconsistency.

No inside or outside barbarians of the world can assume this, and live out the age of mind.

Are secret crimes to beget such artifice ?

What then had Joseph to do with Christ's genealogy ?

Was Mary any direct connexion to David ? Was Mary the mother, less than a vile woman, as none but man ever could be on earth ? As much then as whoredom falls below chastity, so does peculiar faith fall below religion, and so does messiahship fall below the creator. Accursed it lives on earth, blasting mankind by its ignominious degradations.

And king David's was not even pure blood, as Solomon was born of the adulteress. Was this the pretence of oriental assumption, before which mind has been crushed ?

Christ's birth then was an imposition ; his life is described as spent in sectarianism, a very low calling, as the worst of demagogism.

His demonology, if not psychology disguised, proves that he used humbugs and jugglery, that if not of hands, at least of minds, even to this day. But worse than that. His life was not written until many years after he lived, if this was not an entire romance procured by the pious frauds of the priestocracy.

Then it was the worst species of mind-jugglery.

At his death, Christ exclaimed, it is claimed, " My God, why hast thou forsaken me ?" Why did he ask this question without a cause ? Had he not forsaken the best principles of honesty and religion, in assuming to be more than mortal ? But how explain away the great earthquake when Christ was crucified ? If it ever happened, of which there is no true history, and if not a mere coincidence, it proves as much for the consummation of the punishment for his blasphemy. Was any proof given, that it was not a mere coincidence ? But christianity is the guardian of science. It is the obituary maker of philosophical science.

Christianity so far from protecting science, caused the philosophers to be banished Rome by Justinian, and astronomers to be punished for astronomy. She reared up the world-sophists.

It took kings and absolutism to put down God's philosophy, to rear pagan christianity, and deplorable have been the evil consequences to the world therefrom.

It took several centuries for christianity to get a foothold in that country, and it is indebted to Constantine for its establishment by the sword. In becoming the policy of his government, it acquired strength and power by union to state. It has been maintained, by the brute force of usurpation, and whenever expelled, as lately. the pope has been indebted to military power for restoration. Christianity, like all pagan peculiar world faiths, has been smuggled on the world. And such has been the policy of peculiar faith, to hold the world in its grasp and subjection.

The sword is unconscientiously used, if victory can be obtained. Rational mind only stays it to-day, supreme over Christ that came truly " to bring the sword." What is the difference to the world, whether a Constantine or a Mahomet conquers for peculiar faith, that only differs in degree of superstition ? How can this faith be universal and fraternal, when the most powerful nation with its state united to it, usurps the fairest portions of the globe, not to be repressed but by mind and its prowess ?

Some persons undertake to answer for all, because it is booked in the bible, as if the most inconsistent and contradictory, the most inextricable dilemmas were not there presented to its best friends. It involves many arguments that are unanswerable to the shrewdest of them, as what had the genealogy of Joseph to do with Christ's, if Christ was illegitimate ? Again, the apostles are said to have eaten with Christ, after his asserted resurrection.   No spirit can do that, as it is utterly incompatible.   But there was union of body and mind, which was restoration to his original functions, that is, he was made alive as other mortals.   That proves if any thing, that he had never been dead after birth.

All the whims, caprices, and fancies of peculiar faith, whether for Mahomet or Christ, Moses or Bhudd, Brahmin or Mormon, Juggernaut or Lama, end in sophistry and utter perjury, as all have false pretences of damnable character.

Persuasion may ruin, deceive or seduce the world, if mind is not posted up by virtue and intelligence.   It has been thrown off its guard mostly by this very thing.   What had stars, suns of other solar systems to do with individuals of this solar system?   It was the work of astrologers and alchemists, who were the affiliated priestocracy that affected irrational pretensions, as they were the world humbuggers.

But the history of Christ was delayed to be written, it is said, for many years after the supposed transactions.   This implies fraud, for the avoidance of antagonism, that might upset the statement.   No such story could have been valid, unless both sides had been properly reported, and adjudged correctly as verified.

How difficult is it now, in this day and time, with all the light of the press, to get the truth of the very time, published in the immediate circle?   Even in this day, a man by money and power, can get his clan around him, and make out much that is improbable pass for facts.   There is no end to perjury, in the present state of society.

How difficult, if not impossible, is it, to reach the truth and facts after a lapse of time in distant places, where the responsibility personal is not imperative, and the rational standards not the highest.

To obtain Christ, a son should be born of a virgin.   That is the very way that all first children should be born.   Virgins are first mothers that way.

Can partisans be believed in faith, politics, or any matter connected with self-interest?

Admit man has the habit of perverting the truth, constantly declaring the statements of peculiar faith, he will swear to them, particularly if he conceal his disbelief of the bible of tradition privately, while in public he hypocritically professes faith.   Not only was one disciple of Christ a traitor, but another, the chief, was a perjurer, while all were deserters and perjurers.

What confidence can be placed in a world of such cattle?   Who can be safely trusted, after using deceit or forfeiture of his word in serious matters?

The bible of tradition authors were not up to the high and right appreciation of things. What can the inspectors of mind promise themselves, as to the unity of mind on any messiah?   It can be procured on no such bauble, when the prime benefits of God are to be disregarded.   If Christ be adopted, God is left to himself.   Let the world understand this subject perfectly, and it will dismiss all messiahships as frauds on itself.   The hidings of Christ's disciples evince only mortal actions, and the hidings of his father's face evince his own blasphemy.   The whole of it is only a peculiar story unworthy of notice.   We must have a sixth sense to mingle with spirits, as the apostles, as we mortals have to breathe another atmosphere.   The penalty to presume on more is through death.   But so far from the necessity of a sixth sense, whilst some are naturally deprived of a part of their five senses, other persons do not use appropriately all these, most being deprived of the right use of theirs by an interested but' perverted clique of base characters.   How deplorable in both cases!   Are these last duly thankful to see the splendid universe ; to hear the joyful sounds of friendship and love ; to speak the blessed thoughts of mind, yet refuse the proper allegiance to its independence and mighty characteristics in the analysis of truth?

What was the use of the Holy Ghost or Spirit but priest machinery, to circumvent mind's imaginings?

What ignorance has been taught in all bibles of tradition?

The doctrine of demons or spirits, a demoniacal possession, shows affection by epileptic fits, deranged persons, or those affected by numerous diseases.

Mind, the mighty agent for universal action, doubly corrects this wicked pretension.

The pride of reason is the error of opinion, that may mislead into all the puerilities of peculiar faith, as the wonderful visions of dancers, convulsionists, jumpers, jerkers, whippers, shakers, &c.

Fits were supposed, by the ignorant and superstitious ancients, to be a manifestation of actions of demons.

Suppose that the body of Christ had been burnt, as of course it could easily have been, who could have expected to have seen anything but ashes?

Death is the barrier between spirits and mortals.

There can be no visions of all such, no contact, no commerce or intercourse ; as destructive is in antagonism with conservative principles, as evil is so with good, so are spirits and the living eternally separated.

What in the dark ages was Christianity but a darker thing, infuriating the very mind, the beneficiary, that, if perverted, leaves the world a blank?

Under the authority of Gibbon, the historian, the preternatural darkness of the three hours, time, is said to have happened during the lifetime of Seneca and the elder Pliny, not mentioned by them, great natural philosophers as they were, and particularly collecting and describing such remarkable incidents! But it is not proved the Christ arose the third day after his crucifixion; or that his body was in the tomb the second day; or that his spirit could be impeded one moment after death, from its appropriate elements.

"The word for wisdom, in Asia, and in Hebrew, was chest; and when put into Greek, it was christ; and when put into Latin, it was christus."—*Jacobs*.

Incarn was the word. When was Christ born? Was he any but a fictitious personage?

Leo X. said, "it is well known how profitable this fable of Christ has been to us." The gospels were vamped up, at the council of Nice.

What did not these ecclesiastics expect of the world, of Constantine, and all the future?

Had the true Christ been apparent, the Jews would have rushed at the true savior of the world.

All the world never could have been kept back at all, at no time, from that most vital fact.

But in the nature of things of this universe, there can be no Christ, no Savior, if there be a Creator.

You must first uncreate the universe, to make a Christ.

Luke and Matthew differ about the genealogy of Christ, very essentially from each other, and certainly from truth. One having many persons more than the other, having Jacob for Joseph's father, and the other Heli; and both failing to connect Christ with the genealogy of Abraham or David! Now by-the-by, they have no genealogy at all. All are false, faith and Christ.

Kings and priestocracies forced the faith about Christ, supported by ignorant vassals, others knowing better then and now, merely to court popularity, that they have sought through peculiar faith. How servile the sentiment, how ignoble the thought, that when in Rome we must do as the Romans do! They have licked the dust off the Pope's feet! Is that manly; is it not like the beast? What humbugs, peculiar faith, priestocracy, and absolutism: how costly to the sovereign people. Peculiar faith has the road too much to preferment and popularity in the world, and that too most undeserved. Was there ever such a being as Christ? Let all rational beings then investigate, otherwise they will be wofully deceived by the ignorant and impotent priestocracy.

If individuals should be degraded, who violate proper manners, the best that are conventional of society, what can one say of those who violate the first principles of justice to Deity, and impose the deepest frauds on the world?

What power has Christ over sin, more than any other mortal that died? It is not election nor favoritism, but principle, that saves all. Sectarian, the majority of the world invariably dies out of the pale of your peculiar faith. On investigation, who but a coward or slave would own Christ, a most perfect imposition? If the subject were peculiar faiths, I had not written, but they have nothing to do with religion that God requires rational mind to cultivate rightfully.

It is a matter of no moment whether we hear or not of christs or messiahs, who are not available, but stumbling blocks for laity and clergy, while our senses inform us of a God of nature, the majesty of the universe.

As we do not appreciate men by their mere standing alone, but by their life-acts, so no Christ can be verified unless he rule mind through reason and truth, the means that the God of mind uses, an utter impossibility. Christ a God, and let merest mortals conquer him! If God, he could have paralyzed all arms. and convinced all minds. But Christ is dead—what can he do?

The use of such doctrines as Christ uses, not original, not reaching even to God's principles, only proves him a mortal, not a God, and the attempt at miracles lays him and friends low as jugglers, as God's acts universally are conservative, whilst miracles reverse the order of nature, and are destructive.

The use of the doctrines advanced were at best only social principles, used by the world, as China, for centuries. Of course Christ was indebted, though an assumed god, to the supremacy of principles, that are of themselves in abeyance to God, to whom Christ was doubly inferior.

But he even went below them, for he advanced doctrines of blasphemous sectarianism, the lowest of all worldly acts, and expiated therefor with his life.

Of course he was only a man of straw in the hands of blasphemous impostor dramatists, to keep up a degraded game on mind, the main object being vile despotism to defraud and hold mind abject.

Enlightened conscience demands a proved Christ, on certain evidence, properly endorsed, or felony recoils certainly on all offering the bible and doctrine.

Our own mind must have a rightful decision.

If the Jews ever sacrificed Christ, our own sense tells us that he positively was a mortal, for they would not have done it had he proved himself a God.

They would have attempted anything else as soon.   Here is a perfect conclusion to the whole story.

The bible of tradition writers endorse their peculiar faith and their Christ. Who endorse them? They need it above all others, as the veriest world felons, self-evident otherwise. Who came to the rescue? The pulpit priestocracy. The last perjure themselves, the very moment they open their mouth, and of course cannot sustain the bible-perjured authors. What is to be done?

If you believe the book under such inconsistencies, you perjure your mind and soul. The supreme testimony of God's principles excludes all such without mistake. Christ, according to Matthew, c. iv., was said to be led up of the spirit to be tempted of the devil, and was ministered to by angels, neither which can be proved to possibly exist under any circumstances of this universe and God's noblest attributes, much less to have been on our earth.

As to the persecution of Christ so often alluded to, that was sectarian ; on any other a God would have arisen to the dignity of his majesty by that very trial and tribunal, that he would have sought to display his innate greatness. He would have wished it world-wide ; but a mortal would sink, as Christ is said to have done, under it—a mere pagan sectarian.

The world then has not to look at his sectarian persecution so common to the world, but his blasphemy, to assume messiahship, the vilest libel on God.

God never intended that his attributes should be counterfeited. In this all the tinker-cobler dramatists are ever self-evident.

Their hero was to be sacrificed, and some agent had to do it ; but wo to that man! Was there ever such suicidal logic ? Such blasphemous iniquity ? God, perfect purity, had to commit murder to save from sin!

Of all the solecisms of nonsense, this exceeds all.

But they must make him a perpetual drummer travelling agent, to carry out their fooleries.

Such pedant monks had no comprehension of the universe, God or mind, and only looked to their idols of priestocracies. They have committed themselves most hopelessly to inextricable difficulties, and their helpless messiah nobody to nonentity.

Investigation and analysis consign all the peculiar animals to an ignoble position. Their peculiar doctrines place them in peculiar quagmires.

The poor dramatists should have carried him over the converted globe, that had only to see to believe.

As a god of miracles that they claim for Christ, he could have traversed the globe speedily, and have proved then and there, beyond doubt and most convincing to the world, any way desirable to the whole multitude, and done it too like a faithful agent, that mind should not have suffered by delay, neglect or want of the necessary constituent of relief. But messiahship was even ineffectual, a failure, an imposition, incompetent to meet the wants of the world.

What are its wants? Could these infamous daubers tell, or supply if told? They were after making the most out of their ignoble sectarian professions.

Little did these court wily sycophants, who were concocting and writing their schemes for many a year, in their stupidity ever conceive of the sublime intelligence, that rules in the deepest silence and thought the mighty creation, before whom all their innumerable messiahships must sink in the most ignoble insignificance, the most contemptible.

Now the present history of the world proves conclusively, that religious characteristics are a very different thing.

What does Christianity or any peculiar faith avail the world, but enslave it by means of absolutism? At the same time serving to extract the cream of the benefits of the world for the few, but yielding only bitter dregs. The justice that suits the wants of the world is the unadulterated gift of God.

Nations that profess all the pretences of Christian, Mahometan, or any other peculiar policy, do not possess the proper policy of nations of the world of God, as has been proved in India, Palestine, and elsewhere, most abundantly, that have been overrun by several peculiar faiths.

Nor is part of Christian America exempt, when we contemplate the deplorable intoleration that drove the Mormons from several states, and finally to seek the stern injustice of the western wilderness.

The tender mercies of any peculiar faith are tyranny and oppression, that go to extremes, as impunity attends.

The world has its measure of peculiar faith overflowing, without one mark of respect of its intrinsic value, as it trades and speculates on assumed capital.

China has its three hundred millions of people, disposed like the world to be truly and rationally religious, but where is the way ? Would all these be permitted to be lost, if Christ were the only way ? we may well ask the balance of the world. But is not the incarnation of Christ a sublime idea ? It is most ridiculous, and one of the old exploded notions of Eastern Asia. It is said of " The grand Lama, in whom the God of Thibet has just become incarnate." " Vichenou now becoming incarnate in a black shepherd, and under the name of Chrisen, he delivered the world of the venomous serpent Calengarn, and thus crushed his head, after having been wounded by him in the heel." " Bhudd is the ninth incarnation of Vichenou." And the last had priority to Christ's time by many centuries. But it is nothing to the purpose anyway, as they are all fictions of priestocracies. They must stick to their faith, whether their faith sucks to truth.

The Jews or gentiles could not have been chained back from rescuing their savior, who, as God and immortal, could never have been identified with earth or death.

Christ, if equal to God, must have been self-existent, therefore could not be begotten consistently with the prior character of God. This proves his false pretences.

We always wish to be understood, of considering him nothing but a fiction, his claimed functions being never in existence.

Bibles of tradition suggest invariably their true character : Faith novels, fiction and legends, story and history mixed, used as expedient. All pious forgeries, supported by such. The world has been tyrannized over by the peculiar bibles, the peculiar engine of priests. How could Christ, who was begotten, be equal to God, who was unbegotten ?

There can be no true trinity of similar natures, in all this. But his resurrection is certain, says the preacher bigot, who sketches the fictions of faith, over the powers of death, that declares immediate dissolution ?

Hence, they absurdly prove their solecism in language.

Was the body there : Is that certain ?

Who would risk the perjury in swearing it ?

What makes Christ any better, than others of his order ?

He was of the priestocracy. Was he less in collusion than the balance ? There is but one sermon, the main one to be preached about any bible's authenticity, that if established, proves itself for a messiah or any creed necessary.

But all faith creeds have to be peculiar, else none could advance as a system of peculiar faith, and the peculiar interests of the priestocracy.

But christianity claims pre-eminence in eliciting the arts and sciences ! Has the true analysis ever been written ?

Arts and sciences flourish, despite of all peculiar faith christians or any.

Arts and sciences have flourished in lands of superstition, as in Egypt and India. Mind is the thing everywhere.

Distinguished men have been claimed as members of the church? Does that prove any proper conclusion under the true analysis ? Among others, Washington is claimed. Washington was prudent in his faith. He believed in a supreme being, and acted becomingly as a man. He was above the corruption of peculiar or church faith.

If Christ had performed the miracles mentioned, he would have performed all necessary for the world and that age, satisfactory for all minds that could not have been kept back. But then this destroys doubtlessly the original economy of mind, the free agency of which would be absorbed in the defined positions of exact example.

Free agency of mind kills all messiahships.

But all about Christ is mere afterthought, that could not reach any, much less the whole. It cannot take hold of mind at its creation, and therefore is a perfect nullity, and the cobblers ought to be done with this falsity, this ignominious blasphemy. They were stupidly blind.

All minds have resurrection at once and final, till another change of purification, and that dispenses with Christ's peculiar one when all are universal. Mind emanates from God ; peculiar faith and all its peculiar machinery separate it from God as far as in them lies.

Christ a God and son of a God, and still let mortals master him ?   What an imbecile God !   What stupid dramatists—yet what politic priestocracies.

But you may suppose that it is a mere anachronism in regard to the birth of Christ, as detailed by his pretended biographers.   That is not true, for all the particulars are given to destroy that idea.   God who inspires, does not permit anachronisms, that clearly betray that those were not inspired men, but perjurers.

This is the case with all assuming to be inspired, and thereby proving themselves thus.

As Josephus only translated, not wrote his antiquities of the Jews, A. D., 93, how came the famous history of Christ there, if it were not an interpolation ?

Of course these writers are blasphemers of God, plagiarists of Josephus, and degraded before mind, that they impose upon.   We feel perfectly assured, that there never was and never could be such a man as Christ, as endowed with any mission above that of universal mind.   Luke and Matthew, as canonized saints, cut each other's throats.   As to Christ the savior, nothing less than the Almighty creator can be that, at all times and all circumstances, by the nature of creation, the universe, as he must be omniscient, omnipresent and omnipotent.   Now Christ was localized as a mortal on earth, when the functions of a true savior of the universe required absolute omnipresence, and this kills Christ's divine essence altogether.   Now the fact is this, that must not be overlooked, that the bible writers of Moses only had a peculiar god, of one abortion earth, to which he was exclusively devoted, and above all to a peculiar little nation of that little earth, and this is the reason, that through their gross ignorance they displayed themselves as animals, in causing other false faiths, one of which was a Christ for one globe, whereas if any such necessity existed, it prevailed for all ; now this could not be accomplished by any such location as the earth, that cannot possibly be the centre of the universe. But the ignoramuses have omitted, by the most vulgar ignorance, the commission for the whole, and that kills it for one !   Complete in Christ as the priestocracy say, when at the same time, no sane mind can begin to start from him as any part of the godhead, that presides over and comprehends the universe.

We grant you that the Christ spoken of, is a peculiar person in a most peculiar trinity, that cannot possibly be identified with the creator of the universe.

The four-cornered earth-god of Judaism is unknown to us, and would be to all honorable and high-minded committees of the world.   Can any physiologist ever deny the principles of his science, that deny to a mortal all such stuff and nonsense of pedigree ? But you are the very persons that are alarmed about religion !   You could not destroy its elements of any rational mind, do what you will.   But you may rest assured, that you washed your hands of any especial guardianship of rational religion, the very moment you espoused peculiar faith.

Religion is too pure, after such espousals to have you for her patron, be you assured of that, all of you.   If you wish us to adopt your peculiar faith, first destroy our reason. Grace and mind emanate from the same source, and must go together.

But you pretend as if you could decide, that mind is self-confident and relies on itself, because it rejects your peculiar faith errors.   It does no such thing ; it relies on God its author, and to whom it has to alone humble itself, in the glorious principles of causation to the prostration of all atheism, and polytheism, for if there were billions of nature and gods, all are subordinate to the supreme being who rules this universe.

But your pulpit preachers say that the soul that does not look to Christ for salvation, destroys its own peace.   We believe most sincerely that any minds rational enough to ascertain the true position, destroy it as far as in them lies, if they dare look to any such pretence.

But you say, that God is too great and sublime for the soul, not to have an intermediate.   You did not think so, when you adopted the old testament to bolster up the new, in which nearly every page God is made the companion of priests and prophets, his pretended mouth-pieces.   But then this was the peculiar god of the Jews, who like all other ancients, had their peculiar godhead.   And this very peculiar god you adopted, as you have not altered him, by building on Jewish foundation.

The God of the universe inspires mind through science, but the science of these aforesaid, was too small to give character to their inspiration.

We prove that mind, thus exact by science, corrects all the direct pretensions.

Analyze all, and you will find that all else is imposition and fraud.   Show no false colors.

Entrust your mind to God of the universe, and him alone : you may have to pass through many purer spheres in the series of purification, ere you reach the centre of purity and sublimity.   Pulpit preachers, stop.   Let science and philosophy teach mind. Give up your ghostly and gospel stories and fables.

46

In all this disquisition, it is absolutely essential that all should adhere most strictly to the principles of logic, that is, truth. There are minds in the world that are perfectly worthless in ideas, that cannot see an idea in advance, unless their clique-clan faction demagogue, master, say the word.

How is such mind constituted, and what is the mould? Much of it has little or no use of their honest sense, but little principle, so corrupt has it become. Much of the world seems foolish or deranged on peculiar faith. Is there any earthly being worthy of love, who is necessarily an impostor? How can you, pure-minded, love, respect or esteem such a being?

As to Christ's mission to the whole earth, his resurrection should have been before the whole world, for none to doubt, not merely before the affiliated, but all the Jews, and an adequate number of Gentiles. Who can affirm to it at this day, with any honorable truth? No Jews, no nation, could have been committed against such universal interest; that is impossible. All would have declared for it, had this mission been God-sent. Messiahship is too subordinate.

Christ, as messiah, never existed. These events, recorded, were fiction. But as to the testimony-men: they were good and pure men, you assume. Do you endorse all this, like a fanatic, going it blindly?

Do you endorse them? How can you, when the principals destroy each other, belie themselves, disgrace inspirations, and libel God and mind? They are only equal authority to all other pagans.

Miracle proof as clear as creation proofs, would have prevailed. Do not touch this subject, unless you do it justice. Have no vindictive trifling, for you ignorantly degrade yourself, and do not extricate liars. You identify yourself with them.

What else have you to say? You can say nothing, or commit yourself inextricably, as all must that have anything to do with priestocracies.

Mind is to rise to its universal dignity, in asserting all truths at once independent of priestocracies.

Ah! but these good people could not lie! That is the very thing the bible was written for, to uphold priestocracy and absolute government. You are green if you deny this.

Millions upon millions are daily doing that very same thing, and endorsing them on all this point, from emperors, through popes, to the lowest church character.

The world will never be clear of fool-bibles, till it is freed from their priestocracy fabricators.

The proof is essential, for, if wrong, the whole is an awful conspiracy of the priestocracy, to perpetrate the most blasphemous robbery of God. If this be the word of God, then it should rely on proper, self-evident proofs of God, and nothing less.

But are we going to deny the word of God? No, sir; that cannot be done by the universe, which now supports it; for that very reason we deny all such bibles, that God's divine word of creation denies.

But all this is inspiration! The very assertion declares heinous sin of blasphemy. It is the inspiration of priestocracy, to evil. Inspiration does not kill itself and its God, unless it were a fabrication.

But it is hardly to be presumed that the hundred soldiers would have guarded an empty sepulchre. Presumption, and taking for granted, cannot exculpate perjury.

It is hardly to be presumed that a fact-recording author of sound mind, would have omitted all expedient for the verified identification of Christ. The scripture men assume their position.

It devolves on them to prove the affirmative, or it all falls, as it certainly does, to the ground. The mere assertion, written or oral, of any number of men attempting an impossibility as this, is not testimony. Unless the proper proof is adduced, no assertion is testimony for the enlightened conscience of a rational mind.

Had all this been right, the Roman Empire, as well as the world, would have recorded the whole.

The attributes of the God of omniscience, omnipotence, and omnipresence, exclude Christ, and as his function, creation, is not that of procreation, that necessarily excludes all the pretensions of messiahships in birth, and conclusively proves to the whole world all such as most foolish and vain. So Christ is cut out of his pretensions every way.

But this is to be looked at. If Christ had been a God, would the thing have ever come to this, that even his resurrection should be not only doubtful, but impossible, as stated? God does not leave rational mind to doubt what is certain.

There were, if he ever were, as story tells, the sharp-sighted Jews, as sharp as you can be, who were interested, particularly if any, as the best entitled to have Jesus. All the immortal part was paramount to them, as well as the whole world.

Who are the witnesses of Christ's resurrection?

As to John, he gives no statement of a watch, but says : Ch. xx. verse 17, Jesus saith unto her, (Mary,) touch me not, for I am not yet ascended to my Father. Verse 27, he tells Thomas to " reach hither thy hand, and thrust it into my side." Luke xxiv. 39, " Handle me," (said Jesus.) Luke mentions no guard. Mark has no guard. But, no doubt, Matthew wrote to meet the objections to the resurrection, the best his fiction could.

He says Joseph rolled a great stone to the door of the sepulchre, and departed. Did those who came the next day, who " made the sepulchre sure, sealing the stone, and setting a watch," remove the stone to identify the body ? Not they, as the author tells. Alas ! human nature, thou showest thy mortality, thy duplicity !

But the evangelists were good men, who, of course, would not lie. Yet God's whole bible proves them, and all the affiliated, modern and ancient, all perjurers to all time.

Gentlemen must know that mere assertion, backed by all the millions of affiliated, is not proper testimony till properly proved.

Six hundred thousand men, that lost their lives for one of the twenty-four other pagan messiahs, recorded by Buck, would, as millions affiliated with them, have sworn their souls out of them, that theirs was the correct one.

Now, as all messiahships are the rankest perjuries, what prevents these writers—call them by any name, locate them any where at any ancient, corrupt time, give them a century or more to digest their nefarious schemes of governmental priest and despotic policy, unite church and state. emperors and soldiery, to back them—from an equal, if not worse, perjury ?

These few men-writers wrote for one of the priestocracy, and were of the priestocracy, the most corrupt of all belial corruption.

Now honorable, though verdant modern, do not touch this perjury of messiahships.

But the bigot, who has no brains nor principles, no logic nor truth, who cannot prove his position, nor let the proof of yours reach his mind, says you deny Christ; then you must prove the contrary ! O no, fanatic, your logic is as false as your faith. You stand in place of those men ; now prove it.

What can you do with such peculiar minds, that ask for proof of the negative ? It negatives all reason.

Advocates of messiahship forget the principles of logic, in the quagmires of fanaticism, which is abundant now all over the world.

The testimony of the scriptures should be from Christ or God, vouched documents then and now, to possess the proper character and nature of testimony. In whose keeping is all this ? Of course, in the affiliated of peculiar faith, that is itself an imposition. See what are the horrors of sectarianism, between the Christians and Jews, who both differed on this very thing of testimony, which, after all, is no testimony at all, as the whole world of peculiar faith can offer no testimony of truth worthy of a truthful mind. Why is the world cheated, defrauded in this wise, by any peculiar faith, all of which is a false pretence ?

Christ's is not a safe position, as it is not one of principle, for it, as all others, presents sectarianism.

Gratuitous sects are hardly, gratefully received.

A large part of the people is not allowed to read or circulate the word of Moses and Christ, so-called, much less enter into appropriate discussions of the balance. Is the world governed by merits or policy ?

The fictions of peculiar faith go for the last eternally, and are a dangerous game.

What has religion to do with the gospel fiction of St. Matthew, or St. Clement's drama, called once, Euodius ? What was Isaiah, vii. 14, to Ahaz in the sign : " Behold, a virgin shall conceive, and bear a son, and shall call his name Immanuel" ? if that sign was not to be given him (Ahaz) for several centuries after ? How absurd to apply that to a being called Christ ! This is a low way of meeting proof. Whoever advances these, is guilty of the deepest felony by his crimes.

Christ's humanity assuming a godhead, has left a reproachful stigma upon his dramatists.

He had been clothed, fiction as he was, with the highest earthly renown, had he unassumingly died the hero of rational religion. Then, indeed, his triumph had been complete, equal to the crisis. This is all that is wanting now, to cause the world to progress on its right elements to the best appreciation, the best happiness attainable. The world has mind and mind's God, why not act ?

The character of Christ might have been taken from several prototypes years before him. There are many sources to originate such. Is it not a drama, after all ? Were there not many analogous incidents in that play ? But the purity and character of the ancient fathers of the christian church, place them above suspicion and reproach. Let the truth be told of the scenes that occurred at the council of Nice, held in 325 A.D. What was the corruption at that council? Is any mind prepared to endorse it? Disgraceful scenes of persecution followed after the Arian controversy, for much of the balance of the century and long after. Church writers say that councils opposed falsehood to falsehood, fraud to fraud. Deposition and excommunication were decreed on both sides.

The imperial authority obsequiously acquiesced in this struggle of power, as each was triumphant!

Furious rabbles on both sides resorted to riots and massacres. What a state of things under the pretended mantle of holiness. What a desecration!

Christ violated several of the highest duties of religion to God and man, in blasphemy and sectarianism. He is in direct antagonism to God and his principles.

Christ and the Devil were in company with each other, a very suspicious circumstance, as the paternity of both is due to the same priestocracies. Had Christ been a God, he would have performed real miracles as benefiting mankind in all the real blessings of mind, in science, philosophy, and rational religion.

He is claimed as competent to expel devils, the tempters, but we prove that there are no such beings, but in imagination of the dramatists. Consequently, both Christ and the Devil, are nonentities. It is perfect blasphemy to invest any individual with the rights and functions of the Creator. But love your enemies. Yes, but this doctrine could not be upheld by principles at the start, as Christ founded his position on the elements of sectarianism, not universal brotherhood, and the very reverse of such love. He merely superseded the Jewish peculiar faith, by his peculiar faith. Now, as a proof of his doctrines being at variance with principles, the Roman church have destroyed sixty-five millions of people, as affirmed by Buck.

Can there be love between friends, much less enemies. Between those of the same church doctrines under the banner of the cross, literally of blood?

Let us define what is the position of all peculiar faith.

It is comprehended as well by the Romans, as Protestants.

When we advance effectual batteries on either, the most ample protestations are then made, that the position attacked is not christianity. In that way, christianity can be totally disclaimed. Christianity commenced in the very elements of sectarianism, and could not exist one moment without it. In her battlings, she has been parricidal to her own progenital relations. Again, she was in direct antagonism with principles of rational religion. God is unity, and stands on that immutable basis. But she affects to suppose that God has three natures. But supposition will not do, as that has been the world's incendiary. We must go on facts. No one has a right to any such supposition, in contravention of mathematics, an exact science, that teaches three are three, and one is one, the peculiar logic and metaphysics of priestocracies to the contrary. No advocate of peculiar faith can make three natures in Godhead! That unmakes God, by its divisions. There can be no inconsistent nature, as God is unity, and none else on all the highest principles of his own. Yes, but says the advocate, you have two natures, soul and body, yet one being. That proves nothing conclusive against, but all for the unity of God. God can operate best with all his attributes united in him. How absurd to have divided into three separate divisions, none of which can be efficient. All this is man's foolishness. Be done with such idle delusions of priestocracies. But this doctrine is so, says the presumptive vassal, and Christ is an incarnation. Which of the incarnations, as there were nine before him, on the authority of the sacred words of the Bhuddists, who have an equal claim in peculiar faith. So all of this faith is in bad company. Christ was a blasphemous sectarian, in antagonism with the God of nature. The moment that peculiar faith of the christian or any other is advanced, that very moment principles are left behind.

You must look at the nature of mind, that requires principles, not messiahships at all. But in matters of faith other matters cannot come in. That doctrine is Jesuitical, as truth is expedient, and cannot be excluded—therefore, unless we investigate comprehensively, we do no justice to the justice of the whole subject. When we undertake to investigate God's word, we must comprehend the whole universe proof on the best analysis. But the idea is, we must just look at God's book, as it is called, a mere bible of tradition. We go to that, and ask for the proof—the main proof is not there. God has not said it is his book, but man said it. Man wrote it. It is claimed to be inspiration, and must have all truth as God's, else it is entirely false; for God is ever consistent with himself, an immutable being. The consequence is, that we find that we cannot stop short of the whole universe, to get at the appreciation of God's word. The very position that Christ was made to take by his dramatists was necessarily that of a mortal sectarianism. What inhuman persecutions of the Jews have been thereby perpetrated? What principles can you hear from vassal minds? Are they not the affiliated trainbands of unprincipled demagogues, base masters, men of one idea and no principle? The very foundation of Christianity presents no principles, a robbery of God, and a plagiarism on the Jewish bible, in complete rebellious antagonism?

Corrupt man will do anything for money or power. He will invoke all the lies that can be perpetrated on earth; all the perjury to sustain, all the murder and felony to uphold it. The knowing ones that continue it are just as bad as the original perpetrators. From this position are to be excepted all that have had no means to know better.

Christ was born as all other mortals—all else are falsehoods, most clearly.

What good will has the Christian to the Mahometan; nay, let us come nearer home, and to our times; what has he to the Mormons, whom he hath persecuted with the sword?

But the last are fanatics! And what is the Christian? All in the quagmire of superstition. Christ was a man of straw, opposing, as a sectarian, the other sects of the Jews. The best view that can be obtained of him is that he was a blasphemous sectarian. He has left behind him abundant examples. for perverted genius to originate other sectarianisms. The Mormons have done so, as well as the Mahomedans and others. But both are said to practice polygamy. Then they have less principles of religion, as the patriarchs. As polygamists, they are felons.

All the elements of Christianity prove explosion. The only divine grace is of God, which the inalienable rights of creation give to mind, independent of all such pretenders, who are equally indebted. The Christians and Mormons, Jews and Mahometans, have too much enmity ever to be reconciled on this earth. Among them, envy stalks as a puissant evil genius, arousing the worst human passions. Why so? They all are after power.

Their sectarianism has begotten anathemas, curses, excommunications, confiscations, inquisitions, proscriptions, murders, massacres, wars, despotisms, dispensations.

Christ makes the world sectarian, with a wicked derangement, not yet allayed, consequently he is self-condemned, as the most grovelling of mortals.

But his worst position is that he is in blasphemous antagonism with the God of nature; unless this is palliated, that he is so with the peculiar god of the Jews.

All sectarians bend the laws of the God of nature to their notions and self-interests, being the greatest evil.

Fishermen are assumed to have been the writers of the New Testament, when it is clear that the astutest of their stupid priestocracy wrote them. They have lied, and carried by their falsehoods the mass blindly, or the last have been hypocritical. How easy was it to build on the Oriental incarnations! They have made a drama, for the worst of purposes. Tear the mantle of deception from its brow, and give its exposure before the world.

As this drama was written after the destruction of Jerusalem by Titus, how easy was it to prophecy it?

Christ is in an inglorious minority, that will grow beautifully less. God will have to secure the majority, the whole, and he does what he has been always doing, having the universe in his holy protection.

Were there ever blinder dolts than these bigots?

They are deranged with the fascinations and delusions of the world, forgetting mind and its God.

What relation do the Mahometan, Mormon, Christian and Jew bear to each other? They all are the creatures of one creator. They stand to each other by the obligations of universal brotherhood, and yet they all are deadly hostile, and prove it when they have all necessary power. It is utterly impossible for them to be united, under their sectarian banners, only on the standard of Deity alone.

What science we get from priestocracies.

Their devil, who figures so much in the land where the captive Jews abided in the East, was the third power evidently in the world's government. He is equivalent to the Brahmin's destroyer. He caused man's soul to be lost, as their bible-fable pretends, and cost the godhead, in part, his life. He caused Christ to be destroyed. Was this the reason that there were so many foolish subsequent messiahs? Did not messiahship leave the world in a much worse condition than it found it by the loss of its many millions, slaughtered for its follies and crimes?

Let all the messiah-pretenders think that the grace that operated constantly in this one world, necessarily proves that its bounty is adequate for the whole universe, and conversely that the grace that operates for the universe necessarily proves amply abundant for this world.

Yes, that grace that sustains the universe sustains all its parts, this world included, and decides the question fully to the eternal silence of the priestocracy.

We see now that psychology explains something of the acts and admission of minds affected.

We have seen, as the experimentalists, that even seven devils have been admitted to have been taken psychologically from one person, who had previously preached, and who had been inebriated by partaking of water for wine! Depend no longer on the vain pretensions of such messiahship; the only way for you to escape condemnation, is God-intention.

John's epistle is a lie for those believing in Christ. Sectarianism presents the finest character of Christ.

What more enormous iniquity was ever instituted than by the system of Christ, as to forgiveness of sins?

The evil-doers might transgress to an excess and luxuriance, and by all the pious pretences of repentance, they could be saved at once by a conversion.

What does it avail a ruined world, that death-bed repentance should be claimed by its oppressors?

The only pure morals and religion, inculcate a life of best actions and proper responsibility. What has the world to do with a drama that advances Christ as a monk-hero!

What can be worse than the shifting explanations of all the bibles of tradition? At one time Christ is a god, then he is a man! He is the worst anti-god, and this is the position of his followers—all!

As much as the world needed Christ's direct and personal agency, as the priestocracy pretended, he had to give it up unredeemed! Barabbas and Christ—Christ was the worst of the two, as he blasphemously usurped God's rights, and of course then as now, and all the time past as present, the whole world of mind had to improve the God-given faculties. Who can be nearer to mind and the universe than the Creator omnipotent, who is also omnipresent? Who is more their savior than the Almighty? Who more love-giving than the Author of Grace, necessarily resulting from creation? But the advocates claim Christ to be equal to God; that is absurd blasphemy—a mortal to the God of the universe! Well may we ask who are the robbers, but the peculiar faith doctrinists? If the bible's assertions are untrue, they are advocated by falsifiers.

The world of peculiar faith is made a robber by messiahs. Never was there greater need of advocacy of truth—from libels on mind and God in every pulpit-sermon. We might overlook the idle declamation, but for the widespread ruin to the world.

Why was Christ's prayer used? It refers to God as the source of all grace, and absurdly libels him as a tempter.

If addressed to sects, it is wisely spoken.

Let us give no superior title for an inferior one. We must never take anything for granted that is not rational and probable. The advocate of Christ affects to seek nothing grovelling, yet he has taken the most exact pains to reach it, by not considering that God alone exalteth as God! Anything more is not practicable.

Christianity was born of Judaish sectarianism from superstition, and goes against justice, honor and virtue, espousing, as she does, blasphemous antagonism to God the Creator, not god the peculiar.

All these links of peculiar pagan faith went down to the remotest antiquity, to the first sect or peculiar doctrine. Rational religion is the only original, the only one to exist for all time and all eternity.

On due analysis, it will be seen that the more destitute mind was of science, the more superstitious it was, the more polytheism abounded—all departments of nature in her remotest divisions, had peculiar gods or presiding divinities.

Polytheism did preside in all things. Judaism was an improvement, and no more, on its predecessor, as mind improved.

It took the idea of two peculiar gods, but mixed one or both with priestocracy, along with much of their vices.

Everything savored of the priest; he was the first to greet the new born, presiding over birth, marriage, and burial. His was a mighty dynasty, and the fear of superstition, added to his familiarity with his peculiar god or gods, made the little priest-ridden world tremble.

The introduction of Christ was an effort through the priestocracy, who were potent in this matter, at greater improvements; for the mind of the world has been progressive by the innate bounty, grace and science of its Creator, and carried all along with it. This has caused the priestocracy to resort to the most wily duplicity and sophistry, to uphold their ungodly schemes. But they have always been wretchedly short-sighted, in their cunning and artifices.

They have exhausted all the expedients of intrigue and wretched imposition, and yet seek to prop their tottering and base-gotten usurpation.

But what virtue could possibly be in any such imbecility, that betrays at birth, during life and at death, all the signs of a degraded mortal, because he was, or his foster-fathers, blasphemous impostors.

The very moment he or his dramatists affected one function more than mortal, that very moment he was blasphemously antagonistical to God, who is the only creator from the nature of the creation provable, and all else are creatures. All on earth are mortals; and the very moment they assume any other function, they are not gods, however called, but impostors, a step from the sublime to the ridiculous; so Christ, who was necessarily sectarian to all the world in general, and the Jews in particular, in direct antagonism to God, his conservative principles and attributes, having the essential elements of destruction in his own doctrines, sent forth sectarians to cut out from the world particularly all that was God's, to act the veriest robbers, the most imbecile pretenders upheld by the sword that established them.

All this sectarianism has been too long the right arm of arch autocratic despotism, in deception and fraud on the world.

But the followers of Christ disobeyed precepts in the crusades? They did as well as Christ; they followed his example as a sectarian, and could not secure universal brotherhood that was not in his doctrines.

He quarrelled with and reproached the Jews, from whom he was sectarian, deeply antagonistic to God, whose principles do not clash. Christ fell, because it was idle to contend against the world with his few. His followers fought, because the world upheld its course by the sword. What is the difference? Christ used whips in the temple. That was personal violence, compulsion, intoleration as far as he dared. His sectarianism had not the proper elements of peace with God or man. His death was from blasphemy to the first, involving the severest dissension and opposition to the Jews.

He sought to supersede sectarianism, by sectarianism. All such will perish, must go down, ignobly fall to rise no more before the great lights of mind, rational, cultivated by rational, not peculiar education.

Those seeking peace conventions must go home, and first change there all sectarianism. They must first unite the Jew and Mahometan, Christian and Mormon, on the only proper basis of rational mind, and then move forward with the most brilliant prospect of universal brotherhood; as long as sectarianism exists, it being an unholy power, unprincipled and degradingly selfish, give it power, and it will unconscientiously abuse it most assuredly. All this is a most dangerous, vile, and demoralizing evil. But, says the sectarian in his despair, what is the position that puts down sectarianism? It cannot be sectarianism; not at all. It is the God-post of religion, and that between mind alone and God. The suggestion under the noblest toleration and spirit of freedom, is made. Religion is the duty to God. It is not with speculation, and the balance is left where found. With God there is no clash of principle, and his unity absorbs allegiance exclusively. Let bigots learn wisdom by his philosophy, and truth by his works. His functions are alone comprehended in unity, so much so, that the very moment any messiahship is offered, the pretence cuts out proportionately his better power, divests in ratio just that amount of God's perfect attributes. Think of it, a mortal, as all on earth necessarily are, clothed with electricity as part of his duty! The blockhead impostor could not be invested, were God divested, for if God had lost his functions, no less being could assume them. Priestocracy, be done with your perfect nonsense, your craziness. The tinkers knew nothing of the universe: did not know what they pretended to! The miserable botches! But to the objectors, that Christ's followers did not obey precepts: how could they, when he gave them neither precept nor example of religion? What could have been a worse and bloodier proof of Christ's own seed planting, than the butchery and reckless persecution of the Jews by the christians? Did he not invade the sanctity of the Mosaic law, by his own direct sectarianism? Did not the christians necessarily have to involve themselves with all sectarians of any country in which they sojourned?

Did they not involve themselves in bloody antagonism with the prevailing sects of the Roman Empire, and finally usurped their power? This is the history of all sectarianism. The world has not analyzed its position. Masses do not think readily but roughly; they follow file leaders: the thinking mass has been the interested, the deceiving mass. Give us no trammels, no regimes of the schools of the world. Rational religion has modestly bided her time, and raised no world commotion; lovely in her attributes, she upholds her sublime dignity. At no time did the whole world need Christ's mission, much more than at the very time claimed of his being on earth, so far as corruption and ignorance prevailed. None could have filled his own mission better, as he ought to have effected what his disciples could not do. But his dramatists forgot in their stupidity to send him forth to all mankind, and perfect his world's mission by a world's conversions. They were estopped by the world's facts.

The faith of Judaism was peculiar, that of christianity is peculiar; neither mended the matter; both must be cut up as dry weeds that interfere with mind.

All peculiar faiths present sectarianism throughout. Judaism could not answer, being a failure; so is christianity. All peculiar faith, no matter how arrogant by reason of its constituent elements, is void. How can the doctrines of any peculiar faith, christian or not, stand, when their truth is unfounded?

Did not the christians employ known falsehoods in support of their cause? Did they not forge books in support of their doctrine? What is the account of miracles, but forgery? It is nothing, less, or else. Among these forgeries, according to the ancient history of universalism, were the sibylline oracles.

"It appears to have been seized with avidity by the orthodox christians in general; and all their principal writers quoted it as genuine, and urged its testimonies as indubitable evidence. It is mortifying to relate, that not one of them had the honesty to discard the fraud, even when it was detected by their heathen opponents." This is the way a lying and deceitful world is made. Where is the right kind of people to suffer the world so maltreated.

As to the love of the brethren and neighbors of christians, that ought to extend to the love of mankind, a universal brotherhood, of course.

But how can it, when between Romanists, Protestants, and the Greek churches, are arrayed bitter animosities, much less between Christians, Jews, Mahometans, and Mormons. None of these worthies are supreme to the others, as sectarianism was engendered even by Christ, who inveighed against the Jews as vipers, setting himself and sect against them. What virtue has this peculiar faith other, than less alloy which they obtained of mind of civilization? Now, rational religion has no peculiarity, as she universally refers alone to God, with whom she leaves all minds. With the utmost faithfulness, she brings mind to see its chief good. Is there any application of religion to self?' Negative it candidly at once. It meets best all the demands of mind, to reach better what the schools of the world admit satisfactorily. But the christian faith is claimed to be the world guardian of science and invention! Let the sun of the Roman Empire, set in such horrid darkness, and all the rest of the world declare, when this faith found it flourishing. If not accountable for all this, as we think not, then let it not assume to be the world guardian of science, but leave all to mind that it has most ungratefully and scandalously perverted. Not only has Satan, a fourth power in polytheism, been acknowledged, but he is invested as the power and prince of the air, as said by Christ. What part of the gospel is true? It is exploded. No part of the New Testament was written until long after the crucifixion, is even admitted by churchmen. All such gospels are the most untrue of all things; they are any thing but true. The imposition of hands may have been accomplished through the means of psychology, but such explanation is not essential for an exploded imposition.

What determines the fact of regeneration? That of love to all mankind! How can that be, when it embraces sects that are completely at variance with the individual. Christianity, as Christ committed himself, alienated itself from the Jews. Is regeneration peculiar to christianity? No; not even original, as the Brahmins teach regeneration.

Why did Christ affect love at all, when he hated the Jews? Peter could not have become an apostate to God, when impressions would be paramount.

But then Christ told him of his apostacy; but this was after the manner of men, not of God.

Analysis proves Christ a blasphemous culprit, or his dramatists are. Divest this subject of its domestic and educational familiarity, as household matters, heirlooms from parents to children, impressions from superstitious fear, and all rational minds will be struck at the imposition. A correct system of faith, cannot set father against son: God never instituted such sectarianism or heresy, to nature's laws. Christians are of the various forms of superstition, struggling for existence and emolument.

When the chief of the apostles was a perjurer, an equal was a traitor, and the balance deserters! Could they have been unbelievers? The whole field of Palestine was before Christ, and that of the balance of the world was unfilled in his lifetime. Was he not a deserter, in filling this mission of a God? Who so potent to fill it, as he whose mission was thus expressly claimed? Yet after eighteen centuries, more than a majority is leaving the world constantly, to whom this mission neither comes nor benefits, much less convicts and converts. It is entirely incompetent.

In regard to science, claimed exclusively by christianity, where are the noblest orations of Greece and Rome, among the best of the world yet? Where are their poets and historians? Are philosophy and science claimed by christianity, that warred upon them, and is yet most bigotedly hostile in the arena of peculiar faith? Is all claimed yet anything but the triumphant action of mind? Will any anylist risk his reputation to deny this? But christianity is the nearest approach to civilization. Civilization has finally to master all peculiar faiths, and establish a better faith, that spreads its fostering around the world. All these show the triumphs of mind, that responds to God. Do you prove its noblest institution? Do you, sectarian, tell of universal brotherhood, when you must doff your sectarianism, and to do so effectually, you must resort to pure unity of God. This is the highest evidence of science and philosophy to eschew paganism.

In ancient times, men worshipped idols, beasts, vegetables, in all the diversity and excess of polytheism. That showed the ignorance, perversion, corruption and degradation of mind, that has laid aside one error after another, till it has reached the least, the trinity, and its attendants. By this, all disinterested and unaffiliated must see that it is mind, not christian or any peculiar faith, except as to its best action, that is ever through mind, that the world can be set right.

To make trinity unity, and unity trinity, the very essence of science is subverted, and truth is debased, prostituted, and sacrificed, before reason, for the sake of sophistry. Can you look an honest man in the face, when you claim science for christianity?

Christianity has degraded science, and outraged religion. But woman is indebted to christianity; rather, to the blessings of civilization. Rational mind will effect the whole triumph of civilization, constitutional government, and rational religion, exalting the world.

It took centuries to establish this christian faith, among the Roman provinces; and now great divisions of the Protestant churches affect that it is doubtful whether it is the christian faith! In capturing the emperor, it captured the empire, that was universal, as the best civilization of the day. Ingenuity and plausible sophistry, help to uphold it.

It might be asked, Which is less sinful, peculiar faith with all the arts of life, or that in a state of crude nature? The most refined is superstition, dressed up as visionary through dreams, visions, omens and oracles, analogous to auguries. What sort of sectarianism was that of Christ; how destitute of principle to turn the father against the son! Principles unite all in one brotherhood. Christ should have had his resurrection at the very moment that his so-called enemies had sought to slay him.

God made the world right; but the Christ tinkers are too stupid to be enlightened. Joe Smith, Mahomet, and Jesus Christ, are a worthy trinity, and illustrate their own life dramas by their deaths. The worst motives caused their being gotten up. Like the thefts of the Spartans, they sought to deceive and not to be detected.

Indebted to the imperial arms of Rome, introduced as one of her additions of faith and worship, she has been presented the world as of doubtful character.

The ancients, in seeking diamonds, had not crystals.

The language of inferiors, as subject to their king, is no less slavish, than all such doctrines for mind.

As there can be no devils, Christ never performed the miracles, and there is an end to messiahs.

Shall dead nonentities triumph over living rights?

How much is assumed for christianity, that trades on the rich treasures and capital of mind! All science is impudently claimed by her! One of the great changes in the world, for the better, was, the triumph of mind over the barbarity of priestocracies. Had not the abolition of human sacrifices been fully established nearly one hundred years prior to the christian era so called, that might have been claimed as her triumph. We see here one of the most degraded acts of priestocracy expunged by a decree of the Roman Senate, and that by the light of mind. The christian cannot be a divine faith, as such peculiarity can be neither universal nor perpetual, the prerogatives of Deity. No monk, no priestocrat, can ever analyze this subject of the worldly, nor give it its proper solution. Christianity, no more than any other peculiar faith, can stand the proper scrutiny of mind.

Had science been at all indebted to christianity, it had kept science and the world at an advancing progress; but all fell into a worse state, till mind rescued them.

Christianity found what all other peculiar faiths did, the lights and improvement of mind in the world. Upon what prophecies is it founded especially?

If there were any, the Jews would have adopted them.

The hostility of the Jews against christianity, proves it decidedly sectarianism, not religion, in which they, as the world, had an interest too serious to be rejected.

But to the peculiar prophecies. "The sceptre shall not depart from Judah, nor a lawgiver from between his feet, until Shilo come." How often had the sceptre departed previously from the Jews, in their various captivities?

What could have been a more effectual abolition of their power, and what was left when Christ is said to have been born? The manner of their prophecies are expressed enigmatically in time, or mysteriously, like the Delphic oracles. If they were prophecy, truth and fact, all inspiration, and coming from God directly, why did he not come out with all such, especially the fundamental gospels. What can you make out of such pretences? Anything and everything. What were they worth? Nothing to the people, but all to the priestocracy. They were Delphic oracle-capital. There should be no false positions, on this pretended security. Have the Romanists not only been scared off from investigating, but reading the bible? Are the Protestants now prevented, by the sophistry of their priestocracy, from rational discussion, one of the vital essentials of rational religion? Are they fearful of proscription, to do justice to the most important subject? Will they in private declare a candid rejection of the bible, and yet outwardly and most hypocritically affect to adopt it? What kind of a corrupt world do they make? Of what use or value was the mission, when it could not be carried out in full execution, not even to half the world, after more than eighteen centuries? It is the most senseless presumption, that christianity causes science exclusively to flourish. Of course, then, there was no science before christianity?

Where all the ancient arts and sciences of China? Of the world?

Where is the post-office of the ancients, and now of the moderns, the newspaper, the steam-engine, the electric telegraph, representative constitutional government, that ought to shame for mind all usurpation in its place. The mighty stride of civilization is by mind, the God-gift. Where was christianity found, but around the eastern Mediterranean? Where now is it?

Has not the Mahommedan ousted it for more than five hundred years, from its many first strongholds, as Constantinople, Syria, east of that sea and all south? And has not this bled the world? What are her or any other peculiar faith pretensions before the real might of rational mind, that will rule the world, and rule out all peculiar faiths?

After all the pretended divinity established by messiahship, prayer ought to have been effectual for the absent and the distant, if available at all. That of any messiah that pretends to be any god at all, ought to have converted the whole world. That would have shown a God. Even the ministers if properly endowed, should have secured a world's conversion. Were the prayers of Christ so available? If not, why continue this vilest humbug?

How was Jesus Christ of the seed of David?

Christ the pretended messiah was conceived in the brain of man, not in womb of woman.

What can non-resistance do in a wild and reckless community, when law and order are defied? It is a radical defect, a vice, that invokes oppression of the unprincipled. Justice to man, prevents non-resistance. He must not suffer himself to be crushed to the earth; that is a social suicide that must not be, when principles take precedence and will harmonize the whole universe.

You affect to consider Christ as a sacrifice, which however fictitious, you do not analyze; you do not consider how much mind, the world of mind has been tortured, crucified, outraged and sacrificed by his false doctrines. All this must be considered, in its various particulars.

We give credit to the world for wishing well, if all go right with its self-interest, but now it has an opportunity of exhibiting that in execution, in paying due respect to all the known rights of mind.

But the rule of Confucius and the Chinese, as used by Christ, will make man the best of men. That was only a small part of God's code, universal principles. That recognises the first start of faith as wrong, in the necessity pretended of a man-savior. One grand comprehension must be complete and correct on conservative principles, that vindicates a creator-savior.

A false system of faith as all peculiar systems, usurps religion, sophisticates the mind, corrupts and prevents all the nobler sentiments that should be paid wholly to God alone.

When man undertakes to correct God, of course we should revolt at the blasphemy, whether verbal or in mere books called bibles. The heads of all peculiar faiths, vainly and ingloriously aspire to this degradation, as did Christ.

The peculiar people were the very ones gifted with peculiar prophecies, to know this peculiar person, but as they did not, however vital the interest, then the imposition should not be practiced on us. If any mortals are witnesses, then the Jews conclusively rule out Christ, whom truth excludes.

In Christ we can have no honest faith, and shall a dishonest faith save us? This condemns the whole matter of messiahship. But Christ surpasses all others—the world. But analysis of truth, places mind and principles far above his or any, the loftiest pretensions. His is altogether out of sight among the others, before their tribunal. But this is the only way whereby we can be saved. It is one of the very ways, whereby you and the world are damned and cursed to the practicable issue.

But if we doubt, we are damned! Do not all peculiar faiths hold to all such doctrines through the policy of their priestocracy, that theirs is the true and only light? But how can you see by other's eyes, the faith? Who is responsible in all such folly, to help you in your misfortune? Your injury in future cannot be alleviated by their punishment, hence you must judge the case fit for faith, that is truth, else proportionate injury accrues, even to deepest suffering.

It is very rational that christianity should be the especial keeper of the light of science, when she abjures reason, the light of science for faith, the tool of absolutists, kings and priestocrats. Christ is quoted as speaking as man never spake. The bible speaks, man speaks, the affiliated priestocracy speak, and spake for their side of the question, and worse than all, the affiliated puff the speaking, a trick of all tricks.

The bible describes the casting out devils, and that explains it at once to be an imposition, as none are proved in scripture.

In making a devil, they have lowered their god of their heaven to be the keeper of a house of rowdies! And in doing this, they, the bible writers, have degraded themselves to the lowest of all menial offices, perjury perpetrators!

Mark, ch. v. 9., speaks of Christ casting out legion of devils.

First he tells him that had been possessed of the devil, to publish the great things, but in the last part of the same chapter, after arousing the damsel, "he charged them strictly that no man should know it."

Why the inconsistency? He acts like a Jesuit. The bible characters are represented as actors, but this is a misrepresentation. Ch. vi. 13., "And they cast out many devils," &c. These are priest tales and logic. There are so many pretended miracles, and yet unbelief, the thing the peculiar god was trying to overcome. The very terms bespeak ignorance itself—"for the heart was hardened" and faith. What convenient priest machinery. Ch. vii. 21., "For from within, out of the heart of man, proceed evil thoughts, adulteries, fornications, murders," 24, "and (he) entered into a house and would have no man know it; but he could not be hid!" Does the truth slip out at last, though it convict the character of Jesus? 29, "The devil is gone out of thy daughter." And this man should have known that there was no devil: if anything, that it was a disease pretended to be described. All these bible fictions, mind has to wade through. As sure as there is a God-creator, this man-savior was below mind and principle. That, then, kills his messiahship clearly. He a sectarian pagan mortal, not as good as the reformer Socrates, claiming only to be mortal, aiming at a nobler reform, could not be equal to the creator, a perfect savior of all. Whenever a miracle is pretended or spoken of, it is fiction as sure as a priest is about, and that is certain as a bible describes it. The world could not outlie the priestocracies. Who can use more sophistry to sustain them? What greater proof is there of falsehoods, than in these devil matters.

Spake he as man? He did speak as man blasphemously, but only as a man of straw. With this bible drama, and with miracles, the scenes can shift as the puppets are made. No place is too sacred, no theme too powerful.

Ch. ix. 4., "And there appeared—Elias with Moses." Can spirits return?

Who believes it? It is not worth while to use ventriloquism, for there was more powerful machinery, the plastic lies of the priestocracy, v. 29, "And he (Jesus) said unto them, this kind can come forth by nothing, but by prayer and fasting."

And there was such a thing never. 42, "And whosoever shall offend one of these little ones that believe in me, it is better for him that a mill-stone were hanged about his neck, and he were cast into the sea." This was for building up with all deceptive and demagogical means, the priestocracy. 49, "For every one shall be salted with fire, and every sacrifice shall be salted with salt." The time shall come, when all this idle fulmination shall be buried with the inquisition.

Ch. x. 21, "Sell whatsoever thou hast, and give to the poor."

Away with such nonsense and fanaticism, worse than socialism the most radical. 27, "And Jesus saith: for with God all things are possible." That is utterly ridiculous and libelous, of the God of the universe, however it may be with the bibles' peculiar gods. Ch. xi. 12, "He was hungry," 13, "And seeing a fig-tree afar off, having leaves, he came; if haply he might find any thereon; and when he came to it, he found nothing but leaves : for the time of figs was not yet," 14, "And Jesus answered and said unto it, no man eat fruit of thee hereafter forever."

To make a miracle out of this fig-tree, they have unmasked the whole man. They have made this god incompetent to decide whether there was fruit or not on this tree, and as he was so awfully deceived he turned into cursing the innocent tree, "for the time of figs was not yet." And even this, this God forgot through his straw-makers ! He cursed God's own works ! Was this a God who spake as a rational man never spake ? The writers of the drama were nodding. It could be no worse, they were conspiring blasphemously against God. 24, " Therefore I say unto you, what things soever ye desire when ye pray, believe that ye receive them, and ye shall have them." What can advocate the cause of the priests, better ?

Ch. xiii. 10., " And the gospel must be first published among all nations." He should have done this at once himself.

Verse 13. " Ye shall be hated of all men for my name's sake."

This proves sectarianism, antagonism against God, too conclusively to be denied with truth and honesty.

The treasure is too precious to insure hate, if possibly to be appreciated. But the only treasure is of the unity of God.

Verse 25. " And the stars of heaven shall fall." Mark, the speaker was Christ. Inspiration is a true, exact knowledge.

Verse 32. " But of that day and that hour knoweth no man ; no, not the angels which are in heaven, neither the son, but the father."

This is a candid acknowledgment, that the son was not the equal of the father. If not equal, of course he was vastly unequal, as his prayers proved. The efficacy of his own prayers, convicted him, Christ, as a blasphemous impostor.

Christ's heaven and earth shall pass away, but not God's words ! What are they ! Such as the universe, his works—his words proclaim.

Ch. xiv. v. 31. " If I (Peter spake) should die with thee, I will not deny thee in anywise. Likewise also said they all. 50. And they all forsook him and fled." There would have been no perjurers, no deserters, no God-killers, from the impossibility of the thing itself, if Christ had been a God. They could not have been kept from running to him. The thing tells its own tale, too truly. Christ did not act a man of principles, eschew sectarianism. Ch. xvi. v. 15. " And he (Jesus) said unto them, * * * and preach the gospel to every creature." Why had not this God not only done it, but converted all, as that was his mission ? 16. " He that believeth and is baptized shall be saved ; but he that believeth not, shall be damned." If hypocrites, believe ! How if no honest minds can believe, on due analysis of the whole facts submitted ! This proves that fraud is the position, and that the priestocracy manufactured this imposition, to deceive honest minds. 17. " And these signs shall follow them that believe : in my name shall they cast out devils ; they shall speak with new tongues ; they shall take up serpents ; and if they drink any deadly thing, it shall not hurt them ; they shall lay hands on the sick, and they shall recover." This kills the whole, as a false pretence. A want of genealogy proves him a false messiah, and this last chapter of Mark proves him completely a false perjured prophet. Thus ends the whole perjury.

This blasphemous imposition ought to be scouted as the vilest fraud, from the face of the earth. Are there any believers ? All should be brought to this fair test by the world. If they cannot do these signs, they are impostors. Thus the whole are self-convicted. But candor decides, the starters were the impostors.

Let us examine Luke, ch. i. v. 32. " And the Lord God shall give unto him (Jesus) the throne of his father David." How was David his ancestor ? Who can trace that, if the gospel tells the fact ? Here at once is a vile contradiction. Do the pulpit men wish to lay open all the truth, the whole truth, and nothing but the truth, or do they seek to smother up this false pretence ? Do they seek to hold their profession in proved perjury ? 37. " For with God nothing shall be impossible." That is absolutely against all reason and truth. God cannot do anything derogatory to his character, or contrary to his functions. His character is that of virtue, and his function creation, not procreation. 76. " And thou, child, shall be called the prophet of the Highest." One man endorses another in assertion, yet there are no real endorsers at all of the proof : then one perjurer endorses another perjurer, and the preachers preach wilful perjury.

Ch. ii. What an anomaly, a curiosity, that the angel of the Lord could tell shepherds, and could make them believe, and yet did not make the whole world, which was most vitally interested, believe as easily. It was essential, as millions were then dying, or to die, ere their belief.

This one position kills the whole as the vilest imposture. This thing refutes itself; for all the world at that very time was needing the same consolation as Simeon, "a light to lighten the gentiles." The wire-workers caused their bible-heroes to do all they wished. Who to-day can hold them to accountability? Ch. iv. 41. "And devils also came out of many, crying and saying, thou art Christ the son of God. And he, rebuking them, suffered them not to speak : for they knew that he was Christ." Christ seems to have been very familiar with devils. How do you explain? Explain, what never could have happened. 43. "I must preach the kingdom of God to other cities also." If sent by God, and he the Christ, he could have done all, and caused their belief. The people could not have been kept from faith. Ch. vi. 10. "And his hand was restored whole, as the other." This was enough, if it had ever happened. 11. "And they were filled with madness ;" anything else, proper sense decides. This is not human nature at all. What drivelers. 19. "And the whole multitude sought to touch him." Why? Because, or "for there went virtue out of him, and healed them all." What miserable contradictions of reason, with the preceding 11th verse. Ch. vii. 19. "And John, calling unto him two of his disciples, sent them to Jesus, saying, Art thou he that should come? or look we for another?" And John, a prophet, make that inquiry; when Jesus said, 26. "I say unto you, and much more than a prophet (John). 28. "There is not a greater prophet than John the Baptist." Deut. ch. xxxiv. 10. "And there arose not a prophet since in Israel like unto Moses." Who told the truth, Moses or Christ?

Luke, ch. viii. 1. "He went throughout every city and village, preaching." The wonder is, that he did not have more success : he should have performed greater miracles, indeed, to have secured his mission. We would say to the writers, Thrust not mind below priestocracy. Ch. xi. 15. "But some of them said, he casteth out devils through Beelzebub, the chief of devils." He had not any to cast out. Ch. xii. 9. "But he that denieth me, before men, shall be denied before the angels of God." He that shall contravene the truth, to accept of anything less than God, shall suffer proportionately to his knowledge. 51. "Suppose ye that I am come to give peace on earth? I tell you, nay ; but rather division." Here is conclusive argument of sectarianism, that is a peculiar faith, antagonistic to God Almighty. 52. "For from henceforth there shall be five in one house divided, three against two, and two against three." This is an infamous doctrine, that attacks the unity of God, and the universal brotherhood of man on earth. 53. "The father shall be divided against the son, and the son against the father," &c. &c. The hero must be made sectarian and self-condemned ; all one side, egotistical and dictatorial. God save us from such desecration. Upon what authority does Christ, the so-called messiah, come? Upon that of the Mosaic bible? That very book testifies against him. Deuteronomy, ch. xxiv. 16. "The fathers shall not be put to death for the children, neither shall the children be put to death for the fathers ; every man shall be put to death for his own sin." Luke, ch. xiv. 26. "If any man come to me, and hate not his father, and mother, and wife, and children, and brethren, and sisters, yea, and his own life also, he cannot be my disciple." If the priestocracy were the rulers of mind, then we might yield the question : but this premises a most ignominious sectarianism, most hostile to the good of mankind—no religion.

Ch. xvii. 6. "If ye had faith as a grain of mustard seed"—that is, if the people would stupidly throw themselves into the embraces of the priestocracy, their faith would be fine.

Men ought always to act, not to trouble Deity with senseless importunities. God will do justice of his own free will, and by his established providence, less by importunities. Mind must prove itself worthy. God's conservative principles of the universe vindicate his almighty providence.

Ch. xix. 10. "For the son of man is come to seek and to save that which was lost." This is a direct libel on God. His universe is not lost, and all will find mind as God has created it. 27. "But those mine enemies which would not that I should reign over them, bring hither, and slay them before me." Who would have been the enemies of a God? That is impossible. That is false. If Christ had done half of the miracles claimed before the Jews, they could not have been kept from faith in him.

But all the noise about Christ presents the demagogue in all this. But the wonderful incarnation, what an idea! Christians cannot even lay claim to its originality, for the pagans, the heathen, the outside barbarians, as you affect to call all others, had incarnations fourteen hundred years before the Christians, and even the ninth at that. This and all ancient traditions of polytheism, however vamped up, were fabulous, and all pagan. The world makes peculiar deities, and them imbecile. All the legends of antiquity are now before us, in a new mode, but with the old substance and weakness.

But how sublime the thought, that Christ died for us. Did he not die for himself, his own sins, the severe sins of sectarianism, of the sword that he drew. Could God the father sacrifice cruelly and barbarously one of his chief sons, for the balance, an ungodly set? Is not that murder all around?

Is it not most ignominiously worse, only to be conceived of by ungodly stupid priestocracies?

Will that wrong, increased by fornication or adultery, better the case? Is the world any better improved, by Christ? Yes, but there is more peace, and a better state of society? Does not mind govern all this?

There may be no such bloody wars to-day as yesterday, but are there not warriors, and a world full of bloodthirsty sectarians, perfect bloodhounds, ready in every age, if the people permit them, and not see the benefits of pure mind light? But look at Christ's resurrection!

Why not have a resurrection or translation direct, as that of Elijah? Was he less than a God? Ay, less than a man, made by his third day resurrection?

If mind prevaricates about the trinity, and many other mind undigestible monk-tricks, will it not stamp its equivocating character about the balance? The peculiar god permitted a murderous scene, that of the murder of his own son, and could not help him out of the horrible, bloody difficulty. We do not wish to adore such imbecile and murderous god, who sacrificed his chief son for the balance. That, then, is an imbecile god.

How could the God of the universe be pleased with the blood of animals, much less man, or his son, who is man? This was the blasphemous desecration of priestocracy against God; it was consummate folly and degradation. They commenced human sacrifice, and ended with that of God! The dream of Joseph has been lugged in, which proves nothing, only that Mary, the mother of Jesus, was a suspicious and dissolute character, and that Joseph was a bigoted cuckold. It proves too much. Now, it is bad enough for the simple Joseph to have been fooled by his prostitute wife, much less the world! Do you help to aid in that? Are you basely prostituting your mind, your family, to such an ignoble cause?

It was bad enough for those that were injured as to their body; what must it be to those to be defrauded in soul?

Know that bible-statements, and dreams too, are not documents or gospels proved at all, even for the most visionary.

But how noble was the doctrine of non-resistance.

That is the false doctrine, to the world's injury, for it is the sublime one of principle, that governs the universe and rules out that.

Instead of having one Christ, a bungler in morals, and a charlatan on principles, let the world have mind. But he spake, as man never spake? Because he spoke through priestocracies' mouths. "Great is Diana!" was said before, by the affiliated. The bible is one of the same kind of mouth-pieces. He could have made all Nicodemus, if he had been the Christ; but all his disciples were perjurers. Can we believe such? He would have been master of mind, not merely of man. If God, he could have mastered principles, but these he did not, as shall be shown. Luke xxi. 16, "And ye shall be betrayed, both by parents, and brethren, and kinsfolks, and friends; and some of you shall they cause to be put to death." The curse of sectarianism, that he advocated. precluded the principles of universal brotherhood. How came he, a God, to select all his disciples, perjurers? Who can believe such, or the chief of perjurers? Can the fool, abominable priestocracy, not know that the world knows them all to be the worst perjurers? John iii. 5, "Except a man be born of water and of the spirit, he cannot enter into the kingdom of God." The old doctrine of regeneration was among the Brahmins of Asia, fourteen centuries anterior to his pretended mission. If Christ spoke not earthly things true, how could he, the messiah, speak heavenly things true? Verse 16, "Only begotten son." The function of God is to create, not procreate. If you take Christ, you must take the whole family of priestocracy—and if you refuse either, you are damned. You must then take all their damnable perjuries. Verse 18, "But he that believeth not, is condemned already!"

This is the most abominable priest-sophistry, duplicity and craft, which must be truly met by a system of truth, rational religion, the only thing to exclude sectarianism, as good laws exclude bad laws.

The greatest of miracles is to make of Christ a marvellous person on paper. Ch. v. verse 5, "And a certain man was there, which had an infirmity thirty and eight years. Verse 15, The man departed, and told the Jews that it was Jesus which made him whole: verse 16, and therefore did the Jews persecute Jesus, and sought to slay him,

because he had done these things on the Sabbath day." What is this, but the lowest jugglery of mind?
If such things could have been only done on the Sabbath, the world would have besought it, Sabbath or no Sabbath.
If such infirmity had been cured, the people could not have been kept back from the physician. Persecute him! The fellow that would have dared to do it, would have preferred running through the fire, for these very Jews would have mobbed him. No, this is not human nature, ye miserable bunglers: ye lied about the pool, and the angel, and the diseased; above all, ye have lied about this fiction-Christ. Ye have no principles, for ye are caught in your base inconsistencies. Analogous to the waiting at the pool, is that on Christ, by mind, that, in the meantime, if not God-assisted, would be lost.

Ch. vi. verse 44, " No man can come to me, except the Father, which hath sent me, draw him." That decides the whole question of God's ability for conservation. There is no reason of a clumsy machinery of an imbecile, to be in the way of mind and God. Out of his own mouth, the speaker is rebuked and condemned. The highest state of free, not absolute agency of mind, is the purest inspiration of thought. Ch. vii. verse 42, " Christ cometh of the seed of David." Why do not the impostors prove all that? Are they so stupid as not to know that mind will see this, the false Christ?

Why do Luke and Matthew differ so excessively in the genealogy of Joseph, who was no kin to Jesus, by their own confession?

Were they, or their authors rather, such fools that they expected the weak faith of the world could swallow all this falsehood? Verse 39, " Spirit—which they that believe in him, should receive—for the Holy Ghost was not yet given." Which is worse, a priest's ignorance of his own blasphemy, or his falsehood? One of the most heinous of all sins, is peculiar faith. It is the highest sin against God. Did Christ make the seeing, blind? He that giveth not to the Creator all the rights of the Creator, is a traitor to both. Ch. xi. verse 47, " For this man doeth many miracles." All this is false, for there are no miracles. None but stupid ignorance could persist in such a false pretence. The very position is suicidal. Rational mind must see that the council could not have resisted miracles. Verse 48, " If we let him thus alone, all men will believe on him." Of course, the writers violated all principles of human nature, for half of these so-called miracles, one, bringing Lazarus to life, would have converted the whole world.

Of course, they were never performed. This is our sincere knowledge on the best facts of this case, given by the word of God. No proof at all is adduced, that one such miracle ever was wrought. We challenge the proof, that would satisfy a gentleman. Verse 53, " Then, from that day forth, they took counsel together, for to put him to death."

They would have done anything else. Chief priests and pharisees are a part of the human family, and are governed by like passions of interest, analogous to that of the whole world. These writers were the most grovelling animals that ever pretended to sense.

Yet a while, and all the humbuggery of peculiar faith will be done, if mind be right. Ch. xii. verse 39. " Therefore they could not believe, because Esaias had said again." Was bigotry ever more felonious, assumption more blasphemous? The main interest is universal safety, and that the God of the universe, that Christ did not know, alone can give. Vers. 40, " He (God) hath blinded their eyes, and hardened their heart; that they should not see with their eyes, nor understand with their heart, and be converted, and I should heal them"!!!!

What a compound of beastly ignorance about the heart; what ignominious libel of God's attributes and principles! And the saying of a false prophet was to outweigh the conversion of the people. That, religion?

Verse 41, " These things said Esaias, when he saw his glory, and spake of him!" That cannot be proved, on any principle of sound logic; but just reverses it. Ch. xiv. verse 28, " For my Father is greater than I." What could the inferior pretend to? What function, then, was he usurping? Neither mind nor God cared for him. Ch. xv. verse 18, " If the world hate you, ye know that it hated me before it hated you." The world cannot hate God, the Creator; that is impossible; but it hates all impostors as its enemies, and that proves all this a false pretence. Verse 23, " He that hateth me, hateth my Father, also." Is this true? Then his was a peculiar father, offered rational mind. Verse 27, "And ye, also, shall bear witness, because ye have been with me from the beginning!" Who is the witness for us, that these all are not the vilest impostors? We need, absolutely need, their proper endorsement to protect ourselves. We have no such endorsement.

Ch. xvi. verse 7, "It is expedient for you, that I go away." We have Christ talking about himself, most of the time. This is only man's pretences. It is very easy for people to say: I believe, and join the strongest. They can prate as much as they choose, about the spirit. That is their business, and nobody else's, so they take the faith. But, then, they have an ignoble position, that does not avail the creature, of an immortal Creator. God's works only tell of the past, the present, and as much of the future as will be analogous and beneficial for mind to know. About the balance, God has a sublime silence. All his works have rational records. Ask, then, for no faith, where there is no reason or fact. Who knows the depth of priestocracy?

They have given us no sealed and authentic documents, to certify the world of God's archives. God is the keeper of his own archives. All others should be proved, beyond doubt of the world, or they are degraded impostures. Ch. xx. verse 23, "Whosesoever sins ye remit, they are remitted unto them; and whosesoever sins ye retain, they are retained." Long live the priestocracy, says this verse. Verse 29, "Blessed are they that have not seen, and yet have believed." Amended: Foolish are they that have not seen, and yet have believed the most certain falsehoods, intended to catch the world all they could.

Ch. xxi., v. 24. "This is the disciple which testifieth of these things, and wrote these things, and we know that his testimony is true." Who endorses all this? A perfect perjurer proved by the affiliated, even by Mark. It ought to be as clear as the best testimony, in the most approved court of justice.

And there is no novel that is less testimony, if it have rational statements. All are mere statements of the bible, and if any mind adopt them as truth, it is foolish or wicked, one or both. It cannot be any less, if it know what testimony is. No matter what the world thinks, or what we have even previously thought, the comprehension of the whole subject certainly presents the only true exposition. All the principles of logic are violated, when such false pretences are adopted.

ARE THE ACTS OF THE APOSTLES ANY PROOF?

Ch. ii., v. 30. "Therefore (David) being a prophet, and knowing that God had sworn with an oath to him, that of the fruit of his loins, according to the flesh, he would raise up Christ to sit on his throne." Was the fruit of his loins, when Christ and Joseph are no kin? This, then, is a clear perjury. David might have sworn for his descendants to sit on the throne of the Jewish people, but the God of the universe could not possibly swear it, as that would be the division of his own universe.

That would be too small a province, only one world.

This was a compact of the peculiar god of David, and that does not concern the enlightened people of this day, all the monks, priests and preachers to the contrary notwithstanding. 44. "And all that believed were together, and had all things common." Churches, then, are associations of socialists. They were socialists in a measure; mere sectarians; but this was nothing of a brotherhood with the human race.

45. "And sold their possessions and goods, and parted them to all men, as every man had need." Is this a fact confirmed, by the conduct of the Christians of the present day.

Ch. v. The fate of Ananias and Sapphira has not added to the facts of principles, as mortal had no such power claimed; if this is not a blasphemous lie, it is murder. We have no assurance of anything, but that this was an attempt to add to the influence of the priestocracy. This thing of ruling the churches, is one of their great aspirations. As 1st Paul to the Corinthians, ch. i. v, 11. "For it hath been declared unto me, that there are contentions among you." Ch. v., 1. "It is reported commonly that there is fornication among you, and such fornication as is not so much as named among the Gentiles." Well, Paul, was Christian socialism communism? Is this the example for the modern sects? This socialism did not work well, for Acts, ch. vi., 1. "And in those days, when the number of the disciples was multiplied, there arose a murmuring of the Grecians against the Hebrews, because their widows were neglected in the daily ministration." The members of the church, we had thought, were as good when good, as the good of the world, but no worse. But Paul and his dramatists seem to write differently. If Christian advocates tell this, what if the Gentiles could be heard of that day? Though you, churchmen, exert yourselves for ever, yet, having no principles, you cannot flourish. You can get no principles in churches. Rejoice not in sophistry, superstition, nor peculiar faith. Do not believe all things, certainly not without reason, faith or no faith.

Who can prophecy, when all the world knows no such thing, and if it tell the truth it will tell that.

Peculiar faith people can prove anything by faith.

Ch. viii., v. 9. " Simon used sorcery, and bewitched the people of Samaria." Who believes such stuff? Who ever saw a witch or sorcerer? Just about as true as the power of the apostles in giving the Holy Ghost. Who was Saul? V. 1. "And Saul was consenting unto his death (Stephen's)." Was he not a murderer? Ch. ix., v. 21. " Is not this he (Saul) that destroyed them," &c? Ch. x., v. 44. " While Peter yet spake these words, the Holy Ghost fell on all them which heard the word." Do any but the affiliated speak of it? 45. "And they of the circumcision which believed, were astonished, as many as came with Peter, because that on the Gentiles also was poured out the gift of the Holy Ghost." This means as much that the Gentiles were outside barbarians in the opinion of the Jews, and without the protection of their peculiar gods. It seems to us that one of the greatest things is the conservation of the Creator over many minds liable to sin from the bible of tradition, that is filled with falsehood and iniquity from beginning to end, placing devils and angels all over the earth, and polluting all by its unholy pretences   Ch. xiii., v. 23. " Of this man's (David) seed hath God, according to promise, raised unto Israel a saviour, Jesus."

There can be no justification except by the supreme unity of God, for the mind is degraded and vilified, if not permitted to have its dignity and purpose, its liberal, legitimate, free agency.

To damn it because it cannot honestly believe all the absurd and abominable falsehoods about these things, deprives it of all free agency whatever. God, in the sublime silence of his majesty, has truly delineated all practicable free agency, in language most certain to philosophical science. It is not possible that God can overlook his own and mind's supremacy ; but the voice of superstition will be heard in the days of ignorance, and fanaticism will usurp all rightful prerogatives of reason.

Ch. xiv., v. 18. "And with these sayings, scarce restrained they the people, that they had not done sacrifice unto them." And yet Christ scarcely had such honor paid him! When the boundary of truth is overleaped, there are no limits. But all their fine effect is killed in the next verse. 19. "And there came thither certain Jews from Antioch and Iconium, who persuaded the people, and having stoned Paul, (who had healed a cripple impotent in his feet) drew him out of the city, supposing he had been dead." Oh, these Jews! They were not human, or these dramatists considered them not. We must act in part as if some of the probable things might have occurred.

We wish we could pick out all their virtues and bury their vices. But this we cannot do, for reason of their design and employment. This was the kingdom of the people.

Ch. xvi., 6. " And were forbidden of the Holy Ghost to preach the word in Asia." There was one of the most fruitful harvests, as to number of souls, throughout all Asia, teeming with her millions, and her systems of peculiar faith and incarnations. Was this one of the conveniences of the Holy Ghost? But, alas, all these souls had to wait! By rational religion, that is impossible. It was utterly impossible, for God governed mind, after all the false pretences of all the peculiar faiths. But how inconsistent now are these fellows 16 to 23. They were able to stop divination, but were not able to keep off whipping therefor! These lies are so disgustingly stupid, that we could throw down the book, but for our purpose of exposing these reckless pretenders. Cb. xxii., v. 4. "And I (Paul) persecuted this way unto the death." Further proof is furnished of his being a murderer. A fine apostle this.

The two main pillars of the Christian church, one a perjurer, the other a murderer, and propagator of bible perjuries!

Ch. xx., v. 26. " Wherefore I take you to record this day, that I am pure from the blood of all men." What proof is there of this, after the preceding evidence? Does Paul or the bibles lie? Both.

What a singular peculiarity, that any peculiar faith as that of Christianity, is not superstition. Paul, though a Christian, was a murderer for intoleration of faith, a bigot and a fanatic after all. Do we believe that he went to the bible heaven? Christ did not go there direct, we presume, for his blasphemy. But he was the agent for God. If God had not been omnipresent, metaphysics, much less rational religion, would not permit that idea.

If the agent, he could not be principal or equal.

If co-partners, they were co-creators ; but that is impossible. His earthly sojourn kills all that dead, as well as his language. This solar system has only one sun, hence he must have been usurper, but that implies superior power.

Yet, as creature and mortal at that, this is utterly disproved. It is all affected or pretended.

The position of all sinners as murderers and blasphemers, bespeaks atonement by retributive justice. It cannot be anything less. God's mercy is not subordinate to his

47

justice. No one of God's attributes are subordinate. That kills Christ and all the impostor tribe, a universe fold more than all the Jews and Romans did. Purification can be made through retributive justice, and that alone. God is the judge.

There were not less than twenty-five messiahs, and how many more who knows? All blasphemers. This whole subject has been mystified horribly, for the peace and welfare of man.

And we are to have war in families by Christ, the teacher of non-resistance! Will any towering mind be satisfied with this little brief authority, when it can command the whole subject on principles?

This question is not to be skulked.

The idea of a murderer, adulterer, and pirate, a military despot having his sins sponged out in one moment, could only be premised by knaves and impostors, and expected by dolts or knaves. What degraded immorality, though he was a man after God's own heart.

This man was not after the mind of the Supreme Creator of the universe. You act for yourself—mind acts, mind repents, amends. You must reform, not deform mind. Let not the sophist Christ pervert it; that is, do not let his masters, the priestocracy, do it.

Paul and Peter even disagree about circumcision and uncircumcision, proving that their mind had to elicit the most politic—of course, uncircumcision. Paul's Epistle to the Galatians, ch. ii. 11. " But when Peter was come to Antioch, I withstood him to the face, because he was to be blamed." 13 and 14, Paul accuses them of dissimulation, that they did not walk uprightly according to the truth of the gospel!

Was there ever any regeneration of Peter, the rock of churches? After this, what honest mind can say it, after Peter had been caught at this game before? To be proved by his master a perjurer is too bad; to be proved a hypocrite by his holy brother so called, is horrible indeed.

But is Paul any better, sons of civilization?

See Paul to the Romans, ch. iii. v. 7. " For if the truth of God hath more abounded through my lie unto his glory ; why yet am I also judged as a sinner ?"

Which is the best perjurer of the two? Judge ye.

Explanations will push themselves respecting such glaring errors, if mind do justice to itself. The world should not suffer injury, for all such errors or crimes.

The world must from its sad history for thousands of years, exercise the most intellectual caution about all peculiar faiths, and having suffered most woful abuses under their sanction, it must discard them all on the first favorable opportunity.

We cannot reach the blessing of religion, certainly not on any such position, as we have nothing but peculiar faith, though the world know certainly by sad experience that faith is the talisman for all in christianity. Let us hear Paul more, ch. viii. v. 28. " And we know that all things work together for good, to them that love God, to them who are the called according to his purpose. 29, For whom he did foreknow, he also did predestinate to be conformed to the image of his son, that he might be the first-born among many brethren. 30, Moreover. whom he did predestinate, them he also called ; and whom he called, them he also justified ; and whom he justified, them he also glorified. 33, Who shall lay any thing to the charge of God's elect ? It is God that justifieth." Who are the called? All this is the assertion of a man, confessing a lie !

Paul's 2d Epistle to the Thessalonians, ch. ii. v. 11. " And for this cause God shall send them strong delusion, that they should believe a lie." What libels on the God of mind, perjuring the libeler. As v. 12, " That they all might be damned who believed not the truth, but had pleasure in unrighteousness. 13, But we are bound to give thanks alway to God for you, brethren beloved of the Lord, because God hath from the beginning chosen you to salvation through sanctification of the spirit, and belief of the truth."

What libels on God for election, as well as for faith, &c., ch. iii. v. 2, " And that we may be delivered from unreasonable and wicked men : for all men have not faith." Were there ever worse bigotry and bad faith to mind and truth ?

What else are these, but the worst of perjuries ?

Paul's Epistle to Titus, ch. i. v. 1, " According to the faith of God's elect." That is, of the peculiar god ! 3, " But hath (God) in due time manifested his word through preaching, which is committed unto me." Where was preaching that was necessary all time, before ? Every ancient nation had its legends, holy and sacred, as we see with the remotest, the Chinese. The fault with the moderns is, that they do not pass all by as unworthy of their cultivated mind. Instead, they absurdly credit the Jews for one more truthful, as if any legends could be truthful, whereas their priestocracy kept the records which they made in defiance of others, and there is the fraud practiced upon all the world that is verdant enough to take them for granted. The priestocracy have desecrated this whole matter, most ignobly, have falsified God.

Paul in Hebrews, ch. xi. v. 1. "Now faith is the substance of things hoped for, the evidence of things not seen."

What is all priestocracy faith worth? What is all faith worth about the priests, Abel, Enoch, Noah, Abraham, if the pretences are not proved facts? Ch. xii. v. 20, "And if so much as a beast touch the mountain, it shall be stoned, or thrust through with a dart: 21, And so terrible was the sight, that Moses said, I exceedingly fear and quake." These are the playthings of absolutism, to blind the eyes of the people. They are perjury endorsements, by Paul. If any such thing happened as to prevent them going by superstition to the mountain, it was all the tricks of the priestocracy: but it was easier for the false history. When was the Mosaic legend written?

Let the monarchs of all jugglery alone speak. 23, "And to the spirits of just men made perfect," (or all) which are written in the Jewish heaven. What could the monk or priest of a peculiar god know of them, except in his peculiar heaven? What is all that to us? Messiahship presents due humility and reverence before God, not blasphemy. James, ch. v., 15, "And the prayer of faith shall save the sick." 17, "Elias was a man subject to like passions as we are, and he prayed earnestly that it might not rain: and it rained not on the earth by the space of three years and six months." What libels again on God, that prove the worst of human characters affecting to be the purest. II. Peter, ch. ii., v. 7, "And delivered just Lot!" Him, who committed most incest! Well there is such a bible, self-condemned for ever for mind. Ch. iii., v. 7, "But the heavens and earth which are now. by the same word, are kept in store, reserved unto fire against the day of judgment, and perdition of ungodly men." 10, "The heavens shall pass away with a great noise, and the elements shall melt with fervent heat; the earth also, and the works that are therein, shall be burnt up." Peculiar faith, without proof, condemns, in conflict with God's word, confronting. Thou, Peter, art the apostle of peculiar gods, and therefore thou art not licensed to speak with any more truth about the universe, than when thou swore about Christ. Was Peter converted at the time he denied his master and fell back, or converted afterwards? What was his last conversion worth? All the bible advocates relied on revelation of peculiar powers, and Peter's statement alone proves him an ignorant and reckless, unprincipled fanatic. The first epistle general of John, ch. iii., v. 8, "He that committeth sin, is of the devil; for the devil sinneth from the beginning. For this purpose the son of God was manifested, that he might destroy the works of the devil." As it is not provable that there is any devil, it remains therefore to be proved that there ever was any Christ.

Which of these, John or Moses, are to be believed about seeing their god? They are both advanced as inspired men, and affect to tell the exact truth. They are confronted before the whole world. If the last convict the old bible, then it convicts itself. Both are convicted by rational religion.

II. Paul to the Corinthians. Ch. xi., v. 20: "In perils among false brethren." Ch. xii., v. 2: "I knew a man in Christ—such a one caught up to the third heaven." 4, "How that he was caught up into Paradise." Like all such. he has told too much, of heaven and Satan. A faith, by self-humbuggery, is no proof of the scriptures, but everything to condemn them that a rational man could expect.

All such is the faithless legend of the priestocrecy, who have used all ungodly means, to uphold their unprincipled dynasty.

What is a greater piece of sophistry, than St. Paul's article about faith? And yet the world is required, on such faith, to bow to the peculiar bibles of the priestocracy.

The earth shall dissolve, and the elements melt with fervent heat, as much impeach omnipotence as omniscience in God's repenting of having created man.

Peter, or his representative author, was ignorant of the first principles of science, much less of things that inspired minds should have. He was a fanatic, one of the confederate priestocracy. How shall the pretenders dispose of the atmosphere?

The oxygen is a supporter of the combustion, the balance are not combustible. But all nonsense and humbuggery are possible with the priestocracy.

Was Peter a chemist? He was more of a fanatic. It was in the crucible of the priestocracy, that all these things were possible. They could make a caricature of God and creation, and all such dispensation had to be destroyed. Some affect that much of the bible is figures and metaphors. but in the sophists' chancery they carry these figures too high, these metaphors too boldly. They miss a figure, and condemn themselves.

Destroy this earth, and you invade the universe, and all the conservative principles of the Creator. It is time that the world had waked up from the desecrations of all such affiliations.

Priestocracy has thrown around it its superstitious mantles, so much that the people are afraid to look in, like the tabernacle superstition of Moses, &c.

Paul was the worst of sophists and impostors, who supported the miserable humbug. As much as you adopt Christ, so much you remove yourself from God. The messiah is only the shadow, will you take that for the substance, God? The people did not know the month, nor the year of Christ's birth.

The two dispensations comprehend the after-thoughts of mind, not the fore-thoughts of God, who is not identified with either, as he is the creator of mind that looks at principles, not sectarian false doctrines utterly impracticable.

Was not the temple of Jerusalem destroyed by Titus, long before the scene of the drama of Christ was laid? How easy was it, to have it Christ's prophecy antedated! It does not matter whether it was after or before, as we have convicted this character so often. Had the christian been the true faith, the world could not have been kept back at all, by no force or stratagem. Principles will exclude the idea, of mastery of any christ. "Search the Scriptures," is invalid, for they are false and do not comprehend the subject. The justice of penalty cannot be liquidated by vicarious blood. That is impossible in the court of the God of the universe, however it may be ascribed to the peculiar god of a peculiar people. It was of course, only a peculiar mind-facture.

To accomplish any other than a universal system, is to advance man's, and make a peculiar system of gods.

If the peculiar god consent to a bloody, systematic murder and adultery, both impossibilities with the God of the universe, all the perpetrators commit a blasphemy in ascribing such to the creator, and a base libel on his attributes, revolting and disgusting to his principles. But if christianity be the cause of arts and sciences flourishing, how comes it that we are not indebted to it for all the inventions and discoveries of the ancients?

Its head robs God of his functions, and its advocates rob mind of its attributes. The Egyptians and Chaldeans taught the Greeks Pythagoras, Thales, &c., astronomy. That state of science, proves them far before the Jews every way.

As to new birth or regeneration, that is not original, but belongs to the Brahmins of an older date. It is inadmissible in any peculiar faith. The master has to submit to principles, that he was to operate with.

He traded on the capital he found, and that is the province of a mortal. A God creates. All this is no more than myth—mythology varied—mystified by man—in deep insidious collusion—so Mosaic, that you do not know how or when it is done.

But the ancient was not christianity in the crusades?

The modern is a suicidal, subversive of all that is true. It visits continents with military prowess, and extracts conquests and dominion over man and country, while it defends the union of church and state at home, and alienates the rights of citizens, because not of court faith. This doctrine teaches intoleration to those of different opinion, but for mind rationalized. It plants conquest in America, slavery upon Africa, poison in China, and extensive dominion in Asia. The actors are countries coveted by christianity. With the bible it gives wars, takes away the strength and beauty of continents, debases mind, which it deceives and betrays.

But there must be pious frauds practiced, by nations as individuals. But conscience is easy, for the piety of God's service, alias the priestocracy's.

They were the gods: it is polytheism of men.

Who will adopt the base actions of the world, sophisticated as they are? Where there has been an inquisition to force it, wars for centuries to uphold it, kingly and imperial power to sustain it. Insidious have been its enactments. This business will not stand the fair investigation of honest intelligence.

Christians are vindictive, they forswear for each other, and expel numbers on trivial grounds, and retain others that are unworthy members of society. They go more for previous standing, than present impropriety.

Socrates died like a man, but Jesus Christ like a blasphemous culprit. But no great institution of learning, for fifty years has flourished, without the influence of christianity. Where are all the Mahometans, Jews or Chinese, the last of whom constitute nearly one-third of all the world? Is not the balance on the side of a large majority! What produced our republican revolution, that will bury all pagan idolatry at the feet of monotheism? Mind; certainly not christianity, whose church was in union with the state of Britain, with some honorable exceptions on the side of mind. What does the world need of non-resistance, that will not suit for man nor woman, for fortitude or chastity.

Non-resistance will not answer at all for the world, as conservatism must preserve all by constitutional principles. Christians only have the peculiar god of Judaism, involved with their peculiar god. But do we think Christ a master moralist? We do not, for he was a bitter and decided sectarian, drawing the sword instead of promoting peace, setting the family at variance, and deranging God's religion, by telling us that if his faith doctrine was not believed, that the unbeliever should be damned. What principles are in that position?

Principle, is the only safe position. But as he could not be a God, for he was born, lived and died a mortal, and blasphemous at that, an impostor on the world, he was necessarily a perjurer.

An apostate to God is he who does not recognise his exclusive unity, where he has the power of analysis.

A rational being needs rational religion, the highest rational duty to rational society of a rational world, for a rational God. Was Christ then a rational being?

Gratitude is one of the noblest attributes of the human mind or character, to be estimated by action. Did Christ duly exercise it towards his creator, when he or his pretenders assumed for him the regency?

Was he a faithful patriot, leading his country or the world to God by principle, when he dictated by selfishness, and commanded by credulity?

We can only take the whole story of Christ, on analysis of representation.

Is it certain, that christianity furnishes supreme excellence?

What is its moral influence? What can the world do without it? What was the world thousands of years anterior to it? God could not in justice to mankind, preceding the time of the man Christ, have established messiahship, unless he had after-thoughts, a thing impossible—nor could he in justice to himself permit innocent blood to be shed for the guilty, for that causes him to participate in murder, an inconsistency with himself.

But Christ was a God: so much the worse.

Science is aimed to be scowled at by peculiar faith people, as subversive of their plans. Partial success is all that any peculiar faith can ever claim, and that proves nothing essential for christians, as the Mahometans have 140 millions, also victorious they have been over the Christians and Brahmins. But various have been the mutations of war, dependent on mind-skill, not peculiar faith. The christians have conquered much of Asia, where the Mahometan and Brahmin abide.

Christianity was provincial at first, then world travelling, being indebted to the union of state, both of which refer to mind. Instead of pardon of sins, in seeking an intercessor, we commit the most awful blasphemy in such faith.

When we leave creation, we leave the functions of the God of nature, and when we speak of begetting, we at once speak of the functions of creatures clearly proved. All this debits God instead of giving him an elevated credit for creation, and stultifies credulous man. The slow progress of christianity, proves its head a mortal. The man-worship and messiahship of Christ, are in the way of due devotion to God.

God created, not begat the universe ; the science of physiology sets right the stupid blasphemers. We can only have right and justice, by wisdom, truth and science.

Can the birth day of Christ be designated, a day most remarkable of all others. Can even the month? Still worse, can even the year? This proves most conclusively the deepest imposition and fraud on the world. The only way whereby man can be saved, is certainly not by that, not worth a thought beyond its analysis.

It is only by the right action of mind, through the grace of the Creator. Christ never took away sin. There can be no propitiation by blood, only by mind. There can be no other principle, as the analysis of mind discloses. There is no definite prophecy of Isaiah about Christ, nor can Matthew appropriate it. The right functions of time preclude prophecy. All creation is on rational principles; all that mind does then and recognises, is rational, and has to look to rational ways. It is a fine thing that the means have not been in proportion to the ambition of the enterprise. Christ, as created a creature, had no power above a mortal, as his birth, life and death, prove. No special mission on earth, in lieu of the universe, avails, and Christ could only speak of an individual mission, as he was individualized to time, locality, or theatre. This reduces him most clearly and conclusively, to the state analogous to what all souls have by creation right, to which the christian faith is in antagonism.

The christian faith is in antagonism with that of Judaism. How is this, if the last was right? If not right, how can christian faith, that assumes to be founded thereon, be right? The proposition is too clear to be mistaken. If Judaism were ever right, it is so now ; but if false now, it was always false. The proposition is undeniable, consequently all its false positions are inherited by its offspring, Christianity, Mahometanism, and Mormonism, and they are in antagonism to all that is Judaism. The sophistry of three in one, that trinity is unity, is hardly a remove from the first step of ignorance of mind, and certainly bespeaks the lowest state of sophistry. It proves the perjury of undeveloped mind very verdant, but would if it could. It took the sophistry of priestocracy to invent, and the tyranny of the imperial people at Rome to impose, the christian faith on the world.

If Christ advanced new principles, he proved himself a God; as he did not, the failure proves him worse than man, as he was an impostor, and it proves the Creator supreme and sublime in unity, and in supremacy most adequate.

Martyrs are cited as dying, for love of Christ. Millions have died for other christs and messiahs, so that martyrdom is no test of true faith or pure religion.

Of what benefit is Christ to us in the latter days; he is an after-thought. No, he is assumed to be from the foundation. That cannot stand, for there is no foundation to that assertion. The very books that give it, are not proved at all, and ere they be, no such assertion is worth anything with honest or sound truthful minds. People must gullible, go for popularity, not the test of merit and principles, for the master, not principles. The defect of the evangelists, or those who wrote for them, leaves a folly.

Christ's birth-day is unknown! What? The peculiar heavens would have the sign; earth and mortals could not mistake it. The polytheists make God only part of a God, a very small part; the trinitarians only make him one-third of a God. The two attributes, the Holy Ghost and Christ, being absent, how then did he act, when they were on earth? If they have to go to the rest of the universe, for if God be imperfect in this world, he is so in all necessarily, how then is this difficulty to be surmounted? God cannot be a perfect being, when he has others to assist him in his attributes. Of course he lacks those attributes that they have to fulfil. The reason of the second covenant was from the defect of the first, that reflects its defective paternity upon all its progeny. The peculiarity of that matter begets its like. All are peculiar, and all are defective, from that defective peculiarity, most certainly.

If real deism or monotheism had been known to the ancient world, we should now be more exempt from the foul corruptions of Judaism, as God does not beget, but create: then all are his creatures, and Christ is no more than the balance of mortals, and directly proved this by showing his mortality.

What did he do? He left the world worse than he found it, for he proves that a majority has been decidedly against him all the time. In old times, when the mass was ignorant, the cunning impostors had to resort to stratagem, ventriloquism, hand-jugglery, &c., to maintain their doctrines, but all such pretences as these are mind-jugglenes, downright falsehoods, stories.

You claim, by excellence, to be above and separate from the world. By what? On the merits of a redeemer! Why not say the truth—on the false pretences of mortals! A man or mortal savior bespeaks his false position. The error in some church members is thinking themselves above the world. All are of the human family, and can only sin the least. Their very position is very sinful, and should be repented of.

Christ was intolerant to the Pharisees and Jews, like all sectarians. Joseph or any other half-witted cuckold, may have had hundreds of dreams about their faithless spouses, but it would be visionary in any mind to believe it.

John, ch. viii., v. 59: "But Jesus hid himself." What an idea of a God, as Jesus running away. John, ch. x., v. 39: "Therefore they sought again to take him; but he escaped out of their hand." How was the world saved, anterior to Christ, which knew not of him? No faith will do it, for faith could not exist independent of the knowledge of the fact. All this is falsehood! perjury.

Christ was a great reformer, as the bible pretends, but on the whole analysis, he is defiled with sectarianism; thus now we write it out, after a better comprehensive analysis on our own minds, not relying on the defective analysis of the deepest interested priestocracy. Why was not the resurrection of Christ before the whole world, which was to be thereby benefited? Because his mission is an after-thought; God had nothing to do with it. Bad, wicked men, had, and no one else. Bad despotic world-rules, show the reason for such fooleries. This miserable idea is bandied about by weak-minded people, to disturb old imbecile men, weak women, and children. The poor patient is not permitted to die in peace, but his mind is tortured. and he is nearly deranged about this matter that has not the base of satisfaction. But what essential proof of Christ's resurrection is before the world of cotemporary authors? Do Pliny or Seneca, the greatest philosophers of those days. mention the darkness?

But it is claimed by men, assuming to have been deists, that "Celsus, Thallus, Phlegon, Origen, Eusebius, Tertullian and others, some of them christians and some of them pagans, do," and they blame the author, Gibbon, for adverting to the silence of Pliny and Seneca. But one observation will suffice. Were any of these men cotemporaries[1] All that is advanced must relate most powerfully to that point. Constantine, with perjury in his mouth, carried the sword in one hand, and the cross in the other, under the banner of which Popes and their adherents have granted dispensations, for the conquest of the non-christian world, a few centuries back! Could there be a baser system of piracy perpetrated, on the world and mind?

What is trinity? An impossibility, or what is incompatible with reason. Three bodies cannot exist in one and the same space, at the same time, the one omnipotent, the second local, and third imaginary.

God, as immutable, manifests himself uniformly now as previously. There is no change; all else is mere false pretence.

God is not a personal being, because his function pertains to the universe, which premises unity of being and principles, that necessarily impeach all bibles of tradition. We go against the errors of the ignorant, as well as the false pretences of the criminal. Plurality in the godhead, so far from being rational, cannot be reconciled to reason, sound, faithful, truthful, honest sense.

Christ's words are nothing at all, when his actions, birth, life and death, prove him the merest mortal. Christ was a selfish sectarian; he could only have been a rationalist to have been right, but he fell by the ignorance and vices of the times, far below rationalism.

Had Christ been a rationalist, he could have abundantly censured Judaism, one of the pests of sectarianism, and might have asserted the proper position without one iota of reference to the old or new bible of tradition. He might have had it in his power as the greatest reformer, to have carried through the world's reformation on rational principles, but he missed all by the worst of errors, his own sectarianism.

Christ was the greatest of sectarians, as he was granted to have had the greatest power. He sowed the seeds of evil, by his sectarianism.

Trinity is the last relic of polytheism and sectarianism, destroys all the divinity of Christ. Christianity is man and bible worship, pagan idolatry; that is the way to tell it! Our opinion was favorably inclined, as previously recorded, but the comprehension of the whole subject decides the question satisfactorily against any true expounder of religion when identified with sectarianism.

Mark gives us the recital of Christ's commission to his disciples, which completely disproves his divine mission. Ch. xvi. v. 17. "And these signs shall follow them that believe." One of two propositions necessarily follow, either that Christ or his believers are false, and what is inextricable for the poor dupes, christians, their position is false altogether, the rebuke from God's word. If the position were divine, it would be omnipresent wherever mind is; there would be the elements of the christian faith; but it requires a mission that necessarily kills the whole. When we analyze the nature of mind and its duties, we find conclusively that it is not the book that convinces, but it is the actor, God. His deeds are necessary for all cases. Christ's doctrine so far from being a perfect religion, is no religion at all.

Is this true, Mark xvi. v. 20: "They went forth and preached everywhere?" Did they preach in America? What good scholar is not thoroughly convinced, that this is all false? But as to Christ's locality on this one earth, being objectionable, there might have been duplicates on other globes. That implies an Almighty power, that is not to be delegated for the plainest and justest of reasons, as all can be comprehended by God's way. Man's is a botch of after-thoughts, all the time. The christian faith had prevailed for nearly fifteen centuries on the old continent, and might have continued for as many more, but for mind that burst asunder the prison-bars of ignorance. O christianity, then was your time for glory. Columbus stands before all such intellectually, what Socrates does morally. And yet christianity has assumed the guardianship of science and art, genius and discovery. What intelligent, honest mind, can believe this? Christianity is a prostitution of mind that thus loses its dignity.

Who were the council men? "Frail and fallible."

And who empowered them, to make and impose canons for the world? Were rational mind, education, and religion, properly represented?

Constantine and other christian emperors, are said to have had the writings of Porphyry against christianity destroyed. After all, Christ was the reformer of sectarianism, that gives him at the best only mortal existence and fame. Men's minds were not elevated to the demands of the case.

One language that could have been universal to the Apostles, to teach the world, would have benefited them. Was this bestowed by Christ, when he did not possess this himself? God Almighty has proved himself by such, which excludes "the prince of the power of the air." But not so they who give fiction, what does not belong to any but God. What has not been vitiated by the peculiar code of peculiar faith? Having vitiated Josephus, where would they stop?

It is remarkable that Josephus did not write of Jesus, of whom, if so celebrated, he as the whole world would, if he had lived in the age claimed. As there is no genuine document by Josephus, the world must give up the imposition.

Call you christianity a defender of science, a friend to mind, when it excludes religion? When it asserts that those who read must not doubt, as those that doubt will be damned! Is this less tyrannical on mind, than any ukase issued by the most despotic emperor? Is an honest disbelief in matters not and never proved, not possible to be proved, worse than a hypocritical or senseless belief? What virtue is there in all such faith? Christ, a God? It is incompatible with God to abide on earth, most inconsistent with his functions. God would not let mind mistake that, if it had been a mission. Its end proved itself, a blasphemous imposition.

Which of the four gospel writers is right? Two most essentially clash with each other, and all disagree with truth. They have written falsely; Christ could not carry through his own doctrines on account of sectarianism, by which he clearly lost his life. or was victimized. Of course, he had no one to blame but himself. And this is the reason on truthful analysis, that his followers were in antagonism to the world, having the identity of vitiation. What is called martyrdom, results from the persecution of sectarianism of peculiar faith.

In tracing the lineage of Christ from David, the pretenders and advocates of such, ask the people to be fools, to believe the very first item.

Constantine had copies of the scriptures multiplied at the expense of the imperial treasury.

He was smuggler general to this mighty fund of bigotry, and has left a potent curse of absolutism.

Christ could not have been very wise to go for sectarianism, that is necessarily temporary.

His sectarianism, it is true, was the most elaborate of all others. Now all action on principle, will redound to the world's dignity and happiness.

If Christ could not institute any new principles, he could not originate any new functions.

Then he had no divine function, conclusively proving himself a mortal, and necessarily an impostor.

What he taught was incompatible, which solves the main question, that he was mortal. Christ was ambitious, vain and egotistical, reckless of truth. Matthew, ch. xiii. v. 58, "He did not many mighty works then, because of their unbelief." That was the very reason, he should have convinced them. Matthew, xxi. 22, "All things whatsoever ye shall ask in prayer, believing, it shall be done."

Is this honorable truth? What pitiful dramatists!

The people of Palestine did many things incompatible with rational principles, according to Josephus, who in his Antiq., l. xix. c. 8, sec. 2. "They called him (Herod) a God."

But what will the world do for redemption of its sins, for justification by Christ's blood? That position involves murder of all the parties concerned, even of the latest posterity adopting. Who wishes to be involved in such criminal participation, when the bountiful grace of God Almighty is the sustenance of the universe?

We have two points among many that pull down Christ's mortality, his sectarianism, that could not possibly be of God. Christ could not originate any principles, therefore all the work had been done perfect at first, as premised by God's forethought; now, we will defy the world to prove the least necessity of Christ's mission, when he would not originate a single principle, consequently the Almighty had premised all practicable. No two persons, let alone nations, can clash on principles that are truth and fact, which bespeak much sublimer ground than passiveness under aggression, turning the second cheek, and non-resistance. Christ as divine claimed of God, should he divinely inspired when he says, "That the stars shall fall from heaven:" does he speak right?

John vi., 66. "From that time many of his disciples went back, and walked no more with him." If we wished any direct proof of Christ's mortality, we could not have gotten one more direct. If he. with all his pretended miracles, could not retain, but lost many of his own disciples, who turned away from him, how could it be expected that the world since would follow him? How shall it be with his representatives, who have not the works of the signs with them? These many disciples must have best known him, and therefore left him. His own prophecy in Mark proves him a pitiful perjurer. But how about passive obedience? That is most objectionable. How? As it does not promote the dignity and elevation of character. The adoption of principles promotes the world's satisfaction and happiness,—short of that social relations cannot be maintained. Is it possible for two persons of principles to clash? No. If they do, both may be, but one is certainly wrong. Before two individuals or two nations fall out, it becomes them, as rational beings or representatives of rational society, to analyze and correct on that analysis.

The world will never be civilized, till it fully adopts principles. Who, then, gave' Christ his commission? God. What, in antagonism to self? What an idea of a redeemer proceeding from a mortal, sinful woman, both of whom partook of the common lot of humanity in all the just relations of physiology. The woman partook of her sinful earthly attributes, by all the principles of physiology, and her offspring was of the same character. The fact of the impostors offering the genealogy of Joseph, that is totally inapplicable to Christ, in their absurd notions, proves that they must have had misgivings of the position. All shame and sense must have fled them, else they never could have offered, as Matthew is made to say, the most absurd tale of a case transpired centuries before, for that event. How, then, could sinful human nature, as is clearly proved, be a propitiation for what human nature could never command. All is incompatible as mortal, all is impossible as sinful.

A man had better never say one word, if it be attended with such sophistry and perjury, that attend all bibles of tradition in origin and advocacy.

The last dispensation abrogates the first! The abrogations of dispensations conclusively prove their falsity, and identify them as man's. They are all false pretences. To make a messiah, prophet, miracle or mystery-monger, you diminish God more than the universe gains. What can the stupid dolts expect to gain? Horrible would that day be, when expiation by blood could be made! It would be the bloodiest and blackest of all dark days.

Christ had no commission most positively, as he had originated no principles, If you meddle with this subject at all, you may just hold yourself prepared to hear strange questions, for the world will ask you, if you actually believe in a God? Yes, you will tell them, as religion prompts you sincerely in knowledge through science, and that you can believe in nothing else. Then it is mystery to them.

They believe a part of the bible, as far as meets their notions and their faith. All this is abominable. Mind has nothing to do with notions or faith, or its falsities, when exact science bespeaks the reality.

Inspiration speaks through exact science, and answers for all time, never caters to the false taste of superstition, ignorance or error.

As God is perfect in his attributes, no other can show a commission in the universe, as such can originate no new principles, and therefore can only act as a creature. The foulest and blackest ingratitude and blasphemy are perpetrated, in giving away any of God's exclusive jurisdiction.

Why is it that Christ is offered as something for mind, when the most rational being must know that he could not help himself?

The fool-corrupt priestocracy were the blind decoys.

As Christ could not originate new p nc p es and did not advocate rational religion, the only true doctrine, he devised sectarianism. Christ was a sectarian, to have the mission of the second covenant or dispensation as was pretended, abrogating the first.

How comes it, that in this mighty continent, inhabited by so many Indians who comprehended the idea of the Great Spirit, that they excluded, with few exceptions, the doctrine of the trinity, but because it was unreasonable. irrational to the unsophisticated minds of those sons of the forest? Christ, as a man, might have been a reformer, restricted, however, to sectarianism. As a pretended god, he was a blasphemous impostor.

The mission of Christ is predicated on the assumed imperfection of Deity! most clearly involving the crimes of adultery and murder. Christianity in its conception, is involved in the deepest blasphemy, the basest libels on God—nothing short of it.

Apart from false feeling and self-delusion, it could not be believed. What Christ did then was only the result of mind. His brightest thought was taken from men who had preceded centuries upon centuries in the East, and were all predicated on the highest appreciation of social relations.

Confucius had used the sentiment five hundred years before him, and this doctrine of his canonical writings, he acknowledges having copied of legislators, his predecessors for centuries, thus proving a very high antiquity. But the best of all the world does not constitute religion, the consummation of principles.

Do you prefer the trinity to God? Take away the bible, and what would the world do? It would be right so far as that is concerned, and much the best off most assuredly. Arts and sciences flourish where the bible does. Does their whole history, the only current one, inform us of such a state of things? For what was the noblest science of astronomy perverted, but for the infamous lying of that book? To make out the most extraordinary miracles, astronomy was subverted by Joshua or legend writers, and to keep up the fraud, science was corrupted for many centuries, and men of science were infamously treated. Pythagoras, a Grecian, introduced from the East most laudable views of astronomy for his times and means. This was subverted by Ptolemy, and the authority of the Peripatetic school prevailed, that the apparent face in our solar system was the real one. How came the last to have such a hold on the Christian world for so many centuries? Where was the bible then, to correct false pretence of the worst kind in this great science? No, it all more or less conformed to the notions of these bible worthies, and the world might have slept till doomsday thereon. But the son of mind and genius awakes, and yet the mighty Copernicus, the restorer of the Pythagorean system, in place of an hypothesis founded on assumption, withheld his noble system that gave the dawn to astronomical science, for thirty years afraid to publish before the world, that was ingloriously trammelled by the false pretences of the bible.

Yes, his successor, Galileo, was imprisoned, bullied, and forced to recant these facts of science!

Shame upon the bible advocates, to assume the guardianship of science, when they cherished hoary error, nurtured in the priestocracy school. Here then is a sacrifice of science and truth, for the abomination of miracles that cannot exist. If miracles are so false, what must be the pretence of prophecies that are identified? Surely they are equals. Tell us, you who study statistics, how many millions have been sacrificed to these horrible tragedy movers? Tell us how much blood and treasure of the human race their pretension has cost?

But woman is told to look on this triumph of civilization, in place of her degraded condition, especially as to the East, where the light of the gospel is not heard, or does not prevail. No thanks to the gospel, for all this is the light of mind, not the bible. In the East there is a plenty of analogous gospels. This is the pure capital of mind. that is made to do all that can be done for the world under the supervision of Providence. Mind is the agent of Deity.

But we must not reject the overtures of mercy, offered by the bible. Whence are they? What commission has that bible? We merely require its pure proof. We must adopt the path of safety. Is the bible essential, or is God? Where do we find God? Not in the bible. That is the peculiar god. What is christianity of itself? An existence independent? Not an iota. It is due to mind, unfortunately grossly and vulgarly perverted. How modest are those, then, that pretend to claim all that is intellectual for christianity, that itself has not just claims for its own existence! When tried before the only proper, which is a rational tribunal, it is completely reduced to a perfect absurdity. Our American revolution was executed on the principles of mind.

The reformation itself was essentially due to mind.

What did the world gain by exchange of any peculiar faith, only as mind advanced from the inspiration of the cave to that of the bible, the bible of mind?

Rome changed her pagan, for pagan-christian idols. What better proof can be furnished by christianity herself than her ignoble position in regard to the crusades, that for nearly two hundred years spread ruin over half the known world? What sort of arts and sciences did she then furnish, but those of butchery and fanaticism?

Is this civilization of the world? That makes life as agreeable to everybody, all, as practicable.

But, says the priestocracy, what of the ancient Romans or Grecians can compare with the purity of the morals of Christ, especially his sermon on the mount?

That sermon, ascribed to Christ, cannot begin to compare with the light of Godly principles. I have no doubt such sermon, as the boast of the book, refers to the paternity of many fathers, who toiled at it for many a long year.

Let us analyze points, some of which have been previously referred to. This is the sermon of sectarianism, and as such cannot bear the searching analysis of religion. Matt. ch. v. 17. "Think not that I am come to destroy the law, or the prophets: I am not come to destroy, but to fulfil." All this is suicidal, of morals or religion, when such are based on perjury, as already proved. The next verse involves him in a still worse category, as the endorser. The morale then of this sermon is below a religious standard. Ch. vi. 13. "And lead us not into temptation," addressed to the Almighty Creator of the universe, is sacrilegious, blasphemous libel; addressed to the peculiar god of Judaish provincialism, is false pretence, and an outrage most degrading on the people. 24. "No man can serve two masters: for either he will hate the one and love the other; or else he will hold to the one and despise the other.   Ye cannot love God and mammon."   Behold, Christians, the truest mirror of your own position.

In holding to God the creator, rational mind despises the man-savior; and in serving the first, mammon or Christ must be unserved.   If God the supreme be loved as appreciated, the counterfeits all must be hated.   Ch. vii. 11.   " For this is the law and the prophets."   Their law negatived the principles of God by sectarianism, and of course were ruled out, as authority, by religion.

Verse 15. " Beware of false prophets," &c.   And who could be a falser prophet than the preacher, the most demagogical ?   21. " But he that doeth the will of my Father which is in heaven."   That is, as expounded by this rabid sectarian, his mouth-piece pretended.   All this potently and certainly reflect the priestocracy dramatists. 22. " Many will say to me on that day, (that decides the entrance into the kingdom of heaven,) Lord, have we not prophecied in thy name ? and in thy name have cast out devils ? and in thy name done many wonderful works ?"

This is a very Jesuitical piece of monkish demagogism, to catch the verdant world. This is very low, wagish electioneering, but if it were covered with the darkness that Moses affected to mind-facture, it cannot escape due analysis.   It savors of the very hot-bed of all the essence of priestocracy, and is too strong for a pure atmosphere.   No sir, the mount sermon is surmounted by a holier and purer influence, that the priestocracy regime could never attain, never divine.

All their oracles cannot survive, in its presence.   All such bibles are the work of mind, and undeveloped at that; hereafter those of rational mind must take precedence, so far as the last are highest accredited by rational religion.

Isolated cases will not do, however fine morals are presented.   The mens sibi conscia recti. of Horace, will of itself furnish a splendid exhibition of morals, in the briefest space.   So will the moral speech of Confucius, quoted by Christ himself.   But science and philosophy only can irradiate refined civilization.   And do not overlook that the universe was all the time under God, and that rational mind lives.   We must take all Christ's history and its bearings, and that betrays the worst sectarianism and blasphemy. Both sides ought to be discussed.   As it is, it is only one-sided.   Sectarianism killed off Socrates, but Christ killed himself off by his own sectarianism.   When this question is analyzed, we have to recur to a world-wide morals, that a liberal conservation will demonstrate as due to God alone.   What are morals but .the noblest conservative principles, exempt from sectarianism ?

The unity of God alone cuts out this detestable blasphemy.   Why, if christianity be the right way, the true one of mind, that the unsophisticated world has not been converted ?   It is said that the warrior Black Hawk remarked, that the whites showed the path, but they did it for money.

Mind is the only way to produce progress, and its evolution is like the stately oak, the monarch of the forest.

Where, says the preacher, do we find all the blessings of life, but in a christian land ? Are they positively due to christianity ?   Was there not infidelity also prevalent ?   Monotheism did not help the cause ?

Was not the immortal author of the declaration of independence, an infidel ?   Was not the author of influences leading thereto, a pure infidel ?   Was not that independence founded in opposition to a government, that had union of church and state, the very thing. above all others, the most to be deprecated by the world ?

Yet none had morals but christianity.   Where is the first proof of all that ?   Had we the correct history of the past, what a different tale would be told—as that mind had furnished a harvest for excerption in the world ; that patriotism was furnished by several nations, especially the Greeks, Romans, Carthaginians—equal to any of the moderns.   Truth is furnished by some.   That is a constituent of religion.   Was it furnished by the Jews ?   Not at all, though it is the first of religion.

What can be better than honesty ?   Was that honesty, to pirate the country of peaceable citizens ?   Their peculiar god allowed it, but not the God of the universe, whose code of morals is written in eternal principles of justice, not in blood, gory fanaticism, and abominable bigotry.   Can the Christian and Mahommedan be united?   That, as all other unions of mankind, is a chief blessing.

So far from them, that the Latin and Greek churches cannot fraternize.   From whom, christians, did you get your idea of a trinity ?   Is that original, or did you borrow it of Plato, or of the oldest Asiatics ?   Bible advocates condemn philosophy as to their creed, and yet how many ideas have they not borrowed of several so-called philosophers, as Plato, or those that he borrowed from ?

The predecessors of Pythagoras had a sublime idea of astronomy, and that teaches the idea of the Great First Cause, and this teaches to look at the universe as cause and effect, and to rule out superstition.

Does christianity possess this glorious triumph?

As she does not, her undeveloped mind proves her in the barbarous ages of existence, utterly incompetent to advance the world's civilization ; then she is to be led the right way by monotheism.

All this, in process of time, that matures the functions of time, through the phenomena of nature, on which mind reasons. The Christians have introduced Josephus; if they be thereby convicted, then their testimony should be ruled out. Strict justice shall be done them, in due process of this work.

Prayer is communion before God, the confessor of the universe and with one's self, for self-correction and amendment. But God is too elevated above mind, for it to approach such a presence as that of Deity. That pretension, of mind's not approaching Deity, would do, if mind was an alien ; but it is the creation of God, and is identified with his preservation, correspondent to the soul's merits.

How does the silly polytheist mend the matter, by feigning a Mediator, man-savior! Has crazy bible sophistry stultified him? He cannot do so, for there is none other. That position makes it incomparably worse. There is no other way than through mind. The Athenians were superstitious, and so are the Christians ; what is the difference? What wars there were between the Arians and Christians! The Christians became triumphant, by the sword and imperial power. And yet, at the very best, if there were really any difference, the defeat of the Arians proves the Christians the greater pagan idolators!

Christ, a mortal, and also a God! Reason, thou wast then butchered at the shrine of nonsense. Religion, thou wast prostrated at the feet of peculiar faith. Mind, thou wast crushed, under the power of credulity, under the brutality of paganism.

But we must have a messiah to pray to!

By prayer, people correct themselves, not change God, by being raised to the dignity of principles. Do they expect, by prayer, to make a mutable out of an immutable Being? What nonsense! Can a mutable change an immutable Being? Would not the praying undo much, most absurdly by their petitions or prayers? The best would wind up the universe, by their finite minds, if they had their prayers granted.

How many secret infidels are there, even in churches? If they are afraid, even in this free country, to say their souls are God's, how is it in monarchical despotisms, that are united to church hierarchy, which they are sworn to support? How was it in the days of the inquisition?

Mind has advanced to a sublime position of world-congratulation. The pope, that was once superior to monarchs, was humbled, and even expelled by his own people. A few more such deeds, and the victory is the people's. But, then, mind must triumph in its justice, and over social, and all proscriptions.

That triumph is attainable in rational religion, that is the creation birth-right of the world. It is high time that mind and religion should assert their dignity. Those who adjudged heretics, and persecuted them to the death, were the blasphemous heretics against God and mind.

But the house of David was to give the messiah. Then, of course, we have not the true Christ, as his genealogy, nor blood-connection to David, that was absolutely essential to prove, by prophecy, his credentials, is certainly not proved. Did Christ originate any new principles? Yes, in dying for sinners, by his blood-redemption. But the sophists do not know when they are vanquished. They are as ignorant as the priestocracy, of which they form part and parcel. Instead of principles, this was their abrogation by crime in effusion of blood not available. All such premises penalty or murder ; at best only premises the fanaticism of monomania, that blasphemes the creator-savior. How then did he prove his mission? By his miracles. His chief miracles were expulsions of the devil, that could not possibly be in existence, as it was not practicable to get the devil from bible's heaven, and he was not available taken according to the Talmud, by the notions of the Persians, to whom the Jews were indebted for the knowledge thereof. Then Christ's miracles are not only an imposition, but a blasphemy, consequently they cannot furnish credentials, an antagonism to the Creator. All had better honestly and truthfully confess the whole. the sooner the better ; as it has to be done by the world of freemen. The very best proof of the futility of his pretended miracles, and his false position, was, that he could not convert the Jews, who could not have been kept from him, any at all otherwise.

But the apostles risked their lives for him!

Did they at first, when they deserted and perjured themselves on that desertion? In what did they excel the pagan Juggernauts, who martyrize themselves also?

In the greater self-interest, to be realized?

But how came the Jews to reject Christ, if he ever was presented them? Was it not that he was considered to be their mighty leader, to avenge them on the whole tribe of invaders from Babylon to Egypt? Who can be better entitled than the Jews, to interpret their own scriptures? Was an interested party to decide it? What presumption! Mind, under the circumstances of creation that gives the widest legitimate latitude to free moral agency, does away with the fall of man. How could man fall, when God is a perfect being? That position excludes the nonsense and crime of final redemption, and intermediate libels on God, who is not indebted to experience for improvement. All that, is the nonsense of the priestocracy.

Christ only followed Foe, of India, his prototype, and in the most essential particulars. This individual existed, it is pretended, many centuries previously. His was a spiritual empire. He pretended to divinity, and that he was the Savior of men—born to expiate man's sins.

They were to be punished that did not believe in him. He affected many miracles attested in his history, that was written too by several of his disciples. Very many believed in his doctrines.

Christ, of the present New Testament, is conclusively a false messiah, and not the one prophecied of, as descended from David. Then the bible Christ is false. If the advocates of Christ had not done too much, they would have done it better. Had they made him the son of David, they would have had the prophecies, but as it is, they have made him spurious, illegitimate, and false messiah.

Ps. cxxxii. 11. "The Lord hath sworn in truth unto David; he will not turn from it; of the fruit of thy body will I set upon thy throne."

Matt. i. 18. "Now the birth of Jesus Christ was on this wise : when, as his mother Mary was espoused to Joseph, before they came together, she was found with child of the Holy Ghost." If any man assert, as if knowingly, that Christ is the prince, the true messiah, the assertor is an impostor, if he do not prove his position satisfactorily to the principles of reason.

To say that God had need of a Savior, implies his own imbecility in ratio. If God be perfect, no Savior can exist. That is conclusively undeniable, and condemns Christians to eternity.

What merit has Christ to be the redeemer of the world on his own position, when according to Matt., xv. 23, he answered her, (the woman of Canaan who besought him for her daughter, grievously vexed with a devil) not a word. Yet to his disciples, 24, "But he answered and said, I am not sent but unto the lost sheep of the house of Israel." How indignantly did he treat the poor woman, as if a dog!

But the daughter's cure, and the worship by the mother, exalted the priestocracy.

Will anything stop the christian in his false messiahship, but the want of money, that may not be in the treasury? When the people stop supporting all such folly and wickedness, as these exploded doctrines of the ancients, then will all such end and not before. Some know no better, some will not change for interest. We know enough to satisfy the most skeptical, and hold ourselves responsible, to the strict construction of facts, without modification. Sir William Jones, says: "We may fix the time of Buddah, or the ninth great incarnation of Vishnu, in the year 1014, before the birth of Christ." Whence the incarnation of Christ, but from this idea? After all, the priestocracy are preaching a false Christ. Now we can well see, why the Roman Church interdicted the reading of the scriptures.

Is the divinity of Christ, established by God?

If there were ever a preter-natural darkness that prevailed, at the time of the crucifixion of Christ, and identified with it, let alone all the cotemporary miracles, the whole world, Jew and Gentile, would have been converted.

How could they have been kept from it?

People forget what they are at. They commit themselves too plainly. But what object could these good apostles have in lying? The same, that the bigots of every peculiar faith did have and show. They are self-convicted perjurers. If such church had never had inquisitions to enforce the creed, less surprise might be excited. But how many pious frauds from first to last, have been worked in this imposition? Inquisitions never made books?

What tyranny was more ferocious? Was Nero's?

If a God, Christ must have had prescience, if not omniscience, then he must have foreseen the impracticable difficulties, that even now exist, at the distance of more than eighteen centuries, and he would have remedied them. Why did not Christ if God, write his own memoirs as the most capable of fulfilling his whole mission, and fixing God-facts carrying conviction? He had but to act, to speak his miracle, if in char-

acter. If any book of the apostles was expedient, that part was left out undone by him
assuredly, for it was most requisite on his part. Though according to Matthew, xxviii.
18, Jesus claimed all power, as given him in heaven and in earth, yet is that proved?

Missionaries should carry something worthy the attention of mind, to those nations
that they visit, certainly not a false faith of a false messiah. They should learn to carry
out, to the ancient nations of Asia, something of universal faith, to redress the severe
grievances of peculiar pretences, and not leave the world worse than they find it. No
wonder the Chinese scorn the outside barbarians when tested by a faith analogous to
Bhuddism, rejected by them.

So far from doing justice to God, some ministers preach mostly about Christ, and
nearly leave out God. Can their impiety be overlooked? If the redemption of mankind, by any messiah was essential or proved, then a new principle was proved, but as
God's attributes are perfect, he made creation with all essential and necessary principles,
and has left mind untrammelled by the bribe of future rewards, unterrified by future
retributive justice, except by enlightened conscience, since the question of immortality
is to be decided by appropriate functions. It is really disgusting, to see the ministers
of pretended revelation claim possessions, by bible pretences unfounded. How absurd,
for courts to use bibles, that no justice can prove!

From whom did you get your Christian faith directly? From Rome, that had
stretched human vices to their utmost tension: had deified emperors for gods, and
canonized men for saints; whose rule was imperial despotism, that played its last expiring game through the insidious sophistry of a part of the world-governing priestocracy. Her people, sunk to the lowest stretch of mental degradation, ignorant,
vicious, and crushed by assuming power, received any and everything that sophists
could impose.

But mind, the God-made mind, is resilient; but when lately the people had sought to
extricate themselves, here come foreign fanatics, assuming to be republicans, to crush
the popular spirit. It was not enough that inquisitions had luxuriated over the rights
of the people, a military despotism was to crush the soul of liberty. France! your
genuine spirit was not there.

Alas, degraded priestocracy, how much does poor human perverted nature betray
itself, in your pretences. You bring forth a god, but you degrade him below the man.
You expel devils of your creation by him, and you brutalize, then victimize the poor
hogs! Instead of the devil among the hogs, it was the devil among the priestocracy.
that made Christ the devil in the world. Your mock hero does not know whether a
fig-tree is barren, and impiously curses it for his ignorance. Can human blasphemy go
higher, than you have gone? I do not seek to avail myself of the stereotyped idea of
magic perpetrated by Christ, when a much better solution is at hand. I must read
what is so clearly written.

Psychology discloses to us what may be done with the mind, that in a state of passivity
can be mastered, for faith and action. I have caused, as others, subjects to see, feel,
and act, as directed. Water has inebriated, the ghosts have appeared of those long
dead, and the seven devils have been extracted with the utmost facility of theatrical
performance. The main psychology is in the pen of the priests plenipotent.

Jesus has to inquire about the state of the provisions, ere he fed the five thousand!

There might have been an obscure person of the name of Christ, but not such a being
as painted by the priestocracy, who fixed up the whole matter. The conduct of the
Jews about the false Christs, as if there were any other, proves the Jews ready to follow
any that could prove themselves by miracles. But their prophets have deceived them,
and they, poor blockheads, expect some mighty character, even to this day. Reason
asks for consistency, in all things of this universe. What can be more incorrect than
bible language, as well as ideas? We have many expressions of matters about the
heart, that seems to take precedence of the mind, in matters of peculiar faith. Much is
said about love and the heart. What is the physiology of love? Is it an impression
on the heart? Is it not, certainly, on the mind? Derangement of mind takes place:
do we hear of that of the heart, in such matters, any more than of the four corners of
the earth, when the proper language is the circles of the earth?

The world was going just as well when Christ or his fiction-makers came into, as
when he went out of it. What need had the world of him? His death only proves his
own mortality, and his life the false pretences of the priestocracy. Is there anything
remarkable that he, a sectarian, should victimize himself? How many hundreds and
thousands, Christs, Mahomets, and Smiths, have done all this, the world over? How
many millions of followers have martyrized themselves for their peculiar faith? What
has the world to do with any crazy bedlamite named?

How many millions of patriots have fallen, the world over, in defence of all that they held dear, country, faith, and families?

It matters not before how many millions died, as that is of no account. Is the proof before us, of disinterested persons, competent to decide on the truth of their declarations?

Bhudd, Mahomet, are all entitled to credence, if mere book assertions are to be believed; no pagan can take precedence.

I have no need of the ancient opponents of the Christian faith—the advocates of which have to prove their bible authentic, or they, with all pagan thieves, have to die on the cross of faith.

The affiliated only saw Christ after his death.

Cannot we get people to believe anything, even the most absurd, about peculiar faiths?

The world is full of such, to the present Mormons. What was the body of the apostles, as to real respectability of character? I do not mean as to their employment, which has nothing to do with this matter, but their standing on the position of honesty and truth? All were perjurers. Who could safely trust them afterwards, in matters of respectability.

Is Messiahship to stultify or felonize the world?

Were the ancient ages any other than positively lying and perjured ones, for thousands of years? This looks dreadful. No matter how much corruption it depicts, it is necessarily so. The world lied constantly about the various pagan faiths, diversified in every country by peculiar customs and causes. The people of the present age must not overlook how the oracle lies were palmed on kings and people, who sought such humbugs. The world liked, and sought it. It helped, as the moderns, to humbug themselves.

The priestocracy lived by it all their lives. They still batten on the folly of mankind. Dared any man to innovate, death was the result. The murder of Socrates proves that.

More recently, dared any one write or publish, he was burnt at the stake. And how is it now, in this, the finest country on earth, in some respects? The delinquent, as he is considered, cannot be attacked by law, but he is proscribed by social organizations, church policies, bible bullies, and a host of excommunications of usurpation and monopoly. Let the whole world proscribe peculiar domestic education, that makes hypocrites and perjurers, soul-frauds. Can the sovereign people see that oracles were the dynasties of the world?

What difference does it make, whether if booked or verbal? Were there not oracle books?

Have the people forgot all the lies told about superstition? If I help to expose all such, do I not act a most friendly part to the world?

Great empires have state faiths. China and Russia have their pontiffs in their emperors. What important measures were not invoked by Constantine, who helped to propagate the Christian faith? The idea was to concentrate at Rome, the head of the empire, and for the empire, all the divergent faiths into one. What better could unite the people, the world under her dynasty?

This was enough to energize her hundreds of bishops, and all their machinery.

But empires, nor worlds, much less the universe, can be held together, without conservative principles.

And would not books be considered her most powerful energies? Why her councils and imperial edicts, but to evangelize the world? The world has to look at this dynasty-ecclesiastical, that was to contribute all potency in establishing a general empire.

The church and state of Rome, labored to enslave the world. They are being defeated, even in their own circles. The ruins of both are before the world. The christians, or all peculiar sects, are too small for me to have any antagonism with. All such are in the way of religion. Give the aid of an emperor, at this day, even to the Mormons; give them the sword and the purse of a large empire, as that of Rome once was, especially such a superstitious people, and they could go through the world successfully as many other sects. But supposition comes in for Luke's genealogy for Christ, making it that of Mary, instead of Joseph. Why so? Because it differs so much from that of Matthew. But does Luke say, that it is Mary's? Not one word. Then is it supposition that this document, the new testament, is based on, when the whole world was open for the messiah to prove his mission unmistakably? Inspiration and revelation do not depend on supposition, unless they are of men. Rational religion does not depend on supposition. It goes right to reading God's book, from effect to cause, on the principles of causation. The new testament people are horridly hard run, to get the sign of the son Christ from 7 ch. of Isaiah. How foolish is the world to resort to pitiable sophistry for such, when rational religion gives her indisputable facts? The whole plan of salvation, pictured or pretended by Christ, is essentially a futile and worthless perjury. Ask these pretenders, who destroy all mere truth, reason and mind, by their attempt, what is to fill up the chasm of four thousand years for the world so long destitute of Christ. Instead of honorably speaking like honest and truthful men. that God the Creator, who endowed the universe with all the necessary conservative principles, for all time, from its inception to its perpetual eternity, instead of arguing this point on the facts, they sneak off that God is not to be questioned about his system or plan, and that must suffice; that is, the priestocracy say all that, for their false pretences. To say that it is God's plan effectually and truthfully, they must positively prove that theirs is God's. That is impossible, as no planner plans against himself. as this is positively so. How is that? God was supreme, as effect and cause positively proves. and that leaves him in the supremacy of unity. Any invasion of that sovereignty, is the plan of antagonism. God could not commit suicide, however the priestocracy do. But say these wiseacres, if the bible system is broken down, the world has only the system of atheism. That is the worst perjury. Are the people to be for ever gulled and deceived, and that by felon-perjurers?

The world only gets rid of all pagan idolatry, and its abominable priestocracy. If a minister is so ignorant as not to know, so dishonest as to deceive his audience on this important subject, he ought to be excluded from society, whose interests he deserts. whose benefits he forfeits, and of whose confidence he is unworthy. If you do not prove Mary's genealogy from David, there is no true messiah on the position of the bible, and christianity is most truly wound up. The world can decide that part of the question, on the data given.

The idea is advanced in Gen. iii., that there was a fall of man by means of the serpent, and that he had to be regenerated by views altogether as absurd and blasphemous. This is all gratuitous. There was no serpent. It will not do for the world to stand by, and see itself imposed upon in this way about Christ. Why did not the Jews embrace Christ, to whom they had an equal right as any? It is absolutely absurd and most ridiculous, to suppose them stupid and blind to their own god.

What! the chosen people of God, above all other people, to mistake their own chief good, is the most preposterous of all stuff. Either they had the right faith, or they did not. It is claimed by Judaism and Christianity, that an improvement was to be made on Judaism, and that proves that Judaism was deficient. But what filled up this deficit, for thousands and thousands of years? God could not leave a deficit of such time, and then curse the world for refusing to give up what he had given his peculiar people. There are many deep things involved in this statement, that reflect the deficit in the statement, not in God. It is a blasphemous libel.

The Jews had a superstition of faith, and no pure religion any more than the balance of the pagan world. The whole world has never expressed with the Jews, any pure religion. It is all, so far as Judaism is concerned, a bigoted faith, and christianity involves itself in deeper disgustfulness of polytheism. Both have pretended to make gods of mortals, and degraded the pure God to all the brutality of man.

The difference is, Judaism made all her priestocracy God; christianity made one of the priestocracy God, and his officials demi-gods; both made peculiar gods of their priestocracy. Where is the analytic mind of the world?

What absurd things the apostles are made to have written. John xxi. 24: "This is the disciple which testifieth of these things, and wrote these things: and we know that his testimony is true." Who endorses we? What honorable man can? Can rational mind, when he says in the last verse 25, "And there are also many other things which Jesus did, the which, if they should be written every one, I suppose that even the world itself could not contain the books that should be written." Can any rational man believe that when his greatest are recorded in twenty-one chapters of John, a very small volume indeed, that the balance could fill an ordinary sized table?

The perjuries of these perjurers are before us.

What confidence can be put in the so-called fathers or apostles, as Paul or Ireneus. who says, "The gospel was preached throughout the whole world, to the extreme parts of the earth, by the apostles and their disciples." Was America preached to? Who can believe that, any more than the pretended Moses who said that the whole world came to Egypt to buy corn? These are obvious. To reach messiahship by priestocracy or by Christ, weak and corrupt minds will detract from God's universal perfection. The mind-fraud is horrible. All peculiar faiths, as that of christianity, are founded on superstitions, and the whole is a brood of sectarianism, that has to reflect the paternity of a perjured priestocracy.

The first incarnation of Bhudd ought to have been the true one, as he instituted or originated it. Could Christ, the follower, originate any new principles, when Bhudd or Foe did all, if any could, when if God be perfect, he did all at creation. Of course all such false pretences will be brushed away as worthless, before the first great cause. Let mind be mind for once.

Horne says, "There never was a more learned, more philosophical, or more discerning age, than that in which the christian religion was proposed to mankind." Religion is it? Then what becomes of all the refining, humanizing influence of christianity, in the dark ages? After all the vaunts of its advocates, who assert that it was the elevator of mankind? Did it not add the worst quota to the dark ages for two centuries of wars? Did not the infallible head of the church cause one part of the continent to wage war upon the other grand sectarian division, cause a third part to be pirated upon, and the remainder to suffer the extirpation of millions of its people? The world must see the rank imposture of putting it instead of cultivated mind. God has no works of supererogation, for he accomplishes many results by one means. If the solution does not agree in principles, the fault is in mind.

How can christianity or any peculiar faith be the great advancer of civilization, when it arrests from mind its rights, and from rights their freedom? The position is suicidal. What was Christ's mission for? To fulfil the law and the prophets. Mind could only do the first in every land, and therefore most clearly excludes the last. What good was sectarian education to the world, when it propagates such, the most positive and vicious errors? Constitutional government and rational religion, both provide for the improvement and due use of mind and conscience. The world is entitled to them. Shall it be put off by the counterfeits that are impracticable and silly? Constitutional government emanates from mind; all others from power assumed or obstructed. The principles of our government actually shame all peculiar faiths, that are of no value to the people, and self deception to the priestocracy. How could Christ originate any new principles, when his prototype one thousand years—Foe or Bhudd—had instituted all such by his ninth incarnation in the great east? But then, Christ superseded him. On the same logic, Mahomet superseded Christ, and Joe Smith the Mormon or latter day man, superseded all of them. The proper way to tell it is that monotheism is the only religion that was always in rightful existence, without which mind would have been no where, and therefore as the whole brood of peculiar faiths, Judaism, Christianity, Mahomedanism, Mormonism, Bhuddism, &c., are in direct antagonism thereto, they should be made to clear the world by appropriate use of rational mind in double quick time.

Rational religion is the only orthodox, infallible, immutable faith. But christianity is the light of the world, as is assumed by others. To whom do we owe our declaration of independence? To mind of infidels.

An infidel wrote it, and an infidel supported it. That independence to its best triumph, cut loose church and state.

Christ could not unite the Jew and Gentile under one head. Monotheism unites the universe. Atheism is the necessary result of polytheism, as, detract from God's attributes, and we lose that much of respect. Polytheists do this invariably for their detestable profits to the priestocracy.

Christianity violates the first principles of the universe. What is its history up to this time? Its leader defeated in all essentials, resting on a corrupt and rotten foundation. The doctrine nurturing up to the present time. most abominable festering corruption, so degrading that analogous prophecies are used.

But then the poor fishermen had no ambition this way. All they sought, was to be good.

Who swayed the potent sceptre that managed them? Who is the pope? Did the Egyptian priestocracy ever wield greater power? Is he not above law, below principle? Where can despotism be more sacrilegious? Are his secret star chambers no inquisition tribunals? Who has license of crime, and divided the spoils of sin? The man that has the keys of Peter, as is pretended. Now, whence the miracles of his church? Of course from Christ. But the Protestant objects most strenuously to those of the Roman church. Then all the moral religious world can object to those of Christ, whose word is falsified if the church cannot perform them. Truthful people know, that no such miracles are used.

Christianity has retrograded on Judaism, that was bad enough. Judaism was a miserable failure, and has left its curse to the world. It is the most perfect humbug about christianity, possessing all the light of science, when she does not possess the first principle, that of amelioration or advancing to the highest grades of refined civilization by monotheism. All her capital is stolen from rational religion. What sort of justice can we then meet at the hands of an ignorant bigot? How can we possibly expect administrative justice throughout the earth? No peculiar faith is modest, does not defer to the superior and superseding claims of monotheism the only religion, but is in direct antagonism. What could be expected in their exclusive courts? By claims to infallible orthodoxy, they exclude the world that is thus made alien. Where there is room for perjury, is that not used? Christianity in its self-conceitedness, may have never dreamed of exposure. At this day she is neither right in position, nor doctrine. Her doctrine of even passive obedience, is violative of natural laws. That of itself condemns. The greatest light of the age is separation of church and state, and that would be suicidal to christianity. Of course she cannot be entitled to that honor, when known infidels to her superstition instituted it. Never were church and state dissevered till by our country, which clearly is not a christian land. Fidelity to the God of the universe, has excluded the infidelity of christianity. Exodus, xxxiv. 6, 7. Here it is said that God is merciful and gracious, long-suffering, and abundant in goodness and truth, forgiving iniquity and transgression, and sin, how then by the very basis of operations, can they originate any new principles by introduction of any messiahship. What can it do? A work of supererogation? God acts the very reverse of all that. The third gospel dispensation is a clear proof that the first was wofully imperfect, and of course not of God. Where then is the platform for the last? It has got further off the true position. I know God, the Great First Cause, through his universe, and by that I know all that claim a Godship, are impostors. How are you now. priestocracy? The mission of Christ excludes the rights of God; of what avail then is it to man, who is the creature of God? The creature owes all he does owe in religion, to God the creator. What can he owe to Christ, for peculiar faith that is as worthless as counterfeit money? The majority of the world takes no cognisance of Christ for life, do not know of such a character, yet from the nature of existence, all breathe in the creation of God. The world then ought to appreciate what all this is worth. Just appreciation is the most difficult for the world to make: it trusts too much in this to demagogues, who are all the time self-interested in monopoly and usurpation.

The absolute humility engendered by the true appreciation of God, when mind comes to his self-existence, is enough to teach man all that is due God. No other tuition can answer. But we can get no such humility from messiahship, for we cannot truly let our mind down from the sublime eminent perfection of Deity, that thus excludes all such pretensions.

And as to the codes that are affected to be supplied, the self-vindication of principles morally and physically, teach cultivated mind, reason, all that is expedient. What more is needed?

Is man to be unnecessarily rendered dissatisfied by the covetous ambition of paltry, petty priestocracies that the world cannot be rid of too soon? The world has to abjure the very thing Christ started with, sectarianism. Under this dynasty as of Judaism, its pretended teaching: "Thou shalt love thy neighbor as thyself," is utterly impracticable, as it has the elements of its own destruction.

There of course is an end of Christ, who could not originate any principle, as his vile sectarianism was hostile to all social, civil, individual, moral and religious relations. His character was best illustrated in a world's deepest injury, that is yet deeply and poignantly butchered up. He falsified all the noblest characteristics of mind, in its illustrious world theatre.

He murdered the world, as he only taught peculiar faith that has split into fragments. He never touched religion! There it was in its own sublimity, as God gave it to the world, as well before his pretensions as afterwards.

Its power was the same, its magnificence unimpeached. The world-proof is the best.

The great object of all rational bible tuition, that of religion, was never taught by sectarians as Christ, the chief of all such. The dramatists, who, to throw the world off its guard, have been assumed to be fishermen, had the whole world to extract and compile their legend, from the learning of a Confucius, not only long antecedent but rich in treasures of legislative predecessors; in the character of a savior they had a prototype to the very life incarnation of Foe or Bhudd, who had accommodated the world the ninth time; they had the reformer in the example of a Socrates, who willingly suffered death, and their mystical ideas of a trinity could be drawn from the ancient Egyptians, and more recently from the metaphysics of Plato, besides the cunning, the fictions, and systems of all the ancient oracles. How much longer is poor humanity to be racked by all such impositions? It is for the people to see all, but how difficult is it for them to get their ideas up to conservative revolution? What a terrible thing is ignorance, that has absorbed under malign powers all the errors of superstition. It is most difficult to be divested of all the stains and taints. How many believe the character of Christ perfect, yet what sectarian can begin to be in this blasphemy?

How can love be in any peculiar faith, that necessarily has sectarianism, and private, if not public enmity of the other sects? Such, love yields and the Christians have used all the power they could get.

They have created all their most potent influences, a papal empire, spiritual and temporal, to meet the last most comprehensively.

They pay due respect to all temporal matters, their peculiar way. If christianity be the superior light it is claimed for the world, where was its pre-eminent power of science in all the fanaticism that has spread over so many fields of carnage?

It was founded on another sectarianism that knew not mercy, from the Canaanites down to their last devastations and civil wars in Palestine. The many bloody scenes since, assure us that the offspring was true to the nature of the parent. Had Christ been perfect, he had conquered the world's worst enemy, his motto—sectarianism. He was not sent but unto the lost sheep of the house of Israel. That he was sent to the Gentiles, was an after-thought, proving itself most clearly that of a mortal—as God has forethought. Polygamy has been abolished, by the second dispensation. Was it not abolished also at Rome, and in Palestine as part of her empire? Is not all this clearly the result of mind, and not revelation? I speak of the spirit of cultivated mind. Christianity has nothing to do with wars! What should induce a war, for the restoration of the Pope? Has christianity given the highest evidence of religion, in separation of church and state? Did it support the true system of astronomy? Are not the Hindoos ahead, in their peculiar faith, one thousand years, at least, of the Christians? Will not the Hindoos laugh at Christians teaching these doctrines, that they were taught by Bhudd fourteen centuries in advance? All that christianity or any peculiar faith has ever done rightfully, is subsidiary to rational mind. They have become usurpers to mind for themselves—ungrateful assassins in perverting and crushing it.

If the world had been civilised, we never would have had such stuff as christianity, mahommedanism, &c. Judaism was imperfect, then christianity was ineffectual. Mahommed tried his ideas, then Joe Smith his. The world should exclude all such stuff. The only civilizer for the world is rational religion.

Judaism and christianity are woful failures.

Juggernaut beats the world for self-devotion and martyrdom of victims, that devote themselves to death. Yet, christians are committed to the folly and crime of their profession, in pagan idolatry, and are ashamed to retire therefrom. Christ and the woman of Canaan give us to learn, that the last suggested an idea all at once. Like master like man, his disciples wished to drive her away.

How came Christ to say, "My God, my God, why hast thou forsaken me?" Was he not to suffer all that he did suffer? Or was it too late, that he found out his mistake as a false messiah?

As to the Jews, they believed in a temporal king for Christ. All that could flatter the people, alluded to the means of future elevation by some great king at Jerusalem. This was a national vanity. Subsequent priestocracy profited by it, as much as Joe Smith, the shrewd Yankee, did on Judaism, Christianity, and Mahommedanism. They were all reckless of the means, provided the success was there. Joe Smith could innocently invent plates by which he could lie, Mahommed could find an angel to carry him to his heaven, and Christ was as available to a third party, being a second edition of Asiatic faith, all in the chapter of faith perjury. Who believes that the apostles speak many different languages, when Paul lies the most of the difficulty by the Holy Ghost. The Roman, the largest empire, the scene of most if not all their operations, had some common general language, the Greek as well as the Latin. That is the secret. As to their documentary proof, have the Christians any existing manuscripts of the new testament, that can be traced higher than the fourth century? Who is so verdant as to not know, that perjurers availed themselves of all the perjury to the latest period! Christ's prophecy of the temple! Anything else? This is important. The last dispensation, as still of man, most absurd, has to be corrected. The credit of all is impeached as sacred.

As Christ came on earth for a particular mission, as pretended, then he should have written all requisite with certain date, time and circumstance, to insure all needed to mind, and to prevent corruption, which, as a prophet, he should have known. In the absence of all this, it is most fair to conclude that it is an imposition and nothing else, as the Creator wrote all his perfect. How came Christ not to go himself to all the Gentiles, the world, or send his disciples to them or the Samaritans? Matthew, ch. x. v. 5. Jesus commanded them, "Go not into the way of the Gentiles, and into any city

of the Samaritans, enter ye not." He sent them rather to the lost sheep of the house
of Israel. Mat. x., v. 6. What is surprising is, 20. "For it is not ye that speak, but
the spirit of your father which speaketh in you." The spirit of the priestocracy spoke
certainly. The God of the universe is universal, yet how blasphemous is the next, how
abominable to the earth. 21. "And the brother shall deliver up the brother to death,
and the father the child : and the children shall rise up against their parents, and cause
them to be put to death." No, God's principles cannot clash ; of course the preceding
is positively condemned as man's work and writing. Sectarianism is here most prominent, especially in 34. "Think not that I am come to send peace on earth ; I came not
to send peace, but a sword," and 35. "For I am come to set a man at variance against
his father," &c. ; 36. "And a man's foes shall be they of his own household."

The God of the universe is not at variance with his own conservative principles.
All such Christs are horrid impostors.

The fathers of the church were as deep in the mud as any. The council of Laodicea
admitted four of the gospels, and rejected all the rest. All the edicts of Constantine
could not divest christianity of sectarianism. He made it subservient to his ambition
and policy, and affirmed by an oath, of his seeing an illuminated cross in the air, as
Eusebius relates. Now, if any tender conscience doubted my views as too strong, if
he is not convinced by the solemn perjury of Constantine, then he is a hopeless chance.
I do not envy him, his mind or integrity. The trinity in the Godhead, or the Godhead,
originated from the metaphysics of the heathen, the pagans from Egypt, and through
Plato.

Yes, the Christian who, for mere effect, not truth, as he fears for his glass house,
abuses the pagans, the heathens, as ignorant and incapable of giving any ideas of faith,
is indebted actually to them for many particulars, above all, the trinity. The Egyptians
had a trinity, that had in each of its three divisions, separate powers, it is said. The
first was an indivisible unity. Hence Plato's ; but his was a godhead.

Christ's performance of his mission, in gaining proselytes, was not faster than that
of mortals, and confined, too, to a small circle. I presume the prototype of Christ, in
Palestine, might have been the vagrant Jesus spoken of by Josephus. Much of the
pagan systems before the world, have been mere world-explosions. The redemption of
the world, by the blood of Christ ! Were this true, then murder is in it.

But we speak of the might of an Almighty, who not only created the universe, but
all the principles that rule all therein. Can mind ever conceive, much less appreciate,
who the Almighty is ? It has erred, by affecting to alter parts and principles of God's
universe, by bible dispensations, but this vulgar employment of the priestocracy can
avail nothing. Those that I act with, go with me, for the supremacy of God, that
completely silences all messiahships. This is an essential matter for the world, to allay
all agitation, and keep all the peculiar bibles away, and put all the priestocracy to honest
employment, instead of lying.

Was Christ satisfied to die, when he exclaimed : "My God, my God, why hast thou
forsaken me ?" Is not this a part of the author's drama—that of a poor mortal, suffering and afraid to die ?

All the statements made about the deaths of infidels, are on a par with this. How
many females, as well as males, die in this country, without any such change as has
been pretended about a few ? What is all death-bed repentance either way, worth ?
What do the opinions avail ? Is a sick man balanced in mind ?

I say again, as to women and men dying infidels, enough have died, as they lived, in
their pure faith.

Man has been created with intellectual, and moral, rational organs. He has to cultivate these, rationally. What has Christ to do with the cultivation ? To admit him,
defeats the ancient title of God. The world has to come to a whole union or brotherhood. and no peculiar faith, as Christianity, Judaism, or Mahommedanism, will do, having, as all such have, the elements of their own destruction. Is God the Father of all !
Then was there not incest committed in the procreation of Christ ? Was there so much
vile, vicious degradation, in the universe ever conceived ?

Incest had to conceive him, illegitimacy had to sustain him, imposition had to uphold,
and blasphemy had to create the thought ! There were murder and treachery, and
there have been massacres and despotism since, of millions. Where is all this human
tragedy to end ?

Instead of being the redemption, it is the greatest curse that ever was conceived of.
But where can the Christ-messiah be placed, as available, in this part of the universe
of the Creator, who is most perfect ? The creation of man, progressing as all earthly
processes, proves, as the action of the universe declares, one unvaried action of principles, without which chaos and confusion would arise, and by which they are excluded.

Were a Christ introduced as a sun into our solar system, the greatest confusion and disorder would necessarily arise. It would be a work of supererogation, the very reverse of God's deeds, who brings forth many results from the fewest principles. Christ by the side of Washington! How the last towers above the first, as much as patriotism, much less religion, towers above peculiar faith.

In everything of cause and effect, I see so much of God, his perfection so great, his principles so conspicuous, that I cannot possibly see that any other could be admitted. It would be a sacrilege to nature, a libel on God, to do so. Who preserves mankind? God ; who actually protects and defends all who seek after strange godheads, dwarfed peculiarities.

But for him, these small characters, who preach up peculiar faith, would ruin the world and themselves. I cannot possibly believe in them, as they are irrational, crazy. Christ on the earth, yet equal to the Father, a part of the Godhead, and yet die! Of all the metaphysics of sophists, that beats all.

No peculiar faith christianity, or other, can produce pacification, much less the refined civilization to the world, but will exclude them as long as nurtured. The supremacy of the world is that of God, as displayed in the universe ; all else is false pretences. As to the death of Christ being a new principle, the Juggernauts do that plentifully even now.

Where is the operation of mind, for more than half of the world at any one time, for 1800 years, that knew not Christ, or other peculiar faiths, than those of their household? Where was it all the time preceding this mission, for the whole world, thousands of years beyond all bibles ?

Where is it now ? Is the operation of the Creator overlooked in all this matter ? That reflects on the whole tribe of the priestocracy. And shall the word-minds yield up this most important right, without investigation and justice to God of all ?

Mind owes unalloyed, pure, unadulterated allegiance to Almighty God alone. Christ was conceived in sin, and brought forth in iniquity. I had much to satisfy myself that I was not wrong, and was glad to see myself so right.

How can man's soul reach pardon ? By God's grace. The same that has answered for all mankind, before bibles, messiahs, and priestocracies were ever conceived of. Christ adds nothing to God's means, being altogether the available mercenary capital of corrupt men. People, in the world, attribute all, or much, to Christ, whereas, were it not for God, all would be ended, assuredly. What can be worse than the vicious characteristics of Christ's sectarianism? Christ's advice to the harlot was good. But religious principles establish rational education and means for pure justice, before all that. His crime, sectarianism, kills all of the world-good. The greatest despots can do some first-rate acts, as mind dictates.

Christ came to the lost sheep of the house of Israel—and what the Jews would not have, the Gentiles, to whom he did not send his disciples, nor preach himself, at first at least, took him up!

I doubt the propriety of passive toleration, as the proper world-policy. It is not the right position. That would leave moral free agency in abeyance to predestination. When adequate blows are to be received as well as given, when no impunity is established, then the world is brought to its senses.

How came Christ not to write his own laws, and report his own system? Was not that the proper way to have all right, if he was divine ? Who could give a better exposition ? This defect is certain proof that he was only a mere man, and that all about him are impositions. The Christians, as others, say that the world-people must be born again, to be regenerated. What a pagan conception. They have to be anew created, with new organs, and those perfected by rational education of science. What effect can peculiar education produce ?

Mere delusion ? What good does that do ? Christianity does not embrace principles conservative, as evinced by sectarianism, for says the protestant, the Pope has power and uses it iniquitously. And would not any protestant church secure union with government, if it could, and were that the case, power would be only needed to do the balance. Which of peculiar faith, can be trusted with power ? None, each would say of the other. Why does the church organizations differ so much now, about the constitutional laws of this union ? From the relative purity of mind, more or less rational.

But this elevation of life's blessings is not because of christianity, but of mind cultivated, that of science, where bible's explosions must prevail. The lands of the east have been those of despotism of mind, by monarchy and peculiar faith combined. Whereever mind gets freer and more enlightened, there will be the purer rational religion.

What has Joseph, the husband of Mary, to do with the blood relationship of Christ ? If prophecy was ever worth anything, it is here essential, as God swore to David about the seed from his loins. But this Christ is not that seed! There is an awful perjury somewhere. Now christian, what are you going to do about it? You now find that you have been cheated awfully, as to the prophecy. Whose work is all this? That of the priestocracy. Are you going to let them cheat longer and pay them for it, when other genuine claims of philanthropy demand all your benevolence? Are you going to forsake the sublime contemplation of pure religion the God-gift, for the peculiar faith the perversion of degraded priestocracy? I am no free-thinker beyond the limits of rationality, the sacred precincts of mind. I adhere to the correct legitimacy of pure religion as best appreciated, with the brightest lights of the universe. Justification by faith, was the great conservative doctrine taught by Christ. That is the peculiar doctrine of all peculiar faiths, and has no peculiar merit of its own, for the priestocracy down to the Mormon Joe Smith, have appropriated all that as their exclusive property.

How singular is it, that Christ cannot justify faith, in his genealogy.

Do I believe that the apostles were sincere? They started perjurers, all of them, and confiscated their writings, as Constantine swore. They are a part of priestocracy, and act in the same category, and were no more right, than we have a correct genealogy of Christ being lineally descended from the blood of David. The world can only be best governed, by the wisest forecast and independence of rational mind.

The doctrine of passive obedience will not do individually, much less rationally, as the world must stand up for its rights, if it do not, Moses will not, nor Christ, for they take care of their priestocracy. Much is claimed by the advocates of each peculiar faith, that it has such things, that could not have been ever thought of without revelation. Now all this is the stuff of their sophists, that impose it as sound faith on the world, when it is not worth the thought of an honest mind, for any such imposition can damn all such false pretences. All that, and mysteries betray the whole, as alien to mind, that recognises the eternal universal, not peculiar principles of the God of the universe.

The making of one man of fiction a Christ as suffering, and having millions of flesh and blood sacrificed to it, is horrible indeed, and enough to arouse the true sympathy of the religious. Can you sacrifice the world to Christ? That's the question.

Can you, free and intelligent people, stand all this any longer? All superstition, ever a branch of despotism, has pervaded the world. How many little picayune christs, and all the same under different names and dresses, have imposed on the world? The priestocracy are the same in all ages, whether in the form of patriarchs, prophets, martyrs, christs, Smiths, or preachers, and they mind-facture all such. They never learn, and never forget: bound to their car of idolatry and superstition, they enslave the sovereign people, who are bound in the progress of rational education, to hold all professions of medicine, law and faith, in abeyance to principles. Is the great God of the universe to be held in abeyance, to all the dwarf messiahs of man's creation?

What does the world need of a western Christ, a mere copy of the eastern, whose history was given some ten to fourteen centuries before?

The Romanists found customs in China, the prototype of theirs. All priestocracy, is the same folly and crime, only varied in editions.

To put a messiah for nature, the sun, is just as bad—all detract from the functions, potency and rights of the creator. Rational mind is ashamed of all this.

The appropriation of principles, all the property of God their creator, as peculiar discoveries to entitle the party to a godship, is one of the most flagrant breaches of trust on mind, the greatest outrage on its rights.

The principle of doing unto others, as we would have them do unto us in similar circumstances, was notoriously not only previously known to the Chinese, through Confucius and his ancient predecessors, but must have been familiar with any such civilized society, as one of its noblest mind-entitled principles of uniform action and protection.

Carry out all conservative principles, says religion, and the world will be right. Thus where obsolete bibles make world a wild, principles ennoble the whole habitation of mankind.

All sectarianism, as Judaism, christianity, cuts up the highest social feelings, isolates the world into sectional strife, depraves the noblest impulses of mind.

In partially civilized times, the conflict of arms decides for the world, thus governed by force, and necessarily by fraud, sectarianism, whilst in civilized, that is, where mind governs itself, principles peacefully decide through rational mind, that courts and wins the loveliest triumphs of all.

How much of each peculiar leader's views, can be turned against himself? "You cannot serve two masters," teaches his followers, that they cannot have the creator and creature, God and a messiah, that are incompatible and cannot be. They must have no image of idolatry, the messiah or the fleshy one as bad as that of metal or stone, any graven image, or any other made by the priestocraty, or the priestocracy idol.

But Christ inculcated regeneration, being born again, the renovation of the heart! In that he was not original, for that is the doctrine of the Brahmins, and all teach absurdities, for the heart is a mere muscle—and all such stuff is as obsolete as peculiar faith bibles: All sheer ignorance. Cultivation of mind, refined civilization, all under the supremacy of religion, the most rational, produces the best, because the most rational results.

But Christ brought the gospel of glad-tidings. Rational religion is the only true gospel: all else is damnably false. As to testifying about Christ, by four or a dozen disciples or evangelists as they are assumed, that is nothing if there were as many billions of mortals, they pretending to testify to an incredible impracticability, gainsaid by a universe of cause and effect. With the testimony of cause and effect, better heard every day before the tribunal of an enlightened community, against these four evangelists or twelve apostles as they are called, in reality the church advocates of the present day, rather the sticklers for the church profits, paid by the deceived people of the world, were they as many millions, it would only make them perjurers. They cannot upset the eternal truths of the universe. God has written them, and the world of man's bibles is all trash.

No black letter book sovereign, can represent properly a savior, who requires other authentic proofs as adequate as the creator—all else is base imposition.

Universal functions as claimed, require universal proof, but all records show peculiar pretences, that disprove themselves as perjuries, before God and mind.

MATTHEW'S AUTHORITY.

THE whole world cannot trace Jesus to Joseph, and thence to David, the asserted genealogy, taking the Holy Ghost conception!

Ch. i. v. 22, " Now all this was done, that it might be fulfilled which was spoken of the Lord by the prophet, saying, 23, Behold, a virgin shall be with child, and shall bring forth a son, and they shall call his name Emmanuel ; which being interpreted, is, God with us." That proves no prophecy, being only a garbled falsification. This was a sign that the volunteer Isaiah forced on Ahaz, after his absolute refusal. Isaiah, ch. vii. v. 12, " But Ahaz said, I will not ask, neither will I tempt the Lord." And then Isaiah gives the sign in v. 14. And Isaiah says, 16 v., " For before the child shall know to refuse the evil, &c.—the land that thou abhorrest shall be forsaken of both her kings."

' What a stupid set of priestocrats to advance this obsolete explosion! It kills itself dead. Matthew's master should have been at the school of honesty, to learn truth.

Again is Christ descended of David, because Joseph, one of David's descendants, was Mary's husband after she was pregnant with Jesus, by another individual! If this was the Holy Ghost of God, then is God's function changed, for he is Creator, not procreator. Down, Matthew, thou art a degraded libeler. Would an intelligent husband be reconciled to a prostitute wife, by dreams ? Are the world people to be fooled by dreams ? Ch. ii. v. 2, " We have seen his star in the east." The wise men said it ? How is that fact established ? It would be by that star yet most particularly, but there is no such record produced, and that star does not remain. It is then a perjury.

This is a collusion of shrewd priestocracies, instead of wise men, and them too the book, or gospel writers.

John endorses Christ: who endorses John. Matthew. Who endorses him? Faith, wonderful counsellor. And the final endorsers, are priests' collusions. Among them are several applications of the so-called prophecies to Christ. We do not see the first adequate one ; they are as worthless as the sign spoken of by Isaiah.

Ch. iv. v. 24, As to devils, there were none. Though the lunacy and palsy could be affected, yet the general false pretence doctrine covers all that. The world cannot but see the false prophets by the result. Ch. viii. v. 13, " And as thou hast believed." It was not so much the centurion, as the readers or hearers. 10 v. " When Jesus heard it, he marvelled, and said to them that followed, verily I say unto you, I have not found so great faith, no, not in Israel." What pains the priestocracy took to arouse faith, that is credence. As they necessarily lied about curing persons said to be possessed of devils, we must believe that they would lie about all other things. There is no need of the patient affecting palsy, because the masters affected all story of its cure. 34. "And, behold, the whole city came out to meet Jesus: and when they saw him, they besought him that he would depart out of their coasts."

This is self-contradiction—it is not human nature, the gospel writers commit them-selves as stupid dolts, for with such powerful miracle proofs, the people would have believed in him as a God, as he cast out many devils.

Ch. x. v. 14, 15, and 16. The curse of those not receiving the priestocracy, is to be established through the most influential power, an assumed God. 34, "Think not that I am come to send peace on earth ; I came not to send peace. but a sword." It is clear enough that the worst sectarianism in the most blasphemous antagonism, was advocated by Christ in this and several ensuing verses against God of nature, as in 36 v. "And a man's foes shall be they of his own household."

John and Christ were only endorsers for each other, in a priestocracy sense. Too much is proved by the machinery of devils and angels, nonentities.

Ch. xiii. v. 58, "And he did not many mighty works there, because of their unbe-lief!" The very reason he should have done them ; that is then man's idea. If he had been a God, one would been enough. The miracle he could best have performed, was creation of belief. O stupid gospel fabricators, you involve yourselves deeper and deeper.

Ch. xvi. v. 18, "And I say also unto thee, that thou art Peter, and upon this rock I will build my church: and the gates of hell shall not prevail against it." And the rock was proved a perjurer by Christ, who falsifies the statement about hell, and a hypocrite by Paul, himself a murderer. What a family. All the worst against this church next to God's conservative principles, are its own elements of destruction, that are going like St. Peter's church building. 19, "And I will give unto thee the keys of the kingdom of heaven ; and whatsoever thou shalt bind on earth, shall be bound in heaven ; and whatsoever thou shalt loose on earth, shall be loosed in heaven." This is promise of God's functions most blasphemously made, to build up the priest-ocracy. Functions that this one-third character at best, had not. Ch. xxvi. v. 56, "But all this was done, that the scriptures of the prophets might be fulfilled. Then all his disciples forsook him and fled." What prophets are they that need fulfilment ! If crimes of blasphemy and murder are to be fulfilled, better sink prophets and scrip-tures. Prove the very first one. Would the disciples of a God have deserted him ! That is impossible.

This is the book of those, that are bound to prove it satisfactorily. Devils and angels can be no machinery in the functions of the Almighty, hence both bibles libel him.

Mind, not tradition is for man. All such stuff satisfactorily proves that it was the peculiar gods of polytheism.

JOHN.

John, ch. i. v. 18, "No man hath seen God at any time."

29 v., "The next day, John seeth Jesus coming unto him, and saith, Behold the lamb of God, which taketh away the sin of the world!"

This is priest sophistry Jesuiticated. What can beat that?

This is God's word. Of course his word is supreme over man's. Now, prove it by the witness you claim.

You assert, what men assert about God.

Does God confirm that ? No ! not one single word.

Then it is convicted of being the reverse. Next, as God does not speak, which proves as much necessity as when it is claimed, that he first inspired all the bible works, the pretensions are nullified.

An inspiration bible, requires inspiration proof.

As God does not speak, let his works that truly represent him, proclaim the facts, and they do declare him as the Supreme Unit of the universe.

Matthew as Luke, are forgers. Imbecile vassals may adopt the forgeries. In Mark, last chapter, the impostor speaks of preternatural events, that belie him as a prophet, and prove him a lying impostor. These are in the 17th and 18th verses.

They refer to the apostles, says the sophist apologizer, who commits himself most stupidly to arrant imposture. Not at all, as St. Paul refutes that idea. But some wish to deny the plain facts of this quotation, but Paul prevents them, if the inherent proof were wanting that is clearly present.

Thus it is that this Christ is a false messiah and prophet, self-convicted before the God-creator.

Those that espouse such, commit themselves to reckless blasphemy, and brutal pagan idolatry.

Monotheism alone can exalt all to the noblest God-standard, and confer his munificent grace to the soul. The unsolved problem of religion, the consummation of principles, proves pre-eminently immortality of the soul, and if the world adopts any mansavior or messiah, it absurdly drops principles for such that violate all of them.

WAS THERE EVER SUCH A BEING AS CHRIST? IS NOT HIS CRUCIFIXION, A THEOLOGICAL DRAMA?

THE authenticity of all the bibles of tradition rests on no foundation worthy a rational mind ; that of the New Testament is nullified by too many particulars, that cannot be refuted.

We have been induced to notice the authority of Flavius Josephus, by the work of Mr. William Jacobs of New York, and find that Josephus is deserving of especial notice, as he is introduced by the Christians as testimony.

We avail ourselves of Mr. Jacobs' quotations, &c., reducing the extracts to the smallest practicable compass.

The Jerusalem Jews are accused of having scourged, crucified, and nailed to the cross on Mount Calvary, one Jesus of Nazareth, in the 18th year of the reign of Tiberius Cæsar, third emperor of the Romans, when Pontius Pilate was procurator of Judea. This fabricated accusation is put forth by the writers of the gospels, Matthew, Mark, Luke, and John, who state that they were eye-witnesses of the fact, or that they heard the relations from eye-witnesses.

This accusation is stated by Mr. Jacobs to have been first preached in the second century, about A. D. 107, against the Jerusalem Jews. At that time the Romans had dominion over the Jews, who had no temple, and whose high-priesthood was abolished, including the destruction of the principal men of that nation.

Those gospel tales matured for the space of two hundred and eighteen years, from A. D. 107, when Clement was the apostles' amanuensis, just after the death of Flavius Josephus, down to the council of Nice, A. D. 325.

To refute the accusation, many points must be embraced.

At the taking of Jerusalem by Titus Cæsar, A. D. 70, all the Hebrew records were conceded to Josephus.

These records came down until the twelfth year of the reign of Nero, (Jos. Antiq., book xx., ch. xi., sec. 2.) as here ends the taking down of the Hebrew records by the high priests.

Josephus, as he himself informs us, translated, not wrote his Antiquities of the Jews from these very Hebrew records, A. D. 93. Have not some of these works been suppressed, or altered? Who did it? Was it not for the benefit of the New Testament? Where are all the books referred to by Josephus?

To the tribunal of an intelligent world this investigation is submitted. Jacobs claims that the Jews had no longer their original records, to disprove this calumny.

At the council of Nice, A. D. 325, about ninety gospels of tradition were destroyed—when these written gospels were retained and canonized.

In those days the Jews had to submit to awful indignities.

According to the testimony of Matthew, Jesus of Nazareth was born in the days of Herod, the king of Judea—and the same Jesus was put to the crucifixion of the cross, under Pontius Pilate! And this under God's warning, angels' warning, and fulfilment of prophecies, as evidences.

We must advert to the first three chapters, of Luke's Gospel.

ST. LUKE, CHAP. I.

VERSE 1. " Forasmuch as many have taken in hand to set forth, in order, a declaration of those things which are most surely believed amongst us." 2. " Even as they delivered them unto us, which from the beginning were eye-witnesses and ministers of the word."

Verse 5. " There was in the days of Herod, the king of Judea, a certain priest named Zacharias," &c. &c. 26. " And in the sixth month the angel Gabriel was sent from God unto a city of Galilee, named Nazareth. 27. To a virgin espoused," &c.—to verse 36. " And behold thy cousin Elizabeth, she hath also conceived a son in her old age ; and this is the sixth month with her." &c.

The birth of John the Baptist and conception of Jesus are detailed in the first chapter of Luke, and all these things happened " in the days of Herod, the king of Judea." It was in the sixth month of Elizabeth's time, when the angel Gabriel was sent from God to Mary, the mother of Jesus of Nazareth, not yet born ! !

ST. LUKE'S GOSPEL, CHAP. II.

Verse 1. "And it came to pass in those days, that there went out a decree from Cæsar Augustus, that all the world (Syria and Judea) should be taxed."
The second verse designates the most remarkable chronology, the precise period of time when Jesus of Nazareth was born!   2. "And this taxing was first made when Cyrenius was governor of Syria." This whole chapter gives a different relation and evidence from the accounts given by Matthew! Here we see that Jesus of Nazareth was born in Bethlehem of Judea, "when Cyrenius was governor of Syria," and taxing the Jews: &c.   3. "And all went to be taxed, every one to his own city.   4. And Joseph also went up from Galilee, out of the city of Nazareth into Judea, &c.   5. To be taxed, with Mary his espoused wife, being great with child.   6. And so it was, that while they were there, the days were accomplished that she should be delivered.   7. And she brought forth her first born son, and wrapped him in swaddling clothes, and laid him in a manger; because there was no room for them in the inn."

ST. LUKE, CHAP. III.

Verse 1. "Now in the fifteenth year of the reign of Tiberius Cæsar, Pontius Pilate being governor of Judea, and Herod (Antipas,) being tetrarch of Galilee, and his brother (Herod,) Philip tetrarch of Iturea, and of the region of Trachonitis, and Lysanias the tetrarch was of Abilene.   2. Annas and Caiaphas being high-priests; the word of God came unto John the son of Zacharias, in the wilderness," &c.   23. "And Jesus himself began to be about thirty years of age, being, as was supposed, the son of Joseph, which was the son of Heli." &c.
Matthew says Joseph was the son of Jacob.
All the other gospel writers confirm the testimony of Luke, as to his statements concerning both John the Baptist, and Jesus of Nazareth; for all say or imply that John was beheaded by Herod (Antipas,) the tetrarch of Galilee (and Peræa,) in the first or second year, (which was the 16th year of the reign of Tiberius Cæsar!) after Jesus commenced preaching!
Luke only tells us of John the Baptist's conception and birth, and his conception being in the sixth month before the conception of Jesus; therefore, the other three gospel witnesses, one and all, confirm Luke's testimony as to the conception and birth of Jesus of Nazareth.
As the New Testament writers, in their gospel relations, have made reference to Herod, the king of Judea—to Archelaus the son and successor of Herod—to Augustus Cæsar and his decree of taxation—to Herod, the tetrarch of Galilee (and Peræa,) who was one of Herod the king's sons—to Cyrenius governor of Syria—to Tiberius Cæsar—and to Pontius Pilate, procurator of Judea, in the time of whose procuratorship John the Baptist is said to have been beheaded by Herod, the tetrarch of Galilee and Peræa, and Jesus of Nazareth is said to have been put to the crucifixion of the cross by the Jerusalem Jews—it therefore becomes necessary to introduce the best authentic history, to illustrate the subject, now under consideration, and to apply the whole of these things to the rules of historical and chronological criticism.
This testimony is that of Flavius Josephus, respecting the historical records. Whiston's translation of Josephus, from the Greek, is used.
In the first place, are there no interpolations in Josephus? There are three different sections in "the Antiquities of the Jews," considered spurious; to prove which, we must anticipate in other matters. When Herod was first declared king at Rome. (See Antiq. Jews, book xiv. ch. xiv., sec. 5.)
"And thus did this man receive the kingdom, having obtained it on the hundred and eighty-fourth Olympiad, when Caius Domitius Calvinus was consul the second time, and Caius Asinius Polio, the first time." (The Olympiad being a term of four years.)
Herod commenced his reign, upon the taking of Jerusalem from Antigonus—above three years after being declared king at Rome. (Antiq. Jews, book xiv., ch. xvi., sec. 4.) This destruction befell the city of Jerusalem on the hundred and eighty-fifth Olympiad," &c.
This relation concerning Antigonus was recorded in the Jewish (sacred or holy, so called) books, translated A. D. 93, by Josephus, into Greek, who was born 73 years after the record was made, in the first year of the reign of Caius Cæsar. (Antiq. Jews, book xv., ch. v. sec. 1.)

The great battle was fought at Actium, between Octavius Cæsar, (afterwards called Augustus Cæsar) and Antony, for the supreme power of the world, " which fell into the hundred eighty and seventh Olympiad." (Same book and chapter, sec. 2.)

" At this time it was that the fight happened at Actium, in the seventh year of the reign of Herod," &c., counting from the death of Antigonus, not when Herod obtained the kingdom, at Rome, above three years before, according to the translator's note. (Concerning Herod's death, and testament, &c.—Antiq. Jews, book xvii., ch. viii., sec. 1.)

" When he had done these things, he died, the fifth day, after he had caused Antipater (his son) to be slain; having reigned since the death of Antigonus, whom he caused to be slain, thirty-four years; but since he had been declared king by the Romans, thirty-seven years," &c.

Josephus treats in the same book, xvii., &c of Archelaus, Herod's son, as Ethnarch; and in chapter xiii., section 2, he says: " But in the tenth year of Archelaus' government, both his brethren"—Herod Antipas and Herod Philip—observing once for all, that Herod, the king, left but three sons when he died, &c.—accused him before Cæsar, (Augustus.)

Sec. 4. " Glaphyra, his wife, was married while she was a virgin, to Alexander, the son of Herod, and brother of Archelaus. Alexander was slain by his father. She was married to Juba, the king of Lydia, and when he was dead, and she lived in widowhood in Cappadocia with her father, Archelaus (the Ethnarch,) divorced his former wife, Mariamne, and married her." Sec. 5. " So Archelaus' country was laid to the province of Syria; and Cyrenius, one that had been consul, was sent by Cæsar to take an account of the people's effects in Syria, and to sell the house of Archelaus."

When Cyrenius was sent, as compared with Luke's gospel. Antiq. Jews, Book xviii., c. i., sec. 1.

" Cyrenius came himself into Judea, which was now added to the province of Syria, &c., yet there was one Judas,"—of a city whose name was Gamala, &c.—became zealous to draw them (the Jews) to a revolt, &c. The time for this taxation is fixed, when Cyrenius was governor of Syria,

Antiq. Jews, Book xviii., c. ii., sec. 1 :

" When Cyrenius had now disposed of Archelaus' money, and when the taxings were come to a conclusion, which taxings were made or decreed in the thirty-seventh year of Cæsar's victory over Antony, at Actium, he, Cyrenius, deprived Joazer of the high-priesthood," &c.

Concerning the life and reign of Augustus Cæsar—Antiq. Jews, Book xviii., c. ii., sec. 2, (middle of section):

After him came Annius Rufus, under whom died Cæsar Augustus, the second emperor of the Romans, the duration of whose reign was fifty-seven years, besides six months and two days, of which time Antony ruled together with him fourteen years; but the duration of his life was seventy-seven years. upon whose death, Tiberius Nero, (Tiberius Cæsar,) his wife Julia's son, succeeded. He was now the third emperor; and he sent Valerius Gratus to be procurator (governor) of Judea." Gratus deposed and made several high priests, the last was Joseph Caiaphas. " When Gratus had done these things, he went back to Rome, after he had tarried in Judea eleven years, when Pontius Pilate came as his successor."

There was but one high priest at a time.

Under the procuratorship of Pontius Pilate, and reign of Tiberius Cæsar (in " Antiq. Jews",) is found the famous " section" of fourteen lines! concerning Jesus. As this section is spurious, as to be demonstrated, so also is that of John the Baptist and James the Just, the forerunner and brother of Jesus.

The first account, we think, which the world ever had of this famous section, was manifested about 324 A.D.

In 325 A.D. the council of Nice made from the traditions a canon, ever since that time known as the " New Testament." The Hebrew text by Josephus has nothing on the subject concerning Jesus, neither is there anything of the kind in the Greek in Josephus' own translation; neither is John the Baptist or James the Just mentioned.

Antiq. Jews, Book xviii, c. iii., sec. 3 :

" Now, there was about this time Jesus, a wise man, if it be lawful to call him a man," &c. " He was (the) Christ"—" and when Pilate had condemned him to the cross," &c.

When the first whipping and nailing to the cross was done in Judea! Wars of the Jews, Book ii., c. xiv., sec. 9 :

" And what made this calamity the heavier was this new method of Roman barbarity; for Florus ventured then to do what no one had done before, that is, to have men of the equestrian order whipped and nailed to the cross before his tribunal," &c. Under Gessius Florus, was the first whipping and nailing to the cross ever done in Judea, and that, too, in the sixty-sixth year of the present era!

Both whipping and crucifying were old methods. But now " For Florus ventured then to do what no one had done before," &c.

Josephus gives but one more instance, in all his "Antiquities of the Jews," and " Wars of the Jews," of whipping and nailing to the cross, &c. General reference can be made to Josephus, for this authority :

	Yrs.	M.	D.
1. Julius Cæsar commenced and reigned	3	6	00
2. Then Augustus Cæsar succeeded and reigned	57	6	2
3. Tiberius Cæsar " "	22	5	3
4. Caius Cæsar " "	3	8	0
5. Claudius Cæsar	13	8	20
" Nero	13	0	8

And it was in the twelfth year of the reign of Nero, when Florus acted, as we have quoted! See " Antq. Jews," Book xx., c. 11, sec. 1 :

" Now this war began in the second year of the government of Florus, and the twelfth year of the reign of Nero." The falsehood of the gospels can be easily deduced and demonstrated.

Josephus says that Nero sent Portius Festus to succeed Felix. It is written in the " Acts of the Apostles," that it was Festus before whom " St. Paul" was brought.

Luke tells us, in chapter xxv., verse 21st, " But when Paul had appealed to be re-served to the hearing of Augustus." (Cæsar is a generic name, applied to " The Twelve Cæsars," but Augustus is not!) 25. " But when I, Festus, found that he had committed nothing worthy of death, and that he hath appealed to Augustus, I have determined to send him."

Luke makes Portius Festus say that Paul had appealed to Augustus, when he, Augustus had been dead and buried, at this very time, about forty years ; for the acts are said to have been written thirty years from the death of Jesus, in the eighth year of Nero! How could Augustus be appealed to?

Acts, chapter v., verse 34. " Then (A.D. 33) stood there up one in the council—Gamaliel, a doctor of the law—had in reputation among all the people, &c. 35. And said unto them, (that is, unto Annas, the high priest, and Caiaphas, &c.) 36. For before these days (A.D. 33) rose up Theudas, (in the latter part of the fifth year of the reign of Claudius Cæsar! at least twelve years after the reputed A.D. 33 !)—and all were brought to naught. 37. After this man (Theudas) rose up Judas of Galilee in the days of the taxing, (when Cyrenius was governor of Syria, in the fifty-second year of the reign of Augustus Cæsar! !) Is this divine inspiration? Is this a reliable portion of eternal truth?

" Anno Domini" commences, according to common account, in the third year after the death of Herod the Great, and consequently the " Bible Anno Domini 33" brings us to the eighteenth year of the reign of Tiberius Cæsar.

But Luke tells us, in the second chapter of his glad-tidings, that Jesus of Nazareth was born in Bethlehem of Judea, " when Cyrenius was governor of Syria," and taxing the Jews in Judea ; and this was exactly in the fifty-second year of Augustus Cæsar! Then the above " Anno Domini 33" should have been, instead of falling in the eighteenth year of Tiberius Cæsar, in the second year of the reign of Claudius Cæsar! Of Theudas see Antq. Jews, Book xx., c. v., sec. 1—while Fadus was procurator of Judea :

Theudas—a certain magician, (affected) to be a prophet, and many were deluded by his words. They also took Theudas alive, and cut off his head, and carried it to Jerusalem. This was what befell the Jews in the time of Caspius Fadus' government. This is a mere abstract of the whole section. Antiq. Jews, Book xx., c. v., sec. 11 :

The reader will see that Theudas was "brought to naught," instead of the eighteenth year of Tiberius, A.D. 33, in the fifth year of the reign of Claudius Cæsar, A.D. 46.

Upon the authority of the antiquities, we say that Vitellius, the president of Syria, sent Pontius Pilate to Rome, after Pilate had been procurator of Judea exactly ten years ; and that Valerius Gratus had been his predecessor exactly eleven years, as we have already stated. These two procurators occupied twenty-one years of the reign of Tiberius Cæsar ; and this brings us to the twenty-second year of the reign of Tiberius, when Vitellius went, immediately upon the dismissal of Pilate, to Jerusalem, and dismissed Joseph Caiaphas from the high priesthood! So that there now remained of

Tiberius' reign, one year and five months, then the whole reign of Caius Cæsar, three years and eight months, and then five years of the reign of Claudius Cæsar, make ten years one month after Caiaphas was dismissed by Vitellius, before Theudas "was brought to naught."

But, further, the bible A. D. 33, is in the eighteenth year of Tiberius Cæsar; then, to the time of the death of Theudas, is exactly thirteen years, added to A. D. 33, makes exactly A. D. 46. Yet Luke makes Gamaliel, a doctor of the law, say. in "Acts of the Apostles:" "After this man (Theudas!) rose up Judas in the time of the taxing;" which taxing, according to Luke's glad tidings, was, "When Cyrenius was governor of Syria;" and, when, according to the second chapter, Jesus was born! and according to "Antiq. Jews," in the fifty-second year of Augustus Cæsar's reign!

Was Gamaliel Eusebius? Was Eusebius the author of the interpretations in Josephus? Was the author of this pious forgery, the author of the various works under the name of "Paul?"

A great council was convened, A. D. 325, consisting of 318 ecclesiastics, besides presbyters and deacons, under the auspices of Constantine, the first christian emperor, who, "instead of uniting the character of emperor and sovereign pontiff in himself when he became christian, as they were joined in him and all the other emperors in the pagan system of government," gave to this council the seed-plot of "independent wealth and power," to establish the tyranny of the clergy and the servility of the laity. At this council the members retained, from about ninety traditions, only four called the evangelists. These were to be the four witnesses called saints, to testify to the fact of the existence of John the Baptist, and Jesus of Nazareth—and that John the Baptist was beheaded by Herod Antipas, tetrach of Galilee and Perea, in the sixteenth year of the reign of Tiberius Cæsar; and that Jesus of Nazareth was put to the crucifixion of the cross by the Jerusalem Jews, under the procuratorship of Pontius Pilate, in the eighteenth year of the reign of Tiberius Cæsar. The council of Nice was, it would seem, to have this canon called the new testament, in Latin, for "the brethren" only. Was not this drama made not more than five years after the death of Josephus? Did not Matthew or Clement (in his "Euodius") lay the scene with regard to the conception and birth of Jesus of Nazareth in the days of Herod, the King of Judea?

Did Clement retain the holy books conceded to Josephus by Titus Cæsar, after Josephus's death?

What caused the general insurrection of the Jews in all parts of the Roman Empire, but dreadful acts; and for what cause about the ninth year of Trajan, A. D. 107? Were there any apostles of the first century? Were there any such beings, till about the middle of Trajan's reign?

The design of the canonized gospels was to confirm one another's accounts, concerning John the Baptist and Jesus of Nazareth both being preachers! One as having been beheaded by Herod Antipas, tetrarch of Galilee and Perea, in the fifteenth year of the reign of Tiberius Cæsar, because, as these gospels say, John the Baptist had, before the fifteenth year of Tiberius, rebuked Herod Antipas for taking his brother Philip's wife, Herodias, away from Philip, before this same fifteenth year of Tiberius Cæsar!

By reference to the Antiq. Jews, it will be seen that Herod the Great, about three years before his death, betrothed this same Herodias to his son Herod Philip, who was his son by Cleopatra of Jerusalem, and by interpolation in the "Antiquities," called the son of Mariamne!

But by interpolations a Herod and a Philip have been introduced, making two sons each of that name. One of each name has been interpolated, as have been the sections in Josephus concerning Jesus, John the Baptist, and James the Just. Herod the Great's will, will prove interpolation. In his last will it will be seen, that there were, after the death of Antipater, only three sons living, namely, Archelaus, Herod Antipas, and Herod Philip. Herod Philip died in the twentieth year of the reign of Tiberius Cæsar, after having been tetrarch of Batanea, Trachonitis, as well as Auranitis, with a certain part of what was called the house of Zenodorus, (but all which Luke calls Iturea, and the region of Trachonitis!) thirty-seven years. And further, that it was after the death of Herod Philip, in the "Antiq. Jews," as translated from the Hebrew into Greek by Josephus, that Herod Antipas put away Areta's daughter, with whom he had lived a long time, and married Herodias, who was now the widow and not the wife of Philip.

All preachers are now invited by Mr. Jacobs, to show that when Herod the king died, he left more sons than the three whom we have named above?

Well then, in order to show who the writer or revisor of Luke's gospel was; who the writer of the acts of the apostles was; who the writer of the epistles called Paul's was—we think the great Eusebius, according to his own doubtful words, produced the famous section in the Antiq. Jews, concerning Jesus. It seems that he was this very same Saul, alias Paul, alias Terteus, alias Eusebius Pamphili, associated with three hundred and eighteen ecclesiastics, at the council of Nice! The epistles show the great object of the council, that never intended the new testament, which was there made, to be for the people's use and reading. Now for quotations from the epistles. Luke, ch. ix., v. 20, 21 : " He said unto them, but whom say ye that I am ? Peter answering said, the Christ of God. And he straightly charged, and commanded them to tell no man that thing." So St. Matthew or St. Clement, whether his was Romanu's original drama, St. Ignatius's, or St. Euodius's drama, but as revised at the council of Nice. Chap xvi., verses 15 and 16, He, Jesus, is made to say : " But whom say ye (the preachers) that I am ?" 16, "And Simon Peter answered and said, thou art the Christ, the son of the living God." 20th v., "Then charged he his disciples (Simon's preachers) that they should tell no man that he was Jesus the Christ." The heresy was so great, that it had to be exorcised at the council of Nice. The father of this ecclesiastical history, a writer who could write concerning Augustus, Theudas and Judas, in the time of the taxing, as well backwards as forwards, was a miraculous and " inspired writer." Yet Jesus of Nazareth forbids, as the gospels pretend, his apostles so called, to make. him known as the son of God, who was sent into the world to save mankind, and absolutely attributes to God one of the grossest absurdities of which the mind of man can possibly conceive. First Tim. chap. iii, v. 16 : "And without controversy, great is the mystery of godliness," &c. Epistle to the Corinthians, chap. ii., v. 7 : " But we (the preachers) speak the wisdom of God in a mystery, even the hidden wisdom of God, ordained before the world unto our glory."

The world should observe what had been written as to " The wisdom of Jesus, the son of Sirach, or Ecclesiasticus. His prologues," &c.

Did not these furnish the idea of Jesus and Christ?

As Jesus knew the Hebrew well, what motive could Jesus have for making a translation of his own work into another language, for the benefit of strangers ? And why should Jesus himself say, " found a book" in " the time of Euergetes ?" &c., when this very Jesus lived five hundred and twenty years before a. d. commenced !

But to the quotations. First Cor. chap. iv., v. 1 : " Let a man so account of us, (the preachers,) as ministers of Christ, and stewards of the mysteries of God." Second Epistle to the Cor., chap. iv., v. 3 . " But if our gospel be hid, it is hid to them that are lost." Our is what was adopted at the council of Nice. Epistle to the Gal., chap. i., v. 8 : " But though we, or an angel from heaven, preach any other gospel unto you than that which we have preached unto you, let him be accursed." Second Epistle to Thess., chap. ii., v. 15 : " Therefore, brethren, (Preachers,) stand fast, and hold the traditions (of Nice) which ye have been taught, whether by word or our epistle."

Second Epistle to Timothy, chap. i. 14, " That good thing (The New Testament and the mystery of the incarnation of Jesus) which was committed unto thee, keep by the Holy Ghost which dwelleth in us." Chap. ii. 8, " Remember that Jesus Christ, of the seed of David, was raised from the dead, according to my gospel : (the gospel of Nice). Second Peter, ch. i. 15, " Moreover, I will endeavor that ye may be able after my decease, to have these things always in remembrance," verse 20, " Knowing this first, that no prophecy of this scripture is of any private interpretation."

The father is an infinite being, so are the son, and holy ghost. Three infinities are thus involved, the height of all absurdities! Luke, ch. viii. 10 : " And he" (Jesus) " said, unto you," the disciples or preachers, " it is given to know the mysteries," of the kingdom of God ; but to others in parables ; that seeing they might not see, and hearing they might not understand." " The Antiquities of the Jews," the ' Wars of the Jews," " the life of Josephus," and his " Books against Apion," are, in part, the prototype of " The New Testament," &c., see one quotation " Life of Josephus," section 29. " When therefore silence was made by the whole multitude, I spake thus to them : O my countrymen, I refuse not to die, if justice so require." And now see " Acts of the Apostles," chap. xxv, 11, " For if I be an offender, or have committed anything worthy of death, I refuse not to die !"

Josephus' life was written about the last thing he did !—about a. d. 100 ! This the Council of Nice's " Acts of the Apostles"—Matthew, chap. xxvii. 44, " The thieves also, which were crucified with him, cast the same in his teeth."

" Antiquities of the Jews," Book xviii. ch. vi. sec. 2. (latter part) :—

" While Herod hit him in the teeth with his poverty," &c.

Ecclesiasticus, chap. xxxv. 19, "Till he have rendered to every man according to his deeds, and to the works of men according to their devices." &c.

Luke's, Saul's, Paul's, Eusebius's or Council of Nice's Epistle to the Romans :— Chap. ii. 6, " Who will render to every man according to his deeds." Second Esdras, chap. xvi. 44, "They that marry, as they that shall get no children : and they that marry not, as the widowers."

Council of Nice's—First Cor. chap. vii. 29, "But this I say, brethren, the time is short: it remaineth, that both they that have wives be as though they had none."

It is thus demonstrated, that the works of Josephus were in the hands of the writer, or writers of the Books contained in the New Testament; and that the New Testament was written long after the death of Josephus, aided by the sacred books given to Josephus by Titus Cæsar, A. D., 70.

The New Testament was then made, at the Council of Nice. The art of printing, Martin Luther, &c., enabled us to read the scriptures, that were appropriated to the clergy. Then it was that the dawn of science enabled men to advance further, to escape the dark ages—had permission to calculate the time of an eclipse, or measure the circumference of the earth! Romans, ch. iii. 28 :—the writer says, "Therefore we (the preachers,) conclude that man is justified by faith (in Jesus) without the deeds of the law." This is to justify himself and all preachers in future time, for the gospel plan of pious lying! Now for the 7th verse of this same chapter iii., and we think, that no man, in his right reason, can construe the verse in any other sense, than, that he admits his gospels to be a falsehood! "For if the truth of God hath more abounded through my lie (told by me, and my witnesses, Matthew, Mark, and John's traditionary gospels, vamped up at the Council!) unto his glory; why yet am I also judged as a sinner?" Truth and lie are opposites—the one is of God—the other is evil.

If God cannot lie, he never entrusted that power to others. It is an assumption—a falsehood.

But the writer says, in verse 10th, "As it is written, there is none righteous, no, not one."

Now to suppose God capable of lying, would be to suppose him capable of destroying himself!

But Christ is placed as one, "Who being in the likeness of God, thought it no robbery to be equal with God!"

All this is a direct declaration of war against God's moral government over human affairs.

As to John the Baptist's being first shut up in prison, and then beheaded by Herod Antipas, in the fifteenth year of the reign of Tiberius Cæsar, for having, as these gospels say, rebuked Herod for taking his brother Philip's wife, Herodias, away from Philip while living! and that too, before the fifteenth year of Tiberius Cæsar's reign!!

In Josephus' "Antiq. Jews," Book xviii, chapters iv, v, vi, we see that it was after the death of Herod Philip, which happened in the twentieth year of the reign of Tiberius Cæsar; and there we will also see, that it was between the death of Philip and the death of Tiberius, which death happened three years after Philip's, that Herod Antipas, tetrarch of Galilee and Perea, put away his wife, who was the daughter of Aretas, king of Arabia Petrea, with which wife he had lived a long time, and married Herodias, who must to a moral certainty, have been at this very time, Philip's widow, not wife! The amount of argument is by the nature of the testimonies, that Matthew and Luke confute one another, and are confuted by the facts of authentic history.

Jesus of Nazareth could not have been born " in the days of Herod the king of Judea," and also have been born "when Cyrenius was governor of Syria."

Captions.—"Antiq. Jews," by Flavius Josephus, Book xv., "Containing the interval of eighteen years—from the death of Antigonus, to the finishing of the temple by Herod." . . . .   18 years.

Book xvi.—"Containing the interval of twelve years—from the finishing of the temple by Herod, to the death of Alexander and Aristobulus." . . 12 years.

Book xvii.—"Containing the interval of 14 years—from the death of Alexander and Aristobulus, to the banishment of Archelaus." . . . 14 years.

Making together, ...   44 years.

From the taking of Jerusalem from Antigonus, by Herod and Sarius, to the banishment of Archelaus, was just forty-four years. Josephus authorizes us to say, that "Herod the king of Judea," "lived since he had procured Antigonus to be slain, thirty-four years." It has been proved that it was after the banishment of Archelaus to Vienna, a city of Gaul, that Augustus Cæsar sent Cyrenius into Syria and Judea, to make the famous "taxings which were made (decreed) in the thirty-seventh year of Cæsar's victory over Antony at Actium ;" and, when Herod, by the Captions to Books xv, xvi, and xvii, as above, had been dead and buried ten years.

If then Jesus of Nazareth was born as Matthew evidences, when Herod, the king of Judea, was living. Luke's evidence is as large an untruth, and as base a fabrication, as was ever palmed upon the world.

For Luke absolutely says, that Jesus of Nazareth was born "when Cyrenius was governor of Syria," and Judea, taxing the Jews. And Josephus' authentic "Antiquities of the Jews," declares that these " taxings were made (decreed,) in the thirty-seventh (year) of Cæsar's victory over Antony at Actium !" And also, that Cyrenius was sent by Cæsar to make those taxings after the banishment of Archelaus and after Archelaus' country was laid to the province of Syria." Luke, ch. i. 5, "There was in the days of Herod the king of Judea, a certain priest named Zacharias," &c. "John the Baptist" was born in the living days of " Herod the king of Judea ;" and " Jesus of Nazareth" was he begotten in the sixth month after "John the Baptist," " was begotten ?" Luke, ch. 2, Twelve years and nine months after Christ's conception, and upwards of ten years after the death of " Herod the king of Judea," and after the banishment of Archelaus to Vienna, and after Archelaus' country was laid to the province of Syria, and " when Cyrenius was governor of Syria" in the fifty-second year of the reign of Augustus Cæsar, taxing the Jews there, Jesus of Nazareth is at last brought forth, exactly between five years and a half, and six years and a half, before the death of Augustus Cæsar, and therefore, just exactly between five years and a half and six years and a half, before Tiberius Cæsar commenced his reign ? At the time " when Cyrenius was governor of Syria," there was no such man living, as Herod the king of Judea.

Nor any such things as stated in Matthew, ch. ii. v. 1, " Now when Jesus was born in Bethlehem of Judea, in the days of Herod the king, behold, there came wise men from the east to Jerusalem." No such, as in verse 2 : " Saying, where is he that is born king of the Jews? for we (the wise men) have seen his star in the east, and are come to worship him." No such thing, as verse 3 : " When Herod the king had heard these things, he was troubled, and all Jerusalem with him." And all the other matters about Herod the king, even to the end of this whole chapter are contradicted. as if all, were a false statement. But, instead of fleeing into Egypt, and remaining there .ill Archelaus reigned in the room of his father Herod ; and, instead of " Out of Egypt have I called my son ;" and instead of " He turned aside into the parts of Galilee ; and came and dwelt in a city called Nazareth ; that it might be fulfilled which was spoken by the prophets, he shall be called a Nazarene." Luke says, that after the circumcision of the young child : " His parents returned into their own city Nazareth !" And verse 41, he says :—" Now his parents went to Jerusalem, every year at the feast of the passover." And Luke says, verse 2 : that Jesus of Nazareth was born, " when Cyrenius was governor of Syria." The " Antiquities of the Jews," by Flavius Josephus, establish the fact, that Jesus of Nazareth, according to the testimony of Luke, was born exactly between five and a half and six and a half years, before Tiberius Cæsar commenced his reign ! And, when Cyrenius was taxing the Jews, and disposing of Archelaus' house and money ! And now for the angel's assertion to Mary, " For with God, nothing shall be impossible." Shall God, whether he will or not, sanction the truth of Matthew's testimony : thus—" Now when Jesus was born in Bethlehem of Judea, in the days of Herod the king, behold, there came wise men from the east to Jerusalem," &c.

And, also, sanction the truth of Luke's testimony ; thus, chap. ii. v. 9, " And, lo. the angel of the Lord came upon them, and the glory of the Lord shone round about them : and they were sore afraid. 10, And the angel said unto them, fear not : for, behold, I bring you good tidings of great joy, which shall be to all people. 11. For unto you, (when Cyrenius was governor of Syria,) is born this day in the city of David, a savior, which is Christ the Lord." Is it right to suppose or say that God shall be so unlike himself, and so like these two statements as to sanction the truth of any such things ?

Others can decide on this impious boldness of Luke, Saul, Paul, Terteus, alias Eusebius, alias the council of Nice. If there be any error in all this, it is not meant by the reviewers. The fault is in the New Testament. Well, we have the child Jesus, now exactly between five and a half years, and six and a half years old, as we take Luke's 3rd chapter, verse 1, " Now in the fifteenth year of the reign of Tiberius Cæsar, Pontius Pilate being governor of Judea, and Herod (Antipas,) being tetrarch of Galilee. (and Perea,) and his brother (Herod) Philip, tetrarch of Iturea and the region of Trachonitis, and Lysanias the tetrarch of Abilene." There was no such tetrarch as Lysanias, at the time referred to.

Second verse.—" Annas and Caiaphas, (Joseph Caiaphas,) being the high priests ;"

(there never was but one high priest at a time). Verse 23rd : " And Jesus himself began to be about thirty years of age," &c.

	Yrs.	M.	D.
Jesus was six years and six months old the very day that Cyrenius arrived in Judea	6	6	0
Add the whole reign of Tiberius Cæsar	22	5	3
Jesus was when Tiberius Cæsar died, just	28	11	3 old.
Add the whole reign of Caius Cæsar	3	8	0
When Claudius Cæsar's reign commenced, Jesus was	32	7	3 old.

If the evidence of Luke, or the Council of Nice, were the truth as to Jesus' birth, " When Cyrenius was governor of Syria," Jesus could not have commenced " preaching" at the " age of thirty years," until some time in the reign of Caius Cæsar! Nor could he have been " scourged, crucified and nailed to the cross," until about the second year of the reign of Cladius Cæsar, to be thirty-three or thirty-four years old at his crucifixion!

What is the true result ? As Matthew tells the tradition by divine inspiration, that Jesus, and he crucified, under Pontius Pilate, was born in Bethlehem of Judea, at least two years before the death of Herod, the king of Judea, according to ch. ii. v. 16, Matt., " Slew all the children in Bethlehem and all the coasts thereof, from two years and under, according to the time which he (Herod) had diligently enquired of the wise men ;" and, consequently, Jesus was conceived nine months before his birth !

Yet the same God inspires Luke to tell the tradition, that Jesus of Nazareth, and he crucified under Pontius Pilate, was conceived in the days of Herod, the king of Judea, in the sixth month after John the Baptist.

Jesus of Nazareth, and he crucified under Pontius Pilate, was born in Bethlehem, of Judea, when Cyrenius was governor of Syria, and taxing the Jews " in the thirty-seventh (year) of Cæsar's victory over Antony, at Actium," which was after Archelaus had been Ethnarch of Judea, Samaria, and Idumea, ten years from Herod's death, and after Archelaus' country was laid to the province of Syria ! Yet Jesus was also born " when Herod, the king of Judea," was living ! The birth of Christ, according to Luke, is twelve years and nine months after conception, if Luke is right ! As the conception was " in the days of Herod, the king of Judea," and exactly in the sixth month after the conception of John the Baptist, " the days were accomplished that she should be delivered," " when Cyrenius was governer of Syria," in the fifty-second year of the reign of Augustus Cæsar !

Herod lived twenty-seven years, from the fight at Actium.

Josephus says Augustus Cæsar reigned fifty-seven years, six months, and two days, in all, and that of this time, Antony ruled with him fourteen years—to the fight at Actium. Therefore, Augustus Cæsar reigned alone, from the fight at Actium, just forty-three years, six months, and two days.

	Yrs.	M.	D.
Augustus Cæsar reigned, from the fight at Actium,	43	6	2
Herod, the king of Judea, reigned from the fight of Actium,	27	0	0
So Augustus survived king Herod,	16	6	2

Archelaus, successor to his father Herod, ruled as ethnarch over Idumea, Samaria, and Judea, until in the tenth year of his government. Now take these ten years,

	10	0	0
Leaving of Augustus' life at the banishment of Archelaus,	6	6	2

After banishment of Archelaus, Augustus Cæsar sent Cyrenius into Syria and Judea, to make the taxing, &c. Now add the twenty-seven years of Herod's reign to the ten years of Archelaus, equals " the thirty-seventh year of Cæsar's victory over Antony at Actium." Add to these thirty-seven years the seven years back, from the fight at Actium to the taking of Jerusalem from Antigonus, equals forty-four years, equals the amount of the captions of the three books mentioned forty-four years from the taking of Jerusalem from Antigonus to the banishment of Archelaus.

Mathew and Luke destroy each other's testimony.

Matthew says that the birth and time of birth of Jesus of Nazareth, and all other circumstances mentioned by him are true : there being no less than two warnings of God, two warnings of an angel, one advice of an angel, and the absolute fulfilment of five

49

prophecies, in the lifetime of Herod the king of Judea, to prove the statements of him, canonized as a saint.

But Luke says that the conception of Jesus of Nazareth was in the days of Herod the king of Judea, when Cyrenius was governor of Syria, and that it is true : and this is the most astonishing miracle in the New Testament.

Shepherds, angels, and a multitude of the heavenly host, praising God, prove the statement of him a canonized saint. Both prove each other false, and liars.

As to Jesus, mentioned in Josephus, in A.D. 93, Josephus translated from the Hebrew records, " all according to what is written in our sacred books ;" " for this is what I promised to do, in the beginning of this history," the antiquities of the Jews.

Christ's age could not permit any record, by the high priests, during the reign of Tiberius Cæsar.

Joseph Caiaphas was dismissed from the high priesthood, by Vitellius, in the twenty-second year of the reign of Tiberius. Caiaphas could not make that section, of course.

The president, Vitellius, had sent Pilate home to Rome, when Pilate had been in Judea exactly ten years.

As the records were with the high priests and prophets, Caiaphas had nothing to do with them. Of course, Josephus could not translate them when not written.

Eusebius' demonstration of the truth of the Evangelists, &c., to A.D. 324. Certainly the attestation of those I have already produced concerning our Savior, may be sufficient. However, it may not be amiss, if, over and above, we make use of Josephus, the Jew, for further witness ; who, in the eighteenth book of his antiquities, when he was writing the history of what happened under Pilate, makes mention of our Savior in these words," &c. : The council of Nice is the time, A.D. 325, when all this was hatched.

It will be well to observe, " that Eusebius was the renowned father of ecclesiastical history, about the year 313, A.D. At that time christianity first received a full and effectual toleration—still rising in the favor of Constantine, till it was at length declared the established religion of the empire." Soon after that, the Arian controversy involved all Europe and Asia.

The Arians went against consubstantiality, held that Christ was a created being. The most undignified contention arose ; bishops were exiled. There were council after council—the most disgraceful scenes—deliberate falsehoods, and fraud to fraud, perpetrated by them. There were deposition and excommunication, riots and massacre by the rabble of both sides.

Who were the earlier clergy, according to Gregory Nov. ? In the 4th century, they were avaricious, quarrelsome, licentious, and, in one word, unprincipled. The councils instituted miserable persecutions of heretics.

Valmo, the Arian Emperor, drove several orthodox bishops into exile. What could be more relentless than the tyranny of the bishops ?

Josephus has been one of the right hand books of Christians ; and if he be not orthodox, it is not our fault.

But here are four authors, and they saints, against one ; that seems enough to overwhelm, among bigots ; but, with honest minds, one author of veracity outweighs a world full of impostor-priests, if they be affiliated perjurers. If Josephus be wrong, then is the base of the Christian faith wrong, for the books, whence were translated the works of Josephus, were entitled, as so-called sacred books from the priests, to as much weight as any in their archives.

If the archives of Judaism were corrupt, then all sectarian creeds, that build on them, partake of that corruption.

As Josephus has been introduced by the Christians, to prove the supposed eulogium about Christ, it is right that we analyze him there.

The mere adoption of principles proves mortal acts. A co-equal with God creates principles, if he do not he is a degraded impostor. No Christ ever created principles, God did that, and superseded any such pretence. All pretences have accomplished their intended object, to stultify and fleece the poor people. But as to christianity—that is only peculiar faith, which will benefit no country, but will embarrass by its intrigues civilization. Though the world may be considered public property for most to plunder, it will not be yielded to peculiar faith a pirate of society. But this or that supposed great man, believed atheism or polytheism. That very fact detracts from his greatness, proves his error and vitiated opinion, or those of his age and times. All that proves nothing for him, and less for such creed that has to resort to such pitiful pretexts to bolster up its false faith. But what do I think of Christ feeding so many thousands ? That remains to be proved.

God does not lead man into temptation; that is a libel in the prayer of Christ, who is an ignorant but dangerous instrument of straw, in the hands of most artful, designing impostors, unprincipled priestocracies. Now so far from being messiah, he estranges mind from religion and rationality, its noble blessing, from its author God of the universe, and carries mind after strange gods, alien to its creation and preservation.

The whole is the worst state of sophists, idolatry. All this has proved the worst species of mind-cannibalism, a ferocious moloch, a sacrifice of billions upon its most unholy altars.

Christ is the peculiar god's libeller, usurper of his rights, blasphemous defamer of his reputation. The priestocracy knew the calibre of all the peculiar gods, and such petty characters made atheists. I have used my own judgment on the best analysis of this whole subject, else I might have committed myself to Socrates, Bolingbroke and others, who were forced by the vices of polytheism, or the laws of arbitrary force, to acquiesce in much of mind's errors.

Tom Paine is the most philosophical that I have read since I had nearly written this work, but I have not near read all. If christianity depend on the old bible, the new, that supersedes the old dispensation, cannot be true. The immediate resurrection of the spirit must take place, and hence that of Christ is properly disproved, as his petty dramatists were ignorant of what they attempted. In the universe, all phenomena must come under the cognizance of cause and effect, to come under their legitimate designs, the five senses over which reason must preside, to procure rational, not delusive or illusory results.

We ought to be most grateful, that we live in an age and free country, exempt from much of the malign influences of customs and habits of superstition. Christianity is western Buddhism. Both forms have been ejected, by China, very properly. What did this fanatic know of the character of God, with whom he affected familiarity? Prayer, to avoid temptation! All this is the pagan error of superstition, as God has not in his attributes such a quality. Mind has to be strictly guarded against all the besetting errors of life; always, therefore, its best judgment and most innocent action are to be promoted. The noblest views have to be addressed to mind, that mind most rational may rally most rationally against all besetting life difficulties. All systems of christs and messiahships take away from mind, most stupidly, its inherent functions, and cause it to forego all its intrinsic qualities for time, and neglectful of the brightest' hopes for eternity, as far as mind may be concerned. The Creator has, with perfect wisdom, instituted the universe aright. All rational minds have then to appreciate their duty, and perform it excellently. They have to correct themselves, not idly to expect any change in the immutable author of the universe. Such expectation is most superstitious, and detracts abundantly from the best corrections of mind.

By the principles of the universe. all christs must be annunciators of a bible of rational mind and religion, or declare themselves sectarian professors of peculiar faith, all the bibles of which are libels of God, and all the maintainers are libellers.

No amount of disciples of any proposed pretended Christ-messiah could substantiate his mission, as they as mortals have no qualification to entitle mind, that they supplant to credence.

As to the existence of Cæsar, Alexander, or the Jesus, not Christ, the vagrant mentioned by Josephus, they are historical statements that are probable and possible; but no prophecies, miracles, are probable or possible, while the universe exists. All the universe addresses a rational being's senses all the time, and rebukes all the peculiar bibles as utterly false, by the very existence and nature of things.

But you affect that Christ had enough, besides his genealogy, to identify him.

This defect about his genealogy is impracticable, and renders the whole cause hopeless. As to any other evidence, that remains to be fully tested.

The clearest language of God, the Creator of the universe, cause and effect, conclusively contradict all prophecies, miracles. Mysteries and enigmas, are the works of the priestocracy, who fabricate all the necessary machinery of peculiar faith. ·All such is analogous the world over, whether Christian, Jew, or Mormon, or any other pagan; all are to deceive the world, the best being the most artful deception, and the most profitable investment. Names are nothing, faith is nothing, actions prove all, and the thing itself stands out in the boldest relief. Priestcraft and kingcraft put their heads together, complotted in collusion to come it over the world, the sovereign people, who have stood looking on at a vulgar distance, most awfully deceived. For thousands of years the world progressed as God had made, not needing anything but the best light of rational mind, the guardian and protector of the people, till superstition and its myrmidons got the ascendancy. Mind was so constituted that it was to solve the universe problem, but here came the priestocracy and arrested its proper functions of religion, and gave the basest substitute, the worst coin, peculiar faith, that appropriates even God the Creator. Fortunately for mankind, and rational religion, the whole is mockery, a vile pageant, a base imitation. All is contingent and partial. Its bibles have mistranslations, wrong punctuation, the deepest corruptions and falsifications; whereas, God's scriptures are read by all the world, though speaking thousands of different languages, without difficulty, and would have done so to the end of time, but for the most blasphemous corruption of the priestocracy.

Who are the worst sinners of the world? The priestocracy, who mislead the world from religion and God's bible, to their peculiar faiths, bibles and tricks. Whether they be the Incas of Peru, or the Brahmins of Hindoostan, the priestocracy are the same, devoted to their peculiar province. They all have their tradition most peculiar, and seek to be the children of their peculiar god, the sun, and other fancies. All the pretenders have the odious legends of faith, and put their peculiar gods in very bad company. The trinitarians place their best peculiar god in company with an earth-born, a mortal, who died, and make them equal. Now this makes the chief too small for physical or religious competency—most clearly so. But they do worse than all that, for they put both in the worst of bad company, even with the devil, with whom they have familiar conversation. Now all this is the creation of the priestocracy, and proves vitiated taste and miserable morals, no religion. The disciples have not the requisite qualifications of mind in regard to the God-gift functions, as God's word convicts all oracle-mongers as liars, degraded, the vilest of the vile.

As doctrines of sectarianism conclusively clash, those of Christ demonstrate him to be a mortal, and not any intellectual, him or his foster-guardians, coadjutors, and supporters. Christ forgave sins. How blasphemous were the priestocracy, to lie so. How imbecile is mind, or the world, to think so. But these missions captivate. How valuable, when money is the fund. Suppose China or Hindoostan were to send a mission of peculiar faith to this part of the world, which they might reasonably do, inasmuch as western Buddhists had corrupted the faith by idol worship. How could they be successfully met? By faith? That establishes them. By reason? That destroys you, Christians, entirely. You cannot begin to talk of the unity of Catholic faith, for that you have broken into fragments by peculiar views, and you are the younger branch of the same tainted family, nor can you rule out your younger sister. Mormonism, for age makes nothing where all are errors, and as to antiquity, your oldest predecessor is but as to-day compared with rational religion, which all of you basely and ignominiously treacherously deserted, for iniquities of priestocracy.

Now, China or Hindoostan, or their ancient predecessors, may claim justly, for what I know, that christianity was established by their missions, or that all emanated from the East, that it flowed like their acts and science, West. Christ was not identified in the tomb, by disinterested witnesses. His resurrection is plainly disproved. His upholders have undertaken too much, as death separates the dead from the living at once, not after an interval of three days. That is not nature nor the God of nature, and must be the perversion of truth, assuredly. All the lying priestocracy cannot get over this. Their toryism for power and influence is thus annihilated. If the people will only analyze for themselves, the matter is ended.

Had this been a God, instead of three days, he would have triumphed over all the world in less than three seconds. How stupid the dramatists! Christ came to kill the devil, that is, the bible that originates him. A house divided must fall. He could not save himself from the felon's death, as the blasphemer and libeler of his God, the traducer of mankind, greater traitor than Judas to their rights. If anything is claimed for the poor fishermen disciples, it must be that they were very ignorant and stupid, master, wire-workers and all, not to know damnable faith from religion, and I am willing to concede them such characters as they all displayed.

But why not clairvoyant to all other matters, as other world-humbuggers do. O, that is as God' permits. That is as priestocracy, humbuggery, permits—no more or less. Do I believe that Christ was baptized, immersed, or sprinkled? What is that to the purpose? What is that to the world? He was no more than another creature, mortal, person or man. He was born if he ever existed as a man, lived and died as such. But hear the witnesses of Christ. They were all affiliated priestocracy, collusive perjurers. What can all that avail? Do I believe in Christ? What is a dead man? For what? That he was a messiah? An impostor, of course. God's word positively declares God the only Creator, and of course, the only Preserver and Redeemer, the only dispenser of his grace.

If you believe in Christ, you have no religion in that. Peculiar faith it is, and all that is peculiar pagan folly.

If I could not fully prove my position, my confirmed confidence in religion, that requires positively, truth and honesty, I would retire and leave all the vanquished, conquered faiths, as false crystals, and seek where religion is only to be found, not with dead messiahs or affiliated priestocracies, but from God through the highest rationality of my mind. As sure as there is a God, who is as sure as the universe, so surely has he the religion to dispense.

The world-mind cannot learn too much, but bigots and charlatans think themselves above all this. What sort of proof is there, that Christ was born the messiah? Would you let such testimony as you call it, cut you out of your patrimony, your fee simple, and yet let yourself be swindled out of your best perpetual patrimony, incomparably supreme?

The old mythology speaks of gods cohabiting with women. But all this was debased ignorance. Their nature is not compatible.

Christ could never have been foolishly kept here on this earth thirty-three years by his storiographers, had they known of the universe, for unless he is a universal savior, his peculiar mission on this earth does not avail. Now, if he was to remain all the time on all spheres, then he can never accomplish his mission. What foolishness.

Are you a believer? Then you have adopted all the perjuries of the dramatists, and get cut out of religion of course. Mark, ch. xvi., v. 17 and 18. " And these signs shall follow them that believe : in my name shall they cast out devils ; they shall speak with new tongues ; they shall take up serpents ; and if they drink any deadly thing, it shall not hurt them ; they shall lay hands on the sick, and they shall recover." 19. " So then, after the Lord had spoken unto them, he was received up into heaven," &c.

Then, if signs extraordinary do not follow you, you or Christ is an impostor to-day. Either the believer or Christ is an impostor, one or both. Who is the one? Answer, believer, or stand convicted. That question shall be decided on your own bible. So close it, retire in silence, or prove your own documents.

If Christ spoke true, and these signs not following the Christian believer, then the believer is an impostor. But if Christ did not speak truth, then both are impostors. The Christian, whom the signs do not follow, is an impostor any way.

Now, what honorable man would commit himself for such imposition, or stay committed, if deceived into it at first by the fraud of others?

Self-interest is always infatuated ; bigotry is stubborn, short-sighted. Not only take the whole chapter, but author, book, the whole subject of Christian and Jewish peculiar faith. I would not have such a faith, that subjected me to the obloquy of the whole world, the perjury.

The whole Roman church is corrupted by the last chapter of Mark, to meet the impossibilities of the signs that lays the whole Christian world under contribution. The bible condemns the Christian or Christ.

Who is the impostor? Are not both as they stand? The bible of rational mind and religion impeaches both.

The people make themselves impostors unnecessarily any way to be fixed without proper inquiry, for as these signs cannot follow them, they prove by the book they stupidly adopt what is now turned against them, that either they or their Christ was an impostor. If he be an impostor, they are ; and if he be right, and the signs do not follow them, the believers, then they are condemned by their own book. The priestocracy cannot get out of the difficulty. Believers, then, are arrant impostors, unless they prove themselves by miracles. Understand your position relatively to mankind, the world.

John, ch. iii., v. 14. " And as Moses lifted up the serpent in the wilderness, even so must the son of man be lifted up." As Moses' serpent that was worshipped was idolatry, so even was the son of man worshipped by idolatry. Had Christ established rational religion, he would have been the greatest man of the world ; but that was above his comprehension, great as he was assumed. Rational religion is the sublimest action of all the earth. Christs are mere convenient puppets, for absolutists and sophists ; the world does not need grown up children and their false pretences. All the affiliation will avail nothing. Numerous were the ways, means, and times for Christ to have worked mind to be rational, then to the depths of learning and wisdom. Did he show these? No. He whines as well as his sycophants about enemies, who could have been not only silenced but put to the greatest adoration of his superlative greatness.

What dupes, pettifoggers in faith, these dramatists were, that did not know religion. They could not manage the god-drama, as they did not know know to manage human nature. The very condition of human nature, conclusively convicts Christ and his advocacy. It is poor Christ, when the millions have been sacrificed to the false peculiar faiths of the world.

The hundreds of millions of victims are not regarded, as they would have died any how. False faith begets false sympathy most truly. Christ may be what he is, but what self-respect of mind, that God its creator is to respect. Christ showed sectarianism with sectarians, abusing the Jews as hypocrites, &c., and only substituting his pagan peculiar faith for theirs. Was he any better than the Jews? Can I disprove the genealogy of Christ? There is no genealogy proved, and all this perjury of Christ has to be disproved, or he falls to the ground an abortion.

But had not Christ suffered, the scriptures had not been fulfilled!!! Indeed! Then scripture perjury is to fulfil perjury. And the most outrageous blasphemy, involving their God into the worst of crimes, of adultery, murder, &c., are to be perpetrated, to fulfil the scriptures, and rendered neither their peculiar god or Christ worthy of modern, because rational mind. Better damn all these universe firebrands, into non-entity. Before you sacrifice your soul, sacrifice all this. No, they sacrifice no Christ, but an impostor, when a complete failure of prophecy, as usual, is demonstrated that he was descended of David, and he is not identified as a true but false Christ—this the sophisticated priestocracy leave out in their pulpit, knowingly. It takes a perjured priestocracy to affect that prophecies are not perjuries. One-third of their godhead was on earth, and two-thirds were in their heaven. What sort of a godhead was that, when it took all three to make a perfect whole? The whole business needs another dispensation, to clear up the ungodly sophistry.

It is too small a matter to say the disciples stole away the body of Christ, when God raises the soul at once, as soon as the spirit becomes disembodied, which must be at once. The silly dramatists let their dead god lie three days, they lying all the time. You say St. Paul speaks of the perfect revelation, about prophecies; but St. Mark was independent of him. Mark purports to be the reporter of Christ's doctrines absolutely, not as modified by Paul. The 17 and 18 of xvi. of Mark furnish the pivot on which the New Testament turns. Mark has told us a little too much.

The spiritual knockings elicited the aid of several preachers that were protestant, as the Roman story of the blood coming from the picture of Christ. All turn on the pivot of this chaper. To stop all such frauds, estop that bible and all its machinery.

As to the acts of Judas and the devil—God is made indirectly to act by them, which is if he did it himself.

What libels—all show the reproach of stupid libellers. Do the priestocracy tell the truth, the whole truth, and nothing but the truth, when they pretend that Christ is not the false Christ, and stop short of telling that there is a failure of making out the prophecy in the genealogy, that is none at all—that all such prophecy is pretended, the veriest patchwork. Now here is a pretended Christ, that is entirely superfluous, in the way of God the creator and preserver of the universe, without genealogy and resurrection, proved. Will the world-people tolerate this priestocracy fraud any longer? To talk of a Christ proof, there is the preliminary about his genealogy, that estops all the priestocracy forever, unless proved. As to proof by miracles, all the affiliated have to perform them.

They are God's libel, who never created such monsters, identifying himself in their guilt, as his indirect agents, having conservative princ ples in their stead, incomparably better, as all his vicegerents, and helps to mind the mighty object, end and aim of creation.

Clearly, then, the whole bibles of tradition rest not only on degrading ignorance of barbarian ages, but of most corrupt belial ignorance.

Citizen of the fourth, last, and best age of the world, will you not prove yourself worthy of its better light, by discarding all its unenlightened precursors? But Christ, who was a sneak, a god less than a man, what good could he do? The world, that only needs a creator—they are traitors that tell rational mind that more is wanting.

What fine capital for the priestocracy, "that the scriptures might be fulfilled." That is talismanic, no less than "the hardening of the heart," the bad acts, repentance, &c. Who was Christ but a Jew, mutilated by disgusting circumcision? If any thing can kill Christ still more dead, it is the pretended prophecy of Isaiah, whose babble, the refuse of his own king, who knew the hypocritical libeler of his Creator, the priestocracy seek to palm on the moderns.

Christians have their bible idols. They make their Holy Ghost, after all, lower than their bitterest enemies, as they call them. He is a seducer and adulterer, a bad, instead of a good example, and not legitimate; therefore, the position is not tenable before the God of the universe.

If it had been the Holy Ghost, marriage, not adultery, would have been instituted. Guilt, trebly distilled, allied to names not authorized, cannot beget holiness.

Now, did God of creation authorize any persons to use his name in connection with

mistress, peculiar faith, deceives the world with self-delusions and sophistry, and she the foulest bird of the flock in those particulars, is characterized accordingly. You protestants complain of lying Romanists, as if Christians were not in that category. Crime involves crime. The bible fraud involves all subsequent fraud, to keep up the deception. Who would stultify or criminate his mind by any peculiar faith? What sort of morals was the sword of Christ to the people instead of peace, to set the household against itself, and all at variance, and rather to the lost sheep of the house of Israel. If every man have his due, there would have been no preference. But all peculiar faith is below the contempt of mankind, christianity, particularly Christ, as Socrates, Joe Smith, died as innovators—Socrates acted like a man, the other two as malefactors.

Liars, especially those that make Christs and Jew bibles, have necessarily immense memories, not to forget some things, else how came they to overlook his genealogy! Lies cannot be dove-tailed with truth. God created truth, and all the necessary protection. No mortals can alter it, hence all this proves the bible falsehoods. I am perfectly astonished, that any truthful, independent, honest-minded modern clergy, can ally themselves to such a perfectly foolish, rotten false system, when it has so glorious and magnificent a universe book, that needs no edition, no copy, no translation. Which is the worse, their own stupidity in not seeing the last, or correcting the first? But are any clergy honest or truthful-minded? All peculiar faiths are false pretences, and they can only be upheld by those that practice false pretences. How can they be truthful or honest-minded? Then as it is utterly hopeless to expect a proper change in all such, the people who have proper self-respect must do their duty; theirs is the recompense or penalty, not the prince of the power of the air, the devil when personified. What infamous blasphemy. There is no end to the fanatic blasphemy, of all polytheists. When they get started, their limit is in the excess of crime. This is miserable blasphemy. The only prince of the power of the air, is God, who employs no such agent, much less such libeling reporters. Let the God of the universe be correctly represented to mind, that is all that the races of mankind need. All that is of God, must be the God of the universe, and nothing less. Let full justice be done the comprehensive subject, and then these immodest lying priestocracy, whose minds, debauched by their peculiar faith propaganding, would act with all as with the Jews, and if they had the power equal to their wishes, would have murdered the whole world for this object, will be silenced.

A world savior, is it? What absurdity, not so much for the ancients who were ignorant, as the moderns who adopt. He should of necessity have been the universe savior, otherwise there is at once a contradiction. If God was defective in the world, of course he was in the universe, for the messiahship implies imperfection in God. The peculiar god of the Jews and christians, was defective all the time, and no messiahship could ever help him out of the difficulty, that is, the priestocracy. I am of those that go for God exclusively, and cannot go for Christ, therefore as he says himself, through the mouth of the priestocracy, that whoever is not for him, is against him, then he cannot be for the God of the universe, whom I adore.

All the spiritual pretensions, knockings, &c., the derangement of the public mind, clairvoyance, are from Mark's chapter. Why do the people choose the preliminaries, to be humbugged?

All that sustain their bibles by faith and not rationality, are irrational, fanatics, bigots, who impede mind's progress, and sacrifice religion, the highest duty of mind, to public idolatry; the universe God to its peculiar fancy pretences for a pagan god, that makes priests dictate to their idols, in order to dictate to the world. A bible faith bigot, or fanatic, cannot reason—he bolts the whole subject.

The God of the universe does not create any devil, as he does not do by another, what would disgrace him by another. Hence all this priestocracy creation, and their utter disgrace, for to their paternity are due the acts and disgrace of their bantlings. My mind scorns their books, or them as priestocracy, whilst I respect all of them that are respectable men, by monotheism.

Was there such a man as Jesus? I have no doubt but this is the prototype, as furnished in Josephus. "But what is still more terrible, there was one Jesus, the son of Ananus, a plebeian and a husbandman, who, four years before the war began, and at a time when the city was in very great peace and prosperity, came to that feast, whereon it is our custom for every one to make tabernacles to God in the temple, began on a sudden to cry aloud, 'A voice from the east, a voice from the west, a voice from the four winds, a voice against Jerusalem and the holy house, a voice against the bridegrooms and the brides, and a voice against the whole people.' This was his cry, as he went about by day and by night, in all the lanes of the city. However, certain of the most eminent among the populace, had great indignation at this dire cry of his, and took up the man, and gave him a great number of severe stripes; yet did not he either say anything for himself, or anything peculiar to those that chastised him, but still went on with the same words which he cried before. Hereupon our rulers, supposing, as the case proved to be, that this was a sort of divine fury in the man, brought him to the Roman procurator, where he was whipped till his bones were laid bare; yet did he not make any supplication. for himself, nor shed any tears; but turning his voice to the most lamentable tone possible, at every stroke of the whip, his answer was, ' Wo, wo to Jerusalem.' And when Albinus (for he was then our procurator) asked him, ' Who he was? and whence he came? and why he uttered such words?' he made no manner of reply to what he said, but still did not leave off his melancholy ditty, till Albinus took him to be a madman, and dismissed him. Now, during all the time that passed before the war began, this man did not go near any of the citizens, nor was seen by them while he said so, but he every day uttered these lamentable words, as it were his premeditated vow, ' Wo, wo to Jerusalem.' Nor did he give ill words to any of those that beat him every day, nor good words to those that gave him food; but this was his reply to all men, and, indeed. no other than a melancholy presage of what was to come. This cry of his was the loudest at the festivals; and he continued this ditty for seven years and five months, without growing hoarse, or being tired therewith, until the very time that he saw his presage in earnest fulfilled in our seige, when it ceased; for as he was going round upon the wall, he cried out with his utmost force, ' Wo, wo to the city again, and to the people, and to the holy house,' and just as he added at the last, ' wo, wo to myself also,' there came a stone out of one of the engines, and smote him, and killed him immediately; and as he was uttering the very same presages, he gave up the ghost." And what is the most remarkable in Josephus is the statement, "But now, what did the most elevate them in undertaking this war, was an ambiguous oracle that was found also in their sacred writings, how ' about that time one from their country should become governor of the habitable earth.' The Jews took this prediction to belong to themselves in particular, and many of the wise men were thereby deceived in their determination." And this was the war that destroyed the Jews, to the amount of more than a million of people, and broke their spirit as a nation. So much for prophecy, and a messiah.

Now, how can Christ be of God, when he, that is, his priestocracy, libel God? Unless the New Testament is fully proved by the Old, on which it is assumed to be founded, and both demonstrated by God, not man, to be his word, the whole fabric is a false pretence. No second story is good that is not dependent, on the first: and if the New Testament supersede the Old, then God's immutability is superseded, an utter impossibility; therefore the story falls to the ground. Do I admit Josephus? Yes, as far as human testimony has the right and capacity to speak on human affairs, verified and demonstrated by universe facts, no farther.

As to Paul, he is a self-declared subordinate to his master, in sectarianism, and supports Mark's position most strongly. He is an endorser of perjury. He advocates the whole, above all, performs the same, if his account be taken. As to " a more excellent way," when he " now saw through a glass, darkly," he had not reached the balance " then." When his prophecies failed, knowledge vanished away, then the world was in Peter's position. Acts ii. 17, "And it shall come to pass, in the last days, saith God, I will pour out of my spirit upon all flesh: and your sons and your daughters shall prophesy, &c. 19, And I will shew wonders in heaven above, and signs in the earth beneath, &c." Peter tells too much. 20, " The sun shall be turned into darkness, and the moon into blood." Peter knew nothing of the atmosphere producing colors.

By-the-by, which has the best of the truth, the Mormons, Christians, or Jews? Are stone tables of more value than golden plates? The reason, if you please.

Paul was a wily sophist. Could any part of the creation be entrusted to a creature, with a creature's functions?

The idea is absurd. Then all peculiar faith is an imposition. Another blessing of St. Mark's signs, was canonizing Edward by the pope. He received the surname of Confessor, and it was pretended that he was favored with the special privilege of curing the scrofula, or king's evil.

His successors were pretended to have had it, I presume, by the grace of God. All about as strong in truth, as Wesley's knockings, recently imitated in the circle of humbugs. At one time, in England, more than one hundred murders were proved to have been perpetrated by ecclesiastics, of whom none had been punished.

What a scene was there in England, in the cruel persecution of the Reformers. What keeps the same parties, Reformers and Romanists, now down, but the superior state of public mind? What a state of clergy was there, in Elizabeth's reign! They were Protestants or Romanists, as the court was. Is not this the world game? Religion estops this. But the world is told of the communings and feelings of the spirit; all self-delusion. The Juggernauts, Jerkers, all devotees, are enthusiasts, and may be thus psychologized, thereby proving only fanaticism.

All things must have a rational basis, or be nothing but imposition. The enthusiasm of the ancient Pythoness is exactly analogous. Apollo never had but an ideal existence in the minds of the vulgar, or populace, and that is the case about Christ, or any other such pagan polytheism, they are all idols of the world, excluding God Almighty not from his, so far as he is concerned, but so far as the peculiar priestocracy and adherents are identified.

If Christ had had any divine mission, it would have been self-evident as God's facts. whereas the peculiar faith, teaching it by peculiar education, impeaches it, as unworthy the attention of rational mind, especially having its dignity of freedom in constitutional government, and most honorable society, that has no bigotry of proscription.

Now, as Christ, he acted so well his part to aid man, that the world must admire his mission, you say.

Nay, he appears openly confessed and demonstrated an impostor, therefore he cannot command mind's respect, much less love. And now, what is self-evident, he is an impostor of the lowest blasphemy, from the lowest priestocracy, and all those that endorse, with these lights before them, are impostors. Their position they have chosen.

As more than a majority of the world would perjure itself for money, interest of any kind whatever, so all peculiar faith people would necessarily involve themselves in all the worst perjuries for their peculiar faith.

Christ's priestocracy might have been great men; they might have Christ a great man in their drama, but, like Napoleon, both fell short of a Washington. But they started with the Jesus of Josephus, a miserable monomaniac, and have ended with monomania themselves.

But the 17 and 18 of the xvi. of Mark, are metaphors. Then the whole book is metaphor, and worth not the notice of an honorable mind, a moment.

If you say, as the cornered man has said, that it is because the Christians have not full faith, then they are fully decided to be impostors of the worst stamp. As to not having faith to come up to the point of Mark, that kills all dead. But you may pretend that the a e mysteries; then that is a false pretence, and in any way the believers are nonplused. r

So all the quagmires of sophistry do not avail those cornered in the quagmires of any peculiar bible. All such sneak from the honest question. Why not try all, by the principles of truth, and retire from your inglorious position the moment you are not sustained by truth.

Do not resort to all the expedients of vitiated sophists, to sustain what cannot be sustained.

No truth can be advanced by such, all their lifetime, against rational religion.

When any one pretends to stop in investigation of this whole subject, because there are terms used that bespeak its dishonesty and untruth, then he cowardly identifies himself with both, and proclaims himself unworthy of his rational mind. He cheats, defrauds his own mind, and that of the world. Such a character is ignominiously disgraced forever, as long as he is such a debased bigot.

The gospel as it is called of Christ, is an imposition on imposition. Do you adopt and propagate such? Then you are an impostor.

There are two reasons why Christ was a false messiah: he has not the genealogy. The mother of Christ was Mary, of the house of Levi, while David was of the house of Judah. Nor was he a temporal king as pretended to be predicted. He disgraced himself as a false prophet. Either then prophecy is false, or the messiahship. In either case the subject is unworthy rational mind. All the ancients sought superiority through royalty as the height of their ambition, with few exceptions.

Of all the pagans, ancient or modern, Socrates was as far before Christ, as Washington was before Moses, or any other pagan serf-maker. Language has been awfully corrupted.

Socrates died like a philosopher, but Christ like a blasphemous sectarian. Many have assumed the livery of deism, but false books under pagan livery, dictation or restriction, have nothing to do with monotheism.

But what are the gorgeous churches of the moderns?

They are only pagan temples of idolatry.

But the worship of the Almighty God is therein attended to. By those who introduce anti-God pagan idolatry. Let not the purity of language be corrupted; mind prostituted, nor religion be desecrated. Honorable, rational minds cannot possibly want such a system that will heathenize the world, rending it asunder, stultifying more the renovators than the renovated. You pretend how thankful ought I to be, that I was born in a christian country? There it is now, the rankest, most blasphemous idolatry. I thank my God, savior, and creator, that I was born in his universe, and I am grateful to the justice, not charity of monotheism, for the glorious birth-right.

Millions of Christians would be Mahometans, had they been born in the country of that faith. It is then no compliment that they are even christians, pagans as all are, for they are only time-servers, custom-followers, reckless of principle and the sycophants of despotism, identified with the powers that be. Monotheism is of no banner local, but the assertor of perennial principles.

Principles command us not to appreciate the world too highly any way, but to do it justice.

How can you undertake to direct God's plan and system; a creature cannot suggest to a creature? Act intellectually, morally, and religiously up to the dictates of your nature, not over it.

If the voice of principle cannot be justly heard in behalf of any pagan idol, Christ, why should you stultify your mind therefor?

It was a rational finished education that the ancient world needed to rescue itself from pagan barbarism. Rational mind that rules the world at last, must rule out all opposing unprincipled evils. The bible is chief.

Imagine what must be the astonishment of messiahs claiming admission into their bible's heaven, and be told there is no such as depicted.

They cannot be known in their affected character, as that is the very thing to exclude them. They could only be advanced by principles that they had desecrated.

What advantage to the world's principles, is messiahship? Who knows? What can pagan idolatry avail mind?

We need but a right appreciation and duty to God, to whom is due rational mind's constant thanksgiving, the mighty morale of the world, with one harmonious union. All that can be said of Christ's death, the very best is, that it was that of a sectarian, and that has no merit of itself. The untrammelled can say, that he was sacrificed by the Jews, who sought their own profits in protection of their faith.

Christ is only one of the officials of peculiar faith.

The very definition of sin is the transgression of principles that rule out an impracticable interloper as Christ. Touch not this whole peculiar faith no more than any other, for you become a reckless perjurer if you do. All such are anti-God.

The undeveloped mind of the ancients prevented their appreciation of a Creator—savior of the universe, and their abortion, a man savior, is ignominiously advanced by stupid moderns, having a far better light to irradiate rational mind. The modern priestocracy are recreant to rational religion.

Christianity has met the first inherent element of worthy confidence to the world. All her claims are false. Habit is under the rule of principles.

There is a reality in religion that is a universe question, and takes precedence, supremacy over all other vital matters as identifying the soul with its Creator. But all peculiar faiths are impositions, as all are counterfeits of religion. That then is the difference.

Christ proves his incapacity for all the department of religion, by espousing that of faith, and giving the world the evil fruit of his sectarianism. His bad company kills him.

I cannot dwarf my soul to such a pusillanimous view. There can be no man-savior, as there is a creator-savior.

The business of every day life proves religion, that cannot be deferred for preaching or business.

There are no contingencies in religion, which is certain, and only requires mind's best actions to carry out the best requisitions. If there be any faith that is saving, it is that of religion, not of pagan sectarianism. You may mix your pagan faiths and polytheism with the functions of God the universe-creator, still it is only mixed pagan idolatry.

Such can furnish no sudden heart-light or regeneration worthy the attention of a rational world, however it may ruin a fanatic one.

This thing of religion, is of rational culture for man's mortal and immortal exercise. It works at once and for ever, to the best rational appreciation of Deity.

Christ is too low a pagan idol, mixed as you have him, to refine the soul, he being incompetent to command principles, since sectarianism most demoralizing ruled and ruined him.

All sectarianisms debauch and brutalize the soul, and are not of God.

It is not worth while for any part of the world to affect under self-delusion or mercenary bribery, that any part of pagan faith is the thing for the world, that has exclusively to look at religion. The people should rule all such, as false doctrinists and teachers. The world does not need any masters, but principles. If it were not for the priestocracy, we should not have heard of peculiar faiths, messiahs or Christs, and if it were not for speculation, trade, power and all worldly objects, we should never have heard of the priestocracy. There is a whole universe reality in religion, but not one iota of all the priestocracies' claim to it. We can attain no excellence of faith without religion, and for that mind and soul are exclusively indebted to the Creator-savior.

RATIONAL, NOT SECTARIAN DISCUSSION.

WHAT benefit results to religious institutions, when the essential principles are not settled thereby, but warm feelings are aroused, and old opinions, however obsolete, are adhered to about peculiar faith?

Such discussion elicits the position, that baptism or sprinkling is not essential to salvation, as the churches do not agree, having interminable disputes about words never to be settled, and about unimportant rites.

It was important that all this, if necessary, should never have been left to any doubt, when Christ or any vicegerent should be specific and definite, yet deep controversy eliciting talents on both sides, is needlessly and endlessly maintained.

Principles of God are free from all this interminable difficulty, defined by monotheism in rational religion.

The very language of the position is indefinite, it is contended. There can be nothing definite in all such bibles.

If there be no room for doubt, assuredly there is a most awful account for the hosts arrayed against baptism or immersion, even by sophistry.

Can the motives of all such opposition be impure? We cannot think so.

But then, why employ talents and valuable time in useless rites, when the noble principles of Deity furnish the noblest and the only life-subject of religion?

It is like one having a good memory, constantly recurring to deeds of the past, when his highest faculties of judgment and duty are invoked for the present and future.

The advocates of baptism decide immersion to be the rite, and any word vague, if baptize don't mean to immerse.

The converse maintains that baptism is purification, and ceremonious freeing from pollution, and that sprinkling is the rite.

And all this brings in a relative disputation about children, the operations of the Spirit, the Holy Ghost, &c.

Preaching is one thing, and essential practice is another.

The Pedo-Baptists are all hostile to the Baptists.

Of course, it cannot matter as long as such feeling prevails, if spiritual baptism of the Holy Ghost from his heaven, cannot keep the mind from crimes. How can immersion do it? Has God defined it specifically, by his works so unmistakably proved?

What has the mind to do with ceremonies that are nonentities, if their base is a nonentity? But if essential, and the Romanists and Protestants changed the ancient rite, claiming it by church authority, then they can do anything else. The discipline of peculiar churches governs the rites.

It is contended, that if immersion be used, it ought to be thrice done, or triune immersion.

Can all the hosts of discrepancies about church doctrines and rites, ever be reconciled? It is impracticable.

That about infant baptism, is immense. It is contended that the institution of this rite, with exceptions, creates serious difficulties irreconcilable to the laws of nature, and that, if adopted, causes mothers to leave out their children. Then why the base, that is unnatural?

Most of these difficulties have been caused by Christian councils, as that of Carthage, that first announced infant baptism. This is considered a corrupt innovation on the church, that also then received additions to its rites and ceremonies.

The influence of infant baptism is considered by its church opponents, as demoralizing on the world.

Then, how demoralizing all peculiar faiths that originate church corruptions!

How often is it, that rites and ceremonies are impracticable. Rational religion asks for no such mummery as all these.

All must be rational construction as to life's principles.

Who can now deny after all the various discrepancies of peculiar faith, and its irreconcilable differences about rites and ceremonies, but that obscurity to say the least of it, covers the early ages of the church history?

After all the rites and ceremonies of churches, is devotion rendered better and more sacred?

The profession of peculiar faith is only promoted all over the world, by its peculiar tuition.

But science is to be extended to the youthful mind, by appropriate instruction at the proper moment, and then the whole world will do a paramount duty of civilization.

DOCTRINES.

If necessary to baptize infants, what is the error of those rejecting it? If unnecessary, what mummery?

The doctrine of falling from grace is considered demoralizing, and is met by the doctrine of predestination.

Which is freest from error?

Undoubtedly, the Calvinists are in error?

Thus society is cut up into sects and fragments, infallible, yet wrong.

These doctrines just show the libellous assumption of man about God, clashing with principles of reason, and contradictory of God's attributes.

Thus, creeds and articles of peculiar faith are dangerous and demoralizing, especially when directed by inquisitions, the talisman of power, of money, government or hierarchy.

The advocacy of the doctrines, falling from grace and predestination, says enough to cut down Christ at once, as imbecile and incompetent, or self-degraded and unjust.

He who opposes falling from grace, quotes, "But divine grace accompanies passengers to their journey's end, and without aid, so that the meanest pilgrim in Zion, may shout with David, in full certainty of faith, ' surely, goodness and mercy shall follow me all my days, and I shall dwell in the house of the Lord for ever!' " with David who had been pronounced the man after God's own heart, yet became a murderer and adulterer, and not fallen from grace! Then, this grace declares God associated with murder and adultery! O solecism! O vanity of logic!

Again, in opposition to falling from grace, the same author says, "Who will venture with such views of his character, (supposing him, that is, God, incapable of executing what he undertook!) to commit with full faith and interests to his guardianship and fidelity." " The doctrine which tends, in any degree, to impair our confidence in him, we declare that doctrine as demoralizing." That doctrine is, positively, that of messiahship.

A right estimate of human nature will refer to its general frailties, and that perseverance is for all men, whose last end declares the conclusive eulogy of least sin.

We must declare all doctrines that libel man's nature, or that impair God's attributes, as demoralizing or blasphemous.

The pen is so prolific in this theme, that it is difficult to curtail.

The whole subject of religion merges in monotheism, and that discards all the petty conflicts of sectarianism and antagonism of creeds.

The bible of rational mind thus elegantly and substantially sustains itself, while the best advocates involve themselves in inextricable quagmires of the bibles of tradition.

Discuss all things to be right, not vainly to master in words that ought not to be uttered, as valuable time and thoughts are fruitlessly thrown away. Free discussion is to find out only, and adopt all what is right and rational.

We are indebted to rational discussion, for much in life.

Do not decide about faith and religion, till you read and discuss both sides of the question. Who oppose this position? Bigots and sectarians, priests, ministers, and preachers of peculiar faith.

THE DYNASTY OF THE PRIESTOCRACY, CLERGY, PREACHERS, PRIESTS, MINISTERS.

Well may it be asked, if all such people be blasphemous for worldly profit, towards God, how can they be sincere and faithful to man and their own conscience?

Have they hesitated to use all manner of means, bloody as history paints them, to attain all worldly power?

tions, and the people, who lawfully need the light of mind, acquiesce in merited impositions.

How could the priestocracy, at the first or afterwards, with its unjust power, have been competent to bear evidence to truth, that it constantly violated?

Its temporal interest was supreme, and that was enough. It never could be equally involved, with any people that was ruled by bigotry, that is over a companion inseparable of any peculiar faith.

Approach this question, and the alarm is sprung ; to arms, are the cry, the watchword, and the call, from the chiefs and the whole clans ; and the echo is rung among all the affiliated, until fanaticism rears her mob vindictive for blood, slaughter, and conquest, down to the social proscription and ostracism of the very freest.

The intelligent and most refined part of hierarchy do know the awful corruption of hierarchies, and should estimate truly the deplorable condition of mind and country most subject to it. Any, at all subject, should be freed.

The least of the evil is universal freedom.

Not only is its direct power brought to bear, for sinister purposes, but its reflective power is felt in the very vitals of social relations and virtues.

No one, able to obtain his bread by his honest labor, should countenance such a state of things.

Where toleration is the least of all evils, action of mind should not be suspended at any proper moment, that must not be delayed for correction of all these injuries.

Let the world get rid of all state-power unions, of all the profits of professional trade and speculation in the gospel, of all the preferments of worldly honors, and let the word of God stand by itself, for pure results, on its own merits.

Does any intelligent person doubt the protection that mind, cultivated, brings to itself and the world?

Is this doubtful, except to bigots, who especially have but little common sense, and are made more simple by books, who disregard the good of mankind, in their own selfish pretences and professions?

No wonder the impression on those dull plotters, that receive all such as faith that is at their fireside, or at the church, in the state or country.

Stupid, contracted, and bigoted minds are affected to know where can they get any more faith, if that, though false, be removed.

So far from investigating the truth, the inquirers under priestocracy shrink back, with fear, as to other sources.

The bibles of tradition are the word of God, says the priest. What say mind and truth, not man, who is interested? Investigate all aright now, and whatever is by principle, is right ; then all such peculiar gods and priestocracies are synonymous.

We are now in the ages of light, and must read the world by that light, else we are recreant to God's best gifts.

The greatest incentives to idolatry and bad government have been through evil priests and politicians, as Jesuitical, of analogous mould of mind, who sought the profits. What cared they, the worst of demagogues, for the people, but to seek their substance?

Such have caused to be built up creeds of faith, to which mind was to be tortured on the rack, to suit.

Whilst mind can only declare, as truthful and honest, that none but reason can decide faith, the history of her oppression, by all these, is awful and hideous.

The polytheists caused a Socrates to drink poison, because he proclaimed, like a martyr, a better system than theirs. While we cannot portray, by a hundredth part, the iniquitous butchery of priestocracy, all must see the rabid malignity of ferocious, unprincipled opposition, and jealous rivalry for popular and mental tyranny.

The mildest platform of the most provable, has been polluted by reeking blood.

The Romanists excommunicated from church and banished from country, cursed and slayed by all the engines of cruelty, thousands and thousands who refused to assent to their peculiar creeds.

The people on whom all this intolerable evil bore were not bettered, but in despite of all such ignoble creeds of spurious faith, indebted for its hold to sophistry, bigotry, and brute force above all, not on the minds but on the bodies of the people, by the potency of the innate principles of God.

Nothing has been done effectually, but by the very principles so outraged that operated on all for good.

Who were the ancient priests, but the lackey and obsequious subministers of state, to carry out the general policy of superstition throughout the world?

What cared all these arch intriguers for the morals of the people present or of pos-

terity, when the all-absorbing matters of selfish finance and policy were predominant!
It was the universal hold on the world's mind, whereby they could manage it best.

They have managed from the remotest antiquity, by various and adroit devices to the
people's shame, ignominy and bitterest sufferings.

The history of the priests, is the saddest history of humanity, and of its vassal
mind.

But some may affect that the modern priests are better than the ancient.

If we duly estimate the cause of some recent wars, we can hardly think so. Can
you, republican Roman?

Their goodness is due to the general light of minds, and the proper policy-use that
mind has made of its light, but for that blessing the true inspiration of God, inquisitions
and proscriptions would still be the order of the day.

Skepticism, which is nothing but the due effect of the light of liberal mind that philosophy and science have reared, has been sweeping away superstition, the stuff that
makes priestocracy for women and womanish childish men, who are in their first or
second imbecile state.

The history of Alexander furnishes examples enough for the wise, to profit by the
complete instruction.

He was met in his successful career by the Jewish priests, who were willing to do
obeisance to him as a God-sent conqueror! And he affected to have had a dream most
politically devised, to secure the most politic results.

But in Egypt, prolific in craftship, he availed himself of the collusion of the priests
of the Nile, to speculate for more universal conquests. He negotiated for the highest
game.

Alexander affected to be the son of Jupiter Ammon, whose compliant priests gave a
servile response of the oracle to suit the popularity and power of the military hero, and
declared him the son, and "that his father had destined him to become universal lord
of mankind."

"The chief priest addressed him as the son of that God, to which Alexander replied
that he accepted the title."

"And with ready flattery the priests told the followers, that Ammon willingly consented they should adore his son."

But the oracle could not secure from even the vulgar, a full benefit of this organized
imposture.

Superstition and credulity that affect faith, flourish by ignorance. The materials of
this kind were suitable for Mahomet and Christ, but could not succeed with the philosophical pagans, which conclusively proves them the superior of the parties compared.

The political more than faith stratagem was aimed at by this pretence, and answered
to a certain extent.

Alexander, however, was vain enough to enjoy any idolatry, and like the other two,
paid forfeit from his acts by his life.

Poison destroyed two, the cross ends the third god, while shot-guns terminate the
existence of recent prophets and propagators of another form of superstition among
the Mormons. Blasphemy is fatal to most.

Characters base enough can be found as long as false ambition can be nurtured, avarice cherished, and superstition rewarded, to prostitute themselves to the basest assumption and imposition of public opinion, and thereby guide and regulate peculiar faith
opinion. What are the heads of many nations now doing, but thus acting?

Let the people forever examine for themselves ; if they do not befriend themselves,
who will?

They must ever seek the irresistible sway of science-education, as broad as the
lightning's play, to free the human mind from its vulgar and tyrannical prejudices,
created by ignorance of terrestrial wonders, which have been estimated as miracles of
physical nature.

Whoever will not learn from all this, is unworthy of the blessings of mind, a confirmed idolator, a perfect reprobate, he must suffer all its ignominy and penalty.

This now brings us to say boldly, that the God of the universe is too sacred to be
approached by all such priestocracy, but must be appreciated through his works, and
reverenced for his attributes thus evinced.

How could priests win or maintain the confidence of the world, which is the phalanx
of mind, as they lack important characteristics of ability to command time or place, and
of course to dispense favors vouchsafed from their god.

The priests of any peculiar faith can only dispense those peculiar favors, mere trifles
in the universe of God.

Remove, citizens of the world, these difficulties that are in the way of universal pacification, then we are disposed to give credit for such peaceful recognitions, as many unpretending individuals, the ornament of human nature, exhibit now.

What could the world do less than what God purposed it, if placed in the right way, that would enlarge the sphere of action of priestocracy from a very small circle of puny factions, sects, and insignificant creeds, to what could be the highest elevation and perfection of character, in universal redemption, brotherhood and magnanimity, not by priests but by men of mind?

The world needs not the functions of priestocracy.

But the sacred purposes of God have been awfully violated, and that too in the most insidious manner, that adds insult to injury, that deprives the people of all rightful thoughts here of reason, but adds the penalties of imposition from another world; yet all to keep the world in order! Man's infatuation!

Are the men wedded to old professions, bigoted to obsolete notions, influenced by the worldly profits, to be expected to advance first in the progress of revolution?

The quick and ready progress of those untrammelled in mind, will be most to the purpose.

The old dotards will be joined to their errors, and will go down with them unless corrected.

Vice carries in itself as all deceit, the elements of its own destruction, guarded however sagaciously for the moment by cunning, the true solution of which is folly and ruin.

Correct principles are necessarily conservative to all that embrace them to the greatest amount of good, and are self-sustained on their own reward.

The general welfare of the world demands a riddance of all priestocracy, and requires us to get rid of the false impressions created for tithing the people's vineyard.

The real people need the saving, not the expenditure of the many hundreds of millions, in building great churches, palaces and pyramids, much less the originating the wars to support any such evils of absolutism, that pauperize and enslave the world.

Much of this is a false splendor, purchased too dearly when it war with the world's best interests.

Millions of paupers need these expenditures, that do not prevent absolutism from prostration, however protracted. All such will go down, until all travel up to adore a Creator for his attributes, and repel all messiahships and their vicegerents, all such conceptions as impiety towards God, however advanced by lip-worship.

Be these pagan pageants as brilliant as gorgeous vanity can make them, still all faith short of full adoration of the one supreme being are superstition, still disguised by the most consummate art possible.

These things will be as legible as the sunbeams when wise principles govern all.

Contentions without end, strife without shame, and blood shed without apology or remorse, have been the results of peculiar faiths maintained by priestocracy.

What can be the feelings for all their petty benefits, far better done by mind?

Did any civilization ever feel indebted to any such aid of all their faiths?

What did they do ere the dark ages of the world, but still more obscure and desecrate the light?

What have the missionaries done independent of science? Had not science preceded, the balance had been rank superstition; as it is, it is one superstition superseding another.

What shall all just men say in rebuke to present bigots, who would, if they could, enact past scenes, were they not arrested by freedom, sustained in fundamental institutions?

Bigot minds seek to appropriate, in their utter ignorance and corruption, man's rights, but they are bluffed off by the very nature of the case, and the potency of God's noblest veto.

Bigot, stop and learn justice, if you cannot in your little, unbalanced, narrow and contracted mind take in the copious philosophical resources of wisdom.

Do not be the adherents of senseless superstition, however you may have been taught it. Throw away superstition.

Know that you leave a posterity, though you now possess a little brief authority, that must ere long be held up as your reproach if used improperly, and that your descendants will suffer by any folly, crimes, vices or errors of peculiar faith.

Be you emperor or empress, chief of priestocracy, it is all the same before the august imperial tribunal that is no respecter of persons, if they do not respect conservative principles.

The opposers of rational religion can have no advantage before an enlightened people, that must condemn them all for irreligion.

50

All their assertions against the system of rational religion impeach them of untruth and dishonesty, and convict them most successfully of libel.

When you leave the only true God of the universe that is worthy of its reverence, you run after dwarf gods conceived of by man.

This finally dwarfs all virtues, in ways most to be condemned.

Of all tyrannics, hierarchy and priestocracy are the most revolting and flagrant in all forms, when they can command all the potency of force, the seductions of peculiar faith, the mock scruples and incitements of fear, the influence of the fancy punishment foreshadowed for the guilty to eternity, acting on all grades of society and the timid of both sexes, while exercising the most absolute powers and corruptions under the garb of virtues.

All improvers of mind must be accredited by the fruits of their labors, they all then must be teachers of science and philosophy.

What claim then has the apostolic dispensation, or any peculiar dispensation, to the world, if it be not commended by some supreme benefits to mind?

No instructors have occupancy by inherent peculiar supremacy, for they would be then impostors about the innate capacity of mind.

The true God excludes all messiahships; and pure religion, a duty indispensable to God, confirms all such.

How can they possibly face God and man about peculiar faith that has no natural existence?

The statutes of sinful plotters cannot supersede the statute of conscience, the most durable of all statutes, written by Deity, who maintains them by his conservative influence.

Then minds are bound to look to their own intrinsic merits, as well ordered and regulated, and can well and wisely reject those affecting to be ministerial leaders, who have little or no depth of mind or of character, affecting to carry forward what intrinsically ought to prevail by its general good and comprehensive benefits.

What can man expect better than constant deception, when he has to depend on man for the word of God, overlooking all the value of his own means, mind the interpreter, and the holy preachers, God's own works of nature?

If mind could not reach the true philosophy of the subject, then it were well for book directions; but surely, when each can get a living and authentic copy always with him, he will not stupidly refer to the counterfeit, or its upholders.

The copies of mind and of God, by bible tradition, are all counterfeit, and can be nothing else.

As long as there are bibles to support any peculiar faith and government by absolutism of divine rights, so miscalled, mankind will be subject to their malign influence. Take away, sovereign people, the influences foreign to their merit, and they all will perish.

Let absolutists in faith and government act for the mere love of religion and government to the dear people, and we would see all deserting their own standards.

The American United States are not esteemed as a religious country by absolutists, because she does not support an established faith, or order of priestocracy. She is that much advanced in the glorious progress of religion.

If all such faiths were of God, he would uphold them, but as they are of man, assuredly they will go down.

After all the hot-bed of absolutism, and all the appliances of sophistry, still they are going down.

All the oracles of priestocracy, ancient or modern, diversified in numerous editions, in variety of forms, all over the world, are all human devices to gull the people.

It is almost incredible that mind should be so blind and infatuated, to yield credence to any set of impostors affecting to care for the people's souls, at the same time ensnaring them in all the wiles of absolutism, and all the quagmires of sophistry.

All the priest devices can be exposed as the most degrading of superstition and speculation, on the fears and passions of the people.

The oracle at Delphi arose from discovery of gas issuing from the earth, and its effects on those inhaling it, a natural phenomenon.

An enterprising and shrewd Greek appropriated it.

It is the profit all the time, by one power or all powers. Of course, those of that peculiar faith profiting by it reared a tower, and were still more interested in the growing profits, that gave power, bestowed wealth, and increased the consequence of those availing themselves of the stupid superstition of the times.

What can man do for God, better than by doing justice to his fellow-man?

If all do justice to God, they will drop all false faith, and only have one rational religion, that must create one universal brotherhood.

But that faith cannot support the priestocracy in power. But it is for the greatest good of all the people.

Citizen, your vote can decide, for the good of the world, which of the two you prefer, as the proof is positive that all of the priest business is humbuggery, pretence, and fraud, on God and man.

Never say, if you admit the priests, that you are just and honest to the Creator.

It is strange that wise men should forsake the only fountain of wisdom, the only means of understanding, by due process of mind, and go to the set and clique, who, from the earliest times, have been their intentional deceivers, their masters of superstition, and the partakers of the spoils of office.

But all the world is referred, for inquiry, to the scriptures. Are they competent to direct, when they are not authenticated ? Truth, reason, nor philosophical science endorses them. Nothing but an infatuated faith, that is only credulity, upholds this prodigy of false pretences, the work of priestocracy.

Let not good citizens of the world, Jew, Christian, Mahomedan, Pagan, or Mormon, deceive themselves that this bible of mind is against them, as worthy citizens. It is to open all to them, wisely and sincerely, and incite them to secure that, as the world's people, distinct from priests and all humbuggers, which the best cultivated intellects can produce.

The author requests a wiser exposition, suitable to general benefit, if practicable, by a proper system of rational religion, that all the people may participate therein, without priestocracy.

The present state of the world exhibits much of all mankind, in diversified paganism, destitute of proper respect that is due to God and man, and yet under control of priestocracy.

Most of the other sects contend and clash with the great subdivisions and the various sects, yet all professing to worship one God, but under various orders of priestocracy, and in polytheism. The best hope is to begin with that powerful conservative body in the world, ready to do right, and be advised, at mind's tribunal, by reason, who will never be vassals to priestocracy.

Yet most of them have crude notions of religion.

They have never thought maturely on the right analysis, and are too timid to act openly, but, in deference to custom, must sit silent, or not think their own souls God's exclusively. On them the priestocracy's proscription is placed, and what a terror once was that, in the form of excommunication of social rights and comforts.

Then to be an infidel, was once equivalent to outlawry. Ask thousands of these liberal thinking people, afraid to be acting men, what is the real essence of religion, and they will say they cannot believe the bible of tradition : they will not contradict it, because they have been taught it !

We now see the horrid effects of the abominable doctrines of superstition, inculcated by this set of men.

All peculiar beliefs arise from peculiar false education, and the world is injured to that extent by priestocracy.

Their object is not to develope, but conceal truth, while they can grasp power. What do they care for religion, if they can protect peculiar faith by their sophistry ?

The poor craven spirits are actually afraid to contradict what their senses tell them is absolutely untrue, because their education is backed by superstition, and the cringing sycophancy to the times and their tyrants.

We address men, freemen, who care not what leaders of any sect ever said, but decide on the proper position of cultivated minds and facts of nature.

All wise and good men, if true, will reject all fear that promotes base designs of impostors.

All should be strictly without fear and reproach.

The majority of the world, all of us, need reform.

Priests and preachers must be the most degraded of human beings, to prevent, by any means whatever, free or rational discussion to attain all reform necessary, or seek to throw any proscription on its good effects.

Too many self-made ministers have been accredited, to a world's injury and much of its ruin.

As many ministers of God as choose to wisely instruct the people in morals, manners, science, and religious duties, can be hailed with exultation ; but when you raise them for false purposes, an imposition is practiced.

They affect that the prayers of the faithful and pure can only avail. Who are the pure and faithful, and where are they ?

The church guarantees no faithful or pure, hence all such is assumption.

What a complete system of fraud and imposition!

The faithful and pure ministers are mere mortals, and in the category of mortality on earth, and some of them need as much or more regeneration, as laymen, in many respects. Before God, mind at best is only equal to its own duty.

What can make the people so simple, as to credit any such pretences of the priest-ocracy?

Patriotism and humanity demand where all this is to lead?

Upon whose authority is all this pretended to?

· God has certain purposes in creation, and his conservative principles accomplish his will, none of which are varied for accommodation of the evil. His Almighty providence is pre-eminent in general conservation. What more, then, can the good promise themselves?

Whatever establishes man's future happiness best, is not their consideration; if that position conflicts with their order, it is sure to be assailed by them, however unreasonable the objection.

The ancient priestocracy, as the druids and polytheists, assumed to be of the real genuine peculiar faith, and dictated their dogmas then with as much effrontery as the modern priestocracy. All this is despotism.

The right tribunal of mind holds all accountable as intolerant and unreasonable bigots, to be condemned when mind awakes to the appreciation of its true position.

Do they civilize mind when they delude and deceive it?

When worthy citizens, despite of their peculiar profession, which peculiarizes them, they may aid—as all minds bent on good, do—but they avail no more than as far as they go in science and philosophy.

All preachers are involved at once in the absurdest contradictions, by the adoption of any peculiar faith.

If you adopt any bibles of it, you adopt all its false pretences.

Who has analyzed the impiety involved in the legend of the Devil, a fiction that kills all its bibles?

In all such idea, however its peculiar god is helped, the God of the universe is libeled.

Preachers are particularly the aiders and abettors of this libel, and yet they pretend to preach the gospel, which, of course, is anything but the truth.

The worst punishment, no doubt, will pursue those perverting human minds; and preachers, knowingly advancing this poison, ought particularly to suffer the worst of all penalties.

Does the preacher universally adhere to universal principles, to protect benighted minds?

If the love of souls be primary, why is it so often, that when independent in circumstances, that he gives up preaching before he reaches the retiring age?

If principles prevail, how is it that he is so often accused of violation of fundamental rules of chastity of the nuptial bed, and that he triumphs over lay members, equally so respectable, in church trials, however condemned by enlightened public opinion, too often defied by church despotism?

Admit that he should be considered only as human nature; then let all such assume no more than belongs to them, as no more worthy to be separate from general tests. All are protected under the universal God-benefits; why should any claim more!

The present state of things begets corruption, hypocrisy in many church members, it is said. Now, that presupposes perjury, and a most disastrous state of morals to the world.

Can compromise of money alone to the world for social injuries of primary character, exonerate any minds?

Who of mind with least light would be so stupid as to suffer any wolves to visit families and social circles at all times accessible, without the necessary safe guards for universal protection?

What individual exception can be made?

Is any class sounder in morals than others? Where?

There is then a necessity to put religion and freedom on the only right basis, to counteract all perversions of them.

When there is no private or public exemption from responsibility, then all is right.

But the bible of mind gives us the full view of the only safe position in life. It affords an epitome of principles so plain, that all can understand them with common sense, so short that they are written on the tablets of cultivated mind, but too short for speculation and trade of the hierarchal faculty.

We may have its moral and intellectual sermons communing with God, teaching the best science of avoiding evil, and seeking that which is good, availing ourselves of right, and giving the whole world a living chance, never leaving it worse than we find it. It teaches to nurture a liberal and kind spirit towards the world, yet guard against its deepest wiles.

Those fundamental principles that give us rights, making none discontented or miserable with all that cannot be helped, are its precepts.

It teaches to look to reason in our adversity and prosperity.

It guides our minds to scan and look deep into all things, to the necessary depth, and never be deceived by names and professions.

Its tuition is wisdom, to avoid cunning and its results.

In social benevolence it rectifies public morals, and in avoidance of social difficulties it frees from the tax of sharp and trickey pettifoggers and priests.

It proves to us the policy of avoiding trusting to outside appearances.

Its wisest plan is to avoid all practicable in evil—enter into no obligation that sustains no principle, for bible or no bible, if principle be wanting, there can be no soul of religion there.

It teaches man to comprehend safety in principle, and avoid all plans that must result in failure by the inevitable condition of its nature.

It regards the necessity of correct actions, that permit not the world to impose on us at all if practicable to avoid it.

By its admonition, we discover that God's friendship is a jewel invaluable, not to be bought; that incapable and unworthy characters should not be risked for his business, when capable mind can be selected.

That Deity should not be libeled on man's, his construction of his gifts and universal protection, when mind fails to regulate them in the dignity of its most elevated character. Then mind being primarily accountable to God, must prepare and regulate its own best code of ethics as the bible of mind, and seek to avoid all those libels perpetrated by the bibles of tradition on God.

Then all will learn to speak the truth honestly, and reach the highest state of morals.

All professions of peculiar faith intended as all are for speculation, stretch the conscience of the professors to take advantages by many dissembled tricks.

The code of mind, the universal beneficiary, the highest of ethics resting on paramount principles, will not permit the spirit of the people to be crushed by any form of absolutism, and will certainly prevent their debasement by sophistry.

It builds mansions if possible for cultivation of mind, rather than prisons to punish the delinquencies of ignorance, that should have been eradicated by the most liberal systems of rational education.

It takes every necessary opportunity to advance in this age of the world, true religious appreciation and improvement on the inherent elements, the universal dowry of the Creator.

On its basis the pious mother can advance the best catechism for her children, to be aided by the light of rational science attendant in all conditions to raise their character to the best and loftiest aspirations.

All are equal in her view by merit before the God of justice, purity, mercy, and perfection.

Taught by this safe position, the most suitable for man, we go not only for a proper balance of mind, but universal satisfaction on a uniform basis of protection and the loftiest principles of exact justice, not merely preached about, but practiced.

We speak of the action for intelligent, rational freemen, all the time.

As cultivation is the honor of agriculture, not only in evolving the richest harvests, but enriching the soil to the capacity of its faculty; so free agency of mind that endows the world for its best good, must avail itself of all its capabilities for success that comprehends the analysis of a world wide subject that embraces God and the universe.

Mind that is cultivated under the auspices of its own rational bible, must see the folly and criminality of sectarianism of peculiar faiths contending for centuries and thousands of years, about vicegerents and messiahs, showing of course, an earthly unhallowed purpose, but that all true believers in one individual God, having all enlightened principles of intellect and morals, are one brotherhood indivisible and undivided throughout the globe, and above all the universe! What a mighty link, and that through the mighty operations of mind.

The only true rationality will reach us in time, when the mighty action is accomplished by mind!

Pure religionists should never suffer fellow beings to be unrighteously distressed.

They should be sorry in actions, with benevolence aforethought, not in mere words and sympathy, after-thought; responsive to the calls of life, not merely officious at the mere offices of the grave, fully satisfying all the demands of affection and duty.

The world needs codes of par value to suit the dignity of the times, as we see that all past ones are deficient in morals, as they were deficient in philosophy and science. Any bible that does not produce the exalted benefit of mind by religion, is out of its sphere.

He that will exclude all proper basis from the code of the bible of mind, is traitor to humanity and God. We need constitutional codes that will liberate mind from the shackles of preconceived notions and prejudices, a degraded bigotry that will lead him without restraint and social injury, to the soundest legitimate aspirations.

We need every thing pure, conservative, and self vindicatory for free and intelligent people, too intelligent for miracles to be dupes of an ignorant priestocracy and their degraded superstition.

Educated nations of the world, need the proper scope to all this for its full comprehension and satisfaction. A system must be maintained for right action and proper good behavior, for social and rational good extended to the greatest number.

The whole ethics of the world are God-planned, accommodated to man's wants and the treasury of the universe, that is united in one harmonious whole.

Common sense, truth, and honesty, must preside at their selection and theatre.

Man as born a helpless infant, ignorant of the wiles of mind perverted, of evil communications, the poisons of miserable and corrupt education, abiding errors of ignorance, misguided teachings of dolts, dotards and pretenders, invaluable time lost, eternal truths never attained, concealed or mistaught, all the dangers of temptation to ills and evils, only known by physical ruins and despotic tyrannical habits, must have a proper code from the family altar to the boldest communications of good faith, the exertions of genius, and the highest attainment of philosophy for self-defence.

His mind should be duly balanced, and his happiness best promoted by all the fundamental principles that can glorify his perfect Creator.

Then arise the beauties and powers of conscience among the civilized beings taught the ethics inherent to human nature and condition, verified in the illustrious benefits dispensed to the improved world.

But adopt any system of vicegerency of the exploded humbugs, the bibles of tradition, and we take all the evils and conflicts of their absurd contradictions.

Sects and divisions of sects will then espouse neither reason nor truth, but will feel bound when chained to the juggernaut-car of sophistry, the ever constant aid of superstition, to defend all its basest and revolting defects, errors and vices.

The consequence must inevitably be, that it will originate more dark deeds, than it will extinguish.

But the proper, the true system of rational religion dependent on the bible of mind, can stand all proper tests, as all proper principles are inherent to man's nature, and should be evolved by certain education of mind for its present good, and its future happiness.

A neutral state of mind about the proper code of life is a dangerous one.

Man is always a fallen and depraved being, if he do not come up to the proper standard and dignity of his character and capacity of his mental calibre, in all ages.

He perverts his capital into a sad waste, in ratio to his mind's divergence from good.

Already has superstition stalked over every land, rearing her despotism over mind, causing man-worship and idolatry now to flourish.

We have to define the great outlines of our duty, of man to man.

They are to be written more or less in all refined and well-regulated minds, on the tablet of the understanding and memory, ready for constant practice and action.

Man cannot mistake them, imperative as is the obligation, speaking for itself.

There can be no issue on this globe; all rational nations can read them, the language of nature uncorrupted.

Where a correct, moral, and intellectual taste presides, justice governs the world. Where universal good feeling predominates, the innocent do not suffer from the guilty.

Let us not leave a void for any more base systems to enslave, pervert, and corrupt mind in its world's progress, but fill up the space by that system that prevents omissions of duty, and commissions of evil; that establishes true constitutional government of man, and rational religion of God.

A proper code of the bible of mind will cause all to appeal rightly to the dignity of God's conservative principles, that act for him, the Immutable Being, and cause man, the mutable creature, to act for himself.

That code will teach man to be true to God and man, to be true to himself, to avoid all prostitution of his talents and virtues, all habits that enslave with a reckless ruin, all temptation that wisdom shuns, and all communications that are evil.

Where we do not approach the contagion, the poison is wanting.

Human nature in no form, sect, denomination or society is infallible—it therefore must be elevated to its proper dignity by proper education, intellectual and moral, to reach the whole fund of principles, and the whole code of morals and religion.

Let principles of rational religion be discussed, and its virtues be secured by all.

Religion, to be worth anything, must be sincere, of course must be intellectual, of the mind, therefore rational ; all others will be, must be failures.

The question with the world is not as to the bibles of tradition, that became obsolete with their peculiar tradition, but the bible of mind that is always present, the diamond of creation.

How can this be estimated ? Surely not by an interested priestocracy already condemned to complete silence, but by mind, and nothing else, for approval or condemnation on its position.

Mankind may follow the bent of their own evil uncorrected disposition, and must arouse the sleeping lion of bad habits, that their powers can rarely allay if submitted to too long.

Much of the world is propelled to unworthy motives and passions, from the alluring facility of gratifying them.

It is the impunity that allures the warrior to gratify his lust of ambition, through the slaughter of millions. It is the fault of the world, if it will submit to such degradations, when it has the conservation of principles.

Human nature, in all its circumstances and vicissitudes of life, when irrational, is corrupt enough, but its redeeming good quality, if rightly inspired, can cause it to ever respect its bounden duty to commit the least sin, and repent of all misdeeds.

Its inspiration must be from the fountain source of its creation, that can only endow it with the function of timely faculty, which cannot be possessed by any vicarious substitutes from the essential nature of its organization, and that position excludes all creeds of vicegerents that involve themselves forever in contradictions, absurdities and criminalities, and produce an irreparable and greater injury than previously existent.

History tells us what they are, what they say of and do to each other, and their treatment of the world.

Any one that analyzes the deep subject of bible of mind, will acknowledge that the whole code of morals should be systematized for future good as a mirror of mind, that the various nations should throw in their refined science and philosophy for the general good.

All we at present ask for is, that the true system of religion may not be victimized by half mad zealots, deeply self-interested bigots, monomaniac fanatics, who cannot change from interested motives and conceited views.

Let it be certainly known, that rational religion is not only sufficient, but is necessarily all the code that can be possibly realized as the inspiration of God, by the world or people at large.

The bible of mind investigates in some profound inquiries.

Can the prayers of the priests save the souls of people equal, if not superior, to them in purity of conscience ? Why this vassalage of mind ?

This question is not so much the form, as the spirit of government among the people.

The people that can govern themselves, can appreciate the religious part of the question.

If we correct the priestcraftship, we may easily correct a fanatic world.

The very object of the code, the bible of mind, is to elicit appropriate thought, word and action throughout the world.

This code, then, prohibits the faith in dead mortals with all the legions of so-called saints and martyrs, the dregs and vices of bygone days.

Those that hear her rational declaration can feel satisfied to die without being shrived by a priest, or prayed for by a preacher, having posted their life day-book.

They will ask to be delivered from this imposition, that has terrified the credulous part of the world. Will a rational people hold still, and suffer such base imposition and fraud ?

Infants must be christened or probably go to the devil ! Having expelled the last as fiction, the first had best be instructed in the name and virtue of pure religion, that will give wise and virtuous parents enough to do in life.

Nor do people need the aid of the priests or ministers in church-yards, to protect the

dead, that are nuisances to the living in cities, therefore the civilized will have them
removed to some retired rural spot, consecrated to solitude and God's protection.

The code of mind invokes all intellectual freemen, to arrest all damnable frauds on
the pockets, minds, morals, and rational religion of the world.

No peculiar bible can give any idea, but that of a peculiar god, that the universe does
not know.

The priests' bible. god and opinions, are peculiar.

After all, where did they get all these peculiarities, but in the peculiar precincts of
priestocracy.

At this day, we see the most accursed fraud on mind. What was mind for, we ask
you who affect to be holy and divine by excellence, before God and man ?

Are you really so stupid, that you know no better ? Then this is reason enough that
you doff your profession, of which as one from God for man, you are all unworthy. We
this day not only protest against your declarations, before a libeled God and injured man,
but we arraign you as the libelers before God, man and mind.

But you are equally guilty, if you assert this from design, to uphold a book, that is
self-impeached and impeaches you.

The people have submitted most passively and stupidly, to immolate themselves and
freedom on the altar of superstition and absolutism.

The great error has been assumption and usurpation of arrant impostors in their false
pretences, of man degraded and corrupt, in the first place assuming to mediate between
his fellows and God, instead of letting mind, pure and enlightened have its way—the
other is a blind and slavish popular surrender of mind's noblest principles and prerogatives, to all such impostors and pretenders.

In such enormous injustice, we can never yield conservative revolution to imbecile
reformation.

Call you that religion, that asserts faith for reason, and messiahs, necessarily mortal,
for God ?

What a doctrine, that God has entrusted the saving of souls out of his own hands,
into those of the priests and clergy at the death !

We see that a king supporting one state church, when dying take not its eucharist,
caring but little for the established church, but was shrived clandestinely in his dying
couch by the Roman priest !

How much better would it have been, had he submitted his soul directly to his God,
without the intervention of such mummery ?

The priests assumed to be the God-makers, and so far from being the science men and
keepers, they were thereby the science and philosophy corrupters, and are now their
libelers, suppressing free investigation, because these principles interfere with their men-
worship and expose their idolatry.

Treachery, the worst of all ignoble deeds, next to hypocrisy, ever hateful, has been
perpetrated by the priestocracy, from beyond the record of time in fable or story.

The sooner the world is rid of it, the more God will bless mind.

But no little conspicuous is the sophistry of the priests, preachers and all of that tribe
of the world, that after full exposure are still hanging upon the timid credulity of proselytes and the weak-minded, who cannot tell the difference between religion and
superstition. In their defeat they still deceive by pretences.

Priests have used their false pretences, at various ages of the world, to uphold idolatry
or a gross superstition, not to be lightly shaken off, taking advantage of the deplorable
ignorance of the human mind, which they have perverted by all expedients.

Now they should have done better, because they knew better.

They have ignobly degraded man, and themselves.

No wonder that the inside barbarians will not adopt their own codes, returned to them
still more deformed ! Are the Brahmins of Asia, or the priests of China less cunning,
than the priests of Europe ?

Is peculiar faith less odious to monotheists, however disguised in all the expedients
of sophistry and superstition ?

Whenever science and philosophy come to the rescue of mind, a dishonest priestocracy exclaim against them, at the tribunal of a peculiar faith, forever condemned at
the tribunal of reason and reason's God.

Wherever his great principles seem to clash, the definition is due to the finite view
of mortals, consequently, we must correct all such as impious to God, and deceptive to
mind.

No point nor subject is exempt from investigation, and that implies rational mind, and
always implies truth. It is the highest duty of religion, to investigate all presented the
mind to test its honesty, truthfulness in good faith.

All other views of religion are partial, perverted, imperfect, clashing eternally, or their advocates of sectarianism for them, and all such are eternally earthy, and unto mortality they will return.

Let mind, vigorous in health of body, strong in wisdom, and beautiful in innocence, rise triumphantly over all such low elements, guided by the safe pilots, sincerity, truth, and rational education.

What boots the independence of nations, when mind is vassal to superstition, whose priests and preachers denounce its freedom, attained by science and philosophy? All such are impeached before God to-day.

Let not a corrupt priestocracy keep back mind's essential rights, which are the praise and highest reverence of God.

Let not the degraded advocates of peculiar faith pretend that earthly vicegerents are to usurp claims that are individual property of God, for which they are culprits for condign punishment.

If Christ received the reward of his crimes, that of blasphemy, what must they expect sinning against science and philosophy, the best knowledge means?

The world is full of deception, and ever will be, if the people make themselves a herd, to be misled by interested partisans, who become pensioners upon the people's wrongs.

Preachers and priests, as the ancient soothsayers, have lost sight of true analysis, and as the base is sophistry, a base action must result.

What was faith under the soothsayers but an undignified superstition?

What dignity of religion is there now under the present regime?

Who but charlatans in peculiar faith could deny science and philosophy the faculty of correcting all things counterfeit? Who but the followers of spurious faith could deny the test for correct faith?

Sinners, that is those not believing in peculiar faith, are urged to get religion. What more can a conscientious mind do, as it already believes in the God of the universe exclusively, and that embraces the whole subject conclusively, as they reverence him most profoundly?

To go beyond would be treachery to the almighty: to trifle with their creation birth-right religion, is to deal in counterfeits. Can any honest, high-minded man dare open his mouth before this position? Why then, sinners? Is he so stultified by the desire of worldly profits, and influences of petty ambition and avarice, that he should forget proper sense and honesty?

The preachers' is a peculiar faith, that a few may get for peculiar purposes, but God begets a universal belief that all can confide in and enjoy.

How then can the large society of the world get religion on their basis? How absurd to think that it can be really had. Who can give it? Can sinful preachers? Who will swap chances with such?

Are they more truthful and honest than truthful and honest monotheists? Will they prove all that?

As long as the stupid will believe their fables, fanatics will not stop their peculiar faith or cunning stratagems.

If the people believed in one God, then the priestocracy could have no employment for their certificates.

Can preachers call up converts at their bidding; if so, why do they not convert the world?

It is faith of the most peculiar character, that is the main point all the time with the priests and preachers.

But truth and honesty are the main points of religion, that is the main duty to God and man.

What greater benefit can there be than general prosperity of all? At the same time, what but particulars make up the whole? In having each family blessed, the nation, the world, the universe are included.

What then is due the individual must not be withheld from families. What was all this to an ignorant priestocracy, that contracted all to their narrow and bigoted sphere? It is proof undeniable of their selfishness, that the soul of mankind was not cared for on God's principles, but on their degraded position.

It was the absolutism by "divine rights" that was particularly sought. The greatest enemy is the traitor who acts under the guise of friendship; the greatest tyrant is he who affects to rule for the good of the people.

It is for the sovereign people to appreciate and govern, not wait on the actors to reform their abuses.

If reason, truth, science and philosophy flourish, then priests and members of peculiar faith fall as ignorant aiders or abettors, or wilful and knowing impostors. Are preachers called of God! That is, they speak themselves invited if interest invites.

Is their conduct any better than that of others?

We must call things by their right names.

Do the priests and preachers come to us as the apostles of principles, science and philosophy, God's own, or rather of peculiar faith, that refuses these as condemnatory of itself?

Thus we have the strongest proof that the bible of tradition cannot begin to stand up to the demands of popular wants as those of constitutional representative government, that has been sacrificed to peculiar faith of no character in religion, but a strong and insidious copartner of absolutism.

It redounded once to the fame and profits of priestocracy to allay such characters as departed spirits, such as fiction painted disturbed, or to defeat the bad spirits. But that was superstition. Their general acts come under that category.

Now mind, if cultivated, must see that the soothsayers, augurs and priests, all the same, were the base part of mankind, who did many dark deeds, and threw the odium of all that was malign on others not able to answer for themselves, as they had no existence, and of course no responsibility. Their fellow-creatures were deluded on the evolution of such outrages on common sense and honesty, and were victimized abundantly for ages, even in the name of religion! That is the basest piracy on human nature, under the disgraceful and degrading deeds of superstition.

These views, most hostile to the valued actions of sound thought, influence still the mind of all shortsighted people, who follow men and not principles, messiahs and not God, who do not give proper credit to the inherent virtue of enlightened principles, now expanding by their inherent power on the globe, nor to the intrinsic force of circumstances, time and general influence of enlightened countries. The priestocracy are in the way.

All have now to keep pace with the light of mind, or be left in the absolute quagmires of inefficient and murderous actions.

All the machinery of angels, ministers of peculiar faith that relate to vicegerentships, arose from the deep designs of the beneficiary class trespassing, by vile usurpation, on the deep and ignominious ignorance of the people involved in the vassal state of the times, in place of conservative principles. inherent in the universe, that are the only true agencies known to science and philosophy of Deity, who employs all terrestrial agencies only as free agency of mind, that is human, and no more, for universal good.

The whole doctrine about spirits, good and evil, is only from sheer ignorance of principles, that were innate to the universe.

The world must look upon all such as vile imposition, and the agents the most arrant impostors.

Enlightened mind feels for its age and people, to be caught by such vile degradation.

Writers, who might have been the master genius, not only of their day but of future ages, have catered to a morbid taste in this world, parading the heroes of such adventures, who have heard such strange sounds, seen such horrible sights. How they exult in nonsense and folly.

Time, long ago, should have corrected all this.

As to inspiration of preachers and priests, the main question is, are they prepared, by instruction and talents, to teach the principles, not doctrines merely, of God, as evinced through science and philosophy of mind; if not, why should they impose on the world! As proof of their incompetency of teaching, their adherence to the faith of a peculiar god, of peculiar notions, and, above all, of a messiahship, is proof positive that they are peculiarly unfit to teach the world such principles as would suit all mankind. The doctrines of peculiarity are arrant nuisances.

Above all others, they should prize good deeds and proper mind, resulting from proper education, that should elevate the possessor to the head of society.

They, above all others, as teachers of mind, should appreciate an education, liberal enough to master all kinds of difficulties, and therefore it should be properly prepared at all points.

But their peculiar faith steps in and arrests the most material principle, reason of mind, in the most sacred truths.

It is highly important that mind-fund should be preventive of our committing ourselves, by thought, word or deed, improperly, especially by advice. We cannot be too particular with the world, which takes many advantages of mind, that time gives it to correct the judgment.

Truth and honesty can then be estimated by it, as the best policy in all things, especially becoming in rational religion.   But all attempts will be made to let priestocracy down, as if not guilty of enough to eject it forthwith from the pale of all good society.

What a system and machinery that lord it over the mind, the pockets, and the various interests of the mass, the world, and granted indulgences for money, to luxuriate in vices, lust and crime ; for paganism and nothing else !

When the illusion of these impressions of absolutism is destroyed, then mankind will see a monstrous fraud on the world, that ought to appreciate all such now.

How superficial preachers and priests must be, to subscribe to doctrines that disgrace the old soothsayers and augurs.

The only base to build on, is on the supreme power alone.   All else is apostacy, to the unity of God.

How can we reach the worst kind of people, or mind ?

As they have not the prompt remorse that springs from a pure conscience, then such must be reached through penalties that affect their pocket, disgrace, infamy, or ignominy.

The most effectual preacher is he who speaks through certain pains and penalties in this life, a matter of restitution, not deferred to the day of judgment, that some do not appreciate, and others do not expect—a very unsafe, if not bad policy.   Consequently, present and immediate restitution on this earth, and at the time, by wise laws, does its absolute good.

No dynasty of priestocracy can be right, as it is ungodly.

Where do the pretences of priests end ?   In the world's evil.

See the state of the world's classes, embracing particularly the castes of Asia, having the same complexion of priests' abomination.

One of one profession cannot touch those of another, without pollution !   What ungodly mind-pollution, in these faith-bigots.   The difference is indebted to mind, that will necessarily expel the whole fraternity, ere long, as too vile for Asia, even.

Right ordered minds must reject all preachers that seek to arouse excitement, by sulphur and brimstone, as contemptible ; by any peculiar faith, as perjured.

There can be no peculiar preachers, as such are peculiar impostors, for the capital universally is principles.   Those who rightly instruct mind in all proper principles, and their appropriate application, are only entitled as instructors.

Principles are told by their universal, not peculiar effects, as a general rule, and should be faithfully impressed.

Which principles are the best ?   All are equal and essential.   There are none but God's, consequently all are universally good.   Pernicious doctrines, perverted to peculiar faith, mislead the world.

It is not that the people cannot see, it is because the priestocracy, the hierarchy, would find the people as wise as they, and their equals in knowledge would be so in power.

What preacher, more eloquent than his universe, does God the creator, need, for all mankind ?

Certainly not the priestocracy, the counterfeit.

Where God is abundantly proved in his works, Christ or messiahs are disproved altogether by them.

Preachers garble the comprehensive views of science and philosophy about the works of God, and substitute the ignoble libels of peculiar faith.

Better had the people never seen the preachers, if such doctrines of daily blasphemy are to be uttered.

Do they know the secret history of churches, ministers, and priests?   Are they so soft as to believe in them ?

" At Constantinople, the funeral procession may be seen conveying to the cemetery the exposed and richly dressed corpse, with a hurried pace, in order to relieve the soul from the torment it suffers, till the burial of the body."

Now " The Jesuits are omnipotent at Naples."

While the church dignitaries and members, at the best, are no better than other good people of the world, or no worse, unless having hypocrisy, why should mind take this, fallible example, when it has the selection direct of God's infallible principles ?

But some objection may be pretendedly urged, by these partisans of peculiar faith, to reason ; but let us rather have her, with all her blessings, than any of the curses of peculiar faith.

When professors lend their profession to crime, then it is degradation.   Who forgets the adultery recorded by Josephus, as perpetrated at Rome, on a chaste woman, by a base man, who corrupted the priestocracy of the God he assumed to personate ; and polluting, by their agency, their church or temple ?

There is some hope for them; but wo unto those that assume divine rights for insidious purposes.

What order of mankind has ever been more licentious, taken in all their dynasties, than theirs?

It was not safe for the people, in any respect, when there were no limits to their desires, and all to their penalties. For that reason we should have future punishments for those usurping present rights.

In what right of mind have they not only interfered, but sought to crush mind itself?

Their tyranny has been most odious, their iniquity most heinous.

Even at this day, some of them seek to tyrannize over the sacred rites of matrimony, and interrupt what ought to be only a civil ceremony, by arrogating to themselves the only performance of the ceremony for lawful wedlock, and set at defiance and outrage the universal rights of mind.

Who has injured deeper than the so-called divines, in the married circle, if they be perverted?

What is there to prevent excess, when they withhold conservative principles, that the adoration of the true God alone imparts?

But when God alone is adopted, priest-orders are dropped.

No sophistry can exempt them, culpable of vain-glory and demoralization; no priest logic can uphold them in their severest trespasses against all the principles of religious ethics.

Are any preachers of any denomination divested of sophistry and pagan idolatry?

Let them not, whilst thinking that they show divine discipline, disgust mankind by most intolerable errors, with ungodly impudence about worldly matters, under their own weak exposure. They come forward, on superficial systems, to perpetuate priests' power, not mind's energy and elasticity. Can the dogmas of past generations, wofully ignorant and necessarily corrupt, bind the present?

Can the present dynasties of peculiar faith exclude the paramount question of rational religion?

As well say that despotic absolutism is for perpetual government of freemen, who require all the benefits of progressive constitutional rights, as that mind should abide by the bible of tradition and its bigoted expounders.

No matter what be the errors perceivable, no matter how palpable, still we must not get rid of the bible, says bigotry, because we have to get rid of all its expounders. That is the question, the secret, the reason.

It is the highest intellectual tuition to teach children to see for themselves; much more is it to have matured minds perform this world-conservative action.

Ancient priestocrats were derelict in the comprehensive principles of honesty, and were, necessarily, so in religion, pure, vital, and rational, the only religion.

They were ignorant of most of the great and first principles of science and philosophy, ethnology, astronomy, geology, psychology, and political economy, and are self-impeached as impostors, and thus clearly alienate every respect for themselves as religionists.

Now, what must be the condition of the modern minions of priestocracy, who knowingly transgress all the rights and principles of God and mind, to reach their pernicious and degraded actions, trading on such false capital?

Can the world submit much longer to the idolatry of their teaching, when its best happiness is promoted by the exalted sound taste in morals, unperverted by tradition or personal authority?

Have you, in the nothingness and littleness of the creature, forgot the noblest attributes of Deity?

Let neither whim nor caprice, opinionativeness nor procrastination, ruin you, as your predecessors.

Abjure the fashion, ways, and custom that wise men cannot adopt, when such are unreasonable to utilitarians.

Preachers and priests ought to know and do better, than invade God's sacred precincts.

The question is not to popularize opinions, but practice the facts of duty; not to gloss over abominable sophistry, but acknowledge the truth of rational mind; let them not be recreant to God alone for the loaves and fishes.

Who are the preachers and priests, and what are their abilities, to deprive God of his equitable rights?

Do they seek a universal brotherhood, that can only exist on principles of God, as in governments? Then they must overthrow all corruption of peculiar faith.

Instead of missionaries, we must send schoolmasters of rational science to the whole world.

But some may think that, as you are divines, you alone can judge. You have usurped the term, and to you cannot be allowed the term at all of divine.

The sovereign people alone, through mind, have divine rights.

Are the people's by inspiration? No; by creation.

Ministers of mind, to do their whole duty then, as God's works enjoin, cannot be the priestocracy, whom the God of the universe does not know.

The world must be kept clear of acting falsehoods. In faiths peculiar, falsehood will continually be perpetrated.

Without principles of pure religion there can be no truth.

Faith, without God's rights, does not permit the truth.

You cannot be called by patronage at all for God.

But you ask, How comes peculiar faith successful? Peculiar faith follows in the wake of power, and in her, cunning follows in the wake of wisdom.

After all pretensions, is it not mind that does all, yet mind most sadly and ungodly perverted?

The pagan Romans civilized much of the world far better than it had ever been previously; by mind, of course.

By the unity of their empire, many unities succeeded, among them the dynasties of the priests, that had prevailed from the first days of superstition in some form or other. At first they prevailed by deception, and then by government—power. The christians were smuggled into this imperial power. When they did not work the false pretences of miracles on an ignorant people, they worked sophistries on a deceived world.

Miracles and prophecies, in all ages and countries, have been the games of priests and preachers, who have to support their false position by deference to its perjury, that takes precedence of religion.

When the times are too enlightened to practice the fraud, recurrence to the past is had, as if that was more honest, or less fraudulent and false.

One sect has supplanted another sect of impostors, the world over, during its history, all pagan perjury.

All systems of peculiar faith have ever clashed and contradicted each other, keeping the world at perpetual variance and deception, and often in bloodshed.

Their more recent have been their most comprehensive doctrines, accommodated to the advance of mind, when its sophistries can keep it down.

From one step of fraud they have been driven to others. The whole is a story of complete fraud.

The patriarchs were the prophets and priests, the masters and regents of their family circles.

Then comes the order after Melchisedec, who took the tithes, to which they have held fast to the very last, the very cause of all this world-folly and crime.

Inspiration from God is falsely claimed, and for this fraud we have to credit not history, but human story, that reason and rational mind contradict and conquer.

All their scriptures have to be referred to the interpretation of mind, ever cognizant of their truth, that must repel all the bad faith that is peculiar.

The bible of rational mind expels all the mysteries, miracles, prophecies, and their bibles.

Conservative principles prevent all such from action.

The established laws of nature, those of the Creator-savior, reflect the only light, by science and philosophy, that exclude all faiths that contravene them.

Mankind is best reformed as it is enlightened and bettered by their aid, as we all see by the blessings of representative constitutional government.

Asia, Egypt, the world, was full of mysteries of peculiar faith. They have been the hot-beds of iniquities of bigoted priests.

The priestocracy have governed and ruled predominant over the world by their machinery, and corrupted, as all usurpations.

Monarchs have been, and are of that order, having landed possessions in abundance, wealth to extravagance, influence most unbounded, and rule most despotic.

One caste or tribe has had the perpetuity of this power.

What have been their shameful rites and ceremonies, above all, abuse of power, under the dictation of peculiar faith?

They have no allowance for mind, the soul of God's gifts, but fill it with awful delusions.

All their messiahships take away the free agency of mind.

The antagonism to God ought to be cut down, as corrupt must be the mind from peculiar faith.

How full of sophistry, and where is their religion? In irresponsible, ignorant, and corrupt mortals.

What peculiar system of faith in all paganisms does not present messiahships, when carried out by the cunning priests, who rule more absolutely as ignorance between light and darkness prevails?

But if you take away the preachers of peculiar faith, and stop their churches, what will you do for the people's worship? They will then promote rational religion. They are to adore God, that is the purity of mind's offering or office, and all that they can learn by the only pure tuition of rational mind's bible.

People will have bigoted prejudices about peculiar faith from bibles of tradition, but they should modestly investigate the whole history of the world's priestocracy before they decide the question.

Let intelligent mankind rise up with one mind and put down the iniquity of the priests and fanatics. But what shall we do for preaching? That, as organized, is not the world's or mind's functions.

For the balance of time the world can prosper best without any, if we are to have the oracles of superstition and imposition.

The past has been cheated of its life-rights, and most misery has been entailed by the curses of peculiar faith, that impeded the intelligence and happiness of the globe by its firebrands.

Even the best, Judaism or any, reflects the world's darkness.

Are the priestocracy competent then to approach the pure living, eternal, and just God, with their hands stained by corruption, and their minds polluted by iniquity in the very undertaking?

The memorial of God is in the minds of his creatures, and its blessings the vestment of their souls.

All else is vulgar and degrading imposition, of those eating out the substance of the people, who must be rescued by returning to the proper point, the light and purity of mind. Double games in life are played by priestocracy.

It is utterly impossible, for a priest-ridden community to be truly religious, as it is necessarily bigoted, ignorant and superstitious.

It deals in predestination and passive obedience, in the corruption of infallibility of the church, while the most of priestocracy of monarchy play into the hands of absolutism, and understand each other. to continue the abuses of misrule and tyranny.

Therefore we impeach all bibles, but the bible of mind.

How came peculiar faith into the world? It is indebted for its paternity, to the priestocracy.

It is all a fiction, as there can be, as clearly demonstrated, no revealed religion by any means that are not rational.

Peculiar faith was not ushered into the world by good faith, or rational means, and has not the principles of inspiration that bespeak the creator.

All that she offers, we must take as sole authority of man for truth.

What will the priests do if they know better, but still preserve their tenets and peculiar faith?

They cannot leave that profession, though their faith is peculiar, till the people leave them.

But the whole profession of priestocracy, the ministry, preachers, might as well quit, as they do harm clearly, or no good. They have not rational religion, the only thing that is of religion.

The influence of God's spirit, improves the world.

Despite of all the bibles of tradition, and their advancers, arts and science are cultivated, freedom and peace will flourish, and sectarianism will leave the world in quiet possession of a universal brotherhood.

Let God's spirit be hailed triumphantly by rational mind, as that spirit prevailed most clearly, since pagans have instituted by mind, wise laws. But why did they not improve the world more? That question applies to all the operations of mind, that has just commenced rightly the elements of its appropriate rational education.

We believe in the general improvement of the world, but certainly not by sectarianism.

Where are not priests? A universal brotherhood tells.

The history of the world shows one set, against another set.

Emolument determines speculations, in peculiar faith.

It remains for rational mind, to put down all this pest, one of the world's greatest nuisances.

Sacrifice is the trick of priests.

The E   tians are said to have had six hundred and sixty-six different kinds.

There can be no works of supererogation to attain for others, the bounties of providence in grace absolute, universal and eternal, especially by a set of creatures most amenable for their sins.

Trace out the different peculiar faiths, and priestcraft is predominant.   Where can we find in the priestocracy, the least particle of rational religion ?

During the crusades, when men were martyrs in the holy wars ?

"The army of the cross pillaged the very churches, and officers, it is related, danced in the church of St. Sophia, after having robbed the altar and drenched the city of Constantinople in blood. sacked by christians, who had made a vow to fight only against infidels."—*Jones' Church History.*

Shall we look for it, in the persecution of the Albigenses, for many years of their difficulties ?

Shall we find it in wars, the pests of the world ?

No matter for individual persecutions, when peculiar faith has swept the world.

The people were not to be as wise as the priests; that would not answer.

The layman knew at first, as much as the best inspired, then all extraordinary sophistries had to be united, else their vocation might be gone.

All arts and devices were used in various forms.

Romanism presents one undivided whole, but her faith is propagated with a singleness of purpose.

She is not only united in church to state, by all emoluments, powers and preferments. but she, no doubt, subsidizes the press and authors of the tory stamp, especially to carry out her views.

Money and power are at her bidding, at the expense of the rights of the people, who have to pay for the military despotism now over them.

The world has to get rid of all the imposition ; then reformation must not stop short of conservative revolution.

Now in governments of absolutism, the emoluments are so varied, that peculiar faith is preferred to purity of rational religion.

When peculiar faith ceases to be profitable, in trade, speculation and profession, then religion that is rational, will be universal.

Surely in purchasing a fee-simple title to an estate, we would only purchase of the lord of the mansion, not of his retainers, and only pure, not counterfeit coin can be used in payment.

Of this, the mind in its best light, can only take cognizance.   Religion has no hierarchy, no priestocracy.

There can be no means ordained legitimately on this earth, whereby one class of mankind can be more elevated in personal worth, in the sight of God, than others pursuing the true issue, the only path of virtue, and excellence of mind.

There then can be no division of society into castes, in that respect, no orders of hierarchy.   All such is the work of absolutism, in collusion with priestocracy.

As science and philosophy advance, priest faith wanes ; no wonder that the last hates the first, with a bitter and relentless hatred.

When we speak of the first, we include all the rays of light reflective, on the bigotry of the priestocracy.

All things are possible with God, except nonsense and falsehood, all the peculiar bibles of tradition.

He that resorts to by-ways when the way is open, has no respect for himself, and the truth is not in him.

He that resorts to false pretences or perjury, about sacred things, has no justice in his cause.

He that offers bribes through peculiar faith, will not be protected in the days of science. when rational religion shall gather up her jewels, for then all such profligates are degraded.

All corrupt priestocracies shall be scouted before the people, that look in the light of philosophy, as all corrupt governments shall be corrected for the true government, that exalteth and blesseth mind.

The corner and keystones of religion, are honesty, truth, sincerity, fidelity, and integrity of mind, enlightened by reason, that prophecies only by analogy and analysis through the inspiration of wisdom.   Do we know what priestcraft is ?

We have seen some of its effects from the first age of man, through the inquisition, wars and contentions of the world, more extensive than mind can conceive, investing all the relations of society and country.

Whether we turn to the East or the West, we see the condition of human nature in its diversified positions, affected by this world-invader.

The living principle of rational mind is to be presented the present day before the Lord, that supersedes the sacrifices of superstition and the worship of idolatry.

Mind that improves on mind, if conservative principles be advanced all the time, will exclude the priestocracy.

Mind must firmly sustain its proper exalted position above all priest-faith, and hold up its dignity before the world.

What fee simple have they to their pretended heavenly kingdom?

Did God invest them? No: by truth.

Then we all have an equal right through mind, that entitles us all alone by its divine rights, to the choicest attainments of the universe.

On the statute book of nature, an appeal is made to patriots and philanthropists, not to surrender principle, but to hold to cardinal rights unconditionally, as the most auspicious benefit to mind. This brings us to the full point at once for all.

It is high time that the world acted rightly on its own rights, not affirm, craven to pretences, else absolutism will override liberal justice, ungrateful to mind, irreverent to God.

Enthusiasm, not fanaticism, is to act or rule in matters of exalted interest, though it arouses the liveliest sympathies. Mind would be simple to admit that.

In how many points of the world's interest, is authority of supposed great men the standard?

What can be the standard of the world, before all powers, money, or people? What confidence can be put in anything or man, than in the true merits of the question, principle?

But what shall we do with the mighty army of preachers and priests, the hundreds of thousands of retainers, who are supported by contributions, payment of churches, and tithes of the people?

They can elevate themselves to something better, and more useful for God's people.

Cannot we organize something better?

The proper institutions for rational instruction of mind, when generally diffused, will be the best lights of the world.

Truly, we can have days of thanksgiving, to be rid of all others as useless incumbrances, especially, to be rid of all the odious contingency of the inquisitors, that would still tyrannize over the world if they had the power.

But what shall we do for children's sunday schools, to keep them exempt from transgressions?

We will give them a better position for the world.

We can keep them there still, and better direct the first and early impressions of their minds to the nobler principles of science and philosophy, than to grovellings of peculiar faith—a nullity.

We will direct their pure thoughts to the pure fountain, the God of science and philosophy, and have correspondent pure words and actions.

We will pay lecturers, those of talent and worth, of both sexes, who can give us the best views of natural and moral science, and can reward mind, instead of exhausting our means in gorgeous palaces, for stupid superstition, sophists, and bigots.

Let all rational minds seek still more at right, instead of gambling, drinking, and vices, let all proper means for rational religious discussion be established, and let all learn the graceful and ornamental accomplishment of society; let them study all science and literature that are sacred, or any of the noblest subjects.

In this, lovely woman can participate, lovely in the graces of virtue, and who teaches man when she should be treated with the best appreciation.

Who can be more concerned than she, in all the mind-ennobling rationality of action?

Do preachers labor for the good of souls, when their very faith and doctrine deprive God of his exclusive power?

But, cut loose from all the idolized bibles and their expounders, what shall we do for safety in this and the future state?

Rely on God alone, and a proper rational education.

Seek the wise tuition of good parents, friends, and guardians, whose minds have been expanded by the rich treasures that a wise constitutional government bestows, all the legitimate purposes of rational mind.

Seek all the benefits of legislation, a good and true government, a well-balanced head to escape the wiles of the world, the torrent of evil passions, the crash and crush of feelings when avoidable, the intricacies of temptation, the sins that make more and end the victim.

Attend to the monitions of wisdom, sympathy, benevolence, the avoidance of the numerous victimizations of vice, publicly unknown till the suicide arouses our sympathy.

51

Fly all the vices as evils, seek all virtues as good of permanent happiness, and uphold friendship on this basis.

Most paramount points can be effectually met by wise legislation.

Do not cause the world to be corrupt, but exert your benevolence as expansive as the world, and your mind as generous as the universe.

Resolve never to be in the wrong, for life, for ever.

Let the mental remedy be equal to the evil.

Such code and doctrine will engender no strife, possess no ruinous elements, but promote universal blessings.

All peculiar faith codes necessarily unsuccessful, must yield to the elements of rational mind.

Religion is not only an inalienable right, but an indispensable duty, as guardain of all, expelling all the elements of injury.

Rational religion is.due to a free and enlightened people.

All minds have parallel and applicable basis, and need to be risked on no contingency of acting well, and doing no wrong knowingly.

Hierarchies or dynasties of priests of different gods, governed Egypt at least thirty centuries before Christ; they had the third of the uncultivated land.

The system of castes in Egypt and India, has ruined the people, overrun by priests and soldiers, and rendered them in Egypt very abject.

In India, the merchants are forbidden to read the vedas. They can be regenerate or " twice born."

All castes can be degraded by non-compliance with their absurd etiquette, but the priests can be bribed to recover caste.

Among Christians, there are many sects that have bitterly persecuted each other.

Various sects of Brahmins exist, have often persecuted each other with wars of extermination, and " to this day discover a perfect hatred for each other's gods."

In regard to priests, there is nothing new under the sun. The Jews, as well as other nations of antiquity, had their peculiar faiths and gods ; they were selected by the priest-operators, to carry out the full imposture, and if any people are cursed, it is in aiding and abetting.

All the nations of antiquity fell in the lapse of time, and no doubt suffered their share from priestocracy, that oppressed the people, and carried compulsion over them. The ancient nations had no permanent principles.

What have the moderns ?

How can systems of faith other than rational, be built up than by irrational faith and peculiar means ?

What is now presented the world, has cost that world much of its richest blessings.

All adherents are deeply interested in building up their peculiar faith, by which absurd imposition is practiced.

It is imposition all the time, as long as an audience gullible enough to be used up can be got.

Would you select ministers, above all others, for legal, medical, agricultural, and commercial advice ?

Are they wiser and more successful than mankind, to be entitled to the distinction of divine ?

Are they entitled to usurp the province of mind ?

Is it analysis when we are told that science and philosophy do not preside over the whole subject, and that when none can do it better in the department of rational mind ?

Clearly proving the whole corps unworthy of confidence, as incompetent to analyze mind ; of course, we must rely on analysis of mind, if we have mind that is sound. We hold all to analysis and proof.

If now the books of tradition are impeachable, what are those who advocate their false pretenses ?

Many systems of various peculiar faith have flourished for a season, their founder priests referring to auguries, divinations, oracles, and all that could impose on the senses of the people, subverting their rightful appreciation of God and due adoration. Such systems interested governments, and reared military power and the aristocracy of the people, churches and temples. What good will it all do to God's true representation, the sovereign people ?

God must abominate the execrable pretences of priestocracy, that are at enmity to the unity and attributes of the Supreme Being.

Why seek to uphold the corruptions of a rickety priestocracy, that have conspired for thousands of years in their various orders, against the happiness and well being of the people ?

. of the world is enthusiast and credulous, misled by their priests, whom as
-. they stupidly believe inspired of God, and the whole batch use all the false
- to keep up that idea, for their very position bespeaks the height of imposi-
-he public. Why does mind yield its sovereign rights on this question any
-i any other, except from superstitious fear?
-i t to be obtained from mere assertion or tradition, the question had been
-i c negative in the absence of all necessary proof.
-i unmask the world, we shall expose the exploded priestocracy that have
-i. r mind, that vassal to sectarianism, makes cattle of the people.
-i. ev united to state policy, tyrannizes over the world in all its forms, no
- pretensions or name. It is all the same, tyranny first and last.
- against heretics, prove conclusively, the difficulty of propagating peculiar
- r c ional religion propagates itself by civilization.
-i need of priests to do that.
-horrible thing it would be, if only part of mankind, the priests, should be the
- of the religion of the world, when all rational minds are constituted when
-i it very principle.
-i works of the priests of every age, country, and pretension, can be most
-i exposed as false pretences, whether the auguries of the old heathen
- assuming to utter responses of oracular wisdom to the inquiries of the
- or the inspirations of subsequent pretensions affecting to be divine;
-ard all as the fictions of superstition harassing the ignorant and deluded

- the injury to the world is by doctrines that are brutal and degrading,
- ambition, avarice, bigotry, fanaticism, lust for power, usurpation, and mono-
-sophistry.
- re the best of ancient nations but idolators, ignorant and debased murderers;
- and repudiators? What were the priestocracy, that made them so? Then
- could truthfully assume any peculiar prerogatives before God Almighty,
-the greatest good of most is in abeyance to that of one nation of a small
-i absurdity.
-one sin more or less before God, and they are the worst that sin most in the
-i.t and law.
- re better than the great nations, the Greeks and Romans?
- ws? In what? In excess of priest superstition?
- sts look for support to absolutism, where tyranny of the government comes
-i of the church-despotism.
-means did not wish the Pope, whom they expelled; yet even a so-called
-public, comes to the aid of church tyranny, no matter the pretence or excuse.
- not overlook the miseries of the human race, enslaved by this abomination,
-seless and worthless.
-out let mind enlightened be divested of its noblest rights, the proper trust in its
-ce, the Maker and Preserver, Almighty and Omnipotent, to do all that mind

-ells of the ignoble pretence of those assuming, what they more than all others
-or their great sin of blasphemy.
-ogy ought to be wise, liberal and enlightened for all future demands; never
- he defective or destitute of proof most authentic and satisfactory.
-present systems as emanating from priests' pretences, are sadly behind the wants
- people, and the light and spirit of the age, placing dark mysteries of ignorance
- plain wisdom ought to abide. Theology ought to fulfil the world-wide demands
- social wants and morals.
-such systems imbued with peculiar faith, began in fraud, and will end in infamy.
-pure press is most needed in a priestly government; is it there ever free in sub-
-e?
-he people may be excluded in some hierarchies from reading their bibles, which is
-of any consequence, if they had the ability to discuss their demerits, impeach and
-ard them.
-All the bibles' miracles are lying wonders, and saints are impostors and knaves.
-n some countries where the Roman faith prevails, too many are wofully ignorant,
-only taught the poorest elements of common rudiments, and the slavery of mind.
-What is the patronage of priestly pretences worth, when it introduces vassalage of
-ind? Are you, citizen of the world, adding to the imposition of the world, so degrad-
-g to the divine rights of mind? Would you enslave the world ostensibly for a false
-ble, in reality for the power of false government?

You must be aware of the downward tendency of all such malign influence, the bad effects of all such policy of all peculiar faith, Protestant, Greek, Roman, or any supposed better.

God's principles vindicate retributive justice above all for blasphemy of peculiar faith. There is but one sure principle to all this matter : to have all our actions so protected that no injury by bad faith or character can result.

Disguise superstition as sophistry will, still the delusion and perversion cannot escape enlightened mind.

Intellectual freemen must see, that conservative revolution is the antagonistic to the follies and vices of those interested in peculiar faith, too much so, to yield readily to the justice of mankind.

Priestcraft has been imposing on all ages of the world—its pretensions, promises, and curses, pretences and conspiracies ; its power and influences, its means and devices. All have created a fascination and a tyranny, too formidable for the unsuspecting world in most of past circumstances, without a free and enlightened discussion, by inquiring minds, taught to the proper limits of enlightened philosophy.

Who can tell all its insidiousness, faithlessness ?

Priestcraft has exercised all her forces of absolutism, herself the right arm and often the body, to enslave and debase mind with her thousand oppressions. She has resorted to all violence and butcheries ; has silenced all independence, and destroyed all opposition to her assumptions as far as practicable. She has taught mind, by sophistry, to yield up its rights to usurpation.

She burns and lays waste, without hearing reason, that never gave her authority.

She disregards all justice, prejudices before right, and blinds when seen.

After her grand failure in all ages, that she has darkened by her bigotry and usurpation, she tells that the world cannot be governed but by her church influences.

Where are the conservative principles of an all-wise Almighty, that claim the paramount respect of all wise citizens' minds ?

Priestcraft invents and manufactures a thousand fictions, and as many books to support them.

She maligns the authors that advance rational religion, and libels them on their death-bed, though they are countless.

She intrigues with despotism and absolutism, against the divine rights of the people, when she feigns to create the people's good—warring upon, and butchering them.

That is peaceful faith, with a vengeance !

When mind is to be forced to divide its fealty to its Creator and irresponsible bodies. we must look upon all that are concerned as traitors to their God and his supreme rights, as they do not stickle at anything to promote the temporal interests of the priestocracy over all the rights of the people.

Give us, then, God's conservative principles, not perverted mind's degraded tyrants, that enslave.

No one can well appreciate the corruption of mind, until he sees the peculiar faith man tyrannize over his citizens ; like the pettifogger, turn politician.

When pulpit preachings are analyzed, they are found full of sophistry and deceit. Their time is come, if mind be heard.

The Egyptians acknowledged the Supreme in secret, but had a priest-worship of another faith, to carry out the self-interest of the priests, who had one-third of all the cultivated lands, enough to satisfy these rapacious tyrants of the world.

Men that will humbug in one thing, will do it any number of times, if expedient for their self-interests ; the humbuggery of this priestocracy is a fair specimen of all the rest in the world, at any age. As for priestcraft, always read humbuggery and imposition.

And it was from such caste of men that Moses is well considered to have emanated, as having been a priest at Heliopolis.

In his hierarchy, he did not forget the absolutism of the priests, to which he sacrificed the people to the death.

What system of superstition could be imposed successfully on the world, or continued, but for a hell machinery, a picture drawn from volcanoes, with its sulphur and brimstone.

The warring and infidel priests of the world may affect to pour out their malignant vituperation on infidels, but fidelity and reverence to God above, will prevent us from permitting any interlopers.

Infidels ! Who are they, but the priestocracy !

We have no individual conflict, and respect all honest minds. We design to treat priests as other people, on their merits, and respect to principles.

There can be no clash of principles in government and religion, when the God of the universe is considered competent to manage it himself.

Polytheism of any number of gods is as bad as atheism, both excluding the characteristic virtues of the Supreme.

Mind's conception about deity is dwarfed by priest misrule and absolutism, fixed there for time, inconsistently with mind's progress.

It is well for the world to analyze all this, as such a state brings about all the degraded policies of absolutism.

In countries that have state faith, the mass of the sovereign people is divested of their right, and has become very ignorant.

Such are apt to enslave their posterity by national debts, whereas constitutional republics can only guard against that, by wise organic laws, requiring that the people should first decide on all important financial expenditures. To bankrupt posterity, and leave it a perjured faith, is too bad.

Again, their laws of primogeniture decide iniquity, and disseverance of natural ties, among fellow citizens, otherwise on terms of equality.

Such countries have taken advantage of the balance, and perpetrated further wrongs among mankind.

Much of past ages has presented the mere fragments of society, and nearly whole continents have sustained, for centuries, the effects.

The African savages killed their prisoners, taken in war, but afterwards changed the custom, and humanely sold the prisoners into slavery.

By the benignant improvement of mind and its best appreciation, many of that race are returning to Africa with more cultivated intellect, from their associations with more enlightened races, and now dispersing to benighted natives the highest benefits of government and civilization of rationalism.

Another and another wave of conquest has broken over Asia, till at last the most intellectual race has come to supersede the benighted wiles of potent priestcraft. It is to be hoped that the one hundred and forty millions of Hindoos will thus rise superior to their past state, else it may be well asked of that brave nation that has conquered such a mass, after enjoying the rights of their hospitality, what is the difference between national and individual slavery?

The idea of everything possible with God, on man's construction, is to make God the author of the constructor's infinity of follies and crimes.

All impostures, when tolerated, may result in monopolies, because the impostors are most highly presumptuous, not acting on principles conservative of the world's society.

The foggy ignorance of priestocracy creation is advanced for mysteries, not to be understood, and not worth the trouble of investigation and the mind's understanding, but to expose it to a world miserably deluded by it.

Why put the mysteries there, if not to be used by common honest sense, the universal coin and currency of the world, to be at par forever?

The people have sustained the ferocious tribunal, the inquisition, including the most barbarian laws of absolutism. The criminal part of the world that tolerates an inquisition, ought to be sunk under its tyranny, that the balance, the most, may be saved.

The assumptions and pretences of priests result from absolutism, that mind, treacherous to itself, permits.

All such are trades for priests, who are corrupt and vicious. Nearly all priests of all ages are corrupt more or less,—are necessarily and will be forever, all pagans.

The priestocracy are inseparable from paganism!

Be the speculations of the world as to priestocracy what they may, no man should be entrusted with more than defined constitutional delegated powers from the people governed, and only for a few years at most.

If supreme, he will dictate to the constitution.

If moneyed agents, they may not comply, through temptation. What matters it about any faith; that has nothing to do with the matter. It is to be no means before the people. The people have nothing to do with a man's faith speculations, in regard to their business. If this is an age of mind, let mind erect its empire. In its sway, the noblest victories are to be sought. Mind has to triumph in the noblest legitimate direction of passions, without excluding their rightful actions. Passions perverted are evils and curses; when controlled to their legitimate circle, they are God's genuine blessings. They must have power for effectual good.

The world is a matter-of-fact world, and must be taken not as men's fictions pretend, but as God the creator intended, that the radical condition of society be not most perverted.

What an idea, that pretenders in government and religion should appropriate the elementary principles that are universal not individualized, except by mere worshippers, whose grovelling souls will barter all the rights of the world to degraded minds.

How often is it that depraved and corrupt preachers control the church most absolutely—corrupting, if not the whole church, a great part of it, that would not unless by its organization be thus exposed?

But no thanks to church-faith or its preachers, for the rest are honest and truthful in despite of all church-faith corruptions, influence, bigotry—by paramount reason of principles of the only religion that wise, honest, truthful and good citizens can conscientiously believe in.

Then, no mediator but principle can rightly avail between mind and its Creator, and it is absolutely necessary to exclude all others for ever.

The triumph of principles sheds joy throughout the mind, and permits no sacrifice of honor to be made to temporary expediency.

Then industrial labor will have her rewards as her rights.

Then the luxury of rulers and potentates will not be permitted to create unbearable taxes; nor will oppressive burdens of bad government, misrule a people pauperized.

The dispensation of all authors of peculiar faith, as of Moses and Christ, was the oppression and deception of the world. Can we rely on the priestocracy for any correct action about religion? Their very existence implies the exclusion. They present numerous kinds of peculiar faith, but no religion; various messiahs, but no unity of God the Supreme.

Their faith is worthless, and teaches mind to cast down all speculation of clannish societies that disturb the repose of the world, and learn what is universal good.

All such dogmatics must yield to principles, that will rule mankind.

Absolutism, whether of kings or priests, ought to become a curiosity in the world, and enlightened public opinion should rise over all such vulgar ideas, and discard all such creatures.

What have priests to do with the people of the world?

God gave none any such right, title, or dominion over them. Are not most minds of the world to be held their vassals?

Away with all their peculiar books, of Vedas and Menu, Koran and bibles of tradition for miracles, prophecies, mysteries, all false pretences, fables, and engendering sophistries ever in their support.

But where, then, can public morals be?

They must be ever in the securityship and guardianship of mind, enlightened and enlightening the public opinion of an enlightened community, which otherwise becomes corrupted, degraded, debased and enslaved.

What is to teach me my sins, without the preachers and priests? Mind enlightened, for a pure conscience.

All the senses and their relations refer to mind, elegantly proving God's eternal principles, that must not be superseded by such pretenders.

It is mind all the time addressed, invoked and acted on. Mind must be original or reflective; let it not be vassal to priestocracy.

Rational mind having innate faculties to receive correct impressions for the appreciation of ideas of God alone, purified by rational science, can have none for others, as no two bodies can occupy the same space at the same time.

Let reason hold her omnipotent sway.

God's omnipresence excludes that of all others.

Whatever be the theology where it puzzles the mass to distinguish between the Creator and creature, if reason be heard, all false faith now so sneaking cannot be entertained.

The Pope's infallibility, transubstantiation, worship of saints, adoration of relics, all present impostures.

These are no more to be tolerated than their priests playing cards or monté, any games of chance, or any vices of licentiousness.

No such church example is safe, among any sects.

Peculiar faith presents the greatest swindling, especially in confession, where sins have to be acknowledged to Roman and other priests, who alone are considered to be the proper and effectual interceders, at the same time thereby becoming the most blasphemous sinners themselves.

From the author, Christ, to the present propagators, the remission of sins, the part that belongs to mind and God, has been most blasphemously affected.

Peculiar faith or peculiar belief is the blindest of all bigotry, and its practice is the greatest of crimes.

THE DYNASTY OF THE PRIESTOCRACY. 807

It becomes mankind, whether in government or religion, to set the noblest examples
of sinking party, rankship and faction, on the altar of their common country, and exert
a right and patriotic judgment for all.

If any are to be damned bad in the future it must be the priestocracy, who seek to deceive here and damn hereafter. Was there ever any such dynasty, that did not damn
for unbelief of its peculiar doctrine? Was there ever any such despotism, but made
its odious usurpations world-felt if practicable? They have sought to be a distinct
caste the world over. Rational mind cannot recognise any ecclesiastical polity.

The greatest felonies are priestcraft-felonies; their hypocrisy is past redemption.
The people must act.

The priestocracy have always stood, in all lands, on a rotten and corrupt foundation.
They are unjust before the God of the universe, whom their faith and bibles do not permit to be known.

We see, by what Moses imposed on the Jews, how much falsehood priests can impose on the world.

They are prepared to impose any practicable fraud.

The Jews sought abundantly to discard the peculiar faith doctrines of Moses; but he
bound them by laws and rites, selected, no doubt, from revised codes of the chief priestocracies of the world.

The people have become wiser and better, most clearly so, by the master-spirit and
impulse of mind, in its various agencies, progressing to its attainable sublimity.

Mind has to see that these agencies are not corrupt, as they may be subsidized as
the press; therefore, mind must counteract all the malign influences of a corrupt press,
priestocracy, a train-band of vassal retainers, in all the corrupt departments.

It is not faith, but salvation present and future, not the doctrine of priestocracy, but
the whole peoples' safety that is to be promoted, by the improvement of the inherent
elements of religion in each rational mind, by the most rational means and ways.

The history of the world of many nations, as of Great Britain, proves that the clergy,
so-called, was too often plotting and complotting, in their general divisions of Romans
and Protestants, for the ascendency, involving the people in the miserable turmoil, burning them at the stake, destroying them in wars, exiling and banishing them, and overwhelming their sovereign rights. What better to-day is it, but for mind?

The world has been cursed by the clergy many fold, and 'twere better that it had
never known any peculiar faith, as God superintends his universe, whether man knows
it or not. Rational religion is the only thing in faith that will bear examination.

What does mind know, until it learns the elements of science, that introduces mind
supreme, over the dogmas and pretences of superstition, to the only platform of religion,
its rational appreciation?

Has the christian faith any peculiarity of superiority, that gives more principles of
safety than God gave?

What presumption! Does it make people better and wiser than mind's civilization?
Where is the proof? What nonsense, then!

Are any people more truthful, honest, pure, chaste, sincere, without fault, the most
by any peculiar doctrine? That peculiarity makes the falsehood, and of course is a
means of corruption.

If not better, why the peculiar distinction and desertion of God's principles?

There is no bible of tradition worthy to be sworn on in a court of justice. It is a
desecration of God's noblest gift, mind, that should only affirm when necessary to state
solemn facts.

No fictions can prevent the corrupted perjurer; whilst principles of rational religion
will benefit, finally, the whole world, and sustain, as the only means, the cause of truth.

Neither should marriage be valid by a priest, whose functions determine as nonentity;
the magistrate should consummate this civil ceremony. As mind should expel all
dream-books, those of fortune-telling, and all analogous machinery of humbuggery, so
should it expunge all the works of degraded priestocracy.

There is no end to their evil works, the world's age, if mind do not assert its enlightened rights.

Thanks to them for the Mormons, who may give the world a great deal of trouble,
like many other sects that have had their day over its surface.

Thus their thousand forms of peculiar faith may admit hosts of messiahs, affecting
the peace of the world. There is no telling how far their conflicts may lead, as all
messiahs, as their priests, are antagonistic.

As all governments, but constitutional representative republics, are unjust, tyrannical
and inhumane, yet, where the people, in general, is uneducated, you show a mass capable only as wily leaders say: then in all such governments, no matter the name, you

show a mass capable only as wily and corrupt leaders say, a chaos of factions, and is peculiar faith, that claims leaders, not principles, a jumble of fanatics.

A nominal republican, from such schools, can be a fell tyrant. Who loses by his liberality, hardened priestocracy?

One of the great advantages of the present age will be the elements of social and political happiness, security of person as well as of posterity, and the change of the Muftis of Persia, the Brahmins of India, the Christians of Continents, the followers of Confucius, all of idolatry and paganism, into the religious of the world, who will disregard the peculiar doctrines of all these priests, who have been so long misdirected, by self-interest, in their judgment and faith.

How much of their sophistry has influenced the world to join those of peculiar faith churches for sinister objects? Who can honorably call this religion?

Then, O priestocracy of the world, prove your position right, or admit that, heretofore, you have pursued a miserable, bad policy for mankind, and renounce it all as the worst moral poison!

When will this world and circle learn that no man's professions make him a gentleman, and religious?

The highest duty of mind is that of religionists, to maintain, in the utmost purity, the exclusive sovereigns of the Almighty, whose unity is undoubted by reason, and cannot be successfully assailed by sophistry.

The history of nations evinces such a scramble of power among the clergy and absolutists over the people and their divine rights, that it would be impossible that rational mind should ever permit the contaminated hands of such a set, whose base and vicious acts show them the worst of citizens, always struggling for selfish power over the world, enough to convince all unprejudiced realizers of the false position of all peculiar faith, of the necessity to succumb to a rational and just religion, due God exclusively.

But the advocates of peculiar faith doctrines affect that none are converted or sound, but by, or through, the priests! They have not got pure religion themselves, or they never would practice the pretension, the deception to the people, or overlook their baseless position, that confers no honor nor emolument of religion. But Paul was converted otherwise than by the priests. As one of them, his assertion was law and gospel, and that is proved as far as any.

As to his, or any other conversion, who endorses the endorsers?

Paul was elected. That has to be proved, along with the balance of the gospel. But Paul had a vision!

That is impossible, as spirits do not belong to this world or life, being separated therefrom by death, that cannot be approached by mortal vision.

When youths get religion, as it is called, that is, adopt peculiar faith, as told by others, they are not capable, by their unmatured investigations and age, to adopt correct views. Who investigates this subject?

Does not nearly all the world take for granted all that the priestocracy, miscalled divine, tell them about faith, and act as if they had no mind expressly to elucidate this very subject of mind?

Does not the world fall back, when commanded by their divine masters in theology, from investigation, the very thing they ought to do, and adopt, without examination, the false pretences of the worst false pretenders, priestocracy? How can the world get right, when it seeks to proselyte the pre-conceived notions and opinions, not facts, but prejudices, not reason, but faith?

Now what is all the faith of the world worth, without reason, that is ruled by God's spirit, the ruler of the universe? Who made and preserved thee and thy mind, O mortal, but the maker and preserver of the universe? In whose care but his, art thou always? Who watched and preserved the whole universe for all time, but God, when there were no messiahs and priestocracies? What else is peculiar faith but a perjured speculation and trade all over the world, in its various forms, got up to deceive, delude, swindle and cheat, for all practicable time by the priestocracy, all people verdant enough to allow it?

From the popes, bishops and prelates, to the lowest preacher or member, lust, avarice, and perjured, blasphemous sin loom, despite of all professions that therefore cannot protect the world, which is ever best protected by principles.

But does the world expect these characters to be better and above the corruption of perversions?

The world knows, that these are no better than the best of others, and that they have drawn the line of demarkation and distinction improperly, and can justly rebuke them for the vain pretensions.

All minds, the very best, cannot arrogate any peculiar system, to mark them out as the aristocracy of religion—for they thus vainly become the aristocracy of false pretences, the perjured ones.

Of all mankind, that has to be watched in the whole line of their duty, his own eye on himself as best protection, the priestocracy are most to be watched.

In what country are their sinister designs not perpetrated, and that on a confiding world ?

The covenant of death, is an infamous stipulation of the priests to the Chinese, of superstitious rites for another world. Wherever there is money, then the order of Melchisedec prevails, who looks well to the spoils, no matter how derived, and to the tithes, no matter how foully got.

The world rivalry of priestocracy, is now most tremendous—all over the earth, for its spoils. "The opposition of the natives of Madras to christianity, is described as most bitter and unrelenting," &c.

Has not the history of the world proclaimed this, in the most legible characters ?

Millions on millions have been butchered for all this, one peculiar faith superseding another, as peculiar dynasties forced them. The rational world must see and feel all this.

The blackest picture of human nature in its most disgusting features, has been hereby perpetrated.

When the world is liberated from the school of bigots, the most odious dynasty of vassalage, then it may begin a fair race in the brightest day of liberty.

How many of its worthiest citizens have been slaughtered, imprisoned, ruined, outraged, &c., for the infamous cause of brutal bigotry.

If there were no superstitious people, there could be no priests. Consider the ways of these workers of iniquity, and they will fall if mind rises to its dignity. They cannot stand, as they go when man's systems fall, before the majesty of God's religion. Analysis discloses the trickery and fallacy of the priestocracy, in superseding the practice of principles due to religion and God alone, by the pretence which is the least worthy of mind and humanity, of messiahs who died the death of blasphemy, the most ignominious of all deaths before God supreme. We address those of sense, of virtue left in minds, not entirely perverted by polytheism.

If we analyze the priestocracy writers, will they not prove defective in the substantial merits of honesty of mind ? No shrewdness, cunning, device, or design, can finally avail against principles.

Are the world's deceivers wise and good men : much less are they happy and of good fame, on the best philosophical analysis ?

Moses, and all such, have been found out in the proper age of the world, that recognises mind and its field of operations, science and philosophy. In the green age of the world, deception of priestocracy was predominant. Who will dare now uphold the rotten system of priests, but corrupt and ignorant people ?

The religious victory, is the one for life and eternity.

This question belongs to mind, is referred to mind, and must and will be answered by mind most rational.

Priests claimed to be called of God.

What proof can they give, of God's divine authority to them ? It is all pretence; perjury. All teachers of peculiar faith, come of their own design, with various motives of impulse.

All rational beings must believe in principles, when science enlightens them ; then bigotry is at an end, and man's nature is disclosed in truth, not created by mind after its perversion and legend.

The question is not as to man's opinions, influenced by his honors urged by the popular fears and dread of future penalties, but as to the genuine test and truth of this priestly pretence.

Is it not the whole craft of priestocracy to affect, that the world is to be saved by their pretences ?

The evils and abuses from all their peculiar faith, are too plainly evident, all over the world.

Yet some of the shrewdest men have been priests.

But does that prove their profession is right ?

No matter the professions, what are the actions of life ?

How dare any mortal assume the province of a divine creator in religion ? For church or state power, and patronage ? The priestocracy only do it for peculiar faith, as they cannot invade the precincts of religion, that are too sacred for their sacrilegious hands. Impostors will not do to depend on in this life, in any respect to religion, when their motives are so clearly impeachable before the world, as factors of one great clan.

The just law and sense-abiding world, has to pay the spirit of obedience, to the God of the universe.

Those who are called divines, have to yield ecclesiastical influence and power, that are no part of God's religion.

The tithes of priestocracies, all the influences of bigotry, from burning to death at the stake, of thousands of the most innocent, because the most independent people, to all the proscriptions of social relations, have to be obliterated. All such regimes must be annihilated.

The God of principles is to be addressed directly, by all minds of principles, not vicariously by impostors, but with fixed definite and certain principles, that prayer of action, word, and thought may be effectual.

All are ever certain of the efficacy of principles.

But priestocracies affect, that God could not be known without their bibles and aid! How was the God of nature ever purely known in this world, whose rights have been usurped and silenced for a time, by the false pretences of bibles so called?

Rear an infant in the desert, and if of sound mind, he must necessarily find that there is a God, if he find that he has a mind, or as soon as he finds himself as conscious of thought and science.

When mind is found, the God of mind is found.

Hark, there is electricity shot before his vision!

Why that? Does he at first mistake that, for the first great cause? Mind thinks and compares ; it reasons from nature's phenomena to nature's laws, and nature's God, the supreme. Mind corrects itself.

In the savage state, he tells that the Great Spirit weeps through rain : in the most refined, he knows that he rules almighty : has essential purity and perfection.

Science and philosophy correct all his errors, for they are the inspiration of the God of the universe. The wisest of all, is to recognise the character of nature and her legitimate sphere.

What is reason, but the expression of inherent ideas of truth, the holiest inspiration? Can rational mind have inherent ideas of reverence, of any but the supreme, the great first cause?

Rational mind can take cognizance of no other.

Did the stupid priests, with mind undeveloped, authors of the bibles of tradition, ignorant of the plain principles of astronomy, that would disgrace a school-boy now if one of science, ever dream of the universe and its unapproachable author, that can furnish exhaustless position for all the various souls, however distinguished and separated by peculiar and diversified characteristics, appreciate good or bad qualities in reference to their future improvement and happiness?

Yes, this bible of theirs deplorably libels the highest dignity and glory of God, the creator of the universe, who is most deeply interested in the prosperity of all his works. It is a perverted work of minds seeking speculation for self-benefit. It puts a false estimate on the sovereign people, and misdirects their proper directions. It permits mere mortals to usurp God's prerogatives, and appropriate them to the mismanagement of mind on mind. Now, if you adhere to the almighty providence of the God of principles, you will have constantly to do so on his position, that of principle. Mind, that acts thus best to its capacity, makes especial providence.

All honest minds are obliged to acknowledge themselves indebted to mind ; but all the writers of bibles of peculiar faith have committed the worst of all plagiarisms on mind, and have sought to impose these frauds on the world's credulity.

Will the world analyze, or read the analysis, of this fraud? But are the pious frauds committed, no frauds in priests' ethics? What is their bible? It is a work to uphold the assumed divine rights of absolutism. The Greeks even had two kinds of faith, one for the learned, that admitted a Supreme intelligence, a Great First Cause.

The intelligent Persians knew of one supreme God, Mythra, and added two others, Oromasdes, the author of all good; the other, Ariman, the cause of all evil, thus having a trinity. Trinity was the result of the ignorance of the ancients, who could not analyze the complex question of good and evil, and concomitants.

. The priests of Egypt, who knew their power, had a code peculiar for themselves, consecrated in hieroglyphical characters. The Romans had priests and ministers, as the other great nations of antiquity. It was the maintenance of national power and rule.

Romulus, their founder, was chief priest.

The augurs or soothsayers were the prophets.

The high priest not only regulated worship, but was the judge in all matters pertaining to that whole subject. Priests had the most absolute power in some countries. What was the influence of the mysteries of the priests, who had the whole power in their hands? We may judge of the irresistible power of the past, by the tremendous potency of the present. As the mind of the world has become enlightened, the natural result of science, superstition has abated. But man-worship has been left, in even the best of peculiar faiths. Of course the world has only been partially civilized at the best at any time, as all such worships incontestibly prove.

Philosophy is only pure as science is exact, and that is not yet so, for the purity of rational religion among the people.

Those of the ancients who approached nearest to rational religion, pure monotheism, supposed demons to be the inferior agents of Deity, and sacrificed victims on the altars of their gods.

All this is attributable to the want of proper appreciation of the defects of their system, by the want of science and its lights to mind.

But few had a right view of the soul. The Platonists rightly considered the soul incapable of death, and was restored as an emanation from Deity.

Neither Jews nor Greeks had anything like pure monotheism, though they had unity of God; they characterized him by their ignorant fictions, and had belief of demons— also an evil genius. Socrates had a demon.

The condition of the so-called chosen people of God was not equal to some of the unchosen Gentiles.

After all, the sculptured books of mythology, the pyramids of Egypt, and analogous buildings of India, had precedence of antiquity to the bible of the Hebrews, who were no doubt indebted to such institutions for much of the views of Judaism. The history of priestocracies is analogous throughout the world. Of all the felons, they have been the most iniquitous, defrauding mankind. For many centuries they made the people tributary to their rites and power, slaves to their bigotry. With Oriental and Egyptian mysteries they have bound mind vassal, that cannot now be easily rescued. What part of the world is yet rescued?

As the most important literature of the ancients has been lost, or the key to that which is sculptured as the Egyptian, we have but little to truly estimate the past. We know but little of the Persians, Chaldeans, &c. The Jewish literature is imperfectly known. But we are eternally met by the title of inspiration, revelation. All such cannot possibly come, only through rightly cultivated mind, as the mighty deeds of patriots and statesmen, as Washington, and hundreds of others of the world. Whereas the base abuse of mind's privileges are perversions, evinced by the characters of Napoleon, Cæsar: intellectual, but evil.

There cannot possibly be any direct revelation or inspiration. But the ancients were more skilful than the moderns. In what? In pyramids, sphinxes, and other works, for peculiar faith!

May the moderns ever remain ignorant of such art, if they have to submit to the tyranny of priestocracies in raising them, and the object, most miserable, in their execution. The ancients excelled the moderns, then, in all the discoveries of false systems of superstition, and all the deplorable curses growing out of them.

But the useful inventions are predominant among the moderns. The mechanical powers, as the screw, multiplied abundance of times, may suffice to raise the heaviest bodies to a definite extent, while the railroad may convey all such to the point of destination.

It is not the gorgeousness of architecture, with all its millions of expenditure, that distinguishes this or that age by the triumphs of science, as the general light shed among the minds of the world, with all the essentials expedient for life's enjoyment.

All the ancients are clearly excelled in the true science of constitutional freedom and government, one of the most sublime of all sciences, that will bring in its train all that genius can contribute through mind.

Wisdom of the model government of America declares strict responsibility of delegated powers, that the constitution may protect the whole, interpreting itself, or that the interpreters must be silent.

Absolutism compelled the world to allegories, for cover of the true facts. All mysteries arose in the same way, all of which is abhorrent to constitutional freedom, as are all its advocates offensive to the same.

The soul towers far above all such trammels of truth.

What deference has been paid to the world's dynasties by its minions. When Alexander actually retreated before the eastern Asiatics, a flattering world affected that he was the world's conqueror.

Was he not in collusion with the priests?

Instead of flattering the ancients for their superiority to the moderns, we are to consider them as vassals in mind, and inferior in government, their empires destroyed by the heterogeneous materials embraced in three grand divisions of the earth, whilst none were well governed. Had the ancients been equal in the science of mind, the world had not been cursed by priestocracies, so vindictive to each other.

There was no pure religion through monotheism.

Whilst Socrates spoke of a supreme, he as well as Peter were worshippers at the shrine of polytheism. The great principle of toleration had not been truly discovered by the ancients—a great discovery for mind by the moderns, who have it universal as freedom.

The policy of Rome was tolerant, till christianity spoilt it.

The wise world, by toleration, escapes the errors, and profits by the virtues of the ancients. The press is one of the modern characteristics, pre-eminently distinguished for its surpassing greatness over anything of ancient discovery, except of letters themselves. A free press is one of the most substantial blessings of mind ; but trammelled, it corrupts the world. There should be no clerical combinations against the press, permitted by the world.

But their combinations are against mind and the world.

Under the authority of the popes, who ought to have known better, preposterous legends of tutelary saints and martyrs, of demi-gods, the miraculous power of the Virgin Mary, have been advanced for true history.

The monks have established one superstitious faith for another. The real character of mind has been wofully perverted ; the finer feelings of human nature have been lost in the cloisters of deluded or hypocricical devotees.

The wealth of many such fraternities begets a malign influence in the links of society. What injuries and indignities to mind's character, may not be perpetrated in credulous ages of an ignorant world ?

Man-worship has deprived mind of its light, asserted by action of mind on mind, inspired through science and philosophy, the emanations from God Almighty.

Thousands of men of talents have been devoted to the propagation and origination of the main peculiar faiths ; identified in feelings and interests as they are, they are identified essentially with their success.

Absolutism with its power, money with its insidious influence, all the influences of sophistry, have overpowered the world by peculiar faith.

Why do preachers, priests, and hierarchists, spend so much time in proclaiming messiahships, that are entirely worthless from the very nature of things ?

They had better be employed in all the essentials of mind and religion-improvement. Theirs is lost time, in the close of life and its accounts.

They must be utterly reckless of reason and truth, when they advance such pernicious and evil demoralization doctrines. What does not the doctrine of divine rights and passive obedience do, in contravention of popular virtue and freedom ? Shame to you, preachers, priests, and hierarchists, who advance a system of the deepest slavery of vassal mind and its demoralization.

All proselytes seek power for their peculiar faith, of course. Are they very conscientious about the way the object is attained ?

A good government has no triumvirates of cardinals accused of scandalous proceedings.

What are the morals of a preacher or minister worth, who commits himself, as many do, in untruth, lust and infamy ? What is any man's mind worth, when accounted unworthy of credence, or to be relied on by no account, or what is analogous, that advances a cause that it should know is destitute of truth ?

As untrue as the gospels, will yet become a by-word, and their worthless expounders will go with them.

The rising greatness of mighty intellect makes it the bounden duty to take away all ungodly evils, as priestcraft, that lessens the purity and force of mind.

A bigoted Romanist thinks his children, if priests be absent from his circle of residence, cannot be Christians among even Protestants. Why ?

Does he not live among Christians ? Them he calls heathen, that is, inside barbarians !

Thus all sectarians think others fallible and impious, but themselves.

For remorse at their dying hour, some seek to give immense wealth to churches, to gain absolution from their sins ; that has as much potency as amulets and charms, the whole delusions of ignorance.

Can the world be thus ignorant, but for the felony of the priestocracy, that stickle at no means to gain their ends, though they infuriate, with deadly feud, the parts of the world against each other.

Cannot the world rise above such narrow views?

Mind only can enable it to do it properly.

Shame, then, to the ministers, priests and preachers, and all the affiliated partisans ho help keep up the delusion, when all such faith is not obsolete.

Monotheism is the friend of man, but messiahship, alias priestcraft, is anything else.

Do we impute, under any such regime, to God his general influence over the world, uch less the universe?

Do we not thereby sink universal in especial providence?

Sincerity in religion especially demands this assertion.

This tribe must be particularly verdant, if they suppose that their position has not ready been duly appreciated.

They assume to have religion. Are they truthful and just, as truthfulness, honesty, id reason preside over the paramount question of religion? Do they not help rob God his glorious attributes, as far as in them lies?

Then we must next recognise the sources of their faith. They must see, if truthful id honest, that it is absolutely absurd to put faith before reason.

The senses are the only medium through which observation and experience are de- red, and they must be duly regulated, verified, and confirmed by philosophical science, be correct and satisfy the republic of science.

How, then, can any honest men adopt faith without reason?

As rational beings, all must be monotheists.

Let all think, first obey honest thoughts, and then read others that reason approves.

But proselytism' may be the effort, not the truth of mind; hence, mind must be wary pure reason, and reject all that prevails by peculiar education.

The part of the world humbugged, delights in the mystery of that humbug, and seeks hold fast to its profits.

Thus the mere dogmas of such schools and scholars are to be upheld, long after their plosion. Is it nature of mind, to revel in humbugs forever?

This is only of the wilfully perverted; otherwise it is a base libel. Common sense id honesty of the highest order, are the essential organs of God: who, then, authorized oses or any priest to be? The attempt is a felony, black and dark.

Mind's characteristic calibre and integrity decide all matters of sense and honesty.

What good citizen, but has the loftiest aspirations for purest religion, the sublimest duties?

Who will not congratulate himself, on investigation of this mighty subject, which is s sublimest duty to investigate?

Who will be so verdant to entrust it to priestocracies, who have neither the abil- r to decide correctly, nor act honestly?

If the priests have not truth and honesty in profession, they cannot talk of religious iprovement, as all else is dust. It is clear that the profits of the hierarchy, have the ost potential voice in this matter.

One archbishop and nine bishops, in England, have $1,890,000 income yearly, it is serted. Is this true?

The peculiar trammels of education. the dogmas of the schools, the sacrifice to money, wer. and influence of power, of government, cannot be audited at the tribunal of cou- ience.

Liberal minds must base this position most liberally, discarding all the catches of zots and jesuits, most sophisticated. But should not the voice of the priestocracies heard in this matter of religion? Not at all, as they only know superstition, and t religion.

Superstition, not religion, needs priestocracies.

Superstition has given the benefit to them.

All their forms and ceremonies, sacraments and confessions, are for their, not the oples', wants.

The people only need what mind needs, and that is what no priests or preachers have spare.

No matter how much unprincipled opposition to the true faith by these men, still rts will triumph for ever by God's decree over all such that will result as contempti- e. Priests and preachers, if not lost to shame, ought not to present such a theme. ave they analyzed it?

They ought to put all the means of investigation for both sides like honorable men of i ith, in all persons' hands before admission into the church, not suppress rational in- iry basely, ignominiously, and disgracefully.

Now, all rational beings have the innate qualities and faculties of religion, but their ews are not right when perverted to superstition by priests.

Who desires such a position that, adopted by those knowing better, gives the test of their hypocrisy ; if not knowing better, that they are dupes ! All at least ought to be independent. A little more time hence, and the whole peculiar faith of the ignoble priestocracies, will be destroyed before the light of the civilized world.

Would Moses, Mahomet, or Christ-makers use now the means that were adopted by them in their remote ages ? Hardly, if men of sense, as claimed for them by partisans.

Then why should preachers and priests ? Merely to keep up a degraded system of superstition, that however improved upon by all the advantages of mind, is still superstition ?

If those men were to speak as good and wise men of this day, they would bid their followers cease all such superstition, and betake themselves to rational religion. The preachers and ministers do not know what they are about, if they be honest. What they do seals their own condemnation, as felony of the worst sort.

Honorable freemen who have waited with patience to see all this put down, know it to be as mentioned.

How formidable has been the hierarchy of the government of priestocracies ! Where is it now even, that proscription does not prevail against books of free principles ?

The great points of malign overpowering influence, are those of money, church and state power.

Legacies of millions have been left to churches ; even now, Trinity Church of New York has several millions of property, and might, if rightly managed, educate all the poor children of the state in splendid science.

What an engine of power, that might, by its increase of wealth, overrule the city ! All such are soulless corporations.

How came there any saints or sanctification ?

Of course, as God could not possibly make such, they are the last refuges and pretences of peculiar faith.

The laws of life will affirm, that no part of mind can justify such pretences. No pious fraud or lie can avail God, who rules truth and honesty.

The greater and lesser tyrants have abused this world, and libeled the future.

One of the greatest crafts of absolutism of the monarch and priestocracy, was at the Council of Nice. Its deeds were the year before A.D. 325, when there was collusion of state and church, of the emperor Constantine and the priests, the bishops to rule the world, as far as the empire could.

But, thanks to God, there is no restriction of mind, by earthly devices. Customs become obsolete and empires fall, both of emperors and priestocracies. The decree of principles is the only word of God Supreme.

Collusion must attend in all the powers of the craft, and in its government, from conception most ancient to execution most modern.

The pensioners on the supposed bounty are not willing to dissent from the established governmental authority.

See the salaries of the beneficed clergy, with their millions of money.

The clerical peers of the English realm present a road to preferment and of standing, under the banner of perjury nevertheless.

Were it not for the preachers and priests, the hierarchists and ministers, all these lies would perish out forever.

Is the order of priestocracy to be perpetuated through the world ? To be dictatorial ? Puseyism is squinting at Romanism, when the church is made infallible, and the voice of the layman nullified. The principal a cypher.

What state of existence is there so absurd, even of shakerdom, that perverts man's nature and has the fewest claims for legislative protection, but that the votaries of priests will follow to ruin ?

In some countries subject to the Roman faith, figures representing Peter and Mary act the harlequin, for alms. Begging and ignorance prevail in that country !

Does not the clergy seek to keep the people in ignorance, of the main essentials of religion ?

If peculiar faith be right, it ought not to reject reason, nor establish inquisitions about books and opinions of religion, as the bible is that of rational mind.

Now, priestocracies have shown despotism perfect, in asking and forcing credence for irrational faith. They are basely dishonest to do so. If they ask us to believe their proposition, they must give honest and proper reasons, else they are dishonored forever. They are charlatans and triflers with men's souls. No set of men should falsify history. What imposition is practiced by priests, who perjure souls.

But, then, it is the interest the priests take in our immortal souls for glory ! They have no temporal interest for themselves? The priests of Egypt had one-third the produce of all the cultivated land, and peculiar power.

They had what was peculiar people. What did those of Europe and Asia, all over the world, in all their forms and changes from century to century? What possessions and principalities had they not in England and France?

What did they the least have? Religion? No; the people were cheated, for they only had the gift of peculiar faith.

Alas, poor world, you have beeen mistreated your age.

In all ages of the priestocracy-power, whether as druids or augurs, pontiffs or any other, their power predominated, preying upon the sympathies of the people. What awful persecutions—what powerful influence of sects.

Let it not be too late, that you know these things rightly, and do them properly.

How can you believe the priestocracies, as they are temporarily interested? Their testimony is of no account or truth, not trustworthy. People are most verdant to believe them. The world of priestocracies, diversified as they are in both continents by creeds and names, vitiated as a body politic, invested with sovereign power, can never for a moment uphold any bibles of their tradition, as all such are an imposition and fraud on mind.

Absolutism seeks all manner of ways, to deprive mind of its sacred rights, to foil of its due light of rational investigation, or sophisticate all that appears.

Ministers of God will do the thing right, first for their minds, and next trustworthy of freemen.

Shame on the drivellers, who interfere with God's attributes and sovereignty. If crime and Deity are incompatible as purity and impurity, how can the perpetrators of capital-blasphemy-crimes reconcile themselves to the author of their existence and future being?

Do the priestocracies work for nothing? Who is simple enough to believe it, but degraded vassals that are afraid to call their souls God's, and their money their own property?

The curses of the priests have fallen in India, Egypt ánd Chaldea, the world.

When will the day ever come, when those lands will be delivered from the blight of their curses? By christianity? One paganism for another?

Talk of other kinds of slavery, what are they to this slavery? But what right have we to speak? As much as any other of the billion of minds, all of which are the true beneficiaries, and as much as any other patriots, that love truth and reason of all serious propositions submitted. But have not the priestocracies also a right to speak? Certainly, but only as the rights of mind entitle them as men, not the usurpations of mind as impostors.

The sanctity of popes, prelates, bishops, &c.!

For God's sake, and mind's sake, stop that humbuggery.

How long are the preachers and priests, to humbug the world? As long as that world is verdant enough to pay for all such humbugs!!!

Preachers and priests seek to convince the world, and they appeal to reason and faith—sophistry under the garb of reason, and credulity under the garb of faith.

When they pretend that all should "search the scriptures," and "get understanding," they strictly imply reason, which as soon as it is embraced, they rail at and libel most infamously by all the inquisition that universal freedom and toleration permit them, thus most inconsistently convicting and disgracing themselves by bigotry and fanaticism. The proper search of all scriptures of tradition, leads unquestionably to their impeachment and discarding in full.

They cannot stand this test. Of course they are worthless, and the sooner discarded the better, that mind may be rightfully employed.

Truth is immutable, and though suppressed or counterfeited under the pretences of church peculiar faith, yet cannot be annihilated by these deceivers. Many of these people deceive themselves, in keeping up deceptions not recognised now by the whole world. Ministers, you that have minds still unsullied by peculiar faith, you cannot be enraged against us, but will thank us for exposing to you the errors of your ways. It is your duty to renounce them at once and for ever. Preachers, no doubt, preach absurdities and sophistries that they do not believe, and cannot clearly, if intelligent and honest. Josephus (as quoted by Jones' Church History), tells us, "that the high priests of the Jews, were the most abandoned of mortals, and that they generally obtained their dignified stations, either through the influence of money, or court sycophancy; and that they shrank from no species of criminality that might contribute to support them in the possession of an authority thus iniquitously purchased.

"Under a full conviction of the precarious tenure on which they held their situation,

it became a leading object of their concern to accumulate, either by fraud, or force,"
&c. Recollect these were the bible makers!!! Jones says of the Romanists, "that
while they had an interest in disguising the truth, calling them false," &c. These the
pillars of bible advocacy. · What more proof?

What are the immense number of pious frauds perpetrated by this profession in its
various forms?

Observe the Magian rites—Zoroaster to procure the greater veneration for these
sacred fires, pretended to have received fire from heaven.

The fire temple: these Magian rites were built on the Jewish plan.

"The Jews had their sacred fire, which came down from heaven upon the altar of
burnt offerings, which they never suffered to go out, and with which all their sacrifices
and oblations were made." What honest mind believes this lie? "Zoroaster, in like
manner, pretended to have brought his holy fire from heaven." They were all perjuries. The priests of the magi were the scholars and philosophers, and were looked
upon by the vulgar as more than natural, and that they were inspired by superstitious
power." And is not this the world's history?

The Magian priests were all of one tribe, as among the Jews. This became the
national faith.

The royal family were of the priest tribe, to sustain its power of course. This was
supplanted by Mahometanism, another perjury.

The Franciscan and Dominican monks:

"The last adopted fictitious visions and dreams—as dæmons, an imposture of an
opposition. These were impious frauds.

"These monks persecuted Jetser, who heard all the secrets of his life and thoughts,
which the impostors had learned from his confessor."

(The immaculate conception of the Virgin Mary, was adopted by the Franciscans.)
Jetser discovered the plot, and the perpetrator prior.

The Dominicans to prevent exposure of the plot, tried to bribe Jetser to carry on
the cheat, but afterwards as the most effectual way, sought to poison him. The four
friars were burnt. Had this plot not been divulged, it would have been published as a
great miracle. "They were perpetually employed in encroaching upon the rights and
properties of others, to augment their possessions, and in laying the most iniquitous
snares and stratagems for the destruction of their adversaries." They were next to the
Jesuits.

The Jesuits, peculiar like the Jews, were confessors of nearly all the monarchs of
Europe, thus enjoying a great and influential function. The spiritual guides of great
men, "The Jesuits had become the confessors of almost all the monarchs in every
catholic country in Europe: a function of no small importance in any reign, but, under
a weak prince, superior to that of a minister. They were the spiritual guides of almost
every person eminent for rank or power; they possessed the highest degree of confidence and interest with the papal court, as the most zealous and able champions for its
authority; they possessed at different periods, the direction of the most considerable
courts in Europe; they mingled in all affairs, and took part in every intrigue and revolution." They acquired wealth and power. "Unhappily for mankind, their vast
influence has been often exerted with the most fatal effects. They sought to exalt
ecclesiastical power on the ruins of civil government. They incessantly stirred up
against the Protestants, all the rage of ecclesiastical and civil persecutions." And yet
all these people were professed christians, who claim pre-eminently the doctrine of
loving even enemies!

Priestocracy is established under the Grand Lama, the sovereign pontiff or high
priest of Thibetian Tartars. This hierarchy influences much of Asia. It has its
thousands of priests. The Lama is worshipped by the Tartars, most of whom consider him their god. Even the Emperor of China acknowledges him in his peculiar
faith capacity, one of the weakest things in that ruler. His worshippers prostrate
themselves before him. He has unlimited power in his dominions. The inferior
Lamas are the head priests. The country is filled with priests, to whose support Tartary and India contribute. Among their errors, is the doctrine of the transmigration of
the soul.

This peculiar faith is of thousands of years standing, and has temporal and spiritual
influence. Here is the sublime of imposition on the human mind.

The Roman faith seems to be assimilated in its superstitions, so that Asia has not
only furnished the books, but even the rites and ceremonies, &c.

In what does the balance of the world peculiar worship, differ essentially from this?
It is all superstition.

What! says the Protestant. Yes, Mr. Protestant, you are estopped by your brother

Lama priestocracy, on your own position at the very first question of faith. Do you not require this article as essential to your worship, and how dare you hypocritically deny it to the whole world, if you pretend to be sincere?

It matters not what be their rites and ceremonies. You accuse them of worshipping idols of wood! You are worshippers of idols of fiction. Your God has been in dust more than eighteen hundred years, you affirm by statements that unequivocally prove it.

What, sir, is the material difference between dust, and that which will be, in the lapse of time?

You may sophisticate all pagan peculiar worships as you and your priestocracy can, still your quagmire cannot be different from the balance.

It will take lengthy volumes to tell of all the priestocracies of the world. They are the soul of all corrupt peculiar faith, that engendered sectarianism at its conception. What must have been its crimes at birth, and at its maturity? Judaism was a lonely scion from the older dynasties, and she is about to be the mother of a prolific offspring.

But each claims to be a peculiar reformist, still all are alike. In what does one excel the other? All are superstitious. In what did the Roman and Arian disputants differ? Power of the Latins decided for them, and disgraced the excluded Arians, by banishment.

Then arises the Greek on the Roman church, as its "patriarch, who procured the deposition of another official of Jerusalem, was solemnly excommunicated by the patriarch. These churches have insuperable hatred toward each other." All must see that they are just what their priestocracies have made them. "The faith of the Greek church is greatly corrupted in Turkey, being little better than a heap of ridiculous ceremonies and absurdities."—*Buck.*

The patriarchates are sold to the highest bidder. Is it worth a moment's reflection, to know that the Greek church has had its sectarianism too? Superstition, peculiar faith, sectarianism, bigotry, sophistry and fanaticism, are all an ignoble family, that delights in crime, vice, oppression of the world. They characterize the Roman church.

"This church has followers that affect extraordinary piety and devotion, but had little of the power of vital religion, having many follies and superstitions."—*Buck.*

What have not these worthy priestocracies done?

"The first crusade was determined on, in the council of Clermont, in 1095. In this assembly the name of pope was for the first time given to the head of the church, exclusively of the bishops, who used to assume that title."

"The council of Rheims, in 1148, restrained bishops, deacons, sub-deacons, monks, and nuns, from marrying. In this council the doctrine of the trinity was decided." Were the councils divine? If not, they were clearly knaves and impostors.

"In the council of Sutrium, in 1046, three popes who had assumed the chair were deposed."

Plutarch, de Iside, says, "At a certain period, all the Egyptians have animal gods painted. The Thebans are the only people who do not employ painters, because they worship a god whose form comes not under the senses, and cannot be represented."—*Volney's Ruins.*

The ministers of the God of the universe are truly to be admired, as Washington, the father of his country.

But the world needs a priestocracy, an adventitious aid, that may be turned against it!

What protects the world, but its possession of exact science? In days of ignorance, while mind becomes perverted and servile, all kinds of usurpation are arrogated by those in power. Then a Caius Cæsar can make himself a god, and not wait for a posthumous apotheosis. The pretended patrons of learning, who subsidize court parasites and flatterers, instead of being the protectors of science, are the corrupters, forging the fountains. What is the fifth chapter of Acts of the Apostles, but like all the bible priestcraft, to get the people's effects? Do not still persist in your old errors, to make out so erroneous a consistency. You adopted, thoughtlessly, without investigation, all your church-membership and creed, as you thus sincerely believed what an ignorant, stupid, and corrupt priestocracy told you.

They had sinister views in the trade, trick, secrets, mysteries, enigmas, prophecies, and miracles of peculiar faith.

The whole dynasty of priestocracy block the whole game.

What can the world do with its follies and corruptions, if it blindly embrace them?

The conception of the messiahship of Christ bespeaks the low idea of priestocracy all the time; nothing to ennoble or bespeak a god; a fiction that was himself of that order.

It is time that the world had its due, from the moneys expended for despotisms and usurpations, civil, ecclesiastical, and military. Abolish all these. The felons of peculiar faith are counteracting God's decrees, all over the world, for their peculiar benefit. Advantage is taken of the ignorant mass, who know not the first principles of mind, no more than their blind, stupid misleaders. What baseness, when the vassal degraded presses, of degraded felons, assist to overwhelm mind.

What is the difference between priest and preacher, when both are ministers? None. But our priest or preacher is the right one! Who and what made him right? Our peculiar faith and peculiar education. Did robbery of God's functions do that? For that is the position of peculiar priestocracies. Of all corruptions and lies, the priestocracy and gospels are the worst—built up to uphold the most blasphemous. Do not these men deify despots, all mortals; then, can they render sacred their books, one step more in crime of blasphemy?

But the people of the world are good, easy souls; none take the trouble to investigate for themselves. The priests may preach all that. The people view their bible as that of their fathers', and that is enough! This would never have extricated them out of the first barbarian age of the world. Are the people asleep to their own best interests? But they are excited against rational investigators, who, if they set them right, in truth as in God, are not they their friends, and the friends to rational religion?

People do not know what they are doing, when they follow priestocracies. Have you read, or investigated, freemen? It is your duty to do both, most understandingly.

The priestocracies beg your faith, that is, for you to stultify yourself, your mind. They cannot take that citadel, if you do justice to it and God; that is, if you cultivate rational religion, the highest duty to mind and God.

The priestocracies have not a proper comprehensive conception of God, nor pure zeal in preaching the truth.

Are you the representative of a blasphemous priestocracy?

Will you, pulpit-man, trifle your soul away, with such trash? Do you libel God!

Is the people the great leviathan, with hook in jaw, misled by the priestocracy? The people must war, in direct antagonisms. Those, whose profession is for false pretences, should be convicted therefor. Such is the character of the human mind, that becomes fixed on any one opinion or prejudice, through ignorance, that be it a dynasty of error or not, so it be a dynasty, you must not touch it, right or wrong. What is the dynasty of priestocracy, but swindling? Did the people know how to analyze this subject, or have they done it, if they did know?

Oppose the dynasty, and you are opposed powerfully in proportion to its influence, right or wrong. If your acts agree with that dynasty, no matter what it is, all is well, you are welcomed; but if you war upon it, however right you, and wrong it, still you are warred upon by its power, clan, and clique retainers.

But you, for your peculiar policy, affect that God should be sought, through intermediate means. The best way to exalt man, is to bring him directly before God.

But do you believe that faith people can mislead you? That is the most verdant position, when you yourself permit this.

Devils are only the creations of perverted minds.

What a hopeful set, the prophets and priests.

Thousands of these have fashioned the Old Testament; tens of thousands of pulpit people have sustained it, while thousands of despots have aided. Can you trust yourself in the keeping of such a band?

All the pulpit preachers have to carry with them a peculiar god, as if they had the God of the universe. What miserable bigotry and fanaticism, that cannot permit them to see how stupid is their analysis.

All messiahs and priestocracies are lost at the commencement of God's operations, as the most contemptible of all machinery, to becloud, befog, or defraud mind, the beneficiary.

But you cannot head the priestocracy about the authenticity of their bibles, if you, good easy souls, permit them to lay down for granted their own premises.

They take up a partial, not comprehensive authenticity of scriptures, and tell you that Christ's existence and performance of miracles, are as well established as any piece of history, for here is the testimony of the four Evangelists, declaring them to be saints canonized. All that is story, not history. .

Who made them saints? Man, in his power? The saintship belongs to God. Here, at once, is imposition vile.

But this is extraordinary matter and must be met rightly, not by the mere assertion of the pulpit-man, who knows no more than you—and reads from fictions that are not even respectably endorsed for an intellectual freeman!

This age of science cannot be satisfied, that superstition and its perjury should answer for religion.

The man of God is to be appealed to. Who is that man? Let him prove himself divine or otherwise.

If there be children of God, is the rest heathen? Who are the first? Impostors and assumers. Who created the last? The priests have deceived ignorant women and children. Go and locate among church-bigots, if you wish to see for yourself, the curses of society.

I have given audience to all practicable, and sought every opportunity to hear the whole tribe and profession, of vindicating their proper position, but as they had not the elements they could not do so. They cannot do so after a full maturity of time. I will retire from that pulpit-audience after I get through, convert as I am, to rational religion.

You talk about mind not going direct to God, who gives all living beings his grace? How is it with priestocracies and messiahs, that are really so degraded in superstition that they cannot look pure religion in the face? Are these fit to approach God? As liberal as we can be in all this matter, still any party that trespasses on the rights of the world, might be subject to the penitentiary, knowing their pretences to be false. Can you get a fair and impartial tribunal, at all? The partisans are pledged to their side.

They do not act in good, but in peculiar faith, and that universally condemns them.

Consecrate the temple of mind to religion, science, philosophy, truth, and universal brotherhood, then you will renounce peculiar faith and all its inherent sectarianism.

All are students while on earth. How dare the pulpit-men pollute it, with unhallowed peculiar faith?

Why is the pulpit the means yielded by the people to hear the truth so absurdly polluted, by fanatics, who claim an extreme indignation against all those who disbelieve them.

Fanaticism of the pulpit is seen in bitter denunciations. Usurpation of the people's mind's rights, eventuates in their proscription. They have been regarded as the vulgar crowd, by mere usurpers. Where is the hope of correction?

In the rising generation of rational mind, old customs of peculiar faith, dogmatic bigotry and fanaticism, are hard to be eradicated. But all duty, with proper spirit, will rectify through the potency of rational mind.

Christ, you say, is identified with the priestocracy—that is the fact; at the same time, the God of the universe is not complicated at all with them, who have their peculiar gods as a peculiar people.

Mind perverted has made Christianity, Judaism, and all other pagan peculiar faith of the world, what it is.

To call that religion which is peculiar faith, is a base prostitution of the word and language.

The pulpit-man assumes, as if he had thoroughly analyzed mind, when he has not touched the subject.

The rabid fanatic rants in the pulpit, and tells us that all the works on the bibles of tradition have been refuted. He knows he lies, and wishes to estop all inquiring minds from appropriate investigations. Will you believe him: are you so verdant as to rely on his assertion, when he stands in the most equivocal position? You cannot get him to the only thing rational mind should do, namely, reason, for then he flies to the false pretence of faith—credulity. Can you expect the truth from a pulpit-priest? It is their assumed privilege to claim mysteries. They will and must lie outrageously, else they could not deceive the people so exceedingly. The preachers ought not deceive women and children.

The priestocracy could not govern Palestine—they had not mind to unite Israel and Judah, much less the world. A brotherhood is heathen, to such.

Jerusalem was the centre of that country, in regard to priests and kings, yet what advantage did she furnish all?

No, the ancients know not, nor do the moderns take heed, as mind is vassal with mind.

The world has idly, stupidly, ignominiously, left undisturbed, as if entrusted divinely in the hands of the priestocracies, all matters of faith, as if the people were utterly incompetent to perform the functions of mind, the beneficiary of religion. That is the people's duty, as it is mind's functions.

Can we expect the pampered priestocracy to stop, as if convicted of error, unless mind's tribunal force it to that unpleasant, but certain category ?

How much longer, citizens, shall society be swayed, under the tyranny of ignorant, bigoted mind ?

Mind has outlived the priests' crocodile gods—the murder of children by them, by fire ! It will survive all the pagan idolatry.

The most fascinating is power, now, and all its influences over the government of mind.

The Egyptian learning, was building pyramids in part. For what ? Better had mind been liberated from the curses of their priestocracies.

But the preachers go against the unbeliever or disbeliever. It is their duty to prove their gospel, so that an honest mind may believe candidly and honorably, else they are estopped forever in advancing their unendorsed doctrine, much less in inveighing against the last, even skeptics, as they affect. Christians are the last to speak of believers, unless they prove signs.

But then, what is the world to do if all this gospel goes by the board ? The question is not at all with the world, which God governs as the Creator's best right and duty, but with the priestocracy, that are all to be estopped with their estopped gospel, unproved and unendorsed. The gospel had been estopped long ago, if the priestocracy had not to go therewith !

Who are the priestocracies, that they should deceive, oppress, or crush mind ? The mouth-organs of the ancients, the priestocracy could direct public sentiment as it chose nearly ; but how is it now ? The conservative revolution of the world and mind, has materially changed for the better.

The priestocracy absolutely controlled, at one time, the ancient world. The patriarchs of the Jews governed thus their families, and finally, the whole nation.

This is the party most unprincipled in all matters that conflicted with their self-interests, that mind is required to bow to and reverence ! The officials and functionaries of the priestocracy, got up their Israelitish government, a curse to the whole people.

Have mercy on the priestocracies : let them all have mercy on themselves and the world. We have no animosity or ill-will to them, but we act for the principles of patriotism. Some of my best friends are, or were in the church. But we cannot let off the bible of tradition-man easily. The priestocracy bibles of tradition are too small an affair for me : I seek the universal good of mankind—of the world. But for them. public opinion would have become much more enlightened, and had better regulated itself. I wish to be right, and therefore discuss this matter openly and candidly.

How disgusting is pulpit sophistry, how ingenious yet worthless. But, O preachers, how vain are your babblings ! How miserable your pretences, how false, yet how fair. they seem. You pretend to prove your position—your scriptures—you ought not to open them, the way you proceed. Stop all such, and spend the time more usefully to your race, mankind.

The world has seen, without redress, the inutility and degradation of bibles of tradition. It was an anomaly, destitute of proof, that it felt. These bible-men are beyond decent responsibility in rational mind, as they feel justified by the dynasty of superstition and sophistry, to utter all such falsehoods—for mind has been stultified and crushed under their weight. We should never leave it in the province of any functionary of priestocracy, to attempt to supersede mind. Have they ingenuously given to mind its rights ?

Better had it been for the world a billion of times that the priestocracy had never existed, with all their accursed machinery of messiahships, &c. Priestocracy cannot conceive at all of religion, as all peculiar systems' men run into peculiar faith-estimation. The benefits of pure thoughts of religion cannot be put by them above all impure dynasties. They are so bigoted and prejudiced, that it is most difficult to get them to reason even on the subject. They must leave the profession, the first position of reason. They have sought to teach world by the old exploded books, and can hear to nothing like reason.

The world needs rational books and teachers, not the reverse.

What low morals the Jews had under the priestocracy, who were accursed as a body by their own fraternity, as destitute of morals and truth. The priestocracy may affect extraordinary concern for souls, but the world is identified with its good, and will secure it when appreciated.

Who would not glory in exposing priestocracy felony ?

All such will be exposed properly by those not indebted to the loaves and fishes of the church, or unchanged by its morals. All the rabbis, muftis, priestocracies, are to be scouted on the face of the earth.

Now let us see whether the world is hypocritical to discard untried the bible of
mind, or will discuss rationally its merits. By keeping the rest of the world straight,
you are apt to be kept so.

The peculiar god of priestocracy is any and everything every day, that that dynasty
houses. At first, he has permitted man to fall. The priests must atone for him.
Then the covenant of patriarch priests. Then comes a second covenant. All covenants of priests. And sufficient explanations can be given as are available to the
priestocracy.

What can you do with the bigots, that have no exaltation of soul or character, whose
mind is not open to rational education or conviction? It is a hopeless chance when
you see men avoid rational discussion. The pulpit-men do this, pick up isolated points
before their audience, as if they presented the facts.

Any one that proscribes mind, the beneficiary, from all due investigation, is recreant
to justice, honor, truth, virtue, and mind itself; above all, religion. The priestocracy
proscribe even all books that reflect light on the science of religion.

The people could not even get suitable books to read up to the light of the age.
Bigots take the greatest trouble to make the world hate and despise them. Their name
will go down to posterity with its deepest execration and contempt.

If it were not a world of priestocracies and bigots, we should be perfectly astonished
that there was the least foundation for a messiah. Who ever thought of such things
but priests and preachers?

Is a priest anything else than a priest? Can you make anything out of them but
priestly bigots?

They affect to claim all under their bibles, that explanation can make to suit, because
the people mention the wants. There are some minds too rational for the frauds of the
priestocracy to be imposed on them.

What, pulpit-men, will you gospelize falsehoods, and legalize all the injuries resulting
therefrom? Are you possessed of rational minds going to let the priestocracy forever
overwhelm your life-rights, and laugh at you? Are you permitting advantages to
church? Where is the religion in all this? Is this fair and honorable? It may be
christian.

Are you afraid to look the priestocracy or death in the face? Shall a foolish or
designing pulpit man allay your superstitious fears—like an ostrich, stick your eyes in
the bush? Carry out legitimate deductions. But some of the dupes of the world
prefer that false position, for fear it would upset priestocracy, the very essential objection. If you attempt to answer, it must not be partially, but all, and that decides
against you at once. The priestocracy under the old regime, however exploded, are
actually shamed by creation's works of a Creator proved. This position will stop the
fraud, violence, and usurpation of the nations of the world. None but the priestocracy
could have ever made a peculiar god, and bent all their followers to their peculiar
views. The world should be particularly indebted for all exposures of its frauds and
impositions; but can one-fourth of the whole world appreciate truth? How then can
it reflect the true faith? It must be the faith of the prevailing dynasty. The world
must have a head, if it be a demagogue, a radical bigot! It is astonishing to see with
what tenacity bigots will cleave to superstition and its bibles, after all have been most
conclusively exploded. Does a superstitious bigot ever reason? He would rather be
a devil worshipper, and have his old exploded trash of a bible, than see the brilliant
word of God in the mighty orbs of the universe. You cannot beat such out of his
head, because he has been told so, that a senseless book or bible of tradition is the word
of God, when it is positively the word of men, who have got the nearest to be devils
incarnate. God has only left his word where priestocracy cannot disfigure, alloy, counterfeit, or pollute it. They would do so soon enough, if they could. Yes, but the casuist
may pretend that my opinion is worth no more than the opinion of the rest of the
world.

I speak of fixed facts, not opinions. What is the supreme universal standard to a
free mind, but that of rational faith, granted by the Almighty himself, the only head
standard. Parties and partisans that are committed, are not disposed to yield readily.

The first thing the pulpit people have to do, is to prove their position by the
authenticity of their bibles; if they do not, they and their bibles ought and will fall
together, in justice to truth, the emanation of Deity. All such bibles must be subordinate to religion.

Preaching is a contingency, and as long as peculiar faith lasts may never secure the
respectable majority of the world. Sectarians seek to get the cream of the land in all
ages and countries, and the advocates of sectarianism affect to be the most meritorious,
through social offices, the best in the land.

Why is rational discussion of all this subject, even to reading of both sides, proscribed the world by the clergy?

Is the credulous world to be its servant forever?

Whose fault is it that the world is kept in abeyance to this ignoble subject? It is not my fault, as I have besought the pulpit people to prove the authenticity of the scriptures, or be eternally silent thereon. Let the people demand this, or demand an exposure of all impostors. I could not obtain justice; it is the miserable and abominable servitude of the human mind, held in the deepest vassalage to superstition. Why do preachers back out from the proof of the authenticity of the scriptures? Would they do so if they could do better? Yet how much sophistry and falsehood are eternally offered the world instead! Will the stupid mass stop their infamous falsehoods and jugglery? Are you your own worst enemies?

The world is full of intrigue, and this department is saturated with it. All that we can do in this world, is not to arrogate a supremacy in morals or religion, for our own humble selves, but to denounce all peculiar systems and their advocates, that have the elements of corrupting the world. The world will do better, if all such elements are abstracted, and pure, honest mind is left to its intrinsic capacity of seeing its light.

Are preachers any better than the ancient augurs and soothsayers, the Druids? In what respect; let them prove that particular? O but if I affirm anything against the position, I declare God a liar! Was there ever such logic? Who but priests and their vassals, could torture logic to such false pretences! It is only proof of priests being the deepest liars and felons. The God of the universe, has nothing at all to do with such cattle. All that can be claimed at most, is a peculiar god, that the world does not know.

What tricky people all the priestocracy are. They fight for existence, and catch at all manner of expedients.

Peculiar faith is the counterfeit coin of the priestocracy, yet these worthies can descant about or against the heathen. What peculiar privileges have these men-prophets or priests, to assume to be the world's counsellors, &c., when they have no mission proved? In this there must be no degraded charlatanry, not to see what the mind needs; but the cause of the priestocracy is not that of God.

The story of Cain killing Abel, was to fix the idea that the offerings were acceptable to their peculiar god. And all this cause of murder, is the false pretence of the priestocracy.

All this bible is theirs, not the people's nor religion's, concocted and executed by them, brought out for their benefit, and all after the order of Melchisedec. This is part of their funds.

The priestocracy are a libel of religion, well calculated to deceive the world and pervert mind, unless guarded by rational education.

Let not the pulpit people say what sophistry and self interest prompt, but what highminded truth declares, else be silent conscientiously. Better had some never been born, than pervert the world and society so.

Settle this question, at once, and for ever. Infidelity is a robbery, that is the category. How stupid for the priestocracy, to advance books to usurp mind, and yet ask mind to take for granted their false pretences. The prophets, as a great part of this body, wrote for themselves, and availed themselves of the prevailing order of things, to maintain power and the impositions. They are as a mere candle, whilst the sun shines before it in its broadest glare.

Priests, or all that presume to appropriate for granted the statements of bible pretences, are pirates on the world.

All gospels are the results of priestocracy.

If they were honest, they would stop their own sins, the most heinous of all. Such go to the pulpit to sophisticate public morals—rather should they go to the plough, a more honorable business, if they cannot find the eligible modes of teaching rightly the human mind. Nothing equals the sophistry of the priestocracy, but their effrontery and pretences. What else but the deepest corruption of the world, could we expect of them!

Were it not for the sophisticated bigots of the pulpits, the balance might proceed better. In them is a miserable degeneracy of false teaching, to teach the mass! How odious! Teach the mind, and then the errors about the heart would die. All due impressions are to be made in the mind. Is sophistry to do it? The very conduct of priestocracy proves it offensive before mind's rights, in dissuading from rational investigation by absurd theories. What can exceed this felonious deceit in society; such sinister influences?

Let not the world be swindled all around, by these unprincipled men; if we give all the pulpit people the most liberal latitude, even more than they ask, and take them as they mean in the pulpit, most literally, not metaphorically, nor explaining away anything. The faith of the priestocracy begets its sophistry enough. Let us do one good in life, that is, cause the explosion of this profession. Those of you that are affiliated, can hardly, as self-interested, decide this paramount question, as honest truth demands.

The plan of Moses did not make the Jews intellectual and independent, but a nation in abeyance to an imperious priestocracy and their masses vassal.

What confidence can we have in any such, who have thus prostituted mind? Priestocracy is the adjutant-general or chief in absolutism, unworthy of trust, as an usurper or monopolizer forever of popular rights, and is always Jesuitical.

How long will the priestocracy seek to ignobly maintain their ground by sophistry, instead of honorably maintaining the pure cause of religion? We can not be converts to any but God, and anticipate with the most satisfactory complacency, the time of our final change. Who would for all the wealth of the world, be deprived of their position in regard to the rational faith, in adoration of the only perfect God?

The pulpit people are incompetent and faithless to the trust of mind, to act in good faith, to speak the truth.

Is it not almost a waste of time and mind, to expect true thought and liberty, for those plodding priests and politicians to appreciate?

The stupid accrediting the minister's sophistry, that God could not be found out without their bible, is a consummate piece of assurance in these pretenders, all akin with their other idle and vain pretences; when the God of the universe is not there.

They do not state all the propositions, and their people are stupidly credulous, and call it faith! with perfect stupid vassalage of mind. The priests hide their secrets in their sanctuaries. What else do they keep there?

How base is it in them, to exclude mind; how degrading not to revere reason? The greatest fulmination of the priestocracy is eternal damnation and punishment.

What makes the loud calls of the preachers? Money.

How corrupt some of the reviewers, who are creatures to much of the iniquities of peculiar faith.

O credulous multitude, do not be afraid to say, that science is philosophy's, is mind's, and mind God's. Priestocracy has helped to lighten the chains of absolutism. How have these worthies acted? The way to get out of their difficulty, has been to make the deceived hold on, till the deceivers are out of the way. Most actors are the people, but the wire-workers are the priestocrats. Instead of reforming man, they deform their god, by their peculiar pretences.

It has not entered into the mind of man to conceive the iniquities of the priestocracies. The world must not expect the priestocracy to change first; it has to do that. The priestocracy have corrupted man most awfully. They have made him hypocritical by tinkering with him, and produced an antagonism, if not an undying enmity, of man to man, almost to God.

Is it reasonable that mind, educated rationally, would not adopt its Creator, whom to know is to revere beyond all others? It is unreasonable that it should adopt any other. When we suspect ourselves as being too severe against the priestocracy, let us ask ourselves if ever these monsters in human shape ever relented in their encroachments, most foul, on human rights? If they ever sacrificed human beings to appease their angry god of superstition, bigotry, and bloody sacrifice?

At the start the wicked priestocracy of the world vilified, sacrificed mind: got it out of the way for their mental midwifery. Mind was of no account, of no force with them. It had been put into leading-strings, and was misled, blinded to its own power, right and duty.

Never was there such mental vassalage as propagated by the serfs of priestocracy. The belief of gods, or a peculiar god, was inoffensive enough, apparently, but it had to take the priestocracy and all its interests along with it. Wherever priestocracy are, false capital abounds.

What was the custom of all the other priests, soothsayers, and all of that tribe? To lie, and make capital out of it. The sooner this senseless and stupid humbuggery is got rid of, the better; however refined its superstition, still it is a perjured superstition. All this was to blind by the collusion of the priesthood, whose authority was upheld by the bibles of tradition. Who desires priests? None but the victimized. Theirs is dangerous, ruinous error. Do you side with the priestocracy, or reason?

It is the vocation of preachers to uphold their profession. It ought primarily to be to uphold truth and honesty—religion.

Instead of blessing mind by the richest treasures of mind, they are cursing it by the deepest devices of priestocracy.

The priests, preachers, and their vassals, prate about infidelity, and you would think that mind and reason, guides and pilots of God for man, had conspired against them, the priests, rather than that they had done it, a world's age against the world. Let the priestocracy alone for conservative revolution. They are adverse to the noblest dignity of mind, conspiring in fraud, and debased in iniquity; are not trustworthy for mind and reason, as they are traitors to their noblest interests. Instead of freeing, they begin with enslaving it to the worst of superstition and sophistry, enough to ruin a soul, unless the God of the universe had defended it, as great in its conservation as in its creation.

Their piratical fanaticism in the crusades is part of their world-history.

The priests have ruined every country they have mastered, as Mexico, Egypt, Hindostan, and Spain. Their efforts during the crusades were to enslave the world, but their piractical hordes were overwhelmed. The conservative principles of God vindicated themselves. Theirs is the conspiracy against mind and reason, that they so ignominiously hate, as standing in their way.

They misrepresent Deity, mind and reason.

For these noble gifts of God to earth, they give us monomania and their hell in their heaven, expelling therefrom their angels for their devils!

The bigot is joined to his idols, and you will not do anything with him, till his temporal interest moves the animal.

You cannot find his soul in his mind. It is his body you must suspect. We do not oppose truthful and honest people, but all others.

At this day, with all the light of science, and the world in part wide awake on the devices of priestocracy, we cannot get the truth from Rome, where miracles are now claimed, so prone are millions, from the dark ages of antiquity to the present times, to all the forms of self-delusion. What a power and influence the dynasty of the priest-ocracy have wielded.

This dynasty tells more lies about faith, than all the world does about the balance of the subjects of the world; it is the greatest of all earthly tyrannies. It will not let the human mind reason. The following has been advanced as the income of the Spanish clergy, by an English paper :   •

Tithes,	£10,900,000
Fees,	110,000
Alms,	1,950,000
Livings,	1,000,000
Produce of church-yards,	600,000

£14,560,000 annual revenue.

The annual expenditure of the nation is £7,000,000.

The world has surrendered itself to this ignoble excrescence.

Priests have tried human credulity, to see how far they might tinker with the human mind ; they are the insidious offshoots of absolutism, a dead weight to the world.

The after-thoughts of the priestocracy are diametrically opposed to the fore-thoughts of God; the first led to all bibles of tradition, the last to the creation of the universe.

What kindness can the priestocracy, the curse of bigotry, show to the world? Why retain them? Bigotry holds fast to fanaticism. We do not.

Human nature is human nature still, and priestocracy is the same in all ages and all positions of oracles, whether thus saith Apollo, Jupiter, or Jehovah. It is all one on the most intelligent and truthful analysis, as it was the language of peculiar priestocracies. If the priestocracy be not just and truthful to man, how can they be righteous before God? Let the ungodly priestocracy alone.

The profession of the priestocracy has been the best drilled of all for thousands of years : it is the oldest, as it must have commenced with the observation of the elements, leading to its mighty difficulties in superstition. Let us strip the mantle off these hypocrites. And will the priestocracy still persist in bolstering up an exploded, all-perjured book?

Where can they find their locality of a bottomless pit? Not in this earth, whence this very idea originated, as from volcanoes, most superstitiously, of course most ignorantly. The density of the earth proves its solidity. Why should you, priestocracy, place yourselves in antagonism to God and rationality? The pope can get the civil government yet a little longer. But his faith-government is rotten. You should be silent, if your dignity will permit.

Are you, the world-clique, determined to see nothing?

The pulpit-men assume everlastingly, and do not prove.

You talk of Robespierre, Marat, and Danton, enemies of the human race, to hold on to your rottenness a little longer. Did not the dynasty of kings and priestocracies crush the mind of the French people for centuries, brutalize, degrade and barbarize it?

No means for such ungodly collusion or collision should be adopted, or left available on earth by mind, that regards the right culture. The priestocracy should be ashamed by this time, of continuing such felony and devices to defraud their fellow-men. They should resort to the plough, the loom, or the anvil, as an honest means of getting their livelihood, and drop all such idle, false, ungodly pretences. All that were of this faith, that sought to do good, will abhor this as the means to do so.

If the priestocracy persist in their evil ways, let the others serve God Almighty, and seek to reach the pure centre of purity and the universe; but let the world's eyes be upon the perjurers.

Why adhere to a corrupt system of peculiar faith, a counterfeit for God? If people were to turn to their own mind-culture and business to the proper extent, and let God manage his own universe as he desires, the world would be properly governed.

The dynasty of priestocracies has been that of bullies, sophists, and perjurers, all. Has monopoly any conscience?

The greatest vassalage is caused by priestocracies.

The clergy assumed the medical profession. What did they not do, as long as the people permitted them?

Why should they not hold to all the influences that move the world? Surgeons advocated that the royal touch cured scrofula, &c.! Which have been the worst, the meanness and sycophancy of the world, or the pretences of priestocracy?

The sooner you get out of your bibles of tradition, priests, preachers, and dupes, the better. What a puerile sycophancy of professors, to square science with the bibles of ignorant monkish tradition! We are willing to recognise and appreciate, in all professors, all that they can personally claim. It is with them to arrest discussion at the desirable point. If kings can do no wrong, why will not the priestocracy assume more? God will save us, if our minds will do their bounden duty, from the tyranny and seduction of the priestocracy, who have humbugged and tyrannized over the world.

Why do the priestocracy ask of freemen to degrade themselves to superstition, man-worship, for mere pretences?

We think that foul's-day ought to be abolished as superfluous, as there are so many others, since it propagates bad morals, as want of veracity, a serious matter indeed.

All time employed about the priestocracy, comes under this category as most trifling. The priests and preachers must know, if they are smart, that they do wrong.

This is the age that presents the great faculty of reading them thoroughly, whilst it is supposed very verdant.

When the world speaks rightly on this subject, the priestocracy, who are self-imposed impostors, will be nowhere. They will be ashamed of the light, and afraid of their own shadows.

Their great object has been to influence mind for their power, &c. All power, but of the people, has a connective link dovetailed into each other. This is the category and solution of difficulties to be overcome.

While all professions have their humbugs more or less, that of the preachers has the more especially, for it is all humbug. The time will come when they will be panic-struck, in real danger. These ungodly men had better stop.

Preachers, or church-people, are no better, at the best, than good persons out of the church? Yes. Prove them better.

If the priestocracy were the deposit of science and power, they have betrayed that trust. When convicted, they do not wish to be convinced; they do not wish to see right, as they ever misquote. What divine rights have doctors of peculiar faith, to know all about faith?

What unprincipled opposition malignant bigotry can adduce! The edition of priestocracy is analogous, in all ages and places, all over the world. They seek power, impose on the superstitious, increasing ignorant credulity and delusive hopes, causing them to be unreasonable, unjust and sophisticated, making themselves the impostors of the world.

What person, in his senses, will knowingly colleague with them? Self-instituted impostors! Can fanatics absolve themselves from imposition of sin?

Responsibility should attach to all the universe or creation. Will not the preachers and priests be responsible for misleading the people by false pretences of messiahship? They have run riot on vassal mind long enough. It is time that all such frauds be arrested. Do you aim to be right before the world?

We may expect that of the people, but how of the priestocracy in face of facts! They seek to evade, not adopt principles. Their system is bankrupt in principle.

Much of the world assumes to decide this mighty subject, of itself, or by an interested priestocracy. How can it do this honorably, without investigation and proper analysis? What special pleadings have there been, by preachers and priests, to prop up a gone cause.

How is the conservative part of the world to correct them?

How can we get a hearing before bigotry? Every avenue is blocked by money, influence, power, prejudice, and sophistry. The word of the priestocracy is the very last that ought to be taken on this subject, as their self-interest has perverted the subject, for centuries.

The means of the priestocracy are, in all ages, the faith of superstition; otherwise they had, or have, no existence. Instead of teaching mysteries, let science teach all in the tide of time. It is the priestocracy-influence that says: give us the bible of tradition. The word peculiar, belongs to the priestocracy. While others are quick to impose, the people are in the greatest wrong to seek the imposition.

What country should be the refuge of culprits for murder and crime; what country should be the receptacle of their creeds? Is this holy writ? The world yields its power to a set who gives no responsibility.

Who are the real butchers of social life and happiness, friendship of a universal brotherhood?

Do they not cover defeat, as swindlers of popular rights, by doctrines, notoriously the work of mind, perverted by all the corruptions of faith and perjury?

How can you believe the priestocracy, who lie about religion, first to last, all the time?

Fanatics have shut out the light of reason from mind, for pretences of bibles. What felony!

The more ignorant the bigot, the more difficult is he to be corrected. What is that faith worth that pretends that people the worst in the world, at death can be pardoned by a mere act of the priestocracy?

What sin. Confession and forgiveness! What crime in them? What a world-nuisance, to be noticed in rational jurisdiction. Reason is never to be conspired against by any earthly priestocracy, the basest blasphemers, the lowest of the low. What do augury, man-worship, or any of the pagan forms of priestocracy, profit the world? Instead of resisting the blind infatuation of the ignorant multitude, the priestocracy turn deceivers of their countrymen, by an extortion on their credulity, and profit thereby, at the same time claiming, by excellence, to be the means of promoting science and invention in the world.

The priestocracy have been the most degraded, avaricious, deluded, and ignorant. They are one idea people, who cannot analyze that idea. What is messiahship but priestcraft, kept afloat by all kinds of world delusion and iniquity of the inquisition. but if you speak what you know of false pretences of the priestocracy, they will do their worst against you, as you expose them? These professors assume that their profession is superior to the mind, even the soul. At whose tribunal is the responsibility? At God's. Why? By right of creation. The priestocracy play into each other's hands. Do you belong to their dynasty?

What faith, sustained by the doctrine of bibles of tradition, however potent supposed in capacity of saving, can be advanced by any priestocracy, with sincere declarations of infallibility? All their peculiar faith is ruinous to a world's morals, and the soul's happiness. When this profession and vassals are made to speak of it, they are non-plused, and do not wish a fair investigation or rational discussion of the mysteries. The priestocracy have kept back the world from the brightest light, the true analysis of mind.

Cato, the censor, said: "It was surprising that the priests, during the performance of their divine service, could refrain from bursting out into a loud laugh in the faces of their congregation." Is the perjury less?

The sovereign people should not let the priestocracy prejudice them. When faith is mixed up with government—as in China—and absolute dynasties, what a hopeless chance is there for justice to mind!

Bigots! in seeking to convert others, convert yourselves to reason and truth; then you will see justice done.

Ministers, leave that pulpit, seek religion, truth, honesty, and God.

The people are fooled to death by their priestocracy, who try to scare them, as vassals, from reading rational books of religion. What treachery!

The priestocracy cannot answer them honorably and fairly, and have to resort to absolute falsehood to get along. What miserable pious frauds are now being committed to the world in all peculiar faiths.

Were it not for the power, influence and pay, the world would long ago have rejected this, the most abominable curse. There are no hopes of a bigot who acts, by self-interest, not by reason.

But for collusion of the priestocracy and their vassals, the whole of this fable would be done.

No, it is dovetailed in with governments of usurpation, of whatever hierarchy, whether protestant or not, reeking in corruption. To pull it down, you must pull down all absolute governments.

It is shameful that American statesmen should uphold anything of the kind, being bad enough for the vulgar to do so. Why should we have among us men who make false statements about religion?

You rely on the clergy? Can you have proper confidence in them interested to millions of revenue per year, that increases as proselytes increase? Any person or book that proclaims more than the unity of God, libels him most blasphemously. Josephus tells that Ide, the freed woman of Decius Mundus of Rome, corrupted and bribed the priests of Isis to beguile a married woman, Paulina, esteemed a lady, to commit adultery with Mundus, under the disguise of the god Anubis, for which Tiberius ordered the priests as well as Ide to be crucified, and the temple of Isis, &c., to be demolished, only however banishing Mundus. This goes to prove that man, priest, or other, is liable to corruption when he puts himself in the way, which he does by commencing priest, which is the profession of humbuggery.

The priestocracy curse, and lie in that curse. What a position of the class assuming to have all the decency and truth, to be the greatest liars and cursers in the world, that absolutely requires their annihilation.

What does the world wish of false teachers? All their doctrines are perjured.

Are not the preachers concealed infidels? Do not some just believe as far as the money goes?

As to the ancient priestocracy, we may not really blame them so much, considering the disastrous peculiarity of the times, that shaped mind to its sway. We may consider that they sought to escape all the evils of past martial prowess, when slavery or death was too often the result of victory. When we survey the scenes of desolation of ancient ruins, we can best appreciate what peculiar faith and military prowess have done in their reckless fanaticism.

The Jews, whose pagan bible progeny is forced on us, exterminated whole people of all ages and both sexes.

The Romans, whose institutions were apparently best for their own subjects at one time, but which relapsed into the most abject degradation of mind eventually, tyrannized over most of their circle of power.

They spared no city, if expedient, as they massacred a million at a time to subdue it. Military despotism, infuriated by fanatical peculiar faith, carried everything before it. The result of paganism of the whole world is more or less presented us. Will the world most foolishly continue it, the result of undeveloped and vitiated mind, or enjoy the pure religion of rational mind.

We lose valuable time on bigots.

Reformation with such goes on too slowly.

Nothing short of conservative revolution in all things, will meet the purposes of creation.

The union of kings and priests is as old as the bible.

Melchisedec was king and priest, tyrant enough over his country; exclude all the modern Melchisedecs.

Creation shames man, priestocracy, about their bibles, that is so opposed to civilization. What shall the world think of those who mouth the scriptures as the word of God, without any proof at all, but just the reverse is staring them in the face of the universe. Analysis proves the extreme difficulty of escaping the net of the corrupt priestocracy, who introduce all practicable impediments, and not the first one true. Articles of faith are to be signed in England even by the clergy, before undertaking the functions of that faith. That is the act of perjury.

Preachers transgressing the noblest principles of social organization, by the highest treason to God and man, are cloaked up by their partizans, who see their base criminal designs in lust, avarice and ambition, telling on all the world where they can secure power. How important is this thing of advice, that the world absolutely needs. That of the priestocracy cannot be disinterested. Is that of all others? Consider all written or verbal.

What do we want with a pauperized profession?

All, without exception of the priestocracy, should beg at some honest employment of work. They disgrace themselves, and do no good to mind. The way the priestocracy treats the world, proves that they assume to be world guardians, and have the right to dictate their assumption upon it. As Christ had no commission, the priestocracy has none, and should leave the pulpit. The worst self-delusion is seeking to blind the world by words, when actions belie all the time, and when the counterfeits are so worthless, proffered in place of a priceless jewel, rational religion, that gives all a truthful representation. The world would be governed forever by craftship, if it be verdant enough, as in overgrown cities there are professions that live by all the artifice of fraud, and circumvent every, all that they can. Did I say cities: the world is filled with such? In what department of life, is not this sown broad cast? Even in the pearl fishery of Ceylon, two shark charmers are employed to repel the sharks by their charms and potent spells, and they reap an abundant harvest during the fishery. Such is the infatuation of the superstitious divers, that if they did not pay satisfactorily, that a collusion would take place between the charmers and the sharks. Cannot the tender conscience—world-softs see now, that they can trust to none affecting divine missions? Is the hold of the priestocracy any less with their beguiled, befooled superstitious devotees, who are threatened with the weight of eternal damnation by Christ, if the world did not come into his sectarianism? The means of priestocracy are too abundant, too much is appropriated that way to eradicate such a nuisance at once. They as sharks fish the whole world, and get the pearls of value: nature acts best, knowing her own laws, despite of the pretensions of the priestocracy. Priest, priest, it is priestocracy from the first word to the last of all such bibles. Let not the world be deceived any longer. As priestocracies they are dishonored as augurs and oracle-mongers, but as men, when citizens and patriots, they are worthy associates. Why then will they persist in a cause that dishonors them, and corrupts all? The cause of God advocates itself; but that of the priestocracy demands their sophistry and perjury. But the game of the priestocracy is ignoble, to play with souls. Whilst the world must be completely silent in avoiding all calumny, none should be silent in any matter that ought to be made known for the good of society, the world. Most difficult is it for the people, to overcome antiquated notions of the divinity of the priestocracy. This trick, this perjury, has been kept up for many ages, and the mass has stupidly believed it their bounden duty. If the priestocracy have forfeited all claim to the decent respect to the world, by what tenure can they expect it? Do they still take the people for blockheads? The priestocracy are men of one idea, to make all things, even God and nature conform to their exploded antiquated bible! Their actions as sophists most prejudiced, prove, that all should perish at the tribunal of an abominable heresy their faith, as they call it, ere the bible of tradition should receive its just deserts. Gracious God! That millions should have been sacrificed to infamous books, the most counterfeit perjured currency! Has the world lost its senses? Will it hear reason? Will it obey mind? Or will it be vilely cheated; will it cheat itself of all its creation birthrights, to foster the vilest pretensions of imposition, humbug, and chicanery? Were it not for the priestocracy, the world would be done with peculiar faith. Then be done with them. So the priestocracy gained their point, they did not care for temporal gain. Theirs is the most artful and insidious attempt, to rule the world.

If it were not for the fall of man, where would be the rise of priestocracy? Can the world do the doctrine away? You cannot expect that of the priestocracy, to do themselves away?

But was not the serpent, the devil, proof of all that? Was not the serpent worshipped as a symbol of good demon, by the Egyptians, &c., and even of the evil doctrine? Whom do we expect to convince? Bigots? Can we readily eradicate their peculiar faith, one sided preaching, that the mass of the people only hear? Why do not freemen adopt the noble, free, liberal discussion of rational religion? Why do they not elicit the truth, the whole truth, and nothing but the truth?

Why do the priestocracy hate deists, theists or monotheists so? Because they expose on conservative principles, the peculiar and traditional bibles, all fabricated by lying, false pretences, and that cause the world to lie; pollute society, and degrade morals. Keep not back patriots, citizens good and true; take them out of the hands of the unworthy polluters of the world's morals, and invaders of mind's rights, the real culprits of society. They are only the ancient oracle-mongers, modernized. But how could the priestocracy ever corrupt these bibles, that represent such mighty things? That's the very thing the world priestocracy is for, to get power; don't the bible advocates censure the Chinese, Hindoos, and Egyptians, for corrupting their annals, pretending them to be for many thousands of years beyond what Moses' bible says? And the priestocracy of all such, are bible makers. In their own court, all are convicted. To that complexion it has come at last. To sustain the last, pagan priestocracy declare that the Chinese and Hindoo priestocracy, especially, have awfully lied. All lie and perjure themselves. Will the world never learn wisdom? If they had confined this bible and its effects to ancient times, even their killing of witches might have been passed over, but when it has been the means of butchering millions, excluding religion, all the virtues of rationality, imprisoning, banishing and persecuting philosophers, of crushing the best part of the world that is too virtuous to play the hypocrite then it is time to speak out.

The spirit that the sophists showed Socrates, is now displayed by fanatics, who claim the most ungodly bibles.

Why do the priestocracy keep back so much?

Why do the people let them? Has not this country purchased her liberty with blood and treasure enough to fully appreciate its worth and cost?

Brilliant are the efforts of good men everywhere, indeed, but their position is not appropriate and adequate protection at the best. They may wire-draw their ethics, may eschew hilarity, dancing, all the festivities of the ball-room, and the gayest fashionable society by ascetic rules, still their primary defects of peculiar faith kill all the balance.

The best, sincere, honest part of the priestocracy will be highly pleased to find truth, though it be against their faith.

Instead of hunting up materials for sophistry, as the priestocracy are constantly doing, they ought to own the truth at once. We must write things and facts, as they are. The power of the priestocracy can hardly be appreciated. In Ethiopia they commanded kings, until they were commanded by one.

Has not the pope done that abundantly, in Europe? Has not his prototype, the grand lama, operated on Asia? Is not the clergy master, in some churches, of the laity, even in this free country? What good can they do? Are we to be flattered, or wheedled out of our rights? Where are the intellectual patriots of the land? Will they stand by, and do nothing to help put the world right in morals and religion? Are not these momentous enough? Universal justice can only be done, by universal principles.

What a libel on the Creator of the universe, to dwarf him to peculiar views, character, people.

It is the work of the priestocracy, who foist these false pretences on the world. Is it possible that the priestocracy would wish to see truth crushed, for antiquated, exploded faith? Are you prepared, priestocracy, to justify all your actions? The confession of females, to men? The absolutions obtained by money! All the pollutions of mind, by the evil devices of peculiar faith and its sophistry?

Why are the priestocracy afraid to trust the people with the truth, the whole truth, and nothing but the truth? Are they afraid of the truth? Will a free discussion of the whole position vanquish them?

Will the people open their eyes? Will the world-patriots see to it? Priestocracy, if you should attack, with truth, and demolish, you can allay all opposition. But is your situation exempt from censure?

The world overlooks the usurped advantages of the priestocracy of all kinds, that have imposed their false pretences of divinity on it, assuming what now is taken for granted, and yet cannot be proved.

Will the world overlook all this? Will it let all such monopoly pass? It becomes freemen to institute a better course of things. We shall never be freemen till all this is rectified, and both sides of the question are fairly and honorably discussed. And how can this be done, when only one-sided declamation is palmed on the public? The flag of superstition is brought to bear against what is called natural religion, which we are gravely told goes against revealed faith. Is it possible that the words of the priestocracy are to be received for granted, by the people, as the words of the master?

Natural and revealed faith are assuredly incompatibles. How can the people who mean right unmistakably know all this, when all pains are used to keep them from reading any books that shed light on the subject? The position is a false one, to which the priestocracy have no just title at all. If theirs be the true faith, let this be proved properly, and we pledge ourselves to sustain them; but if false, how can any honest, truthful man ask for its maintenance? Can they?

The priestocracy must not think to hold their position by the tenure of sophistry, gained by false pretences, while principles demand their expulsion.

The courtesy of toleration is only extended them until the people see their fault. No title is valid by the little subservient vassalage of mind to their little circle. Priestocracies have tried to see how far they could exert their dynasties over mind. Did the priestocracy, that acted as if God gave the outward garments and regalia for revealed faith, know of a rational religion that would condemn them all, as the most blasphemous impostors?

Who has not heard of human sacrifices? Then you can tell what the priestocracy were up to. These bible men inveigh against heresies, and they are the worst heretics under rational religion. They talk of morals, and their base has none. One sect reproaches another sect about false positions, and the first has as much heresy as any against truth : all peculiar faiths are heresies to the eternal principles of the universe. The priestocracy must be ruled out, as unworthy, after trial of thousands of years. Why should they be treated with more courtesy than other impostors? They were and are usurpers, and must be laid aside as defunct and exploded. But what object could the seemingly good men have, to impose on the world. The very object all the oracle-mongers of antiquity had.

The change of the name did not change their design, object, nor ambition. How verdant must the world be, not to see all this. All the local affiliated cities made a profitable commerce in all this.

Instead of taking rational religion, the priestocracy have given their pretended revelation, that they impiously call the word of God. The world has been witness to all such stuff for thousands of years, to maintain the dynasty of the priestocracy, who rose in proportion as they rendered mind vassal.

As to the peculiar faith revelation of any doctrine, all is worth nothing, but a curse to the world. What then can its advocates avail?

They have acted as if mind was amenable to them, in all the departments of psychology.

The speculation of the priestocracy has corrupted the world, for their age, thousands of years.

They were once truly despotic, but mind is now conquering them. The time will come when the whole world will be ashamed of priestocracies.

It is my duty, as a monotheist, to point out all these things to the sectarians, that they may at once renounce the errors of their ways. The object of the priestocracy is to prejudice the world by all the worst available sophistry, in favor of their book system, against God's, in any form of rational religion.

The common people of the ancient world were most ignorant, the very people for imposition. But what excuse has the free people of this government for such pretences?

One of the greatest outrages on human rights is the interdiction by the priestocracy, to the people, of reading even the books of rational religion. The opposition of the ministry to the advance of rational mind, is bad enough ; but when they set themselves up against constitutional governments, then their functions are not only subversive of all reason, but right. How many have opposed, as ministers of faith, the laws of the United States? Treasonable as all this, it is nothing to their general blasphemy to monotheism.

They pay no respect to the first principles of creation, the proper position of mind, the God-agent, or justify by it the future amelioration. They should not prostitute their talents any more, to those imperfect man's dispensations, and if they can do no better, at least be silent, to let the world recover her lost rights, and a sound state of mind.

Every step in priestocracy, buries them deeper and deeper in the quagmire of blasphemy.

Why do they all misrepresent monotheism? They can neither confute it, nor say anything effectual against it. Honorable people in such circumstances, would be silent. The world has made an awful false step in all priestocracy faith ; no matter how peculiar, how allied to state, it is all false pretence, the veriest trash to mind. But peculiar faith, the priestocracy affect is sacred, and man should be left in his supposed dignity of faith, however false. Truth is too sacred to be sacrificed to the whims or speculations of a bigoted priestocracy.

The idea of heresy separating the world into fragments of a broken brotherhood, never was thought of, till the priestocracy perverted the world, and destroyed the principles of its universality ; now the severance is universal.

This odious heresy on God's and nature's laws, must be cancelled by religion, that all these heresies never knew. Had religion prevailed, these had never been.

So much for the world trusting to the foolish priestocracies of all peculiar faith, the foolish frauds of messiahships, prophecies and miracles.

Who are the priestocracies now? Some of them with their churches are helping to split their unions, and sever that of the United States. They are actually urging the people to disregard constitutional laws! What nuisances to society.

Religion demands, not only to maintain the integrity of constitutional laws, but the right spirit.

The moral obliquity of the priestocracy. in their libels of God, condemns the whole to infamy! It is the most brutal debauchery of mind.

Priestocracy, ministers—ye that declare those that believe in God, but not in creatures, are infidels, are yourselves libelers. That character ye have written, by your own acts.

I have satisfied my own mind, that no one can get the truth out of the priestocracy of any peculiar faith, when the authenticity of that faith or its bible is at stake, as becomes freemen of mind. When will the clergy learn to think, analyze or speak the truth?

Give us always beyond comparison, rather the schoolmaster, than the priestocracy. Apply their immense millions of revenue to extinguishment of national debts, and to national instructions. What a change in the world, since the priestocracy had such sway—now mind has its progressive inherent influence and rights. The products of agriculture, industrial labor, manufactures, commerce, have advanced beyond the conception of their most exalted prophets, priests, and messiahs. Half of the globe has been brought to light, that none of the ancients seemed to know anything at all of. The days that knew of martial prowess, for conquest, priestocracy influence to form world dynasties, are passed, and such things should be exploded.

What does the world possibly need of them?

The great object of the priestocracy, is to establish the worst prejudice of the people against monotheism, which they and all their allies, under all forms can never touch: to terrify them by fear of a future dreadful, to infidels as they call them, being themselves the worst infidels all the time to truth and the facts.

How infatuated are the priestocracy to assail monotheism, because they have assuredly identified themselves with blasphemy! But no persons can become infidel, by investigating the scriptures, say the priestocracy. No intelligent analyst uncommitted to other interests, can do otherwise.

The priestocracy have failed to establish the authenticity of the scriptures, yet will not see their position.

All that mankind wants, is the bible of the universe, merely books in proper agreement with the wisest appreciation thereof.

The moderns ought to declare their independence of mind, from all the ancient trammels of superstition and error. There is no reason why the world should continue to be imposed upon by the priestocracy.

The world has got hold of their prejudiced, stereotyped misrepresentation about monotheism, for which their blasphemous position, pretending that it is infidelity, is not the true issue at all.

How the priestocracy stick out, all the time. They assume as if they were the only expositors of their bibles, and that none others can do. They forget that mind is universal, or that others have mind, which is to solve all solvable problems. In all this pretence, they betray their incompetency to decide, as all they are, and all they got is by usurpation, assumption, superstition, and speculation. They hold fast to all their old exploded errors. They are pretty people, to talk of faith and infidelity, when they cannot establish the first definition of fidelity.

What an absurdity, that the priestocracy blame and libel the people, for unbelief or infidelity in their scriptures, which they cannot begin to prove.

As to preceding rulers stopping such errors, they were too much identified with imposition themselves, and of course feared innovation.

These are the people whose mind should enable them to do right, but they act with the blackest ingratitude to their creator. The world is certainly entitled to a universal brotherhood, which sectarianism, priestocracy, peculiar faith, secret societies, peculiar education and selfish considerations cut out.

Their scriptures violate natural law, yet they assume them authentic, and ask the people to take for granted, what will deprive them of their only legitimate rights, as far as they can divest them. Can the free and intelligent people of the world be kept in abeyance to superstition, or its vassals, the priestocracy?

How long will it take the world to arrive at the right reason, to preserve the union of the world?

The ministry decides cases of mind, as well as conscience. The Romanist prohibits the reading of the bible, the protestant prohibits the reading of infidel books, or what is equal, he proscribes and interdicts them by a vulgar, exclusive criticism. He decides from the pulpit, in one line of excommunication on all such books, and the church members are afraid to be seen reading them, and yet in that pulpit, is the boast of the light of science thus excluded, by the pulpit-bull. It is bad enough when one individual takes ıld of the world's injury, but when collusion prevails with myriads, what can be worse? ᴇᴛ the world can hardly believe, that people who talk so smoothly in the pulpit, can be ᴀınst it! There is nothing plainer. This order of profession through oracles and ᴏᴛhsayings, down to priests and prophets, is the same. The bigot still has his place, ıd the priestocracy still have all the power the people are verdant enough to yield ᴇın. Who have helped to agitate the country more than political priestocracies, ᴘardizing its union?

What would be the peculiar history of much of the priestocracy? Are they exempt ᴏın many of the vices of the world?

The priestocracy are now running from the infidels, and will beg them to let them ᴀᴇ. They would do this fully, if the people were to do justice to themselves. How ᴇᴄh of the world quibbles or equivocates, on what is actually its own rights! Can the world ever learn the truth from monopolists?

The priestocracy overlook the proof of the authenticity of the scriptures, to get at ᴀᴅelity! It is impossible for them to prove the first, without which they have no ᴇᴛᴏnality, as they damn themselves on this basis to all eternity. They are estopped ıı this.

Is it not a burning shame. that the world should be overwhelmed by false messiahs? ᴄho of the church could believe, that a false messiah is preached? Are not the priest-ᴇracy practicing this fraud on an unsuspecting world? Is it possible that bigots have ᴛ die off in the world, before the truth of pure religion can flourish?

The only way to try the sincerity of all the priestocracy, is take their salary away ᴏm them. They forfeit enough by blasphemy, to outrage God's mercy!

If we wish to appreciate rightly the priestocracy, we must estimate them as the ᴀᴄle-mongers, with all their vices—and their own absurd blasphemies besides.

They who utter a counterfeit, knowing it to be so, are not only guilty culprits, but ᴀlpable criminals.

The world of priestocracy cannot exclude mind from reading the universe of God, ᴏᴡever it may direct the minds devoted to peculiar faith, from works commemorative ᴛ the universe.

How is it possible, for the priestocracy to make intercession for any one, when they ᴀve themselves to make expiation for their blasphemy against God?

What false position that they should have any influence with the capital of crimes. ᴛheir capital is verily of this world, which should know all.

The monopolists assume to dictate. We must not expect the peculiar faith people to ᴀy aside their bigoted notions. How presumptuous the blasphemous priestocracy, to ᴇᴄularize God, and vulgarize the people.

Only keep this age in the dark, let the priestocracy escape. The fraud of the world ᴀ deep, therefore the fewest investigate comprehensively, any but the subject imme-ᴅately concerning them.

Ask the thousands of members of churches about the true exposition of the scrip-ᴀres. and when you come to speak of them analytically, the world, the people, are not ᴀnformed. Have they gone it blind? When the priestocracy have got into the pulpit, ᴀve the freemen of the world, purely in defence of mind, interrogated them in their ᴀghtful authority, their commission?

But the world thinks them good men. Yet can it take for granted, and trust any and ıll things from the world, because it thinks, not knows, it good?

It is most ridiculous, that the priestocracy say that God is too high above man, that ᴛhe last must have an intercessor, and yet they themselves mind-facture the pretence ᴀnd the pretender. the imposition and the impostor.

How weak, I might say, how stupid, is that person who defeats his own constitu-tional rights of religion, by the advocacy of the peculiar faith of the priestocracy.

The whole world has to see for itself, their false position, ere the world is right.

If the world listen to them, it will be always in abeyance to degraded vassalage of mind. The mind stands its own sentinel on the watch-tower of its own liberty.

The position of the priestocracy is one of the basest imposition on the people, the most blasphemous libel of Deity. How many of them can justify themselves before the God of the universe? The world must not leave mind, that sacred deposit, to the mercy of the priestocracy, no more than to mere politicians and military chieftains, or despotic monarchs, who all are after selfish gratifications.

What equitable claim have the priestocracy, to any of the rights and titles of religion by peculiar faith?

But few matters are placed on their merits. as evidently, those of peculiar faith, Judaism, Christianity, are all put on intrigue, excluding all the religion practicable, and introducing speculation and trade.

53

Have you, citizen, investigated by the best unobjectionable sources, all this matter?
Do you know what you are doing, when you speak through interested organs, the ministry alone?

What a hard struggle for the mastery; what bitter conflicts, what antagonism have
the priestocracy shown! If their enterprise had depended on merit, what tremendous
power they had. Had this body of people truth on their side, they would have long
since triumphed, and not now sink by an unprincipled opposition to religion. What,
but that, has done the world's mischief? Peculiar faith was a helper. All the peculiar machinery that could be possibly excited was aroused, to break down all pure religion and its proper system. Their position is not maintainable at all—as it involves
necessarily, antagonism with God, mind, principles, religion.

Are the priestocracy so bigoted that they will forget nothing, and learn nothing? Are
the world's brotherhood and its peace, nothing? Is it hopeless to expect the people to
rectify all the errors of the priestocracy?

The longer we tolerate bigots of unprincipled opposition, the more they injure us.
The priestocracy pretend to oppose infidels as they call them, whilst they are the
authors of all infidelity. If they had an honorable proof of their position, there could
be no infidels.

The world's fund, as God's, should not be compromised by the world's cliques and
intrigues. That capital should be appropriated to the noblest purposes of mind and
principles.

Fanatical bigots, the dupes of despotic sway, will rely on men called ministers and
preachers, not on God-given principles. Do the priestocracy prohibit the investigation
of rational religion through their books?

They are tories, traitors to the noblest rights of all these, and mankind in particular.

From the simple tripod, the priestocracy rose to the most gorgeous costly temples,
among which was that of Solomon; that, divine as was pretended, was hewn out by
heathen workmen, as they were called by the Jews, and profaned by sun-worship, by
the same man that had it built, proving that he himself had no confidence in the Jew
peculiar god.

From oracles that were the simplest pretensions of the priestocracy, the world was
introduced to peculiar faith bible prophecies, all equally false and perjured. Can I call
all such serious looking people, hypocrites? No: by no means. I impeach not the
pure motives of the world, but theirs is necessarily all a false position, as all are proved
to be.

Do you wish to test the priestocracy? The proper test is to stop their pay, then, if
they preach for the love of peculiar faith, that is their business, however gratuitous and
false. When the people come to analyze all this matter, and see how they have been
mistreated by the priestocracy, they will be disposed, after looking into it, to exclude
the whole. How much the world that has false taste, desires " to show its little brief
authority." But the priestocracy will keep off the people from reading, by maligning
all the books on rational religion. They cannot do this always. The people must and
will take hold. It is the plan with all the monopolists, to exclude the people from the
rights of mind. Will they dare proscribe the plan and books of reading, discussing
and thinking originally? They seek to bias the world in all this matter, as if theirs
exclusively.

What comparison can be made in regard to the essential difference between the position of the priestocracy, as to mind seeking its Creator through an unauthorized set, or
looking directly through the majesty of his works, as the only representative, up to him!

Only think of it, that the rights and mind of the whole world should be in abeyance
to priestocracies, is too bad indeed. The world should leave all bigots, for honor, profit,
and pleasure. Of all the degraded castes on earth, that of the priestocracy is the worst.
The pettifoggers are contemptible, the charlatan professors, usurpers, are felons, but
the priestocracy defraud God and man. All the world should avoid the appearance of
evil.

Are the people of the world to continue vassals to the priestocracy, bribed by their
own money? Are God's funds, universal brotherhood, to be sacrificed to man's devices,
secret associations, and church machinery? Can freemen speak but under the censorship of the priestocracy, that have usurped the theological opinions of the world?
Where does the divine right come from? From kingly and priest despotism, usurpation, false pretences. Kings must uphold the priestocracy, who uphold their divine
right. It requires much determination, candor and uprightness, to meet all the world-
questions rightly.

The preachers keep out the light, and the world must work out that problem for
itself, as long as it pays preachers to deceive it.

Now the ancient Pythoness was analogous to all since arisen, who are only modified with the times and the astuteness of intellect, seeking all the profit and power for themselves, and the ignoble governments to which they are united. It is all a base speculation. They have perpetrated the most heinous sins, murders and piracy, to overreach the world, of whose confidence they are unworthy.

Where do the priestocracy stand, but on the most abominable rotten platform? We must look at the inherent nature of things. The priestocracy claim precedence in faith, at the risk of blaspheming God. They deny the only rational view of God, as that cuts them and all their tribe out of their profits, however it cuts mind out of its rights. Where is their religion? They have always given us a caricature of the God of the universe.

Religion defines the highest obligations of mind to mind, mankind, the world, princi-ples, to God, their creator.

The priestocracy will howl against my position; the Pythoness or priestess of Apollo would have done the same thing; but the intellectual world ought to see the whole farce and tragedy.

So identified are the participators in the world's frauds, and benefits thereby accruing, that the myrmidons of power bully the world in its own rights with impunity.

The priestocracy corrupt every part about religion. The ancients mixed up peculiar faith government, which was the vice and error of the times. The world was governed by superstition, restricted by bigotry. What can be worse than the rule of priestocra-cy's bibles and statutes?

The world must know what are all the devices of sophistry, and its ruinous perjury. The day will come when all the perjury of priestocracy and their peculiar faiths will be scouted before the world people, as alien and noxious to the popular interests.

Priestocracy are the idols of church-members. They have of course invoked all the expedients of their heaven and earth to aid in their insane and absurd Jesuitical false pretences. Can the priestocracy look an honest, truthful man in the face, and say that any peculiar bible is less than the grossest, most blasphemous libel of the universe Creator?

Can the priestocracy aid the world? If they declare, as honorably bound to God and man, that the bible is all false pretences, and that it ought to go where all dis-honest and fraudulent means ought to go, to annihilation, and the quicker the better.

Where there are bullying clans, the people in their majesty, and by the majesty of the laws, put them down; but what can they do with the most insidious, that ensnare them in all the toils and perjuries of sophistry, by all the terrors of superstition? What confidence can all the peculiar bible advocates inspire the world with, that has been so outraged, deceived, defrauded, bullied, by this tory to the people, the tyrant and cringer to royalty, the dictator of falsehoods and perjuries? If the people fall out with my writings, they side with the priestocracy, recreant themselves to justice and truth.

Are minds of the moderns blinded to the fact that royal and imperial councils, those of the priestocracy, established peculiar bibles and their creeds, a thing more or less executed in every land, a part of the world's governmental machinery, tory to princi-ples and the deceived people?

They divide and subdivide the world's affections, and wrong mind every step, by the grossest and most vulgar tyrannical outrage.

The vulgar blasphemers and presumptuous priestocracy, who could not analyze and see that the effects of violation of conservative principles produced destructive elements. The first bible of Judaism uncreated God to create a devil, and the last capped the climax of uncreating their heaven to finish the horrid picture. How dare the petty priestocracy to interfere with the great world-rights of mind? Let us have the world right, then they may talk of the future.

Before the majesty of mind, freedom and intelligence, the priestocracies are world-nuisances.

Rational religion recognises what is taught consistently with the elements and prin-ciples of religion and mind, not priestocracy gift.

Where are not the priestocracy, and what privileges have they not usurped? In South America they are the children of the sun. All the Oriental priestocracies have assumed all the power practicable. I write now for the positive majority of the world. But for the ecclesiastical state rule of China, the people might have been made ration-alists. But it is the interest of the emperor to be an irresponsible person above the laws and people, chief priest, and his mandarins a graduated priestocracy, to rule the people and extract their profits.

I address the republican part of the priestocracy of the world, not to stand in the way of God's religion.

Rational mind must have no priestocracy exist on the face of the globe. Let no such monstrosity debase mind, their own and the world's. Support all the wisest teachers of principles, philosophy and science, as far as every circle of society can, and let the state do its duty. Have the most elevated organization of mind enlighteners. Credulity is called faith, the gull-trap of the priestocracy, to catch the world-dupes by.

They have taken undue advantage of the generous feelings of the people, and converted them to persuasions for their peculiar interest and ambition.

The present priestocracy are no better than world-sophists, as they desert, tory like, rational religion.

There never was a nation but that had superstition in their faith ; that is, that nation permitted the vile priestocracy to corrupt mind by their stupid sophistry.

If we have a constitutional government, let us have freemen, all the blessings of mind's rationality and freedom. The priestocracy have told us of their martyrs, but have they told us of the millions they and their bibles have martyrized to peculiar systems ? The priestocracy government has been striving, for thousands of years, for mastery.

What will it profit these ignoble men, to create future difficulties for the world ? Do they not involve themselves in all the category of evils, their posterity at least ? And did the priestocracy aspire to the empire rule of the world ?

The people must not leave to the priestocracy the privilege of deciding, exclusively, whether peculiar faith, or monotheism, is right. They are bound to act for themselves, to investigate fully, to decide rightly, for mind and God. The question is, whether they will decide contrary to the wishes of the interested priestocracy, but according to the absolute right and justice of the case. They should be thoroughly certain which side is certainly right, not as man is the exponent, but as justice, truth and reason. If this question of religion is left to the priestocracy, the people never will get right, for self-interest and pride will determine for the priestocracy.

This is not a question of the heart or feeling, but of rational truth, that submits faith to facts. No rational mind ought to leave it undecided a moment ; act rightly, independently of all malign influence.

Constantine, the perjured, enforced what the priestocracy smuggled.

Charlemagne smuggled the pope, who smuggled the inquisition. So there has been a general smuggling, but dangerous to all. All is smuggled. Do you side with the smugglers of absolutists, when you have the ever-living scriptures, never needing a copy of the eternal creator ?

The priestocracy are the most ignorant, stupid, and recreant to all just principles of rational, honorable mind. While I desire the utmost courtesy, I must abide by the most honorable and just equity.

The world goes to them, who feel bound by ignorance, if not from habit, and the spirit of the clique. to uphold and endorse all that their predecessors had fabricated—for all of their bibles are demoralizing fabrications. They have no conscientiousness, and that makes them fanatics. Rational religion cannot go into the first point of fanaticism. The whole universe is eternally addressing the five senses of all rational creatures, who cannot mistake the conclusive supremacy. The people, however, consult the most ignorant and forsworn in ignorance. The devotees speak, in a circle, all that is fiction.

The ignorant, presumptuous world-priestocracy of peculiar faiths, affect to decide the highest of all questions respecting the mind and religion, of which they, by their own chosen position, convict themselves most incompetent of appreciation, for they have crushed the rights of the first by their faiths ; and are they competent to be considered by the world, analysts? They have disproved that, and have proved fully their disqualifications in every respect thereto.

They have acted shamefully for mind, that is now justly exposing them, and ashamed of their nefarious proceedings. These book-serfs have proved themselves every way incompetent of mind's confidence, intellectually or morally, of course religiously.

Who believes clairvoyance, the pretence of a Swedenborg, or any pretending priestocracy ? Let philosophy, with her facts, speak, and astronomy, with her lights, aid in the just cause of humanity. The people are actually scared, afraid to investigate what is their supreme duty, rational religion, because the priestocracy and their clique, their assumed masters in sophists' chancery, have told them not to investigate the subject, for fear of conversion, and that to rational faith. There is rationality for you, a free people! In vain your ancestors of '76, exposed all they had for you. The noblest ancestors, intellectual and brave, left their posterity, the world, the richest legacy and heraldry on earth, compared with which all others pale in vulgar obscurity.

That of priestcraft and kingcraft is the veriest trash to it.

Priestocracy have a bullying sophistry to uphold Jew faith, or their own peculiarities. What a delusion, to attempt to teach the world religion, and their actions incontestibly and most conclusively prove that they did not know what it was.

The church-people speak for their priestocracy and obsolete bible, acting tory to their God of the universe, for the Jew peculiar god. Will you take the Jew peculiar faith, bible, priestocracy, and god, for all go together, in place of rational religion, the bible of rational mind, and the God of the universe?

Religion does not know faith but what is good, founded on truth, honesty, and reason, as peculiar faith does not know good faith, honesty, truth, or reason, for she violates all these at the start, and all the time. Who are the priestocracy? Bible-perjured sophists, tories to mind and God.

Nicholas, if a man, you are my equal; if only one of the priestocracy, you, as the pope of Rome, papa of the Greek church, Grand Lama of Thibet, emperor of China, and the whole clique are all below me, as you are below every honorable monotheist. Know ye that monotheism exalts rational mind to its highest earthly dignity, and renders it the only true dignitary of the world.

You, emperors, seek to govern your people most wisely; then do it most rationally and religiously.

Kings and priests are world-pettifoggers, and below mind's dignity. How basely, tory-like, treacherously, the world priestocracy act, using all their malign influence on the world, to prevent it seeking rational light and religion, because of their base perjuries of peculiar faith. As they are committed to corruption, they ignobly sophisticate the world.

But all priestocracies are similar or analogous editions; in spirit they cannot vary, how much soever they differ in mere forms.

When a conspiracy of moderate collusion is attempted, the world sees through, and condemns it at once as a degradation; but that of peculiar faith, the worst of all, along with that of absolutism, has nonplused untutored mind, and deranged the equilibrium of its justice.

Moderate felony is punished in the world, while the hugest of all is worshipped. Come, preachers, give up your profits, your fat livings, for your faith has given you up, never having had one existence.

The bullying, cunning priestocracy interdict the subject of religion, as if they had any property in the rights of the people, beyond identity of the people.

Rights supreme, over all such stuff, demand the right view of all this subject. Take away this bible of Jewry and Christianity, that has committed petty and grand larceny on God and mind, all the time. The fraud, commenced by it, has been and is to be continued by the priestocracy. Let the pirates restore to God and mind all that are theirs, and the balance will expose the hideousness of this world pirate.

Let principles be properly avenged in this world nuisance.

Let the world look to its own mind all the time; reform and improve that, by the grace of its Author, and not by the absurd notions of any bible clique.

"He that believeth and is baptized, shall be saved; but he that believeth not, shall be damned." Mark, ch. xvi. 16.

"And if any man shall take away from the words of the book of this prophecy, God shall take away his part out of the book of life," &c. Rev. ch. xxii. 19.

Do they speak by authority of their little peculiar god? What's that worth?

The ukase of the belial priestocracy is equal to their blasphemy and ignorance. Not only no toleration, by their despotism, but no religion, under their bible peculiar faith, is to arise. Are they not worse than their own belials?

In their own laboratory, their smuggled councils, did they concoct this curse for mind and world.

The word of God, cause and effect, that graduates the approach of mind, by the self-same deed, to the Great First Cause of the universe, directs necessarily the attention of rational mind to rationality, and no faith can arise except correspondent thereto. Hence, all the priestocracies of all the peculiar faiths, past, present and future, merit the scorn and contempt of mind, to forsake all these facts for their pretences and devices, man-recorded, and kept up by the wiles and false pretences of the priestocracies, who would be expelled the pulpit at once, if the world, the people, rational mind, were to do justice to the universe, God-recorded, ever-living, God-record of facts.

All testimony of such bibles transmitted, is all through the line of interested priestocracy.

Their pulpit sophistry is always an exparte one-sided statement. The world ought not only to analyze, but demand that both sides should be represented. One side might have done for the times of mental obscuration and despotism, when the tripod was the temple, and woman was the priestess. But not now, when monotheism and religion stand invariably on the unrepresented side, omitted by all the ignominious pilferers of God's majesty and attributes. All the priestocracy deal in faith their counterfeit coins—worth nothing to the world, but to seduce, deceive, and injure. For the abuse of mind, whom have the priestocracy to censure but themselves?

Let the five senses rebuke, the light of the universe upbraid, the holy martyrs of mind, liberty, silence them.

Mind has now to conquer the priestocracy. It has to be done.

All this is a very important matter, as sacrifices of all kinds, otherwise, may be the results. All that protects man is rational mind. Any profession, not meeting principles, is unsafe. It is not the name of the thing, but the thing itself. The priestocracy will speak against the God of the universe, till rational mind puts them down, but the mind of the priestocracy is prostituted to miserable peculiar faith. They must retire, and leave their degradation behind them, assume the God-like condition of rational mind—no more to corrupt and debase mind, by a sneaking cunning, that retires behind all false positions and protections, upholding itself; unlike religion, that courts investigation, to be pure and holy, sacred, and innocent.

There are some people so unprincipled, that they would sacrifice the world to their base self-interest. Who are the priestocracy? They go further; they sacrifice your and their souls for this damnable sin, as far as lies in them. What a monster of iniquity are the belials.

The priestocracy could give up the bible, but not their livings.

The gaping crowd congregation receives all the preacher, the pulpit-man, tells it, as true, however false it certainly is; never investigates the outrageous falsehoods of peculiar faith, conspiring all the time to deceive mankind, but hears the sermon, only another name for a full story of perjured sophistry, and praises the man of his peculiar god, his bible, for giving it the most outrageous, nauseous, blasphemous falsehoods. This is the history of the church, of its faith, its preachers. Is the world to be made up of the vilest, most iniquitous humbugs—in the face of mind, that can become rational enough to build on universe conservative principles, that hold the physical and moral creation together, to the highest benefits of rationality? No man, atheist or polytheist, or whatever he calls himself, can cut loose from principles, that keep the universe one mighty unity, without which the whole would fly asunder. The whole universe, then, must ever regard its conservative principles, physically and morally, intellectually and religiously.

No peculiar bibles or priestocracy can pretend to them, destitute of universal character, claiming to be particularly peculiar, for a peculiar people, and all the offsprings of characteristic quality.

When the pulpit sophists tell the people to avoid reading proper books on both sides of the discussion, they fall short of the truth, the whole truth, and nothing but the truth.

Peculiar faith begets the most stupendous faults on the world.

But will not monotheism have its priestocracy?

If it do, that will not be rational religion. It will be a priestocracy speculation. What a sublime position of the world, declaring rational religion. All that can be said for such, is for the God of the universe.

The priestocracy have endeavored to psychologize mind, subvert principles by their doctrines of superstition, using all manner of pious frauds.

What they affect to be piety and charity, heart and getting religion, ought to be banished to the sun-rising country, that will have a sun-set.

The monster superstition, perverted by the priestocracy, has perverted the noblest feelings of humanity, outraged the most refined sentiments of mind, and butchered man. The very existence of the priestocracy is predicated upon the idea most blasphemous, that the Almighty did not make his creation aright, hence the absurd idea of their creation that had to be tinkered and constantly botched to be anyways tolerable. There are many rectifications, but in the mean time you may be ruined, crushed. Where are all the refined right and feelings of humanity, ere they be rightly established? No other standard but the unity of the Almighty, can give a universal comprehension of conservative principles, rational religion.

It is utterly impossible for peculiar faith to do it.

The bible talks of Christ's kingdom, while rational religionists look upon God as instituting his presidency. Bigots, churchmen may talk about their christianity, &c., but they are utterly incompetent to make the world rational, an indispensable essential to its civilization. Religion only does that.

You may be the friend of the priestocracy, if you be their partizan and vassal; but you must not do what religion decides necessary, call in question their acts. No, they affect to be infallible. That they could establish, if they could establish the stupidity of the people.

Have not the priestocracy always assumed the province of mind, by metaphysics, peculiar doctrines, &c.? In what part of the world does not mind find the peculiar faith-fiction of the priestocracy? All ignorant nations have their fanatic creeds, and, strange to say, all such have, though modified to suit the complexion of the times, been retained by the most enlightened part of the world.

It is time that all such superstition should be expunged. Priestocracy that sacrifice human beings in barbarous ages, and cunningly administer sacraments of bread and wine in more refined ones, or of one pretendedly a human sacrifice—all is intolerable butchery of rational religion. What wise patriots of the world at this day, would affiliate with the priestocracy? To have the mind contented, free, happy, satisfied and protected, nothing short of rational religion can do that, which the priestocracy have not and never can get, as they preach up for their faith, not rational religion.

Priestocracies now govern the world, for priests' frauds. Will the world be so superficial as to be thus gulled? Is it never to learn wisdom with all its science and philosophy? Cunning as priest sophistry. its junction with absolutism for both to support the damnable of all the world's curses, peculiar faith, beats all. When absolutism goes, priestocracy goes. Freemen of America, let us free the human mind, to speed that day; then the world will say, Thanks to America, not only for the blessings of constitutional government, but for rational religion. Why stands the world withering under the priestocracy curse, when it might be triumphant in the glories and happiness of rational religion? Will the brute force of absolutism, and the duplicity of wily sophists, thwart mankind?

The apostles prove polytheism, so does Christ, Moses, so do their bibles. Whatever is legitimate is conservative, nothing less. All that is legal is not so—part may be impolitic and unwise, even blasphemous, as the union of church and state. Mind should get rid of all the priestocracy and all their garbled tales, if nothing more to rid the world of the source of dissatisfaction to the people, the spirit of strife. Emperors, lamas, pope, papa and bishops, stop your fanatic peculiar faiths, though united to state; take hold of the strongest link of more rational mind, the most sublime, on God, rational religion, and be greater than all the Mahomets, Christs, Bhudds.

All blasphemers ought to be corrected, whether called Christs or Mahomets, Smiths or Bhudds, lamas or popes, papas, pontiffs or emperors.

" Touch me not," says Christ. My disciples are more holy than the common people. They can touch me. Well done, priestocracy, support your corps: make caste if you can. Give not too much brief authority to any set of people, nothing but constitutional power.

Leave no room to the bigot, polytheist, or atheist.

If the present priestocracy will be so ignobly blind as not to know they are doing wrong, misleading the world, let the wise people act.

Priestocracy, you ought to know, if you know any thing, that you are deluding the people; elevated in your circle of supposed knowledge, you ought to be the light of blessing, not that of curse.

The spirit of priestocracy is a foul spirit. The world is invoked to get rid of its sins. The greatest are committed by mind-perversions of the priestocracy. The world fire-brands are held in one hand, and the dissension of brothers, the world cut up into sectarians in the other.

Usurpation and monopoly are ever unprincipled enough to resort to all necessary expedients. Priestocracy are one of them. The bigot adheres to his sophistry, and does not seek religion, that knows none of it.

Do we know what unlimited despotism the priestocracy have had from time immemorial? And how much now, have they? How much less is it? They exercised it in all departments practicable. Even authors were consecrated or desecrated as they were affiliated to their clique, being either sacred if theirs, or profane if otherwise. The days were in the same category, though all made by the same Almighty, holy if devoted to the priestocracy, but otherwise, not so respected. The whole of the present race of world priestocracy under all names of the five grand divisions and appurtenant islands, ought to go right to the plough at once. They have no honor, truth, nor honesty about their bibles and peculiar faith, acting tory to all the basest indignities of mind, practiced on mind, rights and souls.

The present of Gyges to the Delphic oracle, proves bribery and corruption upheld by monopoly and usurpation. But they were pagans. Indeed. They were not human, if they were unlike the present race of pagan priestocracy. Would the English Episcopalian faithites quarrel with the pope now, for zeal in spreading religion in England? No.

They would be in one universal brotherhood.

But now sectarians, as all Christians are, they contend for the perquisites of office, and the people sovereigns, who should quit their churches in a body, and never look there on such seats of iniquity and mockery, cut each others' throats for all such most contemptible trash. And this is the case all over the world, where popular mind is not qualified to appreciate this God-abhorred state of public feeling. The priestocracy bribed by their faith's profits, with the most miserable bad taste, seek to seduce the world from rational religion, that God the Creator gave the world, mankind, mind. When you have the example of sophists in the pulpit to children, what is all the revelation worth? Does it all amount to any thing? Does it teach mind the first principles of things? Not at all. It is all priestocracy's fabrications, stories. Why do not the bible bigots avail themselves of all other's experience as far as just? The priestocracy talk as familiarly of God, as if they had talked with him, and were his declared agents, peculiarly representing him. That may be all so as to their peculiar god, not the God of the universe.

Atheists affect to believe in no God, while polytheists are foolishly trying to make God no God, as they deal in a messiah. They go back to the pagan heathen, who are all in their category, believing in a number of gods. Do such men know the nature of evidence?

The world demands by its rights, to be freed from sectarianism of all kinds as most corrupt and ungodly, the sooner the better. Keep rid of the speculators in sacred things, the priestocracy.

What a farce, Nicholas, in your sanctuary, and talking about faith. When emperor, you degrade yourself below the man. You can assume nothing about God, no more than your lowest subject, and have no more commission of pontiff. It is your duty to break, not increase as you do, the spell of superstition. That is a miserable prop to absolutism. The world must know that it is the key to absolutism. Stop all this fatal fanaticism to the world. It devolves on emperors, pontiffs, the world patriots, to correct all. When the bible dramatists started it, they did not know the dangerous states of absolutism and fanaticism, backed by superstition and sophistry, enthusiasm and all the rest. The priestocracy are pensioned felons, who should be put out as professors of the world, mind-perversion, rickety, crazy sophistry. The world will not reach rational religion, till it gets rid of all peculiar faiths and its demagogues.

A new era will burst upon the world over these exploded things, and that will be the rationality of mind. The universe of peculiar bibles and priestocracy will do no good, while the creator of that universe is its God. Let the priestocracy be done with their insane, crazy ravings. The priestocracy do not know what they talk of. Take the highest and only legitimate ground, not of the priestocracy. Why? They as impostors, have no ground. Let them prove all their own, otherwise they must be silent. There is but one true position, that is rational religion.

Instead of the vile priestocracy dosing the world or mind with more sophistry, to affect getting on in your bible, faith and church sophistry, think of what will avail you in rational religion.

Bible inspiration mirrors the distorted sense of the priestocracy, who left a memorial of their power and tyranny, in destroying the republican Korah and friends, to the terror of the future, clearly proving that intellect and firmness did speak out like the emanations of mind, not entirely lost.

The statement about Korah is most remarkable, and proves much against Moses. One of the worst things that the world has to contend against, is monopoly and usurpation, in all their forms; and much of this is attempted in all the circles of life. The base and perverted mind, apparently occupying a conspicuous better position, is using it to all the disadvantages in its circle of its fellows, and availing itself of all manner of means to secure their advantages.

The sophists corrupting the frame-works of society, make sycophants of the world, where they make sectarians. Religion holds in abeyance all such things, as she holds in the same category the priestocracy and absolutists. The councils of bible-makers, were self-constituted, and thus may have answered the nefarious ends designed, but not for constitutional freemen who demand mind's highest rationality and supremacy. Now all free, intelligent minds must be self-convicted tories to mind, mankind and God, to acquiesce in such nefarious designs. The height that the priestocracy can go, is to be self-characterized as deluded fanatics.

Deluded fanaticism is the only epitaph that can be truly written, on all the priestocracy of peculiar faith, and this can be written in bold relief.

When every citizen shall be instructed in all proper elements of a rational education, will the rational world consult any ignorant, conceited priestocracy, a deeply interested source, for their order more than religion, to know who God-is, when it has an incomparably better means than they or their absurd bibles, that represent them, ever had, or can have of knowing?

I am not at all surprised at the slaves of absolute governments going for their bibles, a part of their despotism, but it is astonishing, that free people do so.

The greenest thing the world does, is to entrust to ignorant partisans, the priestocracy, to decide about religion for it, what they have not got themselves, farther than mind's elements, and do not know the analysis of. Their views of science and philosophy prove it. Do you, world sophists, think, that rational mind is going to submit to any priestocracy? I charge you in the name of religion, truth, the God of the universe, priestocracy, to cease your false pretences.

The priestocracy must have the paternity of all peculiar bibles. In what part of the world did not they receive the chief spoils, and act brutal murderers, the sycophants, instead of the opposers of brutal idolatry? Have the Mexicans by changing the faith, exchanged the difficulty? Is it not a hopeless vassalage, degrading to popular mind?

Which was worse, the bloody sacrifice of the people to establish the pagan christian, or the human sacrifice of the Indian pagan? Where was there not union of that order, and the civil rulers? Cæsar Augustus, and others of emperors, assumed the office of chief-priest, and gave to Constantine the idea of promoting his views through the christian faith.

Mankind have to make one great move by conservative revolution, and reach rational religion, as the consummation of rational mind.

The pope at the height of the papal power, assumed authority over kings and potentates—Alexander destroyed Callisthenes with the most cruel tortures, because he refused to worship the sot as a god, the philosopher opposing what the African priests admitted!

Will you sacrifice the supremacy of God, religion and mind, to the priestocracy and idle absurd faith?

The very literature of the world is ruined by the priestocracy, as far as they could corrupt it, by helping vitiate it by bible sophistries. They pretend to tell us, that the Jews could not be fooled by their priestocracy. That very statement is the foulest attempt at fooling the modern world. What did they do with the gold, that Aaron got of the Jews to make a calf? Did they not substitute a cheat on the people then, of the worst fraud? Answer, chemists. Could slave Jews resist their despotic masters, who massacred the refractory for centuries in Jewry, killing the priests of each party as victorious. Here were holy wars, with a vengeance.

Psychology of mind prevails in this department, surely. All nations, in every age, are fooled by superstition. Does not the whole world now pay the priestocracy millions yearly, to humbug it with the most blasphemous lies? And is not the whole brood of humbugs hatching all over the world every few months, in saintly knockings, liquefaction, or flowing of blood?

Will you rely on false bibles and faith, when the very foundation, pretended prophecy, ruined the Jewish nation, and caused their deadly million-slaughter at Jerusalem? What nation, on such premises, was ever saved? Did not the popes seek to ruin or rule the world for centuries, and cheat it for all the time of their existence, as far as in them lay? Such characters will strive to ruin it now, at any time. Be silent, or disgraced. If wrong, be set right; do not be fanatics or bigots, that is foolish and criminal.

Act for religion. The majesty of the law and principles is over the bigotry of peculiar priestocracy.

Where the priestocracy cannot bully the world, they defraud it by sophistry. You, priestocracy, are fast approaching your insignificance, to be the scorn and contempt of the world. You compromise with science, that shows your character in all her departments. You do not not go for principles when you go for faith—then of course you do not go for religion.

How much greater power could that of the priestocracy have been in many countries, as India, Thibet, and Egypt? . In the last, whose province was it, but the priestocracy, to take charge of the hieroglyphics, the:very name indicating their functions, which gave, besides their other mighty privileges, vast advantages? What history was not subject to their control, what fiction not in their power? And Moses, or his god-fathers, priestocracy, drank deep enough of its mind-jugglery, beating, if we believe their bible, the Egyptians at their own tricks.

Is it for these that the fires of Smithfield, the butcheries of Paris, of Mexico, of

Salem, and a thousand such scenes, desecrated for thousands of years, should be aroused? Kings have aspired to unite this profession with theirs, to gull and govern the people to their liking. No profession can be more debauched. The kings of Sparta were high priests of the nation ; the emperors of Rome were. What could withstand such formidable power ?

Peculiar faith has been part of the national government of the world ; and as free as America is, still it is a component of more than is estimated.

The influence of the priestocracy is conspicuous throughout Asia, where despotism of mind has too long prevailed.

In ancient Egypt it extended beyond death, and even burial was in abeyance to their courts.

Who but the high priest could enter the interior retreat of the Jewish temple ? Who could detect any deceit there mind-factured ? Priestocracies and astronomers could translate Queen Bernice's hair to become a constellation. Astronomers since have burnt up stars to gratify bibles and their worshippers. What a world !

What nation that had priestocracy but felt the effects of their domineering spirit ? The old Roman high priest had great authority ; has the modern, the pope, any less ? The functions of priestocracy, pagan, always are analogous. What priestocracy have not used the sword when available ? The world has never analyzed this subject comprehensively.

From the contradiction, by God's immutability, of any sight of God by mortals, it is clear demonstration that it was the priestocracy that spoke, with the bible, their mouthpiece, and that it was their peculiar god that was seen. When mind becomes rational on this subject, and these worthies drop their heart-faith, then they will discern clearly. Freemen-priestocracy, act like wise and honest men, for once in your life, and admit that the whole perjury has been your deception ; that henceforth you will not be so degraded as to mislead yourselves, much less, mankind. The world requires your best actions. Give them to the magnificent sublimity of rational religion, that truly represents Deity.

What is more intolerant than bigotry, what more untruthful than peculiar faith, that renders morbidly irritable the mind, and debauches its fairest powers of ratiocination, that leads mind from the humblest effect to the mightiest Great First Cause. Nicholas, and all ye who assume to make capital of this rickety soul-curse, lay aside all faith as totally inefficient—only made for temporal misgovernment. Are the priestocracy more knaves than fools ? What are the absolutists of the world but the wire-workers ?

It is self-evident that the priestocracy have been corrupted by their bibles, that most be perjured, reeking with the abominations of forgery. Yes, the priestocracy forged their bibles, and altered them to suit cases.

From the very first, all these sophists combined and conspired to defraud the whole world with their swindling bible-effronteries and false pretences, that require all the felonious collusions for ever, as long as they last ; thus the world will never be free from base, low intrigues, until it is exempt from all the conspiring causes.

What a miserable state of morals, despotic usurpation presents. The old regime-mind, is hard to operate on. It only thinks, as others before have thought.

World-bigots are stupid. What rational mind have the bigots of one idea ?

Of course, no part of monotheism will suit the monopolizing priestocracy, who desire their own code of usurpation established, to speculate on the world, bribed and seduced by the mercenary advantages.

When the priestocracy shall be no more—and the sooner the better—the world will be at peace that much, and enjoy that much of the sacred gift of religion. There are no functions of the priestocracy pertinent to mind—not one—as all are impositions. The Christians, as much as any, are impostors, blasphemers, being bitter feudal sectarians. Now, the priestocracy may complain that I have been very severe on them. It is they, not I, that are severe, as they have established their position, and I merely expose it as imposition. It was the vices of the times for them to have adopted them, but it will be the crimes of modern times to maintain all such. All peculiar faith priestocracy, and there can be no other, originating from superstition and sophistry, want of philosophical science, and maintaining their course by false pride and bigotry, not having, of course, rational religion, have resorted to bible codes to lie for them. They war for all such, that, if put down, puts down all their infamous propagators and fabricators. That is the reason that the priestocracy perjure themselves constantly, as well as their affiliated minions, for these false conceptions, these bantlings, fire-torches to the whole world. The priestocracy have proved that they did not know God, religion, or morals. That is too clear for a stultified mind to miss. Their bible is a code for petty larceny.

Priestocracy inspiration is it that misleads, at every step in all departments, by their pollutions.

What can render their books holy? Surely, not because kept by such priests?

Faith bibles embody perjuries, and that you call morals and religion?

There is nothing equal to it, except the antagonism of the vulgar priestocracy against rational religion, which they cannot touch with their polluted lips and hands.

Who wrote the peculiar bible? The priestocracy. What sort of government did the Jews have therefrom? The most contemptible, that of the priestocracy, as they were nearly always at civil war, butchering each others' priestocracy; idolatrous, sacrificing their children as burnt offerings, slaves for centuries, by their own confession, and at last winding up the whole national catastrophe by one great, awful million sacrifice at the seige of Jerusalem, on the altar of their superstition, for one oracle or pretended prophecy; and finally, not worth being the notice of the world, that rejected them even as slaves!

Nicholas, you and brother pontiffs, if your people were possessed of rational education, would be laughed to scorn, if you sought to be the mountebanks of the priestocracy.

Why mislead your people in the most essential of all vital subjects, that of religion, which, as rational, you do not possess. You have your mouths full of peculiar faith, but no religion from that source, but the very reverse.

Why, people, do you assent to the priestocracy, as if you belonged to them, rather than God?

No one should affect a department, to which they are unqualified, as the priestocracy. They argue, like monomaniacs, from wrong premises.

Self-interest and peculiar education have blinded and deranged them. Rational education produces the proper equilibrium of mind.

The world should take peculiar faith power out of the hands of the priestocracy, that the people may enjoy the full benefits of God's religion.

Now the dynasty of the priestocracy has had the world long enough in vile vassalage to their peculiar bibles, faith and pretences, all false, that separate mind from religion.

Let all the priestocracy resign their assumed mercenary commissions, that the deceived sovereign people of the world have ignobly surrendered to. The world has need of all the checks and balances that principles bestow, taking nothing for granted from any source, above all of peculiar faith, the theatre of the greatest frauds, where the priestocracy riot over the rights and mind of the whole sovereign people. Religion is for us, to have a right decision, in order that all the balance be right.

Never submit to the tender mercies of any world seducers or pirates—take the only proper stand or platform of principle, and then all is well.

Submit to no ignorant, degraded, because fraudulent priestocracy, to define the rights of soul or mind for the world's people.

Attack all the strongest holds of peculiar faithites by the proper armor of truth, and they will be demolished. They are now upheld by the false aids of malign influence and power.

The priestocracy peculiar god spoke as they dictated, just like the Romans or any others. Whom does monotheism offend, but the priestocracy and their deluded vassals? Who affect to assail this, the God of the universe position, but these short-sighted, sacrilegious blasphemers? Is there aught of beauty in robbery, when the whole is a general smuggle between monarchies and priestocracies, all mind-despots?

"Egypt is a base kingdom." Yes, and what made it a base kingdom? The priestocracy. Who made India the basest of kingdoms, that was not even known to these wiseacres, the pretended prophets?

What is the universal history of all priestocracies in every age and character, but a universal imposition, on citizens as strangers, taking all in, because brief authority can be used.

Slave vassals of superstition! If ignorant, they are unworthy, as they are, to teach the illustrious truths of principles they never knew rightly.

If knowing, they are hypocrites and impostors to religion, for the counterfeit, their supposed temporary benefit. They have no excuse to palliate their blasphemy and perjury, for they have no documents, to talk of God, but what cause and effect present. Always sophists in their theme, because their peculiar faith, as bible, is utterly false.

Monotheism is their teacher, and bids them all silence forever, in the name of the Great First Cause. In peculiar faiths most of the world is outraged, by the barbarous notions of conceited priestocracies. All are pagan fanatics, and most corrupt at that, by their own or others' bigotry.

What despotism they seek to carry out. What millions of bloody murders have been perpetrated for their usurpation, that wars on all sense of religious justice ? In all such there is no rational religion. You prate, Christian, about charity. in the face of all this, and deny justice. Never use the first, as long as your fanaticism in any peculiar shape bible prevents the last.

Your faith annihilation, alone, will only do justice to mind the oppressed. Why nurture any priestocracy, that are the world's nuisances ?

Priestocracies cannot communicate religion : they are a libel on Deity, its author.

Is it not murderous quackery in ecclesiastical, church, and political unions, to prevent the popularizing of religion : it is the depth of dishonesty to wrest such rights from the world, and it is the foulest perjury for them to assume control over mind's department.

Do the clergy correct their mistakes? It is high time that they set about them. myriad as they are. Instead of preaching to congregations, in future, false peculiar faiths, let them absolve themselves from all such heinous sins. and learn to appreciate the Godly and sublime truths of monotheism. What is the vital conservative principle of religion ? Not peculiar faith positively, but principles fully and fairly carried out: Has not the church been kindling all the time high treason to religion, all the element. of civil war and bloodshed ? The sacred preachers, the divines ! Sacred sophists as well, and truthfully said.

I once thought it almost impossible that perjury could be committed, but when I see its platform laid in the pulpit, rational morals and religion both undermined thereby, I am obliged to know that a radical wrong is laid at the framework of society, and the grossest violations of right are perpetrated.

What an absurdity, to damn to all eternity the whole human race, not for the weakness of two fictitious people, but for the wicked mercenariness of the priestocracy, the authors. Adam and Eve do not reach, by thousands of years, the first world people. What is equal to the corruption of the mercenary clergy, who confess dying people, who are thus to go out of the world with perjured lies in their mouths.

Where is the punishment of these soul-assassins ?

It is in mind, enlightened by the liberal principles of monotheism.

This clan and clique have exercised all the despotism that they could get, in all the forms of tyranny. Their social excommunications and proscriptions now, are mere types of their ferocious intention, their will if empowered. No doubt. ancient human victims that were sacrificed on their bloody altars, were such as suited their malignant and fiendish designs.

Priestocracy ! you say you go for your god and gods. How can you go for the Creator of the universe, when your gods are all peculiar ? You act hypocritically and foolishly, when you substitute one for the other.

No sane mind can go for peculiar gods and a universal God at the same time, else the true and counterfeit are all one and the same.

The one has no priestocracy, whilst the others are represented by them, and only breathe in their atmosphere. If their codes, their books were to be blotted out, their existence goes with the books ! O blind and foolish priestocracy, to worship gods that cannot survive man's mind's perverted mementoes of them. Not so, the God of the universe, which endorses its author, and that measures eternity. The union of the whole is pagan mixture.

That these people should stoop so low to pick up the trash of the earth, when they might reap immortal honors in God-given elements.

But the rationalist is to be told, that part of the world must be held subject to fear, not rationality. What stuff, emanating from the same corrupt source. You, citizen, have to be one or the other, a rational or irrational being. No matter your belief or faith, have you acted to the best of your ability? Have you fostered religious sentiments ? Sir, as a good citizen, you are bound to declare for all that promotes the noblest principles.

You have to act for general good.

Monotheism condemns all priestocracy as crazy, if not knaves, and confirms all rational minds in the highest of all allegiance, supreme obligations to Deity. None can revoke, none can secede—all are proved on the highest principles of demonstration to be bound to the commands of monotheism. Hereafter let no polytheist, no atheist, benefited as both are by principles, affect any doctrine that will tolerate brutal indifference, neglect or violation of the religion of principles. Proving such to be universally right, demonstrates the highest obligations of mind universally.

So far from the priestocracy having religion, in that respect they are greatest, merest sophists and oracle-mongers, all mercenary, though they have religion as mind possesses it, whatever they do not neutralize by their profession. The great mistake with all vulgar minds unenlightened is, to suppose that any one peculiar faith, as Christianity, Judaism, or Mormonism is religion, when they do not contain one particle, but trade on a false capital, having all their merits, if any, from monotheism, that their professors most ungratefully libel. This at once proves the folly, infatuation, and bigotry about free agency of mind, that must attain the highest rationality to be a perfect free agent, as legitimately purposed on principles.

The king can do no wrong, is analogous to their divine rights, as those of the priestocracy, who affect to be oracle-makers evinced in their bibles, that cut up all religious wisdom, as all their peculiar doctrines are at war therewith. All this is of a piece, and results from the self-adopting and making of the sovereign people who should never know either more. If there be the best of reasons for getting rid of the odious despotism of one, there is as much in that of the other.

Of the sexes, women take the lead in peculiar faith, acting as if they could not reason, but as the creatures of impulse, complete fanatics, made so by superstition and its peculiar education. This is a part of the world's despotism, that curtailed their rights. Do fears of childbirth increase all this?

Any one that ought to know better by his intelligence, if a legislator, that passes laws to uphold such priestocracy and faith, is traitor to his God and country, the world, mind and truth, above all religion.

There can be no infidelity where there is no truth, except that the advocates are infidel to the Creator of the universe. I would not have bloodshed to promote revolution, all of which can by the will of sovereign mind be conservative and bloodless, much less to oust the priestocracy, as they are included in the category; I leave all remedy fairly, honorably, and properly carried out.

If they do not prove their bible at proper time, they are entitled to no confidence of honest and truthful minds; they never should say another word about their faith, that is utterly faithless, much less show their face in the pulpit, for assuredly such conduct will be felony, treason to honesty and religion, is perjury, and of most corrupt governments. When the world rightly abolishes them, much of despotism is abolished. If any such were abolished by other than legitimate conservative revolution, great evils would be perpetrated probably, though they have debauched mind all over the world.

Who are the priestocracy that they should be consulted in religion, a matter that they nor the bibles, that represent all their vices, follies and crimes, do not, cannot comprehend? There is no such a thing as religion in all the profession and their books. Away with all such impostors and impositions, that go for smuggling all practicable power, and have no compunction of conscience in its use.

When was it ever the case that the priestocracy did not prove themselves the worst of despots? But they excuse themselves under the cloak and pretences of their bible. This is only the circle of despotism, worse and worse, adding sophistry thereto. One set of smugglers forge a bible, and others carry out the despotism. If burial be of any consequence by priests, we see it nullified, compromising their dignity, in refusing to bury those in their claimed consecrated public cemetery who refused to confess to priests. The priestocracy are felons then, to affect peculiar faith for religion. All the priestocracy writers, as preachers, are of the same character.

Swedenborg affects, as is claimed, to have seen three kinds of lights in the celestial and other regions.

The advocates affect to canvass the various conditions of the eye qualified for such vision, absurdly forgetting that the lie is endorsed only by the fabulist.

Do you blame the spiritual knockers and rappers? Dismiss such spiritual visions as this man's, John's, Paul's, and all such fellows, as all such bibles. When this writer tells us that the material and spiritual worlds are separated from each other, he defines his own perjured position, as all other mortals, the utter impossibility of any ingress by the inmates of either.

To freemen belongs the proper adoption of principles that exclude all the priestocracies in the world, and all their stupid inconsistencies—as the first cannot breathe the same atmosphere, and live honorably at least. Their pretences are the most disreputable, taking advantage of religion, and introducing their fanaticism and superstition. Affecting to rebuke sin, the most sinful of all the human race, invading the framework of society by their base corruption; imposing their sophisms on the world, that is bullied and swindled to adopt them.

Organization of society on right basis will exclude all priestocracies. The sacred functions of mind, society, family, man, require it, as they deserve no countenance. They have ruined every nation that they could place a foothold on.

What conscience have they? That of bigots, measured by their own interests.

The priestocracy have mind-factured the peculiar redeemer, and are caught in their perjury, while the Creator is a self-evident universe-conservator.

I am willing to allow all the patriotism, virtue and religion, found in the whole body of the world-priestocracy; but all that is not their fund, but all of mind's fund, and the capital unacknowledged, of rational religion.

How much has the world expiated for the faults, crimes, of its polluted despots? I take the position that all peculiar faith inventors, propagators, aiders and abettors, are impostors, and are amenable to the interdiction of religion.

For parents to give peculiar faith education to children, is to give them mental poison.

Before religion can be properly appreciated, she must be purely rational.

Too much has been left to the barbarian priestocracy, much less should it be to their men of straw, or vassals. They have disunited their own paternal originators, have separated country and world associations. Monotheism, fortunately, has prevented their ruining mankind entirely.

But what will you do for the consecrated rites of religion in the dying hour? Who can impart them of mortals? Can the priestocracy, that pirate on religion? Of all the world pilferers, pirates and swindlers, they cap all, affecting to dispose of wares on false pretences, not in their invoice, without one particle of truth or honesty.

What can we think of the priestocracy, who depart from the conventional rules of reason and civilization, and fly to peculiar faith, that is peculiar falsehood, to subserve their ends?

Elevated mind must detest that mock sentimentalism that will stickle for such myrmidons and their bibles, and sacrifice the world's minds, best and holiest rights, therefor.

What does it avail to bespeak the sympathy, the justice, the religious sentiments of unprincipled desperadoes? They should be exposed and counteracted. What hucksters are the priestocracies of that which does not belong to them.

If they do not believe in the doctrines they preach, they are hypocrites; if they do. they are absurd and ignorant believers. They disown a God in seeking their pretended savior, and discard a conservation higher than a redeemer. They place him on this earth, thereby neutralizing and annihilating his universal character, that renders it effete, if it squinted at diversity, thinking of their little four-cornered earth.

The priestocracy should leave by all means their pulpit, for they belie God's character. This is a perfect world, and presents man as he is, thus gainsaying all their false positions. They put themselves before religion, debasing, as the dirty tools of despotism, mind.

God does not know any priestocracy at all, as he only knows mind and principles.

Why do the priestocracy conspire against universal principles, when they have nothing to palliate their crimes; for instead of upholding religion, they subvert it, and cheat themselves worst of all the world.

Why will they bear false witness against the God of the universe, and spend their life in constant perjury?

Their change from worse to better involves no inconsistency at all, for mind progresses thus in improvement. If the world could see all the schemes of the priestocracy concocted for the promotion of their vile objects, it would be shocked indeed at their iniquity. What if it could only see that which has been suppressed, what would not be disclosed? By their own guarded disclosures, enough of priestocracy revelation is given to prove their ignoble conspiracy on mind, by unmitigated perjuries.

They usurped all practicable to attain power supreme over monarchies, as is most evident by what the popes of Rome did. Down, priestocracies, caterers of despotism of the world—the worst of counterfeiters of religion itself. The priestocracy are nothing compared with the industrious operative. It is horrible that youth of excellent . character should be decoyed into the ministry to be corrupted.

They are to preach morals and religion on a base of world piracy, peculiar faith bibles. That is, their very beginning is a sacrifice of morals and religion, and a perpetration of professional perjury. Deny it if you dare, with truth, and you are the most impudent assassins of truth. All such were ancient soothsayers, augurs, priests, priestesses and oracle-makers. What difference is there between Jew and Jew christian oracles, and theirs? The most truthful analysis, can show none. They are and were all pagans. Is it because the sophist shows towering churches, that the fact is thus disguised? Where are the most splendid temple of Diana of Ephesus, that of Minerva, of Apollo, of Jupiter Olympus? Now in ruins with their worship, because all was destitute of principles, the religion of principles; and thus all paganism will be.

The world needs religion, not faith, nor despotism, nor its vassals, the priestocracy.

THE DYNASTY OF THE PRIESTOCRACY.

Think you, that modern temples and their faiths, are any the better, than the ancients? The world needs no false creeds, bibles or priestocracies, false teachers. It needs correct legislation, action, elevation of character.

Again, too, the great world, the balance, over and above the faithites, that adopts no creeds, needs morals, religion improved as well as the fathites.

None are exempt in creation as rational minds, from their paramount duty and supreme obligation, that must be taught them rightly, by all the best means of enlightened, rational education. Monotheism alone will do, answer for all the world, no matter their creeds or opinions, that must be rightly disciplined, by the supreme standard for rational mind.

You preachers affect, that you are after religion alone—then adopt monotheism, with all its efficient surveillance over the world and all its parts, and drop all your false positions, now, henceforth and evermore. You act the vilest of the vile—for you profess and act perjury.

The caricature of God, booked in your bibles and acts, was their own mind picture self-drawn, daguerreotyped. Little did those fool bigots, know that.

They will die of themselves as all such, a hard, ignominious death. If you go for religion as you say, do not let your hands be polluted once by mercenary rewards, as that is not religion. Come, let your sincerity and motives at least, be above just suspicion. Only give these worthies power, and the darkest ages of bigotry would now prevail,' as with their predecessors, the tools of priestocracies.

But you affect to be useful adjuncts to society. In what way? By prayers and intercessions. Ah, indeed. The universe is fixed on fixed principles, and you ignoramuses, individuals, pretend to alter the universe? Alter your own position, that is the just petition. But is the appeal to your sense of justice, to be as to all other species of despotism, in vain, till the majesty of mind and reason of the people speak in an unmistakable tone in your ears? Beware! Retire—retire all.

These priestocracies that have assumed to talk about infallibility, and orthodoxy in faith, that were befooling and enslaving mind all the time.

Oh! the world-felons. Can it be said, that here are the hirelings at auction, prostituting mind of all to money, the price for corruption? Is not human nature above price, in religion? Yes, she is, for all this is only peculiar faith herself, a prostitute and mistress of priestocracy, the tool of despots.

There are no officials, much less official dignitaries in religion, that presents no such functions, to emperors or their serfs.

Behold your work, clergy, the disastrous effects of bibles. You adopt, and your adoption reflects backwards as forwards. You polytheists, pretend to rebuke and correct sins of the people, before whom with your bible and its abominations, you are too unworthy to appear this day. You affect the province of correcting sin and sinners, and are seeding broadcast in the frame-work of society, the very vilest of all bullion crimes, the deepest soul-corruptions, mind-treacheries, not only in the world, but universe. You think the people simpletons; they know you to be knaves—as an evidence part of them demand of you, as justice to them, to prove your credentials, or resign all at once to the right source, the sovereign people, who are not to be trifled with, as the vassals that had to take what vassals smuggled on them.

Now you ought to know where you are, for the rational people do, and will teach you ere you do justice to justice and its author.

No more of your world corruptions. The pretence that mind rational cannot meet religion by rationality, is the falsest assumption of mind-pirates, whom the world has to punish. You have, priestocracy, to come to the destruction of all false faith, and doctrines of all peculiar bibles. You wait for the effects of bloody revolutions. Monotheism now gives you the most exalted means of a conservative revolution. Speedily adopt it.

For refined, republican minds, to let barbarian ancients, Jew and Jew christian, pagan soothsayers, augurs and priests, get advantage of them, on the score of religion by their positive peculiar sophistry, is too ridiculous to think of, only increased by modern despotism, in all its menial diplomacy of perverted minds. And to hear all the brazen lies of canting hypocrites, in places called pulpits, desecrating what ought to be consecrated, as too holy for such sacrifices. These felon-priestocracies have sacrificed human as brute victims, mind, and now religion to their self-interests. It is too bad. Fly the heathenish, barbarian sacrilege, ye brutal despoilers of mind.

What will not all such ungodly ambition perpetrate? Country, God, the purest of all purity, nothing is too sacred for its vulgar and suicidal desecration. They commence in fraud, end in imbecility and annihilation. Stop, modern augurs, soothsayers, impostors, all. If you do not know it, you are dupes, the weakest of imbecile minds, unworthy to teach ; if you do know it, as mind must, you are the vilest of the vile, unworthy as hypocrites and deceivers to teach, destitute as ye are of integrity. You cannot object to reason or mind, as rational mind has full cognisance, estops and impeaches all such.

If you see errors, are they not of the exposition, and not intrinsic to the subject of monotheism, that is absolutely right. Rationality corrects, while peculiar faith libels. Men of God, is it ?   Men of the priestocracy, and of their gods.

How dare you, priestocracy, to invade with your base false pretences, the sacred precincts of mind ?   Will you desecrate what is sacred of God ?

Do you advise, priestocracy, for the best ?   Are you not libelers of your God, traitors to mind and the people, blasphemers of religion, advancers of tory despotic plagiarisms ?

If you are not certain that you are right, at least be silent. The priestocracy certainly never have truly analyzed their stupid monomaniacal blasphemous anti-god. The moderns have overlooked their duty, and are self-deluded. Can any license the priestocracy to do wrong ?

Why, then, hold themselves exempt from criticism, and that which commands criticism, faith, and all such ?

You, priestocracy, have usurped the province of mind ; you have fallen below its dignity, as its functions. Rational mind cannot recognise such association of priestocracy, unless they give indubitable evidence of their commission and trust ; otherwise it considers them palmed on the public.

All is harmony with God. Why, then, do you pollute your life with such felon antagonisms ?

There should be no antagonism in the world of mankind. Independent of all these evils, exists monotheism ; and yet these conceited beings institute a repulsive antagonism.

It is man that must drop the horrid, iniquitous, peculiar evils, and select universal good. The whole universe, mankind, mind, are all indeed to rational religion as the mighty code to God, she being the proper exponent, exposition of his mighty attributes, character, functions, and principles.

Tell me of priestocracies, and you tell me of a train-band of bigots, conspiring for pagan absurdities, hostile to all that contend for the rights of monotheism over their pretended rights. Hierarchs you may be for a time, but that will more easily expose you.

Instead of sending missions, instituting premiums of peculiar faith, to distant lands, it would be well not to return their own with usury, but to promote rational religion.

Let all be taught to read, and let them have a newspaper of science. O, that will do the world good !

Are these clerical pettifoggers to treat the world like a brute ?   They ask it to believe them implicitly, on faith in their interested declaration. That is, resign its right of judgment, and surrender at discretion.

No wise or honest man asks or does that. But these reverend fathers are such good people, they are for the good of its souls. The name of the thing does not change the nature, the crime. If they have desecrated religion, it is not less a sacrilege, a theft of the worst character. They make out that their creed, their words on a false, perjured bible, is all right. Have they lost their senses ?   They do not ask you, like a man, to stand up to your mind, but an ignominious surrender to not even faith, for it is credulity.

This you call good men ?   They trafficked in the article so grossly, that even their kith and kindred, better raised or worse honored, could not stand it. They sold the thing they called faith, or what not. That is, the poor people were duped ; instead of getting God Almighty's indulgences, they got these pirates, and thus St. Peter was built up on the double theft, and thus to this day. Romanists and Greekists, all pagans, live on theft of mind, soul, religion. Be sure of the sepulchre, not the place for a dead Christ, but a living cheat, and that you do not bury your soul in their sepulchre of their cheat. Priestocracy names do not alter felony.

You do not entrust your fortune to a stranger, in a large city, generally ; how, then, can you resign yourself to this ?

But the man that tells me of all this, is my neighbor. Your neighbor, and seeks to defraud you of your right action of mind ? Rather, a pirate. What right has he to pretend this cheat on you ?   Priestocracy and despotism, the collusive augur, paganism, are before the world, faith, the counterfeit, autocrats, priestocracies, and dupes. But some are excellent men ; granted. They were less corrupt. Here is Father Matthew, who has administered pledges to millions, in general temperance principles. He is in that a monotheist, and not a Romanist. These are the deeds of a man, who, acting on these principles, is a practical monotheist.

All are such from the very nature of their constitutional organization, and that of the mind. Now let them be thoroughly monotheists, for that makes them thoroughly men. Ministers, though arrayed in all the pomp, most gorgeous splendor, and in cathedrals, still the plough-boy is far better off.

Anything that has the priestocracy's stamp, is rankest counterfeit. They have nothing to do in God's temple. They cannot be known at all, in no way, shape or form. They are only of the people, and beyond that are the veriest impostors—most degraded. The affiliated might object to having aught against the poor priests. I have nothing personal with them, but against their doctrines and professions, that are a nuisance to the world. All must be abolished, that religion be progressive to the highest rationality of mind. But, say the advocates, if I cite the past history of their faith, pregnant as it is with iniquity, that was the abuse of such faith by the professors. And pray, special pleaders, is not your whole present and future faith all abuse or usurpation? Show me one iota that is not, and I will yield the victory yours.

Happy would it have been, had the creator endowed mind with perfection. Happy would it be, sophists, if you knew your province, a subaltern of mind, that was appropriately created for its assigned functions.

You have been rebuked, time and again, for all this imperfect attempt at criticism. Mind had not then been a free agent and responsible, and having the highest satisfaction of seeking its acme on its own merit, or sustaining the condemnation on demerits. What have priestocracies to do with religion? Nothing at all.

Are not the pulpit-men ashamed of themselves, of mind, American institutions, to prefer such a miserable subject to an American public, in their platform? Are they stupidly, wilfully blind? Are more victims to be made?

Monotheism never violates any trust; she is all right, and makes all right, never for the sin of priestocracy would she permit to err, whatever else you do.

Is your soul, mind, slave to them, the doer of all work; you, a freeman, thus to become a vassal to despotism?

Who helped despotism? The priestocracy. Who had despotism to slay rival priests? The priestocracy—religion asks.

When you introduce them, she leaves.

The world suffers to this day, from the awful effects of hierarchies, whose corruption was from the priestocracies.

The pretended prophets would sacrifice whole cities, the world, mind, hecatombs to the priestocracy and obsolete bibles. They gloated on kingdoms, as if the earth was never to have constitutional governments, that they were too barbarian to think of. How could preachers go for plastering the pretended prophecies? really it is too bad to hear. What sort of morals, to make sophistry palatable to supersede religion. The generation of all such things! The whole category is spurious.

Americans need monotheism to perfect their institutions and their loveliest magnanimity; but, as for the pusillanimous priestocracy, they should learn of her, and abjure their half-confessed errors. This is the most powerful perversion of misdirected power of the world.

The priestocracy take care of the faith; mind has at last to realize religion, altogether a different affair from that of faith, the capital of the priestocracy.

Instead of the moderns seeking for pure analysis of truth, they darken it the more, and conspire as the affiliated against it, therefore some of them are trustworthy Belial and Baal worshippers.

The idea of a pure, perfect, adorable Creator, supervising with a perfect representation, will, must elevate mind over all the grovelling, low, gross materialism of earth. He meets all the demands that can be made on his providence, universally or especially. He provided at creation—if he had not, creation would have sunk before the priestocracy had been in being, that is too clear. He did most wisely—and it is for mind to furnish itself with the whole—without God's government, who could be safe?—without principles, what mortal could exist? You cannot approach by your words, they are too unholy to be ushered into his holy presence. There is no such proxy recognised. That would reconcile what is incompatible, irreconcilable.

For mind to entrust itself to your impotent position, would be to revolt from the true possession that it already holds, and give a certainty for an uncertainty. God instituted universal brotherhood; will you avow the principles of its order, and enjoy the universal benefits as those of peace and rationality, civilization?

This will make the conservative body in the world, that go for all that is elevated. It will not see it violated by any bibles, which the little brief authority of parents cannot cause children to adopt, when the very first start violates truth and honesty, the base of religion. It will go for expedient, fair, honorable, just, and legitimate possessions.

But you ought not attack the poor priestocracy. Yes, but where are the world's sufferings? Are they not paramount? All this is transplanted Asiatic invention. Put it all aside, as wise and good world-patriots.

But we cannot expect the avaricious, covetous priestocracy, that have such world church possessions, to relax their hold, however convinced. The credulous world has actually paid them, to fasten all the chains practicable. The Brahmins usurped not only the rights of their people, but even of religion, and their worship was part and parcel of their peculiar faith!

They, the slaves of slaves, made their citizens menials to them, and their most degrading faith. They invoked all the thunders of superstition, and prostrated that power, that, armed with its own rationality, rationalized in all legitimate, that masters the universe, would have made these wretches depart as the most vulgar miscreants. They are now, as all such, usurpers.

What is to be done with all the world-bullies, that the demagogues and sycophants call mighty nations, military chieftains, &c.? They are a part of the world's despotism, and must pay forfeit to retributive justice of principles.

I am well assured satisfactorily in my best belief, that none of the priestocracy should delay an honorable and fair justice, in the face of all expedient facts. Equity will certainly bring all to justice, however you delay it.

You have been thought fair and honorable, and how will your house be in excellency without the facts. You have assumed to be the higher law, pretending to be chief justice to justice, and now you are amenable to the religion of principles, whose full power will consign you all to a conspicuous obloquy.

The whole question is definite. you have to ascertain the best that can be done, and that at once. You are to give more than pretences. The great principles of your being, supervised as they are by the functions and attributes of the Creator, no matter in what schools of ethics, varied by peculiar faith, you may have graduated, require it.

· Can you, priestocracy, seek to take advantage of mind by misrepresentation, that peculiar faith is to govern its principles. You ought to be wiser. Do you seek to master deranged minds? Do not interfere with your neighbor's business, much less with his rights. Peculiar faith has interfered with the principles of mind and the world. It is you that have soft heads, in place of hard hearts. You are to consult your own nature; study and correct all your weak points. Free, intelligent minds, need no proscription in republics.

So your case is easy, if you have a living that is predicated on false morals and faith, derogatory to religion, you heed not the ruin of the soul-fabric. You should not foster the opposing elements of rational mind, that is the only legitimate power.

You may rely on it, you acts are meretricious.

Now you will see what can bring you to due responsibility; you cannot escape the tribunal and verdict of principles. You affect that you preach religion; why then do you not begin and end in truth? What mere miserly gain, with no expansive soul of liberty, are you after? Ask yourself, is your soul destitute of one functional duty that can be higher than this you set out your lifetime to violate, and seek to estrange the world from its God?

You have got to do something; you cannot stand at what you are now at. Shame to your peculiar faith or fiction. The pulpit-sophists, to establish preliminaries, must be strictly adjudged vilifiers, libelers of God. When people become the minions of the priestocracy, they cannot get any lower. Will freemen prevaricate to vassals?

Come, do not rely on your supposed strength, for your little brief authority will be annihilated, and your false position and security will be finally nowhere. Depend on it, that monotheism will irradiate the world, that will contemn you the more.

You may rely on it, that monotheism will destroy all your pulpit sophistry. So long as the mind, the soul, is the exponent of principles, you are doomed. So long as the soul is immortal that made this earth, the worthiest that can be devised in God's purpose, you are to be ruled out of your ways. To exclude mind from religion you exclude immortality, all that is worth considering, and not compatible with God. You cannot organize religion. You affect charity, that which belongs to sectarianism, that is to accord credulity to you. Now, religion goes for a certainty, justice, not charity, that is a contingency.

What interest have you, republican, in absolutism? None. Well, what have you to do with a corrupt priestocracy? . None. Well, what have you to do with their ungodly corrupt bibles? . What! their bible ungodly? Yes. Then, least of all—nothing.

If there were millions of writers and advocates, they are all affiliated tribes, hirelings, expectants or identified some way with this foul blot! You cannot mistake wherever the priestocracy have had a hand, that ministers to this world's despotism, ignorance, superstition, and soul-felony.

Hold, citizens, the whole priestocracy to the proper proof of their bible, on the principles of honorable, truthful, honest evidence, and not let them escape it by any manner of means. It is not a question of sophistry, that they are to get over by any special pleading, but one that pure rational religion demands. Let justice, full and satisfactory to all minds on facts, not faith or credulity, be done. You should do justice to your minds. Hold them all responsible at once and all the time, otherwise amenable for disgraceful pretences.

You have not only silenced, but convicted and annihilated the priestocracy. But they will affect to have their pretences taken for granted, as established, if they can get a generation so verdant to trust them, stultify their own minds by credulity, and injure their own souls by an ignoble acquiescence in their impostures.

God save us from the tender mercies of bigots of any kind. The priestocracy are most unprincipled, having a peculiarity that is always in direct antagonism with principles. Their despotism, which unites church and state, is odiously guilty, and directly responsible to religion and God, for the crimes of such ignoble policy. What is the use in having reason, if bigots, aided by government, tory to the sovereign people, is to defeat it?

Rational developed mind learns of God, that the priestocracy are a worthless, tory tribunal. They do not know where they stand. Their orthodoxy and infallibility, are all peculiar. What an inconsistency: the modern priestocracy join the civilized view of God of the universe, indebted to rational mind for the discovery, to the caricature in exploded bibles, whose writers had a peculiar god or gods. What a pagan incongruity: they mix up with oracle-notions, purloined principles from monotheism, and turn about most ungratefully and abuse it, because the purer religion, the more are they exposed and excluded, corrupting or polluting its holy, sacred sanctuaries. Will the monarch set aside his crown, the bigot his church livings, the citizen the peculiar advantages of social sects? Will self-interest permit them for the apparently abstract truths of monotheism? Peculiar faith is peculiar despotism: there is the solution of the whole charm.

The times are not analogous, and the modern priestocracy are absurd to affect to make the two similar. As to monotheists incurring the petty warfare of the world-priestocracy, what less can be expected from the efforts of a dying sworn-band? They are desperate, and still cannot see omnipotent truth for their world speculations, the immense amount of church property and incomes. They cannot well give up all that, court and state power and influence.

From the very organization of the high imperial pontiff powers in Europe and Asia, and correlative prelacies that are identified with governments, all such despotisms will have to be annihilated together. A very small part of what the author has written, in some sections of the world now would cost him his life very speedily, and it cannot be expected that he will escape the fiery ordeal of social proscription. But he abides in the full strength of his principles of truth, religion, and confidence of his God.

The game of despotism has been that of setting the world together by the ears, and avail itself of the feuds, by turning the arms of part against the balance, to conquer and usurp all. What now is the state of its different parts where despotism prevails: brute force, ecclesiastical and civil tyranny? Wedded to superstition, the people have been cursed by the priestocracy, afraid to act independently, as superstition has such fast hold on their minds. Excommunications of perjury still told.

Shrewd and political speculators in human and the world stock of mind, have seized upon peculiar faith as capital. Is the world prepared by its state of mind, civilization for rational religion as far beyond Christ's as the universe is beyond Palestine, to adopt mere feeling, faith, credulity for reason, when all pretenders claim such nonentities? If we advocate religion, the pretended preachers are up in arms. People, mind, are you asleep? To the rescue.

The world is any thing else than indebted to the priestocracy for a correct knowledge of the true God of the universe, as they are eternally foisting and palming on all their false pretences about their peculiar gods, and war on all independents that dare go for the first.

Sophists might as well claim a sixth sense, as the eye of faith, equivalent to knocking, clairvoyance.

But all would not be estimated as any thing, but for all the world resources thereby secured. All this is to the people's injury, and should be ended by the people's voice. Ere long we may see a state of this illustrious union, that will present the Mormon dynasty of peculiar faith. If we trace effects to their causes, we can easily tell what a doleful state of affairs that will be, where fanaticism and bigotry hold the helm. Is it any better with any other variety of peculiar faith? None. All the difference is in mind, that has its best and practical protection of religion.

The very fact or act of a man's becoming a preacher of peculiar faith, no matter what, is conclusive, irrefutable demonstration of his lying that very moment. How can you then with intelligence, expect truth of preachers—the priestocracy? This is certain—undeniable.

How dare any of the preachers or priestocracy assert that the bible Jew, or peculiar god of the priestocracy, was the God of the universe? They cannot palm this on an intelligent nation of freemen. Such is a libel of the Creator, not a description.

Prophecy is a way of blaspheming God, by means of priestocracy's pretences.

Sovereign people who will discard all despotism, do not know in any form whatever the priestocracy in any of their insidious disguises.

Woman, learn of this, you who ask what for morals and religion can you do? You cannot know at all any such profession, and know the God of the universe.

How is it possible that the priestocracy, who are devoted to their peculiar god, can speak of the God of the universe? They are estopped from that, by their own position. There have been various conflicts of peculiar gods, that is, through their representatives, but when the court party rules, the advantage is generally on its side. Thus, Joe Smith suffered, not because the Christian's gods were the best, but because their representatives were. Those who could so easily perjure themselves about their peculiar gods, could lie always to the people for all the vilest purposes, as Moses and clan, who were destitute of the very confidence that their false pretences, miracles, and prophecies were invoked for.

Our very existence is identified with and promises the highest obligations to the Creator, especially gratitude, and the utmost exertion to become worthy of farther introduction, to appreciate the adjourned problem of immortality, that of God.

Rational mind needs the second volume of its existence, the soul organization, and that is too pure for these self-invited officials to affect.

Mind, is eternal as principles, the actor of principles that cannot surrender its protection to such. It cannot submit the matter of faith to them. Man must properly exercise rational mind's function, reason, not only as to the last but the first, to reject the counterfeit and counterfeiters. Otherwise, he might take superstition for religion, and not only make a fool of himself, but seek, as an impostor, to expose his counterfeits to others. Then self-preservation, the very first moral law, precludes his being a blockhead, that he may not become a knave. If he absurdly take man's bibles, and pretend them for God's, he becomes a world's culprit, and is a world's nuisance, and should be abated, if not removed. How will mind get over all this difficulty?

By avoiding all, never taking any step that will identify itself with such associations, that will infect it certainly. The perverse mind may say, I will take the bible. The felon may adopt his profession, but he and all his family will assuredly find an end somewhere; for principles will positively wind him up in this universe.

They are obliged to do it, to do their duty as representatives of the omniscient. His choice will, he thinks, endorse all for him. But all the universe is not blind, though he chooses not to see or reason. He puts on the optical illusions of faith, and thinks he sees all the universe as they misrepresent it. But who endorses the last endorsers, the bible and faith? That is the main question, and that is bottomless and foundationless.

If you take peculiar faith, you must bully or wheedle, to carry out your plans. As much as you affect to deprecate stumbling-blocks, you are one to the whole world, as the whole affair is a stumbling block.

The advocates of peculiar faith had better never have known it; as it is, they, the world, should know it entirely, not as the pulpit sophists premise out of their book, and their versions, through the eye of faith, the people's folly and credulity, but like honest, truthful, and valiant freemen, who should investigate it, and if they find it worthless, palmed on them, the refuse and bantling of royalty, to kick out faith and faith sophists. Happy is mind, to find out in anticipation.

But the advance is rather backwards. In the enlightened metropolis of London, it is estimated that much the largest majority of its citizens do not attend Sabbath worship, as a habitual thing.

The sects are trying to extinguish sects; Romanism and protestantism are pitted against each other, as the court and dissenting faith.

And what difficulties are bred in countries, by the arrogation of Romanism, especially where she has interfered between the head (Elizabeth) of the English government, and her subjects and the bull of her pope—Pius absolving them from allegiance. Surely it is not that the intelligent people of England cannot see that the bible and hierarchies are all excrescences on the world; but royalty has its benefit, as available capital.

Now free Americans, to suffer themselves to be defrauded with such pets of despotism, is beyond endurance. When all this despotic compound goes down, despotism has its fall. Liberalists of the world act, act rightly, and now. Intelligent freemen, yours is the highest duty, to put down all peculiar faiths—the world's follies and curses. The game of Puseyism and anti-puseyism, popery and anti-popery, is too small a calibre for rationalists and liberalists, who can triumphantly point the world to a holier theme.

Peculiar faith extinction will be the only issue of right.

These priestocracies act as if they were the especial guardians of faith. Is faith peculiar? Not at all; that is impossible, as long as the universe hath mind, reason, and honesty, that are universal. It is the false pretence of the priestocracy. For their pretence faith, religion gives her confidence ascertained—her knowledge adoration of God, instead of worship. She commends an independence of speech, as thought and action on the case. Before her, the autocracy of society proscription must decline to utter annihilation, as all of pagan ways. Nobody is safe without the conservative protection, conjoined with its best prudence.

Is there no base lucre behind the confessional, the baptism, indulgences to sins, dispensations for licenses, the quick exit from purgatory; no rich legacies to the churches at death of the deluded?

The whole object of the preaching is to keep out of view the adequacy of monotheism, as if the priestocracy were perjured to be eternal felons on truth and religion, and traitors to mind and God!

The world must not yield an iota of power to any such pretence over the rightful power of mind and the people. What if the pope had power, when he issued his papal bull against Elizabeth, would he not have enforced it? Is this not enough, when he intervened between the people and their government? Has not this been attempted by others, as far as their little brief authority permitted?

The majesty of mind declares that the reason of God is always right and conservative, and mind must elicit that, as all other treasures, by the inquiry.

That is part of his nature. A masterly comprehension and analysis will exclude faith, that does not belong to God's empire, except founded on truth and religion, that no peculiar bibles can fathom. The people only can maintain their supremacy and sovereignty by rational mind education.

You need not advance your peculiar faith—that is reflected by christianity, Mormonism, Judaism, all paganism, that cannot exist a moment in a true constitutional liberty and society.

All the religion of the Creator pre-eminently forbids such materials for the world and mind slavery. If contempt is due the past, must not execration be that of the present priestocracy? The world has pauperized its mind's capacity by faith, in the inexhaustless field of religious action.

It is needless to oppose the progress of rational religion, that never has been, and never can be, assailed justly. All peculiar faiths have had their day, and are now exploded, if mind says so. Where peculiar faith cannot touch, monotheism rules preeminently. The whole reflects the condition of mind, that must inquire in what other school than that of monotheism can one be a perfect gentleman? Let your sons and daughters graduate in that, the best of all on earth.

You send missionaries to China to paganize her and the world. The highest object of religion is to make a decent world, but you cannot thus do it by faithizing, peculiarizing, paganizing it into decency.

Have no clashing interests. Let all have supreme unity of design, conformable to the best constitutional lights of rationality. If China were to send to America to paganize the people, you would ridicule such. Thus these people can do you so. You must first rationalize and religionize yourselves. Cast no bullion sins to the world, to be thrown back upon you; but all the elements of good. The moment you let go principle, you let open the door to the wildest excesses. If you violate principles, the world goes at random in the ordinary operations of life, as in architecture, agriculture; then how, in the noblest of all the soul and mind, can you act with impunity? You are never safe without principles, as you are then at the mercy of the merciless. Is there anything certain in life, but principles and their results, cause and effect, to consummation, religion, that insures conservation.

Do you appreciate truth and honesty in the whole world? You do. Then how comes it you advocate the Jew and Jew-christian bibles, that is founded on lies all the time?

Can you talk of conscience to the fraternity of despotism?

Did not kings, priests, or martial prowess, doff its qualms?

Did Alexander refuse the title of Jupiter's son—God's son—which he had coveted? Did the priestocracy refuse it? Did vassals disobey? Who stayed such but the wise and virtuous of mind, the philosophic Greek?

All faith ends in fanaticism but for rational mind.

We must take away from the world the means and power of hurting itself or others. Principles will be the thing.

Now the acts of rational religion have been going on in every age of the world's humanity, with its silent and lovely modesty, efficient proportionately to mental rationalism; yet the priestocracy has been, and is, one of the worst of professions.

When in the dark ages of the world all things were not appreciated, unappreciated, peculiar faith of course was among them. It is not to be wondered at, when it has been the most available resource of despotism. Unconstitutional power forever precludes due investigation and correction. Appropriate correction can be made by rational mind.

It takes all the sophistry and corrupt false pretences of the moderns, affiliated and leagued together in the worst collusion, to keep their bibles all from sinking together. They have murdered and sacrificed the world, their Creator, and all principles, to uphold it; but all their felonies will not do. They will all sink together. The world, the universe, must have its appropriate motions, time must have its functions, truth must have its facts, religion have its victory, and God his purposes executed.

The lever of the untrammelled press has overcome all the miracles of the dynasty of priestocracies, peculiar gods and all.

But you oppose my definition of pagan, which means a verdant mind, as green as a raw wild countryman, more or less animal, that looks to his master. Now the most unerring is that of a bigot who is an obstinate pagan, who thinks that his custom, his calf called Moses or Aaron, is the best one of the world's team. He will stick to his old daddy's notions, because his dad's register, an old astrological almanac, pretendedly, is the world's register. But he forgets, if he ever knew, to compare dates and matters now obsolete with the universe motions, that he is dreaming of in his blind visions.

Moses made a calf as well as Aaron—his was the bible. Its bleatings are audible in the bestial halls of despotism, and the social proscriptions of republics. It has grown to be a bull, that luxuriates in the halls of papacy, and has gored much of the world, and has tilted many a time, with one of the family bulls, a bigger calf. Which calf can bleat the loudest?

Who can wonder at the present efforts of the modern priestocracy, whose interests, professions and character, are all involved in the support of an exploded bible, that if known fully to the world would involve them all in irremediable ruin?

The most horrid part of the conspiracy is, that moderns, whose mind should have enabled them to meet this loftiest question of religion, have conspired against the peace and dignity of the world in upholding despotism.

Religion does not urge you, who ignorantly adopted a rotten system and bible, to continue foolishly and flagitiously to urge them, after their exposure and explosion, to the people, the world, but to renounce them as derogatory sins, a part of your duty.

The bright light of monotheism will lead you to the pale of universal brotherhood. In that you cannot conflict with the world, but must have the universe with you; starting right in infancy, you will retire with its noblest culmination in old age and the decline of life. That is your only safety and honor.

You should aid the world in all your generous and just resolves; not set it a barbarian and criminal example.

When the lights of religion are before the world, we have the faith of despotism, that prostitutes mind to paganism instead of monotheism.

Who can church religion? Come, mind, you are not linked with any fraudulent priestocracy; but you are with religion, that excludes them. They have only been sustained by the devices of despotism. In this world the soul is interlinked to the universe only by rational mind, and must bespeak an earnest for a substantial and brighter future. It is rational mind that bestows all this, through the inspiration of rationality, the grace of Deity, the Creator.

But where does all the principal fault lie, about impeached bibles, so corrupt, that no honest dupe can now believe them, but corrupt and unworthy of religious audience? It lies in the priestocracy, that are basely corrupt and false to religion, God and mind. Now as the bible is impeached for perjury, the priestocracy have to overcome that successfully the first thing done in the pulpit, or depart perjured themselves.

They will not do service to truth, when they criminate themselves. When the priestocracy affect that such bibles cause nations to flourish, they do not have mind to analyze the facts of the whole case, and place fictitiously bibles for developments of mind. They are unequal as their bibles to the subject of religion, and should, as they will have to, retire ingloriously from the field of mind, and not of bibles except through mind.

Faith has doctrines, but religion has principles.

The priestocracy have had for the age of superstition, time out of mind, beyond all their written bibles, a pet bantling, a rickety concern that they have all tried to keep alive, feeding it on the people's cream all the time, perjuring themselves about it, making pagan houses for it, but it will not all do, for it will die, and its death will be that of an ignominious felon.

What preachers do we want of faith and credulity, ignorant bibles and their ignorant author's creations, when we have religion, the book of God and all that mind ever needed from creation's dawn? We do not need your foolish counterfeits, when we have the richest originals. To take yours, is the deepest sin and blasphemy against the holy creator; to receive his is all that mind can do, in the highest sublimity of justice.

The world cannot take any mere statements of the priestocracy any longer: they have deceived the world, its age. If they have not now facts and truth, proof of their false bibles, then they should seal their false lips forever, and cancel all ingratitude to God their creator, not god the creation.

The very idea of money in religion, presents ungodly corruption, as well as power of any character. That godly possession is only the pure unadulterated boon of the creator, and cannot, must not be defiled by any unchaste speculations of man, clothed with any brief authority whatever. Religion cannot be churched or decked in any ornaments, as they would be those of peculiar faith, meretricious and most mercenary.

Religion has no destructive proscription, a ruthless desecration of all the sanctity of life and mind, the elements of horrid warfare, but rebukes all for their errors, and receives them repentant as members of the human family, and holy brotherhood of God.

The world can march on in beautiful harmony and order, as well as the universe, if rational mind carries out the divine purposes of the creator—as all others have signally failed, it is high time that all such retire, yield precedence to rational mind the Godlike.

The preachers act badly to affect any priestocracy sense. They have a bible sense, that is obsolete, and are obliged to modernize out of obsolete texts, else they would be obsolete. In the pulpit, they are bible demagogues, out of it, they are monotheists, if rational beings. As such, I do justice to their sacred gift, divine mind, and expect them to stop their ungodly deed of paganism. They need not disclaim this term, for they assume miracles, the very thing that a pagan, an ignorant countryman does, when he sees sights of natural phenomena, that the monotheist illustrates of rational principles, and refers on their consummation, rational religion, to the creator.

But tell the people to stop all this paganism, and the corrupt priestocracy who look at the livings, who regard the dollars, affect the reign of terror of atheism in France, as if monotheism was atheism, proving themselves heathen pagans, in not understanding language and acting hypocritically.

All the noise against deists, arose from the glass-houses of polytheists, who were afraid of the full calibre artillery of monotheism. The truth of rational religion, effectually closes the victory.

When bigotry is perjured, will faith do for all things?

On what truth can any peculiar faith rest?

Despotism, ecclesiastical and monarchical, state and church, luxuriates on this degraded infamy.

You must ask the only power on earth that can answer you: rational mind. The world needs mind, rational, to confide in. Are the priestocracies the modern eyes to Moses' bible?

The world must avail itself of all its legitimate full means of protection; among them are full cognizance of all the various forms of peculiar bible frauds, all being gambling speculations on the people. They must not touch one of them, for life and soul. The whole play of the priestocracy is foul, and the most consummate false pretences.

What will not degraded man do, when he gambles on such speculation, for avarice and ambition?

The world will take advantage of us, if we permit it to usurp such principles, no matter who.

No matter the profession, all are tory to mind, if unprincipled in faith. The most absurd thing in the world, is to admit the lovely priestocracy, to defraud it on a baseless foundation. If the world's history was not full of faith speculations for faith's profits, then a few tender conscience-people might affect that some were too good to

mean more than meets the eye. How many people have offered themselves as demagogues, messiahs, involving the deaths of hundreds of thousands of followers?

Who that breaks through the limits of conscience, by ambition, cares for the bloodiest results in its gratification? Does faith furnish limits? She furnishes the very
funds. Moses or Mahomet, Christ or Smith, furnish no exceptions. All were the
basest impostors, and used all available funds of imposition.

Advice is it that is offered? Are the advisers capable in integrity, or capacity?
They affirm their book to be true in the purview of hideous and apparent perjuries.

If sophists, they can add nothing to its proofs; bigotry confirms sophistry, and renders them more odious.

As affiliated, they render themselves amenable to the bible's position, and cannot exculpate themselves.

Their state union only adds to their despotism. The world cannot feel indebted to
them for all this, much less from their treacherous exclusion of monotheism, or rational
religion, the only means of mind's introduction to its Creator. Now, if wise, they
should know that no substitute will answer for the treasure of nature, and they ought
to retire from a theatre, that their whole affiliation, from the first oracle, and soothsaying to the present insidious paganism, has never been able to honor, grace, or benefit.

They are all unworthy the regard of the world, as falsifying religion, and palming
the basest mercenary substitute on it, a credulous people.

The world has nothing at all to do with the works and bibles of priests. That is all
their polity and designs; but it has all to do with religion, and that it has to find of God,
not man.

Think you that the despots of the world would hold their people in such vassalage,
without this means?

When the priestocracy offer us their false bible and machinery, are they held, as they
should be, responsible? Are they not rewarded for perjury, by the suffering world?

The decision of the priestocracy, affiliated in upholding the pagan bible, proves nothing for the bible, but all against themselves, as unworthy of being sustained in what
is so obnoxious.

The priestocracy have assumed, by excellence, to speak authoritatively about the
Jew and Christian bibles, and making them divine, have most positively endorsed their
own pagan characters, instead of changing the character of these pagan books.

What can we expect better of paganism?

All are pagans, of all ages, countries, and governments, that detract that much from
the adoration of one Supreme Creator.

Are church and state ever so merged in one, in any part of the world, that justice, on
any occasion, cannot be rendered; and any one, unconnected with the church, is unsafe,
either as to life or property? This more plainly proves, on my position, that, but for
mind, that peculiar faith, fanaticism, would ruin even the American Union at once. It
is certainly the most dangerous thing on earth. Let the hacks of the priestocracy
order, and the vassals will obey. I willingly yield clergy-preachers all the personal
virtue you claim, all the religion you prove, not on account of names, but of principles.
You can reach the mastery only by, and through, rational religion; no other. She,
given you in elements by the Creator, was exalted therefrom, by the use of rational
mind alone.

The world-despotism, of which the priestocracy are a considerable part, has to go;
and when the world-patriots get rid of that, the balance will be an easier conquest, to
be consummated in one, the present age, if rational mind will it.

The rational part of mankind knows preachers as pulpit perjurers—whether the last
seem to know it—and that all their sermons are perjuries, and can be nothing else. To
be themselves any other, they can forsake such adultery and infamy, and recur to
loveliest protection of monotheism, that points unerringly to the magnificence of the universe, under the providence of its supreme creator, each orb a volume, man a page.
The preachers will hush all inquiring minds, by sophistry, if they cannot usurp the obsolete custom of masters.

But the world needs principles consummated, not pretenders to dictate. Where social
priestocracy-proscription prevails now, in America, would be the most odious despotism
of force extinction, had the proscriptive party power.

Before you committed yourselves to pulpit-perjury, you should have analyzed the
true position of the world's advancing to her proper career of glory, as a constituent of
the universe. You should know that man and earth are destined for appropriate spheres,
both by the refined action of rational mind.

But the priestocracy act in collusion with despotism, in its worst features. Do pure
republicans know what they are doing, what they are at? That they have the concen-

tration of despotism embodiment, controlled only by the potency of mind, that of course should exclude all such? Monotheism is the only beacon-light of liberty for the family of nations; her lustre cannot be excluded. She is the brilliant dispensation of the light of mind, and the blessing of liberty.

You cannot violate any principles, physical, moral, social, or religious, with impunity. How, then, can you promise yourself anything, in this enterprise of an obsolete bible, in its grossest violation?

Make your intellect subservient to your, and the world's, good.

Whenever you quit principles, that moment ou quit your only protection, appointed in the un erse. If you adopt any one called a messiah, you then desert God most certainly. iv

After all said, sung, preached and done, the world's paganism never taught it religion to this time.

If the Jews, as all the ancients, had too little development of rational mind to have rational religion, as is certainly proved, then all their bibles, as books, and all accruing therefrom, are only reflective of that state of mind that is conclusive against the bibles.

The bible is not the throne, but behind it. It is the power that it confers; the mere book is a mere laughing-stock in the hands of the prelates of despotism, who work the wires and set all the strikers in motion.

The priest profession is one thing, a part of government; religion another. Religion gets its bible direct from God, and yields its kindliest influence to man, whilst all peculiar bibles are of the priestocracy in collusion for smuggling mind's rights.

Many people, is it not the majority, go to hear the display, the mind, than the display of bibles?—all such, is the display of monotheism, that gathers her fruits and laurels from a different text, that of rational mind.

The world has to come to the perfect knowledge, that the whole priestocracy are a perfect excrescence on mind, a nullity, and to be dropped at once and forever. Rational mind has to be used in their stead. They are never more to darken the world with their odious twilight-despotism. None but constitutional liberty is allowed to take hold of this matter, and that is going to put down all despotism in all its disguises.

The people have to come to this positively, to treat all the priestocracy as reckless impostors and perjurers, if they will persist in forcing their peculiar faiths, that are perjuries on the world.

When all priestocracies are corrupt, there is no limit to that corruption, and they have left no means unessayed to reach their goal. Their creator has not been too sacred, their own souls and minds have not been too pure for their enormous and iniquitous pollutions.

They should analyze the mighty difference between the exalted firmness of religion, and the fanaticism of pagan faith. All bigots are fanatics. All are pagans that do not take the universal standard, unity of Deity.

Mind, without proper analysis, does not know to what desperate corruption, monopoly and usurpation will lead the perverted, peculiarly educated mind. Make mind vassal, and it will go any lengths, for its despot dictators.

A most masterly victory is due rational religion, over all the perjured pagan faiths of the world, and she will get it, as God rules out all messiahs and their affiliated priestocracies.

Whenever religion is presented for conversion, as it is called, both sides for an honorable soul decision should be investigated.

God Almighty regulates all things, independent of presumptuous priestocracies all, who abstract the rights of mind and the people. The monarchists have minor despotisms to help sustain them. The world needs the noblest, purest motives, to prove the best and noblest attributes of religion. These men do not represent her.

But why not receive the bible and its advocates? Because the adoration to God causes me to do full justice to monotheism, that precludes any charity to any false faith or its followers, pagan and ungodly. Mind cannot alienate to such, anything that it claims.

But horror of all horrors, terror of all terrors, resulted in the reign of terror, when the abstraction of the bible took place in France.

All the overflow came from the bigotry of all bigotries, the reign of bibleocracy. What transpired in France, might be the result to the whole world.

All such is the reign of perverted mind, whether it shows at first in pagan polytheism, and then in pagan atheism, is as bad. God, the Creator, made man a monotheist to be, and nothing less; but perverted, under moral free agency of mind, has made him what irrational mind will ever make him.

His standard for universal safety is in unity of God, and whenever he forsakes that, he goes to the most dangerous pagan idolatry. The whole world has to renounce paganism, and all its appurtenances of bibles and priestocracy.

There are universal reasons for mind ever being a monotheist, as it cannot go through the universe without that passport.

How is it possible for peculiar faithites to write a code of religion, when all theirs is a peculiar world-polity, expressly for their peculiar selfish objects? It was utterly, totally impossible for Moses, or Christ, or any such, to institute the religion of principles, the only religion—they never could, with their universe to teach them.

The faithites seem incompetent to realize the difference between doctrines and principles, faith and religion, the last of which expands man's soul to the enlarged calibre of the universe.

How suspiciously the bible characters are mixed up! The Devil and Christ, priestocracy and despots. How foolish the blood sacrifice of animals, how brutal that of the human. The reign of terror by atheism in France is it? That is nothing to the bloody reign of terror by polytheism in the world. What gave the horrid power to the priestocracy, but the bloody sceptre of human sacrifices? Who could be safe then, as now, where its peculiar power reigns?

But all that comes from Asia, proves mind vagrant, or in the slavery of odious vassalage. On that continent, half of the billion of the whole world, has ostracised the noblest and proper qualities of rational mind, and erected on its ruins all of pagan idolatry. Mind then to that awful extent, is in a deranged state, that of fanatical paganism. The world is ruined by such false, treacherous twilights. This character Christ affected, that faith could remove mountains, but he was wily enough not to undertake that, and Mahomet is said to have gone to the mountain, when it would not come to him. Would you commute your property to-day for bank paper that was counterfeit and worthless? Much worse do you, when you seek to exchange your Creator-savior for man-impostor.

The paramount rights of mind, the world, the soul to such senselessness. The supreme power prevents all that; he inspires with principles to conviction of rationality. The world and bibles must subserve mind, not the last, the first. Monotheism will rectify.

All peculiar faith and its bibles are made of deception, that the priestocrats advocate, and nothing less in all their degradations, the whole of which religion despises. Can illustrious world freemen, adopt any such? While the priestocracy were affecting the devil and pointing the world to his satanic majesty, they were defrauding the people.

Time makes no difference with principles, the majesty of which will reach such.

The right proper use of mind is to be mainly looked at by the whole world of mind, otherwise it is that much deranged from its true state of rationality. As all peculiar faiths are perjuries, whatever part of them the world adopts, that much it has of perjury.

The only standard for the world is that of principle forever, and it cannot know any thing less by custom, habit, or any unprincipled authority.

So the preachers all are sustaining a miserable perjury without any qualification whatever as proved.

They can only retrace their steps. The world must manage its business itself, on right principles, else it will be, that much as its whole history proves, under destructive elements.

How small must American preachers feel in the pulpit when the audience desires to know if they can ask for more than what is rational or reasonable? Will they give less? That very single question winds up forever all bibles of tradition, and all their supporters. Let them give and require all this to and from the world.

Let this be the boldest of all revolutions, still it is conservative. When we speak of religion, the priestocracy fly to faith from truth.

Then that takes away free agency, and leaves the worst state of want of the unity of adaptation.

The history of mind illustrated in the world proves free agency.

The world cannot be offended at me for exposing the bible as perjuries, when it can at once espouse the truth of religion.

What disgrace to rational mind, that peculiar faith-capital should be the governmental policy to tyrannize over the world of mind this day.

I am actually surprised at rational Americans to act thus.

I know no authority of custom, except through principle.

Think of the folly of making a few dictate to millions, when it takes the whole real nation to govern the mighty weal of mankind.

The state of highest civilization asks : Why does not the world speak truly, and speak in the name of religion, not that of its counterfeit, as Christianity, Mohamedanism, Mormonism, or any other paganism of numbers or of place?

But the priestocracy may become indignant at not receiving their due. That would be popular penalty, as malefactors. They had best at once sink all such in the man, and assume no more, but act as real capitalists on monotheism, which capital the world uses most shamefully, without honorable acknowledgment.

Peculiar faith is always conniving at something low against mind, the world, whereas religion exalts the same. Martial, ecclesiastical, or monarchical despotism, has decided no principle. What farces about public chaplains.

What must the people do after having built so many fine churches? Can they leave them? They are only so much the more pagans.

REVELATIONS.

WHAT are the Revelations of John worth, any more than any other oracle-monger? All this, if part of creation, would have started with it, but, as subsequent, violates the certain laws of creation, the immutability of God.

What might, if true, arouse our most certain satisfaction and gratitude most boundless, should, as untrue, cause the deepest disgust. As to the bible saints, as they were not, they were vilest impostors. But John saw war in the bible's heaven, Satan cast out, when he, John, was anticipated by the old bible, that gave Satan long before John. The priestocracy make the devil. God is too good a being to make such a monster of evil his even superior rival. I could not blaspheme God to countenance any such iniquity, such bible or its priestocracy, to libel God in that wise. That is the most outrageous toryism, fraud on mind. Peculiar revelation of faith presents antagonism to universal rights. There can be no faith of sectarians, yet religion has unity under a common faith. Individuals, masses, nations and worlds, must go on principles. How can there be revealed religion? It is an exercise of rational faculties, then it is innate and evolved by reason. I ask all good persons to unite with me to promote principles, of all that are not wedded to bigotry.

Principles beget an immutable morality, a retributive justice for the sovereign people, whose right is divine by mind.

What is all the falsification of all the world's prophecy, all the faiths that pagan idolatry has ever reared through all ancient to Judaism, all modern to Christianity and Mormonism.

Principles are the lofty ambassadors of God, who furnishes the capital of grace to the whole universe thereby.

No pretended revelation can define sin, which it, violating principles, perpetrates What is sin, then, but their violation?

Who can then select the worst, costliest road, but from misdirection? Who but the priestocracy do that?

No bible dramatists could then have understood what they were about, with their undeveloped mind. If their hero was a God, then was he immortal; if he suffered death, it was voluntary, or not a God; and if the last, it was a suicide, and that is the suicide of their drama. Mind has taken the bible along with it, not the bible the mind. When the ancient polytheists fabricated a new divinity of perjury, they were not to be defeated for want of the perjury of the affiliated.

The whole world was to evoke all the best blessings of conservative revolution, and adopt all the position. The desecration of religion is too manifest in the faiths of paganism offered, when it is universe full, the last none of it at all.

A faith of principles is the only faith that mind, in soul-organization, can face Deity with.

All peculiar faiths, as plagiaries by mind most perverted, on mind of the world, are ungodly.

After all, all the ungodly messiahships and revelations, they have all left to God what these world-impostors could not do of themselves, falsely trading on God's capital.

It becomes the free Americans, the only free people if they will erect the banner of rational mind, to banish all such forever, and establish the whole world-blessings, to become the first as the most civilized of humanity.

Christianity cannot perfect man's religious nature, not having the inherent elements itself. This earth is a preparatory state, for the world of mind to operate in its mine.

It is the perpetual development of rational religion ; what foolish thought of peculiar faith suddenly regenerating the heart, much less of sanctification or completion.

FIDELITY AND INFIDELITY—FREE MORAL AGENCY OF MIND.

THERE is every motive for a consistent performance of the requirements, for a commensurate reward.

To whom are fidelity and infidelity referable, when charged on rational religionists? The only characters presented in religion are God and anti-god.

Rational religionists seek, with the most faithful fidelity, to pay their best adoration and loftiest reverence to God alone.

With the utmost fidelity, they consider all vicegerentships hostile to the purity of conscience, and true allegiance and fidelity to God.

With the best fidelity to God and conscience, they consider all vicegerentships prejudicial to the best morals, laws, and well-being of society, and should be read out of all codes of refined minds, distinguished by reason and reason's God.

The infidelity of the anti-god will hence be silenced by the fidelity of rational religionists.

When reason rules mind, all the universe will be ever faithful to omnipotence.

TO FREE AND MORAL AGENCY OF MIND IS DUE THE PROGRESS OF LIBERTY.

A PART of the world has become rational partially, in the right way. That part has commenced rightly in government: all must do it conclusively, in religious faith and action, that must ever agree therewith, as no principles can ever clash at all.

What a great lesson for statesmen, to have correct views of government, firmly and sincerely supported.

What a commentary is at the same time furnished, of the hazard of mind's perversions in government.

Millions of lives have been destroyed, and freely has their blood flown, to rescue liberty's lost rights—rights of the people. These were true martyrs.

How deeply and gratefully, then, ought all the free and wise nations prize their costly acquired blessings.

No country is otherwise herself, as mind is not that noble gift, enriched at a nation's treasury, when lowering governments interdicted its elevated caste in freedom, and give it in mockery even the pretences of constitutional monarchy or absolutism.

All countries, degraded in government less than constitutional republican representation, are necessarily degraded in morals and religion, are only amended when that highest and purest order of government, rightly constituted, and administered without fear and reproach, seeking after popular capital, gives potency and character to mind, and aid to virtue.

When legislators maintain an honest consistency, without retrograding in all the great steps and progress of virtue, they exalt their sublime acts in true government for the people, and their constitutional enactments displayed in numerous wise proceedings, without binding and bankrupting themselves in the tyranny and oppression of mind, will exclude an uncourteous perfidy to sister states possessed of the same principles of government, while the truth and honesty of constitutional principles can be vindicated by the noblest specimens of humanity.

Such governments are truly and only possessed of the potent elements of social and political happiness, and must diffuse the eclipsing light of such lustre over the whole world, winning mind by reason best.

Freedom will wisely exercise the loftiest view, in leading the way to arrest high crimes by statutory punishment, to prevent the indispensable necessity of summary vengeance and retaliation, that are certainly objectionable, if improperly directed and executed.

Every freeman has a direct and abiding interest in his government, and gives a moral potency and validity to the laws of justice.

When constitutional liberty prevails none are above the laws, that should be wisest and wisely instituted to be sacredly respected.

Everything is for mind on this earth, and mind must elicit her wisest institutions for mind.

If the states of the world will justly punish all, in a constitutional way, citizens or aliens amenable, that come rightly under the cognizance of just legislation, then the odious feature of private vengeance, that disgraces any age of laws, always to be the divine agency identified with the best results of principles, that secure the holiest interposition. This is the spirit of religion, and comprehends all practicable duty.

What are you doing individually to help the world. Stop the world-intriguing and deception. Seek a correct knowledge of the world, and a right action thereon. It is most expedient to ascertain what is the highest action that mind can pay to the author of the universe. That cannot be less than the highest-minded adoration, and the exactest duty to the world. What all these are, mind must seek the highest rationality, the most refined civilization to decide.

WHO ARE ANTI-GOD ?

ALL who assume God's attributes to impose on the world, and speculate on its credulity.

Mortals of this age of the world, must have their senses blunted in deep and wilful ignorance and stupidity, to yield credence to pretensions that interfere with Deity's exclusive attributes.

If they have seen such light, original or reflected, and will not acknowledge that which is God's, and assert what is rightful and reasonable, but are wilfully blind, then this position must be applied, in full force and virtue, to all such that refuse that justice.

Their insincerity and bad example will rise up in just judgment against them.

Above all, at first and last, and all the time, they must adore, in full, their Creator, who has endowed all rational minds with the highest proof of an Almighty, referable to their conscience. They cannot now escape this conviction, if they will.

The hand-writing of God can be read and understood by mind, to which he speaks universally, not in mysteries, but in the plainest, soundest proper sense.

If the soul belonged to priests and theologians, then they could implicitly dictate ; but as mind has the keeping of this position, and is responsible, let it have the decision in its own right.

The best proof of irreligion, is adoption of peculiar bibles, and the outrages on the world growing out of them, thus proving them clearly not of a pure source.

Take away my bible, says the pope ?

Do you seek to strip me of my sceptre, my potent temporal power, to guide the world by infallible despotism ? You cannot take my bible, says the autocrat ! I am the head of my empire, and that enables me to rule my serfs most blindly ; for if you take away superstition, the potent charm is broken ; they will then seek the God of the universe.

If you put away that bible, you put away, then, much of the false governments of the world.

Do you, American, wish to retain such false bibles, bloodhound statutes, to murder up and enslave billions of the human race ? To drain their blood, property, liberty, soul, virtue, reputation, life, everything, the whole world as far as can be commanded ?

If perjury can be consecrated, and the clergy be divine, then the world can submit to all the folly and crime of self-delusion.

The whole scheme of the priestocracy is that of ungodly usurpation and monopoly.

The dark ages of malign peculiar faith are about departing, on the approach of brighter rational light.

In all the departments of life, the rational world is progressing, in all that is proper and essential to mind.

The mighty conservative revolution of rational mind is advancing, pregnant with mighty reform, in science, religion and government, exciting the greatest blessings of mind, by its appropriate reward, the meed of merit. The absorption into sectarian and partisan views is diminishing, alike subversive of true dignity, moral worth, and rational greatness. Never, till rational mind is free as air, to seek abroad in the whole world, in all the expanse of its noble theatre-nature, can it reach its proper elevation. Confine it by the trammels of the world's despotic bibles, invade its highest prerogatives by every prejudice that self-interest, most contracted and bigoted, invents ; attempt its acquiescence by force and numbers, it revolts. The God of nature will never permit it. The delusion will be seen, sooner or later, and unless weakness interrupts the decision, the fact will be then recognised, assuredly in the history of mind, the history, then, of the universe, not of this world, to which petty messiahs are dwarfed, by pusillanimous priestocracy.

APHORISMS.

Excel all in politeness and courtesy, the genuine effusions of mind, cultivated in humanity, civilization, and religion.

We ought to be wiser to-day than on yesterday. Then proxy thought for us, now we think for ourselves.

You may injure yourself worse than others can injure you, mentally or bodily, through imprudence.

Counteract all practicable perfidy, by having the right basis.

Wise legislators must counteract private vices and crimes, by removing the necessity that creates them.

How miserable the ignorant often make themselves out of elements that correct science makes most, and rules subservient to man's good, and mind's supremacy.

The miracles of the stupidly ignorant, are the servants of the wise.

Enlightened mind rejects the trammels of partyism, that deprives principles of their legitimate usefulness.

Always act with best humanity, according to the circumstances of the case.

Be no party to any transaction that involves character, therefore revolve in mind your duty first.

The good society citizen seeks to be a gentleman, nature's nobleman, and always aspires to do benevolent acts.

The proffer of the world has honorable exceptions, to being bought and requited by some worldly kindness.

We must watch the world in its intrigues, and counteract its corruptions.

Trust few implicitly, and only those well known, but be just to all.

Who can defend indefensible points; of them we are to be silent—certainly not risk their identification, without proper reasons and exceptions, clearly seen.

Use intelligence—the light of life—the guide of reason and rational mind—above all, virtue, that triumphs over all difficulties, even of defeat.

It is expedient that principles of knowledge and human nature should be exposed to the world, to its best profit.

We all pay dearly for experience. Anticipate that.

We can trust none too far, not even one's self, as self-interest causes much deception.

How many persons have a direct interest in all they advise.

The noblest position of an honorable freeman is not to permit sophistry. He must feel indignant at the propagation of superstition, from peculiar faith to fortune-telling.

A conscientious man governs his impulses; a wise one looks to the remotest consequences.

A proper rational education, to direct all, is an invaluable treasure of the world.

What other protection have we, than from our minds and reason?

Sympathize, but rarely advise, in misfortunes, unless requested; as you may be accountable for what you could not control.

To ask for true confidence is to merit it. This is prayer.

To be independent of the world, is the way to attract its highest respect and regard.

No class or caste of man can possibly be the guide of the world, while principles are of paramount importance.

There are no mysteries, but to ignorance.

Public sentiment, unless enlightened, is a scourge, through opinion, very often.

A gentle but firm handling of all subjects, may do wonders.

We must make no compromise with principles.

Religious fasting is not on the principles of physiology.

Analyze all things, before action.

Nothing is out of date with honesty but low revenge and meanness.

Examine all things, before purchase or adoption, by mind, as mind and investigation, through wise minds, can.

In all cases, the dishonorable view ever recoils on the originator most deservedly, or may rarely, if ever, profit.

The wise man, of well cultivated intellect, makes every day that of judgment.

Never fish with bait more valuable than the fish to be caught, much less be the fish caught, instead of the one hooked.

The conservative companion is that which causes independent thought, for correct action for one's self and age.

While some affect that others cannot honestly rise in the world, they may never rise by their own cunning and deceit.

The promotion of universal good requires the order of universal brotherhood.

Do not ask of your relations more than of others.

Competence saves us independent of the wants of necessities and the world, while wealth, overgrown, enslaves to its absolutism.

People, for riches, look up above them, not down below them. We trust others; who can trust himself?

The machinery of witches is more material than spiritual, as in all such speculations.

Never fish for lost chances, by equal chances.

When a thing is lost, let it go, and consider it lost, nor make the balance of thy possessions a lottery therefor.

Let not the disease of covetousness destroy thy mind, nor envy cause thy flesh to pine away.

The word *No* must be independently spoken forever, when none ought to ask *Yes* of us.

No saves us, where Yes ruins us. But mistake not, also, the functions of Yes.

The greatest cleverness is keeping clear of all avoidable evil, that benefits none in its final results.

The absent agent and security do not often do justice; why is this, but from abundant want of principle?

Hasten not to accumulate riches, that you may regret to leave behind you.

Act so that others cannot hurt you.

Tell no more of your business than absolutely necessary.

Act right, whether popular or not; keep your temper, and restrain your ambition. Emperors had been in peace and life enjoyment, but for that.

Be just all the time—do not defer always.

Carry no revenge to extreme, but in character vindication, and all on approved conservative principles.

Friendship cannot be bought, but may be dearly dealt for, and its appearance rarely retained.

If friendship be bought, it is too dear at any price of money.

A man should not ruin himself, much less his family, by going security, that must be adhered to, invariably, in good faith. *No* is the word, firmly, properly, and speedily spoken.

A liberal and just age requires liberal ideas and policy; an advance on those exploded, however once deemed supreme.

There is but little gratitude after one's best is done, and one's money is gone or obtained.

What imposition is there, in the world's machinery!

Is much of the experience of most, any other than imagination, self-delusion at that?

Where is the honesty, in slanders and libels?

What honor is there in them?

Be just to all, benevolent when necessary, and contentious with none; yet do your duty, and justice to your duty.

Maintain your rights; understand, comprehend them, in their first, their remotest bearing.

It becomes every man to comprehend his best position, commensurately with his talents.

An independence commands the world and riches, and is enslaved by neither. The loftiest and most satisfactory action is the independent one.

The car of covetousness drives recklessly over that of humanity.

Be silent where you cannot praise, that you may be just.

All promises and exactions of promises must be compatible with justice, equity, and truth.

He that respects not the truth cannot merit the respect of the world, that constitutes society.

Falsehood's gains are short-lived, but the disgrace is permanent, as the remorse may be lasting.

Never violate promises, that should not be made till you take all previously into consideration.

Make no extraordinary promises, but perform all punctually.

Return all borrowed, promptly.

Avoid pledging, when it may be forfeited.

Can hierarchies maintain the principles of society, when their very existence or creation contravenes all such? If regular sympathies are to be maintained, antipathies must not be established.

THE SECOND PART,

OR,

THE PRACTICAL SCIENCE FOR MIND.

CIVILIZATION.

THE culture and civilization of mind declare the highest state of mind's activity for the world's appropriate amelioration and employment, over which pre-eminently presides monotheism, or the religion of principles. It is she that declares for the diversity of the human races in regard to their mortal embodiments, while she recognises the illustrious unity of mind, that distinguishes man and itself by immortality.

Physiology cannot prove the unity of the human races under the diversities presented, that are prima facie evidence against it.

All that we appreciate races by is mind, that, however different, is more or less assimilated.

There is a marked diversity in both man and mind, that yet present unity of species only. It is assumed that all races present universal depravity, but all this is an unfair analysis.

Peculiar faith stretches mind's rationality to secure its peculiarity, to fortify the peculiar pretensions of the affiliated, whose platform is raised on man's unity. If the unity of race fall, then the priestocracy's commission and occupation are gone.

All minds are relatively moral, &c., as they are rational, and availed themselves of rational religion. The universality of conscience is relative to mind thus circumstanced, for where mind is there is conscience, graduated from the lowest perverted to the highest rational scale.

The diversity of races demonstrates the illustrious and diverse powers of the Creator.

It is the analysis of mind to be looked at, in regard to its nature and character, that ever refer to the unity of design, that has the richest diversity of means.

It has been claimed by elaborate peculiar faith, that the ten commandments are appreciated by races never having heard of them before.

All that can distinguish any ten commandments is, that they embrace social, moral, and religious laws, as far as peculiar faith permits them.

Now that is the unity of mind, that pre-eminently recognises conservative principles that are pre-eminently universal, bespeaking the highest praise of a perfect God, and referring to the soul-organization, that monotheism demonstrates in her purity.

All the human races, however diversified the body, have unity of mind-organization, and that proves it an element, the recipient of the immortality of the soul, and the universal powers, faculties, functions, and principles of God.

The universality of religious sentiment proves the universality of religion and principles, and that such were never, and never would be, peculiar; certainly not, the unity of the races, an immaterial question. The capacity for improvement is a quality of mind, that we are not to mistake for embodiment.

Rational mind improves only by civilization and religion that is rational. All is by brotherhood of religion.

Religion can only impart its dignity and power, most rational, to the whole human races—the world-universe.

All must be by and through the refined supremacy of mind in this world.

Look at the immense variety of animals, birds, reptiles, fishes, insects, and productions of the world.

Could we see the endless diversity of the universe, mind would be mute at its richness.

The world for centuries of centuries has been squabbling for peculiar faiths, that is, peculiar power, and has lost sight of religion. God has been overlooked for man. bible-images and idols, that are worshipped to secure man's degraded despotism, instead of the bible of mind's system, for the soul's immortal beneficence, happiness, and glory.

Of what use is man if precluded from his society, unprotected from its wiles? Society must present all the blessings of rational civilization. How is that to be attained? The framework of society is so corrupt, that falsehood is mixed too much in peculiar views, that are palmed upon it by the corrupt and vicious, affiliated, as sacred. All peculiar societies break up the good of general society, but are fortunately counteracted frequently by the best efforts of mind.

The sublime history of civilization is one of the greatest moment to earth.

The world is hastening into monotheism. How do I know? It is getting civilized.

Let us make all of the best accomplishments on this earth first, by all the available means of monotheism, then we look for final consummations of the holy centre.

Civilization is looming brighter and brighter, in the world's and mind's horizon. The darkest hour has past, and she is now echoing the bright effulgence of a world's glory.

The best institution of civilization, will be the only course of philanthropy and humanity, and lessen, annihilate the retroactive, retributive justice to prevent criminal cases.

The object is to civilize, religionize the world, not christianize or paganize it. All that is absurd—the world does not need peculiarity, but universality of consecrated principles.

The fourth or last best age of man, can only prove its exalted civilization, by extinction through conservative revolution, of all peculiar faiths of the whole world : all despotisms. Rational mind, bespeaks the religion that flourishes in all constitutional governments, that of pure civilization, that which emanates from the court of God.

Mind has to study the legitimate of the world, and come to that standard.

The present frame-work of the world's society, presents the anomaly of all four states of mind's condition.

It is the noble elevation of mind's development, that the religious have to duly respect.

Religion legitimatizes all life's funds, and promotes the best enjoyment. by adding all the loveliest protection of conservative principles, whilst she does not contract in any.

The very quintessence of civilization requires the highest duty of improvement, the best on that received from ancestors, thereby blessing my right to liberty and their fame. I cannot do higher honor to them ; I dishonor them by continuance in the murky fogs of past incapacitated undeveloped mind.

Peculiar actions always pronounce them pagan, and devoid of exalted civilization.

The world is bound to act up to the proper lights before it, and discard all prejudicial thereto.

The real condition of the world, presents at every epoch, more or less the conflict of undeveloped with developed mind. On this most important point, the whole world must take due cognizance.

The world cannot lose its constitutional rights, by any arrogant custom.

MONEY POWER—BANKING—BANK MANIA—SPECULATION—BANK-RUPTCY—LAW SUITS—DEBTS PUBLIC AND PRIVATE.

Money must be the proper measure of labor, otherwise as in some banks it may be the measure of monopoly and usurpation.

Money power or its equivalent is a necessary constituent of society, as a proper basis and medium of exchange.

Then it is for public utility.

As the measure of property or rewards of labor, analysis shows, that when it aids in truly developing the proper resources of nations, and secures for suitable and extensive prosperity, the blessings of commerce, the advance of manufactures, the industrial pursuits of agriculture, mining, navigation, mechanics and the fisheries, the general enterprises of mankind throughout the globe, that it aids in the potency of civilization.

The real wealth of the world is diffused, by the various operations of man's industry.

This power, the genuine representative and conductor of a world's capital and labor, is one of the potent elements of man's benefit, as nations that are enriched enjoy its exchanges, but may be impoverished by misdirection in its financial regulations.

If permitted a tyrant in society to arouse all the intensest actions, that avarice and passions subversive of virtues can create, instead of the enlarged capacity of its elements, its abuses are to be met by the best morals of society, and its doings must be obviated by the wisest and most comprehensive legislation of statesmen, that embrace in their sphere the interest of the whole world.

The money power is like all great and commanding characters, difficult of reduction to ordinary restriction.

When kept openly before the world, in the universal medium or currency of standard uniform or nearest to that state, its operations are legitimate, not fluctuating or affecting, because the purposes for which it wisely answers are not deranged, nor is general injury the result.

In process of time, in the advance of civilization, the refinements of commerce and the elevation of industry, the best and most extensive facilities of this universal power are solicited.

BANKING.

In the various forms of deposites, exchange and banking, this mighty element has its forces concentrated, and then arose the greater necessity of guardianship for the public good.

The conservative revolutions of society must progress in all the departments, to which the agency of mind is invited by the organic elements of the universe, as an imprescriptible decree of supreme wisdom in its sublime economy, and with their capacity of greater good if rightly advanced and sustained, they have also the inherent element of greater evils, if perverted.

Mind properly rules in the perfection of science.

The injury of banks, like the mighty avalanche, may be precipitated upon the people.

It takes thousands of years schooling in the world's philosophy, ere the people can solve the mighty problem of their own inestimable divine rights.

BANKS

Ought to be predicated on the basis of responsibility of stockholders in personal and real estate for all liabilities of the bank, and a fund reserved in the hands of the comptroller of the government for bank security.

With all the foresight of wisdom that experience has so abundantly proved necessary, banks should ever be the faithful representative on correct principles, to fulfil the important needs, and secure the commercial and financial facilities of the world. The primary and constant paramount security to the note holders, the people of the state, the community at large, and the world in general, in equalizing and not creating fluctuations of the value of property, and exclusion of the state or government from any connection for ever in any way, guise or manner, as an unholy and iniquitous alliance, should be inflexibly pursued in all time to come. Any system of banking that does not save the bill holder harmless, property from fluctuation, and the state—the people from any suffering on its account, is never to be tolerated a moment by honest and free minds.

The violation of this position has spread injury wide over countries at various times, and created a complete mania, that involved myriads in ruin and loss of property, and even of some lives. In the present situation of the commercial world, banks are necessary. Their pernicious effects should be guarded against by all good statesmen. Any country that refuses to bank, but yet uses the paper money of others or foreign states, pays a premium proportionate to the amount and use of that money. It is using a circulation over which it has not the proper control, and is liable to all the contingencies of such currency, without proper redress. A proper currency for the medium of exchange must be adopted, easily transportable for commerce throughout the world.

We should disarm money-power of its malign potency. The condition of the commercial world is such, that bank notes will circulate throughout the civilized world, and each country had best secure all the advantages of sound banks, controlled by satisfactory enactments, and all the bonus arising from such transactions. Secure, universally, the bill-holder, and give liberal charters to capitalists.

THE BEST BANKING SYSTEM

CAN only be instituted upon the true principles of securing the community all the advantages that liberal and enlarged competition produces.

The commercial capital must be adequate for the great law of supply and demand, to command all the sufficiency and advantages of markets, whether in amount or in time.

The ratio must be critically exact between the specie basis and the notes in circulation, and this must be in constant abeyance to recognised certainty of redemption.

According to the best views of free principles, the community may be supplied with all the necessary capital; yet no system can be satisfactory that does not meet the wants of trade, and the mighty interests and security of all bankers and people.

The banker must be fully responsible for his bank liabilities, equally as with his own, and of course he should be equally responsible for fraud and false pretences in such institution, as if committed in any other way, and as amenable to indictment and condign penalty.

The essential protection is in the responsibility, by good faith ownership, of property, limited only by proper resources, and commensurate with appropriate profits.

If we do not have a faithful conduct continued in all such institutions, we had better have none at all.

Bankers should have their own capital truly represented, as banks cannot create capital; if they do, then the people suffer, beyond dispute, proportionately : the banking is a miserable humbug, a nuisance, and the legislation most culpable, that permits any such, always to the injury of the bill and the property holders, and conclusively of the State, whose citizens she is bound to protect from demoralization and imposition.

The science of banking must be backed by the principles of honesty. Public opinion should always be conservative of its evils, to the perfect security of fundamental principles all the time, deep as the roots of these evils may go. The day has arrived, it is now the time of the hour, that mind can counteract rightfully all such unhallowed attempts to get the public's money.

All the most salutary restrictions should be placed on all corporate moneyed institutions that ask for privileges for public confidence, which should never be misplaced, as all false steps are ruinous in the extreme from perversions of great powers.

It is well to restrict inordinate speculations, that become a mania of the wildest character, sweeping over the land, unsettling the value of property, and the morals of the body politic.

When fictitious substitutes supersede the real, the State wakes up from her apathy and bad legislation, drained of her capital, improvidently banked upon by many millions, and her citizens by thousands, "leave their country for their country's good," and see climes more congenial to their nature, in scenes fit for their purloined peculations.

Such means of corruption in banks, to the depth of several millions withdrawn by favoritism, present hardly a redeeming quality of any worthy public improvements of much national value, leaving the State possessed of the deserted homesteads of departed debtors, who forget to settle their bank accounts.

No legislation can put the people out of debt, or render a State a successful banker under intriguing directors. The best directors of capital are those that know the difficulty of its honest acquisition.

The redeeming quality will be in an honest state, that scorns repudiation as the worst corruption to her citizens, whose patriotic honesty prompts the payment of their proportion at once, to extricate the State from her liabilities of millions, incurred by most ignorant and wretched mal-legislation, hoping that no more State banks should ever be known in her limits, if the State be ever so miserably mistreated by her agents.

No State should be involved in a State bank debt of many millions, with nothing to show but ill-requited faith from bank directors, who had seduced some of the legislators by bribes or douceurs, &c.

The individual owners of property can best appreciate it, and as its rightful managers should always be in the majority in all bank regulations.

One of the great staples of the world's commerce is cotton, but a dangerous article for speculation to those seeking its monopoly. This kind of operation is dangerous in most all gigantic speculations, and very rightly from the nature of things, as those in meat and bread-stuffs have recoiled with fearful retribution.

Among other malign influences presented in the winding up, are lawsuits consequent on bankruptcy, arising from wild speculations.

All laws and principles have, by nature, penalties.

The best policy is to check all unwise gigantic speculations, that will finally surely ruin the people at large.

The possession of property, causing the proprietor to be encumbered with debt, produces any other than a pleasant situation. The world should beware of banks as well as lawsuits ; it may be glad to get rid of both.

Swapping debts and compounding interest, do not rid you of debts. Concentrate, not diffuse, your powers.

One of the benefits of wise legislation is to render the circulation of money by banks, equal to the demands of commerce, but not subversive of it.

No legislation should cherish monopolies or factionists.

There must be securities, satisfactory and adequate, for all banks, to make the stockholders responsible, the bill-holders safe, else the people are at their mercy. How many have been reduced to misery and poverty by the bad faith of bankers ?

Terrible is the reaction for morals and principles, that are violated in bank institutions.

Special privileges of banking create obligations for a fixed rate per cent. But individual property-holders, who do not seek corporate powers or special privileges of banks, should be constitutionally exempt from any especial trammels.

Wise legislation can go no farther than see that all branches of business should have the protection from inherent merits, and no more than the wisest organic policy can devise for national benefit.

The safest investment is best guaranteed through self-interest, that sharpens the quickest insight into matters.

The proper bonus is the safest and soundest policy of government, through correct legislation.

I am conscientiously opposed to any union of state, with any but legitimate powers, and those only on equitable satisfaction.

The great principle of supply and demand regulates the world under the supreme law of supreme intelligence, better than all the wisest legislation.

Here then the benefit of mind, that is, proper management of circumstances, displays the best management of the world, decidedly in the best method.

What malign influences money power wields, if perverted. What corruption to mould political and financial sentiments of the people, to bribe them with their own capital, to keep the state of any particular political complexion, and give unworthy members of society accommodations for thousands! When all public faith is violated in entrusting with bank directorships men who embezzle the money by thousands and tens of thousands, defrauding the people whom they bully to overcome, by all the vicious antagonisms possibly to be exerted.

These are the vices of corrupt legislation! God delivers us from the repetition of such evils, if we deliver ourselves from the corrupting influences.

The State should cause not only the greatness, but the purity of mind to stand forth in its boldest relief. What can we think of that community, where the legislators borrow millions to bank on, sanctioned by all the law-making powers, designing this large capital for favorites by the tens of thousands of dollars, a broken bank and a pretended bankrupt community, debtors secreting their property, and the State, if not repudiating, only saved therefrom, by extraordinary exertions of her noblest statesmen and wisest sons!

Does it matter about the name of government, if theft be intended and legalized ?

Surely estimating property many times its realized value for bank funds or security, will never answer for our honest discharge of liabilities.

It is bad enough to have private banks of mere paper character generally bursting, and ruining the parties in fortune and reputation. Those who have seen the evils of fictitious capital, may appreciate in part what is now adverted to.

An honest community cannot escape the moral poison, nor the horrid bankrupt effects.

Statesmen can never overlook these fundamental points.

The interest of the public cannot be duly protected, without concurrent private interest identified.

Thus the officers of a steamer will not risk explosion, when their interest is sufficiently identified in her. No banks should be created as political or legislative engines. Banks well regulated will best discount paper properly drawn, accepted and endorsed, by having it subject to the decision of a majority of private stockholders, who go in for the dividends, not to draw out the capital in larger proportion than they put in, and the bank based not on money-specie in the vaults, but on real and personal property of fictitious and fluctuating value.

No legislature in free governments has any right to make bank paper a legal tender. or bills of state credit. One of the most corrupt means of government, is the management of money matters, regulating the currency through banks. They must not be made political or other machines than called for by their legitimate functions.

The repudiation of banks is one of the world incidents, enough to teach the wisest precaution.

The proper position in banks, is to have them solvent, with guarantees of undoubted character, the notes genuine and promptly redeemed or redeemable. Is any individual opposed to banking, objecting thereto from the superficial knowledge or unfaithfulness of the operators? Let him observe the mighty results through the means of banking to commerce, the trouble and risk of specie and its impracticable narrow limits, and he needs must be a convert to a beneficent, wise and honest system of banking mutually beneficial to all parts of the world.

Whether general or independent banks, the public on which they operate should have undoubted security and safety funds, by deposits in bonds for their circulation.

In this way the State becomes endorser for safety.

Suitable bankrupt laws to secure an honest and good-faith transaction, should be instituted. Bankrupt laws may be prospective, not ex post facto. There must be no cloaking of property, by any means, any evasion of law.

WEALTH—INDEPENDENCE—CONTENT.

WEALTHY persons may be benefited on the reverse by poverty, if they act consistently with wisdom in the trial of their souls.

What a curse is wealth, if it deprive the possessors of the means of independence of time and leisure, of securing or preserving a good constitution, health, or due and desirable improvement of mind.

Wealth should never be the means of injury or aggression to any, much less the poor.

It should be the benefit of mankind, in relief of the oppressed. The best use of wealth is to create the content of independence. Man ought to be content with a rational share of life's blessings.

Man is surrounded by a host of difficulties, that he has to surmount to his glory and reward if wise and firm, well cultivated in mind, especially able to command his passions, that may enslave and oppress him. Fortune or wealth is a curse, if acquired by improper motives and improperly protected. What a fraud in devising a scheme of being reported bankrupt, and then the party to buy up his paper as a bankrupt when full handed.

Property acquired or protected by unprincipled means, gives but little enjoyment. To appreciate the value of money, make it.

There can be no objection to wealth when it enlarges the world's area for progress and improvement, but what misery to be in debt and after riches? It is the legitimate use of money. Lay the proper foundation for a fair fortune.

· The spendthrift does not estimate the value of money, as he has not made it. His parents made it for him to spend. They have not given him business, but spending habits, thus doing him an irreparable injury, especially if they have added to his false peculiar education, thus dwarfing his mind, and all its best impulses and expansions.

To estimate the full value of money, lose all, and then be in a strange land or city. where you can get no accommodation by loan or negotiable paper. You are in a great commercial emporium that looks at money before strangers.

Be able, competent and independent to face the world by the legitimate value of money, that enables man to stand up to his engagements, otherwise he is no man and need not talk of anything. But some people deem themselves nothing, and sink below the actual limit of their own minds; that will not do at all. Have they done the best under their circumstances? They have to fulfil all their engagements in life, expedient for principle.

The mind is apt to be thrown off its guard, but that must never be. To which of the world-sharpers can mind trust? Which has tender mercy on any opportunity presented? Has the pickpocket?

In regard to money, it should only be sought for its real worth, as a subsidiary means to the loftiest attainments, to promote the full and comfortable benefit of mankind, not the enslavement of mind, merely hoarding dollars, and divesting itself of appropriate life.

The desire for immense wealth is positively injurious to individuals and society, detracts from the pleasures of life, the independence of all.

THE WHOLE DRAMA OF GAMBLING, IN ITS COMPREHENSIVE SPECULATION.

Rouse not the sleeping lion in his den.

Conceited and avaricious ignorance misleads its victims, till habit fixes irreclaimable possession and mastery.

The blackleg, with soul and body black even to forgery, has little conscience about the rights of property entrusted to the tender mercies of club laws.

What cares he about the means to insure the game? ·

His character cannot secure the esteem of his citizens, who generally believe that such, part either with reputation and character, or money, and too often with both.

Most of these men are conspicuous before the world, and hold out temptation in alluring forms to seduce mind, and enrich themselves. Can legislation be too just, with such injury? Much of their time is passed on steamers, as cavaliers of clubs, who disseminate property so easily acquired, and morals so hard to be reformed.

Those verdant in the wiles of the world, can hardly suspect in their unsophisticated views, the many resorts to time, place, or modes of this wily fraternity. But the prudent must look for the elephant in his climate, as well as beasts of prey in their lair.

The victims are abundant from the circle of respectable people, who too often involve their more respectable friends in loss of money, and even of reputable characters. When the fiend spirit is aroused, the sleeping evil is unsatisfied with domestic pleasures of wife, family, and friends, who are all resigned to a mortifying close. The dupe may have to submit to the most open frauds, too glaring for stupid ignorance to overlook, but all are to be permitted, unless the last one wishes to be instantly murdered.

If men now read this, previously unsuspecting, and yield, then they go into this iniquity with their eyes open, and their minds self-impeached, as improperly coveting the property of others.

What chance has a verdant youth with the longest purse, and even with that, to escape with safety, amid such people, who are ready for all the diversified and foul scenes of play? At the same time, what could he ordinarily expect from the laws that govern long purses, but that they would be speedily emptied for the benefit of the public?

Gambling involves paramount evils, arouses the worst passions of avarice and its concomitants.

A case is said to have occurred on board a steamer, wherein Poker, the game that decides success by the length of the purse, was introduced. A party of gamblers united their purses to pluck a stranger, who was possessed of money, and incapable of prudently concealing it, as they thought.

These very deep men in cunning, the lowest of intelligence, that becomes antagonistic to the noblest principles of mind, and excites no sympathy for its defeat, finally raised thirty thousand dollars, and gave the forlorn one but few minutes to redeem his supposed best stake, but when, as bank agent, he introduced his valise, with hundreds of thousands in due time, the combination had their game blocked on them without rescue. Yet this was a scene that gave the winner a victory, ruinous to honesty. "The conqueror suffers" at cards, as well as at war. Honesty and honest peace, forever.

Where would the successful party have been, had a heavier sum covered his? Lost and undone, ruined and disgraced, as millions before him in a suicide's grave, or in a felon's life.

If this course of life be not successfully resisted, in vain do its victims resist the most dishonest temptations.

· The history of gambling when given by the reformed, is said to be appalling indeed. The following history has been attributed to Green, whether authentic or fiction, illustrates the severe teachings that it imparts.

A plain looking citizen, introduced himself on board of a western steamer as a master drover, but turned out to be the victor over a band of gamblers then on the alert for such simple people. The game of cards was played, but deeper games were executed. The first character permitted himself to be decoyed, nothing loth by the knowing ones, who sought to operate on the simple countryman.

The stakes were high to five hundred dollars, which when deposited by the gamblers, the other party invariably swapped for his own thousand dollar bill each time.

Finally, the amount staked was enormous, and aroused the attention of the passengers to the game.

The band of gamblers being numerous, deliberately wound up the game by the use of four aces on an ace trump, and took the money. The drover was indignant, but had no redress. The captain was appealed to by the crowd, to expel the gamblers practicing such audacious villany upon a simple countryman, but he forbore, to their renewed indignation. After their arrival at the next landing, and the two gambling parties left the boat, then the captain explained. The master drover was a counterfeiter and pocketed all the genuine cash, good money, while the sharper party had pocketed the worthless counterfeits, by playing five aces. The first history shows success of gambling by the longest purse; the last, by that of the shrewdest villany.

All proper observers must see, that either the purse or the reputation, one, and too often both, are the main stakes at this theatre of corruption and iniquity. Ere the victim is aroused to the fatal coils or fangs of the serpent, its fatal poison has entered his vitals.

What a drama, for a good citizen and an honest man! If enlightened mind cannot counteract the wreck, what can? Enlightened legislation with all her protection, can be successfully invoked along with suitable rational morals.

A gambler oftenest plays to lose money and character: gets into difficulties, fights of killing and murder, and lives an abandoned, wretched life.

We scarcely ever hear of a gambler's losses, but mostly of his winnings, until he himself is lost.

The avoidance of vices, presents an ample payment in a virtuous life. It is said that thirty-five millions of dollars are lost anually, in the gambling houses in London.

The gambler only asks you to play, but if you consent, you are then in his power. If he cheats you in his foul crowd, you may well hesitate to resent it then and there, in his crowd so foul, from which there is no escape with money and life.

Will you go into such position? You, alas, may resign yourself without discretion into many powers scarcely less insidious. Covetousness misleads the world. You should employ your valuable time rationally, not vulgarly, from which you may profit with virtuous intelligence, not vicious cunning. Betting perverted brings in the category of cards, drink, and much general dissipation. But the first false step, ere it be too late, parents, you who are the faithful guardians of your children, must anticipate by that discipline, that the household president originates, ere mind is identified in the grapple of conflicts, utterly incompetent at the tender age of childhood, of self-preservation, because it has never been fortified by the right forewarning, the best forearming, but has to decide for itself the best it can, for many vital contingencies, one of which too often overwhelms miserable verdant youth.

Is there anything in life of secret or open danger, from the first dawn of practical reason, that wise parents can rightly obviate and not do?

The very thing that has to be done, wisely or otherwise?

When a gambler wins, a victim loses.

Recently a swindler was caught stocking the cards, but the hand designed for himself was given another, consequently he was not only loser in money, but was disgraced by the exposure.

When the world adds to this, the conspiracy on the virtue of temperance, of the party to be fleeced, and the various vicious decoys to secure their prey, then we feel that victims are only guarded by innocent ignorance.

The serpent cannot be harmlessly fondled, while enjoying the power of poisonous fangs.

Avarice corrupts minds. Gambling is one of its resorts, blackening the reputation with terms of obloquy and reproach, and the end perdition.

Lucky numbers of lotteries seduce and bankrupt much of the world. With all the public bonus, are any states benefited with such detraction from their morals?

As to the gambler's platform, you never know where to find him, as it embraces a long list of crimes, criminal associations.

The object of this attempt is not to let the world of such people injure us.

The best game, says the gambler, is to know when to stop.

The best, says the rational religionist, is never to know the beginning. The best of life is innocence and independence—never learn this too late. You should know what you are, and capable of being, not of falling from your purest state. The rational promptings of nature bespeak the noblest obligations of bosom friends, to inculcate all that will amply protect us from this whole circle of enormous demoralization.

BETTING ON ELECTIONS.

THIS is most deeply immoral, as it may create improper exertions and unfair proceedings, respecting voting, a freeman's privilege, and is wisely prohibited by legislation ; as all other vicious gambling, lotteries, general piracies, &c.

There will ensue undue excitements, feuds, and animosities, from betting on elections, unquestionably. Betting on elections is a curse to any country. The culprits ought to be disfranchised, and fined the amount bet.

Betting on elections will cause the old gamblers to take all false positions and pretences, and sneak out of any right obligation that they had incurred. They are unworthy of trust and confidence, by good citizens.

FINANCIERING—THE GREAT PRINCIPLES OF FINANCE.

WHEN part of the world gets below the right use of money, it gets below principles. The only real value of money is to secure independence, that secures respect and propriety of the world's department. He is really an independent man who does not give notes or obligations to pay, except under proper circumstances. All indebtedness must be put on a proper sure basis.

The payment of the right interest and value of money, would expedite the payment of debts at the right time, and by the right mode. Money is property, and is worth its current cash value. There can be no wise laws to abrogate nature's laws on this subject.

Fixing interest, except for protection to minors, idiots, &c., is arbitrary and extortion. The legislators might as well fix for other property. There should be no oppression about it either way, but everything should be put on its right basis, amenable to the great law of supply and demand. The rise of property is on price and value. All industrial rewards are predicated rightly on their proper appreciation.

Is it possible that money should be limited in interest by legislators, except in matters that require direct specification ? The enlightened must see that money is property, and its market worth must be governed by the universal law of supply and demand, price and value.

Legal rates per cent. should be fixed for all matters that require law, and no further. Legislation never can define the correct position of the world. Commerce defines that. Stocks of all kinds are only worth their intrinsic value, and no legislation can alter that.

What justice is there in unconstitutional acts ?

If the government license and charter banks, she yields distinct privileges and facilities ; then she has the right to fix the limits and rates of interest.

Banks have caused the people to pay more than all usurious loans besides ; have produced much imposition on the world, and made it pay very dearly.

Why violate constitutional right therefor ?

Good faith must be fully carried out always in all such.

Put all capital on a par on constitutional rights.

The world must negotiate on mercantile commercial principles, and pay always, not have it less than the commercial or fair value. This is a fixed principle in all money matters, to respect the supreme laws of commerce.

Those who borrow must respect the title of property, their own conscience, and constitutional principles.

But not so with individuals who are of sound mind and lawful age, having all the constitutional rights of citizens. The prices of merchandise fluctuate necessarily, according to the supreme law of supply and demand, price and value. All the principle involved is for the capitalist to avoid oppression of the debtor, and especially to secure himself from the loss of his money. Competition saves from oppression.

Some States collect taxes on usury, that they themselves proclaim by unconstitutional laws, and thereby prove the invalidity of such position.

Wise laws should make money property, whether loaned or otherwise used, else where is the consistency of taxing by such laws ? Laws should make all honest, not give any an opportunity to escape from good faith transactions.

States that participate in the profits of what they condemn, are culpable indeed.

As mind is capital in tastes, habits, and customs, legislation must be unconstitutional to trammel by law the value of money, more than that of other kinds of property.

The use is worth what is current value at the time, and no more nor less. It cannot be restricted in this sense to the word usury. Legislators are culpable to license such pretence for obsolete bibles.

It becomes rational man to place all business on the only rational basis of principle most equitable and promotive of justice. No legislation can raise interest above the current value, if below that established by law. Legislation is behind commercial justice. Rescind the obsolete legislation that promotes repudiation of principles.

The rates of interest ought to be a commercial, not legislative matter, as far as the sound minds of adults are concerned. When corporations, minors, and rates not to be fixed by contract, are concerned, then the best protection by wise legislation should be afforded.

Swearing off interest is a premium on dishonesty.

Persons raised in peculiar schools have peculiar notions, destitute of principles. As to keeping their word, some hardly know what that is.

Suppose all were to take advantage of interest contracts by their oaths, for the benefit of their own profits, by means of some absurd law? What a faithless world would we have.

Have proper laws to promote the legitimate claims of nature, on the highest order of taste and justice to all.

The real well disposed cannot in self-defence do half the good practicable, on account of mind's miserable perverseness. There must be no repudiation, no cause for it in this world. If minors get what is absolutely necessary, they should not be allowed the shadow of repudiation.

Let all make principles general, that the benefit may be properly extended to the world.

All the legislative powers in creation, cannot raise per cents any higher, therefore it has no more power to create than lower. Commerce, and the worth of property do that by immutable natural laws.

If petty kings that desired to borrow, would let wise commercial laws of trade be secured the world, then it would be aided in the wisest deeds of existence of enterprise.

Promise nothing without compliance, never violate that promise, hence promise not absolutely or by impulse, but by principle for mutual protection.

The promise to pay money thus obtained is too sacred to be violated by any subsequent act, and legislatures desecrate justice to cause the judicial violations.

He who knowingly violates contracts because not profitable for performance, only needs an opportunity to do worse if possible.

Finance, put on its legitimate natural basis, saves property and feelings, from sacrifices otherwise unavoidable.

It is important that the world attend to best position of money transactions, and secure all that is legitimate.

The forms of notes are important, as if written under hand and seal, they are valid for sixteen years, otherwise they run out of date by ten years sooner. When the debts are due, and the party will not give a bill of exchange or pay, then there is no excuse to sue. Can any wise men ever have made such a law, as that on usury? It does no good to the community, but much harm—it does not prevent honest men from paying their contracts, but helps the unprincipled to repudiate legally all he can contract for. Is there any justice in any such demoralizing laws? Throw open the whole market to honorable and just competition, and let usury and the Jews, their peculiar faith and all, go to kingdom come. What business had borrowers with such property? All is legal repudiation.

In taking hold of what they get under false pretences, they prevent the holders from realizing what is their due—the proper means of realizing the price and value. Now do weak legislators oppose the supreme laws of commerce, to sustain the absurd positions of a Jew peculiar faith bible? Is the enlightened modern world to be tied up, by the vagaries of benighted priestocracies? Are the last to legislate for freemen, when they ruined their own vassals, made them subjects of the world.

When a man agrees to a thing, and then swears against it as a sacred promise, does he not perjure himself to all intents and purposes?

The world should stand up to itself, its principles of conservation, that is the only way to rescue mind from its injuries. Let the pure and rational minded think of all this. As to usury laws they are absurd.

The world does not want legislation, to make repudiators. When any such contract is made in good faith, and for a consideration of current value, on proper competition, nothing better can be done.

Surely property in the form of money, should not be legislated out of possession. Indebtedness should be only yearly, no longer. Have no purchase of notes. Stop such means of law-suit.

But states have to borrow. Let them raise by taxes of the generation that binds itself, not the future—which last is unjust. How came national debts? Do not saddle posterity with impracticable debts. That is the worst despotism.

As to usury laws, the principles of commerce legislate better, than all borrowing legislators of the world. For what benefit is such absurd law, that of usury? The honest man will not begin to avail himself of it: he would scorn such an atrocious bribe, and as to the repudiator, is it proper policy in legislators who affect to be wise ones, to cloak him? If any affect that the ancient law had any virtue, the world should know that ancient laws of the Romans, as well as others, the Jews had the debtors sold for debt, or the debtors became slaves. This was custom, most barbarous. But there is no such thing in civilization. Of course there is no necessity or apology for usury laws. Is there any plea for pleading the just debts of minority or gambling. Honest men will not plead such. Why the benefits to repudiators? To corrupt society that should be entirely renovated on the most honorable basis of rational mind? The party seeks to get the money for years, and then swear all off, deliberately seek this mode of paying debts. Legislation tells him go in court and prove himself a repudiator, to get money under false pretences, the very thing it punishes for. O consistency. When, then, is this perjured man to be believed? What sort of a citizen is he? Will he do to trust, after violating his word, and testifying to his own utter disgrace?

What is to supply the vantage ground lost, by misplaced confidence? Can the injured party be reinstated? There is no need to protect repudiators, who will protect themselves at the expense of honesty and property. Protect honest men against them. The world needs permanently, wise and honest legislation. Carry out principles forever.

Bribery and corruptions can exist in all communities, under their present regime. Can we know how far it goes, to what unlimited extent?

Financiering most elevated, prevents ruinous sacrifices of property, as for instance, cotton or produce falls, by contingent causes in the market, then an honorable loan assists out of all the incidental difficulties, and enables the owner to realize the best market value for his property.

As to the worth of a thing, time proves that what we can fairly get for it.

The value of a thing is what it realizes on fair competition in market. How then should the holders of this kind of property be outlawed in their rights?

But a friend insists on the use of your money; let him have it on proper bills of exchange.

Is he a friend? Then he is entitled to the position of what the money is worth, by what its value commands, otherwise your friendship requires gift to the proper extent. You must decide to give if you lend to doubtful borrowers, without proper bills and nothing else, all fixed up before you act.

The prudent man, whose funds consist alone in money, had best keep them at home, rather than not command them when stipulated, or be compensated for damages.

We must understand always the right position, else we may have to be schooled by loss, that will be no contingency, but a uniform certainty.

The best system is to deal with the whole world at once, rightly and independently.

When a knowledge of human nature declares that much of mankind is made or schooled worthless, however much the world is made to appear proportionately unworthy, we are on the progressive order of improvement, if we rightly appreciate principles.

We can find the world better when mind corrects the positions of the perversion, and that it will best do by science. The greatest study of mankind carries with it in this enlightened age the best amendments by science. Whilst the highest social relations require that all good minds should help protect the world from injury, they require that we should prevent the world from taking advantage of us. We admit the difficulty of knowing the nature of man or woman who studies art, cunning, and duplicity.

As great variety of character is presented, to guard best against all whom it would be best to avoid if we knew them accurately beforehand, but from whom we cannot absolve by promise, test all by firm and adequate obligations, of a bill of exchange, order or draft, duly accepted.

The loan of money is to be predicated on the great law of supply and demand, price and value, that governs the world, and is the only fair principle that is honorable.

The world cannot be hurt by fair analysis.

The world is interested in the welfare not only of an honest, but a generous-minded person. Is it so with the prosperity of the mere miser ?

If you do not have proper stocks for investment of capital, the first thing you know, bankruptcy will be staring you in the face. Now you should do yourself justice as well as the world, and if you have any surplus capital to spare, you can well bestow it on the poor, your own relations and friends, not those who seek to rid you of your own property.

Capitalists must anticipate, ere the explosion point of bankruptcy cuts with impunity. It vexes one too much to pay most of his property, as too many have done, for securityship.

Many in the second circle cannot, after leaving the first, maintain the raising they first had, as public opinion is not chaste enough to sustain them.

In money and security transactions, one should not act till all the documents are fixed right.

There are two things, money loans and securityship, that may derange the world. How many unprincipled people make over their property, and get all they can. All this should be made known, or the fraud should be published. This making over property, having preferred creditors, is fraud, and ought to be treated as such, of the worst kind of felony.

No one ought to do business lightly, loosely. He will be apt if he do to pay for the schooling of the world. What with judgments, executions, making over and away with property, some debtors will be found destitute.

The world can be ruined by following out unprincipled partisans in securityship. No one can be lower than the unprincipled man.

CONSERVATIVE PROTECTION IN TRANSACTIONS.

THE majority of men do not avail themselves of their own great resources and capital. They look to others, when they idly neglect to husband their own mighty, nay, superior resources, of mind and principles, that could elevate them to their loftiest aspirations.

They can justly point to fundamental principles, that reflect conservative benefit universally.

What are those fundamendal errors that the world should avoid, as ruinous transactions, but wild speculations, excessive securities, expensive lawsuits, that are little less than the sleeping lion, if aroused ?

Without financiering or commercial transactions, you will not know mankind, through the best medium knowledge of human nature; therefore, you cannot have an experienced mentor too quick, to guide you at first over difficulties.

When a man's ruin stares him in the face, then his eyes are opened, but he should have wisely used all precautions, to avoid all such forever.

Yet, to whom can he look ?

Upon parents, to counsel and advise him, alas! in matters totally beyond their ability or circle ?

It is well if the world do not pay too dearly for its experience. Some people work for others, with little or no emolument. They had better consider all that beforehand, and take nothing for granted, at all, in money matters, without specific arrangements.

Every man should define his position, and understand that of others, all the right time, and that always at the start, if the party wish to be right.

No false modesty should prevent justice.

Both parties, if honest, owe it to themselves to settle all preliminaries.

The best position for those holding property or wealth, is, never retain that which is due to others, if practicable to pay them, as the best consolation to the mind of an honest man, who does not wish to lose that part in any general wreck. In all business transactions, define the position, if important, in written contracts.

Specify all particulars in business transactions and contracts, securing always, as far as practicable, the most trustworthy, and of principles.

Innocent and pure-minded people, who do not know the world, vainly imagine the world as themselves, whose word is trustworthy ; but they find that others are of different schools of honor from themselves. The world, then, must be uniformly protected, on fixed principles.

No credited accounts of individuals, much less nations, should stand longer than a year, before being audited.

Some people, who prey on the world, only ask to be put in possession of any amount of property, and themselves merely protected by the form, not justice, of law. The world must be appreciated.

Some people cannot be trusted safely with property or life; they care nothing for themselves, how can they do more for others?

In commission and agency business, where there is cause for suspicion of unfaithfulness, the only corrective is to have persons above suspicion, to whom proper and specific written directions, when given, will be the best to obviate the worst difficulties.

In whom can we confide power?

Hardly in any, much less in aliens; therefore we must invariably confide in principles. We must all seek to know rightly the just character of human nature, which we can best know through financial transactions.

Too many agents are indifferent, if not grossly negligent, of their agencies; especially for distant and absent employers.

We should never employ proxy, if practicable to avoid, especially such as this. The practical business man must be convinced of the necessity of one's own immediate attention to his own business, and least of all by proxy.

It is important to analyze the vast difference of the credit and cash systems.

That difference may be bankruptcy with the prodigal. With cash, purchasers can deal understandingly and with correct reference to their absolute wants, many per cent. better. We must give a living, safe price always when we are sure we are right; but that we must ever investigate, or not act.

When we have proper opportunities to know facts and the nature of things, then we should rightly use all such. Take nothing on trust that is suspicious, requires investigation, or can be benefited by it.

It is well for us to deal ever with honest men, but we can only act for self-preservation on principle. Whom can we trust at random in business transactions, when a part of the world avoids payment of just debts contracted for value received? How much false capital is there?

Correct management of the world is the desirable issue.

Individuals seek to repudiate contracts because the price of property has fallen. Would such be anxious to give up the same, had its value risen? The proposition must be honorably fair for both, or it will not be just.

When one recently becomes a citizen, he may not know the people, many local facts, the limits that waters rise and flood the lands, the character of the soil and many essential particulars, therefore he should wait to inquire satisfactorily, and learn by experience, when entering into purchases or any important new business.

Review all sides, the worst, at least the shade, as well as the sunshine. Avoid holding your mind in abeyance to partial views of small circles, when it is worthy of command of circumstances relative to the largest comprehensions, the only safe ones.

Many things, from want of fitness, may produce failure; but many persons do not consider that their own personal unfitness does not arise from intrinsic reasons, but for want of a proper comprehension of the whole world relations to us.

I seek to have all properly protected in the first step, to be not even tempted to wish repudiation of solemn contracts, fair and business-like, in terms troublesome and offensive, in such a way as to create hard and unkind feelings, bitter anguish, sleepless nights, nervousness, severe remarks and nigh approach of actions, but for the mildness of one party. Let both, all parties go into all transactions with their best senses wide awake, to maintain all that is right permanently.

It might be thought that I am too censorious on human nature; I shall be happy to correct myself, but at the whole view it will be found that my strictures are upon the perversions of it from peculiar education, in so peculiar a way that man is taught to look all his way, that is, his self-interest, without respect to the other side, much less to conservative principles of all. It may be said, Yet this is only a certain class. True, but it is the world as far as it goes, and too much of that, which is the worst of all.

Let mind be always our protector, with good faith in business, or all transactions, not to involve the party in insuperable difficulties. Some persons, through ambition, avarice, or envy, do not duly estimate their own resources or capital, mental or pecuniary, but are reckless of calculations that mind demands and reason requires.

We have seen those who, as agents, might be profitably employed instead of principals, thus creating liens on all, though in their possession the owner's property eventually sold for less than the cost on the materials for building, or for less than the third and last payment that they, the nominal purchasers, could not raise, and thus sacrificing all for want of foresight.

When the party does not overreach himself, he may make a competency and live independently, instead of deep depression, anguish and pauperism. Wild speculations are hard to accomplish, and often involve the operators in ruin. What innumerable expedients are resorted to about property !

Contend for your rights withheld, advisedly. All good citizens are concerned in heading false agents and commission merchants. The best policy was evinced in an incident transpired in another continent, where cotton was sold and a loss sustained, but the shipper investigated in person the whole transaction, and received twenty thousand dollars above the account of sales, and the delinquent party was glad to escape further exposure.

If not successful in one business, do not spend all your lifetime and talents fruitlessly, to the benefit of others, who, so far from thanking you for your drudgery, laugh at you for your vain exertions.

Does a man deceive you, by reasons that you can not control ? That is your misfortune, and his fault. If he do it again, that is your fault.

Corrections of errors, in all settlements, should be had for all time that is proper in the utmost courtesy and facility.

In property the first thing is title clear and indisputable, insured by proper documents recorded by a competent office, under no incumbrance of conveyances, deeds of gifts, executions and judgments.

Receive no purchases, especially of estates, for which imperfect titles are given, and the future responsibility may be in bankrupts or irresponsible characters. If administrators sell without validity of will, it will be lawless, and you can receive no rights at all thereby.

In the sale of property, without the whole title is in the party, beyond doubt or cavil, it is a poor business, though indemnifying bonds be attached, as in future days the seller may be dead, insolvent, or in parts unknown, his little property squandered, and all your protection nullified every way. The daily history of the world shows what constant changes are progressing, but few remaining in one place an age !

You may pay all your money to worthless individuals and strangers, &c., who may be bankrupt in character and property, from whom you can not get your own, and may not only have to deliver all that you have bought, but pay for the use of it the whole time, which may be the deepest injury to your purse, and not the most pleasant to your nicest feelings, sentiments and sensibility.

All contracts to be valid, must be for value received. You can take nothing on supposition or granted about the real worth of any individual, unless you know his exact condition and indebtedness or exemptions, and whether and how the debts can be paid.

Some people only pay at the end of the law, which often results in the end of their property. The greatest care should be of honesty, as a real pleasure of life, for then is honesty to console when adversity occupies. Specify all contracts, and all performances of workmanlike skill. All those of importance deferred had better be written, for two reasons, to keep promises sacred, and certify them without danger of misunderstanding and hostile feelings. The world needs the good faith of contracts, veracity in all its circles. Define the position, fix the specific whole.

Who wishes to have his property lost, or be harassed, merely to save a little trouble or duty at first ?

Where there is much public credit and high speculation, there must be a crash. Guard not only against world speculations, but speculators. Do not get your own consent, however specious and fair the bait, till you are not only satisfied, but safe, by the satisfaction of principles.

Speculators may inveigle purchasers into matters to give them ostensibly commissions, or really means to raise capital, to prevent their mercantile houses sinking, and will sell the article in reference to that express view ; not for mutual, reciprocal advantages. There is no position safer than that of principle, that must act every way to present full and fair satisfactory safety, and results final. Sell your property for a fair price, in preference to deferred and uncertain payments. Do not involve yourself by borrowing, but sell for reasonable prices always.

We see fraudulent conveyances, while the owner holds on to the property, in bad faith to honesty and truth and the debts to his creditors, who, in good faith, are the owners.

It is not honest for parties indebted to seek compromise of debts with the least payment, when their funds authorize differently.

What honest man seeks to depreciate, and then buy his depreciated paper in the market ?

It is dishonest to propose compromises, when only partial duty or payment is offered, and withholding the balance. What is the value of money, unless integrity of the world protects property and reputation ?

56

Laws for imprisonment of those fraudulently conveying property till surrendered, should be not only uniformly enacted, but enforced.

Why should it not be a penitentiary offence?

You should not speculate except with your money in hand, nor should you ever risk your whole property in one speculation, lest your adventure be a misadventure and ruin you forever, and you have not wherewith to pay. Do not leave trouble to your friends to settle, after you are dead, what you ought to have settled yourself so much better. If you preserve uniform system in business, it will be much better for you and the world.

Give the world no undue advantage over us, for its history shows that the past has been abused, the present perverted, and the future may be usurped in anticipation. The world will appropriate all kinds of capital in all practicable ways. Do not think of pleasing others at the expense of justice to self. Do not do this at all.

You are requested to promise. Take all matters into consideration and consultation; tell the applicant to wait so many hours necessary, and then decide advisedly. Sometimes people put themselves where justice is satisfied. Patience and perseverance will accomplish much, but do all things perfectly right at first.

The true secret is, to know how to best succeed in this world—not only succeed, but do it as it ought to be done. One of the plans is, to have no antagonism of the world more than the inherent nature of things permits.

We should have no difficulty with any matters, when we can govern all with mastery of mind. The world must have independence of character, know how to act, and with nerve.

Is it safe to buy from an unknown and unknowable operator? Not generally.

Never put it into the power of mortals to injure you by demoralizing causes. Your triumph in this world is complete, if you act honestly, truthfully, faithfully to duty.

1. In the first place, let your contract, verbal or written, be as sacred as life. 2. Let none desecrate this contract, made in good faith, reason and justice. Let truth and honesty be forever sacred, then fire cannot scorch nor ice freeze, in future abodes, the truthful and honest soul, that meets all that is due civil, moral and religious duties.

But rational mind must be properly cultivated, to know all this, and that retribution does not come by miracles, or priests' works or words, but by the intrinsic virtue of self-vindicating principles.

Mind should be duly protected against all the humbugs of the world, all the peculiar mysteries of mock science, emanating from mock bibles and faith.

How difficult is it, for the world to appreciate about property and money power?

It should be American to say and act the negative independently, as well as the affirmative. Many trusts of society are implied. Are you to violate them? You cannot, and maintain an honorable reputation for good faith.

Never promise impracticable or impossible things, or those that do injury. All treaties are to be in good faith, and both are bound, unless one party fails to comply, which absolves all obligations.

Individual and national compacts are to be sacred.

Man must respect the sacred inviolability of good faith contracts. All documents, in trust or otherwise, should be legal, and as they are binding on all parties practicable for good, the parties to the contract can only officially relieve: consequently nothing is valid without their official permission. There can be no violation of word or pledge in money payments, that are practicable, otherwise they should not be given under ordinary or any circumstances.

Put all bids for public labor at the lowest, as base injustice and imposition will be otherwise practiced.

Specific special contracts must be confirmed.

Applicants who seek accommodation in money should pre-pay their debts, or secure them by the best paper—never deferred beyond twelve months.

Never let debts run too deep, either as creditor or debtor.

The unprincipled, reckless, without conscience, will shun their security obligations, if practicable.

When bondsmen suffer tens of thousands, and become bankrupt for others, it is time for self-defence, to institute as great protection as there are temptations.

Some people are harassed all their life by debts, their mind disturbed, estate confiscated to the sheriff. never paying any debts but at the extreme end of the law, paying a fortune in mere costs. They had better sell their property, and be freemen, at once. Then they know what they have to depend on in life.

But this pest of securityship is the thing that perplexes the world to refuse, when otherwise it may have to pay the amount.

The world looks to friendship, that must not, if pure, be violated for dollars and cents.

But as the world has mind to govern it, let all its details be submitted thereto. When required to act, you may decide how much you can give, not sacrifice, to what is called friendship—substantially, mere acquaintance, and made too on interested motives.

Many contract debts never to be paid, as base in the eye of principle as repudiation, and as degraded before God. If the laws had no penalty, all such that resort to this iniquity, however they may affect the best circles, would not prove themselves honest.

To avoid all the liabilities of a promiscuous securityship, mutual friends can select and sign for each other.

Will some aid, who have used up all that you could spare? This address is made to those whose facility of disposition does not urge them to say *no*, in the right place, and at the right time.

Insolvency of estates may often exist, unknown, unless properly investigated. Is the obligation of such worth anything?

Sufficient collateral security should be previously fixed, to prevent accidents by death, &c. Trusteeship and life-insurance, on proper policies, may answer the best purposes.

What little credence can be put in most men, when money is concerned, in bankrupt times!

What an amount of abuse of good faith is there in this respect.

The only safe position is on immutable principle; if you do not thus act, you will soon change your most exalted opinion of the majority, of fair and specious, when nothing is at stake.

Your experience will adequately sustain the question, how is a person known unless previously tried, when you realize what an awful thing it is to some, in stretching one's credit.

One is subject to being victimized, on securityship.

There is no obligation to force friends to tender their fortunes, their all, for mere speculation of others!

True, honorable friendship scorns such ignoble deeds.

At the time that one becomes security, it is too often the case that the payment has to come. Collateral security is due the second, for the preservation of the credit of the first, of good morals generally, every way.

Have the nerve to say *No*, when necessary and proper, beforehand, with forethought, like an intelligent freeman, who looks upon the pliancy of some as most objectionable, then the deed is right.

RELATIVELY TO SECURITYSHIP.

Say that most independent word *No*, on all rightful occasions. Will you go my security? said a merchant to an industrious planter, of good sense, on moderate acquaintance. For how much? Six thousand dollars. No, sir! The merchant was indignant. But the planter firmly said, I made my property by my labor and means, which I can best estimate. Rather than risk my all on your good feelings, I will risk your feelings. In the end, the event proved the value of precaution, the truth of good sense. The merchant ruined his security, obtained elsewhere, leaving speedily and clandestinely for another country; and one of his pupils, an apt scholar, has followed since, violating a generous and sympathising confidence, improperly bestowed, as it was never merited.

How many securities are thus affected? Collateral security is the only defence and forever due, as the rightful ownership is in the person liable—so says my code of ethics. All that intend to do right, and not involve friends, will not hesitate to secure collaterally.

Let every citizen assert his or her own rights, by firm action, with the negative in the right place and time, before, not after damage. Let them observe wisely, act faithfully, to promise consistently with their word and proper decision.

Wealth of dollars too often interrupts happiness.

Sacrifice rightly all that interfere with our best happiness. We need a general system of financiering, to protect ourselves and household rightly, against the sharp part of the world, perfectly reckless of principle, and hostile to all gratitude.

Self-preservation is an important element in this question. Let justice supersede liberality, and take nothing for granted in this matter, as it may be absolutely necessary to have all keep the strait and direct track.

Premising all things right, or never starting, will insure peace and success, and all the suitable independence.

The best dependence is on self, to be independent of others : then you may be best assured of merited success, or see where the fewest errors and faults lie.

You are called upon, by friends and relations, to become security. Have you that certain sum of money that you can—without inconvenience to yourself, and injustice to your own creditors, particularly your own family, and all others that have a direct or immediate and paramount demand on you—spare, for the payment, if called on ?

If not, fulfil the obligations of justice and friendship, by demanding, at the same time, collateral security on enough property, to that value, at least.

The payer ought to own the property. If you pay for it, you are certainly justly entitled to it.

If you do not, all the ends of justice and friendship are rightfully met on both sides.

But the purchaser of a large amount of property refuses collateral security ; then refuse him your friendship, for his object looks sinister, and his conduct is not free from suspicion, if properly honest. He seeks to reach the profits of his speculation at your risk. Is this friendship?

Proper analysis decides it, sordid interest.

Why all this precaution ? To meet the richest feelings of an honest man, that sees thousands of his countrymen fleeing to distant frontier states, running away with their property, or cloaking it with most suspicious appearances that all is not right, when they could have most honorably lived under their own poplars and oaks, on their own broad acres, in the land of their choice, with the contented feelings of all contracts fulfilled, and all the world honestly and cheerfully smiled in the face, had the word *No* been said in the right time, or the word *Yes* been inscribed in the right way. But then this difficulty was for another. It is your own act, just the same ; both are equal. There is no difference between primary and secondary signatures, so far as to be exempt from valid contracts, specifying to be fulfilled.

He who acts by another, acts himself. The rule is general : never purchase beyond your means in speculation, in no respect if you are wise, and wish to abide on the lands you are entitled to by ownership.

Will you permit another to do with yours in reckless gambling speculation, what you will not enact yourself? You have no control over his affairs, then how imperative and incumbent it is on you, to rightly control your own. If you do not, who will ?

Give up no independent comforts, for any prospects however brilliant but unsubstantial.

You may observe only the bright and flourishing view of things, that if reversed, may ruin you speedily.

The reverse has a darker side, than the mind realizes. We must adhere to the legitimate principles of trade, else a mint can be exhausted for speculation.

We may lose all by misfortune, and then the best consolation is, that we have saved by paying our debts. When a merchant is thus overtaken and compounds, assigns or goes into bankruptcy, his books being the regular basis with proper vouchers and documents, he rules the highly dangerous contingency.

The unfortunate man may get into troubles for want of system, firmness, clearness of intellect, decision, and want of guarding against the world's dishonesty and deep intrigues.

Some people may become incapacitated for business, by various habits, that may lead to peculiar state of mind as little removed from mania-a-potu.

What is to protect the helpless, from the rapacity of social pirates ?

You may view the bright and flowery side of human nature, and can never believe in its amount of corruption, until you test it fully in finance and money transactions. The more helpless the proprietor, and the more immunity from penalty, the more are these pirates invited. No circle is too high for dark and corrupt characters to operate therein ; in fact, the greater the stake, the more are such invited in every age and clime, unless principles counteract all of them.

If you should never enter into contract, with any not legally liable and responsible, on account of, aye much less should you do so with those incapacitated from want of principle.

There are some people, whose appreciation of your expression of gratitude for favors from them, will make it all a matter of speculation, and pervert the whole of refined sentiments of mind, to ignoble sensuality and pecuniary profit.

People have told me, that some of their own relations, who were in churches too, would rob their God if they could. Is this too severe a statement? Who will say so!

How many persons who were doing well, have listened to the advice of pretended friendship, and have been used up by so doing ! They have confided in their judgment as best in most business matters, though no better characters than they should be, yet people will follow a leader like sheep or bees, instead of acting like rational men who have intellect to be cultivated, to guard against the adoption of pernicious results by the best use of our matured judgment.

We are bound from the nature of things to analyze all matters, but above all, propositions to benefit the advisers. This rule must be paramount, then you will see all things safe, before your money, your independence and you, part.

The world is ready enough to speculate on you, therefore you must be guarded, especially in insidious attacks on its part, and the weakest one on yours.

Much of the world, no matter how selected, care not for the balance, especially the avaricious and the spendthrift, whose eyes are on money, their immediate advantage, not the other's benefit. Most of these dishonor their own interests, how then in the name of mind can they respect those of other people? It is preposterous to think otherwise. Never then, let the world get the advantage on iniquitous terms, else it will be apt to keep it for life. Only let some people get through life their way, and they will carry all advantages with them. What care unprincipled people for the world, after they are gone, or whilst they are here? If you cannot secure your rights, secure yourself from action with all such. Experience, the wisest professor that has ever yet granted diplomas in the world's school, proves it is idle to trust any further, than the best principles.

Never commit yourself to that fatal word Yes, when you should take time for consideration and mature the facts to estimate the truth.

Say No at the right time, in the right way, and to the right people, rather than Yes in security, and refuse payment because it was security debt, even conveying property.

Act rightly, and then you can act independently, honestly and fearlessly, above reproach or restraint.

Stick up to your word in action, whether security or not.

Be prepared to lose a definite amount for contingencies, as true friends in aiding or lending on trust, the full amount of your friendly deeds. but not to buy your friendship with money. By proper protection of your possessions, you have that proper independence of property that is power, to counteract the arts of base men who take advantage of contingencies and circumstances. How many have been perfectly ruined by securityship? Collateral security should accompany the request, as inability of the one should defeat the speculation, especially if reckless, of the other.

Life insurance might be taken out by married persons, as the best policy for family protection.

The safest plan is for a trio to sign for each other on bills, then they know best how each other stands.

They should confide in each other, and disclose their true situation in life. This is one of the great principles of self-protection and economy.

Going security on blank drafts is enough to ruin any man, as easily as gambling, idling or dissipation. None are so well benefited by experience, as anticipation of difficulties, before the character is shifted and the responsibility lost.

Fewest keep their word about payments to the exact time, unless means are certain and forfeiture is to be sustained. Individuals must invariably comply most punctually with promises, especially in moneyed transactions most promptly, or never make any even to secure any present advantage, as it may turn out to their material disadvantage and injury.

Leave nothing to contingency, but all to uniform principles. Say no, or have collateral security, then all will act honestly and you can guarantee that honesty, for if you hold the world's honor and interest identified, you secure both in the best way.

We can never buy friendship of aliens, when we risk the independence of the family. We must give solution to daily family questions, by saying no, when necessary to those seeking our names. Then we can always stand up to our paper and honor.

The credit system may be disgracefully misused, as its abuse has demoralized many people, and sullied their integrity and veracity.

What right and social law has a pretended friend, to break up any family or individual, by claims for surety in wild and reckless speculation?

The wife has a primary interest, and should have a proper and reasonable veto, to prevent suffering and poverty in all such transactions.

A buys of B, and they are both secured by C, who is not benefited by the security, when he pays and has neither the property secured or the money paid. What reason and honesty are there in all this, must be inquired into previously to the security, for then honesty and honor require full payment.

A must secure or deliver the property to C, if the last pay for it. This law should be instituted, to protect honesty and honest transactions. The wisest legislation is very essential, to individual and universal prosperity and happiness.

Release no security by your facility of disposition, else you may lose the whole debt. Verdant people may lend their name to others, with a blank to be filled up by any amount to be obtained at bank, and before the confiding party knows where he is, a greater obligation is placed over his name than he is solvent for, consequently his family is reduced to hard labor for the balance of their lives, if not absolute want or even genteel beggary.

It alters the case but little, if instead of the particular bank designated, another bank is substituted, a fraud is perpetrated on the innocent stockholders. Such parties go into bankruptcy, and make fortunes by the operation of smuggling property some way or other to relations and friends, who may divide the profits, purchase it for a trifle, and leave the public minus.

Thus the benefit of the bankrupt law is lost in the deepest corruption, and has to be abrogated from the statute books.

Thousands of dollars have been made at one operation, when the whole proceeds should have been paid to honest and suffering creditors. How many are rolling in splendor and luxury, with their thousands made over to secure the use of their property to themselves, and you cannot touch the same. What corruption!

The history of the world bespeaks the utmost importance of attending mainly to the security of property.

The schools of the world require dear sums sometimes for payment of tuition.

Counteract instead of fighting the whole world. There are some cases where the security has to pay the debts of those dishonest men, fraudulently conveying their property; but wise legislation of an honorable community must prevent such nefarious transactions.

Millions of people put all money matters and transactions not on principles, truth or honor, but merely on all points of the law; seek all to the extent of their credit, and never pay if avoidable, acting as public plunderers.

Do we seek to know human nature? We need not ask the sheriff or public officers, when observation and experience in financial operations teach us very clearly. But, then, we ought to anticipate the losses we pay at the school of personal experience. Well then, ask intelligent officers of the land, who see the ways of the world in many of life's vicissitudes.

Men equivocate for dollars all their life, and all your boasted church characters caught in tight places only show what that part of human nature is. Man must inquire of the world, how the world stands. Persons thought good, cannot get credit on loans any way that can be fixed. You must not extend your generosity towards many people, who you expect will reciprocate. You must not depend on public opinion, to cause some people to act right. They may be deficient in all the qualities, and have never learned at any such schools of public sentiment for want of rational education, and public opinion of the right character may be difficult to find in the right place. Public opinion itself is not enlightened even to appreciate what religion is, mistaking peculiar faith for it. Whilst you hold yourself amenable to public opinion, they may have none of the cultivated elements of honesty to compel them to its command. They get your money, goods, credit; you may wait in vain for recompense.

In vain do you invoke the nobler feelings of human natures; it is all the idle wind. If you do not have proper protection always, you have least hold on responsibility.

The more the credit system is licensed, the more injury to the community and morals results.

Counteract all the evils, ills, machinations of perversions, social, civil and national. Permit no wild reckless speculation in security, to render yourself amenable by your whole property.

No honest man should ask of you more in security than is just. If he be a friend, so much the more reason.

How odious is it to sneak out of responsibility, because it can be done by absence, distance, want of technical responsibility. The intention is the thing. Do not keep what is borrowed, the least, even a book, longer than a proper use.

Poor fellow, says the world, he has so much security money to pay. If it were his own debts, he would not mind it. But if security debts are not his, whose are they? What is the difference in conscience? Will he cloak his property, make it over or away, to escape the just demands of the law? Why did he not think of all that before hand, when he came to sign, ere the real owner of the property delivered it up, to him who did not pay therefor? Did he help to perpetrate a fraud, a false pretence, to get the owner's property out of his hand, and then repudiate the debt because he was security, and he says not his own? Then the sympathy of the people permits this character, this fellow, to smuggle his property, himself, to parts unknown, violate the law, and get up in their very community an awful repudiation feeling, instead of asking for the whole support of the law, and helping such poor dolts by subscription, and bidding the world look to the protection, also to the penalty of principles. Just so with culprits, especially if raised in the circle. Pardons must be extended. Instead of the law being vindicated, it is violated under the basest pretences. Give no pardoning power for what is clear violation, and wanton infractions. Give all mercy to the world, but exact justice to the iniquitous culprits. Just so with faith, poor bibles, and priestocracy. But where is the bleeding world, oppressed for thousands of years most awfully by both? Sneak out of all responsibilities, when thou shouldst pay what thou owest. Come up to all that can be justly expected of thee. Be always capable of being depended upon.

Make preliminary arrangements, and deal in those arrangements relatively.

There are people of supposed good authority, whom we cannot take practically—as the credit system, if done on competent basis, will render valuable good to the world, let it be done on a competent security. Some people cannot be classed good or bad. They never pay till forced, nor tell the truth, if avoidable for their interest.

What can the honest part of the world think of those living on property smuggled in the family, and that wrested from poor creditors? Will they not affirm the combination or collusion infamous?

All monotheists will do their very best to pay their debts, and doing justice to man is justice to God. Some circumstances of debt may not be controllable, but honesty can be always exhibited, and the circumstances can prove that much.

Have no preferred creditors. What designates an unprincipled person? One that is derelict in morals, truth, honesty, religion—the less principles, the less rational religion. Let others be base or tyrants, let not others act badly from that cause. Whom can you safely trust? Those that you know possess principles.

NATIONAL OR WORLD-MORALS ARE BASED ON CONSERVATIVE PRINCIPLES.

These promote and require the most honorable possession and protection of property. Wise and just legislation ought to prohibit the least fraud in property, and not protect or oppress any class in preference, either creditor or debtor.

The highest principles must govern.

Murder of the most appalling character is too often committed under specious appearances with entire impunity, especially if the kith or clan can bully the community.

Hardened culprits will affect that they killed in self-defence, but if they provoked the attack by first arrangements, then they committed assassinations.

Some of the world clans, in some few badly organized communities, violate the rights of property, others conceal, and many of the rest perjure themselves for their accomplices' vindication. What can you do with such a community?

You decide to fight fire by fire, and resort to lynch or summary law, yet, ere you are aware of it, that unfortunately takes in the innocent and provokes retaliation.

A better improvement, but objectionable, is a committee of vigilance.

The wisest organizations of social relations, give proper employment of labor and capital.

When constitutions are the sovereigns of the land, the people are rulers, and look to constitutional principles.

All the bodies of society of citizens should be constitutionally united. All sectarianisms are in antagonism with constitutional rights and principles, that look to God alone.

Commerce, industrial labor and civilization of the world are identified with the most substantial cultivation of mind by rational education, to promote national and the world's morals.

This state of things recognises no surplus population, as all is just, adapted for the best state of society, upheld by Deity.

In justice to national morals, resting as they do on constitutional rights, there can be no aristocracy by entail of law—all that is of mind and of its worth, on the best legitimate purposes of God's designs.

The best constituency of society would require of an enlightened criticism, all the original analysis that the highest obligations of truth can impose.

The wisest social organizations must obviate the tyranny as diversified as it may be, assailing the rights of individuals or majorities, as it is still despotism on an analysis. All minds good and true are most profoundly interested in a world's morals as in its welfare.

Its citizens are not only to be apparently better, but must substantially seek for all pertinent to the subject. The time is, when nations' morals are to advance solidly for the world's benefit, and for no peculiar advantage.

The world relies too much on assumed standing, and not conduct, during life.

There is no department, but what civilization will advance the welfare of the world in. She will bring all the commercial parts of the habitable globe into proper communication and amicable trade. The conquests of war, compared to the legitimate benefits of peace, are nothing. The first are degrading, piratical robbery, reducing the world to barbarism; the last are in the highest degree elevating, great, magnanimous, and conservative.

We must have wise legislation and wisely administered, to stop the violence that the people take into their own hands ; the world needs not merely reformation, but conservative revolution.

The people take for granted mere passage of laws, as if they could live by the mere pretences of the Christian or any peculiar faith. No peculiar faith embodies a code of ethics on principles, the only conservation in the world. Mind requires rational education all the time, but then intellect alone will not eradicate errors, unless most rationally comprehensive to embrace and reflect on morals.

Rational mind's due action to man, implies morals.

In past and present ages, only partial views and actions have been embraced, whilst nothing short of full comprehension will answer. What a miserable state of corrupt and perjured morals the world permits in matters of faith about evidence. It takes the codes of priestocracies without proof! What folly, if it were not ruinous injustice. Say what all will, we ask independently, Have any proved anything? No! But it is asserted that all is right. How is that? They imposed on the first, bullied the middle, and demand of the latter ages of the world to persist in their imposition!

To say the least, their position cannot be less than most iniquitous. Their prior acts convict them entirely. Their prior standing in society is beyond endurance. They have built a reputation most factitious through superstition, and the world has gone to sleep on it. The world cannot now say it knows no better. The world cannot maintain a fair and honorable reputation, to give this question the go-by much longer. What is the nature of evidence ? Proof, testimony sufficient and satisfactory.

Well, what is that the world has in regard to faith of bibles of tradition ? Assertion, statement most perjured of its characters, who have the power and authority to place the world right in all such matters. That is the very thing to fix debasing despotism on the minds of the people. Now the priestocracy draw back from honorable proof, instead of seeking, like honest people, to help all investigate. Their platform is a miserable and degraded perjury, instead of taking the legitimate comprehension of the whole subject. The mass of the people is not capable, by their customs and habits, of acting, till revolutionized.

All public matters should be to enlighten mind and better morals, cause truth to be revered as principle, and perjured sophistry to be rejected as falsehood.

The lowest organization of society must have some virtue, or the cement is too defective to last. The law of retaliation, even among humble Indians, exhibits proof of retributive justice. Badly raised people throw their ignominy on the fountain source, and all reflect on the state. When base acts are prominently the effect, the world then acknowledges that the parents should have checked the base thoughts of their offspring. But what if the parents, as is too often the case, should be in the same category ? What will be the result, inevitably, but the worst display of malignant passions ? The world has to reject old regimes of scholastic dogmas not consistent with science, and to correct defects of social organizations that do not execute the requisitions of morals. National morals beget individual correctness. National demoralization should be prevented, estopped, by all wise regulations. The true moral and religious condition of the world constitutes the most elevated standard of taste, virtue, and benefit to mankind, and will vindicate themselves in or out of courts of justice.

The important measure of civilization must be sought in all the essentials. Among the whole, none casts a higher reflection on the elevation of society than true politeness. To be in the company of gentlemen, and have the principles of politeness, is never to permit others to commit an improper or false step. Who ever lost anything by genuine politeness and courtesy ? A true friend, if qualified, should tell in advance all that is expedient, to prevent unsuccessful and bad results, ere victims are committed in public.

But the bold flights of genius cause exceptions, to say the least, of a theatre that may not be comprehended. There should be universal permanent boards of education to promote the enlightened mind of the sovereign people of the world, that is worth all that can be rightly done for them.

The world must be placed in that moral, intellectual, and religious position, that, when principles are duly carried out, there shall be no antagonism thereto.

Nothing protects national morals so much as due justice to all essential points. The honesty of all governmental contracts, and their faithful performance, should be duly exacted. Good faith is due in every public measure, especially in the purity of elections. Nobody is exempt from all his just indebtedness by bankrupt laws, or any other provisions, if he can possibly reach a state in life rendering him competent to the payment. Without good, not peculiar, faith, whose word can we take at all scarcely, when much money is the question? Who of thousands would make a correct rendition, under the present regime of society, but for strict legal exaction? Do nations act justly toward each other without such principle? Is international law on the highest principles? How many collectors prove defaulters; how few act properly! How many public officers fail to do full justice to the public! Thousands are taken out of the public treasury from the dereliction of principle, and yet the class of defaulters are not punished. All this must be effectually met by not only wise legislation, but the most efficient administration, without favor or partiality. No government, no matter the name, is valuable that is not faithfully administered.

Public charters should embrace all comprehensive constitutional powers to provide for all necessary public good, as conservation for public peace, tranquillity and prosperity, and counteract all practicable evils, nuisances, and the like. Counteraction of most evils, and the example of evil men's vices, constitutes a great protection, and even source of happiness, to society and mind.

Pirates, single or in mass, will swarm, if permitted with impunity. Where one evil of perverted mind might exist under law's regulations, thousands would ensue on any other basis. Let there be a proper limit to all things.

After all, the world must yield that mankind has the elements of good, that perverted mind estranges. Many of the class of miseducated people have never had any proper position for rational mind; they do not know that they should never promise unless they complied.

He who studies self-interest rarely looks enough at principle.

Keep out of company that is bad, or where independence and feelings are compromised.

The world must be taught by rational codes, and the beginning must be made at the mother's temple of honor.

Mankind, such as are here portrayed, must be taught principles, and at the earliest periods of mental availability. A large class of the world care nothing for bibles palmed on the world.

All that rationality needs, is what is rational tuition. They must know that all are bound to principle, as the universe, including mind, is bound to its consummation, religion.

If we knew many people, we hardly would have anything to do with them. The clans in society must be rightly met by society.

The world has to get rid of all social and civil circle nuisances. Many people, when they lose their equilibrium of mind, prove themselves nobody, unprincipled, and will take all undue insidious advantages of their opponents.

There are some people palmed on the world presuming on assurance and impudence. Have nothing to do with the really suspicious character. How many of perverted mind can forego present gratification?

Analyze some people, and then you can see man in his abject, contemptible deformity. when you see him in his peculiarity.

No one should get himself into difficulties, neither official nor available. All principles teach this. The highest tuition attainable to man is from that source.

But the world cannot expect regulated order all at once, on its past inefficient regimes of undeveloped mind, that have helped to enlarge the amount of felons and petty larceny people.

Conservative principles for good, and penalties for bad citizens, should be upheld.

Analyze the piracy on the world, national and individual, and it is enough to ask for all the precautions of mind in its deepest thoughts and wisest regulations. See the conflagrations of cities by incendiaries, the stealthy murders and assassinations, robbery and wholesale plunder, the destruction of various kinds of property to obtain the insurance.

There are millions in the world, in whom. though not essentially worthless, I could not possibly have any confidence, where mind vassalage or serfism prevails.

What can the world do with unprincipled people? When we duly analyze society, then we know our own comprehensive rights and duty. A man too often superficially regards himself, whereas he should guard against the whole world in the right way.

For what use or benefit is the long life of some bad people? They use no energy to produce capital from talents or industry, and are apparently a dead weight on society. Their proceeding reflects on the nature of mankind, for want of intelligent use of mind, and, above all, want of gratitude to their creator. No one has any original idea how mean man can be, when the creature or the subject of a clique, or peculiar views. The world must prepare to see many persons in antagonism, not exactly in the penitentiary, but competent to do things that will entitle them to its passport.

The best is, have nothing to do with all such, as far as practicable. But on some occasions you may not help yourself; then bind such party by contracts, before responsible, disinterested witnesses. At first they are drones, and then the curses of society. Society should not be outraged by the evil machination of the bad. The world suffers materially. How can it counteract them?

I have seen the son of him that was in the category of a fraudulent conveyer of property, perjure himself, swearing deliberately to handwriting that was not the one stated.

Can there be any principles anywhere, when they seek to break up their friends by perjury, for securityship which they advanced to gain funds for speculation?

People are not so bad in the majority; but bad associations, peculiar education, and social organizations, may cause deviations from rational rectitude.

Self-interest inspires many tricks. One man smuggles his property, causes his children to cheat and defraud, and become perjurers! How many of these people wind up in houses of refuge, the penitentiary, and prostitution, all to end in a public charity or hospital? The most of these people have peculiar tuition ere they attain to their art.

There are many things, the most important in life, that we may never know of till too late. We can not have a rational code of life, in all the essential departments, too quick.

Can we bind the conscience of an unprincipled man? We must keep the world from hurting us. It is impunity that makes felons of the highest classes.

Some are very bad in the world, without any moral culture. The world must make all due allowance, by due correction, for peculiar education, culture and rearing, that ruin the most.

This class is unfortunately abundant in every circle of the world. Why commute the punishment of those who commit deliberate murder? Let not those in rich or high circles escape, as if the world owed any thing to rank, money and influence. Why should downright, blood-thirsty murderers escape condign punishment? Make an example for the benefit of society.

What does not the world owe to society?

Protection of life, liberty and happiness. Then do not violate her noblest characteristics nor vitiate her highest purity. There is much of low organization that becomes nuisances to society, by perverted state of character.

The State should protect society against all these evils, and prevent, as far as practicable, all felonies. Much of mankind is more animal than mental, and will be, in action, till a right mind-culture is strictly and universally established. Look at the perjurers, in the court cases.

How many millions, in cities and country, are ready for bids and bidding in petty matters of daily business: what shall be the estimate of the many millions to-day willing to commit themselves on peculiar faith, the most dangerous because the most corrupting article the world deals in. The world cannot be involved deeper than it is, except by deeper ignorance by this lower deep, in fanaticism, bigotry and superstition.

Individual sins are bad enough in drunkenness, lust, lying and cheating; but all the imposition of the world is mastered by the preceding, that paves the way for the worst results.

What seems much worse than fraudulent conveyances of property, causing suborning of witnesses, sometimes of the same household, as the son for the father, by perjury, or acts that just graze the penitentiary?

But how can the world make a brotherhood of such degradedly bad men? It is the animal, the hyena untamed, uncivilized, that is thus degraded. Of course, the full comprehension must go to the best light, a rational mind, at once—to the very first germs of thought—to all refined blessings of rational education.

If the germs of thought be perverted by peculiar education, the deformity is conformable thereto.

If the mind be spoiled in the raising, we can not expect the full value of mind. There are some countries that are greater volcanoes of crimes than others. All this appears, on full investigation.

Yet you do not, nor can you, know the world without a life's experience. The best you can do, you must seek the true analysis of others, well versed in world and mind science.

But hell is necessary for such fellows, that pay no respect to the principles of God, or society's best institutions. Whose fault is that, after all the world's proscription by inquisitions, of those very principles? Besides, there is the penitentiary, and still you let them escape. It is the fault of some system, or its administrators; if in the judges or juries, then alter, till mind vanquishes the whole difficulty, which it will have to do to reach proper civilization.

We must all look at the elements of vice, as of cholera, to comprehend the whole relations of creation. We should arrest effectually the least evil productive of murder; to do so, no clan should escape with impunity. Without Lynch Law, the whole community can unite to enforce the due requisitions of wise laws, and be satisfied with no less.

Even the society of Indians, savages they are called, is properly governed by the certainty of their punishments. An Indian may kill, when rendered drunk by the vicious course of the whites, but atones for it when sober. He feels a doomed man, and most rarely seeks to avoid his fate, or punishment, rather. Thus let it be with all guilty of actual murder.

How wantonly rude much of mankind is! What do they care for the rights, much less the feelings, of the world. You will see that their perverted minds have not improved their phrenological deficiencies, who have no suitable equilibrium. There are some dangerous people in the world, a great, vulgar nuisance, drink or no drink, badly, miserably misraised, not raised at all.

When drunk, they are the worst fiends, and often get shot by their equals in excitement. They have little or no chance shown them, in a peaceable community. Their best defence, as the best defence of the world, is principles all the time, not double barreled guns. Such people have actually outlawed themselves in society, which has, in self-defence, to treat them as their demerits require. The statesmen of the world, as well as parents, will think of this; and the wise will be sure to give all practicable and necessary for rational education.

Some of these characters would break up the fountains and functions of justice, so perverted are their minds. They have cliques and clans, even to perjure.

Who is safe? There are two great classes by the organization of the world at present; one is too pure for corruption of this character, to be made no better by bibles of tradition; while the other can be restrained only by the strictest powers of the law, and whom nothing but the penitentiary can keep from all base things.

Proper punishment for these is healthy for the community. No society can exist without it, as we see by the example of the Indians, who punish certainly for all murders. We had better never know some characters, unless it be to know the deformities of human nature. They are the most perverse and degraded; some who would ruin the world any way, surely if they had a chance, and they are of both sexes.

But let not this corrupt class think of escaping, because there is no local hell. They may insure a worse condition, if they provoke it, till their purification comes. That they may and do defer, and may have to encounter all the costs, the wear and tear, the remorse, the corroding canker of a guilty conscience, under the self-vindication of principles.

But there must be a hell for the abandoned. Not necessarily a located hell, as retribution is more successfully left to God and his principles, that vindicate themselves and avenge him. The hell is in the culprit's own mind, and that is too often on this earth.

We have seen the worst results to society from the cunning pirates too wary of the penitentiary. Well is it then that a hell is not located in place after man's thoughts and bible's pretended gospel, but God's more effectual way, in the mind. Peculiar faith cannot fix a hell, a purgatory, or the like. Who has seen in others retributive justice? Let them take care it be not their state. There are some stupid beasts, in man's form, that might be remoulded many times to reach the true standard, to approach God's magnificence and greatness. The misfortune is that they belong even too much to the highest circles, and the world pursues a mistaken policy in regard to making differences as to respect of persons, who violate the laws of the country. Why do republicans act so? Well might the political economist ponder as to the benefits of this class to the community. They can arouse up the latent energies of mind and body of the public to counteract their schemes.

There are some people so lost to sense and modesty of shame, that you cannot get a hold on them by a slight public opinion.

Enlightened public opinion is one of the great conservators of virtue, but then you must have society in a conservative condition. Put then this best brand of society on the delinquent, by proper, wise, and efficient legislation.

Too much of the human life is so perverted by corruption, &c., that man will say, do, and affect any and everything, as immediate self-interest dictates.

Cliques have vassals to obey them, at the expense of mind and principles. Has society been so miserably corrupted, by peculiar faith and its priestocracy? How is the society of worthless people instituted, but of dangerous intrigue against justice? See its perjury, swindling, and collusions.

How many are spoilt in the world by mixed associations, whose licentiousness outrages public morals and opinions? Some of these worthies of the world cannot be reached by law, as in the frontiers, where the froth of the people will work itself off. The world must counteract its cliques and clans.

How many of the world study secret crimes, and aim only not to be caught in secret felony. Is that the creed of a corrupt world?

Keep at a distance from any not possessed of principle, or keep clear of any man that is unprincipled.

Some people's conduct is full of sophistry and corruption. They will jump over or on others' rights, prostrate merit, to seek popularity of self.

The concealment of vice is a secondary consideration with virtuous wisdom, that seeks the avoidance of penalties, as well as anticipate the whole evils otherwise incurred.

Place the vicious in a state of passiveness, as in the penitentiary, to do them good. What can be done with some minds, that have no proper shame of the world, but in the refuge of dark retirement? They have no principle, and have to learn by the severest teachings of experience.

All they do is to pirate on the blessings of society.

They act as if the world was spoils for them.

All that some unprincipled pirates in society study is to get the advantage, get the world's money, power, and influence.

What do the dishonest care for public opinion?

Can it reach them in their circle?

This is an important question about society in general, and may disclose too much of the same quality.

What would the world be, but for the majesty of government, order, and good laws, properly administered?

How many of the world are enslaved to the lowest passions, the lowest state of mind? They are too much of the animal to know or adopt good advice.

The main thing is in the raising. There is where so many minds in this world are ruined.

A man that has no respect for himself, or his word, has but little respect for others, or their word. We lose thousands in the world's schools : for want of rationalized principles. Here religion is needed in rationality. How many are the slaves of habit, custom, and money. How much is sacrificed to these gods of idolatry. Many such get smuggled into good society, that has to be on its proper guard.

The world has to be guarded, from the lowest to the highest circles.

What would the world be, without laws, and their proper execution?

If man or woman turn loose in licentiousness, they can out-do all animals, in that.

The world suffers awfully, by the collusion of cliques and clans for power, to shield vice ; but when such has certain exposure, and no immunity or impunity, then there is the least, or no reckless villany. The power of universal justice is to stop tyranny, oppression, usurpation, and monopoly.

As humble and trifling as each individual may be in the world, still he fills a unit in space and existence, and is missed, when taken away.

What can the world think of the lawless though law-abiding individuals, but that they are worthless?

There are some lawless individuals, who still seek all the law provisions and protections, under the short mantle that veils neither motives nor their dishonesty, much less the assumed garb of their pretensions. Their hypocrisy clearly proves what is their state of morals. They put themselves by all their acts beyond reasonable protection of the world's esteem, in regard to public opinion, alienating all respect in an enlightened community.

In their families they are tyrants to those most needing protection and guardianship, driving them from home desperate, and to be ruined in character, at the mercy of the merciless.

Righteous judgments, vindicative of high-souled principles, must overtake them who sacrifice the feelings of victims suffering in silence, and keeping the burning secrets buried.

In not less culpable state are those who see their dependent friends in abject poverty, without help, almost mocking them, in their plenty and abundance.

Overreaching, by arbitration of interested partisans and meanness, will be attempted in all manner of ways.

In the analysis of first principles, if such be degradation of the mob-spirit, what must be that which creates and arouses its causes? Legislators and law officers cannot do too exactly their duty.

How senseless the multitude must feel, that they should be at warfare about contentious individuals, that have controversies in politics, about the stage, and have seen the community get into a perfect storm, while the two disputants cared only for themselves!

Why not let the two individuals decide the contest for themselves, as the least of all possible evils?

If such proceeding be excited or headed by individuals affecting a better circle of society, then a very signal penalty should be certainly inflicted.

When the money power is prostituted to public bribery, to excite the mob spirit, then the penalty for felony should be visited promptly and adequately.

Very often, lawless men, relying on their cunning and duplicity, adventitious aids, are made to feel the law's penalty, by imprisonment, heavy fines, and damages, that they pay.

The thousand compulsory acts of neighbors, also of debtors, who force creditors to compound, are to be classed in the acts of the dishonest, if not worthless. So many worthless people present a vast theatre, where multitudes could be changed by the right instruction. There is in the world an excess of coarse, vulgar effrontery, that shows the worst perversion of the very highest evidences of mind. Too much of mankind, under the regime of such things, expose their base ingratitude to the noblest gifts. Much allowance is to be made, by the perversion of legitimate taste and refinement. With such men, the most of the wisdom of the law, is possession.

While some friendships cannot be purchased for any price, others are sold too dear at any purchase.

The mere acquaintance with some compromises safety and prudence. Not that money is the only object about worthless people, but the great object is to keep them from transgressing morals. Give away, if you prefer it, all your possessions to the most worthy objects of benevolence, but let not such characters get the advantage of you.

There are certain clans, in all circles, that will domineer over the whole, if the people let them; but it is the interest, and certainly the highest duty, to unite in putting down all such brutes.

Some people know nothing, care for nothing, do nothing, amend nothing, live for nothing, and die nothing.

Where is mind? Are these the guides? How, or where? What good can they do?

ENLIGHTENED PUBLIC OPINION.

This is the representative of the noblest and purest sentiments, if in advance of the age, and guardian of the sublimest public actions, that lead to man's true position. It establishes universal principles to secure the largest amount of happiness.

It is the tribunal at which the world's good has the best audience, and generous actions the best appreciation. It surveys the past with the eye of philosophy, the present with just observation, and the future with the wisest anticipation.

It brings criticism to a right arbitrament, the proper definite views of reason's guide and monitor, and rules out the mock assumptions of custom, and the false pretences of fashion.

It arrests those that are unable to supersede by as good, much less a better, mere radicals or destructives without the virtue of conservatives, acting under the imposition of false criticism, so often foisted with mock dignity on the public.

The best protection of the world from mind, is in an enlightened public opinion. The people are surrounded by supposed evils of magnitude, supreme over their feeble powers of ignorance, in a state less than proper cultivation of intellect. To whom but interested advisers can they apply, when they neglect their own rightful means?

What cannot unprincipled beings do, with power?

What guarantee have the many that their rights are protected, but through mind? And what can mind do, without rightful rational culture?

Unless this great conservative principle prevails, high treason is committed, or the supreme laws are circumvented by collusion.

An enlightened public opinion should speak rightly through the press, by journalism, reviews, and just criticism, as well as in primary assemblies of the people; comprehending the world's relations.

A free and enlightened press must be untrammelled, conservative for good, repellant of evil, and competent to recognise the right, else the seal of silence should be perpetual.

But few editors are qualified for their responsible vocation. Whenever they cater to a vitiated and depraved taste, then public opinion, if enlightened, can be severe in disapprobation.

Organic principles are to be duly respected and evolved, that shall master the rest, and fully command the minutest points.

The true science of the principle of protection is for the ablest minds to consider, in the ablest manner.

What can fortify best of all, more than an enlightened public opinion? The result of reflected light on the globe from universal freedom, dispenses this potent power.

Nearly the people of every nation, with any pretension to civilization, is now appreciating this bright light. With zealous co-operation of continental union, they can attain the great fundamental truths of self-government, the noblest of all. Science may become so exact in all departments, that the actions of enlightened mind may be universally correspondent on inherent principles. A proper code for mind in all its social and religious principles can be secured, because this enlightened state of things will cause their practice, and be satisfied with nothing less.

This code will not be that of a conqueror or civilian, but of exalted mind, evolving its practical benefits.

The greatest good to the greatest number, that is all, embraces a proper enlightened and liberal code, that comes the nearest to exalted practicable and common honest sense purposes of creation.

This position of principles goes against any great public follies or vices, threatening to be national, as repudiation, disunion. There are many things conservative inherent in government, that may become destructive, if not let alone by wise legislation.

We need a general conservatism for best government of the world. If the people be right on principle, and intelligent to keep so, the government partakes of their character, and must be right, without corrupting tendencies any way.

An enlightened public mind will see that there can be no legitimate union of powers, as of church, banks, working-power or aristocracy, with the state. The world has to deplore their corruptions in the social circles of nations, otherwise the freest.

Without equitable principles, the world clashes in the peace of families, much less in the politics of nations.

No republican action can ever be confined to mere names and party, but on honest common sense principles, that take away the causes for the world's antagonism.

Any proper sacrifice of property must be sustained, that repudiation of the state be prevented by wise legislation, that should never involve the public credit at first in inextricable debts.

The great benefit of enlightened public opinion is to comprehend the remotest relations, to establish the most efficient promotion of the best, and the most potent counteraction of the worst effects.

The great question of the world is, to escape the selfish and brutal tyranny of benighted oppression in all its bearings. We need previous instructions by a code from the supreme court in legal wisdom, that will teach the highest practical lessons to mind. It takes the soundest mind to appreciate, and virtuous characters to prevent, with proper independence, the world's malign influence.

Whilst rational mind should contribute its greatest good to, it must be protected against the worst evils of the world. What punishment is worse than a just, enlightened public opinion, that forces any culprit in the community to hang his head, and retire from its just frowns?

The guilty may undertake to deny, but under the cognizance of its facts clearly proved, the effect is withering and lowering, and the culprit cannot dare face its just indignation. Its judgment, as righteous, is forever without appeal; and reformation is best for such a doomed character.

Such never permits the evils of corrupt legislation, but wisely provides constitutional and organic protection.

Even enlightened public opinion is such, that the working-people of London have rebuked the butcheries of despotic monarchs, and reflected back the rights of mind.

As to this thing of public opinion, does it reach near all the world, part of which as yet defies it, or is below it? There is yet such a morbid state from sophistry in high places, that the world's opinion is not right by a great deal.

No tradition of past ages, nor any authority of any age is needed, after mastering the correct principles of reason, to tell us our duty as to omission or commission. Neither priests, preachers, nor clergy, assisting the autocrats, monarchs, and absolutists, of all governments, who have enslaved mind, can direct or mould public sentiment when enlightened.

The highest authority of all doctrines, a cultivated and virtuous intellect, has ever proclaimed and studiously so, by conscience, all that is necessary to the world in the boldest characteristics. Thanks to the Eternal Supreme, our God-given mind is always with us, or under the mind's guardianship, when mind is rational, and government in abeyance thereto.

We may never know any monitor better, for God enlightens and addresses it with all necessary inspiration of reason, wisdom and knowledge.

We are not only led by the force of all such to estimate such momentous decrees, but we are also incited to regard all the higher attributes of man's nature.

The fear of exposure in reputation and all consequent penalties, restrains much of society otherwise reckless of principles. There are many noxious public evils and injuries that the world or national morals must properly meet, that must be recognised through an enlightened public conservative opinion. There are many dangerous writers, who seek to corrupt and are only to be punished this way. Wise legislation should be invoked, in this whole department of public national morals.

The sights of improper pictures, are highly reprehensible. What shall the conservative part of mankind do, to be best protected from the degraded, worthless, unprincipled components of society? We must institute the whole comprehension of principles to embrace the world.

Those false to society, are to be strictly, firmly and consistently dealt with, else Lynch law, another evil of immense magnitude and demoralization, may arise.

There should be a proper surveillance of people's employment, especially in cities.

Hold public officials responsible to the audition of their accounts. There should be no control of prices by cliques, the money market, &c.

Proper competition in principles fix life for the world, and all proper developments. Do not let labor be degraded, but always elevated. Monotheism requires of all appropriate honest labor, for vital maturity with vigor, to do full justice to all the functions of man.

THE PARAMOUNT RIGHTS OF SOCIETY.

ALL its enlightened and honorable governments essential and necessary to its existence, must rest on constitutional popular basis, and universal fundamental principles to be conservative and permanent.

The paramount obligations of society, demand this inalienable and invaluable position. An enlightened public opinion is its best tribunal, and the very soul of the existence of invaluable society.

All else, sooner or later, will be scattered from its inherent elements of destruction, into fragments.

Past history tells the tale of formidable empires, powerful in the hosts of embattled men by land and ocean, but their unprincipled influence yields to pre-eminence of mind devoted to the world's good, not its destruction and conquest attained at the cost of barbarism.

The vital interest of the world, demands the full satisfaction of these rights, when fully prepared for their enjoyment. It is mind raised to the capacity of mind's soul, that best secures it. All violence in such society is nugatory and hurtful to its good, as the law-abiding, order-loving government supporting virtue, is sufficient to shield the world.

The predominance of vice, prevents the realization of this important constituent of man's happiness.

The very existence of enlightened public virtue, constitutes a guardian that repels a thousand evils, creates a negative and a veto to the worst of crimes.

It is the safest element of nations' greatness and vitality, and gives that durability to their existence, that is self-elevated and most self-sustaining. The protection of man's rights includes the social duties, and embraces the highest evidences of rational duties to the creator. The proper foundations of laws, cause them to be no respecter of persons violating them, who should not escape their penalties, nor corrupt their execution.

The voice of the mere politician, must be sunk in the invaluable one of the statesman and patriot. All else are its substitutes for time, and cannot permanently supersede the world's imperial wants, without subterfuge and bad faith.

Such principles contended for, will promote the union of clashing interests, that should be compromised correctly to be permanently directed to the good of all.

All must seek that, which shows the loftiest legitimate freedom. Society must respect self-preservation.

It has to use penitentiaries, the least evil for the greatest good to the greatest number, which should embrace the rarest and most profitable trades and employments, to least affect the good of the community, and less curtail the vital existence of the institution to be supported from the products of its own industry, independent of state taxes.

This system of labor and punishment protects the people, and supersedes the most of even capital punishment. Discipline has to be preserved even with the best, else a degeneracy. Society may yet be so constituted as to found systems of rewards, to be so graduated, that moral delinquents should receive the least possible, for human existence. The culprit of the penitentiary, for the time of confinement, is degraded from participation in the universal enjoyment of liberty. Whipping and branding kill up the sensibilities, and crush the spirit, therefore they should never be used but in the very last resort. As relics of barbarism, let them be superseded by nobler means. Too many efforts are made in this world, to crush the helpless. Most that is done, ought to be done to exalt, and not make people sensible of demerits.

There are thousands of antagonisms in life, that can be illustriously diffused if mind act rightly.

Too often is it the case, that those having power, seek to throw others under obligations, when they are only equals if more than debtors themselves.

When the glorious era of limit to peculiar education and its odious obliquities shall be established, and mind's peculiar perversions directed to their legitimate channel by all the noblest influences of its highest rationality, then the world may expect to see penalties substituted by rewards, and a happier state of human existence shall be announced.

What rational mind is capable of individually, may be anticipated to a great extent in mass, under the most favorable influences invoked.

The world then is bound to elicit all the available means.

To reach the noblest impulses of conscience, mind must be elaborated into its best and most favorable rationality. Are you in want? Work, labor. But there is the difficulty. Who can always command the appropriate employment? The public, statesmanship, must provide for all this.

The position in the world with plenty of valuable business to do, is indeed great.

Let society have bankrupt laws to defeat the corrupt or weak squandering of the debtor, to do justice to all. Something has to be done, as the very first principles of society are most awfully violated, as by murders now constantly being enacted by the world, individually and nationally.

The whole world has to do something, the best under all its circumstances, commensurately with mind and soul's religion.

HUMANITY.

This noble quality of mortals is the qualified claimant for Deity's mercy and justice, and bespeaks man's highest tribute and his most grateful returns in his circle of civilization.

It is profitable for the soul, as a treasure ever equal to all the drafts, and it is the redeeming quality of its many errors. It surveys the past for wise correction, the present for happy enjoyment and tranquillity, and the future for soundest hopes.

Man or beast is safe under its protection ; the tender infant smiles in its sunshine, and old age is happy in its prospects. The longest practicable life and a pleasant one, is its possessions. The slave becomes cheerful and acquiesces in his lot, and adds proper sources of profit, to those that claim them. Proper treatment of brute beasts and animals tell, that become comely in its sight under its superior superintendence when practicable, and proclaim that cruelty is folly and wasteful false economy.

Excess of labor for ordinary purposes is not in its philosophy, as excess of gains is ruled out of its administration on that ground. Overworking, as overcropping, is unwise, as its results are inhumane, and necessarily injurious. Humanity, the interest of all, is united to practical wisdom.

It is a physiological fact, that excessive labor and exercise will stiffen up animal fibre of all kinds, and induce premature decay and injury.

It is told me by intelligent acquaintances that you may run a fox by hounds, till the animal is stiffened to death by the excess of fatigue.

A morbid excessive secretion from all the joints is poured out, beyond tolerance or healthy action. Hence it is that persons unduly exposed and overworked, are lost irrecoverably before a ripe old age.

The influence of severe climates and undue exposure, render healthy persons sickly, and prematurely destroy them. Humanity is then the better part of discretion, and saves many per cent. in the main to all concerned.

There should be little or no night labor for day laborers in appropriate latitudes, or not more than ten hours taken in all the twenty-four.

That labor should be temperate, gentle, and such that the party can be well sustained under its performance.

Let no inhuman task-master presume to exceed this, at his peril. If he violate the laws of humanity, it will be avenged on him many fold.

Let those in power observe the proper rules for rest, and let a wise philosophy direct its whole suspension at least one day in seven, for soul of man, and body of laborers and beasts, that all may be well with them and duly prosper under the best security for universal prosperity.

Let wise legislation give due observance to all such essentials, and enforce the best regulations.

If humanity preside with real character over all governments, mankind will take due care and protection of all servants and animals under their charge.

Animals should not be owned, without the capacity of the owner to do justice to them.

They should not be driven unnecessarily on the Sabbath or by night, nor exposed to injury, poverty, chilling falling weather and piercing cold, or suffocating heat. The horse quickly shows his treatment. If bad, it is cruel.

The iron horse of railroads, the work of mind, has well supplanted the hard-used stage horse, that did not live half his days.

As science improves mind, the last must necessarily become more humane. This is well illustrated in regard to the best treatment of all kinds of stock, that become better and more profitable on improved husbandry. Pedigree and good rearing or breeding, are important combinations.

What has not humane science done for this whole department? By recent distinguished discoveries the best result of the labor of the bees is obtained in glass-houses, of the purest honey without the death of a single bee.

When mind thus throws its humane protection over the parts of creation subject to its rule, imparting a reciprocal agency, then the legitimate results are secured for the good of all.

In regard to laborers, whether in servitude or anyways allied to it by hire or wages, the wisest counsel to each, according to his or her mind, will be decidedly the most humane.

Do not in this particular err; you may estimate too often the character of others' minds by your own. This is not altogether right, as you must not take any such thing for granted at all, since some minds are not enlightened by the proper mental light, yet therein is written a receptacle for light. Do not disregard the elements that merely require the proper evolution.

Yes, counsel all those that work for you when expedient, as it will be better than corporeal chastisement if available, that too often is equivocal in its pretensions.

If you can treat all as rational beings, how much better will it redound to your good, and reflect the noble capacity of your intellect, the refined action of your benignant mind.

Recollect you the old arbitrary mode of government, that applied to nations and individuals? Was that wise or profitable in the end?

Punishment and penalty can be superseded, by reward and reasonable treatment. Public enlightened opinion has now obtained that the sailors of the United Sates navy shall be treated more like rational beings.

The world should seek the abolition of flogging and spirit rations, in the navy, army and all departments. Flogging in our navy has been abolished by act of Congress, except as to any decision of a court-martial. The brutality in the naval and military service has been deplored, as one of the evils of social organization.

Humanity calls for the counteraction of the tyrannies of pedagogues and overseers, superintendents, dynasties of foolish, cruel and corrupt people of either sex assuming dictation.

How repose humanity and moderation, with the corruptions of monarchy and despotism of church and state? Freedom elevates and devotes the human character. Humanity must be protected in all her empire over the world; while no subject is too humble, none are too high to be exempt from her benefit. The most humane are the wisest on earth.

He who acts by another's severity or inhumanity, does the act himself. This principle holds good, as all principles, universally.

Where can mankind go amiss in this world for the objects of humanity, the true test and standard of enlarged humanity? We should not only use no wanton cruelty or destruction in life, but omit no rational opportunity of affording relief to prevent it, in the best sense of the word. This shows refinement, courtesy, humanity, and civilization. Under the auspices of humanity, the gentleman has all that religion can do for him.

A true gentleman respects all others: the rights of the absent stranger, as of the present citizen.

Among its greatest blessings, are her wisest tuitions of duty and justice to the living, and due respect to the burial of the dead.

It has devolved upon mind's reaction to cause the beauty and strength of mind to be seen and felt by the world, the beneficiary, in every department of life.

The true act of government will advance mind to the capacity of happiness, not leave it in the degradation of punishment—never! But will the facts of the case, after all, justify any sentimentality that is not strictly utilitarian? It might seem very questionable, whether duty of sailors can be adequately secured without corporeal compulsion, but the main question of rational mind has not been touched yet.

The highest order of humanity is that of right action of mind, to give the proper employment of time, and not devoting working people in useless, profitless, and injurious employments, that not only keep persons on the stretch all the time, but expose them thereby, killing them up finally.

Humanity and courtesy are dictated as one of the best policies of the whole world, in all climates.

Animals have not the same chance as people. If their mute signs were attended to days before the last stages, generally the first recognised, the cases would not be so fatal from this and other deep-seated congestions and inflammations.

Where is it that humanity and mind do not apply in this wide-world theatre?

A man should seek no more in his household than he can provide for with proper humanity.

The wretch, clothed in little brief authority, absurdly expects immunity in all his unjust and reproachful deeds. But he miscalculates, without rationality. If he permit his ungovernable passions to play the fiend, he is their victim. Short-sighted revenge recoils most powerfully. Barbarous treatment may excite the deepest infliction of injuries of the injured, who may invoke all the deadly potency of the elements on the injurer, who too often finds in a few moments the work of a year destroyed by the fire of the incendiaries. What peaceful emotions are excited by a just and enlightened humanity, that comprehends all the world-relations in its religious benevolence, and that long before the death-bed scene. Does your mind seek to tempt? Avoid all that as the worst taste, the violation of the first principles of humanity. What a sacred thing is feeling: the avenger has an avenging. Do not be inhumane; it is not good for all reasons. Do not presume on impunity, when you have principle that avenges God, as by especial providence; God himself has universal, almighty providence. Do not push inhumanity to that tension, to test the full strength of the camel's back, by breaking it. As to brief authority, be as brief as possible in any abuse. Inhumanity will not do, it ruins the world.

Let the mind, most rational, rejoice that it knows and appreciates humanity and its principles.

Does the world recognise the worth of amiable mind, gentle sensibility, the loveliness of humanity most rational?

SCIENCE.

The world is assumed, by superficial minds, to be not only no better, but worse than that of the ancients.

Then there is less science and more ignorance in general, that produce greater errors, the very reverse of fixed facts. What assurance and impudence, nonsense and ignorance, are expressed in the assertion of the world's present stage being worse than the former.

Mind is so constituted, that its dignity and character rise proportionately to its intelligence diffusion.

The constitution of the world's relations is predicated by the Almighty, to the exaltation of the world's benefit, when mind, rightly directed, rules.

See in past ages what advantages were taken of mind, ignorant, or knowing but little.

Those ages did not prosper, and were amenable to grave and serious charges, of mind's perversions and consequent tyranny.

Then flourished most all the juggleries of hand and mind, through necromancy, divination, oracles—all the psychology that imposition could effect for its sinister purposes.

Then were the days of contingency; but now mind, as in everything, must be man's protection, and necessarily produces more uniform results, the more science directs it. This is conspicuously so in the ennobling qualities of mind, through all the departments of philosophy, and all the permanent mementos of wisdom, up to its highest and most refined rationality.

The world to-day is incomprehensibly advanced in the blessings of civilization, relatively to the predominance of mind's freedom and light, as mind's best developments are now.

Mind is now towering in the science of agriculture, manufactures, navigation, mining, fishing, and commerce, and causes the world to delight in its existence.

Now famine is rarely general in the staple productions of grain and rice, that are adequately supplied for the world's demands, and wisely diffused by a world-wide commerce.

The one article of cotton clothing furnishes the most triumphant pleasures of a civilizing process to the world, while other staples, as sugars, enrich life's choicest viands.

The ignorant state of mind, that was necessarily perverted, made commerce at one time piratical.

The migration of people was on the very basis of piracy. But now science and philosophy interpose their benignant aid, and proclaim that the world is one mighty universal brotherhood, not to be hostilely alienated by race, national interests or bigotry, but united by all the conservation of rational religion.

Science will establish the most enlarged and liberal policy of principles, that rears and rewards men of genius, mind and worth, to their greatest expansion.

Give them only truthful principles, the free play of genius; exercise to invent, but counteract counterfeits.

AN ALMIGHTY.

Providence has amply met all the demands of the mighty increase of the human race as none other could meet it, that has to institute all the agency of science taught to mind by improved means of securing food, &c.

The continents and oceans are yielding their mighty treasures, and acknowledging the triumphant power of enlightened mind!

Now steamers regularly ply over the mightiest Pacific and Atlantic Oceans with expeditious regularity and exact precision, triumphing over the most appalling difficulties, where naught but dangers and impossibilities to all other powers but mind prevailed.

Yet much of the world is in dark ignorance, never to be recovered from but by the genius of mind that speaks, and the power of reason that acts.

The world must be redeemed and disenthralled by the inspirations of genius, the revelations of mind, and the prophecies of time.

Science has to conduct mind to principles, the universe problem solution.

The sacred temple of science is best protected by constitutional rights; its progress best advanced by customs accredited by philosophy, its scope must be free as the air we breathe, and its benefits must be held as sacred as the mind freemen exercise. Time and mind are to reveal, through science, the solution of the balance.

Proper committees might be formed by the people to adequately aid genius and promote its rightful advancement.

The difficulty is often not in the incipient discovery, but in the felon opposition of unprincipled monopolies.

No disciples of philosophical science can be silenced by the world, however they may be hated by the disciples of false sectarian dogmas and usurpations.

The diffusion of science and knowledge is the spread of principles. What is science not evolving?

She now commands the elements, where once ignorance presumed not to go. She is fast advancing in the solution of the world-problems, the very thing that mind had to do to reach the noble standard of reason, and comprehend its vital purpose.

In agriculture, she teaches the world its treasures, that exceed all the magnificence of martial conquests. She teaches subsoil ploughing to reach new materials expedient for the soil, and to fertilize, by returning to the soil through appropriate manures, much that will renew the strength and productive resuscitation. Mind is conservative in the exhaustion of the soil, to afford improvement therefor.

Opposition to science can only be unprincipled from base ignorance or self-interest, and thereby puts all such advocates in false positions; that is, all opposition to science and philosophy results from unprincipled demagogues, who act basely for their own profits and pretensions. The true interests of the world are identified with science, and can present no conflict. When there is especially presented any appearance, the cause is to be regarded as presented by those adverse to both.

Preconceived notions and opinions, prejudices and peculiar faiths, rear their miserable conflicts. The wise of the world should know all this, to appreciate the whole comprehension.

Hail, glorious science! that explodes all the world-humbugs of superstition, and displays all the pretended gods of the world in all ages, and all their worshippers, as degraded impositions.

The great advantages of science in all its departments, as by commerce, will make a universal brotherhood, skilled in philosophy, dignified in mind, and faithful by virtue.

What is science not doing now in the legitimate scope of mind? She is literally mastering the potent elements, that otherwise would overwhelm mind.

Science will disrobe hypocrisy of its pretensions, exciting the world about science, that is supposed to clash with its self-interests in peculiar faith.

Who can wonder that peculiar faith and science should clash, when the last is the only principle? What then remains to be done by the world? To be done with peculiar faith, for science cannot be dispensed with. Science is indispensable to the prosperity of the world, the welfare and happiness of mind.

The great object is to separate science from humbug, that has been practiced beyond appreciation by one part of the world on the other, as if there was one vast conspiracy with but little exception.

To begin then, we must first exclude the ancient mother of humbugs, peculiar faith. It takes all the science that mind can master to read creation right, to which all rational education must best contribute her quota.

See the mighty mineral deposits, in various parts of the world. Can any thing less than science unfold their treasures, or rightly employ them? What exhaustless sea-wealth funds! Are they yet developed? Can we estimate aright all the advantages of the oceans, that modify the temperature of the earth, suitable for all seasons, that bear aloft on their bosoms mind's exhaustless wealth, or that yield their own?

Science now excludes most of life's contingences practicable. What a triumph of mind! It is the great conservative, in eliciting the exhaustless means of industrial labor to promote the welfare of the world's community, until universal principles are established that will be conservative.

Do any pretend to say that science and philosophy can not conduct them best through life to God?

Science enriches the mind and civilizes the soul of man. Bibles of tradition express false theories and delusions of that thing called faith, but science evolves correct thoughts of mind.

Science was meagrely developed in the age of bible writers, consequently they were actually less inspired than the moderns. She truly inspires the mind with faith, causes fanaticism to doff her monstrous delusions and vassalage, making known all facts in time.

All Revelation, to be true, must agree with science, which is the life picture of natural facts.

The scriptures retarded the advance of astronomy, and are in conflict with science. What, better than science, can expose the prophecies pretended of any age of the world? The days of ignorance are necessarily those of miracles. The condition of the world, arising by intrinsic capacity of philosophical science, is the best that God advances. Its beauty will be embellished and its riches evolved in the progress of mind. In the infancy of science, defects of agricultural and commercial, all science, were more frequent, and gave relative injuries by famine, want and suffering.

What would Ireland have done, in the last few years, during her potato rot, but for the aid of commerce and agriculture, and the noble contributions of sympathizing mind? What redress could peculiar faith bring, in such a dilemma? Among industrial pursuits, if agriculture, the lever of life, perish, all perish. Science cherishes it. Analysis, knowledge, science, and wisdom, exalt man to his mental dignity of character.

As science has only partially advanced in some respects, mind unquestionably has to exert itself, to secure the desired triumph for safety, as in regard to the present management of steam, that requires the best prudence which is man's providence.

How far does the present age, by its circle of science, excel the past, by the refinements of its philosophy and the philosophy of its world protection?

The world is indebted to science, in all her departments, whether on land or ocean. Let there be no contingences for exact science.

Ignorance oppresses and enslaves the world, and part of the world takes advantage of the other part.

Why and how is this? What is to prevent all this? Science. What kind? All that is fully comprehensive. Ignorance is the food that the world miracles thrive on. Science proves this, and obviates it.

Independence of mind has to be judged by science, that discloses, every day, more and more the supreme greatness of Deity. She is the true preacher that will convert the infidelity of the bible people, by the intellectual analysis that dignifies man's state. Without her, what is the civilization of the world? The moral must advance with the scientific, as will be necessarily the case on rational organization of society.

Science has enabled the world to reach a high elevation of intellectual benefit, and gives her choice in the selection of patent gifts of nature. Hers is the highway, on ocean or land.

We can only read nature through philosophical science, not by the trammels of the schools, but by the acquisitions and facilities of expansive genius, that looks every way. What changes are in the world by the progress of science!

What gives the chief nations of the world superiority? Theirs is the improvement of science on the gifts of nature. Science is the means to develop mind, that develops the resources of the world. Peculiar faith and education have excited it to hostile animosities, whilst rational education will exalt it to one universal brotherhood. Science reveals the facts of God; her cause is the universal one of truth, to promote the exalted civilization of the world.

She gives the elements of freedom and civilization, improvers of religion, of which God gives the impression to mind. To live above censure, is to have the lights of philosophical science, and be its beneficiary.

Science demands international laws of the justest character.

International copyrights for arts and science must be instituted for good morals. What a guardian of the world is exact science! It is the highest science to be conservative amid most destructive elements.

The advantages of industry, fostered by mind, enrich the world : hence we must have all institutions and rewards for all substantial science.

The industrial pursuits of man are worth more than all the trophies of the sword.

The attainment of modern languages will give mind the requisite discipline, and prepare it for science of mathematics, whilst the knowledge of things and ideas, not words alone, should be fully attended to. The world should attain to original thinking.

CULTIVATION OF INTELLECT—TEACHERS.

The first functionary of the land that comes up to his calling should be the teacher, properly qualified in talents of highest order and acquirements, of elevated refined character for probity and truth, to secure salary and honors of elevated dignity. He should be most satisfactorily competent to command the highest respect of his pupils for his worth, and he should be most amply rewarded.

The education that he should impart must be of sterling worth : while it respects the polite arts and pays due deference to life's courtesies, should uphold all that is substantial and permanent.

A proper rational system, as in all well-directed establishments, should be consistently and uniformly maintained.

A good appreciation of character all the time, referring by circulars daily, weekly, monthly, and semi-annually, to deportment and intellectual progress, will be assuredly best.

These documents may be sent monthly, or as often as expedient. This system can be premised forever with its accompanying rewards, before penalties. The education should have constant reference to higher science, and the institution of the very elements should be consistent to such system, at the same time most assuredly excluding all self-exploded peculiar educational views, whether of bible codes or any other name.

Every rational mind should have correct cultivation in enlightened conservative rational principles, on a suitable code, comprehensive and lucid as light. The mother as well as father, are chiefly responsible for their charge, and particularly for the first six or seven years of age. The first has to form and mould much of the child's character by her looks, voice, words and actions—her conduct the model. What value, then, is attached to that endearing name, around which the heroic and patriotic soul of a Washington placed a garland, ennobling it with his sympathies, sacrificing mere naval ambition to filial affection, refusing rank on royal decks to the gushing tears of a kind mother at the domestic hearth, for which he was compensated by the loftiest triumph of a world's admiration, for deeds done on the holiest theatre, the defence of a nation's rights. Sacred be the emotions in whose defence the philosophic greatness of a Socrates spoke. Let, then, the mother of pure taste, superior to the false notions and fashions of the world, be the mistress of her own nursery, and let no proxy hireling supplant a mother's duty and a mother's care, as wet-nurse or preceptress to a mother's exclusion.

Females should be taught by females.

Teachers fill a mighty duty, next to parents and trusty guardians. Let the best talents conjoined with virtue, be amply requited.

What can be better than to have qualified teachers, satisfactorily imparting the richest science in correct taste, to create a pure refinement, a humanizing civilization. to meet the liberal demands of the world by virtue and mind-fund ? How deficient are most elementary academies in the most important of all principles, those of a right rational education ?

Teachers should possess correct taste in pronunciation, discreet philology, the main feature in reading and speaking. All that speak or read, necessarily address the public, and ought to be heard to the extent of filling, if practicable with their voice, the room in which they are assembled. All should promote the chasteness of language, and accuracy of pronunciation—while all should learn composition with critical accuracy. While ancient and modern languages, geography, &c., train the youthful mind, they also prepare for the matured age suitable for true science that should be profoundly cultivated, in its various departments, mathematical, philosophical, agricultural, chemical, historical, mechanical, through societies, associations, &c., the basis of rational education. It is a moot point whether the ancient languages had not better be displaced by some more useful modern subjects. Where the time of the student is rather limited, they had better be given up. While the learning of languages or the classics may enlarge the capacity and analysis of mental powers, too much time may be consumed in becoming erudite in them.

A suitable library, though a small one, even of one hundred volumes of science and literature well and judiciously selected, will be an invaluable benefit to any literary and thinking reading community. False delicacy has obstructed science.

There is no masculine or feminine science alone, while there may be much to corrupt pervertible minds. All true science is open for all inquiring minds of either sex, while no perversion of knowledge is admissible in the world, that must have its society protected for the good of all.

Formerly stupid adherence to authority of the master was carried to an extent iniquitous to the rights of mind, as to his statement and tuition of science, and was calculated to usurp its progress.

This has been kept up in medicine, and in theology, to the utter disgrace of both, so far as their false masters were concerned. A better light and more liberal policy have attended the system of teaching in most of circles, and better display the mastery of mind, than the mastery of doubtful pretensions, that successive ages have swept away. Some idolatries of books called bibles, and trammels of men called professors, must go by the board, ere the world is conservative.

Mind of the present ages can rightly and justly congratulate itself on the increase of proper facilities of reaching the most desirable object, by increase of books, advantages of journals and newspapers, the works of the press, facilities of commerce, the more general intercourse among all nations, who are improving all the departments of science, by reaction of mind on mind.

Superstition, that darkens and enslaves mind, must yield up finally her degraded pretensions, as the day of more brilliant light approaches, when all assertions, histories and traditions will be only valid, as they coincide with the principles of nature and truth, her best delineators. Then the false pretences of interest and ambition will be reduced to a proper level.

The light of cultivated mind will govern, through reason, the world to her eternal benefit.

Rational education preserves liberty and law, the great conservatives of society.

The world has been misled for thousands of years by mind's perversions, for powers peculiar of money and ambition, government and the priestocracy. It has to plumb the track in the whole legitimate sphere of mind, and must act up to the dictates of nature. This will be done at the proper time, in law, medicine, and theology. The true state of morals is necessarily that of reason, truth and honesty, not faith at all; consequently the world will get wiser as it approaches right, and will be secured in the full adoption of principles.

PROFESSORS.

They should be possessed of analytic minds, capable of reaching the universal facts of nature, rejecting all the sophisticated pedantry of the schools, and renouncing all the pretensions of ancient regimes.

They should be men of the highest order of genius, and should be suitably rewarded by adequate fees. Not only possessed of the highest order of talents, they should endear themselves by the loftiest traits of character to mankind. We have seen some that were possessed of the most degrading points of character, and deprecated their want of honesty, their dereliction in teaching youth, for their equivalent at least. We have seen a junior class swindled out of their medical lectures in midwifery, by the professor taking the senior class to his pavilion, though the junior class had paid for the ticket, thus making private for a few what should have been public to the whole. In this there was no redress of grievances, as the visitors never even had it investigated. The object no doubt being to cause a return of the class by seeking thus to cut them off of *ad eun dem* privileges at other institutions.

We have seen a professor select a private class, thus enabling them to pass off for superiors to their classmates at the examination!

These were false sons of science, raised in a factitious circle of morals, conspiring in collusion for sinister advantages. The facts of such cases impeach these men as opprobrious.

How often are boards of education merely advisory, and appear before the public as nominal inspectors! Many who observe things adverse to public interest and propriety, are not official functionaries, and are therefore ruled out as obtrusive, even for essential information. The world's antagonism is bad enough, but in the effort to do good it is intolerable. With the world's predestinarians, it is all deemed right, any how, however clearly perverted the peculiarly educated mind is.

The world should get rid of all the school trammels of antiquated professors, that are prejudiced to obsolete notions that enslave the world. What shall we say of the mere dogmas of the schools? Are they to restrict mind and restrain genius? Some professors claim all that avarice and despotism of the little brief authority dare assert in this republic.

What can be said of the morals of that professor who imposed pretences to talents by private classes, where they should have been public, to deliver lectures never rendered for money taken therefor?

Worst of all, I have seen perjury perpetrated by cliques of professors to restrict the popular advance of science, the only tenable view that rational mind can accomplish.

The whole framework of society has to be revolutionized, to do justice to conservative principles.

THE UTILITARIAN SCHOOL.

Is that of proper-sense principles, the school of religion?

There is such excess lost by unnecessary professions, waste, extravagance, improvidence, and fines yearly, as would support all the real paupers of the world from first to last.

How much expenditure is lavishly made for the worst of luxuries, as would save the health of the consumers, and promote the blessings of the really poor by mere necessaries.

What is consumed by gorgeous show would *otherwise redound to the world's benefit and happiness.

A small estate in time, is worth a large one out of time. Those rightly independent of poverty or riches, can best enjoy all the smiles of hope and endearments of life's affections, without the failure of reward for proper exertions. This school teaches man to be perfectly independent of the world as far as practicable, and adopt all the exact steps of science to reach that position.

It maintains the noblest aspirations for substantial means to benefit the world. Agriculture is one of its potent elements; its science is particularly regarded, not only as to the immediate best crops, but the best outlays, the best return for the world's wealth, the soil improvement.

Improvers of the soil must see that all crops take away from the soil something, that must be restored by manures of some kind.

One of their important considerations is, to have the consumers brought as near to them, the producers, as practicable. It is false economy to buy cheap articles not worth buying. The world should make legitimate capital out of apparent misfortunes.

Beggars of unworthy merit or suspicious characters should be furnished proper labor, and duly paid therefor. If able to work, and backing out, they can have no proper claim on public sympathy and assistance generally. Some cannot exercise any talents, having never had any active exercise of their faculties that way. Too many have them prematurely directed to cunning, deceit and treachery, and act accordingly correspondent to the great physical principles of matter.

The comprehensive object of this school is to make the world one might family, though placed in five grand divisions and their appurtenant islands of the world. The solution of this world-problem, vast, mighty, and towering in appearance, is attainable in the ethics of rational religion, which premises a perpetual conservative revolution.

Mankind, in obedience to her requisitions, must talk of the principles and practice of a world-expansive justice, of a mind liberalized to its comprehensive mould, before it talks of charity, which is necessarily anticipated by the benevolence of justice.

This school saves the costs of a penitentiary for punishment, and demands the best efforts of the earth, the true strength of the world, to counteract all such by the most comprehensive light of mind.

RATIONAL EDUCATION.

Let every State educate, without failure, her citizens in certain schools of proper order, that the people may always appreciate what is right. Had this prevailed at first, so many conservative revolutions had not been needed, and the world would have been more triumphant in the glories of civilization. Rational education gives proper control, masterly use, and full benefit of mind: builds rightly on its proper funds, takes cognizance of all home raising, renders the parents and friends amenable, and holds the country accountable for what may be responsible to her. Rational education should embrace knowledge and principles of law, for practical life, and render them most available. Why, education, citizen? It is indispensable, to concentrate the powers and virtues of mind. You say that education makes many an individual worse or more vicious.

I must grant that, as the education of the priestocracy has premised the greatest of all demoralizations and vices in the world, for thousands of years. That results from the defects of peculiar education. Education on true, rational principles, embraces the conservative position of the world.

Do you know how to protect yourself? You can not do it effectually short of a mind-fund, liberal as the world's comprehensive principles.

The people have failed, and have to fail, in their most essential rights, because of want of knowledge, that is power. Education, rational to secure wisdom, science, and knowledge, is the world's noblest friend, and is absolutely essential to mind, whilst peculiar education is the world's curse and mind's ruin.

Mankind must embrace what the world needs, to include the right practical view of things.

Individuals and nations have to pay dearly for schooling, in the world's experience.

The public safety binds the world, millions of times, more to support teachers of ‑ational science, than preachers of sectarianism, or peculiar faith ministers, to give the mind fund of analysis of paramount fundamental questions, of constitutional government, and rational religion, that may be perverted, by the prevailing dynasty, to sinister purposes. Truth, reason and science are immutable ; but opinion varies, and must be fixed through rational education that obeys them. You cannot get toleration, much less conservative revolution, unless you obtain it by them.

The world needs the most liberal fund of education, by philosophical science, to be duly exempt from all kinds of imposition and misrule, especially in peculiar faith of bibles of tradition. If we search any of their scriptures or writings diligently, on the conservative principles of rational education, we are compelled to discard them. If the old books or testaments fail for intrinsic deficiency, want of proof of authenticity, so topples the new. What is the new—a patchwork on the old patchwork—worth, if the old be unworthy of confidence ? Physiology, which is rightly embraced by the science of rational education, declares it utterly impossible for any native of the earth to be endowed with a God-birth.

With a liberal and just education, and characteristic freedom, who can be deceived by the miracles of the age ? If the people are predetermined by prejudice and peculiar education, to be deceived, or deceive themselves, then they will be surely, they and their generations, that adhere to the peculiar errors of their fathers.

How much of the world people could be changed to-day, not in intrinsic principles that are immutable, and from which they have strayed, but by the change of ecclesiastical demagogues and sophists, whose interested opinions have misled the world. What is the frame-work of the world society, but of some of the worst delusions and corruptions of mind's peculiar perversions ? But the miserable sophist's followers are scared into all the superstitious fallacies by fears that unbalance mind !

Shame on the supposed lights of the world, that ought to know better, and will not prevent it. Patriots who have the requisite talents and capital, should organize the adequate labor in things so needful. When they deny the world the use of their talents and learning, they do injustice to all. If the world were to exert itself on this point, how many could produce compositions that would commend, not reflect on the capacity, certainly not the want of merit. Rational education will direct properly, talents, capital and labor, otherwise misdirected and misapplied. All this is worthy of deep consideration and correction, as a subject of civil, moral and social economy.

The best of all capital is a character of liberality and justness, of honesty, that yields all right by force of conscience.

Rational education looks to the noblest results of civilization and religion, as it looks essentially to law, order and proper government of principles.

Let us have the era of rational education, to secure the noblest blessing of modern civilization. Rational education enables mind to meet all the most difficult demands made upon it. It is well for the poor and ignorant to have this best defence against the conflict and torment of odd conceits, to conquer which is worth as much as the greatest national or world undertakings. Rational education will enable mind to meet, in suitable dignity, the world-problems to repel those that seek to take all manner of advantages of it. Rational mind cannot trust many of the world, as part are unprincipled, part very weak in intellect, and bad off in education, that has been most miserably perverted by peculiar dogmas.

Rational mind, duly cultivated, can only properly address the Creator, by the sublimity of conservative principles. Rational education can alone impart the true appreciation.

The world should endow with available funds, Universities on rational principles of education.

One of the greatest means and mighty elements of rational education, are the blessings of commerce, that suit for relief in general, famines, pestilence, &c., and that dispenses peace, plenty, and general intelligence. The state governments must direct us to all education that all rational minds must have, under large penalties to the supervisors. There can be but two kinds of education, rational and peculiar, or perverted, that gives peculiar faith, error, vice and crime. In the next step, give all as much independence as practicable, to make them worthy and most useful citizens, that can be the boast, ''.e ornament of the country, the world. All the polite enjoyments of society, as conversation, dancing, music, science, disquisitions, &c., that produce a proper interchange of civilities of the world, between the sexes, are desirable.

Under the right and proper protection of rational education, modest innocence can confront and defy the unprincipled world. Such keeps a healthy state of mind on healthy premises. To confront the unprincipled world immediately by innocence, is to defeat it, and put all on the legitimate purposes of creation.

LIBERAL INSTITUTIONS.

THESE may be classed as moral and intellectual.

Among the first may be placed savings and loan banks, for operatives, various industrial associations for mutual protection, dispensations of contributions to the destitute.

Among them are systems of public lectures, reading rooms, discussion debating societies, the diffusion of rational education to all classes and minds. The people should have free-schools, to the necessary amount, at least.

In the ages of civilization, all things must be referred to protection and science of rational mind. All communities should be furnished with the use of public libraries, association for interchange of ideas, for rational, moral and religious improvement.

The mere pedagogue or priest will not answer the demands of mind. The mere pedant, who affects, is not to direct the immortal mind. Ignorant nations must be taught by national schools. No sectarian missions will meet the case of the world, that should certainly appreciate religion through science, and be taught the eternal law of right is of God, and that no sectarianism can teach, as it cannot touch the subject.

The world has to undergo conservative revolutions in philosophy, government, religion, on rational basis.

It has to discard the errors, vices, and crimes, of all bibles of tradition, atheists, polytheists, or sophists.

Enlightened views must regard the productive agents of wealth and mind, the powers of genius, and the value of industrial labor, rightly directed—giving cardinal and organic developments and regulations, to promote commercial, agricultural, manufacturing, and navigating interests, for the most liberal but just policy of nations.

Some of the highest objects of the world are secured by such institutes as the Smythsonian, for general science of men and the world; Girard's college, for the best liberal commencement of youthful mind, and the library of an Astor, as beneficial to the human race.

The true state of wealth's blessings, is seen in such characteristic advantages. But the foundation must be on the rights and faculties of mind, that must have all rational means to secure the proper expansion of its powers.

There are many institutions that are expedient to carry out the world problem of rational mind, that is to be elevated to its most rational capacity and religious comprehension.

Houses of refuge are essential in cities, for juveniles of both sexes. They may become necessary, in densely populated counties.

They must be considered a necessary expedient, till mind can elicit from its mighty treasury a better means.

The apprentice system must be made available for the millions of youth of country, but of cities especially.

Those deprived of parents should be under proper regulations, especially at night, to preserve morals. The institution of police should be extended to this essential. I have objected to towns, cities, and villages, as they nurture the greatest amount of idle habits. Only think of the rising generation not doing anything, and not able to do so, not knowing, and finally not caring.

Children must not be reared in idleness and ruin, mere loungers. The wisest legislation must counteract all this miserable result. The development of the agricultural resources of the world, of the industrial labor of its citizens, are paramount considerations.

The only proper organization of all societies is on conservative principles, that are as durable as the universe, and indispensable to all society.

MORAL PHILOSOPHY.

WHERE is the standard of morals? Not in selfish ambition and avarice. The acts of the mind in free moral agency may well be compared to the work of laborers in the world, superintended by the chief.

The Creator rightly superintends the universe by his principles, and wisely promotes his necessary purposes. There are many relations of things, that embrace a wide scope.

Does anything go wrong with you? Wait, think, defer, counsel, and ask advice, to avoid all difficulties. You must resort to analysis of all positions legitimate; supply properly the defects by inventions of means ; substitute corrections, to recover the right point ; resort to your genius, for improvement, not to despair.

All moral philosophy must be proved, in the analysis of deportment.

In traffics, dealings, and purchases, in all instances, and in full regard of what is right, just, and correct, give a fair and living price for all ; at the same time receive no statement as true when there is necessity for your own investigation.

Receive no doctrine on trust, as granted, in deference to the mere opinion of man, when you can estimate it by your investigation, much less disseminate any such on your authority as positively right, when others deny the position at all.

Thus it is with all peculiar faith, which monotheists are positively and conscientiously bound to deny as having existence. In discussions use fair principles, without sophistry, else be silent.

Let all professions and creeds be between mind and its Creator, so far as they are a part of republican toleration. Man's works and acts are between mankind, as the best criterion, more or less. A moral and intellectual responsibility rests on all minds, for individual and universal good.

NATURAL PHILOSOPHY.

ALL human knowledge is comparative to its kind, and relative to much of the advantages of the world's age.

Occasionally genius bursts into view of the astonished mind, and wields an importance commensurate with its endowments.

There is too little common sense, and too little exercise of that faculty. Mind, well ordered and self-balanced, can see how well perfected are the Creator's purposes. It will be prepared to acquiesce most wisely in the only dispensations of Providence, not prone to censure or libel the Creator's acts, on imperfect views, that recoil and invariably impeach man.

Man's destiny is his duty to read correctly, and apply the benefit of his observations to his own wisdom and self-improvement, that must operate becomingly in his circle and period. His knowledge must be through science, and give a right direction to the subjects of the world by mind.

What once was superstition's despotism, is now mind's triumph. The mighty storm and tempest subserve the great operations of nature, vivifying and clearing the great ocean masses of water of noxious stagnations and turbid inertness.

How many insects, birds, and animals, are nature's scavengers, all having a useful part and function of life to fulfil, and must be counteracted, if noxiously invasive of man's dominions.

In mastering agriculture, one of the organic levers of vital existence, that raises man in the highest scale of civilization, he must necessarily embrace much of science.

Mind may have ever been disturbed by the hallucinations of superstition, but for the light of philosophical science. Man's fault ought to be remedied by man's mind, not adopt exploded errors much less create censure of Deity. The light of mind declares that any should be rebuked, if not punished by censure, for the nonsense of haunts, ghosts, or spirits, as identified with the world. Only think of the ghosts, spirits, and witches of a bible. What baseness in some who ought to know better, advancing pious frauds to help out the impositions of bibles of traditions !

Among the trophies is geology, that gives us the only true history of the earth, as astronomy will embrace that of the universe. There are many difficult problems to solve in both, that must be in abeyance to the potency of her empire, ruled by enlightened mind.

The atmosphere is the great treasury of nature, for reproduction. How came it so well organized, but by an intellectual, moral, and religious power, of supreme character ?

The excellence of science is to elicit from the world's mighty cabinet all that is suitable for man's use and benefit, to be appropriated on the correct principles of philosophy, and applied on the wisest appreciation of their usefulness.

Geology is essential to philosophical science, to vindicate the truth of natural history, and correct the chronology of tradition and of ignorance, to sustain philosophical principles, architecture, and agriculture.

One of the great conservatives of life, is to identify interest with principle, and render them concomitant, not independent of each other. If officers of vessels, especially of steamers, be made part owners of the stock when paid, the world would secure thereby the best safety and protection, being previously assured of their capacity and integrity.

Public protection is advanced and promoted best, by finances, engineering skill, &c.

What exhaustless stores of knowledge, the cabinet of nature furnishes the philosophical student. All that once were terrors to mind, now fill it with admiration of its adorable author, and the chastest science now repels the most reckless and licentious superstition.

Natural philosophy informs us that continents are separated by oceans to fructify them, and they become more so by means of interior lakes and large rivers. But for these, the earth might be arid and sterile. Water is the solvent of the salts, to fertilize the soil.

The chastest taste results from the philosophical principles of science. By them, all the world difficulties and dangers will be yielded to mind.

One of the most common displays of nature that we are most familiar with, the atmosphere, has never been near appreciated. Philosophical science opens the panorama of nature, and introduces mind into her hall more and more gorgeous.

Its wisest lessons are those of reflection on observation. The nice adjustment of the world productions, is very conformable to climate, and will prevent injurious monopolies in many series of latitude, as cotton is best in one, sugar and coffee in one more south, and the necessary bread-stuffs in those more north, while the necessary grain and fruits may be reared in most.

Mind has many life problems to solve, to promote its own felicitous intelligence, or the elevation of the world.

The laws of physics eminently teach us, that science subserves the great purposes of creation, and overcomes difficulties otherwise impracticable, as the currents of mighty rivers by steamers. Geographers estimate that more than two-thirds of the earth's surface is covered with water, and that declares a vast unexplored field of future operations to man.

NATURE.

The omniscient Deity speaks through nature, and the whole embraces one mighty universe refulgent with his glory. What more can wisdom ask? To look from the realities of this sublimity, to the pretensions of man's books, is a fall from a God to the priestocracy! All nature rejoiceth in the blessings of supreme benefits.

Who can alter for the better, any of nature's operations?

Who can divide the land or water, into more conservative proportions? The limits of climate are clearly wise. The wisest action of mind, is to make the most legitimate capital therefrom.

POPULAR ERRORS AND PREJUDICES.

The condition of ignorant and past ages leaves their sad mementos, and detracts from the value of their true greatness, and the practical results of available capital. They all suffer, by not allowing for the expanse of mind.

The genius of a Milton and a Shakespeare, now sustain these serious difficulties, and present the deformities of peculiar faith doctrines.

The more exact science of the present day, whilst it admires their genius, deplores their machinery of superstition that the school boys of this age laugh at. Their witches and devils belong to impressions, that must now become obsolete.

Man is miserably corrupt by his errors and prejudices, as well as by the peculiar mis-leadings of the world. How often is God's administration libeled by wrong appreciation, or undue attention to world evils.

The world has ventured too far ahead of science, in construction of God's attributes and providence; it must correct and revise after its correction.

What an idea that people should be killed off by war, as they are too thick any how! Is this much less demoralizing than infanticide or fœticide?

The new developments of the future by mind, will unfold and promote the more humane benefits of civilization. The weakness of the people is through want of comprehensive analysis, as they are a prey from miserable policy to the various errors and prejudices of peculiarities.

The work of the devil, analysis tells us, is the work of perverted mind, reflecting too often the state of false faith.

The vulgar mass takes it for granted, that society has a foundation almost unchangeable.

The errors of society, the natural result of mind's incipient ignorance, requires conservative revolution all the while, in the rational progress of mind.

Why are demagogues permitted so much to deceive society by false pretences?

The confiding mass when misled, is senseless enough to bow to its masters, and wai on its deliverers. The right distinction cannot be satisfactorily made in a world, where insidious sophistry has so much the ascendancy.

When the world adopts universal brotherhood, then we may look upon it as truly revolutionized.

The world is so corrupt after all its improvements, from the first hold of errors and prejudices, that a part is not after correcting the old exploded dynasty, but seek to bolster it up by all practicable expedients.

The world looks at stars and fortunes of destiny, instead of principles. The first ruin Napoleons, the last produce Washingtons; the first cause France to fall by the wayside of atheism, the last arouse America to noblest aspirations of rational mind. While the last bows to the majesty of toleration, the former invokes the aid of bristling bayonets to perform the functions of rational mind. All wars on one side or the other, are base means of barbarism, and subserve the interests of piracy. When the world as the universe will be governed by principles, this will be rightly estimated.

The proper cultivation of rational mind and its appropriate sphere, will best civilize and humanize mankind. This is the only mastery of nature's elements.

The individual union of the people of the five grand divisions of the earth, with their appurtenant islands, will put down or an end to all the miserable wars now raging, and will place annexation on the right legitimate constitutional basis.

The mighty fabric will not be complete till all the five be erected, and the universal whole be comprehended. All the prejudices and foibles of nations as individuals, must be turned to the legitimate direction. If the individual youth cannot be governed by the imbecile parent, instead of sending him for further aggression to the ranks of the soldier, the army, to swell the list of drones and lazy officials, let him be placed in the house of refuge, or the county farm.

There, if no otherwise, may be appropriate employment to those inclined to throw themselves away, in not being able to maintain the right equilibrium in doing nothing.

EXPLODED CUSTOMS.

SUPERSTITION ought by this age to have had her day, and ought now to be considered among the things that were. It is high time that mind had asserted its rightful dignity, and done ample justice to the rich means now afforded the world, to reach its high character and beneficiary powers, for the improvement of the entire world. If mind do not accomplish this, there is naught else to expect. All minds, however engaged in life's pursuits, however the adherents of professions whose interest is their support, should consider higher obligations of duty and permanent claims of their Creator, and howevei misled by pre-conceived notions and customs, yet should yield all up as a glorious sacrifice, on the altar of their country's good.

There is no longer any necessity for many of man's devices, among them secret associations and deeds, circumcision of the flesh, &c. Can any rational mind see in any earthly actions of man, any other that the suggestions of mind variously influenced? However viewed as necessary once, reason declares no necessity for their existence.

No form of superstition can abide reason.

Had God decreed any such command, the operations of nature and not of art, would have infallibly dictated it. This is indubitable proof, that any dispensation that declares it, is a false pretence of man. It is strange that the exploded custom of circumcision should be adhered to, in defiance of the prudent suggestions of policy, to a better identity with the nations of the world, among which the Jewish people are so extensively diffused. They are now no longer a nation, and have not been since scattered by the Romans.

It would redound to their high advantage for personal and national considerations, of respect and of improvement by intermarriage for the correction of blood. It is probable, then, that the breach of the custom might be of itself a better state of natural advantages.

There is no peculiarity of any children of men as distinguished by God's peculiar favors, himself the author of universal love and benevolence, and mind should cease

to contract to the narrow limits of its perversions, the universal means of its better
happiness.

The world is slave to custom and habits, that must get out of all such as the very
best at best.

OBSOLETE NOTIONS.

Mind has to take cognizance of many wholesale bubbles and speculations, to sustain
their fearful retributions that are too important to be overlooked in any age, or forgotten
in any life.

Let mind look at the history of bank manias, with millions for capital ostensibly, that
on failure showed but few thousands for assets.

The world has been assailed for indefinite ages, ever since mind has reacted on
mind.

What can mortals say, of all the thousands of despotisms of peculiar faith? How
is it to free itself from these states?

When a man is fanatic or unprincipled, he will do anything commensurate with the
object.

His only palliation is, that he may be incapable of appreciating the ultimate bearing
and object of all conceptions. The world presents many a goldometer expressly for
one's benefit, but assuredly if it were profitable, that one would not have seen it. Look
at all the rappings within the last twelve months, and what are they but a part of that
contemptible machinery that belongs to ghosts and witches, miracles and prophecies,
bibles and their mysteries, their faiths.

Do you suppose that your posterity will reverence you for such piety, as much as it
will deplore the fanaticism and bigotry of their fathers? Divest yourself in time of all
these false pretences, and do some real good to your household by rational religion.

You have been deceived awfully by the priestocracy about their peculiar faith, that
was not worth reception positively.

Some professions are obsolete, to render the world peculiarly imposed upon. The
world has to be governed by conservative principles, the sooner the better for all
rational beings; hence the only proper constitutional government, that helps all mankind,
is the one.

ADVICE.

Advice is a delicate thing, and should be most rarely given, for the result may not
succeed and injury may ensue, then the adviser is blamed. This is often the case in
matrimony. Matches, even by relations, should be rarely interfered with any way.

When necessary, give advice that is manly, wise and proper. Is the adviser to be
benefited, directly or remotely? Then he will volunteer advice surely! Who is
qualified to give advice, that is worthy.

Sheer ignorance and want of particular attention to that subject, perverse and evil
intention to blindly mislead, and interest to defeat the other party, are disqualifying
drawbacks.

The world too often gets the advice of the ignorant, prejudiced, deluded, and above
all, the arrogant and presumptuous.

Neither persuade nor dissuade, but give facts always, and leave the rest to reason
and justice, when not urged to do more.

What avails advice to opinionated persons?

Give them information, and let them use their judgment that God gave them. All
should avoid the antagonism of the world obnoxious to free opinions, no farther than
rights require.

The intelligent are well aware that advice is actually dangerous, coming from interested persons, and that too much caution cannot be exercised on this head.

When asked advice, deal honestly and morally, but if we candidly cannot approve,
tell the parties to see for themselves.

Whom can we trust better, than our own cultivated mind? The errors of other
people often mislead us. Correct ripe right judgment, is a rare and precious jewel.

When individuals wish you to act on their information, you can procure their certifi-
cate of all first, then consult on the propriety with tried and true friends. If your
friend seeks your hospitality in distress, or retiring from his country in ignominy or
disgrace, extend your proper relief to assist his misfortunes, and diminish his afflictions,
but mark you, never commit yourself to any of his misdeeds that reflect dishonor on
principles; advise to justice, and enlighten him in the path of rectitude and probity.

How many in the world might do better, as they could easily with their mind know better, but they are too short-sighted to do the right thing. Before you consult a friend, consult your own best judgment in evoking the best practicable views of the subject, and knowing his capacity for advice, the more important the deeper the enterprise. Many advisers cannot appreciate new conservative revolutions, and thus friendship may be actually lost in the depth of mind, as the advised may be afraid to follow, where his weak advisers forbid, they being monopolists and in antagonism to anything that may benefit others than themselves.

DEMAGOGISM.

THE infusion of demagogism into the mass of the people, is a potent engine and machinery of power. It sacrifices society, and disorganizes the conservative principles of the universe.

To gain its point, it would institute universal psychology in the world, that popular mind might be in abeyance to its exclusive pretensions.

It affects the welfare of all, to promote the selfish views of the conspirators.

The demagogue fears his constituents when he cannot mislead them, the statesman appreciates his conscience, and does his best duty to the Creator.

We must not presume too much on the mass of mankind, as their brains are of such size as to subject them to guidance. They must not be misled by peculiar education, and can only be wisely and efficiently guarded against the demagogue, by rational light. Demagogues of no kind can survive in the atmosphere of rational education. This will break down all the interior walls of China, reared by ignorance, prejudice, or barbarism. What! China ignorant? Yes: she has bigoted ignorance that caused her to stop short of her high attainments, from which she has retrograded. If she do not batter down her walls of ignorance, she will retrograde.

Not that the rich should be upbraided for riches, that is radical; nor the poor for poverty, that is unjust; but that right and justice should be accorded by the wisest of world's statesmen's views.

CRITICISM.

THE world needs master critics, for its universal utility. Many critics cannot generally do more than pander to beaten paths. They are not suited to conservative revolution. How many such critics are incompetent! In old times, they assumed to be masters, now, the principles of God have mastered for mind. Well might wise, candid, honest critics be desired.

A thorough knowledge of language, so very important to chasteness and elevation of thought, correctness of feelings, contracts in business, will be still more advanced in its universal unity.

Those who seek to be the light of the world, must see too, that in the refinements of criticism, that a juster proportion will be established for mind's greatness. Authors have to look at the future evolutions of mind, and relieve the world of all its impracticable peculiarities.

No precedent is good that reason does not sanction; and reason must be qualified like public opinion, by the purest lights of philosophical science. The master teachers of the world, are the authors of brilliant and original genius.

All authors must be in a proper frame of mind or body, to think and write satisfactorily. This is the case with orators, and the effect of their address is proportionate to the state of the audience. The greatest preference, then, should be paid to those that are prompted by the true spirit of action, not forced by the compulsion of want.

The true end of science enables the intelligent world to select systems, not mere professional characters, and escape the precedents of dogmas of the schools.

The hired author is miserably situated. As Emmet said of his epitaph, original authors might say of criticism, much of which cannot be written for that age. Who can review all works satisfactorily? Noble critics' mind can do more good, to protect mind on its merits. The noblest criticism is the correct one, from the strongest opposition of principles. How often does the world have to receive sophistry, instead of criticism.

No review from monopolists or usurpers, can be worth anything. Nothing less than an elevated proper criticism can do justice to any subject.

The master criticism is not of that exalted stand, that the world and mind need.

MODERN CLASSICAL LITERATURE OF THE WORLD.

ALL this must be universal on rational principles, to rationalize mankind.

It is full high time and tide, that the rational popular sovereignty of mind of the world, spoke its rightful code to the whole five grand divisions in a proper way.

Such classical literature is for the moderns to think rightly. To direct a noble criticism is the right culture and decision.

Language is one of man's peculiarity. That must be religionized, scienceized—philosophized.

The world needs a pure and genuine literature that can shed a glory on rational mind, and elevate the chastest genius to the chastest position.

The world's literature is deformed by the peculiar faith obliquities. Give up, unworthy assumed custodians, this charge, to the holy keeping of rational liberalized mind.

The world needs proper reviews with rational sincerity, science, and philosophy—otherwise, it is naught. The trammels of the schools must not dictate to the supremacy of genius, nor the highest requisitions of rational mind.

THE PRESS.

THE press can speak with the power of electricity, and will equal public opinion when both are truly enlightened on proper principles.

The editors should be among the most enlightened citizens, else they may wield an influence that often perverts public taste and morals, and renders the press unprincipled.

Give the world the light and liberty of the press, sustained by a liberal, that is, rational, education.

What can be worse than a mischievous or mercenary press. The court press of monarchy is hireling, and is ever responsible to censorship.

. Tyrants hate a free and intelligent press.

A conservative revolution is demanded, on the most equitable principles of mind, as regards the press, that pours forth much that is obviously derogatory to intelligence. What miserable articles are displayed, of the most ignominious superstition. Is sophistry to be protected by the most degrading machinations against the probity and dignity of truth and science?

God's universal good is promoted only by truth, not falsehoods. If we are to have fiction, let it be so; but the light of the present age requires the proper distinction between them. Let it not be still left to minds to be corrupted, not benefited, by such conceits.

What malign influence has the court press over the people. All presses, as governments, should be the constitutional friend, adviser, and protector of the sovereign people, not its deceiver.

The press may print the laws and all business expedient for governments; but use no sinister influence of any powers. The true principle is, to dissolve all government from church, bank, working, or press-power.

The press managers assume to correct morals, whilst some of them are not exempt from most of human frailties and degraded corruption. What palliation can be offered, when they enjoy the most of light and liberty? Do they refuse to claim justice for public and private oppression for fear of injuring subscription lists? Then that press is servile and degraded.

Rouse up, patriots of the press, for your country and her cause; the dignity and happiness of the world.

Your delay and omission may be even fatal in many of the issues that mind has to present with the sophistry of the world.

The real genuine liberty of mind is to be maintained by its mighty potency in its own best defence. The press aids, and must be ever true to itself, to the equity of laws, and the justice of principles. These are the world-polities, by which nations prosper, and mankind are blessed with glorious and permanent results.

The press needs enlightened editors to keep the heads and the body of the world right, otherwise corruption may ensue, in the heads of government especially.

When partisan and factitious views prevail, from a low train of conduct, then a curse is perpetrated. Republics necessarily require an independent, not a licentious press.

There must be no restriction on the liberty of the press of the world, that it maintain an exalted supremacy, as one of the most potent bulwarks of liberty. This is to expose, with other enlightened means, the defects of old obsolete governments and their rickety plans.

Let the world see the abolition of censorship on the press in all social proscriptions as to its real liberty, and a conservative revolution will have been established worthy of mind most rational. What will elevate the press to its best standard? The right censorship, of rational criticism. No despotic censorship of the press can be tolerated by the world. When the press is fully freed from ignoble censorship, instituted by social proscription, monopoly, and usurpation, our American freedom will be full. Criticism must be as comprehensive as the universe, and the press must be untrammelled by social or professional proscription. What a wretched thing it is to have a press subsidized to political hacks. What shall the world think of those that prostitute themselves to the evil genius of bad, peculiar faith?

But for the press, this Union might have been split into twain, and the intelligence of the people, their patriotism speaking through the press. When it becomes free in this country, then matters will progress better. Let us have a free and enlightened press, based on rational education, the universal accompaniment of rational minds. Let us act worthy of the freedom of rational mind.

What editor in this country can dare resist proscription of society, and act on the principles of rational mind most promptly? Why is the press sneaking from the responsibility of rational mind, by reason of irrational faiths? That is the position, a most ignoble one. Freemen are cheated, fooled, bribed by peculiar faith—a base, degraded means of despotism, mind-toryism. What mind so tory as to receive such? Of all the disgusting fruits of peculiar education, none are so disgusting as peculiar faith.

Are there any heresies in peculiar faith?

They are all heresies, presenting no truth from first to last. Their bibles are no more, not worth any more, than obsolete almanacs, no more truthful than astrological ones. They are all analogous, having the same object in view, imposition. Society cannot be in a worse fix than by peculiar faith. With such bibles, faith, kings, emperors, popes, papas, lamas, priestocracy and laity, and a pliable press, who cannot feel a licentiousness to play the felon on the world?

Constitutional governments demand better things of a servile or cringing press. Let the free voice of a rational people be understood.

VERACITY OR TRUTH, AND EFFECTS OF ITS VIOLATION.

The best social interests of the world and of mankind, require the maintenance of this principle, but by what shall we guard against perjury that is so often involved in its violation? As respectable as the world is professional, or otherwise in talents and integrity, it is apt to run aground, in the abundant violations of veracity.

Adulation must yield to candor, and however prunesome may be by their evil propensities to pervert themselves and the world, jumping into the quagmire of their masters without help to any, the superior taste of wisdom and truth, will counteract this by degrees. They who honor veracity, test its virtue and benefits in their own cases, acting with the best of good faith, that is essential and ever due to God, and man's social relations, in which every human rational being is most deeply interested.

To resign truth, is stupid resignation of her all-important benefits. She is indispensable in the universe, to God and mind as the only exponents of facts.

Truth is ever indispensable in religion.

Truth and honesty are inseparable in religion.

All their codes must be certainly and entirely consistent.

All that look to society, must look to good faith, itself dependent on truth and honesty.

Peculiar faith, not consistent with universal faith of principles, is suicidal as bad faith to the world.

All the blessings that truth procures, are to be sought under her auspices. Under such a conspicuous advantage, man must rely to attain what is just. They who violate serious truth, are dishonored at once most deeply without limits, resign gifts of invaluable character, and impeach their own standing far beyond all the exertions and machinations of their most hostile opponents.

Man's own evil contrivance in his own cunning, kills himself the worst of all.

Short sighted are any to lose the confidence of the public, the avenue to their credence and the only claim to their belief, even when they afterwards speak the truth. Will any adopt any position that impugns reason and expels truth, to gratify his appetite for power, ambition, or love of money?

He creates ignominy and contempt for his word in a court of justice, a barrier to his and others' rights, the scoff of the world, and throws away jewels of the brightest lustre for dross and dust.

He loses his self-respect, the esteem of the virtuous. Here the wise see settled fixed principles, and the penalties of violation. He who loses this pure virtue, has lost a treasure that this world can never supply. Banish this test of fidelity from this globe, and a void is created, that science cannot supply, to disturb the balance of confidence and the pleasures of mind. The mind turns with disgust from the scene, and contemplates the picture with distrust and uncertainty.

Without truth, the universe loses her principles, and principles become chaos and confusion.

Remember that the greatest triumph is the moral after the religious, and above all, over those who have violated truth. Veracity can be best obtained in courts of justice. by affirmation, when all have the true appreciation of morals and religion.

The highest can only be given by a correct appreciation of the great first cause of the universe, whose myriads of suns, with their hosts of planets speak a universal language to the supreme dynasty of mind, which attends the continued succession of the generations of their inhabitants. The revealed faith violates the first principles of evidence and truth, and as vitiated testimony, must be ruled out of the respectable notice of monotheists. Its race is nearly run, and should be at once, as it shocks moral and religious sense and truth.

When man perverts all good actions, speaks falsely and acts so, generally, worshipping cunning instead of adoring wisdom, then if he suffers speedy penalties, who can be surprised ?

Good faith, truth, and honesty, are invaluable to mind, and all are the smartest in the end that use all such. The cunning circumventor is a simpleton and poltroon, afraid to face facts and come to the exact point.

What shall counteract the immense amount of perjury of the day, but the institution of the most exalted principles, that will dignify mind in its most elevated degree ?

Is self-interest to pervert truth ?

Many people think that they may pervert the world their way, but the future penalty is what may disturb them. There is such a thing as one's actions recoiling, such a thing as retributive justice.

What numbers of people are irresponsible for honor of word or system ; their pledges amount to nothing : they do not know the value of a man's word. Their actions do not correspond to promises. Can they be safely trusted?

Their heart is of as much value as their liver or any other vital organ, for their mind has not been duly cultivated, and their conscience has not been awakened.

Mind suffers its most poignant regret, from adequate penalty reaching it.

The respect due ourselves and the world, must be earned, to be deserved amid the conflicts of interest especially, therefore all are concerned in the greatest good to the world.

Truth is truth no matter the authority, and upholds itself. A falsehood, no matter the asserter, destroys itself. Bad citizens will stultify themselves before principles, and prove their corruption by awful falsehoods when expedient, and throw away the confidence of the community, that truth and honesty procure.

Never affect to be above the humble means of honest elevation, whether or not you can prove yourself worthy by merit of rising from obscurity to celebrity. Strong minds do not avoid their history, nor will truthful persons deny it.

What a miserable state of things arises from the habit of not speaking the truth: the person goes from bad to worse, never believed rightfully, but at the hazard of violating all self-respect. The individual is looked upon as a bad member of society.

The conversation of some circles rather reflects on them, for want of the necessary qualities, as truth and honesty. Now what makes the real and essential difference between the respectable and the reverse, but the most universal practice compatible on the adoption of everlasting principles ? All the world has to be estimated alike on its practices and actions, that decide character. We see the least number possible to tell the truth, if their interest misleads, and is supposed to be best promoted the other way.

Many do not appreciate the value of their word, whether in church or out, in all situations even.

Few can say their word is their bond, as only honest men can affirm it. Church membership will not make them do it, if the right principles be not there, consequently we prove that it is not church membership but principles, that operate in religion, and that can only be instituted by God alone, who created the whole subject. On this God-gift, there must be the noblest appreciation through all the blessed lights of rational education.

Damon and Pythias were extraordinary men, performing their word at the hazard of their lives; one no less by his obligation of friendship, the other no less by that of gratitude. There was no influence of peculiar faith to do this. Truth ever depends on principles self-sustaining, not on faith opinions, unless sustained by certain facts. The man that evidently violates the principle of facts, is not to be believed when he asserts general facts on peculiar faith. What claims has he to any gentleman's confidence if he act thus knowingly to the abuse of reason, justice and wisdom? Too late he finds it is his highest honor and interest to speak the whole truth, to obtain what is due as his own: general confidence.

Here, then, intelligence or intellectual sincerity, acknowledges the severe penalty. The shame and ignominy among men, is of itself, no small amount. When, in daily transactions, persons falsify their words all the time when profitable, or even by ruinous habits imposed by false views and bad raising, and even in a court of conscience, then it is plain, they are short-sighted to self-destruction, without one redeeming virtue in such iniquities. This is so dangerously degrading as to little remove the perpetrators from the animal, responsible to neither God nor man.

Credence is best maintained by good faith to all the world's requisitions. In your life make no absolute promise to perform, or require none beyond what is rational or practicable.

If fact be transcended, what malign influence may not arise? We must recollect that habits grow. Obituaries should be true and just, else they are contemptible. Eulogiums should be rarely published of the living, as they may degenerate into flattery and sophistry of morals. Candor in everything is most becoming. Stop short at once, at the noblest word, No, when expedient.

Men who exact impracticable promises, do not comply themselves, if unprincipled, when it does not suit their profits.

SOCIAL RELATIONS AND VIRTUE.

UNDER the auspices of truth and honesty, good faith is due society, to promote the consummation of all the noblest principles.

The preservation promotes the blessings, while the violation of good faith entails the curses on the world. All, then, are enlisted as good and true members, to insure the best for mutual benefit, as well for self as for the whole public.

To advance all the legitimate expectations of the world, each citizen is a self-agent.

The violation of any one relation by any one member, disorganizes the equilibrium.

Any legitimate action of mind transcended, involves difficulties, as well by action as by example, both of which have their influence as good or bad.

The question, then, does not remain with evil tendency in commission, reflecting back on the actor, but also forward on the world.

Each can satisfy himself of the least evils of self, as of the least corruptions of others.

It will be best to review the primary transgressions, and their reaction on society.

The necessary right result will be, to make gentlemen, whose character will be considered the real noblemen of nature. Many mistake that they do not owe civility or courtesy, when they have no affection. The world owes both the first.

In the first rank is that refined sentiment to be ever shown to ladies, who are entitled thereto on all legitimate positions, from the poorest to the richest. Woman's divergence from her appropriate sphere, can be appropriately met. Rebukes can be given the genteelest ladies and the highest functionaries, by the highest counteraction of any machination, in the front rank of which stands a virtuous independence, that retires from any theatre where antagonism would not be satisfactory. Exclusive independence is the course with impracticable people; in fact there is but one way of proceeding rightly, generally, on this earth: by independent action. Not only must we equalize all citizens in securing an education always rational, but time after labor certainly, for recreation and some mental improvement. The vast and unlimited resources of mind as to this earth, will meet this mighty problem in course of time. In filling time with most suitable employment, the world guards best against immoral habits. All rational beings that have necessarily to act on the defensive must do so, as resenting on principles, not for blind vengeance.

The particular, social, civil, and individual protection of the family, is most honorably confided to the nearest relations, as father, brothers, &c.

Religiously uphold your word and faith before the whole world. If you do not disclose at the proper time, all necessary, you may exclude yourself of all that will protect you afterwards.

Firmness is next to conscientiousness, in carrying out all the obligations of society.

THE FIRST PRINCIPLES OF SOCIETY.

CALUMNY and prejudice are abundant world currencies ; but while we may have to hear evil reports mixed up with better, we should not circulate any to the injury of the innocent. Let no punishment or penalty be placed on contingent, arbitrary arrangements, when wise principles should govern.

Let not bible bigots presume upon any policy, on the fear of superstitious minds ; but let wise, rational discussion ever supersede all such abomination. One of the greatest difficulties is to get mind up to its full world duty, in all the circles of social relations. The world needs light of mind, at the right time, and all the buoyant influences. Partial and abstract efforts will not answer.

Legislation is not up to the full demands of justice, or morals of exact science. What an anomaly is presented when an abortionist was convicted of fœticide, and because there was not quickening of the fœtus ; therefore it was only a misdemeanor, and not a felony ! And doctors are said to be engaged in this nefarious business, worse than the unnatural parents. All such is nothing less than murder, and can only be thus treated by wise legislation.

Take not a seducer to your confidence. How do you know all such ? Who is not one ? Those that hold themselves in abeyance to universal principles. Does any person know him or herself ? Those that neglect principles, or the precautions that govern by principles, are liable to the laws of force and impulse. There are people, of both sexes, of so equivocal character, that the genteel, well-ordered world cannot associate with.

Those of principle are bound to assist the world in its ignorance and want, but they cannot trust them to their confidence : if they do, they damn themselves. Analysis of the world is essential to its well-being.

The world must not take advantage of lovely innocence. Those who meet with many poor, ignorant people, who have had no education, must not make these the easy prey to seduction and vice. What, if you are the means of that seduction ? If the world be a thief pirate, are you going to be the conscious receiver ? Let the eye of principle watch for God.

If the world do not act on principle, it degrades itself. On principles you can successfully defend your reputation against all, the most degraded of the human family.

These will institute the best supervision over those cities that adhere to wickedness and are stupid in crime—whose coverts are polluted by corruption—are an abomination to virtue, and whose iniquitous ways pervert the best institutions of the land. Nothing but the greatest amount of practicable independence, can promote the first principles of society. The homestead exemption seems to be one of the blessings of the best of wise governments, in promoting a virtuous independence. Resist no law of the land in execution, unless such position calls for conservative revolution that can be properly encountered. Sense and virtue beget the noblest independence. Man must not make shipwreck of life, but carry out the supremacy of mind, and rise superior to difficulties.

One of the best views in life, is to avoid not only what is sophistry, but all its colorings, as productive of much world difficulties. When we violate any principle, it must react some way or other, on some point of society, with retributive justice. The world must counteract the vile, social machinations, and despotism.

How shall we rectify about persons that are oppressive, and from whom there can be but little or no redress ? They should be exposed, and when public opinion is enlightened and sound, they will be punished.

You should pay all honorable demands, even to taxes, that may look oppressive ; but with a protest, that you may do justice to both sides, in a justifiable way and time.

Have all explanations practicable at the time.

ETIQUETTE.

IT is important that people should conform to the right usages of society, not because sanctioned by time or personal authority, but commended as right. People must dress and adhere to etiquette of society, as a matter of plain sense, virtue and honesty, as marks to distinguish the grades and character of society rightly ; as well as use a courtesy of refined manners, just to nature and conformable to elevation of character. Every man should adapt himself to the disposition of others, as far as principles permit, to do them justice.

The proper way of treating the world, is to prevent its improper liberties. We should make the world estimate us for personal merits.

The greatest impropriety in modest people, is not promptly resenting with the worthless tribe, one's dignity at once and on the spot, not by descending to their level, but of acting on the legitimate principle.

FRIENDSHIP ALIENATED.

If friendship be alienated unintentionally, or by misunderstanding, it may be remedied by proper and skilful management. The character of the notes addressed may be required to be most friendly, as they are between mutual friends.

The strength of sorrow and sympathy must be advocated, at the proper time, by the suitable, tangible test and evident standard, in the overwhelming loss of our friend, thereby evincing the proof of friendship ; and the best evidence of his best actions, is industry and exertion to repair all losses. If a person do you a wanton, intentional injury, prevent the second, any way, of principle. Do not trust him any further, as to leave it in his power to do so again. Beware of such a savage the second time.

SENSE AND CUNNING.

Proper cultivated sense adopts those full comprehensive principles that lead to correct action and sound thought, to secure the best rewards of life.

Cunning devises plans, to escape the penalties for present gratification. The first institutes such a policy as will insure a permanent safety, and prosperous issues as far as mind can influence ; the other hazards much in the contingencies of opinions and the acts of duplicity.

The first acts from reason, the other yields too much to plausible feats, and is more concerned in clever and adroit designs.

The first makes valid contracts and executes them ; the last seeks to avoid them, unless they turn out profitable speculations, then nothing is said against them, as they are then considered fair business transactions.

Cunning lays hold of the rise, but refuses the fall and loss in property. The people of the world have to observe the perversion of mind in its various faces, though nearly all have to pay for that observation by something in experience. The best corrective to counteract perversion of mind in its various shades, will be a liberal education, and all liberal education should be rational.

The world is not safe otherwise with mind of cunning, that tends to display itself in all diversified personifications. The best evidence of the difference is finally seen in transactions of enlarged business. That of insurance offices, that are designed to protect honest sufferers, is certainly not to reward the base designs of cunning and fraud, its late acquaintance, burning up and destroying insured property.

The intellectual safety of proper sense appeals with high-minded satisfaction to the honest policy of an honest world. The people in general should have plain honest sense presented them, as they most rarely understand metaphysical and figurative language, that hides itself for refuge in all the false pretences and devices of mysteries.

How can they decide rightly on mighty questions, that involve in their solution the deepest science, unless properly discussed and fairly represented ?

There are some people very smart in the world by their cunning. They deceive in the end, ruin, as far as in them lies, the world, and deceive themselves.

Cunning has after-thoughts of escaping from incurred difficulties, as the penitentiary and other penalties ; wisdom avoids them by fore-thoughts.

How many seek the world-tact, instead of sterling merit. Cunning often defeats itself by its own means. The greatest opposition may make nations and individuals of talents great indeed, as causing the most enlarged display of nature's greatness.

It is a fact incontestible that rational mind only requires the most appropriate theatre, for the proper exhibition of its qualities.

THE WEAK POINTS OF SOCIETY.

WANT of liberal and philosophical rational education is one, and always will be, yielding the flock to every wolf that enshrouds his ambition in sheep's clothing.

If all free men have a just education that is adorned by science, philosophy and analysis, the sooner and better every rational mind will be competent for its sphere and mission on this earth. Such competency, by analysis of man's inherent condition in the vicissitudes of life, will render the advancement of the greatest happiness of the people, adequate for promotion of their legitimate and necessary demand.

Well bred and liberally educated people of both sexes see and feel the effects of transgression of the great principles, that guide life to its best fruition.

There are many points in the great code of life, that individuals only can recognise, and wisely manage. What a host of duties are brought around the laws of nature, unwritten save in the mind! How can that mind analyze, if unprepared, as it has been by black-letter bibles, for the facts of nature?

The debasement of mind by the subtle policies of the world, is hardly to be estimated by common analysis. Some people have had their minds so miserably perverted, that they would prefer killing a fellow-being for notoriety!

Many would murder, by legally robbing all a man had. Many cowardly, unprincipled wretches, would crush the whole manly spirit of the world, to secure its mastery.

Haggard want has driven men from their high mental estate, and thousands of poor girls are starved and seduced into prostitution. But what are the intermediate steps, for the honor of human nature? How many youthful females are dragged to hopeless misery and degradation, by the wily seductions of more richly endowed acquaintances?

Wise legislation should protect innocence and virtue, against all those who will take advantages in any such way. It must protect the high principles of honor from violation, the debasement of the needy by prostitution, darkening their future perdition.

The strong and wise guardianship of government should be interposed, to prevent the forcing poor fallen sex to a deeper degradation, to hold up mankind the best under the circumstances.

A better order of things will arise to the world universally, when rational mind reaches its mastery.

One of the weakest points in society, is the conduct of frail woman. But is not man as much responsible for his part of virtue, as much as woman?

Many a seduction has been perpetrated not by mere intrinsic frailty, but from want and necessity, that have been taken advantage of by man, who has committed the greatest crime.

Among the baser passions, revenge has been more the instigator than avarice, by woman.

What can sustain woman, in her proper high condition? The world will sincerely be ready to do justice to female chastity, and defend it when necessary, if woman be firm to her own position.

To be that, man must do his duty. Woman must be justly dealt with.

Woman's conduct is her best jewel, that outshines all libels. The line of demarkation is drawn forever, between the virtuous and suspicious of society, for its best protection and defence.

Too late lost woman finds that that line can never be expunged. What profit are all certificates to a woman, more than suspected?

The abandoned should be preserved from lower degradation. The virtuous must not be brought below their own, and only safe standard. It is not the base alloy, the counterfeit, but the genuine currency that wise legislation must seek to preserve. The world must come to its own rescue. Man has an important part in this drama.

Due respect to society has to be inculcated, for it to be protected.

Genius always seems eccentric to the vulgar herd, from pre-conceived views and prejudices, but none other than general good results are to decide the question properly.

What are the ignorant, careless, and exposed, to do?

They should be cared for by the State, to correct their manners and morals, and that in time.

The acquaintance of some people is a constant annoyance and injury. We should be ever watchful in life with many, else we may get more than we ever bargained for.

THE WORLD.

THE world makes the best show and parade, too often with the insidious auctioneer bidding, of seeking popularity and credit, that have been already overstretched.

We often find that the winnings have been recorded, but all the losses are forgotten or omitted.

What is half its authority worth, but a memento of exploded customs, degraded superstitions, and discreditable faiths?

The time is hardly passed when the moon, in her various phases, governed the housewife and husbandman, the mariner and traveller, from whom is never to be excepted the priest, whenever to be turned to account of profit. The less wise the world, the more advice it is offered.

How ignorantly the mass proceeds.

Its leaders have been mostly designing men of every age, assuming popular respect, whose name, character and words, cannot be endorsed.

Where is science, the friend and patron of mind, the world? The ancients did not know half the globe; it was the genius and science of Columbus that gave continents to the circle of man's knowledge. There are some world-problems for solution, as the disposition of rational beings for best rational existence, individuals and nations of the whole world. For this the talents of the world should be concentrated. Thanks to science and mind, above all, the providence of the Creator, no monopoly of the world is practicable.

One of the most tried for dominion has been martial usurpation. But the conquerors, as the conquered, sleep, and their possessions have passed to strangers, men not even thought of in their days.

Nations who have changed the plan of military operations, fond of gunpowder aspirations, ere they reach the height of their wishes of conquest, may be sick at an early period of their designs, that are mere trifles for the good they do the world.

Man's wildest ambition cannot be satiated by all attainable for improper purposes. The most extensive attempts at speculation have been made in articles of diet, that can be easily superseded by others. Most of such articles keep too little time, or the demands of the producer and the profits of the capitalist do not permit it. Climate interferes and puts in her negative.

The world is made right; it is man that misreads and misuses it. Nothing less than the comprehension of the world's subjects can enable mind to keep pace with the age and the civilization of mind.

We should so fix the world that it will subserve the noblest purposes of mind, its master, instead of injuring the great objects of its creation.

The imperial position of the world is in expansive commerce, and proportionate light of freedom.

Great railroads are to unite oceans, and navigation of oceans is to unite continents and islands. All this will further the code that nations of the world will adopt, whereby we shall experience the benefits of one universal brotherhood.

Many crimes that now disfigure the earth's fairest surface will be then obliterated. There will be no inducement for national wars, public or private assassinations, secret misdeeds and crimes of cabinets, when they cannot be committed with impunity, and without the world's rebuke. The pope's excommunication will then be nothing to the moral power of the world, that will reflect blessings on man, honor to God, excommunicating all excommunications.

The world has to be civilized, and all nations are concerned in the solution of that mighty problem.

The most important points, that bear most materially on its evils, should be duly attended to.

TO GOVERN THE·WORLD, AND RIGHTLY MASTER IT.

THE proper position is the best independence, and not till then its unbounded respect and attention can be secured. To keep it getting any undue advantage of us. is to be full master of principles, that lead us safely through life, and never enslave us by imperial powers that bestride the world, nor imprison us in any of the castles or dungeons of evil passions.

How better can we secure proper exemption from exposure to the various tricks in trades, by fair representations on our part, and the fundamental security of best known

characters to deal with? If we allow them invariably a living price, nothing better
tends to insure all this in the very best pledge.

Self-interest, second to not even money power, is the world's first love, and that is to
be primarily regarded. By taking nothing for granted, we may avoid deception of the
many that live on the world, getting their living out of others, who are caused to take
all for granted as right, till the object is accomplished, then no matter about the recompense.

We must not only master the points, but those who abuse the world by their acts,
else any conservative revolution is vain, as it will be presumptive, when it cannot
secure the wise tribunal of reason.

The world can be best managed by a wise independence, the glorious mentality, the
most honorable competition.

Keep the world straight, and act independently of it. Hold it to exact justice.
Dishonesty should not pervade in proper society, under under any forms that tricky
lawyers originate.

Much is often said about false principles, but there can be no such thing, as God
created principles, and all are true; it is man's appreciation of them, that presents a
false position and appreciation.

It is false doctrines and their systems, not principles.

The great questions of the world absorb all, as matters of principle. Commercial
enterprise is one of the great elements of rational education. Principles are the main
points. There is a deep want of courtesy, frankness, in the world. The wisest application of mind is most highly essential. What is there in life that does not demand it
most potently? In the purchase of property, the purchaser may pay all he has, and
then has to yield up all purchased. Is this a proper use of mind? Is it a proper view
of one's duty and action?

Many purchasers of lands and houses on credit have been sold out of all, and all
their other property.

This is ambition, or folly overreached.

How many that are unprincipled, or destitute of intelligence, are incapable of appreciating courtesy. The world must meet, morally and physically, everything at once.

It must understand what are its legitimate resources, and act accordingly. When
things, as gifts, are put into hands, we ought to know the true conditions; not take for
granted, and pay dearly therefor in the end.

Rational mind must look at all the contingencies before promising, and then employ
its best capital in the substantial, not shadowy, pursuits. The uniform protection of
the world's constituency and society, must be sustained on the inherent conservative
principles of the universe. Manage the world by truth and facts. The world may
look upon you as an adventurer, but act independently. Not only false faith, but false
taste, has been engendered in the world. The way to appreciate the world, mind, God,
religion, man, is to put all on their merits and principles. Look through your best
optics, instead of others'.

Make it the best policy as interest to pay, and the honesty of many is secured. How
can that be fully secured in the whole? That is the question with rational religion,
that requires all rational minds to look to principles.

MERCHANTS.

Is it possible, that more than ninety per cent. of merchants fail, in some of the
most respectable cities? Is competition too great, or is it that their system is
deficient?

One of the most important matters with merchants is the proper care of all interests,
as well as principles.

The speediest sales will insure best profits, or, are generally the best. The interest
of the value of goods unsold for years, is to be deeply considered; the expenditures are
another matter of deep interest.

What can prevent many merchants failing, or becoming bankrupt, when they fail
essentially in principle and judgment?

What must be the state of morals in that country, that sees its merchants become
smugglers?

Those possessed of business capacity may succeed, under proper circumstances, with
proper exertions, and a wise prudence or use of mind, in honorable living.

A good and proper sense economy with merchants is worth more than half of all
the profits on their merchandize, to save them from bankruptcy.

Merchants suffer by reckless competition, that ruins all parties, or does but little good ; and above all, by an improper, inconsiderate extension of credit.

To have others' debts to pay, and to be cut off from collections of one's own, by assignment, &c., should be prevented by a bankrupt law, that, if permanently good, would do away with the abuses of the credit system.

Bad men embarrass the rightful action of any good system.

Merchants should particularly regard the interest of idle capital, that might reimburse for subsequent losses, if available.   Re-invest capital constantly and speedily, without permitting it to be idle or dead.   Co-partnerships are very important in the affairs of life, and should be formed on the proper business principles, and no other.   Persons entering old firms have been ruined by their bankruptcy, that was totally unknown to the last party, until too late.

In all business transactions the party should premise his own perfect safety, and take nothing at all for granted, neither trusting to the opinion of others that may be ignorant, or their integrity, that may be deficient in the time of need.   Deal in such a way that none can be injured, and all may have the best chance for benefit.

The world has to notice, even for health, that good be not adulterated, mixed, or injured.   In keeping yourself straight, you will do your part in seeking to keep the world so.   What shall we say of the merchants who have two prices ?   That they are unworthy of public support.   They must have uniform prices.   The highest integrity bespeaks that.

When a messenger is sent to a merchant, for any quantity of goods, wares, or merchandize, why cannot exact justice be done his fellow citizen, as if in his own presence ?

The merchant who sells on credit must be sure that he sells to those competent to pay.   If the goods be gone without the money, and if the money be gone without valid titles, your experience does not avail anything against the collusion.   We cannot trust some people at all, unless we have them bound by interest.

Buy for cash, then you trade independently and with dignity, otherwise you buy at a great disadvantage.   The merchant who exceeds his income, cannot be free from bankruptcy.

A miserable state of world-morals exists, where much of the trading community seek to use the greatest extortions on the ignorant world, in proportion to its ignorance.

None should pledge, as merchants, the quality of their goods, if they do not hold themselves responsible therefor.   Honorable men will hold them responsible in their mind's eye.

This article refers to what is trade, and comprehends the view that is too often unfortunately embraced in speculation, that if recklessly abused, uses up not only the principal, but affects deeply his securities and aiders.   The world is advancing rationally to the position of supervising all departments of self-preservation, that bespeaks the guarantee of best world morals and safety.

Too great calculations are too often made by the world, in future anticipations. Commerce is one of the best practical teachers, and all its regulations must be rationally regarded.   Proper inspection laws for health and security of honesty, even to teas, should be carried out.

Purchasers should have the best supervision of qualities of goods, but should pay a living price.

Inferior prices beget inferior goods.

Who can be more useful than a liberal and enlightened merchant ?

THE RIGHT USE OF TIME AND CAPITAL.

Time, well employed, flies swiftly enough ; but what shall we do when it hangs heavily on us, with nothing to do ?   Really, then, employ the whole time in thinking of some thing to be realized, to be done, and when you attain it, proceed at once to put it into successful operation.   We do not stand still at nothing.

Our function is valuable employment of time, profitably and dutifully.

The negative of ours is evil, by omission as well as by commission.   We should seek more wisdom to-day than we possessed yesterday, a fact identified with constant suitable employment of time.

Better had we left many things undone, and known less of other things.

Repentance bespeaks improvement, as conviction and correction will follow on knowledge and the right appreciation of duty.   All right-minded individuals may acquiesce in what is best principles, presented at the right time ; and the only thing that prevents full success of morals, all the time of life, is the tyranny of habit, a " second nature."

Education, if rational and correct, as it is absolutely essential for pilotage through life, will be the best guarantee, at the right time, of all that is necessary.

When our thoughts get into an improper, uncontrollable current, from vacancy of time, we should strive to do the best actions, something good, at once, as the best prayer at that moment to Almighty God, to arrest them best by this very exclusion.

All mankind, men, women and children, of suitable age, no matter how rich they all are, should use out-door daily exercises,—do something to do right to a proper and necessary extent, for employment of time too. Proper labor is a part component of man's existence.

Most do not employ that time assumed to be employed.

We should never keep capital, mental nor pecuniary, idle ; both, when active, best contribute to our best independence and the world's benefit.

Insurances of life's benefits can be obtained by the proper use of time's functions. As insurance policies are lost by delay and want of good faith, so may the soul's noblest birth-rights.

Self-examination will show time too much misspent or misapplied.

Economy of time and capital, talents and labor, is a noble characteristic, and may be productive of most essential, universal advantages.

Economy, if just, is one of the best to all, and should never be too close nor extravagant. What is economy in some—as, when travelling, sleeping where they best can, eating from their own stock, most commendably—is niggardliness in others. and deprives a useful portion of the community what is due them for public spirit of accommodation.

The public should always justly respond to all just demands upon it.

The world should seek to help sustain the proper institutions of refined civilization.

Extravagance in families may eat up all, principal and interest, the whole capital. The end may be bad. A just liberality may lay a proper foundation in life. Industry and economy are the great talismans to man's temporal happiness.

Mark the benefits of true economy, without mistake. A single man is, apparently, the proper guardian of his own property ; and if he fool it away, then he has none to blame but himself. Yet how awful that censure when he throws himself on friends for support. Let him not condemn the world therefor, but act wisely. The married man is not the exclusive owner of his property, and is responsible to his family.

INDUSTRIAL LABOR.

THIS is one of the most honorable cements of society. No age and country can claim a higher grade in civilization, all other matters being equal, than those that exhibit the appropriate use of the elements of industry and labor ; and no country can be more blessed than that which rewards suitably all such exertions. Both sexes ought to work, or do something equivalent, or their minds may mature evil thoughts, in idle moments, and their bodies engender disease, without the conservation of labor to throw off noxious obstructions.

Governments should give adequate aid to industrial labor, as the means of attainment of dignity, to prevent crime and dissipation. Nothing is so menial as debasement from the effects of non-employment in industrial pursuits. Not only does the race of mankind, but especially women, require good raising of good families, but a continuance of proper labor.

All worthy employments of industry should be equalized as near as possible, and should not have to brook the affectation on a superior footing.

Let all communities, large cities especially, have best general regulations, for all persons competent to the exercise of labor, to have visible and substantial means of subsistence.

The work of honest minds should render them a living. To render the most efficient aid to the industrious-minded or the necessitous, in the absence of governmental grants of land, hereafter to be discussed, large city corporations should remove them to rural districts, that all needing support to be thus benefited.

Free, intelligent minds, must appreciate all such. The union of the good must counteract the bad. No part of professions or labor is to be in disproportion to the whole population, as the agricultural may exceed the mechanics, and an excess of produce may have no suitable market.

There should be industrial exhibitions, as the world has to sustain working associations that should be most elevated, to do away with the apparent necessity of socialism, that may generate many vicious elements. The elements of true enjoyment of life have been dispensed by an all-wise Creator, and must be elicited by the beneficial intercourse of the people for universal amelioration. A proper government sustains all the practicable elements of industrial labor of the free. So much grain is raised in some countries, as wheat in Russia, that much of it has been wasted or destroyed. This seems so much for man's bad management, and improvident government. To remedy all this, tariffs of appropriate revenue character should be adjusted, to bring the consumer by the side of the producer, and equalize in the best manner all industrial labor exertions. Such tariff is best to promote the highest national morals, in preventing smuggling, immorality and dishonesty, by taking away the most formidable means of mind perversion.

The world should patronize the policy that causes the best exertion of labor—that bestows its beneficial blessings on each individual of the world, and overcomes most justly the antagonizing conflicts of particular countries. But let the wisest policies regulate themselves. This is the only wise system to obviate, by the most powerful inherent means, all antagonism. The world has been taught enough to know this. Labor and capital, in a properly organized government, produce a fair organization of society. Monopolies of trade, by government, must be abolished, to do justice to the rights of the sovereign people. The world should have a proper organization of suitable materials, and that position should embrace all the industrial pursuits of agriculture, commerce, navigation, manufactures, mining and fishing. An appropriate industrial equilibrium should be aimed at over the world.

Mind in all its proper facilities will best regulate all such, under the appropriate limitations. What an advance on the errors of the past—now one can count it an honor to have risen by one's own exertions.

We must analyze the position of nations, and see the relative state of their classes, especially landlords and tenantry. This order has to be abolished, by organic conservative principles of the universe.

The world must guard against pauperizing any of mankind.

The necessitous class must be sustained by agricultural labor principally, and that on its best position, the fee-simple of nature. It must go to that kind of labor to elevate it, and the whole community. The question does arise in patriotic minds, to extinguish as early as practicable, the very name of classes and castes, as odious to universal brotherhood? But analysis tells us that many classes are uncaste or made so by vicious habits and customs, often by the poison of alcohol, that affects awfully their whole system, the nerves especially and vital organs, as the liver.

Many are the evils that mind perverted makes out of what was good. They that abide by law so closely, as to wait for all to be decided by lawsuits before even payments of debts, may find themselves in this class. While industry and economy will counteract much of their miseries, an intellectual policy will institute a better position. Mind may be wanting to many, but the proper exercise is neglected by most.

But does the citizen show himself any way a worthy member of society, competent in skill, honest in intention? Let him persevere, and let good citizens aid him, above all, the government, in giving him the surest foundation, a homestead.

Labor ought not to be more than ten hours, temperate at that, in the twenty-four, to give time for daily reading, improvement of mind and recreation.

Many of those most necessitous in cities, may make not only a comfortable but even a genteel living in the country, if placed on their own resources, aided by the amount necessarily expended in cities for their mere existence. It well becomes the community to observe all this subject, and act accordingly. The time may come for the world, when labor may be acknowledged as affording her just share of its benefits, and competent to tell the tale of her own powers. Industrial labor makes nations, the whole world.

The industrious and honest classes will protect themselves almost anywhere; the reverse cannot securely be protected by the wisest laws, that can only promote, not create welfare of the world. It is a deep reflection personally, not to be able to rise by labor in America, from destitution of the actual necessaries of life, when men possess all the healthful vigor of life. What will insure proper employment for labor? Suitable prices. It may be important to institute all expedient organizations of saving institutions and industrial associations. The world should think of a permanent fund, to be raised by all civilized nations, to promote the alleviation of human misery, or the advantages of society. Organic constitutional rights, must first be instituted.

SOCIALISM.

ALL segregated socialism is founded on improper analysis of mind, on the pretence to equalize man, who varies with diversified talents and constitutional characteristics. If you restore to-day the affected equilibrium of property, from the diversity of financial talents, you would speedily see the resulting inequality.

· There cannot possibly be any antagonism of society founded on equitable relations, adverse to the general good. In the great principles of the universe that govern the equilibrium of the planetary bodies, attraction balances repulsion, and the whole is concert of action that is universally harmonized.

Proper and honest sense advises to look eternally at the nature of things, not to our mere wishes or crude opinions. There can be no fanciful Utopia in society, that is necessarily made up of various elements, varied by their several intellectual, moral, physical, contingent and local circumstances, which if arbitrarily equalized by immediate legislation of brute force, must from the very nature of creation be modified by time, and characterized by its eternal revolution among nations, and individuals of those nations.

Her thousand operations by "flood and field," if no other of life's fund was exhibited, meet most fully this interesting question, and cannot fail to satisfy the mind of the philosophic inquirer, of the futility of reaching the solution in any other way, than what nature wills, under the direction of its mighty regulator.

Mind is unsettled by the agitation of unattainable solutions. As the construction, the organization of every person varies enough to characterize the individual, the character of the creation cannot be reduced to his or her subjection, but by principles that recognise that position and that variety.

The world furnishes one great and glorious socialism, only to be realized from rational religion proclaimed in indefinite series in all man's legitimate actions, superior in beauty and loveliness in its world-wide sphere, to any arbitrary arrangement that gratifies man's power, ambition and avarice.

What can governments do, rightly and properly for citizens? They can only put their rights under equal and just protection, else all is union of state and peculiar power, a tyranny and oppression.

The mighty blessings of a consistent government enlightened and free, protect with suitable potency, all classes of citizens. Such government is separate from all but intrinsic power, its own merits, unconnected to all church, bank, money, working people's, all peculiar, social, but the whole rights of the people exclusively, her intrinsic power.

This consistent free government permits only wise legislation, exclusive of pretences to primogeniture, to elevate the accident of birth over the equal rights of many, thus reversing the order of nature that is universal, not peculiar in common rights, beneficial to all, and oppressive to none.

This principle upholds all, but depresses none with crushed spirits. The establishment of the law of primogeniture, is the suppression of free government, causing republicanism to perish.

A state-faith can never be a rational religion, suitable for rationable beings—clearly so. Religion must furnish liberal principles as an institution of mind, not of government, altogether incompatible with other alliances than people's rights.

Religion asks no tithes of the most, to the inconvenience of justice, of home in many instances. Religion does not belong to any circle, and does not permit the destitute, disabled by disease, by imbecility and incapacity, from realizing the state contributions.

Military and naval impressments, when made, are at the expense of popular rights, that guarantee all employments a sufficient payment to insure their prosecution, unless as the least of evils, in cases of necessary and defensive wars.

Good governments seek no wars without principle, and sustain no debts without reason satisfactory to those that pay them, consequently their citizen soldiers ought to be volunteers for all righteous defence. But soldiers and sailors are necessary for a peace establishment, therefore their enlistment should be secured on the prices of competition and rational treatment.

The result of good government is natural and consistent. The world is to be governed on conservative principles, and no other; then let reason legislate.

Deity's attributes will be understood by mind, that seeks to approach the performance of duty.

Having all fundamental points of society right, things must regulate themselves. Legislation is founded on principles that must not be transcended, for if they clash, all good legislation perishes. How then can any class in equitable governments usurp all the common vital benefits over the balance?

All eminently have the election of seeking that road to wealth and honor that best comports with their talents and inclination. This facility of improvement is ample in free republics, so that the mind well balanced and cultivated can secure a good portion of life's benefits in many respects.

The equal division of estates does for individuals or families, what equal governments do for nations.

Such a state of things invalidates serious objections to the permanent state of society as to their rights.

There are certain relations and fitness of things to harmonize prominent difficulties. But there must be the man as well as the government, since success depends as much or more in him, than in the law of the land.

Many employed for daily bread have a hard time of it, but little removed from pauperism, which every state is imperatively bound to provide for directly, and lessen, most legitimately, indirectly.

All free governments, having instituted the first great steps right, wise legislation and union improvements, can look to the blessings of the future.

Union improvements may be designated all those founded on the character of man, and obviously practicable. Benevolent societies and associations are now acting extensively. Man's individual acts, as an exalted being, furnish an important part of this drama; and he has, in his "brief authority" of power, diversified through all the scenes of life, full scope to aid humanity in such a way that rational duty exacts.

Laborers, especially females, destitute orphans, and sickly, helpless children, have a just claim on man's humanity, that must be accredited. Various classes of laborers may have a hard time of their life, females especially, who get but a moderate sum for their work. The merchant pays moderately, as he is thus paid by the purchaser. This can only be corrected by maintenance of the principle of not cheapening below a living price, which should be carried through all the circles, to ratify an equalization of world's labor value. All parties to the social compact must exercise a living, liberal spirit, else they are destitute of the first principles of socialism, that is to be exercised as a conservative in the world, to rescue it from the blights and curses entailed on it improperly, by violation of social relations.

There may, and should be relief committees, to give invariably the various benefits and ablest support to genius and mind. Neither should be ever trammelled in the best exertions for social reforms, nor over-excited by a morbid sentimentality, or mawkish pretensions of demagogism.

Work laws can only be successfully adapted to the general principles of society, and the character of human nature moulded to the highest civilization.

Commerce and industrial labor should be put on an equilibrium for the world.

The operative says, He wishes to enjoy life, have comfort; as he makes money, he must spend it. If he do not, others that do not care for him, will. He does rank injustice to the whole circle, his posterity, his own species, above all, himself. He makes several thousands of dollars clear in the first part of his life, yet he cannot show the same, or the exchange. Now all is expended, and he is left none the wiser, better, happier, or more independent; not able to enjoy life after all; without home, or house, or independence; just missing by that much the whole of life's comforts and enjoyments. He has had his pleasures, but they were sensual, brutal, and now he has their ruinous effects.

As far as socialism rightly protects the community in proper principles, and sustains the rightful means of living, it is right; but not when it presents antagonism of any principles of justice and equity, introducing any *expost facto* law, or anti-rent disturbances.

Associations for architecture, agriculture, may be properly conducted, and redound to the good of the individuals, but they cannot be aggressive upon the rights of any circle.

The world needs no radical agrarian socialism to war on property, and the fair reputation that acquires it, character, family, and man, to dissocialize the world, and break asunder the wise ligaments of best society. The world needs no anti-rent communism to win the battle or conflict by outrage and felony. To make the ultra socialist, unmakes the man.

There is too great a disregard of the sacred rights of property, family, man.

Let irresponsible power be established, and no respect is paid to justice.

Let there be no peculiar parties as factions, revolutionary or others; but let popular world and mind amelioration prevail. Let there be the elevations, not the levellings of society.

Proper competition between labor and capital, as in everything, will insure the right position. There should be no beggars, where the laws can be uniform to prevent them.

There is this about socialism, that freemen have the inalienable right to employ themselves, their time, and talents, exclusively, in seeking that business or profit that they choose, not antagonistic to the principles of social relations.

There are many millions in the world destitute of food and raiment daily. This is a collateral, not paramount question, amid the moral as physical demands of the world. No community, whether of socialism or any other, that presents a licentious or libidinous crowd, can be considered as worthy of public approval. Take away woman's chastity, and one of the noblest of sympathies is torn away, and the brightest of jewels is lost.

We can have no proper legislation for labor direct, to be in union with state; that is absolutism.

Trades union are to protect, on the invasion of deep necessity, and inability of competent support.

But all such must be disconnected with want of morals, community of women.

There must be no shock on public morals, emanating on immutable principles.

Labor associations of working people must and will counteract the direct invasions of poverty.

Shares might be taken through payments, for permanent investments.

Society has certainly to get rid of primary difficulties at the start, then most depends on the individual, not on the nation or government. All nations owe sound constitutional governments to their citizens, who, individually, have thus the best position to prosper.

By the right position in society, a high-toned religion prevails, and high-toned social duties are duly performed. By the law of primogeniture, a few rich are made fewer, but more imbecile and richer; the many, with exceptions, are made poorer. Its abolition pays nature proper tributes, and equalizes life's blessings with proper wisdom.

It is freedom and the intelligence of science that the world needs, not socialism. The luxuries of the world would amply meet the wants of mankind. What a theme for statesmen of the world.

Trades' meetings and associations should be promoted, to prevent over-work, no work, low or reduced wages, to furnish work to all seeking it, diminish oppression, relieve the distressed, promote universal fraternization as far as practicable, universal amelioration of the world—avoid radicalism, impracticable and immoral socialism, terminating in communism.

All citizens should have time for mental improvement and daily recreation, and appropriate means furnished. The world must secure honorable labor.

Socialism of segregation seems folly, not analogous to the first principles of justice to man's nature, or the right organization of society. We permit or sanction no socialism, that is not right.

Socialism, in the patriotic sense of association for labor, may have claims for the respect of the world, so far as its ends are laudable for the good of the whole; but the moment that sectarianism or immoral views are embraced, then it is subject to the general objection to all evils.

As many citizens are suffering from unseen indigence in cities, necessitated for work, they should be provided for in some suitable establishment. The best association is to cause life to be predicated on individual exertions.

Happily for mankind, organic connections may answer the question practically, with the best solution. The Creator has in reserve the rich field of enterprise for the necessitous, meritorious, and industrious, and amply bestows a liberal supply of life's necessaries.

Agricultural labor is open to all, simple to understand, easy and profitable for healthy industry to perform. It may be a wise dispensation, that redundant population should immigrate to more congenial climes. This mighty question is far from exhaustion, as long as mind progresses in improvement. We must admit that every independent mind wishes to be independent of the boons of the world, and only receive, as it merits, its just dues. It may be difficult for the sick and very poor to get a proper start or even support. What is to be done? A healthy, sound man, determined on working his way to an independence, will be very apt to do so. A proper fund should be created in every country, to meet such contingencies as poverty, sickness, or imbecility of age or sex produces.

Under the malign influences of peculiar faith, socialism may be incorporated, offering a nucleus, for weak minds and deranged people to concentrate on a false system, as variance with the laws of nature. It is well that the laws of the country do not lend countenance to such absurdities.

Socialism never will be placed as the conservative principles of society, till society has all proper basis of constitutional government. Of course there can be no monopoly of rulers in essential and necessary articles, as in salt, books, tobacco, &c. None of the money power should exercise dictation, so that capital should own the labor of citizens.

If socialism mean the correct support of industrial labor, then it is laudable and commendable.

Unless the world's society becomes socialism, which seems impossible, then benevolence is reserved to individual justice. I do not wish the world to mistake me. Instead of socialism, the mind of mankind will claim the principle of universal brotherhood. What just claims on the world has any citizen, that is competent, yet will not help himself?

This world at this age needs no ultra radicalism.

Socialism must never be communism, much less dissocial sectarianism, producing the most revolting antagonism. What the rich have, grant that it represents the former labor of predecessors, natural accumulations; capital generally represents the effects of labor, present or past. Now all that is in it, is this, industrial labor of the classes then operating, should be properly protected. All, the most indigent have, it capital, and all such is analogous in the hands of the rich; therefore there can be no natural antagonism of classes, where the government is constitutional, and represents all classes.

The best of good faith must be preserved in society, that demands a perpetual consistent confidence, to uphold its inherent sacredness.

Nothing can be said against money, that is the best medium of exchange. To attack it, when thus society's constitutional representative, is to attack the sacred rights of society, which involves anything else than socialism, a species of agrarianism, that involves the world in perpetual agitation and antagonism. No operatives should seek to pull down the rich or independent, but to raise themselves to their level. This is the highest inculcation of rational religion, that represents the highest rationality attainable by rational mind. If you pull down the soul of the public, who will employ and pay or justly reward you? If you do not analyze this whole position of yours, fairly and honorably, you produce the worst radical revolutions, tainted with the worst corruption and bloodshed. You must comprehend, with true principles only, the exertions. Industrial organizations might answer for a clique, but where is all society in the meantime? All would be in fragments, and each hostile in their little petty circles. Throw open to all liberal and honorable competition; have wise laws or constitutional organic principles, and much of the difficulty is obviated.

We can well ask, will not these industrial organizations produce social antagonisms, a greater evil than any other to be remedied? All such are short-sighted. If merchants are not sustained in their honorable livelihood by industrial operatives, can the last expect in return any work from the first? Have these men analyzed this subject, comprehended the position, and seen at the bottom the lame and impotent unsocial conclusions? It is a dangerous thing in well organized society, to have one set, secret or open, set up for exclusion of the rest.

That will not do good, but originate abundant evils, by the social perversions. Peculiar faith builds on this dogma, even unjustly and unprincipledly expelling rational religion from its God-created position, as far as in it lies, and seeking to substitute her tory brazen impudence therefor. What shameful pretension. This resolves society into its original elements, and excludes all the legitimate basis.

Working men, no more than any exclusive class, do or can alone constitute the quintessence of the whole society. The whole, no matter what the integral part is, must be rightly embraced—that is a vital principle. All improper combinations in society will defeat themselves finally, as they break up the very foundations of all society.

Rational mind is to keep up a proper equilibrium in the social, moral, and religious world. While I exclude all extortion of any circle, I hold that all capital that represents mighty minds' previous exertions, labor, mental or physical, should be duly respected.

Your socialism will render society unsocial, and demoralize it, making it clans and cliques. The world should have a liberal rational education.

Rational education gives mind self-reliance, and makes what would be a blank the greatest power.

The United States have the base constitutional government, to carry out most rightfully all the world-problems, and rational mind will in time present the enlightened solution.

LAND AND A HOMESTEAD FOR ALL FAMILIES OF THE WORLD.

THE idea of religion is to exalt man to his loftiest legitimate world-comprehension. Ought not all mankind, then, to have a homestead? The world is improving by constitutional representative government, and nothing otherwise, by rational progress of enlightened mind, and can give the greatest good to the greatest number, the whole. Mankind must not be crushed in their legitimate rights. Let enlightened public opinion irradiated by principles, illuminate the whole world, and away goes the mixed order of things. All good governments ought to have mind rationally educated, without which the world is barbarian, ready to be duped at all times by the dupers of the world. And yet must it not possess proper means, not such as would be radical, but purely conservative? The way much of the law is managed now, it is but a trickery in most instances for sharp lawyers to carry out their inherent felony. How much property is fraudulently conveyed—assigned. If man could only possess a definite amount, and that a homestead, much of all this would be broken up. What are God's funds? The world problems, among which is the land. How is all that mighty question to be settled? People who come into the world have rights to common property, the atmosphere, oceans, land.

What else, if not land? To guard all popular rights on fixed principles, this world question must be maturely considered with exact justice.

Lands cause much of the world squabble. Our forefathers went on the basis, that land was for mankind.

God created it. Now, how manage this difficult question, which has to be managed? The people are sovereign of the world, and sooner or later mind will assert their supremacy. The essential justice is to do so, with due respect to the constitutional rights of all mankind. Money, nor no other power, should facilitate the world oppression in this respect. Enable every man to keep out of all men's power if avoidable, to be justly independent on the adequate rewards of industrial labor, and then tffe world will see the best organization and guarantee of virtuous deportment. An organic base will then be instituted, for the most expansive happiness and universal peace of rational beings.

For what can they contend? What course of antagonism will there be? Rational mind must remove all the causes of agitation, the bribery of the agitators, and the world will progress in all its legitimate functions.

We have started right, following the standard of God in universal principles of government, but have not carried out all. When we abolished primogeniture and the laws of entail, we advanced much. But we must give every married man a homestead, and then he becomes independent, and declares his adherence for principles, not men nor their miserable time-serving policies.

Man should be protected in his noblest independence, to escape all the obsequious flattery to the world.

Dole out charity, when much that is abstracted is due the beggars or paupers, as they are called.

Proper institutions should never permit the least antagonism between castes, no causes of castes, the most damnable to conservative principles.

Let there be no lazaroni, no landless citizen in any part of the world, without a house to shelter; no mere street beggars for lifetime.

So crushed is mind, that the beneficiaries are not capable of appreciating the deeds of benefactors all at once, but nevertheless let the world solve mind's problem. This position goes for the natural rights of man. There is a highmindedness in all minds properly raised, and of the right stock that cannot be divested of, if they be independent.

Now in the place of charity, an undefined nothing, a contingency, the whole world has the justice of natural rights, which are not to be withheld. All such rights take precedence of peculiar faith, that if taken away, the world-feeling will be right.

All the world has to stand up to conservative revolution, that is absolutely essential to its greatest good.

The people are not to be crushed, but exalted. The lazaroni must have rights. None should be too elevated or degraded. All citizens have equal rights and privileges.

The law must be supreme, to have liberty and freedom, and with all that the noblest conservative principles of order under constitutional government, faithfully administered and carried out.

People may talk of embellishing parks and villas, but can there be a nobler theme than elevating mankind to proper rights and duty?

The houseless and destitute may be eternally in conflict with the supposed rich. If those in purple have any extra privileges, where are constitutional rights? It is desirable to see all prosperous and happy, but the State is more responsible than thought for in regard to rational morals.

All citizens should have not only education, but rational education, and all the birthrights of nature.

The homestead, be it small or great; it is independence that we advocate. Let the occupant say, I am possessor of a homestead, "my right there is none to dispute."

It is the protection of the working man to have him justly independent; none extremely rich, but no degraded lazaroni. The philosophical intelligence of rational mind must counteract all that oppresses mind. What is not accomplished by the foul spirit of intrigue, that deranges the world? If the world get the advantage, it rarely stops or pauses to know whether your rights are incommoded or not. If the unprincipled be at the top of the stairs, what care they about other's heads?

The world has ever been more or less in antagonism about this very principle. The Indian has spoken by his rifle, his war-hatchet, his bow and arrows. But no nation, people, nor individuals should appropriate the soil of the world. There are difficulties to solve, but mind is to solve in its refined civilization, the mightiest problems of the universe. Elevate the condition of popular labor and capital in the world, which must emancipate itself from all monopolies, dynasties, peculiar faiths and their codes or bibles, and subscribe to principles forever. Nothing less than the sovereign rights of the people of the whole world are to predominate, as paramount. All despotisms of monopoly and usurpation must all go by the board, by reason of mind that must regulate all in the legitimate channel. Monopoly and usurpation keep up the corruption, the degradation, the perjury of the world. The great problem of human existence, the natural increase and its happiest support, are all the available means of capital and labor, the due protection of property, life, liberty, reputation and happiness. The home labor and capital will produce the home happiness, give all this legitimate protection—rescue your country, the world from the iron barbarous savage grasp of monopoly and usurpation. How far can public property be established? Shall ferries, wharves, &c., be public as the rivers on which they are located, yielding to the legitimate views of the right possessors when purchased?

When landed property thus becomes public homesteads, there will be no difficulty about the titles, deeds, &c. If all this be rightly established, the world will do away with much useless litigation. This world must have a conservative revolution, over all the frauds and thefts of monopoly and usurpation. The great object is the most honorable elevation of man's true dignity, that will identify mind with its inherent independence and dignity. Make man feel that he is a man, and then you give the world its soul. Make him happy on this earth, to secure the best hopes of the future. If you create lords with privileges above laws, you degrade some to the beggarly elements assuredly below law.

Apply the two hundred millions of dollars annually appropriated for peculiar faith and its priestocracy, a nullity, for the proper relief of all the destitute of the world. This would buy all the destitute homesteads, and instead of false miracles of blood up to the present day, we should have the real results of good deeds for mankind. The whole world needs a beneficial change for the better.

Dependence crushes the soul of man, takes away even the spirit of independence. The Americans have considered themselves entitled to freeholds in regard to the Indians, now let them solve the whole problem.

The landholders are getting fewer in England; it is worse and worse every year. How is it in Italy, as Sardinia, where the labor of the operative could not procure one acre in the lifetime of the indigent?

The world must command its organic powers and principles. When our free government was instituted, the noblest institutions of mind were only commenced. Conservative revolution must carry out the balance.

The indigent cannot abuse the rich for anything predicated on the conservative principles of constitutional government. Let not the world be filled with antagonisms. Let all rational male adults have a foothold, and then their independence will be identified with their and the world's interest to support mind, and its triumphant rights and character, the truth.

Make it the immortal interest and merit of mind to support the truth and principles.

There are other world-wide, paramount, religious principles, that pervade this mighty subject.

The world must be governed on all the highest conservative principles, and those elicited by the most sanctified genius of mind. There is no other way to arrest infra.

ticide of families now going on in China, England, and other countries, but the institution of this most necessary obligation, that will best insure protection against abject want and starvation.

The utilitarian must overcome the fanciful, and the beauty of broad acres must yield to the holiest duty of rational mind throughout the world.

I call upon you, landed aristocrats of the world, whether of England or elsewhere, that seek the annihilation of nature's laws by mind's worst perversions of primogeniture, to attain a false dignity on privileges that cannot supersede rights. You are called upon this day to revoke all abused legislation on this subject, and offer up on your country's altars the noblest of all sacrifices for the best of all good. Your God-given trusts demand all this.

The paramount questions of population require land laws. Our nation acted on the principle of the homestead with the Indians, who were bound to yield a part, thereby acquitting the nation before the world, as far as it acted justly and wisely.

This nation has started right, with pure principles of government, and can best improve on the liberal principles of practical religion. She owes it to herself to carry out the most expansive acts of mind. That idea of the outside barbarians, heathens in all countries but their own, backwoods-men, all exhibits the deepest-rooted prejudices, that a generous and just commerce owes to the world to eradicate, to solve the world-problems. This great land question is a vast world-problem, a paramount one, and must be rightly met by the wisest action of rational mind, in wisest organic legislation. The creative genius of mind originates much capital, as the fisheries, that are a source of immense revenue. A generous protection will enlarge the world's capital; then there must be liberal world-policies, adequate to all legitimate demands. The supervision of rational mind will comprehend the whole agricultural problem, and ultimately rule out the cultivation of needless luxuries, in the place of which all the essentials of life are to be substituted. The utilitarian must prevail. A wise institution of organic principles will rule out loungers, vagabonds, idlers, &c., incompetent to support themselves. The most proper police will be an effectual institution of suitable laws, and their certain execution.

Will not just world-governments appropriate a certain portion, an exact ratio of its land, to the whole denizen constituency? Will the organic constitutional rights of the world tolerate anything less?

Let the enlightened public opinion of the world speak, and rebuke all that contravenes conservative principles.

In China, there are eighty thousand floating huts at Canton alone on its river, a land-excluded caste! These people are not possessed of any land : one step further, had it been practicable, and they had been excluded from atmosphere and water. This position cannot be overlooked. Once the lands were appropriated by military despotisms and primogeniture. All these are now exploded, and the original basis of action must be.

Make it an organic law, that no citizen shall own more than a certain number of acres, proportionate to the family. The first law of rational self-preservation demands this : this is the primary law of religion the most rational, the conservation of rational world-morals. The land fee-simple titles, under a general homestead law, would do away with much legislation.

Mankind should put all organic matters beyond man's whims, his will and devisings. Now a proper portion of land should go to every family. The whole world requires, by the highest of all constitutional laws, this paramount right of mind. Every family must have a homestead, permanent, and exempt from any claim whatever, sacred as the name of the family which owns it.

Here then is the sacred, wise potency of the organic law, that cannot be superseded by mind's follies, perversions, or sycophancy to absolutism.

The world needs no vulgar dissensions and animosities about debt. Put all on the best basis to create the least evils of mind's perversions.

The constitutional laws of states and countries are paramount, and must hold all citizens and rulers in abeyance.

Have all the basis of property right by organic laws.

No citizen should be dispossessed of his just portion of land.

Man should be justly dealt with while on earth.

Leave nothing to uncertainty, contingency, but all to a uniform position. Talk not of charity nor law, when justice will comprehend all the case.

God never made the lazaroni of Naples, much less the inhabitants of eighty thousand water-huts of Canton, not possessed of one foot of earth that nature affords in terra firma.

Give every woman, as well as man, land titles, so that each family may have the benefit of a homestead.

Let the organic law establish, that when a proprietor or proprietress wills at death, that all their children have an equal portion of the land, certainly, of which they cannot be divested, to give the whole world a fair chance to live. All should be compelled to have rational education, and to recover damages of local authorities to the amount of thousands of dollars on failure of the means to impart it, upon the party injured.

There should be proper employment for all capable of industrial labor. The state has to make right views, as to punish for wrong ones. Head all perversions of mind, and reward directly all rationality of mind.

The world should cut loose at once from old obsolete ideas of the old regime of ignorance, and its outrageous concomitants. Law binds man to man; religion binds man to society, and all to God.

The earth owes subsistence to all the people.

The law of nature is no corrupt law. How can kings exist if there be equal portions of land to each citizen? It was not constitutional in the world to yield up organic laws that protect the sovereign people, and it is its duty to re-establish all such by true conservative principles. But if all have homesteads in cities, the cities must be enlarged. Then that will redound to health. A land law has to be made organic, for all families to have a necessary and proportionate ratio. If we fix the world-society and organic constitutional rights right, then the balance of social duties will follow. It must be done by reason of conservative principles, not radical, overturning the existing order of all things, because of opinions. What is justly conservative, may become radical, if aggression be the rule. Is it best to have all debts on honor? This will abrogate much of irresponsible action of agents. What is responsibility, at a distance? It becomes too often irresponsibility. Nothing but principles will put the world aright. They were instituted therefor by the Creator, therefore let the world establish them throughout its whole theatre.

Let not any violate them.

Give every man his proportion of land: make all debts as near matters of honor as practicable; have all laws, the few that remain, simplified, and the world will see or feel but little of law in courts of justice. The whole difficulty will be more than half diminished, for altercation and antagonism in the world. There can be no contention for faith, land or money, if organic action is established by religion. What else can the world contend for? Make all above want.

Let the state be taxed proportionately to purchase, at proper valuation, enough to distribute the necessary homesteads to its own citizens. Abolish poor-houses, the shortcomings and frauds of commission, the deficiencies, and buy homesteads. Let no family be without a homestead. The rights of the world and its citizens are too often crushed by nonentities, that monopolies and usurpations the most abominable may flourish. The problem of socialism is solved not by abstractions, but by contributions universal. To do all this best, tax for homesteads. If the United States grant the balance of her public domain to the States, after proper sales and performance of stipulations, it should be with the express provision, that all the necessitous families of such State shall receive appropriate homesteads from their respective States.

If the world be right, the mind erect, religion and government pure, mankind can be happy.

Let the whole world do justice, and then talk of the future. Let there be no poor-laws, paupers, or poor-houses. Tax relatively to the whole amount, to buy a homestead and proper commencement to start with. But this homestead law may be severe. Yes, but the requisitions of religion demand it of all states and civilized countries of the world. Either a homestead, or a permanent interest in one, to secure proper comforts of life to the people, and proper protection to mind, to put all mankind under the uniform protection of rational religion. For an odious, absurd and tyrannical primogeniture, constitutional governments rear the universal homestead for all families. What a glorious era of rational religion, when rational mind of the world can be independent enough to think for itself, and to think rightly. The universal homestead is adverse to the law, of primogeniture, as much as constitutional government is to monarchy, as rational religion is to peculiar faith.

Give mind adequate protection, by rational education, and uniform means to procure sustenance, as a homestead; then perversion of mind will cease much, and crime will less preponderate. There will be less means to be operated on.

When the real aristocracy of any country arrest the organic rights of the people, that aristocracy render themselves the real culprits, as far as the national and individual perversions go.

In seeking this mighty world subject, nothing of radicalism is permissible, when justice can set the whole right on conservative principles, that balance all on ocean or land.

Rational mind has to carry over and above the weight of the priestocracy and of the debased, to rise.

No one person, clique or clan of persons shall buy up all the land, to the exclusion of the citizens. The purchasers must not transcend the organic laws of the world, which are of nature and nature's God, that cannot permit the proper amount of acres to be exceeded.

All ferries and wharves should be public. I am warmly supported in all this by Mr. F. Walthall, an intelligent citizen of Gainesville.

Are you, aristocracy of the world, desirous of cutting down the vices of the world? Then put man on his rights. Prove all by your actions, the representatives of thought's highest sublimity. Homesteads are expedient to clear the world of guilt,—a savage, unnatural antagonism—to promote the world's rights and redress its wrongs—for early marriages—to go to the deep foundations of virtue—to redress vice—the perversions of mind's habits—to correct man's, mind's evils, by mind's providence.

The Almighty's providence is one thing, mind's providence is another. Do you, world statesmen, see all the infanticides? Why all these, in populous, thickly-settled countries? Not only support that high-toned minded sentiment that will do justice to offspring, but give, yield the means to its complete success. What can be nobler than to support a healthy, virtuous, high-toned, moral and religious sentiment on this subject? The world must do justice to organic elements, that individuals may do strict justice to the human species. Do full and adequate justice to offspring.

What good are the world's laws going to avail man, unless he have some regular means to be identified with them? When one has more land than a proper portion, he has what does not belong to him; he is a monopolizer and usurper. All mankind are entitled to a proper portion, as of fire, air, earth and water—no more, no less: and government is constitutionally correct, that protects their citizens in their just rights and equitable possessions. The homestead is on the side of rational religion; the priestocracy, with their millions of church livings, on the other, a great cancer of demoralization, the worst of all to the world.

Virtue and independence, the strength of the world, are best secured by the homestead, for its honest yeomanry. The other presents a degraded clique, corrupting and defrauding the world of all that rightfully belongs to its legitimate benefits.

God has elegantly divided the earth into five grand divisions, that must cherish appropriate, universal, constitutional governments, to give each state its constituent, equal, maratime and other universal rights and prerogatives; and such government must give or see that each family has a homestead, an indispensable pre-requisite to equal rights and justice. The earth is for the people. There must not be any poor family on earth without a homestead—not one. A homestead must be possessed by all. It must be done; nothing short of it. It will be an everlasting disgrace for any country, not to yield it, as it is to any that the government should not confer equal rights to all citizens, doing "the greatest good to the greatest number."

There is but one kind of government beneficial to the most—the whole, and that is constitutional; that is so, first and last, in sparse or the most compact population, securing the homestead and the inherent honor of the population in all.

Raise all rational minds to practical business, to do themselves justice. Let them not depend on any relations or friends to do them justice, independent of their own high resolves and best exertions.

PUBLIC ECONOMY—GOD'S FUNDS.

But you do not liberally expend on the really indigent, a part of your superfluities. Nations as well as individuals, must seek to do this. The world must institute appropriate organizations therefor.

There are great expenses about matters that are encumbered with needless pomp.

The mind is ever liable, unless guarded by the liberal principles of education, to be perverted by custom, and then the tone of morality will not be up to reason.

The world cannot think or act rightly on its thought, until it waits for others, the leaders, to form a judgment, and then it can follow right or wrong. Those leaders may have self-interest to mislead the world.

We need to be free from the despotism of absolutism and the dynasties of society the greater and less tyrannies.

The world cannot go amiss for lofty enterprises.

The benefits of commerce to Liberia may redound to this country most satisfactorily, and may aid America in carrying out the most beneficent system of liberal constitutional institutions. That is an object of world-importance.

The school-funds should never be misappropriated or misdirected in any country, but should be adequate for all the just demands of universal rational education of the citizens.

This matter should ever be of the first class of relative duties, for mind's consideration.

VICES—EVILS—HABITS, PERVERSIONS OF MIND, THE NEGATIVE OF GOOD.

Who can overlook the effects of vices, in their thousand wiles? How many deceptions are practiced in the world, about its thousand and one influences, especially about money, &c. The very best are apt to deceive themselves and others; money is a power that too many idolators worship.

What does not avarice do in her thousand tricks, reckless of the world's safety, intent most franticly on the degraded gain. She adulterates the choicest viands of nature, to gratify her fiendish appetite of ungodly profit, that oftenest eludes her greedy grasp. She sells grain and meats that are enjoined, that injure the health, and disposes of rotten vessels that destroy life. She sacrifices the world, everything, to her brutal degradation. Void of conscience, which she has buried in her purse, she riots over the world, and binds every interest to her vitiated encroachments.

The acts of those who betray friendships in general practices of every-day life, are false and faithless, and render to the world a false position in society. Trust never to faithless man's promises, but show mind and have no needless proxy. But all this is not practicable in the universal union of society. All that the world can best do is to act on the noblest principles for life, to act for the greatest peace and benefit of the world, to get on without turmoil, trouble, and vexation; to put all things on a firm and uniform, not loose ground of benefit. Much rests with the mind of the individual.

The proper check to ambitious aspirations must be used even in study of science, much less in military glory, when the mind may be inordinately affected, and tranquillity sacrificed to vain and idle triflings never to be gratified. The wisest will take nothing for granted, when science can elucidate the truth and facts of nature. It is the interest of too much of the world to be deceived, or to deceive others. It is one of mind's greatest glories, to expel the world's delusions.

But credence can be entertained in the word of truthful men, who adopt principles, as confidence can be hazarded for their pledges. How can this be known beforehand. Their position is the only one to create a just confidence. They cannot be convicted of treachery to word, or affirmation of word, in their constant conversation. With them all such is sacred, and will be invariably treated as such. The highest obligations, as the marriage vow, will be so held. All such are held subject to principles of God; they know no other.

If rightly directed by the principles of the order of universal brotherhood, they would negative all opposition of accusation of clannish, selfish, and unjust efforts, of siding with secret lodge companions in thwarting justice.

One of the great means of universal conservation, is adequate protection on principles.

Any accused persons, however lowly, are entitled to call for proof of accusation against themselves, else the accused fall otherwise, and society is unhinged. One person is as good as another, no matter how low in worldly possessions, until valid proof is brought; no matter how high the accuser, or lowly the accused, we must have just proof to reach a proper condemnation. Thus, one cannot go to sleep on any reputation, as all are held responsible for good reputation and deportment till death. No kind of peculiar education and habits, its result, can intrinsically excuse interested prejudice and corrupt views. A counteraction of malign influences is the best management in all the circles of one's duties in life.

Most of all social malign influences arise from the peculiar influence of peculiar faith institutions. Abolish all such as world-nuisances.

Many may have not a proper calibre of intellect to resist the delusions of the world, unless duly prepared by a suitable independent code to resist temptation of vice, and the wiles of sophists.

But few can appreciate their absolute world condition.

But steer as clear of vice as you can, still, part of the world extremely corrupt itself, will not do you justice. Then you must do yourself that duty to justice. The best way to counteract libels and calumnies, is to let your actions triumph over all libelers—live them down.

If we study mankind in this unenviable feature, we shall find it one of the worst of perverted mind. It is certain that conservative revolutionists invariably exasperate by their position, the most legitimate of the world, all monopolists of exploded systems that are in antagonism with the world's true interest.

This position of this world, so mixed in ignorance and fraud, that renders perversion of innocent mind, should cause you to define and maintain all your position.

The world affects to treat proper accusations of some people, impugning them as unworthy of credit, as it suits the interest of cabals and factions, because the influence of these people has been in society, factiously great. It does not try the issues on the facts and merits of the case.

If any employment of males or females make them worse, or endangers their morals, drop them entirely. Public sentiment being right in the world, promotes a sound state of morals, religion, and government.

MURDER.

WHEN murder is perpetrated, by insulting the party killed, who may have resisted on the noblest principles of mind, it is nothing but assassination.

The lives of the community should not be sacrificed for the omission of capital punishment by the state, that will find it the least of evils. It cannot be omitted the present age, at the same time all the proper exertions must be made, to elicit the best promotion of the soul-problem. The reward of promotion. solitary confinement, and industrial employment of all classes, may advance the solution.

The murderer causes much perjury, the violation of principles. Murder is only justifiable, when one individual kills another in pure self-defence, that is, to prevent being killed, and this construction involves the noblest principles, not those of provocation.

How often is it, that one provokes another by language, and acts to resent an insult. and then the aggressor takes advantage, planned designedly in his foul crowd, and commits assassination.

But what is the life of such a murderer? Not prepared to die, and unfit to live, abiding a few more years in misery, and dying in horror and remorse.

How often have the innocent been punished, by an imperfect system of jurisprudence. No individual can be presumed murdered, until certain proof of death, by which alone we can convict of murder. What murderer sees peace of mind? Even an Emperor must feel for the wrongs of blood done nations. It is a severe matter of temptation, to be exposed to all the malign influences of power and tyranny that enslave the tyrant and usurper, worse often than his victims.

Provocations of persons to extremes, and then pretendedly killing them in self-defence, is assassination, and must finally produce conscience guilt and remorse.

All the delicate and paramount rights of mind must be duly respected.

RETRIBUTIVE JUSTICE.

WHAT evidences have we of retributive justice? They are too universal over the globe to be misunderstood. We observe many clear facts in the severe domestic tyranny of individuals, who have committed deliberate maiming of subordinates, murdering others, and violation of the nuptial vow, of an unhappy life, and a miserable end, as death by suicide, or by others.

Seduction has rendered all the families unhappy and miserable, the daughter of the seducer a prostitute and an adulteress, the cause of her husband's death, and the eternal disgrace of the best relations.

There are rights and vows that are sacred, and cannot be overlooked but by the worst stock of human nature, of no account to themselves, relations, country, or the world.

In the sacredness of vows, the mind of both parties has to do its part, to render abeyance to the dignity of virtue, above all, duty, and not give an imperfect copy.

Mind owes, above all, justice to itself, that the most exalted thought, habit, and practice bestow.

Prostitution of mind is fearful and retributive, as when the precipice is once passed, the downfall is continuous.

Adultery causes perjury and subornation of perjury, crushed feelings, suicide, murder, misery, strife, contention, iniquity beyond appreciation.

In cases of perverted lust, as that of seduction, the seducer has been involved in suicide, having first failed to produce death upon the unfortunate victim. But what a world of affliction often attends the woman. Many place the account to the seducer, and often very justly. It takes two to confirm and divide all such guilt.

See the withering effects of storms, blighting the various parts of the world, and then observe similar states of moral blights of mind. What was in God's purpose to master creation, mortals cannot say, but his principles are conservative to universal good. Mankind must learn of immortal principles, immortal truths. Too many parents neglect these, unable to teach their children the only means of reaching correct position.

But above all, the state has a higher duty and inquiry in their education, than in their punishment.

The great object of man's congratulation is mind's triumph over all sublunary difficulties, by its inherent faculties rightly called forth by due cultivation, otherwise mind's treasure is inert or misapplied, in inglorious inaction or evil action. The effects of individual and national misdeeds reflect too truly this whole position.

Every age of the world receives its impress of mind's progress, and truly records the necessary results.

Can there be an atheist or polytheist who has comprehended the whole subject, unless monomaniac or unprincipled, when he observes the wisdom of rightly cultivated rational mind's government, in curtailing evil to the narrowest limit?

Mind, that has ignobly surrendered to its own and the frailties of others, the world, tends to degradation, if not perdition. What is to reclaim it?

Peculiar doctrines, those of any peculiar faith?

What inherent peculiar power has that, itself an usurper? Mind can only deal in principles, otherwise peculiar bad effects, retributive, will ensue. The wisest and most comprehensive counteraction is better than all subsequent action in the world's affairs, as who would risk the destruction in the falls of a mighty river, to have the chance of repairing afterwards? Mind can only rejoice in the simple and innocent pleasures of life; beyond the proper limits, families, individuals, nations, the world suffer penalties proportionately to their evil deeds.

The world's history presents much of what is called retaliation, retributive justice that bears often with the heaviest hand. Individual and national retaliation is often excited by the feelings that passions outraged arouse, may not be always wise, is not certainly just, unless facts always warrant.

All this can be referred to the highest earthly tribunal, that of principles, and can yet be better counteracted in the mightier tribunal of conscience.

Patriotic and sound virtues must protect the necessary constituent laws of the land, certainly uphold good and true citizens in what is right and just. All such are of the wise legislation of the world.

The various crimes affect most deeply, and awfully crush the perpetrators, who lose property, caste, character and life in most instances, if amenable for capital offences. In many cases of crimes, retributive justice crushes the soul by the severest inflictions, on both guilty parties. One alone is not guilty. What results from the neglect of becoming virtuous, to individuals and nations? Both lose caste in the world. Neither money nor earthly powers can recall it. The highest appropriate cultivation of intellectual and moral organs alone raises man to his dignity.

Retribution is in the hands of avenging principles. What is repentance in words worth, with no retribution? Where is the remorse of their guilt to end?

Sooner or later retribution will be paid, as principles exact accountability. The guilty party may play a thousand devices before the world, but cunning will not avail; cunning that a wise mind cannot countenance, will not answer the full demands of conscience.

Does the inebriating drink expel man's care, when it drags down his best vitality, and stupifies his feelings? Do cards, that beggar him and others' honesty, avail, when he has none to stake?

Whither can he fly remorse of conscience, the severest retributive justice? As well could he fly from himself. Has he sacrificed all for nothing? Is all this from the smallest commencement of vice, a most irrational violation of innocence and virtue that claimed his best protection, for which life should have been risked, and all his intellectual faculties bravely exerted? Is the woman married? Her anguish knows no cessation, her mind no ease? Is poison or other means to terminate their existence, by ignoble suicide or ignominious vital misery?

Is reckless murder to end this horrible picture?

Who can promise themselves immunity for reckless violation of principles, in a universe that is altogether governed by their conservation?

Pursue the history of one who promised marriage in seduction, at that time making a life competency. After ruin of the woman and injury of his own standing, he changes his abode and pursuits, and amasses an immense fortune. He purchases by the nett proceeds, a landed estate, from which he was ejected by the process of a law-suit, and was then a pauper, as the seller had no title and was a felon in cloaking his property. Considering it collusion, he is tempted to murder, but stays his hand and lets the unprincipled felon, from whom nothing by the laws of his state in which he resides, can be realized, pass. He makes other efforts that are fruitless, to make money, and finally went from compunction of conscience and married the mother of his child, though he had two children to support instead of one, and much intermediate penitence to undergo. What a lesson to the seducer, who had found his false pretences returned home to him with interest. Will any legislator refuse the necessary penalty, for such false pretences? All laws ought to be so founded, as to make the vindication exemplary, and render it the preferable policy to pursue the legitimate actions in life.

What are such frequent consequences, but ignominious compulsion of marriage, or death. These events have transpired. The true philosophical observer will see that many things come home with awful result from vicious habits. The murderer becomes a maniac, in a few days even. Another commits suicide, whilst most suffer the pangs of remorse or have to make restitution by summary punishment to the avenging laws of the country, or the avenging feelings of relations.

Restitution should be made by all delinquents for trespasses and sins surely, as well as bring forgiveness of the Creator. It is impunity that facilitates the perpetration of crime.

Accountability is then the first law of self-preservation of society, and as such is the institution of the Creator. Who can escape it in this life, or in a future state?

The treachery must exact restitution for the crime of the traitor. In how many filial, conjugal and parental, social, moral and religious positions of life is this seen and felt?

The agent, advocate, legislator or magistrate defraud their constituents and usurp their rights, proving themselves unworthy of trust and confidence that is often forfeited never to be recovered!

What a misnomer, that the king can do no wrong; what a fiction, that peculiar faith representatives are infallible and orthodox, when they both are obnoxious to the most positive corrections!

The world abounds in illustrations. History portrays, with faithful picture, the accursed tyranny of absolutism, and exacts the faithful condemnation of future ages against nations as individuals. the rulers more than the people.

The debtors ungratefully defraud their creditors, and teach the world a base peculiar education that perverted minds too quickly learn and pay back with deep retributive justice.

They leave their ill-gotten wealth to their family, which may be defrauded by relatives and false friends, whom their example may have influenced. There is a just God, who rules the world, the universe, all creation by his conservative principles. But why should not the delinquents have been more clearly punished in this world? That, in part, is referable to organic defects of society. That punishment is attainable in God's universe and in his way.

Let all its parts know and appreciate all this most knowingly, ere their sins mislead them to the deepest injury. How many are punished in this world, in most signal manner and ways?

If many are not speedily punished, that punishment may be only mercifully deferred for their amendment and correction.

Even "the conqueror suffers," in the field of battle, and that of his martial glory.

The state awfully suffers for false legislation.

The world awfully suffers, and that most signally, from the demoralization of bibles of tradition, that are idols preferred to the valid principles of mind.

How many evil deeds are perpetrated by cunning, that does not avail, as it recoils on itself.

No man should act as to leave his social circle, as if hurried off by any bad deeds. He should be able to reface it, at any moment of time. How often does adultery present an ignominious death—of course the life must be ignominious. The adulterer, with his dying breath, must often suffer the lie to escape his lips, or be self-condemned. One may be accountable for adultery for life-time.

Fornication and adultery may lead to murder. Avoid them, to escape death, ignominy, detraction, expulsion from society, loss of popular rights. These sins, in their commission, may involve all danger and retributive justice. Where is it to end? In this world? Who that is rational, can think so?

Much adultery is stopped, by direct retributive justice. . The indulgence of bad habits will positively produce retributive justice, unless they are properly resisted and overcome. By their malign influence, many throw themselves away most prematurely, arousing the sleeping tiger of retributive justice, that is not always passive, when they might have done well in marriage, temperance, fortune, fame, usefulness in the whole circle of the world. Some, by the power of vicious habits, cannot live out half their days.

If there be truth in friendship, how simple that person is who throws away reputation, friends, all the elite circle, the ablest advantages of the world, of future best prospects, to reach a mere temporary gratification, in adultery.

Does the world build up the most valued friendship, and then sacrifice it thus?

Seed sown in vice brings a harvest of punishment surely, says enlightened reason. The end will not justify the means, to arrest great evils by violations of proper law. No lynch law meets the case; indignation meetings will do better than indignation actions, the authors of which perpetrate a worse crime, and are doomed to its penalties. We must look to all fundamental principles, to restrict the least evils of society.

The spendthrift is an evidence of strict retributive justice, atoning for principles that he has most grossly violated. What shall the world do, to stay its reckless course? After the flood has poured over the banks, what then can stay its onward and rapid course? The disorganization of morals has been effected. Anticipate all such.

What wrecks of fortune, mind, and character are made, in the abuses of lust!

What sins and crimes has the world to account for, if it yield itself a victim to all such.

The bad habits of human nature lead to retributive justice. How often do penalties recoil on the right spot!

Principles, like ministers, bespeak a master spirit. Whenever proper laws are violated with impunity, the spirit of just retaliation rises on their ruins. We have then the most miserable substitutes. The greatest injury is to oneself for penalties, by self-retribution. The expulsion, by public opinion, from respectable circles, the sacrifice of property by a forced sale; the household participating in all the ignominy of the disgrace, in all the downward habits of dishonesty, plainly prove that the comprehensive view of duty, the whole honest duty, can alone satisfy the full demands of the world justice.

Low revenge, that tramples in the dust, behind as well as before, victimizes often both parties. This thing of proxy vassal dependence, to do the unconscientious bidding of demons in human form, must all have its appropriate retribution.

Moral bravery and intellectual light, with firmness, are what the whole world needs. If you do not stand up to society, who will stand up to you? If you murder, you will catch retributive justice certainly. You cannot miss it, do what you will. If you commit adultery, what will protect you? Thus you may think to violate laws, the principles of society, with impunity; but you can do no such thing. Does one gain anything by selfish advantages, tortures of humanity? No. Retributive justice will prevent him, will recoil on his household. What blockheads are people seeking to keep genius down, when the unprincipled opponents cut themselves out of their proportion of the world's advantages.

In all robberies of the thief, convict and punish him justly. Proper retribution must overtake all who seek to triumph over virtue, the distressed.

To guard best against mobs, Lynch-laws, the violations of laws, let the wisest legislation be instituted, and administered most uniformly.

CAPITAL PUNISHMENT .

CAN hardly be abrogated at this stage of the world. Abolition of capital punishment is not practicable, unless mental discipline be unfailingly adopted in the best, most effectual and conclusive mode; and can only be instituted on conservative revolution of the present social system.

Public exposures should be condemned, as there should be no public executions of criminals. The minds of the spectators are not benefited, but some may be rendered more sanguinary thereby.

The tuition consistent with the best regulations of rational education next to rational religion is the best support, and that ever resorts to the organisation of true government, such as free countries adopt, and that consistently rectifies all that is capital for good, universal success, and insures the highest and just triumphs of mind, in its present emanation and inspiration.

The mind has much civilization and science to reach, ere it can meet this question rightfully. Like that of the peace question, time must best answer it. Prevention of crime, as of disease, is the mighty solution of philosophical science. As the mind has not yet counteracted the direst crimes in individuals or nations, it cannot yet supersede the necessity of self-preservation, by appropriate punishment. Adequate punishment is ever to be contemplated by wise legislators.

The penitentiary presents an important system, though a severe state of existence. It is a necessary evil. It arises, necessarily, from man's perverted nature. This system should restore people to society, if practicable, improved beings, and possessed of some means to enable them to live beyond the oppression of want.

The government is bound to see them start, on a fair and equitable provision, to master the greater difficulties of life.

THE CHARACTER OF MANKIND, KNOWLEDGE OF HUMAN NATURE, THE WORLD AND BUSINESS.

THERE is so much sophistry, professional and general, that we meet with the greatest difficulty in reaching the facts of life, except by the best reasoning.

Man's character, nationally and individually is operated upon, and moulded much by this influence.

There are many men in the world, that we cannot believe on oath. We should trust no farther than we can yield power, that is absolutely necessary.

The doctrine of non-resistance will not suit the world at all, as it requires principles.

What confidence can be placed in mankind, nationally or individually, when self-interest and money are concerned, and there is no counteracting moral or physical power?

All proper confidence can be placed in a proper way with many, but mind has not yet established the universal principles.

Mankind needs rational education, mental and physical employment to nurture a sound state of mind, in the soundest practical constitution, not to thirst for vice and fatten on the spoils of innocence and the world's rights.

Mind rightly directed in conservative principles, will comprehend right with consistent actions to embrace it, resisting temptation, and triumphing over all ignominy. The aristocracy of mind resting on the means of exalting the character of mankind, is the only safe one that will exclude main reliance on force, intrigue, dissimulation and degradation.

Good faith-execution of all essential obligations in life, constitutes one of the best certificates for elevation of character. Punctuality in all serious promises, as payments, renders character conspicuous for honesty and fair honorable dealing.

The present age demands redress, and fundamental correction.

Of the schools of the world, though that of money is great, that of mankind is the greatest, as comprehending all. In this, science decides for all the secret springs of action, and here causes can be duly investigated to cause respect for intrinsic merit.

Mankind is ever disposed to act consistently, but for the world's peculiar education, that has to be conquered. We shall never reach the true analysis of the character of mankind till rational education has the victory. We only see man in peculiar attitudes, but let the school of principles be established, and a mighty conservative revolution will be instituted.

The world would be disposed to do right, were its principles permitted to have free action.

What advantages the mere appearance of character makes, accompanied by good faith. The whole world is captivated by its intrinsic powers.

Then mankind have to nurture truth and honesty, and not only meet all the world's demands upon their purse, but their mind, with exact punctuality, that tells their character to all, in characters unassailable.

All can show an honest action, if such be in their character. Experience can best direct generally, unless peculiar powers of genius can prevail most scientifically.

Proper analysis of the world's subjects is not obtained by faith, or anything short of principles.

It is the duty of the people to awake to a suitable sense of their own case, and its future best correction. When the people are fully enlightened in science and morals, then the most of all world impositions will be assuredly negatived and overthrown. Mind has a high and indispensable duty to perform, and it is essential that there be no defect in this valuable duty.

Some people of supposed good standing, flinch from principle, when they come to speak of money or power. What sort of public morals, and what is the character of public mind, that ought to know better than permit loss of the rule of principles? The knowledge of the world possessed by those that analyze but little, and read little of mankind, is very small. They go for few general principles, seeking by specific peculiar views to govern. Whenever individuals flinch from the test of principles, they may be set down as derelict, in purity of intentions.

We should look at men as they act, not because of their being in any particular circle.

The principle of personal independence is one of the best, that secures the confidence and best respect of the world.

Do you wish to know human nature in its disguises? Money and various trades with the people, in all their diversified business transactions, will impart that knowledge. Look at man, from the diplomacy of state to the pettiest office of the government, then you will find diversity of character.

What principles have some to do justice? But what can we expect, when rational education has hardly dawned on the world's horizon? What a large part of the world wait for the force of the law from a court of justice, ere they can advance the proper position of justice. What part of the world interposes perjury to prevent justice? If you seek to be miserable in your best knowledge of human nature, seek to purchase friendship by money.

If public functionaries lend money that belongs to the public treasury, they will be considered as official robbers, that pretended friends swindle for their own breach of faith. He that would ask a public functionary to lend him of the public treasury, is a traitor to all friendship that is worthy of honor. While our republican views must admit what is expedient and right, our knowledge of human nature requires its treatment according to the best appreciation of its laws. There are many people that it will not answer for them to have any advantage or power over the world, no matter what the pretence, what the name, whether peculiar faith or patriotism, as they will most certainly abuse it. They do not know themselves, how then can the world trust them, when they will be always unprincipled from perversion of mind? Men and women complain of the world-vices or evils; have they not been guilty of bad and pernicious examples? Society is in too artificial a state. Principles must be fixed.

No individual can appreciate man's true character, until the full trial under various vicissitudes; and none can give in the aggregate a better view than financial transactions. Giving, then, full scope in the circle where the best liberal principles of education have not reached and profited, we should find that the least confidence can be truly maintained in a large majority; in other words, that the fewest can be trusted, and that certainly the smallest part of mankind will do the thing that is fully right.

After a long course of observation, the most will be looked upon as unworthy of trust; not exactly worthless, but not exempt from suspicion.

A proper position has to be taken in self-preservation, that the fewest mislead us by sinister designs, that should be invariably counteracted in time.

It is wise to see the plans of all, whether they bring the influence about money or any other power.

It is decidedly the best policy to avoid antagonism; but at the same time, if mind premise suitable principles, we should act most decisively and firmly, for if we do not defend our rights, we forfeit the best right to them. Firmness is a virtue, but sagacity is a necessity, and counteraction a protection against many not trustworthy.

We should beware most clearly in trusting implicitly in any, who have been previously hostile; while we may forgive, we should never forget some unfit to be trusted with power or friendship, or any such thing near as sacred.

Mankind's best actions should show a bright example, and they can never pay too high a tribute to good actions, or reward honorable genius too much, in all her departments. The essence of all practical knowledge furnishes the best fund for a happy passage through the world aright.

Such is the best insured by the truly honest mind, that turns not from its course, but pursues the proper object all lifetime.

Youth should be taught the proper points at the proper time, by all the guardians of nature.

They should never listen to the corrupt advice of companions that does not agree with safe principles, but lay all that is suspicious before their best and worthiest advisers.

Wise parents, friends and guardians, will insure most by prudent persuasion, when they should never govern by mere brief authority, superseding kindness and reason. It is wise instruction that the world needs, and assured of that which is best, most will rush to it with impetuosity in time.

Circumstances of the world can only develop character, and of these, financial business is essential to exhibit it in many varieties. Self-love will be seen predominant in most professions.

So deeply is this characteristic in the mind perverted, as it may be from the correct view, that we should never hasten to commit ourselves in even ordinary business, unless we are perfectly aware that it is the best that can be done.

The wisest maxim will be, to have nothing of important business transactions with any not of approved character, and that of course is the most essential thing to study. Where we may be obliged to suffer if we anticipate this, we can well defer applicants, by taking all important matters into due and proper consideration, to have all right and just.

Selfishness is so often predominant, that myriads of aspiring people are prowling on the world, idle, dissolute, if not abandoned, profligate, vicious and unprincipled, from youth spoilt entirely in their raising, like a crooked, flawed tree, never to be properly mended on this earth, and ask men of truth to commit themselves to their word as their bond, however improperly extracted. The business profits are of course intended for themselves, for if they are to be in for their share of loss, they are not to be found, or found wanting. But their word!

What of that, under the most solemn promises?

They care nothing for their word, nothing for the world's opinion, which at least they will avoid in their way. This is a part of creation, that modest minds must not overlook.

Manly and sincere people promise to comply. Such promise little, but perform enough to the extent of their duty. They live and act prudently, as they desire the wisest position of life.

A true knowledge of the world calls for a guarantee of all things necessary, and leaves nothing for granted, subject to future doubt or cavil, or liable to suffer from the position expedient with all the numerous aspirants of the community, that render themselves unfit to be trusted.

This large portion, if they can compass their object, in getting all the advantages of power, money, and influence, care but little for any tribunal of public opinion, that is too far above them.

If they can retain such possessions, they will usurp all rights, in defiance of reason and reputation, that should control the world.

Does any individual suppose that mankind is known in theory, without financial jurisdiction, in varied money transactions? The proper knowledge of human nature, under the present organization of society, renders it plain, that there can be no fulfilment of contracts generally, where no responsibility can be secured by law. The moral suasion is deficient in too many cases, and proves the defect of untaught, undisciplined mind. For such people it is important to keep receipts, to avoid re-payment. People should learn, as they have to learn the world.

Some have to learn it too dearly, and may be caught for their property, by those schooled in vice and avarice, sharks and sharpers of society—the most corrupt of all the world.

Some individuals will have to adopt a new code of discretion, and trust no more than absolutely obliged; as they, in many instances, may have been the sufferers of ungrateful men taking advantage of their generosity.

There are so many explosions in the world, of all circles and classes, that mankind should be taught in the school of the world's experience.

We may well call money one of the schools of the world.

All then should graduate in the wisdom of this school for human benefit and liberal views, without the specific peculiar losses.

You can never do more strict justice, than when you institute the best security for principles, and, of course, cannot be too much of the adept in the comprehensive acquisitions.

You will surely find that it will not do to trust but a part of all the world, and that part you had better find out beforehand, if practicable.

Judge yourself, as it is a matter of taste and judgment about advising some individuals about others, as the most may be similarly situated.

As to the standards of character and qualification, put all the world upon the broad platform of honesty. Some people mistrust themselves, how then can they do justice to the cause of others?

Man can never know too exactly what principles prevail for best good, throughout his course of life.

The wisest use of man's knowledge is the security of purpose, by definite ends of propriety and fitness.

Some wish to have nothing to do with others, considering rightly that they cannot commit themselves safely to their company, and that the farther off the better. There are picayune great men, that debase human nature, not only with their littleness but baseness. What real good do such men do the world? A suitable knowledge of human nature is one of the momentous questions of the world, to govern which, rightly, you must know all about the bearing of malign influences.

You may be prevented from doing good and kind actions, as this position may be taken advantage of, by false constructions, premises, and pretences, antagonistic to all conservative reformations and revolutions.

Peculiar education, no more than peculiar faith, ever makes man a rational being. The ancients had all the elements of mind's calibre and greatness as the moderns, but they lacked mind cultivated by rational education. As much as we view the elevation of mankind for integrity, there is a sad falling off in this respect in even those, that ought to lead the first circles or morals in their country. Of what use are many public boards in the world, but to deceive it? The subject of inspection is bad, as managed. Some inspectors make things worse, not complying with the proper requisitions of principles.

THE ARMY AND NAVY.

THEY are expedient and essential for mutual protection to all nations, under the present organization of society. The best governments, as the strongest, are those most rational, identified with the affections of the people.

All that the world needs is an adequate police, to protect against piratical tendencies. The paramount question of adequate protection must be maintained, to keep the world right, whose wrongs have taught mankind such awful lessons.

The proper spirit of patriotism will respond to this sentiment. So far from relying on military despotism, neither the character of our institutions nor the advanced progress of the age, will permit the entertaining any such pretence.

The highest functions of enlightened republics would unquestionably respond to this sentiment, and oppose all innovations thereto, from the moral force of enlightened public opinion of the age.

The intellectual world will be duly interested in preservation of peace. The world cannot now have any pitiful excuse for wars on the basis of religion, and never would have had but for the iniquity of hypocrites. Religion cannot fight or contend in any species of antagonism with herself. Her division into parts proves non-existence. If ever there be any dispute about her, it is not religion. How can there be any just war therefore? But mind has been subject to vassalage, by its own weakness. It has sacrificed itself time after time, at the triumphal car of war.

All wars have their inherent evils most justly from the nature of things, the victor suffering even in victory.

Military ambition is a lurid glare—a meteor.

When the world has all the means of promoting peace and friendly relations between nations and individuals, it should endeavor to do so. As toleration of opinion must lead through an enlightened public opinion to freedom universal, as the proper government, that position must lead to universal peace.

We are all frail mortals, and should review nationally as individually our past lives, to amend honorably for the future.

The world should never violate the finer feelings of conscience, that will be always just to protect it better than a bannered army with its hosts.

Wars are objectionable as incompetent to decide principles of justice at least. The evils of wars are at the doors of the usurpers.

All partial and extensive tyrannies, all conquests of war for mere tyranny will fall, as such conquerors are human butchers. The nations of the world must adopt all the practicable safety to country by efficient progress in mind, military engineering science; but, above all, moral and religious science is the best protectress, as preventive of the necessity of the use of the others.

Then the world must advance in ratio with all, by the sublime protection of reason, that createth understanding, and adorneth wisdom, virtue and happiness.

The world has never yet reached the dignity of the world, since it has presented no age that of refined rational civilization.

Have truth, honesty, humanity, and a sound state of enlightened public opinion flourished rightfully ? Have not the wars and violence of the world prevented the consummation of this refined character from being universal, individually and nationally ?

Warfare by the decree of Deity is accompanied by scourges and encompassed by penalties, pestilence and famine. Now the world sees that wars are the most costly games for nations, and that industrial organizations are the most useful to exalt the world's happiness. The wholesale butchery of the people by wars, can be effectually stopped, by suppressing all the State reasons for murders and punishment so abundant among the world's tyrants. Mind will respect mind pre-eminent with statesmen's philosophy, that advances hundreds of years before the people's age, and enkindles their enthusiasm at the time universally to acknowledge the greatness and supremacy of principles, before which potentates are small indeed. Then, and not till then, wars will be no more, and the people's theme will require peace first.

A peace world is expected now, but never will it be attained, till all the elements of antagonism to principles are placed in abeyance to the last. All the present peculiar faith persuasions must be put down and forever silenced, that the only true faith, pure religion due to the omnipotent Lord God, may reign supreme.

The world is filled with clans and sects, some of which will perjure themselves, to rescue members from death deserved, by murder and other crimes.

The secret societies are charitable to their individual members, who raise a proper dividend fund therefor, and keep their members remindful of their peculiar duty and obligations.

Most of them divide and separate the world further apart, by clannish feelings.

The unconditional expulsion of all partial and peculiar tenets can be only attained by general and universal principles, that attest their permanent endurance.

Individual pretensions must be resigned to the benefit of the greatest number, that is, all in such societies, and peculiar faiths must be merged by mankind in general. The world has a paramount claim, that rebukes all secret societies, since a universal brotherhood is absolutely necessary to maintain all its proper relations. The history and analysis of the world teach us certainly that peculiar faith and societies are unsuited to its universal necessities. It well becomes the world to inquire what, if all the means and pains were exercised towards the securing universal brotherhood, as there are to all peculiar faiths and societies, would it not be advanced in its legitimate and dignified worthiest basis ? Assuredly.

The army and navy promote the good of society, embracing the protection of the country and civilization; but when all such are arrayed for mere conquest and dominion, overwhelming mind and civilization, then they are nuisances among nations, and should be accounted as amenable to the just censure of the world.

When opposed to the spirit of free institutions, that must necessarily arise in all countries and supersede any existing government, however sanctified by time—yet not sanctified by its best gifts of blessings to rational mind—then the question of high treason arises, though ostensibly bound to existing orders, as the paramount rights of the citizens place them in that category.

A superior age of civilization has given additional security to the people in their national rights, in which every true patriot soldier or citizen is deeply interested.

Reason and justice must have lost their sway of mind, and mind its right faculties, if war be necessary. War is no more necessary than the belief of the infernal regions, to keep the world in a right state of morals. The defect is in mind, all the time, about all such miserable creeds. The world needs civilization, not war, which is alien to its peace and happiness, and produces barbarism.

Civilization is sustained on universal principles, that must be universally cherished, to reach the brotherhood. The more peculiar the faith, the more nations will be disjunct and their general interests alien.

Any nation alone could not abolish war, but it can place itself ahead of all nations, and an example for their imitation, in constitutional government, rational religion, and the wisest institutions resulting therefrom to mind. What can peace societies avail, if the world does not come up to the dignity and worth of civilization ? The system of national defence embraces much of science and the best precautions of mind, ever ready to assert its independence. Many of the practical principles of life that are identified with so many relations of the universe, are also identified with this whole subject.

Military and naval science, legitimately employed for national defence, yields to none in its potent virtues.

Let the council of the five grand divisions arbitrate it on principles, and settle forever the best practical code under the consummation of the world's rights. The proper development of mind's and the world's resources, will display the advantage unmistakable to maintain universal peace. The world governments should reduce naval and military expenditures to appropriate establishments. Expend all extra naval and military war equipments to the civilization of the world, and to all the paramount demands. The world has to be governed rightly, by proper conformity to the just laws of nature.

Strip war of its absolute self-defence necessity, and it is piracy on the world, and will be so regarded. Parties and their partizans may pretend that it is essential to keep down the human population excess, or the race. That is a libel on Deity. All reflects on mind's perversions and incapacity to appreciate that all of God is right, but all that is not rational; no matter how peculiar, the worse the misconception.

THE COLONIZATION OF AMERICO-AFRICANS.

THE horrible deeds of martial prowess, stained in blood and gore, have changed into the mildness of bondage, and that bondage is raised by education of the savage mind. Africa's races have been exalted by slavery, and the mother country is now being redeemed by their posterity returning, enlightend by the brightest emanations of Anglo-Saxon intellect.

The immutable law of nature shows a superiority in races. The inferior races must have inferior employments, whilst they remain together. With the Caucasian, the African race will be the peasantry.

Colonization, not amalgamation, will be expedient in Liberia; the free colony of Africa will best meet this noblest solution. Slavery will be necessarily limited by the limit of lands and its profits, then it will die out certainly and necessarily.

There are mighty changes going on in the world by emigration. The Americo-Africans, elevated by the proper light of rational education, and transplanted into Africa, will bring, it is hoped, an amelioration of rights and liberty to that grand division of the world.

Civilized colonies, of her own blood and race, have been returned to the bosom of Africa, to arrest more effectually the slave trade, and are now redeeming this fierce country from the deepest vassalage of mind.

While these people have no citizenship among us, let them look to their father-land, where now is reared a home of dignity for the descendants of those, Africa herself enslaved, returning as the freemen of America, that has done a better part by them.

Let the world devote the fees and funds of missionaries to the cause of free black colonization; the main object of all such institutions being the promotion of the world's benefits.

We must expect to avail ourselves of the conservative principles, the best acts of mind being an especial providence, in most instances of life; as there the aid of science enables mind to extract from the richest treasury. Many difficulties are eradicated in time.

Let this matter be taken properly in hand, and let all surplus benevolence be herein concentrated. The benefit will be broadcast in Africa.

A mighty family of confederated states will arise—a free and enlightened nation that will irradiate that vast part of the world.

Colonization associations may advance this magnificent enterprise. An annual appropriation of $30,000 has been made by the Virginia legislature, paying for whatever expense may be incurred by the African Colonization Society in the transportation of free persons of color from the limits of that State. Let us well analyze the suitable means of universal benefits, and shame the feeble and imbecile pretences of bigoted minds, prompt in antagonism with mighty facts that their feeble views cannot comprehend.

There must be no amalgamation of the races, who cannot have equal guarantees of citizenship. Let the free blacks go to Africa, the fairest theatre in the world for intellectual missionaries of refined civilization. They will be worse off in this country, the more dense the population of the whites is. They cannot get citizenship here, but can in Africa carry civilization, science of pure government and mind, and eventually do more for Africa than she ever did for herself.

Their nominal liberty is not freedom, which bespeaks the loftiest rights of the denizen.

Go, free black man, to Africa; there is your noblest theatre for all that a free-man's mind can hold dear; there you can build up the noblest of all freedom, that of mind.

It would be well for this country to appropriate a sinking fund, that is, a certain amount, applied for extinction of any certain debt annually contracted in the Coloniza-tion Society. The abolitionists cannot advance their views but at the expense of dis-union, the ruin of our country. What folly would that be. All such will be best accomplished by the natural result of things, when labor gets profitless. The world will finally come to the right point. Say you that there is no Almighty Providence in all this?

The free blacks are placed as freemen in Africa, to irradiate that benighted land. What a noble destiny is theirs? Instead of wasting their energies here in this country, those who aspire to be men should direct their noblest efforts to that inviting theatre for mind.

Our country and its glorious union, first say all enlightened patriots; then the world. What a gigantic outburst of mind inspiration, through God the Creator, is the solution of the world problem. Africa must and can only best protect herself, as all other coun-tries have to do for themselves. There is no effectual restraint on the African slave trade by the blockading squadrons, and cannot be fairly, till she act herself most effici-ently. The correction applies to the root of the evil. Reaction of mind, as well as of force, must reach her native rulers. The last cover of barbarism is about to be lifted from most of the world, especially Africa, with her intestine wars. What the refined African is, he is indebted to America for; and hereafter he will bear back to his father-land the best impression of America's refined civilization.

Free blacks, who have not the protection of slaves, nor the blessings of liberty to any proper extent in the country of a different race, and cannot have, short of Africa, should never think of remaining out of it as a permanent home.

As a sincere friend to the free black. I suggest that Africa is the only country where they can truly secure their free and best rights. Free negroes should go to Africa, where they can secure all of constitutional government.

Peculiar notions will not answer to extirpate slavery. The world is not to be taken by storm, when rational mind is to promote all that is expedient, for the world's happi-ness and universal good.

The gain of temporary political advantages, pays too dearly for such sacrifices. You lose your country and all its holiest affections, its highest beauties, its firmest strength. You may gain a few isolated points, but you lose a world of freemen. Better sink all your foibles and your crimes in the ocean, or make them a bonfire to your country's good. There are many rectifications, but the beautiful result of time may be expedient.

God made his creation right; it is for rational mind to subserve that paramount idea. The world is not to be forced, reduced, but reasoned with—treated most rationally to be treated most wisely. In this way, the only rational conservative revolutions can be effected, that promote the world's highest, most refined civilization, whereas the revo-lutions of blood may derange all that.

Can you have this reproach that you did that, when you knew better? Are you agitators, so selfish that you are going to throw away your mighty institutions, and involve all the iniquities of military and despotic rule?

The African still has his skin, his peculiar characteristics that distinguish him as a diversity of the human race, the highest proof of God's unlimited creative powers. There is no mark in creation, that can enable rational mind to decide for any peculiar prohibition from his ultimate continental rights in Africa. Let justice be done both sides of the question, to have the world problem rightly solved. Raise a dollar annu-ally for life-time, and let all be faithfully applied to the execution of this plan. Now abolitionists, leave off agitation, and to the practical part.

What is the cost to the different governments, to suppress the slave trade? Can that amount be appropriated to purposes of colonization of the free blacks in Africa? The free blacks need not look for homesteads in America, but you can get them in Africa, and that proves conclusively the necessity of your immediate emigration to that splendid theatre for your best exertions, that await the best display of rational mind.

Free blacks, seek the worthiest theatre, the civilization and rationalization of Africa, a mighty problem. All your acts in this country are puerilities, and your advisers are bigoted What a prospective has the world in recovering Africa from barbarism, through its western coasts, while the eastern, vitiated by peculiar institutions, has shut all that promised mind's elevation. Negroes are assigned inferior places; why do they wish to remain here under such circumstances? If they be civilized, they should give the best proof of it, that of independence.

Have no consolidation of government, but let it be one general government of sovereign states.

Africo-Americans, you hesitate to emigrate to the continent of Africa. Your step will expedite liberation, emancipation and colonization. Interest the world in your illustrious enterprise. Let your thousands rush to her shores, and cause a morale from Africa, that will rouse up the noble spirit of liberation, by the best proof that African descendants are worthy of liberty. The world has to be managed—not forced. Be' done, agitators, and do acts of mind worthy the American Union. Do not be political hacks for partisans to ride. Do not ruin or jeopardize your country's union for all Africa, the world—all. Yours, Americo-Africans, is an excellent theatre to build up a continental republic, greater than, and more durable than that of the Romans, with Cæsar and Pompey at their head, than of Alexander or Napoleon, than all the Ægyptian priestocracy, not to christianize, which is absurd; but civilize and religionize the whole. Here is the munificent and magnificent theatre of your fame, glory and happiness. Leave where you are, uncasted as well unrated, and hasten to your appropriate sphere and rejoice that you can do so.

Come, agitators, political hacks, you tie two knots for one—you are inadequate like all your world-botches, in solution of world problems. Act the right way, only as rationalists.

Save this union from agitation, by colonization principles, that will promote the noblest improvement of Africa through religion and all the attendant blessings of the noblest civilization.

What a benefit, if the world's funds could go to the African Colonization Society and similar associations. Give the preference to Africa over Hungary.

Free blacks, do not listen to your false advisers, as you cannot be free denizens in this country. Before you should be the cause of dividing this union, the Americans would think it the greatest humanity, to see you sink in the ocean. Retire to your proper scene; rush with the greatest joy that you can do so.

To you is reserved the richest of all missions, that of aiding in fully civilizing Africa in process of time—aiding in elevating her to the rank of the fifth grand division, the greatest of all conquest, the fairest field for glory.

The best results can be accomplished—by the best system. You will help to diffuse one universal language, the English, and the highest of all sciences and philosophies.

UNIVERSAL BROTHERHOOD: NO SECRET SOCIETIES.

If any, as the work of man, nurture cabal, faction, unprincipled opposition, antagonism to general good, their policy is too short-sighted to be respectable.

Universal benevolence must be the principle, or they fall short of the best after all.

Is any instituted on sectarianism and clannishness, it then falls short of universal benevolence, as all sectarians do. When any institution premises merely the helping each other, that is, helping themselves alone, that is mere isolated self-preservation. All bodies with the present light before their eyes, cannot seek peculiar faith in any organization, as that is antagonistic to the world's general benefit. They should undoubtedly prefer the world, to any peculiar views that cannot be permanent.

Universal brotherhood alone can only suit the noblest and right position of mind, as it suits best the whole human family. Citizens' rights are now protected in America enough, to advance social rights to an independent universal position, without fear or reproach. States are sovereign, as the mind of the people is prepared. What hero made this country so great and glorious? The free institutions of her citizens, reflecting on and being reflected, from the intelligent mind of freemen. The proper institutions of mind will be promoted by the glorious creator, the magnificent author of mind, to the noblest pinnacle of happiness. Those that were conceived in error or weakness, may fear the light or liberal discussion under the guarantee of liberty, but those that are wise and universally good need not fear the light of the Creator.

Join the universal brotherhood as philosophers, you who are masons and odd-fellows. You have now no longer, as ancient Druids or others who were forced by the despotism of the times, to become secret, to withhold your union to the best efforts of mind.

You can now by universal union more effectually avert the awful calamity of the world, that peculiar education may induce. You can give up all that you devote to this object so partially, especially your money affairs, and let them all go to a general fund if you can do without it, for the benefit of the human family. You can have effectually met all the comprehensive demands of the world by universal brotherhood, that freemasonry and odd-fellowship cannot touch. In this you are placed as you necessarily are in the world, and cannot be excluded from those rights by any petty intrigue.

Do all secret societies nurture clannish notions? Then how long can any such survive and enlarged can such be? Are not all the secret societies and clubs for themselves? That is selfish, clannish, sectarian.

Suffice it for us, the world to know, that it is a case demanding relief, benefit and aid; if so, our brotherhood in that respect is universal.

Let that circle be as comprehensive as the circumference of the earth, as extensive as need, and then the proper requisitions on mind are fulfilled.

Do not trammel your liberty by club-rules, that cut up society, towns and cities, the world, into all the causes and curses of sectional divisions.

The superior interest of the world demands that no secret society should be first, then the world next or not all, to foster the first all, but let the balance starve. All sectional peculiar faiths and societies, abstract from primary universal principles that must have first and last showing all the time, from which the supreme allegiance cannot be ever dissolved.

The interest of secret sectional societies is obsolete, if you follow the noble legitimate principles of approved and refined taste of nature.

Is it not prima facia evidence, that a man has less merit than peculiar motives, to seek and court the popularity and influence of secret societies, to advance his personal pretensions before the world? Why some of these societies? Are they to help uphold the bible? The priestocracy, &c? They will not then uphold themselves, as all such have the elements of their own destruction. Universal brotherhood upholds religion, all that is expedient.

The little peculiar societies of the dark ages, when protection was wanted, are hardly necessary now, when the world is governed better for individual protection, and liberal comprehension of principles.

Which of the secret societies, except those that recognise universal principles, can pretend to reach the points that one universal brotherhood only can? Is the world-society cut up into clans by any society, especial or vice? Counteract all such. You can never identify the majority with any one sectional secret society, as all rational minds are members of universal brotherhood.

We desire no social tyranny, or any malign influence. Bands of secret societies may be dangerous.

All sectarian societies, and all are so that do not admit universal brotherhood, should give up.

Most all secret associations are sectarian, as Masonic and Odd Fellows, and therefore will not answer. We need something of universal brotherhood. How far does the electioneering of secret societies go over personal merits? Does it not prevail, as far as practicable? The attempts of secret societies no doubt originated for certain purposes. If for the best, they must be comprehensive enough to embrace one universal brotherhood. Secret societies are a detraction from part of the world. If some be thus helped, they are so at the expense of others; then injury results. Secret societies should do good to all. There is enough for them to do, if they only prevented strangers from being badly treated.

Why are there secret societies now, in these days of liberty, when one faith is as free as another in respect to worship? By this time we must see that they are incompetent on their present basis of attaining anything like an important point: they will consign themselves to an ignoble position, in face of the progress of universal brotherhood. Behold, what power is in that position! All others are futile, incompetent, and incomprehensive. The Masons were likely the ancient Druids, and may be looked on as one of the world's moderate aids in humanizing the human family, that is, through mind. But it is certainly now an explosion, as too partial. It is not suited to the times. Before the world can accomplish all by peace conventions, it has previously to establish universal brotherhood.

Secret societies have some redeeming quality, but they are strictly sectarian, and their qualities are essentially predicated on that objectionable basis, else they could not exist.

Now the greatest example of the best standard of taste, because the source of excellence in character and action, that of Deity, is a universal benevolence that arises on pure religion that is separate from sects, too plain for any rational being to mistake, as its universal bearing is opposed to such a position. Sects are the antagonism of rational religion, that lies not in fragments, but a universal faculty.

All creeds, notions, and fruits of man's systems, run into peculiarity and partiality; those of God, as displayed in rational religion, are pre-eminently distinguished by the supreme characteristics of universal love and good.

Such transgresses no laws of nature, overwhelms no dignity of justice. Endowed with the true elements of self-exalting greatness, the whole comprehends the world's theatre as her legitimate sphere of best usefulness.

All secret societies are wanting in all the characteristics that will carry us through, and they are essentially deficient in capacity to advance to the lofty heights of rational religion, that has the universal brotherhood united by the indissoluble bonds of all conservative principles.

It is she that prompts the outlay for nations' bounties, a world-wide benevolence, in painful times of famine and disease, and causes nations of the earth to speak in acts of universal beneficence.

She is ever responsible to the deepest sympathies of mind.

Are not God's principles adequate for the universe? If they were not, the universe itself would not exist. Its existence proves God's government.

What general good do secret societies?

Do secret societies create any vices instead of virtues—do no good, but harm more—produce clanships and one-sided views in society? Then such produce disorganization instead of moral dignity.

Can anything be now attained in the present civilized state of the world by secret societies?

Is any partial benefit to be compared to a comprehensive world-wide and expansive liberality?

Is justice defeated, the felon rescued, or favorites benefited; but the opposite party, if not in power, though clothed with triumphant justice in momentous scenes, to be put down by combination and collusion? Is this the way the greatest good to the greatest number in society, the whole, is promoted? What value do all such impart to the strength and intrinsic worth of universal society not previously there? But if it detract from it in any wise, then pause at least.

If a member and the world differ, the secret society is bound, if practicable, to side with the member. Are not the secret societies restricted to the interest of their peculiar order, to help and aid the families of their members? Are there not more than a dozen now? Is society thus properly cut up? There is sectarianism enough in the world. Universal brotherhood embraces all that can be included rightfully, and will heal difficulties impracticable to secret societies. Secret associations disturb the mutual general relations of society, like sectarians of peculiar faith, that go for themselves.

In all such societies the members can only promise themselves partial views and actions, mostly beneficial in their circle, whereas they can be universally so in the great order that embraces all comprehension of the subject. All such fall short of the great principles of the only true society, universal brotherhood of world-civilization. Then there will be no cavil, that men unite to conspire against any part of the whole.

Universal brotherhood will do more good than all secret societies together, as the last can never reach the true position, being of man; the other, of God, and absolutely necessary to exclude all peculiar usurpations, monopolies, and pretensions of peculiar faith, that presents peculiar despotism.

Are not benevolence, mind, &c., world-wide benefits?

Secret society people, do you divide and subdivide the world by secret associations, when you could better facilitate your universal purpose on the noblest principles, and by union of all? Are there not sectarianisms enough in peculiar faith? Do you wish to cut up the whole into the smallest circles?

The junction of the whole grand divisions of all countries will be essentially necessary in self-defence, and of course no partial secret societies can begin to meet the adequate demands of nature. How partial are all secret sectarian societies. All societies, as Masons, Odd Fellows, should take in the whole compass on universal principles, not sectarianism.

You cannot reach the object short of universal principles, which you have not by all your present defective organizations. You have not religious associations, as you confide in sectarian bibles.

All expedients of secret societies are not only superfluous in the existence of the one universal brotherhood, but derogatory to the whole fabric, asking for the substitutes and their idle pretences, instead of God's conservative principles.

All secret societies have sectarianism, that divides and subdivides the world into disorderly and alien petty partisans. Why all this? God needs no such thing. Of course, then, man's general benefit is not concerned when invaded by peculiar devices. We do not want the free or secret Mason's square, when the world has God's principles. Let the last be religiously diffused by rational mind, and the richest fruits will be produced. The superfluities of the world would support all its paupers. What good do these petty societies in the world? Are they not cliques and clans? Affecting universal good, they are sectarian, and the results prove it. If you seek a universal brotherhood, you cannot find it under Masonry, Odd Fellowship, or any peculiar faith doctrines; only on universal conservative principles, established by God himself, who foresaw all the devices of selfish man. Only to think of the petty, inefficient secret societies, when there is one formed by God, and bound by rational religion. What a contrast!

This age must bespeak a different order of things. Let the universal brotherhood hold all the petty secret societies in abeyance. now and forever—looking through universal principles, to a universal standard, Almighty God. Rally under the sublimest of all banners, rational religion, and establish, as world patriots, American liberality, commensurate with the wants of mind.

Religion embraces all the comprehensive principles of universal brotherhood.

All that God has instituted should be most wisely nurtured.

Why then should the whole world waste its most valuable time and talents in any inefficient undertakings? Prove, secret orders, that you are most competent for universal good, otherwise unite in one great brotherhood.

Monotheism demands all, to secure the correct position of the whole, the world.

How, in the name of universal brotherhood, can mankind be properly benefited by sectarian strife? What an amount has been engendered already. Why, secret societies, do you wish to sectarianize the world for? It is bad enough already, by peculiar faith.

THE TEMPLE OF HONOR—TEMPERANCE.

As rational religion is the representative of true religion, then this order of such extensive brotherhood comes in for her estimable qualities, as one of the handmaids, and one of many written in the true deeds of life, that leads to the highest duty of man. This is one of the youngest, but not the least, in this mighty family.

Mind is only prepared to do right, as it is properly instructed.

We most imperfectly understand most of the science of life. We should never waver from the true path of reason, built on facts, for fanciful theories.

The self-balanced mind must appropriate the proper benefits of life, and reject what elicits the evils.

Among the last is intemperance. All good society implores the corrective, and none has been better sustained than this last effort.

Spare not your exertions, ye that labor for man's good in the thousand ways that Deity underwrites.

Let us recollect how many drunkards have been changed into good citizens, and then we can tell what mind's best exertions, in mass, can do for mind's individual good.

But few of the million are up with the immediate benefits of duty, and most are behind the proper dictates of revolution, however urged by discovery; all good men need less thought than action, in this mighty evil of society.

Keep away organic evils, as distilleries, drinkeries, treatings, evil examples—secret actions.

Some citizens exclude all liquor generally from the corporation, which is endowed with that original power, and all fee-simple titles are made with the provision of reversion, if the bond be forfeited.

The conservative order of the temple of honor imparts universal benefit, and is part and parcel of a universal brotherhood. It must begin with domestic education, the best, and change of habits at the hospitable board. Many principles are thus evolved, to the amendment of the world.

This proves the reflective light of an incipient civilized and refined age, the true dignity of mind.

The benefit of science is to supply all necessary defects, by the aid of mind and genius.

All conservative orders must seek the best operations of wise laws, instituted upon the laws of man's nature. Nothing can escape the right capacity of mind. One of the fountain sources of correction is that of the license laws, to arrest the very origin of such things.

The physical and mental functions suffer awfully from organic affections of the head, the stomach and bowels, but much worse of the nervous system shattered, and the circulation obstructed.

Of all the conservative orders of temperance, give us especially the mothers, who form the best views of human character, in all its legitimate comprehension, when the disposition of mind is enthusiastic, and ere the habits are fixed by perversion.

Temperance order is one of the great lights of civilization, and should embrace and command the highest aid of mothers, and females in general, who are deeply interested, and can do much good.

The manufacturers and venders of alcohol are those that injure most.

In the present order of the sons of temperance, we see the effect of mind, patriotism, and humanity—monotheism doing the deed. It is her capital that will reform the whole world.

Poisons will be vended. unless wise legislation seeks to prevent it effectually.

The temperance order has commenced a splendid era, and has the elements of a mighty good, especially of prudence, that constitutes the best individual society.

All such must be adequately comprehensive. else all partial plans will fail. The most comprehensive will be the greatest as most effectual kind of enterprise. The effort, as all the proper efforts of principles, must be followed up, to be eminently successful. A man that forfeits his word, honorably pledged for the proper security and insurance, is no longer trustworthy.

Temperance institution is to secure one general conservation, and must rest on eternal principles, to go successfully to the desired result. Now, had social principles been rightly instituted at first, by proper rational education, then this very institution would have been much superseded by domestic rule, that discards all trifling with principles and mind.

This, and various other institutions of general science, are advanced for man's benefit; for how many parents are entirely competent to govern their families?

Arrest the evil ere it kills the body and injures the soul, and sees the noblest of human nature brutalized into a stupid ferocious beast, the pest and curse of society. If man cannot resolve of himself on his proper duty to self and family, society and country, there is the temple of honor, that reflects the brilliancy of virtue and the worth of mind. The whole principle of temperance is one of many, embraced in the system of rational religion, as universal brotherhood. The system of temperance is founded on universal rational principles.

What is drunkenness? Is it that which destroys mind and its reason, by poison. It is, then, that most of temperance principles are a part of religion.

One of the greatest revolutions in this respect, can be best accomplished by intelligent mothers and temperate fathers. Intemperance is one of the great causes of crime, and much of disease, premature injury, by alcoholic poison on the nervous system.

As bad as drunkenness is, how wretched are the concomitant vices! A drunken man is not to be depended on. What a bore and pest he is!

Drunkenness not only renders a man barbarian, but brutalizes him.

A man's associations decide his fortune very often.

When intoxication is attended with the worst of evils and crimes, what penalty is not due for the perpetration?

What little apology has any member of society, especially parents, if addicted to drunkenness.

How could the offspring be saved from perdition?

See that father with his delirium, seeking to commit suicide. Do you appreciate what are the horrors of delirium tremens, the drunkard's madness, mania-a-potu? You cannot appreciate by description, their dangers and terrors. Even the ordinary regular constant habit of drink, destroys some in a very few years.

How many become paralyzed in part, at least, by this odious and injurious result? How frail and demented others!

Shall reason be humbled at the feet of drunkenness?

Any crime of murder may be the drunkard's. While various passions respect the degrees of murder, this profanes all—none is sacred to its fell abasement. Parricide, the slaughter of children, are perpetrated at its degraded altar.

All the sacredness of society is sacrificed at its bidding, its victims are pauperized, houseless and mindless, involved in crime.

The sellers of liquors run the greatest risk of being the best customers. as well as part of their families, relations, and friends; and what a retributive justice, then!

Drunkenness is the vice of all vices, the crime of crimes. Thy most hostile opponent could wish thee no greater curse, than a drunkard's life and a drunkard's end. Go forth into the world armed with this perversion of thy mind, and the torch of crime will follow you, and proclaim your position that leads to a maniac's dungeon, or suicide, or even worse, even a double murder. Beware of the degrees in means of crime.

Go whither thou wilt, and thy foot-prints will be marked by blood, and reeking, gory degradation, will be there. Thou assertest thy independent aspirations, but it may be fatally too late, for thy powers may be paralyzed.

The first drop will be too much for the fatal contact. as contagion breathes in its cup, and infectious pestilence attends its outpourings.

Be wise at once, and stand firm in the richness of thy richest of all earthly gifts, an unsullied mind.

Beware, you that sell spirits, the evil is domesticated, and you or your family may experience the bitter draught. The habit of drinking will grow. Do not sell the poison, as there is retributive justice in every drop. Before you know the end yourself, prudent and temperate as you now are, you may become the drunkard, and your children may stealthily share in your custom. When you awake to the reality, you will be involved in moral ruin, from which there may be no escape.

CORRECT LEGISLATION.

CORRECT legislation of good and necessary laws with their appropriate execution, is eminently a vast element in mind's mighty duty to the world.

The elevation of every circle benefits the whole. Men in every age and nation have been actors for that one mighty result.

Mankind have an important mission. Humility and modesty must at once convince them that they are only acting instruments in the hands of Deity, for if any assume more at any age of the world, they become monomaniacs or impostors.

They are self-impeached at any time by strict language, even with liberal construction. As the principals are ruled out, so must be their advocates.

All rational religionists are necessarily the boldest advocates for wise and efficient laws having their sway, else the wild terrors of anarchy may arouse the great depth of iniquity, or the horrid cruelties of vindictive aggression of those who take law into their own hands.

Better have no legislation than an unwise and tyrannical one. Wisely have the freemen of 1776 acted for themselves, country, and future generations of the world.

Organic principles were then for the first time rightly established, and enlightened mind must govern the balance. The founders of modern constitutions have a magnificent triumph over past ages, and prove conclusively the advance of mind, and the dignity of man to rationality.

Wise legislation has to premise the proper rational education of all rational minds, in requiring all children capable of instruction to be sent at and for a proper age to suitable schools, and no excuse allowed for their absence, except in busy agricultural seasons of the year.

The morals of the people are the property of the State, to maintain which she has to nurture popular intelligence to the very best of her rational ability.

The district or county should be regularly taxed, and the court required to appropriate the necessary funds to pay for the tuition of all unable to pay.

Competent public teachers should be invariably provided, and no funds appropriated for public schools should be withdrawn by the citizens in pro rata proportions, and thereby break up such schools and inevitably defeat the object of affording public instruction to those who otherwise could not possibly get it. If any such arrangements have been made, they should be cancelled forthwith, and the whole public allowed a fair and proper opportunity of general education. No portion of the community nor section of the country should be independent of responsibility of such jewel trusts.

No rational youth should be permitted to reach the fifteenth year without an ability of reading and writing, if mental and physical endowments entitle to this privilege. All children of proper ages, unable to live otherwise, should be apprenticed as best for their capacity and wishes, faithfully taught some business for a future living, prepared for the world, and all this the court should take regular cognizance of at proper times during each year by regular official superintendents, to prevent poor children from an abuse of brief authority, as servants, cooks and waiters, or general menials, instead of apprentices.

What chance have the destitute minors, especially in some countries, otherwise, with an unprincipled circle?,

Laws should invest a proper part of the estate, as the inalienable rights of the wife and children.

The protection of widows and orphans should be insured, that they be not despoiled of their effects by worthless administrators, who may keep the money for their use and speculation at the most important time of need of body and mind, or that they should be subject to the tender mercies of countless costs, the imbecile protection of magistrates and the irresponsible official cliques.

It is tyranny and dishonesty to restrict the use of. money in contracts, made by persons of sound and mature mind, voluntarily and in good faith.

Usury means oppression. Now surely it is not oppression to sell money for its commercial value, since money is commercial property.

The world will get at the justice of such obligations, when all the exploded systems of absolutism are discarded. If arbitrariness presume to borrow upon its own dictation, to pander to lust and power, then freemen must discard all this abuse too.

The dividends of earned premiums of mutual insurance companies have declared the value of such capital uncontrollable by law of legislation. The wise effects of honorable competition decide the value of money, better than all legislation. Legislation, that is wise, is to universally protect the helpless and minors, provide for all contracts not specifying particulars, whatever is due the industry of the people and enterprise of mind.

There should be no precarious legislation in time, or mode—general acts or statutes should obviate all such contingencies.

Principle is the power that keeps the social circles in their right orbits, that looks higher than laws, far above them in the wise cognizance of efficient legislation. The laws should be reduced to general comprehensive principles in a code so simple, that the intellectual part of the people are considered responsible about all law by a legal fiction, can readily appreciate them, their rights defined and their best duty easily obtained.

The people should have the legitimate result of the great first principles of their rights. Some people plead for legislation—for socialism.

Is this right and just to the whole, who already prove their proportionate aid in the cause of suffering humanity? Legislation has not to embrace Utopian schemes, till they prove themselves consistent with the refined condition of man's independence, universal principles.

Remodel legislation, not at the hazard of speculations of visionary intentions, nor revolutionize the fabric of man's happiness, superseding mind and genius in their appropriate theatres. Wise legislation should never permit either to be trammelled, much less usurped. Effective and uniform laws are needed by the whole world, to protect all mankind. The highest obligation rests by supreme and paramount laws, through their penalties on mind or conscience and body. What observer can miss seeing the legitimate consequences under the penalties of violated law? Though man may be above the laws of the land by temporary power, craft, subterfuge, still he rarely escapes the penalties of violated nature. Providence may have some use for the apparent exception.

Law reform is absolutely needed in the whole circle. There is absolute necessity for law reform, and it should be secured in our country speedily and effectually. Then a straightforward way, principle, and moral justice would prevail for the social, civil and individual rights and benefits of man, and citizens would not be liable to be misled by so many lawyers into greater difficulties than they remedy.

The general principles of civil and common law should be codified by master minds, to reconcile the Roman and Anglo-Norman laws ; or rather, enlightened freemen of the world ought to seek the full establishment of the great principles of law consistent with the best code of refined civilization.

Would the profits of the legal practice fly away too much? What does that weigh with the value of universal good, consequent on the improvement, intellectual, moral, and religious, of the people?

When all laws are consistent with the constitution, no constructive views but what are straightforward can be conscientiously maintained.

It will be most dishonorable to enact any but which are strictly constitutional laws.

Laws are too often made for the benefit of the debtors, the largest class in some circles.

All are presumed to know the laws! Why not then, in justice to this fiction, have a simple code prepared for all citizens? Why is this injury perpetrated, to the reflection on the morals and mind of honest citizens? Why do not citizens see and demand this right?

Citizens lose by not knowing all the points that even lawyers mislead on. Very recently one of many such events has come directly to my notice, that a hard-working man has lost hundreds of dollars, of great consequence to himself and family, by not being informed of the statute of limitations, that prevented his rightful recovery.

Plain citizens go through life without very humble testimonials being yielded them in in any common course of rational education, except the very unpleasant one of law and its experience, or of consequent loss. It is a shame that common justice cannot be done the world in all essential particulars of their best rights.

There remains but little more now to do, than for some intelligent scholar or lawyer meeting this question in a liberal manner. But what prevents the state authorities from having the general principles of the law presented in a small volume, for the good of its citizens? Surely their improvement, intellectual and moral, on such position, will amply repay the elevated design.

The time has arrived that mind of freemen can never be satisfied with any but the correct position, in all the fields of professional science and wise knowledge, however it curtails the profit of a scowling monopoly.

See how the ends of justice are defeated, and a consequent demoralization results in regard to the law's delay.

It is horrible injustice, that a free people will not reach the necessary demands that their glorious governmental benefits entitle them to.

With the errors of a passing age, it is to be hoped that a withering apathy and indifference to our best interests will also depart, and give means to record the progress of the approaching light that gives triumph to its lustre. The people owe it to themselves and their superior governmental institutions, to have all suitable laws, plain and practical, on general principles, and then all public benefit will be promoted well and truly.

The world must seek to put all laws on principles that vindicate themselves, and do not need men to explode diseased gas. The object of all law should be to insure certain responsibility.

When benefits have been conferred upon any property of the rich, though held by the poor, the due liberality of justice should be awarded.

Law revolution demands a proper reform that reduces the practice to plain, honest principles.

Thus the costs of the suit are diminished, justice is expedited, and morals promoted. Simplify law codes, and improve on the basis of a good government. Reform in law is called for most imperatively by the state of free institutions, that require a commensurate advancement in all the blessings that mind can procure.

All laws ought to be predicated on appropriate principles, and all reduced to a practicable circle, whether the interest of judges and lawyers is decisively affected for the good of all, even beyond much of the professional incomes.

When principles are universally applicable, honesty sought, and justice easily secured to all, then what is called law rightfully fulfils its rightful functions. This change should be wisely made, but no less than the conservative wants of the people require. The world needs justice and equity universally, speedily and fully, administered without fear, favor or affection.

The rights of the sovereign people need this. Let rational mind furnish the requisite amendments.

Talk about law—let all be fixed up right at first by mind, on eternal principles; then all will be right, and no difficulty about it. Let the legislators be wise and honorable, upright, talented men; none but those properly nominated in fair conventions, not by caucus. The world should seek to get rid of the sophistry of lawyers. Let master minds simplify and codify the principles of law. All can be done, and this is the government that can enable man to do it.

The great object with wise legislators is to institute better morals of the people, to avoid law-suits, have the costs of collection saved. Debts of honor would accomplish this.

Popular legislation is to prevent crimes, as gambling, seduction, &c., and should concentrate the world's wisdom. One of the worst states of laws that can exist is their feeble execution. How many culprits are pardoned or exonerated by the judiciary and the pardoning powers. If the judge or ruler were willing to take the place of the culprits, then the objection would not be so great.

Suits based on the proper facts may be answered or satisfied by the defendants, properly and promptly. All such suits can go up from courts of conciliation.

Much litigation can be as good as abolished, if the people would, in the main, reform legal proceedings, attend more to the abuses of legislation, have justice better administered, and less vitiated.

What a shame that laws, that are especially essential, should not be faithfully executed.

Many important measures are dependent on them: they have provisions, but the penalties are not enforced. The law for the inspection of steamers yields to none in usefulness, yet is recklessly omitted. There is much local useless and fruitless legislation, when universal principles will best apply. All legislation should be comprehen

sive and wise, to be effectual. It should guard against pauperizing the laboring classes, or permitting licentious evil passions, as jealousy, envy, and ambition, being predominant. No legislation should ever involve bankruptcy of states, and future embarrassment of posterity, any more than dictation of mind what is religion by peculiar faith.

Wise legislation is the wisest exertion of mind, illustrated in the best practical results.

Among the blessings is the progress of mind's benefits, by modern legislation, that rears its loftiest triumph for refined civilization. Rising from the only safe basis, constitutional organic law, the protection of the people, it dispenses light, life, and liberty to mind's energies, and invokes the holiest interests in its welfare. Now the poor are protected, and the weak are upheld. The homestead exemption places the helpless under mind's noble protection. Wise legislation must be permanent : each bill must be put on its relative and intrinsic merits. No sectional, factionist, fanatical, partisan views can be tolerated before the tribunal of principles. The wise exercise of legislation, and its execution in good faith, should be such, that the land of law should hardly be one of lynching or popular fury. Is the police powerless? Is law inefficient to procure protection to life, reputation, and property? Where, then, is an enlightened public opinion? The world should get rid of fruitless legislation, on matters having no equity before that body. Mankind owe allegiance to all the laws of nature and principles, that are paramount; none else in any other than municipal light. Nothing radical, but all conservative, can be permanent.

'Any law to be forever, must be consistent with nature, and conservative. Let the conservative principles of society be carried out right, for uniform protection for life, reputation and property. All laws wisely made, consistently with the immutable decrees of God as evinced in nature, are the ones for the world finally to secure, as only legitimate. Law must go with equity. When it meets lamely, as it now does, the great ends of conservative principles, exalt it to that, the proper standard.

The world must have all just constitutional laws obeyed.

THE COURT OF CONCILIATION.

Such court is to be protected by appropriate judges, properly selected.

Do whatever is right by this institution; act by principles, that vindicate themselves.

Courts of conciliation may become in good faith the best of all means of justice. Who does not wish to escape all the difficulties of lawsuit? Some persons will go to the brink of the precipice in morals, disregarding anything like the spirit, while they have the mere form of law. But as to lawyers, can you expect others, mere agents, to take that interest in your welfare as you would yourself? The wisest action is the prevention of lawsuits.

Advise and reflect; do not give into the hands of others what you can do better yourself. Some people cannot take care of themselves by legal precaution, nor their property; how can they do that for others? Avoid all litigation practicable.

Business may do itself, if the principles be rightly developed. Lawsuits may be generally profitably prevented, by a proper representation and amicable arrangements.

Have as little interference by lawsuits as practicable. Seek to avoid litigation, as one party is worsted always, both injured, and society assailed.

Nothing short of notes written "under hand and seal," should be affected in annual settlements, that will save very great difficulties. All evils ought to be obviated on principles.

The proper avoidance of litigation premises general good to society, in escaping many of its evils, as the sophistry and tricks of small lawyers, and various inroads on good morals, in generating the highest tone to an honorable social condition. Well may the prudent and good citizen avoid lawsuits, unless on principles that are pushed necessarily on him, in defence of his own dearest rights. He may see lawyers foiled in recovery of the most common notes by non-suit, the cost of which falls on the client, unless the lawyer is honest enough to pay it himself, which is not always done if left to the conscience of the lawyer; and he may have to get other lawyers to help the first; of course, at his own cost.

Lawyers have been known, to my certain knowledge, to receive payment for common professional business, required to do it legally right, yet have done it for the benefit of the second party instead of the first, and gave their evidence against the very party employing them, thus perjuring themselves without being exempt from the suspicion of bribery on so glaring an outrage. Where are the responsibility and redress? In this world? In what court? Yet such lawyers pass, especially as belonging to a church. Does the world know its felony? Are the laws always equable and correct, for speedy justice? Are they made to help benefit the community, or for the profession? Do they lead to the creditor's oppression of the debtor, or do they tend to defeat the creditor class, till the debtors escape, making their property over or away, defeating the ends of justice? One of the best attainments of justice, is a speedy promptness in rendering it unto others.

No government is just, that does not secure justice to its citizens in the most expedient legal manner.

What can we say of any system of jurisprudence chancery, or any other, that brings the law's delay for even the best part of a life-time, ere justice is rendered. Is this freedom?

The court of conscience is the best that promptly settles when due, and in the settlement of amounts corrects all errors, and whenever discovered, rectifies them.

In a large majority of cases, the court of conciliation is the court of justice, prompt and comprehensive.

Here are advantages that cannot be overlooked, in the proper maintenance of best feelings in society, and of avoiding evils of greater magnitude.

The party solicits the very means that will free the community from more than half of all vexations, and promote at the same time, a better and higher tone of public sentiment and morals.

Then we shall see or hear more rarely, of many contentions that terminate unpleasantly, not only to the parties immediately interested, but to the chagrin of the public to whom are unnecessarily presented all the foibles of families, with their feuds and defects.

The dignity and sagacity of mind should be competent to parry all the corruptions of lawyers, put all our noble institutions far above their miserable apologies, and law above the pettifogger on its noble principles.

Court of reference or conciliation ought to be instituted with proper appellate functions, otherwise a tyranny and oppression are felt.

ARBITRATION.

CASES of arbitration necessarily occur in all nations, and should be conducted with reference invariably to strict equity and justice, by a right selection of parties well qualified for intellect and probity.

But in arbitration as commonly practiced, anything but an attempt at the right thing is sought by most. A low party whose conscience cannot reach the exact standard of justice, selects a partisan of low views, and imposes him on the other party who earnestly seeks correct principles. No arbitration should be definitely fixed until the arbitrators are at the same time, as well as the whole ground ; any other is an unprincipled imposition. Unless all improper influences be redressed with prudence, and wisely and invariably counteracted by proper guarantees, mock justice and false pretences are imposed on the correct party.

There must be a fixed and full right of protest and appeal to the court, if we can be satisfied that wrong has been awarded, or that rights have been withheld.

Too many referees consider that compromise and not justice, are to be done the subject.

The most are decidedly unqualified for the business, and nothing short of a regular court of conciliation judge can do comprehensive justice.

In most instances, the necessity for all this business emanates from wrong positions, and some parties make assertion in arbitration not warranted by facts, nor the courtesy of such a position, hence the necessity of premising a proper precaution of taking nothing for granted with all suspicious characters, but of having testimony properly authenticated on the party's previous denial or refusal to admit the important facts, which are enough to condemn an arbitration of itself; as all arbitrations ought to be on admitted facts, and simply an inability of the parties contestant, deciding these of themselves. But low cunning that refuses acquiescence in principles will insinuate itself, if not counteracted by preliminaries or first steps, and obviated by full right of protest and appeal, and deferring for important testimony.

The refusal of yielding justice on plain facts, even by arbitration, necessarily compels resort to legal forms.

In reference to arbitration, the least one can do, is to have a gentleman known as such disinterested, of proper approved standing and property, responsible every way, and above all, intelligent and educated liberally, but reserving always the full right to appeal to a higher tribunal. I am well satisfied, that no reference involving much amount can be satisfactorily settled with full justice, unless there be a court for appeal. The right of appeal is a protection for some show of justice. In the way reference or arbitration is had, characters are picked out more like creatures than independent arbitrators.

Such reference must be badly managed. There is too much corruption in most called justice.

Let the system of arbitration be perfected, and all will be satisfactory and right. If there were less law suits, there would be less perjury, less necessity for swearing. Be sure of your tribunal, before which you appear. The arbitrators can be sworn in, as responsible and disinterested. A proper selection of arbitrators is absolutely essential, or it will be a farce or tyranny.

Much litigation can be as good as abolished, if the people in the main would reform their customs and means of appreciation.

The world must require competent tribunals for arbitration, as the most the way it is conducted, is by vassals or partisans. That is worse than no attempt at justice. The great object is to secure exemption from law suits, and if this can be accomplished, a great evil will be remedied.

Let there be no arbitration of partisans to make things worse than better, but courts of conciliation, presided over by judges of consummate abilities, virtue, integrity and honor, amply secured by competent talents.

Partisans may make arbitration the most contemptible counterfeit of justice. Do not go into such at all, without you can secure a tribunal competent, disinterested in every respect, and of the most exalted integrity. In this, be sure to act independently.

This thing of backing out from the decisions of arbitration fairly established, taking advantage every way, presents a dishonest mind. No matter what the friendship and relation, any decision by an exparte arbitration will be most dishonorable, if the parties do not stand exalted in intellect, and possessed of a nice sense of honor. A vengeance to reference without the right to appeal on error, or hindrance of proof at the trial.

Most arbitrators are incompetent, from a fear, a feeling influencing, that is absolutely wrong ; also, from intellectual inability, or want of investigation. Most arbitrations are unjust, generally.

All these must be conducted on the highest principles of honor, and must be sustained by all the aid of highest rationality.

What could the world expect from the tender mercies of a picked body of men, all on one side.

I saw a one-sided pretence of partisanship offered for arbitration ; and, of course, instead of affirming, like gentlemen, they did not know what was proper cognizance—like traitors to mind, they belied mind, honor, and truth ; an adequate reason to convict them of violation of principles.

They had all the defects, that excluded them as a proper tribunal, As church members, they were called on to rescue one that had brought on the difficulty. All was done to smother justice. The whole resulted from betting on an election, that the church-member pledged himself on honor to make good ; but, when the trying hour came, this dishonorable false pretence was to exculpate the criminal parties.

When one man is employed as a tool, his employer must become the dirty tool to extricate him. Can there be any low gambling worse than that on elections ?

A just and comprehensive knowledge of human nature requires that the world should always premise exception to the dishonor of all arbitrations, or anything like them, to hold all such in abeyance.

There can be no greater injustice, than much of apparent arbitration of justice.

As arbitration, it will be a farce, if not from enlightened sources.

A proper selection of two approved discreet men, who may select a third, on disagreement, may institute the jury, who should be enlightened, well qualified, in proper circumstances of life and locality, disjunct from all peculiar interests of business, popularity, church, or any other union or fraternization, except the one of universal brotherhood.

Never trust yourself in the power of a clique. Let arbitrators be invariably named, till adopted by the other party, and let there be no arbitration but on this principle.

Never permit any party by his clique to offer you their indignity of opinion, as if worthy of your serious attention, for it will be a most dishonest sneaking out of all proper responsibility.

You need never expect any honor from one-sided pretences, but dishonorable concealments. I have seen that tried, for that express dishonorable object.

There can be no fair and honorable position, but an equitable adoption of proper, honorable men on both sides.

THE JUDICIARY.

THIS function of government must be respected as worthy of the most scrupulous regard of the world, to be of so illustrious character as intrinsically command at all times, by its merits, the highest tribute of enlightened public opinion. When this position obtains, then one of the highest public guarantees will be permanently secured for the general welfare.

In all departments necessary, the talents and character of the functionary should be elevated to such standard, as at all times secure the full esteem and proper control of the bar, and impart a winning confidence to the people. Such high salary should be invariably paid as will compensate satisfactorily, and be fully competent to enlist the right talents, to speedily dispose of all public business, and that with enlightened justice.

The people should be spared the belief, that collusion can ever stain its ermine, or that incompetency should ever disgrace its sanctuary.

Unfortunately, hitherto, this confidence is sometimes betrayed. " Now it is quite notorious and unquestionable, that for Chancellors to receive presents was customary and common in Bacon's time, and had been so for a hundred years, both in England and in other European states."

Bishop Latimer admits them to be " bribes." !

Now, what man was in the time of Bacon, human nature makes him in every age and nation, under the influence of analogous circumstances.

It is easy for bribery and perjury to prevail, when the proper antagonistic principles do not exist.

If we do not have a correction in enlightened public opinion, that detects, exposes, and punishes these flagrant violations of supreme justice, then the noblest fountains are poisoned at the source, and the corrupting fragments are scattered over society. We cannot secure pure judges at all times, but we have the conservative principles always at hand.

We should seek to select men of best talents and known probity, and pay properly for their life-time, whether in or out of office, if the best part of it has been thus expended.

If imbecility, from old age or decrepitude of mind, exist, such judges should be bound to retire, but on competent life salaries, to sustain them suitably, and return the most grateful tribute of an intellectual republic.

The people should be ever protected, by a proper judiciary, over tyrannical false pretences, under the panoply of virtuous conduct.

No delay should be permitted beyond proper investigations, in chancery or any other system of courts. If justice be promptly and suitably administered, the morals of the people will be exalted, and a high-toned national character will be preserved.

Any deviations from judicial rectitude should be appropriately rebuked.

When legislation has become unconstitutional and corrupt, then it is we must look to an enlightened and virtuous judiciary, to counteract and correct much of such evils, otherwise it is the tool of ignoble tyrants. But an enlightened public opinion must then, forever, keep the morals of the world right.

Jurisprudence ought to meet the demands and wants of the sovereign people—the mainstay of the world.

Laws ought to be consistent with constitutional liberty, and would be, if the people would rise in their majesty, and look at the good of the whole, not that of the legal or judiciary professions. This is the attainment of the dignity of freedom.

What can be worse than a corrupt judiciary?

What are we to think of a judiciary so corrupt and cowardly, as to bend to cliques? An enlightened public opinion towers over the corruptions of such judges and their decisions, and will ultimately expose their true ignominy. What can be more dignified than the virtuous and enlightened judiciary of an enlightened government?

" The chief director of the East India Company expressed in a letter to one who was appointed a judge in India, ' I expect that my will and orders shall be your rule, and not the laws of England.' "

As all popular elections are generally best for the world, the election of judges had best be directly through the people, who are most concerned in their fitness of character.

The people should elect to maintain all appropriate responsibility, as often as necessary their own judges. How much can the citizens of the country or State congratulate themselves on their enlightened judiciary, that prevents unnecessary arguments of counsel, arrests useless and sophisticated pleadings, and brings justice to a proper prompt point.

He rules in a word the lawyers by the best power, that of mind, and gives the best authority by never being at a loss for law. Such should be retained at the satisfactory salary.

The doctrine of popular as personal passive obedience produces impunity, that invites any species of iniquity.

In James II.'s reign there was " the violation of all justice and all law, by judges selected, applauded, and rewarded by him."

" Both in England and Scotland, the judges were his tools." Cannot republics have an honest judiciary to support the principles of honesty ?

Degraded must that judge be that will, in a republic, stoop to cliques, to deny justice to inventive genius. What if he should tolerate perjured banditti, to destroy it ? '

If judges of the highest capacity were presiding over direct rules and lawyers, then we should expect better morals and laws. Now it is a scene for jugglery of mind, to defraud the people by the shrewdest, sharpest sophistry and chicanery. Judges should be men of best mental calibre, to uphold public confidence and morals, the best of lawyers to keep the lawyers straight.

The object is to uphold the dignity and office of the judiciary, by all the best acts of mind.

What could be done with a corrupt judge ?

The same has been one of standing, and has the power of money and friends. And these are to prostrate the majesty of the laws and people ?

The innocent will demand just investigation. The guilty will avoid all such, except through cliques. In some courts, any kind of jury, witnesses and judges can be furnished.

If popular election of judges make them demagogues, then elect by the legislature on approved nominations through the executive.

Some judges might be demagogues, instead of weighing justice impartially ; those too often lean to that side that has political power.

Then those are amenable, and should be adequately rebuked. But the popular voice seems the most effective, renewed as early as practicable.

The judiciary of our free country ought to be pure, independent, free from suspicion, of corruption and bribery, and then we should see that in very large estates it need not take many years before they could be settled, and severe compromises would not have to be made for just rights at ruinous sacrifices. The highest law of the land, a righteous public sentiment, decides corruption somewhere, otherwise.

Elevate the judiciary to the highest degree, as that elevates man and the country of free institutions. Give judges the best of adequate salaries, and best of pensions for those at sixty years of age to retire, to prevent their imbecility.

Why is there so much variation in courts of justice, but from the integrity or capacity of the judges ?

Some judges govern the lawyers, who consume improperly the time of the public.

Small judges are worse than small lawyers, if possible, especially when they identify themselves.

The utmost facility of justice should be ever instituted, to promote good morals. If we act by direction of law under proper judges, we may have all the benefit of law. The redeeming sense through a wise and high-minded judiciary, is the great conservative power next to an enlightened public opinion. Perjury is too abundant over the world.

Principles will best obviate all such, and keep the world straight. It is idle to expect any other to succeed. Courts of justice are too often perverted by the parties not swearing directly to the point of knowledge, but of belief. In this, much latitude for perjury lies.

The sovereign people let all essential matters be handled and directed by professions, as if they were the only beneficiaries, when it is most essential that they should seek diligently to possess the mighty elements of conservative revolution.

The mere profession are not to manage justice as they please. Science, knowledge and wisdom must ever direct mind in all their departments, and the world must seek its own by a just and equitable liberalism, not care for the unprincipled antagonism that comes from those interested in exploded customs.

Justice cannot be legislated defunct, while cultivated mind is just to itself.

The duty of judges in mobs is essentially important. Here is where republics appear less dignified than monarchies, in the suppression. But is not the superiority on the side of republics, for which the affections of good citizens are most elevated? Are not all that feel aught at stake enlisted in its behalf? There arise some evils in all social communities, if the world will give way to the combinations and collusions of men! What set of honorable principles can be fully carried out in any monarchy?

Around the throne always gather parasites, court-flatterers, and corrupt sycophants, the world over.

Can corupt lawyers do much with a corrupt governor, judges, legislature and sheriffs, and too often with supple jurors led by their leaders? Too many of our courts of justice, are a miserable farce. A high intellectual integrity, is worth all the balance of inferior value.

What are our most valuable institutions worth, if our courts of justice defeat that justice, for terms after terms, or your law-makers legislate her defunct, your rulers repudiate her?

THE JURISDICTION OF COURTS.

Courts of justice, whether probate or any other, should primarily protect the weak and helpless widows, orphans and humble citizens with exact and even justice.

No estate should be left without an administratorship, to defend and protect the best interests of the helpless, and promote the faithfulness of society to proper contracts. But the plain citizen may suppose, that the general administrator does all this faithfully. Very clear of it.

Humanity dictates the complete fulfilment of all these obligations.

The world needs no Lynch law of even vigilance committees, when judges are to expedite all that is expedient for law, but not supersede it. Let there be no anti-constitutional resistance to law, no respites and reprieves unless justice demands. If judges cannot meet the demands of the world, let them resign their functions.

Courts of law have been as good as abolished by non-appearance of judges, or the resignation of sheriffs, term after term! Many judges are bribed by the law's delay, when public opinion will not be duped by its perversion. Let there be no rules of court to rule laws, but principles to rule all citizens. Give the world justice, not law. Let not the world quarrel with a packed jury, packed by old dotard judges.

The people of the United States may ruin their liberties, through felonies, clans, cliques, sectional cabals, intrigues, looking yet too slavishly to persons, things, masters, instead of principles.

We need the most talented judges, of upright character and sterling integrity. That is a great point gained.

What avail the best of constitutional governments, if justice be not equity, to prevent the excess of perjury? Consider it, how degrading that strangers cannot get justice done them, because they are unknown or absent.

Have the judiciary been elected for time and manner, as to secure the most elevated action. Have the very best adequate salaries to pay the best talents and most elevated characters, instead of getting pettifogging lawyers, who often disgrace the bench, and bring reproach on free institutions.

What a contemptible character the judiciary presents, when it is mercenary or vassal to cliques or cabals! Have no judiciary, unless enlightened, liberal and elevated. In California, recently on confession of a culprit. "judges and public prosecutors in some portions of the country, were in league with the organization" of felons!

The world's corruption must be defeated.

Some of the judges should be presented to grand juries. The sovereign people, not the servant, should adopt their own choice of judges.

Judges are, at times, and can be, very corrupt indeed. Thomas Jefferson displays "The judiciary of England Forgery," of some half-dozen judges or more about christianity, in upholding the union of church and state.

Who believes that the judges to-day of any government that has union of church and state, but would perjure themselves on preconceived views to sustain that union? What vile elements of popular corruption, is peculiar faith!

How much mockery of justice is exhibited in our courts by perjury, and no radical correction of this organic evil of society ! Men of affected importance, are disgustingly suffered to commit all such deeds with impunity, and even pass celebrated for it, when they should be in the penitentiary.

When the citizens speak of their judiciary being near nobody, full of partiality, that the judge suffers one lawyer to bend him judge, court and jury, with an opinion as law, while some of the lawyers could not tell whether right or wrong, then they may well call for reform, and give all such matters into the appropriate hands.

Justice is a popular question, one that belongs to the people as an inherent right, subject to no fiat of party or clique made supreme.

The magistracy should at least see, that proper legal proceedings are always instituted without equivocation, else they suffer themselves to be made tools of. It is their duty to be properly qualified intellectually for all cases under their cognizance, else justice is a perfect farce.

No sophistry is to be countenanced, as they are sworn to decide according to the law and evidence or testimony. They are to be ever qualified to analyze that testimony, whether it be true or not. They are not only bound to see that all necessary bonds of office are given as the law requires, but that they be fulfilled according to justice.

We should give the election of most officers to the people, of judges especially, and keep all departments separate from, and independent of each other, to preserve the purity and integrity of these offices, and the honesty of the people.

How abominable is it that we should entrust our rights to the miserable contingences, of the disgraces of electioneering, and tricks of log-rolling members of assemblies and representatives of the people ! All such need the highest reforms of the day.

Not only are wise and safe laws to be adhered to, but their best administration insured, and we must present wiser thoughts for advancement and subsequent improvements. What could we think of gerrymandering a state, for election of judges as legislators. What corruption on the purity of elections. What chance would a poor stranger with native wealth and influence have, in any such court of justice ? Are there not glaring bribery and corruption enough, to a vast extent ?

Compromises of ruin to even reputation are made, when some cannot foil the law's delay, and its base iniquitous administration.

Who that observes the sophisticated state of society, will not be more than disgusted, ere he gets through a long life, with the various corruptions of it, that cry aloud to penalty and mind for correction ?

An intelligent free people desires ever to be delivered from corrupt judges, jurists and lawyers ?

If judges be false to their dignity and duty, how can juries be true to their obligations ?

The appointment of judges demands adequate salaries, otherwise how can you insure proper talents of independent mind ? There must be no party spirit in their appointments, as the good of the whole must be regarded.

JURORS—JURIES.

There is too great a partiality in grand jury presentments. Jurors may not be responsible, as their responsibility is diffused in numbers. They are too often hurried, and go too oft as the judge tells them. Many are very ignorant, and are misled by demagogues.

Trial by jury ought to be reformed. In arbitration the jury is looked for, but may not be expedient.

Some judges, as in Kentucky, it is said, rarely charge the jury, to avoid trespass on their province.

A jury should be composed of men of known probity, integrity and talents, and should be amply qualified for all their duties, and properly paid therefor.

Would it not be best to interchange juries in the circuit, as judges, to prevent any sinister malign influences ?

The world has no just or adequate idea of the felony concealed—of the injustice done it judicially ; the miserable complots and collusions for personal popularity. The beauty of the world is nearly ruined by the falsity and sophistry with which it is daubed.

Judges have been the merest tools to all the world despotisms ; and if they carry the juries, they are the tools of tools. No judge or jury should serve in the precinct elected.

Do half of lawyers know the relations of things; or do half do their duty at the start or close of the bearing of the case? How many advantages are taken in law, to the disadvantage of the most honorable justice, by sharp lawyers?

Is this for the benefit of the most?

Too many trust to lawyers, that mislead.

Cannot people do most of their own business, or let it have the principles conservative of it?

We should be freer from much of legal misguidances, and secured from the foul grasp of the self-interested. All of this some have to learn, more or less, in the school of the world, where too many of the people are mere botches, and have to resort to professional business, bankrupt by their own ignoble deeds and folly, and rabid partisans in evil. There are many lawyers who should not be trusted with business, if they paid liberally for it. How many have to learn on the business of the people.

If you seek to advance such into business, you had better give them the amount of fees, and pay a competent and approved lawyer.

Never pay for law friendship, surely.

Experience has fully proved that some have no gratitude, and surely no responsibility, no matter how bad their misleadings, as they were ever ready with sophistry, unprincipled as they were, to get out of the difficulties for themselves, but surely leaving their clients to suffer.

Most of the people lose, before full experience aids them, enough to pay for several codes of proper digested laws. If the people do not protect themselves, how can an irresponsible profession be depended on?

Much of this profession is cunning at its business, incompetent in the performance, and sharp to avoid responsibility. When others turn most to their account, what can the balance do who are without proper advisers?

Freemen wish nothing less than proper protection in business, above mean and dangerous pettifoggers. Do lawyers improve the general morals of the people? Those of elevated character must be an ornament to literature and sound morals. But where they advise only expediency in place of good morals, generally, or success under all manner of sharp, not moral power, may we be saved from all such, whom I could never confide in.

Is the profession predicated on lawyers' moral principles? How much property is cloaked and smuggled by the tricks of pettifoggers?

How much is society disorganized by the harassing delinquencies of parties thus advised!

In the sale of unsound property, thereby invalidating the sale, are the parties promptly advised, beyond what honesty prompts, in taking it back?

Neither moral, intellectual, nor pecuniary responsibility, is advised by the legal profession generally, as becomes a worthy calling. Of course, then, the people suffer.

Responsibility is avoided by too many lawyers, who sneak out of any difficulty, by declaring the litigants have not stated all. The litigants had best give a written document, keeping an exact copy for their protection, otherwise their business may be wretchedly performed by some lawyers.

Of what good account are lawyers, when they get us into more difficulties than they relieve?

The very practice of pettifogging misleads the mind of all professional men, as lawyers, doctors or parsons. We see it in the lawyer, who affects to be essential in saving cases that will save themselves, but is not to be found in bad cases that he brings forward, after the trial and the fees are procured.

Equity and laws most exact could be at once much oftener embraced by juries in most of cases but for pettifoggers. Can man be his own lawyer?

He can be competent for a higher profession, that of avoiding litigation on the highest principles. The profession of the law is most sadly perverted. The pettifoggers who fog up justice, affecting to clear when they muddy the streams of justice, are best avoided. How often do they mislead by their advice, and avoid responsibility by collusion of their tribe?

Is society so pregnant with its own evils, that it cannot deliver itself from those of others?

Lawyers do not intend to have a proper responsibility generally. It is part of their creed, it is certainly part of their practice, to avoid all responsibility. When your business is in a train to do itself, then you may expect it done. What can you do with the most of lawyers? If you have important business to transact, do not select without direct reference to known competency and integrity; otherwise avoid those who call themselves your friends.

How many lawyers have neither integrity nor talents?

The lawyers are more after the clients' money, than after the debtors, too often. Shall justice be in abeyance to the lawyers? There is some legal piracy and felony; beware of them.

There are some lawyers that I should not like to trust my purse, much less my cause in their hands. With the corrupt, every man has his price. Those of integrity are above suspicion. You certainly do not wish to pay away your living for collections. You must not only have a good cause, but fixed up by right testimony and in the right way.

We seek a higher order of justice than lawyers can give; that is, principle.

Justice should not be reduced to mere quibble, extracted by tricks of sharp lawyers.

As to the lawyers in any doubtful case, have the most of them state in writing what they propose to do, and if they cannot be definite, stop all intercourse with them.

Their proceedings may be equivocal, and they may virtually turn against you in the end if necessary, and ascribe their want of success to your not telling them the whole history.

There is but little moral honesty and truth among lawyers, as a class; and it shows the perversion of morals by perversion of mind.

We should best dispense with lawyers, and trust to the equity of principles and wisdom of right, the least to lawyers unless we can secure their intellectual integrity.

Do not go to a lawyer first by any means to settle your business.

What do you say of law? To let it alone, whenever practicable.

The desire of all intelligent citizens, is to be saved from unprincipled lawyers. All should seek to probe to the bottom in all cases, ere we involve ourselves in lawsuits, or take any step not guaranteed by wisdom, and fortified by virtue and innocence.

On what can the whole world better depend, than on just eternal principles?

In law people must adopt proper judgment, to obtain satisfactory justice, otherwise the world may get much more than it is entitled thereto.

The sovereign people must do all business right, at once and on the spot.

Not only pay their debts, but protect themselves on their payment by such proof receipts as will evince honesty, save feelings, and preserve friendship.

If clients were as ready to pay their creditors, what they owe them, as their lawyers to help defeat the proper morals of the world, honesty would be better secured. What does the rational and honorable community need of sharp practice and designing intrigues of pettifoggers, to uphold the felony of those designing the worst infractions in law justice, that ought ever to be comprehended in the same high and honorable court, and will be when the people get the ascendency as world sovereigns for the good of society and virtue. What are lawyers that are pettifoggers and churchmen all, but the rankest sophists? What can the world estimate lawyers who suborn perjurers to obtain success in law, to defend outrageous criminals?

REPUBLICAN INSTITUTIONS.

THE world is now rapidly preparing for them, and the noble position of our glorious country is proof enough that man is qualified for self-government, the best for his happiness. France has had to contend against great odds, peculiarly situated as she is, amid factions and antagonistic interests. She has advanced on her revolution, being taught by the severest lessons of blood addressed to her for half a century.

She will progress in the great battle of mind and freedom, if her position can be rightly secured amid the mighty antagonism of Europe. The whole of Europe must unite for proper government. She, as the world, must become monotheist, ere the crimes of atheism and polytheism will recede for pure government. Obedience to the instructions of constituents, should point kings to their duty. Who are the constituents of kings but the people, that are best qualified to give correction to every age, to the satisfactory amendment of vicious conduct? They should seek to counteract all the intrigues of government by proper principles, that may fully put down all sinister means that are introduced to exalt all improper policies.

The purity of the ballot box is a grand constituent, and is never to be perverted by gerrymandering, local, sectional, or any views of corrupt manœuvre, for corrupt judges or legislators, votes or elections, to create a recoil of national evils.

States are to guard against corrupt legislation as a paramount evil. The sovereign people should correct, not palliate any corruption because of party.

The people must necessarily take cognizance of, and direct the right view of government that becomes republican representation, the only true policy of freedom, just as sure as popular mind rises in the vigor and maturity of manhood. As sure as the sun of our solar system shines, so surely must true popular governments prevail forever.

Many will be the false steps, as much will be the result of unprincipled absolutism advancing all the difficulties vast and numerous in the mazes of sophistry, and the machinations of tyranny, exercising all the delusions, to exclude mind from its true interests. Yet, crushed as mind is, still it will burst its shackles and assert its rights.

It is most important to the world that public opinion be enlightened and just, as all changes for the better even, are accompanied with the means of conservative revolution.

Our great men are too dependent on public opinion, itself dependent on exploded views of past ages, if not enlightened enough to keep in advance of the age, up to it at least, before it if practicable. Why cannot mind properly assert mind's rights and prerogatives, instead of catering to morbid tastes of humanity? It is a disgrace to be behind the essentials of the age.

Mal-administration of government, no matter the name, is very bad, but mal-legislation is the worst.

What boots it to the world, whether in a monarchy, autocracy, or republic, if the proper laws be omitted or violated? When the autocracy commands all emigrants or residents to publish preceding their departure, to satisfy the demands of honest creditors, it excels the republic that overlooks absconding debtors.

No mere partisan elections of mere military chieftains, will advance the true interests of republics.

hoose no man as mere general, and disclaim him from his being a general for civil functions.

Put no candidates for highest offices, especially under pledges, than general principles, else abuses and violations may follow, and the officers of the people become a mockery and corruption.

With nobility, we have violence done to mind and virtue. The laws of nature declare this fact.

Republics have to regard the peculiar faiths of the world, that have rent it for every century of their existence, especially of church and state, as exhibited in the Protestant and Maternal or Roman character. Centuries upon centuries have been disturbed by the bloodiest wars and revolutions of the whole world known at the time.

These are not the results of religion, but the bloody deeds of peculiar faith absolutism. The testimony of affiliated followers decides this for all such.

All are wrong but theirs, and the whole world must be participant thereof. From the most ancient times, through various scenes up to the present, the world must be in abeyance thereto.

The world must look on this republic, that has begun so well, and keep apart politics from state official faith, and all such matters, and have no sectional intrigues for factions to flourish.

Electioneering should not be the order of the day, but on personal merits. It is the duty of citizens to seek modest statesmen. All virtuous citizens should exercise the noblest of all rights and privileges, the elective franchise, in its purity, with proper and correct judgment.

The popular protection is a sacred feature in such institutions. Freedom is asserting her own in establishing the homestead exemption, whereby all destitute families, proprietors, secure a residence free from execution. The whole world must do this. In sustaining the poor independently, the greatest amount of public virtue accrues. The corrupting influences in elections, by drinking and treating, ought to be counteracted by the conservative body of citizens, who should positively vote against the advocates of all such corruption, as directly seeking to bribe the people.

How often is it that candidates have their vices thrown up to them, thereby reflecting the merits of a constitutional government. The severest penalties within the limits of justice should be instituted against all that violate the inestimable benefit of the elective franchise. Its highest purity should be preserved.

Observers can see how far candidates can cater for favoritism, by double dealing. What shall be done against the odious vices of electioneering? How often is it that the manly character, scorning to be the demagogue and sycophant, are foiled in office before the people? Man has to go to executive office candidates to learn the devices of human nature. Some study intrigue and baseness all their life, and never tell the truth, unless to their interest.

We must have all elections official by the people, without gerrymandering, or any such political intrigue, to fix office dynasties throughout the state, an official tyranny and oppression.

Freemen have to guard against the misdeeds and evils of electioneering. No freeman should suffer improper influences to weigh in regard to his vote. He should act exempt from favor or affection in this glorious privilege. Many electioneer to commit the voter prior to election. He should only promise the best consideration of the subject and candidates.

The right of trial by jury does not by a long sight procure the requisite justice. Much depends on the judges.

The people, as they prize all their blessings, must preserve the purity of elections, to keep all matters straight.

Writ of habeas corpus, grand jury, and other blessings, can hardly equal the purity of elections.

Republics have progressed to the best control of their expenses, and should economize in all particulars.

None should long delay or defer public state debts, that should never be contracted without the consent of the constituency, beyond a specified amount.

Office-seeking, and buying at the expense of principles, are the bane of even republics.

That spirit of showing preference to persons once distinguished through their base conceits, is a tribute basely paid.

Republics present the nearest approach of equal rights of citizens; but even here we see, in conflicts where the moneyed power is wielded, that there is but little chance, unless both sides have that power.

If ever treason becomes obsolete, it would be in constitutional republics, and ever green it must be in despotisms; but we would miserably mistake the present organization of the world-safety to reach this as an absolute conclusion.

All representative power is delegated on trust, and when the representative can neither act to instructions and his conscience, then resignation fulfils the best obligations as a republican, I say.

Who can wonder at the revolutions of the world, for government, religion, and science? Most of individuals, as nations, may be surrounded by malign influences. If isolated, mankind, with the lights of the present age before them, would become more republican and liberal; but when surrounded by monarchists, the last must be put down, ere the first can be truly confirmed.

The glorious annexation of enlightened views is spreading in the progress of mind's refined civilization, and is dispensing its glorious benefit to the world.

It is now the march of mind, instead of martial prowess. If the first be rightly dispensed, the last can be dispensed with.

The advocates of monarchy affect that it suits a dense population. It suits none. The constitutional principles of free government only meet the demands of mind, in its amplest requisitions, throughout the world. The Chinese are the very people to have constitutional government. Is England free? Does she keep up that doctrine with the rest of the world? Is she not now acting most unjustly to half the world? To Asia, Africa? As a mighty nation, she has much of the world's, mind's rights, under her dominion. It is monarchy that is radical, and sings the delusive song that the people cannot rule in all the world.

Human nature cannot be worse than the priestocracy make it, for they first libel their Creator, and then turn round and libel mind for not conspiring with them. Were there ever a worse degraded set of those clothed in human flesh, disgracing human nature? Mind, innocent and pure, needs nothing of them, in no respect whatever. Let them stand aside, as impertinent impostors on the rights of free institutions. The consummation of constitutional republican government will elicit the union of the world, and the congratulations of its five organic and appurtenant divisions. A government of constitutional principles demands to be the only one of all. In good faith, the world's five grand divisions must rejoice in the prosperity of the whole.

People of Europe, organize yourselves at once, now and forever, for one grand constitutional union of confederated states. Ask of your agents, the kings, emperors, autocracies, to give you all proper representative government, and to resign as your legitimate trust agents. That they should obey your proper instructions, or else they perjure themselves before the whole world.

Now, what Europe should be, let Asia too.

Australia and Africa will follow America. Let all the world act out, with moral and religious bravery. Let the world be freed from the pernicious malignity of peculiar evils and wrongs, faiths and absolutism the right way.

If these continental unions be promoted, then China may put down effectually the smuggle of India with opium carried on by the imperial power of England, the incursions of the northern barbarians more effectually than by all fleets or walls. Also the southern pirates, especially.

The outsiders and insiders will then unite on honorable terms of conquest, over all the unprincipled pirates of the world, and the whole earth need not fear the conquests of piratical chieftains.

Now, Asiatics, ye see that your governments cannot begin to protect you, uncasting you as citizens, despoiling you as people, and ruining you as nations. You have been the prey of military barbarism too long ; let now the best efforts of rational mind elevate you to its honorable dignity. Renounce forever all the imbecility of your customs and your peculiar faith, and ask of God, in his purity, all that enlightened minds and brave souls can win.

Conservative principles alone will give permanency to national existence.

Liberalists, to the amount of one hundred millions in Europe, speak now by your actions. What are you all about? Organize to-day a constitutional representative government, on conservative, not radical revolution. Do you wish more was diffused over Europe, and millions of the human race butchered? Are you content with the pageantry of military shows to make the demonstration of peculiar power over your best rights? The rights of the world are outraged on land and ocean, enough to cause all monotheists to see the savage and cowardly bullying of large states oppressing the smaller, appropriately arrested : and all that can be only done by continental unions. You cannot reach the noblest of all free triumphs, a liberal conservative revolution, without you rise as one united body, with a due concert of action.

Large nations can act with impunity, what destroys and denationalizes small ones. The whole world needs republican institutions, to put down all the ridiculous, corrupt, rotten systems of the social, political, and national framework of perverted mind.

Why cumber kings and autocrats the chairs of state, that they are unworthy to hold, as they seek to deceive their people by false, bad faith, pretending it to be religion! Let their salaries be for the indigent : let all the excesses of superfluities be to prevent paupers.

Liberalists of Europe, who number more than one hundred millions! You, a majority, speak with all your moral force, for the noblest conservative revolution. Well can the central nation of the earth, so far as her position between the two mightiest oceans make her, be looked to by the whole world.

Let all nations institute systems and means of rational education for all.

It is the world's duty to prevent the five grand divisions from hurting each other, and that can be only accomplished by rational principles of constitutional government. The world should have all things done at the right time. No governmental power must presume on policy, cunning, but on principles. None should commit themselves to any other than principle. Who is up to the civilization of this constitutional government? Civilization of equal magnitude had not dawned among the ancients. Our fathers have only made a beginning, and their posterity has to act equal to the best conservative revolution.

It is not merely to follow what they have done—that is foolish, if the lights of the age add a more brilliant and a nobler light, suitable to originate a better, on their platform. This is the highest of conservatism.

Never fail to vote, citizen. Do not omit that inestimable privilege, as you thereby promote the full success of principles that rightly govern the world.

Let the weaker states, especially, consider of all that is expedient for universal welfare, to be best promoted by continental or grand division unions.

Aristocracy is now superfluous as monarchy, after the people can govern themselves, and that they can, the world proves. Put all nations on equal rights of constitutional government, and who will seek war? Nothing less than international constitutional government can solve the peace problem of the world. All peculiar faith people, now join God's standard, and discard your foolish and corrupt priestocracy, all over the world—and by so doing you drop all your governments false to your good, mind, and its Creator.

Give up the churches, and leave them in their nothingness ; by so doing, you retain your religion, and make it rational.

Leave off all peculiar faith, not only as a nullity but as a world, mind, mankind cause. This is the stronghold of despotism. Let free and intelligent world citizens break this hold, and the theatre is a clear one for rational mind. Let the world know what is religion, that none but free people know now.

Not only justice, but liberality throughout the world, is inculcated, by the universal comity of nations.

The world fighting business is very expensive, and only proves that mind's perversions pay for the evils of its world's creation. When each grand division of the earth has its constitutional government established, then just so much navy and army as will keep down insubordination, smuggling, piracy, mobs, unruly spirits, &c., may be tolerated.

Proper patriotism must never be compromised : proper constitutional laws should be obeyed, administered, and executed, and the world's universal good established.

Come, sovereigns of the earth, it is time for you to resign, and let the true sovereigns be self-governed. Let a star-world imitate a star-nation.

A constitutional government is essentially expedient for all five grand divisions of the earth, to guard and protect, in all the departments of rational mind, as in all great matters of nationality.

Ancestors have no more right to seek to bind posterity, in contracts of debts, by excessive expenditures, than to leave them obsolete bibles and their abominable church despotisms—to curse them with the priestocracy, if they do not believe—at the same time posterity cannot absolve itself from any claims of debts of equitable demands of the nation. The nation knows no ancestors, no posterity, in her debts, that must be paid ; therefore, the most exact justice requires no debts to be contracted that will be national evils. As to not being able to borrow, the rulers have no right to bind the capitalists to usury laws. The rulers are the usurers, and should tax the people for all necessary expedients, not encumber the world with their crimes, and drain continents, and butcher and poison the people, in the draining, to cover the errors of false and fatal ambition. If this be strictly adhered to, the true people will ever seek to be just to themselves, as dictated by their best and vital interests.

They will hardly enter into protracted wars, that beget the heaviest and most onerous taxes, to be paid by themselves, reaping but equivocal glory and no profit. There is a paramount debt due from ancestors to posterity, to leave the expansiveness of a liberal mind the capacity inherent of being rational and civilized, not to be tory to mind, God, and his unmistakable teachings. The priestocracy enter into no such calculations, and are to be forever excluded, as world and mind unworthy.

The hundred millions of freemen in Europe must be rightly invoked, by all rational addresses to their minds. The bribed sophists of sophisticated governments of church and state are not only paid but licensed in their sinful sophistry, to seduce, cheat, and defraud the world, for the sake of false government. China, break down your inside walls of bigotry, and bad government ; call for a union of Asia.

Men of Europe ! Organize, organize, not agitate, openly and above board—assert your inherent rights, that you ought to protect properly, as one hundred millions of liberalists in Europe—a most momentous question. Communicate with each other. Let it be done openly ; ask for a continental convention of all Europe, to establish one universal government. Do so, monotheists of the world. Let emperors know that monotheists are their superiors, as the first dignitaries of the earth.

Nothing can excel this, the most high and pure-minded on earth, in life. The civilizers of the world must not be put back by emperor pontiffs, who tell their vassal bishops about peculiar faith.

All that is folly. Mature your views, liberalists ; do not spill one drop of blood. Who are amenable for the blood of the French revolution ? The whole question must be comprehended most wisely, and the position looked at that crushed mind for centuries. It was the evil genius of peculiar education and government.

Government was instituted for the world's benefit, including all mankind, and is conservative when it embraces principles inherent in proper national, continental and universal basis of permanency. Not because some things are used in monarchies or aristocracies, are they to be rejected by supposed republics, much less adopted because used by the last. Let the progressive light of expansive mind genius, create all the fundamental structure to elicit the mighty world fabric. Conservative principles that will prevent an individual, doing as the world sycophancy directs at Rome or gold mines, are what religion institutes, and when carried out rationally, will secure the world's inherent rights and protection. All necessary governments must be duly amended as requisite, to be duly respected. The conventions of the five grand divisions and appurtenant islands, can meet so as to make the complete circuit, to create a right-toned sentiment throughout the world.

Let the English language become the proper world language. By this world organization, rational mind will seek to embrace and comprehend its liberal expansiveness, and arrest any powerful nation that is after any improper world policy, to bully on the ocean or pirate on the world. Let the world have access to both, through continental constitutional governments. Any nation that is not tried in the various fields of world labor, ocean and land, is not adequate for all man's theatre. Conservative government is that which elicits all the principles conservative to the world's proper government, not because they are used by this or that form of government, but because they were conservative to the proper standard, which protects all properly. No nation or individual should contract any debts, without the means of payment.

They should institute sinking funds, so much per cent. yearly on taxes, to sustain as a sacred fund the most important world's demands.

They should institute an apprentice system, for all needing labor for support, the apprentices the last year to receive wages, and all timely rational education, which must be supervised by responsible citizens, to see that the failure be duly remedied, not afterwards when no pecuniary compensation can make amends for lost rational education. The world needs proper self-protection, which must come by proper instruction. Voters for representations ought to be duly qualified ; property-holders should vote for protection as well as taxation to property. But all this difficulty may be superseded, by the universal homestead to all families needing it. When the world is correctly governed by constitutional governments, the productions of the soil will be appropriately graduated to the proper demands of vital existence. Then luxuries will yield to necessaries, as the sublimity and grandeur of religion are to reach the consummation of appropriate constitutional government. Liberalists, teach your monarchs that they have mistaken the object of their creation, that it was for the holiest, best promotion of rational mind, not act in collusion with false faith and government; that they are bound to give the proper display of rational religion, and its constituent free government, not unite in felonious oppression and see domestic troubles throughout Europe, till the end of time. Tell your miscreant dictators, that without principle, they are nothing, that without principle they have no religion, with all their faithless bad faith.

OFFICE HOLDERS.

INDEPENDENCE of character ought to be the motto of every true-minded man, to the extent that manliness and virtue require. If worthy, his country may well select him from his business or avocation, to represent her properly. He should not permit mere public fame or personal popularity, to usurp his more substantial attributes.

A regular employment, that is calculated to enable man to reach a future competency, is far preferable to office-hunting, as the incumbent may not remain a sufficient time to do justice to his talents as an officer, much less to his condition of life as a man.

All competent men should as rational beings, for proper employment of time, secure a proper business capacity, trade or profession for a permanent living, then they can act as becomes freemen. Office will seek the man, there will be less proscription, the country will be more faithfully and honestly served, patriotism will be duly appreciated, and moral stocks will rise beyond calculation. There will then be no cause for political proscription, and the blessings of a representative government will be best insured.

Appointments by mere political influence, too often detract from the blessings of correct government, and tend to destroy the worth and usefulness of office. Many that have valuable gifts of mind, lose their full value for want of exercising sound judgment, in acquiring an independence of property, to protect themselves against all the vicissitudes of political exposure.

Why then could minds of the right calibre, need office from government generally ? They would be thrown out of regular business, and their affairs might be in a deranged state, unless proper system is maintained by the individuals.

The principal position is, neither seek nor decline proper office generally. When the soldier is needed, all true patriots will rush to the rescue.

How wrong is it, that voters should commit themselves to candidates, prior to investigation of merits in the elective franchise ? History, by the time the election arrives, may show some worthless, unqualified and unworthy of a freeman's vote. All should be cautious in estimating too lightly a freeman's privilege, to secure which, cost so much blood and treasure. None should neglect this invaluable right, none misdirect it.

Patriots have to travel in this life a straight track, and let it be their own track, and no one else's surely, not a demagogue's.

The abuses of government officers, are obvious in all kinds of governments.

The exactions of those in China, are enormous. Are they not so elsewhere ?

The peculations of those in the United States, often go unpunished. We are that much short of proper government. Salaries should be adequate, to secure the best talents and integrity, to prevent peculation and smuggling. There must be no public plunder.

Smuggling in Spain and Portugal, it is said, prevails, and the contrabandists are winked at by the custom house officers, who make all clear that they detect. What venality of public officers and officials! Wise laws, and properly administered by adequately paid officials, are essential to all nations.

What a noble pursuit agriculture is, to render the world independent of the necessity of seeking office. Agricultural societies should be promoted by all the legitimate means of the country and world.

Moreover is needed the assistance of mechanics, mining and manufactures. What value is mind, to secure labor-saving machines? By these advancing with an equal step, a proper relation is maintained for true national independence, and an insurance for adequate markets. Then arises the refining influence of commerce aided by navigation, that embraces the whole world in its beneficial influences. The whole area of mind's employment is thus enlarged to the most liberal comprehension, and the character of the merchant commingles with the world's mighty functionaries.

National legislation that, if wise, diffuses its conservative aid to mankind, can find no department more worthy than national finances. All the great elements embrace principles, and cannot be identified with party, nor be excluded thereby. Whatever is identified with true national prosperity, and especially not in antagonism with the world's welfare, should be accredited as permanent policy.

No system of finance should be instituted that would involve national demoralization. If any should create any tendency to smuggling, it should be forthwith discountenanced.

Mr. Hunt, of congress, is reported as saying: "Under an advalorem duty, insert what guard you please, and still the treasury would be robbed." "Men who regarded their interest only, would get round the law by perjury and fraud. It was a common saying, and a practical principle all over the commercial world, that custom-house oaths had no binding force!" Now we come at world facts. What, then, would be done for peculiar faith, the most influential thing of all mind influences and persuasions? It could enlist nearly a world perjury.

The beauty of correct principles of government is, not to entrust office too long to any, only as best promotive of the good of the whole and the principles that sustain them. This begets a proper national independence that reflects the best patriotism in office, and the best offices on patriotism. The policy of all correct governmental administrations should be, to have no dishonest office-holders, or who do properly punish them for malfeasance in office. What better otherwise is it than absolutism? Living salaries insure fidelity, character and good faith. Give adequate salaries and remuneration. Indifferent candidates run, that would not be nominated if proper salaries were given. Nominations ought to be made or exercised by intelligent freemen, who are the beneficiaries of candidates, not by caucus, without responsibility, but by American spirit, nothing less than proper liberal republicanism. What might not the world stock be to support those really in want, if we could get persons rightfully to disburse all that was entrusted. Why so much defrauding of the public treasury? Are not republics trustworthy? Are monarchies more so than they? Do not create nuisances by low or inadequate salaries. There must be no peculation or embezzlement of government funds. If fraud be committed by officials, punish all, high and low, equally, without obstruction of the supreme rights of the people. Proper rotation in office must be kept up, and offices should be filled by worthy and respectable citizens, not political partizans. Some may regret failure to obtain office, whilst many others may regret getting it, as they fell by temptation, and were crushed in spirit and feelings to death.

The people must familiarize their mind to great, good and virtuous actions, and preserve the guardianship of the best laws. There should be no delay of public justice—no connivance at fraud, peculation or speculation in the wealth of government; but fair and honorable competition.

PARENTS AND CHILDREN.

THE world is most deeply concerned in parental and filial relations. Parents should never let children grow up in ignorance, much less in error; give them no peculiar education but the noble position of rational principles. They wish them to know the world, not only in sunshine, which alone will not answer; but all should seek to know it in the shade, in the storm as calm, adversity as prosperity,—in revolution, conservative, if necessary, as in the mildest stages.

Prepare them for the great scenes of life, to fearlessly originate utilitarian measures, with which those of the world may clash by self-interest-antagonism, where that self-interest cares nothing for principle, the more turbulent the clannish antagonism.

Rich children, at literary institutions, should never have excess of money, that abstracts their mind from study, and carries them on to dissipation and bad habits. Youth can hardly study when the means of temptation are pushed on them. In this particular is more absurd, if not criminal mismanagement, by weak and ignorant parents, than from most other sources.

Yielding to petted children their wrong, headstrong and ruinous way, is reflective on the intelligence and morals of parents, who ought to have guardians themselves, if they will not act the guardians of mind for their own offspring in all vital essentials. They should be taught the proper relation of things by the proper use, not the abuse. The scattering of property speedily scatters the owners, and throws upon them the rebuke of the most poignant reflections. Partiality to children is very wrong.

Some may be raised to spend money, others to make it. Justice is done the last; and if the first become gamblers, spendthrifts and debauchees, most can reproach their parents. Their conduct in life will reflect on parents.

Do parents, by their remiss, loose way of education, bring up their sons to be dissipated, or drunkards? Retributive justice will ensue. No system will be safe but that which recognises mind as identified with soul. The parental and filial relations are most rational the lifetime.

What a mental treasure will children obtain, who are competent, by not only advice, but parental, social and religious training, to possess a reputation that will sustain and carry man where money will not, but endow him with the best appreciation of his future good.

What a blessed thing it is for children to be born of honest and wise parents, whom they can duly respect and love! There is then no danger that their children will be outcasts, when they can be duly enlightened, at the right time and way, by rational principles, that teach mind and correct its errors by rational education.

Such parents will show the right, not refractory spirit—will not outrage feelings, but counteract evil. They will not permit any nursery tales of superstition, all made by pious frauds, or accommodated to the profits of the clergy and the penitentiary. Children's depravity may be increased by idleness. Parents' night police is essential in proper restriction. Parents should never entrust their children to any and every person and company, school and society. Parents, do your children need your aid to give them a proper start in life? You may be too late in assisting your offspring.

Do not have the minds of children crushed or petted—either way spoilt. Parents wish their children to steer clear of drink, lust, crime and vice, then they must all rely on proper, universal tests. Parents should not let children, large enough to work, be idle or lounge about. Children are thus often miseducated, and brought up by parents improperly.

Many parents do not understand to rear children, who are consequently spoilt early in life, and are rendered a curse instead of a blessing to the world. Do they thank their parents, for their treachery to their duty? Parents are thus amenable to their country and the world thereby injured.

There is nothing more important than right rational raising, and yet children are thus ruined abundantly. What can compensate therefor? What a crying shame! It is not for want of bibles of tradition, that never can meet the question, but it is from want of using the appropriate civilization of mind, that thus pays forfeit to society. It is dire neglect, want of cultivation of good qualities, and over-exertion of bad propensities.

Parents must teach children to comprehend and practice all the principles and duties of life and the world; to omit naught of what ought to be, nor commit aught of what ought not to be.

One of the most important things in the world, is society, which the world should properly establish, support, enjoy, and do appropriate justice to. In this, the highest honor is implied or expressed.

Children should thank their God that they are indebted to kind parents or guardians, friends and good citizens, the wisest governmental institutions in the world, and that they have rightly profited therefrom.

They may thank all such for their rational education, for their escapes from the wiles and curses of social harpies. Mind at an early age could not see abstract notions, and include the same duty with attributes and principles. The world cannot obliterate the finer, chaster feelings with impunity; if it produce bad actions, it creates bad habits. All useful accomplishments should be embraced in the plan of rational education — all these rational accomplishments of mind, as music, thorough science, philosophy, sound ratiocination—no treachery to mind, by perversions of faith-sophistry.

Parents must not enslave their children, exhort, not brutally force them to duty, and they will love and reverence you, most preferably to fear. Understand how to raise your children. Do so rightly. If children be badly raised, they may turn against their own parents, and mistreat them for retribution.

Principles will vindicate themselves.

The least that the world should say is, we did our utmost, that the highest filial duty and reverence for parents prompted.

It is essential that parents should excite the highest respect, among their children.

Duty is pleasant, but that of affection bestows a blessing that cannot be surpassed, richer than all of earth. Children should seek the honor of their dying parents. The inculcation of all necessary good habits to children, will be their everlasting good to all.

The good habits of early rising to both sexes create health, pleasure, and wisdom, an exuberance of much that is practicably good.

Children should be caused to cultivate the best disposition, and exercise cheerfulness. The highest object of parents will be attained, by a faithful seeking to make them the ornaments of human nature. The world should be guarded, at once, against all the insidious wiles of mankind.

Do not let you children associate on terms of intimacy or friendship with those that you think they should not marry. What can you expect of human nature? If you do not keep them at first excluded from such companionship, do not stupidly. brutalize nature afterwards, and expose yourself to cruel taunts, or more cruel, if not degrading hazards.

What can the world expect of the insidious seducer? Better had people of virtuous feelings and refined sensibility forego their lifetime, all the supposed advantages of society—better had they see their whole family excluded from the world, and rest on their dignity, than ever know some of the world's wretches.

Are some aware that their own imprudence tempts guilt?

Let every mind be reared on the principle, that a person forfeits his right to the use of speech, when he repeatedly sacrifices and falsifies his word and honor. How easily some people let the most important events pass them without due analysis, which means separating truth from error. The world should see to it, not to have anything in life that would cause a studied violation of veracity.

Next to truth and honesty, teach children the worth of time.

What can compare with invaluable time? What are its appropriate functions? This is one of the world's great problems. If children be lost in the raising, not to estimate either of these, can money compensate parents? All should have proper and full employment. The acts of mind must be truly carried in every department of life, and especially should its guardian care be solicited about youth, who should never be entrusted with any means, as guns, that they hardly know how to manage or load rightly.

Parents should teach their children the invaluable worth of veracity, that is to be maintained with invincible moral firmness. They should be taught a noble and generous piety, and independence. Beware, as you value your soul, of teaching peculiar faith education to children. They must be taught principles, not peculiar faith, else parents may expect to see sorrow, if not disgrace. Principles are the only safety.

When a youth shoots down most wantonly an inoffensive female Indian in the forest, what could be expected short of retributive justice?

What could the father say, when he was forced to see that son skinned alive by the Indians?

Was there not an especial Providence, through principles, that had been grossly abused and violated? What better could have been instituted than a prevention of all this, by the right use of rational mind duly cultivated? All should know that principles, Deity's most faithful representatives in the universe, have a self-vindication somewhere. Children amply repay to parents when they do justice to this position.

They are bound to reverence their parents, respect, cherish, and love them affectionately, to the honorable demands of nature. They must estimate them as duty directs.

Parents will inculcate this in children by supreme care for their minds, and will instil all right principles to lead them aright.

Families should have different rooms for themselves and children, as to sexes, to sleep in.

No house should have less than three rooms, if at all practicable. Good raising is worth more than it can be appreciated, and is inestimable to all good society and honorable states. It is one of the richest jewels.

Parents may teach their children to defraud, and aid them in defrauding others; but such children turn the tables on their parents. The mother teaches her children to steal, and finds them in the penitentiary for their crimes.

What an indissoluble link of morals is there between parents and children!

The duties and affection of parents decide protection to their children, who should be allowed at proper time a decent respect for marriage preferences, and should not be discarded or outlawed, except for disgrace of illegitimate transactions.

They should be rarely, if ever, discarded or renounced altogether, after rightful marriage with those of their choice. How many children have had their spirits crushed by mistreatment of this kind, who might by want be forced, as millions in large, overgrown and vicious cities are, to prostitute and corrupt themselves, and thus indelibly disgrace their whole families.

Wise and generous parents should give them at once a separate, adequate maintenance, if they do not visit them. Justice, if not affection, is due between the parents and children. To renounce it, when needed, is a disgrace to the offending party. In domestic government, honor your children; thus you will honor yourselves, parents, for they will honor you. The legacy of free thought, pure science, and rational education, embodies the honor of mind and God; the slavery of mind is the worst of all curses to country.

Parents should be properly prepared in mind to do justice to the rights and morals of their offspring, as their best natural guardians.

Children are bound, under all rational principles, during their lifetime, to respect their filial duties. Both will feel bound to work for the household, to secure profitable employment of their time, ample fruits of their labor, and adequate improvement of their mind.

Parents have wisely to counteract the vices of perversion, if they wish to be saved from the most withering curses of society. Their paramount duty is the best prayer to be addressed to the Almighty Providence, that cannot be more potently invoked by all in this whole circle.

* This duty forever devolves on them, merely to give the right direction, as principles are ever conservative, characteristic of their most illustrious author. All vices are growing evils, else the constitution of the human mind is wrong. Where would be the basis for mind's improvement, otherwise? The first slight, superficial view of mind might lead to the deepest dissatisfaction; but the deepest analysis corrects all that. Mind must look then forever to principles, as the only safe guardian for parent and child, for all the world.

How, otherwise, can the world be progressive? We recognise all this in our daily transactions and our philosophy. It is the foundation and essence of mind's strength, for if the free agent towering in free principles do not counteract demoralization arising from constant temptation, nothing else can be expected than proportionate suffering. Man is presumed to know and act on this obvious, necessary, and highly important quality of mind given him for his noblest blessing, his greatest good and happiness

The question looks at all future enjoyment, in all the sphere of the soul's action.

Then give the right basis with sufficient cultivation, and the balance rests on supreme power, that none but impious hands arrest and arrogate.

Here are the beauty and strength of the edifice.

Right principles lead man, the actor, safe of penalties in morals. Difficulties make men, if rightly sustained, on this basis.

Then can the smiles of parents arise, for they are blessed by ripe and rich fruits. All else are bad results. Then who will not render themselves suspected by skulking this question, for all these acts are those of honesty? None but the suspected in honesty skulk from all proper questions. Honest minds do not hide under mantles that are deficient, and that must necessarily expose them in their deformities.

Well can freemen gratefully pay homage and their noblest tribute to their country's free institutions, that aid parents and the protectors of mind, in all laudable teachings. If there are to be any confessors of the human mind, parents with the appropriate sex should be of their youthful children, that they may be corrected of secret vices and crimes, ere they fall into numerous ills and deadly penalties.

The sexes certainly can best know appropriate corrections, and can best confide to each other their peculiar cases. A proper right and confiding understanding should prevail between parents, to insure that of the highest respect between themselves and children. Nothing interrupts the proper authority of parents sooner, than the loss of the respect and confidence of their children.

The position of the parent should be firmly defined, but maintained on the best pledges of love and persuasion. Many cases are subject to deepest censure, and some are amenable to presentation before a grand jury; were they not better corrected by the high moral code of the world.

Different sets of children, like different races, are liable to produce alienations and conflicts in the same family, and the whole relations have to be managed with delicate regulations.

Property, the source of much of this evil, had better be under the peculiar care of the best protectors, and when productive of family jars, had better be held inabeyance. The step-son may be hostile to the step-mother, having an interest in securing the property that belongs to his step-mother's children. The step-mother may be hostile to the step-children, wishing to secure the most for her children. Both husband and wife may be unprincipled, and wish to appropriate to their use and profit, to expend the money of their step-children.

A righteous and wise legislation must counteract all these things. Dollars present much of life's difficulties that must be wisely counteracted. The step-mother, when liable to the unprincipled conduct or domestic tyranny of her husband and step-children, must not permit either to trespass on her dignity, as the world can only be rightly managed by a stern, moral firmness, proving one's self right. Bad parents enslave their children to minister to their avarice and ambition. What, then, will an unprincipled world not do, when no relation exists but the securing the greatest profit out of muscular corporeal functions? Children owe it to themselves and parents to govern their own extravagance beyond their income, and amend their economy. Parents should enable their children to learn the use and value of money, and overcome the tendency to its abuse, by making it. Parents will eradicate the latent remnants of superstition and darkness of mind, in any of the exploded doctrines handed down by pious frauds, identified in the propagation of deeper error to render it more plausible.

Parents will object to the affianced feelings of their children, that they have helped to create, despite of all the refined feelings of humanity, and reject their children at the same time that they subject them to an ordeal, that might be too much for most of mankind. The parents are the culpable party, for permission of the association, if there be anything amiss in the other party.

Were parents disgraced by the subsequent conduct of their children, they could not blame them for it, as they have caused it.

Heirs generally cannot take care of property, when they do not know how dearly the same was made. When they are the victims of bad, evil habits, engendered by the profusion of wealth and the temptations of luxuries, so difficult for human nature, early initiated therein to resist, liable to lose all and themselves in endless perdition, then property is a curse. It is cruel to entrust much to a profligate to squander wantonly, when his rightful rational education, including the proper bringing up to habits of industry, economy and reflection of proper thought, as well as action, has been improperly neglected. Parents should invariably provide for their children, at the right time.

Bad children reflect on parents, morally and physically. They can direct them, with proper firmness, and generally success will follow proper training.

Parents should guard their children against evil or vicious habits. Both sexes are amenable to the correction of good taste. Snuff-rubbing is almost enough with some, to break off a match. Ladies should leave all such in the care of the anti-tobacco society, that their life may be pleasant and long.

Parents should never entrust power too soon, to mere children who may act as disposition, not reason, prompts.

Youth could rarely with safety be entrusted with popular government, until their minds are matured in all sound principles.

What children will under the least guide of civilization, ever raise the arm of rebellion against their parents? If they cannot live in peace with them, and maintain an equable and respectful mutual regard, then leave them in peace, but let them not throw themselves away; to spite the world, let them not spite themselves. All minds that reflect the soul's action must rise above the world by mind's merit, and crush all low envy by intrinsic greatness.

No wise parents will make their children suppliant tools, to disgrace them. They will render them, as themselves, worthy of their country, their country worthy of the world, and that of their creator. Such parents and children will not increase the world's stock of vice, but enlarge its virtues. Such parents will not treat youth by peculiar whims and caprices, to become disgusted with family and society, and finally outlaw themselves. Children should receive the rational education, that would cause them to revere their parents—not only love, but look up to them. Principles will cause that.

In family jars, where step-relations are in the way, all proper steps should be taken to prevent any tyranny from that cause, to guard against the future. The character of the parents often decides that of their children generally. Nothing, then, but a differently cultivated intellect can cause posterity to depart from their ancestor's vices, errors, and peculiar faith. Society, then, improves, on each improved age. A worthy husband and virtuous wife can endear themselves to their beloved offspring, and all to the world, by the true course in civilization, the proper rational education of their minds to the legitimate capability.

Do parents make any difference with their children? Spare them that misery of existence! Educate them all rationally and properly. Never give them any peculiar education, that will return you retributive justice.

Parents cannot be too cautious of their children, in overgrown cities, that are most infected with vices. They should not commit themselves about any peculiar faith, so far as to teach children to speak of the contents of bibles by memory, when they can only respond without judgment.

All such is a heinous sin. Have their minds thus been truthfully and honorably exercised?

The height of good taste and avoidance of noxious and bad habits constitute the sublime of domestic tuition, and must gratify the noblest emotions on their attainment. All actions, that do not suit the most approved taste, should be avoided.

The miserable habit of snuff-rubbing, enough to disgust many men of taste against their brides, is pursued by nearly four-fifths of females, in some circles. There should be no immoral speech, sight, taste, or deed, avoidable, to the ears and eyes of youth.

If parents do justice to their children, their children will be apt to do the same in full return. Bad children reflect on parents, say what you will about tender affections. To appreciate the world, mind must have the right science, that by experience is most valuable, if under the right code, the value of things, as money. No one should be left money unless he learns the proper use of it, as it is a lever, otherwise, to corrupt and enslave, probably destroy the possessor. Parents should stimulate the legitimate characteristics, inspirit energy, advise perseverance and industry, in all laudable undertakings. All mankind, no matter who, should be brought up to some business or trade. Piety for parents, to the sublimest, as the highest philanthropy, must be strictly inculcated.

All parents should counteract all the secret vices of their children, by proper, wise instruction on the subject.

The most correct taste of chaste looks, language, conduct, may be most chastely cultivated. In fact, cultivation is the most of all man's duty for himself and others. In regard to children, rational education requires strict attention to the mother's and nurse's department, that influences the character prior to seven years.

Do not confine the young idea merely to letters and books. Teach things, and explain their whole history and philosophy, by not mere words. Much of the difference of the world arises from the character of the race of mankind. No nation can be great without a female morale of superior character—and, of intellectual abilities of the men, resulting from mind and its rational cultivation. It is a wretched policy, to bring up children to spend money, and not make it. They thus are prodigal of immortal time, talents, morals, and the highest obligations of religion. All such prodigality takes away half the worth of man, to raise children, generally, who see vices, and rarely exercise the virtues. Teach your children to have nerve, one of the best parts of mind discipline. This thing of children's wasteful extravagance, is demoralizing in the extreme, nationally and individually.

No matter what the wealth, teach all some business or employment becoming rational minds. Let the world be so taught, that the sexes will properly stimulate, arouse, and refine the highest minded duties of each other.

Right training or bringing up cannot be dispensed with by parents, who ought to be well qualified for all such great duties of life. Mothers have a universal sisterhood, co-equal with the universal brotherhood, both to be as comprehensive as religion. They rear their children at the right time at their bosoms, and can best teach them all the holy principles consecrated in the sacred family circle. Theirs is the holy temple of honor, to teach them temperance and virtue, that is, the practice of principles. Theirs is the sacred duty, and they best secure filial obedience. Then is the time for all efficient action to lay the proper foundation for sincerity, the complete test. What an important commission, to help form the human mind of their offspring, to become statesmen and patriots. Theirs is the world-keeping of rational mind. Surely, their education cannot be too rational, elevated, sublimated.

Parents, do not teach your children to be simple or hypocrites, and they will be one or both if your bible is given them. Monotheism takes all the senses along, and educates them rationally; peculiar faith drops the best, and causes a peculiar perversion of mind in atheists and polytheists, who will be nowhere in the time of triumph of rationality. The mother's temple of honor is to rear children on principles that rule bibles, peculiar faith and the whole machinery.

How few parents are competent to advise, educate mind rationally; How few can comprehend right rational principles! Children should be taught the highest, holiest principles, so as not only not disgrace their relations, but their country and world, their mind, to establish that mind polity, that will not only sustain the best polity for their own support to secure the best comforts of life, but to increase those of others.

Let all families secure the sacred mutual relations, the invaluable amiableness of character.

The parents, withholding patrimony till death from children, whom they doom to struggle for existence, when a proper marriage portion ought always to be given for the independent disposition of mind and its functions, is one of the great errors of conceited and illiberal minds, that must be universally corrected.

There is no comparison of the worth of property then given, to any subsequent remote disposition of it. Children of the rich are kept from the process of financiering, to be finally introduced to that of mere expenditures. Their minds are thus comparatively kept blanks, and a most ungrateful state of things is prepared by the parents themselves. No minds in this world should be exempt from appropriate employment; and if any power on earth prevent this most legitimate rationality, it ought instantly to be sacrificed for public good. The people should become all business people.

Why enjoin the proper care of property? Because money is power, that confers its appropriate independence, that is most valuable for that elevation that it imparts to mind. Beyond a competency, unless legitimately accruing, mind has no need to busy itself, unless for proper employment.

Not only propriety of conduct, but that of language, is to be universally inculcated.

Disobedience, parents, is it you complain of? Whom have you to blame but yourselves?

When principles are desecrated at the family altar, by your faith that has desecrated the family, country, world, can you expect better results?

It is the paramount duty of parents to promote the noblest happiness of their children, by not only inculcating, but securing early marriages. Any other sentiment is derogatory to principle.

Marriage portions should be allotted compatibly with the ability of parents.

WOMAN.

A WOMAN of virtue is beyond esteem, when without it she is utterly contemptible before the world.

The present enlightened free intercourse between the sexes in mind's free improvement, towers over the ancient enslavement. In fact, were not the ancients slaves and vassals to ignorance, prejudice, superstition, customs, and miserable habits?

Half the world, the sex, has been freed since that time.

Correct appreciation by mind's analysis will entrust no females to the control of male teachers, priests or preachers at all, but restraining all classes, sexes, and professions within the appreciation of prudence and suitable restrictions and conduct.

A poor woman's virtue is a jewel, as rich as the richest. In this, all chaste women are equal.

The richest are the poorest if they lose their innocence, and the first step does the irreparable mischief. Innocence cannot be disguised generally. She volunteers to publish wrong, nor skulks behind the times. She cannot be passive in the most fiendish wrongs of the world.

As the high minded value their best views of present and future bliss, they should never resort to any unnatural expedients to gratify lusts. They should discard as brutes, all who plan any illicit gratification any way. The world will put a proper estimate, if all females keep alive self-respect. To insure this, is to insure a correct action of the world itself, that must treat itself with self-respect.

We must duly appreciate the qualities of the world and its best functions.

Woman's virtue only makes her lovely in mind's sight, otherwise she is of no account, an object of disgust. The enlightened society of females, has the conservative kind of moral influence on man. Thus, woman should keep man straight as well as herself, as it is her legitimate province and imperative duty to command him in the best respects.

She can restrain him from approaching her without respect, by her highest self-respect. All conservative prudence requires her to keep him at a distance, unless she can command his respectful attachment, for the moment her virtue becomes easy, man becomes disrespectful of woman, and woman then has no hold on man's respect.

What would be the world, but for woman's virtuous worth? Man would care nothing for himself and society, that is made up of respectable sexual divisions. Does the world as at present organized, give all its protection to female worth?

What shall we think of that of churches when their ministers, arraigned for attack on female virtue, under the influence of the party have actually caused the lady accuser to be expelled the church? No sides in religion can be taken for either sex, but what the justice of the case requires, as there can be no parties when that presides.

Females help to govern morals, and when right, should have the very best protection.

Many females, by the effects of vitiated peculiar education, rely on cunning. intrigue, art, to carry out their designs; but does a chaste woman, or an honest man rely on such ignoble contingencies? They rely on principles that must be uniform. Rational education will give this noble reliance. Who would not save the chastity of a worthy poor female, rather than have built St. Peter's church with the means raised ignobly as they were?

Thanks to the benefits of mind, woman can prove her patriotic, heroic, and domestic virtues as well as man, and that she as well as mind has escaped the degradation of Oriental barbarisms, and western feudalisms.

Rational minds should always recognise principles, and only those as companions who recognise such, male or female, nor suffer any to mislead because the party is female, as that is absurd and truly degrading. The most beautiful romance of refinement of love may be wasted on indifferent callous objects, incompetent to appreciate refined feelings. No suit should be entertained or attempted for a moment, that cannot be reciprocated. No persons of proper culture of mind should put their friends in a false position.

Selfish people ask too much courtesy at the expense of feelings. Flattery ought to be scouted as ignoble for both sexes. It is base coin.

Some busy-body people are always trafficking in matches; they should look to divorces. Pure match-making will often supersede the purest love. There can be no traffic in pure affections. Such will lower the party in estimation of the right thinking.

Let none presume to waive intellect and candor at the expense of self-respect and courtesy.

The world cannot be too much guarded against all mankind, man or woman.

How much is lost about marriage matches.

One of the greatest mistakes of noble human nature, is to permit others to have any power beyond necessity. That is a false position that permits the dynasty of women or woman power.

Both sexes have a claim for what is right, no more.

A lady will never so far forget herself as request any polite gentleman to act in the social circle, what may be done but at the expense of his feelings. Be he the politest man in the world, let him negative any lady's request, that will cause him to feel after the act. Too much of this has been done to gratify the company with a false taste. A lady or gentleman must never forget what they owe themselves in any circle of the whole world. Correct taste must be met, not violated. That is the propriety of courtesy and true politeness. Do ladies expect gentlemen yield to their extravagant requests, that may reflect on the refined feelings of the last? Let the firm refusal be promptly given, and if she be a lady of courteous refinement and principle, as all ladies ought to be, she cannot pretend to urge any request not recognised as satisfactory to the gentleman. Surely, after refusal, she will not seek to have him violate his word—not at all. Then we should have no dynasty of weak or tyrannical women. The wise should submit to none of the various tyrannies and dynasties of the unprincipled in society, nor impose them. In settled communities it should be as much as both sexes' morals are worth, to violate the essential principles of society.

The intelligent must give the negative to all dynasties, weak women especially, who cannot take a hint, and before all of whom the world must act independently. How can ladies be obliged to a man's sorrow, when they exact to the disgust of pure mind? Man should call himself free, to do all that courtesy requires and no more. He should be as ready to negative the folly of dynasties as their crimes. The elevated character of woman reflects on the world, as one of its noblest blessings. It is she, thus refined, that teaches man to beware of being an animal when he should show mind, a mere mass of muscle instead of soul. If ever the presumption of peculiar education is taken for principles, young ladies will find it difficult to sustain their obligation for their share of civilization. How deeply interested are all females in rational education.

The rights of woman have been never yielded by Oriental or any peculiar bibles, but have been respected by American mind the more it respects genuine religion. Here woman can be generally, duly, and rightly estimated, as she respects herself and her elevated position. This part of the world is ever ready to side with woman, that is even accused of high crimes and misdemeanors; but it does so to side with the principles of equal justice.

Let woman prove herself worthy of the American approbation, and she will insure it.

The middle classes of the world are generally those that maintain the most honorable integrity. They are looked upon as most upright in England. There, when a woman of standing uncastes herself, it is then moral death. On the continent of Europe, Asia and Africa, with some exceptions, female modesty is below par, it is said, as most of the governments are below par. This is a sad affair.

The world must look in part to governments in the correction of morals. If the mind and morals of females are naturally defective, or rendered so by defective peculiar education, then their friends and country's laws must afford the highest protection. What souls have women, rational education only can declare. They are creatures of much impulse, and therefore need all the rational aid of intellectual philosophy.

The sex can be most lovely by the triumph of mind, rightly and rationally directed. Woman, with man, makes a whole. Who, when right-minded, properly, rationally educated, and affectionate, can make a truer, juster friend? Foibles are not peculiar to the sex, for those of man may eternally get him into scrapes. They are, then, the result of mind. Man, that has been dissolute, can hardly appreciate a virtuous, chaste woman. He too often dulls his refined sensibility, and mistakes the loveliest part of woman, her virtue.

Women need not seek public action, when private counsel and influence are so sublimely superior. The noblest counsellors of wisdom, virtue and honor, will appear for them, and they need not wish to sacrifice all these at the shrine of unholy ambition and vanity. There should be no dynasty of weak and unprincipled rulers of either sex.

The residence of woman is all the time essentially important. Hotels are generally too public for delicate females to be exposed to public duties. Males should be attended by males, and the sex by females. Each should have their own appropriate department. Woman must look to the fair matter of principles to uphold her best rights.

What can corrupt the female mind worse than peculiar faith? Woman is best protected by rational mind, that makes her equal by principles, virtue, to man. She should instruct her children at the fireside.

Persons may be very sensitive, but they can hardly be too independent in this selfish world. They may be estranged for lifetime by trifles, that if explained at the promptest time, may do justice to the loftiest and purest friendship, and excite no enmity. Have all proper explanations at once and forever. Woman is a man's equal.

Let the interested correct the mistakes of love, and not deplore them. There should be no antagonism between man and woman. Let all mutual explanations and concessions be rightly made. The world when rational, will live for honor, life and love. Before woman must be cherished not only love, but self-respect: both must be cherished and upheld. As to any woman's law for her married protection, there should be reciprocity of course. A woman's law is to protect her rights, those of her children and society, but not make her husband her overseer, much less the scape-goat for swindling property, or enacting any other worthless proceeding to defraud the world.

The world is to be rightly protected, not injured. When mistakes are made, explain ere the feelings are crushed, and sensitiveness is compromised or sacrificed.

It clearly reflects on the character of the libeler's mind, as deficient in moral and intellectual correctness; a libel on human nature, to underrate woman. Who is man or woman until reared in the sublimity of mind's rationality? What cannot woman be, if perverted by peculiar education? Every intelligent woman on earth this day, in her own glorious self-defence, has to declare herself for rational religion, otherwise she is the veriest creature of peculiar monstrosities. Tell us, females who advocate bibles, the peculiar edicts of eastern Asiatic vices, despotisms, to enslave man and woman, soul and body, what was the dignity of the thousand women degraded by the monster Solomon. It is from such felonies, that these vile libels are mind-factured. The whole jugglery of bibles, is mind-jugglery. You say the drama is fine for the world, but if it is purchased at the expense of female morals and virtues, away with it and the corrupt actresses. The victory is not worth the cost. The sacrifice is too great—virtue cannot be exposed to the shambles of a murderous taste.

There is but one proper way to preserve female chastity approvingly, and that is to have it beyond suspicion, chaste as the purest light.

If any employment or faith tend to vitiate mind, what must not that position be but vice or crime?

Will an intelligent, chaste woman, risk her husband's love, friendship, the respect of all? Mothers should guard their offspring on all points of defence. What is that? The sublimest tuition of rational principles.

Woman's education should be liberal, and her protection most comprehensive. It should have the soundest rudiments, to give the profoundest assistance to the rising generation.

MARRIAGE.

MARRIAGE from policy will never do; the fastidious must believe in the proper refinement and sentiments of love, to insure appropriate wedlock.

No institution can be resolved into mere civilized considerations, as none can be more sacred than family alliance. No marriages of blood relations or near degrees can be tolerated, as predicated on the wisest interdictions of nature herself.

Mind has to do its part in the wisest legislation, for the promotion of the highest purposes of existence.

Incest and unnatural alliances are to be most conclusively excluded by all the cogency of social obligations.

The crime of bigamy, polygamy, the relic of barbarous ages of a pretended Abraham and his descendants, is annihilated before the holy precincts of mind and its noblest guardian, Monotheism.

As marriage is invalid on conjugal infidelity, it never would be instituted by high-minded, honorable people, but for the best confidence in conjugal fidelity. This, then, has to be held the most sacred to perpetuate the first of institutions.

Polygamy is incompatible with nature, as the ratio of the sexes prove, being about equalized or balanced; besides, the highest moral position is violated, and natural laws are deranged.

Marriage of blood relations is incompatible with morals and the great laws of nature, that is evidently worsted, as we see in stock, that does not improve in such condition. All animated beings, as far as I know, thus degenerate on the most obvious fundamental principles.

How can we place marriage on proper basis, exempt from most of its contingencies?

Bachelors and maids may have taken too high a position, unless they get their choice. Had they not better sacrifice a little in exchanging their situations of single blessedness?

Marriage, if satisfactorily practicable, is the best. Too many of the world make marriage a very important matter, a mere contingency.

IMPROPER ALLIANCE BY MARRIAGE.

THE world has to avoid all improper alliance by marriage. Intermarriage with blood relations is to be avoided universally, as it has produced defective organizations, physical and mental.

The tainted blood of diseased parents is shown in the offspring abundantly, even to loss of senses, as blindness, imbecility, imperfect physical and mental developments.

Intermarriage of near blood relations, of royal persons, has rendered them idiotic, imbecile and deformed.

The position comprehends physical and moral causes, the first of which has been referred to previously in part.

Parties under consumption, cancer of the system, fungus hematodes, severe scrofula, deep taints of the constitution of the blood by syphilis, habitual fits frequently occurring, irreclaimable drunkards, however great the various charms, are to be avoided as suspicious at least.

What does it profit either party to gain marriage and leave such fatal tendency to a miserable progeny, and themselves left destitute of the object of their choice?

Under these circumstances, matches should be rarely if ever made, while proper alliances ought to be duly promoted. No marriage of those affected by peculiar diseases can be defended.

Some people are but little removed from idiots, varying in all the degrees moral and mental. They are just able to keep from falling into the fire or the penitentiary, and make up by duplicity and cunning what they ostensibly need otherwise, acting under the influence of a perverted mind, weakened in intellect from organic causes, identified with this subject in a line of ancestry or a deficient and vicious education. How far can the state interfere in such positions needing guardianship?

Matrimony never can respond happily to the fraud to obtain it, because it destroys the very foundation, mutual confidence and love. The right time is worth the notice of all mankind, and should be duly inculcated.

The intrigues to interrupt a proper marriage are at war with the best good of society.

Parents should rarely interfere to interrupt any such, and should feel themselves, above all things, compelled to promote the earliest marriages of their children, compatibly with personal and moral merits. They should generally expedite marriage.

Matrimony contemplates no beggared wife of industrious habits, with her destitute small children in pursuit of an absconding, worthless husband. The first step should be the right one, and that one should never be learned too late, when the study of character is accompanied by its loss.

Marriage is on improper base, when disputes for a little property interrupt the peace of those united. The infidelity of women may be risked in part by associations with unprincipled men, miscalled their husbands, who care nothing for the just, legitimate and conservative laws and rules of society. What effect will not such conduct have on the injured purity? They will be degraded with pride-fallen feelings crushed, unless, as is too often the case, restitution be made in blood!

Both parties may resort to expedients that the enlightened, civilized part of the world too often beholds with pity, disgust or contempt.

They may cultivate a cunning that works its own destruction, as it has no principles. The cunning polity will never stand.

The conduct of married people must be honorable and fair. But people badly raised will show it to the last, to the deepest regret of all their friends, and friends who are civil.

Too late it will be seen that good raising is worth most of the balance.

Above all, the deepest injury to society are the immoral taints, unchastity, lying, deceit, fraud, &c.

How often do women resort to shades of character that mislead them to deeper guilt.

How often is it that men perform degrading acts that are considered by some expertness and adroitness, however good faith is violated!

All this position tells at the time of maturity, and reflects on the character of the perpetrator.

THE MARRIAGE VOW.

SOME of the parties to marriage ties are murderers, drunkards and dissolute, wrecked in body, mind, character and property. Many such may not be above the suspicion of violating the marriage vows as adulterers and adulteresses. Freemen are the only people that can understand the rights and blessings of marriage. Aristocracy will pervert this blessing, if the laws of the duel are to decide on claims of the laws of equity.

The duellist becomes assassin, previously lording it over man's rights with impunity. This aggression comes of misrule, from absolute government that sets the most iniquitous examples. The republican takes the matter into his own hands, and avenges in hot haste the taint on his honor, by shooting down the offending party on sight. Married persons may become more unchaste, than those in single life.

To be married to one alienated in affections, deranged in mind, is all very unfortunate, it is true, but then such are life's misfortunes.

All should support the laws of their country, in all valuable customs, as those of marriage, if practicable.

What can the violation of the marriage vow avail most of the guilty parties? If a woman be false to her plighted faith, she will be so to her paramour or seducer. It needs only a better opportunity. What advantage then, can a rational being promise himself, in any such transaction?

The strength and purity of mind ought to be prominent, for security and protection.

Any law, to dissolve the marriage at any time, is legal prostitution and licentiousness. Sacred be the marriage vow to avoid disgrace and reproach to children, relations, friends and self, disunion, ruin, death, and the penalties of an untried being, shot-guns, lies and ignominy.

Marriage, no matter to whom, has a sacred influence, and cannot be dissolved without serious thought by any party that appreciates mind. What confidence can paramours place in the other party, proving false to their plighted pledges? What are degraded parties worth?

What can be better than having virtuous love, at first and always? What but bad and false taste, can cause such violation? The world of those persons thus acting is deeply corrupt, when their minds are thus perverted. Neither revenge nor vindictiveness should have relative sway in this pre-eminent question, but the highest protection of society should be pre-established, and should be held sacred by faithful public guardians. The inviolability and the sacredness of matrimony should be premised, in requiring all, especially females, to start right. All should act to their word, as not needing an oath. The highest appreciation of the world's honorable duty will define, that illicit pleasures are not to be thought of in the pale of matrimony. Have the parties that have pledged their most sacred vows in good faith, ever thought of the real consequences to get at adultery, how they must wade over crimes of dark and malign baseness, falsehood, treachery, and perjury, and the very strong probability and frequent certainty of their landing on the heaviest and most ignominious penalties?

Guardians of a supposed richest treasure are not apt to despise the best means of its protection, and vindication of its violation.

Who can invade its sacred precincts, with impunity? Are there no latent scars of conscience, that will finally harrow up the soul to remorse, and cry aloud for vengeance!

Who would wish any of the blessings of marriage, if to become victims to licentious partners.

Give to newly married people, a proper amount to thrive on, and support hope. Matrimony will protect morals. Every married couple should have a homestead provided for them by state taxes, if its own funds are incompetent.

How bad is interference about marriages, between persons perfectly unobjectionable! What misery is often entailed thereby!

How often is an objection raised, in order to avoid 'giving portions at once, to newly married persons.

What strong affections are often created though misplaced, and how often improperly deferred.

Marriage will enable most, to receive life's appropriate enjoyment.

In marriages, parents that are possessed of a competency, are then obliged by all the paramount obligations of religion, to give a homestead to the son or daughter, as the case may be on the side of one or the other. The object is earthly happiness, in conformity to that supreme law, that God himself has ordained. All this cannot be revoked, but must be wisely sustained. Mind rightly directed with a chaste taste can well correct all such, to a more refined and legitimate department.

Matching or mis-matching in marriage, presents a horrible state of things. This ordinance requires the purest affection, to promote universal happiness. The theatre where the infidelity of married persons is destructive, best displays the character of the virtuous and chaste woman, no less than that of the independent and honorable man.

They fear in bad actions, to arouse the fiery spirit of the sleeping lion, for bad habits grow and enslave proportionately. True heroes and heroines are only made by dangers, and genius is only appreciated where virtues are needed.

How many might see, but how few observe faithfully the upward tendency of good habits. This is the question of their destiny. Is it not that of their decision? Do rational parties mean to act honestly? Where else is the acknowledgment of the means of universal protection? Where can the safety of the married life repose, but in universal chastity, as none are safe without in life? The delinquent's health may be affected from certain ruinous diseases, but the virtuous married are free from sin and all its attending difficulties, dangers and dishonors.

The legitimate results of marriage are generally a family, that unites the social relations.

One of the greatest obligations to society, has been fulfilled by legitimating marriage, and ennobling the matrimonial connection.

The next is, the proper care and support of a family. The most courteous and affectionate regard cannot but be elicited, in the mind that has honorable thoughts. A mutual regard and esteem are expected to arise, to promote the happiest union. Such union should preclude all unkindness. Any personal violence between married persons, must be shameful and barbarous, calculated to crush the spirit or even degrade it indeed. The highest chastity as the highest honor must be maintained, to maintain the elevation suited to such a state. When no grounds exist of unhappy feelings, then the firmest are taken for happiness. The function of reproduction, one of the noblest, may be perverted to a degraded violation of the laws of nature and of virtue. The unity of the marriage vow must not be violated. The marriage institution cannot be too highly protected. No party to this compact should strike the other, but pay the highest deference and respect to each other.

Virtuous wives, when duly appreciated, as universally as they should be, will bless the world as much as wise and honest husbands.

One of the noblest results must be that parental authority will be preserved by wise knowledge, that blesses the world. In such families the life of youth must reach the highest state of innocence, in its morning hours, and maintain the best surety for happiness in its declining moments. There abides the best guarantee for future reformation. Neither husband nor wife should be deceived, nor any of their sacred engagements should be violated. Profligates are apt to put a low estimate on woman or marriage; but neither position can be properly sustained under the sacred sanctions of adequate comprehension.

How much valuable lifetime is thrown away on libertinism, instead of virtuous married life.

Marriage is the sacred institution, that civilized mind estimates as the noblest of social relations.

It cannot be fostered with too pure a spirit.

The utmost respect should be paid to consanguinity, and the greatest regard to avoid the marriage of blood relations.

Do not marry within less than six generations of kindred.

What can you, parents, expect of your children, if you make their marriages without consent of your children, the main parties concerned?

Give them the privilege to marry prudently, but to their wishes. Give them a fair portion of property at the start of married life, as well as of single life, otherwise you may embitter if not crush feelings of the best sympathies of mankind, and may spare yourself many chagrins, of not seeing your sons spendthrifts, and your daughters imprudent.

If the world was more equalized, woman would act better—man would necessarily do better.

Woman, if rightly and rationally educated, cannot but see her proper course, from which she would not swerve. Let her ask herself on what terms man proposes his love, and she can decide whether they be those of honor; for if not, they are unworthy of her attention, and require her, as she values all that is dear to her, to exclude the wretch who would dishonor and disgrace her.

Presume on no alliance through relationship.

There are some persons so degraded and perverted that they are lost, as to their present organization. Some fear to marry, on account of the baseness of woman! This world has to be regenerated by a conservative revolution, to do justice to it, God and mind. Married persons have to bear and forbear, with mutual regard. They should not give each other cause of complaint, but be loving and just to each other. Let those that are in love be not mistaken in any respect.

How foolish is it, that the dying partner should seek to trammel husband or wife about future marriages. No restriction should be put upon the rights of the living about marriage, by the dying. There should be no forced matches: all should be properly married to their wishes, if correct, that no criminal thoughts or actions be excited. But how unprofitable are the love-matches, anything else, brought about by wily relations and scheming friends. A keen merchant, most unprincipled, has his niece, who has property, married to an amorous youth with little brains, and involves him in a few months, to extent of his capital, and beggars both, by having his nephew-in-law to sign his paper. This, of course, was a species of slow murder; but what do unprincipled characters care for principles, if their peculiar education has been to their neglect?

Marriage encounters thousands of divorces, private difficulties, and ruptures. Better never marry, unless you do it right, and then the sooner the better, in reason and justice to the maturity of developments. Some people succeed in life, with any but the main idea of marriage. What would be the misery to a sensitive refined mind, of having an equivocal position by marriage?

There are some things, as death, securityship, and marriage, that require forethoughts.

What are made-up matches generally worth? When an alliance is only respectful to either sex, then it is bereft of its inherent virtue.

Do not force marriages, much less abrogate those of virtuous love. Why are there so many unhappy ones? What is the true conservative conduct? To live happily, above fault, suspicion.

Maids and bachelors have to investigate their most important interest. They should suit themselves in marriage, or live single. One had better be miserable than two. The mishaps of married life may prevent some from marrying. There is risk, and a state of single blessedness might in some respects be the least evil, but rarely so.

Do not marry for money nor ambition. Woman's predominant characteristic is feeling and sympathy, that of man is ratiocination ; and both should act accordingly. The time for marriage is most important. Marriage, when happy, is to be sought for, but when reflected on by the dollars, is to be deprecated, and to be cast off, as a trifle.

We should never give too much personal power to man or woman, and never destroy one's own personal independence merely to please somebody, who usurps and monopolizes, according to concessions.

Of all the entangling alliances, unhappy matrimony may be one, the worst that being about property. To smuggle it entails endless misery and degradation. Better have no property, than be thus involved. Both parties, man and wife, should consult unitedly, with appropriate rule in the sphere of each, with discretion and wisdom.

Bachelordom may have its pains and penalties ; but are there no benefits ? It should not be of voluntary choice. We should seek to obtain the best habits, the noblest benefits of life, in all legitimate things. There is no doubt but that marriage is the proper disposition of ourselves for virtue, and its highest satisfaction.

Under this belief, most must regret a single life. But all conditions, single and married, are bad, if corrupt. What avail marriage, if it do not produce happiness ?

Marriage is to be a civil ceremony for life, unless broken up by extraordinary circumstances, as adultery. Then what can be worse, to all the parties, than that crime ? When we see the wife, with her young offspring, deserted by him whom she had called husband, reckless of nature's ties, we would say that she might congratulate herself, that she had so well escaped the domestic tyranny, if there had been a conspiracy or combination against her ; that she had well escaped from one who was a dead weight on her hands : that the future was not so dark, but she must wait on time, that decided all things best.

The wife might say that she was in her husband's power, and could not help herself. The wise can appreciate much, and the opinion of the balance is worthless.

On the other hand, the wife must not expect to make the home of both disagreeable, and then expect to retain full attraction. Of all positions in the world, antagonism must be avoided in the married state.

There is nothing equal to the pure vows of two worthy people, who should never permit the first step to their violation. What nonsense that domestic feuds should rise about trifles ! What luxuries ever can atone for lost love ? When a separation is wantonly sought, then incalculable injury is done society. An honorable marriage is the sure policy pointed out by nature, that has balanced, or nearly equalized the sexes of each country.

When the world has been put in the wrong by error, it must be made right by science. There is half a million of females left in Great Britain over the amount of males, as estimated, on account of the male emigration and employment in the marine. Some of the females must be colonized where the males have gone.

No individual that seeks marriage should think of courting for mere courtesy, when his conviction goes against it. Woman or man should live above suspicion. There should be no such abuse of public morals as at the capitals and metropolis of some states. Let no vicious fashion, custom, or opinion, flourish with impunity, that is not sound.

Let the sovereign people decide that, on full analysis. Some women may be cunning. Some have been made so by Orientalism, increased by peculiar faith education, by man's brutality. In the name of God, ennoble, not crush, the mother of your children. Spare, not crush woman, the creature, to double brutality. Spare woman, noblest independence, that she may be your refined equal, and aid you in the holiest most refined, civilization of the world.

One of the primary virtues is chastity, for which husbands may overlook many less faults of their wives ; but a transgression in this respect is one of the unpardonable sins, to be washed out by blood alone !! Wives must hold tenaciously to this point, the only one of safety. How horrible is the depravity of its violation. What murder not to individuals, but families.

Intellectual mothers will teach their daughters this, the noblest legacy that they can leave to them. By it they are jewels of the noblest appreciation, above the worth of vulgar men. Without it they disgrace all, and the name of woman. Such chastity, ignobly, illegitimately yielded by the poorest wretch, makes her poorest indeed. Whole hecatombs of worlds cannot atone for this sacrifice. Woman's honor is there doomed, and she is uncasted forever in this world. One such transgression opens the door to her loss on earth. Man as well as woman have to consider in this respect their mighty sacrifices. What shall the world do to stay the spendthrift husband, who cares little or nothing for the family, sells all, and leaves clandestinely ?

The poor newly-married couple should receive portions of the State. It is bad enough to have a bad neighbor, much less a bad conjugal partner.

What teaches the sacredness of blood relationship that must not be united in marriage within certain degrees of consanguinity? The highest of all legislation, the wisest decisions of nature; and the highest moral and religious principles sanction all the relations of affinity as equally sacred.

Men truly represent their character when lovers.

Married parties ought to study what will render each mutually agreeable, not antagonistic. When parties about to marry find that they do not love, they had best stop there; better than seek divorces.

The marriage ceremony should be by a civil magistrate, as none otherwise is valid in the proper sense. Marriage is a means of happiness for life, not for a temporary convenience, or dual conventionality.

The Roman church dissolves the ties of matrimony, and is a world-nuisance. Woman is man's equal, refined civilization tells us all that, but in different spheres of action. No matter how quickly the world refined civilization progresses.

Marriage is held sacred even among savages, so called, so much so, that with many the guilt of violation of the nuptial vow determines the death of the parties. The guilt of violation of female chastity or virtue, is another step of iniquitous magnitude. Assignation in large cities has been supposed to present effectual secrecy; but even there the conspirators of illicit amours have been detected, and signally punished.

There is but one protection in life, and that through principles. Crimination and recrimination rather stultify the parties, when it takes both to commit the crime. Where are mind, principles, religion? Surely not in abeyance to lust.

There should be no advertisement to obtain wife or husband. Proper marriage is the legitimate purpose: it cannot be a mercantile affair.

ADULTERY.

UNDER the snake folds of fornication's corrupt drapery, the fearful crime of adultery lurks, awaiting a punishment that exposes guilt and disgrace in all their horrid deformities, and arousing up fatal retaliations, vindicating itself by fearful retributions, that, if not allied to the vindictiveness of murder because incompetent to execute it, may be participant of equal depths of guilt and iniquity. The marriage vow of conjugal fidelity is sacredly to be observed by both parties to the compact in every respect, else the one violating perpetrates perjury, and is amenable for its commission.

Neither party is exempt from the sacred obligation. The paramount rights of morals hold it sacred. A wise legislation and competent execution of laws, should protect society from all the injuries of illegitimate and inordinate lust, else the laws will be taken into the hands of the injured party.

The days have passed, thanks to mind and mind's associate reason, when tyrants lorded it unprincipled over man's rights and feelings, and the wealthy or potent tyrant of social blessings, luxuriated in all the debaucheries of the age, that presented a hopelessness little short of passive toleration, when virtue was hardly esteemed more by the ude barbarians of the age, than an ignorance of the ways to vice and her prostituted scinations.

'f you play with the rattlesnake, you need not be surprised at receiving the poison.

Does woman come into the conjugal relation, pure and chaste? Then it becomes man to preserve it most sacredly.

What, but misery, is the fruit of adultery, that constitutes a violation of just and most sacred rights, an incurable injury, atoned for very often by blood?

Adultery presents the deepest wounds of conscience, of social, moral, political and religious relations, personal disgrace and infamy. Here ensue the deepest and most poignant misery, and most agonizing remorse. The old, vitiated, and adulterated, debauched companions, are most dearly purchased.

Death is often the penalty from revenge, and that even from the humblest slave who revenges the foul insult and deed done him as a man. Such vice will surrender the culprit into the power of the humblest.

The only safe position of independence is to put one's self into the power of no man. Principles alone will protect.

It is bad business to commit such act, but for the ruined party to be victimized by the poison of such degraded intercourse, the whole life-time is one of the curses of horrid vice. But what refined being desires to live with a party, contaminated in all the depravity of adultery? Which of the injured party likes to submit to the reckless indignity, or dishonorably permit the world to be deceived into social intercourse with such depraved being?

This prostitution, the most heinous that mankind commits, ruins the peace of families, produces certain loss of reputation of the guilty parties in properly elevated circles of society, and frequently, the premature death of one or both, in several ways of penalty, either directly by the hand of man, or indirectly by the vindication of God's principles.

What poor standards are too often presented the world, from frail mortality? Mind ever needs the best from principles, not the copies of poor human nature.

It needs the best guides from the great book of nature, directed by reason and the God of both, consequently, it must reject all the dark spots and precedents attached to dark ages, and their darker bibles of tradition.

No modest female ought to permit herself to be approached by any one that she is not properly certain is a safe companion, or thorough-bred gentleman, in all the senses of the word: a man of strict veracity, honor and virtue.

There are some individuals whose very atmosphere is tainted and poisonous, their looks infectious, and their communications licentious and contagious. What will it profit the world to know such of either sex? It may be the dawn of absolute perdition. Who is more seductive than an artful, insidious libertine, except an intriguing, debauched woman? Neither in thought, word, deed, or looks, are they to be trusted by the pure and upright. The right current of thought has not the right direction with them.

What can compensate for the adulterer's loss of life by his iniquity a moment? None—not even the law can lean to the protection of life or reputation thus forfeited at vice's shrine.

This injury is liable to be vindicated before the highest tribunal of enlightened public opinion.

The freeman's doctrine is now retribution by blood, when the avenger of chastity will keep better faith than all the bibles of tradition. The true position, when defined, requires the whole comprehension of the moral law fully asserted, to be honorably vindicated. Exposition is succeeded by execution. If the principles of the universe, that rule its solar systems and their spheres, are not conservative, the necessary result is that they are destructive.

Cases of adultery ensue, where death follows the paramour, though himself seduced.

Both parties have their part of duty to society to perform. In this matter the receiver is as bad as the thief; both are guilty participants.

If one party escape by courtesy and clemency, peace of mind may be lost forever, the parents become degraded, and die under the reckless stroke of an ungrateful and ignominious child, who lives most often in poignant anguish a living death.

In all these cases, there was originally some great and comprehensive wrong.

Seducers—Hands off! Youth may be injured irrevocably by the base of every society whose look is seductive and whose action is disgrace. What right has any married party to assume that either can act to the crime of lust, that either has less rights, or that both have any rights to commit infractions against the legitimate demands of proper state of society? What can be worse than faith of marriage-vows broken? Do want and worthlessness drive to this ignominy? You that wield money power, or any influence, have you not violated your obligations to society by any infraction on this holy and sacred position? Neither age nor sex, office nor pretences, freedom or slavery, can excuse you before the God of the universe.   •

Some married women may prove false from pure revenge, by the previous disgraceful conduct of their husbands. But with what folly. The action of freemen who have taken the avenging of this iniquity into their own hands, has placed it long before the age of legislation.

My reply to one soliciting my attendance on a meeting to confirm the legal proceedings in the case of him who vindicated the honor of his marriage bed by killing him whom he accused as guilty, was, that the dignity of justice was adequate for her own protection.

Reason permits an acquittal for killing in the act of adultery. If legislators wish to have this question suitably met, let them wisely define by laws all proper penalties. Hardly yet has adultery received its proper counteraction by wise legislation. What subject has?

What argument with all the parties, to complete exhaustion, will cause as much benefit to be the result, the crisis to be met, as wholesome penalties? How would you act, feel, treat the parties identified with your affections, caught in adultery?

You cannot watch the parties always, but you can cause conservative principles to be advanced that always watch, never sleep.

Nothing less than a religious, social, and moral conservative revolution will alter the corruption of the world, as to the infidelity of married persons. Man as well as woman have their parts to act in this matter. The country, the world has its part.

The church furnishes no positive guarantee at all for none of these obligations.

Unchastity in both sexes is better prevented than punished by a right ordering of society, and can be best obviated by adequate laws that public morals will cause to be fully enforced, and will correct the most of the evils at the fountain head, when gunpowder does not fully avail or cannot apply, as when the delinquents become common as brutes. But where was the dignity of character of the other party? Was he wilfully blind to his own honor, and to the respect due good society all this time? Laws are essential, but individual mind's action is absolutely necessary.

Adulterers and adulteresses, seducers and seduceresses, degrade society.

As much as the deep injuries of war fall below the universal blessings of peace that is honorable, so do these characters fall below chaste wives and their worthy husbands. Conscience cannot be appreciated by any such people, who are as reckless as barbarian savages. But they can be made to feel in points most sensitive.

The correct process in society is for all to have a thorough knowledge of its requirements, and of the world's duty. You should know if practicable, human nature, and should rarely have it to say, Did the world ever see such a worthless character as this? The world can make no proper impressions on some of the reckless, whose minds, badly cultivated or not cultivated, are unbalanced by animal passions and depraved tastes. You take it for granted, because they move in the right circle, that they are right.

Their mind has been perverted, and t. :ir improper appreciation of principles unworthy of the world. What can the world be benefited by them, since they are not trustworthy?

Does the adulterer seek to play with the rattlesnake in his bosom? Then his indulgences cannot be bought off with less than life-blood, and the mother may become deranged for the end of such a son, having paid the severest debt of retribution. What can console friends? That they have sanctioned the strictest adherence to virtue? Common sense principles must govern the world. They are its only conservatives. If a man choose to degrade himself by seduction, fornication, and adultery, he would animalize himself easily enough, but man must consider himself a responsible, honorable, and social being. Adultery that leads to lying for the adulteress at the death bed scene, prematurely and forcibly brought about, demands that all should be let alone altogether.

The world's history abounds with such disasters.

It is bad to admit into one's confidence, society, or one's family, a being that turns out degraded, whose habits are of base grovelling sensuality, increased by drunkenness, perfidious or of no proper faith, false to all principles of honor that will deceive and betray. An unfaithful wife or husband, darkens this picture.

In chastity and other virtues, none but an exalted rational education rightly conveyed, can give man or woman, the world, their exalted rank. How often is it that we hear of the false honor and miserable bad faith of the lower orders of the people, the married not adhering to their mates, but basely common, so different from that honorable state of a correct education that prevents such degradation, but teaches all to respect themselves.

This causes the most respectable and refined, the happiest attainable state of the world.

In regard to unchaste women, let adulterers recollect that it is acting in the best of good faith and wisdom, to resist an adulteress, as peace of mind, freedom from vice, and independence of contingent injuries will arise by proper action.

As to temporary possession of such a woman, why not have permanent enjoyment of one to be confided in? Lovely is the modest woman—truly lovely is the chaste one, more honored than all jewels and brilliants. She maketh glad the nation, and is the praise of all. Poor and friendless, her chastity is her strength and glory. When she loses that, she loses the treasure of all price, that if a queen, she is an outcast and beggar.

The adulterer and seducer put their lives at any times in the hands of avengers, who may destroy them at once in the fulness of their sin and iniquity; not only that, but in the power of the laws, risking their own happiness and peace for ever, causing disruptions never to be healed—and disquiet never to be remedied. There could be no adulteress if there were not adulterers; no prostitutes, if the male world would act chastely and virtuously.

History tells the position of adulteresses once having a lofty bearing with character, punished most miserably in a foreign land, forced by opinion to fly the scorn of their own country, living afterwards wretchèd and poor, bereft of necessaries, and worst of all, most pitiable in character and reputation. Such have been the wives of ambassadors, and had brave admirals for their paramours. Some as sirens, have seen their husbands murdered by their paramours, and have had no peace in sleep, screaming out in the agony of their remorseful and punished minds, over which the serpent guilt had triumphed. What was the state of their wakeful moments?

Adultery produces most serious results and evils—among them is disgrace that is proportionate to the refinement of social civilization. Cases have occurred where married men have sought to corrupt ladies that were respectable, and been signally and publicly disgraced. The wise man will not put himself in the power of his punishments, as he will exclude them by the wisest forecast of innocence. What do not adulterers sacrifice? Their disgrace may be so ignominious, that they have no pleasure in their family, and may be obliged to leave. Such have to beware of adultery that may arouse, little as they expect the law of retaliation, brute force, retributive justice, the double barreled gun.

They had cared nothing for the imbecile husband, as they deemed him. But they have to care for principles that vindicate themselves and the God of all. Do they appreciate malign habits, that master and tyrannize to death? They should not put themselves in the power of vice that overrules with an iron despotism, They must fear a violation of principles.

Avoid adultery, though the husband be completely imbecile. The double-barreled gun may miss, but God's eternal principles vindicate themselves with unerring retributive justice.

The murder and assassination for the violation of the nuptial bed must be stopped by the wise precaution of mind. How? By wise legislation. Abolish the law, making killing for adultery excusable homicide. Why not go one step further, and make adultery amenable to capital punishment?

But, then, how can human nature resist temptation? It takes two to commit adultery. Be the position what it may, wise legislation must do away with the necessity of the citizen avenging himself, by excusable homicide. The impulse of passion may be so great in catching in the act of adultery, that the injured party may take vengeance direct on the guilty. Legislation that is wise would fix up the world better about adultery, to prevent it by excusable homicide. Adulterers never know when they are safe. Some debased women may give the first challenge, but man must give the last resistance. Man has his part of social duty to perform, and abstain from this, one of the highest felonies and soul treacheries.

Women might send their compliments and respects, might we say love, to gentlemen. Should that arouse the sleeping lion? For what? Some of the most terrible effects of the human passions are involved in love matters. Wise and prudent men should make no advance in them, other than compatible and congenial. They should assure themselves only of the correct moral position.

What can be more immoral than the custom of pretended fashionable life, visiting after dark, the leaving of one's own wife for another to gallant, and late at night! Who is the best companion, the husband or the stranger? But it looks country-like to gallant one's own wife! The female of course can appropriate right customs and habits, but beyond that she is risking an evil. Is it possible that free republicans. at any city, should adopt the degraded customs of monarchists? Above all, the fashions of pure citizens should take precedence, and will when the world becomes virtuous under wisdom. The imperative obligations of society are to produce virtuous social qualities. When woman, that has pledged her best faith, throws all such away, that woman has thrown her soul away, as far as in her lies. What is worse than a cunning, deceiving woman, whose beautiful body enshrines a soul hideous as sin, and more destructive than the rattlesnake, that warns ere it strikes.

Interference with the domestic social relations in families produces not only bitter prejudices, but vindictive feelings, and just retaliation against the individual reckless of proper principles. The trials of adultery are such, as for refined gold; mankind have to resist temptation. If the first taint be in youth, the corruption is hard to eradicate.

Commission of adultery is commission of perjury. Both parties are amenable, culpable, criminal, guilty.

As to adultery, there are two that play at that game, equally guilty and culpable of perjury. Put every thing on principles, and then they will carry out themselves.

What is virtue but this very thing? The uniform adherence to principle is virtue, that is immutable, has no fashion.

What! the seducer love when he seeks to dishonor? Does the lovely married one stoop to listen? Is she deranged, to believe the false pretence?

DIVORCE.

WHAT horrible iniquity, by disseverance from marriage ties, unless the best of reasons, caused by adultery of the other party, prevail. Old age or death divorces soon enough.

We must recollect that if the wife, the weaker, does not complain of improper treatment of her husband, it is because she prudently chooses the least of evils. The marriage relation, one of chastest virtue, cannot be denounced or violated, but by the vicious or degraded. When one female sues for a divorce from her husband for his bad conduct, well can we appreciate the suggestions to her of her friend, stating that many other females had to bear in silence misdeeds and mistreatment. There are many causes of disagreement laid at the foundation, too often overlooked till the marriage is consummated. When parties are aware of the absence of moral personal worth, an indispensable prerequisite to social happiness, what better can they expect after union? Of the various characters, when a gambler deceives a woman of respectable standing into marriage, starting on gambled money, how can the world expect to see such a union prosperous? Bad people, that wish to dissolve the marriage vow, should be strictly counteracted by the uniform character of all divorces to be granted, on account of the guilt of the party, who is excluded from marriage. The facility of divorce is an evil. Marriage presents the idea of divorce, or shooting down if perverted; but still these evils must be rightly analyzed. It is true the life of single blessedness is very objectionable, and should not be voluntarily chosen, for the best of considerations, of virtue and patriotism, as rational life functions are paramount; but what can be worse than an ill-matched marriage?

There should be no facilities for divorce.

Expulsion of society—is that nothing? What claims have any on society or principles that they recklessly violate?

FORNICATION.

IN fornication, the tendency is of a cast with the circle of principal offences, that exhibit a sad and very often a ruinous result on both parties.

For self-preservation, the first law of nature, a line of demarkation has to be drawn by society, that abides by intellect, in chastity and modesty, the jewels of sex.

The simplest transgression under the influence of inordinate lust, bespeaks the first step of primary evil. The sleeping lion is aroused, and may never be allayed. The most ferocious habit may have been created, that can never be laid aside, till functions or life are extinct.

The least of all evils is, never to tolerate for a moment, any avenue to gratify lust by illegitimate or unnatural means at all.

Ignominy, the loss of self-respect and that of society, may fix the misery on the sex that may uncaste itself, an inextricable position for woman, fixed by the universal laws of violated nature and the best society, and a sad one most often for man who may never recover from habits, that fix the iron grasp of their final tyranny on both.

The loss of health is too often ended in its total sacrifice, with a painful existence of mind and body, the feelings crushed, and the value of life ruined or blasted. The liability to crime, complex and intricate, is easy under its many tortuous wiles, hard indeed, to be rescued from, even to the seduction of innocence and modest virtue, to the agony of soul in its deepest sensibility, down to the excruciating anguish of ruined honor in suicide, for which the seducer is responsible, even to the murder of the offspring, their criminal neglect, contingent injury, exposure to a degraded corruption of mind with shame upon its face, sin and iniquity its example and authority for its constant practice. One deeper step of guilt, places the sinner in the quagmire of adultery.

When man alienates the noble purpose of creation, he becomes identified with the foul outrage.

Who can be less honest and more debased than the designing seducer and adulterer, who destroy the best of public property? Human nature may be so degraded, as to pirate under the domestic protection, against the chastest virtues of woman.

Nothing is sacred to such brutes, who must forget the world-wide benefits of social protection.

They have thus forfeited their claims to such stock, and are amenable to all the forfeits.

How many of the world are unworthy of the trial of friendship of the confiding, that would be degraded and disgraced by such worthless trash of the world.

There are many evils, attending upon fornication unappreciated by the parties, till the sad results burst in upon them. Fornication produces loss of estimation of the virtuous, and an extensive category of crime. If child-bearing ensues, it is prevented, guilt attaches involving mind, relatively to the amount. Murder is attached to fœticide or infanticide.

Do ignorant girls see all this bearing? Their pregnancy involves them in shame, then in guilt to horrible perdition. The first step if false, ruins in the course of iniquity's amount.

Why avoid fornication? The seduction of the parties, leads to misery of relations and friends, destruction of children too often, their victimization of morals, mind and body.

How much is society affected by disorganization, in its essential parts by extreme vices. We have known of arson or house-burning after it was being perpetrated, to exclude vicious characters from a respectable community! Was this wisely done, though self-preservation is the first law of nature? All the wrongs of the universe can never make a right. Due complaints to the governing powers, wisely entrusted with proper authority, might have caused this ejection as nuisances. Wise legislation should then never be neglected, and can only comport with its necessity and suitable execution. Should a grand jury take cognizance of Lynch laws, would perjury of the incendiary if capable of rescue, be left unessayed? The bars of conscience bribed for wretched deeds, are subject to any gust of passion and revenge, and one crime many years afterwards, lands the perpetrator in a penitentiary and a felon's grave.

The poor imbecile never comprehends in his mind's eye, the whole category of crime's circle, for which others are responsible.

What protects any, from a reckless incendiary's torch? In fornication, rational religion looks to the shame of all parties and exempts neither sex, as both are amenable in guilt for exposure of their offspring to the taunts of an unjust world, or the chill penury of its disregard, much more for its murder, moral degradation, life of infamy, and too often of misery.

I call for the returning sense of wisdom and justice, in a free and untrammeled people in seduction, &c. Tell us what the true love of man or woman is worth, ere the flower of innocence be blighted and destroyed?

The seducers may well cause women of respectable feeling and proper breeding, to avoid their company as poisonous contagion; most rightfully so indeed, from the corruption of contact. Their wiles circumvent and prevent escape.

Chastity is founded upon the just action consistent with the true principles of correct systems, and the nature of the universe.

Time has established reforms in the social circles, respecting fornication and adultery, and other analogous crimes, for which better correction will be adopted, when public opinion will be more enlightened on the wrong.

The mind of the public must necessarily be amended, when it reflects on and contemplates the past corruptions of society, yielding to the light of civilization. It is the beautiful discipline of mind, towering in the liberal and rational studies of philosophical science and literature, that can climb to its illustrious position.

The simple but chaste woman, will not believe the most wily man as having any regard for her, when he asks her ever to disregard the principles conservative of life and its blessings.

She can well appreciate at the only right time before hand, the disgust of the parties after fornication and adultery, as there can be no love where inordinate brutal lust misled the guilty parties. The chaste woman will not entrust herself into man's company, much less his protection, unless he can appreciate his past and present standing.

She certainly will not subject herself to the influence of any article conveyed through snuff, diet, drink, confectionary, fruits from a mere stranger, or indeed any whose standing is not well and thoroughly established. She will certainly refuse him, when it is meet that she should have security of principles. Female chastity can be best secured, by supreme care, and respect.

The youth of the country should rely on the country, and avoid all the ills of strange and overgrown cities, if possible to do so. If females seek proper business of the city, they should be certain of persons of proper standing to advise with, ere they expose themselves to the temptations and dangers of cities.

All deviation betrays a stupidity that stultifies the actresses who are involved in all the degradations. The virtuous-minded will neither seek nor suffer seductions. Fornication hath its stings and adultery its ignominy. Both act like slow poisons on many victims. Conspiracy by drugs endangers the life of all engaged therein, both of mother and child, as not only they, but the father, may be victimized by the illegitimate lust, and all overwhelmed in premature death and penalty. How miserably cyprians live!

Is not the whole world still better in the hands of its Creator, where free moral agency of mind is improving mankind by all legitimate means? What else but rational mind can improve the world, that was originally submitted for that very purpose? Where will demoralization end, when the world divests itself of all the inherent potency of managing, and imprudently resigns what best commands it?

Are all the general principles of trusteeship, and agency of rational mind, fairly and honestly executed? What is life, without propriety of conduct?

The wisest action in life is the correct one. In doing correct actions every day, we are doing the wisest. What worse, then, can be the course and wiles of seduction? The world's code demands, to keep sacred its social relations. Above all, the conjugal relations are essentially sacred, as adultery is a sin unatonable, except by blood.

In all infanticides, who of the two can say that they are exempt from an equal participation in the guilt before God's tribunal?

In adultery or fornication, who can promise themselves exemption from capital retribution? Who are they most prone to all the vices of the women of the earth? Are they not the children of extreme want, and a consequent vitiated education? Do not some of the duplicities of peculiar faith that enslaves the public mind over the world, help to debauch the world's chastity? Does not auricular confession do its part? The world should comprehend all that is necessary to protect it.

Poor working women are overwhelmed by poverty, having wretched payments, pittances, and overworked at that. All decent families should be cared for, and the world has to have a living.

Their right cultivated mind will protect women, under proper circumstances, against all false pretences, in teaching them to keep all such characters as seducers at a distance. But is this the case in all ages, governments and courts? Why are the virtues that tower over all evil opposition at so low a value with the world? Why is chastity so slightly cherished in some circles, when fornication has to be avoided, else it may punish as deeply as any vice. It may cause the actor to leave in disgrace, while the other party's friends may vindicate with excess of vindictiveness. Fear, then, habits of fornication, as no one should procreate children, without proper world protection for them in morals, rational education, life support, and, above all, that high-mindedness that is conservative to the refined world.

Who can dare take advantage of defects of mind, or worse, of the poverty of the innocent; or, still worse, the worst of all, the helplessness of those especially under the protection of the violator of all the principles of justice at once?

The duty of man is as paramount as that of woman. Is it not more so?

Simple men will not perceive, and dishonest ones will affect that man, in fornication, is not responsible. How is this? Who thinks of infanticide or fœticide as a lighter matter than murder, and yet your act of fornication may contribute to it? This crime should be rightly prevented by future world morals or alleviated by the wisest legislation. The world should prevent abandoned women from falling lower.

Why is there prostitution? Want of property or decent bringing up, knowledge to counteract the world nuisances. Want and luxury are two extremes that engender crime. Early marriages will prevent much of this. Wise women will ever recollect that base people seek to rise on the ruins of the virtuous.

What associations the world is liable to, unless properly guarded.

WE SHOULD RESPECT CHASTITY, FOR ITS SAKE.

This virtue, as everything else, must be protected by the best care of mind. Corrupt courts of absolutism first often do the fatal deed of corruption of female virtue. The false position of society engenders the facility to much of this corruption.

Why is chastity so low with some women?

Is it that honor is so low with some men?

Are both to blame? The duty of an incorrupt, virtuous woman is clear to herself. She is incorruptible, and therefore a jewel. But how many minds of the world have a defective, because a peculiar education! At best, it may be mixed.

Nothing in this world can atone for innocence and conscience lost.

Parents will be perfectly imbecile or reckless to disregard these wise admonitions.

Let us have all pure things above suspicion.

Woman's part is that of modest virtue, and a silent influence on all around, to calm the boisterous waves of passion and still tumultuous breasts. Man needs her best aid, as he is clearly not always able to command circumstances that expose him to the severest trials of his very nature, that cause him to drink deep of the dregs of the cup of human misery.

Hers may be a difficult part to sustain. It will be well for her if she be rightly imbued in all the principles that adorn the loveliness and innocence of her sex. With no provocation and just cause but the audacity of lawless licentiousness and brute malignity, the offending party, miscalled husband, often invades life's sanctity and disgraces himself beyond redemption, of an honorable position, in points that none but Deity's indignant and justly avenging eye takes cognizance.

Man cannot be too particular in his association, and without doubt must woman, who, as prudent, cannot countenance the bad. The most eligible boarding-houses, if essential, must not only be selected, but in localities that are beyond suspicion or doubt. It is not only or merely the strict rules of propriety in eligible residences must be maintained ; but there must be no mistake that may involve advantages given over virtue difficult to appreciate, till temptation paves the way to perdition.

Woman abused, cannot in justice to the chastity of virtue and decent females, be exalted; but she must be protected with all precaution, by every friend of virtue.

In boarding-schools, the whole subject should be clear and certain. No boarding should commence in anticipation of a suitable age, or of that education secured in the domestic precincts. Ladies should be the head of female academies.

They should be, in midwifery, competent to assist their fellow-ladies in all its proper departments. The radical correction is needed by the imperial power of mind, ere it be too late. The only conservative position is action on principles.

These may look like small matters, but great principles are involved.

The principle of independence is magnificent in woman as well as man, as it is the highest position of virtue.

The brightest jewel of woman is chastity, and she cannot take too much pains to preserve it in its most glorious dignity. The chastity of ladies is to be preserved at all hazards, otherwise the relations of the female are sacrificed. Intellectual, virtuous woman knows well, that one misdeed tending to the suspicion of vice blasts the whole generation, and throws a doubt on all the rest of her actions ; then she should be left to her own wisest expedients to mould the rising sex.

No gentlemen would wish to intrude on chastity—none else ought to be admitted, on terms of proper confidence. No virtuous woman, decently raised, would permit herself to be misled, to uncaste herself, from the very conscientious love of virtue. The best protection for virtue is the greatest remove from vice, with hands and eyes intact, and the mind most firmly fortified in principles. What blessings are secured by the purity of life.

Where is woman to be estimated ? In the place where her kind disposition has been brutalized, her chastity has been perverted ?

The world' is liable to be deceived, in the worst possible way, by the worst of the world.

Does the world analyze much of this imposition, or thank the exposers of half that is practiced on it ?

Who can wonder at the degradation of woman, in countries subject for ages and centuries to the worst species of corruption, of government and peculiar faith, imposed on the sovereign people for religion ? Woman is not only degraded by Eastern despotisms and Oriental ignorance, but she is much disturbed in Europe, which is miserably harrassed by military and ecclesiastical assumptions. But you speak of the corrupt world ! Is there no other locality, by individual aggressions, much over its remotest boundaries ? Have you done nothing to help corrupt it ?

Have you failed to give poor dependent girls a mere pittance, to help keep them from street beggary, exposure, misery, and prostitution ?

Have you not taken advantage of their helpless situation ? Have you left large and pompous legacies to rich corporations, without souls, truth and sincerity, reason and justice ? And have you left disconsolate, lonely, and modest worth, to pass the horrid ordeal of man's crimes, seductions, and intrigues ? Have you aided the brightest jewel of woman's soul, first and last, and all the time, woman's virtue, that honors the world ! You talk of the city—have you done justice to the country, and defended with the purest honor the purest virtue, confided to the world of supposed friends ? Have you upheld her, that was worthy to be sustained, and rescued her that would not have fallen but for the oppressive circumstances of her orphan and bereft condition—deprived of relations, friends, support, and, above all, rational education, that gives the chaste mind its adequate consolation and solace ?

Have you helped to sustain and guard the damsel virgin, and caused all gentlemen to behave to her with propriety? There is no end to the baseness of the unprincipled. With them no chastity is too sacred, no rights too clear.

Woman looks to man, civilized man, for proper protection. If she cannot find it with him, under the circumstances to best call forth his noblest protection, where can she expect it?

She must ever look first to her own mind, under the protection of her Creator, and under the best precepts of rational education, avoid and bid defiance to the unprincipled part of the world.

Man, rightly educated by rational education, will not deceive unprotected woman, as good faith is implied in all this social benefit. Spare woman's modesty and chastity of thought; spare the world, mind, yourself, for the highest duty of religion to God the creator of all mankind.

A lewd woman is dangerous, but have you analyzed the great first causes? Are you not engaged in analogous ones? Fear such that degrade you, from the triumphant faculty of potent mind.

Can you see woman, in her most disgusting seductions, in the purlieus of large cities, at masquerades, you could see what degradation can do for the lovely portion of humanity. When woman becomes debauched, her character may be that of recklessness; then she is prostituted to many crimes indeed. The contrast, with that of virtuous woman's, evinces a direct antagonism.

Where is wise and universal legislation? There must be no bribe for seduction, but all necessary expedients used to counteract it. It is better to defend and protect than to oppress. The best policy of the world is to distribute light and employment of mind in something beneficial. Let all classes have appropriate employment, especially in industrial labor, then much of the world's ills would cease.

The world should be well and properly guarded at the base intrigues of lost and abandoned characters, men and women. Nothing is sacred with them, in the world. They desecrate all that is pure and valuable, and seek to degrade to their degradation all the rest of mankind.

Rational education teaches the world all that is proper to be known and to be guarded against, that informs woman that she uncastes herself, when she steps aside, for a moment, from the autocrat queen to the lowliest beggar-girl.

Rational religion cares for the whole vital wants of virtuous minds, from the first perception of thought, to the noblest appreciation of God. Instead of turning the prostitute out to sin no more, provide for all rightly, in body and mind, anticipate all such ills by a world administration, before complete ruin—nay, before the mind is tainted—by a provision for all, made by justice.

Let the education of rational minds be philosophically rational, that shall guard, warn, protect, and defend, against the world's insidious assaults. What sacrifices are ignominiously made, for lusts? Psychology can explain what effect is made on mind in one branch, by seduction.

The object of the most refined taste is to turn everything into its legitimate channel. That is the paramount duty of mortals.

Where there is much fornication there must be much infanticide. Nothing degrades the world more than the degradation of woman.

Fornication might be excusable, however corrupting to the purity of mind and injurious to health, by disease of prostitution, often incurable or desperately invalidating health and spirits, but how meet the onerous responsibilities of inevitable natural results? In this light fornication is a glaring, damnable crime, for exposures of infants to penury, death, murder, crime, vice, infamy.

Some seek to make the most of life by licentiousness. It is that to secure the most expansive competency. But there are extreme want, wretchedness, with many.

There are in the world, large cities, &c., a band of pirates, that would not give you street-room, if they could profit by it. Why is this? By perversion of mind, and varied abundantly. The world must look at mind's capacity, not at its perversions, as incurable.

It is capable of an elevation in the scale of improvement, by a proper scale of thought, that monotheism elicits.

The prostitute has to make capital, and is reckless of the effects. The highest safeguard of life is in the proper rational use of mind.

How few have that firmness of mind, that drives like a wedge all opposing elements, bad associations. They should avoid all debasing, low associations, but cultivate extensively the society of ladies, whose character is chaste.

But, woman, your diseased mind is worst of all. You must get rid of your innumerable bad, ungodly habits; marriage, alone, will only save you.

Do not go where temptations are, as the explosive train of seduction. What mind, under all its spell-influence, can properly withstand, unless braced by the best rationality? Know your place, and maintain it with dignity.

What can present a more debased sight than that of a drunken woman, who must be utterly lost to the delicate sensibilities of sex?

There is but one effectual way to battle best with all temptation, and the wisest is to get the legitimate hand of principles. The highest principles teach us, never corrupt. Where was the originator of all the evils of the poor debauched?

The woman may act imprudently, but without reproach, yet she endangers her reputation.

Is it impunity alone that warrants them? Impunity when, or where? This thing of violation of principle, is a two-edged sword, that cuts up the active and passive agents. But what care you for principle?

What, then, care you for the universe? What care you for yourself? This question comes home to you and yours, your household, your individuality, and tells with many-times effect the powers of retributive justice and penalty.

Consider you, then: beware. This is a universe of principles. How, then, can you stop short, only in this world? The thing, by this position, is utterly impossible. Monotheism is your supremely wise monitor, and you must conform to its requisitions, that are paramount, supreme—its religion the only one. She cannot be put down or silenced, when she confounds all others, and leaves you your conscience duly informed and adequately enlightened in all its soul duties.

Present, as future enjoyments, must be legitimate.

Whither tends vice? Is the end ever seen? Can you insure on sin of fornication, physically, morally, mentally, or religiously?

All legitimate functions must be schooled and disciplined by principles.

Did woman foresee her wretched destiny, in seduction, she would stop, ere ruin seized the victims of lust, infanticide, and degradation, to relations and friends.

Bring in wise legislation, to arrest the evil that overwhelms much of civilized society. Make it penal for seduction, either way, and also for illegitimate births, by confinement in the penitentiary, and the payment of very adequate sums of money, for the proper support of all such offspring. Wise and effectual legislation, wise execution of wise laws, will advance society, and promote the high attainments of the Creator's purpose.

THE EVILS OF ABSOLUTISM, AS EXAMPLES BEFORE MIND.

WITH impunity, tyrants will act, if the people will let them.

The world has seen the folly and danger of entrusting mortals with any supreme executive power, above the co-ordinate legislative and judicial powers, above the constitution of the country, the rights of the sovereign people, which make all responsible.

The world is taught enough to inquire who can be entrusted with power above the constitutional laws, with safety to the people's rights?

There is but one who is supreme over all, who respects all as they respect themselves.

The highest respect that can be paid to merit, is by the respect and esteem of reason.

Religious philosophy marks the critical index for the soul's happiness.

The human passions are a sacred deposit, and must be touched with masterly hands.

Every mind of male or female must feel itself ever amenable, at the tribunal of an enlightened public opinion, the representative of the Supreme Ruler, whose inspiration is reason through mind.

Enlightened freedom, that looks upon the chastity of woman as one of her greatest blessings, is founded on principles carried to their true issue, and bespeaks an improved age, to take cognizance of such crimes in an enlightened way for their best and organic suppression.

Fundamental principles, when right, keep subordinate results right, and will never endow any man with power over his fellow man to oppress or set at defiance a correct public opinion, that ought to be the basis of a sound elevated state of public benefit.

One of the soundest positions in all society, is the certainty of exposure for violations of its salutary laws, and the inevitable penalties attendant on their violation. It is the immunity that countenances the guilt of vice.

All wise citizens will look to this principle, for the preservation and perpetuity of such public opinion.

Direct penalties oftenest avail, but the religionist asks under the physiological character of man, for the best fixed organic correction, that should be ever faithfully and wisely instituted by the appropriate authorities.

Now, as we prize chastity, one of the highest, we lay the soundest institutions for the rearing of this lovely plant, and must apply the heaviest penalties against those who injure the least its delicate rearing.

Let its protection be commensurate with its invaluable character.

A religious and social conservative revolution is needed, to accomplish all that this world yet requires.

We have spoken of man endowed with all his functions and passions, created for the best of purposes, all the time, if directed to their legitimacy.

This is the matter of primary consideration, to preserve the value of that immortal mind, lest the defect be laid ere mind be capable of acting as mind, but acts as a machine, and the deep and abiding error declares perversions.

It is useless to talk of ideas that degraded mind refuses, rejects, and abuses the worst of purposes.

Mind's perversions must be mastered at the right point.

AN ENLIGHTENED, PHILOSOPHICAL PUBLIC OPINION IS ESSENTIAL, TO CORRECT BAD HABITS, &c.

THE correction of bad habits and training may be often referred to the aid of enlightened philosophical public opinion, whose light it is difficult to revolutionize, to dissipate from the wisest purposes, for the fixedness of reason that commands immortal principles.

What a glorious prospect for the world, if all be right, but they are too often substituted or superseded by sophistry of delusion and false pretences.

If public opinion be not enlightened by the philosophy of science, it may be an average of prejudices and customs, that may take their complexion from the vices or follies of predecessors.

Public opinion may be often wrong, unless it has passed the ordeal of pure reason, that corrects and enlightens it in all respects, pursuing her legitimate function as the highest inspiration of mind from God.

But public opinion by the vices and superstition of the age, may not reach the correction of evils until too late individually—being identified with superstition, it is qualified by superstitious foibles. Tyranny does enslave and suppress it, by all practicable devices.

The only sure foundation for all, is the institution of correct views of education, whereby all more or less. can direct their course aright.

Every wise man will estimate correctly, the whole position of this important subject.

Mind cannot mistake it, if man will, and there is no need to travel out of the way, for then the correction travels to the offender's house and home. Let all wise men recollect this.

The wisest government is admitted to be that of self—over all the passions that ' enslave, if not mastered. These passions are wisely given us for wisdom, not abuse, therefore they should be wisely directed by the best taste and way at the right time.

THE WORLD-GOVERNMENT AND RELIGION.

THE position that our country holds, pre-eminently teaches the world that colonial and all unconstitutional governments should end at the right time and in the right way, else all such may become despotic dynasties, and interfere with the world relations. Parts should be allowed all proper rights, as part of the whole—no more.

All the benefits of mind most rational requires, that colonies should pertain as the sovereign duty to the local division, and no other, by the supreme law of nature.

The paramount rights of religion require the whole world to institute its five great continental constitutional governments, as America, Europe, Asia, Africa, Australia, with their appurtenant islands.

No country can prosper by any spirit of conquest.

Without a suitable and free government, no country has beauty, being cursed with the worst of all deformities, that of misrule of those only interested in subserving their own immediate object.

Let industrial labor supplant the vicious piracy of martial ambition, and let it be cherished as the bulwark of freedom and civilization of the world.

There should be no system of tenantry in the world, by reason of supremacy of homesteads.

Nothing less than an equable right in the possession of the whole soil, can endow mankind with their just titles. Each family claiming must have a homestead, if destitute of the means adequate to its purchase. Nothing less than this will place the world on the right institution of rational religion. This has to be done by the whole world, that is bound to have constituent elements of life.

There can be only two kinds of government in the world, constitutional and unconstitutional, the first of which the rational world is only interested in.

The advocates of the last do not cherish rational philosophy, but err in reckless ambition.

They fix on themselves a national debt, amenable to blood and intrigue.

Do they advance the real greatness of the people? The genuine principles of constitutional government, can meet all this most gloriously, as all the requisitions of peace.

The balance of power in the world's equilibrium can be only won, on the balance of principles that cost the least.

Antagonism of the world can only thus be successfully met, as becomes duty.

The equilibrium of the whole world, absolutely requires the supremacy of constitutional governments.

Will it forego its immediate and permanent self-interest, in this most exalted position? Thus it has it in its power to sustain the noblest attributes of mind.

But no monarchical government has full constitutional freedom, as mind is vassal from union of church and state.

The prelates of the established church only, are peers of the realm. Primogeniture keeps up the aristocracy, all keeping up monarchy, in violation of the great principles of equity and justice to mind. This is the case in the freest of all such, even in Great Britain.

Here great extremes meet in excess of wealth to the few, and pauperism to the millions.

There is something wrong in the elements of such political organization.

It is impossible for any nation to claim national or popular freedom, if all constitutional principles do not harmonize. Can Great Britain be free with her church union, that causes imprisonment of citizens for rational religion?

Shall rational religion be in abeyance to peculiar faith? What a solecism? Reason and mind then are governed by faith and heresy. She construes her constitution then, as the ecclesiastical dynasty declares. From whom does all such come? Asia! So far from Asia even giving the world religion, she has only given us diversities of idol paganism, mixed up in its most nauseous doses.

Constitutional governments can permit no bibles and faiths of despotisms. The last cannot survive in a pure land of freedom. In this country is corruption of the press, by all peculiar bibles and their affiliated priestocracies. Unprincipled men have sought in in every age, to get the most available capital in the world. I hold all responsible, on correct criticism, and therefore protest against all such bibles, not only on principle, but its supreme consummation, religon. This country has yet to learn constitutional government, and above all religion, that excludes bigots, absurd faith and such fallacy.

When monarchy goes down, as all unconstitutional governments will necessarily, peculiar faith, its tool, must die the same death. What is to uphold either? There is no divine right but that of mind, and no substantial power but of the sovereign people.

Britain has taken the lead in many things of mind, but she has stopped short in essentials of freedom.

The want of recognition of God's universal principles, proves the utmost stultification, criminality and obliquity of mind in all the fabricators and adopters of all messiahships. All such are Britain's folly, none but tory mercenary curses of the ignoble priestocracy. All these are theatrical impositions on the world by monarchical pretences.

These are the base restrictions on liberty.

No monarchy can know religion. She is an identity from rational mind existence, therefore no messiahship can do any thing with her. She comprehends all the duties of the universe, and cannot be dwarfed into peculiarities. This age cannot do justice to criticism, most philosophical and religious.

Principles universal have never been defined.

What does the world need of precedents, aught less than principles?

Religion demands all principles, not one idea of fanatic delusion of undeveloped mind.

She is a universe affair, that proves the mind, soul, identified therewith, and most conclusively immortal.

There is nothing in any messiah's teaching to benefit the world. That of passive obedience is degradation that its principles do not allow, nor require, anticipating all as clashing.

Whom can the world apply to, to appreciate religion?

Not to the priestocracy, whose peculiar concern is with peculiar faith. They are mere creatures of despotism, always from the days of superstition, their department. They are mere hirelings to promote the public's morbid taste.

What originality of thought could we expect of serfs? Genius alone can burst all the bars of usurpation and monopoly. Not less than genius can do justice to this universe subject.

No monarchical as unconstitutional government, presents religion. It gives always a part of its own despotism, a most contemptible substitute without truth or reality.

No peculiar faithite can pretend to talk of principles before monotheism: he is estopped thereby, as he has to change his circumscribed position.

Where there is so much violation of all principles by the world, to whose tender mercies of all the profligate, can the world trust?

The world can never trust to any thing less than principles. By this position, is the only responsibility. Hold all the world responsible. As to codifying principles, the more difficulty, the more triumph we secure.

But the world-priestocracy-sophistry is eternally uprising in messiahship fictitious claims.

As to all the blessings of liberty claimed for Christ, where were all such prior to his advent?

The priestocracy fabricate all such. In no respect, priestocracy, can your peculiar faiths, missions, messiahs stand before the brilliant light of rational religion. What do the unprincipled care for bibles, for any thing less than the world police, all instituted by rational mind?

The whole family of priestocracy bibles is as false as they, both creatures of despotism; all will be silenced before the tribunal of principles.

Britain, all monarchies have to look to the destitute, their whole population, to which no monarchy can do justice. This is the point of correction.

What a fine thing is it of creation, that continental empires should be ocean bound.

Come, monarchs of the world, a few short years may be yours, in dominion usurped, and empire monopolized. To continue them you err with your eyes open to the facts, that the good of your people can be thus better advanced.

You were chosen not to oppress but to uphold; not to crush, but to elevate to the sublimest aspiration, your people. Sovereigns now have no excuse. They have been taught a lesson for the world by the statesmen of constitutional government, and they should seek the best lesson of true government, else the people will finally seek them. Monarchs will appreciate the worth of constitutional statesmen, like whom no autocrats were ever in such lustre. They will have to seek out what is true government, for their people will have to do it for themselves. As a conservative revolutionist, I say, the world has to come to this.

I seek to expel anarchy and bestow order, law, and constitutional government for all the world.

Cannot republicanism be established in France?

Why so much faithlessness among the presumed better circles? Is Louis Napoleon the traitor?

Is faithlessness always in the circle of those taught peculiar faith, that has no principle, but always the creature of despots? Is this the very doctrine to forfeit all principles? The world people must be no more gullible, but hold responsible all public officers, who should be at once, on first transgression, impeached or dismissed.

The world must have no superior ranks to adulterate its virtue; no despots to butcher up mankind, but must have all its rational wants supplied.

This is a time in the age of the world whose maturity is reached, and cosmopolitan rights developed, when all nations not recognising this truism should be arraigned before the world. The world has the full right to impeach all aggressive nations, all tyrannies in commanding it, before the enlightened tribunal of rational mind. No one power, or set of powers, have the right, by the prowess of arms and the subtlety of mind, to exhaust the strength of mankind by insidious means and policy.

In the House of Commons, Mr. Bright "looked to the condition of the people of India, which was one of extreme, abject, and almost universal poverty. The East India Company, in fourteen years, had collected a revenue of £316,000,000!"—one and a half billions of dollars.

Spare, Britain, thou first of monarchies, this foul and iniquitous despotism; trample not upon the rights of empires to the bitterest dregs; crush not the souls of so many millions. Call you what you please, it is the most degrading slavery that the most barbarous times have ever seen. Spare this age of the world the accursed sight of such detestable depravity. Be consistent, and what you seem.

Give no such example to posterity, much less the present age, of national depravity.

What have the natives to thank christians for now? For any humble mission, to teach what they have been awfully taught by not less than three dynasties of peculiar faith? Are they to be taught through the loss of all their earthly treasure a poly-theism, whose prototype they had a thousand years in advance of its origin most clearly taught?

Your East India Company has tyrannized over one-eighth of the whole world. What is your peculiar church faith to that world, when it fattens itself on its spoils with worse than priestocracy fury and ferociousness? Has the whole nation turned into a popular priestocracy?

Better had your island sink to the bottom of the ocean, than to give this despotism to the world. Can you escape the recognition of your provincial injuries and suf-ferings?

Is your national justice only measured by the capacity of your provinces to sustain next to the last feather, that broke the camel's back?

Your resources are vast, and your prowess is immense, but let it be a high moral dignity that rules in your realm, to the greatest good of the whole, the world.

The question now arises, which is preferable, the cannabalism of a few savages for food, or the immense butchery of lingering victims by supposed refined civilization. through poison of opium, to create greater wealth, at the expense, too, of the most degrading demoralization, national smuggling, or treaty despotism? What is the differ-ence between cannabalism of the mouth and the sword; between fierce and genteel savages?

A bright and brilliant prospect is yet yours, to master much of the world by the noblest attributes of mind. You have helped to lead the way in arts and science, in commerce and manufactures.

Not only have the conquests of crusades exploded, and their martial prowess faded, but a holier spirit breathes over the enlightened world.

The great channels of commerce are opened, the ruinous policies of perverted mind are being superseded, and the mind is rising to her elevation, dignity, and intended benefits.

England, the duty devolves on you to aid in the union and exaltation of the world, of Asia especially, not that you should gain a greater ascendancy, but that conserva-tive principles should maintain the supremacy.

Tell your rulers, liberalists of the world, that they in good, the only faith, should aid you and all mankind in solving the comprehensive problem of religion, to render it expansive as the world; that they should help perfect the book of monotheism, rational religion, as God wrote it, to the highest that rationality of mind enables.

The time will come when no nation or individual will be entrusted with the little brief authority, as all public trusts must be on constitutional basis. Are not nations now preying on the very soul and marrow of the world, inveigling by their policy, bullying by their brutal force? How many are defrauding the world, worse than that, their citizens, by all the sophistry of peculiar faith? Is the world delusion never to end?

You vainly seek to keep nations of the world at peace, till you seek to make them rational. It is very evident the whole cannot be, when its constituent parts have the elements of disturbance. Tell us what is the relative state even in America, England and France, three of the freest countries on earth? Does not peculiar faith defile the whole? How many general churches have split, or are about to split in two in Amer-ica? Has she not had a war of two faiths, the Christians and Mormons, and has the end yet come?

Where are her riots of Protestants and Romans? Her expulsion of Quakers and Baptists by even brother Protestants? Her witchcraft murders? Where are the English feuds of Episcopalians and Romanists now renovated, more or less continued for centuries? Engrafted on Pagans, the Druids, once the despots of peculiar faith, they have sought as far as mind permitted. What is France, republican France, that has butchered her millions, now doing? Has she not thwarted the Italian republicans and forced them to the despotism of peculiar faith, the worst of all absolutisms? Are these nations holding peace conventions, when they have not established a rational reli-gion, that premises the only proper principles of a world-universal brotherhood? As long as Europe continues as she is, there will be excess of standing armies, and one civilian or citizen will have to work for several—he will have to help pay for his own oppression. Liberalists, do away at once with all these little petty kingdoms, and then you will have one valuable government, that will foster the highest constitutional rights of man. Go for that now, at once and forever, and the day is your own, the sovereign people's.

Why should Europeans, Americans, ask anything of Asia, whose people, men and women, have been so long debauched and enslaved by the worst of all despotisms? The day is the world's, mankind's, if it do justice to religion, that will do the amplest justice to the universe.

With principles, the world can successfully solve its mightiest problem, and can satisfactorily invoke all that is expedient.

The universal brotherhood and sisterhood will be insured the world, by only teaching children rational education, and the aspiration to the practice of conservative principles.

England, for hers is the policy now in Asia, should impart the mighty basis of liberal expansion of mind, then she will have performed the great mission of mind, a duty to God, and a blessing to the world.

England owes one duty to Asia in the name of God, who presides over rational religion, not to let the people supersede one superstition by another.

Hastings was acquitted doubtlessly, from acting in extortion, by the orders of his superiors or employers, the East India Company, who required of him money and power, and in order to get them, he fomented disturbances in a province, and supported the pretender successfully, to whom British bayonets dictated imperiously.

Doubtlessly, Britain would have penetrated to Pekin, and ruled the emperor, but for fear of anarchy in the people, who might have overturned the ruler, and perpetrated a fatal revolution in that vast and populous empire.

Should Japan be treated as India, England would conquer her too. What has British rapacity not done? What has her cruelty not effected? She wades through blood to empires. Her ambition is insatiable. Well for her and the world will it be, to balance the world by equilibrium of principles. The yeomanry of mind in Great Britain can do much, as that country is one of the great lights of the world. As the mother of great nations, she has a mighty influence. Her policy, however, directed by immense power, has not been fruitful to the appropriate intellectual possession. She fought America, like a brave people, and, after failing in her conquest, she was magnanimous to acknowledge her rights as a nation, when this colony, her daughter, became independent. England, influenced by the best appreciation, acquiesced in what was the best policy forever. No less for both than the whole world, is that all should flourish together in the arms of peace and commercial union. Speaking one language, that is spreading with its people over the world, a mighty result must ensue, for the greatest good. Let that be the one universal language of the world.

The sublime existence of freedom arose in Britain, the first of popular rights being wrested by the barons, in magna-charta, from King John, in 1215.

The mighty monarchy of Great Britain, that now holds India, with her one hundred and forty millions of people, by her naval and military prowess, has a vast responsibility on her shoulders.

She should not desolate that immense empire by rapine, plunder, or peculiar faith, that has already ruined so much of this fairest portion of the world.

Let England learn the lesson of human rights, for her greatest glory. All this must redound to the elevation of mankind and the world.

The illustrious advocate of Asia's rights, the noble Burke, has told her what desolation has been in India by British oppression.

Would you, England, for it is you that rules. affect Asia, China and Japan, that way?

Pause and know your right position, before the world's tribunal. You stand conspicuous for mind-power before the world, let your national magnanimity be correlative.

The steam power in Great Britain and Ireland, is now estimated as equivalent to the power of eighteen millions of men! This proves the power of mind. over brute force.

Kings, monarchs and autocrats, all councils of bible tradition men, have all acted in bad faith to their constituency and the world, to monopolize rights that should be constitutionally vindicated, in every age of mankind, to whom all such questions should be submitted forever.

The world now demands the solution of its problems, and commands crowns and sceptres in their abeyance. The world has to seek more equally diffused blessings.

It is advised to have nothing to do with revolution, that is not conservative in its progress or end, if such even be attended with anarchy or disorder or no law, the worst state possible of rational existence.

The world's generosity should now be exerted in behalf of itself, whom it has so mistreated by a policy, that grew up when it was but little civilized.

It now has the means of benefiting itself rightly.

Who to-day is defender of the world's justice? It is high time that all the world was duly regulated. Human nature will wear out, but principles will not. Is brute force to be the law of the world?

It should war no more on distant land.

Come, monarchists, you have a day of reckoning, and act like humanity dictates, while in your power. Rely not on anything less than principles, that will cause you to renounce despotism and all its suicidal doctrines. Rely no more on the military power, for now the stroke of the pen is becoming more potent than the sword. Let the world do justice to itself. Let the year 1852, see the world organized into its five great continental governments, distinguished for principles, brotherhood, and religion.

Then international law and rights will be adjusted.

The internal government of each of the five nations as a unit, must be duly respected and cannot be violated.

No republican is justifiable, by international laws, to interfere.

Good faith in all treaties must be invariably maintained, as the infraction reflects on the deepest immorality of the transgressors.

There will be no cause for intervention, when the whole world shall be rightly installed into its continental governments. Conquests can add nothing, for the uniform permanent policy will ever maintain the integrity of each constitutional governmental union.

Every part of the world furnishes the best of reasons for this most splendid institution, for the general conservation of principles.

It becomes all rational minds to duly estimate the most exalted purposes of creation, and act as speedily as practicable.

The sovereignty, independence, and dignity of constitutional government, legitimately call for the consummation of rational religion. The chaplain of the Revolutionary Congress, implored Washington "to give over the ungodly war in which he was engaged." It never entered into this tory's head, that the illustrious father of his country was contending for the only just principles of government, violated by the aggressor, who refused the proper position of deciding those principles. Peculiar faith is incompetent to the functions of religion in every respect, that must be perfectly fulfilled, as the most sacred obligations of mind, in justice to the world and universe. Had Congress caused this irreligious tory to give over his ungodly profession, then a proper reply had been made by action. There is no sublimity that can compare with the happiness of this union, resulting from the noble constitutional government founded by our illustrious ancestors, the noblest heraldry that the world ever presented.

Agitators are rabid to wish to throw away the third brightest diamond in the universe, and involve all in the category of its destruction. The violation of the first, mind, spirit or soul, transgresses the second, and that of religion which advanced to the rational basis of civilization, witness the third constitutional government, the brightest lustre of which is, that it is clear of all faith.

Faith-bigotry warps the mind in all its circles of duty, political, social and national.

Divide the union, and military misrule flourishes with dictatorships, dissensions and wars. Freedom will have her work to do over again.

But for the press, statesmen and patriots, this nation might have split into fragments. Have not much of the present difficulties in our union grown out of peculiar faith dissensions?

The agitators make false capital. Better had all such sink in the ocean, before disunion is even thought of once.

What is the result but war, then barbarism, let alone military despotism.

Americans are the only people capable by civil blessings to secure those of pure religious liberty, of putting an end for the benefit of the whole world to all the disguises of despotism among them, to lay low all the idle and false pretences of paganism in all the forms and modifications of idolatry. They are to adopt sooner or later the only proper religion of God, monotheism, and will then realize as confer, as the centre of civilization, all the noblest blessings to the world. America will be the favored of nations: nothing less than monotheism will do the world to crush the pusillanimous paganism of all ages, the aiders and abetters of absolutism.

The stars in the flag of the United States present the most liberal comprehension, that they are for universal principles, the most universal polity of rational religion—conservative of the whole world.

The peculiar school doctrine is an outrage.

It remains for free, enlightened Americans to elevate themselves to the highest, that of Monotheism, to take the freedom of mind out of the hands of impostors; the false pretences of an ignoble peculiar faith, palmed on the world for religion, is no more that, than its peculiar gods are like the Creator of the universe.

In a country truly freed by monotheism, rational mind is thrown on its own best resources, free agency. The world has not begun to appreciate the sublime greatness of constitutional liberty, the purity, the elevation, the greatness of rationality. The priestocracy are nowhere—they are incompetent to look religion in the face, creatures as they were and are of debauched despotism.

American clergy ought, in a body, see the despotic infatuation of peculiar faith, and control it. They can now take the noblest stand of patriotism, mind, &c., and assert, as monotheists, that religion is the noblest representative of the Almighty Creator. Nations of the world, prove yourselves worthy of this sublime enjoyment, and render the proper adoration to the Author of Creation.

Civilization proves her benefits through the progress of rational mind, that gives America all the elements of true greatness, durable and eternal, as the Union most sacred, the cement of her majestic liberty.

America is one of the model lights of the world. What had bibles of tradition to do with our revolution? They retarded the execution, asking defenders. Now has mind the ascendancy, and the ballot-box is more powerful than all the artillery of absolutism, and more potent than its sword. America has risen on the best aids of rational mind, that will elevate her to her highest capacity. Her policy must comprehend all its best benefits. What sort of uncivilized country would ours be without our blessed Union? Dissolution of the Union would derange the intellectual and moral world.

Let the light of our counsellors, our chief men, be enlightened and liberal statesmen, of comprehensive mind, duty and patriotism. Be the Constitution the presiding genius —let mutual concessions and compromises be the motto—let justice prevail in her councils, and strength will be in her footprints. Let her flag be the harbinger of joy on the ocean, to the distressed of every land, and the satisfaction of all the wise and true at home.

We must look to America that has enlightened the world on true government, so she must enlighten and bless on rational religion, not the miserable peculiar faith of bibles of tradition, or of imperial dynasties, that rule their world by union of church and state.

Americans owe it to themselves to begin this mighty conservative revolution. But are all our statesmen politicians, that they cannot commit themselves to the justice of rational religion? The American public is the only one that can properly appreciate this position, that no bible of tradition can give the first letters—the elements of pure religion.

The voice of social intellectuality and dignity ought to speak out.

Peculiar faith, as a part and parcel of kingly or papal government, is then notoriously an injurious organ, oppressive to the mind of the sovereign people.

Can the American nation, the whole intellectual world, over-estimate this glorious constitutional government? Can all the beneficiaries duly appreciate the noble Union?

The present age should seek for annexation on the same grand division of the five of the world, not conquest, the moral, not martial influence.

The only universal empire is that of universal brotherhood, founded on the noblest relations of mind, that establishes constitutional governments.

Time was when the old and new continents had no communication. How was this? It was for want of genius, mind, and science, that tower above all faith. Under rational religion the noblest philanthropic associations will grow up.

This Union does hand to the world its constitutional government: let it add also that of rational religion. The banner nation, that gives to the world constitutional government and rational religion, confers a sublime favor that can never be repaid, and will render her the star of light.

Asia is and has been the land of political and faith despotism. It is time that the world caused truth to hold faith in abeyance.

Women, you whose sex has been so long degraded by orientalism, that has taken away or effaced all the noblest traits of soul, and denied even that to you, seek your dignity, and see to the truth and glory of rational religion.

What, then, can be more important to the world, or richer in ennobling materials to its happiness?

The world should now demand as its supreme right, written constitutions of regularly organized conventions, elected by properly constituted electors, as the supreme law of continents. All free intelligent citizens have an interest in constitutional government, rational religion, civilization and universal brotherhood. The permanent, correct

The w...
treated by a ...
It now h...
Who to...
duly regu...
to be the ...
It shoul...
Come, ...
in your p...
nounce ...
for now ...
do justic...
tinental ...
Then ...
The int...
and cannot ...
No reme...
Good ...
the deem...
There ...
insta...
perm...
un...
Ex...
tion for ...
It ...
and ...
...
m...
t...
w...
c...

All the primary and essential points have already been secured the United States of North America, whose natal day of national liberty and freedom should never be given up, if we only celebrate it by reading the Declaration of Independence.

What then can patriots think of the dissolution of this Union, so glorious, so momentous to the world's happiness, much less its own? Traitors to mind may act most irrationally to all the requisitions of the universe. Adulterers may dissolve the sacred union of man and wife, and thus destroy for them forever their domestic happiness! Murderers may destroy the union of soul and body to gratify a fiendish spirit, but what fiend could willingly blast this noblest monument of patriotic genius? Give all your possessions, and work for more to give for this constitutional union. Bury much in the oceans ere disunion. Perish every species, and all the involved interests of political speculation adverse to this glorious Union.

Disunion should be looked upon as the curse awaiting a stupid nation, to be made wretched above all nations at the consummation of such a scene, deplorable to mind forever.

Let patriots sacrifice on the altar of their country all that is needed, to preserve her institutions, that are so magnificently safe, her safety glorious, and her glory permanent. Who can speculate on disunion? Is the union worth preservation, after the spirit and principles of construction are gone?

When party speaks of dissolution of our union, it does not appreciate the character of the world-volcano that will be aroused. But what will not partisanships and factions of party spirit do? Constitutional, not armed mediations, are the available weapons, in wise republics, to secure lasting blessings. The union of the world must be secured.

We should look, at this liberal age, at the unity of countries not only, but of whole grand divisions, as best suited to govern the balances of power, hitherto an unsolved problem, especially in the old continent. The wisest position of peace proclaims this, as imperative. Our views must refer to the earth's circumference, to reach the proper solution.

Who and what are national magistrates?

They are the representatives of a popular constituency—no matter by what name—monarchs, emperors, or presidents. Justice requires that this question be submitted to the sovereign citizens, who should have a voice in all such decisions.

What would we have the monarchs of the world to do, provided that question could be disposed of? They should endow at once the richest means of giving rational education to all rational minds, of their people, and give them all the rightful benefits of a free people, to enjoy mind—that is, all resign for a presidency, elected by the people. All nations that make the least pretensions to culture of mind at this age, should receive, as they are entitled to, constitutional government.

Monarchs, all rulers are only the fiduciaries for the sovereign people. They should not withhold this highest evidence of nations' rights, but impart, as wisdom's best position, the exactest action, resulting on just thoughts, expressed in the fewest words. Monarchy affects to be the natural government, as all, unless the most enlightened, adopt it. The test of nature is the greatest good, and that is by constitutional representation.

The rightful powers of such are the executive, the legislative, and judiciary—all independent of each other, but responsible agents of the sovereign people, who, as mortals, have the only divine rights. This is the beauty of people governing themselves as nations. Such government inculcates the great and necessary duties to the world, country, family, friends, and self, to recognise all important and peaceful science, to advance the improvements and best culture of soils as well as minds, to facilitate the overcoming all obstructions of oceans and continents, all the potent elements of nature, to show mind worthy of its gifts, entitled to its just rewards.

To have the best cultivation of justice, that it be not neglected, for the absent, the weak, the poor, or oppressed; to appreciate a sound and honest judgment of him who might not talk at all, in preference to the flowers of rhetoric or oratory, unsupported by right. To have principle adhered to, and escape all the dangers of factions in faith and government: to elevate the views of the people above the sordid intentions of demagogues, the morbid, rabid taste of customs.

Mankind are the great agents for stirring up the great elements of their improvement, to be followed by the great fruits of repose and happiness, and in none better than in the proper constitutional representative government.

Statesmen and their governments should ever pursue a course of enlightened and peaceful policy towards all the world, and especially all nations at peace with them. They should permit no armament or equipment to be carried from their ports for war purposes, to interfere and conflict with friendly relations. The proper precaution, at first, may prevent the most of the difficulties.

The noble family of free governments and states is increasing ; the dawn has burst upon the world, that is responsive to the brighter light from America. Europe has rekindled, and already Africa is responding.

Absolutism, in all its perversions of government, must yield to true constitutional governments of representative republics, that will give all due in every possible attainment of mind's benefit. God will permit no other, if mind will act up to its own dignity.

Freemen should assert the power that individual knowledge and right give, to attain refined civilization.

Many of the murder class, nationally and individually, could have been arrested, ere the weapons could have been drawn, by arrest of the immoral cause at the bottom of it.

Patriots will not forget the triumph of mind in '76, over absolutism, as to permit Jewish priestocracies, professing peculiar faith, that has entailed difficulties on the world most potent, and that has alienated the fairest portions of the globe from each other, to give us a code of faith, when we reject its legal code.

There is no divine right of government, but by and through the people, who should have rational education, to continue all its rational blessings ; and there certainly is none of church, that abuses pure religion, under its peculiar faith.

As the triumph of mind progresses, so will its proper form of government ; then the offices of absolutism will one day be shunned, more than sought. A statesman seeks to find organic laws, on true government, a proper representative government ! Can he find in any bible of tradition any such authority, but that of the pretended divine rights of kings and the priestocracy ? For their increase of power and privileges ? That kings can do no wrong, under that pretence, as priestocracies commit no error in responsibility, to the sovereign people, their masters ? Thus the progress of mind is impeded, its dignity and worth superseded ; for no innovation can be attempted against absolutism of government, civil and church. What then can be worse than such bibles, that give codes that crush the rights of mind, and that misrule the world ?

How many tribes, races, and nations fail, under weak and bad systems of rule ! Among all, the Jews are most conspicuous.

The time has arrived, when in all nations laws are to be wisely legislated on, and equally and duly administered, otherwise shame and disgrace, for our and all countries, must follow.

There are too many, in all countries, treacherous to just rights, else why oppression on the one, and submission on the other side?

Good governments secure justice, compel redress of grievances and wrongs, and tend to restore a proper estimate of religion, so essential to the universal peace of the world.

Manners are essentially needed, in the best ordered governments, and among the freest people. Annul all laws that give the least complexion to abuses.

The blessings of popular government create good faith among the nations of the world. The world will then safely confide in principles, that will protect it better than all armies and navies, that will eat out its strength and substance.

Under constitutional government rightly administered, our legitimate position being well and truly defined, if we cause others to define their's appropriately, then we can hold all bad characters at command, even without the necessity of arbitration.

But can the people of Europe and other parts of the monarchical world, carry out all the principles of civil and religious freedom?

Most certainly. They have to make their beginning, and the sooner the better ; their leaders if not false, can help them. They are bound in the highest honor to the people, to resign all power unto the sovereign people.

What blessings of our constitution, that gives no citizen supreme power over laws, equity and facts?

Its authors are so superior, when compared to those who formed the hierarchy of the Jews, that were so sadly deficient in popular benefits, that the last appears as schoolboys to the first.

Over priestocracy, by mind, is at once recognised a moral and intellectual victory the highest attainable, and decides conclusively for the highest tribunal, an enlightened public opinion of an enlightened, wise, and virtuous community.

What will not the liberality of free governments do, for the nations of the world, when conservative revolution arises, and tears asunder the mantle of despotism ; then it will be that we shall see the triumph of principles.

The people look now to their government with the deepest interest, and must advance the benefit of free schools to the extent of rational education, and exclude mind's perversions, by expulsion of bibles of tradition and all other abuses. The civilized code of refinement instead of its pretensions, bordering on the barbarian and savage, will expel all noxious evils that destroy mankind prematurely.

Absolutists hold by an uncertain tenure, as they hold without principles ; the more absolute, the sooner the day of retribution may ensue, for retribution comes from the immutable law of principles. Blessed are the republics of the world, whose citizens can amend on the errors of the past, and listen to the voice of reason ; can regulate their organic and constitutional legislation if wrong, and obey their laws if rationally right. Such institutions will speedily limit these old governments that trample on the rights of their citizens, that pollute and violate the dearest interests of mankind.

Principals in power are not put there to corrupt, but protect the sovereign people and their divine rights. Absolutism is the basest for usurpation, in all this. Its wiles may supersede constitutional and imprescriptible freedom in the mass, the judiciary, executive, legislative, political sway.

Beyond principles, nothing can be trustworthy in this world, as the death of many proves how far the passions and prejudices of the mass may be ignobly misled, by the perversion and affectation of knowledge and faith. The crowd that is ignobly misled by demagogues, political or ecclesiastical, is ever ready for corruption, to do wrong in a wrong cause, when light is not beaming to discover it, perfectly unworthy of the injured, hardly fit for subjects to such masters. In just governments only, can mind reach and maintain its supreme goodness, and social rights, their sublime elevation. In such only the supreme excellence of woman, magnificent in her jewels of chastity, is sublimely upheld, by the conservative enlightened opinion of freedom that blesses mankind.

There she is purely above suspicion on the proper basis of mind, high, elevated and great.

There predominates the best taste, to restrain and counteract licentiousness. There reigns the only proper equilibrium, by the justest relation of rights between the sexes, as in the solar system, where each orb maintains its just relations.

None but correct position of mind can do this, where its refined sensitiveness can be heard, and its potency can be justly exerted.

Mind is the impress of the spirit of the age, of the government, of religion, and participates in the blessings of freedom, or sympathizes in the miserable state of the earth.

In the blessings of freedom, it proves the libel on man that all have their price.

Happy America can refute it by her Washington, and unfortunate Hungary can repel it by her Dembinski ! It takes despotism to dishonor and libel mind. Absolutism disgraces mind, by perversions of lust, ambition and avarice, and misleads it into the deepest speculations and gambling of its rights and purity. The proper equilibrium of free government, ennobles mind to its sublimest greatness ; even in its medium, the chastity of woman was proved, by the Roman Lucretia.

Among the blessings of constitutional government, is embraced a jury, that rightly constituted, bestows a practical illustration of cultivated mental light ; but if perverted, this is a perfect nuisance.

Constitutional government is the most appropriate nursery for public spirit and patriotism.

To all this is due proper respect to country, the most enlarged and liberalized spirit that encircles the world and comprehends the universe. It looks to the unity of empire in all the essentials.

It establishes the proper financial system of the country, compatible with its direct interests and the world.

The light of true government bids the mighty conquerors of continents now holding on to their possessions and conquests, which had been previously prey to succession of conquerors, having been ruined by the mal-practices of priestocracies, and all the usurpations over mind, to be now responsible for the improvement of their mighty wards.

All the relative gradations of mind have to be cared for, by the wisest world guardianship. The life-problem is that of mind, responsive to which mankind must ever look. The paramount question, is its right and happiest solution. What if the dissolution of this most exalted model republic should take place ? We ought not and never should hear the last of this catastrophe, the dissolution of the world's freedom. The curses of an injured world would be upon the guilty perpetrators. Down with all such factions and sectional mobs, whose spirit is worse than parricides. All such are to be utterly condemned, without distinction and specific charges. Our union must be preserved, as long as it is honorable and proper.

ᶜ Any other than a constitutional government is as incorrect, as peculiar faith is removed from religion.

We can only have one true government of constitutional freedom for country and mind.

One hundred millions of liberalists could have stood up in Europe, and backed out all the absolutists, had there been a right view taken and upheld. There must be a concentration of all the world's best powers by the liberalists. The people have seen that they have only to look to themselves, not to those alienated from their interests. Does not absolutism of despotism disfranchise most of the rights of man? As much as the ancients missed religion, so have they missed government. Purity of government advances to all mankind the greatest good.

Corruptions of society become more miserable as government is corrupt. The American Union has solved the noblest problem, in the noblest way, of all the social, moral and intellectual relations of the world. Their best problem solution is now that of rational religion.

The nations of the world cannot conceive better than by a conservative revolution, that circumscribes all the ignoble and unprincipled opposition, and proves that without this, no virtue is seen but in self-interest.

The rulers of the world should be constitutional, and recognise their great position, to prevent monopoly being usurpation, and to expel all manner of imposition from the human mind. Theirs is the position to exalt their fellow-citizens to the requisitions of just government. They preside over this great function, and should at once perform it in the most effectual manner. But no! Many of them consider the people, their own people, vulgar, and their rights abstraction. Then it becomes the people to treat them as abstractions and cause them to promptly resign.

Why will kings still persist in popular absolutism; they ought to know that they are usurpers on the divine rights of the people. The votes of the people, and their representation on constitutional principles, are now the proper order of the world.

Monarchies rest on perjuries. They beget mind-vassalage, a subserviency that is degrading. Orientalism has nurtured this to the most abject point. What an amount of imposition begets it. The people, the only sovereigns, are taught to be vassals, bribed, bought and seduced by their own means. Correct government supersedes force and oppression. Every absolute government has a state faith to defraud the deceived people. Nations are degraded by monarchy, and all the appurtenances of absolutism, as Popery. All such brutalize and demoralize the people. Correct minds require such governments as will give best freedom and protection; therefore they cannot, by sovereign and inherent rights, be precluded from selection of matters necessary for comfort of life.

Freemen choose to observe, reflect and select for themselves. They ask for a system not to trust any further than prudent security generally permits.

Trust the least in government when power is delegated. Enlightened mind must see that the pretences of any kind of monarchy cannot for a moment be constitutional government. There can be only one just kind of government, and that constitutional republic.

The example for just, rational government has been given by the United States of America, for three-fourths of a century. A tenth of the world is now enjoying an approach to such blessings and principles.

Even England has the press partially free, when it is not bought, used or employed as the peculiar organ; the right of trial by jury, and an adequate protection to property. But she has not that organic bullion for the full rights of the world, without which the world is necessarily crippled, too often crushed. Her church tyranny is an awful monster of iniquity. Good government, call it by what name you please, gives rational education, security of life, liberty and property, justice to persons and reputation. The world must exclude faction or mere party spirit, and adopt such principles as will insure the good of the most, if not all—not advance mere peculiar interests.

All pure governments that respect their constituency, will revere their constitution and construe it forever with good faith and sense to protect alone thereby. In pure order of government, of liberalism, no power, money or persons get the ascendancy. The world should secure that government that secures amelioration and improvement of social conditions. The best principles of monotheism, rational religion, demand all this.

Such government is needed in the affection, and has won the confidence of the beneficiaries.

What is any government worth, if wise legislation and administration be not secured? Constitutional governments are for the most elevated and beneficial purposes, the independence and purity of officials, the inherent honors of principles.

How much has absolutism, despotism, been a sacrifice of the finest qualities of mind?

The most rational universal governments of the world must be instituted as speedily as practicable.

We must all see by the eye of science, the absolute necessity of having for each of the five grand divisions of the globe, all the national outlets, all the unity of interests; consequently nothing less than a union of all the countries of the same division and appurtenant islands will answer. The sphere of science can now take cognisance of this sublime position of free and intellectual mind.

The greatest and purposed benefits of having continental governments, are full and satisfactory for the world.

Then continental nations, the greatest and most respectable, arise, that may look best at once to all principles the most liberal practicable. Every thing then will be done on a scale commensurate with the mighty interests of the world, and all government operations of that scale, must approach the nearest to the best requirements of universal society, rational mind.

The best outlays of all rational governments, are the elements of rational popular education.

Liberality in most realities of life's expenditures of proper investments, as rational education, oftenest insure the most profitable returns.

Are continental governments the sublime acts of mind, or the Utopias of the imagination ?

Enlightened views show that the largest sources should have general and natural outlets, as large rivers that cannot be safely embanked, but must disembogue themselves by the channels that nature makes and reason observes, not monopoly dictates for universal inundation and ruin.

We must look upon the human family, not in the mere light of politics or partyism alone, unless that particular question comes up in nations whose nationality must be respected and protected when sectional divisions only are regarded. No despots of national circles should affect world-rights.

Annexation of continental nations may now be a happy result, as all may have a purer government and most peaceful relations.

When all become correct representative republican governments, then all conquests must be superseded by nobler means that must be beneficial to the ultimate good of mankind.

Intermixtures of appropriate races, like commercial enterprises, will bring about a higher state of mental elevation, abundance of people of the large divisions of the globe rushing to that point in general, and free intercourse to obtain their purpose, where a vast field of enterprise is excited, the countries will become mighty and settled, and the last great link of commerce will then be complete, the best and brightest of all in refined civilization. Already has the benignity of the supreme kind of government that best gives individual, national and world liberty, that upholds pure rational religion, proved itself, as from a stately bride wooed to be won by the wise of all nations.

The principles of correct government will finally cause all the nations of the same continent, or grand divisions of continent, to be annexed in one indissoluble union, and the continents to be blessed with a world's peace. But how can that be, it may be asked, when our union that is only a part of one continent, has been apparently on the verge of dissolution ? We see the world evils by keeping the union of continents, in the fragments of despotism. Mighty has been the conflict of opposing elements that have tested ours to be the proper government, else it had been shivered into fragments. It is founded in the true affections of the people, and those of cultivated minds. Sane people do not actually know what they are talking of, when they speak of the disunion of this country. They might as well speak of dividing a mighty brilliant, even a principle ! If we were divided, the two divisions would be like the bleeding halves of one body, whose functions were crushed, and whose lustre for ever gone.

Tears of sympathy would be her requiem, or the curses of mankind would be her portion.

Never was suicide so fatal, action so malign.

We will not foster the idea, as long as we can sustain compromise and liberality, justice and patriotism ; all hail our sacred union, blessed with constitutional rights of citizenship. With her we can say all hail the republics of the world, that pour upon the benighted and oppressed, the fruits of light and liberty.

And all hail intellectual freedom, that pours forth on all the continents the wisdom and goodness of an all-wise God.

By this union the safety of the globe is advancing in her dignity, whose desolation has followed the destructions of millions by human butchers.

With her the heroic but feudal ages are passing, while the rational has advanced.

With this glorious union, mind, the noblest endowment of the Creator, has obtained one of the noblest of all acts, self-government, for free and legitimate agency in personal and public affairs.

Nothing but rational education can insure the most appropriate government to man in all the forms of social condition, and parents have to set the best and enlightened example for their children, who are never to be independent of their highest obligations about any duty, and to do all this rightly, all the obsolete pretences of absolutism are to be rejected by the great conservatives of mind through rational education.

The best schools are to be conscientiously maintained in all circles, as one of the very first public duties from parents to their children, the country to its citizens, the world to its people.

Absolutism of all kinds has to be put down, and kept there effectually by the only means, the only legitimate powers of rightly educated mind.

Just governments are shedding their light and blessings, and will wisely precede as the noblest couriers, rational religion purely expressed, that will govern mind, and military power with its fame will be nowhere in the union of all. All the parts of the world cannot have too speedy intercourse with each other, procuring all commercial advantages by rail and plank roads, and steamers, to unite as nations, and unite all nations of the world, that will exchange the surplus produce, and reciprocate all the works of science, art, and manufactures with the world, and the best light of governmental institutions to all, excluding the wretched organizations of absolutism. The world presents a comprehensive theatre, a school for the highest benefit and exercise of mind, not its enslavement or corruption.

The various constitutional governments of nations or continents of nations, will form so many substantial aids to the bible of mind, that the organic and legislative laws, seconded by the irresistible will of the mind, enlightened by refined civilization, will complete this universal object. The five general continental divisions of the earth, must finally be five grand republics of the world. Their code of international law would exclude wars. For what could they fight? As most rationally constituted, they must have one kind of free representative constitutional government, and the moment of their institution also religion, the true faith, not Roman nor universalist, but catholic and universal on true principles of the God of nature, not of any peculiar god of nations. In them rational science and philosophy will flourish. Peace and practicable prosperity will be general. Whose interest then would be peculiar, alien to principles whose influence would be universal? There would be no need of unconstitutional rulers, usurpers and monopolists.

There would be no need of mighty armed powers, to destroy mind's noblest achievements. The triumph would be in the blessing, not in the curse of races, and all peculiar societies would be merged in one universal brotherhood.

The unity of language can be matured through science. Much of mind's benefit, that has been lost in diversity of languages, will then be realized in science.

Genius can reduce language to unity, and the best will be the English, a most comprehensive position of true science.

Enlarged and liberal views to the world's comprehension, are the only just ones, secure the greatest benefit, and require a universal regard, as far as practicable, to its rights.

True citizens of the world, contend for all your principles, and ever obtain them at the tribunal of reason.

Principles do not permit affections nor attributes to be dwarfed. Under them behavior is gentle and courteous, as breeding is correct, and all will tell ultimately on the world and the universe.

The noble principles of liberalism can best preserve the uncorrupt state of society, or correct its downward tendency.

The universal blessing of all nations is through the right exercise of mind's best functions, that cause the light of liberty to flourish.

The light of liberty, of freedom, already irradiates a part of the world, and will cause the best fruit to ripen. The problem of liberty will be solved, when all the world-nations lay proper hold of it. The constitutional representative government has met the mighty unsolved problem most wisely, and that now meets the mightiest of all, that of religion, by a flood of light. In defence of its own divine rights, mind appeals first to constitutional government, to promote the blessings of universal peace, honor, dignity, worth, laws, order of society, and welfare of the world.

Such continental governments will promote the preservation of national treaties, as a matter of general welfare, and exclude the swindling of the rights of the sovereign people by wholesale.

The national vicious characteristics can be got rid of best by continental unions.

The world is concerned in the mighty principles of freedom, and its patriotism must never look at all at any design but in universal good.

A comprehension of the whole category of self-vindication of principles and rational retribution, give this most philosophical forewarning.

Mankind should go the legitimate extent of governmental institutions, to best carry out the world's interests. God has defined them by the existing great local divisions, to be united on international commercial regulations.

The good faith of nations is needed for universal peace, friendly relations and intercourse, and should be universally in unison in religion.

They can only be by rational religion, that excludes all sectarianism.

Under this noble position, what noble triumphs of mind this age has in the thousand inventions and discoveries, the facility of world-mails, the universal lights of the press, the celerity of the telegraph, the great civilizing powers of commerce, the mighty comforts of industrial pursuits, all the advanced developments over past ages!

Mankind must have observed the best inspirations of genius and character through exalted minds, as those of a Columbus, a Washington, and numerous others, who have labored to promote the world's welfare. Having established all primary principles in universal governments of the great divisions of the earth, the whole legitimate benefits will irresistibly result. The principles of universal peace are paramount, because the principles of order are universal in creation. The unity of such country's vast empire, extensive as natural limits either of the continent or its greatest grandest divisions may be, is practicable by the sublime link of principles. None of its parts will gain anything, will do any permanent good to have a disunion, but such part will finally lose everything valuable.

The downfall of empires, as well as their rearing, gives the world some mighty lessons for its profit.

Subdivisions of continents produces nations of unnatural positions, instead of one respectable, reputable great nation, one of the five models of the whole world to respect, admire, and imitate.

Let the lights of true history and judgment be wise teaching to the world. Before universal peace is established in the world, we must establish its noble principles. Many ignorantly descant on all these, as those seeking to build without a proper foundation. If America, in her wisdom and freedom, had not kept peculiar faith apart from government, civil war might have ensued.

Why do the other states of America have civil wars, but from the state of the human mind succumbing to peculiar faith, and its concomitants, ignorance, bigotry, intolerance, and the spirit of persecution? They cannot seek union too speedily for all America.

When nations unite, as the five grand divisions of the world indicate the programme, the thousands of the world-vices will determine.

International congresses of the great five grand divisions of the earth, will add a sublime picture to the world's history and man's happiness.

The state of the world's possessions only justifies the belief that the peace position of the world can be realized, by changes of government on earth's grand divisions, the security of brotherhood.

The mighty difficulties of oceans, deserts, and tyrannies, are best obviated by giving mind right tendencies on its broadest platform, and thus we can best avoid wars, pestilence and famine.

The union of Europe can be secured, as of all others, on right principles, not by the heterogeneous combinations, as in the Roman Empire, with a great central point, that absorbed most of the strength; but on the noble principles of the United States of America.

Then standing armies of half millions to a nation will be dispensed with, and the honest earnings of man be duly rewarded by the blessings of peace. Supreme science, and mighty universal results, are involved in the consummation of a universal brotherhood of nations.

Wars should all be stopped by constitutional continental governments, that when equitably administered, can carry the world through the most trying difficulties, to the highest attainable point of wisdom. There must be good faith toward all nations and countries, and the most practicable means for its security. While the blessings of commerce knit nations into the closest relations, could there be possibly any natural enmity of nations, as England and France, except what is absurdly pretended by absolutism, not certainly between the people? The diplomacy of courts, but another name too often for sophistry, in the action of absolute despotism, may be excluded in this liberal exhibition of mind's right action.

Constitutional organic basis must bind the organic limits of rights. The world has to appeal to its statesmen and patriots, not its warriors, as mind is to govern.

Absolutists, royalists, tories to sovereign rights of the people, may resist, but proper continental annexations and union, the sooner the better, should be instituted, to bring the balance in good government.

Annexation of empires on the same grand division of the same continent, on constitutional principle, and never by conquest, will be the great achievement of mind; hence wars and their injuries will be dispensed with.

We must comprehend universal principles and all world-wide subjects, to do full and comprehensive justice to mankind in all their relations, religious and social.

Broad national, not sectional ground, should invariably be taken, in all co-ordinate departments of free constitutional governments.

The proper view should be that of a world patriotism, to deserve well of our country, of the world, of mankind universally, in its widest scope.

Adequate justice to all citizens, in the best constitutional way, is the primary-object of the world.

Wars for conquest might be otherwise sought for, some longer, but raise the glorious flag of principles, that direct the proper continental union under free constitutional governments, and the balance of that division, sooner or later, will rally to the rescue. Mankind must ever sustain the high duties of the best rational government, the proper enforcement of wise laws, the security and protection to their citizens.

The game of conquest should be an obsolete question, as it is a fearful one, that the whole world can play at most iniquitously, and the sooner given up the better. Commercially, intellectually, and popularly, the light of our constitutional government radiates, to the most civilized portions of the globe. Let it be pure and uneclipsed, universally.

In the solution of this world-interesting question, how great and inherent is its value! How far is it available to a world's prosperity and happiness?

What mighty principles are involved, in national existence! Among them none are more conspicuous than a world's universal brotherhood. The Creator has laid off the world in five grand divisions and appurtenant islands.

True constitutional government, is for their national and individual protection. If they do not thus protect themselves, they never can otherwise. What will protect them, but the most equitable organization, on the noblest comprehension of intelligence? The world must prepare for five grand or great governments, that should be united for general preservation.

Universal principles are essential to the world's society, recognised by mind, from creation.

God instituted this organic position for the best social relations of the world's circle, and free institutions alone can best promote them.

The sooner the better, that we have unions of the five grand divisions of the earth.

They could not be coherent by any other than constitutional governments. Then the mighty highways of nations, oceans and continents, will be filled with the world's blessings, instead of its curses. Then discovery and genius will ennoble each other, and all will redound to universal good, for the institution of honorable policies, primary in all true governments, that will re-act on the whole. What can best counteract the world-piracies? We should institute all comprehensive counteraction of the great first causes.

Nothing is equal to universal rational education of the citizen. If the world be properly instructed in its rights, its duty will best follow for protection, and appropriate governments will adequately meet the whole demands.

When mind obtains its ascendancy over peculiar world despotisms, then the generous rivalry of nations will exist. Time was when priestocracy maintained their government, and monarchs theirs; then came their union, and now only constitutional governments, those of the people, on orthodox principles, will satisfy the world, to supersede all such.

The people of each of the grand divisions must unite for the immediate good of all of that division, then of the world. Escaping from the tyranny of one man and one idea power, they must not plunge into the despotism of the many.

The time has now arrived, when, if the people choose, civil decisions can decide for states, in place of war. The comforts of the world are now promoted by the aid of science and commerce, in their glorious departments, and the manufacturer is fast superseding the warrior.

How superior will the assimilated races become, when an honorable mixture results; and how magnificent the governments that extend to the defined limits of nature.

. Everything can be commensurate with the ocean-bound empires. The people, identified with such magnificent governments, will be correspondently elevated, in social, intellectual, and religious rank.

The world will be exempt from the regime of intrigue, factions, sectional or local, that can have no hope of success.

The Anglo-Saxons will doubtlessly overrun all America ; the English language will prevail over three grand divisions of the globe, and their free institutions will comprehend all mankind, the whole world. The absolutists had best accommodate themselves to this conservative revolution, the sooner the better. Now is the time.

Already enlightened nations are meeting in 'fraternal embrace, and encircling the world by their commerce, arts and sciences, above all, by just constitutional governments.

Who that appreciates the mighty blessings that they enjoy in a land of constitutional laws, morals and order, can forego them ? Such sink to insignificance, the foolish and corrupt administrations of ancient states, and of modern despotisms.

The ignorance and corruption of mind, now only permit them. All is only right that is wise, in just governments. The world will respond to all this.

The world needs good faith in government, and social relations. It has sacrificed its best blood and treasure. All that was becoming in the struggle for its liberty, and possessed of the right intention, will secure it finally. It cannot guard too prudently against the corruptions of government, that beset mind in all the situations of life.

All nations, weak ones especially, have to look to principles, that finally must govern the world. We can well observe now in our own country, a sublime spectacle for the world : settlers from one ocean to another, the great lakes of the north, to the mighty gulf of the south, where once the Indian roamed, now the steamer represents progressive science. America is just emerging from the Pacific Ocean to meet Asia, China, Japan and Siberia. The world's mighty commerce, is telling the value of rationality.

Political science should be eminently philanthropic and philosophical, to benefit the human family by constitutional freedom, that reflects general light of mind, over the world for its loftiest dignity. This will constitute the only permanent basis, to establish those mighty conservative principles intended for enlightened mind. Such divisions represent five unions of brotherhood, all united to one mighty international compact of universal good, illustrative of the true position of peace and fellowship.

All the governments being alike with correct fundamental principles, must produce correspondent beneficial results. Then comes more or less, in process of time, the extinction of thousands of dialects and languages, national vices, narrow prejudices, and evil traits, contracted in narrow bigoted circles. Above the littleness of sectarian faction and faith, will arise the majestic simplicity and unity of rational religion.

Then self will sink into general good, and mind will do itself justice, for the tribunal is that of reason. The true position will blend these principles with reason, duty and religion.

Already philosophical science is the harbinger. The discoveries of genius are ministering to this mighty spectacle. Electric telegraphs now transmit intelligence, on one of Deity's messengers, fast enough for the world. Railroads will conduct from ocean to ocean, across the largest continent, the people, their produce and merchandise, from the ends of any grand division, all the representatives to the central capital, with satisfactory speed of a few days. The press, under its steam improvements, and accelerated transportation, and diffusion of the mails, now informs most distant points, most speedily of the important news.

Civilized man is enlightened to appreciate, that self-government is the only true one, and that conservative principles established by Deity for his universe, are all that are needed for mind on this globe, if wisdom and refinement supersede selfish prejudices and ignorant assumption.

Mind enlightened must consider continental constitutional governments as absolutely necessary, to the right, elevated and peaceable government of all.

We could not desire to displace any supreme powers, until a real conservative constitutional one was established without bloodshed.

Mind owes it to itself, its dignity of supreme earthly character, to master all practicable difficulties, and this among them.

The five grand divisions of the globe, America, Europe, Asia, Africa, Australia and their appurtenant islands, are to be governed with reference to unity entire in each, and all five united on the same general principles of free government, and all the world comprehended in one union predicated on the conservative principles, that will guide it right; a universal union under the supreme ruler God and mind.

Much of the globe is still in antagonism and conflict. All such matters will still prevail, till sects and fragments are superseded by one universal brotherhood in religion, freedom get the ascendancy of absolutism, and intelligence of ignorance.

Absolutism that is above law, is not governed by principles at all, hence all such governments are usurpations where will is law, and faith of will state-faith. All such are in miserable bad taste. All such irrational representations of mind must go down; they will put themselves down at the proper time, as unprincipled; they carry the elements of their own final destruction.

The only proper government is constitutional republicanism, that looks to an executive house of representatives, senate and judiciary, all properly delegated by their constituents, the only real sovereigns, the people. Birthright is not known in this, while talents, virtue or personal meritorious claims may entitle a fair presentation to the elective franchise. The proper government, as all the constituents, are amenable to enlightened public opinion, itself resting on immutable principles. Among some of the most prominent positions of the world, must be observed the various divisions of countries of the same continent.

Those of Europe have harassed her people for many centuries, and their malign influence is felt over the balance of the world.

It is time that they be arrested, on the right basis. Absolutists must go down, before the sovereign people. The petty divisions of Europe, and other grand divisions of continents tend to corrupt the people, by intrigues and cabals, ruin them by wars, and enslave them by conquests. All this is ungodly.

The world's committee of conservative mind must arrest all this. The chief and most powerful liberalists must counteract this tendency.

The world is bound to use good government, the best practicable, on principles amendatory of itself, working out its own best existence. The noble principles of constitutional government advance many lights. Many international matters will be rightly settled by international codes, that will never be fully right till all the world is rightly, constitutionally governed. The benefits of the world should enure on principles.

All of the supposed world evils can be diminished, if not counteracted, by adoption of a wise international code. The most effectual mode of putting down partyism and sectarianism, is to secure all the comprehension of the world. What a clique is to individuals, these are to nations, dwarfing the refined sensibilities of nature. There are one hundred millions of liberalists in Europe, that, if properly organized, might establish a republic of all Europe at once. Where are all the liberalists, that they do not properly organize and demand a proper vindication of their rights? No one country can do it.

Are the soldiers of Europe traitors to Liberty, human rights of their own fellow-citizens?

Of course, the five different governments should not, cannot be consolidated; but they should have federal unions. When the world secures its own right and justice, then is displayed the ripest theatre, the richest arena, for the statesmen of the most admirable calibre of mind and character. Then intellect can luxuriate in all its magnanimity, and genius disport in all its intrinsic greatness.

On this noblest position of world-government all the comprehensive moves of rational mind can be best sustained. It is here statesmen will best find what system of finance will advance the capital, public and private, promote the widest interest, and ever worthy of the deepest consideration. On this, the widest platform of the world, navigation, agriculture, commerce, manufactures, mechanics, mining, and the fisheries, compatible with the best interests of the whole, should be adequately, duly and consistently protected and sustained, and an honorable competition is never to be excluded by the most generous protection.

Capacity, integrity, and honesty, so expedient in all matters, must accompany most conspicuously each other in these enlarged areas, else the patriot may never reach the exalted standard of the finished statesman, and must fall short of that liberalized expansion that belongs to the lights of the age. Enlarged national views, reaching to the circumference of the globe, must prevail. This age requires great railroads, connecting the great oceans, as the Pacific and Atlantic, to be embraced.

Standing armies, as eminently due the world and the equitable conservative principles of mind, must be put down. This is to equalize the cardinal and constitutional principles of proper government, to harmonize the conflicts of interests of the masses, and perpetuate on durable basis the union of free states of the world, on highest equitable principles. The justice of rightful petition will, on the world's platform, be ever respected to the legitimate comprehension, by both parties to the social compact, both the representatives and the people, the constituency, no matter how diversified the interests that are in antagonism with popular rights, those of fellow-citizens of the one common republic. The constitution of the empire has to be duly appreciated, to do exact justice to the whole union.

The plenipotent position of mind is now taken; each great division of the five great sections of the world is now embraced; the march of science has now advanced; civilization begins to complete her most exalted and refined character; the mighty elements of moral and intellectual force are now being developed; the world has just taken a fair and sublime start, and the mighty offspring of a mighty nation is spreading forth the beams of her republican light to all habitable points of the vastest oceans. The intelligence, justice and civilization of the globe betoken the mastery of rational mind.

When the politician yields to the statesman,—the military gives place to the civilian —the sectarian to the religious, and national circles to continental ones, as all are bound to do—the potency of peace measures shall govern the whole world, and mind then will record the mighty triumph. The balance of the world will then be through the equilibrium of God's principles.

The world's legislation forms the world's deepest interest. It must rise to the dignity of its position.

Each of these mighty governments will be a confederation of sovereign states. They will hold the highest national codes, no contracted sectional, but broad platforms of continental empires; no sectarian views that cause internal clashing in the same nation, country, down to the family.

I desire that the world should take hold of constitutional government, through the progress of conservative revolution. The world can well take the example of The North American Union, for constitutional government. This Union was the work of heroes, statesmen and patriots. Sovereigns now will imitate it—patriots can well preserve what their forefathers so gallantly won.

The Union should be preserved as long as it is worth preservation, and its people should make it worth preservation. It is the most glorious country the sun shines on, as its governmental institutions are so illustrious. With the Union, we are all that we are in government—without it, nothing.

. The Union is the richest legacy, not only to us, but to the whole world: better by far than all the mock titles of nobility in heraldry, entailed by primogeniture. It could not have been possible to have created our constitutional union, without the essential articles: the citizens of any section act in bad faith not to uphold most conscientiously all the provisions.

Let nations forgive their foibles, and unite in magnanimous brotherhood. Fair and honorable competition is to be established among all the nations of the world, to live and let live. Such a position of the world will insure the proper management of international affairs. What a sublime spectacle to have constitutional executives over these governments. The purest justice can only be obtained in the constitutional union of confederated states.

In such position conservative revolutions will supersede those of radical revolutions. The glorious constitution of America will be the charter of a world's light; the Declaration of Independence the precursor of a world's liberty; our revolutionary sires, with Washington at their head, will be the noblest sons of freedom's heraldry. Constitutional limits, and express grants of power to all, to the world-governments, are for the world. What advantages will not accrue by such governments, to bring the artizan and the agriculturist together, as a wise world policy?

Such governments will go to put down the practices of a barbarous age, that, if renewed, will renew the barbarity of these ages. There are matters yet in store in the womb of time not yet dreamt of.

These governments will be the noblest asylums of a world's justice, for a world's protection.

Difficulties and delays, amounting too often to a denial of justice, in even this country, governed by constitutional basis, decide that international justice need all the constitutional basis that the enlightened world can comprehend. The income of the world is enough to provide fairly for all its pressing necessities. Let a world morality and intellectuality meet as it ought, all the essential demands. Have not all nations a deep and abiding permanent interest in the prosperity of the whole earth? These mighty governments will furnish constitutional unions, protecting permanently the perpetual rights and feelings of the minority.

Is this constant military excitement in Europe nothing, before the dignity and peace of hundreds of millions of sovereign people? Mind cultivated, rational refined civilized mind, should require not only correct constitutional government, but society of the world. The world is arriving at a new era in its history. America is now destined to take the 'ighest rank among the nations of the world, having won it by intellect, morals, and energectic prowess. Lying between two of the greatest oceans, she must attain therefrom the most commercial importance with the largest mercantile marine in the whole world. Well may she congratulate herself, that her constitutional government is the best adapted to the world's wants.

She needs now rational religion, properly illustrated, to close the moral sublime, for the noblest expansion of civilization. The great defects of world-government must be corrected. Then that pure light of constitutional government, having legitimate constitutional annexations and unions, must go for other things than the pomp and circumstances of war, that renders the world barbarian. Instead of warriors, the destructive, it should have been statemen, the conservative, pacificators of the world, divided into constitutional republics, instead of empires of autocracy.

All such governments will not be antagonistic to each other, but will be conservative of the noblest actions of mind. After rational education, that is so essential to popular instruction, a system of internal improvements will be a universal policy for the world. The people, enlightened by the lights and elements of instruction, will advance to the sublime in philosophical science.

The hundred millions of freemen now of Europe should concentrate their operations, assert their rights. They are citizens, and have the clearest right to constitutional government. If they would only use mind right, they would clearly devise the speedy, effectual, and conservative system for a European union.

Every rational thought conclusively points to that. In detail, they worst themselves by any radical revolution, whereas they can secure all by conservative revolution. This is what the whole world must do.

No perfidy of sovereigns, who act in bad faith any way, can exclude the people, the true sovereigns, forever.

The world needs the proper adjustment of continental governments. Already the balance of power, confined to Europe, looks across oceans to America. The world needs all such for a proper social system.

Sooner or later, the whole of each grand division of the earth should be bound in one indissoluble constitutional government, and each of the parts should be to the whole, as the members of a body are to the whole body. Then every generous impulse, all genius, can be sustained by a proper principle, government.

The Europeans have no need of their many forts and standing armies. Nations that pirate on continents, are world pirates. There are many continental piracies to be stopped.

With such governments, no nation, priding itself on impunity, could ever dare bully on the high seas, plunder and kill, much less subjugate continents.

What is the present condition of the European powers, but an excessive increase of public debt for the people to pay, to be ground down on? The whole world cries aloud for conservative revolution. Mind invokes, society demands, religion will consecrate it.

Where too is ancient Asia, after her protracted sleep of many ages and centuries? Can those ancient people rouse up over Oriental despotisms, to the lustre and utility of rational mind? Can they learn that they have yet, after all the nonsense about peculiar faith and despotic rule, that rational government and religion have in reserve their best blessing for them? Can you, England, in your might, aid this noble cause for its sake? America is advancing, Africa and Australia progressing, it but remains for Europe and Asia to rouse up, and throw off their torpor of many centuries, and act to the just bidding of rational mind.

There must be no piratical nations to enslave and provincialize continents.

However ancient all peculiar faith, all is referable to rationality and utilitarianism.

Let the siren or delusive cry of much of it, that the people cannot do justice to themselves, be forever silenced.

See in China how the mind is crushed, how the body is mistreated. No security for life, reputation, much less property. Mighty continental smuggling, all arising from despotism, should be estopped. I address all nations of the world, that they should not stand in the way of rational mind's highest problems.

Is not man the recipient of as good government as he is entitled to? No, sir, no more than his peculiar faith is religion. The whole world needs a conservative revolution all the time, to carry out the full freedom of the press, put down all monopoly and usurpation, carry out, on the most liberal and expansive theatre, every proper principle in man, legitimatized by religion the most rational.

The very language of China condemns her, as behind the age. Her science was once in advance of the rest of the world, but her miserable selfish home policy ruined that, and puts her behind the capacities of mind.

That will react also on Japan. Asia, once the light of the day in advance, has sunk into inside barbarism, and must shake off the effects of Oriental luxury and mental enervation. China has not less than three peculiar faiths. The Confucian is the state peculiar faith, and the emperor is the head pontiff of that faith. All such states preclude refined civilization of mind. The Chinese are most miserably governed, by the extorting Mandarins. You, China, by my views, will have no need of your monster walls to keep out the northern barbarians. You, India, will not raise opium to poison the Asiatics; and you, England, will not stand before the world the master pirate nation, enslaving, like ungrateful guests, the Hindoos, and smuggling your poison into China, whom you whip to receive it. Let agriculture and commerce be purged of their vile Oriental stains, alien to their God-given character.

In the attainment of constitutional principles of government and rational religion, let all things properly mature, that the revolution may be conservative. The old regime of faith helps to promote a tory government, but rational religion helps support the noblest of all rational, constitutional governments. Nothing but monotheism can give us a true idea of God, religion, and government. Faith itself is an arrant humbug.

A rational government and religion are inseparable when either conflicts with the peculiar book revelations, then bigots, tories to mind, will pretend that the last takes precedence, but rational minds, to which the first are antagonistic, of course will affirm the first is the only universal protection.

Monotheism requires and will secure conservative revolution, guiltless of blood and agitation. Reason can only carry the force of conservation of principles. Peculiar faith and its government are despotic, therefore they must be finally excluded. Constitutional principles can ever organize self-improvement, individually or nationally. Is England free when she excludes the Jew members of parliament, and trammels the Roman and all other churches, for her code of faith and church?

Is France a republic, when she punishes her citizen booksellers by penalties, fines and imprisonments for sales of books subversive of the bad faith of worthless peculiar faiths?

Shall the fire-brands of the peculiar faiths of the world, consume the rights of sovereign people?

False, miserable impeachable pretences are advanced to national preferments, as if peculiar faith in some form, as western Bhuddism or Christianity, had been the only thing to promote the good of the world! And yet all these are the retailed fabricated falsehoods of the priestocracy and their vassals. The world has flourished despite of all such, by all the sovereign potency of mind that has been ignobly betrayed by the ignominious cliques.

Institute, monarchs, the purity of elections, the ballot box at once, to secure the world's and mind's charters of rights. Let mind have the cultivation of all its resources. This is the age for the progress of republican institutions, and the decline and downfall of monarchy.

Monotheism, that despotism of church and state has avoided most curiously, is republican, and is most beneficial as it is universal, and the only faith adapted to mind and its holiest functions, the soul immortal.

The world should declare non-intervention with all peculiar faiths as tory to its rights and benefits.

What mind, indignant at facts, would not exclaim, Down with all churches that are tory to the world. Are they not all so? Their very existence cannot be otherwise. Abolish all churches as inquisitions on the world. Unconditional abrogation of all such tory character, will insure mind its necessary liberty of enlightened conscience.

Churches are the enemies of liberty and comprehensive light of mind. Fair discussion has been crippled all the time, now not even in the freest country permitted without horrid proscriptions.

In Spain, church property, that of course was wrested from the people, has been transferred to the ecclesiastics, and amounts to forty-five millions of pounds sterling; and the salaries of the ministers are even paid by the state. Can there be more flagrant outrages on the people, who pay for all despotisms?

There can be no national independence where church superstition prevails.

Are courts of justice any more courts of justice, by swearing witnesses on perjured bible codes? Are courts of justice less tyrannical to measure conscience the most enlightened by these perjured books?

Look at all the blood of Spain of myriads of her people, that has so freely flowed for years; all her immense sacrifices for the best part of a century. See the deplorable state of Italy. When they, as the world, will rise in their majesty, they will declare their state and church despots as the basest conspirators against religion as liberty.

The world is becoming republican, the only government of principle, that will secure the religion of principles, supreme over unprincipled and reckless speculations of peculiar faith that was mind-factured to suit the despotism and the complexion of the times.

Let the whole people demand this—the resignation of usurped and ill-gotten power. No special pleading of sophistry will answer, that there is doubt or difficulty in the way of popular governments.

Let the vestiges of power remove the supreme difficulty by retiring among the sovereign people. Is kingly government purchased at the expense of the people's rights and constitutional principles?

Away with this foul aspersion on liberty, the world's rights by conservative revolution.

You, monarchs, and peculiar faith people the world over, you are amenable for bloody gory revolutions, if you do not act with conservative revolution to benefit the whole of mankind.

You, peculiar faith people, affect to speak of civil and religious liberty, of the odiousness of despotism. You are amenable for the worst species of it, the despotism of mind in religion, as absurdly ignorant of the first principles of mind and the universe.

For the world, then, to make all best attainable steps in the progress of liberty, let the people renounce now, at once and forever, all communications as evil with all their churches.

To preserve mind's dignity, confer no authority on man but what is purely constitutional.

Monarchy, so far from being right, has no principles, but trades on the borrowed capital of constitutional principles of pure government.

Thus speaks Monotheism, that stops the audacious and impudent sacrilege, under the name of peculiar faiths—their conspiracy with that of monarchy, all despotism against the world's and mind's liberty and light. Monotheism will revolutionize the world on conservative principles.

She looks at the national debts of the world, and asks, why these billions? Why the world impoverished, murdered, oppressed? It is because the evil spirit of piracy is nurtured in the world. Why is this? Have the whole fund of the world's brotherhood, and the annual income that would be hundreds of millions, to civilize, colonize, and emancipate, socialize and humanize mankind. Rush, mind, to the rescue.

You represent the people, and if they desire you to give them a proper constitutional government, and you refuse, then are you felon functionaries. The sophistry of special pleading will not avail you, that is not theirs, but your government.

Conservative revolution will humanize the world faster and better, and if revolution be bloody, then you, not they, are the aggressors.

It well becomes Europeans to avoid the bane, this aid of monarchy, peculiar faithites' peculiar invention. It is the most insidious poison of the world. Discard all such of vile man, that curses all, and adopt the religion of God—that blesses all.

All man's were intended for despotism of unprincipled rulers, not the sovereignty of the world or its people.

Discard all such ignoble encroachments on the liberty of the people—of mind. Vindicate religion and its author in defence of the people.

Have no more to do with peculiar faith, its authors, aiders, or abettors. Leave all such ignoble company, and adopt principles that will promote and mature your noblest aspirations to the most magnificent arch of the universe.

Supersede peculiar faith idolatry by the adoration of the creator of the universe.

Down with all the corrupt presses of despotism, and down with all the servile censorships, the odious proscriptions to a free enlightened and virtuous press. Marshall your forces, Europeans, before you risk inevitably, and go for your universal constitutional independence.

Despots of the world, Europe especially, you owe it to yourselves and people, mind, justice, God, to free your country of all peculiar faith and its false appurtenances, by proper rational conservative revolution, to give your people constitutional governments in their purity, and retire from your monopoly and usurpation.

A correct domestic government, all on rational principles, will rule out the despotism of peculiar education. Without monotheism, liberty at best is licentious.

There must be full organic constitutional liberty, and a police for all communities, counteracting all the evil doers of life; but let not the world be longer mind-led out of its rights.

Let the world be properly enlightened by all proper expedients, and the progress of mind will be exalted.

Let monotheism have her legitimate rule, and mind, the world will go right. Let principle, not despotism, rule.

Recollect that despotism brutalizes all the refined feelings of human nature, and debases their loftiest appreciation, as well the integrity of the man, as the chastity of the woman, the honorable dignity of both. All the billions expended by the dissipation of despotism, are enough to elevate the world, and consecrate the noblest deeds of philanthropy.

To have the law protect any book or scriptures as God's holy word, for fear they may be exposed to contempt or ridicule most justly deserved, is the most absolute despotism on earth.

If lies, they should be exposed—if true, their truths will be self-evident and sustained. To suppress acts of religion is licentiousness.

One of the acts of religion is to establish itself, and suppress by facts, the false pretences of all peculiar faiths.

There has been more despotism for peculiar faith, than all other world-wide calamities together. .

Liberty upholds the good faith of religion, not the peculiar faith of the priestocracy. But no felony, no imposture is legal, because monopoly and usurpation make it so. But despots affect to defend the holy scriptures. What holy scriptures? The creator never wrote but one, the universe, that upholds itself perfectly independent of man.

But they affect, that there is blasphemy somewhere. Truly there is blasphemy, and the degraded wretches should atone therefor. Blasphemy is an attack on religion, by false scriptures of peculiar faith.

Peculiar faith commits blasphemy all the time.

, Let all minds, males and females, regard the universal brotherhood as permanent. superseding all others, available and satisfactory for all the world and mind demands.

The five world-families duly represented at the world's tribunal, must guarantee much better the protection, elevation and felicity of society. Then behold the fruits of constitutional liberty throughout the world. God inspires the universe by principles, truth, honesty and virtue.

Let rational conscience alone, hold the rational mind in abeyance to principles.

The human sacrifices at the altars of ferocious superstitions, are too many. See the human sacrifices now offered up at the dungeons of Roman despotism. How long will these bloody sacrifices be borne? How long will you give aid and comfort to such nefarious bibles that authorize all this iniquity?

Let the watch-word of liberty and religion put a stop to all this world despotism, and mind-sacrilege. There is not the first valid plea for the continuance, as religion discredits all such bloody nuisances, and rationality demands their expulsion by the noblest of all principles.

Shall the priestocracy, who have no commission but that of usurpation and monopoly—who have been smuggled by monarchy, and maintained by reckless, brazen-faced impudence, and the folly of the debased, make prisoner of the human soul, and enslave its very religion?

Civilization and religion are paramount to all such. You, monarchs, must yield up your country or your thrones. Monarchy has no principles. It is usurpation and monopoly at the best, in disguise, and disguised by all the blandishments of peculiar faith, is no less a prostitute and seductress of the rights of the people. No wonder the despotic censorship and corruption of the press, to suppress the liberal advances of religion and liberty.

Conscience, the great directress of mind, that should be supremely enlightened to be the counsellor of the soul, you brutalize.   .

You, monarchs, must bow to the majesty of principles. All peculiar faiths and powers are a larceny on the rights of the people. All peculiar bibles, as peculiar forgeries, are kept up by odious despotism, that has excited fanaticism and superstition.

No nation can be civilized, where peculiar faith abides.

Peculiar faith takes not by open manly argument, but by insidious treachery.

The most brilliant of all victories is not the union of bayonets, but of principles. Sophists of despotism, you are nothing : retire, and let the people organize, with social, legislative, and religious discussions, what mind most rationally elicits. In getting rid of monarchy, you must get rid of all the forms of despotism, as that of peculiar faiths, and their various priestocracy.   .

Rise, in the potency and justice of your brightest luminary, mind, freemen, and make your liberty the most lovely on earth.

Despotism shows billions of debts, millions in standing armies, the people paying for all these, the odious means to crush them to dust, their own money expended in its support, their own blood shed in its defence ; all to fasten the galling chains more brutally.

Despotism has prostituted mind, as harlequin to its all-degraded vitiations!

The society of the world is built of compromises, and can only wisely and justly be elevated by conservative revolutions.

Despotism is bankrupt, and its peculiar faith is obsolete.

Governments, to be properly respected as they ought, should have all the proper elements.

How has the world been worse swindled, than by the brute and sophist force of despotism?

If right, I call in the virtuous world patriotism, to sustain the principles advocated.

Much of South America, Mexico, Central America, seem incompetent to get along, and are falling to pieces. They had better all come in, with the best of good faith, into continental confederacy. Now is the time for all peculiar faith people to seek rational religion, and acquire all the blessings of the universal brotherhood.

Monotheism, with sublimest tuition, greets rational mind, and with magnanimity, liberality, and patriotism, directs nations, worlds, and a universe.

France, you have misconceived your mission. England, you have overlooked your mighty elements, that can yet ennoble and raise you by the side of your eldest daughter, in whom, science and liberty taught, you can amply rejoice.

Nations can learn wisdom of true science, and piety of true religion.

The world owes it to itself to exercise continued conservative revolution, as necessary as continued physical or atmospheric, to produce a healthy, elastic, vital, moral, and religious existence.

This constitutes man what he ought to be, a rigid self-examiner. All is conservative religious revolution.

People of Europe, unite at once, and assert your rights. Let no petty local jealousies prevent it.

Tell your perjured dictators to yield to you, the lawful sovereigns, the arraignment of your own constitutional affairs, and let them faithfully aid you therein. Do not attempt in detail, but have one union of Europe.

All things will regulate themselves. Do not let any local or peculiar difficulties, any such consideration defeat, or put you back from the primary consummation, a single moment. The American people are pre-eminently sovereigns of mind.

The general conservation of truth and honesty, intact before the world, is honored by mind, thus self-blessed.

What is despotism? The power exercised without responsibility, as autocracy, a monarchy. Well, what composes it? The one man. There you mistake most awfully and ignorantly.

The court faith is the greater part. Why? They divide part of the spoils, and better sustain the licentious assumption, monopoly and usurpation. The mighty functions of religion are alien to all such. Part is to promote science. Do professors hold their chairs indebted to Christianity? Has brute force, with its sophistry, mastered science, that the last and mind have been so ignominiously surrendered to peculiar faith and all her debauched, perfidious clan?

Absolutism was in the way of the ancients, who, at best, were only semi-barbarians. There never was an age of the world equal to the present, that history shows, for the light and liberty of mind, that will have its most illustrious beauty and excellence with monotheism.

Peculiar bibles are the codes of absolutism, composed of king, priestocracy and military regimes. The highest dictates of prudence precludes any excess of power, even to one's self.

The wisest mortals can only desire a proper independence as their chief good, the only best for them.

Of all the felonies on earth, the greatest is enjoyed by absolutism in all its departments, rewarded instead of punished for its iniquities.

Surely there is retributive justice for all this. In the holy centre, principles will not distinguish between supreme and petty crimes only bounded by the state of power.

I have a higher object than all the mere gew-gaws of royalty.

Monarchs, do not dwarf mind nor libel religion by peculiar faith. The first runs the greatest risk, in hearing only one side, and that of the peculiar gods, who are the creations of despotism.

My responsibility to the proper construction of language, requires that I oppose the use of the term Christianise, as that and all the department of paganism are too puisne to affect what religionization and its civilization only can effect. The world cannot be peculiarized much longer, even by autocratical despotism. All the peculiar creations of man, from his gods to his own mind subversion, will accompany the association.

Genius cannot be dwarfed, when moral and intellectual force will and must be the essentials of the world-mind.

Monarchs, you can well learn of America, who is now teaching the world her bullion jewels. Her empire is the world-fund.

What gives mind and genius their loftiest triumphs, but the most legitimate expanse of freedom?

Let there be a convention of the nations, in union of the five grand divisions and appurtenant islands, at once, to accustom mind to all the world calibre questions, as religion, the consummation of principles. Let a proper convention of religion of principles be at once instituted, that will be the most august of all, at the best capital of each division, every fifth year interchangeably.

Plain unthinking people might suppose that the world could not reach the zenith of worth personal and manners refined, without court polish, reflecting the jewels of royalty. But in all that, is something identified, that spoils the flavor intrinsically. The world cannot divest it.

With court polish comes court faith, and that is the poison. What, too, is the state of rational, international, as well as mind morals, religion?

Analyze. For court faith, religion demands the superseding by God's faith and courtesy; the full bullion improver. Minds all have, of rational religion, in proportion to their rationality, while they have no peculiar faith that is contingent on peculiar education, and that is furnished in palaces and cathedrals. It is the duty of every age of the world to revise the acts of predecessors, and correct accordingly.

All constitutions that should govern now—mind, the world should be revised by every subsequent age of man—as well as all bibles, in popular or world, not imperial conventions. How can you, republicans, who are to govern this world hereafter by rational mind and principles, stand a book pretence smuggled from despots ecclesiastical and imperial? You would not stand the personifications, much less their bantlings.

Nations must not overlook their high duties. They must maintain inviolate all the relations of non-intervention, though islands encased with diamonds were the conquest.

Constitutional liberty and rational religion, are identified. British bayonets are not for nothing, in sustaining an unsustainable pet faith.

Where is American mind? Captive by sophists?

The worst of all, it surrenders when it has no excuse.

As to the mere results in republics over monarchies, it is only in regard to the legitimate adequate capacities, best insured by constitutional liberty.

The crown sovereigns could not give the people sovereigns peculiar faith for monotheism. It is not whether others are wrong, so much as are we right? That is the question of life. We are obliged to point others out as wrong to put ourselves right, owing to the prevalence of time-pledged customs, that command errors through despotic notions.

The world must meet all on principles, and imperial governments can form no exception.

It is no animosity against people, but professions obnoxious to principles, and injurious to the world.

Brief authority is ever dangerous, especially to the holders, to whom it may bring much remorse individually and nationally.

Sovereigns, do you do all that can be expected of you? Stop your piratical wars, Russia and England. Emperors, lamas, popes, and papas, celestials—all you can reach, teach man's dignity supreme, only by rationality. The whole world is equal by monotheism. Let the rational world legislate against all felons from pagan propagandists, down to the lowest petty larceny man.

What is man even in a republic? I have seen enough to know, that he can play the minion and sycophant to small calibres, in all departments.

Emperors, I will point you to the field of your glory. Nations in this enlightened age, under the appropriate brotherhood of monotheism, can be still more united by annexation. America stands conspicuous in this, as well as by her civil constitutional institutions, to receive the worthy of Europe. No nation should have war, as that is a barbarism, and puts back just that much if no more, the world's civilization. But it may be assumed, that some may take the ascendancy, as England and London. If they are worthy in talents and munificence of means and mind, they can do so. But the whole can be elevated to that scale.

A firm and universal union in Europe, of all the liberalists, will alone do, and solve the problem at once of human liberty. It is idle folly to undertake otherwise. The general pacification of the world requires it.

Every hour is important in the adoption of grand consummation of principles—every moment is pregnant with great results. The genius of the world is directed, to the best discovery of the means of defence, that at the same time is most potent in the destruction of life. We annihilate such means, the necessity of such, by the institution of the mighty principles to be employed by mind, for the best good of mankind. The Creator has most wisely divided the globe in such way, as will conduce best to the greatest good of all.

No one part can subjugate the balance, if mind will only do itself justice. Every moment renders it more expedient to concentrate all the best energies of each grand division and appurtenant islands. Among the speediest means of promoting the world's civilization, it would best comport with the mind's energies, for the best countries to receive and educate some thousand or more of other countries, most destitute of the means of civilization. The United States should set the example, and at once put it into practice, as best comporting with monotheism. The paramount object is to universalize the one language all over the world. Who believes that the priestocracy would aid in Europe, in promoting popular liberty? The people have no need of them, and as the best means to secure the best liberty, will dispense with them, as superfluous and insidious to their rights now, at once, and forever. Let the priestocracy, who can be monotheists, as men ought, aid at once in this glorious world-cause.

Emperors and priestocracies, principals or tools of the world's despotism, you falsify your functions. The world is entitled to the religion of principles instituted by God, and can only thus be properly governed. You falsify every trust, as the best good of all is through constitutional civil and religious liberty. To reach a conservative revolution, the world has to wade through too much of suffering : it is your duty to aid in the best promotion of the first.

The freest nation, even America, does not appreciate, much less enjoy, the full mental repast of liberty ; will not, until the loveliest rectitude of monotheism corrects the foul blurs of social faith proscriptions, and her sovereigns, the earth's sovereigns, the whole free people, the only ones, put down all spurious ones and their more ignoble despotisms.

There is no other sovereignty in the world but that of the whole people, whose rights are divine and sacred ; hence all unconstitutional governments prove high treason to the only sovereigns, the people, whose majesty convicts the perpetrators as pirates, having millions of hireling soldiers as standing armies, seduced by fraud and bribery, debauched by corruption, and influenced by all vitiated machinery of mind's perversions, through the means of the country, that has supreme claims on all citizens ; therefore all soldiers owe paramount allegiance to constitutional governments recognised by the popular will of a free nationality, all other being the perjury of high treason. Conservative revolution, that protects the freest thinking, printing and acting, will terminate all other kinds of revolution.

In the expulsion of world-nuisances, it cannot know the autocrats of usurpation from the lowest petit larceny malefactors. Felony has no royalty, and royalty has no immunity at the tribunal of constitutional principles.

Continental union of the people will alone do full justice to this paramount world-question. The balance of America, Europe, Asia, Africa, and Australia, with all appurtenant islands, can only thus be properly sustained. The sooner the enlightened voice of the people speak, the better for all.

The divine rights of mind of the sovereign people should not be required to play traitors to the dearest interests of their country. Soldiers have inalienable rights, that cannot be transcended by the one-man power, or despotism. What has not despotism debauched? It has debauched faith in every form, to corrupt and defraud the people. If ever there were a favored nation, it is that of these United States, that will grow in the growth, and strengthen in the strength of religion, most rational, civilized, and consummation of principles. They have reached already the intellectual sublime in constitutional government, let it be in the world, universe, and mind and soul-problem. As far above mixed paganism as is rational religion, so far are these states above the Jewish, or any ancient nation in the blessings of the denizen.

The world demands at our hands not the aid of four millions of soldiers ; not that of a marine that exceeds that of any one of all nations, ancient or modern : not the martial prowess that cuts the gordian knot, and destroys all its constituents ; but the most comprehensive illustration of these principles.

No nation ever had the sublime world-action that this Union now has to accomplish.

Talk of the Jews, when the Chinese excelled them in arts and science, that they commenced thousands of years anterior to Christ, intellectually, socially, and morally, and yet never attained a proper calibre, because they moulded mind only to be inside barbarian. Then was the ridiculous of their fall, their dwarfage ; the Jews were worse. Despotism is a dangerous thing, to even those clothed with its brief authority. To sustain itself, it has to perpetrate perjury, and has to sustain its ignoblest doings.

See that the world is guaranteed the rule of the majority, not the misrule.

Despots are world traitors. Religion cannot rise in despotic governments, where court faith flourishes.

The liberalists of the world have to reach constitutional liberty, ere rational religion has her own dear pure chaste reputation, ever. Now she is libeled by the minions of despotism.

The world liberalists, conservative revolutionists must require of despots to restore constitutional and religious liberty, and not palm on them or the world their false pretences of government or faith that are all engines of power intended so to be.

America is to be light to the world's civilization, and to attain it has to give up all vestiges of paganism, and secure the whole benefits of monotheism. The intercourse of the world should be most extensive, and can be when all on continents unite, thus bringing the people together all over the country. The world should review its position, and can only appreciate constitutional liberty, the noblest freedom of rational mind, by justly appreciating monotheism.

All despotism is the world's injury.

If man ever fell, assuredly priestocracy nor their affiliations, messiahships with all their hosts of faiths and bibles, never restored him: that is certain. All such are a world's nuisance. The world must appreciate all such as part and fixture of the world's despots, all traitors. Let priestocrats learn honest logic, and retire to their proper position among the people. Rational mind takes to-day the ascendency, supreme precedence, and with its guardian light and the Creator's universal grace, mercy and omniscience, the whole question will thus and thus only be met, as it can only be most wisely met and closed.

Rational mind is the world guardian in all the supreme rationality. "The French have no religion." That is impossible—as the world has in part. If they had no religion they then would have no principle. But that is impossible. They, as the world, need cultivation of monotheism. The priestocracy must stop all their books of perjury. Resign, unconstitutional rulers of the world. Rational minds of the world, persevere. A curse upon all unconstitutional governments that have to be the foulest living perjury, a perfidy to the people, and as a proof, cannot give them religion, but the vilest perjury. Now we see the base malign brute force to keep down the world spirit in this respect. Come rulers, sacrifice something on your country's altar, and resign your corrupt commissions. Be monotheists, and let the world profit by the best example.

THE WORLD IS ADVANCED ALWAYS PROPERLY, ONLY BY CONSERVATIVE REVOLUTION.

The test now is, by full sincerity of the world-people in thought, word, and action, in the highest evidence of rational mind, in rational science and principle.

Are they prepared for this noble question?

This solution of rational civilization?

The decision is alone with them.

Have we reached the just independence of mind's majesty, enabling the people to be just to themselves, perfectly independent to the proper extent of conservation?

Nothing short of rational independence in conservative revolution will answer.

The full security to-day before the whole world, gives it the glorious triumph of a mastery of obsolete regimes, and of the whole subject.

IMPEACHMENT

OF UNCONSTITUTIONAL GOVERNMENTS OF THE WORLD, PRIESTOCRACY, AND ALL MESSIAHSHIPS—ALL PAGAN NUISANCES.

As excellency of the world-religion can only be consummated by the best cultivation of monotheism, unconstitutional governments must be responsible for popular injury by their innumerable nuisances.

I this day impeach all such, for their butchery of the world's billions, their own sovereigns, as unworthy of the light of mind, most rational. As they interrupt the purest purposes of creation, they are unworthy of its respect.

I this day invoke the world to respect its paramount duty, to extinguish, as a matter of paramount necessity, all unconstitutional governments—as those of autocrats, emperors, monarchs, and aristocrats—those of pontiffs, or defenders of peculiar faith, popes, papas, and lamas—all ·hierarchists and prelates of· paganisms—all messiahships and functionaries, identified with all such felonious impositions, that involve perjury with their bibles, even to oaths on such—amenable all, as world pagan nuisances, by conservative revolution, that will then extinguish the thousand untold other world nuisances, the exemption whereof will glorify and sanctify the world, mankind, mind, most rational.   The question is with the sovereign people, as the mighty purpose of the Almighty Creator of the Universe of Principles.

Lightning Source UK Ltd.
Milton Keynes UK
UKOW01f0746020218

317262UK00008B/357/P